DAS KAPITAL

Karl Marx

INCLUDES VOL I, II AND III

RUPA

Published by
Rupa Publications India Pvt. Ltd 2021
7/16, Ansari Road, Daryaganj
New Delhi 110002

Sales centres:
Bengaluru Chennai
Hyderabad Jaipur Kathmandu
Kolkata Mumbai Prayagraj

P-ISBN: 978-93-5520-098-3
E-ISBN: 978-93-5520-103-4

Third impression 2025

10 9 8 7 6 5 4 3

Printed in India

Contents

VOLUME I
BOOK ONE: THE PROCESS OF PRODUCTION OF CAPITAL

Part I: Commodities and Money

1. Commodities 13
   Section 1: The Two Factors of a Commodity: Use-Value and Value (The Substance of Value and the Magnitude of Value) 13
   Section 2: The Two-Fold Character of the Labour Embodied in Commodities 16
   Section 3: The Form of Value or Exchange Value 19
   Section 4: The Fetishism of Commodities and the Secret Thereof 32
2. Exchange 45
3. Money, Or the Circulation of Commodities 51
   Section 1: The Measure of Values 51
   Section 2: The Medium of Circulation 55
   Section 3: Money 68

Part II: The Transformation of Money into Capital

4. The General Formula for Capital 87
5. Contradictions in the General Formula of Capital 93
6. The Buying and Selling of Labour-Power 100

Part III: The Production of Absolute Surplus-Value

7. The Labour-Process and the Process of Producing Surplus-Value 108
   Section 1: The Labour-Process or the Production of Use-Values 108
   Section 2: The Production Of Surplus-Value 112
8. Constant Capital and Variable Capital 122
9. The Rate of Surplus-Value 129
   Section 1: The Degree of Exploitation of Labour-Power 129
   Section 2: The Representation of the Components of the Value of the Product by Corresponding Proportional Parts of the Product Itself 134
   Section 3: Senior's 'Last Hour' 136
   Section 4: Surplus-Produce 138
10. The Working-Day 141
   Section 1: The Limits of the Working-Day 141
   Section 2: The Greed for Surplus-Labour Manufacturer and Boyard 143
   Section 3: Branches of English Industry without Legal Limits to Exploitation 147
   Section 4: Day and Night Work. The Relay System 153
   Section 5: The Struggle for a Normal Working-Day Compulsory Laws for the Extension of the Working-Day from the Middle of the 14th to the End of the 17th Century 157
   Section 6: The Struggle for the Normal Working-Day. Compulsory Limitation by Law of the Working-Time. The English Factory Acts, 1833 to 1864 162
   Section 7: The Struggle for the Normal Working-Day Re-action of the English Factory Acts on Other Countries 171
11. Rate and Mass of Surplus Value 189

Part IV: Production of Relative Surplus Value

12. The Concept of Relative Surplus Value 196
13. Co-operation 202
14. Division of Labour and Manufacture 211
Section 1: Two-Fold Origin of Manufacture 211
Section 2: The Detail Labourer and his Implements 213
Section 3: The Two Fundamental Forms of Manufacture: Heterogeneous Manufacture, Serial Manufacture 214
Section 4: Division of Labour in Manufacture, and Division of Labour in Society 218
Section 5: The Capitalistic Character of Manufacture 222
15. Machinery and Modern Industry 234
Section 1: The Development of Machinery 234
Section 2: The Value Transferred by Machinery to the Product 241
Section 3: The Proximate Effects of Machinery on the Workman 244
Section 4: The Factory 256
Section 5: The Strife Between Workman and Machine 259
Section 6: The Theory of Compensation as Regards the Work People Displaced by Machinery 265
Section 7: Repulsion and Attraction of Work People by the Factory System. Crises in the Cotton Trade 270
Section 8: Revolution Effected in Manufacture, Handicrafts, and Domestic Industry by Modern Industry 275
Section 9: The Factory Acts. Sanitary and Educational Clauses of the Same. Their General Extension in England 286
Section 10: Modern Industry and Agriculture 299

Part V: The Production of Absolute and of Relative Surplus-Value

16. Absolute and Relative Surplus-Value 327
17. Changes of Magnitude in the Price of Labour-Power and in Surplus-Value 334
Section 1: Length of the Working-Day and Intensity of Labour Constant Productiveness of Labour Variable 334
Section 2: Working-Day Constant. Productiveness of Labour Constant. Intensity of Labour Variable 337
Section 3: Productiveness and Intensity of Labour Constant. Length of the Working-Day Variable 337
Section 4: Simultaneous Variations in the Duration, Productiveness, and Intensity of Labour 338
18. Various Formula for the Rate of Surplus-Value 341

Part VI: Wages

19. The Transformation of the Value (and Respective Price) of Labour-Power into Wages 346
20. Time-Wages 350
21. Piece Wages 356
22. National Differences of Wages 361

Part VII: The Accumulation of Capital

23. Simple Reproduction 366
24. Conversion of Surplus-Value into Capital 375
Section 1: Capitalist Production on a Progressively Increasing Scale. 375

Transition of the Laws of Property that Characterise Production of Commodities into Laws of Capitalist Appropriation
Section 2: Erroneous Conception, by Political Economy, of Reproduction on a Progressively Increasing Scale 380
Section 3: Separation of Surplus-value into Capital and Revenue. The Abstinence Theory 382
Section 4: Circumstances that, Independently of the Proportional Division of Surplus-value into Capital and Revenue, Determine the Amount of Accumulation. Degree of Exploitation of Labour-Power. Productivity of Labour. Growing Difference in Amount between Capital Employed and Capital Consumed. Magnitude of Capital Advanced 385
Section 5: The So-called Labour Fund 390
25. The General Law of Capitalist Accumulation 397
Section 1: The Increased Demand for labour power that Accompanies Accumulation, the Composition of Capital Remaining the Same 397
Section 2: Relative Diminution of the Variable Part of Capital Simultaneously with the Progress of Accumulation and of the Concentration that Accompanies it 401
Section 3: Progressive Production of a Relative surplus population or Industrial Reserve Army 406
Section 4: Different Forms of the Relative surplus population. The General Law of Capitalistic Accumulation 412
Section 5: Illustrations of the General Law of Capitalist Accumulation 416

Part VIII: Primitive Accumulation

26. The Secret of Primitive Accumulation 465
27. Expropriation of the Agricultural Population from the Land 467
28. Bloody Legislation Against the Expropriated, from the End of the 15th Century. Forcing Down of Wages by Acts of Parliament 478
29. Genesis of the Capitalist Farmer 484
30. Reaction of the Agricultural Revolution on Industry. Creation of the Home-Market for Industrial Capital 486
31. Genesis of the Industrial Capitalist 489
32. Historical Tendency of Capitalist Accumulation 496
33. The Modern Theory of Colonisation 498

VOLUME II

BOOK TWO: THE PROCESS OF CIRCULATION OF CAPITAL

Part I: The Metamorphoses of Capital and their Circuits

1. The Circuit of Money Capital 507
Section I. First Stage. M—C[2] 507
Section II. Second Stage. Function of Productive Capital 512
Section III. Third Stage. C'—M' 514
Section IV. The Circuit as a Whole 520
2. The Circuit of Productive Capital 528
Section I. Simple Reproduction 528
Section II. Accumulation and Reproduction on an Extended Scale 537
Section III. Accumulation of Money 539
Section IV. Reserve Fund 540
3. The Circuit of Commodity-Capital 542

4. The Three Formulas of the Circuit 550
5. The Time of Circulation 562
6. The Costs of Circulation 567
Section I. Genuine Costs of Circulation 567
Section II. Costs of Storage 571
Section III. Costs of Transportation 578

Part II: The Turnover of Capital

7. The Turnover Time and the Number of Turnovers 583
8. Fixed Capital and Circulating Capital 585
Section I. Distinctions of Form 585
Section II. Components, Replacements, Repairs and Accumulation of Fixed Capital 592
9. The Aggregate Turnover of Advanced Capital, Cycles of Turnover 601
10. Theories of Fixed and Circulating Capital The Physiocrats and Adam Smith 605
11. Theories of Fixed and Circulating Capital. Ricardo 621
12. The Working Period 629
13. The Time of Production 636
14. The Time of Circulation 642
15. Effect of the Time of Turnover on the Magnitude of Advanced Capital 647
Section I. The Working Period Equal to the Circulation Period 653
Section II. The Working Period Greater than the Period of Circulation 655
Section III. The Working Period Smaller than the Circulation Period 658
Section IV. Conclusion 660
Section V. The Effects of a Change of Prices 664
16. The Turnover of Variable Capital 669
Section I. The Annual Rate of Surplus Value 669
Section II. The Turnover of the Individual Variable Capital 678
Section III. The Turnover of the Variable Capital from the Social Point of View 680
17. The Circulation of Surplus Value 684
Section I. Simple Reproduction 687
Section II. Accumulation and Reproduction on an Extended Scale 699

Part III: The Reproduction and Circulation of the Aggregate Social Capital

18. Introduction 704
Section I. The Subject Investigated 704
Section II. The Role of Money-Capital 705
19. Former Presentations of the Subject 708
Section I. The Physiocrats 708
Section II. Adam Smith 710
Section III. Later Economists 728
20. Simple Reproduction 730
Section I. The Formulation of the Question 730
Section II. The Two Departments of Social Production 732
Section III. Exchange between the Two Departments $I_{(v+s)}$ versus II_c 734
Section IV. Exchange within Department II. Necessities of Life and Articles of Luxury 736
Section V. The Mediation of Exchange by the Circulation of Money 742
Secton VI. The Constant Capital of Department I 748
Section VII. Variable Capital and Surplus-Value in Both Departments 750

Section VIII. The Constant Capital in Both Departments 752
Section IX. A Retrospect to Adam Smith, Storch, and Ramsay 755
Section X. Capital and Revenue: Variable Capital and Wages 757
Section XI. Replacement of the Fixed Capital 764
Section XII. The Reproduction of the Money Material 777
Section XIII. Destutt De Tracy's Theory of Reproduction 784
21. Accumulation and Reproduction on an Extended Scale 790
Section I. Accumulation in Department I 791
Section II. Accumulation in Department II 797
Section III. Schematic Presentation of Accumulation 800
Section IV. Supplementary Remarks 810

VOLUME III

BOOK THREE: THE PROCESS OF CAPITALIST PRODUCTION AS A WHOLE

Part I: The Conversion of Surplus-Value into Profit and of the Rate of Surplus-Value into the Rate of Profit

1. Cost-Price and profit 815
2. The Rate of Profit 823
3. The Relation of the Rate of Profit to the Rate of Surplus-Value 827
4. The Effect of the Turnover on the Rate of Profit 840
5. Economy in the Employment of Constant Capital 845
Section I. In General 845
Section II. Savings in Labour Conditions at the Expense of the Labourers 851
Section III. Economy in the Generation and Transmission of Power, and in Buildings 857
Section IV. Utilisation of the Excretions of Production 860
Section V. Economy Through Inventions 862
6. The Effect of Price Fluctuation 862
Section I. Fluctuations in the Price of Raw Materials, and their Direct Effects on the Rate of Profit 862
Section II. Appreciation, Depreciation, Release and Tie-Up of Capital 865
Section III. General Illustration the Cotton Crisis of 1861-65 873
7. Supplementary Remarks 883

Part II: Conversion of Profit into Average Profit

8. Different Compositions of Capitals in Different Branches of Production and Resulting Differences in Rates of Profit 887
9. Formation of a General Rate of Profit (Average Rate of Profit) and Transformation of the Values of Commodities into Prices of Production 894
10. Equalisation of the General Rate of Profit Through Competition Market-Prices and Market-Values. Surplus-Profit 905
11. Effects of General Wage Fluctuations on Prices of Production 921
12. Supplementary Remarks 923
Section I. Causes Implying a Change in the Price of Production 923
Section II. Price of Production of Commodities of Average Composition 924
Section III. The Capitalist's Grounds for Compensating 925

Part III: The Law of the Tendency of the Rate of Profit to Fall

13. The Law As Such 929
14. Counteracting Influences 941
Section I. Increasing Intensity of Exploitation 941
Section II. Depression of Wages Below the Value of Labour-Power 943
Section III. Cheapening of Elements of Constant Capital 943
Section IV. Relative Over-Population 944
Section V. Foreign Trade 944
Section VI. The Increase of Stock Capital 946
15. Exposition of the Internal Contradictions of the Law 947
Section I. General 947
Section II. Conflict between Expansion of Production and Production of Surplus-Value 950
Section III. Excess Capital and Excess Population 952
Section IV. Supplementary Remarks 958

Part IV: Conversion of Commodity-Capital and Money-Capital into Commercial Capital and Money-Dealing Capital (Merchant's Capital)

16. Commercial Capital 964
17. Commercial Profit 972
18. The Turnover of Merchant's Capital Prices 984
19. Money-Dealing Capital 992
20. Historical Facts about Merchant's Capital 997

Part V: Division of Profit into Interest and Profit of Enterprise. Interest-Bearing Capital

21. Interest-Bearing Capital 1007
22. Division of Profit Rate of Interest Natural Rate of Interest 1018
23. Interest and Profit of Enterprise 1026
24. Externalization of the Relations of Capital in the Form of Interest-Bearing Capital 1039
25. Credit and Fictitious Capital 1044
26. Accumulation of Money-Capital Its Influence on the Interest Rate 1056
27. The Role of Credit in Capitalist Production 1070
28. Medium of Circulation and Capital; Views of Tooke and Fullarton 1075
29. Component Parts of Bank Capital 1087
30. Money-Capital and Real Capital I 1094
31. Money Capital and Real Capital II 1106
32. Money Capital and Real Capital III 1112
33. The Medium of Circulation in the Credit System 1122
34. The Currency Principle and the English Bank Legislation of 1844 1139
35. Precious Metal and Rate of Exchange 1151
Section I. Movement of the Gold Reserve 1151
Section II. The Rate of Exchange 1156
36. Pre-Capitalist Relationships 1169

Part VI: Transformation of Surplus-Profit into Ground-Rent

37. Introduction 1184
38. Differential Rent: General Remarks 1200
39. First Form of Differential Rent (Differential Rent I) 1205
40. Second Form of Differential Rent (Differential Rent II) 1220

41. Differential Rent II First Case: Constant Price of Production 1227
42. Differential Rent II Second Case: Falling Price of Production 1231
Section I. Productivity of the Additional Investment of Capital Remains the Same 1231
Section II. Decreasing Rate of Productivity of the Additional Capital 1236
Section III. Rising Rate of Productivity of the Additional Capital 1237
43. Differential Rent II Third Case: Rising Price of Production 1241
44. Differential Rent Also on the Worst Cultivated Soil 1259
45. Absolute Ground-Rent 1264
46. Building Site Rent. Rent in Mining. Price of Land 1279
47. Genesis of Capitalist Ground-Rent 1284
Section I. Introductory Remarks 1284
Section II. Labour Rent 1289
Section III. Rent In Kind 1291
Section IV. Money-Rent 1293
Section V. Métayage and Peasant Proprietorship of Land Parcels 1296

Part VII: Revenues and their Sources

48. The Trinity Formula 1305
49. Concerning the Analysis of the Process of Production 1315
50. Illusions Created By Competition 1328
51. Distribution Relations and Production Relations 1343
52. Classes 1347

Supplement by Frederick Engels 1349
Section I. Law of Value and Rate of Profit 1349
Section II. The Stock Exchange 1359

VOLUME I

BOOK ONE:
THE PROCESS OF PRODUCTION OF CAPITAL

PART I

COMMODITIES AND MONEY

1

Commodities

Section 1: ***The Two Factors of a Commodity: Use-Value and Value (The Substance of Value and the Magnitude of Value)***

The wealth of those societies in which the capitalist mode of production prevails, presents itself as 'an immense accumulation of commodities,'[1] its unit being a single commodity. Our investigation must therefore begin with the analysis of a commodity.

A commodity is, in the first place, an object outside us, a thing that by its properties satisfies human wants of some sort or another. The nature of such wants, whether, for instance, they spring from the stomach or from fancy, makes no difference.[2] Neither are we here concerned to know how the object satisfies these wants, whether directly as means of subsistence, or indirectly as means of production.

Every useful thing, as iron, paper, &c., may be looked at from the two points of view of quality and quantity. It is an assemblage of many properties, and may therefore be of use in various ways. To discover the various uses of things is the work of history.[3] So also is the establishment of socially-recognized standards of measure for the quantities of these useful objects. The diversity of these measures has its origin partly in the diverse nature of the objects to be measured, partly in convention.

The utility of a thing makes it a use value.[4] But this utility is not a thing of air. Being limited by the physical properties of the commodity, it has no existence apart from that commodity. A commodity, such as iron, corn, or a diamond, is therefore, so far as it is a material thing, a use value, something useful. This property of a commodity is independent of the amount of labour required to appropriate its useful qualities. When treating of use value, we always assume to be dealing with definite quantities, such as dozens of watches, yards of linen, or tons of iron. The use values of commodities furnish the material for a special study, that of the commercial knowledge of commodities.[5] Use values become a reality only by use or consumption: they also constitute the substance of all wealth, whatever may be the social form of that wealth. In the form of society we are about to consider, they are, in addition, the material depositories of exchange value.

Exchange value, at first sight, presents itself as a quantitative relation, as the proportion in which values in use of one sort are exchanged for those of another sort,[6] a relation constantly changing with time and place. Hence exchange value appears to be something accidental and purely relative, and consequently an intrinsic value, *i.e.*, an exchange value that is inseparably connected with, inherent in commodities, seems a contradiction in terms[7] Let us consider the matter a little more closely.

A given commodity, *e.g.*, a quarter of wheat is exchanged for x blacking, y silk, or z gold, &c.—in short, for other commodities in the most different proportions. Instead of one exchange value, the wheat has, therefore, a great many. But since x blacking, y silk, or z gold &c., each represents the exchange value of one quarter of wheat, x blacking, y silk, z gold, &c., must, as exchange values, be replaceable by each other, or equal to each other. Therefore, first: the valid exchange values of a given commodity express something equal; secondly, exchange value, generally, is only the mode of expression, the phenomenal form, of something contained in it, yet distinguishable from it.

Let us take two commodities, *e.g.*, corn and iron. The proportions in which they are exchangeable, whatever those proportions may be, can always be represented by an equation in which a given quantity of corn is equated to some quantity of iron: *e.g.*, 1 quarter corn = x cwt. iron. What does this equation tell us? It tells us that in two different things—in 1 quarter of corn and x cwt. of iron, there exists in equal quantities something common to both. The two things must therefore be equal to a third, which in itself is neither the one nor the other. Each of them, so far as it is exchange value, must therefore be reducible to this third.

A simple geometrical illustration will make this clear. In order to calculate and compare the areas of rectilinear figures, we decompose them into triangles. But the area of the triangle itself is expressed by something totally different from its visible figure, namely, by half the product of the base multiplied by the altitude. In the same way, the exchange values of commodities must be capable of being expressed in terms of something common to them all, of which thing they represent a greater or less quantity.

This common 'something' cannot be either a geometrical, a chemical, or any other natural property of commodities. Such properties claim our attention only in so far as they affect the utility of those commodities, make them use values. But the exchange of commodities is evidently an act characterised by a total abstraction from use value. Then one use value is just as good as another, provided only it be present in sufficient quantity. Or, as old Barbon says,

> one sort of wares are as good as another, if the values be equal. There is no difference or distinction in things of equal value ... An hundred pounds' worth of lead or iron, is of as great value as one hundred pounds' worth of silver or gold.[8]

As use values, commodities are, above all, of different qualities, but as exchange values they are merely different quantities, and consequently do not contain an atom of use value.

If then we leave out of consideration the use value of commodities, they have only one common property left, that of being products of labour. But, even the product of labour itself has undergone a change in our hands. If we make abstraction from its use value, we make abstraction at the same time from the material elements and shapes that make the product a use value; we see in it no longer a table, a house, yarn, or any other useful thing. Its existence as a material thing is put out of sight. Neither can it any longer be regarded as the product of the labour of the joiner, the mason, the spinner, or of any other definite kind of productive labour. Along with the useful qualities of the products themselves, we put out of sight both the useful character of the various kinds of labour embodied in them, and the concrete forms of that labour; there is nothing left but what is common to them all; all are reduced to one and the same sort of labour, human labour in the abstract.

Let us now consider the residue of each of these products; it consists of the same unsubstantial reality in each, a mere congelation of homogeneous human labour, of labour power expended without regard to the mode of its expenditure. All that these things now tell us is, that human labour power has been expended in their production, that human labour is embodied in them. When looked at as crystals of this social substance, common to them all, they are—Values.

We have seen that when commodities are exchanged, their exchange value manifests itself as something totally independent of their use value. But if we abstract from their use value, there remains their Value as defined above. Therefore, the common substance that manifests itself in the exchange value of commodities, whenever they are exchanged, is their value. The progress of our investigation will show that exchange value is the only form in which the value of commodities can manifest itself or be expressed. For the present, however, we have to consider the nature of value independently of this, its form.

A use value, or useful article, therefore, has value only because human labour in the abstract has been embodied or materialised in it. How, then, is the magnitude of this value to be measured? Plainly, by the quantity of the value-creating substance, the labour, contained in the article. The quantity of labour, however, is measured by its duration, and labour time in its turn finds its standard in weeks, days, and hours.

Some people might think that if the value of a commodity is determined by the quantity of labour spent on it, the more idle and unskilful the labourer, the more valuable would his commodity be, because more time would be required in its production. The labour, however, that forms the substance of value, is homogeneous human labour, expenditure of one uniform labour power. The total labour power of society, which is embodied in the sum total of the values of all commodities produced by that society, counts here as one homogeneous mass of human labour power, composed though it be of innumerable individual units. Each of these units is the same as any other, so far as it has the character of the average labour power of society, and takes effect as such; that is, so far as it requires for producing a commodity, no more time than is needed on an average, no more than is socially necessary. The labour time socially necessary is that required to produce an article under the normal conditions of production, and with the average degree of skill and intensity prevalent at the time. The introduction of power-looms into England probably reduced by one-half the labour required to weave a given quantity of yarn into cloth. The hand-loom weavers, as a matter of fact, continued to require the same time as before; but for all that, the product of one hour of their labour represented after the change only half an hour's social labour, and consequently fell to one-half its former value.

We see then that that which determines the magnitude of the value of any article is the amount of labour socially necessary, or the labour time socially necessary for its production.[9] Each individual commodity, in this connexion, is to be considered as an average sample of its class.[10] Commodities, therefore, in which equal quantities of labour are embodied, or which can be produced in the same time, have the same value. The value of one commodity is to the value of any other, as the labour time necessary for the production of the one is to that necessary for the production of the other. 'As values, all commodities are only definite masses of congealed labour time.'[11]

The value of a commodity would therefore remain constant, if the labour time required for its production also remained constant. But the latter changes with every variation in the productiveness of labour. This productiveness is determined by various circumstances, amongst others, by the average amount of skill of the workmen, the state of science, and the degree of its practical application, the social organisation of production, the extent and capabilities of the means of production, and by physical conditions. For example, the same amount of labour in favourable seasons is embodied in 8 bushels of corn, and in unfavourable, only in four. The same labour extracts from rich mines more metal than from poor mines. Diamonds are of very rare occurrence on the earth's surface, and hence their discovery costs, on an average, a great deal of labour time. Consequently much labour is represented in a small compass. Jacob doubts whether gold has ever been paid for at its full value. This applies still more to diamonds. According to Eschwege, the total produce of the Brazilian diamond mines for the eighty years, ending in 1823, had not realised the price of one-and-a-half years' average produce of the sugar and coffee plantations of the same country, although the diamonds cost much more labour, and therefore represented more value. With richer mines, the same quantity of labour would embody itself in more diamonds, and their value would fall. If we could succeed at a small expenditure of labour, in converting carbon into diamonds, their value might fall below that of bricks. In general, the greater the productiveness of labour, the less is the labour time required for the production of an article, the less is the amount of labour crystallised in that article, and the less is its value; and *vice versâ*, the less the productiveness of labour, the greater is the labour time required for the production of an article, and the greater is its value. The value of a commodity, therefore, varies directly as the quantity, and inversely as the productiveness, of the labour incorporated in it.[11(a)]

A thing can be a use value, without having value. This is the case whenever its utility to man is not due to labour. Such are air, virgin soil, natural meadows, &c. A thing can be useful, and the product of human labour, without being a commodity. Whoever directly satisfies his wants with the produce of his own labour, creates, indeed, use values, but not commodities. In order to produce the latter, he must not only produce use values, but use values for others, social use values. (And not only for others, without more. The mediaeval peasant produced quit-rent-corn for his feudal lord and tithe-corn for his parson. But neither the quit-rent-corn nor the tithe-corn became commodities by reason of the fact that they had been produced for others. To become a commodity a product must be transferred to another, whom it will serve as a use value, by means of an exchange.)[12] Lastly nothing can have value, without being an object of utility. If the thing is useless, so is the labour contained in it; the labour does not count as labour, and therefore creates no value.

Section 2: *The Two-Fold Character of the Labour Embodied in Commodities*

At first sight a commodity presented itself to us as a complex of two things—use value and exchange value. Later on, we saw also that labour, too, possesses the same two-fold nature; for, so far as it finds expression in value, it does not possess the same characteristics that belong to it as a creator of use values. I was the first to point out and to examine critically this two-fold nature of the labour contained in commodities. As this point is the pivot on which a clear comprehension of political economy turns, we must go more into detail.

Let us take two commodities such as a coat and 10 yards of linen, and let the former be double the value of the latter, so that, if 10 yards of linen = W, the coat = 2W.

The coat is a use value that satisfies a particular want. Its existence is the result of a special sort of productive activity, the nature of which is determined by its aim, mode of operation, subject, means, and result. The labour, whose utility is thus represented by the value in use of its product, or which manifests itself by making its product a use value, we call useful labour. In this connection we consider only its useful effect.

As the coat and the linen are two qualitatively different use values, so also are the two forms of labour that produce them, tailoring and weaving. Were these two objects not qualitatively different, not produced respectively by labour of different quality, they could not stand to each other in the relation of commodities. Coats are not exchanged for coats, one use value is not exchanged for another of the same kind.

To all the different varieties of values in use there correspond as many different kinds of useful labour, classified according to the order, genus, species, and variety to which they belong in the social division of labour. This division of labour is a necessary condition for the production of commodities, but it does not follow, conversely, that the production of commodities is a necessary condition for the division of labour. In the primitive Indian community there is social division of labour, without production of commodities. Or, to take an example nearer home, in every factory the labour is divided according to a system, but this division is not brought about by the operatives mutually exchanging their individual products. Only such products can become commodities with regard to each other, as result from different kinds of labour, each kind being carried on independently and for the account of private individuals.

To resume, then: In the use value of each commodity there is contained useful labour, *i.e.*, productive activity of a definite kind and exercised with a definite aim. Use values cannot confront each other as commodities, unless the useful labour embodied in them is qualitatively different in each of them. In a community, the produce of which in general takes the form of commodities, *i.e.*, in a community of commodity producers, this qualitative difference between the useful forms of labour that are carried on independently of individual producers, each on their own account, develops into a complex system, a social division of labour.

Anyhow, whether the coat be worn by the tailor or by his customer, in either case it operates as a use value. Nor is the relation between the coat and the labour that produced it altered by the circumstance that tailoring may have become a special trade, an independent branch of the social division of labour. Wherever the want of clothing forced them to it, the human race made clothes for thousands of years, without a single man becoming a tailor. But coats and linen, like every other element of material wealth that is not the spontaneous produce of Nature, must invariably owe their existence to a special productive activity, exercised with a definite aim, an activity that appropriates particular nature-given materials to particular human wants. So far therefore as labour is a creator of use value, is useful labour, it is a necessary condition, independent of all forms of society, for the existence of the human race; it is an eternal nature-imposed necessity, without which there can be no material exchanges between man and Nature, and therefore no life.

The use values, coat, linen, &c., *i.e.*, the bodies of commodities, are combinations of two elements—matter and labour. If we take away the useful labour expended upon them, a material substratum is always left, which is furnished by Nature without the help of man. The latter can work only as Nature does, that is by changing the form of matter.[13] Nay more, in this work of changing the form he is constantly helped by natural forces. We see, then, that labour is not the only source of material wealth, of use values produced by labour. As William Petty puts it, labour is its father and the earth its mother.

Let us now pass from the commodity considered as a use value to the value of commodities.

By our assumption, the coat is worth twice as much as the linen. But this is a mere quantitative difference, which for the present does not concern us. We bear in mind, however, that if the value of the coat is double that of 10 yds of linen, 20 yds of linen must have the same value as one coat. So far as they are values, the coat and the linen are things of a like substance, objective expressions of essentially identical labour. But tailoring and weaving are, qualitatively, different kinds of labour. There are, however, states of society in which one and the same man does tailoring and weaving alternately, in which case these two forms of labour are mere modifications of the labour of the same individual, and not special and fixed functions of different persons, just as the coat which our tailor makes one day, and the trousers which he makes another day, imply only a variation in the labour of one and the same individual. Moreover, we see at a glance that, in our capitalist society, a given portion of human labour is, in accordance with the varying demand, at one time supplied in the form of tailoring, at another in the form of weaving. This change may possibly not take place without friction, but take place it must.

Productive activity, if we leave out of sight its special form, viz., the useful character of the labour, is nothing but the expenditure of human labour power. Tailoring and weaving, though qualitatively different productive activities, are each a productive expenditure of human brains, nerves, and muscles, and in this sense are human labour. They are but two different modes of expending human labour power. Of course, this labour power, which remains the same under all its modifications, must have attained a certain pitch of development before it can be expended in a multiplicity of modes. But the value of a commodity represents human labour in the abstract, the expenditure of human labour in general. And just as in society, a general or a banker plays a great part, but mere man, on the other hand, a very shabby part,[14] so here with mere human labour. It is the expenditure of simple labour power, *i.e.*, of the labour power which, on an average, apart from any special development, exists in the organism of every ordinary individual. Simple average labour, it is true, varies in character in different countries and at different times, but in a particular society it is given. Skilled labour counts only as simple labour intensified, or rather, as multiplied simple labour, a given quantity of skilled being considered equal to a greater quantity of simple labour. Experience shows that this reduction is constantly being made. A commodity may be the product of the most skilled labour, but its value, by equating it to the product of simple unskilled labour, represents a definite quantity of the latter labour alone.[15] The different proportions in which different sorts of labour are reduced to unskilled labour as their standard, are established by a social process that goes on behind the backs of the producers, and, consequently, appear to be fixed by custom. For simplicity's sake, we shall henceforth account every kind of labour to be unskilled, simple labour; by this we do no more than save ourselves the trouble of making the reduction.

Just as, therefore, in viewing the coat and linen as values, we abstract from their different use values, so it is with the labour represented by those values: we disregard the difference between its useful forms, weaving and tailoring. As the use values, coat and linen, are combinations of special productive activities with cloth and yarn, while the values, coat and linen, are, on the other hand, mere homogeneous congelations of undifferentiated labour, so the labour embodied in these latter values does not count by virtue of its productive relation to cloth and yarn, but only as being expenditure of human labour power. Tailoring and weaving are necessary factors in the creation of the use values, coat and linen, precisely because these two kinds of labour are of different qualities; but only in so far as abstraction is made from their special qualities, only in so far as both possess the same quality of being human labour, do tailoring and weaving form the substance of the values of the same articles.

Coats and linen, however, are not merely values, but values of definite magnitude, and according to our assumption, the coat is worth twice as much as the ten yards of linen. Whence this difference in their values? It is owing to the fact that the linen contains only half as much labour as the coat, and consequently, that in the production of the latter, labour power must have been expended during twice the time necessary for the production of the former.

While, therefore, with reference to use value, the labour contained in a commodity counts only qualitatively, with reference to value it counts only quantitatively, and must first be reduced to human labour pure and simple. In the former case, it is a question of How and What, in the latter of How much? How long a time? Since the magnitude of the value of a commodity represents only the quantity of labour embodied in it, it follows that all commodities, when taken in certain proportions, must be equal in value.

If the productive power of all the different sorts of useful labour required for the production of a coat remains unchanged, the sum of the values of the coats produced increases with their number. If one coat represents x days' labour, two coats represent 2x days' labour, and so on. But assume that the duration of the labour necessary for the production of a coat becomes doubled or halved. In the first case one coat is worth as much as two coats were before; in the second case, two coats are only worth as much as one was before, although in both cases one coat renders the same service as before, and the useful labour embodied in it remains of the same quality. But the quantity of labour spent on its production has altered.

An increase in the quantity of use values is an increase of material wealth. With two coats two men can be clothed, with one coat only one man. Nevertheless, an increased quantity of material wealth may correspond to a simultaneous fall in the magnitude of its value. This antagonistic movement has its origin in the two-fold character of labour. Productive power has reference, of course, only to labour of some useful concrete form, the efficacy of any special productive activity during a given time being dependent on its productiveness. Useful labour becomes, therefore, a more or less abundant source of products, in proportion to the rise or fall of its productiveness. On the other hand, no change in this productiveness affects the labour represented by value. Since productive power is an attribute of the concrete useful forms of labour, of course it can no longer have any bearing on that labour, so soon as we make abstraction from those concrete useful forms. However then productive power may vary, the same labour, exercised during equal periods of time, always yields equal amounts of value. But it will yield, during equal periods of time, different quantities of values in use; more, if the productive power rise, fewer, if it fall. The same change in productive power, which increases the fruitfulness of labour, and, in consequence, the quantity of use values produced by that labour, will diminish the total value of this increased quantity of use values, provided such change shorten the total labour time necessary for their production; and *vice versâ*.

On the one hand all labour is, speaking physiologically, an expenditure of human labour power, and in its character of identical abstract human labour, it creates and forms the value of commodities. On the other hand, all labour is the expenditure of human labour power in a special form and with a definite aim, and in this, its character of concrete useful labour, it produces use values.[16]

Section 3: *The Form of Value or Exchange Value*

Commodities come into the world in the shape of use values, articles, or goods, such as iron, linen, corn, &c. This is their plain, homely, bodily form. They are, however, commodities, only because they are something two-fold, both objects of utility, and, at the same time, depositories of value. They manifest themselves therefore as commodities, or have the form of commodities, only in so far as they have two forms, a physical or natural form, and a value form.

The reality of the value of commodities differs in this respect from Dame Quickly, that we don't know 'where to have it.' The value of commodities is the very opposite of the coarse materiality of their substance, not an atom of matter enters into its composition. Turn and examine a single commodity, by itself, as we will, yet in so far as it remains an object of value, it seems impossible to grasp it. If, however, we bear in mind that the value of commodities has a purely social reality, and that they acquire this reality only in so far as they are expressions or embodiments of one identical social substance, viz., human labour, it follows as a matter of course, that value can only manifest itself in the social relation of commodity to commodity. In fact we started from exchange value, or the exchange relation of commodities, in order to get at the value that lies hidden behind it. We must now return to this form under which value first appeared to us.

Every one knows, if he knows nothing else, that commodities have a value form common to them all, and presenting a marked contrast with the varied bodily forms of their use values. I mean their money form. Here, however, a task is set us, the performance of which has never yet even been attempted by *bourgeois* economy, the task of tracing the genesis of this money form, of developing the expression of value implied in the value relation of commodities, from its simplest, almost imperceptible outline, to the dazzling money-form. By doing this we shall, at the same time, solve the riddle presented by money.

The simplest value-relation is evidently that of one commodity to some one other commodity of a different kind. Hence, the relation between the values of two commodities supplies us with the simplest expression of the value of a single commodity.

A. Elementary or Accidental Form f Value

x commodity A = y commodity B, or
x commodity A is worth y commodity B.
20 yards of linen = 1 coat, or
20 Yards of linen are worth 1 coat.

1. *The two poles of the expression of value. Relative form and Equivalent form*

The whole mystery of the form of value lies hidden in this elementary form. Its analysis, therefore, is our real difficulty.

Here two different kinds of commodities (in our example the linen and the coat), evidently play two different parts. The linen expresses its value in the coat; the coat serves as the material in which that value is expressed. The former plays an active, the latter a passive, part. The value of the linen is represented as relative value, or appears in relative form. The coat officiates as equivalent, or appears in equivalent form.

The relative form and the equivalent form are two intimately connected, mutually dependent and inseparable elements of the expression of value; but, at the same time, are mutually exclusive, antagonistic extremes—*i.e.*, poles of the same expression. They are allotted respectively to the two different commodities brought into relation by that expression. It is not possible to express the value of linen in linen. 20 yards of linen = 20 yards of linen is no expression of value. On the contrary, such an equation merely says that 20 yards of linen are nothing else than 20 yards of linen, a definite quantity of the use value linen. The value of the linen can therefore be expressed only relatively—*i.e.*, in some other commodity. The relative form of the value of the linen presupposes, therefore, the presence of some other commodity—here the coat—under the form of an equivalent. On the other hand, the commodity that figures as the equivalent cannot at the same time assume the relative form. That second commodity is not the one whose value is expressed. Its function is merely to serve as the material in which the value of the first commodity is expressed.

No doubt, the expression 20 yards of linen = 1 coat, or 20 yards of linen are worth 1 coat, implies the opposite relation. 1 coat = 20 yards of linen, or 1 coat is worth 20 yards of linen. But, in that case, I must reverse the equation, in order to express the value of the coat relatively; and so soon as I do that the linen becomes the equivalent instead of the coat. A single commodity cannot, therefore, simultaneously assume, in the same expression of value, both forms. The very polarity of these forms makes them mutually exclusive.

Whether, then, a commodity assumes the relative form, or the opposite equivalent form, depends entirely upon its accidental position in the expression of value—that is, upon whether it is the commodity whose value is being expressed or the commodity in which value is being expressed.

2. *The Relative Form of value*

(a) The nature and import of this form

In order to discover how the elementary expression of the value of a commodity lies hidden in the value relation of two commodities, we must, in the first place, consider the latter entirely apart from its quantitative aspect. The usual mode of procedure is generally the reverse, and in the value relation nothing is seen but the proportion between definite quantities of two different sorts of commodities that are considered equal to each other. It is apt to be forgotten that the magnitudes of different things can be compared quantitatively, only when those magnitudes are expressed in terms of the same unit. It is only as expressions of such a unit that they are of the same denomination, and therefore commensurable.[17]

Whether 20 yards of linen = 1 coat or = 20 coats or = x coats—that is, whether a given quantity of linen is worth few or many coats, every such statement implies that the linen and coats, as magnitudes of value, are expressions of the same unit, things of the same kind. Linen = coat is the basis of the equation.

But the two commodities whose identity of quality is thus assumed, do not play the same part. It is only the value of the linen that is expressed. And how? By its reference to the coat as its equivalent, as something that can be exchanged for it. In this relation the coat is the mode of existence of value, is value embodied, for only as such is it the same as the linen. On the other hand, the linen's own value comes to the front, receives independent expression, for it is only as being value that it is comparable with the coat as a thing of equal value, or exchangeable with the coat. To borrow an illustration from chemistry, butyric acid is a different substance from propyl formate. Yet both are made up of the same chemical substances, carbon (C), hydrogen (H), and oxygen (O), and that, too, in like proportions—namely, $C_4H_8O_2$. If now we equate butyric acid to propyl formate, then, in the first place, propyl formate would be, in this relation, merely a form of existence of $C_4H_8O_2$; and in the second place, we should be stating that butyric acid also consists of $C_4H_8O_2$. Therefore, by thus equating the two substances, expression would be given to their chemical composition, while their different physical forms would be neglected.

If we say that, as values, commodities are mere congelations of human labour, we reduce them by our analysis, it is true, to the abstraction, value; but we ascribe to this value no form apart from their bodily form. It is otherwise in the value relation of one commodity to another. Here, the one stands forth in its character of value by reason of its relation to the other.

By making the coat the equivalent of the linen, we equate the labour embodied in the former to that in the latter. Now, it is true that the tailoring, which makes the coat, is concrete labour of a different sort from the weaving which makes the linen. But the act of equating it to the weaving, reduces the tailoring to that which is really equal in the two kinds of labour, to their common character of human labour. In this roundabout way, then, the fact is expressed, that weaving also, in so far as it weaves value, has nothing to distinguish it from tailoring, and, consequently, is abstract human labour. It is the expression of equivalence between different sorts of commodities that alone brings into relief the specific character of value-creating labour, and this it does by actually reducing the different varieties of labour embodied in the different kinds of commodities to their common quality of human labour in the abstract.[18]

There is, however, something else required beyond the expression of the specific character of the labour of which the value of the linen consists. Human labour power in motion, or human labour, creates value, but is not itself value. It becomes value only in its congealed state, when embodied in the form of some object. In order to express the value of the linen as a congelation of human labour, that value must be expressed as having objective existence, as being a something materially different from the linen itself, and yet a something common to the linen and all other commodities. The problem is already solved.

When occupying the position of equivalent in the equation of value, the coat ranks qualitatively as the equal of the linen, as something of the same kind, because it is value. In this position it is a thing in which we see nothing but value, or whose palpable bodily form represents value. Yet the coat itself, the body of the commodity, coat, is a mere use value. A coat as such no more tells us it is value, than does the first piece of linen we take hold of. This shows that when placed in value-relation to the linen, the coat signifies more than when out of that relation, just as many a man strutting about in a gorgeous uniform counts for more than when in mufti.

In the production of the coat, human labour power, in the shape of tailoring, must have been actually expended. Human labour is therefore accumulated in it. In this aspect the coat is a depository of value, but though worn to a thread, it does not let this fact show through. And as equivalent of the linen in the value equation, it exists under this aspect alone, counts therefore as embodied value, as a body that is value. A, for instance, cannot be 'your majesty' to B, unless at the same time majesty in B's eyes assumes the bodily form of A, and, what is more, with every new father of the people, changes its features, hair, and many other things besides.

Hence, in the value equation, in which the coat is the equivalent of the linen, the coat officiates as the form of value. The value of the commodity linen is expressed by the bodily form of the commodity coat, the value of one by the use value of the other. As a use value, the linen is something palpably different from the coat; as value, it is the same as the coat, and now has the appearance of a coat. Thus the linen acquires a value form different from its physical form. The fact that it is value, is made manifest by its equality with the coat, just as the sheep's nature of a Christian is shown in his resemblance to the Lamb of God.

We see, then, all that our analysis of the value of commodities has already told us, is told us by the linen itself, so soon as it comes into communication with another commodity, the coat. Only it betrays its thoughts in that language with which alone it is familiar, the language of commodities. In order to tell us that its own value is created by labour in its abstract character of human labour, it says that the coat, in so far as it is worth as much as the linen, and therefore is value, consists of the same labour as the linen. In order to inform us that its sublime reality as value is not the same as its buckram body, it says that value has the appearance of a coat, and consequently that so far as the linen is value, it and the coat are as like as two peas. We may here remark, that the language of commodities has, besides Hebrew, many other more or less correct dialects. The German 'Wertsein,' to be worth, for instance, expresses in a less striking manner than the Romance verbs 'valere,' 'valer,' 'valoir,' that the equating of commodity B to commodity A, is commodity A's own mode of expressing its value. *Paris vaut bien une messe.* [Paris is certainly worth a mass]

By means, therefore, of the value-relation expressed in our equation, the bodily form of commodity B becomes the value form of commodity A, or the body of commodity B acts as a mirror to the value of commodity A.[19] By putting itself in relation with commodity B, as value *in propriâ personâ*, as the matter of which human labour is made up, the commodity A converts the value in use, B, into the substance in which to express its, A's, own value. The value of A, thus expressed in the use value of B, has taken the form of relative value.

(b) Quantitative determination of Relative value

Every commodity, whose value it is intended to express, is a useful object of given quantity, as 15 bushels of corn, or 100 lbs of coffee. And a given quantity of any commodity contains a definite quantity of human labour. The value form must therefore not only express value generally, but also value in definite quantity. Therefore, in the value relation of commodity A to commodity B, of the linen to the coat, not only is the latter, as value in general, made the equal in quality of the linen, but a definite quantity of coat (1 coat) is made the equivalent of a definite quantity (20 yards) of linen.

The equation, 20 yards of linen = 1 coat, or 20 yards of linen are worth one coat, implies that the same quantity of value substance (congealed labour) is embodied in both; that the two commodities have each cost the same amount of labour or the same quantity of labour time. But the labour time necessary for the production of 20 yards of linen or 1 coat varies with every change in the productiveness of weaving or tailoring. We have now to consider the influence of such changes on the quantitative aspect of the relative expression of value.

I. Let the value of the linen vary,[20] that of the coat remaining constant. If, say in consequence of the exhaustion of flax-growing soil, the labour time necessary for the production of the linen be doubled, the value of the linen will also be doubled. Instead of the equation, 20 yards of linen = 1 coat, we should have 20 yards of linen = 2 coats, since 1 coat would now contain only half the labour time embodied in 20 yards of linen. If, on the other hand, in consequence, say, of improved looms, this labour time be reduced by one-half, the value of the linen would fall by one-half. Consequently, we should have 20 yards of linen = ½ coat. The relative value of commodity A, *i.e.*, its value expressed in commodity B, rises and falls directly as the value of A, the value of B being supposed constant.

II. Let the value of the linen remain constant, while the value of the coat varies. If, under these circumstances, in consequence, for instance, of a poor crop of wool, the labour time necessary for the production of a coat becomes doubled, we have instead of 20 yards of linen = 1 coat, 20 yards of linen = ½ coat. If, on the other hand, the value of the coat sinks by one-half, then 20 yards of linen = 2 coats. Hence, if the value of commodity A remain constant, its relative value expressed in commodity B rises and falls inversely as the value of B.

If we compare the different cases in I and II, we see that the same change of magnitude in relative value may arise from totally opposite causes. Thus, the equation, 20 yards of linen = 1 coat, becomes 20 yards of linen = 2 coats, either, because the value of the linen has doubled, or because the value of the coat has fallen by one-half; and it becomes 20 yards of linen = ½ coat, either, because the value of the linen has fallen by one-half, or because the value of the coat has doubled.

III. Let the quantities of labour time respectively necessary for the production of the linen and the coat vary simultaneously in the same direction and in the same proportion. In this case 20 yards of linen continue equal to 1 coat, however much their values may have altered. Their change of value is seen as soon as they are compared with a third commodity, whose value has remained constant. If the values of all commodities rose or fell simultaneously, and in the same proportion, their relative values would remain unaltered. Their real change of value would appear from the diminished or increased quantity of commodities produced in a given time.

IV. The labour time respectively necessary for the production of the linen and the coat, and therefore the value of these commodities may simultaneously vary in the same direction, but at unequal rates or in opposite directions, or in other ways. The effect of all these possible different variations, on the relative value of a commodity, may be deduced from the results of I, II, and III.

Thus real changes in the magnitude of value are neither unequivocally nor exhaustively reflected in their relative expression, that is, in the equation expressing the magnitude of relative value. The relative value of a commodity may vary, although its value remains constant. Its relative value may remain constant, although its value varies; and finally, simultaneous variations in the magnitude of value and in that of its relative expression by no means necessarily correspond in amount.[21]

3. The Equivalent form of value

We have seen that commodity A (the linen), by expressing its value in the use value of a commodity differing in kind (the coat), at the same time impresses upon the latter a specific form of value, namely that of the equivalent. The commodity linen manifests its quality of having a value by the fact that the coat, without having assumed a value form different from its bodily form, is equated to the linen. The fact that the latter therefore has a value is expressed by saying that the coat is directly exchangeable with it. Therefore, when we say that a commodity is in the equivalent form, we express the fact that it is directly exchangeable with other commodities.

When one commodity, such as a coat, serves as the equivalent of another, such as linen, and coats consequently acquire the characteristic property of being directly exchangeable with linen, we are far from knowing in what proportion the two are exchangeable. The value of the linen being given in magnitude, that proportion depends on the value of the coat. Whether the coat serves as the equivalent and the linen as relative value, or the linen as the equivalent and the coat as relative value, the magnitude of the coat's value is determined, independently of its value form, by the labour time necessary for its production. But whenever the coat assumes in the equation of value, the position of equivalent, its value acquires no quantitative expression; on the contrary, the commodity coat now figures only as a definite quantity of some article.

For instance, 40 yards of linen are worth—what? 2 coats. Because the commodity coat here plays the part of equivalent, because the use-value coat, as opposed to the linen, figures as an embodiment of value, therefore a definite number of coats suffices to express the definite quantity of value in the linen. Two coats may therefore express the quantity of value of 40 yards of linen, but they can never express the quantity of their own value. A superficial observation of this fact, namely, that in the equation of value, the equivalent figures exclusively as a simple quantity of some article, of some use value, has misled Bailey, as also many others, both before and after him, into seeing, in the expression of value, merely a quantitative relation. The truth being, that when a commodity acts as equivalent, no quantitative determination of its value is expressed.

The first peculiarity that strikes us, in considering the form of the equivalent, is this: use value becomes the form of manifestation, the phenomenal form of its opposite, value.

The bodily form of the commodity becomes its value form. But, mark well, that this *quid pro quo* exists in the case of any commodity B, only when some other commodity A enters into a value relation with it, and then only within the limits of this relation. Since no commodity can stand in the relation of equivalent to itself, and thus turn its own bodily shape into the expression of its own value, every commodity is compelled to choose some other commodity for its equivalent, and to accept the use value, that is to say, the bodily shape of that other commodity as the form of its own value.

One of the measures that we apply to commodities as material substances, as use values, will serve to illustrate this point. A sugar-loaf being a body, is heavy, and therefore has weight: but we can neither see nor touch this weight. We then take various pieces of iron, whose weight has been determined beforehand. The iron, as iron, is no more the form of manifestation of weight, than is the sugar-loaf. Nevertheless, in order to express the sugar-loaf as so much weight, we put it into a weight-relation with the iron. In this relation, the iron officiates as a body representing nothing but weight. A certain quantity of iron therefore serves as the measure of the weight of the sugar, and represents, in relation to the sugar-loaf, weight embodied, the form of manifestation of weight. This part is played by the iron only within this relation, into which the sugar or any other body, whose weight has to be determined, enters with the iron. Were they not both heavy, they could not enter into this relation, and the one could therefore not serve as the expression of the weight of the other. When we throw both into the scales, we see in reality, that as weight they are both the same, and that, therefore, when taken in proper proportions, they have the same weight. Just as the substance iron, as a measure of weight, represents in relation to the sugar-loaf weight alone, so, in our expression of value, the material object, coat, in relation to the linen, represents value alone.

Here, however, the analogy ceases. The iron, in the expression of the weight of the sugar-loaf, represents a natural property common to both bodies, namely their weight; but the coat, in the expression of value of the linen, represents a non-natural property of both, something purely social, namely, their value.

Since the relative form of value of a commodity—the linen, for example—expresses the value of that commodity, as being something wholly different from its substance and properties, as being, for instance, coat-like, we see that this expression itself indicates that some social relation lies at the bottom of it. With the equivalent form it is just the contrary. The very essence of this form is that the material commodity itself—the coat—just as it is, expresses value, and is endowed with the form of value by Nature itself. Of course this holds good only so long as the value relation exists, in which the coat stands in the position of equivalent to the linen.[22] Since, however, the properties of a thing are not the result of its relations to other things, but only manifest themselves in such relations, the coat seems to be endowed with its equivalent form, its property of being directly exchangeable, just as much by Nature as it is endowed with the property of being heavy, or the capacity to keep us warm. Hence, the enigmatical character of the equivalent form which escapes the notice of the bourgeois political economist, until this form, completely developed, confronts him in the shape of money. He then seeks to explain away the mystical character of gold and silver, by substituting for them less dazzling commodities, and by reciting, with ever renewed satisfaction, the catalogue of all possible commodities which at one time or another have played the part of equivalent. He has not the least suspicion that the most simple expression of value, such as 20 yds of linen = 1 coat, already propounds the riddle of the equivalent form for our solution.

The body of the commodity that serves as the equivalent, figures as the materialisation of human labour in the abstract, and is at the same time the product of some specifically useful concrete labour. This concrete labour becomes, therefore, the medium for expressing abstract human labour. If on the one hand the coat ranks as nothing but the embodiment of abstract human labour, so, on the other hand, the tailoring which is actually embodied in it, counts as nothing but the form under which that abstract labour is realised. In the expression of value of the linen, the utility of the tailoring consists, not in making clothes, but in making an object, which we at once recognise to be Value, and therefore, to be a congelation of labour, but of labour indistinguishable from that realised in the value of the linen. In order to act as such a mirror of value, the labour of tailoring must reflect nothing besides its own abstract quality of being human labour generally.

In tailoring, as well as in weaving, human labour power is expended. Both, therefore, possess the general property of being human labour, and may, therefore, in certain cases, such as in the production of value, have to be considered under this aspect alone. There is nothing mysterious in this. But, in the expression of value there is a complete turn of the tables. For instance, how is the fact to be expressed that weaving creates the value of the linen, not by virtue of being weaving, as such, but by reason of its general property of being human labour? Simply by opposing to weaving that other particular form of concrete labour (in this instance tailoring), which produces the equivalent of the product of weaving. Just as the coat in its bodily form became a direct expression of value, so now does tailoring, a concrete form of labour, appear as the direct and palpable embodiment of human labour generally.

Hence, the second peculiarity of the equivalent form is, that concrete labour becomes the form under which its opposite, abstract human labour, manifests itself.

But because this concrete labour, tailoring in our case, ranks as, and is directly identified with, undifferentiated human labour, it also ranks as identical with any other sort of labour, and therefore with that embodied in the linen. Consequently, although, like all other commodity-producing labour, it is the labour of private individuals, yet, at the same time, it ranks as labour directly social in its character. This is the reason why it results in a product directly exchangeable with other commodities. We have then a third peculiarity of the equivalent form, namely, that the labour of private individuals takes the form of its opposite, labour directly social in its form.

The two latter peculiarities of the equivalent form will become more intelligible if we go back to the great thinker who was the first to analyse so many forms, whether of thought, society, or Nature, and amongst them also the form of value. I mean Aristotle.

In the first place, he clearly enunciates that the money form of commodities is only the further development of the simple form of value—*i.e.*, of the expression of the value of one commodity in some other commodity taken at random; for he says:

5 beds = 1 house
(χλιναι πεντε αντι οιχιας)

is not to be distinguished from

5 beds = so much money.
(χλιναι πεντε αντι ... οσον αι πεντε χλιναι)

He further sees that the value relation which gives rise to this expression makes it necessary that the house should qualitatively be made the equal of the bed, and that, without such an equalisation, these two clearly different things could not be compared with each other as commensurable quantities. 'Exchange,' he says, 'cannot take place without equality, and equality not without commensurability'.

(ουτ ισοτης μη ουσης συμμετριας). Here, however, he comes to a stop, and gives up the further analysis of the form of value. 'It is, however, in reality, impossible (τη μεν ουν αληθεια αδυνατον), that such unlike things can be commensurable'—*i.e.*, qualitatively equal. Such an equalisation can only be something foreign to their real nature, consequently only 'a makeshift for practical purposes.'

Aristotle therefore, himself, tells us what barred the way to his further analysis; it was the absence of any concept of value. What is that equal something, that common substance, which admits of the value of the beds being expressed by a house? Such a thing, in truth, cannot exist, says Aristotle. And why not? Compared with the beds, the house does represent something equal to them, in so far as it represents what is really equal, both in the beds and the house. And that is—human labour.

There was, however, an important fact which prevented Aristotle from seeing that, to attribute value to commodities, is merely a mode of expressing all labour as equal human labour, and consequently as labour of equal quality. Greek society was founded upon slavery, and had, therefore, for its natural basis, the inequality of men and of their labour powers. The secret of the expression of value, namely, that all kinds of labour are equal and equivalent, because, and so far as they are human labour in general, cannot be deciphered, until the notion of human equality has already acquired the fixity of a popular prejudice. This, however, is possible only in a society in which the great mass of the produce of labour takes the form of commodities, in which, consequently, the dominant relation between man and man, is that of owners of commodities. The brilliancy of Aristotle's genius is shown by this alone, that he discovered, in the expression of the value of commodities, a relation of equality. The peculiar conditions of the society in which he lived, alone prevented him from discovering what, 'in truth,' was at the bottom of this equality.

4. The Elementary Form of value considered as a whole

The elementary form of value of a commodity is contained in the equation, expressing its value relation to another commodity of a different kind, or in its exchange relation to the same. The value of commodity A, is qualitatively expressed, by the fact that commodity B is directly exchangeable with it. Its value is quantitatively expressed by the fact, that a definite quantity of B is exchangeable with a definite quantity of A. In other words, the value of a commodity obtains independent and definite expression, by taking the form of exchange value. When, at the beginning of this chapter, we said, in common parlance, that a commodity is both a use value and an exchange value, we were, accurately speaking, wrong. A commodity is a use value or object of utility, and a value. It manifests itself as this two-fold thing, that it is, as soon as its value assumes an independent form—viz., the form of exchange value. It never assumes this form when isolated, but only when placed in a value or exchange relation with another commodity of a different kind. When once we know this, such a mode of expression does no harm; it simply serves as an abbreviation.

Our analysis has shown, that the form or expression of the value of a commodity originates in the nature of value, and not that value and its magnitude originate in the mode of their expression as exchange value. This, however, is the delusion as well of the mercantilists and their recent revivers, Ferrier, Ganilh,[23] and others, as also of their antipodes, the modern bagmen of Free-trade, such as Bastiat. The mercantilists lay special stress on the qualitative aspect of the expression of value, and consequently on the equivalent form of commodities, which attains its full perfection in money. The modern hawkers of

Free-trade, who must get rid of their article at any price, on the other hand, lay most stress on the quantitative aspect of the relative form of value. For them there consequently exists neither value, nor magnitude of value, anywhere except in its expression by means of the exchange relation of commodities, that is, in the daily list of prices current. Macleod, who has taken upon himself to dress up the confused ideas of Lombard Street in the most learned finery, is a successful cross between the superstitious mercantilists, and the enlightened Free-trade bagmen.

A close scrutiny of the expression of the value of A in terms of B, contained in the equation expressing the value relation of A to B, has shown us that, within that relation, the bodily form of A figures only as a use value, the bodily form of B only as the form or aspect of value. The opposition or contrast existing internally in each commodity between use value and value, is, therefore, made evident externally by two commodities being placed in such relation to each other, that the commodity whose value it is sought to express, figures directly as a mere use value, while the commodity in which that value is to be expressed, figures directly as mere exchange value. Hence, the elementary form of value of a commodity is the elementary form in which the contrast contained in that commodity, between use value and value, becomes apparent.

Every product of labour is, in all states of society, a use value; but it is only at a definite historical epoch in a society's development that such a product becomes a commodity, viz., at the epoch when the labour spent on the production of a useful article becomes expressed as one of the objective qualities of that article, *i.e.*, as its value. It therefore follows that the elementary value form is also the primitive form under which a product of labour appears historically as a commodity, and that the gradual transformation of such products into commodities, proceeds *pari passu* with the development of the value form.

We perceive, at first sight, the deficiencies of the elementary form of value: it is a mere germ, which must undergo a series of metamorphoses before it can ripen into the price form.

The expression of the value of commodity A in terms of any other commodity B, merely distinguishes the value from the use value of A, and therefore places A merely in a relation of exchange with a single different commodity, B; but it is still far from expressing A's qualitative equality, and quantitative proportionality, to all commodities. To the elementary relative value form of a commodity, there corresponds the single equivalent form of one other commodity. Thus, in the relative expression of value of the linen, the coat assumes the form of equivalent, or of being directly exchangeable, only in relation to a single commodity, the linen.

Nevertheless, the elementary form of value passes by an easy transition into a more complete form. It is true that by means of the elementary form, the value of a commodity A, becomes expressed in terms of one, and only one, other commodity. But that one may be a commodity of any kind, coat, iron, corn, or anything else. Therefore, according as A is placed in relation with one or the other, we get for one and the same commodity, different elementary expressions of value.[24] The number of such possible expressions is limited only by the number of the different kinds of commodities distinct from it. The isolated expression of A's value, is therefore convertible into a series, prolonged to any length, of the different elementary expressions of that value.

B. Total or Expanded Form of value

z Com. A = u Com. B or = v Com. C or = w Com. D or = Com. E or = &c. (20 yards of linen = 1 coat or = 10 lbs tea or = 40 lbs. coffee or = 1 quarter corn or = 2 ounces gold or = ½ ton iron or = &c.)

1. The Expanded Relative form of value

The value of a single commodity, the linen, for example, is now expressed in terms of numberless other elements of the world of commodities. Every other commodity now becomes a mirror of the linen's value.[25] It is thus, that for the first time, this value shows itself in its true light as a congelation of undifferentiated human labour. For the labour that creates it, now stands expressly revealed, as labour that ranks equally with every other sort of human labour, no matter what its form, whether tailoring, ploughing, mining, &c., and no matter, therefore, whether it is realised in coats, corn, iron, or gold. The linen, by virtue of the form of its value, now stands in a social relation, no longer with only one other kind of commodity, but with the whole world of commodities. As a commodity, it is a citizen of that world. At the same time, the interminable series of value equations implies, that as regards the value of a commodity, it is a matter of indifference under what particular form, or kind, of use value it appears.

In the first form, 20 yds of linen = 1 coat, it might, for ought that otherwise appears, be pure accident, that these two commodities are exchangeable in definite quantities. In the second form, on the contrary, we perceive at once the background that determines, and is essentially different from, this accidental appearance. The value of the linen remains unaltered in magnitude, whether expressed in coats, coffee, or iron, or in numberless different commodities, the property of as many different owners. The accidental relation between two individual commodity-owners disappears. It becomes plain, that it is not the exchange of commodities which regulates the magnitude of their value; but, on the contrary, that it is the magnitude of their value which controls their exchange proportions.

2. The Particular Equivalent form

Each commodity, such as, coat, tea, corn, iron, &c., figures in the expression of value of the linen, as an equivalent, and, consequently, as a thing that is value. The bodily form of each of these commodities figures now as a particular equivalent form, one out of many. In the same way, the manifold concrete useful kinds of labour, embodied in these different commodities, rank now as so many different forms of the realisation, or manifestation, of undifferentiated human labour.

3. Defects of the Total or Expanded form of Value

In the first place, the relative expression of value is incomplete because the series representing it is interminable. The chain of which each equation of value is a link, is liable at any moment to be lengthened by each new kind of commodity that comes into existence and furnishes the material for a fresh expression of value. In the second place, it is a many-coloured mosaic of disparate and independent expressions of value. And lastly, if, as must be the case, the relative value of each commodity in turn, becomes expressed in this expanded form, we get for each of them a relative value form, different in every case, and consisting of an interminable series of expressions of value. The defects of the expanded relative value form are reflected in the corresponding equivalent form. Since the bodily form of each single commodity is one particular equivalent form amongst numberless others, we have, on the whole, nothing but fragmentary equivalent forms, each excluding the others. In the same way, also, the special, concrete, useful kind of labour embodied in each particular equivalent, is presented only as a particular kind of labour, and therefore not as an exhaustive representative of human labour generally. The latter, indeed, gains adequate manifestation in the totality of its manifold, particular, concrete forms. But, in that case, its expression in an infinite series is ever incomplete and deficient in unity.

The expanded relative value form is, however, nothing but the sum of the elementary relative expressions or equations of the first kind, such as:

20 yards of linen = 1 coat
20 yards of linen = 10 lbs of tea, etc.

Each of these implies the corresponding inverted equation,

1 coat = 20 yards of linen
10 lbs of tea = 20 yards of linen, etc.

In fact, when a person exchanges his linen for many other commodities, and thus expresses its value in a series of other commodities, it necessarily follows, that the various owners of the latter exchange them for the linen, and consequently express the value of their various commodities in one and the same third commodity, the linen. If then, we reverse the series, 20 yards of linen = 1 coat or = 10 lbs of tea, etc., that is to say, if we give expression to the converse relation already implied in the series, we get,

C. The General Form of Value

1	coat	= 20 yards of linen
10	lbs of tea	
40	lbs of coffee	
1	quarter of corn	
2	ounces of gold	
½	a ton of iron	
x	Commodity A, etc.	

1. The altered character of the form of value

All commodities now express their value (1) in an elementary form, because in a single commodity; (2) with unity, because in one and the same commodity. This form of value is elementary and the same for all, therefore general.

The forms A and B were fit only to express the value of a commodity as something distinct from its use value or material form.

The first form, A, furnishes such equations as the following:—1 coat = 20 yards of linen, 10 lbs of tea = ½ a ton of iron. The value of the coat is equated to linen, that of the tea to iron. But, to be equated to linen, and again to iron, is to be as different as are linen and iron. This form, it is plain, occurs practically only in the first beginning, when the products of labour are converted into commodities by accidental and occasional exchanges.

The second form, B, distinguishes, in a more adequate manner than the first, the value of a commodity from its use value, for the value of the coat is there placed in contrast under all possible shapes with the bodily form of the coat; it is equated to linen, to iron, to tea, in short, to everything else, only not to itself, the coat. On the other hand, any general expression of value common to all is directly excluded; for, in the equation of value of each commodity, all other commodities now appear only under the form of equivalents. The expanded form of value comes into actual existence for the first time so soon as a particular product of labour, such as cattle, is no longer exceptionally, but habitually, exchanged for various other commodities.

The third and lastly developed form expresses the values of the whole world of commodities in terms of a single commodity set apart for the purpose, namely, the linen, and thus represents to us their values by means of their equality with linen. The value of every commodity is now, by being equated to linen, not only differentiated from its own use value, but from all other use values generally, and is, by that very fact, expressed as that which is common to all commodities. By this form, commodities are, for the first time, effectively brought into relation with one another as values, or made to appear as exchange values.

The two earlier forms either express the value of each commodity in terms of a single commodity of a different kind, or in a series of many such commodities. In both cases, it is, so to say, the special business of each single commodity to find an expression for its value, and this it does without the help of the others. These others, with respect to the former, play the passive parts of equivalents. The general form of value, C, results from the joint action of the whole world of commodities, and from that alone. A commodity can acquire a general expression of its value only by all other commodities, simultaneously with it, expressing their values in the same equivalent; and every new commodity must follow suit. It thus becomes evident that since the existence of commodities as values is purely social, this social existence can be expressed by the totality of their social relations alone, and consequently that the form of their value must be a socially recognised form.

All commodities being equated to linen now appear not only as qualitatively equal as values generally, but also as values whose magnitudes are capable of comparison. By expressing the magnitudes of their values in one and the same material, the linen, those magnitudes are also compared with each other. For instance, 10 lbs of tea = 20 yards of linen, and 40 lbs of coffee = 20 yards of linen. Therefore, 10 lbs of tea = 40 lbs of coffee. In other words, there is contained in 1 lb of coffee only one-fourth as much substance of value—labour—as is contained in 1 lb of tea.

The general form of relative value, embracing the whole world of commodities, converts the single commodity that is excluded from the rest, and made to play the part of equivalent—here the linen—into the universal equivalent. The bodily form of the linen is now the form assumed in common by the values of all commodities; it therefore becomes directly exchangeable with all and every of them. The substance linen becomes the visible incarnation, the social chrysalis state of every kind of human labour. Weaving, which is the labour of certain private individuals producing a particular article, linen, acquires in consequence a social character, the character of equality with all other kinds of labour. The innumerable equations of which the general form of value is composed, equate in turn the labour embodied in the linen to that embodied in every other commodity, and they thus convert weaving into the general form of manifestation of undifferentiated human labour. In this manner, the labour realised in the values of commodities is presented not only under its negative aspect, under which abstraction is made from every concrete form and useful property of actual work, but its own positive nature is made to reveal itself expressly. The general value form is the reduction of all kinds of actual labour to their common character of being human labour generally, of being the expenditure of human labour power.

The general value form, which represents all products of labour as mere congelations of undifferentiated human labour, shows by its very structure that it is the social resumé of the world of commodities. That form consequently makes it indisputably evident that in the world of commodities the character possessed by all labour of being *human* labour constitutes its specific social character.

2. The Interdependent Development of the Relative Form of Value, and of the Equivalent Form

The degree of development of the relative form of value corresponds to that of the equivalent form. But we must bear in mind that the development of the latter is only the expression and result of the development of the former.

The primary or isolated relative form of value of one commodity converts some other commodity into an isolated equivalent. The expanded form of relative value, which is the expression of the value of one commodity in terms of all other commodities, endows those other commodities with the character of particular equivalents differing in kind. And lastly, a particular kind of commodity acquires the character of universal equivalent, because all other commodities make it the material in which they uniformly express their value.

The antagonism between the relative form of value and the equivalent form, the two poles of the value form, is developed concurrently with that form itself.

The first form, 20 yds of linen = one coat, already contains this antagonism, without as yet fixing it. According as we read this equation forwards or backwards, the parts played by the linen and the coat are different. In the one case the relative value of the linen is expressed in the coat, in the other case the relative value of the coat is expressed in the linen. In this first form of value, therefore, it is difficult to grasp the polar contrast.

Form B shows that only one single commodity at a time can completely expand its relative value, and that it acquires this expanded form only because, and in so far as, all other commodities are, with respect to it, equivalents. Here we cannot reverse the equation, as we can the equation 20 yds of linen = 1 coat, without altering its general character, and converting it from the expanded form of value into the general form of value.

Finally, the form C gives to the world of commodities a general social relative form of value, because, and in so far as, thereby all commodities, with the exception of one, are excluded from the equivalent form. A single commodity, the linen, appears therefore to have acquired the character of direct exchangeability with every other commodity because, and in so far as, this character is denied to every other commodity.[26]

The commodity that figures as universal equivalent, is, on the other hand, excluded from the relative value form. If the linen, or any other commodity serving as universal equivalent, were, at the same time, to share in the relative form of value, it would have to serve as its own equivalent. We should then have 20 yds of linen = 20 yds of linen; this tautology expresses neither value, nor magnitude of value. In order to express the relative value of the universal equivalent, we must rather reverse the form C. This equivalent has no relative form of value in common with other commodities, but its value is relatively expressed by a never ending series of other commodities. Thus, the expanded form of relative value, or form B, now shows itself as the specific form of relative value for the equivalent commodity.

3. Transition from the General form of value to the Money form

The universal equivalent form is a form of value in general. It can, therefore, be assumed by any commodity. On the other hand, if a commodity be found to have assumed the universal equivalent form (form C), this is only because and in so far as it has been excluded from the rest of all other commodities as their equivalent, and that by their own act. And from the moment that this exclusion becomes finally restricted to one particular commodity, from that moment only, the general form of relative value of the world of commodities obtains real consistence and general social validity.

The particular commodity, with whose bodily form the equivalent form is thus socially identified, now becomes the money commodity, or serves as money. It becomes the special social function of that commodity, and consequently its social monopoly, to play within the world of commodities the part of the universal equivalent. Amongst the commodities which, in form B, figure as particular equivalents of the linen, and, in form C, express in common their relative values in linen, this foremost place has been attained by one in particular—namely, gold. If, then, in form C we replace the linen by gold, we get,

D. The Money-Form

20	yards of linen	=	
1	coat	=	
10	lbs of tea	=	
40	lbs of coffee	=	= 2 ounces of gold
1	quarter of corn	=	
2	ounces of gold	=	
½	a ton of iron	=	
x	Commodity A	=	

In passing from form **A** to form **B**, and from the latter to form **C**, the changes are fundamental. On the other hand, there is no difference between forms C and D, except that, in the latter, gold has assumed the equivalent form in the place of linen. Gold is in form D, what linen was in form C—the universal equivalent. The progress consists in this alone, that the character of direct and universal exchangeability—in other words, that the universal equivalent form—has now, by social custom, become finally identified with the substance, gold.

Gold is now money with reference to all other commodities only because it was previously, with reference to them, a simple commodity. Like all other commodities, it was also capable of serving as an equivalent, either as simple equivalent in isolated exchanges, or as particular equivalent by the side of others. Gradually it began to serve, within varying limits, as universal equivalent. So soon as it monopolises this position in the expression of value for the world of commodities, it becomes the money commodity, and then, and not till then, does form **D** become distinct from form **C**, and the general form of value become changed into the money form.

The elementary expression of the relative value of a single commodity, such as linen, in terms of the commodity, such as gold, that plays the part of money, is the price form of that commodity. The price form of the linen is therefore

> 20 yards of linen = 2 ounces of gold, or, if 2 ounces of gold when coined are £2, 20 yards of linen = £2.

The difficulty in forming a concept of the money form, consists in clearly comprehending the universal equivalent form, and as a necessary corollary, the general form of value, form C. The latter is deducible from form **B**, the expanded form of value, the essential component element of which, we saw, is form A, 20 yards of linen = 1 coat or x commodity A = y commodity **B**. The simple commodity form is therefore the germ of the money form.

Section 4: *The Fetishism of Commodities and the Secret Thereof*

A commodity appears, at first sight, a very trivial thing, and easily understood. Its analysis shows that it is, in reality, a very queer thing, abounding in metaphysical subtleties and theological niceties. So far as it is a value in use, there is nothing mysterious about it, whether we consider it from the point of view that by its properties it is capable of satisfying human wants, or from the point that those properties are the product of human labour. It is as clear as noon-day, that man, by his industry, changes the forms of the materials furnished by Nature, in such a way as to make them useful to him. The form of wood, for instance, is altered, by making a table out of it. Yet, for all that, the table continues to be that common, every-day thing, wood. But, so soon as it steps forth as a commodity, it is changed into something transcendent. It not only stands with its feet on the ground, but, in relation to all other commodities, it stands on its head, and evolves out of its wooden brain grotesque ideas, far more wonderful than 'table-turning' ever was.[26(a)]

The mystical character of commodities does not originate, therefore, in their use value. Just as little does it proceed from the nature of the determining factors of value. For, in the first place, however varied the useful kinds of labour, or productive activities, may be, it is a physiological fact, that they are functions of the human organism, and that each such function, whatever may be its nature or form, is essentially the expenditure of human brain, nerves, muscles, &c. Secondly, with regard to that which forms the ground-work for the quantitative determination of value, namely, the duration of that expenditure, or the quantity of labour, it is quite clear that there is a palpable difference between its quantity and quality. In all states of society, the labour time that it costs to produce the means of subsistence, must necessarily be an object of interest to mankind, though not of equal interest in different stages of development.[27] And lastly, from the moment that men in any way work for one another, their labour assumes a social form.

Whence, then, arises the enigmatical character of the product of labour, so soon as it assumes the form of commodities? Clearly from this form itself. The equality of all sorts of human labour is expressed objectively by their products all being equally values; the measure of the expenditure of labour power by the duration of that expenditure, takes the form of the quantity of value of the products of labour; and finally the mutual relations of the producers, within which the social character of their labour affirms itself, take the form of a social relation between the products.

A commodity is therefore a mysterious thing, simply because in it the social character of men's labour appears to them as an objective character stamped upon the product of that labour; because the relation of the producers to the sum total of their own labour is presented to them as a social relation, existing not between themselves, but between the products of their labour. This is the reason why the products of labour become commodities, social things whose qualities are at the same time perceptible and imperceptible by the senses. In the same way, the light from an object is perceived by us not as the subjective excitation of our optic nerve, but as the objective form of something outside the eye itself. But, in the act of seeing, there is at all events, an actual passage of light from one thing to another, from the external object to the eye. There is a physical relation between physical things. But it is different with commodities. There, the existence of the things *quâ* commodities, and the value relation between the products of labour which stamps them as commodities, have absolutely no connection with their physical properties and with the material relations arising therefrom. There it is a definite social relation between men, that assumes, in their eyes, the fantastic form of a relation between things. In order, therefore, to find an analogy, we must have recourse to the mist-enveloped regions of the religious world. In that world the productions of the human brain appear as independent beings endowed with life, and entering into relation both with one another and the human race. So it is in the world of commodities with the products of men's hands. This, I call, the Fetishism which attaches itself to the products of labour, so soon as they are produced as commodities, and which is therefore inseparable from the production of commodities.

This Fetishism of commodities has its origin, as the foregoing analysis has already shown, in the peculiar social character of the labour that produces them.

As a general rule, articles of utility become commodities, only because they are products of the labour of private individuals or groups of individuals who carry on their work independently of each other. The sum total of the labour of all these private individuals forms the aggregate labour of society. Since the producers do not come into social contact with each other until they exchange their products, the specific social character of each producer's labour does not show itself except in the act of exchange. In other words, the labour of the individual asserts itself as a part of the labour of society, only by means of the relations which the act of exchange establishes directly between the products, and indirectly, through them, between the producers. To the latter, therefore, the relations connecting the labour of one individual with that of the rest appear, not as direct social relations between individuals at work, but as what they really are, material relations between persons and social relations between things. It is only by being exchanged that the products of labour acquire, as values, one uniform social status, distinct from their varied forms of existence as objects of utility. This division of a product into a useful thing and a value becomes practically important, only when exchange has acquired such an extension that useful articles are produced for the purpose of being exchanged, and their character as values has therefore to be taken into account, beforehand, during production. From this moment the labour of the individual producer acquires socially a two-fold character. On the one hand, it must, as a definite useful kind of labour, satisfy a definite social want, and thus hold its place as part and parcel of the collective labour of all, as a branch of a social division of labour that has sprung up spontaneously. On the other hand, it can satisfy the manifold wants of the individual producer himself, only in so far as the mutual exchangeability of all kinds of useful private labour is an established social fact, and therefore the private useful labour of each producer ranks on an equality with that of all others. The equalisation of the most different kinds of labour can be the result only of an abstraction from their inequalities, or of reducing them to their common denominator, viz. expenditure of human labour power or human labour in the abstract. The two-fold social character of the labour of the individual appears to him, when reflected in his brain, only under those forms which are impressed upon that labour in every-day practice by the exchange of products. In this way, the character that his own labour possesses of being socially useful takes the form of the condition, that the product must be not only useful, but useful for others, and the social character that his particular labour has of being the equal of all other particular kinds of labour, takes the form that all the physically different articles that are the products of labour, have one common quality, viz., that of having value.

Hence, when we bring the products of our labour into relation with each other as values, it is not because we see in these articles the material receptacles of homogeneous human labour. Quite the contrary: whenever, by an exchange, we equate as values our different products, by that very act, we also equate, as human labour, the different kinds of labour expended upon them. We are not aware of this, nevertheless we do it.[28] Value, therefore, does not stalk about with a label describing what it is. It is value, rather, that converts every product into a social hieroglyphic. Later on, we try to decipher the hieroglyphic, to get behind the secret of our own social products; for to stamp an object of utility as a value, is just as much a social product as language. The recent scientific discovery, that the products of labour, so far as they are values, are but material expressions of the human labour spent in their production, marks, indeed, an epoch in the history of the development of the human race, but, by no means, dissipates the mist through which the social character of labour appears to us to be an objective character of the products themselves. The fact, that in the particular form of production with which we are dealing, viz., the production of commodities, the specific social character of private labour carried on independently, consists in the equality of every kind of that labour, by virtue of its being human labour, which character, therefore, assumes in the product the form of value—this fact appears to the producers, notwithstanding the discovery above referred to, to be just as real and final, as the fact, that, after the discovery by science of the component gases of air, the atmosphere itself remained unaltered.

What, first of all, practically concerns producers when they make an exchange, is the question, how much of some other product they get for their own? In what proportions the products are exchangeable? When these proportions have, by custom, attained a certain stability, they appear to result from the nature of the products, so that, for instance, one ton of iron and two ounces of gold appear as naturally to be of equal value as a pound of gold and a pound of iron in spite of their different physical and chemical qualities appear to be of equal weight. The character of having value, when once impressed upon products, obtains fixity only by reason of their acting and re-acting upon each other as quantities of value. These quantities vary continually, independently of the will, foresight and action of the producers. To them, their own social action takes the form of the action of objects, which rule the producers instead of being ruled by them. It requires a fully developed production of commodities before, from accumulated experience alone, the scientific conviction springs up, that all the different kinds of private labour, which are carried on independently of each other, and yet as spontaneously developed branches of the social division of labour, are continually being reduced to the quantitative proportions in which society requires them. And why? Because, in the midst of all the accidental and ever fluctuating exchange relations between the products, the labour time socially necessary for their production forcibly asserts itself like an over-riding law of Nature. The law of gravity thus asserts itself when a house falls about our ears.[29] The determination of the magnitude of value by labour time is therefore a secret, hidden under the apparent fluctuations in the relative values of commodities. Its discovery, while removing all appearance of mere accidentality from the determination of the magnitude of the values of products, yet in no way alters the mode in which that determination takes place.

Man's reflections on the forms of social life, and consequently, also, his scientific analysis of those forms, take a course directly opposite to that of their actual historical development. He begins, *post festum*, with the results of the process of development ready to hand before him. The characters that stamp products as commodities, and whose establishment is a necessary preliminary to the circulation of commodities, have already acquired the stability of natural, self-understood forms of social life, before man seeks to decipher, not their historical character, for in his eyes they are immutable, but their meaning. Consequently it was the analysis of the prices of commodities that alone led to the determination of the magnitude of value, and it was the common expression of all commodities in money that alone led to the establishment of their characters as values. It is, however, just this ultimate money form of the world of commodities that actually conceals, instead of disclosing, the social character of private labour, and the social relations between the individual producers. When I state that coats or boots stand in a relation to linen, because it is the universal incarnation of abstract human labour, the absurdity of the statement is self-evident. Nevertheless, when the producers of coats and boots compare those articles with linen, or, what is the same thing, with gold or silver, as the universal equivalent, they express the relation between their own private labour and the collective labour of society in the same absurd form.

The categories of bourgeois economy consist of such like forms. They are forms of thought expressing with social validity the conditions and relations of a definite, historically determined mode of production, viz., the production of commodities. The whole mystery of commodities, all the magic and necromancy that surrounds the products of labour as long as they take the form of commodities, vanishes therefore, so soon as we come to other forms of production.

Since Robinson Crusoe's experiences are a favourite theme with political economists,[30] let us take a look at him on his island. Moderate though he be, yet some few wants he has to satisfy, and must therefore do a little useful work of various sorts, such as making tools and furniture, taming goats, fishing and hunting. Of his prayers and the like we take no account, since they are a source of pleasure to him, and he looks upon them as so much recreation. In spite of the variety of his work, he knows that his labour, whatever its form, is but the activity of one and the same Robinson, and consequently, that it consists of nothing but different modes of human labour. Necessity itself compels him to apportion his time accurately between his different kinds of work. Whether one kind occupies a greater space in his general activity than another, depends on the difficulties, greater or less as the case may be, to be overcome in attaining the useful effect aimed at. This, our friend Robinson, soon learns by experience, and having rescued a watch, ledger, and pen and ink from the wreck, commences, like a true-born Briton, to keep a set of books. His stock-book contains a list of the objects of utility that belong to him, of the operations necessary for their production; and lastly, of the labour time that definite quantities of those objects have, on an average, cost him. All the relations between Robinson and the objects that form this wealth of his own creation, are here so simple and clear as to be intelligible without exertion, even to Mr Sedley Taylor. And yet those relations contain all that is essential to the determination of value.

Let us now transport ourselves from Robinson's island bathed in light to the European middle ages shrouded in darkness. Here, instead of the independent man, we find everyone dependent, serfs and lords, vassals and suzerains, laymen and clergy. Personal dependence here characterises the social relations of production just as much as it does the other spheres of life organised on the basis of that production. But for the very reason that personal dependence forms the ground-work of society, there is no necessity for labour and its products to assume a fantastic form different from their reality. They take the shape, in the transactions of society, of services in kind and payments in kind. Here, the particular and natural form of labour, and not, as in a society based on production of commodities, its general abstract form is the immediate social form of labour. Compulsory labour is just as properly measured by time, as commodity-producing labour; but every serf knows that what he expends in the service of his lord, is a definite quantity of his own personal labour power. The tithe to be rendered to the priest is more matter of fact than his blessing. No matter, then, what we may think of the parts played by the different classes of people themselves in this society, the social relations between individuals in the performance of their labour, appear at all events as their own mutual personal relations, and are not disguised under the shape of social relations between the products of labour.

For an example of labour in common or directly associated labour, we have no occasion to go back to that spontaneously developed form which we find on the threshold of the history of all civilised races.[31] We have one close at hand in the patriarchal industries of a peasant family, that produces corn, cattle, yarn, linen, and clothing for home use. These different articles are, as regards the family, so many products of its labour, but as between themselves, they are not commodities. The different kinds of labour, such as tillage, cattle tending, spinning, weaving and making clothes, which result in the various products, are in themselves, and such as they are, direct social functions, because functions of the family, which, just as much as a society based on the production of commodities, possesses a spontaneously developed system of division of labour. The distribution of the work within the family, and the regulation of the labour time of the several members, depend as well upon differences of age and sex as upon natural conditions varying with the seasons. The labour power of each individual, by its very nature, operates in this case merely as a definite portion of the whole labour power of the family, and therefore, the measure of the expenditure of individual labour power by its duration, appears here by its very nature as a social character of their labour.

Let us now picture to ourselves, by way of change, a community of free individuals, carrying on their work with the means of production in common, in which the labour power of all the different individuals is consciously applied as the combined labour power of the community. All the characteristics of Robinson's labour are here repeated, but with this difference, that they are social, instead of individual. Everything produced by him was exclusively the result of his own personal labour, and therefore simply an object of use for himself. The total product of our community is a social product. One portion serves as fresh means of production and remains social. But another portion is consumed by the members as means of subsistence. A distribution of this portion amongst them is consequently necessary. The mode of this distribution will vary with the productive organisation of the community, and the degree of historical development attained by the producers. We will assume, but merely for the sake of a parallel with the production of commodities, that the share of each individual producer in the means of subsistence is determined by his labour time. Labour time would, in that case, play a double part. Its apportionment in accordance with a definite social plan maintains the proper proportion between the different kinds of work to be done and the various wants of the community. On the other hand, it also serves as a measure of the portion of the common labour borne by each individual, and of his share in the part of the total product destined for individual consumption. The social relations of the individual producers, with regard both to their labour and to its products, are in this case perfectly simple and intelligible, and that with regard not only to production but also to distribution.

The religious world is but the reflex of the real world.[note] And for a society based upon the production of commodities, in which the producers in general enter into social relations with one another by treating their products as commodities and values, whereby they reduce their individual private labour to the standard of homogeneous human labour—for such a society, Christianity with its *cultus* of abstract man, more especially in its bourgeois developments, Protestantism, Deism, &c., is the most fitting form of religion. In the ancient Asiatic and other ancient modes of production, we find that the conversion of products into commodities, and therefore the conversion of men into producers of commodities, holds a subordinate place, which, however, increases in importance as the primitive communities approach nearer and nearer to their dissolution. Trading nations, properly so called, exist in the ancient world only in its interstices, like the gods of Epicurus in the Intermundia, or like Jews in the pores of Polish society. Those ancient social organisms of production are, as compared with bourgeois society, extremely simple and transparent. But they are founded either on the immature development of man individually, who has not yet severed the umbilical cord that unites him with his fellowmen in a primitive tribal community, or upon direct relations of subjection. They can arise and exist only when the development of the productive power of labour has not risen beyond a low stage, and when, therefore, the social relations within the sphere of material life, between man and man, and between man and Nature, are correspondingly narrow. This narrowness is reflected in the ancient worship of Nature, and in the other elements of the popular religions. The religious reflex of the real world can, in any case, only then finally vanish, when the practical relations of every-day life offer to man none but perfectly intelligible and reasonable relations with regard to his fellowmen and to Nature.

The life-process of society, which is based on the process of material production, does not strip off its mystical veil until it is treated as production by freely associated men, and is consciously regulated by them in accordance with a settled plan. This, however, demands for society a certain material ground-work or set of conditions of existence which in their turn are the spontaneous product of a long and painful process of development.

Political Economy has indeed analysed, however incompletely,[32] value and its magnitude, and has discovered what lies beneath these forms. But it has never once asked the question why labour is represented by the value of its product and labour time by the magnitude of that value.[33] These formulæ, which bear it stamped upon them in unmistakable letters that they belong to a state of society, in which the process of production has the mastery over man, instead of being controlled by him, such formulæ appear to the bourgeois intellect to be as much a self-evident necessity imposed by Nature as productive labour itself. Hence forms of social production that preceded the bourgeois form, are treated by the bourgeoisie in much the same way as the Fathers of the Church treated pre-Christian religions.[34]

To what extent some economists are misled by the Fetishism inherent in commodities, or by the objective appearance of the social characteristics of labour, is shown, amongst other ways, by the dull and tedious quarrel over the part played by Nature in the formation of exchange value. Since exchange value is a definite social manner of expressing the amount of labour bestowed upon an object, Nature has no more to do with it, than it has in fixing the course of exchange.

The mode of production in which the product takes the form of a commodity, or is produced directly for exchange, is the most general and most embryonic form of bourgeois production. It therefore makes its appearance at an early date in history, though not in the same predominating and characteristic manner as now-a-days. Hence its Fetish character is comparatively easy to be seen through. But when we come to more concrete forms, even this appearance of simplicity vanishes. Whence arose the illusions of the monetary system? To it gold and silver, when serving as money, did not represent a social relation between producers, but were natural objects with strange social properties. And modern economy, which looks down with such disdain on the monetary system, does not its superstition come out as clear as noon-day, whenever it treats of capital? How long is it since economy discarded the physiocratic illusion, that rents grow out of the soil and not out of society?

But not to anticipate, we will content ourselves with yet another example relating to the commodity form. Could commodities themselves speak, they would say: Our use value may be a thing that interests men. It is no part of us as objects. What, however, does belong to us as objects, is our value. Our natural intercourse as commodities proves it. In the eyes of each other we are nothing but exchange values. Now listen how those commodities speak through the mouth of the economist.

'Value'—(*i.e.*, exchange value) 'is a property of things, riches'—(*i.e.*, use value) 'of man. Value, in this sense, necessarily implies exchanges, riches do not.'[35] 'Riches' (use value) 'are the attribute of men, value is the attribute of commodities. A man or a community is rich, a pearl or a diamond is valuable...' A pearl or a diamond is valuable as a pearl or a diamond.[36]

So far no chemist has ever discovered exchange value either in a pearl or a diamond. The economic discoverers of this chemical element, who by-the-bye lay special claim to critical acumen, find however that the use value of objects belongs to them independently of their material properties, while their value, on the other hand, forms a part of them as objects. What confirms them in this view, is the peculiar circumstance that the use value of objects is realised without exchange, by means of a direct relation between the objects and man, while, on the other hand, their value is realised only by exchange, that is, by means of a social process. Who fails here to call to mind our good friend, Dogberry, who informs neighbour Seacoal, that,

'To be a well-favoured man is the gift of fortune; but reading and writing comes by Nature.'[37]

Notes

1. Karl Marx, 'Zur Kritik der Politischen Oekonomie.' Berlin, 1859, p. 3.
2. 'Desire implies want, it is the appetite of the mind, and as natural as hunger to the body... The greatest number (of things) have their value from supplying the wants of the mind.' Nicholas Barbon: 'A Discourse Concerning Coining the New Money Lighter. In Answer to Mr Locke's Considerations, &c.', London, 1696, pp. 2, 3.
3. 'Things have an intrinsick vertue' (this is Barbon's special term for value in use) 'which in all places have the same vertue; as the loadstone to attract iron' (l.c., p. 6). The property which the magnet possesses of attracting iron, became of use only after by means of that property the polarity of the magnet had been discovered.
4. 'The natural worth of anything consists in its fitness to supply the necessities, or serve the

conveniencies of human life.' (John Locke, 'Some Considerations on the Consequences of the Lowering of Interest, 1691,' in Works Edit. Lond., 1777, Vol. II., p. 28.) In English writers of the 17th century we frequently find 'worth' in the sense of value in use, and 'value' in the sense of exchange value. This is quite in accordance with the spirit of a language that likes to use a Teutonic word for the actual thing, and a Romance word for its reflexion.

5. In bourgeois societies the economic *fictio juris* prevails, that every one, as a buyer, possesses an encyclopedic knowledge of commodities.
6. 'La valeur consiste dans le rapport d'échange qui se trouve entre telle chose et telle autre entre telle mesure d'une production et telle mesure d'une autre.' ['Value consists in the exchange relation between one thing and another, between a given amount of one product and a given amount of another'] (Le Trosne: 'De l'Intérêt Social.' Physiocrates, Ed. Daire. Paris, 1846. p. 889.)
7. 'Nothing can have an intrinsick value.' (N. Barbon, l.c., p. 6); or as Butler says—'The value of a thing is just as much as it will bring.'
8. N. Barbon, l.c., p. 53 and 7.
9. 'The value of them (the necessaries of life), when they are exchanged the one for another, is regulated by the quantity of labour necessarily required, and commonly taken in producing them.' ('Some Thoughts on the Interest of Money in General, and Particularly in the Publick Funds, &c.' Lond., p. 36) This remarkable anonymous work written in the last century, bears no date. It is clear, however, from internal evidence that it appeared in the reign of George II, about 1739 or 1740.
10. 'Toutes les productions d'un même genre ne forment proprement qu'une masse, dont le prix se détermine en général et sans égard aux circonstances particulières.' ['Properly speaking, all products of the same kind form a single mass, and their price is determined in general and without regard to particular circumstances'] (Le Trosne, l.c., p. 893.)
11. K. Marx. l.c., p.6.

11a. The following passage occurred only in the first edition.

Now we know the *substance* of value. It is *labour*. We know the *measure of its magnitude*. It is *labour time*. The *form*, which stamps *value* as *exchange-value*, remains to be analysed. But before this we need to develop the characteristics we have already found somewhat more fully.

Taken from the Penguin edition of *Capital*, translated by Ben Fowkes.

12. I am inserting the parenthesis because its omission has often given rise to the misunderstanding that every product that is consumed by some one other than its producer is considered in Marx a commodity. [Engels, 4th German Edition]
13. Tutti i fenomeni dell'universo, sieno essi prodotti della mano dell'uomo, ovvero delle universali leggi della fisica, non ci danno idea di attuale creazione, ma unicamente di una modificazione della materia. Accostare e separare sono gli unici elementi che l'ingegno umano ritrova analizzando l'idea della riproduzione: e tanto e riproduzione di valore (value in use, although Verri in this passage of his controversy with the Physiocrats is not himself quite certain of the kind of value he is speaking of) e di ricchezze se la terra, l'aria e l'acqua ne' campi si trasmutino in grano, come se colla mano dell'uomo il glutine di un insetto si trasmuti in velluto ovvero alcuni pezzetti di metalio si organizzino a formare una ripetizione.' ['All the phenomena of the universe, whether produced by the hand of man or through the universal laws of physics, are not actual new creations, but merely a modification of matter. Joining together and separating are the only elements which the human mind always finds on analysing the concept of reproduction.' and it is just the same with the reproduction of value' (value in use, although Verri in this passage of his controversy with the Physiocrats is not himself quite certain of the kind of value he is speaking of) 'and of wealth, when earth, air and water in the fields are transformed into corn, or when the hand of man transforms the secretions of an insect into silk, or some pieces of metal are arranged

to make the mechanism of a watch.']—Pietro Verri, 'Meditazioni sulla Economia Politica' [first printed in 1773] in Custodi's edition of the Italian Economists, Parte Moderna, t. XV., p. 22.

14. Comp. Hegel, 'Philosophie des Rechts.' Berlin, 1840. p. 250.
15. The reader must note that we are not speaking here of the wages or value that the labourer gets for a given labour time, but of the value of the commodity in which that labour time is materialised. Wages is a category that, as yet, has no existence at the present stage of our investigation.
16. In order to prove that labour alone is that all-sufficient and real measure, by which at all times the value of all commodities can be estimated and compared, Adam Smith says, 'Equal quantities of labour must at all times and in all places have the same value for the labourer. In his normal state of health, strength, and activity, and with the average degree of skill that he may possess, he must always give up the same portion of his rest, his freedom, and his happiness.' ('Wealth of Nations,' b. I. ch. V.) On the one hand, Adam Smith here (but not everywhere) confuses the determination of value by means of the quantity of labour expended in the production of commodities, with the determination of the values of commodities by means of the value of labour, and seeks in consequence to prove that equal quantities of labour have always the same value. On the other hand he has a presentiment, that labour, so far as it manifests itself in the value of commodities, counts only as expenditure of labour power, but he treats this expenditure as the mere sacrifice of rest, freedom, and happiness, not as at the same time the normal activity of living beings. But then, he has the modern wage-labourer in his eye. Much more aptly, the anonymous predecessor of Adam Smith, quoted above in Note 1, p. 39 [note 9 etext]. says 'one man has employed himself a week in providing this necessary of life ... and he that gives him some other in exchange cannot make a better estimate of what is a proper equivalent, than by computing what cost him just as much labour and time; which in effect is no more than exchanging one man's labour in one thing for a time certain, for another man's labour in another thing for the same time.' (l.c., p. 39.) [The English language has the advantage of possessing different words for the two aspects of labour here considered. The labour which creates use value, and counts qualitatively, is Work, as distinguished from Labour, that which creates Value and counts quantitatively, is Labour as distinguished from Work-Engels]
17. The few economists, amongst whom is S. Bailey, who have occupied themselves with the analysis of the form of value, have been unable to arrive at any result, first, because they confuse the form of value with value itself; and second, because, under the coarse influence of the practical bourgeois, they exclusively give their attention to the quantitative aspect of the question. 'The command of quantity ... constitutes value.' ('Money and its Vicissitudes.' London, 1837, p. 11. By S. Bailey.)
18. The celebrated Franklin, one of the first economists, after Wm. Petty, who saw through the nature of value, says: 'Trade in general being nothing else but the exchange of labour for labour, the value of all things is ... most justly measured by labour.' ('The works of B. Franklin, &c.,' edited by Sparks. Boston, 1836, Vol. II., p. 267.) Franklin is unconscious that by estimating the value of everything in labour, he makes abstraction from any difference in the sorts of labour exchanged, and thus reduces them all to equal human labour. But although ignorant of this, yet he says it. He speaks first of 'the one labour,' then of 'the other labour,' and finally of 'labour,' without further qualification, as the substance of the value of everything.
19. In a sort of way, it is with man as with commodities. Since he comes into the world neither with a looking glass in his hand, nor as a Fichtian philosopher, to whom 'I am I' is sufficient, man first sees and recognises himself in other men. Peter only establishes his own identity as a man by first comparing himself with Paul as being of like kind. And thereby Paul, just as he stands in his Pauline personality, becomes to Peter the type of the *genus homo*.
20. Value is here, as occasionally in the preceding pages, used in sense of value determined as to

quantity, or of magnitude of value.

21. This incongruity between the magnitude of value and its relative expression has, with customary ingenuity, been exploited by vulgar economists. For example—'Once admit that A falls, because B, with which it is exchanged, rises, while no less labour is bestowed in the meantime on A, and your general principle of value falls to the ground... If he [Ricardo] allowed that when A rises in value relatively to B, B falls in value relatively to A, he cut away the ground on which he rested his grand proposition, that the value of a commodity is ever determined by the labour embodied in it, for if a change in the cost of A alters not only its own value in relation to B, for which it is exchanged, but also the value of B relatively to that of A, though no change has taken place in the quantity of labour to produce B, then not only the doctrine falls to the ground which asserts that the quantity of labour bestowed on an article regulates its value, but also that which affirms the cost of an article to regulate its value' (J. Broadhurst: 'Political Economy,' London, 1842, pp. 11 and 14.) Mr Broadhurst might just as well say: consider the fractions 10/20, 10/50, 10/100, &c., the number 10 remains unchanged, and yet its proportional magnitude, its magnitude relatively to the numbers 20, 50, 100 &c., continually diminishes. Therefore, the great principle that the magnitude of a whole number, such as 10, is 'regulated' by the number of times unity is contained in it, falls to the ground. [The author explains in section 4 of this chapter, pp. 80-81, note 2 (note 33 etext), what he understands by 'Vulgar Economy.'—Engels]

22. Such expressions of relations in general, called by Hegel reflex categories, form a very curious class. For instance, one man is king only because other men stand in the relation of subjects to him. They, on the contrary, imagine that they are subjects because he is king.

23. F. L. A. Ferrier, sous-inspecteur des douanes, 'Du gouvernement considéré dans ses rapports avec le commerce,' Paris, 1805; and Charles Ganilh, 'Des Systèmes d'Economie Politique,—2nd ed., Paris, 1821.

24. In Homer, for instance, the value of an article is expressed in a series of different things II. VII. 472-475.

25. For this reason, we can speak of the coat value of the linen when its value is expressed in coats, or of its corn value when expressed in corn, and so on. Every such expression tells us, that what appears in the use values, coat, corn, &c., is the value of the linen. 'The value of any commodity denoting its relation in exchange, we may speak of it as ... corn value, cloth value, according to the commodity with which it is compared; and hence there are a thousand different kinds of value, as many kinds of value as there are commodities in existence, and all are equally real and equally nominal.' ('A Critical Dissertation on the Nature, Measures and Causes of Value: chiefly in reference to the writings of Mr Ricardo and his followers.' By the author of 'Essays on the Formation, &c., of Opinions.' London, 1825, p. 39.) S. Bailey, the author of this anonymous work, a work which in its day created much stir in England, fancied that, by thus pointing out the various relative expressions of one and the same value, he had proved the impossibility of any determination of the concept of value. However narrow his own views may have been, yet, that he laid his finger on some serious defects in the Ricardian Theory, is proved by the animosity with which he was attacked by Ricardo's followers. See the *Westminster Review* for example.

26. It is by no means self-evident that this character of direct and universal exchangeability is, so to speak, a polar one, and as intimately connected with its opposite pole, the absence of direct exchangeability, as the positive pole of the magnet is with its negative counterpart. It may therefore be imagined that all commodities can simultaneously have this character impressed upon them, just as it can be imagined that all Catholics can be popes together. It is, of course, highly desirable in the eyes of the petit bourgeois, for whom the production of commodities is the *nec plus ultra* of human freedom and individual independence, that the inconveniences resulting from this character of commodities not being directly exchangeable, should be removed. Proudhon's socialism is a working out of this Philistine

Utopia, a form of socialism which, as I have elsewhere shown, does not possess even the merit of originality. Long before his time, the task was attempted with much better success by Gray, Bray, and others. But, for all that, wisdom of this kind flourishes even now in certain circles under the name of 'science.' Never has any school played more tricks with the word science, than that of Proudhon, for 'wo Begriffe fehlen, Da stellt zur rechten Zeit ein Wort sich ein.' ['Where thoughts are absent, Words are brought in as convenient replacements,' Goethe's, *Faust*, See Proudhon's *Philosophy of Poverty*]

26a. In the German edition, there is the following footnote here: 'One may recall that China and the tables began to dance when the rest of the world appeared to be standing still—*pour encourager les autres* [to encourage the others].' The defeat of the 1848-49 revolutions was followed by a period of dismal political reaction in Europe. At that time, spiritualism, especially table-turning, became the rage among the European aristocracy. In 1850-64, China was swept by an anti-feudal liberation movement in the form of a large-scale peasant war, the Taiping Revolt.—Note by editors of *MECW*.

27. Among the ancient Germans the unit for measuring land was what could be harvested in a day, and was called Tagwerk, Tagwanne (jurnale, or terra jurnalis, or diornalis), Mannsmaad, &c. (See G. L. von Maurer, 'Einleitung zur Geschichte der Mark, &c. Verfassung,' Munchen, 1854, p. 129 sq.)

28. When, therefore, Galiani says: Value is a relation between persons—'La Ricchezza e una ragione tra due persone,'—he ought to have added: a relation between persons expressed as a relation between things. (Galiani: Della Moneta, p. 221, V. III. of Custodi's collection of 'Scrittori Classici Italiani di Economia Politica.' Parte Moderna, Milano 1803.)

29. 'What are we to think of a law that asserts itself only by periodical revolutions? It is just nothing but a law of Nature, founded on the want of knowledge of those whose action is the subject of it.' (Friedrich Engels: 'Umrisse zu einer Kritik der Nationalökonomie,' in the 'Deutsch-Französische Jahrbücher,' edited by Arnold Ruge and Karl Marx. Paris. 1844.)

30. Even Ricardo has his stories *à la Robinson*. 'He makes the primitive hunter and the primitive fisher straightway, as owners of commodities, exchange fish and game in the proportion in which labour time is incorporated in these exchange values. On this occasion he commits the anachronism of making these men apply to the calculation, so far as their implements have to be taken into account, the annuity tables in current use on the London Exchange in the year 1817. The parallelograms of Mr Owen appear to be the only form of society, besides the bourgeois form, with which he was acquainted.' (Karl Marx: 'Zur Kritik, &c.' pp. 38, 39)

31. 'A ridiculous presumption has latterly got abroad that common property in its primitive form is specifically a Slavonian, or even exclusively Russian form. It is the primitive form that we can prove to have existed amongst Romans, Teutons, and Celts, and even to this day we find numerous examples, ruins though they be, in India. A more exhaustive study of Asiatic, and especially of Indian forms of common property, would show how from the different forms of primitive common property, different forms of its dissolution have been developed. Thus, for instance, the various original types of Roman and Teutonic private property are deducible from different forms of Indian common property.' (Karl Marx, 'Zur Kritik, &c.,' p. 10.)

32. The insufficiency of Ricardo's analysis of the magnitude of value, and his analysis is by far the best, will appear from the 3rd and 4th books of this work. As regards value in general, it is the weak point of the classical school of Political Economy that it nowhere expressly and with full consciousness, distinguishes between labour, as it appears in the value of a product, and the same labour, as it appears in the use value of that product. Of course the distinction is practically made, since this school treats labour, at one time under its quantitative aspect, at another under its qualitative aspect. But it has not the least idea, that when the difference between various kinds of labour is treated as purely quantitative, their qualitative unity or equality, and therefore their reduction to abstract human labour, is implied. For instance, Ricardo declares that he agrees with Destutt de Tracy in this proposition: 'As it is certain

that our physical and moral faculties are alone our original riches, the employment of those faculties, labour of some kind, is our only original treasure, and it is always from this employment that all those things are created which we call riches... It is certain, too, that all those things only represent the labour which has created them, and if they have a value, or even two distinct values, they can only derive them from that (the value) of the labour from which they emanate.' (Ricardo, 'The Principles of Pol. Econ.,' 3 Ed. Lond. 1821, p. 334.) We would here only point out, that Ricardo puts his own more profound interpretation upon the words of Destutt. What the latter really says is, that on the one hand all things which constitute wealth represent the labour that creates them, but that on the other hand, they acquire their 'two different values' (use value and exchange value) from 'the value of labour.' He thus falls into the commonplace error of the vulgar economists, who assume the value of one commodity (in this case labour) in order to determine the values of the rest. But Ricardo reads him as if he had said, that labour (not the value of labour) is embodied both in use value and exchange value. Nevertheless, Ricardo himself pays so little attention to the two-fold character of the labour which has a two-fold embodiment, that he devotes the whole of his chapter on 'Value and Riches, Their Distinctive Properties,' to a laborious examination of the trivialities of a J.B. Say. And at the finish he is quite astonished to find that Destutt on the one hand agrees with him as to labour being the source of value, and on the other hand with J. B. Say as to the notion of value.

33. It is one of the chief failings of classical economy that it has never succeeded, by means of its analysis of commodities, and, in particular, of their value, in discovering that form under which value becomes exchange value. Even Adam Smith and Ricardo, the best representatives of the school, treat the form of value as a thing of no importance, as having no connection with the inherent nature of commodities. The reason for this is not solely because their attention is entirely absorbed in the analysis of the magnitude of value. It lies deeper. The value form of the product of labour is not only the most abstract, but is also the most universal form, taken by the product in bourgeois production, and stamps that production as a particular species of social production, and thereby gives it its special historical character. If then we treat this mode of production as one eternally fixed by Nature for every state of society, we necessarily overlook that which is the *differentia specifica* of the value form, and consequently of the commodity form, and of its further developments, money form, capital form, &c. We consequently find that economists, who are thoroughly agreed as to labour time being the measure of the magnitude of value, have the most strange and contradictory ideas of money, the perfected form of the general equivalent. This is seen in a striking manner when they treat of banking, where the commonplace definitions of money will no longer hold water. This led to the rise of a restored mercantile system (Ganilh, &c.), which sees in value nothing but a social form, or rather the unsubstantial ghost of that form. Once for all I may here state, that by classical Political Economy, I understand that economy which, since the time of W. Petty, has investigated the real relations of production in bourgeois society in contradistinction to vulgar economy, which deals with appearances only, ruminates without ceasing on the materials long since provided by scientific economy, and there seeks plausible explanations of the most obtrusive phenomena, for bourgeois daily use, but for the rest, confines itself to systematising in a pedantic way, and proclaiming for everlasting truths, the trite ideas held by the self-complacent bourgeoisie with regard to their own world, to them the best of all possible worlds.

34. 'Les économistes ont une singulière manière de procéder. Il n'y a pour eux que deux sortes d'institutions, celles de l'art et celles de la nature. Les institutions de la féodalité sont des institutions artificielles celles de la bourgeoisie sont des institutions naturelles. Ils ressemblent en ceci aux théologiens, qui eux aussi établissent deux sortes de religions. Toute religion qui n'est pas la leur, est une invention des hommes tandis que leur propre religion est une émanation de Dieu—Ainsi il y a eu de l'histoire, mais il n'y en a plus.'

['Economists have a singular method of procedure. There are only two kinds of institutions for them, artificial and natural. The institutions of feudalism are artificial institutions, those of the bourgeoisie are natural institutions. In this, they resemble the theologians, who likewise establish two kinds of religion. Every religion which is not theirs is an invention of men, while their own is an emanation from God. ... Thus there has been history, but there is no longer any'] (Karl Marx. Misère de la Philosophie. Réponse a la Philosophie de la Misère par M. Proudhon, 1847, p. 113.) Truly comical is M. Bastiat, who imagines that the ancient Greeks and Romans lived by plunder alone. But when people plunder for centuries, there must always be something at hand for them to seize; the objects of plunder must be continually reproduced. It would thus appear that even Greeks and Romans had some process of production, consequently, an economy, which just as much constituted the material basis of their world, as bourgeois economy constitutes that of our modern world. Or perhaps Bastiat means, that a mode of production based on slavery is based on a system of plunder. In that case he treads on dangerous ground. If a giant thinker like Aristotle erred in his appreciation of slave labour, why should a dwarf economist like Bastiat be right in his appreciation of wage labour? I seize this opportunity of shortly answering an objection taken by a German paper in America, to my work, 'Zur Kritik der Pol. Oekonomie, 1859.' In the estimation of that paper, my view that each special mode of production and the social relations corresponding to it, in short, that the economic structure of society, is the real basis on which the juridical and political superstructure is raised and to which definite social forms of thought correspond; that the mode of production determines the character of the social, political, and intellectual life generally, all this is very true for our own times, in which material interests preponderate, but not for the middle ages, in which Catholicism, nor for Athens and Rome, where politics, reigned supreme. In the first place it strikes one as an odd thing for any one to suppose that these well-worn phrases about the middle ages and the ancient world are unknown to anyone else. This much, however, is clear, that the middle ages could not live on Catholicism, nor the ancient world on politics. On the contrary, it is the mode in which they gained a livelihood that explains why here politics, and there Catholicism, played the chief part. For the rest, it requires but a slight acquaintance with the history of the Roman republic, for example, to be aware that its secret history is the history of its landed property. On the other hand, Don Quixote long ago paid the penalty for wrongly imagining that knight errantry was compatible with all economic forms of society.

35. 'Observations on certain verbal disputes in Pol. Econ., particularly relating to value and to demand and supply' Lond., 1821, p. 16.
36. S. Bailey, l.c., p. 165.
37. The author of 'Observations' and S. Bailey accuse Ricardo of converting exchange value from something relative into something absolute. The opposite is the fact. He has explained the apparent relation between objects, such as diamonds and pearls, in which relation they appear as exchange values, and disclosed the true relation hidden behind the appearances, namely, their relation to each other as mere expressions of human labour. If the followers of Ricardo answer Bailey somewhat rudely, and by no means convincingly, the reason is to be sought in this, that they were unable to find in Ricardo's own works any key to the hidden relations existing between value and its form, exchange value.

Note: This oft-quoted aphorism was included in the first English translation prepared by Engels and published in 1887. Readers should note that this observation is consistent with Marx's explanation above. There are numerous divergences between this English edition and the first German edition. [MIA]

2

Exchange

It is plain that commodities cannot go to market and make exchanges of their own account. We must, therefore, have recourse to their guardians, who are also their owners. Commodities are things, and therefore without power of resistance against man. If they are wanting in docility he can use force; in other words, he can take possession of them.[1] In order that these objects may enter into relation with each other as commodities, their guardians must place themselves in relation to one another, as persons whose will resides in those objects, and must behave in such a way that each does not appropriate the commodity of the other, and part with his own, except by means of an act done by mutual consent. They must therefore, mutually recognise in each other the rights of private proprietors. This juridical relation, which thus expresses itself in a contract, whether such contract be part of a developed legal system or not, is a relation between two wills, and is but the reflex of the real economic relation between the two. It is this economic relation that determines the subject-matter comprised in each such juridical act.[2]

The persons exist for one another merely as representatives of, and, therefore, as owners of, commodities. In the course of our investigation we shall find, in general, that the characters who appear on the economic stage are but the personifications of the economic relations that exist between them.

What chiefly distinguishes a commodity from its owner is the fact, that it looks upon every other commodity as but the form of appearance of its own value. A born leveller and a cynic, it is always ready to exchange not only soul, but body, with any and every other commodity, be the same more repulsive than Maritornes herself. The owner makes up for this lack in the commodity of a sense of the concrete, by his own five and more senses. His commodity possesses for himself no immediate use-value. Otherwise, he would not bring it to the market. It has use-value for others; but for himself its only direct use-value is that of being a depository of exchange-value, and, consequently, a means of exchange.[3] Therefore, he makes up his mind to part with it for commodities whose value in use is of service to him. All commodities are non-use-values for their owners, and use-values for their non-owners. Consequently, they must all change hands. But this change of hands is what constitutes their exchange, and the latter puts them in relation with each other as values, and realises them as values. Hence commodities must be realised as values before they can be realised as use-values.

On the other hand, they must show that they are use-values before they can be realised as values. For the labour spent upon them counts effectively, only in so far as it is spent in a form that is useful for others. Whether that labour is useful for others, and its product consequently capable of satisfying the wants of others, can be proved only by the act of exchange.

Every owner of a commodity wishes to part with it in exchange only for those commodities whose use-value satisfies some want of his. Looked at in this way, exchange is for him simply a private transaction. On the other hand, he desires to realise the value of his commodity, to convert it into any other suitable commodity of equal value, irrespective of whether his own commodity has or has not any use-value for the owner of the other. From this point of view, exchange is for him a social transaction of a general character. But one and the same set of transactions cannot be simultaneously for all owners of commodities both exclusively private and exclusively social and general.

Let us look at the matter a little closer. To the owner of a commodity, every other commodity is, in regard to his own, a particular equivalent, and consequently his own commodity is the universal equivalent for all the others. But, since this applies to every owner, there is, in fact, no commodity acting as universal equivalent, and the relative value of commodities possesses no general form under which they can be equated as values and have the magnitude of their values compared. So far, therefore, they do not confront each other as commodities, but only as products or use-values. In their difficulties our commodity owners think like Faust: 'Im Anfang war die Tat.' ['In the beginning was the deed.'—Goethe, *Faust*.] They therefore acted and transacted before they thought. Instinctively they conform to the laws imposed by the nature of commodities. They cannot bring their commodities into relation as values, and therefore as commodities, except by comparing them with some one other commodity as the universal equivalent. That we saw from the analysis of a commodity. But a particular commodity cannot become the universal equivalent except by a social act. The social action therefore of all other commodities, sets apart the particular commodity in which they all represent their values. Thereby the bodily form of this commodity becomes the form of the socially recognised universal equivalent. To be the universal equivalent, becomes, by this social process, the specific function of the commodity thus excluded by the rest. Thus it becomes—money. 'Illi unum consilium habent et virtutem et potestatem suam bestiae tradunt. Et ne quis possit emere aut vendere, nisi qui habet characterem aut nomen bestiae aut numerum nominis ejus.' ['These have one mind, and shall give their power and strength unto the beast.' Revelations, 17:13; 'And that no man might buy or sell, save he that had the mark, or the name of the beast, or the number of his name.' Revelations, 13:17.] (*Apocalypse*.)

Money is a crystal formed of necessity in the course of the exchanges, whereby different products of labour are practically equated to one another and thus by practice converted into commodities. The historical progress and extension of exchanges develops the contrast, latent in commodities, between use-value and value. The necessity for giving an external expression to this contrast for the purposes of commercial intercourse, urges on the establishment of an independent form of value, and finds no rest until it is once for all satisfied by the differentiation of commodities into commodities and money. At the same rate, then, as the conversion of products into commodities is being accomplished, so also is the conversion of one special commodity into money.[4]

The direct barter of products attains the elementary form of the relative expression of value in one respect, but not in another. That form is x Commodity A = y Commodity B. The form of direct barter is x use-value A = y use-value B.[5] The articles A and B in this case are not as yet commodities, but become so only by the act of barter. The first step made by an object of utility towards acquiring exchange-value is when it forms a non-use-value for its owner, and that happens when it forms a superfluous portion of some article required for his immediate wants. Objects in themselves are external to man, and consequently alienable by him. In order that this alienation may be reciprocal, it is only necessary for men, by a tacit understanding, to treat each other as private owners of those alienable objects, and by implication as independent individuals. But such a state of reciprocal independence has no existence in a primitive society based on property in common, whether such a society takes the form of a patriarchal family, an ancient Indian community, or a Peruvian Inca State. The exchange of commodities, therefore, first begins on the boundaries of such communities, at their points of contact with other similar communities, or with members of the latter. So soon, however, as products once become commodities in the external relations of a community, they also, by reaction, become so in its internal intercourse. The proportions in which they are exchangeable are at first quite a matter of chance. What makes them exchangeable is the mutual desire of their owners to alienate them. Meantime the need for foreign objects of utility gradually establishes itself. The constant repetition of exchange makes it a normal social act. In the course of time, therefore, some portion at least of the products of labour must be produced with a special view to exchange. From that moment the distinction becomes firmly established between the utility of an object for the purposes of consumption, and its utility for the purposes of exchange. Its use-value becomes distinguished from its exchange-value. On the other hand, the quantitative proportion in which the articles are exchangeable, becomes dependent on their production itself. Custom stamps them as values with definite magnitudes.

In the direct barter of products, each commodity is directly a means of exchange to its owner, and to all other persons an equivalent, but that only in so far as it has use-value for them. At this stage, therefore, the articles exchanged do not acquire a value-form independent of their own use-value, or of the individual needs of the exchangers. The necessity for a value-form grows with the increasing number and variety of the commodities exchanged. The problem and the means of solution arise simultaneously. Commodity-owners never equate their own commodities to those of others, and exchange them on a large scale, without different kinds of commodities belonging to different owners being exchangeable for, and equated as values to, one and the same special article. Such last-mentioned article, by becoming the equivalent of various other commodities, acquires at once, though within narrow limits, the character of a general social equivalent. This character comes and goes with the momentary social acts that called it into life. In turns and transiently it attaches itself first to this and then to that commodity. But with the development of exchange it fixes itself firmly and exclusively to particular sorts of commodities, and becomes crystallised by assuming the money-form. The particular kind of commodity to which it sticks is at first a matter of accident. Nevertheless there are two circumstances whose influence is decisive. The money-form attaches itself either to the most important articles of exchange from outside, and these in fact are primitive and natural forms in which the exchange-value of home products finds expression; or else it attaches itself to the object of utility that forms, like cattle, the chief portion of indigenous alienable wealth. Nomad races are the first to develop the money-form, because all their worldly goods consist of moveable objects and are therefore directly alienable; and because their mode of life, by continually bringing them into contact with foreign communities, solicits the exchange of products. Man has often made man himself, under the form of slaves, serve as the primitive material of money, but has never used land for that purpose. Such an idea could only spring up in a bourgeois society already well developed. It dates from the last third of the 17th century, and the first attempt to put it in practice on a national scale was made a century afterwards, during the French bourgeois revolution.

In proportion as exchange bursts its local bonds, and the value of commodities more and more expands into an embodiment of human labour in the abstract, in the same proportion the character of money attaches itself to commodities that are by Nature fitted to perform the social function of a universal equivalent. Those commodities are the precious metals.

The truth of the proposition that, 'although gold and silver are not by Nature money, money is by Nature gold and silver,'[6] is shown by the fitness of the physical properties of these metals for the functions of money.[7] Up to this point, however, we are acquainted only with one function of money, namely, to serve as the form of manifestation of the value of commodities, or as the material in which the magnitudes of their values are socially expressed. An adequate form of manifestation of value, a fit embodiment of abstract, undifferentiated, and therefore equal human labour, that material alone can be whose every sample exhibits the same uniform qualities. On the other hand, since the difference between the magnitudes of value is purely quantitative, the money commodity must be susceptible of merely quantitative differences, must therefore be divisible at will, and equally capable of being reunited. Gold and silver possess these properties by Nature.

The use-value of the money-commodity becomes two-fold. In addition to its special use-value as a commodity (gold, for instance, serving to stop teeth, to form the raw material of articles of luxury, &c.), it acquires a formal use-value, originating in its specific social function.

Since all commodities are merely particular equivalents of money, the latter being their universal equivalent, they, with regard to the latter as the universal commodity, play the parts of particular commodities.[8]

We have seen that the money-form is but the reflex, thrown upon one single commodity, of the value relations between all the rest. That money is a commodity[9] is therefore a new discovery only for those who, when they analyse it, start from its fully developed shape. The act of exchange gives to the commodity converted into money, not its value, but its specific value-form. By confounding these two distinct things some writers have been led to hold that the value of gold and silver is imaginary.[10] The fact that money can, in certain functions, be replaced by mere symbols of itself, gave rise to that other mistaken notion, that it is itself a mere symbol. Nevertheless under this error lurked a presentiment that the money-form of an object is not an inseparable part of that object, but is simply the form under which certain social relations manifest themselves. In this sense every commodity is a symbol, since, in so far as it is value, it is only the material envelope of the human labour spent upon it.[11] But if it be declared that the social characters assumed by objects, or the material forms assumed by the social qualities of labour under the régime of a definite mode of production, are mere symbols, it is in the same breath also declared that these characteristics are arbitrary fictions sanctioned by the so-called universal consent of mankind. This suited the mode of explanation in favour during the 18th century. Unable to account for the origin of the puzzling forms assumed by social relations between man and man, people sought to denude them of their strange appearance by ascribing to them a conventional origin.

It has already been remarked above that the equivalent form of a commodity does not imply the determination of the magnitude of its value. Therefore, although we may be aware that gold is money, and consequently directly exchangeable for all other commodities, yet that fact by no means tells how much 10 lbs., for instance, of gold is worth. Money, like every other commodity, cannot express the magnitude of its value except relatively in other commodities. This value is determined by the labour-time required for its production, and is expressed by the quantity of any other commodity that costs the same amount of labour-time.[12] Such quantitative determination of its relative value takes place at the source of its production by means of barter. When it steps into circulation as money, its value is already given. In the last decades of the 17th century it had already been shown that money is a commodity, but this step marks only the infancy of the analysis. The difficulty lies, not in comprehending that money is a commodity, but in discovering how, why, and by what means a commodity becomes money.[13]

We have already seen, from the most elementary expression of value, x commodity A = y commodity B, that the object in which the magnitude of the value of another object is represented, appears to have the equivalent form independently of this relation, as a social property given to it by Nature. We followed up this false appearance to its final establishment, which is complete so soon as the universal equivalent form becomes identified with the bodily form of a particular commodity, and thus crystallised into the money-form. What appears to happen is, not that gold becomes money, in consequence of all other commodities expressing their values in it, but, on the contrary, that all other commodities universally express their values in gold, because it is money. The intermediate steps of the process vanish in the result and leave no trace behind. Commodities find their own value already completely represented, without any initiative on their part, in another commodity existing in company with them. These objects, gold and silver, just as they come out of the bowels of the earth, are forthwith the direct incarnation of all human labour. Hence the magic of money. In the form of society now under consideration, the behaviour of men in the social process of production is purely atomic. Hence, their relations to each other in production assume a material character independent of their control and conscious individual action. These facts manifest themselves at first by products as a general rule taking the form of commodities. We have seen how the progressive development of a society of commodity-producers stamps one privileged commodity with the character of money. Hence, the riddle presented by money is but the riddle presented by commodities; only it now strikes us in its most glaring form.

Notes

1. In the 12th century, so renowned for its piety, they included amongst commodities some very delicate things. Thus a French poet of the period enumerates amongst the goods to be found in the market of Landit, not only clothing, shoes, leather, agricultural implements, &c., but also 'femmes folles de leur corps.'
2. Proudhon begins by taking his ideal of Justice, of 'justice éternelle,' from the juridical relations that correspond to the production of commodities: thereby, it may be noted, he proves, to the consolation of all good citizens, that the production of commodities is a form of production as everlasting as justice. Then he turns round and seeks to reform the actual production of commodities, and the actual legal system corresponding thereto, in accordance with this ideal. What opinion should we have of a chemist, who, instead of studying the actual laws of the molecular changes in the composition and decomposition of matter, and on that foundation solving definite problems, claimed to regulate the composition and decomposition of matter by means of the 'eternal ideas,' of 'naturalité' and 'affinité'? Do we really know any more about 'usury,' when we say it contradicts 'justice éternelle,' équité éternelle,' 'mutualité éternelle,' and other vérités éternelles' than the fathers of the church did when they said it was incompatible with 'grâce éternelle,' 'foi éternelle,' and 'la volonté éternelle de Dieu'?
3. 'For two-fold is the use of every object.... The one is peculiar to the object as such, the other is not, as a sandal which may be worn, and is also exchangeable. Both are uses of the sandal, for even he who exchanges the sandal for the money or food he is in want of, makes use of the sandal as a sandal. But not in its natural way. For it has not been made for the sake of being exchanged.' (Aristoteles, 'De Rep.' l. i. c. 9.)
4. From this we may form an estimate of the shrewdness of the petit-bourgeois socialism, which, while perpetuating the production of commodities, aims at abolishing the 'antagonism' between money and commodities, and consequently, since money exists only by virtue of this antagonism, at abolishing money itself. We might just as well try to retain Catholicism without the Pope. For more on this point see my work, 'Zur Kritik der Pol. Oekon.,' p. 61, sq.
5. So long as, instead of two distinct use-values being exchanged, a chaotic mass of articles are offered as the equivalent of a single article, which is often the case with savages, even the direct barter of products is in its first infancy.
6. Karl Marx, l.c., p. 135. 'I metalli ... naturalmente moneta.' ['The metals ... are by their nature money.'] (Galiani, 'Della moneta' in Custodi's Collection: Parte Moderna t. iii.)
7. For further details on this subject see in my work cited above, the chapter on 'The precious metals.'
8. 'Il danaro è la merce universale»(Verri, l.c., p. 16).
9. 'Silver and gold themselves (which we may call by the general name of bullion) are ... commodities ... rising and falling in ... value ... Bullion, then, may be reckoned to be of higher value where the smaller weight will purchase the greater quantity of the product or manufacture of the countrey,' &c. ('A Discourse of the General Notions of Money, Trade, and Exchanges, as They Stand in Relation each to other.' By a Merchant. Lond., 1695, p. 7.) 'Silver

and gold, coined or uncoined, though they are used for a measure of all other things, are no less a commodity than wine, oil, tobacco, cloth, or stuffs.' ('A Discourse concerning Trade, and that in particular of the East Indies,' &c. London, 1689, p. 2.) 'The stock and riches of the kingdom cannot properly be confined to money, nor ought gold and silver to be excluded from being merchandise.' («The East-India Trade a Most Profitable Trade.' London, 1677, p. 4.)

10. 'L'oro e l'argento hanno valore come metalli anteriore all'esser moneta.' ['Gold and silver have value as metals before they are money'] (Galiani, l.c.) Locke says, 'The universal consent of mankind gave to silver, on account of its qualities which made it suitable for money, an imaginary value.' Law, on the other hand. 'How could different nations give an imaginary value to any single thing... or how could this imaginary value have maintained itself?' But the following shows how little he himself understood about the matter: 'Silver was exchanged in proportion to the value in use it possessed, consequently in proportion to its real value. By its adoption as money it received an additional value (une valeur additionnelle).' (Jean Law: 'Considérations sur le numéraire et le commerce' in E. Daire's Edit. of 'Economistes Financiers du XVIII siècle,' p. 470.)

11. 'L'Argent en (des denrées) est le signe.' ['Money is their (the commodities') symbol'] (V. de Forbonnais: 'Eléments du Commerce, Nouv. Edit. Leyde, 1766,' t. II., p. 143.) 'Comme signe il est attiré par les denrées.' ['As a symbol it is attracted by the commodities'] (l.c., p. 155.) 'L'argent est un signe d'une chose et la représente.' ['Money is a symbol of a thing and represents it'] (Montesquieu: 'Esprit des Lois,' (Oeuvres, Lond. 1767, t. II, p. 2.) 'L'argent n'est pas simple signe, car il est lui-même richesse, il ne représente pas les valeurs, il les équivaut.' ['Money is not a mere symbol, for it is itself wealth; it does not represent the values, it is their equivalents'] (Le Trosne, l.c., p. 910.) 'The notion of value contemplates the valuable article as a mere symbol - the article counts not for what it is, but for what it is worth.' (Hegel, l.c., p. 100.) Lawyers started long before economists the idea that money is a mere symbol, and that the value of the precious metals is purely imaginary. This they did in the sycophantic service of the crowned heads, supporting the right of the latter to debase the coinage, during the whole of the middle ages, by the traditions of the Roman Empire and the conceptions of money to be found in the Pandects. 'Qu'aucun puisse ni doive faire doute,' ['Let no one call into question,'] says an apt scholar of theirs, Philip of Valois, in a decree of 1346, 'que à nous et à notre majesté royale n'appartiennent seulement ... le mestier, le fait, l'état, la provision et toute l'ordonnance des monnaies, de donner tel cours, et pour tel prix comme il nous plait et bon nous semble.' ['that the trade, the composition, the supply and the power of issuing ordinances on the currency ... belongs exclusively to us and to our royal majesty, to fix such a rate and at such price as it shall please us and seem good to us'] It was a maxim of the Roman Law that the value of money was fixed by decree of the emperor. It was expressly forbidden to treat money as a commodity. 'Pecunias vero nulli emere fas erit, nam in usu publico constitutas oportet non esse mercem.' ['However, it shall not be lawful to anyone to buy money, for, as it was created for public use, it is not permissible for it to be a commodity'] Some good work on this question has been done by G. F. Pagnini: 'Saggio sopra il giusto pregio delle cose, 1751'; Custodi 'Parte Moderna,' t. II. In the second part of his work Pagnini directs his polemics especially against the lawyers.

12. 'If a man can bring to London an ounce of Silver out of the Earth in Peru, in the same time that he can produce a bushel of Corn, then the one is the natural price of the other; now, if by reason of new or more easier mines a man can procure two ounces of silver as easily as he formerly did one, the corn will be as cheap at ten shillings the bushel as it was before at five shillings, caeteris paribus.' William Petty. 'A Treatise of Taxes and Contributions.' Lond., 1667, p. 32.

13. The learned Professor Roscher, after first informing us that 'the false definitions of money may be divided into two main groups: those which make it more, and those which make it

less, than a commodity,' gives us a long and very mixed catalogue of works on the nature of money, from which it appears that he has not the remotest idea of the real history of the theory; and then he moralises thus: 'For the rest, it is not to be denied that most of the later economists do not bear sufficiently in mind the peculiarities that distinguish money from other commodities' (it is then, after all, either more or less than a commodity!)... 'So far, the semi-mercantilist reaction of Ganilh is not altogether without foundation.' (Wilhelm Roscher: 'Die Grundlagen der Nationaloekonomie,' 3rd Edn. 1858, pp. 207-210.) More! Less! Not sufficiently! So far! Not altogether! What clearness and precision of ideas and language! And such eclectic professorial twaddle is modestly baptised by Mr Roscher, 'the anatomico-physiological method' of Political Economy! One discovery however, he must have credit for, namely, that money is 'a pleasant commodity.'

3

Money, Or the Circulation of Commodities

Section 1: *The Measure of Values*

Throughout this work, I assume, for the sake of simplicity, gold as the money-commodity.

The first chief function of money is to supply commodities with the material for the expression of their values, or to represent their values as magnitudes of the same denomination, qualitatively equal, and quantitatively comparable. It thus serves as a *universal measure of value*. And only by virtue of this function does gold, the equivalent commodity *par excellence*, become money.

It is not money that renders commodities commensurable. Just the contrary. It is because all commodities, as values, are realised human labour, and therefore commensurable, that their values can be measured by one and the same special commodity, and the latter be converted into the common measure of their values, *i.e.*, into money. Money as a measure of value, is the phenomenal form that must of necessity be assumed by that measure of value which is immanent in commodities, labour-time.[1]

The expression of the value of a commodity in gold—x commodity A = y money-commodity—is its money-form or price. A single equation, such as 1 ton of iron = 2 ounces of gold, now suffices to express the value of the iron in a socially valid manner. There is no longer any need for this equation to figure as a link in the chain of equations that express the values of all other commodities, because the equivalent commodity, gold, now has the character of money. The general form of relative value has resumed its original shape of simple or isolated relative value. On the other hand, the expanded expression of relative value, the endless series of equations, has now become the form peculiar to the relative value of the money-commodity. The series itself, too, is now given, and has social recognition in the prices of actual commodities. We have only to read the quotations of a price-list backwards, to find the magnitude of the value of money expressed in all sorts of commodities. But money itself has no price. In order to put it on an equal footing with all other commodities in this respect, we should be obliged to equate it to itself as its own equivalent.

The price or money-form of commodities is, like their form of value generally, a form quite distinct from their palpable bodily form; it is, therefore, a purely ideal or mental form. Although invisible, the value of iron, linen and corn has actual existence in these very articles: it is ideally made perceptible by their equality with gold, a relation that, so to say, exists only in their own heads. Their owner must, therefore, lend them his tongue, or hang a ticket on them, before their prices can be communicated to the outside world.[2] Since the expression of the value of commodities in gold is a merely ideal act, we may use for this purpose imaginary or ideal money. Every trader knows, that he is far from having turned his goods into money, when he has expressed their value in a price or in imaginary money, and that it does not require the least bit of real gold, to estimate in that metal millions of pounds' worth of goods. When, therefore, money serves as a measure of value, it is employed only as imaginary or ideal money. This circumstance has given rise to the wildest theories.[3] But, although the money that performs the functions of a measure of value is only ideal money, price depends entirely upon the actual substance that is money. The value, or in other words, the quantity of human labour contained in a ton of iron, is expressed in imagination by such a quantity of the money-commodity as contains the same amount of labour as the iron. According, therefore, as the measure of value is gold, silver, or copper, the value of the ton of iron will be expressed by very different prices, or will be represented by very different quantities of those metals respectively.

If, therefore, two different commodities, such as gold and silver, are simultaneously measures of value, all commodities have two prices—one a gold-price, the other a silver-price. These exist quietly side by side, so long as the ratio of the value of silver to that of gold remains unchanged, say, at 15:1. Every change in their ratio disturbs the ratio which exists between the gold-prices and the silver-prices of commodities, and thus proves, by facts, that a double standard of value is inconsistent with the functions of a standard.[4]

Commodities with definite prices present themselves under the form: *a* commodity A = x gold; *b* commodity B = z gold; *c* commodity C = y gold, *&c.*, where *a*, *b*, *c*, represent definite quantities of the commodities A, B, C and x, z, y, definite quantities of gold. The values of these commodities are, therefore, changed in imagination into so many different quantities of gold. Hence, in spite of the confusing variety of the commodities themselves, their values become magnitudes of the same denomination, gold-magnitudes. They are now capable of being compared with each other and measured, and the want becomes technically felt of comparing them with some fixed quantity of gold as a unit measure. This unit, by subsequent division into aliquot parts, becomes itself the standard or scale. Before they become money, gold, silver, and copper already possess such standard measures in their standards of weight, so that, for example, a pound weight, while serving as the unit, is, on the one hand, divisible into ounces, and, on the other, may be combined to make up hundredweights.[5] It is owing to this that, in all metallic currencies, the names given to the standards of money or of price were originally taken from the pre-existing names of the standards of weight.

As *measure of Value*, and as *standard of price*, money has two entirely distinct functions to perform. It is the measure of value inasmuch as it is the socially recognised incarnation of human labour; it is the standard of price inasmuch as it is a fixed weight of metal. As the measure of value it serves to convert the values of all the manifold commodities into prices, into imaginary quantities of gold; as the standard of price it measures those quantities of gold. The measure of values measures commodities considered as values; the standard of price measures, on the contrary, quantities of gold by a unit quantity of gold, not the value of one quantity of gold by the weight of another. In order to make gold a standard of price, a certain weight must be fixed upon as the unit. In this case, as in all cases of measuring quantities of the same denomination, the establishment of an unvarying unit of measure is all-important. Hence, the less the unit is subject to variation, so much the better does the standard of price fulfil its office. But only in so far as it is itself a product of labour, and, therefore, potentially variable in value, can gold serve as a measure of value.[6]

It is, in the first place, quite clear that a change in the value of gold does not, in any way, affect its function as a standard of price. No matter how this value varies, the proportions between the values of different quantities of the metal remain constant. However great the fall in its value, 12 ounces of gold still have 12 times the value of 1 ounce; and in prices, the only thing considered is the relation between different quantities of gold. Since, on the other hand, no rise or fall in the value of an ounce of gold can alter its weight, no alteration can take place in the weight of its aliquot parts. Thus gold always renders the same service as an invariable standard of price, however much its value may vary.

In the second place, a change in the value of gold does not interfere with its functions as a measure of value. The change affects all commodities simultaneously, and, therefore, *caeteris paribus*, leaves their relative values *inter se*, unaltered, although those values are now expressed in higher or lower gold-prices.

Just as when we estimate the value of any commodity by a definite quantity of the use-value of some other commodity, so in estimating the value of the former in gold, we assume nothing more than that the production of a given quantity of gold costs, at the given period, a given amount of labour. As regards the fluctuations of prices generally, they are subject to the laws of elementary relative value investigated in a former chapter.

A general rise in the prices of commodities can result only, either from a rise in their values—the value of money remaining constant—or from a fall in the value of money, the values of commodities remaining constant. On the other hand, a general fall in prices can result only, either from a fall in the values of commodities—the value of money remaining constant—or from a rise in the value of money, the values of commodities remaining constant. It, therefore, by no means follows, that a rise in the value of money necessarily implies a proportional fall in the prices of commodities; or that a fall in the value of money implies a proportional rise in prices. Such change of price holds good only in the case of commodities whose value remains constant. With those, for example, whose value rises, simultaneously with, and proportionally to, that of money, there is no alteration in price. And if their value rise either slower or faster than that of money, the fall or rise in their prices will be determined by the difference between the change in their value and that of money; and so on.

Let us now go back to the consideration of the price-form.

By degrees there arises a discrepancy between the current money-names of the various weights of the precious metal figuring as money, and the actual weights which those names originally represented. This discrepancy is the result of historical causes, among which the chief are:—(1) The importation of foreign money into an imperfectly developed community. This happened in Rome in its early days, where gold and silver coins circulated at first as foreign commodities. The names of these foreign coins never coincide with those of the indigenous weights. (2) As wealth increases, the less precious metal is thrust out by the more precious from its place as a measure of value, copper by silver, silver by gold, however much this order of sequence may be in contradiction with poetical chronology.[7] The word pound, for instance, was the money-name given to an actual pound weight of silver. When gold replaced silver as a measure of value, the same name was applied according to the ratio between the values of silver and gold, to perhaps 1-15th of a pound of gold. The word pound, as a money-name, thus becomes differentiated from the same word as a weight-name.[8] (3) The debasing of money carried on for centuries by kings and princes to such an extent that, of the original weights of the coins, nothing in fact remained but the names.[9]

These historical causes convert the separation of the money-name from the weight-name into an established habit with the community. Since the standard of money is on the one hand purely conventional, and must on the other hand find general acceptance, it is in the end regulated by law. A given weight of one of the precious metals, an ounce of gold, for instance, becomes officially divided into aliquot parts, with legally bestowed names, such as pound, dollar, &c. These aliquot parts, which thenceforth serve as units of money, are then subdivided into other aliquot parts with legal names, such as shilling, penny, &c.[10] But, both before and after these divisions are made, a definite weight of metal is the standard of metallic money. The sole alteration consists in the subdivision and denomination.

The prices, or quantities of gold, into which the values of commodities are ideally changed, are therefore now expressed in the names of coins, or in the legally valid names of the subdivisions of the gold standard. Hence, instead of saying: A quarter of wheat is worth an ounce of gold; we say, it is worth £3 17s. 10 1/2d. In this way, commodities express by their prices how much they are worth, and money serves as *money of account* whenever it is a question of fixing the value of an article in its money-form.[11]

The name of a thing is something distinct from the qualities of that thing. I know nothing of a man, by knowing that his name is Jacob. In the same way with regard to money, every trace of a value-relation disappears in the names pound, dollar, franc, ducat, &c. The confusion caused by attributing a hidden meaning to these cabalistic signs is all the greater, because these money-names express both the values of commodities, and, at the same time, aliquot parts of the weight of the metal that is the standard of money.+12 On the other hand, it is absolutely necessary that value, in order that it may be distinguished from the varied bodily forms of commodities, should assume this material and unmeaning, but, at the same time, purely social form.[13]

Price is the money-name of the labour realised in a commodity. Hence the expression of the equivalence of a commodity with the sum of money constituting its price, is a tautology,[14] just as in general the expression of the relative value of a commodity is a statement of the equivalence of two commodities. But, although price, being the exponent of the magnitude of a commodity's value, is the exponent of its exchange-ratio with money, it does not follow that the exponent of this exchange-ratio is necessarily the exponent of the magnitude of the commodity's value. Suppose two equal quantities of socially necessary labour to be respectively represented by 1 quarter of wheat and £2 (nearly 1/2 oz. of gold), £2 is the expression in money of the magnitude of the value of the quarter of wheat, or is its price. If now circumstances allow of this price being raised to £3, or compel it to be reduced to £1, then although £1 and £3 may be too small or too great properly to express the magnitude of the wheat's value; nevertheless they are its prices, for they are, in the first place, the form under which its value appears, *i.e.*, money; and in the second place, the exponents of its exchange-ratio with money. If the conditions of production, in other words, if the productive power of labour remain constant, the same amount of social labour-time must, both before and after the change in price, be expended in the reproduction of a quarter of wheat. This circumstance depends, neither on the will of the wheat producer, nor on that of the owners of other commodities.

Magnitude of value expresses a relation of social production, it expresses the connexion that necessarily exists between a certain article and the portion of the total labour-time of society required to produce it. As soon as magnitude of value is converted into price, the above necessary relation takes the shape of a more or less accidental exchange-ratio between a single commodity and another, the money-commodity. But this exchange-ratio may express either the real magnitude of that commodity's value, or the quantity of gold deviating from that value, for which, according to circumstances, it may be parted with. The possibility, therefore, of quantitative incongruity between price and magnitude of value, or the deviation of the former from the latter, is inherent in the price-form itself. This is no defect, but, on the contrary, admirably adapts the price-form to a mode of production whose inherent laws impose themselves only as the mean of apparently lawless irregularities that compensate one another.

The price-form, however, is not only compatible with the possibility of a quantitative incongruity between magnitude of value and price, *i.e.*, between the former and its expression in money, but it may also conceal a qualitative inconsistency, so much so, that, although money is nothing but the value-form of commodities, price ceases altogether to express value. Objects that in themselves are no commodities, such as conscience, honour, &c., are capable of being offered for sale by their holders, and of thus acquiring, through their price, the form of commodities. Hence an object may have a price without having value. The price in that case is imaginary, like certain quantities in mathematics. On the other hand, the imaginary price-form may sometimes conceal either a direct or indirect real value-relation; for instance, the price of uncultivated land, which is without value, because no human labour has been incorporated in it.

Price, like relative value in general, expresses the value of a commodity *(e.g.*, a ton of iron), by stating that a given quantity of the equivalent *(e.g.*, an ounce of gold), is directly exchangeable for iron. But it by no means states the converse, that iron is directly exchangeable for gold. In order, therefore, that a commodity may in practice act effectively as exchange-value, it must quit its bodily shape, must transform itself from mere imaginary into real gold, although to the commodity such transubstantiation may be more difficult than to the Hegelian 'concept,' the transition from 'necessity' to 'freedom,' or to a lobster the casting of his shell, or to Saint Jerome the putting off of the old Adam.[15] Though a commodity may, side by side with its actual form (iron, for instance), take in our imagination the form of gold, yet it cannot at one and the same time actually be both iron and gold. To fix its price, it suffices to equate it to gold in imagination. But, to enable it to render to its owner the service of a universal equivalent, it must be actually replaced by gold. If the owner of the iron were to go to the owner of some other commodity offered for exchange, and were to refer him to the price of the iron as proof that it was already money, he would get the same answer as St. Peter gave in heaven to Dante, when the latter recited the creed—

> 'Assai bene è trascorsa d'esta moneta già la lega e 'l peso, ma dimmi se tu l'hai ne la tua borsa.'

A price, therefore, implies both that a commodity is exchangeable for money, and also that it must be so exchanged. On the other hand, gold serves as an ideal measure of value, only because it has already, in the process of exchange, established itself as the money-commodity. Under the ideal measure of values there lurks the hard cash.

Section 2: *The Medium of Circulation*

A. The Metamorphosis of Commodities

We saw in a former chapter that the exchange of commodities implies contradictory and mutually exclusive conditions. The differentiation of commodities into commodities and money does not sweep away these inconsistencies, but develops a *modus vivendi*, a form in which they can exist side by side. This is generally the way in which real contradictions are reconciled. For instance, it is a contradiction to depict one body as constantly falling towards another, and as, at the same time, constantly flying away from it. The ellipse is a form of motion which, while allowing this contradiction to go on, at the same time reconciles it.

In so far as exchange is a process, by which commodities are transferred from hands in which they are non-use-values, to hands in which they become use-values, it is a social circulation of matter. The product of one form of useful labour replaces that of another. When once a commodity has found a resting-place, where it can serve as a use-value, it falls out of the sphere of exchange into that of consumption. But the former sphere alone interests us at present. We have, therefore, now to consider exchange from a formal point of view; to investigate the change of form or metamorphosis of commodities which effectuates the social circulation of matter.

The comprehension of this change of form is, as a rule, very imperfect. The cause of this imperfection is, apart from indistinct notions of value itself, that every change of form in a commodity results from the exchange of two commodities, an ordinary one and the money-commodity. If we keep in view the material fact alone that a commodity has been exchanged for gold, we overlook the very thing that we ought to observe—namely, what has happened to the form of the commodity. We overlook the facts that gold, when a mere commodity, is not money, and that when other commodities express their prices in gold, this gold is but the money-form of those commodities themselves.

Commodities, first of all, enter into the process of exchange just as they are. The process then differentiates them into commodities and money, and thus produces an external opposition corresponding to the internal opposition inherent in them, as being at once use-values and values. Commodities as use-values now stand opposed to money as exchange-value. On the other hand, both opposing sides are commodities, unities of use-value and value. But this unity of differences manifests itself at two opposite poles, and at each pole in an opposite way. Being poles they are as necessarily opposite as they are connected. On the one side of the equation we have an ordinary commodity, which is in reality a use-value. Its value is expressed only ideally in its price, by which it is equated to its opponent, the gold, as to the real embodiment of its value. On the other hand, the gold, in its metallic reality, ranks as the embodiment of value, as money. Gold, as gold, is exchange-value itself. As to its use-value, that has only an ideal existence, represented by the series of expressions of relative value in which it stands face to face with all other commodities, the sum of whose uses makes up the sum of the various uses of gold. These antagonistic forms of commodities are the real forms in which the process of their exchange moves and takes place.

Let us now accompany the owner of some commodity—say, our old friend the weaver of linen—to the scene of action, the market. His 20 yards of linen has a definite price, £2. He exchanges it for the £2, and then, like a man of the good old stamp that he is, he parts with the £2 for a family Bible of the same price. The linen, which in his eyes is a mere commodity, a depository of value, he alienates in exchange for gold, which is the linen's value-form, and this form he again parts with for another commodity, the Bible, which is destined to enter his house as an object of utility and of edification to its inmates. The exchange becomes an accomplished fact by two metamorphoses of opposite yet supplementary character—the conversion of the commodity into money, and the re-conversion of the money into a commodity.[16] The two phases of this metamorphosis are both of them distinct transactions of the weaver—selling, or the exchange of the commodity for money; buying, or the exchange of the money for a commodity; and, the unity of the two acts, selling in order to buy.

The result of the whole transaction, as regards the weaver, is this, that instead of being in possession of the linen, he now has the Bible; instead of his original commodity, he now possesses another of the same value but of different utility. In like manner he procures his other means of subsistence and means of production. From his point of view, the whole process effectuates nothing more than the exchange of the product of his labour for the product of some one else's, nothing more than an exchange of products.

The exchange of commodities is therefore accompanied by the following changes in their form.

Commodity—Money—Commodity.
C——— M ———C.

The result of the whole process is, so far as concerns the objects themselves, C—C, the exchange of one commodity for another, the circulation of materialised social labour. When this result is attained, the process is at an end.

C—M. First metamorphosis, or sale

The leap taken by value from the body of the commodity, into the body of the gold, is, as I have elsewhere called it, the salto mortale of the commodity. If it falls short, then, although the commodity itself is not harmed, its owner decidedly is. The social division of labour causes his labour to be as one-sided as his wants are many-sided. This is precisely the reason why the product of his labour serves him solely as exchange-value. But it cannot acquire the properties of a socially recognised universal equivalent, except by being converted into money. That money, however, is in some one else's pocket. In order to entice the money out of that pocket, our friend's commodity must, above all things, be a use-value to the owner of the money. For this, it is necessary that the labour expended upon it, be of a kind that is socially useful, of a kind that constitutes a branch of the social division of labour. But division of labour is a system of production which has grown up spontaneously and continues to grow behind the backs of the producers. The commodity to be exchanged may possibly be the product of some new kind of labour, that pretends to satisfy newly arisen requirements, or even to give rise itself to new requirements. A particular operation, though yesterday, perhaps, forming one out of the many operations conducted by one producer in creating a given commodity, may to-day separate itself from this connexion, may establish itself as an independent branch of labour and send its incomplete product to market as an independent commodity. The circumstances may or may not be ripe for such a separation. To-day the product satisfies a social want. Tomorrow the article may, either altogether or partially, be superseded by some other appropriate product. Moreover, although our weaver's labour may be a recognised branch of the social division of labour, yet that fact is by no means sufficient to guarantee the utility of his 20 yards of linen. If the community's want of linen, and such a want has a limit like every other want, should already be saturated by the products of rival weavers, our friend's product is superfluous, redundant, and consequently useless. Although people do not look a gift-horse in the mouth, our friend does not frequent the market for the purpose of making presents. But suppose his product turn out a real use-value, and thereby attracts money? The question arises, how much will it attract? No doubt the answer is already anticipated in the price of the article, in the exponent of the magnitude of its value. We leave out of consideration here any accidental miscalculation of value by our friend, a mistake that is soon rectified in the market. We suppose him to have spent on his product only that amount of labour-time that is on an average socially necessary. The price then, is merely the money-name of the quantity of social labour realised in his commodity. But without the leave, and behind the back, of our weaver, the old-fashioned mode of weaving undergoes a change. The labour-time that yesterday was without doubt socially necessary to the production of a yard of linen, ceases to be so to-day, a fact which the owner of the money is only too eager to prove from the prices quoted by our friend's competitors. Unluckily for him, weavers are not few and far between. Lastly, suppose that every piece of linen in the market contains no more labour-time than is socially necessary. In spite of this, all these pieces taken as a whole, may have had superfluous labour-time spent upon them. If the market cannot stomach the whole quantity at the normal price of 2 shillings a yard, this proves that too great a portion of the total labour of the community has been expended in the form of weaving. The effect is the same as if each individual weaver had expended more labour-time upon his particular product than is socially necessary. Here we may say, with the German proverb: caught together, hung together. All the linen in the market counts but as one article of commerce, of which each piece is only an aliquot part. And as a matter of fact, the value also of each single yard is but the materialised form of the same definite and socially fixed quantity of homogeneous human labour.[17]

We see then, commodities are in love with money, but 'the course of true love never did run smooth.' The quantitative division of labour is brought about in exactly the same spontaneous and accidental manner as its qualitative division. The owners of commodities therefore find out, that the same division of labour that turns them into independent private producers, also frees the social process of production and the relations of the individual producers to each other within that process, from all dependence on the will of those producers, and that the seeming mutual independence of the individuals is supplemented by a system of general and mutual dependence through or by means of the products.

The division of labour converts the product of labour into a commodity, and thereby makes necessary its further conversion into money. At the same time it also makes the accomplishment of this transubstantiation quite accidental. Here, however, we are only concerned with the phenomenon in its integrity, and we therefore assume its progress to be normal. Moreover, if the conversion take place at all, that is, if the commodity be not absolutely unsaleable, its metamorphosis does take place although the price realised may be abnormally above or below the value.

The seller has his commodity replaced by gold, the buyer has his gold replaced by a commodity. The fact which here stares us in the face is, that a commodity and gold, 20 yards of linen and £2, have changed hands and places, in other words, that they have been exchanged. But for what is the commodity exchanged? For the shape assumed by its own value, for the universal equivalent. And for what is the gold exchanged? For a particular form of its own use-value. Why does gold take the form of money face to face with the linen? Because the linen's price of £2, its denomination in money, has already equated the linen to gold in its character of money. A commodity strips off its original commodity-form on being alienated, *i.e.*, on the instant its use-value actually attracts the gold, that before existed only ideally in its price. The realisation of a commodity's price, or of its ideal value-form, is therefore at the same time the realisation of the ideal use-value of money; the conversion of a commodity into money, is the simultaneous conversion of money into a commodity. The apparently single process is in reality a double one. From the pole of the commodity-owner it is a sale, from the opposite pole of the money-owner, it is a purchase. In other words, a sale is a purchase, C—M is also M—C.[18]

Up to this point we have considered men in only one economic capacity, that of owners of commodities, a capacity in which they appropriate the produce of the labour of others, by alienating that of their own labour. Hence, for one commodity-owner to meet with another who has money, it is necessary, either, that the product of the labour of the latter person, the buyer, should be in itself money, should be gold, the material of which money consists, or that his product should already have changed its skin and have stripped off its original form of a useful object. In order that it may play the part of money, gold must of course enter the market at some point or other. This point is to be found at the source of production of the metal, at which place gold is bartered, as the immediate product of labour, for some other product of equal value. From that moment it always represents the realised price of some commodity.[19] Apart from its exchange for other commodities at the source of its production, gold, in whose-so-ever hands it may be, is the transformed shape of some commodity alienated by its owner; it is the product of a sale or of the first metamorphosis C—M.[20] Gold, as we saw, became ideal money, or a measure of values, in consequence of all commodities measuring their values by it, and thus contrasting it ideally with their natural shape as useful objects, and making it the shape of their value. It became real money, by the general alienation of commodities, by actually changing places with their natural forms as useful objects, and thus becoming in reality the embodiment of their values. When they assume this money-shape, commodities strip off every trace of their natural use-value, and of the particular kind of labour to which they owe their creation, in order to transform themselves into the uniform, socially recognised incarnation of homogeneous human labour. We cannot tell from the mere look of a piece of money, for what particular commodity it has been exchanged. Under their money-form all commodities look alike. Hence, money may be dirt, although dirt is not money. We will assume that the two gold pieces, in consideration of which our weaver has parted with his linen, are the metamorphosed shape of a quarter of wheat. The sale of the linen, C—M, is at the same time its purchase, M—C. But the sale is the first act of a process that ends with a transaction of an opposite nature, namely, the purchase of a Bible; the purchase of the linen, on the other hand, ends a movement that began with a transaction of an opposite nature, namely, with the sale of the wheat. C—M (linen—money), which is the first phase of C—M—C (linen—money—Bible), is also M—C (money—linen), the last phase of another movement C—M—C (wheat—money—linen). The first metamorphosis of one commodity, its transformation from a commodity into money, is therefore also invariably the second metamorphosis of some other commodity, the retransformation of the latter from money into a commodity.[21]

M—C, or *purchase.*
The second and concluding metamorphosis of a commodity

Because money is the metamorphosed shape of all other commodities, the result of their general alienation, for this reason it is alienable itself without restriction or condition. It reads all prices backwards, and thus, so to say, depicts itself in the bodies of all other commodities, which offer to it the material for the realisation of its own use-value. At the same time the prices, wooing glances cast at money by commodities, define the limits of its convertibility, by pointing to its quantity. Since every commodity, on becoming money, disappears as a commodity, it is impossible to tell from the money itself, how it got into the hands of its possessor, or what article has been changed into it. 'Non olet', from whatever source it may come. Representing on the one hand a sold commodity, it represents on the other a commodity to be bought.[22]

M—C, a purchase, is, at the same time, C—M, a sale; the concluding metamorphosis of one commodity is the first metamorphosis of another. With regard to our weaver, the life of his commodity ends with the Bible, into which he has reconverted his £2. But suppose the seller of the Bible turns the £2 set free by the weaver into brandy M—C, the concluding phase of C—M—C (linen—money—Bible), is also C—M, the first phase of C—M—C (Bible—money—brandy). The producer of a particular commodity has that one article alone to offer; this he sells very often in large quantities, but his many and various wants compel him to split up the price realised, the sum of money set free, into numerous purchases. Hence a sale leads to many purchases of various articles. The concluding metamorphosis of a commodity thus constitutes an aggregation of first metamorphoses of various other commodities.

If we now consider the completed metamorphosis of a commodity, as a whole, it appears in the first place, that it is made up of two opposite and complementary movements, C—M and M—C. These two antithetical transmutations of a commodity are brought about by two antithetical social acts on the part of the owner, and these acts in their turn stamp the character of the economic parts played by him. As the person who makes a sale, he is a seller; as the person who makes a purchase, he is a buyer. But just as, upon every such transmutation of a commodity, its two forms, commodity-form and money-form, exist simultaneously but at opposite poles, so every seller has a buyer opposed to him, and every buyer a seller. While one particular commodity is going through its two transmutations in succession, from a commodity into money and from money into another commodity, the owner of the commodity changes in succession his part from that of seller to that of buyer. These characters of seller and buyer are therefore not permanent, but attach themselves in turns to the various persons engaged in the circulation of commodities.

The complete metamorphosis of a commodity, in its simplest form, implies four extremes, and three dramatic personae. First, a commodity comes face to face with money; the latter is the form taken by the value of the former, and exists in all its hard reality, in the pocket of the buyer. A commodity-owner is thus brought into contact with a possessor of money. So soon, now, as the commodity has been changed into money, the money becomes its transient equivalent-form, the use-value of which equivalent-form is to be found in the bodies of other commodities. Money, the final term of the first transmutation, is at the same time the starting-point for the second. The person who is a seller in the first transaction thus becomes a buyer in the second, in which a third commodity-owner appears on the scene as a seller.[23]

The two phases, each inverse to the other, that make up the metamorphosis of a commodity constitute together a circular movement, a circuit: commodity-form, stripping off of this form, and return to the commodity-form. No doubt, the commodity appears here under two different aspects. At the starting-point it is not a use-value to its owner; at the finishing point it is. So, too, the money appears in the first phase as a solid crystal of value, a crystal into which the commodity eagerly solidifies, and in the second, dissolves into the mere transient equivalent-form destined to be replaced by a use-value.

The two metamorphoses constituting the circuit are at the same time two inverse partial metamorphoses of two other commodities. One and the same commodity, the linen, opens the series of its own metamorphoses, and completes the metamorphosis of another (the wheat). In the first phase or sale, the linen plays these two parts in its own person. But, then, changed into gold, it completes its own second and final metamorphosis, and helps at the same time to accomplish the first metamorphosis of a third commodity. Hence the circuit made by one commodity in the course of its metamorphoses is inextricably mixed up with the circuits of other commodities. The total of all the different circuits constitutes *the circulation of commodities*.

The circulation of commodities differs from the direct exchange of products (barter), not only in form, but in substance. Only consider the course of events. The weaver has, as a matter of fact, exchanged his linen for a Bible, his own commodity for that of some one else. But this is true only so far as he himself is concerned. The seller of the Bible, who prefers something to warm his inside, no more thought of exchanging his Bible for linen than our weaver knew that wheat had been exchanged for his linen. B's commodity replaces that of A, but A and B do not mutually exchange those commodities. It may, of course, happen that A and B make simultaneous purchases, the one from the other; but such exceptional transactions are by no means the necessary result of the general conditions of the circulation of commodities. We see here, on the one hand, how the exchange of commodities breaks through all local and personal bounds inseparable from direct barter, and develops the circulation of the products of social labour; and on the other hand, how it develops a whole network of social relations spontaneous in their growth and entirely beyond the control of the actors. It is only because the farmer has sold his wheat that the weaver is enabled to sell his linen, only because the weaver has sold his linen that our Hotspur is enabled to sell his Bible, and only because the latter has sold the water of everlasting life that the distiller is enabled to sell his *eau-de-vie*, and so on.

The process of circulation, therefore, does not, like direct barter of products, become extinguished upon the use-values changing places and hands. The money does not vanish on dropping out of the circuit of the metamorphosis of a given commodity. It is constantly being precipitated into new places in the arena of circulation vacated by other commodities. In the complete metamorphosis of the linen, for example, linen—money—Bible, the linen first falls out of circulation, and money steps into its place. Then the Bible falls out of circulation, and again money takes its place. When one commodity replaces another, the money-commodity always sticks to the hands of some third person.[24] Circulation sweats money from every pore.

Nothing can be more childish than the dogma, that because every sale is a purchase, and every purchase a sale, therefore the circulation of commodities necessarily implies an equilibrium of sales and purchases. If this means that the number of actual sales is equal to the number of purchases, it is mere tautology. But its real purport is to prove that every seller brings his buyer to market with him. Nothing of the kind. The sale and the purchase constitute one identical act, an exchange between a commodity-owner and an owner of money, between two persons as opposed to each other as the two poles of a magnet. They form two distinct acts, of polar and opposite characters, when performed by one single person. Hence the identity of sale and purchase implies that the commodity is useless, if, on being thrown into the alchemistical retort of circulation, it does not come out again in the shape of money; if, in other words, it cannot be sold by its owner, and therefore be bought by the owner of the money. That identity further implies that the exchange, if it does take place, constitutes a period of rest, an interval, long or short, in the life *of* the commodity. Since the first metamorphosis of a commodity is at once a sale and a purchase, it is also an independent process in itself. The purchaser has the commodity, the seller has the money, *i.e.*, a commodity ready to go into circulation at any time. No one can sell unless some one else purchases. But no one is forthwith bound to purchase, because he has just sold. Circulation bursts through all restrictions as to time, place, and individuals, imposed by direct barter, and this it effects by splitting up, into the antithesis of a sale and a purchase, the direct identity that in barter does exist between the alienation of one's own and the acquisition of some other man's product. To say that these two independent and antithetical acts have an intrinsic unity, are essentially one, is the same as to say that this intrinsic oneness expresses itself in an external antithesis. If the interval in time between the two complementary phases of the complete metamorphosis of a commodity become too great, if the split between the sale and the purchase become too pronounced, the intimate connexion between them, their oneness, asserts itself by producing—a crisis. The antithesis, use-value and value; the contradictions that private labour is bound to manifest itself as direct social labour, that a particularised concrete kind of labour has to pass for abstract human labour; the contradiction between the personification of objects and the representation of persons by things; all these antitheses and contradictions, which are immanent in commodities, assert themselves, and develop their modes of motion, in the antithetical phases of the metamorphosis of a commodity. These modes therefore imply the possibility, and no more than the possibility, of crises. The conversion of this mere possibility into a reality is the result of a long series of relations, that, from our present standpoint of simple circulation, have as yet no existence.[25]

B. The currency[26] of money

The change of form, C—M—C, by which the circulation of the material products of labour is brought about, requires that a given value in the shape of a commodity shall begin the process, and shall, also in the shape of a commodity, end it. The movement of the commodity is therefore a circuit. On the other hand, the form of this movement precludes a circuit from being made by the money. The result is not the return of the money, but its continued removal further and further away from its starting-point. So long as the seller sticks fast to his money, which is the transformed shape of his commodity, that commodity is still in the first phase of its metamorphosis, and has completed only half its course. But so soon as he completes the process, so soon as he supplements his sale by a purchase, the money again leaves the hands of its possessor. It is true that if the weaver, after buying the Bible, sell more linen, money comes back into his hands. But this return is not owing to the circulation of the first 20 yards of linen; that circulation resulted in the money getting into the hands of the seller of the Bible. The return of money into the hands of the weaver is brought about only by the renewal or repetition of the process of circulation with a fresh commodity, which renewed process ends with the same result as its predecessor did. Hence the movement directly imparted to money by the circulation of commodities takes the form of a constant motion away from its starting-point, of a course from the hands of one commodity-owner into those of another. This course constitutes its currency (cours de la monnaie).

The currency of money is the constant and monotonous repetition of the same process. The commodity is always in the hands of the seller; the money, as a means of purchase, always in the hands of the buyer. And money serves as a means of purchase by realising the price of the commodity. This realisation transfers the commodity from the seller to the buyer and removes the money from the hands of the buyer into those of the seller, where it again goes through the same process with another commodity. That this one-sided character of the money's motion arises out of the two-sided character of the commodity's motion, is a circumstance that is veiled over. The very nature of the circulation of commodities begets the opposite appearance. The first metamorphosis of a commodity is visibly, not only the money's movement, but also that of the commodity itself; in the second metamorphosis, on the contrary, the movement appears to us as the movement of the money alone. In the first phase of its circulation the commodity changes place with the money. Thereupon the commodity, under its aspect of a useful object, falls out of circulation into consumption.[27] In its stead we have its value-shape—the money. It then goes through the second phase of its circulation, not under its own natural shape, but under the shape of money. The continuity of the movement is therefore kept up by the money alone, and the same movement that as regards the commodity consists of two processes of an antithetical character, is, when considered as the movement of the money, always one and the same process, a continued change of places with ever fresh commodities. Hence the result brought about by the circulation of commodities, namely, the replacing of one commodity by another, takes the appearance of having been effected not by means of the change of form of the commodities but rather by the money acting as a medium of circulation, by an action that circulates commodities, to all appearance motionless in themselves, and transfers them from hands in which they are non-use-values, to hands in which they are use-values; and that in a direction constantly opposed to the direction of the money. The latter is continually withdrawing commodities from circulation and stepping into their places, and in thus way continually moving further and further from its starting-point. Hence although the movement of the money is merely the expression of the circulation of commodities, yet the contrary appears to be the actual fact, and the circulation of commodities seems to be the result of the movement of the money.[28]

Again, money functions as a means of circulation only because in it the values of commodities have independent reality. Hence its movement, as the medium of circulation, is, in fact, merely the movement of commodities while changing their forms. This fact must therefore make itself plainly visible in the currency of money. Thus the linen for instance, first of all changes its commodity-form into its money-form. The second term of its first metamorphosis, C—M, the money form, then becomes the first term of its final metamorphosis, M—C, its re-conversion into the Bible. But each of these two changes of form is accomplished by an exchange between commodity and money, by their *reciprocal displacement*. The same pieces of coin come into the seller's hand *as the alienated form of the commodity* and leave it as *the absolutely alienable form of the commodity*. They are displaced twice. The first metamorphosis of the linen puts these coins into the weaver's pocket, the second draws them out of it. The two inverse changes undergone by the same commodity are reflected in the displacement, twice repeated, but in opposite directions, of the same pieces of coin.

If, on the contrary, only one phase of the metamorphosis is gone through, if there are only sales or only purchases, then a given piece of money changes its place only once. Its second change of place always expresses the second metamorphosis of the commodity, its re-conversion from money. The frequent repetition of the displacement of the same coins reflects not only the series of metamorphoses that a single commodity has gone through, but also the intertwining of the innumerable metamorphoses in the world of commodities in general. It is a matter of course, that all this is applicable to the simple circulation of commodities alone, the only form that we are now considering.

Every commodity, when it first steps into circulation, and undergoes its first change of form, does so only to fall out of circulation again and to be replaced by other commodities. Money, on the contrary, as the medium of circulation, keeps continually within the sphere of circulation, and moves about in it. The question therefore arises, how much money this sphere constantly absorbs?

In a given country there take place every day at the same time, but in different localities, numerous one-sided metamorphoses of commodities, or, in other words, numerous sales and numerous purchases. The commodities are equated beforehand in imagination, by their prices, to definite quantities of money. And since, in the form of circulation now under consideration, money and commodities always come bodily face to face, one at the positive pole of purchase, the other at the negative pole of sale, it is clear that the amount of the means of circulation required, is determined beforehand by the sum of the prices of all these commodities. As a matter of fact, the money in reality represents the quantity or sum of gold ideally expressed beforehand by the sum of the prices of the commodities. The equality of these two sums is therefore self-evident. We know, however, that, the values of commodities remaining constant, their prices vary with the value of gold (the material of money), rising in proportion as it falls, and falling in proportion as it rises. Now if, in consequence of such a rise or fall in the value of gold, the sum of the prices of commodities fall or rise, the quantity of money in currency must fall or rise to the same extent. The change in the quantity of the circulating medium is, in this case, it is true, caused by the money itself, yet not in virtue of its function as a medium of circulation, but of its function as a measure of value. First, the price of the commodities varies inversely as the value of the money, and then the quantity of the medium of circulation varies directly as the price of the commodities. Exactly the same thing would happen if, for instance, instead of the value of gold falling, gold were replaced by silver as the measure of value, or if, instead of the value of silver rising, gold were to thrust silver out from being the measure of value. In the one case, more silver would be current than gold was before; in the other case, less gold would be current than silver was before. In each case the value of the material of money, *i.e.*, the value of the commodity that serves as the measure of value, would have undergone a change, and therefore so, too, would the prices of commodities which express their values in money, and so, too, would the quantity of money current whose function it is to realise those prices. We have already seen, that the sphere of circulation has an opening through which gold (or the material of money generally) enters into it as a commodity with a given value. Hence, when money enters on its functions as a measure of value, when it expresses prices, its value is already determined. If now its value fall, this fact is first evidenced by a change in the prices of those commodities that are directly bartered for the precious metals at the sources of their production. The greater part of all other commodities, especially in the imperfectly developed stages of civil society, will continue for a long time to be estimated by the former antiquated and illusory value of the measure of value. Nevertheless, one commodity infects another through their common value-relation, so that their prices, expressed in gold or in silver, gradually settle down into the proportions determined by their comparative values, until finally the values of all commodities are estimated in terms of the new value of the metal that constitutes money. This process is accompanied by the continued increase in the quantity of the precious metals, an increase caused by their streaming in to replace the articles directly bartered for them at their sources of production. In proportion therefore as commodities in general acquire their true prices, in proportion as their values become estimated according to the fallen value of the precious metal, in the same proportion the quantity of that metal necessary for realising those new prices is provided beforehand. A one-sided observation of the results that followed upon the discovery of fresh supplies of gold and silver, led some economists in the 17th, and particularly in the 18th century, to the false conclusion, that the prices of commodities had gone up in consequence of the increased quantity of gold and silver serving as means of circulation. Henceforth we shall consider the value of gold to be given, as, in fact, it is momentarily, whenever we estimate the price of a commodity.

On this supposition then, the quantity of the medium of circulation is determined by the sum of the prices that have to be realised. If now we further suppose the price of each commodity to be given, the sum of the prices clearly depends on the mass of commodities in circulation. It requires but little racking of brains to comprehend that if one quarter of wheat costs £2,100 quarters will cost £200, 200 quarters £400, and so on, that consequently the quantity of money that changes place with the wheat, when sold, must increase with the quantity of that wheat.

If the mass of commodities remain constant, the quantity of circulating money varies with the fluctuations in the prices of those commodities. It increases and diminishes because the sum of the prices increases or diminishes in consequence of the change of price. To produce this effect, it is, by no means, requisite that the prices of all commodities should rise or fall simultaneously. A rise or a fall in the prices of a number of leading articles, is sufficient in the one case to increase, in the other to diminish, the sum of the prices of all commodities, and, therefore, to put more or less money in circulation. Whether the change in the price correspond to an actual change of value in the commodities, or whether it be the result of mere fluctuations in market-prices, the effect on the quantity of the medium of circulation remains the same. Suppose the following articles to be sold or partially metamorphosed simultaneously in different localities: say, one quarter of wheat, 20 yards of linen, one Bible, and 4 gallons of brandy. If the price of each article be £2, and the sum of the prices to be realised be consequently £8, it follows that £8 in money must go into circulation. If, on the other hand, these same articles are links in the following chain of metamorphoses: 1 quarter of wheat—£2—20 yards of linen—£2—1 Bible—£2—4 gallons of brandy—£2, a chain that is already well known to us, in that case the £2 cause the different commodities to circulate one after the other, and after realising their prices successively, and therefore the sum of those prices, £8, they come to rest at last in the pocket of the distiller. The £2 thus make four moves. This repeated change of place of the same pieces of money corresponds to the double change in form of the commodities, to their motion in opposite directions through two stages of circulation. and to the interlacing of the metamorphoses of different commodities.[29] These antithetic and complementary phases, of which the process of metamorphosis consists, are gone through, not simultaneously, but successively. Time is therefore required for the completion of the series. Hence the velocity of the currency of money is measured by the number of moves made by a given piece of money in a given time. Suppose the circulation of the 4 articles takes a day. The sum of the prices to be realised in the day is £8, the number of moves of the two pieces of money is four, and the quantity of money circulating is £2. Hence, for a given interval of time during the process of circulation, we have the following relation: the quantity of money functioning as the circulating medium is equal to the sum of the prices of the commodities divided by the number of moves made by coins of the same denomination. This law holds generally.

The total circulation of commodities in a given country during a given period is made up on the one hand of numerous isolated and simultaneous partial metamorphoses, sales which are at the same time purchases, in which each coin changes its place only once, or makes only one move; on the other hand, of numerous distinct series of metamorphoses partly running side by side, and partly coalescing with each other, in each of which series each coin makes a number of moves, the number being greater or less according to circumstances. The total number of moves made by all the circulating coins of one denomination being given, we can arrive at the average number of moves made by a single coin of that denomination, or at the average velocity of the currency of money. The quantity of money thrown into the circulation at the beginning of each day is of course determined by the sum of the prices of all the commodities circulating simultaneously side by side. But once in circulation, coins are, so to say, made responsible for one another. If the one increase its velocity, the other either retards its own, or altogether falls out of circulation; for the circulation can absorb only such a quantity of gold as when multiplied by the mean number of moves made by one single coin or element, is equal to the sum of the prices to be realised. Hence, if the number of moves made by the separate pieces increase, the total number of those pieces in circulation diminishes. If the number of the moves diminish, the total number of pieces increases. Since the quantity of money capable of being absorbed by the circulation is given for a given mean velocity of currency, all that is necessary in order to abstract a given number of sovereigns from the circulation is to throw the same number of one-pound notes into it, a trick well known to all bankers.

Just as the currency of money, generally considered, is but a reflex of the circulation of commodities, or of the antithetical metamorphoses they undergo, so, too, the velocity of that currency reflects the rapidity with which commodities change their forms, the continued interlacing of one series of metamorphoses with another, the hurried social interchange of matter, the rapid disappearance of commodities from the sphere of circulation, and the equally rapid substitution of fresh ones in their places. Hence, in the velocity of the currency we have the fluent unity of the antithetical and complementary phases, the unity of the conversion of the useful aspect of commodities into their value-aspect, and their re-conversion from the latter aspect to the former, or the unity of the two processes of sale and purchase. On the other hand, the retardation of the currency reflects the separation of these two processes into isolated antithetical phases, reflects the stagnation in the change of form, and therefore, in the social interchange of matter. The circulation itself, of course, gives no clue to the origin of this stagnation; it merely puts in evidence the phenomenon itself. The general public, who, simultaneously with the retardation of the currency, see money appear and disappear less frequently at the periphery of circulation, naturally attribute this retardation to a quantitative deficiency in the circulating medium.[30]

The total quantity of money functioning during a given period as the circulating medium, is determined, on the one hand, by the sum of the prices of the circulating commodities, and on the other hand, by the rapidity with which the antithetical phases of the metamorphoses follow one another. On this rapidity depends what proportion of the sum of the prices can, on the average, be realised by each single coin. But the sum of the prices of the circulating commodities depends on the quantity, as well as on the prices, of the commodities. These three factors, however, state of prices, quantity of circulating commodities, and velocity of money-currency, are all variable. Hence, the sum of the prices to be realised, and consequently the quantity of the circulating medium depending on that sum, will vary with the numerous variations of these three factors in combination. Of these variations we shall consider those alone that have been the most important in the history of prices.

While prices remain constant, the quantity of the circulating medium may increase owing to the number of circulating commodities increasing, or to the velocity of currency decreasing, or to a combination of the two. On the other hand, the quantity of the circulating medium may decrease with a decreasing number of commodities, or with an increasing rapidity of their circulation.

With a general rise in the prices of commodities, the quantity of the circulating medium will remain constant, provided the number of commodities in circulation decrease proportionally to the increase in their prices, or provided the velocity of currency increase at the same rate as prices rise, the number of commodities in circulation remaining constant. The quantity of the circulating medium may decrease, owing to the number of commodities decreasing more rapidly; or to the velocity of currency increasing more rapidly, than prices rise.

With a general fall in the prices of commodities, the quantity of the circulating medium will remain constant, provided the number of commodities increase proportionally to their fall in price, or provided the velocity of currency decrease in the same proportion. The quantity of the circulating medium will increase, provided the number of commodities increase quicker, or the rapidity of circulation decrease quicker, than the prices fall.

The variations of the different factors may mutually compensate each other, so that notwithstanding their continued instability, the sum of the prices to be realised and the quantity of money in circulation remain constant; consequently, we find, especially if we take long periods into consideration, that the deviations from the average level, of the quantity of money current in any country, are much smaller than we should at first sight expect, apart of course from excessive perturbations periodically arising from industrial and commercial crises, or less frequently, from fluctuations in the value of money.

The law, that the quantity of the circulating medium is determined by the sum of the prices of the commodities circulating, and the average velocity of currency[31] may also be stated as follows: given the sum of the values of commodities, and the average rapidity of their metamorphoses, the quantity of precious metal current as money depends on the value of that precious metal. The erroneous opinion that it is, on the contrary, prices that are determined by the quantity of the circulating medium, and that the latter depends on the quantity of the precious metals in a country;[32] this opinion was based by those who first held it, on the absurd hypothesis that commodities are without a price, and money without a value, when they first enter into circulation, and that, once in the circulation, an aliquot part of the medley of commodities is exchanged for an aliquot part of the heap of precious metals.[33]

C. Coin and Symbols of Value

That money takes the shape of coin, springs from its function as the circulating medium. The weight of gold represented in imagination by the prices or money-names of commodities, must confront those commodities, within the circulation, in the shape of coins or pieces of gold of a given denomination. Coining, like the establishment of a standard of prices, is the business of the State. The different national uniforms worn at home by gold and silver as coins, and doffed again in the market of the world, indicate the separation between the internal or national spheres of the circulation of commodities, and their universal sphere.

The only difference, therefore, between coin and bullion, is one of shape, and gold can at any time pass from one form to the other.[34] But no sooner does coin leave the mint, than it immediately finds itself on the high-road to the melting pot. During their currency, coins wear away, some more, others less. Name and substance, nominal weight and real weight, begin their process of separation. Coins of the same denomination become different in value, because they are different in weight. The weight of gold fixed upon as the standard of prices, deviates from the weight that serves as the circulating medium, and the latter thereby ceases any longer to be a real equivalent of the commodities whose prices it realises. The history of coinage during the middle ages and down into the 18th century, records the ever renewed confusion arising from this cause. The natural tendency of circulation to convert coins into a mere semblance of what they profess to be, into a symbol of the weight of metal they are officially supposed to contain, is recognised by modern legislation, which fixes the loss of weight sufficient to demonetise a gold coin, or to make it no longer legal tender.

The fact that the currency of coins itself effects a separation between their nominal and their real weight, creating a distinction between them as mere pieces of metal on the one hand, and as coins with a definite function on the other—this fact implies the latent possibility of replacing metallic coins by tokens of some other material, by symbols serving the same purposes as coins. The practical difficulties in the way of coining extremely minute quantities of gold or silver, and the circumstance that at first the less precious metal is used as a measure of value instead of the-more precious, copper instead of silver, silver instead of gold, and that the less precious circulates as money until dethroned by the more precious—all these facts explain the parts historically played by silver and copper tokens as substitutes for gold coins. Silver and copper tokens take the place of gold in those regions of the circulation where coins pass from hand to hand most rapidly, and are subject to the maximum amount of wear and tear. This occurs where sales and purchases on a very small scale are continually happening. In order to prevent these satellites from establishing themselves permanently in the place of gold, positive enactments determine the extent to which they must be compulsorily received as payment instead of gold. The particular tracks pursued by the different species of coin in currency, run naturally into each other. The tokens keep company with gold, to pay fractional parts of the smallest gold coin; gold is, on the one hand, constantly pouring into retail circulation, and on the other hand is as constantly being thrown out again by being changed into tokens.[35]

The weight of metal in the silver and copper tokens is arbitrarily fixed by law. When in currency, they wear away even more rapidly than gold coins. Hence their functions are totally independent of their weight, and consequently of all value. The function of gold as coin becomes completely independent of the metallic value of that gold. Therefore things that are relatively without value, such as paper notes, can serve as coins in its place. This purely symbolic character is to a certain extent masked in metal tokens. In paper money it stands out plainly. In fact, ce n'est que le premier pas qui coûte.

We allude here only to inconvertible paper money issued by the State and having compulsory circulation. It has its immediate origin in the metallic currency. Money based upon credit implies on the other hand conditions, which, from our standpoint of the simple circulation of commodities, are as yet totally unknown to us. But we may affirm this much, that just as true paper money takes its rise in the function of money as the circulating medium, so money based upon credit takes root spontaneously in the function of money as the means of payment.[36]

The State puts in circulation bits of paper on which their various denominations, say £1, £5, &c., are printed. In so far as they actually take the place of gold to the same amount, their movement is subject to the laws that regulate the currency of money itself. A law peculiar to the circulation of paper money can spring up only from the proportion in which that paper money represents gold. Such a law exists; stated simply, it is as follows: the issue of paper money must not exceed in amount the gold (or silver as the case may be) which would actually circulate if not replaced by symbols. Now the quantity of gold which the circulation can absorb, constantly fluctuates about a given level. Still, the mass of the circulating medium in a given country never sinks below a certain minimum easily ascertained by actual experience. The fact that this minimum mass continually undergoes changes in its constituent parts, or that the pieces of gold of which it consists are being constantly replaced by fresh ones, causes of course no change either in its amount or in the continuity of its circulation. It can therefore be replaced by paper symbols. If, on the other hand, all the conduits of circulation were to-day filled with paper money to the full extent of their capacity for absorbing money, they might to-morrow be overflowing in consequence of a fluctuation in the circulation of commodities. There would no longer be any standard. If the paper money exceed its proper limit, which is the amount in gold coins of the like denomination that can actually be current, it would, apart from the danger of falling into general disrepute, represent only that quantity of gold, which, in accordance with the laws of the circulation of commodities, is required, and is alone capable of being represented by paper. If the quantity of paper money issued be double what it ought to be, then, as a matter of fact, £1 would be the money-name not of 1/4 of an ounce, but of 1/8 of an ounce of gold. The effect would be the same as if an alteration had taken place in the function of gold as a standard of prices. Those values that were previously expressed by the price of £1 would now be expressed by the price of £2.

Paper money is a token representing gold or money. The relation between it and the values of commodities is this, that the latter are ideally expressed in the same quantities of gold that are symbolically represented by the paper. Only in so far as paper money represents gold, which like all other commodities has value, is it a symbol of value.[37]

Finally, some one may ask why gold is capable of being replaced by tokens that have no value? But, as we have already seen, it is capable of being so replaced only in so far as it functions exclusively as coin, or as the circulating medium, and as nothing else. Now, money has other functions besides this one, and the isolated function of serving as the mere circulating medium is not necessarily the only one attached to gold coin, although this is the case with those abraded coins that continue to circulate. Each piece of money is a mere coin, or means of circulation, only so long as it actually circulates. But this is just the case with that minimum mass of gold, which is capable of being replaced by paper money. That mass remains constantly within the sphere of circulation, continually functions as a circulating medium, and exists exclusively for that purpose. Its movement therefore represents nothing but the continued alternation of the inverse phases of the metamorphosis C—M—C, phases in which commodities confront their value-forms, only to disappear again immediately. The independent existence of the exchange-value of a commodity is here a transient apparition, by means of which the commodity is immediately replaced by another commodity. Hence, in this process which continually makes money pass from hand to hand, the mere symbolical existence of money suffices. Its functional existence absorbs, so to say, its material existence. Being a transient and objective reflex of the prices of commodities, it serves only as a symbol of itself, and is therefore capable of being replaced by a token.[38] One thing is, however, requisite; this token must have an objective social validity of its own, and this the paper symbol acquires by its forced currency. This compulsory action of the State can take effect only within that inner sphere of circulation which is coterminous with the territories of the community, but it is also only within that sphere that money completely responds to its function of being the circulating medium, or becomes coin.

Section 3: *Money*

The commodity that functions as a measure of value, and, either in its own person or by a representative, as the medium of circulation, is money. Gold (or silver) is therefore money. It functions as money, on the one hand, when it has to be present in its own golden person. It is then the money-commodity, neither merely ideal, as in its function of a measure of value, nor capable of being represented, as in its function of circulating medium. On the other hand, it also functions as money, when by virtue of its function, whether that function be performed in person or by representative, it congeals into the sole form of value, the only adequate form of existence of exchange-value, in opposition to use-value, represented by all other commodities.

A. Hoarding

The continual movement in circuits of the two antithetical metamorphoses of commodities, or the never ceasing alternation of sale and purchase, is reflected in the restless currency of money, or in the function that money performs of a *perpetuum mobile* of circulation. But so soon as the series of metamorphoses is interrupted, so soon as sales are not supplemented by subsequent purchases, money ceases to be mobilised; it is transformed, as Boisguillebert says, from 'meuble' into 'immeuble,' from movable into immovable, from coin into money.

With the very earliest development of the circulation of commodities, there is also developed the necessity, and the passionate desire, to hold fast the product of the first metamorphosis. This product is the transformed shape of the commodity, or its gold-chrysalis.[39] Commodities are thus sold not for the purpose of buying others, but in order to replace their commodity-form by their money-form. From being the mere means of effecting the circulation of commodities, this change of form becomes the end and aim. The changed form of the commodity is thus prevented from functioning as its unconditionally alienable form, or as its merely transient money-form. The money becomes petrified into a hoard, and the seller becomes a hoarder of money.

In the early stages of the circulation of commodities, it is the surplus use-values alone that are converted into money.. Gold and silver thus become of themselves social expressions for superfluity or wealth. This naive form of hoarding becomes perpetuated in those communities in which the traditional mode of production is carried on for the supply of a fixed and limited circle of home wants. It is thus with the people of Asia, and particularly of the East Indies. Vanderlint, who fancies that the prices of commodities in a country are determined by the quantity of gold and silver to be found in it, asks himself why Indian commodities are so cheap. Answer: Because the Hindus bury their money. From 1602 to 1734, he remarks, they buried 150 millions of pounds sterling of silver, which originally came from America to Europe.[40] In the 10 years from 1856 to 1866, England exported to India and China £120,000,000 in silver, which had been received in exchange for Australian gold. Most of the silver exported to China makes its way to India.

As the production of commodities further develops, every producer of commodities is compelled to make sure of the nexus rerum or the social pledge.[41] His wants are constantly making themselves felt, and necessitate the continual purchase of other people's commodities, while the production and sale of his own goods require time, and depend upon circumstances. In order then to be able to buy without selling, he must have sold previously without buying. This operation, conducted on a general scale, appears to imply a contradiction. But the precious metals at the sources of their production are directly exchanged for other commodities. And here we have sales (by the owners of commodities) without purchases (by the owners of gold or silver).[42] And subsequent sales, by other producers, unfollowed by purchases, merely bring about the distribution of the newly produced precious metals among all the owners of commodities. In this way, all along the line of exchange, hoards of gold and silver of varied extent are accumulated. With the possibility of holding and storing up exchange-value in the shape of a particular commodity, arises also the greed for gold. Along with the extension of circulation, increases the power of money, that absolutely social form of wealth ever ready for use. 'Gold is a wonderful thing! Whoever possesses it is lord of all he wants. By means of gold one can even get souls into Paradise.' (Columbus in his letter from Jamaica, 1503.) Since gold does not disclose what has been transformed into it, everything, commodity or not, is convertible into gold. Everything becomes saleable and buyable. The circulation becomes the great social retort into which everything is thrown, to come out again as a gold-crystal. Not even are the bones of saints, and still less are more delicate res sacrosanctae, extra commercium hominum able to withstand this alchemy.[43] Just as every qualitative difference between commodities is extinguished in money, so money, on its side, like the radical leveller that it is, does away with all distinctions.[43a] But money itself is a commodity, an external object, capable of becoming the private property of any individual. Thus, social power becomes the private power of private persons. The ancients therefore denounced money as subversive of the economic and moral order of things.[43b] Modern society, which, soon after its birth, pulled Plutus by the hair of his head from the bowels of the earth,[44] greets gold as its Holy Grail, as the glittering incarnation of the very principle of its own life.

A commodity, in its capacity of a use-value, satisfies a particular want, and is a particular element of material wealth. But the value of a commodity measures the degree of its attraction for all other elements of material wealth, and therefore measures the social wealth of its owner. To a barbarian owner of commodities, and even to a West-European peasant, value is the same as value-form, and therefore to him the increase in his hoard of gold and silver is an increase in value. It is true that the value of money varies, at one time in consequence of a variation in its own value, at another, in consequence of a change in the values of commodities. But this, on the one hand, does not prevent 200 ounces of gold from still containing more value than 100 ounces, nor, on the other hand, does it hinder the actual metallic form of this article from continuing to be the universal equivalent form of all other commodities, and the immediate social incarnation of all human labour. The desire after hoarding is in its very nature unsatiable. In its qualitative aspect, or formally considered, money has no bounds to its efficacy, *i.e.*, it is the universal representative of material wealth, because it is directly convertible into any other commodity. But, at the same time, every actual sum of money is limited in amount, and, therefore, as a means of purchasing, has only a limited efficacy. This antagonism between the quantitative limits of money and its qualitative boundlessness, continually acts as a spur to the hoarder in his Sisyphus-like labour of accumulating. It is with him as it is with a conqueror who sees in every new country annexed, only a new boundary.

In order that gold may be held as money, and made to form a hoard, it must be prevented from circulating, or from transforming itself into a means of enjoyment. The hoarder, therefore, makes a sacrifice of the lusts of the flesh to his gold fetish. He acts in earnest up to the Gospel of abstention. On the other hand, he can withdraw from circulation no more than what he has thrown into it in the shape of commodities. The more he produces, the more he is able to sell. Hard work, saving, and avarice are, therefore, his three cardinal virtues, and to sell much and buy little the sum of his political economy.[45]

By the side of the gross form of a hoard, we find also its aesthetic form in the possession of gold and silver articles. This grows with the wealth of civil society. 'Soyons riches ou paraissons riches' (Diderot).

In this way there is created, on the one hand, a constantly extending market for gold and silver, unconnected with their functions as money, and, on the other hand, a latent source of supply, to which recourse is had principally in times of crisis and social disturbance.

Hoarding serves various purposes in the economy of the metallic circulation. Its first function arises out of the conditions to which the currency of gold and silver coins is subject. We have seen how, along with the continual fluctuations in the extent and rapidity of the circulation of commodities and in their prices, the quantity of money current unceasingly ebbs and flows. This mass must, therefore, be capable of expansion and contraction. At one time money must be attracted in order to act as circulating coin, at another, circulating coin must be repelled in order to act again as more or less stagnant money. In order that the mass of money, actually current, may constantly saturate the absorbing power of the circulation, it is necessary that the quantity of gold and silver in a country be greater than the quantity required to function as coin. This condition is fulfilled by money taking the form of hoards. These reserves serve as conduits for the supply or withdrawal of money to or from the circulation, which in this way never overflows its banks.[46]

B. Means of Payment

In the simple form of the circulation of commodities hitherto considered, we found a given value always presented to us in a double shape, as a commodity at one pole, as money at the opposite pole. The owners of commodities came therefore into contact as the respective representatives of what were already equivalents. But with the development of circulation, conditions arise under which the alienation of commodities becomes separated, by an interval of time, from the realisation of their prices. It will be sufficient to indicate the most simple of these conditions. One sort of article requires a longer, another a shorter time for its production. Again, the production of different commodities depends on different seasons of the year. One sort of commodity may be born on its own market place, another has to make a long journey to market. Commodity-owner No. 1, may therefore be ready to sell, before No. 2 is ready to buy. When the same transactions are continually repeated between the same persons, the conditions of sale are regulated in accordance with the conditions of production. On the other hand, the use of a given commodity, of a house, for instance, is sold (in common parlance, let) for a definite period. Here, it is only at the end of the term that the buyer has actually received the use-value of the commodity. He therefore buys it before he pays for it. The vendor sells an existing commodity, the purchaser buys as the mere representative of money, or rather of future money. The vendor becomes a creditor, the purchaser becomes a debtor. Since the metamorphosis of commodities, or the development of their value-form, appears here under a new aspect, money also acquires a fresh function; it becomes the means of payment.

The character of creditor, or of debtor, results here from the simple circulation. The change in the form of that circulation stamps buyer and seller with this new die. At first, therefore, these new parts are just as transient and alternating as those of seller and buyer, and are in turns played by the same actors. But the opposition is not nearly so pleasant, and is far more capable of crystallisation.[47] The same characters can, however, be assumed independently of the circulation of commodities. The class-struggles of the ancient world took the form chiefly of a contest between debtors and creditors, which in Rome ended in the ruin of the plebeian debtors. They were displaced by slaves. In the middle ages the contest ended with the ruin of the feudal debtors, who lost their political power together with the economic basis on which it was established. Nevertheless, the money relation of debtor and creditor that existed at these two periods reflected only the deeper-lying antagonism between the general economic conditions of existence of the classes in question.

Let us return to the circulation of commodities. The appearance of the two equivalents, commodities and money, at the two poles of the process of sale, has ceased to be simultaneous. The money functions now, first as a measure of value in the determination of the price of the commodity sold; the price fixed by the contract measures the obligation of the debtor, or the sum of money that he has to pay at a fixed date. Secondly, it serves as an ideal means of purchase. Although existing only in the promise of the buyer to pay, it causes the commodity to change hands. It is not before the day fixed for payment that the means of payment actually steps into circulation, leaves the hand of the buyer for that of the seller. The circulating medium was transformed into a hoard, because the process stopped short after the first phase, because the converted shape of the commodity, viz., the money, was withdrawn from circulation. The means of payment enters the circulation, but only after the commodity has left it. The money is no longer the means that brings about the process. It only brings it to a close, by stepping in as the absolute form of existence of exchange-value, or as the universal commodity. The seller turned his commodity into money, in order thereby to satisfy some want, the hoarder did the same in order to keep his commodity in its money-shape, and the debtor in order to be able to pay; if he do not pay, his goods will be sold by the sheriff. The value-form of commodities, money, is therefore now the end and aim of a sale, and that owing to a social necessity springing out of the process of circulation itself.

The buyer converts money back into commodities before he has turned commodities into money: in other words, he achieves the second metamorphosis of commodities before the first. The seller's commodity circulates, and realises its price, but only in the shape of a legal claim upon money. It is converted into a use-value before it has been converted into money. The completion of its first metamorphosis follows only at a later period.[48]

The obligations falling due within a given period, represent the sum of the prices of the commodities, the sale of which gave rise to those obligations. The quantity of gold necessary to realise this sum, depends, in the first instance, on the rapidity of currency of the means of payment. That quantity is conditioned by two circumstances: first the relations between debtors and creditors form a sort of chain, in such a way that A, when he receives money from his debtor B, straightway hands it over to C his creditor, and so on; the second circumstance is the length of the intervals between the different due-days of the obligations. The continuous chain of payments, or retarded first metamorphoses, is essentially different from that interlacing of the series of metamorphoses which we considered on a former page. By the currency of the circulating medium, the connexion between buyers and sellers, is not merely expressed. This connexion is originated by, and exists in, the circulation alone. Contrariwise, the movement of the means of payment expresses a social relation that was in existence long before.

The fact that a number of sales take place simultaneously, and side by side, limits the extent to which coin can be replaced by the rapidity of currency. On the other hand, this fact is a new lever in economising the means of payment. In proportion as payments are concentrated at one spot, special institutions and methods are developed for their liquidation. Such in the middle ages were the *virements* at Lyons. The debts due to A from B, to B from C, to C from A, and so on, have only to be confronted with each other, in order to annul each other to a certain extent like positive and negative quantities. There thus remains only a single balance to pay. The greater the amount of the payments concentrated, the less is this balance relatively to that amount, and the less is the mass of the means of payment in circulation.

The function of money as the means of payment implies a contradiction without a terminus medius. In so far as the payments balance one another, money functions only ideally as money of account, as a measure of value. In so far as actual payments have to be made, money does not serve as a circulating medium, as a mere transient agent in the interchange of products, but as the individual incarnation of social labour, as the independent form of existence of exchange-value, as the universal commodity. This contradiction comes to a head in those phases of industrial and commercial crises which are known as monetary crises.[49] Such a crisis occurs only where the ever-lengthening chain of payments, and an artificial system of settling them, has been fully developed. Whenever there is a general and extensive disturbance of this mechanism, no matter what its cause, money becomes suddenly and immediately transformed, from its merely ideal shape of money of account, into hard cash. Profane commodities can no longer replace it. The use-value of commodities becomes valueless, and their value vanishes in the presence of its own independent form. On the eve of the crisis, the bourgeois, with the self-sufficiency that springs from intoxicating prosperity, declares money to be a vain imagination. Commodities alone are money. But now the cry is everywhere: money alone is a commodity! As the hart pants after fresh water, so pants his soul after money, the only wealth.[50] In a crisis, the antithesis between commodities and their value-form, money, becomes heightened into an absolute contradiction. Hence, in such events, the form under which money appears is of no importance. The money famine continues, whether payments have to be made in gold or in credit money such as bank-notes.[51]

If we now consider the sum total of the money current during a given period, we shall find that, given the rapidity of currency of the circulating medium and of the means of payment, it is equal to the sum of the prices to be realised, plus the sum of the payments falling due, minus the payments that balance each other, minus finally the number of circuits in which the same piece of coin serves in turn as means of circulation and of payment. Hence, even when prices, rapidity of currency, and the extent of the economy in payments, are given, the quantity of money current and the mass of commodities circulating during a given period, such as a day, no longer correspond. Money that represents commodities long withdrawn from circulation, continues to be current. Commodities circulate, whose equivalent in money will not appear on the scene till some future day. Moreover, the debts contracted each day, and the payments falling due on the same day, are quite incommensurable quantities.[52]

Credit-money springs directly out of the function of money as a means of payment. Certificates of the debts owing for the purchased commodities circulate for the purpose of transferring those debts to others. On the other hand, to the same extent as the system of credit is extended, so is the function of money as a means of payment. In that character it takes various forms peculiar to itself under which it makes itself at home in the sphere of great commercial transactions. Gold and silver coin, on the other hand, are mostly relegated to the sphere of retail trade.[53]

When the production of commodities has sufficiently extended itself, money begins to serve as the means of payment beyond the sphere of the circulation of commodities. It becomes the commodity that is the universal subject-matter of all contracts.[54] Rents, taxes, and such like payments are transformed from payments in kind into money payments. To what extent this transformation depends upon the general conditions of production, is shown, to take one example, by the fact that the Roman Empire twice failed in its attempt to levy all contributions in money. The unspeakable misery of the French agricultural population under Louis XIV., a misery so eloquently denounced by Boisguillebert, Marshal Vauban, and others, was due not only to the weight of the taxes, but also to the conversion of taxes in kind into money taxes.[55] In Asia, on the other hand, the fact that state taxes are chiefly composed of rents payable in kind, depends on conditions of production that are reproduced with the regularity of natural phenomena. And this mode of payment tends in its turn to maintain the ancient form of production. It is one of the secrets of the conservation of the Ottoman Empire. If the foreign trade, forced upon Japan by Europeans, should lead to the substitution of money rents for rents in kind, it will be all up with the exemplary agriculture of that country. The narrow economic conditions under which that agriculture is carried on, will be swept away.

In every country, certain days of the year become by habit recognised settling days for various large and recurrent payments. These dates depend, apart from other revolutions in the wheel of reproduction, on conditions closely connected with the seasons. They also regulate the dates for payments that have no direct connexion with the circulation of commodities such as taxes, rents, and so on. The quantity of money requisite to make the payments, falling due on those dates all over the country, causes periodical, though merely superficial, perturbations in the economy of the medium of payment.[56]

From the law of the rapidity of currency of the means of payment, it follows that the quantity of the means of payment required for all periodical payments, whatever their source, is in inverse[57] proportion to the length of their periods.[58]

The development of money into a medium of payment makes it necessary to accumulate money against the dates fixed for the payment of the sums owing. While hoarding, as a distinct mode of acquiring riches, vanishes with the progress of civil society, the formation of reserves of the means of payment grows with that progress.

C. Universal Money

When money leaves the home sphere of circulation, it strips off the local garbs which it there assumes, of a standard of prices, of coin, of tokens, and of a symbol of value, and returns to its original form of bullion. In the trade between the markets of the world, the value of commodities is expressed so as to be universally recognised. Hence their independent value-form also, in these cases, confronts them under the shape of universal money. It is only in the markets of the world that money acquires to the full extent the character of the commodity whose bodily form is also the immediate social incarnation of human labour in the abstract. Its real mode of existence in this sphere adequately corresponds to its ideal concept.

Within the sphere of home circulation, there can be but one commodity which, by serving as a measure of value, becomes money. In the markets of the world a double measure of value holds sway, gold and silver.[59]

Money of the world serves as the universal medium of payment, as the universal means of purchasing, and as the universally recognised embodiment of all wealth. Its function as a means of payment in the settling of international balances is its chief one. Hence the watchword of the mercantilists, balance of trade.[60] Gold and silver serve as international means of purchasing chiefly and necessarily in those periods when the customary equilibrium in the interchange of products between different nations is suddenly disturbed. And lastly, it serves as the universally recognised embodiment of social wealth, whenever the question is not of buying or paying, but of transferring wealth from one country to another, and whenever this transference in the form of commodities is rendered impossible, either by special conjunctures in the markets or by the purpose itself that is intended.[61]

Just as every country needs a reserve of money for its home circulation so, too, it requires one for external circulation in the markets of the world. The functions of hoards, therefore, arise in part out of the function of money, as the medium of the home circulation and home payments, and in part out of its function of money of the world.[62] For this latter function, the genuine money-commodity, actual gold and silver, is necessary. On that account, Sir James Steuart, in order to distinguish them from their purely local substitutes, calls gold and silver 'money of the world.'

The current of the stream of gold and silver is a double one. On the one hand, it spreads itself from its sources over all the markets of the world, in order to become absorbed, to various extents, into the different national spheres of circulation, to fill the conduits of currency, to replace abraded gold and silver coins, to supply the material of articles of luxury, and to petrify into hoards.[63] This first current is started by the countries that exchange their labour, realised in commodities, for the labour embodied in the precious metals by gold and silver-producing countries. On the other hand, there is a continual flowing backwards and forwards of gold and silver between the different national spheres of circulation, a current whose motion depends on the ceaseless fluctuations in the course of exchange.[64]

Countries in which the bourgeois form of production is developed to a certain extent, limit the hoards concentrated in the strong rooms of the banks to the minimum required for the proper performance of their peculiar functions.[65] Whenever these hoards are strikingly above their average level, it is, with some exceptions, an indication of stagnation in the circulation of commodities, of an interruption in the even flow of their metamorphoses.[66]

Notes

1. The question—Why does not money directly represent labour-time, so that a piece of paper may represent, for instance, x hours' labour, is at bottom the same as the question why, given the production of commodities, must products take the form of commodities? This is evident, since their taking the form of commodities implies their differentiation into commodities and money. Or, why cannot private labour—labour for the account of private individuals—be treated as its opposite, immediate social labour? I have elsewhere examined thoroughly the Utopian idea of 'labour-money' in a society founded on the production of commodities (l. c., p. 61, seq.). On this point I will only say further, that Owen's 'labour-money,' for instance, is no more 'money' than a ticket for the theatre. Owen pre-supposes directly associated labour, a form of production that is entirely inconsistent with the production of commodities. The certificate of labour is merely evidence of the part taken by the individual in the common labour, and of his right to a certain portion of the common produce destined for consumption. But it never enters into Owen's head to pre-suppose the production of commodities, and at the same time, by juggling with money, to try to evade the necessary conditions of that production.
2. Savages and half-civilised races use the tongue differently. Captain Parry says of the

inhabitants on the west coast of Baffin's Bay: 'In this case (he refers to barter) they licked it (the thing represented to them) twice to their tongues, after which they seemed to consider the bargain satisfactorily concluded.' In the same way, the Eastern Esquimaux licked the articles they received in exchange. If the tongue is thus used in the North as the organ of appropriation, no wonder that, in the South, the stomach serves as the organ of accumulated property, and that a Kaffir estimates the wealth of a man by the size of his belly. That the Kaffirs know what they are about is shown by the following: at the same time that the official British Health Report of 1864 disclosed the deficiency of fat-forming food among a large part of the working-class, a certain Dr Harvey (not, however, the celebrated discoverer of the circulation of the blood), made a good thing by advertising recipes for reducing the superfluous fat of the bourgeoisie and aristocracy.

3. See Karl Marx: 'Zur Kritik, &c.' 'Theorien von der Masseinheit des Geldes,' p. 53, seq.

4. 'Wherever gold and silver have by law been made to perform the function of money or of a measure of value side by side, it has always been tried, but in vain, to treat them as one and the same material. To assume that there is an invariable ratio between the quantities of gold and silver in which a given quantity of labour-time is incorporated, is to assume in fact, that gold and silver are of one and the same material, and that a given mass of the less valuable metal, silver, is a constant fraction of a given mass of gold. From the reign of Edward III. to the time of George II., the history of money in England consists of one long series of perturbations caused by the clashing of the legally fixed ratio between the values of gold and silver, with the fluctuations in their real values. At one time gold was too high, at another, silver. The metal that for the time being was estimated below its value, was withdrawn from circulation, mated and exported. The ratio between the two metals was then again altered by law, but the new nominal ratio soon came into conflict again with the real one. In our own times, the slight and transient fall in the value of gold compared with silver, which was a consequence of the Indo-Chinese demand for silver, produced on a far more extended scale in France the same phenomena, export of silver, and its expulsion from circulation by gold. During the years 1855, 1856 and 1857, the excess in France of gold-imports over gold-exports amounted to £41,580,000, while the excess of silver-exports over silver-imports was £14,704,000. In fact, in those countries in which both metals are legally measures of value, and therefore both legal tender, so that everyone has the option of paying in either metal, the metal that rises in value is at a premium, and, like every other commodity, measures its price in the over-estimated metal which alone serves in reality as the standard of value. The result of all experience and history with regard to this equation is simply that, where two commodities perform by law the functions of a measure of value, in practice one alone maintains that position.' (Karl Marx, l.c., pp. 52, 53.)

5. The peculiar circumstance, that while the ounce of gold serves in England as the unit of the standard of money, the pound sterling does not form an aliquot part of it, has been explained as follows: 'Our coinage was originally adapted to the employment of silver only, hence, an ounce of silver can always be divided into a certain adequate number of pieces of coin, but as gold was introduced at a later period into a coinage adapted only to silver, an ounce of gold cannot be coined into an aliquot number of pieces.' Maclaren, 'A Sketch of the History of the Currency.' London, 1858, p. 16.

6. With English writers the confusion between measure of value and standard of price (standard of value) is indescribable. Their functions, as well as their names, are constantly interchanged.

7. Moreover, it has not general historical validity.

8. It is thus that the pound sterling in English denotes less than one-third of its original weight; the pound Scot, before the union, only 1-36th; the French livre, 1-74th; the Spanish maravedi, less than 1-1,000th; and the Portuguese rei a still smaller fraction.

9. 'Le monete le quali oggi sono ideal, sono le più antiche d'ogni nazione, e tutte furono un

tempo real, e perche erano reali con esse si contava' ['The coins which today are ideal are the oldest coins of every nation, and all of them were once real, and precisely because they were real they were used for calculation'] (Galiani: Della moneta, l.c., p. 153.)

10. David Urquhart remarks in his 'Familiar Words' on the monstrosity (!) that now-a-days a pound (sterling), which is the unit of the English standard of money, is equal to about a quarter of an ounce of gold. 'This is falsifying a measure, not establishing a standard.' He sees in this 'false denomination' of the weight of gold, as in everything else, the falsifying hand of civilisation.

11. When Anacharsis was asked for what purposes the Greeks used money, he replied, 'For reckoning.' (Ashen. Deipn. 1. iv. 49 v. 2. ed. Schweighauser, 1802.)

12. 'Owing to the fact that money, when serving as the standard of price, appears under the same reckoning names as do the prices of commodities, and that therefore the sum of £3 17s. 10 1/2d. may signify on the one hand an ounce weight of gold, and on the other, the value of a ton of iron, this reckoning name of money has been called its mint-price. Hence there sprang up the extraordinary notion, that the value of gold is estimated in its own material, and that, in contradistinction to all other commodities, its price is fixed by the State. It was erroneously thought that the giving of reckoning names to definite weights of gold, is the same thing as fixing the value of those weights.' (Karl Marx, l.c., p. 52.)

13. See 'Theorien von der Masseinheit des Geldes' in 'Zur Kritik der Poll Oekon. &c.,' p. 53, seq. The fantastic notions about raising or lowering the mint-price of money by transferring to greater or smaller weights of gold or silver, the names already legally appropriated to fixed weights of those metals; such notions, at least in those cases in which they aim, not at clumsy financial operations against creditors, both public and private but at economic quack remedies, have been so exhaustively treated by Wm. Petty in his 'Quantulumcunque concerning money: To the Lord Marquis of Halifax, 1682,' that even his immediate followers, Sir Dudley North and John Locke, not to mention later ones, could only dilute him. 'If the wealth of a nation' he remarks, 'could be decupled by a proclamation, it were strange that such proclamations have not long since been made by our Governors.' (l.c., p. 36.)

14. 'Ou bien, il faut consentir à dire qu'une valeur d'un million en argent vaut plus qu'une valeur égale en marchandises.' ['Or indeed it must be admitted that a million in money is worth more than an equal value in commodities'] (Le Trosne, l.c., p. 919), which amounts to saying 'qu'une valeur vaut plus qu'une valeur égale.' ['that one value is worth more than another value which is equal to it.']

15. Jerome had to wrestle hard, not only in his youth with the bodily flesh, as is shown by his fight in the desert with the handsome women of his imagination, but also in his old age with the spiritual flesh. 'I thought,' he says, 'I was in the spirit before the Judge of the Universe.' 'Who art thou?' asked a voice. 'I am a Christian.' 'Thou liest,' thundered back the great Judge, 'thou art nought but a Ciceronian.'

16. 'eχ sε tou ... puroσ τ'antameeibesqaι panta, jhsiv δ'Hracleitoσ, caι pup apantwv, wopep crusou crhmata caι crhmatwv crusoσ.' ['As Heraclitus says, all things are exchanged for fire and fire for all things, as wares are exchanged for gold and gold for wares.'] (F. Lassalle: 'Die Philosophie Herakleitos des Dunkeln.' Berlin, 1858, Vol. I, p. 222.) Lassalle in his note on this passage, p. 224, n. 3., erroneously makes gold a mere symbol of value.

17. *Note by the Institute of Marxism-Leninism in the Russian edition.*—In his letter of November 28, 1878, to N. F. Danielson (Nikolai-on) Marx proposed that this sentence be corrected to read as follows: 'And, as a matter of fact, the value of each single yard is but the materialised form of a part of the social labour expended on the whole number of yards.' An analogous correction was made in a copy of the second German edition of the first volume of 'Capital' belonging to Marx; however, not in his handwriting.

18. 'Toute vente est achat.' ['Every sale is a purchase.'] (Dr Quesnay: 'Dialogues sur le Commerce et les Travaux des Artisans.' Physiocrates ed. Daire I. Partie, Paris, 1846, p. 170), or as

Quesnay in his 'Maximes générales' puts it, 'Vendre est acheter.' ['To sell is to buy.']

19. 'Le prix d'une marchandise ne pouvant être payé que par le prix d'une autre marchandise' (Mercier de la Rivière: 'L'Ordre naturel et essentiel des sociétés politiques.' ['The price of one commodity can only be paid by the price of another commodity'] Physiocrates, ed. Daire II. Partie, p. 554.)

20. 'Pour avoir cet argent, il faut avoir vendu,' ['In order to have this money, one must have made a sale,'] l.c., p. 543.

21. As before remarked, the actual producer of gold or silver forms an exception. He exchanges his product directly for another commodity, without having first sold it.

22. 'Si l'argent représente, dans nos mains, les choses que nous pouvons désirer d'acheter, il y représente aussi les choses que nous avons vendues pour cet argent.' ['If money represents, in our hands, the things we can wish to buy, it also represents the things we have sold to obtain that money'] (Mercier de la Rivière, l.c., p. 586.)

23. 'Il y a donc ... quatre termes et trois contractants, dont l'un intervient deux fois' ['There are therefore ... four terms and three contracting parties, one of whom intervenes twice'] (Le Trosne, l.c., p. 909.)

24. Self-evident as this may be, it is nevertheless for the most part unobserved by political economists, and especially by the 'Free-trader Vulgaris.'

25. See my observations on James Mill in 'Zur Kritik, &c.,' pp. 74-76. With regard to this subject, we may notice two methods characteristic of apologetic economy. The first is the identification of the circulation of commodities with the direct barter of products, by simple abstraction from their points of difference; the second is, the attempt to explain away the contradictions of capitalist production, by reducing the relations between the persons engaged in that mode of production, to the simple relations arising out of the circulation of commodities. The production and circulation of commodities are however, phenomena that occur to a greater or less extent in modes of production the most diverse. If we are acquainted with nothing but the abstract categories of circulation, which are common to all these modes of production, we cannot possibly know anything of the specific points of difference of those modes, nor pronounce any judgment upon them. In no science is such a big fuss made with commonplace truisms as in Political Economy. For instance, J. B. Say sets himself up as a judge of crises, because, forsooth, he knows that a commodity is a product.

26. *Translator's note.*—This word is here used in its original signification of the course or track pursued by money as it changes from hand to hand, a course which essentially differs from circulation.

27. Even when the commodity is sold over and over again, a phenomenon that at present has no existence for us, it falls, when definitely sold for the last time, out of the sphere of circulation into that of consumption, where it serves either as means of subsistence or means of production.

28. 'Il (l'argent) n'a d'autre mouvement que celui qui lui est imprimé par les productions.' ['It' (money) 'has no other motion than that imparted to it by the products'] (Le Trosne, l.c., p. 885.)

29. 'Ce sont les productions qui le (l'argent) mettent en mouvement et le font circuler ... La célérité de son mouvement (c. de l'argent) supplée à sa quantité. Lorsqu'il en est besoin il ne fait que glisser d'une main dans l'autre sans s'arrêter un instant.' ['It is products which set it' (money) 'in motion and make it circulate ... The velocity of its' (money's) 'motion supplements its quantity. When necessary, it does nothing but slide from hand to hand, without stopping for a moment'] (Le Trosne, l.c.. pp. 915, 916.)

30. 'Money being ... the common measure of buying and selling, everybody who hath anything to sell, and cannot procure chapmen for it, is presently apt to think, that want of money in the kingdom, or country, is the cause why his goods do not go off; and so, want of money

is the common cry; which is a great mistake... What do these people want, who cry out for money? ... The farmer complains ... he thinks that were more money in the country; he should have a price for his goods. Then it seems money is not his want, but a price for his corn and cattel, which he would sell, but cannot... Why cannot he get a price? ... (1) Either there is too much corn and cattel in the country, so that most who come to market have need of selling, as he hath, and few of buying; or (2) There wants the usual vent abroad by transportation..., or (3) The consumption fails, as when men, by reason of poverty, do not spend so much in their houses as formerly they did; wherefore it is not the increase of specific money, which would at all advance the farmer's goods, but the removal of any of these three causes, which do truly keep down the market... The merchant and shopkeeper want money in the same manner, that is, they want a vent for the goods they deal in, by reason that the markets fail' ... [A nation] 'never thrives better, than when riches are tost from hand to hand.' (Sir Dudley North: 'Discourses upon Trade,' Lond. 1691, pp. 11-15, passim.) Herrenschwand's fanciful notions amount merely to this, that the antagonism, which has its origin in the nature of commodities, and is reproduced in their circulation, can be removed by increasing the circulating medium. But if, on the one hand, it is a popular delusion to ascribe stagnation in production and circulation to insufficiency of the circulating medium, it by no means follows, on the other hand, that an actual paucity of the medium in consequence, *e.g.*, of bungling legislative interference with the regulation of currency, may not give rise to such stagnation.

31. 'There is a certain measure and proportion of money requisite to drive the trade of a nation, more or less than which would prejudice the same. Just as there is a certain proportion of farthings necessary in a small retail trade, to change silver money, and to even such reckonings as cannot be adjusted with the smallest silver pieces.... Now, as the proportion of the number of farthings requisite in commerce is to be taken from the number of people, the frequency of their exchanges: as also, and principally, from the value of the smallest silver pieces of money; so in like manner, the proportion of money [gold and silver specie] requisite in our trade, is to be likewise taken from the frequency of commutations, and from the bigness of the payments.' (William Petty, 'A Treatise of Taxes and Contributions.' Lond. 1667, p. 17.) The Theory of Hume was defended against the attacks of J. Steuart and others, by A. Young, in his 'Political Arithmetic,' Lond. 1774, in which work there is a special chapter entitled 'Prices depend on quantity of money, at p. 112, sqq. I have stated in 'Zur Kritik, &c.,' p. 149: 'He (Adam Smith) passes over without remark the question as to the quantity of coin in circulation, and treats money quite wrongly as a mere commodity.' This statement applies only in so far as Adam Smith, ex officio, treats of money. Now and then, however, as in his criticism of the earlier systems of Political Economy, he takes the right view. 'The quantity of coin in every country is regulated by the value of the commodities which are to be circulated by It.... The value of the goods annually bought and sold in any country requires a certain quantity of money to circulate and distribute them to their proper consumers, and can give employment to no more. The channel of circulation necessarily draws to itself a sum sufficient to fill it, and never admits any more.' ('Wealth of Nations.' Bk. IV., ch. 1.) In like manner, ex officio, he opens his work with an apotheosis on the division of labour. Afterwards, in the last book which treats of the sources of public revenue, he occasionally repeats the denunciations of the division of labour made by his teacher, A. Ferguson.

32. 'The prices of things will certainly rise in every nation, as the gold and silver increase amongst the people, and consequently, where the gold and silver decrease in any nation, the prices of all things must fall proportionately to such decrease of money.' (Jacob Vanderlint: 'Money Answers all Things.' Lond. 1734, p. 5.) A careful comparison of this book with Hume's 'Essays,' proves to my mind without doubt that Hume was acquainted with and made use of Vanderlint's work, which is certainly an important one. The opinion that prices are determined by the quantity of the circulating medium, was also held by Barbon and

other much earlier writers. 'No inconvenience,' says Vanderlint, 'can arise by an unrestrained trade, but very great advantage; since, if the cash of the nation be decreased by it, which prohibitions are designed to prevent, those nations that get the cash will certainly find everything advance in price, as the cash increases amongst them. And ... our manufactures, and everything else, will soon become so moderate as to turn the balance of trade in our favour, and thereby fetch the money back again.' (l.c.. pp. 43, 44.)

33. That the price of each single kind of commodity forms a part of the sum of the prices of all the commodities in circulation, is a self-evident proposition. But how use-values which are incommensurable with regard to each other, are to be exchanged, en masse for the total sum of gold and silver in a country, is quite incomprehensible. If we start from the notion that all commodities together form one single commodity, of which each is but an aliquot part, we get the following beautiful result: The total commodity = x cwt. of gold; commodity A = an aliquot part of the total commodity = the same aliquot part of x cwt. of gold. This is stated in all seriousness by Montesquieu: 'Si l'on compare la masse de l'or et de l'argent qui est dans le monde avec la somme des marchandises qui s'y vend il est certain que chaque denrée ou marchandise, en particulier, pourra être comparée à une certaine portion de la masse entière. Supposons qu'il n'y ait qu'une seule denrée ou marchandise dans le monde, ou qu'il n'y ait qu'une seule qui s'achète, et qu'elle se divise comme l'argent: Cette partie de cette marchandise répondra à une partie de la masse de l'argent; la moitié du total de l'une à la moitié du total de l'autre, &c.... L'établissement du prix des choses dépend toujours fondamentalement de la raison du total des choses au total des signes.' ['If one compares the amount of gold and silver in the world with the sum of the commodities available, it is certain that each product or commodity, taken in isolation, could be compared with a certain portion of the total amount of money. Let us suppose that there is only one product, or commodity, in the world, or only one that can be purchased, and that it can be divided in the same way as money: a certain part of this commodity would then correspond to a part of the total amount of money; half the total of the one would correspond to half the total of the other &c. ... the determination of the prices of things always depends, fundamentally, on the relation between the total amount of things and the total amount of their monetary symbols'] (Montesquieu, l.c. t. III, pp. 12, 13.) As to the further development of this theory by Ricardo and his disciples, James Mill, Lord Overstone, and others, see 'Zur Kritik, &c.,' pp. 140-146, and p. 150, sqq. John Stuart Mill, with his usual eclectic logic, understands how to hold at the same time the view of his father, James Mill, and the opposite view. On a comparison of the text of his compendium, 'Principles of Pol. Econ.,' with his preface to the first edition, in which preface he announces himself as the Adam Smith of his day—we do not know whether to admire more the simplicity of the man, or that of the public, who took him, in good faith, for the Adam Smith he announced himself to be, although he bears about as much resemblance to Adam Smith as say General Williams, of Kars, to the Duke of Wellington. The original researches of Mr J. S. Mill which are neither extensive nor profound, in the domain of Political Economy, will be found mustered in rank and file in his little work, 'Some Unsettled Questions of Political Economy,' which appeared in 1844. Locke asserts point blank the connexion between the absence of value in gold and silver, and the determination of their values by quantity alone. 'Mankind having consented to put an imaginary value upon gold and silver ... the intrinsic value, regarded in these metals, is nothing but the quantity." ('Some Considerations,' *&c.*, 1691, Works Ed. 1777, Vol. II., p. 15.)

34. It lies of course, entirely beyond my purpose to take into consideration such details as the seigniorage on minting. I will, however, cite for the benefit of the romantic sycophant, Adam Muller, who admires the 'generous liberality' with which the English Government coins gratuitously, the following opinion of Sir Dudley North: 'Silver and gold, like other commodities, have their ebbings and flowings. Upon the arrival of quantities from Spain ... it is carried into the Tower, and coined. Not long after there will come a demand for bullion

to be exported again. If there is none, but all happens to be in coin, what then? Melt it down again; there's no loss in it, for the coining costs the owner nothing. Thus the nation has been abused, and made to pay for the twisting of straw for asses to eat. If the merchant were made to pay the price of the coinage, he would not have sent his silver to the Tower without consideration, and coined money would always keep a value above uncoined silver.' (North, l.c., p. 18.) North was himself one of the foremost merchants in the reign of Charles II.

35. 'If silver never exceed what is wanted for the smaller payments it cannot be collected in sufficient quantities for the larger payments ... the use of gold in the main payments necessarily implies also its use in the retail trade: those who have gold coin offering them for small purchases, and receiving with the commodity purchased a balance of silver in return; by which means the surplus of silver that would otherwise encumber the retail dealer, is drawn off and dispersed into general circulation. But if there is as much silver as will transact the small payments independent of gold, the retail trader must then receive silver for small purchases, and it must of necessity accumulate in his hands.' (David Buchanan; 'Inquiry into the Taxation and Commercial Policy of Great Britain.' Edinburgh, 1844, pp. 248, 249.)

36. The mandarin Wan-mao-in, the Chinese Chancellor of the Exchequer, took it into his head one day to lay before the Son of Heaven a proposal that secretly aimed at converting the *assignats* of the empire into convertible bank-notes. The assignats Committee, in its report of April, 1854, gives him a severe snubbing. Whether he also received the traditional drubbing with bamboos is not stated. The concluding part of the report is as follows:—'The Committee has carefully examined his proposal and finds that it is entirely in favour of the merchants, and that no advantage will result to the crown.' ('Arbeiten der Kaiserlich Russischen Gesandtschaft zu Peking über China.' Aus dem Russischen von Dr K. Abel und F. A. Mecklenburg. Erster Band. Berlin, 1858, p. 47 sq.) In his evidence before the Committee of the House of Lords on the Bank Acts, a governor of the Bank of England says, with regard to the abrasion of gold coins during currency: 'Every year a fresh class of sovereigns becomes too light. The class which one year passes with full weight, loses enough by wear and tear to draw the scales next year against it.' (House of Lords' Committee, 1848, n. 429.)

37. The following passage from Fullarton shows the want of clearness on the part of even the best writers on money, in their comprehension of its various functions: 'That, as far as concerns our domestic exchanges, all the monetary functions which are usually performed by gold and silver coins, may be performed as effectually by a circulation of inconvertible notes, having no value but that factitious and conventional value they derive from the law, is a fact which admits, I conceive, of no denial. Value of this description may be made to answer all the purposes of intrinsic value, and supersede even the necessity for a standard, provided only the quantity of the issues be kept under due limitation.' (Fullarton: 'Regulation of Currencies,' London, 1845, p. 21.) Because the commodity that serves as money is capable of being replaced in circulation by mere symbols of value, therefore its functions as a measure of value and a standard of prices are declared to be superfluous!

38. From the fact that gold and silver, so far as they are coins, or exclusively serve as the medium of circulation, become mere tokens of themselves, Nicholas Barbon deduces the right of Governments 'to raise money,' that is, to give to the weight of silver that is called a shilling the name of a greater weight, such as a crown; and so to pay creditors shillings, instead of crowns. 'Money does wear and grow lighter by often telling over... It is the denomination and currency of the money that men regard in bargaining, and not the quantity of silver...'Tis the public authority upon the metal that makes it money.' (N. Barbon, l.c., pp. 29, 30, 25.)

39. 'Une richesse en argent n'est que ... richesse en productions, converties en argent.' ['Monetary wealth is nothing but ... wealth in products, transformed into money'] (Mercier de la Rivière, l.c.) 'Une valeur en productions n'a fait que changer de forme.' ['A value in the form of products, which has merely changed its form.'] (Id., p. 486.)

40. 'Tis by this practice' they keep all their goods and manufactures at such low rates.' (Vanderlint, l.c., pp. 95, 96.)

41. 'Money ... is a pledge.' (John Bellers: 'Essays about the Poor, Manufactures, Trade, Plantations, and Immorality,' Lond., 1699, p. 13.)

42. A purchase in a 'categorical' sense, implies that gold and silver are already the converted form of commodities, or the product of a sale.

43. Henry III., most Christian king of France, robbed cloisters of their relics, and turned them into money. It is well known what part the despoiling of the Delphic Temple, by the Phocians, played in the history of Greece. Temples with the ancients served as the dwellings of the gods of commodities. They were 'sacred banks.' With the Phoenicians, a trading people par excellence, money was the transmuted shape of everything. It was, therefore, quite in order that the virgins, who, at the feast of the Goddess of Love, gave themselves up to strangers, should offer to the goddess the piece of money they received.

43a.

'Gold, yellow, glittering, precious gold!
Thus much of this, will make black white; foul, fair;
Wrong, right; base, noble; old, young; coward, valiant.
... What this, you gods? Why, this
Will lug your priests and servants from your sides;
Pluck stout men's pillows from below their heads;
This yellow slave
Will knit and break religions; bless the accurs'd;
Make the hoar leprosy ador'd; place thieves,
And give them title, knee and approbation,
With senators on the bench; this is it,
That makes the wappen'd widow wed again:
... Come damned earth,
Though common whore of mankind.'
(Shakespeare: Timon of Athens.)

43b.

Money! Nothing worse
in our lives, so current, rampant, so corrupting.
Money—you demolish cities, root men from their homes,
you train and twist good minds and set them on
to the most atrocious schemes. No limit,
you make them adept at every kind of outrage,
every godless crimes—money!'
(Sophocles, Antigone.)

44. 'The desire of avarice to draw Pluto himself out of the bowels of the earth.' (The Deipnosophists, VI, 23, Athenaeus)

45. 'Accrescere quanto più si può il numero de'venditori d'ogni merce, diminuere quanto più si puo il numero dei compratori, questi sono i cardini sui quali si raggirano tutte le operazioni di economia politica.' ['These are the pivots around which all the measures of political economy turn: the maximum possible increase in the number of sellers of each commodity, and the maximum possible decrease in the number of buyers'] (Verri, l.c., p. 52.)

46. 'There is required for carrying on the trade of the nation a determinate sum of specifick money which varies, and is sometimes more, sometimes less, as the circumstances we are in require.... This ebbing and flowing of money supplies and accommodates itself, without any aid of Politicians.... The buckets work alternately; when money is scarce, bullion is coined; when bullion is scarce, money is melted.' (Sir D. North, l.c., Postscript, p. 3.) John Stuart Mill, who for a long time was an official of the East India Company, confirms the fact that in

India, silver ornaments still continue to perform directly the functions of a hoard. The silver ornaments are brought out and coined when there is a high rate of interest, and go back again when the rate of interest falls. (1. S. Mill's Evidence 'Reports on Bank Acts,' 1857, 2084.) According to a Parliamentary document of 1864 on the gold and silver import and export of India, the import of gold and silver in 1863 exceeded the export by £19,367,764. During the 8 years immediately preceding 1864, the excess of imports over exports of the precious metals amounted to £109,652,917. During this century far more than £200,000,000 has been coined in India.

47. The following shows the debtor and creditor relations existing between English traders at the beginning of the 18th century. 'Such a spirit of crudity reigns here in England among the men of trade, that is not to be met with in any other society of men, nor in any other kingdom of the world.' ('An Essay on Credit and the Bankrupt Act,' Lond., 1707, p. 2.)

48. It will be seen from the following quotation from my book which appeared in 1859, why I take no notice in the text of an opposite form: 'Contrariwise, in the process in M—C, the money can be alienated as a real means of purchase, and in that way, the price of the commodity can be realised before the use-value of the money is realised and the commodity actually delivered. This occurs constantly under the every-day form of prepayments. And it is under this form, that the English government purchases opium from the ryots of India.... In these cases, however, the money always acts as a means of purchase.... Of course capital also is advanced in the shape of money.... This point of view, however, does not fall within the horizon of simple circulation.' ('Zur Kritik, *&c.*,' pp. 119, 120.)

49. The monetary crisis referred to in the text, being a phase of every crisis, must be clearly distinguished from that particular form of crisis, which also is called a monetary crisis, but; which may be produced by itself as an independent phenomenon in such a way as to react only indirectly on industry and commerce. The pivot of these crises is to be found in moneyed capital, and their sphere of direct action is therefore the sphere of that capital, viz., banking, the stock exchange, and finance.

50. 'The sudden reversion from a system of credit to a system of hard cash heaps theoretical fright on top of the practical panic; and the dealers by whose agency circulation is affected, shudder before the impenetrable mystery in which their own economic relations are involved' (Karl Marx, l.c., p. 126.) 'The poor stand still, because the rich have no money to employ them, though they have the same land and hands to provide victuals and clothes, as ever they had; ...which is the true riches of a nation, and not the money.' John Bellers, *Proposals for Raising a College of Industry*, London, 1696, p3.

51. The following shows how such times are exploited by the 'amis du commerce.' 'On one occasion (1839) an old grasping banker (in the city) in his private room raised the lid of the desk he sat over, and displayed to a friend rolls of bank-notes, saying with intense glee there were £600,000 of them, they were held to make money tight, and would all be let out after three o'clock on the same day.' ('The Theory of Exchanges. The Bank Charter Act of 1844.' Lond. 1864, p. 81). The *Observer*, a semi-official government organ, contained the following paragraph on 24th April, 1864: 'Some very curious rumours are current of the means which have been resorted to; in order to create a scarcity of banknotes.... Questionable as it would seem, to suppose that any trick of the kind would be adopted, the report has been so universal that it really deserves mention.'

52. 'The amount of purchases or contracts entered upon during the course of any given day, will not affect the quantity of money afloat on that particular day, but, in the vast majority of cases, will resolve themselves into multifarious drafts upon the quantity of money which may be afloat at subsequent dates more or less distant.... The bills granted or credits opened, to-day, need have no resemblance whatever, either in quantity, amount or duration, to those granted or entered upon to-morrow or next day, nay, many of today's bills, and credits, when due, fall in with a mass of liabilities whose origins traverse a range of antecedent dates

altogether indefinite, bills at 12, 6, 3 months or 1 often aggregating together to swell the common liabilities of one particular day....' ('The Currency Theory Reviewed; in a Letter to the Scottish People.' By a Banker in England. Edinburgh, 1845, pp. 29, 30 passim.)

53. As an example of how little ready money is required in true commercial operations, I give below a statement by one of the largest London houses of its yearly receipts and payments. Its transactions during the year 1856, extending to many millions of pounds sterling, are here reduced to the scale of one million.

Receipts		*Payments*	
Bankers' and Merchants'	£533,596	Bills payable after date	£302,674
Cheques on Bankers, &c. payable on demand	357,715	Cheques on London Bankers	663,672
Country Notes	9,627	Bank of England Notes	22,743
Bank of England Notes	68,554	Gold	9,427
Gold	28,089	Silver and Copper	1,484
Silver and Copper	1,486		
Post Office Orders	933		
Total £1,000,000		Total £1,000,000	
'Report from the Select Committee on the Bank Acts, July, 1858,' p. lxxi.			

54. 'The course of trade being thus turned, from exchanging of goods for goods, or delivering and taking, to selling and paying, all the bargains ... are now stated upon the foot of a Price in money.' ('An Essay upon Publick Credit.' 3rd Ed. Lond., 1710, p. 8.)

55. 'L'argent ... est devenu le bourreau de toutes choses.' Finance is the 'alambic, qui a fait évaporer une quantité effroyable de biens et de denrées pour faire ce fatal précis.' 'L'argent déclare la guerre à tout le genre humain.' ['Money ... has become the executioner of all things.' Finance is the 'alembic that evaporates a frightful quantity of goods and commodities in order to obtain this fatal extract.' 'Money [...] declares war [...] on the whole human race'] (Boisguillebert: 'Dissertation sur la nature des richesses, de l'argent et des tributs.' Edit. Daire. Economistes financiers. Paris, 1843, t. i., pp. 413, 419, 417.)

56. 'On Whitsuntide, 1824,' says Mr Craig before the Commons' Committee of 1826, 'there was such an immense demand for notes upon the banks of Edinburgh, that by 11 o'clock they had not a note left in their custody. They sent round to all the different banks to borrow, but could not get them, and many of the transactions were adjusted by slips of paper only; yet by three o'clock the whole of the notes were returned into the banks from which they had issued! It was a mere transfer from hand to hand. 'Although the average effective circulation of bank-notes in Scotland is less than three millions sterling, yet on certain pay days in the year, every single note in the possession of the bankers, amounting in the whole to about £7,000,000, is called into activity. On these occasions, the notes have a single and specific function to perform, and so soon as they have performed it, they flow back into the various banks from which they issued. (See John Fullarton, 'Regulation of Currencies.' Lond. 1845, p. 86, note.) In explanation it should be stated, that in Scotland, at the date of Fullarton's work, notes and not cheques were used to withdraw deposits.

57. *Note by the Institute of Marxism-Leninism in the Russian edition:* Apparently a slip of the pen. When writing *inverse* the author evidently meant *direct*.

58. To the question, 'If there were occasion to raise 40 millions p. a., whether the same 6 millions (gold) ... would suffice for such revolutions and circulations thereof, as trade requires,' Petty replies in his usual masterly manner, 'I answer yes: for the expense being 40 millions, if the revolutions were in such short circles, viz., weekly, as happens among poor artisans

and labourers, who receive and pay every Saturday, then 40/52 parts of 1 million of money would answer these ends, but; if the circles be quarterly, according to our custom of paying rent, and gathering taxes, then 10 millions were requisite. Wherefore, supposing payments in general to be of a mixed circle between one week and 13, then add 10 millions to 40/52, the half of which will be 5½, so as if we have 5 1/2 millions we have enough.' (William Petty: 'Political Anatomy of Ireland.' 1672, Edit.: Lond. 1691, pp. 13, 14.)

59. Hence the absurdity of every law prescribing that the banks of a country shall form reserves of that precious metal alone which circulates at home. The 'pleasant difficulties' thus self-created by the Bank of England, are well known. On the subject of the great epochs in the history of the changes in the relative value of gold and silver, see Karl Marx, l.c., p. 136 sq. Sir Robert Peel, by his Bank Act of 1844, sought to tide over the difficulty, by allowing the Bank of England to issue notes against silver bullion, on condition that the reserve of silver should never exceed more than one-fourth of the reserve of gold. The value of silver being for that purpose estimated at its price in the London market.

[*Added in the 4th German edition.*—We find ourselves once more in a period of serious change in the relative values of gold and silver. About 25 years ago the ratio expressing the relative value of gold and silver was 15-1/2:1; now it is approximately 22:1, and silver is still constantly falling as against gold. This is essentially the result of a revolution in the mode of production of both metals. Formerly gold was obtained almost exclusively by washing it out from gold-bearing alluvial deposits, products of the weathering of auriferous rocks. Now this method has become inadequate and has been forced into the background by the processing of the quartz lodes themselves, a way of extraction which formerly was only of secondary importance, although well known to the ancients (Diodorus, III, 12-14) (Diodor's v. Sicilien 'Historische Bibliothek,' book III, 12-14. Stuttgart 1828, pp. 258-261). Moreover, not only were new huge silver deposits discovered in North America, in the Western part of the Rocky Mountains, but these and the Mexican silver mines were really opened up by the laying of railways, which made possible the shipment of modern machinery and fuel and in consequence the mining of silver on a very large scale at a low cost. However there is a great difference in the way the two metals occur in the quartz lodes. The gold is mostly native, but disseminated throughout the quartz in minute quantities. The whole mass of the vein must therefore be crushed and the gold either washed out or extracted by means of mercury. Often 1,000,000 grammes of quartz barely yield 1-3 and very seldom 30-60 grammes of gold. Silver is seldom found native, however it occurs in special quartz that is separated from the lode with comparative ease and contains mostly 40-90% silver; or it is contained, in smaller quantities, in copper, lead and other ores which in themselves are worthwhile working. From this alone it is apparent that the labour expended on the production of gold is rather increasing while that expended on silver production has decidedly decreased, which quite naturally explains the drop in the value of the latter. This fall in value would express itself in a still greater fall in price if the price of silver were not pegged even to-day by artificial means. But America's rich silver deposits have so far barely been tapped, and thus the prospects are that the value of this metal will keep on dropping for rather a long time to come. A still greater contributing factor here is the relative decrease in the requirement of silver for articles of general use and for luxuries, that is its replacement by plated goods, aluminium, etc. One may thus gauge the utopianism of the bimetallist idea that compulsory international quotation will raise silver again to the old value ratio of 1:15-1/2. It is more likely that silver will forfeit its money function more and more in the markets of the world.—*F E.*]

60. The opponents, themselves, of the mercantile system, a system which considered the settlement of surplus trade balances in gold and silver as the aim of international trade, entirely misconceived the functions of money of the world. I have shown by the example of Ricardo in what way their false conception of the laws that regulate the quantity of the circulating medium, is reflected in their equally false conception of the international

movement of the precious metals (l.c., pp. 150 sq.). His erroneous dogma: 'An unfavourable balance of trade never arises but from a redundant currency.... The exportation of the coin is caused by its cheapness, and is not the effect, but the cause of an unfavourable balance,' already occurs in Barbon: 'The Balance of Trade, if there be one, is not the cause of sending away the money out of a nation; but that proceeds from the difference of the value of bullion in every country.' (N. Barbon; l.c., pp. 59, 60.) MacCulloch in 'The Literature of Political Economy, a classified catalogue, Lond. 1845,' praises Barbon for this anticipation, but prudently passes over the naive forms, in which Barbon clothes the absurd supposition on which the 'currency principle' is based. The absence of real criticism and even of honesty, in that catalogue culminates in the sections devoted to the history of the theory of money; the reason is that MacCulloch in this part of the work is flattering Lord Overstone whom he calls 'facile princeps argentanorum.'

61. For instance, in subsidies, money loans for carrying on wars or for enabling banks to resume cash payments, &c., it is the money-form, and no other, of value that may be wanted.

62. 'I would desire, indeed, no more convincing evidence of the competency of the machinery of the hoards in specie-paying countries to perform every necessary office of international adjustment, without any sensible aid from the general circulation, than the facility with which France, when but just recovering from the shock of a destructive foreign invasion, completed within the space of 27 months the payment of her forced contribution of nearly 20 millions to the allied powers, and a considerable proportion of the sum in specie, without any perceptible contraction or derangement of her domestic currency, or even any alarming fluctuation of her exchanges.' (Fullerton, l.c., p. 141.) *[Added in the 4th German edition.*—We have a still more striking example in the facility with which the same France was able in 1871-73 to pay off within 30 months a forced contribution more than ten times as great, a considerable part of it likewise in specie.—*F. E.*]

63. 'L'argent se partage entre les nations relativement au besoin qu'elles en ont ... étant toujours attiré par les productions.' ['Money is shared among the nations in accordance with their need for it ... as it is always attracted by the products'] (Le Trosne, l.c., p. 916.) 'The mines which are continually giving gold and silver, do give sufficient to supply such a needful balance to every nation.' (J. Vanderlint, l.c., p. 40.)

64. 'Exchanges rise and fall every week, and at some particular times in the year run high against a nation, and at other times run as high on the contrary.' (N. Barbon, l.c., p. 39)

65. These various functions are liable to come into dangerous conflict with one another whenever gold and silver have also to serve as a fund for the conversion of bank-notes.

66. 'What money is more than of absolute necessity for a Home Trade, is dead stock ... and brings no profit to that country it's kept in, but as it is transported in trade, as well as imported.' (John Bellers, 'Essays,' p. 13.) 'What if we have too much coin? We may melt down the heaviest and turn it into the splendour of plate, vessels or utensils of gold or silver, or send it out as a commodity, where the same is wanted or desired; or let it out at interest, where interest is high.' (W. Petty: 'Quantulumcunque,' p. 39.) 'Money is but the fat of the Body Politick, whereof too much doth as often hinder its agility, as too little makes it sick ... as fat lubricates the motion of the muscles, feeds in want of victuals, fills up the uneven cavities, and beautifies the body; so doth money in the state quicken its action, feeds from abroad in time of dearth at home, evens accounts ... and beautifies the whole; altho more especially the particular persons that have it in plenty.' (W. Petty, 'Political Anatomy of Ireland,' p. 14.)

PART II

THE TRANSFORMATION OF MONEY INTO CAPITAL

4

The General Formula for Capital

The circulation of commodities is the starting-point of capital. The production of commodities, their circulation, and that more developed form of their circulation called commerce, these form the historical ground-work from which it rises. The modern history of capital dates from the creation in the 16th century of a world-embracing commerce and a world-embracing market.

If we abstract from the material substance of the circulation of commodities, that is, from the exchange of the various use-values, and consider only the economic forms produced by this process of circulation, we find its final result to be money: this final product of the circulation of commodities is the first form in which capital appears.

As a matter of history, capital, as opposed to landed property, invariably takes the form at first of money; it appears as moneyed wealth, as the capital of the merchant and of the usurer.[1] But we have no need to refer to the origin of capital in order to discover that the first form of appearance of capital is money. We can see it daily under our very eyes. All new capital, to commence with, comes on the stage, that is, on the market, whether of commodities, labour, or money, even in our days, in the shape of money that by a definite process has to be transformed into capital.

The first distinction we notice between money that is money only, and money that is capital, is nothing more than a difference in their form of circulation.

The simplest form of the circulation of commodities is C-M-C, the transformation of commodities into money, and the change of the money back again into commodities; or selling in order to buy. But alongside of this form we find another specifically different form: M-C-M, the transformation of money into commodities, and the change of commodities back again into money; or buying in order to sell. Money that circulates in the latter manner is thereby transformed into, becomes capital, and is already potentially capital.

Now let us examine the circuit M-C-M a little closer. It consists, like the other, of two antithetical phases. In the first phase, M-C, or the purchase, the money is changed into a commodity. In the second phase, C-M, or the sale, the commodity is changed back again into money. The combination of these two phases constitutes the single movement whereby money is exchanged for a commodity, and the same commodity is again exchanged for money; whereby a commodity is bought in order to be sold, or, neglecting the distinction in form between buying and selling, whereby a commodity is bought with money, and then money is bought with a commodity.[2] The result, in which the phases of the process vanish, is the exchange of money for money, M-M. If I purchase 2,000 lbs. of cotton for £100, and resell the 2,000 lbs. of cotton for £110, I have, in fact, exchanged £100 for £110, money for money.

Now, it is evident that the circuit M-C-M would be absurd and without meaning if the intention were to exchange by this means two equal sums of money, £100 for £100. The miser's plan would be far simpler and surer; he sticks to his £100 instead of exposing it to the dangers of circulation. And yet, whether the merchant who has paid £100 for his cotton sells it for £110, or lets it go for £100, or even £50, his money has, at all events, gone through a characteristic and original movement, quite different in kind from that which it goes through in the hands of the peasant who sells corn, and with the money thus set free buys clothes. We have therefore to examine first the distinguishing characteristics of the forms of the circuits M-C-M and C-M-C, and in doing this the real difference that underlies the mere difference of form will reveal itself.

Let us see, in the first place, what the two forms have in common.

Both circuits are resolvable into the same two antithetical phases, C-M, a sale, and M-C, a purchase. In each of these phases the same material elements - a commodity, and money, and the same economic dramatis personae, a buyer and a seller - confront one another. Each circuit is the unity of the same two antithetical phases, and in each case this unity is brought about by the intervention of three contracting parties, of whom one only sells, another only buys, while the third both buys and sells.

What, however, first and foremost distinguishes the circuit C-M-C from the circuit M-C-M, is the inverted order of succession of the two phases. The simple circulation of commodities begins with a sale and ends with a purchase, while the circulation of money as capital begins with a purchase and ends with a sale. In the one case both the starting-point and the goal are commodities, in the other they are money. In the first form the movement is brought about by the intervention of money, in the second by that of a commodity.

In the circulation C-M-C, the money is in the end converted into a commodity, that serves as a use-value; it is spent once for all. In the inverted form, M-C-M, on the contrary, the buyer lays out money in order that, as a seller, he may recover money. By the purchase of his commodity he throws money into circulation, in order to withdraw it again by the sale of the same commodity. He lets the money go, but only with the sly intention of getting it back again. The money, therefore, is not spent, it is merely advanced.[3]

In the circuit C-M-C, the same piece of money changes its place twice. The seller gets it from the buyer and pays it away to another seller. The complete circulation, which begins with the receipt, concludes with the payment, of money for commodities. It is the very contrary in the circuit M-C-M. Here it is not the piece of money that changes its place twice, but the commodity. The buyer takes it from the hands of the seller and passes it into the hands of another buyer. Just as in the simple circulation of commodities the double change of place of the same piece of money effects its passage from one hand into another, so here the double change of place of the same commodity brings about the reflux of the money to its point of departure.

Such reflux is not dependent on the commodity being sold for more than was paid for it. This circumstance influences only the amount of the money that comes back. The reflux itself takes place, so soon as the purchased commodity is resold, in other words, so soon as the circuit M-C-M is completed. We have here, therefore, a palpable difference between the circulation of money as capital, and its circulation as mere money.

The circuit C-M-C comes completely to an end, so soon as the money brought in by the sale of one commodity is abstracted again by the purchase of another.

If, nevertheless, there follows a reflux of money to its starting-point, this can only happen through a renewal or repetition of the operation. If I sell a quarter of corn for £3, and with this £3 buy clothes, the money, so far as I am concerned, is spent and done with. It belongs to the clothes merchant. If I now sell a second quarter of corn, money indeed flows back to me, not however as a sequel to the first transaction, but in consequence of its repetition. The money again leaves me, so soon as I complete this second transaction by a fresh purchase. Therefore, in the circuit C-M-C, the expenditure of money has nothing to do with its reflux. On the other hand, in M-C-M, the reflux of the money is conditioned by the very mode of its expenditure. Without this reflux, the operation fails, or the process is interrupted and incomplete, owing to the absence of its complementary and final phase, the sale.

The circuit C-M-C starts with one commodity, and finishes with another, which falls out of circulation and into consumption. Consumption, the satisfaction of wants, in one word, use-value, is its end and aim. The circuit M-C-M, on the contrary, commences with money and ends with money. Its leading motive, and the goal that attracts it, is therefore mere exchange-value.

In the simple circulation of commodities, the two extremes of the circuit have the same economic form. They are both—commodities, and commodities of equal value. But they are also use-values differing in their qualities, as, for example, corn and clothes. The exchange of products, of the different materials in which the labour of society is embodied, forms here the basis of the movement. It is otherwise in the circulation M-C-M, which, at first sight, appears purposeless, because tautological. Both extremes have the same economic form. They are both money, and therefore are not qualitatively different use-values; for money is but the converted form of commodities, in which their particular use-values vanish. To exchange £100 for cotton, and then this same cotton again for £100, is merely a roundabout way of exchanging money for money, the same for the same, and appears to be an operation just as purposeless as it is absurd.[4] One sum of money is distinguishable from another only by its amount. The character and tendency of the process M-C-M, is therefore not due to any qualitative difference between its extremes, both being money, but solely to their quantitative difference. More money is withdrawn from circulation at the finish than was thrown into it at the start. The cotton that was bought for £100 is perhaps resold for £100 + £10 or £110. The exact form of this process is therefore M-C-M›, where M› = M + Δ M = the original sum advanced, plus an increment. This increment or excess over the original value I call 'surplus-value.' The value originally advanced, therefore, not only remains intact while in circulation, but adds to itself a surplus-value or expands itself. It is this movement that converts it into capital.

Of course, it is also possible, that in C-M-C, the two extremes C-C, say corn and clothes, may represent different quantities of value. The farmer may sell his corn above its value, or may buy the clothes at less than their value. He may, on the other hand, 'be done' by the clothes merchant. Yet, in the form of circulation now under consideration, such differences in value are purely accidental. The fact that the corn and the clothes are equivalents, does not deprive the process of all meaning, as it does in M-C-M. The equivalence of their values is rather a necessary condition to its normal course.

The repetition or renewal of the act of selling in order to buy, is kept within bounds by the very object it aims at, namely, consumption or the satisfaction of definite wants, an aim that lies altogether outside the sphere of circulation. But when we buy in order to sell, we, on the contrary, begin and end with the same thing, money, exchange-value; and thereby the movement becomes interminable. No doubt, M becomes M + Δ M, £100 become £110. But, when viewed in their qualitative aspect alone, £110 are the same as £100, namely money; and considered quantitatively, £110 is, like £100, a sum of definite and limited value. If now, the £110 be spent as money, they cease to play their part. They are no longer capital. Withdrawn from circulation, they become petrified into a hoard, and though they remained in that state till doomsday, not a single farthing would accrue to them. If, then, the expansion of value is once aimed at, there is just the same inducement to augment the value of the £110 as that of the £100; for both are but limited expressions for exchange-value, and therefore both have the same vocation to approach, by quantitative increase, as near as possible to absolute wealth. Momentarily, indeed, the value originally advanced, the £100 is distinguishable from the surplus-value of £10 that is annexed to it during circulation; but the distinction vanishes immediately. At the end of the process, we do not receive with one hand the original £100, and with the other, the surplus-value of £10. We simply get a value of £110, which is in exactly the same condition and fitness for commencing the expanding process, as the original £100 was. Money ends the movement only to begin it again.[5] Therefore, the final result of every separate circuit, in which a purchase and consequent sale are completed, forms of itself the starting-point of a new circuit. The simple circulation of commodities - selling in order to buy - is a means of carrying out a purpose unconnected with circulation, namely, the appropriation of use-values, the satisfaction of wants. The circulation of money as capital is, on the contrary, an end in itself, for the expansion of value takes place only within this constantly renewed movement. The circulation of capital has therefore no limits.[6]

As the conscious representative of this movement, the possessor of money becomes a capitalist. His person, or rather his pocket, is the point from which the money starts and to which it returns. The expansion of value, which is the objective basis or main-spring of the circulation M-C-M, becomes his subjective aim, and it is only in so far as the appropriation of ever more and more wealth in the abstract becomes the sole motive of his operations, that he functions as a capitalist, that is, as capital personified and endowed with consciousness and a will. Use-values must therefore never be looked upon as the real aim of the capitalist;[7] neither must the profit on any single transaction. The restless never-ending process of profit-making alone is what he aims at.[8] This boundless greed after riches, this passionate chase after exchange-value[9], is common to the capitalist and the miser; but while the miser is merely a capitalist gone mad, the capitalist is a rational miser. The never-ending augmentation of exchange-value, which the miser strives after, by seeking to save[10] his money from circulation, is attained by the more acute capitalist, by constantly throwing it afresh into circulation.[11]

The independent form, *i.e.*, the money-form, which the value of commodities assumes in the case of simple circulation, serves only one purpose, namely, their exchange, and vanishes in the final result of the movement. On the other hand, in the circulation M-C-M, both the money and the commodity represent only different modes of existence of value itself, the money its general mode, and the commodity its particular, or, so to say, disguised mode.[12] It is constantly changing from one form to the other without thereby becoming lost, and thus assumes an automatically active character. If now we take in turn each of the two different forms which self-expanding value successively assumes in the course of its life, we then arrive at these two propositions: Capital is money: Capital is commodities.[13] In truth, however, value is here the active factor in a process, in which, while constantly assuming the form in turn of money and commodities, it at the same time changes in magnitude, differentiates itself by throwing off surplus-value from itself; the original value, in other words, expands spontaneously. For the movement, in the course of which it adds surplus-value, is its own movement, its expansion, therefore, is automatic expansion. Because it is value, it has acquired the occult quality of being able to add value to itself. It brings forth living offspring, or, at the least, lays golden eggs.

Value, therefore, being the active factor in such a process, and assuming at one time the form of money, at another that of commodities, but through all these changes preserving itself and expanding, it requires some independent form, by means of which its identity may, at any time, be established. And this form it possesses only in the shape of money. It is under the form of money that value begins and ends, and begins again, every act of its own spontaneous generation. It began by being £100, it is now £110, and so on. But the money itself is only one of the two forms of value. Unless it takes the form of some commodity, it does not become capital. There is here no antagonism, as in the case of hoarding, between the money and commodities. The capitalist knows that all commodities, however scurvy they may look, or however badly they may smell, are in faith and in truth, money, inwardly circumcised Jews, and what is more, a wonderful means whereby out of money to make more money.

In simple circulation, C-M-C, the value of commodities attained at the most a form independent of their use-values, *i.e.*, the form of money; but that same value now in the circulation M-C-M, or the circulation of capital, suddenly presents itself as an independent substance, endowed with a motion of its own, passing through a life-process of its own, in which money and commodities are mere forms which it assumes and casts off in turn. Nay, more: instead of simply representing the relations of commodities, it enters now, so to say, into private relations with itself. It differentiates itself as original value from itself as surplus-value; as the father differentiates himself from himself qua the son, yet both are one and of one age: for only by the surplus-value of £10 does the £100 originally advanced become capital, and so soon as this takes place, so soon as the son, and by the son, the father, is begotten, so soon does their difference vanish, and they again become one, £110.

Value therefore now becomes value in process, money in process, and, as such, capital. It comes out of circulation, enters into it again, preserves and multiplies itself within its circuit, comes back out of it with expanded bulk, and begins the same round ever afresh.[14] M-M›, money which begets money, such is the description of Capital from the mouths of its first interpreters, the Mercantilists.

Buying in order to sell, or, more accurately, buying in order to sell dearer, M-C-M', appears certainly to be a form peculiar to one kind of capital alone, namely, merchants' capital. But industrial capital too is money, that is changed into commodities, and by the sale of these commodities, is re-converted into more money. The events that take place outside the sphere of circulation, in the interval between the buying and selling, do not affect the form of this movement. Lastly, in the case of interest-bearing capital, the circulation M-C-M' appears abridged. We have its result without the intermediate stage, in the form M-M', 'en style lapidaire' so to say, money that is worth more money, value that is greater than itself.

M-C-M' is therefore in reality the general formula of capital as it appears prima facie within the sphere of circulation.

Notes

1. The contrast between the power, based on the personal relations of dominion and servitude, that is conferred by landed property, and the impersonal power that is given by money, is well expressed by the two French proverbs, 'Nulle terre sans seigneur,' and 'L'argent n'a pas de maître,'—'No land without its lord,' and 'Money has no master.'
2. 'Avec de l'argent on achète des marchandises et avec des marchandises on achète de l'argent.' ['With money one buys commodities, and with commodities one buys money'] (Mercier de la Rivière: 'L'ordre naturel et essentiel des sociétés politiques,' p. 543.)
3. 'When a thing is bought in order to be sold again, the sum employed is called money advanced; when it is bought not to be sold, it may be said to be expended.'—(James Steuart: 'Works,' &c. Edited by Gen. Sir James Steuart, his son. Lond., 1805, V. I., p. 274.)
4. 'On n'échange pas de l'argent contre de l'argent,' ['One does not exchange money for money,'] says Mercier de la Rivière to the Mercantilists (l.c., p. 486.) In a work, which, ex professo treats of 'trade' and 'speculation,' occurs the following: 'All trade consists in the exchange of things of different kinds; and the advantage' (to the merchant?) 'arises out of this difference. To exchange a pound of bread against a pound of bread ... would be attended with no advantage; ... Hence trade is advantageously contrasted with gambling, which consists in a mere exchange of money for money.' (Th. Corbet, 'An Inquiry into the Causes and Modes of the Wealth of Individuals; or the Principles of Trade and Speculation Explained.' London, 1841, p. 5.) Although Corbet does not see that M-M, the exchange of money for money, is the characteristic form of circulation, not only of merchants' capital but of all capital, yet at least he acknowledges that this form is common to gambling and to one species of trade, viz.; speculation: but then comes MacCulloch and makes out, that to buy in order to sell, is to speculate, and thus the difference between Speculation and Trade vanishes. 'Every transaction in which an individual buys produce in order to sell it again, is, in fact, a speculation.' (MacCulloch: 'A Dictionary Practical, &c., of Commerce.' Lond., 1847, p. 1009.) With much more naiveté, Pinto, the Pindar of the Amsterdam Stock Exchange, remarks, 'Le commerce est un jeu: (taken from Locke) et ce n'est pas avec des gueux qu'on peut gagner. Si l'on gagnait longtemps en tout avec tous, il faudrait rendre de bon accord les plus grandes parties du profit pour recommencer le jeu.' ['Trade is a game, and nothing can be won from

beggars. If one won everything from everybody all the time, it would be necessary to give back the greater part of the profit voluntarily, in order to begin the game again'] (Pinto: 'Traité de la Circulation et du Crédit.' Amsterdam, 1771. p. 231,)

5. 'Capital is divisible ... into the original capital and the profit, the increment to the capital ... although in practice this profit is immediately turned into capital, and set in motion with the original.' (F. Engels, 'Umrisse zu einer Kritik der Nationalökonomie, in: Deutsch-Französische Jahrbücher, herausgegeben von Arnold Ruge und Karl Marx.' Paris, 1844, p. 99.)

6. Aristotle opposes Oeconomic to Chrematistic. He starts from the former. So far as it is the art of gaining a livelihood, it is limited to procuring those articles that are necessary to existence, and useful either to a household or the state. 'True wealth (ο αλεθινοσ πλουτοσ) consists of such values in use; for the quantity of possessions of this kind, capable of making life pleasant, is not unlimited. There is, however, a second mode of acquiring things, to which we may by preference and with correctness give the name of Chrematistic, and in this case there appear to be no limits to riches and possessions. Trade (ε καπελικε is literally retail trade, and Aristotle takes this kind because in it values in use predominate) does not in its nature belong to Chrematistic, for here the exchange has reference only to what is necessary to themselves (the buyer or seller).' Therefore, as he goes on to show, the original form of trade was barter, but with the extension of the latter, there arose the necessity for money. On the discovery of money, barter of necessity developed into καπελικε, into trading in commodities, and this again, in opposition to its original tendency, grew into Chrematistic, into the art of making money. Now Chrematistic is distinguishable from Oeconomic in this way, that 'in the case of Chrematistic circulation is the source of riches ποιετικε χρεματον ... δια χηρεματον διαβολεσ. And it appears to revolve about money, for money is the beginning and end of this kind of exchange (το νομισμα στοιχειον τεσ αλλαγεσ εστιν). Therefore also riches, such as Chrematistic strives for, are unlimited. Just as every art that is not a means to an end, but an end in itself, has no limit to its aims, because it seeks constantly to approach nearer and nearer to that end, while those arts that pursue means to an end, are not boundless, since the goal itself imposes a limit upon them, so with Chrematistic, there are no bounds to its aims, these aims being absolute wealth. Oeconomic not Chrematistic has a limit ... the object of the former is something different from money, of the latter the augmentation of money.... By confounding these two forms, which overlap each other, some people have been led to look upon the preservation and increase of money ad infinitum as the end and aim of Oeconomic.' (Aristoteles, *De Rep.* edit. Bekker, lib. l.c. 8, 9. passim.)

7. 'Commodities (here used in the sense of use-values) are not the terminating object of the trading capitalist, money is his terminating object.' (Th. Chalmers, On Pol. Econ. &c., 2nd Ed., Glasgow, 1832, pp. 165, 166.)

8. 'Il mercante non conta quasi per niente il lucro fatto, ma mira sempre al futuro.' ['The merchant counts the money he has made as almost nothing; he always looks to the future.'] (A. Genovesi, Lezioni di Economia Civile (1765), Custodi's edit. of Italian Economists. Parte Moderna t. viii, p. 139.)

9. 'The inextinguishable passion for gain, the auri sacra fames, will always lead capitalists.' (MacCulloch: 'The Principles of Polit. Econ.' London, 1830, p. 179.) This view, of course, does not prevent the same MacCulloch and others of his kidney, when in theoretical difficulties, such, for example, as the question of over-production, from transforming the same capitalist into a moral citizen, whose sole concern is for use-values, and who even develops an insatiable hunger for boots, hats, eggs, calico, and other extremely familiar sorts of use-values.

10. Σοζειν is a characteristic Greek expression for hoarding. So in English to save has the same two meanings: sauver and *épargner*.

11. 'Questo infinito che le cose non hanno in progresso, hanno in giro.' ['That infinity which things do not possess, they possess in circulation.'] (Galiani.)
12. 'Ce n'est pas la matière qui fait le capital, mais la valeur de ces matières.' ['It is not matter which makes capital, but the value of that matter.'] (J. B. Say: 'Traité d'Econ. Polit.' 3ème éd. Paris, 1817, t. II., p. 429.)
13. 'Currency (!) employed in producing articles... is capital.' (Macleod: 'The Theory and Practice of Banking.' London, 1855, v. 1, ch. i, p. 55.) 'Capital is commodities.' (James Mill: 'Elements of Pol. Econ.' Lond., 1821, p. 74.)
14. Capital: 'portion fructifiante de la richesse accumulée... valeur permanente, multipliante.' (Sismondi: 'Nouveaux Principes d'Econ. Polit.,' t. i., p. 88, 89.)

5

Contradictions in the General Formula of Capital

The form which circulation takes when money becomes capital, is opposed to all the laws we have hitherto investigated bearing on the nature of commodities, value and money, and even of circulation itself. What distinguishes this form from that of the simple circulation of commodities, is the inverted order of succession of the two antithetical processes, sale and purchase. How can this purely formal distinction between these processes change their character as it were by magic?

But that is not all. This inversion has no existence for two out of the three persons who transact business together. As capitalist, I buy commodities from A and sell them again to B, but as a simple owner of commodities, I sell them to B and then purchase fresh ones from A. A and B see no difference between the two sets of transactions. They are merely buyers or sellers. And I on each occasion meet them as a mere owner of either money or commodities, as a buyer or a seller, and, what is more, in both sets of transactions, I am opposed to A only as a buyer and to B only as a seller, to the one only as money, to the other only as commodities, and to neither of them as capital or a capitalist, or as representative of anything that is more than money or commodities, or that can produce any effect beyond what money and commodities can. For me, the purchase from A and the sale to B are part of a series. But the connexion between the two acts exists for me alone. A does not trouble himself about my transaction with B, nor does B about my business with A. And if I offered to explain to them the meritorious nature of my action in inverting the order of succession, they would probably point out to me that I was mistaken as to that order of succession, and that the whole transaction, instead of beginning with a purchase and ending with a sale, began, on the contrary, with a sale and was concluded with a purchase. In truth, my first act, the purchase, was from the standpoint of A, a sale, and my second act, the sale, was from the standpoint of B, a purchase. Not content with that, A and B would declare that the whole series was superfluous and nothing but Hokus Pokus; that for the future A would buy direct from B, and B sell direct to A. Thus the whole transaction would be reduced to a single act forming an isolated, non-complemented phase in the ordinary circulation of commodities, a mere sale from A's point of view, and from B's, a mere purchase. The inversion, therefore, of the order of succession, does not take us outside the sphere of the simple circulation of commodities, and we must rather look, whether there is in this simple circulation anything permitting an expansion of the value that enters into circulation, and, consequently, a creation of surplus-value.

Let us take the process of circulation in a form under which it presents itself as a simple and direct exchange of commodities. This is always the case when two owners of commodities buy from each other, and on the settling day the amounts mutually owing are equal and cancel each other. The money in this case is money of account and serves to express the value of the commodities by their prices, but is not, itself, in the shape of hard cash, confronted with them. So far as regards use-values, it is clear that both parties may gain some advantage. Both part with goods that, as use-values, are of no service to them, and receive others that they can make use of. And there may also be a further gain. A, who sells wine and buys corn, possibly produces more wine, with given labour-time, than farmer B could, and B on the other hand, more corn than wine-grower A could. A, therefore, may get, for the same exchange-value, more corn, and B more wine, than each would respectively get without any exchange by producing his own corn and wine. With reference, therefore, to use-value, there is good ground for saying that 'exchange is a transaction by which both sides gain.'[1] It is otherwise with exchange-value. 'A man who has plenty of wine and no corn treats with a man who has plenty of corn and no wine; an exchange takes place between them of corn to the value of 50, for wine of the same value. This act produces no increase of exchange-value either for the one or the other; for each of them already possessed, before the exchange, a value equal to that which he acquired by means of that operation.'[2] The result is not altered by introducing money, as a medium of circulation, between the commodities, and making the sale and the purchase two distinct acts.[3] The value of a commodity is expressed in its price before it goes into circulation, and is therefore a precedent condition of circulation, not its result.[4]

Abstractedly considered, that is, apart from circumstances not immediately flowing from the laws of the simple circulation of commodities, there is in an exchange nothing (if we except the replacing of one use-value by another) but a metamorphosis, a mere change in the form of the commodity. The same exchange-value, i.e., the same quantity of incorporated social labour, remains throughout in the hands of the owner of the commodity, first in the shape of his own commodity, then in the form of the money for which he exchanged it, and lastly, in the shape of the commodity he buys with that money. This change of form does not imply a change in the magnitude of the value. But the change, which the value of the commodity undergoes in this process, is limited to a change in its money-form. This form exists first as the price of the commodity offered for sale, then as an actual sum of money, which, however, was already expressed in the price, and lastly, as the price of an equivalent commodity. This change of form no more implies, taken alone, a change in the quantity of value, than does the change of a £5 note into sovereigns, half sovereigns and shillings. So far therefore as the circulation of commodities effects a change in the form alone of their values, and is free from disturbing influences, it must be the exchange of equivalents. Little as Vulgar-Economy knows about the nature of value, yet whenever it wishes to consider the phenomena of circulation in their purity, it assumes that supply and demand are equal, which amounts to this, that their effect is nil. If therefore, as regards the use-values exchanged, both buyer and seller may possibly gain something, this is not the case as regards the exchange-values. Here we must rather say, 'Where equality exists there can be no gain.'[5] It is true, commodities may be sold at prices deviating from their values, but these deviations are to be considered as infractions of the laws of the exchange of commodities[6], which in its normal state is an exchange of equivalents, consequently, no method for increasing value.[7]

Hence, we see that behind all attempts to represent the circulation of commodities as a source of surplus-value, there lurks a *quid pro quo*, a mixing up of use-value and exchange-value. For instance, Condillac says: 'It is not true that on an exchange of commodities we give value for value. On the contrary, each of the two contracting parties in every case, gives a less for a greater value. ... If we really exchanged equal values, neither party could make a profit. And yet, they both gain, or ought to gain. Why? The value of a thing consists solely in its relation to our wants. What is more to the one is less to the other, and *vice versâ*. ... It is not to be assumed that we offer for sale articles required for our own consumption. ... We wish to part with a useless thing, in order to get one that we need; we want to give less for more. ... It was natural to think that, in an exchange, value was given for value, whenever each of the articles exchanged was of equal value with the same quantity of gold. ... But there is another point to be considered in our calculation. The question is, whether we both exchange something superfluous for something necessary.'[8] We see in this passage, how Condillac not only confuses use-value with exchange-value, but in a really childish manner assumes, that in a society, in which the production of commodities is well developed, each producer produces his own means of subsistence, and throws into circulation only the excess over his own requirements.[9] Still, Condillac's argument is frequently used by modern economists, more especially when the point is to show, that the exchange of commodities in its developed form, commerce, is productive of surplus-value. For instance, 'Commerce ... adds value to products, for the same products in the hands of consumers, are worth more than in the hands of producers, and it may strictly be considered an act of production.'[10] But commodities are not paid for twice over, once on account of their use-value, and again on account of their value. And though the use-value of a commodity is more serviceable to the buyer than to the seller, its money-form is more serviceable to the seller. Would he otherwise sell it? We might therefore just as well say that the buyer performs 'strictly an act of production,' by converting stockings, for example, into money.

If commodities, or commodities and money, of equal exchange-value, and consequently equivalents, are exchanged, it is plain that no one abstracts more value from, than he throws into, circulation. There is no creation of surplus-value. And, in its normal form, the circulation of commodities demands the exchange of equivalents. But, in actual practice, the process does not retain its normal form. Let us, therefore, assume an exchange of non-equivalents.

In any case, the market for commodities is only frequented by owners of commodities, and the power which these persons exercise over each other, is no other than the power of their commodities. The material variety of these commodities is the material incentive to the act of exchange, and makes buyers and sellers mutually dependent, because none of them possesses the object of his own wants, and each holds in his hand the object of another's wants. Besides these material differences of their use-values, there is only one other difference between commodities, namely, that between their bodily form and the form into which they are converted by sale, the difference between commodities and money. And consequently the owners of commodities are distinguishable only as sellers, those who own commodities, and buyers, those who own money.

Suppose then, that by some inexplicable privilege, the seller is enabled to sell his commodities above their value, what is worth 100 for 110, in which case the price is nominally raised 10%. The seller therefore pockets a surplus-value of 10. But after he has sold he becomes a buyer. A third owner of commodities comes to him now as seller, who in this capacity also enjoys the privilege of selling his commodities 10% too dear. Our friend gained 10 as a seller only to lose it again as a buyer.[11] The net result is, that all owners of commodities sell their goods to one another at 10% above their value, which comes precisely to the same as if they sold them at their true value. Such a general and nominal rise of prices has the same effect as if the values had been expressed in weight of silver instead of in weight of gold. The nominal prices of commodities would rise, but the real relation between their values would remain unchanged.

Let us make the opposite assumption, that the buyer has the privilege of purchasing commodities under their value. In this case it is no longer necessary to bear in mind that he in his turn will become a seller. He was so before he became buyer; he had already lost

10% in selling before he gained 10% as buyer.[12] Everything is just as it was.

The creation of surplus-value, and therefore the conversion of money into capital, can consequently be explained neither on the assumption that commodities are sold above their value, nor that they are bought below their value.[13]

The problem is in no way simplified by introducing irrelevant matters after the manner of Col. Torrens: 'Effectual demand consists in the power and inclination (!), on the part of consumers, to give for commodities, either by immediate or circuitous barter, some greater portion of ... capital than their production costs.'[14] In relation to circulation, producers and consumers meet only as buyers and sellers. To assert that the surplus-value acquired by the producer has its origin in the fact that consumers pay for commodities more than their value, is only to say in other words: The owner of commodities possesses, as a seller, the privilege of selling too dear. The seller has himself produced the commodities or represents their producer, but the buyer has to no less extent produced the commodities represented by his money, or represents their producer. The distinction between them is, that one buys and the other sells. The fact that the owner of the commodities, under the designation of producer, sells them over their value, and under the designation of consumer, pays too much for them, does not carry us a single step further.[15]

To be consistent therefore, the upholders of the delusion that surplus-value has its origin in a nominal rise of prices or in the privilege which the seller has of selling too dear, must assume the existence of a class that only buys and does not sell, i.e., only consumes and does not produce. The existence of such a class is inexplicable from the standpoint we have so far reached, viz., that of simple circulation. But let us anticipate. The money with which such a class is constantly making purchases, must constantly flow into their pockets, without any exchange, gratis, by might or right, from the pockets of the commodity-owners themselves. To sell commodities above their value to such a class, is only to crib back again a part of the money previously given to it.[16] The towns of Asia Minor thus paid a yearly money tribute to ancient Rome. With this money, Rome purchased from them commodities, and purchased them too dear. The provincials cheated the Romans, and thus got back from their conquerors, in the course of trade, a portion of the tribute. Yet, for all that, the conquered were the really cheated. Their goods were still paid for with their own money. That is not the way to get rich or to create surplus-value.

Let us therefore keep within the bounds of exchange where sellers are also buyers, and buyers, sellers. Our difficulty may perhaps have arisen from treating the actors as personifications instead of as individuals.

A may be clever enough to get the advantage of B or C without their being able to retaliate. A sells wine worth £40 to B, and obtains from him in exchange corn to the value of £50. A has converted his £40 into £50, has made more money out of less, and has converted his commodities into capital. Let us examine this a little more closely. Before the exchange we had £40 worth of wine in the hands of A, and £50 worth of corn in those of B, a total value of £90. After the exchange we have still the same total value of £90. The value in circulation has not increased by one iota, it is only distributed differently between A and B. What is a loss of value to B is surplus-value to A; what is 'minus' to one is 'plus' to the other. The same change would have taken place, if A, without the formality of an exchange, had directly stolen the £10 from B. The sum of the values in circulation can clearly not be augmented by any change in their distribution, any more than the quantity of the precious metals in a country by a Jew selling a Queen Anne's farthing for a guinea. The capitalist class, as a whole, in any country, cannot over-reach themselves.[17]

Turn and twist then as we may, the fact remains unaltered. If equivalents are exchanged, no surplus-value results, and if non-equivalents are exchanged, still no surplus-value.[18] Circulation, or the exchange of commodities, begets no value.[19]

The reason is now therefore plain why, in analysing the standard form of capital, the form under which it determines the economic organisation of modern society, we entirely left out of consideration its most popular, and, so to say, antediluvian forms, merchants' capital and money-lenders' capital.

The circuit M-C-M, buying in order to sell dearer, is seen most clearly in genuine merchants' capital. But the movement takes place entirely within the sphere of circulation. Since, however, it is impossible, by circulation alone, to account for the conversion of money into capital, for the formation of surplus-value, it would appear, that merchants' capital is an impossibility, so long as equivalents are exchanged;[20] that, therefore, it can only have its origin in the two-fold advantage gained, over both the selling and the buying producers, by the merchant who parasitically shoves himself in between them. It is in this sense that Franklin says, 'war is robbery, commerce is generally cheating.'[21] If the transformation of merchants' money into capital is to be explained otherwise than by the producers being simply cheated, a long series of intermediate steps would be necessary, which, at present, when the simple circulation of commodities forms our only assumption, are entirely wanting.

What we have said with reference to merchants' capital, applies still more to money-lenders' capital. In merchants' capital, the two extremes, the money that is thrown upon the market, and the augmented money that is withdrawn from the market, are at least connected by a purchase and a sale, in other words by the movement of the circulation. In money-lenders' capital the form M-C-M is reduced to the two extremes without a mean, M-M, money exchanged for more money, a form that is incompatible with the nature of money, and therefore remains inexplicable from the standpoint of the circulation of commodities. Hence Aristotle: 'since chrematistic is a double science, one part belonging to commerce, the other to economic, the latter being necessary and praiseworthy, the former based on circulation and with justice disapproved (for it is not based on Nature, but on mutual cheating), therefore the usurer is most rightly hated, because money itself is the source of his gain, and is not used for the purposes for which it was invented. For it originated for the exchange of commodities, but interest makes out of money, more money. Hence its name ([greek: tokos] interest and offspring). For the begotten are like those who beget them. But interest is money of money, so that of all modes of making a living, this is the most contrary to Nature.'[22]

In the course of our investigation, we shall find that both merchants' capital and interest-bearing capital are derivative forms, and at the same time it will become clear, why these two forms appear in the course of history before the modern standard form of capital.

We have shown that surplus-value cannot be created by circulation, and, therefore, that in its formation, something must take place in the background, which is not apparent in the circulation itself.[23] But can surplus-value possibly originate anywhere else than in circulation, which is the sum total of all the mutual relations of commodity-owners, as far as they are determined by their commodities? Apart from circulation, the commodity-owner is in relation only with his own commodity. So far as regards value, that relation is limited to this, that the commodity contains a quantity of his own labour, that quantity being measured by a definite social standard. This quantity is expressed by the value of the commodity, and since the value is reckoned in money of account, this quantity is also expressed by the price, which we will suppose to be £10. But his labour is not represented both by the value of the commodity, and by a surplus over that value, not by a price of 10 that is also a price of 11, not by a value that is greater than itself. The commodity owner can, by his labour, create value, but not self-expanding value. He can increase the value of his commodity, by adding fresh labour, and therefore more value to the value in hand, by making, for instance, leather into boots. The same material has now more value, because it contains a greater quantity of labour. The boots have therefore more value than the leather, but the value of the leather remains what it was; it has not expanded itself, has not, during the making of the boots, annexed surplus-value. It is therefore impossible that outside the sphere of circulation, a producer of commodities can, without coming into contact with other commodity-owners, expand value, and consequently convert money or commodities into capital.

It is therefore impossible for capital to be produced by circulation, and it is equally impossible for it to originate apart from circulation. It must have its origin both in circulation and yet not in circulation.

We have, therefore, got a double result.

The conversion of money into capital has to be explained on the basis of the laws that regulate the exchange of commodities, in such a way that the starting-point is the exchange of equivalents.[24] Our friend, Moneybags, who as yet is only an embryo capitalist, must buy his commodities at their value, must sell them at their value, and yet at the end of the process must withdraw more value from circulation than he threw into it at starting. His development into a full-grown capitalist must take place, both within the sphere of circulation and without it. These are the conditions of the problem. *Hic Rhodus, hic salta!*[25]

Notes

1. 'L'échange est une transaction admirable dans laquelle les deux contractants gagnent - toujours (!)' ['Exchange is a transaction in which the two contracting parties always gain, both of them (!)'] (Destutt de Tracy: 'Traité de la Volonté et de ses effets.' Paris, 1826, p. 68.) This work appeared afterwards as 'Traité d'Econ. Polit.'
2. 'Mercier de la Rivière,' l. c., p. 544.
3. 'Que l'une de ces deux valeurs soit argent, ou qu'elles soient toutes deux marchandises usuelles, rien de plus indifférent en soi.' ['Whether one of those two values is money, or they are both ordinary commodities, is in itself a matter of complete indifference.'] ('Mercier de la Rivière,' l.c., p. 543.)
4. 'Ce ne sont pas les contractants qui prononcent sur la valeur; elle est décidée avant la convention.' ['It is not the parties to a contract who decide on the value; that has been decided before the contract.'] (Le Trosne, p. 906.)
5. 'Dove è egualità non è lucro.' (Galiani, 'Della Moneta in Custodi, Parte Moderna,' t. iv., p. 244.)
6. 'L'échange devient désavantageux pour l'une des parties, lorsque quelque chose étrangère vient diminuer ou exagérer le prix; alors l'égalité est blessée, mais la lésion procède de cette cause et non de l'échange.' ['The exchange becomes unfavourable for one of the parties when some external circumstance comes to lessen or increase the price; then equality is infringed, but this infringement arises from that cause and not from the exchange itself.'] (Le Trosne, l.c., p. 904.)
7. 'L'échange est de sa nature un contrat d'égalité qui se fait de valeur pour valeur égale. Il n'est donc pas un moyen de s'enrichir, puisque l'on donne autant que l'on reçoit.' ['Exchange is by its nature a contract which rests on equality, i.e., it takes place between two equal values, and it is not a means of self-enrichment, since as much is given as is received.'] (Le Trosne, l.c., p. 903.)
8. Condillac: 'Le Commerce et le Gouvernement' (1776). Edit. Daire et Molinari in the 'Mélanges d'Econ. Polit.' Paris, 1847, pp. 267, 291.
9. Le Trosne, therefore, answers his friend Condillac with justice as follows: 'Dans une ... société formée il n'y a pas de surabondant en aucun genre.' ['In a developed society absolutely nothing is superfluous.'] At the same time, in a bantering way, he remarks: 'If both the persons who exchange receive more to an equal amount, and part with less to an equal amount, they both get the same.' It is because Condillac has not the remotest idea of the nature of exchange-value that he has been chosen by Herr Professor Wilhelm Roscher as a proper person to answer for the soundness of his own childish notions. See Roscher's 'Die Grundlagen der Nationalökonomie, Dritte Auflage,' 1858.

10. S. P. Newman: 'Elements of Polit. Econ.' Andover and New York, 1835, p. 175.
11. 'By the augmentation of the nominal value of the produce... sellers not enriched... since what they gain as sellers, they precisely expend in the quality of buyers.' ('The Essential Principles of the Wealth of Nations.' &c., London, 1797, p. 66.)
12. 'Si l'on est forcé de donner pour 18 livres une quantité de telle production qui en valait 24, lorsqu'on employera ce même argent à acheter, on aura également pour 18 l. ce que l'on payait 24.' ['If one is compelled to sell a quantity of a certain product for 18 livres when it has a value of 24 livres, when one employs the same amount of money in buying, one will receive for 18 livres the same quantity of the product as 24 livres would have bought otherwise.'] (Le Trosne, I. c., p. 897.)
13. 'Chaque vendeur ne peut donc parvenir à renchérir habituellement ses marchandises, qu'en se soumettant aussi à payer habituellement plus cher les marchandises des autres vendeurs; et par la même raison, chaque consommateur ne peut payer habituellement moins cher ce qu'il achète, qu'en se soumettant aussi à une diminution semblable sur le prix des choses qu'il vend.' ['A seller can normally only succeed in raising the prices of his commodities if he agrees to pay, by and large, more for the commodities of the other sellers; and for the same reason a consumer can normally only pay less for his purchases if he submits to a similar reduction in the prices of the things he sells.'] (Mercier de la Rivière, l.c., p. 555.)
14. Torrens. 'An Essay on the Production of Wealth.' London, 1821, p. 349.
15. 'The idea of profits being paid by the consumers, is, assuredly, very absurd. Who are the consumers?' (G. Ramsay: 'An Essay on the Distribution of Wealth.' Edinburgh, 1836, p. 183.)
16. 'When a man is in want of a demand, does Mr Malthus recommend him to pay some other person to take off his goods?' is a question put by an angry disciple of Ricardo to Malthus, who, like his disciple, Parson Chalmers, economically glorifies this class of simple buyers or consumers. (See 'An Inquiry into those Principles Respecting the Nature of Demand and the Necessity of Consumption, lately advocated by Mr Malthus,' &c. Lond., 1821, p. 55.)
17. Destutt de Tracy, although, or perhaps because, he was a member of the Institute, held the opposite view. He says, industrial capitalists make profits because 'they all sell for more than it has cost to produce. And to whom do they sell? In the first instance to one another.' (I. c., p. 239.)
18. 'L'échange qui se fait de deux valeurs égales n'augmente ni ne diminue la masse des valeurs subsistantes dans la société. L'échange de deux valeurs inégales ... ne change rien non plus à la somme des valeurs sociales, bien qu'il ajoute à la fortune de l'un ce qu'il ôte de la fortune de l'autre.' ['The exchange of two equal values neither increases nor diminishes the amount of the values available in society. Nor does the exchange of two unequal values ... change anything in the sum of social values, although it adds to the wealth of one person what it removes from the wealth of another.'] (J. B. Say, l.c., t. II, pp. 443, 444.) Say, not in the least troubled as to the consequences of this statement, borrows it, almost word for word, from the Physiocrats. The following example will show how Monsieur Say turned to account the writings of the Physiocrats, in his day quite forgotten, for the purpose of expanding the 'value' of his own. His most celebrated saying, 'On n'achète des produits qu'avec des produits' ['Products can only be bought with products.'](l.c., t. II. p. 441.) runs as follows in the original physiocratic work: 'Les productions ne se paient qu'avec des productions.' ['Products can only be paid for with products.'] (Le Trosne, l.c., p. 899.)
19. 'Exchange confers no value at all upon products.' (F. Wayland: 'The Elements of Political Economy.' Boston, 1843, p. 169.)
20. Under the rule of invariable equivalents commerce would be impossible. (G. Opdyke: 'A Treatise on Polit. Economy.' New York, 1851, pp. 66-69.) 'The difference between real value and exchange-value is based upon this fact, namely, that the value of a thing is different from the so-called equivalent given for it in trade, i.e., that this equivalent is no equivalent.' (F. Engels, l.c., p. 96).

21. Benjamin Franklin: Works, Vol. II, edit. Sparks in 'Positions to be examined concerning National Wealth,' p. 376.
22. Aristotle, I. c., c. 10.
23. 'Profit, in the usual condition of the market, is not made by exchanging. Had it not existed before, neither could it after that transaction.' (Ramsay, l.c., p. 184.)
24. From the foregoing investigation, the reader will see that this statement only means that the formation of capital must be possible even though the price and value of a commodity be the same; for its formation cannot be attributed to any deviation of the one from the other. If prices actually differ from values, we must, first of all, reduce the former to the latter, in other words, treat the difference as accidental in order that the phenomena may be observed in their purity, and our observations not interfered with by disturbing circumstances that have nothing to do with the process in question. We know, moreover, that this reduction is no mere scientific process. The continual oscillations in prices, their rising and falling, compensate each other, and reduce themselves to an average price, which is their hidden regulator. It forms the guiding star of the merchant or the manufacturer in every undertaking that requires time. He knows that when a long period of time is taken, commodities are sold neither over nor under, but at their average price. If therefore he thought about the matter at all, he would formulate the problem of the formation of capital as follows: How can we account for the origin of capital on the supposition that prices are regulated by the average price, i. e., ultimately by the value of the commodities? I say 'ultimately,' because average prices do not directly coincide with the values of commodities, as Adam Smith, Ricardo, and others believe.
25. See MIA Glossary.

6

The Buying and Selling of Labour-Power

The change of value that occurs in the case of money intended to be converted into capital, cannot take place in the money itself, since in its function of means of purchase and of payment, it does no more than realise the price of the commodity it buys or pays for; and, as hard cash, it is value petrified, never varying.[1] Just as little can it originate in the second act of circulation, the re-sale of the commodity, which does no more than transform the article from its bodily form back again into its money-form. The change must, therefore, take place in the commodity bought by the first act, M-C, but not in its value, for equivalents are exchanged, and the commodity is paid for at its full value. We are, therefore, forced to the conclusion that the change originates in the use-value, as such, of the commodity, i.e., in its consumption. In order to be able to extract value from the consumption of a commodity, our friend, Moneybags, must be so lucky as to find, within the sphere of circulation, in the market, a commodity, whose use-value possesses the peculiar property of being a source of value, whose actual consumption, therefore, is itself an embodiment of labour, and, consequently, a creation of value. The possessor of money does find on the market such a special commodity in capacity for labour or labour-power.

By labour-power or capacity for labour is to be understood the aggregate of those mental and physical capabilities existing in a human being, which he exercises whenever he produces a use-value of any description.

But, in order that our owner of money may be able to find labour-power offered for sale as a commodity, various conditions must first be fulfilled. The exchange of commodities of itself implies no other relations of dependence than those which result from its own nature. On this assumption, labour-power can appear upon the market as a commodity, only if, and so far as, its possessor, the individual whose labour-power it is, offers it for sale, or sells it, as a commodity. In order that he may be able to do this, he must have it at his disposal, must be the untrammelled owner of his capacity for labour, i.e., of his person.[2] He and the owner of money meet in the market, and deal with each other as on the basis of equal rights, with this difference alone, that one is buyer, the other seller; both, therefore, equal in the eyes of the law. The continuance of this relation demands that the owner of the labour-power should sell it only for a definite period, for if he were to sell it rump and stump, once for all, he would be selling himself, converting himself from a free man into a slave, from an owner of a commodity into a commodity. He must constantly look upon his labour-power as his own property, his own commodity, and this he can only do by placing it at the disposal of the buyer temporarily, for a definite period of time. By this means alone can he avoid renouncing his rights of ownership over it.[3]

The second essential condition to the owner of money finding labour-power in the market as a commodity is this—that the labourer—instead of being in the position to sell commodities in which his labour is incorporated, must be obliged to offer for sale as a commodity that very labour-power, which exists only in his living self.

In order that a man may be able to sell commodities other than labour-power, he must of course have the means of production, as raw material, implements, &c. No boots can be made without leather. He requires also the means of subsistence. Nobody—not even 'a musician of the future'—can live upon future products, or upon use-values in an unfinished state; and ever since the first moment of his appearance on the world's stage, man always has been, and must still be a consumer, both before and while he is producing. In a society where all products assume the form of commodities, these commodities must be sold after they have been produced, it is only after their sale that they can serve in satisfying the requirements of their producer. The time necessary for their sale is superadded to that necessary for their production.

For the conversion of his money into capital, therefore, the owner of money must meet in the market with the free labourer, free in the double sense, that as a free man he can dispose of his labour-power as his own commodity, and that on the other hand he has no other commodity for sale, is short of everything necessary for the realisation of his labour-power.

The question why this free labourer confronts him in the market, has no interest for the owner of money, who regards the labour-market as a branch of the general market for commodities. And for the present it interests us just as little. We cling to the fact theoretically, as he does practically. One thing, however, is clear—Nature does not produce on the one side owners of money or commodities, and on the other men possessing nothing but their own labour-power. This relation has no natural basis, neither is its social basis one that is common to all historical periods. It is clearly the result of a past historical development, the product of many economic revolutions, of the extinction of a whole series of older forms of social production.

So, too, the economic categories, already discussed by us, bear the stamp of history. Definite historical conditions are necessary that a product may become a commodity. It must not be produced as the immediate means of subsistence of the producer himself. Had we gone further, and inquired under what circumstances all, or even the majority of products take the form of commodities, we should have found that this can only happen with production of a very specific kind, capitalist production. Such an inquiry, however, would have been foreign to the analysis of commodities. Production and circulation of commodities can take place, although the great mass of the objects produced are intended for the immediate requirements of their producers, are not turned into commodities, and consequently social production is not yet by a long way dominated in its length and breadth by exchange-value. The appearance of products as commodities pre-supposes such a development of the social division of labour, that the separation of use-value from exchange-value, a separation which first begins with barter, must already have been completed. But such a degree of development is common to many forms of society, which in other respects present the most varying historical features. On the other hand, if we consider money, its existence implies a definite stage in the exchange of commodities. The particular functions of money which it performs, either as the mere equivalent of commodities, or as means of circulation, or means of payment, as hoard or as universal money, point, according to the extent and relative preponderance of the one function or the other, to very different stages in the process of social production. Yet we know by experience that a circulation of commodities relatively primitive, suffices for the production of all these forms. Otherwise with capital. The historical conditions of its existence are by no means given with the mere circulation of money and commodities. It can spring into life, only when the owner of the means of production and subsistence meets in the market with the free labourer selling his labour-power. And this one historical condition comprises a world's history. Capital, therefore, announces from its first appearance a new epoch in the process of social production.[4]

We must now examine more closely this peculiar commodity, labour-power. Like all others it has a value.[5] How is that value determined?

The value of labour-power is determined, as in the case of every other commodity, by the labour-time necessary for the production, and consequently also the reproduction, of this special article. So far as it has value, it represents no more than a definite quantity of the average labour of society incorporated in it. Labour-power exists only as a capacity, or power of the living individual. Its production consequently pre-supposes his existence. Given the individual, the production of labour-power consists in his reproduction of himself or his maintenance. For his maintenance he requires a given quantity of the means of subsistence. Therefore, the labour-time requisite for the production of labour-power reduces itself to that necessary for the production of those means of subsistence; in other words, the value of labour-power is the value of the means of subsistence necessary for the maintenance of the labourer. Labour-power, however, becomes a reality only by its exercise; it sets itself in action only by working. But, thereby a definite quantity of human muscle, nerve, brain, &c., is wasted, and these require to be restored. This increased expenditure demands a larger income.[6] If the owner of labour-power works to-day, to-morrow he must again be able to repeat the same process in the same conditions as regards health and strength. His means of subsistence must therefore be sufficient to maintain him in his normal state as a labouring individual. His natural wants, such as food, clothing, fuel, and housing, vary according to the climatic and other physical conditions of his country. On the other hand, the number and extent of his so-called necessary wants, as also the modes of satisfying them, are themselves the product of historical development, and depend therefore to a great extent on the degree of civilisation of a country, more particularly on the conditions under which, and consequently on the habits and degree of comfort in which, the class of free labourers has been formed.[7] In contradistinction therefore to the case of other commodities, there enters into the determination of the value of labour-power a historical and moral element. Nevertheless, in a given country, at a given period, the average quantity of the means of subsistence necessary for the labourer is practically known.

The owner of labour-power is mortal. If then his appearance in the market is to be continuous, and the continuous conversion of money into capital assumes this, the seller of labour-power must perpetuate himself, 'in the way that every living individual perpetuates himself, by procreation.'[8] The labour-power withdrawn from the market by wear and tear and death, must be continually replaced by, at the very least, an equal amount of fresh labour-power. Hence the sum of the means of subsistence necessary for the production of labour-power must include the means necessary for the labourer's substitutes, i.e., his children, in order that this race of peculiar commodity-owners may perpetuate its appearance in the market.[9]

In order to modify the human organism, so that it may acquire skill and handiness in a given branch of industry, and become labour-power of a special kind, a special education or training is requisite, and this, on its part, costs an equivalent in commodities of a greater or less amount. This amount varies according to the more or less complicated character of the labour-power. The expenses of this education (excessively small in the case of ordinary labour-power), enter pro tanto into the total value spent in its production.

The value of labour-power resolves itself into the value of a definite quantity of the means of subsistence. It therefore varies with the value of these means or with the quantity of labour requisite for their production.

Some of the means of subsistence, such as food and fuel, are consumed daily, and a fresh supply must be provided daily. Others such as clothes and furniture last for longer periods and require to be replaced only at longer intervals. One article must be bought or paid for daily, another weekly, another quarterly, and so on. But in whatever way the sum total of these outlays may be spread over the year, they must be covered by the average income, taking one day with another. If the total of the commodities required daily for the production of labour-power = A, and those required weekly = B, and those required quarterly = C, and so on, the daily average of these commodities = (365A + 52B + 4C + &c) / 365. Suppose that in this mass of commodities requisite for the average day there are embodied 6 hours of social labour, then there is incorporated daily in labour-power half a day's average social labour, in other words, half a day's labour is requisite for the daily production of labour-power. This quantity of labour forms the value of a day's labour-power or the value of the labour-power daily reproduced. If half a day's average social labour is incorporated in three shillings, then three shillings is the price corresponding to the value of a day's labour-power. If its owner therefore offers it for sale at three shillings a day, its selling price is equal to its value, and according to our supposition, our friend Moneybags, who is intent upon converting his three shillings into capital, pays this value.

The minimum limit of the value of labour-power is determined by the value of the commodities, without the daily supply of which the labourer cannot renew his vital energy, consequently by the value of those means of subsistence that are physically indispensable. If the price of labour-power fall to this minimum, it falls below its value, since under such circumstances it can be maintained and developed only in a crippled state. But the value of every commodity is determined by the labour-time requisite to turn it out so as to be of normal quality.

It is a very cheap sort of sentimentality which declares this method of determining the value of labour-power, a method prescribed by the very nature of the case, to be a brutal method, and which wails with Rossi that, 'To comprehend capacity for labour (puissance de travail) at the same time that we make abstraction from the means of subsistence of the labourers during the process of production, is to comprehend a phantom (être de raison). When we speak of labour, or capacity for labour, we speak at the same time of the labourer and his means of subsistence, of labourer and wages.'[10] When we speak of capacity for labour, we do not speak of labour, any more than when we speak of capacity for digestion, we speak of digestion. The latter process requires something more than a good stomach. When we speak of capacity for labour, we do not abstract from the necessary means of subsistence. On the contrary, their value is expressed in its value. If his capacity for labour remains unsold, the labourer derives no benefit from it, but rather he will feel it to be a cruel nature-imposed necessity that this capacity has cost for its production a definite amount of the means of subsistence and that it will continue to do so for its reproduction. He will then agree with Sismondi: 'that capacity for labour ... is nothing unless it is sold.'[11]

One consequence of the peculiar nature of labour-power as a commodity is, that its use-value does not, on the conclusion of the contract between the buyer and seller, immediately pass into the hands of the former. Its value, like that of every other commodity, is already fixed before it goes into circulation, since a definite quantity of social labour has been spent upon it; but its use-value consists in the subsequent exercise of its force. The alienation of labour-power and its actual appropriation by the buyer, its employment as a use-value, are separated by an interval of time. But in those cases in which the formal alienation by sale of the use-value of a commodity, is not simultaneous with its actual delivery to the buyer, the money of the latter usually functions as means of payment.[12] In every country in which the capitalist mode of production reigns, it is the custom not to pay for labour-power before it has been exercised for the period fixed by the contract, as for example, the end of each week. In all cases, therefore, the use-value of the labour-power is advanced to the capitalist: the labourer allows the buyer to consume it before he receives payment of the price; he everywhere gives credit to the capitalist. That this credit is no mere fiction, is shown not only by the occasional loss of wages on the bankruptcy of the capitalist,[13] but also by a series of more enduring consequences.[14] Nevertheless, whether money serves as a means of purchase or as a means of payment, this makes no alteration in the nature of the exchange of commodities. The price of the labour-power is fixed by the contract, although it is not realised till later, like the rent of a house. The labour-power is sold, although it is only paid for at a later period. It will, therefore, be useful, for a clear comprehension of the relation of the parties, to assume provisionally, that the possessor of labour-power, on the occasion of each sale, immediately receives the price stipulated to be paid for it.

We now know how the value paid by the purchaser to the possessor of this peculiar commodity, labour power, is determined. The use-value which the former gets in exchange, manifests itself only in the actual utilisation, in the consumption of the labour-power. The money-owner buys everything necessary for this purpose, such as raw material, in the market, and pays for it at its full value. The consumption of labour-power is at one and the same time the production of commodities and of surplus-value. The consumption of labour-power is completed, as in the case of every other commodity, outside the limits of the market or of the sphere of circulation. Accompanied by Mr Moneybags and by the possessor of labour-power, we therefore take leave for a time of this noisy sphere, where everything takes place on the surface and in view of all men, and follow them both into the hidden abode of production, on whose threshold there stares us in the face 'No admittance except on business.' Here we shall see, not only how capital produces, but how capital is produced. We shall at last force the secret of profit making.

This sphere that we are deserting, within whose boundaries the sale and purchase of labour-power goes on, is in fact a very Eden of the innate rights of man. There alone rule Freedom, Equality, Property and Bentham. Freedom, because both buyer and seller of a commodity, say of labour-power, are constrained only by their own free will. They contract as free agents, and the agreement they come to, is but the form in which they give legal expression to their common will. Equality, because each enters into relation with the other, as with a simple owner of commodities, and they exchange equivalent for equivalent. Property, because each disposes only of what is his own. And Bentham, because each looks only to himself. The only force that brings them together and puts them in relation with each other, is the selfishness, the gain and the private interests of each. Each looks to himself only, and no one troubles himself about the rest, and just because they do so, do they all, in accordance with the pre-established harmony of things, or under the auspices of an all-shrewd providence, work together to their mutual advantage, for the common weal and in the interest of all.

On leaving this sphere of simple circulation or of exchange of commodities, which furnishes the 'Free-trader Vulgaris' with his views and ideas, and with the standard by which he judges a society based on capital and wages, we think we can perceive a change in the physiognomy of our dramatis personae. He, who before was the money-owner, now strides in front as capitalist; the possessor of labour-power follows as his labourer. The one with an air of importance, smirking, intent on business; the other, timid and holding back, like one who is bringing his own hide to market and has nothing to expect but—a hiding.

Notes

1. 'In the form of money ... capital is productive of no profit.' (Ricardo: 'Princ. of Pol. Econ.,' p. 267.)
2. In encyclopaedias of classical antiquities we find such nonsense as this—that in the ancient world capital was fully developed, 'except that the free labourer and a system of credit was wanting.' Mommsen also, in his 'History of Rome,' commits, in this respect, one blunder after another.
3. Hence legislation in various countries fixes a maximum for labour-contracts. Wherever free labour is the rule, the laws regulate the mode of terminating this contract. In some States, particularly in Mexico (before the American Civil War, also in the territories taken from Mexico, and also, as a matter of fact, in the Danubian provinces till the revolution effected by Kusa), slavery is hidden under the form of *peonage*. By means of advances, repayable in labour, which are handed down from generation to generation, not only the individual labourer, but his family, become, *de facto*, the property of other persons and their families. Juarez abolished *peonage*. The so-called Emperor Maximilian re-established it by a decree, which, in the House of Representatives at Washington, was aptly denounced as a decree for the re-introduction of slavery into Mexico. 'I may make over to another the use, for a limited time, of my particular bodily and mental aptitudes and capabilities; because in consequence of this restriction, they are impressed with a character of alienation with regard to me as a whole. But by the alienation of all my labour-time and the whole of my work, I should be converting the substance itself, in other words, my general activity and reality, my person, into the property of another.' (Hegel, 'Philosophie des Rechts.' Berlin, 1840, p. 104, § 67.)
4. The capitalist epoch is therefore characterised by this, that labour-power takes in the eyes of the labourer himself the form of a commodity which is his property; his labour consequently becomes wage-labour. On the other hand, it is only from this moment that the produce of labour universally becomes a commodity.
5. 'The value or worth of a man, is as of all other things his price—that is to say, so much as would be given for the use of his power.' (Th. Hobbes: 'Leviathan' in Works, Ed. Molesworth. Lond. 1839-44, v. iii. p. 76.)
6. Hence the Roman Villicus, as overlooker of the agricultural slaves, received 'more meagre fare than working slaves, because his work was lighter.' (Th. Mommsen, Röm. Geschichte, 1856, p. 810.)
7. Compare W. Th. Thornton: 'Over-population and its Remedy,' Lond., 1846.
8. Petty.
9. 'Its (labour's) natural price ... consists in such a quantity of necessaries and comforts of life, as, from the nature of the climate, and the habits of the country, are necessary to support the labourer, and to enable him to rear such a family as may preserve, in the market, an undiminished supply of labour.' (R. Torrens: 'An Essay on the External Corn Trade.' Lond. 1815, p. 62.) The word labour is here wrongly used for labour-power.
10. Rossi: 'Cours d'Econ. Polit.,' Bruxelles, 1842, p. 370.
11. Sismondi: 'Nouv. Princ. etc.,' t. I, p. 112.
12. 'All labour is paid after it has ceased.' ('An Inquiry into those Principles Respecting the

Nature of Demand,' &c., p. 104.) Le crédit commercial a dû commencer au moment où l'ouvrier, premier artisan de la production, a pu, au moyen de ses économies, attendre le salaire de son travail jusqu'à la fin de la semaine, de la quinzaine, du mois, du trimestre, &c.' ['The system of commercial credit had to start at the moment when the labourer, the prime creator of products, could, thanks to his savings, wait for his wages until the end of the week.'] (Ch. Ganilh: 'Des Systèmes d'Econ. Polit.' 2éme édit. Paris, 1821, t. II, p. 150.)

13. 'L'ouvrier prête son industrie,' but adds Storch slyly: he 'risks nothing' except 'de perdre son salaire ... l'ouvrier ne transmet rien de matériel.' ['The labourer lends his industry ... the loss of his wages ... the labourer does not hand over anything of a material nature.'] (Storch: 'Cours d'Econ. Polit.' Pétersbourg, 1815, t. II., p. 37.)

14. One example. In London there are two sorts of bakers, the 'full priced,' who sell bread at its full value, and the 'undersellers,' who sell it under its value. The latter class comprises more than three-fourths of the total number of bakers. (p. xxxii in the Report of H. S. Tremenheere, commissioner to examine into 'the grievances complained of by the journeymen bakers,' &c., Lond. 1862.) The undersellers, almost without exception, sell bread adulterated with alum, soap, pearl ashes, chalk, Derbyshire stone-dust, and such like agreeable nourishing and wholesome ingredients. (See the above cited Blue book, as also the report of 'the committee of 1855 on the adulteration of bread,' and Dr Hassall's 'Adulterations Detected,' 2nd Ed. Lond. 1861.) Sir John Gordon stated before the committee of 1855, that 'in consequence of these adulterations, the poor man, who lives on two pounds of bread a day, does not now get one fourth part of nourishing matter, let alone the deleterious effects on his health.' Tremenheere states (l.c., p. xlviii), as the reason, why a very large part of the working-class, although well aware of this adulteration, nevertheless accept the alum, stone-dust, &c., as part of their purchase: that it is for them 'a matter of necessity to take from their baker or from the chandler's shop, such bread as they choose to supply.' As they are not paid their wages before the end of the week, they in their turn are unable 'to pay for the bread consumed by their families, during the week, before the end of the week,' and Tremenheere adds on the evidence of witnesses, 'it is notorious that bread composed of those mixtures, is made expressly for sale in this manner.' In many English and still more Scotch agricultural districts, wages are paid fortnightly and even monthly; with such long intervals between the payments, the agricultural labourer is obliged to buy on credit.... He must pay higher prices, and is in fact tied to the shop which gives him credit. Thus at Horningham in Wilts, for example, where the wages are monthly, the same flour that he could buy elsewhere at 1s 10d per stone, costs him 2s 4d per stone. ('Sixth Report' on 'Public Health' by 'The Medical Officer of the Privy Council, &c., 1864,' p.264.) 'The block printers of Paisley and Kilmarnock enforced, by a strike, fortnightly, instead of monthly payment of wages.' ('Reports of the Inspectors of Factories for 31st Oct., 1853,' p. 34.) As a further pretty result of the credit given by the workmen to the capitalist, we may refer to the method current in many English coal mines, where the labourer is not paid till the end of the month, and in the meantime, receives sums on account from the capitalist, often in goods for which the miner is obliged to pay more than the market price (Truck-system). 'It is a common practice with the coal masters to pay once a month, and advance cash to their workmen at the end of each intermediate week. The cash is given in the shop' (i.e., the Tommy shop which belongs to the master); 'the men take it on one side and lay it out on the other.' ('Children's Employment Commission, III. Report,' Lond. 1864, p. 38, n. 192.)

PART III

THE PRODUCTION OF ABSOLUTE SURPLUS-VALUE

7

The Labour-Process and the Process of Producing Surplus-Value

Section 1: *The Labour-Process or the Production of Use-Values*

The capitalist buys labour-power in order to use it; and labour-power in use is labour itself. The purchaser of labour-power consumes it by setting the seller of it to work. By working, the latter becomes actually, what before he only was potentially, labour-power in action, a labourer. In order that his labour may re-appear in a commodity, he must, before all things, expend it on something useful, on something capable of satisfying a want of some sort. Hence, what the capitalist sets the labourer to produce, is a particular use-value, a specified article. The fact that the production of use-values, or goods, is carried on under the control of a capitalist and on his behalf, does not alter the general character of that production. We shall, therefore, in the first place, have to consider the labour-process independently of the particular form it assumes under given social conditions.

Labour is, in the first place, a process in which both man and Nature participate, and in which man of his own accord starts, regulates, and controls the material re-actions between himself and Nature. He opposes himself to Nature as one of her own forces, setting in motion arms and legs, head and hands, the natural forces of his body, in order to appropriate Nature's productions in a form adapted to his own wants. By thus acting on the external world and changing it, he at the same time changes his own nature. He develops his slumbering powers and compels them to act in obedience to his sway. We are not now dealing with those primitive instinctive forms of labour that remind us of the mere animal. An immeasurable interval of time separates the state of things in which a man brings his labour-power to market for sale as a commodity, from that state in which human labour was still in its first instinctive stage. We pre-suppose labour in a form that stamps it as exclusively human. A spider conducts operations that resemble those of a weaver, and a bee puts to shame many an architect in the construction of her cells. But what distinguishes the worst architect from the best of bees is this, that the architect raises his structure in imagination before he erects it in reality. At the end of every labour-process, we get a result that already existed in the imagination of the labourer at its commencement. He not only effects a change of form in the material on which he works, but he also realises a purpose of his own that gives the law to his modus operandi, and to which he must subordinate his will. And this subordination is no mere momentary act. Besides the exertion of the bodily organs, the process demands that, during the whole operation, the workman's will be steadily in consonance with his purpose. This means close attention. The less he is attracted by the nature of the work, and the mode in which it is carried on, and the less, therefore, he enjoys it as something which gives play to his bodily and mental powers, the more close his attention is forced to be.

The elementary factors of the labour-process are 1, the personal activity of man, *i.e.*, work itself, 2, the subject of that work, and 3, its instruments.

The soil (and this, economically speaking, includes water) in the virgin state in which it supplies[1] man with necessaries or the means of subsistence ready to hand, exists independently of him, and is the universal subject of human labour. All those things which labour merely separates from immediate connexion with their environment, are subjects of labour spontaneously provided by Nature. Such are fish which we catch and take from their element, water, timber which we fell in the virgin forest, and ores which we extract from their veins. If, on the other hand, the subject of labour has, so to say, been filtered through previous labour, we call it raw material; such is ore already extracted and ready for washing. All raw material is the subject of labour, but not every subject of labour is raw material: it can only become so, after it has undergone some alteration by means of labour.

An instrument of labour is a thing, or a complex of things, which the labourer interposes between himself and the subject of his labour, and which serves as the conductor of his activity. He makes use of the mechanical, physical, and chemical properties of some substances in order to make other substances subservient to his aims.[2] Leaving out of consideration such ready-made means of subsistence as fruits, in gathering which a man's own limbs serve as the instruments of his labour, the first thing of which the labourer possesses himself is not the subject of labour but its instrument. Thus Nature becomes one of the organs of his activity, one that he annexes to his own bodily organs, adding stature to himself in spite of the Bible. As the earth is his original larder, so too it is his original tool house. It supplies him, for instance, with stones for throwing, grinding, pressing, cutting, &c. The earth itself is an instrument of labour, but when used as such in agriculture implies a whole series of other instruments and a comparatively high development of labour.[3] No sooner does labour undergo the least development, than it requires specially prepared instruments. Thus, in the oldest caves we find stone implements and weapons. In the earliest period of human history domesticated animals, *i.e.*, animals which have been bred for the purpose, and have undergone modifications by means of labour, play the chief part as instruments of labour along with specially prepared stones, wood, bones, and shells.[4] The use and fabrication of instruments of labour, although existing in the germ among certain species of animals, is specifically characteristic of the human labour-process, and Franklin therefore defines man as a tool-making animal. Relics of bygone instruments of labour possess the same importance for the investigation of extinct economic forms of society, as do fossil bones for the determination of extinct species of animals. It is not the articles made, but how they are made, and by what instruments, that enables us to distinguish different economic epochs.[5] Instruments of labour not only supply a standard of the degree of development to which human labour has attained, but they are also indicators of the social conditions under which that labour is carried on. Among the instruments of labour, those of a mechanical nature, which, taken as a whole, we may call the bone and muscles of production, offer much more decided characteristics of a given epoch of production, than those which, like pipes, tubs, baskets, jars, &c., serve only to hold the materials for labour, which latter class, we may in a general way, call the vascular system of production. The latter first begins to play an important part in the chemical industries.

In a wider sense we may include among the instruments of labour, in addition to those things that are used for directly transferring labour to its subject, and which therefore, in one way or another, serve as conductors of activity, all such objects as are necessary for carrying on the labour-process. These do not enter directly into the process, but without them it is either impossible for it to take place at all, or possible only to a partial extent. Once more we find the earth to be a universal instrument of this sort, for it furnishes a locus standi to the labourer and a field of employment for his activity. Among instruments that are the result of previous labour and also belong to this class, we find workshops, canals, roads, and so forth.

In the labour-process, therefore, man's activity, with the help of the instruments of labour, effects an alteration, designed from the commencement, in the material worked upon. The process disappears in the product, the latter is a use-value, Nature's material adapted by a change of form to the wants of man. Labour has incorporated itself with its subject: the former is materialised, the latter transformed. That which in the labourer appeared as movement, now appears in the product as a fixed quality without motion. The blacksmith forges and the product is a forging.

If we examine the whole process from the point of view of its result, the product, it is plain that both the instruments and the subject of labour, are means of production,[6] and that the labour itself is productive labour.[7]

Though a use-value, in the form of a product, issues from the labour-process, yet other use-values, products of previous labour, enter into it as means of production. The same use-value is both the product of a previous process, and a means of production in a later process. Products are therefore not only results, but also essential conditions of labour.

With the exception of the extractive industries, in which the material for labour is provided immediately by Nature, such as mining, hunting, fishing, and agriculture (so far as the latter is confined to breaking up virgin soil), all branches of industry manipulate raw material, objects already filtered through labour, already products of labour. Such is seed in agriculture. Animals and plants, which we are accustomed to consider as products of Nature, are in their present form, not only products of, say last year's labour, but the result of a gradual transformation, continued through many generations, under man's superintendence, and by means of his labour. But in the great majority of cases, instruments of labour show even to the most superficial observer, traces of the labour of past ages.

Raw material may either form the principal substance of a product, or it may enter into its formation only as an accessory. An accessory may be consumed by the instruments of labour, as coal under a boiler, oil by a wheel, hay by draft-horses, or it may be mixed with the raw material in order to produce some modification thereof, as chlorine into unbleached linen, coal with iron, dye-stuff with wool, or again, it may help to carry on the work itself, as in the case of the materials used for heating and lighting workshops. The distinction between principal substance and accessory vanishes in the true chemical industries, because there none of the raw material re-appears, in its original composition, in the substance of the product.[8]

Every object possesses various properties, and is thus capable of being applied to different uses. One and the same product may therefore serve as raw material in very different processes. Corn, for example, is a raw material for millers, starch-manufacturers, distillers, and cattlebreeders. It also enters as raw material into its own production in the shape of seed; coal, too, is at the same time the product of, and a means of production in, coal-mining.

Again, a particular product may be used in one and the same process, both as an instrument of labour and as raw material. Take, for instance, the fattening of cattle, where the animal is the raw material, and at the same time an instrument for the production of manure.

A product, though ready for immediate consumption, may yet serve as raw material for a further product, as grapes when they become the raw material for wine. On the other hand, labour may give us its product in such a form, that we can use it only as raw material, as is the case with cotton, thread, and yarn. Such a raw material, though itself a product, may have to go through a whole series of different processes: in each of these in turn, it serves, with constantly varying form, as raw material, until the last process of the series leaves it a perfect product, ready for individual consumption, or for use as an instrument of labour.

Hence we see, that whether a use-value is to be regarded as raw material, as instrument of labour, or as product, this is determined entirely by its function in the labour-process, by the position it there occupies: as this varies, so does its character.

Whenever therefore a product enters as a means of production into a new labour-process, it thereby loses its character of product, and becomes a mere factor in the process. A spinner treats spindles only as implements for spinning, and flax only as the material that he spins. Of course it is impossible to spin without material and spindles; and therefore the existence of these things as products, at the commencement of the spinning operation, must be presumed: but in the process itself, the fact that they are products of previous labour, is a matter of utter indifference; just as in the digestive process, it is of no importance whatever, that bread is the produce of the previous labour of the farmer, the miller, and the baker. On the contrary, it is generally by their imperfections as products, that the means of production in any process assert themselves in their character of products. A blunt knife or weak thread forcibly remind us of Mr A., the cutler, or Mr B., the spinner. In the finished product the labour by means of which it has acquired its useful qualities is not palpable, has apparently vanished.

A machine which does not serve the purposes of labour, is useless. In addition, it falls a prey to the destructive influence of natural forces. Iron rusts and wood rots. Yarn with which we neither weave nor knit, is cotton wasted. Living labour must seize upon these things and rouse them from their death-sleep, change them from mere possible use-values into real and effective ones. Bathed in the fire of labour, appropriated as part and parcel of labour's organism, and, as it were, made alive for the performance of their functions in the process, they are in truth consumed, but consumed with a purpose, as elementary constituents of new use-values, of new products, ever ready as means of subsistence for individual consumption, or as means of production for some new labour-process.

If then, on the one hand, finished products are not only results, but also necessary conditions, of the labour-process, on the other hand, their assumption into that process, their contact with living labour, is the sole means by which they can be made to retain their character of use-values, and be utilised.

Labour uses up its material factors, its subject and its instruments, consumes them, and is therefore a process of consumption. Such productive consumption is distinguished from individual consumption by this, that the latter uses up products, as means of subsistence for the living individual; the former, as means whereby alone, labour, the labour-power of the living individual, is enabled to act. The product, therefore, of individual consumption, is the consumer himself; the result of productive consumption, is a product distinct from the consumer.

In so far then, as its instruments and subjects are themselves products, labour consumes products in order to create products, or in other words, consumes one set of products by turning them into means of production for another set. But, just as in the beginning, the only participators in the labour-process were man and the earth, which latter exists independently of man, so even now we still employ in the process many means of production, provided directly by Nature, that do not represent any combination of natural substances with human labour.

The labour-process, resolved as above into its simple elementary factors, is human action with a view to the production of use-values, appropriation of natural substances to human requirements; it is the necessary condition for effecting exchange of matter between man and Nature; it is the everlasting Nature-imposed condition of human existence, and therefore is independent of every social phase of that existence, or rather, is common to every such phase. It was, therefore, not necessary to represent our labourer in connexion with other labourers; man and his labour on one side, Nature and its materials on the other, sufficed. As the taste of the porridge does not tell you who grew the oats, no more does this simple process tell you of itself what are the social conditions under which it is taking place, whether under the slave-owner's brutal lash, or the anxious eye of the capitalist, whether Cincinnatus carries it on in tilling his modest farm or a savage in killing wild animals with stones.[9]

Let us now return to our would-be capitalist. We left him just after he had purchased, in the open market, all the necessary factors of the labour process; its objective factors, the means of production, as well as its subjective factor, labour-power. With the keen eye of an expert, he has selected the means of production and the kind of labour-power best adapted to his particular trade, be it spinning, bootmaking, or any other kind. He then proceeds to consume the commodity, the labour-power that he has just bought, by causing the labourer, the impersonation of that labour-power, to consume the means of production by his labour. The general character of the labour-process is evidently not changed by the fact, that the labourer works for the capitalist instead of for himself; moreover, the particular methods and operations employed in bootmaking or spinning are not immediately changed by the intervention of the capitalist. He must begin by taking the labour-power as he finds it in the market, and consequently be satisfied with labour of such a kind as would be found in the period immediately preceding the rise of capitalists. Changes in the methods of production by the subordination of labour to capital, can take place only at a later period, and therefore will have to be treated of in a later chapter.

The labour-process, turned into the process by which the capitalist consumes labour-power, exhibits two characteristic phenomena. First, the labourer works under the control of the capitalist to whom his labour belongs; the capitalist taking good care that the work is done in a proper manner, and that the means of production are used with intelligence, so that there is no unnecessary waste of raw material, and no wear and tear of the implements beyond what is necessarily caused by the work.

Secondly, the product is the property of the capitalist and not that of the labourer, its immediate producer. Suppose that a capitalist pays for a day's labour-power at its value; then the right to use that power for a day belongs to him, just as much as the right to use any other commodity, such as a horse that he has hired for the day. To the purchaser of a commodity belongs its use, and the seller of labour-power, by giving his labour, does no more, in reality, than part with the use-value that he has sold. From the instant he steps into the workshop, the use-value of his labour-power, and therefore also its use, which is labour, belongs to the capitalist. By the purchase of labour-power, the capitalist incorporates labour, as a living ferment, with the lifeless constituents of the product. From his point of view, the labour-process is nothing more than the consumption of the commodity purchased, *i. e.*, of labour-power; but this consumption cannot be effected except by supplying the labour-power with the means of production. The labour-process is a process between things that the capitalist has purchased, things that have become his property. The product of this process belongs, therefore, to him, just as much as does the wine which is the product of a process of fermentation completed in his cellar.[10]

Section 2: *The Production Of Surplus-Value*

The product appropriated by the capitalist is a use-value, as yarn, for example, or boots. But, although boots are, in one sense, the basis of all social progress, and our capitalist is a decided 'progressist,' yet he does not manufacture boots for their own sake. Use-value is, by no means, the thing 'qu'on aime pour lui-même' in the production of commodities. Use-values are only produced by capitalists, because, and in so far as, they are the material substratum, the depositories of exchange-value. Our capitalist has two objects in view: in the first place, he wants to produce a use-value that has a value in exchange, that is to say, an article destined to be sold, a commodity; and secondly, he desires to produce a commodity whose value shall be greater than the sum of the values of the commodities used in its production, that is, of the means of production and the labour-power, that he purchased with his good money in the open market. His aim is to produce not only a use-value, but a commodity also; not only use-value, but value; not only value, but at the same time surplus-value.

It must be borne in mind, that we are now dealing with the production of commodities, and that, up to this point, we have only considered one aspect of the process. Just as commodities are, at the same time, use-values and values, so the process of producing them must be a labour-process, and at the same time, a process of creating value.[11]

Let us now examine production as a creation of value.

We know that the value of each commodity is determined by the quantity of labour expended on and materialised in it, by the working-time necessary, under given social conditions, for its production. This rule also holds good in the case of the product that accrued to our capitalist, as the result of the labour-process carried on for him. Assuming this product to be 10 lbs. of yarn, our first step is to calculate the quantity of labour realised in it.

For spinning the yarn, raw material is required; suppose in this case 10 lbs. of cotton. We have no need at present to investigate the value of this cotton, for our capitalist has, we will assume, bought it at its full value, say of ten shillings. In this price, the labour required for the production of the cotton is already expressed in terms of the average labour of society. We will further assume that the wear and tear of the spindle, which, for our present purpose, may represent all other instruments of labour employed, amounts to the value of 2s. If, then, twenty-four hours' labour, or two working-days, are required to produce the quantity of gold represented by twelve shillings, we have here, to begin with, two days' labour already incorporated in the yarn.

We must not let ourselves be misled by the circumstance that the cotton has taken a new shape while the substance of the spindle has to a certain extent been used up. By the general law of value, if the value of 40 lbs. of yarn = the value of 40 lbs. of cotton + the value of a whole spindle, *i. e.*, if the same working-time is required to produce the commodities on either side of this equation, then 10 lbs. of yarn are an equivalent for 10 lbs. of cotton, together with one-fourth of a spindle. In the case we are considering the same working-time is materialised in the 10 lbs. of yarn on the one hand, and in the 10 lbs. of cotton and the fraction of a spindle on the other. Therefore, whether value appears in cotton, in a spindle, or in yarn, makes no difference in the amount of that value. The spindle and cotton, instead of resting quietly side by side, join together in the process, their forms are altered, and they are turned into yarn; but their value is no more affected by this fact than it would be if they had been simply exchanged for their equivalent in yarn.

The labour required for the production of the cotton, the raw material of the yarn, is part of the labour necessary to produce the yarn, and is therefore contained in the yarn. The same applies to the labour embodied in the spindle, without whose wear and tear the cotton could not be spun.

Hence, in determining the value of the yarn, or the labour-time required for its production, all the special processes carried on at various times and in different places, which were necessary, first to produce the cotton and the wasted portion of the spindle, and then with the cotton and spindle to spin the yarn, may together be looked on as different and successive phases of one and the same process. The whole of the labour in the yarn is past labour; and it is a matter of no importance that the operations necessary for the production of its constituent elements were carried on at times which, referred to the present, are more remote than the final operation of spinning. If a definite quantity of labour, say thirty days, is requisite to build a house, the total amount of labour incorporated in it is not altered by the fact that the work of the last day is done twenty-nine days later than that of the first. Therefore the labour contained in the raw material and the instruments of labour can be treated just as if it were labour expended in an earlier stage of the spinning process, before the labour of actual spinning commenced.

The values of the means of production, *i. e.*, the cotton and the spindle, which values are expressed in the price of twelve shillings, are therefore constituent parts of the value of the yarn, or, in other words, of the value of the product.

Two conditions must nevertheless be fulfilled. First, the cotton and spindle must concur in the production of a use-value; they must in the present case become yarn. Value is independent of the particular use-value by which it is borne, but it must be embodied in a use-value of some kind. Secondly, the time occupied in the labour of production must not exceed the time really necessary under the given social conditions of the case. Therefore, if no more than 1 lb. of cotton be requisite to spin 1 lb. of yarn, care must be taken that no more than this weight of cotton is consumed in the production of 1 lb. of yarn; and similarly with regard to the spindle. Though the capitalist have a hobby, and use a gold instead of a steel spindle, yet the only labour that counts for anything in the value of the yarn is that which would be required to produce a steel spindle, because no more is necessary under the given social conditions.

We now know what portion of the value of the yarn is owing to the cotton and the spindle. It amounts to twelve shillings or the value of two days' work. The next point for our consideration is, what portion of the value of the yarn is added to the cotton by the labour of the spinner.

We have now to consider this labour under a very different aspect from that which it had during the labour-process; there, we viewed it solely as that particular kind of human activity which changes cotton into yarn; there, the more the labour was suited to the work, the better the yarn, other circumstances remaining the same. The labour of the spinner was then viewed as specifically different from other kinds of productive labour, different on the one hand in its special aim, viz., spinning, different, on the other hand, in the special character of its operations, in the special nature of its means of production and in the special use-value of its product. For the operation of spinning, cotton and spindles are a necessity, but for making rifled cannon they would be of no use whatever. Here, on the contrary, where we consider the labour of the spinner only so far as it is value-creating, *i.e.*, a source of value, his labour differs in no respect from the labour of the man who bores cannon, or (what here more nearly concerns us), from the labour of the cotton-planter and spindle-maker incorporated in the means of production. It is solely by reason of this identity, that cotton planting, spindle making and spinning, are capable of forming the component parts differing only quantitatively from each other, of one whole, namely, the value of the yarn. Here, we have nothing more to do with the quality, the nature and the specific character of the labour, but merely with its quantity. And this simply requires to be calculated. We proceed upon the assumption that spinning is simple, unskilled labour, the average labour of a given state of society. Hereafter we shall see that the contrary assumption would make no difference.

While the labourer is at work, his labour constantly undergoes a transformation: from being motion, it becomes an object without motion; from being the labourer working, it becomes the thing produced. At the end of one hour's spinning, that act is represented by a definite quantity of yarn; in other words, a definite quantity of labour, namely that of one hour, has become embodied in the cotton. We say labour, *i.e.*, the expenditure of his vital force by the spinner, and not spinning labour, because the special work of spinning counts here, only so far as it is the expenditure of labour-power in general, and not in so far as it is the specific work of the spinner.

In the process we are now considering it is of extreme importance, that no more time be consumed in the work of transforming the cotton into yarn than is necessary under the given social conditions. If under normal, *i.e.*, average social conditions of production, *a* pounds of cotton ought to be made into *b* pounds of yarn by one hour's labour, then a day's labour does not count as 12 hours' labour unless 12 *a* pounds of cotton have been made into 12 *b* pounds of yarn; for in the creation of value, the time that is socially necessary alone counts.

Not only the labour, but also the raw material and the product now appear in quite a new light, very different from that in which we viewed them in the labour-process pure and simple. The raw material serves now merely as an absorbent of a definite quantity of labour. By this absorption it is in fact changed into yarn, because it is spun, because labour-power in the form of spinning is added to it; but the product, the yarn, is now nothing more than a measure of the labour absorbed by the cotton. If, in one hour 1 2/3 lbs. of cotton can be spun into 1 2/3 lbs. of yarn, then 10 lbs. of yarn indicate the absorption of 6 hours' labour. Definite quantities of product, these quantities being determined by experience, now represent nothing but definite quantities of labour, definite masses of crystallised labour-time. They are nothing more than the materialisation of so many hours or so many days of social labour.

We are here no more concerned about the facts, that the labour is the specific work of spinning, that its subject is cotton and its product yarn, than we are about the fact that the subject itself is already a product and therefore raw material. If the spinner, instead of spinning, were working in a coal mine, the subject of his labour, the coal, would be supplied by Nature; nevertheless, a definite quantity of extracted coal, a hundredweight for example, would represent a definite quantity of absorbed labour.

We assumed, on the occasion of its sale, that the value of a day's labour-power is three shillings, and that six hours' labour is incorporated in that sum; and consequently that this amount of labour is requisite to produce the necessaries of life daily required on an average by the labourer. If now our spinner by working for one hour, can convert 1 2/3 lbs. of cotton into 1 2/3 lbs. of yarn,[12] it follows that in six hours he will convert 10 lbs. of cotton into 10 lbs. of yarn. Hence, during the spinning process, the cotton absorbs six hours' labour. The same quantity of labour is also embodied in a piece of gold of the value of three shillings. Consequently, by the mere labour of spinning, a value of three shillings is added to the cotton.

Let us now consider the total value of the product, the 10 lbs. of yarn. Two and a half days' labour has been embodied in it, of which two days were contained in the cotton and in the substance of the spindle worn away, and half a day was absorbed during the process of spinning. This two and a half days' labour is also represented by a piece of gold of the value of fifteen shillings. Hence, fifteen shillings is an adequate price for the 10 lbs. of yarn, or the price of one pound is eighteenpence.

Our capitalist stares in astonishment. The value of the product is exactly equal to the value of the capital advanced. The value so advanced has not expanded, no surplus-value has been created, and consequently money has not been converted into capital. The price of the yarn is fifteen shillings, and fifteen shillings were spent in the open market upon the constituent elements of the product, or, what amounts to the same thing, upon the factors of the labour-process; ten shillings were paid for the cotton, two shillings for the substance of the spindle worn away, and three shillings for the labour-power. The swollen value of the yarn is of no avail, for it is merely the sum of the values formerly existing in the cotton, the spindle, and the labour-power: out of such a simple addition of existing values, no surplus-value can possibly arise.[13] These separate values are now all concentrated in one thing; but so they were also in the sum of fifteen shillings, before it was split up into three parts, by the purchase of the commodities.

There is in reality nothing very strange in this result. The value of one pound of yarn being eighteenpence, if our capitalist buys 10 lbs. of yarn in the market, he must pay fifteen shillings for them. It is clear that, whether a man buys his house ready built, or gets it built for him, in neither case will the mode of acquisition increase the amount of money laid out on the house.

Our capitalist, who is at home in his vulgar economy, exclaims: 'Oh! but I advanced my money for the express purpose of making more money.' The way to Hell is paved with good intentions, and he might just as easily have intended to make money, without producing at all.[14] He threatens all sorts of things. He won't be caught napping again. In future he will buy the commodities in the market, instead of manufacturing them himself. But if all his brother capitalists were to do the same, where would he find his commodities in the market? And his money he cannot eat. He tries persuasion. 'Consider my abstinence; I might have played ducks and drakes with the 15 shillings; but instead of that I consumed it productively, and made yarn with it.' Very well, and by way of reward he is now in possession of good yarn instead of a bad conscience; and as for playing the part of a miser, it would never do for him to relapse into such bad ways as that; we have seen before to what results such asceticism leads. Besides, where nothing is, the king has lost his rights; whatever may be the merit of his abstinence, there is nothing wherewith specially to remunerate it, because the value of the product is merely the sum of the values of the commodities that were thrown into the process of production. Let him, therefore, console himself with the reflection that virtue is its own reward. But no, he becomes importunate. He says: 'The yarn is of no use to me: I produced it for sale.' In that case let him sell it, or, still better, let him for the future produce only things for satisfying his personal wants, a remedy that his physician MacCulloch has already prescribed as infallible against an epidemic of over-production. He now gets obstinate. 'Can the labourer,' he asks, 'merely with his arms and legs, produce commodities out of nothing? Did I not supply him with the materials, by means of which, and in which alone, his labour could be embodied? And as the greater part of society consists of such ne'er-do-wells, have I not rendered society incalculable service by my instruments of production, my cotton and my spindle, and not only society, but the labourer also, whom in addition I have provided with the necessaries of life? And am I to be allowed nothing in return for all this service?' Well, but has not the labourer rendered him the equivalent service of changing his cotton and spindle into yarn? Moreover, there is here no question of service.[15] A service is nothing more than the useful effect of a use-value, be it of a commodity, or be it of labour.[16] But here we are dealing with exchange-value. The capitalist paid to the labourer a value of 3 shillings, and the labourer gave him back an exact equivalent in the value of 3 shillings, added by him to the cotton: he gave him value for value. Our friend, up to this time so purse-proud, suddenly assumes the modest demeanour of his own workman, and exclaims: 'Have I myself not worked? Have I not performed the labour of superintendence and of overlooking the spinner? And does not this labour, too, create value?' His overlooker and his manager try to hide their smiles. Meanwhile, after a hearty laugh, he re-assumes his usual mien. Though he chanted to us the whole creed of the economists, in reality, he says, he would not give a brass farthing for it. He leaves this and all such like subterfuges and juggling tricks to the professors of Political Economy, who are paid for it. He himself is a practical man; and though he does not always consider what he says outside his business, yet in his business he knows what he is about.

Let us examine the matter more closely. The value of a day's labour-power amounts to 3 shillings, because on our assumption half a day's labour is embodied in that quantity of labour-power, *i.e.*, because the means of subsistence that are daily required for the production of labour-power, cost half a day's labour. But the past labour that is embodied in the labour-power, and the living labour that it can call into action; the daily cost of maintaining it, and its daily expenditure in work, are two totally different things. The former determines the exchange-value of the labour-power, the latter is its use-value. The fact that half a day's labour is necessary to keep the labourer alive during 24 hours, does not in any way prevent him from working a whole day. Therefore, the value of labour-power, and the value which that labour-power creates in the labour-process, are two entirely different magnitudes; and this difference of the two values was what the capitalist had in view, when he was purchasing the labour-power. The useful qualities that labour-power possesses, and by virtue of which it makes yarn or boots, were to him nothing more than a conditio sine qua non; for in order to create value, labour must be expended in a useful manner. What really influenced him was the specific use-value which this commodity possesses of being *a source not only of value, but of more value than it has itself.* This is the special service that the capitalist expects from labour-power, and in this transaction he acts in accordance with the 'eternal laws' of the exchange of commodities. The seller of labour-power, like the seller of any other commodity, realises its exchange-value, and parts with its use-value. He cannot take the one without giving the other. The use-value of labour-power, or in other words, labour, belongs just as little to its seller, as the use-value of oil after it has been sold belongs to the dealer who has sold it. The owner of the money has paid the value of a day's labour-power; his, therefore, is the use of it for a day; a day's labour belongs to him. The circumstance, that on the one hand the daily sustenance of labour-power costs only half a day's labour, while on the other hand the very same labour-power can work during a whole day, that consequently the value which its use during one day creates, is double what he pays for that use, this circumstance is, without doubt, a piece of good luck for the buyer, but by no means an injury to the seller.

Our capitalist foresaw this state of things, and that was the cause of his laughter. The labourer therefore finds, in the workshop, the means of production necessary for working, not only during six, but during twelve hours. Just as during the six hours' process our 10 lbs. of cotton absorbed six hours' labour, and became 10 lbs. of yarn, so now, 20 lbs. of cotton will absorb 12 hours' labour and be changed into 20 lbs. of yarn. Let us now examine the product of this prolonged process. There is now materialised in this 20 lbs. of yarn the labour of five days, of which four days are due to the cotton and the lost steel of the spindle, the remaining day having been absorbed by the cotton during the spinning process. Expressed in gold, the labour of five days is thirty shillings. This is therefore the price of the 20 lbs. of yarn, giving, as before, eighteenpence as the price of a pound. But the sum of the values of the commodities that entered into the process amounts to 27 shillings. The value of the yarn is 30 shillings. Therefore the value of the product is 1/9 greater than the value advanced for its production; 27 shillings have been transformed into 30 shillings; a surplus-value of 3 shillings has been created. The trick has at last succeeded; money has been converted into capital.

Every condition of the problem is satisfied, while the laws that regulate the exchange of commodities, have been in no way violated. Equivalent has been exchanged for equivalent. For the capitalist as buyer paid for each commodity, for the cotton, the spindle and the labour-power, its full value. He then did what is done by every purchaser of commodities; he consumed their use-value. The consumption of the labour-power, which was also the process of producing commodities, resulted in 20 lbs. of yarn, having a value of 30 shillings. The capitalist, formerly a buyer, now returns to market as a seller, of commodities. He sells his yarn at eighteenpence a pound, which is its exact value. Yet, for all that he withdraws 3 shillings more from circulation than he originally threw into it. This metamorphosis, this conversion of money into capital, takes place both—within the sphere of circulation and also outside it; within the circulation, because conditioned by the purchase of the labour-power in the market; outside the circulation, because what is done within it is only a stepping-stone to the production of surplus-value, a process which is entirely confined to the sphere of production. Thus 'tout est pour le mieux dans le meilleur des mondes possibles.' ['Everything is for the best in the best of all possible worlds.'—Voltaire, *Candide*]

By turning his money into commodities that serve as the material elements of a new product, and as factors in the labour-process, by incorporating living labour with their dead substance, the capitalist at the same time converts value, *i.e.*, past, materialised, and dead labour into capital, into value big with value, a live monster that is fruitful and multiplies.

If we now compare the two processes of producing value and of creating surplus-value, we see that the latter is nothing but the continuation of the former beyond a definite point. If on the one hand the process be not carried beyond the point, where the value paid by the capitalist for the labour-power is replaced by an exact equivalent, it is simply a process of producing value; if, on the other hand, it be continued beyond that point, it becomes a process of creating surplus-value.

If we proceed further, and compare the process of producing value with the labour-process, pure and simple, we find that the latter consists of the useful labour, the work, that produces use-values. Here we contemplate the labour as producing a particular article; we view it under its qualitative aspect alone, with regard to its end and aim. But viewed as a value-creating process, the same labour-process presents itself under its quantitative aspect alone. Here it is a question merely of the time occupied by the labourer in doing the work; of the period during which the labour-power is usefully expended. Here, the commodities that take part in the process, do not count any longer as necessary adjuncts of labour-power in the production of a definite, useful object. They count merely as depositories of so much absorbed or materialised labour; that labour, whether previously embodied in the means of production, or incorporated in them for the first time during the process by the action of labour-power, counts in either case only according to its duration; it amounts to so many hours or days as the case may be.

Moreover, only so much of the time spent in the production of any article is counted, as, under the given social conditions, is necessary. The consequences of this are various. In the first place, it becomes necessary that the labour should be carried on under normal conditions. If a self-acting mule is the implement in general use for spinning, it would be absurd to supply the spinner with a distaff and spinning wheel. The cotton too must not be such rubbish as to cause extra waste in being worked, but must be of suitable quality. Otherwise the spinner would be found to spend more time in producing a pound of yarn than is socially necessary, in which case the excess of time would create neither value nor money. But whether the material factors of the process are of normal quality or not, depends not upon the labourer, but entirely upon the capitalist. Then again, the labour-power itself must be of average efficacy. In the trade in which it is being employed, it must possess the average skill, handiness and quickness prevalent in that trade, and our capitalist took good care to buy labour-power of such normal goodness. This power must be applied with the average amount of exertion and with the usual degree of intensity; and the capitalist is as careful to see that this is done, as that his workmen are not idle for a single moment. He has bought the use of the labour-power for a definite period, and he insists upon his rights. He has no intention of being robbed. Lastly, and for this purpose our friend has a penal code of his own, all wasteful consumption of raw material or instruments of labour is strictly forbidden, because what is so wasted, represents labour superfluously expended, labour that does not count in the product or enter into its value.[17]

We now see, that the difference between labour, considered on the one hand as producing utilities, and on the other hand, as creating value, a difference which we discovered by our analysis of a commodity, resolves itself into a distinction between two aspects of the process of production.

The process of production, considered on the one hand as the unity of the labour-process and the process of creating value, is production of commodities; considered on the other hand as the unity of the labour-process and the process of producing surplus-value, it is the capitalist process of production, or capitalist production of commodities.

We stated, on a previous page, that in the creation of surplus-value it does not in the least matter, whether the labour appropriated by the capitalist be simple unskilled labour of average quality or more complicated skilled labour. All labour of a higher or more complicated character than average labour is expenditure of labour-power of a more costly kind, labour-power whose production has cost more time and labour, and which therefore has a higher value, than unskilled or simple labour-power. This power being higher-value, its consumption is labour of a higher class, labour that creates in equal times proportionally higher values than unskilled labour does. Whatever difference in skill there may be between the labour of a spinner and that of a jeweller, the portion of his labour by which the jeweller merely replaces the value of his own labour-power, does not in any way differ in quality from the additional portion by which he creates surplus-value. In the making of jewellery, just as in spinning, the surplus-value results only from a quantitative excess of labour, from a lengthening-out of one and the same labour-process, in the one case, of the process of making jewels, in the other of the process of making yarn.[18]

But on the other hand, in every process of creating value, the reduction of skilled labour to average social labour, *e.g.*, one day of skilled to six days of unskilled labour, is unavoidable.[19] We therefore save ourselves a superfluous operation, and simplify our analysis, by the assumption, that the labour of the workman employed by the capitalist is unskilled average labour.

Notes

1. 'The earth's spontaneous productions being in small quantity, and quite independent of man, appear, as it were, to be furnished by Nature, in the same way as a small sum is given to a young man, in order to put him in a way of industry, and of making his fortune.' (James Steuart: 'Principles of Polit. Econ.' edit. Dublin, 1770, v. I, p.116.)
2. 'Reason is just as cunning as she is powerful. Her cunning consists principally in her mediating activity, which, by causing objects to act and re-act on each other in accordance with their own nature, in this way, without any direct interference in the process, carries out reason's intentions.' (Hegel: 'Enzyklopädie, Erster Theil, Die Logik,' Berlin, 1840, p. 382.)
3. In his otherwise miserable work ('Théorie de l'Econ. Polit.' Paris, 1815), Ganilh enumerates in a striking manner in opposition to the 'Physiocrats' the long series of previous processes necessary before agriculture properly so called can commence.
4. Turgot in his 'Réflexions sur la Formation et la Distribution des Richesses' (1766) brings well into prominence the importance of domesticated animals to early civilisation.
5. The least important commodities of all for the technological comparison of different epochs of production are articles of luxury, in the strict meaning of the term. However little our written histories up to this time notice the development of material production, which is the basis of all social life, and therefore of all real history, yet prehistoric times have been classified in accordance with the results, not of so-called historical, but of materialistic investigations. These periods have been divided, to correspond with the materials from which their implements and weapons were made, viz., into the stone, the bronze, and the iron ages.
6. It appears paradoxical to assert, that uncaught fish, for instance, are a means of production in the fishing industry. But hitherto no one has discovered the art of catching fish in waters that contain none.
7. This method of determining, from the standpoint of the labour-process alone, what is productive labour, is by no means directly applicable to the case of the capitalist process of production.
8. Storch calls true raw materials 'matières,' and accessory material 'matériaux.' Cherbuliez describes accessories as 'matières instrumentales.'
9. By a wonderful feat of logical acumen, Colonel Torrens has discovered, in this stone of the savage the origin of capital. 'In the first stone which he [the savage] flings at the wild animal he pursues, in the first stick that he seizes to strike down the fruit which hangs above his reach, we see the appropriation of one article for the purpose of aiding in the acquisition of another, and thus discover the origin of capital.' (R. Torrens: 'An Essay on the Production of Wealth,' &c., pp. 70-71.)
10. 'Products are appropriated before they are converted into capital; this conversion does not secure them from such appropriation.' (Cheibuliez: 'Richesse ou Pauvreté,' edit. Paris, 1841, p. 54.) 'The Proletarian, by selling his labour for a definite quantity of the necessaries of life, renounces all claim to a share in the product. The mode of appropriation of the products

remains the same as before; it is in no way altered by the bargain we have mentioned. The product belongs exclusively to the capitalist, who supplied the raw material and the necessaries of life; and this is a rigorous consequence of the law of appropriation, a law whose fundamental principle was the very opposite, namely, that every labourer has an exclusive right to the ownership of what he produces.' (l.c., p. 58.) 'When the labourers receive wages for their labour ... the capitalist is then the owner not of the capital only' (he means the means of production) 'but of the labour also. If what is paid as wages is included, as it commonly is, in the term capital, it is absurd to talk of labour separately from capital. The word capital as thus employed includes labour and capital both.' (James Mill: 'Elements of Pol. Econ.,' &c., Ed. 1821, pp. 70, 71.)

11. As has been stated in a previous note, the English language has two different expressions for these two different aspects of labour: in the Simple Labour-process, the process of producing Use-Values, it is *Work;* in the process of creation of Value, it is *Labour,* taking the term in its strictly economic sense.—*F. E.*
12. These figures are quite arbitrary.
13. This is the fundamental proposition on which is based the doctrine of the Physiocrats as to the unproductiveness of all labour that is not agriculture: it is irrefutable for the orthodox economist. 'Cette façon d'imputer à une seule chose la valeur de plusieurs autres' (par exemple au lin la consommation du tisserand), 'd'appliquer, pour ainsi dire, couche sur couche, plusieurs valeurs sur une seule, fait que celle-ci grossit d'autant.... Le terme d'addition peint trés bien la maniere dont se forme le prix des ouvrages de main d'oeuvre; ce prix n'est qu'un total de plusieurs valeurs consommées et additionnées ensemble; or, additionner n'est pas multiplier.' ['This method of adding to one particular object the value of a number of others,' (for example, adding the living costs of the weaver to the flax), 'of as it were heaping up various values in layers on top of one single value, has the result that this value grows to the same extent ... The expression 'addition' gives a very clear picture of the way in which the price of a manufactured product is formed; this price is only the sum of a number of values which have been consumed, and it is arrived at by adding them together; however, addition is not the same as multiplication.'] ('Mercier de la Rivière,' l.c., p. 599.)
14. Thus from 1844-47 he withdrew part of his capital from productive employment, in order to throw it away in railway speculations; and so also, during the American Civil War, he closed his factory, and turned his work-people into the streets, in order to gamble on the Liverpool cotton exchange.
15. 'Extol thyself, put on finery and adorn thyself ... but whoever takes more or better than he gives, that is usury, and is not service, but wrong done to his neighbour, as when one steals and robs. All is not service and benefit to a neighbour that is called service and benefit. For an adulteress and adulterer do one another great service and pleasure. A horseman does an incendiary a great service, by helping him to rob on the highway, and pillage land and houses. The papists do ours a great service, in that they don't drown, burn, murder all of them, or let them all rot in prison; but let some live, and only drive them out, or take from them what they have. The devil himself does his servants inestimable service.... To sum up, the world is full of great, excellent, and daily service and benefit.' (Martin Luther: 'An die Pfarrherrn wider den Wucher zu predigen,' Wittenberg, 1540.)
16. In 'Zur Kritik der Pol. Oek.,' p. 14, I make the following remark on this point—'It is not difficult to understand what 'service' the category 'service' must render to a class of economists like J. B. Say and F. Bastiat.'
17. This is one of the circumstances that makes production by slave labour such a costly process. The labourer here is, to use a striking expression of the ancients, distinguishable only as instrumentum vocale, from an animal as instrumentum semi-vocale, and from an implement as instrumentum mutum. But he himself takes care to let both beast and implement feel that he is none of them, but is a man. He convinces himself with immense

satisfaction, that he is a different being, by treating the one unmercifully and damaging the other con amore. Hence the principle, universally applied in this method of production, only to employ the rudest and heaviest implements and such as are difficult to damage owing to their sheer clumsiness. In the slave-states bordering on the Gulf of Mexico, down to the date of the civil war, ploughs constructed on old Chinese models, which turned up the soil like a hog or a mole, instead of making furrows, were alone to be found. Conf. J. E. Cairnes. 'The Slave Power,' London, 1862, p. 46 sqq. In his 'Sea Board Slave States,' Olmsted tells us: 'I am here shown tools that no man in his senses, with us, would allow a labourcr, for whom he was paying wages, to be encumbered with; and the excessive weight and clumsiness of which, I would judge, would make work at least ten per cent greater than with those ordinarily used with us. And I am assured that, in the careless and clumsy way they must be used by the slaves, anything lighter or less rude could not be furnished them with good economy, and that such tools as we constantly give our labourers and find our profit in giving them, would not last out a day in a Virginia cornfield—much lighter and more free from stones though it be than ours. So, too, when I ask why mules are so universally substituted for horses on the farm, the first reason given, and confessedly the most conclusive one, is that horses cannot bear the treatment that they always must get from negroes; horses are always soon foundered or crippled by them, while mules will bear cudgelling, or lose a meal or two now and then, and not be materially injured, and they do not take cold or get sick, if neglected or overworked. But I do not need to go further than to the window of the room in which I am writing, to see at almost any time, treatment of cattle that would ensure the immediate discharge of the driver by almost any farmer owning them in the North.'

18. The distinction between skilled and unskilled labour rests in part on pure illusion, or, to say the least, on distinctions that have long since ceased to be real, and that survive only by virtue of a traditional convention; in part on the helpless condition of some groups of the working-class, a condition that prevents them from exacting equally with the rest the value of their labour-power. Accidental circumstances here play so great a part, that these two forms of labour sometimes change places. Where, for instance, the physique of the working-class has deteriorated, and is, relatively speaking, exhausted, which is the case in all countries with a well developed capitalist production, the lower forms of labour, which demand great expenditure of muscle, are in general considered as skilled, compared with much more delicate forms of labour; the latter sink down to the level of unskilled labour. Take as an example the labour of a bricklayer, which in England occupies a much higher level than that of a damask-weaver. Again, although the labour of a fustian cutter demands great bodily exertion, and is at the same time unhealthy, yet it counts only as unskilled labour. And then, we must not forget, that the so-called skilled labour does not occupy a large space in the field of national labour. Laing estimates that in England (and Wales) the livelihood of 11,300,000 people depends on unskilled labour. If from the total population of 18,000,000 living at the time when he wrote, we deduct 1,000,000 for the 'genteel population,' and 1,500,000 for paupers, vagrants, criminals, prostitutes, &c., and 4,650,000 who compose the middle-class, there remain the above mentioned 11,000,000. But in his middle-class he includes people that live on the interest of small investments, officials, men of letters, artists, schoolmasters and the like, and in order to swell the number he also includes in these 4,650,000 the better paid portion of the factory operatives! The bricklayers, too, figure amongst them. (S. Laing: 'National Distress,' &c., London, 1844). 'The great class who have nothing to give for food but ordinary labour, are the great bulk of the people.' (James Mill, in art.: 'Colony,' Supplement to the Encyclop. Brit., 1831.)

19. 'Where reference is made to labour as a measure of value, it necessarily implies labour of one particular kind ... the proportion which the other kinds bear to it being easily ascertained.' ('Outlines of Pol. Econ.,' Lond., 1832, pp. 22 and 23.)

8

Constant Capital and Variable Capital

The various factors of the labour-process play different parts in forming the value of the product.

The labourer adds fresh value to the subject of his labour by expending upon it a given amount of additional labour, no matter what the specific character and utility of that labour may be. On the other hand, the values of the means of production used up in the process are preserved, and present themselves afresh as constituent parts of the value of the product; the values of the cotton and the spindle, for instance, re-appear again in the value of the yarn. The value of the means of production is therefore preserved, by being transferred to the product. This transfer takes place during the conversion of those means into a product, or in other words, during the labour-process. It is brought about by labour; but how?

The labourer does not perform two operations at once, one in order to add value to the cotton, the other in order to preserve the value of the means of production, or, what amounts to the same thing, to transfer to the yarn, to the product, the value of the cotton on which he works, and part of the value of the spindle with which he works. But, by the very act of adding new value, he preserves their former values. Since, however, the addition of new value to the subject of his labour, and the preservation of its former value, are two entirely distinct results, produced simultaneously by the labourer, during one operation, it is plain that this two-fold nature of the result can be explained only by the two-fold nature of his labour; at one and the same time, it must in one character create value, and in another character preserve or transfer value.

Now, in what manner does every labourer add new labour and consequently new value? Evidently, only by labouring productively in a particular way; the spinner by spinning, the weaver by weaving, the smith by forging. But, while thus incorporating labour generally, that is value, it is by the particular form alone of the labour, by the spinning, the weaving and the forging respectively, that the means of production, the cotton and spindle, the yarn and loom, and the iron and anvil become constituent elements of the product, of a new use-value.[1] Each use-value disappears, but only to re-appear under a new form in a new use-value. Now, we saw, when we were considering the process of creating value, that, if a use-value be effectively consumed in the production of a new use-value, the quantity of labour expended in the production of the consumed article, forms a portion of the quantity of labour necessary to produce the new use-value; this portion is therefore labour transferred from the means of production to the new product. Hence, the labourer preserves the values of the consumed means of production, or transfers them as portions of its value to the product, not by virtue of his additional labour, abstractedly considered, but by virtue of the particular useful character of that labour, by virtue of its special productive form. In so far then as labour is such specific productive activity, in so far as it is spinning, weaving, or forging, it raises, by mere contact, the means of production from the dead, makes them living factors of the labour-process, and combines with them to form the new products.

If the special productive labour of the workman were not spinning, he could not convert the cotton into yarn, and therefore could not transfer the values of the cotton and spindle to the yarn. Suppose the same workman were to change his occupation to that of a joiner, he would still by a day's labour add value to the material he works upon. Consequently, we see, first, that the addition of new value takes place not by virtue of his labour being spinning in particular, or joinering in particular, but because it is labour in the abstract, a portion of the total labour of society; and we see next, that the value added is of a given definite amount, not because his labour has a special utility, but because it is exerted for a definite time. On the one hand, then, it is by virtue of its general character, as being expenditure of human labour-power in the abstract, that spinning adds new value to the values of the cotton and the spindle; and on the other hand, it is by virtue of its special character, as being a concrete, useful process, that the same labour of spinning both transfers the values of the means of production to the product, and preserves them in the product. Hence, at one and the same time there is produced a two-fold result.

By the simple addition of a certain quantity of labour, new value is added, and by the quality of this added labour, the original values of the means of production are preserved in the product. This two-fold effect, resulting from the two-fold character of labour, may be traced in various phenomena.

Let us assume, that some invention enables the spinner to spin as much cotton in 6 hours as he was able to spin before in 36 hours. His labour is now six times as effective as it was, for the purposes of useful production. The product of 6 hours' work has increased six-fold, from 6 lbs. to 36 lbs. But now the 36 lbs. of cotton absorb only the same amount of labour as formerly did the 6 lbs. One-sixth as much new labour is absorbed by each pound of cotton, and consequently, the value added by the labour to each pound is only one-sixth of what it formerly was. On the other hand, in the product, in the 36 lbs. of yarn, the value transferred from the cotton is six times as great as before. By the 6 hours' spinning, the value of the raw material preserved and transferred to the product is six times as great as before, although the new value added by the labour of the spinner to each pound of the very same raw material is one-sixth what it was formerly. This shows that the two properties of labour, by virtue of which it is enabled in one case to preserve value, and in the other to create value, are essentially different. On the one hand, the longer the time necessary to spin a given weight of cotton into yarn, the greater is the new value added to the material; on the other hand, the greater the weight of the cotton spun in a given time, the greater is the value preserved, by being transferred from it to the product.

Let us now assume, that the productiveness of the spinner's labour, instead of varying, remains constant, that he therefore requires the same time as he formerly did, to convert one pound of cotton into yarn, but that the exchange-value of the cotton varies, either by rising to six times its former value or falling to one-sixth of that value. In both these cases, the spinner puts the same quantity of labour into a pound of cotton, and therefore adds as much value, as he did before the change in the value: he also produces a given weight of yarn in the same time as he did before. Nevertheless, the value that he transfers from the cotton to the yarn is either one-sixth of what it was before the variation, or, as the case may be, six times as much as before. The same result occurs when the value of the instruments of labour rises or falls, while their useful efficacy in the process remains unaltered.

Again, if the technical conditions of the spinning process remain unchanged, and no change of value takes place in the means of production, the spinner continues to consume in equal working-times equal quantities of raw material, and equal quantities of machinery of unvarying value. The value that he preserves in the product is directly proportional to the new value that he adds to the product. In two weeks he incorporates twice as much labour, and therefore twice as much value, as in one week, and during the same time he consumes twice as much material, and wears out twice as much machinery, of double the value in each case: he therefore preserves, in the product of two weeks, twice as much value as in the product of one week. So long as the conditions of production remain the same, the more value the labourer adds by fresh labour, the more value he transfers and preserves; but he does so merely because this addition of new value takes place under conditions that have not varied and are independent of his own labour. Of course, it may be said in one sense, that the labourer preserves old value always in proportion to the quantity of new value that he adds. Whether the value of cotton rise from one shilling to two shillings, or fall to sixpence, the workman invariably preserves in the product of one hour only one half as much value as he preserves in two hours. In like manner, if the productiveness of his own labour varies by rising or falling, he will, in one hour, spin either more or less cotton, as the case may be, than he did before, and will consequently preserve in the product of one hour, more or less value of cotton; but, all the same, he will preserve by two hours' labour twice as much value as he will by one.

Value exists only in articles of utility, in objects: we leave out of consideration its purely symbolical representation by tokens. (Man himself, viewed as the impersonation of labour-power, is a natural object, a thing, although a living conscious thing, and labour is the manifestation of this power residing in him.) If therefore an article loses its utility, it also loses its value. The reason why means of production do not lose their value, at the same time that they lose their use-value, is this: they lose in the labour-process the original form of their use-value, only to assume in the product the form of a new use-value. But, however important it may be to value, that it should have some object of utility to embody itself in, yet it is a matter of complete indifference what particular object serves this purpose; this we saw when treating of the metamorphosis of commodities. Hence it follows that in the labour-process the means of production transfer their value to the product only so far as along with their use-value they lose also their exchange-value. They give up to the product that value alone which they themselves lose as means of production. But in this respect the material factors of the labour-process do not all behave alike.

The coal burnt under the boiler vanishes without leaving a trace; so, too, the tallow with which the axles of wheels are greased. Dye stuffs and other auxiliary substances also vanish but re-appear as properties of the product. Raw material forms the substance of the product, but only after it has changed its form. Hence raw material and auxiliary substances lose the characteristic form with which they are clothed on entering the labour-process. It is otherwise with the instruments of labour. Tools, machines, workshops, and vessels, are of use in the labour-process, only so long as they retain their original shape, and are ready each morning to renew the process with their shape unchanged. And just as during their lifetime, that is to say, during the continued labour-process in which they serve, they retain their shape independent of the product, so, too, they do after their death. The corpses of machines, tools, workshops, &c., are always separate and distinct from the product they helped to turn out. If we now consider the case of any instrument of labour during the whole period of its service, from the day of its entry into the workshop, till the day of its banishment into the lumber room, we find that during this period its use-value has been completely consumed, and therefore its exchange-value completely transferred to the product. For instance, if a spinning machine lasts for 10 years, it is plain that during that working period its total value is gradually transferred to the product of the 10 years. The lifetime of an instrument of labour, therefore, is spent in the repetition of a greater or less number of similar operations. Its life may be compared with that of a human being. Every day brings a man 24 hours nearer to his grave: but how many days he has still to travel on that road, no man can tell accurately by merely looking at him. This difficulty, however, does not prevent life insurance offices from drawing, by means of the theory of averages, very accurate, and at the same time very profitable conclusions. So it is with the instruments of labour. It is known by experience how long on the average a machine of a particular kind will last. Suppose its use-value in the labour-process to last only six days. Then, on the average, it loses each day one-sixth of its use-value, and therefore parts with one-sixth of its value to the daily product. The wear and tear of all instruments, their daily loss of use-value, and the corresponding quantity of value they part with to the product, are accordingly calculated upon this basis.

It is thus strikingly clear, that means of production never transfer more value to the product than they themselves lose during the labour-process by the destruction of their own use-value. If such an instrument has no value to lose, if, in other words, it is not the product of human labour, it transfers no value to the product. It helps to create use-value without contributing to the formation of exchange-value. In this class are included all means of production supplied by Nature without human assistance, such as land, wind, water, metals in situ, and timber in virgin forests.

Yet another interesting phenomenon here presents itself. Suppose a machine to be worth £1,000, and to wear out in 1,000 days. Then one thousandth part of the value of the machine is daily transferred to the day's product. At the same time, though with diminishing vitality, the machine as a whole continues to take part in the labour-process. Thus it appears, that one factor of the labour-process, a means of production, continually enters as a whole into that process, while it enters into the process of the formation of value by fractions only. The difference between the two processes is here reflected in their material factors, by the same instrument of production taking part as a whole in the labour-process, while at the same time as an element in the formation of value, it enters only by fractions.[2]

On the other hand, a means of production may take part as a whole in the formation of value, while into the labour-process it enters only bit by bit. Suppose that in spinning cotton, the waste for every 115 lbs. used amounts to 15 lbs., which is converted, not into yarn, but into 'devil's dust.' Now, although this 15 lbs. of cotton never becomes a constituent element of the yarn, yet assuming this amount of waste to be normal and inevitable under average conditions of spinning, its value is just as surely transferred to the value of the yarn, as is the value of the 100 lbs. that form the substance of the yarn. The use-value of 15 lbs. of cotton must vanish into dust, before 100 lbs. of yarn can be made. The destruction of this cotton is therefore a necessary condition in the production of the yarn. And because it is a necessary condition, and for no other reason, the value of that cotton is transferred to the product. The same holds good for every kind of refuse resulting from a labour-process, so far at least as such refuse cannot be further employed as a means in the production of new and independent use-values. Such an employment of refuse may be seen in the large machine works at Manchester, where mountains of iron turnings are carted away to the foundry in the evening, in order the next morning to re-appear in the workshops as solid masses of iron.

We have seen that the means of production transfer value to the new product, so far only as during the labour-process they lose value in the shape of their old use-value. The maximum loss of value that they can suffer in the process, is plainly limited by the amount of the original value with which they came into the process, or in other words, by the labour-time necessary for their production. Therefore, the means of production can never add more value to the product than they themselves possess independently of the process in which they assist. However useful a given kind of raw material, or a machine, or other means of production may be, though it may cost £150, or, say, 500 days' labour, yet it cannot, under any circumstances, add to the value of the product more than £150. Its value is determined not by the labour-process into which it enters as a means of production, but by that out of which it has issued as a product. In the labour-process it only serves as a mere use-value, a thing with useful properties, and could not, therefore, transfer any value to the product, unless it possessed such value previously.[3]

While productive labour is changing the means of production into constituent elements of a new product, their value undergoes a metempsychosis. It deserts the consumed body, to occupy the newly created one. But this transmigration takes place, as it were, behind the back of the labourer. He is unable to add new labour, to create new value, without at the same time preserving old values, and this, because the labour he adds must be of a specific useful kind; and he cannot do work of a useful kind, without employing products as the means of production of a new product, and thereby transferring their value to the new product. The property therefore which labour-power in action, living labour, possesses of preserving value, at the same time that it adds it, is a gift of Nature which costs the labourer nothing, but which is very advantageous to the capitalist inasmuch as it preserves the existing value of his capital.[4] So long as trade is good, the capitalist is too much absorbed in money-grubbing to take notice of this gratuitous gift of labour. A violent interruption of the labour-process by a crisis, makes him sensitively aware of it.[5]

As regards the means of production, what is really consumed is their use-value, and the consumption of this use-value by labour results in the product. There is no consumption of their value,[6] and it would therefore be inaccurate to say that it is reproduced. It is rather preserved; not by reason of any operation it undergoes itself in the process; but because the article in which it originally exists, vanishes, it is true, but vanishes into some other article. Hence, in the value of the product, there is a reappearance of the value of the means of production, but there is, strictly speaking, no reproduction of that value. That which is produced is a new use-value in which the old exchange-value reappears.[7]

It is otherwise with the subjective factor of the labour-process, with labour-power in action. While the labourer, by virtue of his labour being of a specialised kind that has a special object, preserves and transfers to the product the value of the means of production, he at the same time, by the mere act of working, creates each instant an additional or new value. Suppose the process of production to be stopped just when the workman has produced an equivalent for the value of his own labour-power, when, for example, by six hours' labour, he has added a value of three shillings. This value is the surplus, of the total value of the product, over the portion of its value that is due to the means of production. It is the only original bit of value formed during this process, the only portion of the value of the product created by this process. Of course, we do not forget that this new value only replaces the money advanced by the capitalist in the purchase of the labour-power, and spent by the labourer on the necessaries of life. With regard to the money spent, the new value is merely a reproduction; but, nevertheless, it is an actual, and not, as in the case of the value of the means of production, only an apparent, reproduction. The substitution of one value for another, is here effected by the creation of new value.

We know, however, from what has gone before, that the labour-process may continue beyond the time necessary to reproduce and incorporate in the product a mere equivalent for the value of the labour-power. Instead of the six hours that are sufficient for the latter purpose, the process may continue for twelve hours. The action of labour-power, therefore, not only reproduces its own value, but produces value over and above it. This surplus-value is the difference between the value of the product and the value of the elements consumed in the formation of that product, in other words, of the means of production and the labour-power.

By our explanation of the different parts played by the various factors of the labour-process in the formation of the product's value, we have, in fact, disclosed the characters of the different functions allotted to the different elements of capital in the process of expanding its own value. The surplus of the total value of the product, over the sum of the values of its constituent factors, is the surplus of the expanded capital over the capital originally advanced. The means of production on the one hand, labour-power on the other, are merely the different modes of existence which the value of the original capital assumed when from being money it was transformed into the various factors of the labour-process. That part of capital then, which is represented by the means of production, by the raw material, auxiliary material and the instruments of labour does not, in the process of production, undergo any quantitative alteration of value. I therefore call it the constant part of capital, or, more shortly, *constant capital.*

On the other hand, that part of capital, represented by labour-power, does, in the process of production, undergo an alteration of value. It both reproduces the equivalent of its own value, and also produces an excess, a surplus-value, which may itself vary, may be more or less according to circumstances. This part of capital is continually being transformed from a constant into a variable magnitude. I therefore call it the variable part of capital, or, shortly, *variable capital.* The same elements of capital which, from the point of view of the labour-process, present themselves respectively as the objective and subjective factors, as means of production and labour-power, present themselves, from the point of view of the process of creating surplus-value, as constant and variable capital.

The definition of constant capital given above by no means excludes the possibility of a change of value in its elements. Suppose the price of cotton to be one day sixpence a pound, and the next day, in consequence of a failure of the cotton crop, a shilling a pound. Each pound of the cotton bought at sixpence, and worked up after the rise in value, transfers to the product a value of one shilling; and the cotton already spun before the rise, and perhaps circulating in the market as yarn, likewise transfers to the product twice its original value. It is plain, however, that these changes of value are independent of the increment or surplus-value added to the value of the cotton by the spinning itself. If the old cotton had never been spun, it could, after the rise, be resold at a shilling a pound instead of at sixpence. Further, the fewer the processes the cotton has gone through, the more certain is this result. We therefore find that speculators make it a rule when such sudden changes in value occur, to speculate in that material on which the least possible quantity of labour has been spent: to speculate, therefore, in yarn rather than in cloth, in cotton itself, rather than in yarn. The change of value in the case we have been considering, originates, not in the process in which the cotton plays the part of a means of production, and in which it therefore functions as constant capital, but in the process in which the cotton itself is produced. The value of a commodity, it is true, is determined by the quantity of labour contained in it, but this quantity is itself limited by social conditions. If the time socially necessary for the production of any commodity alters—and a given weight of cotton represents, after a bad harvest, more labour than after a good one—all previously existing commodities of the same class are affected, because they are, as it were, only individuals of the species,[8] and their value at any given time is measured by the labour socially necessary, *i.e.*, by the labour necessary for their production under the then existing social conditions.

As the value of the raw material may change, so, too, may that of the instruments of labour, of the machinery, &c., employed in the process; and consequently that portion of the value of the product transferred to it from them, may also change. If, in consequence of a new invention, machinery of a particular kind can be produced by a diminished expenditure of labour, the old machinery becomes depreciated more or less, and consequently transfers so much less value to the product. But here again, the change in value originates outside the process in which the machine is acting as a means of production. Once engaged in this process, the machine cannot transfer more value than it possesses apart from the process.

Just as a change in the value of the means of production, even after they have commenced to take a part in the labour-process, does not alter their character as constant capital, so, too, a change in the proportion of constant to variable capital does not affect the respective functions of these two kinds of capital. The technical conditions of the labour-process may be revolutionised to such an extent, that where formerly ten men using ten implements of small value worked up a relatively small quantity of raw material, one man may now, with the aid of one expensive machine, work up one hundred times as much raw material. In the latter case we have an enormous increase in the constant capital, that is represented by the total value of the means of production used, and at the same time a great reduction in the variable capital, invested in labour-power. Such a revolution, however, alters only the quantitative relation between the constant and the variable capital, or the proportions in which the total capital is split up into its constant and variable constituents; it has not in the least degree affected the essential difference between the two.

Notes

1. 'Labour gives a new creation for one extinguished.' ('An Essay on the Polit. Econ. of Nations,' London, 1821, p. 13.)
2. The subject of repairs of the implements of labour does not concern us here. A machine that is undergoing repair, no longer plays the part of an instrument, but that of a subject of labour. Work is no longer done with it, but upon it. It is quite permissible for our purpose to assume, that the labour expended on the repairs of instruments is included in the labour necessary for their original production. But in the text we deal with that wear and tear, which no doctor can cure, and which little by little brings about death, with 'that kind of wear which cannot be repaired from time to time, and which, in the case of a knife, would ultimately reduce it to a state in which the cutler would say of it, it is not worth a new blade.' We have shewn in the text, that a machine takes part in every labour-process as an integral machine, but that into the simultaneous process of creating value it enters only bit by bit. How great then is the confusion of ideas exhibited in the following extract! 'Mr Ricardo says a portion of the labour of the engineer in making [stocking] machines' is contained for example in the value of a pair of stockings. 'Yet the total labour, that produced each single pair of stockings ... includes the whole labour of the engineer, not a portion; for one machine makes many pairs, and none of those pairs could have been done without any part of the machine.' 'Obs. on Certain Verbal Disputes in Pol. Econ., Particularly Relating to Value,' p. 54. The author, an uncommonly self-satisfied wiseacre, is right in his confusion and therefore in his contention, to this extent only, that neither Ricardo nor any other economist, before or since him, has accurately distinguished the two aspects of labour, and still less, therefore, the part played by it under each of these aspects in the formation of value.
3. From this we may judge of the absurdity of J. B. Say, who pretends to account for surplus-value (Interest, Profit, Rent), by the 'services productifs' which the means of production, soil, instruments, and raw material, render in the labour-process by means of their use-values. Mr Wm. Roscher who seldom loses an occasion of registering, in black and white, ingenious apologetic fancies, records the following specimen: 'J. B. Say (Traité, t. 1, ch. 4) very truly remarks: the value produced by an oil mill, after deduction of all costs, is something new, something quite different from the labour by which the oil mill itself was erected.' (l.c., p. 82, note.) Very true, Mr Professor! the oil produced by the oil mill is indeed something very different from the labour expended in constructing the mill! By value, Mr Roscher understands such stuff as 'oil,' because oil has value, notwithstanding that 'Nature' produces petroleum, though relatively 'in small quantities,' a fact to which he seems to refer in his further observation: 'It (Nature) produces scarcely any exchange-value.' Mr Roscher's 'Nature' and the exchange-value it produces are rather like the foolish virgin who admitted indeed that she had had a child, but 'it was such a little one.' This 'savant sérieux' in continuation remarks: 'Ricardo's school is in the habit of including capital as accumulated labour under the head of labour. This is unskilful work, because, indeed, the owner of capital, after all, does something more than the merely creating and preserving of the same: namely, the abstention from the enjoyment of it, for which he demands, *e.g.*, interest.' (l.c.) How very 'skilful' is this 'anatomico-physiological method' of Political Economy, which, 'indeed,' converts a mere desire 'after all' into a source of value.
4. 'Of all the instruments of the farmers' trade, the labour of man ... is that on which he is most to rely for the repayment of his capital. The other two ... the working stock of the cattle and the ... carts, ploughs, spades, and so forth, without a given portion of the first, are nothing at all.' (Edmund Burke: 'Thoughts and Details on Scarcity, originally presented to the Right Hon. W. Pitt, in the month of November 1795,' Edit. London, 1800, p. 10.)
5. In *The Times* of 26th November, 1862, a manufacturer, whose mill employed 800 hands, and consumed, on the average, 150 bales of East Indian, or 130 bales of American cotton,

complains, in doleful manner, of the standing expenses of his factory when not working. He estimates them at £6,000 a year. Among them are a number of items that do not concern us here, such as rent, rates, and taxes, insurance, salaries of the manager, book-keeper, engineer, and others. Then he reckons £150 for coal used to heat the mill occasionally, and run the engine now and then. Besides this, he includes the wages of the people employed at odd times to keep the machinery in working order. Lastly, he puts down £1,200 for depreciation of machinery, because 'the weather and the natural principle of decay do not suspend their operations because the steam-engine ceases to revolve.' He says, emphatically, he does not estimate his depreciation at more than the small sum of £1,200, because his machinery is already nearly worn out.

6. 'Productive consumption...where the consumption of a commodity is a part of the process of production. ... In these instances there is no consumption of value.' (S. P. Newman, l.c., p. 296.)

7. In an American compendium that has gone through, perhaps, 20 editions, this passage occurs: 'It matters not in what form capital re-appears;' then after a lengthy enumeration of all the possible ingredients of production whose value re-appears in the product, the passage concludes thus: 'The various kinds of food, clothing, and shelter, necessary for the existence and comfort of the human being, are also changed. They are consumed from time to time, and their value re-appears in that new vigour imparted to his body and mind, forming fresh capital, to be employed again in the work of production.' (F. Wayland, l.c., pp. 31, 32.) Without noticing any other oddities, it suffices to observe, that what re-appears in the fresh vigour, is not the bread's price, but its bloodforming substances. What, on the other hand, re-appears in the value of that vigour, is not the means of subsistence, but their value. The same necessaries of life, at half the price, would form just as much muscle and bone, just as much vigour, but not vigour of the same value. This confusion of 'value' and 'vigour' coupled with our author's pharisaical indefiniteness, mark an attempt, futile for all that, to thrash out an explanation of surplus-value from a mere re-appearance of pre-existing values.

8. 'Toutes les productions d'un même genre ne forment proprement qu'une masse, dont le prix se détermine en général et sans égard aux circonstances particulières.' (Le Trosne, l.c., p. 893.) ['Properly speaking, all products of the same kind form a single mass, and their price is determined in general and without regard to particular circumstances.']

9

The Rate of Surplus-Value

Section 1: *The Degree of Exploitation of Labour-Power*

The surplus-value generated in the process of production by C, the capital advanced, or in other words, the self-expansion of the value of the capital C, presents itself for our consideration, in the first place, as a surplus, as the amount by which the value of the product exceeds the value of its constituent elements.

The capital C is made up of two components, one, the sum of money c laid out upon the means of production, and the other, the sum of money v expended upon the labour-power; c represents the portion that has become constant capital, and v the portion that has become variable capital. At first then, C = c + v: for example, if £500 is the capital advanced, its components may be such that the £500 = £410 const. + £90 var. When the process of production is finished, we get a commodity whose value = (c + v) + s, where s is the surplus-value; or taking our former figures, the value of this commodity may be (£410 const. + £90 var.) + £90 surpl. The original capital has now changed from C to C', from £500 to £590. The difference is s or a surplus-value of £90. Since the value of the constituent elements of the product is equal to the value of the advanced capital, it is mere tautology to say, that the excess of the value of the product over the value of its constituent elements, is equal to the expansion of the capital advanced or to the surplus-value produced.

Nevertheless, we must examine this tautology a little more closely. The two things compared are, the value of the product and the value of its constituents consumed in the process of production. Now we have seen how that portion of the constant capital which consists of the instruments of labour, transfers to the production only a fraction of its value, while the remainder of that value continues to reside in those instruments. Since this remainder plays no part in the formation of value, we may at present leave it on one side. To introduce it into the calculation would make no difference. For instance, taking our former example, c = £410: suppose this sum to consist of £312 value of raw material, £44 value of auxiliary material, and £54 value of the machinery worn away in the process; and suppose that the total value of the machinery employed is £1,054. Out of this latter sum, then, we reckon as advanced for the purpose of turning out the product, the sum of £54 alone, which the machinery loses by wear and tear in the process; for this is all it parts with to the product. Now if we also reckon the remaining £1,000, which still continues in the machinery, as transferred to the product, we ought also to reckon it as part of the value advanced, and thus make it appear on both sides of our calculation.[1] We should, in this way, get £1,500 on one side and £1,590 on the other. The difference of these two sums, or the surplus-value, would still be £90. Throughout this Book therefore, by constant capital advanced for the production of value, we always mean, unless the context is repugnant thereto, the value of the means of production actually consumed in the process, and that value alone.

This being so, let us return to the formula C = c + v, which we saw was transformed into C' = (c + v) + s, C becoming C'. We know that the value of the constant capital is transferred to, and merely re-appears in the product. The new value actually created in the process, the value produced, or value-product, is therefore not the same as the value of the product; it is not, as it would at first sight appear (c + v) + s or £410 const. + £90 var. + £90 surpl.; but v + s or £90 var. + £90 surpl., not £590 but £180. If c = 0, or in other words, if there were branches of industry in which the capitalist could dispense with all means of production made by previous labour, whether they be raw material, auxiliary material, or instruments of labour, employing only labour-power and materials supplied by Nature, in that case, there would be no constant capital to transfer to the product. This component of the value of the product, *i.e.*, the £410 in our example, would be eliminated, but the sum of £180, the amount of new value created, or the value produced, which contains £90 of surplus-value, would remain just as great as if c represented the highest value imaginable. We should have C = (0 + v) = v or C' the expanded capital = v + s and therefore C' - C = s as before. On the other hand, if s = 0, or in other words, if the labour-power, whose value is advanced in the form of variable capital, were to produce only its equivalent, we should have C = c + v or C' the value of the product = (c + v) + 0 or C = C'. The capital advanced would, in this case, not have expanded its value.

From what has gone before, we know that surplus-value is purely the result of a variation in the value of v, of that portion of the capital which is transformed into labour-power; consequently, v + s = v + v', or v plus an increment of v. But the fact that it is v alone that varies, and the conditions of that variation, are obscured by the circumstance that in consequence of the increase in the variable component of the capital, there is also an increase in the sum total of the advanced capital. It was originally £500 and becomes £590. Therefore, in order that our investigation may lead to accurate results, we must make abstraction from that portion of the value of the product, in which constant capital alone appears, and consequently must equate the constant capital to zero or make c = 0. This is merely an application of a mathematical rule, employed whenever we operate with constant and variable magnitudes, related to each other by the symbols of addition and subtraction only.

A further difficulty is caused by the original form of the variable capital. In our example, C' = £410 const. + £90 var. + £90 surpl.; but £90 is a given and therefore a constant quantity; hence it appears absurd to treat it as variable. But in fact, the term £90 var. is here merely a symbol to show that this value undergoes a process. The portion of the capital invested in the purchase of labour-power is a definite quantity of materialised labour, a constant value like the value of the labour-power purchased. But in the process of production the place of the £90 is taken by the labour-power in action, dead labour is replaced by living labour, something stagnant by something flowing, a constant by a variable. The result is the reproduction of v plus an increment of v. From the point of view then of capitalist production, the whole process appears as the spontaneous variation of the originally constant value, which is transformed into labour-power. Both the process and its result, appear to be owing to this value. If, therefore, such expressions as '£90 variable capital,' or 'so much self-expanding value,' appear contradictory, this is only because they bring to the surface a contradiction immanent in capitalist production.

At first sight it appears a strange proceeding, to equate the constant capital to zero. Yet it is what we do every day. If, for example, we wish to calculate the amount of England's profits from the cotton industry, we first of all deduct the sums paid for cotton to the United States, India, Egypt and other countries; in other words, the value of the capital that merely re-appears in the value of the product, is put = 0.

Of course the ratio of surplus-value not only to that portion of the capital from which it immediately springs, and whose change of value it represents, but also to the sum total of the capital advanced is economically of very great importance. We shall, therefore, in the third book, treat of this ratio exhaustively. In order to enable one portion of a capital to expand its value by being converted into labour-power, it is necessary that another portion be converted into means of production. In order that variable capital may perform its function, constant capital must be advanced in proper proportion, a proportion given by the special technical conditions of each labour-process. The circumstance, however, that retorts and other vessels, are necessary to a chemical process, does not compel the chemist to notice them in the result of his analysis. If we look at the means of production, in their relation to the creation of value, and to the variation in the quantity of value, apart from anything else, they appear simply as the material in which labour-power, the value-creator, incorporates itself. Neither the nature, nor the value of this material is of any importance. The only requisite is that there be a sufficient supply to absorb the labour expended in the process of production. That supply once given, the material may rise or fall in value, or even be, as land and the sea, without any value in itself; but this will have no influence on the creation of value or on the variation in the quantity of value.[2]

In the first place then we equate the constant capital to zero. The capital advanced is consequently reduced from c + v to v, and instead of the value of the product (c + v) + s we have now the value produced (v + s). Given the new value produced = £180, which sum consequently represents the whole labour expended during the process, then subtracting from it £90 the value of the variable capital, we have remaining £90, the amount of the surplus-value. This sum of £90 or s expresses the absolute quantity of surplus-value produced. The relative quantity produced, or the increase per cent of the variable capital, is determined, it is plain, by the ratio of the surplus-value to the variable capital, or is expressed by s/v. In our example this ratio is 90/90, which gives an increase of 100%. This relative increase in the value of the variable capital, or the relative magnitude of the surplus-value, I call, 'The rate of surplus-value.'[3]

We have seen that the labourer, during one portion of the labour-process, produces only the value of his labour-power, that is, the value of his means of subsistence. Now since his work forms part of a system, based on the social division of labour, he does not directly produce the actual necessaries which he himself consumes; he produces instead a particular commodity, yarn for example, whose value is equal to the value of those necessaries or of the money with which they can be bought. The portion of his day's labour devoted to this purpose, will be greater or less, in proportion to the value of the necessaries that he daily requires on an average, or, what amounts to the same thing, in proportion to the labour-time required on an average to produce them. If the value of those necessaries represent on an average the expenditure of six hours' labour, the workman must on an average work for six hours to produce that value. If instead of working for the capitalist, he worked independently on his own account, he would, other things being equal, still be obliged to labour for the same number of hours, in order to produce the value of his labour-power, and thereby to gain the means of subsistence necessary for his conservation or continued reproduction. But as we have seen, during that portion of his day's labour in which he produces the value of his labour-power, say three shillings, he produces only an equivalent for the value of his labour-power already advanced[4] by the capitalist; the new value created only replaces the variable capital advanced. It is owing to this fact, that the production of the new value of three shillings takes the semblance of a mere reproduction. That portion of the working-day, then, during which this reproduction takes place, I call '*necessary*' labour time, and the labour expended during that time I call '*necessary*' labour.[5] Necessary, as regards the labourer, because independent of the particular social form of his labour; necessary, as regards capital, and the world of capitalists, because on the continued existence of the labourer depends their existence also.

During the second period of the labour-process, that in which his labour is no longer necessary labour, the workman, it is true, labours, expends labour-power; but his labour, being no longer necessary labour, he creates no value for himself. He creates surplus-value which, for the capitalist, has all the charms of a creation out of nothing. This portion of the working-day, I name surplus labour-time, and to the labour expended during that time, I give the name of surplus-labour. It is every bit as important, for a correct understanding of surplus-value, to conceive it as a mere congelation of surplus labour-time, as nothing but materialised surplus-labour, as it is, for a proper comprehension of value, to conceive it as a mere congelation of so many hours of labour, as nothing but materialised labour. The essential difference between the various economic forms of society, between, for instance, a society based on slave-labour, and one based on wage-labour, lies only in the mode in which this surplus-labour is in each case extracted from the actual producer, the labourer.[6]

Since, on the one hand, the values of the variable capital and of the labour-power purchased by that capital are equal, and the value of this labour-power determines the necessary portion of the working-day; and since, on the other hand, the surplus-value is determined by the surplus portion of the working-day, it follows that surplus-value bears the same ratio to variable capital, that surplus-labour does to necessary labour, or in other words, the rate of surplus-value, s/v = (surplus labour)/(necessary labour). Both ratios, s/v and (surplus labour)/(necessary labour), express the same thing in different ways; in the one case by reference to materialised, incorporated labour, in the other by reference to living, fluent labour.

The rate of surplus-value is therefore an exact expression for the degree of exploitation of labour-power by capital, or of the labourer by the capitalist.[7]

We assumed in our example, that the value of the product = £410 const. + £90 var. + £90 surpl., and that the capital advanced = £500. Since the surplus-value = £90, and the advanced capital = £500, we should, according to the usual way of reckoning, get as the rate of surplus-value (generally confounded with rate of profits) 18%, a rate so low as possibly to cause a pleasant surprise to Mr Carey and other harmonisers. But in truth, the rate of surplus-value is not equal to s/C or s/(c+v), but to s/v: thus it is not 90/500 but 90/90 or 100%, which is more than five times the apparent degree of exploitation. Although, in the case we have supposed, we are ignorant of the actual length of the working-day, and of the duration in days or weeks of the labour-process, as also of the number of labourers employed, yet the rate of surplus-value s/v accurately discloses to us, by means of its equivalent expression, surplus-labour/necessary labour the relation between the two parts of the working-day. This relation is here one of equality, the rate being 100%. Hence, it is plain, the labourer, in our example, works one half of the day for himself, the other half for the capitalist.

The method of calculating the rate of surplus-value is therefore, shortly, as follows. We take the total value of the product and put the constant capital which merely re-appears in it, equal to zero. What remains, is the only value that has, in the process of producing the commodity, been actually created. If the amount of surplus-value be given, we have only to deduct it from this remainder, to find the variable capital. And *vice versâ,* if the latter be given, and we require to find the surplus-value. If both be given, we have only to perform the concluding operation, viz., to calculate s/v, the ratio of the surplus-value to the variable capital.

Though the method is so simple, yet it may not be amiss, by means of a few examples, to exercise the reader in the application of the novel principles underlying it.

First we will take the case of a spinning mill containing 10,000 mule spindles, spinning No. 32 yarn from American cotton, and producing 1 lb. of yarn weekly per spindle. We assume the waste to be 6%: under these circumstances 10,600 lbs. of cotton are consumed weekly, of which 600 lbs. go to waste. The price of the cotton in April, 1871, was 7¾d. per lb.; the raw material therefore costs in round numbers £342. The 10,000 spindles, including preparation-machinery, and motive power, cost, we will assume, £1 per spindle, amounting to a total of £10,000. The wear and tear we put at 10%, or £1,000 yearly = £20 weekly. The rent of the building we suppose to be £300 a year, or £6 a week. Coal consumed (for 100 horse-power indicated, at 4 lbs. of coal per horse-power per hour during 60 hours, and inclusive of that consumed in heating the mill), 11 tons a week at 8s. 6d. a ton, amounts to about £4½ a week: gas, £1 a week, oil, &c., £4½ a week. Total cost of the above auxiliary materials, £10 weekly. Therefore the constant portion of the value of the week's product is £378. Wages amount to £52 a week. The price of the yarn is 12¼d. per. lb. which gives for the value of 10,000 lbs. the sum of £510. The surplus-value is therefore in this case £510 - £430 = £80. We put the constant part of the value of the product = 0, as it plays no part in the creation of value. There remains £132 as the weekly value created, which = £52 var. + £80 surpl. The rate of surplus-value is therefore 80/52 = $153^{11}/_{13}$%. In a working-day of 10 hours with average labour the result is: necessary labour = $3^{31}/_{33}$ hours, and surplus-labour = $6^{2}/_{33}$.[8]

One more example. Jacob gives the following calculation for the year 1815. Owing to the previous adjustment of several items it is very imperfect; nevertheless for our purpose it is sufficient. In it he assumes the price of wheat to be 8s. a quarter, and the average yield per acre to be 22 bushels.

VALUE PRODUCED PER ACRE			
Seed	£1 9s. 0d.	Tithes, Rates, and taxes	£1 1s. 0d.
Manure	£2 10s. 0d.	Rent	£1 8s. 0d.
Wages	£3 10s. 0d.	Farmer's Profit and Interest	£1 2s. 0d.
TOTAL	£7 9s. 0d.	TOTAL	£3 11s 0d.

Assuming that the price of the product is the same as its value, we here find the surplus-value distributed under the various heads of profit, interest, rent, &c. We have nothing to do with these in detail; we simply add them together, and the sum is a surplus-value of £3 11s. 0d. The sum of £3 19s. 0d., paid for seed and manure, is constant capital, and we put it equal to zero. There is left the sum of £3 10s. 0d., which is the variable capital advanced: and we see that a new value of £3 10s. 0d + £3 11s. 0d. has been produced in its place. Therefore s/v = £3 11s. 0d. / £3 10s. 0d., giving a rate of surplus-value of more than 100%. The labourer employs more than one half of his working-day in producing the surplus-value, which different persons, under different pretexts, share amongst themselves.[9]

Section 2: *The Representation of the Components of the Value of the Product by Corresponding Proportional Parts of the Product Itself*

Let us now return to the example by which we were shown how the capitalist converts money into capital.

The product of a working-day of 12 hours is 20 lbs. of yarn, having a value of 30s. No less than 8/10ths of this value, or 24s., is due to mere re-appearance in it, of the value of the means of production (20 lbs. of cotton, value 20s., and spindle worn away, 4s.): it is therefore constant capital. The remaining 2/10ths or 6s. is the new value created during the spinning process: of this one half replaces the value of the day's labour-power, or the variable capital, the remaining half constitutes a surplus-value of 3s. The total value then of the 20 lbs. of yarn is made up as follows:

30s. value of yarn = 24s. const. + 3s. var. + 3s. surpl.

Since the whole of this value is contained in the 20 lbs. of yarn produced, it follows that the various component parts of this value, can be represented as being contained respectively in corresponding parts of the product.

If the value of 30s. is contained in 20 lbs. of yarn, then 8/10ths of this value, or the 24s. that form its constant part, is contained in 8/10ths of the product or in 16 lbs. of yarn. Of the latter 13 1/3 lbs. represent the value of the raw material, the 20s. worth of cotton spun, and 2 2/3 lbs. represent the 4s. worth of spindle, &c., worn away in the process.

Hence the whole of the cotton used up in spinning the 20 lbs. of yarn, is represented by 13 1/3 lbs. of yarn. This latter weight of yarn contains, it is true, by weight, no more than 13 1/3 lbs. of cotton, worth 13 1/3 shillings; but the 6 2/3 shillings additional value contained in it, are the equivalent for the cotton consumed in spinning the remaining 6 2/3 lbs. of yarn. The effect is the same as if these 6 2/3 lbs. of yarn contained no cotton at all, and the whole 20 lbs. of cotton were concentrated in the 13 1/3 lbs. of yarn. The latter weight, on the other hand, does not contain an atom either of the value of the auxiliary materials and implements, or of the value newly created in the process.

In the same way, the 2 2/3 lbs. of yarn, in which the 4s., the remainder of the constant capital, is embodied, represents nothing but the value of the auxiliary materials and instruments of labour consumed in producing the 20 lbs. of yarn.

We have, therefore, arrived at this result: although eight-tenths of the product, or 16 lbs. of yarn, is, in its character of an article of utility, just as much the fabric of the spinner's labour, as the remainder of the same product, yet when viewed in this connexion, it does not contain, and has not absorbed any labour expended during the process of spinning. It is just as if the cotton had converted itself into yarn, without help; as if the shape it had assumed was mere trickery and deceit: for so soon as our capitalist sells it for 24s., and with the money replaces his means of production, it becomes evident that this 16 lbs. of yarn is nothing more than so much cotton and spindle-waste in disguise.

On the other hand, the remaining 2/10ths of the product, or 4 lbs of yarn, represent nothing but the new value of 6s.; created during the 12 hours' spinning process. All the value transferred to those 4 lbs, from the raw material and instruments of labour consumed, was, so to say, intercepted in order to be incorporated in the 16 lbs. first spun. In this case, it is as if the spinner had spun 4 lbs. of yarn out of air, or, as if he had spun them with the aid of cotton and spindles, that, being the spontaneous gift of Nature, transferred no value to the product.

Of this 4 lbs. of yarn, in which the whole of the value newly created during the process, is condensed, one half represents the equivalent for the value of the labour consumed, or the 3s. variable capital, the other half represents the 3s. surplus-value.

Since 12 working-hours of the spinner are embodied in 6s., it follows that in yarn of the value of 30s., there must be embodied 60 working-hours. And this quantity of labour-time does in fact exist in the 20 lbs of yarn; for in 8/10ths or 16 lbs there are materialised the 48 hours of labour expended, before the commencement of the spinning process, on the means of production; and in the remaining 2/10ths or 4 lbs there are materialised the 12 hours' work done during the process itself.

On a former page we saw that the value of the yarn is equal to the sum of the new value created during the production of that yarn plus the value previously existing in the means of production.

It has now been shown how the various component parts of the value of the product, parts that differ functionally from each other, may be represented by corresponding proportional parts of the product itself.

To split up in this manner the product into different parts, of which one represents only the labour previously spent on the means of production, or the constant capital, another, only the necessary labour spent during the process of production, or the variable capital, and another and last part, only the surplus-labour expended during the same process, or the surplus-value; to do this, is, as will be seen later on from its application to complicated and hitherto unsolved problems, no less important than it is simple.

In the preceding investigation we have treated the total product as the final result, ready for use, of a working-day of 12 hours. We can however follow this total product through all the stages of its production; and in this way we shall arrive at the same result as before, if we represent the partial products, given off at the different stages, as functionally different parts of the final or total product.

The spinner produces in 12 hours 20 lbs. of yarn, or in 1 hour 1⅔ lbs; consequently he produces in 8 hours 13⅓ lbs., or a partial product equal in value to all the cotton that is spun in a whole day. In like manner the partial product of the next period of 1 hour and 36 minutes, is 2⅔ lbs. of yarn: this represents the value of the instruments of labour that are consumed in 12 hours. In the following hour and 12 minutes, the spinner produces 2 lbs. of yarn worth 3 shillings, a value equal to the whole value he creates in his 6 hours' necessary labour. Finally, in the last hour and 12 minutes he produces another 2 lbs. of yarn, whose value is equal to the surplus-value, created by his surplus-labour during half a day. This method of calculation serves the English manufacturer for every-day use; it shows, he will say, that in the first 8 hours, or ⅔ of the working-day, he gets back the value of his cotton; and so on for the remaining hours. It is also a perfectly correct method: being in fact the first method given above with this difference, that instead of being applied to space, in which the different parts of the completed product lie side by side, it deals with time, in which those parts are successively produced. But, it can also be accompanied by very barbarian notions, more especially in the heads of those who are as much interested, practically, in the process of making value beget value, as they are in misunderstanding that process theoretically. Such people may get the notion into their heads, that our spinner, for example, produces or replaces in the first 8 hours of his working-day the *value* of the cotton; in the following hour and 36 minutes the *value* of the instruments of labour worn away; in the next hour and 12 minutes the *value* of the wages; and that he devotes to the production of surplus-value for the manufacturer, only that well known 'last hour.' In this way the poor spinner is made to perform the two-fold miracle not only of producing cotton, spindles, steam-engine, coal, oil, &c., at the same time that he spins with them, but also of turning one working-day into five; for, in the example we are considering, the production of the raw material and instruments of labour demands four working-days of twelve hours each, and their conversion into yarn requires another such day. That the love of lucre induces an easy belief in such miracles, and that sycophant doctrinaires are never wanting to prove them, is vouched for by the following incident of historical celebrity.

Section 3: *Senior's 'Last Hour'*

One fine morning, in the year 1836, Nassau W. Senior, who may be called the bel-esprit of English economists, well known, alike for his economic 'science,' and for his beautiful style, was summoned from Oxford to Manchester, to learn in the latter place, the Political Economy that he taught in the former. The manufacturers elected him as their champion, not only against the newly passed Factory Act, but against the still more menacing Ten-hours' agitation. With their usual practical acuteness, they had found out that the learned Professor 'wanted a good deal of finishing;' it was this discovery that caused them to write for him. On his side the Professor has embodied the lecture he received from the Manchester manufacturers, in a pamphlet, entitled: 'Letters on the Factory Act, as it affects the cotton manufacture.' London, 1837. Here we find, amongst others, the following edifying passage:

> 'Under the present law, no mill in which persons under 18 years of age are employed, ... can be worked more than 11½ hours a day, that is, 12 hours for 5 days in the week, and nine on Saturday.
>
> 'Now the following analysis (!) will show that in a mill so worked, the whole net profit is derived *from the last hour*. I will suppose a manufacturer to invest £100,000:—£80,000 in his mill and machinery, and £20,000 in raw material and wages. The annual return of that mill, supposing the capital to be turned once a year, and gross profits to be 15 per cent., ought to be goods worth £115,000.... Of this £115,000, each of the twenty-three half-hours of work produces 5-115ths or one twenty-third. Of these 23-23rds (constituting the whole £115,000) twenty, that is to say £100,000 out of the £115,000, simply replace the capital;—one twenty-third (or £5,000 out of the £115,000) makes up for the deterioration of the mill and machinery. The remaining 2-23rds, that is, the last two of the twenty-three half-hours of every day, produce the net profit of 10 per cent. If, therefore (prices remaining the same), the factory could be kept at work thirteen hours instead of eleven and a half, with an addition of about £2,600 to the circulating capital, the net profit would be more than doubled. On the other hand, if the hours of working were reduced by one hour per day (prices remaining the same), the *net* profit would be destroyed—if they were reduced by one hour and a half, even the *gross* profit would be destroyed.'[10]

And the Professor calls this an 'analysis!' If, giving credence to the out-cries of the manufacturers, he believed that the workmen spend the best part of the day in the production, i.e., the reproduction or replacement of the value of the buildings, machinery, cotton, coal, &c., then his analysis was superfluous. His answer would simply have been:—Gentlemen! if you work your mills for 10 hours instead of 11½, then, other things being equal, the daily consumption of cotton, machinery, &c., will decrease in proportion. You gain just as much as you lose. Your work-people will in future spend one hour and a half less time in reproducing or replacing the capital that has been advanced.—If, on the other hand, he did not believe them without further inquiry, but, as being an expert in such matters, deemed an analysis necessary, then he ought, in a question that is concerned exclusively with the relations of net profit to the length of the working-day, before all things to have asked the manufacturers, to be careful not to lump together machinery, workshops, raw material, and labour, but to be good enough to place the constant capital, invested in buildings, machinery, raw material, &c., on one side of the account, and the capital advanced in wages on the other side. If the Professor then found, that in accordance with the calculation of the manufacturers, the workman reproduced or replaced his wages in 2 half-hours, in that case, he should have continued his analysis thus:

According to your figures, the workman in the last hour but one produces his wages, and in the last hour your surplus-value or net profit. Now, since in equal periods he produces equal values, the produce of the last hour but one, must have the same value as that of the last hour. Further, it is only while he labours that he produces any value at all, and the amount of his labour is measured by his labour-time. This you say, amounts to 11½ hours a day. He employs one portion of these 11½ hours, in producing or replacing his wages, and the remaining portion in producing your net profit. Beyond this he does absolutely nothing. But since, on your assumption, his wages, and the surplus-value he yields, are of equal value, it is clear that he produces his wages in 5¾ hours, and your net profit in the other 5¾ hours. Again, since the value of the yarn produced in 2 hours, is equal to the sum of the values of his wages and of your net profit, the measure of the value of this yarn must be 11½ working-hours, of which 5¾ hours measure the value of the yarn produced in the last hour but one, and 5¾, the value of the yarn produced in the last hour. We now come to a ticklish point; therefore, attention! The last working-hour but one is, like the first, an ordinary working-hour, neither more nor less. How then can the spinner produce in one hour, in the shape of yarn, a value that embodies 5¾ hours' labour? The truth is that he performs no such miracle. The use-value produced by him in one hour, is a definite quantity of yarn. The value of this yarn is measured by 5¾ working-hours, of which 4¾ were, without any assistance from him, previously embodied in the means of production, in the cotton, the machinery, and so on; the remaining one hour alone is added by him. Therefore since his wages are produced in 5¾ hours, and the yarn produced in one hour also contains 5¾ hours' work, there is no witchcraft in the result, that the value created by his 5¾ hours' spinning, is equal to the value of the product spun in one hour. You are altogether on the wrong track, if you think that he loses a single moment of his working-day, in reproducing or replacing the values of the cotton, the machinery, and so on. On the contrary, it is because his labour converts the cotton and spindles into yarn, because he spins, that the values of the cotton and spindles go over to the yarn of their own accord. This result is owing to the quality of his labour, not to its quantity. It is true, he will in one hour transfer to the yarn more value, in the shape of cotton, than he will in half an hour; but that is only because in one hour he spins up more cotton than in half an hour. You see then, your assertion, that the workman produces, in the last hour but one, the value of his wages, and in the last hour your net profit, amounts to no more than this, that in the yarn produced by him in 2 working-hours, whether they are the 2 first or the 2 last hours of the working-day, in that yarn, there are incorporated 11½ working-hours, or just a whole day's work, *i.e.*, two hours of his own work and 9½ hours of other people's. And my assertion that, in the first 5¾ hours, he produces his wages, and in the last 5¾ hours your net profit, amounts only to this, that you pay him for the former, but not for the latter. In speaking of payment of labour, instead of payment of labour-power, I only talk your own slang. Now, gentlemen, if you compare the working-time you pay for, with that which you do not pay for, you will find that they are to one another, as half a day is to half a day; this gives a rate of 100%, and a very pretty percentage it is. Further, there is not the least doubt, that if you make your 'hands' toil for 13 hours, instead of 11½, and, as may be expected from you, treat the work done in that extra one hour and a half, as pure surplus-labour, then the latter will be increased from 5¾ hours' labour to 7¼ hours' labour, and the rate of surplus-value from 100% to 126 2/23%. So that you are altogether too sanguine, in expecting that by such an addition of 1½ hours to the working-day, the rate will rise from 100% to 200% and more, in other words that it will be 'more than doubled.' On the other hand—man's heart is a wonderful thing, especially when carried in the purse—you take too pessimist a view, when you fear, that with a reduction of the hours of labour from 11½ to 10, the whole of your net profit will go to the dogs. Not at all. All other conditions remaining the same, the surplus-labour will fall from 5¾ hours to 4¾ hours, a period that still gives a very profitable rate of surplus-value, namely 82 14/23%. But this dreadful 'last hour,' about which you have invented more stories than have the millenarians about the day of judgment, is 'all bosh.' If it goes, it will cost neither you, your net profit, nor the boys and girls whom you employ, their 'purity of mind.'[11] Whenever your 'last hour' strikes in earnest, think of the Oxford Professor. And now, gentlemen, 'farewell, and may we meet again in yonder better world, but not before.'

Senior invented the battle cry of the 'last hour' in 1836.[12] In the London *Economist* of the 15th April, 1848, the same cry was again raised by James Wilson, an economic mandarin of high standing: this time in opposition to the 10 hours' bill.

Section 4: *Surplus-Produce*

The portion of the product that represents the surplus-value, (one tenth of the 20 lbs., or 2 lbs. of yarn, in the example given in Sec. 2) we call 'surplus-produce.' Just as the rate of surplus-value is determined by its relation, not to the sum total of the capital, but to its variable part; in like manner, the relative quantity of surplus-produce is determined by the ratio that this produce bears, not to the remaining part of the total product, but to that part of it in which is incorporated the necessary labour. Since the production of surplus-value is the chief end and aim of capitalist production, it is clear, that the greatness of a man's or a nation's wealth should be measured, not by the absolute quantity produced, but by the relative magnitude of the surplus-produce.[13]

The sum of the necessary labour and the surplus-labour, *i.e.*, of the periods of time during which the workman replaces the value of his labour-power, and produces the surplus-value, this sum constitutes the actual time during which he works, *i.e.*, the working-day.

Notes

1. 'If we reckon the value of the fixed capital employed as a part of the advances, we must reckon the remaining value of such capital at the end of the year as a part of the annual returns.' (Malthus, 'Princ. of Pol. Econ.' 2nd. ed., Lond., 1836, p. 269.)
2. What Lucretius says is self-evident; 'nil posse creari de nihilo,' out of nothing, nothing can be created. Creation of value is transformation of labour-power into labour. Labour-power itself is energy transferred to a human organism by means of nourishing matter.
3. In the same way that the English use the terms 'rate of profit,' 'rate of interest.' We shall see, in Book III, that the rate of profit is no mystery, so soon as we know the laws of surplus-value. If we reverse the process, we cannot comprehend either the one or the other.
4. *Note added in the 3rd German edition.*—The author resorts here to the economic language in current use. It will be remembered that on p. 182 (present edition, p. 174) it was shown that in reality the labourer 'advances' to the capitalist and not the capitalist to the labourer.—*F. E.*
5. In this work, we have, up to now, employed the term 'necessary labour-time,' to designate the time necessary under given social conditions for the production of any commodity. Henceforward we use it to designate also the time necessary for the production of the particular commodity labour-power. The use of one and the same technical term in different senses is inconvenient, but in no science can it be altogether avoided. Compare, for instance, the higher with the lower branches of mathematics.

6. Herr Wilhelm Thucydides Roscher has found a mare's nest. He has made the important discovery that if, on the one hand, the formation of surplus-value, or surplus-produce, and the consequent accumulation of capital, is now-a-days due to the thrift of the capitalist, on the other hand, in the lowest stages of civilisation it is the strong who compel the weak to economise. (l.c., p. 78.) To economise what? Labour? Or superfluous wealth that does not exist? What is it that makes such men as Roscher account for the origin of surplus-value, by a mere rechauffé of the more of less plausible excuses by the capitalist, for his appropriation of surplus-value? It is, besides their real ignorance, their apologetic dread of a scientific analysis of value and surplus-value, and of obtaining a result, possibly not altogether palatable to the powers that be.

7. Although the rate of surplus-value is an exact expression for the degree of exploitation of labour-power, it is, in no sense, an expression for the absolute amount of exploitation. For example, if the necessary labour = 5 hours and the surplus-labour = 5 hours, the degree of exploitation is 100%. The amount of exploitation is here measured by 5 hours. If, on the other hand, the necessary labour = 6 hours and the surplus-labour = 6 hours, the degree of exploitation remains, as before, 100%, while the actual amount of exploitation has increased 20%, namely from five hours to six.

8. The above data, which may be relied upon, were given me by a Manchester spinner. In England, the horse-power of an engine was formerly calculated from the diameter of its cylinder, now the actual horse-power shown by the indicator is taken.

9. The calculations given in the text are intended merely as illustrations. We have in fact. assumed that prices = values. We shall, however, see, in Book III., that even in the case of average prices the assumption cannot be made in this very simple manner.

10. Senior, l.c., pp. 12, 13. We let pass such extraordinary notions as are of no importance for our purpose; for instance, the assertion, that manufacturers reckon as part of their profit, gross or net, the amount required to make good wear and tear of machinery, or in other words, to replace a part of the capital. So, too, we pass over any question as to the accuracy of his figures. Leonard Horner has shown in 'A Letter to Mr Senior,' &c., London, 1837, that they are worth no more than so-called 'Analysis.' Leonard Horner was one of the Factory Inquiry Commissioners in 1833, and Inspector, or rather Censor of Factories till 1859. He rendered undying service to the English working-class. He carried on a life-long contest, not only with the embittered manufacturers, but also with the Cabinet, to whom the number of votes given by the masters in the Lower House, was a matter of far greater importance than the number of hours worked by the 'hands' in the mills.

Apart from efforts in principle, Senior's statement is confused. What he really intended to say was this: The manufacturer employs the workman for 11½ hours or for 23 half-hours daily. As the working-day, so, too, the working year, may be conceived to consist of 11½ hours or 23 half-hours, but each multiplied by the number of working-days in the year. On this supposition, the 23 half-hours yield an annual product of £115,000; one half-hour yields 1/23 × £115,000; 20 half-hours yield 20/23 × £115,000 = £100,000, *i.e.*, they replace no more than the capital advanced. There remain 3 half-hours, which yield 3/23 × £115,000 = £5,000 or the gross profit. Of these 3 half-hours, one yields 1/23 × £115,000 = £15,000; *i.e.*, it makes up for the wear and tear of the machinery; the remaining 2 half-hours, *i.e.*, the last hour, yield 2/23 × £115,000 = £10,000 or the net profit. In the text Senior converts the last 2/23 of the product into portions of the working-day itself.

11. If, on the one hand, Senior proved that the net profit of the manufacturer, the existence of the English cotton industry, and England's command of the markets of the world, depend on 'the last working-hour,' on the other hand, Dr Andrew Ure showed, that if children and young persons under 18 years of age, instead of being kept the full 12 hours in the warm and pure moral atmosphere of the factory, are turned out an hour sooner into the heartless and frivolous outer world, they will be deprived, by idleness and vice, of all hope of salvation for their souls. Since 1848, the factory inspectors have never tired of twitting the masters with this

'last,' this 'fatal hour.' Thus Mr Hovell in his report of the 21st May, 1855: 'Had the following ingenious calculation (he quotes Senior) been correct, every cotton factory in the United Kingdom would have been working at a loss since the year 1850.' (Reports of the Insp. of Fact., for the half-year, ending 30th April, 1855, pp. 19, 20.) In the year 1848, after the passing of the 10 hours' bill, the masters of some flax spinning mills, scattered, few and far between, over the country on the borders of Dorset and Somerset, foisted a petition against the bill on to the shoulders of a few of their work-people. One of the clauses of this petition is as follows: 'Your petitioners, as parents, conceive that an additional hour of leisure will tend more to demoralise the children than otherwise, believing that idleness is the parent of vice.' On this the factory report of 31st Oct., 1848, says: The atmosphere of the flax mills, in which the children of these virtuous and tender parents work, is so loaded with dust and fibre from the raw material, that it is exceptionally unpleasant to stand even 10 minutes in the spinning rooms: for you are unable to do so without the most painful sensation, owing to the eyes, the ears, the nostrils, and mouth, being immediately filled by the clouds of flax dust from which there is no escape. The labour itself, owing to the feverish haste of the machinery, demands unceasing application of skill and movement, under the control of a watchfulness that never tires, and it seems somewhat hard, to let parents apply the term 'idling' to their own children, who, after allowing for meal-times, are fettered for 10 whole hours to such an occupation, in such an atmosphere.... These children work longer than the labourers in the neighbouring villages.... Such cruel talk about 'idleness and vice' ought to be branded as the purest cant, and the most shameless hypocrisy.... That portion of the public, who, about 12 years ago, were struck by the assurance with which, under the sanction of high authority, it was publicly and most earnestly proclaimed, that the whole net profit of the manufacturer flows from the labour of the last hour, and that, therefore, the reduction of the working-day by one hour, would destroy his net profit, that portion of the public, we say, will hardly believe its own eyes, when it now finds, that the original discovery of the virtues of 'the last hour' has since been so far improved, as to include morals as well as profit; so that, if the duration of the labour of children, is reduced to a full 10 hours, their morals, together with the net profits of their employers, will vanish, both being dependent on this last, this fatal hour. (See Repts., Insp. of Fact., for 31st Oct., 1848, p. 101.) The same report then gives some examples of the morality and virtue of these same pure-minded manufacturers, of the tricks, the artifices, the cajoling, the threats, and the falsifications, they made use of, in order, first, to compel a few defenceless workmen to sign petitions of such a kind, and then to impose them upon Parliament as the petitions of a whole branch of industry, or a whole country. It is highly characteristic of the present status of so-called economic science, that neither Senior himself, who, at a later period, to his honour be it said, energetically supported the factory legislation, nor his opponents, from first to last, have ever been able to explain the false conclusions of the 'original discovery.' They appeal to actual experience, but the why and wherefore remains a mystery.

12. Nevertheless, the learned professor was not without some benefit from his journey to Manchester. In the 'Letters on the Factory Act,' he makes the whole net gains including 'profit' and 'interests' and even 'something more,' depend upon a single unpaid hour's work of the labourer. One year previously, in his 'Outlines of Political Economy,' written for the instruction of Oxford students and cultivated Philistines, he had also 'discovered, in opposition to Ricardo's determination of value by labour, that profit is derived from the labour of the capitalist, and interest from his asceticism, in other words, from his abstinence.' The dodge was an old one, but the word 'abstinence' was new. Herr Roscher translates it rightly by 'Enthaltung.' Some of his countrymen, the Browns, Jones, and Robinsons, of Germany, not so well versed in Latin as he, have, monk-like, rendered it by 'Entsagung' (renunciation).

13. 'To an individual with a capital of £20,000, whose profits were £2,000 per annum, it would be a matter quite indifferent whether his capital would employ a 100 or 1,000 men, whether the

commodity produced sold for £10,000 or £20,000, provided, in all cases, his profit were not diminished below £2,000. Is not the real interest of the nation similar? Provided its net real income, its rent and profits, be the same, it is of no importance whether the nation consists of 10 or of 12 millions of inhabitants.' (Ric. l.c.,.p. 416.) Long before Ricardo, Arthur Young, a fanatical upholder of surplus-produce, for the rest, a rambling, uncritical writer, whose reputation is in the inverse ratio of his merit, says, 'Of what use, in a modern kingdom, would be a whole province thus divided [in the old Roman manner, by small independent peasants], however well cultivated, except for the mere purpose of breeding men, which taken singly is a most useless purpose?' (Arthur Young: 'Political Arithmetic, &c.' London, 1774, p. 47.)

Very curious is 'the strong inclination... to represent net wealth as beneficial to the labouring class... though it is evidently not on account of being net.' (Th . Hopkins, 'On Rent of Land, &c.' London, 1828, p. 126.)

10

The Working-Day

Section 1: *The Limits of the Working-Day*

We started with the supposition that labour-power is bought and sold at its value. Its value, like that of all other commodities, is determined by the working-time necessary to its production. If the production of the average daily means of subsistence of the labourer takes up 6 hours, he must work, on the average, 6 hours every day, to produce his daily labour-power, or to reproduce the value received as the result of its sale. The necessary part of his working-day amounts to 6 hours, and is, therefore, *caeteris paribus* [other things being equal], a given quantity. But with this, the extent of the working-day itself is not yet given.

Let us assume that the line A---B represents the length of the necessary working-time, say 6 hours. If the labour be prolonged 1, 3, or 6 hours beyond A—-B, we have 3 other lines:

Working-day I.	Working-day II.	Working-day III.
A---B-C.	A---B--C.	A---B---C.

representing 3 different working-days of 7, 9, and 12 hours. The extension B—-C of the line A—-B represents the length of the surplus-labour. As the working-day is A—-B + B—-C or A—-C, it varies with the variable quantity B—-C. Since A—-B is constant, the ratio of B—-C to A—-B can always be calculated. In working-day I, it is 1/6, in working-day II, 3/6, in working day III 6/6 of A—-B. Since further the ratio (surplus working-time)/(necessary working-time), determines the rate of the surplus-value, the latter is given by the ratio of B—-C to A—-B. It amounts in the 3 different working-days respectively to 16 2/3, 50 and 100 per cent. On the other hand, the rate of surplus-value alone would not give us the extent of the working-day. If this rate, *e.g.*, were 100 per cent., the working-day might be of 8, 10, 12, or more hours. It would indicate that the 2 constituent parts of the working-day, necessary-labour and surplus-labour time, were equal in extent, but not how long each of these two constituent parts was.

The working-day is thus not a constant, but a variable quantity. One of its parts, certainly, is determined by the working-time required for the reproduction of the labour-power of the labourer himself. But its total amount varies with the duration of the surplus-labour. The working-day is, therefore, determinable, but is, *per se*, indeterminate.[1]

Although the working-day is not a fixed, but a fluent quantity, it can, on the other hand, only vary within certain limits. The minimum limit is, however, not determinable; of course, if we make the extension line B—C or the surplus-labour = 0, we have a minimum limit, *i.e.*, the part of the day which the labourer must necessarily work for his own maintenance. On the basis of capitalist production, however, this necessary labour can form a part only of the working-day; the working-day itself can never be reduced to this minimum. On the other hand, the working-day has a maximum limit. It cannot be prolonged beyond a certain point. This maximum limit is conditioned by two things. First, by the physical bounds of labour-power. Within the 24 hours of the natural day a man can expend only a definite quantity of his vital force. A horse, in like manner, can only work from day to day, 8 hours. During part of the day this force must rest, sleep; during another part the man has to satisfy other physical needs, to feed, wash, and clothe himself. Besides these purely physical limitations, the extension of the working-day encounters moral ones. The labourer needs time for satisfying his intellectual and social wants, the extent and number of which are conditioned by the general state of social advancement. The variation of the working-day fluctuates, therefore, within physical and social bounds. But both these limiting conditions are of a very elastic nature, and allow the greatest latitude. So we find working-days of 8, 10, 12, 14, 16, 18 hours, i.e., of the most different lengths.

The capitalist has bought the labour-power at its day-rate. To him its use-value belongs during one working-day. He has thus acquired the right to make the labourer work for him during one day. But, what is a working-day?[2]

At all events, less than a natural day. By how much? The capitalist has his own views of this *ultima Thule* [the outermost limit], the necessary limit of the working-day. As capitalist, he is only capital personified. His soul is the soul of capital. But capital has one single life impulse, the tendency to create value and surplus-value, to make its constant factor, the means of production, absorb the greatest possible amount of surplus-labour.[3]

Capital is dead labour, that, vampire-like, only lives by sucking living labour, and lives the more, the more labour it sucks. The time during which the labourer works, is the time during which the capitalist consumes the labour-power he has purchased of him.[4]

If the labourer consumes his disposable time for himself, he robs the capitalist.[5]

The capitalist then takes his stand on the law of the exchange of commodities. He, like all other buyers, seeks to get the greatest possible benefit out of the use-value of his commodity. Suddenly the voice of the labourer, which had been stifled in the storm and stress of the process of production, rises:

The commodity that I have sold to you differs from the crowd of other commodities, in that its use creates value, and a value greater than its own. That is why you bought it. That which on your side appears a spontaneous expansion of capital, is on mine extra expenditure of labour-power. You and I know on the market only one law, that of the exchange of commodities. And the consumption of the commodity belongs not to the seller who parts with it, but to the buyer, who acquires it. To you, therefore, belongs the use of my daily labour-power. But by means of the price that you pay for it each day, I must be able to reproduce it daily, and to sell it again. Apart from natural exhaustion through age, &c., I must be able on the morrow to work with the same normal amount of force, health and freshness as to-day. You preach to me constantly the gospel of 'saving' and 'abstinence.' Good! I will, like a sensible saving owner, husband my sole wealth, labour-power, and abstain from all foolish waste of it. I will each day spend, set in motion, put into action only as much of it as is compatible with its normal duration, and healthy development. By an unlimited extension of the working-day, you may in one day use up a quantity of labour-power greater than I can restore in three. What you gain in labour I lose in substance. The use of my labour-power and the spoliation of it are quite different things. If the average time that (doing a reasonable amount of work) an average labourer can live, is 30 years, the value of my labour-power, which you pay me from day to day is 1/(365×30) or 1/10950 of its total value. But if you consume it in 10 years, you pay me daily 1/10950 instead of 1/3650 of its total value, *i.e.*, only 1/3 of its daily value, and you rob me, therefore, every day of 2/3 of the value of my commodity. You pay me for one day's labour-power, whilst you use that of 3 days. That is against our contract and the law of exchanges. I demand, therefore, a working-day of normal length, and I demand it without any appeal to your heart, for in money matters sentiment is out of place. You may be a model citizen, perhaps a member of the Society for the Prevention of Cruelty to Animals, and in the odour of sanctity to boot; but the thing that you represent face to face with me has no heart in its breast. That which seems to throb there is my own heart-beating. I demand the normal working-day because I, like every other seller, demand the value of my commodity.[6]

We see then, that, apart from extremely elastic bounds, the nature of the exchange of commodities itself imposes no limit to the working-day, no limit to surplus-labour. The capitalist maintains his rights as a purchaser when he tries to make the working-day as long as possible, and to make, whenever possible, two working-days out of one. On the other hand, the peculiar nature of the commodity sold implies a limit to its consumption by the purchaser, and the labourer maintains his right as seller when he wishes to reduce the working-day to one of definite normal duration. There is here, therefore, an antinomy, right against right, both equally bearing the seal of the law of exchanges. Between equal rights force decides. Hence, is it that in the history of capitalist production, the determination of what is a working-day, presents itself as the result of a struggle, a struggle between collective capital, *i.e.*, the class of capitalists, and collective labour, *i.e.*, the working-class.

Section 2: *The Greed for Surplus-Labour Manufacturer and Boyard*

Capital has not invented surplus-labour. Wherever a part of society possesses the monopoly of the means of production, the labourer, free or not free, must add to the working-time necessary for his own maintenance an extra working-time in order to produce the means of subsistence for the owners of the means of production,[7] whether this proprietor be the Athenian caloς cagaqoς [well-to-do man], Etruscan theocrat, *civis Romanus* [Roman citizen], Norman baron, American slave-owner, Wallachian Boyard, modern landlord or capitalist.[8] It is, however, clear that in any given economic formation of society, where not the exchange-value but the use-value of the product predominates, surplus-labour will be limited by a given set of wants which may be greater or less, and that here no boundless thirst for surplus-labour arises from the nature of the production itself. Hence in antiquity over-work becomes horrible only when the object is to obtain exchange-value in its specific independent money-form; in the production of gold and silver. Compulsory working to death is here the recognised form of over-work. Only read Diodorus Siculus.[9] Still these are exceptions in antiquity. But as soon as people, whose production still moves within the lower forms of slave-labour, corvée-labour, &c., are drawn into the whirlpool of an international market dominated by the capitalistic mode of production, the sale of their products for export becoming their principal interest, the civilised horrors of over-work are grafted on the barbaric horrors of slavery, serfdom, &c. Hence the negro labour in the Southern States of the American Union preserved something of a patriarchal character, so long as production was chiefly directed to immediate local consumption. But in proportion, as the export of cotton became of vital interest to these states, the over-working of the negro and sometimes the using up of his life in 7 years of labour became a factor in a calculated and calculating system. It was no longer a question of obtaining from him a certain quantity of useful products. It was now a question of production of surplus-labour itself: So was it also with the corvée, e.g., in the Danubian Principalities (now Roumania).

The comparison of the greed for surplus-labour in the Danubian Principalities with the same greed in English factories has a special interest, because surplus-labour in the corvée has an independent and palpable form.

Suppose the working-day consists of 6 hours of necessary labour, and 6 hours of surplus-labour. Then the free labourer gives the capitalist every week 6 x 6 or 36 hours of surplus-labour. It is the same as if he worked 3 days in the week for himself, and 3 days in the week gratis for the capitalist. But this is not evident on the surface. Surplus-labour and necessary labour glide one into the other. I can, therefore, express the same relationship by saying, e.g., that the labourer in every minute works 30 seconds for himself, and 30 for the capitalist, etc. It is otherwise with the corvée. The necessary labour which the Wallachian peasant does for his own maintenance is distinctly marked off from his surplus-labour on behalf of the Boyard. The one he does on his own field, the other on the seignorial estate. Both parts of the labour-time exist, therefore, independently, side by side one with the other. In the corvée the surplus-labour is accurately marked off from the necessary labour. This, however, can make no difference with regard to the quantitative relation of surplus-labour to necessary labour. Three days' surplus-labour in the week remain three days that yield no equivalent to the labourer himself, whether it be called corvée or wage-labour. But in the capitalist the greed for surplus-labour appears in the straining after an unlimited extension of the working-day, in the Boyard more simply in a direct hunting after days of corvée.[10]

In the Danubian Principalities the corvée was mixed up with rents in kind and other appurtenances of bondage, but it formed the most important tribute paid to the ruling class. Where this was the case, the corvée rarely arose from serfdom; serfdom much more frequently on the other hand took origin from the corvée.[11] This is what took place in the Roumanian provinces. Their original mode of production was based on community of the soil, but not in the Slavonic or Indian form. Part of the land was cultivated in severalty as freehold by the members of the community, another part—*ager publicus*—was cultivated by them in common. The products of this common labour served partly as a reserve fund against bad harvests and other accidents, partly as a public store for providing the costs of war, religion, and other common expenses. In course of time military and clerical dignitaries usurped, along with the common land, the labour spent upon it. The labour of the free peasants on their common land was transformed into corvée for the thieves of the common land. This corvée soon developed into a servile relationship existing in point of fact, not in point of law, until Russia, the liberator of the world, made it legal under presence of abolishing serfdom. The code of the corvée, which the Russian General Kisseleff proclaimed in 1831, was of course dictated by the Boyards themselves. Thus Russia conquered with one blow the magnates of the Danubian provinces, and the applause of liberal cretins throughout Europe.

According to the 'Règlement organique,' as this code of the corvée is called, every Wallachian peasant owes to the so-called landlord, besides a mass of detailed payments in kind: *(1)*, 12 days of general labour; *(2)*, one day of field labour; *(3)*, one day of wood carrying. In all, 14 days in the year. With deep insight into Political Economy, however, the working-day is not taken in its ordinary sense, but as the working-day necessary to the production of an average daily product; and that average daily product is determined in so crafty a way that no Cyclops would be done with it in 24 hours. In dry words, the Réglement itself declares with true Russian irony that by 12 working-days one must understand the product of the manual labour of 36 days, by 1 day of field labour 3 days, and by 1 day of wood carrying in like manner three times as much. In all, 42 corvée days. To this had to be added the so-called jobagie, service due to the lord for extraordinary occasions. In proportion to the size of its population, every village has to furnish annually a definite contingent to the jobagie. This additional corvée is estimated at 14 days for each Wallachian peasant. Thus the prescribed corvée amounts to 56 working-days yearly. But the agricultural year in Wallachia numbers in consequence of the severe climate only 210 days, of which 40 for Sundays and holidays, 30 on an average for bad weather, together 70 days, do not count. 140 working-days remain. The ratio of the corvée to the necessary labour 56/84 or 66 2/3 % gives a much smaller rate of surplus-value than that which regulates the labour of the English agricultural or factory labourer. This is, however, only the legally prescribed corvée. And in a spirit yet more 'liberal' than the English Factory Acts, the 'Règlement organique' has known how to facilitate its own evasion. After it has made 56 days out of 12, the nominal day's work of each of the 56 corvée days is again so arranged that a portion of it must fall on the ensuing day. In one day, e.g., must be weeded an extent of land, which, for this work, especially in maize plantations, needs twice as much time. The legal day's work for some kinds of agricultural labour is interpretable in such a way that the day begins in May and ends in October. In Moldavia conditions are still harder.

> 'The 12 corvée days of the 'Règlement organique' cried a Boyard drunk with victory, amount to 365 days in the year.'[12]

If the Règlement organique of the Danubian provinces was a positive expression of the greed for surplus-labour which every paragraph legalised, the English Factory Acts are the negative expression of the same greed. These acts curb the passion of capital for a limitless draining of labour-power, by forcibly limiting the working-day by state regulations, made by a state that is ruled by capitalist and landlord. Apart from the working-class movement that daily grew more threatening, the limiting of factory labour was dictated by the same necessity which spread guano over the English fields. The same blind eagerness for plunder that in the one case exhausted the soil, had, in the other, torn up by the roots the living force of the nation. Periodical epidemics speak on this point as clearly as the diminishing military standard in Germany and France.[13]

The Factory Act of 1850 now in force (1867) allows for the average working-day 10 hours, i.e., for the first 5 days 12 hours from 6 a.m. to 6 p.m., including ½ an hour for breakfast, and an hour for dinner, and thus leaving 10½ working-hours, and 8 hours for Saturday, from 6 a.m. to 2 p.m., of which ½ an hour is subtracted for breakfast. 60 working-hours are left, 10½ for each of the first 5 days, 7½ for the last.[14]

Certain guardians of these laws are appointed, Factory Inspectors, directly under the Home Secretary, whose reports are published half-yearly, by order of Parliament. They give regular and official statistics of the capitalistic greed for surplus-labour.

Let us listen, for a moment, to the Factory Inspectors.[15]

> 'The fraudulent mill-owner begins work a quarter of an hour (sometimes more, sometimes less) before 6 a.m., and leaves off a quarter of an hour (sometimes more, sometimes less) after 6 p.m. He takes 5 minutes from the beginning and from the end of the half hour nominally allowed for breakfast, and 10 minutes at the beginning and end of the hour nominally allowed for dinner. He works for a quarter of an hour (sometimes more, sometimes less) after 2 p.m. on Saturday. Thus his gain is —

Before 6 a.m.,	15 minutes.
After 6 p.m.,	15 "
At breakfast time,	10 "
At dinner time,	20 "
Five days—300 minutes,	60 "
On Saturday before 6 a.m.,	15 minutes.
At breakfast time,	10 "
After 2 p.m.,	15 "
	40 minutes.
Total weekly,	340 minutes.

Or 5 hours and 40 minutes weekly, which multiplied by 50 working weeks in the year (allowing two for holidays and occasional stoppages) is equal to 27 working-days.'[16]

'Five minutes a day's increased work, multiplied by weeks, are equal to two and a half days of produce in the year.'[17]

'An additional hour a day gained by small instalments before 6 a.m., after 6 p.m., and at the beginning and end of the times nominally fixed for meals, is nearly equivalent to working 13 months in the year.'[18]

Crises during which production is interrupted and the factories work 'short time,' i.e., for only a part of the week, naturally do not affect the tendency to extend the working-day. The less business there is, the more profit has to be made on the business done. The less time spent in work, the more of that time has to be turned into surplus labour-time.

Thus the Factory Inspector's report on the period of the crisis from 1857 to 1858:

'It may seem inconsistent that there should be any overworking at a time when trade is so bad; but that very badness leads to the transgression by unscrupulous men, they get the extra profit of it. ... In the last half year, says Leonard Horner, 122 mills in my district have been given up; 143 were found standing,' yet, over-work is continued beyond the legal hours.[19]

For a great part of the time,' says Mr Howell, 'owing to the depression of trade, many factories were altogether closed, and a still greater number were working short time. I continue, however, to receive about the usual number of complaints that half, or three-quarters of an hour in the day, are snatched from the workers by encroaching upon the times professedly allowed for rest and refreshment.'[20]

The same phenomenon was reproduced on a smaller scale during the frightful cotton-crises from 1861 to 1865.[21]

'It is sometimes advanced by way of excuse, when persons are found at work in a factory, either at a meal hour, or at some illegal time, that they will not leave the mill at the appointed hour, and that compulsion is necessary to force them to cease work [cleaning their machinery, &c.], especially on Saturday afternoons. But, if the hands remain in a factory after the machinery has ceased to revolve ... they would not have been so employed if sufficient time had been set apart specially for cleaning, &c., either before 6 a.m. *[sic.!]* or before 2 p.m. on Saturday afternoons.'[22]

'The profit to be gained by it (over-working in violation of the Act) appears to be, to many, a greater temptation than they can resist; they calculate upon the chance of not being found out; and when they see the small amount of penalty and costs, which those who have been convicted have had to pay, they find that if they should be detected there will still be a considerable balance of gain....[23] In cases where the additional time is gained by a multiplication of small thefts in the course of the day, there are insuperable difficulties to the inspectors making out a case.'[24]

These 'small thefts' of capital from the labourer's meal and recreation time, the factory inspectors also designate as 'petty pilferings of minutes,'[25] 'snatching a few minutes,'[26] or, as the labourers technically called them, 'nibbling and cribbling at meal-times.'[27]

It is evident that in this atmosphere the formation of surplus-value by surplus-labour, is no secret.

'If you allow me,' said a highly respectable master to me, 'to work only ten minutes in the day over-time, you put one thousand a year in my pocket.'[28] 'Moments are the elements of profit.'[29]

Nothing is from this point of view more characteristic than the designation of the workers who work full time as 'full-timers,' and the children under 13 who are only allowed to work 6 hours as 'half-timers.' The worker is here nothing more than personified labour-time. All individual distinctions are merged in those of 'full-timers' and 'half-timers'[30]

Section 3: ***Branches of English Industry without Legal Limits to Exploitation***

We have hitherto considered the tendency to the extension of the working-day, the were-wolf's hunger for surplus-labour in a department where the monstrous exactions, not surpassed, says an English bourgeois economist, by the cruelties of the Spaniards to the American red-skins,[31] caused capital at last to be bound by the chains of legal regulations. Now, let us cast a glance at certain branches of production in which the exploitation of labour is either free from fetters to this day, or was so yesterday.

> Mr Broughton Charlton, county magistrate, declared, as chairman of a meeting held at the Assembly Rooms, Nottingham, on the 14th January, 1860, 'that there was an amount of privation and suffering among that portion of the population connected with the lace trade, unknown in other parts of the kingdom, indeed, in the civilised world .... Children of nine or ten years are dragged from their squalid beds at two, three, or four o'clock in the morning and compelled to work for a bare subsistence until ten, eleven, or twelve at night, their limbs wearing away, their frames dwindling, their faces whitening, and their humanity absolutely sinking into a stone-like torpor, utterly horrible to contemplate.... We are not surprised that Mr Mallett, or any other manufacturer, should stand forward and protest against discussion.... The system, as the Rev. Montagu Valpy describes it, is one of unmitigated slavery, socially, physically, morally, and spiritually.... What can be thought of a town which holds a public meeting to petition that the period of labour for men shall be diminished to eighteen hours a day? .... We declaim against the Virginian and Carolinian cotton-planters. Is their black-market, their lash, and their barter of human flesh more detestable than this slow sacrifice of humanity which takes place in order that veils and collars may be fabricated for the benefit of capitalists?'[32]

The potteries of Staffordshire have, during the last 22 years, been the subject of three parliamentary inquiries. The result is embodied in Mr Scriven's Report of 1841 to the 'Children's Employment Commissioners,' in the report of Dr Greenhow of 1860 published by order of the medical officer of the Privy Council (Public Health, 3rd Report, 112-113), lastly, in the report of Mr Longe of 1862 in the 'First Report of the Children's Employment Commission, of the 13th June, 1863.' For my purpose it is enough to take, from the reports of 1860 and 1863, some depositions of the exploited children themselves. From the children we may form an opinion as to the adults, especially the girls and women, and that in a branch of industry by the side of which cotton-spinning appears an agreeable and healthful occupation.[33]

William Wood, 9 years old, was 7 years and 10 months when he began to work. He 'ran moulds' (carried ready-moulded articles into the drying-room, afterwards bringing back the empty mould) from the beginning. He came to work every day in the week at 6 a.m., and left off about 9 p.m. 'I work till 9 o'clock at night six days in the week. I have done so seven or eight weeks.'

> Fifteen hours of labour for a child 7 years old! J. Murray, 12 years of age, says: 'I turn jigger, and run moulds. I come at 6. Sometimes I come at 4. I worked all night last night, till 6 o'clock this morning. I have not been in bed since the night before last. There were eight or nine other boys working last night. All but one have come this

morning. I get 3 shillings and sixpence. I do not get any more for working at night. I worked two nights last week.'

Fernyhough, a boy of ten:

> 'I have not always an hour (for dinner). I have only half an hour sometimes; on Thursday, Friday, and Saturday.'[34]

Dr Greenhow states that the average duration of life in the pottery districts of Stoke-on-Trent, and Wolstanton is extraordinarily short. Although in the district of Stoke, only 36.6% and in Wolstanton only 30.4% of the adult male population above 20 are employed in the potteries, among the men of that age in the first district more than half, in the second, nearly 2/5 of the whole deaths are the result of pulmonary diseases among the potters. Dr Boothroyd, a medical practitioner at Hanley, says:

> 'Each successive generation of potters is more dwarfed and less robust than the preceding one.'

In like manner another doctor, Mr M'Bean:

> 'Since he began to practice among the potters 25 years ago, he had observed a marked degeneration especially shown in diminution of stature and breadth.'

These statements are taken from the report of Dr Greenhow in 1860.[35]

From the report of the Commissioners in 1863, the following: Dr J. T. Arledge, senior physician of the North Staffordshire Infirmary, says:

> 'The potters as a class, both men and women, represent a degenerated population, both physically and morally. They are, as a rule, stunted in growth, ill-shaped, and frequently ill-formed in the chest; they become prematurely old, and are certainly short-lived; they are phlegmatic and bloodless, and exhibit their debility of constitution by obstinate attacks of dyspepsia, and disorders of the liver and kidneys, and by rheumatism. But, of all diseases they are especially prone to chest-disease, to pneumonia, phthisis, bronchitis, and asthma. One form would appear peculiar to them, and is known as potter's asthma, or potter's consumption. Scrofula attacking the glands, or bones, or other parts of the body, is a disease of two-thirds or more of the potters .... That the 'degenerescence' of the population of this district is not even greater than it is, is due to the constant recruiting from the adjacent country, and intermarriages with more healthy races.'[36]

Mr Charles Parsons, late house surgeon of the same institution, writes in a letter to Commissioner Longe, amongst other things:

> 'I can only speak from personal observation and not from statistical data, but I do not hesitate to assert that my indignation has been aroused again and again at the sight of poor children whose health has been sacrificed to gratify the avarice of either parents or employers.' He enumerates the causes of the diseases of the potters, and sums them up in the phrase, 'long hours.' The report of the Commission trusts that 'a manufacture which has assumed so prominent a place in the whole world, will not long be subject to the remark that its great success is accompanied with the physical deterioration, widespread bodily suffering, and early death of the workpeople ... by whose labour and skill such great results have been achieved.'[37]
>
> And all that holds of the potteries in England is true of those in Scotland.[38]

The manufacture of lucifer matches dates from 1833, from the discovery of the method of applying phosphorus to the match itself. Since 1845, this manufacture has rapidly developed in England, and has extended especially amongst the thickly populated parts of London as well as in Manchester, Birmingham, Liverpool, Bristol, Norwich, Newcastle and Glasgow. With it has spread the form of lockjaw, which a Vienna physician in 1845 discovered to be a disease peculiar to lucifer-matchmakers. Half the workers are children under thirteen, and young persons under eighteen. The manufacture is on account of its unhealthiness and unpleasantness in such bad odour that only the most miserable part of the labouring class, half-starved widows and so forth, deliver up their children to it, 'the ragged, half-starved, untaught children.'[39]

Of the witnesses that Commissioner White examined (1863), 270 were under 18, 50 under 10, 10 only 8, and 5 only 6 years old. A range of the working-day from 12 to 14 or 15 hours, night-labour, irregular meal-times, meals for the most part taken in the very workrooms that are pestilent with phosphorus. Dante would have found the worst horrors of his Inferno surpassed in this manufacture.

In the manufacture of paper-hangings the coarser sorts are printed by machine; the finer by hand (block-printing). The most active business months are from the beginning of October to the end of April. During this time the work goes on fast and furious without intermission from 6 a.m. to 10 p.m. or further into the night.

J. Leach deposes:

> 'Last winter six out of nineteen girls were away from ill-health at one time from over-work. I have to bawl at them to keep them awake.' W. Duffy: 'I have seen when the children could none of them keep their eyes open for the work; indeed, none of us could.' J. Lightbourne: 'Am 13 ... We worked last winter till 9 (evening), and the winter before till 10. I used to cry with sore feet every night last winter.' G. Apsden: 'That boy of mine when he was 7 years old I used to carry him on my back to and fro through the snow, and he used to have 16 hours a day ... I have often knelt down to feed him as he stood by the machine, for he could not leave it or stop.' Smith, the managing partner of a Manchester factory: 'We (he means his 'hands' who work for 'us') work on with no stoppage for meals, so that day's work of 10½ hours is finished by 4.30 p.m., and all after that is over-time.'[40] (Does this Mr Smith take no meals himself during 10½ hours?) 'We (this same Smith) seldom leave off working before 6 p.m. (he means leave off the consumption of 'our' labour-power machines), so that we (iterum Crispinus) are really working over-time the whole year round. For all these, children and adults alike (152 children and young persons and 140 adults), the average work for the last 18 months has been at the very least 7 days, 5 hours, or 78 1/2 hours a week. For the six weeks ending May 2nd this year (1862), the average was higher—8 days or 84 hours a week.'

Still this same Mr Smith, who is so extremely devoted to the *pluralis majestatis* [the Royal 'we,' i.e., speaking on behalf of his subjects], adds with a smile, "Machine-work is not great.' So the employers in the block-printing say: 'Hand labour is more healthy than machine work.' On the whole, manufacturers declare with indignation against the proposal 'to stop the machines at least during meal-times.'

> 'A clause,' says Mr Otley, manager of a wall-paper factory in the Borough, 'which allowed work between, say 6 a.m. and 9 p.m. in would suit us (!) very well, but the factory hours, 6 a.m. to 6 p.m., are not suitable. Our machine is always stopped for dinner. (What generosity!) There is no waste of paper and colour to speak of. But,' he adds sympathetically, 'I can understand the loss of time not being liked.'

The report of the Commission opines with naïveté that the fear of some 'leading firms' of losing time, *i.e.*, the time for appropriating the labour of others, and thence losing profit is not a sufficient reason for allowing children under 13, and young persons under 18, working 12 to 16 hours per day, to lose their dinner, nor for giving it to them as coal and water are supplied to the steam-engine, soap to wool, oil to the wheel—as merely auxiliary material to the instruments of labour, during the process of production itself.[41]

No branch of industry in England (we do not take into account the making of bread by machinery recently introduced) has preserved up to the present day a method of production so archaic, so—as we see from the poets of the Roman Empire—pre-christian, as baking. But capital, as was said earlier, is at first indifferent as to the technical character of the labour-process; it begins by taking it just as it finds it.

The incredible adulteration of bread, especially in London, was first revealed by the House of Commons Committee 'on the adulteration of articles of food' (1855-56), and Dr Hassall's work, 'Adulterations detected.'[42] The consequence of these revelations was the Act of August 6th, 1860, 'for preventing the adulteration of articles of food and drink,' an inoperative law, as it naturally shows the tenderest consideration for every Free-trader who determines by the buying or selling of adulterated commodities 'to turn an honest penny.'[43] The Committee itself formulated more or less naïvely its conviction that Free-trade meant essentially trade with adulterated, or as the English ingeniously put it, 'sophisticated' goods. In fact this kind of sophistry knows better than Protagoras how to make white black, and black white, and better than the Eleatics how to demonstrate *ad oculos* [before your own eyes] that everything is only appearance.[44]

At all events the Committee had directed the attention of the public to its 'daily bread,' and therefore to the baking trade. At the same time in public meetings and in petitions to Parliament rose the cry of the London journeymen bakers against their over-work, &c. The cry was so urgent that Mr H. S. Tremenheere, also a member of the Commission of 1863 several times mentioned, was appointed Royal Commissioner of Inquiry. His report,[45] together with the evidence given, roused not the heart of the public but its stomach. Englishmen, always well up in the Bible, knew well enough that man, unless by elective grace a capitalist, or landlord, or sinecurist, is commanded to eat his bread in the sweat of his brow, but they did not know that he had to eat daily in his bread a certain quantity of human perspiration mixed with the discharge of abscesses, cobwebs, dead black-beetles, and putrid German yeast, without counting alum, sand, and other agreeable mineral ingredients. Without any regard to his holiness, Free-trade, the free baking-trade was therefore placed under the supervision of the State inspectors (Close of the Parliamentary session of 1863), and by the same Act of Parliament, work from 9 in the evening to 5 in the morning was forbidden for journeymen bakers under 18. The last clause speaks volumes as to the over-work in this old-fashioned, homely line of business.

> 'The work of a London journeyman baker begins, as a rule, at about eleven at night. At that hour he 'makes the dough,'—a laborious process, which lasts from half an hour to three quarters of an hour, according to the size of the batch or the labour bestowed upon it. He then lies down upon the kneading-board, which is also the covering of the trough in which the dough is 'made'; and with a sack under him, and another rolled up as a pillow, he sleeps for about a couple of hours. He is then engaged in a rapid and continuous labour for about five hours—throwing out the dough, 'scaling it off,' moulding it, putting it into the oven, preparing and baking rolls and fancy bread, taking the batch bread out of the oven, and up into the shop, &c., &c. The temperature of a bakehouse ranges from about 75 to upwards of 90 degrees, and in the smaller bakehouses approximates usually to the higher rather than to the lower degree of heat. When the business of making the bread, rolls, &c., is over, that of its distribution begins, and a considerable proportion of the journeymen in the trade, after working hard in the manner described during the night, are upon their legs for many hours during the day, carrying baskets, or wheeling hand-carts, and sometimes again in the bakehouse, leaving off work at various hours between 1 and 6 p.m. according to the

season of the year, or the amount and nature of their master's business; while others are again engaged in the bakehouse in 'bringing out' more batches until late in the afternoon.[46] ... During what is called 'the London season,' the operatives belonging to the 'full-priced' bakers at the West End of the town, generally begin work at 11 p.m., and are engaged in making the bread, with one or two short (sometimes very short) intervals of rest, up to 8 o'clock the next morning. They are then engaged all day long, up to 4, 5, 6, and as late as 7 o'clock in the evening carrying out bread, or sometimes in the afternoon in the bakehouse again, assisting in the biscuit-baking. They may have, after they have done their work, sometimes five or six, sometimes only four or five hours' sleep before they begin again. On Fridays they always begin sooner, some about ten o'clock, and continue in some cases, at work, either in making or delivering the bread up to 8 p.m. on Saturday night, but more generally up to 4 or 5 o'clock, Sunday morning. On Sundays the men must attend twice or three times during the day for an hour or two to make preparations for the next day's bread.... The men employed by the underselling masters (who sell their bread under the 'full price,' and who, as already pointed out, comprise three-fourths of the London bakers) have not only to work on the average longer hours, but their work is almost entirely confined to the bakehouse. The underselling masters generally sell their bread... in the shop. If they send it out, which is not common, except as supplying chandlers' shops, they usually employ other hands for that purpose. It is not their practice to deliver bread from house to house. Towards the end of the week ... the men begin on Thursday night at 10 o'clock, and continue on with only slight intermission until late on Saturday evening.'[47]

Even the bourgeois intellect understands the position of the 'underselling' masters. 'The unpaid labour of the men was made the source whereby the competition was carried on.'[48] And the 'full-priced' baker denounces his underselling competitors to the Commission of Inquiry as thieves of foreign labour and adulterators.

'They only exist now by first defrauding the public, and next getting 18 hours' work out of their men for 12 hours' wages.'[49]

The adulteration of bread and the formation of a class of bakers that sells the bread below the full price, date from the beginning of the 18th century, from the time when the corporate character of the trade was lost, and the capitalist in the form of the miller or flour-factor, rises behind the nominal master baker.[50] Thus was laid the foundation of capitalistic production in this trade, of the unlimited extension of the working-day and of night-labour, although the latter only since 1824 gained a serious footing, even in London.[51]

After what has just been said, it will be understood that the Report of the Commission classes journeymen bakers among the short-lived labourers, who, having by good luck escaped the normal decimation of the children of the working-class, rarely reach the age of 42. Nevertheless, the baking trade is always overwhelmed with applicants. The sources of the supply of these labour-powers to London are Scotland, the western agricultural districts of England, and Germany.

In the years 1858-60, the journeymen bakers in Ireland organised at their own expense great meetings to agitate against night and Sunday work. The public—e.g., at the Dublin meeting in May, 1860—took their part with Irish warmth. As a result of this movement, day-labour alone was successfully established in Wexford, Kilkenny, Clonmel, Waterford, &c.

'In Limerick, where the grievances of the journeymen are demonstrated to be excessive, the movement has been defeated by the opposition of the master bakers, the miller bakers being the greatest opponents. The example of Limerick led to a retrogression in Ennis and Tipperary. In Cork, where the strongest possible demonstration of feeling took place, the masters, by exercising their power of turning the men out of

> employment, have defeated the movement. In Dublin, the master bakers have offered the most determined opposition to the movement, and by discountenancing as much as possible the journeymen promoting it, have succeeded in leading the men into acquiescence in Sunday work and night-work, contrary to the convictions of the men.'[52]

The Committee of the English Government, which Government, in Ireland, is armed to the teeth, and generally knows how to show it, remonstrates in mild, though funereal, tones with the implacable master bakers of Dublin, Limerick, Cork, &c.:

> 'The Committee believe that the hours of labour are limited by natural laws, which cannot be violated with impunity. That for master bakers to induce their workmen, by the fear of losing employment, to violate their religious convictions and their better feelings, to disobey the laws of the land, and to disregard public opinion (this all refers to Sunday labour), is calculated to provoke ill-feeling between workmen and masters, ... and affords an example dangerous to religion, morality, and social order.... The Committee believe that any constant work beyond 12 hours a-day encroaches on the domestic and private life of the working-man, and so leads to disastrous moral results, interfering with each man's home, and the discharge of his family duties as a son, a brother, a husband, a father. That work beyond 12 hours has a tendency to undermine the health of the workingman, and so leads to premature old age and death, to the great injury of families of working-men, thus deprived of the care and support of the head of the family when most required.'[53]

So far, we have dealt with Ireland. On the other side of the channel, in Scotland, the agricultural labourer, the ploughman, protests against his 13-14 hours' work in the most inclement climate, with 4 hours' additional work on Sunday (in this land of Sabbatarians!),[54] whilst, at the same time, three railway men are standing before a London coroner's jury—a guard, an engine-driver, a signalman. A tremendous railway accident has hurried hundreds of passengers into another world. The negligence of the employee is the cause of the misfortune. They declare with one voice before the jury that ten or twelve years before, their labour only lasted eight hours a-day. During the last five or six years it had been screwed up to 14, 18, and 20 hours, and under a specially severe pressure of holiday-makers, at times of excursion trains, it often lasted for 40 or 50 hours without a break. They were ordinary men, not Cyclops. At a certain point their labour-power failed. Torpor seized them. Their brain ceased to think, their eyes to see. The thoroughly 'respectable' British jurymen answered by a verdict that sent them to the next assizes on a charge of manslaughter, and, in a gentle 'rider' to their verdict, expressed the pious hope that the capitalistic magnates of the railways would, in future, be more extravagant in the purchase of a sufficient quantity of labour-power, and more 'abstemious,' more 'self-denying,' more 'thrifty,' in the draining of paid labour-power.[55]

From the motley crowd of labourers of all callings, ages, sexes, that press on us more busily than the souls of the slain on Ulysses, on whom—without referring to the Blue books under their arms—we see at a glance the mark of over-work, let us take two more figures whose striking contrast proves that before capital all men are alike—a milliner and a blacksmith.

In the last week of June, 1863, all the London daily papers published a paragraph with the 'sensational' heading, 'Death from simple over-work.' It dealt with the death of the milliner, Mary Anne Walkley, 20 years of age, employed in a highly-respectable dressmaking establishment, exploited by a lady with the pleasant name of Elise. The old, often-told story,[56] was once more recounted. This girl worked, on an average, 16½ hours, during the season often 30 hours, without a break, whilst her failing labour-power was revived by occasional supplies of sherry, port, or coffee. It was just now the height of the season. It was necessary to conjure up in the twinkling of an eye the gorgeous dresses for the noble ladies bidden to the ball in honour of the newly-imported Princess of Wales. Mary Anne Walkley had worked without intermission for 26½ hours, with 60 other girls, 30 in one room, that only afforded 1/3 of the cubic feet of air required for them. At night, they slept in pairs in one of the stifling holes into which the bedroom was divided by partitions of board.[57] And this was one of the best millinery establishments in London. Mary Anne Walkley fell ill on the Friday, died on Sunday, without, to the astonishment of Madame Elise, having previously completed the work in hand. The doctor, Mr Keys, called too late to the death-bed, duly bore witness before the coroner's jury that

> 'Mary Anne Walkley had died from long hours of work in an over-crowded work-room, and a too small and badly ventilated bedroom.'

In order to give the doctor a lesson in good manners, the coroner's jury thereupon brought in a verdict that

> 'the deceased had died of apoplexy, but there was reason to fear that her death had been accelerated by over-work in an over-crowded workroom, &c.'

'Our white slaves,' cried the *Morning Star*, the organ of the Free-traders, Cobden and Bright, 'our white slaves, who are toiled into the grave, for the most part silently pine and die.'[58]

> 'It is not in dressmakers' rooms that working to death is the order of the day, but in a thousand other places; in every place I had almost said, where 'a thriving business' has to be done.... We will take the blacksmith as a type. If the poets were true, there is no man so hearty, so merry, as the blacksmith; he rises early and strikes his sparks before the sun; he eats and drinks and sleeps as no other man. Working in moderation, he is, in fact, in one of the best of human positions, physically speaking. But we follow him into the city or town, and we see the stress of work on that strong man, and what then is his position in the death-rate of his country. In Marylebone, blacksmiths die at the rate of 31 per thousand per annum, or 11 above the mean of the male adults of the country in its entirety. The occupation, instinctive almost as a portion of human art, unobjectionable as a branch of human industry, is made by mere excess of work, the destroyer of the man. He can strike so many blows per day, walk so many steps, breathe so many breaths, produce so much work, and live an average, say of fifty years; he is made to strike so many more blows, to walk so many more steps, to breathe so many more breaths per day, and to increase altogether a fourth of his life. He meets the effort; the result is, that producing for a limited time a fourth more work, he dies at 37 for 50.'[59]

Section 4: *Day and Night Work. The Relay System*

Constant capital, the means of production, considered from the standpoint of the creation of surplus-value, only exist to absorb labour, and with every drop of labour a proportional quantity of surplus-labour. While they fail to do this, their mere existence causes a relative loss to the capitalist, for they represent during the time they lie fallow, a useless advance of capital. And this loss becomes positive and absolute as soon as the intermission of their employment necessitates additional outlay at the recommencement of work. The prolongation of the working-day beyond the limits of the natural day, into the night, only acts as a palliative. It quenches only in a slight degree the vampire thirst for the living blood of labour. To appropriate labour during all the 24 hours of the day is, therefore, the inherent tendency of capitalist production. But as it is physically impossible to exploit the same individual labour-power constantly during the night as well as the day, to overcome this physical hindrance, an alternation becomes necessary between the workpeople whose powers are exhausted by day, and those who are used up by night. This alternation may be effected in various ways; e.g., it may be so arranged that part of the workers are one week employed on day-work, the next week on night-work. It is well known that this relay system, this alternation of two sets of workers, held full sway in the full-blooded youth-time of the English cotton manufacture, and that at the present time it still flourishes, among others, in the cotton spinning of the Moscow district. This 24 hours' process of production exists to-day as a system in many of the branches of industry of Great Britain that are still 'free,' in the blast-furnaces, forges, plate-rolling mills, and other metallurgical establishments in England, Wales, and Scotland. The working-time here includes, besides the 24 hours of the 6 working-days, a great part also of the 24 hours of Sunday. The workers consist of men and women, adults and children of both sexes. The ages of the children and young persons run through all intermediate grades, from 8 (in some cases from 6) to 18.[60]

In some branches of industry, the girls and women work through the night together with the males.[61]

Placing on one side the generally injurious influence of night-labour,[62] the duration of the process of production, unbroken during the 24 hours, offers very welcome opportunities of exceeding the limits of the normal working-day, e.g., in the branches of industry already mentioned, which are of an exceedingly fatiguing nature; the official working-day means for each worker usually 12 hours by night or day. But the over-work beyond this amount is in many cases, to use the words of the English official report, 'truly fearful.'[63]

> 'It is impossible,' the report continues, 'for any mind to realise the amount of work described in the following passages as being performed by boys of from 9 to 12 years of age ... without coming irresistibly to the conclusion that such abuses of the power of parents and of employers can no longer be allowed to exist.'[64]
>
> 'The practice of boys working at all by day and night turns either in the usual course of things, or at pressing times, seems inevitably to open the door to their not unfrequently working unduly long hours. These hours are, indeed, in some cases, not only cruelly but even incredibly long for children. Amongst a number of boys it will, of course, not unfrequently happen that one or more are from some cause absent. When this happens, their place is made up by one or more boys, who work in the other turn. That this is a well understood system is plain ... from the answer of the manager of some large rolling-mills, who, when I asked him how the place of the boys absent from their turn was made up, 'I daresay, sir, you know that as well as I do,' and admitted the fact.'[65]
>
> 'At a rolling-mill where the proper hours were from 6 a.m. to 5½ p.m., a boy worked about four nights every week till 8½ p.m. at least ... and this for six months. Another, at 9 years old, sometimes made three 12-hour shifts running, and, when 10, has made two days and two nights running.' A third, 'now 10 ... worked from 6 a.m. till 12 p.m. three nights, and till 9 p.m. the other nights.' 'Another, now 13, ... worked from 6 p.m. till 12 noon next day, for a week together, and sometimes for three shifts together, e.g., from Monday morning till Tuesday night.' 'Another, now 12, has worked in an iron foundry at Stavely from 6 a.m. till 12 p.m. for a fortnight on end; could not do it any more.' 'George Allinsworth, age 9, came here as cellar-boy last Friday; next morning we had to begin at 3, so I stopped here all night. Live five miles off. Slept on the floor of the furnace, over head, with an apron under me, and a bit of a jacket over me. The two other days I have been here at 6 a.m. Aye! it *is* hot in here. Before I came here I was nearly a year at the same work at some works in the country. Began there, too, at 3 on Saturday morning—always did, but was very gain [near] home, and could sleep at home. Other days I began at 6 in the morning, and gi'en over at 6 or 7 in the evening,' &c.[66]

Let us now hear how capital itself regards this 24 hours' system. The extreme forms of the system, its abuse in the 'cruel and incredible' extension of the working-day are naturally passed over in silence. Capital only speaks of the system in its 'normal' form.

Messrs. Naylor & Vickers, steel manufacturers, who employ between 600 and 700 persons, among whom only 10 per cent are under 18, and of those, only 20 boys under 18 work in night sets, thus express themselves:

> 'The boys do not suffer from the heat. The temperature is probably from 86° to 90°.... At the forges and in the rolling mills the hands work night and day, in relays, but all the other parts of the work are day-work, *i.e.*, from 6 a.m. to 6 p.m. In the forge the hours are from 12 to 12. Some of the hands always work in the night, without any alternation of day and night work.... We do not find any difference in the health of those who work regularly by night and those who work by day, and probably people can sleep better if they have the same period of rest than if it is changed.... About 20 of the boys under the age of 18 work in the night sets.... We could not well do without lads under 18 working by night. The objection would be the increase in the cost of production.... Skilled hands and the heads in every department are difficult to get, but of lads we could get any number.... But from the small proportion of boys that we employ, the subject *(i.e.*, of restrictions on night-work) is of little importance or interest to us.'[67]

Mr J. Ellis, one of the firm of Messrs. John Brown & Co., steel and iron works, employing about 3,000 men and boys, part of whose operations, namely, iron and heavier steel work, goes on night and day by relays, states 'that in the heavier steel work one or two boys are employed to a score or two men.' Their concern employs upwards of 500 boys under 18, of whom about 1/3 or 170 are under the age of 13. With reference to the proposed alteration of the law, Mr Ellis says:

> 'I do not think it would be very objectionable to require that no person under the age of 18 should work more than 12 hours in the 24. But we do not think that any line could be drawn over the age of 12, at which boys could be dispensed with for night-work. But we would sooner be prevented from employing boys under the age of 13, or even so high as 14, at all, than not be allowed to employ boys that we do have at night. Those boys who work in the day sets must take their turn in the night sets also, because the men could not work in the night sets only; it would ruin their health.... We think, however, that night-work in alternate weeks is no harm.'

(Messrs. Naylor & Vickers, on the other hand, in conformity with the interest of their business, considered that periodically changed night-labour might possibly do more harm than continual night-labour.)

> We find the men who do it, as well as the others who do other work only by day.... Our objections to not allowing boys under 18 to work at night, would be on account of the increase of expense, but this is the only reason.'
>
> (What cynical naïveté!) 'We think that the increase would be more than the trade, with due regard to its being successfully carried out, could fairly bear. (What mealy-mouthed phraseology!) Labour is scarce here, and might fall short if there were such a regulation.' *(i.e.*, Ellis Brown & Co. might fall into the fatal perplexity of being obliged to pay labour-power its full value.)[68]

The 'Cyclops Steel and Iron Works,' of Messrs. Cammell & Co., are concocted on the same large scale as those of the above-mentioned John Brown & Co. The managing director had handed in his evidence to the Government Commissioner, Mr White, in writing. Later he found it convenient to suppress the Ms when it had been returned to him for revision. Mr White, however, has a good memory. He remembered quite clearly that for the Messrs. Cyclops the forbidding of the night-labour of children and young persons 'would be impossible, it would be tantamount to stopping their works,' and yet their business employs little more than 6% of boys under 18, and less than 1% under 13.[69]

On the same subject Mr E. F. Sanderson, of the firm of Sanderson, Bros., & Co., steel rolling-mills and forges, Attercliffe, says:

> 'Great difficulty would be caused by preventing boys under 18 from working at night. The chief would be the increase of cost from employing men instead of boys. I cannot say what this would be, but probably it would not be enough to enable the manufacturers to raise the price of steel, and consequently it would fall on them, as of course the men (what queer-headed folk!) would refuse to pay it.'

Mr Sanderson does not know how much he pays the children, but

> 'perhaps the younger boys get from 4s. to 5s. a week.... The boys' work is of a kind for which the strength of the boys is generally ('generally,' of course not always) quite sufficient, and consequently there would be no gain in the greater strength of the men to counterbalance the loss, or it would be only in the few cases in which the metal is heavy. The men would not like so well not to have boys under them, as men would be less obedient. Besides, boys must begin young to learn the trade. Leaving day-work alone open to boys would not answer this purpose.'

And why not? Why could not boys learn their handicraft in the day-time? Your reason?

> 'Owing to the men working days and nights in alternate weeks, the men would be separated half the time from their boys, and would lose half the profit which they make from them. The training which they give to an apprentice is considered as part of the return for the boys' labour, and thus enables the man to get it at a cheaper rate. Each man would want half of this profit.'

In other words, Messrs. Sanderson would have to pay part of the wages of the adult men out of their own pockets instead of by the night-work of the boys. Messrs. Sanderson's profit would thus fall to some extent, and this is the good Sandersonian reason why boys cannot learn their handicraft in the day.[70] In addition to this, it would throw night-labour on those who worked instead of the boys, which they would not be able to stand. The difficulties in fact would be so great that they would very likely lead to the giving up of night-work altogether, and 'as far as the work itself is concerned,' says E. F. Sanderson, 'this would suit as well, but —' But Messrs. Sanderson have something else to make besides steel. Steel-making is simply a pretext for surplus-value making. The smelting furnaces, rolling-mills, &c., the buildings, machinery, iron, coal, &c., have something more to do than transform themselves into steel. They are there to absorb surplus-labour, and naturally absorb more in 24 hours than in 12. In fact they give, by grace of God and law, the Sandersons a cheque on the working-time of a certain number of hands for all the 24 hours of the day, and they lose their character as capital, are therefore a pure loss for the Sandersons, as soon as their function of absorbing labour is interrupted.

> 'But then there would be the loss from so much expensive machinery, lying idle half the time, and to get through the amount of work which we are able to do on the present system, we should have to double our premises and plant, which would double the outlay.'

But why should these Sandersons pretend to a privilege not enjoyed by the other capitalists who only work during the day, and whose buildings, machinery, raw material, therefore lie 'idle' during the night? E. F. Sanderson answers in the name of all the Sandersons:

> 'It is true that there is this loss from machinery lying idle in those manufactories in which work only goes on by day. But the use of furnaces would involve a further loss in our case. If they were kept up there would be a waste of fuel (instead of, as now, a waste of the living substance of the workers), and if they were not, there would be loss

of time in laying the fires and getting the heat up (whilst the loss of sleeping time, even to children of 8 is a gain of working-time for the Sanderson tribe), and the furnaces themselves would suffer from the changes of temperature.' (Whilst those same furnaces suffer nothing from the day and night change of labour.)[71]

Section 5: *The Struggle for a Normal Working-Day Compulsory Laws for the Extension of the Working-Day from the Middle of the 14th to the End of the 17th Century*

'What is a working-day? What is the length of time during which capital may consume the labour-power whose daily value it buys? How far may the working-day be extended beyond the working-time necessary for the reproduction of labour-power itself?' It has been seen that to these questions capital replies: the working-day contains the full 24 hours, with the deduction of the few hours of repose without which labour-power absolutely refuses its services again. Hence, it is self-evident that the labourer is nothing else, his whole life through, than labour-power, that therefore all his disposable time is by nature and law labour-time, to be devoted to the self-expansion of capital. Time for education, for intellectual development, for the fulfilling of social functions and for social intercourse, for the free-play of his bodily and mental activity, even the rest time of Sunday (and that in a country of Sabbatarians!)[72]—moonshine! But in its blind unrestrainable passion, its were-wolf hunger for surplus-labour, capital oversteps not only the moral, but even the merely physical maximum bounds of the working-day. It usurps the time for growth, development, and healthy maintenance of the body. It steals the time required for the consumption of fresh air and sunlight. It higgles over a meal-time, incorporating it where possible with the process of production itself, so that food is given to the labourer as to a mere means of production, as coal is supplied to the boiler, grease and oil to the machinery. It reduces the sound sleep needed for the restoration, reparation, refreshment of the bodily powers to just so many hours of torpor as the revival of an organism, absolutely exhausted, renders essential. It is not the normal maintenance of the labour-power which is to determine the limits of the working-day; it is the greatest possible daily expenditure of labour-power, no matter how diseased, compulsory, and painful it may be, which is to determine the limits of the labourers' period of repose. Capital cares nothing for the length of life of labour-power. All that concerns it is simply and solely the maximum of labour-power, that can be rendered fluent in a working-day. It attains this end by shortening the extent of the labourer's life, as a greedy farmer snatches increased produce from the soil by robbing it of its fertility.

The capitalistic mode of production (essentially the production of surplus-value, the absorption of surplus-labour), produces thus, with the extension of the working-day, not only the deterioration of human labour-power by robbing it of its normal, moral and physical, conditions of development and function. It produces also the premature exhaustion and death of this labour-power itself.[73] It extends the labourer's time of production during a given period by shortening his actual life-time.

But the value of the labour-power includes the value of the commodities necessary for the reproduction of the worker, or for the keeping up of the working-class. If then the unnatural extension of the working-day, that capital necessarily strives after in its unmeasured passion for self-expansion, shortens the length of life of the individual labourer, and therefore the duration of his labour-power, the forces used up have to be replaced at a more rapid rate and the sum of the expenses for the reproduction of labour-power will be greater; just as in a machine the part of its value to be reproduced every day is greater the more rapidly the machine is worn out. It would seem therefore that the interest of capital itself points in the direction of a normal working-day.

The slave-owner buys his labourer as he buys his horse. If he loses his slave, he loses capital that can only be restored by new outlay in the slave-mart.

> But 'the rice-grounds of Georgia, or the swamps of the Mississippi may be fatally injurious to the human constitution; but the waste of human life which the cultivation of these districts necessitates, is not so great that it cannot be repaired from the teeming preserves of Virginia and Kentucky. Considerations of economy, moreover, which, under a natural system, afford some security for humane treatment by identifying the master's interest with the slave's preservation, when once trading in slaves is practiced, become reasons for racking to the uttermost the toil of the slave; for, when his place can at once be supplied from foreign preserves, the duration of his life becomes a matter of less moment than its productiveness while it lasts. It is accordingly a maxim of slave management, in slave-importing countries, that the most effective economy is that which takes out of the human chattel in the shortest space of time the utmost amount of exertion it is capable of putting forth. It is in tropical culture, where annual profits often equal the whole capital of plantations, that negro life is most recklessly sacrificed. It is the agriculture of the West Indies, which has been for centuries prolific of fabulous wealth, that has engulfed millions of the African race. It is in Cuba, at this day, whose revenues are reckoned by millions, and whose planters are princes, that we see in the servile class, the coarsest fare, the most exhausting and unremitting toil, and even the absolute destruction of a portion of its numbers every year.'[74]

Mutato nomine de te fabula narratur [It is of you that the story is told—Horace]. For slave-trade read labour-market, for Kentucky and Virginia, Ireland and the agricultural districts of England, Scotland, and Wales, for Africa, Germany. We heard how over-work thinned the ranks of the bakers in London. Nevertheless, the London labour-market is always over-stocked with German and other candidates for death in the bakeries. Pottery, as we saw, is one of the shortest-lived industries. Is there any want therefore of potters? Josiah Wedgwood, the inventor of modern pottery, himself originally a common workman, said in 1785, before the House of Commons that the whole trade employed from 15,000 to 20,000 people.[75] In the year 1861, the population alone of the town centres of this industry in Great Britain numbered 101,302.

> 'The cotton trade has existed for ninety years.... It has existed for three generations of the English race, and I believe I may safely say that during that period it has destroyed nine generations of factory operatives.'[76]

No doubt in certain epochs of feverish activity the labour-market shows significant gaps. In 1834, *e.g.* But then the manufacturers proposed to the Poor Law Commissioners that they should send the 'surplus-population' of the agricultural districts to the north, with the explanation 'that the manufacturers would absorb and use it up.'[77]

> Agents were appointed with the consent of the Poor Law Commissioners. ... An office was set up in Manchester, to which lists were sent of those work people in the agricultural districts wanting employment, and their names were registered in books. The manufacturers attended at these offices, and selected such persons as they chose; when they had selected such persons as their 'wants required', they gave instructions to have them forwarded to Manchester, and they were sent, ticketed like bales of goods, by canals, or with carriers, others tramping on the road, and many of them were found on the way lost and half-starved. This system had grown up unto a regular trade. This House will hardly believe it, but I tell them, that this traffic in human flesh was as well kept up, they were in effect as regularly sold to these [Manchester] manufacturers as slaves are sold to the cotton-grower in the United States.... In 1860, 'the cotton trade was at its zenith.' ... The manufacturers again found that they were short of hands.... They applied to the 'flesh agents, as they are called. Those agents sent to the southern downs of England, to the pastures of Dorsetshire, to the glades of Devonshire, to the

people tending kine in Wiltshire, but they sought in vain. The surplus-population was 'absorbed.'

The *Bury Guardian* said, on the completion of the French treaty, that '10,000 additional hands could be absorbed by Lancashire, and that 30,000 or 40,000 will be needed.' After the 'flesh agents and sub-agents' had in vain sought through the agricultural districts,

> 'a deputation came up to London, and waited on the right hon. gentleman [Mr Villiers, President of the Poor Law Board] with a view of obtaining poor children from certain union houses for the mills of Lancashire.'[78]

What experience shows to the capitalist generally is a constant excess of population, i.e., an excess in relation to the momentary requirements of surplus-labour-absorbing capital, although this excess is made up of generations of human beings stunted, short-lived, swiftly replacing each other, plucked, so to say, before maturity.[79] And, indeed, experience shows to the intelligent observer with what swiftness and grip the capitalist mode of production, dating, historically speaking, only from yesterday, has seized the vital power of the people by the very root—shows how the degeneration of the industrial population is only retarded by the constant absorption of primitive and physically uncorrupted elements from the country—shows how even the country labourers, in spite of fresh air and the principle of natural selection, that works so powerfully amongst them, and only permits the survival of the strongest, are already beginning to die off.[80] Capital that has such good reasons for denying the sufferings of the legions of workers that surround it, is in practice moved as much and as little by the sight of the coming degradation and final depopulation of the human race, as by the probable fall of the earth into the sun. In every stockjobbing swindle every one knows that some time or other the crash must come, but every one hopes that it may fall on the head of his neighbour, after he himself has caught the shower of gold and placed it in safety. *Après moi le déluge! [After me, the flood] is* the watchword of every capitalist and of every capitalist nation. Hence Capital is reckless of the health or length of life of the labourer, unless under compulsion from society.[81] To the out-cry as to the physical and mental degradation, the premature death, the torture of over-work, it answers: Ought these to trouble us since they increase our profits? But looking at things as a whole, all this does not, indeed, depend on the good or ill will of the individual capitalist. Free competition brings out the inherent laws of capitalist production, in the shape of external coercive laws having power over every individual capitalist.[82]

The establishment of a normal working-day is the result of centuries of struggle between capitalist and labourer. The history of this struggle shows two opposed tendencies. Compare, e.g., the English factory legislation of our time with the English labour Statutes from the 14th century to well into the middle of the 18th.[83] Whilst the modern Factory Acts compulsorily shortened the working-day, the earlier statutes tried to lengthen it by compulsion. Of course the pretensions of capital in embryo—when, beginning to grow, it secures the right of absorbing a *quantum sufficit* [sufficient quantity] of surplus-labour, not merely by the force of economic relations, but by the help of the State—appear very modest when put face to face with the concessions that, growling and struggling, it has to make in its adult condition. It takes centuries ere the 'free' labourer, thanks to the development of capitalistic production, agrees, *i.e., is* compelled by social conditions, to sell the whole of his active life. his very capacity for work, for the price of the necessaries of life, his birth-right for a mess of pottage. Hence, it is natural that the lengthening of the working-day, which capital, from the middle of the 14th to the end of the 17th century, tries to impose by State-measures on adult labourers, approximately coincides with the shortening of the working-day which, in the second half of the 19th century, has here and there been effected by the State to prevent the coining of children's blood into capital. That which to-day, *e.g.*, in the

State of Massachusetts, until recently the freest State of the North-American Republic, has been proclaimed as the statutory limit of the labour of children under 12, was in England, even in the middle of the 17th century, the normal working-day of able-bodied artisans, robust labourers, athletic blacksmiths.[84]

The first 'Statute of Labourers' (23 Edward III., 1349) found its immediate pretext (not its cause, for legislation of this kind lasts centuries after the pretext for it has disappeared) in the great plague that decimated the people, so that, as a Tory writer says, 'The difficulty of getting men to work on reasonable terms *(i.e.*, at a price that left their employers a reasonable quantity of surplus-labour) grew to such a height as to be quite intolerable.'[85] Reasonable wages were, therefore, fixed by law as well as the limits of the working-day. The latter point, the only one that here interests us, is repeated in the Statute of 1496 (Henry VII.). The working-day for all artificers and field labourers from March to September ought, according to this statute (which, however, could not be enforced), to last from 5 in the morning to between 7 and 8 in the evening. But the meal-times consist of 1 hour for breakfast, 1½ hours for dinner, and ½ an hour for 'noon-meate,' i.e., exactly twice as much as under the factory acts now in force.[86] In winter, work was to last from 5 in the morning until dark, with the same intervals. A statute of Elizabeth of 1562 leaves the length of the working-day for all labourers 'hired for daily or weekly wage' untouched, but aims at limiting the intervals to 2½ hours in the summer, or to 2 in the winter. Dinner is only to last 1 hour, and the 'afternoon-sleep of half an hour' is only allowed between the middle of May and the middle of August. For every hour of absence 1d. is to be subtracted from the wage. In practice, however, the conditions were much more favourable to the labourers than in the statute-book. William Petty, the father of Political Economy, and to some extent the founder of Statistics, says in a work that he published in the last third of the 17th century:

> 'Labouring-men (then meaning field-labourers) work 10 hours per diem, and make 20 meals per week, viz., 3 a day for working-days, and 2 on Sundays; whereby it is plain, that if they could fast on Friday nights, and dine in one hour and an half, whereas they take two, from eleven to one; thereby thus working 1/20 more, and spending 1/20 less, the above-mentioned (tax) might be raised.'[87]

Was not Dr Andrew Ure right in crying down the 12 hours' bill of 1833 as a retrogression to the times of the dark ages? It is true these regulations contained in the statute mentioned by Petty, apply also to apprentices. But the condition of child-labour, even at the end of the 17th century, is seen from the following complaint:

> 'Tis not their practice (in Germany) as with us in this kingdom, to bind an apprentice for seven years; three or four is their common standard: and the reason is, because they are educated from their cradle to something of employment, which renders them the more apt and docile, and consequently the more capable of attaining to a ripeness and quicker proficiency in business. Whereas our youth, here in England, being bred to nothing before they come to be apprentices, make a very slow progress and require much longer time wherein to reach the perfection of accomplished artists.'[88]

Still, during the greater part of the 18th century, up to the epoch of Modern Industry and machinism, capital in England had not succeeded in seizing for itself, by the payment of the weekly value of labour-power, the whole week of the labourer, with the exception, however, of the agricultural labourers. The fact that they could live for a whole week on the wage of four days, did not appear to the labourers a sufficient reason that they should work the other two days for the capitalist. One party of English economists, in the interest of capital, denounces this obstinacy in the most violent manner, another party defends the labourers. Let us listen, *e.g., to* the contest between Postlethwayt whose Dictionary of Trade then had the same reputation as the kindred works of MacCulloch and MacGregor to-day, and the author (already quoted) of the 'Essay on Trade and Commerce.'[89]

Postlethwayt says among other things:

> 'We cannot put an end to those few observations, without noticing that trite remark in the mouth of too many; that if the industrious poor can obtain enough to maintain themselves in five days, they will not work the whole six. Whence they infer the necessity of even the necessaries of life being made dear by taxes, or any other means, to compel the working artisan and manufacturer to labour the whole six days in the week, without ceasing. I must beg leave to differ in sentiment from those great politicians, who contend for the perpetual slavery of the working people of this kingdom; they forget the vulgar adage, all work and no play. Have not the English boasted of the ingenuity and dexterity of her working artists and manufacturers which have heretofore given credit and reputation to British wares in general? What has this been owing to? To nothing more probably than the relaxation of the working people in their own way. Were they obliged to toil the year round, the whole six days in the week, in a repetition of the same work, might it not blunt their ingenuity, and render them stupid instead of alert and dexterous; and might not our workmen lose their reputation instead of maintaining it by such eternal slavery? ... And what sort of workmanship could we expect from such hard-driven animals? ... Many of them will execute as much work in four days as a Frenchman will in five or six. But if Englishmen are to be eternal drudges, 'tis to be feared they will degenerate below the Frenchmen. As our people are famed for bravery in war, do we not say that it is owing to good English roast beef and pudding in their bellies, as well as their constitutional spirit of liberty? And why may not the superior ingenuity and dexterity of, our artists and manufacturers, be owing to that freedom and liberty to direct themselves in their own way, and I hope we shall never have them deprived of such privileges and that good living from whence their ingenuity no less than their courage may proceed.'[90]

Thereupon the author of the 'Essay on Trade and Commerce' replies:

> 'If the making of every seventh day an holiday is supposed to be of divine institution, as it implies the appropriating the other six days to labour' (he means capital as we shall soon see) 'surely it will not be thought cruel to enforce it .... That mankind in general, are naturally inclined to ease and indolence, we fatally experience to be true, from the conduct of our manufacturing populace, who do not labour, upon an average, above four days in a week, unless provisions happen to be very dear.... Put all the necessaries of the poor under one denomination; for instance, call them all wheat, or suppose that ... the bushel of wheat shall cost five shillings and that he (a manufacturer) earns a shilling by his labour, he then would be obliged to work five days only in a week. If the bushel of wheat should cost but four shillings, he would be obliged to work but four days; but as wages in this kingdom are much higher in proportion to the price of necessaries ... the manufacturer, who labours four days, has a surplus of money to live idle with the rest of the week . ... I hope I have said enough to make it appear that the moderate labour of six days in a week is no slavery. Our labouring people do this, and to all appearance are the happiest of all our labouring poor,[91] but the Dutch do this in manufactures, and appear to be a very happy people. The French do so, when holidays do not intervene.[92] But our populace have adopted a notion, that as Englishmen they enjoy a birthright privilege of being more free and independent than in any country in Europe. Now this idea, as far as it may affect the bravery of our troops, may be of some use; but the less the manufacturing poor have of it, certainly the better for themselves and for the State. The labouring people should never) think themselves independent of

> their superiors.... It is extremely dangerous to encourage mobs in a commercial state like ours, where, perhaps, seven parts out of eight of the whole, are people with little or no property. The cure will not be perfect, till our manufacturing poor are contented to labour six days for the same sum which they now earn in four days.'[93]

To this end, and for 'extirpating idleness debauchery and excess,' promoting a spirit of industry, 'lowering the price of labour in our manufactories, and easing the lands of the heavy burden of poor's rates,' our 'faithful Eckart' of capital proposes this approved device: to shut up such labourers as become dependent on public support, in a word, paupers, in 'an *ideal workhouse*.' Such ideal workhouse must be made a 'House of Terror,' and not an asylum for the poor, 'where they are to be plentifully fed, warmly and decently clothed, and where they do but little work.'[94] In this 'House of Terror,' this 'ideal workhouse, the poor shall work 14 hours in a day, allowing proper time for meals, in such manner that there shall remain 12 hours of neat-labour.'[95]

Twelve working-hours daily in the Ideal Workhouse, in the 'House of Terror' of 1770! 63 years later, in 1833, when the English Parliament reduced the working-day for children of 13 to 18, in four branches of industry to 12 full hours, the judgment day of English Industry had dawned! In 1852, when Louis Bonaparte sought to secure his position with the bourgeoisie by tampering with the legal working-day, the French working people cried out with one voice 'the law that limits the working-day to 12 hours is the one good that has remained to us of the legislation of the Republic!'[96] At Zürich the work of children over 10, is limited to 12 hours; in Aargau in 1862, the work of children between 13 and 16, was reduced from 12½ to 12 hours; in Austria in 1860, for children between 14 and 16, the same reduction was made.[97] 'What a progress,' since 1770! Macaulay would shout with exultation!

The 'House of Terror' for paupers of which the capitalistic soul of 1770 only dreamed, was realised a few years later in the shape of a gigantic 'Workhouse' for the industrial worker himself. It is called the Factory. And the ideal this time fades before the reality.

Section 6: *The Struggle for the Normal Working-Day. Compulsory Limitation by Law of the Working-Time. The English Factory Acts, 1833 to 1864*

After capital had taken centuries in extending the working-day to its normal maximum limit, and then beyond this to the limit of the natural day of 12 hours,[98] there followed on the birth of machinism and modern industry in the last third of the 18th century, a violent encroachment like that of an avalanche in its intensity and extent. All bounds of morals and nature, age and sex, day and night, were broken down. Even the ideas of day and night, of rustic simplicity in the old statutes, became so confused that an English judge, as late as 1860, needed a quite Talmudic sagacity to explain 'judicially' what was day and what was night.[99] Capital celebrated its orgies.

As soon as the working-class, stunned at first by the noise and turmoil of the new system of production, recovered, in some measure, its senses, its resistance began, and first in the native land of machinism, in England. For 30 years, however, the concessions conquered by the workpeople were purely nominal. Parliament passed 5 labour Laws between 1802 and 1833, but was shrewd enough not to vote a penny for their carrying out, for the requisite officials, &c.[100]

> They remained a dead letter. 'The fact is, that prior to the Act of 1833, young persons and children were worked all night, all day, or both *ad libitum*.'[101]

A normal working-day for modern industry only dates from the Factory Act of 1833, which included cotton, wool, flax, and silk factories. Nothing is more characteristic of the spirit of capital than the history of the English Factory Acts from 1833 to 1864.

The Act of 1833 declares the ordinary factory working-day to be from half-past five in the morning to half-past eight in the evening and within these limits, a period of 15 hours, it is lawful to employ young persons *(i.e.,* persons between 13 and 18 years of age), at any time of the day, provided no one individual young person should work more than 12 hours in any one day, except in certain cases especially provided for. The 6th section of the Act provided. 'That there shall be allowed in the course of every day not less than one and a half hours for meals to every such person restricted as hereinbefore provided.' The employment of children under 9, with exceptions mentioned later was forbidden; the work of children between 9 and 13 was limited to 8 hours a day, night-work, *i.e.*, according to this Act, work between 8:30 p.m. and 5:30 a.m., was forbidden for all persons between 9 and 18.

The law-makers were so far from wishing to trench on the freedom of capital to exploit adult labour-power, or, as they called it, 'the freedom of labour,' that they created a special system in order to prevent the Factory Acts from having a consequence so outrageous.

> 'The great evil of the factory system as at present conducted,' says the first report of the Central Board of the Commission of June 28th 1833, 'has appeared to us to be that it entails the necessity of continuing the labour of children to the utmost length of that of the adults. The only remedy for this evil, short of the limitation of the labour of adults which would, in our opinion, create an evil greater than that which is sought to be remedied, appears to be the plan of working double sets of children.'

... Under the name of System of Relays, this 'plan' was therefore carried out, so that, e.g., from 5.30 a.m. until 1.30 in the afternoon, one set of children between 9 and 13, and from 1.30 p.m. to 8.30 in the evening another set were 'put to,' &c.

In order to reward the manufacturers for having, in the most barefaced way, ignored all the Acts as to children's labour passed during the last twenty-two years, the pill was yet further gilded for them. Parliament decreed that after March 1st, 1834, no child under 11, after March 1st 1835, no child under 12, and after March 1st, 1836, no child under 13 was to work more than eight hours in a factory. This 'liberalism,' so full of consideration for 'capital,' was the more noteworthy as. Dr Farre, Sir A. Carlisle, Sir B. Brodie, Sir C. Bell, Mr Guthrie, &c., in a word, the most distinguished physicians and surgeons in London, had declared in their evidence before the House of Commons, that there was danger in delay. Dr Farre expressed himself still more coarsely.

> 'Legislation is necessary for the prevention of death, in any form in which it can be prematurely inflicted, and certainly this (i.e., the factory method) must be viewed as a most cruel mode of inflicting it.'

That same 'reformed' Parliament, which in its delicate consideration for the manufacturers, condemned children under 13, for years to come, to 72 hours of work per week in the Factory Hell, on the other hand, in the Emancipation Act, which also administered freedom drop by drop, forbade the planters, from the outset, to work any negro slave more than 45 hours a week.

But, in no wise conciliated, capital now began a noisy agitation that went on for several years. It turned chiefly on the age of those who, under the name of children, were limited to 8 hours' work, and were subject to a certain amount of compulsory education. According to capitalistic anthropology, the age of childhood ended at 10, or at the outside, at 11. The more nearly the time approached for the coming into full force of the Factory Act, the fatal year 1836, the more wildly raged the mob of manufacturers. They managed, in fact, to intimidate the government to such an extent that in 1835 it proposed to lower the limit of the age of childhood from 13 to 12. In the meantime, the pressure from without grew more threatening. Courage failed the House of Commons. It refused to throw children of 13 under the Juggernaut Car of capital for more than 8 hours a day, and the Act of 1833 came into full operation. It remained unaltered until June, 1844.

In the ten years during which it regulated factory work, first in part, and then entirely, the official reports of the factory inspectors teem with complaints as to the impossibility of putting the Act into force. As the law of 1833 left it optional with the lords of capital during the 15 hours, from 5.30 a.m. to 8.30 p.m., to make every 'young person,' and 'every child' begin, break off, resume, or end his 12 or 8 hours at any moment they liked; and also permitted them to assign to different persons, different times for meals, these gentlemen soon discovered a new 'system of relays,' by which the labour-horses were not changed at fixed stations, but were constantly re-harnessed at changing stations. We do not pause longer on the beauty of this system, as we shall have to return to it later. But this much is clear at the first glance: that this system annulled the whole Factory Act, not only in the spirit, but in the letter. How could factory inspectors, with this complex bookkeeping in respect to each individual child or young person, enforce the legally determined work-time and the granting of the legal mealtimes? In a great many of the factories, the old brutalities soon blossomed out again unpunished. In an interview with the Home Secretary (1844), the factory inspectors demonstrated the impossibility of any control under the newly invented relay system.[102] In the meantime, however, circumstances had greatly changed. The factory hands, especially since 1838, had made the Ten Hours' Bill their economic, as they had made the Charter their political, election-cry. Some of the manufacturers, even, who had managed their factories in conformity with the Act of 1833, overwhelmed Parliament with memorials on the immoral competition of their false brethren whom greater impudence, or more fortunate local circumstances, enabled to break the law. Moreover, however much the individual manufacturer might give the rein to his old lust for gain, the spokesmen and political leaders of the manufacturing class ordered a change of front and of speech towards the workpeople. They had entered upon the contest for the repeal of the Corn Laws, and needed the workers to help them to victory. They promised therefore, not only a double-sized loaf of bread, but the enactment of the Ten Hours' Bill in the Free-trade millennium.[103] Thus they still less dared to oppose a measure intended only to make the law of 1833 a reality. Threatened in their holiest interest, the rent of land, the Tories thundered with philanthropic indignation against the 'nefarious practices'[104] of their foes.

This was the origin of the additional Factory Act of June 7th, 1844. It came into effect on September 10th, 1844. It places under protection a new category of workers, viz., the women over 18. They were placed in every respect on the same footing as the young persons, their work time limited to twelve hours, their night-labour forbidden, &c. For the first time, legislation saw itself compelled to control directly and officially the labour of adults. In the Factory Report of 1844-1845, it is said with irony:

> 'No instances have come to my knowledge of adult women having expressed any regret at their *rights* being thus far interfered with.'[105] The working-time of children under 13 was reduced to 6½, and in certain circumstances to 7 hours a-day.[106]

To get rid of the abuses of the 'spurious relay system,' the law established besides others the following important regulations: —

> 'That the hours of work of children and young persons shall be reckoned from the time when any child or young person shall begin to work in the morning.'

So that if A, *e.g.*, begins work at 8 in the morning, and B at 10, B's work-day must nevertheless end at the same hour as A's. 'The time shall be regulated by a public clock,' for example, the nearest railway clock, by which the factory clock is to be set. The occupier is to hang up a 'legible' printed notice stating the hours for the beginning and ending of work and the times allowed for the several meals. Children beginning work before 12 noon may not be again employed after 1 p.m. The afternoon shift must therefore consist of other children than those employed in the morning. Of the hour and a half for meal-times, 'one hour thereof at the least shall be given before three of the clock in the afternoon ... and at the same period of the day. No child or young person shall be employed more than five hours before I p.m. without an interval for meal-time of at least 30 minutes. No child or young person [or female] shall be employed or allowed to remain in any room in which any manufacturing process is then [*i.e.*, at mealtimes] carried on,' &c.

It has been seen that these minutiae, which, with military uniformity, regulate by stroke of the clock the times, limits, pauses of the work were not at all the products of Parliamentary fancy. They developed gradually out of circumstances as natural laws of the modern mode of production. Their formulation, official recognition, and proclamation by the State, were the result of a long struggle of classes. One of their first consequences was that in practice the working-day of the adult males in factories became subject to the same limitations, since in most processes of production the co-operation of the children. young persons, and women is indispensable. On the whole, therefore, during the period from 1844 to 1847, the 12 hours' working-day became general and uniform in all branches of industry under the Factory Act.

The manufacturers, however, did not allow this 'progress' without a compensating 'retrogression.' At their instigation, the House of Commons reduced the minimum age for exploitable children from 9 to 8, in order to assure that additional supply of factory children which is due to capitalists, according to divine and human law.[107]

The years 1846-47 are epoch-making in the economic history of England. The Repeal of the Corn Laws, and of the duties on cotton and other raw material; Free-trade proclaimed as the guiding star of legislation; in a word, the arrival of the millennium. On the other hand, in the same years, the Chartist movement and the 10 hours' agitation reached their highest point. They found allies in the Tories panting for revenge. Despite the fanatical opposition of the army of perjured Free-traders, with Bright and Cobden at their head, the Ten Hours' Bill, struggled for so long, went through Parliament.

The new Factory Act of June 8th, 1847, enacted that on July 1st, 1847, there should be a preliminary shortening of the working-day for 'young persons' (from 13 to 18), and all females to 11 hours, but that on May 1st, 1848, there should be a definite limitation of the working-day to 10 hours. In other respects, the Act only amended and completed the Acts of 1833 and 1844.

Capital now entered upon a preliminary campaign in order to hinder the Act from coming into full force on May 1st, 1848. And the workers themselves, under the presence that they had been taught by experience, were to help in the destruction of their own work. The moment was cleverly chosen.

'It must be remembered, too, that there has been more than two years of great suffering (in consequence of the terrible crisis of 1846-47) among the factory operatives, from many mills having worked short time, and many being altogether closed. A considerable number of the operatives must therefore be in very narrow circumstances many, it is to be feared, in debt; so that it might fairly have been presumed that at the present time they would prefer working the longer time, in order to make up for past losses, perhaps to pay off debts, or get their furniture out of pawn, or replace that sold, or to get a new supply of clothes for themselves and their families.'[108]

The manufacturers tried to aggravate the natural effect of these circumstances by a general reduction of wages by 10%. This was done so to say, to celebrate the inauguration of the new Free-trade era. Then followed a further reduction of 8 1/3% as soon as the working-day was shortened to 11, and a reduction of double that amount as soon as it was finally shortened to 10 hours. Wherever, therefore, circumstances allowed it, a reduction of wages of at least 25% took place.[109] Under such favourably prepared conditions the agitation among the factory workers for the repeal of the Act of 1847 was begun. Neither lies, bribery, nor threats were spared in this attempt. But all was in vain. Concerning the half-dozen petitions in which workpeople were made to complain of 'their oppression by the Act,' the petitioners themselves declared under oral examination, that their signatures had been extorted from them. 'They felt themselves oppressed, but not exactly by the Factory Act.'[110] But if the manufacturers did not succeed in making the workpeople speak as they wished, they themselves shrieked all the louder in press and Parliament in the name of the workpeople. They denounced the Factory Inspectors as a kind of revolutionary commissioners like those of the French National Convention ruthlessly sacrificing the unhappy factory workers to their humanitarian crotchet. This manoeuvre also failed. Factory Inspector Leonard Horner conducted in his own person, and through his sub-inspectors, many examinations of witnesses in the factories of Lancashire. About 70% of the workpeople examined declared in favour of 10 hours, a much smaller percentage in favour of 11, and an altogether insignificant minority for the old 12 hours.[111]

Another 'friendly' dodge was to make the adult males work 12 to 15 hours, and then to blazon abroad this fact as the best proof of what the proletariat desired in its heart of hearts. But the 'ruthless' Factory Inspector Leonard Horner was again to the fore. The majority of the 'over-times' declared:

> 'They would much prefer working ten hours for less wages, but that they had no choice; that so many were out of employment (so many spinners getting very low wages by having to work as piecers, being unable to do better), that if they refused to work the longer time, others would immediately get their places, so that it was a question with them of agreeing to work the longer time, or of being thrown out of employment altogether.'[112]

The preliminary campaign of capital thus came to grief, and the Ten Hours' Act came into force May 1st, 1848. But meanwhile the fiasco of the Chartist party whose leaders were imprisoned, and whose organisation was dismembered, had shaken the confidence of the English working-class in its own strength. Soon after this the June insurrection in Paris and its bloody suppression united, in England as on the Continent, all fractions of the ruling classes, landlords and capitalists, stock-exchange wolves and shop-keepers, Protectionists and Freetraders, government and opposition, priests and freethinkers, young whores and old nuns, under the common cry for the salvation of Property, Religion, the Family and Society. The working-class was everywhere proclaimed, placed under a ban, under a virtual law of suspects. The manufacturers had no need any longer to restrain themselves. They broke out in open revolt not only against the Ten Hours' Act, but against the whole of the legislation that since 1833 had aimed at restricting in some measure the 'free' exploitation of labour-power. It was a pro-slavery rebellion in miniature, carried on for over two years with a cynical recklessness, a terrorist energy all the cheaper because the rebel capitalist risked nothing except the skin of his 'hands.'

To understand that which follows we must remember that the Factory Acts of 1833, 1844, and 1847 were all three in force so far as the one did not amend the other: that not one of these limited the working-day of the male worker over 18, and that since 1833 the 15 hours from 5.30 a.m. to 8.30 p.m. had remained the legal 'day,' within the limits of which at first the 12, and later the 10 hours' labour of young persons and women had to be performed under the prescribed conditions.

The manufacturers began by here and there discharging a part of, in many cases half of the young persons and women employed by them, and then, for the adult males, restoring the almost obsolete night-work. The Ten Hours' Act, they cried, leaves no other alternative.[113]

Their second step dealt with the legal pauses for meals. Let us hear the Factory Inspectors.

'Since the restriction of the hours of work to ten, the factory occupiers maintain, although they have not yet practically gone the whole length, that supposing the hours of work to be from 9 a.m. to 7 p.m. they fulfil the provisions of the statutes by allowing an hour before 9 a.m. and half an hour after 7 p.m. [for meals]. In some cases they now allow an hour, or half an hour for dinner, insisting at the same time, that they are not bound to allow any part of the hour and a half in the course of the factory working-day.'[114] The manufacturers maintained therefore that the scrupulously strict provisions of the Act of 1844 with regard to meal-times only gave the operatives permission to eat and drink before coming into, and after leaving the factory—i.e., at home. And why should not the workpeople eat their dinner before 9 in the morning? The crown lawyers, however, decided that the prescribed meal-times

'must be in the interval during the working-hours, and that it will not be lawful to work for 10 hours continuously, from 9 a.m. to 7 p.m., without any interval.'[115]

After these pleasant demonstrations, Capital preluded its revolt by a step which agreed with the letter of the law of 1844, and was therefore legal.

The Act of 1844 certainly prohibited the employment after 1 p.m. of such children, from 8 to 13, as had been employed before noon. But it did not regulate in any way the 6½ hours' work of the children whose work-time began at 12 midday or later. Children of 8 might, if they began work at noon, be employed from 12 to 1, 1 hour; from 2 to 4 in the afternoon, 2 hours; from 5 to 8.30 in the evening, 3½ hours; in all, the legal 6½ hours. Or better still. In order to make their work coincide with that of the adult male labourers up to 8.30 p.m., the manufacturers only had to give them no work till 2 in the afternoon, they could then keep them in the factory without intermission till 8.30 in the evening.

'And it is now expressly admitted that the practice exists in England from the desire of mill-owners to have their machinery at work for more than 10 hours a-day, to keep the children at work with male adults after all the young persons and women have left, and until 8.30 p.m. if the factory-owners choose.'[116]

Workmen and factory inspectors protested on hygienic and moral grounds, but Capital answered:

'My deeds upon my head! I crave the law,
The penalty and forfeit of my bond.'

In fact, according to statistics laid before the House of Commons on July 26th, 1850, in spite of all protests, on July 15th, 1850, 3,742 children were subjected to this 'practice' in 257 factories.[117] Still, this was not enough. The Lynx eye of Capital discovered that the Act of 1844 did not allow 5 hours' work before mid-day without a pause of at least 30 minutes for refreshment, but prescribed nothing of the kind for work after mid-day. Therefore, it claimed and obtained the enjoyment not only of making children of 8 drudge without intermission from 2 to 8.30 p.m., but also of making them hunger during that time.

'Ay, his heart.
So says the bond.'

This Shylock-clinging[118] to the letter of the law of 1844, so far as it regulated children's labour, was but to lead up to an open revolt against the same law, so far as it regulated the labour of 'young persons and women.' It will be remembered that the abolition of the 'false relay system' was the chief aim and object of that law. The masters began their revolt with the simple declaration that the sections of the Act of 1844 which prohibited the *ad libitum* use of young persons and women in such short fractions of the day of 15 hours as the employer chose, were 'comparatively harmless' so long as the work-time was fixed at 12 hours. But under the Ten Hours' Act they were a 'grievous hardship.'[119] They informed the inspectors in the coolest manner that they should place themselves above the letter of the law, and re-introduce the old system on their own account.[120] They were acting in the interests of the ill-advised operatives themselves, 'in order to be able to pay them higher wages.'

> 'This was the only possible plan by which to maintain, under the Ten Hours' Act, the industrial supremacy of Great Britain.' 'Perhaps it may be a little difficult to detect irregularities under the relay system; but what of that? Is the great manufacturing interest of this country to be treated as a secondary matter in order to save some little trouble to Inspectors and Sub-Inspectors of Factories?'[121]

All these shifts naturally were of no avail. The Factory Inspectors appealed to the Law Courts. But soon such a cloud of dust in the way of petitions from the masters overwhelmed the Home Secretary, Sir George Grey, that in a circular of August 5th, 1848, he recommends the inspectors not

> 'to lay informations against mill-owners for a breach of the letter of the Act, or for employment of young persons by relays in cases in which there is no reason to believe that such young persons have been actually employed for a longer period than that sanctioned by law.' Hereupon, Factory Inspector J. Stuart allowed the so-called relay system during the 15 hours of the factory day throughout Scotland, where it soon flourished again as of old. The English Factory Inspectors, on the other hand, declared that the Home Secretary had no power dictatorially to suspend the law, and continued their legal proceedings against the pro-slavery rebellion.

But what was the good of summoning the capitalists when the Courts in this case the county magistrates—Cobbett's 'Great Unpaid'—acquitted them? In these tribunals, the masters sat in judgment on themselves An example. One Eskrigge, cotton-spinner, of the firm of Kershaw, Leese, & Co., had laid before the Factory Inspector of his district the scheme of a relay system intended for his mill. Receiving a refusal, he at first kept quiet. A few months later, an individual named Robinson, also a cotton-spinner, and if not his Man Friday, at all events related to Eskrigge, appeared before the borough magistrates of Stockport on a charge of introducing the identical plan of relays invented by Eskrigge. Four Justices sat, among them three cottonspinners, at their head this same inevitable Eskrigge. Eskrigge acquitted Robinson, and now was of opinion that what was right for Robinson was fair for Eskrigge. Supported by his own legal decision, he introduced the system at once into his own factory.[122] Of course, the composition of this tribunal was in itself a violation of the law.[123]

> These judicial farces, exclaims Inspector Howell, 'urgently call for a remedy—either that the law should be so altered as to be made to conform to these decisions, or that it should be administered by a less fallible tribunal, whose decisions would conform to the law ... when these cases are brought forward. I long for a stipendiary magistrate.'[124]

The crown lawyers declared the masters' interpretation of the Act of 1848 absurd. But the Saviours of Society would not allow themselves to be turned from their purpose. Leonard Horner reports,

> 'Having endeavoured to enforce the Act ... by ten prosecutions in seven magisterial divisions, and having been supported by the magistrates in one case only ... I considered it useless to prosecute more for this evasion of the law. That part of the Act of 1848 which was framed for securing uniformity in the hours of work, ... is thus no longer in force in my district (Lancashire). Neither have the sub-inspectors or myself any means of satisfying ourselves, when we inspect a mill working by shifts, that the young persons and women are not working more than 10 hours a-day.... In a return

> of the 30th April, ... of millowners working by shifts, the number amounts to 114, and has been for some time rapidly increasing. In general, the time of working the mill is extended to 13½ hours' from 6 a.m. to 7½ p.m., ... in some instances it amounts to 15 hours, from 5½ a.m. to 8½ p.m.'[125]

Already, in December, 1848, Leonard Horner had a list of 65 manufacturers and 29 overlookers who unanimously declared that no system of supervision could, under this relay system, prevent enormous over-work.[126] Now, the same children and young persons were shifted from the spinning-room to the weaving-room, now, during 15 hours, from one factory to another.[127] How was it possible to control a system which,

> 'under the guise of relays, is some one of the many plans for shuffling 'the hands' about in endless variety, and shifting the hours of work and of rest for different individuals throughout the day, so that you may never have one complete set of hands working together in the same room at the same time.'[128]

But, altogether independently of actual over-work, this so-called relay system was an offspring of capitalistic fantasy, such as Fourier, in his humorous sketches of 'Courtes Seances,' has never surpassed, except that the 'attraction of labour' was changed into the attraction of capital. Look, for example, at those schemes of the masters which the 'respectable' press praised as models of 'what a reasonable degree of care and method can accomplish.' The *personnel* of the workpeople was sometimes divided into from 12 to 14 categories, which themselves constantly changed and recharged their constituent parts. During the 15 hours of the factory day, capital dragged in the labourer now for 30 minutes, now for an hour, and then pushed him out again, to drag him into the factory and to thrust him out afresh, hounding him hither and thither, in scattered shreds of time, without ever losing hold of him until the full 10 hours' work was done. As on the stage, the same persons had to appear in turns in the different scenes of the different acts. But as an actor during the whole course of the play belongs to the stage, so the operatives, during 15 hours, belonged to the factory, without reckoning the time for going and coming. Thus the hours of rest were turned into hours of enforced idleness, which drove the youths to the pot-house, and the girls to the brothel. At every new trick that the capitalist, from day to day, hit upon for keeping his machinery going 12 or 15 hours without increasing the number of his hands, the worker had to swallow his meals now in this fragment of time, now in that. At the time of the 10 hours' agitation, the masters cried out that the working mob petitioned in the hope of obtaining 12 hours' wages for 10 hours' work. Now they reversed the medal. They paid 10 hours' wages for 12 or 15 hours' lordship over labour-power.[129] This was the gist of the matter, this the masters' interpretation of the 10 hours' law! These were the same unctuous Free-traders, perspiring with the love of humanity, who for full 10 years, during the Anti-Corn Law agitation, had preached to the operatives, by a reckoning of pounds, shillings, and pence, that with free importation of corn, and with the means possessed by English industry, 10 hours' labour would be quite enough to enrich the capitalists.[130] This revolt of capital, after two years was at last crowned with victory by a decision of one of the four highest Courts of Justice in England, the Court of Exchequer, which in a case brought before it on February 8th, 1850, decided that the manufacturers were certainly acting against the sense of the Act of 1844, but that this Act itself contained certain words that rendered it meaningless. 'By this decision, the Ten Hours' Act was abolished.'[131] A crowd of masters, who until then had been afraid of using the relay system for young persons and women, now took it up heart and soul.[132]

But on this apparently decisive victory of capital, followed at once a revulsion. The workpeople had hitherto offered a passive, although inflexible and unremitting resistance. They now protested in Lancashire and Yorkshire in threatening meetings. The pretended

Ten Hours' Act was thus simple humbug, parliamentary cheating, had never existed! The Factory Inspectors urgently warned the Government that the antagonism of classes had arrived at an incredible tension. Some of the masters themselves murmured:

> 'On account of the contradictory decisions of the magistrates, a condition of things altogether abnormal and anarchical obtains. One law holds in Yorkshire, another in Lancashire, one law in one parish of Lancashire, another in its immediate neighbourhood. The manufacturer in large towns could evade the law, the manufacturer in country districts could not find the people necessary for the relay system, still less for the shifting of hands from one factory to another,' &c.

And the first birthright of capital is equal exploitation of labour-power by all capitalists.

Under these circumstances a compromise between masters and men was effected that received the seal of Parliament in the additional Factory Act of August 5th, 1850. The working-day for 'young persons and women,' was raised from 10 to 10—hours for the first five days of the week, and shortened to 7½ on the Saturday. The work was to go on between 6 a.m. and 6 p.m.,[133] with pauses of not less than 1½ hours for meal-times, these meal-times to be allowed at one and the same time for all, and conformably to the conditions of 1844. By this an end was put to the relay system once for all.[134] For children's labour, the Act of 1844 remained in force.

One set of masters, this time as before, secured to itself special seigneurial rights over the children of the proletariat. These were the silk manufacturers. In 1833 they had howled out in threatening fashion, 'if the liberty of working children of any age for 10 hours a day were taken away, it would stop their works.'[135] It would be impossible for them to buy a sufficient number of children over 13. They extorted the privilege they desired. The pretext was shown on subsequent investigation to be a deliberate lie.[136] It did not, however, prevent them, during 10 years, from spinning silk 10 hours a day out of the blood of little children who had to be placed upon stools for the performance of their work.[137] The Act of 1844 certainly 'robbed' them of the 'liberty' of employing children under 11 longer than 6½ hours a day. But it secured to them, on the other hand, the privilege of working children between 11 and 13, 10 hours a day, and of annulling in their case the education made compulsory for all other factory children. This time the pretext was

> 'the delicate texture of the fabric in which they were employed, requiring a lightness of touch, only to be acquired by their early introduction to these factories.'[138]

The children were slaughtered out-and-out for the sake of their delicate fingers, as in Southern Russia the horned cattle for the sake of their hide and tallow. At length, in 1850, the privilege granted in 1844, was limited to the departments of silk-twisting and silk-winding. But here, to make amends to capital bereft of its 'freedom,' the work-time for children from 11 to 13 was raised from 10 to 10½ hours. Pretext: 'Labour in silk mills was lighter than in mills for other fabrics, and less likely in other respects also to be prejudicial to health.'[139] Official medical inquiries proved afterwards that, on the contrary,

> 'the average death-rate is exceedingly high in the silk districts and amongst the female part of the population is higher even than it is in the cotton districts of Lancashire.'[140]

Despite the protests of the Factory Inspector, renewed every 6 months, the mischief continues to this hour.[141]

The Act of 1850 changed the 15 hours' time from 6 a.m. to 8.30 p.m., into the 12 hours from 6 a.m. to 6 p.m. for 'young persons and women' only. It did not, therefore, affect children who could always be employed for half an hour before and 2½ hours after this period, provided the whole of their labour did not exceed 6½ hours. Whilst the bill was under discussion, the Factory Inspectors laid before Parliament statistics of the infamous abuses due to this anomaly. To no purpose. In the background lurked the intention of screwing up, during prosperous years, the working-day of adult males to 15 hours by the aid of the children. The experience of the three following years showed that such an attempt must come to grief against the resistance of the adult male operatives. The Act of 1850 was therefore finally completed in 1853 by forbidding the 'employment of children in the morning before and in the evening after young persons and women.' Henceforth with a few exceptions the Factory Act of 1850 regulated the working-day of all workers in the branches of industry that come under it.[142] Since the passing of the first Factory Act half a century had elapsed.[143]

Factory legislation for the first time went beyond its original sphere in the 'Printworks' Act of 1845.' The displeasure with which capital received this new 'extravagance' speaks through every line of the Act. It limits the working-day for children from 8 to 13, and for women to 16 hours, between 6 a.m. and 10 p.m., without any legal pause for meal-times. It allows males over 13 to be worked at will day and night.[144] It is a Parliamentary abortion.[145]

However, the principle had triumphed with its victory in those great branches of industry which form the most characteristic creation of the modern mode of production. Their wonderful development from 1853 to 1860, hand-in-hand with the physical and moral regeneration of the factory workers, struck the most purblind. The masters from whom the legal limitation and regulation had been wrung step by step after a civil war of half a century, themselves referred ostentatiously to the contrast with the branches of exploitation still 'free.'[146] The Pharisees of 'Political Economy' now proclaimed the discernment of the necessity of a legally fixed working-day as a characteristic new discovery of their 'science.'[147] It will be easily understood that after the factory magnates had resigned themselves and become reconciled to the inevitable, the power of resistance of capital gradually weakened, whilst at the same time the power of attack of the working-class grew with the number of its allies in the classes of society not immediately interested in the question. Hence the comparatively rapid advance since 1860.

The dye-works and bleach-works all came under the Factory Act of 1850 in 1860;[148] lace and stocking manufactures in 1861.

In consequence of the first report of the Commission on the employment of children (1863) the same fate was shared by the manufacturers of all earthenwares (not merely pottery), Lucifer-matches, percussion caps, cartridges, carpets, fustian-cutting, and many processes included under the name of 'finishing.' In the year 1863 bleaching in the open air[149] and baking were placed under special Acts, by which, in the former, the labour of young persons and women during the night-time (from 8 in the evening to 6 in the morning), and in the latter, the employment of journeymen bakers under 18, between 9 in the evening and 5 in the morning were forbidden. We shall return to the later proposals of the same Commission, which threatened to deprive of their 'freedom' all the important branches of English Industry, with the exception of agriculture, mines, and the means of transport.[150]

Section 7: *The Struggle for the Normal Working-Day Re-action of the English Factory Acts on Other Countries*

The reader will bear in mind that the production of surplus-value, or the extraction of surplus-labour, is the specific end and aim, the sum and substance, of capitalist production, quite apart from any changes in the mode of production, which may arise from the subordination of labour to capital. He will remember that as far as we have at present gone only the independent labourer, and therefore only the labourer legally qualified to act for himself, enters as a vendor of a commodity into a contract with the capitalist. If, therefore, in our historical sketch, on the one hand, modern industry, on the other, the labour of those who are physically and legally minors, play important parts, the former was to us only a special department, and the latter only a specially striking example of labour exploitation. Without, however, anticipating the subsequent development of our inquiry, from the mere connexion of the historic facts before us it follows:

First. The passion of capital for an unlimited and reckless extension of the working-day, is first gratified in the industries earliest revolutionised by water-power, steam, and machinery, in those first creations of the modern mode of production, cotton, wool, flax, and silk spinning, and weaving. The changes in the material mode of production, and the corresponding changes in the social relations of the producers[151] gave rise first to an extravagance beyond all bounds, and then in opposition to this, called forth a control on the part of Society which legally limits, regulates, and makes uniform the working-day and its pauses. This control appears, therefore, during the first half of the nineteenth century simply as exceptional legislation.[152] As soon as this primitive dominion of the new mode of production was conquered, it was found that, in the meantime, not only had many other branches of production been made to adopt the same factory system, but that manufactures with more or less obsolete methods, such as potteries, glass-making, &c., that old-fashioned handicrafts, like baking, and, finally, even that the so-called domestic industries, such as nail-making,[153] had long since fallen as completely under capitalist exploitation as the factories themselves. Legislation was, therefore, compelled to gradually get rid of its exceptional character, or where, as in England, it proceeds after the manner of the Roman Casuists, to declare any house in which work was done to be a factory.[154]

Second. The history of the regulation of the working-day in certain branches of production, and the struggle still going on in others in regard to this regulation, prove conclusively that the isolated labourer, the labourer as 'free' vendor of his labour-power, when capitalist production has once attained a certain stage, succumbs without any power of resistance. The creation of a normal working-day is, therefore, the product of a protracted civil war, more or less dissembled, between the capitalist class and the working-class. As the contest takes place in the arena of modern industry, it first breaks out in the home of that industry—England.[155] The English factory workers were the champions, not only of the English, but of the modern working-class generally, as their theorists were the first to throw down the gauntlet to the theory of capital.[156] Hence, the philosopher of the Factory, Ure, denounces as an ineffable disgrace to the English working-class that they inscribed 'the slavery of the Factory Acts' on the banner which they bore against capital, manfully striving for 'perfect freedom of labour.'[157]

France limps slowly behind England. The February revolution was necessary to bring into the world the 12 hours' law,[158] which is much more deficient than its English original. For all that, the French revolutionary method has its special advantages. It once for all commands the same limit to the working-day in all shops and factories without distinction, whilst English legislation reluctantly yields to the pressure of circumstances, now on this point, now on that, and is getting lost in a hopelessly bewildering tangle of contradictory enactments.[159] On the other hand, the French law proclaims as a principle that which in England was only won in the name of children, minors, and women, and has been only recently for the first time claimed as a general right.[160]

In the United States of North America, every independent movement of the workers was paralysed so long as slavery disfigured a part of the Republic. Labour cannot emancipate itself in the white skin where in the black it is branded. But out of the death of slavery a new life at once arose. The first fruit of the Civil War was the eight hours' agitation, that ran with the seven-leagued boots of the locomotive from the Atlantic to the Pacific, from New England to California. The General Congress of labour at Baltimore (August 16th, 1866) declared:

> 'The first and great necessity of the present, to free the labour of this country from capitalistic slavery, is the passing of a law by which eight hours shall be the normal working-day in all States of the American Union. We are resolved to put forth all our

strength until this glorious result is attained.'[161]

At the same time, the Congress of the International Working Men's Association at Geneva, on the proposition of the London General Council, resolved that 'the limitation of the working-day is a preliminary condition without which all further attempts at improvement and emancipation must prove abortive... the Congress proposes eight hours as the legal limit of the working-day.'

Thus the movement of the working-class on both sides of the Atlantic, that had grown instinctively out of the conditions of production themselves, endorsed the words of the English Factory Inspector, R. J. Saunders

> 'Further steps towards a reformation of society can never be carried out with any hope of success, unless the hours of labour be limited, and the prescribed limit strictly enforced.'[162]

It must be acknowledged that our labourer comes out of the process of production other than he entered. In the market he stood as owner of the commodity 'labour-power' face to face with other owners of commodities, dealer against dealer. The contract by which he sold to the capitalist his labour-power proved, so to say, in black and white that he disposed of himself freely. The bargain concluded, it is discovered that he was no 'free agent,' that the time for which he is free to sell his labour-power is the time for which he is forced to sell it,[163] that in fact the vampire will not lose its hold on him 'so long as there is a muscle, a nerve, a drop of blood to be exploited.'[164] For 'protection' against 'the serpent of their agonies,' the labourers must put their heads together, and, as a class, compel the passing of a law, an all-powerful social barrier that shall prevent the very workers from selling. by voluntary contract with capital, themselves and their families into slavery and death.[165] In place of the pompous catalogue of the 'inalienable rights of man' comes the modest Magna Charta of a legally limited working-day, which shall make clear 'when the time which the worker sells is ended, and when his own begins.' Quantum mutatus ab illo! [What a great change from that time!—Virgil][166]

Notes

1. 'A day's labour is vague, it may be long or short.' ('An Essay on Trade and Commerce, Containing Observations on Taxes, &c.' London. 1770, p. 73.)
2. This question is far more important than the celebrated question of Sir Robert Peel to the Birmingham Chamber of Commerce: What is a pound? A question that could only have been proposed, because Peel was as much in the dark as to the nature of money as the 'little shilling men' of Birmingham.
3. 'It is the aim of the capitalist to obtain with his expended capital the greatest possible quantity of labour (d'obtenir du capital dépense la plus forte somme de travail possible).' J. G. Courcelle-Seneuil. 'Traité théorique et pratique des entreprises industrielles.' 2nd ed. Paris, 1857, p. 63.
4. 'An hour's labour lost in a day is a prodigious injury to a commercial State.... There is a very great consumption of luxuries among the labouring poor of this kingdom: particularly among the manufacturing populace, by which they also consume their time, the most fatal of consumptions.' 'An Essay on Trade and Commerce, &c.,' p. 47, and 15 3.
5. 'Si le manouvrier libre prend un instant de repos, l'économie sordide qui le suit des yeux avec inquiétude, prétend qu'il la vole.' [If the free labourer allows himself an instant of rest, the base and petty management, which follows him with wary eyes, claims he is stealing from it.] N. Linguet, 'Théorie des Lois Civiles. &c.' London, 1767, t. II., p. 466.
6. During the great strike of the London builders, 1860-61, for the reduction of the working-day to 9 hours, their Committee published a manifesto that contained, to some extent, the plea of our worker. The manifesto alludes, not without irony, to the fact, that the greatest profit-monger amongst the building masters, a certain Sir M. Peto, was in the odour of

sanctity (This same Peto, after 1867, came to an end a la Strousberg.)

7. 'Those who labour ... in reality feed both the pensioners ... [called the rich] and themselves.' (Edmund Burke, l.c., p. 2.)

8. Niebuhr in his 'Roman History' says very naively: 'It is evident that works like the Etruscan, which in their ruins astound us, pre-suppose in little (!) states lords and vassals.' Sismondi says far more to the purpose that 'Brussels lace' pre-supposes wage-lords and wage-slaves.

9. 'One cannot see these unfortunates (in the gold mines between Egypt, Ethiopia, and Arabia) who cannot even have their bodies clean, or their nakedness clothed, without pitying their miserable lot. There is no indulgence, no forbearance for the sick, the feeble, the aged, for woman's weakness. All must, forced by blows, work on until death puts an end to their sufferings and their distress.' ('Diod. Sic. Bibl. Hist.,' lib. 2, c. 13.)

10. That which follows refers to the situation in the Rumanian provinces before the change effected since the Crimean war.

11. This holds likewise for Germany, and especially for Prussia east of the Elbe. In the 15th century the German peasant was nearly everywhere a man, who, whilst subject to certain rents paid in produce and labour was otherwise at least practically free. The German colonists in Brandenburg, Pomerania, Silesia, and Eastern Prussia, were even legally acknowledged as free men. The victory of the nobility in the peasants' war put an end to that. Not only were the conquered South German peasants again enslaved. From the middle of the 16th century the peasants of Eastern Prussia, Brandenburg, Pomerania, and Silesia, and soon after the free peasants of Schleswig-Holstein were degraded to the condition of serfs. (Maurer, Fronhöfe iv. vol.,—Meitzen, 'Der Boden des preussischen Staats'—Hanssen, 'Leibeigenschaft in Schleswig-Holstein.'—*F. E.)*

12. Further details are to be found in E. Regnault's 'Histoire politique et sociale des Principautés Danubiennes,' Paris, 1855.

13. 'In general and within certain limits, exceeding the medium size of their kind, is evidence of the prosperity of organic beings. As to man, his bodily height lessens if his due growth is interfered with, either by physical or local conditions. In all European countries in which the conscription holds, since its introduction, the medium height of adult men, and generally their fitness for military service, has diminished. Before the revolution (1789), the minimum for the infantry in France was 165 centimetres; in 1818 (law of March 10th), 157; by the law of March 21, 1832, 156 cm.; on the average in France more than half are rejected on account of deficient height or bodily weakness. The military standard in Saxony was in 1780, 178 cm. It is now 155. In Prussia it is 157. According to the statement of Dr Meyer in the Bavarian Gazette, May 9th, 1862, the result of an average of 9 years is, that in Prussia out of 1,000 conscripts 716 were unfit for military service, 317 because of deficiency in height, and 399 because of bodily defects.... Berlin in 1858 could not provide its contingent of recruits, it was 156 men short.' J. von Liebig: 'Die Chemie in ihrer Anwendung auf Agrikultur und Physiologie. 1862,' 7th Ed., vol. 1, pp. 117, 118.

14. The history of the Factory Act of 1850 will be found in the course of this chapter.

15. I only touch here and there on the period from the beginning of modern industry in England to 1845. For this period I refer the reader to 'Die Lage der arbeitenden Klasse in England,' [Condition of the Working Class in England] von Friedrich Engels, Leipzig, 1845. How completely Engels understood the nature of the capitalist mode of production is shown by the Factory Reports, Reports on Mines, &c., that have appeared since 1845, and how wonderfully he painted the circumstances in detail is seen on the most superficial comparison of his work with the official reports of the Children's Employment Commission, published 18 to 20 years later (1863-1867). These deal especially with the branches of industry in which the Factory Acts had not, up to 1862, been introduced, in fact are not yet introduced. Here, then, little or no alteration had been enforced, by authority, in the conditions painted by Engels. I borrow my examples chiefly from the Free-trade period after

1848, that age of paradise, of which the commercial travellers for the great firm of Free-trade, blatant as ignorant, tell such fabulous tales. For the rest England figures here in the foreground because she is the classic representative of capitalist production, and she alone has a continuous set of official statistics of the things we are considering.

16. 'Suggestions, &c. by Mr L. Horner, Inspector of Factories,' in Factories Regulation Acts. Ordered by the House of Commons to be printed, 9th August, 1859, pp. 4, 5.
17. Reports of the Inspector of Factories for the half year. October, 1856, p. 35.
18. Reports, &c., 30th April, 1858, p. 9.
19. Reports, &c., l.c., p. 10.
20. Reports &c., l.c., p. 25.
21. Reports &c., for the half year ending 30th April, 1861. See Appendix No. 2; Reports, &c., 31st October, 1862, pp. 7, 52, 53. The violations of the Acts became more numerous during the last half year 1863. Cf Reports, &c., ending 31st October, 1863, p. 7.
22. Reports, &c., October 31st, 1860, p. 23. With what fanaticism, according to the evidence of manufacturers given in courts of law, their hands set themselves against every interruption in factory labour, the following curious circumstance shows. In the beginning of June, 1836, information reached the magistrates of Dewsbury (Yorkshire) that the owners of 8 large mills in the neighbourhood of Batley had violated the Factory Acts. Some of these gentlemen were accused of having kept at work 5 boys between 12 and 15 years of age, from 6 a.m. on Friday to 4 p.m. on the following Saturday, not allowing them any respite except for meals and one hour for sleep at midnight. And these children had to do this ceaseless labour of 30 hours in the 'shoddyhole,' as the hole is called, in which the woollen rags are pulled in pieces, and where a dense atmosphere of dust, shreds, &c., forces even the adult workman to cover his mouth continually with handkerchiefs for the protection of his lungs! The accused gentlemen affirm in lieu of taking an oath—as quakers they were too scrupulously religious to take an oath—that they had, in their great compassion for the unhappy children, allowed them four hours for sleep, but the obstinate children absolutely would not go to bed. The quaker gentlemen were mulcted in £20. Dryden anticipated these gentry:

    Fox full fraught in seeming sanctity,
    That feared an oath, but like the devil would lie,
    That look'd like Lent, and had the holy leer,
    And durst not sin! before he said his prayer!'

23. Rep., 31st Oct., 1856, p. 34.
24. l.c., p. 35.
25. l.c., p. 48.
26. l.c., p. 48.
27. l.c., p. 48.
28. l.c., p. 48.
29. Report of the Insp. &c., 30th April 1860, p. 56.
30. This is the official expression both in the factories and in the reports.
31. 'The cupidity of mill-owners whose cruelties in the pursuit of gain have hardly been exceeded by those perpetrated by the Spaniards on the conquest of America in the pursuit of gold.' John Wade, 'History of the Middle and Working Classes,' 3rd Ed. London, 1835, p. 114. The theoretical part of this book, a kind of hand-book of Political Economy, is, considering the time of its publication, original in some parts, *e.g.*, on commercial crises. The historical part is, to a great extent, a shameless plagiarism of Sir F. M. Eden's 'The State of the Poor,' London, 1797.
32. *Daily Telegraph, 17th* January, 1860.
33. Cf. F. Engels 'Lage, etc.' pp. 249-51.
34. Children's Employment Commission. First report., etc., 1863. Evidence. pp. 16, 19, 18.

35. Public Health, 3rd report, etc., pp. 102, 104, 105.
36. Child. Empl. Comm. I. Report, p. 24.
37. Children's Employment Commission, p. 22, and xi.
38. l.c., p. xlviii.
39. l.c., p. liv.
40. This is not to be taken in the same sense as our surplus-labour time. These gentlemen consider 10½ hours of labour as the normal working-day, which includes of course the normal surplus-labour. After this begins 'overtime' which is paid a little better. It will be seen later that the labour expended during the so-called normal day is paid below its value, so that the overtime is simply a capitalist trick in order to extort more surplus-labour, which it would still be, even if the labour-power expended during the normal working-day were properly paid.
41. l.c., Evidence, pp. 123, 124, 125, 140, and 54.
42. Alum finely powdered, or mixed with salt, is a normal article of commerce bearing the significant name of 'bakers' stuff.'
43. Soot is a well-known and very energetic form of carbon, and forms a manure that capitalistic chimney-sweeps sell to English farmers. Now in 1862 the British juryman had in a law-suit to decide whether soot, with which, unknown to the buyer, 90% of dust and sand are mixed, is genuine soot in the commercial sense or adulterated soot in the legal sense. The 'amis du commerce' [friends of commerce] decided it to be genuine commercial soot, and non-suited the plaintiff farmer, who had in addition to pay the costs of the suit.
44. The French chemist, Chevallier, in his treatise on the 'sophistications' of commodities, enumerates for many of the 600 or more articles which he passes in review, 10, 20, 30 different methods of adulteration. He adds that he does not know all the methods and does not mention all that he knows. He gives 6 kinds of adulteration of sugar, 9 of olive oil, 10 of butter, 12 of salt, 19 of milk, 20 of bread, 23 of brandy, 24 of meal, 28 of chocolate, 30 of wine, 32 of coffee, etc. Even God Almighty does not escape this fate. See Rouard de Card, 'On the Falsifications of the materials of the Sacrament.' ('De la falsification des substances sacramentelles,' Paris, 1856.)
45. 'Report, &c., relative to the grievances complained of by the journeymen bakers, &c., London, 1862,' and 'Second Report, &c., London, 1863.'
46. l.c., First Report, &c., p. vi.
47. l.c., p. Ixxi.
48. George Read, 'The History of Baking,' London, 1848, p. 16.
49. Report (First) &c. Evidence of the 'full-priced' baker Cheeseman, p. 108.
50. George Read, l.c. At the end of the 17th and the beginning of the 18th centuries the factors (agents) that crowded into every possible trade were still denounced as 'public nuisances.' Thus the Grand Jury at the quarter session of the Justices of the Peace for the County of Somerset, addressed a presentment to the Lower House which, among other things, states, 'that these factors of Blackwell Hall are a Public Nuisance and Prejudice to the Clothing Trade, and ought to be put down as a Nuisance.' 'The Case of our English Wool., &c.,' London, 1685, pp. 6, 7.
51. First Report, &c.
52. Report of Committee on the Baking Trade in Ireland for 1861.
53. l.c.
54. Public meeting of agricultural labourers at Lasswade, near Edinburgh, January 5th, 1866. (See *Workman's Advocate*, January 13th, 1866.) The formation since the close of 1865 of a Trades' Union among the agricultural labourers at first in Scotland is a historic event. In one of the most oppressed agricultural districts of England, Buckinghamshire, the labourers, in March, 1867, made a great strike for the raising of their weekly wage from 9-10 shillings to 12 shillings. (It will be seen from the preceding passage that the movement of the English

agricultural proletariat, entirely crushed since the suppression of its violent manifestations after 1830, and especially since the introduction of the new Poor Laws, begins again in the sixties, until it becomes finally epoch-making in 1872. I return to this in the 2nd volume, as well as to the Blue books that have appeared since 1867 on the position of the English land labourers. Addendum to the 3rd ed.)

55. *Reynolds' Newspaper*, January, 1866.—Every week this same paper has, under the sensational headings, 'Fearful and fatal accidents,' 'Appalling tragedies,' &c., a whole list of fresh railway catastrophes. On these an employee on the North Staffordshire line comments: 'Everyone knows the consequences that may occur if the driver and fireman of a locomotive engine are not continually on the look-out. How can that be expected from a man who has been at such work for 29 or 30 hours, exposed to the weather, and without rest. The following is an example which is of very frequent occurrence:—One fireman commenced work on the Monday morning at a very early hour. When he had finished what is called a day's work, he had been on duty 14 hours 50 minutes. Before he had time to get his tea, he was again called on for duty.... The next time he finished he had been on duty 14 hours 25 minutes, making a total of 29 hours 15 minutes without intermission. The rest of the week's work was made up as follows:—Wednesday, 15 hours; Thursday, 15 hours 35 minutes; Friday, 14½ hours; Saturday, 14 hours 10 minutes, making a total for the week of 88 hours 30 minutes. Now, sir, fancy his astonishment on being paid 6 1/4 days for the whole. Thinking it was a mistake, he applied to the time-keeper,... and inquired what they considered a day's work, and was told 13 hours for a goods man (*i.e.*, 78 hours).... He then asked for what he had made over and above the 78 hours per week, but was refused. However, he was at last told they would give him another quarter, *i.e.*, 10d.,' l.c., 4th February. 1866.

56. Cf F. Engels, l.c., pp. 253, 254.

57. Dr Letheby, Consulting Physician of the Board of Health, declared: 'The minimum of air for each adult ought to be in a sleeping room 300, and in a dwelling room 500 cubic feet.' Dr Richardson, Senior Physician to one of the London Hospitals: 'With needlewomen of all kinds, including milliners, dressmakers, and ordinary seamstresses, there are three miseries—over-work, deficient air, and either deficient food or deficient digestion.... Needlework, in the main, ... is infinitely better adapted to women than to men. But the mischiefs of the trade, in the metropolis especially, are that it is monopolised by some twenty-six capitalists, who, under the advantages that spring from capital, can bring in capital to force economy out of labour. This power tells throughout the whole class. If a dressmaker can get a little circle of customers, such is the competition that, in her home, she must work to the death to hold together, and this same over-work she must of necessity inflict on any who may assist her. If she fail, or do not try independently, she must join an establishment, where her labour is not less, but where her money is safe. Placed thus, she becomes a mere slave, tossed about with the variations of society. Now at home, in one room, starving, or near to it, then engaged 15, 16, aye, even 18 hours out of the 24, in an air that is scarcely tolerable, and on food which, even if it be good, cannot be digested in the absence of pure air. On these victims, consumption, which is purely a disease of bad air, feeds.' Dr Richardson: 'Work and Over-work,' in 'Social Science Review,' 18th July, 1863.

58. *Morning Star*, 23rd June, 1863.—*The Times* made use of the circumstance to defend the American slave-owners against Bright, &c. 'Very many of us think,' says a leader of July 2nd, 1863, 'that, while we work our own young women to death, using the scourge of starvation, instead of the crack of the whip, as the instrument of compulsion, we have scarcely a right to hound on fire and slaughter against families who were born slave-owners, and who, at least, feed their slaves well, and work them lightly.' In the same manner, the *Standard*, a Tory organ, fell foul of the Rev. Newman Hall: 'He excommunicated the slave-owners, but prays with the fine folk who, without remorse, make the omnibus drivers and conductors of London, &c., work 16 hours a-day for the wages of a dog.' Finally, spake the oracle, Thomas Carlyle, of whom

I wrote, in 1850, 'Zum Teufel ist der Genius, der Kultus ist geblieben.' ['In the cult of genius ... The cult remains,' paraphrasing Schiller] In a short parable, he reduces the one great event of contemporary history, the American Civil War, to this level, that the Peter of the North wants to break the head of the Paul of the South with all his might, because the Peter of the North hires his labour by the day, and the Paul of the South hires his by the life. (*Macmillan's Magazine.* Ilias Americana in nuce. August, 1863.) Thus, the bubble of Tory sympathy for the urban workers—by no means for the rural—has burst at last. The sum of all is—slavery!

59. Dr Richardson, l.c.
60. Children's Employment Commission. Third Report. London, 1864, pp. iv., v., vi.
61. 'Both in Staffordshire and in South Wales young girls and women are employed on the pit banks and on the coke heaps, not only by day but also by night. This practice has been often noticed in Reports presented to Parliament, as being attended with great and notorious evils. These females employed with the men, hardly distinguished from them in their dress, and begrimed with dirt and smoke, are exposed to the deterioration of character, arising from the loss of self-respect, which can hardly fail to follow from their unfeminine occupation.' (l. c., 194, p. xxvi. Cf. Fourth Report (1865), 61, p. xiii.) It is the same in glass-works.
62. A steel manufacturer who employs children in night-labour remarked: 'It seems but natural that boys who work at night cannot sleep and get proper rest by day, but will be running about.' (l.c., Fourth Report, 63, p. xiii.) On the importance of sunlight for the maintenance and growth of the body, a physician writes: 'Light also acts upon the tissues of the body directly in hardening them and supporting their elasticity. The muscles of animals, when they are deprived of a proper amount of light, become soft and inelastic, the nervous power loses its tone from defective stimulation, and the elaboration of all growth seems to be perverted.... In the case of children, constant access to plenty of light during the day, and to the direct rays of the sun for a part of it, is most essential to health. Light assists in the elaboration of good plastic blood, and hardens the fibre after it has been laid down. It also acts as a stimulus upon the organs of sight, and by this means brings about more activity in the various cerebral functions.' Dr W. Strange, Senior Physician of the Worcester General Hospital, from whose work on 'Health' (1864) this passage is taken, writes in a letter to Mr White, one of the commissioners: 'I have had opportunities formerly, when in Lancashire, of observing the effects of nightwork upon children, and I have no hesitation in saying, contrary to what some employers were fond of asserting, those children who were subjected to it soon suffered in their health.' (l.c., 284., p. 55.) That such a question should furnish the material of serious controversy, shows plainly how capitalist production acts on the brain-functions of capitalists and their retainers.
63. l.c., 57, p. xii.
64. l.c.. Fourth Report (1865). 58. p. xii.
65. l.c.
66. l.c., p. xiii. The degree of culture of these 'labour-powers' must naturally be such as appears in the following dialogues with one of the commissioners: Jeremiah Haynes, age 12—'Four times four is 8; 4 fours are 16. A king is him that has all the money and gold. We have a king (told it is a Queen), they call her the Princess Alexandra. Told that she married the Queen's son. The Queen's son is the Princess Alexandra. A Princess is a man.' William Turner, age 12—'Don't live in England. Think it is a country, but didn't know before.' John Morris, age 14—'Have heard say that God made the world, and that all the people was drownded but one, heard say that one was a little bird.' William Smith age 15—'God made man, man made woman.' Edward Taylor, age 15—'Do not know of London.' Henry Matthewman, age 17—'Had been to chapel, but missed a good many times lately. One name that they preached about was Jesus Christ, but I cannot say any others, and I cannot tell anything about him. He was not killed, but died like other people. He was not the same as other people in some ways, because he was religious in some ways and others isn't.' (l.c., p. xv.) 'The devil is a good person. I don't know where he lives.' 'Christ was a wicked man.' 'This girl spelt God as dog, and did not know the name of the

queen.' ('Ch. Employment Comm. V. Report, 1866' p. 55, n. 278.) The same system obtains in the glass and paper works as in the metallurgical, already cited. In the paper factories, where the paper is made by machinery, night-work is the rule for all processes, except rag-sorting. In some cases night-work, by relays, is carried on incessantly through the whole week, usually from Sunday night until midnight of the following Saturday. Those who are on day-work work 5 days of 12, and 1 day of 18 hours; those on night-work 5 nights of 12, and 1 of 6 hours in each week. In other cases each set works 24 hours consecutively on alternate days, one set working 6 hours on Monday, and 18 on Saturday to make up the 24 hours. In other cases an intermediate system prevails, by which all employed on the paper-making machinery work 15 or 16 hours every day in the week. This system, says Commissioner Lord, 'seems to combine all the evils of both the 12 hours' and the 24 hours' relays.' Children under 13, young persons under 18, and women, work under this night system. Sometimes under the 12 hours' system they are obliged, on account of the non-appearance of those that ought to relieve them, to work a double turn of 24 hours. The evidence proves that boys and girls very often work overtime, which, not unfrequently, extends to 24 or even 36 hours of uninterrupted toil. In the continuous and unvarying process of glazing are found girls of 12 who work the whole month 14 hours a day, 'without any regular relief or cessation beyond 2 or, at most, 3 breaks of half an hour each for meals.' In some mills, where regular night-work has been entirely given up, over-work goes on to a terrible extent, 'and that often in the dirtiest, and in the hottest, and in the most monotonous of the various processes.' ('Ch. Employment Comm. Report IV., 1865,' p. xxxviii, and xxxix.)

67. Fourth Report, &c.. 1865, 79, p. xvi.
68. l.c., 80. p. xvi.
69. l.c., 82. p. xvii.
70. In our reflecting and reasoning age a man is not worth much who cannot give a good reason for everything, no matter how bad or how crazy. Everything in the world that has been done wrong has been done wrong for the very best of reasons. (Hegel, l.c., p. 249)
71. l.c., 85, p. xvii. To similar tender scruples of the glass manufacturers that regular meal-times for the children are impossible because as a consequence a certain quantity of heat, radiated by the furnaces, would be 'a pure loss' or 'wasted,' Commissioner White makes answer. His answer is unlike that of Ure, Senior, &c., and their puny German plagiarists à la Roscher who are touched by the 'abstinence,' 'self-denial,' 'saving,' of the capitalists in the expenditure of their gold, and by their Timur-Tamerlanish prodigality of human life! 'A certain amount of heat beyond what is usual at present might also be going to waste, if meal-times were secured in these cases, but it seems likely not equal in money-value to the waste of animal power now going on in glass-houses throughout the kingdom from growing boys not having enough quiet time to eat their meals at ease, with a little rest afterwards for digestion.' (l.c., p. xiv.) And this in the year of progress 1865! Without considering the expenditure of strength in lifting and carrying, such a child, in the sheds where bottle and flint glass are made, walks during the performance of his work 15-20 miles in every 6 hours! And the work often lasts 14 or 15 hours! In many of these glass works, as in the Moscow spinning mills, the system of 6 hours' relays is in force. 'During the working part of the week six hours is the utmost unbroken period ever attained at any one time for rest, and out of this has to come the time spent in coming and going to and from work, washing, dressing, and meals, leaving a very short period indeed for rest, and none for fresh air and play, unless at the expense of the sleep necessary for young boys, especially at such hot and fatiguing work.... Even the short sleep is obviously liable to be broken by a boy having to wake himself if it is night, or by the noise, if it is day.' Mr White gives cases where a boy worked 36 consecutive hours; others where boys of 12 drudged on until 2 in the morning, and then slept in the works till 5 a.m. (3 hours!) only to resume their work. 'The amount of work,' say Tremenheere and Tufnell, who drafted the general report, 'done by boys, youths, girls, and women, in the course of their

daily or nightly spell of labour, is certainly extraordinary.' (l.c., xliii. and xliv.) Meanwhile, late by night, self-denying Mr Glass-Capital, primed with port-wine, reels out of his club homeward droning out idiotically. 'Britons never, never shall be slaves!'

72. In England even now occasionally in rural districts a labourer is condemned to imprisonment for desecrating the Sabbath, by working in his front garden. The same labourer is punished for breach of contract if he remains away from his metal, paper, or glass works on the Sunday, even if it be from a religious whim. The orthodox Parliament will hear nothing of Sabbath-breaking if it occurs in the process of expanding capital. A memorial (August 1863), in which the London day-labourers in fish and poultry shops asked for the abolition of Sunday labour, states that their work lasts for the first 6 days of the week on an average 15 hours a-day, and on Sunday 8-10 hours. From this same memorial we learn also that the delicate gourmands among the aristocratic hypocrites of Exeter Hall, especially encourage this 'Sunday labour.' These 'holy ones,' so zealous *in cute curanda* [in attending to their bodily pleasures], show their Christianity by the humility with which they bear the overwork, the privations, and the hunger of others. *Obsequium ventris istis (the labourers) perniciosius est* [Gluttony is more ruinous to their stomachs—paraphrase of Horace].

73. 'We have given in our previous reports the statements of several experienced manufacturers to the effect that over-hours ... certainly tend prematurely to exhaust the working power of the men.' (l.c., 64. p. xiii.)

74. Cairnes, 'The Slave Power,' pp. 110. 111.

75. John Ward: 'The Borough of Stoke-upon-Trent,' London, 1843, p. 42.

76. Ferrand's Speech in the House of Commons, 27th April, 1863.

77. 'Those were the very words used by the cotton manufacturers.' l.c.

78. l.c. Mr Villiers, despite the best of intentions on his part, was 'legally' obliged to refuse the requests of the manufacturers. These gentlemen, however, attained their end through the obliging nature of the local poor law boards. Mr A. Redgrave, Inspector of Factories, asserts that this time the system under which orphans and pauper children were treated 'legally' as apprentices 'was not accompanied with the old abuses' (on these 'abuses' see Engels, l.c.), although in one case there certainly was 'abuse of this system in respect to a number of girls and young women brought from the agricultural districts of Scotland into Lancashire and Cheshire.' Under this system the manufacturer entered into a contract with the workhouse authorities for a certain period. He fed, clothed and lodged the children, and gave them a small allowance of money. A remark of Mr Redgrave to be quoted directly seems strange, especially if we consider that even among the years of prosperity of the English cotton trade, the year 1860 stands unparalleled, and that, besides, wages were exceptionally high. For this extraordinary demand for work had to contend with the depopulation of Ireland, with unexampled emigration from the English and Scotch agricultural districts to Australia and America, with an actual diminution of the population in some of the English agricultural districts, in consequence partly of an actual breakdown of the vital force of the labourers, partly of the already effected dispersion of the disposable population through the dealers in human flesh. Despite all this Mr Redgrave says: 'This kind of labour, however, would only be sought after when none other could be procured, for it is a high-priced labour. The ordinary wages of a boy of 13 would be about 4s. per week, but to lodge, to clothe, to feed, and to provide medical attendance and proper superintendence for 50 or 100 of these boys, and to set aside some remuneration for them, could not be accomplished for 4s. a-head per week.' (Report of the Inspector of Factories for 30th April, 1860, p. 27.) Mr Redgrave forgets to tell us how the labourer himself can do all this for his children out of their 4s. a-week wages, when the manufacturer cannot do it for the 50 or 100 children lodged, boarded, superintended all together. To guard against false conclusions from the text, I ought here to remark that the English cotton industry, since it was placed under the Factory Act of 1850 with its regulations of labour-time, &c., must be regarded as the model industry of England. The English

cotton operative is in every respect better off than his Continental companion in misery. 'The Prussian factory operative labours at least ten hours per week more than his English competitor, and if employed at his own loom in his own house, his labour is not restricted to even those additional hours. ('Rep. of Insp. of Fact.,' 31st October, 1855, p. 103.) Redgrave, the Factory Inspector mentioned above, after the Industrial Exhibition in 1851, travelled on the Continent, especially in France and Germany, for the purpose of inquiring into the conditions of the factories. Of the Prussian operative he says: 'He receives a remuneration sufficient to procure the simple fare, and to supply the slender comforts to which he has been accustomed ... he lives upon his coarse fare, and works hard, wherein his position is subordinate to that of the English operative.' ('Rep. of Insp. of Fact.' 31st Oct., 1855, p. 85.)

79. The over-worked 'die off with strange rapidity; but the places of those who perish are instantly filled, and a frequent change of persons makes no alteration in the scene.' ('England and America.' London, 1833, vol. I, p. 55. By E. G. Wakefield.)

80. See 'Public Health. Sixth Report of the Medical Officer of the Privy Council, 1863.' Published in London 1864. This report deals especially with the agricultural labourers. 'Sutherland ... is commonly represented as a highly improved county ... but ... recent inquiry has discovered that even there, in districts once famous for fine men and gallant soldiers, the inhabitants have degenerated into a meagre and stunted race. In the healthiest situations, on hill sides fronting the sea, the faces of their famished children are as pale as they could be in the foul atmosphere of a London alley.' (W. Th. Thornton. 'Overpopulation and its Remedy.' l.c., pp. 74, 75.) They resemble in fact the 30,000 'gallant Highlanders' whom Glasgow pigs together in its wynds and closes, with prostitutes and thieves.

81. 'But though the health of a population is so important a fact of the national capital, we are afraid it must be said that the class of employers of labour have not been the most forward to guard and cherish this treasure.... The consideration of the health of the operatives was forced upon the mill-owners.' (*Times*, November 5th, 1861.) 'The men of the West Riding became the clothiers of mankind ... the health of the workpeople was sacrificed, and the lace in a few generations must have degenerated. But a reaction set in. Lord Shaftesbury's Bill limited the hours of children's labour,' &c. ('Report of the Registrar-General,' for October 1861.)

82. We, therefore, find, e.g., that in the beginning of 1863, 26 firms owning extensive potteries in Staffordshire, amongst others, Josiah Wedgwood, & Sons, petition in a memorial for 'some legislative enactment.' Competition with other capitalists permits them no voluntary limitation of working-time for children, &c. 'Much as we deplore the evils before mentioned, it would not be possible to prevent them by any scheme of agreement between the manufacturers. ... Taking all these points into consideration, we have come to the conviction that some legislative enactment is wanted.' ('Children's Employment Comm.' Rep. I, 1863, p. 322.) Most recently a much more striking example offers. The rise in the price of cotton during a period of feverish activity, had induced the manufacturers in Blackburn to shorten, by mutual consent, the working-time in their mills during a certain fixed period. This period terminated about the end of November, 1871. Meanwhile, the wealthier manufacturers, who combined spinning with weaving, used the diminution of production resulting from this agreement, to extend their own business and thus to make great profits at the expense of the small employers. The latter thereupon turned in their extremity to the operatives, urged them earnestly to agitate for the 9 hours' system, and promised contributions in money to this end.

83. The labour Statutes, the like of which were enacted at the same time in France, the Netherlands, and elsewhere, were first formally repealed in England in 1813, long after the changes in methods of production had rendered them obsolete.

84. 'No child under 12 years of age shall be employed in any manufacturing establishment more than 10 hours in one day.' General Statutes of Massachusetts, 63, ch. 12. (The various Statutes were passed between 1836 and 1858.) 'Labour performed during a period of 10 hours on any day in all cotton, woollen, silk, paper, glass, and flax factories, or in manufactories of iron

and brass, shall be considered a legal day's labour. And be it enacted, that hereafter no minor engaged in any factory shall be holden or required to work more than 10 hours in any day,or 60 hours in any week; and that hereafter no minor shall be admitted as a worker under the age of 10 years in any factory within this State.' State of New Jersey. An Act to limit the hours of labour, &c., § 1 and 2. (Law of 18th March, 1851.) 'No minor who has attained the age of 12 years, and is under the age of 15 years, shall be employed in any manufacturing establishment more than 11 hours in any one day, nor before 5 o'clock in the morning, nor after 7.30 in the evening.' ('Revised Statutes of the State of Rhode Island,' &c., ch. 139, § 23, 1st July, 1857.)

85. 'Sophisms of Free Trade.' 7th Ed. London, 1850, p. 205, 9th Ed., p. 253. This same Tory, moreover, admits that 'Acts of Parliament regulating wages, but against the labourer and in favour of the master, lasted for the long period of 464 years. Population grew. These laws were then found, and really became, unnecessary and burdensome.' (l.c., p. 206.)

86. In reference to this statute, J. Wade with truth remarks: 'From the statement above (i.e., with regard to the statute) it appears that in 1496 the diet was considered equivalent to one-third of the income of an artificer and one-half the income of a labourer, which indicates a greater degree of independence among the working-classes than prevails at present; for the board, both of labourers and artificers, would now be reckoned at a much higher proportion of their wages.' (J. Wade, 'History of the Middle and Working Classes,' pp. 24, 25, and 577.) The opinion that this difference is due to the difference in the price-relations between food and clothing then and now is refuted by the most cursory glance at 'Chronicon Preciosum, &c.' By Bishop Fleetwood. 1st Ed., London, 1707; 2nd Ed., London, 1745.

87. W. Petty. 'Political Anatomy of Ireland, Verbum Sapienti,' 1672, Ed. 1691, p. 10.

88. 'A Discourse on the necessity of encouraging Mechanick Industry,' London, 1690, p. 13. Macaulay, who has falsified English history in the interests of the Whigs and the bourgeoisie, declares as follows: 'The practice of setting children prematurely to work ... prevailed in the 17th century to an extent which, when compared with the extent of the manufacturing system, seems almost incredible. At Norwich, the chief seat of the clothing trade, a little creature of six years old was thought fit for labour. Several writers of that time, and among them some who were considered as eminently benevolent, mention with exultation the fact that in that single city, boys and girls of very tender age create wealth exceeding what was necessary for their own subsistence by twelve thousand pounds a year. The more carefully we examine the history of the past, the more reason shall we find to dissent from those who imagine that our age has been fruitful of new social evils.... That which is new is the intelligence and the humanity which remedies them.' ('History of England,' vol. 1., p. 417.) Macaulay might have reported further that 'extremely well-disposed' *amis du commerce* in the 17th century, narrate with 'exultation' how in a poorhouse in Holland a child of four was employed, and that this example of '*vertu mise en pratique*' [applied virtue] passes muster in all the humanitarian works, *à la* Macaulay, to the time of Adam Smith. It is true that with the substitution of manufacture for handicrafts, traces of the exploitation of children begin to appear. This exploitation existed always to a certain extent among peasants, and was the more developed, the heavier the yoke pressing on the husbandman. The tendency of capital is there unmistakably; but the facts themselves are still as isolated as the phenomena of two-headed children. Hence they were noted 'with exultation' as especially worthy of remark and as wonders by the far-seeing '*amis du commerce*,' and recommended as models for their own time and for posterity. This same Scotch sycophant and fine talker, Macaulay, says: 'We hear to-day only of retrogression and see only progress.' What eyes, and especially what ears!

89. Among the accusers of the workpeople, the most angry is the anonymous author quoted in the text of 'An Essay on Trade and Commerce, containing Observations on Taxes, &c.,' London, 1770. He had already dealt with this subject in his earlier work: 'Considerations on Taxes.' London, 1765. On the same side follows Polonius Arthur Young, the unutterable statistical prattler. Among the defenders of the working-classes the foremost are: Jacob Vanderlint, in:

'Money Answers all Things.' London, 1734 the Rev. Nathaniel Forster, D. D., in 'An Enquiry into the Causes of the Present High Price of Provisions,' London, 1767; Dr Price, and especially Postlethwayt, as well in the supplement to his 'Universal Dictionary of Trade and Commerce,' as in his 'Great Bntain's Commercial Interest explained and improved.' 2nd Edition, 1755. The facts themselves are confirmed by many other writers of the time, among others by Josiah Tucker.

90. Postlethwayt, l.c., 'First Preliminary Discourse,' p. 14.

91. 'An Essay,' &c. He himself relates on p. 96 wherein the 'happiness' of the English agricultural labourer already in 1770 consisted. 'Their powers are always upon the stretch, they cannot live cheaper than they do, nor work harder.'

92. Protestantism, by changing almost all the traditional holidays into workdays, plays an important part in the genesis of capital.

93. 'An Essay,' 4c., pp. 15, 41, 96, 97, 55, 57, 69.—Jacob Vanderlint, as early as 1734, declared that the secret of the out-cry of the capitalists as to the laziness of the working people was simply that they claimed for the same wages 6 days' labour instead of 4.

94. l.c., p. 242.

95. l.c. 'The French,' he says, 'laugh at our enthusiastic ideas of liberty.' l.c., p. 78.

96. 'They especially objected to work beyond the 12 hours per day, because the law which fixed those hours, is the only good which remains to them of the legislation of the Republic.' ('Rep. of Insp. of Fact,' 31 st October, 1856, p. 80.) The French Twelve Hours' Bill of September 5th, 1850, a bourgeois edition of the decree of the Provisional Government of March 2nd, 1848, holds in all workshops without exceptions. Before this law the working-day in France was without definite limit. It lasted in the factories 14, 15, or more hours. See 'Des classes ouvrières en France, pendant l'année 1848. Par M. Blanqui.' M. Blanqui the economist, not the Revolutionist, had been entrusted by the Government with an inquiry into the condition of the working-class.

97. Belgium is the model bourgeois state in regard to the regulation of the working-day. Lord Howard of Welden, English Plenipotentiary at Brussels, reports to the Foreign Office May 12th, 1862: 'M. Rogier, the minister, informed me that children's labour is limited neither by a general law nor by any local regulations; that the Government, during the last three years, intended in every session to propose a bill on the subject, but always found an insuperable obstacle in the jealous opposition to any legislation in contradiction with the principle of perfect freedom of labour.'

98. 'It is certainly much to be regretted that any class of persons should toil 12 hours a day, which, including the time for their meals and for going to and returning from their work, amounts, in fact, to 14 of the 24 hours.... Without entering into the question of health, no one will hesitate, I think, to admit that, *in a moral point of view*, so entire an absorption of the time of the working-classes, without intermission, from the early age of 13, and in trades not subject to restriction, much younger, must be extremely prejudicial, and is an evil greatly to be deplored.... For the sake, therefore, of public morals, of bringing up an orderly population, and of giving the great body of the people a reasonable enjoyment of life, it is much to be desired that in all trades some portion of every working-day should be reserved for rest and leisure.' (Leonard Horner in 'Reports of Insp. of Fact. for 31st Dec., 1841.')

99. See 'Judgment of Mr J. H. Otway, Belfast. Hilary Sessions, County Antrim, 1860.'

100. It is very characteristic of the regime of Louis Philippe, the bourgeois king, that the one Factory Act passed during his reign, that of March 22nd, 1841, was never put in force. And this law only dealt with child-labour. It fixed 8 hours a day for children between 8 and 12, 12 hours for children between 12 and 16, &c., with many exceptions which allow night-work even for children 8 years old. The supervision and enforcement of this law are, in a country where every mouse is under police administration, left to the good-will of the *amis du commerce*. Only since 1853, in one single department—the Departement du Nord—has a paid government inspector been appointed. Not less characteristic of the development of French society, generally, is the fact, that Louis Philippe's law stood solitary among the all-

embracing mass of French laws, till the Revolution of 1848.

101. 'Report of Insp. of Fact.' 30th April, 1860, p. 50.
102. 'Rept. of Insp. of Fact.,' 31st October, 1849, p. 6.
103. 'Rept. of Insp. of Fact.,' 31st October, 1848, p. 98.
104. Leonard Horner uses the expression 'nefarious practices' in his official reports. ('Report of Insp. of Fact.,' 31st October, 1859, p. 7.)
105. 'Rept.,' &c., 30th Sept., 1844, p. 15.
106. The Act allows children to be employed for 10 hours if they do not work day after day, but only on alternate days. In the main, this clause remained inoperative.
107. 'As a reduction in their hours of work would cause a larger number (of children) to be employed, it was thought that the additional supply of children from 8 to 9 years of age would meet the increased demand' (l.c., p. 13).
108. 'Rep. of Insp. of Fact.,' 31st Oct., 1848, p. 16.
109. 'I found that men who had been getting 10s. a week, had had 1s. taken off for a reduction in the rate of 10 per cent, and 1s. 6d. off the remaining 9s. for the reduction in time, together 2s. 6d.. and notwithstanding this, many of them said they would rather work 10 hours.' l.c.
110. "Though I signed it [the petition], I said at the time I was putting my hand to a wrong thing.' 'Then why did you put your hand to it?' 'Because I should have been turned off if I had refused.' Whence it would appear that this petitioner felt himself 'oppressed,' but not exactly by the Factory Act.' l.c., p. 102.
111. p. 17, l.c. In Mr Horner's district 10,270 adult male labourers were thus examined in 181 factories. Their evidence is to be found in the appendix to the Factory Reports for the half-year ending October 1848. These examinations furnish valuable material in other connexions also.
112. l.c. See the evidence collected by Leonard Horner himself, Nos. 69, 70, 71, 72, 92, 93, and that collected by Sub-Inspector A., Nos. 51, 52, 58, 59, 62, 70, of the Appendix. One manufacturer, too, tells the plain truth. See No. 14, and No. 265, l.c.
113. Reports, &c., for 31st October, 1848, pp. 133, 134.
114. Reports, &c., for 30th April, 1848, p. 47.
115. Reports, &c., for 31st October, 1848, p. 130.
116. Reports, &c., l.c., p. 142.
117. Reports &c., for 31st October, 1850, pp. 5, 6.
118. The nature of capital remains the same in its developed as in its undeveloped form. In the code which the influence of the slave-owners, shortly before the outbreak of the American Civil War, imposed on the territory of New Mexico, it is said that the labourer, in as much as the capitalist has bought his labour-power, 'is his (the capitalist's) money.' The same view was current among the Roman patricians. The money they had advanced to the plebeian debtor had been transformed via the means of subsistence into the flesh and blood of the debtor. This 'flesh and blood' were, therefore, 'their money.' Hence, the Shylock-law of the Ten Tables. Linguet's hypothesis that the patrician creditors from time to time prepared, beyond the Tiber, banquets of debtors' flesh, may remain as undecided as that of Daumer on the Christian Eucharist.
119. Reports, &c.. for 30th April, 1848, p. 28.
120. Thus, among others, Philanthropist Ashworth to Leonard Horner, in a disgusting Quaker letter. (Reports, &c., April, 1849, p. 4.)
121. l.c., p. 140.
122. Reports, &c., for 30th April, 1849, pp. 21, 22. Cf like examples ibid., pp. 4, 5.
123. By I. and II. Will. IV., ch. 24, s. 10, known as Sir John Hobhouse's Factory Act, it was forbidden to any owner of a cotton-spinning or weaving mill, or the father, son, or brother of such owner, to act as Justice of the Peace in any inquiries that concerned the Factory Act.
124. l.c.
125. Reports, &c., for 30th April, 1849, p. 5.

126. Reports, &c., for 31st October, 1849, p. 6.
127. Reports, &c., for 30th April, 1849, p. 21.
128. Reports, &c., for 31st October, 1848, p. 95.
129. See Reports, &c., for 30th April, 1849, p. 6, and the detailed explanation of the 'shifting system,' by Factory Inspectors Howell and Saunders, in 'Reports, &c., for 31st October, 1848.' See also the petition to the Queen from the clergy of Ashton and vicinity, in the spring of 1849, against the 'shift system.'
130. Cf. for example, 'The Factory Question and the Ten Hours' Bill.', By R. H. Greg, 1837.
131. F. Engels: 'The English Ten Hours' Bill.' (In the 'Neue Rheinische Zeitung. Politisch-oekonomische Revue.' Edited by K. Marx. April number, 1850, p. 13.) The same 'high' Court of Justice discovered, during the American Civil War, a verbal ambiguity which exactly reversed the meaning of the law against the arming of pirate ships.
132. Rep., &c., for 30th April, 1850.
133. In winter, from 7 a.m. to 7 p.m. may be substituted.
134. 'The present law (of 1850) was a compromise whereby the employed surrendered the benefit of the Ten Hours' Act for the advantage of one uniform period for the commencement and termination of the labour of those whose labour is restricted.' (Reports, &c., for 30th April, 1852, p. 14.)
135. Reports, &c., for Sept., 1844, p. 13.
136. l.c.
137. l.c.
138. 'Reports, &c., for 31st Oct., 1846,' p. 20.
139. Reports, &c., for 31st Oct., 1861, p. 26.
140. l.c.,p. 27. On the whole the working population, subject to the Factory Act, has greatly improved physically. All medical testimony agrees on this point, and personal observation at different times has convinced me of it. Nevertheless, and exclusive of the terrible death-rate of children in the first years of their life, the official reports of Dr Greenhow show the unfavourable health condition of the manufacturing districts as compared with 'agricultural districts of normal health.' As evidence, take the following table from his 1861 report:

Percentage of Adult Males Engaged in Manufactures	14.9	42.6	37.3	41.9	31.0	14.9	36.6	30.4	—
Death-rate from Pulmonary Affections per 100,000 Males	598	708	547	611	691	588	721	726	305
Name of District	Wigan	Black-burn	Halifax	Bradford	Maccles-field	Leek	Stoke-upon-Trent	Wools-tanton	Eight healthy agricultural districts
Death-rate from Pulmonary Affections per 100,000 Females	644	734	564	603	804	705	665	727	340
Percentage of Adult Females Engaged in Manufactures	18.0	34.9	20.4	30.0	26.0	17.2	19.3	13.9	—
Kind of Female Occupation	Cotton	Do.	Worsted	Do.	Silk	Do.	Earthen-ware	Do.	—

141. It is well known with what reluctance the English 'Free-traders' gave up the protective duty on the silk manufacture. Instead of the protection against French importation, the absence of protection to English factory children now serves their turn.

142. During 1859 and 1860, the zenith years of the English cotton industry, some manufacturers tried, by the decoy bait of higher wages for over-time, to reconcile the adult male operatives to an extension of the working-day. The hand-mule spinners and self-actor mincers put an end to the experiment by a petition to their employers in which they say, 'Plainly speaking, our lives are to us a burthen; and, while we are confined to the mills *nearly two days a week more* than the other operatives of the country, we feel like helots in the land, and that we are perpetuating a system injurious to ourselves and future generations.... This, therefore, is to give you most respectful notice that when we commence work again after the Christmas and New Year's holidays, we shall work 60 hours per week, and no more, or from six to six, with one hour and a half out.' (Reports, &c., for 30th April, 1860, p. 30.)

143. On the means that the wording of this Act afforded for its violation of the Parliamentary Return 'Factories Regulation Act' (6th August, 1859), and in it Leonard Horner's 'Suggestions for amending the Factory Acts to enable the Inspectors to prevent illegal working, now becoming very prevalent.'

144. 'Children of the age of 8 years and upwards, have, indeed, been employed from 6 a.m. to 9 p.m. during the last half year in my district.' (Reports, &c., for 31st October, 1857, p. 39.)

145. 'The Printworks' Act is admitted to be a failure both with reference to its educational and protective provisions.' (Reports, &c., for 31st October, 1862, p. 52.)

146. Thus, *e.g.*, E. Potter in a letter to the *Times* of March 24th, 1863. The *Times* reminded him of the manufacturers' revolt against the Ten Hours' Bill.

147. Thus, among others, Mr W. Newmarch, collaborator and editor of Tooke's 'History of Prices.' Is it a scientific advance to make cowardly concessions to public opinion?

148. The Act passed in 1860, determined that, in regard to dye and bleachworks, the working-day should be fixed on August 1st, 1861, provisionally at 12 hours, and definitely on August 1st, 1862, at 10 hours, *i.e.*, at 10½ hours for ordinary days, and 7½ for Saturday. Now, when the fatal year, 1862, came, the old farce was repeated. Besides, the manufacturers petitioned Parliament to allow the employment of young persons and women for 12 hours during one year longer. 'In the existing condition of the trade (the time of the cotton famine), it was greatly to the advantage of the operatives to work 12 hours per day, and make wages when they could.' A bill to this effect had been brought in, 'and it was mainly due to the action of the operative bleachers in Scotland that the bill was abandoned.' (Reports, &c., for 31st October, 1862, pp. 14-15.) Thus defeated by the very workpeople, in whose name it pretended to speak, Capital discovered, with the help of lawyer spectacles, that the Act of 1860, drawn up, like all the Acts of Parliament for the 'protection of labour,' in equivocal phrases, gave them a pretext to exclude from its working the calenderers and finishers. English jurisprudence, ever the faithful servant of capital, sanctioned in the Court of Common Pleas this piece of pettifogging. 'The operatives have been greatly disappointed ... they have complained of over-work, and it is greatly to be regretted that the clear intention of the legislature should have failed by reason of a faulty definition.' (l.c., p. 18.)

149. The 'open-air bleachers' had evaded the law of 1860, by means of the lie that no women worked at it in the night. The lie was exposed by the Factory Inspectors, and at the same time Parliament was, by petitions from the operatives, bereft of its notions as to the cool meadow-fragrance, in which bleaching in the open-air was reported to take place. In this aerial bleaching, drying-rooms were used at temperatures of from 90° to 100° Fahrenheit, in which the work was done for the most part by girls. 'Cooling' is the technical expression for their occasional escape from the drying-rooms into the fresh air. 'Fifteen girls in stoves. Heat from 80° to 90° for linens, and 100° and upwards for cambrics. Twelve girls ironing and doing-up in a small room about 10 feet square, in the centre of which is a close stove. The

girls stand round the stove, which throws out a terrific heat, and dries the cambrics rapidly for the ironers. The hours of work for these hands are unlimited. If busy, they work till 9 or 12 at night for successive nights.' (Reports, &c., for 31st October, 1862, p. 56.) A medical man states: 'No special hours are allowed for cooling, but if the temperature gets too high, or the workers' hands get soiled from perspiration, they are allowed to go out for a few minutes.... My experience, which is considerable, in treating the diseases of stove workers, compels me to express the opinion that their sanitary condition is by no means so high as that of the operatives in a spinning factory (and Capital, in its memorials to Parliament, had painted them as floridly healthy after the manner of Rubens.) The diseases most observable amongst them are phthisis, bronchitis, irregularity of uterine functions, hysteria in its most aggravated forms, and rheumatism. All of these, I believe, are either directly or indirectly induced by the impure, overheated air of the apartments in which the hands are employed and the want of sufficient comfortable clothing to protect them from the cold, damp atmosphere, in winter, when going to their homes.' (l.c., pp. 56-57.) The Factory Inspectors remarked on the supplementary law of 1860, torn from these open-air bleachers: 'The Act has not only failed to afford that protection to the workers which it appears to offer, but contains a clause ... apparently so worded that, unless persons are detected working after 8 o'clock at night they appear to come under no protective provisions at all, and if they do so work the mode of proof is so doubtful that a conviction can scarcely follow.' (l.c., p. 52.) 'To all intents and purposes, therefore, as an Act for any benevolent or educational purpose, it is a failure; since it can scarcely be called benevolent to permit, which is tantamount to compelling, women and children to work 14 hours a day with or without meals, as the case may be, and perhaps for longer hours than these, without limit as to age, without reference to sex, and without regard to the social habits of the families of the neighbourhood, in which such works (bleaching and dyeing) are situated.' (Reports, &c., for 30th April, 1863, p. 40.)

150. *Note to the 2nd Ed.* Since 1866, when I wrote the above passages, a reaction has again set in.

151. 'The conduct of each of these classes (capitalists and workmen) has been the result of the relative situation in which they have been placed.' (Reports, &c., for 31st October, 1848, p. 113.)

152. 'The employments, placed under restriction, were connected with the manufacture of textile fabrics by the aid of steam or water-power There were two conditions to which an employment must be subject to cause it to be inspected, viz., the use of steam or waterpower, and the manufacture of certain specified fibre.' (Reports, &c., for 31st October, 1864, p. 8.)

153. On the condition of so-called domestic industries, specially valuable materials are to be found in the latest reports of the Children's Employment Commission.

154. 'The Acts of last Session (1864) ... embrace a diversity of occupations, the customs in which differ greatly, and the use of mechanical power to give motion to machinery is no longer one of the elements necessary, as formerly, to constitute, in legal phrase, a 'Factory.'' (Reports, &c., for 31st Octaber, 1864, p. 8.)

155. Belgium, the paradise of Continental Liberalism, shows no trace of this movement. Even in the coal and metal mines labourers of both sexes, and all ages, are consumed, in perfect 'freedom' at any period and through any length of time. Of every 1,000 persons employed there, 733 are men, 88 women, 135 boys, and 44 girls under 16; in the blast furnaces, &c., of every 1,000, 668 are men, 149 women, 98 boys, and 85 girls under 16. Add to this the low wages for the enormous exploitation of mature and immature labour-power. The average daily pay for a man is 2s. 8d., for a woman, 1s. 8d., for a boy, 1s. 2½d. As a result, Belgium had in 1863, as compared with 1850, nearly doubled both the amount and the value of its exports of coal, iron, &c.

156. Robert Owen, soon after 1810, not only maintained the necessity of a limitation of the working-day in theory, but actually introduced the 10 hours' day into his factory at New Lanark. This was laughed at as a communistic Utopia; so were his 'Combination of children's

education with productive labour and the Co-operative Societies of workingmen, first called into being by him. To-day, the first Utopia is a Factory Act, the second figures as an official phrase in all Factory Acts, the third is already being used as a cloak for reactionary humbug.

157. Ure: 'French translation, Philosophie des Manufactures.' Paris, 1836, Vol. II, pp. 39, 40, 67, 77, &c.

158. In the Compte Rendu of the International Statistical Congress at Paris, 1855, it is stated: 'The French law, which limits the length of daily labour in factories and workshops to 12 hours, does not confine this work to definite fixed hours. For children's labour only the work-time is prescribed as between 5 a.m. and 9 p.m. Therefore, some of the masters use the right which this fatal silence gives them to keep their works going, without intermission, day in, day out, possibly with the exception of Sunday. For this purpose, they use two different sets of workers, of whom neither is in the workshop more than 12 hours at a time, but the work of the establishment lasts day and night. The law is satisfied, but is humanity?' Besides 'the destructive influence or night-labour on the human organism,' stress is also laid upon 'the fatal influence of the association of the two sexes by night in the same badly-lighted workshops.'

159. 'For instance, there is within my district one occupier who, within the same curtilage, is at the same time a bleacher and dyer under the Bleaching and Dyeing Works Act, a printer under the Print Works Act, and a finisher under the Factory Act.' (Report of Mr Baker, in Reports, lic., for October 31st, 1861, p. 20.) After enumerating the different provisions of these Acts, and the complications arising from them, Mr Baker says: 'It will hence appear that it must be very difficult to secure the execution of these three Acts of Parliament where the occupier chooses to evade the law.' But what is assured to the lawyers by this is law-suits.

160. Thus the Factory Inspectors at last venture to say: 'These objections (of capital to the legal limitation of the working-day) must succumb before the broad principle of the rights of labour.... There is a time when the master's right in his workman's labour ceases, and his time becomes his own, even if there were no exhaustion in the question.' (Reports, 8cc., for 31 st Oct., 1862, p. 54.)

161. 'We, the workers of Dunkirk, declare that the length of time of labour required under the present system is too great, and that, far from leaving the worker time for rest and education, it plunges him into a condition of servitude but little better than slavery. That is why we decide that 8 hours are enough for a working-day, and ought to be legally recognised as enough; why we call to our help that powerful lever, the press; ... and why we shall consider all those that refuse us this help as enemies of the reform of labour and of the rights of the labourer.' (Resolution of the Working Men of Dunkirk, New York State, 1866.)

162. Reports, &c., for Oct., 1848, p. 112.

163. 'The proceedings (the manoeuvres of capital, e.g., from 1848-50) have afforded, moreover, incontrovertible proof of the fallacy of the assertion so often advanced, that operatives need no protection, but may be considered as free agents in the disposal of the only property which they possess—the labour of their hands and the sweat of their brows.' (Reports, &c., for April 30th, 1850, p. 45.) 'Free labour (if so it may be termed) even in a free country, requires the strong arm of the law to protect it.' (Reports, &c., for October 31st, 1864, p. 34.) 'To permit, which is tantamount to compelling ... to work 14 hours a day with or without meals,' &c. (Repts., &c., for April 30th, 1863, p. 40.)

164. Friedrich Engels, l.c., p. 5.

165. The 10 Hours' Act has, in the branches of industry that come under it, 'put an end to the premature decrepitude of the former long-hour workers.' (Reports, &c., for 31st Oct., 1859, p. 47.) 'Capital (in factories) can never be employed in keeping the machinery in motion beyond a limited time, without certain injury to the health and morals of the labourers employed; and they are not in a position to protect themselves.' l.c., p. 8)

166. 'A still greater boon is the distinction at last made clear between the worker's own time and

his master's. The worker knows now when that which he sells is ended, and when his own begins; and by possessing a sure foreknowledge of this, is enabled to prearrange his own minutes for his own purposes.' (l.c., p. 52.) 'By making them masters of their own time (the Factory Acts) have given them a moral energy which is directing them to the eventual possession of political power' (l.c., p. 47). With suppressed irony, and in very well weighed words, the Factory Inspectors hint that the actual law also frees the capitalist from some of the brutality natural to a man who is a mere embodiment of capital, and that it has given him time for a little 'culture.' 'Formerly the master had no time for anything but money; the servant had no time for anything but labour' (l.c., p. 48).

11

Rate and Mass of Surplus Value

In this chapter, as hitherto, the value of labour-power, and therefore the part of the working day necessary for the reproduction or maintenance of that labour-power, are supposed to be given, constant magnitudes.

This premised, with the rate, the mass is at the same time given of the surplus-value that the individual labourer furnishes to the capitalist in a definite period of time. If, *e.g.*, the necessary labour amounts to 6 hours daily, expressed in a quantum of gold = 3 shillings, then 3s. is the daily value of one labour-power or the value of the capital advanced in the buying of one labour-power. If, further, the rate of surplus-value be = 100%, this variable capital of 3s. produces a mass of surplus-value of 3s., or the labourer supplies daily a mass of surplus labour equal to 6 hours.

But the variable capital of a capitalist is the expression in money of the total value of all the labour-powers that he employs simultaneously. Its value is, therefore, equal to the average value of one labour-power, multiplied by the number of labour-powers employed. With a given value of labour-power, therefore, the magnitude of the variable capital varies directly as the number of labourers employed simultaneously. If the daily value of one labour-power = 3s., then a capital of 300s. must be advanced in order to exploit daily 100 labour-powers, of n times 3s., in order to exploit daily n labour-powers.

In the same way, if a variable capital of 3s., being the daily value of one labour-power, produce a daily surplus-value of 3s., a variable capital of 300s. will produce a daily surplus-value of 300s., and one of n times 3s. a daily surplus-value of n × 3s. The mass of the surplus-value produced is therefore equal to the surplus-value which the working day of one labourer supplies multiplied by the number of labourers employed. But as further the mass of surplus-value which a single labourer produces, the value of labour-power being given, is determined by the rate of the surplus-value, this law follows: the mass of the surplus-value produced is equal to the amount of the variable capital advanced, multiplied by the rate of surplus-value, in other words: it is determined by the compound ratio between the number of labour-powers exploited simultaneously by the same capitalist and the degree of exploitation of each individual labour-power.

Let the mass of the surplus-value be S, the surplus-value supplied by the individual labourer in the average day s the variable capital daily advanced in the purchase of one individual labour-power v, the sum total of the variable capital V, the value of an average labour-power P, its degree of exploitation (a'/a) (surplus-labour/necessary-labour) and the number of labourers employed n; we have:

$$S = \begin{cases} (s/v) \times V \\ P \times (a'/a) \times n \end{cases}$$

It is always supposed, not only that the value of an average labour-power is constant, but that the labourers employed by a capitalist are reduced to average labourers. There are exceptional cases in which the surplus-value produced does not increase in proportion to the number of labourers exploited, but then the value of the labour-power does not remain constant.

In the production of a definite mass of surplus-value, therefore, the decrease of one factor may be compensated by the increase of the other. If the variable capital diminishes, and at the same time the rate of surplus-value increases in the same ratio, the mass of surplus-value produced remains unaltered. If, on our earlier assumption the capitalist must advance 300s., in order to exploit 100 labourers a day, and if the rate of surplus-value amounts to 50%, this variable capital of 300s. yields a surplus-value of 150s. or of 100 × 3 workinghours. If the rate of surplus-value doubles, or the working day, instead of being extended from 6 to 9, is extended from 6 to 12 hours and at the same time variable capital is lessened by half, and reduced to 150s., it yields also a surplus-value of 150s. or 50 × 6 workinghours. Diminution of the variable capital may therefore be compensated by a proportionate rise in the degree of exploitation of labour-power, or the decrease in the number of the labourers employed by a proportionate extension of the working day. Within certain limits therefore the supply of labour exploitable by capital is independent of the supply of labourers.[1] On the contrary, a fall in the rate of surplus-value leaves unaltered the mass of the surplus-value produced, if the amount of the variable capital, or number of the labourers employed, increases in the same proportion.

Nevertheless, the compensation of a decrease in the number of labourers employed, or of the amount of variable capital advanced by a rise in the rate of surplus-value, or by the lengthening of the working-day, has impassable limits. Whatever the value of labour-power may be, whether the working time necessary for the maintenance of the labourer is 2 or 10 hours, the total value that a labourer can produce, day in, day out, is always less than the value in which 24 hours of labour are embodied, less than 12s., if 12s. is the money expression for 24 hours of realised labour. In our former assumption, according to which 6 working hours are daily necessary in order to reproduce the labour-power itself or to replace the value of the capital advanced in its purchase, a variable capital of 1,500s., that employs 500 labourers at a rate of surplus-value of 100% with a 12 hours' working day, produces daily a surplus-value of 1,500s. or of 6 × 500 working hours. A capital of 300s. that employs 100 labourers a day with a rate of surplus-value of 200% or with a working day of 18 hours, produces only a mass of surplus-value of 600s. or 12 × 100 working hours; and its total value-product, the equivalent of the variable capital advanced plus the surplus-value, can, day in, day out, never reach the sum of 1,200s. or 24 × 100 working hours. The absolute limit of the average working day—this being by nature always less than 24 hours—sets an absolute limit to the compensation of a reduction of variable capital by a higher rate of surplus-value, or of the decrease of the number of labourers exploited by a higher degree of exploitation of labour-power. This palpable law is of importance for the clearing up of many phenomena, arising from a tendency (to be worked out later on) of capital to reduce as much as possible the number of labourers employed by it, or its variable constituent transformed into labour-power, in contradiction to its other tendency to produce the greatest possible mass of surplus-value. On the other hand, if the mass of labour-power employed, or the amount of variable capital, increases, but not in proportion to the fall in the rate of surplus-value, the mass of the surplus-value produced, falls.

A third law results from the determination, of the mass of the surplus-value produced, by the two factors: rate of surplus-value and amount of variable capital advanced. The rate of surplus-value, or the degree of exploitation of labour-power, and the value of labour-power, or the amount of necessary working time being given, it is self evident that the greater the variable capital, the greater would be the mass of the value produced and of the surplus-value. If the limit of the working-day is given, and also the limit of its necessary constituent, the mass of value and surplus-value that an individual capitalist produces, is clearly exclusively dependent on the mass of labour that he sets in motion. But this, under the conditions supposed above, depends on the mass of labour-power, or the number of labourers whom he exploits, and this number in its turn is determined by the amount of the variable capital advanced. With a given rate of surplus-value, and a given value of labour-power, therefore, the masses of surplus-value produced vary directly as the amounts of the variable capitals advanced. Now we know that the capitalist divides his capital into two parts. One part he lays out in means of production. This is the constant part of his capital. The other part he lays out in living labour-power. This part forms his variable capital. On the basis of the same mode of social production, the division of capital into constant and variable differs in different branches of production, and within the same branch of production, too, this relation changes with changes in the technical conditions and in the social combinations of the processes of production. But in whatever proportion a given capital breaks up into a constant and a variable part, whether the latter is to the former as 1:2 or 1:10 or 1:x, the law just laid down is not affected by this. For, according to our previous analysis, the value of the constant capital reappears in the value of the product, but does not enter into the newly produced value, the newly created value product. To employ 1,000 spinners, more raw material, spindles, &c., are, of course, required, than to employ 100. The value of these additional means of production however may rise, fall, remain unaltered, be large or small; it has no influence on the process of creation of surplus-value by means of the labour-powers that put them in motion. The law demonstrated above now, therefore, takes this form: the masses of value and of surplus-value produced by different capitals—the value of labour-power being given and its degree of exploitation being equal—vary directly as the amounts of the variable constituents of these capitals, *i.e.*, as their constituents transformed into living labour-power.

This law clearly contradicts all experience based on appearance. Everyone knows that a cotton spinner, who, reckoning the percentage on the whole of his applied capital, employs much constant and little variable capital, does not, on account of this, pocket less profit or surplus-value than a baker, who relatively sets in motion much variable and little constant capital. For the solution of this apparent contradiction, many intermediate terms are as yet wanted, as from the standpoint of elementary algebra many intermediate terms are wanted to understand that 0/0 may represent an actual magnitude. Classical economy, although not formulating the law, holds instinctively to it, because it is a necessary consequence of the general law of value. It tries to rescue the law from collision with contradictory phenomena by a violent abstraction. It will be seen later[2] how the school of Ricardo has come to grief over this stumbling block. Vulgar economy which, indeed, 'has really learnt nothing,' here as everywhere sticks to appearances in opposition to the law which regulates and explains them. In opposition to Spinoza, it believes that 'ignorance is a sufficient reason.'

The labour which is set in motion by the total capital of a society, day in, day out, may be regarded as a single collective working day. If, *e.g.*, the number of labourers is a million, and the average working-day of a labourer is 10 hours, the social working day consists of ten million hours. With a given length of this working day, whether its limits are fixed physically or socially, the mass of surplus-value can only be increased by increasing the number of labourers, *i.e.*, of the labouring population. The growth of population here forms the mathematical limit to the production of surplus-value by the total social capital. On the contrary, with a given amount of population, this limit is formed by the possible lengthening of the working day.[3] It will, however, be seen in the following chapter that this law only holds for the form of surplus-value dealt with up to the present.

From the treatment of the production of surplus-value, so far, it follows that not every sum of money, or of value, is at pleasure transformable into capital. To effect this transformation, in fact, a certain minimum of money or of exchange-value must be presupposed in the hands of the individual possessor of money or commodities. The minimum of variable capital is the cost price of a single labour-power, employed the whole year through, day in, day out, for the production of surplus-value. If this labourer were in possession of his own means of production, and were satisfied to live as a labourer, he need not work beyond the time necessary for the reproduction of his means of subsistence, say 8 hours a day. He would, besides, only require the means of production sufficient for 8 working-hours. The capitalist, on the other hand, who makes him do, besides these 8 hours, say 4 hours' surplus-labour, requires an additional sum of money for furnishing the additional means of production. On our supposition, however, he would have to employ two labourers in order to live, on the surplus-value appropriated daily, as well as, and no better than a labourer, i.e., to be able to satisfy his necessary wants. In this case the mere maintenance of life would be the end of his production, not the increase of wealth; but this latter is implied in capitalist production. That he may live only twice as well as an ordinary labourer, and besides turn half of the surplus-value produced into capital, he would have to raise, with the number of labourers, the minimum of the capital advanced 8 times. Of course he can, like his labourer, take to work himself, participate directly in the process of production, but he is then only a hybrid between capitalist and labourer, a 'small master.' A certain stage of capitalist production necessitates that the capitalist be able to devote the whole of the time during which he functions as a capitalist, *i.e.*, as personified capital, to the appropriation and therefore control of the labour of others, and to the selling of the products of this labour.[4] The guilds of the middle ages therefore tried to prevent by force the transformation of the master of a trade into a capitalist, by limiting the number of labourers that could be employed by one master within a very small maximum. The possessor of money or commodities actually turns into a capitalist in such cases only where the minimum sum advanced for production greatly exceeds the maximum of the middle ages. Here, as in natural science, is shown the correctness of the law discovered by Hegel (in his 'Logic'), that merely quantitative differences beyond a certain point pass into qualitative changes.[5]

The minimum of the sum of value that the individual possessor of money or commodities must command, in order to metamorphose himself into a capitalist, changes with the different stages of development of capitalist production, and is at given stages different in different spheres of production, according to their special and technical conditions. Certain spheres of production demand, even at the very outset of capitalist production, a minimum of capital that is not as yet found in the hands of single individuals. This gives rise partly to state subsidies to private persons, as in France in the time of Clobber, and as in many German states up to our own epoch, partly to the formation of societies with legal monopoly for the exploitation of certain branches of industry and commerce, the forerunners of our modern joint stock companies.[6]

Within the process of production, as we have seen, capital acquired the command over labour, *i.e.*, over functioning labour-power or the labourer himself. Personified capital, the capitalist takes care that the labourer does his work regularly and with the proper degree of intensity.

Capital further developed into a coercive relation, which compels the working class to do more work than the narrow round of its own life-wants prescribes. As a producer of the activity of others, as a pumper-out of surplus labour and exploiter of labour-power, it surpasses in energy, disregard of bounds, recklessness and efficiency, all earlier systems of production based on directly compulsory labour.

At first, capital subordinates labour on the basis of the technical conditions in which it historically finds it. It does not, therefore, change immediately the mode of production. The production of surplus-value—in the form hitherto considered by us—by means of simple extension of the working day, proved, therefore, to be independent of any change in the mode of production itself. It was not less active in the old-fashioned bakeries than in the modern cotton factories.

If we consider the process of production from the point of view of the simple labour process, the labourer stands in relation to the means of production, not in their quality as capital, but as the mere means and material of his own intelligent productive activity. In tanning, *e.g.*, he deals with the skins as his simple object of labour. It is not the capitalist whose skin he tans. But it is different as soon as we deal with the process of production from the point of view of the process of creation of surplus-value. The means of production are at once changed into means for the absorption of the labour of others. It is now no longer the labourer that employs the means of production, but the means of production that employ the labourer. Instead of being consumed by him as material elements of his productive activity, they consume him as the ferment necessary to their own life-process, and the life-process of capital consists only in its movement as value constantly expanding, constantly multiplying itself. Furnaces and workshops that stand idle by night, and absorb no living labour, are 'a mere loss' to the capitalist. Hence, furnaces and workshops constitute lawful claims upon the night-labour of the work-people. The simple transformation of money into the material factors of the process of production, into means of production, transforms the latter into a title and a right to the labour and surpluslabour of others. An example will show, in conclusion, how this sophistication, peculiar to and characteristic of capitalist production, this complete inversion of the relation between dead and living labour, between value and the force that creates value, mirrors itself in the consciousness of capitalists. During the revolt of the English factory lords between 1848 and 1850, 'the head of one of the oldest and most respectable houses in the West of Scotland, Messrs. Carlile Sons & Co., of the linen and cotton thread factory at Paisley, a company which has now existed for about a century, which was in operation in 1752, and four generations of the same family have conducted it' ... this 'very intelligent gentleman' then wrote a letter[7] in the *Glasgow Daily Mail* of April 25th, 1849, with the title, 'The relay system,' in which among other things the following grotesquely naïve passage occurs: 'Let us now ... see what evils will attend the limiting to 10 hours the working of the factory.... They amount to the most serious damage to the millowner's prospects and property. If he (i.e., his 'hands') worked 12 hours before, and is limited to 10, then every 12 machines or spindles in his establishment shrink to 10, and should the works be disposed of, they will be valued only as 10, so that a sixth part would thus be deducted from the value of every factory in the country.'[8]

To this West of Scotland bourgeois brain, inheriting the accumulated capitalistic qualities of 'four generations,' the value of the means of production, spindles, &c., is so inseparably mixed up with their property, as capital, to expand their own value, and to swallow up daily a definite quantity of the unpaid labour of others, that the head of the firm of Carlile & Co. actually imagines that if he sells his factory, not only will the value of the spindles be paid to him, but, in addition, their power of annexing surplus-value, not only the labour which is embodied in them, and is necessary to the production of spindles of this kind, but also the surpluslabour which they help to pump out daily from the brave Scots of Paisley, and for that very reason he thinks that with the shortening of the working day by 2 hours, the selling-price of 12 spinning machines dwindles to that of 10!

Notes

1. This elementary law appears to be unknown to the vulgar economists, who, upside-down Archimedes, in the determination of the market-price of labour by supply and demand, imagine they have found the fulcrum by means of which, not to move the world, but to stop its motion.
2. Further particulars will be given in Book IV.
3. 'The Labour, that is the economic time, of society, is a given portion, say ten hours a day of a million of people, or ten million hours.... Capital has its boundary of increase. This boundary may, at any given period, be attained in the actual extent of economic time employed.' ('An Essay on the Political Economy of Nations.' London, 1821, pp. 47, 49.)
4. 'The farmer cannot rely on his own labour, and if he does, I will maintain that he is a loser by it. His employment should be a general attention to the whole: his thresher must be watched, or he will soon lose his wages in corn not threshed out, his mowers, reapers, &c., must be looked after; he must constantly go round his fences; he must see there is no neglect; which would be the case if he was confined to any one spot.' ('An Inquiry into the Connexion between the Present Price of Provisions and the Size of Farms, &c. By a Farmer.' London, 1773, p. 12.) This book is very interesting. In it, the genesis of the 'capitalist farmer' or 'merchant farmer,' as he is explicitly called, may be studied, and his self-glorification at the expense of the small farmer who has only to do with bare subsistence, be noted. 'The class of capitalists are from the first partially, and they become ultimately completely, discharged from the necessity of the manual labour.' ('Textbook of Lectures on the Political Economy of Nations. By the Rev. Richard Jones.' Hertford 1852. Lecture III., p. 39.)
5. The molecular theory of modern chemistry first scientifically worked out by Laurent and Gerhardt rests on no other law. (Addition to 3rd Edition.) For the explanation of this statement, which is not very clear to non-chemists, we remark that the author speaks here of the homologous series of carbon compounds, first so named by C. Gerhardt in 1843, each series of which has its own general algebraic formula. Thus the series of paraffins: C_nH_{2n+2}, that of the normal alcohols: $C_nH_{2n+2}O$; of the normal fatty acids: $CnH_{2n}O_2$ and many others. In the above examples, by the simply quantitative addition of CH_2 to the molecular formula, a qualitatively different body is each time formed. On the share (overestimated by Marx) of Laurent and Gerhardt in the determination of this important fact see Kopp, 'Entwicklung der Chemie.' Munchen, 1873, pp. 709, 716, and Schorkmmer, 'The Rise and Development of Organic Chemistry.' London, 1879, p. 54.—*F. E.*. See Letter from Marx to Engels, 22 June 1867

   For Hegel's formulation of the idea in the *Logic*, see Remark: Examples of Such Nodal Lines; the Maxim, 'Nature Does Not Make Leaps.'
6. Martin Luther calls these kinds of institutions: 'The Company Monopolia.'
7. Reports of Insp. of Fact., April 30th, 1849, p. 59.
8. l.c., p. 60. Factory Inspector Stuart, himself a Scotchman, and in contrast to the English Factory Inspectors, quite taken captive by the capitalistic method of thinking, remarks expressly on this letter which he incorporates in his report that it is 'the most useful of the communications which any of the factory-owners working with relays have given to those engaged in the same trade, and which is the most calculated to remove the prejudices of such of them as have scruples respecting any change of the arrangement of the hours of work.'

PART IV

PRODUCTION OF RELATIVE SURPLUS VALUE

12

The Concept of Relative Surplus Value

That portion of the working day which merely produces an equivalent for the value paid by the capitalist for his labour-power, has, up to this point, been treated by us as a constant magnitude, and such in fact it is, under given conditions of production and at a given stage in the economic development of society. Beyond this, his necessary labour-time, the labourer, we saw, could continue to work for 2, 3, 4, 6, &c., hours. The rate of surplus-value and the length of the working day depended on the magnitude of this prolongation. Though the necessary labour-time was constant, we saw, on the other hand, that the total working day was variable. Now suppose we have a working day whose length, and whose apportionment between necessary labour and surplus-labour, are given. Let the whole line a c, a—b—c represent, for example, a working day of 12 hours; the portion of a b 10 hours of necessary labour, and the portion b c 2 hours of surplus-labour. How now can the production of surplus-value be increased, i.e., how can the surplus-labour be prolonged, without, or independently of, any prolongation of a c?

Although the length of a c is given, b c appears to be capable of prolongation, if not by extension beyond its end c, which is also the end of the working day a c, yet, at all events, by pushing back its starting-point b in the direction of a. Assume that b'—b in the line ab'bc is equal to half of b c

a——b'—b—c

or to one hour's labour-time. If now, in a c, the working day of 12 hours, we move the point b to b', b c becomes b' c; the surplus-labour increases by one half, from 2 hours to 3 hours, although the working day remains as before at 12 hours. This extension of the surplus labour-time from b c to b' c, from 2 hours to 3 hours, is, however, evidently impossible, without a simultaneous contraction of the necessary labour-time from a b into a b', from 10 hours to 9 hours. The prolongation of the surplus-labour would correspond to a shortening of the necessary labour; or a portion of the labour-time previously consumed, in reality, for the labourer's own benefit, would be converted into labour-time for the benefit of the capitalist. There would be an alteration, not in the length of the working day, but in its division into necessary labour-time and surplus labour-time.

On the other hand, it is evident that the duration of the surplus-labour is given, when the length of the working day, and the value of labour-power, are given. The value of labour-power, i.e., the labour-time requisite to produce labour-power, determines the labour-time necessary for the reproduction of that value. If one working-hour be embodied in sixpence, and the value of a day's labour-power be five shillings, the labourer must work 10 hours a day, in order to replace the value paid by capital for his labour-power, or to produce an equivalent for the value of his daily necessary means of subsistence. Given the value of these means of subsistence, the value of his labour-power is given;[1] and given the value of his labour-power, the duration of his necessary labour-time is given. The duration of the surplus-labour, however, is arrived at, by subtracting the necessary labour-time from the total working day. Ten hours subtracted from twelve, leave two, and it is not easy to see, how, under the given conditions, the surplus-labour can possibly be prolonged beyond two hours. No doubt, the capitalist can, instead of five shillings, pay the labourer four shillings and sixpence or even less. For the reproduction of this value of four shillings and sixpence, nine hours' labour-time would suffice; and consequently three hours of surplus-labour, instead of two, would accrue to the capitalist, and the surplus-value would rise from one shilling to eighteen-pence. This result, however, would be obtained only by lowering the wages of the labourer below the value of his labour-power. With the four shillings and sixpence which he produces in nine hours, he commands one-tenth less of the necessaries of life than before, and consequently the proper reproduction of his labour-power is crippled. The surplus-labour would in this case be prolonged only by an overstepping of its normal limits; its domain would be extended only by a usurpation of part of the domain of necessary labour-time. Despite the important part which this method plays in actual practice, we are excluded from considering it in this place, by our assumption, that all commodities, including labour-power, are bought and sold at their full value. Granted this, it follows that the labour-time necessary for the production of labour-power, or for the reproduction of its value, cannot be lessened by a fall in the labourer's wages below the value of his labour-power, but only by a fall in this value itself. Given the length of the working day, the prolongation of the surplus-labour must of necessity originate in the curtailment of the necessary labour-time; the latter cannot arise from the former. In the example we have taken, it is necessary that the value of labour-power should actually fall by one-tenth, in order that the necessary labour-time may be diminished by one-tenth, i.e., from ten hours to nine, and in order that the surplus labour may consequently be prolonged from two hours to three.

Such a fall in the value of labour-power implies, however, that the same necessaries of life which were formerly produced in ten hours, can now be produced in nine hours. But this is impossible without an increase in the productiveness of labour. For example, suppose a shoe-maker, with given tools, makes in one working day of twelve hours, one pair of boots. If he must make two pairs in the same time, the productiveness of his labour must be doubled; and this cannot be done, except by an alteration in his tools or in his mode of working, or in both. Hence, the conditions of production, i.e., his mode of production, and the labour-process itself, must be revolutionised. By increase in the productiveness of labour, we mean, generally, an alteration in the labour-process, of such a kind as to shorten the labour-time socially necessary for the production of a commodity, and to endow a given quantity of labour with the power of producing a greater quantity of use-value.[2] Hitherto in treating of surplus-value, arising from a simple prolongation of the working day, we have assumed the mode of production to be given and invariable. But when surplus-value has to be produced by the conversion of necessary labour into surplus-labour, it by no means suffices for capital to take over the labour-process in the form under which it has been historically handed down, and then simply to prolong the duration of that process. The technical and social conditions of the process, and consequently the very mode of production must be revolutionised, before the productiveness of labour can be increased. By that means alone can the value of labour-power be made to sink, and the portion of the working day necessary for the reproduction of that value, be shortened.

The surplus-value produced by prolongation of the working day, I call *absolute surplus-value*. On the other hand, the surplus-value arising from the curtailment of the necessary labour-time, and from the corresponding alteration in the respective lengths of the two components of the working day, I call *relative surplus-value*.

In order to effect a fall in the value of labour-power, the increase in the productiveness of labour must seize upon those branches of industry whose products determine the value of labour-power, and consequently either belong to the class of customary means of subsistence, or are capable of supplying the place of those means. But the value of a commodity is determined, not only by the quantity of labour which the labourer directly bestows upon that commodity, but also by the labour contained in the means of production. For instance, the value of a pair of boots depends not only on the cobbler's labour, but also on the value of the leather, wax, thread, &c. Hence, a fall in the value of labour-power is also brought about by an increase in the productiveness of labour, and by a corresponding cheapening of commodities in those industries which supply the instruments of labour and the raw material, that form the material elements of the constant capital required for producing the necessaries of life. But an increase in the productiveness of labour in those branches of industry which supply neither the necessaries of life, nor the means of production for such necessaries, leaves the value of labour-power undisturbed.

The cheapened commodity, of course, causes only a pro tanto fall in the value of labour-power, a fall proportional to the extent of that commodity's employment in the reproduction of labour-power. Shirts, for instance, are a necessary means of subsistence, but are only one out of many. The totality of the necessaries of life consists, however, of various commodities, each the product of a distinct industry; and the value of each of those commodities enters as a component part into the value of labour-power. This latter value decreases with the decrease of the labour-time necessary for its reproduction; the total decrease being the sum of all the different curtailments of labour-time effected in those various and distinct industries. This general result is treated, here, as if it were the immediate result directly aimed at in each individual case. Whenever an individual capitalist cheapens shirts, for instance, by increasing the productiveness of labour he by no means necessarily aims at reducing the value of labour-power and shortening, pro tanto the necessary labour-time. But it is only in so far as he ultimately contributes to this result, that he assists in raising the general rate of surplus-value.[3] The general and necessary tendencies of capital must be distinguished from their forms of manifestation.

It is not our intention to consider, here, the way in which the laws, immanent in capitalist production, manifest themselves in the movements of individual masses of capital, where they assert themselves as coercive laws of competition, and are brought home to the mind and consciousness of the individual capitalist as the directing motives of his operations. But this much is clear; a scientific analysis of competition is not possible, before we have a conception of the inner nature of capital, just as the apparent motions of the heavenly bodies are not intelligible to any but him, who is acquainted with their real motions, motions which are not directly perceptible by the senses. Nevertheless, for the better comprehension of the production of relative surplus-value, we may add the following remarks, in which we assume nothing more than the results we have already obtained.

If one hour's labour is embodied in sixpence, a value of six shillings will be produced in a working day of 12 hours. Suppose, that with the prevailing productiveness of labour, 12 articles are produced in these 12 hours. Let the value of the means of production used up in each article be sixpence. Under these circumstances, each article costs one shilling: sixpence for the value of the means of production, and sixpence for the value newly added in working with those means. Now let some one capitalist contrive to double the productiveness of labour, and to produce in the working day of 12 hours, 24 instead of 12 such articles. The value of the means of production remaining the same, the value of each article will fall to ninepence, made up of sixpence for the value of the means of production and threepence for the value newly added by the labour. Despite the doubled productiveness of labour, the day's labour creates, as before, a new value of six shillings and no more, which, however, is now spread over twice as many articles. Of this value each article now has embodied in it 1/24th, instead of 1/12th, threepence instead of sixpence; or, what amounts to the same thing, only half an hour's instead of a whole hour's labour-time, is now added to the means of production while they are being transformed into each article. The individual value of these articles is now below their social value; in other words, they have cost less labour-time than the great bulk of the same article produced under the average social conditions. Each article costs, on an average, one shilling, and represents 2 hours of social labour; but under the altered mode of production it costs only ninepence, or contains only 1½ hours' labour. The real value of a commodity is, however, not its individual value, but its social value; that is to say, the real value is not measured by the labour-time that the article in each individual case costs the producer, but by the labour-time socially required for its production. If therefore, the capitalist who applies the new method, sells his commodity at its social value of one shilling, he sells it for threepence above its individual value, and thus realises an extra surplus-value of threepence. On the other hand, the working day of 12 hours is, as regards him, now represented by 24 articles instead of 12. Hence, in order to get rid of the product of one working day, the demand must be double what it was, i.e., the market must become twice as extensive. Other things being equal, his commodities can command a more extended market only by a diminution of their prices. He will therefore sell them above their individual but under their social value, say at tenpence each. By this means, he still squeezes an extra surplus-value of one penny out of each. This augmentation of surplus-value is pocketed by him, whether his commodities belong or not to the class of necessary means of subsistence that participate in determining the general value of labour-power. Hence, independently of this latter circumstance, there is a motive for each individual capitalist to cheapen his commodities, by increasing the productiveness of labour.

Nevertheless, even in this case, the increased production of surplus-value arises from the curtailment of the necessary labour-time, and from the corresponding prolongation of the surplus-labour.[4] Let the necessary labour-time amount to 10 hours, the value of a day's labour-power to five shillings, the surplus labour-time to 2 hours, and the daily surplus-value to one shilling. But the capitalist now produces 24 articles, which he sells at tenpence a-piece, making twenty shillings in all. Since the value of the means of production is twelve shillings, 14 2/5 of these articles merely replace the constant capital advanced. The labour of the 12 hours' working day is represented by the remaining 9 3/5 articles. Since the price of the labour-power is five shillings, 6 articles represent the necessary labour-time, and 3 3/5 articles the surplus-labour. The ratio of the necessary labour to the surplus-labour, which under average social conditions was 5:1, is now only 5:3. The same result may be arrived at in the following way. The value of the product of the working day of 12 hours is twenty shillings. Of this sum, twelve shillings belong to the value of the means of production, a value that merely re-appears. There remain eight shillings, which are the expression in money, of the value newly created during the working day. This sum is greater than the sum in which average social labour of the same kind is expressed: twelve hours of the latter labour are expressed by six shillings only. The exceptionally productive labour operates as intensified labour; it creates in equal periods of time greater values than average social labour of the same kind. (See Ch. I. Sect 2. p. 44.) But our capitalist still continues to pay as before only five shillings as the value of a day's labour-power. Hence, instead of 10 hours, the labourer need now work only 7½ hours, in order to reproduce this value. His surplus-labour is, therefore, increased by 2½ hours, and the surplus-value he produces grows from one, into three shillings. Hence, the capitalist who applies the improved method of production, appropriates to surplus-labour a greater portion of the working day, than the other capitalists in the same trade. He does individually, what the whole body of capitalists engaged in producing relative surplus-value, do collectively. On the other hand, however, this extra surplus-value vanishes, so soon as the new method of production has become general, and has consequently caused the difference between the individual value of the cheapened commodity and its social value to vanish. The law of the determination of value by labour-time, a law which brings under its sway the individual capitalist who applies the new method of production, by compelling him to sell his goods under their social value, this same law, acting as a coercive law of competition, forces his competitors to adopt the new method.[5] The general rate of surplus-value is, therefore, ultimately affected by the whole process, only when the increase in the productiveness of labour, has seized upon those branches of production that are connected with, and has cheapened those commodities that form part of, the necessary means of subsistence, and are therefore elements of the value of labour-power.

The value of commodities is in inverse ratio to the productiveness of labour. And so, too, is the value of labour-power, because it depends on the values of commodities.

Relative surplus-value is, on the contrary, directly proportional to that productiveness. It rises with rising and falls with falling productiveness. The value of money being assumed to be constant, an average social working day of 12 hours always produces the same new value, six shillings, no matter how this sum may be apportioned between surplus-value and wages. But if, in consequence of increased productiveness, the value of the necessaries of life fall, and the value of a day's labour-power be thereby reduced from five shillings to three, the surplus-value increases from one shilling to three. Ten hours were necessary for the reproduction of the value of the labour-power; now only six are required. Four hours have been set free, and can be annexed to the domain of surplus-labour. Hence there is immanent in capital an inclination and constant tendency, to heighten the productiveness of labour, in order to cheapen commodities, and by such cheapening to cheapen the labourer himself.[6]

The value of a commodity is, in itself, of no interest to the capitalist. What alone interests him, is the surplus-value that dwells in it, and is realisable by sale. Realisation of the surplus-value necessarily carries with it the refunding of the value that was advanced. Now, since relative surplus-value increases in direct proportion to the development of the productiveness of labour, while, on the other hand, the value of commodities diminishes in the same proportion; since one and the same process cheapens commodities, and augments the surplus-value contained in them; we have here the solution of the riddle: why does the capitalist, whose sole concern is the production of exchange-value, continually strive to depress the exchange-value of commodities? A riddle with which Quesnay, one of the founders of Political Economy, tormented his opponents, and to which they could give him no answer.

> 'You acknowledge,' he says, 'that the more expenses and the cost of labour can, in the manufacture of industrial products, be reduced without injury to production, the more advantageous is such reduction, because it diminishes the price of the finished article. And yet, you believe that the production of wealth, which arises from the labour of the work people, consists in the augmentation of the exchange-value of their products.'[7]

The shortening of the working day is, therefore, by no means what is aimed at, in capitalist production, when labour is economised by increasing its productiveness.[8] It is only the shortening of the labour-time, necessary for the production of a definite quantity of commodities, that is aimed at. The fact that the workman, when the productiveness of his labour has been increased, produces, say 10 times as many commodities as before, and thus spends one-tenth as much labour-time on each, by no means prevents him from continuing to work 12 hours as before, nor from producing in those 12 hours 1,200 articles instead of 120. Nay, more, his working day may be prolonged at the same time, so as to make him produce, say 1,400 articles in 14 hours. In the treatises, therefore, of economists of the stamp of MacCulloch, Ure, Senior, and *tutti quanti* [the like], we may read upon one page, that the labourer owes a debt of gratitude to capital for developing his productiveness, because the necessary labour-time is thereby shortened, and on the next page, that he must prove his gratitude by working in future for 15 hours instead of 10. The object of all development of the productiveness of labour, within the limits of capitalist production, is to shorten that part of the working day, during which the workman must labour for his own benefit, and by that very shortening, to lengthen the other part of the day, during which he is at liberty to work gratis for the capitalist. How far this result is also attainable, without cheapening commodities, will appear from an examination of the particular modes of producing relative surplus-value, to which examination we now proceed.

Notes

1. The value of his average daily wages is determined by what the labourer requires 'so as to live, labour, and generate.' (Wm. Petty: 'Political Anatomy of Ireland,' 1672, p. 64.) 'The

price of Labour is always constituted of the price of necessaries ... whenever ... the labouring man's wages will not, suitably to his low rank and station, as a labouring man, support such a family as is often the lot of many of them to have,' he does not receive proper wages. (J. Vanderlint, l.c., p. 15.) 'Le simple ouvrier, qui n'a que ses bras et son industrie, n'a rien qu'autant qu'il parvient à vendre à d'autres sa peine... En tout genre de travail il doit arriver, et il arrive en effet, que le salaire de l'ouvrier se borne à ce qui lui est nécessaire pour lui procurer sa subsistance.' [The mere workman, who has only his arms and his industry, has nothing unless he succeeds in selling his labour to others ... In every kind of work it cannot fail to happen, as a matter of fact it does happen, that the wages of the workman are limited to what is necessary to procure him his subsistence.] (Turgot, 'Réflexions, &c.,' *Oeuvres*, éd. Daire t. I, p. 10.) 'The price of the necessaries of life is, in fact, the cost of producing labour.' (Malthus, 'Inquiry into, &c., Rent,' London, 1815, p. 48, note.)

2. 'Quando si perfezionano le arti, che non è altro che la scoperta di nuove vie, onde si possa compiere una manufattura con meno gente o (che è lo stesso) in minor tempo di prima.' (Galiani, l.c., p. 159.) 'L'économie sur les frais de production ne peut donc être autre chose que l'économie sur la quantité de travail employé pour produire.' [Perfection of the crafts means nothing other than the discovery of new ways of making a product with fewer people, or (which is the same thing) in less time than previously] (Sismondi, 'Études,' t. I. p. 22.)

3. 'Let us suppose ... the products ... of the manufacturer are doubled by improvement in machinery ... he will be able to clothe his workmen by means of a smaller proportion of the entire return ... and thus his profit will be raised. But in no other way will it be influenced.' (Ramsay, l.c., pp. 168, 169.)

4. 'A man's profit does not depend upon his command of the produce of other men's labour, but upon his command of labour itself. If he can sell his goods at a higher price, while his workmen's wages remain unaltered, he is clearly benefited.... A smaller proportion of what he produces is sufficient to put that labour into motion, and a larger proportion consequently remains for himself.' ('Outlines of Pol. Econ.' London, 1832, pp. 49, 50.)

5. 'If my neighbour by doing much with little labour, can sell cheap, I must contrive to sell as cheap as he. So that every art, trade, or engine, doing work with labour of fewer hands, and consequently cheaper, begets in others a kind of necessity and emulation, either of using the same art, trade, or engine, or of inventing something like it, that every man may be upon the square, that no man may be able to undersell his neighbour.' ('The Advantages of the East India Trade to England,' London, 1720, p. 67.)

6. 'In whatever proportion the expenses of a labourer are diminished, in the same proportion will his wages be diminished, if the restraints upon industry are at the same time taken off.' ('Considerations Concerning Taking off the Bounty on Corn Exported,' &c., London, 1753, p. 7.) 'The interest of trade requires, that corn and all provisions should be as cheap as possible; for whatever makes them dear, must make labour dear also ... in all countries, where industry is not restrained, the price of provisions must affect the price of labour. This will always be diminished when the necessaries of life grow cheaper.' (I. c., p. 3.) 'Wages are decreased in the same proportion as the powers of production increase. Machinery, it is true, cheapens the necessaries of life, but it also cheapens the labourer.' ('A Prize Essay on the Comparative Merits of Competition and Co-operation.' London, 1834, p. 27.)

7. 'Ils conviennent que plus on peut, sans préjudice, épargner de frais ou de travaux dispendieux dans la fabrication des ouvrages des artisans, plus cette épargne est profitable par la diminution des prix de ces ouvrages. Cependant ils croient que la production de richesse qui résulte des travaux des artisans consiste dans l'augmentation de la valeur vénale de leurs ouvrages.' (Quesnay: 'Dialogues sur le Commerce et les Travaux des Artisans.' pp. 188, 189.)

8. 'Ces spéculateurs si économes du travail des ouvriers qu'il faudrait qu'ils payassent.' [These speculators, who are so economical of the labour of workers they would have to pay] (J.

N. Bidaut: 'Du Monopole qui s'établit dans les arts industriels et le commerce.' Paris, 1828, p. 13.) 'The employer will be always on the stretch to economise time and labour.' (Dugald Stewart: Works ed. by Sir W. Hamilton, Edinburgh, v., viii., 1855. 'Lectures on Polit. Econ.,' p. 318.) 'Their (the capitalists') interest is that the productive powers of the labourers they employ should be the greatest possible. On promoting that power their attention is fixed and almost exclusively fixed.' (R. Jones: l.c., Lecture III.)

13

Co-operation

Capitalist production only then really begins, as we have already seen, when each individual capital employs simultaneously a comparatively large number of labourers; when consequently the labour-process is carried on on an extensive scale and yields, relatively, large quantities of products. A greater number of labourers working together, at the same time, in one place (or, if you will, in the same field of labour), in order to produce the same sort of commodity under the mastership of one capitalist, constitutes, both historically and logically, the starting-point of capitalist production. With regard to the mode of production itself, manufacture, in its strict meaning, is hardly to be distinguished, in its earliest stages, from the handicraft trades of the guilds, otherwise than by the greater number of workmen simultaneously employed by one and the same individual capital. The workshop of the medieval master handicraftsman is simply enlarged.

At first, therefore, the difference is purely quantitative. We have shown that the surplus-value produced by a given capital is equal to the surplus-value produced by each workman multiplied by the number of workmen simultaneously employed. The number of workmen in itself does nor affect, either the rate of surplus-value, or the degree of exploitation of labour-power. If a working-day of 12 hours be embodied in six shillings, 1,200 such days will be embodied in 1,200 times 6 shillings. In one case 12 × 1,200 working-hours, and in the other 12 such hours are incorporated in the product. In the production of value a number of workmen rank merely as so many individual workmen; and it therefore makes no difference in the value produced whether the 1,200 men work separately, or united under the control of one capitalist.

Nevertheless, within certain limits, a modification takes place. The labour realised in value, is labour of an average social quality; is consequently the expenditure of average labour-power. Any average magnitude, however, is merely the average of a number of separate magnitudes all of one kind, but differing as to quantity. In every industry, each individual labourer, be he Peter or Paul, differs from the average labourer. These individual differences, or 'errors' as they are called in mathematics, compensate one another, and vanish, whenever a certain minimum number of workmen are employed together. The celebrated sophist and sycophant, Edmund Burke, goes so far as to make the following assertion, based on his practical observations as a farmer; viz., that 'in so small a platoon' as that of five farm labourers, all individual differences in the labour vanish, and that consequently any given five adult farm labourers taken together, will in the same time do as much work as any other five.[1] But, however that may be, it is clear, that the collective working-day of a large number of workmen simultaneously employed, divided by the number of these workmen, gives one day of average social labour. For example, let the working-day of each individual be 12 hours. Then the collective working-day of 12 men simultaneously employed, consists of 144 hours; and although the labour of each of the dozen men may deviate more or less from average social labour, each of them requiring a different time for the same operation, yet since the working-day of each is one-twelfth of the collective working-day of 144 hours, it possesses the qualities of an average social working-day. From the point of view, however, of the capitalist who employs these 12 men, the working-day is that of the whole dozen. Each individual man's day is an aliquot part of the collective working-day, no matter whether the 12 men assist one another in their work, or whether the connexion between their operations consists merely in the fact, that the men are all working for the same capitalist. But if the 12 men are employed in six pairs, by as many different small masters, it will be quite a matter of chance, whether each of these masters produces the same value, and consequently whether he realises the general rate of surplus-value. Deviations would occur in individual cases. If one workman required considerably more time for the production of a commodity than is socially necessary, the duration of the necessary labour-time would, in his case, sensibly deviate from the labour-time socially necessary on an average; and consequently his labour would not count as average labour, nor his labour-power as average labour-power. It would either be not saleable at all, or only at something below the average value of labour-power. A fixed minimum of efficiency in all labour is therefore assumed, and we shall see, later on, that capitalist production provides the means of fixing this minimum. Nevertheless, this minimum deviates from the average, although on the other hand the capitalist has to pay the average value of labour-power. Of the six small masters, one would therefore squeeze out more than the average rate of surplus-value, another less. The inequalities would be compensated for the society at large, but not for the individual masters. Thus the laws of the production of value are only fully realised for the individual producer, when he produces as a capitalist, and employs a number of workmen together, whose labour, by its collective nature, is at once stamped as average social labour.[2]

Even without an alteration in the system of working, the simultaneous employment of a large number of labourers effects a revolution in the material conditions of the labour-process. The buildings in which they work, the store-houses for the raw material, the implements and utensils used simultaneously or in turns by the workmen; in short, a portion of the means of production, are now consumed in common. On the one hand, the exchange-value of these means of production is not increased; for the exchange-value of a commodity is not raised by its use-value being consumed more thoroughly and to greater advantage. On the other hand, they are used in common, and therefore on a larger scale than before. A room where twenty weavers work at twenty looms must be larger than the room of a single weaver with two assistants. But it costs less labour to build one workshop for twenty persons than to build ten to accommodate two weavers each; thus the value of the means of production that are concentrated for use in common on a large scale does not increase in direct proportion to the expansion and to the increased useful effect of those means. When consumed in common, they give up a smaller part of their value to each single product; partly because the total value they part with is spread over a greater quantity of products, and partly because their value, though absolutely greater, is, having regard to their sphere of action in the process, relatively less than the value of isolated means of production. Owing to this, the value of a part of the constant capital falls, and in proportion to the magnitude of the fall, the total value of the commodity also falls. The effect is the same as if the means of production had cost less. The economy in their application is entirely owing to their being consumed in common by a large number of workmen. Moreover, this character of being necessary conditions of social labour, a character that distinguishes them from the dispersed and relatively more costly means of production of isolated, independent labourers, or small masters, is acquired even when the numerous workmen assembled together do not assist one another, but merely work side by side. A portion of the instruments of labour acquires this social character before the labour-process itself does so.

Economy in the use of the means of production has to be considered under two aspects. First, as cheapening commodities, and thereby bringing about a fall in the value of labour-power. Secondly, as altering the ratio of the surplus-value to the total capital advanced, i.e., to the sum of the values of the constant and variable capital. The latter aspect will not be considered until we come to the third book, to which, with the object of treating them in their proper connexion, we also relegate many other points that relate to the present question. The march of our analysis compels this splitting up of the subject-matter, a splitting up that is quite in keeping with the spirit of capitalist production. For since, in this mode of production, the workman finds the instruments of labour existing independently of him as another man's property, economy in their use appears, with regard to him, to be a distinct operation, one that does not concern him, and which, therefore, has no connexion with the methods by which his own personal productiveness is increased.

When numerous labourers work together side by side, whether in one and the same process, or in different but connected processes, they are said to co-operate, or to work in co-operation.[3]

Just as the offensive power of a squadron of cavalry, or the defensive power of a regiment of infantry is essentially different from the sum of the offensive or defensive powers of the individual cavalry or infantry soldiers taken separately, so the sum total of the mechanical forces exerted by isolated workmen differs from the social force that is developed, when many hands take part simultaneously in one and the same undivided operation, such as raising a heavy weight, turning a winch, or removing an obstacle.[4] In such cases the effect of the combined labour could either not be produced at all by isolated individual labour, or it could only be produced by a great expenditure of time, or on a very dwarfed scale. Not only have we here an increase in the productive power of the individual, by means of co-operation, but the creation of a new power, namely, the collective power of masses.[5]

Apart from the new power that arises from the fusion of many forces into one single force, mere social contact begets in most industries an emulation and a stimulation of the animal spirits that heighten the efficiency of each individual workman. Hence it is that a dozen persons working together will, in their collective working-day of 144 hours, produce far more than twelve isolated men each working 12 hours, or than one man who works twelve days in succession.[6] The reason of this is that man is, if not as Aristotle contends, a political,[7] at all events a social animal.

Although a number of men may be occupied together at the same time on the same, or the same kind of work, yet the labour of each, as a part of the collective labour, may correspond to a distinct phase of the labour-process, through all whose phases, in consequence of co-operation, the subject of their labour passes with greater speed. For instance, if a dozen masons place themselves in a row, so as to pass stones from the foot of a ladder to its summit, each of them does the same thing; nevertheless, their separate acts form connected parts of one total operation; they are particular phases, which must be gone through by each stone; and the stones are thus carried up quicker by the 24 hands of the row of men than they could be if each man went separately up and down the ladder with his burden.[8] The object is carried over the same distance in a shorter time. Again, a combination of labour occurs whenever a building, for instance, is taken in hand on different sides simultaneously; although here also the co-operating masons are doing the same, or the same kind of work. The 12 masons, in their collective working-day of 144 hours, make much more progress with the building than one mason could make working for 12 days, or 144 hours. The reason is, that a body of men working in concert has hands and eyes both before and behind, and is, to a certain degree, omnipresent. The various parts of the work progress simultaneously.

In the above instances we have laid stress upon the point that the men do the same, or the same kind of work, because this, the most simple form of labour in common, plays a great part in co-operation, even in its most fully developed stage. If the work be complicated, then the mere number of the men who co-operate allows of the various operations being apportioned to different hands, and, consequently, of being carried on simultaneously. The time necessary for the completion of the whole work is thereby shortened.[9]

In many industries, there are critical periods, determined by the nature of the process, during which certain definite results must be obtained. For instance, if a flock of sheep has to be shorn, or a field of wheat to be cut and harvested, the quantity and quality of the product depends on the work being begun and ended within a certain time. In these cases, the time that ought to be taken by the process is prescribed, just as it is in herring fishing. A single person cannot carve a working-day of more than, say 12 hours, out of the natural day, but 100 men co-operating extend the working-day to 1,200 hours. The shortness of the time allowed for the work is compensated for by the large mass of labour thrown upon the field of production at the decisive moment. The completion of the task within the proper time depends on the simultaneous application of numerous combined working-days; the amount of useful effect depends on the number of labourers; this number, however, is always smaller than the number of isolated labourers required to do the same amount of work in the same period.[10] It is owing to the absence of this kind of co-operation that, in the western part of the United States, quantities of corn, and in those parts of East India where English rule has destroyed the old communities, quantities of cotton, are yearly wasted.[11]

On the one hand, co-operation allows of the work being carried on over an extended space; it is consequently imperatively called for in certain undertakings, such as draining, constructing dykes, irrigation works, and the making of canals, roads and railways. On the other hand, while extending the scale of production, it renders possible a relative contraction of the arena. This contraction of arena simultaneous with, and arising from, extension of scale, whereby a number of useless expenses are cut down, is owing to the conglomeration of labourers, to the aggregation of various processes, and to the concentration of the means of production.[12]

The combined working-day produces, relatively to an equal sum of isolated working-days, a greater quantity of use-values, and, consequently, diminishes the labour-time necessary for the production of a given useful effect. Whether the combined working-day, in a given case, acquires this increased productive power, because it heightens the mechanical force of labour, or extends its sphere of action over a greater space, or contracts the field of production relatively to the scale of production, or at the critical moment sets large masses of labour to work, or excites emulation between individuals and raises their animal spirits, or impresses on the similar operations carried on by a number of men the stamp of continuity and many-sidedness, or performs simultaneously different operations, or economises the means of production by use in common, or lends to individual labour the character of average social labour whichever of these be the cause of the increase, the special productive power of the combined working-day is, under all circumstances, the social productive power of labour, or the productive power of social labour. This power is due to co-operation itself. When the labourer co-operates systematically with others, he strips off the fetters of his individuality, and develops the capabilities of his species.[13]

As a general rule, labourers cannot co-operate without being brought together: their assemblage in one place is a necessary condition of their co-operation. Hence wage-labourers cannot co-operate, unless they are employed simultaneously by the same capital, the same capitalist, and unless therefore their labour-powers are bought simultaneously by him. The total value of these labour-powers, or the amount of the wages of these labourers for a day, or a week, as the case may be, must be ready in the pocket of the capitalist, before the workmen are assembled for the process of production. The payment of 300 workmen at once, though only for one day, requires a greater outlay of capital, than does the payment of a smaller number of men, week by week, during a whole year. Hence the number of the labourers that co-operate, or the scale of co-operation, depends, in the first instance, on the amount of capital that the individual capitalist can spare for the purchase of labour-power; in other words, on the extent to which a single capitalist has command over the means of subsistence of a number of labourers.

And as with the variable, so it is with the constant capital. For example, the outlay on raw material is 30 times as great, for the capitalist who employs 300 men, as it is for each of the 30 capitalists who employ 10 men. The value and quantity of the instruments of labour used in common do not, it is true, increase at the same rate as the number of workmen, but they do increase very considerably. Hence, concentration of large masses of the means of production in the hands of individual capitalists, is a material condition for the co-operation of wage-labourers, and the extent of the co-operation or the scale of production, depends on the extent of this concentration.

We saw in a former chapter, that a certain minimum amount of capital was necessary, in order that the number of labourers simultaneously employed, and, consequently, the amount of surplus-value produced, might suffice to liberate the employer himself from manual labour, to convert him from a small master into a capitalist, and thus formally to establish capitalist production. We now see that a certain minimum amount is a necessary condition for the conversion of numerous isolated and independent processes into one combined social process.

We also saw that at first, the subjection of labour to capital was only a formal result of the fact, that the labourer, instead of working for himself, works for and consequently under the capitalist. By the co-operation of numerous wage-labourers, the sway of capital develops into a requisite for carrying on the labour-process itself, into a real requisite of production. That a capitalist should command on the field of production, is now as indispensable as that a general should command on the field of battle.

All combined labour on a large scale requires, more or less, a directing authority, in order to secure the harmonious working of the individual activities, and to perform the general functions that have their origin in the action of the combined organism, as distinguished from the action of its separate organs. A single violin player is his own conductor; an orchestra requires a separate one. The work of directing, superintending, and adjusting, becomes one of the functions of capital, from the moment that the labour under the control of capital, becomes co-operative. Once a function of capital, it acquires special characteristics.

The directing motive, the end and aim of capitalist production, is to extract the greatest possible amount of surplus-value,[14] and consequently to exploit labour-power to the greatest possible extent. As the number of the co-operating labourers increases, so too does their resistance to the domination of capital, and with it, the necessity for capital to overcome this resistance by counterpressure. The control exercised by the capitalist is not only a special function, due to the nature of the social labour-process, and peculiar to that process, but it is, at the same time, a function of the exploitation of a social labour-process, and is consequently rooted in the unavoidable antagonism between the exploiter and the living and labouring raw material he exploits.

Again, in proportion to the increasing mass of the means of production, now no longer the property of the labourer, but of the capitalist, the necessity increases for some effective control over the proper application of those means.[15] Moreover, the co-operation of wage labourers is entirely brought about by the capital that employs them. Their union into one single productive body and the establishment of a connexion between their individual functions, are matters foreign and external to them, are not their own act, but the act of the capital that brings and keeps them together. Hence the connexion existing between their various labours appears to them, ideally, in the shape of a preconceived plan of the capitalist, and practically in the shape of the authority of the same capitalist, in the shape of the powerful will of another, who subjects their activity to his aims. If, then, the control of the capitalist is in substance two-fold by reason of the two-fold nature of the process of production itself, which, on the one hand, is a social process for producing use-values, on the other, a process for creating surplus-value in form that control is despotic. As co-operation extends its scale, this despotism takes forms peculiar to itself. Just as at first the capitalist is relieved from actual labour so soon as his capital has reached that minimum amount with which capitalist production, as such, begins, so now, he hands over the work of direct and constant supervision of the individual workmen, and groups of workmen, to a special kind of wage-labourer. An industrial army of workmen, under the command of a capitalist, requires, like a real army, officers (managers), and sergeants (foremen, overlookers), who, while the work is being done, command in the name of the capitalist. The work of supervision becomes their established and exclusive function. When comparing the mode of production of isolated peasants and artisans with production by slave-labour, the political economist counts this labour of superintendence among the *faux frais* of production.[16] But, when considering the capitalist mode of production, he, on the contrary, treats the work of control made necessary by the co-operative character of the labour-process as identical with the different work of control, necessitated by the capitalist character of that process and the antagonism of interests between capitalist and labourer.[17] It is not because he is a leader of industry that a man is a capitalist; on the contrary, he is a leader of industry because he is a capitalist. The leadership of industry is an attribute of capital, just as in feudal times the functions of general and judge, were attributes of landed property.[18]

The labourer is the owner of his labour-power until he has done bargaining for its sale with the capitalist; and he can sell no more than what he has i.e., his individual, isolated labour-power. This state of things is in no way altered by the fact that the capitalist, instead of buying the labour-power of one man, buys that of 100, and enters into separate contracts with 100 unconnected men instead of with one. He is at liberty to set the 100 men to work, without letting them co-operate. He pays them the value of 100 independent labour-powers, but he does not pay for the combined labour-power of the hundred. Being independent of each other, the labourers are isolated persons, who enter into relations with the capitalist, but not with one another. This co-operation begins only with the labour-process, but they have then ceased to belong to themselves. On entering that process, they become incorporated with capital. As co-operators, as members of a working organism, they are but special modes of existence of capital. Hence, the productive power developed by the labourer when working in co-operation, is the productive power of capital. This power is developed gratuitously, whenever the workmen are placed under given conditions, and it is capital that places them under such conditions. Because this power costs capital nothing, and because, on the other hand, the labourer himself does not develop it before his labour belongs to capital, it appears as a power with which capital is endowed by Nature—a productive power that is immanent in capital.

The colossal effects of simple co-operation are to be seen in the gigantic structures of the ancient Asiatics, Egyptians, Etruscans, &c.

> 'It has happened in times past that these Oriental States, after supplying the expenses of their civil and military establishments, have found themselves in possession of a surplus which they could apply to works of magnificence or utility and in the construction of these their command over the hands and arms of almost the entire non-agricultural population has produced stupendous monuments which still indicate their power. The teeming valley of the Nile ... produced food for a swarming non-agricultural population, and this food, belonging to the monarch and the priesthood, afforded the means of erecting the mighty monuments which filled the land.... In

moving the colossal statues and vast masses of which the transport creates wonder, human labour almost alone, was prodigally used.... The number of the labourers and the concentration of their efforts sufficed. We see mighty coral reefs rising from the depths of the ocean into islands and firm land, yet each individual depositor is puny, weak, and contemptible. The non-agricultural labourers of an Asiatic monarchy have little but their individual bodily exertions to bring to the task, but their number is their strength, and the power of directing these masses gave rise to the palaces and temples, the pyramids, and the armies of gigantic statues of which the remains astonish and perplex us. It is that confinement of the revenues which feed them, to one or a few hands, which makes such undertakings possible.'[19]

This power of Asiatic and Egyptian kings, Etruscan theocrats, &c., has in modern society been transferred to the capitalist, whether he be an isolated, or as in joint-stock companies, a collective capitalist.

Co-operation, such as we find it at the dawn of human development, among races who live by the chase,[20] or, say, in the agriculture of Indian communities, is based, on the one hand, on ownership in common of the means of production, and on the other hand, on the fact, that in those cases, each individual has no more torn himself off from the navel-string of his tribe or community, than each bee has freed itself from connexion with the hive. Such co-operation is distinguished from capitalistic co-operation by both of the above characteristics. The sporadic application of co-operation on a large scale in ancient times, in the middle ages, and in modern colonies, reposes on relations of dominion and servitude, principally on slavery. The capitalistic form, on the contrary, pre-supposes from first to last, the free wage-labourer, who sells his labour-power to capital. Historically, however, this form is developed in opposition to peasant agriculture and to the carrying on of independent handicrafts whether in guilds or not.[21] From the standpoint of these, capitalistic co-operation does not manifest itself as a particular historical form of co-operation, but co-operation itself appears to be a historical form peculiar to, and specifically distinguishing, the capitalist process of production.

Just as the social productive power of labour that is developed by co-operation, appears to be the productive power of capital, so co-operation itself, contrasted with the process of production carried on by isolated independent labourers, or even by small employers, appears to be a specific form of the capitalist process of production. It is the first change experienced by the actual labour-process, when subjected to capital. This change takes place spontaneously. The simultaneous employment of a large number of wage-labourers, in one and the same process, which is a necessary condition of this change, also forms the starting-point of capitalist production. This point coincides with the birth of capital itself. If then, on the one hand, the capitalist mode of production presents itself to us historically, as a necessary condition to the transformation of the labour-process into a social process, so, on the other hand, this social form of the labour-process presents itself, as a method employed by capital for the more profitable exploitation of labour, by increasing that labour's productiveness.

In the elementary form, under which we have hitherto viewed it, co-operation is a necessary concomitant of all production on a large scale, but it does not, in itself, represent a fixed form characteristic of a particular epoch in the development of the capitalist mode of production. At the most it appears to do so, and that only approximately, in the handicraft-like beginnings of manufacture,[22] and in that kind of agriculture on a large scale, which corresponds to the epoch of manufacture, and is distinguished from peasant agriculture, mainly by the number of the labourers simultaneously employed, and by the mass of the means of production concentrated for their use. Simple co-operation is always the prevailing form, in those branches of production in which capital operates on a large scale, and division of labour and machinery play but a subordinate part.

Co-operation ever constitutes the fundamental form of the capitalist mode of production, nevertheless the elementary form of co-operation continues to subsist as a particular form of capitalist production side by side with the more developed forms of that mode of production.

Notes

1. 'Unquestionably, there is a good deal of difference between the value of one man's labour and that of another from strength, dexterity, and honest application. But I am quite sure, from my best observation, that any given five men will, in their total, afford a proportion of labour equal to any other five within the periods of life I have stated; that is, that among such five men there will be one possessing all the qualifications of a good workman, one bad, and the other three middling, and approximating to the first, and the last. So that in so small a platoon as that of even five, you will find the full complement of all that five men can earn.' (E. Burke, 1. c., pp. 15, 16.) Compare Quételet on the average individual.
2. Professor Roscher claims to have discovered that one needlewoman employed by Mrs. Roscher during two days, does more work than two needlewomen employed together during one day. The learned professor should not study the capitalist process of production in the nursery, nor under circumstances where the principal personage, the capitalist, is wanting.
3. 'Concours de forces.' (Destutt de Tracy, l.c., p. 80.)
4. 'There are numerous operations of so simple a kind as not to admit a division into parts, which cannot be performed without the co-operation of many pairs of hands. I would instance the lifting of a large tree on to a wain ... everything, in short, which cannot be done unless a great many pairs of hands help each other in the same undivided employment and at the same time.' (E. G. Wakefield: 'A View of the Art of Colonisation.' London, 1849, p. 168.)
5. 'As one man cannot, and ten men must strain to lift a ton of weight, yet 100 men can do it only by the strength of a finger of each of them.' (John Betters: 'Proposals for Raising a Colledge of Industry.' London, 1696, p. 21.)
6. 'There is also' (when the same number of men are employed by one farmer on 300 acres, instead of by ten farmers with 30 acres a piece) 'an advantage in the proportion of servants, which will not so easily be understood but by practical men; for it is natural to say, as 1 is to 4, so are 3 to 12; but this will not hold good in practice; for in harvest time and many other operations which require that kind of despatch by the throwing many hands together, the work is better and more expeditiously done: f i. in harvest, 2 drivers, 2 loaders, 2 pitchers, 2 rakers, and the rest at the rick, or in the barn, will despatch double the work that the same number of hands would do if divided into different gangs on different farms.' ('An Inquiry into the Connexion between the Present Price of Provisions and the Size of Farms.' By a Farmer. London, 1773, pp. 7, 8.)
7. Strictly, Aristotle's definition is that man is by nature a town-citizen. This is quite as characteristic of ancient classical society as Franklin's definition of man, as a tool-making animal, is characteristic of Yankeedom.
8. 'On doit encore remarquer que cette division partielle de travail peut se faire quand même les ouvriers sont occupés d'une même besogne. Des maçons par exemple, occupés à faire passer de mains en mains des briques à un échafaudage supérieur, font tous la même besogne, et pourtant il existe parmi eux une espèce de division de travail, qui consiste en ce que chacun d'eux fait passer la brique par un espace donné, et que tous ensemble la font parvenir beaucoup plus promptement à l'endroit marqué qu'ils ne le feraient si chacun d'eux portait sa brique séparément jusqu'à l'échafaudage supérieur.' [It should be noted further that this partial division of labour can occur even when the workers are engaged in the same task. Masons, for example, engaged in passing bricks from hand to hand to a higher stage of the building, are all performing the same task, and yet there does exist amongst them a sort of

division of labour. This consists in the fact that each of them passes the brick through a given space, and, taken together, they make it arrive much more quickly at the required spot than they would do if each of them carried his brick separately to the upper storey] (F. Skarbek: 'Théorie des richesses sociales.' Paris, 1839, t. I, pp. 97, 98.)

9. 'Est-il question d'exécuter un travail compliqué, plusieurs choses doivent être faites simultanément. L'un en fait une pendant que l'autre en fait une autre, et tous contribuent à l'effet qu'un seul homme n'aurait pu produire. L'un rame pendant que l'autre tient le gouvernail, et qu'un troisième jette le filet on harponne le poisson, et la pêche a un succès impossible sans ce concours.' [Is it a question of undertaking a complex piece of labour? Many things must be done simultaneously. One person does one thing, while another does something else, and they all contribute to an effect that a single man would be unable to produce. One rows while the other holds the rudder, and a third casts the net or harpoons the fish; in this way fishing enjoys a success that would be impossible without this cooperation] (Destutt de Tracy, l.c.)

10. 'The doing of it (agricultural work) at the critical juncture is of so much the greater consequence.' ('An Inquiry into the Connexion between the Present Price,' &c., p. 9.) 'In agriculture, there is no more important factor than that of time.' (Liebig: 'Ueber Theorie und Praxis in der Landwirtschaft.' 1856, p. 23.)

11. 'The next evil is one which one would scarcely expect to find in a country which exports more labour than any other in the world, with the exception, perhaps, of China and England—the impossibility of procuring a sufficient number of hands to clean the cotton. The consequence of this is that large quantities of the crop are left unpicked, while another portion is gathered from the ground when it has fallen, and is of course discoloured and partially rotted, so that for want of labour at the proper season the cultivator is actually forced to submit to the loss of a large part of that crop for which England is so anxiously looking.' ('Bengal Hurkaru.' Bi-Monthly Overland Summary of News, 22nd July, 1861.)

12. In the progress of culture 'all, and perhaps more than all, the capital and labour which once loosely occupied 500 acres, are now concentrated for the more complete tillage of 100.' Although 'relatively to the amount of capital and labour employed, space is concentrated, it is an enlarged sphere of production, as compared to the sphere of production formerly occupied or worked upon by one single independent agent of production.' (R. Jones: 'An Essay on the Distribution of Wealth,' part I. On Rent. London, 1831. p. 191.)

13. 'La forza di ciascuno uomo è minima, ma la riunione delle minime forze forma una forza totale maggiore anche della somma delle forze medesime fino a che le forze per essere riunite possono diminuere il tempo ed accrescere lo spazio della loro azione.' (G. R. Carli, Note to P. Verri, l.c., t. xv., p. 196.)

14. 'Profits ... is the sole end of trade.' (J. Vanderlint, l.c., p. 11.)

15. That Philistine paper, the *Spectator*, states that after the introduction of a sort of partnership between capitalist and workmen in the 'Wirework Company of Manchester,' 'the first result was a sudden decrease in waste, the men not seeing why they should waste their own property any more than any other master's, and waste is, perhaps, next to bad debts, the greatest source of manufacturing loss.' The same paper finds that the main defect in the Rochdale co-operative experiments is this: 'They showed that associations of workmen could manage shops, mills, and almost all forms of industry with success, and they immediately improved the condition of the men; but then they did not leave a clear place for masters.' Quelle horreur!

16. Professor Cairnes, after stating that the superintendence of labour is a leading feature of production by slaves in the Southern States of North America, continues: 'The peasant proprietor (of the North), appropriating the whole produce of his toil, needs no other stimulus to exertion. Superintendence is here completely dispensed with.' (Cairnes, l.c., pp. 48, 49.)

17. Sir James Steuart, a writer altogether remarkable for his quick eye for the characteristic social

distinctions between different modes of production, says: 'Why do large undertakings in the manufacturing way ruin private industry, but by coming nearer to the simplicity of slaves?' ('Prin. of Pol. Econ.,' London, 1767, v. I., pp. 167, 168.)

18. Auguste Comte and his school might therefore have shown that feudal lords are an eternal necessity in the same way that they have done in the case of the lords of capital.
19. R. Jones. 'Textbook of Lectures,' &c., pp. 77, 78. The ancient Assyrian, Egyptian, and other collections in London, and in other European capitals, make us eye-witnesses of the modes of carrying on that co-operative labour.
20. Linguet is improbably right, when in his 'Théorie des Lois Civiles,' he declares hunting to be the first form of co-operation, and man-hunting (war) one of the earliest forms of hunting.
21. Peasant agriculture on a small scale, and the carrying on of independent handicrafts, which together form the basis of the feudal mode of production, and after the dissolution of that system, continue side by side with the capitalist mode, also form the economic foundation of the classical communities at their best, after the primitive form of ownership of land in common had disappeared, and before slavery had seized on production in earnest.
22. 'Whether the united skill, industry, and emulation of many together on the same work be not the way to advance it? And whether it had been otherwise possible for England, to have carried on her Woollen Manufacture to so great a perfection?' (Berkeley. 'The Querist.' London, 1751, p. 56, par. 521.)

14

Division of Labour and Manufacture

Section 1: *Two-Fold Origin of Manufacture*

That co-operation which is based on division of labour, assumes its typical form in manufacture, and is the prevalent characteristic form of the capitalist process of production throughout the manufacturing period properly so called. That period, roughly speaking, extends from the middle of the 16th to the last third of the 18th century.

Manufacture takes its rise in two ways:

1. By the assemblage, in one workshop under the control of a single capitalist, of labourers belonging to various independent handicrafts, but through whose hands a given article must pass on its way to completion. A carriage, for example, was formerly the product of the labour of a great number of independent artificers, such as wheelwrights, harness-makers, tailors, locksmiths, upholsterers, turners, fringe-makers, glaziers, painters, polishers, gilders, &c. In the manufacture of carriages, however, all these different artificers are assembled in one building where they work into one another's hands. It is true that a carriage cannot be gilt before it has been made. But if a number of carriages are being made simultaneously, some may be in the hands of the gilders while others are going through an earlier process. So far, we are still in the domain of simple co-operation, which finds its materials ready to hand in the shape of men and things. But very soon an important change takes place. The tailor, the locksmith, and the other artificers, being now exclusively occupied in carriage-making, each gradually loses, through want of practice, the ability to carry on, to its full extent,

his old handicraft. But, on the other hand, his activity now confined in one groove, assumes the form best adapted to the narrowed sphere of action. At first, carriage manufacture is a combination of various independent handicrafts. By degrees, it becomes the splitting up of carriage-making into its various detail processes, each of which crystallises into the exclusive function of a particular workman, the manufacture, as a whole, being carried on by the men in conjunction. In the same way, cloth manufacture, as also a whole series of other manufactures, arose by combining different handicrafts together under the control of a single capitalist.[1]

2. Manufacture also arises in a way exactly the reverse of this—namely, by one capitalist employing simultaneously in one workshop a number of artificers, who all do the same, or the same kind of work, such as making paper, type, or needles. This is co-operation in its most elementary form. Each of these artificers (with the help, perhaps, of one or two apprentices), makes the entire commodity, and he consequently performs in succession all the operations necessary for its production. He still works in his old handicraft-like way. But very soon external circumstances cause a different use to be made of the concentration of the workmen on one spot, and of the simultaneousness of their work. An increased quantity of the article has perhaps to be delivered within a given time. The work is therefore re-distributed. Instead of each man being allowed to perform all the various operations in succession, these operations are changed into disconnected, isolated ones, carried on side by side; each is assigned to a different artificer, and the whole of them together are performed simultaneously by the co-operating workmen. This accidental repartition gets repeated, develops advantages of its own, and gradually ossifies into a systematic division of labour. The commodity, from being the individual product of an independent artificer, becomes the social product of a union of artificers, each of whom performs one, and only one, of the constituent partial operations. The same operations which, in the case of a papermaker belonging to a German Guild, merged one into the other as the successive acts of one artificer, became in the Dutch paper manufacture so many partial operations carried on side by side by numerous co-operating labourers. The needlemaker of the Nuremberg Guild was the cornerstone on which the English needle manufacture was raised. But while in Nuremberg that single artificer performed a series of perhaps 20 operations one after another, in England it was not long before there were 20 needlemakers side by side, each performing one alone of those 20 operations, and in consequence of further experience, each of those 20 operations was again split up, isolated, and made the exclusive function of a separate workman.

The mode in which manufacture arises, its growth out of handicrafts, is therefore two-fold. On the one hand, it arises from the union of various independent handicrafts, which become stripped of their independence and specialised to such an extent as to be reduced to mere supplementary partial processes in the production of one particular commodity. On the other hand, it arises from the co-operation of artificers of one handicraft; it splits up that particular handicraft into its various detail operations, isolating, and making these operations independent of one another up to the point where each becomes the exclusive function of a particular labourer. On the one hand, therefore, manufacture either introduces division of labour into a process of production, or further develops that division; on the other hand, it unites together handicrafts that were formerly separate. But whatever may have been its particular starting-point, its final form is invariably the same—a productive mechanism whose parts are human beings.

For a proper understanding of the division of labour in manufacture, it is essential that the following points be firmly grasped. First, the decomposition of a process of production into its various successive steps coincides, here, strictly with the resolution of a handicraft into its successive manual operations. Whether complex or simple, each operation has to be done by hand, retains the character of a handicraft, and is therefore dependent on the strength, skill, quickness, and sureness, of the individual workman in handling his tools. The handicraft continues to be the basis. This narrow technical basis excludes a really scientific analysis of any definite process of industrial production, since it is still a condition that each detail process gone through by the product must be capable of being done by hand and of forming, in its way, a separate handicraft. It is just because handicraft skill continues, in this way, to be the foundation of the process of production, that each workman becomes exclusively assigned to a partial function, and that for the rest of his life, his labour-power is turned into the organ of this detail function.

Secondly, this division of labour is a particular sort of co-operation, and many of its advantages* spring from the general character of co-operation, and not from this particular form of it.

Section 2: *The Detail Labourer and his Implements*

If we now go more into detail, it is, in the first place, clear that a labourer who, all his life, performs one and the same simple operation, converts his whole body into the automatic, specialised implement of that operation. Consequently, he takes less time in doing it, than the artificer who performs a whole series of operations in succession. But the collective labourer, who constitutes the living mechanism of manufacture, is made up solely of such specialised detail labourers. Hence, in comparison with the independent handicraft, more is produced in a given time, or the productive power of labour is increased.[2] Moreover, when once this fractional work is established as the exclusive function of one person, the methods it employs become perfected. The workman's continued repetition of the same simple act, and the concentration of his attention on it, teach him by experience how to attain the desired effect with the minimum of exertion. But, since there are always several generations of labourers living at one time, and working together at the manufacture of a given article, the technical skill, the tricks of the trade thus acquired, become established, and are accumulated and handed down.[3]

Manufacture, in fact, produces the skill of the detail labourer, by reproducing, and systematically driving to an extreme within the workshop, the naturally developed differentiation of trades which it found ready to hand in society at large. On the other hand, the conversion of fractional work into the life-calling of one man, corresponds to the tendency shown by earlier societies, to make trades hereditary; either to petrify them into castes, or whenever definite historical conditions beget in the individual a tendency to vary in a manner incompatible with the nature of castes, to ossify them into guilds. Castes and guilds arise from the action of the same natural law, that regulates the differentiation of plants and animals into species and varieties, except that, when a certain degree of development has been reached, the heredity of castes and the exclusiveness of guilds are ordained as a law of society.[4]

> 'The muslins of Dakka in fineness, the calicoes and other piece goods of Coromandel in brilliant and durable colours, have never been surpassed. Yet they are produced without capital, machinery, division of labour, or any of those means which give such facilities to the manufacturing interest of Europe. The weaver is merely a detached individual, working a web when ordered of a customer, and with a loom of the rudest construction, consisting sometimes of a few branches or bars of wood, put roughly together. There is even no expedient for rolling up the warp; the loom must therefore be kept stretched to its full length, and becomes so inconveniently large, that it cannot

be contained within the hut of the manufacturer, who is therefore compelled to ply his trade in the open air, where it is interrupted by every vicissitude of the weather.'[5]

It is only the special skill accumulated from generation to generation, and transmitted from father to son, that gives to the Hindu, as it does to the spider, this proficiency. And yet the work of such a Hindu weaver is very complicated, compared with that of a manufacturing labourer.

An artificer, who performs one after another the various fractional operations in the production of a finished article, must at one time change his place, at another his tools. The transition from one operation to another interrupts the flow of his labour, and creates, so to say, gaps in his working-day. These gaps close up so soon as he is tied to one and the same operation all day long; they vanish in proportion as the changes in his work diminish. The resulting increased productive power is owing either to an increased expenditure of labour-power in a given time i.e., to increased intensity of labour or to a decrease in the amount of labour-power unproductively consumed. The extra expenditure of power, demanded by every transition from rest to motion, is made up for by prolonging the duration of the normal velocity when once acquired. On the other hand, constant labour of one uniform kind disturbs the intensity and flow of a man's animal spirits, which find recreation and delight in mere change of activity.

The productiveness of labour depends not only on the proficiency of the workman, but on the perfection of his tools. Tools of the same kind, such as knives, drills, gimlets, hammers, &c., may be employed in different processes; and the same tool may serve various purposes in a single process. But so soon as the different operations of a labour-process are disconnected the one from the other, and each fractional operation acquires in the hands of the detail labourer a suitable and peculiar form, alterations become necessary in the implements that previously served more than one purpose. The direction taken by this change is determined by the difficulties experienced in consequence of the unchanged form of the implement. Manufacture is characterised by the differentiation of the instruments of labour—a differentiation whereby implements of a given sort acquire fixed shapes, adapted to each particular application, and by the specialisation of those instruments, giving to each special implement its full play only in the hands of a specific detail labourer. In Birmingham alone, 500 varieties of hammers are produced, and not only is each adapted to one particular process, but several varieties often serve exclusively for the different operations in one and the same process. The manufacturing period simplifies, improves, and multiplies the implements of labour, by adapting them to the exclusively special functions of each detail labourer.[6] It thus creates at the same time one of the material conditions for the existence of machinery, which consists of a combination of simple instruments.

The detail labourer and his implements are the simplest elements of manufacture. Let us now turn to its aspect as a whole.

Section 3: *The Two Fundamental Forms of Manufacture: Heterogeneous Manufacture, Serial Manufacture*

The organisation of manufacture has two fundamental forms which, in spite of occasional blending, are essentially different in kind, and, moreover, play very distinct parts in the subsequent transformation of manufacture into modern industry carried on by machinery. This double character arises from the nature of the article produced. This article either results from the mere mechanical fitting together of partial products made independently, or owes its completed shape to a series of connected processes and manipulations.

A locomotive, for instance, consists of more than 5,000 independent parts. It cannot, however, serve as an example of the first kind of genuine manufacture, for it is a structure produced by modern mechanical industry. But a watch can; and William Petty used it to illustrate the division of labour in manufacture. Formerly the individual work of a Nuremberg artificer, the watch has been transformed into the social product of an immense number of detail labourers, such as mainspring makers, dial makers, spiral spring makers, jewelled hole makers, ruby lever makers, hand makers, case makers, screw makers, gilders, with numerous subdivisions, such as wheel makers (brass and steel separate), pin makers, movement makers, acheveur de pignon (fixes the wheels on the axles, polishes the facets, &c.), pivot makers, planteur de finissage (puts the wheels and springs in the works), finisseur de barillet (cuts teeth in the wheels, makes the holes of the right size, &c.), escapement makers, cylinder makers for cylinder escapements, escapement wheel makers, balance wheel makers, raquette makers (apparatus for regulating the watch), the planteur d'échappement (escapement maker proper); then the repasseur de barillet (finishes the box for the spring, &c.), steel polishers, wheel polishers, screw polishers, figure painters, dial enamellers (melt the enamel on the copper), fabricant de pendants (makes the ring by which the case is hung), finisseur de charnière (puts the brass hinge in the cover, &c.), faiseur de secret (puts in the springs that open the case), graveur, ciseleur, polisseur de boîte, &c., &c., and last of all the repasseur, who fits together the whole watch and hands it over in a going state. Only a few parts of the watch pass through several hands; and all these membra disjecta come together for the first time in the hand that binds them into one mechanical whole. This external relation between the finished product, and its various and diverse elements makes it, as well in this case as in the case of all similar finished articles, a matter of chance whether the detail labourers are brought together in one workshop or not. The detail operations may further be carried on like so many independent handicrafts, as they are in the Cantons of Vaud and Neufchâtel; while in Geneva there exist large watch manufactories where the detail labourers directly co-operate under the control of a single capitalist. And even in the latter case the dial, the springs, and the case, are seldom made in the factory itself. To carry on the trade as a manufacture, with concentration of workmen, is, in the watch trade, profitable only under exceptional conditions, because competition is greater between the labourers who desire to work at home, and because the splitting up of the work into a number of heterogeneous processes, permits but little use of the instruments of labour in common, and the capitalist, by scattering the work, saves the outlay on workshops, &c.[7] Nevertheless the position of this detail labourer who, though he works at home, does so for a capitalist (manufacturer, établisseur), is very different from that of the independent artificer, who works for his own customers.[8]

The second kind of manufacture, its perfected form, produces articles that go through connected phases of development, through a series of processes step by step, like the wire in the manufacture of needles, which passes through the hands of 72 and sometimes even 92 different detail workmen.

In so far as such a manufacture, when first started, combines scattered handicrafts, it lessens the space by which the various phases of production are separated from each other. The time taken in passing from one stage to another is shortened, so is the labour that effectuates this passage.[9] In comparison with a handicraft, productive power is gained, and this gain is owing to the general co-operative character of manufacture. On the other hand, division of labour, which is the distinguishing principle of manufacture, requires the isolation of the various stages of production and their independence of each other. The establishment and maintenance of a connexion between the isolated functions necessitates the incessant transport of the article from one hand to another, and from one process to another. From the standpoint of modern mechanical industry, this necessity stands forth as a characteristic and costly disadvantage, and one that is immanent in the principle of manufacture.[10]

If we confine our attention to some particular lot of raw materials, of rags, for instance, in paper manufacture, or of wire in needle manufacture, we perceive that it passes in succession through a series of stages in the hands of the various detail workmen until completion. On the other hand, if we look at the workshop as a whole, we see the raw material in all the stages of its production at the same time. The collective labourer, with one set of his many hands armed with one kind of tools, draws the wire, with another set, armed with different tools, he, at the same time, straightens it, with another, he cuts it, with another, points it, and so on. The different detail processes, which were successive in time, have become simultaneous, go on side by side in space. Hence, production of a greater quantum of finished commodities in a given time.[11] This simultaneity, it is true, is due to the general co-operative form of the process as a whole; but Manufacture not only finds the conditions for co-operation ready to hand, it also, to some extent, creates them by the sub-division of handicraft labour. On the other hand, it accomplishes this social organisation of the labour-process only by riveting each labourer to a single fractional detail.

Since the fractional product of each detail labourer is, at the same time, only a particular stage in the development of one and the same finished article, each labourer, or each group of labourers, prepares the raw material for another labourer or group. The result of the labour of the one is the starting-point for the labour of the other. The one workman therefore gives occupation directly to the other. The labour-time necessary in each partial process, for attaining the desired effect, is learnt by experience; and the mechanism of Manufacture, as a whole, is based on the assumption that a given result will be obtained in a given time. It is only on this assumption that the various supplementary labour-processes can proceed uninterruptedly, simultaneously, and side by side. It is clear that this direct dependence of the operations, and therefore of the labourers, on each other, compels each one of them to spend on his work no more than the necessary time, and thus a continuity, uniformity, regularity, order,[12] and even intensity of labour, of quite a different kind, is begotten than is to be found in an independent handicraft or even in simple co-operation. The rule, that the labour-time expended on a commodity should not exceed that which is socially necessary for its production, appears, in the production of commodities generally, to be established by the mere effect of competition; since, to express ourselves superficially, each single producer is obliged to sell his commodity at its market-price. In Manufacture, on the contrary, the turning out of a given quantum of product in a given time is a technical law of the process of production itself.[13]

Different operations take, however, unequal periods, and yield therefore, in equal times unequal quantities of fractional products. If, therefore, the same labourer has, day after day, to perform the same operation, there must be a different number of labourers for each operation; for instance, in type manufacture, there are four founders and two breakers to one rubber: the founder casts 2,000 type an hour, the breaker breaks up 4,000, and the rubber polishes 8,000. Here we have again the principle of co-operation in its simplest form, the simultaneous employment of many doing the same thing; only now, this principle is the expression of an organic relation. The division of labour, as carried out in Manufacture, not only simplifies and multiplies the qualitatively different parts of the social collective labourer, but also creates a fixed mathematical relation or ratio which regulates the quantitative extent of those parts i.e., the relative number of labourers, or the relative size of the group of labourers, for each detail operation. It develops, along with the qualitative sub-division of the social labour-process, a quantitative rule and proportionality for that process.

When once the most fitting proportion has been experimentally established for the numbers of the detail labourers in the various groups when producing on a given scale, that scale can be extended only by employing a multiple of each particular group.[14] There is this to boot, that the same individual can do certain kinds of work just as well on a large as on a small scale; for instance, the labour of superintendence, the carriage of the fractional product from one stage to the next, &c. The isolation of such functions, their allotment to a particular labourer, does not become advantageous till after an increase in the number of labourers employed; but this increase must affect every group proportionally.

The isolated group of labourers to whom any particular detail function is assigned, is made up of homogeneous elements, and is one of the constituent parts of the total mechanism. In many manufactures, however, the group itself is an organised body of labour, the total mechanism being a repetition or multiplication of these elementary organisms. Take, for instance, the manufacture of glass bottles. It may be resolved into three essentially different stages. First, the preliminary stage, consisting of the preparation of the components of the glass, mixing the sand and lime, &c., and melting them into a fluid mass of glass.[15] Various detail labourers are employed in this first stage, as also in the final one of removing the bottles from the drying furnace, sorting and packing them, &c. In the middle, between these two stages, comes the glass melting proper, the manipulation of the fluid mass. At each mouth of the furnace, there works a group, called 'the hole,' consisting of one bottlemaker or finisher, one blower, one gatherer, one putter-up or whetter-off, and one taker-in. These five detail workers are so many special organs of a single working organism that acts only as a whole, and therefore can operate only by the direct co-operation of the whole five. The whole body is paralysed if but one of its members be wanting. But a glass furnace has several openings (in England from 4 to 6), each of which contains an earthenware melting-pot full of molten glass, and employs a similar five-membered group of workers. The organisation of each group is based on division of labour, but the bond between the different groups is simple co-operation, which, by using in common one of the means of production, the furnace, causes it to be more economically consumed. Such a furnace, with its 4-6 groups, constitutes a glass house; and a glass manufactory comprises a number of such glass houses, together with the apparatus and workmen requisite for the preparatory and final stages.

Finally, just as Manufacture arises in part from the combination of various handicrafts, so, too, it develops into a combination of various manufactures. The larger English glass manufacturers, for instance, make their own earthenware melting-pots, because, on the quality of these depends, to a great extent, the success or failure of the process. The manufacture of one of the means of production is here united with that of the product. On the other hand, the manufacture of the product may be united with other manufactures, of which that product is the raw material, or with the products of which it is itself subsequently mixed. Thus, we find the manufacture of flint glass combined with that of glass cutting and brass founding; the latter for the metal settings of various articles of glass. The various manufactures so combined form more or less separate departments of a larger manufacture, but are at the same time independent processes, each with its own division of labour. In spite of the many advantages offered by this combination of manufactures, it never grows into a complete technical system on its own foundation. That happens only on its transformation into an industry carried on by machinery.

Early in the manufacturing period, the principle of lessening the necessary labour-time in the production of commodities,[16] was accepted and formulated: and the use of machines, especially for certain simple first processes that have to be conducted on a very large scale, and with the application of great force, sprang up here and there. Thus, at an early period in paper manufacture, the tearing up of the rags was done by paper-mills; and in metal works, the pounding of the ores was effected by stamping mills.[17] The Roman Empire had handed down the elementary form of all machinery in the water-wheel.[18]

The handicraft period bequeathed to us the great inventions of the compass, of gunpowder, of type-printing, and of the automatic clock. But, on the whole, machinery played that subordinate part which Adam Smith assigns to it in comparison with division of labour.[19] The sporadic use of machinery in the 17th century was of the greatest importance, because it supplied the great mathematicians of that time with a practical basis and stimulant to the creation of the science of mechanics.

The collective labourer, formed by the combination of a number of detail labourers, is the machinery specially characteristic of the manufacturing period. The various operations that are performed in turns by the producer of a commodity, and coalesce one with another during the progress of production, lay claim to him in various ways. In one operation he must exert more strength, in another more skill, in another more attention; and the same individual does not possess all these qualities in an equal degree. After Manufacture has once separated, made independent, and isolated the various operations, the labourers are divided, classified, and grouped according to their predominating qualities. If their natural endowments are, on the one hand, the foundation on which the division of labour is built up, on the other hand, Manufacture, once introduced, develops in them new powers that are by nature fitted only for limited and special functions. The collective labourer now possesses, in an equal degree of excellence, all the qualities requisite for production, and expends them in the most economical manner, by exclusively employing all his organs, consisting of particular labourers, or groups of labourers, in performing their special functions.[20] The one-sidedness and the deficiencies of the detail labourer become perfections when he is a part of the collective labourer.[21] The habit of doing only one thing converts him into a never failing instrument, while his connexion with the whole mechanism compels him to work with the regularity of the parts of a machine.[22]

Since the collective labourer has functions, both simple and complex, both high and low, his members, the individual labour-powers, require different degrees of training, and must therefore have different values. Manufacture, therefore, develops a hierarchy of labour-powers, to which there corresponds a scale of wages. If, on the one hand, the individual labourers are appropriated and annexed for life by a limited function; on the other hand, the various operations of the hierarchy are parcelled out among the labourers according to both their natural and their acquired capabilities.[23] Every process of production, however, requires certain simple manipulations, which every man is capable of doing. They too are now severed from their connexion with the more pregnant moments of activity, and ossified into exclusive functions of specially appointed labourers. Hence, Manufacture begets, in every handicraft that it seizes upon, a class of so-called unskilled labourers, a class which handicraft industry strictly excluded. If it develops a one-sided speciality into a perfection, at the expense of the whole of a man's working capacity, it also begins to make a speciality of the absence of all development. Alongside of the hierarchic gradation there steps the simple separation of the labourers into skilled and unskilled. For the latter, the cost of apprenticeship vanishes; for the former, it diminishes, compared with that of artificers, in consequence of the functions being simplified. In both cases the value of labour-power falls.[24] An exception to this law holds good whenever the decomposition of the labour-process begets new and comprehensive functions, that either had no place at all, or only a very modest one, in handicrafts. The fall in the value of labour-power, caused by the disappearance or diminution of the expenses of apprenticeship, implies a direct increase of surplus-value for the benefit of capital; for everything that shortens the necessary labour-time required for the reproduction of labour-power, extends the domain of surplus-labour.

Section 4: *Division of Labour in Manufacture, and Division of Labour in Society*

We first considered the origin of Manufacture, then its simple elements, then the detail labourer and his implements, and finally, the totality of the mechanism. We shall now lightly touch upon the relation between the division of labour in manufacture, and the social division of labour, which forms the foundation of all production of commodities.

If we keep labour alone in view, we may designate the separation of social production into its main divisions or *genera*—viz., agriculture, industries, &c., as division of labour in general, and the splitting up of these families into species and sub-species, as division of labour in particular, and the division of labour within the workshop as division of labour in singular or in detail.[25]

Division of labour in a society, and the corresponding tying down of individuals to a particular calling, develops itself, just as does the division of labour in manufacture, from opposite starting-points. Within a family,[26] and after further development within a tribe, there springs up naturally a division of labour, caused by differences of sex and age, a division that is consequently based on a purely physiological foundation, which division enlarges its materials by the expansion of the community, by the increase of population, and more especially, by the conflicts between different tribes, and the subjugation of one tribe by another. On the other hand, as I have before remarked, the exchange of products springs up at the points where different families, tribes, communities, come in contact; for, in the beginning of civilisation, it is not private individuals but families, tribes, &c., that meet on an independent footing. Different communities find different means of production, and different means of subsistence in their natural environment. Hence, their modes of production, and of living, and their products are different. It is this spontaneously developed difference which, when different communities come in contact, calls forth the mutual exchange of products, and the consequent gradual conversion of those products into commodities. Exchange does not create the differences between the spheres of production, but brings what are already different into relation, and thus converts them into more or less inter-dependent branches of the collective production of an enlarged society. In the latter case, the social division of labour arises from the exchange between spheres of production, that are originally distinct and independent of one another. In the former, where the physiological division of labour is the starting-point, the particular organs of a compact whole grow loose, and break off, principally owing to the exchange of commodities with foreign communities, and then isolate themselves so far, that the sole bond, still connecting the various kinds of work, is the exchange of the products as commodities. In the one case, it is the making dependent what was before independent; in the other case, the making independent what was before dependent.

The foundation of every division of labour that is well developed, and brought about by the exchange of commodities, is the separation between town and country.[27] It may be said, that the whole economic history of society is summed up in the movement of this antithesis. We pass it over, however, for the present.

Just as a certain number of simultaneously employed labourers are the material pre-requisites for division of labour in manufacture, so are the number and density of the population, which here correspond to the agglomeration in one workshop, a necessary condition for the division of labour in society.[28] Nevertheless, this density is more or less relative. A relatively thinly populated country, with well-developed means of communication, has a denser population than a more numerously populated country, with badly-developed means of communication; and in this sense the Northern States of the American Union, for instance, are more thickly populated than India.[29]

Since the production and the circulation of commodities are the general pre-requisites of the capitalist mode of production, division of labour in manufacture demands, that division of labour in society at large should previously have attained a certain degree of development. Inversely, the former division reacts upon and develops and multiplies the latter. Simultaneously, with the differentiation of the instruments of labour, the industries that produce these instruments, become more and more differentiated.[30] If the manufacturing system seize upon an industry, which, previously, was carried on in connexion with others, either as a chief or as a subordinate industry, and by one producer, these industries immediately separate their connexion, and become independent. If it seize upon a particular stage in the production of a commodity, the other stages of its production become converted into so many independent industries. It has already been stated, that where the finished article consists merely of a number of parts fitted together, the detail operations may re-establish themselves as genuine and separate handicrafts. In order to carry out more perfectly the division of labour in manufacture, a single branch of production is, according to the varieties of its raw material, or the various forms that one and the same raw material may assume, split up into numerous, and to some extent, entirely new manufactures. Accordingly, in France alone, in the first half of the 18th century, over 100 different kinds of silk stuffs were woven, and, in Avignon, it was law, that 'every apprentice should devote himself to only one sort of fabrication, and should not learn the preparation of several kinds of stuff at once.' The territorial division of labour, which confines special branches of production to special districts of a country, acquires fresh stimulus from the manufacturing system, which exploits every special advantage.[31] The Colonial system and the opening out of the markets of the world, both of which are included in the general conditions of existence of the manufacturing period, furnish rich material for developing the division of labour in society. It is not the place, here, to go on to show how division of labour seizes upon, not only the economic, but every other sphere of society, and everywhere lays the foundation of that all engrossing system of specialising and sorting men, that development in a man of one single faculty at the expense of all other faculties, which caused A. Ferguson, the master of Adam Smith, to exclaim: 'We make a nation of Helots, and have no free citizens.'[32]

But, in spite of the numerous analogies and links connecting them, division of labour in the interior of a society, and that in the interior of a workshop, differ not only in degree, but also in kind. The analogy appears most indisputable where there is an invisible bond uniting the various branches of trade. For instance the cattle-breeder produces hides, the tanner makes the hides into leather, and the shoemaker, the leather into boots. Here the thing produced by each of them is but a step towards the final form, which is the product of all their labours combined. There are, besides, all the various industries that supply the cattle-breeder, the tanner, and the shoemaker with the means of production. Now it is quite possible to imagine, with Adam Smith, that the difference between the above social division of labour, and the division in manufacture, is merely subjective, exists merely for the observer, who, in a manufacture, can see with one glance, all the numerous operations being performed on one spot, while in the instance given above, the spreading out of the work over great areas, and the great number of people employed in each branch of labour, obscure the connexion.[33] But what is it that forms the bond between the independent labours of the cattle-breeder, the tanner, and the shoemaker? It is the fact that their respective products are commodities. What, on the other hand, characterises division of labour in manufactures? The fact that the detail labourer produces no commodities.[34] It is only the common product of all the detail labourers that becomes a commodity.[35] Division of labour in society is brought about by the purchase and sale of the products of different branches of industry, while the connexion between the detail operations in a workshop, is due to the sale of the labour-power of several workmen to one capitalist, who applies it as combined labour-power. The division of labour in the workshop implies concentration of the means of production in the hands of one capitalist; the division of labour in society implies their dispersion among many independent producers of commodities. While within the workshop, the iron law of proportionality subjects definite numbers of workmen to definite functions, in the society outside the workshop, chance and caprice have full play in distributing the producers and their means of production among the various branches of industry. The different spheres of production, it is true, constantly tend to an equilibrium: for, on the one hand, while each producer of a commodity is bound to produce a use-value, to satisfy a particular social want, and while the extent of these wants differs quantitatively, still there exists an inner relation which settles their proportions into a regular system, and that system one of spontaneous growth; and, on the other hand, the law of the value of commodities ultimately determines how much of its disposable working-time society can expend on each particular class of commodities. But this constant tendency to equilibrium, of the various spheres of production, is exercised, only in the shape of a reaction against the constant upsetting of this equilibrium. The *a priori* system on which the division of labour, within the workshop, is regularly carried out, becomes in the division of labour within the society, an *a posteriori*, nature-imposed necessity, controlling the lawless caprice of the producers, and perceptible in the barometrical fluctuations of the market-prices. Division of labour within the workshop implies the undisputed authority of the capitalist over men, that are but parts of a mechanism that belongs to him. The division of labour within the society brings into contact independent commodity-producers, who acknowledge no other authority but that of competition, of the coercion exerted by the pressure of their mutual interests; just as in the animal kingdom, the *bellum omnium contra omnes* [war of all against all—Hobbes] more or less preserves the conditions of existence of every species. The same bourgeois mind which praises division of labour in the workshop, life-long annexation of the labourer to a partial operation, and his complete subjection to capital, as being an organisation of labour that increases its productiveness—that same bourgeois mind denounces with equal vigour every conscious attempt to socially control and regulate the process of production, as an inroad upon such sacred things as the rights of property, freedom and unrestricted play for the bent of the individual capitalist. It is very characteristic that the enthusiastic apologists of the factory system have nothing more damning to urge against a general organisation of the labour of society, than that it would turn all society into one immense factory.

If, in a society with capitalist production, anarchy in the social division of labour and despotism in that of the workshop are mutual conditions the one of the other, we find, on the contrary, in those earlier forms of society in which the separation of trades has been spontaneously developed, then crystallised, and finally made permanent by law, on the one hand, a specimen of the organisation of the labour of society, in accordance with an approved and authoritative plan, and on the other, the entire exclusion of division of labour in the workshop, or at all events a mere dwarflike or sporadic and accidental development of the same.[36]

Those small and extremely ancient Indian communities, some of which have continued down to this day, are based on possession in common of the land, on the blending of agriculture and handicrafts, and on an unalterable division of labour, which serves, whenever a new community is started, as a plan and scheme ready cut and dried. Occupying areas of from 100 up to several thousand acres, each forms a compact whole producing all it requires. The chief part of the products is destined for direct use by the community itself, and does not take the form of a commodity. Hence, production here is independent of that division of labour brought about, in Indian society as a whole, by means of the exchange of commodities. It is the surplus alone that becomes a commodity, and a portion of even that, not until it has reached the hands of the State, into whose hands from time immemorial a certain quantity of these products has found its way in the shape of rent in kind. The constitution of these communities varies in different parts of India. In those of the simplest form, the land is tilled in common, and the produce divided among the members. At the same time, spinning and weaving are carried on in each family as subsidiary industries. Side by side with the masses thus occupied with one and the same work, we find the 'chief inhabitant,' who is judge, police, and tax-gatherer in one; the book-keeper, who keeps the accounts of the tillage and registers everything relating thereto; another official, who prosecutes criminals, protects strangers travelling through and escorts them to the next village; the boundary man, who guards the boundaries against neighbouring communities; the water-overseer, who distributes the water from the common tanks for irrigation; the Brahmin, who conducts the religious services; the schoolmaster, who on the sand teaches the children reading and writing; the calendar-Brahmin, or astrologer, who makes known the lucky or unlucky days for seed-time and harvest, and for every other kind of agricultural work; a smith and a carpenter, who make and repair all the agricultural implements; the potter, who makes all the pottery of the village; the barber, the washerman, who washes clothes, the silversmith, here and there the poet, who in some communities replaces the silversmith, in others the schoolmaster. This dozen of individuals is maintained at the expense of the whole community. If the population increases, a new community is founded, on the pattern of the old one, on unoccupied land. The whole mechanism discloses a systematic division of labour; but a division like that in manufactures is impossible, since the smith and the carpenter, &c., find an unchanging market, and at the most there occur, according to the sizes of the villages, two or three of each, instead of one.[37] The law that regulates the division of labour in the community acts with the irresistible authority of a law of Nature, at the same time that each individual artificer, the smith, the carpenter, and so on, conducts in his workshop all the operations of his handicraft in the traditional way, but independently, and without recognising any authority over him. The simplicity of the organisation for production in these self-sufficing communities that constantly reproduce themselves in the same form, and when accidentally destroyed, spring up again on the spot and with the same name[38]—this simplicity supplies the key to the secret of the unchangeableness of Asiatic societies, an unchangeableness in such striking contrast with the constant dissolution and refounding of Asiatic States, and the never-ceasing changes of dynasty. The structure of the economic elements of society remains untouched by the storm-clouds of the political sky.

The rules of the guilds, as I have said before, by limiting most strictly the number of apprentices and journeymen that a single master could employ, prevented him from becoming a capitalist. Moreover, he could not employ his journeymen in many other handicrafts than the one in which he was a master. The guilds zealously repelled every encroachment by the capital of merchants, the only form of free capital with which they came in contact. A merchant could buy every kind of commodity, but labour as a commodity he could not buy. He existed only on sufferance, as a dealer in the products of the handicrafts. If circumstances called for a further division of labour, the existing guilds split themselves up into varieties, or founded new guilds by the side of the old ones; all this, however, without concentrating various handicrafts in a single workshop. Hence, the guild organisation, however much it may have contributed by separating, isolating, and perfecting the handicrafts, to create the material conditions for the existence of manufacture, excluded division of labour in the workshop. On the whole, the labourer and his means of production remained closely united, like the snail with its shell, and thus there was wanting the principal basis of manufacture, the separation of the labourer from his means of production, and the conversion of these means into capital.

While division of labour in society at large, whether such division be brought about or not by exchange of commodities, is common to economic formations of society the most diverse, division of labour in the workshop, as practised by manufacture, is a special creation of the capitalist mode of production alone.

Section 5: *The Capitalistic Character of Manufacture*

An increased number of labourers under the control of one capitalist is the natural starting-point, as well of co-operation generally, as of manufacture in particular. But the division of labour in manufacture makes this increase in the number of workmen a technical necessity. The minimum number that any given capitalist is bound to employ is here prescribed by the previously established division of labour. On the other hand, the advantages of further division are obtainable only by adding to the number of workmen, and this can be done only by adding multiples of the various detail groups. But an increase in the variable component of the capital employed necessitates an increase in its constant component, too, in the workshops, implements, &c., and, in particular, in the raw material, the call for which grows quicker than the number of workmen. The quantity of it consumed in a given time, by a given amount of labour, increases in the same ratio as does the productive power of that labour in consequence of its division. Hence, it is a law, based on the very nature of manufacture, that the minimum amount of capital, which is bound to be in the hands of each capitalist, must keep increasing; in other words, that the transformation into capital of the social means of production and subsistence must keep extending.[39]

In manufacture, as well as in simple co-operation, the collective working organism is a form of existence of capital. The mechanism that is made up of numerous individual detail labourers belongs to the capitalist. Hence, the productive power resulting from a combination of labours appears to be the productive power of capital. Manufacture proper not only subjects the previously independent workman to the discipline and command of capital, but, in addition, creates a hierarchic gradation of the workmen themselves. While simple co-operation leaves the mode of working by the individual for the most part unchanged, manufacture thoroughly revolutionises it, and seizes labour-power by its very roots. It converts the labourer into a crippled monstrosity, by forcing his detail dexterity at the expense of a world of productive capabilities and instincts; just as in the States of La Plata they butcher a whole beast for the sake of his hide or his tallow. Not only is the detail work distributed to the different individuals, but the individual himself is made the automatic motor of a fractional operation,[40] and the absurd fable of Menenius Agrippa, which makes man a mere fragment of his own body, becomes realised.[41] If, at first, the workman sells his labour-power to capital, because the material means of producing a commodity fail him, now his very labour-power refuses its services unless it has been sold to capital. Its functions can be exercised only in an environment that exists in the workshop of the capitalist after the sale. By nature unfitted to make anything independently, the manufacturing labourer develops productive activity as a mere appendage of the capitalist's workshop.[42] As the chosen people bore in their features the sign manual of Jehovah, so division of labour brands the manufacturing workman as the property of capital.

The knowledge, the judgement, and the will, which, though in ever so small a degree, are practised by the independent peasant or handicraftsman, in the same way as the savage makes the whole art of war consist in the exercise of his personal cunning these faculties are now required only for the workshop as a whole. Intelligence in production expands in one direction, because it vanishes in many others. What is lost by the detail labourers, is concentrated in the capital that employs them.[43] It is a result of the division of labour in manufactures, that the labourer is brought face to face with the intellectual potencies of the material process of production, as the property of another, and as a ruling power. This separation begins in simple co-operation, where the capitalist represents to the single workman, the oneness and the will of the associated labour. It is developed in manufacture which cuts down the labourer into a detail labourer. It is completed in modern industry, which makes science a productive force distinct from labour and presses it into the service of capital.[44]

In manufacture, in order to make the collective labourer, and through him capital, rich in social productive power, each labourer must be made poor in individual productive powers.

> 'Ignorance is the mother of industry as well as of superstition. Reflection and fancy are subject to err; but a habit of moving the hand or the foot is independent of either. Manufactures, accordingly, prosper most where the mind is least consulted, and where the workshop may ... be considered as an engine, the parts of which are men.'[45]

As a matter of fact, some few manufacturers in the middle of the 18th century preferred, for certain operations that were trade secrets, to employ half-idiotic persons.[46]

> 'The understandings of the greater part of men,' says Adam Smith, 'are necessarily formed by their ordinary employments. The man whose whole life is spent in performing a few simple operations ... has no occasion to exert his understanding... He generally becomes as stupid and ignorant as it is possible for a human creature to become.'

After describing the stupidity of the detail labourer he goes on:

> 'The uniformity of his stationary life naturally corrupts the courage of his mind... It corrupts even the activity of his body and renders him incapable of exerting his strength with vigour and perseverance in any other employments than that to which he has been bred. His dexterity at his own particular trade seems in this manner to be acquired at the expense of his intellectual, social, and martial virtues. But in every improved and civilised society, this is the state into which the labouring poor, that is, the great body of the people, must necessarily fall.'[47]

For preventing the complete deterioration of the great mass of the people by division of labour, A. Smith recommends education of the people by the State, but prudently, and in homeopathic doses. G. Garnier, his French translator and commentator, who, under the first French Empire, quite naturally developed into a senator, quite as naturally opposes him on this point. Education of the masses, he urges, violates the first law of the division of labour, and with it

> 'our whole social system would be proscribed.' "Like all other divisions of labour,' he says, 'that between hand labour and head labour[48] is more pronounced and decided in proportion as society (he rightly uses this word, for capital, landed property and their State) becomes richer. This division of labour, like every other, is an effect of past, and a cause of future progress... ought the government then to work in opposition to this division of labour, and to hinder its natural course? Ought it to expend a part of the public money in the attempt to confound and blend together two classes of labour, which are striving after division and separation?'[49]

Some crippling of body and mind is inseparable even from division of labour in society as a whole. Since, however, manufacture carries this social separation of branches of labour much further, and also, by its peculiar division, attacks the individual at the very roots of his life, it is the first to afford the materials for, and to give a start to, industrial pathology.[50]

> 'To subdivide a man is to execute him, if he deserves the sentence, to assassinate him if he does not... The subdivision of labour is the assassination of a people.'[51]

Co-operation based on division of labour, in other words, manufacture, commences as a spontaneous formation. So soon as it attains some consistence and extension, it becomes the recognised methodical and systematic form of capitalist production. History shows how the division of labour peculiar to manufacture, strictly so called, acquires the best adapted form at first by experience, as it were behind the backs of the actors, and then, like the guild handicrafts, strives to hold fast that form when once found, and here and there succeeds in keeping it for centuries. Any alteration in this form, except in trivial matters, is solely owing to a revolution in the instruments of labour. Modern manufacture wherever it arises—I do not here allude to modern industry based on machinery—either finds the disjecta membra poetae ready to hand, and only waiting to be collected together, as is the case in the manufacture of clothes in large towns, or it can easily apply the principle of division, simply by exclusively assigning the various operations of a handicraft (such as book-binding) to particular men. In such cases, a week's experience is enough to determine the proportion between the numbers of the hands necessary for the various functions.[52]

By decomposition of handicrafts, by specialisation of the instruments of labour, by the formation of detail labourers, and by grouping and combining the latter into a single mechanism, division of labour in manufacture creates a qualitative gradation, and a quantitative proportion in the social process of production; it consequently creates a definite organisation of the labour of society, and thereby develops at the same time new productive forces in the society. In its specific capitalist form—and under the given conditions, it could take no other form than a capitalistic one—manufacture is but a particular method of begetting relative surplus-value, or of augmenting at the expense of the labourer the self-expansion of capital—usually called social wealth, 'Wealth of Nations,' &c. It increases the social productive power of labour, not only for the benefit of the capitalist instead of for that of the labourer, but it does this by crippling the individual labourers. It creates new conditions for the lordship of capital over labour. If, therefore, on the one hand, it presents itself historically as a progress and as a necessary phase in the economic development of society, on the other hand, it is a refined and civilised method of exploitation.

Political Economy, which as an independent science, first sprang into being during the period of manufacture, views the social division of labour only from the standpoint of manufacture,[53] and sees in it only the means of producing more commodities with a given quantity of labour, and, consequently, of cheapening commodities and hurrying on the accumulation of capital. In most striking contrast with this accentuation of quantity and exchange-value, is the attitude of the writers of classical antiquity, who hold exclusively by quality and use-value.[54] In consequence of the separation of the social branches of production, commodities are better made, the various bents and talents of men select a suitable field,[55] and without some restraint no important results can be obtained anywhere.[56] Hence both product and producer are improved by division of labour. If the growth of the quantity produced is occasionally mentioned, this is only done with reference to the greater abundance of use-values. There is not a word alluding to exchange-value or to the cheapening of commodities. This aspect, from the standpoint of use-value alone, is taken as well by Plato,[57] who treats division of labour as the foundation on which the division of society into classes is based, as by Xenophon,[58] who with characteristic bourgeois instinct, approaches more nearly to division of labour within the workshop. Plato's Republic, in so far as division of labour is treated in it, as the formative principle of the State, is merely the Athenian idealisation of the Egyptian system of castes, Egypt having served as the model of an industrial country to many of his contemporaries also, amongst others to Isocrates,[59] and it continued to have this importance to the Greeks of the Roman Empire.[60]

During the manufacturing period proper, i.e., the period during which manufacture is the predominant form taken by capitalist production, many obstacles are opposed to the full development of the peculiar tendencies of manufacture. Although manufacture creates, as we have already seen, a simple separation of the labourers into skilled and unskilled, simultaneously with their hierarchic arrangement in classes, yet the number of the unskilled labourers, owing to the preponderating influence of the skilled, remains very limited. Although it adapts the detail operations to the various degrees of maturity, strength, and development of the living instruments of labour, thus conducing to exploitation of women and children, yet this tendency as a whole is wrecked on the habits and the resistance of the male labourers. Although the splitting up of handicrafts lowers the cost of forming the workman, and thereby lowers his value, yet for the more difficult detail work, a longer apprenticeship is necessary, and, even where it would be superfluous, is jealously insisted upon by the workmen. In England, for instance, we find the laws of apprenticeship, with their seven years' probation, in full force down to the end of the manufacturing period; and they are not thrown on one side till the advent of Modern Industry. Since handicraft skill is the foundation of manufacture, and since the mechanism of manufacture as a whole possesses no framework, apart from the labourers themselves, capital is constantly compelled to wrestle with the insubordination of the workmen.

'By the infirmity of human nature,' says friend Ure, 'it happens that the more skilful the workman, the more self-willed and intractable he is apt to become, and of course the less fit a component of a mechanical system in which ... he may do great damage to the whole.'[61]

Hence throughout the whole manufacturing period there runs the complaint of want of discipline among the workmen.[62] And had we not the testimony of contemporary writers, the simple facts, that during the period between the 16th century and the epoch of Modern Industry, capital failed to become the master of the whole disposable working-time of the manufacturing labourers, that manufactures are short-lived, and change their locality from one country to another with the emigrating or immigrating workmen, these facts would speak volumes. 'Order must in one way or another be established,' exclaims in 1770 the oft-cited author of the 'Essay on Trade and Commerce.' 'Order,' re-echoes Dr Andrew Ure 66 years later, 'Order' was wanting in manufacture based on 'the scholastic dogma of division of labour,' and 'Arkwright created order.'

At the same time manufacture was unable, either to seize upon the production of society to its full extent, or to revolutionise that production to its very core. It towered up as an economic work of art, on the broad foundation of the town handicrafts, and of the rural domestic industries. At a given stage in its development, the narrow technical basis on which manufacture rested, came into conflict with requirements of production that were created by manufacture itself.

One of its most finished creations was the workshop for the production of the instruments of labour themselves, including especially the complicated mechanical apparatus then already employed.

A machine-factory, says Ure, 'displayed the division of labour in manifold gradations—the file, the drill, the lathe, having each its different workman in the order of skill.' (P. 21.)

This workshop, the product of the division of labour in manufacture, produced in its turn—machines. It is they that sweep away the handicraftsman's work as the regulating principle of social production. Thus, on the one hand, the technical reason for the life-long annexation of the workman to a detail function is removed. On the other hand, the fetters that this same principle laid on the dominion of capital, fall away.

Notes

1. To give a more modern instance: The silk spinning and weaving of Lyon and Nîmes 'est toute patriarcale; elle emploie beaucoup de femmes et d'enfants, mais sans les épuiser ni les corrompre; elle les laisse dans leur belles valises de la Drôme, du Var, de l'Isère, de Vaucluse, pour y élever des vers et dévider leurs cocons; jamais elle n'entre dans une véritable fabrique. Pour être aussi bien observé ... le principe de la division du travail s'y revêt d'un caractère spécial. Il y a bien des dévideuses, des moulineurs, des teinturiers, des encolleurs, puis des tisserands; mais ils ne sont pas réunis dans un même établissement, ne dépendent pas d'un même maître, tous ils sont indépendants' [... is entirely patriarchal; it employs a large number of women and children, but without exhausting or ruining them; it allows them to stay in their beautiful valleys of the Drôme, the Var, the Isère, the Vaucluse, cultuvating their silkworms and unwinding their cocoons; it never becomes a true factory industry. However, the principle of the division of labour takes on a special character here. There do indeed exist winders, throwsters. dyers, sizers, and finally weavers; but they are not assembled in the same workshop, nor are they dependent on a single master; they are all independent] (A. Blanqui: 'Cours, d'Econ. Industrielle.' Recueilli par A. Blaise. Paris, 1838-39, p. 79.) Since Blanqui wrote this, the various independent labourers have, to some extent, been united in factories.

[And since Marx wrote the above, the power-loom has invaded these factories, and is now 1886 rapidly superseding the hand-loom. (*Added in the 4th German edition*. The Krefeld silk industry also has its tale to tell anent this subject.) F. E.]

2. 'The more any manufacture of much variety shall be distributed and assigned to different artists, the same must needs be better done and with greater expedition, with less loss of time and labour.' ('The Advantages of the East India Trade,' Lond., 1720, p. 71.)
3. 'Easy labour is transmitted skill.' (Th. Hodgskin, 'Popular Political Economy,' p. 48.)
4. 'The arts also have ... in Egypt reached the requisite degree of perfection. For it is the only country where artificers may not in any way meddle with the affairs of another class of citizens, but must follow that calling alone which by law is hereditary in their clan.... In other countries it is found that tradesmen divide their attention between too many objects. At one time they try agriculture, at another they take to commerce, at another they busy themselves with two or three occupations at once. In free countries, they mostly frequent the assemblies of the people.... In Egypt, on the contrary, every artificer is severely punished if he meddles with affairs of State, or carries on several trades at once. Thus there is nothing to disturb their application to their calling.... Moreover, since, they inherit from their forefathers numerous rules, they are eager to discover fresh advantages' (Diodorus Siculus: Bibl. Hist. I. 1. c., 74.)
5. 'Historical and descriptive account of Brit. India, &c.,' by Hugh Murray and James Wilson, &c., Edinburgh 1832, v. II., p. 449. The Indian loom is upright, i.e., the warp is stretched vertically.
6. Darwin in his epoch-making work on the origin of species, remarks, with reference to the natural organs of plants and animals: 'So long as one and the same organ has different kinds of work to perform, a ground for its changeability may possibly be found in this, that natural selection preserves or suppresses each small variation of form less carefully than if that organ were destined for one special purpose alone. Thus, knives that are adapted to cut all sorts of things, may, on the whole, be of one shape; but an implement destined to be used exclusively in one way must have a different shape for every different use.'
7. In the year 1854 Geneva produced 80,000 watches, which is not one-fifth of the production in the Canton of Neufchâtel. La Chaux-de-Fond alone, which we may look upon as a huge watch manufactory, produces yearly twice as many as Geneva. From 1850-61 Geneva produced 720,000 watches. See 'Report from Geneva on the Watch Trade' in 'Reports by H. M.'s Secretaries of Embassy and Legation on the Manufactures, Commerce, &c., No. 6, 1863.' The want of connexion alone, between the processes into which the production of articles that merely consist of parts fitted together is split up, makes it very difficult to convert such a manufacture into a branch of modern industry carried on by machinery; but in the case of a watch there are two other impediments in addition, the minuteness and delicacy of its parts, and its character as an article of luxury. Hence their variety, which is such, that in the best London houses scarcely a dozen watches are made alike in the course of a year. The watch manufactory of Messrs. Vacheron & Constantin, in which machinery has been employed with success, produces at the most three or four different varieties of size and form.
8. In watchmaking, that classical example of heterogeneous manufacture, we may study with great accuracy the above-mentioned differentiation and specialisation of the instruments of labour caused by the sub-division of handicrafts.
9. 'In so close a cohabitation of the people, the carriage must needs be less.' ('The Advantages of the East India Trade,' p. 106.)
10. 'The isolation of the different stages of manufacture, consequent upon the employment of manual labour, adds immensely to the cost of production, the loss mainly arising from the mere removals from one process to another.' ('The Industry of Nations.' Lond., 1855, Part II, p. 200.)
11. 'It (the division of labour) produces also an economy of time by separating the work into its different branches, all of which may be carried on into execution at the same moment....

By carrying on all the different processes at once, which an individual must have executed separately, it becomes possible to produce a multitude of pins completely finished in the same time as a single pin might have been either cut or pointed.' (Dugald Stewart, l.c., p. 319.)

12. 'The more variety of artists to every manufacture... the greater the order and regularity of every work, the same must needs be done in less time, the labour must be less.' ('The Advantages,' &c., p. 68.)
13. Nevertheless, the manufacturing system, in many branches of industry, attains this result but very imperfectly, because it knows not how to control with certainty the general chemical and physical conditions of the process of production.
14. 'When (from the peculiar nature of the produce of each manufactory), the number of processes into which it is most advantageous to divide it is ascertained, as well as the number of individuals to be employed, then all other manufactories which do not employ a direct multiple of this number will produce the article at a greater cost.... Hence arises one of the causes of the great size of manufacturing establishments.' (C. Babbage. 'On the Economy of Machinery,' 1st ed. London. 1832. Ch. xxi, pp. 172-73.)
15. In England, the melting-furnace is distinct from the glass-furnace in which the glass is manipulated. In Belgium, one and the same furnace serves for both processes.
16. This can be seen from W. Petty, John Bellers, Andrew Yarranton, 'The Advantages of the East India Trade,' and J. Vanderlint, not to mention others.
17. Towards the end of the 16th century, mortars and sieves were still used in France for pounding and washing ores.
18. The whole history of the development of machinery can be traced in the history of the corn mill. The factory in England is still a 'mill.' In German technological works of the first decade of this century, the term 'Mühle' is still found in use, not only for all machinery driven by the forces of Nature, but also for all manufactures where apparatus in the nature of machinery is applied.
19. As will be seen more in detail in the fourth book of this work, Adam Smith has not established a single new proposition relating to division of labour. What, however, characterises him as the political economist par excellence of the period of Manufacture, is the stress he lays on division of labour. The subordinate part which he assigns to machinery gave occasion in the early days of modern mechanical industry to the polemic of Lauderdale, and, at a later period, to that of Ure. A. Smith also confounds differentiation of the instruments of labour, in which the detail labourers themselves took an active part, with the invention of machinery; in this latter, it is not the workmen in manufactories, but learned men, handicraftsman, and even peasants (Brindley), who play a part.
20. 'The master manufacturer, by dividing the work to be executed into different processes, each requiring different degrees of skill or of force, can purchase exactly that precise quantity of both which is necessary for each process; whereas, if the whole work were executed by one workman, that person must possess sufficient skill to perform the most difficult, and sufficient strength to execute the most laborious of the operations into which the article is divided.' (Ch. Babbage, l.c., ch. xix.)
21. For instance, abnormal development of some muscles, curvature of bones, &c.
22. The question put by one of the Inquiry Commissioners, How the young persons are kept steadily to their work, is very correctly answered by Mr Wm. Marshall, the general manager of a glass manufactory: 'They cannot well neglect their work; when they once begin, they must go on; they are just the same as parts of a machine.' ('Children's Empl. Comm.,' 4th Rep., 1865, p. 247.)
23. Dr Ure, in his apotheosis of Modern Mechanical Industry, brings out the peculiar character of manufacture more sharply than previous economists, who had not his polemical interest in the matter, and more sharply even than his contemporaries Babbage, e.g., who, though much his superior as a mathematician and mechanician, treated mechanical industry from

the standpoint of manufacture alone. Ure says, 'This appropriation ... to each, a workman of appropriate value and cost was naturally assigned, forms the very essence of division of labour.' On the other hand, he describes this division as 'adaptation of labour to the different talents of men,' and lastly, characterises the whole manufacturing system as 'a system for the division or gradation of labour,' as 'the division of labour into degrees of skill,' &c. (Ure, l.c., pp. 19-23 passim.)

24. 'Each handicraftsman being ... enabled to perfect himself by practice in one point, became ... a cheaper workman.' (Ure, l.c., p. 19.)

25. 'Division of labour proceeds from the separation of professions the most widely different to that division, where several labourers divide between them the preparation of one and the same product, as in manufacture.' (Storch: 'Cours d'Econ. Pol.,' Paris Edn. t. I., p. 173.) 'Nous rencontrons chez les peuples parvenus à un certain degré de civilisation trois genres de divisions d'industrie: la première, que nous nommerons générale, amène la distinction des producteurs en agriculteurs, manufacturiers et commerçants, elle se rapporte aux trois principales branches d'industrie nationale; la seconde qu'on pourrait appeler spéciale, est la division de chaque genre d'industrie en espèces ... la troisième division d'industrie, celle enfin qu'on devrait qualifier de division de la besogne on de travail proprement dit, est celle qui s'établit dans les arts et les métiers séparés ... qui s'établit dans la plupart des manufactures et des ateliers.' [Among peoples which have reached a certain level of civilisation, we meet with three kinds of division of labour: the first, which we shall call general, brings about the division of the producers into agriculturalists, manufacturers, and traders, it corresponds to the three main branches of the nation's labour; the second, which one could call particular, is the division of labour of each branch into species. ... The third division of labour, which one could designate as a division of tasks, or of labour properly so called, is that which grows up in the individual crafts and trades ... which is established in the majority of the manufactories and workshops] (Skarbek, l.c., pp. 84, 85.)

26. *Note to the third edition.* Subsequent very searching study of the primitive condition of man, led the author to the conclusion, that it was not the family that originally developed into the tribe, but that, on the contrary, the tribe was the primitive and spontaneously developed form of human association, on the basis of blood relationship, and that out of the first incipient loosening of the tribal bonds, the many and various forms of the family were afterwards developed. [F. E.]

27. Sir James Steuart is the economist who has handled this subject best. How little his book, which appeared ten years before the 'Wealth of Nations,' is known, even at the present time, may be judged from the fact that the admirers of Malthus do not even know that the first edition of the latter's work on population contains, except in the purely declamatory part, very little but extracts from Steuart, and in a less degree, from Wallace and Townsend.

28. 'There is a certain density of population which is convenient, both for social intercourse, and for that combination of powers by which the produce of labour is increased.' (James Mill, l.c., p. 50.) 'As the number of labourers increases, the productive power of society augments in the compound ratio of that increase, multiplied by the effects of the division of labour.' (Th. Hodgskin, l.c., pp. 125, 126.)

29. In consequence of the great demand for cotton after 1861, the production of cotton, in some thickly populated districts of India, was extended at the expense of rice cultivation. In consequence there arose local famines, the defective means of communication not permitting the failure of rice in one district to be compensated by importation from another.

30. Thus the fabrication of shuttles formed as early as the 17th century, a special branch of industry in Holland.

31. Whether the woollen manufacture of England is not divided into several parts or branches appropriated to particular places, where they are only or principally manufactured; fine cloths in Somersetshire, coarse in Yorkshire, long ells at Exeter, soies at Sudbury, crapes at

Norwich, linseys at Kendal, blankets at Whitney, and so forth.' (Berkeley: 'The Querist,' 1751, § 520.)

32. A. Ferguson: 'History of Civil Society.' Edinburgh, 1767; Part iv, sect. ii., p. 285.

33. In manufacture proper, he says, the division of labour appears to be greater, because 'those employed in every different branch of the work can often be collected into the same workhouse, and placed at once under the view of the spectator. In those great manufactures, (!) on the contrary, which are destined to supply the great wants of the great body of the people, every different branch of the work employs so great a number of workmen, that it is impossible to collect them all into the same workhouse ... the division is not near so obvious.' (A. Smith: 'Wealth of Nations,' bk. i, ch. i.) The celebrated passage in the same chapter that begins with the words, 'Observe the accommodation of the most common artificer or day-labourer in a civilised and thriving country,' &c., and then proceeds to depict what an enormous number and variety of industries contribute to the satisfaction of the wants of an ordinary labourer, is copied almost word for word from B. de Mandeville's Remarks to his 'Fable of the Bees, or Private Vices, Publick Benefits.' (First ed., without the remarks, 1706; with the remarks, 1714.)

34. 'There is no longer anything which we can call the natural reward of individual labour. Each labourer produces only some part of a whole, and each part, having no value or utility in itself, there is nothing on which the labourer can seize, and say: It is my product, this I will keep to myself.' ('Labour Defended against the Claims of Capital.' Lond., 1825, p. 25.) The author of this admirable work is the Th. Hodgskin I have already cited.

35. This distinction between division of labour in society and in manufacture, was practically illustrated to the Yankees. One of the new taxes devised at Washington during the civil war, was the duty of 6% 'on all industrial products.' Question: What is an industrial product? Answer of the legislature: A thing is produced 'when it is made,' and it is made when it is ready for sale. Now, for one example out of many. The New York and Philadelphia manufacturers had previously been in the habit of 'making' umbrellas with all their belongings. But since an umbrella is a *mixtum compositum* of very heterogeneous parts, by degrees these parts became the products of various separate industries, carried on independently in different places. They entered as separate commodities into the umbrella manufactory, where they were fitted together. The Yankees have given to articles thus fitted together, the name of 'assembled articles,' a name they deserve, for being an assemblage of taxes. Thus the umbrella 'assembles,' first, 6% on the price of each of its elements, and a further 6% on its own total price.

36. 'On peut... établir en règle générale, que moins l'autorité préside à la division du travail dans l'intérieur de la société, plus la division du travail se développe dans l'intérieur de l'atelier, et plus elle y est soumise à l'autorité d'un seul. Ainsi l'autorité dans l'atelier et celle dans la société, par rapport à la division du travail, sont en raison inverse l'une de l'autre.' [It can ... be laid down as a general rule that the less authority presides over the division of labour inside society, the more the division of labour develops inside the workshop, and the more it is subjected there to the authority of a single person. Thus authority in the workshop and authority in society in relation to the division of labour, are in inverse ratio to each other] (Karl Marx, 'Misère,' &c., pp. 130-131.)

37. Lieut.-Col. Mark Wilks: 'Historical Sketches of the South of India.' Lond., 1810-17, v. I., pp. 118-20. A good description of the various forms of the Indian communities is to be found in George Campbell's 'Modern India.' Lond., 1852.

38. 'Under this simple form ... the inhabitants of the country have lived from time immemorial. The boundaries of the villages have been but seldom altered; and though the villages themselves have been sometimes injured, and even desolated by war, famine, and disease, the same name, the same limits, the same interests, and even the same families, have continued for ages. The inhabitants give themselves no trouble about the breaking up and division of

kingdoms; while the village remains entire, they care not to what power it is transferred, or to what sovereign it devolves; its internal economy remains unchanged.' (Th. Stamford Raffles, late Lieut. Gov. of Java: 'The History of Java.' Lond., 1817, Vol. I., p. 285.)

39. 'It is not sufficient that the capital' (the writer should have said the necessary means of subsistence and of production) 'required for the subdivision of handicrafts should be in readiness in the society: it must also be accumulated in the hands of the employers in sufficiently large quantities to enable them to conduct their operations on a large scale.... The more the division increases, the more does the constant employment of a given number of labourers require a greater outlay of capital in tools, raw material, &c.' (Storch: 'Cours d'Econ. Polit.' Paris Ed., t. I., pp. 250, 251.) 'La concentration des instruments de production et la division du travail sont aussi inséparables l'une de l'autre que le sont, dans le régime politique, la concentration des pouvoirs publics et la division des intérêts privés.' [The concentration of the instruments of production and the division of labour are as inseparable one from the other, as are, in the political sphere, the concentration of public powers and the division of private interests.] (Karl Marx, l.c., p. 134.)

40. Dugald Stewart calls manufacturing labourers 'living automatons ... employed in the details of the work.' (I. c., p. 318.)

41. In corals, each individual is, in fact, the stomach of the whole group; but it supplies the group with nourishment, instead of, like the Roman patrician, withdrawing it.

42. 'L'ouvrier qui porte dans ses bras tout un métier, peut aller partout exercer son industrie et trouver des moyens de subsister: l'autre (the manufacturing labourer) n'est qu'un accessoire qui, séparé de ses confrères, n'a plus ni capacité, ni indépendance, et qui se trouve force d'accepter la loi qu'on juge à propos de lui imposer.' [The worker who is the master of a whole craft can work and find the means of subsistence anywhere; the other (the manufacturing labourer) is only an appendage who, when he is separated from his fellows, possesses neither capability nor independence, and finds himself forced to accept any law it is thought fit to impose] (Storch, l.c., Petersb. edit., 1815, t. I., p. 204.)

43. A. Ferguson, l.c., p. 281: 'The former may have gained what the other has lost.'

44. 'The man of knowledge and the productive labourer come to be widely divided from each other, and knowledge, instead of remaining the handmaid of labour in the hand of the labourer to increase his productive powers ... has almost everywhere arrayed itself against labour ... systematically deluding and leading them (the labourers) astray in order to render their muscular powers entirely mechanical and obedient.' (W. Thompson: 'An Inquiry into the Principles of the Distribution of Wealth.' London, 1824, p. 274.)

45. A. Ferguson, l.c., p. 280.

46. J. D. Tuckett: 'A History of the Past and Present State of the Labouring Population.' Lond., 1846.

47. A. Smith: 'Wealth of Nations,' Bk. v., ch. i, art. ii. Being a pupil of A. Ferguson who showed the disadvantageous effects of division of labour, Adam Smith was perfectly clear on this point. In the introduction to his work, where he *ex professo* praises division of labour, he indicates only in a cursory manner that it is the source of social inequalities. It is not till the 5th Book, on the Revenue of the State, that he reproduces Ferguson. In my 'Misère de la Philosophie,' I have sufficiently explained the historical connexion between Ferguson, A. Smith, Lemontey, and Say, as regards their criticisms of Division of Labour, and have shown, for the first time, that Division of Labour as practised in manufactures, is a specific form of the capitalist mode of production.

48. Ferguson had already said, l.c., p. 281: 'And thinking itself, in this age of separations, may become a peculiar craft.'

49. G. Garnier, vol. V. of his translation of A. Smith, pp. 4-5.

50. Ramazzini, professor of practical medicine at Padua, published in 1713 his work 'De morbis artificum,' which was translated into French 1781, reprinted 1841 in the 'Encyclopédie

des Sciences Médicales. 7me Dis. Auteurs Classiques.' The period of Modern Mechanical Industry has, of course, very much enlarged his catalogue of labour's diseases. See 'Hygiène physique et morale de l'ouvrier dans les grandes villes en général et dans la ville de Lyon en particulier. Par le Dr A. L. Fonteret, Paris, 1858,' and 'Die Krankheiten, welche verschiednen Ständen, Altern und Geschlechtern eigenthümlich sind. 6 Vols. Ulm, 1860,' and others. In 1854 the Society of Arts appointed a Commission of Inquiry into industrial pathology. The list of documents collected by this commission is to be seen in the catalogue of the 'Twickenham Economic Museum.' Very important are the official 'Reports on Public Health.' See also Eduard Reich, M. D. 'Ueber die Entartung des Menschen,' Erlangen, 1868.

51. (D. Urquhart: 'Familiar Words.' Lond., 1855, p. 119.) Hegel held very heretical views on division of labour. In his 'Rechtsphilosophie' he says: 'By well educated men we understand in the first instance, those who can do everything that others do.'

52. The simple belief in the inventive genius exercised a priori by the individual capitalist in division of labour, exists now-a-days only among German professors, of the stamp of Herr Roscher, who, to recompense the capitalist from whose Jovian head division of labour sprang ready formed, dedicates to him 'various wages' (diverse *Arbeitslöhne*). The more or less extensive application of division of labour depends on length of purse, not on greatness of genius.

53. The older writers, like Petty and the anonymous author of 'Advantages of the East India Trade,' bring out the capitalist character of division of labour as applied in manufacture more than A. Smith does.

54. Amongst the moderns may be excepted a few writers of the 18th century, like Beccaria and James Harris, who with regard to division of labour almost entirely follow the ancients. Thus, Beccaria: 'Ciascuno prova coll'esperienza, che applicando la mano e l'ingegno sempre allo stesso genere di opere e di produtte, egli più facili, più abbondanti e migliori ne traca risultati, di quello che se ciascuno isolatamente le cose tutte a se necessarie soltanto facesse.... Dividendosi in tal maniera per la comune e privata utilità gli uomini in varie classi e condizioni.' [Everyone knows from experience that if the hands and the intelligence are always applied to the same kind of work and the same products, these will be produced more easily, in greater abundance, and in higher quality, than if each individual makes for himself all the things he needs ... In this way, men are divided up into various classes and conditions, to their own advantage and to that of the commodity.](Cesare Beccaria: 'Elementi di Econ: Pubblica,' ed. Custodi, Parte Moderna, t. xi, p. 29.) James Harris, afterwards Earl of Malmesbury, celebrated for the 'Diaries' of his embassy at St. Petersburg, says in a note to his 'Dialogue Concerning Happiness,' Lond., 1741, reprinted afterwards in 'Three Treatises, 3 Ed., Lond., 1772: 'The whole argument to prove society natural (i.e., by division of employments) ... is taken from the second book of Plato's Republic.'

55. Thus, in the Odyssey xiv., 228, ['Alloς gaρ talloisiν aneρ epiterpetaι ergoiς' For different men take joy in different works] and Archilochus in Sextus Empiricus, ['alloς allω επ ergo kardihν iainetaι.' men differ as to things cheer their hearts]

56. ['Polλ hpistaio ergα, cacwς δ hpistano pantα.' He could do many works, but all of them badly—Homer] Every Athenian considered himself superior as a producer of commodities to a Spartan; for the latter in time of war had men enough at his disposal but could not command money, as Thucydides makes Pericles say in the speech inciting the Athenians to the Peloponnesian war: ['swmasι tε etoimoteroι οι autonrgoι twν anthrwpwν η crhmasι polemeiν' people producing for their own consumption will rather let war have their bodies than their money] (Thuc.: 1, I. c. 41.) Nevertheless, even with regard to material production, [autarceia self-sufficiency], as opposed to division of labour remained their ideal, ['parwν gaρ to, eυ, parα toutwν caι to autaresς.' For with the latter there is well-being, but with the former there is independence.] It should be mentioned here that at the date of the fall of the 30 Tyrants there were still not 5,000 Athenians without landed property.

57. With Plato, division of labour within the community is a development from the multifarious requirements, and the limited capacities of individuals. The main point with him is, that the labourer must adapt himself to the work, not the work to the labourer; which latter is unavoidable, if he carries on several trades at once, thus making one or the other of them subordinate. ['Ου gaρ etheleι to prattomenoν teν toυ prattonioσ scholeν perimeneiν, alλ anagkε toν prattontα to prattomeno epakolootheiν mε eν parergoυ mereι. Anagkε. Eκ dε toutoν pleio tε ekastα gignetaι kaι kallioν kaι raoν, otaν eiσ eν kaiα physiν kaι eν kairo scholeν toν alloν agoν, prattε.'] [For the workman must wait upon the work; it will not wait upon his leisure and allow itself to be done in a spare moment.—Yes, he must,— So the conclusion is that more will be produced of every thing and the work will be more easily and better done, when every man is set free from all other occupations to do, at the right time, the one thing for which he is naturally fitted.] (Rep. 1. 2. Ed. Baiter, Orelli, &c.) So in Thucydides, l.c., c. 142: 'Seafaring is an art like any other, and cannot, as circumstances require, be carried on as a subsidiary occupation; nay, other subsidiary occupations cannot be carried on alongside of this one.' If the work, says Plato, has to wait for the labourer, the critical point in the process is missed and the article spoiled, 'ergoυ cairoν diollutaι.' [If someone lets slip ...] The same Platonic idea is found recurring in the protest of the English bleachers against the clause in the Factory Act that provides fixed mealtimes for all operatives. Their business cannot wait the convenience of the workmen, for 'in the various operations of singeing, washing, bleaching, mangling, calendering, and dyeing, none of them can be stopped at a given moment without risk of damage ... to enforce the same dinner hour for all the workpeople might occasionally subject valuable goods to the risk of danger by incomplete operations.' *Le platonisme où va-t-il se nicher!* [Where will Platonism be found next!]

58. Xenophon says, it is not only an honour to receive food from the table of the King of Persia, but such food is much more tasty than other food. 'And there is nothing wonderful in this, for as the other arts are brought to special perfection in the great towns, so the royal food is prepared in a special way. For in the small towns the same man makes bedsteads, doors, ploughs, and tables:' often, too, he builds houses into the bargain, and is quite content if he finds custom sufficient for his sustenance. It is altogether impossible for a man who does so many things to do them all well. But in the great towns, where each can find many buyers, one trade is sufficient to maintain the man who carries it on. Nay, there is often not even need of one complete trade, but one man makes shoes for men, another for women. Here and there one man gets a living by sewing, another by cutting out shoes; one does nothing but cut out clothes, another nothing but sew the pieces together. It follows necessarily then, that he who does the simplest kind of work, undoubtedly does it better than anyone else. So it is with the art of cooking.' (Xen. Cyrop. I. viii., c. 2.) Xenophon here lays stress exclusively upon the excellence to be attained in use-value, although he well knows that the gradations of the division of labour depend on the extent of the market.

59. He (Busiris) divided them all into special castes ... commanded that the same individuals should always carry on the same trade, for he knew that they who change their occupations become skilled in none; but that those who constantly stick to one occupation bring it to the highest perfection. In truth, we shall also find that in relation to the arts and handicrafts, they have outstripped their rivals more than a master does a bungler; and the contrivances for maintaining the monarchy and the other institutions of their State are so admirable that the most celebrated philosophers who treat of this subject praise the constitution of the Egyptian State above all others. (Isocrates, Busiris, c. 8.)

60. Cf. Diodorus Siculus.

61. Ure, l.c., p. 20.

62. This is more the case in England than in France, and more in France than in Holland.

* MECW and Progress Publishers' editions have 'disadvantages,' but the Ben Fowkes

translation in the Penguin edition has 'advantages.' The original German is 'Endlich ist diese Teilung der Arbeit eine besondre Art der Kooperation, und manche ihrer Vorteile entspringen aus dem allgemeinen Wesen, nicht aus dieser besondren Form der Kooperation.'—M.I.A.

15

Machinery and Modern Industry

Section 1: *The Development of Machinery*

John Stuart Mill says in his 'Principles of Political Economy':

> 'It is questionable if all the mechanical inventions yet made have lightened the day's toil of any human being.'[1]

That is, however, by no means the aim of the capitalistic application of machinery. Like every other increase in the productiveness of labour, machinery is intended to cheapen commodities, and, by shortening that portion of the working-day, in which the labourer works for himself, to lengthen the other portion that he gives, without an equivalent, to the capitalist. In short, it is a means for producing surplus-value.

In manufacture, the revolution in the mode of production begins with the labour-power, in modern industry it begins with the instruments of labour. Our first inquiry then is, how the instruments of labour are converted from tools into machines, or what is the difference between a machine and the implements of a handicraft? We are only concerned here with striking and general characteristics; for epochs in the history of society are no more separated from each other by hard and fast lines of demarcation, than are geological epochs.

Mathematicians and mechanicians, and in this they are followed by a few English economists, call a tool a simple machine, and a machine a complex tool. They see no essential difference between them, and even give the name of machine to the simple mechanical powers, the lever, the inclined plane, the screw, the wedge, &c.[2] As a matter of fact, every machine is a combination of those simple powers, no matter how they may be disguised. From the economic standpoint this explanation is worth nothing, because the historical element is wanting. Another explanation of the difference between tool and machine is that in the case of a tool, man is the motive power, while the motive power of a machine is something different from man, as, for instance, an animal, water, wind, and so on.[3] According to this, a plough drawn by oxen, which is a contrivance common to the most different epochs, would be a machine, while Claussen's circular loom, which, worked by a single labourer, weaves 96,000 picks per minute, would be a mere tool. Nay, this very loom, though a tool when worked by hand, would, if worked by steam, be a machine. And since the application of animal power is one of man's earliest inventions, production by machinery would have preceded production by handicrafts. When in 1735, John Wyatt brought out his spinning machine, and began the industrial revolution of the 18th century, not a word did he say about an ass driving it instead of a man, and yet this part fell to the ass. He described it as a machine 'to spin without fingers.'[4]

All fully developed machinery consists of three essentially different parts, the motor mechanism, the transmitting mechanism, and finally the tool or working machine. The motor mechanism is that which puts the whole in motion. It either generates its own motive power, like the steam-engine, the caloric engine, the electromagnetic machine, &c., or it receives its impulse from some already existing natural force, like the water-wheel from a head of water, the wind-mill from wind, &c. The transmitting mechanism, composed of fly-wheels, shafting, toothed wheels, pullies, straps, ropes, bands, pinions, and gearing of the most varied kinds, regulates the motion, changes its form where necessary, as for instance, from linear to circular, and divides and distributes it among the working machines. These two first parts of the whole mechanism are there, solely for putting the working machines in motion, by means of which motion the subject of labour is seized upon and modified as desired. The tool or working machine is that part of the machinery with which the industrial revolution of the 18th century started. And to this day it constantly serves as such a starting-point, whenever a handicraft, or a manufacture, is turned into an industry carried on by machinery.

On a closer examination of the working machine proper, we find in it, as a general rule, though often, no doubt, under very altered forms, the apparatus and tools used by the handicraftsman or manufacturing workman; with this difference, that instead of being human implements, they are the implements of a mechanism, or mechanical implements. Either the entire machine is only a more or less altered mechanical edition of the old handicraft tool, as, for instance, the power-loom,[5] or the working parts fitted in the frame of the machine are old acquaintances, as spindles are in a mule, needles in a stocking-loom, saws in a sawing-machine, and knives in a chopping machine. The distinction between these tools and the body proper of the machine, exists from their very birth; for they continue for the most part to be produced by handicraft, or by manufacture, and are afterwards fitted into the body of the machine, which is the product of machinery.[6] The machine proper is therefore a mechanism that, after being set in motion, performs with its tools the same operations that were formerly done by the workman with similar tools. Whether the motive power is derived from man, or from some other machine, makes no difference in this respect. From the moment that the tool proper is taken from man, and fitted into a mechanism, a machine takes the place of a mere implement. The difference strikes one at once, even in those cases where man himself continues to be the prime mover. The number of implements that he himself can use simultaneously, is limited by the number of his own natural instruments of production, by the number of his bodily organs. In Germany, they tried at first to make one spinner work two spinning-wheels, that is, to work simultaneously with both hands and both feet. This was too difficult. Later, a treddle spinning-wheel with two spindles was invented, but adepts in spinning, who could spin two threads at once, were almost as scarce as two-headed men. The Jenny, on the other hand, even at its very birth, spun with 12-18 spindles, and the stocking-loom knits with many thousand needles at once. The number of tools that a machine can bring into play simultaneously, is from the very first emancipated from the organic limits that hedge in the tools of a handicraftsman.

In many manual implements, the distinction between man as mere motive power, and man as the workman or operator properly so called, is brought into striking contrast. For instance, the foot is merely the prime mover of the spinning-wheel, while the hand, working with the spindle, and drawing and twisting, performs the real operation of spinning. It is this last part of the handicraftsman's implement that is first seized upon by the industrial revolution, leaving to the workman, in addition to his new labour of watching the machine with his eyes and correcting its mistakes with his hands, the merely mechanical part of being the moving power. On the other hand, implements, in regard to which man has always acted as a simple motive power, as, for instance, by turning the crank of a mill,[7] by pumping, by moving up and down the arm of a bellows, by pounding with a mortar, &c., such implements soon call for the application of animals, water[8] and wind as motive powers.

Here and there, long before the period of manufacture, and also, to some extent, during that period, these implements pass over into machines, but without creating any revolution in the mode of production. It becomes evident, in the period of modern industry, that these implements, even under their form of manual tools, are already machines. For instance, the pumps with which the Dutch, in 1836-7, emptied the Lake of Harlem, were constructed on the principle of ordinary pumps; the only difference being, that their pistons were driven by cyclopean steam-engines, instead of by men. The common and very imperfect bellows of the blacksmith is, in England, occasionally converted into a blowing-engine, by connecting its arm with a steam-engine. The steam-engine itself, such as it was at its invention, during the manufacturing period at the close of the 17th century, and such as it continued to be down to 1780,[9] did not give rise to any industrial revolution. It was, on the contrary, the invention of machines that made a revolution in the form of steam-engines necessary. As soon as man, instead of working with an implement on the subject of his labour, becomes merely the motive power of an implement-machine, it is a mere accident that motive power takes the disguise of human muscle; and it may equally well take the form of wind, water or steam. Of course, this does not prevent such a change of form from producing great technical alterations in the mechanism that was originally constructed to be driven by man alone. Now-a-days, all machines that have their way to make, such as sewing-machines, bread-making machines, &c., are, unless from their very nature their use on a small scale is excluded, constructed to be driven both by human and by purely mechanical motive power.

The machine, which is the starting-point of the industrial revolution, supersedes the workman, who handles a single tool, by a mechanism operating with a number of similar tools, and set in motion by a single motive power, whatever the form of that power may be.[10] Here we have the machine, but only as an elementary factor of production by machinery.

Increase in the size of the machine, and in the number of its working tools, calls for a more massive mechanism to drive it; and this mechanism requires, in order to overcome its resistance, a mightier moving power than that of man, apart from the fact that man is a very imperfect instrument for producing uniform continued motion. But assuming that he is acting simply as a motor, that a machine has taken the place of his tool, it is evident that he can be replaced by natural forces. Of all the great motors handed down from the manufacturing period, horse-power is the worst, partly because a horse has a head of his own, partly because he is costly, and the extent to which he is applicable in factories is very restricted.[11] Nevertheless, the horse was extensively used during the infancy of modern industry. This is proved, as well by the complaints of contemporary agriculturists, as by the term 'horse-power,' which has survived to this day as an expression for mechanical force.

Wind was too inconstant and uncontrollable, and besides, in England, the birthplace of modern industry, the use of water power preponderated even during the manufacturing period. In the 17th century attempts had already been made to turn two pairs of millstones with a single water-wheel. But the increased size of the gearing was too much for the water power, which had now become insufficient, and this was one of the circumstances that led to a more accurate investigation of the laws of friction. In the same way, the irregularity caused by the motive power in mills that were put in motion by pushing and pulling a lever, led to the theory, and the application, of the fly-wheel, which afterwards plays so important a part in modern industry.[12] In this way, during the manufacturing period, were developed the first scientific and technical elements of Modern Mechanical Industry. Arkwright's throstle spinning mill was from the very first turned by water. But for all that, the use of water, as the predominant motive power, was beset with difficulties. It could not be increased at will, it failed at certain seasons of the year, and, above all, it was essentially local.[13] Not till the invention of Watt's second and so-called double-acting steam-engine, was a prime mover found, that begot its own force by the consumption of coal and water, whose power was entirely under man's control, that was mobile and a means of locomotion, that was urban and not, like the waterwheel, rural, that permitted production to be concentrated in towns instead of, like the water-wheels, being scattered up and down the country,[14] that was of universal technical application, and, relatively speaking, little affected in its choice of residence by local circumstances. The greatness of Watt's genius showed itself in the specification of the patent that he took out in April, 1784. In that specification his steam-engine is described, not as an invention for a specific purpose, but as an agent universally applicable in Mechanical Industry. In it he points out applications, many of which, as for instance, the steam-hammer, were not introduced till half a century later. Nevertheless he doubted the use of steam-engines in navigation. His successors, Boulton and Watt, sent to the exhibition of 1851 steam-engines of colossal size for ocean steamers.

As soon as tools had been converted from being manual implements of man into implements of a mechanical apparatus, of a machine, the motive mechanism also acquired an independent form, entirely emancipated from the restraints of human strength. Thereupon the individual machine, that we have hitherto been considering, sinks into a mere factor in production by machinery. One motive mechanism was now able to drive many machines at once. The motive mechanism grows with the number of the machines that are turned simultaneously, and the transmitting mechanism becomes a wide-spreading apparatus.

We now proceed to distinguish the co-operation of a number of machines of one kind from a complex system of machinery.

In the one case, the product is entirely made by a single machine, which performs all the various operations previously done by one handicraftsman with his tool; as, for instance, by a weaver with his loom; or by several handicraftsman successively, either separately or as members of a system of Manufacture.[15] For example, in the manufacture of envelopes, one man folded the paper with the folder, another laid on the gum, a third turned the flap over, on which the device is impressed, a fourth embossed the device, and so on; and for each of these operations the envelope had to change hands. One single envelope machine now performs all these operations at once, and makes more than 3,000 envelopes in an hour. In the London exhibition of 1862, there was an American machine for making paper cornets. It cut the paper, pasted, folded, and finished 300 in a minute. Here, the whole process, which, when carried on as Manufacture, was split up into, and carried out by, a series of operations, is completed by a single machine, working a combination of various tools. Now, whether such a machine be merely a reproduction of a complicated manual implement, or a combination of various simple implements specialised by Manufacture, in either case, in the factory, *i.e.*, in the workshop in which machinery alone is used, we meet again with simple co-operation; and, leaving the workman out of consideration for the moment, this co-operation presents itself to us, in the first instance, as the conglomeration in one place of similar and simultaneously acting machines. Thus, a weaving factory is constituted of a number of power-looms, working side by side, and a sewing factory of a number of sewing-machines all in the same building. But there is here a technical oneness in the whole system, owing to all the machines receiving their impulse simultaneously, and in an equal degree, from the pulsations of the common prime mover, by the intermediary of the transmitting mechanism; and this mechanism, to a certain extent, is also common to them all, since only particular ramifications of it branch off to each machine. Just as a number of tools, then, form the organs of a machine, so a number of machines of one kind constitute the organs of the motive mechanism.

A real machinery system, however, does not take the place of these independent machines, until the subject of labour goes through a connected series of detail processes, that are carried out by a chain of machines of various kinds, the one supplementing the other. Here we have again the co-operation by division of labour that characterises Manufacture; only now, it is a combination of detail machines. The special tools of the various detail workmen, such as those of the beaters, cambers, spinners, &c., in the woollen manufacture, are now transformed into the tools of specialised machines, each machine constituting a special organ, with a special function, in the system. In those branches of industry in which the machinery system is first introduced, Manufacture itself furnishes, in a general way, the natural basis for the division, and consequent organisation, of the process of production.[16] Nevertheless, an essential difference at once manifests itself. In Manufacture it is the workmen who, with their manual implements, must, either singly or in groups, carry on each particular detail process. If, on the one hand, the workman becomes adapted to the process, on the other, the process was previously made suitable to the workman. This subjective principle of the division of labour no longer exists in production by machinery. Here, the process as a whole is examined objectively, in itself, that is to say, without regard to the question of its execution by human hands, it is analysed into its constituent phases; and the problem, how to execute each detail process, and bind them all into a whole, is solved by the aid of machines, chemistry, &c.[17] But, of course, in this case also, theory must be perfected by accumulated experience on a large scale. Each detail machine supplies raw material to the machine next in order; and since they are all working at the same time, the product is always going through the various stages of its fabrication, and is also constantly in a state of transition, from one phase to another. Just as in Manufacture, the direct co-operation of the detail labourers establishes a numerical proportion between the special groups, so in an organised system of machinery, where one detail machine is constantly kept employed by another, a fixed relation is established between their numbers, their size, and their speed. The collective machine, now an organised system of various kinds of single machines, and of groups of single machines, becomes more and more perfect, the more the process as a whole becomes a continuous one, i.e., the less the raw material is interrupted in its passage from its first phase to its last; in other words, the more its passage from one phase to another is effected, not by the hand of man, but by the machinery itself. In Manufacture, the isolation of each detail process is a condition imposed by the nature of division of labour, but in the fully developed factory the continuity of those processes is, on the contrary, imperative.

A system of machinery, whether it reposes on the mere co-operation of similar machines, as in weaving, or on a combination of different machines, as in spinning, constitutes in itself a huge automaton, whenever it is driven by a self-acting prime mover. But although the factory as a whole be driven by its steam-engine, yet either some of the individual machines may require the aid of the workman for some of their movements (such aid was necessary for the running in of the mule carriage, before the invention of the self-acting mule, and is still necessary in fine-spinning mills); or, to enable a machine to do its work, certain parts of it may require to be handled by the workman like a manual tool; this was the case in machine-makers' workshops, before the conversion of the slide rest into a self-actor. As soon as a machine executes, without man's help, all the movements requisite to elaborate the raw material, needing only attendance from him, we have an automatic system of machinery, and one that is susceptible of constant improvement in its details. Such improvements as the apparatus that stops a drawing frame, whenever a sliver breaks, and the self-acting stop, that stops the power-loom so soon as the shuttle bobbin is emptied of weft, are quite modern inventions. As an example, both of continuity of production, and of the carrying out of the automatic principle, we may take a modern paper mill. In the paper industry generally, we may advantageously study in detail not only the distinctions between modes of production based on different means of production, but also the connexion of the social conditions of production with those modes: for the old German paper-making furnishes us with a sample of handicraft production; that of Holland in the 17th and of France in the 18th century with a sample of manufacturing in the strict sense; and that of modern England with a sample of automatic fabrication of this article. Besides these, there still exist, in India and China, two distinct antique Asiatic forms of the same industry.

An organised system of machines, to which motion is communicated by the transmitting mechanism from a central automaton, is the most developed form of production by machinery. Here we have, in the place of the isolated machine, a mechanical monster whose body fills whole factories, and whose demon power, at first veiled under the slow and measured motions of his giant limbs, at length breaks out into the fast and furious whirl of his countless working organs.

There were mules and steam-engines before there were any labourers, whose exclusive occupation it was to make mules and steam-engines; just as men wore clothes before there were such people as tailors. The inventions of Vaucanson, Arkwright, Watt, and others, were, however, practicable, only because those inventors found, ready to hand, a considerable number of skilled mechanical workmen, placed at their disposal by the manufacturing period. Some of these workmen were independent handicraftsman of various trades, others were grouped together in manufactures, in which, as before-mentioned, division of labour was strictly carried out. As inventions increased in number, and the demand for the newly discovered machines grew larger, the machine-making industry split up, more and more, into numerous independent branches, and division of labour in these manufactures was more and more developed. Here, then, we see in Manufacture the immediate technical foundation of modern industry. Manufacture produced the machinery, by means of which modern industry abolished the handicraft and manufacturing systems in those spheres of production that it first seized upon. The factory system was therefore raised, in the natural course of things, on an inadequate foundation. When the system attained to a certain degree of development, it had to root up this ready-made foundation, which in the meantime had been elaborated on the old lines, and to build up for itself a basis that should correspond to its methods of production. Just as the individual machine retains a dwarfish character, so long as it is worked by the power of man alone, and just as no system of machinery could be properly developed before the steam-engine took the place of the earlier motive powers, animals, wind, and even water; so, too, modern industry was crippled in its complete development, so long as its characteristic instrument of production, the machine, owed its existence to personal strength and personal skill, and depended on the muscular development, the keenness of sight, and the cunning of hand, with which the detail workmen in manufactures, and the manual labourers in handicrafts, wielded their dwarfish implements. Thus, apart from the dearness of the machines made in this way, a circumstance that is ever present to the mind of the capitalist, the expansion of industries carried on by means of machinery, and the invasion by machinery of fresh branches of production, were dependent on the growth of a class of workmen, who, owing to the almost artistic nature of their employment, could increase their numbers only gradually, and not by leaps and bounds. But besides this, at a certain stage of its development, modern industry became technologically incompatible with the basis furnished for it by handicraft and Manufacture. The increasing size of the prime movers, of the transmitting mechanism, and of the machines proper, the greater complication, multiformity and regularity of the details of these machines, as they more and more departed from the model of those originally made by manual labour, and acquired a form, untrammelled except by the conditions under which they worked,[18] the perfecting of the automatic system, and the use, every day more unavoidable, of a more refractory material, such as iron instead of wood—the solution of all these problems, which sprang up by the force of circumstances, everywhere met with a stumbling-block in the personal restrictions, which even the collective labourer of Manufacture could not break through, except to a limited extent. Such machines as the modern hydraulic press, the modern power-loom, and the modern carding engine, could never have been furnished by Manufacture.

A radical change in the mode of production in one sphere of industry involves a similar change in other spheres. This happens at first in such branches of industry as are connected together by being separate phases of a process, and yet are isolated by the social division of labour, in such a way, that each of them produces an independent commodity. Thus, spinning by machinery made weaving by machinery a necessity, and both together made the mechanical and chemical revolution that took place in bleaching, printing, and dyeing, imperative. So too, on the other hand, the revolution in cotton-spinning called forth the invention of the gin, for separating the seeds from the cotton fibre; it was only by means of this invention, that the production of cotton became possible on the enormous scale at present required.[19] But more especially, the revolution in the modes of production of industry and agriculture made necessary a revolution in the general conditions of the social process of production, i.e., in the means of communication and of transport. In a society whose pivot, to use an expression of Fourier, was agriculture on a small scale, with its subsidiary domestic industries, and the urban handicrafts, the means of communication and transport were so utterly inadequate to the productive requirements of the manufacturing period, with its extended division of social labour, its concentration of the instruments of labour, and of the workmen, and its colonial markets, that they became in fact revolutionised. In the same way the means of communication and transport handed down from the manufacturing period soon became unbearable trammels on modern industry, with its feverish haste of production, its enormous extent, its constant flinging of capital and labour from one sphere of production into another, and its newly-created connexions with the markets of the whole world. Hence, apart from the radical changes introduced in the construction of sailing vessels, the means of communication and transport became gradually adapted to the modes of production of mechanical industry, by the creation of a system of river steamers, railways, ocean steamers, and telegraphs. But the huge masses of iron that had now to be forged, to be welded, to be cut, to be bored, and to be shaped, demanded, on their part, cyclopean machines, for the construction of which the methods of the manufacturing period were utterly inadequate.

Modern industry had therefore itself to take in hand the machine, its characteristic instrument of production, and to construct machines by machines. It was not till it did this, that it built up for itself a fitting technical foundation, and stood on its own feet. Machinery, simultaneously with the increasing use of it, in the first decades of this century, appropriated, by degrees, the fabrication of machines proper. But it was only during the decade preceding 1866, that the construction of railways and ocean steamers on a stupendous scale called into existence the cyclopean machines now employed in the construction of prime movers.

The most essential condition to the production of machines by machines was a prime mover capable of exerting any amount of force, and yet under perfect control. Such a condition was already supplied by the steam-engine. But at the same time it was necessary to produce the geometrically accurate straight lines, planes, circles, cylinders, cones, and spheres, required in the detail parts of the machines. This problem Henry Maudsley solved in the first decade of this century by the invention of the slide rest, a tool that was soon made automatic, and in a modified form was applied to other constructive machines besides the lathe, for which it was originally intended. This mechanical appliance replaces, not some particular tool, but the hand itself, which produces a given form by holding and guiding the cutting tool along the iron or other material operated upon. Thus it became possible to produce the forms of the individual parts of machinery

> 'with a degree of ease, accuracy, and speed, that no accumulated experience of the hand of the most skilled workman could give.'[20]

If we now fix our attention on that portion of the machinery employed in the construction of machines, which constitutes the operating tool, we find the manual implements re-appearing, but on a cyclopean scale. The operating part of the boring machine is an immense drill driven by a steam-engine; without this machine, on the other hand, the cylinders of large steam-engines and of hydraulic presses could not be made. The mechanical lathe is only a cyclopean reproduction of the ordinary foot-lathe; the planing machine, an iron carpenter, that works on iron with the same tools that the human carpenter employs on wood; the instrument that, on the London wharves, cuts the veneers, is a gigantic razor; the tool of the shearing machine, which shears iron as easily as a tailor's scissors cut cloth, is a monster pair of scissors; and the steam-hammer works with an ordinary hammer head, but of such a weight that not Thor himself could wield it.[21] These steam-hammers are an invention of Nasmyth, and there is one that weighs over 6 tons and strikes with a vertical fall of 7 feet, on an anvil weighing 36 tons. It is mere child's-play for it to crush a block of granite into powder, yet it is no less capable of driving, with a succession of light taps, a nail into a piece of soft wood.[22]

The implements of labour, in the form of machinery, necessitate the substitution of natural forces for human force, and the conscious application of science, instead of rule of thumb. In Manufacture, the organisation of the social labour-process is purely subjective; it is a combination of detail labourers; in its machinery system, modern industry has a productive organism that is purely objective, in which the labourer becomes a mere appendage to an already existing material condition of production. In simple co-operation, and even in that founded on division of labour, the suppression of the isolated, by the collective, workman still appears to be more or less accidental. Machinery, with a few exceptions to be mentioned later, operates only by means of associated labour, or labour in common. Hence the co-operative character of the labour-process is, in the latter case, a technical necessity dictated by the instrument of labour itself.

Section 2: *The Value Transferred by Machinery to the Product*

We saw that the productive forces resulting from co-operation and division of labour cost capital nothing. They are natural forces of social labour. So also physical forces, like steam, water, &c., when appropriated to productive processes, cost nothing. But just as a man requires lungs to breathe with, so he requires something that is work of man's hand, in order to consume physical forces productively. A water-wheel is necessary to exploit the force of water, and a steam-engine to exploit the elasticity of steam. Once discovered, the law of the deviation of the magnetic needle in the field of an electric current, or the law of the magnetisation of iron, around which an electric current circulates, cost never a penny.[23] But the exploitation of these laws for the purposes of telegraphy, &c., necessitates a costly and extensive apparatus. The tool, as we have seen, is not exterminated by the machine. From being a dwarf implement of the human organism, it expands and multiplies into the implement of a mechanism created by man. Capital now sets the labourer to work, not with a manual tool, but with a machine which itself handles the tools. Although, therefore, it is clear at the first glance that, by incorporating both stupendous physical forces, and the natural sciences, with the process of production, modern industry raises the productiveness of labour to an extraordinary degree, it is by no means equally clear, that this increased productive force is not, on the other hand, purchased by an increased expenditure of labour. Machinery, like every other component of constant capital, creates no new value, but yields up its own value to the product that it serves to beget. In so far as the machine has value, and, in consequence, parts with value to the product, it forms an element in the value of that product. Instead of being cheapened, the product is made dearer in proportion to the value of the machine. And it is clear as noon-day, that machines and systems of machinery, the characteristic instruments of labour of Modern Industry, are incomparably more loaded with value than the implements used in handicrafts and manufactures.

In the first place, it must be observed that the machinery, while always entering as a whole into the labour-process, enters into the value-begetting process only by bits. It never adds more value than it loses, on an average, by wear and tear. Hence there is a great difference between the value of a machine, and the value transferred in a given time by that machine to the product. The longer the life of the machine in the labour-process, the greater is that difference. It is true, no doubt, as we have already seen, that every instrument of labour enters as a whole into the labour-process, and only piece-meal, proportionally to its average daily loss by wear and tear, into the value-begetting process. But this difference between the instrument as a whole and its daily wear and tear, is much greater in a machine than in a tool, because the machine, being made from more durable material, has a longer life; because its employment, being regulated by strictly scientific laws, allows of greater economy in the wear and tear of its parts, and in the materials it consumes; and lastly, because its field of production is incomparably larger than that of a tool. After making allowance, both in the case of the machine and of the tool, for their average daily cost, that is for the value they transmit to the product by their average daily wear and tear, and for their consumption of auxiliary substance, such as oil, coal, and so on, they each do their work gratuitously, just like the forces furnished by Nature without the help of man. The greater the productive power of the machinery compared with that of the tool, the greater is the extent of its gratuitous service compared with that of the tool. In modern industry, man succeeded for the first time in making the product of his past labour work on a large scale gratuitously, like the forces of Nature.[24]

In treating of Co-operation and Manufacture, it was shown that certain general factors of production, such as buildings, are, in comparison with the scattered means of production of the isolated workman, economised by being consumed in common, and that they therefore make the product cheaper. In a system of machinery, not only is the framework of the machine consumed in common by its numerous operating implements, but the prime mover, together with a part of the transmitting mechanism, is consumed in common by the numerous operative machines.

Given the difference between the value of the machinery, and the value transferred by it in a day to the product, the extent to which this latter value makes the product dearer, depends in the first instance, upon the size of the product; so to say, upon its area. Mr Baynes, of Blackburn, in a lecture published in 1858, estimates that:

> 'each real mechanical horse-power[25] will drive 450 self-acting mule spindles, with preparation, or 200 throstle spindles, or 15 looms for 40 inch cloth with the appliances for warping, sizing, &c.'

In the first case, it is the day's produce of 450 mule spindles, in the second, of 200 throstle spindles, in the third, of 15 power-looms, over which the daily cost of one horse-power, and the wear and tear of the machinery set in motion by that power, are spread; so that only a very minute value is transferred by such wear and tear to a pound of yarn or a yard of cloth. The same is the case with the steam-hammer mentioned above. Since its daily wear and tear, its coal-consumption, &c., are spread over the stupendous masses of iron hammered by it in a day, only a small value is added to a hundred weight of iron; but that value would be very great, if the cyclopean instrument were employed in driving in nails.

Given a machine's capacity for work, that is, the number of its operating tools, or, where it is a question of force, their mass, the amount of its product will depend on the velocity of its working parts, on the speed, for instance, of the spindles, or on the number of blows given by the hammer in a minute. Many of these colossal hammers strike seventy times in a minute, and Ryder's patent machine for forging spindles with small hammers gives as many as 700 strokes per minute.

Given the rate at which machinery transfers its value to the product, the amount of value so transferred depends on the total value of the machinery.[26] The less labour it contains, the less value it imparts to the product. The less value it gives up, so much the more productive it is, and so much the more its services approximate to those of natural forces. But the production of machinery by machinery lessens its value relatively to its extension and efficacy.

An analysis and comparison of the prices of commodities produced by handicrafts or manufactures, and of the prices of the same commodities produced by machinery, shows generally, that, in the product of machinery, the value due to the instruments of labour increases relatively, but decreases absolutely. In other words, its absolute amount decreases, but its amount, relatively to the total value of the product, of a pound of yarn, for instance, increases.[27]

It is evident that whenever it costs as much labour to produce a machine as is saved by the employment of that machine, there is nothing but a transposition of labour; consequently the total labour required to produce a commodity is not lessened or the productiveness of labour is not increased. It is clear, however, that the difference between the labour a machine costs, and the labour it saves, in other words, that the degree of its productiveness does not depend on the difference between its own value and the value of the implement it replaces. As long as the labour spent on a machine, and consequently the portion of its value added to the product, remains smaller than the value added by the workman to the product with his tool, there is always a difference of labour saved in favour of the machine. The productiveness of a machine is therefore measured by the human labour-power it replaces. According to Mr Baynes, 2 operatives are required for the 450 mule spindles, inclusive of preparation machinery,[28] that are driven by one-horse power; each self-acting mule spindle, working ten hours, produces 13 ounces of yarn (average number of thickness); consequently 2½ operatives spin weekly 365 5/8 lbs. of yarn. Hence, leaving waste on one side, 366 lbs. of cotton absorb, during their conversion into yarn, only 150 hours' labour, or fifteen days' labour of ten hours each. But with a spinning-wheel, supposing the hand-spinner to produce thirteen ounces of yarn in sixty hours, the same weight of cotton would absorb 2,700 days' labour of ten hours each, or 27,000 hours' labour.[29] Where blockprinting, the old method of printing calico by hand, has been superseded by machine printing, a single machine prints, with the aid of one man or boy, as much calico of four colours in one hour, as it formerly took 200 men to do.[30] Before Eli Whitney invented the cotton gin in 1793, the separation of the seed from a pound of cotton cost an average day's labour. By means of his invention one negress was enabled to clean 100 lbs. daily; and since then, the efficacy of the gin has been considerably increased. A pound of cotton wool, previously costing 50 cents to produce, included after that invention more unpaid labour, and was consequently sold with greater profit, at 10 cents. In India, they employ for separating the wool from the seed, an instrument, half machine, half tool, called a churka; with this one man and a woman can clean 28 lbs. daily. With the churka invented some years ago by Dr Forbes, one man and a boy produce 250 lbs. daily. If oxen, steam, or water, be used for driving it, only a few boys and girls as feeders are required. Sixteen of these machines driven by oxen do as much work in a day as formerly 750 people did on an average.[31]

As already stated, a steam-plough does as much work in one hour at a cost of three-pence, as 66 men at a cost of 15 shillings. I return to this example in order to clear up an erroneous notion. The 15 shillings are by no means the expression in money of all the labour expended in one hour by the 66 men. If the ratio of surplus-labour to necessary labour were 100%, these 66 men would produce in one hour a value of 30 shillings, although their wages, 15 shillings, represent only their labour for half an hour. Suppose, then, a machine cost as much as the wages for a year of the 150 men it displaces, say £3,000; this £3,000 is by no means the expression in money of the labour added to the object produced by these 150 men before the introduction of the machine, but only of that portion of their year's labour which was expended for themselves and represented by their wages. On the other hand, the £3,000, the money-value of the machine, expresses all the labour expended on its production, no matter in what proportion this labour constitutes wages for the workman, and surplus-value for the capitalist. Therefore, though a machine cost as much as the labour-power displaced by it costs, yet the labour materialised in it is even then much less than the living labour it replaces.[32]

The use of machinery for the exclusive purpose of cheapening the product, is limited in this way, that less labour must be expended in producing the machinery than is displaced by the employment of that machinery, For the capitalist, however, this use is still more limited. Instead of paying for the labour, he only pays the value of the labour-power employed; therefore, the limit to his using a machine is fixed by the difference between the value of the machine and the value of the labour-power replaced by it. Since the division of the day's work into necessary and surplus-labour differs in different countries, and even in the same country at different periods, or in different branches of industry; and further, since the actual wage of the labourer at one time sinks below the value of his labour-power, at another rises above it, it is possible for the difference between the price of the machinery and the price of the labour-power replaced by that machinery to vary very much, although the difference between the quantity of labour requisite to produce the machine and the total quantity replaced by it, remain constant.[33] But it is the former difference alone that determines the cost, to the capitalist, of producing a commodity, and, through the pressure of competition, influences his action. Hence the invention now-a-days of machines in England that are employed only in North America; just as in the sixteenth and seventeenth centuries, machines were invented in Germany to be used only in Holland, and just as many a French invention of the eighteenth century was exploited in England alone. In the older countries, machinery, when employed in some branches of industry, creates such a redundancy of labour in other branches that in these latter the fall of wages below the value of labour-power impedes the use of machinery, and, from the standpoint of the capitalist, whose profit comes, not from a diminution of the labour employed, but of the labour paid for, renders that use superfluous and often impossible. In some branches of the woollen manufacture in England, the employment of children has during recent years been considerably diminished, and in some cases has been entirely abolished. Why? Because the Factory Acts made two sets of children necessary, one working six hours, the other four, or each working five hours. But the parents refused to sell the 'half-timers' cheaper than the 'full-timers.' Hence the substitution of machinery for the 'half-timers.'[34] Before the labour of women and of children under 10 years of age was forbidden in mines, capitalists considered the employment of naked women and girls, often in company with men, so far sanctioned by their moral code, and especially by their ledgers, that it was only after the passing of the Act that they had recourse to machinery. The Yankees have invented a stone-breaking machine. The English do not make use of it, because the 'wretch'[35] who does this work gets paid for such a small portion of his labour, that machinery would increase the cost of production to the capitalist.[36] In England, women are still occasionally used instead of horses for hauling canal boats,[37] because the labour required to produce horses and machines is an accurately known quantity, while that required to maintain the women of the surplus-population is below all calculation. Hence nowhere do we find a more shameful squandering of human labour-power for the most despicable purposes than in England, the land of machinery.

Section 3: *The Proximate Effects of Machinery on the Workman*

The starting-point of modern industry is, as we have shown, the revolution in the instruments of labour, and this revolution attains its most highly developed form in the organised system of machinery in a factory. Before we inquire how human material is incorporated with this objective organism, let us consider some general effects of this revolution on the labourer himself.

A. Appropriation of Supplementary Labour-power by Capital. The Employment of Women and Children

In so far as machinery dispenses with muscular power, it becomes a means of employing labourers of slight muscular strength, and those whose bodily development is incomplete, but whose limbs are all the more supple. The labour of women and children was, therefore, the first thing sought for by capitalists who used machinery. That mighty substitute for labour and labourers was forthwith changed into a means for increasing the number of wage-labourers by enrolling, under the direct sway of capital, every member of the workman's family, without distinction of age or sex. Compulsory work for the capitalist usurped the place, not only of the children's play, but also of free labour at home within moderate limits for the support of the family.[38]

The value of labour-power was determined, not only by the labour-time necessary to maintain the individual adult labourer, but also by that necessary to maintain his family. Machinery, by throwing every member of that family on to the labour-market, spreads the value of the man's labour-power over his whole family. It thus depreciates his labour-power. To purchase the labour-power of a family of four workers may, perhaps, cost more than it formerly did to purchase the labour-power of the head of the family, but, in return, four days' labour takes the place of one, and their price falls in proportion to the excess of the surplus-labour of four over the surplus-labour of one. In order that the family may live, four people must now, not only labour, but expend surplus-labour for the capitalist. Thus we see, that machinery, while augmenting the human material that forms the principal object of capital's exploiting power,[39] at the same time raises the degree of exploitation.

Machinery also revolutionises out and out the contract between the labourer and the capitalist, which formally fixes their mutual relations. Taking the exchange of commodities as our basis, our first assumption was that capitalist and labourer met as free persons, as independent owners of commodities; the one possessing money and means of production, the other labour-power. But now the capitalist buys children and young persons under age. Previously, the workman sold his own labour-power, which he disposed of nominally as a free agent. Now he sells wife and child. He has become a slave-dealer.[40] The demand for children's labour often resembles in form the inquiries for negro slaves, such as were formerly to be read among the advertisements in American journals.

> 'My attention,' says an English factory inspector, 'was drawn to an advertisement in the local paper of one of the most important manufacturing towns of my district, of which the following is a copy: Wanted, 12 to 20 young persons, not younger than what can pass for 13 years. Wages, 4 shillings a week. Apply &c.'[41]

The phrase 'what can pass for 13 years,' has reference to the fact, that by the Factory Act, children under 13 years may work only 6 hours. A surgeon officially appointed must certify their age. The manufacturer, therefore, asks for children who look as if they were already 13 years old. The decrease, often by leaps and bounds in the number of children under 13 years employed in factories, a decrease that is shown in an astonishing manner by the English statistics of the last 20 years, was for the most part, according to the evidence of the factory inspectors themselves, the work of the certifying surgeons, who overstated the age of the children, agreeably to the capitalist's greed for exploitation, and the sordid trafficking needs of the parents. In the notorious district of Bethnal Green, a public market is held every Monday and Tuesday morning, where children of both sexes from 9 years of age upwards, hire themselves out to the silk manufacturers. "The usual terms are 1s. 8d. a week (this belongs to the parents) and '2d. for myself and tea.' The contract is binding only for the week. The scene and language while this market is going on are quite disgraceful.'[42] It has also occurred in England, that women have taken 'children from the workhouse and let any one have them out for 2s. 6d. a week.'[43] In spite of legislation, the number of boys sold in Great Britain by their parents to act as live chimney-sweeping machines (although there exist plenty of machines to replace them) exceeds 2,000.[44] The revolution effected by machinery in the juridical relations between the buyer and the seller of labour-power, causing the transaction as a whole to lose the appearance of a contract between free persons, afforded the English Parliament an excuse, founded on juridical principles, for the interference of the state with factories. Whenever the law limits the labour of children to 6 hours in industries not before interfered with, the complaints of the manufacturers are always renewed. They allege that numbers of the parents withdraw their children from the industry brought under the Act, in order to sell them where 'freedom of labour' still rules, i.e., where children under 13 years are compelled to work like grown-up people, and therefore can be got rid of at a higher price. But, since capital is by nature a leveller, since it exacts in every sphere of production equality in the conditions of the exploitation of labour, the limitation by law of children's labour, in one branch of industry, becomes the cause of its limitation in others.

We have already alluded to the physical deterioration as well of the children and young-persons as of the women, whom machinery, first directly in the factories that shoot up on its basis, and then indirectly in all the remaining branches of industry, subjects to the exploitation of capital. In this place, therefore, we dwell only on one point, the enormous mortality, during the first few years of their life, of the children of the operatives. In sixteen of the registration districts into which England is divided, there are, for every 100,000 children alive under the age of one year, only 9,000 deaths in a year on an average (in one district only 7,047); in 24 districts the deaths are over 10,000, but under 11,000; in 39 districts, over 11,000, but under 12,000; in 48 districts over 12,000, but under 13,000; in 22 districts over 20,000; in 25 districts over 21,000; in 17 over 22,000; in 11 over 23,000; in Hoo, Wolverhampton, Ashton-under-Lyne, and Preston, over 24,000; in Nottingham, Stockport, and Bradford, over 25,000; in Wisbeach, 16,000; and in Manchester, 26,125.[45] As was shown by an official medical inquiry in the year 1861, the high death-rates are, apart from local causes, principally due to the employment of the mothers away from their homes, and to the neglect and maltreatment, consequent on her absence, such as, amongst others, insufficient nourishment, unsuitable food, and dosing with opiates; besides this, there arises an unnatural estrangement between mother and child, and as a consequence intentional starving and poisoning of the children.[46] In those agricultural districts, 'where a minimum in the employment of women exists, the death-rate is on the other hand very low.'[47] The Inquiry Commission of 1861 led, however, to the unexpected result, that in some purely agricultural districts bordering on the North Sea, the death-rate of children under one year old almost equalled that of the worst factory districts. Dr Julian Hunter was therefore commissioned to investigate this phenomenon on the spot. His report is incorporated with the 'Sixth Report on Public Health.'[48] Up to that time it was supposed, that the children were decimated by malaria, and other diseases peculiar to low-lying and marshy districts. But the inquiry showed the very opposite, namely, that the same cause which drove away malaria, the conversion of the land, from a morass in winter and a scanty pasture in summer, into fruitful corn land, created the exceptional death-rate of the infants.[49] The 70 medical men, whom Dr Hunter examined in that district, were 'wonderfully in accord' on this point. In fact, the revolution in the mode of cultivation had led to the introduction of the industrial system.

> Married women, who work in gangs along with boys and girls, are, for a stipulated sum of money, placed at the disposal of the farmer, by a man called the 'undertaker,' who contracts for the whole gang. 'These gangs will sometimes travel many miles from their own village; they are to be met morning and evening on the roads, dressed in short petticoats, with suitable coats and boots, and sometimes trousers, looking wonderfully strong and healthy, but tainted with a customary immorality and heedless

> of the fatal results which their love of this busy and independent life is bringing on their unfortunate offspring who are pining at home."[50]

Every phenomenon of the factory districts is here reproduced, including, but to a greater extent, ill-disguised infanticide, and dosing children with opiates.[51]

> 'My knowledge of such evils,' says Dr Simon, the medical officer of the Privy Council and editor in chief of the Reports on Public Health, 'may excuse the profound misgiving with which I regard any large industrial employment of adult women.'[52]

'Happy indeed,' exclaims Mr Baker, the factory inspector, in his official report, 'happy indeed will it be for the manufacturing districts of England, when every married woman having a family is prohibited from working in any textile works at all.'[53]

The moral degradation caused by the capitalistic exploitation of women and children has been so exhaustively depicted by F. Engels in his 'Lage der Arbeitenden Klasse Englands,' and other writers, that I need only mention the subject in this place. But the intellectual desolation artificially produced by converting immature human beings into mere machines for the fabrication of surplus-value, a state of mind clearly distinguishable from that natural ignorance which keeps the mind fallow without destroying its capacity for development, its natural fertility, this desolation finally compelled even the English Parliament to make elementary education a compulsory condition to the 'productive' employment of children under 14 years, in every industry subject to the Factory Acts. The spirit of capitalist production stands out clearly in the ludicrous wording of the so-called education clauses in the Factory Acts, in the absence of an administrative machinery, an absence that again makes the compulsion illusory, in the opposition of the manufacturers themselves to these education clauses, and in the tricks and dodges they put in practice for evading them.

> 'For this the legislature is alone to blame, by having passed a delusive law, which, while it would seem to provide that the children employed in factories shall be *educated,* contains no enactment by which that professed end can be secured. It provides nothing more than that the children shall on certain days of the week, and for a certain number of hours (three) in each day, be inclosed within the four walls of a place called a school, and that the employer of the child shall receive weekly a certificate to that effect signed by a person designated by the subscriber as a schoolmaster or schoolmistress.'[54]

Previous to the passing of the amended Factory Act, 1844, it happened, not unfrequently, that the certificates of attendance at school were signed by the schoolmaster or schoolmistress with a cross, as they themselves were unable to write.

> 'On one occasion, on visiting a place called a school, from which certificates of school attendance, had issued, I was so struck with the ignorance of the master, that I said to him: 'Pray, sir, can you read?' His reply was: 'Aye, summat!' and as a justification of his right to grant certificates, he added: 'At any rate, I am before my scholars.'

The inspectors, when the Bill of 1844 was in preparation, did not fail to represent the disgraceful state of the places called schools, certificates from which they were obliged to admit as a compliance with the laws, but they were successful only in obtaining thus much, that since the passing of the Act of 1845,

> the figures in the school certificate must be filled up in the handwriting of the schoolmaster, who must also sign his Christian and surname in full.'[55]

Sir John Kincaid, factory inspector for Scotland, relates experiences of the same kind.

> 'The first school we visited was kept by a Mrs. Ann Killin. Upon asking her to spell her name, she straightway made a mistake, by beginning with the letter C, but correcting

herself immediately, she said her name began with a K. On looking at her signature, however, in the school certificate books, I noticed that she spelt it in various ways, while her handwriting left no doubt as to her unfitness to teach. She herself also acknowledged that she could not keep the register ... In a second school I found the schoolroom 15 feet long, and 10 feet wide, and counted in this space 75 children, who were gabbling something unintelligible'[56] But it is not only in the miserable places above referred to that the children obtain certificates of school attendance without having received instruction of any value, for in many schools where there is a competent teacher, his efforts are of little avail from the distracting crowd of children of all ages, from infants of 3 years old and upwards; his livelihood, miserable at the best, depending on the pence received from the greatest number of children whom it is possible to cram into the space. To this is to be added scanty school furniture, deficiency of books, and other materials for teaching, and the depressing effect upon the poor children themselves of a close, noisome atmosphere. I have been in many such schools, where I have seen rows of children doing absolutely nothing; and this is certified as school attendance, and, in statistical returns, such children are set down as being educated.'[57]

In Scotland, the manufacturers try all they can to do without the children that are obliged to attend school.

> 'It requires no further argument to prove that the educational clauses of the Factory Act, being held in such disfavour among mill-owners, tend in a great measure to exclude that class of children alike from the employment and the benefit of education contemplated by this Act.'[58]

Horribly grotesque does this appear in print works, which are regulated by a special Act. By that Act,

> 'every child, before being employed in a print work must have attended school for at least 30 days, and not less than 150 hours, during the six months immediately preceding such first day of employment, and during the continuance of its employment in the print works, it must attend for a like period of 30 days, and 150 hours during every successive period of six months.... The attendance at school must be between 8 a.m. and 6 p.m. No attendance of less than 2½ hours, nor more than 5 hours on any one day, shall be reckoned as part of the 150 hours. Under ordinary circumstances the children attend school morning and afternoon for 30 days, for at least 5 hours each day, and upon the expiration of the 30 days, the statutory total of 150 hours having been attained, having, in their language, made up their book, they return to the print work, where they continue until the six months have expired, when another instalment of school attendance becomes due, and they again seek the school until the book is again made up.... Many boys having attended school for the required number of hours, when they return to school after the expiration of their six months' work in the print work, are in the same condition as when they first attended school as print-work boys, that they have lost all they gained by their previous school attendance.... In other print works the children's attendance at school is made to depend altogether upon the exigencies of the work in the establishment. The requisite number of hours is made up each six months, by instalments consisting of from 3 to 5 hours at a time, spreading over, perhaps, the whole six months.... For instance, the attendance on one day might be from 8 to 11 a.m., on another day from I p.m. to 4 p.m., and the child might not appear at school again for several days, when it would attend from 3 p.m. to 6 p.m.; then it might attend for 3 or 4 days consecutively, or for a week, then it would not appear in school for 3 weeks or a month, after that upon some odd days at some odd hours when the operative who

employed it chose to spare it; and thus the child was, as it were, buffeted from school to work, from work to school, until the tale of 150 hours was told.'[59]

By the excessive addition of women and children to the ranks of the workers, machinery at last breaks down the resistance which the male operatives in the manufacturing period continued to oppose to the despotism of capital.[60]

B. Prolongation of the Working-Day

If machinery be the most powerful means for increasing the productiveness of labour—i.e., for shortening the working-time required in the production of a commodity, it becomes in the hands of capital the most powerful means, in those industries first invaded by it, for lengthening the working-day beyond all bounds set by human nature. It creates, on the one hand, new conditions by which capital is enabled to give free scope to this its constant tendency, and on the other hand, new motives with which to whet capital's appetite for the labour of others.

In the first place, in the form of machinery, the implements of labour become automatic, things moving and working independent of the workman. They are thenceforth an industrial *perpetuum mobile*, that would go on producing forever, did it not meet with certain natural obstructions in the weak bodies and the strong wills of its human attendants. The automaton, as capital, and because it is capital, is endowed, in the person of the capitalist, with intelligence and will; it is therefore animated by the longing to reduce to a minimum the resistance offered by that repellent yet elastic natural barrier, man.[61] This resistance is moreover lessened by the apparent lightness of machine work, and by the more pliant and docile character of the women and children employed on it.[62]

The productiveness of machinery is, as we saw, inversely proportional to the value transferred by it to the product. The longer the life of the machine, the greater is the mass of the products over which the value transmitted by the machine is spread, and the less is the portion of that value added to each single commodity. The active lifetime of a machine is, however, clearly dependent on the length of the working-day, or on the duration of the daily labour-process multiplied by the number of days for which the process is carried on.

The wear and tear of a machine is not exactly proportional to its working-time. And even if it were so, a machine working 16 hours daily for 7½ years, covers as long a working period as, and transmits to the total product no more value than, the same machine would if it worked only 8 hours daily for 15 years. But in the first case the value of the machine would be reproduced twice as quickly as in the latter, and the capitalist would, by this use of the machine, absorb in 7½ years as much surplus-value as in the second case he would in 15.

The material wear and tear of a machine is of two kinds. The one arises from use, as coins wear away by circulating, the other from non-use, as a sword rusts when left in its scabbard. The latter kind is due to the elements. The former is more or less directly proportional, the latter to a certain extent inversely proportional, to the use of the machine.[63]

But in addition to the material wear and tear, a machine also undergoes, what we may call a moral depreciation. It loses exchange-value, either by machines of the same sort being produced cheaper than it, or by better machines entering into competition with it.[64] In both cases, be the machine ever so young and full of life, its value is no longer determined by the labour actually materialised in it, but by the labour-time requisite to reproduce either it or the better machine. It has, therefore, lost value more or less. The shorter the period taken to reproduce its total value, the less is the danger of moral depreciation; and the longer the working-day, the shorter is that period. When machinery is first introduced into an industry, new methods of reproducing it more cheaply follow blow upon blow,[65] and so do improvements, that not only affect individual parts and details of the machine, but its entire build. It is, therefore, in the early days of the life of machinery that this special incentive to the prolongation of the working-day makes itself felt most acutely.[66]

Given the length of the working-day, all other circumstances remaining the same, the exploitation of double the number of workmen demands, not only a doubling of that part of constant capital which is invested in machinery and buildings, but also of that part which is laid out in raw material and auxiliary substances. The lengthening of the working-day, on the other hand, allows of production on an extended scale without any alteration in the amount of capital laid out on machinery and buildings.[67] Not only is there, therefore, an increase of surplus-value, but the outlay necessary to obtain it diminishes. It is true that this takes place, more or less, with every lengthening of the working-day; but in the case under consideration, the change is more marked, because the capital converted into the instruments of labour preponderates to a greater degree.[68] The development of the factory system fixes a constantly increasing portion of the capital in a form, in which, on the one hand, its value is capable of continual self-expansion, and in which, on the other hand, it loses both use-value and exchange-value whenever it loses contact with living labour. 'When a labourer,' said Mr Ashworth, a cotton magnate, to Professor Nassau W. Senior, 'lays down his spade, he renders useless, for that period, a capital worth eighteen-pence. When one of our people leaves the mill, he renders useless a capital that has cost £100,000.'[69] Only fancy! making 'useless' for a single moment, a capital that has cost £100,000! It is, in truth, monstrous, that a single one of our people should ever leave the factory! The increased use of machinery, as Senior after the instruction he received from Ashworth clearly perceives, makes a constantly increasing lengthening of the working-day 'desirable.'[70]

Machinery produces relative surplus-value; not only by directly depreciating the value of labour-power, and by indirectly cheapening the same through cheapening the commodities that enter into its reproduction, but also, when it is first introduced sporadically into an industry, by converting the labour employed by the owner of that machinery, into labour of a higher degree and greater efficacy, by raising the social value of the article produced above its individual value, and thus enabling the capitalist to replace the value of a day's labour-power by a smaller portion of the value of a day's product. During this transition period, when the use of machinery is a sort of monopoly, the profits are therefore exceptional, and the capitalist endeavours to exploit thoroughly 'the sunny time of this his first love,' by prolonging the working-day as much as possible. The magnitude of the profit whets his appetite for more profit.

As the use of machinery becomes more general in a particular industry, the social value of the product sinks down to its individual value, and the law that surplus-value does not arise from the labour-power that has been replaced by the machinery, but from the labour-power actually employed in working with the machinery, asserts itself. Surplus-value arises from variable capital alone, and we saw that the amount of surplus-value depends on two factors, viz., the rate of surplus-value and the number of the workmen simultaneously employed. Given the length of the working-day, the rate of surplus-value is determined by the relative duration of the necessary labour and of the surplus-labour in a day. The number of the labourers simultaneously employed depends, on its side, on the ratio of the variable to the constant capital. Now, however much the use of machinery may increase the surplus-labour at the expense of the necessary labour by heightening the productiveness of labour, it is clear that it attains this result, only by diminishing the number of workmen employed by a given amount of capital. It converts what was formerly variable capital, invested in labour-power, into machinery which, being constant capital, does not produce surplus-value. It is impossible, for instance, to squeeze as much surplus-value out of 2 as out of 24 labourers. If each of these 24 men gives only one hour of surplus-labour in 12, the 24 men give together 24 hours of surplus-labour, while 24 hours is the total labour of the two men. Hence, the application of machinery to the production of surplus-value implies a contradiction which is immanent in it, since of the two factors of the surplus-value created by a given amount of capital, one, the rate of surplus-value, cannot be increased, except by diminishing the other, the number of workmen. This contradiction comes to light, as soon as by the general employment of machinery in a given industry, the value of the machine-produced commodity regulates the value of all commodities of the same sort; and it is this contradiction, that in its turn, drives the capitalist, without his being conscious of the fact,[71] to excessive lengthening of the working-day, in order that he may compensate the decrease in the relative number of labourers exploited, by an increase not only of the relative, but of the absolute surplus-labour.

If, then, the capitalistic employment of machinery, on the one hand, supplies new and powerful motives to an excessive lengthening of the working-day, and radically changes, as well the methods of labour, as also the character of the social working organism, in such a manner as to break down all opposition to this tendency, on the other hand it produces, partly by opening out to the capitalist new strata of the working-class, previously inaccessible to him, partly by setting free the labourers it supplants, a surplus working population,[72] which is compelled to submit to the dictation of capital. Hence that remarkable phenomenon in the history of modern industry, that machinery sweeps away every moral and natural restriction on the length of the working-day. Hence, too, the economic paradox, that the most powerful instrument for shortening labour-time, becomes the most unfailing means for placing every moment of the labourer's time and that of his family, at the disposal of the capitalist for the purpose of expanding the value of his capital. 'If,' dreamed Aristotle, the greatest thinker of antiquity, 'if every tool, when summoned, or even of its own accord, could do the work that befits it, just as the creations of Daedalus moved of themselves, or the tripods of Hephaestos went of their own accord to their sacred work, if the weavers' shuttles were to weave of themselves, then there would be no need either of apprentices for the master workers, or of slaves for the lords.'[73] And Antipatros, a Greek poet of the time of Cicero, hailed the invention of the water-wheel for grinding corn, an invention that is the elementary form of all machinery, as the giver of freedom to female slaves, and the bringer back of the golden age.[74] Oh! those heathens! They understood, as the learned Bastiat, and before him the still wiser MacCulloch have discovered, nothing of Political Economy and Christianity. They did not, for example, comprehend that machinery is the surest means of lengthening the working-day. They perhaps excused the slavery of one on the ground that it was a means to the full development of another. But to preach slavery of the masses, in order that a few crude and half-educated parvenus, might become 'eminent spinners,' 'extensive sausage-makers,' and 'influential shoe-black dealers,' to do this, they lacked the bump of Christianity.

C. Intensification of Labour

The immoderate lengthening of the working-day, produced by machinery in the hands of capital, leads to a reaction on the part of society, the very sources of whose life are menaced; and, thence, to a normal working-day whose length is fixed by law. Thenceforth, a phenomenon that we have already met with, namely, the intensification of labour, develops into great importance. Our analysis of absolute surplus-value had reference primarily to the extension or duration of the labour, its intensity being assumed as given. We, now, proceed to consider the substitution of a more intensified labour for labour of more extensive duration, and the degree of the former.

It is self-evident, that in proportion as the use of machinery spreads, and the experience of a special class of workmen habituated to machinery accumulates, the rapidity and intensity of labour increase as a natural consequence. Thus in England, during half a century, lengthening of the working-day went hand in hand with increasing intensity of factory labour. Nevertheless the reader will clearly see, that where we have labour, not carried on by fits and starts, but repeated day after day with unvarying uniformity, a point must inevitably be reached, where extension of the working-day and intensity of the labour mutually exclude one another, in such a way that lengthening of the working-day becomes compatible only with a lower degree of intensity, and a higher degree of intensity, only with a shortening of the working-day. So soon as the gradually surging revolt of the working-class compelled Parliament to shorten compulsorily the hours of labour, and to begin by imposing a normal working-day on factories proper, so soon consequently as an increased production of surplus-value by the prolongation of the working-day was once for all put a stop to, from that moment capital threw itself with all its might into the production of relative surplus-value, by hastening on the further improvement of machinery. At the same time a change took place in the nature of relative surplus-value. Generally speaking, the mode of producing relative surplus-value consists in raising the productive power of the workman, so as to enable him to produce more in a given time with the same expenditure of labour. Labour-time continues to transmit as before the same value to the total product, but this unchanged amount of exchange-value is spread over more use-value; hence the value of each single commodity sinks. Otherwise, however, so soon as the compulsory shortening of the hours of labour takes place. The immense impetus it gives the development of productive power, and to economy in the means of production, imposes on the workman increased expenditure of labour in a given time, heightened tension of labour-power, and closer filling up of the pores of the working-day, or condensation of labour to a degree that is attainable only within the limits of the shortened working-day. This condensation of a greater mass of labour into a given period thenceforward counts for what it really is, a greater quantity of labour. In addition to a measure of its extension, i.e., duration, labour now acquires a measure of its intensity or of the degree of its condensation or density.[75] The denser hour of the ten hours' working-day contains more labour, i.e., expended labour-power than the more porous hour of the twelve hours' working-day. The product therefore of one of the former hours has as much or more value than has the product of 1 1/5 of the latter hours. Apart from the increased yield of relative surplus-value through the heightened productiveness of labour, the same mass of value is now produced for the capitalist say by 3 1/3 hours of surplus-labour, and 6 2/3 hours of necessary labour, as was previously produced by four hours of surplus-labour and eight hours of necessary labour.

We now come to the question: How is the labour intensified?

The first effect of shortening the working-day results from the self-evident law, that the efficiency of labour-power is in an inverse ratio to the duration of its expenditure. Hence, within certain limits what is lost by shortening the duration is gained by the increasing tension of labour-power. That the workman moreover really does expend more labour-power, is ensured by the mode in which the capitalist pays him.[76] In those industries, such as potteries, where machinery plays little or no part, the introduction of the Factory Acts has strikingly shown that the mere shortening of the working-day increases to a wonderful degree the regularity, uniformity, order, continuity, and energy of the labour.[77] It seemed, however, doubtful whether this effect was produced in the factory proper, where the dependence of the workman on the continuous and uniform motion of the machinery had already created the strictest discipline. Hence, when in 1844 the reduction of the working-day to less than twelve hours was being debated, the masters almost unanimously declared

> 'that their overlookers in the different rooms took good care that the hands lost no time,' that 'the extent of vigilance and attention on the part of the workmen was hardly capable of being increased,' and, therefore, that the speed of the machinery and other conditions remaining unaltered, 'to expect in a well-managed factory any important result from increased attention of the workmen was an absurdity.'[78]

This assertion was contradicted by experiments. Mr Robert Gardner reduced the hours of labour in his two large factories at Preston, on and after the 20th April, 1844, from twelve to eleven hours a day. The result of about a year's working was that 'the same amount of product for the same cost was received, and the workpeople as a whole earned in eleven hours as much wages as they did before in twelve.'[79] I pass over the experiments made in the spinning and carding rooms, because they were accompanied by an increase of 2% in the speed of the machines. But in the weaving department, where, moreover, many sorts of figured fancy articles were woven, there was not the slightest alteration in the conditions of the work. The result was: 'From 6th January to 20th April, 1844, with a twelve hours' day, average weekly wages of each hand 10s. 1½d., from 20th April to 29th June, 1844, with day of eleven hours, average weekly wages 10s. 3½d.'[80] Here we have more produced in eleven hours than previously in twelve, and entirely in consequence of more steady application and economy of time by the workpeople. While they got the same wages and gained one hour of spare time, the capitalist got the same amount produced and saved the cost of coal, gas, and other such items, for one hour. Similar experiments, and with the like success, were carried out in the mills of Messrs. Horrocks and Jacson.[81]

The shortening of the hours of labour creates, to begin with, the subjective conditions for the condensation of labour, by enabling the workman to exert more strength in a given time. So soon as that shortening becomes compulsory, machinery becomes in the hands of capital the objective means, systematically employed for squeezing out more labour in a given time. This is effected in two ways: by increasing the speed of the machinery, and by giving the workman more machinery to tent. Improved construction of the machinery is necessary, partly because without it greater pressure cannot be put on the workman, and partly because the shortened hours of labour force the capitalist to exercise the strictest watch over the cost of production. The improvements in the steam-engine have increased the piston speed, and at the same time have made it possible, by means of a greater economy of power, to drive with the same or even a smaller consumption of coal more machinery with the same engine. The improvements in the transmitting mechanism have lessened friction, and, what so strikingly distinguishes modern from the older machinery, have reduced the diameter and weight of the shafting to a constantly decreasing minimum. Finally, the improvements in the operative machines have, while reducing their size, increased their speed and efficiency, as in the modern power-loom; or, while increasing the size of their framework, have also increased the extent and number of their working parts, as in spinning-mules, or have added to the speed of these working parts by imperceptible alterations of detail, such as those which ten years ago increased the speed of the spindles in self-acting mules by one-fifth.

The reduction of the working-day to 12 hours dates in England from 1832. In 1836 a manufacturer stated:

> 'The labour now undergone in the factories is much greater than it used to be ... compared with thirty or forty years ago ... owing to the greater attention and activity required by the greatly increased speed which is given to the machinery.'[82]

In the year 1844, Lord Ashley, now Lord Shaftesbury, made in the House of Commons the following statements, supported by documentary evidence:

> 'The labour performed by those engaged in the processes of manufacture, is three times as great as in the beginning of such operations. Machinery has executed, no doubt, the work that would demand the sinews of millions of men; but it has also prodigiously multiplied the labour of those who are governed by its fearful movements.... In 1815, the labour of following a pair of mules spinning cotton of No. 40—reckoning 12 hours to the working-day—involved a necessity of walking 8 miles. In 1832, the distance travelled in following a pair of mules, spinning cotton yarn of the same number, was

> 20 miles, and frequently more. In 1835' (query—1815 or 1825?) 'the spinner put up daily, on each of these mules, 820 stretches, making a total of 1,640 stretches in the course of the day. In 1832, the spinner put up on each mule 2,200 stretches, making a total of 4,400. In 1844, 2,400 stretches, making a total of 4,800; and in some cases the amount of labour required is even still greater.... I have another document sent to me in 1842, stating that the labour is progressively increasing—increasing not only because the distance to be travelled is greater, but because the quantity of goods produced is multiplied, while the hands are fewer in proportion than before; and, moreover, because an inferior species of cotton is now often spun, which it is more difficult to work.... In the carding-room there has also been a great increase of labour. One person there does the work formerly divided between two. In the weaving-room, where a vast number of persons are employed, and principally females ... the labour has increased within the last few years fully 10 per cent., owing to the increased speed of the machinery in spinning. In 1838, the number of hanks spun per week was 18,000, in 1843 it amounted to 21,000. In 1819, the number of picks in power-loom-weaving per minute was 60—in 1842 it was 140, showing a vast increase of labour.'[83]

In the face of this remarkable intensity of labour which had already been reached in 1844 under the Twelve Hours' Act, there appeared to be a justification for the assertion made at that time by the English manufacturers, that any further progress in that direction was impossible, and therefore that every further reduction of the hours of labour meant a lessened production. The apparent correctness of their reasons will be best shown by the following contemporary statement by Leonard Horner, the factory inspector, their ever watchful censor.

> 'Now, as the quantity produced must, in the main, be regulated by the speed of the machinery, it must be the interest of the mill-owner to drive it at the utmost rate of speed consistent with these following conditions, viz., the preservation of the machinery from too rapid deterioration; the preservation of the quality of the article manufactured; and the capability of the workman to follow the motion without a greater exertion than he can sustain for a constancy. One of the most important problems, therefore, which the owner of a factory has to solve is to find out the maximum speed at which he can run, with a due regard to the above conditions. It frequently happens that he finds he has gone too fast, that breakages and bad work more than counterbalance the increased speed, and that he is obliged to slacken his pace. I therefore concluded, that as an active and intelligent mill-owner would find out the safe maximum, it would not be possible to produce as much in eleven hours as in twelve. I further assumed that the operative paid by piecework, would exert himself to the utmost consistent with the power of continuing at the same rate.'[84]
>
> Horner, therefore, came to the conclusion that a reduction of the working hours below twelve would necessarily diminish production.[85] He himself, ten years later, cites his opinion of 1845 in proof of how much he under-estimated in that year the elasticity of machinery, and of man's labour-power, both of which are simultaneously stretched to an extreme by the compulsory shortening of the working-day.

We now come to the period that follows the introduction of the Ten Hours' Act in 1847 into the English cotton, woollen, silk, and flax mills.

'The speed of the spindles has increased upon throstles 500, and upon mules 1,000 revolutions a minute, i.e., the speed of the throstle spindle, which in 1839 was 4,500 times a minute, is now (1862) 5,000; and of the mule spindle, that was 5,000, is now 6,000 times a minute, amounting in the former case to one-tenth, and in the second case to one-fifth additional increase.'[86]

James Nasmyth, the eminent civil engineer of Patricroft, near Manchester, explained in a letter to Leonard Horner, written in 1852, the nature of the improvements in the steam-engine that had been made between the years 1848 and 1852. After remarking that the horse-power of steam-engines, being always estimated in the official returns according to the power of similar engines in 1828,[87] is only nominal, and can serve only as an index of their real power, he goes on to say:

> 'I am confident that from the same weight of steam-engine machinery, we are now obtaining at least 50 per cent. more duty or work performed on the average, and that in many cases the identical steam-engines which in the days of the restricted speed of 220 feet per minute, yielded 50 horsepower, are now yielding upwards of 100...' 'The modern steam-engine of 100 horse-power is capable of being driven at a much greater force than formerly, arising from improvements in its construction, the capacity and construction of the boilers, &c....' 'Although the same number of hands are employed in proportion to the horse-power as at former periods, there are fewer hands employed in proportion to the machinery.'[88] 'In the year 1850, the factories of the United Kingdom employed 134,217 nominal horse-power to give motion to 25,638,716 spindles and 301,445 looms. The number of spindles and looms in 1856 was respectively 33,503,580 of the former, and 369,205 of the latter, which, reckoning the force of the nominal horse-power required to be the same as in 1850, would require a force equal to 175,000 horses, but the actual power given in the return for 1856 is 161,435, less by above 10,000 horses than, calculating upon the basis of the return of 1850, the factories ought to have required in 1856.'[89] 'The facts thus brought out by the Return (of 1856) appear to be that the factory system is increasing rapidly; that although the same number of hands are employed in proportion to the horse-power as at former periods, there are fewer hands employed in proportion to the machinery; that the steam-engine is enabled to drive an increased weight of machinery by economy of force and other methods, and that an increased quantity of work can be turned off by improvements in machinery, and in methods of manufacture, by increase of speed of the machinery, and by a variety of other causes.'[90]
>
> 'The great improvements made in machines of every kind have raised their productive power very much. Without any doubt, the shortening of the hours of labour... gave the impulse to these improvements. The latter, combined with the more intense strain on the workman, have had the effect, that at least as much is produced in the shortened (by two hours or one-sixth) working-day as was previously produced during the longer one.'[91]

One fact is sufficient to show how greatly the wealth of the manufacturers increased along with the more intense exploitation of labour-power. From 1838 to 1850, the average proportional increase in English cotton and other factories was 32%, while from 1850 to 1856 it amounted to 86%.

But however great the progress of English industry had been during the 8 years from 1848 to 1856 under the influence of a working-day of 10 hours, it way far surpassed during the next period of 6 years from 1856 to 1862. In silk factories, for instance, there were in 1856, spindles 1,093,799; in 1862, 1,388,544; in 1856, looms 9,260; in 1862, 10,709. But the number of operatives was, in 1856, 56,131; in 1862, 52,429. The increase in the spindles was therefore 26.9% and in the looms 15.6%, while the number of the operatives decreased 7%. In the year 1850 there were employed in worsted mills 875,830 spindles; in 1856, 1,324,549 (increase 51.2%), and in 1862, 1,289,172 (decrease 2.7%). But if we deduct the doubling spindles that figure in the numbers for 1856, but not in those for 1862, it will be found that after 1856 the number of spindles remained nearly stationary. On the other hand, after 1850, the speed of the spindles and looms was in many cases doubled.

The number of power-looms in worsted mills was, in 1850, 32,617; in 1856, 38,956; in 1862, 43,048. The number of the operatives was, in 1850, 79,737; in 1856, 87,794; in 1862, 86,063; included in these, however, the children under 14 years of age were, in 1850, 9,956; in 1856, 11,228; in 1862, 13,178. In spite, therefore, of the greatly increased number of looms in 1862, compared with 1856, the total number of the workpeople employed decreased, and that of the children exploited increased.[92]

On the 27th April, 1863, Mr Ferrand said in the House of Commons:

> 'I have been informed by delegates from 16 districts of Lancashire and Cheshire, in whose behalf I speak, that the work in the factories is, in consequence of the improvements in machinery, constantly on the increase. Instead of as formerly one person with two helps tenting two looms, one person now tents three looms without helps, and it is no uncommon thing for one person to tent four. Twelve hours' work, as is evident from the facts adduced, is now compressed into less than 10 hours. It is therefore self-evident, to what an enormous extent the toil of the factory operative has increased during the last 10 years.'[93]

Although, therefore, the Factory Inspectors unceasingly and with justice, commend the results of the Acts of 1844 and 1850, yet they admit that the shortening of the hours of labour has already called forth such an intensification of the labour as is injurious to the health of the workman and to his capacity for work.

> 'In most of the cotton, worsted, and silk mills, an exhausting state of excitement necessary to enable the workers satisfactorily to mind the machinery, the motion of which has been greatly accelerated within the last few years, seems to me not unlikely to be one of the causes of that excess of mortality from lung disease, which Dr Greenhow has pointed out in his recent report on this subject.'[94]

There cannot be the slightest doubt that the tendency that urges capital, so soon as a prolongation of the hours of labour is once for all forbidden, to compensate itself, by a systematic heightening of the intensity of labour, and to convert every improvement in machinery into a more perfect means of exhausting the workman, must soon lead to a state of things in which a reduction of the hours of labour will again be inevitable.[95] On the other hand, the rapid advance of English industry between 1848 and the present time, under the influence of a day of 10 hours, surpasses the advance made between 1833 and 1847, when the day was 12 hours long, by far more than the latter surpasses the advance made during the half century after the first introduction of the factory system, when the working-day was without limits.[96]

Section 4: *The Factory*

At the commencement of this chapter we considered that which we may call the body of the factory, i.e., machinery organised into a system. We there saw how machinery, by annexing the labour of women and children, augments the number of human beings who form the material for capitalistic exploitation, how it confiscates the whole of the workman's disposable time, by immoderate extension of the hours of labour, and how finally its progress, which allows of enormous increase of production in shorter and shorter periods, serves as a means of systematically getting more work done in a shorter time, or of exploiting labour-power more intensely. We now turn to the factory as a whole, and that in its most perfect form.

Dr Ure, the Pindar of the automatic factory, describes it, on the one hand, as

> 'Combined co-operation of many orders of workpeople, adult and young, in tending

with assiduous skill, a system of productive machines, continuously impelled by a central power' (the prime mover); on the other hand, as 'a vast automaton, composed of various mechanical and intellectual organs, acting in uninterrupted concert for the production of a common object, all of them being subordinate to a self-regulated moving force.'

These two descriptions are far from being identical. In one, the collective labourer, or social body of labour, appears as the dominant subject, and the mechanical automaton as the object; in the other, the automaton itself is the subject, and the workmen are merely conscious organs, co-ordinate with the unconscious organs of the automaton, and together with them, subordinated to the central moving-power. The first description is applicable to every possible employment of machinery on a large scale, the second is characteristic of its use by capital, and therefore of the modern factory system. Ure prefers therefore, to describe the central machine, from which the motion comes, not only as an automaton, but as an autocrat. 'In these spacious halls the benignant power of steam summons around him his myriads of willing menials.'[97]

Along with the tool, the skill of the workman in handling it passes over to the machine. The capabilities of the tool are emancipated from the restraints that are inseparable from human labour-power. Thereby the technical foundation on which is based the division of labour in Manufacture, is swept away. Hence, in the place of the hierarchy of specialised workmen that characterises manufacture, there steps, in the automatic factory, a tendency to equalise and reduce to one and the same level every kind of work that has to be done by the minders of the machines;[98] in the place of the artificially produced differentiations of the detail workmen, step the natural differences of age and sex.

So far as division of labour re-appears in the factory, it is primarily a distribution of the workmen among the specialised machines; and of masses of workmen, not however organised into groups, among the various departments of the factory, in each of which they work at a number of similar machines placed together; their co-operation, therefore, is only simple. The organised group, peculiar to manufacture, is replaced by the connexion between the head workman and his few assistants. The essential division is, into workmen who are actually employed on the machines (among whom are included a few who look after the engine), and into mere attendants (almost exclusively children) of these workmen. Among the attendants are reckoned more or less all 'Feeders' who supply the machines with the material to be worked. In addition to these two principal classes, there is a numerically unimportant class of persons, whose occupation it is to look after the whole of the machinery and repair it from time to time; such as engineers, mechanics, joiners, &c. This is a superior class of workmen, some of them scientifically educated, others brought up to a trade; it is distinct from the factory operative class, and merely aggregated to it.[99] This division of labour is purely technical.

To work at a machine, the workman should be taught from childhood, in order that he may learn to adapt his own movements to the uniform and unceasing motion of an automaton. When the machinery, as a whole, forms a system of manifold machines, working simultaneously and in concert, the co-operation based upon it, requires the distribution of various groups of workmen among the different kinds of machines. But the employment of machinery does away with the necessity of crystallising this distribution after the manner of Manufacture, by the constant annexation of a particular man to a particular function.[100] Since the motion of the whole system does not proceed from the workman, but from the machinery, a change of persons can take place at any time without an interruption of the work. The most striking proof of this is afforded by the *relays system*, put into operation by the manufacturers during their revolt from 1848-1850. Lastly, the quickness with which machine work is learnt by young people, does away with the necessity of bringing up for exclusive employment by machinery, a special class of operatives.[101] With regard to the work of the mere attendants, it can, to some extent, be replaced in the mill by machines,[102] and owing to its extreme simplicity, it allows of a rapid and constant change of the individuals burdened with this drudgery.

Although then, technically speaking, the old system of division of labour is thrown overboard by machinery, it hangs on in the factory, as a traditional habit handed down from Manufacture, and is afterwards systematically re-moulded and established in a more hideous form by capital, as a means of exploiting labour-power. The life-long speciality of handling one and the same tool, now becomes the life-long speciality of serving one and the same machine. Machinery is put to a wrong use, with the object of transforming the workman, from his very childhood, into a part of a detail-machine.[103] In this way, not only are the expenses of his reproduction considerably lessened, but at the same time his helpless dependence upon the factory as a whole, and therefore upon the capitalist, is rendered complete. Here as everywhere else, we must distinguish between the increased productiveness due to the development of the social process of production, and that due to the capitalist exploitation of that process. In handicrafts and manufacture, the workman makes use of a tool, in the factory, the machine makes use of him. There the movements of the instrument of labour proceed from him, here it is the movements of the machine that he must follow. In manufacture the workmen are parts of a living mechanism. In the factory we have a lifeless mechanism independent of the workman, who becomes its mere living appendage.

> 'The miserable routine of endless drudgery and toil in which the same mechanical process is gone through over and over again, is like the labour of Sisyphus. The burden of labour, like the rock, keeps ever falling back on the worn-out labourer.'[104]

At the same time, that factory work exhausts the nervous system to the uttermost, it does away with the many-sided play of the muscles, and confiscates every atom of freedom, both in bodily and intellectual activity.[105] The lightening of the labour, even, becomes a sort of torture, since the machine does not free the labourer from work, but deprives the work of all interest. Every kind of capitalist production, in so far as it is not only a labour-process, but also a process of creating surplus-value, has this in common, that it is not the workman that employs the instruments of labour, but the instruments of labour that employ the workman. But it is only in the factory system that this inversion for the first time acquires technical and palpable reality. By means of its conversion into an automaton, the instrument of labour confronts the labourer, during the labour-process, in the shape of capital, of dead labour, that dominates, and pumps dry, living labour-power. The separation of the intellectual powers of production from the manual labour, and the conversion of those powers into the might of capital over labour, is, as we have already shown, finally completed by modern industry erected on the foundation of machinery. The special skill of each individual insignificant factory operative vanishes as an infinitesimal quantity before the science, the gigantic physical forces, and the mass of labour that are embodied in the factory mechanism and, together with that mechanism, constitute the power of the 'master.' This 'master,' therefore, in whose brain the machinery and his monopoly of it are inseparably united, whenever he falls out with his 'hands,' contemptuously tells them:

> 'The factory operatives should keep in wholesome remembrance the fact that theirs is really a low species of skilled labour; and that there is none which is more easily acquired, or of its quality more amply remunerated, or which by a short training of the least expert can be more quickly, as well as abundantly, acquired.... The master's machinery really plays a far more important part in the business of production than the labour and the skill of the operative, which six months' education can teach, and a common labourer can learn.'[106]

The technical subordination of the workman to the uniform motion of the instruments of labour, and the peculiar composition of the body of workpeople, consisting as it does of individuals of both sexes and of all ages, give rise to a barrack discipline, which is elaborated into a complete system in the factory, and which fully develops the before mentioned labour of overlooking, thereby dividing the workpeople into operatives and overlookers, into private soldiers and sergeants of an industrial army. 'The main difficulty [in the automatic factory] ... lay ... above all in training human beings to renounce their desultory habits of work, and to identify themselves with the unvarying regularity of the complex automaton. To devise and administer a successful code of factory discipline, suited to the necessities of factory diligence, was the Herculean enterprise, the noble achievement of Arkwright! Even at the present day, when the system is perfectly organised and its labour lightened to the utmost, it is found nearly impossible to convert persons past the age of puberty, into useful factory hands.'[107] The factory code in which capital formulates, like a private legislator, and at his own good will, his autocracy over his workpeople, unaccompanied by that division of responsibility, in other matters so much approved of by the bourgeoisie, and unaccompanied by the still more approved representative system, this code is but the capitalistic caricature of that social regulation of the labour-process which becomes requisite in co-operation on a great scale, and in the employment in common, of instruments of labour and especially of machinery. The place of the slave-driver's lash is taken by the overlooker's book of penalties. All punishments naturally resolve themselves into fines and deductions from wages, and the law-giving talent of the factory Lycurgus so arranges matters, that a violation of his laws is, if possible, more profitable to him than the keeping of them.[108] We shall here merely allude to the material conditions under which factory labour is carried on. Every organ of sense is injured in an equal degree by artificial elevation of the temperature, by the dust-laden atmosphere, by the deafening noise, not to mention danger to life and limb among the thickly crowded machinery, which, with the regularity of the seasons, issues its list of the killed and wounded in the industrial battle.[109] Economy of the social means of production, matured and forced as in a hothouse by the factory system, is turned, in the hands of capital, into systematic robbery of what is necessary for the life of the workman while he is at work, robbery of space, light, air, and of protection to his person against the dangerous and unwholesome accompaniments of the productive process, not to mention the robbery of appliances for the comfort of the workman.[110] Is Fourier wrong when he calls factories 'tempered bagnos'?[111]

Section 5: *The Strife Between Workman and Machine*

The contest between the capitalist and the wage-labourer dates back to the very origin of capital. It raged on throughout the whole manufacturing period.[112] But only since the introduction of machinery has the workman fought against the instrument of labour itself, the material embodiment of capital. He revolts against this particular form of the means of production, as being the material basis of the capitalist mode of production.

In the 17th century, nearly all Europe experienced revolts of the workpeople against the ribbon-loom, a machine for weaving ribbons and trimmings, called in Germany Bandmühle, Schnurmühle, and Mühlenstuhl. These machines were invented in Germany. Abbé Lancellotti, in a work that appeared in Venice in 1636, but which was written in 1579, says as follows:

> 'Anthony Müller of Danzig saw about 50 years ago in that town, a very ingenious machine, which weaves 4 to 6 pieces at once. But the Mayor being apprehensive that this invention might throw a large number of workmen on the streets, caused the inventor to be secretly strangled or drowned.'

In Leyden, this machine was not used till 1629; there the riots of the ribbon-weavers at length compelled the Town Council to prohibit it.

> 'In hac urbe,' says Boxhorn (Inst. Pol., 1663), referring to the introduction of this machine into Leyden, 'ante hos viginti circiter annos instrumentum quidam invenerunt textorium, quo solus plus panni et facilius conficere poterat, quan plures aequali tempore. Hinc turbae ortae et querulae textorum, tandemque usus hujus instrumenti a magistratu prohibitus est.'
>
> [In this town, about twenty years ago certain people invented an instrument for weaving, with which a single person could weave more cloth, and more easily, than many others in the same length of time. As a result there arose disturbances and complaints from the weavers, until the Town Council finally prohibited the use of this instrument.]

After making various decrees more or less prohibitive against this loom in 1632, 1639, &c., the States General of Holland at length permitted it to be used, under certain conditions, by the decree of the 15th December, 1661. It was also prohibited in Cologne in 1676, at the same time that its introduction into England was causing disturbances among the workpeople. By an imperial Edict of 19th Feb., 1685, its use was forbidden throughout all Germany. In Hamburg it was burnt in public by order of the Senate. The Emperor Charles VI., on 9th Feb., 1719, renewed the edict of 1685, and not till 1765 was its use openly allowed in the Electorate of Saxony. This machine, which shook Europe to its foundations, was in fact the precursor of the mule and the power-loom, and of the industrial revolution of the 18th century. It enabled a totally inexperienced boy, to set the whole loom with all its shuttles in motion, by simply moving a rod backwards and forwards, and in its improved form produced from 40 to 50 pieces at once.

About 1630, a wind-sawmill, erected near London by a Dutchman, succumbed to the excesses of the populace. Even as late as the beginning of the 18th century, sawmills driven by water overcame the opposition of the people, supported as it was by Parliament, only with great difficulty. No sooner had Everet in 1758 erected the first wool-shearing machine that was driven by water-power, than it was set on fire by 100,000 people who had been thrown out of work. Fifty thousand workpeople, who had previously lived by carding wool, petitioned Parliament against Arkwright's scribbling mills and carding engines. The enormous destruction of machinery that occurred in the English manufacturing districts during the first 15 years of this century, chiefly caused by the employment of the power-loom, and known as the Luddite movement, gave the anti-Jacobin governments of a Sidmouth, a Castlereagh, and the like, a pretext for the most reactionary and forcible measures. It took both time and experience before the workpeople learnt to distinguish between machinery and its employment by capital, and to direct their attacks, not against the material instruments of production, but against the mode in which they are used.[113]

The contests about wages in Manufacture, pre-suppose manufacture, and are in no sense directed against its existence. The opposition against the establishment of new manufactures, proceeds from the guilds and privileged towns, not from the workpeople. Hence the writers of the manufacturing period treat the division of labour chiefly as a means of virtually supplying a deficiency of labourers, and not as a means of actually displacing those in work. This distinction is self-evident. If it be said that 100 millions of people would be required in England to spin with the old spinning-wheel the cotton that is now spun with mules by 500,000 people, this does not mean that the mules took the place of those millions who never existed. It means only this, that many millions of workpeople would be required to replace the spinning machinery. If, on the other hand, we say, that in England the power-loom threw 800,000 weavers on the streets, we do not refer to existing machinery, that would have to be replaced by a definite number of workpeople, but to a number of weavers in existence who were actually replaced or displaced by the looms. During the manufacturing period, handicraft labour, altered though it was by division of labour, was yet the basis. The demands of the new colonial markets could not be satisfied owing to the relatively small number of town operatives handed down from the middle ages, and the manufactures proper opened out new fields of production to the rural population, driven from the land by the dissolution of the feudal system. At that time, therefore, division of labour and co-operation in the workshops, were viewed more from the positive aspect, that they made the workpeople more productive.[114] Long before the period of modern industry, co-operation and the concentration of the instruments of labour in the hands of a few, gave rise, in numerous countries where these methods were applied in agriculture, to great, sudden and forcible revolutions in the modes of production, and consequentially, in the conditions of existence, and the means of employment of the rural populations. But this contest at first takes place more between the large and the small landed proprietors, than between capital and wage labour; on the other hand, when the labourers are displaced by the instruments of labour, by sheep, horses, &c., in this case force is directly resorted to in the first instance as the prelude to the industrial revolution. The labourers are first driven from the land, and then come the sheep. Land grabbing on a great scale, such as was perpetrated in England, is the first step in creating a field for the establishment of agriculture on a great scale.[115] Hence this subversion of agriculture puts on, at first, more the appearance of a political revolution.

The instrument of labour, when it takes the form of a machine, immediately becomes a competitor of the workman himself.[116] The self-expansion of capital by means of machinery is thenceforward directly proportional to the number of the workpeople, whose means of livelihood have been destroyed by that machinery. The whole system of capitalist production is based on the fact that the workman sells his labour-power as a commodity. Division of labour specialises this labour-power, by reducing it to skill in handling a particular tool. So soon as the handling of this tool becomes the work of a machine, then, with the use-value, the exchange-value too, of the workman's labour-power vanishes; the workman becomes unsaleable, like paper money thrown out of currency by legal enactment. That portion of the working-class, thus by machinery rendered superfluous, i.e., no longer immediately necessary for the self-expansion of capital, either goes to the wall in the unequal contest of the old handicrafts and manufactures with machinery, or else floods all the more easily accessible branches of industry, swamps the labour-market, and sinks the price of labour-power below its value. It is impressed upon the workpeople, as a great consolation, first, that their sufferings are only temporary ('a temporary inconvenience"), secondly, that machinery acquires the mastery over the whole of a given field of production, only by degrees, so that the extent and intensity of its destructive effect is diminished. The first consolation neutralises the second. When machinery seizes on an industry by degrees, it produces chronic misery among the operatives who compete with it. Where the transition is rapid, the effect is acute and felt by great masses. History discloses no tragedy more horrible than the gradual extinction of the English hand-loom weavers, an extinction that was spread over several decades, and finally sealed in 1838. Many of them died of starvation, many with families vegetated for a long time on 2½ d. a day.[117] On the other hand, the English cotton machinery produced an acute effect in India. The Governor General reported 1834-35:

> 'The misery hardly finds a parallel in the history of commerce. The bones of the cotton-weavers are bleaching the plains of India.'

No doubt, in turning them out of this 'temporal' world, the machinery caused them no more than 'a temporary inconvenience.' For the rest, since machinery is continually seizing upon new fields of production, its temporary effect is really permanent. Hence, the character of independence and estrangement which the capitalist mode of production as a whole gives to the instruments of labour and to the product, as against the workman, is developed by means of machinery into a thorough antagonism.[118] Therefore, it is with the advent of machinery, that the workman for the first time brutally revolts against the instruments of labour.

The instrument of labour strikes down the labourer. This direct antagonism between the two comes out most strongly, whenever newly introduced machinery competes with handicrafts or manufactures, handed down from former times. But even in modern industry the continual improvement of machinery, and the development of the automatic system, has an analogous effect.

> 'The object of improved machinery is to diminish manual labour, to provide for the performance of a process or the completion of a link in a manufacture by the aid of an iron instead of the human apparatus.'[119] 'The adaptation of power to machinery heretofore moved by hand, is almost of daily occurrence ... the minor improvements in machinery having for their object economy of power, the production of better work, the turning off more work in the same time, or in supplying the place of a child, a female, or a man, are constant, and although sometimes apparently of no great moment, have somewhat important results.'[120] 'Whenever a process requires peculiar dexterity and steadiness of hand, it is withdrawn, as soon as possible, from the cunning workman, who is prone to irregularities of many kinds, and it is placed in charge of a peculiar mechanism, so self-regulating that a child can superintend it.'[121] 'On the automatic plan skilled labour gets progressively superseded.'[122] 'The effect of improvements in machinery, not merely in superseding the necessity for the employment of the same quantity of adult labour as before, in order to produce a given result, but in substituting one description of human labour for another, the less skilled for the more skilled, juvenile for adult, female for male, causes a fresh disturbance in the rate of wages.'[123] 'The effect of substituting the self-acting mule for the common mule, is to discharge the greater part of the men spinners, and to retain adolescents and children.'[124]

The extraordinary power of expansion of the factory system owing to accumulated practical experience, to the mechanical means at hand, and to constant technical progress, was proved to us by the giant strides of that system under the pressure of a shortened working-day. But who, in 1860, the Zenith year of the English cotton industry, would have dreamt of the galloping improvements in machinery, and the corresponding displacement of working people, called into being during the following 3 years, under the stimulus of the American Civil War? A couple of examples from the Reports of the Inspectors of Factories will suffice on this point. A Manchester manufacturer states:

> 'We formerly had 75 carding engines, now we have 12, doing the same quantity of work.... We are doing with fewer hands by 14, at a saving in wages of £10 a-week. Our estimated saving in waste is about 10% in the quantity of cotton consumed.' 'In another fine-spinning mill in Manchester, I was informed that through increased speed and the adoption of some self-acting processes, a reduction had been made, in number, of a fourth in one department, and of above half in another, and that the introduction of the combing machine in place of the second carding, had considerably reduced, the number of hands formerly employed in the carding-room.'

Another spinning-mill is estimated to effect a saving of labour of 10%. The Messrs. Gilmour, spinners at Manchester, state: 'In our blowing-room department we consider our expense with new machinery is fully one-third less in wages and hands ... in the jack-frame and drawing-frame room, about one-third less in expense, and likewise one-third less in hands; in the spinning room about one-third less in expenses. But this is not all; when our yarn goes to the manufacturers, it is so much better by the application of our new machinery, that they will produce a greater quantity of cloth, and cheaper than from the yarn produced by old machinery.'[125] Mr Redgrave further remarks in the same Report:

> 'The reduction of hands against increased production is, in fact, constantly taking place, in woollen mills the reduction commenced some time since, and is continuing; a few days since, the master of a school in the neighbourhood of Rochdale said to me, that the great falling off in the girls' school is not only caused by the distress, but by the changes of machinery in the woollen mills, in consequence of which a reduction of 70 short-timers had taken place.'[126]

The following table shows the total result of the mechanical improvements in the English cotton industry due to the American Civil War.

Number of Factories	*1857*	*1861*	*1868*
England and Wales	2,046	2,715	2,405
Scotland	152	163	131
Ireland	12	9	13
United Kingdom	2,210	2,887	2,549
Number of Power Looms	**1857**	**1861**	**1868**
England and Wales	275,590	368,125	344,719
Scotland	21,624	30,110	31,864
Ireland	1,633	1,757	2,746
United Kingdom	298,847	399,992	379,329
Number of Spindles	**1857**	**1861**	**1868**
England and Wales	25,818,576	28,352,125	30,478,228
Scotland	2,041,129	1,915,398	1,397,546
Ireland	150,512	119,944	124,240
United Kingdom	28,010,217	30,387,467	32,000,014
Number of Persons Employed	**1857**	**1861**	**1868**
England and Wales	341,170	407,598	357,052
Scotland	34,698	41,237	39,809
Ireland	3,345	2,734	4,203
United Kingdom	379,213	452,569	401,064

Hence, between 1861 and 1868, 338 cotton factories disappeared, in other words more productive machinery on a larger scale was concentrated in the hands of a smaller number of capitalists. The number of power-looms decreased by 20,663; but since their product increased in the same period, an improved loom must have yielded more than an old one. Lastly the number of spindles increased by 1,612,541, while the number of operatives decreased by 50,505. The 'temporary' misery inflicted on the workpeople by the cotton-crisis, was heightened, and from being temporary made permanent, by the rapid and persistent progress of machinery.

But machinery not only acts as a competitor who gets the better of the workman, and is constantly on the point of making him superfluous. It is also a power inimical to him, and as such capital proclaims it from the roof tops and as such makes use of it. It is the most powerful weapon for repressing strikes, those periodical revolts of the working-class against the autocracy of capital.[127] According to Gaskell, the steam-engine was from the very first an antagonist of human power, an antagonist that enabled the capitalist to tread under foot the growing claims of the workmen, who threatened the newly born factory system with a crisis.[128] It would be possible to write quite a history of the inventions, made since 1830, for the sole purpose of supplying capital with weapons against the revolts of the working-class. At the head of these in importance, stands the self-acting mule, because it opened up a new epoch in the automatic system.[129]

Nasmyth, the inventor of the steam-hammer, gives the following evidence before the Trades' Union Commission, with regard to the improvements made by him in machinery and introduced in consequence of the wide-spread and long strikes of the engineers in 1851.

> 'The characteristic feature of our modern mechanical improvements, is the introduction of self-acting tool machinery. What every mechanical workman has now to do, and what every boy can do, is not to work himself but to superintend the beautiful labour of the machine. The whole class of workmen that depend exclusively on their skill, is now done away with. Formerly, I employed four boys to every mechanic. Thanks to these new mechanical combinations, I have reduced the number of grown-up men from 1,500 to 750. The result was a considerable increase in my profits.'

Ure says of a machine used in calico printing:

> 'At length capitalists sought deliverance from this intolerable bondage' [namely the, in their eyes, burdensome terms of their contracts with the workmen] 'in the resources of science, and were speedily re-instated in their legitimate rule, that of the head over the inferior members.'

Speaking of an invention for dressing warps:

> 'Then the combined malcontents, who fancied themselves impregnably entrenched behind the old lines of division of labour, found their flanks turned and their defences rendered useless by the new mechanical tactics, and were obliged to surrender at discretion.'

With regard to the invention of the self-acting mule, he says:

> 'A creation destined to restore order among the industrious classes.... This invention confirms the great doctrine already propounded, that when capital enlists science into her service, the refractory hand of labour will always be taught docility.'130

Although Ure's work appeared 30 years ago, at a time when the factory system was comparatively but little developed, it still perfectly expresses the spirit of the factory, not only by its undisguised cynicism, but also by the naïveté with which it blurts out the stupid contradictions of the capitalist brain. For instance, after propounding the 'doctrine' stated above, that capital, with the aid of science taken into its pay, always reduces the refractory hand of labour to docility, he grows indignant because

> 'it (physico-mechanical science) has been accused of lending itself to the rich capitalist as an instrument for harassing the poor.'

After preaching a long sermon to show how advantageous the rapid development of machinery is to the working-classes, he warns them, that by their obstinacy and their strikes they hasten that development.

> 'Violent revulsions of this nature,' he says, 'display short-sighted man in the contemptible character of a self-tormentor.'

A few pages before he states the contrary.

> 'Had it not been for the violent collisions and interruptions resulting from erroneous views among the factory operatives, the factory system would have been developed still more rapidly and beneficially for all concerned.' Then he exclaims again: 'Fortunately

> for the state of society in the cotton districts of Great Britain, the improvements in machinery are gradual.' 'It' (improvement in machinery) 'is said to lower the rate of earnings of adults by displacing a portion of them, and thus rendering their number superabundant as compared with the demand for their labour. It certainly augments the demand for the labour of children and increases the rate of *their* wages.'

On the other hand, this same dispenser of consolation defends the lowness of the children's wages on the ground that it prevents parents from sending their children at too early an age into the factory. The whole of his book is a vindication of a working-day of unrestricted length; that Parliament should forbid children of 13 years to be exhausted by working 12 hours a day, reminds his liberal soul of the darkest days of the Middle Ages. This does not prevent him from calling upon the factory operatives to thank Providence, who by means of machinery has given them the leisure to think of their 'immortal interests.'[131]

Section 6: *The Theory of Compensation as Regards the Work People Displaced by Machinery*

James Mill, MacCulloch, Torrens, Senior, John Stuart Mill, and a whole series besides, of bourgeois political economists, insist that all machinery that displaces workmen, simultaneously and necessarily sets free an amount of capital adequate to employ the same identical workmen.[132]

Suppose a capitalist to employ 100 workmen, at £30 a year each, in a carpet factory. The variable capital annually laid out amounts, therefore, to £3,000. Suppose, also, that he discharges 50 of his workmen, and employs the remaining 50 with machinery that costs him £1,500. To simplify matters, we take no account of buildings, coal, &c. Further suppose that the raw material annually consumed costs £3,000, both before and after the change.[133] Is any capital set free by this metamorphosis? Before the change, the total sum of £6,000 consisted half of constant, and half of variable capital. After the change it consists of £4,500 constant (£3,000 raw material and £1,500 machinery), and £1,500 variable capital. The variable capital, instead of being one half, is only one quarter, of the total capital. Instead of being set free, a part of the capital is here locked up in such a way as to cease to be exchanged against labour-power: variable has been changed into constant capital. Other things remaining unchanged, the capital of £6,000, can, in future, employ no more than 50 men. With each improvement in the machinery, it will employ fewer. If the newly introduced machinery had cost less than did the labour-power and implements displaced by it, if, for instance, instead of costing £1,500, it had cost only £1,000, a variable capital of £1,000 would have been converted into constant capital, and locked up; and a capital of £500 would have been set free. The latter sum, supposing wages unchanged, would form a fund sufficient to employ about 16 out of the 50 men discharged; nay, less than 16, for, in order to be employed as capital, a part of this £500 must now become constant capital, thus leaving only the remainder to be laid out in labour-power.

But, suppose, besides, that the making of the new machinery affords employment to a greater number of mechanics, can that be called compensation to the carpet-makers, thrown on the streets? At the best, its construction employs fewer men than its employment displaces. The sum of £1,500 that formerly represented the wages of the discharged carpet-makers, now represents in the shape of machinery: (1) the value of the means of production used in the construction of that machinery, (2) the wages of the mechanics employed in its construction, and (3) the surplus-value falling to the share of their 'master.' Further, the machinery need not be renewed till it is worn out. Hence, in order to keep the increased number of mechanics in constant employment, one carpet manufacturer after another must displace workmen by machines.

As a matter of fact the apologists do not mean this sort of setting free.

They have in their minds the means of subsistence of the liberated work-people. It cannot be denied, in the above instance, that the machinery not only liberates 50 men, thus placing them at others' disposal, but, at the same time, it withdraws from their consumption, and sets free, means of subsistence to the value of £1,500. The simple fact, by no means a new one, that machinery cuts off the workmen from their means of subsistence is, therefore, in economic parlance tantamount to this, that machinery liberates means of subsistence for the workman, or converts those means into capital for his employment. The mode of expression, you see, is everything. Nominibus mollire licet mala.

This theory implies that the £1,500 worth of means of subsistence was capital that was being expanded by the labour of the 50 men discharged. That, consequently, this capital falls out of employment so soon as they commence their forced holidays, and never rests till it has found a fresh investment, where it can again be productively consumed by these same 50 men. That sooner or later, therefore, the capital and the workmen must come together again, and that, then, the compensation is complete. That the sufferings of the workmen displaced by machinery are therefore as transient as are the riches of this world.

In relation to the discharged workmen, the £1,500 worth of means of subsistence never was capital. What really confronted them as capital, was the sum of £1,500, afterwards laid out in machinery. On looking closer it will be seen that this sum represented part of the carpets produced in a year by the 50 discharged men, which part they received as wages from their employer in money instead of in kind. With the carpets in the form of money, they bought means of subsistence to the value of £1,500. These means, therefore, were to them, not capital, but commodities, and they, as regards these commodities, were not wage-labourers, but buyers. The circumstance that they were 'freed' by the machinery, from the means of purchase, changed them from buyers into non-buyers. Hence a lessened demand for those commodities—voilà tout. If this diminution be not compensated by an increase from some other quarter, the market price of the commodities falls. If this state of things lasts for some time, and extends, there follows a discharge of workmen employed in the production of these commodities. Some of the capital that was previously devoted to production of necessary means of subsistence, has to become reproduced in another form. While prices fall, and capital is being displaced, the labourers employed in the production of necessary means of subsistence are in their turn 'freed' from a part of their wages. Instead, therefore, of proving that, when machinery frees the workman from his means of subsistence, it simultaneously converts those means into capital for his further employment, our apologists, with their cut-and-dried law of supply and demand, prove, on the contrary, that machinery throws workmen on the streets, not only in that branch of production in which it is introduced, but also in those branches in which it is not introduced.

The real facts, which are travestied by the optimism of economists, are as follows: The labourers, when driven out of the workshop by the machinery, are thrown upon the labour market, and there add to the number of workmen at the disposal of the capitalists. In Part VII of this book it will be seen that this effect of machinery, which, as we have seen, is represented to be a compensation to the working class, is on the contrary a most frightful scourge. For the present I will only say this: The labourers that are thrown out of work in any branch of industry, can no doubt seek for employment in some other branch. If they find it, and thus renew the bond between them and the means of subsistence, this takes place only by the intermediary of a new and additional capital that is seeking investment; not at all by the intermediary of the capital that formerly employed them and was afterwards converted into machinery. And even should they find employment, what a poor look-out is theirs! Crippled as they are by division of labour, these poor devils are worth so little outside their old trade, that they cannot find admission into any industries, except a few of inferior kind, that are over-supplied with underpaid workmen.[134] Further, every branch of industry attracts each year a new stream of men, who furnish a contingent from which to fill up vacancies, and to draw a supply for expansion. So soon as machinery sets free a part of the workmen employed in a given branch of industry, the reserve men are also diverted into new channels of employment, and become absorbed in other branches; meanwhile the original victims, during the period of transition, for the most part starve and perish.

It is an undoubted fact that machinery, as such, is not responsible for 'setting free' the workman from the means of subsistence. It cheapens and increases production in that branch which it seizes on, and at first makes no change in the mass of the means of subsistence produced in other branches. Hence, after its introduction, the society possesses as much, if not more, of the necessaries of life than before, for the labourers thrown out of work; and that quite apart from the enormous share of the annual produce wasted by the non-workers. And this is the point relied on by our apologists! The contradictions and antagonisms inseparable from the capitalist employment of machinery, do not exist, they say, since they do not arise out of machinery, as such, but out of its capitalist employment! Since therefore machinery, considered alone, shortens the hours of labour, but, when in the service of capital, lengthens them; since in itself it lightens labour, but when employed by capital, heightens the intensity of labour; since in itself it is a victory of man over the forces of Nature, but in the hands of capital, makes man the slave of those forces; since in itself it increases the wealth of the producers, but in the hands of capital, makes them paupers—for all these reasons and others besides, says the bourgeois economist without more ado, it is clear as noon-day that all these contradictions are a mere semblance of the reality, and that, as a matter of fact, they have neither an actual nor a theoretical existence. Thus he saves himself from all further puzzling of the brain, and what is more, implicitly declares his opponent to be stupid enough to contend against, not the capitalistic employment of machinery, but machinery itself.

No doubt he is far from denying that temporary inconvenience may result from the capitalist use of machinery. But where is the medal without its reverse! Any employment of machinery, except by capital, is to him an impossibility. Exploitation of the workman by the machine is therefore, with him, identical with exploitation of the machine by the workman. Whoever, therefore, exposes the real state of things in the capitalistic employment of machinery, is against its employment in any way, and is an enemy of social progress![135] Exactly the reasoning of the celebrated Bill Sykes. 'Gentlemen of the jury, no doubt the throat of this commercial traveller has been cut. But that is not my fault, it is the fault of the knife. Must we, for such a temporary inconvenience, abolish the use of the knife? Only consider! where would agriculture and trade be without the knife? Is it not as salutary in surgery, as it is knowing in anatomy? And in addition a willing help at the festive board? If you abolish the knife—you hurl us back into the depths of barbarism.'[136]

Although machinery necessarily throws men out of work in those industries into which it is introduced, yet it may, notwithstanding this, bring about an increase of employment in other industries. This effect, however, has nothing in common with the so-called theory of compensation. Since every article produced by a machine is cheaper than a similar article produced by hand, we deduce the following infallible law: If the total quantity of the article produced by machinery, be equal to the total quantity of the article previously produced by a handicraft or by manufacture, and now made by machinery, then the total labour expended is diminished. The new labour spent on the instruments of labour, on the machinery, on the coal, and so on, must necessarily be less than the labour displaced by the use of the machinery; otherwise the product of the machine would be as dear, or dearer, than the product of the manual labour. But, as a matter of fact, the total quantity of the article produced by machinery with a diminished number of workmen, instead of remaining equal to, by far exceeds the total quantity of the hand-made article that has been displaced. Suppose that 400,000 yards of cloth have been produced on power-looms by fewer weavers than could weave 100,000 yards by hand. In the quadrupled product there lies four times as much raw material. Hence the production of raw material must be quadrupled.

But as regards the instruments of labour, such as buildings, coal, machinery, and so on, it is different; the limit up to which the additional labour required for their production can increase, varies with the difference between the quantity of the machine-made article, and the quantity of the same article that the same number of workmen could make by hand.

Hence, as the use of machinery extends in a given industry, the immediate effect is to increase production in the other industries that furnish the first with means of production. How far employment is thereby found for an increased number of men, depends, given the length of the working-day and the intensity of labour, on the composition of the capital employed, i.e., on the ratio of its constant to its variable component. This ratio, in its turn, varies considerably with the extent to which machinery has already seized on, or is then seizing on, those trades. The number of the men condemned to work in coal and metal mines increased enormously owing to the progress of the English factory system; but during the last few decades this increase of number has been less rapid, owing to the use of new machinery in mining.[137] A new type of workman springs into life along with the machine, namely, its maker. We have already learnt that machinery has possessed itself even of this branch of production on a scale that grows greater every day.[138] As to raw material,[139] there is not the least doubt that the rapid strides of cotton spinning, not only pushed on with tropical luxuriance the growth of cotton in the United States, and with it the African slave trade, but also made the breeding of slaves the chief business of the border slave-states. When, in 1790, the first census of slaves was taken in the United States, their number was 697,000; in 1861 it had nearly reached four millions. On the other hand, it is no less certain that the rise of the English woollen factories, together with the gradual conversion of arable land into sheep pasture, brought, about the superfluity of agricultural labourers that led to their being driven in masses into the towns. Ireland, having during the last twenty years reduced its population by nearly one half, is at this moment undergoing the process of still further reducing the number of its inhabitants, so as exactly to suit the requirements of its landlords and of the English woollen manufacturers.

When machinery is applied to any of the preliminary or intermediate stages through which the subject of labour has to pass on its way to completion, there is an increased yield of material in those stages, and simultaneously an increased demand for labour in the handicrafts or manufactures supplied by the produce of the machines. Spinning by machinery, for example, supplied yarn so cheaply and so abundantly that the hand-loom weavers were, at first, able to work full time without increased outlay. Their earnings accordingly rose.[140] Hence a flow of people into the cotton-weaving trade, till at length the 800,000 weavers, called into existence by the Jenny, the throstle and the mule, were overwhelmed by the power-loom. So also, owing to the abundance of clothing materials produced by machinery, the number of tailors, seamstresses and needlewomen, went on increasing until the appearance of the sewing-machine.

In proportion as machinery, with the aid of a relatively small number of workpeople, increases the mass of raw materials, intermediate products, instruments of labour, &c., the working-up of these raw materials and intermediate products becomes split up into numberless branches; social production increases in diversity. The factory system carries the social division of labour immeasurably further than does manufacture, for it increases the productiveness of the industries it seizes upon, in a far higher degree.

The immediate result of machinery is to augment surplus-value and the mass of products in which surplus-value is embodied. And, as the substances consumed by the capitalists and their dependents become more plentiful, so too do these orders of society. Their growing wealth, and the relatively diminished number of workmen required to produce the necessaries of life beget, simultaneously with the rise of new and luxurious wants, the means of satisfying those wants. A larger portion of the produce of society is changed into surplus-produce, and a larger part of the surplus-produce is supplied for consumption in a multiplicity of refined shapes. In other words, the production of luxuries increases.[141] The refined and varied forms of the products are also due to new relations with the markets of the world, relations that are created by modern industry. Not only are greater quantities of foreign articles of luxury exchanged for home products, but a greater mass of foreign raw materials, ingredients, and intermediate products, are used as means of production in the home industries. Owing to these relations with the markets of the world, the demand for labour increases in the carrying trades, which split up into numerous varieties.[142]

The increase of the means of production and subsistence, accompanied by a relative diminution in the number of labourers, causes an increased demand for labour in making canals, docks, tunnels, bridges, and so on, works that can only bear fruit in the far future. Entirely new branches of production, creating new fields of labour, are also formed, as the direct result either of machinery or of the general industrial changes brought about by it. But the place occupied by these branches in the general production is, even in the most developed countries, far from important. The number of labourers that find employment in them is directly proportional to the demand, created by those industries, for the crudest form of manual labour. The chief industries of this kind are, at present, gas-works, telegraphs, photography, steam navigation, and railways. According to the census of 1861 for England and Wales, we find in the gas industry (gas-works, production of mechanical apparatus, servants of the gas companies, &c), 15,211 persons; in telegraphy, 2,399; in photography, 2,366; steam navigation, 3,570; and in railways, 70,599, of whom the unskilled 'navvies,' more or less permanently employed, and the whole administrative and commercial staff, make up about 28,000. The total number of persons, therefore, employed in these five new industries amounts to 94,145.

Lastly, the extraordinary productiveness of modern industry, accompanied as it is by both a more extensive and a more intense exploitation of labour-power in all other spheres of production, allows of the unproductive employment of a larger and larger part of the working-class, and the consequent reproduction, on a constantly extending scale, of the ancient domestic slaves under the name of a servant class, including men-servants, women-servants, lackeys, &c. According to the census of 1861, the population of England and Wales was 20,066,244; of these, 9,776,259 males, and 10,289,965 females. If we deduct from this population all who are too old or too young for work, all unproductive women, young persons and children, the 'ideological' classes, such as government officials, priests, lawyers, soldiers, &c.; further, all who have no occupation but to consume the labour of others in the form of rent, interest, &c.; and, lastly, paupers, vagabonds, and criminals, there remain in round numbers eight millions of the two sexes of every age, including in that number every capitalist who is in any way engaged in industry, commerce, or finance. Among these 8 millions are:

	Persons
Agricultural labourers (including shepherds, farm servants, and maidservants living in the houses of farmers)	1,098,261
All who are employed in cotton, woollen, worsted, flax, hemp, silk, and jute factories, in stocking making and lace making by machinery	[143]642,607
All who are employed in coal mines and metal mines	565,835
All who are employed in metal works (blastfurnaces, rolling mills, &c.), and metal manufactures of every kind	[144]396,998
The servant class	[145]1,208,648

All the persons employed in textile factories and in mines, taken together, number 1,208,442; those employed in textile factories and metal industries, taken together, number 1,039,605; in both cases less than the number of modern domestic slaves. What a splendid result of the capitalist exploitation of machinery!

All political economists of any standing admit that the introduction of new machinery has a baneful effect on the workmen in the old handicrafts and manufactures with which this machinery at first competes. Almost all of them bemoan the slavery of the factory operative. And what is the great trump-card that they play? That machinery, after the horrors of the period of introduction and development have subsided, instead of diminishing, in the long run increases the number of the slaves of labour! Yes, Political Economy revels in the hideous theory, hideous to every 'philanthropist' who believes in the eternal Nature-ordained necessity for capitalist production, that after a period of growth and transition, even its crowning success, the factory system based on machinery, grinds down more workpeople than on its first introduction it throws on the streets.[146]

It is true that in some cases, as we saw from instances of English worsted and silk factories, an extraordinary extension of the factory system may, at a certain stage of its development, be accompanied not only by a relative, but by an absolute decrease in the number of operatives employed. In the year 1860, when a special census of all the factories in the United Kingdom was taken by order of Parliament, the factories in those parts of Lancashire, Cheshire, and Yorkshire, included in the district of Mr Baker, the factory inspector, numbered 652; 570 of these contained 85,622 power-looms, 6,819,146 spindles (exclusive of doubling spindles), employed 27,439 horse-power (steam), and 1,390 (water), and 94,119 persons. In the year 1865, the same factories contained, looms 95,163, spindles 7,025,031, had a steam-power of 28,925 horses, and a water-power of 1,445 horses, and employed 88,913 persons. Between 1860 and 1865, therefore, the increase in looms was 11%, in spindles 3%, and in engine-power 3%, while the number of persons employed decreased 5½%.[147] Between 1852 and 1862, considerable extension of the English woollen manufacture took place, while the number of hands employed in it remained almost stationary,

> 'showing how greatly the introduction of new machines had superseded the labour of preceding periods.'[148]

In certain cases, the increase in the number of hands employed is only apparent; that is, it is not due to the extension of the factories already established, but to the gradual annexation of connected trades; for instance, the increase in power-looms, and in the hands employed by them between 1838 and 1856, was, in the cotton trade, simply owing to the extension of this branch of industry; but in the other trades to the application of steam-power to the carpet-loom, to the ribbon-loom, and to the linen-loom, which previously had been worked by the power of men.[149] Hence the increase of the hands in these latter trades was merely a symptom of a diminution in the total number employed. Finally, we have considered this question entirely apart from the fact, that everywhere, except in the metal industries, young persons (under 18), and women and children form the preponderating element in the class of factory hands.

Nevertheless, in spite of the mass of hands actually displaced and virtually replaced by machinery, we can understand how the factory operatives, through the building of more mills and the extension of old ones in a given industry, may become more numerous than the manufacturing workmen and handicraftsman that have been displaced. Suppose, for example, that in the old mode of production, a capital of £500 is employed weekly, two-fifths being constant and three-fifths variable capital, *i.e.*, £200 being laid out in means of production, and £300, say £1 per man, in labour-power. On the introduction of machinery the composition of this capital becomes altered. We will suppose it to consist of four-fifths constant and one-fifth variable, which means that only £100 is now laid out in labour-power. Consequently, two-thirds of the workmen are discharged. If now the business extends, and the total capital employed grows to £1,500 under unchanged conditions, the number of operatives employed will increase to 300, just as many as before the introduction of the machinery. If the capital further grows to £2,000, 400 men will be employed, or one-third more than under the old system. Their numbers have, in point of fact, increased by 100, but relatively, i.e., in proportion to the total capital advanced, they have diminished by 800, for the £2,000 capital would, in the old state of things, have employed 1,200 instead of 400 men. Hence, a relative decrease in the number of hands is consistent with an actual increase. We assumed above that while the total capital increases, its composition remains the same, because the conditions of production remain constant. But we have already seen that, with every advance in the use of machinery, the constant component of capital, that part which consists of machinery, raw material, &c., increases, while the variable component, the part laid out in labour-power, decreases. We also know that in no other system of production is improvement so continuous, and the composition of the capital employed so constantly changing as in the factory system. These changes are, however, continually interrupted by periods of rest, during which there is a mere quantitative extension of the factories on the existing technical basis. During such periods the operatives increase in number. Thus, in 1835, the total number of operatives in the cotton, woollen, worsted, flax, and silk factories of the United Kingdom was only 354,684; while in 1861 the number of the power-loom weavers alone (of both sexes and of all ages, from eight years upwards), amounted to 230,654. Certainly, this growth appears less important when we consider that in 1838 the hand-loom weavers with their families still numbered 800,000,[150] not to mention those thrown out of work in Asia, and on the Continent of Europe.

In the few remarks I have still to make on this point, I shall refer to some actually existing relations, the existence of which our theoretical investigation has not yet disclosed.

So long as, in a given branch of industry, the factory system extends itself at the expense of the old handicrafts or of manufacture, the result is as sure as is the result of an encounter between an army furnished with breach-loaders, and one armed with bows and arrows. This first period, during which machinery conquers its field of action, is of decisive importance owing to the extraordinary profits that it helps to produce. These profits not only form a source of accelerated accumulation, but also attract into the favoured sphere of production a large part of the additional social capital that is being constantly created, and is ever on the look-out for new investments. The special advantages of this first period of fast and furious activity are felt in every branch of production that machinery invades. So soon, however, as the factory system has gained a certain breadth of footing and a definite degree of maturity, and, especially, so soon as its technical basis, machinery, is itself produced by machinery; so soon as coal mining and iron mining, the metal industries, and the means of transport have been revolutionised; so soon, in short, as the general conditions requisite for production by the modern industrial system have been established, this mode of production acquires an elasticity, a capacity for sudden extension by leaps and bounds that finds no hindrance except in the supply of raw material and in the disposal of the produce. On the one hand, the immediate effect of machinery is to increase the supply of raw material in the same way, for example, as the cotton gin augmented the production of cotton.[151] On the other hand, the cheapness of the articles produced by machinery, and the improved means of transport and communication furnish the weapons for conquering foreign markets. By ruining handicraft production in other countries, machinery forcibly converts them into fields for the supply of its raw material. In this way East India was compelled to produce cotton, wool, hemp, jute, and indigo for Great Britain.[152] By constantly making a part of the hands 'supernumerary,' modern industry, in all countries where it has taken root, gives a spur to emigration and to the colonisation of foreign lands, which are thereby converted into settlements for growing the raw material of the mother country; just as Australia, for example, was converted into a colony for growing wool.[153] A new and international division of labour, a division suited to the requirements of the chief centres of modern industry springs up, and converts one part of the globe into a chiefly agricultural field of production, for supplying the other part which remains a chiefly industrial field. This revolution hangs together with radical changes in agriculture which we need not here further inquire into.[154]

On the motion of Mr Gladstone, the House of Commons ordered, on the 17th February, 1867, a return of the total quantities of grain, corn, and flour, of all sorts, imported into, and exported from, the United Kingdom, between the years 1831 and 1866. I give below a summary of the result. The flour is given in quarters of corn. (See the Table on p. 532.)

The enormous power, inherent in the factory system, of expanding by jumps, and the dependence of that system on the markets of the world, necessarily beget feverish production, followed by over-filling of the markets, whereupon contraction of the markets brings on crippling of production. The life of modern industry becomes a series of periods of moderate activity, prosperity, over-production, crisis and stagnation. The uncertainty and instability to which machinery subjects the employment, and consequently the conditions of existence, of the operatives become normal, owing to these periodic changes of the industrial cycle. Except in the periods of prosperity, there rages between the capitalists the most furious combat for the share of each in the markets. This share is directly proportional to the cheapness of the product. Besides the rivalry that this struggle begets in the application of improved machinery for replacing labour-power, and of new methods of production, there also comes a time in every industrial cycle, when a forcible reduction of wages beneath the value of labour-power, is attempted for the purpose of cheapening commodities.[156]

A necessary condition, therefore, to the growth of the number of factory hands, is a proportionally much more rapid growth of the amount of capital invested in mills. This growth, however, is conditioned by the ebb and flow of the industrial cycle. It is, besides, constantly interrupted by the technical progress that at one time virtually supplies the place of new workmen, at another, actually displaces old ones. This qualitative change in mechanical industry continually discharges hands from the factory, or shuts its doors against the fresh stream of recruits, while the purely quantitative extension of the factories absorbs not only the men thrown out of work, but also fresh contingents. The workpeople are thus continually both repelled and attracted, hustled from pillar to post, while, at the same time, constant changes take place in the sex, age, and skill of the levies.

The lot of the factory operatives will be best depicted by taking a rapid survey of the course of the English cotton industry.

From 1770 to 1815, this trade was depressed or stagnant for 5 years only. During this period of 45 years the English manufacturers had a monopoly of machinery and of the markets of the world. From 1815 to 1821 depression; 1822 and 1823 prosperity; 1824 abolition of the laws against Trades' Unions, great extension of factories everywhere; 1825 crisis; 1826 great misery and riots among the factory operatives; 1827 slight improvement; 1828 great increase in power-looms, and in exports; 1829 exports, especially to India, surpass all former years; 1830 glutted markets, great distress; 1831 to 1833 continued depression, the monopoly of the trade with India and China withdrawn from the East India Company; 1834 great increase of factories and machinery, shortness of hands. The new poor law furthers the migration of agricultural labourers into the factory districts. The country districts swept of children. White slave trade; 1835 great prosperity, contemporaneous starvation of the hand-loom weavers; 1836 great prosperity; 1837 and 1838 depression and crisis; 1839 revival; 1840 great depression, riots, calling out of the military; 1841 and 1842 frightful suffering among the factory operatives; 1842 the manufacturers lock the hands out of the factories in order to enforce the repeal of the Corn Laws. The operatives stream in thousands into the towns of Lancashire and Yorkshire, are driven back by the military, and their leaders brought to trial at Lancaster; 1843 great misery; 1844 revival; 1845 great prosperity; 1846 continued improvement at first, then reaction. Repeal of the Corn Laws; 1847 crisis, general reduction of wages by 10 and more per cent. in honour of the 'big loaf"; 1848 continued depression; Manchester under military protection; 1849 revival; 1850 prosperity; 1851 falling prices, low wages, frequent strikes; 1852 improvement begins, strikes continue, the manufacturers threaten to import foreign hands; 1853 increasing exports. Strike for 8 months, and great misery at Preston; 1854 prosperity, glutted markets; 1855 news of failures stream in from the United States, Canada, and the Eastern markets; 1856 great prosperity; 1857 crisis; 1858 improvement; 1859 great prosperity, increase in factories; 1860 Zenith of the English cotton trade, the Indian, Australian, and other markets so glutted with goods that even in 1863 they had not absorbed the whole lot; the French Treaty of Commerce, enormous growth of factories and machinery; 1861 prosperity continues for a time, reaction, the American Civil War, cotton famine: 1862 to 1863 complete collapse.

The history of the cotton famine is too characteristic to dispense with dwelling upon it for a moment. From the indications as to the condition of the markets of the world in 1860 and 1861, we see that the cotton famine came in the nick of time for the manufacturers, and was to some extent advantageous to them, a fact that was acknowledged in the reports of the Manchester Chamber of Commerce, proclaimed in Parliament by Palmerston and Derby, and confirmed by events.[157] No doubt, among the 2,887 cotton mills in the United Kingdom in 1861, there were many of small size. According to the report of Mr A. Redgrave, out of the 2,109 mills included in his district, 392, or 19% employed less than ten horse-power each; 345, or 16% employed 10 H. P., and less than 20 H. P.; while 1,372 employed upwards of 20 H. P.[158] The majority of the small mills were weaving sheds, built during the period of prosperity after 1858, for the most part by speculators, of whom one supplied the yarn, another the machinery, a third the buildings, and were worked by men who had been overlookers, or by other persons of small means. These small manufacturers mostly went to the wall. The same fate would have overtaken them in the commercial crisis that was staved off only by the cotton famine. Although they formed one-third of the total number of manufacturers, yet their mills absorbed a much smaller part of the capital invested in the cotton trade. As to the extent of the stoppage, it appears from authentic estimates, that in October 1862, 60.3% of the spindles, and 58% of the looms were standing. This refers to the cotton trade as a whole, and, of course, requires considerable modification for individual districts. Only very few mills worked full time (60 hours a week), the remainder worked at intervals. Even in those few cases where full time was worked, and at the customary rate of piece-wage, the weekly wages of the operatives necessarily shrank, owing to good cotton being replaced by bad, Sea Island by Egyptian (in fine spinning mills), American and Egyptian by Surat, and pure cotton by mixings of waste and Surat. The shorter fibre of the Surat cotton and its dirty condition, the greater fragility of the thread, the substitution of all sorts of heavy ingredients for flour in sizing the warps, all these lessened the speed of the machinery, or the number of the looms that could be superintended by one weaver, increased the labour caused by defects in the machinery, and reduced the piece-wage by reducing the mass of the product turned off. Where Surat cotton was used, the loss to the operatives when on full time, amounted to 20, 30, and more per cent. But besides this, the majority of the manufacturers reduced the rate of piece-wage by 5, 7½, and 10 per cent. We can therefore conceive the situation of those hands who were employed for only 3, 3½ or 4 days a week, or for only 6 hours a day. Even in 1863, after a comparative improvement had set in, the weekly wages of spinners and of weavers were 3s. 4d., 3s. 10d., 4s. 6d. and 5s. 1d.[159] Even in this miserable state of things, however, the inventive spirit of the master never stood still, but was exercised in making deductions from wages. These were to some extent inflicted as a penalty for defects in the finished article that were really due to his bad cotton and to his unsuitable machinery. Moreover, where the manufacturer owned the cottages of the workpeople, he paid himself his rents by deducting the amount from these miserable wages. Mr Redgrave tells us of self-acting minders (operatives who manage a pair of self-acting mules) 'earning at the end of a fortnight's full work 8s. 11d., and that from this sum was deducted the rent of the house, the manufacturer, however, returning half the rent as a gift. The minders took away the sum of 6s. 11d. In many places the self-acting minders ranged from 5s. to 9s. per week, and the weavers from 2s. to 6s. per week, during the latter part of 1862.'[160]

Even when working short time the rent was frequently deducted from the wages of the operatives.[161] No wonder that in some parts of Lancashire a kind of famine fever broke out. But more characteristic than all this, was, the revolution that took place in the process of production at the expense of the workpeople. Experimenta in corpore vili, like those of anatomists on frogs, were formally made.

'Although,' says Mr Redgrave, 'I have given the actual earnings of the operatives in the several mills, it does not follow that they earn the same amount week by week. The operatives are subject to great fluctuation from the constant experimentalising of the manufacturers ... the earnings of the operatives rise and fall with the quality of the cotton mixings; sometimes they have been within 15 per cent. of former earnings, and then, in a week or two, they have fallen off from 50 to 60 per cent.'[162]

These experiments were not made solely at the expense of the workman's means of subsistence. His five senses also had to pay the penalty.

'The people who are employed in making up Surat cotton complain very much. They inform me, on opening the bales of cotton there is an intolerable smell, which causes sickness.... In the mixing, scribbling and carding rooms, the dust and dirt which are disengaged, irritate the air passages, and give rise to cough and difficulty of breathing. A disease of the skin, no doubt from the irritation of the dirt contained in the Surat cotton, also prevails.... The fibre being so short, a great amount of size, both animal and vegetable, is used.... Bronchitis is more prevalent owing to the dust. Inflammatory sore throat is common, from the same cause. Sickness and dyspepsia are produced by the frequent breaking of the weft, when the weaver sucks the weft through the eye of the shuttle.' On the other hand, the substitutes for flour were a Fortunatus' purse to the manufacturers, by increasing the weight of the yarn. They caused '15 lbs. of raw material to weigh 26 lbs. after it was woven.'[163]

In the Report of Inspectors of Factories for 30th April, 1864, we read as follows:

'The trade is availing itself of this resource at present to an extent which is even discreditable. I have heard on good authority of a cloth weighing 8 lbs. which was made of 5 1/4 lbs. cotton and 2 3/4 lbs. size; and of another cloth weighing 5 1/4 lbs., of which 2 lbs. was size. These were ordinary export shirtings. In cloths of other descriptions, as much as 50 per cent. size is sometimes added; so that a manufacturer may, and does truly boast, that he is getting rich by selling cloth for less money per pound than he paid for the mere yarn of which they are composed.'[164]

But the workpeople had to suffer, not only from the experiments of the manufacturers inside the mills, and of the municipalities outside, not only from reduced wages and absence of work, from want and from charity, and from the eulogistic speeches of lords and commons.

'Unfortunate females who, in consequence of the cotton famine, were at its commencement thrown out of employment, and have thereby become outcasts of society; and now, though trade has revived, and work is plentiful, continue members of that unfortunate class, and are likely to continue so. There are also in the borough more youthful prostitutes than I have known for the last 25 years.'[165]

We find then, in the first 45 years of the English cotton trade, from 1770 to 1815, only 5 years of crisis and stagnation; but this was the period of monopoly. The second period from 1815 to 1863 counts, during its 48 years, only 20 years of revival and prosperity against 28 of depression and stagnation. Between 1815 and 1830 the competition with the continent of Europe and with the United States sets in. After 1833, the extension of the Asiatic markets is enforced by 'destruction of the human race' (the wholesale extinction of Indian hand-loom weavers). After the repeal of the Corn Laws, from 1846 to 1863, there are 8 years of moderate activity and prosperity against 9 years of depression and stagnation. The condition of the adult male operatives, even during the years of prosperity, may be judged from the note subjoined.[166]

Section 8: *Revolution Effected in Manufacture, Handicrafts, and Domestic Industry by Modern Industry*

A. Overthrow of Co-operation Based on Handicraft, and on the Division of Labour

We have seen how machinery does away with co-operation based on handicrafts, and with manufacture based on the division of handicraft labour. An example of the first sort is the mowing-machine; it replaces co-operation between mowers. A striking example of the second kind, is the needle-making machine. According to Adam Smith, 10 men, in his day, made in co-operation, over 48,000 needles a-day. On the other hand, a single needle-machine makes 145,000 in a working-day of 11 hours. One woman or one girl superintends four such machines, and so produces near upon 600,000 needles in a day, and upwards of 3,000,000 in a week.[167] A single machine, when it takes the place of co-operation or of manufacture, may itself serve as the basis of an industry of a handicraft character. Still, such a return to handicrafts is but a transition to the factory system, which, as a rule, makes its appearance so soon as the human muscles are replaced, for the purpose of driving the machines, by a mechanical motive power, such as steam or water. Here and there, but in any case only for a time, an industry may be carried on, on a small scale, by means of mechanical power. This is effected by hiring steam-power, as is done in some of the Birmingham trades, or by the use of small caloric-engines, as in some branches of weaving.[168] In the Coventry silk weaving industry the experiment of 'cottage factories' was tried. In the centre of a square surrounded by rows of cottages, an engine-house was built and the engine connected by shafts with the looms in the cottages. In all cases the power was hired at so much per loom. The rent was payable weekly, whether the looms worked or not. Each cottage held from 2 to 6 looms; some belonged to the weaver, some were bought on credit, some were hired. The struggle between these cottage factories and the factory proper, lasted over 12 years. It ended with the complete ruin of the 300 cottage factories.[169] Wherever the nature of the process did not involve production on a large scale, the new industries that have sprung up in the last few decades, such as envelope making, steel-pen making, &c., have, as a general rule, first passed through the handicraft stage, and then the manufacturing stage, as short phases of transition to the factory stage. The transition is very difficult in those cases where the production of the article by manufacture consists, not of a series of graduated processes, but of a great number of disconnected ones. This circumstance formed a great hindrance to the establishment of steel-pen factories. Nevertheless, about 15 years ago, a machine was invented that automatically performed 6 separate operations at once. The first steel-pens were supplied by the handicraft system, in the year 1820, at £7 4s. the gross; in 1830 they were supplied by manufacture at 8s., and today the factory system supplies them to the trade at from 2 to 6d. the gross.[170]

B. Reaction of the Factory System on Manufacture and Domestic Industries

Along with the development of the factory system and of the revolution in agriculture that accompanies it, production in all the other branches of industry not only extends, but alters its character. The principle, carried out in the factory system, of analysing the process of production into its constituent phases, and of solving the problems thus proposed by the application of mechanics, of chemistry, and of the whole range of the natural sciences, becomes the determining principle everywhere. Hence, machinery squeezes itself into the manufacturing industries first for one detail process, then for another. Thus the solid crystal of their organisation, based on the old division of labour, becomes dissolved, and makes way for constant changes. Independently of this, a radical change takes place in the composition of the collective labourer, a change of the persons working in combination. In contrast with the manufacturing period, the division of labour is thenceforth based, wherever possible, on the employment of women, of children of all ages, and of unskilled labourers, in one word, on cheap labour, as it is characteristically called in England. This is the case not only with all production on a large scale, whether employing machinery or not, but also with the so-called domestic industry, whether carried on in the houses of the workpeople or in small workshops. This modern so-called domestic industry has nothing, except the name, in common with the old-fashioned domestic industry, the existence of which pre-supposes independent urban handicrafts, independent peasant farming, and above all, a dwelling-house for the labourer and his family. That old-fashioned industry has now been converted into an outside department of the factory, the manufactory, or the warehouse. Besides the factory operatives, the manufacturing workmen and the handicraftsman, whom it concentrates in large masses at one spot, and directly commands, capital also sets in motion, by means, of invisible threads, another army; that of the workers in the domestic industries, who dwell in the large towns and are also scattered over the face of the country. An example: The shirt factory of Messrs. Tillie at Londonderry, which employs 1,000 operatives in the factory itself, and 9,000 people spread up and down the country and working in their own houses.[171]

The exploitation of cheap and immature labour-power is carried out in a more shameless manner in modern Manufacture than in the factory proper. This is because the technical foundation of the factory system, namely, the substitution of machines for muscular power, and the light character of the labour, is almost entirely absent in Manufacture, and at the same time women and over-young children are subjected, in a most unconscionable way, to the influence of poisonous or injurious substances. This exploitation is more shameless in the so-called domestic industry than in manufactures, and that because the power of resistance in the labourers decreases with their dissemination; because a whole series of plundering parasites insinuate themselves between the employer and the workman; because a domestic industry has always to compete either with the factory system, or with manufacturing in the same branch of production; because poverty robs the workman of the conditions most essential to his labour, of space, light and ventilation; because employment becomes more and more irregular; and, finally, because in these the last resorts of the masses made 'redundant' by modern industry and Agriculture, competition for work attains its maximum. Economy in the means of production, first systematically carried out in the factory system, and there, from the very beginning, coincident with the most reckless squandering of labour-power, and robbery of the conditions normally requisite for labour—this economy now shows its antagonistic and murderous side more and more in a given branch of industry, the less the social productive power of labour and the technical basis for a combination of processes are developed in that branch.

C. Modern Manufacture

I now proceed, by a few examples, to illustrate the principles laid down above. As a matter of fact, the reader is already familiar with numerous instances given in the chapter on the working-day. In the hardware manufactures of Birmingham and the neighbourhood, there are employed, mostly in very heavy work, 30,000 children and young persons, besides 10,000 women. There they are to be seen in the unwholesome brass-foundries, button factories, enamelling, galvanising, and lackering works.[172] Owing to the excessive labour of their workpeople, both adult and non-adult, certain London houses where newspapers and books are printed, have got the ill-omened name of 'slaughterhouses.'[173] Similar excesses are practised in book-binding, where the victims are chiefly women, girls, and children; young persons have to do heavy work in rope-walks and night-work in salt mines, candle manufactories, and chemical works; young people are worked to death at turning the looms in silk weaving, when it is not carried on by machinery.[174] One of the most shameful, the most dirty, and the worst paid kinds of labour, and one on which women and young girls are by preference employed, is the sorting of rags. It is well known that Great Britain, apart from its own immense store of rags, is the emporium for the rag trade of the whole world. They flow in from Japan, from the most remote States of South America, and from the Canary Islands. But the chief sources of their supply are Germany, France, Russia, Italy, Egypt, Turkey, Belgium, and Holland. They are used for manure, for making bedflocks, for shoddy, and they serve as the raw material of paper. The rag-sorters are the medium for the spread of small-pox and other infectious diseases, and they themselves are the first victims.[175] A classical example of over-work, of hard and inappropriate labour, and of its brutalising effects on the workman from his childhood upwards, is afforded not only by coal-mining and miners generally, but also by tile and brick making, in which industry the recently invented machinery is, in England, used only here and there. Between May and September the work lasts from 5 in the morning till 8 in the evening, and where the drying is done in the open air, it often lasts from 4 in the morning till 9 in the evening. Work from 5 in the morning till 7 in the evening is considered 'reduced' and 'moderate.' Both boys and girls of 6 and even of 4 years of age are employed. They work for the same number of hours, often longer, than the adults. The work is hard and the summer heat increases the exhaustion. In a certain tile-field at Mosley, e.g., a young woman, 24 years of age, was in the habit of making 2,000 tiles a day, with the assistance of 2 little girls, who carried the clay for her, and stacked the tiles. These girls carried daily 10 tons up the slippery sides of the clay pits, from a depth of 30 feet, and then for a distance of 210 feet.

> 'It is impossible for a child to pass through the purgatory of a tile-field without great moral degradation... the low language, which they are accustomed to hear from their tenderest years, the filthy, indecent, and shameless habits, amidst which, unknowing, and half wild, they grow up, make them in after-life lawless, abandoned, dissolute.... A frightful source of demoralisation is the mode of living. Each moulder, who is always a skilled labourer, and the chief of a group, supplies his 7 subordinates with board and lodging in his cottage. Whether members of his family or not, the men, boys, and girls all sleep in the cottage, which contains generally two, exceptionally 3 rooms, all on the ground floor, and badly ventilated. These people are so exhausted after the day's hard work, that neither the rules of health, of cleanliness, nor of decency are in the least observed. Many of these cottages are models of untidiness, dirt, and dust.... The greatest evil of the system that employs young girls on this sort of work, consists in this, that, as a rule, it chains them fast from childhood for the whole of their after-life to the most abandoned rabble. They become rough, foul-mouthed boys, before Nature has taught them that they are women. Clothed in a few dirty rags, the legs naked far above the knees, hair and face besmeared with dirt, they learn to treat all feelings of decency and of shame with contempt. During meal-times they lie at full length in the fields, or watch the boys bathing in a neighbouring canal. Their heavy day's work at length completed, they put on better clothes, and accompany the men to the public houses.'

That excessive insobriety is prevalent from childhood upwards among the whole of this class, is only natural.

> 'The worst is that the brickmakers despair of themselves. You might as well, said one of the better kind to a chaplain of Southallfield, try to raise and improve the devil as a brickie, sir!'[176]

As to the manner, in which capital effects an economy in the requisites of labour, in modern Manufacture (in which I include all workshops of larger size, except factories proper), official and most ample material bearing on it is to be found in the Public Health Reports IV. (1863) and VI. (1864). The description of the workshops, more especially those of the London printers and tailors, surpasses the most loathsome phantasies of our romance writers. The effect on the health of the workpeople is self-evident. Dr Simon, the chief medical officer of the Privy Council and the official editor of the 'Public Health Reports,' says:

> 'In my fourth Report (1863) I showed, how it is practically impossible for the workpeople to insist upon that which is their first sanitary right, viz., the right that, no matter what the work for which their employer brings them together, the labour, so far as it depends upon him, should be freed from all avoidably unwholesome conditions. I pointed out, that while the workpeople are practically incapable of doing themselves this sanitary justice, they are unable to obtain any effective support from the paid administrations of the sanitary police.... The life of myriads of workmen and workwomen is now uselessly tortured and shortened by the never-ending physical suffering that their mere occupation begets.'[177]

In illustration of the way in which the workrooms influence the state of health Dr Simon gives the following table of mortality.[178]

Number of persons of all ages employed in the respective industries.	*Industries compared as regards health.*	*Death-rate per 100,000 men in the respective industries between the stated ages*		
		Age 25-35	*Age 35-45*	*Age 45-55*
958,265	Agriculture in England & Wales	743	805	1,145
22,301 men 12,379 women	London tailors	958	1,262	2,093
13,803	London printers	894	1,747	2,367

D. Modern Domestic Industry

I now come to the so-called domestic industry. In order to get an idea of the horrors of this sphere, in which capital conducts its exploitation in the background of modern mechanical industry, one must go to the apparently quite idyllic trade of nail-making,[179] carried on in a few remote villages of England. In this place, however, it will be enough to give a few examples from those branches of the lace-making and straw-plaiting industries that are not yet carried on by the aid of machinery, and that as yet do not compete with branches carried on in factories or in manufactories.

Of the 150,000 persons employed in England in the production of lace, about 10,000 fall under the authority of the Factory Act, 1861. Almost the whole of the remaining 140,000 are women, young persons, and children of both sexes, the male sex, however, being weakly represented. The state of health of this cheap material for exploitation will be seen from the following table, computed by Dr Trueman, physician to the Nottingham General Dispensary.

Out of 686 female patients who were lace-makers, most of them between the ages of 17 and 24, the number of consumptive ones were:

1852.—1 in 45.	**1857.—1 in 13.**
1853.—1 in 28.	**1858.—1 in 15.**
1854.—1 in 17.	**1859.—1 in 9.**
1856.—1 in 15.	**1861.—1 in 8.**[180]

This progress in the rate of consumption ought to suffice for the most optimist of progressists, and for the biggest hawker of lies among the Free-trade bagmen of Germany.

The Factory Act of 1861 regulates the actual making of the lace, so far as it is done by machinery, and this is the rule in England. The branches that we are now about to examine, solely with regard to those of the workpeople who work at home, and not those who work in manufactories or warehouses, fall into two divisions, viz. (1), finishing; (2), mending. The former gives the finishing touches to the machine-made lace, and includes numerous sub-divisions.

The lace finishing is done either in what are called 'mistresses' houses,' or by women in their own houses, with or without the help of their children. The women who keep the 'mistresses' houses' are themselves poor. The workroom is in a private house. The mistresses take orders from manufacturers, or from warehousemen, and employ as many women, girls, and young children as the size of their rooms and the fluctuating demand of the business will allow. The number of the workwomen employed in these workrooms varies from 20 to 40 in some, and from 10 to 20 in others. The average age at which the children commence work is six years, but in many cases it is below five. The usual working-hours are from 8 in the morning till eight in the evening, with 1½ hours for meals, which are taken at irregular intervals, and often in the foul workrooms. When business is brisk, the labour frequently lasts from 8 or even 6 o'clock in the morning till 10, 11, or 12 o'clock at night. In English barracks the regulation space allotted to each soldier is 500-600 cubic feet, and in the military hospitals 1,200 cubic feet. But, in those finishing sties there are but 67 to 100 cubic feet to each person. At the same time the oxygen of the air is consumed by gas-lights. In order to keep the lace clean, and although the floor is tiled or gagged, the children are often compelled, even in winter, to pull off their shoes.

> 'It is not at all uncommon in Nottingham to find 14 to 20 children huddled together in a small room, of, perhaps, not more than 12 feet square, and employed for 15 hours out of the 24, at work that of itself is exhausting, from its weariness and monotony, and is besides carried on under every possible unwholesome condition.... Even the very youngest children work with a strained attention and a rapidity that is astonishing, hardly ever giving their fingers rest or glowering their motion. If a question be asked them, they never raise their eyes from their work from fear of losing a single moment.'

The 'long stick' is used by the mistresses as a stimulant more and more as the working hours are prolonged.

> 'The children gradually tire and become as restless as birds towards the end of their long detention at an occupation that is monotonous, eye-straining, and exhausting from the uniformity in the posture of the body. Their work is like slavery.'[181]

When women and their children work at home, which now-a-days means in a hired room, often in a garret, the state of things is, if possible, still worse. This sort of work is given out within a circle of 80 miles radius from Nottingham. On leaving the warehouses at 9 or 10 o'clock at night, the children are often given a bundle of lace to take home with them and finish. The Pharisee of a capitalist represented by one of his servants, accompanies this action, of course, with the unctuous phrase: 'That's for mother,' yet he knows well enough that the poor children must sit up and help.[182]

Pillow lace-making is chiefly carried on in England in two agricultural districts; one, the Honiton lace district, extending from 20 to 30 miles along the south coast of Devonshire, and including a few places in North Devon; the other comprising a great part of the counties of Buckingham, Bedford, and Northampton, and also the adjoining portions of Oxfordshire and Huntingdonshire. The cottages of the agricultural labourers are the places where the work is usually carried on. Many manufacturers employ upwards of 3,000 of these lace-makers, who are chiefly children and young persons of the female sex exclusively. The state of things described as incidental to lace finishing is here repeated, save that instead of the 'mistresses' houses,' we find what are called 'lace-schools,' kept by poor women in their cottages. From their fifth year and often earlier, until their twelfth or fifteenth year, the children work in these schools; during the first year the very young ones work from four to eight hours, and later on, from six in the morning till eight and ten o'clock at night.

> 'The rooms are generally the ordinary living rooms of small cottages, the chimney stopped up to keep out draughts, the inmates kept warm by their own animal heat alone, and this frequently in winter. In other cases, these so-called school-rooms are like small store-rooms without fire-places.... The over-crowding in these dens and the consequent vitiation of the air are often extreme. Added to this is the injurious effect of drains, privies, decomposing substances, and other filth usual in the purlieus of the smaller cottages.' With regard to space: 'In one lace-school 18 girls and a mistress, 35 cubic feet to each person; in another, where the smell was unbearable, 18 persons and 24½ cubic feet per head. In this industry are to be found employed children of 2 and 2½ years.'[183]

Where lace-making ends in the counties of Buckingham and Bedford, straw-plaiting begins, and extends over a large part of Hertfordshire and the westerly and northerly parts of Essex. In 1861, there were 40,043 persons employed in straw-plaiting and straw-hat making; of these 3,815 were males of all ages, the rest females, of whom 14,913, including about 7,000 children, were under 20 years of age. In the place of the lace-schools we find here the 'straw-plait schools.' The children commence their instruction in straw-plaiting generally in their 4th, often between their 3rd and 4th year. Education, of course, they get none. The children themselves call the elementary schools, 'natural schools,' to distinguish them from these blood-sucking institutions, in which they are kept at work simply to get through the task, generally 30 yards daily, prescribed by their half-starved mothers. These same mothers often make them work at home, after school is over, till 10, 11, and 12 o'clock at night. The straw cuts their mouths, with which they constantly moisten it, and their fingers. Dr Ballard gives it as the general opinion of the whole body of medical officers in London, that 300 cubic feet is the minimum space proper for each person in a bedroom or workroom. But in the straw-plait schools space is more sparingly allotted than in the lace-schools, '12 2/3, 17, 18½ and below 22 cubic feet for each person.'

> 'The smaller of these numbers, says one of the commissioners, Mr White, represents less space than the half of what a child would occupy if packed in a box measuring 3 feet in each direction.'

Thus do the children enjoy life till the age of 12 or 14. The wretched half-starved parents think of nothing but getting as much as possible out of their children. The latter, as soon as they are grown up, do not care a farthing, and naturally so, for their parents, and leave them.

> 'It is no wonder that ignorance and vice abound in a population so brought up.... Their morality is at the lowest ebb,... a great number of the women have illegitimate

children, and that at such an immature age that even those most conversant with criminal statistics are astounded.'[184]

And the native land of these model families is the pattern Christian country for Europe; so says at least Count Montalembert, certainly a competent authority on Christianity!

Wages in the above industries, miserable as they are (the maximum wages of a child in the straw-plait schools rising in rare cases to 3 shillings), are reduced far below their nominal amount by the prevalence of the truck system everywhere, but especially in the lace districts.[185]

E. Passage of Modern Manufacture, an Domestic Industry into Modern Mechanical Industry. The Hastening of This Revolution by the Application of the Factory Acts to those Industries

The cheapening of labour-power, by sheer abuse of the labour of women and children, by sheer robbery of every normal condition requisite for working and living, and by the sheer brutality of overwork and night-work, meets at last with natural obstacles that cannot be overstepped. So also, when based on these methods, do the cheapening of commodities and capitalist exploitation in general. So soon as this point is at last reached—and it takes many years—the hour has struck for the introduction of machinery, and for the thenceforth rapid conversion of the scattered domestic industries and also of manufactures into factory industries.

An example, on the most colossal scale, of this movement is afforded by the production of wearing apparel. This industry, according to the classification of the Children's Employment Commission, comprises straw-hat makers, ladies'-hat makers, cap-makers, tailors, milliners and dressmakers, shirt-makers, corset-makers, glove-makers, shoemakers, besides many minor branches, such as the making of neck-ties, collars, &c. In 1861, the number of females employed in these industries, in England and Wales, amounted to 586,299, of these 115,242 at the least were under 20, and 16,650. under 15 years of age. The number of these workwomen in the United Kingdom in 1861, was 750,334. The number of males employed in England and Wales, in hat-making, shoemaking, glove-making and tailoring was 437,969; of these 14,964 under 15 years, 89,285 between 15 and 20, and 333,117 over 20 years. Many of the smaller branches are not included in these figures. But take the figures as they stand; we then have for England and Wales alone, according to the census of 1861, a total of 1,024,277 persons, about as many as are absorbed by agriculture and cattle breeding. We begin to understand what becomes of the immense quantities of goods conjured up by the magic of machinery, and of the enormous masses of workpeople, which that machinery sets free.

The production of wearing apparel is carried on partly in manufactories in whose workrooms there is but a reproduction of that division of labour, the membra disjecta of which were found ready to hand; partly by small master-handicraftsmen; these, however, do not, as formerly, work for individual consumers, but for manufactories and warehouses, and to such an extent that often whole towns and stretches of country carry on certain branches, such as shoemaking, as a speciality; finally, on a very great scale by the so-called domestic workers, who form an external department of the manufactories, warehouses, and even of the workshops of the smaller masters.[186]

The raw material, &c., is supplied by mechanical industry, the mass of cheap human material (taillable à merci et miséricorde) is composed of the individuals 'liberated' by mechanical industry and improved agriculture. The manufactures of this class owed their origin chiefly to the capitalist's need of having at hand an army ready equipped to meet any increase of demand.[187] These manufactures, nevertheless, allowed the scattered handicrafts and domestic industries to continue to exist as a broad foundation. The great production of surplus-value in these branches of labour, and the progressive cheapening of their articles, were and are chiefly due to the minimum wages paid, no more than requisite for a miserable vegetation, and to the extension of working-time up to the maximum endurable by the human organism. It was in fact by the cheapness of the human sweat and the human blood, which were converted into commodities, that the markets were constantly being extended, and continue daily to be extended; more especially was this the case with England's colonial markets, where, besides, English tastes and habits prevail. At last the critical point was reached. The basis of the old method, sheer brutality in the exploitation of the workpeople, accompanied more or less by a systematic division of labour, no longer sufficed for the extending markets and for the still more rapidly extending competition of the capitalists. The hour struck for the advent of machinery. The decisively revolutionary machine, the machine which attacks in an equal degree the whole of the numberless branches of this sphere of production, dressmaking, tailoring, shoemaking, sewing, hat-making, and many others, is the sewing-machine.

Its immediate effect on the workpeople is like that of all machinery, which, since the rise of modern industry, has seized upon new branches of trade. Children of too tender an age are sent adrift. The wage of the machine hands rises compared with that of the house-workers, many of whom belong to the poorest of the poor. That of the better situated handicraftsman, with whom the machine competes, sinks. The new machine hands are exclusively girls and young women. With the help of mechanical force, they destroy the monopoly that male labour had of the heavier work, and they drive off from the lighter work numbers of old women and very young children. The overpowering competition crushes the weakest of the manual labourers. The fearful increase in death from starvation during the last 10 years in London runs parallel with the extension of machine sewing.[188] The new workwomen turn the machines by hand and foot, or by hand alone, sometimes sitting, sometimes standing, according to the weight, size, and special make of the machine, and expend a great deal of labour-power. Their occupation is unwholesome, owing to the long hours, although in most cases they are not so long as under the old system. Wherever the sewing-machine locates itself in narrow and already over-crowded workrooms, it adds to the unwholesome influences.

> 'The effect,' says Mr Lord, 'on entering low-ceiled workrooms in which 30 to 40 machine hands are working is unbearable.... The heat, partly due to the gas stoves used for warming the irons, is horrible.... Even when moderate hours of work, i.e., from 8 in the morning till 6 in the evening, prevail in such places, yet 3 or 4 persons fall into a swoon regularly every day.'[189]

The revolution in the industrial methods which is the necessary result of the revolution in the instruments of production, is effected by a medley of transition forms. These forms vary according to the extent to which the sewing-machine has become prevalent in one branch, of industry or the other, to the time during which it has been in operation, to the previous condition of the workpeople, to the preponderance of manufacture, of handicrafts or of domestic industry, to the rent of the workrooms,[190] &c. In dressmaking, for instance, where the labour for the most part was already organised, chiefly by simple co-operation, the sewing-machine at first formed merely a new factor in that manufacturing industry. In tailoring, shirtmaking, shoemaking, &c., all the forms are intermingled. Here the factory system proper. There middlemen receive the raw material from the capitalist *en chef*, and group around their sewing-machines, in 'chambers' and 'garrets,' from 10 to 50 or more workwomen. Finally, as is always the case with machinery when not organised into a system, and when it can also be used in dwarfish proportions, handicraftsman and domestic workers, along with their families, or with a little extra labour from without, make use of their own sewing-machines.[191] The system actually prevalent in England is, that the capitalist concentrates a large number of machines on his premises, and then distributes the produce of those machines for further manipulation amongst the domestic workers.[192] The variety of the transition forms, however, does not conceal the tendency to conversion into the factory system proper. This tendency is nurtured by the very nature of the sewing-machine, the manifold uses of which push on the concentration, under one roof, and one management, of previously separated branches of a trade. It is also favoured by the circumstance that preparatory needlework, and certain other operations, are most conveniently done on the premises where the machine is at work; as well as by the inevitable expropriation of the hand sewers, and of the domestic workers who work with their own machines. This fate has already in part overtaken them. The constantly increasing amount of capital invested in sewing-machines,[193] gives the spur to the production of, and gluts the markets with, machine-made articles, thereby giving the signal to the domestic workers for the sale of their machines. The overproduction of sewing-machines themselves, causes their producers, in bad want of a sale, to let them out for so much a week, thus crushing by their deadly competition the small owners of machines.[194] Constant changes in the construction of the machines, and their ever-increasing cheapness, depreciate day by day the older makes, and allow of their being sold in great numbers, at absurd prices, to large capitalists, who alone can thus employ them at a profit. Finally, the substitution of the steam-engine for man gives in this, as in all similar revolutions, the finishing blow. At first, the use of steam power meets with mere technical difficulties, such as unsteadiness in the machines, difficulty in controlling their speed, rapid wear and tear of the lighter machines, &c., all of which are soon overcome by experience.[195] If, on the one hand, the concentration of many machines in large manufactories leads to the use of steam power, on the other hand, the competition of steam with human muscles hastens on the concentration of workpeople and machines in large factories. Thus, England is at present experiencing, not only in the colossal industry of making wearing apparel, but in most of the other trades mentioned above, the conversion of manufacture, of handicrafts, and of domestic work into the factory system, after each of those forms of production, totally changed and disorganised under the influence of modern industry, has long ago reproduced, and even overdone, all the horrors of the factory system, without participating in any of the elements of social progress it contains.[196]

This industrial revolution which takes place spontaneously, is artificially helped on by the extension of the Factory Acts to all industries in which women, young persons and children are employed. The compulsory regulation of the working-day as regards its length, pauses, beginning and end, the system of relays of children, the exclusion of all children under a certain age, &c., necessitate on the one hand more machinery[197] and the substitution of steam as a motive power in the place of muscles.[198] On the other hand, in order to make up for the loss of time, an expansion occurs of the means of production used in common, of the furnaces, buildings, &c., in one word, greater concentration of the means of production and a correspondingly greater concourse of workpeople. The chief objection, repeatedly and passionately urged on behalf of each manufacture threatened with the Factory Act, is in fact this, that in order to continue the business on the old scale a greater outlay of capital will be necessary. But as regards labour in the so-called domestic industries and the intermediate forms between them and Manufacture, so soon as limits are put to the working-day and to the employment of children, those industries go to the wall. Unlimited exploitation of cheap labour-power is the sole foundation of their power to compete.

One of the essential conditions for the existence of the factory system, especially when the length of the working-day is fixed, is certainty in the result, i.e., the production in a given time of a given quantity of commodities, or of a given useful effect. The statutory pauses in the working-day, moreover, imply the assumption that periodical and sudden cessation of the work does no harm to the article undergoing the process of production. This certainty in the result, and this possibility of interrupting the work are, of course, easier to be attained in the purely mechanical industries than in those in which chemical and physical processes play a part; as, for instance, in the earthenware trade, in bleaching, dyeing, baking, and in most of the metal industries. Wherever there is a working day without restriction as to length, wherever there is night-work and unrestricted waste of human life, there the slightest obstacle presented by the nature of the work to a change for the better is soon looked upon as an everlasting barrier erected by Nature. No poison kills vermin with more certainty than the Factory Act removes such everlasting barriers. No one made a greater outcry over 'impossibilities' than our friends the earthenware manufacturers. In 1864, however, they were brought under the Act, and within sixteen months every 'impossibility' had vanished.

> 'The improved method,' called forth by the Act, 'of making slip by pressure instead of by evaporation, the newly-constructed stoves for drying the ware in its green state, &c., are each events of great importance in the pottery art, and mark an advance which the preceding century could not rival.... It has even considerably reduced the temperature of the stoves themselves with a considerable saving of fuel, and with a readier effect on the ware.'[199]

In spite of every prophecy, the cost-price of earthenware did not rise, but the quantity produced did, and to such an extent that the export for the twelve months, ending December, 1865, exceeded in value by £138,628 the average of the preceding three years. In the manufacture of matches it was thought to be an indispensable requirement, that boys, even while bolting their dinner, should go on dipping the matches in melted phosphorus, the poisonous vapour from which rose into their faces. The Factory Act (1864) made the saving of time a necessity, and so forced into existence a dipping machine, the vapour from which could not come in contact with the workers.[200] So, at the present time, in those branches of the lace manufacture not yet subject to the Factory Act, it is maintained that the meal-times cannot be regular owing to the different periods required by the various kinds of lace for drying, which periods vary from three minutes up to an hour and more. To this the Children's Employment Commissioners answer:

> 'The circumstances of this case are precisely analogous to that of the paper-stainers, dealt with in our first report. Some of the principal manufacturers in the trade urged that in consequence of the nature of the materials used, and their various processes, they would be unable, without serious loss, to stop for meal-times at any given moment. But it was seen from the evidence that, by due care and previous arrangement, the apprehended difficulty would be got over; and accordingly, by clause 6 of section 6 of the Factory Acts Extension Act, passed during this Session of Parliament, an interval of eighteen months is given to them from the passing of the Act before they are required to conform to the meal hours, specified by the Factory Acts.'[201]

Hardly had the Act been passed when our friends the manufacturers found out:

> 'The inconveniences we expected to arise from the introduction of the Factory Acts into our branch of manufacture, I am happy to say, have not arisen. We do not find the production at all interfered with; in short, we produce more in the same time.'[202]

It is evident that the English legislature, which certainly no one will venture to reproach with being overdosed with genius, has been led by experience to the conclusion that a simple compulsory law is sufficient to enact away all the so-called impediments, opposed by the nature of the process, to the restriction and regulation of the working-day. Hence, on the introduction of the Factory Act into a given industry, a period varying from six to eighteen months is fixed within which it is incumbent on the manufacturers to remove all technical impediments to the working of the Act. Mirabeau's 'Impossible! ne me dites jamais ce bête de mot!' is particularly applicable to modern technology. But though the

Factory Acts thus artificially ripen the material elements necessary for the conversion of the manufacturing system into the factory system, yet at the same time, owing to the necessity they impose for greater outlay of capital, they hasten on the decline of the small masters, and the concentration of capital.[203]

Besides the purely technical impediments that are removable by technical means, the irregular habits of the workpeople themselves obstruct the regulation of the hours of labour. This is especially the case where piece-wage predominates, and where loss of time in one part of the day or week can be made good by subsequent over-time, or by night-work, a process which brutalises the adult workman, and ruins his wife and children.[204] Although this absence of regularity in the expenditure of labour-power is a natural and rude reaction against the tedium of monotonous drudgery, it originates, also, to a much greater degree from anarchy in production, anarchy that in its turn pre-supposes unbridled exploitation of labour-power by the capitalist. Besides the general periodic changes of the industrial cycle, and the special fluctuations in the markets to which each industry is subject, we may also reckon what is called 'the season,' dependent either on the periodicity of favourable seasons of the year for navigation; or on fashion, and the sudden placing of large orders that have to be executed in the shortest possible time. The habit of giving such orders becomes more frequent with the extension of railways and telegraphs.

> 'The extension of the railway system throughout the country has tended very much to encourage giving short notice. Purchasers now come up from Glasgow, Manchester, and Edinburgh once every fortnight or so to the wholesale city warehouses which we supply, and give small orders requiring immediate execution, instead of buying from stock as they used to do. Years ago we were always able to work in the slack times, so as to meet demand of the next season, but now no one can say beforehand what will be the demand then.'[205]

In those factories and manufactories that are not yet subject to the Factory Acts, the most fearful over-work prevails periodically during what is called the season, in consequence of sudden orders. In the outside department of the factory, of the manufactory, and of the warehouse, the so-called domestic workers, whose employment is at the best irregular, are entirely dependent for their raw material and their orders on the caprice of the capitalist, who, in this industry, is not hampered by any regard for depreciation of his buildings and machinery, and risks nothing by a stoppage of work, but the skin of the worker himself. Here then he sets himself systematically to work to form an industrial reserve force that shall be ready at a moment's notice; during one part of the year he decimates this force by the most inhuman toil, during the other part, he lets it starve for want of work.

> 'The employers avail themselves of the habitual irregularity in the homework, when any extra work is wanted at a push, so that the work goes on till 11, and 12 p.m. or 2 a.m., or as the usual phrase is, 'all hours,' and that in localities where 'the stench is enough to knock you down, you go to the door, perhaps, and open it, but shudder to go further.'[206] 'They are curious men,' said one of the witnesses, a shoemaker, speaking of the masters, 'they think it does a boy no harm to work too hard for half the year, if he is nearly idle for the other half.'[207]

In the same way as technical impediments, so, too, those 'usages which have grown with the growth of trade' were and still are proclaimed by interested capitalists as obstacles due to the nature of the work. This was a favourite cry of the cotton lords at the time they were first threatened with the Factory Acts. Although their industry more than any other depends on navigation, yet experience has given them the lie. Since then, every pretended obstruction to business has been treated by the Factory inspectors as a mere sham.[208] The thoroughly conscientious investigations of the Children's Employment Commission prove that the effect of the regulation of the hours of work, in some industries, was to spread the mass of labour previously employed more evenly over the whole year[208a] that this regulation was the first rational bridle on the murderous, meaningless caprices of fashion,[208b] caprices that consort so badly with the system of modern industry; that the development of ocean navigation and of the means of communication generally, has swept away the technical basis on which season-work was really supported,[209] and that all other so-called unconquerable difficulties vanish before larger buildings, additional machinery, increase in the number of workpeople employed,[210] and the alterations caused by all these in the mode of conducting the wholesale trade.[211] But for all that, capital never becomes reconciled to such changes—and this is admitted over and over again by its own representatives—except 'under the pressure of a General Act of Parliament'[212] for the compulsory regulation of the hours of labour.

Section 9: *The Factory Acts. Sanitary and Educational Clauses of the Same. Their General Extension in England*

Factory legislation, that first conscious and methodical reaction of society against the spontaneously developed form of the process of production, is, as we have seen, just as much the necessary product of modern industry as cotton yarn, self-actors, and the electric telegraph. Before passing to the consideration of the extension of that legislation in England, we shall shortly notice certain clauses contained in the Factory Acts, and not relating to the hours of work.

Apart from their wording, which makes it easy for the capitalist to evade them, the sanitary clauses are extremely meagre, and, in fact, limited to provisions for whitewashing the walls, for insuring cleanliness in some other matters, for ventilation, and for protection against dangerous machinery. In the third book we shall return again to the fanatical opposition of the masters to those clauses which imposed upon them a slight expenditure on appliances for protecting the limbs of their workpeople, an opposition that throws a fresh and glaring light on the Free-trade dogma, according to which, in a society with conflicting interests, each individual necessarily furthers the common weal by seeking nothing but his own personal advantage! One example is enough. The reader knows that during the last 20 years, the flax industry has very much extended, and that, with that extension, the number of scutching mills in Ireland has increased. In 1864, there were in that country 1,800 of these mills. Regularly in autumn and winter women and 'young persons,' the wives, sons, and daughters of the neighbouring small farmers, a class of people totally unaccustomed to machinery, are taken from field labour to feed the rollers of the scutching mills with flax. The accidents, both as regards number and kind, are wholly unexampled in the history of machinery. In one scutching mill, at Kildinan, near Cork, there occurred between 1852 and 1856, six fatal accidents and sixty mutilations; every one of which might have been prevented by the simplest appliances, at the cost of a few shillings. Dr W. White, the certifying surgeon for factories at Downpatrick, states in his official report, dated the 15th December, 1865:

> 'The serious accidents at the scutching mills are of the most fearful nature. In many cases a quarter of the body is torn from the trunk, and either involves death, or a future of wretched incapacity and suffering. The increase of mills in the country will, of course, extend these dreadful results, and it will be a great boon if they are brought under the legislature. I am convinced that by proper supervision of scutching mills a vast sacrifice of life and limb would be averted.'[213]

What could possibly show better the character of the capitalist mode of production, than the necessity that exists for forcing upon it, by Acts of Parliament, the simplest appliances for maintaining cleanliness and health? In the potteries the Factory Act of 1864 'has whitewashed and cleansed upwards of 200 workshops, after a period of abstinence from any such cleaning, in many cases of 20 years, and in some, entirely,' (this is the 'abstinence' of the capitalist!) 'in which were employed 27,800 artisans, hitherto breathing through protracted days and often nights of labour, a mephitic atmosphere, and which rendered an otherwise comparatively innocuous occupation, pregnant with disease and death. The Act has improved the ventilation very much.'[214]

At the same time, this portion of the Act strikingly shows that the capitalist mode of production, owing to its very nature, excludes all rational improvement beyond a certain point. It has been stated over and over again that the English doctors are unanimous in declaring that where the work is continuous, 500 cubic feet is the very least space that should be allowed for each person. Now, if the Factory Acts, owing to their compulsory provisions, indirectly hasten on the conversion of small workshops into factories, thus indirectly attacking the proprietary rights of the smaller capitalists, and assuring a monopoly to the great ones, so, if it were made obligatory to provide the proper space for each workman in every workshop, thousands of small employers would, at one full swoop, be expropriated directly! The very root of the capitalist mode of production, i.e., the self-expansion of all capital, large or small, by means of the 'free' purchase and consumption of labour-power, would be attacked. Factory legislation is therefore brought to a deadlock before these 500 cubic feet of breathing space. The sanitary officers, the industrial inquiry commissioners, the factory inspectors, all harp, over and over again, upon the necessity for those 500 cubic feet, and upon the impossibility of wringing them out of capital. They thus, in fact, declare that consumption and other lung diseases among the workpeople are necessary conditions to the existence of capital.[215]

Paltry as the education clauses of the Act appear on the whole, yet they proclaim elementary education to be an indispensable condition to the employment of children.[216] The success of those clauses proved for the first time the possibility of combining education and gymnastics[217] with manual labour, and, consequently, of combining manual labour with education and gymnastics. The factory inspectors soon found out by questioning the schoolmasters, that the factory children, although receiving only one half the education of the regular day scholars, yet learnt quite as much and often more.

> 'This can be accounted for by the simple fact that, with only being at school for one half of the day, they are always fresh, and nearly always ready and willing to receive instruction. The system on which they work, half manual labour, and half school, renders each employment a rest and a relief to the other; consequently, both are far more congenial to the child, than would be the case were he kept constantly at one. It is quite clear that a boy who has been at school all the morning, cannot (in hot weather particularly) cope with one who comes fresh and bright from his work.'[218]

Further information on this point will be found in Senior's speech at the Social Science Congress at Edinburgh in 1863. He there shows, amongst other things, how the monotonous and uselessly long school hours of the children of the upper and middle classes, uselessly add to the labour of the teacher, 'while he not only fruitlessly but absolutely injuriously, wastes the time, health, and energy of the children.'[219] From the Factory system budded, as Robert Owen has shown us in detail, the germ of the education of the future, an education that will, in the case of every child over a given age, combine productive labour with instruction and gymnastics, not only as one of the methods of adding to the efficiency of production, but as the only method of producing fully developed human beings.

Modern industry, as we have seen, sweeps away by technical means the manufacturing division of labour, under which each man is bound hand and foot for life to a single detail-operation. At the same time, the capitalistic form of that industry reproduces this same division of labour in a still more monstrous shape; in the factory proper, by converting the workman into a living appendage of the machine; and everywhere outside the Factory, partly by the sporadic use of machinery and machine workers,[220] partly by re-establishing the division of labour on a fresh basis by the general introduction of the labour of women and children, and of cheap unskilled labour.

The antagonism between the manufacturing division of labour and the methods of modern industry makes itself forcibly felt. It manifests itself, amongst other ways, in the frightful fact that a great part of the children employed in modern factories and manufactures, are from their earliest years riveted to the most simple manipulations, and exploited for years, without being taught a single sort of work that would afterwards make them of use, even in the same manufactory or factory. In the English letter-press printing trade, for example, there existed formerly a system, corresponding to that in the old manufactures and handicrafts, of advancing the apprentices from easy to more and more difficult work. They went through a course of teaching till they were finished printers. To be able to read and write was for every one of them a requirement of their trade. All this was changed by the printing machine. It employs two sorts of labourers, one grown up, renters, the other, boys mostly from 11 to 17 years of age whose sole business is either to spread the sheets of paper under the machine, or to take from it the printed sheets. They perform this weary task, in London especially, for 14, 15, and 16 hours at a stretch, during several days in the week, and frequently for 36 hours, with only 2 hours' rest for meals and sleep.[221] A great part of them cannot read, and they are, as a rule, utter savages and very extraordinary creatures.

> 'To qualify them for the work which they have to do, they require no intellectual training; there is little room in it for skill, and less for judgment; their wages, though rather high for boys, do not increase proportionately as they grow up, and the majority of them cannot look for advancement to the better paid and more responsible post of machine minder, because while each machine has but one minder, it has at least two, and often four boys attached to it.'[222]

As soon as they get too old for such child's work, that is about 17 at the latest, they are discharged from the printing establishments. They become recruits of crime. Several attempts to procure them employment elsewhere, were rendered of no avail by their ignorance and brutality, and by their mental and bodily degradation.

As with the division of labour in the interior of the manufacturing workshops, so it is with the division of labour in the interior of society. So long as handicraft and manufacture form the general groundwork of social production, the subjection of the producer to one branch exclusively, the breaking up of the multifariousness of his employment,[223] is a necessary step in the development. On that groundwork each separate branch of production acquires empirically the form that is technically suited to it, slowly perfects it, and, so soon as a given degree of maturity has been reached, rapidly crystallises that form. The only thing, that here and there causes a change, besides new raw material supplied by commerce, is the gradual alteration of the instruments of labour. But their form, too, once definitely settled by experience, petrifies, as is proved by their being in many cases handed down in the same form by one generation to another during thousands of years. A characteristic feature is, that, even down into the eighteenth century, the different trades were called 'mysteries' (mystères);[224] into their secrets none but those duly initiated could penetrate. modern industry rent the veil that concealed from men their own social process of production, and that turned the various, spontaneously divided branches of production into so many riddles, not only to outsiders, but even to the initiated. The principle which it pursued, of resolving each process into its constituent movements, without any regard to their possible execution by the hand of man, created the new modern science of technology. The varied, apparently unconnected, and petrified forms of the industrial processes now resolved themselves into so many conscious and systematic applications of natural science to the attainment of given useful effects. Technology also discovered the few main fundamental forms of motion, which, despite the diversity of the instruments used, are necessarily taken by every productive action of the human body; just as the science of mechanics sees in the most complicated machinery nothing but the continual repetition of the simple mechanical powers.

Modern industry never looks upon and treats the existing form of a process as final. The technical basis of that industry is therefore revolutionary, while all earlier modes of production were essentially conservative.[225] By means of machinery, chemical processes and other methods, it is continually causing changes not only in the technical basis of production, but also in the functions of the labourer, and in the social combinations of the labour-process. At the same time, it thereby also revolutionises the division of labour within the society, and incessantly launches masses of capital and of workpeople from one branch of production to another. But, if modern industry, by its very nature, therefore necessitates variation of labour, fluency of function, universal mobility of the labourer, on the other hand, in its capitalistic form, it reproduces the old division of labour with its ossified particularisations. We have seen how this absolute contradiction between the technical necessities of modern industry, and the social character inherent in its capitalistic form, dispels all fixity and security in the situation of the labourer; how it constantly threatens, by taking away the instruments of labour, to snatch from his hands his means of subsistence,[226] and, by suppressing his detail-function, to make him superfluous, we have seen, too, how this antagonism vents its rage in the creation of that monstrosity, an industrial reserve army, kept in misery in order to be always at the disposal of capital; in the incessant human sacrifices from among the working-class, in the most reckless squandering of labour-power and in the devastation caused by a social anarchy which turns every economic progress into a social calamity. This is the negative side. But if, on the one hand, variation of work at present imposes itself after the manner of an overpowering natural law, and with the blindly destructive action of a natural law that meets with resistance[227] at all points, modern industry, on the other hand, through its catastrophes imposes the necessity of recognising, as a fundamental law of production, variation of work, consequently fitness of the labourer for varied work, consequently the greatest possible development of his varied aptitudes. It becomes a question of life and death for society to adapt the mode of production to the normal functioning of this law. Modern Industry, indeed, compels society, under penalty of death, to replace the detail-worker of to-day, grappled by life-long repetition of one and the same trivial operation, and thus reduced to the mere fragment of a man, by the fully developed individual, fit for a variety of labours, ready to face any change of production, and to whom the different social functions he performs, are but so many modes of giving free scope to his own natural and acquired powers.

One step already spontaneously taken towards effecting this revolution is the establishment of technical and agricultural schools, and of 'écoles d'enseignement professionnel,' in which the children of the working-men receive some little instruction in technology and in the practical handling of the various implements of labour. Though the Factory Act, that first and meagre concession wrung from capital, is limited to combining elementary education with work in the factory, there can be no doubt that when the working-class comes into power, as inevitably it must, technical instruction, both theoretical and practical, will take its proper place in the working-class schools. There is also no doubt that such revolutionary ferments, the final result of which is the abolition of the old division of labour, are diametrically opposed to the capitalistic form of production, and to the economic status of the labourer corresponding to that form. But the historical development of the antagonisms, immanent in a given form of production, is the only way in which that form of production can be dissolved and a new form established. 'Ne sutor ultra crepidam'—this nec plus ultra of handicraft wisdom became sheer nonsense, from the moment the watchmaker Watt invented the steam-engine, the barber Arkwright, the throstle, and the working-jeweller, Fulton, the steamship.[228]

So long as Factory legislation is confined to regulating the labour in factories, manufactories, &c., it is regarded as a mere interference with the exploiting rights of capital. But when it comes to regulating the so-called 'home-labour,'[229] it is immediately viewed as a direct attack on the patria potestas, on parental authority. The tender-hearted English Parliament long affected to shrink from taking this step. The force of facts, however, compelled it at last to acknowledge that modern industry, in overturning the economic foundation on which was based the traditional family, and the family labour corresponding to it, had also unloosened all traditional family ties. The rights of the children had to be proclaimed. The final report of the Ch. Empl. Comm. of 1866, states:

> 'It is unhappily, to a painful degree, apparent throughout the whole of the evidence, that against no persons do the children of both sexes so much require protection as against their parents.' The system of unlimited exploitation of children's labour in general and the so-called home-labour in particular is "maintained only because the parents are able, without check or control, to exercise this arbitrary and mischievous power over their young and tender offspring.... Parents must not possess the absolute power of making their children mere 'machines to earn so much weekly wage....' The children and young persons, therefore, in all such cases may justifiably claim from the legislature, as a natural right, that an exemption should be secured to them, from what destroys prematurely their physical strength, and lowers them in the scale of intellectual and moral beings.'[230]

It was not, however, the misuse of parental authority that created the capitalistic exploitation, whether direct or indirect, of children's labour; but, on the contrary, it was the capitalistic mode of exploitation which, by sweeping away the economic basis of parental authority, made its exercise degenerate into a mischievous misuse of power. However terrible and disgusting the dissolution, under the capitalist system, of the old family ties may appear, nevertheless, modern industry, by assigning as it does an important part in the process of production, outside the domestic sphere, to women, to young persons, and to children of both sexes, creates a new economic foundation for a higher form of the family and of the relations between the sexes. It is, of course, just as absurd to hold the Teutonic-Christian form of the family to be absolute and final as it would be to apply that character to the ancient Roman, the ancient Greek, or the Eastern forms which, moreover, taken together form a series in historical development. Moreover, it is obvious that the fact of the collective working group being composed of individuals of both sexes and all ages, must necessarily, under suitable conditions, become a source of humane development; although in its spontaneously developed, brutal, capitalistic form, where the labourer exists for the process of production, and not the process of production for the labourer, that fact is a pestiferous source of corruption and slavery.[231]

The necessity for a generalisation of the Factory Acts, for transforming them from an exceptional law relating to mechanical spinning and weaving—those first creations of machinery—into a law affecting social production as a whole, arose, as we have seen, from the mode in which modern industry was historically developed. In the rear of that industry, the traditional form of manufacture, of handicraft, and of domestic industry, is entirely revolutionised; manufactures are constantly passing into the factory system, and handicrafts into manufactures; and lastly, the spheres of handicraft and of the domestic industries become, in a, comparatively speaking, wonderfully short time, dens of misery in which capitalistic exploitation obtains free play for the wildest excesses. There are two circumstances that finally turn the scale: first, the constantly recurring experience that capital, so soon as it finds itself subject to legal control at one point, compensates itself all the more recklessly at other points;[232]

secondly, the cry of the capitalists for equality in the conditions of competition, i.e., for equal restrain on all exploitation of labour.[233] On this point let us listen to two heart-broken cries. Messrs. Cooksley of Bristol, nail and chain, &c., manufacturers, spontaneously introduced the regulations of the Factory Act into their business.

> 'As the old irregular system prevails in neighbouring works, the Messrs. Cooksley are subject to the disadvantage of having their boys enticed to continue their labour elsewhere after 6 p.m. 'This,' they naturally say, 'is an unjustice and loss to us, as it exhausts a portion of the boy's strength, of which we ought to have the full benefit'.'[234]

Mr J. Simpson (paper box and bagmaker, London) states before the commissioners of the Ch. Empl. Comm.:

> 'He would sign any petition for it' (legislative interference)... 'As it was, he always felt restless at night, when he had closed his place, lest others should be working later than him and getting away his orders.'[235]

Summarising, the Ch. Empl. Comm. says:

> 'It would be unjust to the larger employers that their factories should be placed under regulation, while the hours of labour in the smaller places in their own branch of business were under no legislative restriction. And to the injustice arising from the unfair conditions of competition, in regard to hours, that would be created if the smaller places of work were exempt, would be added the disadvantage to the larger manufacturers, of finding their supply of juvenile and female labour drawn off to the places of work exempt from legislation. Further, a stimulus would be given to the multiplication of the smaller places of work, which are almost invariably the least favourable to the health, comfort, education, and general improvement of the people.'[236]

In its final report the Commission proposes to subject to the Factory Act more than 1,400,000 children, young persons, and women, of which number about one half are exploited in small industries and by the so-called home-work.[237] It says,

> 'But if it should seem fit to Parliament to place the whole of that large number of children, young persons and females under the protective legislation above adverted to ... it cannot be doubted that such legislation would have a most beneficent effect, not only upon the young and the feeble, who are its more immediate objects, but upon the still larger body of adult workers, who would in all these employments, both directly and indirectly, come immediately under its influence. It would enforce upon them regular and moderate hours; it would lead to their places of work being kept in a healthy and cleanly state; it would therefore husband and improve that store of physical strength on which their own well-being and that of the country so much depends; it would save the rising generation from that overexertion at an early age which undermines their constitutions and leads to premature decay; finally, it would ensure them—at least up to the age of 13—the opportunity of receiving the elements of education, and would put an end to that utter ignorance ... so faithfully exhibited in the Reports of our Assistant Commissioners, and which cannot be regarded without the deepest pain, and a profound sense of national degradation.'[238]

The Tory Cabinet[239] announced in the Speech from the Throne, on February 5, 1867, that it had framed the proposals of the Industrial Commission of Inquiry[240] into Bills. To get that far, another twenty years of *experimentum in corpore vili* had been required. Already in 1840 a Parliamentary Commission of Inquiry on the labour of children had been appointed. Its Report, in 1842, unfolded, in the words of Nassau W. Senior, 'the most frightful picture of avarice, selfishness and cruelty on the part of masters and of parents, and of juvenile and infantile misery, degradation and destruction ever presented.... It may be supposed that it describes the horrors of a past age. But there is unhappily evidence that those horrors continue as intense as they were. A pamphlet published by Hardwicke about 2 years ago states that the abuses complained of in 1842, are in full bloom at the present day. It is a strange proof of the general neglect of the morals and health of the children of the working-class, that this report lay unnoticed for 20 years, during which the children, 'bred up without the remotest sign of comprehension as to what is meant by the term morals, who had neither knowledge, nor religion, nor natural affection,' were allowed to become the parents of the present generation.'[241]

The social conditions having undergone a change, Parliament could not venture to shelve the demands of the Commission of 1862, as it had done those of the Commission of 1840. Hence in 1864, when the Commission had not yet published more than a part of its reports, the earthenware industries (including the potteries), makers of paperhangings, matches, cartridges, and caps, and fustian cutters were made subject to the Acts in force in the textile industries. In the Speech from the Throne, on 5th February, 1867, the Tory Cabinet of the day announced the introduction of Bills, founded on the final recommendations of the Commission, which had completed its labours in 1866.

On the 15th August, 1867, the Factory Acts Extension Act, and on the 21st August, the Workshops' Regulation Act received the Royal Assent; the former Act having reference to large industries, the latter to small.

The former applies to blast-furnaces, iron and copper mills, foundries, machine shops, metal manufactories, gutta-percha works, paper mills, glass-works, tobacco manufactories, letter-press printing (including newspapers), book-binding, in short to all industrial establishments of the above kind, in which 50 individuals or more are occupied simultaneously, and for not less than 100 days during the year.

To give an idea of the extent of the sphere embraced by the Workshops' Regulation Act in its application, we cite from its interpretation clause, the following passages:

'*Handicraft* shall mean any manual labour exercised by way of trade, or for purposes of gain in, or incidental to, the making any article or part of an article, or in, or incidental to, the altering, repairing, ornamenting, finishing, or otherwise adapting for sale any article.'

'*Workshop* shall mean any room or place whatever in the open air or undercover, in which any handicraft is carried on by any child, young person, or woman, and to which and over which the person by whom such child, young person, or woman is employed, has the right of access and control.'

'*Employed* shall mean occupied in any handicraft, whether for wages or not, under a master or under a parent as herein defined.'

'*Parent* shall mean parent, guardian, or person, having the custody of, or control over, any... child or young person.'

Clause 7, which imposes a penalty for employment of children, young persons, and women, contrary to the provisions of the Act, subjects to fines, not only the occupier of the workshop, whether parent or not, but even

'the parent of, or the person deriving any direct benefit from the labour of, or having the control over, the child, young person or woman.'

The Factory Acts Extension Act, which affects the large establishments, derogates from the Factory Act by a crowd of vicious exceptions and cowardly compromises with the masters.

The Workshops' Regulation Act, wretched in all its details, remained a dead letter in the hands of the municipal and local authorities who were charged with its execution. When, in 1871, Parliament withdrew from them this power, in order to confer it on the Factory Inspectors, to whose province it thus added by a single stroke more than one hundred thousand workshops, and three hundred brickworks, care was taken at the same time not to add more than eight assistants to their already undermanned staff.[242]

What strikes us, then, in the English legislation of 1867, is, on the one hand, the necessity imposed on the parliament of the ruling classes, of adopting in principle measures so extraordinary, and on so great a scale, against the excesses of capitalistic exploitation; and on the other hand, the hesitation, the repugnance, and the bad faith, with which it lent itself to the task of carrying those measures into practice.

The Inquiry Commission of 1862 also proposed a new regulation of the mining industry, an industry distinguished from others by the exceptional characteristic that the interests of landlord and capitalist there join hands. The antagonism of these two interests had been favourable to Factory legislation, while on the other hand the absence of that antagonism is sufficient to explain the delays and chicanery of the legislation on mines.

The Inquiry Commission of 1840 had made revelations so terrible, so shocking, and creating such a scandal all over Europe, that to salve its conscience Parliament passed the Mining Act of 1842, in which it limited itself to forbidding the employment underground in mines of children under 10 years of age and females.

Then another Act, The Mines' Inspecting Act of 1860, provides that mines shall be inspected by public officers nominated specially for that purpose, and that boys between the ages of 10 and 12 years shall not be employed, unless they have a school certificate, or go to school for a certain number of hours. This Act was a complete dead letter owing to the ridiculously small number of inspectors, the meagreness of their powers, and other causes that will become apparent as we proceed.

One of the most recent Blue books on mines is the 'Report from the Select Committee on Mines, together with &c. Evidence, 23rd July, 1866.' This Report is the work of a Parliamentary Committee selected from members of the House of Commons, and authorised to summon and examine witnesses. It is a thick folio volume in which the Report itself occupies only five lines to this effect; that the committee has nothing to say, and that more witnesses must be examined!

The mode of examining the witnesses reminds one of the cross-examination of witnesses in English courts of justice, where the advocate tries, by means of impudent, unexpected, equivocal and involved questions, put without connexion, to intimidate, surprise, and confound the witness, and to give a forced meaning to the answers extorted from him. In this inquiry the members of the committee themselves are the cross-examiners, and among them are to be found both mine-owners and mine exploiters; the witnesses are mostly working coal miners. The whole farce is too characteristic of the spirit of capital, not to call for a few extracts from this Report. For the sake of conciseness I have classified them. I may also add that every question and its answer are numbered in the English Blue books.

1. Employment in mines of boys of 10 years and upwards: In the mines the work, inclusive of going and returning, usually lasts 14 or 15 hours, sometimes even from 3, 4 and 5 o'clock a.m., till 5 and 6 o'clock p.m. (n. 6, 452, 83). The adults work in two shifts, of eight hours each; but there is no alternation with the boys, on account of the expense (n. 80, 203, 204). The younger boys are chiefly employed in opening and shutting the ventilating doors in the various parts of the mine; the older ones are employed on heavier work, in carrying coal, &c. (n. 122, 739, 1747). They work these long hours underground until their 18th or 22nd year, when they are put to miner's work proper (n. 161). Children and young persons are at present worse treated, and harder worked than at any previous period (n. 1663-1667). The miners demand almost unanimously an act of Parliament prohibiting the employment in mines of children under 14. And now Hussey Vivian (himself an exploiter of mines) asks:

> 'Would not the opinion of the workman depend upon the poverty of the workman's family?' Mr Bruce: 'Do you not think it would be a very hard case, where a parent had been injured, or where he was sickly, or where a father was dead, and there was only a mother, to prevent a child between 12 and 14 earning 1s. 7d. a day for the good of the family? ... You must lay down a general rule? ... Are you prepared to recommend legislation which would prevent the employment of children under 12 and 14, whatever the state of their parents might be?' 'Yes.' (ns. 107-110). Vivian: 'Supposing that an enactment were passed preventing the employment of children under the age of 14, would it not be probable that ... the parents of children would seek employment for their children in other directions, for instance, in manufacture?' 'Not generally I think' (n. 174). Kinnaird: 'Some of the boys are keepers of doors?' 'Yes.' 'Is there not generally a very great draught every time you open a door or close it?' 'Yes, generally there is.' 'It sounds a very easy thing, but it is in fact rather a painful one?' 'He is imprisoned there just the same as if he was in a cell of a gaol.' Bourgeois Vivian: 'Whenever a boy is furnished with a lamp cannot he read?' 'Yes, he can read, if he finds himself in candles.... I suppose he would be found fault with if he were discovered reading; he is there to mind his business, he has a duty to perform, and he has to attend to it in the first place, and I do not think it would be allowed down the pit.' (ns. 139, 141, 143, 158, 160).

II. Education: The working miners want a law for the compulsory education of their children, as in factories. They declare the clauses of the Act of 1860, which require a school certificate to be obtained before employing boys of 10 and 12 years of age, to be quite illusory. The examination of the witnesses on this subject is truly droll.

> 'Is it (the Act) required more against the masters or against the parents?' 'It is required against both I think.' 'You cannot say whether it is required against one more than against the other?' 'No; I can hardly answer that question.' (ns. 115, 116). 'Does there appear to be any desire on the part of the employers that the boys should have such hours as to enable them to go to school?' 'No; the hours are never shortened for that purpose.' (n. 137) Mr Kinnaird: 'Should you say that the colliers generally improve their education; have you any instances of men who have, since they began to work, greatly improved their education, or do they not rather go back, and lose any advantage that they may have gained?' 'They generally become worse: they do not improve; they acquire bad habits; they get on to drinking and gambling and such like, and they go completely to wreck.' (n. 211.) 'Do they make any attempt of the kind (for providing instruction) by having schools at night?' 'There are few collieries where night schools are held, and perhaps at those collieries a few boys do go to those schools; but they are so physically exhausted that it is to no purpose that they go there.' (n. 454.) 'You are then,' concludes the bourgeois, 'against education?' 'Most certainly not; but,' &c. (n. 443.) 'But are they (the employers) not compelled to demand them (school certificates)?' 'By law they are; but I am not aware that they are demanded by the employers.' 'Then it is your opinion, that this provision of the Act as to requiring certificates, is not generally carried out in the collieries?' 'It is not carried out.' (ns. 443, 444.) 'Do the men take a great interest in this question (of education)?' 'The majority of them do.' (n. 717.) 'Are they very anxious to see the law enforced?' 'The majority are.' (n. 718.) 'Do you think that in this country any law that you pass ... can really be effectual unless the population themselves assist in putting it into operation?' 'Many a man might wish to object to employing a boy, but he would perhaps become marked by it.' (n. 720.) 'Marked by whom?' 'By his employers.' (n. 721.) 'Do you think that the employers would find any fault with a man who obeyed the

law... ?' 'I believe they would.' (n. 722.) 'Have you ever heard of any workman objecting to employ a boy between 10 and 12, who could not write or read?' 'It is not left to men's option.' (n. 123.) 'Would you call for the interference of Parliament?' 'I think that if anything effectual is to be done in the education of the colliers' children, it will have to be made compulsory by Act of Parliament.' (n. 1634.) 'Would you lay that obligation upon the colliers only, or all the workpeople of Great Britain?' 'I came to speak for the colliers.' (n. 1636.) 'Why should you distinguish them (colliery boys) from other boys?' 'Because I think they are an exception to the rule.' (n. 1638.) 'In what respect?' 'In a physical respect.' (n. 1639.) 'Why should education be more valuable to them than to other classes of lads?' 'I do not know that it is more valuable; but through the over-exertion in mines there is less chance for the boys that are employed there to get education, either at Sunday schools, or at day schools.' (n. 1640.) 'It is impossible to look at a question of this sort absolutely by itself?' (n. 1644.) 'Is there a sufficiency of schools?'—'No"... (n. 1646). 'If the State were to require that every child should be sent to school, would there be schools for the children to go to?' 'No; but I think if the circumstances were to spring up, the schools would be forthcoming.' (n. 1647.) 'Some of them (the boys) cannot read and write at all, I suppose?' 'The majority cannot... The majority of the men themselves cannot.' (ns. 705, 725.)

III. Employment of women: Since 1842, women are no more employed underground, but are occupied on the surface in loading the coal, &c., in drawing the tubs to the canals and railway waggons, in sorting, &c. Their numbers have considerably increased during the last three or four years. (n. 1727.) They are mostly the wives, daughters, and widows of the working miners, and their ages range from 12 to 50 or 60 years. (ns. 645, 1779.)

'What is the feeling among the working miners as to the employment of women?' 'I think they generally condemn it.' (n. 648.) 'What objection do you see to it?' 'I think it is degrading to the sex.' (n. 649.) 'There is a peculiarity of dress?' 'Yes ... it is rather a man's dress, and I believe in some cases, it drowns all sense of decency.' 'Do the women smoke?' 'Some do.' 'And I suppose it is very dirty work?' 'Very dirty.' 'They get black and grimy?' 'As black as those who are down the mines ... I believe that a woman having children (and there are plenty on the banks that have) cannot do her duty to her children.' (ns. 650-654, 701.) 'Do you think that those widows could get employment anywhere else, which would bring them in as much wages as that (from 8s. to 10s. a week)?' 'I cannot speak to that.' (n. 709.) 'You would still be prepared, would you,' (flint-hearted fellow!) 'to prevent their obtaining a livelihood by these means?' 'I would.' (n. 710.) 'What is the general feeling in the district ... as to the employment of women?' 'The feeling is that it is degrading; and we wish as miners to have more respect to the fair sex than to see them placed on the pit bank... Some part of the work is very hard; some of these girls have raised as much as 10 tons of stuff a day.' (ns. 1715,1717.) 'Do you think that the women employed about the collieries are less moral than the women employed in the factories?' '. ..the percentage of bad ones may be a little more ... than with the girls in the factories.' (n. 1237.) 'But you are not quite satisfied with the state of morality in the factories?' 'No.' (n. 1733.) 'Would you prohibit the employment of women in factories also?' 'No, I would not.' (n. 1734.) 'Why not?' 'I think it a more honourable occupation for them in the mills.' (n. 1735.) 'Still it is injurious to their morality, you think?' 'Not so much as working on the pit bank; but it is more on the social position I take it; I do not take it on its moral ground alone. The degradation, in its social bearing on the girls, is deplorable in the extreme. When these 400 or 500 girls become colliers' wives, the men suffer greatly from this degradation, and it causes them to leave their homes and drink.' (n. 1736.) 'You would be obliged to stop the employment of women in the ironworks as well, would you not, if you stopped it in the

> collieries?' 'I cannot speak for any other trade.' (n. 1737.) 'Can you see any difference in the circumstances of women employed in ironworks, and the circumstances of women employed above ground in collieries?' 'I have not ascertained anything as to that.' (n. 1740.) 'Can you see anything that makes a distinction between one class and the other?' 'I have not ascertained that, but I know from house to house visitation, that it is a deplorable state of things in our district....' (n. 1741.) 'Would you interfere in every case with the employment of women where that employment was degrading?' 'It would become injurious, I think, in this way: the best feelings of Englishmen have been gained from the instruction of a mother. ...' (n. 1750.) 'That equally applies to agricultural employments, does it not?' 'Yes, but that is only for two seasons, and we have work all the four seasons.' (n. 1751.) 'They often work day and night, wet through to the skin, their constitution undermined and their health ruined.' 'You have not inquired into that subject perhaps?' 'I have certainly taken note of it as I have gone along, and certainly I have seen nothing parallel to the effects of the employment of women on the pit bank.... It is the work of a man... a strong man.' (ns. 1753, 1793, 1794.) 'Your feeling upon the whole subject is that the better class of colliers who desire to raise themselves and humanise themselves, instead of deriving help from the women, are pulled down by them?' 'Yes.' (n. 1808.) After some further crooked questions from these bourgeois, the secret of their 'sympathy' for widows, poor families, &c., comes out at last. 'The coal proprietor appoints certain gentlemen to take the oversight of the workings, and it is their policy, in order to receive approbation, to place things on the most economical basis they can, and these girls are employed at from 1s. up to 1s. 6d. a day, where a man at the rate of 2s. 6d. a day would have to be employed.' (n. 1816.)

IV. Coroner's inquests:
'With regard to coroner's inquests in your district, have the workmen confidence in the proceedings at those inquests when accidents occur?' 'No; they have not.' (n. 360.) 'Why not?' 'Chiefly because the men who are generally chosen, are men who know nothing about mines and such like.' 'Are not workmen summoned at all upon the juries?' 'Never but as witnesses to my knowledge.' 'Who are the people who are generally summoned upon these juries?' 'Generally tradesmen in the neighbourhood ... from their circumstances they are sometimes liable to be influenced by their employers ... the owners of the works. They are generally men who have no knowledge, and can scarcely understand the witnesses who are called before them, and the terms which are used and such like.' 'Would you have the jury composed of persons who had been employed in mining?' 'Yes, partly... they (the workmen) think that the verdict is not in accordance with the evidence given generally.' (ns. 361, 364, 366, 368, 371, 375.) 'One great object in summoning a jury is to have an impartial one, is it not?' 'Yes, I should think so.' 'Do you think that the juries would be impartial if they were composed to a considerable extent of workmen?' 'I cannot see any motive which the workmen would have to act partially ... they necessarily have a better knowledge of the operations in connexion with the mine.' 'You do not think there would be a tendency on the part of the workmen to return unfairly severe verdicts?' 'No, I think not.' (ns. 378, 379, 380.)

V. False weights and measures: The workmen demand to be paid weekly instead of fortnightly, and by weight instead of by cubical contents of the tubs; they also demand protection against the use of false weights, &c. (n. 1071.)

> 'If the tubs were fraudulently increased, a man could discontinue working by giving 14 days' notice?' 'But if he goes to another place, there is the same thing going on there.' (n. 1071.) 'But he can leave that place where the wrong has been committed?' 'It is general; wherever he goes, he has to submit to it.' (n. 1072.) 'Could a man leave by giving 14 days' notice?' 'Yes.' (n. 1073.) And yet they are not satisfied!

VI. Inspection of mines: Casualties from explosions are not the only things the workmen suffer from. (n. 234, sqq.)

> 'Our men complained very much of the bad ventilation of the collieries ... the ventilation is so bad in general that the men can scarcely breathe; they are quite unfit for employment of any kind after they have been for a length of time in connexion with their work; indeed, just at the part of the mine where I am working, men have been obliged to leave their employment and come home in consequence of that ... some of them have been out of work for weeks just in consequence of the bad state of the ventilation where there is not explosive gas ... there is plenty of air generally in the main courses, yet pains are not taken to get air into the workings where men are working.' 'Why do you not apply to the inspector?' 'To tell the truth there are many men who are timid on that point; there have been cases of men being sacrificed and losing their employment in consequence of applying to the inspector.' 'Why is he a marked man for having complained?' 'Yes...... And he finds it difficult to get employment in another mine?' 'Yes.' 'Do you think the mines in your neighbourhood are sufficiently inspected to insure a compliance with the provisions of the Act?' 'No; they are not inspected at all ... the inspector has been down just once in the pit, and it has been going seven years.... In the district to which I belong there are not a sufficient number of inspectors. We have one old man more than 70 years of age to inspect more than 130 collieries.' 'You wish to have a class of sub-inspectors?' 'Yes.' (ns. 234, 241, 251, 254, 274, 275, 554, 276, 293.) 'But do you think it would be possible for Government to maintain such an army of inspectors as would be necessary to do all that you want them to do, without information from the men?' 'No, I should think it would be next to impossible....' 'It would be desirable the inspectors should come oftener?' 'Yes, and without being sent for.' (n. 280, 277.) 'Do you not think that the effect of having these inspectors examining the collieries so frequently would be to shift the responsibility (!) of supplying proper ventilation from the owners of the collieries to the Government officials?' 'No, I do not think that, I think that they should make it their business to enforce the Acts which are already in existence.' (n. 285.) 'When you speak of sub-inspectors, do you mean men at a less salary, and of an inferior stamp to the present inspectors?' 'I would not have them inferior, if you could get them otherwise.' (n. 294.) 'Do you merely want more inspectors, or do you want a lower class of men as an inspector?' 'A man who would knock about, and see that things are kept right; a man who would not be afraid of himself.' (n. 295.) 'If you obtained your wish in getting an inferior class of inspectors appointed, do you think that there would be no danger from want of skill, &c?' 'I think not, I think that the Government would see after that, and have proper men in that position.' (n. 297.)

This kind of examination becomes at last too much even for the chairman of the committee, and he interrupts with the observation:

> 'You want a class of men who would look into all the details of the mine, and would go into all the holes and corners, and go into the real facts ... they would report to the chief inspector, who would then bring his scientific knowledge to bear on the facts they have stated?' (ns. 298, 299.) 'Would it not entail very great expense if all these old workings were kept ventilated?' 'Yes, expense might be incurred, but life would be at the same time protected.' (n. 531.)

A working miner objects to the 17th section of the Act of 1860; he says,

> 'At the present time, if the inspector of mines finds a part of the mine unfit to work in, he has to report it to the mine-owner and the Home Secretary. After doing that,

> there is given to the owner 20 days to look over the matter; at the end of 20 days he has the power to refuse making any alteration in the mine; but, when he refuses, the mine-owner writes to the Home Secretary, at the same time nominating five engineers, and from those five engineers named by the mine-owner himself, the Home Secretary appoints one, I think, as arbitrator, or appoints arbitrators from them; now we think in that case the mine-owner virtually appoints his own arbitrator.' (n. 581.)

Bourgeois examiner, himself a mine-owner:

> 'But ... is this a merely speculative objection?' (n. 586.) 'Then you have a very poor opinion of the integrity of mining engineers?' 'It is most certainly unjust and inequitable.' (n. 588.) 'Do not mining engineers possess a sort of public character, and do not you think that they are above making such a partial decision as you apprehend?' 'I do not wish to answer such a question as that with respect to the personal character of those men. I believe that in many cases they would act very partially indeed, and that it ought not to be in their hands to do so, where men's lives are at stake.' (n. 589.)

This same bourgeois is not ashamed to put this question: 'Do you not think that the mine-owner also suffers loss from an explosion?' Finally, 'Are not you workmen in Lancashire able to take care of your own interests without calling in the Government to help you?' 'No.' (n. 1042.)

In the year 1865 there were 3,217 coal mines in Great Britain, and 12 inspectors. A Yorkshire mine-owner himself calculates (*Times*, 26th January, 1867), that putting on one side their office work, which absorbs all their time, each mine can be visited but once in ten years by an inspector. No wonder that explosions have increased progressively, both in number and extent (sometimes with a loss of 200-300 men), during the last ten years. These are the beauties of 'free' capitalist production! *[This sentence has been added to the English text in conformity with the 4th German edition.—Ed.]*

The very defective Act, passed in 1872, is the first that regulates the hours of labour of the children employed in mines, and makes exploiters and owners, to a certain extent, responsible for so-called accidents.

The Royal Commission appointed in 1867 to inquire into the employment in agriculture of children, young persons, and women, has published some very important reports. Several attempts to apply the principles of the Factory Acts, but in a modified form, to agriculture have been made, but have so far resulted in complete failure. All that I wish to draw attention to here is the existence of an irresistible tendency towards the general application of those principles.

If the general extension of factory legislation to all trades for the purpose of protecting the working-class both in mind and body has become inevitable, on the other hand, as we have already pointed out, that extension hastens on the general conversion of numerous isolated small industries into a few combined industries carried on upon a large scale; it therefore accelerates the concentration of capital and the exclusive predominance of the factory system. It destroys both the ancient and the transitional forms, behind which the dominion of capital is still in part concealed, and replaces them by the direct and open sway of capital; but thereby it also generalises the direct opposition to this sway. While in each individual workshop it enforces uniformity, regularity, order, and economy, it increases by the immense spur which the limitation and regulation of the working-day give to technical improvement, the anarchy and the catastrophes of capitalist production as a whole, the intensity of labour, and the competition of machinery with the labourer. By the destruction of petty and domestic industries it destroys the last resort of the 'redundant population,' and with it the sole remaining safety-valve of the whole social mechanism. By maturing the material conditions, and the combination on a social scale of the processes of production, it matures the contradictions and antagonisms of the capitalist form of production, and thereby provides, along with the elements for the formation of a new society, the forces for exploding the old one.[243]

Section 10: *Modern Industry and Agriculture*

The revolution called forth by modern industry in agriculture, and in the social relations of agricultural producers, will be investigated later on. In this place, we shall merely indicate a few results by way of anticipation. If the use of machinery in agriculture is for the most part free from the injurious physical effect it has on the factory operative, its action in superseding the labourers is more intense, and finds less resistance, as we shall see later in detail. In the counties of Cambridge and Suffolk, for example, the area of cultivated land has extended very much within the last 20 years (up to 1868), while in the same period the rural population has diminished, not only relatively, but absolutely. In the United States, it is as yet only virtually that agricultural machines replace labourers; in other words, they allow of the cultivation by the farmer of a larger surface, but do not actually expel the labourers employed. In 1861, the number of persons occupied in England and Wales in the manufacture of agricultural machines was 1,034, whilst the number of agricultural labourers employed in the use of agricultural machines and steam-engines did not exceed 1,205.

In the sphere of agriculture, modern industry has a more revolutionary effect than elsewhere, for this reason, that it annihilates the peasant, that bulwark of the old society, and replaces him by the wage-labourer. Thus the desire for social changes, and the class antagonisms are brought to the same level in the country as in the towns. The irrational, old-fashioned methods of agriculture are replaced by scientific ones. Capitalist production completely tears asunder the old bond of union which held together agriculture and manufacture in their infancy. But at the same time it creates the material conditions for a higher synthesis in the future, viz., the union of agriculture and industry on the basis of the more perfected forms they have each acquired during their temporary separation. Capitalist production, by collecting the population in great centres, and causing an ever-increasing preponderance of town population, on the one hand concentrates the historical motive power of society; on the other hand, it disturbs the circulation of matter between man and the soil, i.e., prevents the return to the soil of its elements consumed by man in the form of food and clothing; it therefore violates the conditions necessary to lasting fertility of the soil. By this action it destroys at the same time the health of the town labourer and the intellectual life of the rural labourer.[244] But while upsetting the naturally grown conditions for the maintenance of that circulation of matter, it imperiously calls for its restoration as a system, as a regulating law of social production, and under a form appropriate to the full development of the human race. In agriculture as in manufacture, the transformation of production under the sway of capital, means, at the same time, the martyrdom of the producer; the instrument of labour becomes the means of enslaving, exploiting, and impoverishing the labourer; the social combination and organisation of labour-processes is turned into an organised mode of crushing out the workman's individual vitality, freedom, and independence. The dispersion of the rural labourers over larger areas breaks their power of resistance while concentration increases that of the town operatives. In modern agriculture, as in the urban industries, the increased productiveness and quantity of the labour set in motion are bought at the cost of laying waste and consuming by disease labour-power itself. Moreover, all progress in capitalistic agriculture is a progress in the art, not only of robbing the labourer, but of robbing the soil; all progress in increasing the fertility of the soil for a given time, is a progress towards ruining the lasting sources of that fertility. The more a country starts its development on the foundation of modern industry, like the United States, for example, the more rapid is this process of destruction.[245] Capitalist production, therefore, develops technology, and the combining together of various processes into a social whole, only by sapping the original sources of all wealth—the soil and the labourer.

Notes

1. Mill should have said, 'of any human being not fed by other people's labour,' for, without doubt, machinery has greatly increased the number of well-to-do idlers.
2. See, for instance, Hutton: 'Course of Mathematics.'
3. 'From this point of view we may draw a sharp line of distinction between a tool and a machine: spades, hammers, chisels, &c., combinations of levers and of screws, in all of which, no matter how complicated they may be in other respects, man is the motive power, ... all this falls under the idea of a tool; but the plough, which is drawn by animal power, and wind-mills, &c., must be classed among machines.' (Wilhelm Schulz: 'Die Bewegung der Produktion.' Zürich, 1843, p. 38.) In many respects a book to be recommended.
4. Before his time, spinning machines, although very imperfect ones, had already been used, and Italy was probably the country of their first appearance. A critical history of technology would show how little any of the inventions of the 18th century are the work of a single individual. Hitherto there is no such book. Darwin has interested us in the history of Nature's Technology, i.e., in the formation of the organs of plants and animals, which organs serve as instruments of production for sustaining life. Does not the history of the productive organs of man, of organs that are the material basis of all social organisation, deserve equal attention? And would not such a history be easier to compile, since, as Vico says, human history differs from natural history in this, that we have made the former, but not the latter? Technology discloses man's mode of dealing with Nature, the process of production by which he sustains his life, and thereby also lays bare the mode of formation of his social relations, and of the mental conceptions that flow from them. Every history of religion, even, that fails to take account of this material basis, is uncritical. It is, in reality, much easier to discover by analysis the earthly core of the misty creations of religion, than, conversely, it is, to develop from the actual relations of life the corresponding celestialised forms of those relations. The latter method is the only materialistic, and therefore the only scientific one. The weak points in the abstract materialism of natural science, a materialism that excludes history and its process, are at once evident from the abstract and ideological conceptions of its spokesmen, whenever they venture beyond the bounds of their own speciality.
5. Especially in the original form of the power-loom, we recognise, at the first glance, the ancient loom. In its modern form, the power-loom has undergone essential alterations.
6. It is only during the last 15 years (i.e., since about 1850), that a constantly increasing portion of these machine tools have been made in England by machinery, and that not by the same manufacturers who make the machines. Instances of machines for the fabrication of these mechanical tools are, the automatic bobbin-making engine, the cardsetting engine, shuttle-making machines, and machines for forging mule and throstle spindles.
7. Moses says: 'Thou shalt not muzzle the ox that treads the corn.' The Christian philanthropists of Germany, on the contrary, fastened a wooden board round the necks of the serfs, whom they used as a motive power for grinding, in order to prevent them from putting flour into their mouths with their hands.
8. It was partly the want of streams with a good fall on them, and partly their battles with superabundance of water in other respects, that compelled the Dutch to resort to wind as a motive power. The wind-mill itself they got from Germany, where its invention was the origin of a pretty squabble between the nobles, the priests, and the emperor, as to which of those three the wind 'belonged.' The air makes bondage, was the cry in Germany, at the same time that the wind was making Holland free. What it reduced to bondage in this case, was not the Dutchman, but the land for the Dutchman. In 1836, 12,000 windmills of 6,000

horse-power were still employed in Holland, to prevent two-thirds of the land from being reconverted into morasses.

9. It was, indeed, very much improved by Watt's first so-called single acting engine; but, in this form, it continued to be a mere machine for raising water, and the liquor from salt mines.

10. 'The union of all these simple instruments, set in motion by a single motor, constitutes a machine.' (Babbage, l.c.)

11. In January, 1861, John C. Morton read before the Society of Arts a paper on 'The forces employed in agriculture.' He there states: 'Every improvement that furthers the uniformity of the land makes the steam-engine more and more applicable to the production of pure mechanical force.... Horse-power is requisite wherever crooked fences and other obstructions prevent uniform action. These obstructions are vanishing day by day. For operations that demand more exercise of will than actual force, the only power applicable is that controlled every instant by the human mind-in other words, man-power.' Mr Morton then reduces steam-power, horse-power, and man-power, to the unit in general use for steam-engines, namely, the force required to raise 33,000 lbs. one foot in one minute, and reckons the cost of one horse-power from a steam-engine to be 3d., and from a horse to be 5½d. per hour. Further, if a horse must fully maintain its health, it can work no more than 8 hours a day. Three at the least out of every seven horses used on tillage land during the year can be dispensed with by using steam-power, at an expense not greater than that which, the horses dispensed with, would cost during the 3 or 4 months in which alone they can be used effectively. Lastly, steam-power, in those agricultural operations in which it can be employed, improves, in comparison with horse-power, the quality of the work. To do the work of a steam-engine would require 66 men, at a total cost of 15s. an hour, and to do the work of a horse, 32 men, at a total cost of 8s. an hour.

12. Faulhaber, 1625; De Caus, 1688.

13. The modern turbine frees the industrial exploitation of water-power from many of its former fetters.

14. 'In the early days of textile manufactures, the locality of the factory depended upon the existence of a stream having a sufficient fall to turn a water-wheel; and, although the establishment of the water-mills was the commencement of the breaking up of the domestic system of manufacture, yet the mills necessarily situated upon streams, and frequently at considerable distances the one from the other, formed part of a rural, rather than an urban system; and it was not until the introduction of the steam-power as a substitute for the stream that factories were congregated in towns, and localities where the coal and water required for the production of steam were found in sufficient quantities. The steam-engine is the parent of manufacturing towns.' (A. Redgrave in 'Reports of the Insp. of Fact., 30th April, 1860,' p. 36.)

15. From the standpoint of division of labour in Manufacture, weaving was not simple, but, on the contrary, complicated manual labour; and consequently the power-loom is a machine that does very complicated work. It is altogether erroneous to suppose that modern machinery originally appropriated those operations alone, which division of labour had simplified. Spinning and weaving were, during the manufacturing period, split up into new species, and the implements were modified and improved; but the labour itself was in no way divided, and it retained its handicraft character. It is not the labour, but the instrument of labour, that serves as the starting-point of the machine.

16. Before the epoch of Mechanical Industry, the wool manufacture was the predominating manufacture in England. Hence it was in this industry that, in the first half of the 18th century, the most experiments were made. Cotton, which required less careful preparation for its treatment by machinery, derived the benefit of the experience gained on wool, just as afterwards the manipulation of wool by machinery was developed on the lines of cotton-spinning and weaving by machinery. It was only during the 10 years immediately

preceding 1866, that isolated details of the wool manufacture, such as woolcombing, were incorporated in the factory system. 'The application of power to the process of combing wool ... extensively in operation since the introduction of the combingmachine, especially Lister's ... undoubtedly had the effect of throwing a very large number of men out of work. Wool was formerly combed by hand, most frequently in the cottage of the comber. It is now very generally combed in the factory, and hand-labour is superseded, except in some particular kinds of work, in which hand-combed wool is still preferred. Many of the hand-combers found employment in the factories, but the produce of the hand-combers bears so small a proportion to that of the machine, that the employment of a very large number of combers has passed away.' ('Rep. of lnsp. of Fact. for 31st Oct., 1856,' p. 16.)

17. 'The principle of the factory system, then, is to substitute ... the partition of a process into its essential constituents, for the division or graduation of labour among artisans.' (Andrew Ure: 'The Philosophy of Manufactures,' Lond., 1835, p. 20.)

18. The power-loom was at first made chiefly of wood; in its improved modern form it is made of iron. To what an extent the old forms of the instruments of production influenced their new forms at first starting, is shown by, amongst other things, the most superficial comparison of the present power-loom with the old one, of the modern blowing apparatus of a blast-furnace with the first inefficient mechanical reproduction of the ordinary bellows, and perhaps more strikingly than in any other way, by the attempts before the invention of the present locomotive, to construct a locomotive that actually had two feet, which after the fashion of a horse, it raised alternately from the ground. It is only after considerable development of the science of mechanics, and accumulated practical experience, that the form of a machine becomes settled entirely in accordance with mechanical principles, and emancipated from the traditional form of the tool that gave rise to it.

19. Eli Whitney's cotton gin had, until very recent times, undergone less essential changes than any other machine of the 18th century. It is only during the last decade (i.e., since 1856) that another American, Mr Emery, of Albany, New York, has rendered Whitney's gin antiquated by an improvement as simple as it is effective.

20. 'The Industry of Nations,' Lond., 1855, Part II., p. 239. This work also remarks: 'Simple and outwardly unimportant as this appendage to lathes may appear, it is not, we believe, averring too much to state, that its influence in improving and extending the use of machinery has been as great as that produced by Watt's improvements of the steam-engine itself. Its introduction went at once to perfect all machinery, to cheapen it, and to stimulate invention and improvement.'

21. One of these machines, used for forging paddle-wheel shafts in London, is called 'Thor.' It forges a shaft of 16½ tons with as much ease as a blacksmith forges a horseshoe.

22. Wood-working machines that are also capable of being employed on a small scale are mostly American inventions.

23. Science, generally speaking, costs the capitalist nothing, a fact that by no means hinders him from exploiting it. The science of others is as much annexed by capital as the labour of others. Capitalistic appropriation and personal appropriation, whether of science or of material wealth, are, however, totally different things. Dr Ure himself deplores the gross ignorance of mechanical science existing among his dear machinery-exploiting manufacturers, and Liebig can a tale unfold about the astounding ignorance of chemistry displayed by English chemical manufacturers.

24. Ricardo lays such stress on this effect of machinery (of which, in other connexions, he takes no more notice than he does of the general distinction between the labour process and the process of creating surplus-value), that he occasionally loses sight of the value given up by machines to the product, and puts machines on the same footing as natural forces. Thus 'Adam Smith nowhere undervalues the services which the natural agents and machinery perform for us, but he very justly distinguishes the nature of the value which they add to

commodities... as they perform their work gratuitously, the assistance which they afford us, adds nothing to value in exchange.' (Ric., l.c., pp. 336, 337.) This observation of Ricardo is of course correct in so far as it is directed against J. B. Say, who imagines that machines render the 'service' of creating value which forms a part of 'profits.'

25. A horse-power is equal to a force of 33,000 foot-pounds per minute, i.e., to a force that raises 33,000 pounds one foot in a minute, or one pound 33,000 feet. This is the horse power meant in the text. In ordinary language, and also here and there in quotations in this work, a distinction is drawn between the 'nominal' and the 'commercial' or 'indicated' horse-power of the same engine. The old or nominal horse-power is calculated exclusively from the length of piston-stroke, and the diameter of the cylinder, and leaves pressure of steam and piston speed out of consideration. It expresses practically this: This engine would be one of 50 horse-power, if it were driven with the same low pressure of steam, and the same slow piston speed, as in the days of Boulton and Watt. But the two latter factors have increased enormously since those days. In order to measure the mechanical force exerted today by an engine, an indicator has been invented which shows the pressure of the steam in the cylinder. The piston speed is easily ascertained. Thus the 'indicated' or 'commercial' horse-power of an engine is expressed by a mathematical formula, involving diameter of cylinder, length of stroke, piston speed, and steam pressure, simultaneously, and showing what multiple of 33,000 pounds is really raised by the engine in a minute. Hence, one 'nominal' horse-power may exert three, four, or even five 'indicated' or 'real' horse-powers. This observation is made for the purpose of explaining various citations in the subsequent pages.—*F. E.*

26. The reader who is imbued with capitalist notions will naturally miss here the 'interest' that the machine, in proportion to its capital value, adds to the product. It is, however, easily seen that since a machine no more creates new value than any other part of constant capital, it cannot add any value under the name of 'interest.' It is also evident that here, where we are treating of the production of surplus-value, we cannot assume *a priori* the existence of any part of that value under the name of interest. The capitalist mode of calculating, which appears, *primâ facie*, absurd, and repugnant to the laws of the creation of value, will be explained in the third book of this work.

27. This portion of value which is added by the machinery, decreases both absolutely and relatively, when the machinery does away with horses and other animals that are employed as mere moving forces, and not as machines for changing the form of matter. It may here be incidentally observed, that Descartes, in defining animals as mere machines, saw with eyes of the manufacturing period, while to eyes of the middle ages, animals were assistants to man, as they were later to Von Haller in his 'Restauration der Staatswissenschaften.' That Descartes, like Bacon, anticipated an alteration in the form of production, and the practical subjugation of Nature by Man, as a result of the altered methods of thought, is plain from his 'Discours de la Méthode.' He there says: 'Il est possible (by the methods he introduced in philosophy) de parvenir à des connaissances fort utiles à la vie, et qu'au lieu de cette philosophie spéculative qu'on enseigne dans les écoles, on en peut trouver une pratique, par laquelle, connaissant la force et les actions du feu, de l'eau, de l'air, des astres, et de tous les autres corps qui nous environnent, aussi distinctement que nous connaissons les divers métiers de nos artisans, nous les pourrions employer en même façon à tous les usages auxquels ils sont propres, et ainsi nous rendre comme maîtres et possesseurs de la nature' and thus 'contribuer au perfectionnement de la vie humaine.' [It is possible to attain knowledge very useful in life and, in place of the speculative philosophy taught in the schools, one can find a practical philosophy by which, given that we know the powers and the effectiveness of fire, water, air, the stars, and all the other bodies that surround us, as well and as accurately as we know the various trades of our craftsmen, we shall be able to employ them in the same manner as the latter to all uses to which they are adapted, and thus as it were make ourselves the masters and possessors of nature, and thus contributing

to the perfection of human life.] In the preface to Sir Dudley North's 'Discourses upon Trade' (1691) it is stated, that Descartes' method had begun to free Political Economy from the old fables and superstitious notions of gold, trade, &c. On the whole, however, the early English economists sided with Bacon and Hobbes as their philosophers; while, at a later period, the philosopher [...] of Political Economy in England, France, and Italy, was Locke.

28. According to the annual report (1863) of the Essen chamber of commerce, there was produced in 1862, at the cast-steel works of Krupp, with its 161 furnaces, thirty-two steam-engines (in the year 1800 this was about the number of all the steam-engines working in Manchester), and fourteen steam-hammers (representing in all 1,236 horse-power) forty-nine forges, 203 tool-machines, and about 2,400 workmen—thirteen million pounds of cast steel. Here there are not two workmen to each horse-power.
29. Babbage estimates that in Java the spinning labour alone adds 117% to the value of the cotton. At the same period (1832) the total value added to the cotton by machinery and labour in the fine-spinning industry, amounted to about 33% of the value of the cotton. ('On the Economy of Machinery,' pp. 165, 166.)
30. Machine printing also economises colour.
31. See Paper read by Dr Watson, Reporter on Products to the Government of India, before the Society of Arts, 17th April, 1860.
32. 'These mute agents (machines) are always the produce of much less labour than that which they displace, even when they are of the same money-value.' (Ricardo, l.c., p. 40.)
33. Hence in a communistic society there would be a very different scope for the employment of machinery than there can be in a bourgeois society.
34. 'Employers of labour would not unnecessarily retain two sets of children under thirteen.... In fact one class of manufacturers, the spinners of woollen yarn, now rarely employ children under thirteen years of age, i.e., half-timers. They have introduced improved and new machinery of various kinds, which altogether supersedes the employment of children (i.e., under 13 years); f. i., I will mention one process as an illustration of this diminution in the number of children, wherein by the addition of an apparatus, called a piecing machine, to existing machines, the work of six or four half-timers, according to the peculiarity of each machine, can be performed by one young person (over 13 years)... the half-time system 'stimulated' the invention of the piecing machine.' (Reports of Insp. of Fact. for 31st Oct., 1858.)
35. 'Wretch' is the recognised term in English Political Economy for the agricultural labourer.
36. 'Machinery ... can frequently not be employed until labour (he means wages) rises.' (Ricardo, l.c., p. 479.)
37. See 'Report of the Social Science Congress, at Edinburgh.' Oct., 1863.
38. Dr Edward Smith, during the cotton crisis caused by the American Civil War, was sent by the English Government to Lancashire, Cheshire, and other places, to report on the sanitary condition of the cotton operatives. He reported, that from a hygienic point of view, and apart from the banishment of the operatives from the factory atmosphere, the crisis had several advantages. The women now had sufficient leisure to give their infants the breast, instead of poisoning them with 'Godfrey's cordial.' They had time to learn to cook. Unfortunately the acquisition of this art occurred at a time when they had nothing to cook. But from this we see how capital, for the purposes of its self-expansion, has usurped the labour necessary in the home of the family. This crisis was also utilised to teach sewing to the daughters of the workmen in sewing schools. An American revolution and a universal crisis, in order that the working girls, who spin for the whole world, might learn to sew!
39. 'The numerical increase of labourers has been great, through the growing substitution of female for male, and above all, of childish for adult labour. Three girls of 13, at wages of from 6 shillings to 8 shillings a week, have replaced the one man of mature age, of wages varying

from 18 shillings to 45 shillings.' (Th. de Quincey: 'The Logic of Political Econ.,' London, 1844. Note to p. 147.) Since certain family functions, such as nursing and suckling children, cannot be entirely suppressed, the mothers confiscated by capital, must try substitutes of some sort. Domestic work, such as sewing and mending, must be replaced by the purchase of ready-made articles. Hence, the diminished expenditure of labour in the house is accompanied by an increased expenditure of money. The cost of keeping the family increases, and balances the greater income. In addition to this, economy and judgment in the consumption and preparation of the means of subsistence becomes impossible. Abundant material relating to these facts, which are concealed by official Political Economy, is to be found in the Reports of the Inspectors of Factories, of the Children's Employment Commission, and more especially in the Reports on Public Health.

40. In striking contrast with the great fact, that the shortening of the hours of labour of women and children in English factories was exacted from capital by the male operatives, we find in the latest reports of the Children's Employment Commission traits of the operative parents in relation to the traffic in children, that are truly revolting and thoroughly like slave-dealing. But the Pharisee of a capitalist, as may be seen from the same reports, denounces this brutality which he himself creates, perpetuates, and exploits, and which he moreover baptises 'freedom of labour.' 'Infant labour has been called into aid ... even to work for their own daily bread. Without strength to endure such disproportionate toil, without instruction to guide their future life, they have been thrown into a situation physically and morally polluted. The Jewish historian has remarked upon the overthrow of Jerusalem by Titus that it was no wonder it should have been destroyed, with such a signal destruction, when an inhuman mother sacrificed her own offspring to satisfy the cravings of absolute hunger.' ('Public Economy Concentrated.' Carlisle, 1833, p. 66.)

41. A. Redgrave in 'Reports of lnsp. of Fact. for 31st October, 1858,' pp. 40, 41.

42. 'Children's Employment Commission, Fifth Report,' London, 1866, p. 81, n. 31. *[Added in the 4th German edition.—The Bethnal Green silk industry is now almost destroyed.—F. E.]*

43. 'Children's Employment Commission, Third Report,' London, 1864, p. 53, n. 15.

44. l.c., Fifth Report, p. 22, n. 137.

45. 'Sixth Report on Public Health,' Lond., 1864, p. 34.

46. 'It (the inquiry of 1861)... showed, moreover, that while, with the described circumstances, infants perish under the neglect and mismanagement which their mothers' occupations imply, the mothers become to a grievous extent denaturalised towards their offspring—commonly not troubling themselves much at the death, and even sometimes... taking direct measures to insure it.' (l.c.)

47. l.c., p. 454.

48. l.c., pp. 454-463. 'Report by Dr Henry Julian Hunter on the excessive mortality of infants in some rural districts of England.'

49. l.c., p. 35 and pp. 455, 456.

50. l.c., p. 456.

51. In the agricultural as well as in the factory districts the consumption of opium among the grown-up labourers, both male and female, is extending daily. 'To push the sale of opiate... is the great aim of some enterprising wholesale merchants. By druggists it is considered the leading article.' (l.c., p. 459.) Infants that take opiates 'shrank up into little old men,' or 'wizened like little monkeys.' (l.c., p. 460.) We here see how India and China avenged themselves on England.

52. l.c., p. 37.

53. 'Rep. of Insp. of Fact. for 31st Oct., 1862,' p. 59. Mr Baker was formerly a doctor.

54. L. Horner in 'Reports of Insp. of Fact. for 30th June, 1857,' p. 17.

55. L. Horner in 'Rep. of lnsp. of Fact. for 31st Oct., 1855,' pp. 18, 19.

56. Sir John Kincaid in 'Rep. of Insp. of Fact. for 31st Oct., 1858,' pp. 31, 32.

57. L. Horner in 'Reports, &c., for 31st Oct., 1857,' pp. 17, 18.

58. Sir J. Kincaid in 'Reports, &c., 31st Oct., 1856,' p. 66.

59. A. Redgrave in 'Rep. of Insp. of Fact., 31st. Oct., 1857,' pp. 41-42. In those industries where the Factory Act proper (not the Print Works Act referred to in the text) has been in force for some time, the obstacles in the way of the education clauses have, in recent years, been overcome. In industries not under the Act, the views of Mr J. Geddes, a glass manufacturer, still extensively prevail. He informed Mr White, one of the Inquiry Commissioners: 'As far as I can see, the greater amount of education which a part of the working-class has enjoyed for some years past is an evil. It is dangerous, because it makes them independent.' ('Children's Empl. Comm., Fourth Report,' Lond., 1865, p. 253.)

60. 'Mr E., a manufacturer ... informed me that he employed females exclusively at his power-looms ... gives a decided preference to married females, especially those who have families at home dependent on them for support; they are attentive, docile, more so than unmarried females, and are compelled to use their utmost exertions to procure the necessaries of life. Thus are the virtues, the peculiar virtues of the female character to be perverted to her injury—thus all that is most dutiful and tender in her nature is made a means of her bondage and suffering.' (Ten Hours' Factory Bill. The Speech of Lord Ashley, March 15th, Lond., 1844, p. 20.)

61. 'Since the general introduction of machinery, human nature has been forced far beyond its average strength.' (Rob. Owen: 'Observations on the Effects of the Manufacturing System,' 2nd Ed., London, 1817.)

62. The English, who have a tendency to look upon the earliest form of appearance of a thing as the cause of its existence, are in the habit of attributing the long hours of work in factories to the extensive kidnapping of children, practised by capitalists in the infancy of the factory system, on workhouses and orphanages, by means of which robbery, unresisting material for exploitation was procured. Thus, for instance, Ficiden, himself a manufacturer, says: 'It is evident that the long hours of work were brought about by the circumstance of so great a number of destitute children being supplied from different parts of the country, that the masters were independent of the hands, and that having once established the custom by means of the miserable materials they had procured in this way, they could impose it on their neighbours with the greater facility.' (J. Ficiden: 'The Curse of the Factory System,' Lond., 1836, p. 11.) With reference to the labour of women, Saunders, the factory inspector, says in his report of 1844: 'Amongst the female operatives there are some women who, for many weeks in succession, except for a few days, are employed from 6 a.m. till midnight, with less than 2 hours for meals, so that on 5 days of the week they have only 6 hours left out of the 24, for going to and from their homes and resting in bed.'

63. 'Occasion... injury to the delicate moving parts of metallic mechanism by inaction.' (Ure, l.c., p. 281.)

64. The Manchester Spinner (*Times*, 26th Nov., 1862) before referred to says in relation to this subject: 'It (namely, the 'allowance for deterioration of machinery") is also intended to cover the loss which is constantly arising from the superseding of machines before they are worn out, by others of a new and better construction.'

65. 'It has been estimated, roughly, that the first individual of a newly-invented machine will cost about five times as much as the construction of the second.' Babbage, l.c., p. 349.

66. 'The improvements which took place not long ago in frames for making patent net were so great that a machine in good repair which had cost £1,200, sold a few years after for £60 ... improvements succeeded each other so rapidly, that machines which had never been finished were abandoned in the hands of their makers, because new improvements had superseded their utility.' (Babbage, l.c., p. 233.) In these stormy, go-ahead times, therefore, the tulle manufacturers soon extended the working-day, by means of double sets of hands, from the original 8 hours to 24.

67. 'It is self-evident, that, amid the ebbings and flowings of the markets and the alternate expansions and contractions of demand, occasions will constantly recur, in which the manufacturer may employ additional floating capital without employing additional fixed capital... if additional quantities of raw material can be worked up without incurring an additional expense for buildings and machinery.' (R. Torrens: 'On Wages and Combination.' London, 1834, p. 64.)

68. This circumstance is mentioned only for the sake of completeness, for I shall not consider the rate of profit, i.e., the ratio of the surplus-value to the total capital advanced, until I come to the third book.

69. Senior, 'Letters on the Factory Act.' London, 1837, pp. 13, 14.

70. 'The great proportion of fixed to circulating capital ... makes long hours of work desirable.' With the increased use of machinery, &c., 'the motives to long hours of work will become greater, as the only means by which a large proportion of fixed capital can be made profitable.' (l.c., pp. 11-13.) 'There are certain expenses upon a mill which go on in the same proportion whether the mill be running short or full time, as, for instance, rent rates, and taxes, insurance against fire, wages of several permanent servants, deterioration of machinery, with various other charges upon a manufacturing establishment, the proportion of which to profits increases as the production decreases.' ('Rep. of Insp. of Fact. for 31st Oct., 1862,' p. 19.)

71. Why it is, that the capitalist, and also the political economists who are imbued with his views, are unconscious of this immanent contradiction, will appear from the first part of the third book.

72. It is one of the greatest merits of Ricardo to have seen in machinery not only the means of producing commodities, but of creating a 'redundant population.'

73. F. Biese. 'Die Philosophie des Aristoteles,' Vol. 2. Berlin, 1842, p. 408.

74. I give below the translation of this poem by Stolberg, because it brings into relief, quite in the spirit of former quotations referring to division of labour, the antithesis between the views of the ancients and the moderns. 'Spare the hand that grinds the corn, Oh, miller girls, and softly sleep. Let Chanticleer announce the morn in vain! Deo has commanded the work of the girls to be done by the Nymphs, and now they skip lightly over the wheels, so that the shaken axles revolve with their spokes and pull round the load of the revolving stones. Let us live the life of our fathers, and let us rest from work and enjoy the gifts that the Goddess sends us.'

'Schonet der mahlenden Hand, o Müllerinnen, und schlafet
Sanft! es verkünde der Hahn euch den Morgen umsonst!
Däo hat die Arbeit der Midchen den Nymphen befohlen,
Und itzt hüpfen sic leicht über die Räder dahin,
Daß die erschütterten Achsen mit ihren Speichen sich wälzen,
Und im Kreise die Last drehen des wälzenden Steins.
Laßt uns leben das Leben der Väter, und laBt uns der Gaben
Arbeitslos uns freun, welche die Göttin uns schenkt.'
(Gedichte aus dem Griechischen übersetzt von Christian Graf zu Stolberg, Hamburg, 1782.)

75. There are, of course, always differences, in the intensities of the labour in various industries. But these differences are, as Adam Smith has shown, compensated to a partial extent by minor circumstances, peculiar to each sort of labour. Labour-time, as a measure of value, is not, however, affected in this case, except in so far as the duration of labour, and the degree of its intensity, are two antithetical and mutually exclusive expressions for one and the same quantity of labour.

76. Especially by piece-work, a form we shall investigate in Part VI. of this book.

77. See 'Rep. of Insp. of Fact. for 31st October, 1865.'
78. Rep. of Insp. of Fact. for 1844 and the quarter ending 30th April, 1845, pp. 20-21.
79. l.c., p. 19. Since the wages for piece-work were unaltered, the weekly wages depended on the quantity produced.
80. l.c., p. 20.
81. The moral element played an important part in the above experiments. The workpeople told the factory inspector: 'We work with more spirit, we have the reward ever before us of getting away sooner at night, and one active and cheerful spirit pervades the whole mill, from the youngest piecer to the oldest hand, and we can greatly help each other.' (l.c., p. 21.)
82. John Fielden, l.c., p. 32.
83. Lord Ashley, l.c., pp. 6-9, passim.
84. Rep. of Insp. of Fact. for Quarter ending 30th September, 1844, and from 1st October, 1844, to 30th April, 1845, p. 20.
85. l.c., p. 22.
86. 'Rep. of Insp. of Fact. for 31st October, 1862,' p. 62.
87. This was altered in the 'Parliamentary Return' of 1862. In it the actual horse-power of the modern steam engines and water wheels appears in place of the nominal. The doubling spindles, too, are no longer included in the spinning spindles (as was the case in the 'Returns' of 1839, 1850, and 1856); further, in the case of woollen mills, the number of 'gigs' is added, a distinction made between jute and hemp mills on the one hand and flax mills on the other, and finally stocking-weaving is for the first time inserted in the report.
88. 'Rep. of Insp. of Fact. for 31st October, 1856,' pp. 13-14, 20 and 1852, p. 23.
89. l.c., pp. 14-15.
90. l.c., P. 20.
91. 'Reports, &c., for 31st October, 1858,' pp. 9-10. Compare 'Reports, &c., for 30th April, 1860,' p. 30, sqq.
92. 'Reports of Insp. of Fact. for 31st Oct., 1862,' pp. 100 and 130.
93. On 2 modern power-looms a weaver now makes in a week of 60 hours 26 pieces of certain quality, length, and breadth; while on the old power-looms he could make no more than 4 such pieces. The cost of weaving a piece of such cloth had already soon after 1850 fallen from 2s. 9d. to 5 1/8d.

    'Thirty years ago (1841) one spinner with three placers was not required to attend to more than one pair of mules with 300-324 spindles. At the present time (1871) he has to mind with the help of 5 piecers 2,200 spindles, and produces not less than seven times as much yarn as in 1841.' (Alex. Redgrave, Factory Inspector—in the *Journal of Arts*, 5th January, 1872.)

94. 'Rep. of Insp. of Fact. for 31st Oct., 1861,' pp. 25, 26.
95. The agitation for a working-day of 8 hours has now (1867) begun in Lancashire among the factory operatives.
96. The following few figures indicate the increase in the 'factories' of the United Kingdom since 1848:

	Quantity Exported 1848	*Quantity Exported 1851*	*Quantity Exported 1860*	*Quantity Exported 1865*
		COTTON		
Cotton yarn	lbs. 135,831,162	lbs. 143,966,106	lbs. 197,343,655	lbs. 103,751,455
Sewing thread	—	lbs. 4,392,176	lbs. 6,297,554	lbs. 4,648,611

Cotton cloth	yds. 1,091,373,930	yds. 1,543,161,789	yds. 2,776,218,427	yds. 2,015,237,851
FLAX & HEMP				
Yarn	lbs. 11,722,182	lbs. 18,841,326	lbs. 31,210,612	lbs. 36,777,334
Cloth	yds. 88,901,519	yds. 129,106,753	yds. 143,996,773	yds. 247,012.529
SILK				
Yarn	lbs. 466,825	lbs. 462,513	lbs. 897,402	lbs. 812,589
Cloth	—	yds. 1,181,455	yds. 1,307,293	yds. 2,869,837
WOOL				
Woollen and Worsted yarns	—	lbs. 14,670,880	lbs. 27,533,968	lbs. 31,669,267
Cloth	—	yds. 151,231,153	yds. 190,371,507	yds. 278,837,418
	Value Exported. 1848. £	**Value Exported. 1851. £**	**Value Exported. 1860. £**	**Value Exported. 1865. £**
COTTON				
Yarn	5,927,831	6,634,026	9,870,875	10,351,049
Cloth	16,753,369	23,454,810	42,141,505	46,903,796
FLAX & HEMP				
Yarn	493,449	951,426	1,801,272	2,505,497
Cloth	2,802,789	4,107,396	4,804,803	9,155,358
SILK				
Yarn	77,789	196,380	826,107	768,064
Cloth	—	1,130,398	1,587,303	1,409,221
WOOL				
Yarn	776,975	1,484,544	3,843,450	5,424,047
Cloth	5,733,828	8,377,183	12,156,998	20,102,259

See the Blue books 'Statistical Abstract of the United Kingdom,' Nos. 8 and 13. Lond., 1861 and 1866. In Lancashire the number of mills increased only 4 per cent. between 1839 and 1850; 19 per cent. between 1850 and 1856; and 33 per cent. between 1856 and 1862; while the persons employed in them during each of the above periods of It years increased absolutely, but diminished relatively. (See 'Rep. of Insp. of Fact., for 31st Oct., 1862,' p. 63.) The cotton trade preponderates in Lancashire. We may form an idea of the stupendous nature of the cotton trade in that district when we consider that, of the gross number of textile factories in the United Kingdom, it absorbs 45.2 per cent., of the spindles 83.3 per cent., of the power-looms 81.4 per cent., of the mechanical horse-power 72.6 per cent., and of the total number of persons employed 58.2 per cent. (l.c., pp. 62-63.)

97. Ure, l.c., p. 18.
98. Ure, l.c., P. 3 1. See Karl Marx, l.c., pp. 140-141.
99. It looks very like intentional misleading by statistics (which misleading it would be possible to prove in detail in other cases too), when the English factory legislation excludes from its operation the class of labourers last mentioned in the text, while the parliamentary returns expressly include in the category of factory operatives, not only engineers, mechanics, &c., but also managers, salesmen, messengers, warehousemen, packers, &c., in short everybody, except the owner of the factory himself.

100. Ure grants this. He says, 'in case of need,' the workmen can be moved at the will of the manager from one machine to another, and he triumphantly exclaims: 'Such a change is in flat contradiction with the old routine, that divides the labour, and to one workman assigns the task of fashioning the head of a needle, to another the sharpening of the point.' He had much better have asked himself, why this 'old routine' is departed from in the automatic factory, only 'in case of need.'

101. When distress is very great, as, for instance, during the American Civil War, the factory operative is now and then set by the Bourgeois to do the roughest of work, such as road-making, &c.. The English 'ateliers nationaux' [national workshops] of 1862 and the following years, established for the benefit of the destitute cotton operatives, differ from the French of 1848 in this, that in the latter the workmen had to do unproductive work at the expense of the state, in the former they had to do productive municipal work to the advantage of the bourgeois, and that, too, cheaper than the regular workmen, with whom they were thus thrown into competition. 'The physical appearance of the cotton operatives is unquestionably improved. This I attribute ... as to the men, to outdoor labour on public works.' ('Rep. of Insp. of Fact., 31st Oct., 1863,' p. 59.) The writer here alludes to the Preston factory operatives, who were employed on Preston Moor.

102. An example: The various mechanical apparatus introduced since the Act of 1844 into woollen mills, for replacing the labour of children. So soon as it shall happen that the children of the manufacturers themselves have to go through a course of schooling as helpers in the mill, this almost unexplored territory of mechanics will soon make remarkable progress. 'Of machinery, perhaps self-acting mules are as dangerous as any other kind. Most of the accidents from them happen to little children, from their creeping under the mules to sweep the floor whilst the mules are in motion. Several 'minders' have been fined for this offence, but without much general benefit. If machine makers would only invent a self-sweeper, by whose use the necessity for these little children to creep under the machinery might be prevented, it would be a happy addition to our protective measures.' ('Reports of Insp. of Fact. for 31st. Oct., 1866,' p. 63.)

103. So much then for Proudhon's wonderful idea: he 'construes' machinery not as a synthesis of instruments of labour, but as a synthesis of detail operations for the benefit of the labourer himself.

104. F. Engels, l.c., p. 217. Even an ordinary and optimist Free-trader, like Mr Molinari, goes so far as to say, 'Un homme s'use plus vite en surveillant, quinze heures par jour, l'évolution uniforme d'un mécanisme, qu'en exercant, dans le même espace de temps, sa force physique. Ce travail de surveillance qui servirait peut-être d'utile gymnastique à l'intelligence, s'il n'était pas trop prolongé, détruit à la longue, par son excès, et l'intelligence, et le corps même.' [A man becomes exhausted more quickly when he watches over the uniform motion of mechanism for fifteen hours a day, than when he applies his physical strength over the same period of time. This labour of surveillance, which might perhaps serve as a useful exercise for the mind, if it did not go on too long, destroys both the mind and the body in the long run, through excessive application] (G. de Molinari: 'Études Économiques.' Paris, 1846.)

105. F. Engels, l.c., p. 216.

106. 'The Master Spinners' and Manufacturers' Defence Fund. Report of the Committee.' Manchester, 1854, p. 17. We shall see hereafter, that the 'master' can sing quite another song, when he is threatened with the loss of his 'living' automaton.

107. Ure, l.c., p. 15. Whoever knows the life history of Arkwright, will never dub this barber-genius 'noble.' Of all the great inventors of the 18th century, he was incontestably the greatest thiever of other people's inventions and the meanest fellow.

108. 'The slavery in which the bourgeoisie has bound the proletariat, comes nowhere more plainly into daylight than in the factory system. In it all freedom comes to an end both at law and in fact. The workman must be in the factory at half past five. If he come a few

minutes late, he is punished; if he come 10 minutes late, he is not allowed to enter until after breakfast, and thus loses a quarter of a day's wage. He must eat, drink and sleep at word of command.... The despotic bell calls him from his bed, calls him from breakfast and dinner. And how does he fare in the mill? There the master is the absolute law-giver. He makes what regulations he pleases; he alters and makes additions to his code at pleasure; and if he insert the veriest nonsense, the courts say to the workman: Since you have entered into this contract voluntarily, you must now carry it out .... These workmen are condemned to live, from their ninth year till their death, under this mental and bodily torture.' (F. Engels, l.c., p. 217, sq.) What, 'the courts say,' I will illustrate by two examples. One occurs at Sheffield at the end of 1866. In that town a workman had engaged himself for 2 years in a steelworks. In consequence of a quarrel with his employer he left the works, and declared that under no circumstances would he work for that master any more. He was prosecuted for breach of contract, and condemned to two months' imprisonment. (If the master break the contract, he can be proceeded against only in a civil action, and risks nothing but money damages.) After the workman has served his two months, the master invites him to return to the works, pursuant to the contract. Workman says: No, he has already been punished for the breach. The master prosecutes again, the court condemns again, although one of the judges, Mr Shee, publicly denounces this as a legal monstrosity, by which a man can periodically, as long as he lives, be punished over and over again for the same offence or crime. This judgment was given not by the 'Great Unpaid,' the provincial Dogberries, but by one of the highest courts of justice in London.—[Added *in the 4th German edition.—This* has now been done away with. With few exceptions, e.g., when public gas-works are involved, the worker in England is now put on an equal footing with the employer in case of breach of contract and can be sued only civilly.—F. E.] The second case occurs in Wiltshire at the end of November 1863. About 30 power-loom weavers, in the employment of one Harrup, a cloth manufacturer at Leower's Mill, Westbury Leigh, struck work because master Harrup indulged in the agreeable habit of making deductions from their wages for being late in the morning; 6d. for 2 minutes; 1s. for 3 minutes, and 1s. 6d. for ten minutes. This is at the rate of 9s. per hour, and £4 10s. 0d. per diem; while the wages of the weavers on the average of a year, never exceeded 10s. to 12s. weekly. Harrup also appointed a boy to announce the starting time by a whistle, which he often did before six o'clock in the morning: and if the hands were not all there at the moment the whistle ceased, the doors were closed, and those hands who were outside were fined: and as there was no clock on the premises, the unfortunate hands were at the mercy of the young Harrup-inspired time-keeper. The hands on strike, mothers of families as well as girls, offered to resume work if the timekeeper were replaced by a clock, and a more reasonable scale of fines were introduced. Harrup summoned I9 women and girls before the magistrates for breach of contract. To the utter indignation of all present, they were each mulcted in a fine of 6d. and 2s. 6d. for costs. Harrup was followed from the court by a crowd of people who hissed him. A favourite operation with manufacturers is to punish the workpeople by deductions made from their wages on account of faults in the material worked on. This method gave rise in 1866 to a general strike in the English pottery districts. The reports of the Ch. Empl. Com. (1863-1866), give cases where the worker not only receives no wages, but becomes, by means of his labour, and of the penal regulations, the debtor to boot, of his worthy master. The late cotton crisis also furnished edifying examples of the sagacity shown by the factory autocrats in making deductions from wages. Mr R. Baker, the Inspector of Factories, says, 'I have myself had lately to direct prosecutions against one cotton mill occupier for having in these pinching and painful times deducted 10d. a piece from some of the young workers employed by him, for the surgeon's certificate (for which he himself had only paid 6d.), when only allowed by the law to deduct 3d., and by custom nothing at all .... And I have been informed of another, who, in order to keep without the law, but to attain the same object, charges the poor children who work for him a shilling each, as a fee for learning them the art and mystery of cotton spinning, so soon as they are declared by the surgeon fit and proper persons for that occupation. There may therefore be undercurrent causes for such extraordinary exhibitions as strikes, not only wherever they arise, but particularly at such times as the present, which without explanation, render them inexplicable to the public understanding.' He alludes here to a strike of power-loom weavers at Darwen, June, 1863. ('Reports of Insp. of Fact. for 30 April, 1863,' pp. 50-51.) The reports always go beyond their official dates.

109. The protection afforded by the Factory Acts against dangerous machinery has had a beneficial effect. 'But ... there are other sources of accident which did not exist twenty years since; one especially, viz., the increased speed of the machinery. Wheels, rollers, spindles and shuttles are now propelled at increased and increasing rates; fingers must be quicker and defter in their movements to take up the broken thread, for, if placed with hesitation or carelessness, they are sacrificed.... A large number of accidents are caused by the eagerness of the workpeople to get through their work expeditiously. It must be remembered that it is of the highest importance to manufacturers that their machinery should be in motion, i.e., producing yarns and goods. Every minute's stoppage is not only a loss of power, but of production, and the workpeople are urged by the overlookers, who are interested in the quantity of work turned off, to keep the machinery in motion, and it is no less important to those of the operatives who are paid by the weight or piece, that the machines should be kept in motion. Consequently, although it is strictly forbidden in many, nay in most factories, that machinery should be cleaned while in motion, it is nevertheless the constant practice in most, if not in all, that the workpeople do, unreproved, pick out waste, wipe rollers and wheels, &c., while their frames are in motion. Thus from this cause only, 906 accidents have occurred during the six months.... Although a great deal of cleaning is constantly going on day by day, yet Saturday is generally the day set apart for the thorough cleaning of the machinery, and a great deal of this is done while the machinery is in motion.' Since cleaning is not paid for, the workpeople seek to get done with it as speedily as possible. Hence 'the number of accidents which occur on Fridays, and especially on Saturdays, is much larger than on any other day. On the former day the excess is nearly 12 per cent. over the average number of the four first days of the week, and on the latter day the excess is 25 per cent. over the average of the preceding five days; or, if the number of working-hours on Saturday being taken into account—7½ hours on Saturday as compared with 10½ on other days—there is an excess of 65 per cent. on Saturdays over the average of the other five days.' ('Rep. of Insp. of Fact., 31st Oct., 1866,' pp. 9, 15, 16, 17.)

110. In Part I. of Book III. I shall give an account of a recent campaign by the English manufacturers against the Clauses in the Factory Acts that protect the 'hands' against dangerous machinery. For the present, let this one quotation from the official report of Leonard Horner suffice: 'I have heard some mill-owners speak with inexcusable levity of some of the accidents; such, for instance, as the loss of a finger being a trifling matter. A working-man's living and prospects depend so much upon his fingers, that any loss of them is a very serious matter to him. When I have heard such inconsiderate remarks made, I have usually put this question: Suppose you were in want of an additional workman, and two were to apply, both equally well qualified in other respects, but one had lost a thumb or a forefinger, which would you engage? There never was a hesitation as to the answer....' The manufacturers have 'mistaken prejudices against what they have heard represented as a pseudo-philanthropic legislation.' ('Rep. of Insp. of Fact., 31st Oct., 1855.») These manufacturers are clever folk, and not without reason were they enthusiastic for the slave-holders' rebellion.

111. In those factories that have been longest subject to the Factory Acts, with their compulsory limitation of the hours of labour, and other regulations, many of the older abuses have vanished. The very improvement of the machinery demands to a certain extent 'improved

construction of the buildings,' and this is an advantage to the workpeople. (See 'Rep. of Insp. of Fact. for 31st Oct., 1863,' p. 109.)

112. See amongst others, John Houghton: 'Husbandry and Trade Improved.' London, 1727. 'The Advantages of the East India Trade, 1720.' John Bellers, l.c. 'The masters and their workmen are, unhappily, in a perpetual war with each other. The invariable object of the former is to get their work done as cheaply as possible; and they do not fail to employ every artifice to this purpose, whilst the latter are equally attentive to every occasion of distressing their masters into a compliance with higher demands.' ('An Enquiry into the Causes of the Present High Price of Provisions,' pp. 61-62. Author, the Rev. Nathaniel Forster, quite on the side of the workmen.)

113. In old-fashioned manufactures the revolts of the workpeople against machinery, even to this day, occasionally assume a savage character, as in the case of the Sheffield file cutters in 1865.

114. Sir James Steuart also understands machinery quite in this sense. 'Je considère donc les machines comme des moyens d'augmenter (virtuellement) le nombre des gens industrieux qu'on n'est pas obligé de nourrir.... En quoi l'effet d'une machine diffère-t-il de celui de nouveaux habitants?' (French trans. t. I., l. I., ch. XIX.) More naïve is Petty, who says, it replaces 'Polygamy.' The above point of view is, at the most, admissible only for some parts of the United States. On the other hand, 'machinery can seldom be used with success to abridge the labour of an individual; more time would be lost in its construction than could be saved by its application. It is only really useful when it acts on great masses, when a single machine can assist the work of thousands. It is accordingly in the most populous countries, where there are most idle men, that it is most abundant.... It is not called into use by a scarcity of men, but by the facility with which they can be brought to work in masses.' (Piercy Ravenstone: 'Thoughts on the Funding System and its Effects.' London, 1824, p. 45.)

115. *[Note in the 4th German edition.*—This applies to Germany too. Where in our country agriculture on a large scale exists, hence particularly in the East, it has become possible only in consequence of the clearing of the estates ('Bauernlegen»), a practice which became widerspread in the 16th century and was particularly so since 1648.—*F. E.*]

116. 'Machinery and labour are in constant competition.' Ricardo, l.c., p. 479.

117. The competition between hand-weaving and power-weaving in England, before the passing of the Poor Law of 1833, was prolonged by supplementing the wages, which had fallen considerably below the minimum, with parish relief. 'The Rev. Mr Turner was, in 1827, rector of Wilmslow in Cheshire, a manufacturing district. The questions of the Committee of Emigration, and Mr Turner's answers, show how the competition of human labour is maintained against machinery. 'Question: Has not the use of the power-loom superseded the use of the hand-loom? Answer: Undoubtedly; it would have superseded them much more than it has done, if the hand-loom weavers were not enabled to submit to a reduction of wages.' 'Question: But in submitting he has accepted wages which are insufficient to support him, and looks to parochial contribution as the remainder of his support? Answer: Yes, and in fact the competition between the hand-loom and the power-loom is maintained out of the poor-rates.' Thus degrading pauperism or expatriation, is the benefit which the industrious receive from the introduction of machinery, to be reduced from the respectable and in some degree independent mechanic, to the cringing wretch who lives on the debasing bread of charity. This they call a temporary inconvenience.' ('A Prize Essay on the Comparative Merits of Competition and Co-operation.' Lond., 1834, p. 29.)

118. 'The same cause which may increase the revenue of the country' (i.e., as Ricardo explains in the same passage, the revenues of landlords and capitalists, whose wealth, from the economic point of view, forms the Wealth of the Nation), 'may at the same time render the population redundant and deteriorate the condition of the labourer.' (Ricardo, l.c., p. 469.) 'The constant aim and the tendency of every improvement in machinery is, in fact, to do away entirely with the labour of man, or to lessen its price by substituting the labour of women and children for that of grown-up men, or of unskilled for that of skilled workmen.' (Ure, l.c., t. I., p. 35.)

119. 'Rep. Insp. Fact. for 31st October, 1858,' p. 43.
120. 'Rep. lnsp. Fact. for 31st October, 1856,' p. 15.
121. Ure, l.c., p. 19. 'The great advantage of the machinery employed in brick-making consists in this, that the employer is made entirely independent of skilled labourers.' ('Ch. Empl. Comm. V. Report,' Lond., 1866, p. 130, n. 46.) Mr A. Sturrock, superintendent of the machine department of the Great Northern Railway, says, with regard to the building of locomotives, &c.: 'Expensive English workmen are being less used every day. The production of the workshops of England is being increased by the use of improved tools and these tools are again served by a low class of labour.... Formerly their skilled labour necessarily produced all the parts of engines. Now the parts of engines are produced by labour with less skill, but with good tools. By tools, I mean engineer's machinery, lathes, planing machines, drills, and so on.' ('Royal Com. on Railways,' Lond., 1867, Minutes of Evidence, n. 17, 862 and 17, 863.)
122. Ure, l.c., p. 20.
123. Ure, l.c., p. 321.
124. Ure, l.c., p. 23.
125. 'Rep. Insp. Fact., 31st Oct., 1863,' pp. 108,109.
126. l.c., p. 109. The rapid improvement of machinery, during the crisis, allowed the English manufacturers, immediately after the termination of the American Civil War, and almost in no time, to glut the markets of the world again. Cloth, during the last six months of 1866, was almost unsaleable. Thereupon began the consignment of goods to India and China, thus naturally making the glut more intense. At the beginning of 1867 the manufacturers resorted to their usual way out of the difficulty, viz., reducing wages 5 per cent. The workpeople resisted, and said that the only remedy was to work short time, 4 days a-week; and their theory was the correct one. After holding out for some time, the self-elected captains of industry had to make up their minds to short time, with reduced wages in some places, and in others without.
127. 'The relation of master and man in the blown-flint bottle trades amounts to a chronic strike.' Hence the impetus given to the manufacture of pressed glass, in which the chief operations are done by machinery. One firm in Newcastle, who formerly produced 350,000 lbs. of blown-flint glass, now produces in its place 3,000,500 lbs. of pressed glass. ('Ch. Empl. Comm., Fourth Rep.,' 1865, pp. 262-263.)
128. Gaskell. 'The Manufacturing Population of England,' London, 1833, pp. 3, 4.
129. W. Fairbairn discovered several very important applications of machinery to the construction of machines, in consequence of strikes in his own workshops.
130. Ure, l.c., pp. 368-370
131. Ure, l.c., pp. 368, 7, 370, 280, 281, 321, 370, 475.
132. Ricardo originally was also of this opinion, but afterwards expressly disclaimed it with the scientific impartiality and love of truth characteristic of him. See l.c., ch. xxxi. 'On Machinery.'
133. *Nota bene.* My illustration is entirely on the lines of those given by the above named economists.
134. A disciple of Ricardo, in answer to the insipidities of J. B. Say, remarks on this point: 'Where division of labour is well developed, the skill of the labourer is available only in that particular branch in which it has been acquired; he himself is a sort of machine. It does not therefore help matters one jot, to repeat in parrot fashion, that things have a tendency to find their level. On looking around us we cannot but see, that they are unable to find their level for a long time; and that when they do find it, the level is always lower than at the commencement of the process.' ('An Inquiry into those Principles Respecting the Nature of Demand,' &c., Lond. 1821, p. 72.)
135. MacCulloch, amongst others, is a past master in this pretentious cretinism. 'If,' he says, with the affected naïveté of a child of 8 years, 'if it be advantageous, to develop the skill of the workman more and more, so that he is capable of producing, with the same or with

a less quantity of labour, a constantly increasing quantity of commodities, it must also be advantageous, that he should avail himself of the help of such machinery as will assist him most effectively in the attainment of this result.' (MacCulloch: 'Princ. of Pol. Econ.,' Lond. 1830, p. 166.)

136. 'The inventor of the spinning machine has ruined India, a fact, however, that touches us but little.' A. Thiers: De la propriété.—M. Thiers here confounds the spinning machine with the power-loom, 'a fact, however, that touches us but little.'

137. According to the census of 1861 (Vol. II., Lond., 1863), the number of people employed in coal mines in England and Wales, amounted to 246,613 of which 73,545 were under, and 173,067 were over 20 years. Of those under 20, 835 were between 5 and 10 years, 30,701 between 10 and 15 years, 42,010 between 15 and 19 years. The number employed in iron, copper, lead, tin, and other mines of every description, was 319, 222.

138. In England and Wales, in 1861, there were employed in making machinery, 60,807 persons, including the masters and their clerks, &c., also all agents and business people connected with this industry, but excluding the makers of small machines, such as sewing-machines, &c., as also the makers of the operative parts of machines, such as spindles. The total number of civil engineers amounted to 3,329.

139. Since iron is one of the most important raw materials; let me here state that, in 1861, there were in England and Wales 125,771 operative iron founders, of whom 123,430 were males, 2,341 females. Of the former 30,810 were under, and 92,620 over 20 years.

140. 'A family of four grown-up persons, with two children as winders, earned at the end of the last, and the beginning of the present century, by ten hours' daily labour, £4 a week. If the work was very pressing, they could earn more.... Before that, they had always suffered from a deficient supply of yarn.' (Gaskell, l.c., pp. 25-27.)

141. F. Engels, in 'Lage, &c.,' points out the miserable condition of a large number of those who work on these very articles of luxury. See also numerous instances in the 'Reports of the Children's Employment Commission.'

142. In 1861, in England and Wales, there were 94,665 sailors in the merchant service.

143. Of these only 177,596 are males above 13 years of age.

144. Of these, 30,501 are females.

145. Of these, 137,447 males. None are included in the 1,208,648 who do not serve in private houses. Between 1861 and 1870, the number of male servants nearly doubled itself. It increased to 267,671. In the year 1847 there were 2,694 gamekeepers (for the landlords' preserves), in 1869 there were 4,921. The young servant girls in the houses of the London lower middle class are in common parlance called 'slaveys.'

146. Ganilh, on the contrary, considers the final result of the factory system to be an absolutely less number of operatives, at whose expense an increased number of 'gens honnêtes' live and develop their well-known 'perfectibilité perfectible.' Little as he understands the movement of production, at least he feels, that machinery must needs be a very fatal institution, if its introduction converts busy workmen into paupers, and its development calls more slaves of labour into existence than it has suppressed. It is not possible to bring out the cretinism of his standpoint, except by his own words: 'Les classes condamnées à produire et à consommer diminuent, et les classes qui dirigent le travail, qui soulagent, consolent, et éclairent toute la population, se multiplient ... et s'approprient tous les bienfaits qui résultent de la diminution des frais du travail, de l'abondance des productions, et du bon marché des consommations. Dans cette direction, l'espéce humaine s'élève aux plus hautes conceptions du génie, pénètre dans les profoundeurs mystérieuses de la religion, établit les principes salutaires de la morale (which consists in 's'approprier tous les beinfaits,' &c.), les lois tutélaires de la liberté (liberty of 'les classes condamnées à produire?') et du pouvoir, de l'obéissance et de la justice, du devoir et de la l'humanité.' [The classes condemned to produce and to consume diminish, and the classes which direct labour, which relieve, console and enlighten the whole

population, multiply ... and appropriate all the benefits which result from the diminution of the costs of labour, from the abundance of products and the cheapness of consumer goods. In this way, the human species rises to the highest creations of genius, penetrates the mysterious depths of religion, and establishes the salutory principles of morality, the laws for the protection of liberty, and power, of obedience and justice, of obligation and humanity] For this twaddle, see 'Des Systèmes d'Economie Politique, &c., Par M. Ch. Ganilh,' 2ème ed., Paris, 1821, t. I, p. 224, and see p. 212.

147. 'Reports of Insp. of Fact., 31 Oct., 1865,' p. 58, sq. At the same time, however, means of employment for an increased number of hands was ready in 110 new mills with 11,625 looms, 628,576 spindles and 2,695 total horse-power of steam and water (l.c.).

148. 'Reports, &c., for 31 Oct., 1862,' p. 79. At the end of 1871, Mr A. Redgrave, the factory inspector, in a lecture given at Bradford, in the New Mechanics' Institution, said: 'What has struck me for some time past is the altered appearance of the woollen factories. Formerly they were filled with women and children, now machinery seems to do all the work. At my asking for an explanation of this from a manufacturer, he gave me the following: 'Under the old system I employed 63 persons; after the introduction of improved machinery I reduced my hands to 33, and lately, in consequence of new and extensive alterations, I have been in a position to reduce those 33 to 13.'

149. See 'Reports, &c., 31 Oct., 1856,' p. 16.

150. 'The sufferings of the hand-loom weavers were the subject of an inquiry by a Royal Commission, but although their distress was acknowledged and lamented, the amelioration of their condition was left, and probably necessarily so, to the chances and changes of time, which it may now be hoped' [20 years later!] 'have nearly obliterated those miseries, and not improbably by the present great extention of the power-loom.' ('Rep. Insp. of Fact., 31 Oct., 1856,' p. 15.)

151. Other ways in which machinery affects the production of raw material will be mentioned in the third book.

152.

Export of Cotton From India to Great Britain	
1846. —	34,540,143 lbs.
1860. —	204,141,168 lbs.
1865. —	445,947,600 lbs.
Export of Wool From India to Great Britain	
1846. —	4,570,581 lbs.
1860. —	20,214,173 lbs.
1865. —	20,679,111 lbs.

153.

Export of Wool From the Cape to Great Britain	
1846. —	2,958,457 lbs.
1860. —	16,574,345 lbs.
1865. —	29,920,623 lbs.
Export of Wool from Australia to Great Britain	
1846. —	21,789,346 lbs.
1860. —	59,166,616 lbs.
1865. —	109,734,261 lbs.

154. The economic development of the United States is itself a product of European, more especially of English modern industry. In their present form (1866) the States must still be considered a European colony. [*Added in the 4th German edition.—'Since then they have developed into country whose industry holds second place in the world, without on that account entirely losing their colonial character.'—F. E.*]

Export of Cotton from the United States to Great Britain	
1846. —	401,949,393 lbs.
1852. —	765,630,543 lbs.
1859. —	961,707,264 lbs.
1860. —	1,115,890,608 lbs.

Export of Corn, &C., from the United States to Great Britain 1862		
Wheat, cwts	16,202,312	41,033,503
Barley, cwts	3,669,653	6,624,800
Oats, cwts	3,174,801	4,496,994
Rye, cwts	388,749	7,108
Flour, cwts	3,819,440	7,207,113
Buckwheat, cwts	1,054	19,571
Maize, cwts	5,473,161	11,694,818
Bere or Bigg (a sort of Barley), cwts	2,039	7,675
Peas, cwts	811,620	1,024,722
Beans, cwts	1,822,972	2,037,137
Total exports	—	74,083,441

156. In an appeal made in July, 1866, to the Trade Societies of England, by the shoemakers of Leicester, who had been thrown on the streets by a lock-out, it is stated: 'Twenty years ago the Leicester shoe trade was revolutionised by the introduction of riveting in the place of stitching. At that time good wages could be earned. Great competition was shown between the different firms as to which could turn out the neatest article. Shortly afterwards, however a worse kind of competition sprang up, namely, that of underselling one another in the market. The injurious consequences soon manifested themselves in reductions of wages, and so sweepingly quick was the fall in the price of labour, that many firms now pay only one half of the original wages. And yet, though wages sink lower and lower, profits appear, with each alteration in the scale of wages, to increase.' Even bad times are utilised by the manufacturers, for making exceptional profits by excessive lowering of wages, i.e., by a direct robbery of the labourer's means of subsistence. One example (it has reference to the crisis in the Coventry silk weaving): 'From information I have received from manufacturers as well as workmen, there seems to be no doubt that wages have been reduced to a greater extent than either the competition of the foreign producers, or other circumstances have rendered necessary ... the majority of weavers are working at a reduction of 30 to 40 per cent. in their wages. A piece of ribbon for making which the weaver got 6s. or 7s. five years back, now only brings them 3s. 3d. or 3s. 6d.; other work is now priced at 2s. and 2s. 3d. which was formerly priced at 4s. and 4s. 3d. The reduction in wage seems to have been carried to a greater extent than is necessary for increasing demand. Indeed, the reduction in the cost of weaving, in the case of many descriptions of ribbons, has not been accompanied by any corresponding reduction in the selling price of the manufactured article.' (Mr F. D. Longe's Report. 'Ch. Emp. Com., V. Rep., 1866,' p. 114, 1.)

157. Conf 'Reports of Insp. of Fact., 31st October, 1862,' p. 30.
158. l.c., p. 19.
159. 'Rep. Insp. of Fact., 31st October, 1863,' pp. 41-45.
160. l.c., pp. 41-42
161. l.c., p. 57.
162. l.c., pp. 50-51.
163. l.c., pp. 62-63.
164. 'Rep. &c., 30th April, 1864,' p. 27.
165. From a letter of Mr Harris, Chief Constable of Bolton, in 'Rep. of Insp. of Fact., 31st October, 1865,' pp. 61-62.
166. In an appeal, dated 1863, of the factory operatives of Lancashire, &c., for the purpose of forming a society for organised emigration, we find the following: 'That a large emigration of factory workers is now absolutely essential to raise them from their present prostrate condition, few will deny; but to show that a continuous stream of emigration is at all times demanded, and, without which it is impossible for than to maintain their position in ordinary times, we beg to call attention to the subjoined facts:—In 1814, the official value of cotton goods exported was £17,665,378, whilst the real marketable value was £20,070,824. In 1858, the official value of cotton goods exported, was £182,221,681; but the real or marketable value was only £43,001,322, being a ten-fold quantity sold for little more than double the former price. To produce results so disadvantageous to the country generally, and to the factory workers in particular, several causes have cooperated, which, had circumstances permitted, we should have brought more prominently under your notice; suffice it for the present to say that the most obvious one is the constant redundancy of labour, without which a trade so ruinous in its effects never could have been carried on, and which requires a constantly extending market to save it from annihilation. Our cotton mills may be brought to a stand by the periodical stagnations of trade, which, under present arrangements, are as inevitable as death itself; but the human mind is constantly at work, and although we believe we are under the mark in stating that six millions of persons have left these shores during the last 25 years, yet, from the natural increase of population, and the displacement of labour to cheapen production, a large percentage of the male adults in the most prosperous times find it impossible to obtain work in factories on any conditions whatever.' ('Reports of Insp. of Fact., 30th April 1863,' pp. 51-52.) We shall, in a later chapter, see how our friends, the manufacturers, endeavoured, during the catastrophe in the cotton trade, to prevent by every means, including State interference, the emigration of the operatives.
167. 'Ch. Empt. Comm. III. Report, 1864,' p. 108, n. 447.
168. In the United States the restoration, in this way, of handicrafts based on machinery is frequent; and therefore, when the inevitable transition to the factory system shall take place, the ensuing concentration will, compared with Europe and even with England, stride on in seven-league boots.
169. See 'Rep. of Insp. of Fact., 31st Oct., 1865,' p. 64.
170. Mr Gillott erected in Birmingham the first steel-pen factory on a large scale. It produced, so early as 1851, over 180,000,000 of pens yearly, and consumed 120 tons of steel. Birmingham has the monopoly of this industry in the United Kingdom, and at present produces thousands of millions of steel-pens. According to the Census of 1861, the number of persons employed was 1,428, of whom 1,268 females from 5 years of age upwards.
171. 'Ch. Empl. Comm. II. Rep. 1864,' p. LXVIII., n. 415.
172. And now forsooth children are employed at file-cutting in Sheffield.
173. 'Ch. Empl. Comm., V. Rep. 1866,' p. 3, n. 24; p. 6, n. 55, 56; p. 7, n. 59, 60.
174. l.c., pp. 114, 115, n. 6, 7. The commissioner justly remarks that though as a rule machines take the place of men, here literally young persons replace machines.

175. See the Report on the rag trade, and numerous details in 'Public Health, VIII. Rep.' Lond. 1866, app., pp. 196, 208.
176. 'Ch. Empl. Comm. V. Rep., 1866,' pp. xvi-xviii, n. 86-97, and pp. 130-133, n. 39-71. See also III. Rep., 1864, pp. 48, 56.
177. 'Public Health. Sixth Rep.,' Lond. 1864, pp. 29, 31.
178. l.c., p. 30. Dr Simon remarks that the mortality among the London tailors and printers between the ages of 25 and 35 is in fact much greater, because the employers in London obtain from the country a great number of young people up to 30 years of age, as 'apprentices' and 'improvers,' who come for the purpose of being perfected in their trade. These figure in the census as Londoners, they swell out the number of heads on which the London death-rate is calculated, without adding proportionally to the number of deaths in that place. The greater part of them in fact return to the country, and especially in cases of severe illness. (l.c.)
179. I allude here to hammered nails, as distinguished from nails cut out and made by machinery. See 'Child. Empl. Comm., Third Rep.,' pp. xi., xix., n. 125-130, p. 52, n. 11, p. 114, n. 487, p. 137, n. 674.
180. 'Ch. Empl. Comm., II. Rep.,' p. xxii, n. 166.
181. 'Ch. Empl. Comm., II. Rep., 1864,' pp. xix., xx., xxi.
182. l.c., pp. xxi.. xxii.
183. l.c., pp. xxix., xxx.
184. l.c., pp. xi., xii.
185. 'Child. Empl. Comm., I. Rep. 1863,' p. 185.
186. In England, millinery and dressmaking are for the most part carried on, on the premises of the employer, partly by workwomen who live there, partly by women who live off the premises.
187. Mr White, a commissioner, visited a military clothing manufactory that employed 1,000 to 1,200 persons, almost all females, and a shoe manufactory with 1,300 persons; of these nearly one half were children and young persons.
188. An instance. The weekly report of deaths by the Registrar-General dated 26th Feb., 1864, contains 5 cases of death from starvation. On the same day *The Times* reports another case. Six victims of starvation in one week!
189. 'Child. Empl. Comm., Second Rep., 1864,' p. lxvii., n. 406-9, p. 84, n. 124, p. lxxiii, n. 441, p. 68, n. 6, p. 84, n. 126, p. 78, n. 85, p. 76, n. 69, p. lxxii, n. 483.
190. 'The rental of premises required for workrooms seems the element which ultimately determines the point; and consequently it is in the metropolis, that the old system of giving work out to small employers and families has been longest retained, and earliest returned to.' (l.c., p. 83, n. 123.) The concluding statement in this quotation refers exclusively to shoemaking.
191. In glove-making and other industries where the condition of the work-people is hardly distinguishable from that of paupers, this does not occur.
192. l.c., p. 83, n. 122.
193. In the wholesale boot and shoe trade of Leicester alone, there were in 1864, 800 sewing-machines already in use.
194. l.c., p. 84, n. 124.
195. Instances: The Army Clothing Depot at Pimlico, London, the Shirt factory of Tillie and Henderson at Londonderry, and the clothes factory of Messrs. Tait at Limerick which employs about 1,200 hands.
196. 'Tendency to Factory System' (l.c., p. lxvii). 'The whole employment is at this time in a state of transition, and is undergoing the same Change as that effected in the lace trade, weaving, &c.' (l.c., n. 405.) 'A complete revolution' (l.c., p. xlvi., n. 318). At the date of the Child. Empl. Comm. of 1840 stocking making was still done by manual labour. Since 1846,

various sorts of machines have been introduced, which are now driven by steam. The total number of persons of both sexes and of all ages from 3 years upwards, employed in stocking making in England, was in 1862 about 129,000. Of these only 4,063 were, according to the Parliamentary Return of the 11th February, 1862, working under the Factory Acts.

197. Thus, e.g., in the earthenware trade, Messrs. Cochrane, of the Britain Pottery, Glasgow, report: 'To keep up our quantity we have gone extensively into machines wrought by unskilled labour, and every day convinces us that we can produce a greater quantity than by the old method.' ('Rep. of Insp. of Fact., 31st Oct., 1865,' p. 13.) 'The effect of the Fact. Acts is to force on the further introduction of machinery' (l.c., pp. 13-14).

198. Thus, after the extension of the Factory Act to the potteries, great increase of powerjiggers in place of hand-moved jiggers.

199. 'Report of lnsp. of Fact., 31st Oct., 1865,' pp. 96 and 127.

200. The introduction of this and other machinery into match-making caused in one department alone 230 young persons to be replaced by 32 boys and girls of 14 to 17 years of age. This saving in labour was carried still further in 1865, by the employment of steam power.

201. 'Ch. Empl. Comm., 11. Rep., 1864,' p. ix., n. 50.

202. 'Rep. of Insp. of Fact., 31st Oct., 1865,' p..22.

203. 'But it must be borne in mind that those improvements, though carried out fully in some establishments, are by no means general, and are not capable of being brought into use in many of the old manufactories without an expenditure of capital beyond the means of many of the present occupiers.' 'I cannot but rejoice,' writes Sub-Insp. May, 'that notwithstanding the temporary disorganisation which inevitably follows the introduction of such a measure (as the Factory Act Extension Act), and is, indeed, directly indicative of the evils which it was intended to remedy, &c.' (Rep. of Insp. of Fact., 31st Oct., 1865.)

204. With blast furnaces, for instance, 'work towards the end of the week being generally much increased in duration in consequence of the habit of the men of idling on Monday and occasionally during a part or the whole of Tuesday also.' ('Child. Empl. Comm., III. Rep.,' p. vi.) 'The little masters generally have very irregular hours. They lose two or three days, and then work all night to make it up.... They always employ their own children, if they have any.' (l.c., p. vii.) 'The want of regularity in coming to work, encouraged by the possibility and practice of making up for this by working longer hours.' (l.c., p. xviii.) 'In Birmingham ... an enormous amount of time is lost ... idling part of the time, slaving the rest.' (l.c., p. xi.)

205. 'Child. Empl. Comm., IV., Rep.,' p. xxxii., 'The extension of the railway system is said to have contributed greatly to this custom of giving sudden orders, and the consequent hurry, neglect of meal-times, and late hours of the workpeople.' (l.c., p. xxxi.)

206. 'Ch. Empl. Comm, IV. Rep.,' pp. xxxv., n. 235, 237.

207. 'Ch. Empl. Comm. IV. Rep.,' p. 127, n. 56.

208. 'With respect to the loss of trade by non-completion of shipping orders in time, I remember that this was the pet argument of the factory masters in 1832 and 1833. Nothing that can be advanced now on this subject, could have the force that it had then, before steam had halved all distances and established new regulations for transit. It quite failed at that time of proof when put to the test, and again it will certainly fail should it have to be tried.' ('Reports of Insp. of Fact., 31 Oct., 1862,' pp. 54, 55.)

208 (a) 'Ch. Empl. Comm. IV. Rep.,' p. xviii, n. 118.

208 (b) John Bellers remarked as far back as 1699: 'The uncertainty of fashions does increase necessitous poor. It has two great mischiefs in it. 1st, The journeymen are miserable in winter for want of work, the mercers and master-weavers not daring to lay out their stocks to keep the journeymen employed before the spring comes, and they know what the fashion will then be; 2ndly, In the spring the journeymen are not sufficient, but the master-weavers must draw in many prentices, that they may supply the trade of the kingdom in a quarter or half a year, which robs the plough of hands, drains the country of labourers, and in a great part

stocks the city with beggars, and starves some in winter that are ashamed to beg.' ('Essays about the Poor, Manufactures, &c.,' p. 9.)

209. 'Ch. Empl. Comm. V. Rep.,' p. 171, n. 34.

210. The evidence of some Bradford export-houses is as follows: 'Under these circumstances, it seems clear that no boys need be worked longer than from 8 a.m. to 7 or 7.30 p.m., in making up. It is merely a question of extra hands and extra outlay. If some masters were not so greedy, the boys would not work late; an extra machine costs only £16 or £18; much of such over-time as does occur is to be referred to an insufficiency of appliances, and a want of space.' 'Ch. Empl, Comm. V. Rep.,' p. 171, n. 35, 36, 38.

211. l.c. A London manufacturer, who in other respects looks upon the compulsory regulation of the hours of labour as a protection for the workpeople against the manufacturers, and for the manufacturers themselves against the wholesale trade, states: 'The pressure in our business is caused by the shippers, who want, e.g., to send the goods by sailing vessel so as to reach their destination at a given season, and at the same time want to pocket the difference in freight between a sailing vessel and a steamship, or who select the earlier of two steamships in order to be in the foreign market before their competitors.'

212. 'This could be obviated,' says a manufacturer, 'at the expense of an enlargement of the works under the pressure of a General Act of Parliament.' l.c., p. x., n. 38.

213. l.c., p. xv., n. 72. sqq.

214. 'Rep. Insp. Fact., 31st October, 1865,' p. 127.

215. It has been found out by experiment, that with each respiration of average intensity made by a healthy average individual, about 25 cubic inches of air are consumed, and that about 20 respirations are made in each minute. Hence the air inhaled in 24 hours by each individual is about 720,000 cubic inches, or 416 cubic feet. It is clear, however, that air which has been once breathed, can no longer serve for the same process until it has been purified in the great workshop of Nature. According to the experiments of Valentin and Brunner, it appears that a healthy man gives off about 1,300 cubic inches of carbonic acid per hour; this would give about 8 ounces of solid carbon thrown off from the lungs in 24 hours. 'Every man should have at least 800 cubic feet.' (Huxley.)

216. According to the English Factory Act, parents cannot send their children under 14 years of age into Factories under the control of the Act, unless at the same time they allow them to receive elementary education. The manufacturer is responsible for compliance with the Act. 'Factory education is compulsory, and it is a condition of labour.' ('Rep. Insp. Fact., 31st Oct., 1865,' p. 111.)

217. On the very advantageous results of combining gymnastics (and drilling in the case of boys) with compulsory education for factory children and pauper scholars, see the speech of N. W. Senior at the seventh annual congress of 'The National Association for the Promotion of Social Science,' in 'Report of Proceedings, &c.,' Lond. 1863, pp. 63, 64, also the 'Rep. Insp. Fact., 31st Oct., 1865,' pp. 118, 119, 120, 126, sqq.

218. 'Rep. Insp. Fact., 31st Oct., 1865,' p. 118. A silk manufacturer naively states to the Children's Employment Commissioners: 'I am quite sure that the true secret of producing efficient workpeople is to be found in uniting education and labour from a period of childhood. Of course the occupation must not be too severe, nor irksome, or unhealthy. But of the advantage of the union I have no doubt. I wish my own children could have some work as well as play to give variety to their schooling.' ('Ch. Empl. Comm. V. Rep.,' p. 82, n. 36.)

219. Senior, l.c., p. 66. How modern industry, when it has attained to a certain pitch, is capable, by the revolution it effects in the mode of production and in the social conditions of production, of also revolutionising people's minds, is strikingly shown by a comparison of Senior's speech in 1863, with his philippic against the Factory Act of 1833; or by a comparison, of the views of the congress above referred to, with the fact that in certain country districts of England poor parents are forbidden, on pain of death by starvation,

to educate their children. Thus, e.g., Mr Snell reports it to be a common occurrence in Somersetshire that, when a poor person claims parish relief, he is compelled to take his children from school. Mr Wollarton, the clergyman at Feltham, also tells of cases where all relief was denied to certain families 'because they were sending their children to school!'

220. Wherever handicraft-machines, driven by men, compete directly or indirectly with more developed machines driven by mechanical power, a great change takes place with regard to the labourer who drives the machine. At first the steam-engine replaces this labourer, afterwards he must replace the steam-engine. Consequently the tension and the amount of labour-power expended become monstrous, and especially so in the case of the children who are condemned to this torture. Thus Mr Longe; one of the commissioners, found in Coventry and the neighbourhood boys of from 10 to 15 years employed in driving the ribbon-looms, not to mention younger children who had to drive smaller machines. 'It is extraordinarily fatiguing work. The boy is a mere substitute for steam power.' ('Ch. Empl. Comm. V, Rep. 1866;' p. 114, n. 6.) As to the fatal consequences of 'this system of slavery,' as the official report styles it, see l.c., p. 114 sqq.

221. l.c., p. 3, n. 24.

222. l.c., P. 7, n. 60.

223. 'In some parts of the Highlands of Scotland, not many years ago, every peasant, according to the Statistical Account, made his own shoes of leather tanned by himself. Many a shepherd and cottar too, with his wife and children, appeared at Church in clothes which had been touched by no hands but their own, since they were shorn from the sheep and sown in the flaxfield. In the preparation of these. it is added, scarcely a single article had been purchased, except the awl, needle, thimble, and a very few parts of the iron-work employed in the weaving. The dyes, toci, were chiefly extracted by the women from trees, shrubs and herbs.' (Dugald Stewart's 'Works,' Hamilton's Ed., Vol. viii., pp. 327-328.)

224. In the celebrated 'Livre des métiers' of Etienne Boileau, we find it prescribed that a journeyman on being admitted among the masters had to swear 'to love his brethren with brotherly love, to support them in their respective trades, not wilfully to betray the secrets of the trade, and besides, in the interests of all, not to recommend his own wares by calling the attention of the buyer to defects in the articles made by others.'

225. 'The bourgeoisie cannot exist without continually revolutionising the instruments of production, and thereby the relations of production and all the social relations. Conservation, in an unaltered form, of the old modes of production was on the contrary the first condition of existence for all earlier industrial classes. Constant revolution in production, uninterrupted disturbance of all social conditions, everlasting uncertainty and agitation, distinguish the bourgeois epoch from all earlier ones. All fixed, fast-frozen relations, with their train of ancient and venerable prejudices and opinions, are swept away, all new formed ones become antiquated before they can ossify. All that is solid melts into air, all that is holy is profaned, and man is at last compelled to face with sober senses his real conditions of life, and his relations with his kind.' (F. Engels und Karl Marx: 'Manifest der Kommunistischen Partei.' Lond. 1848, p. 5.)

226.

'You take my life
When you do take the means whereby I live.'
Shakespeare.

227. A French workman, on his return from San-Francisco, writes as follows: 'I never could have believed, that I was capable of working at the various occupations I was employed on in California. I was firmly convinced that I was fit for nothing but letter-press printing.... Once in the midst of this world of adventurers, who change their occupation as often as they do their shirt, egad, I did as the others. As mining did not turn out remunerative enough, I left it for the town, where in succession I became typographer, slater, plumber, &c. In consequence

of thus finding out that I am fit to any sort of work, I feel less of a mollusk and more of a man.' (A. Corbon, 'De l'enseignement professionnel,' 2ème ed., p. 50.)

228. John Bellers, a very phenomenon in the history of Political Economy, saw most clearly at the end of the 17th century, the necessity for abolishing the present system of education and division of labour, which beget hypertrophy and atrophy at the two opposite extremities of society. Amongst other things he says this: 'An idle learning being little better than the learning of idleness.... Bodily labour, it's a primitive institution of God.... Labour being as proper for the bodies' health as eating is for its living; for what pains a man saves by ease, he will find in disease.... Labour adds oil to the lamp of life, when thinking inflames it.... A childish silly employ' (a warning this, by presentiment, against the Basedows and their modern imitators) 'leaves the children's minds silly,' ('Proposals for Raising a Colledge of Industry of all Useful Trades and Husbandry.' Lond., 1696, pp. 12, 14, 18.)

229. This sort of labour goes on mostly in small workshops, as we have seen in the lacemaking and straw-plaiting trades, and as could be shown more in detail from the metal trades of Sheffield, Birmingham, &c.

230. 'Ch. Empl. Comm., V. Rep.,' p. xxv., n. 162, and II. Rep., p. xxxviii., n, 285, 289, p. xxv., xxvi., n. 191.

231. 'Factory labour may be as pure and as excellent as domestic labour, and perhaps more so.' ('Rep. Insp. of Fact., 31st October, 1865,' p. 129.)

232. 'Rep. Insp. of Fact., 31st October, 1865,' pp. 27-32.

233. Numerous instances will be found in 'Rep. of Insp. of Fact.'

234. 'Ch. Empl. Comm., V. Rep.,' p. x., n. 35.

235. 'Ch. Empl. Comm., V. Rep.,' p. ix., n. 28.

236. l.c., p. xxv., n. 165-167. As to the advantages of large scale, compared with small scale, industries, see 'Ch. Empl. Comm., III. Rep.,' p. 13, n. 144, p. 25, n. 121, p. 26, n. 125, p. 27, n. 140, &c.

237. The trades proposed to be brought under the Act were the following: Lace-making, stocking-weaving, straw-plaiting, the manufacture of wearing apparel with its numerous sub-divisions, artificial flower-making, shoemaking, hat-making, glove-making, tailoring, all metal works, from blast furnaces down to needleworks, &c., paper-mills, glassworks, tobacco factories, India-rubber works, braid-making (for weaving), hand-carpetmaking, umbrella and parasol making, the manufacture of spindles and spools, letterpress printing, book-binding, manufacture of stationery (including paper bags, cards, coloured paper, &c.), rope-making, manufacture of jet ornaments, brick-making, silk manufacture by hand, Coventry weaving, salt works, tallow chandlers, cement works, sugar refineries, biscuit-making, various industries connected with timber, and other mixed trades.

238. l.c., p. xxv., n. 169.

239. Here (from 'The Tory Cabinet...... to 'Nassau W. Senior") the English text has been altered in conformity with the 4th German edition.—Ed.

240. The Factory Acts Extension Act was passed on August 12, 1867. It regulates all foundries, smithies, and metal manufactories, including machine shops; furthermore glass-works, paper mills, gutta-percha and India-rubber works, tobacco manufactories, letter-press printing and book-binding works, and, lastly, all workshops in which more than 50 persons are employed. The Hours of Labour Regulation Act, passed on August 17, 1867, regulates the smaller workshops and the so-called domestic industries.

I shall revert to these Acts and to the new Mining Act of 1872 in Volume II.

241. Senior, 'Social Science Congress,' pp. 55-58.

242. The 'personnel' of this staff consisted of 2 inspectors, 2 assistant inspectors and 41 sub-inspectors. Eight additional sub-inspectors were appointed in 1871. The total cost of administering the Acts in England, Scotland, and Ireland amounted for the year 1871-72 to

no more than £25,347, inclusive of the law expenses incurred by prosecutions of offending masters.

243. Robert Owen, the father of Co-operative Factories and Stores, but who, as before remarked, in no way shared the illusions of his followers with regard to the bearing of these isolated elements of transformation, not only practically made the factory system the sole foundation of his experiments, but also declared that system to be theoretically the starting-point of the social revolution. Herr Vissering, Professor of Political Economy in the University of Leyden, appears to have a suspicion of this when, in his 'Handboek van Practische Staatshuishoudkunde, 1860-62,' which reproduces all the platitudes of vulgar economy, he strongly supports handicrafts against the factory system.

[*Added in the 4th German edition*—The 'hopelessly bewildering tangle of contradictory enactments' (S. 314) (present volume, p. 284) which English legislation called into life by means of the mutually conflicting Factory Acts, the Factory Acts Extension Act and the Workshops' Act, finally became intolerable, and thus all legislative enactments on this subject were codified in the Factory and Workshop Act of 1878. Of course no detailed critique of this English industrial code now in effect can be presented here. The following remarks will have to suffice. The Act comprises:

1) **Textile Mills.** Here everything remains about as it was: children more than 10 years of age may work 5½ hours a day; or 6 hours and Saturday off; young persons and women, 10 hours on 5 days, and at most 6½ on Saturday.
2) **Non-Textile Factories.** Here the regulations are brought closer than before to those of No. 1, but there are still several exceptions which favour the capitalists and which in certain cases may be expanded by special permission of the Home Secretary.
3) **Workshops**, defined approximately as in the former Act; as for the children, young workers and women employed there, the workshops are about on a par with the non-textile factories, but again conditions are easier in details.
4) **Workshops** in which no children or young workers are employed, but only persons of both sexes above the age of 18; this category enjoy still easier conditions.
5) **Domestic Workshops**, where only members of the family are employed, in the family dwelling: still more elastic regulations and simultaneously the restriction that the inspector may, without special permission of the ministry or a court, enter only rooms not used also for dwelling purposes; and lastly unrestricted freedom for straw-plaiting and lace and glove-making by members of the family. With all its defects this Act, together with the Swiss Federal Factory Law of March 23, 1877, is still by far the best piece of legislation in this field. A comparison of it with the said Swiss federal law is of particular interest because it clearly demonstrates the merits and demerits of the two legislative methods—the English, 'historical' method, which intervenes when occasion requires, and the continental method, which is built up on the traditions of the French Revolution and generalises more. Unfortunately, due to insufficient inspection personnel, the English code is still largely a dead letter with regard to its application to workshops.—*F. E.*]

244. 'You divide the people into two hostile camps of clownish boors and emasculated dwarfs. Good heavens! A nation divided into agricultural and commercial interests, calling itself sane; nay, styling itself enlightened and civilised, not only in spite of, but in consequence of this monstrous and unnatural division.' (David Urquhart, l.c., p. 119.) This passage shows, at one and the same time, the strength and the weakness of that kind of criticism which knows how to judge and condemn the present, but not how to comprehend it.

245. See Liebig: 'Die Chemie in ihrer Anwendung auf Agricultur und Physiologie,' 7. Auflage, 1862, and especially the 'Einleitung in die Naturgesetze des Feldbaus,' in the 1st Volume. To have developed from the point of view of natural science, the negative, i.e., destructive side of modern agriculture, is one of Liebig's immortal merits. His summary, too, of the

history of agriculture, although not free from gross errors, contains flashes of light. It is, however, to be regretted that he ventures on such haphazard assertions as the following: 'By greater pulverising and more frequent ploughing, the circulation of air in the interior of porous soil is aided, and the surface exposed to the action of the atmosphere is increased and renewed; but it is easily seen that the increased yield of the land cannot be proportional to the labour spent on that land, but increases in a much smaller proportion. This law,' adds Liebig, 'was first enunciated by John Stuart Mill in his 'Principles of Pol. Econ.,' Vol. 1, p. 17, as follows: 'That the produce of land increases, *caeteris paribus*, in a diminishing ratio to the increase of the labourers employed' (Mill here introduces in an erroneous form the law enunciated by Ricardo's school, for since the 'decrease of the labourers employed,' kept even pace in England with the advance of agriculture, the law discovered in, and applied to, England, could have no application to that country, at all events), 'is the universal law of agricultural industry.' This is very remarkable, since Mill was ignorant of the reason for this law.' (Liebig, l.c., Bd. I., p. 143 and Note.) Apart from Liebig's wrong interpretation of the word 'labour,' by which word he understands something quite different from what Political Economy does, it is, in any case, 'very remarkable' that he should make Mr John Stuart Mill the first propounder of a theory which was first published by James Anderson in A. Smith's days, and was repeated in various works down to the beginning of the 19th century; a theory which Malthus, that master in plagiarism (the whole of his population theory is a shameless plagiarism), appropriated to himself in 1815; which West developed at the same time as, and independently of, Anderson; which in the year 1817 was connected by Ricardo with the general theory of value, then made the round of the world as Ricardo's theory, and in 1820 was vulgarised by James Mill, the father of John Stuart Mill; and which, finally, was reproduced by John Stuart Mill and others, as a dogma already quite commonplace, and known to every schoolboy. It cannot be denied that John Stuart Mill owes his, at all events, 'remarkable' authority almost entirely to such *quid-pro-quos*.

PART V

THE PRODUCTION OF ABSOLUTE AND OF RELATIVE SURPLUS-VALUE

16

Absolute and Relative Surplus-Value

In considering the labour-process, we began (see Chapter VII.) by treating it in the abstract, apart from its historical forms, as a process between man and Nature. We there stated, 'If we examine the whole labour-process, from the point of view of its result, it is plain that both the instruments and the subject of labour are means of production, and that the labour itself is productive labour.' And in Note 2, same page, we further added: 'This method of determining, from the standpoint of the labour-process alone, what is productive labour, is by no means directly applicable to the case of the capitalist process of production.' We now proceed to the further development of this subject.

So far as the labour-process is purely individual, one and the same labourer unites in himself all the functions, that later on become separated. When an individual appropriates natural objects for his livelihood, no one controls him but himself. Afterwards he is controlled by others. A single man cannot operate upon Nature without calling his own muscles into play under the control of his own brain. As in the natural body head and hand wait upon each other, so the labour-process unites the labour of the hand with that of the head. Later on they part company and even become deadly foes. The product ceases to be the direct product of the individual, and becomes a social product, produced in common by a collective labourer, *i.e.*, by a combination of workmen, each of whom takes only a part, greater or less, in the manipulation of the subject of their labour. As the co-operative character of the labour-process becomes more and more marked, so, as a necessary consequence, does our notion of productive labour, and of its agent the productive labourer, become extended. In order to labour productively, it is no longer necessary for you to do manual work yourself; enough, if you are an organ of the collective labourer, and perform one of its subordinate functions. The first definition given above of productive labour, a definition deduced from the very nature of the production of material objects, still remains correct for the collective labourer, considered as a whole. But it no longer holds good for each member taken individually.

On the other hand, however, our notion of productive labour becomes narrowed. Capitalist production is not merely the production of commodities, it is essentially the production of surplus-value. The labourer produces, not for himself, but for capital. It no longer suffices, therefore, that he should simply produce. He must produce surplus-value. That labourer alone is productive, who produces surplus-value for the capitalist, and thus works for the self-expansion of capital. If we may take an example from outside the sphere of production of material objects, a schoolmaster is a productive labourer when, in addition to belabouring the heads of his scholars, he works like a horse to enrich the school proprietor. That the latter has laid out his capital in a teaching factory, instead of in a sausage factory, does not alter the relation. Hence the notion of a productive labourer implies not merely a relation between work and useful effect, between labourer and product of labour, but also a specific, social relation of production, a relation that has sprung up historically and stamps the labourer as the direct means of creating surplus-value. To be a productive labourer is, therefore, not a piece of luck, but a misfortune. In Book IV. which treats of the history of the theory, it will be more clearly seen, that the production of surplus-value has at all times been made, by classical political economists, the distinguishing characteristic of the productive labourer. Hence their definition of a productive labourer changes with their comprehension of the nature of surplus-value. Thus the Physiocrats insist that only agricultural labour is productive, since that alone, they say, yields a surplus-value. And they say so because, with them, surplus-value has no existence except in the form of rent.

The prolongation of the working-day beyond the point at which the labourer would have produced just an equivalent for the value of his labour-power, and the appropriation of that surplus-labour by capital, this is production of absolute surplus-value. It forms the general groundwork of the capitalist system, and the starting-point for the production of relative surplus-value. The latter presupposes that the working-day is already divided into two parts, necessary labour, and surplus-labour. In order to prolong the surplus-labour, the necessary labour is shortened by methods whereby the equivalent for the wages is produced in less time. The production of absolute surplus-value turns exclusively upon the length of the working-day; the production of relative surplus-value, revolutionises out and out the technical processes of labour, and the composition of society. It therefore presupposes a specific mode, the capitalist mode of production, a mode which, along with its methods, means, and conditions, arises and develops itself spontaneously on the foundation afforded by the formal subjection of labour to capital. In the course of this development, the formal subjection is replaced by the real subjection of labour to capital.

It will suffice merely to refer to certain intermediate forms, in which surplus-labour is not extorted by direct compulsion from the producer, nor the producer himself yet formally subjected to capital. In such forms capital has not yet acquired the direct control of the labour-process. By the side of independent producers who carry on their handicrafts and agriculture in the traditional old-fashioned way, there stands the usurer or the merchant, with his usurer's capital or merchant's capital, feeding on them like a parasite. The predominance, in a society, of this form of exploitation excludes the capitalist mode of production; to which mode, however, this form may serve as a transition, as it did towards the close of the Middle Ages. Finally, as is shown by modern 'domestic industry,' some intermediate forms are here and there reproduced in the background of Modern Industry, though their physiognomy is totally changed.

If, on the one hand, the mere formal subjection of labour to capital suffices for the production of absolute surplus-value, if, *e.g.*, it is sufficient that handicraftsmen who previously worked on their own account, or as apprentices of a master, should become wage labourers under the direct control of a capitalist; so, on the other hand, we have seen, how the methods of producing relative surplus-value, are, at the same time, methods of producing absolute surplus-value. Nay, more, the excessive prolongation of the working-day turned out to be the peculiar product of Modern Industry. Generally speaking, the specifically capitalist mode of production ceases to be a mere means of producing relative surplus-value, so soon as that mode has conquered an entire branch of production; and still more so, so soon as it has conquered all the important branches. It then becomes the general, socially predominant form of production. As a special method of producing relative surplus-value, it remains effective only, first, in so far as it seizes upon industries that previously were only formally subject to capital, that is, so far as it is propagandist; secondly, in so far as the industries that have been taken over by it, continue to be revolutionised by changes in the methods of production.

From one standpoint, any distinction between absolute and relative surplus-value appears illusory. Relative surplus-value is absolute, since it compels the absolute prolongation of the working-day beyond the labour-time necessary to the existence of the labourer himself. Absolute surplus-value is relative, since it makes necessary such a development of the productiveness of labour, as will allow of the necessary labour-time being confined to a portion of the working-day. But, if we keep in mind the behaviour of surplus-value, this appearance of identity vanishes. Once the capitalist mode of production is established and become general, the difference between absolute and relative surplus-value makes itself felt, whenever there is a question of raising the rate of surplus-value. Assuming that labour-power is paid for at its value, we are confronted by this alternative: given the productiveness of labour and its normal intensity, the rate of surplus-value can be raised only by the actual prolongation of the working-day; on the other hand, given the length of the working-day, that rise can be effected only by a change in the relative magnitudes of the components of the working-day, viz., necessary labour and surplus-labour; a change which, if the wages are not to fall below the value of labour-power, presupposes a change either in the productiveness or in the intensity of the labour.

If the labourer wants all his time to produce the necessary means of subsistence for himself and his race, he has no time left in which to work gratis for others. Without a certain degree of productiveness in his labour, he has no such superfluous time at his disposal; without such superfluous time, no surplus-labour, and therefore no capitalists, no slave-owners, no feudal lords, in one word, no class of large proprietors.[1]

Thus we may say that surplus-value rests on a natural basis; but this is permissible only in the very general sense, that there is no natural obstacle absolutely preventing one man from disburdening himself of the labour requisite for his own existence, and burdening another with it, any more, for instance, than unconquerable natural obstacle prevent one man from eating the flesh of another.[2] No mystical ideas must in any way be connected, as sometimes happens, with this historically developed productiveness of labour. It is only after men have raised themselves above the rank of animals, when therefore their labour has been to some extent socialised, that a state of things arises in which the surplus-labour of the one becomes a condition of existence for the other. At the dawn of civilisation the productiveness acquired by labour is small, but so too are the wants which develop with and by the means of satisfying them. Further, at that early period, the portion of society that lives on the labour of others is infinitely small compared with the mass of direct producers. Along with the progress in the productiveness of labour, that small portion of society increases both absolutely and relatively.[3] Besides, capital with its accompanying relations springs up from an economic soil that is the product of a long process of development. The productiveness of labour that serves as its foundation and starting-point, is a gift, not of nature, but of a history embracing thousands of centuries.

Apart from the degree of development, greater or less, in the form of social production, the productiveness of labour is fettered by physical conditions. These are all referable to the constitution of man himself (race, &c.), and to surrounding nature. The external physical conditions fall into two great economic classes, (1) Natural wealth in means of subsistence, *i.e.*, a fruitful soil, waters teeming with fish, &c., and (2), natural wealth in the instruments of labour, such as waterfalls, navigable rivers, wood, metal, coal, &c. At the dawn of civilisation, it is the first class that turns the scale; at a higher stage of development, it is the second. Compare, for example, England with India, or in ancient times, Athens and Corinth with the shores of the Black Sea.

The fewer the number of natural wants imperatively calling for satisfaction, and the greater the natural fertility of the soil and the favourableness of the climate, so much less is the labour-time necessary for the maintenance and reproduction of the producer. So much greater therefore can be the excess of his labours for others over his labour for himself. Diodorus long ago remarked this in relation to the ancient Egyptians.

> 'It is altogether incredible how little trouble and expense the bringing up of their children causes them. They cook for them the first simple food at hand; they also give them the lower part of the papyrus stem to eat, so far as it can be roasted in the fire, and the roots and stalks of marsh plants, some raw, some boiled and roasted. Most of the children go without shoes and unclothed, for the air is so mild. Hence a child, until he is grown up, costs his parents not more, on the whole, than twenty drachmas. It is this, chiefly, which explains why the population of Egypt is so numerous, and, therefore, why so many great works can be undertaken.'[4]

Nevertheless the grand structures of ancient Egypt are less due to the extent of its population than to the large proportion of it that was freely disposable. Just as the individual labourer can do more surplus-labour in proportion as his necessary labour-time is less, so with regard to the working population. The smaller the part of it which is required for the production of the necessary means of subsistence, so much the greater is the part that can be set to do other work.

Capitalist production once assumed, then, all other circumstances remaining the same, and given the length of the working day, the quantity of surplus-labour will vary with the physical conditions of labour, especially with the fertility of the soil. But it by no means follows from this that the most fruitful soil is the most fitted for the growth of the capitalist mode of production. This mode is based on the dominion of man over nature. Where nature is too lavish, she 'keeps him in hand, like a child in leading-strings.' She does not impose upon him any necessity to develop himself.[5] It is not the tropics with their luxuriant vegetation, but the temperate zone, that is the mother-country of capital. It is not the mere fertility of the soil, but the differentiation of the soil, the variety of its natural products, the changes of the seasons, which form the physical basis for the social division of labour, and which, by changes in the natural surroundings, spur man on to the multiplication of his wants, his capabilities, his means and modes of labour. It is the necessity of bringing a natural force under the control of society, of economising, of appropriating or subduing it on a large scale by the work of man's hand, that first plays the decisive part in the history of industry. Examples are, the irrigation works in Egypt,[6] Lombardy, Holland, or in India and Persia where irrigation by means of artificial canals, not only supplies the soil with the water indispensable to it, but also carries down to it, in the shape of sediment from the hills, mineral fertilisers. The secret of the flourishing state of industry in Spain and Sicily under the dominion of the Arabs lay in their irrigation works.[7]

Favourable natural conditions alone, give us only the possibility, never the reality, of surplus-labour, nor, consequently, of surplus-value and a surplus-product. The result of difference in the natural conditions of labour is this, that the same quantity of labour satisfies, in different countries, a different mass of requirements,[8] consequently, that under circumstances in other respects analogous, the necessary labour-time is different. These conditions affect surplus-labour only as natural limits, *i.e.*, by fixing the points at which labour for others can begin. In proportion as industry advances, these natural limits recede. In the midst of our West European society, where the labourer purchases the right to work for his own livelihood only by paying for it in surplus-labour, the idea easily takes root that it is an inherent quality of human labour to furnish a surplus-product.[9] But consider, for example, an inhabitant of the eastern islands of the Asiatic Archipelago, where sago grows wild in the forests.

> 'When the inhabitants have convinced themselves, by boring a hole in the tree, that the pith is ripe, the trunk is cut down and divided into several pieces, the pith is extracted, mixed with water and filtered: it is then quite fit for use as sago. One tree commonly yields 300 lbs., and occasionally 500 to 600 lbs. There, then, people go into the forests, and cut bread for themselves, just as with us they cut fire-wood.'[10]

Suppose now such an eastern bread-cutter requires 12 working hours a week for the satisfaction of all his wants. Nature's direct gift to him is plenty of leisure time. Before he can apply this leisure time productively for himself, a whole series of historical events is required; before he spends it in surplus-labour for strangers, compulsion is necessary. If capitalist production were introduced, the honest fellow would perhaps have to work six days a week, in order to appropriate to himself the product of one working day. The bounty of Nature does not explain why he would then have to work 6 days a week, or why he must furnish 5 days of surplus-labour. It explains only why his necessary labour-time would be limited to one day a week. But in no case would his surplus-product arise from some occult quality inherent in human labour.

Thus, not only does the historically developed social productiveness of labour, but also its natural productiveness, appear to be productiveness of the capital with which that labour is incorporated.

Ricardo never concerns himself about the origin of surplus-value. He treats it as a thing inherent in the capitalist mode of production, which mode, in his eyes, is the natural form of social production. Whenever he discusses the productiveness of labour, he seeks in it, not the cause of surplus-value, but the cause that determines the magnitude of that value. On the other hand, his school has openly proclaimed the productiveness of labour to be the originating cause of profit (read: Surplus-value). This at all events is a progress as against the mercantilists who, on their side, derived the excess of the price over the cost of production of the product, from the act of exchange, from the product being sold above its value. Nevertheless, Ricardo's school simply shirked the problem, they did not solve it. In fact these bourgeois economists instinctively saw, and rightly so, that it is very dangerous to stir too deeply the burning question of the origin of surplus-value. But what are we to think of John Stuart Mill, who, half a century after Ricardo, solemnly claims superiority over the mercantilists, by clumsily repeating the wretched evasions of Ricardo's earliest vulgarisers?

Mill says:

> 'The cause of profit is that labour produces more than is required for its support.'

So far, nothing but the old story; but Mill wishing to add something of his own, proceeds:

> 'To vary the form of the theorem; the reason why capital yields a profit, is because food, clothing, materials and tools, last longer than the time which was required to produce them.'

He here confounds the duration of labour-time with the duration of its products. According to this view, a baker whose product lasts only a day, could never extract from his workpeople the same profit, as a machine maker whose products endure for 20 years and more. Of course it is very true, that if a bird's nest did not last longer than the time it takes in building, birds would have to do without nests.

This fundamental truth once established, Mill establishes his own superiority over the mercantilists.

> 'We thus see,' he proceeds, 'that profit arises, not from the incident of exchange, but from the productive power of labour; and the general profit of the country is always what the productive power of labour makes it, whether any exchange takes place or not. If there were no division of employments, there would be no buying or selling, but there would still be profit.'

For Mill then, exchange, buying and selling, those general conditions of capitalist production, are but an incident, and there would always be profits even without the purchase and sale of labour-power!

> 'If,' he continues, 'the labourers of the country collectively produce twenty per cent more than their wages, profits will be twenty per cent, whatever prices may or may not be.' This is, on the one hand, a rare bit of tautology; for if labourers produce a surplus-value of 20% for the capitalist, his profit will be to the total wages of the labourers as 20:100. On the other hand, it is absolutely false to say that 'profits will be 20%.' They will always be less, because they are calculated upon the *sum total* of the capital advanced. If, for example, the capitalist have advanced £500, of which £400 is laid out in means of production and £100 in wages, and if the rate of surplus-value be 20%, the rate of profit will be 20:500, *i.e.*, 4% and not 20%.

Then follows a splendid example of Mill's method of handling the different historical forms of social production.

> 'I assume, throughout, the state of things which, where the labourers and capitalists are separate classes, prevails, with few exceptions, universally; namely, that the capitalist advances the whole expenses, including the entire remuneration of the labourer.'

Strange optical illusion to see everywhere a state of things which as yet exists only exceptionally on our earth.[11] But let us finish—Mill is willing to concede,

> 'that he should do so is not a matter of inherent necessity.' On the contrary: 'the labourer might wait, until the production is complete, for all that part of his wages which exceeds mere necessaries: and even for the whole, if he has funds in hand sufficient for his temporary support. But in the latter case, the labourer is to that extent really a capitalist in the concern, by supplying a portion of the funds necessary for carrying it on.'

Mill might have gone further and have added, that the labourer who advances to himself not only the necessaries of life but also the means of production, is in reality, nothing but his own wage-labourer. He might also have said that the American peasant proprietor is but a serf who does enforced labour for himself instead of for his lord.

After thus proving clearly, that even if capitalist production had no existence, still it would always exist, Mill is consistent enough to show, on the contrary, that it has no existence, even when it does exist.

> 'And even in the former case' (when the workman is a wage labourer to whom the capitalist advances all the necessaries of life, he the labourer), 'may be looked upon in the same light,' (i.e., as a capitalist), 'since, contributing his labour at less than the market-price, (!) he may be regarded as lending the difference (?) to his employer and receiving it back with interest, &c.'[12]

In reality, the labourer advances his labour gratuitously to the capitalist during, say one week, in order to receive the market price at the end of the week, &c., and it is this which, according to Mill, transforms him into a capitalist. On the level plain, simple mounds look like hills; and the imbecile flatness of the present bourgeoisie is to be measured by the altitude of its great intellects.

Notes

1. 'The very existence of the master-capitalists, as a distinct class, is dependent on the productiveness of industry.' (Ramsay, l.c., p. 206.) 'If each man's labour were but enough to produce his own food, there could be no property.' (Ravenstone, l.c. p. 14, 15.)
2. According to a recent calculation, there are yet at least 4,000,000 cannibals in those parts of the earth which have already been explored.
3. 'Among the wild Indians in America, almost everything is the labourer's, 99 parts of a hundred are to be put upon the account of labour. In England, perhaps, the labourer has not 2/3.' (The Advantages of the East India Trade, &c., p. 73.)
4. Diodorus, l.c., l. I., c. 80.
5. 'The first (natural wealth) as it is most noble and advantageous, so doth it make the people careless, proud, and given to all excesses; whereas the second enforceth vigilancy, literature, arts and policy.' (England's Treasure by Foreign Trade. Or the Balance of our Foreign Trade is the Rule of our Treasure. Written by Thomas Mun of London, merchant, and now published for the common good by his son John Mun. London, 1669, p. 181, 182.) 'Nor can I conceive a greater curse upon a body of people, than to be thrown upon a spot of land, where the productions for subsistence and food were, in great measure, spontaneous, and the climate

required or admitted little care for raiment and covering... there may be an extreme on the other side. A soil incapable of produce by labour is quite as bad as a soil that produces plentifully without any labour.' (An Inquiry into the Present High Price of Provisions. Lond. 1767, p. 10.)

6. The necessity for predicting the rise and fall of the Nile created Egyptian astronomy, and with it the dominion of the priests, as directors of agriculture. 'Le solstice est le moment de l'année ou commence la crue du Nil, et celui que les Egyptiens ont du observer avec le plus d'attention.... C'était cette année tropique qu'il leur importait de marquer pour se diriger dans leurs opérations agricoles. Ils durent donc chercher dans le ciel un signe apparent de son retour.' [The solstice is the moment of the year when the Nile begins to rise, and it is the moment the Egyptians have had to watch for with the greatest attention ... It was the evolution of the tropical year which they had to establish firmly so as to conduct their agricultural operations in accordance with it. They therefore had to search the heavens for a visible sign of the solstice's return.] (Cuvier: Discours sur les révolutions du globe, ed. Hoefer, Paris, 1863, p. 141.)

7. One of the material bases of the power of the state over the small disconnected producing organisms in India, was the regulation of the water supply. The Mahometan rulers of India understood this better than their English successors. It is enough to recall to mind the famine of 1866, which cost the lives of more than a million Hindus in the district of Orissa, in the Bengal presidency.

8. 'There are no two countries which furnish an equal number of the necessaries of life in equal plenty, and with the same quantity of labour. Men's wants increase or diminish with the severity or temperateness of the climate they live in; consequently, the proportion of trade which the inhabitants of different countries are obliged to carry on through necessity cannot be the same, nor is it practicable to ascertain the degree of variation farther than by the degrees of Heat and Cold; from whence one may make this general conclusion, that the quantity of labour required for a certain number of people is greatest in cold climates, and least in hot ones; for in the former men not only want more clothes, but the earth more cultivating than in the latter.' (An Essay on the Governing Causes of the Natural Rate of Interest. Lond. 1750. p. 60.) The author of this epoch-making anonymous work is J. Massy. Hume took his theory of interest from it.

9. 'Chaque travail doit (this appears also to be part of the *droits et devoirs du citoyen* [rights and duties of the citizen]) laisser un excédent.' [All labour must leave a surplus] Proudhon.

10. F. Schouw: 'Die Erde, die Pflanze und der Mensch,' 2. Ed. Leipz. 1854, p. 148.

11. In earlier editions of *Capital* the quotation from John Stuart Mill, 'I assume throughout...of the labourer,' had been given incorrectly, the words 'where the labourers and capitalists are separate classes' having been left out. Marx, in a letter dated November 28, 1878, pointed this out to Danielson, the Russian translator of *Capital*, adding:

    'The next two sentences, viz. 'Strange optical illusion to see everywhere a state of things which as yet exists only exceptionally on our earth. But let us finish' - should be deleted and the following sentence substituted:

    'Mr Mill is good enough to believe that this state of things is not an absolute necessity, even in that economic system in which 'labourers and capitalists are separate classes.'

    The substance of this note has been taken from the *Volksausgabe*. The quotation from Mill is from his *Principles of Political Economy*, Book II, Chap XV, 5.

12. J. St. Mill. Principles of Pol. Econ. Lond. 1868, p. 252-53 passim.

17

Changes of Magnitude in the Price of Labour-Power and in Surplus-Value

The value of labour-power is determined by the value of the necessaries of life habitually required by the average labourer. The quantity of these necessaries is known at any given epoch of a given society, and can therefore be treated as a constant magnitude. What changes, is the value of this quantity. There are, besides, two other factors that enter into the determination of the value of labour-power. One, the expenses of developing that power, which expenses vary with the mode of production; the other, its natural diversity, the difference between the labour-power of men and women, of children and adults. The employment of these different sorts of labour-power, an employment which is, in its turn, made necessary by the mode of production, makes a great difference in the cost of maintaining the family of the labourer, and in the value of the labour-power of the adult male. Both these factors, however, are excluded in the following investigation.[1]

I assume (1) that commodities are sold at their value; (2) that the price of labour-power rises occasionally above its value, but never sinks below it.

On this assumption we have seen that the relative magnitudes of surplus-value and of price of labour-power are determined by three circumstances; (1) the length of the working-day, or the extensive magnitude of labour; (2) the normal intensity of labour, its intensive magnitude, whereby a given quantity of labour is expended in a given time; (3) the productiveness of labour, whereby the same quantum of labour yields, in a given time, a greater or less quantum of product, dependent on the degree of development in the conditions of production. Very different combinations are clearly possible, according as one of the three factors is constant and two variable, or two constant and one variable, or lastly, all three simultaneously variable. And the number of these combinations is augmented by the fact that, when these factors simultaneously vary, the amount and direction of their respective variations may differ. In what follows the chief combinations alone are considered.

Section 1: *Length of the Working-Day and Intensity of Labour Constant Productiveness of Labour Variable*

On these assumptions the value of labour-power, and the magnitude of surplus-value, are determined by three laws.

1. A working day of given length always creates the same amount of value, no matter how the productiveness of labour, and, with it, the mass of the product, and the price of each single commodity produced, may vary.

   If the value created by a working-day of 12 hours be, say, six shillings, then, although the mass of the articles produced varies with the productiveness of labour, the only result is that the value represented by six shillings is spread over a greater or less number of articles.

2. Surplus-value and the value of labour-power vary in opposite directions. A variation in the productiveness of labour, its increase or diminution, causes a variation in the opposite direction in the value of labour-power, and in the same direction in surplus-value.

   The value created by a working day of 12 hours is a constant quantity, say, six shillings. This constant quantity is the sum of the surplus-value plus the value of the labour-power, which latter value the labourer replaces by an equivalent. It is self-evident, that if a constant quantity consists of two parts, neither of them can increase without the other diminishing. Let the two parts at starting be equal; 3 shillings value of labour-power, 3 shillings surplus-value. Then the value of the labour-power cannot rise from three shillings to four, without the surplus-value falling from three shillings to two; and the surplus-value cannot rise from three shillings to four, without the value of labour-power falling from three shillings to two. Under these circumstances, therefore, no change can take place in the absolute magnitude, either of the surplus-value, or of the value of labour-power, without a simultaneous change in their relative magnitudes, *i.e.*, relatively to each other. It is impossible for them to rise or fall simultaneously.

Further, the value of labour-power cannot fall, and consequently surplus-value cannot rise, without a rise in the productiveness of labour. For instance, in the above case, the value of the labour-power cannot sink from three shillings to two, unless an increase in the productiveness of labour makes it possible to produce in 4 hours the same quantity of necessaries as previously required 6 hours to produce. On the other hand, the value of the labour-power cannot rise from three shillings to four, without a decrease in the productiveness of labour, whereby eight hours become requisite to produce the same quantity of necessaries, for the production of which six hours previously sufficed. It follows from this, that an increase in the productiveness of labour causes a fall in the value of labour-power and a consequent rise in surplus-value, while, on the other hand, a decrease in such productiveness causes a rise in the value of labour-power, and a fall in surplus-value.

In formulating this law, Ricardo overlooked one circumstance; although a change in the magnitude of the surplus-value or surplus-labour causes a change in the opposite direction in the magnitude of the value of labour-power, or in the quantity of necessary labour, it by no means follows that they vary in the same proportion. They do increase or diminish by the same quantity. But their proportional increase or diminution depends on their original magnitudes before the change in the productiveness of labour took place. If the value of the labour-power be 4 shillings, or the necessary labour time 8 hours, and the surplus-value be 2 shillings, or the surplus-labour 4 hours, and if, in consequence of an increase in the productiveness of labour, the value of the labour-power fall to 3 shillings, or the necessary labour to 6 hours, the surplus-value will rise to 3 shillings, or the surplus-labour to 6 hours. The same quantity, 1 shilling or 2 hours, is added in one case and subtracted in the other. But the proportional change of magnitude is different in each case. While the value of the labour-power falls from 4 shillings to 3, *i.e.*, by 1/4 or 25%, the surplus-value rises from 2 shillings to 3, *i.e.*, by 1/2 or 50%. It therefore follows that the proportional increase or diminution in surplus-value, consequent on a given change in the productiveness of labour, depends on the original magnitude of that portion of the working day which embodies itself in surplus-value; the smaller that portion, the greater is the proportional change; the greater that portion, the less is the proportional change.

3. Increase or diminution in surplus-value is always consequent on, and never the cause of, the corresponding diminution or increase in the value of labour-power.[2]

Since the working-day is constant in magnitude, and is represented by a value of constant magnitude, since, to every variation in the magnitude of surplus-value, there corresponds an inverse variation in the value of labour-power, and since the value of labour-power cannot change, except in consequence of a change in the productiveness of labour, it clearly follows, under these conditions, that every change of magnitude in surplus-value arises from an inverse change of magnitude in the value of labour-power. If, then, as we have already seen, there can be no change of absolute magnitude in the value of labour-power, and in surplus-value, unaccompanied by a change in their relative magnitudes, so now it follows that no change in their relative magnitudes is possible, without a previous change in the absolute magnitude of the value of labour-power.

According to the third law, a change in the magnitude of surplus-value, presupposes a movement in the value of labour-power, which movement is brought about by a variation in the productiveness of labour. The limit of this change is given by the altered value of labour-power. Nevertheless, even when circumstances allow the law to operate, subsidiary movements may occur. For example: if in consequence of the increased productiveness of labour, the value of labour-power falls from 4 shillings to 3, or the necessary labour time from 8 hours to 6, the price of labour-power may possibly not fall below 3s. 8d., 3s. 6d., or 3s. 2d., and the surplus-value consequently not rise above 3s. 4d., 3s. 6d., or 3s. 10d. The amount of this fall, the lowest limit of which is 3 shillings (the new value of labour-power), depends on the relative weight, which the pressure of capital on the one side, and the resistance of the labourer on the other, throws into the scale.

The value of labour-power is determined by the value of a given quantity of necessaries. It is the value and not the mass of these necessaries that varies with the productiveness of labour. It is, however, possible that, owing to an increase of productiveness, both the labourer and the capitalist may simultaneously be able to appropriate a greater quantity of these necessaries, without any change in the price of labour-power or in surplus-value. If the value of labour-power be 3 shillings, and the necessary labour time amount to 6 hours, if the surplus-value likewise be 3 shillings, and the surplus-labour 6 hours, then if the productiveness of labour were doubled without altering the ratio of necessary labour to surplus-labour, there would be no change of magnitude in surplus-value and price of labour-power. The only result would be that each of them would represent twice as many use-values as before; these use-values being twice as cheap as before. Although labour-power would be unchanged in price, it would be above its value. If, however, the price of labour-power had fallen, not to 1s. 6d., the lowest possible point consistent with its new value, but to 2s. 10d. or 2s. 6d., still this lower price would represent an increased mass of necessaries. In this way it is possible with an increasing productiveness of labour, for the price of labour-power to keep on falling, and yet this fall to be accompanied by a constant growth in the mass of the labourer's means of subsistence. But even in such case, the fall in the value of labour-power would cause a corresponding rise of surplus-value, and thus the abyss between the labourer's position and that of the capitalist would keep widening.[3]

Ricardo was the first who accurately formulated the three laws we have above stated. But he falls into the following errors: (1) he looks upon the special conditions under which these laws hold good as the general and sole conditions of capitalist production. He knows no change, either in the length of the working-day, or in the intensity of labour; consequently with him there can be only one variable factor, viz., the productiveness of labour; (2), and this error vitiates his analysis much more than (1), he has not, any more than have the other economists, investigated surplus-value as such, *i.e.*, independently of its particular forms, such as profit, rent, &c. He therefore confounds together the laws of the rate of surplus-value and the laws of the rate of profit. The rate of profit is, as we have already said, the ratio of the surplus-value to the total capital advanced; the rate of surplus-value is the ratio of the surplus-value to the variable part of that capital. Assume that a capital C of £500 is made up of raw material, instruments of labour, &c. (c) to the amount of £400; and of wages (v) to the amount of £100; and further, that the surplus-value (s) = £100. Then we have rate of surplus-value s/v = £100/£100 = 100%. But the rate of profit s/c = £100/£500 = 20%. It is, besides, obvious that the rate of profit may depend on circumstances that in no way affect the rate of surplus-value. I shall show in Book III that, with a given rate of surplus-value, we may have any number of rates of profit, and that various rates of surplus-value may, under given conditions, express themselves in a single rate of profit.

Section 2: *Working-Day Constant. Productiveness of Labour Constant. Intensity of Labour Variable*

Increased intensity of labour means increased expenditure of labour in a given time. Hence a working-day of more intense labour is embodied in more products than is one of less intense labour, the length of each day being the same. Increased productiveness of labour also, it is true, will supply more products in a given working-day. But in this latter case, the value of each single product falls, for it costs less labour than before; in the former case, that value remains unchanged, for each article costs the same labour as before. Here we have an increase in the number of products, unaccompanied by a fall in their individual prices: as their number increases, so does the sum of their prices. But in the case of increased productiveness, a given value is spread over a greater mass of products. Hence the length of the working-day being constant, a day's labour of increased intensity will be incorporated in an increased value, and, the value of money remaining unchanged, in more money. The value created varies with the extent to which the intensity of labour deviates from its normal intensity in the society. A given working-day, therefore, no longer creates a constant, but a variable value; in a day of 12 hours of ordinary intensity, the value created is, say 6 shillings, but with increased intensity, the value created may be 7, 8, or more shillings. It is clear that, if the value created by a day's labour increases from, say, 6 to 8 shillings then the two parts into which this value is divided, viz., price of labour-power and surplus-value, may both of them increase simultaneously, and either equally or unequally. They may both simultaneously increase from 3 shillings to 4. Here, the rise in the price of labour-power does not necessarily imply that the price has risen above the value of labour-power. On the contrary, the rise in price may be accompanied by a fall in value. This occurs whenever the rise in the price of labour-power does not compensate for its increased wear and tear.

We know that, with transitory exceptions, a change in the productiveness of labour does not cause any change in the value of labour-power, nor consequently in the magnitude of surplus-value, unless the products of the industries affected are articles habitually consumed by the labourers. In the present case, this condition no longer applies. For when the variation is either in the duration or in the intensity of labour, there is always a corresponding change in the magnitude of the value created, independently of the nature of the article in which that value is embodied.

If the intensity of labour were to increase simultaneously and equally in every branch of industry, then the new and higher degree of intensity would become the normal degree for the society, and would therefore cease to be taken account of. But still, even then, the intensity of labour would be different in different countries, and would modify the international application of the law of value. The more intense working-day of one nation would be represented by a greater sum of money than would the less intense day of another nation.[4]

Section 3: *Productiveness and Intensity of Labour Constant. Length of the Working-Day Variable*

The working-day may vary in two ways. It may be made either longer or shorter. From our present data, and within the limits of the assumptions made on p. 487 [v. 35 MECW p. 520] we obtain the following laws:

1. The working-day creates a greater or less amount of value in proportion to its length—thus, a variable and not a constant quantity of value.
2. Every change in the relation between the magnitudes of surplus-value and of

the value of labour-power arises from a change in the absolute magnitude of the surplus-labour, and consequently of the surplus-value.

3. The absolute value of labour-power can change only in consequence of the reaction exercised by the prolongation of surplus-labour upon the wear and tear of labour-power. Every change in this absolute value is therefore the effect, but never the cause, of a change in the magnitude of surplus-value.

We begin with the case in which the working-day is shortened.

1. A shortening of the working-day under the conditions given above, leaves the value of labour-power, and with it, the necessary labour time, unaltered. It reduces the surplus-labour and surplus-value. Along with the absolute magnitude of the latter, its relative magnitude also falls, *i.e.*, its magnitude relatively to the value of labour-power whose magnitude remains unaltered. Only by lowering the price of labour-power below its value could the capitalist save himself harmless.

   All the usual arguments against the shortening of the working-day, assume that it takes place under the conditions we have here supposed to exist; but in reality the very contrary is the case: a change in the productiveness and intensity of labour either precedes, or immediately follows, a shortening of the working-day.[5]

2. Lengthening of the working-day. Let the necessary labour time be 6 hours, or the value of labour-power 3 shillings; also let the surplus-labour be 6 hours or the surplus-value 3 shillings. The whole working-day then amounts to 12 hours and is embodied in a value of 6 shillings. If, now, the working-day be lengthened by 2 hours and the price of labour-power remain unaltered, the surplus-value increases both absolutely and relatively. Although there is no absolute change in the value of labour-power, it suffers a relative fall. Under the conditions assumed in 1. there could not be a change of relative magnitude in the value of labour-power without a change in its absolute magnitude. Here, on the contrary, the change of relative magnitude in the value of labour-power is the result of the change of absolute magnitude in surplus-value.

   Since the value in which a day's labour is embodied, increases with the length of that day, it is evident that the surplus-value and the price of labour-power may simultaneously increase, either by equal or unequal quantities. This simultaneous increase is therefore possible in two cases, one, the actual lengthening of the working-day, the other, an increase in the intensity of labour unaccompanied by such lengthening.

   When the working-day is prolonged, the price of labour-power may fall below its value, although that price be nominally unchanged or even rise. The value of a day's labour-power is, as will be remembered, estimated from its normal average duration, or from the normal duration of life among the labourers, and from corresponding normal transformations of organised bodily matter into motion,[6] in conformity with the nature of man. Up to a certain point, the increased wear and tear of labour-power, inseparable from a lengthened working-day, may be compensated by higher wages. But beyond this point the wear and tear increases in geometrical progression, and every condition suitable for the normal reproduction and functioning of labour-power is suppressed. The price of labour-power and the degree of its exploitation cease to be commensurable quantities.

Section 4: *Simultaneous Variations in the Duration, Productiveness, and Intensity of Labour*

It is obvious that a large number of combinations are here possible. Any two of the factors may vary and the third remain constant, or all three may vary at once. They may vary either in the same or in different degrees, in the same or in opposite directions, with the result that the variations counteract one another, either wholly or in part. Nevertheless the analysis of every possible case is easy in view of the results given in I., II., and III. The effect of every possible combination may be found by treating each factor in turn as variable, and the other two constant for the time being. We shall, therefore, notice, and that briefly, but two important cases.

A. Diminishing productiveness of labour with a simultaneous lengthening of the working-day.

In speaking of diminishing productiveness of labour, we here refer to diminution in those industries whose products determine the value of labour-power; such a diminution, for example, as results from decreasing fertility of the soil, and from the corresponding dearness of its products. Take the working-day at 12 hours and the value created by it at 6 shillings, of which one half replaces the value of the labour-power, the other forms the surplus-value. Suppose, in consequence of the increased dearness of the products of the soil, that the value of labour-power rises from 3 shillings to 4, and therefore the necessary labour time from 6 hours to 8. If there be no change in the length of the working-day, the surplus-labour would fall from 6 hours to 4, the surplus-value from 3 shillings to 2. If the day be lengthened by 2 hours, *i.e.*, from 12 hours to 14, the surplus-labour remains at 6 hours, the surplus-value at 3 shillings[note], but the surplus-value decreases compared with the value of labour-power, as measured by the necessary labour time. If the day be lengthened by 4 hours, viz., from 12 hours to 16, the proportional magnitudes of surplus-value and value of labour-power, of surplus-labour and necessary labour, continue unchanged, but the absolute magnitude of surplus-value rises from 3 shillings to 4, that of the surplus-labour from 6 hours to 8, an increment of 33 1/3%. Therefore, with diminishing productiveness of labour and a simultaneous lengthening of the working-day, the absolute magnitude of surplus-value may continue unaltered, at the same time that its relative magnitude diminishes; its relative magnitude may continue unchanged, at the same time that its absolute magnitude increases; and, provided the lengthening of the day be sufficient, both may increase.

In the period between 1799 and 1815, the increasing price of provisions led in England to a nominal rise in wages, although the real wages, expressed in the necessaries of life, fell. From this fact West and Ricardo drew the conclusion, that the diminution in the productiveness of agricultural labour had brought about a fall in the rate of surplus-value, and they made this assumption of a fact that existed only in their imaginations, the starting-point of important investigations into the relative magnitudes of wages, profits, and rent. But, as a matter of fact, surplus-value had at that time, thanks to the increased intensity of labour, and to the prolongation of the working-day, increased both in absolute and relative magnitude. This was the period in which the right to prolong the hours of labour to an outrageous extent was established;[7] the period that was especially characterised by an accelerated accumulation of capital here, by pauperism there.[8]

B. Increasing intensity and productiveness of labour with simultaneous shortening of the working-day

Increased productiveness and greater intensity of labour, both have a like effect. They both augment the mass of articles produced in a given time. Both, therefore, shorten that portion of the working-day which the labourer needs to produce his means of subsistence or their equivalent. The minimum length of the working-day is fixed by this necessary but contractile portion of it. If the whole working-day were to shrink to the length of this portion, surplus-labour would vanish, a consummation utterly impossible under the régime of capital. Only by suppressing the capitalist form of production could the length of the working-day be reduced to the necessary labour time. But, even in that case, the latter would extend its limits. On the one hand, because the notion of 'means of subsistence' would considerably expand, and the labourer would lay claim to an altogether different standard of life. On the other hand, because a part of what is now surplus-labour, would then count as necessary labour; I mean the labour of forming a fund for reserve and accumulation.

The more the productiveness of labour increases, the more can the working-day be shortened; and the more the working-day is shortened, the more can the intensity of labour increase. From a social point of view, the productiveness increases in the same ratio as the economy of labour, which, in its turn, includes not only economy of the means of production, but also the avoidance of all useless labour. The capitalist mode of production, while on the one hand, enforcing economy in each individual business, on the other hand, begets, by its anarchical system of competition, the most outrageous squandering of labour-power and of the social means of production, not to mention the creation of a vast number of employments, at present indispensable, but in themselves superfluous.

The intensity and productiveness of labour being given, the time which society is bound to devote to material production is shorter, and as a consequence, the time at its disposal for the free development, intellectual and social, of the individual is greater, in proportion as the work is more and more evenly divided among all the able-bodied members of society, and as a particular class is more and more deprived of the power to shift the natural burden of labour from its own shoulders to those of another layer of society. In this direction, the shortening of the working-day finds at last a limit in the generalisation of labour. In capitalist society spare time is acquired for one class by converting the whole life-time of the masses into labour time.

Notes

1. *Note in the 3rd German edition.*—The case considered at pages 321-324 is here of course omitted.—*F. E.*
2. To this third law MacCulloch has made, amongst others, this absurd addition, that a rise in surplus-value, unaccompanied by a fall in the value of labour-power, can occur through the abolition of taxes payable by the capitalist. The abolition of such taxes makes no change whatever in the quantity of surplus-value that the capitalist extorts at first-hand from the labourer. It alters only the proportion in which that surplus-value is divided between himself and third persons. It consequently makes no alteration whatever in the relation between surplus-value and value of labour-power. MacCulloch's exception therefore proves only his misapprehension of the rule, a misfortune that as often happens to him in the vulgarisation of Ricardo, as it does to J. B. Say in the vulgarisation of Adam Smith.
3. 'When an alteration takes place in the productiveness of industry, and that either more or less is produced by a given quantity of labour and capital, the proportion of wages may obviously vary, whilst the quantity, which that proportion represents, remains the same, or the quantity may vary, whilst the proportion remains the same.' ('Outlines of Political Economy, &c.,' p. 67.)
4. 'All things being equal, the English manufacturer can turn out a considerably larger amount of work in a given time than a foreign manufacturer, so much as to counterbalance the difference of the working-days, between 60 hours a week here, and 72 or 80 elsewhere.' (Rep. of Insp. of Fact. for 31st Oct., 1855, p. 65.) The most infallible means for reducing this qualitative difference between the English and Continental working hour would be a law shortening quantitatively the length of the working-day in Continental factories.
5. 'There are compensating circumstances ... which the working of the Ten Hours› Act has brought to light.' ('Rep. of Insp. of Fact. for 31st Oct. 1848,' p. 7.)
6. 'The amount of labour which a man had undergone in the course of 24 hours might be

approximately arrived at by an examination of the chemical changes which had taken place in his body, changed forms in matter indicating the anterior exercise of dynamic force.' (Grove: 'On the Correlation of Physical Forces.')

7. 'Corn and labour rarely march quite abreast; but there is an obvious limit, beyond which they cannot be separated. With regard to the unusual exertions made by the labouring classes in periods of dearness, which produce the fall of wages noticed in the evidence' (namely, before the Parliamentary Committee of Inquiry, 1814-15), 'they are most meritorious in the individuals, and certainly favour the growth of capital. But no man of humanity could wish to see them constant and unremitted. They are most admirable as a temporary relief; but if they were constantly in action, effects of a similar kind would result from them, as from the population of a country being pushed to the very extreme limits of its food.' (Malthus: 'Inquiry into the Nature and Progress of Rent,' Lond., 1815, p. 48, note.) All honour to Malthus that he lays stress on the lengthening of the hours of labour, a fact to which he elsewhere in his pamphlet draws attention, while Ricardo and others, in face of the most notorious facts, make invariability in the length of the working-day the groundwork of all their investigations. But the conservative interests, which Malthus served, prevented him from seeing that an unlimited prolongation of the working-day, combined with an extraordinary development of machinery, and the exploitation of women and children, must inevitably have made a great portion of the working-class 'supernumerary,' particularly whenever the war should have ceased, and the monopoly of England in the markets of the world should have come to an end. It was, of course, far more convenient, and much more in conformity with the interests of the ruling classes, whom Malthus adored like a true priest, to explain this 'over-population' by the eternal laws of Nature, rather than by the historical laws of capitalist production.

8. 'A principal cause of the increase of capital, during the war, proceeded from the greater exertions, and perhaps the greater privations of the labouring classes, the most numerous in every society. More women and children were compelled by necessitous circumstances, to enter upon laborious occupations, and former workmen were, from the same cause, obliged to devote a greater portion of their time to increase production.' (Essays on Pol. Econ., in which are illustrated the principal causes of the present national distress. Lond., 1830, p. 248.)

18

Various Formula for the Rate of Surplus-Value

We have seen that the rate of surplus-value is represented by the following formulae:

$$\text{I.}\quad \frac{\text{Surplus-value}}{\text{Variable Capital}}\left(\frac{s}{v}\right) = \frac{\text{Surplus-value}}{\text{Value of labour-power}} = \frac{\text{Surplus-labour}}{\text{Necessary labour}}$$

The two first of these formulae represent, as a ratio of values, that which, in the third, is represented as a ratio of the times during which those values are produced. These formulae, supplementary the one to the other, are rigorously definite and correct. We therefore find them substantially, but not consciously, worked out in classical Political Economy. There we meet with the following derivative formulae.

$$\text{II.}\quad \frac{\text{Surplus-labour}}{\text{Working-day}} = \frac{\text{Surplus-value}}{\text{Value of the Product}} = \frac{\text{Surplus-product}}{\text{Total Product}}$$

One and the same ratio is here expressed as a ratio of labour-times, of the values in which those labour-times are embodied, and of the products in which those values exist. It is of course understood that, by 'Value of the Product,' is meant only the value newly created in a working-day, the constant part of the value of the product being excluded.

In all of these formulae (II.), the actual degree of exploitation of labour, or the rate of surplus-value, is falsely expressed. Let the working-day be 12 hours. Then, making the same assumptions as in former instances, the real degree of exploitation of labour will be represented in the following proportions.

$$\frac{\text{6 hours surplus-labour}}{\text{6 hours necessary labour}} = \frac{\text{Surplus-value of 3 sh.}}{\text{Variable Capital of 3 sh.}} = 100\%$$

From formulae II. we get very differently,

$$\frac{\text{6 hours surplus-labour}}{\text{Working-day of 12 hours}} = \frac{\text{Surplus-value of 3 sh.}}{\text{Value created of 6 sh.}} = 50\%$$

These derivative formulae express, in reality, only the proportion in which the working-day, or the value produced by it, is divided between capitalist and labourer. If they are to be treated as direct expressions of the degree of self-expansion of capital, the following erroneous law would hold good: Surplus-labour or surplus-value can never reach 100%.[1] Since the surplus-labour is only an aliquot part of the working-day, or since surplus-value is only an aliquot part of the value created, the surplus-labour must necessarily be always less than the working-day, or the surplus-value always less than the total value created. In order, however, to attain the ratio of 100:100 they must be equal. In order that the surplus-labour may absorb the whole day (i.e., an average day of any week or year), the necessary labour must sink to zero. But if the necessary labour vanish, so too does the surplus-labour, since it is only a function of the former. The ratio

$$\frac{\text{Surplus-labour}}{\text{Working-day}} \text{ or } \frac{\text{Surplus-value}}{\text{Value created}}$$

can therefore never reach the limit 100/100, still less rise to 100 + x/100. But not so the rate of surplus-value, the real degree of exploitation of labour. Take, e.g., the estimate of L. de Lavergne, according to which the English agricultural labourer gets only 1/4, the capitalist (farmer) on the other hand 3/4 of the product[2] or its value, apart from the question of how the booty is subsequently divided between the capitalist, the landlord, and others. According to this, this surplus-labour of the English agricultural labourer is to his necessary labour as 3:1, which gives a rate of exploitation of 300%.

The favorite method of treating the working-day as constant in magnitude became, through the use of formulae II., a fixed usage, because in them surplus-labour is always compared with a working-day of given length. The same holds good when the repartition of the value produced is exclusively kept in sight. The working-day that has already been realized in given value, must necessarily be a day of given length.

The habit of representing surplus-value and value of labour-power as fractions of the value created—a habit that originates in the capitalist mode of production itself, and whose import will hereafter be disclosed—conceals the very transaction that characterizes capital, namely the exchange of variable capital for living labour-power, and the consequent exclusion of the labourer from the product. Instead of the real fact, we have false semblance of an association, in which labourer and capitalist divide the product in proportion to the different elements which they respectively contribute towards its formation. [3]

Moreover, the formulae II. can at any time be reconverted into formulae I. If, for instance, we have

$$\frac{\text{Surplus-labour of 6 hours}}{\text{Working-day of 12 hours}}$$

then the necessary labour-time being 12 hours less the surplus-labour of 6 hours, we get the following result,

$$\frac{\text{Surplus-labour of 6 hours}}{\text{Necessary labour of 6 hours}} = \frac{100}{100}$$

There is a third formula which I have occasionally already anticipated; it is

$$\text{III.} \quad \frac{\text{Surplus-value}}{\text{Value of labour-power}} = \frac{\text{Surplus-labour}}{\text{Necessary labour}} = \frac{\text{Unpaid labour}}{\text{Paid labour}}$$

After the investigations we have given above, it is no longer possible to be misled, by the formula

$$\frac{\text{Unpaid labour,}}{\text{Paid labour}}$$

into concluding, that the capitalist pays for labour and not for labour-power. This formula is only a popular expression for

$$\frac{\text{Surplus-labour,}}{\text{Necessary labour}}$$

The capitalist pays the value, so far as price coincides with value, of the labour-power, and receives in exchange the disposal of the living labour-power itself. His usufruct is spread over two periods. During one the labourer produces a value that is only equal to the value of his labour-power; he produces its equivalent. This the capitalist receives in return for his advance of the price of the labour-power, a product ready made in the market. During the other period, the period of surplus-labour, the usufruct of the labour-power creates a value for the capitalist, that costs him no equivalent. [4] This expenditure of labour-power comes to him gratis. In this sense it is that surplus-labour can be called unpaid labour.

Capital, therefore, is not only, as Adam Smith says, the command over labour. It is essentially the command over unpaid labour. All surplus-value, whatever particular form (profit, interest, or rent), it may subsequently crystallize into, is in substance the materialization of unpaid labour. The secret of the self-expansion of capital resolves itself into having the disposal of a definite quantity of other people's unpaid labour.

Notes

1. Thus, e.g., in 'Dritter Brief an v. Kirchmann von Rodbertus. Widerlegung der Ricardo'schen Lehre von der Grundrente und Begrundung einer neuen Rententheorie'. Berlin, 1851. I shall return to this letter later on; in spite of its erroneous theory of rent, it sees through the nature of capitalist production.
   NOTE ADDED IN THE 3RD GERMAN EDITION: It may be seen from this how favorably Marx judged his predecessors, whenever he found in them real progress, or new and sound ideas. The subsequent publications of Robertus' letters to Rud. Meyer has shown that the

above acknowledgement by Marx wants restricting to some extent. In those letters this passage occurs:

> 'Capital must be rescued not only from labour, but from itself, and that will be best effected, by treating the acts of the industrial capitalist as economic and political functions, that have been delegated to him with his capital, and by treating his profit as a form of salary, because we still know no other social organization. But salaries may be regulated, and may also be reduced if they take too much from wages. The irruption of Marx into Society, as I may call his book, must be warded off.... Altogether, Marx's book is not so much an investigation into capital, as a polemic against the present form of capital, a form which he confounds with the concept itself of capital.'

('Briefe, &c., von Dr Robertus-Jagetzow, herausgg. von Dr Rud. Meyer,' Berlin, 1881, I, Bd. P.111, 46. Brief von Rodbertus.) To such ideological commonplaces did the bold attack by Robertus in his 'social letters' finally dwindle down.—*F.E.*

2. That part of the product which merely replaces the constant capital advanced is of course left out in this calculation. Mr L. de Lavergne, a blind admirer of England, is inclined to estimate the share of the capitalist too low, rather than too high.
3. All well-developed forms of capitalist production being forms of cooperation, nothing is, of course, easier, than to make abstraction from their antagonistic character, and to transform them by a word into some form of free association, as is done by A. de labourde in 'De l'Esprit d'Association dans tous les intérêts de la communauté». Paris 1818. H. Carey, the Yankee, occasionally performs this conjuring trick with like success, even with the relations resulting from slavery.
4. Although the Physiocrats could not penetrate the mystery of surplus-value, yet this much was clear to them, viz., that it is 'une richesse indépendante et disponible qu'il (the possessor) n'a point achetée et qu'il vend.' [a wealth which is independent and disposable, which he ... has not bought and which he sells] (Turgot: 'Réflexions sur la Formation et la Distribution des Richesses,' p.11.)

PART VI

WAGES

19

The Transformation of the Value (and Respective Price) of Labour-Power into Wages

On the surface of bourgeois society the wage of the labourer appears as the price of labour, a certain quantity of money that is paid for a certain quantity of labour. Thus people speak of the value of labour and call its expression in money its necessary or natural price. On the other hand they speak of the market-prices of labour, i.e., prices oscillating above or below its natural price.

But what is the value of a commodity? The objective form of the social labour expended in its production. And how do we measure the quantity of this value? By the quantity of the labour contained in it. How then is the value, e.g., of a 12 hour working-day to be determined? By the 12 working-hours contained in a working-day of 12 hours, which is an absurd tautology.[1]

In order to be sold as a commodity in the market, labour must at all events exist before it is sold. But, could the labourer give it an independent objective existence, he would sell a commodity and not labour.[2]

Apart from these contradictions, a direct exchange of money, i.e., of realized labour, with living labour would either do away with the law of value which only begins to develop itself freely on the basis of capitalist production, or do away with capitalist production itself, which rests directly on wage-labour. The working-day of 12 hours embodies itself, e.g., in a money-value of 6s. Either equivalents are exchanged, and then the labourer receives 6s, for 12 hours' labour; the price of his labour would be equal to the price of his product. In this case he produces no surplus-value for the buyer of his labour, the 6s. are not transformed into capital, the basis of capitalist production vanishes. But it is on this very basis that he sells his labour and that his labour is wage-labour. Or else he receives for 12 hours' labour less than 6s., i.e., less than 12 hours' labour. Twelve hours' labour are exchanged against 10, 6, &c., hours' labour. This equalization of unequal quantities not merely does away with the determination of value. Such a self-destructive contradiction cannot be in any way even enunciated or formulated as a law.[3]

It is of no avail to deduce the exchange of more labour against less, from their difference of form, the one being realized, the other living.[4] This is the more absurd as the value of a commodity is determined not by the quantity of labour actually realized in it, but by the quantity of living labour necessary for its production. A commodity represents, say, 6 working-hours. If an invention is made by which it can be produced in 3 hours, the value, even of the commodity already produced, falls by half. It represents now 3 hours of social labour instead of the 6 formerly necessary. It is the quantity of labour required for its production, not the realized form of that labour, by which the amount of the value of a commodity is determined.

That which comes directly face to face with the possessor of money on the market, is in fact not labour, but the labourer. What the latter sells is his labour-power. As soon as his labour actually begins, it has already ceased to belong to him; it can therefore no longer be sold by him. Labour is the substance, and the immanent measure of value, but has itself no value.[5]

In the expression 'value of labour,' the idea of value is not only completely obliterated, but actually reversed. It is an expression as imaginary as the value of the earth. These imaginary expressions, arise, however, from the relations of production themselves. They are categories for the phenomenal forms of essential relations. That in their appearance things often represent themselves in inverted form is pretty well known in every science except Political Economy.[6]

Classical Political Economy borrowed from every-day life the category 'price of labour' without further criticism, and then simply asked the question, how is this price determined? It soon recognized that the change in the relations of demand and supply explained in regard to the price of labour, as of all other commodities, nothing except its changes i.e., the oscillations of the market-price above or below a certain mean. If demand and supply balance, the oscillation of prices ceases, all other conditions remaining the same. But then demand and supply also cease to explain anything. The price of labour, at the moment when demand and supply are in equilibrium, is its natural price, determined independently of the relation of demand and supply. And how this price is determined is just the question. Or a larger period of oscillations in the market-price is taken, e.g., a year, and they are found to cancel one the other, leaving a mean average quantity, a relatively constant magnitude. This had naturally to be determined otherwise than by its own compensating variations. This price which always finally predominates over the accidental market-prices of labour and regulates them, this 'necessary price' (Physiocrats) or 'natural price' of labour (Adam Smith) can, as with all other commodities, be nothing else than its value expressed in money. In this way, Political Economy expected to penetrate athwart the accidental prices of labour, to the value of labour. As with other commodities, this value was determined by the cost of production. But what is the cost of production—of the labourer, i.e., the cost of producing or reproducing the labourer himself? This question unconsciously substituted itself in Political Economy for the original one; for the search after the cost of production of labour as such turned in a circle and never left the spot. What economists therefore call value of labour, is in fact the value of labour-power, as it exists in the personality of the labourer, which is as different from its function, labour, as a machine is from the work it performs. Occupied with the difference between the market-price of labour and its so-called value, with the relation of this value to the rate of profit, and to the values of the commodities produced by means of labour, &c., they never discovered that the course of the analysis had led not only from the market-prices of labour to its presumed value, but had led to the resolution of this value of labour itself into the value of labour-power. Classical economy never arrived at a consciousness of the results of its own analysis; it accepted uncritically the categories 'value of labour', 'natural price of labour,' &c., as final and as adequate expressions for the value-relation under consideration, and was thus led, as will be seen later, into inextricable confusion and contradiction, while it offered to the vulgar economists a secure basis of operations for their shallowness, which on principle worships appearances only.

Let us next see how value (and price) of labour-power, present themselves in this transformed condition as wages.

We know that the daily value of labour-power is calculated upon a certain length of the labourer's life, to which, again, corresponds a certain length of working-day. Assume the habitual working-day as 12 hours, the daily value of labour-power as 3s., the expression in money of a value that embodies 6 hours of labour. If the labourer receives 3s., then he receives the value of his labour-power functioning through 12 hours. If, now, this value of a day's labour-power is expressed as the value of a day's labour itself, we have the formula: Twelve hours' labour has a value of 3s. The value of labour-power thus determines the value of labour, or, expressed in money, its necessary price. If, on the other hand, the price of labour-power differs from its value, in like manner the price of labour differs from its so-called value.

As the value of labour is only an irrational expression for the value of labour-power, it follows, of course, that the value of labour must always be less than the value it produces, for the capitalist always makes labour-power work longer than is necessary for the reproduction of its own value. In the above example, the value of the labour-power that functions through 12 hours is 3s., a value for the reproduction of which 6 hours are required. The value which the labour-power produces is, on the other hand, 6s., because it, in fact, functions during 12 hours, and the value it produces depends, not on its own value, but on the length of time it is in action. Thus, we have a result absurd at first sight that labour which creates a value of 6s. possesses a value of 3s.[7]

We see, further: The value of 3s. by which a part only of the working-day—i.e., 6 hours' labour-is paid for, appears as the value or price of the whole working-day of 12 hours, which thus includes 6 hours unpaid for. The wage form thus extinguishes every trace of the division of the working-day into necessary labour and surplus-labour, into paid and unpaid labour. All labour appears as paid labour. In the corvée, the labour of the worker for himself, and his compulsory labour for his lord, differ in space and time in the clearest possible way. In slave labour, even that part of the working-day in which the slave is only replacing the value of his own means of existence, in which, therefore, in fact, he works for himself alone, appears as labour for his master. All the slave's labour appears as unpaid labour.[8] In wage labour, on the contrary, even surplus-labour, or unpaid labour, appears as paid. There the property-relation conceals the labour of the slave for himself; here the money-relation conceals the unrequited labour of the wage labourer.

Hence, we may understand the decisive importance of the transformation of value and price of labour-power into the form of wages, or into the value and price of labour itself. This phenomenal form, which makes the actual relation invisible, and, indeed, shows the direct opposite of that relation, forms the basis of all the juridical notions of both labourer and capitalist, of all the mystifications of the capitalistic mode of production, of all its illusions as to liberty, of all the apologetic shifts of the vulgar economists.

If history took a long time to get at the bottom of the mystery of wages, nothing, on the other hand, is more easy to understand than the necessity, the raison d'etre, of this phenomenon.

The exchange between capital and labour at first presents itself to the mind in the same guise as the buying and selling of all other commodities. The buyer gives a certain sum of money, the seller an article of a nature different from money. The jurist's consciousness recognizes in this, at most, a material difference, expressed in the juridically equivalent formula: 'Do ut des, do ut facias, facio ut des, facio ut facias.'[9]

Furthermore, exchange-value and use-value, being intrinsically incommensurable magnitudes, the expressions 'value of labour,' 'price of labour,' do not seem more irrational than the expressions 'value of cotton,' 'price of cotton.' Moreover, the labourer is paid after he has given his labour. In its function of means of payment, money realizes subsequently the value or price of the article supplied—i.e., in this particular case, the value or price of the labour supplied. Finally, the use-value supplied by the labourer to the capitalist is not, in fact, his labour-power, but its function, some definite useful labour, the work of tailoring, shoemaking, spinning, &c. That this same labour is, on the other hand, the universal value-creating element, and thus possesses a property by which it differs from all other commodities, is beyond the cognizance of the ordinary mind.

Let us put ourselves in the place of the labourer who receives for 12 hours' labour, say the value produced by 6 hours' labour, say 3s. For him, in fact, his 12 hours' labour is the means of buying the 3s. The value of his labour-power may vary, with the value of his usual means of subsistence, from 3 to 4 shillings, or from 3 to 2 shillings; or, if the value of his labour-power remains constant, its price may, in consequence of changing relations of demand and supply, rise to 4s. or fall to 2s. He always gives 12 hours of labour. Every change in the amount of the equivalent that he receives appears to him, therefore, necessarily as a change in the value or price of his 12 hours' work. This circumstance misled Adam

Smith, who treated the working-day as a constant quantity,[10] to the assertion that the value of labour is constant, although the value of the means of subsistence may vary, and the same working-day, therefore, may represent itself in more or less money for the labourer.

Let us consider, on the other hand, the capitalist. He wishes to receive as much labour as possible for as little money as possible. Practically, therefore, the only thing that interests him is the difference between the price of labour-power and the value which its function creates. But, then, he tries to buy all commodities as cheaply as possible, and always accounts for his profit by simple cheating, by buying under, and selling over the value. Hence, he never comes to see that, if such a thing as the value of labour really existed, and he really paid this value, no capital would exist, his money would not be turned into capital.

Moreover, the actual movement of wages presents phenomena which seem to prove that not the value of labour-power is paid, but the value of its function, of labour itself. We may reduce these phenomena to two great classes: 1) Change of wages with the changing length of the working-day. One might as well conclude that not the value of a machine is paid, but that of its working, because it costs more to hire a machine for a week than for a day. 2) The individual difference in the wages of different labourers who do the same kind of work. We find this individual difference, but are not deceived by it, in the system of slavery, where, frankly and openly, without any circumlocution, labour-power itself is sold. Only, in the slave system, the advantage of a labour-power above the average, and the disadvantage of a labour-power below the average, affects the slave-owner; in the wage-labour system, it affects the labourer himself, because his labour-power is, in the one case, sold by himself, in the other, by a third person.

For the rest, in respect to the phenomenal form, 'value and price of labour,' or 'wages,' as contrasted with the essential relation manifested therein, viz., the value and price of labour-power, the same difference holds that holds in respect to all phenomena and their hidden substratum. The former appear directly and spontaneously as current modes of thought; the latter must first be discovered by science. Classical Political Economy nearly touches the true relation of things, without, however, consciously formulating it. This it cannot, so long as it sticks in its bourgeois skin.

Notes

1. 'Mr Ricardo ingeniously enough avoids a difficulty which, on a first view, threatens to encumber his doctrine—that value depends on the quantity of labour employed in production. If this principle is rigidly adhered to, it follows that the value of labour depends on the quantity of labour employed in producing it—which is evidently absurd. By a dexterous turn, therefore, Mr Ricardo makes the value of labour depend on the quantity of labour required to produce wages; or, to give him the benefit of his own language, he maintains, that the value of labour is to be estimated by the quantity of labour required to produce wages; by which he means the quantity of labour required to produce the money or commodities given to the labourer. This is similar to saying, that the value of cloth is estimated, not by the quantity of labour bestowed on its production, but by the quantity of labour bestowed on the production of the silver, for which the cloth is exchanged.'—'A Critical Dissertation on the Nature, &c., of Value,' pp. 50, 51.
2. 'If you call labour a commodity, it is not like a commodity which is first produced in order to exchange, and then brought to market where it must exchange with other commodities according to the respective quantities of each which there may be in the market at the time; labour is created the moment it is brought to market; nay, it is brought to market before it is created.'—'Observations on Certain Verbal Disputes,' &c., pp. 75, 76.
3. 'Treating labour as a commodity, and capital, the produce of labour, as another, then, if the values of these two commodities were regulated by equal quantities of labour, a given

amount of labour would ... exchange for that quantity of capital which had been produced by the same amount of labour; antecedent labour would ... exchange for the same amount as present labour. But the value of labour in relation to other commodities ... is determined not by equal quantities of labour.'—E. G. Wakefield in his edition of Adam Smith's 'Wealth of Nations,' Vol. I., London, 1836, p. 231, note.

4. 'There has to be a new agreement' (a new edition of the social contract!) 'that whenever there is an exchange of work done for work to be done, the latter' (the capitalist) 'is to receive a higher value than the former' (the worker).—Simonde (de Sismondi), 'De la Richesse Commerciale,' Geneva, 1803, Vol I, p. 37.
5. 'Labour the exclusive standard of value ... the creator of all wealth, no commodity.' Thomas Hodgskin, 'Popul. Polit. Econ.,' p. 186.
6. On the other hand, the attempt to explain such expressions as merely poetic license only shows the impotence of the analysis. Hence, in answer to Proudhon's phrase; 'Labour is called value, not as being a commodity itself, but in view of the values supposed to be potentially embodied in it. The value of labour is a figurative expression,' &c. I have remarked: 'In labour, commodity, which is a frightful reality, he (Proudhon) sees nothing but a grammatical ellipsis. The whole of existing society, then, based upon labour commodity, is henceforth based upon a poetic license, on a figurative expression. Does society desire to eliminate all the inconveniences which trouble it, it has only to eliminate all the ill-sounding terms. Let it change the language, and for that it has only to address itself to the Academy and ask it for a new edition of its dictionary.' (Karl Marx, 'Misère de la Philosophie,' pp. 34, 35.) It is naturally still more convenient to understand by value nothing at all. Then one can without difficulty subsume everything under this category. Thus, e.g., J. B. Say: 'What is value?' Answer: 'That which a thing is worth"; and what is 'price"? Answer: 'The value of a thing expressed in money.' And why has agriculture a value? Answer: 'Because one sets a price on it.' Therefore value is what a thing is worth, and the land has its 'value,' because its value is 'expressed in money.' This is, anyhow, a very simple way of explaining the why and the wherefore of things.
7. Cf. 'Zur Kritik &c.,' p. 40, where I state that, in the portion of that work that deals with Capital, this problem will be solved: 'How does production, on the basis of exchange-value determined simply by labour-time, lead to the result that the exchange-value of labour is less than the exchange-value of its product?'
8. The 'Morning Star,' a London Free-trade organ, naif to silliness, protested again and again during the American Civil War, with all the moral indignation of which man is capable, that the Negro in the 'Confederate States' worked absolutely for nothing. It should have compared the daily cost of such a Negro with that of the free workman in the East-end of London.
9. I give in order that you may give; I give in order that you may produce; I produce so that you may give; I produce so that you may produce.
10. Adam Smith only accidentally alludes to the variation of the working-day when he is referring to piece-wages.

20

Time-Wages

Wages themselves again take many forms, a fact not recognizable in the ordinary economic treatises which, exclusively interested in the material side of the question, neglect every difference of form. An exposition of all these forms however, belongs to the special study of wage labour, not therefore to this work. Still the two fundamental forms must be briefly worked out here.

The sale of labour-power, as will be remembered, takes place for a definite period of time. The converted form under which the daily, weekly, &c., value of labour-power presents itself, is hence that of time-wages, therefore day-wages, &c.

Next it is to be noted that the laws set forth, in the 17th chapter, on the changes in the relative magnitudes of price of labour-power and surplus-value, pass by a simple transformation of form, into laws of wages. Similarly the distinction between the exchange-value of labour power, and the sum of the necessaries of life into which this value is converted, now reappears as the distinction between nominal and real wages. It would be useless to repeat here, with regard to the phenomenal form, what has been already worked out in the substantial form. We limit ourselves therefore to a few points characteristic of time-wages.

The sum of money[1] which the labourer receives for his daily or weekly labour, forms the amount of his nominal wages, or of his wages estimated in value. But it is clear that according to the length of the working-day, that is, according to the amount of actual labour daily supplied, the same daily or weekly wage may represent very different prices of labour, i.e., very different sums of money for the same quantity of labour.[2] We must, therefore, in considering time-wages, again distinguish between the sum-total of the daily or weekly wages, &c., and the price of labour. How then, to find this price, i.e., the money-value of a given quantity of labour? The average price of labour is found, when the average daily value of the labour-power is divided by the average number of hours in the working-day. If, e.g., the daily value of labour-power is 3 shillings, the value of the product of 6 working-hours, and if the working-day is 12 hours, the price of 1 working hour is 3/12 shillings = 3d. The price of the working-hour thus found serves as the unit measure for the price of labour.

It follows therefore that the daily and weekly wages, &c., may remain the same, although the price of labour falls constantly. If, e.g., the habitual working-day is 10 hours and the daily value of the labour-power 3s., the price of the working-hour is 3 3/5d. It falls to 3d. as soon as the working-day rises to 12 hours, to 2 2/5d as soon as it rises to 15 hours. Daily or weekly wages remain, despite all this, unchanged. On the contrary, the daily or weekly wages may rise, although the price of labour remains constant or even falls. If, e.g., the working-day is 10 hours, and the daily value of labour-power 3 shillings, the price of one working-hour is 3 3/5d. If the labourer, in consequence of increase of trade, works 12 hours, the price of labour remaining the same, his daily wage now rises to 3 shillings 7 1/5 d. without any variation in the price of labour. The same result might follow if, instead of the extensive amount of labour, its intensive amount increased.[3] The rise of the nominal daily or weekly wages may therefore be accompanied by a price of labour that remains stationary or falls. The same holds as to the income of the labourer's family, as soon as the quantity of labour expended by the head of the family is increased by the labour of the members of his family. There are, therefore, methods of lowering the price of labour independent of the reduction of the nominal daily or weekly wages.[4]

As a general law it follows that, given the amount of daily or weekly labour, &c., the daily or weekly wages depend on the price of labour which itself varies either with the value of labour-power, or with the difference between its price and its value. Given, on the other hand, the price of labour, the daily or weekly wages depend on the quantity of the daily or weekly labour.

The unit-measure for time-wages, the price of the working-hour, is the quotient of the value of a day's labour-power, divided by the number of hours of the average working-day. Let the latter be 12 hours, and the daily value of labour-power 3 shillings, the value of the product of 6 hours of labour. Under these circumstances the price of a working hour is 3d.; the value produced in it is 6d. If the labourer is now employed less than 12 hours (or less than 6 days in the week), e.g., only 6 or 8 hours, he receives, with this price of labour, only 2s. or 1s. 6d. a day.[5] As on our hypothesis he must work on the average 6 hours daily, in order to produce a day's wage corresponding merely to the value of his labour power, as according to the same hypothesis he works only half of every hour for himself, and half for the capitalist, it is clear that he cannot obtain for himself the value of the product of 6 hours if he is employed less than 12 hours. In previous chapters we saw the destructive consequences of over-work; here we find the sources of the sufferings that result to the labourer from his insufficient employment.

If the hour's wage is fixed so that the capitalist does not bind himself to pay a day's or a week's wage, but only to pay wages for the hours during which he chooses to employ the labourer, he can employ him for a shorter time than that which is originally the basis of the calculation of the hour-wage, or the unit-measure of the price of labour. Since this unit is determined by the ratio

$$\frac{\text{daily value of labour-power}}{\text{working-day of a given number of hours}},$$

it, of course, loses all meaning as soon as the working-day ceases to contain a definite number of hours. The connection between the paid and the unpaid labour is destroyed. The capitalist can now wring from the labour a certain quantity of surplus-labour without allowing him the labour-time necessary for his own subsistence. He can annihilate all regularity of employment, and according to his own convenience, caprice, and the interest of the moment, make the most enormous overwork alternate with relative or absolute cessation of work. He can, under the pretense of paying 'the normal price of labour,' abnormally lengthen the working-day without any corresponding compensation to the labourer. Hence the perfectly rational revolt in 1860 of the London labourers, employed in the building trades, against the attempt of the capitalists to impose on them this sort of wage by the hour. The legal limitation of the working-day puts an end to such mischief, although not, of course, to the diminution of employment caused by the competition of machinery, by changes in the quality of the labourers employed, and by crises partial or general.

With an increasing daily or weekly wage the price of labour may remain nominally constant, and yet may fall below its normal level. This occurs every time that, the price of labour (reckoned per working-hour) remaining constant, the working-day is prolonged beyond its customary length. If in the fraction:

$$\frac{\text{daily value of labour power}}{\text{working-day}}$$

the denominator increases, the numerator increases yet more rapidly. The value of labour-power, as dependent on its wear and tear, increases with the duration of its functioning, and in more rapid proportion than the increase of that duration. In many branches of industry where time-wage is the general rule without legal limits to the working-time, the habit has, therefore, spontaneously grown up of regarding the working day as normal only up to a certain point, e.g., up to the expiration of the tenth hour ('normal working-day,' 'the day's work,' 'the regular hours of work'). Beyond this limit the working-time is over-time, and is, taking the hour as unit-measure, paid better ('extra pay'), although often in a proportion ridiculously small.[6] The normal working-day exists here as a fraction of the actual working-day, and the latter, often during the whole year, lasts longer than the former.[7] The increase in the price of labour with the extension of the working-day beyond a certain normal limit, takes such a shape in various British industries that the low price of labour during the so-called normal time compels the labourer to work during the better paid over-time, if he wishes to obtain a sufficient wage at all.[8] Legal limitation of the working-day puts an end to these amenities.[9]

It is a fact generally known that, the longer the working-days, in any branch of industry, the lower are the wages.[10] A. Redgrave, factory inspector, illustrates this by a comparative review of the 20 years from 1839-1859, according to which wages rose in the factories under the 10 Hours Law, whilst they fell in the factories in which the work lasted 14 to 15 hours daily.[11]

From the law, 'the price of labour being given, the daily or weekly wage depends on the quantity of labour expended,' it follows, first of all, that the lower the price of labour, the greater must be the quantity of labour, or the longer must be the working-day for the labourer to secure even a miserable average wage. The lowness of the price of labour acts here as a stimulus to the extension of the labour-time.[12]

On the other hand, the extension of the working-time produces, in its turn, a fall in the price of labour, and with this a fall in the day's or week's wages.

The determination of the price of labour by:

$$\frac{\text{daily value of labour power}}{\text{working day of a given number of hours}}$$

shows that a mere prolongation of the working-day lowers the price of labour, if no compensation steps in. But the same circumstances which allow the capitalist in the long run to prolong the working-day, also allow him first, and compel him finally, to nominally lower the price of labour until the total price of the increased number of hours is lowered, and, therefore, the daily or weekly wage. Reference to two circumstances is sufficient here. If one man does the work of 1½ or 2 men, the supply of labour increases, although the supply of labour-power on the market remains constant. The competition thus created between the labourers allows the capitalist to beat down the price of labour, whilst the falling price of labour allows him, on the other hand, to screw up still further the working-time.[13] Soon, however, this command over abnormal quantities of unpaid labour, i.e., quantities in excess of the average social amount, becomes a source of competition amongst the capitalists themselves. A part of the price of the commodity consists of the price of labour. The unpaid part of the labour-price need not be reckoned in the price of the commodity. It may be presented to the buyer. This is the first step to which competition leads. The second step to which it drives is to exclude also from the selling price of the commodity at least a part of the abnormal surplus-value created by the extension of the working-day. In this way, an abnormally low selling price of the commodity arises, at first sporadically, and becomes fixed by degrees; a lower selling price which henceforward becomes the constant basis of a miserable wage for an excessive working-time, as originally it was the product of these very circumstances. This movement is simply indicated here, as the analysis of competition does not belong to this part of our subject. Nevertheless, the capitalist may, for a moment, speak for himself. 'In Birmingham there is so much competition of masters one against another that many are obliged to do things as employers that they would otherwise be ashamed of; and yet no more money is made, but only the public gets the benefit.'[14] The reader will remember the two sorts of London bakers, of whom one sold the bread at its full price (the 'full-priced' bakers), the other below its normal price ('the under-priced,' 'the undersellers'). The 'full-priced' denounced their rivals before the Parliamentary Committee of Inquiry: 'They only exist now by first defrauding the public, and next getting 18 hours' work out of their men for 12 hours' wages.... The unpaid labour of the men was made ... the source whereby the competition was carried on, and continues so to this day.... The competition among the master bakers is the cause of the difficulty in getting rid of night-work. An underseller, who sells his bread below the cost-price according to the price of flour, must make it up by getting more out of the labour of the men.... If I got only 12 hours' work out of my men, and my neighbor got 18 or 20, he must beat me in the selling price. If the men could insist on payment for over-work, this would be set right.... A large number of those employed by the undersellers are foreigners and youths, who are obliged to accept almost any wages they can obtain.'[15]

This jeremiad is also interesting because it shows how the appearance only of the relations of production mirrors itself in the brain of the capitalist. The capitalist does not know that the normal price of labour also includes a definite quantity of unpaid labour, and that this very unpaid labour is the normal source of his gain. The category of surplus labour-time does not exist at all for him, since it is included in the normal working-day, which he thinks he has paid for in the day's wages. But over-time does exist for him, the prolongation of the working-day beyond the limits corresponding with the usual price of labour. Face to face with his underselling competitor, he even insists upon extra pay for this over-time. He again does not know that this extra pay includes unpaid labour, just as well as does the price of the customary hour of labour. For example, the price of one hour of the 12 hours' working-day is 3d., say the value-product of half a working-hour, whilst the price of the over-time working-hour is 4d., or the value-product of 2/3 of a working hour. In the first case the capitalist appropriates to himself one-half, in the second, one-third of the working-hour without paying for it.

Notes

1. The value of money itself is here always supposed constant.
2. 'The price of labour is the sum paid for a given quantity of labour.' (Sir Edward West, 'Price of Corn and Wages of Labour,' London, 1836, p. 67.) West is the author of the anonymous 'Essay on the Application of Capital to Land.' by a Fellow of the University College of Oxford, London, 1815. An epoch-making work in the history of Political Economy.
3. 'The wages of labour depend upon the price of labour and the quantity of labour performed.... An increase in the wages of labour does not necessarily imply an enhancement of the price of labour. From fuller employment, and greater exertions, the wages of labour may be considerably increased, while the price of labour may continue the same.' (West, op. cit., pp. 67, 68, 112.) The main question: 'How is the price of labour determined?' West, however, dismisses with mere banalities.
4. This is perceived by the fanatical representative of the industrial bourgeoisie of the 18th century, the author of the 'Essay on Trade and Commerce' often quoted by us, although he puts the matter in a confused way: 'It is the quantity of labour and not the price of it' (he means by this the nominal daily or weekly wages) 'that is determined by the price of provisions and other necessaries: reduce the price of necessaries very low, and of course you reduce the quantity of labour in proportion. Master manufacturers know that there are various ways of raising and felling the price of labour, besides that of altering its nominal amount.' (op. cit., pp. 48, 61.) In his 'Three Lectures on the Rate of Wages,' London, 1830, in which N. W. Senior uses West's work without mentioning it, he says: 'The labourer is principally interested in the amount of wages' (p. 14), that is to say, the labourer is principally interested in what he receives, the nominal sum of his wages, not in that which he gives, the amount of labour!
5. The effect of such an abnormal lessening of employment is quite different from that of a general reduction of the working-day, enforced by law. The former has nothing to do with the absolute length of the working-day, and may occur just as well in a working-day of 15, as of 6 hours. The normal price of labour is in the first case calculated on the labourer working 15 hours, in the second case on his working 6 hours a day on the average. The result is therefore the same, if he in the one case is employed only for 7½, in the other only for 3 hours.
6. 'The rate of payment for overtime (in lace-making) is so small, from ½ d. and ¾ d. to 2d. per hour, that it stands in painful contrast to the amount of injury produced to the health and stamina of the workpeople.... The small amount thus earned is also often obliged to be spent in extra nourishment.' ('Child.Empl.Com., II. Rep.,' p. xvi., n. 117.)

7. E.g., in paper-staining before the recent introduction into this trade of the Factory Act. 'We work on with no stoppage for meals, so that the day's work of 10½ hours is finished by 4:30 p.m., and all after that is over-time, and we seldom leave off working before 6 p.m., so that we are really working over-time the whole year round.' (Mr Smith's 'Evidence in Child. Empl. Com., 1. Rep.,' p. 125.)

8. E.g., in the Scotch bleaching-works. 'In some parts of Scotland this trade' (before the introduction of the Factory Act in 1862) 'was carried on by a system of over-time, i.e., ten hours a day were the regular hours of work, for which a nominal wage of 1s. 2d. per day was paid to a man, there being every day over-time for three or four hours, paid at the rate of 3d. per hour. The effect of this system ... a man could not earn more than 8s. per week when working the ordinary hours ... without over-time they could not earn a fair day's wages.' ('Rept. of Insp. of Factories,' April 30th, 1863, p. 10.) 'The higher wages, for getting adult males to work longer hours, are a temptation too strong to be resisted.' ('Rept. of Insp. of Fact.,' April 30th, 1848, p. 5.) The book-binding trade in the city of London employs very many young girls from 14 to 15 years old, and that under indentures which prescribe certain definite hours of labour. Nevertheless, they work in the last week of each month until 10, 11, 12, or 1 o'clock at night, along with the older labourers, in a very mixed company. 'The masters tempt them by extra pay and supper,' which they eat in neighboring public houses. The great debauchery thus produced among these 'young immortals' ('Children's Employment Comm., V. Rept.,' p. 44, n. 191) is compensated by the fact that among the rest many Bibles and religious books are bound by them.

9. See 'Reports of Insp. of Fact.,' 30th April, 1863, p. 10. With very accurate appreciation of the state of things, the London labourers employed in the building trades declared, during the great strike and lock-out of 1860, that they would only accept wages by the hour under two conditions: (1), that, with the price of the working-hour, a normal working day of 9 and 10 hours respectively should be fixed, and that the price of the hour for the 10 hours' working-day should be higher than that for the hour of the 9 hours working-day; (2), that every hour beyond the normal working-day should be reckoned as over-time and proportionally more highly paid.

10. 'It is a very notable thing, too, that where long hours are the rule, small wages are also so.' ('Report of Insp. of Fact.,' 31st. Oct., 1863, p. 9.) 'The work which obtains the scanty pittance of food, is, for the most part, excessively prolonged.' ('Public Health, Sixth Report,' 1864, p. 15.)

11. 'Report of Inspectors of Fact.,' 30th April, 1860, pp. 31, 32.

12. The hand nail-makers in England, e.g., have, on account of the low price of labour, to work 15 hours a day in order to hammer out their miserable weekly wage. 'It's a great many hours in a day (6 a.m. to 8 p.m.), and he has to work hard all the time to get 11 d. or 1s., and there is the wear of the tools, the cost of firing, and something for waste iron to go out of this, which takes off altogether 2½d. or 3d.' ('Children's Employment Com., III. Report,' p. 136, n. 671.) The women earn by the same working-time a week's wage of only 5 shillings. (l.c., p. 137, n. 674.)

13. If a factory-hand, e.g., refused to work the customary long hours, 'he would very shortly be replaced by somebody who would work any length of time, and thus be thrown out of employment.' ('Reports of Inspectors of Factories,' 30th April, 1848. Evidence, p. 39, n. 58.) 'If one man performs the work of two... the rate of profits will generally be raised ... in consequence of the additional supply of labour having diminished its price.' (Senior, l.c., p. 15.)

14. 'Children's Employment Com., III Rep.,' Evidence, p. 66, n. 22.

15. 'Report, &c., Relative to the Grievances Complained of by the Journeymen Bakers.' London, 1862, p. 411, and ib. Evidence, notes 479, 359, 27. Anyhow the full-priced bakers, as was mentioned above, and as their spokesman, Bennett, himself admits, make their men 'generally begin work at 11 p.m. ... up to 8 o'clock the next morning.... They are then engaged all day long ... as late as 7 o'clock in the evening.' (l.c., p. 22.)

21

Piece Wages

Wages by the piece are nothing else than a converted form of wages by time, just as wages by time are a converted form of the value or price of labour-power.

In piece wages it seems at first sight as if the use-value bought from the labourer was, not the function of his labour-power, living labour, but labour already realized in the product, and as if the price of this labour was determined, not as with time-wages, by the fraction

$$\frac{\text{daily value of labour-power}}{\text{the working day of a given number of hours}}$$

but by the capacity for work of the producer.[1]

The confidence that trusts in this appearance ought to receive a first severe shock from the fact that both forms of wages exist side by side, simultaneously, in the same branches of industry; e.g.,

> 'the compositors of London, as a general rule, work by the piece, time-work being the exception, while those in the country work by the day, the exception being work by the piece. The shipwrights of the port of London work by the job or piece, while those of all other parts work by the day.'[2]

In the same saddlery shops of London, often for the same work, piece wages are paid to the French, time-wages to the English. In the regular factories in which throughout piece wages predominate, particular kinds of work are unsuitable to this form of wage, and are therefore paid by time.[3] But it is, moreover, self-evident that the difference of form in the payment of wages alters in no way their essential nature, although the one form may be more favorable to the development of capitalist production than the other.

Let the ordinary working-day contain 12 hours of which 6 are paid, 6 unpaid. Let its value-product be 6 shillings, that of one hour's labour therefore 6d. Let us suppose that, as the result of experience, a labourer who works with the average amount of intensity and skill, who, therefore, gives in fact only the time socially necessary to the production of an article, supplies in 12 hours 24 pieces, either distinct products or measurable parts of a continuous whole. Then the value of these 24 pieces, after. subtraction of the portion of constant capital contained in them, is 6 shillings, and the value of a single piece 3d. The labourer receives 1 ½d. per piece, and thus earns in 12 hours 3 shillings. Just as, with time-wages, it does not matter whether we assume that the labourer works 6 hours for himself and 6 hours for the capitalist, or half of every hour for himself, and the other half for the capitalist, so here it does not matter whether we say that each individual piece is half paid, and half unpaid for, or that the price of 12 pieces is the equivalent only of the value of the labour-power, whilst in the other 12 pieces surplus-value is incorporated.

The form of piece wages is just as irrational as that of time-wages. Whilst in our example two pieces of a commodity, after subtraction of the value of the means of production consumed in them, are worth 6d. as being the product of one hour, the labourer receives for them a price of 3d. Piece wages do not, in fact, distinctly express any relation of value. It is not, therefore, a question of measuring the value of the piece by the working-time incorporated in it, but on the contrary, of measuring the working-time the labourer has expended by the number of pieces he has produced. In time-wages, the labour is measured by its immediate duration; in piece wages, by the quantity of products in which the labour has embodied itself during a given time.[4] The price of labour time itself is finally determined by the equation: value of a day's labour = daily value of labour-power. Piece-wage is, therefore, only a modified form of time-wage.

Let us now consider a little more closely the characteristic peculiarities of piece wages.

The quality of the labour is here controlled by the work itself, which must be of average perfection if the piece-price is to be paid in full. Piece wages become, from this point of view, the most fruitful source of reductions of wages and capitalistic cheating.

They furnish to the capitalist an exact measure for the intensity of labour. Only the working-time which is embodied in a quantum of commodities determined beforehand, and experimentally fixed, counts as socially necessary working-time, and is paid as such. In the larger workshops of the London tailors, therefore, a certain piece of work, a waistcoat, e.g., is called an hour, or half an hour, the hour at 6d. By practice it is known how much is the average product of one hour. With new fashions, repairs, &c., a contest arises between master and labourer as to whether a particular piece of work is one hour, and so on, until here also experience decides. Similarly in the London furniture workshops, &c. If the labourer does not possess the average capacity, if he cannot in consequence supply a certain minimum of work per day, he is dismissed.[5]

Since the quality and intensity of the work are here controlled by the form of wage itself, superintendence of labour becomes in great part superfluous. Piece wages therefore lay the foundation of the modern 'domestic labour,' described above, as well as of a hierarchically organized system of exploitation and oppression. The latter has two fundamental forms. On the one hand, piece wages facilitate the interposition of parasites between the capitalist and the wage-labourer, the 'sub-letting of labour.' The gain of these middlemen comes entirely from the difference between the labour-price which the capitalist pays, and the part of that price which they actually allow to reach the labourer.[6] In England, this system is characteristically called the 'sweating system.' On the other hand, piece-wage allows the capitalist to make a contract for so much per piece with the head labourer—in manufactures with the chief of some group, in mines with the extractor of the coal, in the factory with the actual machine-worker—at a price for which the head labourer himself undertakes the enlisting and payment of his assistant work people. The exploitation of the labourer by capital is here effected through the exploitation of the labourer by the labourer.[7]

Given piece-wage, it is naturally the personal interest of the labourer to strain his labour-power as intensely as possible; this enables the capitalist to raise more easily the normal degree of intensity of labour.[8] It is moreover now the personal interest of the labourer to lengthen the working-day, since with it his daily or weekly wages rise.[9] This gradually brings on a reaction like that already described in time-wages, without reckoning that the prolongation of the working-day, even if the piece wage remains constant, includes of necessity a fall in the price of the labour.

In time-wages, with few exceptions, the same wage holds for the same kind of work, whilst in piece wages, though the price of the working time is measured by a certain quantity of product, the day's or week's wage will vary with the individual differences of the labourers, of whom one supplies in a given time the minimum of product only, another the average, a third more than the average. With regard to actual receipts there is, therefore, great variety according to the different skill, strength, energy, staying-power, &c., of the individual labourers.[10] Of course this does not alter the general relations between capital and wage-labour. First, the individual differences balance one another in the workshop as a whole, which thus supplies in a given working-time the average product, and the total wages paid will be the average wages of that particular branch of industry. Second, the proportion between wages and surplus-value remains unaltered, since the mass of surplus labour supplied by each particular labourer corresponds with the wage received by him. But the wider scope that piece-wage gives to individuality tends to develop on the one hand that individuality, and with it the sense of liberty, independence, and self-control of the labourers, and on the other, their competition one with another. Piece-work has, therefore, a tendency, while raising individual wages above the average, to lower this average itself. But where a particular rate of piece-wage has for a long time been fixed by tradition, and its lowering, therefore, presented especial difficulties, the masters, in such exceptional cases, sometimes had recourse to its compulsory transformation into time-wages. Hence, e.g., in 1860, a great strike among the ribbon-weavers of Coventry.[11] Piece-wage is finally one of the chief supports of the hour-system described in the preceding chapter.[12]

From what has been shown so far, it follows that piece-wage is the form of wages most in harmony with the capitalist mode of production. Although by no means new—it figures side by side with time-wages officially in the French and English labour statutes of the 14th century—it only conquers a larger field for action during the period of manufacture, properly so-called. In the stormy youth of modern industry, especially from 1797 to 1815, it served as a lever for the lengthening of the working-day, and the lowering of wages. Very important materials for the fluctuation of wages during that period are to be found in the Blue books: 'Report and Evidence from the Select Committee on Petitions respecting the Corn Laws' (Parliamentary Session of 1813-14), and 'Report from the Lords' Committee, on the State of the Growth, Commerce, and Consumption of Grain, and all Laws relating thereto' (Session of 1814-15). Here we find documentary evidence of the constant lowering of the price of labour from the beginning of the anti-Jacobin War. In the weaving industry, e.g., piece wages had fallen so low that, in spite of the very great lengthening of the working-day, the daily wages were then lower than before.

> 'The real earnings of the cotton weaver are now far less than they were; his superiority over the common labourer, which at first was very great, has now almost entirely ceased. Indeed... the difference in the wages of skillful and common labour is far less now than at any former period.'[13]

How little the increased intensity and extension of labour through piece wages benefited the agricultural proletariat, the following passage borrowed from a work on the side of the landlords and farmers shows:

> 'By far the greater part of agricultural operations is done by people who are hired for the day or on piece-work. Their weekly wages are about 12s., and although it may be assumed that a man earns on piece-work under the greater stimulus to labour, 1s. or perhaps 2s. more than on weekly wages, yet it is found, on calculating his total income, that his loss of employment, during the year, outweighs this gain...Further, it will generally be found that the wages of these men bear a certain proportion to the price of the necessary means of subsistence, so that a man with two children is able to bring up his family without recourse to parish relief.'[14]

Malthus at that time remarked with reference to the facts published by Parliament:

> 'I confess that I see, with misgiving, the great extension of the practice of piece-wage. Really hard work during 12 or 14 hours of the day, or for any longer time, is too much for any human being.'[15]

In the workshops under the Factory Acts, piece wages become the general rule, because capital can there only increase the efficacy of the working-day by intensifying labour.[16]

With the changing productiveness of labour the same quantum of product represents a varying working-time. Therefore, piece-wage also varies, for it is the money expression of a determined working-time. In our example above, 24 pieces were produced in 12 hours, whilst the value of the product of the 12 hours was 6s., the daily value of the labour-power 3s., the price of the labour-hour 3d., and the wage for one piece ½d. In one piece half-an-hour's labour was absorbed. If the same working-day now supplies, in consequence of the doubled productiveness of labour, 48 pieces instead of 24, and all other circumstances remain unchanged, then the piece-wage falls from 1 ½d. to 3/4d., as every piece now only represents 1/4, instead of ½ of a working-hour. 24 by 1½d. = 3s., and in like manner 48 by 3/4d. = 3s. In other words, piece-wage is lowered in the same proportion as the number of the pieces produced in the same time rises,[17] and, therefore, as the working time spent on the same piece falls. This change in piece-wage, so far purely nominal, leads to constant battles between capitalist and labour. Either because the capitalist uses it as a pretext for actually lowering the price of labour, or because increased productive power of labour is accompanied by an increased intensity of the same. Or because the labourer takes seriously the appearance of piece wages (viz., that his product is paid for, and not his labour-power) and therefore revolts against a lowering of wages, unaccompanied by a lowering in the selling price of the commodity.

> 'The operatives...carefully watch the price of the raw material and the price of manufactured goods, and are thus enabled to form an accurate estimate of their master's profits.'[18]

The capitalist rightly knocks on the head such pretensions as gross errors as to the nature of wage-labour.[19] He cries out against this usurping attempt to lay taxes on the advance of industry, and declares roundly that the productiveness of labour does not concern the labourer at all.[20]

Notes

1. 'The system of piece-work illustrates an epoch in the history of the working-man; it is halfway between the position of the mere day-labourer depending upon the will of the capitalist and the co-operative artisan, who in the not distant future promises to combine the artisan and the capitalist in his own person. Piece-workers are in fact their own masters, even whilst working upon the capital of the employer.' (John Watts: 'Trade Societies and Strikes, Machinery and Co-operative Societies.' Manchester, 1865, pp. 52, 53.) I quote this little work because it is a very sink of all long-ago-rotten, apologetic commonplaces. This same Mr Watts earlier traded in Owenism and published in 1842 another pamphlet: 'Facts and Fictions of Political Economists,' in which among other things he declares that 'property is robbery.' That was long ago.
2. T. J. Dunning: 'Trades' Unions and Strikes,' Lond., 1860, p. 22.
3. How the existence, side by side and simultaneously, of these two forms of wage favors the masters' cheating: 'A factory employs 400 people, the half of which work by the piece, and have a direct interest in working longer hours. The other 200 are paid by the day, work equally long with the others, and get no more money for their over-time.... The work of these 200 people for half an hour a day is equal to one person's work for 50 hours, or 5/6's of one person's labour in a week, and is a positive gain to the employer.' ('Reports of Insp. of Fact., 31st Oct., 1860,' p. 9.) 'Over-working to a very considerable extent still prevails; and, in most instances, with that security against detection and punishment which the law itself affords. I have in many former reports shown ... the injury to workpeople who are not employed on piece-work, but receive weekly wages.' (Leonard Horner in 'Reports of Insp. of Fact.,' 30th April, 1859, pp. 8, 9.)
4. 'Wages can be measured in two ways: either by the duration of the labour, or by its product.' ('Abrégé élémentaire des principes de l'économie politique.' Paris, 1796, p. 32.) The author of this anonymous work: G. Garnier.
5. 'So much weight of cotton is delivered to him' (the spinner), 'and he has to return by a certain time, in lieu of it, a given weight of twist or yarn, of a certain degree of fineness, and he is paid so much per pound for all that he so returns. If his work is defective in quality, the penalty falls on him, if less in quantity than the minimum fixed for a given time, he is dismissed and an

abler operative procured.' (Ure, l.c., p. 317.)

6. 'It is when work passes through several hands, each of which is to take its share of profits, while only the last does the work, that the pay which reaches the workwoman is miserably disproportioned.' ('Child. Emp. Comm. II Report,' p. 1xx., n. 424.)
7. Even Watts, the apologetic, remarks: 'It would be a great improvement to the system of piece-work, if all the men employed on a job were partners in the contract, each according to his abilities, instead of one man being interested in over-working his fellows for his own benefit.' (l.c., p. 53.) On the vileness of this system, cf. 'Child. Emp. Comm., Rep. III.,' p. 66, n. 22, p. 11, n. 124, p. xi, n. 13, 53, 59, &c.
8. This spontaneous result is often artificially helped along, e.g., in the Engineering Trade of London, a customary trick is 'the selecting of a man who possesses superior physical strength and quickness, as the principal of several workmen, and paying him an additional rate, by the quarter or otherwise, with the understanding that he is to exert himself to the utmost to induce the others, who are only paid the ordinary wages, to keep up to him ... without any comment this will go far to explain many of the complaints of stinting the action, superior skill, and working-power, made by the employers against the men' (in Trades-Unions. Dunning, l.c., pp. 22, 23). As the author is himself a labourer and secretary of a Trades' Union, this might be taken for exaggeration. But the reader may compare the 'highly respectable' 'Cyclopedia of Agriculture' of J. C. Morton, Art., the article 'Labourer,' where this method is recommended to the farmers as an approved one.
9. 'All those who are paid by piece-work ... profit by the transgression of the legal limits of work. This observation as to the willingness to work over-time is especially applicable to the women employed as weavers and reelers.' ('Rept. of Insp. of Fact., 30th April, 1858,' p. 9.) 'This system' (piece-work), 'so advantageous to the employer ... tends directly to encourage the young potter greatly to over-work himself during the four or five years during which he is employed in the piece-work system, but at low wages.... This is ... another great cause to which the bad constitutions of the potters are to be attributed.' ('Child. Empl. Comm. 1. Rept.,' p. xiii.)
10. 'Where the work in any trade is paid for by the piece at so much per job ... wages may very materially differ in amount.... But in work by the day there is generally an uniform rate ... recognized by both employer and employed as the standard of wages for the general run of workmen in the trade.' (Dunning, l.c., p. 17.)
11. 'The work of the journeyman-artisans will be ruled by the day or by the piece. These master-artisans know about how much work a journeyman-artisan can do per day in each craft, and often pay them in proportion to the work which they do; the journey men, therefore, work as much as they can, in their own interest, without any further inspection.' (Cantillon, 'Essai sur la Nature du Commerce en général,' Amst. Ed., 1756, pp. 185 and 202. The first edition appeared in 1755.) Cantillon, from whom Quesnay, Sir James Steuart & A. Smith have largely drawn, already here represents piece-wage as simply a modified form of time-wage. The French edition of Cantillon professes in its title to be a translation from the English, but the English edition: 'The Analysis of Trade, Commerce, &c.,' by Philip Cantillon, late of the city of London, Merchant, is not only of later date (1759), but proves by its contents that it is a later and revised edition: e.g., in the French edition, Hume is not yet mentioned, whilst in the English, on the other hand, Petty hardly figures any longer. The English edition is theoretically less important, but it contains numerous details referring specifically to English commerce, bullion trade, &c., that are wanting in the French text. The words on the title-page of the English edition, according to which the work is 'taken chiefly from the manuscript of a very ingenious gentleman, deceased, and adapted, &c.,' seem, therefore, a pure fiction, very customary at that time.
12. 'How often have we seen, in some workshops, many more workers recruited than the work actually called for? On many occasions, workers are recruited in anticipation of future work, which may never materialize. Because they are paid by piece wages, it is said that no risk is

incurred, since any loss of time will be charged against the unemployed.' (H. Gregoir: 'Les Typographes devant le Tribunal correctionnel de Bruxelles,' Brusseles, 1865, p. 9.)

13. 'Remarks on the Commercial Policy of Great Britain,' London, 1815.
14. 'A Defense of the Landowners and Farmers of Great Britain,' 1814, pp. 4, 5.
15. Malthus, 'Inquiry into the Nature and Progress of Rent,' Lond., 1815.
16. 'Those who are paid by piece-work ... constitute probably four-fifths of the workers in the factories.' 'Report of Insp. of Fact.,' 30th April, 1858.
17. 'The productive power of his spinning-machine is accurately measured, and the rate of pay for work done with it decreases with, though not as, the increase of its productive power.' (Ure, l.c., p. 317.) This last apologetic phrase Ure himself again cancels. The lengthening of the mule causes some increase of labour, he admits. The labour does therefore not diminish in the same ratio as its productivity increases. Further: 'By this increase the productive power of the machine will be augmented one-fifth. When this event happens the spinner will not be paid at the same rate for work done as he was before, but as that rate will not be diminished in the ratio of one-fifth, the improvement will augment his money earnings for any given number of hours' work,' but 'the foregoing statement requires a certain modification.... The spinner has to pay something additional for juvenile aid out of his additional sixpence, accompanied by displacing a portion of adults' (l.c., p. 321), which has in no way a tendency to raise wages.
18. H. Fawcett: 'The Economic Position of the British labourer.' Cambridge and London, 1865, p. 178.
19. In the 'London Standard' of October 26, 1861, there is a report of proceedings of the firm of John Bright & Co., before the Rochdale magistrates 'to prosecute for intimidation the agents of the Carpet Weavers Trades' Union. Bright's partners had introduced new machinery which would turn out 240 yards of carpet in the time and with the labour (!) previously required to produce 160 yards. The workmen had no claim whatever to share in the profits made by the investment of their employer's capital in mechanical improvements. Accordingly, Messrs. Bright proposed to lower the rate of pay from 1½d. per yard to 1d., leaving the earnings of the men exactly the same as before for the same labour. But there was a nominal reduction, of which the operatives, it is asserted, had not fair warning beforehand.'
20. 'Trades' Unions, in their desire to maintain wages, endeavor to share in the benefits of improved machinery.' (Quelle horreur!) '... the demanding higher wages, because labour is abbreviated, is in other words the endeavor to establish a duty on mechanical improvements.' ('On Combination of Trades,' new ed., London, 1834, p. 42.)

22

National Differences of Wages

In the 17th chapter we were occupied with the manifold combinations which may bring about a change in magnitude of the value of labour-power—this magnitude being considered either absolutely or relatively, i.e., as compared with surplus-value; whilst on the other hand, the quantum of the means of subsistence in which the price of labour is realized might again undergo fluctuations independent of, or different from, the changes of this price.[1] As has been already said, the simple translation of the value, or respectively of the price, of labour-power into the exoteric form of wages transforms all these laws into laws of the fluctuations of wages. That which appears in these fluctuations of wages within a single country as a series of varying combinations, may appear in different countries as contemporaneous difference of national wages. In the comparison of the wages in different nations, we must therefore take into account all the factors that determine changes in the amount of the value of labour-power; the price and the extent of the prime necessaries of life as naturally and historically developed, the cost of training the labourers, the part played by the labour of women and children, the productiveness of labour, its extensive and intensive magnitude. Even the most superficial comparison requires the reduction first of the average day-wage for the same trades, in different countries, to a uniform working-day. After this reduction to the same terms of the day-wages, time-wage must again be translated into piece-wage, as the latter only can be a measure both of the productivity and the intensity of labour.

In every country there is a certain average intensity of labour below which the labour for the production of a commodity requires more than the socially necessary time, and therefore does not reckon as labour of normal quality. Only a degree of intensity above the national average affects, in a given country, the measure of value by the mere duration of the working-time. This is not the case on the universal market, whose integral parts are the individual countries. The average intensity of labour changes from country to country; here it is greater, there less. These national averages form a scale, whose unit of measure is the average unit of universal labour. The more intense national labour, therefore, as compared with the less intense, produces in the same time more value, which expresses itself in more money.

But the law of value in its international application is yet more modified by the fact that on the world-market the more productive national labour reckons also as the more intense, so long as the more productive nation is not compelled by competition to lower the selling price of its commodities to the level of their value.

In proportion as capitalist production is developed in a country, in the same proportion do the national intensity and productivity of labour there rise above the international level.[2] The different quantities of commodities of the same kind, produced in different countries in the same working-time, have, therefore, unequal international values, which are expressed in different prices, i.e., in sums of money varying according to international values. The relative value of money will, therefore, be less in the nation with more developed capitalist mode of production than in the nation with less developed. It follows, then, that the nominal wages, the equivalent of labour-power expressed in money, will also be higher in the first nation than in the second; which does not at all prove that this holds also for the real wages, i.e., for the means of subsistence placed at the disposal of the labourer.

But even apart from these relative differences of the value of money in different countries, it will be found, frequently, that the daily or weekly, &tc., wage in the first nation is higher than in the second, whilst the relative price of labour, i.e., the price of labour as compared both with surplus-value and with the value of the product, stands higher in the second than in the first.[3]

J. W. Cowell, member of the Factory Commission of 1833, after careful investigation of the spinning trade, came to the conclusion that

> 'in England wages are virtually lower to the capitalist, though higher to the operative than on the Continent of Europe.'[4]

The English Factory Inspector, Alexander Redgrave, in his report of Oct. 31st, 1866, proves by comparative statistics with continental states, that in spite of lower wages and much longer working-time, continental labour is, in proportion to the product, dearer than English. An English manager of a cotton factory in Oldenburg declares that the working time there lasted from 5:30 a.m. to 8 p.m., Saturdays included, and that the workpeople there, when under English overlookers, did not supply during this time quite so much product as the English in 10 hours, but under German overlookers much less. Wages are much lower than in England, in many cases 50%, but the number of hands in proportion to the machinery was much greater, in certain departments in the proportion of 5:3.

Mr Redgrave gives very full details as to the Russian cotton factories. The data were given him by an English manager until recently employed there. On this Russian soil, so fruitful of all infamies, the old horrors of the early days of English factories are in full swing. The managers are, of course, English, as the native Russian capitalist is of no use in factory business. Despite all over-work, continued day and night, despite the most shameful under-payment of the workpeople, Russian manufacture manages to vegetate only by prohibition of foreign competition.

I give, in conclusion, a comparative table of Mr Redgrave's, on the average number of spindles per factory and per spinner in the different countries of Europe. He himself remarks that he had collected these figures a few years ago, and that since that time the size of the factories and the number of spindles per labourer in England has increased. He supposes, however, an approximately equal progress in the continental countries mentioned, so that the numbers given would still have their value for purposes of comparison.

Average Number of Spindles Per Factory	
England, average of spindles per factory	12,600
France, *average of spindles per factory*	1,500
Prussia, *average of spindles per factory*	1,500
Belgium, *average of spindles per factory*	4,000
Saxony, *average of spindles per factory*	4,500
Austria, *average of spindles per factory*	7,000
Switzerland, *average of spindles per factory*	8,000
Average Number of Persons Employed to Spindles	
France	*one person to* 14 spindles
Russia	*one person to* 28 spindles
Prussia	*one person to* 37 spindles
Bavaria	*one person to* 46 spindles
Austria	*one person to* 49 spindles
Belgium	*one person to* 50 spindles
Saxony	*one person to* 50 spindles
Switzerland	*one person to* 55 spindles
Smaller States of Germany	*one person to* 55 spindles
Great Britain	*one person to* 74 spindles

> 'This comparison,' says Mr Redgrave, 'is yet more unfavorable to Great Britain, inasmuch as there is so large a number of factories in which weaving by power is carried on in conjunction with spinning' (whilst in the table the weavers are not deducted), 'and the factories abroad are chiefly spinning factories; if it were possible to compare like with like, strictly, I could find many cotton spinning factories in my district in which mules containing 2,200 spindles are minded by one man (the minder) and two assistants only, turning off daily 220 lbs. of yarn, measuring 400 miles in length.'[5]

It is well known that in Eastern Europe, as well as in Asia, English companies have undertaken the construction of railways, and have, in making them, employed side by side with the native labourers, a certain number of English working-men. Compelled by practical necessity, they thus have had to take into account the national difference in the intensity of labour, but this has brought them no loss. Their experience shows that even if the height of wages corresponds more or less with the average intensity of labour, the relative price of labour varies generally in the inverse direction.

In an 'Essay on the Rate of Wages,'[6] one of his first economic writings, H. Carey tries to prove that the wages of the different nations are directly proportional to the degree of productiveness of the national working-days, in order to draw from this international relation the conclusion that wages everywhere rise and fall in proportion to the productiveness of labour. The whole of our analysis of the production of surplus-value shows the absurdity of this conclusion, even if Carey himself had proved his premises instead of, after his usual uncritical and superficial fashion, shuffling to and fro a confused mass of statistical materials. The best of it is that he does not assert that things actually are as they ought to be according to his theory. For State intervention has falsified the natural economic relations. The different national wages must be reckoned, therefore, as if that part of each that goes to the State in the form of taxes, came to the labourer himself. Ought not Mr Carey to consider further whether those 'State expenses' are not the 'natural' fruits of capitalistic development? The reasoning is quite worthy of the man who first declared the relations of capitalist production to be eternal laws of nature and reason, whose free, harmonious working is only disturbed by the intervention of the State, in order afterwards to discover that the diabolical influence of England on the world market (an influence which, it appears, does not spring from the natural laws of capitalist production) necessitates State intervention, i.e., the protection of those laws of nature and reason by the State, alias the System of Protection. He discovered further that the theorems of Ricardo and others, in which existing social antagonisms and contradictions are formulated, are not the ideal product of the real economic movement, but on the contrary, that the real antagonisms of capitalist production in England and elsewhere are the result of the theories of Ricardo and others! Finally he discovered that it is, in the last resort, commerce that destroys the inborn beauties and harmonies of the capitalist mode of production. A step further and he will, perhaps, discover that the one evil in capitalist production is capital itself. Only a man with such atrocious want of the critical faculty and such spurious erudition deserved, in spite of his Protectionist heresy, to become the secret source of the harmonious wisdom of a Bastiat, and of all the other Free-trade optimists of today.

Notes

1. 'It is not accurate to say that wages' (he deals here with their money expression) 'are increased, because they purchase more of a cheaper article.' (David Buchanan in his edition of Adam Smith's 'Wealth of Nations,' 1814, Vol. 1, p. 417, note.)
2. We shall inquire, in another place, what circumstances in relation to productivity may modify this law for individual branches of industry.
3. James Anderson remarks in his polemic against Adam Smith: 'It deserves, likewise, to be remarked, that although the apparent price of Labour is usually lower in poor countries, where the produce of the soil, and grain in general, is cheap; yet it is in fact for the most part really higher than in other countries. For it is not the wages that is given to the labourer per day that constitutes the real price of labour, although it is its apparent price. The real price is that which a certain quantity of work performed actually costs the employer; and considered in this light, labour is in almost all cases cheaper in rich countries than in those that are poorer, although the price of grain and other provisions is usually much lower in the last than in the first.... Labour estimated by the day is much lower in Scotland than in England.... Labour by the piece is generally cheaper in England.' (James Anderson, 'Observations on the Means of Exciting a Spirit of National Industry,' &tc., Edin. 1777, pp. 350, 351.) On the contrary, lowness of wages produces, in its turn, dearness of labour. 'Labour being dearer in Ireland than it is in England ... because the wages are so much lower.' (N. 2079 in 'Royal Commission on Railways, Minutes,' 1867.)
4. (Ure, op. cit., p. 314.)
5. ('Reports of Insp. of Fact.,' 31st Oct., 1866, pp. 31-37, passim.)
6. 'Essay on the Rate of Wages, with an Examination of the Causes of the Differences in the Condition of the Labouring Population throughout the World,' Philadelphia, 1835.

PART VII

THE ACCUMULATION OF CAPITAL

The conversion of a sum of money into means of production and labour-power, is the first step taken by the quantum of value that is going to function as capital. This conversion takes place in the market, within the sphere of circulation. The second step, the process of production, is complete so soon as the means of production have been converted into commodities whose value exceeds that of their component parts, and, therefore, contains the capital originally advanced, plus a surplus-value. These commodities must then be thrown into circulation. They must be sold, their value realised in money, this money afresh converted into capital, and so over and over again. This circular movement, in which the same phases are continually gone through in succession, forms the circulation of capital.

The first condition of accumulation is that the capitalist must have contrived to sell his commodities, and to reconvert into capital the greater part of the money so received. In the following pages we shall assume that capital circulates in its normal way. The detailed analysis of the process will be found in Book II.

The capitalist who produces surplus-value—*i.e.*, who extracts unpaid labour directly from the labourers, and fixes it in commodities, is, indeed, the first appropriator, but by no means the ultimate owner, of this surplus-value. He has to share it with capitalists, with landowners, &c., who fulfil other functions in the complex of social production. Surplus-value, therefore, splits up into various parts. Its fragments fall to various categories of persons, and take various forms, independent the one of the other, such as profit, interest, merchants' profit, rent, &c. It is only in Book III. that we can take in hand these modified forms of surplus-value.

On the one hand, then, we assume that the capitalist sells at their value the commodities he has produced, without concerning ourselves either about the new forms that capital assumes while in the sphere of circulation, or about the concrete conditions of reproduction hidden under these forms. On the other hand, we treat the capitalist producer as owner of the entire surplus-value, or, better perhaps, as the representative of all the sharers with him in the booty. We, therefore, first of all consider accumulation from an abstract point of view—*i.e.*, as a mere phase in the actual process of production.

So far as accumulation takes place, the capitalist must have succeeded in selling his commodities, and in reconverting the sale-money into capital. Moreover, the breaking-up of surplus-value into fragments neither alters its nature nor the conditions under which it becomes an element of accumulation. Whatever be the proportion of surplus-value which the industrial capitalist retains for himself, or yields up to others, he is the one who, in the first instance, appropriates it. We, therefore, assume no more than what actually takes place. On the other hand, the simple fundamental form of the process of accumulation is obscured by the incident of the circulation which brings it about, and by the splitting up of surplus-value. An exact analysis of the process, therefore, demands that we should, for a time, disregard all phenomena that hide the play of its inner mechanism.

23

Simple Reproduction

Whatever the form of the process of production in a society, it must be a continuous process, must continue to go periodically through the same phases. A society can no more cease to produce than it can cease to consume. When viewed, therefore, as a connected whole, and as flowing on with incessant renewal, every social process of production is, at the same time, a process of reproduction.

The conditions of production are also those of reproduction. No society can go on producing, in other words, no society can reproduce, unless it constantly reconverts a part of its products into means of production, or elements of fresh products. All other circumstances remaining the same, the only mode by which it can reproduce its wealth, and maintain it at one level, is by replacing the means of production—*i.e.*, the instruments of labour, the raw material, and the auxiliary substances consumed in the course of the year—by an equal quantity of the same kind of articles; these must be separated from the mass of the yearly products, and thrown afresh into the process of production. Hence, a definite portion of each year's product belongs to the domain of production. Destined for productive consumption from the very first, this portion exists, for the most part, in the shape of articles totally unfitted for individual consumption.

If production be capitalistic in form, so, too, will be reproduction. Just as in the former the labour process figures but as a means towards the self-expansion of capital, so in the latter it figures but as a means of reproducing as capital—*i.e.*, as self-expanding value—the value advanced. It is only because his money constantly functions as capital that the economic guise of a capitalist attaches to a man. If, for instance, a sum of £100 has this year been converted into capital, and produced a surplus-value of £20, it must continue during next year, and subsequent years, to repeat the same operation. As a periodic increment of the capital advanced, or periodic fruit of capital in process, surplus-value acquires the form of a revenue flowing out of capital.[1]

If this revenue serve the capitalist only as a fund to provide for his consumption, and be spent as periodically as it is gained, then, *caeteris paribus*, simple reproduction will take place. And although this reproduction is a mere repetition of the process of production on the old scale, yet this mere repetition, or continuity, gives a new character to the process, or, rather, causes the disappearance of some apparent characteristics which it possessed as an isolated discontinuous process.

The purchase of labour-power for a fixed period is the prelude to the process of production; and this prelude is constantly repeated when the stipulated term comes to an end, when a definite period of production, such as a week or a month, has elapsed. But the labourer is not paid until after he has expended his labour-power, and realised in commodities not only its value, but surplus-value. He has, therefore, produced not only surplus-value, which we for the present regard as a fund to meet the private consumption of the capitalist, but he has also produced, before it flows back to him in the shape of wages, the fund out of which he himself is paid, the variable capital; and his employment lasts only so long as he continues to reproduce this fund. Hence, that formula of the economists, referred to in Chapter XVIII, which represents wages as a share in the product itself.[2] What flows back to the labourer in the shape of wages is a portion of the product that is continuously reproduced by him. The capitalist, it is true, pays him in money, but this money is merely the transmuted form of the product of his labour. While he is converting a portion of the means of production into products, a portion of his former product is being turned into money. It is his labour of last week, or of last year, that pays for his labour-power this week or this year. The illusion begotten by the intervention of money vanishes immediately, if, instead of taking a single capitalist and a single labourer, we take the class of capitalists and the class of labourers as a whole. The capitalist class is constantly giving to the labouring class order-notes, in the form of money, on a portion of the commodities produced by the latter and appropriated by the former. The labourers give these order-notes back just as constantly to the capitalist class, and in this way get their share of their own product. The transaction is veiled by the commodity form of the product and the money form of the commodity.

Variable capital is therefore only a particular historical form of appearance of the fund for providing the necessaries of life, or the labour-fund which the labourer requires for the maintenance of himself and family, and which, whatever be the system of social production, he must himself produce and reproduce. If the labour-fund constantly flows to him in the form of money that pays for his labour, it is because the product he has created moves constantly away from him in the form of capital. But all this does not alter the fact, that it is the labourer's own labour, realised in a product, which is advanced to him by the capitalist.[3] Let us take a peasant liable to do compulsory service for his lord. He works on his own land, with his own means of production, for, say, 3 days a week. The 3 other days he does forced work on the lord's domain. He constantly reproduces his own labour-fund, which never, in his case, takes the form of a money payment for his labour, advanced by another person. But in return, his unpaid forced labour for the lord, on its side, never acquires the character of voluntary paid labour. If one fine morning the lord appropriates to himself the land, the cattle, the seed, in a word, the, means of production of this peasant, the latter will thenceforth be obliged to sell his labour-power to the lord. He will, *ceteris paribus*, labour 6 days a week as before, 3 for himself, 3 for his lord, who thenceforth becomes a wages-paying capitalist. As before, he will use up the means of production as means of production, and transfer their value to the product. As before, a definite portion of the product will be devoted to reproduction. But, from the moment that the forced labour is changed into wage labour, from that moment the labour-fund, which the peasant himself continues as before to produce and reproduce, takes the form of a capital advanced in the form of wages by the lord. The bourgeois economist whose narrow mind is unable to separate the form of appearance from the thing that appears, shuts his eyes to the fact, that it is but here and there on the face of the earth, that even nowadays the labour fund crops up in the form of capital.[4]

Variable capital, it is true, only then loses its character of a value advanced out of the capitalist's funds,[5] when we view the process of capitalist production in the flow of its constant renewal. But that process must have had a beginning of some kind. From our present standpoint it therefore seems likely that the capitalist, once upon a time, became possessed of money, by some accumulation that took place independently of the unpaid labour of others, and that this was, therefore, how he was enabled to frequent the market as a buyer of labour-power. However this may be, the mere continuity of the process, the simple reproduction, brings about some other wonderful changes, which affect not only the variable, but the total capital.

If a capital of £1,000 beget yearly a surplus-value of £200, and if this surplus-value be consumed every year, it is clear that at the end of 5 years the surplus-value consumed will amount to 5 × £200 or the £1,000 originally advanced. If only a part, say one half, were consumed, the same result would follow at the end of 10 years, since 10 × £100= £1,000. General Rule: The value of the capital advanced divided by the surplus-value annually consumed, gives the number of years, or reproduction periods, at the expiration of which the capital originally advanced has been consumed by the capitalist and has disappeared. The capitalist thinks, that he is consuming the produce of the unpaid labour of others, *i.e.*, the surplus-value, and is keeping intact his original capital; but what he thinks cannot alter facts. After the lapse of a certain number of years, the capital value he then possesses is equal to the sum total of the surplus-value appropriated by him during those years, and the total value he has consumed is equal to that of his original capital. It is true, he has in hand a capital whose amount has not changed, and of which a part, viz., the buildings, machinery, &c., were already there when the work of his business began. But what we have to do with here, is not the material elements, but the value, of that capital. When a person gets through all his property, by taking upon himself debts equal to the value of that property, it is clear that his property represents nothing but the sum total of his debts. And so it is with the capitalist; when he has consumed the equivalent of his original capital, the value of his present capital represents nothing but the total amount of the surplus-value appropriated by him without payment. Not a single atom of the value of his old capital continues to exist.

Apart then from all accumulation, the mere continuity of the process of production, in other words simple reproduction, sooner or later, and of necessity, converts every capital into accumulated capital, or capitalised surplus-value. Even if that capital was originally acquired by the personal labour of its employer, it sooner or later becomes value appropriated without an equivalent, the unpaid labour of others materialised either in money or in some other object. We saw in Chapt. IV.-VI. that in order to convert money into capital something more is required than the production and circulation of commodities. We saw that on the one side the possessor of value or money, on the other, the possessor of the value-creating substance; on the one side, the possessor of the means of production and subsistence, on the other, the possessor of nothing but labour-power, must confront one another as buyer and seller. The separation of labour from its product, of subjective labour-power from the objective conditions of labour, was therefore the real foundation in fact, and the starting-point of capitalist production.

But that which at first was but a starting-point, becomes, by the mere continuity of the process, by simple reproduction, the peculiar result, constantly renewed and perpetuated, of capitalist production. On the one hand, the process of production incessantly converts material wealth into capital, into means of creating more wealth and means of enjoyment for the capitalist. On the other hand, the labourer, on quitting the process, is what he was on entering it, a source of wealth, but devoid of all means of making that wealth his own. Since, before entering on the process, his own labour has already been alienated from himself by the sale of his labour-power, has been appropriated by the capitalist and incorporated with capital, it must, during the process, be realised in a product that does not belong to him. Since the process of production is also the process by which the capitalist consumes labour-power, the product of the labourer is incessantly converted, not only into commodities, but into capital, into value that sucks up the value-creating power, into means of subsistence that buy the person of the labourer, into means of production that command the producers.[6] The labourer therefore constantly produces material, objective wealth, but in the form of capital, of an alien power that dominates and exploits him; and the capitalist as constantly produces labour-power, but in the form of a subjective source of wealth, separated from the objects in and by which it can alone be realised; in short he produces the labourer, but as a wage labourer.[7] This incessant reproduction, this perpetuation of the labourer, is the sine quâ non of capitalist production.

The labourer consumes in a two-fold way. While producing he consumes by his labour the means of production, and converts them into products with a higher value than that of the capital advanced. This is his productive consumption. It is at the same time consumption of his labour-power by the capitalist who bought it. On the other hand, the labourer turns the money paid to him for his labour-power, into means of subsistence: this is his individual consumption. The labourer's productive consumption, and his individual consumption, are therefore totally distinct. In the former, he acts as the motive power of capital, and belongs to the capitalist. In the latter, he belongs to himself, and performs his necessary vital functions outside the process of production. The result of the one is, that the capitalist lives; of the other, that the labourer lives.

When treating of the working day, we saw that the labourer is often compelled to make his individual consumption a mere incident of production. In such a case, he supplies himself with necessaries in order to maintain his labour-power, just as coal and water are supplied to the steam-engine and oil to the wheel. His means of consumption, in that case, are the mere means of consumption required by a means of production; his individual consumption is directly productive consumption. This, however, appears to be an abuse not essentially appertaining to capitalist production.[8]

The matter takes quite another aspect, when we contemplate, not the single capitalist, and the single labourer, but the capitalist class and the labouring class, not an isolated process of production, but capitalist production in full swing, and on its actual social scale. By converting part of his capital into labour-power, the capitalist augments the value of his entire capital. He kills two birds with one stone. He profits, not only by what he receives from, but by what he gives to the labourer. The capital given in exchange for labour-power is converted into necessaries, by the consumption of which the muscles, nerves, bones, and brains of existing labourers are reproduced, and new labourers are begotten. Within the limits of what is strictly necessary, the individual consumption of the working class is, therefore, the reconversion of the means of subsistence given by capital in exchange for labour-power, into fresh labour-power at the disposal of capital for exploitation. It is the production and reproduction of that means of production so indispensable to the capitalist: the labourer himself. The individual consumption of the labourer, whether it proceed within the workshop or outside it, whether it be part of the process of production or not, forms therefore a factor of the production and reproduction of capital; just as cleaning machinery does, whether it be done while the machinery is working or while it is standing. The fact that the labourer consumes his means of subsistence for his own purposes, and not to please the capitalist, has no bearing on the matter. The consumption of food by a beast of burden is none the less a necessary factor in the process of production, because the beast enjoys what it eats. The maintenance and reproduction of the working class is, and must ever be, a necessary condition to the reproduction of capital. But the capitalist may safely leave its fulfilment to the labourer's instincts of self-preservation and of propagation. All the capitalist cares for, is to reduce the labourer's individual consumption as far as possible to what is strictly necessary, and he is far away from imitating those brutal South Americans, who force their labourers to take the more substantial, rather than the less substantial, kind of food.[9]

Hence, both, the capitalist and his ideological representative, the political economist, consider that part alone of the labourer's individual consumption to be productive, which is requisite for the perpetuation of the class, and which therefore must take place in order that the capitalist may have labour-power to consume; what the labourer consumes for his own pleasure beyond that part, is unproductive consumption.[10] If the accumulation of capital were to cause a rise of wages and an increase in the labourer's consumption, unaccompanied by increase in the consumption of labour-power by capital, the additional capital would be consumed unproductively.[11] In reality, the individual consumption of the labourer is unproductive as regards himself, for it reproduces nothing but the needy individual; it is productive to the capitalist and to the State, since it is the production of the power that creates their wealth.[12]

From a social point of view, therefore, the working class, even when not directly engaged in the labour process, is just as much an appendage of capital as the ordinary instruments of labour. Even its individual consumption is, within certain limits, a mere factor in the process of production. That process, however, takes good care to prevent these self-conscious instruments from leaving it in the lurch, for it removes their product, as fast as it is made, from their pole to the opposite pole of capital. Individual consumption provides, on the one hand, the means for their maintenance and reproduction: on the other hand, it secures by the annihilation of the necessaries of life, the continued re-appearance of the workman in the labour-market. The Roman slave was held by fetters: the wage labourer is bound to his owner by invisible threads. The appearance of independence is kept up by means of a constant change of employers, and by the fictio juris of a contract.

In former times, capital resorted to legislation, whenever necessary, to enforce its proprietary rights over the free labourer. For instance, down to 1815, the emigration of mechanics employed in machine making was, in England, forbidden, under grievous pains and penalties.

The reproduction of the working class carries with it the accumulation of skill, that is handed down from one generation to another.[13] To what extent the capitalist reckons the existence of such a skilled class among the factors of production that belong to him by right, and to what extent he actually regards it as the reality of his variable capital, is seen so soon as a crisis threatens him with its loss. In consequence of the civil war in the United States and of the accompanying cotton famine, the majority of the cotton operatives in Lancashire were, as is well known, thrown out of work. Both from the working class itself, and from other ranks of society, there arose a cry for State aid, or for voluntary national subscriptions, in order to enable the 'superfluous' hands to emigrate to the colonies or to the United States. Thereupon, *The Times* published on the 24th March, 1863, a letter from Edmund Potter, a former president of the Manchester Chamber of Commerce. This letter was rightly called in the House of Commons, the manufacturers' manifesto.[14] We cull here a few characteristic passages, in which the proprietary rights of capital over labour-power are unblushingly asserted.

> 'He' (the man out of work) 'may be told the supply of cotton-workers is too large ... and ... must ... in fact be reduced by a third, perhaps, and that then there will be a healthy demand for the remaining two-thirds.... Public opinion... urges emigration.... The master cannot willingly see his labour supply being removed; he may think, and perhaps justly, that it is both wrong and unsound.... But if the public funds are to be devoted to assist emigration, he bas a right to be heard, and perhaps to protest.'

Mr Potter then shows how useful the cotton trade is, how the 'trade has undoubtedly drawn the surplus-population from Ireland and from the agricultural districts', how immense is its extent, how in the year 1860 it yielded 5/13 ths of the total English exports, how, after a few years, it will again expand by the extension of the market, particularly of the Indian market, and by calling forth a plentiful supply of cotton at 6d. per lb. He then continues:

> 'Some time ...,one, two, or three years, it may be, will produce the quantity.... The question I would put then is this—Is the trade worth retaining? Is it worth while to keep the machinery (he means the living labour machines) in order, and is it not the greatest folly to think of parting with that? I think it is. I allow that the workers are not a property, not the property of Lancashire and the masters; but they are the strength of both; they are the mental and trained power which cannot be. replaced for a generation; the mere machinery which they work might much of it be beneficially replaced, nay improved, in a twelvemonth[15] Encourage or allow (!) the working-power to emigrate, and what of the capitalist?... Take away the cream of the workers, and fixed capital will depreciate in a great degree, and the floating will not subject itself to a struggle with the short supply of inferior labour.... We are told the workers wish it' (emigration). 'Very natural it is that they should do so.... Reduce, compress the cotton trade by taking away its working power and reducing their wages expenditure, say one-fifth, or five millions, and what then would happen to the class above, the small shopkeepers; and what of the rents, the cottage rents.... Trace out the effects upwards to the small farmer, the better householder, and ... the landowner, and say if there could be any suggestion more suicidal to all classes of the country than by enfeebling a nation by exporting the best of its manufacturing population, and destroying the value of some of its most productive capital and enrichment .... I advise a loan (of five or six millions sterling), ... extending it may be over two or three years, administered by special commissioners added to the Boards of Guardians in the cotton districts, under special legislative regulations, enforcing some occupation or labour, as a means of keeping up at least the moral standard of the recipients of the loan... can anything be worse for landowners or masters than parting with the best of the workers, and demoralising and disappointing the rest by an extended depletive emigration, a depletion of capital and value in an entire province?'

Potter, the chosen mouthpiece of the manufacturers, distinguishes two sorts of 'machinery,' each of which belongs to the capitalist, and of which one stands in his factory, the other at night-time and on Sundays is housed outside the factory, in cottages. The one is inanimate, the other living. The inanimate machinery not only wears out and depreciates from day to day, but a great part of it becomes so quickly superannuated, by constant technical progress, that it can be replaced with advantage by new machinery after a few months. The living machinery, on the contrary gets better the longer it lasts, and in proportion as the skill, handed from one generation to another, accumulates. *The Times* answered the cotton lord as follows:

> 'Mr Edmund Potter is so impressed with the exceptional and supreme importance of the cotton masters that, in order to preserve this class and perpetuate their profession, he would keep half a million of the labouring class confined in a great moral workhouse against their will. 'Is the trade worth retaining?' asks Mr Potter. 'Certainly by all honest means it is,' we answer. 'Is it worth while keeping the machinery in order?' again asks Mr Potter. Here we hesitate. By the 'machinery' Mr Potter means the human machinery, for he goes on to protest that he does not mean to use them as an absolute property. We must confess that we do not think it 'worth while,' or even possible, to keep the human machinery in order-that is to shut it up and keep it oiled till it is wanted. Human machinery will rust under inaction, oil and rub it as you may. Moreover, the human machinery will, as we have just seen, get the steam up of its own accord, and burst or run amuck in our great towns. It might, as Mr Potter says, require some time to reproduce the workers, but, having machinists and capitalists at hand, we could always find thrifty, hard, industrious men wherewith to improvise more master manufacturers than we can ever want. Mr Potter talks of the trade reviving 'in one, two, or three years,' and he asks us not 'to encourage or allow (!) the working power to emigrate.'[16] He says that it is very natural the workers should wish to emigrate; but he thinks that in spite of their desire, the nation ought to keep this half million of workers with their 700,000 dependents, shut up in the cotton districts; and as a necessary consequence, he must of course think that the nation ought to keep down their discontent by force, and sustain them by alms—and upon the chance that the cotton masters may some day want them.... The time is come when the great public opinion of these islands must operate to save this 'working power' from those who would deal with it as they would deal with iron, and coal, and cotton.'

The Times' article was only a jeu d'esprit. The 'great public opinion' was, in fact, of Mr Potter's opinion, that the factory operatives are part of the movable fittings of a factory. Their emigration was prevented. They were locked up in that 'moral workhouse,' the cotton districts, and they form, as before, 'the strength' of the cotton manufacturers of Lancashire.

Capitalist production, therefore, of itself reproduces the separation between labour-power and the means of labour. It thereby reproduces and perpetuates the condition for exploiting the labourer. It incessantly forces him to sell his labour-power in order to live, and enables the capitalist to purchase labour-power in order that he may enrich himself.[17] It is no longer a mere accident, that capitalist and labourer confront each other in the market as buyer and seller. It is the process itself that incessantly hurls back the labourer on to the market as a vendor of his labour-power, and that incessantly converts his own product into a means by which another man can purchase him. In reality, the labourer belongs to capital before he has sold himself to capital. His economic bondage[18] is both brought about and concealed by the periodic sale of himself, by his change of masters, and by the oscillations in the market-price of labour-power.[19]

Capitalist production, therefore, under its aspect of a continuous connected process, of a process of reproduction, produces not only commodities, not only surplus-value, but it also produces and reproduces the capitalist relation; on the one side the capitalist, on the other the wage labourer.[20]

Notes

1. 'Mais ces riches, qui consomment les produits du travail des autres, ne peuvent les obtenir que par des échanges [purchases of commodities]. S'ils donnent cependant leur richesse acquise et accumulée en retour contre ces produits nouveaux qui sont l'objet de leur fantaisie, ils semblent exposés à épuiser bientôt leur fonds de réserve; ils ne travaillent point, avons-nous dit, et ils ne peuvent même travailler; on croirait donc que chaque jour doit voir diminuer leurs vieilles richesses, et que lorsqu'il ne leur en restera plus, rien ne sera offert en échange aux ouvriers qui travaillent exclusivement pour eux.... Mais dans l'ordre social, la richesse a acquis la propriété de se reproduire par le travail d'autrui, et sans que son propriétaire y concoure. La richesse, comme le travail, et par le travail, donne un fruit annuel qui peut être détruit chaque année sans que le riche en devienne plus pauvre. Ce fruit est le *revenu* qui naît du *capital*.' [The rich, who consume the labour of others, can only obtain them by making exchanges ... By giving away their acquired and accumulated wealth in exchange for the new products which are the object of their capricious wishes, they seem to be exposed to an early exhaustion of their reserve fund; we have already said that they do not work and are unable to work; therefore it could be assumed with full justification that their former wealth would be diminishing with every day and that, finally, a day would come when they would have nothing, and they would have nothing to offer to the workers, who work exclusively for them. ... But, in the social order, wealth has acquired the power of reproducing itself through the labour of others, without the help of its owners. Wealth, like labour, and by means of labour, bears fruit every year, but this fruit can be destroyed every year without making the rich man any poorer thereby. This fruit is the *revenue* which arises our of *capital*.] (Sismondi: 'Nouv. Princ. d'Econ. Pol.' Paris, 1819, t. I, pp. 81-82.)
2. 'Wages as well as profits are to be considered, each of them, as really a portion of the finished product.' (Ramsay, l. c., p. 142.) 'The share of the product which comes to the labourer in the form of wages.' (J. Mill, 'Eléments, &c.' Translated by Parissot. Paris, 1823, p. 34.)
3. 'When capital is employed in advancing to the workman his wages, it adds nothing to the funds for the maintenance of labour.' (Cazenove in note to his edition of Malthus' 'Definitions in Pol. Econ.' London, 1853, p. 22.)
4. 'The wages of labour are advanced by capitalists in the case of less than one fourth of the labourers of the earth.' (Rich. Jones: 'Textbook of Lectures on the Pol. Econ. of Nations.' Hertford, 1852, p. 36.)
5. 'Though the manufacturer' (i.e., the labourer) 'has his wages advanced to him by his master, he in reality costs him no expense, the value of these wages being generally reserved, together with a profit, in the improved value of the subject upon which his labour is bestowed.' (A. Smith, l. c., Book II. ch. III, p. 311.)
6. 'This is a remarkably peculiar property of productive labour. Whatever is productively consumed is capital and it becomes capital by consumption.' (James Mill, l. c., p. 242.) James Mill, however, never got on the track of this 'remarkably peculiar property.'
7. 'It is true indeed, that the first introducing a manufacture employs many poor, but they cease not to be so, and the continuance of it makes many.' ('Reasons for a Limited Exportation of Wool.' London, 1677, p. 19.) 'The farmer now absurdly asserts, that he keeps the poor. They are indeed kept in misery.' ('Reasons for the Late Increase of the Poor Rates: or a Comparative View of the Prices of Labour and Provisions.' London, 1777, p. 31.)
8. Rossi would not declaim so emphatically against this, had he really penetrated the secret of 'productive consumption.'

9. 'The labourers in the mines of S. America, whose daily task (the heaviest perhaps in the world) consists in bringing to the surface on their shoulders a load of metal weighing from 180 to 200 pounds, from a depth of 450 feet, live on bread and beans only; they themselves would prefer the bread alone for food, but their masters, who have found out that the men cannot work so hard on bread, treat them like horses, and compel them to eat beans; beans, however, are relatively much richer in bone-earth (phosphate of lime) than is bread.' (Liebig, l. c., vol. 1., p. 194, note.)
10. James Mill, l. c., p. 238.
11. 'If the price of labour should rise so high that, notwithstanding the increase of capital, no more could be employed, I should say that such increase of capital would be still unproductively consumed.' (Ricardo, l. c., p. 163.)
12. 'The only productive consumption, properly so called, is the consumption or destruction of wealth' (he alludes to the means of production) 'by capitalists with a view to reproduction.... The workman ... is a productive consumer to the person who employs him, and to the State, but not, strictly speaking, to himself.' (Malthus' 'Definitions, &c.,' p. 30.)
13. 'The only thing, of which one can say, that it is stored up and prepared beforehand, is the skill of the labourer.... The accumulation and storage of skilled labour, that most important operation, is, 'as regards the great mass of labourers, accomplished without any capital whatever.' (Th. Hodgskin: 'Labour Defended, &c.,' p. 13.)
14. 'That letter might be looked upon as the manifesto of the manufacturers.' (Ferrand: 'Motion on the Cotton Famine.' H.o.C., 27th April, 1863.)
15. It will not be forgotten that this same capital sings quite another song, under ordinary circumstances, when there is a question of reducing wages. Then the masters exclaim with one voice: 'The factory operatives should keep in wholesome remembrance the fact that theirs is really a low species of skilled labour, and that there is none which is more easily acquired, or of its quality more amply remunerated, or which, by a short training of the least expert, can be more quickly, as well as abundantly, acquired ... The master's machinery' (which we now learn can be replaced with advantage in 12 months,) 'really plays a far more important part in the business of production than the labour and skill of the operative' (who cannot now be replaced under 30 years), 'which six months' education can reach, and a common labourer can learn.' (See ante, p. 423.)
16. Parliament did not vote a single farthing in aid of emigration, but simply passed some Acts empowering the municipal corporations to keep the operatives in a half-starved state, *i.e.*, to exploit them at less than the normal wages. On the other hand, when 3 years later, the cattle disease broke out, Parliament broke wildly through its usages and voted, straight off, millions for indemnifying the millionaire landlords, whose farmers in any event came off without loss, owing to the rise in the price of meat. The bull-like bellow of the landed proprietors at the opening of Parliament, in 1866, showed that a man can worship the cow Sabala without being a Hindu, and can change himself into an ox without being a Jupiter.
17. 'L'ouvrier demandait de la subsistence pour vivre, le chef demandait du travail pour gagner.' [The worker required the means of subsistence to live, the boss required labour to make a profit] (Sismondi, l. c., p. 91.)
18. A boorishly clumsy form of this bondage exists in the county of Durham. This is one of the few counties, in which circumstances do not secure to the farmer undisputed proprietary rights over the agricultural labourer. The mining industry allows the latter some choice. In this county, the farmer, contrary to the custom elsewhere, rents only such farms as have on them labourers' cottages. The rent of the cottage is a part of the wages. These cottages are known as 'hinds' houses.' They are let to the labourers in consideration of certain feudal services, under a contract called 'bondage,' which, amongst other things, binds the labourer, during the time he is employed elsewhere, to leave some one, say his daughter, &c., to supply his place. The labourer himself is called a 'bondsman.' The relationship here set up also shows

how individual consumption by the labourer becomes consumption on behalf of capital—or productive consumption—from quite a new point of view: 'It is curious to observe that the very dung of the hind and bondsman is the perquisite of the calculating lord ... and the lord will allow no privy but his own to exist in the neighbourhood, and will rather give a bit of manure here and there for a garden than bate any part of his seigneurial right.' ('Public Health, Report VII., 1864,' p. 188.)

19. It will not be forgotten, that, with respect to the labour of children, &c., even the formality of a voluntary sale disappears.

20. 'Capital pre-supposes wage labour, and wage labour pre-supposes capital. One is a necessary condition to the existence of the other; they mutually call each other into existence. Does an operative in a cotton-factory produce nothing but cotton goods? No, he produces capital. He produces values that give fresh command over his labour, and that, by means of such command, create fresh values.' (Karl Marx: 'Lohnarbeit und Kapital,' in the *Neue Rheinische Zeitung*: No. 266, 7th April, 1849.) The articles published under the above title in the *N. Rh. Z.* are parts of some lectures given by me on that subject, in 1847, in the German 'Arbeiter-Verein' at Brussels, the publication of which was interrupted by the revolution of February.

24

Conversion of Surplus-Value into Capital

Section 1: *Capitalist Production on a Progressively Increasing Scale. Transition of the Laws of Property that Characterise Production of Commodities into Laws of Capitalist Appropriation*

Hitherto we have investigated how surplus-value emanates from capital; we have now to see how capital arises from surplus-value. Employing surplus-value as capital, reconverting it into capital, is called accumulation of capital.[1]

First let us consider this transaction from the standpoint of the individual capitalist. Suppose a spinner to have advanced a capital of £10,000, of which four-fifths (£8,000) are laid out in cotton, machinery, &c., and one-fifth (£2,000) in wages. Let him produce 240,000 lbs. of yarn annually, having a value of £12,000. The rate of surplus-value being 100%, the surplus-value lies in the surplus or net product of 40,000 lbs. of yarn, one-sixth of the gross product, with a value of £2,000 which will be realised by a sale. £2,000 is £2,000. We can neither see nor smell in this sum of money a trace of surplus-value. When we know that a given value is surplus-value, we know how its owner came by it; but that does not alter the nature either of value or of money.

In order to convert this additional sum of £2,000 into capital, the master-spinner will, all circumstances remaining as before, advance four-fifths of it (£1,600) in the purchase of cotton, &c., and one-fifth (£400) in the purchase of additional spinners, who will find in the market the necessaries of life whose value the master has advanced to them.

Then the new capital of £2,000 functions in the spinning mill, and brings in, in its turn, a surplus-value of £400.

The capital value was originally advanced in the money form. The surplus-value on the contrary is, originally, the value of a definite portion of the gross product. If this gross product be sold, converted into money, the capital value regains its original form. From this moment the capital value and the surplus-value are both of them sums of money, and their reconversion into capital takes place in precisely the same way. The one, as well as the other, is laid out by the capitalist in the purchase of commodities that place him in a position to begin afresh the fabrication of his goods, and this time, on an extended scale. But in order to be able to buy those commodities, he must find them ready in the market.

His own yarns circulate, only because he brings his annual product to market, as all other capitalists likewise do with their commodities. But these commodities, before coming to market, were part of the general annual product, part of the total mass of objects of every kind, into which the sum of the individual capitals, *i.e.*, the total capital of society, had been converted in the course of the year, and of which each capitalist had in hand only an aliquot part. The transactions in the market effectuate only the interchange of the individual components of this annual product, transfer them from one hand to another, but can neither augment the total annual production, nor alter the nature of the objects produced. Hence the use that can be made of the total annual product, depends entirely upon its own composition, but in no way upon circulation.

The annual production must in the first place furnish all those objects (use values) from which the material components of capital, used up in the course of the year, have to be replaced. Deducting these there remains the net or surplus-product, in which the surplus-value lies. And of what does this surplus-product consist? Only of things destined to satisfy the wants and desires of the capitalist class, things which, consequently, enter into the consumption fund of the capitalists? Were that the case, the cup of surplus-value would be drained to the very dregs, and nothing but simple reproduction would ever take place.

To accumulate it is necessary to convert a portion of the surplus-product into capital. But we cannot, except by a miracle, convert into capital anything but such articles as can be employed in the labour process (*i.e.*, means of production), and such further articles as are suitable for the sustenance of the labourer (*i.e.*, means of subsistence). Consequently, a part of the annual surplus-labour must have been applied to the production of additional means of production and subsistence, over and above the quantity of these things required to replace the capital advanced. In one word, surplus-value is convertible into capital solely because the surplus-product, whose value it is, already comprises the material elements of new capital.[2]

Now in order to allow of these elements actually functioning as capital, the capitalist class requires additional labour. If the exploitation of the labourers already employed do not increase, either extensively or intensively, then additional labour-power must be found. For this the mechanism of capitalist production provides beforehand, by converting the working class into a class dependent on wages, a class whose ordinary wages suffice, not only for its maintenance, but for its increase. It is only necessary for capital to incorporate this additional labour-power, annually supplied by the working class in the shape of labourers of all ages, with the surplus means of production comprised in the annual produce, and the conversion of surplus-value into capital is complete. From a concrete point of view, accumulation resolves itself into the reproduction of capital on a progressively increasing scale. The circle in which simple reproduction moves, alters its form, and, to use Sismondi's expression, changes into a spiral.[3]

Let us now return to our illustration. It is the old story: Abraham begat Isaac, Isaac begat Jacob, and so on. The original capital of £10,000 brings in a surplus-value of £2,000, which is capitalised. The new capital of £2,000 brings in a surplus-value of £400, and this, too, is capitalised, converted into a second additional capital, which, in its turn, produces a further surplus-value of £80. And so the ball rolls on.

We here leave out of consideration the portion of the surplus-value consumed by the capitalist. Just as little does it concern us, for the moment, whether the additional capital is joined on to the original capital, or is separated from it to function independently; whether the same capitalist, who accumulated it, employs it, or whether he hands it over to another.

This only we must not forget, that by the side of the newly-formed capital, the original capital continues to reproduce itself, and to produce surplus-value, and that this is also true of all accumulated capital, and the additional capital engendered by it.

The original capital was formed by the advance of £10,000. How did the owner become possessed of it? 'By his own labour and that of his forefathers,' answer unanimously the spokesmen of Political Economy. [4] And, in fact, their supposition appears the only one consonant with the laws of the production of commodities.

But it is quite otherwise with regard to the additional capital of £2,000. How that originated we know perfectly well. There is not one single atom of its value that does not owe its existence to unpaid labour. The means of production, with which the additional labour-power is incorporated, as well as the necessaries with which the labourers are sustained, are nothing but component parts of the surplus-product, of the tribute annually exacted from the working class by the capitalist class. Though the latter with a portion of that tribute purchases the additional labour-power even at its full price, so that equivalent is exchanged for equivalent, yet the transaction is for all that only the old dodge of every conqueror who buys commodities from the conquered with the money he has robbed them of.

If the additional capital employs the person who produced it, this producer must not only continue to augment the value of the original capital, but must buy back the fruits of his previous labour with more labour than they cost. When viewed as a transaction between the capitalist class and the working class, it makes no difference that additional labourers are employed by means of the unpaid labour of the previously employed labourers. The capitalist may even convert the additional capital into a machine that throws the producers of that capital out of work, and that replaces them by a few children. In every case the working class creates by the surplus-labour of one year the capital destined to employ additional labour in the following year.[5] And this is what is called: creating capital out of capital.

The accumulation of the first additional capital of £2,000 presupposes a value of £10,000 belonging to the capitalist by virtue of his 'primitive labour,' and advanced by him. The second additional capital of £400 presupposes, on the contrary, only the previous accumulation of the £2,000, of which the £400 is the surplus-value capitalised. The ownership of past unpaid labour is thenceforth the sole condition for the appropriation of living unpaid labour on a constantly increasing scale. The more the capitalist has accumulated, the more is he able to accumulate.

In so far as the surplus-value, of which the additional capital, No. 1, consists, is the result of the purchase of labour-power with part of the original capital, a purchase that conformed to the laws of the exchange of commodities, and that, from a legal standpoint, presupposes nothing beyond the free disposal, on the part of the labourer, of his own capacities, and on the part of the owner of money or commodities, of the values that belong to him; in so far as the additional capital, No. 2, &c., is the mere result of No. 1, and, therefore, a consequence of the above conditions; in so far as each single transaction invariably conforms to the laws of the exchange of commodities, the capitalist buying labour-power, the labourer selling it, and we will assume at its real value; in so far as all this is true, it is evident that the laws of appropriation or of private property, laws that are based on the production and circulation of commodities, become by their own inner and inexorable dialectic changed into their very opposite. The exchange of equivalents, the original operation with which we started, has now become turned round in such a way that there is only an apparent exchange. This is owing to the fact, first, that the capital which is exchanged for labour-power is itself but a portion of the product of others' labour appropriated without an equivalent; and, secondly, that this capital must not only be replaced by its producer, but replaced together with an added surplus. The relation of exchange subsisting between capitalist and labourer becomes a mere semblance appertaining to the process of circulation, a mere form, foreign to the real nature of the transaction, and only mystifying it. The ever repeated purchase and sale of labour-power is now the mere form; what really takes place is this—the capitalist again and again appropriates, without equivalent, a portion of the previously materialised labour of others, and exchanges it for a greater quantity of living labour. At first the rights of property seemed to us to be based on a man's own labour. At least, some such assumption was necessary since only commodity-owners with equal rights confronted each other, and the sole means by which a man could become possessed of the commodities of others, was by alienating his own commodities; and these could be replaced by labour alone. Now, however, property turns out to be the right, on the part of the capitalist, to appropriate the unpaid labour of others or its product, and to be the impossibility, on the part of the labourer, of appropriating his own product. The separation of property from labour has become the necessary consequence of a law that apparently originated in their identity.[6]

Therefore,[7] however much the capitalist mode of appropriation may seem to fly in the face of the original laws of commodity production, it nevertheless arises, not from a violation, but, on the contrary, from the application of these laws. Let us make this clear once more by briefly reviewing the consecutive phases of motion whose culminating point is capitalist accumulation.

We saw, in the first place, that the original conversion of a sum of values into capital was achieved in complete accordance with the laws of exchange. One party to the contract sells his labour-power, the other buys it. The former receives the value of his commodity, whose use value—labour—is thereby alienated to the buyer. Means of production which already belong to the latter are then transformed by him, with the aid of labour equally belonging to him, into a new product which is likewise lawfully his.

The value of this product includes: first, the value of the used-up means of production. Useful labour cannot consume these means of production without transferring their value to the new product, but, to be saleable, labour-power must be capable of supplying useful labour in the branch of industry in which it is to be employed.

The value of the new product further includes: the equivalent of the value of the labour-power together with a surplus-value. This is so because the value of the labour-power—sold for a definite length of time, say a day, a week, etc.—is less than the value created by its use during that time. But the worker has received payment for the exchange-value of his labour-power and by so doing has alienated its use value—this being the case in every sale and purchase.

The fact that this particular commodity, labour-power, possesses the peculiar use value of supplying labour, and therefore of creating value, cannot affect the general law of commodity production. If, therefore, the magnitude of value advanced in wages is not merely found again in the product, but is found there augmented by a surplus-value, this is not because the seller has been defrauded, for he has really received the value of his commodity; it is due solely to the fact that this commodity has been used up by the buyer.

The law of exchange requires equality only between the exchange-values of the commodities given in exchange for one another. From the very outset it presupposes even a difference between their use values and it has nothing whatever to do with their consumption, which only begins after the deal is closed and executed.

Thus the original conversion of money into capital is achieved in the most exact accordance with the economic laws of commodity production and with the right of property derived from them. Nevertheless, its result is:

1. that the product belongs to the capitalist and not to the worker;
2. that the value of this product includes, besides the value of the capital advanced, a surplus-value which costs the worker labour but the capitalist nothing, and which none the less becomes the legitimate property of the capitalist;
3. that the worker has retained his labour-power and can sell it anew if he can find a buyer.

Simple reproduction is only the periodical repetition of this first operation; each time money is converted afresh into capital. Thus the law is not broken; on the contrary, it is merely enabled to operate continuously. 'Several successive acts of exchange have only made the last represent the first' (Sismondi, 'Nouveaux Principes, etc.,' p. 70).

And yet we have seen that simple reproduction suffices to stamp this first operation, in so far as it is conceived as an isolated process, with a totally changed character. 'Of those who share the national income among themselves, the one side (the workers) acquire every year a fresh right to their share by fresh work; the others (the capitalists) have already acquired, by work done originally, a permanent right to their share' (Sismondi, l. c., pp. 110, 111). It is indeed notorious that the sphere of labour is not the only one in which primogeniture works miracles.

Nor does it matter if simple reproduction is replaced by reproduction on an extended scale, by accumulation. In the former case the capitalist squanders the whole surplus-value in dissipation, in the latter he demonstrates his bourgeois virtue by consuming only a portion of it and converting the rest into money.

The surplus-value is his property; it has never belonged to anyone else. If he advances it for the purposes of production, the advances made come from his own funds, exactly as on the day when he first entered the market. The fact that on this occasion the funds are derived from the unpaid labour of his workers makes absolutely no difference. If worker B is paid out of the surplus-value which worker A produced, then, in the first place, A furnished that surplus-value without having the just price of his commodity cut by a half-penny, and, in the second place, the transaction is no concern of B's whatever. What B claims, and has a right to claim, is that the capitalist should pay him the value of his labour-power. 'Both were still gainers: the worker because he was advanced the fruits of his labour' (should read: of the unpaid labour of other workers) 'before the work was done' (should read: before his own labour had borne fruit); 'the employer *(le maître),* because the labour of this worker was worth more than his wages' (should read: produced more value than the value of his wages). (Sismondi, l. c., p. 135.)

To be sure, the matter looks quite different if we consider capitalist production in the uninterrupted flow of its renewal, and if, in place of the individual capitalist and the individual worker, we view in their totality, the capitalist class and the working class confronting each other. But in so doing we should be applying standards entirely foreign to commodity production.

Only buyer and seller, mutually independent, face each other in commodity production. The relations between them cease on the day when the term stipulated in the contract they concluded expires. If the transaction is repeated, it is repeated as the result of a new agreement which has nothing to do with the previous one and which only by chance brings the same seller together again with the same buyer.

If, therefore, commodity production, or one of its associated processes, is to be judged according to its own economic laws, we must consider each act of exchange by itself, apart from any connexion with the act of exchange preceding it and that following it. And since sales and purchases are negotiated solely between particular individuals, it is not admissible to seek here for relations between whole social classes.

However long a series of periodical reproductions and preceding accumulations the capital functioning today may have passed through, it always preserves its original virginity. So long as the laws of exchange are observed in every single act of exchange the mode of appropriation can be completely revolutionised without in any way affecting the property rights which correspond to commodity production. These same rights remain in force both at the outset, when the product belongs to its producer, who, exchanging equivalent for equivalent, can enrich himself only by his own labour, and also in the period of capitalism, when social wealth becomes to an ever-increasing degree the property of those who are in a position to appropriate continually and ever afresh the unpaid labour of others.

This result becomes inevitable from the moment there is a free sale, by the labourer himself, of labour-power as a commodity. But it is also only from then onwards that commodity production is generalised and becomes the typical form of production; it is only from then onwards that, from the first, every product is produced for sale and all wealth produced goes through the sphere of circulation. Only when and where wage labour is its basis does commodity production impose itself upon society as a whole; but only then and there also does it unfold all its hidden potentialities. To say that the supervention of wage labour adulterates commodity production is to say that commodity production must not develop if it is to remain unadulterated. To the extent that commodity production, in accordance with its own inherent laws, develops further, into capitalist production, the property laws of commodity production change into the laws of capitalist appropriation.[8]

We have seen that even in the case of simple reproduction, all capital, whatever its original source, becomes converted into accumulated capital, capitalised surplus-value. But in the flood of production all the capital originally advanced becomes a vanishing quantity *(magnitudo evanescens,* in the mathematical sense), compared with the directly accumulated capital, *i.e.*, with the surplus-value or surplus-product that is reconverted into capital, whether it functions in the hands of its accumulator, or in those of others. Hence, Political Economy describes capital in general as 'accumulated wealth' (converted surplus-value or revenue), 'that is employed over again in the production of surplus-value,'[9] and the capitalist as 'the owner of surplus-value.'[10] It is merely another way of expressing the same thing to say that all existing capital is accumulated or capitalised interest, for interest is a mere fragment of surplus-value.[11]

Section 2: *Erroneous Conception, by Political Economy, of Reproduction on a Progressively Increasing Scale*

Before we further investigate accumulation or the reconversion of surplus-value into capital, we must brush on one side an ambiguity introduced by the classical economists.

Just as little as the commodities that the capitalist buys with a part of the surplus-value for his own consumption, serve the purpose of production and of creation of value, so little is the labour that he buys for the satisfaction of his natural and social requirements, productive labour. Instead of converting surplus-value into capital, he, on the contrary, by the purchase of those commodities and that labour, consumes or expends it as revenue. In the face of the habitual mode of life of the old feudal nobility, which, as Hegel rightly says, 'consists in consuming what is in hand,' and more especially displays itself in the luxury of personal retainers, it was extremely important for bourgeois economy to promulgate the doctrine that accumulation of capital is the first duty of every citizen, and to preach without ceasing, that a man cannot accumulate, if he eats up all his revenue, instead of spending a good part of it in the acquisition of additional productive labourers, who bring in more than they cost. On the other hand the economists had to contend against the popular prejudice, that confuses capitalist production with hoarding,[12] and fancies that accumulated wealth is either wealth that is rescued from being destroyed in its existing form, *i.e.*, from being consumed, or wealth that is withdrawn from circulation. Exclusion of money from circulation would also exclude absolutely its self-expansion as capital, while accumulation of a hoard in the shape of commodities would be sheer tomfoolery.[13] The accumulation of commodities in great masses is the result either of over-production or of a stoppage of circulation.[14] It is true that the popular mind is impressed by the sight, on the one hand, of the mass of goods that are stored up for gradual consumption by the rich,[15] and on the other hand, by the formation of reserve stocks; the latter, a phenomenon that is common to all modes of production, and on which we shall dwell for a moment, when we come to analyse circulation. Classical economy is therefore quite right, when it maintains that the consumption of surplus-products by productive, instead of by unproductive labourers, is a characteristic feature of the process of accumulation. But at this point the mistakes also begin. Adam Smith has made it the fashion, to represent accumulation as nothing more than consumption of surplus products by productive labourers, which amounts to saying, that the capitalising of surplus-value consists in merely turning surplus-value into labour-power.

Let us see what Ricardo, *e.g.*, says:

> 'It must be understood that all the productions of a country are consumed; but it makes the greatest difference imaginable whether they are consumed by those who reproduce, or by those who do not reproduce another value. When we say that revenue is saved, and added to capital, what we mean is, that the portion of revenue, so said to be added to capital, is consumed by productive instead of unproductive labourers. There can be no greater error than in supposing that capital is increased by non-consumption.'[16]

There can be no greater error than that which Ricardo and all subsequent economists repeat after A. Smith, viz., that

> 'the part of revenue, of which it is said, it has been added to capital, is consumed by productive labourers.'

According to this, all surplus-value that is changed into capital becomes variable capital. So far from this being the case, the surplus-value, like the original capital, divides itself into constant capital and variable capital, into means of production and labour-power. Labour-power is the form under which variable capital exists during the process of production. In this process, the labour-power is itself consumed by the capitalist while the means of production are consumed by the labour-power in the exercise of its function, labour. At the same time, the money paid for the purchase of the labour-power, is converted into necessaries, that are consumed, not by 'productive labour,' but by the 'productive labourer.' Adam Smith, by a fundamentally perverted analysis, arrives at the absurd conclusion, that even though each individual capital is divided into a constant and a variable part, the capital of society resolves itself only into variable capital, *i.e.*, is laid out exclusively in payment of wages. For instance, suppose a cloth manufacturer converts £2,000 into capital. One portion he lays out in buying weavers, the other in woollen yarn, machinery, &c. But the people, from whom he buys the yarn and the machinery, pay for labour with a part of the purchase money, and so on until the whole £2,000 are spent in the payment of wages, *i.e.*, until the entire product represented by the £2,000 has been consumed by productive labourers. It is evident that the whole gist of this argument lies in the words 'and so on,' which send us from pillar to post. In truth, Adam Smith breaks his investigation off, just where its difficulties begin.[17]

The annual process of reproduction is easily understood, so long as we keep in view merely the sum total of the year's production. But every single component of this product must be brought into the market as a commodity, and there the difficulty begins. The movements of the individual capitals, and of the personal revenues, cross and intermingle and are lost in the general change of places, in the circulation of the wealth of society; this dazes the sight, and propounds very complicated problems for solution. In the third part of Book II. I shall give the analysis of the real bearings of the facts. It is one of the great merits of the Physiocrats, that in their *Tableau économique* they were the first to attempt to depict the annual production in the shape in which it is presented to us after passing through the process of circulation.[18]

For the rest, it is a matter of course, that Political Economy, acting in the interests of the capitalist class, has not failed to exploit the doctrine of Adam Smith, viz., that the whole of that part of the surplus-product which is converted into capital, is consumed by the working class.

In the last preceding chapter, we treated surplus-value (or the surplus-product) solely as a fund for supplying the individual consumption of the capitalist. In this chapter we have, so far, treated it solely as a fund for accumulation. It is, however, neither the one nor the other, but is both together. One portion is consumed by the capitalist as revenue,[19] the other is employed as capital, is accumulated.

Given the mass of surplus-value, then, the larger the one of these parts, the smaller is the other. *Caeteris paribus*, the ratio of these parts determines the magnitude of the accumulation. But it is by the owner of the surplus-value, by the capitalist alone, that the division is made. It is his deliberate act. That part of the tribute exacted by him which he accumulates, is said to be saved by him, because he does not eat it, *i.e.*, because he performs the function of a capitalist, and enriches himself.

Except as personified capital, the capitalist has no historical value, and no right to that historical existence, which, to use an expression of the witty Lichnowsky, 'hasn't got no date.' And so far only is the necessity for his own transitory existence implied in the transitory necessity for the capitalist mode of production. But, so far as he is personified capital, it is not values in use and the enjoyment of them, but exchange-value and its augmentation, that spur him into action. Fanatically bent on making value expand itself, he ruthlessly forces the human race to produce for production's sake; he thus forces the development of the productive powers of society, and creates those material conditions, which alone can form the real basis of a higher form of society, a society in which the full and free development of every individual forms the ruling principle. Only as personified capital is the capitalist respectable. As such, he shares with the miser the passion for wealth as wealth. But that which in the miser is a mere idiosyncrasy, is, in the capitalist, the effect of the social mechanism, of which he is but one of the wheels. Moreover, the development of capitalist production makes it constantly necessary to keep increasing the amount of the capital laid out in a given industrial undertaking, and competition makes the immanent laws of capitalist production to be felt by each individual capitalist, as external coercive laws. It compels him to keep constantly extending his capital, in order to preserve it, but extend it he cannot, except by means of progressive accumulation.

So far, therefore, as his actions are a mere function of capital—endowed as capital is, in his person, with consciousness and a will—his own private consumption is a robbery perpetrated on accumulation, just as in book-keeping by double entry, the private expenditure of the capitalist is placed on the debtor side of his account against his capital. To accumulate, is to conquer the world of social wealth, to increase the mass of human beings exploited by him, and thus to extend both—the direct and the indirect sway of the capitalist.[20]

But original sin is at work everywhere. As capitalist production, accumulation, and wealth, become developed, the capitalist ceases to be the mere incarnation of capital. He has a fellow-feeling for his own Adam, and his education gradually enables him to smile at the rage for asceticism, as a mere prejudice of the old-fashioned miser. While the capitalist of the classical type brands individual consumption as a sin against his function, and as 'abstinence' from accumulating, the modernised capitalist is capable of looking upon accumulation as 'abstinence' from pleasure.

> 'Two souls, alas, do dwell with in his breast;
> The one is ever parting from the other.'[21]

At the historical dawn of capitalist production,—and every capitalist upstart has personally to go through this historical stage—avarice, and desire to get rich, are the ruling passions. But the progress of capitalist production not only creates a world of delights; it lays open, in speculation and the credit system, a thousand sources of sudden enrichment. When a certain stage of development has been reached, a conventional degree of prodigality, which is also an exhibition of wealth, and consequently a source of credit, becomes a business necessity to the 'unfortunate' capitalist. Luxury enters into capital's expenses of representation. Moreover, the capitalist gets rich, not like the miser, in proportion to his personal labour and restricted consumption, but at the same rate as he squeezes out the labour-power of others, and enforces on the labourer abstinence from all life's enjoyments. Although, therefore, the prodigality of the capitalist never possesses the bona fide character of the open-handed feudal lord's prodigality, but, on the contrary, has always lurking behind it the most sordid avarice and the most anxious calculation, yet his expenditure grows with his accumulation, without the one necessarily restricting the other. But along with this growth, there is at the same time developed in his breast, a Faustian conflict between the passion for accumulation, and the desire for enjoyment.

Dr Aikin says in a work published in 1795:

> 'The trade of Manchester may be divided into four periods. First, when manufacturers were obliged to work hard for their livelihood.'

They enriched themselves chiefly by robbing the parents, whose children were bound as apprentices to them; the parents paid a high premium, while the apprentices were starved. On the other hand, the average profits were low, and to accumulate, extreme parsimony was requisite. They lived like misers and were far from consuming even the interest on their capital.

> 'The second period, when they had begun to acquire little fortunes, but worked as hard as before,'—for direct exploitation of labour costs labour, as every slave-driver knows—'and lived in as plain a manner as before.... The third, when luxury began, and the trade was pushed by sending out riders for orders into every market town in the Kingdom.... It is probable that few or no capitals of £3,000 to £4,000 acquired by trade existed here before 1690. However, about that time, or a little later, the traders had got money beforehand, and began to build modern brick houses, instead of those of wood and plaster.'

Even in the early part of the 18th century, a Manchester manufacturer, who placed a pint of foreign wine before his guests, exposed himself to the remarks and headshakings of all his neighbours. Before the rise of machinery, a manufacturer's evening expenditure at the public house where they all met, never exceeded sixpence for a glass of punch, and a penny for a screw of tobacco. It was not till 1758, and this marks an epoch, that a person actually engaged in business was seen with an equipage of his own.

> 'The fourth period,' the last 30 years of the 18th century, 'is that in which expense and luxury have made great progress, and was supported by a trade extended by means of riders and factors through every part of Europe.'[22]

What would the good Dr Aikin say if he could rise from his grave and see the Manchester of today?

Accumulate, accumulate! That is Moses and the prophets! 'Industry furnishes the material which saving accumulates.'[23] Therefore, save, save, *i.e.*, reconvert the greatest possible portion of surplus-value, or surplus-product into capital! Accumulation for accumulation's sake, production for production's sake: by this formula classical economy expressed the historical mission of the bourgeoisie, and did not for a single instant deceive itself over the birth-throes of wealth.[24] But what avails lamentation in the face of historical necessity? If to classical economy, the proletarian is but a machine for the production of surplus-value; on the other hand, the capitalist is in its eyes only a machine for the conversion of this surplus-value into additional capital. Political Economy takes the historical function of the capitalist in bitter earnest. In order to charm out of his bosom the awful conflict between the desire for enjoyment and the chase after riches, Malthus, about the year 1820, advocated a division of labour, which assigns to the capitalist actually engaged in production, the business of accumulating, and to the other sharers in surplus-value, to the landlords, the place-men, the beneficed clergy, &c., the business of spending. It is of the highest importance, he says,

> 'to keep separate the passion for expenditure and the passion for accumulation.'[25]

The capitalists having long been good livers and men of the world, uttered loud cries. What, exclaimed one of their spokesmen, a disciple of Ricardo, Mr Malthus preaches high rents, heavy taxes, &c., so that the pressure of the spur may constantly be kept on the industrious by unproductive consumers! By all means, production, production on a constantly increasing scale, runs the shibboleth; but

> 'production will, by such a process, be far more curbed in than spurred on. Nor is it quite fair thus to maintain in idleness a number of persons, only to pinch others, who are likely, from their characters, if you can force them to work, to work with success.'[26]

Unfair as he finds it to spur on the industrial capitalist, by depriving his bread of its butter, yet he thinks it necessary to reduce the labourer's wages to a minimum "to keep him industrious.' Nor does he for a moment conceal the fact, that the appropriation of unpaid labour is the secret of surplus-value.

> 'Increased demand on the part of the labourers means nothing more than their willingness to take less of their own product for themselves, and leave a greater part of it to their employers; and if it be said, that this begets glut, by lessening consumption' (on the part of the labourers), 'I can only reply that glut is synonymous with large profits.'[27]

The learned disputation, how the booty pumped out of the labourer may be divided, with most advantage to accumulation, between the industrial capitalist and the rich idler, was hushed in face of the revolution of July. Shortly afterwards, the town proletariat at Lyons sounded the tocsin of revolution, and the country proletariat in England began to set fire to farm-yards and corn-stacks. On this side of the Channel Owenism began to spread; on the other side, St. Simonism and Fourierism. The hour of vulgar economy had struck. Exactly a year before Nassau W. Senior discovered at Manchester, that the profit (including interest) of capital is the product of the last hour of the twelve, he had announced to the world another discovery.

> 'I substitute,' he proudly says, 'for the word capital, considered as an instrument of production, the word abstinence.'

An unparalleled sample this, of the discoveries of vulgar economy! It substitutes for an economic category, a sycophantic phrase—*voilà tout.* [that's all]

> 'When the savage,' says Senior, 'makes bows, he exercises an industry, but he does not practise abstinence.'[28]

This explains how and why, in the earlier states of society, the implements of labour were fabricated without abstinence on the part of the capitalist.

> 'The more society progresses, the more abstinence is demanded,'[29]

Namely, from those who ply the industry of appropriating the fruits of others' industry. All the conditions for carrying on the labour process are suddenly converted into so many acts of abstinence on the part of the capitalist. If the corn is not all eaten, but part of it also sown—abstinence of the capitalist. If the wine gets time to mature—abstinence of the capitalist.[30] The capitalist robs his own self, whenever he 'lends (!) the instruments of production to the labourer,' that is, whenever by incorporating labour-power with them, he uses them to extract surplus-value out of that labour-power, instead of eating them up, steam-engines, cotton, railways, manure, horses, and all; or as the vulgar economist childishly puts it, instead of dissipating 'their value' in luxuries and other articles of consumption.[31] How the capitalists as a class are to perform that feat, is a secret that vulgar economy has hitherto obstinately refused to divulge. Enough, that the world still jogs on, solely through the self-chastisement of this modern penitent of Vishnu, the capitalist. Not only accumulation, but the simple 'conservation of a capital requires a constant effort to resist the temptation of consuming it.' [32] The simple dictates of humanity therefore plainly enjoin the release of the capitalist from this martyrdom and temptation, in the same way that the Georgian slave-owner was lately delivered, by the abolition of slavery, from the painful dilemma, whether to squander the surplus-product, lashed out of his niggers, entirely in champagne, or whether to reconvert a part of it into more niggers and more land.

In economic forms of society of the most different kinds, there occurs, not only simple reproduction, but, in varying degrees, reproduction on a progressively increasing scale. By degrees more is produced and more consumed, and consequently more products have to be converted into means of production. This process, however, does not present itself as accumulation of capital, nor as the function of a capitalist, so long as the labourer's means of production, and with them, his product and means of subsistence, do not confront him in the shape of capital.[33] Richard Jones, who died a few years ago, and was the successor of Malthus in the chair of Political Economy at Haileybury College, discusses this point well in the light of two important facts. Since the great mass of the Hindu population are peasants cultivating their land themselves, their products, their instruments of labour and means of subsistence never take 'the shape of a fund saved from revenue, which fund has, therefore, gone through a previous process of accumulation.'[34] On the other hand, the non-agricultural labourers in those provinces where the English rule has least disturbed the old system, are directly employed by the magnates, to whom a portion of the agricultural surplus-product is rendered in the shape of tribute or rent. One portion of this product is consumed by the magnates in kind, another is converted, for their use, by the labourers, into articles of luxury and such like things, while the rest forms the wages of the labourers, who own their implements of labour. Here, production and reproduction on a progressively increasing scale, go on their way without any intervention from that queer saint, that knight of the woeful countenance, the capitalist 'abstainer.'

Section 4: *Circumstances that, Independently of the Proportional Division of Surplus-value into Capital and Revenue, Determine the Amount of Accumulation. Degree of Exploitation of Labour-Power. Productivity of Labour. Growing Difference in Amount between Capital Employed and Capital Consumed. Magnitude of Capital Advanced*

The proportion in which surplus-value breaks up into capital and revenue being given, the magnitude of the capital accumulated clearly depends on the absolute magnitude of the surplus-value. Suppose that 80 per cent. were capitalised and 20 per cent. eaten up, the accumulated capital will be £2,400 or £200, according as the total surplus-value has amounted to £3,000 or £500. Hence all the circumstances that determine the mass of surplus-value operate to determine the magnitude of the accumulation. We sum them up once again, but only in so far as they afford new points of view in regard to accumulation.

It will be remembered that the rate of surplus-value depends, in the first place, on the degree of exploitation of labour-power. Political Economy values this fact so highly, that it occasionally identifies the acceleration of accumulation due to increased productiveness of labour, with its acceleration due to increased exploitation of the labourer.[35] In the chapters on the production of surplus-value it was constantly presupposed that wages are at least equal to the value of labour-power. Forcible reduction of wages below this value plays, however, in practice too important a part, for us not to pause upon it for a moment. It, in fact, transforms, within certain limits, the labourer's necessary consumption fund into a fund for the accumulation of capital.

> 'Wages,' says John Stuart Mill, 'have no productive power; they are the price of a productive power. Wages do not contribute, along with labour, to the production of commodities, no more than the price of tools contributes along with the tools themselves. If labour could be had without purchase, wages might be dispensed with.'[36]

But if the labourers could live on air they could not be bought at any price. The zero of their cost is therefore a limit in a mathematical sense, always beyond reach, although we can always approximate more and more nearly to it. The constant tendency of capital is to force the cost of labour back towards this zero. A writer of the 18th century, often quoted already, the author of the 'Essay on Trade and Commerce,' only betrays the innermost secret soul of English capitalism, when he declares the historic mission of England to be the forcing down of English wages to the level of the French and the Dutch.[37] With other things he says naively:

> 'But if our poor' (technical term for labourers) 'will live luxuriously ... then labour must, of course, be dear ... When it is considered what luxuries the manufacturing populace consume, such as brandy, gin, tea, sugar, foreign fruit, strong beer, printed linens, snuff, tobacco, &C.'[38]

He quotes the work of a Northamptonshire manufacturer, who, with eyes squinting heavenward moans:

> 'Labour is one-third cheaper in France than in England; for their poor work hard, and fare hard, as to their food and clothing. Their chief diet is bread, fruit, herbs, roots, and dried fish; for they very seldom eat flesh; and when wheat is dear, they eat very little bread.'[39] 'To which may be added,' our essayist goes on, 'that their drink is either water or other small liquors, so that they spend very little money.... These things are very difficult to be brought about; but they are not impracticable, since they have been effected both in France and in Holland.'[40]

Twenty years later, an American humbug, the baronised Yankee, Benjamin Thompson (*alias* Count Rumford) followed the same line of philanthropy to the great satisfaction of God and man. His 'Essays' are a cookery book with receipts of all kinds for replacing by some succedaneum the ordinary dear food of the labourer. The following is a particularly successful receipt of this wonderful philosopher:

> '5 lbs. of barleymeal, 7½d.; 5 lbs. of Indian corn, 6¼d.; 3d. worth of red herring, 1d. salt, 1d. vinegar, 2d. pepper and sweet herbs, in all 20¾.; make a soup for 64 men, and at the medium price of barley and of Indian corn ... this soup may be provided at ¼d., the portion of 20 ounces.[41]

With the advance of capitalistic production, the adulteration of food rendered Thompson's ideal superfluous.[42] At the end of the 18th and during the first ten years of the 19th century, the English farmers and landlords enforced the absolute minimum of wage, by paying the agricultural labourers less than the minimum in the form of wages, and the remainder in the shape of parochial relief. An example of the waggish way in which the English Dogberries acted in their 'legal' fixing of a wages tariff:

> 'The squires of Norfolk had dined, says Mr Burke, when they fixed the rate of wages; the squires of Berks evidently thought the labourers ought not to do so, when they fixed the rate of wages at Speenhamland, 1795.... There they decide that 'income (weekly) should be 3s. for a man,' when the gallon or half-peck loaf of 8 lbs. 11 oz. is at 1s., and increase regularly till bread is 1s. 5d.; when it is above that sum decrease regularly till it be at 2s., and then his food *should be* 1/5 th less.'[43]

Before the Committee of Inquiry of the House of Lords, 1814, a certain A. Bennett, a large farmer, magistrate, poor-law guardian, and wage-regulator, was asked:

> 'Has any proportion of the value of daily labour been made up to the labourers out of the poors' rate?' Answer: 'Yes, it has; the weekly income of every family is made up to the gallon loaf (8 lbs. 11 oz.), and 3d. per head!... The gallon loaf per week is what we suppose sufficient for the maintenance of every person in the family for the week; and the 3d. is for clothes, and if the parish think proper to find clothes; the 3d. is deducted. This practice goes through all the western part of Wiltshire, and, I believe, throughout the country.'[44] 'For years,' exclaims a bourgeois author of that time, 'they (the farmers) have degraded a respectable class of their countrymen, by forcing them to have recourse to the workhouse ... the farmer, while increasing his own gains, has prevented any accumulation on the part of his labouring dependents.'[45]

The part played in our days by the direct robbery from the labourer's necessary consumption fund in the formation of surplus-value, and, therefore, of the accumulation fund of capital, the so-called domestic industry has served to show. (Ch. xv., sect. 8, c.) Further facts on this subject will be given later.

Although in all branches of industry that part of the constant capital consisting of instruments of labour must be sufficient for a certain number of labourers (determined by the magnitude of the undertaking), it by no means always necessarily increases in the same proportion as the quantity of labour employed. In a factory, suppose that 100 labourers working 8 hours a day yield 800 working-hours. If the capitalist wishes to raise this sum by one half, he can employ 50 more workers; but then he must also advance more capital, not merely for wages, but for instruments of labour. But he might also let the 100 labourers work 12 hours instead of 8, and then the instruments of labour already to hand would be enough. These would then simply be more rapidly consumed. Thus additional labour, begotten of the greater tension of labour-power, can augment surplus-product and surplus-value (i.e., the subject-matter of accumulation), without corresponding augmentation in the constant part of capital.

In the extractive industries, mines, &c., the raw materials form no part of the capital advanced. The subject of labour is in this case not a product of previous labour, but is furnished by Nature gratis, as in the case of metals, minerals, coal, stone, &c. In these cases the constant capital consists almost exclusively of instruments of labour, which can very well absorb an increased quantity of labour (day and night shifts of labourers, *e.g.*). All other things being equal, the mass and value of the product will rise in direct proportion to the labour expended. As on the first day of production, the original produce-formers, now turned into the creators of the material elements of capital—man and Nature—still work together. Thanks to the elasticity of labour-power, the domain of accumulation has extended without any previous enlargement of constant capital.

In agriculture the land under cultivation cannot be increased without the advance of more seed and manure. But this advance once made, the purely mechanical working of the soil itself produces a marvellous effect on the amount of the product. A greater quantity of labour, done by the same number of labourers as before, thus increases the fertility, without requiring any new advance in the instruments of labour. It is once again the direct action of man on Nature which becomes an immediate source of greater accumulation, without the intervention of any new capital.

Finally, in what is called manufacturing industry, every additional expenditure of labour presupposes a corresponding additional expenditure of raw materials, but not necessarily of instruments of labour. And as extractive industry and agriculture supply manufacturing industry with its raw materials and those of its instruments of labour, the additional product the former have created without additional advance of capital, tells also in favour of the latter.

General result: by incorporating with itself the two primary creators of wealth, labour-power and the land, capital acquires a power of expansion that permits it to augment the elements of its accumulation beyond the limits apparently fixed by its own magnitude, or by the value and the mass of the means of production, already produced, in which it has its being.

Another important factor in the accumulation of capital is the degree of productivity of social labour.

With the productive power of labour increases the mass of the products, in which a certain value, and, therefore, a surplus-value of a given magnitude, is embodied. The rate of surplus-value remaining the same or even falling, so long as it only falls more slowly, than the productive power of labour rises, the mass of the surplus-product increases. The division of this product into revenue and additional capital remaining the same, the consumption of the capitalist may, therefore, increase without any decrease in the fund of accumulation. The relative magnitude of the accumulation fund may even increase at the expense of the consumption fund, whilst the cheapening of commodities places at the disposal of the capitalist as many means of enjoyment as formerly, or even more than formerly. But hand-in-hand with the increasing productivity of labour, goes, as we have seen, the cheapening of the labourer, therefore a higher rate of surplus-value, even when the real wages are rising. The latter never rise proportionally to the productive power of labour. The same value in variable capital therefore sets in movement more labour-power, and, therefore, more labour. The same value in constant capital is embodied in more means of production, *i.e.*, in more instruments of labour, materials of labour and auxiliary materials; it therefore also supplies more elements for the production both of use value and of value, and with these more absorbers of labour. The value of the additional capital, therefore, remaining the same or even diminishing, accelerated accumulation still takes place. Not only does the scale of reproduction materially extend, but the production of surplus-value increases more rapidly than the value of the additional capital.

The development of the productive power of labour reacts also on the original capital already engaged in the process of production. A part of the functioning constant capital consists of instruments of labour, such as machinery, &c., which are not consumed, and therefore not reproduced, or replaced by new ones of the same kind, until after long periods of time. But every year a part of these instruments of labour perishes or reaches the limit of its productive function. It reaches, therefore, in that year, the time for its periodical reproduction, for its replacement by new ones of the same kind. If the productiveness of labour has, during the using up of these instruments of labour, increased (and it develops continually with the uninterrupted advance of science and technology), more efficient and (considering their increased efficiency), cheaper machines, tools, apparatus, &c., replace the old. The old capital is reproduced in a more productive form, apart from the constant detail improvements in the instruments of labour already in use. The other part of the constant capital, raw material and auxiliary substances, is constantly reproduced in less than a year; those produced by agriculture, for the most part annually. Every introduction of improved methods, therefore, works almost simultaneously on the new capital and on that already in action. Every advance in Chemistry not only multiplies the number of useful materials and the useful applications of those already known, thus extending with the growth of capital its sphere of investment. It teaches at the same time how to throw the excrements of the processes of production and consumption back again into the circle of the process of reproduction, and thus, without any previous outlay of capital, creates new matter for capital. Like the increased exploitation of natural wealth by the mere increase in the tension of labour-power, science and technology give capital a power of expansion independent of the given magnitude of the capital actually functioning. They react at the same time on that part of the original capital which has entered upon its stage of renewal. This, in passing into its new shape, incorporates gratis the social advance made while its old shape was being used up. Of course; this development of productive power is accompanied by a partial depreciation of functioning capital. So far as this depreciation makes itself acutely felt in competition, the burden falls on the labourer, in the increased exploitation of whom the capitalist looks for his indemnification.

Labour transmits to its product the value of the means of production consumed by it. On the other hand, the value and mass of the means of production set in motion by a given quantity of labour increase as the labour becomes more productive. Though the same quantity of labour adds always to its products only the same sum of new value, still the old capital value, transmitted by the labour to the products, increases with the growing productivity of labour.

An English and a Chinese spinner, e.g., may work the same number of hours with the same intensity; then they will both in a week create equal values. But in spite of this equality, an immense difference will obtain between the value of the week's product of the Englishman, who works with a mighty automaton, and that of the Chinaman, who has but a spinning-wheel. In the same time as the Chinaman spins one pound of cotton, the Englishman spins several hundreds of pounds. A sum, many hundred times as great, of old values swells the value of his product, in which those re-appear in a new, useful form, and can thus function anew as capital.

> 'In 1782,' as Frederick Engels teaches us, 'all the wool crop in England of the three preceding years, lay untouched for want of labourers, and so it must have lain, if newly invented machinery had not come to its aid and spun it.'[46]

Labour embodied in the form of machinery of course did not directly force into life a single man, but it made it possible for a smaller number of labourers, with the addition of relatively less living labour, not only to consume the wool productively, and put into it new value, but to preserve in the form of yarn, &c., its old value. At the same time, it caused and stimulated increased reproduction of wool. It is the natural property of living labour, to transmit old value, whilst it creates new. Hence, with the increase in efficacy, extent and value of its means of production, consequently with the accumulation that accompanies the development of its productive power, labour keeps up and eternises an always increasing capital value in a form ever new.'[47] This natural power of labour takes the appearance of an intrinsic property of capital, in which it is incorporated, just as the productive forces of social labour take the appearance of inherent properties of capital, and as the constant appropriation of surplus-labour by the capitalists, takes that of a constant self-expansion of capital.

With the increase of capital, the difference between the capital employed and the capital consumed increases. In other words, there is increase in the value and the material mass of the instruments of labour, such as buildings, machinery, drain-pipes, working-cattle, apparatus of every kind that function for a longer or shorter time in processes of production constantly repeated, or that serve for the attainment of particular useful effects, whilst they themselves only gradually wear out, therefore only lose their value piecemeal, therefore transfer that value to the product only bit by bit. In the same proportion as these instruments of labour serve as product-formers without adding value to the product, *i.e.*, in the same proportion as they are wholly employed but only partly consumed, they perform, as we saw earlier, the same gratuitous service as the natural forces, water, steam, air, electricity, etc. This gratuitous service of past labour, when seized and filled with a soul by living labour, increases with the advancing stages of accumulation.

Since past labour always disguises itself as capital, *i.e.*, since the passive of the labour of A, B, C, etc., takes the form of the active of the non-labourer X, bourgeois and political economists are full of praises of the services of dead and gone labour, which, according to the Scotch genius MacCulloch, ought to receive a special remuneration in the shape of interest, profit, etc.[48] The powerful and ever-increasing assistance given by past labour to the living labour process under the form of means of production is, therefore, attributed to that form of past labour in which it is alienated, as unpaid labour, from the worker himself, *i.e.*, to its capitalistic form. The practical agents of capitalistic production and their pettifogging ideologists are as unable to think of the means of production as separate from the antagonistic social mask they wear today, as a slave-owner to think of the worker himself as distinct from his character as a slave.

With a given degree of exploitation of labour-power, the mass of the surplus-value produced is determined by the number of workers simultaneously exploited; and this corresponds, although in varying proportions, with the magnitude of the capital. The more, therefore, capital increases by means of successive accumulations, the more does the sum of the value increase that is divided into consumption fund and accumulation fund. The capitalist can, therefore, live a more jolly life, and at the same time show more 'abstinence.' And, finally, all the springs of production act with greater elasticity, the more its scale extends with the mass of the capital advanced.

Section 5: *The So-called Labour Fund*

It has been shown in the course of this inquiry that capital is not a fixed magnitude, but is a part of social wealth, elastic and constantly fluctuating with the division of fresh surplus-value into revenue and additional capital. It has been seen further that, even with a given magnitude of functioning capital, the labour-power, the science, and the land (by which are to be understood, economically, all conditions of labour furnished by Nature independently of man), embodied in it, form elastic powers of capital, allowing it, within certain limits, a field of action independent of its own magnitude. In this inquiry we have neglected all effects of the process of circulation, effects which may produce very different degrees of efficiency in the same mass of capital. And as we presupposed the limits set by capitalist production, that is to say, presupposed the process of social production in a form developed by purely spontaneous growth, we neglected any more rational combination, directly and systematically practicable with the means of production, and the mass of labour-power at present disposable. Classical economy always loved to conceive social capital as a fixed magnitude of a fixed degree of efficiency. But this prejudice was first established as a dogma by the arch-Philistine, Jeremy Bentham, that insipid, pedantic, leather-tongued oracle of the ordinary bourgeois intelligence of the 19th century.[49] Bentham is among philosophers what Martin Tupper is among poets. Both could only have been manufactured in England.[50] In the light of his dogma the commonest phenomena of the process of production, as, *e.g.*, its sudden expansions and contractions, nay, even accumulation itself, become perfectly inconceivable.[51] The dogma was used by Bentham himself, as well as by Malthus, James Mill, MacCulloch, etc., for an apologetic purpose, and especially in order to represent one part of capital, namely, variable capital, or that part convertible into labour-power, as a fixed magnitude. The material of variable capital, *i.e.*, the mass of the means of subsistence it represents for the labourer, or the so-called labour fund, was fabled as a separate part of social wealth, fixed by natural laws and unchangeable. To set in motion the part of social wealth which is to function as constant capital, or, to express it in a material form, as means of production, a definite mass of living labour is required. This mass is given technologically. But neither is the number of labourers required to render fluid this mass of labour-power given (it changes with the degree of exploitation of the individual labour-power), nor is the price of this labour-power given, but only its minimum limit, which is moreover very variable. The facts that lie at the bottom of this dogma are these: on the one hand, the labourer has no right to interfere in the division of social wealth into means of enjoyment for thc non-labourer and means of production. [52] On the other hand, only in favourable and exceptional cases, has he the power to enlarge the so-called labour fund at the expense of the 'revenue' of the wealthy.

What silly tautology results from the attempt to represent the capitalistic limits of the labour fund as its natural and social limits may be seen, e.g., in Professor Fawcett.[53]

'The circulating capital of a country,' he says, 'is its wage-fund. Hence, if we desire to calculate the average money wages received by each labourer, we have simply to divide the amount of this capital by the number of the labouring population.'[54]

That is to say, we first add together the individual wages actually paid, and then we affirm that the sum thus obtained, forms the total value of the 'labour fund' determined and vouchsafed to us by God and Nature. Lastly, we divide the sum thus obtained by the number of labourers to find out again how much may come to each on the average. An uncommonly knowing dodge this. It did not prevent Mr Fawcett saying in the same breath:

'The aggregate wealth which is annually saved in England, is divided into two portions; one portion is employed as capital to maintain our industry, and the other portion is exported to foreign countries... Only a portion, and perhaps, not a large portion of the wealth which is annually saved in this country, is invested in our own industry.[55]

The greater part of the yearly accruing surplus-product, embezzled, because abstracted without return of an equivalent, from the English labourer, is thus used as capital, not in England, but in foreign countries. But with the additional capital thus exported, a part of the 'labour fund' invented by God and Bentham is also exported.[56]

Notes

1. 'Accumulation of capital; the employment of a portion of revenue as capital.' (Malthus: 'Definitions, &c.,' ed. Cazenove, p. 11.) 'Conversion of revenue into capital,' (Malthus: 'Princ. of Pol. Econ '2nd Ed., Lond.. 1836, p. 320.)
2. We here take no account of export trade, by means of which a nation can change articles of luxury either into means of production or means of subsistence, and *vice versà*. In order to examine the object of our investigation in its integrity, free from all disturbing subsidiary circumstances, we must treat the whole world as one nation, and assume that capitalist production is everywhere established and has possessed itself of every branch of industry.
3. Sismondi's analysis of accumulation suffers from the great defect, that he contents himself, to too great an extent, with the phrase 'conversion of revenue into capital,' without fathoming the material conditions of this operation.
4. 'Le travail primitif auquel son capital a dû sa naissance.' [the original labour, to which his capital owed its origin] Sismondi, l. c., ed. Paris, t. I., p. 109.
5. 'Labour creates capital before capital employs labour.' E. G. Wakefield, 'England and America,' Lond., 1833, Vol. II, p. 110.
6. The property of the capitalist in the product of the labour of others 'is a strict consequence of the law of appropriation, the fundamental principle of which was, on the contrary, the exclusive title of every labourer to the product of his own labour.' (Cherbuliez, 'Richesse ou Pauvreté,' Paris, 1841, p. 58, where, however, the dialectical reversal is not properly developed.)
7. The following passage (to p. 551 'laws of capitalist appropriation.') has been added to the English text in conformity with the 4th German edition.

8. We may well, therefore, feel astonished at the cleverness of Proudhon, who would abolish capitalistic property by enforcing the eternal laws of property that are based on commodity production!
9. 'Capital, viz., accumulated wealth employed with a view to profit.' (Malthus, l. c.) 'Capital ... consists of wealth saved from revenue, and used with a view to profit.' (R. Jones: 'An Introductory Lecture on Polit. Econ.,' Lond., 1833, p. 16.)
10. 'The possessors of surplus-produce or capital.' ('The Source and Remedy of the National Difficulties. A Letter to Lord John Russell.' Lond., 1821.)
11. 'Capital, with compound interest on every portion of capital saved, is so all engrossing that all the wealth in the world from which income is derived, has long ago become the interest on capital.' (London, *Economist*, 19th July, 1851.)
12. 'No political economist of the present day can by saving mean mere hoarding: and beyond this contracted and insufficient proceeding, no use of the term in reference to the national wealth can well be imagined, but that which must arise from a different application of what is saved, founded upon a real distinction between the different kinds of labour maintained by it.' (Malthus, l. c., pp. 38, 39.)
13. Thus for instance, Balzac, who so thoroughly studied every shade of avarice, represents the old usurer Gobseck as in his second childhood when he begins to heap up a hoard of commodities.
14. 'Accumulation of stocks ... non-exchange ... over-production.' (Th. Corbet. l. c., p. 104.)
15. In this sense Necker speaks of the 'objets de faste et de somptuosité,' [things of pomp and luxury] of which 'le temps a grossi l'accummulation,' [accumulation has grown with time] and which 'les lois de propriété ont rassemblés dans une seule classe de la société.' [the laws of property have brought into the hands of one class of society alone] (*Oeuvres de M. Necker*, Paris and Lausanne, 1789, t. ii., p. 291.)
16. Ricardo, l.c., p. 163, note.
17. In spite of his 'Logic,' John St. Mill never detects even such faulty analysis as this when made by his predecessors, an analysis which, even from the bourgeois standpoint of the science, cries out for rectification. In every case he registers with the dogmatism of a disciple, the confusion of his master's thoughts. So here: 'The capital itself in the long run becomes entirely wages, and when replaced by the sale of produce becomes wages again.'
18. In his description of the process of reproduction, and of accumulation, Adam Smith, in many ways, not only made no advance, but even lost considerable ground, compared with his predecessors, especially by the Physiocrats. Connected with the illusion mentioned in the text, is the really wonderful dogma, left by him as an inheritance to Political Economy, the dogma, that the price of commodities is made up of wages, profit (interest) and rent, *i.e.*, of wages and surplus-value. Starting from this basis, Storch naively confesses, 'Il est impossible de résoudre le prix nécessaire dans ses éléments les plus simples.' [... it is impossible to resolve the necessary price into its simplest elements] (Storch, l. c., Petersb. Edit., 1815, t. ii., p. 141, note.) A fine science of economy this, which declares it impossible to resolve the price of a commodity into its simplest elements! This point will be further investigated in the seventh part of Book iii.
19. The reader will notice, that the word revenue is used in a double sense: first, to designate surplus-value so far as it is the fruit periodically yielded by capital; secondly, to designate the part of that fruit which is periodically consumed by the capitalist, or added to the fund that supplies his private consumption. I have retained this double meaning because it harmonises with the language of the English and French economists.
20. Taking the usurer, that old-fashioned but ever renewed specimen of the capitalist for his text, Luther shows very aptly that the love of power is an element in the desire to get rich. 'The heathen were able, by the light of reason, to conclude that a usurer is a double-dyed thief and murderer. We Christians, however, hold them in such honour, that we fairly worship them

for the sake of their money.... Whoever eats up, robs, and steals the nourishment of another, that man commits as great a murder (so far as in him lies) as he who starves a man or utterly undoes him. Such does a usurer, and sits the while safe on his stool, when he ought rather to be hanging on the gallows, and be eaten by as many ravens as he has stolen guilders, if only there were so much flesh on him, that so many ravens could stick their beaks in and share it. Meanwhile, we hang the small thieves.... Little thieves are put in the stocks, great thieves go flaunting in gold and silk.... Therefore is there, on this earth, no greater enemy of man (after the devil) than a gripe-money, and usurer, for he wants to be God over all men. Turks, soldiers, and tyrants are also bad men, yet must they let the people live, and Confess that they are bad, and enemies, and do, nay, must, now and then show pity to some. But a usurer and money-glutton, such a one would have the whole world perish of hunger and thirst, misery and want, so far as in him lies, so that he may have all to himself, and every one may receive from him as from a God, and be his serf for ever. To wear fine cloaks, golden chains, rings, to wipe his mouth, to be deemed and taken for a worthy, pious man .... Usury is a great huge monster, like a werewolf, who lays waste all, more than any Cacus, Gerion or Antus. And yet decks himself out, and would be thought pious, so that people may not see where the oxen have gone, that he drags backwards into his den. But Hercules shall hear the cry of the oxen and of his prisoners, and shall seek Cacus even in cliffs and among rocks, and shall set the oxen loose again from the villain. For Cacus means the villain that is a pious usurer, and steals, robs, eats everything. And will not own that he has done it, and thinks no one will find him out, because the oxen, drawn backwards into his den, make it seem, from their foot-prints, that they have been let out. So the usurer would deceive the world, as though he were of use and gave the world oxen, which he, however, rends, and eats all alone... And since we break on the wheel, and behead highwaymen, murderers and housebreakers, how much more ought we to break on the wheel and kill.... hunt down, curse and behead all usurers.' (Martin Luther, l. c.)

21. See Goethe's 'Faust.'
22. Dr Aikin: 'Description of the Country from 30 to 40 miles round Manchester.' Lond., 1795, p. 182, sq.
23. A. Smith, l. c., bk. iii., ch. iii.
24. Even J. B. Say says: 'Les épargnes des riches se font aux dépens des pauvres.' [the savings of the rich are made at the expense of the poor] 'The Roman proletarian lived almost entirely at the expense of society.... It can almost be said that modern society lives at the expense of the proletarians, on what it keeps out of the remuneration of labour.' (Sismondi: 'études, &c.,' t. i., p. 24.)
25. Malthus, l. c., pp. 319, 320.
26. 'An Inquiry into those Principles Respecting the Nature of Demand, &c.,' p. 67.
27. l. c., p. 59.
28. (Senior, 'Principes fondamentaux del'Écon. Pol.' trad. Arrivabene. Paris, 1836, p. 308.) This was rather too much for the adherents of the old classical school. 'Mr Senior has substituted for it' (the expression, labour and profit) 'the expression labour and Abstinence. He who converts his revenue abstains from the enjoyment which its expenditure would afford him. It is not the capital, but the use of the capital productively, which is the cause of profits.' (John Cazenove, l. c., p. 130, Note.) John St. Mill, on the contrary, accepts on the one hand Ricardo's theory of profit, and annexes on the other hand Senior's 'remuneration of abstinence.' He is as much at home in absurd contradictions, as he feels at sea in the Hegelian contradiction, the source of all dialectic. It has never occurred to the vulgar economist to make the simple reflexion, that every human action may be viewed, as 'abstinence' from its opposite. Eating is abstinence from fasting, walking, abstinence from standing still, working, abstinence from idling, idling, abstinence from working, &c. These gentlemen would do well, to ponder, once in a while, over Spinoza's: 'Determinatio est Negatio.'
29. Senior, l. c., p. 342.

30. 'No one ... will sow his wheat, for instance, and allow it to remain a twelvemonth in the ground, or leave his wine in a cellar for years, instead of consuming these things or their equivalent at once ... unless he expects to acquire additional value, &c.' (Scrope, 'Polit. Econ.,' edit. by A. Potter, New York, 1841, pp. 133-134.)
31. 'La privation que s'impose le capitalisté, en prêtant [The deprivation the capitalist imposes on himself by lending ...] (this euphemism used, for the purpose of identifying, according to the approved method of vulgar economy, the labourer who is exploited, with the industrial capitalist who exploits, and to whom other capitalists lend money) ses instruments de production au travailleur, au lieu d'en consacrer la valeur à son propre usage, en la transforment en objets d'utilité ou d'agrément.' [his instruments of production to the worker, instead of devoting their value to his own consumption, by transforming them into objects of utility or pleasure] (G. de Molinari, l. c., p. 36.)
32. 'La conservation d'un capital exige ... un effort constant pour résister a la tentation de le consommer.' (Courcelle-Seneuil, l. c., p. 57.)
33. 'The particular classes of income which yield the most abundantly to the progress of national capital, change at different stages of their progress, and are, therefore, entirely different in nations occupying different positions in that progress.... Profits ... unimportant source of accumulation, compared with wages and rents, in the earlier stages of society.... When a considerable advance in the powers of national industry has actually taken place, profits rise into comparative importance as a source of accumulation.' (Richard Jones, 'Textbook, &c.,' pp. 16, 21.)
34. l. c., p. 36, sq.
35. 'Ricardo says: 'In different stages of society the accumulation of capital or of the means of employing' (i.e., exploiting) 'labour is more or less rapid, and must in all cases depend on the productive powers of labour. The productive powers of labour are generally greatest where there is an abundance of fertile land.' If, in the first sentence, the productive powers of labour mean the smallness of that aliquot part of any produce that goes to those whose manual labour produced it, the sentence is nearly identical, because the remaining aliquot part is the fund whence capital can, if the *owner pleases*, be accumulated. But then this does not generally happen, where there is most fertile land.' ('Observations on Certain Verbal Disputes, &c.' pp. 74, 75.)
36. J. Stuart Mill: 'Essays on Some Unsettled Questions of Political Economy,' Lond., 1844, p. 90.
37. 'An Essay on Trade and Commerce,' Lond., 1770, P. 44. *The Times* of December, 1866, and January, 1867, in like manner published certain outpourings of the heart of the English mine-owner, in which the happy lot of the Belgian miners was pictured, who asked and received no more than was strictly necessary for them to live for their 'masters.' The Belgian labourers have to suffer much, but to figure in *The Times* as model labourers! In the beginning of February, 1867, came the answer: strike of the Belgian miners at Marchienne, put down by powder and lead.
38. l. c., pp. 44, 46.
39. The Northamptonshire manufacturer commits a pious fraud, pardonable in one whose heart is so full. He nominally compares the life of the English and French manufacturing labourer, but in the words just quoted he is painting, as he himself confesses in his confused way, the French agricultural labourers.
40. l. c., pp. 70, 71. *Note in the 3rd German edition:* today, thanks to the competition on the world-market, established since then, we have advanced much further. 'If China,' says Mr Stapleton, M.P., to his constituents, 'should become a great manufacturing country, I do not see how the manufacturing population of Europe could sustain the contest without descending to the level of their competitors.' (*Times,* Sept. 3, 1873, p. 8.) The wished-for goal of English capital is no longer Continental wages but Chinese.
41. Benjamin Thompson: 'Essays, Political, Economical, and Philosophical, &c.,' 3 vols., Lond,

1796-1802, vol. i., p. 294. In his 'The State of the Poor, or an History of the Labouring Classes in England, &c.,' Sir F. M. Eden strongly recommends the Rumfordian beggar-soup to workhouse overseers, and reproachfully warns the English labourers that 'many poor people, particularly in Scotland, live, and that very comfortably, for months together, upon oat-meal and barley-meal, mixed with only water and salt.' (l. c., vol. i, book i., ch. 2, p. 503.) The same sort of hints in the 19th century. 'The most wholesome mixtures of flour having been refused (by the English agricultural labourer)... in Scotland, where education is better, this prejudice is, probably, unknown.' (Charles H. Parry, M. D., 'The Question of the Necessity of the Existing Corn Laws Considered.' London, 1816, p. 69.) This same Parry, however, complains that the English labourer is now (1815) in a much worse condition than in Eden's time (1797.)

42. From the reports of the last Parliamentary Commission on adulteration of means of subsistence, it will be seen that the adulteration even of medicines is the rule, not the exception in England. E.g., the examination of 34 specimens of opium, purchased of as many different chemists in London, showed that 31 were adulterated with poppy heads, wheat-flour, gum, clay, sand, &c. Several did not contain an atom of morphia.

43. G. B. Newnham (barrister-at-law): 'A Review of the Evidence before the Committee of the two Houses of Parliament on the Corn Laws.' Lond., 1815, p. 20, *note.*

44. l. c., pp. 19, 20.

45. C. H. Parry, l. c., pp. 77, 69. The landlords, on their side, not only 'indemnified' themselves for the Anti-Jacobin War, which they waged in the name of England, but enriched themselves enormously. Their rents doubled, trebled, quadrupled, 'and in one instance, increased sixfold in eighteen years.' (I. c., pp. 100, 101.)

46. Friedrich Engels, 'Lage der arbeitenden Klasse in England,' p. 20.

47. Classic economy has, on account of a deficient analysis of the labour process, and of the process of creating value, never properly grasped this weighty element of reproduction, as may be seen in Ricardo; he says, *e.g.*, whatever the change in productive power, 'a million men always produce in manufactures the same value.' This is accurate, if the extension and degree of intensity of their labour are given. But it does not prevent (this Ricardo overlooks in certain conclusions he draws) a million men with different powers of productivity in their labour, turning into products very different masses of the means of production, and therefore preserving in their products very different masses of value; in consequence of which the values of the products yielded may vary considerably. Ricardo has, it may be noted in passing, tried in vain to make clear to J. B. Say, by that very example, the difference between use value (which he here calls wealth or material riches) and exchange-value. Say answers: 'Quant à la difficulté qu'élève Mr Ricardo en disant que, par des procédés mieux entendus un million de personnes peuvent produire deux fois, trois fois autant de richesses, sans produire plus de valeurs, cette difficulté n'est pas une lorsque l'on considére, ainsi qu'on le doit, la production comme un échange dans lequel on donne les services productifs de son travail, de sa terre, et de ses capitaux, pour obtenir des produits. C'est par le moyen de ces services productifs, que nous acquérons tous les produits qui sont au monde. Or... nous sommes d'autant plus riches, nos services productifs ont d'autant plus de valeur qu'ils obtiennent dans l'échange appelé production une plus grande quantité de choses utiles.' [As for the difficulty raised by Ricardo when he says that, by using better methods of production, a million people can produce two or three times as much wealth, without producing any more value, this difficulty disappears when one bears in mind, as one should, that production is like an exchange in which a man contributes the productive services of his labour, his land, and his capital, in order to obtain products. It is by means of these productive services that we acquire all the products existing in the world. Therefore ... we are richer, our productive services have the more value, the greater the quantity of useful things they bring in through the exchange which is called production] (J. B. Say, 'Lettres à M. Malthus,' Paris, 1820, pp. 168, 169.) The 'difficulté'—it exists for him, not

for Ricardo—that Say means to clear up is this: Why does not the exchange-value of the use values increase, when their quantity increases in consequence of increased productive power of labour? Answer: the difficulty is met by calling use value, exchange-value, if you please. Exchange-value is a thing that is connected one way or another with exchange. If therefore production is called an exchange of labour and means of production against the product, it is clear as day that you obtain more exchange-value in proportion as the production yields more use value. In other words, the more use values, e.g., stockings, a working-day yields to the stocking-manufacturer, the richer is he in stockings. Suddenly, however, Say recollects that 'with a greater quantity' of stockings their 'price' (which of course has nothing to do with their exchange-value!) falls 'parce que la concurrence les (les producteurs) oblige à donner les produits pour ce qu'ils leur coûtent... [because competition obliges them (the producers) to sell their products for what they cost to make] But whence does the profit come, if the capitalist sells the commodities at cost-price? Never mind! Say declares that, in consequence of increased productivity, every one now receives in return for a given equivalent two pairs of stockings instead of one as before. The result he arrives at, is precisely that proposition of Ricardo that he aimed at disproving. After this mighty effort of thought, he triumphantly apostrophises Malthus in the words: 'Telle est, monsieur, la doctrine bien liée, sans laquelle il est impossible, je le déclare, d'expliquer les plus grandes difficultés de l'économie politique, et notamment, comment il se peut qu'une nation soit plus riche lorsque ses produits diminuent de valeur, quoique la richesse soit de la valeur.' [This, Sir, is the well-founded doctrine without which it is impossible, I say, to explain the greatest difficulties in political economy, and, in particular, to explain why it is that a nation can be richer when its products fall in value, even though wealth is value] (l. c., p. 170.) An English economist remarks upon the conjuring tricks of the same nature that appear in Say's 'Lettres': 'Those affected ways of talking make up in general that which M. Say is pleased to call his doctrine and which he earnestly urges Malthus to teach at Hertford, as it is already taught 'dans plusieurs parties de l'Europe.' He says, 'Si vous trouvez une physionomie de paradoxe à toutes ces propositions, voyez les choses qu'elles expriment, et j'ose croire qu'elles vous paraîtront fort simples et fort raisonnables.' [in numerous parts of Europe ... If all those propositions appear paradoxical to you, look at the things they express, and I venture to believe that they will then appear very simple and very rational] Doubtless, and in consequence of the same process, they will appear everything else, except original.' ('An Inquiry into those Principles Respecting the Nature of Demand, &c.,' pp. 116, 110.)

48. MacCulloch took out a patent for 'wages of past labour,' long before Senior did for 'wages of abstinence.'

49. Compare among others, Jeremy Bentham: 'Théorie des Peines et des Récompenses,' traduct. d'Et. Dumont, 3ème édit. Paris, 1826, t. II, L. IV., ch. II.

50. Bentham is a purely English phenomenon. Not even excepting our philosopher, Christian Wolff, in no time and in no country has the most homespun commonplace ever strutted about in so self-satisfied a way. The principle of utility was no discovery of Bentham. He simply reproduced in his dull way what Helvétius and other Frenchmen had said with esprit in the 18th century. To know what is useful for a dog, one must study dog-nature. This nature itself is not to be deduced from the principle of utility. Applying this to man, he that would criticise all human acts, movements, relations, etc., by the principle of utility, must first deal with human nature in general, and then with human nature as modified in each historical epoch. Bentham makes short work of it. With the driest naiveté he takes the modern shopkeeper, especially the English shopkeeper, as the normal man. Whatever is useful to this queer normal man, and to his world, is absolutely useful. This yard-measure, then, he applies to past, present, and future. The Christian religion, e.g., is 'useful,' 'because it forbids in the name of religion the same faults that the penal code condemns in the name of the law.' Artistic criticism is 'harmful,' because it disturbs worthy people in their enjoyment of Martin Tupper, etc. With such rubbish has the brave fellow, with his motto, 'nuila dies sine

line!,' piled up mountains of books. Had I the courage of my friend, Heinrich Heine, I should call Mr Jeremy a genius in the way of bourgeois stupidity.

51. 'Political economists are too apt to consider a certain quantity of capital and a certain number of labourers as productive instruments of uniform power, or operating with a certain uniform intensity.... Those... who maintain ... that commodities are the sole agents of production ... prove that production could never be enlarged, for it requires as an indispensable condition to such an enlargement that food, raw materials, and tools should be previously augmented; which is in fact maintaining that no increase of production can take place without a previous increase, or, in other words, that an increase is impossible.' (S. Bailey: 'Money and its Vicissitudes,' pp. 58 and 70.) Bailey criticises the dogma mainly from the point of view of the process of circulation.
52. John Stuart Mill, in his 'Principles of Political Economy,' says: 'The really exhausting and the really repulsive labours instead of being better paid than others, are almost invariably paid the worst of all.... The more revolting the occupation, the more certain it is to receive the minimum of remuneration.... The hardships and the earnings, instead of being directly proportional, as in any just arrangements of society they would be, are generally in an inverse ratio to one another.' To avoid misunderstanding, let me say that although men like John Stuart Mill are to blame for the contradiction between their traditional economic dogmas and their modern tendencies, it would be very wrong to class them with the herd of vulgar economic apologists.
53. H. Fawcett, Professor of Political Economy at Cambridge. 'The Economic position of the British labourer.' London, 1865, p. 120.
54. I must here remind the reader that the categories, 'variable and constant capital,' were first used by me. Political Economy since the time of Adam Smith has confusedly mixed up the essential distinctions involved in these categories, with the mere formal differences, arising out of the process of circulation, of fixed and circulating capital. For further details on this point, see Book II., Part II.
55. Fawcett, l. c., pp. 122, 123.
56. It might be said that not only capital, but also labourers, in the shape of emigrants, are annually exported from England. In the text, however, there is no question of the peculium of the emigrants, who are in great part not labourers. The sons of farmers make up a great part of them. The additional capital annually transported abroad to be put out at interest is in much greater proportion to the annual accumulation than the yearly emigration is to the yearly increase of population.

25

The General Law of Capitalist Accumulation

Section 1: *The Increased Demand for labour power that Accompanies Accumulation, the Composition of Capital Remaining the Same*

In this chapter we consider the influence of the growth of capital on the lot of the labouring class. The most important factor in this inquiry is the composition of capital and the changes it undergoes in the course of the process of accumulation.

The composition of capital is to be understood in a two-fold sense. On the side of value, it is determined by the proportion in which it is divided into constant capital or value of the means of production, and variable capital or value of labour power, the sum total of wages. On the side of material, as it functions in the process of production, all capital is divided into means of production and living labour power. This latter composition is determined by the relation between the mass of the means of production employed, on the one hand, and the mass of labour necessary for their employment on the other. I call the former the *value-composition*, the latter the *technical composition* of capital.

Between the two there is a strict correlation. To express this, I call the value composition of capital, in so far as it is determined by its technical composition and mirrors the changes of the latter, the *organic composition* of capital. Wherever I refer to the composition of capital, without further qualification, its organic composition is always understood.

The many individual capitals invested in a particular branch of production have, one with another, more or less different compositions. The average of their individual compositions gives us the composition of the total capital in this branch of production. Lastly, the average of these averages, in all branches of production, gives us the composition of the total social capital of a country, and with this alone are we, in the last resort, concerned in the following investigation.

Growth of capital involves growth of its variable constituent or of the part invested in labour power. A part of the surplus-value turned into additional capital must always be re-transformed into variable capital, or additional labour fund. If we suppose that, all other circumstances remaining the same, the composition of capital also remains constant (*i.e.*, that a definite mass of means of production constantly needs the same mass of labour power to set it in motion), then the demand for labour and the subsistence-fund of the labourers clearly increase in the same proportion as the capital, and the more rapidly, the more rapidly the capital increases. Since the capital produces yearly a surplus-value, of which one part is yearly added to the original capital; since this increment itself grows yearly along with the augmentation of the capital already functioning; since lastly, under special stimulus to enrichment, such as the opening of new markets, or of new spheres for the outlay of capital in consequence of newly developed social wants, &c., the scale of accumulation may be suddenly extended, merely by a change in the division of the surplus-value or surplus-product into capital and revenue, the requirements of accumulating capital may exceed the increase of labour power or of the number of labourers; the demand for labourers may exceed the supply, and, therefore, wages may rise. This must, indeed, ultimately be the case if the conditions supposed above continue. For since in each year more labourers are employed than in its predecessor, sooner or later a point must be reached, at which the requirements of accumulation begin to surpass the customary supply of labour, and, therefore, a rise of wages takes place. A lamentation on this score was heard in England during the whole of the fifteenth, and the first half of the eighteenth centuries. The more or less favourable circumstances in which the wage working class supports and multiplies itself, in no way alter the fundamental character of capitalist production. As simple reproduction constantly reproduces the capital relation itself, *i.e.*, the relation of capitalists on the one hand, and wage workers on the other, so reproduction on a progressive scale, *i.e.*, accumulation, reproduces the capital relation on a progressive scale, more capitalists or larger capitalists at this pole, more wage workers at that. The reproduction of a mass of labour power, which must incessantly re-incorporate itself with capital for that capital's self-expansion; which cannot get free from capital, and whose enslavement to capital is only concealed by the variety of individual capitalists to whom it sells itself, this reproduction of labour power forms, in fact, an essential of the reproduction of capital itself. Accumulation of capital is, therefore, increase of the proletariat.[1]

Classical economy grasped this fact so thoroughly that Adam Smith, Ricardo, &c., as mentioned earlier, inaccurately identified accumulation with the consumption, by the productive labourers, of all the capitalised part of the surplus-product, or with its transformation into additional wage labourers. As early as 1696 John Bellers says:

'For if one had a hundred thousand acres of land and as many pounds in money, and as many cattle, without a labourer, what would the rich man be, but a labourer? And as the labourers make men rich, so the more labourers there will be, the more rich men ... the labour of the poor being the mines of the rich.'[2]

So also Bernard de Mandeville at the beginning of the eighteenth century:

> 'It would be easier, where property is well secured, to live without money than without poor; for who would do the work? ... As they [the poor] ought to be kept from starving, so they should receive nothing worth saving. If here and there one of the lowest class by uncommon industry, and pinching his belly, lifts himself above the condition he was brought up in, nobody ought to hinder him; nay, it is undeniably the wisest course for every person in the society, and for every private family to be frugal; but it is the interest of all rich nations, that the greatest part of the poor should almost never be idle, and yet continually spend what they get.... Those that get their living by their daily labour ... have nothing to stir them up to be serviceable but their wants which it is prudence to relieve, but folly to cure. The only thing then that can render the labouring man industrious, is a moderate quantity of money, for as too little will, according as his temper is, either dispirit or make him desperate, so too much will make him insolent and lazy.... From what has been said, it is manifest, that, in a free nation, where slaves are not allowed of, the surest wealth consists in a multitude of laborious poor; for besides, that they are the never-failing nursery of fleets and armies, without them there could be no enjoyment, and no product of any country could be valuable. 'To make the society' [which of course consists of non-workers] 'happy and people easier under the meanest circumstances, it is requisite that great numbers of them should be ignorant as well as poor; knowledge both enlarges and multiplies our desires, and the fewer things a man wishes for, the more easily his necessities may be supplied.'[3]

What Mandeville, an honest, clear-headed man, had not yet seen, is that the mechanism of the process of accumulation itself increases, along with the capital, the mass of 'labouring poor,' *i.e.*, the wage labourers, who turn their labour power into an increasing power of self-expansion of the growing capital, and even by doing so must eternise their dependent relation on their own product, as personified in the capitalists. In reference to this relation of dependence, Sir F. M. Eden in his 'The State of the Poor, an History of the Labouring Classes in England,' says,

> 'the natural produce of our soil is certainly not fully adequate to our subsistence; we can neither be clothed, lodged nor fed but in consequence of some previous labour. A portion at least of the society must be indefatigably employed .... There are others who, though they 'neither toil nor spin,' can yet command the produce of industry, but who owe their exemption from labour solely to civilisation and order .... They are peculiarly the creatures of civil institutions,[4] which have recognised that individuals may acquire property by various other means besides the exertion of labour.... Persons of independent fortune ... owe their superior advantages by no means to any superior abilities of their own, but almost entirely ... to the industry of others. It is not the possession of land, or of money, but the command of labour which distinguishes the opulent from the labouring part of the community .... This [scheme approved by Eden] would give the people of property sufficient (but by no means too much) influence and authority over those who ... work for them; and it would place such labourers, not in an abject or servile condition, but in such a state of easy and liberal dependence as all who know human nature, and its history, will allow to be necessary for their own comfort.'[5]

Sir F. M. Eden, it may be remarked in passing, is the only disciple of Adam Smith during the eighteenth century that produced any work of importance.[6]

Under the conditions of accumulation supposed thus far, which conditions are those most favourable to the labourers, their relation of dependence upon capital takes on a form endurable or, as Eden says: 'easy and liberal.' Instead of becoming more intensive with the growth of capital, this relation of dependence only becomes more extensive, *i.e.*, the sphere of capital's exploitation and rule merely extends with its own dimensions and the number of its subjects. A larger part of their own surplus-product, always increasing and continually transformed into additional capital, comes back to them in the shape of means of payment, so that they can extend the circle of their enjoyments; can make some additions to their consumption-fund of clothes, furniture, &c., and can lay by small reserve funds of money. But just as little as better clothing, food, and treatment, and a larger peculium, do away with the exploitation of the slave, so little do they set aside that of the wage worker. A rise in the price of labour, as a consequence of accumulation of capital, only means, in fact, that the length and weight of the golden chain the wage worker has already forged for himself, allow of a relaxation of the tension of it. In the controversies on this subject the chief fact has generally been overlooked, viz., the *differentia specifica* {defining characteristic} of capitalistic production. Labour power is sold today, not with a view of satisfying, by its service or by its product, the personal needs of the buyer. His aim is augmentation of his capital, production of commodities containing more labour than he pays for, containing therefore a portion of value that costs him nothing, and that is nevertheless realised when the commodities are sold. Production of surplus-value is the absolute law of this mode of production. Labour power is only saleable so far as it preserves the means of production in their capacity of capital, reproduces its own value as capital, and yields in unpaid labour a source of additional capital.[7] The conditions of its sale, whether more or less favourable to the labourer, include therefore the necessity of its constant re-selling, and the constantly extended reproduction of all wealth in the shape of capital. Wages, as we have seen, by their very nature, always imply the performance of a certain quantity of unpaid labour on the part of the labourer. Altogether, irrespective of the case of a rise of wages with a falling price of labour, &c., such an increase only means at best a quantitative diminution of the unpaid labour that the worker has to supply. This diminution can never reach the point at which it would threaten the system itself. Apart from violent conflicts as to the rate of wages (and Adam Smith has already shown that in such a conflict, taken on the whole, the master is always master), a rise in the price of labour resulting from accumulation of capital implies the following alternative:

Either the price of labour keeps on rising, because its rise does not interfere with the progress of accumulation. In this there is nothing wonderful, for, says Adam Smith, 'after these (profits) are diminished, stock may not only continue to increase, but to increase much faster than before.... A great stock, though with small profits, generally increases faster than a small stock with great profits.' (l. c., ii, p. 189.) In this case it is evident that a diminution in the unpaid labour in no way interferes with the extension of the domain of capital.—Or, on the other hand, accumulation slackens in consequence of the rise in the price of labour, because the stimulus of gain is blunted. The rate of accumulation lessens; but with its lessening, the primary cause of that lessening vanishes, *i.e.*, the disproportion between capital and exploitable labour power. The mechanism of the process of capitalist production removes the very obstacles that it temporarily creates. The price of labour falls again to a level corresponding with the needs of the self-expansion of capital, whether the level be below, the same as, or above the one which was normal before the rise of wages took place. We see thus: In the first case, it is not the diminished rate either of the absolute, or of the proportional, increase in labour power, or labouring population, which causes capital to be in excess, but conversely the excess of capital that makes exploitable labour power insufficient. In the second case, it is not the increased rate either of the absolute, or of the proportional, increase in labour power, or labouring population, that makes capital insufficient; but, conversely, the relative diminution of capital that causes the exploitable labour power, or rather its price, to be in excess. It is these absolute movements of the accumulation of capital which are reflected as relative movements of the mass of exploitable labour power, and therefore seem produced by the latter's own independent movement. To put it mathematically: the rate of accumulation is the independent, not the dependent, variable; the rate of wages, the dependent, not the independent, variable. Thus, when the industrial cycle is in the phase of crisis, a general fall in the price of commodities is expressed as a rise in the value of money, and, in the phase of prosperity, a general rise in the price of commodities, as a fall in the value of money. The so-called currency school concludes from this that with high prices too much, with low prices too little[8] money is in circulation. Their ignorance and complete misunderstanding of facts[9] are worthily paralleled by the economists, who interpret the above phenomena of accumulation by saying that there are now too few, now too many wage labourers.

The law of capitalist production, that is at the bottom of the pretended 'natural law of population,' reduces itself simply to this: The correlation between accumulation of capital and rate of wages is nothing else than the correlation between the unpaid labour transformed into capital, and the additional paid labour necessary for the setting in motion of this additional capital. It is therefore, in no way, a relation between two magnitudes, independent one of the other: on the one hand, the magnitude of the capital; on the other, the number of the labouring population; it is rather, at bottom, only the relation between the unpaid and the paid labour of the same labouring population. If the quantity of unpaid labour supplied by the working class, and accumulated by the capitalist class, increases so rapidly that its conversion into capital requires an extraordinary addition of paid labour, then wages rise, and, all other circumstances remaining equal, the unpaid labour diminishes in proportion. But as soon as this diminution touches the point at which the surplus labour that nourishes capital is no longer supplied in normal quantity, a reaction sets in: a smaller part of revenue is capitalised, accumulation lags, and the movement of rise in wages receives a check. The rise of wages therefore is confined within limits that not only leave intact the foundations of the capitalistic system, but also secure its reproduction on a progressive scale. The law of capitalistic accumulation, metamorphosed by economists into pretended law of Nature, in reality merely states that the very nature of accumulation excludes every diminution in the degree of exploitation of labour, and every rise in the price of labour, which could seriously imperil the continual reproduction, on an ever-enlarging scale, of the capitalistic relation. It cannot be otherwise in a mode of production in which the labourer exists to satisfy the needs of self-expansion of existing values, instead of, on the contrary, material wealth existing to satisfy the needs of development on the part of the labourer. As, in religion, man is governed by the products of his own brain, so in capitalistic production, he is governed by the products of his own hand.[10]

Section 2: *Relative Diminution of the Variable Part of Capital Simultaneously with the Progress of Accumulation and of the Concentration that Accompanies it*

According to the economists themselves, it is neither the actual extent of social wealth, nor the magnitude of the capital already functioning, that lead to a rise of wages, but only the constant growth of accumulation and the degree of rapidity of that growth. (Adam Smith, Book I., chapter 8.) So far, we have only considered one special phase of this process, that in which the increase of capital occurs along with a constant technical composition of capital. But the process goes beyond this phase.

Once given the general basis of the capitalistic system, then, in the course of accumulation, a point is reached at which the development of the productivity of social labour becomes the most powerful lever of accumulation.

> 'The same cause,' says Adam Smith, 'which raises the wages of labour, the increase of stock, tends to increase its productive powers, and to make a smaller quantity of labour produce a greater quantity of work.'[11]

Apart from natural conditions, such as fertility of the soil, &c., and from the skill of independent and isolated producers (shown rather qualitatively in the goodness than quantitatively in the mass of their products), the degree of productivity of labour, in a given society, is expressed in the relative extent of the means of production that one labourer, during a given time, with the same tension of labour power, turns into products. The mass of the means of production which he thus transforms, increases with the productiveness of his labour. But those means of production play a double part. The increase of some is a consequence, that of the others a condition of the increasing productivity of labour. *E.g.*, with the division of labour in manufacture, and with the use of machinery, more raw material is worked up in the same time, and, therefore, a greater mass of raw material and auxiliary substances enter into the labour process. That is the consequence of the increasing productivity of labour. On the other hand, the mass of machinery, beasts of burden, mineral manures, drain-pipes, &c., is a condition of the increasing productivity of labour. So also is it with the means of production concentrated in buildings, furnaces, means of transport, &c. But whether condition or consequence, the growing extent of the means of production, as compared with the labour power incorporated with them, is an expression of the growing productiveness of labour. The increase of the latter appears, therefore, in the diminution of the mass of labour in proportion to the mass of means of production moved by it, or in the diminution of the subjective factor of the labour process as compared with the objective factor.

This change in the technical composition of capital, this growth in the mass of means of production, as compared with the mass of the labour power that vivifies them, is reflected again in its value composition, by the increase of the constant constituent of capital at the expense of its variable constituent. There may be, *e.g.*, originally 50 per cent. of a capital laid out in means of production, and 50 per cent. in labour power; later on, with the development of the productivity of labour, 80 per cent. in means of production, 20 per cent. in labour power, and so on. This law of the progressive increase in constant capital, in proportion to the variable, is confirmed at every step (as already shown) by the comparative analysis of the prices of commodities, whether we compare different economic epochs or different nations in the same epoch. The relative magnitude of the element of price, which represents the value of the means of production only, or the constant part of capital consumed, is in direct, the relative magnitude of the other element of price that pays labour (the variable part of capital) is in inverse proportion to the advance of accumulation.

This diminution in the variable part of capital as compared with the constant, or the altered value-composition of the capital, however, only shows approximately the change in the composition of its material constituents. If, *e.g.*, the capital-value employed today in spinning is 7/8 constant and 1/8 variable, whilst at the beginning of the 18th century it was ½ constant and ½ variable, on the other hand, the mass of raw material, instruments of labour, &c., that a certain quantity of spinning labour consumes productively today, is many hundred times greater than at the beginning of the 18th century. The reason is simply that, with the increasing productivity of labour, not only does the mass of the means of production consumed by it increase, but their value compared with their mass diminishes. Their value therefore rises absolutely, but not in proportion to their mass. The increase of the difference between constant and variable capital, is, therefore, much less than that of the difference between the mass of the means of production into which the constant, and the mass of the labour power into which the variable, capital is converted. The former difference increases with the latter, but in a smaller degree.

But, if the progress of accumulation lessens the relative magnitude of the variable part of capital, it by no means, in doing this, excludes the possibility of a rise in its absolute magnitude. Suppose that a capital-value at first is divided into 50 per cent. of constant and 50 per cent. of variable capital; later into 80 per cent. of constant and 20 per cent. of variable. If in the meantime the original capital, say £6,000, has increased to £18,000, its variable constituent has also increased. It was £3,000, it is now £3,600. But where as formerly an increase of capital by 20 per cent. would have sufficed to raise the demand for labour 20 per cent., now this latter rise requires a tripling of the original capital.

In Part IV, it was shown, how the development of the productiveness of social labour presupposes co-operation on a large scale; how it is only upon this supposition that division and combination of labour can be organised, and the means of production economised by concentration on a vast scale; how instruments of labour which, from their very nature, are only fit for use in common, such as a system of machinery, can be called into being; how huge natural forces can be pressed into the service of production; and how the transformation can be effected of the process of production into a technological application of science. On the basis of the production of commodities, where the means of production are the property of private persons, and where the artisan therefore either produces commodities, isolated from and independent of others, or sells his labour power as a commodity, because he lacks the means for independent industry, co-operation on a large scale can realise itself only in the increase of individual capitals, only in proportion as the means of social production and the means of subsistence are transformed into the private property of capitalists. The basis of the production of commodities can admit of production on a large scale in the capitalistic form alone. A certain accumulation of capital, in the hands of individual producers of commodities, forms therefore the necessary preliminary of the specifically capitalistic mode of production. We had, therefore, to assume that this occurs during the transition from handicraft to capitalistic industry. It may be called primitive accumulation, because it is the historic basis, instead of the historic result of specifically capitalist production. How it itself originates, we need not here inquire as yet. It is enough that it forms the starting point. But all methods for raising the social productive power of labour that are developed on this basis, are at the same time methods for the increased production of surplus-value or surplus-product, which in its turn is the formative element of accumulation. They are, therefore, at the same time methods of the production of capital by capital, or methods of its accelerated accumulation. The continual re-transformation of surplus-value into capital now appears in the shape of the increasing magnitude of the capital that enters into the process of production. This in turn is the basis of an extended scale of production, of the methods for raising the productive power of labour that accompany it, and of accelerated production of surplus-value. If, therefore, a certain degree of accumulation of capital appears as a condition of the specifically capitalist mode of production, the latter causes conversely an accelerated accumulation of capital. With the accumulation of capital, therefore, the specifically capitalistic mode of production develops, and with the capitalist mode of production the accumulation of capital. Both these economic factors bring about, in the compound ratio of the impulses they reciprocally give one another, that change in the technical composition of capital by which the variable constituent becomes always smaller and smaller as compared with the constant.

Every individual capital is a larger or smaller concentration of means of production, with a corresponding command over a larger or smaller labour-army. Every accumulation becomes the means of new accumulation. With the increasing mass of wealth which functions as capital, accumulation increases the concentration of that wealth in the hands of individual capitalists, and thereby widens the basis of production on a large scale and of the specific methods of capitalist production. The growth of social capital is effected by the growth of many individual capitals. All other circumstances remaining the same, individual capitals, and with them the concentration of the means of production, increase in such proportion as they form aliquot parts of the total social capital. At the same time portions of the original capitals disengage themselves and function as new independent capitals. Besides other causes, the division of property, within capitalist families, plays a great part in this. With the accumulation of capital, therefore, the number of capitalists grows to a greater or less extent. Two points characterise this kind of concentration which grows directly out of, or rather is identical with, accumulation. First: The increasing concentration of the social means of production in the hands of individual capitalists is, other things remaining equal, limited by the degree of increase of social wealth. Second: The part of social capital domiciled in each particular sphere of production is divided among many capitalists who face one another as independent commodity-producers competing with each other. Accumulation and the concentration accompanying it are, therefore, not only scattered over many points, but the increase of each functioning capital is thwarted by the formation of new and the sub-division of old capitals. Accumulation, therefore, presents itself on the one hand as increasing concentration of the means of production, and of the command over labour; on the other, as repulsion of many individual capitals one from another.

This splitting-up of the total social capital into many individual capitals or the repulsion of its fractions one from another, is counteracted by their attraction. This last does not mean that simple concentration of the means of production and of the command over labour, which is identical with accumulation. It is concentration of capitals already formed, destruction of their individual independence, expropriation of capitalist by capitalist, transformation of many small into few large capitals. This process differs from the former in this, that it only presupposes a change in the distribution of capital already to hand, and functioning; its field of action is therefore not limited by the absolute growth of social wealth, by the absolute limits of accumulation. Capital grows in one place to a huge mass in a single hand, because it has in another place been lost by many. This is centralisation proper, as distinct from accumulation and concentration.

The laws of this centralisation of capitals, or of the attraction of capital by capital, cannot be developed here. A brief hint at a few facts must suffice. The battle of competition is fought by cheapening of commodities. The cheapness of commodities demands, *caeteris paribus,* on the productiveness of labour, and this again on the scale of production. Therefore, the larger capitals beat the smaller. It will further be remembered that, with the development of the capitalist mode of production, there is an increase in the minimum amount of individual capital necessary to carry on a business under its normal conditions. The smaller capitals, therefore, crowd into spheres of production which Modern Industry has only sporadically or incompletely got hold of. Here competition rages in direct proportion to the number, and in inverse proportion to the magnitudes, of the antagonistic capitals. It always ends in the ruin of many small capitalists, whose capitals partly pass into the hands of their conquerors, partly vanish. Apart from this, with capitalist production an altogether new force comes into play—the credit system, which in its first stages furtively creeps in as the humble assistant of accumulation, drawing into the hands of individual or associated capitalists, by invisible threads, the money resources which lie scattered, over the surface of society, in larger or smaller amounts; but it soon becomes a new and terrible weapon in the battle of competition and is finally transformed into an enormous social mechanism for the centralisation of capitals.

Commensurately with the development of capitalist production and accumulation there develop the two most powerful levers of centralisation—competition and credit. At the same time the progress of accumulation increases the material amenable to centralisation, *i.e.,* the individual capitals, whilst the expansion of capitalist production creates, on the one hand, the social want, and, on the other, the technical means necessary for those immense industrial undertakings which require a previous centralisation of capital for their accomplishment. Today, therefore, the force of attraction, drawing together individual capitals, and the tendency to centralisation are stronger than ever before. But, if the relative extension and energy of the movement towards centralisation is determined, in a certain degree, by the magnitude of capitalist wealth and superiority of economic mechanism already attained, progress in centralisation does not in any way depend upon a positive growth in the magnitude of social capital. And this is the specific difference between centralisation and concentration, the latter being only another name for reproduction on an extended scale. Centralisation may result from a mere change in the distribution of capitals already existing, from a simple alteration in the quantitative grouping of the component parts of social capital. Here, capital can grow into powerful masses in a single hand because there it has been withdrawn from many individual hands. In any given branch of industry centralisation would reach its extreme limit if all the individual capitals invested in it were fused into a single capital.[12] In a given society the limit would be reached only when the entire social capital was united in the hands of either a single capitalist or a single capitalist company.

Centralisation completes the work of accumulation by enabling industrial capitalists to extend the scale of their operations. Whether this latter result is the consequence of accumulation or centralisation, whether centralisation is accomplished by the violent method of annexation—when certain capitals become such preponderant centres of attraction for others that they shatter the individual cohesion of the latter and then draw the separate fragments to themselves—or whether the fusion of a number of capitals already formed or in process of formation takes place by the smoother process of organising joint-stock companies—the economic effect remains the same. Everywhere the increased scale of industrial establishments is the starting point for a more comprehensive organisation of the collective work of many, for a wider development of their material motive forces—in other words, for the progressive transformation of isolated processes of production, carried on by customary methods, into processes of production socially combined and scientifically arranged.

But accumulation, the gradual increase of capital by reproduction as it passes from the circular to the spiral form, is clearly a very slow procedure compared with centralisation, which has only to change the quantitative groupings of the constituent parts of social capital. The world would still be without railways if it had had to wait until accumulation had got a few individual capitals far enough to be adequate for the construction of a railway. Centralisation, on the contrary, accomplished this in the twinkling of an eye, by means of joint-stock companies. And whilst centralisation thus intensifies and accelerates the effects of accumulation, it simultaneously extends and speeds those revolutions in the technical composition of capital which raise its constant portion at the expense of its variable portion, thus diminishing the relative demand for labour.

The masses of capital fused together overnight by centralisation reproduce and multiply as the others do, only more rapidly, thereby becoming new and powerful levers in social accumulation. Therefore, when we speak of the progress of social accumulation we tacitly include—today—the effects of centralisation.

The additional capitals formed in the normal course of accumulation (see Chapter XXIV, Section 1) serve particularly as vehicles for the exploitation of new inventions and discoveries, and industrial improvements in general. But in time the old capital also reaches the moment of renewal from top to toe, when it sheds its skin and is reborn like the others in a perfected technical form, in which a smaller quantity of labour will suffice to set in motion a larger quantity of machinery and raw materials. The absolute reduction in the demand for labour which necessarily follows from this is obviously so much the greater the higher the degree in which the capitals undergoing this process of renewal are already massed together by virtue of the centralisation movement.

On the one hand, therefore, the additional capital formed in the course of accumulation attracts fewer and fewer labourers in proportion to its magnitude. On the other hand, the old capital periodically reproduced with change of composition, repels more and more of the labourers formerly employed by it.

Section 3: *Progressive Production of a Relative surplus population or Industrial Reserve Army*

The accumulation of capital, though originally appearing as its quantitative extension only, is effected, as we have seen, under a progressive qualitative change in its composition, under a constant increase of its constant, at the expense of its variable constituent.[13]

The specifically capitalist mode of production, the development of the productive power of labour corresponding to it, and the change thence resulting in the organic composition of capital, do not merely keep pace with the advance of accumulation, or with the growth of social wealth. They develop at a much quicker rate, because mere accumulation, the absolute increase of the total social capital, is accompanied by the centralisation of the individual capitals of which that total is made up; and because the change in the technological composition of the additional capital goes hand in hand with a similar change in the technological composition of the original capital. With the advance of accumulation, therefore, the proportion of constant to variable capital changes. If it was originally say 1:1, it now becomes successively 2:1, 3:1, 4:1, 5:1, 7:1, &c., so that, as the capital increases, instead of ½ of its total value, only 1/3, 1/4, 1/5, 1/6, 1/8, &c., is transformed into labour-power, and, on the other hand, 2/3, 3/4, 4/5, 5/6, 7/8 into means of production. Since the demand for labour is determined not by the amount of capital as a whole, but by its variable constituent alone, that demand falls progressively with the increase of the total capital, instead of, as previously assumed, rising in proportion to it. It falls relatively to the magnitude of the total capital, and at an accelerated rate, as this magnitude increases. With the growth of the total capital, its variable constituent or the labour incorporated in it, also does increase, but in a constantly diminishing proportion. The intermediate pauses are shortened, in which accumulation works as simple extension of production, on a given technical basis. It is not merely that an accelerated accumulation of total capital, accelerated in a constantly growing progression, is needed to absorb an additional number of labourers, or even, on account of the constant metamorphosis of old capital, to keep employed those already functioning. In its turn, this increasing accumulation and centralisation becomes a source of new changes in the composition of capital, of a more accelerated diminution of its variable, as compared with its constant constituent. This accelerated relative diminution of the variable constituent, that goes along with the accelerated increase of the total capital, and moves more rapidly than this increase, takes the inverse form, at the other pole, of an apparently absolute increase of the labouring population, an increase always moving more rapidly than that of the variable capital or the means of employment. But in fact, it is capitalistic accumulation itself that constantly produces, and produces in the direct ratio of its own energy and extent, a relatively redundant population of labourers, *i.e.*, a population of greater extent than suffices for the average needs of the self-expansion of capital, and therefore a surplus population.

Considering the social capital in its totality, the movement of its accumulation now causes periodical changes, affecting it more or less as a whole, now distributes its various phases simultaneously over the different spheres of production. In some spheres a change in the composition of capital occurs without increase of its absolute magnitude, as a consequence of simple centralisation; in others the absolute growth of capital is connected with absolute diminution of its variable constituent, or of the labour power absorbed by it; in others again, capital continues growing for a time on its given technical basis, and attracts additional labour power in proportion to its increase, while at other times it undergoes organic change, and lessens its variable constituent; in all spheres, the increase of the variable part of capital, and therefore of the number of labourers employed by it, is always connected with violent fluctuations and transitory production of surplus population, whether this takes the more striking form of the repulsion of labourers already employed, or the less evident but not less real form of the more difficult absorption of the additional labouring population through the usual channels.[14] With the magnitude of social capital already functioning, and the degree of its increase, with the extension of the scale of production, and the mass of the labourers set in motion, with the development of the productiveness of their labour, with the greater breadth and fulness of all sources of wealth, there is also an extension of the scale on which greater attraction of labourers by capital is accompanied by their greater repulsion; the rapidity of the change in the organic composition of capital, and in its technical form increases, and an increasing number of spheres of production becomes involved in this change, now simultaneously, now alternately. The labouring population therefore produces, along with the accumulation of capital produced by it, the means by which it itself is made relatively superfluous, is turned into a relative surplus population; and it does this to an always increasing extent.[15] This is a law of population peculiar to the capitalist mode of production; and in fact every special historic mode of production has its own special laws of population, historically valid within its limits and only in so far as man has not interfered with them.

But, if a surplus labouring population is a necessary product of accumulation or of the development of wealth on a capitalist basis, this surplus population becomes, conversely, the lever of capitalistic accumulation, nay, a condition of existence of the capitalist mode of production. It forms a disposable industrial reserve army, that belongs to capital quite as absolutely as if the latter had bred it at its own cost. Independently of the limits of the actual increase of population, it creates, for the changing needs of the self-expansion of capital, a mass of human material always ready for exploitation. With accumulation, and the development of the productiveness of labour that accompanies it, the power of sudden expansion of capital grows also; it grows, not merely because the elasticity of the capital already functioning increases, not merely because the absolute wealth of society expands, of which capital only forms an elastic part, not merely because credit, under every special stimulus, at once places an unusual part of this wealth at the disposal of production in the form of additional capital; it grows, also, because the technical conditions of the process of production themselves—machinery, means of transport, &c.—now admit of the rapidest transformation of masses of surplus-product into additional means of production. The mass of social wealth, overflowing with the advance of accumulation, and transformable into additional capital, thrusts itself frantically into old branches of production, whose market suddenly expands, or into newly formed branches, such as railways, &c., the need for which grows out of the development of the old ones. In all such cases, there must be the possibility of throwing great masses of men suddenly on the decisive points without injury to the scale of production in other spheres. Overpopulation supplies these masses. The course characteristic of modern industry, *viz.*, a decennial cycle (interrupted by smaller oscillations), of periods of average activity, production at high pressure, crisis and stagnation, depends on the constant formation, the greater or less absorption, and the re-formation of the industrial reserve army or surplus population. In their turn, the varying phases of the industrial cycle recruit the surplus population, and become one of the most energetic agents of its reproduction. This peculiar course of modern industry, which occurs in no earlier period of human history, was also impossible in the childhood of capitalist production. The composition of capital changed but very slowly. With its accumulation, therefore, there kept pace, on the whole, a corresponding growth in the demand for labour. Slow as was the advance of accumulation compared with that of more modern times, it found a check in the natural limits of the exploitable labouring population, limits which could only be got rid of by forcible means to be mentioned later. The expansion by fits and starts of the scale of production is the preliminary to its equally sudden contraction; the latter again evokes the former, but the former is impossible without disposable human material, without an increase, in the number of labourers independently of the absolute growth of the population. This increase is effected by the simple process that constantly 'sets free' a part of the labourers; by methods which lessen the number of labourers employed in proportion to the increased production. The whole form of the movement of modern industry depends, therefore, upon the constant transformation of a part of the labouring population into unemployed or half-employed hands. The superficiality of Political Economy shows itself in the fact that it looks upon the expansion and contraction of credit, which is a mere symptom of the periodic changes of the industrial cycle, as their cause. As the heavenly bodies, once thrown into a certain definite motion, always repeat this, so is it with social production as soon as it is once thrown into this movement of alternate expansion and contraction. Effects, in their turn, become causes, and the varying accidents of the whole process, which always reproduces its own conditions, take on the form of periodicity. When this periodicity is once consolidated, even Political Economy then sees that the production of a relative surplus population—*i.e.*, surplus with regard to the average needs of the self-expansion of capital—is a necessary condition of modern industry.

> 'Suppose,' says H. Merivale, formerly Professor of Political Economy at Oxford, subsequently employed in the English Colonial Office, 'suppose that, on the occasion of some of these crises, the nation were to rouse itself to the effort of getting rid by emigration of some hundreds of thousands of superfluous arms, what would be the consequence? That, at the first returning demand for labour, there would be a deficiency. However rapid reproduction may be, it takes, at all events, the space of a generation to replace the loss of adult labour. Now, the profits of our manufacturers depend mainly on the power of making use of the prosperous moment when demand is brisk, and thus compensating themselves for the interval during which it is slack. This power is secured to them only by the command of machinery and of manual labour. They must have hands ready by them, they must be able to increase the activity of their operations when required, and to slacken it again, according to the state of the market, or they cannot possibly maintain that pre-eminence in the race of competition on which the wealth of the country is founded.'[16]

Even Malthus recognises overpopulation as a necessity of modern industry, though, after his narrow fashion, he explains it by the absolute over-growth of the labouring population, not by their becoming relatively supernumerary. He says:

> 'Prudential habits with regard to marriage, carried to a considerable extent among the labouring class of a country mainly depending upon manufactures and commerce, might injure it.... From the nature of a population, an increase of labourers cannot be brought into market in consequence of a particular demand till after the lapse of 16 or 18 years, and the conversion of revenue into capital, by saving, may take place much more rapidly: a country is always liable to an increase in the quantity of the funds for the maintenance of labour faster than the increase of population.'[17]

After Political Economy has thus demonstrated the constant production of a relative surplus population of labourers to be a necessity of capitalistic accumulation, she very aptly, in the guise of an old maid, puts in the mouth of her 'beau ideal' of a capitalist the following words addressed to those supernumeraries thrown on the streets by their own creation of additional capital:

> 'We manufacturers do what we can for you, whilst we are increasing that capital on which you must subsist, and you must do the rest by accommodating your numbers to the means of subsistence.'[18]

Capitalist production can by no means content itself with the quantity of disposable labour power which the natural increase of population yields. It requires for its free play an industrial reserve army independent of these natural limits.

Up to this point it has been assumed that the increase or diminution of the variable capital corresponds rigidly with the increase or diminution of the number of labourers employed.

The number of labourers commanded by capital may remain the same, or even fall, while the variable capital increases. This is the case if the individual labourer yields more labour, and therefore his wages increase, and this although the price of labour remains the same or even falls, only more slowly than the mass of labour rises. Increase of variable capital, in this case, becomes an index of more labour, but not of more labourers employed. It is the absolute interest of every capitalist to press a given quantity of labour out of a smaller, rather than a greater number of labourers, if the cost is about the same. In the latter case, the outlay of constant capital increases in proportion to the mass of labour set in action; in the former that increase is much smaller. The more extended the scale of production, the stronger this motive. Its force increases with the accumulation of capital.

We have seen that the development of the capitalist mode of production and of the productive power of labour—at once the cause and effect of accumulation—enables the capitalist, with the same outlay of variable capital, to set in action more labour by greater exploitation (extensive or intensive) of each individual labour power. We have further seen that the capitalist buys with the same capital a greater mass of labour power, as he progressively replaces skilled labourers by less skilled, mature labour power by immature, male by female, that of adults by that of young persons or children.

On the one hand, therefore, with the progress of accumulation, a larger variable capital sets more labour in action without enlisting more labourers; on the other, a variable capital of the same magnitude sets in action more labour with the same mass of labour power; and, finally, a greater number of inferior labour powers by displacement of higher.

The production of a relative surplus population, or the setting free of labourers, goes on therefore yet more rapidly than the technical revolution of the process of production that accompanies, and is accelerated by, the advance of accumulation; and more rapidly than the corresponding diminution of the variable part of capital as compared with the constant. If the means of production, as they increase in extent and effective power, become to a less extent means of employment of labourers, this state of things is again modified by the fact that in proportion as the productiveness of labour increases, capital increases its supply of labour more quickly than its demand for labourers. The overwork of the employed part of the working class swells the ranks of the reserve, whilst conversely the greater pressure that the latter by its competition exerts on the former, forces these to submit to overwork and to subjugation under the dictates of capital. The condemnation of one part of the working class to enforced idleness by the overwork of the other part, and the converse, becomes a means of enriching the individual capitalists,[19] and accelerates at the same time the production of the industrial reserve army on a scale corresponding with the advance of social accumulation. How important is this element in the formation of the relative surplus population, is shown by the example of England. Her technical means for saving labour are colossal. Nevertheless, if to-morrow morning labour generally were reduced to a rational amount, and proportioned to the different sections of the working class according to age and sex, the working population to hand would be absolutely insufficient for the carrying on of national production on its present scale. The great majority of the labourers now 'unproductive' would have to be turned into 'productive' ones.

Taking them as a whole, the general movements of wages are exclusively regulated by the expansion and contraction of the industrial reserve army, and these again correspond to the periodic changes of the industrial cycle. They are, therefore, not determined by the variations of the absolute number of the working population, but by the varying proportions in which the working class is divided into active and reserve army, by the increase or diminution in the relative amount of the surplus population, by the extent to which it is now absorbed, now set free. For Modern Industry with its decennial cycles and periodic phases, which, moreover, as accumulation advances, are complicated by irregular oscillations following each other more and more quickly, that would indeed be a beautiful law, which pretends to make the action of capital dependent on the absolute variation of the population, instead of regulating the demand and supply of labour by the alternate expansion and contraction of capital, the labour-market now appearing relatively under-full, because capital is expanding, now again over-full, because it is contracting. Yet this is the dogma of the economists. According to them, wages rise in consequence of accumulation of capital. The higher wages stimulate the working population to more rapid multiplication, and this goes on until the labour-market becomes too full, and therefore capital, relatively to the supply of labour, becomes insufficient. Wages fall, and now we have the reverse of the medal. The working population is little by little decimated as the result of the fall in wages, so that capital is again in excess relatively to them, or, as others explain it, falling wages and the corresponding increase in the exploitation of the labourer again accelerates accumulation, whilst, at the same time, the lower wages hold the increase of the working class in check. Then comes again the time, when the supply of labour is less than the demand, wages rise, and so on. A beautiful mode of motion this for developed capitalist production! Before, in consequence of the rise of wages, any positive increase of the population really fit for work could occur, the time would have been passed again and again, during which the industrial campaign must have been carried through, the battle fought and won.

Between 1849 and 1859, a rise of wages practically insignificant, though accompanied by falling prices of corn, took place in the English agricultural districts. In Wiltshire, *e.g.*, the weekly wages rose from 7s. to 8s.; in Dorsetshire from 7s. or 8s., to 9s., &c. This was the result of an unusual exodus of the agricultural surplus population caused by the demands of war, the vast extension of railroads, factories, mines, &c. The lower the wages, the higher is the proportion in which ever so insignificant a rise of them expresses itself. If the weekly wage, *e.g.*, is 20s. and it rises to 22s., that is a rise of 10 per cent.; but if it is only 7s. and it rises to 9s., that is a rise of 28 4/7 per cent., which sounds very fine. Everywhere the farmers were howling, and the London *Economist*, with reference to these starvation-wages, prattled quite seriously of 'a general and substantial advance.'[20] What did the farmers do now? Did they wait until, in consequence of this brilliant remuneration, the agricultural labourers had so increased and multiplied that their wages must fall again, as prescribed by the dogmatic economic brain? They introduced more machinery, and in a moment the labourers were redundant again in a proportion satisfactory even to the farmers. There was now 'more capital' laid out in agriculture than before, and in a more productive form. With this the demand for labour fell, not only relatively, but absolutely.

The above economic fiction confuses the laws that regulate the general movement of wages, or the ratio between the working class—*i.e.*, the total labour power—and the total social capital, with the laws that distribute the working population over the different spheres of production. If, *e.g.*, in consequence of favourable circumstances, accumulation in a particular sphere of production becomes especially active, and profits in it, being greater than the average profits, attract additional capital, of course the demand for labour rises and wages also rise. The higher wages draw a larger part of the working population into the more favoured sphere, until it is glutted with labour power, and wages at length fall again to their average level or below it, if the pressure is too great. Then, not only does the immigration of labourers into the branch of industry in question cease; it gives place to their emigration. Here the political economist thinks he sees the why and wherefore of an absolute increase of workers accompanying an increase of wages, and of a diminution of wages accompanying an absolute increase of labourers. But he sees really only the local oscillation of the labour-market in a particular sphere of production—he sees only the phenomena accompanying the distribution of the working population into the different spheres of outlay of capital, according to its varying needs.

The industrial reserve army, during the periods of stagnation and average prosperity, weighs down the active labour-army; during the periods of over-production and paroxysm, it holds its pretensions in check. Relative surplus population is therefore the pivot upon which the law of demand and supply of labour works. It confines the field of action of this law within the limits absolutely convenient to the activity of exploitation and to the domination of capital.

This is the place to return to one of the grand exploits of economic apologetics. It will be remembered that if through the introduction of new, or the extension of old, machinery, a portion of variable capital is transformed into constant, the economic apologist interprets this operation which 'fixes' capital and by that very act sets labourers 'free,' in exactly the opposite way, pretending that it sets free capital for the labourers. Only now can one fully understand the effrontery of these apologists. What are set free are not only the labourers immediately turned out by the machines, but also their future substitutes in the rising generation, and the additional contingent, that with the usual extension of trade on the old basis would be regularly absorbed. They are now all 'set free,' and every new bit of capital looking out for employment can dispose of them. Whether it attracts them or others, the effect on the general labour demand will be nil, if this capital is just sufficient to take out of the market as many labourers as the machines threw upon it. If it employs a smaller number, that of the supernumeraries increases; if it employs a greater, the general demand for labour only increases to the extent of the excess of the employed over those 'set free.' The impulse that additional capital, seeking an outlet, would otherwise have given to the general demand for labour, is therefore in every case neutralised to the extent of the labourers thrown out of employment by the machine. That is to say, the mechanism of capitalistic production so manages matters that the absolute increase of capital is accompanied by no corresponding rise in the general demand for labour. And this the apologist calls a compensation for the misery, the sufferings, the possible death of the displaced labourers during the transition period that banishes them into the industrial reserve army! The demand for labour is not identical with increase of capital, nor supply of labour with increase of the working class. It is not a case of two independent forces working on one another. Les dés sont pipés.

Capital works on both sides at the same time. If its accumulation, on the one hand, increases the demand for labour, it increases on the other the supply of labourers by the 'setting free' of them, whilst at the same time the pressure of the unemployed compels those that are employed to furnish more labour, and therefore makes the supply of labour, to a certain extent, independent of the supply of labourers. The action of the law of supply and demand of labour on this basis completes the despotism of capital. As soon, therefore, as the labourers learn the secret, how it comes to pass that in the same measure as they work more, as they produce more wealth for others, and as the productive power of their labour increases, so in the same measure even their function as a means of the self-expansion of capital becomes more and more precarious for them; as soon as they discover that the degree of intensity of the competition among themselves depends wholly on the pressure of the relative surplus population; as soon as, by Trades' Unions, &c., they try to organise a regular co-operation between employed and unemployed in order to destroy or to weaken the ruinous effects of this natural law of capitalistic production on their class, so soon capital and its sycophant, Political Economy, cry out at the infringement of the 'eternal' and so to say 'sacred' law of supply and demand. Every combination of employed and unemployed disturbs the 'harmonious' action of this law. But, on the other hand, as soon as (in the colonies, *e.g.*) adverse circumstances prevent the creation of an industrial reserve army and, with it, the absolute dependence of the working class upon the capitalist class, capital, along with its commonplace Sancho Panza, rebels against the 'sacred' law of supply and demand, and tries to check its inconvenient action by forcible means and State interference.

Section 4: *Different Forms of the Relative surplus population. The General Law of Capitalistic Accumulation*

The relative surplus population exists in every possible form. Every labourer belongs to it during the time when he is only partially employed or wholly unemployed. Not taking into account the great periodically recurring forms that the changing phases of the industrial cycle impress on it, now an acute form during the crisis, then again a chronic form during dull times—it has always three forms, the floating, the latent, the stagnant.

In the centres of modern industry—factories, manufactures, ironworks, mines, &c.—the labourers are sometimes repelled, sometimes attracted again in greater masses, the number of those employed increasing on the whole, although in a constantly decreasing proportion to the scale of production. Here the surplus population exists in the floating form.

In the automatic factories, as in all the great workshops, where machinery enters as a factor, or where only the modern division of labour is carried out, large numbers of boys are employed up to the age of maturity. When this term is once reached, only a very small number continue to find employment in the same branches of industry, whilst the majority are regularly discharged. This majority forms an element of the floating surplus population, growing with the extension of those branches of industry. Part of them emigrates, following in fact capital that has emigrated. One consequence is that the female population grows more rapidly than the male, *teste* England. That the natural increase of the number of labourers does not satisfy the requirements of the accumulation of capital, and yet all the time is in excess of them, is a contradiction inherent to the movement of capital itself. It wants larger numbers of youthful labourers, a smaller number of adults. The contradiction is not more glaring than that other one that there is a complaint of the want of hands, while at the same time many thousands are out of work, because the division of labour chains them to a particular branch of industry.[21]

The consumption of labour power by capital is, besides, so rapid that the labourer, half-way through his life, has already more or less completely lived himself out. He falls into the ranks of the supernumeraries, or is thrust down from a higher to a lower step in the scale. It is precisely among the work-people of modern industry that we meet with the shortest duration of life. Dr Lee, Medical Officer of Health for Manchester, stated:

> 'that the average age at death of the Manchester ... upper middle class was 38 years, while the average age at death of the labouring class was 17; while at Liverpool those figures were represented as 35 against 15. It thus appeared that the well-to-do classes had a lease of life which was more than double the value of that which fell to the lot of the less favoured citizens.'[22]

In order to conform to these circumstances, the absolute increase of this section of the proletariat must take place under conditions that shall swell their numbers, although the individual elements are used up rapidly. Hence, rapid renewal of the generations of labourers (this law does not hold for the other classes of the population). This social need is met by early marriages, a necessary consequence of the conditions in which the labourers of modern industry live, and by the premium that the exploitation of children sets on their production.

As soon as capitalist production takes possession of agriculture, and in proportion to the extent to which it does so, the demand for an agricultural labouring population falls absolutely, while the accumulation of the capital employed in agriculture advances, without this repulsion being, as in non-agricultural industries, compensated by a greater attraction. Part of the agricultural population is therefore constantly on the point of passing over into an urban or manufacturing proletariat, and on the look-out for circumstances favourable to this transformation. (Manufacture is used here in the sense of all non-agricultural industries.)[23] This source of relative surplus population is thus constantly flowing. But the constant flow towards the towns pre-supposes, in the country itself, a constant latent surplus population, the extent of which becomes evident only when its channels of outlet open to exceptional width. The agricultural labourer is therefore reduced to the minimum of wages, and always stands with one foot already in the swamp of pauperism.

The third category of the relative surplus population, the stagnant, forms a part of the active labour army, but with extremely irregular employment. Hence it furnishes to capital an inexhaustible reservoir of disposable labour power. Its conditions of life sink below the average normal level of the working class; this makes it at once the broad basis of special branches of capitalist exploitation. It is characterised by maximum of working-time, and minimum of wages. We have learnt to know its chief form under the rubric of 'domestic industry.' It recruits itself constantly from the supernumerary forces of modern industry and agriculture, and specially from those decaying branches of industry where handicraft is yielding to manufacture, manufacture to machinery. Its extent grows, as with the extent and energy of accumulation, the creation of a surplus population advances. But it forms at the same time a self-reproducing and self-perpetuating element of the working class, taking a proportionally greater part in the general increase of that class than the other elements. In fact, not only the number of births and deaths, but the absolute size of the families stand in inverse proportion to the height of wages, and therefore to the amount of means of subsistence of which the different categories of labourers dispose. This law of capitalistic society would sound absurd to savages, or even civilised colonists. It calls to mind the boundless reproduction of animals individually weak and constantly hunted down.[24]

The lowest sediment of the relative surplus population finally dwells in the sphere of pauperism. Exclusive of vagabonds, criminals, prostitutes, in a word, the 'dangerous' classes, this layer of society consists of three categories. First, those able to work. One need only glance superficially at the statistics of English pauperism to find that the quantity of paupers increases with every crisis, and diminishes with every revival of trade. Second, orphans and pauper children. These are candidates for the industrial reserve army, and are, in times of great prosperity, as 1860, *e.g.*, speedily and in large numbers enrolled in the active army of labourers. Third, the demoralised and ragged, and those unable to work, chiefly people who succumb to their incapacity for adaptation, due to the division of labour; people who have passed the normal age of the labourer; the victims of industry, whose number increases with the increase of dangerous machinery, of mines, chemical works, &c., the mutilated, the sickly, the widows, &c. Pauperism is the hospital of the active labour-army and the dead weight of the industrial reserve army. Its production is included in that of the relative surplus population, its necessity in theirs; along with the surplus population, pauperism forms a condition of capitalist production, and of the capitalist development of wealth. It enters into the *faux frais* of capitalist production; but capital knows how to throw these, for the most part, from its own shoulders on to those of the working class and the lower middle class.

The greater the social wealth, the functioning capital, the extent and energy of its growth, and, therefore, also the absolute mass of the proletariat and the productiveness of its labour, the greater is the industrial reserve army. The same causes which develop the expansive power of capital, develop also the labour power at its disposal. The relative mass of the industrial reserve army increases therefore with the potential energy of wealth. But the greater this reserve army in proportion to the active labour army, the greater is the mass of a consolidated surplus population, whose misery is in inverse ratio to its torment of labour. The more extensive, finally, the lazarus layers of the working class, and the industrial reserve army, the greater is official pauperism. *This is the absolute general law of capitalist accumulation.* Like all other laws it is modified in its working by many circumstances, the analysis of which does not concern us here.

The folly is now patent of the economic wisdom that preaches to the labourers the accommodation of their number to the requirements of capital. The mechanism of capitalist production and accumulation constantly effects this adjustment. The first word of this adaptation is the creation of a relative surplus population, or industrial reserve army. Its last word is the misery of constantly extending strata of the active army of labour, and the dead weight of pauperism.

The law by which a constantly increasing quantity of means of production, thanks to the advance in the productiveness of social labour, may be set in movement by a progressively diminishing expenditure of human power, this law, in a capitalist society—where the labourer does not employ the means of production, but the means of production employ the labourer—undergoes a complete inversion and is expressed thus: the higher the productiveness of labour, the greater is the pressure of the labourers on the means of employment, the more precarious, therefore, becomes their condition of existence, *viz.*, the sale of their own labour power for the increasing of another's wealth, or for the self-expansion of capital. The fact that the means of production, and the productiveness of labour, increase more rapidly than the productive population, expresses itself, therefore, capitalistically in the inverse form that the labouring population always increases more rapidly than the conditions under which capital can employ this increase for its own self-expansion.

We saw in Part IV., when analysing the production of relative surplus-value: within the capitalist system all methods for raising the social productiveness of labour are brought about at the cost of the individual labourer; all means for the development of production transform themselves into means of domination over, and exploitation of, the producers; they mutilate the labourer into a fragment of a man, degrade him to the level of an appendage of a machine, destroy every remnant of charm in his work and turn it into a hated toil; they estrange from him the intellectual potentialities of the labour process in the same proportion as science is incorporated in it as an independent power; they distort the conditions under which he works, subject him during the labour process to a despotism the more hateful for its meanness; they transform his life-time into working-time, and drag his wife and child beneath the wheels of the Juggernaut of capital. But all methods for the production of surplus-value are at the same time methods of accumulation; and every extension of accumulation becomes again a means for the development of those methods. It follows, therefore, that in proportion as capital accumulates, the lot of the labourer, be his payment high or low, must grow worse. The law, finally, that always equilibrates the relative surplus population, or industrial reserve army, to the extent and energy of accumulation, this law rivets the labourer to capital more firmly than the wedges of Vulcan did Prometheus to the rock. It establishes an accumulation of misery, corresponding with accumulation of capital. Accumulation of wealth at one pole is, therefore, at the same time accumulation of misery, agony of toil slavery, ignorance, brutality, mental degradation, at the opposite pole, *i.e.*, on the side of the class that produces its own product in the form of capital.[25] This antagonistic character of capitalistic accumulation is enunciated in various forms by political economists, although by them it is confounded with phenomena, certainly to some extent analogous, but nevertheless essentially distinct, and belonging to pre-capitalistic modes of production.

The Venetian monk Ortes, one of the great economic writers of the 18th century, regards the antagonism of capitalist production as a general natural law of social wealth.

> 'In the economy of a nation, advantages and evils always balance one another (il bene ed il male economico in una nazione sempre all, istessa misura): the abundance of wealth with some people, is always equal to the want of it with others (la copia dei beni in alcuni sempre eguale alia mancanza di essi in altri): the great riches of a small

number are always accompanied by the absolute privation of the first necessaries of life for many others. The wealth of a nation corresponds with its population, and its misery corresponds with its wealth. Diligence in some compels idleness in others. The poor and idle are a necessary consequence of the rich and active,' &c.[26]

In a thoroughly brutal way about 10 years after Ortes, the Church of England parson, Townsend, glorified misery as a necessary condition of wealth.

> 'Legal constraint (to labour) is attended with too much trouble, violence, and noise, whereas hunger is not only a peaceable, silent, unremitted pressure, but as the most natural motive to industry and labour, it calls forth the most powerful exertions.'

Everything therefore depends upon making hunger permanent among the working class, and for this, according to Townsend, the principle of population, especially active among the poor, provides.

> 'It seems to be a law of Nature that the poor should be to a certain degree improvident' [*i.e.*, so improvident as to be born *without* a silver spoon in the mouth], 'that there may always be some to fulfil the most servile, the most sordid, and the most ignoble offices in the community. The stock of human happiness is thereby much increased, whilst the more delicate are not only relieved from drudgery ... but are left at liberty without interruption to pursue those callings which are suited to their various dispositions ... it' [the Poor Law] 'tends to destroy the harmony and beauty, the symmetry and order of that system which God and Nature have established in the world.'[27] If the Venetian monk found in the fatal destiny that makes misery eternal, the *raison d'être* of Christian charity, celibacy, monasteries and holy houses, the Protestant prebendary finds in it a pretext for condemning the laws in virtue of which the poor possessed a right to a miserable public relief.
>
> 'The progress of social wealth,' says Storch, 'begets this useful class of society ... which performs the most wearisome, the vilest, the most disgusting functions, which takes, in a word, on its shoulders all that is disagreeable and servile in life, and procures thus for other classes leisure, serenity of mind and conventional' [c'est bon!] 'dignity of character.'[28]

Storch asks himself in what then really consists the progress of this capitalistic civilisation with its misery and its degradation of the masses, as compared with barbarism. He finds but one answer: security!

> 'Thanks to the advance of industry and science,' says Sismondi, 'every labourer can produce every day much more than his consumption requires. But at the same time, whilst his labour produces wealth, that wealth would, were he called on to consume it himself, make him less fit for labour.' According to him, 'men' [*i.e.*, non-workers] 'would probably prefer to do without all artistic perfection, and all the enjoyments that manufacturers procure for us, if it were necessary that all should buy them by constant toil like that of the labourer.... Exertion today is separated from its recompense; it is not the same man that first works, and then reposes; but it is because the one works that the other rests.... The indefinite multiplication of the productive powers of labour can then only have for result the increase of luxury and enjoyment of the idle rich.'[29]

Finally Destutt de Tracy, the fish-blooded bourgeois doctrinaire, blurts out brutally:

> 'In poor nations the people are comfortable, in rich nations they are generally poor.'[30]

A. England from 1846-1866

No period of modern society is so favourable for the study of capitalist accumulation as the period of the last 20 years. It is as if this period had found Fortunatus' purse. But of all countries England again furnishes the classical example, because it holds the foremost place in the world-market, because capitalist production is here alone completely developed, and lastly, because the introduction of the Free-trade millennium since 1846 has cut off the last retreat of vulgar economy. The titanic advance of production—the latter half of the 20 years' period again far surpassing the former—has been already pointed out sufficiently in Part IV.

Although the absolute increase of the English population in the last half century was very great, the relative increase or rate of growth fell constantly, as the following table borrowed from the census shows.

Annual increase per cent of the population of England and Wales in decimal numbers:

1811-1821	1.533 per cent.
1821-1831	1.446 per cent.
1831-1841	1.326 per cent.
1841-1851	1.216 per cent.
1851-1861	1.141 per cent.

Let us now, on the other hand, consider the increase of wealth. Here, the movement of profit, rent of land, &c., that come under the income tax, furnishes the surest basis. The increase of profits liable to income tax (farmers and some other categories not included) in Great Britain from 1853 to 1864 amounted to 50.47% or 4.58% as the annual average,[31] that of the population during the same period to about 12%. The augmentation of the rent of land subject to taxation (including houses, railways, mines, fisheries, &c.), amounted for 1853 to 1864 to 38% or 3 5/12% annually. Under this head the following categories show the greatest increase:

Excess of annual income of 1864 over that of 1853		*Increase per year*
Houses	38.60%	3.50%
Quarries	84.76%	7.70%
Mines	68.85%	6.26%
Ironworks	39.92%	3.63%
Fisheries	57.37%	5.21%
Gasworks	126.02%	11.45%
Railways	83.29%	7.57%

If we compare the years from 1853 to 1864 in three sets of four consecutive years each, the rate of augmentation of the income increases constantly.[32] It is, *e.g.*, for that arising from profits between 1853 to 1857, 1.73% yearly; 1857-1861, 2.74%, and for 1861-64, 9.30% yearly. The sum of the incomes of the United Kingdom that come under the income tax was in 1856, £307,068,898; in 1859, £328,127,416; in 1862, £351,745,241; in 1863, £359,142,897; in 1864, £362,462,279; in 1865, £385,530,020.[33]

The accumulation of capital was attended at the same time by its concentration and centralisation. Although no official statistics of agriculture existed for England (they did for Ireland), they were voluntarily given in 10 counties. These statistics gave the result that from 1851 to 1861 the number of farms of less than 100 acres had fallen from 31,583 to 26,597, so that 5,016 had been thrown together into larger farms.[34] From 1815 to 1825, no personal estate of more than £1,000,000 came under the succession duty; from 1825 to

1855, however, 8 did; and 4 from 1856 to June, 1859, *i.e.*, in 4½ years.[35] The centralisation will, however, be best seen from a short analysis of the Income Tax Schedule D (profits, exclusive of farms, &c.), in the years 1864 and 1865. I note beforehand that incomes from this source pay income tax on everything over £60. These incomes liable to taxation in England, Wales and Scotland, amounted in 1864 to £95,844,222, in 1865 to £105,435,579.[36] The number of persons taxed were in 1864, 308,416, out of a population of 23,891,009; in 1865, 332,431 out of a population of 24,127,003. The following table shows the distribution of these incomes in the two years:

	Year ending April 5th, 1864.		*Year ending April 5th, 1865.*	
	Income from Profits	*Income from People*	*Income from Profits*	*Income from People*
Total Income	£95,844,222	308,416	105,435,738	332,431
of these	57,028,289	23,334	64,554,297	24,265
of these	36,415,225	3,619	42,535,576	4,021
of these	22,809,781	832	27,555,313	973
of these	8,744,762	91	11,077,238	107

In 1855, there were produced in the United Kingdom 61,453,079 tons of coal, of value £16,113,167; in 1864, 92,787,873 tons, of value £23,197,968; in 1855, 3,218,154 tons of pig-iron, of value £8,045,385; 1864, 4,767,951 tons, of value £11,919,877. In 1854, the length of the railroads worked in the United Kingdom was 8,054 miles, with a paid-up capital of £286,068,794; in 1864 the length was 12,789 miles, with capital paid up of £425,719,613. In 1854 the total sum of the exports and imports of the United Kingdom was £268,210,145; in 1865, £489,923,285. The following table shows the movement of the exports:

1846	£58,842,377
1849	63,596,052
1856	115,826,948
1860	135,842,817
1865	165,862,402
1866[37]	188,917,563

After these few examples one understands the cry of triumph of the Registrar-General of the British people:

> 'Rapidly as the population has increased, it has not kept pace with the progress of industry and wealth.'[38]

Let us turn now to the direct agents of this industry, or the producers of this wealth, to the working class.

> 'It is one of the most melancholy features in the social state of this country,' says Gladstone, 'that while there was a decrease in the consuming powers of the people, and while there was an increase in the privations and distress of the labouring class and operatives, there was at the same time a constant accumulation of wealth in the upper classes, and a constant increase of capital.'[39]

Thus spake this unctuous minister in the House of Commons of February 13th, 1843. On April 16th, 1863, 20 years later, in the speech in which he introduced his Budget:

'From 1842 to 1852 the taxable income of the country increased by 6 per cent.... In the 8 years from 1853 to 1861 it had increased from the basis taken in 1853 by 20 per cent.! The fact is so astonishing as to be almost incredible ... this intoxicating augmentation of wealth and power ... entirely confined to classes of property ... must be of indirect benefit to the labouring population, because it cheapens the commodities of general consumption. While the rich have been growing richer, the poor have been growing less poor. At any rate, whether the extremes of poverty are less, I do not presume to say.'[40]

How lame an anti-climax! If the working class has remained 'poor,' only 'less poor' in proportion as it produces for the wealthy class 'an intoxicating augmentation of wealth and power,' then it has remained relatively just as poor. If the extremes of poverty have not lessened, they have increased, because the extremes of wealth have. As to the cheapening of the means of subsistence, the official statistics, *e.g.*, the accounts of the London Orphan Asylum, show an increase in price of 20% for the average of the three years 1860-1862, compared with 1851-1853. In the following three years, 1863-1865, there was a progressive rise in the price of meat, butter, milk, sugar, salt, coals, and a number of other necessary means of subsistence.[41] Gladstone's next Budget speech of April 7th, 1864, is a Pindaric dithyrambus on the advance of surplus-value-making and the happiness of the people 'tempered by poverty.' He speaks of masses 'on the border' of pauperism, of branches of trade in which 'wages have not increased,' and finally sums up the happiness of the working class in the words:

'human life is but, in nine cases out of ten, a struggle for existence.'[42]

Professor Fawcett, not bound like Gladstone by official considerations, declares roundly:

'I do not, of course, deny that money wages have been augmented by this increase of capital (in the last ten years), but this apparent advantage is to a great extent lost, because many of the necessaries of life are becoming dearer' (he believes because of the fall in value of the precious metals)..."the rich grow rapidly richer, whilst there is no perceptible advance in the comfort enjoyed by the industrial classes.... They (the labourers) become almost the slaves of the tradesman, to whom they owe money.'[43]

In the chapters on the 'working-day' and 'machinery,' the reader has seen under what circumstances the British working class created an 'intoxicating augmentation of wealth and power' for the propertied classes. There we were chiefly concerned with the social functioning of the labourer. But for a full elucidation of the law of accumulation, his condition outside the workshop must also be looked at, his condition as to food and dwelling. The limits of this book compel us to concern ourselves chiefly with the worst paid part of the industrial proletariat, and with the agricultural labourers, who together form the majority of the working class.

But first, one word on official pauperism, or on that part of the working class which has forfeited its condition of existence (the sale of labour power), and vegetates upon public alms. The official list of paupers numbered in England[44] 851,369 persons; in 1856, 877,767; in 1865, 971,433. In consequence of the cotton famine, it grew in the years 1863 and 1864 to 1,079,382 and 1,014,978. The crisis of 1866, which fell most heavily on London, created in this centre of the world market, more populous than the kingdom of Scotland, an increase of pauperism for the year 1866 of 19.5% compared with 1865, and of 24.4% compared with 1864, and a still greater increase for the first months of 1867 as compared with 1866. From the analysis of the statistics of pauperism, two points are to be taken. On the one hand, the fluctuation up and down of the number of paupers, reflects the periodic changes of the industrial cycle. On the other, the official statistics become more and more misleading as to the actual extent of pauperism in proportion as, with the accumulation of capital, the class-struggle, and, therefore, the class consciousness of the working men, develop. *E.g.*, the barbarity in the treatment of the paupers, at which the English Press (*The Times, Pall Mall Gazette,* etc.) have cried out so loudly during the last two years, is of ancient date. F. Engels showed in 1844 exactly the same horrors, exactly the same transient canting outcries of 'sensational literature.' But frightful increase of 'deaths by starvation' in London during the last ten years proves beyond doubt the growing horror in which the working-people hold the slavery of the workhouse, that place of punishment for misery.[45]

B. The Badly Paid Strata of the British Industrial Class

During the cotton famine of 1862, Dr Smith was charged by the Privy Council with an inquiry into the conditions of nourishment of the distressed operatives in Lancashire and Cheshire. His observations during many preceding years had led him to the conclusion that 'to avert starvation diseases,' the daily food of an average woman ought to contain at least 3,900 grains of carbon with 180 grains of nitrogen; the daily food of an average man, at least 4,300 grains of carbon with 200 grains of nitrogen; for women, about the same quantity of nutritive elements as are contained in 2 lbs. of good wheaten bread, for men 1/9 more; for the weekly average of adult men and women, at least 28,600 grains of carbon and 1,330 grains of nitrogen. His calculation was practically confirmed in a surprising manner by its agreement with the miserable quantity of nourishment to which want had forced down the consumption of the cotton operatives. This was, in December, 1862, 29,211 grains of carbon, and 1,295 grains of nitrogen weekly.

In the year 1863, the Privy Council ordered an inquiry into the state of distress of the worst-nourished part of the English working class. Dr Simon, medical officer to the Privy Council, chose for this work the above-mentioned Dr Smith. His inquiry ranges on the one hand over the agricultural labourers, on the other, over silk-weavers, needlewomen, kid-glovers, stocking-weavers, glove-weavers, and shoemakers. The latter categories are, with the exception of the stocking-weavers, exclusively town-dwellers. It was made a rule in the inquiry to select in each category the most healthy families, and those comparatively in the best circumstances.

As a general result it was found that:

> 'in only one of the examined classes of in-door operatives did the average nitrogen supply just exceed, while in another it nearly reached, the estimated standard of bare sufficiency [*i.e.*, sufficient to avert starvation diseases], and that in two classes there was defect—in one, a very large defect—of both nitrogen and carbon. Moreover, as regards the examined families of the agricultural population, it appeared that more than a fifth were with less than the estimated sufficiency of carbonaceous food, that more than one-third were with less than the estimated sufficiency of nitrogenous food, and that in three counties (Berkshire, Oxfordshire, and Somersetshire), insufficiency of nitrogenous food was the average local diet.'[46]

Among the agricultural labourers, those of England, the wealthiest part of the United Kingdom, were the worst fed.[47] The insufficiency of food among the agricultural labourers, fell, as a rule, chiefly on the women and children, for 'the man must eat to do his work.' Still greater penury ravaged the town-workers examined.

> 'They are so ill fed that assuredly among them there must be many cases of severe and injurious privation.'[48]

('Privation' of the capitalist all this! *i.e.*, 'abstinence' from paying for the means of subsistence absolutely necessary for the mere vegetation of his 'hands.')[49]

The following table shows the conditions of nourishment of the above-named categories of purely town-dwelling work-people, as compared with the minimum assumed by Dr Smith, and with the food-allowance of the cotton operatives during the time of their greatest distress:

Both Sexes	*Average weekly carbon*	*Average weekly nitrogen*
Five in-door occupations	28,876 grains	1,192 grains
Unemployed Lancashire Operatives	28,211 grains	1,295 grains
Minimum quantity to be allowed to the Lancashire Operatives, equal number of males and females	28,600 grains	1,330 grains

One half, or 60/125, of the industrial labour categories investigated, had absolutely no beer, 28% no milk. The weekly average of the liquid means of nourishment in the families varied from seven ounces in the needle-women to 24¾ ounces in the stocking-makers. The majority of those who did not obtain milk were needle-women in London. The quantity of bread-stuffs consumed weekly varied from 7¾ lbs. for the needle-women to 11½ lbs. for the shoemakers, and gave a total average of 9.9 lbs. per adult weekly. Sugar (treacle, etc.) varied from 4 ounces weekly for the kid-glovers to 11 ounces for the stocking-makers; and the total average per week for all categories was 8 ounces per adult weekly. Total weekly average of butter (fat, etc.) 5 ounces per adult. The weekly average of meat (bacon, etc.) varied from 7¼ ounces for the silk-weavers, to 18¼ ounces for the kid-glovers; total average for the different categories 13.6 ounces. The weekly cost of food per adult, gave the following average figures; silk-weavers 2s. 2½d., needle-women 2s. 7d., kid-glovers 2s. 9½d., shoemakers 2s 7¾d., stocking-weavers 2s. 6¼d. For the silk-weavers of Macclesfield the average was only 1s. 8½d. The worst categories were the needle-women, silk-weavers and kid-glovers.[50] Of these facts, Dr Simon in his General Health Report says:

> 'That cases are innumerable in which defective diet is the cause or the aggravator of disease, can be affirmed by any one who is conversant with poor law medical practice, or with the wards and out-patient rooms of hospitals.... Yet in this point of view, there is, in my opinion, a very important sanitary context to be added. It must be remembered that privation of food is very reluctantly borne, and that as a rule great poorness of diet will only come when other privations have preceded it. Long before insufficiency of diet is a matter of hygienic concern, long before the physiologist would think of counting the grains of nitrogen and carbon which intervene between life and starvation, the household will have been utterly destitute of material comfort; clothing and fuel will have been even scantier than food—against inclemencies of weather there will have been no adequate protection—dwelling space will have been stinted to the degree in which overcrowding produces or increases disease; of household utensils and furniture there will have been scarcely any—even cleanliness will have been found costly or difficult, and if there still be self-respectful endeavours to maintain it, every such endeavour will represent additional pangs of hunger. The home, too, will be where shelter can be cheapest bought; in quarters where commonly there is least fruit of sanitary supervision, least drainage, least scavenging, least suppression of public nuisances, least or worst water supply, and, if in town, least light and air. Such are the sanitary dangers to which poverty is almost certainly exposed, when it is poverty enough to imply scantiness of food. And while the sum of them is of terrible magnitude against life, the mere scantiness of food is in itself of very serious moment.... These are painful reflections, especially when it is remembered that the poverty to which they

> advert is not the deserved poverty of idleness. In all cases it is the poverty of working populations. Indeed, as regards the in-door operatives, the work which obtains the scanty pittance of food, is for the most part excessively prolonged. Yet evidently it is only in a qualified sense that the work can be deemed self-supporting.... And on a very large scale the nominal self-support can be only a circuit, longer or shorter, to pauperism.'[51]

The intimate connexion between the pangs of hunger of the most industrious layers of the working class, and the extravagant consumption, coarse or refined, of the rich, for which capitalist accumulation is the basis, reveals itself only when the economic laws are known. It is otherwise with the 'housing of the poor.' Every unprejudiced observer sees that the greater the centralisation of the means of production, the greater is the corresponding heaping together of the labourers, within a given space; that therefore the swifter capitalistic accumulation, the more miserable are the dwellings of the working-people. 'Improvements' of towns, accompanying the increase of wealth, by the demolition of badly built quarters, the erection of palaces for banks, warehouses, &c., the widening of streets for business traffic, for the carriages of luxury, and for the introduction of tramways, &c., drive away the poor into even worse and more crowded hiding places. On the other hand, every one knows that the dearness of dwellings is in inverse ratio to their excellence, and that the mines of misery are exploited by house speculators with more profit or less cost than ever were the mines of Potosi. The antagonistic character of capitalist accumulation, and therefore of the capitalistic relations of property generally,[52] is here so evident, that even the official English reports on this subject teem with heterodox onslaughts on 'property and its rights.' With the development of industry, with the accumulation of capital, with the growth and 'improvement' of towns, the evil makes such progress that the mere fear of contagious diseases which do not spare even 'respectability,' brought into existence from 1847 to 1864 no less than 10 Acts of Parliament on sanitation, and that the frightened bourgeois in some towns, as Liverpool, Glasgow, &c., took strenuous measures through their municipalities. Nevertheless Dr Simon, in his report of 1865, says:

> 'Speaking generally, it may be said that the evils are uncontrolled in England.'

By order of the Privy Council, in 1864, an inquiry was made into the conditions of the housing of the agricultural labourers, in 1865 of the poorer classes in the towns. The results of the admirable work of Dr Julian Hunter are to be found in the seventh (1865) and eighth (1866) reports on 'Public Health.' To the agricultural labourers, I shall come later. On the condition of town dwellings, I quote, as preliminary, a general remark of Dr Simon.

> 'Although my official point of view,' he says, 'is one exclusively physical, common humanity requires that the other aspect of this evil should not be ignored .... In its higher degrees it [*i.e.*, over-crowding] almost necessarily involves such negation of all delicacy, such unclean confusion of bodies and bodily functions, such exposure of animal and sexual nakedness, as is rather bestial than human. To be subject to these influences is a degradation which must become deeper and deeper for those on whom it continues to work. To children who are born under its curse, it must often be a very baptism into infamy. And beyond all measure hopeless is the wish that persons thus circumstanced should ever in other respects aspire to that atmosphere of civilisation which has its essence in physical and moral cleanliness.'[53]

London takes the first place in over-crowded habitations, absolutely unfit for human beings.

> 'He feels clear,' says Dr Hunter, 'on two points; first, that there are about 20 large colonies in London, of about 10,000 persons each, whose miserable condition exceeds almost anything he has seen elsewhere in England, and is almost entirely the result of their bad house accommodation; and second, that the crowded and dilapidated condition of the

houses of these colonies is much worse than was the case 20 years ago.'[54] 'It is not too much to say that life in parts of London and Newcastle is infernal.'[55]

Further, the better-off part of the working class, together with the small shopkeepers and other elements of the lower middle class, falls in London more and more under the curse of these vile conditions of dwelling, in proportion as 'improvements,' and with them the demolition of old streets and houses, advance, as factories and the afflux of human beings grow in the metropolis, and finally as house rents rise with the ground-rents.

> 'Rents have become so heavy that few labouring men can afford more than one room.'[56]

There is almost no house-property in London that is not overburdened with a number of middlemen. For the price of land in London is always very high in comparison with its yearly revenue, and therefore every buyer speculates on getting rid of it again at a jury price (the expropriation valuation fixed by jurymen), or on pocketing an extraordinary increase of value arising from the neighbourhood of some large establishment. As a consequence of this there is a regular trade in the purchase of 'fag-ends of leases.'

> 'Gentlemen in this business may be fairly expected to do as they do—get all they can from the tenants while they have them, and leave as little as they can for their successors.'[57]

The rents are weekly, and these gentlemen run no risk. In consequence of the making of railroads in the City,

> 'the spectacle has lately been seen in the East of London of a number of families wandering about some Saturday night with their scanty worldly goods on their backs, without any resting place but the workhouse.'[58]

The workhouses are already over-crowded, and the 'improvements' already sanctioned by Parliament are only just begun. If labourers are driven away by the demolition of their old houses, they do not leave their old parish, or at most they settle down on its borders, as near as they can get to it.

> 'They try, of course, to remain as near as possible to their workshops. The inhabitants do not go beyond the same or the next parish, parting their two-room tenements into single rooms, and crowding even those.... Even at an advanced rent, the people who are displaced will hardly be able to get an accommodation so good as the meagre one they have left.... Half the workmen ... of the Strand ... walked two miles to their work.'[59]

This same Strand, a main thoroughfare which gives strangers an imposing idea of the wealth of London, may serve as an example of the packing together of human beings in that town. In one of its parishes, the Officer of Health reckoned 581 persons per acre, although half the width of the Thames was reckoned in. It will be self-understood that every sanitary measure, which, as has been the case hitherto in London, hunts the labourers from one quarter, by demolishing uninhabitable houses, serves only to crowd them together yet more closely in another.

> 'Either,' says Dr Hunter, 'the whole proceeding will of necessity stop as an absurdity, or the public compassion (!) be effectually aroused to the obligation which may now be without exaggeration called national, of supplying cover to those who by reason of their having no capital, cannot provide it for themselves, though they can by periodical payments reward those who will provide it for them.'[60]

Admire this capitalistic justice! The owner of land, of houses, the businessman, when expropriated by 'improvements' such as railroads, the building of new streets, &c., not only receives full indemnity. He must, according to law, human and divine, be comforted for his enforced 'abstinence' over and above this by a thumping profit. The labourer, with his wife and child and chattels, is thrown out into the street, and—if he crowds in too large numbers towards quarters of the town where the vestries insist on decency, he is prosecuted in the name of sanitation!

Except London, there was at the beginning of the 19th century no single town in England of 100,000 inhabitants. Only five had more than 50,000. Now there are 28 towns with more than 50,000 inhabitants.

> 'The result of this change is not only that the class of town people is enormously increased, but the old close-packed little towns are now centres, built round on every side, open nowhere to air, and being no longer agreeable to the rich are abandoned by them for the pleasanter outskirts. The successors of these rich are occupying the larger houses at the rate of a family to each room [... and find accommodation for two or three lodgers ...] and a population, for which the houses were not intended and quite unfit, has been created, whose surroundings are truly degrading to the adults and ruinous to the children.'[61]

The more rapidly capital accumulates in an industrial or commercial town, the more rapidly flows the stream of exploitable human material, the more miserable are the improvised dwellings of the labourers.

Newcastle-on-Tyne, as the centre of a coal and iron district of growing productiveness, takes the next place after London in the housing inferno. Not less than 34,000 persons live there in single rooms. Because of their absolute danger to the community, houses in great numbers have lately been destroyed by the authorities in Newcastle and Gateshead. The building of new houses progresses very slowly, business very quickly. The town was, therefore, in 1865, more full than ever. Scarcely a room was to let. Dr Embleton, of the Newcastle Fever Hospital, says:

> 'There can be little doubt that the great cause of the continuance and spread of the typhus has been the over-crowding of human beings, and the uncleanliness of their dwellings. The rooms, in which labourers in many cases live, are situated in confined and unwholesome yards or courts, and for space, light, air, and cleanliness, are models of insufficiency and insalubrity, and a disgrace to any civilised community; in them men, women, and children lie at night huddled together: and as regards the men, the night-shift succeed the day-shift, and the day-shift the night-shift in unbroken series for some time together, the beds having scarcely time to cool; the whole house badly supplied with water and worse with privies; dirty, unventilated, and pestiferous.'[62]

The price per week of such lodgings ranges from 8d. to 3s.

> 'The town of Newcastle-on-Tyne,' says Dr Hunter, 'contains a sample of the finest tribe of our countrymen, often sunk by external circumstances of house and street into an almost savage degradation.'[63]

As a result of the ebbing and flowing of capital and labour, the state of the dwellings of an industrial town may today be bearable, tomorrow hideous. Or the aedileship of the town may have pulled itself together for the removal of the most shocking abuses. Tomorrow, like a swarm of locusts, come crowding in masses of ragged Irishmen or decayed English agricultural labourers. They are stowed away in cellars and lofts, or the hitherto respectable labourer's dwelling is transformed into a lodging house whose *personnel* changes as quickly as the billets in the 30 years' war. Example: Bradford (Yorkshire). There the municipal philistine was just busied with urban improvements. Besides, there were still in Bradford, in 1861, 1,751 uninhabited houses. But now comes that revival of trade which the mildly liberal

Mr Forster, the negro's friend, recently crowed over with so much grace. With the revival of trade came of course an overflow from the waves of the ever fluctuating 'reserve army' or 'relative surplus population.' The frightful cellar habitations and rooms registered in the list,[64] which Dr Hunter obtained from the agent of an Insurance Company, were for the most part inhabited by well-paid labourers. They declared that they would willingly pay for better dwellings if they were to be had. Meanwhile, they become degraded, they fall ill, one and all, whilst the mildly liberal Forster, M. P., sheds tears over the blessings of Free Trade, and the profits of the eminent men of Bradford who deal in worsted. In the Report of September, 1865, Dr Bell, one of the poor law doctors of Bradford, ascribes the frightful mortality of fever-patients in his district to the nature of their dwellings.

> 'In one small cellar measuring 1,500 cubic feet ... there are ten persons .... Vincent Street, Green Aire Place, and the Leys include 223 houses having 1,450 inhabitants, 435 beds, and 36 privies.... The beds—and in that term I include any roll of dirty old rags, or an armful of shavings—have an average of 3.3 persons to each, many have 5 and 6 persons to each, and some people, I am told, are absolutely without beds; they sleep in their ordinary clothes, on the bare boards—young men and women, married and unmarried, all together. I need scarcely add that many of these dwellings are dark, damp, dirty, stinking holes, utterly unfit for human habitations; they are the centres from which disease and death are distributed amongst those in better circumstances, who have allowed them thus to fester in our midst.'[65]

Bristol takes the third place after London in the misery of its dwellings.

> 'Bristol, where the blankest poverty and domestic misery abound in the wealthiest town of Europe.'[66]

C. The Nomad Population

We turn now to a class of people whose origin is agricultural, but whose occupation is in great part industrial. They are the light infantry of capital, thrown by it, according to its needs, now to this point, now to that. When they are not on the march, they 'camp.' Nomad labour is used for various operations of building and draining, brick-making, lime-burning, railway-making, &c. A flying column of pestilence, it carries into the places in whose neighbourhood it pitches its camp, small-pox, typhus, cholera, scarlet fever, &c.[67] In undertakings that involve much capital outlay, such as railways, &c., the contractor himself generally provides his army with wooden huts and the like, thus improvising villages without any sanitary provisions, outside the control of the local boards, very profitable to the contractor, who exploits the labourers in two-fold fashion—as soldiers of industry and as tenants. According as the wooden hut contains 1, 2, or 3 holes, its inhabitant, navvy, or whatever he may be, has to pay 1, 3, or 4 shillings weekly.[68] One example will suffice. In September, 1864, Dr Simon reports that the Chairman of the Nuisances Removal Committee of the parish of Sevenoaks sent the following denunciation to Sir George Grey, Home Secretary:

> 'Small-pox cases were rarely heard of in this parish until about twelve months ago. Shortly before that time, the works for a railway from Lewisham to Tunbridge were commenced here, and, in addition to the principal works being in the immediate neighbourhood of this town, here was also established the depôt for the whole of the works, so that a large number of persons was of necessity employed here. As cottage accommodation could not be obtained for them all, huts were built in several places along the line of the works by the contractor, Mr Jay, for their especial occupation. These huts possessed no ventilation nor drainage, and, besides, were necessarily over-

crowded, because each occupant had to accommodate lodgers, whatever the number in his own family might be, although there were only two rooms to each tenement. The consequences were, according to the medical report we received, that in the night-time these poor people were compelled to endure all the horror of suffocation to avoid the pestiferous smells arising from the filthy, stagnant water, and the privies close under their windows. Complaints were at length made to the Nuisances Removal Committee by a medical gentleman who had occasion to visit these huts, and he spoke of their condition as dwellings in the most severe terms, and he expressed his fears that some very serious consequences might ensue, unless some sanitary measures were adopted. About a year ago, Mr Jay promised to appropriate a hut, to which persons in his employ, who were suffering from contagious diseases, might at once be removed. He repeated that promise on the 23rd July last, but although since the date of the last Promise there have been several cases of small-pox in his huts, and two deaths from the same disease, yet he has taken no steps whatever to carry out his promise. On the 9th September instant, Mr Kelson, surgeon, reported to me further cases of small-pox in the same huts, and he described their condition as most disgraceful. I should add, for your (the Home Secretary's) information that an isolated house, called the Pest-house, which is set apart for parishioners who might be suffering from infectious diseases, has been continually occupied by such patients for many months past, and is also now occupied; that in one family five children died from small-pox and fever; that from the 1st April to the 1st September this year, a period of five months, there have been no fewer than ten deaths from small-pox in the parish, four of them being in the huts already referred to; that it is impossible to ascertain the exact number of persons who have suffered from that disease although they are known to be many, from the fact of the families keeping it as private as possible.'[69]

The labourers in coal and other mines belong to the best paid categories of the British proletariat. The price at which they buy their wages was shown on an earlier page.[70] Here I merely cast a hurried glance over the conditions of their dwellings. As a rule, the exploiter of a mine, whether its owner or his tenant, builds a number of cottages for his hands. They receive cottages and coal for firing 'for nothing'—*i.e.*, these form part of their wages, paid in kind. Those who are not lodged in this way receive in compensation £4 per annum. The mining districts attract with rapidity a large population, made up of the miners themselves, and the artisans, shopkeepers, &c., that group themselves around them. The ground-rents are high, as they are generally where population is dense. The master tries, therefore, to run up, within the smallest space possible at the mouth of the pit, just so many cottages as are necessary to pack together his hands and their families. If new mines are opened in the neighbourhood, or old ones are again set working, the pressure increases. In the construction of the cottages, only one point of view is of moment, the 'abstinence' of the capitalist from all expenditure that is not absolutely unavoidable.

'The lodging which is obtained by the pitman and other labourers connected with the collieries of Northumberland and Durham,' says Dr Julian Hunter, 'is perhaps, on the whole, the worst and the dearest of which any large specimens can be found in England, the similar parishes of Monmouthshire excepted.... The extreme badness is in the high number of men found in one room, in the smallness of the ground-plot on which a great number of houses are thrust, the want of water, the absence of privies, and the frequent placing of one house on the top of another, or distribution into flats, ... the lessee acts as if the whole colony were encamped, not resident.'[71]

'In pursuance of my instructions,' says Dr Stevens, 'I visited most of the large colliery villages in the Durham Union.... With very few exceptions, the general statement that no means are taken to secure the health of the inhabitants would be true of all of them.... All colliers are bound ['bound,' an expression which, like bondage, dates from the age of serfdom] to the colliery lessee or owner for twelve months.... If the colliers express discontent, or in any way annoy the 'viewer,' a mark of memorandum is made against their names, and, at the annual 'binding,' such men are turned off... It appears to me that no part of the 'truck system' could be worse than what obtains in these densely-populated districts. The collier is bound to take as part of his hiring a house surrounded with pestiferous influences; he cannot help himself, and it appears doubtful whether anyone else can help him except his proprietor (he is, to all intents and purposes, a serf), and his proprietor first consults his balance-sheet, and the result is tolerably certain. The collier is also often supplied with water by the proprietor, which, whether it be good or bad, he has to pay for, or rather he suffers a deduction for from his wages.'[72]

In conflict with 'public opinion,' or even with the Officers of Health, capital makes no difficulty about 'justifying' the conditions partly dangerous, partly degrading, to which it confines the working and domestic life of the labourer, on the ground that they are necessary for profit. It is the same thing when capital 'abstains' from protective measures against dangerous machinery in the factory, from appliances for ventilation and for safety in mines, &c. It is the same here with the housing of the miners. Dr Simon, medical officer of the Privy Council, in his official Report says:

'In apology for the wretched household accommodation ... it is alleged that miners are commonly worked on lease; that the duration of the lessee's interest (which in collieries is commonly for 21 years), is not so long that he should deem it worth his while to create good accommodation for his labourers, and for the tradespeople and others whom the work attracts; that even if he were disposed to act liberally in the matter, this disposition would commonly be defeated by his landlord's tendency to fix on him, as ground-rent, an exorbitant additional charge for the privilege of having on the surface of the ground the decent and comfortable village which the labourers of the subterranean property ought to inhabit, and that prohibitory price (if not actual prohibition) equally excludes others who might desire to build. It would be foreign to the purpose of this report to enter upon any discussion of the merits of the above apology. Nor here is it even needful to consider where it would be that, if decent accommodation were provided, the cost ... would eventually fall—whether on landlord, or lessee, or labourer, or public. But in presence of such shameful facts as are vouched for in the annexed reports [those of Dr Hunter, Dr Stevens, &c.] a remedy may well be claimed.... Claims of landlordship are being so used as to do great public wrong. The landlord in his capacity of mine-owner invites an industrial colony to labour on his estate, and then in his capacity of surface-owner makes it impossible that the labourers whom he collects, should find proper lodging where they must live. The lessee [the capitalist exploiter] meanwhile has no pecuniary motive for resisting that division of the bargain; well knowing that if its latter conditions be exorbitant, the consequences fall, not on him, that his labourers on whom they fall have not education enough to know the value of their sanitary rights, that neither obscenest lodging nor foulest drinking water will be appreciable inducements towards a 'strike."[73]

D. Effect of Crises on the Best Paid Part of the Working Class

Before I turn to the regular agricultural labourers, I may be allowed to show, by one example, how industrial revulsions affect even the best-paid, the aristocracy, of the working class. It will be remembered that the year 1857 brought one of the great crises with which the industrial cycle periodically ends. The next termination of the cycle was due in 1866. Already discounted in the regular factory districts by the cotton famine, which threw much capital from its wonted sphere into the great centres of the money-market, the crisis assumed, at this time, an especially financial character. Its outbreak in 1866 was signalised by the failure of a gigantic London Bank, immediately followed by the collapse of countless swindling companies. One of the great London branches of industry involved in the catastrophe was iron shipbuilding. The magnates of this trade had not only over-produced beyond all measure during the overtrading time, but they had, besides, engaged in enormous contracts on the speculation that credit would be forthcoming to an equivalent extent. Now, a terrible reaction set in, that even at this hour (the end of March, 1867) continues in this and other London industries.[74] To show the condition of the labourers, I quote the following from the circumstantial report of a correspondent of the *Morning Star*, who, at the end of 1866, and beginning of 1867, visited the chief centres of distress:

> 'In the East End districts of Poplar, Millwall, Greenwich, Deptford, Limehouse and Canning Town, at least 15,000 workmen and their families were in a state of utter destitution, and 3,000 skilled mechanics were breaking stones in the workhouse yard (after distress of over half a year's duration).... I had great difficulty in reaching the workhouse door, for a hungry crowd besieged it.... They were waiting for their tickets, but the time had not yet arrived for the distribution. The yard was a great square place with an open shed running all round it, and several large heaps of snow covered the paving-stones in the middle. In the middle, also, were little wicker-fenced spaces, like sheep pens, where in finer weather the men worked; but on the day of my visit the pens were so snowed up that nobody could sit in them. Men were busy, however, in the open shed breaking paving-stones into macadam. Each man had a big paving-stone for a seat, and he chipped away at the rime-covered granite with a big hammer until he had broken up, and think! five bushels of it, and then he had done his day's work, and got his day's pay—threepence and an allowance of food. In another part of the yard was a rickety little wooden house, and when we opened the door of it, we found it filled with men who were huddled together shoulder to shoulder for the warmth of one another's bodies and breath. They were picking oakum and disputing the while as to which could work the longest on a given quantity of food—for endurance was the point of honour. Seven thousand ... in this one workhouse ... were recipients of relief ... many hundreds of them ... it appeared, were, six or eight months ago, earning the highest wages paid to artisans.... Their number would be more than doubled by the count of those who, having exhausted all their savings, still refuse to apply to the parish, because they have a little left to pawn. Leaving the workhouse, I took a walk through the streets, mostly of little one-storey houses, that abound in the neighbourhood of Poplar. My guide was a member of the Committee of the Unemployed.... My first call was on an ironworker who had been seven and twenty weeks out of employment. I found the man with his family sitting in a little back room. The room was not bare of furniture, and there was a fire in it. This was necessary to keep the naked feet of the young children from getting frost bitten, for it was a bitterly cold day. On a tray in front of the fire lay a quantity of oakum, which the wife and children were picking in return for their allowance from the parish. The man worked in the stone yard of the workhouse for a certain ration of food, and threepence per day. He had now come home to dinner quite hungry, as he told us with a melancholy smile, and his dinner consisted of a couple of slices of bread and dripping, and a cup of milkless tea.... The next door at which we knocked was opened by a middle-aged woman, who, without saying a word, led us into a little back parlour, in which sat all her family, silent and fixedly staring at a rapidly dying fire. Such desolation, such hopelessness was about these people and their little room, as I should not care to witness again. 'Nothing have they done, sir,' said the woman, pointing to her boys, 'for six and twenty weeks; and

all our money gone—all the twenty pounds that me and father saved when times were better, thinking it would yield a little to keep us when we got past work. Look at it,' she said, almost fiercely, bringing out a bank-book with all its well kept entries of money paid in, and money taken out, so that we could see how the little fortune had begun with the first five shilling deposit, and had grown by little and little to be twenty pounds, and how it had melted down again till the sum in hand got from pounds to shillings, and the last entry made the book as worthless as a blank sheet. This family received relief from the workhouse, and it furnished them with just one scanty meal per day.... Our next visit was to an iron labourer's wife, whose husband had worked in the yards. We found her ill from want of food, lying on a mattress in her clothes, and just covered with a strip of carpet, for all the bedding had been pawned. Two wretched children were tending her, themselves looking as much in need of nursing as their mother. Nineteen weeks of enforced idleness had brought them to this pass, and while the mother told the history of that bitter past, she moaned as if all her faith in a future that should atone for it were dead.... On getting outside a young fellow came running after us, and asked us to step inside his house and see if anything could be done for him. A young wife, two pretty children, a cluster of pawn-tickets, and a bare room were all he had to show.'

On the after pains of the crisis of 1866, the following extract from a Tory newspaper. It must not be forgotten that the East-end of London, which is here dealt with, is not only the seat of the iron shipbuilding mentioned above, but also of a so-called 'home-industry' always underpaid.

> 'A frightful spectacle was to be seen yesterday in one part of the metropolis. Although the unemployed thousands of the East-end did not parade with their black flags *en masse,* the human torrent was imposing enough. Let us remember what these people suffer. They are dying of hunger. That is the simple and terrible fact. There are 40,000 of them.... In our presence, in one quarter of this wonderful metropolis, are packed—next door to the most enormous accumulation of wealth the world ever saw—cheek by jowl with this are 40,000 helpless, starving people. These thousands are now breaking in upon the other quarters; always half-starving, they cry their misery in our ears, they cry to Heaven, they tell us from their miserable dwellings, that it is impossible for them to find work, and useless for them to beg. The local ratepayers themselves are driven by the parochial charges to the verge of pauperism.'—(*Standard,* 5th April, 1867.)

As it is the fashion amongst English capitalists to quote Belgium as the Paradise of the labourer because 'freedom of labour,' or what is the same thing, 'freedom of capital,' is there limited neither by the despotism of Trades' Unions, nor by Factory Acts, a word or two on the 'happiness' of the Belgian labourer. Assuredly no one was more thoroughly initiated in the mysteries of this happiness than the late M. Ducpétiaux, inspector-general of Belgian prisons and charitable institutions, and member of the central commission of Belgian statistics. Let us take his work: 'Budgets économiques des classes ouvrières de la Belgique,' Bruxelles, 1855. Here we find among other matters, a normal Belgian labourer's family, whose yearly income and expenditure he calculates on very exact data, and whose conditions of nourishment are then compared with those of the soldier, sailor, and prisoner. The family 'consists of father, mother, and four children.' Of these 6 persons 'four may be usefully employed the whole year through.' It is assumed that 'there is no sick person nor one incapable of work, among them,' nor are there 'expenses for religious, moral, and intellectual purposes, except a very small sum for church sittings,' nor 'contributions to savings banks or benefit societies,' nor 'expenses due to luxury or the result of improvidence.' The father and eldest son, however, allow themselves 'the use of tobacco,' and on Sundays 'go to the *cabaret,*' for which a whole 86 centimes a week are reckoned.

'From a general compilation of wages allowed to the labourers in different trades, it follows that the highest average of daily wage is 1 franc 56c., for men, 89 centimes for women, 56 centimes for boys, and 55 centimes for girls. Calculated at this rate, the resources of the family would amount, at the maximum, to 1,068 francs a-year.... In the family ... taken as typical we have calculated all possible resources. But in ascribing wages to the mother of the family we *raise the question of the direction of the household.* How will its internal economy be cared for? Who will look after the young children? Who will get ready the meals, do the washing and mending? This is the dilemma incessantly presented to the labourers.'

According to this the budget of the family is:

The father	300 working-days at fr. 1.56	fr. 468
mother	300 working-days at fr. 0.89	fr. 267
boy	300 working-days at fr. 0.56	fr. 168
girl	300 working-days at fr. 0.55	fr. 165
		Total fr. 1,068

The annual expenditure of the family would cause a deficit upon the hypothesis that the labourer has the food of:

The man-of-war's man	fr. 1,828	Deficit fr. 760
The soldier	fr. 1,473	Deficit fr. 405
The prisoner	fr. 1,112	Deficit fr. 44

'We see that few labouring families can reach, we will not say the average of the sailor or soldier, but even that of the prisoner. The general average (of the cost of each prisoner in the different prisons during the period 1847-1849), has been 63 centimes for all prisons. This figure, compared with that of the daily maintenance of the labourer, shows a difference of 13 centimes. It must be remarked further, that if in the prisons it is necessary to set down in the account the expenses of administration and surveillance, on the other hand, the prisoners have not to pay for their lodging; that the purchases they make at the canteens are not included in the expenses of maintenance, and that these expenses are greatly lowered in consequence of the large number of persons that make up the establishments, and of contracting for or buying wholesale, the food and other things that enter into their consumption.... How comes it, however, that a great number, we might say, a great majority, of labourers, live in a more economical way? It is ... by adopting expedients, the secret of which only the labourer knows; by reducing his daily rations; by substituting rye-bread for wheat; by eating less meat, or even none at all, and the same with butter and condiments; by contenting themselves with one or two rooms where the family is crammed together, where boys and girls sleep side by side, often on the same pallet; by economy of clothing, washing, decency; by giving up the Sunday diversions; by, in short, resigning themselves to the most painful privations. Once arrived at this extreme limit, the least rise in the price of food, stoppage of work, illness, increases the labourer's distress and determines his complete ruin; debts accumulate, credit fails, the most necessary clothes and furniture are pawned, and finally, the family asks to be enrolled on the list of paupers.' (Ducpétiaux, l. c., pp. 151, 154, 155.)

In fact, in this 'Paradise of capitalists' there follows, on the smallest change in the price of the most essential means of subsistence, a change in the number of deaths and crimes! (See Manifesto of the Maatschappij: 'De Vlamingen Vooruit!' Brussels, 1860, pp. 15, 16.)

In all Belgium are 930,000 families, of whom, according to the official statistics, 90,000 are wealthy and on the list of voters = 450,000 persons; 390,000 families of the lower middle-class in towns and villages, the greater part of them constantly sinking into the proletariat, = 1,950,000 persons. Finally, 450,000 working class families = 2,250,000 persons, of whom the model ones enjoy the happiness depicted by Ducpétiaux. Of the 450,000 working class families, over 200,000 are on the pauper list.

E. The British Agricultural Proletariat

Nowhere does the antagonistic character of capitalistic production and accumulation assert itself more brutally than in the progress of English agriculture (including cattle-breeding) and the retrogression of the English agricultural labourer. Before I turn to his present situation, a rapid retrospect. Modern agriculture dates in England from the middle of the 18th century, although the revolution in landed property, from which the changed mode of production starts as a basis, has a much earlier date.

If we take the statements of Arthur Young, a careful observer, though a superficial thinker, as to the agricultural labourer of 1771, the latter plays a very pitiable part compared with his predecessor of the end of the 14th century,

> 'when the labourer ... could live in plenty, and accumulate wealth,'[75]

not to speak of the 15th century, 'the golden age of the English labourer in town and country.' We need not, however, go back so far. In a very instructive work of the year 1777 we read:

> 'The great farmer is nearly mounted to a level with him [the gentleman]; while the poor labourer is depressed almost to the earth. His unfortunate situation will fully appear, by taking a comparative view of it, only forty years ago, and at present.... Landlord and tenant ... have both gone hand in hand in keeping the labourer down.'[76]

It is then proved in detail that the real agricultural wages between 1737 and 1777 fell nearly ¼ or 25 per cent.

> 'Modern policy,' says Dr Richard Price also, 'is, indeed, more favourable to the higher classes of people; and the consequences may in time prove that the whole kingdom will consist of only gentry and beggars, or of grandees and slaves.'[77]

Nevertheless, the position of the English agricultural labourer from 1770 to 1780, with regard to his food and dwelling, as well as to his self-respect, amusements, &c., is an ideal never attained again since that time. His average wage expressed in pints of wheat was from 1770 to 1771, 90 pints, in Eden's time (1797) only 65, in 1808 but 60.[78]

The state of the agricultural labourer at the end of the Anti-Jacobin War, during which landed proprietors, farmers, manufacturers, merchants, bankers, stockbrokers, army-contractors, &c., enriched themselves so extraordinarily, has been already indicated above. The nominal wages rose in consequence partly of the bank-note depreciation, partly of a rise in the price of the primary means of subsistence independent of this depreciation. But the actual wage-variation can be evidenced in a very simple way, without entering into details that are here unnecessary. The Poor Law and its administration were in 1795 and 1814 the same. It will be remembered how this law was carried out in the country districts: in the form of alms the parish made up the nominal wage to the nominal sum required for the simple vegetation of the labourer. The ratio between the wages paid by the farmer, and the wage-deficit made good by the parish, shows us two things. First, the falling of wages below their minimum; second, the degree in which the agricultural labourer was a compound of wage labourer and pauper, or the degree in which he had been turned into a serf of his parish. Let us take one county that represents the average condition of things in all counties. In Northamptonshire, in 1795, the average weekly wage was 7s. 6d.; the total yearly expenditure of a family of 6 persons, £36 12s. 5d.; their total income, £29 18s.; deficit made good by the parish, £6 14s. 5d. In 1814, in the same county, the weekly wage was 12s. 2d.; the total yearly expenditure of a family of 5 persons, £54 18s. 4d.; their total income, £36, 2s.; deficit made good by the parish, £18 6s. 4d.[79] In 1795, the deficit was less than 1/4 the wage, in 1814, more than half. It is self-evident that, under these circumstances, the meagre comforts that Eden still found in the cottage of the agricultural labourer, had vanished by 1814.[80] Of all the animals kept by the farmer, the labourer, the *instrumentum vocale*, was, thenceforth, the most oppressed, the worst nourished, the most brutally treated.

The same state of things went on quietly until

> 'the Swing riots, in 1830, revealed to us (*i.e.*, the ruling classes) by the light of blazing corn-stacks, that misery and black mutinous discontent smouldered quite as fiercely under the surface of agricultural as of manufacturing England.'[81]

At this time, Sadler, in the House of Commons, christened the agricultural labourers 'white slaves,' and a Bishop echoed the epithet in the Upper House. The most notable political economist of that period—E. G. Wakefield—says:

> 'The peasant of the South of England ... is not a freeman, nor is he a slave; he is a pauper.'[82]

The time just before the repeal of the Corn Laws threw new light on the condition of the agricultural labourers. On the one hand, it was to the interest of the middle-class agitators to prove how little the Corn Laws protected the actual producers of the corn. On the other hand, the industrial bourgeoisie foamed with sullen rage at the denunciations of the factory system by the landed aristocracy, at the pretended sympathy with the woes of the factory operatives, of those utterly corrupt, heartless, and genteel loafers, and at their 'diplomatic zeal' for factory legislation. It is an old English proverb that 'when thieves fall out, honest men come by their own,' and, in fact, the noisy, passionate quarrel between the two fractions of the ruling class about the question, which of the two exploited the labourers the more shamefully, was on each hand the midwife of the truth. Earl Shaftesbury, then Lord Ashley, was commander-in-chief in the aristocratic, philanthropic, anti-factory campaign. He was, therefore, in 1845, a favourite subject in the revelations of the *Morning Chronicle* on the condition of the agricultural labourers. This journal, then the most important Liberal organ, sent special commissioners into the agricultural districts, who did not content themselves with mere general descriptions and statistics, but published the names both of the labouring families examined and of their landlords. The following list gives the wages paid in three villages in the neighbourhood of Blanford, Wimbourne, and Poole. The villages are the property of Mr G. Bankes and of the Earl of Shaftesbury. It will be noted that, just like Bankes, this 'low church pope,' this head of English pietists, pockets a great part of the miserable wages of the labourers under the pretext of house-rent:

FIRST VILLAGE						
(a) Children	2	3	2	2	6	3
(b) Number of Members in Family	4	5	4	4	8	5
(c) Weekly Wage of the Men	8s. 0d.	8s. 0d.	8s. 0d.	8s. 0d.	7s. 0d.	7s. 0d.
(d) Weekly Wage of the Children	—	—	—	—	1/-, 1/6	1/-, 2/-
(e) Weekly Income of the whole Family	8s. 0d.	8s. 0d.	8s. 0d.	8s. 0d.	10s. 6d.	7s. 0d.
(f) Weekly Rent	2s. 0d.	1s. 6d.	1s. 0d.	1s. 0d.	2s. 0d.	1s. 4d.
(g) Total Weekly wage after deduction of Rent	6s. 0d.	6s. 6d.	7s. 0d.	7s. 0d.	8s. 6d.	5s. 8d.
(h) Weekly income per head	1s. 6d.	1s. 3½d.	1s. 9d.	1s. 9d.	1s. 0 3/4d.	1s. 1½d.

SECOND VILLAGE						
(a) Children	6	6	8	4	3	
(b) Number of Members in Family	8	8	10	6	5	
(c) Weekly Wage of the Men	7s. 0d.	7s. 0d.	7s. 0d.	7s. 0d.	7s. 0d.	
(d) Weekly Wage of the Children	1/-, 1/6	1/-, 1/6	—	—	—	
(e) Weekly Income of the whole Family	10s. 0d.	7s. 0d.	7s. 0d.	7s. 0d.	7s. 0d.	
(f) Weekly Rent	1s. 6d.	1s. 3½d.	1s. 3½d.	1s. 6½d.	1s. 6½d.	
(g) Total Weekly wage after deduction of Rent	8s. 6d.	5s. 8½d.	5s. 8½d.	5s. 5½d.	5s. 5½d.	
(h) Weekly income per head	1s. 0 3/4d.	0s. 8½d.	0s. 7d.	0s. 11d.	1s. 1d.	
THIRD VILLAGE						
(a) Children	4	3	0			
(b) Number of Members in Family	6	5	2			
(c) Weekly Wage of the Men	7s. 0d.	7s. 0d.	5s. 0d.			
(d) Weekly Wage of the Children	-	1/- 2/-	1/- 2/6			
(e) Weekly Income of the whole Family	7s. 0d.	11s. 6d.	5s. 0d.			
(f) Weekly Rent	1s. 0d.	0s. 10d.	1s. 0d.			
(g) Total Weekly wage after deduction of Rent	6s. 0d.	10s. 8d.	4s. 0d.			
(h) Weekly income per head[83]	1s. 0d.	2s. 1 3/5d.	2s. 0d.			

The repeal of the Corn Laws gave a marvellous impulse to English agriculture.[84] Drainage on the most extensive scale, new methods of stall-feeding, and of the artificial cultivation of green crops, introduction of mechanical manuring apparatus, new treatment of clay soils, increased use of mineral manures, employment of the steam-engine, and of all kinds of new machinery, more intensive cultivation generally, characterised this epoch. Mr Pusey, Chairman of the Royal Agricultural Society, declares that the (relative) expenses of farming have been reduced nearly one half by the introduction of new machinery. On the other hand, the actual return of the soil rose rapidly. Greater outlay of capital per acre, and, as a consequence, more rapid concentration of farms, were essential conditions of the new method.[85] At the same time, the area under cultivation increased, from 1846 to 1856, by 464,119 acres, without reckoning the great area in the Eastern Counties which was transformed from rabbit warrens and poor pastures into magnificent corn-fields. It has already been seen that, at the same time, the total number of persons employed in agriculture fell. As far as the actual agricultural labourers of both sexes and of all ages are concerned, their number fell from 1,241,396, in 1851, to 1,163, 217 in 1861.[86] If the English Registrar-General, therefore, rightly remarks:

'The increase of farmers and farm-labourers, since 1801, bears no kind of proportion ... to the increase of agricultural produce,'[87]

> this disproportion obtains much more for the last period, when a positive decrease of the agricultural population went hand in hand with increase of the area under cultivation, with more intensive cultivation, unheard-of accumulation of the capital incorporated with the soil, and devoted to its working, an augmentation in the products of the soil without parallel in the history of English agriculture, plethoric rent-rolls of landlords, and growing wealth of the capitalist farmers. If we take this, together with the swift, unbroken extension of the markets, *viz.*, the towns, and the reign of Free Trade, then the agricultural labourer was at last, *post tot discrimina rerum,* placed in circumstances that ought, *secundum artem,* to have made him drunk with happiness.

But Professor Rogers comes to the conclusion that the lot of the English agricultural labourer of today, not to speak of his predecessor in the last half of the 14th and in the 15th century, but only compared with his predecessor from 1770 to 1780, has changed for the worse to an extraordinary extent, that 'the peasant has again become a serf,' and a serf worse fed and worse clothed.[88] Dr Julian Hunter, in his epochmaking report on the dwellings of the agricultural labourers, says:

> 'The cost of the hind' (a name for the agricultural labourer, inherited from the time of serfdom) 'is fixed at the lowest possible amount on which he can live ... the supplies of wages and shelter are not calculated on the profit to be derived from him. He is a zero in farming calculations ...[89] The means [of subsistence] being always supposed to be a fixed quantity.[90] As to any further reduction of his income, he may say, *nihil habeo nihil curo.* He has no fears for the future, because he has now only the spare supply necessary to keep him. He has reached the zero from which are dated the calculations of the farmer. Come what will, he has no share either in prosperity or adversity.'[91]

In the year 1863, an official inquiry took place into the conditions of nourishment and labour of the criminals condemned to transportation and penal servitude. The results are recorded in two voluminous Blue books. Among other things it is said:

> 'From an elaborate comparison between the diet of convicts in the convict prisons in England, and that of paupers in workhouses and of free labourers in the same country ... it certainly appears that the former are much better fed than either of the two other classes,'[92] whilst 'the amount of labour required from an ordinary convict under penal servitude is about one half of what would be done by an ordinary day-labourer.'[93]

A few characteristic depositions of witnesses: John Smith, governor of the Edinburgh prison, deposes:

> No. 5056. 'The diet of the English prisons [is] superior to that of ordinary labourers in England.' No 50. 'It is the fact ... that the ordinary agricultural labourers in Scotland very seldom get any meat at all.' Answer No. 3047. 'Is there anything that you are aware of to account for the necessity of feeding them very much better than ordinary labourers?—Certainly not.' No. 3048. 'Do you think that further experiments ought to be made in order to ascertain whether a dietary might not be hit upon for prisoners employed on public works nearly approaching to the dietary of free labourers? ...'[94] 'He [the agricultural labourer] might say: 'I work hard, and have not enough to eat, and when in prison I did not work harder where I had plenty to eat, and therefore it is better for me to be in prison again than here.''[95]

From the tables appended to the first volume of the Report I have compiled the annexed comparative summary.

WEEKLY AMOUNT OF NUTRIENTS				
	Quantity of Nitrogenous Ingredients	*Quantity of Non-Nitrogenous Ingredients*	*Quantity of Mineral Matter*	*TOTAL*
	Ounces	*Ounces*	*Ounces*	*Ounces*
Portland (convict)	28.95	150.06	4.68	183.69
Sailor in the Navy	29.63	152.91	4.52	187.06
Soldier	25.55	114.49	3.94	143.98
Working Coachmaker	24.53	162.06	4.23	190.82
Compositor	21.24	100.83	3.12	125.19
Agricultural labourer[96]	17.73	118.06	3.29	139.08

The general result of the inquiry by the medical commission of 1863 on the food of the lowest fed classes, is already known to the reader. He will remember that the diet of a great part of the agricultural labourers' families is below the minimum necessary 'to arrest starvation diseases.' This is especially the case in all the purely rural districts of Cornwall, Devon, Somerset, Wilts, Stafford, Oxford, Berks, and Herts.

> 'The nourishment obtained by the labourer himself,' says Dr E. Smith, 'is larger than the average quantity indicates, since he eats a larger share ... necessary to enable him to perform his labour ... of food than the other members of the family, including in the poorer districts nearly all the meat and bacon.... The quantity of food obtained by the wife and also by the children at the period of rapid growth, is in many cases, in almost every county, deficient, and particularly in nitrogen.'[97]

The male and female servants living with the farmers themselves are sufficiently nourished. Their number fell from 288,277 in 1851, to 204,962 in 1861.

> 'The labour of women in the fields,' says Dr Smith, 'whatever may be its disadvantages, ... is under present circumstances of great advantage to the family, since it adds that amount of income which ... provides shoes and clothing and pays the rent, and thus enables the family to be better fed.'[98]

One of the most remarkable results of the inquiry was that the agricultural labourer of England, as compared with other parts of the United Kingdom, 'is considerably the worst fed,' as the appended table shows:

Quantities of Carbon and Nitrogen weekly consumed by an average agricultural adult:

	Carbon, grains	*Nitrogen, grains*
England	46,673	1,594
Wales	48,354	2,031
Scotland	48,980	2,348
Ireland[99]	43,366	2,434

> 'To the insufficient quantity and miserable quality of the house accommodation generally had,' says Dr Simon, in his official Health Report, 'by our agricultural labourers, almost every page of Dr Hunter's report bears testimony. And gradually, for many years past, the state of the labourer in these respects has been deteriorating, house-room being now greatly more difficult for him to find, and, when found, greatly less suitable to his needs than, perhaps, for centuries had been the case. Especially within the last twenty or thirty years, the evil has been in very rapid increase, and the household circumstances of the labourer are now in the highest degree deplorable. Except in so far as they whom his labour enriches, see fit to treat him with a kind of pitiful indulgence, he is quite peculiarly helpless in the matter. Whether he shall find house-room on the land which he contributes to till, whether the house-room which he gets shall be human or swinish, whether he shall have the little space of garden that so vastly lessens the pressure of his poverty—all this does not depend on his willingness and ability to pay reasonable rent for the decent accommodation he requires, but depends on the use which others may see fit to make of their 'right to do as they will with their own.' However large may be a farm, there is no law that a certain proportion of labourers' dwellings (much less of decent dwellings) shall be upon it; nor does any law reserve for the labourer ever so little right in that soil to which his industry is as needful as sun and rain.... An extraneous element weighs the balance heavily against him ... the influence of the Poor Law in its provisions concerning settlement and chargeability.[100] Under this influence, each parish has a pecuniary interest in reducing to a minimum the number of

its resident labourers:—for, unhappily, agricultural labour instead of implying a safe and permanent independence for the hardworking labourer and his family, implies for the most part only a longer or shorter circuit to eventual pauperism—a pauperism which, during the whole circuit, is so near, that any illness or temporary failure of occupation necessitates immediate recourse to parochial relief—and thus all residence of agricultural population in a parish is glaringly an addition to its poor-rates .... Large proprietors[101] ... have but to resolve that there shall be no labourers' dwellings on their estates, and their estates will thenceforth be virtually free from half their responsibility for the poor. How far it has been intended, in the English constitution and law, that this kind of unconditional property in land should be acquirable, and that a landlord 'doing as he wills with his own,' should be able to treat the cultivators of the soil as aliens, whom he may expel from his territory, is a question which I do not pretend to discuss.... For that (power) of eviction ... does not exist only in theory. On a very large scale it prevails in practice—prevails ... as a main governing condition in the household circumstances of agricultural labour.... As regards the extent of the evil, it may suffice to refer to the evidence which Dr Hunter has compiled from the last census, that destruction of houses, notwithstanding increased local demands for them, had, during the last ten years, been in progress in 821 separate parishes or townships of England, so that irrespectively of persons who had been forced to become non-resident (that is in the parishes in which they work), these parishes and townships were receiving in 1861, as compared with 1851, a population 5 1/3 per cent. greater, into houseroom 4½ per cent. less... When the process of depopulation has completed itself, the result, says Dr Hunter, is a show-village where the cottages have been reduced to a few, and where none but persons who are needed as shepherds, gardeners, or game-keepers, are allowed to live; regular servants who receive the good treatment usual to their class.[102] But the land requires cultivation, and it will be found that the labourers employed upon it are not the tenants of the owner, but that they come from a neighbouring open village, perhaps three miles off, where a numerous small proprietary had received them when their cottages were destroyed in the close villages around. Where things are tending to the above result, often the cottages which stand, testify, in their unrepaired and wretched condition, to the extinction to which they are doomed. They are seen standing in the various stages of natural decay. While the shelter holds together, the labourer is permitted to rent it, and glad enough he will often be to do so, even at the price of decent lodging. But no repair, no improvement shall it receive, except such as its penniless occupants can supply. And when at last it becomes quite uninhabitable—uninhabitable even to the humblest standard of serfdom—it will be but one more destroyed cottage, and future poor-rates will be somewhat lightened. While great owners are thus escaping from poor-rates through the depopulation of lands over which they have control, the nearest town or open village receive the evicted labourers: the nearest, I say, but this 'nearest' may mean three or four miles distant from the farm where the labourer has his daily toil. To that daily toil there will then have to be added, as though it were nothing, the daily need of walking six or eight miles for power of earning his bread. And whatever farmwork is done by his wife and children, is done at the same disadvantage. Nor is this nearly all the toil which the distance occasions him. In the open village, cottage-speculators buy scraps of land, which they throng as densely as they can with the cheapest of all possible hovels. And into those wretched habitations (which, even if they adjoin the open country, have some of the worst features of the worst town residences) crowd the agricultural labourers of England.[103] .... Nor on the other hand must it be supposed that even when the labourer is housed upon the lands which he cultivates, his household circumstances are generally such as his life of productive industry would seem to deserve. Even on princely estates ... his cottage ... may be of the meanest description. There are landlords who deem any stye good enough for their labourer and his family, and who yet do not disdain to drive with him the hardest possible bargain for rent.[104] It may be but a ruinous one-bedroomed hut, having no fire-grate, no privy, no opening window, no water supply but the ditch, no garden—but the labourer is helpless against the wrong.... And the Nuisances Removal Acts ... are ... a mere dead letter ... in great part dependent for their working on such cottage-owners as the one from whom his (the labourer's) hovel is rented.... From brighter, but exceptional scenes, it is requisite in the interests of justice, that attention should again be drawn to the overwhelming preponderance of facts which are a reproach to the civilisation of England. Lamentable indeed, must be the case, when, notwithstanding all that is evident with regard to the quality of the present accommodation, it is the common conclusion of competent observers that even the general badness of dwellings is an evil infinitely less urgent than their mere numerical insufficiency. For years the over-crowding of rural labourers' dwellings has been a matter of deep concern, not only to persons who care for sanitary good, but to persons who care for decent and moral life. For, again and again in phrases so uniform that they seem stereotyped, reporters on the spread of epidemic disease in rural districts, have insisted on the extreme importance of that over-crowding, as an influence which renders it a quite hopeless task, to attempt the limiting of any infection which is introduced. And again and again it has been pointed out that, notwithstanding the many salubrious influences which there are in country life, the crowding which so favours the extension of contagious disease, also favours the origination of disease which is not contagious. And those who have denounced the over-crowded state of our rural population have not been silent as to a further mischief. Even where their primary concern has been only with the injury to health, often almost perforce they have referred to other relations on the subject. In showing how frequently it happens that adult persons of both sexes, married and unmarried, are huddled together in single small sleeping rooms, their reports have carried the conviction that, under the circumstances they describe, decency must always be outraged, and morality almost of necessity must suffer.[105] Thus, for instance, in the appendix of my last annual report, Dr Ord, reporting on an outbreak of fever at Wing, in Buckinghamshire, mentions how a young man who had come thither from Wingrave with fever, 'in the first days of his illness slept in a room with nine other persons. Within a fortnight several of these persons were attacked, and in the course of a few weeks five out of the nine had fever, and one died...' From Dr Harvey, of St. George's Hospital, who, on private professional business, visited Wing during the time of the epidemic, I received information exactly in the sense of the above report.... 'A young woman having fever, lay at night in a room occupied by her father and mother, her bastard child, two young men (her brothers), and her two sisters, each with a bastard child—10 persons in all. A few weeks ago 13 persons slept in it.'[106]

Dr Hunter investigated 5,375 cottages of agricultural labourers, not only in the purely agricultural districts, but in all counties of England. Of these, 2,195 had only one bedroom (often at the same time used as living-room), 2,930 only two, and 250, more than two. I will give a few specimens culled from a dozen counties.

(1) Bedfordshire

Wrestlingworth. Bedrooms about 12 feet long and 10 broad, although many are smaller than this. The small, one-storied cots are often divided by partitions into two bedrooms, one bed frequently in a kitchen, 5 feet 6 inches in height. Rent, £3 a year. The tenants have to make their own privies, the landlord only supplies a hole. As soon as one has made a privy, it is made use of by the whole neighbourhood. One house, belonging to a family called Richardson, was of quite unapproachable beauty. 'Its plaster walls bulged very like a lady's dress in a curtsey. One gable end was convex, the other concave, and on this last, unfortunately, stood the chimney, a curved tube of clay and wood like an elephant's trunk. A long stick served as prop to prevent the chimney from falling. The doorway and window were rhomboidal.' Of 17 houses visited, only 4 had more than one bedroom, and those four overcrowded. The cots with one bedroom sheltered 3 adults and 3 children, a married couple with 6 children, &c.

Dunton. High rents, from £4 to £5; weekly wages of the man, 10s. They hope to pay the rent by the straw-plaiting of the family. The higher the rent, the greater the number that must work together to pay it. Six adults, living with 4 children in one sleeping apartment, pay £3 10s. for it. The cheapest house in Dunton, 15 feet long externally, 10 broad, let for £3. Only one of the houses investigated had 2 bedrooms. A little outside the village, a house whose 'tenants dunged against the house-side,' the lower 9 inches of the door eaten away through sheer rottenness; the doorway, a single opening closed at night by a few bricks, ingeniously pushed up after shutting and covered with some matting. Half a window, with glass and frame, had gone the way of all flesh. Here, without furniture, huddled together were 3 adults and 5 children. Dunton is not worse than the rest of Biggleswade Union.

(2) Berkshire

Beenham. In June, 1864, a man, his wife and 4 children lived in a cot (one-storied cottage). A daughter came home from service with scarlet fever. She died. One child sickened and died. The mother and one child were down with typhus when Dr Hunter was called in. The father and one child slept outside, but the difficulty of securing isolation was seen here, for in the crowded market of the miserable village lay the linen of the fever-stricken household, waiting for the wash. The rent of H.'s house, 1s. a-week; one bedroom for man, wife, and 6 children. One house let for 8d. a-week, 14 feet 6 inches long, 7 feet broad, kitchen, 6 feet high; the bedroom without window, fire-place, door, or opening, except into the lobby; no garden. A man lived here for a little while, with two grown-up daughters and one grown-up son; father and son slept on the bed, the girls in the passage. Each of the latter had a child while the family was living here, but one went to the workhouse for her confinement and then came home.

(3) Buckinghamshire

30 cottages—on 1,000 acres of land—contained here about 130-140 persons. The parish of *Bradenham* comprises 1,000 acres; it numbered, in 1851, 36 houses and a population of 84 males and 54 females. This inequality of the sexes was partly remedied in 1861, when they numbered 98 males and 87 females; increase in 10 years of 14 men and 33 women. Meanwhile, the number of houses was one less.

Winslow. Great part of this newly built in good style; demand for houses appears very marked, since very miserable cots let at 1s. to 1s. 3d. per week.

Water Eaton. Here the landlords, in view of the increasing population, have destroyed about 20 per cent. of the existing houses. A poor labourer, who had to go about 4 miles to his work, answered the question, whether he could not find a cot nearer: 'No; they know better than to take a man in with my large family.'

Tinker's End, near Winslow. A bedroom in which were 4 adults and 4 children; 11 feet long, 9 feet broad, 6 feet 5 inches high at its highest part; another 11 feet 3 inches by 9 feet, 5 feet 10 inches high, sheltered 6 persons. Each of these families had less space than is considered necessary for a convict. No house had more than one bedroom, not one of them a back-door; water very scarce; weekly rent from 1s. 4d. to 2s. In 16 of the houses visited, only 1 man that earned 10s. a-week. The quantity of air for each person under the circumstances just described corresponds to that which he would have if he were shut up in a box of 4 feet measuring each way, the whole night. But then, the ancient dens afforded a certain amount of unintentional ventilation.

(4) Cambridgeshire

Gamblingay belongs to several landlords. It contains the wretchedest cots to be found anywhere. Much straw-plaiting. 'A deadly lassitude, a hopeless surrendering up to filth,' reigns in Gamblingay. The neglect in its centre, becomes mortification at its extremities, north and south, where the houses are rotting to pieces. The absentee landlords bleed this poor rookery too freely. The rents are very high; 8 or 9 persons packed in one sleeping apartment, in 2 cases 6 adults, each with 1 or 2 children in one small bedroom.

(5) Essex

In this county, diminutions in the number of persons and of cottages go, in many parishes, hand in hand. In not less than 22 parishes, however, the destruction of houses has not prevented increase of population, or has not brought about that expulsion which, under the name 'migration to towns,' generally occurs. In Fingringhoe, a parish of 3,443 acres, were in 1851, 145 houses; in 1861, only 110. But the people did not wish to go away, and managed even to increase under these circumstances. In 1851, 252 persons inhabited 61 houses, but in 1861, 262 persons were squeezed into 49 houses. In Basilden, in 1851, 157 persons lived on 1,827 acres, in 35 houses; at the end of ten years, 180 persons in 27 houses. In the parishes of Fingringhoe, South Fambridge, Widford, Basilden, and Ramsden Crags, in 1851, 1,392 persons were living on 8,449 acres in 316 houses; in 1861, on the same area, 1,473 persons in 249 houses.

(6) Herefordshire

This little county has suffered more from the 'eviction-spirit' than any other in England. At Nadby, overcrowded cottages generally, with only 2 bedrooms, belonging for the most part to the farmers. They easily let them for £3 or £4 a-year, and paid a weekly wage of 9s.

(7) Huntingdon

Hartford had, in 1851, 87 houses; shortly after this, 19 cottages were destroyed in this small parish of 1,720 acres; population in 1831, 452; in 1852, 382; and in 1861, 341. 14 cottages, each with 1 bedroom, were visited. In one, a married couple, 3 grown-up sons, 1 grown-up daughter, 4 children—in all 10 in another, 3 adults, 6 children. One of these rooms, in which 8 people slept, was 12 feet 10 inches long, 12 feet 2 inches broad, 6 feet 9 inches high: the average, without making any deduction for projections into the apartment, gave about 130 cubic feet per head. In the 14 sleeping rooms, 34 adults and 33 children. These cottages are seldom provided with gardens, but many of the inmates are able to farm small allotments at 10s. or 12s. per rood. These allotments are at a distance from the houses, which are without privies. The family 'must either go to the allotment to deposit their ordures,' or, as happens in this place, saving your presence, 'use a closet with a trough set like a drawer in a chest of drawers, and drawn out weekly and conveyed to the allotment to be emptied where its contents were wanted.' In Japan, the circle of life-conditions moves more decently than this.

(8) Lincolnshire

Langtoft. A man lives here, in Wright's house, with his wife, her mother, and 5 children; the house has a front kitchen, scullery, bedroom over the front kitchen; front kitchen and bedroom, 12 feet 2 inches by 9 feet 5 inches; the whole ground floor, 21 feet 2 inches by 9 feet 5 inches. The bedroom is a garret: the walls run together into the roof like a sugar-loaf, a dormer-window opening in front. 'Why did he live here? On account of the garden? No; it is very small. Rent? High, 1s. 3d. per week. Near his work? No; 6 miles away, so that he walks daily, to and fro, 12 miles. He lived there, because it was a tenantable cot,' and because he wanted to have a cot for himself alone, anywhere, at any price, and in any conditions. The following are the statistics of 12 houses in Langtoft, with 12 bedrooms, 38 adults, and 36 children.

TWELVE HOUSES IN LANGTOFT												
House	*No. 1.*	*No. 2.*	*No. 3.*	*No. 4.*	*No. 5.*	*No. 6.*	*No. 7.*	*No. 8.*	*No. 9.*	*No. 10.*	*No. 11.*	*No. 12.*
Bedrooms	1	1	1	1	1	1	1	1	1	1	1	1
Adults.	3	4	4	5	2	5	3	3	2	2	3	2
Children.	5	3	4	4	2	3	3	2	0	3	3	4
Number of Persons.	8	7	8	9	4	8	6	5	2	.5	6	6

(9) Kent

Kennington, very seriously over-populated in 1859, when diphtheria appeared, and the parish doctor instituted a medical inquiry into the condition of the poorer classes. He found that in this locality, where much labour is employed, various cots had been destroyed and no new ones built. In one district stood four houses, named birdcages; each had 4 rooms of the following dimensions in feet and inches:

Kitchen:	9 ft. 5 by 8 ft. 11 by 6 ft. 6
Scullery:	8 ft. 6 by 4 ft. 6 by 6 ft. 6
Bedroom:	8 ft. 5 by 5 ft. 10 by 6 ft. 3
Bedroom:	8 ft. 3 by 8 ft. 4 by 6 ft. 3

(10) Northamptonshire

Brinworth, Pickford and Floore: in these villages in the winter 20-30 men were lounging about the streets from want of work. The farmers do not always till sufficiently the corn and turnip lands, and the landlord has found it best to throw all his farms together into 2 or 3. Hence want of employment. Whilst on one side of the wall, the land calls for labour, on the other side the defrauded labourers are casting at it longing glances. Feverishly overworked in summer, and half-starved in winter, it is no wonder if they say in their peculiar dialect, 'the parson and gentlefolk seem frit to death at them.'

At Floore, instances, in one bedroom of the smallest size, of couples with 4, 5, 6 children; 3 adults with 5 children; a couple with grandfather and 6 children down with scarlet fever, &c.; in two houses with two bedrooms, two families of 8 and 9 adults respectively.

(11) Wiltshire

Stratton. 31 houses visited, 8 with only one bedroom. Pentill, in the same parish: a cot let at Is. 3d. weekly with 4 adults and 4 children, had nothing good about it, except the walls, from the floor of rough-hewn pieces of stones to the roof of worn-out thatch.

(12) Worcestershire

House-destruction here not quite so excessive; yet from 1851 to 1861, the number of inhabitants to each house on the average, has risen from 4.2 to 4.6.

Badsey. Many cots and little gardens here. Some of the farmers declare that the cots are 'a great nuisance here, because they bring the poor.' On the statement of one gentleman:

'The poor are none the better for them; if you build 500 they will let fast enough, in fact, the more you build, the more they want'

(according to him the houses give birth to the inhabitants, who then by a law of Nature press on 'the means of housing'). Dr Hunter remarks:

'Now these poor must come from somewhere, and as there is no particular attraction, such as doles, at Badsey, it must be repulsion from some other unfit place, which will send them here. If each could find an allotment near his work, he would not prefer Badsey, where he pays for his scrap of ground twice as much as the farmer pays for his.'

The continual emigration to the towns, the continual formation of surplus population in the country through the concentration of farms, conversion of arable land into pasture, machinery, &c., and the continual eviction of the agricultural population by the destruction of their cottages, go hand in hand. The more empty the district is of men, the greater is its 'relative surplus population,' the greater is their pressure on the means of employment, the greater is the absolute excess of the agricultural population over the means for housing it, the greater, therefore, in the villages is the local surplus population and the most pestilential packing together of human beings. The packing together of knots of men in scattered little villages and small country towns corresponds to the forcible draining of men from the surface of the land. The continuous superseding of the agricultural labourers, in spite of their diminishing number and the increasing mass of their products, gives birth to their pauperism. Their pauperism is ultimately a motive to their eviction and the chief source of their miserable housing which breaks down their last power of resistance, and makes them more slaves of the landed proprietors and the farmers.[107] Thus the minimum of wages becomes a law of Nature to them. On the other hand, the land, in spite of its constant 'relative surplus population,' is at the same time underpopulated. This is seen, not only locally at the points where the efflux of men to towns, mines, railroad-making, &c., is most marked. It is to be seen everywhere, in harvest-time as well as in spring and summer, at those frequently recurring times when English agriculture, so careful and intensive, wants extra hands. There are always too many agricultural labourers for the ordinary, and always too few for the exceptional or temporary needs of the cultivation of the soil.[108] Hence we find in the official documents contradictory complaints from the same places of deficiency and excess of labour simultaneously. The temporary or local want of labour brings about no rise in wages, but a forcing of the women and children into the fields, and exploitation at an age constantly lowered. As soon as the exploitation of the women and children takes place on a larger scale, it becomes in turn a new means of making a surplus population of the male agricultural labourer and of keeping down his wage. In the east of England thrives a beautiful fruit of this vicious circle—the so-called gang-system, to which I must briefly return here.[109]

The gang-system obtains almost exclusively in the counties of Lincoln, Huntingdon, Cambridge, Norfolk, Suffolk, and Nottingham, here and there in the neighbouring counties of Northampton, Bedford, and Rutland. Lincolnshire will serve us as an example. A large part of this county is new land, marsh formerly, or even, as in others of the eastern counties just named, won lately from the sea. The steam-engine has worked wonders in the way of drainage. What were once fens and sandbanks, bear now a luxuriant sea of corn and the highest of rents. The same thing holds of the alluvial lands won by human endeavour, as in the island of Axholme and other parishes on the banks of the Trent. In proportion as the new farms arose, not only were no new cottages built: old ones were demolished, and the supply of labour had to come from open villages, miles away, by long roads that wound along the sides of the hills. There alone had the population formerly found shelter from the incessant floods of the winter-time. The labourers that dwell on the farms of

400-1,000 acres (they are called 'confined labourers') are solely employed on such kinds of agricultural work as is permanent, difficult, and carried on by aid of horses. For every 100 acres there is, on an average, scarcely one cottage. A fen farmer, e.g., gave evidence before the Commission of Inquiry:

> 'I farm 320 acres, all arable land. I have not one cottage on my farm. I have only one labourer on my farm now. I have four horsemen lodging about. We get light work done by gangs.'[110]

The soil requires much light field labour, such as weeding, hoeing, certain processes of manuring, removing of stones, &c. This is done by the gangs, or organised bands that dwell in the open villages.

The gang consists of 10 to 40 or 50 persons, women, young persons of both sexes (13-18 years of age, although the boys are for the most part eliminated at the age of 13), and children of both sexes (6-13 years of age). At the head is the gang-master, always an ordinary agricultural labourer, generally what is called a bad lot, a scapegrace, unsteady, drunken, but with a dash of enterprise and *savoir-faire*. He is the recruiting-sergeant for the gang, which works under him, not under the farmer. He generally arranges with the latter for piece-work, and his income, which on the average is not very much above that of an ordinary agricultural labourer,[111] depends almost entirely upon the dexterity with which he manages to extract within the shortest time the greatest possible amount of labour from his gang. The farmers have discovered that women work steadily only under the direction of men, but that women and children, once set going, impetuously spend their life-force—as Fourier knew—while the adult male labourer is shrewd enough to economise his as much as he can. The gang-master goes from one farm to another, and thus employs his gang from 6 to 8 months in the year. Employment by him is, therefore, much more lucrative and more certain for the labouring families, than employment by the individual farmer, who only employs children occasionally. This circumstance so completely rivets his influence in the open villages that children are generally only to be hired through his instrumentality. The lending out of these individually, independently of the gang, is his second trade.

The 'drawbacks' of the system are the overwork of the children and young persons, the enormous marches that they make daily to and from the farms, 5, 6, and sometimes 7 miles distant, finally, the demoralisation of the gang. Although the gang-master, who, in some districts is called 'the driver,' is armed with a long stick, he uses it but seldom, and complaints of brutal treatment are exceptional. He is a democratic emperor, or a kind of Pied Piper of Hamelin. He must therefore be popular with his subjects, and he binds them to himself by the charms of the gipsy life under his direction. Coarse freedom, a noisy jollity, and obscenest impudence give attractions to the gang. Generally the gangmaster pays up in a public house; then he returns home at the head of the procession reeling drunk, propped up right and left by a stalwart virago, while children and young persons bring up the rear, boisterous, and singing chaffing and bawdy songs. On the return journey what Fourier calls 'phanerogamie,' is the order of the day. The getting with child of girls of 13 and 14 by their male companions of the same age, is common. The open villages which supply the contingent of the gang, become Sodoms and Gomorrahs,[112] and have twice as high a rate of illegitimate births as the rest of the kingdom. The moral character of girls bred in these schools, when married women, was shown above. Their children, when opium does not give them the finishing stroke, are born recruits of the gang.

The gang in its classical form just described, is called the public, common, or tramping gang. For there are also private gangs. These are made up in the same way as the common gang, but count fewer members, and work, not under a gang-master, but under some old farm servant, whom the farmer does not know how to employ in any better way. The gipsy fun has vanished here, but according to all witnesses, the payment and treatment of the children is worse.

The gang-system, which during the last years has steadily increased,[113] clearly does not exist for the sake of the gang-master. It exists for the enrichment of the large farmers,[114] and indirectly of the landlords.[115] For the farmer there is no more ingenious method of keeping his labourers well below the normal level, and yet of always having an extra hand ready for extra work, of extracting the greatest possible amount of labour with the least possible amount of money[116] and of making adult male labour 'redundant.' From the exposition already made, it will be understood why, on the one hand, a greater or less lack of employment for the agricultural labourer is admitted, while on the other, the gang-system is at the same time declared 'necessary' on account of the want of adult male labour and its migration to the towns.[117] The cleanly weeded land, and the uncleanly human weeds, of Lincolnshire, are pole and counterpole of capitalistic production.[118]

F. Ireland

In concluding this section, we must travel for a moment to Ireland. First, the main facts of the case.

The population of Ireland had, in 1841, reached 8,222,664; in 1851, it had dwindled to 6,623,985; in 1861, to 5,850,309; in 1866, to 5½ millions, nearly to its level in 1801. The diminution began with the famine year, 1846, so that Ireland, in less than twenty years, lost more than 5/16 ths of its people.[119] Its total emigration from May, 1851, to July, 1865, numbered 1,591,487: the emigration during the years 1861-1865 was more than half-a-million. The number of inhabited houses fell, from 1851-1861, by 52,990. From 1851-1861, the number of holdings of 15 to 30 acres increased 61,000, that of holdings over 30 acres, 109,000, whilst the total number of all farms fell 120,000, a fall, therefore, solely due to the suppression of farms under 15 acres—*i.e.*, to their centralisation.

TABLE A
LIVE-STOCK

Year	*Horses*		*Cattle*			*Sheep*			*Pigs*		
	Total Number	*Decrease*	*Total Number*	*Decrease*	*Increase*	*Total Number*	*Decrease*	*Increase*	*Total Number*	*Decrease*	*Increase*
1860	619,811	—	3,606,374	—	—	3,542,080	—	—	1,271,072	—	—
1861	614,232	5,579	3,471,688	134,686	—	3,556,050	—	13,970	1,102,042	169,030	—
1862	602,894	11,338	3,254,890	216,798	—	3,456,132	99,918	—	1,154,324	—	52,282
1863	579,978	22,916	3,144,231	110,659	—	3,308,204	147,982	—	1,067,458	86,866	—
1864	562,158	17,820	3,262,294	—	118,063	3,366,941	—	58,737	1,058,480	8,978	—
1865	547,867	14,291	3,493,414	—	231,120	3,688,742	—	321,801	1,299,893	—	241,413

The decrease of the population was naturally accompanied by a decrease in the mass of products. For our purpose, it suffices to consider the 5 years from 1861-1865 during which over half-a-million emigrated, and the absolute number of people sank by more than 1/3 of a million. From the above table it results:

Horses	*Cattle*	*Sheep*	*Pigs*
Absolute Decrease	*Absolute Decrease*	*Absolute Increase*	*Absolute Increase*
71,944	112,960	146,662	28,8211120

Let us now turn to agriculture, which yields the means of subsistence for cattle and for men. In the following table is calculated the decrease or increase for each separate year, as compared with its immediate predecessor. The Cereal Crops include wheat, oats, barley, rye, beans, and peas; the Green Crops, potatoes, turnips, marigolds, beet-root, cabbages, carrots, parsnips, vetches. &c.

In the year 1865, 127,470 additional acres came under the heading 'grass land,' chiefly because the area under the heading of 'bog and waste unoccupied,' decreased by 101,543 acres. If we compare 1865 with 1864, there is a decrease in cereals of 246,667 qrs., of which 48,999 were wheat, 160,605 oats, 29,892 barley, &c.: the decrease in potatoes was 446,398 tons, although the area of their cultivation increased in 1865.

From the movement of population and the agricultural produce of Ireland, we pass to the movement in the purse of its landlords, larger farmers, and industrial capitalists. It is reflected in the rise and fall of the Income-tax. It may be remembered that Schedule D. (profits with the exception of those of farmers), includes also the so-called, 'professional' profits—*i.e.*, the incomes of lawyers, doctors, &c.; and the Schedules C. and E., in which no special details are given, include the incomes of employees, officers, State sinecurists, State fundholders, &c.

TABLE D

THE INCOME-TAX ON THE SUBJOINED INCOMES IN POUNDS STERLING

(Tenth Report of the Commissioners of Inland Revenue, Lond. 1866.)

	1860	*1861*	*1862*	*1863*	*1864*	*1865*
Schedule A. Rent of Land	13,893,829	13,003,554	13,398,938	13,494,091	13,470,700	13,801,616
Schedule B. Farmers' Profits.	2,765,387	2,773,644	2,937,899	2,938,923	2,930,874	2,946,072
Schedule D. Industrial, &c., Profits	4,891,652	4,836,203	4,858,800	4,846,497	4,546,147	4,850,199
Total Schedules A to E	22,962,885	22,998,394	23,597,574	23,658,631	23,236,298	23,930,340

Under Schedule D., the average annual increase of income from 1853-1864 was only 0.93; whilst, in the same period, in Great Britain, it was 4.58. The following table shows the distribution of the profits (with the exception of those of farmers) for the years 1864 and 1865:

TABLE E.[122]

SCHEDULE D

INCOME FROM PROFITS (OVER £6O) IN IRELAND

	1864 £	*1865* £
Total yearly income of	4,368,610 divided among 17,467 persons.	4,669,979 divided among 18,081 persons.
Yearly income over £60 and under £100	238,726 divided among 5,015 persons.	222,575 divided among 4,703 persons.
Of the yearly total income	1,979,066 divided among 11,321 persons.	2,028,571 divided among 12,184 persons.
Remainder of the total yearly income	2,150,818 divided among 1,131 persons.	2,418,833 divided among 1,194 persons.

Of these		
	1,073,906 divided among 1,010 persons.	1,097,927 divided among 1,044 persons.
	1,076,912 divided among 121 persons.	1,320,906 divided among 150 persons.
	430,535 divided among 95 persons.	584,458 divided among 2 persons.
	646,377divided among 26	736,448 divided among 28
	262,819 divided among 3	274,528 divided among 3

England, a country with fully developed capitalist production, and pre-eminently industrial, would have bled to death with such a drain of population as Ireland has suffered. But Ireland is at present only an agricultural district of England, marked off by a wide channel from the country to which it yields corn, wool, cattle, industrial and military recruits.

The depopulation of Ireland has thrown much of the land out of cultivation, has greatly diminished the produce of the soil,[123] and, in spite of the greater area devoted to cattle breeding, has brought about, in some of its branches, an absolute diminution, in others, an advance scarcely worthy of mention, and constantly interrupted by retrogressions. Nevertheless, with the fall in numbers of the population, rents and farmers' profits rose, although the latter not as steadily as the former. The reason of this is easily comprehensible. On the one hand, with the throwing of small holdings into large ones, and the change of arable into pasture land, a larger part of the whole produce was transformed into surplus-produce. The surplus-produce increased, although the total produce, of which it formed a fraction, decreased. On the other hand, the money value of this surplus-produce increased yet more rapidly than its mass, in consequence of the rise in the English market price of meat, wool, &c., during the last 20, and especially during the last 10, years.

The scattered means of production that serve the producers themselves as means of employment and of subsistence, without expanding their own value by the incorporation of the labour of others, are no more capital than a product consumed by its own producer is a commodity. If, with the mass of the population, that of the means of production employed in agriculture also diminished, the mass of the capital employed in agriculture increased, because a part of the means of production that were formerly scattered, was concentrated and turned into capital.

The total capital of Ireland outside agriculture, employed in industry and trade, accumulated during the last two decades slowly, and with great and constantly recurring fluctuations; so much the more rapidly did the concentration of its individual constituents develop. And, however small its absolute increase, in proportion to the dwindling population it had increased largely.

Here, then, under our own eyes and on a large scale, a process is revealed, than which nothing more excellent could be wished for by orthodox economy for the support of its dogma: that misery springs from absolute surplus population, and that equilibrium is re-established by depopulation. This is a far more important experiment than was the plague in the middle of the 14th century so belauded of Malthusians. Note further: If only the naïveté of the schoolmaster could apply, to the conditions of production and population of the nineteenth century, the standard of the 14th, this naïveté, into the bargain, overlooked the fact that whilst, after the plague and the decimation that accompanied it, followed on this side of the Channel, in England, enfranchisement and enrichment of the agricultural population, on that side, in France, followed greater servitude and more misery.[124]

The Irish famine of 1846 killed more than 1,000,000 people, but it killed poor devils only. To the wealth of the country it did not the slightest damage. The exodus of the next 20 years, an exodus still constantly increasing, did not, as, *e.g.*, the Thirty Years' War, decimate, along with the human beings, their means of production. Irish genius discovered an altogether new way of spiriting a poor people thousands of miles away from the scene of its misery. The exiles transplanted to the United States, send home sums of money every year as travelling expenses for those left behind. Every troop that emigrates one year, draws another after it the next. Thus, instead of costing Ireland anything, emigration forms one of the most lucrative branches of its export trade. Finally, it is a systematic process, which does not simply make a passing gap in the population, but sucks out of it every year more people than are replaced by the births, so that the absolute level of the population falls year by year.[125]

What were the consequences for the Irish labourers left behind and freed from the surplus population? That the relative surplus population is today as great as before 1846; that wages are just as low, that the oppression of the labourers has increased, that misery is forcing the country towards a new crisis. The facts are simple. The revolution in agriculture has kept pace with emigration. The production of relative surplus population has more than kept pace with the absolute depopulation. A glance at table C shows that the change of arable to pasture land must work yet more acutely in Ireland than in England. In England the cultivation of green crops increases with the breeding of cattle; in Ireland, it decreases. Whilst a large number of acres, that were formerly tilled, lie idle or are turned permanently into grass-land, a great part of the waste land and peat bogs that were unused formerly, become of service for the extension of cattle-breeding. The smaller and medium farmers—I reckon among these all who do not cultivate more than 100 acres—still make up about 8/10ths of the whole number.[126] They are one after the other, and with a degree of force unknown before, crushed by the competition of an agriculture managed by capital, and therefore they continually furnish new recruits to the class of wage labourers. The one great industry of Ireland, linen-manufacture, requires relatively few adult men and only employs altogether, in spite of its expansion since the price of cotton rose in 1861-1866, a comparatively insignificant part of the population. Like all other great modern industries, it constantly produces, by incessant fluctuations, a relative surplus population within its own sphere, even with an absolute increase in the mass of human beings absorbed by it. The misery of the agricultural population forms the pedestal for gigantic shirt-factories, whose armies of labourers are, for the most part, scattered over the country. Here, we encounter again the system described above of domestic industry, which in underpayment and overwork, possesses its own systematic means for creating supernumerary labourers. Finally, although the depopulation has not such destructive consequences as would result in a country with fully developed capitalistic production, it does not go on without constant reaction upon the home-market. The gap which emigration causes here, limits not only the local demand for labour, but also the incomes of small shopkeepers, artisans, tradespeople generally. Hence the diminution in incomes between £60 and £100 in Table E.

A clear statement of the condition of the agricultural labourers in Ireland is to be found in the Reports of the Irish Poor Law Inspectors (1870).[127] Officials of a government which is maintained only by bayonets and by a state of siege, now open, now disguised, they have to observe all the precautions of language that their colleagues in England disdain. In spite of this, however, they do not let their government cradle itself in illusions. According to them the rate of wages in the country, still very low, has within the last 20 years risen 50-60 per cent., and stands now, on the average, at 6s. to 9s. per week. But behind this apparent rise, is hidden an actual fall in wages, for it does not correspond at all to the rise in price of the necessary means of subsistence that has taken place in the meantime. For proof, the following extract from the official accounts of an Irish workhouse.

AVERAGE WEEKLY COST PER HEAD			
Year ended	*Provisions and Necessaries*	*Clothing.*	*Total*
29th Sept., 1849.	1s. 3 1/4d.	3d.	1s. 6 1/4d.
29th Sept., 1869.	2s. 7 1/4d.	6d.	3s. 1 1/4d.

The price of the necessary means of subsistence is therefore fully twice, and that of clothing exactly twice, as much as they were 20 years before.

Even apart from this disproportion, the mere comparison of the rate of wages expressed in gold would give a result far from accurate. Before the famine, the great mass of agricultural wages were paid in kind, only the smallest part in money; today, payment in money is the rule. From this it follows that, whatever the amount of the real wage, its money rate must rise.

> 'Previous to the famine, the labourer enjoyed his cabin ... with a rood, or half-acre or acre of land, and facilities for ... a crop of potatoes. He was able to rear his pig and keep fowl.... But they now have to buy bread, and they have no refuse upon which they can feed a pig or fowl, and they have consequently no benefit from the sale of a pig, fowl, or eggs.'[128]

In fact, formerly, the agricultural labourers were but the smallest of the small farmers, and formed for the most part a kind of rear-guard of the medium and large farms on which they found employment. Only since the catastrophe of 1846 have they begun to form a fraction of the class of purely wage labourers, a special class, connected with its wage-masters only by monetary relations.

We know what were the conditions of their dwellings in 1846. Since then they have grown yet worse. A part of the agricultural labourers, which, however, grows less day by day, dwells still on the holdings of the farmers in over-crowded huts, whose hideousness far surpasses the worst that the English agricultural labourers offered us in this way. And this holds generally with the exception of certain tracts of Ulster; in the south, in the counties of Cork, Limerick, Kilkenny, &c.; in the east, in Wicklow, Wexford, &c.; in the centre of Ireland, in King's and Queen's County, Dublin, &c.; in the west, in Sligo, Roscommon, Mayo, Galway, &c.

> 'The agricultural labourers' huts,' an inspector cries out, 'are a disgrace to the Christianity and to the civilisation of this country.'[129]

In order to increase the attractions of these holes for the labourers, the pieces of land belonging thereto from time immemorial, are systematically confiscated.

> 'The mere sense that they exist subject to this species of ban, on the part of the landlords and their agents, has ... given birth in the minds of the labourers to corresponding sentiments of antagonism and dissatisfaction towards those by whom they are thus led to regard themselves as being treated as ... a proscribed race.'[130]

The first act of the agricultural revolution was to sweep away the huts situated on the field of labour. This was done on the largest scale, and as if in obedience to a command from on high. Thus many labourers were compelled to seek shelter in villages and towns. There they were thrown like refuse into garrets, holes, cellars and corners, in the worst back slums. Thousands of Irish families, who according to the testimony of the English, eaten up as these are with national prejudice, are notable for their rare attachment to the domestic hearth, for their gaiety and the purity of their home-life, found themselves suddenly transplanted into hotbeds of vice. The men are now obliged to seek work of the neighbouring farmers and are only hired by the day, and therefore under the most precarious form of wage. Hence 'they sometimes have long distances to go to and from work, often get wet, and suffer much hardship, not unfrequently ending in sickness, disease and want.'[131]

'The towns have had to receive from year to year what was deemed to be the surplus-labour of the rural division;'[132] and then people still wonder 'there is still a surplus of labour in the towns and villages, and either a scarcity or a threatened scarcity in some of the country divisions.'[133] The truth is that this want only becomes perceptible 'in harvest-time, or during spring, or at such times as agricultural operations are carried on with activity; at other periods of the year many hands are idle;'[134] that 'from the digging out of the main crop of potatoes in October until the early spring following ... there is no employment for them;'[135] and further, that during the active times they 'are subject to broken days and to all kinds of interruptions.'[136]

These results of the agricultural revolution—*i.e.*, the change of arable into pasture land, the use of machinery, the most rigorous economy of labour, &c., are still further aggravated by the model landlords, who, instead of spending their rents in other countries, condescend to live in Ireland on their demesnes. In order that the law of supply and demand may not be broken, these gentlemen draw their

> 'labour-supply ... chiefly from their small tenants, who are obliged to attend when required to do the landlord's work, at rates of wages, in many instances, considerably under the current rates paid to ordinary labourers, and without regard to the inconvenience or loss to the tenant of being obliged to neglect his own business at critical periods of sowing or reaping.'[137]

The uncertainty and irregularity of employment, the constant return and long duration of gluts of labour, all these symptoms of a relative surplus population, figure therefore in the reports of the Poor Law administration, as so many hardships of the agricultural proletariat. It will be remembered that we met, in the English agricultural proletariat, with a similar spectacle. But the difference is that in England, an industrial country, the industrial reserve recruits itself from the country districts, whilst in Ireland, an agricultural country, the agricultural reserve recruits itself from the towns, the cities of refuge of the expelled agricultural labourers. In the former, the supernumeraries of agriculture are transformed into factory operatives; in the latter, those forced into the towns, whilst at the same time they press on the wages in towns, remain agricultural labourers, and are constantly sent back to the country districts in search of work.

The official inspectors sum up the material condition of the agricultural labourer as follows:

> 'Though living with the strictest frugality, his own wages are barely sufficient to provide food for an ordinary family and pay his rent' and he depends upon other sources for the means of clothing himself, his wife, and children.... The atmosphere of these cabins, combined with the other privations they are subjected to, has made this class particularly susceptible to low fever and pulmonary consumption.'[138]

After this, it is no wonder that, according to the unanimous testimony of the inspectors, a sombre discontent runs through the ranks of this class, that they long for the return of the past, loathe the present, despair of the future, give themselves up 'to the evil influence of agitators,' and have only one fixed idea, to emigrate to America. This is the land of Cockaigne, into which the great Malthusian panacea, depopulation, has transformed green Erin.

What a happy life the Irish factory operative leads one example will show:

> 'On my recent visit to the North of Ireland,' says the English Factory Inspector, Robert Baker, 'I met with the following evidence of effort in an Irish skilled workman

to afford education to his children; and I give his evidence verbatim, as I took it from his mouth. That he was a skilled factory hand, may be understood when I say that he was employed on goods for the Manchester market. 'Johnson.—I am a beetler and work from 6 in the morning till 11 at night, from Monday to Friday. Saturday we leave off at 6 p. m., and get three hours of it (for meals and rest). I have five children in all. For this work I get 10s. 6d. a week; my wife works here also, and gets 5s. a week. The oldest girl who is 12, minds the house. She is also cook, and all the servant we have. She gets the young ones ready for school. A girl going past the house wakes me at half past five in the morning. My wife gets up and goes along with me. We get nothing (to eat) before we come to work. The child of 12 takes care of the little children all the day, and we get nothing till breakfast at eight. At eight we go home. We get tea once a week; at other times we get stirabout, sometimes of oat-meal, sometimes of Indian meal, as we are able to get it. In the winter we get a little sugar and water to our Indian meal. In the summer we get a few potatoes, planting a small patch ourselves; and when they are done we get back to stirabout. Sometimes we get a little milk as it may be. So we go on from day to day, Sunday and week day, always the same the year round. I am always very much tired when I have done at night. We may see a bit of flesh meat sometimes, but very seldom. Three of our children attend school, for whom we pay 1d. a week a head. Our rent is 9d. a week. Peat for firing costs 1s. 6d. a fortnight at the very lowest."[139]

Such are Irish wages, such is Irish life!

In fact the misery of Ireland is again the topic of the day in England. At the end of 1866 and the beginning of 1867, one of the Irish land magnates, Lord Dufferin, set about its solution in *The Times*. 'Wie menschlich von solch grossem Herrn!'

From Table E. we saw that, during 1864, of £4,368,610 of total profits, three surplus-value makers pocketed only £262,819; that in 1865, however, out of £4,669,979 total profits, the same three virtuosi of 'abstinence' pocketed £274,528; in 1864, 26 surplus-value makers reached to £646,377; in 1865, 28 surplus-value makers reached to £736,448; in 1864, 121 surplus-value makers, £1,076,912; in 1865, 150 surplus-value makers, £1,320,906; in 1864, 1,131 surplus-value makers £2,150,818, nearly half of the total annual profit; in 1865, 1,194 surplus-value makers, £2,418,833, more than half of the total annual profit. But the lion's share, which an inconceivably small number of land magnates in England, Scotland and Ireland swallow up of the yearly national rental, is so monstrous that the wisdom of the English State does not think fit to afford the same statistical materials about the distribution of rents as about the distribution of profits. Lord Dufferin is one of those land magnates. That rent-rolls and profits can ever be 'excessive,' or that their plethora is in any way connected with plethora of the people's misery is, of course, an idea as 'disreputable' as 'unsound.' He keeps to facts. The fact is that, as the Irish population diminishes, the Irish rent-rolls swell; that depopulation benefits the landlords, therefore also benefits the soil, and, therefore, the people, that mere accessory of the soil. He declares, therefore, that Ireland is still over-populated, and the stream of emigration still flows too lazily. To be perfectly happy, Ireland must get rid of at least one-third of a million of labouring men. Let no man imagine that this lord, poetic into the bargain, is a physician of the school of Sangrado, who as often as he did not find his patient better, ordered phlebotomy and again phlebotomy, until the patient lost his sickness at the same time as his blood. Lord Dufferin demands a new blood-letting of one-third of a million only, instead of about two millions; in fact, without the getting rid of these, the millennium in Erin is not to be. The proof is easily given.

NUMBER AND EXTENT OF FARMS IN IRELAND IN 1864[140]

	No.	*Acres*
(1) Farms not over 1 acre.	48,653	25,394
(2) Farms over 1, not over 5 acres.	82,037	288,916
(3) Farms over 5, not over 15 acres.	176,368	1,836,310
(4) Farms over 15, not over 30 acres.	136,578	3,051,343
(5) Farms over 30, not over 50 acres.	71,961	2,906,274
(6) Farms over 50, not over 100 acres.	54,247	3,983,880
(7) Farms over 100 acres.	31,927	8,227,807
(8) TOTAL AREA.	—	26,319,924

Centralisation has, from 1851 to 1861, destroyed principally farms of the first three categories, under 1 and not over 15 acres. These above all must disappear. This gives 307,058 'supernumerary' farmers, and reckoning the families the low average of 4 persons, 1,228,232 persons. On the extravagant supposition that, after the agricultural revolution is complete one-fourth of these are again absorbable, there remain for emigration 921,174 persons. Categories 4, 5, 6, of over 15 and not over 100 acres, are, as was known long since in England, too small for capitalistic cultivation of corn, and for sheep-breeding are almost vanishing quantities. On the same supposition as before, therefore, there are further 788,761 persons to emigrate; total, 1,709,532. And as l'appétit vient en mangeant, Rentroll's eyes will soon discover that Ireland, with 3½ millions, is still always miserable, and miserable because she is overpopulated. Therefore her depopulation must go yet further, that thus she may fulfil her true destiny, that of an English sheep-walk and cattle-pasture.'[141]

Like all good things in this bad world, this profitable method has its drawbacks. With the accumulation of rents in Ireland, the accumulation of the Irish in America keeps pace. The Irishman, banished by sheep and ox, re-appears on the other side of the ocean as a Fenian, and face to face with the old queen of the seas rises, threatening and more threatening, the young giant Republic:

> *Acerba fata Romanos agunt Scelusque fraternae necis.*
> [A cruel fate torments the Romans, and the crime of fratricide]

Notes

1. Karl Marx, l. c., 'A égalité d'oppression des masses, plus un pays a de prolétaires et plus il est riche.' (Colins, 'L'Economie Politique. Source des Révolutions et des Utopies, prétendues Socialistes.' Paris, 1857, t. III., p. 331.) Our 'prolétarian' is economically none other than the wage labourer, who produces and increases capital, and is thrown out on the streets, as soon as he is superfluous for the needs of aggrandisement of 'Monsieur capital,' as Pecqueur calls this person. 'The sickly proletarian of the primitive forest,' is a pretty Roscherian fancy. The primitive forester is owner of the primitive forest, and uses the primitive forest as his property with the freedom of an orang-outang. He is not, therefore, a proletarian. This would only be the case, if the primitive forest exploited him, instead of being exploited by him. As far as his health is concerned, such a man would well bear comparison, not only with the modern proletarian, but also with the syphilitic and scrofulous upper classes. But, no doubt, Herr Wilhelm Roscher, by 'primitive forest' means his native heath of Lüneburg.
2. John Bellers, l. c., p. 2.
3. Bernard de Mandeville: 'The Fable of the Bees,' 5th edition, London, 1728. Remarks, pp. 212, 213, 328. 'Temperate living and constant employment is the direct road, for the poor, to

rational happiness' [by which he most probably means long working-days and little means of subsistence], 'and to riches and strength for the state' (*viz.*, for the landlords, capitalists, and their political dignitaries and agents). ('An Essay on Trade and Commerce,' London, 1770, p. 54.)

4. Eden should have asked, whose creatures then are 'the civil institutions»? From his standpoint of juridical illusion, he does not regard the law as a product of the material relations of production, but conversely the relations of production as products of the law. Linguet overthrew Montesquieu's illusory 'Esprit des lois' with one word: ' L'esprit des lois, c'est la propriété.' [The spirit of laws is property]
5. Eden, l. c., Vol. 1, book I., chapter 1, pp. 1, 2, and preface, p. xx.
6. If the reader reminds me of Malthus, whose 'Essay on Population' appeared in 1798, I remind him that this work in its first form is nothing more than a schoolboyish, superficial plagiary of De Foe, Sir James Steuart, Townsend, Franklin, Wallace, &c., and does not contain a single sentence thought out by himself. The great sensation this pamphlet caused, was due solely to party interest. The French Revolution had found passionate defenders in the United Kingdom; the 'principle of population,' slowly worked out in the eighteenth century, and then, in the midst of a great social crisis, proclaimed with drums and trumpets as the infallible antidote to the teachings of Condorcet, &c., was greeted with jubilance by the English oligarchy as the great destroyer of all hankerings after human development. Malthus, hugely astonished at his success, gave himself to stuffing into his book materials superficially compiled, and adding to it new matter, not discovered but annexed by him. Note further: Although Malthus was a parson of the English State Church, he had taken the monastic vow of celibacy—one of the conditions of holding a Fellowship in Protestant Cambridge University: 'Socios collegiorum maritos esse non permittimus, sed statim postquam quis uxorem duxerit socius collegii desinat esse.' ('Reports of Cambridge University Commission,' p. 172.) This circumstance favourably distinguishes Malthus from the other Protestant parsons, who have shuffled off the command enjoining celibacy of the priesthood and have taken, 'Be fruitful and multiply,' as their special Biblical mission in such a degree that they generally contribute to the increase of population to a really unbecoming extent, whilst they preach at the same time to the labourers the 'principle of population.' It is characteristic that the economic fall of man, the Adam's apple, the urgent appetite, 'the checks which tend to blunt the shafts of Cupid,' as Parson Townsend waggishly puts it, that this delicate question was and is monopolised by the Reverends of Protestant Theology, or rather of the Protestant Church. With the exception of the Venetian monk, Ortes, an original and clever writer, most of the population theory teachers are Protestant parsons. For instance, Bruckner, 'Théorie du Système animal,' Leyde, 1767, in which the whole subject of the modern population theory is exhausted, and to which the passing quarrel between Quesnay and his pupil, the elder Mirabeau, furnished ideas on the same topic; then Parson Wallace, Parson Townsend, Parson Malthus and his pupil, the arch-Parson Thomas Chalmers, to say nothing of lesser reverend scribblers in this line. Originally, Political Economy was studied by philosophers like Hobbes, Locke, Hume; by businessmen and statesmen, like Thomas More, Temple, Sully, De Witt, North, Law, Vanderlint, Cantillon, Franklin; and especially, and with the greatest success, by medical men like Petty, Barbon, Mandeville, Quesnay. Even in the middle of the eighteenth century, the Rev. Mr Tucker, a notable economist of his time, excused himself for meddling with the things of Mammon. Later on, and in truth with this very 'Principle of population,' struck the hour of the Protestant parsons. Petty, who regarded the population as the basis of wealth, and was, like Adam Smith, an outspoken foe to parsons, says, as if he had a presentiment of their bungling interference, 'that Religion best flourishes when the Priests are most mortified, as was before said of the Law, which best flourisheth when lawyers have least to do.' He advises the Protestant priests, therefore, if they, once for all, will not follow the Apostle Paul and 'mortify' themselves by celibacy, 'not to breed more Churchmen than

the Benefices, as they now stand shared out, will receive, that is to say, if there be places for about twelve thousand in England and Wales, it will not be safe to breed up 24,000 ministers, for then the twelve thousand which are unprovided for, will seek ways how to get themselves a livelihood, which they cannot do more easily than by persuading the people that the twelve thousand incumbents do poison or starve their souls, and misguide them in their way to Heaven.' (Petty: 'A Treatise of Taxes and Contributions,' London, 1667, p. 57.) Adam Smith's position with the Protestant priesthood of his time is shown by the following. In 'A Letter to A. Smith, L.L.D. On the Life, Death, and Philosophy of his Friend, David Hume. By one of the People called Christians,' 4th Edition, Oxford, 1784, Dr Horne, Bishop of Norwich, reproves Adam Smith, because in a published letter to Mr Strahan, he 'embalmed his friend David' (sc. Hume); because he told the world how 'Hume amused himself on his deathbed with Lucian and Whist,' and because he even had the impudence to write of Hume: 'I have always considered him, both in his life-time and since his death, as approaching as nearly to the idea of a perfectly wise and virtuous man, as, perhaps, the nature of human frailty will permit.' The bishop cries out, in a passion: 'Is it right in you, Sir, to hold up to our view as 'perfectly wise and virtuous,' the *character* and *conduct* of one, who seems to have been possessed with an incurable antipathy to all that is called *Religion;* and who strained every nerve to explode, suppress and extirpate the spirit of it among men, that its very name, if he could effect it, might no more be had in remembrance?' (l. c., p. 8.) 'But let not the lovers of truth be discouraged. Atheism cannot be of long continuance.' (P. 17.) Adam Smith, 'had the atrocious wickedness to propagate atheism through the land (viz., by his 'Theory of Moral Sentiments'). Upon the whole, Doctor, your meaning is good; but I think you will not succeed this time. You would persuade us, by the example of *David Hume, Esq.*, that atheism is the only cordial for low spirits, and the proper antidote against the fear of death.... You may smile over *Babylon* in ruins and congratulate the hardened *Pharaoh* on his overthrow in the Red Sea.' (l. c., pp. 21, 22.) One orthodox individual, amongst Adam Smith's college friends, writes after his death: 'Smith's well-placed affection for Hume ... hindered him from being a Christian.... When he met with honest men whom he liked ... he would believe almost anything they said. Had he been a friend of the worthy ingenious Horrox he would have believed that the moon some times disappeared in a clear sky without the interposition of a cloud.... He approached to republicanism in his political principles.' ('The Bee.' By James Anderson, 18 Vols., Vol. 3, pp. 166, 165, Edinburgh, 1791-93.) Parson Thomas Chalmers has his suspicions as to Adam Smith having invented the category of 'unproductive labourers,' solely for the Protestant parsons, in spite of their blessed work in the vineyard of the Lord.

7. 'The limit, however, to the employment of both the operative and the labourer is the same; namely, the possibility of the employer realising a *profit* on the produce of their industry. If the rate of wages is such as to reduce the master's gains below the average profit of capital, he will cease to employ them, or he will only employ them on condition of submission to a reduction of wages.' (John Wade, l. c., p. 241.)
8. Note by the Institute of Marxism-Leninism to the Russian edition: The MS in the first case says 'little' and in the second case 'much'; the correction has been introduced according to the authorised French translation.
9. Cf. Karl Marx: 'Zur Kritik der Politischen Oekonomie,' pp. 166, seq.
10. 'If we now return to our first inquiry, wherein it was shown that capital itself is only the result of human labour... it seems quite incomprehensible that man can have fallen under the domination of capital, his own product; can be subordinated to it; and as in reality this is beyond dispute the case, involuntarily the question arises: How has the labourer been able to pass from being master of capital—as its creator—to being its slave?' (Von Thünen, 'Der isolierte Staat' Part ii., Section ii., Rostock, 1863, pp. 5, 6.) It is Thünen's merit to have asked this question. His answer is simply childish.
11. From Adam Smith, *Enquiry into the Nature of....*, Volume I.

12. *Note in the 4th German edition.*—The latest English and American 'trusts' are already striving to attain this goal by attempting to unite at least all the large-scale concerns in one branch of industry into one great joint-stock company with a practical monopoly. *F. E.*

13. *Note in the 3rd German edition.*—In Marx's copy there is here the marginal note: 'Here note for working out later; if the extension is only quantitative, then for a greater and a smaller capital in the same branch of business the profits are as the magnitudes of the capitals advanced. If the quantitative extension induces qualitative change, then the rate of profit on the larger capital rises simultaneously.' *F. E.*

14. The census of England and Wales shows: all persons employed in agriculture (landlords, farmers, gardeners, shepherds, &c., included): 1851, 2,011,447; 1861, 1,924,110. Fall, 87,337. Worsted manufacture: 1851, 102,714 persons; 1861, 79,242. Silk weaving: 1851, 111,940; 1861, 101,678. Calico-printing: 1851, 12,098; 1861, 12,556. A small rise that, in the face of the enormous extension of this industry and implying a great fall proportionally in the number of labourers employed. Hat-making: 1851, 15,957; 1861, 13,814. Straw-hat and bonnet-making: 1851, 20,393; 1861, 18,176. Malting: 1851, 10,566; 1861, 10,677. Chandlery, 1851, 4,949; 1861, 4,686. This fall is due, besides other causes, to the increase in lighting by gas. Comb-making: 1851, 2,038; 1861, 1,478. Sawyers: 1851, 30,552; 1861, 31,647—a small rise in consequence of the increase of sawing-machines. Nail-making: 1851, 26,940; 1861, 26,130—fall in consequence of the competition of machinery. Tin and copper-mining: 1851, 31,360; 1861, 32,041. On the other hand: Cotton-spinning and weaving: 1851, 371,777; 1861, 456,646. Coal-mining: 1851, 183,389, 1861, 246,613, 'The increase of labourers is generally greatest, since 1851, in such branches of industry in which machinery has not up to the present been employed with success.' (Census of England and Wales for 1861. Vol. III. London, 1863, p. 36.)

15. *Added in the 4th German edition.*—The law of progressive diminution of the relative magnitude of variable capital and its effect on the condition of the class of wage workers is conjectured rather than understood by some of the prominent economists of the classical school. The greatest service was rendered here by John Barton, although he, like all the rest, lumps together constant and fixed capital, variable and circulating capital. He says:

> 'The demand for labour depends on the increase of circulating, and not of fixed capital. Were it true that the proportion between these two sorts of capital is the same at all times, and in all circumstances, then, indeed, it follows that the number of labourers employed is in proportion to the wealth of the state. But such a proposition has not the semblance of probability. As arts are cultivated, and civilisation is extended, fixed capital bears a larger and larger proportion to circulating capital. The amount of fixed capital employed in the production of a piece of British muslin is at least a hundred, probably a thousand times greater than that employed in a similar piece of Indian muslin. And the proportion of circulating capital is a hundred or thousand times less ... the whole of the annual savings, added to the fixed capital, would have no effect in increasing the demand for labour.' (John Barton, 'Observations on the Circumstances which Influence the Condition of the Labouring Classes of Society.' London, 1817, pp. 16, 17.) 'The same cause which may increase the net revenue of the country may at the same time render the population redundant, and deteriorate the condition of the labourer.' (Ricardo, l. c., p. 469.) With increase of capital, 'the demand [for labour] will be in a diminishing ratio.' (Ibid., p. 480, Note.) 'The amount of capital devoted to the maintenance of labour may vary, independently of any changes in the whole amount of capital.... Great fluctuations in the amount of employment, and great suffering may become more frequent as capital itself becomes more plentiful.' (Richard Jones, 'An Introductory Lecture on Pol. Econ.,' Lond. 1833, p. 13) 'Demand [for labour] will rise ... not in proportion to the accumulation of the general capital. ... Every augmentation, therefore, in the national

stock destined for reproduction, comes, in the progress of society, to have less and less influence upon the condition of the labourer.' (Ramsay, l. c., pp. 90, 91.)

16. H. Merivale. 'Lectures on Colonisation and Colonies,' 1841, Vol. I , p. 146.
17. Malthus, 'Principles of Political Economy,' pp. 215, 319, 320. In this work, Malthus finally discovers, with the help of Sismondi, the beautiful Trinity of capitalistic production: over-production, over-population, over-consumption—three very delicate monsters, indeed. Cf. F. Engels, 'Umrisse zu einer Kritik der Nationalökonomie,' l. c., p, 107, et seq.
18. Harriet Martineau, 'A Manchester Strike,' 1832, p. 101.
19. Even in the cotton famine of 1863 we find, in a pamphlet of the operative cotton-spinners of Blackburn, fierce denunciations of overwork, which, in consequence of the Factory Acts, of course only affected adult male labourers. 'The adult operatives at this mill have been asked to work from 12 to 13 hours per day, while there are hundreds who are compelled to be idle who would willingly work partial time, in order to maintain their families and save their brethren from a premature grave through being overworked.... We,' it goes on to say, 'would ask if the practice of working overtime by a number of hands, is likely to create a good feeling between masters and servants. Those who are worked overtime feel the injustice equally with those who are condemned to forced idleness. There is in the district almost sufficient work to give to all partial employment if fairly distributed. We are only asking what is right in requesting the masters generally to pursue a system of short hours, particularly until a better state of things begins to dawn upon us, rather than to work a portion of the hands overtime, while others, for want of work, are compelled to exist upon charity.' ('Reports of Insp. of Fact., Oct. 31, 1863,' p. 8.) The author of the 'Essay on Trade and Commerce' grasps the effect of a relative surplus population on the employed labourers with his usual unerring bourgeois instinct. 'Another cause of idleness in this kingdom is the want of a sufficient number of labouring hands .... Whenever from an extraordinary demand for manufactures, labour grows scarce, the labourers feel their own consequence, and will make their masters feel it likewise—it is amazing; but so depraved are the dispositions of these people, that in such cases a set of workmen have combined to distress the employer by idling a whole day together.' ('Essay, &c.,' pp. 27, 28.) The fellows in fact were hankering after a rise in wages.
20. *Economist*, Jan. 21. 1860.
21. Whilst during the last six months of 1866, 80-90,000 working people in London were thrown out of work, the Factory Report for that same half year says: 'It does not appear absolutely true to say that demand will always produce supply just at the moment when it is needed. It has not done so with labour, for much machinery has been idle last year for want of hands.' ('Rep. of Insp. of Fact., 31st Oct., 1866,' p. 81.)
22. Opening address to the Sanitary Conference, Birmingham, January 15th, 1875, by J. Chamberlain, Mayor of the town, now (1883) President of the Board of Trade.
23. 781 towns given in the census for 1861 for England and Wales 'contained 10,960,998 inhabitants, while the villages and country parishes contained 9,105,226. In 1851, 580 towns were distinguished, and the population in them and in the surrounding country was nearly equal. But, while in the subsequent ten years the population in the villages and the country increased half a million, the population in the 580 towns increased by a million and a half (1,554,067). The increase of the population of the country parishes is 6.5 per cent., and of the towns 17.3 per cent. The difference in the rates of increase is due to the migration from country to town. Three-fourths of the total increase of population has taken place in the towns.' ('Census. &c.,' pp. 11 and 12.)
24. 'Poverty seems favourable to generation.' (A. Smith.) This is even a specially wise arrangement of God, according to the gallant and witty Abbé Galiani 'Iddio af che gli uomini che esercitano mestieri di prima utilità nascono abbondantemente.' (Galiani, l. c., p. 78.) [God ordains that men who carry on trades of primary utility are born in abundance]

'Misery up to the extreme point of famine and pestilence, instead of checking, tends to increase population.' (S. Laing, 'National Distress,' 1844, p. 69.) After Laing has illustrated this by statistics, he continues: 'If the people were all in easy circumstances, the world would soon be depopulated.'

25. 'De jour en jour il devient donc plus clair que les rapports de production dans lesquels se meut la bourgeoisie n'ont pas un caractère un, un caractère simple, mais un caractère de duplicité; que dans les mêmes rapports dans lesquels se produit la richesse, la misère se produit aussi; que dans les mêmes rapports dans lesquels il y a développement des forces productives, il y a une force productive de répression; que ces rapports ne produisent la richesse bourgeoise, c'est-à-dire la richesse de la classe bourgeoise, qu'en anéantissant continuellement la richesse des membres intégrants de cette classe et en produisant un prolétariat toujours croissant.' [From day to day it thus becomes clearer that the production relations in which the bourgeoisie moves have not a simple, uniform character, but a dual character; that in the selfsame relations in which wealth is produced, poverty is produced also; that in the selfsame relations in which there is a development of productive forces, there is also a force producing repression; that there relations produce bourgeois wealth, i.e., the wealth of the bourgeois class, only by continually annihilating the wealth of the individual members of this class and by producing an evergrowing proletariat] (Karl Marx: 'Misère de la Philosophie,' p. 116.)

26. G. Ortes: 'Delia Economia Nazionale libri sei, 1777,' in Custodi, Parte Moderna, t. xxi, pp. 6, 9, 22, 25, etc. Ortes says, l. c., p. 32: 'In luoco di progettar sistemi inutili per la felicità de'popoli, mi limiterò a investigare la regione della loro infelicità.' [Instead of projecting useless systems for achieving the happiness of people, I shall limit myself to investigating the reasons for their unhappiness]

27. 'A Dissertation on the Poor Laws. By a Well-wisher of Mankind. (The Rev. J. Townsend) 1786,' republished Lond. 1817, pp. 15, 39, 41. This 'delicate' parson, from whose work just quoted, as well as from his 'Journey through Spain,' Malthus often copies whole pages, himself borrowed the greater part of his doctrine from Sir James Steuart, whom he however alters in the borrowing. *E.g.*, when Steuart says: 'Here, in slavery, was a forcible method of making mankind diligent,' [for the non-workers] ... 'Men were then forced to work' [*i.e.*,to work gratis for others], 'because they were slaves of others; men are now forced to work' [*i.e.*, to work gratis for non-workers] 'because they are the slaves of their necessities,' he does not thence conclude, like the fat holder of benefices, that the wage labourer must always go fasting. He wishes, on the contrary, to increase their wants and to make the increasing number of their wants a stimulus to their labour for the 'more delicate.'

28. Storch, l. c., t. iii, p. 223.

29. Sismondi, l. c., pp. 79, 80, 85.

30. Destutt de Tracy, l. c., p. 231: 'Les nations pauvres, c'est là où le peuple est à son aise; et les nations riches, c'est là où il est ordinairement pauvre.' [The poor nations are those where the people are comfortably off; and the rich nations, those where the people are generally poor]

31. 'Tenth Report of the Commissioners of H. M. Inland Revenue.' Lond., 1866. p. 38.

32. lbidem.

33. These figures are sufficient for comparison, but, taken absolutely, are false, since, perhaps, £100,000,000 of income are annually not declared. The complaints of the Inland Revenue Commissioners of systematic fraud, especially on the part of the commercial and industrial classes, are repeated in each of their reports. So *e.g.*, 'A Joint-stock company returns £6,000 as assessable profits, the surveyor raises the amount to £88,000, and upon that sum duty is ultimately paid. Another company which returns £190,000 is finally compelled to admit that the true return should be £250,000.' (Ibid., p, 42.)

34. 'Census, &c.,' l. c., p. 29. John Bright's assertion that 150 landlords own half of England, and 12 half the Scotch soil, has never been refuted.

35. 'Fourth Report, &c., of Inland Revenue.' Lond., 1860, p. 17.
36. These are the net incomes after certain legally authorised abatements.
37. At this moment, March, 1867, the Indian and Chinese market is again overstocked by the consignments of the British cotton manufacturers. In 1866, a reduction in wages of 5 per cent. took place amongst the cotton operatives. In 1867, as consequence of a similar operation, there was a strike of 20,000 men at Preston. *[Added in the 4th German* edition.—That was the prelude to the crisis which broke out immediately afterwards.—*F. E.]*
38. 'Census, &C.,' l. c., P. 11.
39. Gladstone in the House of Commons, Feb. 13th, 1843. *Times,* Feb. 14th, 1843—'It is one of the most melancholy features in the social state of this country that we see, beyond the possibility of denial, that while there is at this moment a decrease in the consuming powers of the people, an increase of the pressure of privations and distress; there is at the same time a constant accumulation of wealth in the upper classes, an increase of the luxuriousness of their habits, and of their means of enjoyment.' (Hansard, 13th Feb.)
40. Gladstone in the House of Commons, April 16th, 1863. *Morning Star,* April 17th.
41. See the official accounts in the Blue book: 'Miscellaneous Statistics of the United Kingdom,' Part vi., London, 1866, pp. 260-273, passim. Instead of the statistics of orphan asylums, &c., the declamations of the ministerial journals in recommending dowries for the Royal children might also serve. The greater dearness of the means of subsistence is never forgotten there.
42. Gladstone, House of Commons, 7th April, 1864.—'The Hansard version runs: 'Again, and yet more at large—what is human life, but, in the majority of cases, a struggle for existence.' The continual crying contradictions in Gladstone's Budget speeches of 1863 and 1864 were characterised by an English writer by the following quotation from Boileau:

'Voilà l'homme en effet. Il va du blanc au noir,
Il condamne au matin ses sentiments du soir.
Importun à tout autre, à soi-même incommode,
Il change à tout moment d'esprit comme de mode.'
[Such is the man: he goes from black to white. / He condemns in the morning what he felt in the evening. / A nuisance to everyone else, and an inconvenience to himself, / he changes his way of thinking as easily as he changes his way of dressing]
('The Theory of Exchanges, &c.,' London, 1864, p. 135.)

43. H. Fawcett, l. c., pp. 67-82. As to the increasing dependence of labourers on the retail shopkeepers, this is the consequence of the frequent oscillations and interruptions of their employment.
44. Wales here is always included in England.
45. A peculiar light is thrown on the advance made since the time of Adam Smith, by the fact that by him the word 'workhouse' is still occasionally used as synonymous with 'manufactory'; *e.g.*, the opening of his chapter on the division of labour; 'those employed in every different branch of the work can often be collected into the same workhouse.'
46. 'Public Health. Sixth Report, 1864,' p. 13.
47. l. c., p. 17.
48. l. c., p. 13.
49. l. c., Appendix, p. 232.
50. l. c., pp. 232, 233.
51. l. c., pp. 14, 15.
52. 'In no particular have the rights of *persons* been so avowedly and shamefully sacrificed to the rights of *property* as in regard to the lodging of the labouring class. Every large town may be looked upon as a place of human sacrifice, a shrine where thousands pass yearly through the fire as offerings to the moloch of avarice,' S. Laing, l. c., p. 150.
53. 'Public Health, Eighth Report. 1866.' p. 14, note.

54. l. c., p. 89. With reference to the children in these colonies, Dr Hunter says: 'People are not now alive to tell us how children were brought up before this age of dense agglomerations of poor began, and he would be a rash prophet who should tell us what future behaviour is to be expected from the present growth of children, who, under circumstances probably never before paralleled in this country, are now completing their education for future practice, as 'dangerous classes' by sitting up half the night with persons of every age, half naked, drunken, obscene, and quarrelsome.' (l. c., p. 56.)
55. l. c., p. 62.
56. 'Report of the Officer of Health of St. Martins-in-the-Fields, 1865.'
57. 'Public Health, Eighth Report, 1866,' p. 91.
58. l. c., p. 88.
59. l. c., p. 88.
60. l. c., p. 89.
61. l. c., p. 55 and 56.
62. l. c., p. 149.
63. l. c., p. 50.
64.

COLLECTING AGENTS LIST (BRADFORD).		
	Houses	
Vulcan Street, No. 122	1 room	16 persons
Lumiev Street, No. 13	1 room	11 persons
Bower Street, No. 41	1 room	11 persons
Portland Street. No. 112	1 room	10 persons
Hardy Street, No. 17	1 room	10 persons
North Street, No. 18	1 room	16 persons
North Street, No. 17	1 room	13 persons
Wymer Street, No. 19	1 room	8 adults
Jowett Street, No. 56	1 room	12 persons
George Street, No. 150	1 room	3 families
Rifle Court Marygate, No. 11	1 room	11 persons
Marshall Street, No. 28	1 room	10 persons
Marshall Street, No. 49	1 room	3 families
George Street, No. 128	1 room	18 persons
George Street, No. 130	1 room	16 persons
Edward Street, No. 4	1 room	17 persons
George Street, No. 49	1 room	2 families
York Street, No. 34	1 room	2 families
Salt Pie Street (bottom)	2 room	26 persons
	Cellars	
Regent Square	1 cellar	8 persons
Acre Street	1 cellar	7 persons
33 Roberts Court	1 cellar	7 persons
Back Pratt Street used as a brazier's shop	1 cellar	7 persons
27 Ebenezer Street	1 cellar	6 persons
l. c.,	p. 111.	(no male above 18).

65. l. c., p. 114.
66. l. c., p. 50.
67. 'Public Health. Seventh Report. 1865,' p. 18.

68. l. c., p. 165.
69. l. c., p. 18, Note.—The Relieving Officer of the Chapel-en-le-Frith Union reported to the Registar-General as follows:—'At Doveholes, a number of small excavations have been made into a large hillock of lime ashes (the refuse of lime-kilns), and which are used as dwellings, and occupied by labourers and others employed in the construction of a railway now in course of construction through that neighbourhood. The excavations are small and damp, and have no drains or privies about them, and not the slightest means of ventilation except up a hole pulled through the top, and used for a chimney. In consequence of this defect, small-pox has been raging for some time, and some deaths [amongst the troglodytes] have been caused by it.' (l. c., note 2.)
70. The details given at the end of Part IV. refer especially to the labourers in coal mines. On the still worse condition in metal mines, see the very conscientious Report of the Royal Commission of 1864.
71. l. c., pp. 180, 182.
72. l. c., pp. 515, 517.
73. l. c., p. 16.
74. 'Wholesale starvation of the London Poor.... Within the last few days the walls of London have been placarded with large posters, bearing the following remarkable announcement:—'Fat oxen! Starving men! The fat oxen from their palace of glass have gone to feed the rich in their luxurious abode, while the starving men are left to rot and die in their wretched dens.' The placards bearing these ominous words are put up at certain intervals. No sooner has one set been defaced or covered over, than a fresh set is placarded in the former, or some equally public place.... This ... reminds one of the secret revolutionary associations which prepared the French people for the events of 1789.... At this moment, while English workmen with their wives and children are dying of cold and hunger, there are millions of English gold—the produce of English labour—being invested in Russian, Spanish, Italian, and other foreign enterprises.' —*Reynolds' Newspaper,* January 20th, 1867.
75. James E. Thorold Rogers. (Prof. of Polit. Econ. in the University of Oxford.) 'A History of Agriculture and Prices in England.' Oxford, 1866, v. 1, p. 690. This work, the fruit of patient and diligent labour, contains in the two volumes that have so far appeared, only the period from 1259 to 1400. The second volume contains simply statistics. It is the first authentic 'History of Prices' of the time that we possess.
76. 'Reasons for the Late Increase of the Poor-Rates: or a comparative view of the prices of labour and provisions.' Lond., 1777, pp. 5, 11.
77. Dr Richard Price: 'Observations on Reversionary Payments,' 6th Ed. By W. Morgan, Lond., 1803, v. II., pp. 158, 159. Price remarks on p. 159: 'The nominal price of day-labour is at present no more than about four times, or, at most, five times higher than it was in the year 1514. But the price of corn is seven times, and of flesh-meat and raiment about fifteen times higher. So far, therefore, has the price of labour been even from advancing in proportion to the increase in the expenses of living, that it does not appear that it bears now half the proportion to those expenses that it did bear.'
78. Barton, l. c., p. 26. For the end of the 18th century cf. Eden, l. c.
79. Parry, l. c., p. 86.
80. id., p. 213.
81. S. Laing, l. c., p. 62.
82. 'England and America.' Lond., 1833, Vol. 1, p. 47.
83. The landed aristocracy advanced themselves to this end, of course per Parliament, funds from the State Treasury, at a very low rate of interest, which the farmers have to make good at a much higher rate.
84. London *Economist,* May 29th, 1845, p. 290.
85. The decrease of the middle-class farmers can be seen especially in the census category:

'Farmer's son, grandson, brother, nephew, daughter, granddaughter, sister, niece»; in a word, the members of his own family, employed by the farmer. This category numbered, in 1851, 216,851 persons; in 1861, only 176,151. From 1851 to 1871, the farms under 20 acres fell by more than 900 in number; those between 50 and 75 acres fell from 8,253 to 6,370; the same thing occurred with all other farms under 100 acres. On the other hand, during the same twenty years, the number of large farms increased; those of 300-500 acres rose from 7,771 to 8,410, those of more than 500 acres from 2,755 to 3,914, those of more than 1,000 acres from 492 to 582.

86. The number of shepherds increased from 12,517 to 25,559.
87. Census, l. c., p. 36.
88. Rogers, l. c., p. 693, p. 10. Mr Rogers belongs to the Liberal School, is a personal friend of Cobden and Bright, and therefore no *laudator temporis acti.*
89. 'Public Health. Seventh Report,' 1865, p. 242. It is therefore nothing unusual either for the landlord to raise a labourer's rent as soon as he hears that he is earning a little more, or for the farmer to lower the wage of the labourer, 'because his wife has found a trade,' l. c.
90. l. c., p. 135.
91. l. c., p. 134.
92. 'Report of the Commissioners ... relating to Transportation and Penal Servitude,' Lond., 1863, pp. 42, 50.
93. l. c., p. 77. 'Memorandum by the Lord Chief Justice.'
94. l. c., Vol. II, Minutes of Evidence.
95. l. c., Vol. 1. Appendix, p. 280.
96. l. c., pp. 274, 275.
97. 'Public Health, Sixth Report,' 1864, pp. 238, 249, 261, 262.
98. l. c., p. 262.
99. l. c., p. 17. The English agricultural labourer receives only 1/4 as much milk, and 1/2 as much bread as the Irish. Arthur Young in his 'Tour in Ireland,' at the beginning of this century, already noticed the better nourishment of the latter. The reason is simply this, that the poor Irish farmer is incomparably more humane than the rich English. As regards Wales, that which is said in the text holds only for the southwest. All the doctors there agree that the increase of the death-rate through tuberculosis, scrofula, etc., increases in intensity with the deterioration of the physical condition of the population, and all ascribe this deterioration to poverty. 'His (the farm labourer's) keep is reckoned at about five pence a day, but in many districts it was said to be of much less cost to the farmer' [himself very poor].... 'A morsel of the salt meat or bacon, ... salted and dried to the texture of mahogany, and hardly worth the difficult process of assimilation ... is used to flavour a large quantity of broth or gruel, of meal and leeks, and day after day this is the labourer's dinner.' The advance of industry resulted for him, in this harsh and damp climate, in 'the abandonment of the solid homespun clothing in favour of the cheap and so-called cotton goods,' and of stronger drinks for so-called tea. 'The agriculturist, after several hours' exposure to wind and rain, pins his cottage to sit by a fire of peat or of balls of clay and small coal kneaded together, from which volumes of carbonic and sulphurous acids are poured forth. His walls are of mud and stones, his floor the bare earth which was there before the hut was built, his roof a mass of loose and sodden thatch. Every crevice is topped to maintain warmth, and in an atmosphere of diabolic odour, with a mud floor, with his only clothes drying on his back, he often sups and sleeps with his wife and children. Obstetricians who have passed parts of the night in such cabins have described how they found their feet sinking in the mud of the floor, and they were forced (easy task) to drill a hole through the wall to effect a little private respiration. It was attested by numerous witnesses in various grades of life, that to these insanitary influences, and many more, the underfed peasant was nightly exposed, and of the result, a debilitated and scrofulous people, there was no want of evidence.... The statements of the relieving officers of Carmarthenshire

and Cardiganshire show in a striking way the same state of things. There is besides 'a plague more horrible still, the great number of idiots.' Now a word on the climatic conditions. 'A strong south-west wind blows over the whole country for 8 or 9 months in the year, bringing with it torrents of rain, which discharge principally upon the western slopes of the hills. Trees are rare, except in sheltered places, and where not protected, are blown out of all shape. The cottages generally crouch under some bank, or often in a ravine or quarry, and none but the smallest sheep and native cattle can live on the pastures.... The young people migrate to the eastern mining districts of Glamorgan and Monmouth. Carmarthenshire is the breeding ground of the mining population and their hospital. The population can therefore barely maintain its numbers.' Thus in Cardiganshire:

	1851	*1861*
Males	45,155	44,446
Females	52,459	52,955
	97,614	97,401

Dr Hunter's Report in 'Public Health, Seventh Report. 1865,' pp. 498-502, passim.

100. In 1865, this law was improved to some extent. It will soon be learnt from experience that tinkering of this sort is of no use.
101. In order to understand that which follows, we must remember that 'Close Villages' are those whose owners are one or two large landlords. 'Open villages,' those whose soil belongs to many smaller landlords. It is in the latter that building speculators can build cottages and lodging-houses.
102. A show-village of this kind looks very nice, but is as unreal as the villages that Catherine II. saw on her journey to the Crimea. In recent times the shepherd also has often been banished from these show-villages; *e.g.*, near Market Harboro is sheep-farm of about 500 acres, which only employs the labour of one man. To reduce the long trudges over these wide plains, the beautiful pastures of Leicester and Northampton, the shepherd used to get a cottage on the farm. Now they give him a thirteenth shilling a week for lodging, that he must find far away in an open village.
103. 'The labourers' houses (in the open villages, which, of course, are always overcrowded) are usually in rows, built with their backs against the extreme edge of the plot of land which the builder could call his, and on this account are not allowed light and air, except from the front.' (Dr Hunter's Report, l. c., p. 135.) Very often the beerseller or grocer of the village is at the same time the letter of its houses. In this case, the agricultural labourer finds in him a second master, besides the farmer. He must be his customer as well as his tenant. 'The hind with his 10s. a week, minus a rent of £4 a year ... is obliged to buy at the seller's own terms, his modicum of tea, sugar, flour, soap, candles, and beer.' (l. c., p. 132.) These open villages form, in fact, the 'penal settlements' of the English agricultural proletariat. Many of the cottages are simply lodging-houses, through which all the rabble of the neighbourhood passes. The country labourer and his family who had often, in a way truly wonderful, preserved, under the foulest conditions, a thoroughness and purity of character, go, in these, utterly to the devil. It is, of course, the fashion amongst the aristocratic shylocks to shrug their shoulders pharisaically at the building speculators, the small landlords, and the open villages. They know well enough that their 'close villages' and 'show-villages' are the birth-places of the open villages, and could not exist without them. 'The labourers ... were it not for the small owners, would, for by far the most part, have to sleep under the trees of the farms on which they work.' (l. c., p. 135.) The system of 'open' and 'closed' villages obtains in all the Midland counties and throughout the East of England.
104. 'The employer ... is ... directly or indirectly securing to himself the profit on a man employed at 10s. a week, and receiving from this poor hind £4 or £5 annual rent for houses not worth

£20 in a really free market, but maintained at their artificial value by the power of the owner to say 'Use my house, or go seek a hiring elsewhere without a character from me....' Does a man wish to better himself, to go as a plate-layer on the railway, or to begin quarry-work, the same power is ready with 'Work for me at this low rate of wages or begone at a week's notice; take your pig with you, and get what you can for the potatoes growing in your garden.' Should his interest appear to be better served by it, an enhanced rent is sometimes preferred in these cases by the owner (*i.e.*, the farmer) as the penalty for leaving his service.' (Dr Hunter, l. c., p. 132.)

105. 'New married couples are no edifying study for grown-up brothers and sisters: and though instances must not be recorded, sufficient data are remembered to warrant the remark, that great depression and sometimes death are the lot of the female participator in the offence of incest.' (Dr Hunter, l. c., p. 137.) A member of the rural police who had for many years been a detective in the worst quarters of London, says of the girls of his village: 'their boldness and shamelessness I never saw equalled during some years of police life and detective duty in the worst parts of London .... They live like pigs, great boys and girls, mothers and fathers, all sleeping in one room, in many instances.' ('Child. Empl. Com. Sixth Report, 1867,' p. 77 sq. 155.)

106. 'Public Health. Seventh Report, 1865,' pp. 9, 14 passim.

107. 'The heaven-born employment of the hind gives dignity even to his position. He is not a slave, but a soldier of peace, and deserves his place in married men's quarters to be provided by the landlord, who has claimed a power of enforced labour similar to that the country demands of the soldier. He no more receives market-price for his work than does the soldier. Like the soldier he is caught young, ignorant, knowing only his own trade, and his own locality. Early marriage and the operation of the various laws of settlement affect the one as enlistment and the Mutiny Act affect the other.' (Dr Hunter, l. c., p. 132.) Sometimes an exceptionally soft-hearted landlord relents as the solitude he has created. 'It is a melancholy thing to stand alone in one's country,' said Lord Leicester, when complimented on the completion of Hookham. 'I look around and not a house is to be seen but mine. I am the giant of Giant Castle, and have eat up all my neighbours.'

108. A similar movement is seen during the last ten years in France; in proportion as capitalist production there takes possession of agriculture, it drives the 'surplus' agricultural population into the towns. Here also we find deterioration in the housing and other conditions at the source of the surplus population. On the special 'prolétariat foncier,' to which this system of parcelling out the land has given rise, see, among others, the work of Colins, already quoted, and Karl Marx 'Der Achtzehnte Brumaire des Louis Bonaparte.' 2nd edition. Hamburg, 1869, pp. 56, &c. In 1846, the town population in France was represented by 24.42, the agricultural by 75.58; in 1861, the town by 28.86, the agricultural by 71.14 per cent. During the last 5 years, the diminution of the agricultural percentage of the population has been yet more marked. As early as 1846, Pierre Dupont in his 'Ouvriers' sang:

Mal vêtus, logés dans des trous,
Sous les combles, dans les décombres,
Nous vivons avec les hiboux
Et les larrons, amis des ombres.
[Badly clothed, living in holes, under the eaves, in the ruins, with the owls and the thieves, companions of the shadows]

109. 'Sixth and last Report of the Children's Employment Commission,' published at the end of March, 1867. It deals solely with the agricultural gang-system.

110. 'Child. Emp. Comm., VI. Report.» Evidence 173, p. 37.

111. Some gang-masters, however, have worked themselves up to the position of farmers of 500 acres, or proprietors of whole rows of houses.

112. 'Half the girls of Ludford have been ruined by going out' (in gangs). l. c., p. 6, § 32.

113. 'They (gangs) have greatly increased of late years. In some places they are said to have been introduced at comparatively late dates; in others where gangs ... have been known for many years ... more and younger children are employed in them.' (l. c., p. 79, § 174).

114. 'Small farmers never employ gangs.' 'It is not on poor land, but on land which affords rent of from 40 to 50 shillings, that women and children are employed in the greatest numbers.' (l. c., pp. 17, 14.)

115. To one of these gentlemen the taste of his rent was so grateful that he indignantly declared to the Commission of Inquiry that the whole hubbub was only due to the name of the system. If instead of 'gang' it were called 'the Agricultural Juvenile Industrial Self-supporting Association,' everything would be all right.

116. 'Gang work is cheaper than other work; that is why they are employed,' says a former gang-master (l. c., p. 17, § 14).»The gang-system is decidedly the cheapest for the farmer, and decidedly the worst for the children,' says a farmer (l. c., p. 16, § 3.)

117. 'Undoubtedly much of the work now done by children in gangs used to be done by men and women. More men are out of work now where children and women are employed than formerly.' (l. c., p. 43, n. 202.) On the other hand, 'the labour question in some agricultural districts, particularly the arable, is becoming so serious in consequence of emigration, and the facility afforded by railways for getting to large towns that I (the 'I' is the steward of a great lord) think the services of children are most indispensable,' (l. c., p. 80, n. 180.) For the 'labour question' in English agricultural districts, differently from the rest of the civilised world, means the landlords' and farmers' question, *viz.*, how is it possible, despite an always increasing exodus of the agricultural folk, to keep up a sufficient relative surplus population in the country, and by means of it keep the wages of the agricultural labourer at a minimum?

118. The 'Public Health Report,' where in dealing with the subject of children's mortality, the gang-system is treated in passing, remains unknown to the press, and, therefore, to the English public. On the other hand, the last report of the 'Child. Empl. Comm.' afforded the press sensational copy always welcome. Whilst the Liberal press asked how the fine gentlemen and ladies, and the well-paid clergy of the State Church, with whom Lincolnshire swarms, could allow such a system to arise on their estates, under their very eyes, they who send out expressly missions to the Antipodes, 'for the improvement of the morals of South Sea Islanders'—the more refined press confined itself to reflections on the coarse degradation of the agricultural population who are capable of selling their children into such slavery! Under the accursed conditions to which these 'delicate' people condemn the agricultural labourer, it would not be surprising if he ate his own children. What is really wonderful is the healthy integrity of character, he has, in great part, retained. The official reports prove that the parents, even in the gang districts, loathe the gang-system. 'There is much in the evidence that shows that the parents of the children would, in many instances, be glad to be aided by the requirements of a legal obligation, to resist the pressure and the temptations to which they are often subject. They are liable to be urged, at times by the parish officers, at times by employers, under threats of being themselves discharged, to be taken to work at an age when ... school attendance ... would be manifestly to their greater advantage.... All that time and strength wasted; all the suffering from extra and unprofitable fatigue produced to the labourer and to his children; every instance in which the parent may have traced the moral ruin of his child to the undermining of delicacy by the over-crowding of cottages, or to the contaminating influences of the public gang, must have been so many incentives to feelings in the minds of the labouring poor which can be well understood, and which it would be needless to particularise. They must be conscious that much bodily and mental pain has thus been inflicted upon them from causes for which they were in no way answerable; to which, had it been in their power, they would have in no way consented; and against which they were powerless to struggle.' (l. c., p. xx., § 82, and xxiii., n. 96.)

119. Population of Ireland, 1801, 5,319,867 persons; 1811, 6,084,996; 1821, 6,869,544; 1831, 7,828,347; 1841, 8,222,664.

120. The result would be found yet more unfavourable if we went further back. Thus: Sheep in 1865, 3,688,742, but in 1856, 3,694,294. Pigs in 1865, 1,299,893, but in 1858, 1,409,883.

121. The data of the text are put together from the materials of the 'Agricultural Statistics, Ireland, General Abstracts, Dublin,' for the years 1860, *et seq.*, and 'Agricultural Statistics, Ireland. Tables showing the estimated average produce, &c., Dublin, 1866.' These statistics are official, and laid before Parliament annually.

Note to 2nd edition. The official statistics for the year 1872 show, as compared with 1871, a decrease in area under cultivation of 134,915 acres. An increase occurred in the cultivation of green crops, turnips, mangold-wurzel, and the like; a decrease in the area under cultivation for wheat of 16,000 acres; oats, 14,000; barley and rye, 4,000; potatoes, 66,632; flax, 34,667; grass, clover, vetches, rape-seed, 30,000. The soil under cultivation for wheat shows for the last 5 years the following stages of decrease:—1868, 285,000 acres; 1869, 280,000; 1870, 259,000; 1871, 244,000; 1872, 228,000. For 1872 we find, in round numbers, an increase of 2,600 horses, 80,000 horned cattle, 68,609 sheep, and a decrease of 236,000 pigs.

122. The total yearly income under Schedule D. is different in this table from that which appears in the preceding ones, because of certain deductions allowed by law.

123. If the product also diminishes relatively per acre, it must not be forgotten that for a century and a half England has indirectly exported the soil of Ireland, without as much as allowing its cultivators the means for making up the constituents of the soil that had been exhausted.

124. As Ireland is regarded as the promised land of the 'principle of population,' Th. Sadler, before the publication of his work on population, issued his famous book, 'Ireland, its Evils and their Remedies.' 2nd edition, London, 1829. Here, by comparison of the statistics of the individual provinces, and of the individual counties in each province, he proves that the misery there is not, as Malthus would have it, in proportion to the number of the population, but in inverse ratio to this.

125. Between 1851 and 1874, the total number of emigrants amounted to 2,325,922.

126. According to a table in Murphy's 'Ireland Industrial, Political and Social,' 1870, 94.6 per cent. of the holdings do not reach 100 acres, 5.4 exceed 100 acres.

127. 'Reports from the Poor Law Inspectors on the Wages of Agricultural Labourers in Dublin,' 1870. See also 'Agricultural labourers (Ireland). Return, etc.' 8 March, 1861, London, 1862.

128. l. c., pp. 29, 1.

129. l. c., p. 12.

130. l. c., p. 12.

131. l. c., p. 25.

132. l. c., p. 27.

133. l. c., p. 25.

134. l. c., p. 1.

135. l. c., pp. 31, 32.

136. l. c., p. 25.

137. l. c., p. 30.

138. l. c., pp. 21, 13.

139. 'Rept. of Insp. of Fact., 31st Oct., 1866,' p. 96.

140. The total area includes also peat, bogs, and waste land.

141. How the famine and its consequences have been deliberately made the most of, both by the individual landlords and by the English legislature, to forcibly carry out the agricultural revolution and to thin the population of Ireland down to the proportion satisfactory to the landlords, I shall show more fully in Vol. III. of this work, in the section on landed property. There also I return to the condition of the small farmers and the agricultural labourers. At

present, only one quotation. Nassau W. Senior says, with other things, in his posthumous work, 'Journals, Conversations and Essays relating to Ireland.' 2 vols. London, 1868; Vol. II., p. 282. 'Well,' said Dr G., 'we have got our Poor Law and it is a great instrument for giving the victory to the landlords. Another, and a still more powerful instrument is emigration.... No friend to Ireland can wish the war to be prolonged [between the landlords and the small Celtic farmers]—still less, that it should end by the victory of the tenants. The sooner it is over—the sooner Ireland becomes a grazing country, with the comparatively thin population which a grazing country requires, the better for all classes.' The English Corn Laws of 1815 secured Ireland the monopoly of the free importation of corn into Great Britain. They favoured artificially, therefore, the cultivation of corn. With the abolition of the Corn Laws in 1846, this monopoly was suddenly removed. Apart from all other circumstances, this event alone was sufficient to give a great impulse to the turning of Irish arable into pasture land, to the concentration of farms, and to the eviction of small cultivators. After the fruitfulness of the Irish soil had been praised from 1815 to 1846, and proclaimed loudly as by Nature herself destined for the cultivation of wheat, English agronomists, economists, politicians, discover suddenly that it is good for nothing but to produce forage. M. Léonce de Lavergne has hastened to repeat this on the other side of the Channel. It takes a 'serious' man, à la Lavergne, to be caught by such childishness.

PART VIII

PRIMITIVE ACCUMULATION

26

The Secret of Primitive Accumulation

We have seen how money is changed into capital; how through capital surplus-value is made, and from surplus-value more capital. But the accumulation of capital presupposes surplus-value; surplus-value presupposes capitalistic production; capitalistic production presupposes the pre-existence of considerable masses of capital and of labour power in the hands of producers of commodities. The whole movement, therefore, seems to turn in a vicious circle, out of which we can only get by supposing a primitive accumulation (previous accumulation of Adam Smith) preceding capitalistic accumulation; an accumulation not the result of the capitalistic mode of production, but its starting point.

This primitive accumulation plays in Political Economy about the same part as original sin in theology. Adam bit the apple, and thereupon sin fell on the human race. Its origin is supposed to be explained when it is told as an anecdote of the past. In times long gone by there were two sorts of people; one, the diligent, intelligent, and, above all, frugal elite; the other, lazy rascals, spending their substance, and more, in riotous living. The legend of theological original sin tells us certainly how man came to be condemned to eat his bread in the sweat of his brow; but the history of economic original sin reveals to us that there are people to whom this is by no means essential. Never mind! Thus it came to pass that the former sort accumulated wealth, and the latter sort had at last nothing to sell except their own skins. And from this original sin dates the poverty of the great majority that, despite all its labour, has up to now nothing to sell but itself, and the wealth of the few that increases constantly although they have long ceased to work. Such insipid childishness is every day preached to us in the defence of property. M. Thiers, *e.g.*, had the assurance to repeat it with all the solemnity of a statesman to the French people, once so *spirituel*. But as soon as the question of property crops up, it becomes a sacred duty to proclaim the intellectual food of the infant as the one thing fit for all ages and for all stages of development. In actual history it is notorious that conquest, enslavement, robbery, murder, briefly force, play the great part. In the tender annals of Political Economy, the idyllic reigns from time immemorial. Right and 'labour' were from all time the sole means of enrichment, the present year of course always excepted. As a matter of fact, the methods of primitive accumulation are anything but idyllic.

In themselves money and commodities are no more capital than are the means of production and of subsistence. They want transforming into capital. But this transformation itself can only take place under certain circumstances that centre in this, viz., that two very different kinds of commodity-possessors must come face to face and into contact; on the one hand, the owners of money, means of production, means of subsistence, who are eager to increase the sum of values they possess, by buying other people's labour power; on the other hand, free labourers, the sellers of their own labour power, and therefore the sellers of labour. Free labourers, in the double sense that neither they themselves form part and parcel of the means of production, as in the case of slaves, bondsmen, &c., nor do the means of production belong to them, as in the case of peasant-proprietors; they are, therefore, free from, unencumbered by, any means of production of their own. With this polarization of the market for commodities, the fundamental conditions of capitalist production are given. The capitalist system presupposes the complete separation of the labourers from all property in the means by which they can realize their labour. As soon as capitalist production is once on its own legs, it not only maintains this separation, but reproduces it on a continually extending scale. The process, therefore, that clears the way for the capitalist system, can be none other than the process which takes away from the labourer the possession of his means of production; a process that transforms, on the one hand, the social means of subsistence and of production into capital, on the other, the immediate producers into wage labourers. The so-called primitive accumulation, therefore, is nothing else than the historical process of divorcing the producer from the means of production. It appears as primitive, because it forms the prehistoric stage of capital and of the mode of production corresponding with it.

The economic structure of capitalist society has grown out of the economic structure of feudal society. The dissolution of the latter set free the elements of the former.

The immediate producer, the labourer, could only dispose of his own person after he had ceased to be attached to the soil and ceased to be the slave, serf, or bondsman of another. To become a free seller of labour power, who carries his commodity wherever he finds a market, he must further have escaped from the regime of the guilds, their rules for apprentices and journeymen, and the impediments of their labour regulations. Hence, the historical movement which changes the producers into wage-workers, appears, on the one hand, as their emancipation from serfdom and from the fetters of the guilds, and this side alone exists for our bourgeois historians. But, on the other hand, these new freedmen became sellers of themselves only after they had been robbed of all their own means of production, and of all the guarantees of existence afforded by the old feudal arrangements. And the history of this, their expropriation, is written in the annals of mankind in letters of blood and fire.

The industrial capitalists, these new potentates, had on their part not only to displace the guild masters of handicrafts, but also the feudal lords, the possessors of the sources of wealth. In this respect, their conquest of social power appears as the fruit of a victorious struggle both against feudal lordship and its revolting prerogatives, and against the guilds and the fetters they laid on the free development of production and the free exploitation of man by man. The chevaliers d'industrie, however, only succeeded in supplanting the chevaliers of the sword by making use of events of which they themselves were wholly innocent. They have risen by means as vile as those by which the Roman freedman once on a time made himself the master of his *patronus*.

The starting point of the development that gave rise to the wage labourer as well as to the capitalist, was the servitude of the labourer. The advance consisted in a change of form of this servitude, in the transformation of feudal exploitation into capitalist exploitation. To understand its march, we need not go back very far. Although we come across the first beginnings of capitalist production as early as the 14th or 15th century, sporadically, in certain towns of the Mediterranean, the capitalistic era dates from the 16th century. Wherever it appears, the abolition of serfdom has been long effected, and the highest development of the middle ages, the existence of sovereign towns, has been long on the wane.

In the history of primitive accumulation, all revolutions are epoch-making that act as levers for the capital class in course of formation; but, above all, those moments when great masses of men are suddenly and forcibly torn from their means of subsistence, and hurled as free and 'unattached' proletarians on the labour-market. The expropriation of the agricultural producer, of the peasant, from the soil, is the basis of the whole process. The history of this expropriation, in different countries, assumes different aspects, and runs through its various phases in different orders of succession, and at different periods. In England alone, which we take as our example, has it the classic form.[1]

Notes

1. In Italy, where capitalistic production developed earliest, the dissolution of serfdom also took place earlier than elsewhere. The serf was emancipated in that country before he had acquired any prescriptive right to the soil. His emancipation at once transformed him into a free proletarian, who, moreover, found his master ready waiting for him in the towns, for

the most part handed down as legacies from the Roman time. When the revolution of the world-market, about the end of the 15th century, annihilated Northern Italy's commercial supremacy, a movement in the reverse direction set in. The labourers of the towns were driven *en masse* into the country, and gave an impulse, never before seen, to the *petite culture*, carried on in the form of gardening.

27

Expropriation of the Agricultural Population from the Land

In England, serfdom had practically disappeared in the last part of the 14th century. The immense majority of the population[1] consisted then, and to a still larger extent, in the 15th century, of free peasant proprietors, whatever was the feudal title under which their right of property was hidden. In the larger seignorial domains, the old bailiff, himself a serf, was displaced by the free farmer. The wage labourers of agriculture consisted partly of peasants, who utilised their leisure time by working on the large estates, partly of an independent special class of wage labourers, relatively and absolutely few in numbers. The latter also were practically at the same time peasant farmers, since, besides their wages, they had allotted to them arable land to the extent of 4 or more acres, together with their cottages. Besides they, with the rest of the peasants, enjoyed the usufruct of the common land, which gave pasture to their cattle, furnished them with timber, fire-wood, turf, &c.[2] In all countries of Europe, feudal production is characterised by division of the soil amongst the greatest possible number of subfeudatories. The might of the feudal lord, like that of the sovereign, depended not on the length of his rent roll, but on the number of his subjects, and the latter depended on the number of peasant proprietors.[3] Although, therefore, the English land, after the Norman Conquest, was distributed in gigantic baronies, one of which often included some 900 of the old Anglo-Saxon lordships, it was bestrewn with small peasant properties, only here and there interspersed with great seignorial domains. Such conditions, together with the prosperity of the towns so characteristic of the 15th century, allowed of that wealth of the people which Chancellor Fortescue so eloquently paints in his 'Laudes legum Angliae;' but it excluded the possibility of capitalistic wealth.

The prelude of the revolution that laid the foundation of the capitalist mode of production, was played in the last third of the 15th, and the first decade of the 16th century. A mass of free proletarians was hurled on the labour market by the breaking-up of the bands of feudal retainers, who, as Sir James Steuart well says, 'everywhere uselessly filled house and castle.' Although the royal power, itself a product of bourgeois development, in its strife after absolute sovereignty forcibly hastened on the dissolution of these bands of retainers, it was by no means the sole cause of it. In insolent conflict with king and parliament, the great feudal lords created an incomparably larger proletariat by the forcible driving of the peasantry from the land, to which the latter had the same feudal right as the lord himself, and by the usurpation of the common lands. The rapid rise of the Flemish wool manufactures, and the corresponding rise in the price of wool in England, gave the direct impulse to these evictions. The old nobility had been devoured by the great feudal wars. The new nobility was the child of its time, for which money was the power of all powers. Transformation of arable land into sheep-walks was, therefore, its cry. Harrison, in his 'Description of England, prefixed to Holinshed's Chronicles,' describes how the expropriation of small peasants is ruining the country. 'What care our great encroachers?' The dwellings of the peasants and the cottages of the labourers were razed to the ground or doomed to decay. 'If,' says Harrison, 'the old records of euerie manour be sought... it will soon appear that in some manour seventeene, eighteene, or twentie houses are shrunk... that England was neuer less furnished with people than at the present... Of cities and townes either utterly decaied or more than a quarter or half diminished, though some one be a little increased here or there; of townes pulled downe for sheepe-walks, and no more but the lordships now standing in them... I could saie somewhat.' The complaints of these old chroniclers are always exaggerated, but they reflect faithfully the impression made on contemporaries by the revolution in the conditions of production. A comparison of the writings of Chancellor Fortescue and Thomas More reveals the gulf between the 15th and 16th century. As Thornton rightly has it, the English working class was precipitated without any transition from its golden into its iron age.

Legislation was terrified at this revolution. It did not yet stand on that height of civilization where the 'wealth of the nation' (i.e., the formation of capital, and the reckless exploitation and impoverishing of the mass of the people) figure as the *ultima Thule* of all state-craft. In his history of Henry VII., Bacon says: 'Inclosures at that time (1489) began to be more frequent, whereby arable land (which could not be manured without people and families) was turned into pasture, which was easily rid by a few herdsmen; and tenancies for years, lives, and at will (whereupon much of the yeomanry lived) were turned into demesnes. This bred a decay of people, and (by consequence) a decay of towns, churches, tithes, and the like... In remedying of this inconvenience the king's wisdom was admirable, and the parliament's at that time... they took a course to take away depopulating enclosures, and depopulating pasturage.' An Act of Henry VII., 1489, cap. 19, forbad the destruction of all 'houses of husbandry' to which at least 20 acres of land belonged. By an Act, 25 Henry VIII., the same law was renewed. It recites, among other things, that many farms and large flocks of cattle, especially of sheep, are concentrated in the hands of a few men, whereby the rent of land has much risen and tillage has fallen off, churches and houses have been pulled down, and marvellous numbers of people have been deprived of the means wherewith to maintain themselves and their families. The Act, therefore, ordains the rebuilding of the decayed farmsteads, and fixes a proportion between corn land and pasture land, &c. An Act of 1533 recites that some owners possess 24,000 sheep, and limits the number to be owned to 2,000.[4] The cry of the people and the legislation directed, for 150 years after Henry VII., against the expropriation of the small farmers and peasants, were alike fruitless. The secret of their inefficiency Bacon, without knowing it, reveals to us. 'The device of King Henry VII.,' says Bacon, in his 'Essays, Civil and Moral,' Essay 29, 'was profound and admirable, in making farms and houses of husbandry of a standard; that is, maintained with such a proportion of land unto them as may breed a subject to live in convenient plenty, and no servile condition, and to keep the plough in the hands of the owners and not mere hirelings.'[5] What the capitalist system demanded was, on the other hand, a degraded and almost servile condition of the mass of the people, the transformation of them into mercenaries, and of their means of labour into capital. During this transformation period, legislation also strove to retain the 4 acres of land by the cottage of the agricultural wage labourer, and forbad him to take lodgers into his cottage. In the reign of James I., 1627, Roger Crocker of Front Mill, was condemned for having built a cottage on the manor of Front Mill without 4 acres of land attached to the same in perpetuity. As late as Charles I.'s reign, 1638, a royal commission was appointed to enforce the carrying out of the old laws, especially that referring to the 4 acres of land. Even in Cromwell's time, the building of a house within 4 miles of London was forbidden unless it was endowed with 4 acres of land. As late as the first half of the 18th century complaint is made if the cottage of the agricultural labourer has not an adjunct of one or two acres of land. Nowadays he is lucky if it is furnished with a little garden, or if he may rent, far away from his cottage, a few roods. 'Landlords and farmers,' says Dr Hunter, 'work here hand in hand. A few acres to the cottage would make the labourers too independent.'[6]

The process of forcible expropriation of the people received in the 16th century a new and frightful impulse from the Reformation, and from the consequent colossal spoliation of the church property. The Catholic church was, at the time of the Reformation, feudal proprietor of a great part of the English land. The suppression of the monasteries, &c., hurled their inmates into the proletariat. The estates of the church were to a large extent given away to rapacious royal favourites, or sold at a nominal price to speculating farmers and citizens, who drove out, *en masse,* the hereditary sub-tenants and threw their holdings into one. The legally guaranteed property of the poorer folk in a part of the church's tithes was tacitly confiscated.[7] 'Pauper ubique jacet,' cried Queen Elizabeth, after a journey through England. In the 43rd year of her reign the nation was obliged to recognise pauperism officially by the introduction of a poor-rate. 'The authors of this law seem to have been ashamed to state the grounds of it, for [contrary to traditional usage] it has no preamble whatever.'[8] By the 16th of Charles I., ch. 4, it was declared perpetual, and in fact only in 1834 did it take a new and harsher form.[9] These immediate results of the Reformation were not its most lasting ones. The property of the church formed the religious bulwark of the traditional conditions of landed property. With its fall these were no longer tenable.[10]

Even in the last decade of the 17th century, the yeomanry, the class of independent peasants, were more numerous than the class of farmers. They had formed the backbone of Cromwell's strength, and, even according to the confession of Macaulay, stood in favourable contrast to the drunken squires and to their servants, the country clergy, who had to marry their masters' cast-off mistresses. About 1750, the yeomanry had disappeared,[11] and so had, in the last decade of the 18th century, the last trace of the common land of the agricultural labourer. We leave on one side here the purely economic causes of the agricultural revolution. We deal only with the forcible means employed.

After the restoration of the Stuarts, the landed proprietors carried, by legal means, an act of usurpation, effected everywhere on the Continent without any legal formality. They abolished the feudal tenure of land, *i.e.*, they got rid of all its obligations to the State, 'indemnified' the State by taxes on the peasantry and the rest of the mass of the people, vindicated for themselves the rights of modern private property in estates to which they had only a feudal title, and, finally, passed those laws of settlement, which, *mutatis mutandis*, had the same effect on the English agricultural labourer, as the edict of the Tartar Boris Godunof on the Russian peasantry.

The 'glorious Revolution' brought into power, along with William of Orange, the landlord and capitalist appropriators of surplus-value.[12] They inaugurated the new era by practising on a colossal scale thefts of state lands, thefts that had been hitherto managed more modestly. These estates were given away, sold at a ridiculous figure, or even annexed to private estates by direct seizure.[13] All this happened without the slightest observation of legal etiquette. The Crown lands thus fraudulently appropriated, together with the robbery of the Church estates, as far as these had not been lost again during the republican revolution, form the basis of the today princely domains of the English oligarchy.[14] The bourgeois capitalists favoured the operation with the view, among others, to promoting free trade in land, to extending the domain of modern agriculture on the large farm-system, and to increasing their supply of the free agricultural proletarians ready to hand. Besides, the new landed aristocracy was the natural ally of the new bankocracy, of the newly-hatched *haute finance,* and of the large manufacturers, then depending on protective duties. The English bourgeoisie acted for its own interest quite as wisely as did the Swedish bourgeoisie who, reversing the process, hand in hand with their economic allies, the peasantry, helped the kings in the forcible resumption of the Crown lands from the oligarchy. This happened since 1604 under Charles X. and Charles XI.

Communal property—always distinct from the State property just dealt with—was an old Teutonic institution which lived on under cover of feudalism. We have seen how the forcible usurpation of this, generally accompanied by the turning of arable into pasture land, begins at the end of the 15th and extends into the 16th century. But, at that time, the process was carried on by means of individual acts of violence against which legislation, for a hundred and fifty years, fought in vain. The advance made by the 18th century shows itself in this, that the law itself becomes now the instrument of the theft of the people's land, although the large farmers make use of their little independent methods as well.[15] The parliamentary form of the robbery is that of Acts for enclosures of Commons, in other words, decrees by which the landlords grant themselves the people's land as private property, decrees of expropriation of the people. Sir F. M. Eden refutes his own crafty special pleading, in which he tries to represent communal property as the private property of the great landlords who have taken the place of the feudal lords, when he, himself, demands a 'general Act of Parliament for the enclosure of Commons' (admitting thereby that a parliamentary *coup d'état* is necessary for its transformation into private property), and moreover calls on the legislature for the indemnification for the expropriated poor.[16]

Whilst the place of the independent yeoman was taken by tenants at will, small farmers on yearly leases, a servile rabble dependent on the pleasure of the landlords, the systematic robbery of the Communal lands helped especially, next to the theft of the State domains, to swell those large farms, that were called in the 18th century capital farms[17] or merchant farms,[18] and to 'set free' the agricultural population as proletarians for manufacturing industry.

The 18th century, however, did not yet recognise as fully as the 19th, the identity between national wealth and the poverty of the people. Hence the most vigorous polemic, in the economic literature of that time, on the 'enclosure of commons.' From the mass of materials that lie before me, I give a few extracts that will throw a strong light on the circumstances of the time. 'In several parishes of Hertfordshire,' writes one indignant person, '24 farms, numbering on the average 50-150 acres, have been melted up into three farms.'[19] 'In Northamptonshire and Leicestershire the enclosure of common lands has taken place on a very large scale, and most of the new lordships, resulting from the enclosure, have been turned into pasturage, in consequence of which many lordships have not now 50 acres ploughed yearly, in which 1,500 were ploughed formerly. The ruins of former dwelling-houses, barns, stables, &c.,' are the sole traces of the former inhabitants. 'An hundred houses and families have in some open-field villages dwindled to eight or ten.... The landholders in most parishes that have been enclosed only 15 or 20 years, are very few in comparison of the numbers who occupied them in their open-field state. It is no uncommon thing for 4 or 5 wealthy graziers to engross a large enclosed lordship which was before in the hands of 20 or 30 farmers, and as many smaller tenants and proprietors. All these are hereby thrown out of their livings with their families and many other families who were chiefly employed and supported by them.'[20] It was not only the land that lay waste, but often land cultivated either in common or held under a definite rent paid to the community, that was annexed by the neighbouring landlords under pretext of enclosure. 'I have here in view enclosures of open fields and lands already improved. It is acknowledged by even the writers in defence of enclosures that these diminished villages increase the monopolies of farms, raise the prices of provisions, and produce depopulation ... and even the enclosure of waste lands (as now carried on) bears hard on the poor, by depriving them of a part of their subsistence, and only goes towards increasing farms already too large.'[21] 'When,' says Dr Price, 'this land gets into the hands of a few great farmers, the consequence must be that the little farmers' (earlier designated by him 'a multitude of little proprietors and tenants, who maintain themselves and families by the produce of the ground they occupy by sheep kept on a common, by poultry, hogs, &c., and who therefore have little occasion to purchase any of the means of subsistence') 'will be converted into a body of men who earn their subsistence by working for others, and who will be under a necessity of going to market for all they want.... There will, perhaps, be more labour, because there will be more compulsion to it.... Towns and manufactures will increase, because more will be driven to them in quest of places and employment. This is the way in which the engrossing of farms naturally operates. And this is the way in which, for many years, it has been actually operating in this kingdom.'[22] He sums up the effect of the enclosures thus: 'Upon the whole, the circumstances of the lower ranks of men are altered in almost every respect for the worse. From little occupiers of land, they are reduced to the state of day-labourers and hirelings; and, at the same time, their subsistence in that state has become more difficult.'[23] In fact, usurpation of the common lands and the revolution in agriculture accompanying this, told so acutely on the agricultural labourers that, even according to Eden, between 1765 and 1780, their wages began to fall below the minimum, and to be supplemented by official poor-law relief. Their wages, he says, 'were not more than enough for the absolute necessaries of life.'

Let us hear for a moment a defender of enclosures and an opponent of Dr Price. 'Not is it a consequence that there must be depopulation, because men are not seen wasting their labour in the open field.... If, by converting the little farmers into a body of men who must work for others, more labour is produced, it is an advantage which the nation' (to which, of course, the 'converted' ones do not belong) 'should wish for ... the produce being greater when their joint labours are employed on one farm, there will be a surplus for manufactures, and by this means manufactures, one of the mines of the nation, will increase, in proportion to the quantity of corn produced.'[24]

The stoical peace of mind with which the political economist regards the most shameless violation of the 'sacred rights of property' and the grossest acts of violence to persons, as soon as they are necessary to lay the foundations of the capitalistic mode of production, is shown by Sir F. M. Eden, philanthropist and tory to boot. The whole series of thefts, outrages, and popular misery, that accompanied the forcible expropriation of the people, from the last third of the 15th to the end of the 18th century, lead him merely to the comfortable conclusion: 'The due proportion between arable land and pasture had to be established. During the whole of the 14th and the greater part of the 15th century, there was one acre of pasture to 2, 3, and even 4 of arable land. About the middle of the 16th century the proportion was changed of 2 acres of pasture to 2, later on, of 2 acres of pasture to one of arable, until at last the just proportion of 3 acres of pasture to one of arable land was attained.'

In the 19th century, the very memory of the connexion between the agricultural labourer and the communal property had, of course, vanished. To say nothing of more recent times, have the agricultural population received a farthing of compensation for the 3,511,770 acres of common land which between 1801 and 1831 were stolen from them and by parliamentary devices presented to the landlords by the landlords?

The last process of wholesale expropriation of the agricultural population from the soil is, finally, the so-called clearing of estates, *i.e.*, the sweeping men off them. All the English methods hitherto considered culminated in 'clearing.' As we saw in the picture of modern conditions given in a former chapter, where there are no more independent peasants to get rid of, the 'clearing' of cottages begins; so that the agricultural labourers do not find on the soil cultivated by them even the spot necessary for their own housing. But what 'clearing of estates' really and properly signifies, we learn only in the promised land of modern romance, the Highlands of Scotland. There the process is distinguished by its systematic character, by the magnitude of the scale on which it is carried out at one blow (in Ireland landlords have gone to the length of sweeping away several villages at once; in Scotland areas as large as German principalities are dealt with), finally by the peculiar form of property, under which the embezzled lands were held.

The Highland Celts were organised in clans, each of which was the owner of the land on which it was settled. The representative of the clan, its chief or 'great man,' was only the titular owner of this property, just as the Queen of England is the titular owner of all the national soil. When the English government succeeded in suppressing the intestine wars of these 'great men,' and their constant incursions into the Lowland plains, the chiefs of the clans by no means gave up their time-honored trade as robbers; they only changed its form. On their own authority they transformed their nominal right into a right of private property, and as this brought them into collision with their clansmen, resolved to drive them out by open force. 'A king of England might as well claim to drive his subjects into the sea,' says Professor Newman.[25] This revolution, which began in Scotland after the last rising of the followers of the Pretender, can be followed through its first phases in the writings of Sir James Steuart[26] and James Anderson.[27] In the 18th century the hunted-out Gaels were forbidden to emigrate from the country, with a view to driving them by force to Glasgow and other manufacturing towns.[28] As an example of the method[29] obtaining in the 19th century, the 'clearing' made by the Duchess of Sutherland will suffice here. This person, well instructed in economy, resolved, on entering upon her government, to effect a radical cure, and to turn the whole country, whose population had already been, by earlier processes of the like kind, reduced to 15,000, into a sheep-walk. From 1814 to 1820 these 15,000 inhabitants, about 3,000 families, were systematically hunted and rooted out. All their villages were destroyed and burnt, all their fields turned into pasturage. British soldiers enforced this eviction, and came to blows with the inhabitants. One old woman was burnt to death in the flames of the hut, which she refused to leave. Thus, this fine lady appropriated 794,000 acres of land that had from time immemorial belonged to the clan. She assigned to the expelled inhabitants about 6,000 acres on the sea-shore—2 acres per family. The 6,000 acres had until this time lain waste, and brought in no income to their owners. The Duchess, in the nobility of her heart, actually went so far as to let these at an average rent of 2s. 6d. per acre to the clansmen, who for centuries had shed their blood for her family. The whole of the stolen clanland she divided into 29 great sheep farms, each inhabited by a single family, for the most part imported English farm-servants. In the year 1835, the 15,000 Gaels were already replaced by 131,000 sheep. The remnant of the aborigines flung on the sea-shore tried to live by catching fish. They became amphibious and lived, as an English author says, half on land and half on water, and withal only half on both.[30]

But the brave Gaels must expiate yet more bitterly their idolatry, romantic and of the mountains, for the 'great men' of the clan. The smell of their fish rose to the noses of the great men. They scented some profit in it, and let the sea-shore to the great fishmongers of London. For the second time the Gaels were hunted out.[31]

But, finally, part of the sheep-walks are turned into deer preserves. Every one knows that there are no real forests in England. The deer in the parks of the great are demurely domestic cattle, fat as London aldermen. Scotland is therefore the last refuge of the 'noble passion.' 'In the Highlands,' says Somers in 1848, 'new forests are springing up like mushrooms. Here, on one side of Gaick, you have the new forest of Glenfeshie; and there on the other you have the new forest of Ardverikie. In the same line you have the Black Mount, an immense waste also recently erected. From east to west—from the neighbourhood of Aberdeen to the crags of Oban—you have now a continuous line of forests; while in other parts of the Highlands there are the new forests of Loch Archaig, Glengarry, Glenmoriston, &c. Sheep were introduced into glens which had been the seats of communities of small farmers; and the latter were driven to seek subsistence on coarser and more sterile tracks of soil. Now deer are supplanting sheep; and these are once more dispossessing the small tenants, who will necessarily be driven down upon still coarser land and to more grinding penury. Deer-forests[32] and the people cannot co-exist. One or other of the two must yield. Let the forests be increased in number and extent during the next quarter of a century, as they have been in the last, and the Gaels will perish from their native soil... This movement among the Highland proprietors is with some a matter of ambition... with some love of sport... while others, of a more practical cast, follow the trade in deer with an eye solely to profit. For it is a fact, that a mountain range laid out in forest is, in many cases, more profitable to the proprietor than when let as a sheep-walk. ... The huntsman who wants a deer-forest limits his offers by no other calculation than the extent of his purse.... Sufferings have been inflicted in the Highlands scarcely less severe than those occasioned by the policy of the Norman kings. Deer have received extended ranges, while men have been hunted within a narrower and still narrower circle.... One after one the liberties of the people have been cloven down.... And the oppressions are daily on the increase.... The clearance and dispersion of the people is pursued by the proprietors as a settled principle, as an agricultural necessity, just as trees and brushwood are cleared from the wastes of America or Australia; and the operation goes on in a quiet, business-like way, &c.'[33]

The spoliation of the church's property, the fraudulent alienation of the State domains, the robbery of the common lands, the usurpation of feudal and clan property, and its transformation into modern private property under circumstances of reckless terrorism, were just so many idyllic methods of primitive accumulation. They conquered the field for capitalistic agriculture, made the soil part and parcel of capital, and created for the town industries the necessary supply of a 'free' and outlawed proletariat.

Notes

1. 'The petty proprietors who cultivated their own fields with their own hands, and enjoyed a modest competence.... then formed a much more important part of the nation than at present. If we may trust the best statistical writers of that age, not less than 160,000 proprietors who, with their families, must have made up more than a seventh of the whole population, derived their subsistence from little freehold estates. The average income of these small landlords... was estimated at between £60 and £70 a year. It was computed that the number of persons who tilled their own land was greater than the number of those who farmed the land of others.' Macaulay: 'History of England,' 10th ed., 1854, I. pp. 333, 334. Even in the last third of the 17th century, 4/5 of the English people were agricultural. (l. c., p. 413.) I quote Macaulay, because as systematic falsifier of history he minimises as much as possible facts of this kind.
2. We must never forget that even the serf was not only the owner, if but a tribute-paying owner, of the piece of land attached to his house, but also a co-possessor of the common land. 'Le paysan (in Silesia, under Frederick II.) est serf.' Nevertheless, these serfs possess common lands. 'On n'a pas pu encore engager les Silésiens au partage des communes, tandis que dans la Nouvelle Marche, il n'y a guère de village où ce partage ne soit exécuté avec le plus grand succès.' [The peasant ... is a serf. ... It has not yet been possible to persuade the Silesians to partition the common lands, whereas in the Neumark there is scarcely a village where the partition has not been implemented with very great success] (Mirabeau: 'De la Monarchie Prussienne.' Londres, 1788, t. ii, pp. 125, 126.)
3. Japan, with its purely feudal organisation of landed property and its developed *petite culture*, gives a much truer picture of the European middle ages than all our history books, dictated as these are, for the most part, by bourgeois prejudices. It is very convenient to be 'liberal' at the expense of the middle ages.
4. In his 'Utopia,' Thomas More says, that in England 'your shepe that were wont to be so meke and tame, and so smal eaters, now, as I heare saye, be become so great devourers and so wylde that they eate up, and swallow downe, the very men themselfes.' 'Utopia,' transl. by Robinson, ed. Arber, Lond., 1869, p. 41.
5. Bacon shows the connexion between a free, well-to-do peasantry and good infantry. 'This did wonderfully concern the might and mannerhood of the kingdom to have farms as it

were of a standard sufficient to maintain an able body out of penury, and did in effect amortise a great part of the lands of the kingdom unto the hold and occupation of the yeomanry or middle people, of a condition between gentlemen, and cottagers and peasants.... For it hath been held by the general opinion of men of best judgment in the wars.... that the principal strength of an army consisteth in the infantry or foot. And to make good infantry it requireth men bred, not in a servile or indigent fashion, but in some free and plentiful manner. Therefore, if a state run most to noblemen and gentlemen, and that the husbandman and ploughmen be but as their workfolk and labourers, or else mere cottagers (which are but hous'd beggars), you may have a good cavalry, but never good stable bands of foot.... And this is to be seen in France, and Italy, and some other parts abroad, where in effect all is noblesse or peasantry.... insomuch that they are inforced to employ mercenary bands of Switzers and the like, for their battalions of foot; whereby also it comes to pass that those nations have much people and few soldiers.' ('The Reign of Henry VII.' Verbatim reprint from Kennet's England. Ed. 1719. Lond., 1870, p. 308.)

6. Dr Hunter, l. c., p. 134. 'The quantity of land assigned (in the old laws) would now be judged too great for labourers, and rather as likely to convert them into small farmers.' (George Roberts: 'The Social History of the People of the Southern Counties of England in Past Centuries.' Lond., 1856, pp. 184-185.)
7. 'The right of the poor to share in the tithe, is established by the tenour of ancient statutes.' (Tuckett, l. c., Vol. II., pg. 804-805.)
8. William Cobbett: 'A History of the Protestant Reformation,' § 471.
9. The 'spirit' of Protestantism may be seen from the following, among other things. In the south of England certain landed proprietors and well-to-do farmers put their heads together and propounded ten questions as to the right interpretation of the poor-law of Elizabeth. These they laid before a celebrated jurist of that time, Sergeant Snigge (later a judge under James I.) for his opinion. 'Question 9—Some of the more wealthy farmers in the parish have devised a skilful mode by which all the trouble of executing this Act (the 43rd of Elizabeth) might be avoided. They have proposed that we shall erect a prison in the parish, and then give notice to the neighbourhood, that if any persons are disposed to farm the poor of this parish, they do give in sealed proposals, on a certain day, of the lowest price at which they will take them off our hands; and that they will be authorised to refuse to any one unless he be shut up in the aforesaid prison. The proposers of this plan conceive that there will be found in the adjoining counties, persons, who, being unwilling to labour and not possessing substance or credit to take a farm or ship, so as to live without labour, may be induced to make a very advantageous offer to the parish. If any of the poor perish under the contractor's care, the sin will lie at his door, as the parish will have done its duty by them. We are, however, apprehensive that the present Act (43rd of Elizabeth) will not warrant a prudential measure of this kind; but you are to learn that the rest of the freeholders of the county, and of the adjoining county of B, will very readily join in instructing their members to propose an Act to enable the parish to contract with a person to lock up and work the poor; and to declare that if any person shall refuse to be so locked up and worked, he shall be entitled to no relief. This, it is hoped, will prevent persons in distress from wanting relief, and be the means of keeping down parishes.' (R. Blakey: 'The History of Political Literature from the Earliest Times.' Lond., 1855, Vol. II., pp. 84-85.) In Scotland, the abolition of serfdom took place some centuries later than in England. Even in 1698, Fletcher of Saltoun, declared in the Scotch parliament, 'The number of beggars in Scotland is reckoned at not less than 200,000. The only remedy that I, a republican on principle, can suggest, is to restore the old state of serfdom, to make slaves of all those who are unable to provide for their own subsistence.' Eden, l. c., Book I., ch. 1, pp. 60-61, says, 'The decrease of villenage seems necessarily to have been the era of the origin of the poor. Manufactures and commerce are the two parents of our national poor.' Eden, like our Scotch republican on principle, errs only in this: not the abolition of villenage, but the abolition of the property of

the agricultural labourer in the soil made him a proletarian, and eventually a pauper. In France, where the expropriation was effected in another way, the ordonnance of Moulins, 1571, and the Edict of 1656, correspond to the English poor-laws.

10. Professor Rogers, although formerly Professor of Political Economy in the University of Oxford, the hotbed of Protestant orthodoxy, in his preface to the 'History of Agriculture' lays stress on the fact of the pauperisation of the mass of the people by the Reformation.
11. 'A Letter to Sir T. C. Bunbury, Bart., on the High Price of Provisions. By a Suffolk Gentleman.' Ipswich, 1795, p. 4. Even the fanatical advocate of the system of large farms, the author of the 'Inquiry into the Connexion between the Present Price of Provisions,' London, 1773, p. 139, says: 'I most lament the loss of our yeomanry, that set of men who really kept up the independence of this nation; and sorry I am to see their lands now in the hands of monopolising lords, tenanted out to small farmers, who hold their leases on such conditions as to be little better than vassals ready to attend a summons on every mischievous occasion.'
12. On the private moral character of this bourgeois hero, among other things: 'The large grant of lands in Ireland to Lady Orkney, in 1695, is a public instance of the king's affection, and the lady's influence... Lady Orkney's endearing offices are supposed to have been—fœda labiorum ministeria.' (In the Sloane Manuscript Collection, at the British Museum, No. 4224. The Manuscript is entitled: 'The character and behaviour of King William, Sunderland, etc., as represented in Original Letters to the Duke of Shrewsbury from Somers Halifax, Oxford, Secretary Vernon, etc.' It is full of curiosa.)
13. 'The illegal alienation of the Crown Estates, partly by sale and partly by gift, is a scandalous chapter in English history... a gigantic fraud on the nation.' (F. W. Newman, 'Lectures on Political Economy.' London, 1851, pp. 129, 130.) [For details as to how the present large landed proprietors of England came into their possessions see 'Our Old Nobility. By Noblesse Oblige.' London, 1879.—*F. E.*]
14. Read, *e.g.*, E. Burke's Pamphlet on the ducal house of Bedford, whose offshoot was Lord John Russell, the 'tomtit of Liberalism.'
15. 'The farmers forbid cottagers to keep any living creatures besides themselves and children, under the pretence that if they keep any beasts or poultry, they will steal from the farmers' barns for their support; they also say, keep the cottagers poor and you will keep them industrious, &c., but the real fact I believe, is that the farmers may have the whole right of common to themselves.' ('A Political Inquiry into the Consequences of Enclosing Waste Lands.' London, 1785, p. 75.)
16. Eden, l. c., preface.
17. 'Capital Farms.' Two letters on the Flour Trade and the Dearness of Corn. By a person in business. London, 1767, pp. 19, 20.
18. 'Merchant Farms.' 'An Enquiry into the Causes of the Present High Price of Provisions.' London, 1767, p. 11. Note.— This excellent work, that was published anonymously, is by the Rev. Nathaniel Forster.
19. Thomas Wright: 'A Short Address to the Public on the Monopoly of Large Farms,' 1779, pp. 2, 3.
20. Rev. Addington: 'Inquiry into the Reasons for or against Enclosing Open Fields,' London, 1772, pp. 37, 43 passim.
21. Dr R. Price, l. c., v. ii., p. 155, Forster, Addington, Kent, Price, and James Anderson, should be read and compared with the miserable prattle of Sycophant MacCulloch in his catalogue: 'The Literature of Political Economy,' London, 1845.
22. Price, l. c., p. 147.
23. Price, l. c., p. 159. We are reminded of ancient Rome. 'The rich had got possession of the greater part of the undivided land. They trusted in the conditions of the time, that these possessions would not be again taken from them, and bought, therefore, some of the pieces of land lying near theirs, and belonging to the poor, with the acquiescence of their owners,

and took some by force, so that they now were cultivating widely extended domains, instead of isolated fields. Then they employed slaves in agriculture and cattle-breeding, because freemen would have been taken from labour for military service. The possession of slaves brought them great gain, inasmuch as these, on account of their immunity from military service, could freely multiply and have a multitude of children. Thus the powerful men drew all wealth to themselves, and all the land swarmed with slaves. The Italians, on the other hand, were always decreasing in number, destroyed as they were by poverty, taxes, and military service. Even when times of peace came, they were doomed to complete inactivity, because the rich were in possession of the soil, and used slaves instead of freemen in the tilling of it.' (Appian: 'Civil Wars,' I.7.) This passage refers to the time before the Licinian rogations. Military service, which hastened to so great an extent the ruin of the Roman plebeians, was also the chief means by which, as in a forcing-house, Charlemagne brought about the transformation of free German peasants into serfs and bondsmen.

24. 'An Inquiry into the Connexion between the Present Price of Provisions, &c.,' pp. 124, 129. To the like effect, but with an opposite tendency: 'Working-men are driven from their cottages and forced into the towns to seek for employment; but then a larger surplus is obtained, and thus capital is augmented.' ('The Perils of the Nation,' 2nd ed. London., 1843, p. 14.)
25. l. c., p. 132.
26. Steuart says: 'If you compare the rent of these lands' (he erroneously includes in this economic category the tribute of the taskmen to the clanchief) 'with the extent, it appears very small. If you compare it with the numbers fed upon the farm, you will find that an estate in the Highlands maintains, perhaps, ten times as many people as another of the same value in a good and fertile province.' (l. c., vol. i., ch. xvi., p. 104.)
27. James Anderson: 'Observations on the Means of Exciting a Spirit of National Industry, &c.,' Edinburgh, 1777.
28. In 1860, the people expropriated by force were exported to Canada under false pretences. Some fled to the mountains and neighbouring islands. They were followed by the police, came to blows with them and escaped.
29. 'In the Highlands of Scotland,' says Buchanan, the commentator on Adam Smith, 1814, 'the ancient state of property is daily subverted.... The landlord, without regard to the hereditary tenant (a category used in error here), now offers his land to the highest bidder, who, if he is an improver, instantly adopts a new system of cultivation. The land, formerly overspread with small tenants or labourers, was peopled in proportion to its produce, but under the new system of improved cultivation and increased rents, the largest possible produce is obtained at the least possible expense: and the useless hands being, with this view, removed, the population is reduced, not to what the land will maintain, but to what it will employ. 'The dispossessed tenants either seek a subsistence in the neighbouring towns,' &c. (David Buchanan: 'Observations on, &c., A. Smith's Wealth of Nations.' Edinburgh, 1814, vol. iv., p. 144.) 'The Scotch grandees dispossessed families as they would grub up coppice-wood, and they treated villages and their people as Indians harassed with wild beasts do, in their vengeance, a jungle with tigers.... Man is bartered for a fleece or a carcase of mutton, nay, held cheaper.... Why, how much worse is it than the intention of the Moguls, who, when they had broken into the northern provinces of China, proposed in council to exterminate the inhabitants, and convert the land into pasture. This proposal many Highland proprietors have effected in their own country against their own countrymen.' (George Ensor: 'An Inquiry Concerning the Population of Nations.' Lond,. 1818, pp. 215, 216.)
30. When the present Duchess of Sutherland entertained Mrs. Beecher Stowe, authoress of 'Uncle Tom's Cabin,' with great magnificence in London to show her sympathy for the Negro slaves of the American republic—a sympathy that she prudently forgot, with her fellow-aristocrats, during the civil war, in which every 'noble' English heart beat for the slave-owner—I gave in the *New York Tribune* the facts about the Sutherland slaves. (Epitomised in part by Carey in 'The

Slave Trade.' Philadelphia, 1853, pp. 203, 204.) My article was reprinted in a Scotch newspaper, and led to a pretty polemic between the latter and the sycophants of the Sutherlands.

31. Interesting details on this fish trade will be found in Mr David Urquhart's Portfolio, new series.—Nassau W. Senior, in his posthumous work, already quoted, terms 'the proceedings in Sutherlandshire one of the most beneficent clearings since the memory of man.' (l. c.)

32. The deer-forests of Scotland contain not a single tree. The sheep are driven from, and then the deer driven to, the naked hills, and then it is called a deer-forest. Not even timber-planting and real forest culture.

33. Robert Somers: 'Letters from the Highlands: or the Famine of 1847.' London, 1848, pp. 12-28 passim. These letters originally appeared in *The Times*. The English economists of course explained the famine of the Gaels in 1847, by their over-population. At all events, they 'were pressing on their food-supply.' The 'clearing of estates,' or as it is called in Germany, 'Bauernlegen,' occurred in Germany especially after the 30 years' war, and led to peasant-revolts as late as 1790 in Kursachsen. It obtained especially in East Germany. In most of the Prussian provinces, Frederick II. for the first time secured right of property for the peasants. After the conquest of Silesia he forced the landlords to rebuild the huts, barns, etc., and to provide the peasants with cattle and implements. He wanted soldiers for his army and tax-payers for his treasury. For the rest, the pleasant life that the peasant led under Frederick's system of finance and hodge-podge rule of despotism, bureaucracy and feudalism, may be seen from the following quotation from his admirer, Mirabeau: 'Le lin fait donc une des grandes richesses du cultivateur dans le Nord de l'Allemagne. Malheureusement pour l'espèce humaine, ce n'est qu'une ressource contre la misère et non un moyen de bien-être. Les impôts directs, les corvées, les servitudes de tout genre, écrasent le cultivateur allemand, qui paie encore des impôts indirects dans tout ce qu'il achète.... et pour comble de ruine, il n'ose pas vendre ses productions où et comme il le veut; il n'ose pas acheter ce dont il a besoin aux marchands qui pourraient le lui livrer au meilleur prix. Toutes ces causes le ruinent insensiblement, et il se trouverait hors d'état de payer les impôts directs à l'échéance sans la filerie; elle lui offre une ressource, en occupant utilement sa femme, ses enfants, ses servants, ses valets, et lui-même; mais quelle pénible vie, même aidée de ce secours. En été, il travaille comme un forçat au labourage et à la récolte; il se couche à 9 heures et se lève à deux, pour suffire aux travaux; en hiver il devrait réparer ses forces par un plus grand repos; mais il manquera de grains pour le pain et les semailles, s'il se défait des denrées qu'il faudrait vendre pour payer les impôts. Il faut donc filer pour suppléer à ce vide.... il faut y apporter la plus grande assiduité. Aussi le paysan se couche-t-il en hiver à minuit, une heure, et se lève à cinq ou six; ou bien il se couche à neuf, et se lève à deux, et cela tous les jours de la vie si ce n'est le dimanche. Ces excès de veille et de travail usent la nature humaine, et de là vient qu'hommes et femmes vieillissent beaucoup plutôt dans les campagnes que dans les villes.' [Flax represents one of the greatest sources of wealth for the peasant of North Germany. Unfortunately for the human race, this is only a resource against misery and not a means towards well-being. Direct taxes, forced labour service, obligations of all kinds crush the German peasant, especially as he still has to pay indirect taxes on everything he buys, ... and to complete his ruin he dare not sell his produce where and as he wishes; he dare not buy what he needs from the merhcants who could sell it to him at a cheaper price. He is slowly ruined by all those factors, and when the dirct taxes fall due, he would find himself incapable of paying them without his spinning-wheel; it offers him a last resort, while providing useful occupation for his wife, his children, his maids, his farm-hands, and himself; but what a painful life he leads, even with this extra resource! In summer, he works like a convict with the plough and at harvest; he goes to bed at nine o'clock and rises at two to get through all his work; in winter he ought to be recovering his strength by sleeping longer; but he would run short of corn for his bread and next year's sowing if he got rid of the products that he needs to sell in order to pay the taxes. He therefore has to spin to fill up this gap ... and indeed he

must do so most assiduously. Thus, the peasant goes to bed at midnight or one o'clock in winter, and gets up at five or six; or he goes to bed at nine and gets up at two, and this he does every day of his life except Sundays. These excessively short hours of sleep and long hours of work consume a person's strength and hence it happens that men and women age much more in the country than in the towns] (Mirabeau, l. c., t.III. pp. 212 sqq.)

Note to the second edition. In April 1866, 18 years after the publication of the work of Robert Somers quoted above, Professor Leone Levi gave a lecture before the Society of Arts on the transformation of sheep-walks into deer-forest, in which he depicts the advance in the devastation of the Scottish Highlands. He says, with other things: 'Depopulation and transformation into sheep-walks were the most convenient means for getting an income without expenditure... A deer-forest in place of a sheep-walk was a common change in the Highlands. The landowners turned out the sheep as they once turned out the men from their estates, and welcomed the new tenants—the wild beasts and the feathered birds.... One can walk from the Earl of Dalhousie's estates in Forfarshire to John O'Groats, without ever leaving forest land.... In many of these woods the fox, the wild cat, the marten, the polecat, the weasel and the Alpine hare are common; whilst the rabbit, the squirrel and the rat have lately made their way into the country. Immense tracts of land, much of which is described in the statistical account of Scotland as having a pasturage in richness and extent of very superior description, are thus shut out from all cultivation and improvement, and are solely devoted to the sport of a few persons for a very brief period of the year.' The London *Economist* of June 2, 1866, says, 'Amongst the items of news in a Scotch paper of last week, we read... 'One of the finest sheep farms in Sutherlandshire, for which a rent of £1,200 a year was recently offered, on the expiry of the existing lease this year, is to be converted into a deer-forest.' Here we see the modern instincts of feudalism ... operating pretty much as they did when the Norman Conqueror... destroyed 36 villages to create the New Forest.... Two millions of acres... totally laid waste, embracing within their area some of the most fertile lands of Scotland. The natural grass of Glen Tilt was among the most nutritive in the county of Perth. The deer-forest of Ben Aulder was by far the best grazing ground in the wide district of Badenoch; a part of the Black Mount forest was the best pasture for black-faced sheep in Scotland. Some idea of the ground laid waste for purely sporting purposes in Scotland may be formed from the fact that it embraced an area larger than the whole county of Perth. The resources of the forest of Ben Aulder might give some idea of the loss sustained from the forced desolations. The ground would pasture 15,000 sheep, and as it was not more than one-thirtieth part of the old forest ground in Scotland ... it might, &c., ... All that forest land is as totally unproductive.... It might thus as well have been submerged under the waters of the German Ocean.... Such extemporised wildernesses or deserts ought to be put down by the decided interference of the Legislature.'

28

Bloody Legislation Against the Expropriated, from the End of the 15th Century. Forcing Down of Wages by Acts of Parliament

The proletariat created by the breaking up of the bands of feudal retainers and by the forcible expropriation of the people from the soil, this 'free' proletariat could not possibly be absorbed by the nascent manufactures as fast as it was thrown upon the world. On the other hand, these men, suddenly dragged from their wonted mode of life, could not as suddenly adapt themselves to the discipline of their new condition. They were turned *en masse* into beggars, robbers, vagabonds, partly from inclination, in most cases from stress of circumstances. Hence, at the end of the 15th and during the whole of the 16th century, throughout Western Europe a bloody legislation against vagabondage. The fathers of the present working class were chastised for their enforced transformation into vagabonds and paupers. Legislation treated them as 'voluntary' criminals, and assumed that it depended on their own good will to go on working under the old conditions that no longer existed.

In England this legislation began under Henry VII.

Henry VIII. 1530: Beggars old and unable to work receive a beggar's licence. On the other hand, whipping and imprisonment for sturdy vagabonds. They are to be tied to the cart-tail and whipped until the blood streams from their bodies, then to swear an oath to go back to their birthplace or to where they have lived the last three years and to 'put themselves to labour.' What grim irony! In 27 Henry VIII. the former statute is repeated, but strengthened with new clauses. For the second arrest for vagabondage the whipping is to be repeated and half the ear sliced off; but for the third relapse the offender is to be executed as a hardened criminal and enemy of the common weal.

Edward VI.: A statute of the first year of his reign, 1547, ordains that if anyone refuses to work, he shall be condemned as a slave to the person who has denounced him as an idler. The master shall feed his slave on bread and water, weak broth and such refuse meat as he thinks fit. He has the right to force him to do any work, no matter how disgusting, with whip and chains. If the slave is absent a fortnight, he is condemned to slavery for life and is to be branded on forehead or back with the letter 'S'; if he runs away thrice, he is to be executed as a felon. The master can sell him, bequeath him, let him out on hire as a slave, just as any other personal chattel or cattle. If the slaves attempt anything against the masters, they are also to be executed. Justices of the peace, on information, are to hunt the rascals down. If it happens that a vagabond has been idling about for three days, he is to be taken to his birthplace, branded with a red-hot iron with the letter V on the breast and be set to work, in chains, in the streets or at some other labour. If the vagabond gives a false birthplace, he is then to become the slave for life of this place, of its inhabitants, or its corporation, and to be branded with an 'S.' All persons have the right to take away the children of the vagabonds and to keep them as apprentices, the young men until the 24th year, the girls until the 20th. If they run away, they are to become up to this age the slaves of their masters, who can put them in irons, whip them, &c., if they like. Every master may put an iron ring round the neck, arms or legs of his slave, by which to know him more easily and to be more certain of him. [1] The last part of this statute provides, that certain poor people may be employed by a place or by persons, who are willing to give them food and drink and to find them work. This kind of parish slaves was kept up in England until far into the 19th century under the name of 'roundsmen.'

Elizabeth, 1572: Unlicensed beggars above 14 years of age are to be severely flogged and branded on the left ear unless some one will take them into service for two years; in case of a repetition of the offence, if they are over 18, they are to be executed, unless some one will take them into service for two years; but for the third offence they are to be executed without mercy as felons. Similar statutes: 18 Elizabeth, c. 13, and another of 1597.[2]

James 1: Any one wandering about and begging is declared a rogue and a vagabond. Justices of the peace in petty sessions are authorised to have them publicly whipped and for the first offence to imprison them for 6 months, for the second for 2 years. Whilst in prison they are to be whipped as much and as often as the justices of the peace think fit... Incorrigible and dangerous rogues are to be branded with an R on the left shoulder and set to hard labour, and if they are caught begging again, to be executed without mercy. These statutes, legally binding until the beginning of the 18th century, were only repealed by 12 Anne, c. 23.

Similar laws in France, where by the middle of the 17th century a kingdom of vagabonds (truands) was established in Paris. Even at the beginning of Louis XVI.'s reign (Ordinance of July 13th, 1777) every man in good health from 16 to 60 years of age, if without means of subsistence and not practising a trade, is to be sent to the galleys. Of the same nature are the statute of Charles V. for the Netherlands (October, 1537), the first edict of the States and Towns of Holland (March 10, 1614), the 'Plakaat' of the United Provinces (June 26, 1649), &c.

Thus were the agricultural people, first forcibly expropriated from the soil, driven from their homes, turned into vagabonds, and then whipped, branded, tortured by laws grotesquely terrible, into the discipline necessary for the wage system.

It is not enough that the conditions of labour are concentrated in a mass, in the shape of capital, at the one pole of society, while at the other are grouped masses of men, who have nothing to sell but their labour-power. Neither is it enough that they are compelled to sell it voluntarily. The advance of capitalist production develops a working class, which by education, tradition, habit, looks upon the conditions of that mode of production as self-evident laws of Nature. The organisation of the capitalist process of production, once fully developed, breaks down all resistance. The constant generation of a relative surplus-population keeps the law of supply and demand of labour, and therefore keeps wages, in a rut that corresponds with the wants of capital. The dull compulsion of economic relations completes the subjection of the labourer to the capitalist. Direct force, outside economic conditions, is of course still used, but only exceptionally. In the ordinary run of things, the labourer can be left to the 'natural laws of production,' *i.e.*, to his dependence on capital, a dependence springing from, and guaranteed in perpetuity by, the conditions of production themselves. It is otherwise during the historic genesis of capitalist production. The bourgeoisie, at its rise, wants and uses the power of the state to 'regulate' wages, *i.e.*, to force them within the limits suitable for surplus-value making, to lengthen the working-day and to keep the labourer himself in the normal degree of dependence. This is an essential element of the so-called primitive accumulation.

The class of wage labourers, which arose in the latter half of the 14th century, formed then and in the following century only a very small part of the population, well protected in its position by the independent peasant proprietary in the country and the guild-organisation in the town. In country and town master and workmen stood close together socially. The subordination of labour to capital was only formal—*i.e.*, the mode of production itself had as yet no specific capitalistic character. Variable capital preponderated greatly over constant. The demand for wage labour grew, therefore, rapidly with every accumulation of capital, whilst the supply of wage labour followed but slowly. A large part of the national product, changed later into a fund of capitalist accumulation, then still entered into the consumption-fund of the labourer.

Legislation on wage labour (from the first, aimed at the exploitation of the labourer and, as it advanced, always equally hostile to him),[3] is started in England by the Statute of Labourers, of Edward III., 1349. The ordinance of 1350 in France, issued in the name of King John, corresponds with it. English and French legislation run parallel and are identical in purport. So far as the labour-statutes aim at compulsory extension of the working-day, I do not return to them, as this point was treated earlier (Chap. X., Section 5).

The Statute of Labourers was passed at the urgent instance of the House of Commons. A Tory says naively:

> 'Formerly the poor demanded such *high* wages as to threaten industry and wealth. Next, their wages are so *low* as to threaten industry and wealth equally and perhaps more, but in another way.'[4]

A tariff of wages was fixed by law for town and country, for piece-work and day-work. The agricultural labourers were to hire themselves out by the year, the town ones 'in open market.' It was forbidden, under pain of imprisonment, to pay higher wages than those fixed by the statute, but the taking of higher wages was more severely punished than the giving them. [So also in Sections 18 and 19 of the Statute of Apprentices of Elizabeth, ten days' imprisonment is decreed for him that pays the higher wages, but twenty-one days for him that receives them.] A statute of 1360 increased the penalties and authorised the masters to extort labour at the legal rate of wages by corporal punishment. All combinations, contracts, oaths, &c., by which masons and carpenters reciprocally bound themselves, were declared null and void. Coalition of the labourers is treated as a heinous crime from the 14th century to 1825, the year of the repeal of the laws against Trades' Unions. The spirit of the Statute of Labourers of 1349 and of its offshoots comes out clearly in the fact, that indeed a maximum of wages is dictated by the State, but on no account a minimum.

In the 16th century, the condition of the labourers had, as we know, become much worse. The money wage rose, but not in proportion to the depreciation of money and the corresponding rise in the prices of commodities. Wages, therefore, in reality fell. Nevertheless, the laws for keeping them down remained in force, together with the ear-clipping and branding of those 'whom no one was willing to take into service.' By the Statute of Apprentices 5 Elizabeth, c. 3, the justices of the peace were empowered to fix certain wages and to modify them according to the time of the year and the price of commodities. James I. extended these regulations of labour also to weavers, spinners, and all possible categories of workers.[5] George II. extended the laws against coalitions of labourers to manufactures. In the manufacturing period *par excellence*, the capitalist mode of production had become sufficiently strong to render legal regulation of wages as impracticable as it was unnecessary; but the ruling classes were unwilling in case of necessity to be without the weapons of the old arsenal. Still, 8 George II. forbade a higher day's wage than 2s. 7½d. for journeymen tailors in and around London, except in cases of general mourning; still, 13 George III., c. 68, gave the regulation of the wages of silk-weavers to the justices of the peace; still, in 1706, it required two judgments of the higher courts to decide, whether the mandates of justices of the peace as to wages held good also for non-agricultural labourers; still, in 1799, an act of Parliament ordered that the wages of the Scotch miners should continue to be regulated by a statute of Elizabeth and two Scotch acts of 1661 and 1671. How completely, in the meantime, circumstances had changed, is proved by an occurrence unheard-of before in the English Lower House. In that place, where for more than 400 years laws had been made for the maximum, beyond which wages absolutely must not rise, Whitbread in 1796 proposed a legal minimum wage for agricultural labourers. Pitt opposed this, but confessed that the 'condition of the poor was cruel.' Finally, in 1813, the laws for the regulation of wages were repealed. They were an absurd anomaly, since the capitalist regulated his factory by his private legislation, and could by the poor-rates make up the wage of the agricultural labourer to the indispensable minimum. The provisions of the labour statutes as to contracts between master and workman, as to giving notice and the like, which only allow of a civil action against the contract-breaking master, but on the contrary permit a criminal action against the contract-breaking workman, are to this hour (1873) in full force. The barbarous laws against Trades' Unions fell in 1825 before the threatening bearing of the proletariat. Despite this, they fell only in part. Certain beautiful fragments of the old statute vanished only in 1859. Finally, the act of Parliament of June 29, 1871, made a pretence of removing the last traces of this class of legislation by legal recognition of Trades' Unions. But an act of Parliament of the same date (an act to amend the criminal law relating to violence, threats, and molestation), re-established, in point of fact, the former state of things in a new shape. By this Parliamentary escamotage the means which the labourers could use in a strike or lock-out were withdrawn from the laws common to all citizens, and placed under exceptional penal legislation, the interpretation of which fell to the masters themselves in their capacity as justices of the peace. Two years earlier, the same House of Commons and the same Mr Gladstone in the well-known straightforward fashion brought in a bill for the abolition of all exceptional penal legislation against the working class. But this was never allowed to go beyond the second reading, and the matter was thus protracted until at last the 'great Liberal party,' by an alliance with the Tories, found courage to turn against the very proletariat that had carried it into power. Not content with this treachery, the 'great Liberal party' allowed the English judges, ever complaisant in the service of the ruling classes, to dig up again the earlier laws against 'conspiracy,' and to apply them to coalitions of labourers. We see that only against its will and under the pressure of the masses did the English Parliament give up the laws against Strikes and Trades' Unions, after it had itself, for 500 years, held, with shameless egoism, the position of a permanent Trades' Union of the capitalists against the labourers.

During the very first storms of the revolution, the French bourgeoisie dared to take away from the workers the right of association but just acquired. By a decree of June 14, 1791, they declared all coalition of the workers as 'an attempt against liberty and the declaration of the rights of man,' punishable by a fine of 500 livres, together with deprivation of the rights of an active citizen for one year. [6] This law which, by means of State compulsion, confined the struggle between capital and labour within limits comfortable for capital, has outlived revolutions and changes of dynasties. Even the Reign of Terror left it untouched. It was but quite recently struck out of the Penal Code. Nothing is more characteristic than the pretext for this bourgeois *coup d'état*. 'Granting,' says Chapelier, the reporter of the Select Committee on this law, 'that wages ought to be a little higher than they are, ... that they ought to be high enough for him that receives them, to be free from that state of absolute dependence due to the want of the necessaries of life, and which is almost that of slavery,' yet the workers must not be allowed to come to any understanding about their own interests, nor to act in common and thereby lessen their 'absolute dependence, which is almost that of slavery;' because, forsooth, in doing this they injure 'the freedom of their cidevant masters, the present entrepreneurs,' and because a coalition against the despotism of the quondam masters of the corporations is—guess what!—is a restoration of the corporations abolished by the French constitution.[7]

Notes

1. The author of the 'Essay on Trade, etc.,' 1770, says, 'In the reign of Edward VI. indeed the English seem to have set, in good earnest, about encouraging manufactures and employing the poor. This we learn from a remarkable statute which runs thus: 'That all vagrants shall be branded, &c." l. c., p. 5.
2. Thomas More says in his 'Utopia»: 'Therfore that on covetous and unsatiable cormaraunte and very plage of his native contrey maye compasse aboute and inclose many thousand akers of grounde together within one pale or hedge, the husbandman be thrust owte of their owne, or els either by coneyne and fraude, or by violent oppression they be put besydes it, or by wrongs and iniuries thei be so weried that they be compelled to sell all: by one meanes, therfore, or by other, either by hooke or crooke they muste needes departe awaye, poore, selye, wretched soules, men, women, husbands, wiues, fatherlesse children, widowes, wofull mothers with their yonge babes, and their whole household smal in substance, and muche in numbre, as husbandrye requireth many handes. Awaye thei trudge, I say, owte of their knowen accustomed houses, fyndynge no place to reste in. All their housholde stuffe, which is very little woorthe, thoughe it might well abide the sale: yet beeynge sodainely thruste owte, they be constrayned to sell it for a thing of nought. And when they haue wandered abrode tyll that be spent, what cant they then els doe but steale, and then iustly pardy be hanged, or els go about beggyng. And yet then also they be caste in prison as vagaboundes, because they go

aboute and worke not: whom no man wyl set a worke though thei neuer so willyngly profre themselues therto.' Of these poor fugitives of whom Thomas More says that they were forced to thieve, '7,200 great and petty thieves were put to death,' in the reign of Henry VIII. (Holinshed, 'Description of England,' Vol. 1, p. 186.) In Elizabeth's time, 'rogues were trussed up apace, and that there was not one year commonly wherein three or four hundred were not devoured and eaten up by the gallowes.' (Strype's 'Annals of the Reformation and Establishment of Religion and other Various Occurrences in the Church of England during Queen Elizabeth's Happy Reign.' Second ed., 1725, Vol. 2.) According to this same Strype, in Somersetshire, in one year, 40 persons were executed, 35 robbers burnt in the hand, 37 whipped, and 183 discharged as 'incorrigible vagabonds.' Nevertheless, he is of opinion that this large number of prisoners does not comprise even a fifth of the actual criminals, thanks to the negligence of the justices and the foolish compassion of the people; and the other counties of England were not better off in this respect than Somersetshire, while some were even worse.

3. 'Whenever the legislature attempts to regulate the differences between masters and their workmen, its counsellors are always the masters,' says A. Smith. 'L'esprit des lois, c'est la propriété,' says Linguet.
4. 'Sophisms of Free Trade.' By a Barrister. Lond., 1850, p. 206. He adds maliciously: 'We were ready enough to interfere for the employer, can nothing now be done for the employed?'
5. From a clause of Statute 2 James I., c. 6, we see that certain clothmakers took upon themselves to dictate, in their capacity of justices of the peace, the official tariff of wages in their own shops. In Germany, especially after the Thirty Years' War, statutes for keeping down wages were general. 'The want of servants and labourers was very troublesome to the landed proprietors in the depopulated districts. All villagers were forbidden to let rooms to single men and women; all the latter were to be reported to the authorities and cast into prison if they were unwilling to become servants, even if they were employed at any other work, such as sowing seeds for the peasants at a daily wage, or even buying and selling corn. (Imperial privileges and sanctions for Silesia, I., 25.) For a whole century in the decrees of the small German potentates a bitter cry goes up again and again about the wicked and impertinent rabble that will not reconcile itself to its hard lot, will not be content with the legal wage; the individual landed proprietors are forbidden to pay more than the State had fixed by a tariff. And yet the conditions of service were at times better after war than 100 years later; the farm servants of Silesia had, in 1652, meat twice a week, whilst even in our century, districts are known where they have it only three times a year. Further, wages after the war were higher than in the following century.' (G. Freytag.)
6. Article I. of this law runs: 'L'anéantissement de toute espèce de corporations du même état et profession étant l'une des bases fondamentales de la constitution française, il est défendu de les rétablir de fait sous quelque prétexte et sous quelque forme que ce soit.' Article IV. declares, that if 'des citoyens attachés aux mêmes professions, arts et métiers prenaient des délibérations, faisaient entre eux des conventions tendantes à refuser de concert ou à n'accorder qu'à un prix déterminé le secours de leur industrie ou de leurs travaux, les dites délibérations et conventions... seront déclarées inconstitutionnelles, attentatoires à la liberté et à la declaration des droits de l'homme, &c.;' felony, therefore, as in the old labour-statutes. [As the abolition of any form of association between citizens of the same estate and profession is one of the foundations of the French constitution, it is forbidden to re-establish them under any pretext or in any form, whatever they might be. ... citizens belonging to the same profession, craft or trade have joint discussions and make joint decisions with the intention of refusing together to perform their trade or insisting together on providing the services of their trade or their labours only at a particular price, then the said deliberations and agreements ... shall be declared unconstitutional, derogatory to liberty and the declaration of the rights of man, etc.] ('Révolutions de Paris,' Paris, 1791, t. III, p. 523.)
7. Buchez et Roux: 'Histoire Parlementaire,' t. x., p. 195.

29

Genesis of the Capitalist Farmer

Now that we have considered the forcible creation of a class of outlawed proletarians, the bloody discipline that turned them into wage labourers, the disgraceful action of the State which employed the police to accelerate the accumulation of capital by increasing the degree of exploitation of labour, the question remains: whence came the capitalists originally? For the expropriation of the agricultural population creates, directly, none but the greatest landed proprietors. As far, however, as concerns the genesis of the farmer, we can, so to say, put our hand on it, because it is a slow process evolving through many centuries. The serfs, as well as the free small proprietors, held land under very different tenures, and were therefore emancipated under very different economic conditions. In England, the first form of the farmer is the bailiff, himself a serf. His position is similar to that of the old Roman *villicus*, only in a more limited sphere of action. During the second half of the 14th century he is replaced by a farmer, whom the landlord provided with seed, cattle and implements. His condition is not very different from that of the peasant. Only he exploits more wage labour. Soon he becomes a metayer, a half-farmer. He advances one part of the agricultural stock, the landlord the other. The two divide the total product in proportions determined by contract. This form quickly disappears in England, to give the place to the farmer proper, who makes his own capital breed by employing wage labourers, and pays a part of the surplus-product, in money or in kind, to the landlord as rent. So long, during the 15th century, as the independent peasant and the farm-labourer working for himself as well as for wages, enriched themselves by their own labour, the circumstances of the farmer, and his field of production, were equally mediocre. The agricultural revolution which commenced in the last third of the 15th century, and continued during almost the whole of the 16th (excepting, however, its last decade), enriched him just as speedily as it impoverished the mass of the agricultural people.[1]

The usurpation of the common lands allowed him to augment greatly his stock of cattle, almost without cost, whilst they yielded him a richer supply of manure for the tillage of the soil. To this was added in the 16th century a very important element. At that time the contracts for farms ran for a long time, often for 99 years. The progressive fall in the value of the precious metals, and therefore of money, brought the farmers golden fruit. Apart from all the other circumstances discussed above, it lowered wages. A portion of the latter was now added to the profits of the farm. The continuous rise in the price of corn, wool, meat, in a word of all agricultural produce, swelled the money capital of the farm without any action on his part, whilst the rent he paid (being calculated on the old value of money) diminished in reality.[2] Thus they grew rich at the expense both of their labourers and their landlords. No wonder, therefore, that England, at the end of the 16th century, had a class of capitalist farmers, rich, considering the circumstances of the time.[3]

Notes

1. Harrison in his 'Description of England,' says 'although peradventure foure pounds of old rent be improved to fortie, toward the end of his term, if he have not six or seven yeares rent lieng by him, fiftie or a hundred pounds, yet will the farmer thinke his gaines verie small.'
2. On the influence of the depreciation of money in the 16th century, on the different classes of society, see 'A Compendium of Briefe Examination of Certayne Ordinary Complaints of Divers of our Countrymen in these our Days,' by W. S. Gentleman (London 1581). The

dialogue form of this work led people for a long time to ascribe it to Shakespeare, and even in 1751, it was published under his name. Its author is William Stafford. In one place the knight reasons as follows: *Knight*: You, my neighbor, the husbandman, you Maister Mercer, and you Goodman Cooper, with other artificers, may save yourselves metely well. For as much as all things are dearer than they were, so much do you arise in the pryce of your wares and occupations that ye sell agayne. But we have nothing to sell whereby we might advance ye price there of, to countervaile those things that we must buy agayne.' In another place, the knight asks the doctor: 'I pray you, what be those sorts that ye meane. And first, of those that ye thinke should have no losse thereby? *Doctor*: I mean all those that live by buying and selling, for as they buy deare, they sell thereafter. *Knight*: What is the next sort that ye say would win by it? *Doctor*: Marry, all such as have takings of fearmes in their owne manurance [cultivation] at the old rent, for where they pay after the olde rate they sell after the newe—that is, they paye for theire lande good cheape, and sell all things growing thereof deare. *Knight*: What sorte is that which, ye sayde should have greater losse hereby, than these men had profit? *Doctor*: It is all noblemen, gentlemen, and all other that live either by a stinted rent or stypend, or do not manure [cultivate] the ground, or doe occupy no buying and selling.'

3. In France, the régisseur, steward, collector of dues for the feudal lords during the earlier part of the middle ages, soon became an homme d›affaires, who by extortion, cheating, &c., swindled himself into a capitalist. These régisseurs themselves were sometimes noblemen. *E.g.*, 'C'est li compte que messire Jacques de Thoraine, chevalier chastelain sor Besançon rent és-seigneur tenant les comptes à Dijon pour monseigneur le duc et comte de Bourgoigne, des rentes appartenant à la dite chastellenie, depuis xxve jour de décembre MCCCLIX jusqu'au xxviiie jour de décembre MCCCLX.' [This is the account given by M. Jacques de Thoraisse, knight, and Lord of a manor near Besançon, to the lord who administers the accounts at Dijon for his highness the Duke and Count of Burgundy, of the rents appurtenant to the above-mentioned manor, from the 25th day of December 1359 to the 28th day of December 1360] (Alexis Monteil: 'Traité de Matériaux Manuscrits etc.,' pp. 234, 235.) Already it is evident here how in all spheres of social life the lion's share falls to the middleman. In the economic domain, *e.g.*, financiers, stock-exchange speculators, merchants, shopkeepers skim the cream; in civil matters, the lawyer fleeces his clients; in politics the representative is of more importance than the voters, the minister than the sovereign; in religion, God is pushed into the background by the 'Mediator,' and the latter again is shoved back by the priests, the inevitable middlemen between the good shepherd and his sheep. In France, as in England, the great feudal territories were divided into innumerable small homesteads, but under conditions incomparably more favorable for the people. During the 14th century arose the farms or *terriers*. Their number grew constantly, far beyond 100,000. They paid rents varying from 1/12 to 1/5 of the product in money or in kind. These farms were fiefs, sub-fiefs, &c., according the value and extent of the domains, many of them only containing a few acres. But these farmers had rights of jurisdiction in some degree over the dwellers on the soil; there were four grades. The oppression of the agricultural population under all these petty tyrants will be understood. Monteil says that there were once in France 160,000 judges, where today, 4,000 tribunals, including justices of the peace, suffice.

30

Reaction of the Agricultural Revolution on Industry. Creation of the Home-Market for Industrial Capital

The expropriation and expulsion of the agricultural population, intermittent but renewed again and again, supplied, as we saw, the town industries with a mass of proletarians entirely unconnected with the corporate guilds and unfettered by them; a fortunate circumstance that makes old A. Anderson (not to be confounded with James Anderson), in his 'History of Commerce,' believe in the direct intervention of Providence. We must still pause a moment on this element of primitive accumulation. The thinning-out of the independent, self-supporting peasants not only brought about the crowding together of the industrial proletariat, in the way that Geoffrey Saint Hilaire explained the condensation of cosmical matter at one place, by its rarefaction at another.[1] In spite of the smaller number of its cultivators, the soil brought forth as much or more produce, after as before, because the revolution in the conditions of landed property was accompanied by improved methods of culture, greater co-operation, concentration of the means of production, &c., and because not only were the agricultural wage labourers put on the strain more intensely[2], but the field of production on which they worked for themselves became more and more contracted. With the setting free of a part of the agricultural population, therefore, their former means of nourishment were also set free. They were now transformed into material elements of variable capital. The peasant, expropriated and cast adrift, must buy their value in the form of wages, from his new master, the industrial capitalist. That which holds good of the means of subsistence holds with the raw materials of industry dependent upon home agriculture. They were transformed into an element of constant capital. Suppose, *e.g.*, a part of the Westphalian peasants, who, at the time of Frederick II, all span flax, forcibly expropriated and hunted from the soil; and the other part that remained, turned into day labourers of large farmers. At the same time arise large establishments for flax-spinning and weaving, in which the men 'set free' now work for wages. The flax looks exactly as before. Not a fibre of it is changed, but a new social soul has popped into its body. It forms now a part of the constant capital of the master manufacturer. Formerly divided among a number of small producers, who cultivated it themselves and with their families spun it in retail fashion, it is now concentrated in the hand of one capitalist, who sets others to spin and weave it for him. The extra labour expended in flax-spinning realised itself formerly in extra income to numerous peasant families, or maybe, in Frederick II's time, in taxes pour le roi de Prusse. It realises itself now in profit for a few capitalists. The spindles and looms, formerly scattered over the face of the country, are now crowded together in a few great labour-barracks, together with the labourers and the raw material. And spindles, looms, raw material, are now transformed from means of independent existence for the spinners and weavers, into means for commanding them and sucking out of them unpaid labour.[3] One does not perceive, when looking at the large manufactories and the large farms, that they have originated from the throwing into one of many small centres of production, and have been built up by the expropriation of many small independent producers. Nevertheless, the popular intuition was not at fault. In the time of Mirabeau, the lion of the Revolution, the great manufactories were still called manufactures réunies, workshops thrown into one, as we speak of fields thrown into one. Says Mirabeau:

'We are only paying attention to the grand manufactories, in which hundreds of men work under a director and which are commonly called *manufactures réunies*. Those where a very large number of labourers work, each separately and on his own account, are hardly considered; they are placed at an infinite distance from the others. This is a great error, as the latter alone make a really important object of national prosperity.... The large workshop (manufacture réunie) will enrich prodigiously one or two entrepreneurs, but the labourers will only be journeymen, paid more or less, and will not have any share in the success of the undertaking. In the discrete workshop (manufacture separée), on the contrary, no one will become rich, but many labourers will be comfortable; the saving and the industrious will be able to amass a little capital, to put by a little for a birth of a child, for an illness, for themselves or their belongings. The number of saving and industrious labourers will increase, because they will see in good conduct, in activity, a means of essentially bettering their condition, and not of obtaining a small rise in wages that can never be of any importance of the future, and whose sole result is to place men in the position to live a little better, but only from day to day.... The large workshops, undertakings of certain private persons who pay labourers from day to day to work for their gain, may be able to put these private individuals at their ease, but they will never be an object worth the attention of governments. Discrete workshops, for the most part combined with cultivation of small holdings, are the only free ones.'[4] The expropriation and eviction of a part of the agricultural population not only set free for industrial capital, the labourers, their means of subsistence, and material for labour; it also created the home-market.

In fact, the events that transformed the small peasants into wage labourers, and their means of subsistence and of labour into material elements of capital, created, at the same time, a home-market for the latter. Formerly, the peasant family produced the means of subsistence and the raw materials, which they themselves, for the most part, consumed. These raw materials and means of subsistence have now become commodities; the large farmer sells them, he finds his market in manufactures. Yarn, linen, coarse woollen stuffs—things whose raw materials had been within the reach of every peasant family, had been spun and woven by it for its own use—were now transformed into articles of manufacture, to which the country districts at once served for markets. The many scattered customers, whom stray artisans until now had found in the numerous small producers working on their own account, concentrate themselves now into one great market provided for by industrial capital.[5] Thus, hand in hand with the expropriation of the self-supporting peasants, with their separation from their means of production, goes the destruction of rural domestic industry, the process of separation between manufacture and agriculture. And only the destruction of rural domestic industry can give the internal market of a country that extension and consistence which the capitalist mode of production requires. Still the manufacturing period, properly so called, does not succeed in carrying out this transformation radically and completely. It will be remembered that manufacture, properly so called, conquers but partially the domain of national production, and always rests on the handicrafts of the town and the domestic industry of the rural districts as its ultimate basis. If it destroys these in one form, in particular branches, at certain points, it calls them up again elsewhere, because it needs them for the preparation of raw material up to a certain point. It produces, therefore, a new class of small villagers who, while following the cultivation of the soil as an accessary calling, find their chief occupation in industrial labour, the products of which they sell to the manufacturers directly, or through the medium of merchants. This is one, though not the chief, cause of a phenomenon which, at first, puzzles the student of English history.[6] From the last third of the 15th century he finds continually complaints, only interrupted at certain intervals, about the encroachment of capitalist farming in the country districts, and the progressive destruction of the peasantry. On the other hand, he always finds this peasantry turning up again, although in diminished number, and always under worse conditions. The chief reason is: England is at one time chiefly a cultivator of corn, at another chiefly a breeder of cattle, in alternate periods, and with these the extent of peasant cultivation fluctuates. Modern Industry alone, and finally, supplies, in machinery, the lasting basis of capitalistic agriculture, expropriates radically the enormous majority of the agricultural population, and completes the separation between agriculture and rural domestic industry, whose roots—spinning and weaving—it tears up.[7] It therefore also, for the first time, conquers for industrial capital the entire home market.[8]

Notes

1. In his 'Notions de Philosophie Naturelle.' Paris, 1838.
2. A point that Sir James Steuart emphasises.
3. 'Je permettrai,' says the capitalist, 'que vous ayez l'honneur de me servir, à condition que vous me donnez le peu qui vous reste pour la peine que je prends de vous commander.' [I will allow you ... to have the honour of serving me, on condition that, in return for the pains I take in commanding you, you give me the little that remains to you] (J. J. Rousseau: 'Discours sur l'Economie Politique.')
4. Mirabeau, l.c., t.III, pp.20-109 passim. That Mirabeau considers the separate workshops more economical and productive than the 'combined,' and sees in the latter merely artificial exotics under government cultivation, is explained by the position at that time of a great part of the continental manufactures.
5. 'Twenty pounds of wool converted unobtrusively into yearly clothing of a labourer's family by its own industry in the intervals of other works—this makes no show; but bring it to market, send it to the factory, thence to the broker, thence to the dealer, and you will have great commercial operations, and nominal capital engaged to the amount of twenty times its value.... The working-class is thus emersed to support a wretched factory population, a parastical shop-keeping class, and a fictitious commercial, monetary, and financial system.' (David Urquhart, l.c., p.120.)
6. Cromwell's time forms an exception. So long as the Republic lasted, the mass of the English people of all grades rose from the degradation into which they had sunk under the Tudors.
7. Tuckett is aware that the modern woollen industry has sprung, with the introduction of machinery, from manufacture proper and from the destruction of rural and domestic industries.

   'The plough, the yoke, were 'the invention of gods, and the occupation of heroes'; are the loom, the spindle, the distaff, of less noble parentage. You sever the distaff and the plough, the spindle and the yoke, and you get factories and poor-houses, credit and panics, two hostile nations, agriculture and commercial.' (David Urquhart, l.c., p.122.)

   But now comes Carey, and cries out upon England, surely not with unreason, that it is trying to turn every other country into a mere agricultural nation, whose manufacturer is to be England. He pretends that in this way Turkey has been ruined, because 'the owners and occupants of land have never been permitted by England to strengthen themselves by the formation of that natural alliance between the plough and the loom, the hammer and the harrow.' ('The Slave Trade,' p.125.) According to him, Urquhart himself is one of the chief agents in the ruin of Turkey, where he had made Free-trade propaganda in the English interest. The best of it is that Carey, a great Russophile by the way, wants to prevent the process of separation by that very system of protection which accelerates it.
8. Philanthropic English economists, like Mill, Rogers, Goldwin Smith, Fawcett, &c., and liberal manufacturers like John Bright & Co., ask the English landed proprietors, as God asked Cain after Abel, Where are our thousands of freeholders gone? But where do *you* come from, then? From the destruction of those freeholders. Why don't you ask further, where are the independent weavers, spinners, and artisans gone?

31

Genesis of the Industrial Capitalist

The genesis of the industrial* capitalist did not proceed in such a gradual way as that of the farmer. Doubtless many small guild-masters, and yet more independent small artisans, or even wage labourers, transformed themselves into small capitalists, and (by gradually extending exploitation of wage labour and corresponding accumulation) into full-blown capitalists. In the infancy of capitalist production, things often happened as in the infancy of medieval towns, where the question, which of the escaped serfs should be master and which servant, was in great part decided by the earlier or later date of their flight. The snail's pace of this method corresponded in no wise with the commercial requirements of the new world market that the great discoveries of the end of the 15th century created. But the middle ages had handed down two distinct forms of capital, which mature in the most different economic social formations, and which before the era of the capitalist mode of production, are considered as capital quand même [all the same]—usurer's capital and merchant's capital.

> 'At present, all the wealth of society goes first into the possession of the capitalist ... he pays the landowner his rent, the labourer his wages, the tax and tithe gatherer their claims, and keeps a large, indeed the largest, and a continually augmenting share, of the annual produce of labour for himself. The capitalist may now be said to be the first owner of all the wealth of the community, though no law has conferred on him the right to this property... this change has been effected by the taking of interest on capital ... and it is not a little curious that all the law-givers of Europe endeavoured to prevent this by statutes, viz., statutes against usury.... The power of the capitalist over all the wealth of the country is a complete change in the right of property, and by what law, or series of laws, was it effected?'[2]

The author should have remembered that revolutions are not made by laws.

The money capital formed by means of usury and commerce was prevented from turning into industrial capital, in the country by the feudal constitution, in the towns by the guild organisation. [3] These fetters vanished with the dissolution of feudal society, with the expropriation and partial eviction of the country population. The new manufactures were established at sea-ports, or at inland points beyond the control of the old municipalities and their guilds. Hence in England an embittered struggle of the corporate towns against these new industrial nurseries.

The discovery of gold and silver in America, the extirpation, enslavement and entombment in mines of the aboriginal population, the beginning of the conquest and looting of the East Indies, the turning of Africa into a warren for the commercial hunting of black-skins, signalised the rosy dawn of the era of capitalist production. These idyllic proceedings are the chief momenta of primitive accumulation. On their heels treads the commercial war of the European nations, with the globe for a theatre. It begins with the revolt of the Netherlands from Spain, assumes giant dimensions in England's Anti-Jacobin War, and is still going on in the opium wars against China, &c.

The different momenta of primitive accumulation distribute themselves now, more or less in chronological order, particularly over Spain, Portugal, Holland, France, and England. In England, at the end of the 17th century, they arrive at a systematical combination, embracing the colonies, the national debt, the modern mode of taxation, and the protectionist system. These methods depend in part on brute force, *e.g.*, the colonial system. But, they all employ the power of the State, the concentrated and organised force of society, to hasten, hot-house fashion, the process of transformation of the feudal mode of production into the capitalist mode, and to shorten the transition. Force is the midwife of every old society pregnant with a new one. It is itself an economic power.

Of the Christian colonial system, W. Howitt, a man who makes a speciality of Christianity, says:

> 'The barbarities and desperate outrages of the so-called Christian race, throughout every region of the world, and upon every people they have been able to subdue, are not to be paralleled by those of any other race, however fierce, however untaught, and however reckless of mercy and of shame, in any age of the earth.'[4]

The history of the colonial administration of Holland—and Holland was the head capitalistic nation of the 17th century —

> 'is one of the most extraordinary relations of treachery, bribery, massacre, and meanness'[5]

Nothing is more characteristic than their system of stealing men, to get slaves for Java. The men stealers were trained for this purpose. The thief, the interpreter, and the seller, were the chief agents in this trade, native princes the chief sellers. The young people stolen, were thrown into the secret dungeons of Celebes, until they were ready for sending to the slave-ships. An official report says:

> 'This one town of Macassar, *e.g.*, is full of secret prisons, one more horrible than the other, crammed with unfortunates, victims of greed and tyranny fettered in chains, forcibly torn from their families.'

To secure Malacca, the Dutch corrupted the Portuguese governor. He let them into the town in 1641. They hurried at once to his house and assassinated him, to 'abstain' from the payment of £21,875, the price of his treason. Wherever they set foot, devastation and depopulation followed. Banjuwangi, a province of Java, in 1750 numbered over 80,000 inhabitants, in 1811 only 18,000. Sweet commerce!

The English East India Company, as is well known, obtained, besides the political rule in India, the exclusive monopoly of the tea-trade, as well as of the Chinese trade in general, and of the transport of goods to and from Europe. But the coasting trade of India and between the islands, as well as the internal trade of India, were the monopoly of the higher employés of the company. The monopolies of salt, opium, betel and other commodities, were inexhaustible mines of wealth. The employés themselves fixed the price and plundered at will the unhappy Hindus. The Governor-General took part in this private traffic. His favourites received contracts under conditions whereby they, cleverer than the alchemists, made gold out of nothing. Great fortunes sprang up like mushrooms in a day; primitive accumulation went on without the advance of a shilling. The trial of Warren Hastings swarms with such cases. Here is an instance. A contract for opium was given to a certain Sullivan at the moment of his departure on an official mission to a part of India far removed from the opium district. Sullivan sold his contract to one Binn for £40,000; Binn sold it the same day for £60,000, and the ultimate purchaser who carried out the contract declared that after all he realised an enormous gain. According to one of the lists laid before Parliament, the Company and its employés from 1757-1766 got £6,000,000 from the Indians as gifts. Between 1769 and 1770, the English manufactured a famine by buying up all the rice and refusing to sell it again, except at fabulous prices.[6]

The treatment of the aborigines was, naturally, most frightful in plantation-colonies destined for export trade only, such as the West Indies, and in rich and well-populated countries, such as Mexico and India, that were given over to plunder. But even in the colonies properly so called, the Christian character of primitive accumulation did not belie itself. Those sober virtuosi of Protestantism, the Puritans of New England, in 1703, by decrees of their assembly set a premium of £40 on every Indian scalp and every captured red-skin: in 1720 a premium of £100 on every scalp; in 1744, after Massachusetts-Bay had proclaimed a certain tribe as rebels, the following prices: for a male scalp of 12 years and upwards £100 (new currency), for a male prisoner £105, for women and children prisoners £50, for scalps of women and children £50. Some decades later, the colonial system took its revenge on the descendants of the pious pilgrim fathers, who had grown seditious in the meantime. At English instigation and for English pay they were tomahawked by red-skins. The British Parliament proclaimed bloodhounds and scalping as 'means that God and Nature had given into its hand.'

The colonial system ripened, like a hot-house, trade and navigation. The 'societies Monopolia' of Luther were powerful levers for concentration of capital. The colonies secured a market for the budding manufactures, and, through the monopoly of the market, an increased accumulation. The treasures captured outside Europe by undisguised looting, enslavement, and murder, floated back to the mother-country and were there turned into capital. Holland, which first fully developed the colonial system, in 1648 stood already in the acme of its commercial greatness. It was

> 'in almost exclusive possession of the East Indian trade and the commerce between the south-east and north-west of Europe. Its fisheries, marine, manufactures, surpassed those of any other country. The total capital of the Republic was probably more important than that of all the rest of Europe put together.' Gülich forgets to add that by 1648, the people of Holland were more over-worked, poorer and more brutally oppressed than those of all the rest of Europe put together.

Today industrial supremacy implies commercial supremacy. In the period of manufacture properly so called, it is, on the other hand, the commercial supremacy that gives industrial predominance. Hence the preponderant rôle that the colonial system plays at that time. It was 'the strange God' who perched himself on the altar cheek by jowl with the old Gods of Europe, and one fine day with a shove and a kick chucked them all of a heap. It proclaimed surplus-value making as the sole end and aim of humanity.

The system of public credit, *i.e.*, of national debts, whose origin we discover in Genoa and Venice as early as the Middle Ages, took possession of Europe generally during the manufacturing period. The colonial system with its maritime trade and commercial wars served as a forcing-house for it. Thus it first took root in Holland. National debts, *i.e.*, the alienation of the state—whether despotic, constitutional or republican—marked with its stamp the capitalistic era. The only part of the so-called national wealth that actually enters into the collective possessions of modern peoples is their national debt. [7] Hence, as a necessary consequence, the modern doctrine that a nation becomes the richer the more deeply it is in debt. Public credit becomes the *credo* of capital. And with the rise of national debt-making, want of faith in the national debt takes the place of the blasphemy against the Holy Ghost, which may not be forgiven.

The public debt becomes one of the most powerful levers of primitive accumulation. As with the stroke of an enchanter's wand, it endows barren money with the power of breeding and thus turns it into capital, without the necessity of its exposing itself to the troubles and risks inseparable from its employment in industry or even in usury. The state creditors actually give nothing away, for the sum lent is transformed into public bonds, easily negotiable, which go on functioning in their hands just as so much hard cash would. But further, apart from the class of lazy annuitants thus created, and from the improvised wealth of the financiers, middlemen between the government and the nation—as also apart from the tax-farmers, merchants, private manufacturers, to whom a good part of every national loan renders the service of a capital fallen from heaven—the national debt has given rise to joint-stock companies, to dealings in negotiable effects of all kinds, and to agiotage, in a word to stock-exchange gambling and the modern bankocracy.

At their birth the great banks, decorated with national titles, were only associations of private speculators, who placed themselves by the side of governments, and, thanks to the privileges they received, were in a position to advance money to the State. Hence the accumulation of the national debt has no more infallible measure than the successive rise in the stock of these banks, whose full development dates from the founding of the Bank of England in 1694. The Bank of England began with lending its money to the Government at 8%; at the same time it was empowered by Parliament to coin money out of the same capital, by lending it again to the public in the form of banknotes. It was allowed to use these notes for discounting bills, making advances on commodities, and for buying the precious metals. It was not long ere this credit-money, made by the bank itself, became. The coin in which the Bank of England made its loans to the State, and paid, on account of the State, the interest on the public debt. It was not enough that the bank gave with one hand and took back more with the other; it remained, even whilst receiving, the eternal creditor of the nation down to the last shilling advanced. Gradually, it became inevitably the receptacle of the metallic hoard of the country, and the centre of gravity of all commercial credit. What effect was produced on their contemporaries by the sudden uprising of this brood of bankocrats, financiers, rentiers, brokers, stock-jobbers, &c., is proved by the writings of that time, *e.g.*, by Bolingbroke's.[8]

With the national debt arose an international credit system, which often conceals one of the sources of primitive accumulation in this or that people. Thus the villainies of the Venetian thieving system formed one of the secret bases of the capital-wealth of Holland to whom Venice in her decadence lent large sums of money. So also was it with Holland and England. By the beginning of the 18th century the Dutch manufactures were far outstripped. Holland had ceased to be the nation preponderant in commerce and industry. One of its main lines of business, therefore, from 1701-1776, is the lending out of enormous amounts of capital, especially to its great rival England. The same thing is going on today between England and the United States. A great deal of capital, which appears today in the United States without any certificate of birth, was yesterday, in England, the capitalised blood of children.

As the national debt finds its support in the public revenue, which must cover the yearly payments for interest, &c., the modern system of taxation was the necessary complement of the system of national loans. The loans enable the government to meet extraordinary expenses, without the tax-payers feeling it immediately, but they necessitate, as a consequence, increased taxes. On the other hand, the raising of taxation caused by the accumulation of debts contracted one after another, compels the government always to have recourse to new loans for new extraordinary expenses. Modern fiscality, whose pivot is formed by taxes on the most necessary means of subsistence (thereby increasing their price), thus contains within itself the germ of automatic progression. Overtaxation is not an incident, but rather a principle. In Holland, therefore, where this system was first inaugurated, the great patriot, DeWitt, has in his 'Maxims' extolled it as the best system for making the wage labourer submissive, frugal, industrious, and overburdened with labour. The destructive influence that it exercises on the condition of the wage labourer concerns us less however, here, than the forcible expropriation, resulting from it, of peasants, artisans, and in a word, all elements of the lower middle class. On this there are not two opinions, even among the bourgeois economists. Its expropriating efficacy is still further heightened by the system of protection, which forms one of its integral parts.

The great part that the public debt, and the fiscal system corresponding with it, has played in the capitalisation of wealth and the expropriation of the masses, has led many writers, like Cobbett, Doubleday and others, to seek in this, incorrectly, the fundamental cause of the misery of the modern peoples.

The system of protection was an artificial means of manufacturing manufacturers, of expropriating independent labourers, of capitalising the national means of production and subsistence, of forcibly abbreviating the transition from the medieval to the modern mode of production. The European states tore one another to pieces about the patent of this invention, and, once entered into the service of the surplus-value makers, did not merely lay under contribution in the pursuit of this purpose their own people, indirectly through protective duties, directly through export premiums. They also forcibly rooted out, in their dependent countries, all industry, as, *e.g.*, England did. with the Irish woollen manufacture. On the continent of Europe, after Colbert's example, the process was much simplified. The primitive industrial capital, here, came in part directly out of the state treasury. 'Why,' cries Mirabeau, 'why go so far to seek the cause of the manufacturing glory of Saxony before the war? 180,000,000 of debts contracted by the sovereigns!'[9]

Colonial system, public debts, heavy taxes, protection, commercial wars, &c., these children of the true manufacturing period, increase gigantically during the infancy of Modem Industry. The birth of the latter is heralded by a great slaughter of the innocents. Like the royal navy, the factories were recruited by means of the press-gang. Blasé as Sir F. M. Eden is as to the horrors of the expropriation of the agricultural population from the soil, from the last third of the 15th century to his own time; with all the self-satisfaction with which he rejoices in this process, 'essential' for establishing capitalistic agriculture and 'the due proportion between arable and pasture land'—he does not show, however, the same economic insight in respect to the necessity of child-stealing and child-slavery for the transformation of manufacturing exploitation into factory exploitation, and the establishment of the 'true relation' between capital and labour-power. He says:

> 'It may, perhaps, be worthy the attention of the public to consider, whether any manufacture, which, in order to be carried on successfully, requires that cottages and workhouses should be ransacked for poor children; that they should be employed by turns during the greater part of the night and robbed of that rest which, though indispensable to all, is most required by the young; and that numbers of both sexes, of different ages and dispositions, should be collected together in such a manner that the contagion of example cannot but lead to profligacy and debauchery; will add to the sum of individual or national felicity?'[10]
>
> 'In the counties of Derbyshire, Nottinghamshire, and more particularly in Lancashire,' says Fielden, 'the newly-invented machinery was used in large factories built on the sides of streams capable of turning the water-wheel. Thousands of hands were suddenly required in these places, remote from towns; and Lancashire, in particular, being, till then, comparatively thinly populated and barren, a population was all that she now wanted. The small and nimble fingers of little children being by very far the most in request, the custom instantly sprang up of procuring *apprentices* from the different parish workhouses of London, Birmingham, and elsewhere. Many, many thousands of these little, hapless creatures were sent down into the north, being from the age of 7 to the age of 13 or 14 years old. The custom was for the master to clothe his apprentices and to feed and lodge them in an 'apprentice house' near the factory; overseers were appointed to see to the works, whose interest it was to work the children to the utmost, because their pay was in proportion to the quantity of work that they could exact. Cruelty was, of course, the consequence. ... In many of the manufacturing districts, but particularly, I am afraid, in the guilty county to which I belong [Lancashire], cruelties the most heart-rending were practised upon the unoffending and friendless creatures who were thus consigned to the charge of master-manufacturers; they were harassed to the brink of death by excess of labour ... were flogged, fettered and tortured in the most exquisite refinement of cruelty; ... they

> were in many cases starved to the bone while flogged to their work and ... even in some instances ... were driven to commit suicide.... The beautiful and romantic valleys of Derbyshire, Nottinghamshire and Lancashire, secluded from the public eye, became the dismal solitudes of torture, and of many a murder. The profits of manufacturers were enormous; but this only whetted the appetite that it should have satisfied, and therefore the manufacturers had recourse to an expedient that seemed to secure to them those profits without any possibility of limit; they began the practice of what is termed 'night-working,' that is, having tired one set of hands, by working them throughout the day, they had another set ready to go on working throughout the night; the day-set getting into the beds that the night-set had just quitted, and in their turn again, the night-set getting into the beds that the day-set quitted in the morning. It is a common tradition in Lancashire, that the beds *never get cold.*'

With the development of capitalist production during the manufacturing period, the public opinion of Europe had lost the last remnant of shame and conscience. The nations bragged cynically of every infamy that served them as a means to capitalistic accumulation. Read, *e.g.*, the naïve Annals of Commerce of the worthy A. Anderson. Here it is trumpeted forth as a triumph of English statecraft that at the Peace of Utrecht, England extorted from the Spaniards by the Asiento Treaty the privilege of being allowed to ply the negro trade, until then only carried on between Africa and the English West Indies, between Africa and Spanish America as well. England thereby acquired the right of supplying Spanish America until 1743 with 4,800 negroes yearly. This threw, at the same time, an official cloak over British smuggling. Liverpool waxed fat on the slave trade. This was its method of primitive accumulation. And, even to the present day, Liverpool 'respectability' is the Pindar of the slave trade which—compare the work of Aikin [1795] already quoted—'has coincided with that spirit of bold adventure which has characterised the trade of Liverpool and rapidly carried it to its present state of prosperity; has occasioned vast employment for shipping and sailors, and greatly augmented the demand for the manufactures of the country' (p. 339). Liverpool employed in the slave-trade, in 1730, 15 ships; in 1751, 53; in 1760, 74; in 1770, 96; and in 1792, 132.[12]

Whilst the cotton industry introduced child-slavery in England, it gave in the United States a stimulus to the transformation of the earlier, more or less patriarchal slavery, into a system of commercial exploitation. In fact, the veiled slavery of the wage workers in Europe needed, for its pedestal, slavery pure and simple in the new world.

Tantae molis erat, to establish the 'eternal laws of Nature' of the capitalist mode of production, to complete the process of separation between labourers and conditions of labour, to transform, at one pole, the social means of production and subsistence into capital, at the opposite pole, the mass of the population into wage labourers, into 'free labouring poor,' that artificial product of modern society.[13] If money, according to Augier,[14] 'comes into the world with a congenital blood-stain on one cheek,' capital comes dripping from head to foot, from every pore, with blood and dirt.[15]

Notes

1. Industrial here in contradistinction to agricultural. In the 'categoric' sense the farmer is an industrial capitalist as much as the manufacturer.
2. 'The Natural and Artificial Rights of Property Contrasted.' Lond., 1832, pp. 98-99. Author of the anonymous work: 'Th. Hodgskin.'
3. Even as late as 1794, the small cloth-makers of Leeds sent a deputation to Parliament, with a petition for a law to forbid any merchant from becoming a manufacturer. (Dr Aikin, l. c.)
4. William Howitt: 'Colonisation and Christianity: A Popular History of the Treatment of the Natives by the Europeans in all their Colonies.' London, 1838, p. 9. On the treatment of the slaves there is a good compilation in Charles Comte, 'Traité de la Législation.' 3me éd.

Bruxelles, 1837. This subject one must study in detail, to see what the bourgeoisie makes of itself and of the labourer, wherever it can, without restraint, model the world after its own image.

5. Thomas Stamford Raffles, late Lieut-Gov. of that island: 'The History of Java,' Lond., 1817.
6. In the year 1866 more than a million Hindus died of hunger in the province of Orissa, alone. Nevertheless, the attempt was made to enrich the Indian treasury by the price at which the necessaries of life were sold to the starving people.
7. William Cobbett remarks that in England all public institutions are designated 'royal'; as compensation for this, however, there is the 'national' debt.
8. 'Si les Tartares inondaient l'Europe aujourd'hui, il faudrait bien des affaires pour leur faire entendre ce que c'est qu'un financier parmi nous.' [if the Tartars were to flood into Europe today, it would be a difficult job to make them understand what a financier is with us] Montesquieu, 'Esprit des lois,' t. iv., p. 33, ed. Londres, 1769.
9. Mirabeau, l. c., t. vi., p. 101.
10. Eden, l. c., Vol. I., Book II., Ch. 1., p. 421.
11. John Fielden, l. c., pp. 5, 6. On the earlier infamies of the factory system, cf. Dr Aikin (1795), l. c., p. 219. and Gisborne: 'Enquiry into the Duties of Men,' 1795 Vol. II. When the steam-engine transplanted the factories from the country waterfalls to the middle of towns, the 'abstemious' surplus-value maker found the child-material ready to his hand, without being forced to seek slaves from the workhouses. When Sir R. Peel (father of the 'minister of plausibility»), brought in his bill for the protection of children, in 1815, Francis Homer, lumen of the Billion Committee and intimate friend of Ricardo, said in the House of Commons: 'It is notorious, that with a bankrupt's effects, a gang, if he might use the word, of these children had been put up to sale, and were advertised publicly as part of the property. A most atrocious instance had been brought before the Court of King's Bench two years before, in which a number of these boys, apprenticed by a parish in London to one manufacturer, had been transferred to another, and had been found by some benevolent persons in a state of absolute famine. Another case more horrible had come to his knowledge while on a [Parliamentary] Committee ... that not many years ago, an agreement had been made between a London parish and a Lancashire manufacturer, by which it was stipulated, that with every 20 sound children one idiot should be taken.'
12. In 1790, there were in the English West Indies ten slaves for one free man, in the French fourteen for one, in the Dutch twenty-three for one. (Henry Brougham: 'An Inquiry into the Colonial Policy of the European Powers.' Edin. 1803, vol. II., p. 74.)
13. The phrase, 'labouring poor,' is found in English legislation from the moment when the class of wage labourers becomes noticeable. This term is used in opposition, on the one hand, to the 'idle poor,' beggars, etc., on the other to those labourers, who, pigeons not yet plucked, are still possessors of their own means of labour. From the Statute Book it passed into Political Economy, and was handed down by Culpeper, J. Child, etc., to Adam Smith and Eden. After this, one can judge of the good faith of the 'execrable political cant-monger,' Edmund Burke, when he called the expression, 'labouring poor,'—'execrable political cant.' This sycophant who, in the pay of the English oligarchy, played the romantic laudator temporis acti against the French Revolution, just as, in the pay of the North American Colonies, at the beginning of the American troubles, he had played the Liberal against the English oligarchy, was an out and out vulgar bourgeois. 'The laws of commerce are the laws of Nature, and therefore the laws of God.' (E. Burke, l. c., pp. 31, 32.) No wonder that, true to the laws of God and of Nature, he always sold himself in the best market. A very good portrait of this Edmund Burke, during his liberal time, is to be found in the writings of the Rev. Mr Tucker. Tucker was a parson and a Tory, but, for the rest, an honourable man and a competent political economist. In face of the infamous cowardice of character that reigns today, and believes most devoutly in 'the laws of commerce,' it is our bounden duty again and

again to brand the Burkes, who only differ from their successors in one thing—talent.

14. Marie Angier: 'Du Crédit Public.' Paris, 1842.
15. 'Capital is said by a Quarterly Reviewer to fly turbulence and strife, and to be timid, which is very true; but this is very incompletely stating the question. Capital eschews no profit, or very small profit, just as Nature was formerly said to abhor a vacuum. With adequate profit, capital is very bold. A certain 10 per cent. will ensure its employment anywhere; 20 per cent. certain will produce eagerness; 50 per cent., positive audacity; 100 per cent. will make it ready to trample on all human laws; 300 per cent., and there is not a crime at which it will scruple, nor a risk it will not run, even to the chance of its owner being hanged. If turbulence and strife will bring a profit, it will freely encourage both. Smuggling and the slave-trade have amply proved all that is here stated.' (T. J. Dunning, l. c., pp. 35, 36.)

32

Historical Tendency of Capitalist Accumulation

What does the primitive accumulation of capital, *i.e.*, its historical genesis, resolve itself into? In so far as it is not immediate transformation of slaves and serfs into wage labourers, and therefore a mere change of form, it only means the expropriation of the immediate producers, *i.e.*, the dissolution of private property based on the labour of its owner. Private property, as the antithesis to social, collective property, exists only where the means of labour and the external conditions of labour belong to private individuals. But according as these private individuals are labourers or not labourers, private property has a different character. The numberless shades, that it at first sight presents, correspond to the intermediate stages lying between these two extremes. The private property of the labourer in his means of production is the foundation of petty industry, whether agricultural, manufacturing, or both; petty industry, again, is an essential condition for the development of social production and of the free individuality of the labourer himself. Of course, this petty mode of production exists also under slavery, serfdom, and other states of dependence. But it flourishes, it lets loose its whole energy, it attains its adequate classical form, only where the labourer is the private owner of his own means of labour set in action by himself: the peasant of the land which he cultivates, the artisan of the tool which he handles as a virtuoso. This mode of production presupposes parcelling of the soil and scattering of the other means of production. As it excludes the concentration of these means of production, so also it excludes cooperation, division of labour within each separate process of production, the control over, and the productive application of the forces of Nature by society, and the free development of the social productive powers. It is compatible only with a system of production, and a society, moving within narrow and more or less primitive bounds. To perpetuate it would be, as Pecqueur rightly says, 'to decree universal mediocrity". At a certain stage of development, it brings forth the material agencies for its own dissolution. From that moment new forces and new passions spring up in the bosom of society; but the old social organisation fetters them and keeps them down. It must be annihilated; it is annihilated. Its annihilation, the transformation of the individualised and scattered means of production into socially concentrated ones, of the pigmy property of the many into the huge property of the few, the expropriation of the great mass of the people from the soil, from the means of subsistence, and from the means of labour, this fearful and painful expropriation of the mass of the people forms the prelude to the history of capital. It comprises a series of forcible methods, of which we have passed in review only those that have been epoch-making as methods of the primitive accumulation of capital. The expropriation of the immediate producers was accomplished with merciless Vandalism, and under the stimulus of passions the most infamous, the most sordid, the pettiest, the most meanly odious. Self-earned private property, that is based, so to say, on the fusing together of the isolated, independent labouring individual with the conditions of his labour, is supplanted by capitalistic private property, which rests on exploitation of the nominally free labour of others, *i.e.*, on wage labour.[1]

As soon as this process of transformation has sufficiently decomposed the old society from top to bottom, as soon as the labourers are turned into proletarians, their means of labour into capital, as soon as the capitalist mode of production stands on its own feet, then the further socialisation of labour and further transformation of the land and other means of production into socially exploited and, therefore, common means of production, as well as the further expropriation of private proprietors, takes a new form. That which is now to be expropriated is no longer the labourer working for himself, but the capitalist exploiting many labourers. This expropriation is accomplished by the action of the immanent laws of capitalistic production itself, by the centralisation of capital. One capitalist always kills many. Hand in hand with this centralisation, or this expropriation of many capitalists by few, develop, on an ever-extending scale, the cooperative form of the labour process, the conscious technical application of science, the methodical cultivation of the soil, the transformation of the instruments of labour into instruments of labour only usable in common, the economising of all means of production by their use as means of production of combined, socialised labour, the entanglement of all peoples in the net of the world market, and with this, the international character of the capitalistic regime. Along with the constantly diminishing number of the magnates of capital, who usurp and monopolise all advantages of this process of transformation, grows the mass of misery, oppression, slavery, degradation, exploitation; but with this too grows the revolt of the working class, a class always increasing in numbers, and disciplined, united, organised by the very mechanism of the process of capitalist production itself. The monopoly of capital becomes a fetter upon the mode of production, which has sprung up and flourished along with, and under it. Centralisation of the means of production and socialisation of labour at last reach a point where they become incompatible with their capitalist integument. This integument is burst asunder. The knell of capitalist private property sounds. The expropriators are expropriated.

The capitalist mode of appropriation, the result of the capitalist mode of production, produces capitalist private property. This is the first negation of individual private property, as founded on the labour of the proprietor. But capitalist production begets, with the inexorability of a law of Nature, its own negation. It is the negation of negation. This does not re-establish private property for the producer, but gives him individual property based on the acquisition of the capitalist era: *i.e.*, on cooperation and the possession in common of the land and of the means of production.

The transformation of scattered private property, arising from individual labour, into capitalist private property is, naturally, a process, incomparably more protracted, violent, and difficult, than the transformation of capitalistic private property, already practically resting on socialised production, into socialised property. In the former case, we had the expropriation of the mass of the people by a few usurpers; in the latter, we have the expropriation of a few usurpers by the mass of the people.[2]

Notes

1. 'Nous sommes dans une condition tout-à-fait nouvelle de la societé... nous tendons a séparer toute espèce de propriété d'avec toute espèce de travail.' [We are in a situation which is entirely new for society ... we are striving to separate every kind of property from every kind of labour] (Sismondi: 'Nouveaux Principes d'Econ. Polit.' t.II, p.434.)

2. The advance of industry, whose involuntary promoter is the bourgeoisie, replaces the isolation of the labourers, due to competition, by their revolutionary combination, due to association. The development of Modern Industry, therefore, cuts from under its feet the very foundation on which the bourgeoisie produces and appropriates products. What the bourgeoisie, therefore, produces, above all, are its own grave-diggers. Its fall and the victory of the proletariat are equally inevitable.... Of all the classes that stand face-to-face with the bourgeoisie today, the proletariat alone is a really revolutionary class. The other classes perish and disappear in the face of Modern Industry, the proletariat is its special and essential product.... The lower middle classes, the small manufacturers, the shopkeepers, the artisan, the peasant, all these fight against the bourgeoisie, to save from extinction their existence as fractions of the middle class... they are reactionary, for they try to roll back the wheel of history. Karl Marx and Friedrich Engels, 'Manifest der Kommunistischen Partei,' London, 1848, pp. 9, 11.

33

The Modern Theory of Colonisation[1]

Political economy confuses on principle two very different kinds of private property, of which one rests on the producers' own labour, the other on the employment of the labour of others. It forgets that the latter not only is the direct antithesis of the former, but absolutely grows on its tomb only. In Western Europe, the home of Political Economy, the process of primitive accumulation is more of less accomplished. Here, the capitalist regime has either directly conquered the whole domain of national production, or, where economic conditions are less developed, it, at least, indirectly controls those strata of society which, though belonging to the antiquated mode of production, continue to exist side by side with it in gradual decay. To this ready-made world of capital, the political economist applies the notions of law and of property inherited from a pre-capitalistic world with all the more anxious zeal and all the greater unction, the more loudly the facts cry out in the face of his ideology. It is otherwise in the colonies. There the capitalist regime everywhere comes into collision with the resistance of the producer, who, as owner of his own conditions of labour, employs that labour to enrich himself, instead of the capitalist. The contradiction of these two diametrically opposed economic systems, manifests itself here practically in a struggle between them. Where the capitalist has at his back the power of the mother-country, he tries to clear out of his way by force the modes of production and appropriation based on the independent labour of the producer. The same interest, which compels the sycophant of capital, the political economist, in the mother-country, to proclaim the theoretical identity of the capitalist mode of production with its contrary, that same interest compels him in the colonies to make a clean breast of it, and to proclaim aloud the antagonism of the two modes of production. To this end, he proves how the development of the social productive power of labour, co-operation, division of labour, use of machinery on a large scale, &c., are impossible without the expropriation of the labourers, and the corresponding transformation of their means of production into capital. In the interest of the so-called national wealth, he seeks for artificial means to ensure the poverty of the people. Here his apologetic armor crumbles off, bit by bit, like rotten touchwood. It is the great merit of E.G. Wakefield to have discovered, not anything new about the Colonies[2], but to have discovered in the Colonies the truth as to the conditions of capitalist production in the mother country.

As the system of protection at its origin[3] attempted to manufacture capitalists artificially in the mother-country, so Wakefield's colonisation theory, which England tried for a time to enforce by Acts of Parliament, attempted to effect the manufacture of wage-workers in the Colonies. This he calls 'systematic colonisation.'

First of all, Wakefield discovered that in the Colonies, property in money, means of subsistence, machines, and other means of production, does not as yet stamp a man as a capitalist if there be wanting the correlative—the wage-worker, the other man who is compelled to sell himself of his own free will. He discovered that capital is not a thing, but a social relation between persons, established by the instrumentality of things.[4] Mr Peel, he moans, took with him from England to Swan River, West Australia, means of subsistence and of production to the amount of £50,000. Mr Peel had the foresight to bring with him, besides, 300 persons of the working class, men, women, and children. Once arrived at his destination, 'Mr Peel was left without a servant to make his bed or fetch him water from the river.'[5] Unhappy Mr Peel who provided for everything except the export of English modes of production to Swan River!

For the understanding of the following discoveries of Wakefield, two preliminary remarks: We know that the means of production and subsistence, while they remain the property of the immediate producer, are not capital. They become capital only under circumstances in which they serve at the same time as means of exploitation and subjection of the labourer. But this capitalist soul of theirs is so intimately wedded, in the head of the political economist, to their material substance, that he christens them capital under all circumstances, even when they are its exact opposite. Thus is it with Wakefield. Further: the splitting up of the means of production into the individual property of many independent labourers, working on their own account, he calls equal division of capital. It is with the political economist as with the feudal jurist. The latter stuck on to pure monetary relations the labels supplied by feudal law.

'If,' says Wakefield, 'all members of the society are supposed to possess equal portions of capital... no man would have a motive for accumulating more capital than he could use with his own hands. This is to some extent the case in new American settlements, where a passion for owning land prevents the existence of a class of labourers for hire.'[6] So long, therefore, as the labourer can accumulate for himself—and this he can do so long as he remains possessor of his means of production—capitalist accumulation and the capitalistic mode of production are impossible. The class of wage labourers, essential to these, is wanting. How, then, in old Europe, was the expropriation of the labourer from his conditions of labour, i.e., the co-existence of capital and wage labour, brought about? By a social contract of a quite original kind. 'Mankind have adopted a... simple contrivance for promoting the accumulation of capital,' which, of course, since the time of Adam, floated in their imagination, floated in their imagination as the sole and final end of their existence: 'they have divided themselves into owners of capital and owners of labour.... The division was the result of concert and combination.' [7] In one word: the mass of mankind expropriated itself in honor of the 'accumulation of capital.' Now, one would think that this instinct of self-denying fanaticism would give itself full fling especially in the Colonies, where alone exist the men and conditions that could turn a social contract from a dream to a reality. But why, then, should 'systematic colonisation' be called in to replace its opposite, spontaneous, unregulated colonisation? But - but - 'In the Northern States of the American Union; it may be doubted whether so many as a tenth of the people would fall under the description of hired labourers.... In England... the labouring class compose the bulk of the people.'[8] Nay, the impulse to self-expropriation on the part of labouring humanity for the glory of capital, exists so little that slavery, according to Wakefield himself, is the sole natural basis of Colonial wealth. His systematic colonisation is a mere *pis aller*, since he unfortunately has to do with free men, not with slaves. 'The first Spanish settlers in Saint Domingo did not obtain labourers from Spain. But, without labourers, their capital must have perished, or at least, must soon have been diminished to that small amount which each individual could employ with his own hands. This has actually occurred in the last Colony founded by England—the Swan River Settlement—where a great mass of capital, of seeds, implements, and cattle, has perished for want of labourers to use it, and where no settler has preserved much more capital than he can employ with his own hands.'[9]

We have seen that the expropriation of the mass of the people from the soil forms the basis of the capitalist mode of production. The essence of a free colony, on the contrary, consists in this—that the bulk of the soil is still public property, and every settler on it therefore can turn part of it into his private property and individual means of production, without hindering the later settlers in the same operation.[10] This is the secret both of the prosperity of the colonies and of their inveterate vice—opposition to the establishment of capital. 'Where land is very cheap and all men are free, where every one who so pleases can easily obtain a piece of land for himself, not only is labour very dear, as respects the labourer's share of the produce, but the difficulty is to obtain combined labour at any price.'[11]

As in the colonies the separation of the labourer from the conditions of labour and their root, the soil, does not exist, or only sporadically, or on too limited a scale, so neither does the separation of agriculture from industry exist, nor the destruction of the household industry of the peasantry. Whence then is to come the internal market for capital? 'No part of the population of America is exclusively agricultural, excepting slaves and their employers who combine capital and labour in particular works. Free Americans, who cultivate the soil, follow many other occupations. Some portion of the furniture and tools which they use is commonly made by themselves. They frequently build their own houses, and carry to market, at whatever distance, the produce of their own industry. They are spinners and weavers; they make soap and candles, as well as, in many cases, shoes and clothes for their own use. In America the cultivation of land is often the secondary pursuit of a blacksmith, a miller or a shopkeeper.'[12] With such queer people as these, where is the 'field of abstinence' for the capitalists?

The great beauty of capitalist production consists in this—that it not only constantly reproduces the wage-worker as wage-worker, but produces always, in proportion to the accumulation of capital, a relative surplus-population of wage-workers. Thus the law of supply and demand of labour is kept in the right rut, the oscillation of wages is penned within limits satisfactory to capitalist exploitation, and lastly, the social dependence of the labourer on the capitalist, that indispensable requisite, is secured; an unmistakable relation of dependence, which the smug political economist, at home, in the mother-country, can transmogrify into one of free contract between buyer and seller, between equally independent owners of commodities, the owner of the commodity capital and the owner of the commodity labour. But in the colonies, this pretty fancy is torn asunder. The absolute population here increases much more quickly than in the mother-country, because many labourers enter this world as ready-made adults, and yet the labour-market is always understocked. The law of supply and demand of labour falls to pieces. On the one hand, the old world constantly throws in capital, thirsting after exploitation and 'abstinence'; on the other, the regular reproduction of the wage labourer as wage labourer comes into collision with impediments the most impertinent and in part invincible. What becomes of the production of wage-labourers, supernumerary in proportion to the accumulation of capital? The wage-worker of to-day is to-morrow an independent peasant, or artisan, working for himself. He vanishes from the labour-market, but not into the workhouse. This constant transformation of the wage-labourers into independent producers, who work for themselves instead of for capital, and enrich themselves instead of the capitalist gentry, reacts in its turn very perversely on the conditions of the labour-market. Not only does the degree of exploitation of the wage labourer remain indecently low. The wage labourer loses into the bargain, along with the relation of dependence, also the sentiment of dependence on the abstemious capitalist. Hence all the inconveniences that our E. G. Wakefield pictures so doughtily, so eloquently, so pathetically. The supply of wage labour, he complains, is neither constant, nor regular, nor sufficient. 'The supply of labour is always not only small but uncertain.'[13] 'Though the produce divided between the capitalist and the labourer be large, the labourer takes so great a share that he soon becomes a capitalist.... Few, even those whose lives are unusually long, can accumulate great masses of wealth.'[14] The labourers most distinctly decline to allow the capitalist to abstain from the payment of the greater part of their labour. It avails him nothing, if he is so cunning as to import from Europe, with his own capital, his own wage-workers. They soon 'cease... to be labourers for hire; they... become independent landowners, if not competitors with their former masters in the labour-market.'[15] Think of the horror! The excellent capitalist has imported bodily from Europe, with his own good money, his own competitors! The end of the world has come! No wonder Wakefield laments the absence of all dependence and of all sentiment of dependence on the part of the wage-workers in the colonies. On account of the high wages, says his disciple, Merivale, there is in the colonies 'the urgent desire for cheaper and more subservient labourers—for a class to whom the capitalist might dictate terms, instead of being dictated to by them.... In ancient civilised countries the labourer, though free, is by a law of Nature dependent on capitalists; in colonies this dependence must be created by artificial means.'[16]

What is now, according to Wakefield, the consequence of this unfortunate state of things in the colonies? A 'barbarising tendency of dispersion' of producers and national wealth.[17] The parcelling-out of the means of production among innumerable owners, working on their own account, annihilates, along with the centralisation of capital, all the foundation of combined labour. Every long-winded undertaking, extending over several years and demanding outlay of fixed capital, is prevented from being carried out. In Europe, capital invests without hesitating a moment, for the working class constitutes its living appurtenance, always in excess, always at disposal. But in the colonies! Wakefield tells an extremely doleful anecdote. He was talking with some capitalists of Canada and the state of New York, where the immigrant wave often becomes stagnant and deposits a sediment of 'supernumerary' labourers. 'Our capital,' says one of the characters in the melodrama, 'was ready for many operations which require a considerable period of time for their completion; but we could not begin such operations with labour which, we knew, would soon leave us. If we had been sure of retaining the labour of such emigrants, we should have been glad to have engaged it at once, and for a high price: and we should have engaged it, even though we had been sure it would leave us, provided we had been sure of a fresh supply whenever we might need it.'[18]

After Wakefield has constructed the English capitalist agriculture and its 'combined' labour with the scattered cultivation of American peasants, he unwittingly gives us a glimpse at the reverse of the medal. He depicts the mass of the American people as well-to-do, independent, enterprising, and comparatively cultured, whilst 'the English agricultural labourer is miserable wretch, a pauper.... In what country, except North America and some new colonies, do the wages of free labour employed in agriculture much exceed a bare subsistence for the labourer? ... Undoubtedly, farm-horses in England, being a valuable property, are better fed than English peasants.'[19] But, never mind, national wealth is, once again, by its very nature, identical with misery of the people.

How, then, to heal the anti-capitalistic cancer of the colonies? If men were willing, at a blow, to turn all the soil from public into private property, they would destroy certainly the root of the evil, but also—the colonies. The trick is how to kill two birds with one stone. Let the Government put upon the virgin soil an artificial price, independent of the law of supply and demand, a price that compels the immigrant to work a long time for wages before he can earn enough money to buy land, and turn himself into an independent peasant.[20] The fund resulting from the sale of land at a price relatively prohibitory for the wage-workers, this fund of money extorted from the wages of labour by violation of the sacred law of supply and demand, the Government is to employ, on the other hand, in proportion as it grows; to import have-nothings from Europe into the colonies, and thus keep the wage labour market full for the capitalists. Under these circumstances, tout sera pour le mieux dans le meilleur des mondes possibles. This is the great secret of 'systematic colonisation.' By this plan, Wakefield cries in triumph, 'the supply of labour *must* be constant and regular, because, first, as no labourer would be able to procure land until he had worked for money, all immigrant labourers, working for a time for wages and in combination, would produce capital for the employment of more labourers; secondly, because every labourer who left off working for wages and became a landowner would, by purchasing land, provide a fund for bringing fresh labour to the colony.'[21] The price of the soil imposed by the State must, of course, be a 'sufficient price'—*i.e.*, so high 'as to prevent the labourers from becoming independent landowners until others had followed to take their place.'[22] This 'sufficient price for the land' is nothing but a euphemistic circumlocution for the ransom which the labourer pays to the capitalist for leave to retire from the wage labour market to the land. First, he must create for the capitalist 'capital,' with which the latter may be able to exploit more labourers; then he must place, at his own expense, a *locum tenens* [placeholder] on the labour market, whom the Government forwards across the sea for the benefit of his old master, the capitalist.

It is very characteristic that the English Government for years practised this method of 'primitive accumulation' prescribed by Mr Wakefield expressly for the use of the colonies. The fiasco was, of course, as complete as that of Sir Robert Peel's Bank Act. The stream of emigration was only diverted from the English colonies to the United States. Meanwhile, the advance of capitalistic production in Europe, accompanied by increasing Government pressure, has rendered Wakefield's recipe superfluous. On the one hand, the enormous and ceaseless stream of men, year after year driven upon America, leaves behind a stationary sediment in the east of the United States, the wave of immigration from Europe throwing men on the labour-market there more rapidly than the wave of emigration westwards can wash them away. On the other hand, the American Civil War brought in its train a colossal national debt, and, with it, pressure of taxes, the rise of the vilest financial aristocracy, the squandering of a huge part of the public land on speculative companies for the exploitation of railways, mines, &c., in brief, the most rapid centralisation of capital. The great republic has, therefore, ceased to be the promised land for emigrant labourers. Capitalistic production advances there with giant strides, even though the lowering of wages and the dependence of the wage-worker are yet far from being brought down to the normal European level. The shameless lavishing of uncultivated colonial land on aristocrats and capitalists by the Government, so loudly denounced even by Wakefield, has produced, especially in Australia[23], in conjunction with the stream of men that the gold diggings attract, and with the competition that the importation of English-commodities causes even to the smallest artisan, an ample 'relative surplus labouring population,' so that almost every mail brings the Job's news of a 'glut of the Australia labour-market,' and the prostitution in some places flourishes as wantonly as in the London Haymarket.

However, we are not concerned here with the conditions of the colonies. The only thing that interests us is the secret discovered in the new world by the Political Economy of the old world, and proclaimed on the housetops: that the capitalist mode of production and accumulation, and therefore capitalist private property, have for their fundamental condition the annihilation of self-earned private property; in other words, the expropriation of the labourer.

Notes

1. We treat here of real Colonies, virgins soils, colonised by free immigrants. The United States are, speaking economically, still only a Colony of Europe. Besides, to this category belong such old plantations as those in which the abolition of slavery has completely altered the earlier conditions.
2. Wakefield's few glimpses on the subject of Modern Colonisation are fully anticipated by Mirabeau Pere, the physiocrat, and even much earlier by English economists.
3. Later, it became a temporary necessity in the international competitive struggle. But, whatever its motive, the consequences remain the same.
4. 'A negro is a negro. In certain circumstances he becomes a slave. A mule is a machine for spinning cotton. Only under certain circumstances does it become capital. Outside these circumstances, it is no more capital than gold is intrinsically money, or sugar is the price of sugar.... Capital is a social relation of production. It is a historical relation of production.' (Karl Marx, 'Lohnarbeit und Kapital,' *N. Rh. Z.*, No.266, April 7, 1849.)
5. E. G. Wakefield: 'England and America,' vol.ii. p.33.
6. l.c., p.17.
7. l.c., vol.i, p.18.
8. l.c., pp.42, 43, 44.
9. l.c., vol.ii, p.5.
10. 'Land, to be an element of colonisation, must not only be waste, but it must be public property, liable to be converted into private property.' (l.c., Vol.II, p.125.)
11. l.c., Vol.I, p.247.
12. l.c., pp.21, 22.
13. l.c., Vol.II, p.116.
14. l.c., Vol.I, p.131.
15. l.c., Vol.II, p.5.
16. Merivale, l.c., Vol.II, pp.235-314 passim. Even the mild, Free Trade, vulgar economist, Molinari, says: 'Dans les colonies où l'esclavage a été aboli sans que le travail forcé se trouvait remplacé par une quantité équivalente de travail libre, on a vu s'opérer la contre-partie du fait qui se réalise tous les jours sous nos yeux. On a vu les simples travailleurs exploiter à leur tour les entrepreneurs d'industrie, exiger d'eux des salaires hors de toute proportion avec la part légitime qui leur revenait dans le produit. Les planteurs, ne pouvant obtenir de leurs sucres un prix suffisant pour couvrir la hausse de salaire, ont été obligés de fournir l'excédant, d'abord sur leurs profits, ensuite sur leurs capitaux mêmes. Une foule de planteurs ont été ruinés de la sorte, d'autres ont fermé leurs ateliers pour échapper à une ruine imminente.... Sans doute, il vaut mieux voir périr des accumulations de capitaux que des générations d'hommes [how generous Mr Molinari!]: mais ne vaudrait-il pas mieux que ni les uns ni les autres périssent? [In the colonies where slavery has been abolished without the compulsory labour being replaced with an equivalent quantity of free labour, there has occurred the opposite of what happens every day before our eyes. Simple workers have been seen to exploit in their turn the industrial entrepreneurs, demanding from them wages which bear absolutely no relation to the legitimate share in the product which they ought to receive. The planters were unable to obtain for their sugar for a sufficent price to cover the increase in wages, and were obliged to furnish the extra amount, at first out of their profits, and then out of their very capital. A considerable amount of planters have been ruined as a result, while others have closed down their businesses in order to avoid the ruin which threatened them ... It is doubtless better that these accumulations of capital should be destroyed than that generations of men should perish ... but would it not be better if both survived?] (Molinari, l.c., pp.51,52.) Mr Molinari, Mr Molinari! What then becomes of the ten commandments, of Moses and the prophets, of the law of supply and demand, if in Europe the 'entrepreneur' can cut down the labourer's legitimate part, and in

the West Indies, the labourer can cut down the entrepreneur's? And what, if you please, is this 'legitimate part,' which on your own showing the capitalist in Europe daily neglects to pay? Over yonder, in the colonies where the labourers are so 'simple' as to 'exploit' the capitalist, Mr Molinari feels a strong itching to set the law of supply and demand, that works elsewhere automatically, on the right road by means of the police.

17. Wakefield, l.c., Vol.II, p.52.
18. l.c., pp.191, 192.
19. l.c., Vol.I, p.47, 246.
20. 'C'est, ajoutez-vous, grâce à l'appropriation du sol et des capitaux que l'homme, qui n'a que ses bras, trouve de l'occupation et se fait un revenu... c'est au contraire, grâce à l'appropriation individuelle du sol qu'il se trouve des hommes n'ayant que leurs bras.... Quand vous mettez un homme dans le vide, vous vous emparez de l'atmosphère. Ainsi faites-vous, quand vous vous emparez du sol.... C'est le mettre dans le vide le richesses, pour ne la laisser vivre qu'à votre volonté.' [It is, you add, a result of the appropriation of the soil and of capital that the man who has nothing but the strength of his arms finds employment and creates an income for himself ... but the opposite is true, it is thanks to the individual appropriation of the soil that there exist men who only possess the strength of their arms ... When you put a man in a vacuum, you rob him of the air. You do the same, when you take away the soil from him ... for you are putting him in a space void of wealth, so as to leave him no way of living except according to your wishes] (Collins, l.c. t.III, pp.268-71, passim.)
21. Wakefield, l.c., Vol.II, p.192.
22. l.c., p.45.
23. As soon as Australia became her own law-giver, she passed, of course, laws favorable to the settlers, but the squandering of the land, already accomplished by the English Government, stands in the way. 'The first and main object at which new Land Act of 1862 aims is to give increased facilities for the settlement of the people.' ('The Land Law of Victoria,' by the Hon. C. G. Duffy, Minister of Public Lands, Lond., 1862.)

VOLUME II

BOOK TWO:
THE PROCESS OF CIRCULATION OF CAPITAL

PART I

THE METAMORPHOSES OF CAPITAL AND THEIR CIRCUITS

1

The Circuit of Money Capital

The circular movement[1] of capital takes place in three stages, which, according to the presentation in Volume I, form the following series:

First stage: The capitalist appears as a buyer on the commodity- and the labour-market; his money is transformed into commodities, or it goes through the circulation act M—C.

Second Stage: Productive consumption of the purchased commodities by the capitalist. He acts as a capitalist producer of commodities; his capital passes through the process of production. The result is a commodity of more value than that of the elements entering into its production.

Third Stage: The capitalist returns to the market as a seller; his commodities are turned into money; or they pass through the circulation act C—M.

Hence the formula for the circuit of money-capital is: M—C ... P ... C'—M', the dots indicating that the process of circulation is interrupted, and C' and M' designating C and M increased by surplus-value.

The first and third stages were discussed in Book I only in so far as this was necessary for the understanding of the second stage, the process of production of capital. For this reason, the various forms which capital takes on in its different stages, and which now assumes and now strips off in the repetition of its circuit, were not considered. These forms are now the direct object of our study.

In order to conceive these forms in their pure state, one must first of all discard all factors which have nothing to do with the changing or building of forms as such. It is therefore taken for granted here not only that the commodities are sold at their values but also that this takes place under the same conditions throughout. Likewise disregarded therefore are any changes of value which might occur during the movement in circuits.

Section I. *First Stage. M—C*[2]

M—C represents the conversion of a sum of money into a sum of commodities; the purchaser transforms his money into commodities, the sellers transform their commodities into money. What renders this act of the general circulation of commodities simultaneously a functionally definite section in independent circuit of some individual capital is primarily not the form of the act but its material content, the specific use-character of the commodities which change places with the money. These commodities are on the one hand means of production, on the other labour-power, material and personal factors in the production of commodities whose specific nature must of course correspond to the special kind of articles to be manufactured. If we call labour-power L, and the means of production MP, then the sum of commodities to be bought, C, is equal to L + MP, or more briefly $C<^{L}_{MP}$. M—C, considered as to its substance is therefore represented by M—$C<^{L}_{MP}$, that is to say M—C is composed of M—L and M—MP. The sum of money M is separated into two parts, one of which buys labour-power, the other means of production. These two series of purchases belong to entirely different markets, the one to the commodity-market proper, the other to the labour-market.

Aside from this qualitative division of the sum of commodities into which M is transformed, the formula M—$C<^{L}_{MP}$ also represents a most characteristic quantitative relation.

We know that the value, or price, of labour-power is paid to its owner, who offers it for sale as a commodity, in the form of wages, that is to say as the price of a sum of labour containing surplus-labour. For instance, if the daily value of labour-power is equal to the product of five hours labour valued at three shillings, this sum figures in the contract between the buyer and seller as the price, or wages, for, say, ten hours of labour. If such a contract is made for instance with 50 labourers, they are supposed to work altogether 500 hours per day for the purchaser, and one half of this time, or 250 hours equal to 25 days of labour of 10 hours each, represents nothing but surplus labour. The quantity and the volume of the means of production to be purchased must be sufficient for the utilisation of this mass of labour.

M—C$<^{L}_{MP}$, then, does not merely express the qualitative relation indicating that a certain sum of money, say £422, is exchanged for a corresponding sum of means of production and labour-power, but also a quantitative relation between L, the part of the money spent for labour-power, and MP, the part spent for means of production. This relation is determined at the outset by the quantity of excess labour, of surplus-labour to be expended by a certain number of labourers.

If for instance in a spinning-mill the weekly wage of its 50 labourers amounts to £50, £372 must be spent for means of production, if this is the value of the means of production which a weekly labour of 3,000 hours, 1,500 of which are surplus-labour, transforms into yarn.

It is immaterial here how much additional value in the form of means of production is required in the various lines of industry by the utilisation of additional labour. The point merely is that the part of the money spent for means of production—the means of production bought in M—MP—must absolutely suffice, i.e., must at the outset be calculated accordingly, must be procured in corresponding proportion. To put it another way, the quantity of means of production must suffice to absorb the amount of labour, to be transformed by it into products. If the means of production at hand were insufficient, the excess labour at the disposal of the purchaser could not be utilised; his right to dispose of it is futile. If there were more means of production than available labour, they would not be saturated with labour, would not be transformed into products.

As soon as M—C$<^{L}_{MP}$ is completed, the purchaser has at his disposal more than simply the means of production and labour-power required for the production of some useful article. He disposes of a greater capacity to render labour-power fluent, or a greater quantity of labour than is necessary for the replacement of the value of this labour-power, and he has at the same time the means of production requisite for the realisation or materialisation of this quantity of labour. In other words, he has at his disposal the factors making for the production of articles of a greater value than that of the elements of production—the factors of production of a mass of commodities containing surplus-value. The value advanced by him in money-form has now assumed a bodily form in which it can be incarnated as a value generating surplus-value (in the shape of commodities). In brief, value exists here in the condition or form of *productive capital*, which has the factor of creating value and surplus-value. Let us call capital in this form P.

Now the value of P is equal to that of L + MP, it is equal to M exchanged for L and MP. M is the same capital-value as P, only it has a different mode of existence, it is capital-value in the state or form of money—*money-capital.*

M—C$<^{L}_{MP}$, or its general form M—C, a sum of purchases of commodities, an act of the general circulation of commodities, is therefore at the same time—as a stage in the independent circuit of capital—a transformation of capital-value from its money-form into its productive form. More briefly, it is the transformation of *money-capital* into *productive capital.* In the diagram of the circuit which we are here discussing, money appears as the first depository of capital-value, and money-capital therefore represents the form in which capital is advanced.

Capital in the form of money-capital is in a state in which it can perform the functions of money, in the present case the functions of a universal means of purchase and universal means of payment. (The last-named inasmuch as labour-power though first bought is not paid for until it has been put into operation. To the extent that the means of production are not found ready on the market but have to be ordered first, money in M—MP likewise serves as a means of payment.) This capacity is not due to the fact that money-capital is capital but that it is money.

On the other hand capital-value in the form of money cannot perform any other functions but those of money. What turns the money-functions into functions of capital is the definite role they play in the movement of capital, and therefore also the interrelation of the stage in which these functions are performed with the other stages of the circuit of capital. Take, for instance, the case with which we are here dealing. Money is here converted into commodities the combination of which represents the bodily form of productive capital, and this form already contains latently, potentially, the result of the process of capitalist production.

A part of the money performing the function of money-capital in $M—C<^{L}_{MP}$ assumes, by consummating the act of circulation, a function in which it loses its capital character but preserves its money-character. The circulation of money-capital M is divided into M—MP and M—L, into the purchase of means of production and the purchase of labour-power. Let us consider the last-named process by itself. M—L is the purchase of labour-power by the capitalist. It is also the sale of labour-power—we may here say of labour, since the form of wages is assumed—by the laborer who owns it. What is M—C (= M—L) for the buyer is here, as in every other purchase, L—M (= C—M) for the seller (the laborer). It is the sale of his labour-power. This is the first stage of circulation, or the first metamorphosis, of the commodity (Buch I, Kap. III, 2a).[English edition: Ch. III, 2a—*Ed.*] It is for the seller of labour a transformation of his commodity into the money-form. The laborer spends the money so obtained gradually for a number of commodities required for the satisfaction of his needs, for articles of consumption. The complete circulation of his commodity therefore appears as L—M—C, that is to say first as L—M (= C—M) and secondly as M—C; hence in the general form of the simple circulation of commodities, C—M—C. Money is in this case merely a passing means of circulation, a mere medium in the exchange of one commodity for another.

M—L is the characteristic moment in the transformation of money-capital into productive capital, because it is the essential condition for the real transformation of value advanced in the form of money into capital, into a value producing surplus-value. M—MP is necessary only for the purpose of realising the quantity of labour bought in the process M—L, which was discussed from this point of view in Book I, Part II, under the head of 'The Transformation of Money into Capital.' We shall have to consider the matter at this point also from another angle, relating especially to money-capital the form in which capital manifests itself.

Generally M—L is regarded as characteristic of the capitalist mode of production. However not at all for the reason given above, that the purchase of labour-power represents a contract of purchase which stipulates for the delivery of a quantity of labour in excess of that needed to replace the price of the labour-power, the wages; hence delivery of surplus-labour, the fundamental condition for the capitalisation of the value advanced, or for the production of surplus-value, which is the same thing. On the contrary, it is so regarded because of its form, since *money* in the form of wages buys labour, and this is the characteristic mark of the money system.

Nor is it the irrationality of the form which is taken as characteristic. On the contrary, one overlooks the irrational. The irrationality consists in the fact that labour itself as a value-creating element cannot have any value, nor can therefore any definite amount of labour have any value expressed in its price, in its equivalence to a definite quantity of money. But we know that wages are but a disguised form, a form in which for instance the price of one day's labour-power presents itself as the price of the labour rendered fluent by this labour-power in one day. The value produced by this labour-power in, say, six hours of labour is thus expressed as the value of twelve hours' functioning or operation of the labour-power.

M—L is regarded as the characteristic feature, the hallmark of the so-called money system, because labour there appears as the commodity of its owner, and money therefore as the buyer—hence on account of the money-relation (i.e., the sale and purchase of human activity). Money however appears very early as a buyer of so-called services, without the transformation of M into money-capital, and without any change in the general character of the economic system.

It makes no difference to money into what sort of commodities it is transformed. It is the universal equivalent of all commodities which show, if only by their prices, that ideally they represent a certain sum of money, anticipate their transformation into money, and do not acquire the form in which they may be converted into use-values for their owners until they change places with money. Once labour-power has come into the market as the commodity of its owner and its sale takes the form of payment for labour, assumes the shape of wages, its purchase and sale is no more startling than the purchase and sale of any other commodity. The characteristic thing is not that the commodity labour-power is purchasable but that labour-power appears as a commodity.

By means of M—C$<^{L}_{MP}$, the transformation of money-capital into productive capital, the capitalist effects the combination of the objective and personal factors of production so far as they consist of commodities. If money is transformed into productive capital for the first time or if it performs for the first time the function of money-capital for its owner, he must begin by buying means of production, such as buildings, machinery, etc., before he buys any labour-power. For as soon as he compels labour-power to act in obedience to his sway, he must have means of production to which he can apply it as labour-power.

This is the capitalist's presentation of the case.

The labourer's case is as follows: The productive application of his labour-power is not possible until it is sold and brought into connection with means of production. Before its sale, labour-power exists therefore separately from the means of production, from the material conditions of its application. In this state of separation it cannot be used either directly for the production of use-values for its owner or for the production of commodities, by the sale of which he could live. But from the moment that as a result of its sale it is brought into connection with means of production, it forms part of the productive capital of its purchaser, the same as the means of production.

True, in the act M—L the owner of money and the owner of labour-power enter only into the relation of buyer and seller, confront one another only as money-owner and commodity-owner. In this respect they enter merely into a money-relation. Yet at the same time the buyer appears also from the outset in the capacity of an owner of means of production, which are the material conditions for the productive expenditure of labour-power by its owner. In other words, these means of production are in opposition to the owner of the labour-power, being property of another. On the other hand the seller of labour faces its buyer as labour-power of another which must be made to do his bidding, must be integrated into his capital, in order that it may really become productive capital. The class relation between capitalist and wage-laborer therefore exists, is presupposed from the moment the two face each other in the act M—L (L—M on the part of the laborer). It is a purchase and sale, a money-relation, but a purchase and sale in which the buyer is assumed to be a capitalist and the seller a wage-laborer. And this relation arises out of the fact that the conditions required for the realisation of labour-power, viz., means of subsistence and means of production, are separated from the owner of labour-power, being the property of another.

We are not concerned here with the origin of this separation. It exists as soon as M—L goes on. The thing which interests us here is this: If M—L appears here as a function of money-capital or money as the form of existence of capital, the sole reason that money here assumes the role of a means of paying for a useful human activity or service; hence by no means in consequence of the function of money as a means of payment. Money can be expended in this form only because labour-power finds itself in a state of separation from its means of production (including the means of subsistence as means of production of the labour-power itself), and because this separation can be overcome only by the sale of the labour-power to the owner of the means of production; because therefore the functioning of labour-power, which is not at all limited to the quantity of labour required for the reproduction of its own price, is likewise the concern of its buyer. The capital-relation during the process of production arises only because it is inherent in the act of circulation, in the different fundamental economic conditions in which buyer and seller confront each other, in their class relation. It is not money which by its nature creates this relation; it is rather the existence of this relation which permits of the transformation of a mere money-function into a capital-function.

In the conception of money-capital (for the time being we deal with the latter only within the confines of the special function in which it faces us here) two errors run parallel to each other or cross each other. In the first place the functions performed by capital-value in its capacity as money-capital, which it can perform precisely owing to its money-form, are erroneously derived from its character as capital, whereas they are due only to the money-form of capital-value, to its form of appearance as money. In the second place, on the contrary, the specific content of the money-function, which renders it simultaneously a capital-function, is traced to the nature of money (money being here confused with capital), while the money function premises social conditions, such as are here indicated by the act M—L, which do not at all exist in the mere circulation of commodities and the corresponding circulation of money.

The purchase and sale of slaves is formally also a purchase and sale of commodities. But money cannot perform this function without the existence of slavery. If slavery exists, then money can be invested in the purchase of slaves. On the other hand the mere possession of money cannot make slavery possible.

In order that the sale of one's own labour-power (in the form of the sale of one's own labour or in the form of wages) may constitute not an isolated phenomenon but a socially decisive premise for the production of commodities, in order that money-capital may therefore perform, on a social scale , the above-discussed function M—C$<^{L}_{MP}$, historical processes are assumed by which the original connection of the means of production with labour-power was dissolved—processes in consequence of which the mass of the people, the labourers, have, as non-owners, come face to face with non-labourers as the owners of these means of production. It makes no difference in this case whether the connection before its dissolution was such in form that the laborer, being himself a means of production, belonged to the other means of production or whether he was their owner.

What lies back of M—C$<^{L}_{MP}$ is distribution; not distribution in the ordinary meaning of a distribution of articles of consumption, but the distribution of the elements of production itself, the material factors of which are concentrated on one side, and labour-power, isolated, on the other.

The means of production, the material part of productive capital, must therefore face the laborer as such, as capital, before the act M—L can become a universal, social one.

We have seen on previous occasions [English edition: Karl Marx, *Capital*, Vol. I, Part VII, Moscow, 1954.—*Ed.*] that in its further development capitalist production, once it is established, not only reproduces this separation but extends its scope further and further until it becomes the prevailing condition. However, there is still another side to this question. In order that capital may be able to arise and take control of production, a definite stage in the development of trade is assumed. This applies therefore also to the circulation of commodities, and hence to the production of commodities; for no articles can enter circulation as commodities unless they are produced for sale, hence as commodities. But the production of commodities does not become the normal, dominant type of production until capitalist production serves as its basis.

The Russian landowners, who as a result of the so-called emancipation of the peasants are now compelled to carry on agriculture with the help of wage-labourers instead of the forced labour of serfs, complain about two things: First, about the lack of money-capital. They say for instance that comparatively large sums must be paid to wage-labourers before the crops are sold, and just then there is a dearth of ready cash, the prime condition. Capital in the form of money must always be available, particularly for the payment of wages, before production can be carried on capitalistically. But the landowners may take hope. Everything comes to those who wait, and in due time the industrial capitalist will have at his disposal not alone his own money but also that of others.

The second complaint is more characteristic. It is to the effect that even if one has money, not enough labourers are to be had at any time. The reason is that the Russian farm-laborer, owing to the common ownership of land in the village community, has not yet been fully separated from his means of production and hence is not yet a 'free wage-laborer' in the full sense of the word. But the existence of the latter on a social scale is a *sine qua non* for M—C, the conversion of money into commodities, to be able to represent the transformation of money-capital into productive capital.

It is therefore quite clear that the formula for the circuit of money-capital, M—C ... C'—M', is the matter-of-course form of the circuit of capital only on the basis of already developed capitalist production, because it presupposes the existence of a class of wage-labourers on a social scale. We have seen that capitalist production does not only create commodities and surplus-value, but also reproduces to an ever increasing extent the class of wage-labourers, into whom it transforms the vast majority of direct producers. Since the first condition for its realisation is the permanent existence of a class of wage-labourers, M—C ... P ... C'—M' presupposes a capital in the form of productive capital, and hence the form of the circuit of productive capital.

Section II. *Second Stage. Function of Productive Capital*

The circuit of capital, which we have here considered, begins with the act of circulation M—C, the transmutation of money into commodities—purchase. Circulation must therefore be complemented by the antithetical metamorphosis C—M, the transformation of commodities into money—sale. But the direct result of $M—C<^{L}_{MP}$ is the interruption of the circulation of the capital-value advanced in the form of money. By the transformation of money-capital into productive capital the capital-value has acquired a bodily form in which it cannot continue to circulate but must enter into consumption, viz., into productive consumption. The use of labour-power, labour, can be materialised only in the labour-process. The capitalist cannot resell the laborer as a commodity because he is not his chattel slave and the capitalist has not bought anything except the right to use his labour-power for a certain time. On the other hand the capitalist cannot use this labour-power in any other way than by utilising means of production to create commodities with its help. The result of the first stage is therefore entrance into the second, the productive stage of capital.

This movement is represented by $M—C<^{L}_{MP}$ ... P, in which the dots indicate that the circulation of capital is interrupted, while its circular movement continues, since it passes from the sphere of circulation of commodities into that of production. The first stage, the transformation of money-capital into productive capital, is therefore merely the harbinger and introductory phase of the second stage, the functioning of productive capital.

M—C<$^{L}_{MP}$ presupposes that the individual performing this act not only has at his disposal values in any use-form, but also that he has them in the form of money, that he is the owner of money. But as the act consists precisely in giving away money, the individual can remain the owner of money only in so far as the act of giving away implies a return of money. But money can return to him only through the sale of commodities. Hence the above act assumes him to be a producer of commodities.

M—L. The wage-laborer lives only by the sale of his labour-power. Its preservation—his preservation—requires daily consumption. Hence payment for it must be continuously repeated at rather short intervals in order that he may be able to repeat acts L—M—C or C—M—C, repeat the purchases needed for his self-preservation. For this reason the capitalist must always meet the wage-laborer in the capacity of a money-capitalist, and his capital as money-capital. On the other hand if the wage-labourers, the mass of direct producers, are to perform the act L—M—C, they must constantly be faced with the necessary means of subsistence in purchasable form, i.e., in the form of commodities. This state of affairs necessitates a high degree of development of the circulation of products in the form of commodities, hence also of the volume of commodities produced. When production by means of wage-labour becomes universal, commodity production is bound to be the general form of production. This mode of production, once it is assumed to be general, carries in its wake an ever increasing division of social labour, that is to say an ever growing differentiation of the articles which are produced in the form of commodities by a definite capitalist, ever greater division of complementary processes of production into independent processes. M—MP therefore develops to the same extent as M—L does, that is to say the production of means of production is divorced to that extent from the production of commodities whose means of production they are. And the latter then stand opposed to every producer of commodities which he does not produce but buys for his particular process of production. They come from branches of production which, operated independently, are entirely divorced from his own, enter into his own branch as commodities, and must therefore be bought. The material conditions of commodity production face him more and more as products of other commodity producers, as commodities. And to the same extent the capitalist must assume the role of money-capitalist, in other words there is an increase in the scale on which his capital must assume the functions of money-capital.

On the other hand, the same conditions which give rise to the basic condition of capitalist production, the existence of a class of wage-workers, facilitate the transition of all commodity production to capitalist commodity production. As capitalist production develops, it has a disintegrating, resolvent effect on all older forms of production, which, designed mostly to meet the direct needs of the producer, transform only the excess produced into commodities. Capitalist production makes the sale of products the main interest, at first apparently without affecting the mode of production itself. Such was for instance the first effect of capitalist world commerce on such nations as the Chinese, Indians, Arabs, etc. But, secondly, wherever it takes root capitalist production destroys all forms of commodity production which are based either on the self-employment of the producers, or merely on the sale of the excess product as commodities. Capitalist production first makes the production of commodities general and then, by degrees, transforms all commodity production into capitalist commodity production.[3]

Whatever the social form of production, labourers and means of production always remain factors of it. But in a state of separation from each other either of these factors can be such only potentially. For production to go on at all they must unite. The specific manner in which this union is accomplished distinguishes the different economic epochs of the structure of society from one another. In the present case, the separation of the free worker from his means of production is the starting-point given, and we have seen how and under what conditions these two elements are united in the hands of the capitalist, namely, as the productive mode of existence of his capital. The actual process which the personal and material creators of commodities enter upon when thus brought together, the process of production, becomes therefore itself a function of capital, the capitalist process of production, the nature of which has been fully analysed in the first book of this work. Every enterprise engaged in commodity production becomes at the same time an enterprise exploiting labour-power. But only the capitalist production of commodities has become an epoch-making mode of exploitation, which, in the course of its historical development, revolutionises, through the organisation of the labour-process and the enormous improvement of technique, the entire structure of society in a manner eclipsing all former epochs.

The means of production and labour-power, in so far as they are forms of existence of advanced capital-value, are distinguished by the different roles assumed by them during the process of production in the creation of value, hence also of surplus-value, into constant and variable capital. Being different components of productive capital they are furthermore distinguished by the fact that the means of production in the possession of the capitalist remain his capital even outside of the process of production, while labour-power becomes the form of existence of an individual capital only within this process. Whereas labour-power is a commodity only in the hands of its seller, the wage-labourer, it becomes capital only in the hands of its buyer, the capitalist who acquires the temporary use of it. The means of production do not become the material forms of productive capital, or productive capital, until labour-power, the personal form of existence of productive capital, is capable of being embodied in them. Human labour-power is by nature no more capital than by means of production. They acquire this specific social character only under definite, historically developed conditions, just as only under such conditions the character of money is stamped upon precious metals, or that of money-capital upon money.

Productive capital, in performing its functions, consumes its own component parts for the purpose of transforming them into a mass of products of a higher value. Since labour-power acts merely as one of its organs, the excess of the product's value engendered by its surplus-labour over and above the value of productive capital's constituent elements is also the fruit of capital. The surplus-labour of labour-power is the gratuitous labour performed for capital and thus forms surplus-value for the capitalist, a value which costs him no equivalent return. The product is therefore not only a commodity, but a commodity pregnant with surplus-value. Its value is equal to P + s, that is to say equal to the value of the productive capital P consumed in the production of the commodity plus the surplus values created by it. Let us assume that this commodity consists of 10,000 lbs. of yarn, and that means of production worth £372 and labour power worth £50 were consumed in the fabrication of this quantity of yarn. During the process of spinning, the spinners transmitted to the yarn the value of the means of production consumed by their labour, amounting to £372, and at the same time they created, in proportion with the labour-power expended by them, new value to the amount of, say, £128. The 10,000 lbs. of yarn therefore represent a value of £500.

Section III. *Third Stage. C'—M'*

Commodities become *commodity-capital* as a functional form of existence—stemming directly from the process of production itself—of capital-value which has already produced surplus-value. If the production of commodities were carried on capitalistically throughout society, all commodities would be elements of commodity-capital from the outset, whether they were crude iron, Brussels lace, sulphuric acid or cigars. The problem of what kinds of commodities, is one of the self-created lovely ills of scholastic political economy.

Capital in the form of commodities has to perform the function of commodities. The articles of which capital is composed are produced especially for the market and must be sold, transformed into money, hence go through the process C—M.

Suppose the commodity of the capitalist to consist of 10,000 lbs. of cotton yarn. If £372 represent the value of the means of production consumed in the spinning process, and new value to the amount of £128 has been created, the yarn has a value of £500, which is expressed in its price of the same amount. Suppose further that this price is realised by the sale C—M. What is it that makes of this simple act of all commodity circulation at the same time a capital-function? No change that takes place inside of it, neither in the use-character of the commodity—for it passes into the hands of the buyer as an object of use—nor in its value, for this value has not experienced any change of magnitude, but only of form. It first existed in the form of yarn, while now it exists in the form of money. Thus a substantial distinction is evident between the first stage M—C and the last stage C—M. There the advanced money functions as money-capital, because it is transformed by means of the circulation into commodities of a specific use-value. Here the commodities can serve as capital only to the extent that they bring this character with them in ready shape from the process of production before their circulation begins. During the spinning process, the spinners create yarn value to the amount of £128. Of this sum, say £50 represent to the capitalist merely an equivalent for his outlay for labour-power, while £78—when the degree of exploitation of labour-power is 156 per cent—form surplus-value. The value of the 10,000 lbs. of yarn therefore embodies first the value of the consumed productive capital P, the constant part of which amounts to £372 and the variable to £50, their sum being £422, equal to 8,440 lbs. of yarn. Now the value of the productive capital P is equal to C, the value of its constituent elements, which in the stage M—C confronted the capitalist as commodities in the hands of their sellers.

In the second place, however, the value of the yarn contains a surplus-value of £78, equal to 1,560 lbs. of yarn. C as an expression of the value of the 10,000 lbs. of yarn is therefore equal to C plus DC, or C plus an increment of C (equal to £78), which we shall call c, since it exists in the same commodity-form as now the original value C. The value of the 10,000 lbs. of yarn, equal to £500, is therefore represented by C + c = C'. What turns C, the expression of the value of 10,000 lbs. of yarn, into C' is not the absolute magnitude of its value (£500), for that is determined, as in the case of any other C standing for the expression of the value of some other sum of commodities, by the quantity of labour embodied in it. It is its relative value-magnitude, its value-magnitude as compared with that of capital P consumed in its production. This value is contained in it plus the surplus-value supplied by the productive capital. Its value is greater, exceeds that of the capital-value by this surplus-value c. The 10,000 lbs. of yarn are the bearers of the capital-value expanded, enriched by this surplus-value, and they are so by virtue of being the product of the capitalist process of production. C' expresses a value-relation, the relation of the value of the commodities produced to that of the capital spent on their production, in other words, expresses the fact that its value is composed of capital-value and surplus-value. The 10,000 lbs. of yarn represent commodity capital, C', only because they are a converted form of the productive capital P, hence in a connection which exists originally only in the circuit of this individual capital, or only for the capitalist who produced the yarn with the help of his capital. It is, so to say, only an internal, not an external relation that turns the 10,000 lbs. of yarn in their capacity of vehicles of value into a commodity-capital. They exhibit their capitalist birthmark not in the absolute magnitude of their value but in its relative magnitude, in the magnitude of their value as compared with that possessed by the productive capital embodied in them before it was transformed into commodities. If, then, these 10,000 lbs. of yarn are sold at their value of £500, this act of circulation, considered by itself, is identical with C—M, a mere transformation of an unchanging value from the form of a commodity into that of money. But as a special stage in the circuit of an individual capital, the same act is a realisation of the capital-value embodied in the commodity to the amount of £422 plus the surplus-value, likewise embodied in it, of £78. That is to say it represents C'—M', the transformation of the commodity-capital from its commodity-form into the money form.[4]

The function of C' is now that of all commodities, viz.: to transform itself into money, to be sold, to go through the circulation stage C—M. So long as the capital, now expanded, remains in the form of commodity-capital, lies immovable in the market, the process of production is at rest. The commodity-capital acts neither as a creator of products nor as a creator of value. A given capital-value will serve, in widely different degrees, as a creator of products and value, and the scale of reproduction will be extended or reduced commensurate with the particular speed with which that capital throws off its commodity-form and assumes that of money, or with the rapidity of the sale. It was shown in Book I that the degree of efficiency of any given capital is conditional on the potentialities of the productive process, which to a certain extent are independent of the magnitude of its own value. [English edition: Karl Marx, *Capital*, Vol. I, pp. 602-08.—*Ed.*] Here it appears that the process of circulation sets in motion new forces independent of the capital's magnitude of value and determining its degree of efficiency, its expansion and contraction.

The mass of commodities C', being the depository of the expanded capital, must furthermore pass in its entirety through the metamorphosis C'—M'. The quantity sold is here a main determinant. The individual commodity figures only as an integral part of the total mass. The £500 worth of value exists in the 10,000 lbs. of yarn. If the capitalist succeeds in selling only 7,440 lbs. at their value of £372, he has replaced only the value of his constant capital, the value of the expanded means of production. If he sells 8,440 lbs. he recovers only the value of the total capital advanced. He must sell more in order to realise some surplus-value, and he must sell the entire 10,000 lbs. in order to realise the surplus-value of £78 (1,560 lbs. of yarn). In £500 in money he receives merely an equivalent for the commodity sold. His transaction within the circulation is simply C—M. If he had paid his labourers £64 in wages instead of £50 his surplus-value would only be £64 instead of £78, and the degree of exploitation would have been only 100 per cent instead of 156. But the value of the yarn would not change; only the relation between its component parts would be different. The circulation act C—M would still represent the sale of 10,000 lbs. of yarn for £500, their value.

C' is equal to C + c (or £422 at £78). C equals the value of P, the productive capital, and this equals the value of M, the money advanced in M—C, the purchase of the elements of production, amounting to £422 in our example. If the mass of commodities is sold at its value, then C equals £422 and c equals £78, the value of the surplus-product of 1,560 lbs. of yarn. If we call c, expressed in money, m, then C'—M' = (C + c) - (M + m), and the circuit M—C ... P ... C'—M', in its expanded form, is therefore represented by M—C$<^{L}_{MP}$ ... P ... (C + c) - (M + m).

In the first stage the capitalist takes articles of consumption out of the commodity-market proper and the labour-market. In the third stage he throws commodities back, but only into one market, the commodity-market proper. However the fact that he extracts from the market, by means of his commodities, a greater value than he threw upon it originally is due only to the circumstance that he throws more commodity-value back upon it than he first drew out of it. He threw value M upon it and drew out of it the equivalent C; he throws C + c back upon it, and draws out of it the equivalent M + m.

M was in our example equal to the value of 8,440 lbs. of yarn. But he throws 10,000 lbs. of yarn on the market, consequently he returns a greater value than he took from it. On the other hand he threw this increased value on the market only because through the exploitation of labour-power in the process of production he had created surplus-value (as an aliquot part of the product expressed in surplus-product). It is only by virtue of being the product of this process that the mass of commodities becomes commodity-capital, the bearer of the expanded capital-value. By performing C'—M' the advanced capital-value as well as the surplus-value are realised. The realisation of both takes place simultaneously in a series of sales or in a lump sale of the entire mass of commodities which is expressed by C'—M'. But the same circulation act C'—M' is different for capital-value and surplus-value, as it expresses for each of them a different stage of their circulation, a different section of the series of metamorphoses through which they must pass in the sphere of circulation. The surplus-value c came into the world only during the process of production. It appeared for the first time in the commodity-market, in the form of commodities. This is its first form of circulation, hence the act c—m is its first circulation act, or its first metamorphosis, which remains to be supplemented by the antithetical act of circulation, or the reverse metamorphosis, m—c.[5]

It is different with the circulation which the capital-value C performs in the same circulation act C'—M', and which constitutes for the circulation act C—M, in which C is equal to P, equal to the M originally advanced. Capital-value has opened its first circulation act in the form of M, money-capital, and returns through the act C—M to the same form. It has therefore passed through the two antithetical stages of circulation, first M—C, second C—M, and finds itself once more in the form in which it can begin its circular movement anew. What for surplus-value constitutes the first transformation of the commodity-form into that of money, constitutes for capital-value in return, or retransformation, into its original money-form.

By means of $M—C<^{L}_{MP}$ money capital is transformed into an equivalent mass of commodities, L and MP. These commodities no longer perform the function of commodities, of articles for sale. Their value is now in the hands of the capitalist who bought them; they represent the value of his productive capital P. And in the function of P, productive consumption, they are transformed into a kind of commodity differing materially from the means of production, into yarn, in which their value is not only preserved but increased, from £422 to £500. By means of this real metamorphosis, the commodities taken from the market in the first stage, M—C, are replaced by commodities of different substance and value, which now must perform the function of commodities, must be transformed into money and sold. The process of production therefore appears to be only an interruption of the process of circulation of capital-value, of which up to that point only the first phase, M—C, has been passed through. It passes through the second and concluding phase, C—M, after C has been altered in substance and value. But so far as capital-value, considered by itself, is concerned, it has merely suffered an alteration of its use-form in the process of production. It existed in the form of £422 worth of L and MP, while now it exists in the form of £422 worth of, or 8,440 lbs. of yarn. If we therefore consider merely the two circulation phases of capital-value, apart from its surplus-value, we find that it passes through 1) M—C and 2) C—M, in which the second C has a different use-form but the same value as the first C. Hence it passes through M—C—M, a form of circulation which, because the commodity here changes place twice and in the opposite direction—transformation from money into commodities and from commodities into money—necessitates the return of the value advanced in the form of money to its money-form—its reconversion into money.

The same circulation act C'—M' that constitutes the second and concluding metamorphosis, a return to the money-form, for the capital-value advanced in money, represents for the surplus-value—borne along by the commodity-capital and simultaneously realised by its change into the money-form—its first metamorphosis, its transformation from the commodity- to the money-form, C—M, its first circulation phase.

We have, then, two kinds of observations to make here. First, the ultimate reconversion of capital-value into its original money-form is a function of commodity-capital. Secondly, this function includes the first transformation of surplus-value from its original commodity-form to its money-form. The money-form, then, plays a double role here. On the one hand it is the form to which a value originally advanced in money returns, hence a return to the form of value which opened the process. On the other hand it is the first converted form of a value which originally enters the circulation in commodity-form. If the commodities composing the commodity-capital are sold at their values, as we assume, then C plus c is transformed into M plus m, its equivalent. The realised commodity-capital now exists in the hands of the capitalist in this form: M plus m (£422 plus £78 = £500). Capital-value and surplus-value are now present in the form of money, the form of the universal equivalent.

At the conclusion of the process capital-value has therefore resumed the form in which it entered it, and as money-capital can now open and go through a new process. Just because the initial and final forms of this process are those of money-capital, M, we call this form of the circulation process the circuit of money-capital. It is not the form but merely the magnitude of the advanced value that is changed at the close.

M plus m is nothing but a sum of money of a definite magnitude, in this case £500. But as a result of the circulation of capital, as realised commodity-capital, this sum of money contains the capital-value and the surplus-value. And these values are now no longer inseparably united as they were in the yarn; they now lie side by side. Their sale has given both of them an independent money-form; 211/250 of this money represent the capital-value of £422 and 39/250 constitute the surplus-value of £78. This separation, effected by the realisation of the commodity-capital, has not only the formal content to which we shall refer presently. It becomes important in the process of the reproduction of capital, depending on whether m is entirely or partially or not at all lumped together with M, i.e., depending on whether or not it continues to function as a component part of the advanced capital-value. Both m and M may pass through quite different processes of circulation.

In M' capital has returned to its original form M, to its money-form, a form however in which it is materialised as capital.

There is in the first place a difference of quantity. It was M, £422. It is now M', £500, and this difference is expressed by M ... M', the quantitatively different extremes of the circuit, whose movement is indicated only by the three dots. M' > M, and M' - M = s, the surplus-value. But as a result of this circular movement M ... M' it is only M' which exists now; it is the product in which its process of formation has become extinct. M' now exists by itself, independently of the movement which brought it into existence. That movement is gone; M' is there in its place.

But M', being M plus m, £500, composed of £422 advanced capital plus an increment of the same amounting to £78, represents at the same time a qualitative relation, although this qualitative relation itself exists only as a relation between the parts of one and the same sum, hence as a quantitative relation. M, the advanced capital, which is now once more present in its original form (£422), exists as realised capital. It has not only preserved itself but also realised itself as capital by being distinguished as such from m (£78), to which it stands in the same relation as to an increase *of its own*, to a fruit *of its own*, to an increment to which it has given birth itself. It has been realised as capital because it has been realised as a value which has created value. M' exists as a capital-relation. M no longer appears as mere money, but expressly plays the part of money-capital, expressed as a self-expanded value, hence possessing the property of self-expansion, of hatching a higher value than it itself has. M became capital by virtue of its relation to the other part of M', which it has brought about, which has been effected by it as the cause, which is the consequence of it as the ground. Thus M' appears as the sum of values differentiated within itself, functionally (conceptually) distinguished within itself, expressing the capital-relation.

But this is expressed only as a result, without the intervention of the process of which it is the result.

Parts of value as such are not qualitatively different from one another, except in so far as they appear as values of different articles, of concrete things, hence in various use-forms and therefore as values of different commodities—a difference which does not originate with them themselves as mere parts of value. In money all differences between commodities are extinguished, because it is the equivalent form common to all of them. A sum of money in the amount of £500 consists solely of uniform elements of £1 each. Since the intermediate links of its origin are obliterated in the simple existence of this sum of money and every trace has been lost of the specific difference between the different component parts of capital in the process of production, there exists now only the distinction between the conceptual form of a **principal** equal to £422, the capital advanced, and an excess value of £78. Let M› be equal to, say, £110, of which £100 may be equal to M, the principal, and 10 equal to s, the surplus-value. There is an absolute homogeneity, an absence of conceptual distinctions, between the two constituent parts of the sum of £110. Any £10 of this sum always constitute 1/11 of the total sum of £1/10, whether they are 1/10 of the advanced principal of £100 or the excess of £10 above it. Principal and excess sum, capital and surplus-sum, may therefore be expressed as fractional parts of the total sum. In our illustration, 10/11 form the principal, or the capital, and 1/11 the surplus sum. In its money-expression realised capital appears therefore at the end of its process as an irrational expression of the capital-relation.

True, this applies also to C' (C plus c). But there is this difference: that C', of which C and c are only proportional value-parts of the same homogeneous mass of commodities, indicates its origin P, whose immediate product it is, while in M', a form derived directly from circulation, the direct relation to P is obliterated.

The irrational distinction between the principal and the incremental sum, which is contained in M', so far as that expresses the result of the movement M ... M', disappears as soon as it once more functions actively as money-capital and is therefore not fixed as a money-expression of expanded industrial capital. The circuit of capital can never begin with M' (although M' now performs the function of M). It can begin only with M, that is to say it can never begin as an expression of the capital-relation, but only as a form of advance of capital-value. As soon as the £500 are once more advanced as capital, in order again to produce s, they constitute a point of departure, not one of return. Instead of a capital of £422, a capital of £500 is now advanced. It is more money than before, more capital-value, but the relation between its two constituent parts has disappeared. In fact a sum of £500 instead of the £422 might originally have served as capital.

It is not an active function of money-capital to appear as M'; to appear as M' is rather a function of C'. Even in the simple circulation of commodities, first in C_1—M, secondly in M—C_2, money M does not figure actively until the second act, M—C_2. Its appearance in the form of M is only the result of the first act, by virtue of which it only then appears as a converted form of C_1. True, the capital-relation contained in M', the relation of one of its parts as the capital-value to the other as its value increment, acquires functional importance in so far as, with the constantly repeated circuit M ... M', M' splits into two circulations, one of them a circulation of capital, the other of surplus-value. Consequently these two parts perform not only quantitatively but also qualitatively different functions, M others than m. But considered by itself, the form M ... M' does not include what the capitalist consumes, but explicitly only the self-expansion and accumulation, so far as the latter expresses itself above all as a periodical augmentation of ever renewed advances of money-capital.

Although M', equal to M plus m, is the irrational form of capital, it is at the same time only money-capital in its realised form, in the form of money which has generated money. But this is different from the function of money-capital in the first stage, M—C<$^{L}_{MP}$. In the first stage, M circulates as money. It assumes the functions of money-capital because only in its money state can it perform a money-function, can it transform itself into the elements of P, into L and MP, which stand opposed to it as commodities. In this circulation act it functions only as money. But as this act is the first stage of capital-value in process, it is simultaneously a function of money-capital, by virtue of the specific use-form of the commodities L and MP which are bought. M' on the other hand, composed of M, the capital-value, and m, the surplus-value begotten of M, stands for self-expanded capital-value—the purpose and the outcome, the function of the total circuit of capital. The fact that it expresses this outcome in the form of money, as realised money-capital, does not derive from its being the money-form of capital, *money-capital*, but on the contrary from its being *money-capital*, capital in the form of money, from capital having opened the process in this form, from its having been advanced in the money-form. Its reconversion into the money-form is, as we have seen, a function of commodity-capital C', not of money-capital. As for the difference between M and M', it (m) is simply the money-form of c, the increment of C. M' is composed of M plus m only because C' was composed of C plus c. In C' therefore this difference and the relation of the capital-value to the surplus-value generated by it is present and expressed before both of them are transformed into M', into a sum of money in which both parts of the value come face to face with each other independently and may, therefore, be employed in separate and distinct functions.

M' is only the result of the realisation of C'. Both M' and C' are merely different forms of self-expanded capital-value, one of them the commodity-form, the other the money-form. Both of them have this in common: that they are self-expanded capital-value. Both of them are materialised capital, because capital-value as such exists here together with the surplus-value, the fruit obtained through it and differing from it, although this relation is expressed only in the irrational form of the relation between two parts of a sum of money or of a commodity-value. But as expressions of capital in relation and contradistinction to the surplus-value produced by it, hence as expressions of self-expanded value, M' and C' are the same and express the same thing, only in different forms. They do not differ as money-capital and commodity-capital but as money and commodities. In so far as they represent self-expanded value, capital acting as capital, they only express the result of the functioning of productive capital, the only function in which capital-value generates value. What they have in common is that both of them, money-capital as well as commodity-capital, are modes of existence of capital. The one is capital in money-form, the other in commodity-form. The specific functions that distinguish them cannot therefore be anything else but differences between the functions of money and of commodities. Commodity-capital, the direct product of the capitalist process of production, is reminiscent of its origin and is therefore more rational and less incomprehensible in form than money-capital, in which every trace of this process has vanished, as in general all special use-forms of commodities disappear in money. It is therefore only when M' itself functions as commodity-capital, when it is the direct product of a productive process instead of being the converted form of this product, that it loses its bizarre form, that is to say, in the production of the money material itself. In the production of gold for instance the formula would be $M—C<^{L}_{MP}$ ... P ... M› (M plus m), where M› would figure as a commodity product, because P furnishes more gold than was advanced for the elements of production of the gold in the first M, the money-capital. In this case the irrational nature of the expression M ... M› (M plus m) disappears. Here a part of a sum of money appears as the mother of another part of the same sum of money.

Section IV. *The Circuit as a Whole*

We have seen that the process of circulation is interrupted at the end of its first phase, $M—C<^{L}_{MP}$, by P, in which the commodities L and MP bought in the market are consumed as the material and value components of productive capital. The product of this consumption is a new commodity, C', altered in respect of substance and value. The interrupted process of circulation, M—C, must be completed by C—M. But the bearer of this second and concluding phase of circulation is C', a commodity different in substance and value from the original C. The circulation series therefore appears as 1) M—C_1; 2) C'_2—M›, where in the second phase of the first commodity, C_1, another commodity of greater value and different use-form, C'_2, is substituted during the interruption caused by the functioning of P, the production of C' from the elements of C, the forms of existence of productive capital P. However, the first form of appearance in which capital faced us (Buch. I, Kap. IV, 1), [English edition: Ch. IV.—*Ed.*] viz., M—C—M' (extended: 1) M—C_1; 2) C_1—M›) shows the same commodity twice. Both times it is the same commodity into which money is transformed in the first phase and reconverted into more money in the second phase. In spite of this essential difference, both circulations share this much: that in their first phase money is transformed into commodities, and in the second commodities into money, that the money spent in the first phase returns in the second. On the one hand both have in common this reflux of the money to its starting-point, on the other hand also the excess of the returning money over the money advanced. To that extent the formula M—C ... C›—M› is contained in the general formula M—C—M›.

It follows furthermore that each time equally great quantities of simultaneously existing values face and replace each other in the two metamorphoses M—C and C'—M' belonging in circulation. The change in value pertains exclusively to the metamorphosis P, the process of production, which thus appears as a real metamorphosis of capital, as compared with the merely metamorphosis of circulation.

Let us now consider the total movement, M—C ... P ... C'—M', or, M—C<$^{L}_{MP}$ ... P ... C› (C + c)—M› (M + m), its more expanded form. Capital here appears as a value which goes through a series of interconnected, interdependent transformations, a series of metamorphoses which form just as many phases, or stages, of the process as a whole. Two of these phases belong in the sphere of circulation, one of them in that of production. In each one of these phases capital-value has a different form for which there is a correspondingly different, special function. Within this movement the advanced value does not only preserve itself but grows, increases in magnitude. Finally, in the concluding stage, it returns to the same form which it had at the beginning of the process as a whole. This process as a whole constitutes therefore the process of moving in circuits.

The two forms assumed by capital-value at the various stages of its circulation are those of *money-capital* and *commodity-capital*. The form pertaining to the stage of production is that of *productive capital*. The capital which assumes these forms in the course of its total circuit and then discards them and in each of them performs the function corresponding to the particular form, is *industrial capital*, industrial here in the sense it comprises every branch of industry run on a capitalist basis.

Money-capital, commodity-capital and productive capital, do not therefore designate independent kinds of capital whose functions form the content of likewise independent branches of industry separated from one another. They denote here only special functional forms of industrial capital, which assumes all three of them one after the other.

Capital describes its circuit normally only so long as its various phases pass uninterruptedly into one another. If capital stops short in the first phase M—C, money-capital assumes the rigid form of a hoard; if it stops in the phase of production, the means of production lie without functioning on the one side, while labour-power remains unemployed on the other; and if capital stops short in the last phase C'—M', piles of unsold commodities accumulate and clog the flow of circulation.

However, it is in the nature of things that the circuit itself necessitates the fixation of capital for certain lengths of time in its various phases. In each of its phases industrial capital is tied up with a definite form: money-capital, productive capital, commodity-capital. It does not acquire the form in which it may enter a new transformation phase until it has performed the function corresponding to each particular form. To make this plain, we have assumed in our illustration that the capital-value of the quantity of commodities created at the stage of production is equal to the total sum of the value originally advanced in the form of money; or, in other words, that the entire capital-value advanced in the form of money passes on in bulk from one stage to the next. But we have seen (Buch I, Kap. VI) [English edition: Ch. VIII.—*Ed.*] that a part of constant capital, the labour instruments proper (e.g., machinery), continually serve anew, with more or less numerous repetitions of the same process of production, hence transfer their values piecemeal to the products. It will be seen later to what extent this circumstance modifies the circular movement of capital. For the present the following suffices: In our illustration the value of productive capital amounting to £422 contained only the average wear and tear of factory buildings, machinery, etc., that is to say only that part of value which they transferred to the yarn in the transformation of 10,600 lbs. of cotton into 10,000 lbs. of yarn, which represented the product of one week's spinning of 60 hours. In the means of production, into which the advanced constant capital of £372 was transformed, the instruments of labour, buildings, machinery, etc., figured as if they had only been rented in the market at a weekly rate. But this does not change the gist of the matter in any way. We have but to multiply the quantity of yarn produced in one week, i.e., 10,000 lbs. of yarn, by the number of weeks contained in a certain number of years, in order to transfer to the yarn the entire value of the instruments of labour bought and consumed during this period. It is then plain that the advanced money-capital must first be transformed into these instruments, hence must have gone through the first phase M—C before it can function as productive capital P. And it is likewise plain in our illustration that the capital value of £422, embodied in the yarn during the process of production, cannot be part of the value of the 10,000 lbs. of yarn and enter the circulation phase C'—M' until it is ready. It cannot be sold until it has been spun.

In the general formula the product P is regarded as a material thing different from the elements of the productive capital, as an object existing apart from the process of production and having a use-form different from that of the elements of production. This is always the case when the result of the productive process assumes the form of a thing, even when a part of the product re-enters the resumed production as one of its elements. Grain for instance serves as seed for its own production, but the product consists only of grain and hence has a shape different from those of related elements such as labour-power, implements, fertiliser. But there are certain independent branches of industry in which the product of the productive process is not a new material product, is not a commodity. Among these only the communications industry, whether engaged in transportation proper, of goods and passengers, or in the mere transmission of communications, letters, telegrams, etc., is economically important.

A. Chuprov[6] says on this score:

> 'The manufacturer may first produce articles and then look for consumers'

[his product, thrust out of the process of production when finished, passes into circulation as a commodity separated from it].

> 'Production and consumption thus appear as two acts separated in space and time. In the transportation industry, which does not create any new products but merely transfer men and things, these two acts coincide; its services' [change of place] 'are consumed the moment they are produced. For this reason the area within which railways can sell their services extends at best 50 versts (53 kilometres) on either side of their tracks.'

The result, whether men or goods are transported, is a change in their whereabouts. Yarn, for instance, may now be in India instead of in England, where it was produced.

However, what the transportation industry sells is change of location. The useful effect is inseparably connected with the process of transportation, i.e., the productive process of the transport industry. Men and goods travel together with the means of transportation, and their traveling, this locomotion, constitutes the process of production effected by these means. The useful effect can be consumed only during this process of production. It does not exist as a utility different from this process, a use-thing which does not function as an article of commerce, does not circulate as a commodity, until after it has been produced. But the exchange-value of this useful effect is determined, like that of any other commodity, by the value of the elements of production (labour-power and means of production) consumed in it plus the surplus-value created by the surplus-labour of the labourers employed in transportation. This useful effect also entertains the very same relations to consumption that other commodities do. If it is consumed individually its value disappears during its consumption; if it is consumed productively so as to constitute by itself a stage in the production of the commodities being transported, its value is transferred as an additional value to the commodity itself. The formula for the transport industry would therefore be M—C$<^{L}_{MP}$ ... P—M›, since it is the process of production itself that is paid for and consumed, not a product separate and distinct from it. Hence this formula has almost the same form as that of the production of precious metals, the only difference being that in this case M› represents the converted form of the useful effect created during the process of production, and not the bodily form of the gold or silver produced in this process and extruded from it.

Industrial capital is the only mode of existence of capital in which not only the appropriation of surplus-value, or surplus-product, but simultaneously its creation is a function of capital. Therefore with it the capitalist character of production is a necessity. Its existence implies the class antagonism between capitalists and wage-labourers. To the extent that it seizes control of social production, the technique and social organisation of the labour-process are revolutionised and with them the economico-historical type of society. The other kinds of capital, which appeared before industrial capital amid conditions of social production that have receded into the past or are now succumbing, are not only subordinated to it and the mechanism of their functions altered in conformity with it, but move solely with it as their basis, hence live and die, stand and fall with this basis. Money-capital and commodity-capital, so far as they function as vehicles of particular branches of business, side by side with industrial capital, are nothing but modes of existence of the different functional forms now assumed, now discarded by industrial capital in the sphere of circulation—modes which, due to social division of labour, have attained independent existence and been developed one-sidedly.

The circuit M ... M' on the one hand intermingles with the general circulation of commodities, proceeds from it and flows back into it, is a part of it. On the other hand it forms an independent movement of the capital-value for the individual capitalist, a movement of its own which takes place partly within the general circulation of commodities, partly outside of it, but which always preserves its independent character. First, because its two phases that take place in the sphere of circulation, M—C and C'—M', being phases of the movement of capital, have functionally definite characters. In M—C, C is materially determined as labour-power and means of production; in C'—M' the capital-value is realised plus the surplus-value. Secondly, because P, the process of production, embraces productive consumption. Thirdly, because the return of the money to its starting-point makes of the movement M ... M' a circuit complete in itself.

Every individual capital is therefore, on the one hand, in its two circulation-halves M—C and C'—M', an agent of the general circulation of commodities, in which it either functions or lies concatenated as money or as a commodity, thus forming a link in the general chain of metamorphoses taking place in the world of commodities. On the other hand it describes within the general circulation its own independent circuit in which the sphere of production forms a transitional stage and in which this capital returns to its starting-point in the same form in which it left that point. Within its own circuit, which includes its real metamorphosis in the process of production, it changes at the same time the magnitude of its value. It returns not simply as money-value, but as augmented, increased money-value.

Let us finally consider M—C ... P ... C'—M' as a special form of the circular course of capital, alongside the other forms which we shall analyse later. We shall find that it is distinguished by the following features:

1. It appears as the circuit of *money-capital*, because industrial capital in its *money-form*, as money-capital, forms the starting-point and the point of return of its total process. The formula itself expresses the fact that the money is not expended here as money but is merely advanced, hence is merely the money-form of capital, money-capital. It expresses furthermore that exchange-value, not use-value, is the determining aim of this movement. Just because the money-form of value is the independent, tangible form in which value appears, the form of circulation M ... M', the initial and terminal points of which are real money, expresses most graphically the compelling motive of capitalist production—money-making. The process of production appears merely as an unavoidable intermediate link, as a necessary evil for the sake of money-making. All nations with a capitalist mode of production are therefore seized periodically by a feverish attempt to make money without the intervention of the process of production.
2. The stage of production, the function of P, represents in this circuit an interruption between the two phases of circulation M—C ... C'—M', which in its turn represents only the intermediate link in the simple circulation M—C—M'. The process of production appears in the form of a circuit-describing process, formally and explicitly as that which it is in the capitalist mode of production, as a mere means of expanding the advanced value, hence enrichment as such as the purpose of production.
3. Since the series of phases is opened by M—C, the second link of the circulation is C'—M'. In other words, the starting-point is M, the money-capital that is to be self-expanded; the terminal point is M', the self-expanded money-capital M plus m, in which M figures as realised capital along with its offspring m. This distinguishes the circuit of M from that of the two other circuits P and C', and does so in two ways. On the one hand by the money-form of the two extremes. And money is the independent, tangible form of existence of value, the value of the product in its independent value-form, in which every trace of the use-value of the commodities has been extinguished. On the other hand the form P ... P does not necessarily become P ... P' (P plus p), and in the form C ... C' no difference whatever in value is visible between the two extremes. It is therefore characteristic of the formula M—M' that for one thing capital-value is its starting-point and expanded capital-value its point of return, so that the advance of capital-value appears as the means and expanded capital-value as the end of the entire operation; and that for another thing this relation is expressed in money-form, in the independent value-form, hence money-capital as money begetting money. The generation of surplus-value by value is not only expressed as the Alpha and Omega of the process, but explicitly in the form of glittering money.
4. Since M', the money-capital realised as a result of C'—M', the complementary and concluding phase of M—C, has absolutely the same form as that in which it began its first circuit, it can, as soon as it emerges from the latter, begin the same circuit over again as an increased (accumulated) money-capital; M' = M + m. And at

least it is not expressed in the form M ... M' that, in the repetition of the circuit, the circulation of m separates from that of M. Considered in its one-time form, formally, the circuit of money-capital expresses therefore simply the process of self-expansion and of accumulation. Consumption is expressed in it only as productive consumption, by M—C<$^{L}_{MP}$, and it is only this consumption that is included in this circuit of individual capital. M—L is L—M or C—M on the part of the labourer. It is therefore the first phase of circulation which brings about his individual consumption, thus: L—M—C (means of subsistence). The second phase M—C, no longer falls within the circuit of individual capital, but is initiated and premised by it, since the labourer must above all live, hence maintain himself by individual consumption, in order to always be in the market as material that the capitalist can exploit. But this consumption itself is here only assumed as a condition for the productive consumption of labour-power by capital, hence only to the extent that the worker maintains and reproduces himself as labour-power by means of his individual consumption. However the MP, the commodities proper which enter into the circuit of capital, are nutriment for the productive consumption only. The act L—M promotes the individual consumption of the labourer, the transformation of the means of subsistence into his flesh and blood. True, the capitalist must also be there, must also live and consume to be able to perform the function of a capitalist. To this end, he has, indeed, to consume only as much as the labourer, and that is all this form of the circulation process presupposes. But even this is not formally expressed, since the formula concludes with M', i.e., a result which can at once resume its function as money-capital, now augmented.

C'—M' directly contains the sale of C'; but C'—M', a sale on the one part, is M—C, a purchase, on the other part, and in the last analysis a commodity is bought only for its use-value, in order to enter (leaving intermediate sales out of consideration) the process of consumption, whether this is individual or productive, according to the nature of the article bought. But this consumption does not enter the circuit of individual capital, the product of which is C'. This product is eliminated from the circuit precisely because it is a commodity for sale. C' is expressly designed for consumption by others than the producer. Thus we find that certain exponents of the mercantile system (which is based on the formula M—C ... P ... C'—M') deliver lengthy sermons to the effect that the individual capitalist should consume only as much as the labourer, that the nation of capitalists should leave the consumption of their own commodities, and the consumption process in general, to the other, less intelligent nations but that they themselves should make productive consumption their life's task. These sermons frequently remind one in form and content of analogous ascetic expostulations of the fathers of the church.

Capital's movement in circuits is therefore the unity of circulation and production; it includes both. Since the two phases M—C and C'—M' are acts of circulation, the circulation of capital is a part of the general circulation of commodities. But as functionally they are definite sections, stages in capital's circuit, which pertains not only to the sphere of circulation but also to that of production, capital goes through its own circuit in the general circulation of commodities. The general circulation of commodities serves capital in the first stage as a means of assuming that shape in which it can perform the function of productive capital; in the second stage it serves to strip off the commodity-function in which capital cannot renew its circuit; at the same time it opens up to capital the possibility of separating its own circuit from the circulation of the surplus-value that accrued to it.

The circuit made by money-capital is therefore the most one-sided, and thus the most striking and typical form in which the circuit of industrial capital appears, the capital whose aim and compelling motive—the self-expansion of value, the making of money, and accumulation—is thus conspicuously revealed (buying to sell dearer). Owing to the fact that the first phase is M—C it is also revealed that the constituents of productive capital originate in the commodity-market, and in general that the capitalist process of production depends on circulation, on commerce. The circuit of money-capital is not merely the production of commodities; it is itself possible only through circulation and presupposes it. This is plain, if only from the fact that the form M belonging in circulation appears as the first and pure form of advanced capital-value, which is not the case in the other two circuit forms.

The money-capital circuit always remains the general expression of industrial capital, because it always includes the self-expansion of the advanced value. In P ... P, the money-expression of capital appears only as the price of the elements of production, hence only as a value expressed in money of account and is fixed in this form in book-keeping.

M ... M' becomes a special form of the industrial capital circuit when newly active capital is first advanced in the form of money and then withdrawn in the same form, either in passing from one branch of industry to another or in retiring industrial capital from a business. This includes the functioning as capital of the surplus-value first advanced in the form of money, and becomes most evident when surplus-value functions in some other business than the one in which it originated. M ... M' may be the first circuit of a certain capital; it may be the last; it may be regarded as the form of the total social capital; it is the form of capital that is newly invested, either as capital recently accumulated in the form of money, or as some old capital which is entirely transformed into money for the purpose of transfer from one branch of industry to another.

Being a form always contained in all circuits, money-capital performs this circuit precisely for that part of capital which produces surplus-value, viz., variable capital. The normal form of advancing wages is payment in money; this process must be renewed in comparatively short intervals, because the labourer lives from hand to mouth. The capitalist must therefore always confront the labourer as money-capitalist, and his capital as money-capital. There can be no direct or indirect balancing of accounts in this case such as we find in the purchase of means of production and in the sale of produced commodities (so that the greater part of the money-capital actually figures only in the form of commodities, money only in the form of money of account and finally in cash only in the balancing of accounts). On the other hand, a part of the surplus-value arising out of variable capital is spent by the capitalist for his individual consumption, which pertains to the retail trade and, however circuitous the route may be, this part is always spent in cash, in the money-form of surplus-value. Variable capital always appears anew as money-capital invested in wages (M—L) and m as surplus-value to defray the cost of individual consumption of the capitalist. Hence M, advanced variable capital-value, and m, its increment, are necessarily held in the form of money to be spent in this form.

The formula M—C ... P ... C'—M', with its result M' = M + m, is deceptive in form, is illusory in character, owing to the existence of the advanced and self-expanded value in its equivalent form, money. The emphasis is not on the self-expansion of value but on the *money-form* of this process, on the fact that more value in money-form is finally drawn out of the circulation than was originally advanced to it; hence on the multiplication of the mass of gold and silver belonging to the capitalist. The so-called monetary system is merely an expression of the irrational form M—C—M›, a movement which takes place exclusively in circulation and therefore can explain the two acts M—C and C—M› in no other way than as a sale of C above its value in the second act and therefore as C drawing more money out of the circulation than was put into it by its purchase. On the other hand M—C ... P ... C›—M›, fixed as the exclusive form, constitutes the basis of the more highly developed mercantile system, in which not only the circulation of commodities but also their production appears as a necessary element.

The illusory character of M—C ... P ... C'—M' and the correspondingly illusory interpretation exists whenever this form is fixed as occurring once, not as fluent and ever renewed; hence whenever this form is considered not as one of the forms of the circuit but as its exclusive form. But it itself points toward other forms.

In the first place this entire circuit is premised on the capitalist character of the process of production, and therefore considers this process together with the specific social conditions brought about by it as the basis. M—C = M—C$<^{L}_{MP}$; but M—L assumes the existence of the wage-labourer, and hence the means of production as part of productive capital. It assumes, therefore, that the process of labour and self-expansion, the process of production, is a function of capital.

In the second place, if M ... M' is repeated, the return to the money-form appears just as evanescent as the money-form in the first stage. M—C disappears to make room for P. The constantly recurrent advance in the form of money and its constant return in the form of money appear merely as fleeting moments in the circuit.

In the third place

M C... P... C'—M' M—C... P... C' M' M—C... P... etc

Beginning with the second repetition of the circuit, the circuit P ... C'—M'. M—C ... P appears before the second circuit of M is completed, and all subsequent circuits may thus be considered under the form of P ... C'—M—C ... P, so that M—C, being the first phase of the first circuit, is merely the passing preparation for the constantly repeated circuit of the productive capital. And this indeed is so in the case of industrial capital invested for the first time in the form of money-capital.

On the other hand before the second circuit of P is completed, the first circuit, that of commodity-capital, C'—M'.M—C ... P ... C' (abridged C' ... C') has already been made. Thus the first form already contains the other two, and the money-form thus disappears, so far as it is not merely an expression of value but an expression of value in the equivalent form, in money.

Finally, if we consider some newly invested individual capital describing for the first time the circuit M—C ... P ... C'—M', then M—C is the preparatory phase, the forerunner of the first process of production gone through by this individual capital. This phase M—C is consequently not presupposed but rather called for or necessitated by the process of production. But this applies only to this individual capital. The general form of the circuit of industrial capital is the *circuit of money-capital*, whenever the capitalist mode of production is taken for granted, hence in social conditions determined by capitalist production. Therefore the capitalist process of production is assumed as a pre-condition, if not in the first circuit of the money-capital of a newly invested industrial capital, then outside of it. The continuous existence of this process of production presupposes the constantly renewed circuit P ... P. Even in the first stage, M—C$<^{L}_{MP}$, this premise plays a part, for this assumes on the one hand the existence of the class of wage-labourers; and then, on the other, that which is M—C, the first stage, for the buyer of means of production, is C'—M' for their seller; hence C' presupposes commodity-capital, and thus the commodities themselves as a result of capitalist production, and thereby the function of productive capital.

Notes

1. From Manuscript II.—*F.E.*
2. Beginning of Manuscript VII, started July 1878.
3. End of Manuscript VII. Beginning of Manuscript VI.—*F.E.*
4. End of Manuscript VI. Beginning of Manuscript V.—*F.E.*

5. This is true no matter how we separate capital-value and surplus-value. 10,000 lbs. of yarn contain 1,560 lbs., or £78 worth of surplus-value; likewise, one lb., or one shilling's worth of yarn, contains 2.496 ounces, or 1.872 pence worth, of surplus-value.
6. A. Chuprov, *Railroading*, Moscow, 1875, pp. 69 and 70.

2

The Circuit of Productive Capital

The circuit of productive capital has the general formula P ... C'—M'—C ... P. It signifies the periodical renewal of the functioning of productive capital, hence its reproduction, or its process of production as a process of reproduction aiming at the self-expansion of value; not only production but a periodical reproduction of surplus-value; the function of industrial capital in its productive form, and this function performed not once but periodically repeated, so that the renewal is determined by the starting-point. A portion of C' may (in certain cases, in various branches of industrial capital) re-enter directly as means of production into the same labour-process out of which it came in the shape of a commodity. This merely saves the transformation of the value of this portion into real money or token-money or else the commodity finds an independent expression only as money of account. This part of value does not enter into the circulation. Thus values enter into the process of production which do not enter into the process of circulation. The same is true of that part of C' which is consumed by the capitalist in kind as part of the surplus-product. But this is insignificant for capitalist production. It deserves consideration, if at all, only in agriculture.

Two things are at once strikingly apparent in this form.

For one thing, while in the first form, M ... M', the process of production, the function of P, interrupts the circulation of money-capital and acts only as a mediator between its two phases M—C and C'—M', here the entire circulation process of industrial capital, its entire movement within the phase of circulation, constitutes only an interruption and consequently only the connecting link between the productive capital, which as the first extreme opens the circuit, and that which closes it as the other extreme in the same form, hence in the form in which it starts again. Circulation proper appears but as an instrument promoting the periodically renewed reproduction, rendered continuous by the renewal.

For another thing, the entire circulation presents itself in a form which is the opposite of that which it has in the circuit of money-capital. There it was: M—C—M (M—C. C—M), apart from the determination of value; here it is, again apart from the value determination: C—M—C (C—M. M—C), i.e., the form of the simple circulation of commodities.

Section I. *Simple Reproduction*

Let us first consider the process C'—M'—C, which takes place in the sphere of circulation between the two extremes P ... P.

The starting-point of this circulation is commodity-capital; C' = C + c = P + c. The function of commodity-capital C'—M' (the realisation of the capital-value contained in it equals P, which now exists as the constituent part C of C', as well as of the surplus-value contained in it, which exists as a constituent part of the same quantity of commodities and has the value c) was examined in the first form of the circuit. But there this function formed the second phase of the interrupted circulation and the concluding phase of the entire circuit. Here it forms the second phase of the circuit but the first phase of the circulation. The first circuit ends with M', and since M' as well as the original M can again open the second circuit as money-capital, it was not necessary at first to see whether M and m (surplus-value) contained in M' continue in their course together or whether each of them pursues its own course. This would only have become necessary if we had followed up further the first circuit in its renewed course. But this point must be decided in the circuit of the productive capital, because the determination of its very first circuit depends on it and because C'—M' appears in it as the first phase of the circulation, which has to be complemented by M—C. It depends on this decision whether the formula represents simple reproduction or reproduction on an extended scale. The character of the circuit changes according to the decision made.

Let us, then, consider first the simple reproduction of productive capital, assuming that, as in the first chapter, conditions remain constant and that commodities are bought and sold at their values.

On this assumption the entire surplus-value enters into the individual consumption of the capitalist. As soon as the transformation of the commodity-capital C' into money has taken place, that part of the money which represents the capital-value continues to circulate in the circuit of industrial capital; the other part, which is surplus-value changed into money, enters into the general circulation of commodities, constitutes a circulation of money emanating from the capitalist but taking place outside of the circulation of his individual capital.

In our illustration we had a commodity-capital C' of 10,000 lbs. of yarn, valued at £500; £422 of this represent the value of the productive capital and continue, as the money-form of 8,440 lbs. of yarn, the capital circulation begun by C', while the surplus value of £78, the money-form of 1,560 lbs. of yarn, the excess of the commodity-product, leaves this circulation and describes a separate course within the general circulation of commodities.

$$C' \begin{Bmatrix} C \\ + \\ c \end{Bmatrix} \begin{matrix} — \\ — \\ — \end{matrix} M' \begin{Bmatrix} M \\ + \\ m \end{Bmatrix} \begin{matrix} — \quad C < \begin{matrix} L \\ MP \end{matrix} \\ \\ — \quad c \end{matrix}$$

m—c represents a series of purchases by means of money which the capitalist spends either for commodities proper or for personal services to his cherished self or family. These purchases are made piecemeal at various times. The money therefore exists temporarily in the form of a supply, or hoard, destined for current consumption, since money whose circulation has been interrupted assumes the form of a hoard. Its function as a medium of circulation, which includes its transient form of a hoard, does not enter the circulation of capital in its money-form M. This money is not advanced but spent.

We have assumed that the total advanced capital always passes wholly from one of its phases to the other; and so here too we assume that the commodities produced by P represent the total value of the productive capital P, or £422 plus £78 of surplus-value created in the process of production. In our illustration, which deals with a discrete commodity, the surplus-value exists in the form of 1,560 lbs. of yarn; if computed on the basis of one pound of yarn, it would exist in the form of 2.496 ounces of yarn. But, if the commodity were for instance a machine valued at £500 and having the same value-composition, one a part of the value of this machine, £78, would be surplus-value, but these £78 would exist only in the machine as a whole. This machine cannot be divided into capital-value and surplus-value without breaking it to pieces and thus destroying its value together with its use-value. For this reason the two value-components can be represented only ideally as components of the commodity, not as independent elements of the commodity C', like any pound of yarn, which represents a separable independent element of the 10,000 lbs. of commodity. In the first case the aggregate commodity, the commodity-capital, the machine, must be sold in its entirety before m can enter upon its separate circulation. On the other hand when the capitalist has sold 8,440 lbs., the sale of the remaining 1,560 lbs. would represent a wholly separate circulation of the surplus-value in the form of c (1,560 lbs. of yarn)—m (£78)—c (articles of consumption). But the elements of value of each individual portion of the 10,000 lbs. of yarn, the product, can be represented by parts of the product as well as by the total product. Just as the latter, 10,000 lbs. of yarn, the product, can be represented by parts of the product as well as by the total product. Just as the latter, 10,000 lbs. of yarn, can be divided into the value of the constant capital (c), 7,440 lbs. of yarn worth £372, variable capital-value (v) of 1,000 lbs. of yarn worth £50, and surplus-value (s) of 1,560 lbs. of yarn worth £78, so every pound of yarn may be divided into c, equal to 11.904 ounces worth 8.928 d., v equal to 1.600 ounces of yarn worth 1.200 d., and s equal to 2.496 ounces of yarn worth 1.872 d. The capitalist might also sell various portions of the 10,000 lbs. of yarn successively and successively consume successive portions of the surplus-value elements contained in them, thus realising, also successively, the sum of c plus v. But in the final analysis this operation likewise premises the sale of the entire lot of 10,000 lbs., that therefore the value of c and v will be replaced by the sale of 8,440 lbs. (Buch I, Kap. VII, 2.) [English edition: Ch. IX, 2.—*Ed.*]

However that may be, by means of C'—M' both the capital-value and surplus-value contained in C' acquire a separable existence, the existence of different sums of money. In both cases M and m are really a converted form of the value which originally in C' had only a peculiar, an ideal expression as the price of the commodity.

c—m—c represents the simple circulation of commodities, the first phase of which, c—m, is included in the circulation of commodity-capital, C'—M', i.e., included in the circuit of capital; its complementary phase m—c falls, on the contrary, outside of this circuit, being a separate act in the general circulation of commodities. The circulation of C and c, of capital-value and surplus-value, splits after the transformation of C' into M'. Hence it follows:

First, while the commodity-capital is realised by C'—M' = C'—(M + m), the movement of capital-value and surplus-value, which in C'—M' is still united and carried on by the same quantity of commodities, becomes separable, both of them henceforth possessing independent forms as separate sums of money.

Secondly, if this separation takes place, m being spent as the revenue of the capitalist, while M as a functional form of capital-value continues its course determined by the circuit, the first act, C'—M', in connection with the subsequent acts, M—C and m—c, may be represented as two different circulations C—M—C and c—m—c; and both of these series, so far as their general form is concerned, belong in the usual circulation of commodities.

By the way, in the case of the continuous, indivisible commodities, it is a matter of practice to isolate the value constituents ideally. For instance, in the London building-business, which is carried on mainly on credit, the building contractor receives advances in accordance with the stage of construction reached. None of these stages is a house, but only a really existing constituent part of an inchoate future house; hence, in spite of its reality, it is but an ideal fraction of the entire house, but real enough to serve as security for an additional advance. (See on this point Chapter XII below.) [See pp. 237-38 of this book.—*Ed.*]

Thirdly, if the movement of capital-value and surplus-value, which still proceeds unitedly in C and M, is separated only in part (a portion of the surplus-value not being spent as revenue) or not at all, a change takes place in the capital-value itself within its circuit, before it is completed. In our illustration the value of the productive capital was equal to £422. If that capital continues M—C, as, say, £480 or £500, then it strides through the latter stages of its circuit with an increase of £58 or £78 over its initial value. This may also go hand in hand with a change in the composition of its value.

C'—M', the second stage of the circulation and the final stage of circuit I (M ... M'), is the second stage in our circuit and the first in the circulation of commodities. So far as the circulation is concerned, it must be complemented by M'—C'. But not only has C'—M' the process of self-expansion already behind it (in this case the function of P, the first stage), but its result, the commodity C'; has already been realised. The process of the self-expansion of capital and the realisation of the commodities representing the expanded capital-value are therefore completed in C'—M'.

And so we have premised simple reproduction, i.e., that m—c separates entirely from M—C. Since both circulations, c—m—c as well as C—M—C, belong in the circulation of commodities, so far as their general form is concerned (and for this reason do not show only value differences in their extremes), it is easy to conceive the process of capitalist production, after the manner of vulgar economy, as a mere production of commodities, of use-values designed for consumption of some sort, which the capitalist produces for no other purpose than that of getting in their place commodities with different use-values, or of exchanging them for such, as vulgar economy erroneously states.

C' acts from the very outset as commodity-capital, and the purpose of the entire process, enrichment (the production of surplus-value), does not, by any means, exclude increasing consumption on the part of the capitalist as his surplus-value (and hence his capital) increases; on the contrary, it emphatically includes it.

Indeed, in the circulation of the revenue of the capitalist, the produced commodity c (or the fraction of the produced commodity C' ideally corresponding to it) serves only to transform it, first into money, and from money into a number of other commodities serving private consumption. But we must not, at this point, overlook the trifling circumstance that c is commodity-value which did not cost the capitalist anything, an incarnation of surplus-labour, for which reason it originally stepped on the stage as a component part of commodity-capital C'. This c is, by the very nature of its existence, bound to the circuit of capital-value in process and if this circuit begins to stagnate or is otherwise disturbed, not only the consumption of c restricted or entirely arrested, but also the disposal of that series of commodities which serve to replace c. The same is true when C'—M' ends in failure, or only a part of C' can be sold.

We have seen that c—m—c, representing the circulation of the revenue of the capitalist, enters into the circulation of capital only so long as c is a part of the value of C', of capital in its functional form of commodity-capital; but, as soon as it acquires independence from m—c, hence throughout the form c—m—c, the circulation of that revenue does not enter into the movement of the capital advanced by the capitalist, although it stems from it. This circulation is connected with the movement of advanced capital inasmuch as the existence of capital presupposes the existence of the capitalist, and his existence is conditioned on his consuming surplus-value.

Within the general circulation C', for example yarn, functions only as a commodity; but as an element in the circulation of capital it performs the function of *commodity-capital*, a form which capital-value alternately assumes and discards. After the sale of the yarn to a merchant, it is extruded out of the circular movement of capital whose product it is, but nevertheless, as a commodity, it moves always in the sphere of the general circulation. The circulation of one and the same mass of commodities continues, in spite of the fact that it has ceased to be a phase in the independent circuit of the spinner's capital. Hence the real definitive metamorphosis of the mass of commodities thrown into circulation by the capitalist, C—M, their final exit into consumption may be completely separated in time and space from that metamorphosis in which this mass of commodities functions as his commodity-capital. The same metamorphosis which has been accomplished in the circulation of capital still remains to be accomplished in the sphere of the general circulation.

This state of things is not changed a bit if this yarn enters the circuit of some other industrial capital. The general circulation comprises as much the intertwining of the circuits of the various independent fractions of social capital, i.e., the totality of the individual capitals, as the circulation of those values which are not thrown on the market as capital but enter into individual consumption.

The relation between a circuit of capital forming part of a general circulation and a circuit forming links in an independent circuit is shown further on when we examine the circulation of M, which is equal to M plus m. M as money-capital continues capital's circuit; m, being spent as revenue (m—c), enters into the general circulation, but comes flying out of the circuit of capital. Only that part enters the latter circuit which performs the function of additional money-capital. In c—m—c money serves only as coin; the object of this circulation is the individual consumption of the capitalist. It is typical of the idiocy of vulgar economy that it gives out this circulation, which does not enter into the circuit of capital—the circulation of that part of the value produced which is consumed as revenue—as the characteristic circuit of capital.

In the second phase M—C, the capital-value M, which is equal to P (the value of the productive capital that at this point opens the circuit of industrial capital), is again present, delivered of its surplus-value, therefore having the same magnitude of value as it had in the first stage of the circuit of money-capital M—C. In spite of the difference in place the function of the money-capital into which the commodity-capital has now been transformed is the same: its transformation into MP and L, into means of production and labour-power.

In the functioning of commodity-capital C'—M', the capital-value, simultaneously with c—m, has consequently gone through the phase C—M and enters now into the complementary phase M—C$<^{L}_{MP}$. Its complete circulation is therefore C—M— C$<^{L}_{MP}$.

First: Money-capital M appeared in Form I (circuit M ... M') as the original form in which capital-value is advanced; it appears here from the outset as a part of that sum of money into which commodity-capital transformed itself in the first circulation phase C'—M', therefore from the outset as the transformation of P, the productive capital, through the medium of the sale of commodities, into the money-form. Money-capital exists here from the outset as that form of capital-value which is neither its original nor its final one, since the phase M—C, which concludes the phase C—M, can only be performed by again discarding the money-form. Therefore that part of M—C which is at the same time M—L appears now no longer as a mere advance of money by the purchase of labour-power, but as an advance by means of which the same 1,000 lbs. of yarn, valued at £50, which form a part of the commodity-value created by labour-power, are advanced to labour-power in the form of money. The money advanced here to the labourer is only a converted equivalent form of a part of the commodity-value produced by himself. And for that reason if no other the act M—C, so far as it means M—L, is by no means simply a replacement of a commodity in the form of money by a commodity in the use-form, but it includes other elements which are independent of the general commodity circulation as such.

M' appears as a converted form of C', which is itself a product of a previous function of P, the process of production. The entire sum of money M' is therefore a money-expression of past labour. In our illustration, 10,000 lbs. of yarn worth £500 are the product of the spinning process. Of this quantity, 7,440 lbs. of yarn are equal to the advanced constant capital c worth £372; 1,000 lbs. of yarn are equal to the advanced variable capital v worth £50; and 1,560 lbs. of yarn represent the surplus-value s worth £78. If of M' only the original capital of £422 is again advanced, other conditions remaining the same, then the labourer is advanced the following week, in M—L, only a part of the 10,000 lbs. of yarn produced in the given week (the money-value of 1,000 lbs. of yarn). As a result of C—M, money is always the expression of past labour. If the complementary act M—C takes place at once in the commodity-market, i.e., M is given in return for commodities existing in the market, this is again a transformation of past labour, from one form (money) into another form (commodities). But M—C differs in the matter of time from C—M. They may exceptionally take place at the same time, for instance when the capitalist who performs M—C and the capitalist to whom this act means C—M ship their commodities to each other at the same time and M is used only to square the balance. The difference in time between the performance of M—C and C—M may be more or less considerable. Although M, as the result of C—M, represents past labour, it may, in the act M—C, represent the converted form of commodities which are not as yet in the market, but will be thrown upon it in the future, since M—C need not take place until C has been produced anew. M may likewise stand for commodities which are produced simultaneously with the C whose money-expression it is. For instance in the exchange M—C (purchase of means of production) coal may be bought before it has been mined. In so far as m figures as an accumulation of money, is not spent as revenue, it may stand for cotton which will not be produced until the following year. The same holds good on spending the revenue of the capitalist, m—c. It also applies to wages, to L equal to £50. This money is not only the money-form of past labour of the labourers but at the same time a draft on simultaneous and future labour which is just being realised or should be realised in the future. The labourer may buy with his wages a coat which will not be made until the following week. This applies especially to the vast number of necessary means of subsistence which must be consumed almost as soon as they have been produced to prevent spoilage. Thus the labourer receives, in the money which is paid to him in wages, the converted form of his own future labour or that of other labourers. By giving the labourer a part of his past labour, the capitalist gives him a draft on his own future labour. It is the labourer's own simultaneous or future labour that constitutes the not yet existing supply out of which he will be paid for his past labour. In this case the idea of hoarding disappears altogether. [Here Marx made the following note in the manuscript: 'All this, however, belongs to the last part of Book Two.'—*Ed.*]

Secondly: In the circulation C—M—C$<^{L}_{MP}$ the same money changes place twice; the capitalist first receives it as a seller and passes it on as a buyer; the transformation of commodities into the money-form serves only for the purpose of retransforming it from the money-form into the commodity-form; the money-form of capital, its existence as money-capital, is only a transient phase in this movement; or, so far as the movement is fluent, money-capital appears only as a medium of circulation when it serves as a means of purchase; it acts as a paying medium proper when capitalists buy from one another and therefore only have to square accounts.

Thirdly, the function of money-capital, whether it is a mere circulating medium or a paying medium, effects only the replacement of C by L and MP, i.e., the replacement of the yarn, the commodity which represents the result of the productive capital (after deducting the surplus-value to be used as revenue), by its elements of production, in other words, the retransformation of capital-value from its form as a commodity into the elements that build this commodity. In the last analysis, the function of money-capital promotes only the retransformation of commodity-capital into productive capital.

In order that the circuit may be completed normally, C' must be sold at its value and in its entirety. Furthermore C—M—C includes not merely replacement of one commodity by another, but replacement with value-relations remaining the same. We assume that this takes place here. As a matter of fact, however, the value of the means of production vary. It is precisely capitalist production to which continuous change of value-relations is peculiar, if only because of the ever changing productivity of labour that characterises this mode of production. This change in the value of the elements of production will be discussed later on, [See Section V of Chapter XV of this volume.—*Ed.*] and we merely mention it here.

The transformation of the elements of production into commodity-products, of P into C', takes place in the sphere of production, while the transformation from C' into P occurs in the sphere of circulation. It is brought about by a simple metamorphosis of commodities, but its content is a phase in the process of reproduction, regarded as a whole. C—M—C, being a form of circulation of capital, involves a functionally determined exchange of matter. The transformation C—M—C requires further that C should be equal to the elements of production of the commodity-quantum C', and that these elements should retain their original value-relations to one another. It is therefore assumed that the commodities are not only bought at their respective values, but also do not undergo any change of value during the circular movement. Otherwise this process cannot run normally.

In M ... M', M represents the original form of the capital-value, which is discarded only to be resumed. In P ... C'—M'—C ... P, M represents a form which is only assumed in the process and which is discarded before this process is over. The money-form appears here only as a transient independent form of capital-value. Capital in the form of C' is just as anxious to assume the money-form as it is to discard it in M', after barely assuming that garb in order again to transform itself into productive capital. So long as it remains in the garb of money, it does not function as capital and its value does not therefore expand. The capital lies fallow. M serves here as a circulating medium, but as a circulating medium of capital. [Here Marx made the following note in the manuscript: 'Against Tooke.'—*Ed.*] The semblance of independence which the money-form of capital-value possesses in the first form of its circuit (the form of money-capital) disappears in this second form, which thus is a criticism of Form I and reduces it to merely a special form. If the second metamorphosis, M—C, meets with any obstacles—for instance if there are no means of production in the market—the circuit, the flow of the process of reproduction, is interrupted quite as much as when capital is held fast in the form of commodity-capital. But there is this difference: It can remain longer in the money-form than in the transitory form of commodities. It does not cease to be money, if it does not perform the functions of money-capital; but it does cease to be a commodity, or a use-value in general, if it is delayed too long in the exercise of its function of commodity-capital. Furthermore, in its money-form it is capable of assuming another form in the place of its original one of productive capital while it cannot budge at all if held in the form of C'.

C'—M'—C includes acts of circulation only for C' in accordance with its form, acts which are phrases of its reproduction; but the real reproduction of C, into which C' transforms itself, is necessary for the performance of C'—M'—C. This however is conditioned on processes of reproduction which lie outside of the process of reproduction of the individual capital represented by C'.

In Form I the act M—C$<^{L}_{MP}$ prepares on the first transformation of money-capital into productive capital; in Form II it prepares the retransformation from commodity-capital into productive capital; that is to say, so far as the investment of industrial capital remains the same, retransformation of the commodity-capital into the same elements of production as those from which it originated. Consequently here as well as in Form I, the act appears as a preparatory phase of the process of production, but as a return to it, as a renewal of it, hence as a precursor of the process of reproduction, hence also of a repetition of the process of self-expansion of value.

It must be noted once more that M—L is not a simple exchange of commodities but the purchase of a commodity, L, which is to serve for the production of surplus-value, just as M—MP is only a procedure which is materially indispensable for the attainment of this end.

With the completion of M—C$<^{L}_{MP}$ M is reconverted into productive capital, into P, and the circuit begins anew.

The expanded form of P ... C'—M'—C ... P is therefore:

$$P \ldots C' \begin{bmatrix} C \\ + \\ c \end{bmatrix} \begin{matrix} - \\ \\ - \end{matrix} M' \begin{bmatrix} M \\ + \\ m \end{bmatrix} \begin{matrix} - C < \begin{matrix} L \\ MP \ldots P \end{matrix} \\ \\ - c \end{matrix}$$

The transformation of money-capital into productive capital is the purchase of commodities for the production of commodities. Consumption falls within the circuit of capital itself only in so far as it is productive consumption; its premise is that surplus-value is produced by means of the commodities so consumed. And this is something very different from production and even commodity production, which has for its end the existence of the producer. A replacement—commodity by commodity—thus contingent on the production of surplus-value is quite a different matter from the bare exchange of products brought about merely by means of money. But the economists take this matter as proof that no overproduction is possible.

Apart from the productive consumption of M, which is transformed into L and MP, the circuit contains the first member M—L, which signifies, from the standpoint of the labourer, L—M, which equals C—M. In the labourer's circulation, L—M—C, which includes his consumption, only the first member falls within the circuit of the capital as a result of M—L. The second act, M—C, does not fall within the circulation of individual capital, although it springs from it. But the continuous existence of the working class is necessary for the capitalist class, and so is therefore the consumption of the labourer made possible by M—C.

The only condition which the act C'—M' stipulates for capital-value to continue its circuit and for surplus-value to be consumed by the capitalist is that C' shall have been converted into money, shall have been sold. Of course, C' is bought only because the article is a use-value, hence serviceable for consumption of any kind, productive or individual. But if C' continues to circulate for instance in the hands of the merchant who bought the yarn, this at first does not in the least affect the continuation of the circuit of the individual capital which produced the yarn and sold it to the merchant. The entire process continues and with it the individual consumption of the capitalist and the labourer made necessary by it. This point is important in a discussion of crises.

For as soon as C' has been sold, been converted into money, it can be reconverted into the real factors of the labour process, and thus of the reproductive process. Whether C' is bought by the ultimate consumer or by a merchant for resale does not affect the case. The quantity of commodities created in masses by capitalist production depends on the scale of production and on the need for constantly expanding this production, and not on a predestined circle of supply and demand, on wants that have to be satisfied. Mass production can have no other direct buyer, apart from other industrial capitalists, than the wholesaler. Within certain limits, the process of reproduction may take place on the same or on an increased scale even when the commodities expelled from it did not really enter individual or productive consumption. The consumption of commodities is not included in the circuit of the capital from which they originated. For instance, as soon as the yarn is sold the circuit of the capital value represented by the yarn may begin anew, regardless of what may next become of the sold yarn. So long as the product is sold, everything is taking its regular course from the standpoint of the capitalist producer. The circuit of capital-value he is identified with is not interrupted. And if this process is expanded—which includes increased productive consumption of the means of production—this reproduction of capital may be accompanied by increased individual consumption (hence demand) on the part of the labourers, since this process is initiated and effected by productive consumption. Thus the production of surplus-value, and with it the individual consumption of the capitalist, may increase, the entire process of reproduction may be in a flourishing condition, and yet a large part of the commodities may have entered into consumption only apparently, while in reality they may still remain unsold in the hands of dealers, may in fact still be lying in the market. Now one stream of commodities follows another, and finally it is discovered that the previous streams had been absorbed only apparently by consumption. The commodity-capitals compete with one another for a place in the market. Late-comers, to sell at all, sell at lower prices. The former streams have not yet been disposed of when payment for them falls due. Their owners must declare their insolvency or sell at any price to meet their obligations. This sale has nothing whatever to do with the actual state of the demand. It only concerns the *demand for payment*, the pressing necessity of transforming commodities into money. Then a crisis breaks out. It becomes visible not in the direct decrease of consumer demand, the demand for individual consumption, but in the decrease of exchanges of capital for capital, of the reproductive process of capital.

If the commodities MP and L, into which M is transformed to perform its function of money-capital, of capital-value destined to be retransformed into productive capital—if those commodities are to be bought or paid for on different terms, so that M—C represents a series of purchases and payments, then a part of M performs the act M—C, while another part persists in the form of money and does not serve to perform simultaneous or successive acts of M—C until such time as the conditions of this process itself may determine. This part is only temporarily withheld from circulation, in order to go into action, perform its function, in due time. This storing of it is then in its turn a function determined by its circulation and intended for circulation. Its existence as a fund for purchase and payment, the suspension of its movement, the interrupted state of its circulation, will then constitute a state in which money exercises one of its functions as money-capital. As money-capital; for in this case the money temporarily remaining at rest is itself a part of money-capital M (of M' minus m, equal to M), of that portion of the value of commodity-capital which is equal to P, to that value of productive capital from which the circuit starts. On the other hand all money withdrawn from circulation has the form of a hoard. Money in the form of a hoard therefore becomes here a function of money-capital, just as in M—C the function of money as a means of purchase or payment becomes a function of money-capital. This is so because capital-value exists here in the form of money, because the money state here is a state in which industrial capital finds itself at one of its stages and which is prescribed by the interconnections within the circuit. At the same time it is here proved true once more that money-capital within the circuit of industrial capital performs no other functions than those of money and that these money-functions assume the significance of capital-functions only by virtue of their interconnections with the other stages of this circuit.

The representation of M' as a relation of m to M, as a capital-relation, is not directly a function of money-capital but of commodity-capital C', which in its turn, as a relation of c and C, expresses but the result of the process of production, of the self-expansion of capital-value which took place in it.

If the continuation of the process of circulation meets with obstacles, so that M must suspend its function M—C on account of external circumstances, such as the conditions of the market, etc., and if it therefore remains for a shorter or longer time in its money-form, then we have once more money in the form of a hoard, which happens also in simple commodity circulation whenever the transition from C—M to M—C is interrupted by external circumstances. It is an involuntary formation of a hoard. In the case at hand money has the form of fallow, latent money-capital. But we will not discuss this point any further for the present.

In either case however persistence of capital in its money state appears as the result of interrupted movement, no matter whether this is expedient or inexpedient, voluntary or involuntary, in accordance with its functions or contrary to them.

Since the proportions which the expansion of the productive process may assume are not arbitrary but prescribed by technology, the realised surplus-value, though intended for capitalisation, frequently can only by dint of several successive circuits attain such a size (and until then must therefore be accumulated) as will suffice for its effective functioning as additional capital or for entrance into the circuit of functioning capital-value. Surplus-value thus congeals into a hoard and in this form constitutes latent money-capital—latent because it cannot act as capital so long as it persists in the money-form.[1] The formation of a hoard thus appears here as a factor included in the process of capitalist accumulation, accompanying it but nevertheless essentially differing from it; for the process of reproduction itself is not expanded by the formation of latent money-capital. On the contrary, latent money-capital is formed here because the capitalist producer cannot directly expand the scale of his production. If he sells his surplus-product to a producer of gold or silver, who puts new gold or silver into circulation or, what amounts to the same thing, to a merchant who imports additional gold or silver from foreign countries for a part of the national surplus-product, then his latent money-capital forms an increment of the national gold or silver hoard. In all other cases, the £78 for instance, which were a circulating medium in the hands of the purchaser, assume only the form of a hoard in the hands of the capitalist. Hence all that has taken place is a different distribution of the national gold or silver hoard.

If in the transaction of our capitalist the money serves as a means of payment (the commodities having to be paid for by the buyer on longer or shorter terms), then the surplus-product intended for capitalisation is not transformed into money but into creditor's claims, into titles of ownership of an equivalent which the buyer may already have in his possession or which he may expect to possess. It does not enter into the reproductive process of the circuit any more than does money in invested in interest-bearing securities, etc., although it may enter into the circuits of other individual industrial capitals.

The entire character of capitalist production is determined by the self-expansion of the advanced capital-value, that is to say, in the first instance by the production of as much surplus-value as possible; in the second place however (see Buch I, Kap. XXII) [English edition: Ch. XXIV.—*Ed.*] by the production of capital, hence by the transformation of surplus-value into capital. Accumulation, or production on an extended scale, which appears as a means for constantly more expanded production of surplus-value—hence for the enrichment of the capitalist, as his personal aim—and is comprised in the general tendency of capitalist production, becomes later, however, as was shown in Book I, by virtue of its development, a necessity for every individual capitalist. The constant augmentation of his capital becomes a condition of its preservation. But we need not revert more fully to what was previously expounded.

We considered first simple reproduction, assuming that the entire surplus-value is spent as revenue. In reality, under normal conditions a part of the surplus-value must always be spent as revenue, and another part must be capitalised. And it is quite immaterial whether a certain surplus-value produced in any particular period is entirely consumed or entirely capitalised. On the average—the general formula can represent only the average movement—both cases occur. But in order not to complicate the formula, it is better to assume that the entire surplus-value is accumulated. The formula: P ... C'—M'—C'<$^{L}_{MP}$ ... P› stands for productive capital, which is reproduced on an enlarged scale and with greater value, and which as augmented productive capital begins its second circuit, or, what amounts to the same, renews its first circuit. As soon as this second circuit is begun, we once more have P as the starting-point; only this P is a larger productive capital than the first P was. Hence, if in the formula M ... M› the second circuit begins with M›, M› functions as M, as an advanced money-capital of a definite magnitude. It is a larger money-capital than the one with which the first circular movement was opened, but all reference to its augmentation by the capitalisation of surplus-value ceases as soon as it assumes the function of advanced money-capital. This origin is expunged in its form of money-capital, which begins its circuit. This also applies to P' as soon as it functions as the starting-point of a new circuit.

If we compare P ... P' with M ... M', or with the first circuit, we find that they have not the same significance at all. M ... M' taken by itself as an isolated circuit, expresses only that M, the money-capital (or industrial capital in its circuit as money-capital), is money generating money, value generating value, in other words, produces surplus-value. But in the P circuit the process of producing surplus-value is already completed upon the termination of the first stage, the process of production, and after going through the second stage (the first stage of the circulation), C'—M', the capital-value plus surplus-value already exist as realised money-capital, as M', which appeared as the last extreme in the first circuit. That surplus-value has been produced is depicted in the first-considered formula P ... P (see expanded formula, [M—C<$^{L}_{MP}$ ... P ... (C + c) - (M + m)]) by c—m—c, which, in its second stage, falls outside of the circulation of capital and represents the circulation of surplus-value as revenue. In this form, where the entire movement is represented by P ... P, where consequently there is no difference in value between the two extremes, the self-expansion of the advanced value the production of surplus-value, is therefore represented in the same way as in M ... M›, except that the act C›—M›, which appears as the last stage in M ... M›, and as the second stage of the circuit, serves as the first stage of the circulation in P ... P.

In P ... P', P' does not indicate that the surplus-value has been produced but that the produced surplus-value has been capitalised, hence that capital has been accumulated and that therefore P', in contrast to P, consists of the original capital-value plus the value of the capital accumulated because of the capital-value's movement.

M', as the simple close of M ... M', and also C', as it appears within all these circuits, do not if taken by themselves express the movement but its result: the self-expansion of capital-value realised in the form of commodities or money, and hence, capital-value as M plus m, or C plus c, as a relation of capital-value to its surplus-value, as its offspring. They express this result as various circulation forms of the self-expanded capital-value. But neither in the form of C' nor of M' is the self-expansion which has taken place itself a function of money-capital or of commodity-capital. As special, differentiated forms, modes of existence corresponding to special functions of industrial capital, money-capital can perform only money-functions and commodity-capital only commodity-functions, the difference between them being merely that between money and commodity. Similarly industrial capital in its form of productive capital can consist only of the same elements as those of any other labour-process which creates products: on the one hand objective conditions of labour (means of production), on the other productively (purposively) functioning labour-power. Just as industrial capital can exist in the sphere of production only in a composition which meets the requirements of the production process in general, hence also of the non-capitalist production process, so it can exist in the sphere of circulation only in the two forms corresponding to it, viz., that of a commodity and of money. But just as the totality of the elements of production announces itself at the outset as productive capital by the fact that the labour-power is labour-power that belongs to others and that the capitalist purchased it from its proprietor, just as he purchased his means of production from other commodity-owners; just as therefore the process of production itself appears as a productive function of industrial capital, so money and commodities appear as forms of circulation of the same industrial capital, hence their functions appear as the functions of circulation, which either introduce the functions of productive capital or emanate from them. Here the money-function and the commodity-function are at the same time functions of commodity-capital, but solely because they are interconnected as forms of functions which industrial capital has to perform at the different stages of its circuit. It is therefore wrong to attempt to derive the specific properties and functions which characterise money as money and commodities as commodities from their quality as capital, and it is equally wrong to derive on the contrary the properties of productive capital from its mode of existence in means of production.

As soon as M' or C' have become fixed as M plus m or C plus c, i.e., as the relation between the capital-value and surplus-value, its offspring, this relation is expressed in both of them, in the first case in the money-form, in the second case in the commodity-form, which does not change matters in the least. Consequently this relation does not have its origin in any properties or functions inherent in money as such or commodities as such. In both cases the characteristic property of capital, that of being a value, is expressed only as a result. C' is always the product of the function of P, and M' is always merely the form of C' changed in the circuit of industrial capital. As soon therefore as the realised money-capital resumes its special function of money capital, it ceases to express the capital-relation contained in M' = M plus m. After M ... M' has been passed through and M' begins the circuit anew, it does not figure as M even if the entire surplus-value contained in M' is capitalised. The second circuit begins in our case with a money-capital of £500, instead of £422, as in the first circuit. The money-capital, which opens the circuit, is £78 larger than before. This difference exists on comparing the one circuit with the other, but no such comparison is made within each particular circuit. The £500 advanced as money-capital, £78 which formerly existed as surplus-value, do not play any other role than would some other £500 with which another capitalist inaugurates his first circuit. The same happens in the circuit of the productive capital. The increased P' acts as P on recommencing, just as P did in the simple reproduction P ... P.

In the stage $M'—C'<^{L}_{MP}$, the augmented magnitude is indicated only by C', but not by L' or MP'. Since C is the sum of L and MP, C' indicates sufficiently that the sum of L and MP contained in it is greater than the original P. In the second place, the terms L' and MP' would be incorrect, because we know that the growth of capital involves a change in the constitution of its value and that as this change progresses the value of MP increases, that of L always decreasing relatively and often absolutely.

Section III. *Accumulation of Money*

Whether or not m, the surplus-value turned into money, is immediately added to the capital-value in process and is thus enabled to enter the circuit together with capital M now having the magnitude M', depends on circumstances which are independent of the mere existence of m. If m is to serve as money-capital in a second independent business, to be run side by side with the first, it is evident that it cannot be used for this purpose unless it is of the minimum size required for it. And if it is intended to be used for the expansion of the original business, the relations between the material factors of P and their value-relations likewise demand a minimum magnitude for m. All the means of production employed in this business have not only a qualitative but also a definite quantitative relation to one another, are proportionate in quantity. These material relations as well as the pertinent value-relations of the factors entering into the productive capital determine the minimum magnitude m must possess to be capable of transformation into additional means of production and labour-power, or only into the former, as an accretion to the productive capital. Thus the owner of a spinning-mill cannot increase the number of his spindles without at the same time purchasing a corresponding number of carders and roving frames, apart from the increased expenditure for cotton and wages which such an expansion of his business demands. To carry this out, the surplus-value must therefore have reached a considerable figure (generally calculated to be £1 per newly installed spindle). If m does not reach this minimum size the circuit of capital must be repeated until the sum of m successively produced by it can function together with M, hence $M'—C'<^{L}_{MP}$. Even mere changes of detail, for instance in the spinning machinery, introduced to make it more productive, require greater expenditures for spinning material, more roving machinery, etc. In the meantime m is accumulated, and its accumulation is not its own function but the result of repeated P ... P. Its own function consists in persisting in the money state until it receives sufficient increment from the repeated surplus-value-creating circuits, i.e., from outside, to possess the minimum magnitude necessary for its active function, the magnitude in which alone it can really enter as money-capital—in the case at hand as the accumulated part of the functioning of money-capital M—into the functioning of M. But in the interim it is accumulated and exists only in the shape of a hoard in process of formation, of growth. Hence, the accumulation of money, hoarding, appears here as a process by which real accumulation, the extension of the scale on which industrial capital operates, is temporarily accompanied. Temporarily, for so long as the hoard remains in the condition of a hoard, it does not function as capital, does not take part in the process of creating surplus-value, remains a sum of money which grows only because money, come by without its doing anything, is thrown in the same coffer.

The form of a hoard is simply the form of money not in circulation, of money whose circulation has been interrupted and which is therefore fixed in its money-form. As for the process of hoarding, it is common to all commodity production and figures as an end in itself only in the undeveloped, pre-capitalist forms of this production. In the present case, however, the hoard appears as a form of money-capital and the formation of a hoard as a process which temporarily accompanies the accumulation of capital because and so far as the money here figures as *latent money-capital*; because the formation of a hoard, the state of being a hoard, in which the surplus-value existing in money-form finds itself, is a functionally determined preparatory stage gone through outside of the circuit described by the capital and required for the transformation of the surplus-value into really functioning capital. By its definition it is therefore latent money-capital. Hence the size it must acquire before it can take part in the process is determined in each case by the value constitution of the productive capital. But so long as it remains in the condition of a hoard it does not yet perform the functions of money-capital but is still idle money-capital; not money-capital whose function has been interrupted, as was the case before, but money-capital not yet capable of performing it.

We are here discussing the accumulation of money in its original real form of an actual hoard of money. It may also exist in the form of a mere outstanding money, of claims on debtors by capitalists who have sold C'. As for other forms in which this latent money-capital may exist in the meantime even in the shape of money-breeding money, such as interest-bearing bank deposits, bills of exchange or securities of any description, these do not belong here. Surplus-value realised in the form of money in such cases performs special capital-functions outside the circuit described by the industrial capital which originated it—functions which in the first place have nothing to do with that circuit as such but which in the second place presuppose capital-functions which differ from the functions of industrial capital and which have not yet been developed here.

Section IV. *Reserve Fund*

In the form in which we have just discussed, the hoard, as which the surplus-value exists, is a fund for the accumulation of money, the money-form temporarily assumed by capital accumulation and to that extent a condition of this accumulation. However, this accumulation-fund can also perform special services of a subordinate nature, that is to say can enter into capital's movement in circuits without this process assuming the form of P ... P', hence without an expansion of capitalist reproduction.

If the process C'—M' is prolonged beyond its normal duration, if therefore the commodity capital is abnormally delayed in its transformation into the money-form or if, for instance, after the completion of this transformation the price of the means of production into which the money-capital must be transformed has risen above the level prevailing at the beginning of the circuit, the hoard functioning as accumulation-fund can be used in the place of money-capital or of part of it. Thus the money-accumulation fund serves as a reserve fund for counter-balancing disturbances in the circuit.

As such a reserve fund it differs from the fund of purchasing or paying media discussed in the circuit P ... P. These media are a part of functioning money-capital (hence forms of existence of a part of capital-value in general going through the process) whose parts enter upon their functions only at different times, successively. In the continuous process of production, reserve-money capital is always formed, since one day money is received and no payments have to be made until later, and another day large quantities of goods are sold while other large quantities are not due to be bought until a subsequent date. In these intervals—a part of the circulating capital exists continuously in the form of money. A reserve fund on the other hand is not a part of constituent capital already performing its functions, or, to be more exact, of money-capital. It is rather a part of capital in a preliminary stage of its accumulation, of surplus-value not yet transformed into active capital. As for the rest, it needs no explaining that a capitalist in financial straits does not concern himself about what the particular functions of the money he has on hand are. He simply employs whatever money he has for the purpose of keeping his capital circulating. For instance in our illustration M is equal to £422, M' to £500. If a part of the capital of £422 exists as a fund of means of payment and purchase, as a money reserve, it is intended, other conditions remaining the same, that it should enter wholly into the circuit, and besides should suffice for this purpose. The reserve fund however is a part of the £78 of surplus-value. It can enter the circular course of the capital worth £422 only to the extent that this circuit takes place under conditions not remaining the same; for it is a part of the accumulation-fund, and figures here without any extension of the scale of reproduction.

Money-accumulation fund implies the existence of latent money-capital, hence the transformation of money into money-capital.

The following is the general formula for the circuit of productive capital. It combines simple reproduction and reproduction on a progressively increasing scale:

$$P \ldots \overbrace{C' \ - \ M'}^{1}. \qquad \overbrace{M \ - \ C}^{2} < \begin{matrix} L \\ MP \ldots P\ (P') \end{matrix}$$

If P equals P, then M in 2) equals M' minus m; if P equals P', then M in 2) is greater than M' minus m; that is to say m has been completely or partially transformed into money-capital.

The circuit of productive capital is the form in which classical Political Economy examines the circular movement of industrial capital.

Note

1. The term 'latent' is borrowed from the idea of latent heat in physics, which has now been almost replaced by the theory of the transformation of energy. Marx therefore uses in the third part (a later version), another term, borrowed from the idea of potential energy, viz.: 'potential' or analogous to the virtual velocities of D'Alembert, 'virtual capital.'—*Ed.*

3

The Circuit of Commodity-Capital

The general formula for the circuit of commodity-capital is:

C'—M'—C ... P ... C'.

C' appears not alone as the product but also as the premise of the two previous circuits, since that which M—C means for the one capital C'—M' means for the other, inasmuch as at least a part of the means of production is itself the commodity-product of other individual capitals describing their circuits. In our case, for instance, coal, machinery, etc., represent the commodity-capital of the mine-owner, of the capitalist machine-manufacturer, etc. Furthermore we have shown in Chapter 1.4, that not only the circuit P ... P but also the circuit C' ... C' is assumed even in the first repetition of M ... M', before this second circuit of money-capital is completed.

If reproduction takes place on an extended scale, then the final C' is greater than the initial C' and should therefore be designated here as C".

The difference between the third form and the first two is as follows: First, in this case the total circulation with its two antithetical phases opens the circuit, while in the Form I the circulation is interrupted by the process of production and in Form II the total circulation with its two complementary phases appears merely as a means of effecting the process of reproduction and therefore constitutes the movement mediating between P ... P. In the case of M ... M', the form of circulation is M—C ... C'—M' = M—C—M. In the case of P ... P it has the inverted form C'—M'. M—C = C—M—C. In the case of C'—C' it likewise has this form.

Secondly, when circuits I and II are repeated, even if the final points M' and P' form the starting-points of the renewed circuit, the form in which M' and P' were produced disappears. M' = M plus m and P' = P plus p begin the new process as M and P. But in the form III the starting-point C must be designated as C', even if the circuit is renewed on the same scale, for the following reason. In Form I, as soon as M' as such opens a new circuit it functions as money-capital M, as an advance in money-form of the capital-value that is to produce surplus-value. The size of the advanced money-capital, augmented by the accumulation achieved during the first circuit, has increased. But whether the size of the advanced money-capital is £422 or £500 does not alter the fact that it appears as simple capital-value. M' no longer exists as self-expanded capital or a capital pregnant with surplus-value, as a capital-relation. Indeed, it is to expand itself only during its process. The same is true of P ... P'; P' must steadily continue to function as P, as capital-value which is to produce surplus-value, and must renew its circuit.

The commodity-capital circuit, on the contrary, does not open with just capital-value but with capital-value augmented in the commodity-form. Hence it includes from the start the circuit of not only capital-value existing in the form of commodities, but also of surplus-value. Consequently if simple reproduction takes place in this form, the C' at the terminal point is equal in size to the C' at the starting-point. If a part of the surplus-value enters into the capital circuit, C", an enlarged C', appears at the close instead of C'. This is merely a larger C' than that of the proceeding circuit, with a larger accumulated capital-value. Hence it begins its new circuit with a relatively larger, newly created surplus-value. In any event C' always inaugurates the circuit as a commodity-capital which is equal to capital-value plus surplus-value.

C' as C does not appear in the circuit of an individual industrial capital as a form of this capital but as a form of some other industrial capital, so far as the means of production are the product of the latter. The act M—C (i.e., M—MP) of the first capital is C'—M' for this second capital.

In the circulation act M—C$<^{L}_{MP}$ L and MP bear identical relations, as they are commodities in the hands of their sellers—on the one hand the labourers who sell their labour-power, on the other the owner of the means of production, who sells these. For the purchaser, whose money here functions as money-capital, L and MP function merely as commodities until he has bought them, hence so long as they confront his capital, existing in the form of money, as commodities of others. MP and L differ here only in this respect, that MP may be C›, hence capital, in the hands of its seller, if MP is the commodity-form of his capital, while L is always nothing else but a commodity for the labourer and becomes capital only in the hands of its purchaser as a constituent part of P.

For this reason C' can never open any circuit as a mere C, as a mere commodity-form of capital-value. As commodity-capital it is always two-fold. From the point of view of use-value it is the product, in the present case yarn, of the functioning of P whose elements L and MP, coming as commodities from the sphere of circulation, have functioned only as factors in the creation of this product. Secondly, from the point of view of value, it is the capital-value P plus the surplus-value s produced by the functioning of P.

It is only in the circuit described by C' itself that C equal to P and equal to the capital-value can and must separate from that part of C' in which the surplus-value is lodged. It does not matter whether the two things can be actually separated, as in the case of yarn, or whether they cannot, as in the case of a machine. They always become separable as soon as C' is transformed into M'.

If the entire commodity-product can be separated into independent homogeneous partial products, as in the case of our 10,000 lbs. of yarn, and if therefore the act C'—M' can be represented by a number of successive sales, then the capital-value in the form of commodities can function as C, can be separated from C', before the surplus-value, hence before C' in its entirety, has been realised.

Of the 10,000 lbs. of yarn worth £500, the value of 8,440 lbs., equal to £422, is equal to the capital-value less the surplus-value. If the capitalist sells first 8,440 lbs. of yarn at £422, then these 8,440 lbs. of yarn represent C, the capital-value in commodity-form. The surplus-product of 1,560 lbs. of yarn, contained besides in C' and equal to a surplus value of £78, does not circulate until later. The capitalist could get through C—M—C$<^{L}_{MP}$ before the circulation of the surplus-product c—m—c is accomplished.

Or if he sells 7,440 lbs. of yarn worth £372, and then 1,000 lbs. of yarn worth £50, he might replace the means of production (the constant capital c) with the first part of C, and the variable capital v, the labour-power, with the second part of C, and then proceed as before.

But if such successive sales take place and the conditions of the circuit permit it, the capitalist, instead of separating C' into c + v + s, may make such a preparation also in the case of aliquot parts of C'.

For example the 7,440 lbs. of yarn equal at £372, which as parts of C' (10,000 lbs. of yarn worth £500) represent the constant part of capital, may themselves be separated into 5,535.360 lbs. of yarn worth £276.768, which replace only the constant part, the value of the means of production used up in producing 7,440 lbs. of yarn; 744 lbs. of yarn worth £37.200, which replace only the variable capital; and 1,160.640 lbs. of yarn worth £58.032, which, being surplus-product, are the depositories of surplus-value. Consequently on selling the 7,440 lbs. of yarn, he can replace the capital value contained in them out of the sale of 6,279.360 lbs. of yarn at the price of £313.968, and he can spend as his revenue the value of the surplus-product amounting to 1,160.640 lbs., or £58.032.

In the same way, he may divide up another 1,000 lbs. of yarn equal to £50, equal to the variable capital-value, and sell them accordingly; 744 lbs. of yarn worth £37.200, constant capital-value contained in 1,000 lbs. of yarn; finally, 100 lbs. of yarn worth £5.000, variable capital-value ditto; hence 844 lbs. of yarn worth £42.200, replacement of the capital-value contained in the 1,000 lbs. of yarn; finally 156 lbs. of yarn worth £7.800, representing the surplus-product contained in it, which may be consumed as such.

Finally, he may divide the remaining 1,560 lbs. of yarn worth £78, in such a way, provided he succeeds in selling them, that the sale of 1,160.640 lbs. of yarn, worth £58.032, replaces the value of the means of production contained in those 1,560 lbs. of yarn, and that 156 lbs. of yarn worth £7.800, replaces the variable capital-value; altogether 1,316.640 lbs. of yarn equal to £65.832, replacement of the total capital-value; finally the surplus-product of 243.360 lbs., equal to £12.168, remains to be spent as revenue.

All the elements—c, v and s—contained in the yarn are divisible into the same component parts, and so is every individual pound of yarn, worth 1 s., or 12 d.

c	=	0.744	lbs. of yarn	=	8.928 d.
v	=	0.100	lbs. of yarn	=	1.200 d.
s	=	0.156	lbs. of yarn	=	1.872 d.
c + v + s = 1 lb. of yarn = 12 d.					

If we add the results of the above three partial sales we obtain the same result on selling the entire 10,000 lbs. at one sweep.

We have of constant capital:

at the first sale:	5,535.360	lbs. of yarn	=	£276.768
at the second sale:	744.000	lbs. of yarn	=	£ 37.200
at the third sale:	1,160.640	lbs. of yarn	=	£ 58.032
Total	7,440	lbs. of yarn	=	£372

Of variable capital:

at the first sale:	744.000	lbs. of yarn	=	£37.200
at the second sale:	100.000	lbs. of yarn	=	£ 5.000
at the third sale:	156.000	lbs. of yarn	=	£ 7.800
Total	1,000	lbs. of yarn	=	£50

Of surplus-value:

at the first sale:	1,160.640	lbs. of yarn = £58.032
at the second sale:	156.000	lbs. of yarn = £ 7.800
at the third sale:	243.360	lbs. of yarn = £ 12.168
Total	1,560	lbs. of yarn = £78

Grand Total:

Constant capital .... 7,440 lbs. of yarn = £372
Variable capital ....1,000 lbs. of yarn = £ 57
Surplus-value .... 1,560 lbs. of yarn = £ 78
Total .... 10,000 lbs. of yarn = £500

C'—M' in itself stands merely for the sale of 10,000 lbs. of yarn. These 10,000 lbs. of yarn, like all other yarn, are a commodity. The purchaser is interested in the price of 1 s. per lb., or of £500 for 10,000 lbs. If during the negotiations he goes into the value-composition of the yarn, he does so simply with the insidious intention of proving that it could be sold at less than 1 s. per pound and would still be a good bargain for the seller. But the quantity purchased by him depends on his requirements. If he is, for example, the owner of a weaving-mill, it depends on the composition of his own capital functioning in this enterprise, not on the composition of the spinner's of whom he buys. The proportions in which C' has to replace on the one hand the capital used up in its production (or the various component parts of this capital), and on the other to serve as surplus-product either for the spending of the surplus-value or for the accumulation of capital, exist only in the circuit of capital which has as its commodity-form the 10,000 lbs. of yarn. These proportions have nothing to do with the sale as such. In the present case it is assumed besides that C' is sold at its value, so that it is only a question of its transformation from the commodity-form into the money-form. It is of course of decisive importance with regard to C', the functional form in the circuit of this individual capital out of which the productive capital is to be replaced, to what extent, if at all, there is a discrepancy between price and value in the sale. But this does not concern us here in the examination of mere distinctions of form.

In Form I, or M ... M', the process of production intervenes midway between the two complementary and mutually opposite phases of the circulation of capital. It is past before the concluding phase C'—M' begins. Money is advanced as capital, is first transformed into the elements of production and from these into the commodity-product, and this commodity-product in its turn is changed back into money. It is a full and complete business cycle that results in money, something everyone can use for everything. A new start is therefore only a possibility. M ... P ... M' may be either be the last circuit that concludes the functioning of some individual capital being withdrawn from business, or the first circuit of some new capital entering upon its function. The general movement is here M ... M', from money to more money.

In Form II, P ... C'—M'—C ... P (P'), the entire circulation process follows after the first P and precedes the second P; but it takes place in the opposite order from that of Form I. The first P is the productive capital, and its function is the productive process, the prerequisite of the succeeding circulation process. The concluding P on the other hand is not the productive process; it is only the renewed existence of the industrial capital in its form of productive capital. And it is such as a result of the transformation, during the last phase of circulation, of the capital-value into L plus MP, into the subjective and objective factors which by combining constitute the form of existence of the productive capital. The capital, whether P or P', is at the end once more present in a form in which it must function anew as productive capital, must again perform the productive process. The general form of the movement P ... P is the form of reproduction and, unlike M ... M', does not indicate the self-expansion of value as the object of the process. This form makes it therefore so much easier for classical Political Economy to ignore the definite capitalistic form of the process of production and to depict production as such as the purpose of this process; namely that as much as possible must be produced and as cheaply as possible, and that the product must be exchanged for the greatest variety of other products, partly for the renewal of production (M—C), partly for consumption (m—c). It is then possible to overlook the peculiarities of money and money-capital, for M and m appear here merely as transient media of circulation. The entire process seems simple and natural, i.e., possesses the naturalness of a shallow rationalism. In the same way profit is occasionally forgotten in commodity-capital and the latter figures merely as a commodity when the production circuit as a whole is under discussion. But as soon as the constituents of value are debated, commodity-capital figures as commodity-capital. Accumulation, of course, is seen in the same light as production.

In Form III, C'—M'—C .... P ... C', the two phases of the circulation process open the circuit, and do so in the same order which obtains in Form II, P ... P; next follows P, with its function, the productive process, the same as in Form I; the circuit closes with the result of the process of production, C'. Just as in Form II the circuit closes with P, the merely renewed existence of productive capital, so here it closes with C', the renewed existence of commodity-capital. Just as in Form II capital, in its concluding form P, must start the process over again as a process of production, so here upon the reappearance of industrial capital in the form of commodity-capital the circuit must re-open with the circulation phase C'—M'.

Both forms of the circuit are incomplete because they do not close with M', the capital-value retransformed into *money* and self-expanded. Both must therefore be continued and consequently include the reproduction. The total circuit in Form III is C› ... C›.

The third form is distinguished from the first two by the fact that it is only in this circuit that the self-expanded capital-value—and not the original one, the capital-value that must still produce surplus-value—appears as the starting point of its self-expansion. C as a capital-relation is here the starting point and as such relation has a determining influence on the entire circuit because it includes the circuit of the capital-value as well as that of the surplus-value in its first phase, and because the surplus-value must at least in the average, if not in every single circuit, be expended partly as revenue, go through the circulation c—m—c, and must perform the function of an element of capital accumulation.

In the form C' ... C' the consumption of the entire commodity-product is assumed as the condition of the normal course of the circuit of capital itself. The individual consumption of the labourer and the individual consumption of the unaccumulated part of the surplus-product comprise the entire individual consumption. Hence consumption in its totality—individual as well as productive—enters into circuit C' as a condition of it. Productive consumption (which essentially includes the individual consumption of the labourer, since labour-power is a continuous product, with certain limits, of the labourer's individual consumption) is carried on by every individual capital. Individual consumption, except in so far as it is required for the existence of the individual capitalist, is here assumed to be only a social act, but by no means an act of the individual capitalist.

In Forms I and II the aggregate movement appears as a movement of advanced capital-value. In Form III the self-expanded capital, in the shape of the total commodity-product, forms the starting-point and has the form of moving capital, commodity-capital. Not until its transformation into money has been accomplished does the movement branch out into movements of capital and of revenue. The distribution of the total social product, as well as the special distribution of the product for each individual commodity-capital, into an individual consumption-fund on the one hand and into reproduction fund on the other is included in this form in the circuit of capital.

In M... M' possible enlargement of the circuit is included, depending on the volume of m entering into the renewed circuit.

In P ... P the new circuit may be started by P with the same or perhaps even a smaller value and yet may represent a reproduction on an extended scale, for instance when certain elements of commodities become cheaper on account of increased productivity of labour. Vice versa, a productive capital which has increased in value may, in a contrary case, represent reproduction on a materially contracted scale as for instance when elements of production have become dearer. The same is true of C' ... C'.

In C' ... C' capital in the form of commodities is the premise of production. It re-appears as a premise within this circuit in the second C. If this C has not yet been produced or reproduced the circuit is obstructed. This C must be reproduced, for the greater part of as C' of some other industrial capital. In this circuit C' exists as the point of departure, of transition, and of the conclusion of the movement; hence it is always there. It is a permanent condition of the process of reproduction.

C' ... C' is distinguished from Forms I and II by still another feature. All three circuits have this in common, that capital begins its circular course in the same form in which it concludes it, and thus finds itself in the initial form in which it opens the circuit anew. The initial form M, P or C' is always the one in which capital-value (in III augmented by its surplus-value) is advanced, in other words its original form in regard to the circuit. The concluding form M', P or C' is always a changed form of a functional form which preceded in the circuit and is not the original form.

Thus M' in I is a changed form of C', the final P in II is a changed form of M (and this transformation is accomplished in I and II by a simple act of commodity circulation, by a formal change of position of commodity and money); in III, C' is a changed form of the productive capital P. But here, in III, the transformation, in the first place, does not merely concern the functional form of capital but also the magnitude of its value; in the second place, however, the transformation is not the result of a merely formal change in position pertaining to the circulation process, but of a real transformation experienced by the use-form and value of the commodity constituents of the productive capital in the process of production.

The form of the initial extreme M, P or C' is the premise of the corresponding circuit I, II or III. The form returning in the final extreme is premised and consequently brought about by the series of metamorphoses of the circuit itself. C', as the terminal point in the circuit of an individual industrial capital, presupposes only the non-circulation form P of the same industrial capital of which it is the product. M', as the terminal point of I, as the converted form of C' (C'—M'), presupposes that M is in the hands of the buyer, exists outside of the circuit M ... M', and is drawn into it and made its own terminal form by the sale of C'. Thus the terminal P in II presupposes that L and MP (C) exist outside and are incorporated in it as its terminal form by means of M—C. But apart from the last extreme, the circuit of individual money-capital does not presuppose the existence of money-capital in general, nor does the circuit of individual productive capital presuppose the existence of productive capital. In I, M may be the first money-capital; in II, P may be the first productive capital appearing on the historical scene. But in III,

$$C' \begin{cases} C - \\ -M' \\ C - \end{cases} \begin{cases} M - C <^{L}_{MP \ldots P \ldots C'} \\ \\ m - c \end{cases}$$

C is presupposed twice outside the circuit. The first time in the circuit $C'—M'—C<^{L}_{MP}$. This C, so far as it consists of MP, is commodity in the hands of the seller; it is itself commodity-capital, so far as it is the product of a capitalist process of production; and even if it is not, it appears as commodity-capital in the hands of the merchant. The second time, in the second c of c—m—c, which must likewise be at hand as a commodity so that it can be bought. At any rate, whether they are commodity-capital or not, L and MP are just as much commodities as is C› and bear to each other the relation of commodities. The same is true of the second c in c—m—c. Inasmuch therefore as C› is equal to C (L plus MP), it has commodities as elements for its own production and must be replaced by the same commodities in the circulation. In the same way the second c in c—m—c must be replaced by similar commodities in the circulation.

On the basis that the capitalist mode of production is the prevailing mode, all commodities in the hands of the seller must, besides, be commodity-capital. And they continue to be so in the hands of the merchant or become such if they were not such before. Or they have to be commodities—such as imported articles—which replace original commodity-capital and hence bestow upon it merely another form of existence.

As forms of existence of P the commodity-elements L and MP, of which the productive capital P consists, do not possess the same form as in the various commodity markets where they are fetched. They are now united, and so combined they can perform the functions of productive capital.

That C appears as the premise of C only in this Form III, within the circuit itself, is due to capital in commodity-form being its starting point. The circuit is opened by the transformation of C' (in so far as it functions as capital-value, regardless of whether it has been increased by the addition of surplus-value or not) into those commodities which are its elements of production. But this transformation comprises the entire process of circulation, C—M—C (equal to L plus MP), and is its result. C here stands at both extremes, but the second extreme, which receives its form C by means of M—C from outside, the commodity-market, is not the last extreme of the circuit but only of its first two stages comprising the process of circulation. Its result is P, which then performs its function, the process of production. It is only as the result of this process, hence not as that of the circulation process, that C' appears as the terminal point of the circuit and in the same form as the starting-point, C'. On the other hand in M ... M' and P ... P, the final extremes M' and P are the direct results of the process of circulation. Here therefore it is presupposed only at the end that one time M' and the other time P exist in the hands of others. In so far as the circuit is made between the extremes, neither M in the one case nor P in the other—the existence of M as the money of another person and of P as the production process of another capital—appears as the premise of these circuits. C' ... C' on the contrary presupposes the existence of C (equal to L plus MP) as commodities of others in the hands of others—commodities drawn into the circuit by the introductory process of circulation and transformed into productive capital, as a result of whose functioning C' once more becomes the concluding form of the circuit.

But just because the circuit C' ... C' presupposes within its sphere the existence of other industrial capital in the form of C (equal to L + MP)—and MP comprises diverse other capitals, in our case for instance machinery, coal, oil, etc.—it clamours to be considered not only as the *general* form of the circuit, i.e., not only as a social form in which every single industrial capital (except when first invested) can be studied, hence not merely as a form of movement common to all individual industrial capitals, but simultaneously also as a form of movement of the sum of the individual capitals, consequently of the aggregate capital of the capitalist class, a movement in which that of each individual industrial capital appears as only a partial movement which intermingles with the other movements and is necessitated by them. For instance if we regard the aggregate of commodities annually produced in a certain country and analyse the movement by which a part of it replaces the productive capital in all individual businesses, while another part enters into the individual consumption of the various classes, then we consider C› ... C› as a form of movement of social capital as well as of the surplus-value, or surplus-product, generated by it. The fact that the social capital is equal to the sum of the individual capitals (including the joint-stock capital or the state capital, so far as governments employ productive wage-labour in mines, railways, etc., perform the function of industrial capitalists), and that the aggregate movement of social capital is equal to the algebraic sum of the movements of the individual capitals, does not in any way preclude the possibility that this movement as the movement of a single individual capital, may present other phenomena than the same movement does when considered from the point of view of a part of the aggregate movement of social capital, hence in its interconnections with the movements of its other parts, and that the movement simultaneously solves problems the solution of which must be assumed when studying the circuit of a separate, individual capital instead of being the result of such study.

C' ... C' is the sole circuit in which the originally advanced capital-value consists only a part of the extreme that opens the movement and in which the movement from its inception thus reveals itself as the total movement of the industrial capital—as the movement of that part of the product which replaces the productive capital as well as of that part which forms surplus-product and which on the average is spent in part as revenue and employed in part as an element of accumulation. Included in this circuit is the expenditure of surplus-value as revenue and to that extent individual consumption is likewise included. The latter is furthermore included for the reason that the starting-point C, commodity, exists in the form of some utility; but every article produced by capitalist methods is commodity-capital, no matter whether its use-form destines it for productive or for individual consumption, or for both. M ... M' indicates only the value side, the self-expansion of the advanced capital-value, as the purpose of the entire process; P ... P (P') indicates the process of production of capital as a process of reproduction with a productive capital of the same or of increasing magnitude (accumulation). Revealing itself already in its initial extreme as a form of capitalist commodity production, C' ... C' comprises productive and individual consumption from the start; productive consumption and the self-expansion of value therein included appear only as a branch of its movement. Finally, since C' may exist in a use-form which cannot enter any more into any process of production, it is indicated at the outset that C''s various constituents of value expressed by parts of the product must occupy a different position, according to whether C' ... C' is regarded as the form of the movement of the total social capital or as the independent movement of an individual industrial capital. All these peculiarities of the circuit lead us beyond its own confines as an isolated circuit of some merely individual capital.

In the formula C' ... C', the movement of the commodity-capital, that is to say, of the total product created capitalistically, appears not only as the premise of the independent circuit of the individual capital but also as required by it. If the formula and its peculiarities are grasped, it is no longer sufficient to confine oneself to indicating that the metamorphoses C'—M' and M—C are on the one hand functionally defined sections in the metamorphoses of capital, on the other are links in the general circulation of commodities. It becomes necessary to elucidate the intertwining of the metamorphoses of one individual capital with those of other individual capitals and with that part of the total product which is intended for individual consumption. On analysing the circuit of an individual industrial capital, we therefore base our studies mainly on the first two forms.

The circuit C' ... C' appears as a form of a single individual capital, for instance in agriculture, where calculations are made from crop to crop. In Formula II, the sowing is the starting-point, in Formula III the harvest, or, to speak with the physiocrats, Formula II starts out with the *avance*, and Formula III with the *reprises*. The movement of capital-value appears in III from the outset only as a part of the movement of the general mass of products, while in I and II the movement of C' constitutes only a phase of the movement of some isolated capital.

In Formula III commodities in the market are the continuous premise of the process of production and reproduction. Hence, if attention is fixed exclusively on this formula all elements of the process of production seem to originate in commodity circulation and to consist only of commodities. This one-sided conception overlooks those elements of the process of production which are independent of the commodity-elements.

Since in C' ... C' the starting-point is the total product (total value), it turns out that (if foreign trade is disregarded) reproduction on an extended scale, productivity remaining otherwise constant, can take place only when the part of the surplus-product to be capitalised already contains the material elements of the additional productive capital; that therefore, so far as the production of one year serves as the premise of the following year's production or so far as this can take place simultaneously with the process of simple reproduction within one year, surplus-product is at once produced in a form which enables it to perform the functions of additional capital. Increased productivity can increase only the substance of capital but not its value; but therewith it creates additional material for the self-expansion of that value.

C' ... C' is the groundwork for Quesnay's *Tableau économique*, and it shows great and true discretion on his part that in contrast to M ... M' (the isolatedly and rigidly retained form of the mercantile system) he selected this form and not P ... P.

4

The Three Formulas of the Circuit

The three formulas may be set down in the following manner, using Tc for 'total circulation process':

I. M—C ... P ... C'—M'
II. P ... Tc ... P
III. Tc ... P (C')

If we combine all three forms, all premises of the process appear as its result, as a premise produced by it itself. Every element appears as a point of departure, of transit, and of return. The total process presents itself as the unity of the processes of production and circulation. The process of production becomes the mediator of the process of circulation and vice versa.

All three circuits have the following in common: The self-expansion of value as the determining purpose, as the compelling motive. In I this is expressed in its form. Formula II begins with P, the very process of creating surplus-value. In III the circuit begins with the self-expanded value, even if the movement is repeated on the same scale.

As C—M means M—C for the buyer, and M—C means C—M for the seller, the circulation of capital presents only the ordinary metamorphosis of commodities, and the laws evolved with regard to it (Buch I, Kap. III, 2) [English edition: Ch. III, 2.—*Ed.*] on the mass of money in circulation are valid here. However, if we do not cling to this formal aspect but rather consider the actual connection between the metamorphoses of the various individual capitals, in other words, if we study the connection between the circuits of individual capitals as partial movements of the process of reproduction of the total social capital, then the mere change of form of money and commodities cannot explain the connection.

In a constantly revolving circle every point is simultaneously a point of departure and a point of return. If we interrupt the rotation, not every point of departure is a point of return. Thus we have seen that not only does every individual circuit presuppose (*implicite*) the others, but also that the repetition of the circuit in one form comprises the performance of the circuit in the other forms. The entire difference thus appears to be a merely formal one, or as a merely subjective distinction existing solely for the observer.

Since every one of these circuits is considered a special form of this movement in which various individual industrial capitals are engaged, this difference exists only as an individual one. But in reality every individual industrial capital is present simultaneously in all three circuits. These three circuits, the forms of reproduction assumed by the three forms of capital, are made continuously side by side. For instance, one part of the capital-value, which now performs the function of commodity-capital, is transformed into money-capital, but at the same time another part leaves the process of production and enters the circulation as a new commodity-capital. The circuit form C' ... C' is thus continuously described; and so are the other two forms. The reproduction of capital in each one of its forms and stages is just as continuous as the metamorphosis of these forms and the successive passage through the three stages. The entire circuit is thus a unity of its three forms.

We assumed in our analysis that capital-value in its entire magnitude acts as money-capital, productive-capital or commodity-capital. For instance, we had those £422 first entirely as money-capital, then we transformed them wholly into productive capital, and finally into commodity-capital, into yarn of the value of £500 (containing £78 worth of surplus-value). Here the various stages are just so many interruptions. So long as, e.g., those £422 retain their money-form, that is to say, until the purchases M—C (L plus MP) are made, the entire capital exists and functions only as money-capital. As soon as it is transformed into productive capital, it performs neither the function of money-capital nor of commodity-capital. Its entire process of circulation is interrupted, as soon as it functions in one of its two circulation stages, either as M or as C'. Consequently, the circuit P ... P would represent not only a periodical renewal of the productive capital but also the interruption of its function, the process of production, up to the time when the process of circulation is completed. Instead of proceeding continuously, production would take place in jerks and would be renewed only in periods of accidental duration, according to whether the two stages of the process of circulation are got through with quickly or slowly. This would apply for instance to a Chinese artisan who works only for private customers and whose process of production ceases until he receives a new order.

This is indeed true of every single part of capital that is in motion, and all parts of capital go through this motion in succession. Suppose that the 10,000 lbs. of yarn are the weekly product of some spinner. These 10,000 lbs. of yarn leave the sphere of production entirely and enter the sphere of circulation; the capital-value contained in it must all be converted into money-capital, and so long as this value continues in the form of money-capital it cannot enter anew into the process of production. It must first go into circulation and be reconverted into the elements of productive capital, L plus MP. The circuit-describing process of capital means constant interruption, the leaving of one stage and the entering into the next, the discarding of one form and the assuming of another. Each one of these stages not only presupposes the next but also excludes it.

But continuity is the characteristic mark of capitalist production, necessitated by its technical basis, although not always absolutely attainable. Let us see then what happens in reality. While, e.g., the 10,000 lbs. of yarn appear in the market as commodity-capital and are transformed into money (regardless of whether it is a paying or purchasing medium or only money of account), new cotton, coal, etc., take the place of the yarn in the process of production, have therefore, already been reconverted from the money-form and commodity-form into that of productive capital, and begin to function as such. At the same time that these 10,000 lbs. of yarn are being reconverted into money, the preceding 10,000 lbs. of yarn are going through the second stage of their circulation and are being reconverted from money into the elements of productive capital. All parts of capital successively describe circuits, are simultaneously at its different stages. The industrial capital, continuously progressing along its orbit, thus exists simultaneously at all its stages and in the diverse functional forms corresponding to these stages. That part of industrial capital which is converted for the first time from commodity-capital into money begins the circuit C' ... C', while industrial capital as a moving whole has already passed through that circuit. One hand advances money, the other receives it. The inauguration of the circuit M ... M' at one place coincides with the return of the money at another place. The same is true of productive capital.

The actual circuit of industrial capital in its continuity is therefore not alone the unity of the processes of circulation and production but also the unity of all its three circuits. But it can be such a unity only if all the different parts of capital can go through the successive stages of the circuit, can pass from one phase, from one functional form to another, so that the industrial capital, being the whole of all these parts, exists simultaneously in its various phases and functions and thus describes all three circuits at the same time. The succession]*das Nacheinander*] of these parts is here governed by their co-existence [*das Nebeneinander*], that is to say, by the division of capital. In a ramified factory system the product is constantly in the various stages of its process of formation and constantly passes from one phase of production to another. As the individual industrial capital has a definite size which depends on the means of the capitalist and which has a definite minimum magnitude for every branch of industry, it follows that its division must proceed according to definite proportions. The magnitude of the available capital determines the dimensions of the process of production, and this again determines the dimensions of the commodity-capital and money-capital in so far as they perform their functions parallel with the process of production. However co-existence, by which continuity of production is determined, is only due to the movement of those parts of capital in which they successively pass through their different stages. Co-existence is itself merely the result of succession. If for instance C'—M' as far as one part is concerned, if the commodity cannot be sold, then the circuit of this part is interrupted and no replacement by its means of reproduction takes place; the succeeding parts, which emerge from the process of production in the shape of C', find the change of their functions blocked by their predecessors. If this lasts for some time, production is restricted and the entire process brought to a halt. Every stagnation in succession carries disorder into co-existence, every stagnation in one stage causes more or less stagnation in the entire circuit of not only the stagnant part of capital but also of the total individual capital.

The next form in which the process presents itself is that of a succession of phases, so that the transition of capital into a new phase is made necessary by its departure from another. Every separate circuit has therefore one of the functional forms of capital for its point of departure and point of return. On the other hand the aggregate process is in fact the unity of the three circuits, which are the different forms in which the continuity of the process expresses itself. The aggregate circuit presents itself to every functional form of capital as its specific circuit and every one of these circuits is a condition of the continuity of the total process. The cycle of each functional form is dependent upon the others. It is a necessary prerequisite of the aggregate process of production, especially for the social capital, that it is at the same time a process of reproduction and hence a circuit of each one of its elements. Various fractional parts of capital pass successively through the various stages and functional forms. Thanks to this every functional form passes simultaneously with the others through its own circuit, although always a different part of capital finds its expression in it. One part of capital, continually changing, continually reproduced, exists as a commodity-capital which is converted into money; another as money-capital which is converted into productive capital; and a third as productive capital which is transformed into commodity-capital. The continuous existence of all three forms is brought about by the circuit the aggregate capital describes in passing through precisely these three phases.

Capital as a whole, then, exists simultaneously, spatially side by side, in its different phases. But every part passes constantly and successively from one phase, from one functional form, into the next and thus functions in all of them in turn. Its forms are hence fluid and their simultaneousness is brought about by their succession. Every form follows another and precedes it, so that the return of one capital part to a certain form is necessitated by the return of the other part to some other form. Every part describes continuously its own cycle, but it is always another part of capital which exists in this form, and these special cycles form only simultaneous and successive elements of the aggregate process.

The continuity—instead of the above-described interruption—of the aggregate process is achieved only in the unity of the three circuits. The aggregate social capital always has this continuity and its process always exhibits the unity of the three circuits.

The continuity of the reproduction is at times more or less interrupted so far as individual capitals are concerned. In the first place the masses of value are frequently distributed at various periods in unequal portions over the various stages and functional forms. In the second place these portions may be differently distributed, according to the character of the commodity to be produced, hence according to the particular sphere of production in which the capital is invested. In the third place the continuity may be more or less broken in those branches of production which are dependent on the seasons, either on account of natural conditions (agriculture, herring catch, etc.) or on account of conventional circumstances, as for instance in so-called seasonal work. The process goes on most regularly and uniformly in the factories and mines. But this difference in the various branches of production does not cause any difference in the general forms of the circular process.

Capital as self-expanding value embraces not only class relations, a society of a definite character resting on the existence of labour in the form of wage-labour. It is a movement, a circuit-describing process going through various stages, which itself comprises three different forms of circuit-describing process. Therefore it can be understood only as a motion, not as a thing at rest. Those who regard the gaining by value of independent existence as a mere abstraction forget that the movement of industrial capital is this abstraction in *actu*. Value here passes through various forms, various movements in which it maintains itself and at the same time expands, augments. As we are here concerned primarily with the mere form of this movement, we shall not take into consideration the revolutions which capital-value may undergo during its circuit. But it is clear that in spite of all the revolutions of value, capitalist production exists and can endure only so long as capital-value is made to create surplus-value, that is, so long as it describes its circuit as a value that has gained independence, so long therefore as the revolutions in value are overcome and equilibrated in some way. The movements of capital appear as the action of some individual industrial capitalist who performs the functions of a buyer of commodities and labour, a seller of commodities, and an owner of productive capital, who therefore promotes the circuit by this activity. If social capital experiences a revolution in value, it may happen that the capital of the individual capitalist succumbs to it and fails, because it cannot adapt itself to the conditions of this movement of values. The more acute and frequent such revolutions in value become, the more does the automatic movement of the now independent value operate with the elemental force of a natural process, against the foresight and calculation of the individual capitalist, the more does the course of normal production become subservient to abnormal speculation, and the greater is the danger that threatens the existence of the individual capitals. These periodical revolutions in value therefore corroborate what they are supposed to refute, namely, that value as capital acquires independent existence, which it maintains and accentuates through its movement.

This succession of the metamorphoses of capital in process includes continuous comparison of the change in the magnitude of value of the capital brought about in the circuit with the original value. If value's acquisition of independence of the value-creating power, labour-power, is inaugurated by the act M—L (purchase of labour-power) and is effected during the process of production as exploitation of labour-power, this acquisition of independence on the part of value does not re-appear in that circuit, in which money, commodities, and elements of production are merely alternating forms of capital-value in process, and the former magnitude of value is compared with capital's present changed magnitude of value.

> 'Value,' argues Bailey against the acquisition of independence by value, an independence which is characteristic of the capitalist mode of production and which he treats as an illusion of certain economists; 'value is a relation between contemporary commodities, because such only admit of being exchanged for each other.' [See Bailey, Samuel, *A Critical Dissertation on the Nature, Measures, and Causes of Value; Chiefly in Reference to the Writings of Mr. Ricardo and His Followers By the Author of Essays on the Formation and Publication of Opinions*, London, 1825, p. 72.—*Ed.*]

This he says against the comparison of commodity-values of different epochs, a comparison which amounts only to comparing the expenditure of labour required in various periods for the production of the same sort of commodities, once the value of money has been fixed for every period. This comes from his general misunderstanding, for he thinks that exchange-value is equal to value, that the form if value is value itself; consequently commodity-value can no longer be compared, if they do not function actively as exchange-values and thus cannot actually be exchanged for one another. He has not the least inkling of the fact that value functions as capital-value or capital only in so far as it remains identical with itself and is compared with itself in the different phases of its circuit, which are not at all '**contemporary**' but succeed one another.

In order to study the formula of the circuit in its purity it is not sufficient to postulate that commodities are sold at their value; it must also be assumed that this takes place with other things being equal. Take for instance the form P ... P, disregarding all technical revolutions within the process of production by which the productive capital of a certain capitalist might be depreciated; disregarding furthermore all reactions which a change in the elements of value of the productive capital might have on the value of the existing commodity-capital, which might appreciate or depreciate if a stock of it is on hand. Suppose the 10,000 lbs. of yarn, C', have been sold at their value of £500; 8,440 lbs. equal to £422, replace the capital-value contained in C'. But if the value of cotton, coal, etc., has increased (we do not consider mere fluctuations in price), these £422 may not suffice for the full replacement of the elements of productive capital; additional money-capital is required, money-capital is tied up. The opposite takes place when those prices fall. Money-capital is set free. The process takes a wholly normal course only when the value-relations remain constant; its course is practically normal so long as the disturbances during the repetitions of the circuit balance one another. But the greater these disturbances the greater the money-capital which the industrial capitalist must possess to tide over the period of readjustment; and as the scale of each individual process of production and with it the minimum size of the capital to be advanced increases in the process of capitalist production, we have here another circumstance to be added to those others which transform the function of the industrial capitalist more and more into a monopoly of big money-capitalists, who may operate singly or in association.

We remark incidentally that if a change in the value of the elements of production occurs a difference appears between the form M...M' on one side and of P ... P and C' ... C' on the other.

In M ... M', the formula of newly-invested capital, which first appears as money-capital, a fall in the value of the means of production, such as raw material, auxiliary material, etc., will permit of a smaller expenditure of money-capital than before this fall for the purpose of starting a business of a definite size, because the scale of the process of production (productive power development remaining the same) depends on the mass and volume of the means of production which a given quantity of labour-power can cope with; but it does not depend on the value of these means of production nor on that of the labour-power (the latter value affects only the magnitude of self-expansion). Take the reverse case. If there is a rise in the value of the elements of production of the commodities which constitute the elements of the productive capital, then more money-capital is needed for the establishment of a business of definite proportions. In both cases it is only the amount of the money-capital required for new investment that is affected. In the former case money-capital becomes surplus, in the latter it is tied up, provided the accession of new individual industrial capital proceeds in the usual way in a given branch of production.

The circuits P ... P and C' ... C' present themselves as M ... M' only to the extent that the movement of P and C' is at the same time accumulation, hence to the extent that additional m, money, is converted into money-capital; here, too, we do not take into consideration the reaction of such changes in value on those constituent parts of capital which are engaged in the process of production. It is not the original expenditure which is directly affected here, but an industrial capital engaged in its process of reproduction and not in its first circuit; i.e., C' ... $C<^{L}_{MP}$, the reconversion of commodity-capital into its elements of production, so far as they are composed of commodities. When value (prices) fall three cases are possible: The process of reproduction is continued on the same scale; in that event a part of the money-capital existing hitherto is set free and money-capital is accumulated, although no real accumulation (production on an extended scale) or transformation of m (surplus-value) into an accumulation-fund initiating and accompanying such accumulation has previously taken place. Or the process of reproduction is carried on a more extensive scale than ordinarily would have been the case, provided the technical proportions admit it. Or, finally, a larger stock of raw materials, etc., is laid in.

The opposite occurs if the value of the elements of replacement of a commodity-capital increases. In that case reproduction no longer takes place on its normal scale (e.g., the working-day gets shorter); or additional money-capital must be employed in order to maintain the old volume of work (money-capital is tied up); or the money-fund for accumulation, when one exists, is employed entirely or partially for the operation of the process of reproduction on its old scale instead of for the enlargement of this process. This is also tying up money-capital, except that here the additional money-capital does not come from the outside, from the money-market, but from the means of the industrial capitalist himself.

However, there may be modifying circumstances in P ... P and C' ... C'. If our spinning-mill proprietor for example has a large stock of cotton (a large proportion of his productive capital in the form of a stock of cotton), a part of his productive capital is depreciated by a fall in the prices of cotton; but if on the contrary these prices rise, this part of his productive capital appreciates. On the other hand, if he has tied up huge quantities in the form of commodity-capital, for instance of cotton yarn, a part of his commodity-capital, hence of his circuit describing capital in general, is depreciated by a fall of cotton, or appreciated by a rise in its prices. Finally take the process C'—M—C$<^{L}_{MP}$. If C'—M, the realisation of the commodity-capital, has taken place before a change in the value of the elements of C, then capital is affected only in the way indicated in the first case, namely in the second act of circulation, M—C$<^{L}_{MP}$; but if such a change has occurred before C'—M has been effected, then, other conditions remaining equal, a fall in the price of cotton causes a corresponding fall in the price of yarn, and a rise in the price of cotton means conversely a rise in the price of yarn. The effect on the various individual capitals invested in the same branch of production may differ widely, according to the circumstances in which they find themselves.

Money-capital may also be set free or tied up on account of differences in the duration of the process of circulation, hence also in the speed of circulation. But this belongs in the discussion on turnover. At this point we are only interested in the real difference that becomes evident, with regard to changes of values of the elements of productive capital, between M ... M' and the other two circuit forms.

In the circulation section M—C$<^{L}_{MP}$, in the epoch of the already developed and hence prevailing capitalist mode of production, a large portion of the commodities composing MP, the means of production, is itself functioning as the commodity-capital of someone else. From the standpoint of the seller, therefore, C'—M', the transformation of commodity-capital into money-capital, takes place. But this is not an absolute rule. On the contrary. Within its process of circulation, in which industrial capital functions either as money or as commodities, the circuit of industrial capital, whether as money-capital or as commodity-capital, crosses the commodity circulation of the most diverse modes of social production, so far as they produce commodities. No matter whether commodities are the output of production based on slavery, of peasants (Chinese, Indian ryots). of communes (Dutch East Indies), of state enterprise (such as existed in former epochs of Russian history on the basis of serfdom) or of half-savage hunting tribes, etc.—as commodities and money they come face to face with the money and commodities in which the industrial capital presents itself and enter as much into its circuit as into that of the surplus-value borne in the commodity-capital, provided the surplus-value is spent as revenue; hence they enter in both branches of circulation of commodity-capital. The character of the process of production from which they originate is immaterial. They function as commodities in the market, and as commodities they enter into the circuit of industrial capital as well as into the circulation of the surplus-value incorporated in it. It is therefore the universal character of the origin of the commodities, the existence of the market as world-market, which distinguishes the process of circulation of industrial capital. What is true of the commodities of others is also true of the money of others. Just as commodity-capital faces money only as commodities, so this money functions vis-à-vis commodity-capital only as money. Money here performs the functions of world-money.

However two points must be noted here.

First: as soon as act M—MP is completed, the commodities (MP) cease to be such and become one of the modes of existence of industrial capital in its functional form of P, productive capital. Thereby however their origin is obliterated. They exist henceforth only as forms of existence of industrial capital, are embodied in it. However it still remains true that to replace them they must be reproduced, and to this extent the capitalist mode of production is conditional on modes of production lying outside of its own stage of development. But it is the tendency of the capitalist mode of production to transform all production as much as possible into commodity production. The mainspring by which this is accomplished is precisely the involvement of all production into the capitalist circulation process. And developed commodity production itself is capitalist commodity production. The intervention of industrial capital promotes this transformation everywhere, but with it also the transformation of all direct producers into wage-labourers.

Secondly: the commodities entering into the circulation of industrial capital (including the requisite means of subsistence into which variable capital, after being paid to the labourers, is transformed for the purpose of reproducing their labour-power), regardless of their origin and of the social form of the productive process by which they were brought into existence, come face to face with industrial capital itself already in the form of commodity-capital, in the form of commodity-dealer's or merchant's capital. And merchant's capital, by its very nature comprises commodities of all modes of production.

The capitalist mode of production presupposes not only large-scale production but also, and necessarily so, sales on a large scale, hence sale to the merchant, not to the individual consumer. If this consumer is himself a productive consumer, hence an industrial capitalist, i.e., if the industrial capital of one branch of production supplies some other branch of industry with means of production, direct sale by one industrial capitalist to many others take place (in the form of orders, etc.). To this extent every industrial capitalist is a direct seller and his own merchant, which by the way is when he sells to a merchant.

Trading in commodities as the function of merchant's capital is a premise of capitalist production and develops more and more in the course of development of such production. Therefore we occasionally take its existence for granted to illustrate particular aspects of the process of capitalist circulation; but in the general analysis of this process we assume direct sale, without the intervention of a merchant, because this intervention obscures various facets of the movement.

Cf. Sismondi, who presents the matter somewhat naively:

> 'Commerce employs considerable capital, which at first sight does not seem to be a part of that capital whose movement we have described. The value of the cloth accumulated in the stores of the cloth-merchant seems at first to be entirely foreign to that part of the annual production which the rich gives to the poor as wages in order to make him work. However this capital has simply replaced the other of which we have spoken.

For the purpose of clearly understanding the progress of wealth, we have begun with its creation and followed it to its consumption. Then the capital employed in cloth manufacturing, for instance, always seemed the same to us; it was exchanged for the revenue of the consumer, it was divided into only two parts, one of them serving as revenue of the manufacturer in the form of the profit, the other serving as revenue of the labourers in the form of wages for the time they were manufacturing new cloth.

'But it was soon found that it would be to the advantage of all if the different parts of this capital were to replace one another and that, if 100,000 ècus were sufficient for the entire circulation between the manufacturer and the consumer, they should be divided equally between the manufacturer, the wholesale merchant, and the retail merchant. The first then did with only one-third of this capital the same work as he had done with the entire capital, because as soon as his work of manufacturing was completed he found out that a merchant would rather buy from him than a consumer would. On the other hand the capital of the wholesaler was much sooner replaced by that of the retailer... The difference between the sums advanced for wages and the purchase price paid by the ultimate consumer was considered the profit of those capitals. It was divided between the manufacturer, the merchant and the retailer, from the moment that they had divided their functions among themselves, and the work performed was the same, although it had required three persons and three parts of capital instead of one.' (*Nouveaux Principes*, I, pages 139-140.)

'All of them [the merchants] contributed indirectly to the production; for having consumption for its object, production cannot be regarded as completed until the thing produced is placed within the reach of the consumer.' (*Ibid*., p. 137)

In the discussion of the general forms of the circuit and in the entire second book in general, we take money to mean metallic money, with the exception of symbolic money, mere tokens of value, which are designed for specific use in certain states, and of credit-money, which is not yet developed. In the first place, this is the historical order; credit-production plays only a very minor role, or none at all, during the first epoch of capitalist production. In the second place, the necessity of this order is demonstrated theoretically by the fact that everything of a critical nature which Tooke and others hitherto expounded in regard to the circulation of credit-money compelled them to hark back again and again to the question of what would be the aspect of the matter if nothing but metal-money were in circulation. But it must not be forgotten that metal-money may serve as a purchasing medium and also as a paying medium. For the sake of simplicity, we consider it in this second book generally only in its first functional form.

The process of circulation of industrial capital, which is only a part of its individual circuit, is determined by the general laws previously set forth (Buch I, Kap. III), [English edition: Ch. III.—*Ed.*] in so far as it is only a series of acts within the general circulation of commodities. The greater the velocity of the currency of money, the more rapidly therefore every individual capital passes through the series of its commodity or money metamorphoses, the more numerous are the industrial capitals (or individual capitals in the form of commodity-capitals) started circulating successively by a given mass of money, for example £500. The more the money functions as a paying medium, the more therefore—for instance in the replacement of some commodity-capital by its means of production—nothing but balances have to be squared, and the shorter the periods of time when payments fall due, as for instance in paying wages, the less money a given mass of capital-value therefore requires for its circulation. On the other hand, assuming that the velocity of the circulation and all other conditions remain the same, the amount of money required to circulate as money-capital is determined by the sum of the prices of the commodities (price multiplied by the volume of commodities), or, if the quantity and value of the commodities are fixed, by the value of the money itself.

But the laws of the general circulation of commodities are valid only when capital's circulation process consists of a series of simple acts of circulation; they do not apply when the latter constitute functionally determined sections of the circuit of individual industrial capitals.

In order to make this plain, it is best to study the process of circulation in its uninterrupted interconnection, such as it appears in the following two forms:

$$\text{II)}\quad P\ldots C' \left\{ \begin{array}{l} C- \\ -M' \\ C- \end{array} \right. \left\{ \begin{array}{l} M-C < \begin{array}{l} L \\ MP\ldots P(P') \end{array} \\ \\ m-c \end{array} \right.$$

$$\text{III)}\quad C' \left\{ \begin{array}{l} C- \\ -M' \\ C- \end{array} \right. \left\{ \begin{array}{l} M-C < \begin{array}{l} L \\ MP\ldots P\ldots C' \end{array} \\ \\ m-c \end{array} \right.$$

As series of acts of circulation in general, the process of circulation (whether in the form of C—M—C or of M—C—M) represents the two antithetical series of commodity metamorphoses, every single one of which in its turn implies an opposite metamorphosis on the part of the alien commodity or alien money confronting the commodity.

C—M on the part of the owner of a commodity means M—C on the part of its buyer; the first metamorphosis of the commodity appearing in the form of M; the opposite applies to M—C. What has been shown concerning the intertwining of the metamorphosis of a certain commodity in one stage with that of another in another stage applies to the circulation of capital so far as the capitalist functions as a buyer and seller of commodities, and his capital on that account functions in the form of money opposed to the commodities of another. But this intertwining is not to be identified with the intertwining of the metamorphoses of capitals.

In the first place M—C (MP), as we have seen, may represent an intermingling of the metamorphoses of different individual capitals. For instance the commodity-capital of the spinning-mill owner, yarn is partly replaced by coal. One part of his capital exists in the form of money and is converted into the form of commodities, while the capital of the capitalist producer of coal is in the form of commodities and is therefore converted into the form of money; the same act of circulation represents in this case opposite metamorphoses of two industrial capitals (in different branches of production), hence an intertwining of the series of metamorphoses of these capitals. But as we have seen the MP into which M is transformed need not be commodity-capital in the categorical sense, i.e., need not be a functional form of industrial capital, need not be produced by a capitalist. It is always M—C on one side and C—M on the other, but not always an intermingling of metamorphoses of capitals. Furthermore M—L, the purchase of labour-power, is never an intermingling of metamorphoses of capitals, for labour-power, though the commodity of the labourer, does not become capital until it is sold to the capitalist. On the other hand in the process C'—M', it is not necessary that M' should represent converted commodity-capital; it may be the realisation in money of the commodity labour-power (wages), or of the product of some independent labourer, slave, serf, or community.

In the second place however it is not at all required for the discharge of the functionally determined role played by every metamorphosis occurring within the process of circulation of some individual capital that this metamorphosis should represent the corresponding opposite metamorphosis in the circuit of the other capital, provided we assume that the entire production of the world-market is carried on capitalistically. For instance in the circuit P ... P, the M which converts C' into money may be to the buyer only the realisation in money of his surplus-value (if the commodity is an article of consumption); or in M'—C'$<^{L}_{MP}$ (where therefore already accumulated capital enters) M› may, as far as the vendor of MP is concerned, enter into the circulation of his capital only to replace his advanced capital or it may not re-enter at all by being diverted into revenue expenditure.

Therefore the manner in which the various component parts of the aggregate social capital, of which the individual capitals are but constituents functioning independently, mutually replace one another in the process of circulation—in regard to capital as well as surplus-value—is not ascertained from the simple intertwinings of the metamorphoses in the circulation of commodities—intertwinings which the acts of capital circulation have in common with all other circulation of commodities. That requires a different method of investigation. Hitherto one has been satisfied with uttering phrases which upon closer analysis are found to contain nothing but indefinite ideas borrowed from the intertwining of metamorphoses common to all commodity circulation.

Natural Money and Credit Economy

One of the most obvious peculiarities of the movement in circuits of industrial capital, and therefore also of capitalist production, is the fact that on one hand the component elements of productive capital are derived from the commodity-market and must be continually renewed out of it, bought as commodities; and that on the other hand the product of the labour-process emerges from it as a commodity and must be continually sold anew as a commodity. Compare for instance a modern farmer of the Scotch lowlands with an old-fashioned small peasant on the Continent. The former sells his entire product and has therefore to replace all its elements, even his seed, in the market; the latter consumes the greater part of his product directly, buys and sells as little as possible, fashions tools, makes clothing, etc., so far as possible himself.

Natural economy, money-economy, and credit-economy have therefore been placed in opposition to one another as being the three characteristic economic forms of movement in social production.

In the first place these three forms do not represent equivalent phases of development. The so-called credit-economy is merely a form of the money-economy, since both terms express functions or modes of exchange among the producers themselves. In developed capitalist production, the money-economy appears only as the basis of the credit-economy. The money-economy and credit-economy thus correspond only to different stages in the development of capitalist production, but they are by no means independent forms of exchange vis-à-vis natural economy. With the same justification one might contrapose as equivalents the very different forms of natural economy to those two economies.

In the second place, since it is not the economy, i.e., the process of production itself that is emphasised as the distinguishing mark of the two categories, money-economy and credit-economy, but rather the mode of exchange—corresponding to that economy—between the various agents of production, or producers, the same should apply to the first category. Hence exchange economy instead of natural economy. A completely isolated natural economy, such as the Inca state of Peru, would not come under any of these categories.

In the third place, the money-economy is common to all commodity production and the product appears as a commodity in the most varied organisms of social production. Consequently what characterises capitalist production would then be only the extent to which the product is created as an article of commerce, as a commodity, and hence the extent also to which its own constituent elements must enter again as articles of commerce, as commodities, into the economy from which it emerges.

As a matter of fact capitalist production is commodity production as the general form of production. But it is so and becomes so more and more in the course of its development only because labour itself appears here as a commodity, because the labourer sells his labour, that is, the function of his labour-power, and our assumption is that he sells it at its value, determined by its cost of reproduction. To the extent that labour becomes wage-labour, the producer becomes an industrial capitalist. For this reason capitalist production (and hence also commodity production) does not reach its full scope until the direct agricultural producer becomes a wage-labourer. In the relation of capitalist and wage-labourer, the money-relation, the relation between the buyer and the seller, becomes a relation inherent in production. But this relation has its foundation in the social character of production, not in the mode of exchange. The latter conversely emanates from the former. It is, however, quite in keeping with the bourgeois horizon, everyone being engrossed in the transaction of shady business, not to see in the character of the mode of production the basis of the mode of exchange corresponding to it, but vice versa.[1]

The Meeting of Demand and Supply

The capitalist throws less value in the form of money into the circulation than he draws out of it, because he throws into it more value in the form of commodities than he withdrew from it in the form of commodities. Since he functions simply as a personification of capital, as an industrial capitalist, his supply of commodity-value is always greater than his demand for it. If his supply and demand in this respect covered each other it would mean that his capital had not produced any surplus-value, that it had not functioned as productive capital, that the productive capital had been converted into commodity-capital not big with surplus-value; that it had not drawn any surplus-value in commodity form out of labour-power during the process of production, had not functioned at all as capital. The capitalist must indeed 'sell dearer than he has bought, ' but he succeeds in doing so only because the capitalist process of production enables him to transform the cheaper commodity he bought—cheaper because it contains less value—into a commodity of greater value, hence a dearer one. He sells dearer, not because he sells above the value of his commodity, but because his commodity contains value in excess of that contained in the ingredients of its production.

The rate at which the capitalist makes the value of his capital expand is the greater, the greater the difference between his supply and his demand, i.e., the greater the excess of the commodity-value he supplies over the commodity-value he demands. His aim is not to equalize his supply and demand, but to make the inequality between them, the excess of his supply over his demand, as great as possible.

What is true of the individual capitalist applies to the capitalist class.

In so far as the capitalist merely personifies industrial capital, his own demand is confined to means of production and labour-power. In point of value, his demand for MP is smaller than his advanced capital; he buys means of production of a smaller value than that of his capital, and therefore of a still smaller value than that of the commodity-capital which he supplies.

As regards his demand for labour-power, it is determined in point of value by the relation of his variable capital to his total capital, hence equals v : C. In capitalist production this demand thereby grows smaller than his demand for means of production. His purchases of MP steadily rise above his purchases of L.

Since the labourer generally converts his wages into means of subsistence, and for the overwhelmingly larger part into absolute necessities, the demand of the capitalist for labour-power is indirectly also a demand for the articles of consumption essential to the working-class. But this demand is equal to v and not one iota greater (if the labourer saves a part of his wages—we necessarily discard here all credit relations—he converts part of his wages into a hoard and to that extent does not act as a bidder, a purchaser). The upper limit of a capitalist's demand is C, equal to c + v, but his supply is equal to c + v + s. Consequently if the composition of his commodity-capital is $80_c + 20_v + 20_s$, his demand is equal to $80_c + 20_v$, hence, considered from the angle of the value it contains, one-fifth smaller than his supply. The greater the percentage of the mass of surplus-value produced by him (his rate of profit) the smaller becomes his demand in relation to his supply. Although with the further development of production the demand of the capitalist for labour-power, and thus indirectly for necessary means of subsistence, steadily decreases compared with his demand for means of production, it must not be forgotten on the other hand that his demand for MP is always smaller than his capital. His demand for means of production must therefore always be smaller in value than the commodity-product of the capitalist who, working with a capital of equal value and under equal conditions, furnishes him with those means of production. That many capitalists and not only one do the furnishing does not alter the case. Take it that his capital is £1,000, and its constant part £800; then his demand on all these capitalists is equal to £800. Together they supply means of production worth £1,200 for each £1,000 (regardless of what share in each £1,000 may fall to each one of them and of the fraction of his total capital which the share of each may represent), assuming that the rate of profit is the same. Consequently his demand covers only two-thirds of their supply, while his own total demand amounts to only four-fifths of his own supply, measured in value.

It still remains for us, incidentally, to investigate the problem of turnover. Let the total capital of the capitalist be £5,000, of which £4,000 is fixed and £1,000 circulating capital; let this 1,000 be composed of 800_c plus 200_v, as assumed above. His circulating capital must be turned over five times a year for his total capital to turn over once. His commodity-product is then equal to £6,000, i.e., £1,000 more than his advanced capital, which results in the same ratio of surplus-value as above:

$$5{,}000\ C : 1{,}000_{(c+v)} : 20_s$$

This turnover therefore does not change anything in the ratio of his total demand to his total supply. The former remains one-fifth smaller than the latter.

Suppose his fixed capital has to be renewed in 10 years. So the capitalist pays every year one-tenth, or £400, into a sinking fund and thus has only a value of £3,600 of fixed capital left plus £400 in money. If the repairs are necessary and do not exceed the average, they represent nothing but capital invested later. We may look at the matter the same as if he had allowed for the cost of repairs beforehand, when calculating the value of his investment capital, so far as this enters into the annual commodity-product, so that it is included in the one-tenth sinking fund payment. (If his need for repairs is below average he is so much money to the good, and the reverse if above. But this evens out for the entire class of capitalists engaged in the same branch of industry.) At any rate, although his annual demand still remains £5,000, equal to the original capital-value he advanced (assuming his total capital is turned over once a year), this demand increases with regard to the circulating part of the capital, while it steadily decreases with regard to its fixed part.

We now come to reproduction. Let us assume that the capitalist consumes the entire surplus-value m and reconverts only capital C of the original magnitude into productive capital. Then the demand of the capitalist is equal in value to his supply; but this does not refer to the movement of his capital. As a capitalist he exercises a demand for only four-fifths of his supply (in terms of value). He consumes one-fifth as a non-capitalist, not in his function as capitalist but for his private requirements or pleasures.

His calculation, expressed in percentages, is then as follows:

Demand as capitalist	100,
supply	120
Demand as man about town	20,
supply	—
Total demand	120,
supply	120

This assumption is tantamount to assuming that capitalist production does not exist, and therefore that the industrial capitalist himself does not exist. For capitalism is abolished root and branch by the bare assumption that it is personal consumption and not enrichment that works as the compelling motive.

But such an assumption is impossible also technically. The capitalist must not only form a reserve capital to cushion price fluctuations and enable him to wait for favorable buying and selling conditions. He must accumulate capital in order to extend his production and build technical progress into his productive organism.

In order to accumulate capital he must first withdraw in money-form from circulation a part of the surplus-value which he obtained from that circulation, and must hoard it until it has increased sufficiently for the extension of his old business or the opening of a side-line. So long as the formation of the hoard continues, it does not increase the demand of the capitalist. The money is immobilised. It does not withdraw from the commodity-market any equivalent in commodities for the money equivalent withdrawn from it for commodities supplied.

Credit is not considered here. And credit includes for example deposits by the capitalist of accumulating money in a bank on current account paying interest.

Note

1. End of Manuscript V. What follows to the end of the chapter, is a note contained in a notebook of 1877 or 1878 amid extracts from various books.—F.E.

5

The Time of Circulation[1]

We have seen that the movement of capital through the sphere of production and the two phases of the sphere of circulation takes place in a series of periods of time. The duration of its sojourn in the sphere of production is its time of production, that of its stay in the sphere of circulation its time of circulation. The total time during which it describes its circuit is therefore equal to the sum of its time of production and its time of circulation.

The time of production naturally comprises the period of the labour-process, but is not comprised in it. It will be remembered first of all that a part of the constant capital exists in the form of instruments of labour, such as machinery, buildings, etc., which serve the same constantly repeated labour-processes until they are worn out. Periodical interruptions of the labour-process, by night for instance, interrupt the functioning of these instruments of labour, but not their stay at the place of production. They belong to this place when they are in function as well as when they are not. On the other hand the capitalist must have a definite supply of raw material and auxiliary material in readiness, in order that the process of production may take place for a longer or shorter time on a previously determined scale, without being dependent on the accidents of daily supply from the market. This supply of raw material, etc., is productively consumed only by degrees. There is, therefore, a difference between its time of production[2] and its time of functioning. The time of production of the means of production in general comprises, therefore, 1) the time during which they function as means of production, hence serve in the productive process; 2) the stops during which the process of production, and thus the functioning of the means of production embodied in it, are interrupted; 3) the time during which they are held in readiness as prerequisites of that process, hence already represent productive capital but have not yet entered into the process of production.

The difference so far considered has in each case been the difference between the time which the productive capital stays in the sphere of production and that it stays in the process of production. But the process of production may itself be responsible for interruptions of the labour-process, and hence of the labour-time—intervals during which the subject of labour is exposed to the action of physical processes without the further intervention of human labour. The process of production, and thus the functioning of the means of production, continue in this case, although the labour-process, and thus the functioning of the means of production as instruments of labour, have been interrupted. This applies, for instance, to the grain, after it has been sown, the wine fermenting in the cellar, the labour-material of many factories, such as tanneries, where the material is exposed to the action of chemical processes. The time of production is here longer than the labour-time. The difference between the two consists in an excess of the production time over the labour-time. This excess always arises from the *latent* existence of productive capital in the sphere of production without functioning in the process of production itself or from its functioning in the productive process without taking part in the labour-process.

That part of the latent productive capital is held in readiness only as a requisite for the productive process, such as cotton, coal, etc., in a spinning-mill, acts as a creator of neither products nor value. It is fallow capital, although its fallowness is essential for the uninterrupted flow of the process of production. The buildings, apparatus, etc., necessary for the storage of the productive supply (latent capital) are conditions of the productive process and therefore constitute component parts of the advanced productive capital. They perform their function as conservators of the productive components in the preliminary stage. Inasmuch as labour-processes are necessary in this stage, they add to the cost of raw material, etc., but are productive labour and productive surplus-value, because a part of this labour, like of all other wage-labour, is not paid for. The normal interruptions of the entire process of production, the intermissions during which the productive capital does not function, create neither value nor surplus-value. Hence the desire to the work going at night, too. (Buch I, Kap. VIII, 4.) [English edition: Ch. X, 4.—*Ed.*]

The intervals in the labour-time which the subject of labour must endure in the process of production itself create neither value nor surplus-value. But they advance the product, form a part of its life, a process through which it must pass. The value of the apparatus, etc., is transferred to the product in proportion to the entire time during which they perform their function; the product is brought to this stage by labour itself, and the employment of these apparatus is as much a condition of production as is the reduction to dust of a part of the cotton which does not enter into the product but nevertheless transfers its value to the product. The other part of the latent capital, such as buildings, machinery, etc., the instruments of labour whose functioning is interrupted only by the regular pauses of the productive process—irregular interruptions caused by the restriction of production, crises, etc., are total losses—adds value without entering into the creation of the product. The total value which this part of capital adds to the product is determined by its average durability; it loses value, because it loses its use-value, both during the time that it performs its functions as well as during that in which it does not.

Finally the value of the constant part of capital, which continues in the productive process although the labour-process is interrupted, re-appears in the result of the productive process. Labour itself has here placed the means of production in conditions under which they pass of themselves through certain natural processes, the result of which is a definite useful effect or a change in the form of their use-value. Labour always transfers the value of the means of production to the product, in so far as it really consumes them in a suitable manner, as means of production. And it does not change the matter whether labour has to bear continually on its subject by means of the instruments of labour in order to produce this effect or whether it merely needs to give the first impulse by providing the means of production with conditions under which they undergo the intended alteration of themselves, in consequence of natural processes, without the further assistance of labour.

Whatever may be the reason for the excess of production time over the labour-time—whether the circumstance that means of production constitute only latent productive capital and hence are still in a stage preliminary to the actual productive process or that their own functioning is interrupted within the process of production by its pauses or finally that the process of production itself necessitates interruptions of the labour-process—in none of these cases do the means of production function as absorbers of labour. And if they do not absorb labour, they do not absorb surplus-labour, either. Hence there is no expansion of the value of productive capital so long as it stays in that part of its production time which exceeds the labour-time, no matter how inseparable from these pauses the carrying on of the process of self-expansion may be. It is plain that the more the production time and labour-time cover each other the greater is the productivity and self-expansion of a given productive capital in a given space of time. Hence the tendency of the capitalist production to reduce the excess of the production time over the labour-time as much as possible. But while the time of production of a certain capital may differ from its labour-time, it always comprises the latter, and this excess is itself a condition of the process of production. The time of production, then, is always that time in which a capital produces use-values and expands, hence functions as productive capital, although it includes time in which it is either latent or produces without expanding its value.

Within the sphere of circulation, capital abides as commodity-capital and money-capital. Its two processes of circulation consist in its transformation from the commodity-form into that of money and from the money-form into that of commodities. The circumstance that the transformation of commodities into money is here at the same time a realisation of the surplus-value embodied in the commodities, and that the transformation of money into commodities is at the same time a conversion or reconversion of capital-value into the form of its elements of production does not in the least alter the fact that these processes, as processes of circulation, are processes of the simple metamorphosis of commodities.

Time of circulation and time of production mutually exclude each other. During its time of circulation capital does not perform the functions of productive capital and therefore produces neither commodities nor surplus-value. If we study the circuit in its simplest form, as when the entire capital-value passes in one bulk from one phase into another, it becomes palpably evident that the process of production and therefore also the self-expansion of capital-value are interrupted so long as its time of circulation lasts, and that the renewal of the process of production will proceed at a faster or a slower pace depending on the length of the circulation time. But if on the contrary the various parts of capital pass through the circuit one after another, so that the circuit of the entire capital-value is accomplished successively in the circuits of its various component parts, then it is evident that the longer its aliquot parts stay in the sphere of circulation the smaller must be the part functioning in the sphere of production. The expansion and contraction of the time of circulation operate therefore as negative limits to the contraction or expansion of the time of production or of the extent to which a capital of a given size functions as productive capital. The more the metamorphoses of circulation of a certain capital are only ideal, i.e., the more the time of circulation is equal to zero, or approaches zero, the more does capital function, the more does its productivity and the self-expansion of its value increase. For instance, if a capitalist executes an order by the terms of which he receives payment on delivery of the product, and if this payment is made in his own means of production, the time of circulation approaches zero.

A capital's time of circulation therefore limits, generally speaking, its time of production and hence its process of generating surplus-value. And it limits this process in proportion to its own duration. This duration may considerably increase or decrease and hence may restrict capital's time of production in a widely varying degree. But Political Economy sees only what is apparent, namely the effect of the time of circulation on capital's process of the creation of surplus-value in general. It takes this negative effect for a positive one, because its consequences are positive. It clings the more tightly to this appearance since it seems to furnish proof that capital possesses a mystic source of self-expansion independent of its process of production and hence of the exploitation of labour, a spring which flows to it from the sphere of circulation. We shall see later that even scientific Political Economy has been deceived by this appearance of things. Various phenomena, it will turn out, give color to this semblance: 1) The capitalist method of calculating profit, in which the negative cause figures a positive one, since with capitals in different spheres of investment, where only the time of circulation are different, a longer time of circulation tends to bring about an increase in prices, in short, serves as one of the causes of equalising profits. 2) The time of circulation is but a phase of the time of turnover; the latter however includes the time of production or reproduction. What is really due to the latter seems to be due to the time of circulation. 3) The conversion of commodities into variable capital (wages) is necessitated by their previous conversion into money. In the accumulation of capital, the conversion into additional variable capital therefore takes place in the sphere of circulation, or during the time of circulation. Consequently it seems that the accumulation thus achieved is owed to the latter.

Within the sphere of circulation capital passes through the two antithetical phases C—M and M—C; it is immaterial in what order. Hence its time of circulation is likewise divided into two parts, viz.: the time it requires for its conversion from commodities into money, and that which it requires for its conversion from money into commodities. We have already learned from the analysis of simple circulation of commodities (Buch I, Kap. III) [English edition: Ch. III.—*Ed.*] that C—M, the sale, is the most difficult part of its metamorphosis and that therefore under ordinary conditions it takes up the greater part of its time of circulation. As money, value exists in its always convertible form. As a commodity it must first be transformed into money before it can assume this form of direct convertibility and hence of constant readiness for action. However, in capital's process of circulation, its phase M—C has to do with its transformation into commodities which constitute definite elements of productive capital in a given enterprise. The means of production may not be available in the market and must first be produced or they must be procured from distant markets or their ordinary supply has become irregular or prices have changed, etc., in short there are a multitude of circumstances which are not noticeable in the simple change of form M—C, but which nevertheless requires now more, now less time also for this part of the circulation phase. C—M and M—C may be separate not only in time but also in space; the market for buying and the market for selling may be located apart. In the case of factories for instance buyer and seller are frequently different persons. In the production of commodities, circulation is as necessary as production itself, so that circulation agents are just as much needed as production agents. The process of reproduction includes both functions of capital, therefore it includes the necessity of having representatives of these functions, either in the person of the capitalist himself or of wage-labourers, his agents. But this furnishes no ground for confusing the agents of circulation with those of production, any more than it furnishes ground for confusing the functions of commodity-capital and money-capital with those of productive capital. The agents of circulation must be paid by the agents of production. But the capitalists, who sell to and buy from one another, create neither values nor products by these acts, this state of affairs is not changed if they are enabled or compelled by the volume of their business to shift this function on to others. In some businesses the buyers and sellers get paid in the form of percentages on the profits. All talk about their being paid by the consumer does not help matters. The consumers can pay only in so far as they, as agents of production, produce an equivalent in commodities for themselves or appropriate it from production agents either on the basis of some legal title (as their co-partners, etc.) or by personal services.

There is a difference between C—M and M—C which has nothing to do with the difference in forms of commodities and money but arises from the capitalist character of production. Intrinsically both C—M and M—C are mere conversions of given values from one form into another. But C'—M' is at the same time a realisation of the surplus-value contained in C'. M—C however is not. Hence selling is more important than buying. Under normal conditions M—C is an act necessary for the self-expansion of the value expressed in M, but it is not a realisation of surplus-value; it is the introduction to its production, not an afterword.

The form in which a commodity exists, its existence as a use-value, sets definite limits to the circulation of commodity capital C'—M'. Use-values are perishable by nature. Hence if they are not productively or individually consumed within a certain time, depending on what they are intended for, in other words, if they are not sold within a certain period, they spoil and lose with their use-value the property of being vehicles of exchange-value. The capital-value contained in them, hence also the surplus-value accrued in it, gets lost. The use-values do not remain the carriers of perennial self-expanding capital-value unless they are constantly renewed and reproduced, are replaced by new use-values of the same or of some other order. The sale of the use-values in the form of commodities, hence their entry into productive or individual consumption effected through this sale is however the ever recurring condition of their reproduction. They must change their old use-form within a definite time in order to continue their existence in a new form. Exchange-value maintains itself only by means of this constant renewal of its body. The use-values of various commodities spoil sooner or later; the interval between their production and consumption may therefore be comparatively long or short; hence they can persist without spoiling in the circulation phase C—M for a shorter or longer term in the form of commodity-capital, can endure a shorter or a longer time of circulation as commodities. The limit of the circulation time of a commodity-capital imposed by the spoiling of the body of the commodity is the absolute limit of this part of the time of circulation, or of the time of circulation of commodity-capital as such. The more perishable a commodity and the sooner after its production it must therefore be consumed and hence sold, the more restricted is its capacity for removal from its place of production, the narrower therefore is the spatial sphere of its circulation, the more localised are the markets where it can be sold. For this reason the more perishable a commodity is and the greater the absolute restriction of its time of circulation as commodity on account of its physical properties, the less is it suited to be an object of capitalist production. Such a commodity can come within its grasp only in thickly populated districts or to the extent that improved transportation eliminate distance. But the concentration of the production of any article in the hands of a few and in a populous district may create a relatively large market even for such articles as are the products of large breweries, dairies, etc.

Notes

1. Beginning of Manuscript IV.—*F.E.*
2. Time of production is here used in the active sense: The time of production of the means of production does not mean in this case the time required for their production, but the time during which they take part in the process of production of a certain commodity.—*F.E.*

6

The Costs of Circulation

Section I. *Genuine Costs of Circulation*

(a) The Time of Purchase and Sale

The transformations of the forms of capital from commodities into money and from money into commodities are at the same time transactions of the capitalist, acts of purchase and sale. The time in which these transformations of forms take place constitutes subjectively, from the standpoint of the capitalist, the time of purchase and sale; it is the time during which he performs the functions of a seller and buyer in the market. Just as the time of circulation of capital is a necessary segment of its time of reproduction, so the time in which the capitalist buys and sells and scours the market is a necessary part of the time in which he functions as a capitalist, i.e., as personified capital. It is a part of his business hours.

[Since we have assumed that commodities are bought and sold at their values, these acts constitute merely the conversion of a certain value from one form into another, from the commodity-form into the money-form or from the money-form into the commodity-form—a change in the state of being. If commodities are sold at their values, then the magnitudes of value in the hands of the buyer and seller remain unchanged. Only the form of existence of value is changed. If the commodities are not sold at their values, then the sum of the converted values remains unchanged; the plus on one side is a minus on the other.

The metamorphoses C—M and M—C are transactions between buyers and sellers; they require time to conclude bargains, the more so as the struggle goes on in which each seeks to get the best of the other, and it is businessmen who face one another here; and **'when Greek meets Greek then comes the tug of war.'** [A paraphrase of words from the 17th century tragedy *The Rival Queens, or the Death of Alexander the Great by Nathaniel Lee.—Ed.*] To effect a change in the state of being costs of time and labour-power, not for the purpose of creating value, however, but in order to accomplish the conversion of value from one form into another. The mutual attempt to appropriate an extra slice of this value on this occasion changes nothing. This labour, increased by the evil designs on either side, creates no value, any more than the work performed in a judicial proceeding increases the value of the subject matter of the suit. Matters stand with this labour—which is a necessary element in the capitalist process of production as a whole, including circulation or included by it—as they stand, say, with the work of combustion of some substance used for the generation of heat. This work of combustion does not generate any heat, although it is a necessary element in the process of combustion. In order, e.g., to consume coal as fuel, I must combine it with oxygen, and for this purpose must transform it from the solid into the gaseous state (for in the carbonic acid gas, the result of the combustion, coal is in the gaseous state); consequently, I must bring about a physical change in the form of its existence or in its state of being. The separation of carbon molecules, which are united into a solid mass, and the splitting up of these molecules into their separate atoms must precede the new combination, and this requires a certain expenditure of energy which thus is not transformed into heat but taken from it. Therefore, if the owners of the commodities are not capitalists but independent direct producers, the time employed in buying and selling is a diminution of their labour-time, and for this reason such transactions used to be deferred (in ancient and medieval times) to holidays.

Of course the dimensions assumed by the conversion of commodities in the hands of the capitalists cannot transform this labour—which does not create any value—into labour productive of value. Nor can the miracle of this transubstantiation be accomplished by a transposition, i.e., by the industrial capitalist making this 'work of combustion' the exclusive business of third persons, who are paid by them, instead of performing it themselves. This third persons will of course not tender their labour-power to the capitalist out of sheer love for them. It is a matter of indifference to the rent collector of a real-estate owner or the messenger of a bank that their labour does not add one iota or tittle to the value of either the rent or the gold pieces carried to another bank by the bagful.][1]

To the capitalist who has others working for him, buying and selling becomes a primary function. Since he appropriates the product of many on a large social scale, he must sell it on the same scale and then reconvert it from money into elements of production. Now as before neither the time of purchase nor of sale creates any value. The function of merchant's capital gives rise to an illusion. But without going into this at length here this much is plain from the start: If by a division of labour a function, unproductive in itself although a necessary element of reproduction, is transformed from an incidental occupation of many into an exclusive occupation of a few, into their special business, the nature of this function itself is not changed. *One* merchant (here considered a mere agent attending to the change of form of commodities, a mere buyer and seller) may by his operations shorten the time of purchase and sale for *many* producers. In such case he should be regarded as a machine which reduces useless expenditure of energy or helps to set production time free.[2]

In order to simplify the matter (since we shall not discuss the merchant as a capitalist and merchant's capital until later) we shall assume that this buying and selling agent is a man who sells his labour. He expends his labour-power and labour-time in the operations C—M and M—C. And he makes his living that way, just as another does by spinning or making pills. He performs a necessary function, because the process of reproduction itself includes unproductive functions. He works as well as the next man, but intrinsically his labour creates neither value nor product. He belongs himself to the *faux frais* of production. His usefulness does not consist in transforming an unproductive function into a productive one, nor unproductive into productive labour. It would be a miracle if such transformation could be accomplished by the mere transfer of a function. His usefulness consists rather in the fact that a smaller part of society's labour-power and labour-time is tied up in this unproductive function. More. We shall assume that he is a mere wage-labourer, even one of the better paid, for all the difference it makes. Whatever his pay, as a wage-labourer he works part of his time for nothing. He may receive daily the value of the product of eight working-hours, yet functions ten. But the two hours of surplus-labour he performs do not produce value anymore than his eight hours of necessary labour, although by means of the latter a part of the social product is transferred to him. In the first place, looking at it from the standpoint of society, labour-power is used up now as before for ten hours in a mere function of circulation. It cannot be used for anything else, not for productive labour. In the second place however society does not pay for those two hours of surplus-labour, although they are spent by the individual who performs this labour. Society does not appropriate any extra product or value thereby. But the costs of circulation, which he represents, are reduced by one-fifth, from ten hours to eight. Society does not pay any equivalent for one-fifth of this active time of circulation, of which he is the agent. But if this man is employed by a capitalist, then the non-payment of these two hours reduces the cost of circulation of *his* capital, which constitutes a deduction from his income. For the capitalist this is a positive gain, because the negative limit for the self-expansion of his capital-value is thereby reduced. So long as small independent producers of commodities spend a part of their own time in buying and selling, this represents nothing but time spent during the intervals between their productive function or diminution of their time of production.

At all events, the time consumed for this purpose constitutes one of the costs of circulation which adds nothing to the converted values. It is the cost of converting them from the commodity-form into the money-form. The capitalist producer of commodities acting as an agent of circulation differs from the direct producer of commodities only in the fact that he buys and sells on a larger scale and therefore his function as such agent assumes greater dimensions. And if the volume of his business compels or enables him to buy (hire) circulation agents of his own to serve as wage-labourers, the nature of the case is not changed thereby. A certain amount of labour-power and labour-time must be expended in the process of circulation (so far as it is merely a change of form). But this now appears as an additional investment of capital. A part of the variable capital must be laid out in the purchase of this labour-power functioning only in circulation. This advance capital creates neither product nor value. It reduces *pro tanto* the dimensions in which the advanced capital functions productively. It is as though one part of the product were transformed into a machine which buys and sells the rest of the product. This machine brings about a reduction of the product. It does not participate in the productive process, although it can diminish the labour-power, etc., spent on circulation. It constitutes merely a part of the costs of circulation.

(b) Book-keeping

Apart from the actual buying and selling, labour-time is expended on book-keeping, which besides absorbs materialised labour such as pens, ink, paper, desks, office paraphernalia. This function, therefore, exacts the expenditure on the one hand of labour-power and on the other of instruments of labour. It is the same condition of things as obtained in the case of the time of purchase and sale.

As unity within its circuits, as value in motion, whether in the sphere of production or in either phase of the sphere of circulation, capital exists ideally only in the form of money of account, primarily in the mind of the producer of commodities, the capitalist producer of commodities. This movement is fixed and controlled by book-keeping, which includes the determination of prices, or the calculation of the prices of commodities. The movement of production, especially of the production of surplus-value—in which the commodities figure only as depositories of value, as the names of things whose ideal existence as values is crystallised in money of account—thus is symbolically reflected in imagination. So long as the individual producer of commodities keeps account only in his head (for instance, a peasant; the book-keeping tenant-farmer was not produced until the rise of capitalist agriculture), or books his expenditures, receipts, due dates of payments, etc., only incidentally, outside of his production time, it is palpably clear that this function and the instruments of labour consumed by it, such as paper, etc., represent additional consumption of labour-time and instruments which are necessary, but constitute a deduction from the time available for productive consumption as well as from the instruments of labour which functions in the real process of production, enter into the creation of products and value.[3] The nature of the function is not changed—neither by the dimensions which it assumes on account of its concentration in the hands of the capitalist producer of commodities and the fact that instead of appearing as the function of many small commodity-producers it appears as the function of *one* capitalist, as a function within a process of large-scale production; nor is it altered by its divorcement from those productive functions of which it formed an appendage, nor by its conversion into an independent function of special agents exclusively entrusted with it.

Division of labour and assumption of independence do not make a function one that creates products and value if it was not so intrinsically, hence before it became independent. If a capitalist invests his capital anew, he must invest a part of it in hiring a book-keeper, etc., and in the wherewithal of book-keeping. If his capital is already functioning, is engaged in the process of its own constant reproduction, he must continually reconvert a part of his product into a book-keeper, clerks, and the like, by transforming that part into money. That part of his capital is withdrawn from the process of production and belongs in the costs of circulation, deductions from the total yield (including the labour-power itself that is expended exclusively for this function).

But there is a certain difference between the costs incidental to book-keeping, or the unproductive expenditure of labour-time on the one hand and those of mere buying and selling time on the other. The latter arise only from the definite social form of the process of production, from the fact that it is the process of production of commodities. Book-keeping, as the control and ideal synthesis of the process, becomes the more necessary the more the process assumes a social scale and loses its purely individual character. It is therefore more necessary in capitalist production than in the scattered production of handicraft and peasant economy, more necessary in collective production than in capitalist production. But the costs of book-keeping drop as production becomes concentrated and book-keeping becomes social.

We are concerned here only with the general character of the costs of circulation, which arise out of the metamorphosis of forms alone. It is superfluous to discuss here all their forms in detail. But how forms which belong in the sphere of pure changes of the form of value and hence originate from the particular social form of the process of production, forms which in the case of the individual commodity-producer are only transient, barely perceptible elements, run alongside his productive functions or become intertwined with them—how these can strike the eye as the huge costs of circulation can be seen from just the money taken in and paid out when these operations have become independent and concentrated on a large scale as the exclusive function of banks, etc., or of cashiers in individual businesses. But it must be firmly borne in mind that these costs of circulation are not changed in character by their change in appearance.

(c) Money

Whether a product is fabricated as a commodity or not, it is always a material form of wealth, a use-value intended for individual or productive consumption. Its value as a commodity is ideally expressed in its price, which does not change its actual use-form in the least. But the fact that certain commodities like gold and silver function as money and as such reside exclusively in the process of circulation (even in the form of hoards, reserve funds, etc., they remain in the sphere of circulation, although latently) is a pure product of the particular social form of the process of production, the process of production of commodities. Since under capitalist production products assume the general form of commodities, and the overwhelming mass of products is created as commodities and must therefore assume the form of money, and since the vast bulk of commodities, the part of social wealth functioning as commodities, grows continually, it follows that the quantity of gold and silver functioning as means of circulation, paying medium, reserve fund, etc., likewise increases. These commodities performing the function of money enter into neither individual nor productive consumption. They represent social labour in a fixed form in which it serves as a mere circulation machine. Besides the fact that a part of social wealth has been condemned to assume this unproductive form, the wearing down of the money demands its constant replacement, or the conversion of more social labour, in the form of products, into more gold and silver. These replacement costs are considerable in capitalistically developed nations, because in general the portion of wealth tied up in the form of money is tremendous. Gold and silver as money-commodities mean circulation costs to society which arise solely out of the social form of production. They are *faux frais* of commodity production in general, and they increase with the development of this production, especially of capitalist production. They represent a part of the social wealth that must be sacrificed to the process of circulation.[4]

Section II. *Costs of Storage*

Costs of circulation, which originate in a mere change of form of value, in circulation, ideally considered, do not enter into the value of commodities. The parts of capital expended as such costs are merely deductions from the productively expended capital so far as the capitalist is concerned. The costs of circulation which we shall consider now are of a different nature. They may arise from processes of production which are only continued in circulation, the productive character of which is hence merely concealed by the circulation form. On the other hand they may be, from the standpoint of society, mere costs, unproductive expenditure of living or materialised labour, but for that very reason they become productive of value for the individual capitalist, may constitute an addition to the selling price of his commodities. This already follows from the fact that these costs are different in different spheres of production, and here and there even for different individual capitals in one and the same sphere of production. By being added to the prices of commodities they are distributed in proportion to the amount to be borne by each individual capitalist. But all labour which adds value can also add surplus-value, and will always add surplus-value under capitalist production, as the value created by labour depends on the amount of the labour itself, whereas the surplus-value created by it depends on the extent to which the capitalist pays for it. Consequently, costs which enhance the price of a commodity without adding to its use-value, which therefore are to be classed as unproductive expenses so far as society is concerned, may be a source of enrichment to the individual capitalist. On the other hand, as this addition to the price of the commodity merely distributes these costs of circulation equally, they do not thereby cease to be unproductive in character. For instance, insurance companies divide the losses of individual capitalists among the capitalist class. But this does not prevent these equalised losses from remaining losses so far as the aggregate social capital is concerned.

(a) Formation of Supply in General

During its existence as commodity-capital or its stay in the market, in other words, during the interval between the process of production, from which it emerges, and the process of consumption, into which it enters, the product constitutes a commodity supply. As a commodity in the market, and therefore in the shape of a supply, commodity-capital figures in a dual capacity in each circuit: one time as the commodity-product of that capital in process whose circuit is being examined; the other time however as the commodity-product of another capital, which must be available in the market to be bought and converted into productive capital. It is, indeed, possible that this last-named commodity-capital is not produced until ordered. In that event an interruption occurs until it has been produced. But the flow of the process of production and reproduction requires that a certain mass of commodities (means of production) should always be in the market, should therefore form a supply. Productive capital likewise comprises the purchase of labour-power, and the money-form is here only the value-form of the means of subsistence, the greater part of which the labourer must find at hand in the market. We shall discuss this more in detail further on in this paragraph. But at this point the following is already clear: As far as concerns capital-value in process which has been transformed into a commodity and must now be sold or reconverted into money, which therefore functions for the moment as commodity-capital in the market, the condition in which it constitutes a supply is to be described as an inexpedient, involuntary stay there. The quicker the sale is effected the more smoothly runs the process of reproduction. Delay in the form of conversion of C'—M' impedes the real exchange of matter which must take place in the circuit of capital, as well as its further functioning as productive capital. On the other hand, so far as M—C is concerned, the constant presence of commodities in the market, commodity-supply, appears as a condition of the flow of the process of reproduction and of the investment of new or additional capital.

The abidance of the commodity-capital as a commodity-supply in the market requires buildings, stores, storage places, warehouses, in other words, an expenditure of constant capital; furthermore the payment of labour-power for placing the commodities in storage. Besides, commodities spoil and are exposed to the injurious influences of the elements. Additional capital must be invested, partly in instruments of labour, in material form, and partly in labour-power to protect the commodities against the above.[5]

Thus the existence of capital in its form of commodity-capital and hence of commodity-supply gives rise to costs which must be classed as costs of circulation, since they do not come within the sphere of production. These costs of circulation differ from those mentioned under I by the fact that they enter to a certain extent into the value of the commodities, i.e., they increase the prices of commodities. At all events the capital and labour-power which serve the need of preserving and storing the commodity-supply are withdrawn from the direct process of production. On the other hand, the capitals thus employed, including labour-power as a constituent of capital, must be replaced out of the social product. Their expenditure has therefore the effect of diminishing the productive power of labour, so that a greater amount of capital and labour is required to obtain a particular useful effect. They are *unproductive costs.*

As the costs of circulation necessitated by the formation of a commodity-supply are due merely to the time required for the conversion of existing values from the commodity-form into the money-form, hence merely to the particular social form of the production process (i.e., are due only to the fact that the product is brought forth as a commodity and must therefore undergo the transformation into money), these costs completely share the character of the circulation costs enumerated under I. On the other hand, the value of the commodities is here preserved or increased only because the use-value, the product itself, is placed in definite material conditions which cost capital outlay and is subjected to operations which bring additional labour to bear on the use-values. However the computation of the values of commodities, the book-keeping incidental to this process, the transactions of purchase and sale, do not affect the use-value in which the commodity-value exists. They have to do only with the form of the commodity-value. Although in the case submitted [i.e., Corbet's calculations given in Footnote 14.—*Ed.*] the costs of forming a supply (which is here done involuntarily) arise only from a delay in the change of form and from its necessity, still these costs differ from those mentioned under I, in that their purpose is not a change in the form of the value, but the preservation of the value existing in the commodity as a product, a utility, and which cannot be preserved in any other way than by preserving the product, the use-value, itself. The use-value is neither raised nor increased here; on the contrary, it diminishes. But its diminution is restricted and it is preserved. Neither is the advanced value contained in the commodity increased here; but new labour, materialised and living, is added.

We have now to investigate furthermore to what extent these costs arise from the peculiar nature of commodity production in general and from commodity production in its general, absolute form, i.e., capitalist commodity production; and to what extent on the other hand they are common to all social production and merely assume a special shape, a special form of appearance, in capitalist production.

Adam Smith entertained the splendid notion that the formation of a supply was a phenomenon peculiar to capitalist production.[6] More recent economists, for instance Lalor, insist on the contrary that it declines with the development of capitalist production. [See: J. Lalor, Money and Morals: A Book for the Times, London, 1852, pp. 43-44.—*Ed.*] Sismondi even regards it as one of the drawbacks of the latter. [See: J.C.L. Sismonde de Sismondi, *Etudes sur l'èconomie politique*, Tome I. Bruxelles, 1837, p. 49, etc.—*Ed.*]

As a matter of fact, supplies exist in three forms: in the form of productive capital, in the form a fund for individual consumption, and in the form of a commodity-supply or commodity-capital. The supply in one form decreases relatively when it increases in another, although its quantity may increase absolutely in all three forms simultaneously.

It is plain from the outset that wherever production is carried on for the direct satisfaction of the needs of the producer and only to a minor extent for exchange or sale, hence where the social product does not assume the form of commodities at all or only to a rather small degree, the supply in the form of commodities, or commodity-supply, forms only a small and insignificant part of wealth. But here the consumption-fund is relatively large, especially that of the means of subsistence proper. One need but take a look at old-fashioned peasant economy. There the overwhelming part of the product is transformed directly into supplies of means of production or means of subsistence, without becoming supplies of commodities, for the very reason that it remains in the hands of its owner. It does not assume the form of a commodity-supply and for this reason Adam Smith declares that there is no supply in societies based on this mode of production. He confuses the form of the supply with the supply itself and believes that society hitherto lived from hand to mouth or trusted to the hap of the morrow.[7] This is a naive misunderstanding.

A supply in the form of productive capital exists in the shape of means of production, which already are in the process of production or at least in the hands of the producer, hence latently already in the process of production. It was seen previously that with the development of the productivity of labour and therefore also with the development of the capitalist mode of production—there is a steady increase in the mass of means of production (buildings, machinery, etc.) which are embodied once and for all in the process in the form of instruments of labour, and perform with steady repetition their function in it for a longer or shorter time. It was also observed that this increase is at the same time the premise and consequence of the development of the social productive power of labour. The growth, not only absolute but relative, of wealth in this form (cf. Buch I, Kap XXIII, 2) [English edition: Ch. XXV, 2.—*Ed.*] is characteristic above all of the capitalist mode of production. The material forms of existence of constant capital, the means of production, do not however consist only of such instruments of labour but also of materials of labour in various stages of processing, and of auxiliary materials. With the enlargement of the scale of production and the increase in the productive power of labour through co-operation, division of labour, machinery, etc., grows the quantity of raw materials, auxiliary materials, etc., entering into the daily process of reproduction. These elements must be ready at hand in the place of production. The volume of this supply existing in the form of productive capital increases therefore absolutely, in order that the process may keep going—apart from the fact whether this supply can be renewed daily or only at fixed intervals—there must always be a greater accumulation of ready raw material, etc., at the place of production than is used up, say, daily or weekly. The continuity of the process requires that the presence of its conditions should not be jeopardised by possible interruptions when making purchases daily, nor depend on whether the product is sold daily or weekly, and hence is reconvertible into its elements of production only irregularly. But it is evident that productive capital may be latent or form a supply in quite different proportions. There is for instance a great difference whether the spinning-mill owner must have on hand a supply of cotton or coal for three months or for one. Patently this supply, while increasing absolutely, may decrease relatively.

This depends on various conditions, all of which practically amount to a demand for greater rapidity, regularity, and reliability in furnishing the necessary amount of raw material, so that no interruption will ever occur. The less these conditions are complied with, hence the less rapid, regular and reliable the supplies, the greater must be the latent part of the productive capital, that is to say, the supply of raw material, etc., in the hands of the producer waiting to be worked up. These conditions are inversely proportional to the degree of development of capitalist production, and hence of the productive power of social labour. The same applies therefore to the supply in this form.

However that which appears here as a decrease of the supply (for instance, in Lalor) is in part merely a decrease of the supply in the form of commodity-capital, or of the commodity-supply proper; it is consequently only a change of form of the same supply. If for instance the quantity of coal daily produced in a certain country, and therefore the scale and energy of operation of the coal industry, are great, the spinner does not need a large store of coal in order to ensure the continuity of his production. The steady and certain renewal of his coal supply makes this unnecessary. In the second place, the rapidity with which the product of one process may be transferred as means of production to another process depends on the development of the transport and communication facilities. The cheapness of transportation is of great importance in this question. The continually renewed transport of coal from the mine to the spinning-mill for instance would be more expensive than the storing up of a larger supply of coal for a longer time when the price of transportation is relatively cheaper. These two circumstances examined so far arise from the process of production itself. In the third place the development of the credit-system also exerts an influence. The less the spinner is dependent on the direct sale of his yarn for the renewal of his supply of cotton, coal, etc.—and this direct dependence will be the smaller, the more developed the credit-system is—the smaller relatively these supplies can be and yet ensure a continuous production of yarn on a given scale, a production independent of the hazards of the sale of yarn. In the fourth place, however, many raw materials, semi-finished goods, etc., require long periods of time for their production. This applies especially to all raw materials furnished by agriculture. If no interruption of the process of production is to take place, a certain amount of raw materials must be on hand for the entire period in which no new products can take the place of the old. If this supply decreases in the hands of the industrial capitalist, it proves merely that it increases in the hands of the merchant in the form of commodity-supply. The development of transportation, for instance, makes it possible rapidly to ship the cotton lying, say, in Liverpool's import warehouses to Manchester, so that the manufacturer can renew his supply in comparatively small portions, as and when needed. But in that case the cotton remains in so much larger quantities as commodity-supply in the hands of the Liverpool merchants. It is therefore merely a change in the form of the supply, and this Lalor and others overlooked. And if you consider the social capital, the same quantity of products exists in either case in the form of supply. The quantity required for a single country during the period of, say, one year decreases as transportation improves. If a large number of sailing vessels and steamers ply between America and England, England's opportunities to renew its cotton supply are increased while the average quantity to be held in storage in England decreases. The same effect is produced by the development of the world market and the consequent multiplication of the sources of supply of the same merchandise. The article is supplied piecemeal from various countries and at various intervals.

(b) The Commodity-Supply Proper

We have already seen that under capitalist production the product assumes the general form of a commodity, and the more so the more that production grows in size and depth. Consequently, even if production retains the same volume, the far greater part of the products exists in the shape of commodities, compared with either the former modes of production or the capitalist mode of production at a less developed stage. And every commodity—therefore, also every commodity-capital, which is only commodities, but commodities serving as the form of existence of capital-value—constitutes an element of the commodity-supply, unless it passes immediately from its sphere of production into productive or individual consumption, that is, does not lie in the market in the interval. If the volume of production remains the same, the commodity-supply (i.e., this isolation and fixation of the commodity-form of the product) grows therefore of itself concomitantly with capitalist production. We have seen above that this is merely a change of form of the supply, that is to say, the supply in the form of commodities increases on the one hand because on the other the supply in the form intended directly for production or consumption decreases. It is merely a changed social form of the supply. If at the same time it is not only the relative magnitude of the commodity-supply compared with the aggregate social product that increases but also its absolute magnitude, that is so because the mass of the aggregate product grows with the growth of capitalist production.

With the development of capitalist production, the scale of production is determined less and less by the direct demand for the product and more and more by the amount of capital available in the hands of the individual capitalist, by the urge of self-expansion inherent in his capital and by the need of continuity and expansion of the process of production. Thus in each particular branch of production there is a necessary increase in the mass of products available in the market in the shape of commodities, i.e., in search of buyers. The amount of capital fixed for a shorter or longer period in the form of commodity-capital grows. Hence the commodity-supply also grows.

Finally the majority of the members of society are transformed into wage-labourers, into people who live from hand to mouth, who receive their wages weekly and spend them daily, who therefore must have their means of subsistence made available to them in the shape of a supply. Although the separate elements of this supply may be in continuous flow, a part of them must always stagnate in order that the supply as a whole may remain in a state of flux.

All these characteristics have their origin in the form of production and in the incident change of form which the product must undergo in the process of circulation.

Whatever may be the social form of the products-supply, its preservation requires outlays for buildings, vessels, etc., which are facilities for storing the product; also for means of production and labour, more or less of which must be expended, according to the nature of the product, in order to combat injurious influences. The more concentrated socially the supply is, the smaller relatively are the costs. These outlays always constitute a part of the social labour, in either materialised or living form—hence in the capitalist form outlays of capital—which do not enter into the formation of the product itself and thus are deductions from the product. They are necessary, these unproductive expenses of social wealth. They are the costs of preserving the social product regardless of whether its existence as an element of the commodity-supply stems merely from the social form of production, hence from the commodity-form and its necessary change of form, or whether we regard the commodity-supply merely as a special form of the supply of products, which is common to all societies, although not in the form of a *commodity*-supply that form of products-supply belonging in the process of circulation.

It may now be asked to what extent these costs enhance the value of commodities.

If the capitalist has converted the capital advanced by him in the form of means of production and labour-power into a product, into a definite quantity of commodities ready for sale, and these commodities remain in stock unsold, then we have a case of not only the stagnation of the process of self-expansion of his capital-value during this period. The costs of preserving this supply in buildings, of additional labour, etc., mean a positive loss. The buyer he would ultimately find would laugh in his face if he were to say to him: 'I could not sell my goods for six months, and their preservation during that period did not only keep so and so much of my capital idle, but also cost me so and so much extra expense.' '*Tant pis pour vous!*' the buyer would say. 'Right here alongside of you is another seller whose wares were completed only the day before yesterday. Your articles are shop-worn and probably more or less damaged by the ravages of time. Therefore you will have to sell cheaper than your competitor.'

The conditions under which a commodity exists are not in the least affected by whether its producer is the real producer or a capitalist producer, hence actually only a representative of the real producer. He has to turn his product into money. The expenses incurred by him because of the fixation of the product in the form of commodities are a part of his individual speculations with which the buyer of the commodities has no concern. The latter does not pay him for the time of circulation of his commodities. Even when the capitalist keeps his goods intentionally off the market, in times of an actual or anticipated revolution of values, it depends on the advent of this revolution of values, on the correctness or incorrectness of his speculation, whether he will recover his additional costs or not. But the revolution in values does not ensue in consequence of his additional costs. Hence in so far as the formation of a supply entails a stagnation of circulation, the expense incurred thereby does not add to the value of the commodities. On the other hand, there cannot be any supply without a stay in the sphere of circulation, without capital staying for a longer or shorter time in its commodity-form; hence no supply without stagnation of circulation, just as no money can circulate without the formation of a money-reserve. Hence no commodity circulation without commodity-supply. If the capitalist does not come face to face with this necessity in C'—M', he will encounter it in M—C; if not with regard to his own commodity-capital, then with regard to that of other capitalists, who produce means of production for him and means of subsistence for his labourers.

Whether the formation of a supply is voluntary or involuntary, that is to say, whether the commodity-producer keeps a supply intentionally or whether his products form a supply in consequence of the sales resistance offered by the conditions of the process of circulation itself cannot effect the matter essentially, it would seem. But for the solution of this problem it is useful to know what distinguishes voluntary from involuntary supply formation. Involuntary formation arises from, or is identical with, a stagnation of the circulation which is independent of the knowledge of the commodity-producer and thwarts his will. And what characterises the voluntary formation of a supply? In both instances the seller seeks to get rid of his commodity as fast as ever. He always offers his product for sale as a commodity. If he were to withdraw it from sale, it would be only a potential (δυνάμει), not an actual (ἐναγεία) element of the commodity-supply. To him the commodity as such is as much a depository of exchange-value as ever and as such can act only by and after stripping off its commodity-form and assuming the money-form.

The commodity-supply must be of a certain volume in order to satisfy the demand during a given period. A continual extension of the circle of buyers is counted upon. For instance, in order to last for one day, a part of the commodities in the market must constantly remain in the commodity-form while the remainder is fluent, turns into money. True, the part which stagnates while the rest is fluent decreases steadily, just as the size of the supply itself decreases until it is all sold. The stagnation of commodities thus counts as a requisite condition of their sale. The volume must furthermore be larger than the average sale or the average demand. Otherwise the excess over these averages could not be satisfied. On the other hand the supply must constantly be renewed, because it is constantly being drawn on. This renewal cannot come from anywhere in the last instance except from production, from a supply of commodities. It is immaterial whether this comes from abroad or not. The renewal depends on the periods required by the commodities for their reproduction. The commodity-supply must last the whole time. The fact that it does not remain in the hands of the original producer but passes through various reservoirs, from the wholesaler to the retailer, changes merely the appearance and not the nature of the thing. From the point of view of society, a part of the capital retains in both instances the form of a commodity-supply until the commodities enter productive or individual consumption. The producer tries to keep a stock corresponding to his average demand in order not to depend directly on production and to ensure for himself a steady clientele. Purchase periods corresponding to the periods of production are formed and the commodities constitute supplies for longer or shorter time, until they can be replaced by new commodities of the same kind. Constancy and continuity of the process of circulation, and therefore of the process of reproduction, which includes the process of circulation, are safeguarded only by the formation of such supplies.

It must be remembered that C'—M' may have been transacted for the producer of C, even if C is still in the market. If the producer were to keep his own commodities in stock until they are sold to the ultimate consumer, he would have to set two capitals in motion, one as the producer of the commodities and one as a merchant. As far as the commodity itself is concerned, whether we look upon it as an individual commodity or as a component part of social capital, it is immaterial whether the costs of forming the supply must be borne by its producer or by a series of merchants from A to Z.

Since the commodity-supply is nothing but the commodity-form of the product which at a particular level of social production would exist either as a productive supply (latent production fund) or as a consumption-fund (reserve of means of consumption) if it did not exist as a commodity-supply, the expenses required for its preservation, that is, the costs of supply formation—i.e., materialised or living labour spent for this purpose—are merely expenses incurred for maintaining either the social fund for production or the social fund for consumption. The increase in the value of commodities caused by them distributes these costs simply *pro rata* over the different commodities, since the costs differ with different kinds of commodities. And the costs of supply formation are as much as ever deductions from the social wealth, although they constitute one of the conditions of its existence.

Only to the extent that the commodity-supply is a premise of commodity circulation and is itself a form necessarily arising in commodity circulation, only in so far as this apparent stagnation is therefore a form of the movement itself, just as the formation of a money-reserve is a premise of money circulation—only to that extent is such stagnation normal. But as soon as the commodities lying in the reservoirs of circulation do not make room for the swiftly succeeding wave of production, so that the reservoirs become overstocked, the commodity-supply expands in consequence of the stagnation in circulation just as the hoards increase when money-circulation is clogged. It does not make any difference whether this jam occurs in the warehouses of the industrial capitalist or in the storerooms of the merchant. The commodity-supply is in that case not a prerequisite of uninterrupted sale, but a consequence of the impossibility of selling the goods. The costs are the same, but since they now arise purely out of the form, that is to say, out of the necessity of transforming the commodities into money and out of the difficulty of going through this metamorphosis, they do not enter into the values of the commodities but constitute deductions, losses of value in the realisation of the value. Since the normal and abnormal forms of the supply do not differ in form and both clog circulation, these phenomena may be confused and deceive the agent of production himself so much the more since for the producer the process of circulation of his capital may continue while that of his commodities which have changed hands and now belong to merchants may be arrested. If production and consumption swell, other things being equal, then the commodity-supply swells likewise. It is renewed and absorbed just as fast, but its size is greater. Hence the bulging size of the commodity-supply, for which stagnant circulation is responsible, may be mistaken for a symptom of the expansion of the process of reproduction, especially when the development of the credit-system makes it possible to wrap the real movement in mystery.

The costs of supply formation consist: 1) of a quantitative diminution of the mass of the products (for instance in the case of a flour supply; 2) of a deterioration of quality; 3) of the materialised and living labour required for the preservation of the supply.

Section III. *Costs of Transportation*

It is not necessary to go here into all the details of the costs of circulation, such as packing, sorting, etc. The general law is that *all costs of circulation, which arise only from changes in the forms of commodities do not add to their value*. They are merely expenses incurred in the realisation of the value or in its conversion from one form into another. The capital spent to meet those costs (including the labour done under its control) belongs among the *faux frais* of capitalist production. They must be replaced from the surplus-product and constitute, as far as the entire capitalist class is concerned, a deduction from the surplus-value or surplus-product, just as the time a labourer needs for the purchase of his means of subsistence is lost time. But the costs of transportation play a too important part to pass them by without a few brief remarks.

Within the circuit of capital and the metamorphosis of commodities, which forms a part of the circuit, an interchange of matter takes place in social labour. This interchange of matter may necessitate a change of location of products, their real motion from one place to another. Still, circulation of commodities can take place without physical motion by them, and there can be transportation of products without circulation of commodities, and even without a direct exchange of products. A house sold by A to B does not wander from one place to another, although it circulates as a commodity. Movable commodity-values, such as cotton or pig iron, may lie in the same storage dump at a time when they are passing through dozens of circulation processes, are bought and resold by speculators.[8] What really does move here is the title of ownership in goods, not the goods themselves. On the other hand, transportation played a prominent role in the land of the Incas, although the social product neither circulated as a commodity nor was distributed by means of barter.

Consequently, although the transportation industry when based on capitalist production appears as a cause of circulation costs, this special form of appearance does not alter the matter in the least.

Quantities of products are not increased by transportation. Nor, with a few exceptions, is the possible alteration of their natural qualities, brought about by transportation, an intentional useful effect; it is rather an unavoidable evil. But the use-value of things is materialised only in their consumption, and their consumption may necessitate a change of location of these things, hence may require an additional process of production, in the transport industry. The productive capital invested in this industry imparts value to the transported products, partly by transferring value from the means of transportation, partly by adding value through the labour performed in transport. This last-named increment of value consists, as it does in all capitalist production, of a replacement of wages and of surplus-value.

Within each process of production, a great role is played by the change of location of the subject of labour and the required instruments of labour and labour-power—such as cotton trucked from the carding to the spinning room or coal hoisted from the shaft to the surface. The transition of the finished product as finished goods from one independent place of production to another located at a distance shows the same phenomenon, only on a larger scale. The transport of products from one productive establishment to another is furthermore followed by the passage of the finished products from the sphere of production to that of consumption. The product is not ready for consumption until it has completed these movements.

As was shown above, the general law of commodity production holds: The productivity of labour is inversely proportional to the value created by it. This is true of the transport industry as well as of any other. The smaller the amount of dead and living labour required for the transportation of commodities over a certain distance, the greater the productive power of labour, and vice versa.[9]

The absolute magnitude of the value which transportation adds to the commodities stands in inverse proportion to the productive power of the transport industry and in direct proportion to the distance traveled, other conditions remaining the same.

The relative part of the value added to the prices of commodities by the costs of transportation, other conditions remaining the same, is directly proportional to their cubic content and weight, and inversely proportional to their value. But there are many modifying factors. Transportation requires, for instance, more or less important precautionary measures, and therefore more or less expenditure of labour and instruments of labour, depending on how fragile, perishable, explosive, etc., the articles are. Here the railway kings show greater ingenuity in the invention of fantastic species than do botanists and zoologists. The classification of goods on English railways, for example, fills volumes and, in principle, rests on the general tendency to transform the diversified natural properties of goods into just as many ills of transportation and routine pretexts for fraudulent charges.

> 'Glass, which was formerly worth £11 per crate, is now worth only £2 since the improvements which have taken place in manufactures, and since the abolition of the duty; but the rate for carriage is the same as it was formerly, and higher than it was previously, when carried by canal. Formerly, manufacturers inform me that they had glass and glass wares for the plumbers' trade carried at about 10 s. per ton, within 50 miles of Birmingham. At the present time, the rate to cover risk of breakage is three times that amount... The companies always resist any claim that is made for breakages.'[10]

The fact that furthermore the part of the value added to an article by the costs of transportation is inversely proportional to its value furnishes special grounds to the railway kings to tax articles in direct proportion to their values. The complaints of the industrialists and merchants on this score are found on every page of the testimony given in the report quoted.

The capitalist mode of production reduces the costs of transportation of the individual commodity by the development of the means of transportation and communication, as well as by concentration—increasing scale—of transportation. It increases that part of the living and materialised social labour which is expended in the transport of commodities, firstly by converting the great majority of all products into commodities, secondly, by substituting distant for local markets.

The circulation, i.e., the actual locomotion of commodities in space, resolves itself into the transport of commodities. The transport industry forms on the one hand an independent branch of production and thus a separate sphere of investment of productive capital. On the other hand its distinguishing feature is that it appears as a continuation of a process of production *within* the process of circulation and *for* the process of circulation.

Notes

1. The bracketed text is taken from a note at the end of Manuscript VIII.—*F.E.*
2. 'The costs of commerce, although necessary, must be regarded as an onerous outlay.' (Quesnay, *Analyse du Tableau économique*, in Daire, *Physiocrates*, Part I, Paris, 1846, p. 71.) According to Quesnay, the 'profit' which the competition among merchants produces, in that it compels them to 'content themselves with a smaller reward or gain ... is, strictly speaking, nothing but a *prevention of loss* (privation de perte) for the seller at first hand and for the buyer-consumer. Now, a prevention of loss on the costs of commerce is not a *real product* or an accession of wealth through commerce. If considered simply as an exchange, whether with or without the cost of transportation.' (pp. 145 and 146.) 'The costs of commerce are always paid by those who sell the products and who would enjoy the full prices paid for them by the buyers, if there were no intermediate expenses.' (p. 163.) The proprietors and producers are '*salariants*' (payers of wages), the merchants are '*salariès*' (recipients of wages). (p.164, Quesnay, *Dialogues sur le Commerce et sur les Travaux des Artisans*. In Daire, *Physiocrates*, Part I, Paris, 1846.)
3. In the Middle Ages we find book-keeping for agriculture only in the monasteries. But we have seen (Buch I, p. 343 [English edition: p. 357,—*Ed.*]) that a book-keeper was installed for agriculture as early as the primitive Indian communities. Book-keeping is there made the independent and exclusive function of the communal officer. This division of labour saves time, effort and expense, but production and book-keeping in the sphere of production remain as much two different things as the cargo of a ship and the bill of lading. In the person of the book-keeper, a part of the labour-power of the community is withdrawn from production, and the costs of his function are not made good by his own labour but by a deduction from the communal product. What is true of the book-keeper of an Indian community is true *mutatis mutandis* of the book-keeper of the capitalist. (From Manuscript II).
4. 'The money circulating in a country is a certain portion of the capital of the country, absolutely withdrawn from productive purposes, in order to facilitate or increase the productiveness of the remainder. A certain amount of wealth is, therefore, as necessary in order to adopt gold as a circulating medium, as it is to make a machine, in order to facilitate any other production.' (*Economists*, Vol. V, p. 520.)
5. Corbet calculates, in 1841, that the cost of storing wheat for a season of nine months amounts to a loss of ½ per cent in quantity, 3 per cent for interest on the price of wheat, 2 percent for warehouse rental, 1 percent for sifting and drayage, ½ percent for delivery, together 7 percent, or 3s. 6d. on a price of 50s. per quarter. (Th. Corbet, *An Inquiry into the Causes and Modes of Wealth of Individuals, etc.*, London, 1841.) According to the testimony of Liverpool merchants before the Railway Commission, the (net) costs of grain storage in 1865 amounted to about 2d. per quarter per month, or 9d. or 10d. a ton. (*Royal Commission on Railways*, 1867. Evidence, p. 19, No. 331.)
6. Book II. Introduction. [A. Smith, *An Inquiry into the Nature and Causes of the Wealth of Nations*. A new edition in four volumes, London, 1843, Vol. II, pp. 249-52.—*Ed.*]
7. Instead of a supply arising only upon and from the conversion of the product into a commodity, and of the consumption-supply into a commodity-supply, as Adam Smith wrongly imagines, this change of form, on the contrary, causes most violent crises in the economy of the producers during the transition from production for one's own needs to commodity production. In India, for instance, 'the disposition to hoard largely the grain for which little could be got in years of abundance' was observed until very recent times. (Return. *Bengal and Orissa Famine H. of C., 1867*, I, pp. 230-31, No. 74.) The sudden increase in the demand for cotton, jute, etc., due to the American Civil War led in many parts of India to a severe restriction of rice culture, a rise in the price of rice, and a sale of

the producers' old rice supplies. To this must be added the unexampled export of rice to Australia, Madagascar, etc., after 1864-66. This accounts for the acute character of Orissa alone (loc. cit., 174, 175, 213, 214, and III: *Papers relating to the famine in Behar*, pp. 32, 33, where the '**drain of old stocks**' is emphasised as one of the causes of the famine). (From Manuscript II.)

8. Storch calls this 'circulation factice' (fictitious circulation).
9. Ricardo quotes Say, who considers it one of the blessings of commerce that by means of the costs of transportation it increases the price, or the value, of products. 'Commerce,' writes Say, 'enables us to obtain a commodity in the place where it is to be found, and to convey it to another where it is to be consumed; it therefore gives us the power of increasing the value of the commodity, by the whole difference between its price in the first of these places, and its price in the second.' [J.B. Say, *Traitè d'ѐconomie politique*, Troisième edition, Paris, 1817, Tome II, p. 433.—*Ed.*] Ricardo remarks with reference to this: 'True, but how is this additional value given to it? By adding to the cost of production, first, the expenses of conveyance; secondly, the profit on the advances of capital made by the merchant. The commodity is only more valuable, for the same reason that every other commodity may become more valuable, because more labour is expended on its production and conveyance before it is purchased by the consumer. This must not be mentioned as one of the advantages of commerce.' (Ricardo, *Principles of Political Economy*, 3rd. ed., London, 1821, pp. 309, 310.)
10. Royal Commission on Railways, p. 31, No. 630.

PART II

THE TURNOVER OF CAPITAL

7

The Turnover Time and the Number of Turnovers

We have seen that the entire time of turnover of a given capital is equal to the sum of its time of circulation and its time of production. It is the period of time from the moment of the advance of capital-value in a definite form to the return of the functioning capital-value in the same form.

The compelling motive of capitalist production is always the creation of surplus-value by means of the advanced value, no matter whether this value is advanced in its independent form, i.e., in the money-form, or in commodities, in which case its value-form possesses only ideal independence in the price of the advanced commodities. In both cases this capital-value passes through various forms of existence during its circular movement. Its identity with itself is fixed in the books of the capitalists, or in the form of money of account.

Whether we take the form of M ... M' or the form P ... P, the implication is (1) that the advanced value performs the function of capital-value and has created surplus-value; (2) that after completing its process it has returned to the form in which it began it. The self-expansion of the advanced value M and at the same time the return of capital to this form (the money-form) is plainly visible in M ... M'. But the same takes place in the second form. For the starting-point of P is the existence of the elements of production, of commodities having a given value. The form includes the self-expansion of this value (C' and M') and the return to the original form, for in the second P the advanced value has again the form of the elements of production in which it was originally advanced.

We have seen previously: 'If production be capitalistic in form, so, too, will be reproduction. Just as in the former the labour-process figures but as a means towards the self-expansion of capital, so in the latter it figures but as a means of reproducing as capital—*i.e.*, as self-expanding value—the value advanced.' (Buch I, Kap. XXI, S. 588.) [English edition: Ch. XXIII, p. 566.—*Ed.*]

The three forms (I) M ... M' (II) P ... P, and (III) C' ... C', present the following distinctions: in form II, P ... P, the renewal of the process, the process of reproduction, is expressed as a reality, while in form I only as a potentiality. But both differ from form III in that with them the advanced capital-value—advanced either in the form of money or of material elements of production—is the starting-point and therefore also the returning point. In M ... M' the return is expressed by M' = M + m. If the process is renewed on the same scale, M is again the starting-point and m does not enter into it, but shows merely that M has self-expanded as capital and hence created a surplus-value, m, but cast it off. In the form P ... P capital-value P advanced in the form of elements of production is likewise the starting-point. This form includes its self-expansion. If simple reproduction takes place, the same capital-value renews the same process in the same form P. If accumulation takes place, then P' (equal in magnitude of value to M', equal to C') reopens the process as an expanded capital-value. But the process begins again with the advanced capital-value in its initial form, although with a greater capital-value than before. In form III, on the contrary, the capital-value does not begin the process as an advance, but as a value already expanded, as the aggregate wealth existing in the form of commodities, of which the advanced capital-value is but a part. This last form is important for Part III, in which the movements of the individual capitals are discussed in connection with the movement of the aggregate social capital. But it is not to be used in connection with the turnover of capital, which always begins with the advance of capital-value, whether in the form of money or commodities, and which always necessitates the return of the rotating capital-value in the form in which it was advanced. Of the circuits I and II, the former is of service in a study primarily of the influence of the turnover on the formation of surplus-value and the latter in a study of its influence on the creation of the product.

Economists have little distinguished between the different forms of circuits, nor have they examined them individually with relation to the turnover of capital. They generally consider the form M ... M', because it dominates the individual capitalist and aids him in his calculations, even if money is the starting-point only in the shape of money of account. Others start with outlays in the form of elements of production to the point when returns are received, without alluding at all to the form of the returns, whether made in commodities or money. For instance,

> 'the Economic Cycle, ... the whole course of production, from the time that outlays are made till returns are received. In agriculture, seedtime is its commencement, and harvesting its ending.' S. P. Newman, *Elements of Political Economy*, Andover and New York, p. 81.

Others begin with C' (the third form): Says Th. Chalmers, in his work *On Political Economy*, 2nd ed., Glasgow, 1832, p. 85 et seq.:

> 'The world of trade may be conceived to revolve in what we shall call an economic cycle, which accomplishes one revolution by business, coming round again, through its successive transactions, to the point from which it set out. Its commencement may be dated from the point at which the capitalist has obtained those returns by which his capital is replaced to him: whence he proceeds anew to engage his workmen; to distribute among them, in wages, their maintenance, or rather, the power of lifting it; to obtain from them, in finished work, the articles in which he specially deals; to bring these articles to market and there terminate the orbit of one set of movements, by effecting a sale, and receiving, in its proceeds, a return for the whole outlays of the period.'

As soon as the entire capital-value invested by some individual capitalist in any branch of production whatever has described its circuit, it finds itself once more in its initial form and can now repeat the same process. It must repeat it, if the value is to perpetuate itself as a capital-value and to create surplus-value. An individual circuit is but a constantly repeated section in the life of a capital; hence a period. At the end of the period M ... M' capital has once more the form of money-capital, which passes anew through that series of changes of form in which its process of reproduction, or self-expansion, is included. At the end of the period P ... P capital resumes the form of elements of production, which are the prerequisites for a renewal of its circuit. A circuit performed by a capital and meant to be a periodical process, not an individual act, is called its turnover. The duration of this turnover is determined by the sum of its time of production and its time of circulation. This time total constitutes the time of turnover of the capital. It measures the interval of time between one circuit period of the entire capital-value and the next, the periodicity in the process of life of capital or, if you like, the time of the renewal, the repetition, of the process of self-expansion, or production, of one and the same capital-value.

Apart from the individual adventures which may accelerate or shorten the time of turnover of certain capitals, this time differs in the different spheres of investment. Just as the working day is the natural unit for measuring the function of labour-power, so the year is the natural unit for measuring the turnovers of functioning capital. The natural basis of this unit is the circumstance that the most important crops of the temperate zone, which is the mother country of capitalist production, are annual products. If we designate the year as the unit of measure of the turnover time by T, the time of turnover of a given capital by t, and the number of its turnovers by n, then n = T/t. If, for instance, the time of turnover t is 3 months, then n is equal to 12/3, or 4; capital is turned over four times per year. If t = 18 months, then n = 12/18 = ⅔, or capital completes only two-thirds of its turnover in one year. If its time of turnover is several years, it is computed in multiples of one year.

From the point of view of the capitalist, the time of turnover of his capital is the time for which he must advance his capital in order to create surplus-value with it and receive it back in its original shape.

Before examining more closely the influence of the turnover on the processes of production and self-expansion, we must investigate two new forms which accrue to capital from the process of circulation and affect the form of its turnover.

8

Fixed Capital and Circulating Capital

Section I. *Distinctions of Form*

We have seen (Buch I, Kap. VI) [English edition: Ch. VIII.—*Ed.*] that, in relation to the products toward the creation of which it contributes, a portion of the constant capital retains that definite use-form in which it enters into the process of production. Hence it performs the same functions for a longer or shorter period, in ever repeated labour-processes. This applies for instance to industrial buildings, machinery, etc.—in short to all things which we comprise under the name of *instruments of labour*. This part of constant capital yields up value to the product in proportion as it loses its own exchange-value together with its own use-value. This delivery of value, or this transition of the value of such a means of production to the product which it helps to create is determined by a calculation of averages. It is measured by the average duration of its function, from the moment that the means of production enters into the process of production to the moment that it is completely spent, dead and gone, and must be replaced by a new sample of the same kind, or reproduced.

This, then, is the peculiarity of this part of constant capital, of the labour instruments proper:

A part of capital has been advanced in the form of constant capital, i.e., of means of production, which function as factors of the labour-process so long as they retain the independent use-form in which they enter this process. The finished product, and therefore also the creators of the product, so far as they have been transformed into product, is thrust out of the process of production and passes as a commodity from the sphere of production to the sphere of circulation. But the instruments of labour never leave the sphere of production, once they have entered it. Their function holds them there. A portion of the advanced capital-value becomes *fixed* in this form determined by the function of the instruments of labour in the process. In the performance of this function, and thus by the wear and tear of the instruments of labour, a part of their value passes on to the product, while the other remains fixed in the instruments of labour and thus in the process of production. The value fixed in this way decreases steadily, until the instrument of labour is worn out, its value having been distributed during a shorter or longer period over a mass of products originating from a series of constantly repeated labour-processes. But so long as they are still effective as instruments of labour and need not yet be replaced by new ones of the same kind, a certain amount of constant capital-value remains fixed in them, while the other part of the value originally fixed in them is transferred to the product and therefore circulates as a component part of the commodity-supply. The longer an instrument lasts, the slower it wears out, the longer will its constant capital-value remains fixed in this use-form. But whatever may be its durability, the proportion in which it yields value is always inverse to the entire time it functions. If of two machines of equal value one wears out in five years and the other in ten, then the first yields twice as much value in the same time as the second.

This portion of the capital-value fixed in the instrument of labour circulates as well as any other. We have seen in general that all capital-value is constantly in circulation, and that in this sense all capital is circulating capital. But the circulation of the portion of capital which we are now studying is peculiar. In the first place it does not circulate in its use-form, but it is merely its value that circulates, and this takes place gradually, piecemeal, in proportion as it passes from it to the product, which circulates as a commodity. During the entire period of its functioning, a part of its value always remain fixed in it, independently of the commodities which it helps to produce. It is this peculiarity which gives to this portion of constant capital the form of *fixed capital.* All the other material parts of capital advanced in the process of production form by way of contrast the *circulating,* or *fluid, capital.*

Some means of production do not enter materially into the product. Such are auxiliary materials, which are consumed by the instruments of labour themselves in the performance of their functions, like coal consumed by a steam-engine; or which merely assist in the operation, like gas for lighting, etc. It is only their value which forms a part of the value of the products. The product circulates in its own circulation the value of these means of production. This feature they have in common with fixed capital. But they are entirely consumed in every labour-process which they enter and must therefore be wholly replaced by new means of production of the same kind in every new labour-process. They do not preserve their independent use-form while performing their function. Hence while they function no portion of capital-value remains fixed in their old use-form, their bodily form, either. The circumstance that this portion of the auxiliary materials does not pass bodily into the product but enters into the value of the product only according to its own value, as a portion of that value, and what hangs together with this, namely, that the function of these substances is strictly confined to the sphere of production, has misled economists like Ramsay (who at the same time got fixed capital mixed up with constant capital) to classify them as fixed capital. [Karl Marx, *Theorien über den Mehrwert* (Vierter Band des Kapitals), 3. Teil, Berlin, 1962, SS. 323-25.—*Ed.*]

That part of the means of production which bodily enters into the product, i.e., raw materials, etc., thus assumes in part forms which enable it later to enter into individual consumption as articles of use. The instruments of labour properly so called, the material vehicles of the fixed capital, are consumed only productively and cannot enter into individual consumption, because they do not enter into the product, or the use-value, which they held to create but retain their independent form with reference to it until they are completely worn out. The means of transportation are an exception to this rule. The useful effect which they produce during the performance of their productive function, hence during their stay in the sphere of production, the change of location, passes simultaneously into the individual use in the same way in which he pays for the use of other articles of consumption. We have seen [Karl Marx, *Capital,* Vol. I, pp. 181-82.—*Ed.*] that for instance in chemical manufacture raw and auxiliary materials blend. The same applies to instruments of labour and auxiliary and raw materials. Similarly in agriculture the substances added for the improvement of the soil pass partly into the plants raised and help to form the product. On the other hand, their effect is distributed over a lengthy period, say four or five years. A portion of them therefore passes bodily into the product and thus transfers its value to the product while the other portion remains fixed in its old use-form and retains its value. It persists as a means of production and consequently keeps the form of fixed capital. As a beast of toil an ox is fixed capital. If he is eaten, he no longer functions as an instrument of labour, nor as fixed capital either.

What determines that a portion of the capital-value invested in means of production is endowed with the character of fixed capital is exclusively the peculiar manner in which this value circulates. This specific manner of circulation arises from the specific manner in which the instrument of labour transmits its value to the product, or in which it behaves as a creator of values during the process of production. This manner again arises from the special way in which the instruments of labour function in the labour-process.

We know that a use-value which emerges as a product from one labour-process enters into another as a means of production. [Karl Marx, *Capital*, Vol. I, p. 181.—*Ed.*] It is only the functioning of a product as an instrument of labour in the process of production that makes it fixed capital. But when it itself only just emerges from a process, it is by no means fixed capital. For instance a machine, as a product or commodity of the machine-manufacturer, belongs to his commodity-capital. It does not become fixed capital until it is employed productively in the hands of its purchaser, the capitalist.

All other circumstances being equal, the degree of fixity increases with the durability of the instrument of labour. It is this durability that determines the magnitude of the difference between the capital-value fixed in instruments of labour and that part of its value which it yields to the product in repeated labour-processes. The slower this value is yielded—and value is given up by the instrument of labour in every repetition of the labour-process—the larger is the fixed capital and the greater the difference between the capital employed in the process of production and the capital consumed in it. As soon as this difference has disappeared the instrument of labour has outlived its usefulness and has lost with its use-value also its value. It has ceased to be the depository of value. Since an instrument of labour, like every other material carrier of constant capital, parts with value to the product only to the extent that together with its use-value it loses its value, it is evident that the more slowly its use-value is lost, the longer it lasts in the process of production, the longer is the period in which constant capital-value remains fixed in it.

If a means of production which is not an instrument of labour strictly speaking, such as auxiliary substances, raw material, partly finished articles, etc., behaves with regard to value yield and hence manner of circulation of its value in the same way as the instruments of labour, then it is likewise a material depository, a form of existence, of fixed capital. This is the case with the above-mentioned improvements of the soil, which add to it chemical substances whose influence is distributed over several periods of production or years. Here a portion of the value continues to exist alongside the product, in its independent form or in the form of fixed capital, while the other portion of the value has been delivered to the product and therefore circulates with it. In this case it is not alone a portion of the value of the fixed capital which enters into the product, but also the use-value, the substance, in which this portion of value exists.

Apart from the fundamental mistake—the mixing up of the categories 'fixed' and 'circulating capital' with the categories 'constant' and 'variable capital'—the confusion of the economists hitherto in the definitions of concepts is based first of all on the following points:

One turns certain properties materially inherent in instruments of labour into direct properties of fixed capital; for instance physical immobility, say, of a house. However it is always easy to prove in such case that other instruments of labour, which as such are likewise fixed capital, possess the opposite property: for instance physical mobility, say, of a ship.

Or one confuses the economic definiteness of form which arises from the circulation of value with an objective property; as if objects which in themselves are not capital at all but rather become so only under definite social conditions could *in themselves* and in their very nature be capital in some definite form, fixed or circulating. We have seen (Buch I, Kap. V) [English edition: Ch. VII.—*Ed.*] that the means of production in every labour-process, regardless of the social conditions in which it takes place, are divided into instruments of labour and subjects of labour. But both of them become capital only under the capitalist mode of production, when they become 'productive capital,' as shown in the preceding part. Thus the distinction between instruments of labour and subject of labour, which is grounded on the nature of the labour-process, is reflected in a new form: the distinction between fixed capital and circulating capital. It is only then that a thing which performs the function of an instrument of labour becomes fixed capital. If owing to its material properties it can function also in other capacities than that of instrument of labour, it may be fixed capital or not, depending on the specific function it performs. Cattle as beasts of toil are fixed capital; as beef cattle they are raw material which finally enters into circulation as a product; hence they are circulating, not fixed capital.

The mere fixation of a means of production for a considerable length of time in repeated labour-processes, which however are connected, continuous, and therefore form a production period—i.e., the entire time of production required to finish a certain product—obliges the capitalist, just as fixed capital does, to make his advances for a longer or shorter term, but this does not make his capital fixed capital. Seeds for instance are not fixed capital, but only raw material which is held for about a year in the process of production. All capital is held in the process of production so long as it functions as productive capital, and so are therefore all elements of productive capital, whatever their material forms, their functions and the modes of circulation of their values. Whether this period of fixation lasts a long or a short time—a matter depending on the kind of process of production involved or the useful effect aimed at—this does not effect the distinction between fixed and circulating capital.[1]

A part of the instruments of labour, which includes the general instruments of labour, is either localised as soon as it enters the process of production as an instrument of labour, i.e., is prepared for its productive function, such as for instance machinery, or is produced from the outset in its immovable, localised form, such as improvements of the soil, factory buildings, blast furnaces, canals, railways, etc. The constant attachment of the instrument of labour to the process of production in which it is to function is here also due to its physical mode of existence. On the other hand an instrument of labour may physically change continually from place to place, may move about, and nevertheless be constantly in the process of production; for instance a locomotive, a ship, beasts of burden, etc. Neither does immobility in the one case bestow upon it the character of fixed capital, nor does mobility in the other case deprive it of this character. But the fact that some instruments of labour are localised, attached to the soil by their roots, assigns to this portion of fixed capital a peculiar role in the economy of nations. They cannot be sent abroad, cannot circulate as commodities in the world-market. Title to this fixed capital may change, it may be bought and sold, and to this extent may circulate ideally. These titles of ownership may even circulate in foreign markets, for instance in the form of stocks. But a change of the persons owning this class of fixed capital does not alter the relation of the immovable, materially fixed part of the national wealth to its immovable part.[2]

The peculiar circulation of fixed capital results in a peculiar turnover. That part of the value which it loses in its bodily form by wear and tear circulates as a part of the value of the product. The product converts itself by means of its circulation from commodities into money; hence the same applies to the value-part of the instrument of labour circulated by the product, and this value drips down in the form of money from the process of circulation in proportion as this instrument of labour ceases to be a depository of value in the process of production. Its value thus acquires a double existence. One part of it remains attached to its use-form or bodily form belonging in the process of production. The other part detaches itself from that form in the shape of money. In the performance of its function that part of the value of an instrument of labour which exists in its bodily form constantly decreases, while that which is transformed into money constantly increases until the instrument is at last exhausted and its entire value, detached from its corpse, is converted into money. Here the peculiarity of the turnover of this element of productive capital becomes apparent. The transformation of its value into money keeps pace with the pupation into money of the commodity which is the carrier of its value. But its reconversion from the money-form into a use-form proceeds separately from the reconversion of the commodities into other elements of their production and is determined rather by its own period of reproduction, that is, by the time during which the instrument of labour wears out and must be replaced by another of the same kind. If a machine worth £10,000 lasts for, say, a period of ten years, then the period of turnover of the value originally advanced for it amounts to ten years. It need not be renewed and continues to function in its bodily form until this period has expired. In the meantime its value circulates piecemeal as a part of the value of the commodities whose continuous production it serves and it is thus gradually transformed into money until finally at the end of ten years it entirely assumes the form of money and is reconverted from money into a machine, in other words, has completed its turn-over. Until this time of reproduction arrives, its value is gradually accumulated, in the form of a money reserve fund to start with.

The remaining elements of productive capital consist partly of those elements of constant capital which exist as auxiliary and raw materials, partly of variable capital invested in labour-power.

The analysis of the labour-process and of the process of producing surplus-value (Buch I, Kap. V) [English edition: Ch. VII.—*Ed.*] showed that these different components behave quite differently as creators of products and as creators of values. The value of that part of constant capital which consists of auxiliary and raw materials—the same as of that part which consists of instruments of labour—re-appears in the value of the product as only transferred value, while labour-power adds an equivalent of its value to the product by means of the labour-process, in other words, actually reproduces its value. Furthermore, one part of the auxiliary substances—fuel, lighting gas, etc.—is consumed in the process of labour without entering bodily into the product, while the other part of them enters bodily into the product and forms its material substance. But all these differences are immaterial so far as the circulation and therefore the mode of turnover is concerned. Since auxiliary and raw materials are entirely consumed in the creation of the product, they transfer their value entirely to the product. Hence this value is circulated in its entirety by the product, transforms itself into money and from money back into the elements of production of the commodity. Its turnover is not interrupted, as is that of fixed capital, but passes uninterruptedly through the entire circuit of its forms, so that these elements of productive capital are continually renewed in kind.

As for the variable component of productive capital, which is invested in labour-power, be it noted that labour-power is purchased for a definite period of time. As soon as the capitalist has bought it and embodied it in the process of production, it forms a component part of his capital, its variable component. Labour-power acts daily during the period of time in which it adds to the product not only its own value for the whole day but also a surplus-value in excess of it. We shall not consider this surplus-value for the present. After labour-power has been bought and it has performed its function, say for a week, its purchase must be constantly renewed within the customary intervals of time. The equivalent of its value, which the labour-power adds to the product during its functioning and which is transformed into money in consequence of the circulation of the product, must continually be reconverted from money into labour-power or continually pass through the complete circuit of its forms, that is, must be turned over, if the circuit of continuous production is not to be interrupted.

Hence that part of the value of the productive capital which has been advanced for labour-power is entirely transferred to the product (we constantly leave the question of surplus-value out of consideration here), passes with it through the two metamorphoses belonging in the sphere of circulation and always remains incorporated in the process of production by virtue of this continuous renewal. Hence, however different otherwise may be the relation between labour-power, so far as the creation of value is concerned, and the component parts of constant capital which *do not constitute fixed* capital, this kind of turnover of its value labour-power shares with them, in contradistinction to fixed capital. These components of the productive capital—the parts of its value invested in labour-power and in means of production which do not constitute fixed capital—by reason of their common turnover characteristics confront the fixed capital as *circulating* or *fluent* capital.

We have already shown [Karl Marx, *Capital*, Vol. I, Ch. VI, pp. 167-76.—*Ed.*] that the money which the capitalist pays to the labourer for the use of his labour-power is nothing more or less than the form of the general equivalent for the means of subsistence required by the labourer. To this extent, the variable capital consists in substance of means of subsistence. But in this case, where we are discussing turnover, it is a question of form. The capitalist does not buy the labourer's means of subsistence but his labour-power. And that which forms the variable part of his capital is not the labourer's means of subsistence but his labour-power in action. What the capitalist consumes productively in the labour-process is the labour-power itself and not the labourer's means of subsistence. It is the labourer himself who converts the money received for his labour-power into means of subsistence, in order to reconvert them into labour-power, to keep alive, just as the capitalist for instance converts a part of the surplus-value of the commodities he sells for money into means of subsistence for himself without thereby warranting the statement that the purchaser of his commodities pays him in means of subsistence. Even if the labourer is paid a part of his wages in means of subsistence, in kind, this nowadays amounts to a second transaction. He sells his labour-power at a certain price, with the understanding that he shall receive a part of this price in means of subsistence. This changes merely the form of the payment, but not the fact that what he actually sells is his labour-power. It is a second transaction, which does not take place between the labourer and the capitalist, but between the labourer as a buyer of commodities and the capitalist as a seller of commodities, while in the first transaction the labourer is a seller of a commodity (his labour-power) and the capitalist its buyer. It is exactly the same as if a capitalist, on selling his commodity, say, a machine, to an iron works, has it replaced by some other commodity, say, iron. It is therefore not the labourer's means of subsistence which acquire the definite character of circulating capital as opposed to fixed capital. Nor is it his labour-power. It is rather that part of the value of productive capital which is invested in labour-power and which, by virtue of the form of its turnover, receives this character in common with some, and in contrast with other, component parts of the constant capital.

The value of the circulating capital—in labour-power and means of production—is advanced only for the time during which the product is in process of production, in accordance with the scale of production determined by the volume of the fixed capital. This value enters entirely into the product, is therefore fully returned by its sale from the sphere of circulation, and can be advanced anew. The labour-power and means of production, in which the circulating component of capital exists, are withdrawn from circulation to the extent required for the creation and sale of the finished product, but they must be continually replaced and renewed by purchasing them back, by reconverting them from the money-form into the elements of production. They are withdrawn from the market in smaller quantities at a time than the elements of fixed capital, but they must be withdrawn again from it so much the more frequently and the advance of capital invested in them must be renewed at shorter intervals. This constant renewal is effected by the continuous conversion of the product which circulates their entire value. And finally, they pass through the entire circuit of metamorphoses, not only so far as their value is concerned but also their material form. They are perpetually reconverted from commodities into the elements of production of the same commodities.

Together with its own value, labour-power always adds to the product surplus-value, the embodiment of unpaid labour. This is continuously circulated by the finished product and converted into money just as are other elements of its value. But here, where we are primarily concerned with the turnover of capital-value, and not with that of the surplus-value occurring at the same time, we dismiss the latter for the present.

From the foregoing one may conclude the following:

1. The definiteness of form of fixed and circulating capital arises merely from the different turnovers of the capital-value, functioning in the process of production, or of the *productive capital*. This difference in turnover arises in its turn from the different manner in which the various components of productive capital transfer their value to the product; it is not due to the different parts played by these components in the generation of product value, nor to their characteristic behaviour in the process of self-expansion. Finally the difference in the delivery of value to the product—and therefore the different manner in which this value is circulated by the product and is renewed in its original bodily form through the metamorphoses of the product—arises from the difference of the material shapes in which the productive capital exists, one portion of it being entirely consumed during the creation of an individual product and the other being used up only gradually. Hence it is only the productive capital which can be divided into fixed and circulating capital. But this antithesis does not apply to the other two modes of existence of industrial capital, that is to say, commodity-capital and money-capital, nor does it exist as an antithesis of these two modes to productive capital. It exists *only for productive capital and within its sphere*. No matter how much money-capital and commodity-capital may function as capital and no matter how fluently they may circulate, they cannot become circulating capital as distinct from fixed capital until they are transformed into circulating components of productive capital. But because these two forms of capital dwell in the sphere of circulation, Political Economy as we shall see has been misled since the time of Adam Smith into lumping them together with the circulating part of productive capital and assigning them to the category of circulating capital. They are indeed circulation capital in contrast to productive capital, but they are not circulating capital in contrast to fixed capital.
2. The turnover of the fixed component part of capital, and therefore also the time of turnover necessary for it, comprises several turnovers of the circulating constituents of capital. In the time during which the fixed capital turns over once, the circulating capital turns over several times. One of the component parts of the value of the productive capital acquires the definiteness of form of fixed capital only in case the means of production in which it exists is not wholly worn out in the time required for the fabrication of the product and its expulsion from the process of production as a commodity. One part of its value must remain tied up in the form of the still preserved old use-form, while the other part is circulated by the finished product, and this circulation on the contrary simultaneously circulates the entire value of the fluent component parts of the capital.
3. The value-part of the productive capital, the part invested in fixed capital, is advanced in one lump sum for the entire period of employment of that part of the means of production of which the fixed capital consists. Hence this value is

thrown into the circulation by the capitalist all at one time. But it is withdrawn again from the circulation only piecemeal and gradually by realising the parts of value which the fixed capital adds piecemeal to the commodities. On the other hand the means of production themselves, in which a component part of the productive capital becomes fixed, are withdrawn from the circulation all at one time to be embodied in the process of production for the entire period in which they function. But they do not require for this period any replacement by new samples of the same kind, do not require reproduction. They continue for a longer or shorter period to contribute to the creation of the commodities thrown into circulation without withdrawing from circulation the elements of their own renewal. Hence they do not require from the capitalist a renewal of his advance during this period. Finally the capital-value invested in fixed capital does not pass bodily through the circuit of its forms, during the functioning period of the means of production in which this capital-value exists, but only as concerns its value, and even this it does only parts and gradually. In other words, a portion of its value is continually circulated and converted into money as a part of the value of the commodities, without being reconverted from money into its original bodily form. This reconversion of money into the bodily form of the means of production does not take place until the end of its functioning period, when the means of production has been completely consumed.

4. The elements of circulating capital are as permanently fixed in the process of production—if it is to be uninterrupted—as the elements of fixed capital. But the elements of circulating capital thus fixed are continually renewed in kind (the means of production by new products of the same kind, labour-power by constantly renewed purchases) while in the case of the elements of fixed capital neither they themselves are renewed nor need their purchases be renewed so long as they continue to exist. There are always raw and auxiliary materials in the process of production, but always new products of the same kind, after the old elements have been consumed in the creation of the finished product. Labour-power likewise always exists in the process of production, but only by means of ever new purchases, frequently involving changes of persons. But the same identical buildings, machines, etc., continue to function, during repeated turnovers of the circulating capital, in the same repeated processes of production.

Section II. *Components, Replacements, Repairs and Accumulation of Fixed Capital*

In any investment of capital the separate elements of the fixed capital have different lifetimes, and therefore different turnover times. In a railway, for instance, the rails, sleepers, earthworks, terminals, bridges, tunnels, locomotives, and carriages have different functional periods and times of reproduction, hence the capital advanced for them has different times of turnover. For a great number of years, buildings, platforms, water tanks, viaducts, tunnels, cuttings, dams, in short everything called '**works of art**' in English railroading, do not require any renewal. The things which wear out most are the tracks and **rolling stock**.

Originally in the construction of modern railways it was the prevailing opinion, nursed by the most prominent practical engineers, that a railway would last a century and that the wear and tear of the rails was so imperceptible that it could be ignored for all financial and other practical purposes; 100 to 150 years was supposed to be the life of good rails. But it was soon found that the life of a rail, which naturally depends on the speed of the locomotives, the weight and number of trains, the diameter of the rails, and on a multitude of other attendant circumstances, did not exceed an average of 20 years. In some railway terminals, great traffic centres, the rails even wear out every year. About 1867 began the introduction of steel rails, which cost about twice as much as iron rails but which last more than twice as long. The life-time of wooden sleepers was from 12 to 15 years. It was also ascertained with regard to the rolling stock that freight cars wear out faster than passenger cars. The life of a locomotive was estimated in 1867 to be about 10 to 12 years.

The wear and tear is first of all a result of use. As a rule 'the wear of the rails is proportionate to the number of trains.' (R.C., No. 17645.)[3] With increased speed the wear and tear of a railway increased in a higher ratio than the square of the speed; that is to say, if you doubled the speed of the engine, you more than quadrupled the cost of wear and tear of the road. (R.C., No. 17046.)

Wear and tear is furthermore caused by the action of natural forces. For instance sleepers suffer not only from actual wear but also from rot.

> 'The cost of maintaining the road does not depend so much upon the wear and tear of the traffic passing over it, as upon the quality of wood, iron, bricks and mortars exposed to the atmosphere. A month of severe water would do not more damage to the road of a railway than a year's traffic.' (R. P. Williams; 'On the Maintenance of Permanent Way,' Paper read at the Institute of Civil Engineers, Autumn, 1867. [R. P. Williams's paper was published in Money Market Review of December 2, 1867.—*Ed.*])

Finally, here as everywhere else in modern industry, the moral depreciation plays a role. After the lapse of ten years, one can generally buy the same number of cars and locomotives for £30,000 that would previously have cost £40,000. Depreciation in the rolling stock must be set at 25 per cent of the market price even when there is no depreciation whatever in its use-values. (Lardner, *Railway Economy*.)

> 'Tube bridges will not be replaced in their present form.'

(Because now there are better forms for such bridges.)

> 'Ordinary repairs, taking away gradually, and replacing are not practicable.' (W. P. Adams, *Roads and Rails*, London, 1862.)

The instruments of labour are largely modified all the time by the progress of industry. Hence they are not replaced in their original, but in their modified form. On the one hand the mass of the fixed capital invested in a certain bodily form and endowed in that form with a certain average life constitutes one reason for the only gradual pace of the introduction of new machinery, etc., and therefore an obstacle to the rapid general introduction of improved instruments of labour. On the other hand competition compels the replacement of the old instruments of labour by new ones before the expiration of their natural life, especially when decisive changes occur. Such premature renewals of factory equipment on a rather large social scale are mainly enforced by catastrophes or crises.

By wear and tear (moral depreciation excepted) is meant that part of value which the fixed capital, on being used, gradually transmits to the product, in proportion to its average loss of use-value.

This wear and tear takes place partly in such a way that the fixed capital has a certain average durability. It is advanced for this entire period in one sum. After the termination of this period it must be totally replaced. So far as living instruments of labour are concerned, for instance horses, their reproduction is timed by nature itself. Their average lifetime as instruments of labour is determined by laws of nature. As soon as this term has expired they must be replaced by new ones. A horse cannot be replaced piecemeal; it must be replaced by another horse.

Other elements of fixed capital permit of a periodical or partial renewal. In this instance partial or periodical replacement must be distinguished from gradual extension of the business.

The fixed capital consists in part of homogeneous constituents which do not however last the same length of time but are renewed piecemeal at various intervals. This is true for instance of the rails and railway stations, which must be replaced more often than those of the remainder of the trackage. It also applies to the sleepers, which on the Belgian railways had to be renewed in the forties at the rate of 8 per cent annually, according to Lardner, so that all the sleepers were renewed in the course of 12½ years. Hence we have here the following situation: a certain sum is advanced for a certain kind of fixed capital for say ten years. This expenditure is made at one time. But a definite part of this fixed capital, the value of which has entered into the value of the product and been converted with it into money, is replaced in kind every year, while the remainder continues to exist in its original body form. It is this advance in one sum and the only partial reproduction in bodily form which distinguish this capital, as fixed, from circulating capital.

Other pieces of the fixed capital consist of heterogeneous components, which wear out in unequal periods of time and must so be replaced. This applies particularly to machines. What we have just said concerning the different durabilities of different constituent parts of a fixed capital applies in this case to the durability of different component parts of any machine figuring as a piece of this fixed capital.

With regard to the gradual extension of the business in the course of the partial renewal, we make the following remarks: Although, as we have seen, the fixed capital continues to perform its functions in the process of production in kind, a part of its value, proportionate to the average wear and tear, has circulated with the product, has been converted into money, and forms an element in the money reserve fund intended for the replacement of the capital pending its reproduction in kind. This part of the value of the fixed capital transformed into money may serve to extend the business or to make improvements in the machinery which will increase the efficiency of the latter. Thus reproduction takes place in larger or smaller periods of time, and this is, from the standpoint of society, reproduction on an enlarged scale—extensive if the means of production is extended; intensive if the means of production is made more effective. This reproduction on an extended scale does not result from accumulation—transformation of surplus-value into capital—but from the reconversion of the value which has branched off, detached itself in the form of money from the body of the fixed capital into new additional or at least more effective fixed capital of the same kind. Of course it depends partly on the specific nature of the business, to what extent and in what proportions it is capable of such gradual addition, hence also in what amount a reserve fund must be collected to be reinvested in this way, and what period of time this requires. To what extent furthermore improvements in the details of existing machinery can be made, depends of course on the nature of these improvements and the construction of the machine itself. How well this point is considered at the very outset in the construction of railways is shown by Adams:

> 'The whole structure should be set out on the principle which governs the beehive—capacity for indefinite extension. Any fixed and decided symmetrical structure is to be deprecated, as needing subsequent pulling down in case of enlargement.' (p. 123.)

This depends largely on the available space. In the case of some buildings additional storeys may be built; in the case of others lateral extension, hence more land, is required. Within capitalist production there is on the one side much waste of material, on the other much impracticable lateral extension of this sort (partly to the injury of the labour-power) in the gradual expansion of the business, because nothing is undertaken according to a social plan, but everything depends on the infinitely different conditions, means, etc., with which the individual capitalist operates. This results in a great waste of the productive forces.

This piecemeal reinvestment of the money reserve fund (i.e., of that part of the fixed capital which has been reconverted into money) is easiest in agriculture. A field of production of a given area is here capable of the greatest possible gradual absorption of capital. The same applies to where there is natural reproduction as in cattle breeding.

Fixed capital entails special maintenance costs. A part of this maintenance is provided by the labour-process itself; fixed capital spoils, if it is not employed in the labour-process (Buch I, Kap. VI, S. 196 and Kap. XIII, S. 423, [English edition: Ch. VIII and XV.—*Ed.*] on wear and tear of machinery when not in use). The English law therefore explicitly treats it as **waste**, if rented lands are not cultivated according to the custom of the land. (W. A. Holdsworth, Barrister at Law, *The Law of Landlord and Tenant*, London, 1857, p. 96.)

This maintenance resulting from use in the labour-process is a free gift inherent in the nature of living labour. Moreover the preservative power of labour is of a two-fold character. On the one hand it preserves the value of the materials of labour by transferring it to the product, on the other hand it preserves the value of the instruments of labour without transferring this value to the product, by preserving their use-value through their activity in the process of production.

The fixed capital however requires also a positive expenditure of labour for its maintenance in good repair. The machinery must be cleaned from time to time. It is a question here of additional labour without which the machinery becomes useless, of merely warding off the noxious influences of the elements, which are inseparable from the process of production; hence it is a question of keeping the machinery literally in working order. It goes without saying that the normal durability of fixed capital is calculated on the supposition that all the conditions which it can perform its functions normally during that time are fulfilled, just as we assume, in placing a man's life at 30 years on the average, that he will wash himself. It is here not a question of replacing the labour contained in the machine, but of constant additional labour made necessary by its use. It is not a question of labour performed by the machine, but of labour spent on it, of labour which it is not an agent of production but raw material. The capital expended for this labour must be classed as circulating capital, although it does not enter into the labour-process proper to which the product owes its existence. This labour must be continually expended in production, hence its value must be continually replaced by that of the product. The capital invested in it belongs in that part of circulating capital which has to cover the unproductive costs and is to be distributed over the produced values according to an annual average calculation. We have seen [Karl Marx, *Capital*, Vol. I, p. 426, Note 1.—*Ed.*] that in industry proper this labour of cleaning is performed by the workingmen gratis, during the rest periods, and for that very reason often also during the process of production itself, and most accidents can be traced to this source. This labour does not figure in the price of the product. As far as that goes the consumer receives it gratis. On the other hand, the capitalist thus does not pay the maintenance costs of the machine. The labourer pays *in persona*, and this is one of the mysteries of the self-preservation of capital, which in point of fact constitute a legal claim by the labourer on the machinery, on the strength of which he is a co-owner of the machine even from the standpoint of bourgeois law. However, in various branches of production, in which the machinery must be removed from the process of production for the purpose of cleaning and where therefore the cleaning cannot be performed in between, as for instance in the case of locomotives, this maintenance work counts as current expenses and is therefore an element of circulating capital. For instance a goods engine should not run more than 3 days without being kept one day in the shed. If you attempt to wash out the boiler before it has cooled down that is very injurious. (R.C., No. 17823.)

The actual repairs or patchwork require expenditures of capital and labour which are not contained in the originally advanced capital and cannot therefore be replaced and covered, at least not always, by the gradual replacement of the value of the fixed capital. For instance, if the value of the fixed capital is £10,000 and its total life of 10 years, then these £10,000, having been entirely converted into money after the lapse of ten years, will replace only the value of the capital originally invested, but they do not replace the capital, or labour, added in the meantime for repairs. This is an additional component part of the value, which is not advanced all at one time but whenever a need for it arises, and the various times for advancing it are in the very nature of things accidental. All fixed capital demands such subsequent, dosed out, additional outlay of capital for instruments of labour and labour-power.

The damage which separate parts of the machinery, etc., may incur is naturally accidental and so are therefore the repairs involved. Nevertheless two kinds of repairs are to be distinguished in the general mass, which are of a more or less fixed character and fall within various periods of the life of fixed capital. These are the ailments of childhood and the far more numerous ailments of the post-middle durability period. A machine for instance may be commissioned in ever so perfect a condition, still actual use will reveal shortcomings which must be remedied by subsequent labour. On the other hand the more a machine passes beyond the mid-durability point, the more therefore the normal wear and tear has accumulated and the more the material of which it consists has been worn out and become decrepit, the more numerous and considerable will be the repairs required to keep it going for the remainder of its average durability. It is the same with an old man, who incurs more medical expenses to keep from dying prematurely than a young and strong man. So in spite of its accidental character repair work is unevenly distributed over the various periods of life of fixed capital.

From the foregoing and from the generally accidental character of repair work on machines its follows:

In one respect the actual expenditure of labour-power and instruments of labour on repairs is accidental, like the circumstances which necessitate these repairs; the amount of the repairs needed is unevenly distributed over the different periods of fixed capital's life. In other respects, it is taken for granted in estimating the average life of fixed capital that it is constantly kept in good working order, partly by cleaning (including the cleaning of the premises), partly by repairs as often as required. The transfer of value through wear and tear of fixed capital is calculated on its average life, but this average life itself is based on the assumption that the additional capital required for maintenance purposes is continually advanced.

But then it is also evident that the value added by this extra expenditure of capital and labour cannot enter into the price of the commodities concerned at the same time as it is incurred. For example, a manufacturer of yarn cannot sell his yarn dearer this week than last, merely because one of his wheels broke or a belt tore this week. The general costs of spinning have not been changed in any way by this accident in some individual factory. Here, as in all determinations of value, the average decides. Experience shows the average occurrence of such accidents and the average volume of the maintenance and repair work necessary during the average life of the fixed capital invested in a given branch of business. This average expense is distributed over the average life and added to the price of the product in corresponding aliquot parts; hence it is replaced by means of its sale.

The additional capital which is thus replaced belongs to the circulating capital, although the manner of its expenditure is irregular. As it is of paramount importance to remedy every damage to machinery immediately, every comparatively large factory employs in addition to the regular factory force special personnel—engineers, carpenters, mechanics, locksmiths, etc. Their wages are a part of the variable capital and the value of their labour is distributed over the product. On the other hand, the expenses for means of production are calculated on the basis of the above-mentioned average, according to which they form continually a part of the value of the product, although they are actually advanced in irregular periods and therefore enter into the product or the fixed capital in irregular periods. This capital, expended in repairs properly so called, is in many respects a capital *sui generis*, which can be classed neither as circulating nor as fixed capital, but belongs with greater justification to the former, since it figures among the running expenses.

The manner of book-keeping does not of course change in any way the actual state of affairs booked. But it is important to note that customarily many lines of business figure the costs of repairs together with the actual wear and tear of the fixed capital in the following manner: Let the advanced fixed capital be £10,000 and its durability 15 years. The annual wear and tear is then £666⅔. But the depreciation is calculated on a durability of only ten years; in other words, £1,000 are added annually to the price of the produced commodities for wear and tear of the fixed capital, instead of £666⅔. Thus £333⅓ are reserved for repairs, etc. (The figures 10 and 15 are chosen only by way of illustration.) This amount is spent on an average for repairs, so that the fixed capital may last 15 years. Such a calculation naturally does not prevent the fixed capital and the additional capital spent on repairs from belonging to different categories. On the strength of this mode of calculation it was assumed for instance that the lowest cost estimate for the maintenance and replacement of steamships was 15 per cent annually the time of reproduction being therefore 6⅔ years. In the sixties, the English government indemnified the Peninsular and Oriental Co. at the annual rate of 16 percent, corresponding to a reproduction time of 6¼ years. On railways the average life of a locomotive is 10 years, but the depreciation, counting in repairs is taken as 12½ per cent, which brings down its durability to 8 years. In the case of passenger and goods cars, the estimate is 9 per cent, or a durability of 11 1/9 years.

Legislation has everywhere drawn a distinction, in leases of houses and other objects which represent fixed capital to their owners and are leased as such, between normal depreciation, which is the result of time, the action of the elements, and normal wear on the one hand and on the other those occasional repairs which are required from time to time for maintenance during the normal life of the house and during its normal use. As a rule, the former are borne by the owner, the latter by the tenant. Repairs are further divided into ordinary and substantial ones. The last-named are partly a renewal of the fixed capital in its bodily form, and they fall likewise on the shoulders of the owner, unless the lease explicitly states the contrary. Take for instance the English law:

> 'A tenant from year to year, on the other hand, is not bound to do more than keep the premises wind and watertight, when that can be done without 'substantial' repairs; and generally to do repairs coming fairly under the head 'ordinary.' Even with respect to those parts of the premises which are the subject of 'ordinary' repairs, regard must be had to their age and general state, and condition, when he took possession, for he is not bound to replace old and worn-out materials with new ones, nor to make good the inevitable depreciation resulting from time and ordinary wear and tear.' (Holdsworth, *Law of Landlord and Tenant*, pp. 90 and 91.)

Entirely different from the replacement of wear and tear and from the work of maintenance and repair is *insurance*, which relates to destruction caused by extraordinary phenomena of nature, fire, flood, etc. This must be made good out of the surplus-value and is a deduction from it. Or, considered from the point of view of society as a whole, there must be continuous over-production, that is, production on a larger scale than is necessary for the simple replacement and reproduction of the existing wealth, quite apart from the increase in population, so as to be in possession of the means of production required to compensate for the extraordinary destruction caused by accidents and natural forces.

In point of fact only the smallest part of the capital needed for replacement consists of the money reserve fund. The most substantial part consists in the extension of the scale of production itself, which partly is actual expansion and partly belongs to the normal volume of production in those branches of industry which produce the fixed capital. For instance, a machine factory must arrange things so that the factories of its customers can annually be extended and that a number of them will always stand in need of total or partial reproduction.

On determining the wear and tear as well as the costs of repairs, according to the social average, great disparity necessarily appears, even in the case of capital investments of equal size, operating otherwise under equal conditions and in the same branch of industry. In practice a machine, etc., lasts with one capitalist longer than the average period, while with another it does not last so long. With the one the costs of repairs are above, with the other below average, etc. But the addition to the price of the commodities resulting from wear and tear and from costs of repairs is the same and is determined by the average. The one therefore gets more out of this additional price than he really added, the other less. This circumstance as well as all others which result in different gains for different capitalists in the same line of business with the same degree of exploitation of labour-power tends to enhance the difficulty of understanding the true nature of surplus-value.

The line between repairs proper and replacement, between costs of maintenance and costs of renewal, is rather flexible. Hence the eternal dispute, for instance in railroading, whether certain expenses are for repairs or for replacement, whether they must be defrayed from current expenditures or from the original stock. A transfer of expenses for repairs to capital account instead of revenue account is the familiar method by which railway boards of directors artificially inflate their dividends. However, experience has already furnished the most important clues for this. According to Lardner, the subsequent labour required during the early life of a railway for example

> 'ought not to be denominated repairs, but should be considered as an essential part of the construction of the railway, and in the financial accounts should be debited to capital, and not to revenue, not being expenses due to wear and tear, or to the legitimate operation of the traffic, but to the original and inevitable incompleteness of the construction of the line.' (Lardner, loc. cit., p. 40.)
>
> 'The only sound way is to charge each year's revenue with the depreciation necessarily suffered to earn the revenue, whether the amount is actually spent or not.' (Captain Fitzmaurice, 'Committee of Inquiry on Caledonian Railway,' published in *Money Market Review*, 1867.)

The separation of the replacement and maintenance of fixed capital become practically impossible and purposeless in agriculture, at least when not operated by steam. According to Kirchhof (*Handbuch der landwirthschaftlichen Betriebslehre*, Dresden, 1852, p. 137),

> 'wherever there is a complete, though not excessive, supply of implements (of agricultural and other implements and farm appliances of every description) it is the custom to estimate the annual wear and tear and maintenance of the implements, according to the different existing conditions, at a general average of 15 to 25 per cent of the original stock.'

In the case of the rolling stock of a railway, repairs and replacement cannot be separated at all.

> 'We maintain our stock by number. Whatever number of engines we have we maintain that. If one is destroyed by age, and it is better to build a new one, we build it at the expense of revenue, of course, taking credit for the materials of the old one as far as they go.... there is a great deal left; there are the wheels, the axles, the boilers, and in fact a great deal of the old engine is left.' (T. Gooch, Chairman of Great Western Railway Co., R. C. on Railways, p. 858, Nos. 17327-17329.) '...Repairing means renewing; I do not believe in the word replacement...; once a railway company has bought a vehicle or an engine, it ought to be repaired, and in that way admit of

going on for ever.' (No. 17784.) '...The engines are maintained for ever out of this 8½ d. We rebuild our engines. If you purchase an engine entirely it would be spending more money than is necessary ... yet there is always a pair of wheels or an axle or some portion of the engine which comes in, and hence it cheapens the cost of producing a practically new engine.' (No. 17790.) 'I am at this moment turning out a new engine every week, or practically a new engine, for it has a new boiler, cylinder, or framing.' (No. 17823. Archibald Sturrock, **Locomotive Superintendent of Great Northern Railway, in** R. C., 1867.)

The same with coaches:

> 'In the course of time the stock of engines and vehicles is continually repaired. New wheels are put on at one time, and a new body at another. The different moving parts most subject to wear are gradually renewed; and the engines and vehicles may be conceived even to be subject to such a succession of repairs, that in many of them not a vestige of the original materials remains.... Even in this case, however, the old materials of coaches or engines are more or less worked up into other vehicles or engines, and never totally disappear from the road. The movable capital therefore may be considered to be in a state of continual reproduction; and that which, in the case of the permanent way, must take place altogether at a future epoch, when the entire road will have to be relaid, takes place in the rolling stock gradually from year to year. Its existence is perennial, and it is in a constant state of rejuvenescence.' (Lardner, *op. cit.*, pp. 115-16.)

This process, which Lardner here describes relative to a railway, does not fit the case of an individual factory, but may well serve as an illustration of continuous, partial reproduction of fixed capital intermingled with repairs within an entire branch of industry or even within the aggregate production considered on a social scale.

Here is proof of the lengths to which adroit boards of directors may go in manipulating the terms repairs and replacement for the purpose of extracting dividends. According to the above-quoted paper read by R. P. Williams, various English railway companies wrote off the following sums from the revenue account, as averages over a number of years, for repairs and maintenance of the permanent way and buildings (per English mile of track annually).

London & North Western	£370
Midland	£225
London & South Western	£257
Great Northern	£360
Lancashire & Yorkshire	£377
South Eastern	£263
Brighton	£266
Manchester & Sheffield	£200

These differences arise only to a very minor degree from differences in the actual expenses; they are due almost exclusively to different methods of calculation, according to whether items of expenses are debited to the capital or the revenue account. Williams says so in so many words that a lesser charge is booked because this is necessary for a good dividend, and a higher charge is booked because there is a greater revenue which can bear it.

In certain cases the wear and tear, and therefore its replacement, is practically infinitesimal so that nothing but costs of repairs have to be charged. Lardner's statements below relative to works of art in railroading apply in general to all such durable structures as docks, canals, iron and stone bridges, etc.

> 'That wear and tear which, being due to the slow operation of time acting upon the more solid structures, produces an effect altogether insensible when observed through short periods, but which, after a long interval of time, such, for example, as centuries, must necessitate the reconstruction of some or all even of the most solid structures. These changes may not unaptly be assimilated to the periodical and secular inequalities which take place in the movements of the great bodies of the universe. The operation of time upon the more massive works of art upon the railway, such as the bridges, tunnels, viaducts, etc., afford examples of what may be called the secular wear and tear. The more rapid and visible deterioration, which is made good by repairs or reconstruction effected at shorter intervals, is analogous to the periodic inequalities. In the annual repairs is included the casual damage which the exterior of the more solid and durable works may from time to time sustain; but, independently of these repairs, age produces its effects even on these structures, and an epoch must arrive, however remote it be, at which they would be reduced to a state which will necessitate their reconstruction. For financial and economic purposes such an epoch is perhaps too remote to render it necessary to bring it into practical calculation, and therefore it need here only be noticed in passing.' (Lardner, loc. cit., pp., 38, 39.)

This applies to all similar structures of secular duration, in which cases therefore the capital advanced need not be gradually replaced commensurate with their wear and tear, but only the annual average costs of maintenance and repair need be transferred to the prices of the product.

Although, as we have seen, a greater part of the money returning for the replacement of the wear and tear of the fixed capital is annually, or even in shorter intervals, reconverted into its bodily form, nevertheless every single capitalist requires a sinking fund for that part of his fixed capital which falls due for reproduction only after a lapse of years but must then be entirely replaced. A considerable component part of the fixed capital precludes gradual reproduction because of its peculiar properties. Besides, in cases where the reproduction takes place piecemeal in such a way that at short intervals new stock is added to the depreciated old stock, a previous accumulation of money of a greater or smaller amount, depending on the specific character of the branch of industry, is necessary before the replacement can be effected. Not just any sum of money will suffice for this purpose; a definite amount is needed.

If we study this question on the assumption of simple circulation of money, without regard to the credit system, of which we shall treat later, [The capitalist credit system is treated in parts IV and V of the third volume of Capital.—*Ed.*] then the mechanism of this movement is as follows: It was shown (Buch I, Kap. III, 3a) [English edition: Volume I, Ch. III, 3a,—*Ed.*] that the proportion in which the aggregate mass of money is distributed over a hoard and means of circulation varies steadily, if one part of the money available in society constantly lies fallow as a hoard, while another performs the functions of a medium of circulation or of an immediate reserve fund of the directly circulating money. Now, in our case, money that must be accumulated as a hoard in the hands of a relatively big capitalist in rather large amounts is thrown all at once into circulation on the purchase of the fixed capital. It then divides again in society into medium of circulation and hoard. By means of the sinking fund, in which the value of the fixed capital flows back to its starting-point in proportion to its wear and tear, a part of the circulating money again forms a hoard, for a longer or shorter period, in the hands of the same capitalist whose hoard had, upon the purchase of the fixed capital, been transformed into a medium of circulation and passed away from him. It is a continually changing distribution of the hoard which exists in society and alternately functions as a medium of circulation and then is separated again, as a hoard, from the mass of the circulating money. With the development of the credit system, which necessarily runs parallel with the development of modern industry and capitalist production, this money no longer serves as a hoard but as capital; however not in the hands of its owner but of other capitalists at whose disposal it has been placed.

Notes

1. On account of the difficulty of determining what is fixed and what circulating capital, Herr Lorenz Stein thinks that this distinction is meant only to facilitate the treatment of the subject.
2. End of Manuscript IV, beginning of Manuscript II.—*Ed.*
3. The quotations marked R. C. are from: *Royal Commission on Railways. Minutes of Evidence taken before the Commissioners. Presented to both Houses of Parliament*, London, 1867.—The questions and answers are numbered and the numbers given here.

9

The Aggregate Turnover of Advanced Capital, Cycles of Turnover

We have seen that the fixed and circulating component parts of productive capital are turned over in various ways and at various periods, also that the different constituents of the fixed capital of a business have different periods of turnover, depending on their different durabilities and therefore on their different times of reproduction. (On the real or apparent difference in the turnover of different constituents of circulating capital in the same business, see the close of this chapter, under 6.)

1. The aggregate turnover of an advanced capital is the average turnover of its various constituent parts; the mode of its calculation is given later. Inasmuch as it is merely a question of different periods of time, nothing is easier than to compute their average. But
2. We have here not alone quantitative but also qualitative difference.

   The circulating capital entering into the process of production transfers its entire value to the product and must therefore be continually replaced in kind by the sale of the product, if the process of production is to proceed without interruption. The fixed capital entering into the process of production transfers only a part of its value (the wear and tear) to the product and despite this wear and tear continues functioning in the process of production. Therefore it need not be replaced in kind until the lapse of intervals of various duration, at any rate not as frequently as the circulating capital. This necessity of replacement, the reproduction term, is not only quantitatively different for the various constituent parts of fixed capital, but, as we have seen, a part of the perennial fixed capital, that which lasts longer, may be replaced annually or at shorter intervals and added in kind to the old fixed capital. In the case of fixed capital of different properties the replacement can take place only all at once at the end of its period of durability.

   It is therefore necessary to reduce the specific turnovers of the various parts of fixed capital to a homogeneous form of turnover, so that they will remain different only quantitatively, namely, according to duration of turnover.

The qualitative identity does not come about if we take as our starting-point P ... P, the form of the continuous process of production. For definite elements of P must be constantly replaced in kind while others need not. However the form M ... M' undoubtedly yields this identity of turnover. Take for instance a machine worth £10,000, which lasts ten years of which one-tenth, or £1,000, is annually reconverted into money. These £1,000 have been converted in the course of one year from money-capital into productive capital and commodity-capital, and then reconverted from this into money-capital. They have returned to their original form, the money-form, just like the circulating capital, if we study the latter in this form, and it is immaterial whether this money-capital of £1,000 is once more converted at the end of the year into the bodily form of a machine or not. In calculating the aggregate turnover of the advanced productive capital we therefore fix all its elements in the money-form, so that the return to that form concludes the turnover. We assume that value is always advanced in money, even in the continuous process of production, where this money-form of value is only that of money of account. Thus we can compute the average.

3. It follows that even if by far the greater part of the advanced productive capital consists of fixed capital whose period of reproduction, hence also of turnover, comprises a cycle of many years, the capital-value turned over during the year may, on account of the repeated turnovers of the circulating capital within the same year, be larger than the aggregate value of the advanced capital.

Suppose the fixed capital is £80,000 and its period of reproduction 10 years, so that £8,000 of it annually return to their money-form, or it completes one-tenth of its turnover. Suppose further the circulating capital is £20,000, and its turnover is completed five times per year. The total capital would then be £100,000. The turned-over fixed capital is £8,000, the turned-over circulating capital five times £20,000, or £100,000. Then the capital turned over during one year is £108,000, or £8,000 more than the advanced capital. 1 + 2/25 of the capital have been turned over.

4. Therefore the *turnover time of the value* of the advanced capital differs from its actual time of reproduction or from the actual time of turnover of its component parts. Take for instance a capital of £4,000 and let it turn over, say, five times a year. The turned-over capital is then five times £4,000, or £20,000. But what returns at the end of each turnover to be advanced anew is the originally advanced capital of £4,000. Its magnitude is not changed by the number of turnover periods, during which it performs anew its functions as capital. (Apart from surplus-value.)

In the illustration under No. 3, then, the sums assumedly returned into the hands of the capitalist at the end of one year are (a) a sum of value amounting to £20,000 which he invests again in the circulating constituents of the capital, and (b) a sum of £8,000 which has been set free by wear and tear from the value of the advanced fixed capital; simultaneously this same fixed capital remains in the process of production, but with the reduced value of £72,000 instead of £80,000. The process of production therefore would have to be continued for nine years more, before the advanced fixed capital outlived its term and ceased to function as a creator of products and values, so that it would have to be replaced. The advanced capital-value, then, has to pass through a cycle of turnovers, in the present case a cycle of ten annual ones, and this cycle is determined by the life, hence the reproduction or turnover time of the applied fixed capital.

As the magnitude of the value and the durability of the applied fixed capital develop with the development of the capitalist mode of production, the lifetime of industry and of industrial capital lengthens in each particular field of investment to a period of many years, say of ten years on an average. Whereas the development of fixed capital extends the length of this life on the one hand it is shortened on the other by the continuous revolution in the means of production, which likewise incessantly gains momentum with the development of the capitalist mode of production. This involves a change in the means of production and the necessity of their constant replacement, on account of moral depreciation, long before they expire physically. One may assume that in the essential branches of modern industry this life-cycle now averages ten years. However we are not concerned here with the exact figure. This much is evident: the cycle of interconnected turnovers embracing a number of years, in which capital is held fast by its fixed constituent part, furnishes a material basis for the periodic crises. During this cycle business undergoes successive periods of depression, medium activity, precipitancy, crisis. True, periods in which capital is invested differ greatly and far from coincide in time. But a crisis always forms the starting-point of large new investments. Therefore, from the point of view of society as a whole, more or less, a new material basis for the next turnover cycle.[1]

5. On the way to calculate the turnovers, an American economist states:

'In some trades the whole capital embarked is turned or circulated several times within the year. In others a part is turned oftener than once a year, another part less often. It is the average period which his entire capital takes in passing through his hands, or making one revolution, from which a capitalist must calculate his profits. Suppose for example that a person engaged in a particular business has one half of his capital invested in buildings and machinery; so as to be turned only once in ten years; that one-fourth more, the cost of his tools, etc., is turned once in two years; and the remaining fourth, employed in paying wages and purchasing material, is turned twice in one year. Say that his entire capital is \$50,000. Then his annual expenditure will be,

\$25,000	:	10	=	\$ 2,500
12,500	:	2	=	6,500
12,500	×	2	=	25,000
\$33,750				

... the mean term in which his capital is turned being about sixteen months [In the manuscript Marx points out the fallacy of such a method of calculating the period of the turnover of capital. The mean term of turnover (16 months) given in the quotation was calculated with account taken of a profit of 7.5 per cent on the aggregate capital of \$50,000. Profit discounting, the turnover of capital is equal to 18 months.—*Ed.*]

'... Take another case, ... say that one-fourth of the entire capital circulates in ten years, one-fourth in one year, and one half twice in the year. Then the annual expenditure will be,

\$12,500	:	10	=	\$ 1,250
12,500			=	12,500
25,000	×	2	=	50,000
Turned over in 1 year \$63,750				

(Scrope, *Pol. Econ.*, edit. Alonzo Potter, New York, 1841, pp. 142, 143.) [The book referred to is A. Potter's *Political Economy, Its Objects, Uses, and Principles*, New York, 1840. According to the author's 'Advertisement', the second part of the book is substantially a reprint (with many alterations made by A. Potter) of G.J.P. Scrope's *The Principles of Political Economy*, London, 1833.—*Ed.*]

6. Real and apparent differences in the turnover of the various parts of capital.

The same Scrope says in the same passage:

> 'The capital laid out by a manufacturer, farmer, or tradesman in the payment of his labourer's wages, circulates most rapidly, being turned perhaps once a week (if his men are paid weekly), by the weekly receipts on his bills or sales. That invested in his materials and stock in hand circulates less quickly, being turned perhaps twice, perhaps four times in the year, according to the time consumed between his purchases of the one and sales of the other, supposing him to buy and sell on equal credits. The capital invested in his implements and machinery circulates still more slowly, being turned, that is, consumed and renewed, on the average, perhaps but once in five or ten years; though there are many tools that are worn out in one set of operations. The capital which is embarked in buildings, as mills, shops, warehouses, barns, in roads, irrigation, etc., may appear scarcely to circulate at all. But, in truth, these things are, to the full, as much as those we have enumerated, consumed in contributing to production, and must be reproduced in order to enable the producer to continue his operations; with this only difference, that they are consumed and reproduced by slower degrees than the rest ... and the capital invested in them may be turned perhaps every twenty of fifty years.' [pp. 141-42.]

Scrope confuses here the difference in the flow of certain parts of the circulating capital, brought about for the individual capitalist by terms of payment and conditions of credit, with the difference in the turnovers due to the nature of capital. He says that wages must be paid weekly out of the weekly receipts from paid sales or bills. It must be noted here in the first place that certain differences occur relative to wages themselves, depending on the length of the term of payment, that is, the length of time for which the labourer must give credit to the capitalist, whether wages are payable every week, month, three months, six months, etc. In this case, the law expounded before, holds good, to the effect that 'the quantity of the means of payment required for all periodical payments' (hence of the money-capital to be advanced at one time) 'is in inverse [This is evidently a slip of the pen, the proportion being direct and not inverse.—*Ed.*] proportion to the length of their periods.' (Buch I, Kap. III, 3b, Seite 124.) [English edition: Ch. III, 3b, p. 141.—*Ed.*]

In the second place, it is not only the new value added in the process of production by the week's labour which enters completely into the weekly product, but also the value of the raw and auxiliary materials consumed by the weekly product. This value circulates with the product containing it. It assumes the form of money through the sale of the product and must be reconverted into the same elements of production. This applies as much to the labour-power as to the raw and auxiliary materials. But we have already seen (Chapter VI, II, 1) that continuity of production requires a supply of means of production different for different branches of industry, and different within one and the same branch of business for different component parts of this element of the circulating capital, for instance, for coal and cotton. Hence, although these materials must be continually replaced in kind, they need not always be bought anew. The frequency of purchases depends on the size of the available stock, on the time it takes to exhaust it. In the case of labour-power there is no such storing of a supply. The reconversion into money of the part of capital laid out in labour-power goes hand in hand with that of the capital invested in raw and auxiliary materials. But the reconversion of the money, on the one hand into labour-power, on the other into raw materials, proceeds separately on account of the special terms of purchase and payment of these two constituents, one of them being bought as a productive supply for long periods, the other, labour-power, for shorter periods, for instance a week. On the other hand the capitalist must keep a stock of finished commodities besides a stock of materials for production. Let us leave sales difficulties aside. A certain quantity of goods must be produced, say, on order. While the last portion of this lot is being produced, the finished products are waiting in the warehouse until the order can be completely filled. Other differences in the turnover of circulating capital arise whenever some of its separate elements must stay in some preliminary stage of the process of production (drying of wood, etc.) longer than others.

The credit system, to which Scrope here refers, as well as commercial capital, modifies the turnover for the individual capitalist. On a social scale it modifies the turnover only in so far as it does not accelerate merely production but also consumption.

Note

1. 'Urban production is bound to a cycle of days, rural production on the contrary to one of years.' (Adam G. Müller, *Die Elemente der Staatskunst*, Berlin, 1809, III, p. 178.) this is the naive conception of industry and agriculture held by the romantic school.

10

Theories of Fixed and Circulating Capital The Physiocrats and Adam Smith

In Quesnay the distinction between fixed and circulating capital presents itself as *avances primitives* and *avances annuelles*. He correctly represents this distinction as one existing within productive capital, capital directly engaged in the process of production. As he regards the capital employed in agriculture, the capital of the farmer, as the only really productive capital, he draws these distinctions only for the capital of the farmer. This also accounts for the annual period of turnover of one part of the capital, and the more than annual (decennial) period of the other part. In the course of the development the physiocrats incidentally applied these distinctions also to other kinds of capital and to industrial capital in general. The distinction between annual advances and others of longer duration has retained such importance for society that many economists, even after Adam Smith, return to this definition.

The difference between these two kinds of advances does not arise until advanced money has been transformed into the elements of productive capital. It is a difference that exists solely within productive capital. It therefore never occurs to Quesnay to classify money either among the original or the annual advances. As advances for production, i.e., as productive capital, both of them stand opposed to money as well as the commodities existing in the market. Furthermore the difference between these two elements of productive capital is correctly reduced in Quesnay to the different manner in which they enter into the value of the finished product, hence to the different manner in which their values are circulated together with those of the products, and hence to the different manner of their replacement or their reproduction, the value of the one being wholly replaced annually, that of the other partly and at longer intervals.[1]

The only progress made by Adam Smith is the generalisation of the categories. With him it no longer applies to one special form of capital, the farmer's capital, but to every form of productive capital. Hence it follows as a matter of course that the distinction derived from agriculture between an annual turnover and one of two or more years' duration is superseded by the general distinction into different periods of turnover, one turnover of the fixed capital always comprising more than one turnover of the circulating capital, regardless of the periods of turnover of the circulating capital; whether they be annual, more than annual, or less than annual. Thus in Adam Smith the *avances annuelles* transform themselves into circulating capital, and the *avances primitives* into fixed capital. But his progress is confined to this generalisation of the categories. His implementation is far inferior to that of Quesnay.

The crudely empirical manner in which Smith broaches the investigation engenders at the very outset a lack of clarity:

> 'There are two different ways in which a capital may be employed so as to yield a revenue or profit to its employer.' (*Wealth of Nations*, Book II, Chap. I, p. 189, Aberdeen edition, 1848. [Wherever Marx did not give a page reference to quotations from Smith's work, editorial page references are given in square brackets to the London 1843 edition of *An Inquiry into the Nature and Causes of the Wealth of Nations, A new edition in four volumes*. This and all the following quotations from Smith have been checked with this edition.—*Ed.*]

The ways in which value may be invested so as to perform the functions of capital, to yield surplus value to its owner, are as different and varied as the spheres of investment of capital. It is a question of the different branches of production in which capital may be invested. If put in this way, the question implies still more. It includes the question of the way in which value, even if it is not invested as productive capital, can function as capital for its owner, for instance as interest-bearing capital, merchants' capital, etc. At this point we are already miles away from the real subject of the analysis, viz., the question of how the division of *productive* capital into its different elements, apart from their different spheres of investment, affects their turnover.

Adam Smith immediately continues:

> 'First, it may be employed in raising, manufacturing, or purchasing goods, and selling them again with a profit.' [Vol. II, p. 254.]

He does not tell us anything else here than that capital may be employed in agriculture, manufacture, and commerce. He speaks therefore only of the different spheres of investment of capital, including such in which, as in commerce, capital is not directly embodied in the process of production, hence does not function as productive capital. In so doing he abandons the foundation on which the physiocrats base the distinctions within productive capital and their effect on the turnover. More. He uses merchant's capital as an illustration in a problem which concerns exclusively differences within the *productive* capital in the product and value-creating process, which in turn cause differences in its turnover and reproduction.

He continues:

> 'The capital employed in this manner yields no revenue or profit to its employer, while it either remains in his possession or continues in the same shape.' [Vol. II, p. 254.]

'The capital employed in this manner!' But Smith speaks of capital invested in agriculture, in industry, and he tells us later that a capital so employed divides into fixed and circulating capital! Hence investment of capital in this manner cannot make fixed or circulating capital of it.

Or does he mean to say that capital employed in order to produce goods and to sell these at a profit must be sold after its transformation into goods and by means of the sale must in the first place pass from the possession of the seller into that of the buyer, and in the second place change from its bodily form, goods, into its money-form, so that it is of no use to its owner so long as it either remains in his possession or continues in the same shape? In that case, the whole thing amounts to this: The capital-value that formerly functioned in the form of productive capital, in a form peculiar to the process of production, now functions as commodity-capital and money-capital, in forms peculiar to the process of circulation, where it is no longer either fixed or circulating capital. And this applies equally to those elements of value which are added by raw and auxiliary material, i.e., by circulating capital, and to those which are added by the wear and tear of instruments of labour hence by fixed capital. We do not get any nearer to the difference between fixed and circulating capital in this way.

Further:

> 'The goods of the merchant yield him no revenue or profit till he sells them for money, and the money yields him as little till it is again exchanged for goods. His capital is continually going from him in one shape, and returning to him in another, and it is only by means of such circulation, or successive exchanges, that it can yield him any profit. Such capitals therefore may very properly be called circulating capitals.' [Vol. II, p. 254.]

What Adam Smith here defines as circulating capital is what I want to call *capital of circulation*, capital in a form pertinent to the process of circulation, to a change of form by means of exchange (a change of substance and change of hands), hence commodity-capital and money-capital, as distinguished from its form pertinent to the process of production, that of productive capital. These are not different kinds into which the industrial capitalist divides his capital, but different forms over and over again assumed and stripped off successively by the same advanced capital-value during its *curriculum vitae*. Adam Smith lumps this together—and this is a big step back compared to the physiocrats—with the distinctions in form which arise in the sphere of circulation of capital-value, in its circular course through its successive forms, while the capital-value exists in the form of *productive* capital; and they arise because of the different ways in which the different elements of productive capital take part in the formation of values and transfer their value to the product. We shall see below the consequences of this basic confusion of productive capital and capital in the sphere of circulation (commodity-capital and money-capital) on the one hand, with fixed and circulating capital on the other. The capital-value advanced in fixed capital is as much circulated by the product as that which has been advanced in the circulating capital, and both are equally converted into money-capital by the circulation of the commodity-capital. The difference evolves only from the fact that the value of the fixed capital circulates piece-meal and therefore must likewise be replaced piecemeal, at shorter or longer intervals, must be reproduced in its bodily form.

That by circulating capital Adam Smith means here nothing but capital of circulation, i.e., capital-value in the forms pertaining to the process of circulation (commodity capital and money-capital) is shown by his singularly ill-chosen illustration. He selects for this purpose a kind of capital which does not belong at all in the process of production, but whose abode is exclusively the sphere of circulation, which consists solely of capital of circulation—merchant's capital.

How absurd it is to start out with an illustration in which capital does not figure altogether as productive capital is stated right afterwards by him himself:

> 'The capital of a merchant, for example, is altogether a circulating capital.'

[Vol. II, p. 255.] Yet we are told later on that the difference between circulating and fixed capital evolves out of essential differences within the productive capital itself. On the one hand Adam Smith has the distinction of the physiocrats in mind, on the other the different forms assumed by capital-value in its circuit. And both these things are higgledy-piggledy jumbled together.

But how a profit is to come into existence by changes of form of money and commodities, by a mere transmutation of value from one of these forms into another, is more than anyone can tell. And an explanation becomes absolutely impossible because he starts out here with merchants' capital, which moves only in the sphere of circulation. We shall return to this later. Let us first hear what he has to say about fixed capital. [Vol. II, pp. 254-55.]

> 'Secondly, it (capital) may be employed in the improvement of land, in the purchase

> of useful machines and instruments of trade, or in suchlike things as yield a revenue or profit without changing masters, or circulating any further. Such capitals therefore may very properly be called fixed capitals. Different occupations require very different proportions between the fixed and circulating capitals employed in them. ... Some part of the capital of every master artificer or manufacturer be fixed in the instruments of his trade. This part, however, is very small in some, and very great in others. ... The far greater part of the capital of all such master artificers (such as tailors, shoemakers, weavers) however is circulated, either in the wages of their workmen, or in the price of their materials, and to be repaid with a profit by the price of work.'

Apart from the naïve determination of the source of profit weakness and confusion become at once apparent from the following: To a machine manufacturer for example the machine is his product, which circulates as commodity-capital, or in Adam Smith's words, 'is parted with, changes masters, circulates further.' According to his own definition therefore this machine would not be fixed but circulating capital. This confusion is again due to the fact that Smith mixes up the distinction between fixed and circulating capital evolved out of the manifold circulation of the various elements of productive capital, with differences in the form assumed by the same capital which functions as productive capital within the process of production and as circulation capital, that is to say, as commodity-capital or as money-capital, within the sphere of circulation. Consequently with Adam Smith things can function as fixed capital (as instruments of labour, elements of productive capital), or as 'circulating' capital, commodity-capital (as products thrust out of the sphere of production into that of circulation), all depending on the position they occupy in the life-process of capital.

But Adam Smith suddenly changes the entire basis of his classification, and contradicts the text with which he had opened the entire investigation a few lines previously. This refers particularly to the statement: 'There are two different ways in which a capital may be employed so as to yield a revenue or a profit to its employer,' [Vol. II, p. 254] namely, as circulating or as fixed capital. According to that these are therefore different methods of employing different capitals independent of one another, such as capitals that can be employed either in industry or in agriculture. And then we read [Vol. II, p. 255]:

> 'Different occupations require very different proportions between the fixed and circulating capitals employed in them.'

Fixed and circulating capital are now no longer different, independent investments of capital, but different portions of the same productive capital, which form different parts of the total value of this capital in different spheres of investment. Hence we have here differences arising from an appropriate division of the *productive* capital itself and therefore valid only with respect to it. But this runs counter to the circumstance that merchants' capital, being merely circulating capital, is opposed to fixed capital, for Adam Smith says himself: 'The capital of a merchant for example is altogether a circulating capital.' [Vol. II, p. 255.] It is indeed a capital performing its functions solely within the sphere of circulation and as such stands opposed in general to productive capital, the capital embodied in the process of production. But for this very reason it cannot be contrasted, as the circulating component part of productive capital, to its fixed component part.

In the illustrations Smith gives he designates the 'instruments of trade' as fixed capital, and the portion of capital laid out in wages and raw materials, including auxiliary materials, as circulating capital ('repaid with a profit by the price of the work').

And so he starts out, in the first place, from the various constituents of the labour-process, from labour-power (labour) and raw materials on the one hand, and instruments of labour on the other. But these are constituents of capital, because a sum of value which is to function as capital is invested in them. To this extent they are material elements, modes of existence of *productive* capital, that is to say, of capital functioning in the process of production. But why is one of these parts called fixed? Because

> 'some parts of the capital must be fixed in the instruments of trade.' [Vol. II, p. 254.]

But the other part is also fixed—in wages and raw materials. Machines however and

> 'instruments of trade ... or suchlike things ... yield a revenue or profit without changing masters, or circulating any further. Such capitals, therefore, may very properly be called fixed capitals.' [Vol. II, p. 254.]

Take for instance the mining industry. No raw material at all is used there, because the subject of labour, such as copper, is a product of nature, which must first be appropriated by labour. The copper to be first appropriated, the product of the process, which circulates later as a commodity, or commodity-capital, does not form an element of productive capital. No part of its value is invested in it. On the other hand the other elements of the productive process, labour-power and auxiliary materials such as coal, water, etc., do not enter materially into the product, either. The coal is entirely consumed and only its value enters into the product, just as a part of the value of the machine, etc., enters into it. Finally, the labourer remains as independent vis-à-vis the product, the copper, as the machine; except that the value which he produces by, means of his labour is now a component part of the value of the copper. Hence in this illustration not a single constituent of productive capital changes 'masters,' nor is any of them circulated further, because none of them enter materially into the product. What becomes of the circulating capital in this case? According to Adam Smith's own definition the entire capital employed in a copper mine consists of fixed capital and nothing else.

Let us take on the other hand a different industry, one which utilises raw materials that form the substance of its product, and auxiliary materials that enter into the product bodily and not only as so much value, as is the case with fuel coal. The product, for instance the yarn, changes hands together with the raw material, the cotton, composing it, and passes from the process of production into that of consumption. But so long as the cotton functions as an element of productive capital, its master does not sell it, but processes it, has it made into yarn. He does not part with it. Or, to use Smith's crudely erroneous and trivial terms, he does not make any profit 'by parting with it, by its changing masters, or by circulating it.' He does not permit his materials to circulate any more than his machines. They are fixed in the process of production, the same as the spinning machines and the factory buildings. Indeed, a part of the productive capital must be just as continually fixed in the form of coal, cotton, etc., as in the form of instruments of labour. The difference is only that for instance the cotton, coal, etc., required for one week's yarn production, are always entirely consumed in the manufacture of the weekly product, so that new cotton, coal, etc., must be supplied in their place; in other words, these elements of productive capital, although remaining identical in kind, always consist of new specimens of the same kind, while the same individual spinning machine or the same individual factory building continues its participation in a whole series of weekly productions without being replaced by a new specimen of its kind. As elements of the productive capital all its constituent parts are continually fixed in the process of production, for it cannot proceed without them. And all the elements of productive capital, whether fixed or circulating, equally confront, as productive capital, the capital of circulation, i.e., commodity-capital and money-capital.

It is the same with labour-power. A part of the productive capital must be continually fixed in it, and it is the same identical labour-powers, just as it is the same machines, that are everywhere employed for a certain length of time by the same capitalist. The difference between labour-power and machines in this case is not that the machines are bought once and for all (which is not so when they are paid for in instalments), while the labourer is not. The difference is rather that the labour expended by the labourer enters wholly into the value of the product, while the value of the machines enters only piecemeal.

Smith confuses different definitions when he says of circulating capital as opposed to fixed:

> 'The capital employed in this manner yields no revenue or profit to its employer, while it either remains in his possession or continues in the same shape.'

[Vol. II, p. 254.] He places the merely formal metamorphosis of the commodity, which the product, the commodity-capital, undergoes in the sphere of circulation and which brings about the change of hands of the commodities, on the same level as the bodily metamorphosis, which the various elements of productive capital undergo during the process of production. He indiscriminately jumbles together the transformation of commodities into money and of money into commodities, or purchase and sale, with the transformation of elements of production into products. His illustration for circulating capital is merchants' capital, which is converted from commodities into money and from money into commodities—the change of form C—M—C pertaining to the circulation of commodities. But this change of form within the circulation signifies for the industrial capital in action that the commodities into which the money is reconverted are elements of production (instruments of labour and labour-power), that, therefore, the change of form renders the function of industrial capital continuous, renders the process of production a continuous one, or a process of reproduction. This entire change of form takes place in circulation. It is this change of form that brings about the real passage of the commodities from hand to hand. But the metamorphoses gone through by productive capital within its process of production are on the contrary metamorphoses that pertain to the *labour-process* and are necessary to transform the elements of production into the desired product. Adam Smith clings to the fact that a part of the means of production (the instruments of labour proper) serve in the labour-process ('yield a profit to their master,' as he erroneously expresses it) without changing their bodily form and wear out only by degrees; while the other part, the materials, change and by virtue of this very change attain their destination as means of production. This difference in the behaviour of the elements of productive capital in the labour-process forms however only the point of departure of the difference between fixed and non-fixed capital, not this difference itself. That follows from the fact alone that this different behaviour exists in equal measure under all modes of production, capitalist and non-capitalist. To this different behaviour of material elements corresponds however the *transmission of value* to the product, and to this in turn corresponds the replacement of value by the sale of the product. That and that alone is what constitutes the difference in question. Hence capital is not called fixed because it is fixed in the instruments of labour but because a part of its value laid out in instruments of labour remains fixed in them, while the other part circulates as a component part of the value of the product.

> 'If it (the stock) is employed in procuring future profit, it must procure this profit either by staying with him (the employer), or by going from him. In the one case it is a fixed, in the other it is a circulating capital.' (p. 189.)

What strikes one here above all is that the crudely empirical conception of profit derived from the outlook of the ordinary capitalist, which wholly contradicts the better esoteric understanding of Adam Smith. Not only the price of materials and that of the labour-power is replaced in the price of the product, but also that part of value which is transferred by wear and tear from the instruments of labour to the product. Under no circumstances does this replacement yield profit. Whether a value advanced for the production of a commodity is replaced entirely or piecemeal, at one time or gradually, by the sale of that commodity, cannot change anything except the manner and time of replacement. But in no event can it transform that which is common to both, the replacement of value, into a creation of surplus-value. At the bottom of it all lies the commonly held idea that, because surplus-value is not realised until the product is sold, until it circulates, it originates only from sales, from the circulation. Indeed the different manner of origination of profit is in this case but a wrong way of expressing the fact that the different elements of productive capital serve differently, that as productive elements they act differently in the labour-process. In the end, the difference is not derived from the process of labour or self-expansion, not from the function of productive capital itself, but it is supposed to apply only subjectively to the individual capitalist, to whom one part of capital serves a useful purpose in one way, while another part does so in another way.

Quesnay, on the other hand, had derived these differences from the process of reproduction and its necessities. In order that this process may be continuous, the value of the annual advances must annually be replaced in full out of the value of the annual product, while the value of the investment capital need be replaced only piecemeal, so that it requires complete replacement and therefore complete reproduction only in a period of, say, ten years (by a new material of the same kind). Consequently Adam Smith falls far below Quesnay.

So there is therefore absolutely nothing left to Adam Smith for a definition of fixed capital except that it is instruments of labour which do not change their shape in the process of production and continue to serve in production until they are worn out, as opposed to the products in the formation of which they assist. He forgets that all elements of productive capital continually confront in their bodily form (as instruments of labour, materials, and labour-power) the product and the product circulating as a commodity, and that the difference between the part consisting of materials and labour-power and that consisting of instruments of labour is only this: with regard to labour-power, that it is always purchased afresh (not bought for the time it lasts, as are the instruments of labour); with regard to the materials, that it is not the same identical materials that function in the labour-process throughout, but always new materials of the same kind. At the same time the false impression is created that the value of the fixed capital does not participate in the circulation, although of course Adam Smith previously explained the wear and tear of fixed capital as a part of the price of the product.

In opposing circulating capital to fixed, no emphasis is placed on the fact that this opposition exists solely because it is that constituent part of productive capital which must be *wholly* replaced out of the value of the product and must therefore fully share in its metamorphoses, while this is not so in the case of the fixed capital. Instead the circulating capital is jumbled together with those forms which capital assumes on passing from the sphere of production to that of circulation, as commodity-capital and money-capital. But both forms, commodity-capital as well as money-capital, are carriers of the value of both the fixed and the circulating component parts of productive capital. Both of them are capital of circulation, as distinguished from productive capital, but not circulating (fluent) capital as distinguished from fixed capital.

Finally, owing to the wholly erroneous explanation that profit is made by fixed capital staying in the process of production, and by circulating capital leaving it and being circulated, and also on account of the identity of form assumed in the *turnover* by the variable capital and the circulating constituent of the constant capital, their essential difference in the *process of self-expansion* and of the formation of surplus-value is hidden, so that the entire secret of capitalist production is obscured still more. The common designation 'circulating capital' abolishes this essential difference. Political Economy subsequently went still farther by holding fast not to the antithesis between variable and constant capital but to the antithesis between fixed and circulating capital as the essential and sole delimitation.

After Adam Smith has designated fixed and circulating capital as two particular ways of investing capital, each of which yields a profit by itself, he says:

> 'No fixed capital can yield any revenue but by means of a circulating capital. The most useful machines and instruments of trade will produce nothing without the circulating capital which affords the materials they are employed upon, the maintenance of the workmen who employ them.' (P. 188.)

Here it becomes apparent what the previously used expressions 'yield a revenue,' 'make a profit,' etc., signify, viz., that both parts of capital serve as creators of product.

Adam Smith then gives the following illustration:

> 'That part of the capital of the farmer which is employed in the instruments of agriculture is a fixed, that which is employed in the wages and maintenance of his labouring servants is a circulating capital.'

(Here the difference between fixed and circulating capital is correctly applied only to difference in circulation, to the turnovers of different constituent parts of productive capital.)

> 'He makes a profit of the one by keeping it in his own possession, and of the other by parting with it. The price or value of his labouring cattle is a fixed capital'

(here he is again correct when he says it is the value, not the material element, to which the difference applies)

> 'in the same manner as that of the instruments of husbandry; their maintenance' (that of the labouring cattle) 'is a circulating capital in the same manner as that of the labouring servants. The farmer makes his profit by keeping the labouring cattle, and by parting with their maintenance.'

(The farmer keeps the fodder of the cattle, he does not sell it. He uses it to feed the cattle, while he uses us the cattle themselves as instruments of labour. The difference is only this: The fodder that goes for the maintenance of the labouring cattle is consumed wholly and must be continually replaced by new cattle fodder out of the products of agriculture or by their sale; the cattle themselves are replaced only as each head becomes incapacitated for work.)

> 'Both the price and the maintenance of the cattle which are bought in and fattened, not for labour but for sale, are a circulating capital. The farmer makes his profit by parting with them.' [Vol. II, pp. 255-56.]

(Every producer of commodities, hence likewise the capitalist producer, sells his product, the result of his process of production, but this is no reason why this product should form a part of either the fixed or the circulating component of his *productive* capital. The product now exists rather in that form in which it is thrust out of the process of production and must function as commodity-capital. The fattened stock function in the process of production as raw material, not as instruments of labour like the labouring cattle. Hence the fattened cattle enter into the product as substance, and their whole value enters into it, just as that of the auxiliary material [its fodder]. The fattened cattle are therefore a circulating part of the productive capital, but not because the sold product, the fattened cattle, have the same bodily form as the raw material, the cattle not yet fattened. This is accidental. At the same time Adam Smith might have seen by this illustration that it is not the material form of the element of production but its function within the process of production that determines the value contained in it as fixed or circulating.)

> 'The whole value of the seed too is properly a fixed capital. Though it goes backwards and forwards between the ground and the granary, it never changes masters, and

therefore it does not properly circulate. The farmer makes his profit not by its sale, but by its increase.' [Vol. II, p. 256.]

At this point the utter thoughtlessness of the Smithian distinction reveals itself. According to him seed would be fixed capital, if there would be no 'change of masters,' that is to say, if the seed is directly replaced out of the annual product, is deducted from it. On the other hand it would be circulating capital, if the entire product were sold and with a part of its value seed of another owner were bought. In the one case there is a 'change of masters,' in the other there is not. Smith once more confuses here circulating and commodity-capital. The product is the material vehicle of the commodity-capital, but of course only that part of it which actually enters into the circulation and does not re-enter directly into the process of production from which it emerged as a product.

Whether the seed is directly deducted from the product as a part of it or the entire product is sold and a part of its value converted in the purchase of another man's seed—in either case it is mere replacement that takes place and no profit is made by this replacement. In the one case the seed enters into circulation as a commodity together with the remainder of the product; in the other it figures only in book-keeping as a component part of the value of the advanced capital. But in both cases it remains a circulating constituent of the productive capital. The seed is entirely consumed to get the product ready, and it must be entirely replaced out of the product to make reproduction possible.

'Hence raw material and auxiliary substances lose the characteristic form with which they are clothed on entering the labour-process. It is otherwise with the instruments of labour. Tools, machines, workshops, and vessels, are of use in the labour-process, only so long as they retain their original shape, and are ready each morning to renew the process, with their shape unchanged. And just as during their lifetime, that is to say, during the continued labour-process in which they serve, they retain their shape independent of the product, so too, they do after their death. The corpses of machines, tools, workshops, etc., are always separate and distinct from the product they helped to turn out.' (Buch I, Kap. VI, S. 192.) [English edition: Volume I, Ch. VIII, p. 203.—*Ed.*]

These different ways in which means of production are consumed to form the product, some of them preserving their independent shape vis-à-vis the product, others changing or losing it entirely—this difference pertaining to the labour-process as such and therefore just as well to the labour-processes aimed at satisfying merely one's own needs, e.g., the needs of the patriarchal family, without any exchange, without production of commodities—are falsified by Adam Smith. He does so 1) by introducing here the totally irrelevant definition of profit, claiming that some of the means of production yield a profit to their owner by preserving their form, while the others do so by losing it; 2) by jumbling together the alterations of a part of the elements of production in the labour-process with the change of form (purchase and sale) that is characteristic of the exchange of products, of commodity circulation, and which at the same time includes a change in the ownership of the circulating commodities.

The turnover presupposes reproduction effected by circulation, hence by the sale of the product, by its conversion into money and its reconversion from money into its elements of production. But, since a part of the capitalist producer's own product serves him directly as means of production, he appears as a seller of it to himself, and that is how the matter figures in his books. In that case, this part of the reproduction is not brought about by circulation but proceeds directly. However the part of the product thus serving again as means of production replaces circulating, not fixed capital, since 1) its value passes wholly into the product, and 2) it itself has been wholly replaced in kind by a new specimen out of the new product.

Adam Smith tells us now what circulating and fixed capital consist of. He enumerates the things, the material elements, which form fixed, and those which form circulating capital, as if this definiteness were inherent in these things materially, by nature, and did not rather spring from their definite function within the capitalist process of production. And yet in the same chapter (Book II, Chapter I) he makes the remark that although a certain thing, e.g., a dwelling, which is reserved as 'stock' for 'immediate consumption,'

> 'may yield a revenue to its proprietor, and thereby serve *in the function of a capital* to him, it cannot yield any to the public, nor serve in the function of a capital to it, and the revenue of the whole body of the people can never be in the smallest degree increased by it.' (p. 186.)

Here, then, Adam Smith clearly states that the property of being capital is not inherent in things as such and in any case, but is a function with which they may or may not be invested, according to circumstances. But what is true of capital in general is also true of its subdivisions.

Things form constituent parts of the circulating or fixed capital, depending on what function they perform in the labour-process. A head of cattle for instance, as labouring cattle (instrument of labour), represents the material mode of existence of fixed capital, while as cattle for fattening (raw material) it is a constituent part of the farmer's circulating capital. On the other hand the same thing may now function as a constituent part of productive capital and now belong to the fund for direct consumption. A house for instance when performing the function of a workshop, is a fixed component part of productive capital; when serving as a dwelling it is in no wise a form of capital. The same instruments of labour may, in many cases, serve either as means of production or as means of consumption.

It was one of the errors following from Adam Smith's idea that the property of being fixed or circulating capital was conceived as inherent in the things themselves. The mere analysis of the labour-process (Buch I, Kap. V) [English edition: Volume I, Ch. VII.—*Ed.*] shows that the definitions of instruments of labour, materials of labour, and product change according to the various roles played by one and the same thing in the process. The definitions of fixed and non-fixed capital are based in their turn on the definite roles played by these elements in the labour-process, and therefore also in the value formation process.

In the second place, on enumerating the things fixed and circulating capitals consist of, it becomes fully apparent that Smith lumps together the distinction—valid and making sense only with regard to productive capital (capital in its productive form)—between the fixed and circulating components of the same, with the distinction between productive capital and those forms which pertain to capital in its process of circulation, viz., commodity-capital and money-capital. He says in the same passage (pp. 187 and 188):

> 'The circulating capital consists ... of the provisions, materials, and finished work of all kinds that are in the hands of their respective dealers, and of the money that is necessary for circulating and distributing them, etc.'

Indeed, if we look more closely we observe that here, contrary to his previous statements, circulating capital is again equated to commodity-capital and money-capital, that is to say, to two forms of capital which do not belong in the process of production at all, which do not form circulating (fluent) capital as opposed to fixed, but capital of circulation as opposed to productive capital. It is only *alongside* these that the constituents of productive capital advanced in materials (raw materials or semi-finished products) and really incorporated in the process of production then play a role again. He says:

> '... The third and last of the three portions into which the general stock of the society naturally divides itself, is the circulating capital, of which the characteristic is, that it affords a revenue only by circulating or changing masters. It is composed likewise of four parts: first of the money ...'

(but money is never a form of productive capital, of capital functioning in the productive process; it is always only one of the forms assumed by capital within its process of circulation);

> 'secondly, of the stock of provisions which are in the possession of the butcher, the grazier, the farmer ... from the sale of which they expect to derive a profit ... Fourthly and lastly, of the work which is made up and completed, but which is still in the hands of the merchant and manufacturer. And, thirdly, of the materials, whether altogether rude, or more or less manufactured, of clothes, furniture, and buildings, which are not yet made up into any of those three shapes, but which remain in the hands of the growers, the manufacturers, the mercers and drapers, the timber-merchants, the carpenters and jointers, the brick-makers, etc.'

Nos. 2 and 4 contain nothing but products which have been thrust out as such from the process of production and must be sold, in short, which now function as commodities, hence as commodity-capital, and which therefore have a form and occupy a place in the process in which they are not elements of productive capital, no matter what may be their eventual destination, i.e., whether, in order to answer their purpose (use-value), they should finally be allotted to individual or productive consumption. The products mentioned in 2 are foodstuffs, in 4 all other finished products, which in turn consist only of finished instruments of labour or finished articles of consumption (foodstuffs other than those mentioned under 2).

The fact that Smith at the same time speaks of the merchant shows his confusion. Once the producer sells his product to the merchant, it no longer constitutes any form of his capital. From the point of view of society, it is indeed still commodity-capital, although in other hands than those of its producer; but for the very reason that it is a commodity-capital it is neither fixed nor circulating capital.

In every kind of production not meant for the satisfaction of the producer's direct needs, the product must circulate as a commodity, i.e., it must be sold, not in order to make a profit on it, but that the producer may be able to live at all. Under capitalist production, there is to be added the circumstance that when a commodity is sold the surplus-value embodied in it is also realised. The product emerges as a commodity from the process of production and is therefore neither a fixed nor a circulating element of this process.

Incidentally, Smith here argues against himself. The finished products, whatever their material form or their use-value, their useful effect, are all commodity-capital here, hence capital in a form characteristic of the process of circulation. Being in this form, they are not constituent parts of any productive capital their owner may have. This does not in the least prevent them from becoming, right after their sale, in the hands of their purchaser, constituent parts of productive capital, either fixed or circulating. Here it is evident that things which for a certain time appear in the market as commodity-capital, as opposed to productive capital, may or may not function as circulating or fixed constituents of productive capital after they have been removed from the market.

The product of the cotton spinner, yarn, is the commodity-form of his capital, is commodity-capital as far as he is concerned. It cannot function again as a constituent part of his productive capital, neither as material of labour nor as an instrument of labour. But in the hands of the weaver who buys it it is incorporated in the productive capital of the latter as one of its circulating constituent parts. For the spinner, however, the yarn is the depository of the value of part of his fixed as well as circulating capital (apart from the surplus-value). In the same way a machine, the product of a machine-manufacturer, is the commodity-form of his capital, is commodity-capital to him. And so long as it stays in this form it is neither circulating nor fixed capital. But if sold to a manufacturer for use it becomes a fixed component part of a productive capital. Even if by virtue of its use-form the product can partly re-enter as means of production into the process from which it originated, e.g., coal into coal production, precisely that part of the output of coal which is intended for sale represents neither circulating nor fixed capital but commodity-capital.

On the other hand a product, due to its use-form, may be wholly incapable of forming any element of productive capital, either as material of labour or as an instrument of labour. For instance any means of subsistence. Nevertheless it is commodity-capital for its producer, is the carrier of the value of his fixed as well as circulating capital; and of the one or the other according to whether the capital employed in its production has to be replaced in whole or in part, has transferred its value to the product in whole or in part.

With Smith, in No. 3, the raw material (material not worked up, semi-finished products, auxiliary substances) does not figure on the one hand as a component part embodied in the productive capital, but actually only as a special kind of use-values of which the social product can at all consist, as a special kind of commodities existing alongside the other material constituent parts, means of subsistence, etc., enumerated under Nos. 2 and 4. On the other hand, these materials are indeed cited as incorporated in the productive capital and therefore as elements of it in the hands of the producer. The confusion is evidenced by the fact that they are partly conceived as functioning in the hands of the producer ('in the hands of the growers, the manufacturers, etc.'), and partly in the hands of merchants ('mercers, drapers, timber-merchants'), where they are merely commodity-capital, not component parts of productive capital.

Indeed, Adam Smith wholly forgets here, in enumerating the elements of circulating capital, the distinction—applying only to the productive capital—between fixed and circulating capital. He rather places commodity-capital and money-capital, i.e., the two forms of capital typical of the process of circulation, in opposition to the productive capital, but that quite unconsciously.

Finally, it is a striking fact that Adam Smith forgets to mention labour-power when counting off the constituent parts of circulating capital. There are two reasons for this.

We have just seen that, apart from money-capital, circulating capital is only another name for commodity-capital. But to the extent that labour-power circulates in the market, it is not capital, no form of commodity-capital. It is not capital at all; the labourer is not a capitalist, although he brings a commodity to market, namely his own skin. Not until labour-power has been sold, been incorporated in the process of production, hence not until it has ceased to circulate as a commodity, does it become a constituent of productive capital—variable capital as the source of surplus-value, a circulating component part of productive capital with reference to the turnover of the capital-value invested in it. Since Smith here confuses the circulating capital with commodity-capital, he cannot bring labour-power under the head of circulating capital. Hence the variable capital here appears in the form of the commodities the labourer buys with his wages, viz., means of subsistence. In this form the capital-value invested in wages is supposed to belong to circulating capital. That which is incorporated in the process of production is labour-power, the labourer himself, not the means of subsistence wherewith the labourer maintains himself. True, we have seen (Buch I, Kap. XXI) [English edition: Volume I, Ch. XXIII.—*Ed.*] that from the point of view of society the reproduction of the labourer himself by means of his individual consumption is likewise part of the process of reproduction of social capital. But this does not apply to the individual, isolated process of production which we are studying here. The 'acquired and useful abilities' (p. 187) which Smith mentions under the head of fixed capital are on the contrary component parts of circulating capital, since they are 'abilities' of the wage-labourer and he has sold his labour together with its 'abilities.'

It is a great mistake on the part of Adam Smith to divide the entire social wealth into 1) a fund for immediate consumption, 2) fixed capital, and 3) circulating capital. According to the above, wealth would have to be divided into 1) a consumption-fund which does not form any part of functioning social capital although parts of it *can* continually function as capital; and 2) capital. Accordingly one part of the wealth functions as capital, the other as non-capital, or consumption-fund. And here appears the absolute necessity that all capital be either fixed or circulating somewhat like the natural necessity that a mammal be male or female. But we have seen that the antithesis between fixed and circulating capital applies solely to the elements of *productive* capital, that consequently there is besides these a considerable amount of capital—commodity-capital and money-capital—exists in a form in which it *can be* neither fixed nor circulating.

Inasmuch as under capitalist production the entire mass of social products circulates in the market as commodity-capital, with the exception of that part of the products which is directly used up again by the individual capitalist producers in its bodily form as means of production without being sold or bought, it is evident that not only the fixed and circulating elements of productive capital, but likewise all the elements of the consumption-fund are derived from the commodity-capital. This is tantamount to saying that on the basis of capitalist production both means of production and articles of consumption first appear as commodity-capital, even though they are intended for later use as means of production or articles of consumption, just as labour-power itself is found in the market as a commodity, although not as commodity-capital.

This accounts for the following new confusion in Adam Smith. He says:

> 'Of these four parts'

(of the 'circulating' capital, i.e., of capital in its forms of commodity-capital and money-capital belonging in the process of circulation, two parts which are turned into four by the material distinctions Adam Smith makes between the constituent parts of commodity-capital)

> 'three—provisions, materials, and finished work, are either annually or in a longer or shorter period, regularly withdrawn from it and placed either in the fixed capital, or in the stock reserved for immediate consumption. Every fixed capital is both originally derived from, and requires to be continually supported by, a circulating capital. All useful machines and instruments of trade are originally derived from a circulating capital which furnishes the materials of which they are made and the maintenance of the workmen who make them. They require, too, a capital of the same kind to keep them in constant repair.' (p. 188.)

With the exception of that part of the product which is constantly consumed again as means of production directly by its producers, the following general proposition applies to capitalist production: All products reach the market as commodities and therefore circulate for the capitalist as the commodity-form of his capital, as commodity-capital, regardless of whether these products must or can function in their bodily form, in accordance with their use-values, as elements of productive capital (of the process of production), as means of production and therefore as fixed or circulating elements of productive capital; or whether they can serve only as means of individual, not of productive, consumption. All products are thrown upon the market as commodities; all means of production or consumption, all elements of productive and individual consumption, must therefore be extracted from the market by purchasing them as commodities. This truism is of course correct. It applies for this reason to the fixed as well as the circulating elements of productive capital, to instruments of labour as well as material of labour in all forms. (This, moreover, ignores the fact that there are elements of productive capital which are furnished by nature, are not products.) A machine is bought in the market, as is cotton. But it does not follow from this by any means that every fixed capital stems originally from some circulating capital; that follows only from the Smithian confusion of capital of circulation with circulating or fluent, i.e., non-fixed capital. Besides, Smith actually refutes himself. According to him himself, machines, as commodities, form a part of No. 4 of the circulating capital. Hence to say that they come from the circulating capital means only that they functioned as commodity-capital before they functioned as machines, but that materially they are derived from themselves; so is cotton, as the circulating element of some spinner's capital, derived from the cotton in the market. But, if Adam Smith in his further exposition derives fixed capital from circulating capital for the reason that labour and raw material are required to build machines, it must be borne in mind that in the first place, instruments of labour, hence fixed capital, are also required to build machines, and in the second place fixed capital, such as machinery, etc., is likewise required to make raw materials, since productive capital always includes instruments of labour, but not always material of labour. He himself says immediately afterwards:

> 'Land, mines, and fisheries, require all both a fixed and a circulating capital to cultivate them;'

(thus he admits that not only circulating but also fixed capital is required for the production of raw material)

> 'and' (new error at this point) 'their produce replaces with a profit, not only those capitals, but *all the others in the society*.' (p. 188.)

This is entirely wrong. Their produce furnishes the raw material, auxiliary material, etc., for all other branches of industry. But their value does not replace the value of all other social capitals; it replaces only their own capital-value (plus the surplus-value). Adam Smith is here again in the grip of his physiocratic reminiscences.

Considered socially it is true that the part of the commodity-capital which consists of products that can serve only as instruments of labour must—unless they have been produced to no purpose, cannot be sold—sooner or later function as instruments of labour, i.e., with capitalist production as their basis, they must, whenever they cease to be commodities, form real, as before they formed prospective, elements of the fixed part of the social productive capital.

But there is a distinction here, arising from the bodily form of the product.

A spinning machine for instance has no use-values, unless it is used for spinning, unless therefore it functions as an element of production and consequently, from the point of view of the capitalist, as a fixed component part of a productive capital. But a spinning machine is movable. It may be exported from the country in which it was produced and sold abroad directly or indirectly for raw materials, etc., or for champagne. In that case it has functioned only as a commodity-capital in the country in which it was produced, but never as fixed capital, not even after its sale.

Products however which are localised by being anchored in the soil, and can therefore be used only locally, such as factory buildings, railways, bridges, tunnels, docks, etc., soil improvements, etc., cannot be exported bodily, neck and crop. They are not movable. They are either useless, or as soon as they have been sold must function as fixed capital in the country that produced them. To their capitalist producer, who builds factories or improves land for speculative sale, these things are forms of his commodity-capital, or, according to Adam Smith, forms of circulating capital. But viewed socially these things—if they are not to be useless—must ultimately function as fixed capital in that very country, in some local process of production. From this it does not follow in the least that immovables are in themselves fixed capital. They may belong, as dwelling houses, etc., to the consumption-fund, and in that case they are not part whatever of the social capital, although they constitute an element of the social wealth of which capital is only a part. The producer of these things, to speak in the language of Adam Smith, makes a profit by their sale. And so they are circulating capital! Their practical utiliser, their ultimate purchaser, can use them only by applying them in the process of production, and so they are fixed capital!

Titles to property, for instance railway shares, may change hands every day, and their owner may make a profit by their sale even in foreign countries, so that titles to property are exportable, although the railway itself is not. Nevertheless these things must either lie fallow in the very country in which they are localised, or function as a fixed component of some productive capital. In the same way manufacturer A may make a profit by selling his factory to manufacturer B, but this does not prevent the factory from functioning as fixed capital the same as before.

Therefore, while the locally fixed instruments of labour, which cannot be detached from the soil, will nevertheless, in all probability, have to function as commodity-capital for their producer and not constitute any elements of his fixed capital (which is made up as far as he is concerned of the instruments of labour he needs for the construction of buildings, railways, etc.), one should not by any means draw the contrary conclusion that fixed capital necessarily consists of immovables. A ship and a locomotive are effective only through their motion; yet they function, not for him who produced them, but for him who applies them as fixed capital. On the other hand things which are most decidedly fixed in the process of production, live and die in it and never leave it any more after once entering it, are circulating component parts of the productive capital. Such are for instance the coal consumed to drive the machine in the process of production, the gas used to light the factory, etc. They are circulating capital not because they bodily leave the process of production together with the product and circulate as commodities, but because their value enters wholly into that of the commodity which they help to produce and which therefore must be entirely replaced out of the proceeds of the sale of the commodity.

In the passage last quoted from Adam Smith, notice must also be taken of the following phrase:

> 'A circulating capital which furnishes ... the maintenance of the workmen who make them' (machines, etc.).

With the physiocrats that part of capital which is advanced for wages figures correctly under the avances annuelles as distinguished from the avances primitives. On the other hand, it is not he labour-power itself that appears with them as a constituent part of the productive capital employed by the farmer, but the means of subsistence (the maintenance of the workmen, as Smith calls it) given to the farm-labourers. This hangs together exactly with their specific doctrine. For according to them the value-part added to the product by labour (quite like the value-part added to the product by raw material, instruments of labour, etc., in short, by all the material components of constant capital) is equal only to the value of the means of subsistence paid to the labourers and necessarily consumed for the maintenance of their ability to function as labour-power. Their very doctrine stands in the way of their discovering the distinction between constant and variable capital. If it is labour that produces surplus-value (in addition to reproducing its own price), then it does so in industry as well as in agriculture. But since, according to their system, labour produces surplus-value only in one branch of production, namely agriculture, it does not arise out of labour but out of the special activity (assistance) of nature in this branch. And only for this reason agricultural labour is to them productive labour, as distinct from other kinds of labour.

Adam Smith classifies the means of subsistence of labourers as circulating capital in contradistinction to fixed capital:

1. Because he confuses circulating as distinguished from fixed capital with forms of capital pertaining to the sphere of circulation, with capital of circulation—a confusion uncritically accepted. He therefore mixes up commodity-capital and the circulating component of productive capital, and in that case it is a matter of course that whenever the social product assumes the form of commodities, the

means of subsistence of the labourers as well as those of the non- labourers, the materials as well as the instruments of labour themselves, must be supplied out of the commodity capital.

2. But the physiocratic conception too lurks in Smith's analysis, although it contradicts the esoteric—really scientific—part of his own exposition.

Generally speaking, the advanced capital is converted into productive capital, i.e., it assumes the form of elements of production which are themselves the products of past labour. (Among them labour-power.) Capital can function in the process of production only in this form. Now, if instead of labour-power itself, into which the variable part of capital has been converted, we take the labourer's means of subsistence, it is evident that these means as such do not differ, so far as the formation of value is concerned, from the other elements of productive capital, from the raw materials and the food of the labouring cattle, on which ground Smith in one of the passages quoted above places them, after the manner of the physiocrats, on the same level. The means of subsistence cannot themselves expand their own value or add any surplus-value to it. Their value, like that of the other elements of the productive capital, can re-appear only in the value of the product. They cannot add any more to its value than they have themselves. Like raw materials, semi-finished goods, etc., they differ from fixed capital composed of instruments of labour only in that they are entirely consumed in the product (at least as far as concerns the capitalist who pays for them) in the formation of which they participate and that therefore their value must be replaced as a whole, while in the case of the fixed capital this takes place only gradually, piecemeal. The part of productive capital advanced in labour-power (or in the labourer's means of subsistence) differs here only materially and not in respect of the process of labour and production of surplus-value from the other material elements of productive capital. It differs only in so far as it falls into the category of circulating capital together with one part of the objective creators of the product ('materials' Adam Smith calls them generally), as opposed to the other part of these objective product creators, which belong in the category of fixed capital.

The fact that the capital laid out in wages belongs in the circulating part of productive capital and, unlike the fixed component of productive capital, shares the quality of fluency with a part of the objective product creators, the raw materials, etc., has nothing whatever to do with the role played in the process of self-expansion by this variable part, as distinct from the constant part of capital. This refers only to how this part of the advanced capital-value is to be replaced, renewed, hence reproduced out of the value of the product of means of the circulation. The purchase and repurchase of labour-power belong in the process of circulation. But it is only within the process of production that the value laid out in labour-power is converted (not for the labourer but for the capitalist) from a definite, constant magnitude into a variable one, and only thus the advanced value is converted altogether into capital-value, into capital, into self-expanding value. But by classing, like Smith, the value expended for the means of subsistence of the labourers, instead of value laid out in labour-power, as the circulating component of productive capital, the understanding of the distinction between variable and constant capital, and thus the understanding of the capitalist process of production in general, is rendered impossible. The determination that this part of capital is variable capital in contrast to the constant capital, spent for material creators of the product, is buried beneath the determination that the part of the capital invested in labour-power belongs, as far as the turnover is concerned, in the circulating part of productive capital. And the burial is brought to completion by enumerating the labourer's means of subsistence instead of his labour-power as an element of productive capital. It is immaterial whether the value of the labour-power is advance in money or directly in means of subsistence. However under capitalist production the latter can be but an exception.[2]

By thus establishing the definition of circulating capital as being the determinant of the capital value laid out for labour-power—this physiocratic definition without the premise of the physiocrats—Adam Smith fortunately killed among his followers the understanding that that part of capital which is spent on labour-power is variable capital. The more profound and correct ideas developed by him elsewhere did not prevail, but this blunder of his did. Indeed, other writers after him went even further. They were not content to make it the decisive definition of the part of capital invested in labour-power to be circulating as opposed to fixed capital; they made it the essential definition of circulating capital to be invested in labour-power to be circulating as opposed to fixed capital; they made it the essential definition of circulating capital to be invested in means of subsistence for labourers. Naturally associated with this is the doctrine that the labour-fund, [Karl Marx, *Capital*, Vol. I, pp. 609-11.—*Ed.*] consisting of the necessary means of subsistence, is of a definite magnitude, which on the one hand physically limits the share of the labourers in the social product, but on the other has to be fully expended in the purchase of labour-power.

Notes

1. Cf. Quesnay, *Analyse du Tableau Economique* (*Physiocrates*, èd. Daire, 1. partie, Paris, 1846). There we read, for instance: 'The annual advances consist of the expenses incurred annually for the labour of cultivation; these advances must be distinguished from the original advances, which form the fund for the establishment of the farming enterprise.' (P. 59.) In the works of the later physiocrats these advances are sometimes termed directly capital: *Capital ou avances* Dupont de Nemours, *Maximes du Docteur Quesnay, ou Rèsumè de ses Principes d'Economie Sociale* (Daire, I, p. 391); furthermore Le Trosne writes: 'As a result of the greater or smaller durability of the works of human labour, a nation possesses a substantial fund of wealth independent of its annual reproduction, this fund forming a capital—accumulated over a long period and originally paid with products—which is continually preserved and augmented.' (Daire, II, pp. 928-29.) Turgot employs the term capital more regularly for *avances*, and identifies the *avances* of the manufacturers still more with those of the farmers. (Turgot, *Rèflexions surla Formation et la Distribution des Richesses*, 1766.)
2. To what extent Adam Smith has blocked his own way to an understanding of the role of labour-power in the process of self-expansion of value is proven by the following sentence, which in the manner of the physiocrats places the labour of labourers on a level with that of labouring cattle. 'Not only his (the farmer's) labouring servants, but his labouring cattle are productive labourers.' (Book II, Ch. V, p. 243.)

11

Theories of Fixed and Circulating Capital. Ricardo

Ricardo introduces the distinction between fixed and circulating capital merely for the purpose of illustrating the exceptions to the rule of value, namely, cases where the rate of wages affects prices. The discussion of this point is reserved for Book III. [Karl Marx, *Capital*, Vol. III, Ch. XI, pp. 196-200.—*Ed.*]

But the original lack of clarity is apparent at the outset in the following immaterial juxtaposition:

'This difference in the degree of durability of fixed capital, *and* this variety in the proportions in which the two sorts of capital may be combined.'[1]

And if we ask him which two sorts of capital he is referring to, we are told:

'The proportions, too, in which the capital that is to support labour, and the capital that is invested in tools, machinery, and buildings, may be variously combined.'[2]

In other words, fixed capital equals instruments of labour and circulating capital equals capital laid out in labour. 'Capital that is to support labour' is a senseless term culled from Adam Smith. On the one hand the circulating capital is here lumped together with the variable capital, i.e., with that part of productive capital which is laid out in labour. But on the other hand, doubly erroneous definitions arise for the reason that the antithesis is not derived from the process of self-expansion of value—constant and variable capital—but from the process of circulation (Adam Smith's old confusion).

First: The differences in the degree of durability of fixed capital and the difference arising from capital being composed of constant and variable capital are conceived as being of equal significance. But the last-named difference determines the difference in the production of surplus-value; the first named on the other hand, so far as the process of self-expansion is concerned, refers only to the manner in which a particular value is transferred from a means of production to the product; so far as the process of circulation is concerned, this difference refers only to the period of the renewal of the expended capital, or, from another point of view, to the time for which it has been advanced. If instead of seeing through the internal machinery of the capitalist process of production one considers merely the accomplished phenomena, then these distinctions actually coincide. In the distribution of the social surplus-value among the various capitals invested in different branches of industry, the differences in the different periods of time for which capital is advanced (for instance the various degrees of durability of fixed capital) and the different organic compositions of capital (and therefore also the different circulations of constant and variable capital) contribute equally toward an equalisation of the general rate of profit and the conversion of values into prices of production.

Secondly: From the point of view of the process of circulation, we have on one side the instruments of labour—fixed capital, on the other the material of labour and wages—circulating capital. But from the point of view of the process of labour and self-expansion, we have on the one side means of production (instruments of labour and material of labour)—constant capital; on the other, labour-power—variable capital. It is wholly immaterial for the organic composition of capital (Buch I, Kap. XXIII, 2, p. 647) [English edition, Volume I, Ch. XXV, 2, pp. 622-23.—*Ed.*] whether a specified quantity of value of constant capital consists of many instruments of labour and little material of labour or of much material of labour and few instruments of labour, while everything depends on the ratio of the capital laid out in means of production to that laid out in labour-power. Vice versa: from the point of view of the process of circulation, of the distinction between fixed and circulating capital, it is just as immaterial in what proportions a particular quantity of value circulating capital divides into material of labour and wages. From one of these points of view the material of labour is classed in the same category with the instruments of labour, as opposed to the capital-value laid out in labour-power; from the other view-point the part of capital laid out in labour-power ranges with that laid out in material of labour, as opposed to that laid out in instruments of labour.

For this reason the part of the capital-value laid out in material of labour (raw and auxiliary materials) does not appear on either side in Ricardo. It disappears entirely; for it will not do to class it with fixed capital, because its mode of circulation coincides entirely with that of the part of capital laid out in labour-power. And on the other hand it should not be placed alongside circulating capital, because in that event the identification of the antithesis of fixed and circulating capital with that of constant and variable capital, which had been handed down by Adam Smith and is tacitly retained, would abolish itself. Ricardo has too much logical instinct not to feel this, and for this reason that part of capital vanishes entirely from his sight.

It is to be noted at this point that the capitalist, to use the jargon of Political Economy, advances the capital laid out in wages for various periods of time, according to whether he pays these wages weekly, monthly, or quarterly. But as a matter of fact the reverse takes place. It is the labourer who advances his labour to the capitalist for a week, a month, or three months, according to whether he is paid by the week, by the month, or every three months. If the capitalist *bought* labour-power instead of paying for it, in other words, if he paid the labourer his wages in advance for a day, a week, a month, or a quarter, he would be justified in claiming that he advanced wages for those periods. But since he pays after the labour *has* lasted for days, weeks, or months, instead of buying it and paying for the time which it is to last, the whole thing amounts to a capitalist *quid pro quo*, and the advance which the labour gives to the capitalist in labour is turned into an advance of money given to the labourer by the capitalist. It does not alter the case in the least that the capitalist gets back the product itself or its value (together with the surplus-value embodied in it) from circulation, or realises it, only after a relatively long or short period of time, according to the different periods required for its manufacture or for its circulation. The seller of a commodity does not care a rap what its buyer is going to do with it. The capitalist does not get a machine cheaper because he must advance its entire value at one shot, while this value returns to him only gradually and piecemeal from circulation; nor does he pay more for cotton because its value enters entirely into the value of the product into which it is made and is therefore replaced fully and at one time by the sale of the product.

Let us return to Ricardo.

Firstly: The characteristic feature of variable capital is that a definite, given (and as such constant) part of capital, a given sum of values (assumed to be equal in value to the labour-power, although it does not matter here whether the wages are equal, more or less than the value of the labour-power) is exchanged for a self-expanding, value-creating power, viz., labour-power, which not only reproduces its value, paid by the capitalist, but simultaneously produces a surplus-value, a value not existing previously and not paid for by any equivalent. This characteristic property of the part of capital laid out for wages, which distinguishes it *toto coelo* as variable capital from constant capital, disappears whenever the part of capital expended on wages is considered solely from the point of view of the process of circulation and thus appears as circulating capital in contradistinction to the fixed capital laid out in instruments of labour. This is apparent if only from the fact that it is then brought under one head—that of circulating capital—together with the component part of the constant capital laid out in material of labour and opposed to the other component of the constant capital—that laid out in instruments of labour. Surplus-value, hence the very circumstance which converts the laid-out sum of value into capital, is entirely ignored thereby. Similarly the fact is ignored that the part of the value added to the product by the capital laid out in wages is newly produced (and therefore really reproduced), while the part of the value which the raw material adds to the product is not newly produced, not really reproduced, but only preserved in the value of the product, conserved, and hence merely reappears as a component part of the value of the product. The distinction, as now seen from the point of view of the contrast between fixed and circulating capital, consists simply in this: The value of the instruments of labour used for the production of a commodity enters only partially into the value of the commodity and is therefore only partially replaced by its sale, hence is replaced altogether only piecemeal and gradually. On the other hand the value of the labour-power and subjects of labour (raw materials, etc.) used for the production of a commodity entirely enters into it and is therefore entirely replaced by its sale. In this respect, as far as the process of circulation is concerned, one part of capital presents itself as fixed, the other as fluent, or circulating. In both cases it is a matter of transferring given, advanced values to the product and of their replacement by the sale of the product. The difference now depends only on whether the transfer of value, and consequently the replacement of the value, takes place piecemeal and gradually, or in bulk. By this means the distinction between the variable and constant capital, which decides everything, is blotted out, hence the whole secret of the production of surplus-value and of capitalist production, the circumstances which transform certain values and the things in which they present themselves into capital, are obliterated. All constituent parts of capital are then distinguished merely by their mode of circulation (and, of course, circulation of commodities concerns itself solely with already existing given values); and the capital laid out in wages shares a peculiar mode of circulation with the part of capital laid out in raw materials, semi-finished products, auxiliary materials, as opposed to the part of capital laid out in instruments of labour.

It is therefore understandable why bourgeois Political Economy instinctively clung to Adam Smith's confusion of the categories 'constant and variable capital' with the categories 'fixed and circulating,' and repeated it parrotlike, without criticism, from generation to generation for a century. The part of capital laid out for wages is no longer in the least distinguished by bourgeois Political Economy from the part of capital laid out for raw materials, and differs only formally from constant capital—on the point of whether it is circulated piecemeal or in one lump by the product. Thereby the basis for an understanding of the real movement of capitalist production, and hence of capitalist exploitation, is buried at one stroke. It is but a question of the reappearance of advanced values.

In Ricardo the uncritical adoption of the Smithian confusion is more disturbing not only than in the later apologists, in whom the confusion of ideas is rather something not disturbing, but than in Adam Smith himself, because Ricardo, in contrast to the latter, is more consistent and incisive in his analysis of value and surplus-value, and indeed upholds the esoteric Adam Smith against the exoteric Adam Smith.

Among the physiocrats there is no such confusion. The distinction between *avances annuelles* and *avances primitives* refers only to the different periods of reproduction of the different component of capital, especially of agricultural capital, while their views on the production of surplus-value form a part of their theory that is independent of these distinctions, a part they hold up as the strong point of the theory. The formation of surplus-value is not explained as originating from capital as such, but is attributed to one particular sphere of the production of capital, agriculture.

Secondly: The essential point in the definition of variable capital—and therefore for the conversion of any sum of values into capital—is that the capitalist exchanges a definite, given (and in this sense constant) magnitude of value for value-creating power, a magnitude of value for the production, self-expansion, of value. Whether the capitalist pays the labourer in money or in means of subsistence does not affect this basic definition. It only alters the mode of existence of the value advanced by the capitalist which in one case exists in the form of money for which the labourer buys himself his means of subsistence in the market, in the other case in the form of means of subsistence which he consumes directly. Developed capitalist production rests indeed on the assumption that the labourer is paid in money, just as in general it presupposes the process of production brought about by the process of circulation, hence presupposes the monetary system. But the creation of surplus-value—and consequently the capitalisation of the advanced sum of values—has its source neither in the money-form of wages nor in the form of wages paid in kind, nor in the capital laid out in the purchase of labour-power. It arises out of the exchange of value for value-creating power, out of the conversion of a constant into a variable magnitude.

The greater or smaller fixity of the instruments of labour depends on their degree of durability, hence on a physical property. Other circumstances being equal, they will wear out sooner or later, will therefore function a longer or a shorter time as fixed capital, according to their durability. But it is by no means solely on account of this physical property of durability that they function as fixed capital. The raw material in metal factories is just as durable as the machines used in manufacturing, and more durable than many component parts of these machines, such as leather and wood. Nevertheless the metal serving as raw materials forms a part of the circulating capital, while the instrument of labour, although probably built of the same metal, is a part of the fixed capital when in use. Consequently it is not because of the material, physical nature, nor the relatively great or small speed with which it wears out that a metal is put now in the category of fixed, now in that of circulating capital. This distinction is rather due to the role played by it in the process of production, being a subject of labour in one case and an instrument of labour in the other.

The function of an instrument of labour in the process of production requires that on the average it should serve for a longer or shorter period in ever renewed labour-processes. Its very function therefore prescribes that the stuff of which it is composed should be more or less durable. But it is not the durability of the material of which it is fabricated that by itself makes it fixed capital. The same stuff, when raw material, becomes circulating capital, and among economists who confuse the distinction between commodity-capital and productive capital with the distinction between circulating and fixed capital, the same stuff, the same machine, is circulating capital as product and fixed capital as instrument of labour.

Although it is not the durability of the material of which it is fabricated that makes an instrument of labour fixed capital, nevertheless its role as such an instrument requires that it should be composed of relatively durable material. The durability of its material is therefore a condition of its function as an instrument of labour, and consequently the material basis of the mode of circulation which renders it fixed capital. Other things being equal, the higher or lower degree of wear and tear of the stuff it is made of impresses upon it in a higher or lower degree the stamp of fixedness, is therefore very closely interwoven with the quality of being fixed capital.

If the part of capital laid out in labour-power is considered exclusively from the point of view of circulating capital, hence in contrast with fixed capital, and if consequently the distinctions between constant and variable capital are lumped with those between fixed and circulating capital, then it is natural—supposing that material reality of the instrument of labour forms an essential basis of its character of fixed capital—to derive its character of circulating capital, in contrast with the fixed capital, from the material reality of the capital invested in labour-power, and then again to determine the circulating capital with the aid of the material reality of the variable capital.

The real substance of the capital laid out in wages is labour itself, active, value-creating labour-power, living labour, which the capitalist exchanges for dead, materialised labour and embodies in his capital, by which means, and by which alone, the value in his hands turns into self-expanding value. But this power of self-expansion is not sold by the capitalist. It is always only a constituent part of his productive capital, the same as his instruments of labour; it is never a part of his commodity-capital, as for instance the finished product which he sells. In the process of production the instruments of labour, as components of the productive capital, are not opposed to labour-power as fixed capital any more than materials of labour and auxiliary substances are identified with it as circulating capital. Labour-power confronts both of them as a personal factor, while those are objective factors—speaking from the point of view of the labour-process. Both of them stand opposed to labour-power, as constant capital to variable capital—speaking from the point of view of the process of self-expansion of value. Or, if mention is to be made here of a material difference, so far as it affects the process of circulation, it is only this: It follows from the nature of value, which is nothing but materialised labour, and from the nature of active labour-power, which is nothing but labour in process of materialisation, that labour-power continually creates value and surplus-value during the time it functions; that what on the part of labour-power appears as motion, as a creation of value, appears on the part of its product in a state of rest, as created value. If the labour-power has performed its function, capital no longer consists of labour-power on the one side and means of production on the other. The capital-value that was invested in labour-power is now value which (+ surplus-value) was added to the product. In order to repeat the process, the product must be sold and new labour-power constantly bought with the proceeds and incorporated in the productive capital. This then gives to the part of capital invested in labour-power, and to that invested in material of labour, etc., the character of circulating capital as opposed to the capital remaining fixed in the instruments of labour.

But if, on the contrary, the secondary definition of the circulating capital, which it shares with a part of the constant capital (raw and auxiliary materials), is made the essential definition of the part of capital laid out in labour-power, to wit, that the value laid out in it is transferred in full to the product in whose creation it is consumed, and not gradually and piecemeal as in the case of the fixed capital, and that consequently it must be replaced in full by the sale of the product—then the part of the capital laid out in wages must likewise consist, materially, not of active labour-power but of the material elements which the labourer buys with his wages, i.e., it must consist of that part of the social commodity-capital which passes into the consumption of the labourer, viz., of means of subsistence. In that case the fixed capital consists of the more slowly perishable instruments of labour which therefore have to be replaced more slowly, and the capital laid out in labour-power consists of the means of subsistence, which must be replaced more rapidly.

However, the border-line between greater or lesser perishableness is very vague and indistinct.

> 'The food and clothing consumed by the labourer, the buildings in which he works, the implements with which his labour is assisted, are all of a perishable nature. There is however a vast difference in the time for which these different capitals will endure: a steam-engine will last longer than a ship, a ship than the clothing of the labourer, and the clothing of the labourer longer than the food which he consumes.'[3]

Ricardo forgets to mention the house in which the labourer lives, his furniture, his tools of consumption, such as knives, forks, dishes, etc., all of which have the same quality of durability as the instruments of labour. The same things, the same kinds of things, appear in one place as articles of consumption and in another as instruments of labour.

The difference, as stated by Ricardo, is this:

> 'According as capital is rapidly perishable and requires to be frequently reproduced, or is of slow consumption, it is classed under the heads of circulating or fixed capital.'[4]

And he adds this note:

> 'A division not essential, and in which the line of demarcation cannot be accurately drawn.'[5]

Thus we have once more happily arrived in the camp of the physiocrats, where the distinction between *avances annuelles* and *avances primitives* was one referring to the time of consumption, and consequently also to the different times of reproduction of the capital employed. Only, what with them constitutes an important phenomenon of social production and is described in the *Tableau Économique* in connection with the process of circulation, becomes here a subjective and, in Ricardo's own words, superfluous distinction.

Once the part of capital invested in labour differs from that invested in instruments of labour only by its period of reproduction and hence its term of circulation, and once one part consists of means of subsistence and the other of instruments of labour so that those differ from these only in being more rapidly perishable, there being various degrees of durability within the first group itself, all *differentia specifica* between capital invested in labour-power and capital invested in means of production is naturally obliterated.

This wholly contradicts Ricardo's doctrine of value, likewise his theory of profit, which is in fact a theory of surplus-value. In general he considers the distinction between fixed and circulating capital only to the extent that different proportions of both of them in equally large capitals invested in different branches of production influence the law of value, particularly the extent to which an increase or decrease of wages in consequence of these conditions affects prices. But even within this restricted investigation he commits the gravest errors on account of his confusing fixed and circulating with constant and variable capital. Indeed, he starts his analysis on an entirely wrong basis. In the first place, in so far as the part of the capital-value laid out in labour-power has to be classified under the head of circulating capital, the definitions of circulating capital itself are wrongly developed, particularly the circumstances which place the part of capital laid out in labour under this head. In the second place there is a confusion of the definition according to which the part of capital invested in labour is variable capital with the definition according to which it is circulating capital, as opposed to fixed capital.

It is evident at the outset that the definition of capital invested in labour-power as circulating or fluent capital is a secondary one, obliterating its *differentia specifica* in the process of production. For in this definition, on the one hand, the capitals invested in labour are of the same importance as those invested in raw material, etc. A classification which identifies a part of the constant capital with the variable capital does not deal with the *differentia specifica* of variable capital in opposition to constant capital. On the other hand, the parts of capital laid out in labour are indeed opposed to those invested in instruments of labour, but not in the least with reference to the fact that these parts enter into the production of value in quite different ways, but with reference to the fact that both transfer their value to the product, but in different periods of time.

In all of these cases the point at issue is *how* a given value, laid out in the process of production of commodities, whether it be wages, the price of raw materials, or that of instruments of labour, is transferred to the product, hence is circulated by the product, and returned to its starting-point by the sale of the product, or is replaced. The only difference lies here in the '*how*,' in the particular manner of the transfer, and therefore also of the circulation of this value.

Whether the price of labour-power previously stipulated by contract in each individual case is paid in money or means of subsistence does not alter in any way its character of being a fixed price. However it is evident in the case of wages paid in money that the money itself does not pass into the process of production in the way that the value as well as the material of the means of production do. But, if on the other hand, the means of subsistence which the labourer buys with his wages are directly classed in the same category, alongside raw materials, etc., as the material form of circulating capital and are opposed to the instruments of labour, then the matter assumes a different aspect. If the value of these things, of the means of production, is transferred to the product in the labour-process, the value of those other things, the means of subsistence, reappears in the labour-power that consumes them and is likewise transferred to the product by the functioning of this power. In both these cases it is equally a question of the mere reappearance, in the product, of the values advanced during production. (The physiocrats took this seriously and therefore denied that industrial labour created surplus-value.) Thus the previously quoted [Karl Marx, *Capital*, Vol. I, p. 207, Note 3.—*Ed.*] passage from Wayland.

> 'The form, however, is of no consequence... The various kinds of food, clothing, and shelter, necessary for the existence and comfort of the human being, are also changed.

> They are consumed, from time to time, and their value reappears...' (*Elements of Pol. Econ.*, pp. 31, 32.)

The capital-values advanced for production in the form of both means of production and means of subsistence reappear here equally in the value of the product. Thus the transformation of the capitalist process of production into a complete mystery is happily accomplished and the origin of the surplus-value existing in the product is entirely withdrawn from view.

Furthermore this brings to completion the fetishism peculiar to bourgeois Political Economy, the fetishism which metamorphoses the social, economic character impressed on things in the process of social production into a natural character stemming from the material nature of those things. For instance, 'instruments of labour are fixed capital,' is a scholastic definition, which leads to contradictions and confusion. Just as was demonstrated in the case of the labour-process (Buch I, Kap. V), [English edition: Ch. VII.—*Ed.*] that it depends wholly on the role which the material components play in a particular labour-process, on their function—whether they function as instruments of labour, material of labour, or products—so instruments of labour are fixed capital only if the process of production is really a capitalist process of production and the means of production are therefore really capital and possess economic definiteness, the social character of capital. And in the second place, they are fixed capital only if they transfer their value to the product in a particular way. If not, they remain instruments of labour without being fixed capital. In the same way, if auxiliary materials like manure give up value in the same peculiar manner as the greater part of the instruments of labour, they become fixed capital although they are not instruments of labour. It is not a question here of definitions, which things must be made to fit. We are dealing here with definite functions which must be expressed in definite categories.

If to be capital laid out in wages is considered one of the qualities of means of subsistence as such under all circumstances, then it will also be a quality of this 'circulating' capital '**to support labour**.' (Ricardo, p. 25.) If the means of subsistence were not 'capital' they would not support labour-power; whereas it is precisely their quality of capital that endows them with the faculty of supporting *capital by foreign labour*.

If means of subsistence as such are circulating capital—after the latter had been converted into wages—it follows further that the magnitude of wages depends on the ratio of the number of labourers to the given amount of circulating capital—a favourite economic proposition—while as a matter of fact the quantity of means of subsistence withdrawn from the market by the labourer, and the quantity of means of subsistence available for the consumption of the capitalist, depend on the ratio of the surplus-value to the price of labour.

Ricardo, like Barton,[6] everywhere confounds the relation of variable to constant capital with that of circulating to fixed capital. We shall see later to what extent this vitiates his investigation of the rate of profit. [Karl Marx, *Capital*, Vol. III, Ch. I-III.—*Ed.*]

Ricardo furthermore identifies the differences which arise in the turnover from other causes than the distinction between fixed and circulating capital with this distinction:

> 'It is also to be observed that the circulating capital may circulate, or be returned to its employer, in very unequal times. The wheat bought by a farmer to sow is comparatively a fixed capital to the wheat purchased by a baker to make into loaves. The one leaves it in the ground, and can obtain no return for a year; the other can get it ground into flour, sell it as bread to his customers, and have his capital free, to renew the same, or commence any other employment in a week.'[7]

It is characteristic here that wheat, although not serving as a means of subsistence but as raw material when used for sowing, is in the first place circulating capital, because in itself it is a means of subsistence, and in the second placed fixed capital, because its return takes over a year. However it is not only the more or less slow or rapid return which makes a fixed capital of a means of production, but also the definite manner in which it transfers its value to the product.

The confusion created by Adam Smith has brought about the following results:

1. The distinction between fixed and circulating capital is confused with that between productive capital and commodity-capital. For instance a machine is considered circulating capital when in the market as a commodity, and fixed capital when incorporated in the process of production. Moreover, it is absolutely impossible to ascertain why one kind of capital should be more fixed or circulating than another.
2. All circulating capital is identified with capital laid out or to be laid out in wages. This is so in John Stewart Mill, [J. St. Mill, *Essays on Some Unsettled Questions of Political Economy*, London, 1844, p. 164.—*Ed.*] and others.
3. The distinction between variable and constant capital, which was previously mistaken by Barton, Ricardo, and others for that between circulating and fixed capital, is finally wholly reduced to this last-named distinction, for instance in Ramsay, where all means of production, raw materials, etc., as well as instruments of labour are fixed capital, and only capital laid out in wages is circulating capital. [G. Ramsay, *An Essay on the Distribution of Wealth*, Edinburgh, 1833, pp. 21-24.—*Ed.*] But because the reduction takes place in this form, the real distinction between constant and variable capital is not understood.
4. The latter-day British, especially Scotch, economists, who look upon all things from the inexpressibly narrow-minded point of view of a bank clerk, such as MacLeod, [H. D. MacLeod, *The Elements of Political Economy*, London, 1858, pp. 76-80.—*Ed.*] Patterson, [R. H. Patterson, *The Science of Finance. A Practical Treatise*, Edinburgh and London, 1868, pp. 129-44.—*Ed.*] and others, transform the distinction between fixed and circulating capital into one between **money at call** and **money not at call**.

Notes [1]

1. Ricardo, *Principles*, etc., p. 25.
2. *Loc. cit.*
3. Ricardo, *Principles*, etc., p. 26.
4. *Ibid.*
5. *Ibid.*
6. *Observations on the Circumstances Which Influence the Condition of the Labouring Classes of Society*, London, 1817. A pertinent passage is quoted in Book I, p. 655, Note 79. [English edition: p. 631, Note 1.]
7. *Principles*, etc., pp. 26 and 27.

12

The Working Period

Let us take two branches of business with working-days of equal length, say, of ten hours each, one of them a cotton spinning-mill, the other a locomotive works. In one of these branches a definite quantity of finished product, cotton yarn, is turned out daily or weekly; in the other, the labour-process has to be repeated for perhaps three months in order to manufacture a finished product, a locomotive. In one case the product is discrete in nature; and each day or week the same labour starts over again. In the other case the labour-process is continuous and extends over a rather great number of daily labour-processes which, in their interconnection, in the continuity of their operation, bring forth a finished product only after a rather long period of time. Although the duration of the daily labour-process is the same here, there is a very marked difference in the duration of the productive act, i.e., in the duration of the repeated labour-processes required to get out a finished product, to market it as a commodity, hence to convert it from productive to commodity-capital. The distinction between fixed and circulating capital has nothing to do with this. The distinction indicated would exist even if the very same proportions of fixed and circulating capital were employed in both branches of production.

These differences in the duration of the productive act can be observed not alone between different spheres of production, but also within one and the same sphere of production, depending on the amount of product to be turned out. An ordinary dwelling house is built in less time than a large factory and therefore requires fewer continuous labour-processes. While the building of a locomotive takes three months, that of an armoured man-of-war requires one year or more. It takes nearly a year to produce grain and several years to raise big cattle, while timber-growing needs from twelve to one hundred years. A few months will suffice for a country road, while a railway is a job of years. An ordinary carpet is made in about a week, but a *Gobelin* takes years, etc. Hence the time consumed in the performance of the productive act varies infinitely.

The difference in the duration of the productive act must evidently give rise to a difference in the velocity of the turnover, if invested capitals are equal, in other words, must make a difference in the time for which a certain capital is advanced. Assume that a spinning-mill and a locomotive works employ the same amount of capital, that the ratio of their constant to their variable capital is the same, likewise the proportion between the fixed and circulating parts of the capitals, and that lastly their working-day is of equal length and its division into necessary and surplus-labour the same. In order to eliminate, furthermore, all the circumstances arising out of the process of circulation and having no bearing on the present case, let us suppose that both the yarn and the locomotive are made to order and will be paid on delivery of the finished product. At the end of the week, on delivery of the finished yarn, the spinning-mill owner recovers his outlay for circulating capital (leaving the surplus-value out of consideration), likewise the fixed capital's wear and tear incorporated in the value of the yarn. He can therefore repeat the same circuit anew with the same capital. It has completed its turnover. The locomotive manufacturer on the other hand must lay out ever new capital for wages and raw material every week for three months in succession, and it is only after three months, after the delivery of the locomotive, that the circulating capital, meanwhile gradually laid out in one and the same productive act for the manufacture of one and the same commodity, once more exists in a form in which it can renew its circuit. The wear and tear of his machinery during these three months is likewise replaced only now. The expenditure of the one is made for one week, that of the other is the weekly expenditure multiplied by twelve. All other circumstances being assumed as equal, the one must have twelve times as much circulating capital at his disposal as the other.

It is however immaterial here that the capitals advanced weekly are equal. Whatever the amount of the advanced capital, it is advanced for only one week in the one case and for twelve weeks in the other, and the above periods must respectively elapse before it can be used for a new operation, before the same operation can be repeated with it, or a different one inaugurated.

The difference in the velocity of the turnover, or in the length of time for which the individual capital must be advanced before the same capital-value can be employed in a new labour- or self-expansion process, arises here from the following circumstances:

Granted the manufacture of a locomotive or of any other machine requires 100 working-days. So far as the labourers employed in the manufacture of yarn or the building of locomotives are concerned, 100 working-days constitute in either case a discontinuous (discrete) magnitude, consisting, according to our assumption, of 100 consecutive separate ten-hour labour-processes. But so far as the product—the machine—is concerned, these 100 working-days form a continuous magnitude, a working-day of 1,000 working-hours, one single connected act of production. I call such a working-day which is composed of a more or less numerous succession of connected working days a *working period*. When we speak of a working-day we mean the length of working time during which the labourer must daily spend his labour-power, must work day by day. But when we speak of a working period we mean the number of connected working-days required in a certain branch of industry for the manufacture of a finished product. In this case the product of every working-day is but a partial one, which is further worked upon from day to day and only at the end of the longer or shorter working period receives its finished form, is a finished use-value.

Interruptions, disturbances of the process of social production, in consequence for instance of crises, have therefore very different effects on labour-products of a discrete nature and on those that require for their production a prolonged connected period. In the one case all that happens is that today's production of a certain quantity of yarn, coal, etc., is not followed by tomorrow's new production of yarn, coal, etc. Not so in the case of ships, buildings, railways, etc. Here it is not only the day's work but an entire connected act of production that is interrupted. If the job is not continued, the means of production and labour already consumed in its production are wasted. Even if it is resumed, a deterioration has inevitably set in in the meantime.

For the entire length of the working period, the part of the value daily transferred to the product by the fixed capital accumulates in layers, as it were, until the product is finished. And here the difference between fixed and circulating capital is revealed at the same time in its practical significance. Fixed capital is advanced in the process of production for a comparatively long period; it need not be renewed until after the expiration of perhaps a period of several years. Whether a steam-engine transfers its value daily piecemeal to some yarn, the product of a discrete labour-process, or for three months to a locomotive, the product of a continuous act of production, is immaterial as far as laying out the capital required for the purchase of the steam-engine is concerned. In the one case its value flows back in small doses, for instance weekly, in the other case in larger quantities, for instance quarterly. But in either case the renewal of the steam-engine may take place only after twenty years. So long as every individual period within which the value of the steam-engine is returned piecemeal by the sale of the product is shorter than the lifetime of the engine itself, the latter continues to function in the process of production for several working periods.

It is different with the circulating components of the advanced capital. The labour-power bought for a definite week is expended in the course of the same week and is materialised in the product. It must be paid for at the end of the week. And this investment of capital in labour-power is repeated every week during the three months; yet the expenditure of this part of the capital during the week does not enable the capitalist to settle for the purchase of the labour the following week. Every week additional capital must be expended to pay for labour-power, and, leaving aside the question of credit, the capitalist must be able to lay out wages for three months, even if he pays them only in weekly doses. It is the same with the other portion of circulating capital, the raw and auxiliary materials. One layer of labour after another is piled up on the product. It is not alone the value of the expended labour-power that is continually being transferred to the product during the labour-process, but also surplus-value. This product, however, is unfinished, it has not yet the form of a finished commodity, hence it cannot yet circulate. This applies likewise to the capital-value transferred in layers from the raw and auxiliary materials to the product.

Depending on the length of the working period exacted by the specific nature of the product or by the useful effect to be achieved in its manufacture, a continuous additional investment of circulating capital (wages and raw and auxiliary materials) is required, no part of which is in a form capable of circulation and hence of promoting a renewal of the same operation. Every part is, on the contrary, held fast successively in the sphere of production as a component of the nascent product, tied up in the form of productive capital. Now, the time of turnover is equal to the sum of the time of production and the time of circulation of the capital. Hence a prolongation of the time of production reduces the velocity of the turnover quite as much as a prolongation of the time of circulation. In the present case however the following two points must be noted:

Firstly: The prolonged stay in the sphere of production. The capital advanced for instance for labour, raw material, etc., during the first week, as well as the portions of value transferred to the product by the fixed capital, are held fast in the sphere of production for the entire term of three months, and, being incorporated in an only nascent, still unfinished product, cannot pass into circulation as commodities.

Secondly: Since the working period required for the performance of the productive act lasts three months, and forms in fact only one connected labour-process, a new dose of circulating capital must be continually added week after week to the preceding amount. The total of the successively advanced additional capital grows therefore with the length of the working period.

We have assumed that capitals of equal size are invested in spinning and machine-building, that these capitals contain equal proportions of constant and variable, fixed and circulating capital, that the working-days are of equal length, in brief, that all conditions are equal except the duration of the working period. In the first week, the outlay for both is the same, but the product of the spinner can be sold and the proceeds of the sale used to buy new labour-power, new raw materials, etc.; in short, production can be resumed on the same scale. The machine-manufacturer on the other hand cannot reconvert the circulating capital expended in the first week into money and resume operations with it until three months later, when his product is finished. There is therefore first a difference in the return of the identical quantities of capital invested. But in the second place identical amounts of productive capital are employed during the three months in both spinning and machine-building. However the magnitude of the outlay of capital in the case of the yarn manufacturer is quite different from that of the machine-builder; for in the one case the same capital is rapidly renewed and the same operation can therefore be repeated, while in the other case the renewal of the capital is relatively slow, so that ever new quantities of capital must be added to the old up to the time of its renewal. Consequently there is a difference not only in the length of time of renewal of definite portions of capital, or in the length of time for which the capital is advanced, but also in the quantity of the capital to be advanced according to the duration of the labour-process (although the capitals employed daily or weekly are equal). This circumstance is worthy of note for the reason that the term of the advance may be prolonged, as we shall see in the cases treated in the next chapter, without thereby necessitating a corresponding increase in the amount of the capital to be advanced. The capital must be advanced for a longer time, and a larger amount of capital is tied up in the form of productive capital.

At the less developed stages of capitalist production, undertakings requiring a long working period, and hence a large investment of capital for a long time, such as the building of roads, canals, etc., especially when they can be carried out only on a large scale, are either not carried out on a capitalist basis at all, but rather at communal or state expense (in earlier times generally by forced labour, so far as the labour-power was concerned). Or objects whose production requires a lengthy working period are fabricated only for the smallest part by recourse to the private means of the capitalist himself. For instance, in the building of a house, the private person for whom it is built makes a number of partial advance payments to the building contractor. He therefore actually pays for the house piecemeal, in proportion as the productive process progresses. But in the advanced capitalist era, when on the one hand huge capitals are concentrated in the hands of single individuals, while on the other the associated capitalist (joint-stock companies) appears side by side with the individual capitalist and a credit system has simultaneously been developed, a capitalist building contractor builds only in exceptional cases on the order of private individuals. His business nowadays is to build whole rows of houses and entire sections of cities for the market, just as it is the business of individual capitalists to build railways as contractors.

To what extent capitalist production has revolutionised the building of houses in London is shown by the testimony of a builder before the banking committee of 1857. When he was young, he said, houses were generally built to order and the payments made in instalments to the contractor as certain stages of the building were being completed. Very little was built on speculation. Contractors used to assent to such operations mainly to keep their men in constant employment and thus hold them together. In the last forty years all that has changed. Very little is now built to order. Anyone wanting a new house picks one from among those built on speculation or still in process of construction. The builder no longer works for his customers but for the market. Like every other industrial capitalist he is compelled to have finished articles in the market. While formerly a builder had perhaps three or four houses building at a time for speculation, he must now buy a large plot of ground (which in continental language means rent it for ninety-nine years, as a rule), build from 100 to 200 houses on it, and thus embark on an enterprise which exceeds his resources twenty to fifty times. The funds are procured through mortgaging and the money is placed at the disposal of the contractor as the buildings proceed. Then, if a crisis comes along and interrupts the payment of the advance instalments, the entire enterprise generally collapses. At best, the houses remain unfinished until better times arrive; at the worst they are sold at auction for half their cost. Without speculative building, and on a large scale at that, no contractor can get along today. The profit from just building is extremely small. His main profit comes from raising the ground-rent, from careful selection and skilled utilisation of the building terrain. It is by this method of speculation anticipating the demand for houses that almost the whole Belgravia and Tyburnia, and the countless thousands of villas round London have been built. (Abbreviated from the Report of the Select Committee on Bank Acts, Part I, 1857, Evidence, Questions 5413-18; 5435-36.)

The execution of enterprises requiring working periods of considerable length and operations on a large scale does not fall fully within the province of capitalist production until the concentration of capital becomes very pronounced, and the development of the credit system offers to the capitalist, on the other hand, the convenient expedient of advancing and thus risking other people's capital instead of his own. It goes without saying that whether the capital advanced in production belongs to him who uses it or does not has no effect on the velocity or time of turnover.

Conditions such as cooperation, division of labour, application of machinery, which augment the product of the individual working-day, shorten at the same time the working period of connected acts of production. Thus machinery shortens the building time of houses, bridges, etc.; mowers and threshers reduce the working period required to transform ripe grain into the finished product. Greater speed due to improved shipbuilding cuts the turnover time of capital invested in shipping. But improvements that shorten the working period and thereby the time during which circulating capital must be advanced generally go hand in hand with an increased outlay of fixed capital.

On the other hand the working period in certain branches of production may be diminished by the mere extension of cooperation. The completion of a railway is expedited by setting afoot huge armies of labourer and thus tackling the job in many spots at once. The time of turnover is lessened in that case by an increase of the advanced capital. More means of production and more labour-power must be united under the command of the capitalist.

Whereas the shortening of the working period is thus mostly connected with an increase of the capital advanced for this abbreviated time—the shorter the term of advance the greater the capital advanced—it must here be recalled that regardless of the existing amount of social capital, the essential point is the degree in which the means of production and subsistence, or the disposal of them, are scattered or concentrated in the hands of individual capitalists, in other words, the degree of concentration of capitals already attained. Inasmuch as credit promotes, accelerates and enhances the concentration of capital in one hand, it contributes to the shortening of the working period and thus of the turnover time.

In branches of production in which the working period, whether continuous or discontinuous, is prescribed by definite natural conditions, no shortening by the above-mentioned means can take place. Says W. Walter Good, in his *Political, Agricultural, and Commercial Fallacies* (London, 1866, p. 325):

> 'In regard to quicker returns, this term cannot be made to apply to corn crops, as one return only can be made per annum. In respect to stock, we will simply ask, how is the return of two- and three-year-old sheep, and four- and five-year-old oxen to be quickened.'

The necessity of securing ready money as soon as possible (for instance to meet fixed obligations, such as taxes, ground-rent, etc.) solves this problem, e.g., by selling or slaughtering cattle before they have reached the economically normal age, to the great detriment of agriculture. This also brings about in the end a rise in the price of meat.

> 'Men who have mainly reared cattle for supplying the pastures of the Midland counties in summer, and the yards of the eastern counties in winter ... have become so crippled through the uncertainty and lowness in the prices of corn that they are glad to take advantage of the high prices of butter and cheese; the former they take to market weekly to help to pay current expenses, and draw on the other from some factor, who takes the cheese when fit to move, and, of course, nearly at his own price. For this reason, remembering that farming is governed by the principles of Political Economy, the calves which used to come south from the dairying counties for rearing, are now largely sacrificed at times at a week and ten days old, in the shambles of Birmingham, Manchester, Liverpool, and other large neighbouring towns. If, however, malt had been free from duty, not only would farmers have made more profit and therefore been able to keep their stock till it got older and heavier, but it would have been substituted for milk for rearing by men who did not keep cows, and thus the present alarming scarcity of young cattle which has befallen the nation would have been largely averted. What these little men now say, in reply to recommendations to rear, is, 'We know very well it would pay to rear on milk, but it would first require us to put our hands in our purse, which we cannot do, and then we should have to wait a long time for a return, instead of getting it at once by dairying.' (*Ibid*., pp. 11 and 12.)

If the prolongation of the turnover has such consequences for the small English farmers, it is easy to see what disarrangement it must produce among the small peasants of the continent.

The part of the value transferred in layers by the fixed capital to the product accumulates, and the return of this part is delayed, in proportion to the length of the working period and thus, also of the period of time required for the completion of the commodity capable of circulation. But this delay does not cause a renewed outlay of fixed capital. The machine continues to function in the process of production, whether the replacement of its wear and tear in the form of money returns slowly or rapidly. It is different with the circulating capital. Not only must capital be tied up for a rather long time, in proportion to the length of the working period, but new capital must be continually advanced in the shape of wages, and raw and auxiliary materials. A delayed return has therefore a different effect on each. No matter whether the return is rapid or slow, the fixed capital continues to function. But the circulating capital becomes unable to perform its functions, if the return is delayed, if it is tied up in the form of unsold, or unfinished and as yet unsaleable products, and if no additional capital is at hand for its renewal in kind.

> 'While the peasant farmer starves, his cattle thrive. Repeated showers had fallen in the country, and the forage was abundant. The Hindoo peasant will perish by hunger beside a fat bullock. The prescriptions of superstition, which appear cruel to the individual, are conservative for the community; and the preservation of the labouring cattle secures the power of cultivation, and the sources of future life and wealth. It may sound harsh and sad to say so, but in India it is more easy to replace a man than an ox.' (Return, East India, Madras and Orissa Famine. No. 4, p. 44.)

Compare with the preceding the utterance of Manava Dharma Sastra, [Manava Dharma Sastra or Manu laws—an ancient Indian religious, legal and ritual code which determined the duties of every Hindu in keeping with the tenets of Brahmanism. The compilation of these laws is traditionally attributed to Manu, the mythical progenitor of man. Marx quotes from Manava Dharma Sastra, or the Institutes of Manu According to the Gloss of Kulluka, Comprising the Indian System of Duties, Religious and Civil, third edition, Madras, 1863, p. 281.—*Ed.*] Chapter X, $ 62.

> 'Desertion of life, without reward, for the sake of preserving a priest or a cow ... may cause the beatitude of those base-born tribes.'

Naturally, it is impossible to deliver a five-year-old animal before the lapse of five years. But what is possible, within certain limits, is getting animals ready for their destination in less time by changing the way of treating them. This is precisely what Bakewell accomplished. Formerly English sheep, like the French as late as 1855, were not fit for the butcher until four or five years old. According to the Bakewell system, sheep may be fattened when only one year old and in every case have reached their full growth before the end of the second year. By careful selection, Bakewell, a Dishley Grange farmer, reduced the skeleton of sheep to the minimum required for their existence. His sheep are called the New Leicesters.

> '... the breeder can now sent three to market in the same space of time that it formerly took him to prepare one; and if they are not taller, they are broader, rounder, and have a greater development in those parts which give most flesh. Of bone, they have absolutely no greater amount than is necessary to support them, and almost all their weight is pure meat.' (Lavergne, *The Rural Economy of England, etc.*, 1855, p. 20.)

The methods which shorten the working periods are applicable in various branches of industry to a widely varying extent and do not eliminate the time differences of the various working periods. To stick to our illustration, the working period required for the building of a locomotive may be absolutely shortened by the employment of new machine-tools. But if at the same time the finished product turned out daily or weekly by a cotton-spinning mill is still more rapidly increased by improved processes, then the working period in machine-building, compared with that in spinning, has nevertheless grown relatively in length.

13

The Time of Production

Working time is always production time, that is to say, time during which capital is held fast in the sphere of production. But vice versa, not all time during which capital is engaged in the process of production is necessarily working time.

It is here not a question of interruptions of the labour-process necessitated by natural limitations of the labour-power itself, although we have seen to what extent the mere circumstance that fixed capital—factory buildings, machinery, etc.—lies idle during pauses in the labour-process, [See: Karl Marx, *Capital*, Vol. I, pp. 256-63.—*Ed.*] became one of the motives for an unnatural prolongation of the labour-process and for day-and-night work. We are dealing here rather with interruptions independent of the length of the labour-process, brought about by the very nature of the product and its fabrication, during which the subject of labour is for a longer or shorter time subjected to natural processes, must undergo physical, chemical and physiological changes, during which the labour-process is entirely or partially suspended.

For instance grape after being pressed must ferment awhile and then rest for some time in order to reach a certain degree of perfection. In many branches of industry the product must pass through a drying process, for instance in pottery, or be exposed to certain conditions in order to change its chemical properties, as for instance in bleaching. Winter grain needs about nine months to mature. Between the time of sowing and harvesting the labour-process is almost entirely suspended. In timber-raising, after the sowing and the incidental preliminary work are completed, the seed requires about 100 years to be transformed into a finished product and during all that time it stands in comparatively very little need of the action of labour.

In all these cases additional labour is drawn on only occasionally during a large portion of the time of production. The condition described in the previous chapter, where additional capital and labour must be supplied to the capital already tied up in the process of production, obtains here only with longer or shorter intervals.

In all these cases therefore the production time of the advanced capital consists of two periods: one period during which the capital is engaged in the labour-process and a second period during which its form of existence—that of an unfinished product—is abandoned to the sway of natural processes, without being at that time in the labour-process. Nor does it matter in the least here and there. The working period and the production period do not coincide in these cases. The production period is longer than the working period. But the product is not finished, not ready, hence not fit to be converted from the form of productive into that of commodity-capital until the production period is completed. Consequently the length of the turnover period increases in proportion to the length of the production time that does not consist of working time. In so far as the production time in excess of the working time is not fixed by natural laws given once and for all, such as govern the maturing of grain, the growth of an oak, etc., the period of turnover can often be more or less shortened by an artificial reduction of the production time. Such instances are the introduction of chemical bleaching instead of bleaching on the green and more efficient drying apparatus. Or, in tanning, where the penetration of the tannic acid into the skins, by the old method, took from six to eighteen months, while the new method, by means of an air-pump, does it in only one and a half to two months. (J. G. Courcelle-Seneuil, *Traitè thèorique et pratique des entreprises industrielles, etc.*, Paris, 1857, 2-me èd.) The most magnificent illustration of an artificial abbreviation of the time of production taken up exclusively with natural processes is furnished by the history of iron manufacture, more especially the conversion of pig iron into steel during the last 100 years, from the puddling process discovered about 1780 to the modern Bessemer process and the latest methods introduced since. The time of production has been brought down tremendously, but the investment of fixed capital has increased in proportion.

A peculiar illustration of the divergence of the production time from the working time is furnished by the American manufacture of shoe-lasts. In this case a considerable portion of the unproductive costs arises from having to hold the timber at least eighteen months before it is dry enough to work, so as to prevent subsequent warping. During this time the wood does not pass through any other labour-process. The period of turnover of the invested capital is therefore not determined solely by the time required for the manufacture of the lasts but also by the time during which it lies unproductive in the shape of drying wood. It stays 18 months in the process of production before it can enter into the labour-process proper. This example shows at the same time that the times of turnover of different parts of the aggregate circulating capital may differ in consequence of conditions which do not arise within the sphere of circulation but owe their origin to the production process.

The difference between production time and working time becomes especially apparent in agriculture. In our moderate climates the land bears grain once a year. Shortening or lengthening the period of production (for winter grain it averages nine months) itself depends on the alternation of good and bad seasons, and for this reason cannot be accurately determined and controlled beforehand as in industry proper. Only such by-products as milk, cheese, etc., can steadily be produced and sold in comparatively short periods. On the other hand, working time data are as follows:

> 'The number of working-days in the various regions of Germany, with due regard to the climatic and other determining conditions, will for the three main working periods presumably be: For the spring period, from the middle of March or beginning of April to the middle of May, about 50 to 60 working-days; for the summer period, from the beginning of June to the end of August, 65 to 80; and for the autumn period, from the beginning of September to the end of October, or the middle or end of November, 55 to 75 working-days. For the winter, only the jobs market goods, building materials, etc., are to be noted.' (F. Kirchhof, *Handbuch der landwirthschaftlichen Betriebslehre*, Dessau, 1852, S. 160.)

The more unfavourable the climate, the more congested is the working period in agriculture, and hence the shorter is the time in which capital and labour are expended. Take Russia for instance. In some of the northern districts of that country field labour is possible only from 130 to 150 days throughout the year, and it may be imagined what a loss Russia would sustain if 50 out of the 65 millions of her European population remained without work during the six or eight months of the winter, when agricultural labour is at a standstill. Apart from the 200,000 peasants who work in the 10,500 factories of Russia, local domestic industries have everywhere developed in the villages. There are villages in which all the peasants have been for generations weavers, tanners, shoemakers, locksmiths, cutlers, etc. This is particularly the case in the gubernias of Moscow, Vladimir, Kaluga, Kostroma, and Petersburg. By the way, this domestic industry is being pressed more and more into the service of capitalist production. The weavers for instance are supplied with warp and woof directly by merchants or through middlemen. (Abbreviated from the Reports by H. M. Secretaries of Embassy and Legation, on the Manufactures, Commerce, etc., No. 8, 1865, pp. 86 and 87.) We see here that the divergence of the production period from the working period, the latter being but a part of the former, constitutes the natural basis for the combination of agriculture with subsidiary rural industries, and that these subsidiary industries in turn offer points of vantage to the capitalist, who intrudes first in the person of the merchant. When capitalist production later accomplishes the separation of manufacture and agriculture, the rural labourer becomes ever more dependent on merely casual accessory employment and his condition deteriorates thereby. For capital, as will be seen later, all differences in the turnover are evened out. Not so for the labourer.

In most branches of industry proper, of mining, transportation, etc., operations proceed evenly, the working time being the same year in year out and the outlay of capital passing daily into the circulation process being uniformly distributed, apart from such abnormal interruptions as fluctuations of prices, business dislocations, etc. Likewise the return of the circulating capital or its renewal is evenly distributed throughout the year, market conditions otherwise remaining the same. Yet there is in the course of the various periods of the year the greatest inequality in the outlay of circulating capital in such capital investments in which the working time constitutes only a part of the production time, while the return takes place only in bulk at a time fixed by natural conditions. If the scale of business is the same, i.e., if the amount of advanced circulating capital is the same, it must be advanced in larger quantities at a time and for longer periods than in enterprises with continuous working periods. There is also a considerably greater difference here between the life of the fixed capital and the time in which it really functions productively. Due to the difference between working time and production time, the time of employment of the applied fixed capital is of course likewise continually interrupted for a longer or shorter time, for instance in agriculture in the case of working cattle, implements and machines. In so far as this fixed capital consists of draught animals, it requires continually the same, or nearly the same, expenditure for feed, etc., as it does during the time they work. In the case of dead stock non-use also brings on a certain amount of depreciation. Hence the product is in general increasing in price, since the transfer of value to it is not calculated according to the time during which the fixed capital functions but according to the time during which it depreciates in value. In branches of production such as these, the idling of the fixed capital, whether combined with current expenses or not, forms as much a condition of its normal employment as for instance the loss of a certain quantity of cotton in spinning; and in the same way the labour-power expended unproductively but unavoidably in any labour-process under normal technical conditions counts just as well as that expended productively. Every improvement which reduces the unproductive expenditure of instruments of labour, raw material, and labour-power also reduces the value of the product.

In agriculture we have a combination of both the longer working period and the great difference between working time and production time. Hodgskin rightly remarks:

> 'The difference of time' (although he does not differentiate here between working time and production time) 'required to complete the products of agriculture, and of other species of labour,' is 'the main cause of the great dependence of the agriculturists. They cannot bring their commodities to market in less time than a year. For that whole period they are obliged to borrow of the shoemaker, the tailor, the smith, the wheelwright, and the various other labourers, whose products they cannot dispense with, but which are completed in a few days or weeks. Owing to this natural circumstance, and owing to the more rapid increase of the wealth produced by other labour than that of agriculture, the monopolisers of all the land, though they have also monopolised legislation, have not been able to save themselves and their servants, the farmers, from becoming the most dependent class of men in the community.' (Thomas Hodgskin, *Popular Political Economy*, London, 1827, p. 147. note.)

All methods by which in agriculture on the one hand the expenditures for wages and instruments of labour are distributed more evenly over the entire year, while on the other the turnover is shortened by raising a greater variety of crops, thus making different harvests possible throughout the year, require an increase of the circulating capital advanced in production, invested in wages, fertilisers, seed, etc. This is the case in the transition from the three-field system with fallow land to the system of crop rotation without fallow. It applies furthermore to the *cultures dèrobèes* of Flanders.

> 'The root crops are planted in *culture dèrobèe*; the same field yields in succession first grain, flax, colza, for the wants of man, and after they are harvested root crops are sown for the maintenance of cattle. This system, which permits the keeping of horned cattle in the stables, yields a considerable amount of manure and thus becomes the pivot of crop rotation. More than a third of the cultivated area in sandy districts is taken up with *cultures dèrobèes*; it is just as if the cultivated area had been increased by one-third.'

Apart from root crops, clover and other fodder plants are likewise used for this purpose.

> 'Agriculture, being thus carried to a point where it turns into horticulture, naturally requires a considerable investment of capital. This capital, estimated in England at 250 francs per hectare, must be almost 500 francs in Flanders, a figure which good farmers will undoubtedly consider far too low, judging by their own lands.' (Émile de Laveleye, *Essais sur l'èconomie rurale de la Belgique*, Paris, 1863, pp. 45, 46 and 48.)

Take finally timber-growing.

> 'The production of timber differs from most of the other branches of production essentially in that here the forces of nature act independently and do not require the power of man or capital when the increase is natural. Even in places where forests are propagated artificially the expenditure of human and capital energy is inconsiderable compared with the action of the natural forces. Besides, a forest will still thrive in soils and on sites where grain no longer gets along or where its cultivation no longer pays. Furthermore forestry engaged in as a regular economy requires a larger area than grain culture, because small plots do not permit of proper forestry methods, largely prevent the enjoyment of the secondary uses to which the land can be put, make forest protection more difficult, etc. But the productive process extends over such long periods that it exceeds the planning of an individual farm and in certain cases surpasses the entire span of a human life. The capital invested in the purchase of forest land'

(in the case of communal production this capital becomes unnecessary, the question then being simply what acreage the community can spare from its sowing and grazing area for forestry)

> 'will not yield substantial returns until after a long period, and even then is turned over only partially. With forests producing certain species of trees the complete turnover takes as much as 150 years. Besides, a properly managed timber-growing establishment itself demands a supply of standing timber which amounts to ten to forty times the annual yield. Unless a man has therefore still other sources of income and owns vast tracts of forest land, he cannot engage in regular forestry.' (Kirchhof, p. 58.)

The long production time (which comprises a relatively small period of working time) and the great length of the periods of turnover entailed make forestry an industry of little attraction to private and therefore capitalist enterprise, the latter being essentially private even if the associated capitalist takes the place of the individual capitalist. The development of culture and of industry in general has evinced itself in such energetic destruction of forest that everything done by it conversely for their preservation and restoration appears infinitesimal.

The following passage in the above quotation from Kirchhof in particularly worthy of note:

> 'Besides, a properly managed timber-growing establishment itself demands a supply of standing timber which amounts to ten to forty times the annual yield.'

In other words, a turnover occurs once in ten to forty or more years.

The same applies to stock raising. A part of the herd (supply of cattle) remains in the process of production, while another part is sold annually as a product. In this case only a part of the capital is turned over every year, just as in the case of fixed capital: machinery, working cattle, etc. although this capital is a capital fixed in the process of production for a long time, and thus prolongs the turnover of the total capital, it is not a fixed capital in the strict definition of the term.

What is here called a supply—a certain amount of standing timber or livestock—exists relatively in the process of production (simultaneously as instruments of labour and material of labour); in accordance with the natural conditions of its reproduction under proper management, a considerable part of this supply must always be available in this form.

A similar influence on the turnover is exerted by another kind of supply, which is productive capital only potentially, but which owing to the nature of this economy, must be accumulated in more or less considerable quantities and hence advanced for purposes of production for a long term, although it enters into the actual process of production only gradually. In this class belongs, for instance, manure before it is hauled to the field, furthermore grain, hay, etc., and such supplies of means of subsistence as are employed in the production of cattle.

> 'A considerable part of the working capital is contained in the farm's supplies. But these may lose more or less of their value, if the precautionary measures necessary for their preservation in good condition are not properly observed. Lack of attention may even result in the total loss of a part of the produce supplies for the farm. For this reason, a careful inspection of the barns, feed and grain lofts, and cellars becomes indispensable, the store rooms must always be well closed, kept clean, ventilated, etc. The grain and other crops held in storage must be thoroughly turned over from time to time, potatoes and beets must be protected against frost, rain and rot.' (Kirchhof, p. 292.) 'In calculating one's own requirements, especially for the keeping of cattle, the distribution must be made according to the product obtained and its intended use. One must not only consider covering one's ordinary needs but also see to it that there is a proportionate reserve for extraordinary cases. If it is then found that the demand cannot be fully met by one's own production, it becomes necessary to reflect first whether the deficiency cannot be covered by other products (substitutes), or by the cheaper procurement of such in place of the deficient ones. For instance if there should happen to be a shortage of hay, this might be made good by roots and an admixture of straw. In general, the intrinsic value and market-price of the various crops must always be kept in mind in such cases, and consumption regulated accordingly. If, for instance, oats are high, while peas and rye are relatively low, it will pay to substitute peas or rye for a part of the oats intended for horses and to sell the oats thus saved.' (*Ibid.*, p. 300.)

It was previously stated, when discussing the formation of a supply, [See pp. 140-146 of this book.—Ed.] that a definite quantity, big or small, of potential productive capital is required, i.e., of means of production intended for use in production, which must be available in bigger or smaller quantities for the purpose of entering by and by into the productive process. The remark was incidentally made that, given a certain business or capitalist enterprise of definite proportions, the magnitude of this productive supply depends on the greater or lesser difficulties of its renewal, the relative nearness of markets of supply, the development of transportation and communication facilities, etc. All these circumstances affect the minimum of capital which must be available in the form of a productive supply, hence affect the length of time for which the capital must be advanced and the amount of capital to be advanced at one time. This amount, which affects also the turnover, is determined by the longer or shorter time during which a circulating capital is tied up in the form of a productive supply as merely potential productive capital. On the other hand, inasmuch as this stagnation depends on the greater or smaller possibility of rapid replacement, on market conditions, etc., it arises itself out of the time of circulation, out of circumstances that belong in the sphere of circulation.

> 'Furthermore, all such implements and accessories as hand tools, sieves, baskets, ropes, wagon grease, nails, etc., must be the more available for immediate replacement, the less there is opportunity for purchasing them nearby without delay. Finally, the entire supply of implements must be carefully overhauled every winter, and new purchases or repairs found necessary must be provided for at once. Whether or not one is to keep a great or small supply of articles of equipment is to be settled mainly by local conditions. Wherever there are no artisans or stores in the vicinity, it is necessary to keep larger supplies than in places where these are to be had on the spot or nearby. But if the necessary supplies are procured in large quantities at a time, then other circumstances being equal, one generally gets the benefit of cheaper purchases, provided an appropriate time has been chosen to make them. True, the rotating working capital is thereby shorn of a correspondingly larger sum, all at once, which cannot always be well spared in the business.' (Kirchhof, p. 301.)

The difference between production time and working time admits of many variations, as we have seen. For the circulating capital it may be production time before it enters into the labour-process proper (production of lasts); or it may be production time after it has passed through the labour-process proper (wine, seed grain); or the production time is occasionally interrupted by working time (agriculture, timber-growing). A large portion of the product fit for circulation remains incorporated in the active process of production, while a much smaller part enters into annual circulation (timber-growing and cattle raising); the longer or shorter period of time for which a circulating capital must be invested in the form of potential productive capital, hence also the larger or smaller amount of this capital to be advanced at one time, depends partly on the kind of productive process (agriculture), and partly on the proximity of markets, etc., in short, on circumstances pertinent to the sphere of circulation.

We shall see later (Volume III), what senseless theories MacCulloch, James Mill, etc., arrived at as a result of the attempt to identify the production time diverging from working time with the latter, an attempt which in turn is due to a misapplication of the theory of value.

The turnover cycle which we considered above is determined by the durability of the fixed capital advanced for the process of production. Since this cycle extends over a number of years it comprises a series of either annual turnovers of fixed capital or of turnovers repeated during the year.

In agriculture such a cycle of turnovers arises out of the system of crop rotation.

> 'The duration of the lease must in no case be less than the time of completion of the adopted system of crop rotation. Hence one always calculates 3, 6, 9, etc., in the three-field system. In that system with clean fallow, a field is cultivated only four times in six years, being sown to winter and summer grain in the years of cultivation, and, if the properties of the soil require or permit it, to wheat and rye, barley and oats successively. Every species of grain differs in its yield from the others on the same soil, every one of them has a different value and is sold at a different price. For this reason the yield of a field is different every year it is cultivated, and different in the first half of the rotation (the first three years) from that of the second. Even the average yield of one period of rotation is not equal to that of another, for fertility does not depend solely on the good quality of the soil, but also on the weather each year, just as prices depend on a multitude of changing conditions. If one now calculates the income from a field by

taking into account the average fertility and the average prices for the entire six-year rotation period, one finds the total income of one year in either period of the rotation. But this is not so if the proceeds are calculated only for half of the time rotation, that is to say, for three years; for then the total income figures would not coincide. It follows from the foregoing that a lease of land worked by the three-field system should run for at least six years. It is however always still more desirable for lessor and lessee that the duration of the lease should be multiple of the duration of the lease (*sic!*); hence that it should be 12, 18, and ever more years instead of 6 years in a system of three fields and 14, 28 years instead of 7 in a system of seven fields.' (Kirchhof, pp. 117, 118.)

(At this place the manuscript contains the note: 'The English system of crop rotation. Give a note here.')

14

The Time of Circulation

All circumstances considered so far which distinguish the periods of turnover of different capitals invested in different branches of industry and hence also the periods for which capital must be advanced, originate in the process of production itself, such as the difference between fixed and circulating capital, the difference in the working periods, etc. But the time of turnover of capital is equal to the sum of its production time plus its circulation, or rotation, time. It is therefore a matter of course that a difference in the time of circulation causes a difference in the time of turnover and hence in the length of the period of turnover. This becomes more evident either on comparing two different investments of capital in which all circumstances modifying the turnover are equal except the time of circulation, or on selecting a given capital with a given proportion of fixed and circulating capital, a given working period, etc., with only the times of circulation varying, hypothetically.

One of the sections of the time of circulation—relatively the most decisive—consists of the time of selling, the period during which capital exists in the state of commodity-capital. The time of circulation, and hence the period of turnover in general, are long or short depending on the relative length of this selling time. An additional outlay of capital may become necessary as a result of expenses of storage, etc. It is clear at the very start that the time required for the sale of finished goods may differ considerably for the individual capitalists in one and the same branch of industry. Hence it may differ not only for the aggregate capitals invested in the various branches of industry, but also for the various independent capitals, which are in fact merely parts of the aggregate capital invested in the same sphere of production but which have made themselves independent. Other circumstances remaining equal, the period of selling will vary for the same individual capital with the general fluctuations of the market or with its fluctuations in that particular line of business. We shall not dwell on this point any longer. We merely state this simple fact: All circumstances which in general give rise to differences in the periods of turnover of the capitals invested in different branches of industry bring in their train differences also in the turnover of the various individual capitals operating in the same business, provided these circumstances operate individually (for instance, if one capitalist has an opportunity to sell more rapidly than his competitor, if one employs more methods shortening the working periods than the other, etc.)

One cause which acts permanently in differentiating the times of selling, and thus the periods of turnover in general, is the distance of the market in which a commodity is sold from its place of production. During the entire trip to the market, capital finds itself fettered in the state of commodity-capital. If goods are made to order, up to the time of delivery; if they are not made to order, there must be added to the time of the trip to the market the time during which the goods are in the market waiting to be sold. The improvement of the means of communication and transportation cuts down absolutely the wandering period of the commodities but does not eliminate the relative difference in the time of circulation of different commodity-capitals arising from their peregrinations, nor that of different portions of the same commodity-capital which migrate to different markets. For instance, the improved sailing vessels and steamships, which shorten travelling, do so equally for near and distant ports. The relative difference remains, although often diminished. But the relative difference may be shifted about by the development of the means of transportation and communication in a way that does not correspond to the geographical distances. For instance a railway which leads from a place of production to an inland centre of population may relatively or absolutely lengthen the distance to a nearer inland point not connected by rail, as compared to the one which geographically is more remote. In the same way the same circumstances may alter the relative distance of places of production from the larger markets, which explains the deterioration of old and the rise of new centres of production because of changes in communication and transportation facilities. (To this must be added the circumstances that long hauls are relatively cheaper than short ones.) Moreover with the development of transport facilities not only is the velocity of movement in space accelerated and thereby the geographic distance shortened in terms of time. Not only is there a development of the mass of communication facilities so that for instance many vessels sail simultaneously for the same port, or several trains travel simultaneously on different railways between the same two points, but freight vessels may clear on consecutive days of the same week from Liverpool for New York, or goods trains may start at different hours of the same day from Manchester to London. True, the absolute velocity—hence this part of the time of circulation—is not altered by this latter circumstance, a certain definite capacity of the means of transportation being given. But successive shipments of commodities can start their passage at shorter intervals of time and thus reach the market one after another without accumulating in large quantities as potential commodity-capital before actual shipment. Hence the return of capital likewise is distributed over shorter successive periods of time, so that a part is continually transformed into money-capital, while the other circulates as commodity-capital. By spreading the return over several successive periods the total time of circulation and hence also the turnover are abridged. The first to increase is the frequency with which the means of transportation function, for instance the number of railway trains, as existing places of production produce more, become greater centres of production. The development tends in the direction of the already existing market, that is to say, towards the great centres of production and population, towards ports of exports, etc. On the other hand these particularly great traffic facilities and the resultant acceleration of the capital turnover (since it is conditional on the time of circulation) give rise to quicker concentration of both the centres of production and the markets. Along with this concentration of masses of men and capital thus accelerated at certain points, there is the concentration of these masses of capital in the hands of a few. Simultaneously, one may note again a shifting and relocation of places of production and of markets as a result of the changes in their relative positions caused by the transformations in transport facilities. A place of production which once had a special advantage by being located on some highway or canal may now find itself relegated to a single side-track, which runs trains only at a relatively long intervals, while another place, which formerly was remote from the main arteries of traffic, may now be situated at the junction of several railways. This second locality is on the upgrade, the former on the downgrade. Changes in the means of transportation thus engender local differences in the time of circulation of commodities, in the opportunity to buy, sell, etc., or an already existing local differentiation is distributed differently. The importance of this circumstance for the turnover of capital is evidenced by the wrangling of the commercial and industrial representatives of the various localities with the railway managements. (See for instance the above-quoted Bluebook of the Railway Committee. [See p. 154 of this book.—*Ed.*])

All branches of production which, by the nature of their product, are dependent mainly on local consumption, such as breweries, are therefore developed to the greatest extent in the principal centres of population. The more rapid turnover of capital compensates here in part for the circumstance that a number of conditions of production, building lots, etc., are more expensive.

Whereas on the one hand, the improvement of the means of transportation and communication brought about by the progress of capitalist production reduces the time of circulation of particular quantities of commodities, the same progress and the opportunities created by the development of transport and communication facilities make it imperative, conversely, to work for ever more remote markets, in a word—for the world-market. The mass of commodities in transit for distant places grows enormously, and with it therefore grows, both absolutely and relatively, that part of social capital which remains continually for long periods in the stage of commodity-capital, within the time of circulation. There is a simultaneous growth of that portion of social wealth which, instead of serving as direct means of production, is invested in means of transportation and communication and in the fixed and circulating capital required for their operation.

The mere relative length of the transit of the commodities from their place of production to their market produces a difference not only in the first part of the circulation time, the selling time, but also in its second part, the reconversion of the money into the elements of the productive capital, the buying time. Suppose a commodity is shipped to India. This requires, say, four months. Let us assume that the selling time is equal to zero, i.e., the commodities are made to order and are paid for on delivery to the agent of the producer. The return of the money (no matter in what form) requires another four months. Thus it takes altogether eight months before a capital can again function as productive capital, renew the same operation. The differences in the turnover thus occasioned form one of the material bases of the various terms of credit, just as overseas commerce in general, for instance in Venice and Genoa, is one of the sources of the credit system, properly speaking.

> 'The crisis of 1847 enabled the banking and mercantile community of that time to reduce the India and China usance' (time allowed for the currency of bills of exchange between there and Europe) 'from ten months' date to six months' sight, and the lapse of twenty years with all the accelerations of speed and establishment of telegraphs ... renders necessary ... a further reduction' from six months' sight to four months' date as a first step to four months' sight. 'The voyage of a sailing vessel *via* the Cape from Calcutta to London is on the average under 90 days. A usance of four months' sight would be equal to a currency of say 150 days. The present usance of six months' sight is equal to a currency of say 210 days.' (*London Economist*, June 16, 1866.)

On the other hand:

> 'The Brazilian usance remains at two and three months' sight, bills from Antwerp are drawn' (on London) 'at three months' date, and even Manchester and Bradford draw upon London at three months and longer dates. By tacit consent, a fair opportunity is afforded to the merchant of realising the proceeds of his merchandise, not indeed before, but within a reasonable time of, the bills drawn against it falling due. In this view, the present usance for Indian bills cannot be considered excessive. Indian produce

> for the most part being sold in London with three months' prompt, and allowing for loss of time in effecting sales, cannot be realised much within five months, while another period of five months will have previously elapsed (on an average) between the time of purchase in India and of delivery in the English warehouse. We have here a period of ten months, whereas the bill drawn against the goods does not live beyond seven months.' (*Ibid.*, June 30, 1866.)
>
> 'On July 2, 1866, five big London banks dealing mainly with India and China, and the Paris *Comptoir d'Escompte*, gave notice that from the 1st January, 1867, their branches and agencies in the East will only buy and sell bills of exchange at a term not exceeding four months' sight.' (*Ibid.*, July 7, 1866.)

However this reduction miscarried and had to be abandoned. (Since then the Suez Canal has revolutionized all this.)

It is a matter of course that with the longer time of commodity circulation the risk of a change of prices in the market increases, since the period in which price changes can take place is lengthened.

Differences in the time of circulation, partly individual between the various separate capitals of the same branch of business, partly between different branches of business according to the different usances, when payment is not made in spot cash, arise from the different terms of payment in buying and selling. We shall not dwell any longer here on this point which is of importance to the credit system.

Differences in the turnover time arise also from the size of contracts for the delivery of goods, and their size grows with the extent and scale of capitalist production. A contract of delivery, being a transaction between buyer and seller, is an operation pertaining to the market, the sphere of circulation. The differences in the time of turnover arising here stem therefore from the sphere of circulation, but react immediately on the sphere of production, and do so apart from all terms of payment and conditions of credit, hence also in the case of cash payment. For instance coal, cotton, yarn, etc., are discrete products. Every day supplies its quantum of finished product. But, if the master-spinner or the mine-owner accepts contracts for the delivery of such large quantities of products as require, say, a period of four or six weeks of consecutive working-days, then this is quite the same, so far as the time of advancement of capital is concerned, as if a continuous working period of four or six weeks had been introduced in this labour-process. It is of course assumed here that the entire quantity ordered is to be delivered in one bulk, or at least is paid for only after total delivery. Individually considered, every day has thus furnished its definite quantum of finished product. But this finished quantum is only a part of the quantity contracted for. While in this case the portion finished so far is no longer in the process of production, still it lies in the warehouse as potential capital only.

Now let us take up the second stage of the time of circulation, the buying time, or that period in which capital is reconverted from the money-form into the elements of productive capital. During this period it must persist for a shorter or longer time in its condition of money-capital, hence a certain portion of the total capital advanced must all the time be in the condition of money-capital, although this portion consists of constantly changing elements. For instance, of the total capital advanced in a certain business, *n* times £100 must be available in the form of money-capital, so that, while all the constituent parts of these *n* times £100 are continually converted into productive capital, this sum is nevertheless just as continually replenished by the influx from the circulation, from the realised commodity-capital. A definite part of the advanced capital-value is therefore continually in the condition of money-capital, i.e., a form not pertaining to its sphere of production but its sphere of circulation.

We have already seen that the prolongation of the time for which capital is fettered in the form of commodity-capital on account of the distance of the market results in direct delay of the return of the money and consequently also the transformation of the capital from money-capital into productive capital.

We have furthermore seen (Chapter VI) with reference to the purchase of commodities, that the time of buying, the greater or smaller distance from the main sources of the raw material, makes it necessary to purchase raw material for a longer period and have it available in the form of a productive supply, of latent or potential productive capital; that in consequence it increases the amount of capital to be advanced at one time, and the time for which it must be advanced, if the scale of production remains otherwise the same.

A similar effect is produced in various branches of business by the more or less prolonged periods in which rather large quantities of raw material are thrown on the market. In London, for example, great auction sales of wool take place every three months, and the wool market is controlled by them. The cotton market on the other hand is on the whole restocked continuously, if not uniformly, from harvest to harvest. Such periods determine the principal dates when these raw materials are bought. Their effect is particularly great on speculative purchases necessitating advances for longer or shorter periods for these elements of production, just as the nature of the produced commodities acts on the speculative, intentional withholding of a product for a longer or shorter term in the form of potential commodity-capital.

> 'The agriculturist must also be a speculator to a certain extent and therefore hold back the sale of his products if prevailing conditions so suggest...'

Here follow a few general rules.

> '...However in the sale of the products, it all depends mainly on the person, the product itself, and the locality. Anyone who, besides being skilful and lucky (!), is provided with sufficient working capital will not be blamed if for once he keeps his grain crop stored as long as a year when prices are unusually low. On the other hand a man who lacks working capital or is altogether devoid (!) of speculative spirit will try to get the current average prices and will be compelled to sell as soon and as often as opportunity presents itself. It will almost always mean a loss to keep wool stored longer than a year, while corn and oil seed may be stored for several years without detriment to their properties and high quality. Products generally subject to severe fluctuation at short intervals, for instance oil seed, hops, teasel and the like, may be stored to good advantage during years in which the selling price is far below the price of production. It is least permissible to postpone the sale of articles whose preservation involves daily expense, such as fatted cattle, or which are perishable, such as fruit, potatoes, etc. In various localities a certain product fetches its lowest average price in certain seasons, its highest in others. Thus, in some parts the average price of corn is lower around St. Martin's Day than between Christmas and Easter. Furthermore some products sell well in certain localities only at certain times, as is the case with wool in the wool markets of those localities where the wool trade at other times is dull, etc.' (Kirchhof, p. 302.)

In the study of the second half of the time of circulation, during which the money is reconverted into the elements of productive capital, it is not only this transformation, taken by itself, that should be given consideration, not only the time within which the money returns, according to the distance of the market in which the product is sold. What must also be considered, and primarily so, is the amount of that part of the advanced capital which is always to be available in the form of money, in the condition of money-capital.

Apart from all speculation, the volume of the purchases of those commodities which must always be available as a productive supply depends on the times of the renewal of this supply, hence on circumstances which in their turn are dependent on market conditions and which therefore are different for different raw materials. In these cases, money must be advanced from time to time in rather large quantities and in lump sums. It returns more or less rapidly, but always in instalments, according to the turnover of capital. One portion of it, namely the part reconverted into wages, is just as continually expended again at short intervals. But another portion, namely that which is to be reconverted into raw material, etc., must be accumulated for rather long periods, as a reserve fund for either buying or paying. Therefore it exists in the form of money-capital, although the volume in which it exists as such, changes.

We shall see in the next chapter that other circumstances arising either from the process of production or that of circulation make it necessary for a certain portion of the advanced capital to be available in the form of money. In general it must be noted that the economists are very prone to forget not only that a part of the capital required in a business passes successively through the three stages of money-capital, productive capital, and commodity-capital, but also that different portions of it continuously and simultaneously possess these forms, although the relative magnitudes of these portions vary all the time. It is especially the part always available as money-capital that is forgotten by the economists, although precisely this circumstance is highly essential for an understanding of bourgeois economy and consequently makes its importance felt as such also in practice.

15

Effect of the Time of Turnover on the Magnitude of Advanced Capital

In this chapter and in the next, the sixteenth, we shall treat of the influence of the time of turnover on the self-expansion of capital.

Take the commodity-capital which is the product of a working period of, say, nine weeks. Let us, for the time being, leave aside that portion of the value of the product which is added to it by the average wear and tear of the fixed capital, and also the surplus-value added to the product during the process of production. The value of this product is then equal to that of the circulating capital, advanced for its production, i.e., of the wages and the raw and auxiliary materials consumed in its production. Let this value be £900, so that the weekly outlay is £100. The period of production, which here coincides with the working period, is therefore nine weeks. It is immaterial whether it is assumed that this is the working period of a continuous product, or whether it is a continuous working period for a discrete product, so long as the quantity of discrete product brought to market at one time costs nine weeks' labour. Let the time of circulation be three weeks. Then the entire period of turnover is twelve weeks. At the end of nine weeks the advanced productive capital is converted into commodity-capital, but now it stays for three weeks in the period of circulation. The new period of production therefore cannot start before the beginning of the thirteenth week, and production would be at a standstill for three weeks, or for a quarter of the entire period of turnover. It again does not make any difference whether it is assumed that it takes so long on an average to sell the product, or that this length of time is bound up with the remoteness of the market or the terms of payment for the goods sold. Production would be standing still for three weeks every three months, making it four times three, or twelve weeks in a year, which means three months, or one-quarter, of the annual period of turnover. Hence, if production is to be continuous and carried along the same scale week after week, there is only this alternative:

Either the scale of production must be reduced, so that the £900 suffice to keep the work going both during the working period and the time of circulation of the first turnover, is then commenced with the tenth week, before the first period of turnover is completed, for the period of turnover is twelve weeks, and the working period nine weeks. A sum of £900 distributed over twelve weeks makes £75 per week. It is evident in the first place that such a reduced scale of business presupposes changed dimensions of the fixed capital and therefore, on the whole, a curtailment of the business. In the second place, it is questionable whether such a reduction can take place at all, for in each business there exists, commensurate with the development of its production, a normal minimum of invested capital essential to maintain its capacity to complete. This normal minimum grows steadily with the advance of capitalist production, and hence it is not fixed. There are numerous intermediate grades between the normal minimum existing at any particular time and the ever increasing normal maximum, a medium which permits of many different scales of capital investment. Within the limits of this medium reductions may take place, their lowest limit being the prevailing normal minimum.

When there is a hitch in production, when the markets are overstocked, and when raw materials rise in price, etc., the normal outlay of circulating capital is restricted—once the pattern of the fixed capital has been set—by cutting down working time to, say, one half. On the other hand, in times of prosperity, the pattern of the fixed capital given, there is an abnormal expansion of the circulating capital, partly through the extension of working time and partly through its intensification. In businesses which have, from the outset, to reckon with such fluctuations, the situation is relieved partly by recourse to the above measures and partly by employing simultaneously a greater number of labourers, in combination with the application of reserve fixed capital, such as reserve locomotives on railways, etc. However, such abnormal fluctuations are not considered here, where we assume normal conditions.

In order to make production continuous, therefore, the expenditure of the same circulating capital is here distributed over a longer period, over twelve weeks instead of nine. In every section of time there consequently functions a reduced productive capital. The circulating portion of the productive capital is reduced from 100 to 75, or one-quarter. The total amount by which the productive capital functioning for a working period of nine weeks is reduced equals 9 times 25, or £225, or one-quarter of £900. But the ratio of the time of circulation to that of turnover is likewise three-twelfths, or one-quarter. It follows therefore: circulation of the productive capital transformed into commodity-capital, if it is rather to be carried on simultaneously and continuously week after week, and if no special circulating capital is available for this purpose, it can be done only by curtailing productive operations, by reducing the circulating component of the functioning productive capital. The portion of circulating capital thus set free for production during the time of circulation is to the total advanced circulating capital as the time of circulation is to the period of turnover. This applies, as has already been stated, only to branches of production in which the labour-process is carried on in the same scale week after week, where therefore no varying amounts of capital are to be invested in different working periods, as for instance in agriculture.

If on the other hand we assume that the nature of the business excludes a reduction of the scale of production, and thus of the circulating capital to be advanced each week, then continuity of production can be secured only by additional circulating capital, in the above-named case of £300. During the twelve-week turnover period, £1,200 are successively invested, and £300 is one-quarter of this sum as three weeks is of twelve. At the end of the working time of nine weeks the capital-value of £900 has been converted from the form of productive into that of commodity-capital. Its working period is concluded, but it cannot be re-opened with the same capital. During the three weeks in which it stays in the sphere of circulation, functioning as commodity-capital, it is in the same state, so far as the process of production is concerned, as if it did not exist at all. We rule out in the present case all credit relations and take for granted that the capitalist operates only with his own money. But during the time the capital advanced for the first working period, having completed its process of production, stays three weeks in the process of circulation, there functions an additional capital investment of £300, so that the continuity of production is not broken.

Now, the following must be noted in this connection:

Firstly: The working period of the capital of £900 first advanced is completed at the close of nine weeks and it does not return until after three weeks are up, that is to say, at the beginning of the thirteenth week. But a new working period is immediately begun with the additional capital of £300. By this means continuity of production is maintained.

Secondly: The functions of the original capital of £900 and of the capital of £300 newly added at the close of the first nine-week working period, inaugurating the second working period after the conclusion of the first without any interruption, are, or at least could be, clearly distinguished in the first period of turnover, while they cross each other each other in the course of the second period of turnover.

Let us make this matter plainer.

First period of turnover of 12 weeks: First working period of 9 weeks; the turnover of the capital advanced for this is completed at the beginning of the 13th week. During the last 3 weeks the additional capital of £300 functions, opening the second working period of 9 weeks.

Second period of turnover: At the beginning of the 13th week, £900 have returned and are able to begin a new turnover. But the second working period has already been opened in the 10th week by the additional £300. At the start of the 13th week, thanks to this, one-third of the working period is already over and £300 has been converted from productive capital into product. Since only 6 weeks more are required for the completion of the second working period, only two-thirds of the returned capital of £900, or only £600, can enter into the productive process of the second working period. £300 of the original £900 are set free to play the same role which the additional capital of £300 played in the first working period. At the close of the 6th week of the second period of turnover the second working period is up. The capital of £900 advanced in it returns after 3 weeks, or at the end of the 9th week of the second, 12-week period of turnover. During the 3 weeks of its period of circulation, the freed capital of £300 comes into action. This begins the third working period of a capital of 900 in the 7th week of the second period of turnover, or the 19th week of the year.

Third period of turnover: At the close of the 9th week of the second period of turnover there is a new reflux of £900. But the third working period has already commenced in the 7th week of the previous period of turnover and 6 weeks have already elapsed. The third working period, then, lasts only another 3 weeks. Hence only £300 of the returned £900 enter into the productive process. The fourth working period fills out the remaining 9 weeks of this period of turnover and thus the 37th week of the year begins simultaneously the fourth period of turnover and the fifth working period.

In order to simplify the calculation in this case let us assume a working period of 5 weeks and a period of circulation of 5 weeks, making a turnover period of 10 weeks. Figure the year as composed of fifty weeks and the capital outlay per week as £100. A working period then requires a circulating capital of £500 and the time of circulation an additional capital of £500. The working periods and times of turnover then are as follows:

1st wrkg. period	1st-5th wk.	(£500 in goods) returned end of 10th wk.
2nd wrkg. period	6th-10th wk.	(£500 in goods) returned end of 15th wk.
3rd wrkg. period	11th-15th wk.	(£500 in goods) returned end of 20th wk.
4th wrkg. period	16th-20th wk.	(£500 in goods) returned end of 25th wk.
5th wrkg. period	21st-25th wk.	(£500 in goods) returned end of 30th wk.
		and so forth.

If the time of circulation is zero, so that the period of turnover is equal to the working period, then the number of turnovers is equal to the number of working periods of the year. In the case of a 5-week working period this would make 50/5, or 10, periods of turnover per year, and the value of the capital turned over would be 500 times 10, or 5,000. In our table, in which we have assumed a circulation time of 5 weeks, the total value of the commodities produced per year would also be £5,000, but one-tenth of this, or £500, would always be in the form of commodity-capital, and would not return until after 5 weeks. At the end of the year the product of the tenth working period (the 46th to the 50th working week) would have completed its time of turnover only by half, and its time of circulation would fall within the first five weeks of the next year.

Now let us take a third illustration: Working period 6 weeks time of circulation 3 weeks, weekly advance during labour-process £100.

1st working period: 1st-6th week. At the end of the 6th week a commodity-capital of £600, returned at the end of the 9th week.

2nd working period: 7th-12th week. During the 7th-9th week £300 of additional capital is advanced. At the end of the 9th week, return of £600. Of this, £300 are advanced during the 10th-12th week. At the end of the 12th week therefore £300 are free and £600 are in the form of commodity-capital, returnable at the end of the 15th week.

3rd working period: 13th-18th week. During the 13th-15th week, advance of above £300, then reflux of £600, of which 300 are advanced for the 16th-18th week. At the end of the 18th week, £300 are free in money-form, £600 on hand as commodity-capital which returns at the end of the 21st week. (See the more detailed presentation of this case under II, below.)

In other words, during 9 working periods (54 weeks) a total of 600 times 9 or £5,400 worth of commodities are produced. At the end of the ninth working period the capitalist has £300 in money and £600 in commodities which have not yet completed their term of circulation.

A comparison of these three illustrations shows, first, that a successive release of capital I of £500 and of additional capital II of likewise £500 takes place only in the second illustration, so that these two portions of capital move separately and apart from each other. But this is so only because we have made the very exceptional assumption that the working period and the time of circulation form two equal halves of the turnover period. In all other cases, whatever the difference between the two constituents of the period of turnover, the movements of the two capitals cross each other, as in illustrations I and III, beginning with the second period of turnover. The additional capital II, with a portion of capital I, then forms the capital functioning in the second turnover period, while the remainder of capital I is set free to perform the original function of capital II. The capital operating during the circulation time of the commodity-capital is not identical, in this case, with the capital II originally advanced for this purpose, but it is of the same value and forms the same aliquot part of the total capital advanced.

Secondly: The capital which functioned during the working period lies idle during the time of circulation. In the second illustration the capital functions during the 5 weeks of the working period and lies idle during the 5 weeks of the circulation period. Therefore the entire time during which capital I lies idle here amounts to one half of the year. It is the additional capital II that appears during this time having, in the case before us, also in its turn lain idle half a year. But the additional capital required to ensure the continuity of production during the time of circulation is not determined by the aggregated amount, or sum total, of the times of circulation during the year, but only by the ratio of the time of circulation to the period of turnover. (We assume, of course, that all the turnovers take place under the same conditions.) For this reason £500 of additional capital, and not £2,500, are required in the second illustration. This is simply due to the fact that the additional capital enters just as well into the turnover as the capital originally advanced, and that it therefore makes up its magnitude just as the other by the number of its turnovers.

Thirdly: The circumstances here considered are not affected by whether the time of production is longer than the working time or not. True, the aggregate of the periods of turnover is prolonged thereby, but this extension does not necessitate any additional capital for the labour-process. The additional capital serves merely the purpose of filling the gaps in the labour-process that arise on account of the time of circulation. Hence it is there simply to protect production against interruptions, originating in the time of circulation. Interruptions arising from the specific conditions of production are to be eliminated in another way, which need not be discussed at this point. There are, however, establishments in which work is carried on only intermittently, to order, so that there may be intervals between the working periods. In such cases, the need for additional capital is *pro tanto* eliminated. On the other hand in most cases of seasonal work there is a certain limit for the time of reflux. The same work cannot be renewed next year with the same capital, if the circulation time of this capital has not, in the meantime, run out. On the other hand, the time of circulation may also be shorter than the interval between two periods of production. In that event the capital lies fallow, unless it is meanwhile employed otherwise.

Fourthly: The capital advanced for a certain working period—for instance the £600 in the third illustration—is invested partly in raw and auxiliary materials, in a productive supply for the working period, in constant circulating capital, and partly in variable circulating capital, in the payment of labour itself. The portion laid out in constant circulating capital, may not exist for the same length of time in the form of a productive supply; the raw material for instance may not be on hand for the entire working period, coal may be procured only every two weeks. However, as credit is still out of the question here, this portion of capital, in so far as it is not available in the form of a productive supply, must be kept on hand in the form of money so that it can be converted into a productive supply as and when needed. This does not alter the magnitude of the constant circulating capital-value advanced for 6 weeks. On the other hand—regardless of the money-supply for unforeseen expenses, the reserve fund proper for the elimination of disturbances—wages are paid in shorter intervals, mostly weekly. Therefore, unless the capitalist compels the labourer to advance his labour for a longer time, the capital required for wages must be on hand in the form of money. During the reflux of the capital a portion must therefore be retained in money-form for the payment of the labour, while the remaining portion may be converted into productive supply.

The additional capital is divided exactly like the original. But it is distinguished from capital I by the fact that (apart from credit relations) in order to be available for its own working period it must advanced during the entire duration of the first working period of capital I, into which it does not enter. During this time it can already be converted, at least in part, into constant circulating capital, having been advanced for the entire period of turnover. To what extent it assumes this form or persists in the form of additional money-capital until this conversion becomes necessary, will depend partly on the special conditions of production of definite lines of business, partly on local conditions, partly on the price fluctuations of raw material, etc. If social capital is viewed in its entirety, a more or less considerable part of this additional capital will always be for a rather long time in the state of money-capital. But as for that portion of capital II which is to be advanced for wages, it is always converted only gradually into labour-power, as small working periods expire and are paid for. This portion of capital II, then, is available in the form of money-capital during the entire working period, until by its conversion into labour-power it take part in the function of productive capital.

Consequently, the accession of the additional capital required for the transformation of the circulation time of capital I into time of production, increases not only the magnitude of the advanced capital and the length of time for which the aggregate capital must necessarily be advanced, but also, and specifically so, that portion of the advanced capital which exists as money-supply, which hence exists in the state of money-capital and has the form of potential money-capital.

The same thing also takes place—as far as it concerns both the advance in the form of a productive supply and in that of a money-supply—when the separation of capital into two parts made necessary by the time of circulation, namely into capital for the first working period and replacement capital for the time of circulation, is not caused by the increase of the capital laid out but by a decrease of the scale of production. The amount of capital tied up in the money-form grows here still more in relation to the scale of production.

What is achieved in general by this separation of capital into an originally productive and an additional capital is a continuous succession of the working periods, the constant function of an equal portion of the advanced capital as productive capital.

Let us look at the second illustration. The capital continuously employed in the process of production amounts to £500. As the working period is 5 weeks it operates ten times during 50 weeks (taken as a year). Hence its product, apart from surplus-value, is 10 times £500, or £5,000. From the standpoint of a capital working directly and uninterruptedly in the process of production—a capital-value of £500—the time of circulation seems to be brought to nought. The period of turnover coincides with the working period, and the time of circulation is assumed to be equal to zero.

But, if the capital of £500 were regularly interrupted in its productive activity by a 5-week circulation time, so that it would again become capable of production only after the close of the entire 10-week turnover period, we should have 5 turnovers of ten weeks each in the 50 weeks of the year. These would comprise five 5-week periods of production, or a sum of 25 productive weeks with a total product worth 5 times £500 or £2,500, and five 5-week periods of circulation, or a total circulation time of likewise 25 weeks. If we say, in this case, that the capital of £500 has been turned over 5 times in the year, it will be clear and obvious that during half of each period of turnover this capital of £500 did not function at all as a production capital and that, all in all, it performed its functions only during one half of the year, but did not function at all during the other half.

In our illustration the replacement capital of £500 appears on the scene during those five periods of circulation and the turnover is thus expanded from £2,500 to £5,000. But now the advanced capital is £1,000 instead of £500. 5,000 divided by 1,000 is 5. Hence, there are five turnovers instead of ten. And that is just the way people figure. But when it is said that the capital of £1,000 has been turned over five times during the year, the recollection of the time of circulation disappears from the hollow skulls of the capitalists and a confused idea is formed that this capital has served continuously in the production process during the five successive turnovers. But, if we say that the capital of £1,000 has been turned over five times this includes both the time of circulation and the time of production. Indeed, if £1,000 had really been continuously active in the process of production, the product would, according to our assumptions, have to be £10,000 instead of £5,000. But in order to have £1,000 continuously in the process of production, £2,000 would have to be advanced. The economists, who as a general rule have nothing clear to say in reference to the mechanism of the turnover, always overlook this main point, to wit, that only a part of the industrial capital can actually be engaged in the process of production if production is to proceed uninterruptedly. While one part is in the period of production, another must always be in the period of circulation. Or in other words, one part can perform the function of productive capital only on condition that another part is withdrawn from production proper in the form of commodity- or money-capital. In overlooking this, the significance and role of money-capital is entirely ignored.

We have now to ascertain what differences in the turnover arise if the two sections of the period of turnover, the working period and the circulation period, are equal, or if the working period is greater or smaller than the circulation period, and, furthermore, what effect this has on the tie-up of capital in the form of money-capital.

We assume the capital advanced weekly to be in all cases £100, and the period of turnover 9 weeks, so that the capital to be advanced in each period of turnover is £900.

Section I. *The Working Period Equal to the Circulation Period*

Although this case occurs in reality only as an accidental exception, it must serve as our point of departure in this investigation, because here relations shape themselves in the simplest and most intelligible way.

The two capitals (capital I advanced for the first working period, and supplemental capital II, which functions during the circulation period of capital I) relieve one another in their movements without crossing. With the exception of the first period, either of the two capitals is therefore advanced only for its own period of turnover. Let the period of turnover be 9 weeks, as indicated in the following illustrations, so that the working period and the circulation period are each 4½ weeks. Then we have the following annual diagram.

TABLE 1

CAPITAL I			
Periods of Turnover	*Working Periods*	*Advance*	*Periods of Circulation*
I. 1st-9th week	1st-4th ½ week	£450	4th ½-9th week
II. 10th-18th "	10th-13th ½ "	£450	13th ½-18th "
III. 19th-27th "	19th-22nd ½ "	£450	22nd ½-27th "
IV. 28th-36th "	28th-31st ½ "	£450	31st ½-36th "
V. 37th-45th "	37th-40th ½ "	£450	40th ½-45th "
VI. 46th-[54th]	46th-49th ½ "	£450	49th ½-[54th] "[1]
CAPITAL II			
I. 1st-9th week	4th ½-9th week	£450	10th-13th ½ week
II. 10th-18th "	13th ½-18th "	£450	19th-22nd ½ "
III. 19th-27th "	22nd ½-27th "	£450	28th-31st ½ "
IV. 28th-36th "	31st ½-36th "	£450	37th-40th ½ "
V. 37th-45th "	40th ½-45th "	£450	46th-49th ½ "
VI. 46th-[54th] "	49th ½-[54th] "	£450	[55th-58th ½] "

Within the 51 weeks which here stand for one year, capital I runs through six full working periods, producing 6 times 450, or £2,700 worth of commodities, and capital II producing in five full working periods 5 times £450, or £2,250 worth of commodities. In addition, capital II produced, within the last one and a half weeks of the year (middle of the 50th to the end of the 51st week), an extra £150 worth. The aggregate product in 51 weeks is worth £5,100. So far as the direct production of surplus-value is concerned, which takes place only during the working period, the aggregate capital of £900 would have been turned over 5⅔ times

(5⅔ times 900 equals £5,100)). But if we consider the real turnover, capital I has been turned over 5⅔ times, since at the close of the 51st week it still has 3 weeks to go of its sixth period of turnover; 5⅔ times 450 makes £2,550; and capital II turned over 5 1/6 times, since it has completed only 1½ weeks of its sixth period of turnover, so that 7½ weeks of it run into the next year; 5 1/6 times 450 makes £2,325; real aggregate turnover: £4,875.

Let us consider capital I and capital II as two capitals wholly independent of one another. They are entirely independent in their movements; these movements complement one another merely because their working and circulating periods directly relieve one another. They may be regarded as two totally independent capitals belonging to different capitalists.

Capital I has completed five full turnovers and two-thirds of its sixth turnover period. At the end of the year it has the form of commodity-capital, which is three weeks short of its normal realisation. During this time it cannot enter into the process of production. It functions as commodity-capital, it circulates. It has completed only two-thirds of its last period of turnover. This is expressed as follows: It has been turned over only two-thirds of a time, only two-thirds of its total value have performed a complete turnover. We say that £450 complete their turnover in 9 weeks, hence £300 do in 6 weeks. But in this mode of expression the organic relations between the two specifically different components of the turnover time are ignored. The exact meaning of the expression that the advanced capital of £450 has made 5⅔ turnovers is merely that it has accomplished five turnovers fully and only two-thirds of the sixth. On the other hand, the expression that the turned-over capital equals 5⅔ times the advanced capital—hence, in the above case, 5⅔ times £450, making £2,550—is correct, meaning that unless this capital of £450 were complemented by another capital of £450, one portion of it would have to be in the process of production while another in the process of circulation. If the time of turnover is to be expressed in terms of the capital turned over, it can always be expressed only in terms of existing value (in fact, of finished product). The circumstance that the advanced capital is not in a condition in which it may re-open the process of production finds expression in the fact that only a part of it is in a state capable of production or that, in order to be in a state of uninterrupted production, the capital would have to be divided into a portion which would be continually in the period of production and into another which would be continually in the period of circulation, depending upon the relation of these periods to each other. It is the same law which determines the quantity of the constantly functioning productive capital by the ratio of the time of circulation to the time of turnover.

By the end of the 51st week, which we regard here as the end of the year, £150 of capital II have been advanced to the production of an unfinished lot of goods. Another part of it exists in the form of circulating constant capital—raw materials, etc.—i.e., in a form in which it can function as productive capital in the production process. But a third part of it exists in the form of money, at least the amount of the wages for the remainder of the working period (3 weeks), which is not paid, however, until the end of each week. Now, although at the beginning of a new year, hence of a new turnover cycle, this portion of the capital is not in the form of productive capital but in that of money-capital, in which it cannot take part in the process of production, at the opening of the new turnover circulating variable capital, i.e., living labour-power, is nevertheless active in the process of production. This is due to the fact that labour-power is not paid until the end of the week, although bought at the beginning of the working period, say, per week, and so consumed. Money serves here as a means of payment. For this reason it is still as money in the hands of the capitalist, on the one hand, while, on the other hand, labour-power, the commodity into which money is being transformed, is already active in the process of production, so that the same capital-value appears here doubly.

If we look merely at the working periods,

capital I produces	6	times	450,	or	£2,700
capital II produces	5⅓	times	450,	or	£2,400
Hence together	5⅓	times	900,	or	£5,100

Hence the total advanced capital of £900 has functioned 5⅔ times throughout the year as productive capital. It is immaterial for the production of the surplus-value whether there are always £450 in the production process and always £450 in the circulation process, or whether £900 function 4½ weeks in the process of production and the following 4½ weeks in the process of circulation.

On the other hand, if we consider the periods of turnover, there has been turned over:

capital I,	5⅔	times	450,	or	£2,550
capital II,	5 1/6	times	450,	or	£2,325
Hence the total capital	5 5/12	times	900,	or	£4,875.

For the number of turnovers of the total capital is equal to the sum of the amounts turned over by I and II, divided by the sum of I and II.

It is to be noted that if capitals I and II were independent of each other they would nevertheless form merely different independent portions of the social capital advanced in the same sphere of production. Hence if the social capital within this sphere of production were composed *solely* of I and II, the same calculation would apply to the turnover of the social capital in this sphere as applies here to the constituent parts I and II of the same private capital. Going further, every portion of the entire social capital invested in any particular sphere of production may be so calculated. But in the last analysis, the number of turnovers made by the entire social capital is equal to the sum of the capitals turned over in the various spheres of production divided by the sum of the capitals advanced in those spheres.

It must further be noted that just as capitals I and II in the same private business have here strictly speaking different turnover years (the cycle of turnover of capital II beginning 4½ weeks later than that of capital I, so that the year of I ends 4½ weeks earlier than that of II), so the various private capitals in the same sphere of production begin their operations at totally different periods and therefore conclude their turnover years at different times of the year. The same calculation of averages that we employed above for I and II suffices also here to bring down the turnover years of the various independent portions of the social capital to one uniform turnover year.

Section II. *The Working Period Greater than the Period of Circulation*

The working and turnover periods of capitals I and II cross one another instead of relieving one another. Simultaneously some capital is set free. This was not so in the previously considered case.

But this does not alter the fact that, as before, 1) the number of working periods of the total capital advanced is equal to the sum of the value of the annual product of both advanced portions of capital divided by the total capital advanced, and 2) the number of turnovers made by the total capital is equal to the sum of the two amounts turned over divided by the sum of the two advanced capitals. Here too we must consider both portions of capital as if they performed turnover movements entirely independent of each other.

Thus, we assume once more, that £100 are to be advanced weekly to the labour-process. Let the working period last 6 weeks, requiring therefore every time an advance of £600 (capital I). Let the time of circulation be 3 weeks, so that the period of turnover is 9 weeks, as before. Let capital II of £300 step in during the three-week circulation period of capital I. Considering both capitals as independent of each other, we find the schedule of the annual turnover to be as follows:

TABLE II

CAPITAL I, £600			
Periods of Turnover	*Working Periods*	*Advance*	*Periods of Circulation*
I. 1st-9th week	1st-6th week	£600	7th-9th week
II. 10th-18th "	10th-15th "	£600	16th-18th"
III. 19th-27th "	19th-24th "	£600	25th-27th "
IV. 28th-36th "	28th-33rd "	£600	34th-36th "
V. 37th-45th "	37th-42nd "	£600	43rd-45th "
VI. 46th-[54th] "	46th-51st "	£600	[52nd-54th] "
ADDITIONAL CAPITAL II, £300			
I. 7th-15th week	7th-9th week	£300	10th-15th week
II. 16th-24th "	16th-18th "	£300	19th-24th "
III. 25th-33rd "	25th-27th "	£300	28th-33rd "
IV. 34th-42nd "	34th-36th "	£300	37th-42nd "
V. 43rd-51st "	43rd-45th "	£300	46th-51st "

The process of production continues uninterruptedly the whole year round on the same scale. The two capitals I and II remain entirely separate. But in order to represent them as separate, we had to tear apart their real intersections and intertwinings, and thus also to change the number of turnovers. For according to the above table the amounts turned over would be:

by capital I,	5⅔	times	600,	or	£3,400 and
by capital II,	5	times	300,	or	£1,500
Hence by the total capital	5 4/9	times	900,	or	£4,900.

But this is not correct, for, as we shall see, the actual periods of production and circulation do not absolutely coincide with those of the above schedule, in which it was mainly a question of presenting capitals I and II as independent of each other.

In reality, capital II has no working and circulating periods separate and distinct from those of capital I. The working period is 6 weeks, the circulation period 3 weeks. Since capital II amounts to only £300, it can suffice only for a part of the working period. This is indeed the case. At the end of the 6th week a product valued at £600 passes into circulation and returns in money-form at the close of the 9th week. Then, at the opening of the 7th week, capital II begins its activity, and covers the requirements of the next working period, the 7th to 9th week. But according to our assumption the working period is only half up at the end of the 9th week. Hence capital I of £600 having just returned, at the beginning of the 10th week, once more enters into operation and with its £300 supplies the advances needed for the 10th to 12th week. This disposes of the second working period. A product value of £600 is in circulation and will return at the close of the 15th week. At the same time, £300, the amount of the original capital II, are set free and are able to function in the first half of the following working period, that is to say, in the 13th to 15th week. After the lapse of these weeks the £600 return; £300 of them suffice for the remainder of the working period, and £300 remain for the following working period.

The thing therefore works as follows:

First period of turnover: 1st-9th week.
1st working period: 1st-6th week. Capital I, £600, performs its function.
1st period of circulation: 7th-9th week. End of 9th week, £600 return.

Second period of turnover: 7th-15th week.
2nd working period: 7th-12th week.

First half: 7th-9th week. Capital II, £300, performs its function.
End of 9th week, £600 return in money-form (capital I).
Second half: 10th-12th week. £300 of capital I perform their function. The other £300 of capital I remain freed.
2nd period of circulation: 13th-15th week.
End of 15th week, £600 (half taken from capital I, half from capital II) return in the form of money.

Third period of turnover; 13-21st week.

3rd working period: 13th-18th week.
First half: 13th-15th week. The freed £300 perform their function. End of 15th week, £600 return in money-form.
Second half: 16th-18th week, £300 of the returned £600 function, the other £300 again remain freed.
3rd period of circulation: 19th-21st week at the close of which £600 again return in money-form. In these £600 capital I and capital II are now indistinguishably fused.

And so there are eight full turnover periods of a capital of £600 (I: 1st-9th week; II: 7th-15th week; III: 13th-21st; IV: 19th-27th; V: 25th-33rd; VI: 31st-39th; VII: 37th-45th; VIII: 43rd-51st week) to the end of the 51st week. But as the 49th-51st weeks fall within the eighth period of circulation, the £300 of freed capital must step in and keep production going. Thus the turnover at the end of the year is as follows: £600 have completed their circuit eight times, making £4,800. In addition we have the product of the last 3 weeks (49th-51st), which, however, has completed only one-third of its circuit of 9 weeks, so that in the sum turned over it counts for only one-third of its amount, £100. If, then, the annual product of 51 weeks is £5,100, the capital turned over is only 4,800 plus 100, or £4,900. The total capital advanced, £900, has therefore been turned over 5 4/9 times, a trifle more than in the first case.

In the present example we assumed a case in which the working time was ⅔ and the circulation time ⅓ of the period of turnover, i.e., the working time was a simple multiple of the circulation time. The question now is whether capital is likewise set free, in the way shown above, when this assumption is not made.

Let us assume a working time of 5 weeks, a circulation time of 4 weeks, and a capital advance of £100 per week.

First period of turnover: 1st-9th week.

1st working period: 1st-5th week. Capital I, or £500, performs its function.

1st circulation period: 6th-9th week. End of 9th week, £500 return in money-form.

Second period of turnover: 6th-14th week.

2nd working period: 6th-10th week.
First section: 6th-9th week. Capital II, of £400, performs its function. End of 9th week, capital I of £500 returns in money-form.
Second section: 10th week. £100 of the returned £500 perform their function. The remaining £400 are set free for the following working period.
2nd circulation period: 11th-14th week. End of 14th week. £500 return in money-form.

Up to the end of the 14th week (11th-14th), the £400 set free above perform their function; £100 of the £500 then returned fill the requirements of the third working period (11th-15th week) so that £400 are once more released for the fourth working period. The same thing is repeated in every working period; at its beginning £40 are ready at hand, sufficing for the first 4 weeks. End of the 4th week, £500 return in money-form, only £100 of which are needed for the last week, while the other £400 remain free for the next working period.

Let us further assume a working period of 7 weeks, with a capital I of £700; a circulation period of 2 weeks, with a capital II of £200.

In that case the first period of turnover lasts from the 1st to the 9th week; its first working period from the 1st to the 7th week, with an advance of £700, its first circulation period from the 8th to the 9th week. End of the 9th week, £700 flow back in money-form.

The second period of turnover, from the 8th to the 16th week, contains the second working period of the 8th to the 14th week. The requirements of the 8th and 9th weeks of this period are covered by capital II. End of the 9th week, the above £700 return. Up to the close of this working period (10th-14th week), £500 of this sum are used up; £200 remain free for the next working period. The second circulation period lasts from the 15th to the 16th week. End of the 16th week £700 return once more. From now on, the same thing is repeated in every working period. The need for capital during the first two weeks is covered by the £200 set free at the close of the preceding working period; at the close of the second week £700 return; but only 5 weeks remain of the working period, so that it can consume only £500; therefore £200 always remain free for the next working period.

We find, then, that in the given case, where the working period has been assumed to be greater than the circulation period, a money-capital will at all events have been set free at the close of each working period, which is of the same magnitude as capital II advanced for the circulation period. In our three illustrations capital II was £300 in the first, £400 in the second, and £200 in third. Accordingly, the capital set free at the close of each working period was £300, £400 and £200 respectively.

Section III. *The Working Period Smaller than the Circulation Period*

We begin by assuming once more a period of turnover of 9 weeks, of which 3 weeks are assigned to the working period with an available capital I of £300. Let the circulation period be 6 weeks. For these 6 weeks, an additional capital of £600 is required, which we may divide in turn into two capitals of £300, each of them meeting the requirements of one working period. We then have three capitals of £300 each, of which £300 are always engaged in production, while £600 circulate.

TABLE III

CAPITAL I		
Periods of Turnover	*Working Periods*	*Periods of Circulation*
I. 1st-9th week	1st-3rd week	4th-9th week
II. 10th-18th "	10th-12th "	13th-18th "
III. 19th-27th "	19th-21st "	22nd-27th "
IV. 28th-36th "	28th-30th "	31st-36th "
V. 37th-45th "	37th-39th "	40th-45th "
VI. 46th-[54th] "	46th-48th "	49th-[54th] "
CAPITAL II		
I. 1st-9th week	4th-6th week	7th-12th week
II. 10th-18th "	13th-15th "	16th-21st "
III. 19th-27th "	22nd-24th "	25th-30th "
IV. 28th-36th "	31st-33rd "	34th-39th "
V. 37th-45th "	40th-42nd "	43rd-48th "
VI. 46th-[54th] "	49th-51st "	51st-[57th] "

CAPITAL III		
I. 7th-15th week	7th-9th week	10th-15th week
II. 16th-24th "	16th-18th "	19th-24th "
III. 25th-33rd "	25th-27th "	28th-33rd "
IV. 34th-42nd "	34th-36th "	37th-42nd "
V. 43rd-51st "	43rd-45th "	46th-51st "

We have here the exact counterpart of Case I, with the only difference that now three capitals relieve one another instead of two. There is no intersection or intertwining of capitals. Each one of them can be traced separately to the end of the year. Just as in Case I, no capital is set free at the close of a working period, Capital I is completely laid out at the end of the 3rd week, returns entirely at the end of the 9th, and resumes its functions at the beginning of the 10th week. Similarly with capitals II and III. The regular and complete relief excludes any release of capital.

The total turnover is as follows:

capital	I,	£300 times 5⅔,	or £1,700
capital	II,	£300 times 5⅓,	or £1,600
capital	III,	£300 times 5,	or £1,500
Total capital,		£900 times 5⅓,	or £4,800

Let us now also take an illustration in which the circulation period is not an exact multiple of the working period. For instance, working period—4 weeks, circulation period—5 weeks. The corresponding amounts of capital would then be: capital I—£400; capital II—£400; capital III—£100. We present only the first three turnovers.

TABLE IV

CAPITAL I		
Periods of Turnover	*Working Periods*	*Periods of Circulation*
I. 1st-9th week	1st-4th week	5th-9th week
II. 9th-17th "	9. 10th-12th "	13th-17th "
III. 18th-25th "	17. 18th-20th "	21st-25th "
CAPITAL I		
I. 5th-13th week	5th-8th week	9th-13th week
II. 13th-21st "	13. 14th-16th "	17th-21st "
III. 21st-29th "	21. 22nd-24th "	25th-29th "
CAPITAL III		
I. 9th-17th week	9th week	10th-17th week
II. 17th-25th "	17th "	18th-25th "
III. 25th-33rd "	25th "	26th-33rd "

There is in this case an intertwining of capitals in so far as the working period of capital II, which has no independent working period, because it suffices for only one week, coincides with the first working week of capital I. On the other hand an amount of £100, equal to capital III, is set free at the close of the working period of both capital I and II. For if capital III fills up the first week of the second and all succeeding working periods of capital I and £400, the entire capital I, return at the close of this first week, then only 3 weeks and a corresponding capital investment of £300 will remain for the rest of the working period of capital I. The £200 thus set free suffice for the first week of the immediately following working period of capital

II; at the end of that week the entire capital II of £400 returns. But since the working period already started can absorb only another £300, £100 are once more disengaged at its close. And so forth. We have, then, a release of capital at the close of a working period whenever the circulation period is not a simple multiple of the working period. And this liberated capital is equal to that portion of the capital which has to fill up the excess of the circulation period over the working period or over a multiple of working periods.

In all cases investigated it was assumed that both the working period and the circulation period remain the same throughout the year in any of the businesses here examined. This assumption was necessary if we wished to ascertain the influence of the time of circulation on the turnover and advancement of capital. That in reality this assumption is not so unconditionally valid, and that it frequently is not valid at all does not alter the case in the least.

In this entire section we have discussed only the turnovers of the circulating capital, not those of the fixed, for the simple reason that the question at issue has nothing to do with fixed capital. The instruments of labour, etc., employed in the process of production form only fixed capital, inasmuch as their time of employment exceeds the period of turnover of the circulating capital; inasmuch as the period of time during which these instruments of labour continue to serve in perpetually repeated labour-processes is greater than the period of turnover of the circulating capital, and hence equal to the *n* periods of turnover of the circulating capital. Regardless of whether the total time represented by these n periods of turnover of the circulating capital is longer or shorter, that portion of the productive capital which was advanced for this time in fixed capital is not advanced anew during its course. It continues its functions in its old use-form. The difference is merely this: In proportion to the varying length of a single *working period* of each period of turnover of the circulating capital, the fixed capital gives up a greater or smaller part of its original value to the product of that working period, and proportionally to the duration of the circulation time of each period of turnover this value-part of the fixed capital given up to the product returns quicker or slower in money-form. The nature of the subject we are discussing in this section—the turnover of the circulating portion of productive capital—derives from the very nature of this portion. The circulating capital employed in a working period cannot be applied in a new working period until it has completed its turnover, until it has been transformed into commodity-capital, from that into money-capital, and from that back into productive capital. Hence, in order that the first working period may be immediately followed by a second, capital must be advanced anew and converted into the circulating elements of productive capital, and its quantity must be sufficient to fill the void occasioned by the circulation period of the circulating capital advanced or the first working period. This is the source of the influence exerted by the length of the working period of the circulating capital over the scale of the labour-process and the division of the advanced capital or the addition of new portions of capital. This was precisely what we had to examine in this section.

Section IV. *Conclusion*

From the preceding investigation it follows that

A. The different portions into which capital must be divided in order that one part of it may be continually in the working period while others are in the period of circulation, relieve one another, like different independent individual capitals, in two cases: (1) when the working period is equal to the period of circulation, so that the period of turnover is divided into two equal sections; (2) when the period of circulation is longer than the working period, but at the same time is a simple multiple of the working period, so that one period of circulation is equal to *n* working periods, in which case *n* must be a whole number. In these cases no portion of the successively advanced capital is set free.

B. On the other hand in all cases in which (1) the period of circulation is longer than the working period without being a simple multiple of it, and (2) in which the working period is longer than the circulation period, a portion of the total circulating capital is set free continually and periodically at the close of each working period, beginning with the second turnover. This freed capital is equal to that portion of the total capital which has been advanced for the circulation period, provided the working period is longer than the period of circulation; and equal to that portion of the capital which has to fill up the excess of the circulation period over the working period or over a multiple of working periods, provided the circulation period is longer than the working period.

C. It follows that for the aggregate social capital, so far as its circulating part is concerned, the release of capital must be the rule, while the mere alternation of portions of capital functioning successively in the production process must be the exception. For the equality of the working and circulation periods, or the equality of the period of circulation and a simple multiple of the working period, this regular proportionality of the two components of the period of turnover has absolutely nothing to do with the nature of the case and for this reason it can occur on the whole only as a matter of exception.

A very considerable portion of the social circulating capital, which is turned over several times a year, will therefore periodically exist in the form of released capital during the annual turnover cycle.

It is furthermore evident that, all other circumstances being equal, the magnitude of the released capital grows with the volume of the labour-process or with the scale of production, hence with the development of capitalist production in general. In the case cited under *B*, (2), because the total advanced capital increases; in *B* (1), because with the development of capitalist production the length of the period of circulation grows, hence also the period of turnover in those cases where the working period is less than the period of circulation, and there is no regular ratio between the two periods.

In the first case for instance we had to invest £100 per week. This required £600 for a working period of 6 weeks, £300 for a circulation period of 3 weeks, totalling £900. In that case £300 are released continually. On the other hand if £300 are invested weekly, we have £1,800 for the working period and £900 for the circulation period. Hence £900 for the circulation period. Hence £900 instead of £300 are periodically set free.

D. A total capital of, say £900 must be divided into two portions, as above, £600 for the working period and £300 for the period of circulation. That portion which is really invested in the labour-process is thus reduced by one-third, from £900 to £600; consequently, the scale of production is diminished by one-third. On the other hand, the £300 function only to make the working period continuous, in order that £100 may be invested every week of the year in the labour-process.

Abstractly speaking, it is all the same whether £600 work during 6 times 8, or 48, weeks (product £4,800) or whether the total capital of £900 is expended during 6 weeks in the labour-process and then lies idle during the 3-week period of circulation. In the latter case, it would be working, in the course of the 48 weeks, 5⅓ times 6, or 32 weeks (product 5⅓ times 900, or £4,800), and lie idle for 16 weeks. But, apart from the greater spoilage of the fixed capital during the idle 16 weeks and apart from the appreciation of labour, which must be paid during the entire year, even if employed only during a part of it, such a regular interruption of the process of production is altogether irreconcilable with the operations of modern big industry. This continuity is itself a productive power of labour.

Now, if we take a closer look at the released, or rather suspended, capital, we find that a considerable part of it must always be in the form of money-capital. Let us adhere to our illustration: Working period—6 weeks, period of circulation—3 weeks, investment per week—£100. In the middle of the second working period, end of the 9th week, £600 return, and only £300 of them must be invested for the remainder of the working period. At the end of the second working period, £300 are therefore released. In what state are these £300? We shall assume that ⅓ is invested for wages and ⅔ are for raw and auxiliary materials. Then £200 of the returned £600 exist in the form of money for wages and £400 in the form of productive supply, in the form of elements of the constant circulating productive capital. But since only one half of this productive supply is required for the second half of the second working period, the other half exists for 3 weeks in the form of a surplus productive supply, i.e., of a supply exceeding the requirements of one working period. But the capitalist knows that he needs only one half, or £200, of this portion (£400) of the returned capital for the current working period. It will therefore depend on market conditions whether he will immediately reconvert these £200, in whole or in part, into a surplus productive supply, or keep them entirely or partially in the form of money-capital in anticipation of a more favourable market. On the other hand it goes without saying that the portion to be laid out for wages (£200) is retained in the form of money. The capitalist cannot store labour-power in warehouses after he has bought it, as he may do with the raw material. He must incorporate it in the process of production and pay for it at the end of the week. At any rate these £100 of the released capital of £300 will therefore have the form of money-capital set free, i.e., not required for the working period. The capital released in the form of money-capital must therefore be at least equal to the variable portion of capital invested in wages. At a maximum, it may comprise the entire released capital. In reality it fluctuates constantly between this minimum and maximum.

The money-capital thus released by the mere mechanism of the turnover movement (together with that freed by the successive reflux of fixed capital and that required in every labour-process for variable capital) must play an important role as soon as the credit system develops and must at the same time form one of the latter's foundations.

Let us assume that the time of circulation in our illustration is shortened from 3 to 2 weeks. This is not to be a normal change, but due, say, to prosperous times, shorter terms of payment, etc. The capital of £600, which is laid out during the working period, returns one week earlier than needed. It is therefore released for this week. Furthermore, in the middle of the working period, as before, £300 are released (a portion of those £600), but for 4 weeks instead of 3. There are then, on the money-market £600 for one week and £300 for 4 instead of 3 weeks. As this concerns not one capitalist alone but many and occurs in various periods in different businesses, more available money-capital makes its appearance in the market. If this condition lasts for some time, production will be expanded wherever feasible. Capitalists operating on borrowed money will exercise less demand on the money-market, which eases it as much as increased supply; or finally the sums which have become superfluous for the mechanism are thrown definitely on the money-market.

In consequence of the contraction of the time of circulation from 3 weeks to 2, and consequently of the period of turnover from 9 weeks to 8, one-ninth of the total capital advanced becomes superfluous. The 6-week working period can now be kept going as continuously with £800 as formerly with £900. One portion of the value of the commodity-capital, equal to £100, once it has been reconverted into money, persists therefore in the state of money-capital without performing any more functions as a part of the capital advanced for the process of production. While the scale of production and other conditions, such as prices, etc., remain the same, the sum of value of the advanced capital is reduced from £900 to £800. The remainder of the originally advanced value amounting to £100 is eliminated in the form of money-capital. As such it enters the money-market and forms an additional portion of the capitals functioning here.

This shows the way in which a plethora of money-capital may arise—and not only in the sense that the supply of money-capital is greater than the demand; this is always only a relative plethora, which occurs for instance in the 'melancholy period' opening a new cycle after the end of a crisis. But also in the sense that a definite portion of the capital-value advanced becomes superfluous for the operation of the entire process of social reproduction which includes the process of circulation and is therefore eliminated in the form of money-capital—a plethora brought about by the mere contraction of the period of turnover, while the scale of production and prices remain the same. The amount of money in circulation, whether great or small, did not influence it in the least.

Let us assume on the contrary that the period of circulation is prolonged from, say, 3 weeks to 5. In that case at the very next turnover the reflux of the advanced capital takes place 2 weeks too late. The last part of the process of production of this working period cannot be carried on further by the mechanism of the turnover of the advanced capital itself. Should this condition last any length of time, a contraction of the process of production, a reduction of its volume, might take place, just as an extension occurred in the previous case. But in order to continue the process on the same scale, the advanced capital would have to be increased by 2/9, or £200, for the entire term of the prolongation of the circulation period. This additional capital can be obtained only from the money-market. If the lengthening of the period of circulation applies to one or several big branches of business, it may exert pressure on the money-market, unless this effect is paralysed by some counter-effect. In this case it is likewise evident and obvious that this pressure, like that plethora before, had nothing whatever to do with a movement either of prices of the commodities or the mass of existing circulating medium.

[The preparation of this chapter for publication presented no small number of difficulties. Firmly grounded as Marx was in algebra, he did not get the knack of handling figures, particularly commercial arithmetic, although there exists a thick batch of copybooks containing numerous examples of all kinds of commercial computations which he had solved himself. But knowledge of the various methods of calculation and exercise in daily practical commercial arithmetic are by no means the same, and consequently Marx got so tangled up in his computations of turnovers that besides places left uncompleted a number of things were incorrect and contradictory. In the tables reproduced above I have preserved only the simplest and arithmetically correct data. My reason for doing so was mainly the following:

The uncertain results of these painstaking calculations led Marx to attach unwarranted importance to a circumstance, which in my opinion, has actually little significance. I refer to what he calls the 'release' of money-capital. The actual state of affairs, based on the above assumptions, is this:

No matter what may be the ratio between the working period and circulation time, hence between capital I and capital II, there is returned to the capitalist, in the form of money, after the end of the first turnover and thereafter at regular intervals equal to the duration of one working period, the capital required for one working period, i.e., a sum equal to capital I.

If the working period is 5 weeks, the circulation time 4 weeks, and capital I £500, then a sum of money equal to £500 returns each time at the end of the 9th, 14th, 19th, 24th, 29th week, etc.

If the working period is 6 weeks, the circulation time 3 weeks, and capital I £600, then £600 return at the end of the 9th, 15th, 21st, 27th, 33rd week, etc.

Finally, if the working period is 4 weeks, the circulation time 5 weeks, and capital I £400, then £400 are returned at the end of the 9th, 13th, 17th, 21st, 25th week, etc.

Whether any, and if so how much, of this returned money is superfluous and thus released for the current working period is immaterial. It is assumed that production continues uninterruptedly on the current scale, and in order that this may come about money must be available and must therefore return, whether 'released' or not. If production is interrupted, release stops likewise.

In other words: There is indeed a release of money, a formation therefore of latent, merely potential, capital in the form of money. But it takes place under all circumstances and not only under the special conditions set forth in the text; and it comes about on a larger scale than that assumed in the text. So far as circulating capital I is concerned, the industrial capitalist is in the same situation at the end of each turnover as when he established his business: he has all of it in one bulk, while he can convert it back into productive capital only gradually.

The essential point in the text is the proof that on the one hand a considerable portion of the industrial capital must always be available in the form of money and that on the other hand a still more considerable portion must temporarily assume the form of money. The proof is, if anything, rendered stronger by these additional remarks of mine.—*F. E.*]

Section V. *The Effects of a Change of Prices*

We have, on the one hand, just assumed unaltered prices and an unaltered scale of production, and a contraction or expansion of the time of circulation on the other. Now let us suppose, on the contrary, an unaltered period of turnover and an unaltered scale of production, and on the other hand price changes, i.e., rise or fall of prices of raw materials, auxiliary substances, and labour, or of the two first-named elements alone. Take it that the price of raw and auxiliary materials, as well as wages, fall by one half. In that case the capital to be advanced in our example would be £50 instead of £100 per week, and that for the 9-week turnover period would be £450 instead of £900. £450 of the advanced capital-value are eliminated first of all in the form of money-capital, but the process of production continues on the same scale, with the same period of turnover, and with the previous division of the latter. The annual output likewise remains the same but its value has been cut in half. This change, which is accompanied by a change in the supply and demand of money-capital, is brought about neither by an acceleration of the circulation, nor by a change in the quantity of circulating money. On the contrary. A fall by half in the value, or price, of the elements of productive capital would first have the effect of diminishing by half the capital-value to be advanced for the continuation of Business X on the same scale as before, and hence only one half of the money would have to be thrown on the market by Business X, since Business X advances this capital-value first in the form of money, i.e., as money-capital. The amount of money thrown into circulation would decrease because the prices of the elements of production fell. This would be the first effect.

In the second place however one half of the originally advanced capital-value of £900, or £450, which (a) passed successively through the forms of money-capital, productive capital, and commodity-capital, and (b) existed simultaneously and constantly side by side partly in the form of money-capital, partly in that of productive capital, and partly in that of commodity-capital, would be eliminated from the circuit of Business X, and thus come into the money-market as additional money-capital, affecting it as an additional constituent. These released £450 act as money-capital, not because they have become superfluous money for the operation of Business X but because they are a constituent part of the original capital-value, and hence are intended to function further as capital and not to be expended as mere means of circulation. The best method of letting them operate as capital is that of throwing them as money-capital on the money-market. On the other hand the scale of production (apart from fixed capital) might be doubled. In that case a productive process of double the previous volume would be carried on with the same advanced capital of £900.

If, on the other hand, the prices of the circulation elements of productive capital were to increase by one half, £1500 instead of £100 or £1,350 instead of £900 would be required per week. It would take an additional capital of £450 to carry on the business on the same scale, and this would exert a *pro tanto* pressure on the money-market, big or small depending on its condition. If all the capital available on this market were then already engaged, there would be increased competition for available capital. If a portion of it were unemployed, it would *pro tanto* be called into action.

But, in the third place, given a certain scale of production, the turnover velocity and the prices of the elements of the circulating productive capital remaining the same, the price of the products of Business X may rise or fall. If the price of the commodities supplied by Business X falls, the price of its commodity-capital of £600, which it constantly threw into circulation, drops to, say, £500. Hence one-sixth of the value of the advanced capital does not return from the process of circulation. (The surplus-value contained in the commodity-capital is not considered here.) It is lost in that process. But since the value, or price, of the elements of production remains the same, this reflux of £500 suffices only to replace 5/6 of the capital of £600 constantly engaged in the process of production. It would therefore require an additional money-capital of £100 to continue production on the same scale.

Vice versa, if the price of the product of Business X were to rise, then the price of the £600 commodity-capital would be increased, say, to £700. One-seventh of this price, or £100, does not originate in the process of production, is not advanced in this process, but derives from the process of circulation. But only £600 are needed to replace the elements of production. Hence, the release of £100.

It does not fall within the scope of the investigation hitherto made to ascertain why, in the first case, the period of turnover is shortened or lengthened, and why in the second case the prices of raw materials and labour, and in the third, the prices of the products supplied, rise or fall.

But the following does belong in it:

First case: ***Unchanged Scale of Production, Unchanged Prices of the Elements of Production and of Products, and a Change in the Period of Circulation and Thus of Turnover***

According to the assumptions of our example, one-ninth less of the total advanced capital is needed as a result of the contraction of the period of circulation, so that the total capital is reduced from £900 to £800 and £100 of money-capital is eliminated.

Business X supplies, just as before, the same six weeks' product of the same value of £600, and as work continues year in year out without interruption, it supplies in 51 weeks the same quantity of products, valued at £5,100. There is, then, no change so far as the quantity and price of the product thrown into circulation by this business are concerned, nor in the times when it throws its product on the market. But £100 are eliminated because due to the contraction of the circulation period the requirements of the process are satisfied with only £800 instead of the former £900. The £100 eliminated capital exist in the form of money-capital. But they do not by any means represent that portion of the advanced capital which would have to function constantly in the form of money-capital. Let us assume that 4/5, or £480, of the advanced circulating capital I of £600 are constantly invested in productive materials and 1/5, or £120, in wages. Then the weekly investment in materials of production would be £80 and in wages £20. Capital II, amounting to £300, should then also be divided into 4/5, or £240, for materials of production and 1/5, or £60, for wages. The capital invested in wages must always be advanced in the form of money. As soon as the commodity-product, worth £600, has been reconverted into the money-form, or sold, £480 of it can be transformed into materials of production (productive supply), but £120 retain their money-form in order to serve for the payment of wages for six weeks. These £120 are the minimum of the returning capital of £600 which must always be renewed and replaced in the form of money-capital and therefore must always be kept on hand as that portion of the advanced capital which functions in the form of money.

Now, if £100 of the £300 periodically released for three weeks, and likewise divisible into £240 for productive supply and £60 for wages, is entirely eliminated, completely thrust out of the turnover mechanism, in the form of money-capital by shortening the circulation time, where does the money for this money-capital of £100 come from? Only one-fifth of this amount consists of money-capital periodically set free within the turnovers. But four-fifths, or £80, are already replaced by an additional productive supply of the same value. In what manner is this additional productive supply converted into money, and where does the money for this conversion come from?

If the abridged period of circulation has become a fact, then only £400 of the above £600, instead of £480, are reconverted into productive supply. The remainder, £80, is retained in its money-form and constitutes, together with the above £20 for wages, the £100 of eliminated capital. Although these £100 come from the sphere of circulation through the sale of the £600 worth of commodity-capital and are now withdrawn from it by not being reinvested in wages and elements of production, it must not be forgotten that, being in the money-form, they are once more in that form in which they were originally thrown into circulation. In the beginning £900 were invested in productive supply and wages. Now only £800 are necessary to carry out the same productive process. The £100 thus released in money now form a new, employment-seeking money-capital, a new constituent part of the money-market. True, they have already previously been periodically in the form of released money-capital and of additional productive capital, but these latent states were themselves the requisites for the execution of the process of production, because they were the requisites for its continuity. Now they are no longer needed for that purpose and for this reason form new money-capital and a constituent part of the money-market, although they, by no means, form either an additional element of the available social money-supply (for they existed at the beginning of the business and were thrown by it into the circulation), or a newly accumulated hoard.

These £100 are now in actual fact withdrawn from circulation inasmuch as they are a part of the advanced money-capital that is no longer employed in the same business. But this withdrawal is possible only because the conversion of the commodity-capital into money, and of this money into productive capital, C'—M—C, is accelerated by one week, so that the circulation of the money operating in this process is likewise hastened. They have been withdrawn from it because they are no longer needed for the turnover of capital X.

It has been assumed here that the advanced capital belongs to him who employs it. Had he borrowed it nothing would be changed. With the shortening of the time of circulation he would have to borrow only £800 instead of £900. The £100, if returned to the lender, would as before form £100 of new money-capital, only in the hands of Y instead of X. Should capitalist X receive £480 worth of materials of production on credit, so that he has to advance only £210 in money for wages out of his own pocket, he would now have to procure £80 worth of materials less on credit and this sum would constitute superfluous commodity-capital for the capitalist granting the credit, while capitalist X would have eliminated £20 in money.

The additional supply for production is now reduced by one-third. It consisted of £240 constituting four-fifths of £300, the additional capital II, but now it is only £160, i.e., additional supply for 2 instead of 3 weeks. It is now renewed every 2 weeks instead of every 3, but only for 2 instead of 3 weeks. The purchases, for instance in the cotton market, are thus more frequent and smaller. The same amount of cotton is withdrawn from the market, for the quantity of the product remains the same. But the withdrawals are distributed differently in time, extending over a longer period. Supposing that it is a question of 3 months or 2. If the annual consumption of cotton amounts to 1,200 bales, the sales in the first case will be:

January 1,	300 bales, left in storage	900 bales
April 1,	300 " " " "	600 "
July 1,	300 " " " "	300 "
October 1,	300 " " " "	0 "

But in the second case:

January 1, sold	200, in storage	1,000 bales
March 1, "	200, " "	800 "
May 1, "	200, " "	600 "
July 1, "	200, " "	400 "
September 1, "	200, " "	200 "
November 1, "	200, " "	0 "

So the money invested in cotton only returns completely one month later, in November instead of October. If, therefore, one-ninth of the advanced capital, or £100, is eliminated in the form of money-capital by the contraction of the circulation time and thus of the turnover and if these £100 are composed of £20 worth of periodically superfluous money-capital for the payment of weekly wages, and of £80 which existed as periodically superfluous productive supply for one week, then the diminished superfluous productive supply in the hands of the manufacturer corresponds, so far as these £80 are concerned, to an enlarged commodity-supply in the hands of the cotton dealer. The longer this cotton lies in the latter's warehouse as a commodity, the less it lies in the storeroom of the manufacturer as a productive supply.

Hitherto we presupposed that the contraction of the time of circulation in Business X was due to the fact that X sold his articles quicker, received his money for them sooner, or, in the event of credit, was given shorter terms of payment. The contraction was therefore attributed to a quicker sale of the commodities, to a quicker transformation of commodity-capital into money-capital, C'—M, the first phase of the process of circulation. But it might also derive from the second phase, M—C, and hence from a simultaneous change, be it in the working period or in the time of circulation of capitals Y, Z, etc., which supply capitalist X with the productive elements of his circulating capital.

For instance if cotton, coal, etc., with the old methods of transport, are three weeks in transit from their place of production or storage to the place of production of capitalist X, then X's productive supply must last at least for three weeks, until the arrival of new supplies. So long as cotton and coal are in transit, they cannot serve as means of production. They are then rather a subject of labour for the transport industry and the capital employed in it; they are also commodity-capital in the process of circulation for the producer of coal or the dealer in cotton. Suppose improvements in transport reduce the transit to two weeks. Then the productive supply can be changed from a three-weekly into a fortnightly supply. This releases the additional advanced capital £80 set aside for this purpose and likewise the £20 for wages, because the turned-over capital of £600 returns one week sooner.

On the other hand if for instance the working period of the capital which supplies the raw materials is cut down (examples of which were given in the preceding chapters), so that the possibility arises of renewing the supply of raw materials in less time, then the productive supply may be reduced and the interval between periods of renewal shortened.

If, vice versa, the time of circulation, and thus the period of turnover, are prolonged, then it is necessary to advance additional capital. This must come out of the pocket of the capitalist himself if he has any additional capital. But it will then be invested in some form or other as a part of the money-market. To make it available, it must be pried loose from its old form. For instance stocks must be sold, deposits withdrawn, so that in this case too the money-market is indirectly affected. Or he must borrow it. As for that part of the additional capital which is needed for wages, it must under normal conditions always be advanced in the form of money-capital, and for that purpose the capitalist X exerts his share of direct pressure on the money-market. But this is indispensable for the part which must be invested in materials of production only if he must pay for them in cash. If he can get them on credit, this does not have any direct influence on the money-market, because the additional capital is then advanced directly as a productive supply and not in the first instance as money-capital. But if the lender throws the bill of exchange received from X directly on the market, discounts it, etc., this would influence the money-market indirectly, through someone else. If, however, he uses this note to cover a debt not yet due for instance, this additional advanced capital does not affect the money-market either directly or indirectly.

Second Case: ***A Change in the Price of Materials of Production, All Other Circumstances Remaining the Same.***

We just assumed that the total capital of £900 was four-fifths invested in materials of production (equalling £720) and one-fifth in wages (equalling £180).

If the materials of production drop to half, they require for the 6-week period only £240 instead of £480, and for the additional capital No. II only £120 instead of £240. Capital I is thus reduced from £600 to £240 plus £120, or £360, and capital II from £300 to £120 plus £60, or £180. The total capital of £900 is therefore reduced to £360 plus £180, or £540. A sum of £360 is therefore released.

This eliminated and now unemployed capital, or money-capital, seeking employment in the money-market, is nothing but a portion of the capital of £900 originally advanced as money-capital, which, due to the fall in the prices of the materials of production, into which it is periodically reconverted, has become superfluous if the business is not to be expanded but carried on in the same scale. If this fall in prices were not due to accidental circumstances (a particularly rich harvest, over-supply, etc.) but to an increase of productive power in the branch of production which furnishes the raw materials, then this money-capital would be an absolute addition to the money-market, and to the capital available in the form of money-capital in general, because it would no longer constitute an integral part of the capital already invested.

Third Case: ***A Change in the Market Price of the Product Itself.***

In the case of a fall in prices a portion of the capital is lost, and must consequently be made good by a new advance of money-capital. This loss of the seller may be a gain to the buyer. Directly, if the market price of the product has fallen merely because of an accidental fluctuation, and afterwards rises once more to its normal level. Indirectly, if the change of prices is caused by a change of value reacting on the old product and if this product passes again, as an element of production, into another sphere of production and there releases capital *pro tanto*. In either case the capital lost by X, and for whose replacement he exerts pressure on the money-market, may be supplied to him by his business friends as new additional capital. All that takes place then is a transfer.

If, on the contrary, the price of the product rises, a portion of the capital which was not advanced is taken out of circulation. This is not an organic part of the capital advanced in the process of production and unless production is expanded therefore constitutes money-capital eliminated. As we have assumed that the prices of the elements of the product were given before it was brought to market as commodity-capital, a real change of value might have caused the rise of prices since it acted retroactively, causing a subsequent rise in the price of, say, raw materials. In that event capitalist X would realise a gain on his product circulating as commodity-capital and on his available productive supply. This gain would give him an additional capital, which would now be needed for the continuation of his business with the new and higher prices of the elements of production.

Or the rise of prices is but temporary. What capitalist X then needs by way of additional capital becomes released capital for the other side, insofar as X's product forms an element of production for other branches of business. What the one has lost the other has gained.

Note

1. The weeks falling within the second year of turnover are put in parenthesis.

16

The Turnover of Variable Capital

Section I. *The Annual Rate of Surplus Value*

Let us assume a circulating capital of £2,500, four-fifths of which, or £2,000, are constant capital (materials of production) and one-fifth, or £500, is variable capital invested in wages.

Let the period of turnover be 5 weeks: the working period 4 weeks, the period of circulation 1 week. Then capital I is £2,000, consisting of £1,600 of constant capital and £400 of variable capital; capital II is £500, £400 of which are constant and £100 variable. In every working week a capital of £500 is invested. In a year of 50 weeks an annual product of 50 times 500, or £2,500, is manufactured. Capital I of £2,000, constantly employed in the working period, is therefore turned over 12½ times. 12½ times 2,000 makes £25,000. Of these £25,000 four-fifths, or £20,000, are constant capital laid out in means of production, and one-fifth, or £5,000 is variable capital laid out in wages. The total capital of £25,000 is thus turned over 25,000/2,500, or 10 times.

The variable circulating capital expended in production can serve afresh in the process of circulation only to the extent that the product in which its value is reproduced has been sold, converted from a commodity-capital into a money-capital, in order to be once more laid out in payment of labour-power. But the same is true of the constant circulating capital (materials of production) invested in production, the value of which reappears in the product as a portion of its value. What these two portions—the variable and the constant part of the circulating capital—have in common and what distinguishes them from the fixed capital is not that the value transferred from them to the product is circulated by the commodity-capital, i.e., through the circulation of the product as a commodity. One portion of the value of the product, and thus of the product circulating as a commodity, of the commodity-capital, always consists of the wear and tear of the fixed capital, that is to say, of that portion of the value of the fixed capital which is transferred to the product during the process of production. The difference is really this: The fixed capital continues to function in the process of production in its old use-form for a longer or shorter cycle of turnover periods of the circulating capital (equal to constant circulating plus variable circulating capital), while every single turnover is conditioned on the replacement of the entire circulating capital passing from the sphere of production—in the form of commodity-capital—into the sphere of circulation. The constant circulating and variable circulating capital have the first phase of circulation, C'—M, in common. In the second phase they separate. The money into which the commodity is reconverted is in part transformed into a productive supply (constant circulating capital). Depending on the different terms of purchase of its constituent parts, one portion of the money may sooner, another later, be converted from money into materials of production, but finally it is wholly consumed that way. Another portion of the money realised by the sale of the commodity is held in the form of a money-supply, in order to be gradually expended in the payment of the labour-power incorporated in the process of production. This part constitutes the variable circulating capital. Nevertheless the entire replacement of either portion always originates from the turnover of capital, from its conversion into a product, from a product into a commodity, from a commodity into money. This is the reason why, in the preceding chapter, the turnover of the circulating capital, constant and variable, was treated jointly and separately without paying any regard to the fixed capital.

In the question which we shall now take up, we must go a step farther and proceed with the variable portion of the circulating capital as though it along constituted the circulating capital. In other words, we leave out of consideration the constant circulating capital which is turned over together with it.

A sum of £2,500 has been advanced and the value of the annual product is £25,000. But the variable portion of the circulating capital is £500; therefore the variable capital contained in £25,000 amounts to 25,000 divided by 5, or £5,000. If we divide these £5,000 by £500, we find the number of turnovers is 10, just as it is in the case of the total capital of £2,500.

Here, where it is only a question of the production of surplus-value, it is absolutely correct to make this average calculation, according to which the value of the annual product is divided by the value of the advanced capital and not by the value of that portion of this capital which is employed constantly in one working period (thus, in the present case not by 400 but by 500, not by capital I but by capital I plus capital II). We shall see later that, from another point of view, the calculation is not quite exact, just as this average calculation generally is not quite exact. That is to say, it serves well enough for the practical purposes of the capitalist, but it does not express exactly or properly all the real circumstances of the turnover.

We have hitherto ignored one part of the value of the commodity-capital, namely the surplus-value contained in it, which was produced during the process of production and incorporated in the product. To this we have now to direct our attention.

Suppose the variable capital of £100 invested weekly produces a surplus-value of 100%, or £100, then the variable capital of £500 invested over a 5-week turnover period produces £500 of surplus-value, i.e., one half of the working day consists of surplus-labour.

If £500 of variable capital produce a surplus-value of £500, then £5,000 produce ten times £500, or £5,000 in surplus-value. But the advanced variable capital amounts to £500. The ratio of the total surplus-value produced during one year to the sum of value of the advanced variable capital is what we call the annual rate of surplus-value. In the case at hand it is 5,000 to 500 or 1,000%. If we analyse this rate more closely, we find that it is equal to the rate of surplus-value produced by the advanced variable capital during one period of turnover, multiplied by the number of turnovers of the variable capital (which coincides with the number of turnovers of the entire circulating capital).

The variable capital advanced in the case before us for one period of turnover is £500. The surplus-value produced during this period is likewise £500. The rate of surplus-value for one period of turnover is therefore 500s/500v or 100%. This 100%, multiplied by 10, the number of turnovers in one year, makes 5,000s/500v, or 1,000%.

That refers to the annual rate of surplus-value. As for the amount of surplus-value obtained during a specified period of turnover, it is equal to the value of the variable capital advanced during this period, of £500 in the present case, multiplied by the rate of surplus-value, in the present case therefore 500 times 100/100, or 500 times 1, or £500. If the advanced variable capital were £1,500, then with the same rate of the surplus-value the amount of surplus-value would be 1,500 times 100/100, or £1,500.

We shall apply the term capital A to the variable capital of £500, which is turned over ten times per year, producing an annual surplus-value of £5,000 for which, therefore, the yearly rate of surplus-value is 1,000%.

Now let us assume that another variable capital, B, of £5,000, is advanced for one whole year (i.e., here for 50 weeks), so that it is turned over only once a year. We assume furthermore that at the end of the year the product is paid for on the same day that it is finished, so that the money-capital, into which it is converted, returns on the same day. The circulation period is then zero, the period of turnover equals the working period, namely, one year. As in the preceding case there is to be found in the labour-process each week a variable capital of £100, or of £5,000 in 50 weeks. Let the rate of surplus-value be the same, or 100%, i.e., let one half of the working-day of the same length consist of surplus-labour. If we consider 5 weeks, the invested variable capital is £500, the rate of surplus-value 100% and therefore the amount of surplus-value produced in 5 weeks £500. The quantity of labour-power here exploited, and the intensity of its exploitation, are assumed to be exactly the same as those of capital A.

Each week the invested variable capital of £100 produces a surplus-value of £100, hence in 50 weeks the invested capital of 50 × 100 = £5,000 produces a surplus-value of £5,000. The amount of surplus-value produced annually is the same as in the previous case, £5,000, but the yearly rate of surplus-value is entirely different. It is equal to the surplus-value produced in one year divided by the advanced variable capital: 5,000s/5,000v, or 100%, while in the case of capital A it was 1,000%.

In the case of both capitals A and B, we have invested a variable capital of £100 a week. The degree of self-expansion, or the rate of surplus-value, is likewise the same, 100%, and so is the magnitude of the variable capital, £100. The same quantity of labour-power is exploited, the volume and degree of exploitation are equal in both cases, the working-days are the same and equally divided into necessary labour and surplus-labour. The amount of variable capital employed in the course of the year is £5,000 in either case; it sets the same amount of labour in motion, and extracts the same amount of surplus-value, £5,000, from the labour-power set in motion by these two equal capitals. Nevertheless there is a difference of 900% in the annual rate of surplus-value of the two capitals A and B.

This phenomenon creates the impression, at all events, that the rate of surplus-value depends not only on the quantity and intensity of exploitation of the labour-power set in motion by the variable capital, but besides on inexplicable influences arising from the process of circulation. And it has indeed been so interpreted, and has—if not in this its pure form, then at least in its more complicated and disguised form, that of the annual rate of profit—completely routed the Ricardian school since the beginning of the twenties.

The strangeness of this phenomenon disappears at once when we place capitals A and B in exactly the same conditions, not only seemingly but actually. These equal conditions exist only when the variable capital B in its entire volume is expended for the payment of labour-power in the same period of time as capital A.

In that case the £5,000 of capital B are invested for 5 weeks, £1,000 per week makes an investment of £50,000 per year. The surplus-value is then likewise £50,000, according to our premises. The turned-over capital of £50,000 divided by the advanced capital of £5,000 makes the number of turnovers 10. The rate of surplus-value, 5,000s/5,000v, or 100%, multiplied by the number of turnovers, 10, makes the annual rate of surplus-value 50,000s/5,000v, or 10/1, or 1,000%. Now the annual rate of surplus-value are alike for A and B, namely 1,000%, but the amounts of the surplus-value are £50,000 in the case of B, and £5,000 in the case of A. The amounts of the surplus-value produced are now in the same proportion to one another as the advanced capital-values B and A, to wit: 5,000:500 = 10:1. But capital B has set in motion ten times as much labour-power as capital A within the same time.

Only the capital actually employed in the labour-power produces surplus-value and to it apply all laws relating to surplus-value, including therefore the law according to which the quantity of surplus-value, its rate being given, is determined by the relative magnitude of the variable capital. [See Karl Marx, *Capital*, Ch. XI.—*Ed.*]

The labour-process itself is measured by time. If the length of the working-day is given (as here, where we assume all conditions relating to A and B to be equal, in order to elucidate the difference in the annual rate of surplus-value), the working week consists of a definite number of working-days. Or we may consider any working period, for instance this working period of 5 weeks, as one single working-day of, say, 300 hours, if the working-day has 10 hours and the week 6 days. We must further multiply this number by the number of labourers who are employed conjointly every day simultaneously in the same labour-process. If that number is taken as 10, there will be 60 times 10 or 600 hours in one week, and a working period of 5 weeks would have 600 times 5, or 3,000 hours. The rate of surplus-value and the length of the working-day being the same, variable capitals of equal magnitude are therefore employed, if equal quantities of labour-power (a labour-power of the same price multiplied by the number of labourers) are set in motion in the same time.

Let us now return to our original examples. In both cases, A and B, equal variable capitals of £100 per week are invested every week throughout the year. The invested variable capitals actually functioning in the labour-process are therefore equal, but the advanced variable capitals are very unequal. In the case of A, £500 are advanced for every 5 weeks, of which £100 are employed every week. In the case of B, £5,000 must be advanced for the first 5-week period, of which only £100 per week, or £500 in 5 weeks, or one-tenth of the advanced capital, is employed. In the second 5-week period £4,500 must be advanced, but only £500 of this is employed, etc. The variable capital advanced for a definite period of time is converted into employed, hence actually functioning and operative variable capital only to the extent that it really steps into the sections of that period of time taken up by the labour-process, to the extent that it really functions in the labour-process. In the intermediate time, in which a portion of it is advanced in order to be employed later, this portion is practically non-existent for the labour-process and has therefore no influence on the formation of either value or surplus-value. Take for instance capital A, of £500. It is advanced for 5 weeks, but every week only £100 enter successively into the labour-process. In the first week one-fifth of this capital is employed; four-fifths are advanced without being employed, although they must be in stock, and therefore advanced, for the labour-processes of the following 4 weeks.

The circumstances which differentiate the relation between the advanced and the employed variable capital affect the production of surplus-value—the rate of surplus-value being given—only to the extent, and only by reason of the fact that they differentiate the quantity of variable capital which can be really employed in a stated period of time, for instance in one week, 5 weeks, etc. The advanced variable capital functions as variable capital only to the extent and only during the time that it is actually employed, and not during the time in which it remains in stock, is advanced, without being employed. But all the circumstances which differentiate the relation between the advanced and the employed variable capital come down to the difference of the periods of turnover (determined by the difference of either the working period, or the circulation period, or both). The law of production of surplus-value states that equal quantities of functioning variable capital produce equal quantities of surplus-value if the rate of surplus-value is the same. If then, equal quantities of variable capital are employed by the capitals A and B in equal periods of time with equal rates of surplus-value, they must generate equal quantities of surplus-value in equal periods of time, no matter how different the ratio of this variable capital employed during a definite period of time to the variable capital advanced during the same time, and no matter therefore how different the ratio of the quantities of surplus-value produced, not to the employed but to the advanced variable capital in general. The difference of this ratio, far from contradicting the laws of the production of surplus-value that have been demonstrated, rather corroborates them and is one of their inevitable consequences.

Let us consider the first 5-week productive period of capital B. At the end of the fifth week £500 have been employed and consumed. The value of the product is £1,000, hence 500s/500v = 100%. Just the same as with capital A. The fact that, in the case of capital A, the surplus-value is realised together with the advanced capital, while in the case of B it is not, does not concern us here, where it is only a question of the production of surplus-value and of its ratio to the variable capital advanced during its production. But if on the contrary we calculate the ratio of surplus-value in B, not to that portion of the advanced capital of £5,000 which has been employed and hence consumed during its production, but to this total advanced capital itself, we find that it is 500s/5,000v of 1/10, or 10%. Hence it is 10% for capital B and 100% for capital A, i.e., ten-fold. If it were said that this difference in the rate of surplus-value for equal capitals, which have set in motion equal quantities of labour equally divided at that into paid and unpaid labour, is contrary to the laws of the production of surplus-value, the answer would be simple and prompted by a mere glance at the actual relations: In the case of A, the actual rate of surplus-value is expressed, i.e., the relation of a surplus-value produced in 5 weeks by a variable capital of £500, to the variable capital of £500. In the case of B, on the other hand, the calculation is of a kind which has nothing to do either with the production of surplus-value or with the determination of its corresponding rate of surplus-value. For the £500 of surplus-value produced by a variable capital of £500 of variable capital advanced during their production, but with reference to a capital of £5,000, nine-tenths of which, or £4,500, have nothing whatever to do with the production of this surplus-value of £500, but are on the contrary intended to function gradually in the course of the following 45 weeks, so that they do not exist at all so far as the production of the first 5 weeks is concerned, which alone is at issue in this instance. Hence in this case the difference in the rates of surplus-value of A and B presents no problem at all.

Let us now compare the annual rates of surplus-value for capitals B and A. For capital B it is 500s/500v = 100%; for capital A it is 5,000s/500v = 1,000%. But the ratio of the rates of surplus-value is the same as before. There we had

$$\frac{\text{(Rate of Surplus-Value of Capital B)}}{\text{Rate of Surplus-Value of Capital A)}} = 10\% \,/\, 100\%$$

Now we have

$$\frac{\text{(Annual Rate of Surplus-Value of Capital B)}}{\text{(Annual Rate of Surplus-Value of Capital A)}} = \frac{100\%}{1{,}000\%}$$

But 10% : 100% = 100% : 1,000%, so that the proportion is the same.

But now the problem has changed. The annual rate of capital B, 5,000s/5,000v = 100%, offers not the slightest deviation—not even the semblance of a deviation—from the laws of production known to us and of the rate of surplus-value corresponding to this production. During the year 5,000v have been advanced and productively consumed, and they have produced 5,000s. The rate of surplus-value therefore equals the above fraction, 5,000s/5,000v = 100%. The annual rate agrees with the actual rate of surplus-value. In this case it is therefore not capital B but capital A which presents the anomaly that has to be explained.

We have here the rate of surplus-value 5,000s/500v = 1,000%. But while in the first case 500s, the product of 5 weeks, was calculated for an advanced capital of £5,000, nine-tenths of which were not employed by its production, we have now 5,000s calculated for 500v, i.e., for only one-tenth of the variable capital actually employed in the production of 5,000s; for the 5,000s are the product of a variable capital of £5,000 productively consumed during 50 weeks, not that of a capital of £500 consumed in one single period of 5 weeks. In the first case the surplus-value produced in 5 weeks had been calculated for a capital advanced for 50 weeks, a capital ten times as large as the one consumed during the 5 weeks. Now the surplus-value produced in 50 weeks is calculated for a capital advanced for 5 weeks, a capital ten times smaller than the one consumed in 50 weeks.

Capital A, of £500, is never advanced for more than 5 weeks. At the end of this time it returns and can renew the same process in the course of the year ten times, as it makes ten turnovers. Two conclusions follow from this:

Firstly: The capital advanced in the case of A is only five times larger than that portion of capital which is constantly employed in the productive process of one week. On the other hand capital B which is turned over only once in 50 weeks and must therefore be advanced for 50 weeks, is fifty times larger than that one of its portions which can constantly be employed for one week. The turnover therefore modifies the relation between the capital advanced during the year for the process of production and the capital constantly employable for a definite period of production, say, a week. Here we have, then, the first case, in which the surplus-value of 5 weeks is not calculated for the capital employed during these 5 weeks, but for a capital ten times larger, employed for 50 weeks.

Secondly: The 5-week period of turnover of capital A comprises only one-tenth of the year, so that one year contains ten such turnover periods, in which capital A of £500 is successively re-invested. The employed capital is here equal to the capital advanced for 5 weeks, multiplied by the number of periods of turnover per year. The capital employed during the year is 500 times 10, or £5,000. The capital advanced during the year is 5,000/10, or £500. Indeed, although the £500 are always re-employed, the sum advanced every 5 weeks never exceeds these same £500. On the other hand in case of capital B only £500 are employed during 5 weeks and advanced for these 5 weeks. But as the period of turnover in this case is 50 weeks, the capital employed in one year is equal to the capital advanced for 50 weeks and not to that advanced for every 5 weeks. The annually produced quantity of surplus-value, given the rate of surplus-value, is however commensurate with the capital employed during the year, not with the capital advanced during the year. Hence it is not larger for this capital of £5,000, which is turned over once a year, than it is for the capital of £500, which is turned over ten times a year. And it is so big only because the capital turned over once a year is itself ten times larger than the capital turned over ten times a year.

The variable capital turned over during one year—hence the portion of the annual product, or of the annual expenditure equal to that portion—is the variable capital actually employed, productively consumed, during that year. It follows therefore that if the variable capital A turned over annually and the variable capital B turned over annually are equal and the employed under equal conditions of self-expansion, so that the rate of surplus-value is the same for both of them, then the quantity of surplus-value produced annually must likewise be the same for both of them. Hence the rate of surplus-value calculated for a year must also be the same, since the amounts of capital employed are the same, so far as the rate is expressed by (quantity of surplus-value produced annually) / (variable capital turned over annually). Or, expressed generally: Whatever the relative magnitude of the turned-over variable capitals, the rate of the surplus-value produced by them in the course of the year is determined by the rate of surplus-value at which the respective capitals have worked in average periods (say, the average of a week or day).

This is the only consequence of the laws of production of surplus-value and of the determination of the rate of surplus-value.

Let us see further what is expressed by the ratio

$$\frac{\text{(Capital turned over annually)}}{\text{(capital advanced)}}$$

(taking into account, as we have said before, only the variable capital). The division shows the number of turnovers made by the capital advanced in one year.

In the case of capital A we have:

$$\frac{\text{(£5,000 of capital turned over annually)}}{\text{(£500 of capital advanced)}}$$

In the case of capital B we have:

$$\frac{\text{(£5,000 of capital turned over annually)}}{\text{(£5,000 of capital advanced)}}$$

In both ratios the numerator expressed the advanced capital multiplied by the *number* of turnovers; in the case of A, 500 times 10; in the case of B, 5,000 times 1. Or it may be multiplied by the inverted *time* of turnover calculated for one year. The time of turnover for A is 1/10 of a year; the inverted time of turnover is 10/1 years; hence 500 times 10/1, or 5,000. In the case of B, 5,000 times 1/1, or 5,000. The denominator expresses the turned-over capital multiplied by the inverted *number* of turnovers; in the case of A, 5,000 times 1/10; in the case of B, 5,000 times 1/1.

The respective quantities of labour (the sum of the paid and unpaid labour), which are set in motion by the two variable capitals turned over annually, are equal in this case, because the turned-over capitals themselves are equal and their rates of self-expansion are likewise equal.

The ratio of variable capital turned over annually to the variable capital advanced indicates 1) the ratio of the capital to be advanced to the variable capital employed during a definite working period. If the number of turnovers is 10, as in the case of A, and the year assumed to have 50 weeks, then the period of turnover is 5 weeks. For these 5 weeks variable capital must be advanced and the capital advanced for 5 weeks must be 5 times as large as the variable capital employed during one week. That is to say, only one-fifth of the advanced capital (in this case £500) can be employed in the course of one week. On the other hand, in the case of capital B, where the number of turnovers is 1/1, the time of turnover is 1 year, or 50 weeks. The ratio of the advanced capital to the capital employed weekly is therefore 50 : 1. If matters were the same for B as they are for A, then B would have to invest £1,000 per week instead of £100. 2) It follows that B has employed ten times as much capital (£5,000) as A to set in motion the same quantity of variable capital and hence—the rate of surplus-value being given—of labour (paid and unpaid), and thus to produce also the same quantity of surplus-value during the year. The real rate of surplus-value expresses nothing but the ratio of the variable capital employed during a definite period to the surplus-value produced in the same time; or the quantity of unpaid labour set in motion by the variable capital employed during this time. It has absolutely nothing to do with that portion of the variable capital which is advanced during the time in which it is not employed. Hence it has likewise nothing to do with the ratio between that portion of capital which is advanced during a definite period of time and that portion which is employed during the same period of time—a ratio that is modified and differentiated for different capitals by the turnover period.

It follows rather from what has been set forth above that the annual rate of surplus-value coincides only in one single case with the real rate of surplus-value which expresses the degree of exploitation of labour; namely in the case when the advanced capital is turned over only once a year and the capital advanced is thus equal to the capital turned over in the course of the year, when therefore the ratio of the quantity of the surplus-value produced during the year to the capital employed during the year in this production coincides and is identical with the ratio of the quantity of surplus-value produced during the year to the capital advanced during the year.

A. The annual rate of surplus-value is equal to the

$$\frac{\text{(quantity of surplus-value produced during the year)}}{\text{(variable capital advanced)}}$$

But the quantity of the surplus-value produced during the year is equal to the real rate of surplus-value multiplied by the variable capital employed in its production. The capital employed in the production of the annual quantity of surplus-value is equal to the advanced capital multiplied by the number of its turnovers, which we shall call n. Formula A is therefore transformed into the following:

B. The annual rate of surplus-value is equal to the

$$\frac{\text{(real rate of surplus-value} \times \text{variable capital advanced} \times n)}{\text{(variable capital advanced)}}$$

For instance, in the case of capital B = 100 × 5,000 × 1 / 5,000, or 100%.

Only when *n* is equal to 1, that is, when the variable capital advanced is turned over only once a year, and hence equal to the capital employed or turned over during a year, the annual rate of surplus-value is equal to its real rate.

Let us call the annual rate of surplus-value S', the real rate of surplus-value s', the advanced variable capital v, the number of turnovers *n*. Then S' = s'v*n*/v = s'*n*. In other words, S' is equal to s'*n*, and it is equal to s' only when *n* = 1, and hence S› = s› times 1, or s›.

It follows furthermore that the annual rate of surplus-value is always equal to s'*n*, i.e., to the real rate of surplus-value produced in one period of turnover by the variable capital consumed during that period, multiplied by the number of turnovers of this variable capital during one year, or (what amounts to the same) multiplied by its inverted *time* of turnover calculated for one year. (If the variable capital is turnover over ten times per year, then its time of turnover is 1/10 of a year; its inverted time of turnover therefore 10/1 or 10.)

It follows furthermore that S' = s' when *n* is equal to 1. S› is greater than s› when *n* is greater than 1; i.e., when the advanced capital is turned over more than once a year or the turned-over capital is greater than the capital advanced.

Finally, S' is smaller than s' when *n* is smaller than 1, that is, when the capital turned over during the year is only a part of the advanced capital, so that the period of turnover is longer than one year.

Let us dwell a moment on this last case.

We retain all the premises of our former illustration, except that the period of turnover is lengthened to 55 weeks. The labour-process requires a variable capital of £100 per week, hence £5,500 for the period of turnover, and produces every week 100s; s' is therefore 100%, as before. The number of turnovers, *n*, is here 50/55 or 10/11, because the time of turnover is 1 plus 1/10 of the year (of 50 weeks), or 11/10 years.

S' = 100% × 5,500 × 10/11 / 5,500 = 100 × 10/11 = 1000/11 = 90 10/11%. It is therefore smaller than 100%.

Indeed, if the annual rate of surplus-value were 100%, then during the year 5,500v would produce 5,500s, whereas 10/11 years are required for that. The 5,500v produce only 5,000s during one year, therefore the annual rate of surplus-value is 5,000s/5,500v, or 10/11 or 90 10/11%.

The annual rate of surplus-value, or the comparison between the surplus-value produced during one year and the variable capital *advanced* in general (as distinguished from the variable capital *turned over* during the year), is therefore not merely subjective comparison; the actual movement of the capital itself gives rise to this contraposition. So far as the owner of capital A is concerned, his advanced variable capital of £500 has returned to him at the end of the year, and £5,000 of surplus-value in addition. It is not the quantity of capital employed by him during the year, but the quantity returning to him periodically that expresses the magnitude of his advanced capital. It is immaterial for the present issue whether at the end of the year the capital exists partly as a productive supply, or partly as money- or commodity-capital, and in what proportions it may have been divided into these different parts. So far as the owner of capital B is concerned, £5,000, his advanced capital, has returned to him besides £5,000 in surplus-value. For the owner of capital C (the last considered, worth £5,500) surplus-value to the amount of £5,000 has been produced during the year (£5,000 invested and rate of surplus-value 100%), but his advanced capital has not yet returned to him, nor has his produced surplus-value.

S' = s'*n* indicates that the rate of surplus-value valid for the variable capital employed during one period of turnover, to wit,

$$\frac{\text{(quantity of s produced in one turnover period)}}{\text{(variable capital employed in one turnover period)}}$$

must be multiplied by the number of turnover periods, or of the periods of reproduction of the advanced variable capital, by the number of periods in which it renews its circuit.

We have already seen (Buch I, Kap. IV [English edition: Part II.—*Ed.*]) (The Transformation of Money into Capital), and furthermore (Buch I, Kap. XXI [English edition: Ch. XXIII.—*Ed.*]) (Simple Reproduction), that the capital-value is in general advanced, not expended, as this value, having passed through the various phases of its circuit, returns to its point of departure, and at that enriched by surplus-value. This characterises it as advanced. The time that elapses from the moment of its departure to the moment of its return is the time for which it was advanced. The entire circular movement described by capital-value, measured by the time from its advance to its return, constitutes its turnover, and the duration of this turnover is a period of turnover. When this period has expired and the circuit is completed, the same capital-value can renew the same circuit, can therefore expand anew, can create surplus-value. If the variable capital is turned over ten times in one year, as in the case of capital A, then the same advance of capital begets in the course of one year ten times the quantity of surplus-value that corresponds to one period of turnover.

One must get a clear conception of the nature of this advance from the standpoint of capitalist society.

Capital A, which is annually turned over ten times, is advanced ten times during one year. It is advanced anew for every new period of turnover. But at the same time, during the year A never advances more than this same capital-value of £500 and in actual fact never disposes of more than these £500 for the productive process examined by us. As soon as these £500 have completed one circuit A makes them start anew the same circuit; by its very nature capital preserves its character of capital only because it always functions as capital in successive production processes. It is, moreover, never advanced for more than five weeks. Should the turnover last longer, it proves inadequate. Should the turnover be curtailed, a part becomes superfluous. Not ten capitals of £500 are advanced, but *one* capital of £500 is advanced ten times at successive intervals. The annual rate of surplus-value is therefore not calculated for ten advances of a capital of £500 or for £5,000, but for one advance of a capital of £500. It is the same as if one shilling circulates ten times and yet never represents more than one single shilling in circulation, although it performs the function of 10 shillings. But in the pocket which holds it after each change of hands it retains the same identical value of one shilling as before.

In the same way, capital A indicates at each successive return, and likewise on its return at the end of the year, that its owner has operated always with the same capital-value of £500. Hence only £500 return to him each time. His advanced capital is therefore never more than £500. Hence the advanced capital of £500 forms the denominator of the fraction which expresses the annual rate of surplus-value. We had for it the above formula $S' = s'vn/v = s'n$. Since the real rate of surplus-value, s', equals s/v, the quantity of surplus-value divided by the variable capital which produced it, we may substitute s/v for the value of s' in $s'n$, and get the other formula $S' = sn/v$.

But by its ten-fold turnover and thus the ten-fold renewal of its advance, the capital of £500 performs the function of a ten times larger capital, of a capital of £5,000, just as 500 shillings which circulate ten times per year perform the same function as 5,000 shillings which circulate only once.

'Whatever the form of the process of production in a society, it must be a continuous process, must continue to go periodically through the same phases... When viewed therefore as a connected whole and as flowing on with incessant renewal, every social process of production is, at the same time, a process of reproduction... As a periodic increment of the capital advanced, or periodic fruit of capital in process, surplus-value acquires the form of a *revenue* flowing out of capital.' (Buch I, Kap. XXI, pp. 588, 589.) [English edition: pp. 566 and 567.—*Ed.*]

In the case of capital A we have 10 five-week turnover periods. In the first period of turnover £500 of variable capital are advanced; i.e., £100 are weekly converted into labour-power, so that £500 are spent on labour-power at the end of the first turnover period. These £500, originally a part of the total capital advanced, have ceased to be capital. They are paid out in wages. The labourers in their turn pay them out in the purchase of means of subsistence, consuming means of subsistence worth £500. A quantity of commodities of that value is therefore annihilated; (what the labourer may save up in money, etc., is not capital either). As far as concerns the labourer, this quantity of commodities has been consumed unproductively, except inasmuch as it preserves the efficacy of his labour-power, an instrument indispensable to the capitalist.

In the second place, however, these £500 have been transformed, for the capitalist, into labour-power of the same value (or price). Labour-power is consumed by him productively in the labour-process. At the end of 5 weeks a product valued at £1,000 has been created. Half of this, £500, is the reproduced value of the variable capital expended in payment of labour-power. The other half, £500, is newly produced surplus-value. But the 5-weekly labour-power, through exchange for which a portion of the capital was converted into variable capital, is likewise expended, consumed, although productively. The labour which was active yesterday is not the same that is active today. Its value plus that of surplus-value created by it exists now as the value of a thing distinct from labour-power, to wit, of a product. But by converting the product into money, that portion of its value which is equal to the value of variable capital advanced can once more be exchanged for labour-power and thus again function as variable capital. The fact that the same workmen, i.e., the same bearers of labour-power, are given employment not only by the reproduced capital-value but also by that which has been reconverted into the form is immaterial. It is possible for the capitalist to hire different workmen for the second period of turnover.

In actual fact therefore a capital of £5,000, and not of £500, is expended successively in wages during the ten periods of turnover of 5 weeks each, and these wages will again be spent by the labourers to buy means of subsistence. The capital of £5,000 so advanced is consumed. It ceases to exist. On the other hand labour-power worth £5,000, not £500, is incorporated successively in the productive process and reproduces not only its own value of £5,000, but produces over and above that a surplus-value of £5,000. The variable capital of £500 advanced during the second period of turnover is not the identical capital of £500 that had been advanced during the first period of turnover. That has been consumed, spent in wages. But it is *replaced* by new variable capital of £500, which was produced in the first period of turnover in the form of commodities, and reconverted into money. This new money-capital of £500 is therefore the money-form of the quantity of commodities newly produced in the first period of turnover. The fact that an identical sum of money, £500, is again in the hands of the capitalist, i.e., apart from the surplus-value, precisely as much money-capital as he had originally advanced, conceals the circumstance that he is operating with newly produced capital. (As for the other constituents of value of the commodity-capital, which replace the constant parts of capital, their value is not newly produced, but only the form is changed in which this value exists.)

Let us take the third period of turnover. Here it is evident that the capital of £500, advanced for a third time, is not an old but a newly produced capital, for it is the money-form of the quantity of commodities produced in the second, not the first, period of turnover, i.e., of that portion of this quantity of commodities whose value is equal to that of the advanced variable capital. The quantity of commodities produced in the first period of turnover is sold. A part of its value equal to the variable portion of the value of the advanced capital was transformed into the new labour-power of the second period of turnover; it produced a new quantity of commodities, which were sold in their turn and a portion of whose value constitutes the capital of £500 advanced in the third turnover period.

And so forth during the ten periods of turnover. In the course of these, newly produced quantities of commodities (whose value, inasmuch as it replaces variable capital, is also newly produced, and does not merely re-appear as in the case of the constant circulating part of the capital) are thrown upon the market every 5 weeks, in order to incorporate ever new labour-power in the process of production.

Therefore what is accomplished by the ten-fold turnover of the advanced variable capital of £500 is not that this capital of £500 can be productively consumed ten times, or that a variable capital lasting for 5 weeks can be employed for 50 weeks. Rather, ten times £500 of variable capital is employed in the 50 weeks, and the capital of £500 always lasts only for 5 weeks and must be replaced at the end of the 5 weeks by a newly produced capital of £500. This applies equally to capitals A and B. But at this point the difference begins.

At the end of the first period of 5 weeks a variable capital of £500 has been advanced and expended by B as well as A. Both A and B have converted its value into labour-power and replaced it by that portion of the value of the product newly created by this labour-power which is equal to the value of the advanced variable capital of £500. For both B and A the labour-power has not only replaced the value of the expended variable capital of £500 by a new value of the same amount, but also added a surplus-value which, according to our assumption, is of the same magnitude.

But in the case of B the value-product, which replaces the advanced variable capital and adds to it a surplus-value, is not in the form in which it can function anew as productive, or variable, capital. It is in such a form in the case of A. And up to the end of the year B does not possess the variable capital expended in the first 5 and every subsequent 5 weeks (although it has been replaced by newly produced value plus surplus-value) in the form in which it can again function as productive, or variable, capital. True, its *value* is replaced by new value, hence renewed, but the *form* of its value (in this case the absolute form of value, its money-form) is not renewed.

For the second period of 5 weeks (and thus for every succeeding 5 weeks of the year) another £500 must again be available, the same as for the first period. Hence, regardless of credit conditions, £5,000 must be available at the beginning of the year as a latent advanced money-capital, although they are really expended, turned into labour-power, only gradually, in the course of the year.

But because in the case of A the circuit, the turnover of the advanced capital, is consummated, the replacement value after the lapse of the first 5 weeks is already in the form in which it can set new labour-power in motion for a term of 5 weeks—in its original form, the money-form.

In cases of both A and B new labour-power is consumed in the second 5-week period and a new capital of £500 is spent in payment of this labour-power. The means of subsistence of the labourers, paid with the first £500, are gone; at all events their value has vanished from the hands of the capitalist. With the second £500 new labour-power is bought, new means of subsistence withdrawn from the market. In short, it is a new capital of £500 that is being expended, not the old. But in the case of A this new capital of £500 is the money-form of the newly produced substitute for the value of the formerly expended £500, while in the case of B, this substitute is in a form in which it cannot function as variable capital. It is there, but not in the form of variable capital. For the continuation of the process of production for the next 5 weeks an additional capital of £500 must therefore be available and advanced in the here indispensable form of money. Thus, during 50 weeks, both A and B expend an equal amount of variable capital, pay for and consume an equal quantity of labour-power. Only, B must pay for it with an advanced capital equal to its total value of £5,000, while A pays for it successively with the ever renewed money-form of the value-substitute, produced every 5 weeks, for the capital of £500 advanced for every 5 weeks, i.e., never more than that advanced for the first 5 weeks, viz., £500. These £500 last for the entire year. It is therefore clear that, the degree of exploitation of labour and the real rate of surplus-value being the same, the annual rates (of surplus-value) of A and B must be inversely proportional to the magnitudes of the variable money-capitals which have to be advanced in order to set in motion the same amount of labour-power during the year.

A: 5,000s/500v = 1,000%; B: 5,000s/5,000v = 100%.

But 500v : 5,000v = 1 : 10 = 100% : 1,000%.

The difference is due to the difference in the periods of turnover, i.e., the periods in which the value-substitute of the variable capital employed for a definite time can function anew as capital, hence as new capital. In the case of B as well as A, there is the same replacement of value for the variable capital employed during the same periods. There is also the same increment of surplus-value during the same periods. But in the case of B, while every 5 weeks there is a replacement of the value of £500 and a surplus-value of £500, this value-substitute does not constitute new capital, because it does not exist in the form of money. In the case of A the old capital-value is not only replaced by a new one, but is rehabilitated in its money-form, hence replaced as a new capital capable of performing its function.

The conversion, sooner or later, of the value-substitute into money, and thus into the form in which variable capital is advanced, is obviously an immaterial circumstance, so far as the production of surplus-value itself is concerned. This production depends on the magnitude of variable capital employed and the degree of exploitation of labour. But that circumstance modifies the magnitude of the money-capital which must be advanced in order to set a definite quantum of labour-power in motion during the year, and therefore it determines the annual rate of surplus-value.

Section III. *The Turnover of the Variable Capital from the Social Point of View*

Let us look at this matter for a moment from the point of view of society. Let the wages of one labourer be £1 per week, the working-day 10 hours. In case of A as well as B, 100 labourers are employed during a year (£100 for 100 labourers per week, or £500 for 5 weeks, or £5,000 for 50 weeks), and each one of them works 60 hours per week of 6 days. So 100 labourers work 6,000 hours per week and 300,000 hours in 50 weeks. This labour-power is taken hold of by A and B and therefore cannot be expended by society for anything else. To this extent the matter is the same socially with both A and B. Furthermore: In the cases of both A and B, the 100 labourers employed by either side receive a yearly wage of £5,000 (or, together for the 200 labourers, £10,000) and withdraw from society means of subsistence to that amount. So far the matter is therefore socially the same in the case of both A and B. Since the labourers in either case are paid by the week, they weekly withdraw their means of subsistence from society and, in either case, throw a weekly equivalent in money into circulation. But here the difference begins.

First. The money which the A labourer throws into circulation is not only, as it is for the B labourer, the money-form of the value of his labour-power (in fact a means of payment for labour already performed); it is, counting from the second turnover period after the opening of the business, the money-form *of his own value* (equal to the price of the labour-power plus the surplus-value) created during the first period of turnover, by which his labour is paid during the second period of turnover. This is not the case with the B labourer. As far as the latter is concerned, the money is here, true enough, a medium of payment for work already done by him, but this work done is not paid for with the value which it itself produced and which was turned into money (not with the money-form of the value of the labour itself has produced). This cannot be done until the beginning of the second year, when the B labourer is paid with the value produced by him in the preceding year and turned into money.

The shorter the period of turnover of capital—the shorter therefore the intervals at which it is reproduced throughout the year—the quicker is the variable portion of the capital, originally advanced by the capitalist in the form of money, transformed into the money-form of the value (including, besides, surplus-value) created by the labourer to replace this variable capital; the shorter is the time for which the capitalist must advance money out of his own funds, and the smaller is the capital advanced by him in general in proportion to the given scale of production; and the greater comparatively is the quantity of surplus-value which he extracts during the year with a given rate of surplus-value, because he can buy the labourer so much more frequently with the money-form of the value created by that labourer and can so much more frequently set his labour into motion again.

If the scale of production is given, the absolute magnitude of the advanced variable money-capital (and of the circulating capital in general) decreased proportionately to the decrease of the turnover period, while the annual rate of surplus-value increases. If the magnitude of the advanced capital is given, the scale of production grows; hence, if the rate of surplus-value is given, the absolute quantity of surplus-value created in one period of turnover likewise grows, simultaneously with the rise in the annual rate of surplus-value effected by the shortening of the periods of reproduction. It generally follows from the foregoing investigation that the different lengths of the turnover periods make it necessary for money-capital to be advanced in very different amounts in order to set in motion the same quantity of productive circulating capital and the same quantity of labour with the same degree of exploitation of labour.

Second—and this is interlinked with the first difference—the B and A labourers pay for the means of subsistence which they buy with the variable capital that has been transformed in their hands into a medium of circulation. For instance, they not only withdraw wheat from the market, but they also replace it with an equivalent in money. But, since the money wherewith the B labourer pays for his means of subsistence, which he withdraws from the market, is not the money-form of a value produced and thrown by him on the market during the year, as it is in the case of the A labourer, he supplies the seller of the means of subsistence with money, but not with commodities—be they means of production or means of subsistence—which this seller could buy with the proceeds of the sale, as he can in the case of A. The market is therefore stripped of labour-power, means of subsistence for this labour-power, fixed capital in the form of instruments of labour used in the case of B, and of materials of production, and to replace them an equivalent in money is thrown on the market; but during the year no product is thrown on the market with which to replace the material elements of productive capital withdrawn from it. If we conceive society as being not capitalistic but communistic, there will be no money-capital at all in the first place, not the disguises cloaking the transactions arising on account of it. The question then comes down to the need of society to calculate beforehand how much labour, means of production, and means of subsistence it can invest, without detriment, in such lines of business as for instance the building of railways, which do not furnish any means of production or subsistence, nor produce any useful effect for a long time, a year or more, while they extract labour, means of production and means of subsistence from the total annual production. In capitalist society, however, where social reason always asserts itself only *post festum* great disturbances may and must constantly occur. On the one hand, pressure is brought to bear on the money-market, while on the other, an easy money-market calls such enterprises into being *en masse*, thus creating the very circumstances which later give rise to pressure on the money-market. Pressure is brought to bear on the money-market, since large advances of money-capital are constantly needed here for long periods of time. And this regardless of the fact that industrialists and merchants throw the money-capital necessary to carry on their business into speculative railway schemes; etc., and make it good by borrowing in the money-market.

On the other hand, pressure on society's available productive capital. Since elements of productive capital are for ever being withdrawn from the market and only an equivalent in money is thrown on the market in their place, the effective demand rises without itself furnishing any element of supply. Hence a rise in the prices of productive materials as well as means of subsistence. To this must be added that stock-jobbing is a regular practice and capital is transferred on a large scale. A band of speculators, contractors, engineers, lawyers, etc., enrich themselves. They create a strong demand for articles of consumption on the market, wages rising at the same time. So far as foodstuffs are involved, agriculture too is stimulated. But as these foodstuffs cannot be suddenly increased in the course of the year, their import grows, just as that of exotic foods in general (coffee, sugar, wine, etc.) and of articles of luxury. Hence excessive imports and speculation in this line of the import business. Meanwhile, in those branches of industry in which production can be rapidly expanded (manufacture proper, mining, etc.), climbing prices give rise to sudden expansion soon followed by collapse. The same effect is produced in the labour-market, attracting great numbers of the latent relative surplus-population, and even of the employed labourers, to the new lines of business. In general such large-scale undertakings as railways withdraw a definite quantity of labour-power from the labour-market, which can come only from such lines of business as agriculture, etc., where only strong lads are needed. This still continues even after the new enterprises have become established lines of business and the migratory working-class needed for them has already been formed, as for instance in the case of temporary rise above the average in the scale of railway construction. A portion of the reserve army of labourers, which keep wages down, is absorbed. A general rise in wages ensues, even in the hitherto well employed sections of the labour-market. This lasts until the inevitable crash again releases the reserve army of labour and wages are once more depressed to their minimum, and lower.[1]

Inasmuch as the length, great or small, of the period of turnover depends on the working period proper, that is, the period necessary to get the product ready for the market, it is based on the existing material conditions of production specific for the various investments of capital. In agriculture they assume more of the character of natural conditions of production, in manufacture and the greater part of the mining industry they vary with the social development of the process of production itself.

Inasmuch as the length of the working period depends on the size of the supply (the quantitative volume in which the product is generally thrown upon the market as commodities), it is conventional in character. But the convention itself has its material basis in the scale of production, and is therefore accidental only when examined singly.

Finally, inasmuch as the length of the turnover period hinges on that of the period of circulation, it is partly dependent on the incessant change of market conditions, the greater or lesser ease of selling, and the resultant necessity of disposing of part of the product in nearer or remoter markets. Apart from the volume of the demand in general, the movement of prices is here of cardinal importance since sales are intentionally restricted when prices are falling, while production proceeds; vice versa, production and sales keep pace when prices are rising or sales can be made in advance. But we must consider the actual distance of the place of production from the market as the real material basis.

For instance, English cotton goods or yarn are sold to India. Suppose the exporter himself pays the English cotton manufacturer (the exporter does so willingly only if the money-market is strong. But when the manufacturer himself replaces his money-capital by some credit transaction, things are not so good). The exporter sells his cotton goods later in the Indian market, from where his advanced capital is remitted to him. Up to this remittance the case runs the very same course as when the length of the working period necessitated the advance of new money-capital to maintain the production process on a given scale. The money-capital with which the manufacturer pays his labourers and renews the other elements of his circulating capital is not the money-form of the yarn produced by him. This cannot be the case until the value of this yarn has returned to England in the form of money or products. It is additional money-capital as before. The only difference is that instead of the manufacturer, it is advanced by the merchant, who in turn may well have obtained it by means of credit operations. Similarly, before this money is thrown on the market, or simultaneously with this, no additional product has been put on the English market that could be bought with this money and would enter the sphere of productive or individual consumption. If this situation continues for a rather long period of time and on a rather large scale, it must have the same effect as the previously mentioned prolongation of the working period.

Now it may be that in India the yarn is again sold on credit. With this credit products are bought in India and sent as return shipment to England or drafts remitted for this amount. If this condition is protracted, the Indian money-market comes under pressure and the reaction on England may here produce a crisis. This crisis, in its turn, even if connected with bullion export to India, calls forth a new crisis in that country on account of the bankruptcy of English firms and their Indian branches, which had received credit from Indian banks. Thus a crisis occurs simultaneously in the market in which the balance of trade is *favourable*, as well as in the one in which it is *unfavourable*. This phenomenon may be still more complicated. Assume for instance that England has sent silver bullion to India but India's English creditors are not urgently collecting their debts in that country, and India will soon after have to ship its silver bullion back to England.

It is possible that the export trade to India and the import trade from India may approximately balance each other, although the volume of the import trade (except under special circumstances, such as a scarcity of cotton, etc.) is determined and stimulated by the export trade. The balance of trade between England and India may seem equilibrated or may disclose slight oscillations in either direction. But as soon as the crisis breaks out in England it turns out that unsold cotton goods are stored in India (hence have not been transformed from commodity-capital into money-capital—an over-production to this extent), and that on the other hand there are stored up in England unsold supplies of Indian goods, and moreover, a great portion of the sold and consumed supplies is not yet paid. Hence what appears as a crisis on the money-market is in reality an expression of abnormal conditions in the very process of production and reproduction.

Third. So far as the employed circulating capital itself (constant and variable) is concerned, the length of the period of turnover, since it derives from the working period, makes this difference: In the case of several turnovers during one year, an element of the variable or constant circulating capital may be supplied through its own product, for instance in the production of coal, the ready-made clothes business, etc. In other cases this cannot occur, at least not within the same year.

Note

1. In the manuscript, the following note is here inserted for future amplification: 'Contradiction in the capitalist mode of production: the labourers as buyers of commodities are important for the market. But as sellers of their own commodity—labour-power—capitalist society tends to keep them down to the minimum price.

—Further contradiction: the periods in which capitalist production exerts all its forces regularly turn out to be periods of over-production, because production potentials can never be utilised to such an extent that more value may not only be produced but also realised; but the sale of commodities, the realisation of commodity-capital and thus of surplus-value, is limited, not by the consumer requirements of society in general, but by the consumer requirements of a society in which the vast majority are always poor and must always remain poor. However, this pertains to the next part.

17

The Circulation of Surplus Value

We have just seen that a difference in the period of turnover causes a difference in the annual rate of surplus-value, even if the mass of the annually produced surplus-value is the same.

But there are furthermore necessarily differences in the capitalisation of surplus-value, in *accumulation*, and also in the quantity of surplus-value produced during the year, while the rate of surplus-value remains the same.

To begin with, we note that capital A (in the illustration of the preceding chapter) has a current periodical revenue, so that with the exception of the period of turnover inaugurating the business, it pays for its own consumption within the year out of its production of surplus-value, and need not cover it by advances out of its own funds. But the latter has to be done in the case of B. While it produces as much surplus-value in the same intervals of time as A, the surplus-value is not realised and therefore cannot be consumed either productively or individually. So far as individual consumption is concerned, the surplus-value is anticipated. Funds for that purpose must be advanced.

One portion of the productive capital, which it is difficult to classify namely the additional capital required for the repair and maintenance of the fixed capital, is now likewise seen in a new light.

In the case of A, this portion of capital is not advanced—in full or for the greater part—at the beginning of production. It need not be available or even in existence. It comes out of the business itself by a direct transformation of surplus-value into capital, i.e., by its direct employment as capital. A part of the surplus-value which is not only periodically generated but also realised during the year can defray the expenditures that must be incurred for repairs, etc. A portion of the capital needed to carry on the business on its original scale is thus produced in the course of business by the business itself by means of capitalising part of the surplus-value. This is impossible for capital B. The portion of capital in question must in his case form a part of the capital originally advanced. In both cases this portion will figure in the books of the capitalists as an advanced capital, which it really is, since according to our assumption it forms a part of the productive capital required for maintaining the business on a certain scale. But it makes all the difference in the world out of which funds it is advanced. In the case of B it is really a part of the capital to be originally advanced or held available. In the case of A, on the other hand, it is a part of the surplus-value used as capital. This last case shows that not only the accumulated capital but also a portion of the originally advanced capital may simply be capitalised surplus-value.

As soon as the development of credit interferes, the relation between originally advanced capital and capitalised surplus-value becomes still more complicated. For instance, from not having sufficient capital of his own at the very outset for this purpose, A borrows from banker C a portion of the productive capital with which he starts in business or continues it during the year. Banker C lends him a sum of money which consists only of surplus-value deposited with the banker by capitalists D, E, F, etc. As far as A is concerned there is as yet no question of accumulated capital. But with regard to D, E, F, etc., A is, in fact, nothing but an agent capitalising surplus-value appropriated by them.

We have seen (Buch I, Kap. XXII) [English edition: Ch. XXIV.—*Ed.*] that accumulation, the conversion of surplus-value into capital, is essentially a process of reproduction on a progressively increasing scale, whether this expansion is expressed extensively in the form of an addition of new factories to the old, or intensively by the enlargement of the existing scale of operation.

The expansion of the scale of production may proceed in small portions, a part of the surplus-value being used for improvements which either simply increase the productive power of the labour employed or permit at the same time of its more intensive exploitation. Or, where the working-day is not legally limited, an additional expenditure of circulating capital (in materials of production and wages) suffices to enhance the production scale without an expansion of the fixed capital, whose daily time of employment is thus merely lengthened, while its period of turnover is correspondingly shortened. Or the capitalised surplus-value may, under favourable market conditions, permit of speculation in raw materials, operations for which the capital originally advanced would not have been sufficient, etc.

However, it is clear that in cases where the greater number of periods of turnover brings with it a more frequent realisation of surplus-value during the year, there will be periods in which there can be neither a prolongation of the working-day nor an introduction of improvements in details; on the other hand a proportional expansion of the whole business, partly by expanding its entire plant, the buildings for example, partly by enlarging the cultivated areas in agriculture, is possible only within certain more or less narrow limits and, besides, requires such a volume of additional capital as can be supplied only by several years' accumulation of surplus-value.

Along with the real accumulation or conversion of surplus-value into productive capital (and a corresponding reproduction on an extended scale), there is, then, an accumulation of money, a raking together of a portion of the surplus-value in the form of latent money-capital, which is not intended to function as additional active capital until later, when it swells to a certain volume.

That is how the matter looks from the standpoint of the individual capitalist. But simultaneously with the development of capitalist production the credit system also develops. The money-capital which the capitalist cannot as yet employ in his own business is employed by others, who pay him interest for its use. It serves him as money-capital in its specific meaning, as a kind of capital distinguished from productive capital. But it serves as capital in another's hands. It is plain that with the more frequent realisation of surplus-value and the rising scale on which it is produced, there is an increase in the proportion of new money-capital or money as capital thrown upon the money-market and then absorbed—at least the greater part of it—by extended production.

The simplest form in which the additional latent money-capital may be represented is that of a hoard. It may be that this hoard is additional gold or silver secured directly or indirectly in exchange with countries producing precious metals. And only in this manner does the hoarded money in a country grow absolutely. On the other hand it may be—and is so in the majority of cases—that this hoard is nothing but money which has been withdrawn from circulation at home and has assumed the form of a hoard in the hands of individual capitalists. It is furthermore possibly that this latent money-capital consists only of tokens of value—we still ignore credit-money at this point—or of mere claims of capitalists (titles) against third persons conferred by legal documents. In all such cases, whatever may be the form of existence of this additional money-capital, it represents, so far as it is capital *in spe*, nothing but additional and reserved legal titles of capitalists to future annual additional social production.

> 'The mass of real accumulated wealth, in point of magnitude ... is so utterly insignificant when compared with the powers of production of the same society in whatever state of civilisation, or even compared with the actual consumption for even a few years of that society, that the great attention of legislators and political economists should be directed to 'productive powers' and their future free development, and not, as hitherto, to the mere accumulated wealth that strikes the eye. Of what is called accumulated wealth, by far the greater part is only nominal, consisting not of any real things, ships, houses, cottons, improvements on land, but of mere demands on the future annual productive powers of society, engendered and perpetuated by the expedients or institutions of insecurity ... The use of such articles (accumulations of physical things or actual wealth) as a mere means of appropriating to their possessors the wealth to be created by the future productive powers of society, being that alone of which the natural laws of distribution would, without force, gradually deprive them, or, if aided by cooperative labour, would in a very few years deprive them.' (William Thompson, *An Inquiry into the Principles of the Distribution of Wealth*, London, 1850, p. 453. This book originally appeared in 1824.)
>
> 'It is little thought, by most persons not at all suspected, how very small a proportion, either in extent or influence, the actual accumulations of society bear to human productive powers, even to the ordinary consumption of a few years of a single generation. The reason is obvious; but the effect very pernicious. The wealth that is annually consumed, disappearing with its consumption, is seen but for a moment, and makes no impression but during the act of enjoyment or use. But that part of wealth which is of slow consumption, furniture, machinery, buildings, from childhood to old age stand out before the eye, the durable monuments of human exertion. By means of the possession of this fixed, permanent, or slowly consumed, part of national wealth, of the land and materials to work upon, the tools to work with, the houses to shelter whilst working, the holders of these articles command for their own benefit the yearly productive powers of all the really efficient productive labourers of society, though these articles may bear ever so small a proportion to the recurring products of that labour. The population of Britain and Ireland being twenty millions, the average consumption of each individual, man, woman, and child, is probably about twenty pounds, making four hundred millions of wealth, the product of labour annually consumed. The whole amount of the accumulated capital of these countries, it has been estimated, does not exceed twelve hundred millions, or three times the year's labour of the community; or, if equally divided, sixty pounds capital for every individual. 'Tis with the proportions, rather than with the absolute accurate amount of these estimated sums, we are concerned. The interest of this capital stock would support the whole population in the same comfort in which they now exist, for about two months of one year, the whole accumulated capital itself would maintain them in idleness (could purchasers be found) for three years! at the end of which time, without houses, clothes, or food, they must starve, or become the slaves of those who supported them in the three years idleness. As three years to the life of one healthy generation, say forty years, so is the magnitude and importance of the actual wealth, the accumulated capital of even the wealthiest community, to the productive powers of only one generation; not of what, under judicious arrangements of equal security, they might produce, particularly with the aid of cooperative labour, but of what, under the defective and depressing expedients of insecurity, they do absolutely produce!.. The seeming mighty mass of existing capital to maintain and perpetuate which (or rather the command of the

> products of yearly labour which it serves as the means of engrossing) ... in its present state of forced division, are all the horrible machinery, the vices, crimes, and miseries of insecurity, sought to be perpetuated. As nothing can be accumulated without first supplying necessaries, and as the great current of human inclination is to enjoyment; hence the comparatively trifling amount of the actual wealth of society at any particular moment. 'Tis an eternal round of production and consumption. From the amount of this immense mass of annual consumption and production, the handful of actual accumulation would hardly be missed; and yet it is to this handful, and not to the mass of productive powers that attention has chiefly been directed. This handful, however, having been seized upon by a few, and been made the instrument of converting to their use the constantly recurring annual products of the labour of the great majority of their fellow-creatures; hence, in the opinion of these few, the paramount importance of such an instrument... About one-third part of the annual products of the labour of these countries is now abstracted from the producers, under the name of public burdens, and unproductively consumed by those who give no equivalent, that is to say, none satisfactory to the producers... With the accumulated masses, particularly when held forth in the hands of a few individuals, the vulgar eye has been always struck. The annually produced and consumed masses, like the eternal and incalculable waves of a mighty river, roll on and are lost in the forgotten ocean of consumption. On this eternal consumption, however, are dependent, not only for almost all gratifications, but even for existence, the whole human race. The quantity and distribution of these yearly products ought to be the paramount objects of consideration. The actual accumulation is altogether of secondary importance, and derives almost the whole of that importance from its influence on the distribution of the yearly productions... Actual accumulations and distributions have been always considered' (in Thompson's works) 'in reference, and subordinate to actual accumulations, and to the perpetuating of the existing modes of distribution. In comparison to the preservation of the actual distribution, the ever recurring misery of happiness of the whole human race has been considered as unworthy of regard. To perpetuate the results of force, fraud, and chance, has been called security; and to the support of this spurious security, have all the productive powers of the human race been unrelentingly sacrificed.' (*Ibid*., pp. 440-43.)

For reproduction only two normal cases are possible, apart from disturbances, which interfere with reproduction even on a fixed scale.

There is either reproduction on a simple scale.

Or there is capitalisation of surplus-value, accumulation.

Section I. *Simple Reproduction*

In the case of simple reproduction the surplus-value produced and realised annually, or periodically, if there are several turnovers during the year, is consumed individually, that is to say, unproductively, by its owner, the capitalist.

The circumstance that the value of the product consists in part of surplus-value and in part of that portion of value which is formed by the variable capital reproduced in the product plus the constant capital consumed by it, does not alter anything whatever either in the quantity or in the value of the total product, which constantly steps into circulation as commodity-capital and is just as constantly withdrawn from it, in order to be productively or individually consumed, i.e., to serve as means of production or consumption. If constant capital is left aside, only the distribution of the annual product between the labourers and the capitalists is affected thereby.

Even if simple reproduction is assumed, a portion of the surplus-value must therefore always exist in the form of money and not of products, because otherwise it could not be converted for purposes of consumption from money into products. This conversion of the surplus-value from its original commodity-form into money must be further analysed at this place. In order to simplify the matter, we shall presuppose the most elementary form of the problem, namely the exclusive circulation of metal coin, of money which is a real equivalent.

According to the laws of the simple circulation of commodities (developed in Buch I, Kap. III), [English edition: Volume I, Ch. III.—*Ed.*] the mass of the metal coin existing in a country must not only be sufficient to circulate the commodities, but must also suffice to meet the currency fluctuations, which arise partly from fluctuations in the velocity of the circulation, partly from a change in the prices of commodities, partly from the various and varying proportions in which the money functions as a medium of payment or as a medium of circulation proper. The proportion in which the existing quantity of money is split into a hoard and money in circulation varies continually, but the total quantity of money is always equal to the sum of the money hoarded and the money circulating. This quantity of money (quantity of precious metal) is a gradually accumulated hoard of society. Since a portion of this hoard is consumed by wear and tear, it must be replaced annually, the same as any other product. This takes place in reality by a direct or indirect exchange of a part of the annual product of a particular country for the product of countries producing gold and silver. However, this international character of the transaction conceals its simple course. In order to reduce the problem to its simplest and most lucid expression, it must be assumed that the production of gold and silver takes place in that particular country itself, that therefore the production of gold and silver constitutes a part of the total social production within every country.

Apart from the gold and silver produced for articles of luxury, the minimum of their annual production must be equal to the wear of metal coin annually occasioned by the circulation of money. Furthermore, if the sum of the values of the annually produced and circulating quantity of commodities increases, the annual production of gold and silver must likewise increase, inasmuch as the increased sum of values of the circulating commodities and the quantity of money required for their circulation (and the corresponding formation of a hoard) are not made good by a greater velocity of money currency and a more comprehensive function of money as a medium of payment, i.e., by a greater mutual balancing of purchases and sales without the intervention of actual money.

A portion of the social labour-power and a portion of the social means of production must therefore be expended annually in the production of gold and silver.

The capitalists who are engaged in the production of gold and silver and who, according to our assumption of simple reproduction, carry on their production only within the bounds of the annual average wear and tear and the annual average consumption of gold and silver entailed thereby throw their surplus-value—which they consume annually, according to our assumption, without capitalising any of it—directly into circulation in the money-form, which is its natural form; unlike the other branches of production, where it is the converted form of the product.

Furthermore, as far as wages are concerned—the money-form in which the variable capital is advanced—they are also not replaced by the sale of the product, by its conversion into money, but by a product itself whose natural form is from the outset that of money.

Finally, the same applies also to that portion of the product of precious metals which is equal to the value of the periodically consumed constant capital, both the constant circulating and constant fixed capital consumed during the year.

Let us consider the circuit, or turnover, of the capital invested in the production of precious metals first in the form of M—C ... P ... M'. Since C in M—C consists not only of labour-power and means of production but also of fixed capital, only a part of whose value is consumed in P, it is evident that M', the product, is a sum of money equal to the variable capital laid out in wages plus the circulating constant capital laid out in means of production plus a portion of the value equivalent to the worn-out fixed capital plus the surplus-value. If the sum were smaller, the general value of gold remaining the same, then the mine would be unproductive or, if this got to be generally the case, the value of gold compared with the value of commodities that remains unchanged would subsequently rise; i.e., the prices of commodities would fall, so that henceforth the amount of money laid out in M—C would be smaller.

If we consider at first only the circulating portion of capital advanced in M, the starting-point of M—C ... P ... M', we find that a certain sum of money is advanced, thrown into circulation for the payment of labour-power and the purchase of materials of production. But this sum is not withdrawn from circulation by the circuit of *this* capital, in order to be thrown into it anew. The product is money even in its bodily form; there is no need therefore of transforming it into money by means of exchange, by a process of circulation. It passes from the process of production into the sphere of circulation, not in the form of commodity-capital which has to be reconverted in money-capital, but as money-capital which is to be reconverted into productive capital, i.e., which is to buy fresh labour-power and materials of production. The money-form of the circulating capital consumed in labour-power and means of production is replaced, not by the sale of the product, but by the bodily form of the product itself; hence, not by once more withdrawing its value from circulation in money-form, but by additional newly produced money.

Let us suppose that this circulating capital is £500, the period of turnover 5 weeks, the working period 4 weeks, the period of circulation only 1 week. From the outset, money for 5 weeks must be partly advanced for a productive supply, and partly be ready to be paid out gradually in wages. At the beginning of the 6th week, £400 will have returned and £100 will have been released. This is constantly repeated. Here, as in previous cases, £100 will always be found in released form during a certain time of the turnover. But they consist of additional, newly produced, money, the same as the other £400. We have in this case 10 turnovers per year and the annual product is £5,000 in gold. (The period of circulation is not constituted, in this case, by the time required for the conversion of commodities into money, but by that required for the conversion of money into the elements of production.)

In the case of every other capital of £500 turned over under the same conditions, the ever renewed money-form is the converted form of the commodity-capital produced and thrown into circulation every 4 weeks and which by its sale—that is to say, by a periodical withdrawal of the quantity of money it represented when it originally entered into the process—assumes this money-form anew over and over again. Here, on the contrary, in every turnover period a new additional £500 in money is thrown from the process of production itself into circulation, in order to withdraw from it continually materials of production and labour-power. This money thrown into circulation is not withdrawn from it again by the circuit which this capital describes, but is rather increased by quantities of gold constantly produced anew.

Let us look at the variable portion of this circulating capital, and assume that it is, as before, £100. Then these £100 would be sufficient in the ordinary production of these commodities, with 10 turnovers, to pay continually for the labour-power. Here, in the production of gold, the same amount is sufficient. But the £100 of the reflux, with which the labour-power is paid every 5 weeks, are not a converted form of its product but a portion of this ever renewed product itself. The producer of gold pays his labourers directly with a portion of the gold they themselves produced. The £1,000 thus expended annually in labour-power and thrown by the labourers into circulation do not return therefore via this circulation to their starting-point.

Furthermore, so far as the fixed capital is concerned, it requires the investment of a comparatively large money-capital on the original establishment of the business, and this capital is thus thrown into circulation. Like all fixed capital it returns only piecemeal in the course of years. But it returns as a direct portion of the product, of the gold, not by the sale of the product and its consequent conversion into money. In other words, it gradually assumes its money-form not by a withdrawal of money from the circulation but by an accumulation of a corresponding portion of the product. The money-capital so restored is not a quantity of money gradually withdrawn from the circulation to compensate for the sum originally thrown into it for the fixed capital. It is an additional sum of money.

Finally, as concerns the surplus-value, it is likewise equal to a certain portion of the new gold product, which is thrown into the circulation in every new period of turnover in order to be unproductively expended, according to our assumption, on means of subsistence and articles of luxury.

But according to our assumption, the entire annual production of gold—which continually withdraws labour-power and materials of production, but no money, from the market, while continuously adding fresh quantities of money to it—merely replaces the money worn out during the year, hence only keeps intact the quantity of social money which exists constantly, although in varying portions, in the two forms of hoarded money and money in circulation.

According to the law of the circulation of commodities, the quantity of money must be equal to the amount of money required for circulation plus a certain amount held in the form of a hoard, which increases or decreases as the circulation contracts or expands, and serves especially for the formation of the requisite reserve funds of means of payment. What must be paid in money in so far as there is no balancing of accounts—is the value of the commodities. The fact that a portion of this value consists of surplus-value, that is to say, did not cost the seller of the commodities anything, does not alter the matter in any way. Let us suppose that the producers are all independent owners of their means of production, so that circulation takes place between the immediate producers themselves. Apart from the constant portion of their capital, their annual value-product might then be divided into two parts, analogous with capitalist conditions: Part a, replacing only the necessary means of subsistence, and part b, consumed partly in articles of luxury, partly for an expansion of production. Part a then represents the variable capital, part b the surplus-value. But this division would remain without influence on the magnitude of the sum of money required for the circulation of their total product. Other circumstances remaining equal, the value of the circulating mass of commodities would be the same, and thus also the amount of money required for that value. They would also have to have the same money-reserves if the turnover periods are equally divided, i.e., the same portion of their capital would always have to be held in the form of money, because their production, according to our assumption, would be commodity production, the same as before. Hence the fact that a portion of the value of the commodities consists of surplus-value would change absolutely nothing in the quantity of the money required for the running of the business.

An opponent of Tooke, who clings to the formula M—C—M', asks him how the capitalist manages always to withdraw more money from circulation than he throws into it. Mind you! The question at issue here is not the *formation* of surplus-value. This, the only secret, is a matter of course from the capitalist standpoint. The sum of values employed would not be capital if it did not enrich itself by means of surplus-value. But as it is capital by assumption, surplus-value is taken for granted.

The question, then, is not where the surplus-value comes from but whence the money comes into which it is turned.

But in bourgeois economics, the existence of surplus-value is self-understood. It is therefore not only assumed but also connected with the further assumption that a part of the mass of commodities thrown into circulation is a surplus-product, hence representing a value which the capitalist did not throw into circulation as part of his capital; that, consequently, with his product the capitalist throws into circulation a surplus over and above his capital, and that he withdraws this surplus from it.

The commodity-capital, which the capitalist throws into circulation, has a greater value (it is not explained and remains obscure where this comes from, but the above Political Economy considers it a fact) than the productive capital which he withdrew from circulation in the form of labour-power plus means of production. On the basis of this assumption it is evident why not only capitalist A, but also B, C, D, etc., are always able to withdraw more value from circulation by the exchange of their commodities than the value of the capital originally and repeatedly advanced by them. A, B, C, D, and the rest continuously throw a greater commodity-value into circulation in the form of commodity-capital—this operation is as many-sided as the various independently functioning capitals—than they withdraw from it in the form of productive capital. Hence they have constantly to divide among themselves a sum of values (i.e., everyone, on his part, has to withdraw from circulation a productive capital) equal to the sum of values of the productive capitals they respectively advanced; and just as constantly they have to divide among themselves a sum of values which they all, from all sides, throw into circulation in the form of commodities representing the respective excesses of the commodity-values above the values of their elements of production.

But the commodity-capital must be turned into money before its reconversion into productive capital and before the surplus-value contained in it is spent. Where does the money for this purpose come from? This question seems difficult at the first glance and neither Tooke nor any one else has answered it so far.

Let the circulating capital of £500 advanced in the form of money-capital, whatever its period of turnover, now stand for the total circulating capital of society, that is, of the capitalist class. Let the surplus-value be £100. How can the entire capitalist class manage to draw continually £600 out of circulation, when it continually throws only £500 into it?

After the money-capital of £500 has been converted into productive capital, the latter transforms itself within the process of production into commodities worth £600 and there are in circulation not only commodities valued at £500, equal to the money-capital originally advanced, but also a newly produced surplus-value of £100.

This additional surplus-value of £100 is thrown into circulation in the form of commodities. No doubt about that. But such an operation does not by any means furnish the additional money for the circulation of this additional commodity-value.

It will not do to obviate this difficulty by plausible subterfuges.

For instance: So far as the constant circulating capital is concerned, it is obvious that not all invest it simultaneously. While capitalist A sells his commodities, so that his advanced capital assumes the form of money, there is on the other hand the available money-capital of the buyer B which assumes the form of his means of production—precisely what A is producing. By the same act through which A restores the money-form to his produced commodity-capital, B returns his capital to its productive form, transforms it from money-form into means of production and labour-power; the same amount of money functions in the two-sided process as in every simple purchase C—M. On the other hand, when A reconverts his money into means of production, he buys from C, and this man pays B with it, etc., and thus the transaction would be explained. But:

None of the laws established with reference to the quantity of the circulating money in the circulation of commodities (Buch I, Kap. III), [English edition: Volume I, Ch. III.—*Ed.*] are changed in any way by the capitalist character of the process of production.

Hence, when one says that the circulating capital of society to be advanced in the form of money amounts to £500, one has already taken into account that this is on the one hand the sum simultaneously advanced, and that on the other hand it sets in motion more productive capital than £500 because it serves alternately as the money-form of various productive capitals. This manner of explanation, then, assumes the money, whose existence it is called upon to explain, as already existing.

It might be further said: Capitalist A produces articles which capitalist B consumes individually, unproductively. B's money therefore turns A's commodity-capital into money and thus the same sum of money serves to realise B's surplus-value and A's circulating constant capital. But in that case the question that still awaits solution is assumed still more directly to have been solved, namely: where does B get the money that makes up his revenue? How did he himself realise this portion of the surplus-value of his product?

It might also be said that the part of the circulating variable capital which A steadily advances to his labourers returns to him steadily from the circulation, and only a varying part of it always stays with him for the payment of wages. But a certain time elapses between the expenditure and the reflux, and meanwhile the money paid out for wages might, among other uses, serve for the realisation of surplus-value.

But we know in the first place that the longer this time the greater must be the supply of money which capitalist A must keep constantly *in petto*. In the second place, the labourer spends the money, buys commodities for it and thus converts into money *pro tanto* the surplus-value contained in them. Consequently the same money that is advanced in the form of variable capital serves *pro tanto* also the purpose of turning surplus-value into money. Without penetrating any further into the question at this point, let this suffice: the consumption of the entire capitalist class and its retainers keeps step with that of the working-class; hence simultaneously with the money thrown into circulation by the labourers the capitalists too must throw money into it, in order to spend their surplus-value as revenue. Hence money must be withdrawn from circulation for it. This explanation would serve merely to reduce, but not eliminate, the quantity of money required.

Finally, it might be said: A large amount of money is constantly thrown into circulation when fixed capital is first invested, and it is recovered from the circulation only gradually, piecemeal, after a lapse of years, by him who threw it into circulation. Cannot this sum suffice to convert the surplus-value into money?

The answer to this must be that perhaps the sum of £500 (which includes hoard formation for needed reserve funds) implies its employment as fixed capital, if not by him who threw it into circulation, then by somebody else. Besides, it is already assumed in regard to the amount expended for the procurement of products serving as fixed capital that the surplus-value contained in them is also paid, and the question is precisely where this money comes from.

The general reply has already been given: If a mass of commodities worth x times £1,000 has to circulate, it changes absolutely nothing in the quantity of the money required for this circulation whether the value of this mass of commodities has been produced capitalistically or not. *The problem itself therefore does not exist.* All other conditions being given, such as velocity of the currency of money, etc., a definite sum of money is required in order to circulate commodities worth x times £1,000 quite independently of how much or how little of this value falls to the share of the direct producers of these commodities. So far as any problem exists here, it coincides with the general problem: Where does the money required for the circulation of the commodities of a country come from?

However, from the point of view of capitalist production, the *semblance* of a special problem does indeed exist. In the present case it is the capitalist who appears as the point of departure, who throws money into circulation. The money which the labourer expends for the payment of his means of subsistence existed previously as the money-form of the variable capital and was therefore thrown originally into circulation by the capitalist as a means of buying or paying for the labour-power. The capitalist furthermore throws into circulation the money which constitutes originally the money-form of his constant, fixed and circulating, capital; he expends it as a means of purchase or payment for instruments of labour and materials of production. But beyond this the capitalist no longer appears as the starting-point of the quantity of money in circulation. Now, there are only two points of departure: the capitalist and the labourer. All third categories of persons must either receive money for their services from these two classes or, to the extent that they receive it without any services in return, they are joint owners of the surplus-value in the form of rent, interest, etc. That the surplus-value does not all stay in the pocket of the industrial capitalist but must be shared by him with other persons, has nothing to do with the present question. The question is how he turns his surplus-value into money, not how the proceeds are later divided. For our purposes the capitalist may as well still be regarded as the sole owner of the surplus-value. As for the labourer, it has already been said that he is but the secondary, while the capitalist is the primary, starting-point of the money thrown by the labourer into circulation. The money first advanced as variable capital is going through its second circulation when the labourer spends it to pay for means of subsistence.

The capitalist class remains consequently the sole point of departure of the circulation of money. If they need £400 for the payment of means of production and £100 for the payment of labour-power, they throw £500 into circulation. But the surplus-value incorporated in the product, with a rate of surplus-value incorporated in the product, with a rate of surplus-value of 100%, is equal in value to £100. How can they continually draw £600 out of circulation, when they continually throw only £500 into it? Nothing comes from nothing. The capitalist class as a whole cannot draw out of circulation what was not previously thrown into it.

We disregard here the fact that the sum of £400 may suffice, when turned over ten times, to circulate means of production valued at £4,000 and labour-power valued at £1,000, and that the other £100 may likewise suffice for the circulation of £1,000 worth of surplus-value. The ratio of the sum of money to the value of commodities circulated by it is immaterial here. The problem remains the same. Unless the same pieces of money circulate several times, a capital of £5,000 must be thrown into circulation, and £1,000 is required to convert the surplus-value into money. The question is where this money comes from, whether it is £1,000 or £100. In any event it is in excess of the money-capital thrown into the circulation.

Indeed, paradoxical as it may appear at first sight, it is the capitalist class itself that throws the money into circulation which serves for the realisation of the surplus-value incorporated in the commodities. But, *nota bene*, it does not throw it into circulation as advanced money, hence not as capital. It spends it as a means of purchase for its individual consumption. The money is not therefore advanced by the capitalist class, although it is the point of departure of its circulation.

Let us take some individual capitalist who is starting in business, a farmer for instance. During the first year, he advances a money-capital of, say, £5,000, paying £4,000 for means of production, and £1,000 for labour-power. Let the rate of surplus-value be 100%, the amount of surplus-value appropriated by him £1,000. The above £5,000 comprise all the money he advances as money-capital. But the man must also live, and he does not take in any money until the end of the year. Take it that his consumption amounts to £1,000. These he must have in his possession. He may say that he has to advance himself these £1,000 during the first year. But this advance, which here has only a subjective meaning, denotes nothing else but that he must pay for his individual consumption during the first year out of his own pocket instead of defraying it out of the gratuitous production of his labourers. He does not advance this money as capital. He spends it, pays it out for an equivalent in means of subsistence which he consumes. This value has been spent by him in money, thrown into circulation and withdrawn from it in the form of commodity-values. These commodity-values he has consumed. He has thus ceased to bear any relation to their value. The money with which he paid for this value exists now as an element of the circulating money. But he has withdrawn the value of this money from circulation in the form of products; and this value is now destroyed together with the products in which it existed. It's all gone. But at the end of the year he throws commodities worth £6,000 into circulation and sells them. By this means he recovers: 1) his advanced money-capital of £5,000; 2) the realised surplus-value of £1,000. He has advanced as capital, has thrown into circulation, £5,000, and he withdraws from it £6,000—£5,000 of which cover his capital, and £1,000 his surplus-value. The last £1,000 are turned into money with the money which he himself has thrown into circulation, which he did not advance, but spent as a consumer, not as a capitalist. They now return to him as the money-form of the surplus-value produced by him. And henceforth this operation is repeated every year. But beginning with the second year, the £1,000 which he spends are constantly the converted form, the money-form, of the surplus-value produced by him. He spends them annually and they return to him annually.

If his capital were turned over more frequently a year, it would not alter this state of affairs, but would affect the length of time, and hence the amount which he would have to throw into circulation for his individual consumption over and above his advanced money-capital.

This money is not thrown into circulation by the capitalist as capital. But it is a decided trait of the capitalist to be able to live on means in his possession until surplus-value begins to return.

In the present case we assumed that the sum of money which the capitalist throws into circulation to pay for his individual consumption until the first returns of his capital is exactly equal to the surplus-value which he produced and hence must turn into money. This is obviously an arbitrary assumption so far as the individual capitalist is concerned. But it must be correct when applied to the entire capitalist class as simple reproduction is assumed. It only expresses the same thing as the assumption; namely, that the entire surplus-value, and it alone—hence no fraction of the original capital stock—is consumed unproductively.

It had been previously assumed that the total production of precious metals (taken to be equal to £500) sufficed only for the replacement of the wear and tear of the money.

The capitalists producing gold possess their entire product in gold—that portion which replaces constant capital as well as that which replaces variable capital, and also that consisting of surplus-value. A portion of the social surplus-value therefore consists of gold, and not of a product which is turned into gold only in the process of circulation. It consists from the outset of gold and is thrown into circulation in order to draw products out of it. The same applies here to wages to variable capital, and to the replacement of the advanced constant capital. Hence, whereas one part of the capitalist class throws into circulation commodities greater in value (greater by the amount of the surplus-value) than the money-capital advanced by them, another part of the capitalists throws into circulation money of greater value (greater by the amount of surplus-value) than that of the commodities which they constantly withdraw from circulation for the production of gold. Whereas one part of the capitalists constantly pumps more money out of the circulation than it pours into it, the part that produces gold constantly pumps more money into it than it takes out in means of production.

Although a part of this product of £500 in gold is surplus-value of the gold-producers, the entire sum is, nonetheless, intended only to replace the money necessary for the circulation of commodities. It is immaterial for this purpose how much of this gold turns into money the surplus-value incorporated in the commodities, and how much of it their other value constituents.

Transferring the production of gold from one country to another produces no change whatever in the matter. One part of the social labour-power and the social means of production of country A is converted into a product, for instance linen, valued at £500, which is exported to country B in order to buy gold there. The productive capital thus employed in the country A throws no more commodities—as distinct from money—upon the market of country A than it would it if were employed directly in the production of gold. This product of A represents £500 in gold and enters into the circulation of this country only as money. That portion of the social surplus-value which is contained in this product exists for country A directly in the form of money, and never in any other form. Although for the gold-producing capitalists only a part of the product represents surplus-value, and another part of the replacement capital, still the question of how much of this gold, outside the circulating constant capital, replaces variable capital and how much of it represents surplus-value depends exclusively on the respective ratios of wages and surplus-value to the value of the circulating commodities. The part which forms surplus-value is distributed among the diverse members of the capitalist class. Although that part is continually spent by them for individual consumption and recovered by the sale of new products—it is precisely this purchase and sale that circulates among them the money required for the conversion of the surplus-value into money—there is nevertheless a portion of the social surplus-value, in the form of money, even if in varying proportions, in the pockets of the capitalists, just as a portion of the wages stays at least during part of the week in the pockets of the labourers in the form of money. And this part is not limited by that part of the money product which originally forms the surplus-value of the gold-producing capitalists, but, as we have said, is limited by the proportion in which the above product of £500 is generally distributed between capitalists and labourers, and in which the commodity-supply to be circulated consists of surplus-value and the other constituents of value.

However, that portion of surplus-value which does not exist in other commodities but alongside of them in the form of money, consists of a portion of the annually produced gold only to the extent that a portion of the annual production of gold circulates for the realisation of the surplus-value. The other portion of money, which is continually in the hands of the capitalist class in varying portions, as the money-form of their surplus-value, is not an element of the annually produced gold, but of the mass of money previously accumulated in the country.

According to our assumption the annual production of gold, £500, just covers the annual wear of money. If we keep in mind only these £500 and ignore that portion of the annually produced mass of commodities which is circulated by means of previously accumulated money, the surplus-value produced in commodity-form will find in the circulation process money for its conversion into money for the simple reason that on the other side surplus-value is annually produced in the form of gold. The same applies to the other parts of the gold product of £500 which replace the advanced money-capital.

Now, two things are to be noted here.

In the first place, it follows that the surplus-value spent by the capitalists as money, as well as the variable and other productive capital advanced by them in money, is actually the product of labourers, namely of the labourers engaged in the production of gold. They produce anew not only that portion of the gold product which is 'advanced' to them as wages but also that portion of the gold product in which the surplus-value of the capitalist gold-producers is directly represented. Finally, as for that portion of the gold product which replaces only the constant capital-value advanced for its production, it re-appears in the form of money (or product in general) only through the annual work of the labourers. When the business started, it was originally expended by the capitalist in the form of money, which was not newly produced but formed a part of the circulating mass of social money. But to the extent that it is replaced by a new product, by additional gold, it is the annual product of the labourer. The advance on the part of the capitalist appears here, too, merely as a form which owes its existence to the fact that the labourer is neither the owner of his own means of production nor able to command, during production, the means of subsistence produced by other labourers.

In the second place however, as far as concerns that mass of money which exists independently of his annual replacement of £500, partly in the form of a hoard and partly in the form of circulating money, things must be, or rather must have been originally with it just as they are annually with regard to these £500. We shall return to this point at the close of this sub-section. [See: pp. 347-48 of this book.—*Ed.*] But before then we wish to make a few additional remarks.

We have seen during our study of the turnover that, other circumstances remaining equal, changes in the length of the periods of turnover require changes in the amounts of money-capital, in order to carry on production on the same scale. The elasticity of the money-circulation must therefore be sufficient to adapt itself to this alternation of expansion and contraction.

If we furthermore assume other circumstances as remaining equal—including the length, intensity, and productivity of the working-day—but *a different division of the value of the product* between wages and surplus-value, so that either the former rises and the latter falls, or vice versa, the mass of the circulating money is not affected thereby. This change can take place without any expansion or contraction of the money currency. Let us consider particularly the case in which there is a general rise in wages, so that, under the assumptions made, there will be a general fall in the rate of surplus-value, but besides this, also according to our assumption, there will be no change in the value of the circulating mass of commodities. In this case there naturally is an increase in the money-capital which must be advanced as variable capital, hence in the amount of money which performs this function. But the surplus-value, and therefore also the amount of money required for its realisation, decreases by exactly the same amount by which the amount of money required for the function of variable capital increases. The amount of money required for the realisation of the commodity-value is not affected thereby, any more than this commodity-value itself. The cost price of the commodity rises for the individual capitalist but its social price of production remains unchanged. What is changed is the proportion in which, apart from the constant part of the value, the price of production of commodities is divided into wages and profit.

But, it is argued, a greater outlay of variable money-capital (the value of the money is, of course, considered constant) implies a larger amount of money in the hands of the labourers. This causes a greater demand for commodities on the part of the labourers. This, in turn, leads to a rise in the price of commodities.—Or it is said: If wages rise, the capitalists raise the prices of their commodities.—In either case, the general rise in wages causes a rise in commodity prices. Hence a greater amount of money is needed for the circulation of the commodities, no matter how the rise in prices is explained.

Reply to the first formulation: in consequence of a rise in wages, the demand of the labourers for the necessities of life will rise particularly. Their demand for articles of luxury will increase to a lesser degree, or a demand will develop for things which formerly did not come within the scope of their consumption. The sudden and large-scale increase in the demand for the indispensable means of subsistence will doubtless raise their prices immediately. The consequence: a greater part of the social capital will be employed in the production of necessities of life and a smaller in the production of luxuries, since these fall in price on account of the decrease in surplus-value and the consequent decrease in the demand of the capitalists for these articles. On the other hand as the labourers themselves buy articles of luxury, the rise in their wages does not promote an increase in the prices of the necessities of life but simply displaces buyers of luxuries. More luxuries than before are consumed by labourers, and relatively fewer by capitalists. *Voilà tout.* After some oscillations the value of the mass of circulating commodities is the same as before. As for the momentary fluctuations, they will not have any other effect than to throw unemployed money-capital into domestic circulation, capital which hitherto sought employment in speculative deals on the stock-exchange or in foreign countries.

Reply to the second formulation: If it were in the power of the capitalist producers to raise the prices of their commodities at will, they could and would do so without a rise in wages. Wages would never rise if commodity prices fell. The capitalist class would never resist the trades' unions, if it could always and under all circumstances do what it is now doing by way of exception, under definite, special, so to say local, circumstances, to wit, avail itself of every rise in wages in order to raise prices of commodities much higher yet and thus pocket greater profits.

The assertion that the capitalists can raise the prices of luxuries, because the demand for them decreases (in consequence of the reduced demand of the capitalists whose means of purchasing such articles has decreased) would be a very unique application of the law of supply and demand. Since it is not a mere displacement of luxury buyers, a displacement of capitalists by labourers—and so far as this displacement does occur, the demand of the labourers does not stimulate a rise in the prices of necessities, for the labourers cannot spend that portion of their increased wages for necessities which they spend for luxuries—the prices of luxuries fall in consequence of reduced demand. Capital is therefore withdrawn from the production of luxury articles, until their supply is reduced to dimensions corresponding to their altered role in the process of social production. With their production thus reduced, they rise in price—their value otherwise unchanged—to their normal level. So long as this contraction, or this process of levelling, lasts and the prices of necessities rise, as much capital is supplied to the production of the latter as is withdrawn from other branches of production, until the demand is satisfied. Then the equilibrium is restored and the end of the whole process is that the social capital, and therefore also the money-capital, is divided in a different proportion between the production of the necessities of life and that of luxury articles.

The entire objection is a bugbear set up by the capitalists and their economic sycophants. The facts which serve as the pretext for this bugbear are of three kinds:

1. It is a general law of money circulation that, other things being equal, the quantity of money in circulation increases with a rise in the sum of the prices of circulating commodities, irrespective of whether this augmentation of the totality of prices applies to the same quantity of commodities or to a greater quantity. The effect is then confused with the cause. Wages rise (although the rise is rare, and proportional only in exceptional cases) with the rising prices of the necessities of life. Wage advances are the consequence, not the cause, of advances in the prices of commodities.
2. In the case of a partial, or local, rise of wages—that is, a rise only in some branches of production—a local rise in the prices of the products of these branches may follow. But even this depends on many circumstances. For instance that wages were not abnormally depressed and that therefore the rate of profit was not abnormally high; that the market for these goods is not narrowed by the rise in prices (hence a contraction of their supply previous to raising their prices is not necessary), etc.
3. In the case of a general rise in wages the price of the produced commodities rises in branches of industry where the variable capital preponderates, but falls on the other hand in branches where the constant, or fixed, capital preponderates.

We found in our study of the simple circulation of commodities (Buch I, Kap. III, 2) [English edition: Ch. III.—*Ed.*] that, though the money-form of any definite quantity of commodities is only transient within the sphere of circulation, still the money transiently in the hands of one man during the metamorphosis of a certain commodity necessarily passes into the hands of another, so that in the first instance commodities are not only exchanged all-sidedly, or replace one another, but this replacement is promoted and accompanied by an all-sided precipitation of money. 'When one commodity replaces another, the money-commodity always sticks to the hands of some third person. Circulation sweats money from every pore.' (Buch I, S. 92.) [English edition: p. 113.—*Ed.*] The same identical fact is expressed, on the basis of the capitalist production of commodities, by a portion of capital constantly existing in the form of money-capital, and a portion of surplus-value constantly being found in the hands of its owners, likewise in the form of money.

Apart from this, the *circuit of money*—that is, the *return* of money to its point of departure—being a phase of the turnover of capital, is a phenomenon entirely differently from, and even the opposite of, the *currency of money*,[1] which expresses its steady departure from the starting-point by changing hands again and again. (Buch I, S. 94.) [English edition: pp. 114-15.—*Ed.*] Nevertheless, an accelerated turnover implies *eo ipso* an accelerated currency.

First concerning the variable capital: If a certain money-capital of, say, £500 is turned over the form of variable capital ten times a year, it is evident that this aliquot part of the quantity of money in circulation circulates ten times its value, or £5,000. It circulates ten times a year between the capitalist and the labourer. The labourer is paid, and pays, ten times a year with the same aliquot part of the circulating quantity of money. If the same variable capital were turned over only once a year, the scale of production remaining the same, there would be only one capital turnover of £5,000.

Furthermore: Let the constant portion of the circulating capital be equal to £1,000. If the capital is turned over ten times, the capitalist sells his commodity, and therefore also the constant circulating portion of its value, ten times a year. The same aliquot part of the circulating quantity of money (equal to £1,000) passes ten times per annum from the hands of its owners into those of the capitalist. This money changes hands ten times. Secondly, the capitalist buys means of production ten times a year. This again makes ten circulations of money from one hand into another. With a sum of money amounting to £1,000, the industrial capitalist sells £10,000 worth of commodities, and again buys £10,000 worth of commodities. By means of 20 circulations of £1,000 in money a commodity-supply of £20,000 is circulated.

Finally, with an acceleration of the turnover, the portion of money with realises the surplus-value also circulates faster.

But, conversely, an acceleration of money-circulation does not necessarily imply a more rapid turnover of capital, and therefore of money; that is, it does not necessarily imply a contraction and more rapid renewal of the reproduction process.

A more rapid circulation of money takes place whenever a larger number of transactions are performed with the same amount of money. This may also take place under the same periods of capital reproduction as a result of changes in the technical facilities for the circulation of money. Furthermore, there may be an increase in the number of transactions in which money circulates without representing actual exchanges of commodities (marginal transactions on the stock-exchange, etc.). On the other hand, some circulations of money may be entirely eliminated, as for instance where the agriculturist is himself a landowner, there is no circulation of money between the farmer and the landlord; where the industrial capitalist is himself the owner of the capital, there is no circulation of money between him and the creditors.

As for the primitive formation of a money-hoard in a country, and its appropriation by a few, it is unnecessary to discuss it in detail at this point.

The capitalist mode of production—its basis being wage-labour, the payment of the labourer in money, and in general the transformation of payments in kind into money payments—can assume greater dimensions and achieve greater perfection only where there is available in the country a quantity of money sufficient for circulation and the formation of a hoard (reserve fund, etc.) promoted by it. This is the historical premise, although it is not to be taken to mean that first a sufficient hoard is formed and then capitalist production begins. It develops simultaneously with the development of the conditions necessary for it, and one of these conditions is a sufficient supply of precious metals. Hence the increased supply of precious metals since the sixteenth century is an essential element in the history of the development of capitalist production. But so far as the necessary further supply of money material on the basis of capitalist production is concerned, we see surplus-value incorporated in products thrown into circulation without the money required for their conversion into money, on the one hand, and on the other surplus-value in the form of gold without previous transformation of products into money.

The additional commodities to be converted into money find the necessary amount of money at hand, because on the other side additional gold (and silver) intended for conversion into commodities is thrown into circulation, not by means of exchange, but by production itself.

Section II. *Accumulation and Reproduction on an Extended Scale*

Since accumulation takes place in the form of extended reproduction, it is evident that it does not offer any new problem with regard to money-circulation.

In the first place, as far as the additional money-capital required for the functioning of the increasing productive capital is concerned, that is supplied by the portion of the realised surplus-value thrown into circulation by the capitalists as money-capital, not as the money-form of the revenue. The money is already in the hands of the capitalists. Only its employment is different.

Now however in consequence of the additional productive capital, its product, an additional mass of commodities is thrown into circulation. Together with this additional quantity of commodities, a part of the additional money needed for its realisation is thrown into circulation, inasmuch as the value of this mass of commodities is equal to that of the productive capital consumed in their production. This additional amount of money has been advanced precisely as additional money-capital, and therefore returns to the capitalist through the turnover of his capital. Here the same question as above re-appears. Where does the additional money come from with which to realise the additional surplus-value now contained in the form of commodities?

The general reply is again the same. The sum total of the prices of the circulating commodities has been increased, not because the prices of a given quantity of commodities have risen, but because the mass of commodities now circulating is greater than that of the previously circulating commodities, without it being offset by a fall in prices. The additional money required for the circulation of this greater quantity of commodities of greater value must be secured either by greater economy in the use of the circulating quantity of money—whether by balancing the payments, etc., by measures which accelerate the circulation of the same coins—or by the transformation of money from the form of a hoard into that of a circulating medium. The latter does not only imply that idle money-capital begins to function as a means of purchase or payment, or that money-capital already functioning as a reserve fund while performing this function for its owner, actively circulates for society (as is the case with bank deposits which are continually lent), thus performing a double function. It also implies that the stagnating reserve funds of coins are economised.

'In order that money should flow continuously as coin, coin must constantly coagulate as money. The continual currency of coin depends on its continual stagnation, in greater or smaller quantities, in reserve funds of coin which spring up throughout the sphere of circulation and also necessitate it; the formation, distribution, dissolution, and re-formation of these reserve funds are constantly alternating, their existence constantly disappears, their disappearance constantly exists. Adam Smith expressed this never-ceasing transformation of coin into money and of money into coin by saying that every owner of commodities must always keep in supply, aside from the particular commodity which he sells, a certain quantity of the universal commodity with which he buys. We saw that in the circulation C—M—C the second member M—C splits up constantly into a series of purchases which do not take place at once but at successive intervals of time, so that one part of M is current as coin while the other rests as money. As a matter of fact money is in that case only suspended coin and the separate parts of the current mass of coins continuously appear now in the one form, and now in the other, alternating constantly. This first transformation of the medium of circulation into money represents, therefore, but a technical aspect of money-circulation itself.' (Karl Marx, *Zur Kritik der Politischen Oekonomie*, 1859, pp. 105, 106.) ('Coin' as distinguished from money is here employed to indicate money in its function of a mere medium of circulation in contrast with its other functions.)

When all these measures do not suffice, additional gold must be produced, or, what amounts to the same, a part of the additional product exchanged, directly or indirectly, for gold—the product of countries in which precious metals are mined.

The entire amount of labour-power and social means of production expended in the annual production of gold and silver intended as instruments of circulation constitutes a bulky item of the *faux frais* of the capitalist mode of production, of the production of commodities in general. It is an equivalent abstraction from social utilisation of as many additional means of production and consumption as possible, i.e., of real wealth. To the extent that the costs of this expensive machinery of circulation are decreased, the given scale of production or the given degree of its extension remaining constant, the productive power of social labour is *eo ipso* increased. Hence, so far as the expediencies developing with the credit system have this effect, they increase capitalist wealth directly, either by performing a large portion of the social production and labour-power without any intervention of real money, or by raising the functional capacity of the quantity of money really functioning.

This disposes also of the absurd question whether capitalist production in its present volume would be possible without the credit system (even if regarded only from this point of view), that is, with the circulation of metallic coin alone. Evidently this is not the case. It would rather have encountered barriers in the volume of production of precious metals. On the other hand one must not entertain any fantastic illusions on the productive power of the credit system, so far as it supplies or sets in motion money-capital. A further analysis of this question is out of place here.

We have now to investigate the case in which there takes place no real accumulation, i.e., no direct expansion of the scale of production, but where a part of the realised surplus-value is accumulated for a longer or shorter time as a money-reserve fund, in order to be transformed later into productive capital.

Inasmuch as the money so accumulating is additional money, the matter needs no explanation. It can only be a portion of the surplus-gold brought from gold-producing countries. In this connection it must be noted that the home product, in exchange for which this gold is imported, is no longer in the country in question. It has been exported to foreign countries in exchange for gold.

But if we assume that the same amount of money is still in the country as before, then the accumulated and accumulating money has accrued from the circulation. Only its function is changed. It has been converted from money in currency into latent money-capital gradually taking shape.

The money which is accumulated in this case is the money-form of sold commodities, and moreover of that part of their value which constitutes surplus-value for their owner. (The credit system is here assumed to be non-existent.) The capitalist who accumulates this money has sold *pro tanto* without buying.

If we look upon this process merely as an individual phenomenon, there is nothing to explain. A part of the capitalists keeps a portion of the money realised by the sale of its product without withdrawing products from the market in return. Another part of them on the other hand transforms its money wholly into products, with the exception of the constantly recurring money-capital required for running the business. One portion of the products thrown upon the market as vehicles of surplus-value consists of means of production, or of the real elements of variable capital, the necessary means of subsistence. It can therefore serve immediately for the expansion of production. For it has not been premised in the least that one part of the capitalists accumulates money-capital, while the other consumes its surplus-value entirely, but only that one part does its accumulating in the shape of money, forms latent money-capital, while the other part accumulates genuinely, that is to say, enlarges the scale of production, genuinely expands its productive capital. The available quantity of money remains sufficient for the requirements of circulation, even if, alternately, one part of the capitalists accumulates money, while the other enlarges the scale of production, and vice versa. Moreover, the accumulation of money on one side may proceed even without cash money by the mere accumulation of outstanding claims.

But the difficulty arises when we assume not an individual, but a general accumulation of money-capital on the part of the capitalist class. Apart from this class, according to our assumption—the general and exclusive domination of capitalist production—there is no other class at all except the working-class. All that the working-class buys is equal to the sum total of its wages, equal to the sum total of the variable capital advanced by the entire capitalist class. This money flows back to the capitalist class by the sale of its product to the working-class. Its variable capital thus resumes its money-form. Let the sum total of the variable capital be x times £100, i.e., the sum total of the variable capital employed, not advanced, during the year. The question now under consideration is not affected by how much or how little money, depending on the velocity of the turnover, is needed to advance this variable capital-value during the year. The capitalist class buys with these x times £100 of capital a certain amount of labour-power, or pays wages to a certain number of labourers—first transaction. The labourers buy with this same sum a certain quantity of commodities from the capitalists, whereby the sum of x times £100 flows back into the hands of the capitalists—second transaction. And this is constantly repeated. This amount of x times £100, therefore, can never enable the working-class to buy the part of the product which represents the constant capital, not to mention the part which represents the surplus-value of the capitalist class. With these x times £100 the labourers can never buy more than a part of the value of the social product equal to that part of the value which represents the value of the advanced variable capital.

Apart from the case in which this universal accumulation of money expresses nothing but the distribution of the precious metal additionally introduced, in whatever proportion, among the various individual capitalists, how is the entire capitalist class then supposed to accumulate money?

They would all have to sell a portion of their product without buying anything in return. There is nothing mysterious about the fact that they all have a certain fund of money which they throw into circulation as a medium of circulation for their consumption, and a certain portion of which returns to each one of them from the circulation. But in that case this money-fund exists precisely as a fund for circulation, as a result of the conversion of the surplus-value into money, and does not by any means exist as latent money-capital.

If we view the matter as it takes place in reality, we find that the latent money-capital, which is accumulated for future use, consists:

1. Of deposits in banks; and it is a comparatively trifling sum which is really at the disposal of the bank. Money-capital is accumulated here only nominally. What is actually accumulated is outstanding claims which can be converted into money (if ever) only because a certain balance arises between the money withdrawn and the money deposited. It is only a relatively small sum that the bank holds in its hands in money.

2. Of government securities. These are not capital at all, but merely outstanding claims on the annual product of the nation.
3. Of stocks. Those which are not fakes are titles of ownership of some corporative real capital and drafts on the surplus-value accruing annually from it.

There is no accumulation of money in any of these cases. What appears on the one side as an accumulation of money-capital appears on the other as a continual actual expenditure of money. It is immaterial whether the money is spent by him who owns it, or by others, his debtors.

On the basis of capitalist production the formation of a hoard as such is never an end in itself but the result either of a stagnation of the circulation—larger amounts of money than is generally the case assuming the form of a hoard—or of accumulations necessitated by the turnover; or, finally, the hoard is merely the creation of money-capital existing temporarily in latent form and intended to function as productive capital.

If therefore on the one hand a portion of the surplus-value realised in money is withdrawn from circulation and accumulated as a hoard, another part of the surplus-value is at the same time continually converted into productive capital. With the exception of the distribution of additional precious metals among the members of the capitalist class, accumulations in the form of money never takes place simultaneously at all points.

What is true of the portion of the annual product which represents surplus-value in the form of commodities, is also true of the other portion of it. A certain sum of money is required for its circulation. This sum of money belongs to the capitalist class quite as much as the annually produced quantity of commodities which represents surplus-value. It is originally thrown into circulation by the capitalist class itself. It is constantly redistributed among its members by means of the circulation itself. Just as in the case of circulation of coin in general, a portion of this sum stagnates at ever varying points, while another portion continually circulates. Whether a part of this accumulation is intentional, for the purpose of forming money-capital, or not, does not alter things.

No notice has been taken here of those adventures of circulation in which one capitalist grasps a portion of the surplus-value, or even of the capital, of another, thereby bringing about one-sided accumulation and centralisation of money-capital as well as of productive capital. For instance a part of the snatched surplus-value accumulated by A as money-capital may be a part of the surplus-value of B which does not return to him.

Note

1. Although the physiocrats still confuse these two phenomena, they were the first to emphasise the reflux of money to its starting-point as the essential form of circulation of capital, as that form of circulation which promotes reproduction. 'Cast a glance at the *Tableau Économique* and you will see that the productive class provides the money with which the other classes buy products from it, and that they return this money to it when they come back next year to make the same purchases... You see, then, no other circle here but that of expenditure followed by reproduction, and of reproduction followed by expenditure, a circle described by the circulation of money, which measures expenditure and reproduction.' (Quesnay, *Dialogues sur le Commerce et sur les Travaux des Artisans*, Daire édition, Physiocrats, I, pp. 208, 209.) 'It is this continual advance and return of capitals which should be called the circulation of money, this useful and fertile circulation which gives life to all the labours of society, which maintains the activity and life of the body politic, and which is quite rightly compared to the circulation of blood in the animal body.' (Turgot, *Réflexions, etc., Oeuvres*, Daire édition, I, p. 45.)

PART III

THE REPRODUCTION AND CIRCULATION OF THE AGGREGATE SOCIAL CAPITAL

18

Introduction

Section I. *The Subject Investigated*

The direct process of the production of capital is its labour and self-expansion process, the process whose result is the commodity-product and whose compelling motive is the production of surplus-value.

The process of reproduction of capital comprises this direct process of production as well as the two phases of the circulation process proper, i.e., the entire circuit which, as a periodic process—a process which constantly repeats itself in definite periods—constitutes the turnover of capital.

Whether we study the circuit in the form of M ... M' or that of P ... P, the direct process of production P itself always forms but one link in this circuit. In the one form it appears as a promoter of the process of circulation; in the other the process of circulation appears as its promoter. Its continuous renewal, the continuous re-appearance of capital as productive capital, is in either case determined by its transformations in the process of circulation. On the other hand the continuously renewed process of production is the condition of the transformations which the capital undergoes ever anew in the sphere of circulation, of its alternate appearance as money-capital and commodity-capital.

Every individual capital forms, however, but an individualised fraction, a fraction endowed with individual life, as it were, of the aggregate social capital, just as every individual capitalist is but an individual element of the capitalist class. The movement of the social capital consists of the totality of the movements of its individualised fractional parts, the turnovers of the individual capitals. Just as the metamorphosis of the individual commodity is a link in the series of metamorphoses of the commodity-world—the circulation of commodities—so the metamorphosis of the individual capital, its turnover, is a link in the circuit described by social capital.

This total process comprises both the productive consumption (the direct process of production) together with the conversions of form (materially considered, exchanges) which bring it about, and the individual consumption together with the conversions of form or exchanges by which it is brought about. It includes on the one hand the conversion of variable capital into labour-power, and therefore the incorporation of labour-power in the process of capitalist production. Here the labourer acts as the seller of his commodity, labour-power, and the capitalist as its buyer. But on the other hand the sale of the commodities embraces also their purchase by the working-class appears as buyer and the capitalists as sellers of commodities to the labourers.

The circulation of the commodity-capital includes the circulation of surplus-value, hence also the purchases and sales by which the capitalist effect their individual consumption, the consumption of surplus-value.

The circuit of the individual capitals in their aggregate as social capital, hence considered in its totality, comprises not only the circulation of capital but also the general circulation of commodities. The latter can originally consist of only two components: 1) The circuit of capital proper and 2) the circuit of the commodities which enter into individual consumption, consequently of the commodities for which the labourer expends his wages and the capitalist his surplus-value (or a part of it). At any rate, the circuit of capital comprises also the circulation of the surplus-value, since the latter is a part of the commodity capital, and likewise the conversion of the variable capital into labour-power, the payment of wages. But the expenditure of this surplus-value and wages for commodities does not form a link in the circulation of capital, although at least the expenditure of wages is essential for this circulation.

In Volume I the process of capitalist production was analysed as an individual act as well as a process of reproduction: the production of surplus-value and the production of capital itself. The changes of form and substance experienced by capital in the sphere of circulation were assumed without dwelling upon them. It was presupposed that on the one hand the capitalist sells the product at its value and on the other that he finds within the sphere of circulation the objective means of production for restarting or continuing the process. The only act within the sphere of circulation on which we have dwelt was the purchase and sale of labour-power as the fundamental condition of capitalist production.

In the first part of this Book II, the various forms were considered which capital assumes its circular movement, and the various forms of this movement itself. The circulation time must now be added to the working times discussed in Volume I.

In the second Part, the circuit was studied as being periodic, i.e., as a turnover. It was shown on the one hand in what manner the various constituents of capital (fixed and circulating) accomplish the circuit of forms in different periods of time and in different ways; on the other hand the circumstances were examined by which the different lengths of the working period and circulation period are conditioned. The influence was shown which the period of the circuit and the different proportions of its component parts exert upon the dimensions of the production process itself and upon the annual rate of surplus-value. Indeed, while it was the successive forms continually assumed and discarded by capital in its circuit that were studied in Part I, it was shown in Part II how a capital of a given magnitude is simultaneously, though in varying proportions, divided, within this flow and succession of forms, into different forms: productive capital, money-capital, and commodity-capital, so that they not only alternate with one another, but different portions of the total capital-value are constantly side by side and function in these different states. Especially money-capital came forward with distinctive features not shown in Volume I. Certain laws were found according to which diverse large components of a given capital must be continually advanced and renewed—depending on the conditions of the turnover—in the form of money-capital in order to keep a productive capital of a given size constantly functioning.

But in both the first and the second Parts it was always only a question of some individual capital, of the movement of some individualised part of social capital.

However, the circuits of the individual capitals intertwine, presuppose and necessitate one another, and form, precisely in this interlacing, the movement of the total social capital. Just as in the simple circulation of commodities the total metamorphosis of a commodity appeared as a link in the series of metamorphoses of the world of commodities, so now the metamorphosis of the individual capital appears as a link in the series of metamorphoses of the social capital. But, while simple commodity circulation by no means necessarily comprises the circulation of capital—since it may take place on the basis of non-capitalist production—the circuit of the aggregate social capital, as was noted, comprises also the commodity circulation lying outside the circuit of individual capital, i.e., the circulation of commodities which do not represent capital.

We have now to study the process of circulation (which in its entirety is a form of the process of reproduction) of the individual capitals as components of the aggregate social capital, that is to say, the process of circulation of this aggregate social capital.

Section II. *The Role of Money-Capital*

[Although the following belongs in a later section of this Part, we shall analyse it immediately, namely, the money-capital considered as a constituent part of the aggregate social capital.]

In the study of the turnover of the individual capital money-capital revealed two aspects.

In the first place it constitutes the form in which every individual capital appears upon the scene and opens its process as capital. It therefore appears as the *primus motor*, lending impetus to the entire process.

In the second place, that portion of the advanced capital-value which must be continually advanced and renewed in the form of money differs in its ratio to the productive capital which it sets in motion, i.e., in its ratio to the continuous scale of production, depending on the particular length of the period of turnover and the particular ratio between its two component parts—the working period and the period of circulation. But whatever this ratio may be, the portion of the capital-value in process which can continually function as productive capital is limited in any event by that portion of the advanced capital-value which must always exist beside the productive capital in the form of money. It is here merely a question of the normal turnover, an abstract average. Additional money-capital required to compensate for interruptions of the circulation is excepted.

As to the first point: commodity production presupposes commodity circulation, and commodity circulation presupposes the expression of commodities in money, the circulation of money; the splitting of a commodity into commodity and money is law of the expression of the product as a commodity. Similarly the capitalist production of commodities—whether considered socially or individually—presupposes capital in the form of money, or money-capital, both as the *primus motor* of every incipient business, and as its continual motor. The circulating capital especially implies that the money-capital acts with constant repetition at short intervals as a motor. The entire advanced capital-value, that is to say, all the elements of capital, consisting of commodities, labour-power, instruments of labour, and materials of production, must be bought over and over again with money. What is true here of the individual capital is also true of the social capital, which functions only in the form of many individual capitals. But as we showed in Volume I, it does not at all follow from this that capital's field of operation, the scale of production, depends—even on a capitalist basis—for its *absolute* limits on the amount of functioning money-capital.

Incorporated in capital are elements of production whose expansion within certain limits is independent of the magnitude of the advanced money-capital. Though payment of labour-power be the same, it can be exploited more or less extensively or intensively. If the money-capital is increased with this greater exploitation (that is, if wages are raised), it is not increased proportionately, hence not at all *pro tanto*.

The productively exploited nature-given materials—the soil, the seas, ores, forests, etc.—which do not constitute elements of capital-value, are more intensively or extensively exploited with a greater exertion of the same amount of labour-power, without an increased advance of money-capital. The real elements of productive capital are thus multiplied without requiring an additional money-capital. But so far as such an addition becomes necessary for additional auxiliary materials, the money-capital in which the capital-value is advanced is not increased proportionately to the augmented effectiveness of the productive capital, hence is *pro tanto* not at all increased.

The same instruments of labour, and thus the same fixed capital, can be used more effectively by an extension of the time they are daily used and by a greater intensity of employment, without an additional outlay of money for fixed capital. There is, in that case, only a more rapid turnover of the fixed capital, but then the elements of its reproduction are supplied more rapidly.

Apart from the natural substances, it is possible to incorporate in the productive process natural forces, which do not cost anything, to act as agents with more or less heightened effect. The degree of their effectiveness depends on methods and scientific developments which cost the capitalist nothing.

The same is true of the social combination of labour-power in the process of production and of the accumulated skill of the individual labourers. Carey calculates that the landowner never receives enough, because he is not paid for all the capital or labour put into the soil since time immemorial in order to give it its present productivity. (Of course, no mention is made of the productivity of which the soil is robbed.) According to that, each individual labourer would have to paid according to the work which it cost the entire human race to evolve a modern mechanic out of a savage. On the contrary, one should think that if all the unpaid labour put into the soil and converted into money by the landowner and capitalist is totalled up, all the capital ever invested in this soil has been paid back over and over again with usurious interest, so that society has long ago redeemed landed property over and over again.

True enough, the increase in the productive power of labour, so far as it does not imply an additional investment of capital-value, augments in the first instance only the quantity of the product, not its value, except insofar as it makes it possible to reproduce more constant capital with the same labour and thus to preserve its value. But it forms at the same time new material for capital, hence the basis of increased accumulation of capital.

So far as the organisation of social labour itself, and thus the increase in the social productive power of labour, requires large-scale production and therefore the advance of large quantities of money-capital by individual capitalists, we have shown in Book I [From Manuscript II.—*F. E.*] that this is accomplished in part by the centralisation of capitals in a few hands, without necessitating an absolute increase in the magnitude of the functioning capital-values, and consequently also in the magnitude of the money-capital in which they are advanced. The magnitude of the individual capitals can increase by centralisation in the hands of a few without a growth of their social sum total. It is only a changed distribution of the individual capitals.

Finally, we have shown in the preceding Part that a shortening of the period of turnover permits of setting in motion either the same productive capital with less money-capital or more productive capital with the same money-capital. [English edition: Vol. I, pp. 624-28, 761-64.—*Ed.*]

But evidently all this has nothing to do with the question of money-capital itself. It shows only that the advanced capital—a given sum of values consisting in its free form, in its value-form, of a certain sum of money—includes, after its conversion into productive capital, productive powers whose limits are not set by the limits of its value, but which on the contrary may operate within certain bounds with differing degrees of extensiveness or intensiveness. If the prices of the elements of production—the means of production and labour-power—are given, the magnitude of the money-capital required for the purchase of a definite quantity of these elements of production existing as commodities is determined. Or the magnitude of value of the capital to be advanced is determined. But the extent to which this capital acts as a creator of values and products is elastic and variable.

As to the second point: it is self-evident that part of the social labour and means of production which must be annually expended for the production or purchase of money in order to replace worn-off coin is *pro tanto* a diminution of the volume of social production. But as for the money-value which functions partly as a medium of circulation, partly as a hoard, it is simply there, acquired, present alongside the labour-power, the produced means of production, and the natural sources of wealth. It cannot be regarded as a limit set to these things. By its transformation into elements of production, by its exchange with other nations, the scale of production might be extended. This presupposes, however, that money plays its role of world-money the same as ever.

To set the productive capital in motion requires more or less money-capital, depending on the length of the period of turnover. We have also seen that the division of the period of turnover into working time and circulation time requires an increase of the capital latent or suspended in the form of money.

Inasmuch as the period of turnover is determined by the length of the working period, it is determined, other conditions remaining equal, by the material nature of the process of production, hence not by the specific social character of this process of production. However, on the basis of capitalist production, more extensive operations of comparatively long duration necessitate large advances of money-capital for a rather long time. Production in such spheres depends therefore on the magnitude of the money-capital which the individual capitalist has at his disposal. This barrier is broken down by the credit system and the associations connected with it, e.g., the stock companies. Disturbances in the money-market therefore put such establishments out of business, while these same establishments, in their turn, produce disturbances in the money-market.

On the basis of socialised production the scale must be ascertained on which those operations—which withdraw labour-power and means of production for a long time without supplying any product as a useful effect in the interim—can be carried on without injuring branches of production which not only withdraw labour-power and means of production continually, or several times a year, but also supply means of subsistence and of production. Under socialised as well as capitalist production, the labourers in branches of business with shorter working periods will as before withdraw products only for a short time without giving any products in return; while branches of business with long working periods continually withdraw products for a longer time before they return anything. This circumstance, then, arises from the material character of the particular labour-process, not from its social form. In the case of socialised production the money-capital is eliminated. Society distributes labour-power and means of production to the different branches of production. The producers may, for all it matters, receive paper vouchers entitling them to withdraw from the social supplies of consumer goods a quantity corresponding to their labour-time. These vouchers are not money. They do not circulate.

We see that inasmuch as the need for money-capital originates in the length of the working period, it is conditioned by two things: *First*, that money in general is the form in which every individual capital (apart from credit) must make its appearance in order to transform itself into productive capital; this follows from the nature of capitalist production and commodity-production in general. *Second*, the magnitude of the required money advance is due to the circumstance that labour-power and means of production are continually withdrawn from society for a comparatively long time without any return to it, during that period, of products convertible into money. The first condition, that the capital to be advanced must be advanced in the form of money, is not eliminated by the form of this money itself, whether it is metal-money, credit-money, token-money, etc. The second condition is in no way affected by what money-medium or in what form of production labour, means of subsistence, and means of production are withdrawn without the return of some equivalent to the circulation.

19[1]

Former Presentations of the Subject

Section I. *The Physiocrats*

Quesnay's *Tableau Économique* shows in a few broad outlines how the annual result of the national production, representing a definite value, is distributed by means of the circulation in such a way that, other things being equal, simple reproduction, i.e., reproduction on the same scale, can take place. The starting-point of the period of production is properly the preceding year's harvest. The innumerable individual acts of circulation are at once brought together in their characteristic social mass movement—the circulation between great functionally determined economic classes of society. We are here interested in the following: A portion of the total product—being, like every other portion of it, a use-object, it is a new result of last year's labour—is at the same time only the depository of old capital-value re-appearing in the same bodily form. It does not circulate but remains in the hands of its producers, the class of farmers, in order to resume there its service as capital. In this portion of the year's product, the constant capital, Quesnay includes impertinent elements, but he strikes upon the main thing, thanks to the limitations of his horizon, within which agriculture is the only sphere of investment of human labour producing surplus-value, hence the only really productive one from the capitalist point of view. The economic process of reproduction, whatever may be its specific social character, always becomes intertwined in this sphere (agriculture) with a natural process of reproduction. The obvious conditions of the latter throw light on those of the former, and keep off a confusion of thought which is called forth by the mirage of circulation.

The label of a system differs from that of other articles, among other things, by the fact that it cheats not only the buyer but often also the seller. Quesnay himself and his immediate disciples believed in their feudal shop-sign. So do our grammarians even this day and hour. But as a matter of fact the system of the physiocrats is the first systematic conception of capitalist production. The representative of industrial capital—the class of tenants—directs the entire economic movement. Agriculture is carried on capitalistically, that is to say, it is the enterprise of a capitalist farmer on a large scale; the direct cultivator of the soil is the wage-labourer. Production creates not only articles of use but also their value; its compelling motive is the procurement of surplus-value, whose birth-place is the sphere of production, not of circulation. Among the three classes which figure as the vehicles of the social process of reproduction brought about by the circulation, the immediate exploiter of 'productive' labour, the producer of surplus-value, [Marx analyses Quesnay's *Tableau Économique* in greater detail in his *Theories of Surplus-Value* (see English edition: Karl Marx, *Theories of Surplus-Value* [Volume IV of Capital], Part I, Moscow, 1963, pp. 299-333 and 367-69).—*Ed.*] the capitalist farmer, is distinguished from those who merely appropriate the surplus-value.

The capitalist character of the physiocratic system excited opposition even during its florescence: on the one side it was challenged by Linguet and Mably, on the other by the champions of the small freeholders.

Adam Smith's retrogression[2] in the analysis of the process of reproduction is so much the more remarkable because he not only elaborates upon Quesnay's correct analyses, generalising his '*avances primitives*' and '*avances annuelles*' for instance and calling them respectively 'fixed' and 'circulating' capital[3], but even relapses in spots entirely into physiocratic errors. For instance in order to demonstrate that the farmer produces more value than any other sort of capitalist, he says:

> 'No equal capital puts into motion a greater quantity of productive labour than that of the farmer. Not only his labouring servants, but his labouring cattle are productive labourers.' (Fine compliment for the labouring servants!) 'In agriculture too nature *labours* along with man; and though *her labour costs no expense*, its produce has *its value, as well as that of the most expensive workmen*. The most important operations of agriculture seem intended not so much to increase, though they do that too, as to direct the fertility of nature towards the production of the plants most profitable to man. A field overgrown with briars and brambles may frequently produce as great a quantity of vegetables as the best cultivated vineyard or corn field. Planting and tillage frequently regulate more

than they animate the active fertility of nature; and after all their labour, a great part of the work always remains to be done by her. The labourers and labouring cattle (*sic*!), therefore, employed in agriculture, not only occasion, like the workmen in manufactures, the reproduction of a value equal to their own consumption, or to the capital which employs them, together with its owners' profits; but of a much greater value. Over and above the capital of the farmer and all its profits, they regularly occasion the reproduction of the rent of the landlord. This rent may be considered as the produce of those powers of nature the use of which the landlord lends to the farmer. It is greater or smaller according to the supposed extent of those powers, or, in other words, according to the supposed natural or improved fertility of the land. It is the work of nature which remains after deducting or compensating everything which can be regarded as the work of man. It is seldom less than a fourth, and frequently more than a third of the whole produce. No equal quantity of productive labour employed in manufactures can ever occasion so great a reproduction. In them nature does nothing; man does all; and the reproduction must always be in proportion to the strength of the agents that occasion it. The capital employed in agriculture, therefore, not only puts into motion a greater quantity of productive labour than any equal capital employed in manufactures, but in proportion too to the quantity of productive labour which it employs, it adds a much greater value to the annual produce of the land and labour of the country, to the real wealth and revenue of its inhabitants.' (Book II, Ch. 5, p. 242.)

Adam Smith says in Book II, Ch. 1:

> 'The whole value of the seed, too, is properly a fixed capital.'

Here, then, capital equals capital-value; it exists in a 'fixed' form.

> 'Though it (the seed) goes backwards and forwards between the ground and the granary, it never changes masters, and therefore does not properly circulate. The farmer makes his profit, not by its sale, but by its increase.' (p. 186.)

The absurdity of the thing lies here in the fact that Smith does not, like Quesnay before him, see the re-appearance of the value of constant capital in a renewed form, and hence fails to see an important element of the process of reproduction, but merely offers one more illustration, and a wrong one at that, of his distinctions between circulating and fixed capital. In Smith's translation of '*avances primitives*' and '*avances annuelles*' as 'fixed capital' and 'circulating capital,' the progress consists in the term 'capital,' the concept of which is generalised, and becomes independent of the special consideration for the 'agricultural' sphere of application of the physiocrats; the retrogression consists in the fact that 'fixed' and 'circulating' are regarded as the overriding distinction, and are so maintained.

Section II. *Adam Smith*

1. Smith's General Points of View

Adam Smith says in Book I, Ch. 6, page 42:

> 'In every society the price of every commodity finally resolves itself into some one or other, or all of those three parts (wages, profit, rent); and in every improved society, all the three enter more or less, as component parts, into the price of the far greater part of commodities.'[4]

Or, as he continues, page 43:

> 'Wages, profit, and rent, are the *three original sources* of all revenue as well as of *all exchangeable value*.'

Below we shall discuss in greater detail this doctrine of Adam Smith concerning 'the component parts of the price of commodities,' or of 'all exchangeable value.'

He says furthermore:

> 'Since this is the case, it has been observed, with regard to every particular commodity, taken separately; it must be so with regard to all the commodities which compose the *whole annual produce* of the land and labour of every country, taken complexly. The *whole price or exchangeable value* of that annual produce, must *resolve* itself into the same three parts, and *be parcelled out* among the different inhabitants of the country, either as the *wages* of their labour, the *profits* of their stock, or the *rent* of their land. (Book II, Ch. 2, p. 190.)

After Adam Smith has thus resolved the price of all commodities individually, as well as 'the whole price or exchangeable value ... of the annual produce of the land and labour of every country,' into wages, profit and rent, the three sources of revenue for wage-labourers, capitalists, and landowners, he must needs smuggle in a fourth element by circuitous route, namely the element of capital. This is accomplished by drawing a distinction between gross and net revenue:

> 'The *gross* revenue of all the inhabitants of a great country comprehends the *whole annual produce* of their land and labour; the *neat* revenue, what remains free to them *after deducting the expense of maintaining*; first, their *fixed*; and secondly, their *circulating capital*; or what, without encroaching upon their capital, they can place in their stock reserved for immediate consumption, or spend upon their subsistence, conveniences, and amusements. Their real wealth too is in proportion, not to their gross, but to their neat revenue.' (*Ibid*., p. 190.)

On this we comment as follows:

1. Adam Smith expressly deals here only with simple reproduction, not reproduction on an extended scale, or accumulation. He speaks only of expenses for 'maintaining' the capital in operation. The 'neat' income is equal to that portion of the annual product, whether of society or of the individual capitalist, which can pass into the 'fund for consumption,' but the size of this fund must not 'encroach upon capital' in operation. One portion of the value of both the individual and the social product, then, is resolved neither into wages nor into profit nor into rent, but into capital.
2. Adam Smith flees from his own theory by means of a play upon words, the distinction between 'gross and neat revenue.' The individual capitalist as well as the entire capitalist class, or the so-called nation, receive in place of the capital consumed in production a commodity-product whose value—it can be represented by the proportional parts of this product—replaces on the one hand the expended capital-value and thus forms an income, or still more literally, revenue (*revenue*, pp. of *revenir*—to come back), but, *nota bene*, a revenue upon capital, or income upon capital; on the other hand components of value which are 'parcelled out among the different inhabitants of the country, either as the wages of their labour, the profits of their stock, or the rent of their land', a thing commonly called income. Hence the value of the entire product constitutes somebody's income—either of the individual capitalist or of the whole country, but it is on the one hand an income upon capital, and on the other a 'revenue' different from the latter. Consequently, the thing which is eliminated in the analysis of the value of the commodity into its component parts is brought back through a side door—the ambiguity of the word 'revenue.' But only such value constituents of the product

can be 'taken in' as already exist in it. If the *capital* is to come in as revenue, capital must first have been expended.

Adam Smith says furthermore:

> 'The lowest ordinary rate of profit must always be something more than what is sufficient to compensate the occasional losses to which every employment of stock is exposed. It is this surplus only which is neat or clear profit.'

[What capitalist understands by profit, necessary expenditure of capital?]

> 'What is called gross profit comprehends frequently, not only this surplus, but what is retained for compensating such extraordinary losses.' (Book I, Ch. 9, p. 72.)

This means nothing else than that a part of the surplus-value, considered as a part of the gross profit, must form an insurance-fund for the production. This insurance-fund is created by a portion of the surplus-labour, which to that extent produces capital directly, that is to say, the fund intended for reproduction. As regards the expense for 'maintaining' the fixed capital, etc. (see the above quotations), the replacement of the consumed fixed capital by a new one is not a new outlay of capital, but only a renewal of the old capital-value in new form. And as far as the repair of the fixed capital is concerned, which Adam Smith counts likewise among the costs of maintenance, this expense goes in with the price of the capital advance. The fact that the capitalist, instead of having to invest this all at one time invests it gradually, as required, during the functioning of the capital, and can invest it out of profits already pocketed, does not change the source of this profit. The value constituent of which it consists proves only that the labourer delivers surplus-labour for the insurance-fund as well as for the repair fund.

Adam Smith then tells us that one should exclude from the net revenue, i.e., from the revenue in its specific meaning, the entire fixed capital, and also the entire portion of the circulating capital which is required for the maintenance and repair of the fixed capital, and for its renewal, in fact all capital not in a bodily form intended for the consumption-fund.

> 'The whole expense of maintaining the fixed capital, must evidently be excluded from the neat revenue of the society. Neither the materials necessary for supporting their useful machines and instruments of trade ... nor the produce of the labour necessary for fashioning those materials into the proper form, can ever make a part of it. The *price* of that labour may indeed make a part of it; as the workmen so employed may place the whole value of their wages in their stock reserved for immediate consumption. But in other sorts of labour, both the *price* [i.e., the wages paid for this labour] and the *produce* [in which this labour is incorporated] go to this stock, the price to that of the workmen, the produce to that of other people, whose subsistence, conveniences, and amusements, are augmented by the labour of those workmen.' (Book II, Ch. 2, pp. 190, 191.)

Adam Smith comes here upon a very important distinction between the labourers employed in the production of *means of production* and those employed in the immediate production of *articles of consumption*. The value of the commodities produced by the first-named contains a constituent part which is equal to the sum of the wages, i.e., equal to the value of the part of capital invested in the purchase of labour-power. This part of value exists bodily as a certain quota of the means of production produced by the labourers. The money received by them as wages is their revenue, but their labour has not produced any goods which are consumable, either for themselves or for others. Hence these products are not an element of that part of the annual product which is intended to form a social consumption-fund, in which alone a 'neat revenue' can be realised. Adam Smith forgets to add here that the same thing that applies to wages is also true of that constituent of the value of the means of production which, being surplus-value, forms the revenues (first and foremost) of the industrial capitalist under the categories of profit and rent. These value-components likewise exist in means of production, articles which cannot be consumed. They cannot raise articles of consumption produced by the second kind of labourers in a quantity corresponding to their price until they have been converted into money; only then can they transfer those articles to the individual consumption-fund of their owners. But so much the more should Adam Smith have seen that that part of the value of the annually begotten means of production which is equal to the value of the means of production functioning within this sphere of production—the means of production with which means of production are made—hence a portion of value equal to the value of the constant capital employed here, cannot possibly be a value constituent forming revenue, not only on account of the bodily form in which it exists, but also on account of its functioning as capital.

With regard to the second kind of labourers—who directly produce articles of consumption—Adam Smith's definitions are not quite exact. For he says that in these kinds of labour, both the price of labour and the product '**go to**' the stock reserved for immediate consumption,

> 'the *price*' (i.e., the money received in wages) 'to that of the *workmen*, the *produce* to **that of *other people***, whose subsistence, conveniences and amusements, are augmented by the labour of these workmen.'

But the labourer cannot live on the '*price*' of his labour, the money in which his wages are paid; he realises this money by buying articles of consumption with it. These may in part consist of classes of commodities produced by himself. On the other hand his own product may be such as goes only into the consumption of the exploiters of labour.

After Adam Smith has thus entirely excluded the fixed capital from the 'net revenue' of a country, he continues:

> 'But though the whole expense of maintaining the fixed capital is thus necessarily excluded from the neat revenue of the society, it is not the same case with that of maintaining the circulating capital. Of the four parts of which this latter capital is composed, money, provisions, materials, and finished work, the three last, it has already been observed, are regularly withdrawn from it, and placed either in the fixed capital of the society, or in their stock reserved for immediate consumption. Whatever portion of those consumable goods is not employed in maintaining the former' [the fixed capital] 'goes all to the latter' [the fund for immediate consumption], 'and makes a part of the neat revenue of the society. The maintenance of those three parts of the circulating capital, therefore, withdraws no portion of the annual produce from the neat revenue of the society, besides what is necessary for maintaining the fixed capital.' Book II, Ch. 2, p. 192.)

It is sheer tautology to say that that portion of the circulating capital which does not serve for the production of means of production goes into that of articles of consumption, in other words, into that part of the annual product which is intended to form society's consumption-fund. However, the immediately following passage is important:

> 'The circulating capital of a society is in this respect different from that of an individual. That of an individual is totally excluded from making any part of his neat revenues, which must consist altogether in his profits. But though the circulating capital of every individual makes a part of that of the society to which he belongs, it is not upon that account totally excluded from making a part likewise of their neat revenue. Though the whole goods in a merchant's shop must by no means be placed in his own stock reserved for immediate consumption, they may in that of other people, who, from a revenue

derived form other funds, may regularly replace their value to him, together with its profits, without occasioning any diminution either of his capital or of theirs.' (*Ibid.*)

And so we learn hear that:

1. Just as the fixed capital, and the circulating capital required for its reproduction (he forgets the function) and maintenance, are totally excluded from the *net* revenue of every individual capitalist, which can consist only of his profit, so is the circulating capital employed in the production of articles of consumption. Hence that portion of his commodity-product which replaces his capital cannot resolve itself into constituents of value which form any revenue for him.
2. The circulating capital of each individual capitalist constitutes a part of society's circulating capital the same as every individual fixed capital.
3. The circulating capital of society, while representing only the sum of the individual circulating capitals, has a character different from that of the circulating capital of every individual capitalist. The latter circulating capital can never form a part *of his own revenue*; however a portion of the first-named circulating capital (namely that consisting of consumable goods) may at the same time form a portion of the *revenue of society* or, as he had expressed it above, it must not necessarily reduce the net revenue of society by a portion of the annual product. Indeed, that which Adam Smith here calls circulating capital consists of the annually produced commodity-capital, which is thrown into circulation annually by the capitalists producing articles of consumption. This entire annual commodity product of theirs consists of consumable goods and therefore forms the fund in which the net revenues of society (including wages) are realised or expended. Instead of choosing for his illustration the goods in a merchant's shop, Adam Smith should have selected the masses of goods stored away in the warehouses of the industrial capitalists.

Now if Adam Smith had welded together the snatches of thought which forced themselves upon him at first in the study of the reproduction of that which he calls fixed, and now of that which he calls circulating capital, he would have arrived at the following result:

I. The annual product of society consists of two departments: one of them comprises the means of production, the other the articles of consumption. Each must be treated separately.

II. The aggregate value of that part of the annual product which consists of *means of production* is divided as follows: One portion of the value represents only the value of the means of production consumed in the fabrication of these means of production; it is but capital-value re-appearing in a renewed form; another portion is equal to the value of the capital laid out in labour-power, or equal to the sum of wages paid by the capitalists in this sphere of production. Finally, a third portion of value is the source of profits, including ground-rent, of the industrial capitalists in this category.

The first constituent part, according to Adam Smith the reproduced portion of the fixed capital of all the individual capitalists employed in this first section, is 'totally excluded from making any part of the neat revenue,' either of the individual capitalist or of society. It always functions as capital, never as revenue. To that extent the 'fixed capital' of every individual capitalist is in no way different from the fixed capital of society. But the other portions of value of the annual product of society consisting of means of production—portions of value which therefore exist in aliquot parts of this aggregate quantity of means of production—form indeed simultaneously *revenues for all agents engaged in this production*, wages for the labourers, profits and ground-rents for the capitalists. But they form *capital*, not revenue, *for society*, although the annual product of society consists only of the sums of the products of the individual capitalists who belong to that society. By nature they are generally fit to function only as means of production, and even those which, if need be, might be able to function as articles of consumption are intended for service as raw or auxiliary materials of new production. But they serve as such—hence as capital—not in the hands of their producers, but in those of their users, namely:

III. The capitalists of the second department, the direct producers of *articles of consumption*. They replace for these capitalists the capital consumed in the production of articles of consumption (so far as this capital is not converted into labour-power, and hence is not the sum of the wages of the labourers of this second department), while this consumed capital, which now exists in the form of articles of the consumption in the hands of the capitalist producing them—socially speaking—in its turn *forms the consumption-fund in which the capitalists and labourers of the first department realise their revenue.*

If Adam Smith had continued his analysis to this point, but little would have been lacking for the solution of the whole problem. He almost hit the nail on the head, for he had already observed that certain value-parts of *one* kind (means of production) of the commodity-capitals constituting the total annual product of society indeed form revenue for the individual labourers and capitalists engaged in their production, but do not form a constituent part of the revenue of society; while a value-part of the *other* kind (articles of consumption), although representing capital-value for its individual owners, the capitalists engaged in this sphere of investment, is only a part of the social revenue.

But this much is evident from the foregoing:

First: Although the social capital is only equal to the sum of the individual capitals and for this reason the annual commodity-product (or commodity-capital) of society is equal to the sum of commodity-products of these individual capitals; and although therefore the analysis of the value of the commodities into its component parts, valid for every individual commodity-capital, must also be valid for the commodity-capital of all society—and actually proves valid in the end—the form of appearance which these component parts assume in the aggregate social process of reproduction is *different*.

Second: Even on the basis of simple reproduction there takes place not merely a production of wages (variable capital) and surplus-value, but direct production of new constant capital-value, although the working-day consists of only two parts, one in which the labourer replaces the variable capital, in fact producing an equivalent for the purchase of his labour-power, and another in which he produces surplus-value (profit, rent, etc.).

The daily labour which is expended in the reproduction of means of production—and whose value is composed of wages and surplus-value—realises itself in new means of production which replace the constant part of capital laid out in the production of articles of consumption.

The main difficulties, the greater part of which has been solved in the preceding text, are not encountered in studying accumulation but simple reproduction. For this reason, Adam Smith (Book II) and Quesnay (*Tableau Économique*) before him make simple reproduction their starting-point, whenever it is a question of the movement of the annual product of society and its reproduction through circulation.

2. Adam Smith Resolves Exchange Value into v + s

Adam Smith's dogma that the price, or '**exchangeable value**,' of any single commodity—and therefore of all commodities in the aggregate constituting the annual product of society (he rightly assumes capitalist production everywhere)—is made up of three '**component parts**,' or '**resolves itself into**' wages, profit, and rent, can be reduced to this: that the commodity-value is equal to v + s, i.e., equal to the value of the advanced variable capital plus the surplus-value. And we may undertake this reduction of profit and rent to a common unit called s with the express permission of Adam Smith, as shown by the following quotations, in which we at first leave aside all minor points, i.e., any apparent or real deviation from the dogma that commodity-value consists exclusively of those elements which we call v + s.

In manufacture:

> 'The value which the workmen add to the materials ... resolves itself ... into two parts, of which the one pays their wages, the other the profits of their employer upon the whole stock of materials and wages which he advanced.' (Book I, Ch. 6, p. 41.)
>
> 'Though the manufacturer has his wages advanced to him by his master, he, in reality, costs him no expense, the value of those wages being generally **restored**, together with a profit, in the improved value of the subject upon which his labour is bestowed.' (Book II, Ch. 3, p. 221.)

That portion of the **stock** which is laid out

> 'in maintaining productive hands ... after having served in the function of a capital to him (the employer) ...constitutes a revenue to them' (the labourers). (Book II, Ch. 3 p. 223.)

Adam Smith says explicitly in the chapter just quoted:

> 'The whole annual produce of the land and labour of every country ... **naturally** divides itself into two parts. One of them, and frequently the largest, is in the first place, destined for replacing a capital, or for renewing the provisions, materials, and finished work, which had been withdrawn from a capital; the other for constituting a revenue either to the owner of this capital, as the *profit of his stock*; or to some other person, as the rent of his *land*.' (p. 222.)

Only one part of the capital, so Adam Smith just informed us, forms at the same time a revenue for somebody, namely that which is invested in the purchase of productive hands. This portion—the variable capital—first 'serves in the function of a capital' in the hands of its employer and for him and then it 'constitutes a revenue' for the productive labourer himself. The capitalist transforms a portion of his capital-value into labour-power and precisely thereby into variable capital; it is only due to this transformation that not alone this portion of capital but his entire capital functions as industrial capital. The labourer—the seller of labour-power—receives its value in the form of wages. In his hands labour-power is but a saleable commodity, a commodity by the sale of which he lives, which therefore is the sole source of his revenue; labour-power functions as a variable capital only in the hands of its buyer, the capitalist, and the capitalist advances its purchase price only apparently, since its value has been previously supplied to him by the labourer.

After Adam Smith has thus shown that the value of a product in manufacture is equal to v + s (s standing for the profit of the capitalist), he tells us that in agriculture the labourers besides

> 'the reproduction of a value equal to their own consumption, or to the [variable] capital which employs them, together with its owners' profits ...'—furthermore, 'over and above the capital of the farmer and all its *profits* regularly occasion the reproduction of the *rent* of the landlord.' (Book II, Ch. 5, p. 243.)

The fact that the rent passes into the hands of the landlord is wholly immaterial for the question under consideration. Before it can pass into his hands, it must be in those of the farmer, i.e., of the industrial capitalist. It must form a component part of the value of the product before it becomes a revenue for anyone. Rent as well as profit are therefore, according to Adam Smith himself, but component parts of surplus-value and these the productive labourer reproduces continually together with his own wages, i.e., with the value of the variable capital. Hence rent and profit are parts of the surplus-value s, and thus, with Adam Smith, the price of all commodities resolves itself into v + s.

The dogma that the price of all commodities (hence also of the annual commodity-product) resolves itself into wages plus profit plus ground-rent, assumes even in the intermittent esoteric constituents of Smith's work the form that the value of every commodity, hence also that of society's annual commodity-product, is equal to v + s, or equal to the capital-value laid out in labour-power and continually reproduced by the labourers, plus the surplus-value added by the labourers through their work.

This final result of Adam Smith reveals to us at the same time—see further down—the source of his one-sided analysis of the component parts into which the value of a commodity resolves sources of revenue for different classes engaged in production has nothing to do with the determination of the magnitude of each of these component parts and of the sum of their values.

All kinds of *quid pro quo*'s are jumbled together when Adam Smith says:

> 'Wages, profit, and rent, are the three original sources of all revenue as well as of all exchangeable value. All other revenue is ultimately derived from some one or other of these.' (Book I, Ch. 6, p. 48.)

1. All member of society not directly engaged in reproduction, with or without labour, can obtain their share of the annual commodity-product—in other words, their articles of consumption—primarily out of the hands of those classes to which the product first accrues—productive labourers, industrial capitalists, and landlords. To that extent their revenues are materially derived from wages (of the productive labourers), profit, and rent, and appear therefore as derivative vis-à-vis those primary revenues. But on the other hand the recipients of these revenues, derived in this sense, draw them by virtue of their social functions—as a king, priest, professor, prostitute, soldier, etc., and they may, therefore, regard these functions as the original sources of their revenue.
2. —and here Adam Smith's ridiculous blunder reaches its climax. After starting by correctly defining the component parts of the value of the commodities and the sum of the value-product incorporated in them, and then demonstrating how these component parts form so many different sources of revenue,[5] after thus deriving the revenues from the value, he proceeds in the opposite direction—and this remains the predominant conception with him—and turns the revenues from '**component parts**' into '*original sources* of all exchangeable value,' thereby throwing the doors wide open to vulgar economy. (See our Roscher. [Marx has in mind W. Roscher's *System der Vokswirtschaft. Band I: Die Grundlagen der Nationalökonomie*. Dritte, vermehrte und verbesserte Auflage. Stuttgart und Augsburg, 1858.—*Ed.*])

3. The Constant Part of Capital

Let us now see how Adam Smith tries to spirit the constant part of the capital-value away from the commodity-value.

> 'In the price of corn, for example, one part pays the rent of the landlord.'

The origin of this constituent of value has no more to do with the circumstance that it is paid to the landlord and forms a revenue for him in the shape of rent than the origin of the other constituents of value has to do with the fact that as profit and wages they form sources of revenue.

> 'Another [portion] pays the wages or maintenance of the labourers' ['and labouring cattle,' he adds] 'employed in producing it, and the third pays the profit of the farmer. These three parts seem' [they seem indeed] 'either immediately or ultimately to make up the whole price of corn.'[6]

This entire price, i.e., the determination of its magnitude, is absolutely independent of its distribution among three kinds of people.

> 'A fourth part, it may perhaps be thought, is necessary for replacing the stock of the farmer, or for compensating the wear and tear of his labouring cattle, and other instruments of husbandry. But it must be considered that the price of any instrument of husbandry, such as a labouring horse, is itself made up of the same three parts: the rent of the land upon which he is reared, the labour of tending and rearing him, and the profits of the farmer who advances both the rent of this land, and the wages of this labour. Though the price of the corn, therefore, may pay the price as well as the maintenance of the horse, the whole price still resolves itself either immediately or ultimately into the same three parts of rent, labour' (he means wages), 'and profit.' (Book I, Ch. 6, p. 42.)

This is verbatim all that Adam Smith has to say in support of his astonishing doctrine. His proof consists simply in the repetition of the same assertion. He admits, for instance, that the price of corn does not only consist of v + s, but also of the price of the means of production consumed in the production of corn, hence of a capital-value not invested in labour-power by the farmer. But, he says, the prices of all these means of production resolve themselves into v + s, the same as the price of corn. He forgets, however, to add: and, moreover, into the prices of the means of production consumed in their own creation. He refers us from one branch of production to another, and from that to a third. The contention that the entire price of commodities resolves itself 'immediately' or '**ultimately**' into v + s would not be a hollow subterfuge only if he were able to demonstrate that the commodities whose price resolves itself immediately into c (price of consumed means of production) + v + s, are ultimately compensated by commodities which completely replace those 'consumed means of production,' and which are themselves produced by the mere outlay of variable capital, i.e., by a mere investment of capital in labour-power. The price of these last commodity-products would then be immediately v + s. Consequently the price of the former, c + v + s, where c stands for the constant part of capital, would also be ultimately resolvable into v + s. Adam Smith himself did not believe that he had furnished such a proof by his example of the collectors of **Scotch pebbles**, who, according to him 1) do not generate surplus-value of any description, but produce only their own wages, and 2) do not employ any means of production (they do, however, employ them, such as baskets, sacks, and other containers for carrying the pebbles).

We have already seen above that Adam Smith himself later on overthrows his own theory, without however being conscious of his contradictions. But their source is to be found precisely in his scientific premises. The capital converted into labour produces a greater value than its own. How? Says Adam Smith: by the labourers imparting during the process of production to the things on which they work a value which forms not only an equivalent for their own purchase price, but also a surplus-value (profit and rent) apportioned not to them but to their employers. That is all they accomplish, and all they can accomplish. And what is true of the industrial labour of one day is true of the labour set in motion by the entire capitalist class during one year. Hence the aggregate mass of the annual value produced by society can resolve itself only into v + s, into an equivalent by which the labourers replace the capital-value expended for the purchase of their own labour-power, and into an additional value which they must deliver over and above this to their employers. But these two elements of commodity-value form at the same time sources of revenue for the various classes engaged in reproduction: the first is the source of wages, the revenue of the labourers; the second that of surplus-value, a portion of which is retained by the industrial capitalist in the form of profit, while another is given up by him as rent, the revenue of the landlord. Where, then, should another portion of value come from, when the annual value-product contains no other elements than v + s? We are proceeding here from simple reproduction. Since the entire quantity of annual labour resolves itself into labour needed for the reproduction of the capital-value laid out in labour-power, and into labour needed for the creation of surplus-value, where should the labour for the production of a capital-value not laid out in labour-power come from?

The case is as follows:

1. Adam Smith determines the value of a commodity by the amount of labour which the wage-labourer adds to the subject of labour. He calls it literally 'materials,' since he is dealing with manufacture, which itself is working up products of labour. But this does not alter the matter. The value which the labourer adds to a thing (and this '**adds**' is the expression of Adam Smith) is entirely independent of whether or not this object to which value is added had itself any value *before* this addition. The labourer therefore produces a value in the form of a commodity. This, according to Adam Smith, is partly an equivalent for his wages, and this part, then, is determined by the magnitude of value of his wages; depending on that magnitude he has to add labour in order to produce or reproduce a value equal to that of his wages. On the other hand, the labourer adds more labour over and above the limit so drawn, and this creates surplus-value for the capitalist employing him. Whether this surplus-value remains entirely in the hands of the capitalist or parts of it are yielded by him to third persons, does not in the least alter either the qualitative (that is at all surplus-value) or the quantitative (magnitude) determination of the surplus-value added by the wage-labourer. It is value the same as any other portion of the value of the product, but it differs in that the labourer has not received any equivalent for it, nor will receive any later on, in that, on the contrary, this value is appropriated by the capitalist without any equivalent. The total value of a commodity is determined by the quantity of labour expended by the labourer in its production; one portion of this total value is determined by the fact that it is equal to the value of the wages, i.e., an equivalent for them. The second part, the surplus-value, is, therefore, necessarily likewise determined as equal to the total value of the product minus that part of its value which is equivalent to the wages; hence equal to the excess of the value produced in the making of the commodity over that part of the value contained in it which is an equivalent for his wages.
2. That which is true of a commodity produced in some individual industrial establishment by any individual labourer is true of the annual product of all branches of business as a whole. That which is true of the day's work of some individual productive labourer is true of the year's work set in motion by the entire class of productive labourers. It 'fixes' (Adam Smith's expression) in the annual product of a total value determined by the quantity of the annual labour expended, and this total value resolves itself into one portion determined by that part of the annual labour wherewith the working-class creates an equivalent of its annual wages, in fact, these wages themselves; and into another portion determined by the additional annual labour by which the labourer creates surplus-value for the capitalist class. The annual value-product contained in the annual product consists therefore of but two elements: namely, the equivalent of the annual wages received by the working-class, and the

surplus-value annually provided for the capitalist class. Now, the annual wages are the revenue of the working-class, and the annual quantity of surplus-value the revenue of the capitalist class; hence both of them represent the relative shares in the annual fund for consumption (this view is correct when describing simple reproduction) and are realised in it. There is, then, no room left anywhere for the constant capital-value, for the reproduction of the capital functioning in the form of means of production. And Adam Smith states explicitly in the introduction to his work that all portions of the value of commodities which serve as revenue coincide with the annual product of labour intended for the social fund for consumption:

> 'To explain in what has consisted the revenue of the great body of the people, or what has been the nature of those funds, which, in different ages and nations, have supplied their annual consumption, is the object of these first Four Books.' (p. 12.)

And in the very first sentence of the introduction we read:

> 'The annual labour of every nation is the fund, which originally supplies it with all the necessaries and conveniences of life which it annually consumes, and which consists always either in the immediate produced of that labour, or in what is purchased with that produce from other nations.' (p. 11.)

Now Adam Smith's first mistake consists in equating the *value* of the *annual product* to the *newly produced annual value*. The latter is *only* the product of labour of the past year, the former includes besides all elements of value consumed in the making of the annual product, but which *were produced in the preceding and partly even earlier years*: means of production whose value merely *re-appears*—which, as far as their value is concerned, have been neither produced nor reproduced by the labour expended in the past year. By this confusion Adam Smith spirits away the constant portion of the value of the annual product. This confusion rests on another error in his fundamental conception: He does not distinguish the two-fold nature of labour itself: of labour which creates value by expending labour-power, and of labour as concrete, useful work, which creates articles of use (use-values). The total quantity of the commodities fabricated annually, in other words, the *total annual product* is the product of the *useful* labour active during the past year; it is only due to the fact that socially employed labour was spent in a ramified system of useful kinds of labour that all these commodities exist; it is due to this fact alone that the value of the means of production consumed in the production of commodities and reappearing in a new bodily form is preserved in their total value. The total *annual product*, then, is the result of the *useful* labour expended during the year; but only a part of the *value* of the annual *product* has been created during the year; this portion is the annual *value-product*, in which the quantity of labour set in motion during the year is represented.

Hence, if Adam Smith says in the passage just cited:

> 'The annual labour of every nation is the fund which originally supplies it with all the necessaries and conveniences of life which it annually consumes, etc.,'

he takes the one-sided standpoint of solely useful labour, which has indeed given all these means of subsistence their consumable form. But he forgets that this was impossible without the assistance of instruments and subjects of labour supplied by former years, and that, therefore, the 'annual labour,' while it created value, did not create all the value of the products fabricated by it; that the value newly produced is smaller than the value of the product.

While we cannot reproach Adam Smith for going in this analysis no farther than all his successors (although a step in the right direction could already be discerned among the physiocrats), he subsequently gets lost in a chaos and this mainly because his 'esoteric' conception of the value of commodities in general is constantly contravened by exoteric conceptions, which on the whole prevail with him, and yet his scientific instinct permits the esoteric standpoint to re-appear from time to time.

4. Capital and Revenue in Adam Smith

That portion of the value of every commodity (and therefore also of the annual product) which is but an equivalent of the wages, is equal to the capital advanced by the capitalist for labour-power; i.e., is equal to the variable portion of the total capital advanced. The capitalist recovers this portion of the total capital through a portion of the newly produced value of the commodities supplied by the wage-labourers. Whether the variable capital is advanced in the sense that the capitalist pays the labourer in money for his share in a product which is not yet ready for sale or which, though ready, has not yet been sold by the capitalist, or whether he pays him with money already obtained by the sale of commodities previously supplied by the labourer, or whether he has drawn this money in advance by means of credit—in all these cases the capitalist expends variable capital, which passes into the hands of the labourers in the form of money, and on the other hand he possesses the equivalent of this capital-value in that portion of the value of his commodities in which the labourer has produced anew his share of its total value, in other words, in which he has produced the value of his own wages. Instead of giving him this portion of the value in the bodily form of his own product, the capitalist pays it to him in money. For the capitalist the variable portion of his advanced capital-value now exists in the form of commodities, while the labourer has received the equivalent for his sold labour-power in the form of money.

Now while that portion of the capital advanced by the capitalist, which has been converted by the purchase of labour-power into variable capital, functions in the process of production itself as operative labour-power and by the expenditure of this power is produced anew as a new value, in the form of commodities, i.e., is reproduced—hence a reproduction, or new production, of advanced capital-value—the labourer spends the value, or price, of his sold labour-power on means of subsistence, on means for the reproduction of his labour-power. An amount of money equal to the variable capital forms his income, hence his revenue, which lasts only so long as he can sell his labour-power to the capitalist.

The commodity of the wage-labourer—his labour power—serves as a commodity only to the extent that it is incorporated in the capital of the capitalist, acts as capital; on the other hand the capital expended by the capitalist as money-capital in the purchase of labour-power functions as a revenue in the hands of the seller of labour-power, the wage labourer.

Various processes of circulation and production intermingle here, which Adam Smith does not distinguish.

First: Acts pertaining to the process of *circulation*. The labourer sells his commodity—labour-power—to the capitalist; the money with which the capitalist buys it is from his point of view money invested for the production of surplus-value, hence money-capital; it is not spent but advanced. (This is the real meaning of 'advance'—the *avance* of the physiocrats—no matter where the capitalist gets the money. Every value which the capitalist pays out for the purposes of the productive process is advanced from his point of view, regardless of whether this takes place before or *post festum*; it is advanced to the process of production itself.) The same takes place here as in every other sale of commodities: The seller gives away a use-value (in this case his labour-power) and receives its value (realises its price) in money; the buyer gives away his money and receives in return the commodity itself—in this case labour-power.

Second: In the process of *production* the purchased labour-power now forms a part of the functioning capital, and the labourer himself serves here merely as a special bodily form of this capital, distinguished from its elements existing in the bodily form of means of production. During the process, by expending his labour-power, the labourer adds value to the means of production which he converts into products equal to the value of his labour-power (exclusive of surplus-value); he therefore reproduces for the capitalist in the form of commodities that portion of his capital which has been, or has to be, advanced by him for wages, produces for him an equivalent of the latter; hence he reproduces for the capitalist that capital which the latter can 'advance' once more for the purchase of labour-power.

Third: In the sale of a commodity one portion of its selling price replaces the variable capital advanced by the capitalist, whereby on the one hand he is enabled anew to buy labour-power, and the labourer on the other to sell it anew.

In all purchases and sales of commodities—so far as only these transactions are under discussion—it is quite immaterial what becomes of the proceeds the seller receives for his commodities, and what becomes of the bought articles of use in the hands of the buyer. Hence, so far as the mere process of circulation is concerned, it is quite immaterial that the labour-power bought by the capitalist reproduces capital-value for him, and that on the other hand the money received by the labourer as the purchase-price of his labour-power constitutes his revenue. The magnitude of value of the labourer's article of commerce, his labour-power, is not affected either by its forming 'revenue' for him or by the fact that the use of this article of commerce by the buyer reproduces capital-value for this buyer.

Since the value of labour-power—i.e., the adequate selling price of this commodity—is determined by the quantity of labour required for its reproduction, and this quantity of labour itself is here determined by that needed for the production of the necessary means of subsistence of the labourer, hence for the maintenance of his existence, the wages become the revenue on which the labourer has to live.

It is entirely wrong, when Adam Smith says (p. 223):

> '*That portion of the stock* which is laid out in maintaining productive hands ... after having served in the function of a capital to him [the capitalist] ... constitutes a revenue to them' [the labourers].

The *money* with which the capitalist pays for the labour-power purchased by him 'serves in the function of a capital to him,' since he thereby incorporates labour-power in the material constituents of his capital and thus enables his capital to function altogether as productive capital. We must make this distinction: The labour-power is a *commodity*, not capital, in the hands of the labourer, and it constitutes for him a revenue so long as he can continuously repeat its sale; it functions as capital *after* its sale, in the hands of the capitalist, during the process of production itself. That which here serves twice is labour-power: as a commodity which is sold at its value, in the hands of the labourer; as a power-producing value and use-value, in the hands of the capitalist who has bought it. But the labourer does not receive the money from the capitalist until after he has given him the use of his labour-power, after it has already been realised in the value of the product of labour. The capitalist possesses this value before he pays for it. Hence, it is not the money which functions twice: first, as the money-form of the variable capital, and then as wages. On the contrary it is labour-power which has functioned twice: first, as a *commodity* in the sale of labour-power (in stipulating the amount of wages to be paid, money acts merely as an ideal measure of value and need not even be in the hands of the capitalist); secondly, in the process of production, in which it functions as *capital*, i.e., as an element, in the hands of the capitalist, creating use-value and value. Labour-power already supplied, in the form of commodities, the equivalent which is to be paid to the labourer, before it is paid by the capitalist to the labourer in money-form. Hence the labourer himself creates the fund out of which the capitalist pays him. But this is not all.

The money which the labourer receives is spent by him in order to preserve his labour-power, or—viewing the capitalist class and the working-class in their totality—in order to preserve for the capitalist the instrument by means of which alone he can remain a capitalist.

Thus the continuous purchase and sale of labour-power perpetuates on the one hand labour-power as an element of capital, by virtue of which the latter appears as the creator of commodities, articles of use having value, by virtue of which, furthermore, that portion of capital which buys labour-power is continually restored by labour-power's own product, and consequently the labourer himself constantly creates the fund of capital out of which he is paid. On the other hand, the constant sale of labour-power becomes the source, ever renewing itself, of the maintenance of the labourer and hence his labour-power appears as that faculty through which he secures the revenue by which he lives. Revenue in this case signifies nothing else than a appropriation of values effected by ever repeated sales of a commodity (labour-power), these values serving only for the continual reproduction of the commodity to be sold. And to this extent Smith is right when he says that the portion of the value of the product created by the labourer himself for which the capitalist pays him an equivalent in the form of wages, becomes the source of revenue for the labourer. But this does not alter the nature or magnitude of this portion of the value of the commodity any more than the value of the means of production is changed by the fact that they function as capital-values, or the nature and magnitude of a straight line are changed by the fact that it serves as the base of some triangle or as the diameter of some ellipse. The value of labour-power remains quite as independently definite as that of those means of production. This portion of the value of a commodity neither *consists of* revenue as an independent factor constituting this value-part nor does it *resolve itself* into revenue. While this new value constantly reproduced by the labourer constitutes a source of revenue for him, his revenue conversely is not a constituent of the new value produced by him. The magnitude of the share paid to him of the new value created by him determines the value-magnitude of his revenue, not vice versa. The fact that this part of the newly created value forms a revenue for him, indicates merely what becomes of it, shows the character of its application, and has no more to do with its formation than with that of any other value. If my receipts are ten shillings a week that changes nothing in the *nature* of the value of the ten shillings, nor in the *magnitude* of their value. As in the case of every other commodity so in that of labour-power its value is determined by the amount of this labour is necessary for its reproduction; that the amount of this labour is determined by the value of the labourer's necessary means of subsistence, hence is equal to the labour required for the reproduction of the very conditions of his life—that is peculiar for this commodity (labour-power), but no more peculiar than the fact that the value of labouring cattle is determined by the value of the means of subsistence necessary for its maintenance, i.e., by the amount of human labour necessary to produce these means of subsistence.

But it is this category of 'revenue' which is to blame for all the harmful confusion in Adam Smith. The various kinds of revenue form with him the '**component parts**' of the annually produced, newly created commodity-value, while, vice versa, the two parts into which this commodity-value resolves itself *for the capitalist*—the equivalent of his variable capital advanced in the form of money when purchasing labour, and the other portion of the value, the surplus- value, which likewise belongs to him but did not cost him anything—form sources of revenue. The equivalent of the variable capital is advanced again for labour-power and to that extent forms a revenue for the labourer in the shape of wages; since the other portion, the surplus-value, does not serve to replace any advance of capital for the capitalist, it may be spent by him in articles of consumption (both necessities and luxuries) or consumed as revenue instead of forming capital-value of any description. Commodity-value itself is the preliminary condition of this revenue and its component parts differ, from the point of view of the capitalist, only to the extent that they constitute either an equivalent for an excess *over* the variable capital-value advanced by him. Both of them consist of nothing but labour-power expended during the production of commodities, rendered fluent in labour. They consist of outlay, not income or revenue—of outlay of labour.

In accordance with the *quid pro quo*, by which the revenue becomes the source of commodity-value instead of the commodity-value being the source of revenue, the value of commodities new has the appearance of being 'composed' of the various kinds of revenue; these revenues are determined independently of one another, and the total value of commodities is determined by the addition of the values of these revenues. But now the question is how to determine the value of each of these revenues which are supposed to form commodity-value. In the case of wages it can be done, for wages represent the value of their commodity, labour-power, and this value is determinable (the same as that of all other commodities) by the labour required for the reproduction of this commodity. But surplus-value, or, as Adam Smith has it, its two forms, profit and rent, how are they determined? Here Adam Smith has but empty phrases to offer. At one time he represents wages and surplus-value (or wages and profit) as component parts of the value, or price, of commodities; at another, and almost in the same breath, as parts into which the price of commodities '**resolves itself**'; but this means on the contrary that the commodity-value is the thing given first and that different parts of this given value fall in the form of different revenues to the share of different persons engaged in the productive process. This is, by no means, identical with the notion that value is 'composed' of these three 'component parts.' If I determine the lengths of three different straight lines independently, and then form out of these three lines as 'component parts' a fourth straight line equal to their sum, it is by no means the same procedure as when I have some given straight line before me and for some purpose divide it, 'resolve' it, so to say, into three different parts. In the first case, the length of the line changes throughout with the lengths of the three lines whose sum it is; in the second case, the lengths of the three parts of the line are from the outset limited by the fact that they are parts of a line of given length.

As a matter of fact, if we adhere to that part of Smith's exposition which is correct, namely, that *the value newly created by the annual labour* and contained in the annual social commodity-product (the same as in every individual commodity, or every daily, weekly, etc., product) is equal to the value of the variable capital advanced (i.e., to the value-part intended to purchase new labour-power) plus the surplus-value which the capitalist can realise in means of his individual consumption—simple reproduction being assumed and other circumstances remaining the same; if we furthermore keep in mind that Adam Smith lumps together labour, so far as it creates value and is an expenditure of labour-power, and labour, so far as it creates use value, i.e., is expended in a useful, appropriate manner—then the entire conception amounts to this: The value of every commodity is the product of labour; hence this is also true of the value of the product of the annual labour or of the value of society's annual commodity-product. But, since all labour resolves itself 1) into necessary labour-time, in which the labourer reproduces merely an equivalent for the capital advanced in the purchase of his labour-power, and 2) into surplus-labour, by which he supplies the capitalist with a value for which the latter does not give any equivalent, hence surplus-value, it follows that all commodity value can resolve itself only into these two component parts, so that ultimately it forms a revenue for the working-class in the form of wages, and for the capitalist class in the form of surplus-value. As for the constant capital-value, i.e., the value of the means of production consumed in the creation of the annual product, it cannot be explained how this value gets into that of the new product (except for the phrase that the capitalist charges the buyer with it in the sale of his goods), but **ultimately**, since the means of production are themselves products of labour, this portion of value can, in turn, consist only of an equivalent of the variable capital and of surplus-value, of a product of necessary labour and of surplus-labour. The fact that the values of these means of production function in the hands of their employers as capital-values does not prevent them from having 'originally,' in the hands of others if we go to the bottom of the matter—even though at some previous time—resolved themselves into the same two portions of value, hence into two different sources of revenue.

One point herein is correct: that the matter presents itself differently in the movement of social capital, i.e., of the totality of individual capitals, from the way it presents itself for each individual capital considered separately, hence from the standpoint of each individual capitalist. For the latter the value of commodities resolves itself into 1) a constant element (a fourth one, as Adam Smith says), and 2) the sum of wages and surplus-value, or wages, profit and rent. But from the point of view of society the fourth element of Adam Smith, the constant capital-value, disappears.

5. Recapitulation

The absurd formula that the three revenues, wages, profit and rent, form the three 'component parts' of the value of commodities originates with Adam Smith from the more plausible idea that the value of commodities '**resolves itself**' into these three component parts. This is likewise incorrect, even granted that the value of commodities is divisible only into an equivalent of the consumed labour-power and the surplus-value created by it. But the mistake rests here too on a deeper, a true foundation. Capitalist production is based on the fact that the productive labourer sells his own labour-power, as his commodity, to the capitalist, in whose hands it then functions merely as an element of his productive capital. This transaction, which pertains to circulation—the sale and purchase of labour-power—not only inaugurates the process of production, but also determines implicitly its specific character. The production of a use-value, and even that of a commodity (for this can be carried on also by independent productive labourers), is here only a means of producing absolute and relative surplus-value for a capitalist. For this reason we have seen in the analysis of the process of production that the production of absolute and relative surplus-value determines 1) the duration of the daily labour-process and 2) the entire social and technical configuration of the capitalist process of production. Within this process there is realised the distinction between the mere conservation of value (of the constant capital-value), the actual reproduction of advanced value (equivalent of labour-power), and the production of surplus-value, i.e., of value for which the capitalist has neither advanced an equivalent previously nor will advance one *post festum*.

The appropriation of surplus-value—a value in excess of the equivalent of the value advanced by the capitalist—although inaugurated by the purchase and sale of labour-power, is an act performed within the process of production itself, and forms an essential element of it.

The introductory act, which constitutes an act of circulation—the purchase and sale of labour-power—itself rests on a distribution of the *elements* of production which preceded and presupposed the distribution of the social *products*, namely on the separation of labour-power as a commodity of the labourer from the means of production as the property of non-labourers.

However, this appropriation of surplus-value, or this separation of the production of value into a reproduction of advanced value and a production of new value (surplus-value) which does not replace any equivalent, does not alter in any way the substance of value itself or the nature of the production of value. The substance of value is and remains nothing but expended labour-power—labour independent of the specific, useful character of this expenditure. A serf for instance expends his labour-power for six days, labours for six days, and the fact of this expenditure as such is not altered by the circumstance that he may be working three days for himself, on his own field, and three days for his lord, on the field of the latter. Both his voluntary labour for himself and his forced labour for his lord are equally labour; so far as this labour is considered with reference to the values, or to the useful articles created by it, there is no difference in his six days of labour. The difference refers merely to the different conditions by which the expenditure of his labour-power during both halves of his labour-time of six days is called forth. The same applies to the necessary and surplus-labour of the wage-labourer.

The process of production expires in the commodity. The fact that labour-power was expended in its fabrication now appears as a material property of the commodity, as the property of possessing value. The magnitude of this value is measured by the amount of labour expended; the value of a commodity resolves itself into nothing else besides and is not composed of anything else. If I have drawn a straight line of definite length, I have, to start with, 'produced' a straight line (true, only symbolically, as I know beforehand) by resort to the art of drawing, which is practised in accordance with certain rules (laws) independent of myself. If I divide this line into three sections (which may correspond to a certain problem), every one of these sections remains a straight line, and the entire line, whose sections they are, does not resolve itself by this division into anything different from a straight line, for instance into some kind of curve. Neither can I divide a line of a given length in such a way that the sum of its parts is greater than the undivided line itself; hence the length of the undivided line is not determined by any arbitrarily fixed lengths of its parts. Vice versa, the relative lengths of these parts are limited from the outset by the size of the line whose parts they are.

In this, a commodity produced by a capitalist does not differ in any way from that produced by an independent labourer or by communities of working-people or by slaves. But in the present case the entire product of labour, as well as its entire value, belongs to the capitalist. Like every other producer he has to convert his commodity by sale into money before he can manipulate it further; he must convert it into the form of the universal equivalent.

Let us examine the commodity-product before it is converted into money. It belongs wholly to the capitalist. On the other hand, as a useful product of labour, a use-value, it is entirely the product of a past labour-process. Not so its value. One portion of this value is but the value of the means of production expended in the production of this commodity and re-appearing in a new form. This value has not been produced during the process of production of this commodity, for the means of production possessed this value before the process of production, independently of it; they entered into this process as the vehicles of this value; it is only its form of appearance that has been renewed and altered. This portion of the value of the commodity constitutes for the capitalist an equivalent of the portion of the constant capital-value advanced and consumed in the production of the commodity. It existed previously in the form of means of production; it exists now as a component part of the value of the newly produced commodity. As soon as this commodity has been turned into money, the value now existing in the form of money must be reconverted into means of production, into its original form determined by the process of production and its function in it. Nothing is altered in the character of the value of a commodity by the function of this value as capital.

A second portion of the value of a commodity is the value of the labour-power which the wage-worker sells to the capitalist. It is determined, the same as that of the means of production, independently of the process of production into which labour-power is to enter, and it is fixed in an act of circulation, the purchase and sale of labour-power, before the latter enters the process of production. By means of his function—the expenditure of labour-power—the wage-labourer produces a commodity-value equal to the value which the capitalist has to pay him for the use of his labour-power. He gives this value to the capitalist in the form of a commodity and is paid for it by him in money. That this portion of the commodity-value is for the capitalist but an equivalent for the variable capital which he has to advance in wages does not alter in any way the fact that it is a commodity-value newly created during the process of production and consisting of nothing but what surplus-value consists of, namely, past expenditure of labour-power. Nor is this truth affected by the fact that the value of the labour-power paid by the capitalist to the labourer in the form of wages and assumes the form of a revenue for the labourer, and that not only labour-power is continually reproduced thereby but also the class of wage-labourers as such, and thus the basis of the entire capitalist production.

However, the sum of these two portions of value does not comprise the whole of commodity-value. There remains an excess over both of them—the surplus-value. This, like the portion of value which replaces the variable capital advanced in wages, is a value newly created by the labourer during the process of production—congealed labour. But it does not cost the owner of the entire product, the capitalist, anything. This circumstance actually permits the capitalist to consume the surplus-value entirely as revenue, unless he has to surrender parts of it to other participants—such as ground-rent to the landlord, in which case such portions constitute a revenue of such third persons. This same circumstance was the compelling motive that induced our capitalist to engage at all in the manufacture of commodities. But neither his original benevolent intention of snatching surplus-value, nor its subsequent expenditure as revenue by him or others affects the surplus-value as such. They do not impair the fact that it is congealed unpaid labour, nor the magnitude of this surplus-value, which is determined by entirely different conditions.

However, if Adam Smith wanted to occupy himself, as he did, with the role of the various parts of this value in the total process of reproduction, even while he was investigating the value of commodities, it would be evident that while some particular parts function as revenue, others function just as continually as capital—and consequently, according to his logic, should have been designated as constituent parts of the commodity-value, or parts into which this value resolves itself.

Adam Smith identifies the production of commodities in general with capitalist commodity production; the means of production are to him from the outset 'capital,' labour is from the outset wage-labour, and therefore

> 'the number of useful and productive labourers ... is everywhere in proportion **to the quantity of capital stock which employed in setting them to work**.' (Introduction, p. 12.)

In short, the various factors of the labour-process—both objective and personal—appear from the first with the masks characteristic of the period of capitalist production. The analysis of the value of commodities therefore coincides directly with the consideration of the extent to which this value is, on the one hand, a mere equivalent of capital laid out, and on the other, to what extent it forms 'free' value, value not replacing any advanced capital-value, or surplus-value. Compared from this point of view, parts of commodity-value thus transform themselves imperceptibly into its independent 'component parts,' and finally into the 'sources of all value.' A further conclusion is that commodity-value is composed of, or 'resolves itself' into, revenues of various kinds, so that the revenues do not consist of commodity-values but the commodity-value consists of 'revenues.' As little, however, as the nature of a commodity-value as such, or of money as such, is changed through their functioning as capital-value, just so little is the nature of a commodity-value as capital-value, just so little is the nature of a commodity-value changed on account of its functioning later as a revenue for some particular person. The commodity with which Adam Smith has to deal is from the outset commodity-capital (which comprises surplus-value in addition to the capital-value consumed in the production of the commodity); it is therefore a commodity produced capitalistically, the result of the capitalist process of production. It would have been necessary, then, to analyse first this process, and also the process of self-expansion and of the formation of value, which it includes. Since this process is in its turn premised by the circulation of commodities, its description requires also a preliminary and independent analysis of the commodity. However, even where Adam Smith at times hits 'esoterically' upon the correct thing he always takes into consideration the formation of value only as incidental to the analysis of commodities, i.e., to the analysis of commodity-capital.

Ricardo reproduces the theory of Adam Smith almost verbatim:

> 'It must be understood that all the productions of a country are consumed; but it makes the greatest difference imaginable whether they are consumed by those who reproduced, or by those who do not reproduce another value. When we say that revenue is saved, and added to capital, what we mean is, that the portion of revenue, so said to be added to the capital, is consumed by productive instead of unproductive labourers.' (*Principles*, p. 163.)

In fact Ricardo fully accepted the theory of Adam Smith concerning the resolution of the price of commodities into wages and surplus-value (or variable capital and surplus-value). The points of dispute with him are 1) the component parts of the surplus-value: he eliminates ground-rent as an essential element of it; 2) Ricardo *splits* the price of the commodity into these component parts. The magnitude of value is, then, the *prius*. The sum of component parts is assumed as a given magnitude, it is the starting point, while Adam Smith frequently acts to the contrary, against his own better judgement, by subsequently deducing the magnitude of value of the commodity through the sum of the component parts.

Ramsay makes the following remark against Ricardo:

> '... He seems always to consider the whole produce as divided between wages and profits, forgetting the part necessary for replacing fixed capital.' (*An Essay on the Distribution of Wealth*, Edinburgh, 1836, p. 174.)

By fixed capital Ramsay means the same thing that I mean by constant capital:

> 'Fixed capital exists in a form in which, though assisting to raise the future commodity, it does not maintain labourers.' (*Ibid.*, p. 59.)

Adam Smith opposed the necessary conclusion of his resolution of the value of commodities, and therefore also of the value of the social annual product into wages and surplus-value and therefore into mere revenue—the conclusion that in this event the entire annual product might be consumed. It is never the original thinkers that draw the absurd conclusions. They leave that to the Says and MacCullochs.

Say, indeed, settles the matter easy enough. That which is an advance of capital for one, is or was a revenue and net product for another. The difference between the gross and the net product is purely subjective, and

> 'thus the total value of all products, has been distributed in society as revenue.' (Say, *Traitè d'Economie Politique*, 1817, II, p. 64.) 'The total value of every product is composed of the profits of the landowners, the capitalists, and those who ply industrial trades' [wages figure here as *profits des industrieux*!] 'who have contributed towards its production. This makes the revenue of society equal to the *gross value produced*, not equal to the net products of the soil, as was believed by the sect of the economists' [the physiocrats]. (p. 63.)

Among others, Proudhon has appropriated this discovery of Say.

Storch, who likewise accepts Adam Smith's doctrine in principle, finds however that Say's practical application of it does not hold water.

> 'If it is admitted that the revenue of a nation is equal to its gross product, i.e., that no capital' [it should say: no constant capital] 'is to be deducted, then it must also be admitted that this nation may consume unproductively the entire value of its annual product without the least detriment to its future revenue.... The products

which represent the' [constant] 'capital of a nation are not consumable.' (Storch, *Considérations sur la nature du revenu national*, Paris, 1824, pp. 147, 150.)

However, Storch forgot to tell us how the existence of this constant portion of capital harmonises with the Smithian analysis of prices accepted by him, according to which the value of commodities contains only wages and surplus-value, but no part of any constant capital. He realises only through Say that this analysis of prices leads to absurd results, and his own last word on the subject is

'that it is impossible to resolve the necessary price into its simplest elements.' (*Cours d'Économie Politique*, Petersburg, 1815, II, p. 141.)

Sismondi, who occupies himself particularly with the relation of capital to revenue, and in actual fact makes the peculiar formulation of this relation the *differentia specifica* of his *Nouveaux Principes*, did not say *one* scientific word, did not contribute one iota to the clarification of the problem.

Barton, Ramsay, and Cherbuliez attempt to go beyond the formulation of Adam Smith. They founder because they pose the problem one-sidedly from the outset by failing to make clear the distinction between constant and variable capital-value and between fixed and circulating capital.

John Stuart Mill likewise reproduces, with his usual pomposity, the doctrine handed down by Adam Smith to his followers. As a result, the Smithian confusion of thought persists to this hour and his dogma is one of the orthodox articles of faith of Political Economy.

Notes

1. Beginning of Manuscript VIII.—*F. E.*
2. *Kapital*, Band I, 2. Ausgabe, S. 612, Note 32. [Eng. ed., Moscow, 1954, p. 591, Note 1.]
3. Some physiocrats had paved the way for him even here, especially Turgot. The latter uses the term capital for *avances* more frequently than Quesnay and the other physiocrats and identifies still more the *avances*, or *capitaux*, of the manufacturers with those of the farmers. For instance: 'Like these (the entrepreneurs-manufacturers), they (*les fermiers*, i.e., the capitalist farmers) must receive in addition to returning capitals, etc.' (Turgot, *Oeuvres*, Daire edition, Paris, 1844, Vol. I, p. 40.)
4. In order that the reader may not misconstrue the meaning of the phrase 'the price of the far greater part of commodities,' the following shows how Adam Smith himself explains this term. For instance, no rent enters into the price of sea fish, only wages and profit, only wages enter into the price of Scotch pebbles. He says: 'In some parts of Scotland a few poor people make a trade of gathering, along the sea-shore, those little variegated stones commonly known by the name of Scotch pebbles. The price which is paid to them by the stone-cutter is altogether the wages of their labour; neither rent nor profit makes any part of it.'
5. I reproduce this sentence verbatim from the manuscript, although it seems to contradict, in its present context, both what precedes and immediately follow. This apparent contradiction is resolved further down in No. 4: Capital and Revenue in Adam Smith.—*F. E.*
6. We ignore the fact that Adam Smith was here particularly unfortunate in the choice of his example. The value of the corn resolves itself into wages, profit, and rent only because the food consumed by the labouring cattle is depicted as wages of the labouring cattle, and the labouring cattle as wage-labourers, so that the wage-labourer on his part is also depicted as labouring cattle. (Added from the Manuscript II.—*F. E.*)
7. From here to the end of the chapter, a supplement from Manuscript II.—*F. E.*

20

Simple Reproduction

PART 1

Section I. *The Formulation of the Question*

If we study the annual function of social capital—hence of the total capital of which the individual capitals form only fractional parts, whose movement is their individual movement and simultaneously integrating link in the movement of the total capital—and its results, i.e., if we study the commodity-product furnished by society during the year, then it must become apparent how the process of reproduction of the social capital takes place, what characteristics distinguish this process of reproduction from the process of reproduction of an individual capital, and what characteristics are common to both. The annual product includes those portions of the social product which replace capital, namely social reproduction, as well as those which go to the consumption-fund, those which are consumed by labourers and capitalists, hence both productive and individual consumption. It comprises also the reproduction (i.e., maintenance) of the capitalist class and the working-class, and thus the reproduction of the capitalist character of the entire process of production.

It is evidently the circulation formula

$$C' - \begin{cases} M—C\ldots P\ldots C' \\ \\ M—C \end{cases}$$

which we have to analyse, and consumption necessarily plays a role in it; for the point of departure, C' = C + c, the commodity-capital embraces both the constant and variable capital-value, and the surplus-value. Its movement therefore includes both individual and productive consumption. In the circuits M—C ... P... C'— M' and P ... C'— M'— C ... P, the movement of the *capital* is the starting and finishing point. And of course this includes consumption, for the commodity, the product, must be sold. When this has assumedly been done it is immaterial for the movement of the individual capital what becomes of the commodities subsequently. On the other hand in the movement of C› ... C› the conditions of social reproduction are discernible precisely from the fact that it must be shown what becomes of every portion of value of this total product, C›. In this case the total process of reproduction includes the process of consumption brought about by the circulation quite as much as the process of reproduction of the capital itself.

For our present purpose, this process of reproduction must be studied from the point of view of the replacement of the value as well as the substance of the individual component parts of C'. We cannot rest content any longer, as we did in the analysis of the value of the product of the individual capital, with the *assumption* that the individual capitalist can first convert the component parts of his capital into money by the sale of his commodities, and then reconvert them into productive capital by renewed purchase of the elements of production in the commodity-market. Inasmuch as those elements of production are by nature material, they represent as much a constituent of the social capital as the individual finished product, which is exchanged for them and replaced by them. Contrariwise the movement of that portion of the social commodity-product which is consumed by the labourer in expending his wages, and by the capitalist in expending his surplus-value, not only forms an integral part of the movement of the total product but intermingles with the movements of the individual capitals, and therefore this process cannot be explained by merely assuming it.

The question that confronts us directly is this: How is the *capital* consumed in production replaced in value out of the annual product and how does the movement of this replacement intertwine with the consumption of the surplus-value by the capitalists and of the wages by the labourers? It is then first a matter of reproduction on a simple scale. It is furthermore assumed that products are exchanged at their values and also that there is no revolution in the values of the component parts of productive capital. The fact that prices diverge from values cannot, however, exert any influence on the movements of the social capital. On the whole, there is the same exchange of the same quantities of products, although the individual capitalists are involved in value-relations no longer proportional to their respective advances and to the quantities of surplus-value produced singly by every one of them. As for revolutions in value, they do not alter anything in the relations between the value-components of the total annual product, provided they are universally and evenly distributed. To the extent however that they are partially and unevenly distributed, they represent disturbances which, in the *first* place, can be understood as such only as far as they are regarded as *divergences* from unchanged value-relations, but in the *second* place, once there is proof of the law according to which one portion of the value of the annual product replaces constant, and another portion variable capital, a revolution either in the value of the constant or that of the variable capital would not alter anything in this law. It would change merely the relative magnitudes of the portions of value which function in the one or the other capacity, because other values would have taken the places of the original ones.

So long as we looked upon the production of value and the value of the product of capital individually, the bodily form of the commodities produced was wholly immaterial for the analysis, whether it was machines, for instance, corn, or looking glasses. It was always but a matter of illustration, and any branch of production could have served that purpose equally well. What we dealt with was the immediate process of production itself, which presents itself at every point as the process of some individual capital. So far as the reproduction of capital was concerned, it was sufficient to assume that that portion of the product in commodities which represents capital-value finds an opportunity in the sphere of circulation to reconvert itself into its elements of production and thus into its form of productive capital; just as it sufficed to assume that both the labourer and the capitalist find in the market those commodities on which they spend their wages and the surplus-value. This merely formal manner of presentation is no longer adequate in the study of the total social capital and of the value of its products. The reconversion of one portion of the value of the product into capital and the passing of another portion into the individual consumption of the capitalist as well as the working-class form a movement within the value of the product itself in which the result of the aggregate capital finds expression; and this movement is not only a replacement of value, but also a replacement in material and is therefore as much bound up with the relative proportions of the value-components of the total social product as with their use-value, their material shape. Simple reproduction, reproduction on the same scale, appears as an abstraction, inasmuch as on the one hand the absence of all accumulation or reproduction on an extended scale is a strange assumption in capitalist conditions, and on the other hand conditions of production do not remain exactly the same in different years (and this is assumed). The assumption is that a social capital of a given magnitude produces the same quantity of commodity-value this year as last, and supplies the same quantum of wants, although the forms of the commodities may change in the process of reproduction. However, as far as accumulation does take place, simple reproduction is always a part of it, and can therefore be studied by itself, and is an actual factor of accumulation. The value of the annual product may decrease, although the quantity of use-values may remain the same; or the value may remain the same although the quantity of the use-values may decrease; or the quantity of value and of the reproduced use-values may decrease simultaneously. All this amounts to reproduction taking place either under more favourable conditions than before or under more difficult ones, which may result in imperfect—defective—reproduction. All this can refer only to the quantitative aspect of the various elements of reproduction, not to the role which they play as reproducing capital or as a reproduced revenue in the entire process.

Section II. *The Two Departments of Social Production*

The total product, and therefore the total production, of society may be divided into two major departments:

I. ***Means of Production***, commodities having a form in which they must, or at least may, pass into productive consumption.
II. ***Articles of Consumption***, commodities having a form in which they pass into the individual consumption of the capitalist and the working-class.

All the various branches of production pertaining to each of these two departments form one single great branch of production, that of the means of production in the one case, and that of articles of consumption in the other. The aggregate capital employed in each of these two branches of production constitutes a separate large department of the social capital.

In each department the capital consists of two parts:

1. ***Variable Capital.*** This capital, so far as its *value* is concerned, is equal to the value of the social labour-power employed in this branch of production; in other words, it is equal to the sum of the wages paid for this labour-power. So far as its substance is concerned, it consists of the labour-power in action, i.e., of the living labour set in motion by this capital-value.
2. ***Constant Capital.*** This is the value of all the means of production employed for productive purposes in this branch. These, again, are divided into *fixed capital*, such as machines, instruments of labour, buildings, labouring animals, etc., and *circulating* constant capital, such as materials of production: raw and auxiliary materials, semi-finished products, etc.

The value of the total annual product created with the aid of this capital in each of the two departments consists of one portion which represents the constant capital c consumed in the process of production and only transferred to the product in accordance with its value, and of another portion added by the entire labour of the year. This latter portion is divided in turn into the replacement of the advanced variable capital v and the excess over and above it, which forms the surplus-value s. And just as the value of every individual commodity, that of the entire annual product of each department consists of c + v + s.

Portion c of the value, representing the constant capital *consumed* in production, does not coincide with the value of the constant capital *employed* in production. True, the materials of production are entirely consumed and their values completely transferred to the product. But only a portion of the employed *fixed* capital is wholly consumed and its value thus transferred to the product. Another part of the fixed capital, such as machines, buildings, etc., continues to exist and function the same as before, though depreciated to the extent of the annual wear and tear. This persistent portion of the fixed capital does not exist for us, when we consider the value of the product. It is a portion of the capital-value, which exists independently and alongside of this newly produced commodity-value. This was shown previously in the analysis of the value of the product of individual capital (Vol. I, Ch. VIII.). However, for the present we must leave aside the method of analysis employed there. We saw in the study of the value of the product of individual capital that the value of which the fixed capital was shorn through wear and tear is transferred to the product created during the time of wear, irrespective of whether or not any portion of this fixed capital is replaced in kind during this time out of the value thus transferred. At this point in the study of the total social product and of its value, however, we are compelled, at least for the present, to leave out of account that portion of value which is transferred from the fixed capital to the annual product by wear and tear, unless fixed capital is replaced in kind during the year. In one of the following sections of this chapter we shall discuss this point in particular.

We shall base our study of simple reproduction on the following scheme, in which c stands for constant capital, v for variable capital, and s for surplus-value, assuming the rate of surplus-value s/v to be 100 per cent. The figures may indicate millions of marks, francs, or pounds sterling.

I. Production of Means of Production:
Capital. . . . . $4{,}000_c + 1{,}000_v = 5{,}000$
Commodity-Product . . . $4{,}000_c + 1{,}000_v + 1{,}000_s = 6{,}000$, existing in means of production.

II. Production of Articles of Consumption:
Capital . . . . $2{,}000_c + 500_v = 2{,}500$
Commodity-Product . . $2{,}000_c + 500_v + 500_s = 3{,}000$, existing in articles of consumption.

Recapitulation: Total annual commodity-product:

I. $4{,}000_c + 1{,}000_v + 1{,}000_s = 6{,}000$ means of production
II. $2{,}000_c + 500_v + 500_s = 3{,}000$ articles of consumption.

Total value 9,000, exclusive of the fixed capital persisting in its natural form, according to our assumption.

If we were now to examine the transformations necessary on the basis of simple reproduction, where the entire surplus-value is unproductively consumed, and leave aside for the present the money-circulation that brings them about, we should obtain at the outset three great points of support.

1. The 500_v, representing wages of the labourers, and 500_s, representing surplus-value of the capitalists, in department II, must be spent for articles of consumption. But their value exists in articles of consumption worth 1,000, held by the capitalists of department II, which replace the advanced 500_v and represent the 500_s. Consequently the wages and surplus-value of department II are exchanged within this department for products of this same department. Thereby articles of consumption to the amount of $(500_v + 500_s)$ II = 1,000, drop out of the total product.
2. The $1{,}000_v$ plus $1{,}000_s$ of department I must likewise be spent for articles of consumption; in other words, for products of department II. Hence they must be exchanged for the remainder of this product equal to the constant capital part, $2{,}000_c$. Department II receives in return an equal quantity of means of production, the product of I, in which the value of $1{,}000_v + 1{,}000_s$ of I is incorporated. Thereby 2,000 II_c and $(1{,}000_v + 1{,}000_s)$ I drop out of the calculation.
3. There still remain 4,000 I_c. These consist of means of production which can be used only in department I to replace its consumed constant capital, and are

therefore disposed of by mutual exchange between the individual capitalists of I, just as the ($500_v + 500_s$) II by an exchange between the labourers and capitalists, or between the individual capitalists of II.

Let this serve for the moment to facilitate the understanding of what follows.

Section III. *Exchange between the Two Departments* $I_{(v+s)}$ *versus* II_c

We begin with the great exchange between the two classes. ($1{,}000_v + 1{,}000_s$) I—these values consisting, in the hands of their producers, of means of production in their natural form, are exchanged for 2,000 II_c, for values consisting of articles of consumption in their bodily form. The capitalist class of II thereby reconverts its constant capital of 2,000 from the form of articles of consumption into that of means of production of articles of consumption, into a form in which it can once more function as a factor of the labour-process and for purposes of self-expansion of value as constant capital-value. On the other hand the equivalent of the labour-power of I ($1{,}000_v$) and the surplus-value of the capitalists of I ($1{,}000_s$) are realised thereby in articles of consumption; both of them are converted from their bodily form of means of production into a bodily form in which they can be consumed as revenue.

Now, this mutual exchange is accomplished by means of a circulation of money, which promotes it just as much as it renders its understanding difficult, but which is of decisive importance because the variable portion of capital must ever resume the form of money, as money-capital converting itself from the form of money into labour-power. The variable capital must be advanced in the form of money in all branches of production carried on at the entire periphery of society simultaneously alongside each other, regardless of whether they belong to category I or II. The capitalist buys the labour-power before it enters into the process of production, but pays for it only at stipulated times, after it has been expended in the production of use-values. He owns, together with the remainder of the value of the product, also that portion of it which is only an equivalent for the money expended in the payment of labour-power, that portion of the value of the product which represents variable capital. In this portion of value the labourer has already supplied the capitalist with the equivalent of his wages. But it is the reconversion of commodities into money, their sale, which restores to the capitalist his variable capital in the form of money-capital, which he may advance once more for the purchase of labour-power.

In department I, then, the aggregate capitalist has paid £1,000 (I say £ solely to indicate that it is value in the *form of money*), equal to $1{,}000_v$, to the labourers for the value of product I already existing as the v-portion, i.e., of the means of production created by them. With these £1,000 the labourers buy articles of consumption of the same value from capitalists II, thereby converting one half of the constant capital II into money; capitalists II, in their turn, buy with these £1,000 means of production, valued at 1,000, from capitalists I; thereby, as far as the latter are concerned, the variable capital-value equal to $1{,}000_v$, which, being part of their product, existed in the bodily form of means of production, is thus reconverted into money and can now function anew in the hands of capitalists I as money-capital, which is transformed into labour-power, hence into the most essential element of productive capital. In this way, their variable capital flows back to them in the form of money, as a result of the realisation of some of their commodity-capital.

As for the money required to exchange the s-portion of commodity-capital I for the second half of constant capital II, it may be advanced in various ways. In reality this circulation embraces innumerable separate purchases and sales by the individual capitalists of both categories, the money coming in any event from these capitalists, since we have already accounted for the money put into circulation by the labourers. A capitalist of category II can buy, with the money-capital he has besides his productive capital, means of production from capitalists of category I, and, vice versa, a capitalist of category I can buy, with money-funds assigned for personal and not for capital expenditure, articles of consumption from capitalists of category II. A certain supply of money, to be used either for the advancement of capital or for the expenditure of revenue must under all circumstances be assumed to exist beside the productive capital in the hands of the capitalists, as we have shown above in parts I and II. Let us assume—the proportion is wholly immaterial for our purpose—that one half of the money is advanced by capitalists II in the purchase of means of production for the replacement of their constant capital, while the other half is spent by capitalists I for articles of consumption. In that case department II advances £500 for the purchase of means of production from department I, thereby replacing (inclusive of the above £1,000 coming from the labourers of department I) three-quarters of its constant capital in kind, with the £500 so obtained department I buys articles of consumption from II, thereby completing for one half of the s-portion of its commodity-capital the circulation c—m—c, and thus realising its product in the consumption-fund. By means of this second process the £500 return to the hands of II as money-capital existing beside its productive capital. On the other hand I expends money to the amount of £500 for the purchase of II's articles of consumption in anticipation of the sale of that half of the s-portion of its commodity-capital which is still lying in store as product. With the same £500 II buys from I means of production, thereby replacing in kind its entire constant capital (1,000 + 500 + 500 = 2,000) while I realises its entire surplus-value in articles of consumption. On the whole, the entire exchange of commodities in the amount of £4,000 would be effected with a money-circulation of £2,000 which amount is attained only because the entire annual product is described as exchanged in bulk, in a few large lots. The important point here is that II has not only reconverted its constant capital reproduced in the form of articles of consumption, into the form of means of production, but has besides recovered the £500 which it had advanced to the circulation for the purchase of means of production; and that, similarly, I again possesses not only its variable capital, which it had reproduced in the form of means of production, in money-form, as money-capital once more directly convertible into labour-power, but also the £500 expended in the purchase of articles of consumption in anticipation of the sale of the s-portion of its capital. These £500 flow back to it not because of the expenditure incurred, but because of the subsequent sale of a part of its commodity-product incorporating one half of its surplus-value.

In both cases, it is not only that the constant capital of II is reconverted from the form of a product into the bodily form of means of production, in which alone it can function as capital; and likewise it is not only that the variable portion of the capital of I is converted into its money-form, and the surplus-value portion of the means of production of I into its consumable form, the form in which it can be used as revenue. It is also that the £500 of money-capital, advanced by II in the purchase of means of production prior to selling the corresponding compensating portion of the value of its constant capital – existing in the form of means of consumption – flow back to II; and furthermore back to I flow the £500 which were expended *anticipando* by it for the purchase of articles of consumption. If the money advanced by II at the expense of the constant portion of its commodity-product, and by I at the expense of the surplus-value portion of its commodity-product, flows back to them, this is solely because the one class of capitalists throws £500 into circulation over and above the constant capital existing in the form of commodities in II, and the other class a like amount over and above the surplus-value existing in the form of commodities in I. In the last analysis the two departments have mutually paid one another in full by the exchange of equivalents in the shape of their respective commodities. The money thrown into circulation by them in excess of the values of their commodities, as a means of effecting the exchange of these commodities, returns to each one of them out of the circulation in proportion to the quota which each of the two had thrown into circulation.

Neither has grown a farthing richer thereby. I possessed a constant capital of 2,000 in the form of articles of consumption plus 500 in money; now it possesses 2,000 in means of production plus 500 in money, the same as before; in the same way I possesses, as before, a surplus-value of 1,000 (consisting of commodities, means of production, now converted into a consumption-fund) plus 500 in money. The general conclusion is this: Of the money which the industrial capitalists throw into circulation to accomplish their own commodity circulation, whether at the expense of the constant part of the commodity-value or at the expense of the surplus-value existing in the commodities to the extent that it is laid out as revenue, as much returns into the hands of the respective capitalists as was advanced by them for the money-circulation.

As for the reconversion of the variable capital of class I into the form of money, this capital, after the capitalists of I invested it in wages, exists for them first in the form of commodities in which the labourers delivered it to them. They paid this capital in the form of money to these labourers as the price of their labour-power. To this extent the capitalists have paid for that constituent part of the value of their commodity-product which is equal to the variable capital expended in the form of money. They are, for this reason, the owners of this portion of the commodity-product as well. But that part of the working-class which is employed by them does not buy the means of production created by it; these labourers buy articles of consumption produced by II. Hence, the variable capital advanced by the capitalists of I in the payment of labour-power does not return to them directly. It passes by means of purchases made by the labourers into the hands of the capitalist producers of the commodities necessary for and within the reach of working folks; in other words, it passes into the hands of capitalists II. And not until these expend the money in the purchase of means of production does it return by this circuitous route into the hands of capitalists I. It follows that, on the basis of simple reproduction, the sum of the values of v + s of the commodity-capital of I (and therefore a corresponding proportional part of the total commodity-product of I) must be equal to the constant capital II_c, which is likewise taken as a proportional part of the total commodity-product of department II; or $I_{(v + s)} = II_c$.

Section IV. *Exchange within Department II. Necessities of Life and Articles of Luxury*

Of the value of the commodity-product of department II there still remain to be studied the constituents v plus s. This analysis has nothing to do with the most important question which occupies our attention here, namely to what extent the division of the value of every individual capitalist commodity-product into c + v + s—even if brought about by different forms of appearance—applies also to the value of the total annual product. This question finds its answers on the one hand in the exchange of $I_{(v + s)}$ for II_c, and on the other hand in the investigation, to be made later, of the reproduction of I in the annual product of I. Since $II_{(v + s)}$ exists in the bodily form of articles of consumption; since the variable capital advanced to the labourers in payment of their labour-power must generally speaking be spent by them for articles of consumption; and since the s-portion of the value of commodities, on the assumption of simple reproduction, is practically spent as revenue for articles of consumption, it is *prima facie* evident that the labourers II buy back, with the wages received from the capitalists II, a portion of their own product, corresponding to the amount of the money-value received as wages. Thereby the capitalist class II reconverts the money-capital advanced by it in the payment of labour-power into the form of money. It is quite the same as if it had paid the labourers in mere value tokens. As soon as the labourers would realise these value tokens by the purchase of a part of the commodities produced by them but belonging to the capitalists, these tokens would return into the hands of the capitalists. Only, these tokens do not merely represent value but possess it, in golden or silver embodiment. We shall analyse in greater detail later on this sort of reflux of variable capital advanced in the form of money by means of a process in which the working-class appears as the purchaser and the capitalist class as the seller. Here however a different point is at issue, which must be discussed in connection with this return of the variable capital to its point of departure.

Category II of the annual production of commodities consists of a great variety of branches of production, which may, however, be divided into two great sub-divisions by their products.

a) Articles of consumption, which enter into the consumption of the working-class, and, to the extent that they are necessities of life—even if frequently different in quality and value from those of the labourers—also form a portion of the consumption of the capitalist class. For our purposes we may call this entire sub-division consumer *necessities*, regardless of whether such a product as tobacco is really a consumer necessity from the physiological point of view. It suffices that it is habitually such.

b) Articles of *luxury*, which enter into the consumption of only the capitalist class and can therefore be exchanged only for spent surplus-value, which never falls to the share of the labourer.

As far as the first category is concerned it is obvious that the variable capital advanced in the production of the commodities belonging in it must flow back in money-form directly to that portion of the capitalist class II (i.e., the capitalists IIa) who have produced these necessities of life. They sell them to their own labourers to the amount of the variable capital paid to them in wages. This reflux is *direct* so far as this entire sub-division a of capitalist class I is concerned, no matter how numerous the transactions may be between the capitalists of the various pertinent branches of industry, by means of which the returning variable capital is distributed *pro rata*. These are processes of circulation, whose means of circulation are supplied directly by the money expended by the labourers. It is different, however, with sub-division IIb. The entire portion of the value produced in this sub-division, $IIb_{(v + s)}$, exists in the bodily form of articles of luxury, i.e., articles which the labouring class can buy no more than it can buy commodity-value I existing in the form of means of production, notwithstanding the fact that both the articles of luxury and the means of production are the products of these labourers.

Hence the reflux by which the variable capital advanced in this subdivision returns to the capitalist producers in its money-form cannot be direct but must be mediated, as in the case of I_v.

Let us assume for instance that v = 500 and s = 500, as they did in the case of the entire class II; but that the variable capital and the corresponding surplus-value are distributed as follows:

Sub-division a, Necessities of Life: v = 400; s = 400; hence a quantity of commodities in consumer necessities of the value of 400 v + 400_s = 800, or IIa (400_v + 400_s).

Sub-division b, Articles of Luxury: of the value of 100 v + l00 s = 200, or IIb ($L00_v$ + 100_s).

The labourers of IIb have received 100 in money as payment for their labour-power, or say £100. With this money they buy articles of consumption from capitalists IIa to the same amount. This class of capitalists buys with the same money £100 worth of the IIb commodities, and in this way the variable capital of capitalists IIb flows back to them in the form of money.

In IIa there are available once more 400_v in money, in the hands of the capitalists, obtained by exchange with their own labourers. Besides, a fourth of the part of the product representing surplus-value has been transferred to the labourers of IIb, and in exchange IIb (100_v) have been received in the form of articles of luxury.

Now, assuming that the capitalists of IIa and IIb divide the expenditure of their revenue in the same proportion between necessities of life and luxuries—three-fifths for necessities for instance and two-fifths for luxuries—the capitalists of sub-class IIa will spend three-fifths of their revenue from surplus-value, amounting to 400_s, or 240, for their own products, necessities of life, and two-fifths, or 160, for articles of luxury. The capitalists of sub-class IIb will divide their surplus-value of 100_s in the same way: three-fifths, or 60, for necessities, and two-fifths, or 40, for articles of luxury, the latter being produced and exchanged in their own sub-class.

The 160 in articles of luxury received by $(IIa)_s$ pass into the hands of the IIa capitalists in the following manner: As we have seen, 100 of the (IIa) 400_s were exchanged in the form of necessities of life for an equal amount of $(IIb)_v$, which exists as articles of luxury, and another 60, consisting of necessities of life, for (IIb) 60_s, consisting of luxuries. The total calculation then stands as follows:

IIa: $400_v + 400_s$; IIb: $100_v + 100_s$

1. 400_v (a) are consumed by the labourers of IIa, a part of whose product (necessities of life) they form. The labourers buy them from the capitalist producers of their own sub-division. These capitalists thereby recover £400 in money, which is the value of their variable capital of 400 paid by them to these same labourers as wages. They can now once more buy labour-power with it.
2. A part of the 400_s (a), equal to the 100_v (b), one-fourth of the surplus-value (a), is realised in luxuries in the following way: The labourers (b) received from the capitalists of their sub-division (b) £100 in wages. With this amount they buy one-fourth of the surplus-value (a), i.e., commodities consisting of necessities of life. With this money the capitalists of (a) buy articles of luxury to the same amount, which equals 100_v (b), or one half of the entire output of luxuries. In this way the b capitalists get back their variable capital in the form of money and are enabled to resume reproduction by again purchasing labour-power, since the entire constant capital of the whole category II has already been replaced by the exchange of $I_{(v+s)}$ for II_c. The labour-power of the luxury workers is therefore saleable anew only because the part of their own product created as an equivalent for their wages is drawn by capitalists IIa into their consumption-fund, is turned into money. (The same applies to the sale of the labour-power of I, since the II for which $I_{(v+s)}$ is exchanged, consists of both articles of luxury and necessities of life, and that which is renewed by means of $I_{(v+s)}$ constitutes the means of production of both luxuries and necessities.)
3. We now come to the exchange between a and b, which is merely exchange between the capitalists of the two sub-divisions. So far we have disposed of the variable capital (400_v) and part of the surplus-value (100_s) in a, and the variable capital (100_v) in b. We have furthermore assumed that the average proportion of the expenditure of the capitalist revenue was in both classes two-fifths for luxuries and three-fifths for necessities. Apart from the 100 already expended for luxuries, the entire subdivision a still has to be allotted 60 for luxuries, and b has proportionately to be allotted 40.

$(IIa)_s$ is then divided into 240 for necessities and 160 for luxuries, or 240 + 160 = 400, (IIa).

$(IIb)_s$ is divided into 60 for necessities and 40 for luxuries; 60 + 40 = 100, (IIb). The last 40 are consumed by this class out of its own product (two-fifths of its surplus-value); the 60 in necessities are obtained by this class through the exchange of 60 of its surplus-value for 60, (a).

We have, then, for the entire capitalist class II the following (v plus s in sub-division [a] consisting of necessities, in [b] of luxuries): IIa ($400_v + 400_s$) + IIb ($100_v + 100_s$) = 1,000;

by this movement there is thus realised: 500_v (a + b) [realised in 400_v (a) and 100_s (a)] + 500_s (a + b) [realised in 300_s (a) + 100_v (b) + 100_s (b)] =1,000. For a and b, each considered by itself, we obtain the following realisation:

a) $v / (400_v(a)) + s / (240_s(a) + 100_s(a) + 60_s(b)) = 800$
b) $v / (100_s(a)) + s / (60_s(a) + 40_s(a) + ...) = (200 / 1000)$

If, for the sake of simplicity, we assume the same proportion between the variable and constant capital (which, by the way, is not at all necessary), we obtain for 400_v (a) a constant capital of 1,600, and for 100_v (b) a constant capital of 400. We then have the following two subdivisions, a and b, in II:

IIa) $1{,}600_c + 400_v + 400_s = 2{,}400$
IIb) $400_c + 100_v + 100_s = 600$

adding up to

$2{,}000_c + 500_v + 500_s = 3{,}000$

Accordingly, 1,600 of the 2,000 II_c in articles of consumption, which are exchanged for 2,000 $I_{(v + s)}$, are exchanged for means of production of necessities of life and 400 for means of production of luxurites.

The 2,000 $I_{(v + s)}$ would therefore break up into (800_v + 800_s) I for a, equal to 1,600 means of production of necessities of life, and (200_v + 200_s) I for b, equal to 400 means of production of luxuries.

A considerable part of the instruments of labour as such, as well as of the raw and auxiliary materials, etc., is the same for both departments. But so far as the exchange of the various portions of value of the total product $I_{(v + s)}$ is concerned, such a division would be wholly immaterial. Both the above 800_v of I and the 200_v of I are realised because the wages are spent for articles of consumption 1,000 II_c; hence the money-capital advanced for this purpose is distributed evenly on its return among the capitalist producers of I, their advanced variable capital is replaced *pro rata* in money. On the other hand, so far as the realisation of the 1,000 I_s is concerned, the capitalists will here likewise draw uniformly (in proportion to the magnitude of their s) 600 IIa and 400 IIb in means of consumption out of the entire second half of II_c, equal to 1,000; consequently those who replace the constant capital of IIa will draw.

480 (three-fifths) out of 600_c (IIa) and 320 (two-fifths) out of 400_c (IIb), a total of 800; those who replace the constant capital of IIb will draw.

120 (three-fifths) out of 600_c (IIa) and 80 (two-fifths) out of 400_c (IIb), which equals 200. Grand total, 1,000.

What is arbitrary here is the ratio of the variable to the constant capital of both I and II and so is the identity of this ratio for I and II and their sub-divisions. As for this identity, it has been assumed here merely for the sake of simplification, and it would not alter in any way the conditions of the problem and its solution if we were to assume different proportions. However, the necessary result of all this, on the assumption of simple reproduction, is the following.

1. That the new value created by the labour of one year (divisible into v + s) in the bodily form of means of production is equal to the value of the constant capital c contained in the value of the product created by the other part of the annual labour and reproduced in the form of articles of consumption. If it were smaller than II_c, it would be impossible for II to replace its constant capital entirely; if it were greater, a surplus would remain unused. In either case, the assumption of simple reproduction would be violated.

2. That in the case of annual product which is reproduced in the form of articles of consumption, the variable capital v advanced in the form of money can be realised by its recipients, inasmuch as they are labourers producing luxuries, only in that portion of the necessities of life which embodies for their capitalist producers *prima facie* their surplus-value; hence that v, laid out in the production of luxuries, is equal in value to a corresponding portion of s produced in the form of necessities of life, and hence must be smaller than the whole of this s, namely $(IIa)_s$, and that the variable capital advanced by the capitalist producers of luxuries returns to them in the form of money only by means of the realisation of that v in this portion of s. This phenomenon is quite analogous to the realisation of $I_{(v+s)}$ in II_c, except that in the second case $(IIb)_v$ realizes itself in a *part* of $(IIa)_s$ of the same value. These proportions remain qualitatively determinant in every distribution of the total annual product, since it actually enters into the process of the annual reproduction brought about by circulation. $I_{(v+s)}$ can be realised only in II_c, just as II_c can only be renewed in function as a component part of productive capital by means of this realisation; in the same way, $(IIb)_v$ can be realised only in a portion of $(IIa)_s$ and $(IIb)_v$ can only thus be reconverted into the form of money-capital. It goes without saying that this applies only to the extent that it all is really a result of the process of reproduction itself, i.e., to the extent that the capitalists of IIb, for instance, do not obtain money-capital for v on credit from others. Quantitatively however the exchanges of the various portions of the annual product can take place in the proportions indicated above only so long as the scale and value-relations in production remain stationary and so long as these strict relations are not altered by foreign commerce.

Now, if we were to say after the manner of Adam Smith that $I_{(v+s)}$ resolve themselves into II_c, and II_c resolves itself into $I_{(v+s)}$, or, as he used to say more frequently and still more absurdly, $I_{(v+s)}$ constitute component parts of the price (or 'value in exchange,' as he has it) of II and II constitutes the entire component part of the value of $I_{(v+s)}$, then one could and should likewise say that $(IIb)_v$ resolves itself into $(IIa)_s$, or $(IIa)_s$ into $(IIb)_v$, or $(IIb)_v$ forms a component part of the surplus-value of IIa, and, vice versa, the surplus-value thus resolves itself into wages, or into variable capital, and the variable capital forms a 'component part' of the surplus-value. This absurdity is indeed found in Adam Smith, since with him wages are determined by the value of the necessities of life, and these commodity-values in their turn by the value of the wages (variable capital) and surplus-value contained in them. He is so absorbed in the fractional parts into which the value-product of one working-day is divided on the basis of capitalism—namely into v plus s—that he quite forgets that it is immaterial in simple commodity exchange whether the equivalents existing in various bodily forms consist of paid or unpaid labour, since their production costs in either case the same amount of labour; and that it is also immaterial whether the commodity of A is a means of production and that of B an article of consumption and whether one commodity has to serve as a component part of capital after its sale while another passes into the consumption-fund and, *secundum* Adam, is consumed as revenue. The use to which the individual buyer puts his commodity does not come within the scope of commodity-exchange, the sphere of circulation, and does not affect the value of the commodity. This is in no wise altered by the fact that in the analysis of the circulation of the total annual social product, the definite use for which it is intended, the factor of consumption of the various component parts of that product, must be taken into consideration.

In the exchange established above of $(IIb)_v$ for a portion of $(IIa)_s$ of the same value, and in the further exchanges between (IIa), and (IIb), it is by no means assumed that either the individual capitalists of IIa and IIb or their respective totalities divide their surplus-value in the same proportion between necessary articles of consumption and articles of luxury. The one may spend more on this consumption, the other more on that. On the basis of simple reproduction, it is merely assumed that a sum of values equal to the entire surplus-value is realised in the consumption-fund. The limits are thus given. Within each department, the one may spend more in a, the other in b. But this may compensate itself mutually, so that the capitalist groups of a and b, taken as a whole, each participate in the same proportion in both. The value-relations—the proportional shares of the two kinds of producers, a and b in the total value of product II—consequently also a definite quantitative relation between the branches of production supplying those products—are however necessarily given in each concrete case; only the proportion chosen as an illustration is a hypothetical one. It would not alter the qualitative aspects if another illustration were selected; only the quantitative determinations would be altered. But, if on account of any circumstances there arises an actual change in the relative magnitude of a and b, the conditions of simple reproduction would also change accordingly.

Since $(IIb)_v$ is realised in an equivalent part of $(IIa)_s$, it follows that in proportion as the luxury part of the annual product grows, as therefore an increasing share of the labour-power is absorbed in the production of luxuries, the reconversion of the variable capital advanced in $(IIb)_v$ into money-capital functioning anew as the money-form of the variable capital, and thereby the existence and reproduction of the part of the working-class employed in IIb—the supply to them of consumer necessities—depends upon the prodigality of the capitalist class, upon the exchange of a considerable portion of their surplus-value for articles of luxury.

Every crisis at once lessens the consumption of luxuries. It retards, delays the reconversion of $(IIb)_v$ into money-capital, permitting it only partially and thus throwing a certain number of the labourers employed in the production of luxuries out of work, while on the other hand it thus clogs the sale of consumer necessities and reduces it. And this without mentioning the unproductive labourers who are dismissed at the same time, labourers who receive for their services a portion of the capitalists' luxury expense fund (these labourers are themselves *pro tanto* luxuries), and who take part to a very considerable extent in the consumption of the necessities of life, etc. The reverse takes place in periods of prosperity, particularly during the times of bogus prosperity, in which the relative value of money, expressed in commodities, decreases also for other reasons (without any actual revolution in values), so that the prices of commodities rise independently of their own values. It is not alone the consumption of necessities of life which increases. The working-class (now actively reinforced by its entire reserve army) also enjoys momentarily articles of luxury ordinarily beyond its reach, and those articles which at other times constitute for the greater part consumer 'necessities' only for the capitalist class. This on its part calls forth a rise in prices.

It is sheer tautology to say that crises are caused by the scarcity of effective consumption, or of effective consumers. The capitalist system does not know any other modes of consumption than effective ones, except that of *sub forma pauperis* or of the swindler. That commodities are unsaleable means only that no effective purchasers have been found for them, i.e., consumers (since commodities are bought in the final analysis for productive or individual consumption). But, if one were to attempt to give this tautology the semblance of a profounder justification by saying that the working-class receives too small a portion of its own product and the evil would be remedied as soon as it receives a larger share of it and its wages increase in consequence, one could only remark that crises are always prepared by precisely a period in which wages rise generally and the working-class actually gets a larger share of that part of the annual product which is intended for consumption. From the point of view of these advocates of sound and 'simple' (!) common sense, such a period should rather remove the crisis. It appears, then, that capitalist production comprises conditions independent of good or bad will, conditions which permit the working-class to enjoy that relative prosperity only momentarily, and at that always only as the harbinger of a coming crisis. [*Ad notam* for possible followers of the Rodbertian theory of crises.—F.E.]

We saw a while ago that the proportion between the production of consumer necessities and that of luxuries requires the division of $II_{(v+s)}$ between IIa and IIb, and thus of II_c between $(IIa)_c$ and $(IIb)_c$. Hence this division affects the character and the quantitative relations of production to their very roots, and is an essential determining factor of its general structure.

Simple reproduction is essentially directed toward consumption as an end, although the grabbing of surplus-value appears as the compelling motive of the individual capitalists; but surplus-value, whatever its relative magnitude may be, is after all supposed to serve here only for the individual consumption of the capitalist.

As simple reproduction is a part, and the most important one at that, of all annual reproduction on an extended scale, this motive remains as an accompaniment of and contrast to the self-enrichment motive as such. In reality the matter is more complicated, because **partners** in the loot—the surplus-value of the capitalist—figure as consumers independent of him.

Section V. *The Mediation of Exchange by the Circulation of Money*

So far as we have analysed circulation up to the present, it proceeded between the various classes of producers as indicated in the following scheme:

1. Between class I and class II:

$$\text{I. } 4{,}000_c + 1{,}000_v + 1{,}000_s$$
$$\text{II. . . } 2{,}000_c \text{ . . . . . } + 500_v + 500_s.$$

This disposes of the circulation of II_c, equal to 2,000, which is exchanged for I $(1{,}000_v + 1{,}000_s)$.

Leaving aside for the present the 4,000 I_c there still remains the circulation of v + s within class II. Now $II_{(v+s)}$ is divided between the sub-classes IIa and IIb in the following manner:

2. $\text{II. } 500_v + 500_s = \text{a } (400_v + 400_s) + \text{b } (100_v + 100_s).$

The 400_v (a) circulates within its own sub-class; the labourers paid with it buy from their employers, the capitalists IIa, necessary means of subsistence produced by themselves.

Since the capitalists of both sub-classes spend three-fifths of their surplus-value in products of IIa (necessities) and two-fifths in products of IIb (luxuries), the three-fifths of the surplus-value of a, or 240, are consumed within the sub-class IIa itself; likewise, two-fifths of the surplus-value of b (produced and existing in the form of articles of luxury), within the sub-class IIb.

There remains to be exchanged between IIa and IIb: On the side of IIa: 160_s;

On the side of IIb: $100_v + 60_s$. These cancel each other. With their 100, received in the form of money wages, the labourers of IIb buy necessities of life in that amount from IIa. The IIb capitalists likewise buy necessities from IIa to the amount of three-fifths of their surplus-value, or 60. The IIa capitalists thus obtain the money required for investing, as above assumed, two-fifths of their surplus-value, or 160_s, in luxuries produced by IIb (100, held by the IIb capitalists as a product replacing the wages paid by them, and 60_s). The scheme for this is therefore:

3. II a. // 400v // + // <u>160s</u>
240s // +
b. . . . . 100v + 60s + //40s// the bracketed items circulating and being consumed only within their own sub-class.

The direct reflux of the money-capital advanced in variable capital, which takes place only in the case of the capitalist department IIa which produces necessities of life, is but an expression, modified by special conditions, of the previously mentioned general law that money advanced to the circulation by producers of commodities returns to them in the normal course of commodity circulation. From this, it incidentally follows that if any money-capitalist at all stands behind the producer of commodities and advances to the industrial capitalist money-capital (in the strictest meaning of the word, i.e., capital-value in the form of money), the real point of reflux for this money is the pocket of this money-capitalist. Thus the mass of the circulating money belongs to that department of money-capital which is organised and concentrated in the form of banks, etc., although the money circulates more or less through all hands. The way in which this department advances its capital necessitates the continual final reflux to it in the form of money, although this is once again brought about by the reconversion of the industrial capital into money-capital.

The circulation of commodities always requires two things: Commodities which are thrown into circulation and money which is likewise thrown into it. 'The process of circulation ... does not, like direct barter of products, become extinguished upon the use-values changing places and hands. The money does not vanish on dropping out of the circuit of the metamorphosis of a given commodity. It is constantly being precipitated into new places in the arena of circulation vacated by other commodities,' etc. (Vol. I, Ch. III.).

For instance in the circulation between II_c and $I_{(v+s)}$ we assumed that II had advanced £500 in money for it. In the innumerable processes of circulation, into which the circulation between large social groups of producers resolves itself, representatives of the various groups will, at various times, be the first to appear as buyers, and hence throw money into circulation. Quite apart from particular circumstances, this is necessitated by the difference, if nothing else, in the periods of production, and thus of the turnovers, of the various commodity-capitals. So with these £500 II buys from I means of production of the same value and I buys from II articles of consumption valued at £500. Hence the money flows back to II, but this department does not in any way grow richer by this reflux. It had first thrown £500 in money into circulation and drew commodities of the same value out of it; then it sells £500 worth of commodities and draws the same amount of money out of circulation; thus the £500 flow back to it. As a matter of fact, II has thrown into circulation £500 in money and £500 in commodities, which is equal to £1,000. It draws out of the circulation £500 in commodities and £500 in money. The circulation requires for the handling of £500 in I commodities and £500 in II commodities only £500 in money; hence whoever advanced the money in the purchase of commodities from other producers recovers it when selling his own. Consequently, if I had at first bought commodities from II for £500, and later sold to II commodities of the value of £500, these £500 would have returned to I instead of to II.

In class I the money invested in wages, i.e., the variable capital advanced in the form of money, does not return directly in this form but indirectly, by a detour. But in II the £500 of wages return directly from the labourers to the capitalists, and this return is always direct in the case where purchase and sale take place repeatedly between the same persons in such a way that they are acting alternately as buyers and sellers of commodities. The capitalist of II pays for the labour-power in money; he thereby incorporates labour-power in his capital and assumes the role of an industrial capitalist in relation to his labourers as wage-earners, but does so only by means of this act of circulation, which is for him merely a conversion of money-capital into productive capital. Thereupon the labourer, who in the first instance was a seller, a dealer in his own labour-power, appears in the second instance as a buyer, a possessor of money, in relation to the capitalist, who now acts as a seller of commodities. In this way, the capitalist recovers the money invested by him in wages. As the sale of these commodities does not imply cheating, etc., but is an exchange of equivalents in commodities and money, it is not a process by which the capitalist enriches himself. He does not pay the labourer twice, first in money and then in commodities. His money returns to him as soon as the labourer exchanges it for his commodities.

However, the money-capital converted into variable capital, i.e., the money advanced for wages, plays a prominent role in the circulation of money itself, since the labourers must live from hand to mouth and cannot give the industrial capitalists credit for any length of time. For this reason variable capital must be advanced in the form of money simultaneously at innumerable territorially different points in society at certain short intervals, such as a week, etc.—in periods of time that repeat themselves rather quickly (and the shorter these periods, the smaller relatively is the total amount of money thrown at one time into circulation through this channel)—whatever the various periods of turnover of the capitals in the different branches of industry. In every country with a capitalist production the money-capital so advanced constitutes a relatively decisive share of the total circulation, the more so as the same money, before its reflux to its point of departure, passes through the most diverse channels and functions as a medium of circulation for countless other businesses.

Now let us consider the circulation between $I_{(v+s)}$ and II from a different angle.

Capitalists I advance £1,000 in the payment of wages. With this money the labourers buy £1,000 worth of means of subsistence from capitalists II. These in turn buy for the same money means of production from capitalists I. Capitalists I thus get back their variable capital in the form of money, while capitalists II have reconverted one half of their constant capital from the form of commodity-capital into that of productive capital. Capitalists II advance another £500 in money to get means of production from I. The capitalists I spend this money on articles of consumption from II. These £500 thus return to capitalists II. They advance this amount again in order to reconvert the last quarter of their constant capital, converted into commodities, into its productive bodily form. This money flows back to I and once more withdraws articles of consumption of the same amount from II. Thus the £500 return to II. The capitalists II are now as before in possession of £500 in money and £2,000 in constant capital, the latter having been newly converted from the form of commodity-capital into that of productive capital. By means of £1,500 a quantity of commodities worth £5,000 has been circulated. Namely: 1) I pays £1,000 to his labourers for their labour-power of the same value; 2) With these same £1,000 the labourers buy means of subsistence from II; 3) With the same money II buys means of production from I, thereby restoring to I variable capital to the amount of £1,000 in the form of money; 4) II buys £500 worth of means of production from I; 5) With the same £500 I buys articles of consumption from II; 6) With the same £500 II buys means of production from I; 7) With the same £500 I buys means of subsistence from II. Thus £500 have returned to II, which had thrown them into circulation besides its £2,000 in commodities and for which it did not withdraw from circulation any equivalent in commodities.

The exchange therefore takes the following course:

1. I pays £1,000 in money for labour-power, hence for commodities equal to £1,000.
2. The labourers buy with their wages amounting in money to £1,000 articles of consumption from II; hence commodities equal to £1,000.
3. With the £1,000 received from the labourers II buys means of production of the same value from I; hence commodities equal to £1,000.

   In this way the £1,000 have returned to I as the money-form of its variable capital.
4. II buys £500 worth of means of production from I, hence commodities equal to £500.
5. With the same £500 I buys articles of consumption from II; hence commodities equal to £500.

6. With the same £500 II buys means of production from I; hence commodities equal to £500.
7. With the same £500 I buys articles of consumption from II; hence commodities equal to £500.

   Total amount of commodity-values exchanged: £5,000.

   The £500 advanced by II for the purchase have returned to it.

The result is as follows:

1. I possesses variable capital in the form of money to the amount of £1,000, which it originally advanced to the circulation. It furthermore expended £1,000 for its individual consumption, in the shape of its own products; i.e., it has spent the money which it had received for the sale of means of production to the amount of £1,000.

   On the other hand, the bodily form into which the variable capital existing in the form of money must be transformed, i.e., labour-power, has been maintained, reproduced and again made available by consumption as the sole article of trade of its owners, which they must sell in order to live. The relation of wage-labourers and capitalists has likewise been reproduced.
2. The constant capital of II is replaced in kind, and the £500 advanced by the same II to the circulation have returned to it. As for the labourers I, the circulation is the simple one of C—M—C:C' (labour-power) —M^2 (£1,000, money-form of variable capital I) —C^3 (necessities of life to the amount of £1,000); these £1,000 convert into money to the same amount of value the constant capital II existing in the form of commodities, of means of subsistence.

As for the capitalists II, the process is C— M, the transformation of a portion of their commodity-product into the money-form, from which it is reconverted into the constituents of productive capital, namely into a portion of the means of production required by them. In the money advance (£500) made by capitalists II for the purchase of the other parts of the means of production, the money-form of that portion of II which exists as yet in the form of commodities (articles of consumption) is anticipated; in the act M—C, in which II buys with M, and C is sold by I, the money (II) is converted into a portion of the productive capital, while C (I) passes through the act C—M, changes into money, which however does not represent any component part of capital-value for I, but surplus-value converted into money and expended solely for articles of consumption.

In the circuit M—C ... P ... C'—M', the first act, M—C, is that of one capitalist, the last, C'—M' (or part of it), is that of another; whether the C, by which M is converted into productive capital, represents a component of constant capital, of variable capital, or surplus-value for the seller of C (who exchanges this C for money), is wholly immaterial for the commodity circulation itself.

Class I, so far as concerns the component v + s of its commodity-product, draws more money out of the circulation than it has thrown in. In the first place, the £1,000 of variable capital return to it; in the second place, it sells means of production worth £500 (see above, exchange No. 4); one half of its surplus-value is thus turned into money; then (exchange No. 6) it sells once more £500 worth of means of production, the second half of its surplus-value, and thus the entire surplus-value is withdrawn from circulation in the shape of money. Hence in succession: 1) variable capital reconverted into money, equal to £1,000; 2) one half of the surplus-value turned into money, equal to £500; 3) the other half of the surplus-value, equal to £500; altogether $1{,}000_v + 1{,}000_s$ turned into money, equal to £2,000. Although I threw only £1,000 into circulation (aside from those exchanges which promote the reproduction of I and which we shall have to analyse later), it has withdrawn double that amount from it. Of course s passes into other hands, (II), as soon as it has been converted into money, by being spent for articles of consumption. The capitalists of I withdrew only as much in money as they threw into it in value in the form of commodities; the fact that this value is surplus-value, i.e., that it does not cost the capitalists anything, does not alter the value of these commodities in any way; so far as the exchange of values in commodity circulation is concerned, that fact is of no consequence at all. The existence of surplus-value in money is of course transient, the same as all other forms which the advanced capital assumes in its metamorphoses. It lasts no longer than the interval between the conversion of commodities I into money and the subsequent conversion of the money I into commodities II.

If the turnovers had been assumed to be shorter—or, from the point of view of the simple circulation of commodities, the circulation of money more rapid—even less money would be ample to circulate the exchanged commodity-values; the amount is always determined—if the number of successive exchanges is given—by the sum of the prices, or the sum of values, of the circulating commodities. It is immaterial in what proportion this sum of values consists of surplus-value on the one hand, and of capital-value on the other.

If the wages of I, in our illustration, were paid four times per year, we should have 4 times 250, or 1,000. Hence £250 in money would suffice for the circulation I_v—½ II_c, and for that between the variable capital I_v and the labour-power I. Likewise, if the circulation between I and II were to take place in four turnovers, it would require only £250, or in the aggregate a sum of money, or a money-capital, of £500 for the circulation of commodities amounting to £5,000. In that case, the surplus-value would be converted into money four times successively, one-quarter each time, instead of twice successively, one half each time.

If I instead of II should act as buyer in exchange No. 4 and expend £500 for articles of consumption of the same value, II would buy means of production with the same £500 in exchange No. 5; 6) I buys articles of consumption with the same £500; 7) II buys means of production with the same £500 so that the £500 finally return to I, the same as before to II. The surplus-value is here converted into money by means of the money spent by the capitalist producers themselves for their individual consumption. This money represents the anticipated revenue, the anticipated receipts from the surplus-value contained in the commodities still to be sold. The surplus-value is not converted into money by the reflux of the £500; for aside from £1,000 in the form of commodities I_v, I threw £500 in money into circulation at the close of exchange No. 4, and this was additional money, so far as we know, and not the proceeds from the sale of commodities. If this money flows back to I, I merely gets back its additional money, and does not thereby convert its surplus-value into money. The conversion of the surplus-value I into money takes place only by the sale of the commodities I_s, in which it is incorporated, and lasts each time only until the money obtained by the sale of the commodities is expended anew in the purchase of articles of consumption.

With additional money (£500) I buys articles of consumption from II; this money was spent by I, which holds its equivalent in II commodities; the money returns for the first time by the purchase from I by II of commodities to the amount of £500; in other words, it returns as the equivalent of the commodities sold by I, but these commodities do not cost I anything, they constitute surplus-value for I, and *thus the money thrown into circulation by this very department turns its own surplus-value into money.* On buying for the second time (No. 6) I has likewise obtained its equivalent in II commodities. Take it, now, that II does not buy (No. 7) means of production from I. In that case, I would have actually paid £1,000 for articles of consumption, thereby consuming its entire surplus-value as revenue; namely, 500 in its own I commodities (means of production) and 500 in money: on the other hand, it would still have £500 in its own commodities (means of production) in stock, and would have got rid of £500 in money.

On the contrary II would have reconverted three-fourths of its constant capital from the form of commodity-capital into that of productive capital; but one-fourth (£500) would be held by it in the form of money-capital, actually in the form of idle money, or of money which has suspended its function and is held in abeyance. Should this state of affairs last for any length of time, II would have to cut down its scale of reproduction by one-fourth.

However the 500 in means of production, which I has on its hands, are not surplus-value existing in the form of commodities; they occupy the place of the £500 advanced in money, which I possessed aside from its £1,000 of surplus-value in commodity-form. In the form of money, they are always convertible; as commodities they are momentarily unsaleable. So much is evident: that simple reproduction—in which every element of productive capital must be replaced in both II and I—remains possible in this case only if the 500 golden birds, which I first sent flying, return to it.

If a capitalist (we have only industrial capitalists still to deal with here, who are the representatives of all others) spends money for articles of consumption, he is through with it, it goes the way of all flesh. It can flow back to him only if he fishes it out of circulation in exchange for commodities, i.e., for his commodity-capital. As the value of his entire annual commodity-product (his commodity-capital), so that of every one of its elements, i.e., the value of every individual commodity, is divisible, as far as he is concerned, into constant capital-value, variable capital-value, and surplus-value. The conversion into money of every individual commodity (as elements constituting the commodity-product) is consequently at the same time such a conversion of a certain portion of the surplus-value contained in the entire commodity-product. In this case, then, it is literally true that the capitalist himself threw the money into circulation—when he spent it on articles of consumption—by which his surplus-value is converted into money, or realised. Of course it is not a question of the identical coins but of a certain amount of hard cash equal to the one (or to a portion of the one) which he had previously thrown into circulation to satisfy his personal wants.

In practice this occurs in two ways. If the business has just been opened, in the current year, it will take quite a while, at least a few months, before the capitalist is able to use any portion of the receipts of his business for his personal consumption. But for all that he does not suspend his consumption for a single moment. He advances to himself (immaterial whether out of his own pocket or by means of credit from the pocket of somebody else) money in anticipation of surplus-value still to be snatched by him; but in doing so he also advances a circulating medium for the realisation of surplus-value to be realised later. If, on the contrary, the business has been running regularly for a longer period payments and receipts are distributed over different terms throughout the year. But one thing continues uninterruptedly, namely, the consumption of the capitalist, which anticipates, and whose volume is computed on a definite proportion of, the customary or estimated revenue. With every portion of commodities sold, a portion of the surplus-value to be produced annually is also realised. But, if during the entire year only as much of the produced commodities is sold as is required to replace the constant and variable capital-values contained in them, or if prices were to fall to such an extent that only the advanced capital-value contained in the entire annual commodity-product should be realised on its sale, then the anticipatory character of the expenditure of money in expectation of future surplus-value would be clearly revealed. If our capitalist fails, his creditors and the court investigate whether his anticipated private expenditures were in proper proportion to the volume of his business and to the receipt of surplus-value usually or normally corresponding to it.

So far as the entire capitalist class is concerned, the proposition that it must itself throw into circulation the money required for the realisation of its surplus-value (correspondingly also for the circulation of its capital, constant and variable) not only fails to appear paradoxical, but stands forth as a necessary condition of the entire mechanism. For there are here only two classes: the working-class disposing only of its labour-power, and the capitalist class, which has a monopoly of the social means of production and money. It would rather be a paradox if the working-class were to advance in the first instance from its own resources the money required for the realisation of the surplus-value contained in the commodities. But the individual capitalist makes this advance only by acting as a buyer, *expending* money in the purchase of articles of consumption or *advancing* money in the purchase of elements of his productive capital, whether of labour-power or means of production. He never parts with his money unless he gets an equivalent for it. He advances money to the circulation only in the same way as he advances commodities to it. He acts in both instances as the initial point of their circulation.

The actual process is obscured by two circumstances:

1. The appearance in the process of circulation of industrial capital of *merchant's capital* (the first form of which is always money, since the merchant as such does not create any 'product' or 'commodity') and of *money-capital* as an object of manipulation by a special kind of capitalists.
2. The division of surplus-value—which must always be first in the hands of the industrial capitalist—into various categories, as vehicles of which there appear, aside from the industrial capitalist, the landlord (for ground-rent), the usurer (for interest), etc., furthermore the government and its employees, rentiers, etc. These gentry appear as buyers vis-à-vis the industrial capitalist and to that extent as converters of his commodities into money; they too throw 'money' *pro parte* into the circulation and he gets it from them. But it is always forgotten from what source they derived it originally, and continue deriving it ever anew.

PART 2

Secton VI. *The Constant Capital of Department I*

It remains for us to analyse the constant capital of department I, amounting to $4{,}000_c$. This value is equal to the value—appearing anew in the commodity-product I—of the means of production consumed in the creation of this quantity of commodities. This re-appearing value, which was not produced in the process of production of I, but entered into it during the preceding year as constant value, as the given value of its means of production, exists now in the entire part of commodity mass I not absorbed by category II. And the value of this quantity of commodities thus left in the hands of the I capitalists equals two-thirds of the value of their entire annual commodity-product. In the case of the individual capitalist producing some particular means of production we could say: He sells his commodity-product; he converts it into money. By converting it into money he has also reconverted into money the constant portion of the value of his product. With this portion of value converted into money, he then buys his means of production once more from other sellers of commodities or transforms the constant portion of the value of his product into a bodily form in which it can resume its function of productive constant capital. But now this assumption becomes impossible. The capitalist class of I comprises the totality of the capitalists producing means of production. Besides, the commodity-product of 4,000, which is left on their hands, is a portion of the social product which cannot be exchanged for any other, because no such other portion of the annual product remains. With the exception of these 4,000, all the remainder has been disposed of. One portion has been absorbed by the social consumption-fund, and another portion has to replace the constant capital of department II, which has already exchanged everything it could dispose of in an exchange with department I.

The difficulty is solved very easily if we remember that the entire commodity-product I in its bodily form consists of means of production, i.e., of the material elements of the constant capital itself. We meet here the same phenomenon which we witnessed before under II, only in a different aspect. In the case of II the entire commodity-product consisted of articles of consumption. Hence one portion of it, measured by the wages plus surplus-value contained in this product, could be consumed by its own producers. Here, in the case of I, the entire product consists of means of production, of buildings, machinery, vessels, raw and auxiliary materials, etc. One portion of them, namely that replacing the constant capital employed in this sphere, can therefore immediately function anew in its bodily form as a component of the productive capital: So far as it goes into circulation, it circulates within class I. In II a part of the commodity-product is individually consumed in kind by its own producers while in I a portion of the product is productively consumed in kind by its capitalist producers.

In the part of the commodity-product I equal to $4,000_c$ the capital-value consumed in this category re-appears, and does so in a bodily form in which it can immediately resume its function of productive constant capital. In II that portion of the commodity-product of 3,000 whose value is equal to the wages plus the surplus-value (equal to 1,000) passes directly into the individual consumption of the capitalists and labourers of II, while on the other hand the constant capital-value of this commodity-product (equal to 2,000) cannot re-enter the productive consumption of the II capitalists but must be replaced by exchange with I.

In I, on the contrary, that portion of its commodity-product of 6,000 whose value is equal to the wages plus the surplus-value (equal to 2,000) does not pass into the individual consumption of its producers, and cannot do so on account of its bodily form. It must first be exchanged with II. Contrariwise, the constant portion of the value of this product, equal to 4,000, exists in a bodily form in which—taking the capitalist class I as a whole—it can immediately resume its function of constant capital of that class. In other words, the entire product of department I consists of use-values which, on account of their bodily form, can under a capitalist mode of production serve only as elements of constant capital. Hence one-third (2,000) of this product of 6,000 replaces the constant capital of department II, and the other two thirds the constant capital of department I.

The constant capital I consists of a great number of different groups of capital invested in the various branches of production of means of production, so much in iron works, so much in coal-mines, etc. Every one of these groups of capital, or every one of these social group capitals, is in its turn composed of a larger or smaller number of independently functioning individual capitals. In the first place, the capital of society, for instance 7,500 (which may mean millions, etc.) is composed of various groups of capital; the social capital of 7,500 is divided into separate parts, every one of which is invested in a special branch of production; each portion of the social capital-value invested in some particular branch of production consists, so far as its bodily form is concerned, partly of means of production required in that particular sphere of production, partly of the labour-power needed in that business and trained accordingly, variously modified by division of labour, according to the specific kind of labour to be performed in each individual sphere of production. Each portion of social capital invested in any particular branch of production in its turn consists of the sum of the individual capitals invested in it and functioning independently. This patently applies to both departments, I as well as II.

As for the constant capital-value re-appearing in I in the form of its commodity-product, it re-enters in part as means of production into the particular sphere of production (or even into the individual business) from which it emerges as product; for instance corn into the production of corn, coal into the production of coal, iron in the form of machines into the production of iron, etc.

However, since the partial products constituting the constant capital-value I do not return directly to their particular or individual sphere of production, they merely change their place. They pass in their bodily form to some other sphere of production of department I, while the product of other spheres of production of department I replaces them in kind. It is merely a change of place of these products. All of them re-enter as factors replacing constant capital in I, only instead of the same group of I they enter another. Since an exchange takes place here between the individual capitalist of I, it is an exchange of one bodily form of constant capital for another bodily form of constant capital, of one kind of means of production for other kinds of means of production. It is an exchange of the different individual parts of constant capital I among themselves. Products which do not serve directly as means of production in their own sphere are transferred from their place of production to another and thus mutually replace one another. In other words (similarly to what we saw in the case of the surplus-value II), every capitalist I draws from this quantity of commodities, proportionally to his share in the constant capital of 4,000, the means of production required by him. If production were socialised instead of capitalistic, these products of department I would evidently just as regularly be redistributed as means of production to the various branches of this department, for purposes of reproduction, one portion remaining directly in that sphere of production from which it emerged as a product, another passing over to other places of production, thereby giving rise to a constant to-and-fro movement between the various places of production in this department.

Section VII. *Variable Capital and Surplus-Value in Both Departments*

The total value of the annually produced articles of consumption is thus equal to the variable capital-value II reproduced during the year plus the newly produced surplus-value II (i.e., equal to the value produced by II during the year) plus the variable capital-value I reproduced during the year and the newly produced surplus-value I (i.e., plus the value created by I during the year).

On the assumption of simple reproduction the total value of the annually produced articles of consumption is therefore equal to the annual value-product, i.e., equal to the total value produced during the year by social labour, and this must be so, because in simple reproduction this entire value is consumed.

The total social working-day is divided into two parts: 1) Necessary labour which creates in the course of the year a value of $1{,}500_v$; 2) surplus-labour, which creates an additional value, or surplus-value, of $1{,}500_s$. The sum of these values, 3,000, is equal to the value of the annually produced articles of consumption—3,000. The total value of the articles of consumption produced during the year is therefore equal to the total value produced by the total social working-day during the year, equal to the value of the social variable capital plus the social surplus-value, equal to the total new product of the year.

But we know that although these two magnitudes of value are equal the total value of commodities II, the articles of consumption, is not produced in this department of social production. They are equal because the constant capital-value re-appearing in II is equal to the value newly produced by I (value of variable capital plus surplus-value); therefore $I_{(v + s)}$ can buy the part of the product of II which represents the constant capital-value for its producers (in department II). This shows, then, why the value of the product of capitalists II, from the point of view of society, may be resolved into v + s although for these capitalists it is divided into c + v + s. This is so only because II_c is here equal to $I_{(v + s)}$, and because these two components of the social product interchange their bodily forms by exchange, so that after this transformation II exists once more in means of production and $I_{(v + s)}$ in articles of consumption.

And it is this circumstance which induced Adam Smith to maintain that the value of the annual product resolves itself into v + s. This is true 1) only for that part of the annual product which consists of articles of consumption; and 2) it is not true in the sense that this total value is produced in II and that the value of its product is equal to the value of the variable capital advanced in II plus the surplus-value produced in II. It is true only in the sense that $II_{(c + v + s)}$ is equal to $II_{(v + s)} + I_{(v + s)}$, or because II is equal to $I_{(v + s)}$.

It follows furthermore:

> The social working-day (i.e., the labour expended by the entire working-class during the whole year), like every individual working-day, breaks up into only two parts, namely into necessary labour and surplus-labour, and the value produced by this working-day consequently likewise resolves itself into only two parts, namely into the value of the variable capital, or that portion of the value with which the labourer buys the means of his own reproduction, and the surplus-value which the capitalist may spend for his own individual consumption. Nevertheless, from the point of view of society, one part of the social working-day is spent exclusively on the *production of new constant capital*, namely of products exclusively intended to function as means of production in the labour-process and hence as constant capital in the accompanying process of self-expansion of value. According to our assumption, the total social working-day presents itself as a money-value of 3,000, only one-third of which, or 1,000, is produced in department II which manufactures articles of consumption, that is, the commodities in which the entire value of the variable capital and the entire surplus-value of society are ultimately realised. Thus, according to this assumption, two-thirds of the social working-day are employed in the production of new constant capital. Although, from the standpoint of the individual capitalists and labourers of department I, these two-thirds of the social working-day serve merely for the production of variable capital-value plus surplus-value, the same as the last third of the social working-day in department II, still from the point of view of society and likewise of the use-value of the product, these two-thirds of the social working-day produce only replacement of constant capital in the process of productive consumption or already so consumed. Also when viewed individually these two-thirds of the working-day, while producing a total value equal only to the value of the variable capital plus surplus-value for the producer, nevertheless do not produce any use-values of a kind on which wages or surplus-value could be expended; for their products are means of production.

It must be noted in the first place that no portion of the social working-day, whether in I or in II, serves for the production of the value of the constant capital employed and functioning in these two great spheres of production. They produce only additional value, 2,000 $I_{(v + s)}$ + 1,000 $II_{(v + s)}$, in addition to the value of the constant capital equal to 4,000 I_c + 2,000 II_c. The new value produced in the form of means of production is not yet constant capital. It merely is intended to function as such in the future.

The entire product of II—the articles of consumption—viewed concretely as a use-value, in its bodily form, is a product of the one-third of the social working-day spent by II. It is the product of labour in its concrete form—such as the labour of weaving, baking, etc., performed in this department—the product of this labour, inasmuch as it functions as the subjective element of the labour-process. As to the constant portion of the value of this product II, it re-appears only in a new use-value, in a new bodily form, the form of articles of consumption, while it existed previously in the form of means of production. Its value has been transferred by the labour-process from its old bodily form to its new bodily form. But the *value* of these two-thirds of the product-value, equal to 2,000, has not been produced in this year's self-expansion process of II.

Just as from the point of view of the labour-process, the product of II is the result of newly functioning living labour and of the assumed means of production assigned to it, in which that labour materialises itself as in its objective conditions, so, from the point of view of the process of self-expansion, the value of the product of II, equal to 3,000, is composed of a new value ($500_v + 500_s = 1{,}000$) produced by the newly added one-third of the social working-day and of a constant value in which are embodied two-thirds of a past social working-day that had elapsed before the present process of production of II here under consideration. This portion of the value of the II product finds expression in a portion of the product itself. It exists in a quantity of articles of consumption worth 2,000, or two-thirds of a social working-day. This is the new use-form in which this value-portion re-appears. The exchange of part of the articles of consumption equal to 2,000 II_c for means of production of I equal to I ($1{,}000_v + 1{,}000_s$) thus really represents an exchange of two-thirds of an aggregate working-day—which do not constitute any portion of this year's labour, and elapsed before this year—for two-thirds of the working-day newly added this year. Two-thirds of this year's social working-day could not be employed in the production of constant capital and at the same time constitute variable capital-value plus surplus-value for their own producers unless they were to be exchanged for a portion of the value of the annually consumed articles of consumption, in which are incorporated two-thirds of a working-day spent and realised before this year. It is an exchange of two-thirds of this year's working-day for two-thirds of a working-day spent before this year, an exchange of this year's labour-time for last year's. This explains the riddle of how the value-product of an entire social working-day can resolve itself into variable capital-value plus surplus-value, although two-thirds of this working-day were not expended in the production of articles in which variable capital or surplus-value can be realised, but rather in the production of means of production for the replacement of the capital consumed during the year. The explanation is simply that two-thirds of the value of the product of II, in which the capitalists and labourers of I realise the variable capital-value plus surplus-value produced by them (and which constitute two-ninths of the value of the entire annual product), are, so far as their value is concerned, the product of two-thirds of a social working-day of a year prior to the current one.

The sum of the social product I and II—means of production and articles of consumption—is indeed, viewed from the standpoint of their use-value, in their concrete, bodily form, the product of this year's labour, but only to the extent that this labour itself is regarded as useful and concrete and not as an expenditure of labour-power, as value-creating labour. And even the first is true only in the sense that the means of production have transformed themselves into new products, into this year's products solely by dint of the living labour added on to them, operating on them. On the contrary, this year's labour could not have transformed itself into products without means of production independent of it, without instruments of labour and materials of production.

Section VIII. *The Constant Capital in Both Departments*

The analysis of the total value of the product of 9,000, and of the categories into which it is divided, does not present any greater difficulty than that of the value produced by an individual capital. On the contrary, they are identical.

The entire annual social product here contains three social working-days, each of one year. The value expressed by each one of these working-days is 3,000, so that the value expressed by the total product is equal to 3 × 3,000, or 9,000.

Furthermore, the following portions of this working time have elapsed *prior* to the one-year process of production, the product of which we are now analysing: In department I- four-thirds of a working-day (with a product worth 4,000), and in department II- two-thirds of a working-day (with a product worth 2,000), making a total of two social working-days with a product worth 6,000. For this reason $4{,}000\ I_c + 2{,}000\ II_c = 6{,}000_c$ figure as the value of the means of production, or the constant capital-value re-appearing in the total value of the social product. Furthermore, one-third of the social working-day of one year newly added in department I is necessary labour, or labour replacing the value of the variable capital of 1,000 I and paying the price of the labour employed by I. In the same way, one-sixth of a social working-day in II is necessary labour with a value of 500. Hence 1,000 I_v + 500 II_v = $1{,}500_v$, expressing the value of one half of the social working-day, is the value-expression of the first half of the aggregate working-day added this year and consisting of necessary labour.

Finally, in department I- one-third of the aggregate working-day, with a product worth 1,000, is surplus-labour, and in department II- one-sixth of the working-day, with a product worth 500, is surplus-labour.

Together they constitute the other half of the added aggregate working-day. Hence the total surplus-value produced is equal to 1,000 I_s + 500 II_s, or $1{,}500_s$.

Thus:

The constant capital portion of the value of the social product (c):

Two working-days expended prior to the process of production; expression of value = 6,000.

Necessary labour (v) expended during the year:

One half of a working-day expended on the annual production; expression of value 1,500.

Surplus-labour (s) expended during the year:

One half of a working-day expended on the annual production; expression of value = 1,500.

Value produced by annual labour (v + s) = 3,000.

Total value of product (c + v + s) = 9,000.

The difficulty, then, does not consist in the analysis of the *value* of the social product itself. It arises in the comparison of the component parts of the value of the social product with its *material* constituents.

The constant, merely re-appearing portion of value is equal to the value of that part of this product which consists of means of *production* and is incorporated in that part.

The new value-product of the year, equal to v + s, is equal to the value of that part of this product which consists of *articles of consumption* and is incorporated in it.

But with exceptions of no consequence here, means of production and articles of consumption are wholly different kinds of commodities, products of entirely different bodily or use-forms, and, therefore, products of wholly different classes of concrete labour. The labour which employs machinery in the production of means of subsistence is vastly different from the labour which makes machinery. The entire aggregate annual working-day, whose value-expression is 3,000, seems spent in the production of articles of consumption equal to 3,000, in which no constant portion of value re-appears, since these 3,000, equal to $1{,}500_v$ + $1{,}500_s$, resolve themselves only into variable capital-value and surplus-value. On the other hand, the constant capital-value of 6,000 re-appears in a class of products quite different from articles of consumption, namely in means of production, while as a matter of fact no part of the social working-day seems spent in the production of these new products. It seems rather that the entire working-day consists only of classes of labour which do not result in means of production but in articles of consumption. This mystery has already been cleared up. The value-product of the year's labour is equal to the value of the products of department II, to the total value of the newly produced articles of consumption. But the value of these products is greater by two-thirds than that portion of the annual labour which has been expended in the sphere of production of articles of consumption (department II). Only one-third of the annual labour has been expended in their production. Two-thirds of this annual labour have been expended in the production of means of production, that is to say, in department I. The value-product created during this time in I, equal to the variable capital-value plus surplus-value produced in I, is equal to the constant-capital-value of II re-appearing in articles of consumption of II. Hence they may be mutually exchanged and replaced in kind. The total value of the articles of consumption of II is therefore equal to the sum of the new value-product of I and II, or $II_{(c+v+s)}$ equal to $I_{(v+s)} + II_{(v+s)}$, hence equal to the sum of the new values produced by the year's labour in the form of v plus s.

On the other hand, the total value of the means of production (I) is equal to the sum of the constant capital-value re-appearing in the form of means of production (I) and in that of articles of consumption (II); in other words, equal to the sum of the constant capital-value re-appearing in the total product of society. This total value is equal in terms of value to four-thirds of a working-day preceding the process of production of I and two-thirds of a working-day preceding the process of production of II, in all equal to two aggregate working-days.

The difficulty with the annual social product arises therefore from the fact that the constant portion of value is represented by a wholly different class of products—means of production—than the new value v + s added to this constant portion of value and represented by articles of consumption. Thus the appearance is created, so far as value is concerned, that two-thirds of the consumed mass of products are found again in a new form as new product, without any labour having been expended by society in their production. This is not so in the case of an individual capital. Every individual capitalist employs some particular concrete kind of labour, which transforms the means of production peculiar to it into a product. Let, for instance, the capitalist be a machine-builder, the constant capital expended during the year $6{,}000_c$, the variable $1{,}500_v$, the surplus-value $1{,}500_s$, the product 9,000, the product, say, 18 machines of 500 each. The entire product here exists in the same form, that of machines. (If he produces various kinds, each kind is calculated separately.) The entire commodity-product is the result of the labour expended during the year in machine-building; it is a combination of the same concrete kind of labour with the same means of production. The various portions of the value of the product therefore present themselves in the same bodily form: 12 machines embody $6{,}000_c$, 3 machines $1{,}500_v$, 3 machines $1{,}500_s$. In the present case it is evident that the value of the 12 machines is equal to $6{,}000_c$, not because there is incorporated in these 12 machines only labour performed previously to the manufacture of these machines and not labour expended on building them. The value of the means of production for 18 machines did not of itself become transformed into 12 machines but the value of these 12 machines (consisting itself of $4{,}000_c + 1{,}000_v + 1{,}000_s$) is equal to the total value of the constant capital contained in the 18 machines. The machine-manufacturer must therefore sell 12 of the 18 machines in order to replace his expended constant capital, which he requires for the reproduction of 18 new machines. On the contrary, the thing would be inexplicable if in spite of the fact that the labour expended was employed solely in the manufacture of machines, the result were to be: On the one hand, 6 machines equal to $1{,}500_v + 1{,}500_s$, on the other iron, copper, screws, belts, etc., of a value amounting to $6{,}000_c$, i.e., the means of production of the machines in their bodily form, which, as we know, the individual machine-building capitalist does not produce himself but must replace by way of the process of circulation. And yet it seems at first glance that the reproduction of the annual product of society takes place in this absurd way.

The product of an individual capital, i.e., of every fraction of the social capital endowed with a life of its own and functioning independently, has a bodily form of one kind or another. The only condition is that this product must really have a use-form, a use-value, which gives it the imprint of a member of the world of commodities capable of circulation. It is immaterial and accidental whether or not it can re-enter as a means of production into the same process of production from which it emerged as a product; in other words, whether the portion of its value representing the constant part of the capital has a bodily form in which it can actually function again as constant capital. If not, this portion of the value of the product is reconverted into the form of its material elements of production by means of sale and purchase and thus the constant capital is reproduced in the bodily form capable of functioning.

It is different with the product of the aggregate social capital. All the material elements of reproduction must in their bodily form constitute parts of this product. The consumed constant part of capital can be replaced by the aggregate production only to the extent that the entire constant part of the capital reappearing in the product re-appears in the bodily form of new means of production which can really function as constant capital. Hence, simple reproduction being assumed, the value of that portion of the product which consists of means of production must be equal to the constant portion of the value of social capital.

Furthermore: Considered individually, the capitalist produces in the value of his product by means of the newly added labour only his variable capital plus surplus-value, while the constant part of the value is transferred to the product owing to the concrete character of the newly added labour.

Considered socially that portion of the social working-day which produces means of production, hence adding new value to them as well as transferring to them the value of the means of production consumed in their manufacture, creates nothing but new *constant capital* intended to replace that consumed in the shape of old means of production in both departments I and II. It creates only product intended for productive consumption. The entire value of this product, then, is only value which can function anew as constant capital, which can only buy back constant capital in its bodily form, and which, for this reason, resolves itself, considered socially, neither into variable capital nor surplus-value. On the other hand, that part of the social working-day which produces articles of consumption does not create any portion of the social replacement capital. It creates only products intended, in their bodily form, to realise the value of the variable capital and surplus-value of I and II.

Speaking of the point of view of society, and therefore considering the aggregate product of society, which comprises both the reproduction of social capital and individual consumption, we must not lapse into the manner copied by Proudhon from bourgeois economy and look upon this matter as though a society with a capitalist mode of production, if viewed *en bloc*, as a totality, would lose this its specific historical and economic character. No, on the contrary. We have, in that case, to deal with the aggregate capitalist. The aggregate capital appears as the capital stock of all individual capitalists combined. This joint-stock company has in common with many other stock companies that everyone knows what he puts in, but not what he will get out of it.

Section IX. *A Retrospect to Adam Smith, Storch, and Ramsay*

The aggregate value of the social product amounts to 9,000, equal to $6{,}000_c + 1{,}500_c + 1{,}500_s$, i.e., 6,000 reproduce the value of the means of production and 3,000 that of the articles of consumption. The value of the social revenue (v + s) amounts therefore to only one-third of the value of the aggregate product, and the totality of consumers, labourers as well as capitalists, can draw commodities, products out of the total social product and incorporate them in their consumption-fund only to the amount of this one-third. On the other hand 6,000, or two-thirds, of the value of the product, are the value of the constant capital which must be replaced in kind. Means of production to this amount must, therefore, again be incorporated in the production-fund. Storch recognised this as essential without being able to prove it:

> 'It is clear that the value of the annual product is divided partly into capital and partly into profits, and that each one of these portions of the value of the annual product is regularly employed in buying the products which the nation needs both for the

> maintenance of its capital and for replenishing its consumption-fund... . The products which constitute the *capital* of a nation *are not to be consumed*.' (Storch, *Considèrations sur la nature du revenu national Paris*, 1824, pp. 134-35, 150.)

Adam Smith, however, has promulgated this astounding dogma, which is believed to this day, not only in the previously mentioned form, according to which the entire value of the social product resolves itself into revenue, into wages plus surplus-value, or, as he expresses it, into wages plus profit (interest) plus ground-rent, but also in the still more popular form, according to which the *consumers* must '**ultimately**' pay to the producers the *entire value of the product*. This is to this day one of the best-established commonplaces, or rather eternal truths, of the so-called science of political economy. This is illustrated in the following plausible manner: Take any article, for instance a linen shirt. First, the spinner of linen yarn has to pay the flax-grower the entire value of the flax, i.e., the value of flax-seed, fertilisers, labouring cattle feed, etc., plus that part of the value which the fixed capital, such as buildings, agricultural implements, etc., of the flax-grower gives up to the product; the wages paid in the production of the flax; the surplus-value (profit, ground-rent) embodied in the flax; finally the carriage costs of the flax from its place of production to the spinnery. Next, the weaver has to reimburse the spinner of the linen yarn not only for the price of the flax, but also for that portion of the value of machinery, buildings, etc., in short of the fixed capital, which is transferred to the flax; furthermore, all the auxiliary materials consumed in the spinning process, the wages of the spinners, the surplus-value, etc., and so the thing goes on with the bleacher, the transportation costs of the finished linen, and finally the shirtmaker, who has to pay the entire price of all preceding producers, who supplied him only with his raw material. In his hands a further addition of value takes place, partly through the value of constant capital consumed in the manufacture of shirts in the shape of instruments of labour, auxiliary materials, etc., and partly through the labour expended, which adds the value of the shirtmakers' wages plus the surplus-value of the shirt manufacturer. Now let this entire product in shirts cost ultimately £100 and let this be the aliquot part of the value of the total annual product expended by society on shirts. The consumers of the shirts pay these £100, i.e., the value of all the means of production contained in the shirts, and of the wages plus surplus-value of the flax-grower, spinner, weaver, bleacher, shirt manufacturer, and all carriers. This is absolutely correct. Indeed, every child can see that. But then it says: that's how matters stand with regard to the value of all other commodities. It should say: That's how matters stand with regard to the value of *all articles of consumption*, with regard to the value of that portion of the social product which passes into the consumption-fund, i.e., with regard to that portion of the value of the social product which can be expended as revenue. True enough, the sum of the values of all these commodities is equal to the value of all the means of production (constant portions of capital) used up in them plus the value created by the labour last added (wages plus surplus-value). Hence the totality of the consumers can pay for this entire sum of values because, although the value of each individual commodity is made up of $c + v + s$, nevertheless the sum of the values of all commodities passing into the consumption-fund, taken at its maximum, can be equal only to that portion of the value of the social product which resolves itself into $v + s$, in other words, equal to that value which the labour expended during the year has added to the existing means of production—i.e., to the value of the constant capital. As for the value of the constant capital, we have seen that it is replaced out of the mass of social products in a two-fold way. First, through an exchange by capitalists II, who produce articles of consumption, with capitalists I, who produce the means of production for them. And here is the source of the saying that what is capital for the one is revenue for the other. But this is not the actual state of affairs. The 2,000 II_c existing in the shape of articles of consumption worth 2,000 constitute a constant capital-value for the capitalist class of II. They therefore cannot consume this value themselves, although the product in accordance with its bodily form is intended for consumption. On the other hand, the 2,000 $I_{(v+s)}$ are wages plus surplus-value produced by capitalist and working-class I. They exist in the bodily form of means of production, of things in which their own value cannot be consumed. We have here, then, a sum of values to the amount of 4,000, one half of which, before and after the exchange, replaces only constant capital, while the other half forms only revenue.

In the second place the constant capital of department I is replaced in kind, partly by exchange among capitalists I, partly by replacement in kind in each individual business.

The phrase that the value of the entire annual product must ultimately be paid by the consumer would be correct only if consumer were taken to comprise two vastly different kinds: individual consumers and productive consumers. However, that one portion of the product must be consumed *productively* means nothing but that it must *function as capital* and not be *consumed as revenue*.

If we divide the value of the aggregate product, equal to 9,000, into $6{,}000_c + 1{,}500_v + 1{,}500_s$ and look upon the $3{,}000_{(v+s)}$ only in its quality of revenue, then, on the contrary, the variable capital seems to disappear and capital, socially speaking, to consist only of constant capital. For that which appeared originally as $1{,}500_v$ has resolved itself into a portion of the social revenue, into wages, the revenue of the working-class, and its character of capital has thus vanished. This conclusion is actually drawn by Ramsay. According to him, capital, socially considered, consists only of fixed capital, but by fixed capital be means the constant capital, that quantity of values which consists of means of production, whether these means of production are instruments or materials of labour, such as raw materials, semi-finished products, auxiliary materials, etc. He calls the variable capital circulating capital:

> 'Circulating capital consists exclusively of subsistence and other necessaries advanced to the workmen, previous to the completion of the produce of their labour... Fixed capital alone, not circulating, is properly speaking a source of national wealth... Circulating capital is not an immediate agent in production, nor even essential to it at all, but merely a convenience rendered necessary by the deplorable poverty of the mass of the people... Fixed capital alone constitutes an element of cost of production in a national point of view.' (Ramsay, l.c., pp. 23 to 26, *passim.*)

Ramsay defines fixed capital, by which he means constant capital, more closely in the following words:

> 'On the length of time during which any portion of the product of that labour' (namely **labour bestowed on any commodity**) 'has existed as fixed capital; that is, in a form in which, though assisting to raise the future commodity, *it does not maintain labourers*.' Ibid., p. 59.)

Here we see once more the calamity Adam Smith brings on by submerging the distinction between constant and variable capital in that between fixed capital and circulating capital. Ramsay's constant capital consists of instruments of labour, his circulating capital of means of subsistence. Both of them are commodities of a given value. The one can no more create surplus-value than the other.

Section X. *Capital and Revenue: Variable Capital and Wages*

The entire annual reproduction, the entire product of a year is the product of the useful labour of that year. But the value of this total product is greater than that portion of the value in which the annual labour, the labour-power expended during the current year, is incorporated. The *value-product* of this year, the value newly created during this period in the form of commodities, is smaller than the *value of the product*, the aggregate value of the mass of commodities fabricated during the entire year. The difference obtained by deducting from the total value of the annual product that value which was added to it by the labour of the current year, is not really reproduced value but only value re-appearing in a new form of existence. It is value transferred to the annual product from value existing prior to it, which may be of an earlier or later date, according to the durability of the components of the constant capital which have participated in that year's social labour-process, a value which may originate from the value of means of production which came into the world the previous year or in a number of years even previous to that. It is, by all means, a value transferred from means of production of former years to the product of the current year.

Take our scheme. We have, after the exchange of the elements hitherto considered between I and II, and within II.

I) $4,000_c + 1,000_v + 1,000_s$ (the latter 2,000 realised in articles of consumption of II_c) = 6,000.

II) $2,000_c$ (reproduced by exchange with $I_{(v+s)}$ + $500_v + 500_s$ = 3,000.
Sum of values = 9,000.

Value newly produced during the year is contained only in v and s. The sum of the value-product of this year is therefore equal to the sum of v + s, or 2,000 $I_{(v+s)}$ + 1,000 $II_{(v+s)}$ = 3,000. All remaining value-parts of the product of this year are merely value transferred from the value of earlier means of production consumed in the annual production. The current annual labour has not produced any value other than that of 3,000. That represents its entire annual value-product.

Now, as we have seen, the 2,000 $I_{(v+s)}$ replace for class II its 2,000 II_c in the bodily form of means of production. Two-thirds of the annual labour, then, expended in category I, have newly produced constant capital II, both its entire value and its bodily form. From the standpoint of society, two-thirds of the labour expended during the year have created new constant capital-value realised in the bodily form appropriate for department II. Thus the greater portion of the annual labour of society has been spent in the production of new constant capital (capital-value existing in the form of means of production) in order to replace the value of the constant capital expended in the production of articles of consumption. What distinguishes capitalist society in this case from the savage is not, as Senior[1] thinks, the privilege and peculiarity of the savage to expend his labour at times in a way that does not procure him any products resolvable (exchangeable) into revenue, i.e., into articles of consumption. No, the distinction consists in the following.

a) Capitalist society employs more of its available annual labour in the production of means of production (ergo, of constant capital) which are not resolvable into revenue in the form of wages or surplus-value, but can function only as capital.

b) When a savage makes bows, arrows, stone hammers, axes, baskets, etc., he knows very well that he did not spend the time so employed in the production of articles of consumption, but that he has thus stocked up the means of production he needs, and nothing else. Furthermore, a savage commits a grave economic sin by his utter indifference to waste of time, and, as Tylor[2] tells us, takes sometimes a whole month to make one arrow.

The current conception whereby some political economists seek to extricate themselves from the theoretical difficulty, i.e., the understanding of the real interconnections—that what is capital to one is revenue to another, and vice versa—is only partially correct and becomes utterly wrong (harbours therefore a complete misunderstanding of the entire process of exchange taking place in annual reproduction, hence also a misunderstanding of the actual basis of the partially correct) as soon as the character of universality is attributed to it.

We now summarise the actual relations on which the partial correctness of this conception rests, and in doing so the wrong conception of these relations will come to the surface.

1. The variable capital functions as capital in the hands of the capitalist and as revenue in the hands of the wage-worker.

   The variable capital exists at first in the hands of the capitalist as *money-capital*; and it performs the function of *money-capital*, by his buying labour-power with it. So long as it persists in his hands in the form of money, it is nothing but a given value existing in the form of money; hence a constant and not a variable magnitude. It is a variable capital only potentially, owing to its convertibility into labour-power. It becomes real variable capital only after divesting itself of its money-form, after being converted into labour-power functioning as a component part of productive capital in the capitalist process.

   Money, which first functioned as the money-form of the variable capital for the capitalist, now functions in the hands of the labourer as the money-form of his wages, which he exchanges for means of subsistence; i.e., as the money-form of *revenue* derived from the constantly repeated sale of his labour-power.

   We have here but the simple fact that the money of the buyer, in this case the capitalist, passes from his hands into those of the seller, in this case the seller of labour-power, the labourer. It is not a case of the variable *capital* functioning in a dual capacity, as capital for the capitalist and as revenue for the labourer. It is the same *money* which exists first in the hands of the capitalist as the money-form of his variable capital, hence as potential variable capital, and which serves in the hands of the labourer as an equivalent for sold labour-power as soon as the capitalist converts it into labour-power. But the fact that the same money serves another useful purpose in the hands of the seller than in those of the buyer is a phenomenon peculiar to the purchase and sale of all commodities.

   Apologetic economists present the matter in a wrong light, as is best seen if we keep our eyes fixed exclusively, without taking for the time being any notice of what follows, on the act of circulation M—L (equal to M—C), the conversion of money into labour-power on the part of the capitalist buyer, which is L—M (equal to C—M), the conversion of the commodity labour-power into money on the part of the seller, the labourer. They say: Here the same money realises two capitals; the buyer—the capitalist—converts his money-capital into living labour-power, which he incorporates in his productive capital; on the other hand the seller, the labourer, converts his commodity, labour-power, into money, which he spends as revenue, and this enables him to keep on reselling his labour-power and thereby to maintain it. His labour-power, then, represents his capital in commodity-form, which yields him a continuous revenue. Labour-power is indeed his property (ever self-renewing, reproductive), not his capital. It is the only commodity which he can and must sell continually in order to live, and which acts as capital (variable) only in the hands of the buyer, the capitalist. The fact that a man is continually compelled to sell his labour-power, i.e., himself, to another man proves, according to those economists, that he is a capitalist, because he constantly has 'commodities' (himself) for sale. In that sense a slave is also a capitalist, although he is sold by another once and for all as a commodity; for it is in the nature of this commodity, a labouring slave, that its buyer does not only make it work anew every day, but also provides it with the means of subsistence that enable it to work ever anew. (Compare on this point Sismondi and Say in the letters to Malthus.[3])

2. And so, in the exchange of 1,000 I_v + 1,000 I_s for 2,000 II_c, what is constant capital for some (2,000 II_c) becomes variable capital and surplus-value, hence generally revenue, for the others; and what is variable capital and surplus-value (2,000 $I_{(v+s)}$), hence generally revenue for some becomes constant capital for the others.

Let us first look at the exchange of I_v for II_c, beginning with the point of view of the labourer.

The collective labourer of I has sold his labour-power to the collective capitalist of I for 1,000; he receives this value in money, paid in the form of wages. With this money he buys from II articles of consumption for the same amount of value. Capitalist II confronts him only as a seller of commodities, and nothing else, even if the labourer buys from his own capitalist, as he does for instance in the exchange of 500 II_v, as we have seen above (Part IV, present chapter). The form of circulation through which his commodity, labour-power, passes, is that of the simple circulation of commodities for the mere satisfaction of needs, for the purpose of consumption: C (labour-power)—M—C (articles of consumption, commodities II). The result of this act of circulation is that the labourer maintains himself as labour-power for capitalist I, and in order to continue maintaining himself as such he must continually renew the process L(C)—M—C. His wages are realised in articles of consumption, they are spent as revenue, and, taking the working-class as a whole, are spent again and again as revenue.

Now let us look at the same exchange of I_v for II_c, from the point of view of the capitalist. The entire commodity-product of II consists of articles of consumption, hence of things intended to enter into annual consumption, hence to serve in the realisation of revenue for someone, in the present case for the collective labourer I. But for the collective capitalist II one portion of his commodity-product, equal to 2,000, is now the form of the constant capital-value of his productive capital converted into commodities. This productive capital must be reconverted from this commodity-form into its bodily form, in which it may act again as the constant portion of a productive capital. What capitalist II has accomplished so far is that he has reconverted by means of sales to labourers I one half (equal to 1,000) of his constant capital-value, which had been reproduced in the shape of commodities (articles of consumption), into the form of money. Hence it is not the variable capital I_v, which has been converted into this first half of the constant capital-value II_c, but simply the money which functioned for I as money-capital in the exchange for labour-power and thus came into the possession of the seller of labour-power, to whom it does not represent capital but revenue in the form of money, i.e., it is spent as a means of purchase of articles of consumption. Meanwhile, the money amounting to 1,000, which has come into the hands of the II capitalists from labourers of I, cannot function as the constant element of productive capital II. It is only as yet the money-form of his commodity-capital to be commuted into fixed or circulating constituents of constant capital. So II buys with the money received from the labourers of I, the buyers of its commodities, means of production from I to the amount of 1,000. In this way, the constant capital-value II is renewed to the extent of one half of its total amount in its bodily form, in which it can function once more as an element of productive capital II. The circulation in this instance took the course C—M—C: articles of consumption worth 1,000—money to the amount of 1,000—means of production worth 1,000.

But C—M—C represents here the movement of capital. C, when sold to the labourers, is converted into M, and this M is converted into means of production. It is the reconversion of commodities into the material elements of which this commodity is made. On the other hand just as capitalist II acts vis-à-vis I only as a buyer of commodities, so capitalist I acts only as a seller of commodities vis-à-vis II. I originally bought labour-power worth 1,000 with 1,000 in money intended to function as variable capital. It has therefore received an equivalent for the $1,000_v$ which it expended in money-form. This money now belongs to the labourer who spends it in purchases from II. I cannot get back this money, which thus found its way into the II treasury unless it fishes its way out of it again by the sale of commodities of the same value.

I first had a definite sum of money amounting to 1,000 destined to function as variable capital. The money functions as such by its conversion into labour-power of the same value. But the labourer supplied it as a result of the process of production with a quantity of commodities (means of production) worth 6,000, of which one-sixth, or 1,000, are equivalent to the variable portion of capital advanced in money. The variable capital-value functions no more as variable capital now in its commodity-form than it did before in its form of money. It can do so only after its conversion into living labour-power, and only so long as this labour-power functions in the process of production. As money, the variable capital-value was only potential variable capital. But it had a form in which it was directly convertible into labour-power. As a commodity the same variable capital-value is still potential money-value, it is restored to its original money-form only by the sale of the commodities, and therefore by II buying for 1,000 commodities from I. The movement of the circulation is here as follows: $1{,}000_v$ (money)—labour-power worth 1,000—1,000 in commodities (equivalent of the variable capital)—$1{,}000_v$ (money); hence M—C... C—M (equal to M—L ... C—M). The process of production intervening between C ... C does not itself belong in the sphere of circulation. It does not figure in the mutual exchange of the various elements of the annual reproduction, although this exchange includes the reproduction of all the elements of productive capital, the constant elements as well as the variable element (labour-power). All the participants in this exchange appear either as buyers or sellers or both. The labourers appear only as buyers of commodities, the capitalists alternately as buyers and sellers, and within certain limits either only as buyers of commodities or only as sellers of commodities.

Result: I possesses once more the variable value-constituent of its capital in the form of money, from which alone it is directly convertible into labour-power, i.e., it once more possesses the variable capital-value in the sole form in which it can really be advanced as a variable element of its productive capital. On the other hand, the labourer must again act as a seller of commodities, of his labour-power, before he can act again as a buyer of commodities.

So far as the variable capital of category II (500 II_v) is concerned, the process of circulation between the capitalists and labourers of the same class of production takes place directly, since we look upon it as taking place between the collective capitalist II and the collective labourer II.

The collective capitalist II advances 500_v for the purchase of labour-power of the same value. In this case, the collective capitalist is a buyer, the collective labourer a seller. Thereupon the labourer appears with the proceeds of the sale of his labour-power to act as a buyer of a part of the commodities produced by himself. Here the capitalist is therefore a seller. The labourer has replaced to the capitalist the money paid in the purchase of his labour-power by means of a portion of commodity-capital II produced, namely 500_v in commodities. The capitalist now holds in the form of commodities the same v which he had in the form of money before its conversion into labour-power, while the labourer on the other hand has realised the value of his labour-power in money and now, in his turn, realises this money by spending it as his revenue to defray his consumption in the purchase of part of the articles of consumption produced by himself. It is an exchange of the revenue of the labourer in money for a portion of commodities he has himself reproduced, namely 500_v of the capitalist. In this way this money returns to capitalist II as the money-form of his variable capital. An equivalent value of revenue in the form of money here replaces variable capital-value in the form of commodities.

The capitalist does not increase his wealth by taking away again the money paid by him to the labourer in the purchase of labour-power when he sells him an equivalent quantity of commodities. He would indeed be paying the labourer twice if he were to pay him first 500 in the purchase of his labour-power, and then in addition give him gratis a quantity of commodities worth 500, which the labourers produced for him. Vice versa, if the labourer were to produce for him nothing but an equivalent in commodities worth 500 for the price of his labour-power of 500, the capitalist would be no better off after the transaction than before. But the labourer has reproduced a product of 3,000. He has preserved the constant portion of the value of the product, i.e., the value of the means of production used up in it to the amount of 2,000 by converting them into a new product. He has furthermore added to this given value a value of $1{,}000_{(v + s)}$. (The idea that the capitalist grows richer in the sense that he wins a surplus-value by the reflux of the 500 in money is developed by Destutt de Tracy, as shown in detail in section XIII of this chapter.)

Through the purchase of 500 worth of articles of consumption by labourer II, capitalist II recovers the value of 500 II_v—which he just possessed in commodities—in money, the form in which he advanced it originally. The immediate result of this transaction, as of any other sale of commodities, is the conversion of a given value from the form of commodities into that of money. Nor is there anything special in the reflux thus effected of the money to its point of departure. If capitalist II had bought, with 500 in money, commodities from capitalist I, and then in turn sold to capitalist I commodities to the amount of 500, 500 would have likewise returned to him in money. This sum of 500 in money would merely have served for the circulation of a quantity of commodities (1,000), and according to the general law previously expounded, the money would have returned to the one who put it into circulation for the purpose of exchanging this quantity of commodities.

But the 500 in money which flowed back to capitalist II are at one and the same time renewed potential variable capital in money-form. Why is this so? Money, and therefore money-capital, is potential variable capital only because and to the extent that it is convertible into labour-power. The return of £500 in money to capitalist II is accompanied by the return of labour-power II to the market. The return of both of these at opposite poles—hence also the re-appearance of 500 in money, not only as money but also as variable capital in the form of money—is conditional on one and the same process. The money equal to 500 returns to capitalist II because he sold to labourers II articles of consumption amounting to 500, i.e., because the labourer spends his wages to maintain himself and his family and thus his labour-power. In order to be able to live on and act again as a buyer of commodities he must again sell his labour-power. The return of 500 in money to capitalist II is therefore at the same time a return, or an abiding, of the labour-power in the capacity of a commodity purchasable with 500 in money, and thereby a return of 500 in money as potential variable capital.

As for category IIb, which produces articles of luxury, the case with v—$(IIb)_v$—is the same as with I_v. The money, which renews for capitalists IIb their variable capital in the form of money, flows back to them in a round-about way through capitalists IIa. But it nevertheless makes a difference whether the labourers buy their means of subsistence directly from the capitalist producers to whom they sell their labour-power or whether they buy them from capitalists of another category, through whose agency the money returns to the former only by a circuitous route. Since the working-class lives from hand to mouth, it buys as long as it has the means to buy. It is different with the capitalists, as for instance in the exchange of 1,000 II_c for 1,000 I_v. The capitalist does not live from hand to mouth. His compelling motive is the utmost self-expansion of his capital. Now, if circumstances of any description seem to promise greater advantages to capitalist II in case he holds on to his money, or to part of it at least, for a while, instead of immediately renewing his constant capital, then the return of 1,000 II_c (in money) to I is delayed; and so is the restoration of $1{,}000_v$ to the form of money, and capitalist I can continue his business on the same scale only if he disposes of reserve money; and, generally speaking, reserve capital in the form of money is necessary to be able to work without interruption, regardless of the rapid or slow reflux of the variable capital-value in money.

If the exchange of the various elements of the current annual reproduction is to be investigated, so are the results of the labour of the preceding year, of the labour of the year that has already come to a close. The process of production which resulted in this yearly product lies behind us; it is a thing of the past, incorporated in its product, and so much the more is this the case with the process of circulation, which precedes the process of production or runs parallel with it, the conversion of potential into real variable capital, i.e., the sale and purchase of labour-power. The labour-market is no longer a part of the commodity-market, such as we have here before us. The labourer has here not only already sold his labour-power, but besides the surplus-value also supplied an equivalent of the price of his labour-power in the shape of commodities. He has furthermore pocketed his wages and figures during the exchange only as a buyer of commodities (articles of consumption). On the other hand the annual product must contain all the elements of reproduction, restore all the elements of productive capital, above all its most important element, the variable capital. And we have seen indeed that the result of the exchange in regard to the variable capital is this: By spending his wages and consuming the purchased commodities, the labourer as a buyer of commodities maintains and reproduces his labour-power, this being the only commodity which he has to sell. Just as the money advanced by the capitalist in the purchase of his labour-power returns to him, so labour-power returns to the labour-market in its capacity of a commodity exchangeable for money. The result in the special case of 1,000 I_v is that the capitalists of I hold $1{,}000_v$ in money and the labourers of I offer them 1,000 in labour-power, so that the entire process of reproduction of I can be renewed. This is one result of the process of exchange.

On the other hand, the expenditure of the wages of the labourers of I relieved II of articles of consumption to the amount of $1{,}000_c$, thus transforming them from the commodity-form into the money-form. Department II reconverted them into the bodily form of its constant capital by purchasing from I commodities equal to $1{,}000_v$ and thus restoring to I in money-form the value of its variable capital. The variable capital of I passes through three metamorphoses, which do not appear at all in the exchange of the annual product or do so only suggestively.

1. The first form is 1,000 I_v in money, which is converted into labour-power of the same value. This conversion does not itself appear in the exchange of commodities between I and II, but its result is seen in the fact that working-class I confronts commodity seller II with 1,000 in money, just as working-class II with 500 in money confronts commodity seller of 500 II_v in commodity-form.
2. The second form, the only one in which variable capital actually varies, functions as variable capital, where value-creating force appears in the place of given value exchanged for it; it belongs exclusively to the process of production which is behind us.
3. The third form, in which the variable capital has justified itself as such in the result of the process of production, is the annual value-product, which in the case of I is equal to $1{,}000_v$ plus $1{,}000_s$, or 2,000 $I_{(v+s)}$. In the place of its original value of 1,000 in money we have a value of double this amount, or 2,000, in commodities. The variable capital-value of 1,000 in commodities is therefore only one half of the value produced by the variable capital as an element of the productive capital. The 1,000 I_v in commodities are an exact equivalent of the 1,000 in money originally advanced by I and intended to be the variable part of the aggregate capital. But in the form of commodities they are money only potentially (they do not become so actually until they are sold), and still less directly are they variable money-capital. They eventually become variable money-capital by the sale of the commodity 1,000 I_v to II_c, and by the early re-appearance of labour-power as a purchasable commodity, as a material for which 1,000 in money may be exchanged.

During all these transformations capitalist I continually holds the variable capital in his hands; 1) to start with as money-capital; 2) then as an element of his productive capital;

3) still later as a portion of the value of his commodity-capital, hence in the form of commodity-value; 4) finally once more in money which is again confronted by the labour-power for which it can be exchanged. During the labour-process the capitalist is in possession of the variable capital as active value-creating labour-power, but not as a value of a given magnitude. But since he never pays the labourer until his power has acted for a certain length of time, he already has in hand the value created by that power to replace itself plus the surplus-value before he pays him.

As the variable capital always stays in the hands of the capitalist in some form or other, it cannot be claimed in any way that it converts itself into revenue for anyone. On the contrary, 1,000 I_v in commodities converts itself into money by its sale to II half of whose constant capital it replaces in kind.

What resolves itself into revenue is not variable capital I, or $1{,}000_v$ in money. This money has ceased to function as the money-form of variable capital I as soon as it is converted into labour-power, just as the money of any other buyer of commodities has ceased to represent anything belonging to him as soon as he has exchanged it for commodities of still other sellers. The conversions which the money received in wages goes through in the hands of the working-class are not conversions of variable capital, but of the value of their labour-power converted into money; just as the conversion of the value (2,000 $I_{(v+s)}$) created by the labourer is only the conversion of a commodity belonging to the capitalist, which does not concern the labourer. However, the capitalist, and still more his theoretical interpreter, the political economist, can rid himself only with the greatest difficulty of the idea that the money paid to the labourer is still his, the capitalist's. If the capitalist is a producer of gold, then the variable portion of value—i.e., the equivalent in commodities which replaces for him the purchasing price of the labour—appears itself directly in the form of money and can therefore function anew as variable money-capital without the circuitous route of a reflux. But so far as labourer II is concerned—aside from the labourer who produces articles of luxury—500 v exists in commodities intended for the consumption of the labourer which he, considered as the collective labourer, buys directly again from the same collective capitalist to whom he sold his labour-power. The variable portion of capital-value II, so far as its bodily form is concerned, consists of articles of consumption intended mostly for consumption by the working-class. But it is not the variable capital which is spent in this form by the labourer, it is the wages, the money of the labourer, which precisely by its realisation in these articles of consumption restores to the capitalist the variable capital 500 II_v in its money-form. The variable capital II_v is reproduced in articles of consumption, the same as the constant capital 2,000 II_c. The one resolves itself no more into revenue than the other does. In either case it is the wages which resolve themselves into revenue.

However it is a momentous fact in the exchange of the annual product that by the expenditure of the wages as revenue there is restored to the form of money-capital in the one case 1,000 II_c, likewise, by this circuitous route, 1,000 I_v and ditto 500 II_v, hence constant and variable capital. (In the case of the variable capital partly by means of a direct and partly by means of an indirect reflux.)

PART 3

Section XI. *Replacement of the Fixed Capital*

In the analysis of the exchanges of the annual reproduction the following presents great difficulty. If we take the simplest form in which the matter may be presented, we get:

I. $4{,}000_c + 1{,}000_v + 1{,}000_s +$

II. $2{,}000_c + 500_v + 500_s = 9{,}000$. This resolves itself finally into: $4{,}000\ I_c + 2{,}000\ II_c + 1{,}000\ I_v + 500\ II_v + 1{,}000\ I_s + 500\ II_s = 6{,}000_c + 1{,}500_v + 1{,}500_s = 9{,}000$

One portion of the value of the constant capital, which consists of instruments of labour in the strict meaning of the term (as a distinct section of the means of production) is transferred from the instruments of labour to the product of labour (the commodity); these instruments of labour continue to function as elements of the productive capital, doing so in their old bodily form. It is their wear and tear, the depreciation gradually experienced by them during their continual functioning for a definite period which re-appears as an element of value of the commodities produced by means of them, which is transferred from the instrument of labour to the product of labour. With regard to the annual reproduction therefore only such component parts of fixed capital will from the first be given consideration as last longer than a year. If they are completely worn out within the year they must be completely replaced and renewed by the annual reproduction, and the point at issue does not concern them at all. It may happen in the case of machines and other more durable forms of fixed capital—and it frequently does happen—that certain parts of them must be replaced lock, stock and barrel within one year, although the building or machine in its entirety lasts much longer. These parts belong in one category with the elements of fixed capital which are to be replaced within one year.

This element of the value of commodities must not be confused with the costs of repair. If a commodity is sold, this value-element is turned into money, the same as all others. But after it has been turned into money, its difference from the other elements of value becomes apparent. The raw and auxiliary materials consumed in the production of commodities must be replaced in kind in order that the reproduction of commodities may begin (or that the process of production of commodities in general may be continuous). The labour-power spent on them must also be renewed by fresh labour-power. Consequently, the money realised on the commodities must be continually reconverted into these elements of the productive capital, from the money-form into the commodity-form. It does not alter the matter if raw and auxiliary materials, for instance, are bought at certain intervals in larger quantities—so that they constitute productive supplies—and need not be bought anew during certain periods; and therefore—as long as they last—the money coming in through the sale of commodities, inasmuch as it is meant for this purpose, may accumulate and this portion of constant capital thus appears temporarily as money-capital whose active function has been suspended. It is not a revenue-capital; it is productive capital suspended in the form of money. The renewal of the means of production must go on all the time, although the form of this renewal—with reference to the circulation—may vary. The new purchases, the circulation operation by which they are renewed or replaced, may take place at more or at less prolonged intervals: then a large amount may be invested at one stroke, compensated by a corresponding productive supply. Or the intervals between purchases may be small: then follows a rapid succession of money expenditures in small doses, of small productive supplies. This does not alter the matter itself. The same applies to labour-power. Where production is carried on continuously throughout the year on the same scale—continuous replacement of consumed labour-power by new. Where work is seasonable, or different portions of labour are applied at different periods, as in agriculture—corresponding purchases of labour-power, now in small, now in large amounts. But the money proceeds realised from the sale of commodities, so far as they turn into money that part of the commodity-value which is equal to the wear and tear of fixed capital, are not re-converted into that component part of the productive capital whose diminution in value they cover. They settle down beside the productive capital and persist in the form of money. This precipitation of money is repeated, until the period of reproduction consisting of great or small numbers of years has elapsed, during which the fixed element of constant capital continues to function in the process of production in its old bodily form. As soon as the fixed element, such as buildings, machinery, etc., has been worn out, and can no longer function in the process of production, its value exists alongside it fully replaced by money, by the sum of money precipitations, the values which had been gradually transferred from the fixed capital to the commodities in whose production it participated and which had assumed the form of money as a result of the sale of these commodities. This money then serves to replace the fixed capital (or its elements, since its various elements have different durabilities) in kind and thus really to renew this component part of the productive capital. This money is therefore the money-form of a part of the constant capital-value, namely of its fixed part. The formation of this hoard is thus itself an element of the capitalist process of reproduction; it is the reproduction and storing up—in the form of money—of the value of fixed capital, or its several elements, until the fixed capital has ceased to live and in consequence has given off its full value to the commodities produced and must now be replaced in kind. But this money loses only its form of a hoard and hence resumes its activity in the process of reproduction of capital brought about by the circulation as soon as it is reconverted into new elements of fixed capital to replace those that died off.

Just as simple commodity circulation is in no way identical with a bare exchange of products, the conversion of the annual commodity-product can in no way resolve itself into a mere unmediated mutual exchange of its various components. Money plays a specific role in it, which finds expression particularly in the manner in which the value of the fixed capital is reproduced. (How different the matter would present itself if production were collective and no longer possessed the form of commodity production is left to a later analysis.)

Should we now return to our fundamental scheme, we shall get the following for class II: $2{,}000_c + 500_v + 500_s$. All the articles of consumption produced in the course of the year are in that case equal in value to 3,000; and every one of the different commodity elements in the total sum of the commodities is composed, so far as its value is concerned, of $⅔_c + 1/6_v + 1/6_s$, or, in percentages, $66⅔_c + 16⅔_v + 16⅔_s$. The various kinds of commodities of class II may contain different proportions of constant capital. Likewise the fixed portion of the constant capital may be different. The duration of the parts of the fixed capital and hence the annual wear and tear, or that portion of value which they transfer *pro rata* to the commodities in the production of which they participate, may also differ. But that is immaterial here. As to the process of social reproduction, it is only a question of exchange between classes II and I. These two classes here confront each other only in their social, mass relations. Therefore, the proportional magnitude of part c of the value of commodity-product II (the only one of consequence in the question now being discussed) gives the average proportion if all the branches of production classed under II are embraced.

Every kind of commodity (and they are largely the same kinds) whose aggregate value is classed under $2{,}000_c + 500_v + 500_s$ is therefore equal in value to $66⅔\%_c + 16⅔\%_v + 16⅔\%_s$. This applies to every 100 of the commodities, whether classed under c, v or s.

The commodities in which the $2{,}000_c$ are incorporated may be further divided, in value, into:

1. $1{,}333⅓_c + 333⅓_v + 333⅓_s = 2{,}000_c$; similarly 500_v may be divided into:
2. $333⅓_c + 83⅓_v + 83⅓_s = 500_v$; and finally 500_s may be divided into:
3. $333⅓_c + 83⅓_v + 83⅓_s = 500_s$

Now, if we add the c's in 1), 2), and 3) we get $1{,}333⅓_c + 333⅓_c + 333⅓_c = 2{,}000$. Furthermore $333⅓_v + 83⅓_v + 83⅓_v = 500$.

And the same in the case of s. The addition gives the same total value of 3,000, as above.

The entire constant capital-value contained in the commodity mass II representing a value of 3,000 is therefore comprised in $2{,}000_c$, and neither 500_v nor 500_s hold an atom of it. The same is true of v and s respectively.

In other words, the entire share of commodity mass II that represents constant capital-value and therefore is reconvertible either into its bodily or its money-form, exists in $2,000_c$. Everything referring to the exchange of the constant value of commodities II is therefore confined to the movement of 2,000 II_c. And this exchange can be made only with I ($1,000_v$ + $1,000_s$).

Similarly, as regards class I, everything that bears in the exchange of the constant capital-value of that class is to be confined to a consideration of 4,000 I_c.

1. Replacement of the Wear and Tear Portion of the Value in the Form of Money

Now, if to start with we take

I. 4,000c + 1,000v + 1,000s

II. .... 2,000c + 500v + 500s,

the exchange of the commodities 2,000 II_c for commodities of the same value I ($1,000_v$ + $1,000_s$) would presuppose that the entire 2,000 II_c are reconverted in kind into the natural elements of the constant capital of II, produced by I. But the commodity-value of 2,000, in which the latter exists, contains an element making good the depreciation in value of the fixed capital, which is not to be replaced immediately in kind but converted into money, which gradually accumulates into a sum total until the time for the renewal of the fixed capital in its bodily form arrives. Every year registers the demise of fixed capital which must be replaced in this or that individual business, or in this or that branch of industry. In the case, of one and the same individual capital, this or that portion of its fixed capital must be replaced, since its different parts have different durabilities. On examining annual reproduction, even on a simple scale, i.e., disregarding all accumulation, we do not begin *ab ovo*. The year which we study is one in the course of many; it is not the first year after the birth of capitalist production. The various capitals invested in the manifold lines of production of class II therefore differ in age. Just as people functioning in these lines of production die annually, so a host of fixed capitals expire annually and must be renewed in kind out of the accumulated money-fund. Therefore the exchange of 2,000 II_c for 2,000 $I_{(v+s)}$ includes a conversion of 2,000 II_c from its commodity-form (articles of consumption) into natural elements which consist not only of raw and auxiliary materials but also of natural elements of fixed capital, such as machinery, tools, buildings, etc. The wear and tear, which must be replaced in money in the value of 2,000 II_c, therefore by no means corresponds to the amount of the functioning fixed capital, since a portion of this must be replaced in kind every year. But this assumes that the money necessary for this replacement was accumulated in former years by the capitalists of class II. However that very condition holds good in the same measure for the current year as for the preceding ones.

In the exchange between I ($1,000_v$ + $1,000_s$) and 2,000 II_c it must be first noted that the sum of values $I_{(v+s)}$ does not contain any constant element of value, hence also no element of value to replace wear and tear, i.e., value that has been transmitted from the fixed component of the constant capital to the commodities in whose bodily form v + s exist. On the other hand, this element exists in II_c, and it is precisely a part of this value-element that owes its existence to fixed capital which is not to be converted immediately from the money-form into its bodily form, but has first to persist in the form of money. The exchange between I ($1,000_v$ + $1,000_s$) and 2,000 II_c, therefore, at once presents the difficulty that the means of production of I, in whose bodily form the $2,000_{(v+s)}$ exist, are to be exchanged to the full value of 2,000 for an equivalent in articles of consumption II, while on the other hand the 2,000 II_c of articles of consumption cannot be exchanged at their full value for means of production I ($1,000_v$ + $1,000_s$) because an aliquot part of their value—equal to the wear and tear, or the value depreciation of the fixed capital that is to be replaced—must first be precipitated in the form of money that will not function any more as a medium of circulation during the current period of annual reproduction, which alone we are examining. But the money paying for this element of wear and tear incorporated in the commodity-value 2,000 II_c can come only from department I, since II cannot pay for itself but effects payment precisely by selling its goods, and since presumably $I_{(v+s)}$ buys the whole of the commodities 2,000 II_c. Hence class I must, by means of this purchase, convert that wear and tear into money for II. But according to the law previously evolved, money advanced to the circulation returns to the capitalist producer who later on throws an equal amount of commodities into circulation. It is evident that in buying II_c, I cannot give II commodities worth 2,000 and a surplus amount of money on top of that once and for all (without any return of the same by way of the operation of exchange). Otherwise, I would buy the commodity mass II above its value. If II actually exchanges its $2{,}000_c$ for I ($1{,}000_v$ + $1{,}000_s$), it has no further claims on I, and the money circulating in this exchange returns to either I or II, depending on which of them threw it into circulation, i.e., which of them acted first as buyer. At the same time, II would have reconverted the entire value of its commodity-capital into the bodily form of means of production, while our assumption is that after its sale it would not reconvert an aliquot portion of it during the current period of annual reproduction from money into the bodily form of fixed components of its constant capital. A money balance in favour of II could arise only if it sold 2,000 worth to I and bought less than 2,000 from I, say only 1,800. In that case, I would have to make good the debit balance by 200 in money, which would not flow back to it, because it would not have withdrawn from circulation the money it had advanced to it by throwing into it commodities equal to 200. In such an event we would have a money-fund for II, placed to the credit of the wear and tear of its fixed capital. But then we would have an over-production of means of production in the amount of 200 on the other side, the side of I, and the basis of our scheme would be destroyed, namely reproduction on the same scale, where complete proportionality between the various systems of production is assumed. We would only have done away with one difficulty in order to create another one much worse.

As this problem offers peculiar difficulties and has hitherto not been treated at all by the political economists, we shall examine *seriatim* all possible (at least seemingly possible) solutions, or rather formulations of the problem.

In the first place, we have just assumed that II sells commodities of the value of 2,000 to I, but buys from it only 1,800 worth. The commodity-value 2,000 II_c contains 200 for replacement of wear and tear, which must be stored up in the form of money. The value of 2,000 II_c would thus be divided into 1,800, to be exchanged for means of production I, and 200, to replace wear and tear, which are to be kept in the form of money (after the sale of the $2{,}000_c$ to I). Expressed in terms of value, 2,000 II_c equals $1{,}800_c$ + 200_c(d), this d standing for *déchet.* [*Wear and tear.—Ed.*]

We would then have to study exchange

I. $1{,}000_v + 1{,}000_s$
II. $1{,}800_c + 200_c$(d).

I buys with £1,000, which has gone to the labourers in wages for their labour-power, 1,000 II_c of articles of consumption. II buys with the same £1,000 means of production 1,000 I_v. Capitalists I thus recover their variable capital in the form of money and can employ it next year in the purchase of labour power to the same amount, i.e., they can replace the variable portion of their productive capital in kind.

Furthermore, II buys with advanced £400 means of production I_s, and I_s buys with the same £400 articles of consumption II_c. The £400 advanced to the circulation by the capitalists of II have thus returned to them, but only as an equivalent for sold commodities. I now buys articles of consumption for advanced £400; II buys from I £400 worth of means of production, whereupon these £400 flow back to I. So far, then, the account is as follows:

I. throws into circulation $1{,}000_v$ + 800_s in commodities; it furthermore throws into circulation, in money, £1,000 in wages and £400 for exchange with II. After the exchange has been made, I has $1{,}000_v$ in money, 800_s exchanged for 800 II_c (articles of consumption) and £400 in money.

II. throws into circulation $1{,}800_c$ in commodities (articles of consumption) and £400 in money. On the completion of the exchange it has 1,800 in commodities I (means of production) and £400 in money.

There still remain, on the side of I, 200_s (in means of production) and, on the side of II, 200_c(d) (in articles of consumption).

According to our assumption I buys with £200 the articles of consumption c (d) of the value of 200. But II holds on to these £200 since 200 c (d) represent wear and tear, and are not to be immediately reconverted into means of production. Therefore 200 I_s cannot be sold. One-fifth of the surplus-value I to be replaced cannot be realised, or converted, from its bodily form of means of production into that of articles of consumption.

This not only contradicts our assumption of reproduction on a simple scale; it is by itself not a hypothesis which would explain the transformation of 200_c(d) into money. It means rather that it cannot be explained. Since it cannot be demonstrated in what manner 200_c(d) can be converted into money, it is assumed that I is obliging enough to do the conversion just because it is not able to convert its own remainder of 200_s into money. To conceive this as a normal operation of the exchange mechanism is tantamount to the notion that £200 fall every year from the clouds in order regularly to convert 200_c(d) into money.

But the absurdity of such a hypothesis does not strike one at once if I_s, instead of appearing, as it does in this case, in its primitive mode of existence—namely as a component part of the value of means of production, hence as a component part of the value of commodities which their capitalist producers must convert into money by sale—appears in the hands of the partners of the capitalists, for instance as ground-rent in the hands of landowners or as interest in the bands of moneylenders. But, if that portion of the surplus-value of commodities which the industrial capitalist has to yield as ground-rent or interest to other co-owners of the surplus-value cannot be realised for a long time by the sale of the commodities, then there is also an end to the payment of rent and interest, and the landowners or recipients of interest cannot therefore serve as *dei ex machina* to convert at pleasure definite portions of the annual reproduction into money by spending rent and interest. The same is true of the expenditures of all so-called unproductive labourers—government officials, physicians, lawyers, etc., and others who as members of the 'general public' 'serve' the political economists by explaining what they left unexplained.

Nor does it improve matters if instead of direct exchange between I and II—between the two major departments of capitalist producers—the merchant is drawn in as mediator and helps to overcome all difficulties with his 'money.' In the present case for instance, 200 I_s must be definitively disposed of to the industrial capitalists of II. It may pass through the hands of a number of merchants, but the last of them will find himself, according to the hypothesis, in the same predicament, vis- à-vis II, in which the capitalist producers of I were at the outset, i.e., they cannot sell the 200 I_s to II. And this stalled purchase sum cannot renew the same process with I.

We see here that, aside from our real purpose, it is absolutely necessary to view the process of reproduction in its basic form—in which obscuring minor circumstances have been eliminated—in order to get rid of the false subterfuges which furnish the semblance of 'scientific' analysis when the process of social reproduction is immediately made the subject of the analysis in its complicated concrete form.

The law that when reproduction proceeds normally (whether it be on a simple or on an extended scale) the money advanced by the capitalist producer to the circulation must return to its point of departure (whether the money is his own or borrowed) excludes once and for all the hypothesis that 200 II_c(d) is converted into money by means of money advanced by I.

2. Replacement of Fixed Capital in Kind

Having disposed of the hypothesis considered above, only such possibilities remain as, besides replacing the wear-and-tear portion in money, include also the replacement in kind of the wholly defunct fixed capital.

We assumed hitherto

a) that £1,000 paid in wages by I are spent by the labourers for II_c to the same amount, i.e., that they buy articles of consumption with them. It is merely a statement of fact that these £1,000 are advanced by I in money. Wages must be paid in money by the respective capitalist producers. This money is then spent by the labourers for articles of consumption and serves the sellers of the articles of consumption as a medium of circulation in the conversion of their constant capital from commodity-capital into productive capital. True, it passes through many channels (shopkeepers, house owners, tax collectors, unproductive labourers, such as physicians, etc., who are needed by the labourer himself) and hence it flows only in part directly from the hands of labourers I into those of capitalist class II. Its flow may be retarded more or less and the capitalist may therefore require a new money-reserve. All this does not come under consideration in this basic form.

b) We assumed that at one time I advances another £400 in money for purchases from II and that this money returns to it, while at some other time II advances £400 for purchases from I and likewise recovers this money. This assumption must be made, for it would be arbitrary to presuppose the contrary, that capitalist class I or II should one-sidedly advance to the circulation of the money necessary for the exchange of their commodities. Since we have shown under subtitle 1 that one should reject as absurd the hypothesis that I would throw additional money into the circulation in order to turn 200 II_c(d) into money, it would appear that there was left only the seemingly still more absurd hypothesis that II itself was throwing the money into circulation, by which that constituent portion of the value of its commodities is converted into money which has to compensate the wear and tear of its fixed capital. For instance, that portion of value which is lost by the spinning-machine of Mr. X in the process of production re-appears as a portion of the value of the yarn. The loss which his spinning-machine suffers in value, i.e., in wear and tear, on the one hand, should accumulate in his hands as money on the other. Now supposing that X buys £200 worth of cotton from Y and thus advances to the circulation £200 in money. Y then buys from him £200 worth of yarn, and these £200 now serve X as a fund to compensate the wear and tear of his machine. The thing would simply come down to this—that X, aside from his production, its product, and the sale of this product, keeps £200 *in petto* to make good to himself the depreciation of his spinning-machine, i.e., that in addition to losing £200 through the depreciation of his machine, he must also put up another £200 in money every year out of his own pocket in order to be able eventually to buy a new spinning-machine.

But the absurdity is only apparent. Class II consists of capitalists whose fixed capital is in the most diverse stages of its reproduction. In the case of some of them it has arrived at the stage where it must be entirely replaced in kind. In the case of the others it is more or less remote from that stage. All the members of the latter group have this in common, that their fixed capital is not actually reproduced, i.e., is not renewed *in natura* by a new specimen of the same kind, but that its value is successively accumulated in money. The first group is in quite the same (or almost the same, it does not matter here) position as when it started in business, when it came on the market with its money-capital in order to convert it into constant (fixed and circulating) capital on the one hand and into labour-power, into variable capital, on the other. They have once more to advance this money-capital to the circulation, i.e., the value of constant fixed capital as well as that of the circulating and variable capital.

Hence, if we assume that half of the £400 thrown into circulation by capitalist class II for exchange with I comes from those capitalists of II who have to renew not only by means of their commodities their means of production pertaining to the circulating capital, but also, by means of their money, their fixed capital in kind, while the other half of capitalists II replaces in kind with its money only the circulating portion of its constant capital, but does not renew in kind its fixed capital, then there is no contradiction in the statement that these returning £400 (returning as soon as I buys articles of consumption for it) are variously distributed among these two sections of II. They return to class II, but they do not come back into the same hands and are distributed variously within this class, passing from one of its sections to another.

One section of II has, besides the part of the means of production covered in the long run by its commodities, converted £200 in money into new elements of fixed capital in kind. As was the case at the start of the business the money thus spent returns to this section from the circulation only gradually over a number of years as the wear-and-tear portion of the value of the commodities to be produced by this fixed capital.

The other section of II however did not get any commodities from I for £200. But I pays it with the money which the first section of II spent for elements of its fixed capital. The first section of II has its fixed capital-value once more in renewed bodily form, while the second section is still engaged in accumulating it in money-form for the subsequent replacement of its fixed capital in kind.

The basis on which we now have to proceed after the previous exchanges is the remainder of the commodities still to be exchanged by both sides: 400_s on the part of I, and 400_c on the part of II.[4] We assume that II advances 400 in money for the exchange of these commodities amounting to 800. One half of the 400 (equal to 200) must be laid out under all circumstances by that section of II_c which has accumulated 200 in money as the wear-and-tear value and which has to reconvert this money into the bodily form of its fixed capital.

Just as constant capital-value, variable capital-value, and surplus-value—into which the value of commodity-capital II as well as I is divisible—may be represented by special proportional shares of commodities II and I respectively, so may, within the value of the constant capital itself, that portion of the value which is not yet to be converted into the bodily form of the fixed capital, but is rather to be accumulated for the time being in the form of money. A certain quantity of commodities II (in the present case therefore one half of the remainder, or 200) is here only a vehicle of this wear-and-tear value, which has to be precipitated in money by means of exchange. (The first section of capitalists II, which renews fixed capital in kind, may already have realised in this way—with the wear-and-tear part of the mass of commodities of which here only the rest still figures—a part of its wear-and-tear value, but it still has to realise 200 in money.)

As for the second half (equal to 200) of the £400 thrown into circulation by II in this final operation, it buys circulating components of constant capital from I. A portion of these £200 may be thrown into circulation by both sections of II, or only by the one which does not renew its fixed component of value in kind.

With these £400 there is thus extracted from I: 1) commodities amounting to £200, consisting only of elements of fixed capital; 2) commodities amounting to £200, replacing only natural elements of the circulating portion of the constant capital of II. So I has sold its entire annual product, so far as it is to be sold to II; but the value of one-fifth of it, £400, is now held by I in the form of money. This money however is surplus-value converted into money which must be spent as revenue for articles of consumption. Thus I buys with its £400 II's entire commodity-value equal to 400; hence this money flows back to II by setting its commodities in motion.

We shall now suppose three cases, in which we shall call the section of capitalists II which replaces its fixed capital in kind 'section 1,' and that section which stores up depreciation-value from fixed capital in money-form, 'section 2.' The three cases are the following: a) that a share of the 400 still existing with II as a remnant in the shape of commodities must replace certain shares of the circulating parts of the constant capital for sections 1 and 2 (say, one half for each); b) that section 1 has already sold all its commodities, while section 2 still has to sell 400; c) that section 2 has sold all but the 200 which are the bearers of the depreciation value.

Then we have the following distributions:

(a) Of the commodity-value 400_c, still in the hands of II, section 1 holds 100 and section 2—300; 200 out of the 300 represent depreciation. In that case, section 1 originally laid out 300 of the £400 in money now returned by I to get commodities from II, namely 200 in money, for which it secured elements of fixed capital in kind from I, and 100 in money for the promotion of its exchange of commodities with I. Section 2, on the other hand, advanced only ¼ of the 400, i.e., 100, likewise for the promotion of its commodity-exchange with I.

Section 1, then, advanced 300, and section 2—100 of the 400 in money.

Of these 400 there return however:

To section 1—100 i.e., only one-third of the money advanced by it. But it has in place of the other ⅔ a renewed fixed capital to the value of 200. Section 1 has given money to I for this element of fixed capital to the value of 200, but no subsequent commodities. So far as the 200 in money are concerned, section 1 confronts department I only as buyer, but not later on as seller. This money cannot therefore return to section 1; otherwise it would have received the elements of fixed capital from I as a gift.

With reference to the last third of the money advanced by it, section 1 first acted as a buyer of circulating constituent parts of its constant capital. With the same money I buys from it the remainder of its commodities worth 100. This money, then, flows back to it (section 1 of department II) because it acts as a vendor of commodities directly after having acted as a buyer. If this money did not return, then II (section 1) would have given to I, for commodities amounting to 100, first 100 in money, and then into the bargain, 100 in commodities, i.e., II would have given away its commodities to I as a present.

On the other hand, section 2, which laid out 100 in money receives back 300 in money: 100 because first as a buyer it threw 100 in money into circulation, and receives them back as a seller; 200, because it functions only as a seller of commodities to that amount, but not as a buyer. Hence the money cannot flow back to I. The fixed capital depreciation is thus balanced by the money thrown into circulation by II (section 1) in the purchase of elements of fixed capital. But it reaches the hands of section 2 not as money of section 1, but as money belonging to class I.

(b) On this assumption the remainder of II is so distributed that section 1 has 200 in money and section 2 has 400 in commodities.

Section 1 has sold all of its commodities, but 200 in money are a transformed shape of the fixed component part of its constant capital which it has to renew in kind. Hence it acts here only as a buyer and receives instead of its money commodity I to the same value in natural elements of its fixed capital. Section 2 has to throw only £200 into circulation, as a maximum (if I does not advance any money for commodity-exchange between I and II), since for half of its commodity-value it is only a seller to I, not a buyer from I.

There return to section 2 from the circulation £400: 200, because it has advanced them as a buyer and receives them back as a seller of 200 in commodities; 200, because it sells commodities to the value of 200 to I without obtaining an equivalent in commodities from I.

(c) Section 1 has 200 in money and 200 in commodities. Section 2 has 200 c (d) in commodities.

On this supposition section 2 does not have any advance to make in money, because vis-à-vis I it no longer acts at all as buyer but only as seller, hence has to wait until someone buys from it.

Section 1 advances £400 in money: 200 for mutual commodity-exchange with I, 200 as mere buyer from I. With the last £200 in money it purchases the elements of fixed capital.

With £200 in money I buys from section 1 commodities for 200, so that the latter thus recovers the £200 in money it had advanced for this commodity-exchange. And I buys with the other £200, which it has likewise received from section 1, commodities to the value of 200 from section 2, whereby the latter's wear and tear of fixed capital is precipitated in the form of money.

The matter is not altered in the least if it is assumed that, in case c), class I instead of II (section 1) advances the 200 in money to promote the exchange of the existing commodities. If I buys in that event first 200 in commodities from II, section 2, on the assumption that this section has only this commodity remnant left to sell—then the £200 do not return to I, since II, section 2, does not act again as buyer. But II, section 1, has in that case £200 in money to spend in buying and 200 in commodities for exchange purposes, thus making a total of 400 for trading with I, £200 in money then return to I from II, section 1. If I again lays them out in the purchase of 200 in commodities from II, section 1, they return to I as soon as II, section 1, takes the second half of the 400 in commodities off I's hands. Section 1 (II) has spent £200 in money as a mere buyer of elements of fixed capital; they therefore do not return to it, but serve to turn the 200_c, the commodity remnant of II, section 2, into money, while the £200, the money laid out by I for the exchange of commodities, return to I via II, section 1, not via II, section 2. In the place of its commodities of 400 there has returned to it a commodity equivalent amounting to 400; the £200 in money advanced by it for the exchange of 800 in commodities have likewise returned to it. Everything is therefore all right.

The difficulty encountered in the exchange

$$\text{I.}\quad \underbrace{1000_V + 1{,}000_S}_{2{,}000_C}$$

was reduced to the difficulty on exchanging remainders:

I. ....400_s.

II. (1) 200 in money + 200_c in commodities + (2) 200_c in commodities. Or, to make the matter still clearer:

I. $200_s + 200_s$.

II. (1) 200 in money + 200_c in commodities + (2) 200_c in commodities.

Since in II, section 1, 200_c in commodities are exchanged for 200 I_s (in commodities) and since all the money circulating in this exchange of 400 in commodities between I and II returns to him who advanced it, I or II, this money, being an element of the exchange between I and II, is actually not an element of the problem which is troubling us here. Or, to present it differently: Supposing in the exchange between 200 I_s (commodities) and 200 II_c (commodities of II, section 1) the money functions as a means of payment, not as a means of purchase and therefore also not as a 'medium of circulation,' in the strictest sense of the words. It is then clear, since the commodities 200 I_s and 200 II_c (section 1) are equal in magnitude of value, that means of production worth 200 are exchanged for articles of consumption worth 200, that money functions here only ideally, and that neither side really has to throw any money into the circulation for the payment of any balance. Hence the problem presents itself in its pure form only when we strike off on both sides, I and II, the commodities 200 I_s and their equivalent, the commodities 200 II_c (section 1).

After the elimination of these two amounts of commodities of equal value (I and II), which balance each other, there is left for exchange a remainder in which the problem evinces its pure form, namely,

I. 200_s in commodities.
II. (1) 200_c in money plus (2) 200_c in commodities.

It is evident here that II, section 1, buys with 200 in money the component parts of its fixed capital, 200 I_s. The fixed capital of II, section 1, is thereby renewed in kind and the surplus-value of I, worth 200, is converted from the commodity-form (means of production, or, more precisely, elements of fixed capital) into the money-form. With this money I buys articles of consumption from II, section 2, and the result for II is that for section I a fixed component part of its constant capital has been renewed in kind, and that for section 2 another component part (which compensates for the depreciation of its fixed capital) has been precipitated in money-form. And this continues every year until this last component part, too, has to be renewed in kind.

The condition precedent is here evidently that this fixed component part of constant capital II, which is reconverted into money to the full extent of its value and therefore must be renewed in kind each year (section 1), should be equal to the annual depreciation of the other fixed component part of constant capital II, which continues to function in its old bodily form and whose wear and tear, depreciation in value, which it transfers to the commodities in whose production it is engaged, is first to be compensated in money. Such a balance would seem to be a law of reproduction on the same scale. This is equivalent to saying that in class I, which puts out the means of production, the proportional division of labour must remain unchanged, since it produces on the one hand circulating and on the other fixed component parts of the constant capital of department II.

Before we analyse this more closely we must see what turn the matter takes if the remainder of II_c (1) is not equal to the remainder of II_c (2), and may be larger or smaller. Let us study the two cases one after the other.

First Case

I. 200_s.
II. (1) 220_c (in money) plus (2) 200_c (in commodities).

In this case II_c (1) buys with £200 in money the commodities 200 I_s, and I buys with the same money the commodities 200 II_c (2), i.e., that portion of the fixed capital which is to be precipitated in money. This portion is thus converted into money. But 20 II_c (1) in money cannot be reconverted into fixed capital in kind.

It seems this misfortune can be remedied by setting the remainder of I_s at 220 instead of at 200, so that only 1,780 instead of 1,800 of the 2,000 I would be disposed of by former exchange. We should then have:

I. 220_s.

II. (1) 220_c (in money) plus (2) 200_c (in commodities).

II_c, section 1, buys with £220 in money the 220 I_s and I buys then with £200 the 200 II_c (2) in commodities. But now £20 in money remain on the side of I, a portion of surplus-value which it can hold on to only in the form of money, without being able to spend it for articles of consumption. The difficulty is thus merely transferred from II_c, section 1, to I_s.

Let us now assume on the other hand that II_c, section 1, is smaller than II_c, section 2: then we have the

Second Case

I. 200_s (in commodities).
I. (1) 180_c (in money) plus (2) 200_c (in commodities).

With £180 in money II (section 1) buys commodities, 180 I_s. With this money I buys commodities of the same value from II (section 2), hence 180 II_c (2). There remain 20 I_s unsaleable on one side, and also 20 II_c (2) on the other—commodities worth 40, not convertible into money.

It would not help us to make the remainder of I equal to 180. True, no surplus would then be left in 1, but now as before a surplus of 20 would remain in II_c (section 2), unsaleable, inconvertible into money. In the first case, where II (1) is greater than II (2), there remains on the side of II_c (1) a surplus in money-form not reconvertible into fixed capital; or, if the remainder I_s is assumed to be equal to II_c (1), there remains on the side of I_s the same surplus in money-form, not convertible into articles of consumption.

In the second case, where II_c (1) is smaller than II_c (2), there remains a money deficit on the side of 200 I_s and II_c (2), and an equal surplus of commodities on both sides, or, if the remainder of I_s is assumed to be equal to II_c (1), there remains a money deficit and a surplus of commodities on the side of II_c (2).

If we assume the remainders of I, always to be equal to II_c (1)—since production is determined by orders and reproduction is not altered in any way if one year there is a greater output of fixed component parts and the next a greater output of circulating component part of constant capitals II and I—then in the first case I_s can be reconverted into articles of consumption only if I buys with it a portion of the surplus-value of II and II accumulates it in money instead of consuming it; and in the second case matters can be remedied only if I spends the money itself, an assumption we have already rejected.

If II_c (1) is greater than II_c (2), foreign commodities must be imported to realise the money-surplus in I_s. If, conversely, II_c (1) is smaller than II_c (2), commodities II (articles of consumption) will have to be exported to realise the depreciation part of II_c in means of production. Consequently, in either case foreign trade is necessary.

Even granted that for a study of reproduction on an unchanging scale it is to be supposed that the productivity of all lines of industry, hence also the proportional value-relations of their commodities, remain constant, the two last-named cases, in which II_c (1) is either greater or smaller than II_c (2), will nevertheless always be of interest for production on an enlarged scale where these cases may infallibly be encountered.

3. Results

The following is to be noted with reference to replacement of fixed capital:

If—all other things, and not only the scale of production, but above all the productivity of labour, remaining the same—a greater part of the fixed element of II_c expires than did the year before, and hence a greater part must be renewed in kind, then that part of the fixed capital which is as yet only on the way to its demise and is to be replaced meanwhile in money until its day of expiry, must shrink in the same proportion, inasmuch as it was assumed that the sum (and the sum of the value) of the fixed part of capital functioning in II remains the same. This, however, brings with it the following circumstances. *First*: If the greater part of commodity-capital I consists of elements of the fixed capital of II_c, then a correspondingly smaller portion consists of circulating component parts of II_c, because the total production of I for II_c remains unchanged. If one of these parts increases the other decreases, and vice versa. On the other hand, the total production of class II also retains the same volume. But how is this possible if its raw materials, semi-finished products, and auxiliary materials (i.e., the circulating elements of constant capital II) decrease? *Second*: the greater part of fixed capital II_c, restored in its money-form, flows to I to be reconverted from its money-form into its bodily form. So there is a greater flow of money to I, aside from the money circulating between I and II merely for the exchange of their commodities; more money which is not instrumental in effecting mutual commodity exchange, but acts only one-sidedly in the function of a means of purchase. But then the mass of commodities of II_c, which is the bearer of the wear-and-tear equivalent—and thus the mass of commodities II that must only be exchanged for money I and not for commodities I—would also shrink proportionately. More money would have flown from II to I as mere means of purchase, and there would be fewer commodities II in relation to which I would have to function as a mere buyer. A greater portion of I_s—for I_v is already converted into commodities II—would not therefore be convertible into commodities II, but would persist in the form of money.

The opposite case, in which the reproduction of demises of fixed capital II in a certain year is less and on the contrary the depreciation part greater, needs no further discussion.

There would be a crisis—a crisis of over-production—in spite of reproduction on an unchanging scale.

In short, if under simple reproduction and other unchanged conditions—particularly under unchanged productive power, total volume and intensity of labour—no constant proportion is assumed between expiring fixed capital (to be renewed) and fixed capital still continuing to function in its old bodily form (merely adding to the products value in compensation of its depreciation), then, in the one case the mass of circulating component parts to be reproduced would remain the same while the mass of fixed component parts to be reproduced would be increased. Therefore the total production I would have to grow or, even aside from money-relations, there would be a deficit in reproduction.

In the other case, if the size of fixed capital II to be reproduced in kind should proportionately decrease and hence the component part of fixed capital II, which must now be replaced only in money, should increase in the same ratio, then the quantity of the circulating component parts of constant capital II reproduced by I would remain unchanged, while that of the fixed component parts to be reproduced would decrease. Hence either decrease in aggregate production of I, or surplus (as previously deficit) and surplus that is not to be converted into money.

True, the same labour can, in the first case, turn out a greater product through increasing productivity, extension or intensity, and the deficit could thus be covered in that case. But such a change would not take place without a shifting of capital and labour from one line of production of I to another, and every such shift would call forth momentary disturbances. Furthermore (in so far as extension and intensification of labour would mount), I would have for exchange more of its own value for less of II's value. Hence there would be a depreciation of the product of I.

The reverse would take place in the second case, where I must curtail its production, which implies a crisis for its labourers and capitalists, or produce a surplus, which again spells crisis. Such surplus is not an evil in itself, but an advantage; however it is an evil under capitalist production.

Foreign trade could help out in either case: in the first case in order to convert commodities I held in the form of money into articles of consumption, and in the second case to dispose of the commodity surplus. But since foreign trade does not merely replace certain elements (also with regard to value), it only transfers the contradictions to a wider sphere and gives them greater latitude.

Once the capitalist form of reproduction is abolished, it is only a matter of the volume of the expiring portion—expiring and therefore to be reproduced in kind—of fixed capital (the capital which in our illustration functions in the production of articles of consumption) varying in various successive years. If it is very large in a certain year (in excess of the average mortality, as is the case with human beings), then it is certainly so much smaller in the next year. The quantity of raw materials, semi-finished products, and auxiliary materials required for the annual production of the articles of consumption—provided other things remain equal—does not decrease in consequence. Hence the aggregate production of means of production would have to increase in the one case and decrease in the other. This can be remedied only by a continuous relative over-production. There must be, on the one hand, a certain quantity of fixed capital produced in excess of that which is directly required; on the other hand, and particularly, there must be a supply of raw materials, etc., in excess of the direct annual requirements (this applies especially to means of subsistence). This sort of over-production is tantamount to control by society over the material means of its own reproduction. But within capitalist society it is an element of anarchy.

This illustration of fixed capital, on the basis of an unchanged scale of reproduction, is striking. A disproportion of the production of fixed and circulating capital is one of the favourite arguments of the economists in explaining crises. That such a disproportion can and must arise even when the fixed capital is merely preserved, that it can and must do so on the assumption of ideal normal production on the basis of simple reproduction of the already functioning social capital is something new to them.

PART 4

Section XII. *The Reproduction of the Money Material*

One factor has so far been entirely disregarded, namely the annual reproduction of gold and silver. As mere material for articles of luxury, gilding, etc., there is as little occasion for special mention of them as there is of mentioning any other products. But they play an important role as money material and hence as potential money. For the sake of simplicity we here regard only gold as material for money.

According to older data, the entire annual production of gold amounted to 800,000-900,000 lbs., equal roundly to 1,100 or 1,250 million marks. But according to Soetbeers it amounted to only 170,675 kilograms, valued at roundly 476 million marks, based on the average for 1871 to 1875. Of this amount Australia supplied roundly 167, the United States 166, and Russia 93 million marks. The remainder is distributed over various countries in amounts of less than 10 million marks each. During the same period, the annual production of silver amounted to somewhat less than 2 million kilograms, valued at 354½ million marks. Of this amount, Mexico supplied roundly 108, the United States 102, South America 67, Germany 26 million, etc.

Among the countries with predominantly capitalist production only the United States is a producer of gold and silver. The capitalist countries of Europe obtain almost all their gold, and by far the greater part of their silver, from Australia, the United States, Mexico, South America, and Russia.

But we take it that the gold mines are in a country with capitalist production whose annual reproduction we are here analysing, and for the following reasons:

Capitalist production does not exist at all without foreign commerce. But when one assumes normal annual reproduction on a given scale one also assumes that foreign commerce only replaces home products by articles of other use or bodily form, without affecting value-relations, hence without affecting either the value-relations in which the two categories 'means of production' and 'articles of consumption' mutually exchange, or the relations between constant capital, variable capital, and surplus-value, into which the value of the product of each of these categories may be divided. The involvement of foreign commerce in analysing the annually reproduced value of products can therefore only confuse without contributing any new element of the problem, or of its solution. For this reason it must be entirely discarded. And consequently gold too is to be treated here as a direct element of annual reproduction and not as a commodity element imported from abroad by means of exchange.

The production of gold, like that of metals generally, belongs in class I, the category which embraces the production of means of production. Supposing the annual production of gold is equal to 30 (for convenience's sake; actually the figure is much too high compared to the other figures of our scheme). Let this value be divisible into $20_c + 5_v + 5_s$; 20_c is to be exchanged for other elements of I_c and this is to be studied later; but the $5_v + 5_s$ (I) are to be exchanged for elements of II_c, i.e., articles of consumption.

As for the 5_v, every gold-producing establishment begins by buying labour-power. This is done not with gold produced by this particular enterprise, but with a portion of the money-supply in the land. The labourers buy with this 5_v articles of consumption from II, and that buys with this money means of production from I. Let II buy gold from I to the amount of 2 as commodity material, etc. (component part of its constant capital), then 2_v flow back to gold producers I in money which has already belonged to the circulation. If II does not buy any more material from I, then I buys from II by throwing its gold into circulation as money, since gold can buy any commodity. The difference is only that I does not act here as a seller, but only as a buyer. Gold miners I can always get rid of their commodity; it is always in a directly exchangeable form.

Let us assume that some producer of yarn has paid 5_v to his labourers, who create for him in return—aside from the surplus-value—a yarn product equal to 5. For 5 the labourers buy from II_c, and the latter buys yarn from I for 5 in money, and thus 5 flows back in money to the spinner of yarn. Now in the case assumed I g (as we shall designate the producers of gold) advances to its labourers 5_v in money which previously belonged to the circulation. The labourers spend it for articles of consumption, but only 2 of the 5 return from II to I g. However I g can begin the process of reproduction anew, just as well as the producer of yarn. For his labourers have supplied him with 5 in gold, 2 of which he sold and 3 of which he still has, so that he has but to coin[5] them, or turn them into bank-notes to have his entire variable capital again directly in his hands in money-form, without the further intervention of II.

Even this first process of annual reproduction has wrought a change in the quantity of money actually or virtually belonging to the circulation. We assumed that II_c bought 2_v (I g) as material, and that I g has again laid out 3—as the money-form of its variable capital—within II. Hence 3 of the mass of money supplied by the new gold production remained within II and did not return to I. According to our assumption II has satisfied its requirements in gold material. The 3 remain in its hands as a gold hoard. Since they cannot constitute any element of its constant capital, and since II had previously enough money-capital for the purchase of labour-power; since furthermore these additional 3 g, with the exception of the depreciation element, have no function to perform within II_c, for a portion of which they were exchanged (they could only serve to cover the depreciation element *pro tanto*, if II_c (1) should be smaller than II_c (2), which would be accidental); on the other hand, however, namely with the exception of the depreciation element, the entire commodity-product II_c must be exchanged for means of production $I_{(v+s)}$—this money must be transferred in its entirety from II_c to II_s, no matter whether it exists in necessities of life or articles of luxury, and vice versa corresponding commodity-value must be transferred from II_s to II_c. Result: A portion of the surplus-value is stored up as a money-hoard.

In the second year of reproduction, provided the same proportion of annually produced gold continues to be used as material, 2 will again flow back to I g, and 3 will be replaced in kind, i.e., will be released again in II as a hoard, etc.

With reference to the variable capital in general: The capitalist I g, like every other capitalist, must continually advance this capital in money for the purchase of labour-power. But so far as this v is concerned, it is not he but his labourers who have to buy from II. It can therefore never happen that he should act as a buyer, throwing gold into II without the initiative of II. But to the extent that II buys material from him, and must convert constant capital II c into gold material, a portion of $(I\ g)_v$ flows back to him from II in the same way that it does to other capitalists of I. And so far as this is not the case, he replaces his v in gold directly from his product. But to the extent that the v advanced in money does not flow back to him from II, a portion of the already available means of circulation (received from I and not returned to I) is converted in II into a hoard and for that reason a portion of its surplus-value is not expended for articles of consumption. Since new gold-mines are continually opened or old ones re-opened, a certain portion of the money to be laid out by I g in v is always part of the money existing prior to the new gold production; it is thrown by I g through its labourers into II, and unless it returns from II to I g it forms there an element of hoard formation.

But as for $(I\ g)_s$, I g can always act here as buyer. He throws his s in the shape of gold into circulation and withdraws from it in return articles of consumption II_c. In II the gold is used in part as material, and thus functions as a real element of the constant constituent portion c of the productive capital. When this is not the case it becomes once more an element of hoard formation as a part of II_s persisting in the form of money. We see, then, aside from I_c which we reserve for a later analysis,[6] that even simple reproduction, excluding accumulation proper, namely reproduction on an extended scale, necessarily includes the storing up, or hoarding, of money. And as this is annually repeated, it explains the assumption from which we started in the analysis of capitalist production, namely, that at the beginning of the reproduction a supply of money corresponding to the exchange of commodities is in the hands of capitalist classes I and II. Such an accumulation takes place even after deducting the amount of gold being lost through the depreciation of money in circulation.

It goes without saying that the more advanced capitalist production, the more money is accumulated in all hands, and therefore the smaller the quantity annually added to this hoard by the production of new gold, although the absolute quantity thus added may be considerable. We revert once more in general terms to the objection raised against Tooke; how is it possible that every capitalist draws a surplus-value in money out of the annual product, i.e., draws more money out of the circulation than he throws into it, since in the long run the capitalist class itself must be regarded as the source of all the money thrown into circulation?

We reply by summarising the ideas developed previously (in Chapter XVII):

1. The only assumption essential here, namely, that in general there is money enough for the exchange of the various elements of the mass of the annual reproduction, is not affected in any way by the fact that a portion of the commodity-value consists of surplus-value. Supposing that the entire production belonged to the labourers themselves and that their surplus-labour were therefore only surplus-labour for themselves, not for the capitalists, then the quantity of circulating commodity-values would be the same and, other things being equal, would require the same amount of money for their circulation. The question in either case is therefore only: Where does the money come from to make possible the exchange of this total of commodity-values? It is not at all: where does the money come from to turn

the surplus-value into money? It is true, to revert to it once more, that every individual commodity consists of c + v + s, and the circulation of the entire quantity of commodities therefore requires on the one hand a definite sum of money for the circulation of the capital c + v and on the other hand another sum for the circulation of the revenue of the capitalists, the surplus-value s. For the individual capitalist, as well as for the entire capitalist class; the money in which they advance capital is different from the money in which they spend their revenue. Where does the latter money come from? Simply from the mass of money in the hands of the capitalist class, hence by and large from the total mass of money in society, a portion of which circulates the revenue of the capitalists. We have seen above that every capitalist establishing a new business recoups the money which he spent for his maintenance in articles of consumption as money serving to convert his surplus-value into money, once his business is fairly under way. But generally speaking the whole difficulty has two sources:

> In the first place, if we analyse only the circulation and the turnover of capital, thus regarding the capitalist merely as a personification of capital, not as a capitalist consumer and man about town, we see indeed that he is continually throwing surplus-value into circulation as a component part of his commodity-capital, but we never see money as a form of revenue in his hands. We never see him throwing money into circulation for the consumption of his surplus-value.

In the second place, if the capitalist class throws a certain amount of money into circulation in the shape of revenue, it looks as if it were paying an equivalent for this portion of the total annual product, and this portion thereby ceases to represent surplus-value. But the surplus-product in which the surplus-value is represented does not cost the capitalist class anything. As a class, the capitalists possess and enjoy it gratuitously, and the circulation of money cannot alter this fact. The alteration brought about by this circulation consists merely in the fact that every capitalist, instead of consuming his surplus-product in kind, a thing which is generally impossible, draws commodities of all sorts up to the amount of the surplus-value he has appropriated out of the general stock of the annual surplus-product of society and appropriates them. But the mechanism of the circulation has shown that while the capitalist class throws money into circulation for the purpose of spending its revenue, it also withdraws this money from the circulation, and can continue the same process over and over again; so that, considered as a class, capitalists remain as before in possession of the amount of money necessary for the conversion of surplus-value into money. Hence, if the capitalist not only withdraws his surplus-value from the commodity-market in the form of commodities for his consumption-fund, but at the same time gets back the money with which he has paid for these commodities, he has evidently withdrawn the commodities from circulation without paying an equivalent for them. They do not cost him anything, although he pays money for them. If I buy commodities for one pound sterling and the seller of the commodities gives me the pound back for surplus-product which I got for nothing, it is obvious that I received the commodities gratis. The constant repetition of this operation does not alter the fact that I constantly withdraw commodities and constantly remain in possession of the pound, although I part with it temporarily to purchase commodities. The capitalist constantly gets this money back as a money equivalent of surplus-value that has not cost him anything.

We have seen that with Adam Smith the entire value of the social product resolves itself into revenue, into v + s, so that the constant capital-value is set down as zero. It follows necessarily that the money required for the circulation of the yearly revenue must also suffice for the circulation of the entire annual product, that therefore in our illustration the money required for the circulation of the articles of consumption worth 3,000 also suffices for the circulation of the entire annual product worth 9,000. This is indeed the opinion of Adam Smith, and it is repeated by Th. Tooke. This erroneous conception of the ratio of the quantity of money required for the realisation of revenue to the quantity of money required to circulate the entire social product is the necessary result of the uncomprehended, thoughtlessly conceived manner in which the various elements of material and value of the total annual product are reproduced and annually replaced. It has therefore already been refuted.

Let us listen to Smith and Tooke themselves.

Smith says in Book II, Ch. 2:

> 'The circulation of every country may be considered as divided into two different branches: the circulation of the dealers with one another, and the circulation between the dealers and the consumers. Though the same pieces of money, whether paper or metal, may be employed sometimes in the one circulation and sometimes in the other; yet as both are constantly going on at the same time, each requires a certain stock of money of one kind or another, to carry it on. The value of the goods circulated between the different dealers, never can exceed the value of those circulated between the dealers and the consumers; whatever is bought by the dealers, being ultimately destined to be sold to the consumers. The circulation between the dealers, as it is carried on by wholesale, requires generally a pretty large sum for every particular transaction. That between the dealers and the consumers, on the contrary, as it is generally carried on by retail, frequently requires but very small ones, a shilling, or even a halfpenny, being often sufficient. But small sums circulate much faster than large ones... Though the annual purchases of all the consumers, therefore, are at least' [this 'at least' is rich] 'equal in value to those of all the dealers, they can generally be transacted with a much smaller quantity of money;' etc.

Th. Tooke remarks to this passage from Adam Smith (in *An Inquiry into the Currency Principle*, London, 1844, pp. 34 to 36 *passim*):

> 'There can be no doubt that the distinction here made is substantially correct ... the interchange between dealers and consumers including the payment of wages, which constitute the **principal means** of the consumers... All the transactions between dealers and dealers, by which are to be understood all sales from the producer or importer, through all the stages of intermediate processes of manufacture or otherwise to the retail dealer or the exporting merchant, are resolvable into movements or transfers of capital. Now transfers of capital do not necessarily suppose, nor do actually as a matter of fact entail, in the great majority of transactions, a passing of money, that is, bank-notes or coin—I mean bodily, and not by fiction—at the time of transfer... The total amount of the transactions between dealers and dealers must, in the last resort, be determined and limited by the amount of those between dealers and consumers.'

If this last sentence stood by itself, one might think Tooke simply stated the fact that there was a ratio between the exchanges among dealers and those among dealers and consumers, in other words, between the value of the total annual revenue and the value of the capital with which it is produced. But this is not the case. He explicitly endorses the view of Adam Smith. A special criticism of his theory of circulation is therefore superfluous.

2. Every industrial capital, on beginning its career, throws at one fling money into circulation for its entire fixed constituent part, which it recovers but gradually, in the course of years, by the sale of its annual products. Thus it throws at first more money into circulation than it draws from it. This is repeated at every renewal of the entire capital in kind. It is repeated every year for a certain number of enterprises whose fixed capital is to be renewed in kind. It is repeated piecemeal at every repair, every only partial renewal of the fixed capital. While, then, on the one hand more money is withdrawn from circulation than is thrown into it, the

opposite takes place on the other hand.

In all lines of industry whose production period—as distinguished from its working period—extends over a long term, money is continually thrown into circulation during this period by the capitalist producers, partly in payment for labour-power employed, partly in the purchase of means of production to be consumed. Means of production are thus directly withdrawn from the commodity-market, and articles of consumption, partly indirectly, by the labourers spending their wages, and partly directly, by the capitalists, who do not by any means suspend their consumption, although they do not simultaneously throw any equivalent in commodities on the market. During this period the money thrown by them into circulation serves to convert commodity value, including the surplus-value embodied in it, into money. This factor becomes very important in an advanced stage of capitalist production in the case of long-drawn out enterprises, such as are undertaken by stock companies, etc., for instance the construction of railways, canals, docks, large municipal buildings, iron shipbuilding, large-scale drainage of land, etc.

3. While the other capitalists, aside from the investment in fixed capital, draw more money out of the circulation than they threw into it on purchasing the labour-power and the circulating elements, the gold- and silver-producing capitalists throw only money into the circulation, aside from the precious metal which serves as raw material, while they withdraw only commodities from it. The constant capital, with the exception of the depreciated portion, the greater portion of the variable capital and the entire surplus-value, save the hoard which may be accumulating in their own hands, are all thrown into circulation as money.

4. On the one hand, all kinds of things circulate as commodities which were not produced during the given year, such as land lots, houses, etc.; furthermore goods whose period of production exceeds one year, such as cattle, timber, wine, etc. For this and other phenomena, it is important to establish that aside from the quantity of money required for the immediate circulation there is always a certain quantity in a latent non-functioning state which may start functioning if the impulse is given. Furthermore, the value of such products circulates often piecemeal and gradually, like the value of houses in the rents over a number of years.

On the other hand, not all movements of the process of reproduction are effected through the circulation of money. The entire process of production, once its elements have been procured, is excluded from circulation. All products which the producer himself consumes directly, whether individually or productively, are also excluded. Under this head comes also the feeding of agricultural labourers in kind.

Therefore, the quantity of money which circulates the annual product, exists in society, having been gradually accumulated. It does not belong to the value produced during the given year, except perhaps the gold used to make good the loss of depreciated coins.

This exposition presupposes the exclusive circulation of precious metals as money, and in this circulation the simplest form of cash purchases and sales; although money can function also as a means of payment, and has actually done so in the course of history, even on the basis of circulating plain metal coin, and though a credit system and certain aspects of its mechanism have developed upon that basis. This assumption is not made from mere considerations of method, although these are important enough, as demonstrated by the fact that Tooke and his school, as well as their opponents, were continually compelled in their controversies concerning the circulation of bank-notes to revert to the hypothesis of a purely metallic circulation. They were forced to do so *post festum* and did so very superficially, which was unavoidable, because the point of departure in their analysis thus played merely the role of an incidental point.

But the simplest study of money—circulation presented in its *primitive* form—and this is here an immanent element of the process of annual reproduction—demonstrates:

a) Advanced capitalist production, and hence the domination of the wage system, being assumed, money-capital obviously plays a prominent role, since it is the form in which the variable capital is advanced. In step with the development of the wage system, all products are transformed into commodities and must therefore—with a few important exceptions—pass in their entirety through the transformation into money as one phase of their movement. The quantity of circulating money must suffice for this conversion of commodities into money, and the greater part of this mass is furnished in the form of wages, of the money advanced by the industrial capitalists as the money-form of the variable capital in payment for labour-power, and which functions in the hands of the labourers, generally speaking, only as a medium of circulation (means of purchase). It is quite the opposite of natural economy such as is predominant under every form of bondage (including serfdom), and still more so in more or less primitive communities, whether or not they are attended by conditions of bondage or slavery.

In the slave system, the money-capital invested in the purchase of labour-power plays the role of the money-form of the fixed capital, which is but gradually replaced as the active period of the slave's life expires. Among the Athenians therefore, the gain realised by a slave owner directly through the industrial employment of his slave, or indirectly by hiring him out to other industrial employers (e.g., for mining), was regarded merely as interest (plus depreciation allowance) on the advanced money-capital, just as the industrial capitalist under capitalist production places a portion of the surplus-value plus the depreciation of his fixed capital to the account of interest and replacement of his fixed capital. This is also the rule with capitalists offering fixed capital (houses, machinery, etc.) for rent. Mere household slaves, whether they perform necessary services or are kept as luxuries for show, are not considered here. They correspond to the modern servant class. But the slave system too—so long as it is the dominant form of productive labour in agriculture, manufacture, navigation, etc., as it was in the advanced states of Greece and Rome—preserves an element of natural economy. The slave market maintains its supply of the commodity labour-power by war, piracy, etc., and this rapine is not promoted by a process of circulation, but by the actual appropriation of the labour-power of others by direct physical compulsion. Even in the United States, after the conversion of the buffer territory between the wage-labour states of the North and the slavery states of the South into a slave-breeding region for the South, where the slave thrown on the market thus became himself an element of the annual reproduction, this did not suffice for a long time, so that the African slave trade was continued as long as possible to satisfy the market.

b) The fluxes and refluxes of money taking place spontaneously on the basis of capitalist production in the exchange of the annual products; the one-time advances of fixed capitals to the full extent of their value and the successive extraction of this value from the circulation in the course of years, in other words, their gradual reconstitution in money-form by the annual formation of hoards, a hoarding which is essentially different from the parallel accumulation of hoards based on the annual production of new gold; the different lengths of time for which, depending on the duration of the production period of the commodities, money must be advanced, and consequently always hoarded anew before it can be recovered from the circulation by the sale of the commodities; the different lengths of time for which money must be advanced, if only resulting from the different distances of the places of production from their markets; furthermore the differences in the magnitude and period of the reflux according to the condition or relative size of the productive supplies in the various lines of business and in the individual businesses of the same line, and hence the lengths of periods for which the elements of constant capital are bought, and all this during the year of reproduction—all these different aspects of spontaneous movement had only to be noted, and made conspicuous, through experience, in order to give rise to a methodical use of the mechanical appliances of the credit system and to a real fishing out of available loanable capitals.

To this must be added the difference between those lines of business whose production proceeds under otherwise normal conditions continuously on the same scale, and those which apply varying quantities of labour-power in different periods of the year, such as agriculture.

Section XIII. *Destutt De Tracy's Theory of Reproduction*

Let us illustrate the confused and at the same time boastful thoughtlessness of political economists analysing social reproduction, with the example of the great logician Destutt de Tracy (Vol. 1, Ch. V, Note), whom even Ricardo took seriously and called a **very distinguished writer**. (*Principles*, p. 333.)

This 'distinguished writer' gives the following explanations concerning the entire process of social reproduction and circulation:

> 'I shall be asked how these industrial entrepreneurs can make such large profits and out of whom they can draw them. I reply that they do so by selling everything which they produce for more than it has cost to produce; and that they sell:
>
> '1. to one another for the entire portion of their consumption intended for the satisfaction of their needs, which they pay with a portion of their profits;
>
> '2. to the wage-labourers, both those whom they pay and those whom the idle capitalists pay; from these wage-labourers they thus extract their entire wages except perhaps their small savings;
>
> '3. to the idle capitalists who pay them with the portion of their revenue which they have not yet given to the wage-labourers employed by them directly; so that the entire rent which they pay them annually flows back to them in this way or the other.' (Destutt de Tracy, *Traité de la volonté et de ses effets*, Paris, 1826, p. 239.)

In other words, the capitalists enrich themselves by mutually getting the best of one another in the exchange of that portion of their surplus-value which they set apart for their individual consumption or consume as revenue. For instance, if this portion of their surplus-value or of their profits is equal to £400, this sum of £400 is supposed to grow to, say, £500 by each stockholder of the £400 selling his share to another 25 per cent in excess. But since all do the same, the result will be the same as if they had sold to one another at the real values. They merely need £500 in money for the circulation of commodities worth £400, and this would seem to be rather a method of impoverishing than of enriching themselves since it compels them to keep a large portion of their total wealth unproductively in the useless form of circulation media. The whole thing boils down to this, that despite the all-round nominal rise in the price of their commodities the capitalist class has only £400 worth of commodities to divide among themselves for their individual consumption, but that they do one another the favour of circulating £400 worth of commodities by means of a quantity of money which is required to circulate £500 worth of commodities.

And this quite aside from the fact that a 'portion of their profits,' and therefore, in general, a supply of commodities in which there exist profits, is here assumed. But Destutt undertook precisely to tell us where those profits come from. The quantity of money required to circulate the profit is a very subordinate question. The quantity of commodities in which the profit is represented seems to have its origin in the circumstance that the capitalists not only sell these commodities to one another, although even this much is quite fine and profound, but sell them to one another at prices which are too high. So we now know one source of the enrichment of the capitalists. It is on a par with the secret of the 'Entspektor Bräsig'[7] that the great poverty is due to the great '*pauvreté*.'

2) The same capitalists furthermore sell

> 'to the wage-labourers, both those whom they pay and those whom the idle capitalists pay; from these wage-labourers they thus recover their entire wages, except perhaps their small savings.'

According to Monsieur Destutt, then, the reflux of the money-capital, the form in which the capitalists have advanced wages to the labourers, is the second source of the enrichment of these capitalists. If, therefore, the capitalists paid for instance £100 to their labourers as wages and if these same labourers then buy from the same capitalists commodities of this same value, of £100, so that the sum of £100 which the capitalists had advanced as buyers of labour-power returns to the capitalists when they sell to the labourers £100 worth of commodities, the capitalists *get richer* thereby. It would appear to anyone endowed with ordinary common sense that they only find themselves once more in possession of their £100, which they owned before this procedure. At the beginning of the procedure they have £100 in money. For these £100 they buy labour-power. The labour bought produces for these £100 in money commodities of a value which, so far as we now know, amounts to £100. By selling the £100 worth of commodities to their labourers the capitalists recover £100 in money. The capitalists then have once more £100 in money, and the labourers have £100 worth of commodities which they have themselves produced. It is hard to understand how that can make the capitalists any richer. If the £100 in money did not flow back to them they would first have to pay to the labourers £100 in money for their labour and secondly to give them the product of this labour, £100 worth of articles of consumption, for nothing. The reflux of this money might therefore at best explain why the capitalists do not get poorer by this transaction, but by no means why they get richer by it.

To be sure it is another question how the capitalists came into possession of the £100 and why the labourers, instead of producing commodities for their own account, are compelled to exchange their labour-power for these £100. But this, for a thinker of Destutt's calibre, is self-explanatory.

Destutt himself is not quite satisfied with the solution. After all, he did not tell us that one gets richer by spending a sum of money, a hundred pounds, and then taking in again a sum of money amounting to £100; hence, by the reflux of £100 in money, which merely shows why the £100 in money do not get lost. He tells us that the capitalists get richer

> 'by selling everything which they produce for more than it has cost to produce.'

Consequently, the capitalists must get richer also in their transactions with the labourers by selling to them too dear. Very well!

> 'They pay wages ... and all this flows back to them through the expenditures of all these people who pay them more' [for the products] 'than they cost them [the capitalists] in wages.' (Ibid., p. 240.)

In other words, the capitalists pay £100 in wages to the labourers, and then they sell to these labourers their own product at £120, so that they not only recover their £100 but also gain £20? That is impossible. The labourers can pay only with the money which they have received in the form of wages. If they get £100 in wages from the capitalists they can buy only £100 worth, not £120 worth. So this will not work. But there is still another way. The labourers buy from the capitalists commodities for £100, but actually receive commodities worth only £80. Then they are absolutely cheated out of £20. And the capitalist has absolutely gained £20, because he actually paid for the labour-power 20 per cent less than its value, or cut nominal wages 20 per cent by a circuitous route.

The capitalist class would accomplish the same end if it paid the labourers at the start only £80 in wages and afterwards gave them for these £80 in money actually £80 worth of commodities. This seems to be the normal way, considering the class of capitalists as a whole, for according to Monsieur Destutt himself the labouring class must receive a 'sufficient wage' (p. 219), since their wages must at least be adequate to maintain their existence and capacity to work, 'to procure the barest subsistence.' (p. 180). If the labourers do not receive such sufficient wages, that means, according to the same Destutt, 'the death of industry' (p. 208), which does not seem therefore to be a way in which the capitalists can get richer. But whatever may be the scale of wages paid by the capitalists to the working-class, they have a definite value, e.g., £80. If the capitalist class pays the labourers £80, then it has to supply them with commodities worth £80 for these £80 and the reflux of the £80 does not enrich it. If it pays them £100 in money, and sells them £80 worth of commodities for £100 it pays them in money 25 per cent more than their normal wage and supplies them in return with 25 per cent less in commodities.

In other words, the fund from which the capitalist class in general derives its profits is supposedly made up of deductions from the normal wages by paying less than its value for labour-power, i.e., less than the value of the means of subsistence required for their normal reproduction as wage-labourers. If therefore normal wages were paid, which is supposed to be the case according to Destutt, there could be no profit fund for either the industrial or the idle capitalists.

Hence Destutt should have reduced the entire secret of how the capitalist class gets richer to the following: by a deduction from wages. In that case the other surplus-value funds, which he mentions under 1) and 3), would not exist.

Hence in all countries, in which the money wages of the labourers should be reduced to the value of the articles of consumption necessary for their subsistence as a class, there would be no consumption-fund and no accumulation-fund for the capitalists, and hence also no existence-fund for the capitalist class, and hence also no capitalist class. And, according to Destutt, this should be the case in all wealthy and developed countries with an old civilisation, for in them,

> 'in our ancient societies, the fund for the maintenance of wage-labourers is ... an almost constant magnitude.' (Ibid., p. 202.)

Even with a deduction from the wages, the capitalist does not enrich himself by first paying the labourer £100 in money and then supplying him with £80 worth of commodities for these £100, thus actually circulating £80 worth of commodities by means of £100, an excess of 25 per cent. The capitalist gets richer by appropriating, besides the surplus-value—that portion of the product in which surplus-value is represented—25 per cent of that portion of the product which the labourer should receive in the form of wages. The capitalist class would not gain anything by the silly method Destutt conceived. It pays £100 in wages and gives back to the labourer for these £100 £80 worth of his own product. But, in the next transaction it must again advance £100 for the same procedure. It would thus be indulging in the useless sport of advancing £100 in money and giving in exchange £80 in commodities, instead of advancing £80 in money and supplying in exchange for it £80 in commodities. That is to say, it would be continually advancing to no purpose a money-capital which is 25 per cent in excess of that required for the circulation of its variable capital, which is a very peculiar method of getting rich.

3) Finally the capitalist class sells

> 'to the idle capitalists, who pay them with the portion of their revenue which they have not yet given to the wage-labourers employed by them directly; so that the entire rent, which they pay them (the idle ones) annually, flows back to them in this way or the other.'

We have seen above that the industrial capitalists

> 'pay with a portion of their profits the entire portion of their consumption intended for the satisfaction of their needs.'

Take it, then, that their profits are equal to £200. And let them use up, say, £100 of this in their individual consumption. But the other half, or £100, does not belong to them; it belongs to the idle capitalists, i.e., to those who receive the ground-rent, and to capitalists who lend money on interest. So they have to pay £100 to these gentry. Let us assume that these gentry need £80 of this money for their individual consumption, and £20 for the hire of servants, etc. With those £80 they buy articles of consumption from the industrial capitalists. Thus while these capitalists part with commodities to the value of £80, they receive back £80 in money, or four-fifths of the £100 paid by them to the idle capitalists under the name of rent, interest, etc.

Furthermore the servant class, the direct wage-labourers of the idle capitalists, have received £20 from their masters. These servants likewise buy articles of consumption from the industrial capitalists to the amount of £20. In this way, while parting with commodities worth £20, these capitalists have £20 in money flow back to them, the last fifth of the £100 which they paid to the idle capitalists for rent, interest, etc. At the close of the transaction the industrial capitalists have recovered in money the £100 which they remitted to the idle capitalists in payment of rent, interest, etc. But one half of their surplus-product, equal to £100, passed meanwhile from their hands into the consumption-fund of the idle capitalists.

It is evidently quite superfluous for the question now under discussion to bring in somehow or other the division of the £100 between the idle capitalists and their direct wage-labourers. The matter is simple: their rent, interest, in short, their share in the surplus-value equal to £200, is paid to them by the industrial capitalists in money to the amount of £100. With these £100 they buy directly or indirectly articles of consumption from the industrial capitalists. Thus they pay back to them the £100 in money and take from them articles of consumption worth £100.

This completes the reflux of the £100 paid by the industrial capitalists in money to the idle capitalists. Is this reflux of money a means of enriching the industrial capitalists, as Destutt imagines? Before the transaction they had a sum of values amounting to £200, 100 being money and 100 articles of consumption. After the transaction they have only one half of the original sum of values. They have once more the £100 in money, but they have lost the £100 in articles of consumption which have passed into the hands of the idle capitalists. Hence they are poorer by £100 instead of richer by £100. If instead of taking the circuitous route of first paying out £100 in money and then receiving this £100 in money back in payment of articles of consumption worth £100, they had paid rent, interest, etc., directly in the bodily form of their products, there would be no £100 in money flowing back to them from the circulation, because they would not have thrown that amount of money into the circulation. *Via* payment in kind the matter would simply have taken this course: they would keep one half of the surplus-product worth £200 for themselves and give the other half to the idle capitalists without any equivalent in return. Even Destutt would not have been tempted to declare this a means of getting richer. Of course the land and capital borrowed by the industrial capitalists from the idle capitalists and for which they have to pay a portion of their surplus-value in the form of ground-rent, interest, etc., are profitable for them, for this constitutes one of the conditions of production of commodities in general and of that portion of the product which constitutes surplus-product or in which surplus-value is represented. This profit accrues from the use of the borrowed land and capital, not from the price paid for them. This price rather constitutes a deduction from it. Otherwise, one would have to contend that the industrial capitalists would not get richer but poorer, if they were able to keep the other half of their surplus-value for themselves instead of having to give it away. This is the confusion which results from mixing up such phenomena of circulation as a reflux of money with the distribution of the product, which is merely promoted by these phenomena of circulation.

And yet the same Destutt is shrewd enough to remark:

> 'Whence come the revenues of these idle gentry? Do the revenues not come out of the rent paid to them out of their profits by those who put the capitals of the former to work, i.e., by those who pay with the funds of the former a labour which produces more than it costs, in a word, the industrial capitalists? It is always necessary to hark back to them to find the source of all wealth. It is they who in reality feed the wage-labourers employed by the former.' (p. 246.)

So now the payment of this rent, etc., is a deduction from the profit of the industrial capitalists. Before it was a means wherewith they could enrich themselves.

But at least one consolation is left to our Destutt. These good industrialists handle the idle capitalists the same way they have been handling one another and the labourers. They sell them all commodities too dear, for instance, by 20 per cent. Now there are two possibilities. The idle capitalists either have other money resources aside from the £100 which they receive annually from the industrial capitalists, or they have not. In the first case the industrial capitalists sell them commodities worth £100 at a price of, say, £120. Consequently, on selling their commodities they recover not only the £100 paid to the idlers but £20 besides, which constitute really new value for them. How does the account look now? They have given away £100 in commodities for nothing, because the £100 in money that they were paid in part for their commodities were their own money. Thus their own commodities have been paid with their own money. Hence they have lost £100. But they have also received an excess of £20 in the price of their commodities over and above their value, which makes £20 to the good. Balance this against the loss of £100, and you still have a loss of £80. Never a plus, always a minus. The cheating practised against the idle capitalists has reduced the loss of the industrial capitalists, but for all that it has not transformed a diminution of their wealth into a means of enrichment. But this method cannot go on indefinitely, for the idle capitalists cannot possibly pay year after year £120 in money if they take in only £100 in money year after year.

There remains the other approach: The industrial capitalists sell commodities worth £80 in exchange for the £100 in money they paid to the idle capitalists. In this case, the same as before, they still give away £80 for nothing, in the form of rent, interest, etc. By this fraudulent means the industrial capitalists have reduced their tribute to the idlers, but it still exists nevertheless and the idlers are in a position—according to the same theory proclaiming that prices depend on the good will of the sellers—to demand in the future £120 instead of £100, as formerly, for rent, interest, etc., on their land and capital.

This brilliant analysis is quite worthy of that deep thinker who copies on the one hand from Adam Smith that

> 'labour is the source of all wealth' (p. 242)

that the industrial capitalists

> 'employ their capital to pay for labour that reproduces it with a profit' (p. 246)

and who concludes on the other hand that these industrial capitalists 'feed all the other people, are the only ones who increase the public wealth, and create all our means of enjoyment' (p. 242)

that it is not the capitalists who are fed by the labourers, but the labourers who are fed by the capitalists, for the brilliant reason that the money with which the labourers are paid does not remain in their hands, but continually returns to the capitalists in payment of the commodities produced by the labourers.

'All they do is receive with one hand and return with the other. Their consumption must therefore be regarded as engendered by those who hire them.' (p. 235.)

After this exhaustive analysis of social reproduction and consumption, as being brought about by the circulation of money, Destutt continues:

'This is what perfects this *perpetuum mobile* of wealth, a movement which, though badly understood' (*mal connu*, I should say so!), 'has justly been named circulation. For it is indeed a circuit and always returns to its point of departure. This is the point where production is consummated.' (pp. 239 and 240.)

Destutt, that very distinguished writer, *membre de l'Institut de France et de la Société Philosophique de Philadelphie,* and in fact to a certain extent a luminary among the vulgar economists, finally requests his readers to admire the wonderful lucidity with which he has presented the course of social process, the flood of light which he has poured over the matter, and is even condescending enough to communicate to his readers, where all this light comes from. This must be read in the original:

'It will be noted, I hope, how much this manner of viewing the consummation of our wealth is in accord with all we have been saying concerning its production and distribution, and at the same time how much light it throws on the entire course of society. Whence this accord and this lucidity? From the fact that we have met truth face to face. This recalls the effect of those mirrors in which things are reflected accurately and in their true proportions when correctly focussed, but in which everything appears confused and disjointed when one is too close or too far away from them.' (pp. 242 and 243.)

Voilà le crétinisme bourgeois dans toute sa béatitude! [There you have the bourgeois idiocy in all its beatitude!]

Notes

1. 'When the savage makes bows, he exercises an industry, but he does not practise abstinence.' (Senior, *Principes fondamentaux de l'Économie Politique,* trad. Arrivabene, Paris, 1836, pp. 342-43.) 'The more society progresses, the more abstinence is demanded.' (Ibid., p. 312). (Cf. *Capital*, Ch. XXIV, 3.]
2. E.B. Tylor, *Researches into the Early History of Mankind*, etc., London, 1865, pp. 198-99.
3. Marx has in mind J. B. Say's *Lettres à M. Malthus sur différents sujets d'économie politique, notamment sur les causes de la stagnation générale du commerce,* Paris, 1820.—Ed.
4. These figures again do not coincide with those previously assumed. But this is immaterial since it is merely a question of proportions.—*F.E.*
5. 'A considerable quantity of **gold bullion** ... is taken direct to the mint at San Francisco by the owners.' *Reports of H. M. Secretaries of Embassy and Legation*, 1879, Part III, p. 337.
6. The study of the exchange of newly produced gold within the constant capital of department I is not contained in the manuscript.—*F.E.*
7. A character in a number of works by the German humorist Fritz Reuter (1810-74).—**Ed.**

21

Accumulation and Reproduction on an Extended Scale

PART 1

It has been shown in Book I how accumulation works in the case of the individual capitalist. By the conversion of the commodity-capital into money the surplus-product, in which the surplus-value is represented, is also turned into money. The capitalist reconverts the so metamorphosed surplus-value into additional natural elements of his productive capital. In the next cycle of production the increased capital furnishes an increased product. But what happens in the case of the individual capital must also show in the annual reproduction as a whole, just as we have seen it happen on analysing simple reproduction, namely, that the successive precipitation – in the case of individual capital – of its used-up fixed component parts in money which is being hoarded, also finds expression in the annual reproduction of society. If a certain individual capital is equal to 400 c + 100 v, and the annual surplus-value is equal to 100, then the commodity-product amounts to 400 c + 100 v + 100 s. These 600 are converted into money. Of this money, again, 400 c are converted into the natural form of constant capital, 100 v into labour-power, and – provided the entire surplus-value is being accumulated – 100 s are converted besides into additional constant capital by transformation into natural elements of the productive capital. It is assumed in this case: 1) that this amount is sufficient under the given technical conditions either to expand the functioning constant capital or to establish a new industrial business. But it may also happen that surplus-value must be converted into money and this money hoarded for a much longer time before this process, i.e., before real accumulation, expansion of production, can take place; 2) that production on an extended scale has actually been in process previously. For in order that the money (the surplus-value hoarded in money-form) may be converted into elements of productive capital, one must be able to buy these elements on the market as commodities. It makes no difference if they are not bought as finished products but made to order. They are not paid for until they are in existence and at any rate not until actual reproduction on an extended scale, an expansion of hitherto normal production, has taken place so far as they are concerned. They had to exist potentially, i.e., in their elements, as it requires only the impulse of an order, that is, the purchase of commodities before they actually exist and their anticipated sale, for their production really to take place. The money on the one side then calls forth extended reproduction on the other, because the possibility of it exists without money. For money in itself is not an element of real reproduction.

For instance capitalist A, who sells during one year or during a number of years certain quantities of commodities successively produced by him, thereby converts into money also that portion of the commodities which is the vehicle of surplus-value – the surplus-product – or in other words the very surplus-value produced by him in commodity-form, accumulates it gradually, and thus forms for himself new potential money-capital – potential because of its capacity and mission to be converted into elements of productive capital. But in actual fact he only engages in simple hoarding, which is not an element of actual reproduction. His activity at first consists only in successively withdrawing circulating money out of the circulation. Of course it is not impossible that the circulating money thus kept under lock and key by him was itself, before it entered into circulation, a portion of some other hoard. This hoard of A, which is potentially new money-capital, is not additional social wealth, any more than it would be if it were spent in articles of consumption. But money withdrawn from circulation, which therefore previously existed in circulation, may have been stored up at some prior time as a component part of a hoard, may have been the money-form of wages, may have converted means of production or other commodities into money or may have circulated portions of constant capital or the revenue of some capitalist. It is no more new wealth than money, considered from the standpoint of the simple circulation of commodities, is the vehicle not only of its actual value but also of its ten-fold value, because it was turned over ten times a day, realised ten different commodity-values. The commodities exist without it, and it itself remains what it is (or becomes even less by depreciation) whether in one turnover or in ten. Only in the production of gold – inasmuch as the gold product contains a surplus-product, a depository of surplus-value – is new wealth (potential money) created, and it increases the money material of new potential money-capitals only so far as the entire money-product enters into circulation.

Although this surplus-value hoarded in the form of money is not additional new social wealth, it represents new potential money-capital, on account of the function for which it is hoarded. (We shall see later that new money-capital may arise also in a way other than the gradual conversion of surplus-value into money.)

Money is withdrawn from circulation and stored up as a hoard by selling commodities without subsequent buying. If this operation is therefore conceived as a general process, it seems inexplicable where the buyers are to come from, since in that process everybody would want to sell in order to hoard, and none would want to buy. And it must be conceived generally, since every individual capital may be in the process of accumulation.

If we were to conceive the process of circulation between the various parts of the annual reproduction as taking place in a straight line-which would be wrong as it always consists with a few exceptions of mutually opposite movements-then we should have to start from the producer of gold (or silver) who buys without selling, and to assume that all others sell to him. In that case the entire yearly social surplus-product (the bearer of the entire surplus-value) would pass into his hands, and all the other capitalists would distribute among themselves pro rata his surplus-product, which naturally exists in the form of money, the natural embodiment in gold of his surplus-value. For that portion of the product of the gold producer which has to make good his active capital is already tied up and disposed of. The surplus-value of the gold producer, created in the form of gold, would then be the sole fund from which all other capitalists would draw the material for the conversion of their annual surplus-product into money. The magnitude of its value would then have to be equal to the entire annual surplus-value of society, which must first assume the guise of a hoard. Absurd as these assumptions would be, they would do nothing more than explain the possibility of a universal simultaneous formation of a hoard, and would not get reproduction itself one step further, except on the part of the gold producer.

Before we resolve this seeming difficulty we must distinguish between the accumulation in department I (production of means of production) and in department II (production of articles of consumption). We shall start with I.

Section I. *Accumulation in Department I*

1. The Formation of a Hoard

It is evident that both the investments of capital in the numerous lines of industry constituting class I and the different individual investments of capital within each of these lines of industry, according to their age, i.e., the space of time during which they already have functioned, quite aside from their volumes, technical conditions, market conditions, etc., are in different stages of the process of successive transformation from surplus-value into potential money-capital, whether this money-capital is to serve for the expansion of the active capital or for the establishment of new industrial enterprises – the two forms of expansion of production. One part of the capitalists is continually converting its potential money-capital, grown to an appropriate size, into productive capital, i.e., with the money hoarded by the conversion of surplus-value into money they buy means of production, additional elements of constant capital. Another part of the capitalists is meanwhile still engaged in hoarding its potential money-capital. Capitalists belonging to these two categories confront each other: some as buyers, the others as sellers, and each one of the two exclusively in one of these roles.

For instance, let A sell 600 (equal to 400 c + 100 v + 100 s) to B (who may represent more than one buyer). A sells 600 in commodities for 600 in money, of which 100 are surplus-value which he withdraws from circulation and hoards in the form of money. But these 100 in money are but the money-form of the surplus-product, which was the bearer of a value of 100. The formation of a hoard is no production at all, hence not an increment of production, either. The action of the capitalist consists here merely in withdrawing from circulation the 100 in money he grabbed by the sale of his surplus-product, holding on to it and impounding it. This operation is carried on not alone by A, but at numerous points along the periphery of circulation by other capitalists, A', A", A"', all of them working with equal zeal at this sort of hoard formation. These numerous points at which money is withdrawn from circulation and accumulated in numerous individual hoards or potential money-capitals appear as so many obstacles to circulation, because they immobilise the money and deprive it of its capacity to circulate for a certain length of time. But it must be borne in mind that hoarding takes place in the simple circulation of commodities long before this is based on capitalist commodity production. The quantity of money existing in society is always greater than the part of it in actual circulation, although this swells or subsides according to circumstances. We find here again the same hoards, and the same formation of hoards, but now as an element immanent in the capitalist process of production.

One can understand the pleasure experienced when all these potential capitals within the credit system, by their concentration in the hands of banks, etc., become disposable, 'loanable capital,' money-capital, which indeed is no longer passive and music of the future, but active capital growing rank.

However, A accomplishes the formation of a hoard only to the extent that he acts only as a seller, so far as his surplus-product is concerned, and not afterward as a buyer. His successive production of surplus-products, the vehicles of his surplus-value to be converted into money, is therefore the premise of his forming a hoard. In the present case, where we are examining only the circulation within category I, the bodily form of the surplus-product, as that of the total product of which it is a part, is the bodily form of an element of constant capital I, that is to say, it belongs in the category of means of production creating means of production. We shall see presently what becomes of it, what function it performs, in the hands of buyers B, B', B", etc.

It must be noted at this point first and foremost that although withdrawing money to the amount of his surplus-value from circulation and hoarding it, A on the other hand throws commodities into it without withdrawing other commodities in return. The capitalists B, B', B", etc., are thereby enabled to throw money into circulation and withdraw only commodities from it. In the present case these commodities, according to their bodily form and their destination, enter into the constant capital of B, B', etc., as fixed or circulating element. We shall hear more about this anon when we deal with the buyer of the surplus-product, with B, B', etc.

Let us note by the way: Once more we find here, as we did in the case of simple reproduction, that the exchange of the various component parts of the annual product, i.e., their circulation (which must comprise at the same time the reproduction of the capital, and indeed its restoration in its various determinations, such as constant, variable, fixed, circulating, money- and commodity-capital) does not, by any means, presuppose mere purchase of commodities supplemented by a subsequent sale, or a sale supplemented by a subsequent purchase, so that there would actually be a bare exchange of commodity for commodity, as Political Economy assumes, especially the free-trade school since the physiocrats and Adam Smith. We know that the fixed capital, once the expenditure for it is made, is not replaced during the entire period of its function, but continues to act in its old form, while its value is gradually precipitated in the form of money. Now we have seen that the periodical renewal of fixed capital II (the entire capital-value II being converted into elements worth $I_{(v+s)}$) presupposes on the one hand the mere purchase of the fixed part of II c, reconverted from the form of money into its bodily form, to which corresponds the mere sale of I s ; and presupposes on the other hand the mere sale on the part of II c, the sale of its fixed (depreciation) part of the value precipitated in money, to which corresponds the mere purchase of I,. In order that the exchange may take place normally in this case, it must be assumed that the mere purchase on the part of II c is equal in magnitude of value to the mere sale on the part of II c, and that in the same way the mere sale of I s to II c, section 1, is equal to its mere purchase from II c, section 2. Otherwise simple reproduction is disturbed. Mere purchase here must be offset by a mere sale there. It must likewise be assumed in this case that the mere sale of that portion of I s which forms the hoards of A, A›, A›› is balanced by the mere purchase of that portion of I s which converts the hoards of B, B›, and B›› into elements of additional productive capital.

So far as the balance is restored by the fact that the buyer acts later on as a seller to the same amount of value, and vice versa, the money returns to the side that advanced it on purchasing, and which sold before it bought again. But the actual balance, so far as the exchange of commodities itself, the exchange of the various portions of the annual product is concerned, demands that the values of the commodities exchanged for one another be equal.

But inasmuch as only one-sided exchanges are made, a number of mere purchases on the one hand, a number of mere sales on the other – and we have seen that the normal exchange of the annual product on the basis of capitalism necessitates such one-sided metamorphoses – the balance can be maintained only on the assumption that in amount the value of the one-sided purchases and that of the one-sided sales tally. The fact that the production of commodities is the general form of capitalist production implies the role which money is playing in it not only as a medium of circulation, but also as money-capital, and engenders certain conditions of normal exchange peculiar to this mode of production and therefore of the normal course of reproduction, whether it be on a simple or on an extended scale – conditions which change into so many conditions of abnormal movement, into so many possibilities of crises, since a balance is itself an accident owing to the spontaneous nature of this production.

We have also seen that in the exchange of I v for a corresponding amount of value of II c, there takes place in the end, precisely for II c, a replacement of commodities II by an equivalent commodity-value I, that therefore on the part of aggregate capitalist II the sale of his own commodities is subsequently supplemented by the purchase of commodities from I of the same amount of value. This replacement takes place. But what does not take place is an exchange between capitalists I and II of their respective goods. II sells its commodities to working-class I. The latter confronts it one-sidedly, as a buyer of commodities, and it confronts that class one-sidedly as a seller of commodities. With the money proceeds so obtained II c confronts aggregate capitalist I one-sidedly as a buyer of commodities, and aggregate capitalist I confronts it one-sidedly as a seller of commodities up to the amount of I v. It is only by means of this sale of commodities that I finally reproduces its variable capital in the form of money-capital. If capital I faces that of II one-sidedly as a seller of commodities to the amount of I v, it faces working-class I as a buyer of commodities purchasing their labour-power. And if working-class I faces capitalist II one-sidedly as a buyer of commodities (namely, as a buyer of means of subsistence), it faces capitalist I one-sidedly as a seller of commodities, namely, as a seller of its labour-power.

The constant supply of labour-power on the part of working-class I, the reconversion of a portion of commodity-capital I into the money-form of variable capital, the replacement of a portion of commodity-capital II by natural elements of constant capital II c – all these necessary premises demand one another, but they are brought about by a very complicated process, including three processes of circulation which occur independently of one another but intermingle. This process is so complicated that it offers ever so many occasions for running abnormally.

2. The Additional Constant Capital

The surplus-product, the bearer of surplus-value, does not cost its appropriators, capitalists I, anything. They are, by no manner of means, obliged to advance any money or commodities in order to obtain it. Even among the physiocrats an advance was the general form of value embodied in elements of productive capital. Hence what capitalists I advance is nothing but their constant and variable capital. The labourer not only preserves by his labour their constant capital; he not only replaces the value of their variable capital by a corresponding newly created portion of value in the form of commodities; by his surplus-labour he supplies them with a surplus-value existing in the form of surplus-product. By the successive sale of this surplus-product they form a hoard, additional potential money-capital. In the case under consideration, this surplus-product consists from the outset of means of production of means of production. It is only when it reaches the hands of B, B', B", etc. (I) that this surplus-product functions as additional constant capital. But it is this *virtualiter* even before it is sold, even in the hands of the accumulators of hoards, A, A›, A›› (I). If we consider merely the amount of value of the reproduction on the part of I, we are still moving within the bounds of simple reproduction, for no additional capital has been set in motion to create this *virtualiter* additional constant capital (the surplus-product), nor has any greater amount of surplus-labour been expended than that on the basis of simple reproduction. The difference is here only in the form of the surplus-labour performed, in the concrete nature of its particular useful character. It has been expended in means of production for I c instead of II c, in means of production of means of production instead of means of production of articles of consumption. In the case of simple reproduction it was assumed that the entire surplus-value I is spent as revenue, hence in commodities II. Hence the surplus-value consisted only of such means of production as have to replace constant capital II in its bodily form. In order that the transition from simple to extended reproduction may take place, production in department I must be in a position to fabricate fewer elements of constant capital for II and so many the more for I. This transition, which does not always take place without difficulties, is facilitated by the fact that some of the products of I may serve as means of production in either department.

It follows, then, that, considering the matter merely from the angle of volume of values, the material substratum of extended reproduction is produced within simple reproduction. It is simply surplus-labour of working-class I expended directly in the production of means of production, in the creation of virtual additional capital I. The formation of virtual additional money-capital on the part of A, A' and A" (1) – by the successive sale of their surplus-product which was formed without any capitalist expenditure of money – is therefore simply the money-form of additionally produced means of production 1.

Consequently, production of virtual additional capital expresses in our case (we shall see that it may also be formed in a quite different way) nothing but a phenomenon of the process of production itself, production, in a particular form, of elements of productive capital.

The production of additional virtual money-capital on a large scale, at numerous points of the periphery of circulation, is therefore but a result and expression of multifarious production of virtually additional productive capital, whose rise does not itself require additional expenditure of money on the part of the industrial capitalist. The successive transformation of this virtually additional productive capital into virtual money-capital (hoard) on the part of A, A', A", etc. (I), occasioned by the successive sale of their surplus-product – hence by repeated one-sided sale of commodities without a supplementing purchase – is accomplished by a repeated withdrawal of money from circulation and a corresponding formation of a hoard. Except in the case where the buyer is a gold producer, this hoarding does not in any way imply additional wealth in precious metals, but only a change in the function of money previously circulating. A while ago it functioned as a medium of circulation, now it functions as a hoard, as virtually new money-capital in the process of formation. Thus the formation of additional money-capital and the quantity of the precious metals existing in a country are not in any causal relation to each other.

Hence it follows furthermore: The greater the productive capital already functioning in a country (including the labour-power, the producer of the surplus-product, incorporated in it), the more developed the productive power of labour and thereby also the technical means for the rapid expansion of the production of means of production – the greater therefore the quantity of the surplus-product both as to its value and as to the quantity of use-values in which it is represented – so much the greater is

1. the virtually additional productive capital in the form of surplus-product in the hands of A, A', A", etc., and
2. the quantity of this surplus-product transformed into money, and hence that of the virtually additional money-capital in the hands of A, A', A". The fact that Fullarton for instance does not want to hear of over-production in the ordinary sense but only of the over-production of capital, meaning money-capital, again shows how extremely little of the mechanism of their own system even the best bourgeois economists understand.

Whereas the surplus-product, directly produced and appropriated by the capitalists A, A', A" (I), is the real basis of the accumulation of capital, i.e., of extended reproduction, although it does not actually function in this capacity until it reaches the hands of B, B', B", etc. (I), it is on the contrary absolutely unproductive in its chrysalis stage of money – as a hoard and virtual money-capital in process of gradual formation – runs parallel with the process of production in this form, but lies outside of it. It is a dead weight of capitalist production. The eagerness to utilise this surplus-value accumulating as virtual money-capital for the purpose of deriving profits or revenue from it finds its object accomplished in the credit system and 'papers.' Money-capital thereby gains in another form an enormous influence on the course and the stupendous development of the capitalist system of production. The surplus-product converted into virtual money-capital will grow so much more in volume, the greater was the total amount of already functioning capital whose functioning brought it into being. With the absolute increase of the volume of the annually reproduced virtual money-capital its segmentation also becomes easier, so that it is more rapidly invested in any particular business, either in the hands of the same capitalist or in those of others (for instance members of the family, in the case of a partition of inherited property, etc.). By segmentation of money-capital is meant here that it is wholly detached from the parent stock in order to be invested as a new money-capital in a new and independent business.

While the sellers of the surplus-product, A, A', A", etc. (I), have obtained it as a direct outcome of the process of production, which does not envisage any additional acts of circulation except the advance of constant and variable capital required also in simple reproduction; and while they thereby construct the real basis for reproduction on an extended scale, and in actual fact manufacture virtually additional capital, the attitude of B, B', B", etc. (I), is different. 1) Not until it reaches the hands of B, B', B", etc. (I), will the surplus-product of A, A', A", etc., actually function as additional constant capital (we leave out of consideration for the present the other element of productive capital, the additional labour-power, in other words, the additional variable capital).

2) In order that that surplus-product may reach their hands an act of circulation is wanted – they must buy it.

In regard to point 1 it should be noted here that a large portion of the surplus-product (virtually additional constant capital), although produced by A, A', A" (I) in a given year, may not function as industrial capital in the hands of B, B', B" (I) until the following year or still later. With reference to point 2, the question arises: Whence comes the money needed for the process of circulation?

Since the products created by B, B', B", etc. (I), re-enter in kind into their own process, it goes without saying that *pro tanto* a portion of their own surplus-product is transferred directly (without any intervention of circulation) to their productive capital and becomes an additional element of constant capital. And pro tanto they do not effect the conversion of the surplus-product of A, A›, etc. (I), into money. Aside from this, where does the money come from? We know that B, B›, B››, etc. (I) have formed their hoard in the same way as A, A›, etc., by the sale of their respective surplus-products. Now they have arrived at the point where their hoarded, only virtual, money-capital is to function effectively as additional money-capital. But this is merely going round in circles. The question still remains: Where does the money come from which the B›s (I) before withdrew from circulation and accumulated? We know from the analysis of simple reproduction that capitalists I and II must have a certain amount of money at hand in order to be able to exchange their surplus-product. In that case the money which served only as revenue to be spent for articles of consumption returned to the capitalists in the same measure in which they had advanced it for the exchange of their respective commodities. Here the same money re-appears, but performing a different function. The A›s and B›s (I) supply one another alternately with the money for converting surplus-product into additional virtual money-capital, and throw the newly formed money-capital alternately back into circulation as a means of purchase. The only assumption made in this case is that the amount of money in the country in question (the velocity of circulation, etc., being constant) should suffice for both the active circulation and the reserve hoard. As we have seen this is the same assumption as had to be made in the case of the simple circulation of commodities. Only the function of the hoards is different in the present case. Furthermore, the available amount of money must be larger, first, because under capitalist production all the products (with the exception of newly produced precious metals and the few products consumed by the producer himself) are created as commodities and must therefore pass through the pupation stage of money; secondly, because on a capitalist basis the quantity of the commodity-capital and the magnitude of its value is not only absolutely greater but also grows with incomparably greater rapidity; thirdly, because an ever expanding variable capital must always be converted into money-capital; fourthly, because the formation of new money-capitals keeps pace with the extension of production, so that the material for corresponding hoard formation must be available.

This is generally true of the first phase of capitalist production, in which even the credit system is mostly accompanied by metallic circulation, and it applies to the most developed phase of the credit system as well, to the extent that metallic circulation remains its basis. On the one hand an additional production of precious metals, being alternately abundant or scarce, may here exert a disturbing influence on the prices of commodities not only at long, but also at very short intervals. On the other hand, the entire credit mechanism is continually occupied in reducing the actual metallic circulation to a relatively more and more decreasing minimum by means of sundry operations, methods, and technical devices.

The artificiality of the entire machinery and the possibility of disturbing its normal course increase to the same extent.

The different B's, B"s, B"'s, etc. (I), whose virtual new money-capital enters upon its function as active capital, may have to buy their products (portions of their surplus-product) from one another, or to sell them to one another. Pro tanto the money advanced by them for the circulation of their surplus-product flows back under normal conditions to the different B's in the same proportion in which they had advanced it for the circulation of their respective commodities. If the money circulates as a means of payment, then only balances are to be squared so far as the mutual purchases and sales do not cover one another. But it is important first and foremost to assume here, as everywhere, metallic circulation in its simplest, most primitive form, because then the flux and reflux, the squaring of balances, in short all elements appearing under the credit system as consciously regulated processes present themselves as existing independently of the credit system, and the matter appears in primitive form instead of the later, reflected form.

3. The Additional Variable Capital

Hitherto we have been dealing only with additional constant capital. Now we must direct our attention to a consideration of the additional variable capital.

We have explained at great length in Book I that labour-power is always available under the capitalist system of production, and that more labour can be rendered fluent, if necessary, without increasing the number of labourers or the quantity of labour-power employed. We therefore need not go into this any further, but shall rather assume that the portion of the newly created money-capital capable of being converted into variable capital will always find at hand the labour-power into which it is to transform itself. It has also been explained in Book I that a given capital may expand its volume of production within certain limits without any accumulation. But here we are dealing with the accumulation of capital in its specific meaning, so that the expansion of production implies the conversion of surplus-value into additional capital, and thus also an expansion of the capital forming the basis of production.

The gold producer can accumulate a portion of his golden surplus- value as virtual money-capital. As soon as it becomes sufficient in amount, he can transform it directly into new variable capital, without first having to sell his surplus-product. He can likewise convert it into elements of the constant capital. But in the latter case he must find at hand the material elements of his constant capital. It is immaterial whether, as was assumed in our presentation hitherto, each producer works to stock up and then brings his finished product to the market or fills orders. The actual expansion of production, i.e., the surplus-product, is assumed in either case, in the one case as actually available, in the other as virtually available, capable of delivery.

Section II. *Accumulation in Department II*

We have hitherto assumed that A, A', A" (I) sell their surplus-product to B, B', B", etc., who belong to the same department I. But supposing A (I) converts his surplus-product into money by selling it to one B in department II. This can be done only by A (I) selling means of production to B (II) without subsequently buying articles of consumption, i.e., only by a one-sided sale on A's part. Now whereas II c cannot be converted from the commodity-capital form into the bodily form of productive constant capital unless not only I but also at least a portion of I, is exchanged for a portion of II c, which II exists in the form of articles of consumption; but now A converts his I into money by not making this exchange but rather withdrawing from circulation the money obtained from II on the sale of his I s instead of exchanging it in the purchase of articles of consumption II c – then what we have on the part of A (I) is indeed a formation of additional virtual money-capital, but on the other hand a portion of the constant capital of B (II) of equal magnitude of value is tied up in the form of commodity-capital, unable to transform itself into the bodily form of productive, constant capital. In other words, a portion of the commodities of B (II), and indeed primo facie a portion without the sale of which he cannot reconvert his constant capital entirely into its productive form, has become unsaleable. As far as this portion is concerned there is therefore an over-production, which, likewise as far as the same portion is concerned, clogs reproduction, even on the same scale.

In this case, the additional virtual money-capital on the side of A (I) is indeed a moneyed form of surplus-product (surplus-value), but the surplus-product (surplus-value) considered as such is here a phenomenon of simple reproduction, not yet of reproduction on an extended scale. $I_{(v+s)}$ for which this is true at all events of one portion of s, must ultimately be exchanged for II c, in order that the reproduction of II c may take place on the same scale. By the sale of his surplus-product to B(II), A(I) has supplied to the latter a corresponding portion of the value of constant capital in its bodily form. But at the same time he has rendered an equivalent portion of the commodities of B (II) unsaleable by withdrawing the money from circulation – by failing to complement his sale through subsequent purchase. Hence, if we survey the entire social reproduction, which comprises the capitalists of both I and II, the conversion of the surplus-product of A (I) into virtual money-capital expresses the impossibility of reconverting commodity-capital of B (II) representing an equal amount of value into productive (constant) capital; hence not virtual production on an extended scale but an obstruction of simple reproduction, and so a deficit in simple reproduction. As the formation and sale of the surplus-product of A (I) are normal phenomena of simple reproduction, we have here even on the basis of simple reproduction the following interdependent phenomena: Formation of virtual additional money-capital in class I (hence under-consumption from the view-point of II); piling up of commodity-supplies in class II which cannot be reconverted into productive capital (hence relative over-production in II); surplus of money-capital in I and reproduction deficit in II.

Without pausing any longer at this point, we simply remark that we had assumed in the analysis of simple reproduction that the entire surplus-value of I and II is spent as revenue. As a matter of fact however one portion of the surplus-value is spent as revenue, and the other is converted into capital. Actual accumulation can take place only on this assumption. That accumulation should take place at the expense of consumption is, couched in such general terms, an illusion contradicting the nature of capitalist production. For it takes for granted that the aim and compelling motive of capitalist production is consumption, and not the snatching of surplus-value and its capitalisation, i.e., accumulation.

Let us now take a closer look at the accumulation in department II.

The first difficulty with reference to II c, i.e., its reconversion from a component part of commodity-capital II into the bodily form of constant capital II, concerns simple reproduction. Let us take the former scheme: (1,000 v + 1,000 s) I are exchanged for 2,000 II c.

Now, if for instance one half of the surplus-product of I, hence 1,000/2 s or 500 I s is reincorporated in department I as constant capital, then this portion of the surplus-product, being detained in I, cannot replace any part of II c. Instead of being converted into articles of consumption (and here in this section of the circulation between I and II the exchange is actually mutual, that is, there is a double change of position of the commodities, unlike the replacement of 1,000 II c by 1,000 I v effected by the labourers of I), it is made to serve as an additional means of production in I itself. It cannot perform this function simultaneously in I and II. The capitalist cannot spend the value of his surplus-product for articles of consumption and at the same time consume the surplus-product itself productively, i.e., incorporate it in his productive capital. Instead of 2,000 $I_{(v+s)}$, only 1,500, namely (1,000 v

+ 500 s) I, are therefore exchangeable for 2,000 II c ; 500 II c cannot be reconverted from the commodity-form into productive (constant) capital

II. Hence there would be an over-production in II, exactly equal in volume to the expansion of production in I. This over-production in II might react to such an extent on I that even the reflux of the 1,000 spent by the labourers of I for articles of consumption of II might take place but partially, so that these 1,000 would not return to the hands of capitalists I in the form of variable money-capital. These capitalists would thus find themselves hampered even in reproduction on an unchanging scale, and this by the bare attempt to expand it. And in this connection it must be taken into consideration that in I only simple reproduction had actually taken place and that its elements, as represented in our scheme, are only differently grouped with a view to expansion in the future, say, next year.

One might attempt to circumvent this difficulty in the following way: Far from being over-production, the 500 II c which are kept in stock by the capitalists and cannot be immediately converted into productive capital represent, on the contrary, a necessary element of reproduction, which we have so far neglected. We have seen that a money-supply must be accumulated at many points, hence money must be withdrawn from circulation, partly for the purpose of making it possible to form new money-capital in I, and partly to hold fast temporarily the value of the gradually depreciating fixed capital in the form of money. But, since we placed all money and commodities from the very start exclusively into the hands of capitalists I and II when we drew up our scheme and since neither merchants, nor money-changers, nor bankers, nor merely consuming and not directly producing classes exist here, it follows that the constant formation of commodity stores in the hands of their respective producers is here indispensable to keep the machinery of reproduction going. The 500 II c held in stock by capitalists II therefore represent the commodity-supply of articles of consumption which ensures the continuity of the process of consumption implied in reproduction, here meaning the passage of one year to the next. The consumption-fund, which is as yet in the hands of its sellers who are at the same time its producers, cannot fall one year to the point of zero in order to begin the next with zero, any more than such a thing can take place in the transition from today to tomorrow. Since such supplies of commodities must constantly be built up anew, though varying in volume, our capitalist producers II must have a reserve money-capital, which enables them to continue their process of production although one portion of their productive capital is temporarily tied up in the shape of commodities. Our assumption is that they combine the whole business of trading with that of producing. Hence they must also have at their disposal the additional money-capital, which is in the hands of the merchants when the individual functions in the process of reproduction are separated and distributed among the various kinds of capitalists.

To this one may object:

1. That the forming of such supplies and the necessity of doing so applies to all capitalists, those of I as well as of II. Considered as mere sellers of commodities, they differ only in that they sell different kinds of commodities. A supply of commodities II implies a previous supply of commodities I. If we neglect this supply on one side, we must also do so on the other. But if we take them into account on both sides, the problem is not altered in any way.
2. Just as a certain year closes on the part of II with a supply of commodities for the following year, so it was opened with a supply of commodities on the same part, taken over from the preceding year. In an analysis of annual reproduction, reduced to its most abstract form, we must therefore strike it out in both cases. If we leave to the given year its entire production, including the commodity-supply to be yielded up for next year, and simultaneously take from it the supply

of commodities transferred to it from the preceding year, we have before us the actual aggregate product of an average year as the subject of our analysis.

3. The simple circumstance that in the analysis of simple reproduction we did not stumble across the difficulty which is now to be surmounted proves that we are confronted by a specific phenomenon due solely to the different grouping (with reference to reproduction) of elements I, a changed grouping without which reproduction on an extended scale cannot take place at all.

PART 2

Section III. *Schematic Presentation of Accumulation*

We shall now study reproduction according to the following scheme.

Scheme a)	I. 4,000c + 1,000v + 1,000s	= 6,000
	II. 1,500c + 376v + 376s	= 2,252
		= 8,252 Total

We note in the first place that the sum total of the annual social product, or 8,252, is smaller than that of the first scheme, where it was 9,000. We might just as well assume a much larger sum, for instance one ten times larger. We have chosen a smaller sum than in our scheme I in order to make it conspicuously clear that reproduction on an enlarged scale (which is here regarded merely as production carried on with a larger investment of capital) has nothing to do with the absolute volume of the product, that for a given quantity of commodities it implies merely a different arrangement or a different definition of the functions of the various elements of a given product, so that it is but a simple reproduction so far as the value of the product is concerned. It is not the quantity but the qualitative determination of the given elements of simple reproduction which is changed, and this change is the material premise of a subsequent reproduction on an extended scale.[1]

We might vary the scheme by changing the ratio between the variable and constant capital. For instance as follows:

Scheme b)	I. 4,000c + 875v + 875s	= 5,750
	II. 1,750c + 376v + 376s	= 2,502
		= 8,252 Total

This scheme seems arranged for reproduction on a simple scale, the surplus-value being entirely consumed as revenue and not accumulated. In either case, both a) and b), we have an annual product of the same magnitude of value, only under b) functionally its elements are grouped in such a way that reproduction is resumed on the same scale, while under a) the functional grouping forms the material basis of reproduction on an extended scale. Under b) ($875_v + 875_s$) I, or 1,750 $I_{(v+s)}$, are exchanged without any surplus for 1,750 II_c while under a) the exchange of ($1{,}000_v + 1{,}000_s$) I, equal to 2,000 $I_{(v+s)}$, for 1,000 II_c leaves a surplus of 500 I_s for accumulation in class I.

Now let us analyse scheme a) more closely. Let us suppose that both I and II accumulate one half of their surplus-value, that is to say, convert it into an element of additional capital, instead of spending it as revenue. As one half of 1,000 I_s, or 500, are to be accumulated in one form or another, invested as additional money-capital, i.e., converted into additional productive capital, only ($1{,}000_v + 500_s$) I are spent as revenue. Hence only 1,500 figures here as the normal size of II_c. We need not further examine the exchange between 1,500 $I_{(v+s)}$ and 1,500 II_c, because this has already been done under the head of process of simple reproduction. Nor does 4,000 I_c require any attention, since its re-arrangement for the newly commencing reproduction (which this time will occur on an extended scale) was likewise discussed as a process of simple reproduction.

The only thing that remains to be examined by us is 500 I_s and (376_v + 376_s) II, inasmuch as it is a matter on the one hand of the internal relations of both I and II and on the other of the movement between them. Since we have assumed that in II likewise one half of the surplus-value is to be accumulated, 188 are to be converted here into capital, of which one-fifth, or 47, or, to round it off, 48, are to be variable capital, so that 140 remain to be converted into constant capital.

Here we come across a new problem, whose very existence must appear strange to the current view that commodities of one kind are exchanged for commodities of another kind, or commodities for money and the same money again for commodities of another kind. The 140 II_s can be converted into productive capital only by replacing them with commodities of I_s of the same value. It is a matter of course that that portion of I_s which must be exchanged for II_s must consist of means of production, which may enter either into the production of both I and II, or exclusively into that of II. This replacement can be made feasible only by means of a one-sided purchase on the part of II, as the entire surplus-product of 500 I_s, which we still have to examine, is to serve the purposes of accumulation within I, hence cannot be exchanged for commodities II; in other words, it cannot be simultaneously accumulated and consumed by I. Therefore II must buy 140 I_s for cash without recovering this money by a subsequent sale of its commodities to I. And this is a process which is continually repeating itself in every new annual production, so far as it is reproduction on an extended scale. Where in II is the source of the money for this?

It would rather seem that II is a very unprofitable field for the formation of new money-capital which accompanies actual accumulation and necessitates it under capitalist production, and which at first actually presents itself as simple hoarding.

We have first 376 II_v. The money-capital of 376, advanced in labour-power, continually returns through the purchase of commodities II as variable capital in money-form to capitalist II. This constant repetition of departure from and return to the starting-point, the pocket of the capitalist, does not add in any way to the money roving over this circuit. This, then, is not a source of the accumulation of money. Nor can this money be withdrawn from circulation in order to form hoarded, virtually new, money-capital.

But stop! Isn't there a chance here to make a little profit?

We must not forget that class II has this advantage over class I, that its labourers have to buy back from it the commodities produced by themselves. Class II is a buyer of labour-power and at the same time a seller of the commodities to the owners of the labour-power employed by it. Class II can therefore:

1. —and this it shares with the capitalists of class I—simply depress wages below their normal average level. By this means a portion of the money functioning as the money-form of variable capital is released, and if this process is continually repeated, it might become a normal source of hoarding, and thus of virtually additional money-capital in class II. Of course we are not referring to a casual swindle profit here, since we are treating of a normal formation of capital. But it must not be forgotten that the normal wages actually paid (which *ceteris paribus* determine the magnitude of the variable capital) are not paid by the capitalists but of the goodness of their hearts, but must he paid under given relations. This eliminates the above method of explanation. If we assume that 376_v is the variable capital to be laid out by class II, we have no right suddenly to sneak in the hypothesis that it may pay only 350_v instead of 376_v, merely to elucidate a problem that has newly arisen.

2. On the other hand class II, taken as a whole, has the above-mentioned advantage over I that it is at the same time a buyer of labour-power and a seller of its commodities to its own labourers. Every industrial country (for instance Britain and the U.S.A.) furnishes the most tangible proofs of the way in which this advantage may be exploited—by paying nominally the normal wages but grabbing, alias stealing, back part of them without an equivalent in commodities; by accomplishing the same thing either through the truck system or through a falsification of the medium of circulation (perhaps in a way too elusive for the law). (Take this opportunity to expatiate on this idea with some appropriate examples.) This is the same operation as under 1), only disguised and carried out by a detour. Therefore it must likewise be rejected, the same as the other. We are dealing here with actually paid, not nominally paid wages.

We see that in an objective analysis of the mechanism of capitalism certain stains still sticking to it with extraordinary tenacity cannot be used as a subterfuge to get over some theoretical difficulties. But strange to say, the great majority of my bourgeois critics upbraid me as though I have wronged the capitalists by assuming, for instance in Book I of *Capital*, that the capitalist pays labour-power at its real value, a thing which he mostly does not do! (Here, exercising some of the magnanimity attributed to me, it would be appropriate to quote Schäffle.)

So with the 376 II_v we cannot get any nearer the goal we have mentioned.

But the 376 II_v seem to be in a still more precarious position. Here only capitalists of the same class, mutually buying and selling the articles of consumption they produced, confront one another. The money required for these transactions functions only as a medium of circulation and in the normal course of things must flow back to the interested parties in the same portion in which they advanced it to the circulation, in order to cover the same route over and over again.

There seem to be only two ways by which this money can be withdrawn from circulation to form virtually additional money-capital. Either one part of capitalists II cheats the other and thus robs them of their money. We know that no preliminary expansion of the circulating medium is necessary for the formation of new money-capital. All that is necessary is that the money should be withdrawn from circulation by certain parties and hoarded. It would not alter the case if this money were stolen, so that the formation of additional money-capital by one part of capitalists II would entail a positive loss of money by another part. The cheated capitalists II would have to live a little less gaily, that would be all.

Or a part of II represented by necessities of life is directly converted into new variable capital within department II. How that is done we shall examine at the close of this chapter (under No. IV).

1. First Illustration

A. Scheme of Simple Reproduction

I. $4{,}000_c + 1{,}000_v + 1{,}000_s$ = 6,000

II. $2{,}000_c + 500_v + 500_s$ =3,000

= 9,000 Total

B. Initial Scheme for Reproduction on an Extended Scale

I. $4{,}000_c + 1{,}000_v + 1{,}000_s$ = 6,000

II. $1{,}500_c + 750_v + 750_s$ = 3,000

= 9,000 Total

Assuming that in scheme B one half of surplus-value I, i.e., 500, is accumulated, we first receive ($1,000_v$ + 500_s) I, or 1,500 $I_{(v+s)}$ to be replaced by 1,500 II_c. There then remains in I:$4,000_c$ and 500_s, the latter having to be accumulated. The replacement of ($1,000_v$ + 500_s) I by 1,500 II_c is a process of simple reproduction, which has been examined previously.

Let us now assume that 400 of the 500 I_s are to be converted into constant capital, and 100 into variable capital. The exchange within I of the 400_s, which are thus to be capitalised, has already been discussed. They can therefore be annexed to I_c, without more ado and in that case we get for I:

$4,400_c$ + $1,000_v$ + 100_s (the latter to be converted into 100_v).

II in turn buys from I for the purpose of accumulation the 100 I_s (existing in means of production) which now form additional constant capital II, while the 100 in money which it pays for them are converted into the money-form of the additional variable capital of I. We then have for I a capital of $4,400_c$ + $1,100_v$ (the latter in money), equaling 5,500.

II has now $1,600_c$ for its constant capital. In order to put them to work, it must advance a further 50_v in money for the purchase of new labour-power, so that its variable capital grows from 750 to 800. This expansion of the constant and variable capital of II by a total of 150 is supplied out of its surplus-value. Hence only 600_s of the 750 II_s remain as a consumption-fund for capitalists II, whose annual product is now distributed as follows:

II. $1,600_c$ + 800_v + 600_s (consumption-fund), equal to 3,000.

The 150_s produced in articles of consumption, which have been converted here into (100_c + 50_v) II, go entirely in their bodily form for the consumption of the labourers, 100 being consumed by the labourers of I (100 I_v), and 50 by the labourers of II (50 II_v), as explained above. As a matter of fact in II, where its total product is prepared in a form suitable for accumulation, a part greater by 100 of the surplus-value in the form of *necessary* articles of consumption must be reproduced. If reproduction really starts on an extended scale, then the 100 of variable money-capital I flow back through the hands of its working-class to II, while II transfers 100_s in commodity-supply to I and at the same time 50 in commodity-supply to its own working-class.

The arrangement changed for the purpose of accumulation is now as follows:

I.	$4,400_c$ + $1,100_s$ + 500 consumption-fund	= 6,000
II.	$1,600_c$ + 800_v + 600 consumption-fund	= 3,000
		= 9,000 Total, as before

Of these amounts, the following are capital:

I.	$4,400_c$ + $1,100_v$ (money)	= 5,500
II.	$1,600_c$ + 800_v (money)	= 2,400
		= 7,900

while production started out with

I.	$4,000_c$ + $1,000_v$	= 5,000
II.	$1,500_c$ + 750_v	= 2,250
		= 7,250

Now, if actual accumulation takes place on this basis, that is to say, if production really goes on with this augmented capital, we obtain at the end of the following year:

I. $4,400_c + 1,100_v + 1,100_s$ $= 6,600$

II. $1,600_c + 800_v + 800_v$ $= 3,200$

$= 9,800$

Then let accumulation in I continue in the same proportion, so that 550_s are spent as revenue and 550_s accumulated. In that case 1,100 I_v are first replaced by 1,100 II_c, and 550 I_s must be realised in an equal amount of commodities of II, making a total of 1,650 $I_{(v+s)}$. But the constant capital II, which is to be replaced, is equal to only 1,600; hence the remaining 50 must be supplemented out of 800 II_s. Leaving aside the money aspect for the present, we have as a result of this transaction:

I. $4,400_c + 550_s$ (to be capitalised); furthermore, realised in commodities II_c, the consumption-fund of the capitalists and labourers $1,650_{(v+s)}$.

II. $1,650_c$ (50 added from II_s as indicated above) $+ 800_v + 750_s$ (consumption-fund of the capitalists).

But, if the old ratio of v:s is maintained in II, then additional 25_v must be laid out for 50_c, and these are to be taken from the 750_s. Then we have

II. $1,650_c + 825_v + 725_s$.

In I, 550_s must be capitalised. If the former ratio is maintained, 440 of this amount form constant capital and 110 variable capital. These 110 might be taken out of the 725 II_s, i.e., articles of consumption to the value of 110 are consumed by labourers I instead of capitalists II, so that the latter are compelled to capitalise these 110_s which they cannot consume. This leaves 615 II_s of the 725 II_s. But if II thus converts these 110 into additional constant capital, it requires an additional variable capital of 55. This again must be supplied by its surplus-value. Subtracting this amount from 615 II_s leaves 560 for the consumption of capitalists II, and we now obtain the following capital-value after accomplishing all actual and potential transfers:

I. $(4,400_c + 440_c) + (1,100_v + 110_v) = 4,840_c + 1,210_v = 6,050$

II. $(1,600_c + 50_c + 110_c) + (800_v + 25_v + 55_v) = 1760_c + 880_v = 2,640/8,690$

If things are to proceed normally, accumulation in II must take place more rapidly than in I, because otherwise the portion $I_{(v+s)}$ which must be converted into commodities II will grow more rapidly than II_c, for which alone it can be exchanged.

If reproduction is continued on this basis and conditions otherwise remain unchanged we obtain at the end of the succeeding year:

I. $4,840_c + 1,210_v + 1,210_s$ $= 7,260$

II. $1,760_c + 880_v + 880_s$ $= 3,520$

$= 10,780$

If the rate of division of the surplus-value remains unchanged, there is first to be expended as revenue by I: $1,210_v$ and one half of s, or 605, a total of 1,815. This consumption-fund is again larger than II_c by 55. These 55 must be deducted from 880_s, leaving 825. Furthermore, the conversion of 55 II_s into II implies another deduction from II_s for a corresponding variable capital of 27½, leaving for consumption 797½ II_s.

I has now to capitalise 605_s. Of these 484 are constant and 121 variable. The last named are to be deducted from II_s, which is still equal to 797½, leaving 676½ II_s. II, then, converts another 121 into constant capital and requires another variable capital of 60½ for it, which likewise comes out of 676½, leaving 616 for consumption.

Then we have the following capitals:

I.	Constant:	4,840 + 484 = 5,324
	Variable:	1,210 + 121 = 1,331
II.	Constant:	1,760 + 55 + 121 = 1,936
	Variable:	880 + 27½ + 60½ = 968

Totals: I. $5{,}324_c + 1{,}331_v = 6{,}655$

II. $1{,}936_s + 968_v = 2{,}904$

$= 9{,}559$

And at the end of the year the product is

I. $5{,}324_c + 1{,}331_v + 1{,}331_s = 7{,}986$

II. $1{,}936_c + 968_v + 968_s = 3{,}872$

$= 11{,}858$

Repeating the same calculation and rounding off the fractions, we get at the end of the succeeding year the following product:

I. $5{,}856_c + 1{,}464_v + 1{,}464_s = 8{,}784$

II. $2{,}129_c + 1{,}065_v + 1{,}065_c = 4{,}259$

$= 13{,}043$

And at the end of the next succeeding year:

I. $6{,}442_c + 1{,}610_v + 1{,}610_s = 9{,}662$

II. $2{,}342_c + 1{,}172_v + 1{,}172_s = 4{,}686$

$= 14{,}348$

In the course of five years of reproduction on an extended scale the aggregate capital of I and II has risen from $5{,}500_c + 1{,}750_v = 7{,}250$ to $8{,}784_c + 2{,}782_v = 11{,}566$; in other words in the ratio of 100:160. The total surplus-value was originally 1,750; it is now 2,782. The consumed surplus-value was originally 500 for I and 600 for II, a total of 1,100. The previous year it was 732 for I and 745 for II, a total of 1,477. It has therefore grown in the ratio of 100:134.

2. Second Illustration

Now take the annual product of 9,000, which is altogether a commodity-capital in the hands of the class of industrial capitalists in a form in which the general average ratio of the variable to the constant capital is that of 1:5. This presupposes a considerable development of capitalist production and accordingly of the productivity of social labour, a considerable previous increase in the scale of production, and finally a development of all the circumstances which produce a relative surplus-population among the working-class. The annual product will then be divided as follows, after rounding off the various fractions:

I. $5{,}000_c + 1{,}000_v + 1{,}000_s = 7{,}000$

II. $1{,}430_c + 285_v + 285_s = 2{,}000$

$= 9{,}000$

Now take it that capitalist class I consumes one half of its surplus-value, or 500, and accumulates the other half. In that case $(1{,}000_v + 500_s)$ I, or 1,500, would have to be converted into 1,500 II_c. Since II_c here amounts to only 1,430, it is necessary to add 70 from the surplus-value. Subtracting this sum from 285 II_s leaves 215 II_s. Then we have:

I. $5{,}000_c + 500_s$ (to be capitalised) $+ 1{,}500_{(v+s)}$ in the consumption-fund of the capitalists and labourers.

II. $1{,}430_c + 70_s$ (to be capitalised) $+ 285_v + 215_s$.

As 70 II_s are directly annexed here to II_c, a variable capital of 70/5, or 14, is required to set this additional constant capital in motion. These 14 must also come out of the 215 II_s, so that 201 II_s remain, and we have:

II. $(1{,}430_c + 70_c) + (285_v + 14_v) + 201_s$.

The exchange of 1,500 $I_{(v + ½s)}$ for 1,500 II_c is a process of simple reproduction, and nothing further need be said about it. However a few peculiarities remain to be noted here, which arise from the fact that in accumulating reproduction $I_{(v + ½s)}$ is not replaced solely by II_c, but by II_c plus a portion of II_s.

It goes without saying that as soon as we assume accumulation, $I_{(v+s)}$ is greater than II_c, not equal to II_c, as in simple reproduction. For in the first place, I incorporates a portion of its surplus-product in its own productive capital and converts five-sixths of it into constant capital, therefore cannot replace these five-sixths simultaneously by articles of consumption II. In the second place I has to supply out of its surplus-product the material for the constant capital required for accumulation within II, just as II has to supply I with the material for the variable capital, which is to set in motion the portion of I's surplus-product employed by I itself as additional constant capital. We know that the actual, and therefore also the additional, variable capital consists of labour-power. It is not capitalist I who buys from II a supply of necessities of life or accumulates them for the additional labour-power to be employed by him, as the slaveholder had to do. It is the labourers themselves who trade with II. But this does not prevent the articles of consumption of his additional labour-power from being viewed by the capitalist as only so many means of production and maintenance of his eventual additional labour-power, hence as the bodily form of his variable capital. His own immediate operation, in the present case that of I, consists in merely storing up the new money-capital required for the purchase of additional labour-power. As soon as he has incorporated this in his capital, the money becomes a means of purchase of commodities II for this labour-power, which must find these articles of consumption at hand.

By the by. The capitalist, as well as his press, is often dissatisfied with the way in which the labour-power spends its money and with the commodities II in which it realises this money. On such occasions he philosophises, babbles of culture, and dabbles in philanthropical talk, for instance after the manner of Mr. Drummond, the Secretary of the British Embassy in Washington. According to him, *The Nation* (a journal) carried last October 1879, an interesting article, which contained among other things the following passages:

> 'The working-people have not kept up in culture with the growth of invention, and they have had things showered on them which they do not know how to use, and thus make no market for.' [Every capitalist naturally wants the labourer to buy his commodities.] 'There is no reason why the working man should not desire as many comforts as the minister, lawyer, and doctor, who is earning the same amount as himself.' [This class of lawyers, ministers and doctors have indeed to be satisfied with the mere desire of many comforts!] 'He does not do so, however. The problem remains, how to raise him as a consumer by rational and healthful processes, not an easy one, as his ambition does not go beyond a diminution of his hours of labour, the demagogues rather inciting him to this than to raising his condition by the improvement of his mental and moral powers.' (*Reports of H. M.'s Secretaries of Embassy and Legation on the Manufactures, Commerce, etc., of the Countries in which they reside*. London, 1879, p. 404.)

Long hours of labour seem to be the secret of the rational and healthful processes, which are to raise the condition of the labourer by an improvement of his mental and moral powers and to make a rational consumer of him. In order to become a rational consumer of the commodities of the capitalist, he should above all begin to let his own capitalist consume his labour-power irrationally and unhealthfully—but the demagogue prevents him! What the capitalist means by a rational consumption is evident wherever he is condescending enough to engage directly in the trade with his own labourers, in the truck system, which includes also the supplying of homes to the labourers, so that the capitalist is at the same time a landlord for them—a branch of business among many others.

The same Drummond, whose beautiful soul is enamoured of the capitalist attempts to uplift the working-class, tells in the same report among other things of the cotton goods manufacture of the Lowell and Lawrence Mills. The boarding and lodging houses for the factory girls belong to the corporation or company owning the mills. The stewardesses of these houses are in the employ of the same company which prescribes them rules of conduct. No girl is permitted to stay out after 10 p.m. Then comes a gem: a special police patrol the grounds for the purpose of guarding against an infringement of those rules. After 10 p. m. no girl can leave or enter. No girl may live anywhere but on the premises of the company, and every house on it brings the company about 10 dollars per week in rent. And now we see the rational consumer in his full glory:

> 'As the ever present piano is however to be found in many of the best appointed working girls' boarding houses, music, song, and dance come in for a considerable share of the operatives' attention at least among those who, after 10 hours' steady work at the looms, need more relief from monotony than actual rest.' (p. 412.)

But the main secret of making a rational consumer out of the labourer is yet to be told. Mr. Drummond visits the cutlery works of Turner's Falls (Connecticut River), and Mr. Oakman, the treasurer of the concern, after telling him that especially American table cutlery beat the English in quality, continues:

> 'The time is coming that we will beat England as to prices also, we are ahead in quality now, that is acknowledged, but we must have lower prices, and shall have it the moment we get our steel at lower prices and have our labour down.' (p. 427.)

A reduction of wages and long hours of labour—that is the essence of the rational and healthful processes which are to uplift the labourer to the dignity of a rational consumer, so that 'they make a market for things showered upon them' by culture and growth of invention.

Consequently, just as I has to supply the additional constant capital of II out of its surplus-product, so II likewise supplies the additional variable capital for I. II accumulates for I and for itself, so far as the variable capital is concerned, by reproducing a greater portion of its total product, and hence especially of its surplus-product, in the shape of necessary articles of consumption.

In production on the basis of increasing capital, $I_{(v + s)}$ must be equal to II plus that portion of the surplus-product which is re-incorporated as capital, plus the additional portion of constant capital required for the expansion of the production in II; and the minimum of this expansion is that without which real accumulation, i.e., a real expansion of production in I itself, is unfeasible.

Reverting now to the case which we examined last, we find in it the peculiarity that II is smaller than $I_{(v + ½s)}$, than that portion of product I which is spent as revenue for articles of consumption, so that on exchanging the 1,500 $I_{(v + s)}$ a portion of surplus-product II, equal to 70, is at once realised. As for II_c, equal to 1,430, it must, all other conditions remaining the same, be replaced by an equal magnitude of value out of $I_{(v + s)}$, in order that simple reproduction may take place in II, and to that extent we need not pay any more attention to it here. It is different with the additional 70 II_s. What for I is merely a replacement of revenue by articles of consumption, merely commodity-exchange meant for consumption, is for II not a mere reconversion of its constant capital from the form of commodity-capital into its bodily form, as it is in simple reproduction, but a direct process of accumulation, a transformation of a part of its surplus-product from the form of articles of consumption into that of constant capital. If with £70 in money (money-reserve for the conversion of surplus-value) I buys the 70 II_s, and if II does not buy in exchange 70 I_s, but accumulates the £70 as money-capital, then the latter is indeed always an expression of additional product (precisely of the surplus-product of II, of which it is an aliquot part), although this is not a product which re-enters production; but in that case this accumulation of money on the part of II would at the same time express that 70 I_s in means of production are unsaleable. There would be a relative overproduction in I, corresponding to the simultaneous non-expansion of reproduction on the part of II.

But apart from this: Until the 70 in money, which came from I, return to it, wholly or in part, through the purchase of 70 I_s by II, this 70 in money figures wholly or in part as additional virtual money-capital in the hands of II. This is true of every exchange between I and II, until the mutual replacement of their respective commodities has effected the return of the money to its starting-point. But in the normal course of things the money figures here only transiently in this role. In the credit system, however, where all temporarily released additional money is supposed to function at once actively as an additional money-capital, such only temporarily released money-capital may be enthralled, for instance, serve in new enterprises of I, while it should have to realise surplus-products held there in other enterprises. It must also be noted that the annexation of 70 I_s to constant capital II requires at the same time an expansion of variable capital II by 14. This implies—about the way it did in I, in the direct incorporation of surplus-product I_s in capital I_c—that the reproduction in II is already in process with a tendency toward further capitalisation; in other words, it implies expansion of that portion of the surplus-product which consists of necessary means of subsistence.

The product of 9,000 in the second illustration must, as we have seen, be distributed in the following manner for the purpose of reproduction, if 500 I_s is to be capitalised. In doing so we merely consider the commodities and neglect the money-circulation.

I. $5{,}000_c + 500_s$ (to be capitalised) + $1{,}500_{(v + s)}$ consumption-fund equals 7,000 in commodities.

II. $1{,}500_c + 299_v + 201_s$ equals 2,000 in commodities. Grand total, 9,000 in commodities.

Capitalisation takes place in the following manner:

In I the 500_s which are being capitalised divide into five-sixths, or 417_c plus one-sixth, or 83_v. The 83_v draw an equal amount out of II_s, which buys elements of constant capital and adds them to II_c. An increase of II_c by 83 implies an increase of II_v by one-fifth of 83, or 17.

We have, then, after this exchange

I. $(5{,}000_c + 417_{s})_c + (1{,}000_v + 83_{s})_v = 5{,}417_c + 1{,}083_v = 6{,}500$

II. $(1{,}500_c + 83_{s})_c + (299_v + 17_{s})_v = 1{,}583_c + 316_v = 1{,}899$ Total... 8,399.

The capital in I has grown from 6,000 to 6,500, or by 1/12. That of II has grown from 1,715 to 1,899, or by not quite 1/9.

The reproduction on this basis in the second year brings the capital at the end of that year to

I. $(5{,}417_c + 452_{s})_c + (1{,}083_v + 90_{s})_v = 5{,}869_c + 1{,}173_v = 7{,}042$

II. $(1{,}583_c + 42_s + 90_{s})_c + (316_v + 8_s + 18_{s})_v = 1{,}715_c + 342_v = 2{,}057.$

And at the end of the third year, we have a product of

I. $5{,}869_c + 1{,}173_v + 1{,}173_s$
II. $1{,}715_c + 342_v + 342_s$.

If I accumulates one half of its surplus-value, as before, we find that $I_{(v + ½s)}$ yields $1{,}173_v$ + $587_{(½s)}$, equal to 1,760, more than the entire 1,715 II_c, an excess of 45. This must again be balanced by transferring an equal amount of means of production to II_c, which thus grows by 45, necessitating an addition of one-fifth, or 9, to II_v. Furthermore, the capitalised 587 I_s divide into five-sixths and one-sixth, i.e., 489_c and 98_v. The 98 imply in II a new addition of 98 to the constant capital, and this again an increase of variable capital II by one-fifth, or 20. Then we have:

I. $(5{,}869_c + 489_s)_c + (1{,}173_v + 98_s)_v = 6{,}358_s + 1{,}271_v = 7{,}629$
II. $(1{,}715_c + 45_s + 98_s)_c + (342_v + 9_s + 20_s)_v = 1{,}858_c + 371_v = 2{,}229$
Total capital = 9,858.

In three years of growing reproduction the total capital of I has increased from 6,000 to 7,629 and that of II from 1,715 to 2,229, the aggregate social capital from 7,715 to 9,858.

3. Replacement of II_c in Accumulation

In the exchange of $I_{(v+s)}$ for II_c we thus meet with various cases. In simple reproduction both of them must be equal and replace one another, since otherwise simple reproduction cannot proceed without disturbance, as we have seen above.

In accumulation it is above all the rate of accumulation that must be considered. In the preceding cases we assumed that the rate of accumulation in I was equal to ½s I, and also that it remained constant from year to year. We changed only the proportion in which this accumulated capital was divided into variable and constant capital. We then had three cases:

1. $I_{(v + ½s)}$ equals II_c, which is therefore smaller than $I_{(v + s)}$. This must always be so, otherwise I does not accumulate.
2. $I_{(v + ½s)}$ is greater than II_c. In this case the replacement is effected by adding a corresponding portion of II_s to II_c, so that this sum becomes equal to $I_{(v + ½s)}$. Here the replacement for II is not a simple reproduction of its constant capital, but accumulation, an augmentation of its constant capital by that portion of its surplus-product which it exchanges for means of production of I. This augmentation implies at the same time a corresponding addition to variable capital II out of its own surplus-product.
3 $I_{(v + ½s)}$ is smaller than II_c. In this case II does not fully reproduce its constant capital by means of exchange and must make good the deficit by purchase from I. But this does not entail any further accumulation of variable capital II, since its constant capital is fully reproduced only by this operation. On the other hand that part of capitalists I who accumulate only additional money-capital, have already accomplished a portion of this accumulation by this transaction.

The premise of simple reproduction, that $I_{(v + s)}$ is equal to II_c, is not only incompatible with capitalist production, although this does not exclude the possibility that in an industrial cycle of 10-11 years some year may show a smaller total production than the preceding year, so that not even simple reproduction takes place compared to the preceding year. Besides that, considering the natural annual increase in population simple reproduction could take place only to the extent that a correspondingly larger number of unproductive servants would partake of the 1,500 representing the aggregate surplus-value. But accumulation of capital, real capitalist production, would be impossible under such circumstances. The fact of capitalist accumulation therefore excludes the possibility of II_c being equal to $I_{(v+s)}$. Nevertheless, it might occur even with capitalist accumulation that in consequence of the course taken by the processes of accumulation during a preceding series of periods of production II_c might become not only equal but even bigger than $I_{(v+s)}$. This would mean an over-production in II and could not be adjusted in any other way than by a great crash, in consequence of which some capital of II would get transferred to I.

Nor does it alter the relation of $I_{(v+s)}$ to II_c if a portion of constant capital II reproduces itself, as happens for instance in the use of home-grown seeds in agriculture. This portion of II_c is no more to be taken into consideration in the exchange between I and II than is I_c. Nor does it change matters if a part of the products of II is capable of entering into I as means of production. It is covered by a part of the means of production supplied by I, and this portion must be deducted on both sides at the outset, if we wish to examine in pure and unobscured form the exchange between the two large classes of social production, the producers of means of production and the producers of articles of consumption.

Hence, under capitalist production $I_{(v+s)}$ cannot be equal to II_c, in other words, the two cannot balance in mutual exchange. On the other hand, if $I_{(s/x)}$ is taken as that portion of I_s which is spent by capitalists I as revenue, $I_{(v+s/x)}$ may be equal to, larger, or smaller than, II_c. But $I_{(v+s/x)}$ must always be smaller than $II_{(c+s)}$ by as much as that portion of II_s which must be consumed under all circumstances by capitalist class II.

It must be noted that in this exposition of accumulation the value of the constant capital is not presented accurately so far as that capital is a part of the value of the commodity-capital it helped to produce. The fixed portion of the newly accumulated constant capital enters into the commodity-capital only gradually and periodically, according to the different natures of these fixed elements. Therefore, whenever raw materials, semi-finished goods, etc., enter in huge quantities into the production of commodities, the commodity-capital consists for the most part of replacements of the circulating constant components and of the variable capital. (On account of the specific turnover of the circulating component parts this way of presenting the matter may nevertheless be adopted. It is then assumed that the circulating portion together with the portion of value of the fixed capital transferred to it is turned over so often during the year that the aggregate sum of the commodities supplied is equal in value to all the capital entering into the annual production.) But wherever only auxiliary materials are used for mechanical industry, and no raw material, there the labour element, equal to v, must reappear in the commodity-capital as its larger constituent. While in the calculation of the rate of profit the surplus-value is figured on the total capital, regardless of whether the fixed components periodically transfer much or little value to the product, the fixed portion of constant capital is to be included in the calculation of the value of any periodically created commodity-capital only to the extent that on an average it yields value to the product on account of wear and tear.

Section IV. *Supplementary Remarks*

The original source of the money for II is v + s of the gold industry I exchanged for a part of II_c. The v + s of the producer of gold does not enter into II only to the extent that he accumulates surplus-value or converts it into means of production I, i.e., to the extent that he expands his production. On the other hand, since the accumulation of money on the part of the gold producer himself leads ultimately to reproduction on an extended scale, a portion of the surplus-value of gold production not spent as revenue passes as additional variable capital of the gold producer into II, promotes here the formation of new hoards or supplies new means with which to buy from I without selling to it direct. From the money derived from this $I_{(v+s)}$ of the production of gold that portion of the gold must be deducted which certain branches of production II need as raw material, etc., in short as an element for the replacement of their constant capital. An element for the preliminary formation of hoards—for the purpose of future extended reproduction—exists in the exchange between I and II: for I only if part of I_s is sold one-sidedly, without a balancing purchase, to II and serves there as additional constant capital II; for II, when the same is the case on the part of I for additional variable capital; furthermore, if a part of the surplus-value spent by I as revenue is not covered by II_c, hence a part of II_s is bought with it and thus converted into money. If $I_{(v + s/x)}$ is greater than II_c, then II_c need not for its simple reproduction replace in commodities from I what I consumed out of II_s. The question arises to what extent hoarding can take place within the sphere of exchange of capitalists II among themselves, an exchange which can consist only of a mutual exchange of II_s. We know that direct accumulation takes place within II by the direct conversion of a portion of II s into variable capital (just as in I a portion of I_s is directly converted into constant capital). In the various age categories of accumulation within the various lines of business of II, and for the individual capitalists in each line of business, the matter is explained *mutatis mutandis* in the same way as in I. Some are still in the stage of hoarding, and sell without buying; the others are on the point of actual expansion of reproduction, and buy without selling. The additional variable money-capital is, true enough, first invested in additional labour-power, but this buys means of subsistence from the hoarding owners of the additional articles of consumption entering into the consumption of the labourers. From these owners, *pro rata* to their hoard formation, the money does not return to its point of departure. They hoard it.

Note

1. This puts an end, once and for all, to the feud over the accumulation of capital between James Mill and S. Bailey, which we have discussed from another point of view in Book I, Ch. XXIV, 5, Note, namely, the feud concerning the possibility of extending the operation of industrial capital without changing its magnitude. We shall revert to this later.

VOLUME III

BOOK THREE: THE PROCESS OF CAPITALIST PRODUCTION AS A WHOLE

PART i

THE CONVERSION OF SURPLUS-VALUE INTO PROFIT AND OF THE RATE OF SURPLUS-VALUE INTO THE RATE OF PROFIT

1

Cost-Price and Profit

In Book I we analysed the phenomena which constitute the *process of capitalist production* as such, as the immediate productive process, with no regard for any of the secondary effects of outside influences. But this immediate process of production does not exhaust the life span of capital. It is supplemented in the actual world by the *process of circulation*, which was the object of study in Book II. In the latter, namely in Part III, which treated the process of circulation as a medium for the process of social reproduction, it developed that the capitalist process of production taken as a whole represents a synthesis of the processes of production and circulation. Considering what this third book treats, it cannot confine itself to general reflection relative to this synthesis. On the contrary, it must locate and describe the concrete forms which grow out of the *movements of capital as a whole*. In their actual movement, capitals confront each other in such concrete shape, for which the form of capital in the immediate process of production, just as its form in the process of circulation, appear only as special instances. The various forms of capital, as evolved in this book, thus approach step by step the form which they assume on the surface of society, in the action of different capitals upon one another, in competition, and in the ordinary consciousness of the agents of production themselves.

The value of every commodity produced in the capitalist way is represented in the formula: C = c + v + s. If we subtract surplus-values from this value of the product there remains a bare equivalent or a substitute value in goods, for the capital-value c + v expended in the elements of production.

For example, if the production of a certain article requires a capital outlay of £500, of which £20 are for the wear and tear of instruments of production, £380 for the materials of production, and £100 for labour-power, and if the rate of surplus-value is 100%, then the value of the product = $400_c + 100_v + 100_s$ = £600.

After deducting the surplus-value of £100, there remains a commodity-value of £500 which only replaces the expended capital of £500. This portion of the value of the commodity, which replaces the price of the consumed means of production and labour-power, only replaces what the commodity costs the capitalist himself. For him it, therefore, represents the cost-price of the commodity.

What the commodity costs the capitalist and its actual production cost are two quite different magnitudes. That portion of the commodity-value making up the surplus-value does not cost the capitalist anything simply because it costs the labourer unpaid labour. Yet, on the basis of capitalist production, after the labourer enters the production process he himself constitutes an ingredient of operating productive capital, which belongs to the capitalist. Therefore, the capitalist is the actual producer of the commodity. For this reason, the cost-price of the commodity necessarily appears to the capitalist as the actual cost of the commodity. If we take k to be the cost-price, the formula C = c + v + s turns into the formula C = k + s, that is, the commodity-value = cost-price + surplus-value.

The grouping of the various value portions of a commodity which only replace the value of the capital expended in its production under the head of cost-price expresses, on the one hand, the specific character of capitalist production. The capitalist cost of the commodity is measured by the expenditure of *capital*, while the actual cost of the commodity is measured by the expenditure of *labour*. Thus, the capitalist cost-price of the commodity differs in quantity from its value, or its actual cost-price. It is smaller than the value of the commodity, because, with C = k + s, it is evident that k = C - s. On the other hand, the cost-price of a commodity is by no means simply a category which exists only in capitalist book-keeping. The individualisation of this portion of value is continually manifest in practice in the actual production of the commodity, because it has ever to be reconverted from its commodity-form by way of the process of circulation into the form of productive capital, so that the cost-price of the commodity always must repurchase the elements of production consumed in its manufacture.

The category of cost-price, on the other hand, has nothing to do with the formation of commodity-value, or with the process of self-expansion of capital. When I know that of the value of a commodity worth £600, five-sixths, or £500, represent no more than an equivalent of the capital of £500 consumed in its production and that it can therefore suffice only to repurchase the material elements of this capital, I know nothing as yet either of the way in which these five-sixths of the value of the commodity, which represent its cost-price, are produced, or about the way in which the last sixth, which constitutes its surplus-value, was produced. The investigation will show, however, that in capitalist economics the cost-price assumes the false appearance of a category of value production itself.

To return to our example. Suppose the value produced by one labourer during an average social working-day is represented by a money sum of 6s. = 6M. Then the advanced capital of £500 = $400_c + 100_v$ represents a value produced in 1,666⅔ ten-hour working-days, of which 1,333⅓ working-days are crystallised in the value of the means of production = 400_c, and 333⅓ are crystallised in the value of labour-power = 100_v. Having assumed a rate of surplus-value of 100%, the production of the commodity to be newly formed entails a labour expenditure = $100_v + 100_s$ = 666⅔ ten-hour working-days.

We know, then (see Buch 1, Kap. VII, S. 201/193) [English edition: Ch. IX, p. 212.-*Ed.*] that the value of the newly created product of £600 is composed of 1) the reappearing value of the constant capital of £400 expended for means of production, and 2) a newly produced value of £200. The cost-price of the commodity = £500 comprises the reappearing 400_c and one-half of the newly produced value of £200 (= 100_v), that is, two elements of the commodity-value which are of entirely different origin.

Owing to the purposive nature of the labour expended during 666⅔ ten-hour working-days, the value of the consumed means of production amounting to £400 is transferred from these means of production to the product. This previously existing value thus reappears as a component part of the value of the product, but is not created in the process of production of *this* commodity. It exists as a component of the value of the commodity only because it previously existed as an element of the invested capital. The expended constant capital is therefore replaced by that portion of the value of the commodity which this capital itself adds to that value. This element of the cost-price, therefore, has a double meaning. On the one hand, it goes into the cost-price of the commodity, because it is part of the commodity-value which replaces consumed capital. And on the other hand, it forms an element of the commodity-value only because it is the value of expended capital or because the means of production cost so and so much.

It is quite the reverse in the case of the other element of the cost-price. The 666⅔ working-days expended in the production of the commodity create a new value of £200. One portion of this new value merely replaces the advanced variable capital of £100, or the price of the labour-power employed. But this advanced capital-value does not in any way go into the creation of the new value. So far as the advance of capital is concerned, labour-power counts as a *value*. But in the process of production, it acts as the *creator* of value. The place of the value of the labour-power that obtains within the advanced capital is taken in the actually *functioning* productive capital by living value-creating labour-power itself.

The difference between these various elements of the commodity-value, which together make up the cost-price, leaps to the eye whenever a change takes place in the size of the value of either the expended constant, or the expended variable, part of the capital. Let the price of the same means of production, or of the constant part of capital, rise from £400 to £600, or, conversely, let it fall to £200. In the first case it is not only the cost-price of the commodity which rises from £500 to $600_c + 100_v$ = £700, but also the value of the commodity which rises from £600 to $600_c + 100_v + 100_s$ = £800. In the second case, it is not only the cost-price which falls from £500 to 200_c+100_v = £300, but also the value of the commodity which falls from £600 to $200_c + 100_v + 100_s$ = £400. Since the expended constant capital transfers its own value to the product, the value of the product rises or falls with the absolute magnitude of that capital-value, other conditions remaining equal. Assume, on the other hand, that, other circumstances remaining unchanged, the price of the same amount of labour-power rises from £100 to £150, or, conversely, that it falls from £100 to £50. In the first case, the cost-price rises from £500 to $400_c + 150_v$ = £550, and falls in the second case from £500 to $400_c + 50_v$ = £450. But in either case the commodity-value remains unchanged = £600; one time it is $400_c + 150_v + 50_s$, and the other time, $400_c + 50_v + 150_s$. The advanced variable capital does not add its own value to the product. The place of its value is taken in the product rather by a new value created by labour. Therefore, a change in the absolute magnitude of the variable capital, so far as it expresses merely a change in the price of labour-power, does not in the least alter the absolute magnitude of the commodity-value, because it does not alter anything in the absolute magnitude of the new value created by living labour-power. Such a change rather affects only the relative proportion of the two component parts of the new value, of which one forms surplus-value and the other makes good the variable capital and therefore passes into the cost-price of the commodity.

The two elements of the cost-price, in the present case $400_c + 100_v$, have only this in common that they are both parts of the commodity-value that replace advanced capital.

But this true state of affairs necessarily appears reversed from the standpoint of capitalist production.

The capitalist mode of production differs from the mode of production based on slavery, among other things, by the fact that in it the value, and accordingly the price, of labour-power appears as the value, or price, of labour itself, or as wages (Buch 1, Kap. XVII) [English edition: Ch. XIX.—*Ed.*]. The variable part of the advanced capital, therefore, appears as capital expended in wages, as a capital-value which pays for the value, and accordingly the price, of all the labour expended in production. Let us assume, for instance, that an average ten-hour social working-day is incorporated in a sum of money amounting to 6 shillings. In that case, the advance of a variable capital of £100 represents the money expression of a value produced in 333 ⅓; ten-hour working-days. But this value, representing purchased labour-power in the capital advanced, does not, however, form a part of the actually functioning productive capital. Its place in the process of production is taken by living labour-power. If, as in our illustration, the degree of exploitation of the latter is 100%, then it is expended during 666⅔ ten-hour working-days, and thereby adds to the product a new value of £200. But in the capital advanced the variable capital of £100 figures as capital invested in wages, or as the price of labour performed during 666⅔ ten-hour days. The sum of £100 divided by 666⅔ gives us 3 shillings as the price of a ten-hour working-day, which is equal in value to the product of five hours' labour.

Now, if we compare the capital advanced on the one hand with the commodity-value on the other, we find:

I. Capital advanced £500 = £400 of capital expended in means of production (price of means of production) + £100 of capital expended in labour (price of 666⅔ working-days, or wages for same).

II. Value of commodities £600 = £500 representing the cost-price (£400 price of expended means of production + £100 price of expended 666⅔; working-days) + £100 surplus-value.

In this formula, the portion of capital invested in labour-power differs from that invested in means of production, such as cotton or coal, only by serving as payment for a materially different element of production, but not by any means because it serves a functionally different purpose in the process of creating commodity-value, and thereby also in the process of the self-expansion of capital. The price of the means of production reappears in the cost-price of the commodities, just as it figured in the capital advanced, and it does so because these means of production have been purposively consumed. The price, or wages, for the 666⅔ working-days consumed in the production of these commodities likewise reappears in the cost-price of the commodities just as it has figured in the capital advanced, and also because this amount of labour has been purposively expended. We see only finished and existing values—the portions of the value of the advanced capital which go into the making of the value of the product—but not the element creating new values. The distinction between constant and variable capital has disappeared. The entire cost-price of £500 now has the double meaning that, first, it is that portion of the commodity-value of £600 which replaces the capital of £500 expended in the production of the commodity; and that, secondly, this component of the commodity-value exists only because it existed previously as the cost-price of the elements of production employed, namely means of production and labour, i.e., as advanced capital. The capital-value reappears as the cost-price of a commodity because, and in so far as, it has been expended as a capital-value.

The fact that the various components of the value of the advanced capital have been expended for materially different elements of production, namely for instruments of labour, raw materials, auxiliary materials, and labour, requires only that the cost-price of the commodity must buy back these materially different elements of production. So far as the formation of the cost-price is concerned, however, only one distinction is appreciable, namely that between fixed and circulating capital. In our example, we have set down £20 for wear and tear of instruments of labour (400_c = £20 for depreciation of instruments of labour + £380 for materials of production). Before the productive process, the value of these instruments of labour was, say, £1,200. After the commodities have been produced it exists in two forms, the £20 as part of the value of the commodity, and 1,200 - 20, or £1,180, as the remaining value of the instruments of labour which, as before, are in the possession of the capitalist; in other words, as an element of his productive, not of his commodity-capital. Materials of production and wages, as distinct from means of labour, are entirely consumed in the production of the commodity and thus their entire value goes into that of the produced commodity. We have seen how these various components of the advanced capital assume the forms of fixed and circulating capital in relation to the turnover.

Accordingly, the capital advanced = £1,680: fixed capital = £1,200 + circulating capital = £480 (= £380 in materials of production plus £100 in wages).

But the cost-price of the commodity only = £500 (£20 for the wear and tear of the fixed capital, and £480 for circulating capital).

This difference between the cost-price of the commodity and the capital advanced merely proves, however, that the cost-price of the commodity is formed exclusively by the capital actually consumed in its production.

Means of production valued at £1,200 are employed in producing the commodity, but only £20 of this advanced capital-value are lost in production. Thus, the employed fixed capital goes only partially into the cost-price of the commodity, because it is only partially consumed in its production. The employed circulating capital goes entirely into the cost-price of the commodity, because it is entirely consumed in production. But does not this only prove that the consumed portions of the fixed and circulating capital pass uniformly, *pro rata* to the magnitude of their values, into the cost-price of the commodity and that this component of the value of the commodity originates solely with the capital expended in its production? If this were not so, it would be inexplicable why the advanced fixed capital of £1,200 should not, aside from the £20 which it loses in the productive process, also contribute the other £1,180 which it does not lose.

This difference between fixed and circulating capital with reference to the calculation of the cost-price, therefore, only confirms the seeming origination of the cost-price from the expended capital-value, or the price paid by the capitalist himself for the expended elements of production, including labour. On the other hand, so far as the formation of value is concerned, the variable portion of capital invested in labour-power is here emphatically identified under the head of circulating capital with constant capital (that part of capital which consists of materials of production), and this completes the mystification of the self-expansion process of capital.[1]

So far we have considered just one element of the value of commodities, namely the cost-price. We must now turn also to the other component of the value of commodities, namely the excess over the cost-price, or the surplus-value. In the first place, then, surplus-value is the excess value of a commodity over and above its cost-price. But since the cost-price equals the value of the consumed capital, into whose material elements it is continually reconverted, this excess value is an accretion in the value of the capital expended in the production of the commodity and returning by way of its circulation.

We have already seen earlier that, though s, the surplus-value, springs merely from a change in the value of the variable capital v and is, therefore, originally but an increment of variable capital, after the process of production is over it nevertheless also forms an increment of c + v, the expended total capital. The formula c + (v + s), which indicates that s is produced through the conversion of a definite capital-value v advanced for labour-power into a fluctuating magnitude, i.e., of a constant magnitude into a variable one, may also be represented as (c + v) + s. Before production took place we had a capital of £500. After production is completed we have the capital of £500 plus a value increment of £100.[2]

However, surplus-value forms an increment not only of the portion of the advanced capital which goes into the self-expansion process, but also of the portion which does not go into it. In other words, it is an accretion not only to the consumed capital made good out of the cost-price of the commodity, but to all the capital invested in production. Before the production process, we had a capital valued at £1,680, namely £1,200 of fixed capital invested in means of production, only £20 of which go into the value of the commodity for wear and tear, plus £480 of circulating capital in materials of production and wages. After the production process, we have £1,180 as the constituent element of the value of the productive capital plus a commodity-capital of £600. By adding these two sums of value we find that the capitalist now has a value of £1,780. After deducting his advanced total capital of £1,680 there remains a value increment of £100. The £100 of surplus-value thus form as much of an increment in relation to the invested £1,680 as to its fraction of £500 expended during production.

It is now clear to the capitalist that this increment of value springs from the productive processes undertaken with the capital, that it therefore, springs from the capital itself, because it is there after the production process, while it is not there before it. As for the capital consumed in production, the surplus-value seems to spring equally from all its different elements of value consisting of means of production and labour. For all these elements contribute equally to the formation of the cost-price. All of them add their values, obtaining as advanced capital, to the value of the product, and are not differentiated as constant and variable magnitudes of value. This becomes obvious if we assume for a moment that all the expended capital consisted either exclusively of wages, or exclusively of the value of the means of production. In the first case, we should then have the commodity-value of $500_v + 100_s$ instead of the commodity-value of $400_c + 100_v + 100_s$. The capital of £500 laid out in wages represents the value of all the labour expended in the production of the commodity-value of £600, and for just this reason forms the cost-price of the entire product. But the formation of this cost-price, whereby the value of the expended capital is reproduced as a constituent part of the value of the product, is the only process in the formation of this commodity-value that is known to us. We do not know how its surplus-value portion of £100 is formed. The same is true in the second case, in which the commodity-value = $500_c + 100_s$. We know in both cases that surplus-value is derived from a given value, because this value was advanced in the form of productive capital, be it in the form of labour or of means of production. On the other hand, this advanced capital-value cannot form surplus-value for the reason that it has been expended and therefore constitutes the cost-price of the commodity. Precisely because it forms the cost-price of the commodity, it does not form any surplus-value, but merely an equivalent, a value replacing the expended capital. So far, therefore, as it forms surplus-value, it does so not in its specific capacity as expended, but rather as advanced, and hence utilised, capital. For this reason, the surplus-value arises as much out of the portion of the advanced capital which goes into the cost-price of the commodity, as out of the portion which does not. In short, it arises equally out of the fixed and the circulating components of the utilised capital. The aggregate capital serves materially as the creator of products, the means of labour as well as the materials of production, and the labour. The total capital materially enters into the actual labour-process, even though only a portion of it enters the process of self-expansion. This is, perhaps, the very reason why it contributes only in part to the formation of the cost-price, but totally to the formation of surplus-value. However that may be, the outcome is that surplus-value springs simultaneously from all portions of the invested capital. This deduction may be substantially abbreviated, by saying pointedly and concisely in the words of Malthus:

> The capitalist ... *expects* an equal profit upon all the parts of the capital which he advances.[3]

In its assumed capacity of offspring of the aggregate advanced capital, surplus-value takes the converted form of *profit*. Hence, a certain value is capital when it is invested with a view to producing profit[4], or, there is profit because a certain value was employed as capital. Suppose profit is p. Then the formula C = c + v + s = k + s turns into the formula C = k + p, or the *value of a commodity = cost-price + profit.*

The profit, such as it is represented here, is thus the same as surplus-value, only in a mystified form that is nonetheless a necessary outgrowth of the capitalist mode of production. The genesis of the mutation of values that occurs in the course of the production process, must be transferred from the variable portion of the capital to the total capital, because there is no apparent distinction between constant and variable capital in the assumed formation of the cost-price. Because at one pole the price of labour-power assumes the transmuted form of wages, surplus-value appears at the opposite pole in the transmuted form of profit.

We have seen that the cost-price of a commodity is smaller than its value. Since C = k + s, it follows that k = C - s. The formula C = k + s reduces itself to C = k, or commodity-value = commodity cost-price only if s = 0, a case which never occurs on the basis of capitalist production, although peculiar market conditions may reduce the selling price of commodities to the level of, or even below, their cost-price.

Hence, if a commodity is sold at its value, a profit is realised which is equal to the excess of its value over its cost-price, and therefore equal to the entire surplus-value incorporated in the value of the commodity. But the capitalist may sell a commodity at a profit even when he sells it below its value. So long as its selling price is higher than its cost-price, though it may be lower than its value, a portion of the surplus-value incorporated in it is always realised, thus always yielding a profit. In our illustration, the value of the commodity is £600, and the cost-price is £500. If the commodity is sold at £510, 520, 530, 560 or 590, it is sold respectively £90, 80, 70, 40, or 10 below its value. Yet a profit of £10, 20, 30, 60, or 90 respectively is realised in its sale. There is obviously an indefinite number of selling prices possible between the value of a commodity and its cost-price. The greater the surplus-value element of the value of a commodity, the greater the practical range of these intermediate prices.

This explains more than just the everyday phenomena of competition, such as certain cases of underselling, abnormally low commodity-prices in certain lines of industry[5], etc. The fundamental law of capitalist competition, which political economy had not hitherto grasped, the law which regulates the general rate of profit and the so-called prices of production determined by it, rests, as we shall later see, on this difference between the value and the cost-price of commodities, and on the resulting possibility of selling a commodity at a profit under its value.

The minimal limit of the selling price of a commodity is its cost-price. If it is sold under its cost-price, the expended constituent elements of productive capital cannot be fully replaced out of the selling price. If this process continues, the value of the advanced capital disappears. From this point of view alone, the capitalist is inclined to regard the cost-price as the true *inner* value of the commodity, because it is the price required for the bare conservation of his capital. But there is also this, that the cost-price of a commodity is the purchase price paid by the capitalist himself for its production, therefore the purchase price determined by the production process itself. For this reason, the excess value, or the surplus-value, realised in the sale of a commodity appears to the capitalist as an excess of its selling price over its value, instead of an excess of its value over its cost-price, so that accordingly the surplus-value incorporated in a commodity is not realised through its sale, but springs out of the sale itself. We have given this illusion closer consideration in Book I (Kap. IV, 2) [English edition: Ch. V, 2.—*Ed.*] ("Contradictions in the General Formula of Capital"), but revert here for a moment to the form in which it was reaffirmed by Torrens, among others, as an advance of political economy beyond Ricardo.

> The natural price, consisting of the cost of production, or, in other words, of the capital expended in raising or fabricating commodities, cannot include the profit.... The farmer, we will suppose, expends one hundred quarters of corn in cultivating his fields, and obtains in return one hundred and twenty quarters. In this case, twenty quarters, being the excess of produce above expenditure, constitute the farmer's profit; but it would be absurd to call this excess, or profit, a part of the expenditures... The master manufacturer expends a certain quantity of raw material, of tools and implements of trade, and of subsistence for labour, and obtains in return a quantity of finished work. This finished work must possess a higher exchangeable value than the materials, tools, and subsistence, by the advance of which it was obtained.

Torrens concludes therefrom that the excess of the selling price over the cost-price, or profit, is derived from the fact that the consumers,

> [E]ither by immediate or circuitous barter give some greater portion of all the ingredients of capital than their production costs.[6]

Indeed, the excess over a given magnitude cannot form a part of this magnitude, and therefore the profit, the excess value of a commodity over the capitalist's expenditures, cannot form a part of these expenditures. Hence, if no other element than the value advance of the capitalist enters into the formation of the value of a commodity, it is inexplicable how more value should come out of production than went into it, for something cannot come out of nothing. But Torrens only evades this creation out of nothing by transferring it from the sphere of commodity-production to that of commodity-circulation. Profit cannot come out of production, says Torrens, for otherwise it would already be contained in the cost of production, and there would not be a surplus over this cost. Profit cannot come out of the exchange of commodities, replies Ramsay, unless it already existed before this exchange. The sum of the value of the exchanged products is evidently not altered in the exchange of these products, whose sum of value it is. It is the same before and after the exchange. It should be noted here that Malthus refers expressly to the authority of Torrens[7] although he himself has a different explanation for the sale of commodities above their value, or rather has no explanation at all, since all arguments of this sort never, in effect, fail to be reduced to the same thing as the once-famed negative weight of phlogiston.

In a social order dominated by capitalist production, even the non-capitalist producer is gripped by capitalist conceptions. Balzac, who is generally remarkable for his profound grasp of reality, aptly describes in his last novel, *Les Paysans*, how a petty peasant performs many small tasks gratuitously for his usurer, whose goodwill he is eager to retain, and how he fancies that he does not give the latter something for nothing because his own labour does not cost him any cash outlay. As for the usurer, he thus fells two dogs with one stone. He saves the cash outlay for wages and enmeshes the peasant, who is gradually ruined by depriving his own field of labour, deeper and deeper in the spider-web of usury.

The thoughtless conception that the cost-price of a commodity constitutes its actual value, and that surplus-value springs from selling the product above its value, so that commodities would be sold at their value if their selling price were to equal their cost-price, i.e., if it were to equal the price of the consumed means of production plus wages, has been heralded to the world as a newly discovered secret of socialism by Proudhon with his customary quasi-scientific chicanery. Indeed, this reduction of the value of commodities to their cost-price is the basis of his People's Bank. It was earlier shown that the various constituent elements of the value of a product may be represented in proportional parts of the product itself. For instance (Buch I, Kap. VI 1, 2, S. 211/203) [English edition: Ch. IX, 2, pp. 220-21.—*Ed.*] if the value of 20 lbs. of yarn is 30 shillings—namely 24 shillings of means of production, 3 shillings of labour-power, and 3 shillings of surplus-value—then this surplus-value may be represented as 1/10 of the product=2 lbs. of yarn. Should these 20 lbs. of yarn now be sold at their cost-price, at 27 shillings, then the purchaser receives 2 lbs. of yarn for nothing, or the article is sold 1/10 below its value. But the labourer has, as before, performed his surplus-labour, only this time for the purchaser of the yarn instead of the capitalist yarn producer. It would be altogether wrong to assume that if all commodities were sold at their cost-price, the result would really be the same as if they had all been sold above their cost-price, but at their value. For even if the value of the labour-power, the length of the working-day, and the degree of exploitation of labour were the same everywhere, the quantities of surplus-value contained in the values of the various kinds of commodities would be unequal, depending on the different organic composition of the capitals advanced for their production.[8]

Notes

1. In Book I (Kap. VII, 3, S. 216/206 ff.) [English edition: Ch. IX, 3, 225 ff.—*Ed.*] we have given the example of N. W. Senior to show what confusion this may create in the mind of the economist.
2. 'From what has gone before, we know that surplus-value is purely the result of a variation in the value of v, of that portion of the capital which is transformed into labour-power; consequently, v + s = v + Dv (or v plus an increment of v). But the fact that it is v alone that varies, and the conditions of that variation, are obscured by the circumstance that in consequence of the increase in the variable component of the capital, there is also an increase in the sum total of the advanced capital. It was originally £500, and becomes £590.' (Buch I, Kap. VI I, 1, S. 203/195.) [English edition: Ch. IX, 1, p. 214.—*Ed.*]
3. Malthus, *Principles of Political Economy*, 2nd ed., London, 1836, p. 268.
4. 'Capital is that which is expended with a view to profit.' Malthus, *Definitions in Political Economy*, London, 1827, p. 86.

5. Cf. Buch I. Kap. XVIII, 1, S. 571/561 ff. [English edition: Ch. XX, 1, p. 549 ff.—*Ed.*]
6. R. Torrens, *An Essay on the Production of Wealth*, London, 1821, pp. 51-53, and 349.
7. Malthus, *Definitions in Political Economy*, London, 1853, pp. 70, 71.
8. 'The masses of value and of surplus-value produced by different capitals—the value of labour-power being given and its degree of exploitation being equal—vary directly as the amounts of the variable constituents of these capitals, i.e., as their constituents transformed into living labour-power.' (Buch 1, Kap. IX. S. 312/303.) [English edition: Ch. XI, pp. 306/307.—*Ed.*]

2

The Rate of Profit

The general formula of capital is M-C-M'. In other words, a sum of value is thrown into circulation to extract a larger sum out of it. The process which produces this larger sum is capitalist production. The process that realises it is circulation of capital. The capitalist does not produce a commodity for its own sake, nor for the sake of its use-value, or his personal consumption. The product in which the capitalist is really interested is not the palpable product itself, but the excess value of the product over the value of the capital consumed by it. The capitalist advances the total capital without regard to the different roles played by its components in the production of surplus-value. He advances all these components uniformly, not just to reproduce the advanced capital, but rather to produce value in excess of it. The only way in which he can convert the value of his advanced variable capital into a greater value is by exchanging it for living labour and exploiting living labour. But he cannot exploit this labour unless he makes a simultaneous advance of the conditions for performing this labour, namely means of labour and subjects of labour, machinery and raw materials, i.e., unless he converts a certain amount of value in his possession into the form of conditions of production; for he is a capitalist and can undertake the process of exploiting labour only because, being the owner of the conditions of labour, he confronts the labourer as the owner of only labour-power. As already shown in the first book [English edition: Vol. 1, pp. 168-69. 714-16.—*Ed.*], it is precisely the fact that non-workers own the means of production which turns labourers into wage-workers and non-workers into capitalists.

The capitalist does not care whether it is considered that he advances constant capital to make a profit out of his variable capital, or that he advances variable capital to enhance the value of the constant capital; that he invests money in wages to raise the value of his machinery and raw materials, or that he invests money in machinery and raw materials to be able to exploit labour. Although it is only the variable portion of capital which creates surplus-value, it does so only if the other portions, the conditions of production, are likewise advanced. Seeing that the capitalist can exploit labour only by advancing constant capital and that he can turn his constant capital to good account only by advancing variable capital, he lumps them all together in his imagination, and much more so since the actual rate of his gain is not determined by its proportion to the variable, but to the total capital, not by the rate of surplus-value, but by the rate of profit. And the latter, as we shall see, may remain the same and yet express different rates of surplus-value.

The costs of the product include all the elements of its value paid by the capitalist or for which he has thrown an equivalent into production. These costs must be made good to preserve the capital or to reproduce it in its original magnitude.

The value contained in a commodity is equal to the labour-time expended in its production, and the sum of this labour consists of paid and unpaid portions. But for the capitalist, the costs of the commodity consist only of that portion of the labour materialised in it for which he has paid. The surplus-labour contained in the commodity costs the capitalist nothing, although, like the paid portion, it costs the labourer his labour, and although it creates value and enters into the commodity as a value-creating element quite like paid labour. The capitalist's profit is derived from the fact that he has something to sell for which he has paid nothing. The surplus-value, or profit, consists precisely in the excess value of a commodity over its cost-price, i.e., the excess of the total labour embodied in the commodity over the paid labour embodied in it. The surplus-value, whatever its origin, is thus a surplus over the advanced total capital. The proportion of this surplus to the total capital is therefore expressed by the fraction s/C, in which C stands for total capital. We thus obtain the *rate of profit* s/C=s/(c+v), as distinct from the rate of surplus-value s/v.

The rate of surplus-value measured against the variable capital is called rate of surplus-value. The rate of surplus-value measured against the total capital is called rate of profit. These are two different measurements of the same entity, and owing to the difference of the two standards of measurement they express different proportions or relations of this entity.

The transformation of surplus-value into profit must be deduced from the transformation of the rate of surplus-value into the rate of profit, not vice versa. And in fact, it was rate of profit which was the historical point of departure. Surplus-value and rate of surplus-value are, relatively, the invisible and unknown essence that wants investigating, while rate of profit and therefore the appearance of surplus-value in the form of profit are revealed on the surface of the phenomenon.

So far as the individual capitalist is concerned, it is evident that he is only interested in the relation of the surplus-value, or the excess value at which he sells his commodities, to the total capital advanced for the production of the commodities, while the specific relationship and inner connection of this surplus with the various components of capital fail to interest him, and it is, moreover, rather in his interests to draw the veil over this specific relationship and this intrinsic connection.

Although the excess value of a commodity over its cost-price is shaped in the immediate process of production, it is realised only in the process of circulation, and appears all the more readily to have arisen from the process of circulation, since in reality, under competition, in the actual market, it depends on market conditions whether or not and to what extent this surplus is realised. There is no need to waste words at this point about the fact that if a commodity is sold above or below its value, there is merely another kind of division of surplus-value, and that this different division, this changed proportion in which various persons share in the surplus-value, does not in any way alter either the magnitude or the nature of that surplus-value. It is not alone the metamorphoses discussed by us in Book II that take place in the process of circulation; they fall in with actual competition, the sale and purchase of commodities above or below their value, so that the surplus-value realised by the individual capitalist depends as much on the sharpness of his business wits as on the direct exploitation of labour.

In the process of circulation the time of circulation comes to exert its influence alongside the working-time, thereby limiting the amount of surplus-value realisable within a given time span. Still, other elements derived from circulation intrude decisively into the actual production process. The actual process of production and the process of circulation intertwine and intermingle continually, and thereby invariably adulterate their typical distinctive features. The production of surplus-value, and of value in general, receives new definition in the process of circulation, as previously shown. Capital passes through the circuit of its metamorphoses. Finally, stepping beyond its inner organic life, so to say, it enters into relations with outer life, into relations in which it is not capital and labour which confront one another, but capital and capital in one case, and individuals, again simply as buyers and sellers, in the other. The time of circulation and working-time cross paths and thus both seem to determine the surplus-value. The original form in which capital and wage-labour confront one another is disguised through the intervention of relationships seemingly independent of it. Surplus-value itself does not appear as the product of the appropriation of labour-time, but as an excess of the selling price of commodities over their cost-price, the latter thus being easily represented as their actual value (*valeur intrinsèque*), while profit appears as an excess of the selling price of commodities over their immanent value.

True, the nature of surplus-value impresses itself constantly upon the consciousness of the capitalist during the process of production, as his greed for the labour-time of others, etc., has revealed in our analysis of surplus-value. But: 1) The actual process of production is only a fleeting stage which continually merges with the process of circulation, just as the latter merges with the former, so that in the process of production, the more or less clearly dawning notion of the source of the gain made in it, i.e., the inkling of the nature of surplus-value, stands at best as a factor equally valid as the idea that the realised surplus originates in a movement that is independent of the production process, that it arises in circulation, and that it belongs to capital irrespective of the latter's relation to labour. Even such modern economists as Ramsay, Malthus, Senior, Torrens, etc., identify these phenomena of circulation directly as proofs that capital in its bare material existence, independent of its social relation to labour which makes capital of it, is, as it were, an independent source of surplus-value alongside labour and independent of labour. 2) Under the item of expenses, which embrace wages as well as the price of raw materials, wear and tear of machinery, etc., the extortion of unpaid labour figures only as a saving in paying for an article which is included in expenses, only as a smaller payment for a certain quantity of labour, similar to the saving when raw materials are bought more cheaply, or the depreciation of machinery decreases. In this way, the extortion of surplus-labour loses its specific character. Its specific relationship to surplus-value is obscured. This is greatly furthered and facilitated, as shown in Book I (Abschn. VI) [English edition: Part VI, pp. 535-43.—*Ed.*], by representing the value of labour-power in the form of wages.

The relationships of capital are obscured by the fact that all parts of capital appear equally as the source of excess value (profit).

The way in which surplus-value is transformed into the form of profit by way of the rate of profit is, however, a further development of the inversion of subject and object that takes place already in the process of production. In the latter, we have seen, the subjective productive forces of labour appear as productive forces of capital. [English edition: Vol. 1, pp. 332-33.—*Ed.*] On the one hand, the value, or the past labour, which dominates living labour, is incarnated in the capitalist. On the other hand, the labourer appears as bare material labour-power, as a commodity. Even in the simple relations of production this inverted relationship necessarily produces certain correspondingly inverted conceptions, a transposed consciousness which is further developed by the metamorphoses and modifications of the actual circulation process.

It is altogether erroneous, as a study of the Ricardian school shows, to try to identify the laws of the rate of profit with the laws of the rate of surplus-value, or vice versa. The capitalist naturally does not see the difference between them. In the formula s/C the surplus-value is measured by the value of the total capital advanced for its production, of which a part was totally consumed in this production and a part was merely employed in it. In fact, the formula s/C expresses the degree of self-expansion of the total capital advanced, or, taken in conformity with inner conceptual connections and the nature of surplus-value, it indicates the ratio of the amount of variation of variable capital to the magnitude of the advanced total capital.

In itself, the magnitude of value of total capital has no inner relationship to the magnitude of surplus-value, at least not directly. So far as its material elements are concerned, the total capital minus the variable capital, that is, the constant capital, consists of the material requisites—the means of labour and materials of labour—needed to materialise labour. It is necessary to have a certain quantity of means and materials of labour for a specific quantity of labour to materialise in commodities and thereby to produce value. A definite technical relation depending on the special nature of the labour applied is established between the quantity of labour and the quantity of means of production to which this labour is to be applied. Hence there is also to that extent a definite relation between the quantity of surplus-value, or surplus-labour, and the quantity of means of production. For instance, if the labour necessary for the production of the wage amounts to a daily 6 hours, the labourer must work 12 hours to do 6 hours of surplus-labour, or produce a surplus-value of 100%. He uses up twice as much of the means of production in 12 hours as he does in 6. Yet this is no reason for the surplus-value produced by him in 6 hours to be directly related to the value of the means of production used up in those 6, or in 12 hours. This value is here altogether immaterial; it is only a matter of the technically required quantity. It does not matter whether the raw materials or means of labour are cheap or dear, as long as they have the required use-value and are available in technically prescribed proportion to the labour to be applied. If I know that x lbs. of cotton are consumed in an hour of spinning and that they cost a shillings, then, of course, I also know that 12 hours' spinning consumes 12x lbs. of cotton = 12 a shillings, and can then calculate the proportion of the surplus-value to the value of the 12 as well as to that of the 6. But the relation of living labour to the *value* of means of production obtains here only to the extent that a shillings serve as a name for x lbs. of cotton; because a definite quantity of cotton has a definite price, and therefore, conversely, a definite price may also serve as an index for a definite quantity of cotton, so long as the price of cotton does not change. If I know that the labourer must work 12 hours for me to appropriate 6 hours of surplus-labour, that therefore I must have a 12-hour supply of cotton ready for use, and if I know the price of this quantity of cotton needed for 12 hours, then I have an indirect relation between the price of cotton (as an index of the required quantity) and the surplus-value. But, conversely, I can never conclude the quantity of the raw material that may be consumed in, say, one hour, and not 6, of spinning from the price of the raw material. There is, then, no necessary inner relation between the value of the constant capital, nor, therefore, between the value of the total capital (=c+v) and the surplus-value.

If the rate of surplus-value is known and its magnitude given, the rate of profit expresses nothing but what it actually is, namely a different way of measuring surplus-value, its measurement according to the value of the total capital instead of the value of the portion of capital from which surplus-value directly originates by way of its exchange for labour. But in reality (i.e., in the world of phenomena) the matter is reversed. Surplus-value is given, but given as an excess of the selling price of the commodity over its cost-price; and it remains a mystery where this surplus originated—from the exploitation of labour in the process of production, or from outwitting the purchaser in the process of circulation, or from both. What is also given is the proportion of this surplus to the value of the total capital, or the rate of profit. The calculation of this excess of the selling price over the cost-price in relation to the value of the advanced total capital is very important and natural, because in effect it yields the ratio in which total capital has been expanded, i.e., the degree of its self-expansion. If we proceed from this rate of profit, we cannot therefore conclude the specific relations between the surplus and the portion of capital invested in wages. We shall see in a subsequent chapter [K. Marx, *Theorien über den Mehrwert*. K. Marx/F. Engels, *Werke*, Band 26, Teil 3, S. 25-28 .—*Ed.*] what amusing somersaults Malthus makes when he tries in this way to get at the secret of the surplus-value and of its specific relation to the variable part of the capital. What the rate of profit actually shows is rather a uniform relation of the surplus to equal portions of the total capital, which, from this point of view, does not show any inner difference at all, unless it be between the fixed and circulating capital. And it shows this difference, too, only because the surplus is calculated in two ways; namely, first, as a simple magnitude—as excess over the cost-price. In this, its initial, form, the entire circulating capital goes into the cost-price, while of the fixed capital only the wear and tear goes into it. Second, the relation of this excess in value to the total value of the advanced capital. In this case, the value of the total fixed capital enters into the calculation, quite the same as the circulating capital. Therefore, the circulating capital goes in both times in the same way, while the fixed capital goes in differently the first time, and in the same way as circulating capital the second time. Under the circumstances the difference between fixed and circulating capital is the only one which obtrudes itself.

If, as Hegel would put it, the surplus, therefore, re-reflects itself in itself out of the rate of profit, or, put differently, the surplus is more closely characterised by the rate of profit, it appears as a surplus produced by capital above its own value over a year, or in a given period of circulation.

Although the rate of profit thus differs numerically from the rate of surplus-value, while surplus-value and profit are actually the same things and numerically equal, profit is nevertheless a converted form of surplus-value, a form in which its origin and the secret of its existence are obscured and extinguished. In effect, profit is the form in which surplus-value presents itself to the view, and must initially be stripped by analysis to disclose the latter. In surplus-value, the relation between capital and labour is laid bare; in the relation of capital to profit, i.e., of capital to surplus-value that appears on the one hand as an excess over the cost-price of commodities realised in the process of circulation and, on the other, as a surplus more closely determined by its relation to the total capital, *the capital* appears *as a relation to itself*, a relation in which it, as the original sum of value, is distinguished from a new value which it generated. One is conscious that capital generates this new value by its movement in the processes of production and circulation. But the way in which this occurs is cloaked in mystery and appears to originate from hidden qualities inherent in capital itself.

The further we follow the process of the self-expansion of capital, the more mysterious the relations of capital will become, and the less the secret of its internal organism will be revealed.

In this part, the rate of profit is numerically different from the rate of surplus-value; while profit and surplus-value are treated as having the same numerical magnitude but only a different form. In the next part, we shall see how the alienation goes further, and how profit represents a magnitude differing also numerically from surplus-value.

3

The Relation of the Rate of Profit to the Rate of Surplus-Value

Here, as at the close of the preceding chapter, and generally in this entire first part, we presume the amount of profit falling to a given capital to be equal to the total amount of surplus-value produced by means of this capital during a certain period of circulation. We thus leave aside for the present the fact that, on the one hand, this surplus-value may be broken up into various sub-forms, such as interest on capital, ground-rent, taxes, etc., and that, on the other, it is not, as a rule, identical with profit as appropriated by virtue of a general rate of profit, which will be discussed in the second part.

So far as the quantity of profit is assumed to be equal to that of surplus-value, its magnitude, and that of the rate of profit, is determined by ratios of simple figures given or ascertainable in every individual case. The analysis, therefore, first is carried on purely in the mathematical field.

We retain the designations used in Books I and II. Total capital C consists of constant capital c and variable capital v, and produces a surplus-value s. The ratio of this surplus-value to the advanced variable capital, or s/v, is called the rate of surplus-value and designated s'. Therefore s/v = s', and consequently s = s'v. If this surplus-value is related to the total capital instead of the variable capital, it is called profit, p, and the ratio of the surplus-value s to the total capital C, or s/C, is called the rate of profit, p'. Accordingly,

$$p' = s/C = s/(c + v)$$

Now, substituting for s its equivalent s'v, we find

$$p' = s' (v/C) = s' v/(c + v)$$

which equation may also be expressed by the proportion

$$p' : s' = v : C ;$$

the rate of profit is related to the rate of surplus-value as the variable capital is to the total capital.

It follows from this proportion that the rate of profit, p', is always smaller than s', the rate of surplus-value, because v, the variable capital, is always smaller than C, the sum of v + c, or the variable plus the constant capital; the only, practically impossible case excepted, in which v = C, that is, no constant capital at all, no means of production, but only wages are advanced by the capitalist.

However, our analysis also considers a number of other factors which have a determining influence on the magnitude of c, v, and s, and must therefore be briefly examined.

First, the *value of money*. We may assume this to be constant throughout.

Second, the *turnover*. We shall leave this factor entirely out of consideration for the present, since its influence on the rate of profit will be treated specially in a later chapter. [Here we anticipate just one point, that the formula p' = s' (v/C) is strictly correct only for *one* period of turnover of the variable capital. But we may correct it for an annual turnover by substituting for the simple rate of surplus-value, s›, the annual rate of surplus-value, s›n. In this, n is the number of turnovers of the variable capital within one year. (Cf. Book II, Chapter XVI, 1)—F. E.]

Third, due consideration must be given to *productivity of labour*, whose influence on the rate of surplus-value has been thoroughly discussed in Book I (Abschnitt IV). [English edition: Part IV.—Ed.] Productivity of labour may also exert a direct influence on the rate of profit, at least of an individual capital, if, as has been demonstrated in Book I (Kap. X, S. 323/324 [= MEW 23, S.335/336]) [English edition: Ch. XII, pp. 316-17.—Ed.] this individual capital operates with a higher than the average social productivity and produces commodities at a lower value than their average social value, thereby realising an extra profit. However, this case will not be considered for the present, since in this part of the work we also proceed from the premise that commodities are produced under normal social conditions and are sold at their values. Hence, we assume in each case that the productivity of labour remains constant. In effect, the value-composition of a capital invested in a branch of industry, that is, a certain proportion between the variable and constant capital, always expresses a definite degree of labour productivity. As soon, therefore, as this proportion is altered by means other than a mere change in the value of the material elements of the constant capital, or a change in wages, the productivity of labour must likewise undergo a corresponding change, and we shall often enough see, for this reason, that changes in the factors c, v, and s also imply changes in the productivity of labour.

The same applies to the three remaining factors—the *length of the working-day, intensity of labour, and wages*. Their influence on the quantity and rate of surplus-value has been exhaustively discussed in Book I [English edition: Vol. 1, pp. 519-30.—Ed.] It will be understood, therefore, that notwithstanding the assumption, which we make for the sake of simplicity, that these three factors remain constant, the changes that occur in v and s may nevertheless imply changes in the magnitude of these, their determining elements. In this respect, we must briefly recall that the wage influences the quantity of surplus-value and the rate of surplus-value in inverse proportion to the length of the working-day and the intensity of labour; that an increase in wages reduces the surplus-value, while a lengthening of the working-day and an increase in the intensity of labour add to it.

Suppose a capital of 100 produces a surplus-value of 20 employing 20 labourers working a 10-hour day for a total weekly wage of 20. Then we have:

$$80_c + 20_v + 20_s;\ s' = 100\%,\ p' = 20\%.$$

Now the working-day is lengthened to 15 hours without raising the wages. The total value produced by the 20 labourers will thereby increase from 40 to 60 (10 : 15 = 40 : 60). Since v, the wages paid to the labourers, remains the same, the surplus-value rises from 20 to 40, and we have:

$$80_c + 20_v + 40_s;\ s' = 200\%,\ p' = 40\%.$$

If, conversely, the ten-hour working-day remains unchanged, while wages fall from 20 to 12, the total value-product amounts to 40 as before, but is differently distributed; v falls to 12, leaving a remainder of 28 for s. Then we have:

$$80_c + 12_v + 28_s;\ s' = 233\tfrac{1}{3}\%,\ p' = 28/92 = 30\ 10/23\ \%.$$

Hence, we see that a prolonged working-day (or a corresponding increase in the intensity of labour) and a fall in wages both increase the amount, and thus the rate, of surplus-value. Conversely, a rise in wages, other things being equal, would lower the rate of surplus-value. Hence, if v rises through a rise in wages, it does not express a greater, but only a dearer quantity of labour, in which case s' and p' do not rise, but fall.

This indicates that changes in the working-day, intensity of labour and wages cannot take place without a simultaneous change in v and s and their ratio, and therefore also p', which is the ratio of s to the total capital c + v. And it is also evident that changes in the ratio of s to v also imply corresponding changes in at least one of the three above-mentioned labour conditions.

Precisely this reveals the specific organic relationship of variable capital to the movement of the total capital and to its self-expansion, and also its difference from constant capital. So far as generation of value is concerned, the constant capital is important only for the value it has. And it is immaterial to the generation of value whether a constant capital of £1,500 represents 1,500 tons of iron at, say, £1, or 500 tons of iron at £3. The quantity of actual material, in which the value of the constant capital is incorporated, is altogether irrelevant to the formation of value and the rate of profit, which varies inversely to this value no matter what the ratio of the increase or decrease of the value of constant capital to the mass of material use-value which it represents.

It is different with variable capital. It is not the value it has, not the labour incorporated in it, that matter at this point, but this value as a mere index of the total labour that it sets in motion and which is not expressed in it—the total labour, whose difference from the labour expressed in that value, hence the paid labour, i.e., that portion of the total labour which produces surplus-value, is all the greater, the less labour is contained in that value itself. Suppose, a ten-hour working-day is equal to ten shillings = ten marks. If the labour necessary to replace the wages, and thus the variable capital = 5 hours = 5 shillings, then the surplus-labour = 5 hours and the surplus-value = 5 shillings. Should the necessary labour = 4 hours = 4 shillings, then the surplus-labour = 6 hours and the surplus-value = 6 shillings.

Hence, as soon as the value of the variable capital ceases to be an index of the quantity of labour set in motion by it, and, moreover, the measure of this index is altered, the rate of surplus-value will change in the opposite direction and inversely.

Let us now go on to apply the above-mentioned equation of the rate of profit, $p' = s'(v/C)$, to the various possible cases. We shall successively change the value of the individual factors of $s'(v/C)$ and determine the effect of these changes on the rate of profit. In this way, we shall obtain different series of cases, which we may regard either as successive altered conditions of operation for one and the same capital, or as different capitals existing side by side and introduced for the sake of comparison, taken, as it were, from different branches of industry or different countries. In cases, therefore, where the conception of some of our examples as successive conditions for one and the same capital appears to be forced or impracticable, this objection falls away the moment they are regarded as comparisons of independent capitals.

Hence, we now separate the product $s'(v/C)$ into its two factors s' and v/C. At first, we shall treat s' as constant and analyse the effect of the possible variations of v/C. After that, we shall treat the fraction v/C as constant and let s' pass through its possible variations. Finally, we shall treat all factors as variable magnitudes and thereby exhaust all the cases from which laws concerning the rate of profit may be derived.

I. s' constant, v/C variable

This case, which embraces a number of subordinate cases, may be covered by a general formula. Take two capitals, C and C_1, with their respective variable components, v and v_1, with a common rate of surplus-value, s', and rates of profit p' and p'_1. Then:

$$p' = s'(v/C)\ ;\ p'_1 = s'(v_1/C_1)$$

Now let us make a proportion of C and C_1, and of v and v_1. For instance, let the value of the fraction $C_1/C = E$, and that of $v_1/v = e$. Then $C_1 = EC$, and $v_1 = ev$. Substituting in the above equation these values for p_1, C_1 and v_1, we obtain

$$p'_1 = s'\,ev/EC$$

Again, we may derive a second formula from the above two equations by transforming them into the proportion:

$$p' : p'_1 = s'(v/C) : s'(v_1/C_1) = (v/C) : v_1/C_1 .$$

Since the value of a fraction is not changed if we multiply or divide its numerator and denominator by the same number, we may reduce v/C and v_1/C_1 to percentages, that is, we may make C and C_1 both = 100. Then we have $v/C = v/100$ and $v_1/C_1 = v_1/100$, and may then drop the denominators in the above proportion, obtaining:

$$p' : p'_1 = v : v_1, \text{ or:}$$

Taking any two capitals operating with the same rate of surplus-value, the rates of profit are to each other as the variable portions of the capitals calculated as percentages of their respective total capitals.

These two formulas embrace all the possible variations of v/C.

One more remark before we analyse these various cases singly. Since C is the sum of c and v, of the constant and variable capitals, and since the rates of surplus-value, as of profit, are usually expressed in percentages, it is convenient to assume that the sum of c + v is also equal to 100, i.e., to express c and v in percentages. For the determination of the rate of profit, if not of the amount, it is immaterial whether we say that a capital of 15,000, of which 12,000 is constant and 3,000 is variable, produces a surplus-value of 3,000, or whether we reduce this capital to percentages:

$$15{,}000\ C = 12{,}000_c + 3{,}000_v\ (+\ 3{,}000_s)$$
$$100\ C = 80_c + 20_v\ (+\ 20_s).$$

In either case the rate of surplus-value s' = 100%, and the rate of profit = 20%.

The same is true when we compare two capitals, say, the foregoing capital with another, such as

$$12{,}000\ C = 10{,}800_c + 1{,}200_v\ (+\ 1{,}200_s)$$
$$100\ C = 90_c + 10_v\ (+\ 10_s).$$

in both of which s' = 100%, p' = 10%, and in which the comparison with the foregoing capital is clearer in percentage form.

On the other hand, if it is a matter of changes taking place in one and the same capital, the form of percentages is rarely to be used, because it almost always obscures these changes. If a capital expressed in the form of percentages:

$$80_c + 20_v + 20_s$$

assumes the form of percentages:

$$90_c + 10_v + 10_s,$$

we cannot tell whether the changed composition in percentages, $90_v + 10_c$, is due to an absolute decrease of v or an absolute increase of c, or to both. We would need the absolute magnitudes in figures to ascertain this. In the analysis of the following individual cases of variation, however, everything depends on how these changes have come about; whether $80_v + 20_c$ changed into $90_c + 10_v$ through an increase of the constant capital without any change in the variable capital, for instance, through $12{,}000_c + 3{,}000_v$ changing into $27{,}000_c + 3{,}000_v$ (corresponding to a percentage of $90_c + 10_v$); or whether they took this form through a reduction of the variable capital, with the constant capital remaining unchanged, that is, through a change into $12{,}000_c + 1{,}333⅓_v$ (also corresponding to a percentage of $90_c + 10_v$); or, lastly, whether both of the terms changed into $13{,}500_c + 1{,}500_v$ (corresponding once more to a percentage of $90_c + 10_v$). But it is precisely these cases which we shall have to successively analyse, and in so doing dispense with the convenient form of percentages, or at least employ these only as a secondary alternative.

1) s' and C constant, v variable

If v changes in magnitude, C can remain unaltered only if c, the other component of C, that is, the constant capital, changes by the same amount as v, but in the opposite direction.

If C originally = $80_c + 20_v$ = 100, and if v is then reduced to 10, then C can = 100 only if c is increased to 90; $90_c + 10_v$ = 100. Generally speaking, if v is transformed into v ± d, into v increased or decreased by d, then c must be transformed into c ± d, into c varying by the same amount, but in the opposite direction, so that the conditions of the present case are satisfied.

Similarly, if the rate of surplus-value s' remains the same, while the variable capital v changes, the amount of surplus-value s must change, since s = s'v, and since one of the factors of s'v, namely v, is given another value.

The assumptions of the present case produce, alongside the original equation,

$$p' = s'\ (v/C)\ ,$$

still another equation through the variation of v:

$$p'_1 = s' (v_1/C)$$

in which v has become v_1 and p'_1, the resultant changed rate of profit, is to be found.

It is determined by the following proportion:

$$p' : p'_1 = s' (v/C) : s' (v_1/C) = v : v_1$$

Or: with the rate of surplus-value and total capital remaining the same, the original rate of profit is to the new rate of profit produced by a change in the variable capital as the original variable capital is to the changed variable capital.

If the original capital was, as above:

I. 15,000 C = $12{,}000_c + 3{,}000_v$ (+ $3{,}000_s$), and if it is now:

II. 15,000 C = $13{,}000_c + 2{,}000_v$ (+ $2{,}000_s$), then C = 15,000 and s' = 100% in either case, and the rate of profit of I, 20%, is to that of II, 13⅓%, as the variable capital of I, 3,000, is to that of II, 2,000, i.e., 20% : 13⅓% = 3,000 : 2,000.

Now, the variable capital may either rise or fall. Let us first take an example in which it rises. Let a certain capital be originally constituted and employed as follows:

I. $100_c + 20_v + 10_s$; C = 120, s' = 50%, p' = 8⅓%.

Now let the variable capital rise to 30. In that case, according to our assumption, the constant capital must fall from 100 to 90 so that total capital remains unchanged at 120. The rate of surplus-value remaining constant at 50%, the surplus-value produced will then rise from 10 to 15. We shall then have:

II. $90_c + 30_v + 15_s$; C = 120, s' = 50%, p' = 12½%.

Let us first proceed from the assumption that wages remain unchanged. Then the other factors of the rate of surplus-value, i.e., the working-day and the intensity of labour, must also remain unchanged. In that event, the rise of v (from 20 to 30) can signify only that another half as many labourers are employed. Then the total value produced also rises one-half, from 30 to 45, and is distributed, just as before, ⅔ for wages and ⅓ for surplus-value. But at the same time, with the increase in the number of labourers, the constant capital, the value of the means of production, has fallen from 100 to 90. We have, then, a case of decreasing productivity of labour combined with a simultaneous shrinkage of constant capital. Is such a case economically possible?

In agriculture and the extractive industries, in which a decrease in labour productivity and, therefore, an increase in the number of employed labourers is quite comprehensible, this process is on the basis and within the scope of capitalist production attended by an increase, instead of a decrease, of constant capital. Even if the above fall of c were due merely to a fall in prices, an individual capital would be able to accomplish the transition from I to II only under very exceptional circumstances. But in the case of two independent capitals invested in different countries, or in different branches of agriculture or extractive industry, it would be nothing out of the ordinary if in one of the cases more labourers (and therefore more variable capital) were employed and worked with less valuable or scantier means of production than in the other case.

But let us drop the assumption that the wage remains the same, and let us explain the rise of the variable capital from 20 to 30 through a rise of wages by one-half. Then we shall have an entirely different case. The same number of labourers—say, twenty—continue to work with the same or only slightly reduced means of production. If the working-day remains unchanged—say, 10 hours—then the total value produced also remains unchanged. It was and remains = 30. But all of this 30 is now required to make good the advanced variable capital of 30; the surplus-value would disappear. We have assumed, however, that the rate of surplus-value should remain constant, that is, the same as in I, at 50%. This is possible only if the working-day is prolonged by one-half to 15 hours. Then the 20 labourers would produce a total value of 45 in 15 hours, and all conditions would be satisfied:

II. $90_c + 30_v + 15_s$; C = 120, s' = 50%, p' = 12½%.

In this case, the 20 labourers do not require any more means of labour, tools, machines, etc., than in case I. Only the raw materials or auxiliary materials would have to be increased by one-half. In the event of a fall in the prices of these materials, the transition from I to II might be more possible economically, even for an individual capital, in keeping with our assumption. And the capitalist would be somewhat compensated by increased profits for any loss incurred through the depreciation of his constant capital.

Now let us assume that the variable capital falls, instead of rising. Then we have but to reverse our example, taking II as the original capital, and passing from II to I.

II. $90_c + 30_v + 15_s$, then changes into I. $100_c + 20_v + 10_s$, and it is evident that this transposition does not in the least alter any of the conditions regulating the respective rates of profit and their mutual relation.

If v falls from 30 to 20 because ⅓ fewer labourers are employed with the growing constant capital, then we have before us the normal case of modern industry, namely, an increasing productivity of labour, and the operation of a larger quantity of means of production by fewer labourers. That this movement is necessarily connected with a simultaneous drop in the rate of profit will be developed in the third part of this book.

If, on the other hand, v falls from 30 to 20, because the same number of labourers is employed at lower wages, the total value produced would, with the working-day unchanged, as before = $30_v + 15_s$ = 45. Since v fell to 20, the surplus-value would rise to 25, the rate of surplus-value from 50% to 125%, which would be contrary to our assumption. To comply with the conditions of our case, the surplus-value, with its rate at 50%, must rather fall to 10, and the total value produced must, therefore, fall from 45 to 30, and this is possible only if the working-day is reduced by ⅓. Then, as before, we have:

$100_c + 20_v + 10_s$; s' = 50%, p' = 8⅓%.

It need hardly be said that this reduction of the working-time, in the case of a fall in wages, would not occur in practice. But that is immaterial. The rate of profit is a function of several variable magnitudes, and if we wish to know how these variables influence the rate of profit, we must analyse the individual effect of each in turn, regardless of whether such an isolated effect is economically practicable with one and the same capital.

2) s' constant, v variable, C changes through the variation of v.

This case differs from the preceding one only in degree. Instead of decreasing or increasing by as much as v increases or decreases, c remains constant. Under present-day conditions in the major industries and agriculture, the variable capital is only a relatively small part of the total capital. For this reason, its increase or decrease, so far as either is due to changes in the variable capital, are likewise relatively small.

Let us again proceed with a capital:

I. $100_c + 20_v + 10_s$; C = 120, s' = 50%, p' = 8⅓%.

which would then change, say, into:

II. $100_c + 30_v + 15_s$; C = 130, s' = 50%, p' = $11^7/_{13\%}$.

The opposite case, in which the variable capital decreases, would again be illustrated by the reverse transition from II to I.

The economic conditions would be essentially the same as in the preceding case, and therefore they need not be discussed again. The transition from I to II implies a decrease in the productivity of labour by one-half; for II the utilisation of 100 requires an increase of labour by one-half over that of I. This case may occur in agriculture.[1]

But while the total capital remains constant in the preceding case, owing to the conversion of constant into variable capital, or vice versa, there is in this case, a tie-up of additional capital if the variable capital increases, and a release of previously employed capital if the variable capital decreases.

3) s' and v constant, c and therefore C variable.

In this case the equation changes from:

$$p' = s' (v/C) \text{ into } p' = s' (v/C_1),$$

and after reducing the same factors on both sides, we have:

$$p'_1 : p' = C : C_1;$$

with the same rate of surplus-value and equal variable capitals, the rates of profit are inversely proportional to the total capitals.

Should we, for example, have three capitals, or three different conditions of the same capital:

I. $80_c + 20_v + 20_s$; C = 100, s' = 100%, p' = 20%;
II. $100_c + 20_v + 20_s$; C = 120, s' = 100%, p' = 16⅔%;
III. $60_c + 20_v + 20_s$; C = 80, s' = 100%, p' = 25%.

Then we obtain the proportions:

20% : 16⅔% = 120 : 100 and 20% : 25% = 80 : 100.

The previously given general formula for variations of v/C with a constant s' was:

$$p'_1 = s' \, ev/EC \text{ ; now it becomes: } p'_1 = s' \, v/EC,$$

since v does not change, the factor $e = v_1/v$, becomes = 1.

Since s'v = s, the quantity of surplus-value, and since both s' and v remain constant, it follows that s, too, is not affected by any variation of C. The amount of surplus-value is the same after the change as it was before it.

If c were to fall to zero, p' would = s', i.e., the rate of profit would equal the rate of surplus-value.

The alteration of c may be due either to a mere change in the value of the material elements of constant capital, or to a change in the technical composition of the total capital, that is, a change in the productivity of labour in the given branch of industry. In the latter case, the productivity of social labour mounting due to the development of modern industry and large-scale agriculture would bring about a transition (in the above illustration) in the sequence from III to I and from I to II. A quantity of labour which is paid with 20 and produces a value of 40 would first utilise means of labour to a value of 60; if productivity mounted and the value remained the same, the used up means of labour would rise first to 80, and then to 100. An inversion of this sequence would imply a decrease in productivity. The same quantity of labour would put a smaller quantity of means of production into motion, and the operation would be curtailed, as may occur in agriculture, mining, etc.

A saving in constant capital increases the rate of profit on the one hand, and, on the other, sets free capital, for which reason it is of importance to the capitalist. We shall make a closer study of this, and likewise of the influence of a change in the prices of the elements of constant capital, particularly of raw materials, at a later point. [Present edition:

Ch. V, VI.—Ed.]

It is again evident here that a variation of the constant capital equally affects the rate of profit, regardless of whether this variation is due to an increase or decrease of the material elements of c, or merely to a change in their value.

4) s' constant, v, c and C all variable

In this case, the general formula for the changed rate of profit, given at the outset, remains in force:

$$p'_1 = s› ev/EC .$$

It follows from this that with the rate of surplus-value remaining the same:

a) The rate of profit falls if E is greater than e, that is, if the constant capital is augmented to such an extent that the total capital grows at a faster rate than the variable capital. If a capital of $80_c + 20_v + 20_s$ changes into $170_c + 30_v + 30_s$, then s' remains = 100%, but v/C falls from 20/100 to 30/100, in spite of the fact that both v and C have grown, and the rate of profit falls correspondingly from 20% to 15%.

b) The rate of profit remains unchanged only if e = E, that is, if the fraction v/C retains the same value in spite of a seeming change, i.e., if its numerator and denominator are multiplied or divided by the same factor. The capitals $80_c + 20_v + 20_s$ and $160_c + 40_v + 40_s$ obviously have the same rate of profit of 20%, because s› remains = 100% and v/C = 20/100 = 40/200 represents the same value in both examples.

c) The rate of profit rises when e is greater than E, that is, when the variable capital grows at a faster rate than the total capital. If $80_c + 20_v + 20_s$ turns into $120_c + 40_v + 40_s$, the rate of profit rises from 20% to 25%, because with an unchanged s' (v/C) = 20/100 rises to 40/160, or from 1/5 to 1/4.

If the changes of v and C are in the same direction, we may view this change of magnitude as though, to a certain extent, both of them varied in the same proportion, so that v/C remained unchanged up to that point. Beyond this point, only one of them would vary, and we shall have thereby reduced this complicated case to one of the preceding simpler ones.

Should, for instance, $80_c + 20_v + 20_s$ become $100_c + 30_v + 30_s$, then the proportion of v to c, and also to C, remains the same in this variation up to : $100_c + 25_v + 25_s$. Up to that point, therefore, the rate of profit likewise remains unchanged. We may then take $100_c + 25_v + 25_s$ as our point of departure; we find that v increased by 5 to become 30_v, so that C rose from 125 to 130, thus giving us the second case, that of the simple variation of v and the consequent variation of C. The rate of profit, which was originally 20%, rises through this addition of 5_v to 23 1/13 %, provided the rate of surplus-value remains the same.

The same reduction to a simpler case can also take place if v and C change their magnitudes in opposite directions. For instance, let us again start with $80_c + 20_v + 20_s$, and let this become: $110_c + 10_v + 10_s$. In that case, with the change going as far as $40_c + 10_v + 10_s$, the rate of profit would remain the same 20%. By adding 70_c to this intermediate form, it will drop to 8⅓%. Thus, we have again reduced the case to an instance of change of one variable, namely of c.

Simultaneous variation of v, c, and C, does not, therefore, offer any new aspects and in the final analysis leads back to a case in which only one factor is a variable.

Even the sole remaining case has actually been exhausted, namely that in which v and C remain numerically the same, while their material elements undergo a change of value, so that v stands for a changed quantity of labour put in motion and c for a changed quantity of means of production put in motion.

In $80_c + 20_v + 20_s$, let 20_v originally represent the wages of 20 labourers working

10 hours daily. Then let the wages of each rise from 1 to 1 ¼. In that case the 20_v will pay only 16 labourers instead of 20. But if 20 labourers produce a value of 40 in 200 working-hours, 16 labourers working 10 hours daily will in 160 working-hours produce a value of only 32. After deducting 20_v for wages, only 12 of the 32 would then remain for surplus-value. The rate of surplus-value would have fallen from 100% to 60%. But since we have assumed the rate of surplus-value to be constant, the working-day would have to be prolonged by one-quarter, from 10 to 12½ hours. If 20 labourers working 10 hours daily = 200 working-hours produce a value of 40, then 16 labourers working 12½ hours daily = 200 hours will produce the same value, and the capital of $80_c + 20_v$ would as before yield the same surplus-value of 20.

Conversely, if wages were to fall to such an extent that 20v would represent the wages of 30 labourers, then s would remain constant only if the working-day were reduced from 10 to 6⅔ hours. For 20 × 10 = 30 × 6⅔ = 200 working-hours.

We have already in the main discussed to what extent c may in these divergent examples remain unchanged in terms of value expressed in money and yet represent different quantities of means of production changed in accordance with changing conditions. In its pure form, this case would be possible only by way of an exception.

As for a change in the value of the elements of c which increases or decreases their mass but leaves the sum of the value of c unchanged, it does not affect either the rate of profit or the rate of surplus-value, so long as it does not lead to a change in the magnitude of v.

We have herewith exhausted all the possible cases of variation of v, c, and C in our equation. We have seen that the rate of profit may fall, remain unchanged, or rise, while the rate of surplus-value remains the same, with the least change in the proportion of v to c or to C, being sufficient to change the rate of profit as well.

We have seen, furthermore, that in variations of v there is a certain limit everywhere beyond which it is economically impossible for s' to remain constant. Since every one-sided variation of c must also reach a certain limit where v can no longer remain unchanged, we find that there are limits for every possible variation of v/C, beyond which s' must likewise become variable. In the variations of s' which we shall now discuss, this interaction of the different variables of our equation will stand out still clearer.

II. s' variable

We obtain a general formula for the rates of profit with different rates of surplus-value, no matter whether v/C remains constant or not, by converting the equation:

$$p' = s' (v/C)$$

into

$$p'_1 = s'_1 (v_1/C_1),$$

in which p'_1, s'_1, v_1 and C_1 denote the changed values of p', s', v and C. Then we have:

$$p' : p'_1 = s'_1 (v/C) : s'_1 (v_1/C_1),$$

and hence:

$$p'_1 = (s'_1/s_1) \times v_1/v \times C/C_1 \times p'.$$

1) s' variable, v/C constant.

In this case we have the equations:

$$p' = s' (v/C); p'_1 = s' (v/C),$$

in both of which v/C is equal. Therefore:

$$p' : p'_1 = s' : s'_1$$

The rates of profit of two capitals of the same composition are to each other as the two corresponding rates of surplus-value. Since in the fraction v/C it is not a question of the absolute magnitudes of v and C, but only of their ratio, this applies to all capitals of equal composition whatever their absolute magnitude.

$80_c + 20_v + 20_s$; C = 100, s' = 100%, p' = 20%
$160_c + 40_v + 20_s$; C = 200, s' = 50%, p' = 10%
100% : 50% = 20% : 10%.

If the absolute magnitudes of v and C are the same in both cases, the rates of profit are moreover also related to one another as the amounts of surplus-value:

$$p' : p'_1 = s'v : s'_1v = s : s_1.$$

For instance:

$80_c + 20_v + 20_s$; s' = 100%, p' = 20%
$80_c + 20_v + 10_s$; s' = 50%, p' = 10%
20% : 10% = 100 × 20 : 50 × 20 = $20_s : 10_s$.

It is now clear that with capitals of equal absolute or percentage composition the rate of surplus-value can differ only if either the wages, or the length of the working-day, or the intensity of labour, differ. In the following three cases:

I. $80_c + 20_v + 10_s$; s' = 50%, p' = 10%
II. $80_c + 20_v + 20_s$; s' = 100%, p' = 20%
III. $80_c + 20_v + 40_s$; s' = 200%, p' = 40%

the total value produced in I is 30 ($20_v + 10_s$); in II it is 40; in III it is 60. This may come about in three different ways.

First, if the wages are different, and 20_v stands for a different number of labourers in every individual case. Suppose capital I employs 15 labourers 10 hours daily at a wage of £1⅓, who produce a value of £30, of which £20 replace the wages and £10 are surplus-value. If wages fall to £1, then 20 labourers may be employed for 10 hours; they will produce a value of £40, of which £20 will replace the wages, and £20 will be surplus-value. Should wages fall still more, to £⅔, thirty labourers may be employed for 10 hours. They will produce a value of £60, of which £20 will be deducted for wages, and £40 will represent surplus-value.

This case—a constant composition of capital in per cent, a constant working-day and constant intensity of labour, and the rate of surplus-value varying because of variation in wages—is the only one in which Ricardo's assumption is correct:

> Profit would be high or low, *exactly in proportion* as wages were low or high. (*Principles*, Ch. I, Sect. III, p. 18 of the *Works* of D. Ricardo, ed. by MacCulloch, 1852.)

Or *second*, if the intensity of labour varies. In that case, say, 20 labourers working 10 hours daily with the same means of production produce 30 pieces of a certain commodity in I, 40 in II, and 60 in III, of which every piece, aside from the value of the means of production incorporated in it, represents a new value of £1. Since every 20 pieces = £20 make good the wages, there remain 10 pieces = £10 for surplus-value in I, 20 pieces = £20 in II, and 40 pieces = £40 in III.

Or *third*, the working-day differs in length. If 20 labourers work with the same intensity for 9 hours in I, 12 hours in II, and 18 hours in III, their total products, 30 : 40 : 60 vary as 9 : 12 : 18. And since wages = 20 in every case, 10, 20, and 40 respectively again remain as surplus-value.

A rise or fall in wages, therefore, influences the rate of surplus-value inversely, and a rise or fall in the intensity of labour, and a lengthening or shortening of the working-day, act the same way on the rate of surplus-value and thereby, with v/C constant, on the rate of profit.

2) s' and v variable, C constant.

The following proportion applies in this case:

$$p' : p'_1 = s› (v/C) : s› (v_1/C) = s'v : s'_1v_1 = s : s_1.$$

The rates of profit are related to one another as the respective amounts of surplus-value.

Changes in the rate of surplus-value with the variable capital remaining constant meant a change in the magnitude and distribution of the produced value. A simultaneous variation of v and s' also always implies a different distribution, but not always a change in the magnitude of the produced value. Three cases are possible:

a) Variation of v and s' takes place in opposite directions, but by the same amount; for instance:

   I. $80_c + 20_v + 10_s$; s' = 50%, p' = 10%
   II. $90_c + 10_v + 20_s$; s' = 200%, p' = 20%

   The produced value is equal in both cases, hence also the quantity of labour performed; $20_v + 10_s = 10_v + 20_s = 30$. The only difference is that in the first case 20 is paid out for wages and 10 remains as surplus-value, while in the second case wages are only 10 and surplus-value is therefore 20. This is the only case in which the number of labourers, the intensity of labour, and the length of the working-day remain unchanged, while v and s› vary simultaneously.

b) Variation of s' and v also takes place in opposite directions, but not by the same amount. In that case the variation of either v or s' outweighs the other.

   I. $80_c + 20_v + 20_s$; s' = 100%, p' = 20%
   II. $72_c + 28_v + 20_s$; s' = 71 3/7%, p' = 20%
   III. $84_c + 16_v + 20_s$; s' = 125%, p' = 20%.

   Capital I pays for produced value amounting to 40 with 20v, II a value of 48 with 28_v, and III a value of 36 with 16_v. Both the produced value and the wages have changed. But a change in the produced value means a change in the amount of labour performed, hence a change either in the number of labourers, the hours of labour, the intensity of labour, or in more than one of these.

c) Variation of s' and v takes place in the same direction. In that case the one intensifies the effect of the other.
   $90_c + 10_v + 10_s$; s' = 100%, p' = 10%
   $80_c + 20_v + 30_s$; s' = 150%, p' = 30%
   $92_c + 8_v + 6_s$; s' = 75%, p' = 6%.

Here too the three values produced are different, namely 20, 50, and 14. And this difference in the magnitude of the respective quantities of labour reduces itself once more to a difference in the number of labourers, the hours of labour, and the intensity of labour, or several or all of these factors.

3) s', v and C variable.

This case offers no new aspects and is solved by the general formula given under II, in which s' is variable.

The effect of a change in the magnitude of the rate of surplus-value on the rate of profit hence yields the following cases:

1. p' increases or decreases in the same proportion as s' if v/C remains constant.
   $80_c + 20_v + 20_s$; s' = 100%, p' = 20%
   $80_c + 20_v + 10_s$; s' = 50%, p' = 10%
   100% : 50% = 20% : 10%.
2. p' rises or falls at a faster rate than s' if v/C moves in the same direction as s', that is, if it increases or decreases when s' increases or decreases.
   $80_c + 20_v + 10_s$; s' = 50%, p' = 10%
   $70_c + 30_v + 20_s$; s' = 66⅔%, p' = 10%
   50% : 66⅔% < 10% : 20%.
3. p' rises or falls at a slower rate than s' if v/C changes inversely to s', but at a slower rate.
   $80_c + 20_v + 10_s$; s' = 50%, p' = 10%
   $90_c + 10_v + 15_s$; s' = 150%, p' = 15%
   50% : 150% > 10% : 15%.
4. p' rises while s' falls, or falls while s' rises if v/C changes inversely to, and at, a faster rate than, s'.
   $80_c + 20_v + 20_s$; s' = 100%, p' = 20%
   $90_c + 10_v + 15_s$; s' = 150%, p' = 15%.
   s' has risen from 100% to 150%, p' has fallen from 20% to 15%.
5. Finally, p' remains constant whereas s' rises or falls, while v/C changes inversely to, but in exactly the same proportion as, s'.

It is only this last case which still requires some explanation. We have observed earlier in the variations of v/C that one and the same rate of surplus-value may be expressed in very much different rates of profit. Now we see that one and the same rate of profit may be based on very much different rates of surplus-value. But while any change in the proportion of v to C is sufficient to produce a difference in the rate of profit so long as s is constant, a change in the magnitude of s must lead to a corresponding inverse change of v/C in order that the rate of profit remains the same. In the case of one and the same capital, or in that of two capitals in one and the same country, this is possible but in exceptional cases. Assume, for example, that we have a capital of

$$80_c + 20_v + 20_s; C = 100, s' = 100\%, p' = 20\%;$$

and let us suppose that wages fall to such an extent that the same number of labourers is obtainable for 16v instead of 20v. Then, other things being equal, and 4v being released, we shall have:

$$80_c + 16_v + 24_s; C = 96, s' = 150\%, p' = 25\%.$$

In order that p' may now = 20% as before, the total capital would have to increase to 120, the constant capital therefore rising to 104:

$$104_c + 16_v + 24_s; C = 120, s' = 150\%, p' = 20\%.$$

This would only be possible if the fall in wages were attended simultaneously by a change in the productivity of labour which required such a change in the composition of capital. Or, if the value in money of the constant capital increased from 80 to 104. In short, it would require an accidental coincidence of conditions such as occurs in exceptional cases. In fact, a variation of s' that does not call for the simultaneous variation of v, and thus of v/C, is conceivable only under very definite conditions, namely in such branches of industry in which only fixed capital and labour are employed, while the materials of labour are supplied by Nature.

But this is not so when the rates of profit of two different countries are compared. For in that case the same rate of profit is, in effect, based largely on different rates of surplus-value.

It follows from all of these five cases, therefore, that a rising rate of profit may correspond to a falling or rising rate of surplus-value, a falling rate of profit to a rising or falling rate of surplus-value, and a constant rate of profit to a rising or falling rate of surplus-value. And we have seen in I that a rising, falling, or constant rate of profit may also accord with a constant rate of surplus-value.

The rate of profit, therefore, depends on two main factors—the rate of surplus-value and the value-composition of capital. The effects of these two factors may be briefly summed up as follows, by giving the composition in per cent, for it is immaterial which of the two portions of the capital causes the variation:

The rates of profit of two different capitals, or of one and the same capital in two successive different conditions,

are equal

1. if the per cent composition of the capitals is the same and their rates of surplus-value are equal;
2. if their per cent composition is not the same, and the rates of surplus-value are unequal, provided the products of the rates of surplus-value by the percentages of the variable portions of capitals (s' by v) are the same, i.e., if the *masses* of surplus-value (s = s›v) calculated in per cent of the total capital are equal; in other words, if the factors s' and v are inversely proportional to one another in both cases.

They are unequal

1. if the per cent composition is equal and the rates of surplus-value are unequal, in which case they are related as the rates of surplus-value;
2. if the rates of surplus-value are the same and the per cent composition is unequal, in which case they are related as the variable portions of the capitals;
3. if the rates of surplus-value are unequal and the per cent composition not the same, in which case they are related as the products s'v, i.e., as the quantities of surplus-value calculated in per cent of the total capital.[2]

Notes

1. The manuscript has the following note at this point: 'Investigate later in what manner this case is connected with ground-rent.' *F. E.*
2. The manuscript contains also very detailed calculations of the difference between the rate of surplus-value and the rate of profit (s'-p'), which has very interesting peculiarities, and whose movement indicates where the two rates draw apart or approach one another. These movements may also be represented by curves. I am not reproducing this material, because it is of less importance to the immediate purposes of this work, and because it is enough here to call attention to this fact for readers who wish to pursue this point further.—*F.E.*

4

The Effect of the Turnover on the Rate of Profit

The effect of the turnover on the production of surplus-value, and consequently of profit, has been discussed in Book II. Briefly summarised, it signifies that owing to the time span required for turnover, not all the capital can be employed all at once in production; some of the capital always lies idle, either in the form of money-capital, of raw material supplies, of finished but still unsold commodity-capital, or of outstanding claims; that the capital in active production, i.e., in the production and appropriation of surplus-value, is always short by this amount, and that the produced and appropriated surplus-value is always curtailed to the same extent. The shorter the period of turnover, the smaller this idle portion of capital as compared with the whole, and the larger, therefore, the appropriated surplus-value, provided other conditions remain the same.

It has already been shown in detail in Book II [English edition: Vol. II, pp. 293-98.—*Ed.*] how the quantity of produced surplus-value is augmented by reductions in the period of turnover, or of one of its two sections, in the time of production and the time of circulation. But since the rate of profit only expresses the relation of the produced quantity of surplus-value to the total capital employed in its production, it is evident that any such reduction increases the rate of profit. Whatever has been said earlier in Part II of Book II in regard to surplus-value, applies equally to profit and the rate of profit and needs no repetition here. We wish only to stress a few of the principal points.

The chief means of reducing the time of production is higher labour productivity, which is commonly called industrial progress. If this does not involve a simultaneous considerable increase in the outlay of total capital resulting from the installation of expensive machinery, etc., and thus a reduction of the rate of profit, which is calculated on the total capital, this rate must rise. And this is decidedly true in the case of many of the latest improvements in metallurgy and in the chemical industry. The recently discovered methods of producing iron and steel, such as the processes of Bessemer, Siemens, Gilchrist-Thomas, etc., cut to a minimum at relatively small costs the formerly arduous processes. The making of alizarin, a red dye-stuff extracted from coal-tar, requires but a few weeks, and this by means of already existing coal-tar dye-producing installations, to yield the same results which formerly required years. It took a year for the madder to mature, and it was customary to let the roots grow a few years more before they were processed.

The chief means of reducing the time of circulation is improved communications. The last fifty years have brought about a revolution in this field, comparable only with the industrial revolution of the latter half of the 18th century. On land, the macadamized road has been displaced by the railway, on sea, the slow and irregular sailing vessel has been pushed into the background by the rapid and dependable steamboat line, and the entire globe is being girdled by telegraph wires. The Suez Canal has fully opened East Asia and Australia to steamer traffic. The time of circulation of a shipment of commodities to East Asia, at least twelve months in 1847 (cf. Buch II, S. 235 [English edition: Karl Marx, *Capital*, Vol. II, pp. 251-52.—*Ed.*]), has now been reduced to almost as many weeks. The two large centres of the crises of 1825-57, America and India, have been brought from 70 to 90 per cent nearer to the European industrial countries by this revolution in transport, and have thereby lost a good deal of their explosive nature. The period of turnover of the total world commerce has been reduced to the same extent, and the efficacy of the capital involved in it has been more than doubled or trebled. It goes without saying that this has not been without effect on the rate of profit.

To single out the effect of the turnover of total capital on the rate of profit, we must assume all other conditions of the capitals to be compared as equal. Aside from the rate of surplus-value and the working-day it is also notably the per cent composition which we must assume to be the same. Now let us take a capital A composed of $80_c + 20_v = 100$ C, which makes two turnovers yearly at a rate of surplus-value of 100%. The annual product is then:

$160_c + 40_v + 40_s$. However, to determine the rate of profit we do not calculate the 40s on the turned-over capital-value of 200, but on the advanced capital of 100, and thus obtain p' = 40%.

Now let us compare this with a capital B = $160_c + 40_v = 200$ C, which has the same rate of surplus-value of 100%, but which is turned over only once a year. The annual product of this capital is, therefore, the same as that of A:

$160_c + 40_v + 40_s$. But this time the 40s are to be calculated on an advance of capital amounting to 200, which yields a rate of profit of only 20%, or one-half that of A.

We find, then, that for capitals with an equal per cent composition, with equal rates of surplus-value and equal working-days, the rates of profit of the two capitals are related inversely as their periods of turnover. If either the composition, the rates of surplus-value, the working-day, or the wages, are unequal in the two compared cases, this would naturally produce further differences in the rates of profit; but these are independent of the turnover and, for this reason, do not concern us at this point. They have already been discussed in Chapter III.

The direct effect of a reduced period of turnover on the production of surplus-value, and consequently of profit, consists of an increased efficiency imparted thereby to the variable portion of capital, as shown in Book II, Chapter XVI, 'The Turnover of Variable Capital'. This chapter demonstrated that a variable capital of 500 turned over ten times a year produces as much surplus-value in this time as a variable capital of 5,000 with the same rate of surplus-value and the same wages, turned over just once a year.

Take capital I, consisting of 10,000 fixed capital whose annual depreciation is 10% = 1,000, of 500 circulating constant and 500 variable capital. Let the variable capital turn over ten times per year at a 100% rate of surplus-value. For the sake of simplicity, we assume in all the following examples that the circulating constant capital is turned over in the same time as the variable, which is generally the case in practice. Then the product of one such period of turnover will be:

100_c (depreciation) $+ 500_c + 500_v + 500_s = 1{,}600$

and the product of one entire year, with ten such turnovers, will be

$1{,}000_c$ (depreciation) $+ 5{,}000_c + 5{,}000_v + 5{,}000_s = 16{,}000$,
$C = 11{,}000$, $s = 5{,}000$, $p' = 5{,}000/11{,}000 = 45\ 5/11\ \%$.

Now, let us take capital II: 9,000 fixed capital, 1,000 annual wear and tear, 1,000 circulating constant capital, 1,000 variable capital, 100% rate of surplus-value, 5 turnovers of variable capital per year. Then the product of each of the turnovers of the variable capital will be:

200_c (depreciation) $+ 1{,}000_c + 1{,}000_v + 1{,}000_s = 3{,}200$,

and the total annual product after five turnovers:

$1{,}000_c$ (depreciation) $+ 5{,}000_c + 5{,}000_v + 5{,}000_s = 16{,}000$,
$C = 11{,}000$, $s = 5{,}000$, $p' = 5{,}000/11{,}000 = 45\ 5/11\ \%$

Further, take capital III with no fixed capital, 6,000 circulating constant capital and 5,000 variable capital. Let there be one turnover per year at a 100% rate of surplus-value. Then the total annual product is:

$6{,}000_c + 5{,}000_v + 5{,}000_s = 16{,}000$,
$= 11{,}000$, $s = 5{,}000$, $p' = 5{,}000/11{,}000 = 45\ 5/11\%$.

In all the three cases we therefore have the same annual quantity of surplus-value = 5,000, and, since the total capital is likewise equal in all three cases, namely = 11,000, also the same rate of profit of 45 5/11%.

But should capital I have only 5 instead of 10 turnovers of its variable part per year, the result would be different. The product of one turnover would then be:

200_c (depreciation) $+ 500_c + 500_v + 500_s = 1{,}700$.

And the annual product:

$$1{,}000_c \text{ (depreciation)} + 2{,}500_c + 2{,}500_v + 2{,}500_s = 8{,}500,$$
$$C = 11{,}000,\ s = 2{,}500;\ p' = 2{,}500/11{,}000 = 22\ 8/11\%.$$

The rate of profit has fallen one-half, because the period of turnover has doubled.

The quantity of surplus-value appropriated in one year is therefore equal to the quantity of surplus-value appropriated in one turnover of the *variable* capital multiplied by the number of such turnovers per year. Suppose we call the surplus-value, or profit, appropriated in one year S, the surplus-value appropriated in one period of turnover s, the number of turnovers of the variable capital in one year n, then S = sn, and the annual rate of surplus-value S› = s›n, as already demonstrated in Book II, Chapter XVI, I. [English edition: Vol. II, p. 305.—*Ed.*]

It goes without saying that the formula p' = s' (v/C) = s' v/(c + v) is correct only so long as the v in the numerator is the same as that in the denominator. In the denominator, v stands for the entire portion of the total capital used on an average as variable capital for the payment of wages. The v of the numerator is primarily only determined by the fact that a certain quantity of surplus-value = s is produced and appropriated by it, whose relation to it s/v, is m', the rate of surplus-value. It is only along these lines that the formula p' = s/(c + v) is transformed into the other: p' = s' v/(c + v). The v of the numerator will now be more accurately determined by the fact that it must equal the v of the denominator, that is, the entire variable portion of capital C. In other words, the equation p' = (s/C) may be correctly transformed into the equation p' = s' v/(c + v) only if s stands for surplus-value produced in one turnover of the variable capital. Should s be only a portion of this surplus-value, then s = s'v is still correct, but this v is then smaller than the v in C = c + v, because it is smaller than the entire variable capital expended for wages. But should s stand for more than the surplus-value of one turnover of v, then a portion of this v, or perhaps the whole of it, serves twice, namely in the first and in the second turnover, and eventually in subsequent turnovers. The v, which produces the surplus-value and represents the sum of all paid wages, is therefore, greater than the v in c + v and the calculation falls into error.

To make the formula precise for the annual rate of profit, we must substitute the annual rate of surplus-value for the simple rate of surplus-value, that is, substitute S' or s'n for s'. In other words, we must multiply the rate of surplus-value s', or, what amounts to the same thing, the variable capital v contained in C, by n, the number of turnovers of this variable capital in one year. Thus we obtain p' = s'n (v/C), which is the formula for the annual rate of profit.

The amount of variable capital invested in his business is something the capitalist himself does not know in most cases. We have seen in Chapter VIII of Book II, and shall see further along, that the only essential distinction within his capital which impresses itself upon the capitalist is that of fixed and circulating capital. He takes money to pay wages from his cash-box containing the part of the circulating capital he has on hand in the form of money, so far as it is not deposited in a bank; he takes money from the same cash-box for raw and auxiliary materials, and credits both items to the same cash-account. And even if he should keep a separate account for wages, at the close of the year this would only show the sum paid out for this item, hence vn, but not the variable capital v itself. In order to ascertain this, he would have to make a special calculation, of which we propose here to give an illustration.

For this purpose we select the cotton spinnery of 10,000 mule spindles described in Book I (S. 209/201) [English edition: p. 219.—*Ed.*] and assume that the data given there for one week of April 1871, are in force during the whole year. The fixed capital incorporated in the machinery was £10,000. The circulating capital was not given. We assume it to have been £2,500. This is a rather high estimate, but justified by the assumption, which we must always make here, that no credit operations were effected, hence no permanent or temporary employment of other people's capital. The value of the weekly product was composed of £20 for depreciation of machinery, £358 circulating constant advanced capital (rent £6; cotton £342; coal, gas, oil, £10), £52 variable capital paid out for wages, and £80 surplus-value. Therefore,

$$20_c \text{ (depreciation)} + 358_c + 52_v + 80_s = 510.$$

The weekly advance of circulating capital, therefore, was $358_c + 52_v = 410$. In terms of per cent, this was $87.3_c + 12.7_v$. For the entire circulating capital of £2,500 this would be £2,182 constant and £318 variable capital. Since the total expenditure for wages in one year was 52 times £52, or £2,704, it follows that in a year the variable capital of £318 was turned over almost exactly 8½ times. The rate of surplus-value was 80/52 = 153 11/13. We calculate the rate of profit on the basis of these elements by inserting the above values in the formula p' = s'n (v/C) : s' = 153 11/13, n = 8½, v = 318, C = 12,500; hence:

$$p' = 153\ 11/13 \times 8½ \times 318/12{,}500 = 33.27\%.$$

We test this by means of the simple formula p' = (s/C). The total annual surplus-value or profit amounts to 52 times £80, or £4,160, and this divided by the total capital of £12,500 gives us 33.28%, or almost an identical result. This is an abnormally high rate of profit, which may only be explained by extraordinarily favourable conditions of the moment (very low prices of cotton along with very high prices of yarn), and could certainly not have obtained throughout the year.

The s'n in the formula p' = s'n (v/C) stands, as has been said, for the thing called in Book II [English edition: Vol. II, p. 295.—*Ed.*] the annual rate of surplus-value. In the above case, it is 153 11/13% multiplied by 8½ or in exact figures, 1,307 9/18%. Thus, if a certain Biedermann [Biedermann—Philistine. A pun, being also the name of the editor of the *Deutsche Allgemeine Zeitung.—Ed.*] was shocked by the abnormity of an annual rate of surplus-value of 1,000% used as an illustration in Book II, he will now perhaps be pacified by this annual rate of surplus-value of more than 1,300% taken from the living experience of Manchester. In times of greatest prosperity, such as we have not indeed seen for a long time, such a rate is by no means a rarity.

For that matter, we have here an illustration of the actual composition of capital in modern large-scale industry. The total capital is broken up into £12,182 constant and £318 variable capital, a sum of £12,500. In terms of percent this is 97½c + 2½v = 100 C. Only one-fortieth of the total, but in more than an eight-fold annual turnover, serves for the payment of wages.

Since very few capitalists ever think of making calculations of this sort with reference to their own business, statistics is almost completely silent about the relation of the constant portion of the total social capital to its variable portion. Only the American census gives what is possible under modern conditions, namely the sum of wages paid in each line of business and the profits realised. Questionable as they may be, being based on the capitalist's own uncontrolled statements, they are nevertheless very valuable and the only records available to us on this subject. [In Europe we are far too delicate to expect such revelations from our major capitalists.—*F.E.*]

5

Economy in the Employment of Constant Capital

Section I. *In General*

The increase of absolute surplus-value, or the prolongation of surplus-labour, and thus of the working-day, while the variable capital remains the same and thus employs the same number of labourers at the same nominal wages, regardless of whether overtime is paid or not, reduces the relative value of the constant capital as compared to the total and the variable capital, and thereby increases the rate of profit, again irrespective of the growth of the quantity of surplus-value and a possibly rising rate of surplus-value. The volume of the fixed portion of constant capital, such as factory buildings, machinery, etc., remains the same, no matter whether these serve the labour-process 16 or 12 hours. A prolongation of the working-day does not entail any fresh expenditures in this, the most expensive portion of constant capital. Furthermore, the value of the fixed capital is thereby reproduced in a smaller number of turnover periods, so that the time for which it must be advanced to make a certain profit is abbreviated. A prolongation of the working-day therefore increases the profit, even if overtime is paid, or even if, up to a certain point, it is better paid than the normal hours of labour. The ever-mounting need to increase fixed capital in modern industry was, therefore, one of the main reasons prompting profit-mad capitalists to lengthen the working-day.[1] The same conditions do not obtain if the working-day is constant. Then it is necessary either to increase the number of labourers, and with them to a certain extent the amount of fixed capital, the buildings, machinery, etc., in order to exploit a greater quantity of labour (for we leave aside deductions from wages or the depression of wages below their normal level), or, if the intensity and, consequently, the productivity of labour, increase and, generally, more relative surplus-value is produced, the magnitude of the circulating portion of constant capital increases in such industrial branches which use raw materials, since more raw material, etc., is processed in a given time; and, secondly, the amount of machinery set in motion by the same number of labourers, therefore also this part of constant capital, increases as well. Hence, an increase in surplus-value is accompanied by an increase in constant capital, and the growing exploitation of labour by greater outlays of the means of production through which labour is exploited, i.e., by a greater investment of capital. Therefore, the rate of profit is thereby reduced on the one hand while it increases on the other.

Quite a number of current expenses remain almost or entirely the same whether the working-day is longer or shorter. The cost of supervision is less for 500 working-men during 18 working-hours than for 750 working-men during 12 working-hours.

> The expense of working a factory 10 hours almost equals that of working it 12. (Reports of Insp. of Fact., October 1848, p. 37.)

State and municipal taxes, fire insurance, wages of various permanent employees, depreciation of machinery, and various other expenses of a factory, remain unchanged whether the working-time is long or short. To the extent to which production decreases, these expenses rise as compared to the profit. (Reports of Insp. of Fact., October 1862, p. 19.)

The period in which the value of the machinery and of the other components of fixed capital is reproduced is determined in practice not by their mere lifetime, but by the duration of the entire labour-process during which they serve and wear out. If the labourers must work 18 instead of 12 hours, this makes a difference of three days more per week, so that one week is stretched into one and a half, and two years into three. If this overtime is unpaid the labourers give away gratis a week out of every three and a year out of every three on top of the normal surplus-labour time. In this way, the reproduction of the value of the machinery is speeded up 50% and accomplished in ⅔ of the usually required time.

To avoid useless complications, we proceed in this analysis, and in that of price fluctuations for raw materials (Chap. VI), from the assumption that the mass and rate of surplus-value are given.

As already shown in the presentation of co-operation, division of labour and machinery, the economy of production conditions [English edition: Vol. I, pp. 324-25—*Ed.*] found in large-scale production is essentially due to the fact that these conditions prevail as conditions of social, or socially combined, labour, and therefore as social conditions of labour. They are commonly consumed in the process of production by the aggregate labourer, instead of being consumed in small fractions by a mass of labourers operating disconnectedly or, at best, directly co-operating on a small scale. In a large factory with one or two central motors the cost of these motors does not increase in the same ratio as their horse-power and, hence, their possible sphere of activity. The cost of the transmission equipment does not grow in the same ratio as the total number of working machines which it sets in motion. The frame of a machine does not become dearer in the same ratio as the mounting number of tools which it employs as its organs, etc. Furthermore, the concentration of means of production yields a saving on buildings of various kinds not only for the actual workshops, but also for storage, etc. The same applies to expenditures for fuel, lighting, etc. Other conditions of production remain the same, whether used by many or by few.

This total economy, arising as it does from the concentration of means of production and their use *en masse*, imperatively requires, however, the accumulation and co-operation of labourers, i.e., a social combination of labour. Hence, it originates quite as much from the social nature of labour, just as surplus-value originates from the surplus-labour of the individual labourer considered singly. Even the continual improvements, which are here possible and necessary, are due solely to the social experience and observation ensured and made possible by production of aggregate labour combined on a large scale.

The same is true of the second big source of economy in the conditions of production. We refer to the reconversion of the excretions of production, the so-called waste, into new elements of production, either of the same, or of some other line of industry; to the processes by which this so-called excretion is thrown back into the cycle of production and, consequently, consumption, whether productive or individual. This line of savings, which we shall later examine more closely, is likewise the result of large-scale social labour. It is the attendant abundance of this waste which renders it available again for commerce and thereby turns it into new elements of production. It is only as waste of combined production, therefore, of large-scale production, that it becomes important to the production process and remains a bearer of exchange-value. This waste, aside from the services which it performs as new element of production, reduces the cost of the raw material to the extent to which it is again saleable, for this cost always includes the normal waste, namely the quantity ordinarily lost in processing. The reduction of the cost of this portion of constant capital increases *pro tanto* the rate of profit, assuming the magnitude of the variable capital and the rate of surplus-value to be given.

If the surplus-value is given, the rate of profit can be increased only by reducing the value of the constant capital required for commodity-production. So far as constant capital enters into the production of commodities, it is not its exchange-value, but its use-value alone, which matters. The quantity of labour which flax can absorb in a spinnery does not depend on its value, but on its quantity, assuming the productivity of labour, i.e., the level of technical development, to be given. In like manner, the assistance rendered by a machine to, say, three labourers does not depend on its value, but on its use-value as a machine. On one level of technical development, a bad machine may be expensive and on another a good machine may be cheap.

The increased profit received by a capitalist through the cheapening of, say, cotton and spinning machinery, is the result of higher labour productivity; not in the spinnery, to be sure, but in cotton cultivation and construction of machinery. It requires smaller outlays of the conditions of labour to incorporate a given quantity of labour, and hence to extract a given quantity of surplus-labour. The costs required to appropriate a certain quantity of surplus-labour diminish.

We have already mentioned savings yielded in the production process through co-operative use of means of production by the aggregate, or socially combined, labour. Other savings of constant capital arising from the shortening of the time of circulation in which the development of means of communication is a dominant material factor will be discussed later. At this point, we shall deal with the savings yielded by continuous improvements of machinery, namely 1) of its material, e.g., the substitution of iron for wood; 2) the cheapening of machinery due to the general improvement of machine-building; so that, although the value of the fixed portion of constant capital increases continually with the development of labour on a large scale, it does not increase at the same rate[2]; 3) special improvements enabling existing machinery to work more cheaply and effectively; for instance, improvements of steam-boilers, etc., which will be discussed later on in greater detail; 4) reduction of waste through better machinery.

Whatever reduces the wear of machinery, and of fixed capital in general, for any given period of production, cheapens not only the individual commodity, in view of the fact that in its price every individual commodity reproduces its aliquot share of this depreciation, but reduces also the aliquot portion of the invested capital for this period. Repair work, etc., to the extent that it becomes necessary, is added to the original cost of the machinery. A reduction in repair costs, due to greater durability of the machinery, lowers *pro tanto* the price of this machinery.

It may again be said of all these savings that they are largely possible only for combined labour, and are often not realised until production is carried forward on a still larger scale, so that they require an even greater combination of labour in the immediate process of production.

However, on the other hand the development of the productive power of labour in any *one* line of production, e.g., the production of iron, coal, machinery, in architecture, etc., which may again be partly connected with progress in the field of intellectual production, notably natural science and its practical application, appears to be the premise for a reduction of the value, and consequently of the cost, of means of production in *other* lines of industry, e.g., the textile industry, or agriculture. This is self-evident, since a commodity which is the product of a certain branch of industry enters another as a means of production. Its greater or lesser price depends on the productivity of labour in the line of production from which it issues as a product, and is at the same time a factor that not only cheapens the commodities into whose production it goes as a means of production, but also reduces the value of the constant capital whose element it here becomes, and thereby one that increases the rate of profit.

The characteristic feature of this kind of saving of constant capital arising from the progressive development of industry is that the rise in the rate of profit in *one* line of industry depends on the development of the productive power of labour in *another*. Whatever falls to the capitalist's advantage in this case is once more a gain produced by social labour, if not a product of the labourers he himself exploits. Such a development of productive power is again traceable in the final analysis to the social nature of the labour engaged in production; to the division of labour in society; and to the development of intellectual labour, especially in the natural sciences. What the capitalist thus utilises are the advantages of the entire system of the social division of labour. It is the development of the productive power of labour in its exterior department, in that department which supplies it with means of production, whereby the value of the constant capital employed by the capitalist is relatively lowered and consequently the rate of profit is raised.

Another rise in the rate of profit is produced, not by savings in the labour creating the constant capital, but by savings in the application of this capital itself. On the one hand, the concentration of labourers, and their large-scale co-operation, saves constant capital. The same buildings, and heating and lighting appliances, etc., cost relatively less for the large-scale than for small-scale production. The same is true of power and working machinery. Although their absolute value increases, it falls in comparison to the increasing extension of production and the magnitude of the variable capital, or the quantity of labour-power set in motion. The economy realised by a certain capital within its own line of production is first and foremost an economy in labour, i.e., a reduction of the paid labour of its own labourers. The previously mentioned economy, on the other hand, is distinguished from this one by the fact that it accomplishes the greatest possible appropriation of other people's unpaid labour in the most economical way, i.e., with as little expense as the given scale of production will permit. Inasmuch as this economy does not rest with the previously mentioned exploitation of the productivity of the social labour employed in the production of constant capital, but with the economy in the constant capital itself, it springs either directly from the co-operation and social form of labour within a certain branch of production, or from the production of machinery, etc., on a scale in which its value does not grow at the same rate as its use-value.

Two points must be borne in mind here: It the value of c = zero, then p' = s', and the rate of profit would be at its maximum. Second, however, the most important thing for the direct exploitation of labour itself is not the value of the employed means of exploitation, be they fixed capital, raw materials or auxiliary substances. In so far as they serve as means of absorbing labour, as media in or by which labour and, hence, surplus-labour are materialised, the exchange-value of machinery, buildings, raw materials, etc., is quite immaterial. What is ultimately essential is, on the one hand, the quantity of them technically required for combination with a certain quantity of living labour, and, on the other, their suitability, i.e., not only good machinery, but also good raw and auxiliary materials. The rate of profit depends partly on the good quality of the raw material. Good material produces less waste. Less raw materials are then needed to absorb the same quantity of labour. Furthermore, the resistance to be overcome by the working machine is also less. This partly affects even the surplus-value and the rate of surplus-value. The labourer needs more time when using bad raw materials to process the same quantity. Assuming wages remain the same, this causes a reduction in surplus-labour. This also substantially affects the reproduction and accumulation of capital, which depend more on the productivity than on the amount of labour employed, as shown in Book I (S. 627/619ff.) [English edition: p. 603.—*Ed.*].

The capitalist's fanatical insistence on economy in means of production is therefore quite understandable. That nothing is lost or wasted and the means of production are consumed only in the manner required by production itself, depends partly on the skill and intelligence of the labourers and partly on the discipline enforced by the capitalist for the combined labour. This discipline will become superfluous under a social system in which the labourers work for their own account, as it has already become practically superfluous in piece-work. This fanatical insistence comes to the surface also conversely in the adulteration of the elements of production, which is one of the principal means of lowering the relation of the value of the constant capital to the variable capital, and thus of raising the rate of profit. Whereby the sale of these elements of production above their value, so far as this reappears in the product, acquires a marked element of cheating. This practice plays an essential part particularly in German industry, whose maxim is: People will surely appreciate if we send them good samples at first, and then inferior goods afterward. However, as these matters belong to the sphere of competition, they do not concern us here.

It should be noted that this raising of the rate of profit by means of lowering the value of the constant capital, i.e., by reducing its expensiveness, does not in any way depend on whether the branch of industry in which it takes place produces luxuries, or necessities for the consumption of labourers, or means of production generally. This last circumstance would only be of material importance if it were a question of the rate of surplus-value, which depends essentially on the value of labour-power, i.e., on the value of the customary necessities of the labourer. But in the present case, the surplus-value and the rate of surplus-value have been assumed as given. The relation of surplus-value to total capital—and this determines the rate of profit—depends under these circumstances exclusively on the value of the constant capital, and in no way on the use-value of the elements of which it is composed.

A relative cheapening of the means of production does not, of course, exclude the possible increase of their absolute aggregate value, for the absolute volume in which they are employed grows tremendously with the development of the productive power of labour and the attendant growth of the level of production. Economy, in the use of constant capital, from whatever angle it may be viewed, is, in part, the exclusive result of the fact that the means of production function and are consumed as joint means of production of the combined labourer, so that the resulting saving appears as a product of the social nature of directly productive labour; in part, however, it is the result of developing productivity of labour in spheres which supply capital with its means of production, so that if we view the total labour in relation to total capital, and not simply the labourers employed by capitalist X in relation to capitalist Y, this economy presents itself once more as a product of the development of the productive forces of social labour, with the only difference that capitalist X enjoys the advantage not only of the productivity of labour in his own establishment, but also of that in other establishments. Yet the capitalist views economy of his constant capital as a condition wholly independent of, and entirely alien to, his labourers. He is always well aware, however, that the labourer has something to do with the employer buying much or little labour with the same amount of money (for this is how the transaction between the capitalist and labourer appears in his mind). This economy, in the application of the means of production, this method of obtaining a certain result with a minimum outlay appears more than any other inner power of labour as an inherent power of capital and a method peculiar and characteristic of the capitalist mode of production.

This conception is so much the less surprising since it appears to accord with fact, and since the relationship of capital actually conceals the inner connection behind the utter indifference, isolation, and alienation in which they place the labourer vis-à-vis the means incorporating his labour.

First, the means of production that make up the constant capital represent only the money belonging to the capitalist (just as the body of the Roman debtor represented the money of his creditor, according to Linguet [*Théorie des loix civiles, ou principes fondamentaux de la société*, tome II, Londres, 1767, livre V, chapitre XX.—*Ed.*]) and are related to him alone, while the labourer, who comes in contact with them only in the direct process of production, deals with them as use-values of production only as means of labour and materials of production. Increase or decrease of their value, therefore, has as little bearing on his relations to the capitalist as the circumstance whether he may be working with copper or iron. For that matter, the capitalist likes to view this point differently, as we shall later indicate, whenever the means of production gain in value and thereby reduce his rate of profit.

Second, in so far as these means of production in the capitalist production process are at the same time means of exploiting labour, the labourer is no more concerned with their relative dearness or cheapness than a horse is concerned with the dearness or cheapness of its bit and bridle.

Finally, we have earlier [English edition: Vol. 1, p. 325.—*Ed.*] seen that, in fact, the labourer looks at the social nature of his labour, at its combination with the labour of others for a common purpose, as he would at an alien power; the condition of realising this combination is alien property, whose dissipation would be totally indifferent to him if he were not compelled to economise with it. The situation is quite different in factories owned by the labourers themselves, as in Rochdale, for instance.

It scarcely needs to be mentioned, then, that as far as concerns the productivity of labour in one branch of industry as a lever for cheapening and improving the means of production in another, and thereby raising the rate of profit, the general interconnection of social labour affects the labourers as a matter alien to them, a matter that actually concerns the capitalist alone, since it is he who buys and appropriates these means of production. The fact that he buys the product of labourers in another branch of industry with the product of labourers in his own, and that he, therefore, disposes of the product of the labourers of another capitalist only by gratuitously appropriating that of his own, is a development that is fortunately concealed by the process of circulation, etc.

Moreover, since production on a large scale develops for the first time in its capitalist form, the thirst for profits on the one hand, and competition on the other, which compels the cheapest possible production of commodities, make this economy in the employment of constant capital appear as something peculiar to the capitalist mode of production and therefore as a function of the capitalist.

Just as the capitalist mode of production promotes the development of the productive powers of social labour, on the one hand, so does it whip on to economy in the employment of constant capital on the other.

However, it is not only the alienation and indifference that arise between the labourer, the bearer of living labour, and the economical, i.e., rational and thrifty, use of the material conditions of his labour. In line with its contradictory and antagonistic nature, the capitalist mode of production proceeds to count the prodigious dissipation of the labourer's life and health, and the lowering of his living conditions, as an economy in the use of constant capital and thereby as a means of raising the rate of profit.

Since the labourer passes the greater portion of his life in the process of production, the conditions of the production process are largely the conditions of his active living process, or his living conditions, and economy in these living conditions is a method of raising the rate of profit; just as we saw earlier [English edition: Vol. I, pp. 231-302.—*Ed.*] that overwork, the transformation of the labourer into a work horse, is a means of increasing capital, or speeding up the production of surplus-value. Such economy extends to overcrowding close and unsanitary premises with labourers, or, as capitalists put it, to space saving; to crowding dangerous machinery into close quarters without using safety devices; to neglecting safety rules in production processes pernicious to health, or, as in mining, bound up with danger, etc. Not to mention the absence of all provisions to render the production process human, agreeable, or at least bearable. From the capitalist point of view, this would be quite a useless and senseless waste. The capitalist mode of production is generally, despite all its niggardliness, altogether too prodigal with its human material, just as, conversely, thanks to its method of distribution of products through commerce and manner of competition, it is very prodigal with its material means, and loses for society what it gains for the individual capitalist.

Just as capital has the tendency to reduce the direct employment of living labour to no more than the necessary labour, and always to cut down the labour required to produce a commodity by exploiting the social productiveness of labour and thus to save a maximum of directly applied living labour, so it has also the tendency to employ this labour, reduced to a minimum, under the most economical conditions, i.e., to reduce to its minimum the value of the employed constant capital. If it is the necessary labour-time which determines the value of commodities, instead of all the labour-time contained in them, so it is the capital which realises this determination and, at the same time, continually reduces the labour-time socially necessary to produce a given commodity. The price of the commodity is thereby lowered to its minimum since every portion of the labour required for its production is reduced to its minimum.

We must make a distinction in economy as regards use of constant capital. If the quantity, and consequently the sum of the value of employed capital, increases, this is primarily only a concentration of more capital in a single hand. Yet it is precisely this greater quantity applied by a single source—attended, as a rule, by an absolutely greater but relatively smaller amount of employed labour—which permits economy of constant capital. To take an individual capitalist, the volume of the necessary investment of capital, especially of its fixed portion, increases. But its value decreases relative to the mass of worked-up materials and exploited labour.

This is now to be briefly illustrated by a few examples. We shall begin at the end—the economy in the conditions of production, in so far as these also constitute the living conditions of the labourer.

Section II. *Savings in Labour Conditions at the Expense of the Labourers*

Coal mines. Neglect of indisputable outlays

> Under the competition which exists among the coal-owners and coal-proprietors ... no more outlay is incurred than is sufficient to overcome the most obvious physical difficulties; and under that which prevails among the labouring colliers, who are ordinarily more numerous than the work to be done requires, a large amount of danger and exposure to the most noxious influences will gladly be encountered for wages a little in advance of the agricultural population round them, in an occupation, in which they can moreover make a profitable use of their children. This double competition is quite sufficient ... to cause a large proportion of the pits to be worked with the most imperfect drainage and ventilation; often with ill-constructed shafts, bad gearing, incompetent engineers, and ill-constructed and ill-prepared bays and roadways; causing a destruction of life, and limb, and health, the statistics of which would present an appalling picture. (First Report on Children's Employment in Mines and Collieries, etc., April 21, 1829, p. 102.)

Around 1860, a weekly average of 15 men lost their lives in the English collieries. According to the report on Coal Mines Accidents (February 6, 1862), a total of 8,466 were killed in the ten years 1852-61. But the report admits that this number is far too low, because in the first few years, when the inspectors had just been installed and their districts were far too large, a great many accidents and deaths were not reported. The very fact that the number of accidents, though still very high, has decreased markedly since the inspection system was established, and this in spite of the limited powers and insufficient numbers of the inspectors, demonstrates the natural tendency of capitalist exploitation. These human sacrifices are mostly due to the inordinate avarice of the mine owners. Very often, they had only one shaft sunk, so that apart from the lack of effective ventilation there was no escape were this shaft to become obstructed.

Capitalist production, when considered in isolation from the process of circulation and the excesses of competition, is very economical with the materialised labour incorporated in commodities. Yet, more than any other mode of production, it squanders human lives, or living-labour, and not only blood and flesh, but also nerve and brain. Indeed, it is only by dint of the most extravagant waste of individual development that the development of the human race is at all safeguarded and maintained in the epoch of history immediately preceding the conscious reorganisation of society. Since all of the economising here discussed arises from the social nature of labour, it is indeed just this directly social nature of labour which causes the waste of life and health. The following question suggested by factory inspector R. Baker is characteristic in this respect:

> The whole question is one for serious consideration, and in what way *this sacrifice of infant life occasioned by congregational labour* can be best averted? (Reports of Insp. of Fact., October 1863, p. 157.)

Factories

Under this heading there is covered the disregard for safety measures to ensure the security, comfort, and health of labourers also in the actual factories. It is to blame for a large portion of the casualty lists containing the wounded and killed industrial workers (cf. the annual factory reports). Similarly, lack of space, ventilation, etc.

As far back as October 1855, Leonard Horner complained about the resistance of very many manufacturers to the legal requirements concerning safety devices on horizontal shafts, although the danger was continually emphasised by accidents, many of them fatal, and although these safety devices did not cost much and did not interfere with production. (Reports of Insp. of Fact., October 1855, p. 6.) In their resistance against these and other legal requirements, the manufacturers were openly seconded by the unpaid justices of the peace, who were themselves mostly manufacturers or friends of manufacturers, and handed down their decisions accordingly. What sort of verdicts these gentlemen handed down was revealed by Superior Judge Campbell, who said with reference to one of them, against which an appeal had been made to him:

> It is not an interpretation of the Act of Parliament, it is a repeal of the Act of Parliament (*loc. cit.*, p. 11).

Horner states in the same report that in many factories, labourers are not warned when machinery is about to be started up. Since there is always something to be done about machinery even when it is not operating, fingers and hands are always occupied with it, and accidents happen continually due to the mere omission of a warning signal (*loc. cit.*, p. 44). The manufacturers had a trades-union at the time to oppose factory legislation, the so-called National Association for the Amendment of the Factory Laws in Manchester, which in March 1855 collected more than £50,000 by assessing 2 shillings per horse-power, to pay for the court proceedings against its members started by factory inspectors, and to conduct the cases in the name of the union. It was a matter of proving that killing was no murder [Allusion to the pamphlet 'Killing no Murder' which appeared in England in 1657. Its author was the leveller Edward Sexby.—*Ed.*] when it occurred for the sake of profit. A factory inspector for Scotland, Sir John Kincaid, tells about a certain firm in Glasgow which used the iron scrap at its factory to make protective shields for all its machinery, the cost amounting to £9 1s. Joining the manufacturers' union would have cost it an assessment of £11 for its 110 horse-power, which was more than the cost of all its protective appliances. But the National Association had been organised in 1854 for the express purpose of opposing the law which prescribed such protection. The manufacturers had not paid the least heed to it during the whole period from 1844 to 1854. When the factory inspectors, at instructions from Palmerston, then informed the manufacturers that the law would be enforced in earnest, the manufacturers instantly founded their association, many of whose most prominent members were themselves justices of the peace and in this capacity were supposed to enforce the law. When in April 1855 the new Minister of the Interior, Sir George Grey, offered a compromise under which the government would be content with practically nominal safety appliances, the Association indignantly rejected even this. In various lawsuits the famous engineer William Fairbairn threw the weight of his reputation behind the principle of economy and in defence of the freedom of capital which had been violated. The head of factory inspection, Leonard Horner, was persecuted and maligned by the manufacturers in every conceivable manner.

But the manufacturers did not rest until they obtained a writ of the Court of Queen's Bench, according to which the Law of 1844 did not prescribe protective devices for horizontal shafts installed more than seven feet above the ground and, finally, in 1856, they succeeded in securing an Act of Parliament entirely satisfactory to them in the circumstances, through the services of the bigot Wilson Patten, one of those pious souls whose display of religion is always ready to do the dirty work for the knights of the money-bag. This Act practically deprived the labourers of all special protection and referred them to the common courts for compensation in the event of industrial accidents (sheer mockery in view of the excessive cost of English lawsuits), while it made it almost impossible for the manufacturer to lose the lawsuit by providing in a finely-worded clause for expert testimony. The result was a rapid increase of accidents. In the six months from May to October 1858, Inspector Baker reported that accidents increased by 21% compared with the preceding half-year. In his opinion, 36.7% of these accidents might have been avoided. It is true that the number of accidents in 1858 and 1859 was considerably below that of 1845 and 1846. It was actually 29% less although the number of labourers in the industries subject to inspection had increased 20%. But what was the reason for this? In so far as this issue has been settled now (1865), it was mainly accomplished through the introduction of new machinery already provided with safety devices to which the manufacturer did not object because they cost him no extra expense. Furthermore, a few labourers succeeded in securing heavy damages for their lost arms, and had this judgement upheld even by the highest courts. (Reports of Insp. of Fact., April 30, 1861, p. 31, ditto April 1862, p. 17.)

So much for economy in devices protecting the life and limbs of labourers (among whom many children) against the dangers of handling and operating machinery.

Work in Enclosed Places Generally

It is well known to what extent economy of space, and thus of buildings, crowds labourers into close quarters. In addition, there is also economy in means of ventilation. Coupled with the long working-hours, the two cause a large increase in diseases of the respiratory organs, and an attendant increase in the death-rate. The following illustrations have been taken from Reports on Public Health, 6th report, 1863. This report was compiled by Dr John Simon, well known from our Book I.

Just as combination and co-operation of labour permits large-scale employment of machinery, concentration of means of production, and economy in their use, it is this very working together *en masse* in enclosed places and under conditions rather determined by ease of manufacture than by health requirements—it is this mass concentration in one and the same workshop that acts, on the one hand, as a source of greater profits for the capitalist and, on the other, unless counteracted by a reduced number of hours and special precautions, as the cause of the squandering of the lives and health of the labourers.

Dr Simon formulates the following rule and backs it up with abundant statistics:

> In proportion as the people of a district are attracted to any collective indoor occupation, in such proportion, other things being equal, the district death-rate by lung diseases will be increased' (p. 23). The cause is bad ventilation. 'And probably in all England there is no exception to the rule, that, in every district which has a large indoor industry, the increased mortality of the workpeople is such as to colour the death-return of the whole district with a marked excess of lung disease (p. 23).

Mortality figures for industries carried on in enclosed places, collected by the Board of Health in 1860 and 1861, indicate that for the same number of men between the ages of 15 and 55, for which the death-rate from consumption and other pulmonary diseases in English agricultural districts is 100, the death-rate in Coventry is 163, in Blackburn and Skipton 167, Congleton and Bradford 168, Leicester 171, Leek 182, Macclesfield 184, Bolton 190, Nottingham 192, Rochdale 193, Derby 198, Salford and Ashton-under-Lyne 203, Leeds 218, Preston 220, and Manchester 263 (p. 24). The following table presents a still more striking illustration.

District	*Chief industry*	*Deaths from pulmonary diseases between the ages of 15 and 25, per 100,000 population*	
		Men	*Women*
Berkhampstead	Straw plaiting (women)	219	578
Leighton Buzzard	Straw plaiting (women)	309	554
Newport Pagnell	Lace manufacture (women)	301	617
Towcester	Lace manufacture (women)	239	577
Yeovil	Manufacture of gloves (mainly women)	280	409
Leek	Silk industry (predominantly women)	437	856
Congleton	Silk industry (predominantly women)	566	790
Macclesfield	Silk industry (predominantly women)	593	890
Healthy country district	Agriculture	331	333

It shows the death-rate for pulmonary diseases separately for both sexes between the ages of 15 and 25 computed for every 100,000 population. In the districts selected, only women are employed in industries carried on in enclosed places, while men work in all other possible lines.

In the silk districts, where more men are employed in the factory, their mortality is also higher. The death-rate from consumption, etc., for both sexes, reveals, as the report says,

> 'the atrocious sanitary circumstances under which much of our silk industry is conducted'.

And it is in this same silk industry that the manufacturers, pleading exceptionally favourable and sanitary conditions in their establishments, demanded by way of an exception, and partially obtained, long working-hours for children under 13 years of age (Buch I, Kap. VIII, 6, S. 296/286) [English edition: Ch. X, 6, p. 293.—*Ed.*]

> Probably no industry which has yet been investigated has afforded a worse picture than that which Dr Smith gives of tailoring: 'Shops vary much in their sanitary conditions, but almost universally are overcrowded and ill-ventilated, and in a high degree unfavourable to health.... Such rooms are necessarily warm; but when the gas is lit, as during the day-time on foggy days, and at night during the winter, the heat increases to 80° and even to upwards of 90°, causing profuse perspiration, and condensation of vapour upon the panes of glass, so that it runs down in streams or drops from the roof, and the operatives are compelled to keep some windows open, at whatever risk to themselves of taking cold.' And he gives the following account of what he found in 16 of the most important West End shops. 'The largest cubic space in these ill-ventilated rooms allowed to each operative is 270 feet, and the least 105 feet, and in the whole

> averages only 156 feet per man. In one room, with a gallery running round it, and lighted only from the roof, from 92 to upwards of 100 men are employed, where a large number of gaslights burn, and where the urinals are in the closest proximity, the cubic space does not exceed 150 feet per man. In another room, which can only be called a kennel in a yard, lighted from the roof, and ventilated by a small skylight opening, five to six men work in a space of 112 cubic feet per man.' ... Tailors, in those atrocious workshops which Dr Smith describes, work generally for about 12 or 13 hours a day, and at some times the work will be continued for 15 or 16 hours. (pp. 25, 26, 28)

Numbers of persons employed	*Branches of industry and locality*	*Death-rate per 100,000 between the ages of*		
		25-35	*35-45*	*45-55*
958,265	Agriculture, England and Wales	743	805	1,145
22,301 men and	Tailoring, London	958	1,262	2,093
12,377 women				
13,803	Type-setters and printers, London	894	1,747	2,367

(p. 30). It must be noted, and has in fact been remarked by John Simon, chief of the Medical Department and author of the report, that the mortality-rate for tailors, type-setters, and printers of London between the ages of 25 and 35 was cited lower than the real figure, because London employers in both lines of business have a large number of young people (probably up to 30 years of age) from the country engaged as apprentices and 'improvers', i.e., men getting additional training. These swell the number of hands for which the London industrial death-rates are computed. But they do not proportionally contribute to the number of deaths in London because their stay there is only temporary. If they fall ill during this period, they return to their homes in the country, where their death is registered if they die. This circumstance affects the earlier ages still more and renders the London death-rates for these age groups completely valueless as indexes of the ill-effects of industry on health (p. 30).

The case of the type-setters is similar to that of the tailors. In addition to lack of ventilation, to poisoned air, etc., there is still night-work to be mentioned. Their regular working-time is 12 to 13 hours, sometimes 15 to 16.

> Great heat and foulness which begin when the gas-jets are lit. ... It not infrequently happens that fumes from a foundry, or foul odours from machinery or sinks, rise from the lower room, and aggravate the evils of the upper one. The heated air of the lower rooms always tends to heat the upper by warming the floor, and when the rooms are low, and the consumption of gas great, this is a serious evil, and one only surpassed in the case where the steam-boilers are placed in the lower room, and supply unwished-for heat to the whole house.... As a general expression, it may be stated that universally the ventilation is defective, and quite insufficient to remove the heat and the products of the combustion of gas in the evening and during the night, and that in many offices, and particularly in those made from dwelling-houses, the condition is most deplorable. ... And in some offices (especially those of weekly newspapers) there will be work—work too, in which boys between 12 and 16 years of age take equal part of or almost uninterrupted periods of two days and a night at a time;—while, in other printing-offices which lay themselves out for the doing of 'urgent' business, Sunday gives no relaxation to the workman, and his working-days become seven instead of six in every week. (pp. 26, 28)

The milliners and dress-makers have already attracted our attention in Book I (Kap. VIII, 3, S. 249/241) [English edition: Ch. X, 3, pp. 254-55.—*Ed.*] in respect to overwork. Their workshops are described in our report by Dr Ord. Even if better during the day, they become overheated, foul, and unhealthy during the hours in which gas is burned. Dr Ord found in 34 shops of the better sort that the average number of cubic feet per worker was as follows:

> ... In four cases more than 500, in four other cases from 400 to 500, ... in seven others from 200 to 250, in four others from 150 to 200, and in nine others only from 100 to 150. The largest of these allowances would but be scanty for continuous work, unless the space were thoroughly well ventilated; and, except with extraordinary ventilation, its atmosphere could not be tolerably wholesome during gas light.

And here is Dr Ord's remark about one of the minor workshops which he visited, operated for the account of a middleman:

> One room area in cubical feet, 1,280; persons present, 14; area to each, in cubical feet, 91.5. The women here were weary-looking and squalid; their earnings were stated to be 7s. to 15s. a week, and their tea. ... Hours 8 a. m. to 8 p. m. The small room into which these 14 persons were crowded was ill-ventilated. There were two movable windows and a fire-place, but the latter was blocked up and there was no special ventilation of any kind. (p. 27)

The same report states with reference to the overwork of milliners and dress-makers:

> ... The overwork of the young women in fashionable dress-making establishments does not, for more than about four months of the year, prevail in that monstrous degree which has on many occasions excited momentary public surprise and indignation; but for the indoor hands during these months it will, as a rule, be of full 14 hours a day, and will, when there is pressure, be, for days together, of 17 or even 18 hours. At other times of the year the work of the indoor hands ranges probably from 10 to 14 hours; and uniformly the hours for outdoor hands are 12 or 13. For mantle-makers, collar-makers, shirt-makers, and various other classes of needleworkers (including persons who work at the sewing-machine) the hours spent in the common workroom are fewer—generally not more than 10 to 12 hours; but, says Dr Ord, the regular hours of work are subject to considerable extension in certain houses at certain times, by the practice of working extra hours for extra pay, and in other houses by the practice of taking work away from houses of business, to be done after hours at home, both practices being, it may be added, often compulsory. (p. 28)

John Simon remarks in a footnote to this page:

> Mr Radcliffe, ... the Honorary Secretary of the Epidemiological Society, ... happening to have unusual opportunities for questioning the young women employed in first-class houses of business ... has found that in only one out of twenty girls examined who called themselves 'quite well' could the state of health be pronounced good; the rest exhibiting in various degrees evidences of depressed physical power, nervous exhaustion, and numerous functional disorders thereupon dependent. He attributes these conditions in the first place to the length of the hours of work—the minimum of which he estimates at 12 hours a day out of the season; and secondarily to ... crowding and bad ventilation of workrooms, gas-vapours, insufficiency or bad quality of food, and inattention to domestic comfort.

The conclusion arrived at by the chief of the English Board of Health is that

> [I]t is practically impossible for workpeople to insist upon that which in theory is their first sanitary right—the right that whatever work their employer assembles them to do, shall, so far as depends upon him, be, at his cost, divested of all needlessly unwholesome circumstances; ... while workpeople are practically unable to exact that

> sanitary justice for themselves, they also (notwithstanding the presumed intentions of the law) cannot expect any effectual assistance from the appointed administrators of the Nuisances Removal Acts (p. 29). Doubtless there may be some small technical difficulty in defining the exact line at which employers shall become subject to regulation. But ... in principle, the sanitary claim is universal. And in the interest of myriads of labouring men and women, whose lives are now needlessly afflicted and shortened by the infinite physical suffering which their mere employment engenders, I would venture to express my hope, that universally the sanitary circumstances of labour may, at least so far, be brought within appropriate provisions of law, that the effective ventilation of all indoor workplaces may be ensured, and that in every naturally insalubrious occupation the specific health-endangering influence may as far as practicable be reduced. (p. 31)

Section III. *Economy in the Generation and Transmission of Power, and in Buildings*

In his October 1852 report L. Horner quotes a letter of the famous engineer James Nasmyth of Patricroft, the inventor of the steam-hammer, which, among other things, contains the following:

> ...The public are little aware of the vast increase in driving power which has been obtained by such changes of system and improvements (of steam-engines) as I allude to. The engine power of this district (Lancashire) lay under the incubus of timid and prejudiced traditions for nearly forty years, but now we are happily emancipated. During the last fifteen years, but more especially in the course of the last four years (since 1848), some very important changes have taken place in the system of working condensing steam-engines. ... The result ... has been to realise a much greater amount of duty or work performed by the identical engines, and that again at a very considerable reduction of the expenditure of fuel. ... For a great many years after the introduction of steam-power into the mills and manufactories of the above-named districts, the velocity of which, it was considered proper to work condensing steam-engines was about 220 feet per minute of the piston; that is to say, an engine with a 5-feet stroke was restricted by 'rule' to make 22 revolutions of the crankshaft per minute. Beyond this speed it was not considered prudent or desirable to work the engine; and as all the mill gearing ... were made suitable to this 220 feet per minute speed of piston, this slow and absurdly restricted velocity ruled the working of such engines for many years. However, at length, either through fortunate ignorance of the 'rule', or by better reasons on the part of some bold innovator, a greater speed was tried, and as the result was highly favourable, others followed the example, by, as it is termed, 'letting the engine away', namely, by so modifying the proportions of the first motion wheels of the mill gearing as to permit the engine to run at 300 feet and upwards per minute, while the mill gearing generally was kept at its former speed.... This 'letting the engine away'... has led to the almost universal 'speeding' of engines, because it was proved that not only was there available power gained from the identical engines, but also as the higher velocity of the engine yielded a greater momentum in the fly-wheel the motion was found to be much more regular.... We ... obtain more power from a steam-engine by simply permitting its piston to move at a higher velocity (pressure of steam and vacuum in the condenser remaining the same).... Thus, for example, suppose any given engine yields 40 horse-power when its piston is travelling at 200 feet per minute, if by suitable arrangement or modification we can permit this same engine to run at such a speed as that its piston will travel through space at 400 feet per minute (pressure of steam and vacuum, as before said, remaining the same), we shall then have just double the power ... and as the pressure by steam

and vacuum is the same in both cases, the strain upon the parts of this engine will be no greater at 400 than at 200 feet speed of piston, so that the risk of 'break-down' does not materially increase with the increase of speed. All the difference is, that we shall in such case consume steam at a rate proportional to the speed of piston, or nearly so; and there will he some small increase in the wear and tear of 'the brasses' or rubbing-parts, but so slight as to be scarcely worth notice.... But in order to obtain increase of power from the same engine by permitting its piston to travel at a higher velocity it is requisite ... to bum more coal per hour under the same boiler, or employ boilers of greater evaporating capabilities, i.e., greater steam-generating powers. This accordingly was done, and boilers of greater steam-generating or water-evaporating powers were supplied to the old 'speeded' engines, and in many cases near 100 per cent more work was got out of the identical engines by means of such changes as above named. About ten years ago the extraordinary economical production of power as realised by the engines employed in the mining operations of Cornwall began to attract attention; and as competition in the spinning trade forced manufacturers to look to 'savings' as the chief source of profits, the remarkable difference in the consumption of coal per horsepower per hour, as indicated by the performance of the Cornish engines, as also the extraordinary economical performance of Woolf's double-cylinder engines, began to attract increased attention to the subject of economy of fuel in this district, and as the Cornish and double-cylinder engines gave a horse-power for every 3½ to 4 lbs of coal per hour, while the generality of cotton-mill engines were consuming 8 or 12 pounds per horse per hour, so remarkable a difference induced mill-owners and engine-makers in this district to endeavour to realise, by the adoption of similar means, such extraordinary economical results as were proved to be common in Cornwall and France, where the high price of coal had compelled manufacturers to look more sharply to such costly departments of their establishments. The result of this increased attention to economy of fuel has been most important in many respects. In the first place, many boilers, the half of whose surface had been in the good old times of high profits left exposed quite naked to the cold air, began to get covered with thick blankets of felt, and brick and plaster, and other modes and means whereby to prevent the escape of that heat from their exposed surface which had cost so much fuel to maintain. Steam-pipes began to be 'protected' in the same manner, and the outside of the cylinder of the engine felted and cased in with wood in like manner. Next came the use of 'high steam', namely, instead of having the safety-valve loaded so as to blow off at 4, 6, or 8 lbs to the square inch, it was found that by raising the pressure to 14 or 20 lbs ... a very decided economy of fuel resulted; in other words, the work of the mill was performed by a very notable reduced consumption of coals, ... and those who had the means and the boldness carried the increased pressure and 'expansion system' of working to the full extent, by employing properly constructed boilers to supply steam of 30, 40, 50, 60, and 70 lbs to the square inch; pressures which would have frightened an engineer of the old school out of his wits. But as the economic results of so increasing the pressure of steam... soon appeared in most unmistakable £ s. d. forms, the use of high-pressure steam-boilers for working condensing engines became almost general. And those who desired to go to the full extent ... soon adopted the employment of the Woolf engine in its full integrity, and most of our mills lately built are worked by the Woolf engines, namely, those on which there are two cylinders to each engine, in one of which the high-pressure steam from the boiler exerts or yields power by its excess of pressure over that of the atmosphere, which, instead of the said high-pressure steam being let pass off at the end of each stroke free into the atmosphere, is caused to pass into a low-pressure cylinder of about four times the area of the former, and after due expansion passes to the condenser, the economic result obtained from engines of this class is such that the consumption of fuel is at the

> rate of from 3½ to 4 lbs. of coal per horse per hour; while in the engines of the old system the consumption used to be on the average from 12 to 14 lbs. per horse per hour. By an ingenious arrangement, the Woolf system of double cylinder or combined low- and high-pressure engine has been introduced extensively to already existing engines, whereby their performance has been increased both as to power and economy of fuel. The same result ... has been in use these eight or ten years, by having a high-pressure engine so connected with a condensing engine as to enable the waste steam of the former to pass on to and work the latter. This system is in many cases very convenient.
>
> 'It would not be very easy to get an exact return as to the increase of performance or work done by the identical engines to which some or all of these improvements have been applied; I am confident, however, ... that from the same weight of steam-engine machinery we are now obtaining at least 50 per cent more duty or work performed on the average, and that in many cases, the identical steam-engines which in the days of the restricted speed of 220 feet per minute yielded 50 horse-power, are now yielding upwards of 100. The very economical results derived from the employment of high-pressure steam in working condensing steam-engines, together with the much higher power required by mill extensions from the same engines, has within the last three years led to the adoption of tubular boilers, yielding a much more economical result than those formerly employed in generating steam for mill engines. (Reports of Insp. of Fact., October 1852, pp. 23-27.)

What applies to power generation also applies to power transmission and working machinery.

> The rapid strides with which improvement in machinery has advanced within these few years have enabled manufacturers to increase production without additional moving power. The more economical application of labour has been rendered necessary by the diminished length of the working-day, and in most well-regulated mills an intelligent mind is always considering in what manner production can be increased with decreased expenditure. I have before me a statement, kindly prepared by a very intelligent gentleman in my district, showing the number of hands employed, their ages, the machines at work, and the wages paid from 1840 to the present time. In October 1840, his firm employed 600 hands, of whom 200 were under 13 years of age. In October last, 350 hands were employed, of whom 60 only were under 13; the same number of machines, within very few, were at work, and the same sum in wages was paid at both periods. (Redgrave's Report in Reports of Insp. of Fact., Oct. 1852, pp. 58-59.)

These improvements of the machinery do not show their full effect until they are used in new, appropriately arranged factories.

> As regards the improvement made in machinery, I may say in the first place that a great advance has been made in the construction of mills adapted to receive improved machinery.... In the bottom room I double all my yarn, and upon that single floor I shall put 29,000 doubling spindles. I effect a saving of labour in the room and shed of at least 10 per cent, not so much from any improvement in the principle of doubling yarn, but from a concentration of machinery under a single management; and I am enabled to drive the said number of spindles by one single shaft, a saving in shafting, compared with what other firms have to use to work the same number of spindles, of 60 per cent, in some cases 80 per cent. There is a large saving in oil, and shafting, and in grease.... With superior mill arrangements and improved machinery, at the lowest estimate I have effected a saving in labour of 10 per cent, a great saving in power, coal, oil, tallow, shafting and strapping. (Evidence of a cotton spinner, Reports of Insp. of Fact., Oct. 1863, pp. 109, 110.)

The capitalist mode of production extends the utilisation of the excretions of production and consumption. By the former, we mean the waste of industry and agriculture, slid by the latter partly the excretions produced by the natural exchange of matter in the human body and partly the form of objects that remains after their consumption. In the chemical industry, for instance, excretions of production are such by-products as are wasted in production on a smaller scale; iron filings accumulating in the manufacture of machinery and returning into the production of iron as raw material, etc. Excretions of consumption are the natural waste matter discharged by the human body, remains of clothing in the form of rags, etc. Excretions of consumption are of the greatest importance for agriculture. So far as their utilisation is concerned, there is an enormous waste of them in the capitalist economy. In London, for instance, they find no better use for the excretion of four and a half million human beings than to contaminate the Thames with it at heavy expense.

Rising prices of raw materials naturally stimulate the utilisation of waste products.

The general requirements for the re-employment of these excretions are: large quantities of such waste, such as are available only in large-scale production; improved machinery whereby materials, formerly useless in their prevailing form, are put into a state fit for new production; scientific progress, particularly of chemistry, which reveals the useful properties of such waste. It is true that great savings of this sort are also observed in small-scale agriculture, as prevails in, say, Lombardy, southern China, and Japan. But on the whole, the productivity of agriculture under this system obtains from the prodigal use of human labour-power, which is withheld from other spheres of production.

The so-called waste plays an important role in almost every industry. Thus, the Factory Report for December 1863 mentions as one of the principal reasons why the English and many of the Irish farmers do not like to grow flax, or do so but rarely,

> [T]he great waste ... which has taken place at the little water scutch mills ... the waste in cotton is comparatively small, but in flax very large. The efficiency of water steeping and of good machine scutching will reduce this disadvantage very considerably.... Flax, scutched in Ireland in a most shameful way, and a large percentage actually lost by it, equal to 28 or 30 percent. (Reports of Insp. of Fact., Dec. 1863, pp. 139, 142)

whereas all this might be avoided through the use of better machinery. So much tow fell by the wayside that the factory inspector reports:

> I have been informed with regard to some of the scutch mills in Ireland, that the waste made at them has often been used by the scutchers to burn on their fires at home, and yet it is very valuable. (p. 140 of the above report)

We shall speak of cotton waste later, when we deal with the price fluctuations of raw materials.

The wool industry was shrewder than the flax manufacturers.

> It was once the common practice to decry the preparation of waste and woollen rags for re-manufacture, but the prejudice has entirely subsided as regards the shoddy trade, which has become an important branch of the woollen trade of Yorkshire, and doubtless the cotton waste trade will be recognised in the same manner as supplying an admitted want. Thirty years since, woollen rags, i.e., pieces of cloth, old clothes, etc., of nothing but wool, would average about £4 4s. per ton in price: within the last few years they have become worth £44 per ton, and the demand for them has so increased that means have been found for utilising the rags of fabrics of cotton and wool mixed by destroying the cotton and leaving the wool intact, and now thousands of operatives are engaged in the manufacture of shoddy, from which the consumer has greatly benefited

in being able to purchase cloth of a fair and average quality at a very moderate price. (Reports of Insp. of Fact., Oct. 1863, p. 107.)

By the end of 1862 the rejuvenated shoddy made up as much as one-third of the entire consumption of wool in English industry. (Reports of Insp. of Fact., October 1862, p. 81.) The 'big benefit' for the 'consumer' is that his shoddy clothes wear out in just one-third of the previous time and turn threadbare in one-sixth of this time.

The English silk industry moved along the same downward path. The consumption of genuine raw silk decreased somewhat between 1839 and 1862, while that of silk waste doubled. Improved machinery helped to manufacture a silk useful for many purposes from this otherwise rather worthless stuff.

The most striking example of utilising waste is furnished by the chemical industry. It utilises not only its own waste, for which it finds new uses, but also that of many other industries. For instance, it converts the formerly almost useless gas-tar into aniline dyes, alizarin, and, more recently, even into drugs.

This economy of the excretions of production through their re-employment is to be distinguished from economy through the prevention of waste, that is to say, the reduction of excretions of production to a minimum, and the immediate utilisation to a maximum of all raw and auxiliary materials required in production.

Reduction of waste depends in part on the quality of the machinery in use. Economy in oil, soap, etc., depends on how well the mechanical parts are machined and polished. This refers to the auxiliary materials. In part, however, and this is most important, it depends on the quality of the employed machines and tools whether a larger or smaller portion of the raw material is turned into waste in the production process. Finally, this depends on the quality of the raw material itself. This, in turn, depends partly on the development of the extractive industry and agriculture which produce the raw material (strictly speaking on the progress of civilisation), and partly on the improvement of processes through which raw materials pass before they enter into manufacture.

> Parmentier has demonstrated that the art of grinding grain has improved very materially in France since a none too distant epoch, for instance the time of Louis XIV, so that the new mills, compared to the old, can make up to half as much more bread from the same amount of grain. The annual consumption of a Parisian, indeed, has first been estimated at 4 *setiers* of grain, then at 3, finally at 2, while nowadays it is only 1⅓ *setiers*, or about 342 lbs per capita.... In the Perche, where I have lived for a long time, the crude mills of granite and trap rock millstones have been mostly rebuilt according to the rules of mechanics which has made such rapid progress in the last 30 years. They have been provided with good millstones from La Ferté, have ground the grain twice, the milling sack has been given a circular motion, and the output of flour from the same amount of grain has increased 1/6. The enormous discrepancy between the daily grain consumption of the Romans and ourselves is therefore easily explained. It is due simply to imperfect methods of milling and bread-making. This is the way I feel I must explain a remarkable observation made by Pliny, XVIII, Ch. 20, 2: ..., 'The flour was sold in Rome, depending on its quality, at 40, 48 or 96 *as* per modius. These prices, so high in proportion to the contemporaneous grain prices, are due to the imperfect state of the mills of that period, which were still in their infancy, and the resultant heavy cost of milling.' (Dureau de la Malle, *Économie Politique des Romains*, Paris, 1840, I, pp. 280-81.)

These savings in the application of fixed capital are, we repeat, due to the employment of the conditions of labour on a large scale; in short, are due to the fact that these serve as conditions of directly social, or socialised labour or direct co-operation within the process of production. On the one hand, this is the indispensable requirement for the utilisation of mechanical and chemical inventions without increasing the price of the commodity, and this is always the *conditio sine qua non*. On the other hand, only production on a large scale permits the savings derived from co-operative productive consumption. Finally, it is only the experience of the combined labourer which discovers and reveals the where and how of saving, the simplest methods of applying the discoveries, and the ways to overcome the practical frictions arising from carrying out the theory—in its application to the production process—etc.

Incidentally, a distinction should be made between universal labour and co-operative labour. Both kinds play their role in the process of production; both flow one into the other, but both are also differentiated. Universal labour is all scientific labour, all discovery and all invention. This labour depends partly on the co-operation of the living, and partly on the utilisation of the labours of those who have gone before. Co-operative labour, on the other hand, is the direct co-operation of individuals.

The foregoing is corroborated by frequent observation, to wit:

1. The great difference in the cost of the first model of a new machine and that of its reproduction (regarding which, see Ure [*The Philosophy of Manufactures*, Second edition, London, 1855.—*Ed.*] and Babbage [*On the Economy of Machinery and Manufactures*, London, 1832, pp. 280-81.—*Ed.*]).
2. The far greater cost of operating an establishment based on a new invention as compared to later establishments arising *ex suis ossibus*. This is so very true that the trail-blazers generally go bankrupt, and only those who later buy the buildings, machinery, etc., at a cheaper price, make money out of it. It is, therefore, generally the most worthless and miserable sort of money-capitalists who draw the greatest profit out of all new developments of the universal labour of the human spirit and their social application through combined labour.

Notes

1. 'Since in all factories there is a very large amount of fixed capital in buildings and machinery, the greater the number of hours that machinery can be kept at work the greater will be the return.' (Reports of Insp. of Fact., 31st October, 1858, p. 8.)
2. Cf. Ure on the progress in factory construction.

6

The Effect of Price Fluctuation

Section I. *Fluctuations in the Price of Raw Materials, and their Direct Effects on the Rate of Profit*

The assumption in this case, as in previous ones, is that no change takes place in the rate of surplus-value. It is necessary to analyse the case in its pure form. However, it might be possible for a specific capital, whose rate of surplus-value remains unchanged, to employ an increasing or decreasing number of labourers, in consequence of contraction or expansion caused by such fluctuations in the price of raw materials as we are to analyse here. In that case, the quantity of surplus-value might vary, while the rate of surplus-value remains the same. Yet this should also be disregarded here as a side-issue. If improvements of machinery and changes in the price of raw materials simultaneously influence either the number of labourers employed by a definite capital, or the level of wages, one has but to put together 1) the effect caused by the variations of constant capital on the rate of profit, and 2) the effect caused by variations in wages on the rate of profit. The result is then obtained of itself.

But in general, it should be noted here, as in the previous case, that if variations take place, either due to savings in constant capital, or due to fluctuations in the price of raw materials, they always affect the rate of profit, even if they leave the wage, hence the rate and amount of surplus-value, untouched. They change the magnitude of C in s' (v/C) and thus the value of the whole fraction. It is therefore immaterial, in this case as well—in contrast to what we found in our analysis of surplus-value—in which sphere of production these variations occur; whether or not the production branches affected by them produce necessities for labourers, or constant capital for the production of such necessities. The deductions made here are equally valid for variations occurring in the production of luxury articles, and by luxury articles we here mean all production that does not serve the reproduction of labour-power.

The raw materials here include auxiliary materials as well, such as indigo, coal, gas, etc. Furthermore, so far as machinery is concerned under this head, its own raw material consists of iron, wood, leather, etc. Its own price is therefore affected by fluctuations in the price of raw materials used in its construction. To the extent that its price is raised through fluctuations, either in the price of the raw materials of which it consists, or of the auxiliary materials consumed in its operation, the rate of profit falls *pro tanto*. And vice versa.

In the following analysis, we shall confine ourselves to fluctuations in the price of raw materials, not so far as they go to make up the raw materials of machinery serving as means of labour or as auxiliary materials applied in its operation, but in so far as they enter the process in which commodities are produced. There is just one thing to be noted here: the natural wealth in iron, coal, wood, etc., which are the principal elements used in the construction and operation of machinery, presents itself here as a natural fertility of capital and is a factor determining the rate of profit irrespective of the high or low level of wages.

Since the rate of profit is s/C, or s/(c + v), it is evident that every thing causing a variation in the magnitude of c, and thereby of C, must also bring about a variation in the rate of profit, even if s and v, and their mutual relation, remain unaltered. Now, raw materials are one of the principal components of constant capital. Even in industries which consume no actual raw materials, these enter the picture as auxiliary materials or components of machinery, etc., and their price fluctuations thus accordingly influence the rate of profit. Should the price of raw material fall by an amount = d, then s/C, or s/(c + v) becomes s/(C - d), or s/((c - d) + v). Thus, the rate of profit rises. Conversely, if the price of raw material rises, then s/C, or s/(c + v), becomes s/(C + d), or s/((c + d) + v), and the rate of profit falls. Other conditions being equal, the rate of profit, therefore, falls and rises inversely to the price of raw material. This shows, among other things, how important the low price of raw material is for industrial countries, even if fluctuations in the price of raw materials are not accompanied by variations in the sales sphere of the product, and thus quite aside from the relation of demand to supply. It follows furthermore that foreign trade influences the rate of profit, regardless of its influence on wages through the cheapening of the necessities of life. The point is that it affects the prices of raw or auxiliary materials consumed in industry and agriculture. It is due to an as yet imperfect understanding of the nature of the rate of profit and of its specific difference from the rate of surplus-value that, on the one hand, economists (like Torrens [R. Torrens, *An Essay on the Production of Wealth*, London, 1821, p. 28 et seq.—*Ed.*]) wrongly explain the marked influence of the prices of raw material on the rate of profit, which they note through practical experience, and that, on the other, economists like Ricardo [D. Ricardo, *On the Principles of Political Economy, and Taxation*, Third edition, London, 1821, pp. 131-138.—*Ed.*], who cling to general principles, do not recognise the influence of, say, world trade on the rate of profit.

This makes clear the great importance to industry of this elimination or reduction of customs duties on raw materials. The rational development of the protective tariff system made the utmost reduction of import duties on raw materials one of its cardinal principles. This, and the abolition of the duty on corn, was the main object of the English free-traders, who were primarily concerned with having the duty on cotton lifted as well.

The use of flour in the cotton industry may serve as an illustration of the importance of a price reduction for an article which is not strictly a raw material but an auxiliary and at the same time, one of the principal elements of nourishment. As far back as 1837, R. H. Greg[1] calculated that the 100,000 power-looms and 250,000 hand-looms then operating in the cotton-mills of Great Britain annually consumed 41 million lbs of flour to smooth the warp. He added a third of this quantity for bleaching and other processes, and estimated the total annual value of the flour so consumed at £342,000 for the preceding ten years. A comparison with flour prices on the continent showed that the higher flour price forced upon manufacturers by corn tariffs alone amounted to £170,000 per year. Greg estimated the sum at a minimum of £200,000 for 1837 and cited a firm for which the flour price difference amounted to £1,000 annually. As a result,

> great manufacturers, thoughtful, calculating men of business, have said that ten hours' labour would be quite sufficient, if the Corn Laws were repealed. (Reports of Insp. of Fact., Oct. 1848, p. 98.)

The Corn Laws were repealed. So were the duties on cotton and other raw materials. But no sooner had this been accomplished than the opposition of the manufacturers to the Ten Hours' Bill became more violent than ever. And when the ten-hour factory day nevertheless became a law soon after, the first result was a general attempt to reduce wages.

The value of raw and auxiliary materials passes entirely and all at one time into the value of the product in the manufacture of which they are consumed, while the elements of fixed capital transfer their value to the product only gradually in proportion to their wear and tear. It follows that the price of the product is influenced far more by the price of raw materials than by that of fixed capital, although the rate of profit is determined by the total value of the capital applied no matter how much of it is consumed in the making of the product. But it is evident—although we merely mention it in passing, since we here still assume that commodities are sold at their values, so that price fluctuations caused by competition do not as yet concern us—that the expansion or contraction of the market depends on the price of the individual commodity and is inversely proportional to the rise or fall of this price. It actually develops, therefore, that the price of the product does not rise in proportion to that of the raw material, and that it does not fall in proportion to that of raw material. Consequently, the rate of profit falls lower in one instance, and rises higher in the other than would have been the case if products were sold at their value.

Further, the quantity and value of the employed machinery grows with the development of labour productivity but not in the same proportion as this productivity, i.e., not in the proportion in which this machinery increases its output. In those branches of industry, therefore, which do consume raw materials, i.e., in which the subject of labour is itself a product of previous labour, the growing productivity of labour is expressed precisely in the proportion in which a larger quantity of raw material absorbs a definite quantity of labour, hence in the increasing amount of raw material converted in, say, one hour into products, or processed into commodities. The value of raw material, therefore, forms an ever-growing component of the value of the commodity-product in proportion to the development of the productivity of labour, not only because it passes wholly into this latter value, but also because in every aliquot part of the aggregate product the portion representing depreciation of machinery and the portion formed by the newly added labour—both continually decrease. Owing to this falling tendency, the other portion of the value representing raw material increases proportionally, unless this increase is counterbalanced by a proportionate decrease in the value of the raw material arising from the growing productivity of the labour employed in its own production.

Further, raw and auxiliary materials, just like wages, form parts of the circulating capital and must, therefore, be continually replaced in their entirety through the sale of the product, while only the depreciation is to be renewed in the case of machinery, and first of all in the form of a reserve fund. It is, moreover, in no way essential for each individual sale to contribute its share to this reserve fund, so long as the total annual sales contribute their annual share. This shows again how a rise in the price of raw material can curtail or arrest the entire process of reproduction if the price realised by the sale of the commodities should not suffice to replace all the elements of these commodities. Or, it may make it impossible to continue the process on the scale required by its technical basis, so that only a part of the machinery will remain in operation, or all the machinery will work for only a fraction of the usual time.

Finally, the expense incurred through waste varies in direct proportion to the price fluctuations of the raw material, rising, when they rise and falling when they fall. But there is a limit here as well. The Factory Report for April 1850 maintained:

> One source of considerable loss arising from an advance in the price of the raw material would hardly occur to any one but a practical spinner, viz., that from waste. I am informed that when cotton advances, the cost to the spinner, of the lower qualities especially, is increased in a ratio beyond the advance actually paid, because the waste made in spinning coarse yarns is fully 15 per cent; and this rate, while it causes a loss of ½d. per lb. on cotton at 3½d. per lb., brings up the loss to 1d. per lb. when cotton advances to 7d. (Reports of Insp. of Fact., April 1850, p. 17.)

But when, as a result of the American Civil War, the price of cotton rose to a level unequalled in almost 100 years, the report read differently:

> The price now given for waste, and its re-introduction in the factory in the shape of cotton waste, go some way to compensate for the difference in the loss by waste, between Surat cotton and American cotton, about 12½ per cent.
>
> The waste in working Surat cotton being 25 per cent, the cost of the cotton to the spinner is enhanced one-fourth before he has manufactured it. The loss by waste used not to be of much moment when American cotton was 5d. or 6d. per lb., for it did not exceed ¾d. per lb., but it is now of great importance when upon every lb. of cotton which costs 2s. there is a loss by waste equal to 6d.[2] (Reports of Insp. of Fact., Oct. 1863, p. 106.)

Section II. *Appreciation, Depreciation, Release and Tie-Up of Capital*

The phenomena analysed in this chapter require for their full development the credit system and competition on the world-market, the latter being the basis and the vital element of capitalist production. These more definite forms of capitalist production can only be comprehensively presented, however, after the general nature of capital is understood. Furthermore, they do not come within the scope of this work and belong to its eventual continuation. Nevertheless, the phenomena listed in the above title may be discussed in a general way at this stage. They are interrelated, first with one another and, secondly, also with the rate and amount of profit. They are to be briefly discussed here if only because they create the impression that not only the rate, but also the amount of profit—which is actually identical with the amount of surplus-value—could increase or decrease independently of the movements of the quantity or rate of surplus-value.

Are we to consider release and tie-up of capital, on the one hand, and its appreciation and depreciation, on the other, as different phenomena?

The question is, what we mean by release and tie-up of capital? Appreciation and depreciation are self-explanatory. All they mean is that a given capital increases or decreases in value as a result of certain general economic conditions, for we are not discussing the particular fate of an individual capital. All they mean, therefore, is that the value of a capital invested in production rises or falls, irrespective of its self-expansion by virtue of the surplus-labour employed by it.

By tie-up of capital, we mean that certain portions of the total value of the product must be reconverted into elements of constant and variable capital if production is to proceed on the same scale. By release of capital we mean that a portion of the total value of the product which had to be reconverted into constant or variable capital up to a certain time, becomes disposable and superfluous, should production continue on the previous scale. This release or tie-up of capital is different from the release or tie-up of revenue. If the annual surplus-value of an individual capital C is, let us say, equal to x, then a reduction in the price of commodities consumed by the capitalists would make x—a sufficient to procure the same enjoyments, etc., as before. A portion of the revenue = a is released, therefore, and may serve either to increase consumption or to be reconverted into capital (for the purpose of accumulation). Conversely, if x + a is needed to continue to live as before, then this standard of living must either be reduced or a portion of the previously accumulated income = a, expended as revenue.

Appreciation and depreciation may affect either constant or variable capital, or both, and in the case of constant capital, it may, in turn, affect either the fixed, or the circulating portion, or both.

Under constant capital, we must consider the raw and auxiliary materials, including semi-finished products, all of which we here include under the term of raw materials, machinery, and other fixed capital.

In the preceding analysis we referred especially to variations in the price, or the value, of raw materials in respect to their influence on the rate of profit, and determined the general law that with other conditions being equal, the rate of profit is inversely proportional to the value of the raw materials. This is absolutely true for capital newly invested in a business enterprise, in which the investment, i.e., the conversion of money into productive capital, is only just taking place.

But aside from this capital, which is being newly invested, a large portion of the already functioning capital is in the sphere of circulation, while another portion is in the sphere of production. One portion is in the market in the shape of commodities waiting to be converted into money; another is on hand as money, in whatever form, waiting to be reconverted into elements of production; finally, a third portion is in the sphere of production, partly in its original form of means of production such as raw and auxiliary materials, semi-finished products purchased in the market, machinery and other fixed capital, and partly in the form of products which are in the process of manufacture. The effect of appreciation or depreciation depends here to a great extent on the relative proportion of these component parts. Let us, for the sake of simplicity, leave aside all fixed capital and consider only that portion of constant capital which consists of raw and auxiliary materials, and semi-finished products, and both finished commodities in the market and commodities still in the process of production.

If the price of raw material, for instance of cotton, rises, then the price of cotton goods—both semi-finished goods like yarn and finished goods like cotton fabrics—manufactured while cotton was cheaper, rises also. So does the value of the unprocessed cotton held in stock, and of the cotton in the process of manufacture. The latter because it comes to represent more labour-time in retrospect and thus adds more than its original value to the product which it enters, and more than the capitalist paid for it.

Hence, if the price of raw materials rises, and there is a considerable quantity of available finished commodities in the market, no matter what the stage of their manufacture, the value of these commodities rises, thereby enhancing the value of the existing capital. The same is true for the supply of raw materials, etc., in the hands of the producer. This appreciation of value may compensate, or more than compensate, the individual capitalist, or even an entire separate sphere of capitalist production, for the drop in the rate of profit attending a rise in the price of raw materials. Without entering into the detailed effects of competition, we might state for the sake of thoroughness that 1) if available, supplies of raw material are considerable, they tend to counteract the price increase which occurred at the place of their origin; 2) if the semi-finished and finished goods press very heavily upon the market, their price is thereby prevented from rising proportionately to the price of their raw materials.

The reverse takes place when the price of raw material falls. Other circumstances remaining the same, this increases the rate of profit. The commodities in the market, the articles in the process of production, and the available supplies of raw material, depreciate in value and thereby counteract the attendant rise in the rate of profit.

The effect of price variations for raw materials is the more pronounced, the smaller the supplies available in the sphere of production and in the market at, say, the close of a business year, i.e., after the harvest in agriculture, when great quantities of raw materials are delivered anew.

We proceed in this entire analysis from the assumption that the rise or fall in prices expresses actual fluctuations in value. But since we are here concerned with the effects such price variations have on the rate of profit, it matters little what is at the bottom of them. The present statements apply equally if prices rise or fall under the influence of the credit system, competition, etc., and not on account of fluctuations in value.

Since the rate of profit equals the ratio of the excess over the value of the product to the value of the total capital advanced, a rise caused in the rate of profit by a depreciation of the advanced capital would be associated with a loss in the value of capital. Similarly, a drop caused in the rate of profit by an appreciation of the advanced capital might possibly be associated with a gain.

As for the other portion of constant capital, such as machinery and fixed capital in general, the appreciation of value taking place in it with respect mainly to buildings, real estate, etc., cannot be discussed without the theory of ground-rent, and does not, therefore, belong in this chapter. But of a general importance to the question of depreciation are:

The continual improvements which lower the use-value, and therefore the value, of existing machinery, factory buildings, etc. This process has a particularly dire effect during the first period of newly introduced machinery, before it attains a certain stage of maturity, when it continually becomes antiquated before it has time to reproduce its own value. This is one of the reasons for the flagrant prolongation of the working-time usual in such periods, for alternating day and night-shifts, so that the value of the machinery may be reproduced in a shorter time without having to place the figures for wear and tear too high. If, on the other hand, the short period in which the machinery is effective (its short life vis-à-vis the anticipated improvements) is not compensated in this manner, it gives up so much of its value to the product through moral depreciation that it cannot compete even with hand-labour.[3]

After machinery, equipment of buildings, and fixed capital in general, attain a certain maturity, so that they remain unaltered for some length of time, at least in their basic construction, there arises a similar depreciation due to improvements in the methods of reproducing this fixed capital. The value of the machinery, etc., falls in this case not so much because the machinery is rapidly crowded out and depreciated to a certain degree by new and more productive machinery, etc., but because it can be reproduced more cheaply. This is one of the reasons why large enterprises frequently do not flourish until they pass into other hands, i.e., after their first proprietors have been bankrupted, and their successors, who buy them cheaply, therefore begin from the outset with a smaller outlay of capital.

It leaps to the eye, particularly in the case of agriculture, that the causes which raise or lower the price of a product, also raise or lower the value of capital, since the latter consists to a large degree of this product, whether as grain, cattle, etc. (Ricardo [D. Ricardo, *On the Principles of Political Economy, and Taxation*, Third edition, London, 1821, Chapter II.—*Ed.*]).

There is still variable capital to be considered.

Inasmuch as the value of labour-power rises because there is a rise in the value of the means of subsistence required for its reproduction, or falls because there is a reduction in their value—and the appreciation and depreciation of variable capital are really nothing more than expressions of these two cases—a drop in surplus-value corresponds to such appreciation and an increase in surplus-value to such depreciation, provided the length of the working-day remains the same. But other circumstances—the release and tie-up of capital—may also be associated with such cases, and since we have not analysed them so far, we shall briefly mention them now.

If wages fall in consequence of a depreciation in the value of labour-power (which may even be attended by a rise in the real price of labour), a portion of the capital hitherto invested in wages is released. Variable capital is set free. In the case of new investments of capital, this has simply the effect of its operating with a higher rate of surplus-value. It takes less money than before to set in motion the same amount of labour, and in this way, the unpaid portion of labour increases at the expense of the paid portion. But in the case of already invested capital, not only does the rate of surplus-value rise, but a portion of the capital previously invested in wages is also released. Until this time, it was tied up and formed a regular portion which had to be deducted from the proceeds for the product and advanced for wages, acting as variable capital if the business were to continue on its former scale. Now this portion is set free and may be used as a new investment, be it to extend the same business or to operate in some other sphere of production.

Let us assume, for instance, that £500 per week were required at first to employ 500 labourers, and that now only £400 are needed for the same purpose. If the quantity of value produced in either case = £1,000, the amount of weekly surplus-value in the first case = £500, and the rate of surplus-value 500/500 = 100%. But after the wage reduction, the quantity of surplus-value £1,000 - £400 = £600, and its rate 600/400 = 150%. And this increase in the rate of surplus-value is the only effect for one who starts a new enterprise in this sphere of production with a variable capital of £400 and a corresponding constant capital. But when this takes place in a business already in operation, the depreciation of the variable capital does not only increase the quantity of surplus-value from £500 to £600, and the rate of surplus-value from 100 to 150%, but releases £100 of the variable capital for the further exploitation of labour. Hence, the same amount of labour is exploited to greater advantage, and, what is more, the release of £100 makes it possible to exploit more labourers than before at the higher rate with the same variable capital of £500.

Now, the reverse situation. Suppose, with 500 employed labourers, the original proportion in which the product is divided = 400v + 600s = 1,000, making the rate of surplus-value = 150%. In that case, the labourer receives £4/5, or 16 shillings per week.

Should 500 labourers cost £500 per week, due to an appreciation of variable capital, each one of them will receive a weekly wage = £1, and £400 can employ only 400 labourers. If the same number of labourers as before is put to work, therefore, we have $500_v + 500_s = 1{,}000$. The rate of surplus-value would fall from 150 to 100%, which is ⅓. In the case of new capital, the only effect would be this lower rate of surplus-value. Other conditions being equal, the rate of profit would also have fallen accordingly, although not in the same proportion. For instance, if c = 2,000, we have in the one case $2{,}000_c + 400_v + 600_s = 3{,}000$. The rate of surplus-value = 150%, the rate of profit = 600/2,400 = 25%. In the second case, $2{,}000_c + 500_v + 500_s = 3{,}000$. The rate of surplus-value = 100%, the rate of profit = 500/2,500 = 20%. In the case of already invested capital, however, there would be a dual effect. Only 400 labourers could be employed with a £400 variable capital, and that at a rate of surplus-value of 100%. They would therefore produce an aggregate surplus-value of only £400. Furthermore, since a constant capital of £2,000 requires 500 labourers for its operation, 400 labourers can put into motion only a constant capital of £1,600. For production to continue on the same scale so that 1/5 of the machinery does not stand idle, £100 must be added to the variable capital in order to employ 500 labourers as before. And this can be accomplished only by tying up hitherto disposable capital, so that part of the accumulation intended to extend production serves merely to stop a gap, or a portion reserved for revenue is added to the old capital. Then a variable capital increased by £100 produces £100 less surplus-value. More capital is required to employ the same number of labourers, and at the same time, the surplus-value produced by each labourer is reduced.

The advantages resulting from a release and the disadvantages resulting from a tie-up of variable capital both exist only for capital already engaged and reproducing itself under certain given conditions. For newly invested capital the advantages on the one hand, and the disadvantages on the other, are confined to an increase or drop in the rate of surplus-value, and to a corresponding, if in no way proportionate, change in the rate of profit.

The release and tie-up of variable capital, just analysed, is the result of a depreciation or appreciation of the elements of variable capital, that is, of the cost of reproducing labour-power.

But variable capital could also be released if, with the wage rate unchanged, fewer labourers were required due to the development of labour productivity to set in motion the same amount of constant capital. In like manner, there may reversely be a tie-up of additional variable capital if more labourers are required for the same quantity of constant capital due to a drop in productivity. If, on the other hand, a portion of capital formerly employed as variable capital is employed in the form of constant capital, so that merely a different distribution exists between the components of the same capital, this has an influence on both the rate of surplus-value and the rate of profit, but does not belong under the heading of tie-up and release of capital, which is here being discussed.

We have already seen that constant capital may also be tied up or released by the appreciation or depreciation of its component elements. Aside from this, it can be tied up only if the productive power of labour increases (provided a portion of the variable is not converted into constant capital) so that the same amount of labour creates a greater product and therefore sets in motion a larger constant capital. The same may occur under certain circumstances if productivity decreases, for instance, in agriculture, so that the same quantity of labour requires more means of production, such as seeds or manure, drainage, etc., in order to produce the same output. Constant capital may be released without depreciation if improvements, utilisation of the forces of Nature, etc., enable a constant capital of smaller value to technically perform the same services as were formerly performed by a constant capital of greater value.

We have seen in Book II [English edition: Vol. II, Part III.—*Ed.*] that once commodities have been converted into money, or sold, a certain portion of this money must be reconverted into the material elements of constant capital, and in the proportions required by the technical nature of the particular sphere of production. In this respect, the most important element in all branches—aside from wages, i.e., variable capital—is raw material, including auxiliary material, which is particularly important in such lines of production as do not involve raw materials in the strict sense of the term, for instance in mining and the extractive industries in general. That portion of the price which is to make good the wear and tear of machinery enters the accounts chiefly nominally so long as the machinery is at all in an operating condition. It does not greatly matter whether it is paid for and replaced by money one day or the next or at any other stage of the period of turnover of the capital. It is quite different in the case of the raw material. If the price of raw material rises, it may be impossible to make it good fully out of the price of the commodities after wages are deducted. Violent price fluctuations, therefore, cause interruptions, great collisions, even catastrophes, in the process of reproduction. It is especially agricultural produce proper, i.e., raw materials taken from organic nature, which—leaving aside the credit system for the present—is subject to such fluctuations of value in consequence of changing yields, etc. Due to uncontrollable natural conditions, favourable or unfavourable seasons, etc., the same quantity of labour may be represented in very different quantities of use-values, and a definite quantity of these use-values may therefore have very different prices. If the value x is represented by 100 lbs of the commodity a, then the price of one lb. of a = x/100; if it is represented by 1,000 lbs of a, the price of one lb. of a = x/1,000, etc. This is, therefore, one of the elements of these fluctuations in the price of raw materials. A second element, mentioned at this point only for the sake of completeness—since competition and the credit system are still outside the scope of our analysis—is this: It is, in the nature of things that vegetable and animal substances whose growth and production are subject to certain organic laws and bound up with definite natural time periods, cannot be suddenly augmented in the same degree as, for instance, machines and other fixed capital, or coal, ore, etc., whose reproduction can, provided the natural conditions do not change, be rapidly accomplished in an industrially developed country. It is therefore quite possible, and under a developed system of capitalist production even inevitable, that the production and increase of the portion of constant capital consisting of fixed capital, machinery, etc., should considerably outstrip the portion consisting of organic raw materials, so that demand for the latter grows more rapidly than their supply, causing their price to rise. Rising prices actually cause 1) these raw materials to be shipped from greater distances, since the mounting prices suffice to cover greater freight rates; 2) an increase in their production, which circumstance, however, will probably not, for natural reasons, multiply the quantity of products until the following year; 3) the use of various previously unused substitutes and greater utilisation of waste. When this rise of prices begins to exert a marked influence on production and supply, it indicates in most cases that the turning point has been reached at which demand drops on account of the protracted rise in the price of the raw material and of all commodities of which it is an element, causing a reaction in the price of raw material. Aside from the convulsions which this causes in various forms through depreciation of capital, there are also other circumstances, which we shall mention shortly.

But so much is already evident from the foregoing: The greater the development of capitalist production, and, consequently, the greater the means of suddenly and permanently increasing that portion of constant capital consisting of machinery, etc., and the more rapid the accumulation (particularly in times of prosperity), so much greater the relative over-production of machinery and other fixed capital, so much more frequent the relative under-production of vegetable and animal raw materials, and so much more pronounced the previously described rise of their prices and the attendant reaction. And so much more frequent are the convulsions caused as they are by the violent price fluctuations of one of the main elements in the process of reproduction.

If, however, a collapse of these high prices occurs because their rise caused a drop in demand on the one hand, and, on the other, an expansion of production in one place and in another importation from remote and previously less resorted to, or entirely ignored, production areas, and, in both cases, a supply of raw materials exceeding the demand—particularly at the old high prices—then the result may be considered from different points of view. The sudden collapse of the price of raw materials checks their reproduction, and the monopoly of the original producing countries, which enjoy the most favourable conditions of production, is thereby restored—possibly with certain limitations, but restored nevertheless. True, due to the impetus it has had, reproduction of raw material proceeds on an extended scale, especially in those countries which more or less possess a monopoly of this production. But the basis on which production carries on after the extension of machinery, etc., and which, after some fluctuations, is to serve as the new normal basis, the new point of departure, is very much extended by the developments in the preceding cycle of turnover. In the meantime, the barely increased reproduction again experiences considerable impediments in some of the secondary sources of supply. For instance, it is easily demonstrated on the basis of the export tables that in the last thirty years (up to 1865), the production of cotton in India increases whenever there has been a drop in American production, and subsequently it drops again more or less permanently. During the period in which raw materials become dear, industrial capitalists join hands and form associations to regulate production. They did so after the rise of cotton prices in 1848 in Manchester, for example, and similarly in the case of flax production in Ireland. But as soon as the immediate impulse is over and the general principle of competition to 'buy in the cheapest market' (instead of stimulating production in the countries of origin, as the associations attempt to do, without regard to the immediate price at which these may happen at that time to be able to supply their product)—as soon as the principle of competition again reigns supreme, the regulation of the supply is left once again to 'prices'. All thought of a common, all-embracing and far-sighted control of the production of raw materials gives way once more to the faith that demand and supply will mutually regulate one another. And it must be admitted that such control is on the whole irreconcilable with the laws of capitalist production, and remains forever a pious wish, or is limited to exceptional co-operation in times of great stress and confusion.[4] The superstition of the capitalists in this respect is so deep that in their reports even factory inspectors, again and again, throw up their hands in astonishment. The alternation of good and bad years naturally also provides for cheaper raw materials. Aside from the direct effect this has on raising the demand, there is also the added stimulus of the previously mentioned influence on the rate of profit. The aforesaid process of production of raw materials being gradually overtaken by the production of machinery, etc., is then repeated on a larger scale. An actual improvement of raw materials satisfying not only the desired quantity, but also the quality desired, such as cotton from India of American quality, would require a prolonged, regularly growing and steady European demand (regardless of the economic conditions under which the Indian producer labours in his country). As it is, however, the sphere of production of raw materials is, by fits, first suddenly enlarged, and then again violently curtailed. All this, and the spirit of capitalist production in general, may be very well studied in the cotton shortage of 1861-65, further characterised as it was by the fact that a raw material, one of the principal elements of reproduction, was for a time entirely unavailable. To be sure, the price may also rise in the event of an abundant supply, provided the conditions for this abundance are more knotty. Or, there may be an actual shortage of raw material. It was this last situation which originally prevailed in the cotton crisis.

The closer we approach our own time in the history of production, the more regularly do we find, especially in the essential lines of industry, the ever-recurring alternation between relative appreciation and the subsequent resulting depreciation of raw materials obtained from organic nature. What we have just analysed will be illustrated by the following examples taken from reports of factory inspectors.

The moral of history, also to be deduced from other observations concerning agriculture, is that the capitalist system works against a rational agriculture, or that a rational agriculture is incompatible with the capitalist system (although the latter promotes technical improvements in agriculture) and needs either the hand of the small farmer living by his own labour or the control of associated producers.

Herewith follow the illustrations referred to above, taken from the English Factory Reports.

> The state of trade is better; but the cycle of good and bad times diminishes as machinery increases, and the changes from the one to the other happen oftener, as the demand for raw materials increases with it... At present, confidence is not only restored after the panic of 1857, but the panic itself seems to be almost forgotten. Whether this improvement will continue or not depends greatly upon the price of raw materials. There appear to me evidences already, that in some instances the maximum has been reached, beyond which their manufacture becomes gradually less and less profitable, till it ceases to be so altogether. If we take, for instance, the lucrative years in the worsted trade of 1849 and 1850, we see that the price of English combing wool stood at 1s. 1d., and of Australian at between 1s. 2d. and 1s. 5d. per lb., and that on the average of the ten years from 1841 to 1850, both inclusive, the average price of English wool never exceeded 1s. 2d. and of Australian wool 1s. 5d. per lb. But that in the commencement of the disastrous year of 1857, the price of Australian wool began with 1s. 11d., falling to 1s. 6d. in December, when the panic was at its height, but has gradually risen again to 1s. 9d. through 1858, at which it now stands; whilst that of English wool, commencing with 1s. 8d., and rising in April and September 1857 to 1s. 9d., falling in January 1858 to 1s. 2d., has since risen to 1s. 5d., which is 3d. per lb. higher than the average of the ten years to which I have referred... This shows, I think, one of three things—either that the bankruptcies which similar prices occasioned in 1857 are forgotten; or that there is barely the wool grown which the existing spindles are capable of consuming; or else, that the prices of manufactured articles are about to be permanently higher... And as in past experience I have seen spindles and looms multiply both in numbers and speed in an incredibly short space of time, and our exports of wool to France increase in an almost equal ratio, and as both at home and abroad the age of sheep seems to be getting less and less, owing to increasing populations and to what the agriculturalists call 'a quick return in stock', so I have often felt anxious for persons whom, without this knowledge, I have seen embarking skill and capital in undertakings, wholly reliant for their success on a product which can only be increased according to organic laws. ... The same state of supply and demand of all raw materials ... seems to account for many of the fluctuations in the cotton trade during past periods, as well as for the condition of the English wool market in the autumn of 1857, with its overwhelming consequences.[5] (R. Baker in Reports of Insp. of Fact., Oct. 1858, pp. 56-61.)

The halcyon days of the West-Riding worsted industry, of Yorkshire, were 1849-50. This industry employed 29,246 persons in 1838; 37,000 persons in 1843; 48,097 in 1845; and 74,891 in 1850. The same district had 2,768 mechanical looms in 1838; 11,458 in 1841; 16,870 in 1843; 19,121 in 1845 and 29,539 in 1850. (Reports of Insp. of Fact., 1850, p. 60.) This prosperity of the carded wool industry excited certain forebodings as early as October 1850. In his report for April 1851, Sub-Inspector Baker said in regard to Leeds and Bradford:

> The state of trade is, and has been for some time, very unsatisfactory. The worsted spinners are fast losing the profits of 1850, and, in the majority of cases, the manufacturers are not doing much good. I believe, at this moment, there is more

woollen machinery standing than I have almost ever known at one time, and the flax spinners are also turning off hands and stopping frames. The cycles of trade, in fact, in the textile fabrics, are now extremely uncertain, and I think we shall shortly find to be true ... that there is no comparison made between the producing power of the spindles, the quantity of raw material, and the growth of the population. (p. 52)

The same is true of the cotton industry. In the cited report for October 1858, we read:

> Since the hours of labour in factories have been fixed, the amounts of consumption, produce, and wages in all textile fabrics have been reduced to a rule of three. ... I quote from a recent lecture delivered by ... the present Mayor of Blackburn, Mr Baynes, on the cotton trade, who by such means has reduced the cotton statistics of his own neighbourhood to the closest approximation:
>
> > 'Each real and mechanical horse-power will drive 450 self-acting mule spindles with preparation, or 200 throstle spindles, or 15 looms for 40 inches cloth, with winding, warping, and sizing. Each horse-power in spinning will give employment to 2½ operatives, but in weaving to 10 persons, at wages averaging full 10s. 6d. a week to each person. ... The average counts of yarn spun and woven are from 30s. to 32s. twist, and 34s. to 36s. weft yarns; and taking the spinning production at 13 ounces per spindle per week, will give 824,700 lbs yarn spun per week, requiring 970,000 lbs or 2,300 bales of cotton, at a cost of £28,300... The total cotton consumed in this district (within a five-mile radius round Blackburn) per week is 1,530,000 lbs, or 3,650 bales, at a cost of £44,625... This is one-eighteenth of the whole cotton spinning of the United Kingdom, and one-sixth of the whole power-loom weaving.'
>
> Thus we see that, according to Mr Baynes's calculations, the total number of cotton spindles in the United Kingdom is 28,800,000, and supposing these to be always working full time, that the annual consumption of cotton ought to be 1,432,080,000 lbs. But as the import of cotton, less the export in 1856 and 1857, was only 1,022,576,832 lbs, there must necessarily be a deficiency of supply equal to 409,503,168 lbs. Mr Baynes, however, who has been good enough to communicate with me on this subject, thinks that an annual consumption of cotton based upon the quantity used in the Blackburn district would be liable to be overcharged, owing to the difference, not only in the counts spun, but in the excellence of the machinery. He estimates the total annual consumption of cotton in the United Kingdom at 1,000,000,000 lbs. But if he is right, and there really is an excess of supply equal to 22,576,832 lbs, supply and demand seem to be nearly balanced already, without taking into consideration those additional spindles and looms which Mr Baynes speaks of as getting ready for work in his own district, and, by parity of reasoning, probably in other districts also. (pp. 59, 60)

Section III. *General Illustration the Cotton Crisis of 1861-65*

Preliminary History. 1845-60

1845. The golden age of cotton industry. Price of cotton very low. L. Horner says on this point:

> For the last eight years I have not known so active a state of trade as has prevailed during the last summer and autumn, particularly in cotton spinning. Throughout the half-year I have been receiving notices every week of new investments of capital in factories, either in the form of new mills being built, of the few that were untenanted

finding occupiers, of enlargements of existing mills, of new engines of increased power, and of manufacturing machinery. (Reports of Insp. of Fact., Oct. 1845, p. 13.)

1846. The complaints begin:

> For a considerable time past I have heard from the occupiers of cotton mills very general complaints of the depressed state of their trade... for within the last six weeks several mills have begun to work short time, usually eight hours a day instead of twelve; this appears to be on the increase... There has been a great advance in the price of the raw material... there has been not only no advance in the manufactured articles, but ... prices are lower than they were before the rise in cotton began. From the great increase in the number of cotton mills within the last four years, there must have been, on the one hand, a greatly increased demand for the raw material, and, on the other, a greatly increased supply in the market of the manufactured articles; causes that must concurrently have operated against profits, supposing the supply of the raw material and the consumption of the manufactured article to have remained unaltered; but, of course, in the greater ratio by the late short supply of cotton, and the falling off in the demand for the manufactured articles in several markets, both home and foreign. (Reports of Insp. of Fact., Oct. 1846, p. 10.)

The rising demand for raw materials naturally went hand in hand with a market flooded with manufactures. By the way, the expansion of industry at that time and the subsequent stagnation were not confined to the cotton districts. The carded wool district of Bradford had only 318 factories in 1836 and 490 in 1846. These figures do not by any means express the actual growth of production, since the existing factories were also considerably enlarged. This was particularly true of the flax spinning-mills.

> All have contributed more or less, during the last ten years, to the overstocking of the market, to which a great part of the present stagnation of trade must be attributed... The depression... naturally results from such rapid increase of mills and machinery. (Reports of Insp. of Fact., Oct. 1846, p. 30.)

1847. In October, a money panic. Discount 8%. This was preceded by the debacle of the railway swindle and the East Indian speculation in accommodation bills. But:

> 'Mr Baker enters into very interesting details respecting the increased demand, in the last few years, for cotton, wool, and flax, owing to the great extension of these trades. He considers the increased demand for these raw materials, occurring, as it has, at a period when the produce has fallen much below an average supply, as almost sufficient, even without reference to the monetary derangement, to account for the present state of these branches. This opinion is fully confirmed, by my own observations, and conversation with persons well acquainted with trade. Those several branches were all in a very depressed state, while discounts were readily obtained at and under 5 per cent. The supply of raw silk has, on the contrary, been abundant, the prices moderate, and the trade, consequently, very active, till ... the last two or three weeks, when there is no doubt the monetary derangement has affected not only the persons actually engaged in the manufacture, but more extensively still, the manufacturers of fancy goods, who were great customers to the throwster. A reference to published returns shows that the cotton trade had increased nearly 27 per cent in the last three years. Cotton has consequently increased, in round numbers, from 4d. to 6d. per lb., while twist, in consequence of the increased supply, is yet only a fraction above its former price. The woollen trade began its increase in 1836, since which Yorkshire has increased its manufacture of this article 40 per cent, but Scotland exhibits a yet greater increase. The increase of the worsted trade is still larger. Calculations give a result of upwards of 74 per cent increase within the same period. The consumption

of raw wool has therefore been immense. Flax has increased since 1839 about 25 per cent in England, 22 per cent in Scotland, and nearly 90 per cent in Ireland[7]; the consequence of this, in connexion with bad crops, has been that the raw material has gone up £10 per ton, while the price of yarn has fallen 6d. a bundle.[6] (Reports of Insp. of Fact., Oct. 1847, pp. 30-31.)

1849. Since late in 1848 business revived.

> The price of flax which has been so low as to almost guarantee a reasonable profit under any future circumstances, has induced the manufacturers to carry on their work very steadily.... The woollen manufacturers were exceedingly busy for a while in the early part of the year.... I fear that consignments of woollen goods often take the place of real demand, and that periods of apparent prosperity, i.e., of full work, are not always periods of legitimate demand. In some months the worsted has been exceedingly good, in fact flourishing.... At the commencement of the period referred to, wool was exceedingly low; what was bought by the spinners was well bought, and no doubt in considerable quantities. When the price of wool rose with the spring wool sales, the spinner had the advantage, and the demand for manufactured goods becoming considerable and imperative, they kept it. (Reports of Insp. of Fact., April 1849, p. 42.)
>
> If we look at the variations in the state of trade, which have occurred in the manufacturing districts of the kingdom for a period now of between three and four years, I think we must admit the existence of a great disturbing cause somewhere ... but may not the immensely productive power of increased machinery have added another element to the same cause? (Reports of Insp. of Fact., April 1849, pp. 42, 43.)

In November 1848, and in May and summer of 1849, right up to October, business flourished.

> The worsted stuff of trade, of which Bradford and Halifax are the great hives of industry, has been the one most active; this trade has never before reached anything like the extent, to which it has now attained. Speculation, and uncertainty as to the probable supply of cotton wool, have ever had the effect of causing greater excitement, and more frequent alterations in the state of that branch of manufacture, than any other. There is ... at present an accumulation in stock of the coarser kinds of cotton goods, which creates anxiety on the part of the smaller spinners, and is already acting to their detriment, having caused several of them to work their mills short time. (Reports of Insp. of Fact., Oct. 1849, pp. 64-65.)

1850. April. Business continued brisk. The exception:

> The great depression in a part of the cotton trade ... attributable to the scarcity in the supply of the raw material more especially adapted to the branch engaged in spinning low numbers of cotton yarns, or manufacturing heavy cotton goods. A fear is entertained that the increased machinery built recently for the worsted trade, may be followed with a similar reaction. Mr Baker computes that in the year 1849 alone the worsted looms have increased their produce 40 per cent, and the spindles 25 or 30 per cent, and they are still increasing at the same rate. (Reports of Insp. of Fact., April 1850, p. 54.)

1850. October.

> The high price of raw cotton continues ... to cause a considerable depression in this branch of manufacture, especially in those descriptions of goods in which the raw material constitutes a considerable part of the cost of production.... The great advance in the price of raw silk has likewise caused a depression in many branches of that manufacture. (Reports. of Insp. of Fact., Oct. 1850, p. 14.)

And on pages 31 and 33 of the same report we learn that the Committee of the Royal Society for the Promotion and Improvement of the Growth of Flax in Ireland predicted that the high price of flax, together with the low level of prices for other agricultural products, ensured a considerable increase in flax production in the ensuing year.

1853. April. Great prosperity. L. Horner says in his report:

> At no period during the last seventeen years that I have been officially acquainted with the manufacturing districts in Lancashire have I known such general prosperity; the activity in every branch is extraordinary. (Reports of Insp. of Fact., April 1853, p. 19.)

1853. October. Depression in the cotton industry. 'Over-production.' (Reports of Insp. of Fact., Oct. 1853, p. 15.)

1854. April.

> The woollen trade, although not brisk, has given full employment to all the factories engaged upon that fabric, and a similar remark applies to the cotton factories. The worsted trade generally has been in an uncertain and unsatisfactory condition during the whole of the last half-year. The manufacture of flax and hemp are more likely to be seriously impeded, by reason of the diminished supplies of the raw materials from Russia due to the Crimean war. (Reports of Insp. of Fact., April 1854, p. 37.)

1859.

> 'The trade in the Scottish flax districts still continues depressed—the raw material being scarce, as well as high in price; and the inferior quality of the last year's crop in the Baltic, from whence come our principal supplies, will have an injurious effect on the trade of the district; jute, however, which is gradually superseding flax in many of the coarser fabrics, is neither unusually high in price, nor scarce in quantity ... about one-half of the machinery in Dundee is now employed in jute spinning.' (Reports of Insp. of Fact., April 1859, p. 19.)—'Owing to the high price of the raw material, flax spinning is still far from remunerating, and while all the other mills are going full time, there are several instances of the stoppage of flax machinery.... Jute spinning is ... in a rather more satisfactory state, owing to the recent decline in the price of material, which has now fallen to a very moderate point.' (Reports of Insp. of Fact., Oct. 1859, p. 20.)

1861-64. American Civil War. Cotton Famine. The Greatest Example of an Interruption in the Production Process through Scarcity and Dearness of Raw Material

1860. April.

> With respect to the state of trade, I am happy to be able to inform you that, notwithstanding the high price of raw material, all the textile manufactures, with the exception of silk, have been fairly busy during the past half-year.... In some of the cotton districts hands have been advertised for, and have migrated thither from Norfolk and other rural counties. There appears to be, in every branch of trade, a great scarcity of raw material. It is ... the want of it alone, which keeps us within bounds. In the cotton trade, the erection of new mills, the formation of new systems of extension, and the demand for hands, can scarcely, I think, have been at any time exceeded. Everywhere there are new movements in search of raw material. (Reports of Insp. of Fact., April 1860, p. 57.)

1860. October.

> The state of trade in the cotton, woollen, and flax districts as been good; indeed in Ireland, it is stated to have been 'very good' for now more than a year; and that it would have been still better, but for the high price of raw material. The flax spinners appear to be looking with more anxiety than ever to the opening out of India by railways, and

to the development of its agriculture, for a supply of flax which may be commensurate with their wants. (Reports of Insp. of Fact., Oct. 1860, p. 37.)

1861. April.

The state of trade is at present depressed.... A few cotton mills are running short time, and many silk mills are only partially employed. Raw material is high. In almost every branch of textile manufacture it is above the price at which it can be manufactured for the masses of the consumers. (Reports of Insp. of Fact., April 1861, p. 33.)

It had become evident that in 1860 the cotton industry had overproduced. The effect of this made itself felt during the next few years.

'It has taken between two and three years to absorb the over-production of 1860 in the markets of the world.' (Reports of Insp. of Fact., December 1863, p. 127.) 'The depressed state of the markets for cotton manufactures in the East, early in 1860, had a corresponding effect upon the trade of Blackburn, in which 30,000 power-looms are usually employed almost exclusively in the production of cloth to be consumed in the East. There was consequently but a limited demand for labour for many months prior to the effects of the cotton blockade being felt.... Fortunately this preserved many of the spinners and manufacturers from being involved in the common ruin. Stocks increased in value so long as they were held, and there had been consequently nothing like that alarming depreciation in the value of property which might not unreasonably have been looked for in such a crisis.' (Reports of Insp. of Fact., Oct. 1862, pp. 29, 31.)

1861. October.

'Trade has been for some time in a very depressed state. It is not improbable indeed that during the winter months many establishments will be found to work very short time. This might, however, have been anticipated ... irrespective of the causes which have interrupted our usual supplies of cotton from America and our exports, short time must have been kept during the ensuing winter in consequence of the great increase of production during the last three years, and the unsettled state of the Indian and Chinese markets.' (Reports of Insp. of Fact., Oct. 1861, p. 19.)

Cotton Waste. East Indian Cotton (Surat). Influence on the Wages of Labourers. Improvement of Machinery. Adding Starch Flour and Mineral Substitutes to Cotton. Effect of Starch Flour Sizing on Labourers. Manufacturers of Finer Yarn Grades. Manufacturers' Fraud.

'A manufacturer writes to me thus: "As to estimates of consumption per spindle, I doubt if you take sufficiently into calculation the fact that when cotton is high in price, every spinner of ordinary yarns (say up to 40s.) (principally 12s. to 32s.) will raise his counts as much as he can, that is, will spin 16s. where he used to spin 12s., or 22s. in the place of 16s., and so on; and the manufacturer using these fine yarns will make his cloth the usual weight by the addition of so much more size. The trade is availing itself of this resource at present to an extent which is even discreditable. I have heard on good authority of ordinary export shirting weighing 8 lbs which was made of 5¼ lbs. cotton and 2¾ lbs size.... In cloths of other descriptions as much as 50 per cent size is sometimes added; so that a manufacturer may and does truly boast that he is getting rich by selling cloth for less money per pound than he paid for the mere yarn of which they are composed." (Reports of Insp. of Fact., April 1864, p. 27.)

'I have also received statements that the weavers attribute increased sickness to the size which is used in dressing the warps of Surat cotton, and which is not made of the same material as formerly, viz., flour. This substitute for flour is said, however, to have the very important advantage of increasing greatly the weight of the cloth manufactured, making 15 lbs of the raw material to weigh 20 lbs when woven into cloth.' (Reports of Insp. of Fact., Oct. 1863. This substitute was ground talcum, called China clay, or gypsum, called French chalk.) 'The earnings of the weavers (meaning the operatives) are much reduced from the employment of substitutes for flour as sizing for warps. This sizing, which gives weight to the yarn, renders it hard and brittle. Each thread of the warp in the loom passes through a part of the loom called 'a heald', which consists of strong threads to keep the warp in its proper place, and the hard state of the warp causes the threads of the heald to break frequently; and it is said to take a weaver five minutes to tie up the threads every time they break; and a weaver has to piece these ends at least ten times as often as formerly, thus reducing the productive powers of the loom in the working-hours. ' (*Ibid.*, pp. 42-43.)

'In Ashton, Stalybridge, Mossley, Oldham, etc., the reduction of the time has been fully one-third, and the hours are lessening every week.... Simultaneously with this diminution of time there is also a reduction of wages in many departments.' (Reports of Insp. of Fact., Oct. 1861, pp. 12-13.)

Early in 1861 there was a strike among the mechanical weavers in some parts of Lancashire. Several manufacturers had announced a wage reduction of 5 to 7.5%. The operatives insisted that the wage scale remain the same while working-hours were reduced. This was not granted, and a strike was called. A month later, the operatives had to give in. But then they got both.

In addition to the reduction of wages to which the operatives at last consented, many mills are now running short time. (Reports of Insp. of Fact., April 1861, p. 23)

1862. April.

'The sufferings of the operatives since the date of my last report have greatly increased; but at no period of the history of manufactures, have sufferings so sudden and so severe been borne with so much silent resignation and so much patient self-respect.' (Reports of Insp. of Fact., April 1862, p. 10.) 'The proportionate number of operatives wholly out of employment at this date appears not to be much larger than it was in 1848, when there was an ordinary panic of sufficient consequences to excite alarm amongst the manufacturers, so much as to warrant the collection of similar statistics of the state of the cotton trade as are now issued weekly.... In May 1848, the proportion of cotton operatives out of work in Manchester out of the whole number usually employed was 15 per cent, on short time 12 per cent, whilst 70 per cent were in full work. On the 28th of May of the present year, of the whole number of persons usually employed 15 per cent were out of work, 35 per cent were on short time, and 49 per cent were working full time.... In some other places, Stockport for example, the averages of short time and of non-employment are higher, whilst those of full time are less', because coarser numbers are spun there than in Manchester'. (p. 16)

1862. October.

I find by the last return to Parliament that there were 2,887 cotton factories in the United Kingdom in 1861, 2,109 of them being in my district (Lancashire and Cheshire). I was aware that a very large proportion of the 2,109 factories in my district were small establishments, giving employment to few persons, but I have been surprised to find how large that proportion is. In 392, or 19 per cent, the steam-engine or waterwheel is under 10 horse-power; in 345, or 16 per cent, the horsepower is above 10 and under 20; and in 1,372 the power is 20 horses and more.... A very large proportion of these small manufacturers—being more than a third of the whole number—were operatives themselves at no distant period; they are men without command of capital. The brunt of the burden then would have to be borne by the remaining two-thirds. (Reports of Insp. of Fact., Oct. 1862, pp. 18, 19.)

According to the same report, 40,146, or 11.3%, of the cotton employees in Lancashire and Cheshire were then working full time; 134,767, or 38%, were working short time; and 179,721, or 50.7%, were unemployed. After deducting the returns from Manchester and Bolton, where mainly fine grades were spun, a line relatively little affected by the cotton famine, the matter looks still more unfavourable; namely, fully employed 8.5%, partly employed 38%, and unemployed 53.5% (pp. 19 and 20).

> Working up good or bad cotton makes a material difference to the operative. In the earlier part of the year, when manufacturers were endeavouring to keep their mills at work by using up all the moderately priced cotton they could obtain, much bad cotton was brought into mills in which good cotton was ordinarily used, and the difference to the operatives in wages was so great that many strikes took place on the ground that they could not make a fair day's wages at the old rates.... In some cases, although working full time, the difference in wages from working bad cotton was as much as one-half. (p. 27)

1863. April.

> 'During the present year there will not be full employment for much more than one-half of the cotton operatives in the country.' (Reports of Insp. of Fact., April 1863, p. 14.)
>
> 'A very serious objection to the use of Surat cotton, as manufacturers are now compelled to use it, is that the speed of the machinery must be greatly reduced in the processes of manufacture. For some years past every effort has been made to increase the speed of machinery, in order to make the same machinery produce more work; and the reduction of the speed becomes therefore a question which affects the operative as well as the manufacturer; for the chief part of the operatives are paid by the work done; for instance, spinners are paid per lb. for the yarn spun, weavers per piece for the number of pieces woven; and even with the other classes of operatives paid by the week there would be a diminution of wages in consideration of the less amount of goods produced. From inquiries I have made, and statements placed in my hands, of the earnings of cotton operatives during the present year, I find there is a diminution averaging 20 per cent upon their former earnings, in some instances the diminution has been as much as 50 per cent, calculated upon the same rate of wages as prevailed in 1861' (p. 13). '...The sum earned depends upon ... the nature of the material operated upon.... The position of the operatives in regard to the amount of their earnings is very much better now (October 1863) than it was this time last year. Machinery has improved, the material is better understood, and the operatives are able better to overcome the difficulties they had to contend with at first. I remember being in a sewing school (a charity institution for unemployed) at Preston last spring, when two young women, who had been sent to work at a weaving shed the day before, upon the representation of the manufacturer that they could earn 4s. per week, returned to the school to be readmitted, complaining that they could not have earned 1s. per week. I have been informed of 'self-acting minders' ... men who manage a pair of self-acting mules, earning at the end of a fortnight's full work 8s. 11d., and that from this sum was deducted the rent of the house, the manufacturer, however, returning half the rent as a gift. (How generous!) The minders took away the sum of 6s. 11d. In many places the self-acting minders ranged from 5s. to 9s. per week, and the weavers from 2s. to 6s. per week in the last months of 1862.... At the present time a much more healthy state of things exists, although there is still a great decrease in the earnings in most districts.... There are several causes which have tended to the reduction of earnings, besides the shorter staple of the Surat cotton and its dirty condition; for instance, it is now the

> practice to mix 'waste' largely with Surat, which consequently increases the difficulties of the spinner or minder. The threads, from their shortness of fibre, are more liable to break in the drawing out of the mule and in the twisting of the yarn, and the mule cannot be kept so continuously in motion.... Then, from the great attention required in watching the threads in weaving, many weavers can only mind one loom, and very few can mind more than two looms.... There has been a direct reduction of 5, 7½ and 10 per cent upon the wages of the operatives.... In the majority of cases the operative has to make the best of his material, and to earn the best wages he can at the ordinary rates.... Another difficulty the weavers have sometimes to contend with is, that they are expected to produce well-finished cloth from inferior materials, and are subject to fine for the flaws in their work.' (Reports of Insp. of Fact., Oct. 1863, pp. 41-43.)

Wages were miserable, even where work was full time. The cotton workers willingly offered themselves for all public works such as drainage, road-building, stone-breaking and street-paving, in which they were employed, to get their keep from the authorities (although this practically amounted to assistance to the manufacturer. See Book I, S. 598/589 [English edition: pp. 574-75.—*Ed.*]). The whole bourgeoisie stood guard over the labourers. Were the worst dog's wages offered, and a labourer refused to accept them, the Relief Committee would strike him from its lists. It was in a way a golden age for the manufacturers, for the labourers had either to starve or work at a price most profitable for the bourgeois. The Relief Committees acted as watch-dogs. At the same time, the manufacturers acted in secret agreement with the government to hinder emigration as much as possible, partly to retain in readiness the capital invested in the flesh and blood of the labourers, and partly to safeguard the house-rent squeezed out of the labourers.

> The Relief Committees acted with great strictness upon this point. If work was offered, the operatives to whom it was proposed were struck off the lists, and thus compelled to accept the offer. When they objected to accept work... the cause has been that their earnings would have been merely nominal, and the work exceedingly severe. (Reports of Insp. of Fact., Oct. 1863, p. 97.)

The operatives were willing to perform any work given to them under the Public Works Act.

> The principle upon which industrial employments were organised varied considerably in different towns, but in those places even in which the outdoor work was not absolutely a labour test the manner in which labour was remunerated by its being paid for either at the exact rate of relief, or closely approximating the rate, it became in fact a labour test (p. 69). The Public Works Act of 1863 was intended to remedy this inconvenience, and to enable the operative to earn his day's wages as an independent labourer. The purpose of this Act was three-fold: firstly, to enable local authorities to borrow money of the Exchequer Loan Commissioners (with consent of the President of the Central Relief Committee); secondly, to facilitate the improvement of the towns of the cotton districts; thirdly, to provide work and remunerative wages to the unemployed operatives.

Loans to the amount of £883,700 had been granted under this Act up to the end of October 1863 (p. 70). The works undertaken were mainly canalisation, road-building, street-paving, water-works reservoirs, etc.

Mr Henderson, president of the committee in Blackburn, wrote with reference to this to factory inspector Redgrave:

> Nothing in my experience, during the present period of suffering and distress, has struck me more forcibly or given me more satisfaction, than the cheerful alacrity with which the unemployed operatives of this district have accepted of the work offered to them through the adoption of the Public Works Act, by the Corporation of Blackburn.

> A greater contrast than that presented between the cotton spinner as a skilled workman in a factory, and as a labourer in a sewer 14 or 18 feet deep, can scarcely be conceived.

(Depending on the size of his family, he earned 4 to 12s. per week, this enormous amount providing sometimes for a family of eight. The towns-men derived a double profit from this. In the first place, they secured money to improve their smoky and neglected cities at exceptionally low interest rates. In the second place, they paid the labourers far less than the regular wage.)

> Accustomed as he had been to a temperature all but tropical, to work at which agility and delicacy of manipulation availed him infinitely more than muscular strength and to double and sometimes treble the remuneration which it is possible for him now to obtain, his ready acceptance of the proffered employment involved an amount of self-denial and consideration the exercise of which is most creditable. In Blackburn the men have been tested at almost every variety of outdoor work; in excavating a stiff heavy clay soil to a considerable depth, in draining, in stone-breaking, in road-making, and in excavating for street sewers to a depth of 14, 16, and sometimes 20 feet. In many cases while thus employed they are standing in mud and water to the depth of 10 or 12 inches, and in all they are exposed to a climate which, for chilly humidity is not surpassed I suppose, even if it is equalled, by that of any district in England' (pp. 91-92). 'The conduct of the operatives has been almost blameless, and their readiness to accept and make the best of outdoor labour. (p. 69)

1864. April.

> Complaints are occasionally made in different districts at the scarcity of hands, but this deficiency is chiefly felt in particular departments, as, for instance of weavers.... These complaints have their origin as much from the low rate of wages which the hands can earn owing to the inferior qualities of yarn used, as from any positive scarcity of work-people even in that particular department. Numerous differences have taken place during the past month between the masters of particular mills and their operatives in respect of the wages. Strikes, I am sorry to say, are but too frequently resorted to. ... The effect of the Public Works Act is felt as a competition by the mill-owners. The local committee at Bacup has suspended operations, for although all the mills are not running, yet a scarcity of hands has been experienced. (Reports of Insp. of Fact., April 1864, pp. 9, 10.)

It was indeed high time for the manufacturers. Due to the Public Works Act the demand for labour grew so strong that many a factory hand was earning 4 to 5 shillings daily in the quarries of Bacup. And so the public works were gradually suspended—this new edition of the *Ateliers nationaux* of 1848, but this time instituted in the interests of the bourgeoisie.

Experiments in corpore vili

> Although I have given the actual earnings of the operatives (fully employed) in several mills, it does not follow that they earn the same amount week by week. The operatives are subject to great fluctuation, from the constant experimentalising of the manufacturers upon different kinds and proportions of cotton and waste in the same mill, the 'mixings' as it is called, being frequently changed; and the earnings of the operatives rise and fall with the quality of the cotton mixings; sometimes they have been within 15 per cent of former earnings, and then in a week or two, they have fallen from 50 to 60 per cent.

Inspector Redgrave, who makes this report, then proceeds to cite wage figures taken from actual practice, of which the following examples may suffice:

A, weaver, family of 6, employed 4 days a week, 6s. 8.5d.; B, twister, employed 4.5 days a week, 6s.; C, weaver, family of 4, employed 5 days a week, 5s. 1d.; D, slubber, family of

6, employed 4 days a week, 7s. 10d.; E, weaver, family of 7, employed 3 days a week, 5s., etc. Redgrave continues:

> The above returns are deserving of consideration, for they show that work would become a misfortune in many a family, as it not merely reduces the income, but brings it so low as to be utterly insufficient to provide more than a small portion of the absolute wants, were it not that supplemental relief is granted to operatives when the wages of the family do not reach the sum that would be given to them as relief, if they were all unemployed. (Reports of Insp. of Fact., Oct. 1863, pp. 50-53.)
>
> In no week since the 5th of June last was there more than two days seven hours and a few minutes employment for all the workers. (*Ibid.*, p. 121.)

From the beginning of the crisis to March 25, 1863, nearly three million pounds sterling were expended by the guardians, the Central Relief Committee, and the Mansion House Committee. (*Ibid.*, p. 13.)

> In a district in which the finest yarn is spun ... the spinners suffer an indirect reduction of 15 per cent in consequence of the change from South Sea Island to Egyptian cotton. In an extensive district, in many parts of which waste is largely used as a mixture with Surat ... the spinners have had a reduction of 5 per cent, and have lost from 20 to 30 per cent in addition, through working Surat and waste. The weavers are reduced from 4 looms to 2 looms. In 1860, they averaged 5s. 7d. per loom, in 1863, only 3s. 4d. The fines, which formerly varied from 3d. to 6d. (for the weaver) on American, now run up to from 1s. to 3s. 6d.

In one district, where Egyptian cotton was used with an admixture of East Indian

> The average of the mule spinners, which was in 1860 18s. to 25s., now averages from 10s. to 18s. per week, caused, in addition to inferior cotton, by the reduction of the speed of the mule to put an extra amount of twist in the yarn, which in ordinary times would be paid for according to list (pp. 43, 44). Although the Indian cotton may have been worked to profit by the manufacturer, it will be seen (see the wage list on p. 53) that the operatives are sufferers compared with 1861, and if the use of Surat be confirmed, the operatives will want to earn the wages of 1861, which would seriously affect the profits of the manufacturer, unless he obtain compensation either in the price of the raw cotton or of his products. (p. 105)

House-Rent.

> 'The rent is frequently deducted from the wages of operatives, even when working short time, by the manufacturers whose cottages they may be occupying. Nevertheless the value of this class of property has diminished, and houses may be obtained at a reduction of from 25 to 50 per cent upon the rent of the houses in ordinary times; for instance, a cottage which would have cost 3s. 6d. per week can now be had for 2s. 4d. per week, and sometimes even for less' (p. 57).

Emigration. The employers were naturally opposed to emigration of labourers, because, on the one hand,

> [L]ooking forward to the recovery of the cotton trade from its present depression, they keep within their reach the means whereby their mills can be worked in the most advantageous manner'. On the other hand, 'many manufacturers are owners of the houses in which operatives employed in their mills reside, and some unquestionably expect to obtain a portion of the back rent owing. (p. 96)

Mr Bernall Osborne said in a speech to his parliamentary constituents on October 22, 1864, that the labourers of Lancashire had behaved like the ancient philosophers—(Stoics). Not like sheep?

Notes

1. *The Factory Question and the Ten Hours' Bill* by R. H. Greg, London, 1837, p. 115.
2. The report errs in the final sentence. Instead of 6d. it should be 3d. for loss through waste. This loss amounts to 25% in the case of Surat, and only 12½ to 15% in the case of American cotton, and this latter is meant, the same percentage having been correctly calculated for the price of 5 to 6d. It is true, however, that also in the case of American cotton brought to Europe during the latter years of the Civil War the proportion of waste often rose considerably higher than before.—*F. E.*
3. For examples see Babbage [*On the Economy of Machinery and Manufactures*, London, 1832, pp. 280-81.—*Ed.*], among others. The usual expedient—a reduction of wages—is also employed in this instance, so that this continual depreciation acts quite contrary to the dreams of Mr Carey's 'harmonious brain'.
4. Since the above was written (1865), competition on the world-market has been considerably intensified by the rapid development of industry in all civilised countries, especially in America and Germany. The fact that the rapidly and enormously expanding productive forces today outgrow the control of the laws of the capitalist mode of commodity exchange, within which they are supposed to operate, impresses itself more and more even on the minds of the capitalists. This is disclosed especially by two symptoms. First, by the new general mania for a protective tariff, which differs from the old protectionism in that now articles fit for export are those best protected. And secondly, by the trusts of manufacturers of whole spheres of production which regulate production, and thus prices and profits. It goes without saying that these experiments are practicable only so long as the economic climate is relative favourable. The first storm must upset them and prove that, although production assuredly needs regulation, it is certainly not the capitalist class which is fitted for that task. Meanwhile, the trusts have no other mission but to see to it that the little fish are swallowed by the big fish still more rapidly than before.—*F.E.*
5. It goes without saying that we do not, like Mr Baker, *explain* the wool crisis of 1857 on the basis of the disproportion between the prices of raw material and product. This disproportion was itself but a symptom, and the crisis was a general one.—*F.E.*
6. A sharp distinction is made in England between woollen manufacture, which spins carded yarn from short wool and weaves it (main centre Leeds), and worsted manufacture, which makes worsted yarn from long wool and weaves it (main seat Bradford, in Yorkshire).—*F.E.*
7. This rapid expansion of output of machine-made linen yarn in Ireland dealt a death-blow to exports of linen made of hand-made yarn in Germany (Silesia, Lusatia, and Westphalia).—*F.E.*

7

Supplementary Remarks

Suppose, as is assumed in this part, the amount of profit in any particular sphere of production equals the sum of the surplus-value produced by the total capital invested in that sphere. Even then the bourgeois will not consider his profit as identical with surplus-value, i.e., with unpaid surplus-labour, and, to be sure, for the following reasons:

1. In the process of circulation he forgets the process of production. He thinks that surplus-value is made when he realises the value of commodities, which includes realisation of their surplus-value. [A blank space which follows in the manuscript, indicates that Marx intended to dwell in greater detail on this point. – *F. E.*]
2. Assuming a uniform degree of exploitation, we have seen that regardless of all modifications originating in the credit system, regardless of the capitalists' efforts to outwit and cheat one another, and, lastly, regardless of any favourable choice of the market – the rate of profit may differ considerably, depending on the low or high prices of raw materials and the experience of the buyer, on the relative productivity, efficiency and cheapness of the machinery, on the greater or lesser efficiency of the aggregate arrangement in the various stages of the productive process, elimination of waste, the simplicity and efficiency of management and supervision, etc. In short, given the surplus-value for a certain variable capital, it still depends very much on the individual business acumen of the capitalist, or of his managers and salesmen, whether this same surplus-value is expressed in a greater or smaller rate of profit, and accordingly yields a greater or smaller amount of profit. Let the same surplus-value of £1,000, the product of £1,000 in wages, obtain in enterprise A for a constant capital of £9,000, and in enterprise B, for £11,000. In case A, we have p' = 1,000/10,000 or 10%. In case B we have p' = 1,000/12,000, or 8⅓%. The total capital produces relatively more profit in enterprise A than in B, because of a higher rate of profit, although the variable capital advanced in both cases = £1,000 and the surplus-value produced by each likewise = £1,000, so that in both cases there exists the same degree of exploitation of the same number of labourers. This difference in the presentation of the same mass of surplus-value, or the difference in the rates of profit, and therefore in the profit itself, while the exploitation of labour is the same, may also be due to other causes. Still, it may also be due wholly to a difference in the business acumen with which both establishments are run. And this circumstance misleads the capitalist, convinces him that his profits are not due to exploiting labour, but, at least in part, to other independent circumstances, and particularly his individual activity.

The analyses in this first part demonstrate the incorrectness of the view (Rodbertus [*Sociale Briefe an von Kirchmann, Dritter Brief: Widerlegung der Ricardo'schen Lehre von der Grundrente und Begründung einer neuen Rententheorie*, Berlin, 1851, S. 125. – *Ed.*]) according to which (as distinct from ground-rent, in which case, for example, the area of real estate remains the same and yet the rent rises) a change in the magnitude of an individual capital is supposed to have no influence on the ratio of profit to capital, and thus on the rate of profit, because if the mass of profit should grow, so does the mass of capital upon which it is calculated, and vice versa.

This is true only in two cases. First, when – assuming that all other circumstances, especially the rate of surplus-value, remain unchanged—there is a change in the value of that commodity which is a money-commodity. (The same occurs in a merely nominal change of value, the rise or fall of more tokens of value, other conditions being equal.) Let the total capital = £100, and the profit = £20, the rate of profit being = 20%. Should gold fall by half, or double, the same capital previously worth only £100, will be worth £200 if it falls, and the profit will be worth £40, i.e., it will be expressed in so much money instead of the former £20; if it rises, the capital of £100 will be worth only £50, and the profit will be represented by a product, whose value will be £10. But in either case 200:40 = 50:10 = 100:20 = 20%. In all these examples, there would, however, have been no actual change in the magnitude of capital-value, and only in the money-expression of the same value and the same surplus-value. For this reason, s/C, or the rate of profit, could not be affected.

In the second case, there is an actual change of magnitude in the value, but unaccompanied by a change in the ratio of v to c; in other words, with a constant rate of surplus-value the relation of capital invested in labour-power (variable capital considered as an index of the amount of labour-power set in motion) to the capital invested in means of production remains the same. Under these circumstances, no matter whether we have C, or nC, or C/n, e.g., 1,000, or 2,000, or 500, and the rate of profit being 20%, the profit = 200 in the first case, = 400 in the second and = 100 in the third. But 200:1,000 = 400:2,000 = 100:500 = 20%. That is to say, the rate of profit is unchanged, because the composition of capital remains the same and is not affected by the change in magnitude. Therefore, an increase or decrease in the amount of profit shows merely an increase or decrease in the magnitude of the invested capital.

In the first case, there is, therefore, but the appearance of a change in the magnitude of the employed capital, while in the second case there is an actual change in magnitude, but no change in the organic composition of the capital, i.e., in the relative proportions of its variable and constant portions. But with the exception of these two cases, a change in the magnitude of the employed capital is either the *result* of a preceding change in the value of one of its components, and therefore of a change in the relative magnitude of these components (as long as the surplus-value itself does not change with the variable capital); or, this change of magnitude (as in labour-processes on a large scale, introduction of new machinery, etc.) is the *cause* of a change in the relative magnitude of its two organic components. In all these cases, other circumstances remaining the same, a change in the magnitude of the employed capital must therefore be accompanied simultaneously by a change in the rate of profit.

A rise in the rate of profit is always due to a relative or absolute increase of the surplus-value in relation to its cost of production, i.e., to the advanced total capital, or to a decrease in the difference between the rate of profit and the rate of surplus-value.

Fluctuations in the rate of profit may occur irrespective of changes in the organic components of the capital, or of the absolute magnitude of the capital, through a rise or fall in the value of the fixed or circulating advanced capital caused by an increase or a reduction of the working-time required for its reproduction, this increase or reduction taking place independently of the already existing capital. The value of every commodity—thus also of the commodities making up the capital—is determined not by the necessary labour-time contained in it but by the social labour-time required for its reproduction. This reproduction may take place under unfavourable or under propitious circumstances, distinct from the conditions of original production. If, under altered conditions, it takes double or, conversely, half the time, to reproduce the same material capital, and if the value of money remains unchanged, a capital formerly worth £100 would be worth £200, or £50 respectively. Should this appreciation or depreciation affect all parts of capital uniformly, then the profit would also be accordingly expressed in double, or half, the amount of money. But if it involves a change in the organic composition of the capital, if the ratio of the variable to the constant portion of capital rises or falls, then, other circumstances remaining the same, the rate of profit will rise with a relatively rising variable capital and fall with a relatively falling one. If only the money-value of the advanced capital rises or falls (in consequence of a change in the value of money), then the money-expression of the surplus-value rises or falls in the same proportion. The rate of profit remains unchanged.

PART II

CONVERSION OF PROFIT INTO AVERAGE PROFIT

8

Different Compositions of Capitals in Different Branches of Production and Resulting Differences in Rates of Profit

In the preceding part, we demonstrated, among other things, that the rate of profit may vary—rise or fall—while the rate of surplus-value remains the same. In the present chapter, we assume that the intensity of labour exploitation, and therefore the rate of surplus-value and the length of the working-day, are the same in all the spheres of production into which the social labour of a given country is divided. Adam Smith has already comprehensively shown that the numerous differences in the exploitation of labour in various spheres of production balance one another by means of all kinds of existing compensations, or compensations accepted as such on the basis of current prejudice, so that they are merely evanescent distinctions and are of no moment in a study of the general relations. Other differences, for instance, those in the wage scale, rest largely on the difference between simple and complicated labour mentioned in the beginning of Book I (p. 19), and have nothing to do with the intensity of exploitation in the different spheres of production, although they render the lot of the labourer in those spheres very unequal. For instance, if the labour of a goldsmith is better paid than that of a day-labourer, the former's surplus-labour produces proportionately more surplus-value than the latter's. And although the equalizing of wages and working-days, and thereby of the rates of surplus-value, among different spheres of production, and even among different investments of capital in the same sphere of production, is checked by all kinds of local obstacles, it is nevertheless taking place more and more with the advance of capitalist production and the subordination of all economic conditions to this mode of production. The study of such frictions, while important to any special work on wages, may be dispensed with as incidental and irrelevant in a general analysis of capitalist production. In a general analysis of this kind, it is usually always assumed that the actual conditions correspond to their conception, or, what is the same, that actual conditions are represented only to the extent that they are typical of their own general case.

The difference in the rates of surplus-value in different countries, and consequently the national differences in the degree of exploitation of labour, are immaterial for our present analysis. What we want to show in this part is precisely the way in which a general rate of profit takes shape in any given country. It is evident, however, that a comparison of the various national rates of profit requires only a collation of the previously studied with that which is here to be studied. First one should consider the differences in the national rates of surplus-value, and then, on the basis of these given rates, a comparison should be made of the differences in the national rates of profit. In so far as those differences are not due to differences in the national rates of surplus-value, they must be due to circumstances in which the surplus-value is assumed, just as in the analysis of this chapter, to be universally the same, i.e., constant.

We demonstrated in the preceding chapter that, assuming the rate of surplus-value to be constant, the rate of profit obtaining for a given capital may rise or fall in consequence of circumstances which raise or lower the value of one or the other portion of constant capital, and so affect the proportion between the variable and constant components of capital. We further observed that circumstances which prolong or reduce the time of turnover of an individual capital may similarly influence the rate of profit. Since the mass of the profit is identical with the mass of the surplus-value, and with the surplus-value itself, it was also seen that the *mass* of the profit—as distinct from the *rate* of profit—is not affected by the aforementioned fluctuations of value. They only modify the rate in which a given surplus-value, and therefore a profit of a given magnitude, express themselves; in other words, they modify only the relative magnitude of profit, i.e., its magnitude compared with the magnitude of the advanced capital. Inasmuch as capital was tied up or released by such fluctuations of value, it was not only the rate of profit, but the profit itself, which was likely to be affected in this indirect manner. However, this has then always applied only to such capital as was already invested, and not to new investments. Besides, the increase or reduction of profit always depended on the extent to which the same capital could, in consequence of such fluctuation of value, set in motion more or less labour; in other words, it depended on the extent to which the same capital could, with the rate of surplus-value remaining the same, obtain a larger or smaller amount of surplus-value. Far from contradicting the general rule, or from being an exception to it, this seeming exception was really but a special case in the application of the general rule.

It was seen in the preceding part that the degree of exploitation remaining constant, changes in the value of the component parts of constant capital and in the time of turnover of capital are attended by changes in the rate of profit. The obvious conclusion is that the rates of profit in different spheres of production existing side by side have to differ when, other circumstances remaining unchanged, the time of turnover of capitals employed in the different spheres differs, or when the value-relation of the organic components of these capitals differs in the various branches of production. What we previously regarded as changes occurring successively with one and the same capital is now to be regarded as simultaneous differences among capital investments existing side by side in different spheres of production.

In these circumstances, we shall have to analyze: 1) the difference in the *organic composition* of capitals, and 2) the difference in their period of turnover.

The premise in this entire analysis is naturally that by speaking of the composition or turnover of a capital in a certain line of production, we always mean the average normal proportions of capital invested in this sphere, and generally the average in the total capital employed in that particular sphere, and not the accidental differences of the individual capitals.

Since it is further assumed that the rate of surplus-value and the working-day are constant, and since this assumption also implies constant wages, a certain quantity of variable capital represents a definite quantity of labour-power set in motion, and therefore a definite quantity of materialized labour. If, therefore, £100 represent the weekly wage of 100 labuorers, indicating 100 actual labour-powers, then n times £100 indicate the labour-powers of n times 100 labourers, and £100/n those of 100/n labourers. The variable capital thus serves here (as is always the case when the wage is given) as an index of the amount of labour set in motion by a definite total capital. Differences in the magnitude of the employed variable capitals serve, therefore, as indexes of the difference in the amount of employed labour-power. If £100 indicate 100 labourers per week, and represent 6,000 working-hours at 60 working-hours per week, then £200 represent 12,000, and £50 only 3,000 working-hours.

By composition of capital, we mean, as stated in Book I, the proportion of its active and passive components, i.e., of variable and constant capital. Two proportions enter into consideration under this heading. They are not equally important, although they may produce similar effects under certain circumstances.

The first proportion rests on a technical basis and must be regarded as given at a certain stage of development of the productive forces. A definite quantity of labour-power represented by a definite number of labourers is required to produce a definite quantity of products in, say, one day, and—what is self-evident—thereby to consume productively, i.e., to set in motion, a definite quantity of means of production, machinery, raw materials, etc. A definite number of labourers corresponds to a definite quantity of means of production, and hence a definite quantity of living labour to a definite quantity of labour materialized in means of production. This proportion differs greatly in different spheres of production and frequently even in different branches of one and the same industry, although it may by coincidence be entirely or approximately the same in entirely separate lines of industry.

This proportion forms the technical composition of capital and is the real basis of its organic composition.

However, it is also possible that this first proportion may be the same in different lines of industry, provided variable capital is merely an index of labour-power and constant capital merely an index of the mass of means of production set in motion by this labour-power. For instance, certain work in copper and iron may require the same ratio of labour-power to mass of means of production. But since copper is more expensive than iron, the value-relation between variable and constant capital is different in each case, and hence also the value-composition of the two total capitals. The difference between the technical composition and the value composition is manifested in each branch of industry in that the value-relation of the two portions of capital may vary while the technical composition is constant, and the value-relation may remain the same while the technical composition varies. The latter case will, of course, be possible only if the change in the ratio of the employed masses of means of production and labour-power is compensated by a reverse change in their values.

The value-composition of capital, inasmuch as it is determined by, and reflects, its technical composition, is called the *organic* composition of capital.

In the case of variable capital, therefore, we assume that it is the index of a definite quantity of labour-power, or of a definite number of labourers, or a definite quantity of living labour set in motion. We have seen in the preceding part that a change in the magnitude of the value of variable capital might eventually indicate nothing but a higher or lower price of the same mass of labour. But here, where the rate of surplus-value and the working-day are taken to be constant, and the wages for a definite working period are given, this is out of the question. On the other hand, a difference in the magnitude of the constant capital may likewise be an index of a change in the mass of means of production set in motion by a definite quantity of labour-power. But it may also stem from a difference in value between the means of production set in motion in one sphere and those of another. Both points of view must therefore be examined here.

Finally, we must take note of the following essential facts:

Let £100 be the weekly wage of 100 labourers. Let the weekly working-hours = 60. Furthermore, let the rate of surplus-value = 100%. In this case, the labourers work 30 of the 60 hours for themselves and 30 hours gratis for the capitalist. In fact, the £100 of wages represent just the 30 working-hours of 100 labourers, or altogether 3,000 working-hours, while the other 3,000 hours worked by the labourers are incorporated in the £100 of surplus-value, or in the profit pocketed by the capitalist. Although the wage of £100 does not, therefore, express the value in which the weekly labour of the 100 labourers is materialized, it indicates nevertheless (since the length of the working-day and the rate of surplus-value are given) that this capital sets in motion 100 labourers for 6,000 working-hours. The capital of £100 indicates this, first, because it indicates the number of labourers set in motion, with £1 = 1 labourer per week, hence £100 = 100 labourers; and, secondly, because, since the rate of surplus-value is given as 100%, each of these labourers performs twice as much work as is contained in his wages, so that £1, i.e., his wage, which is the expression of half a week of labour, actuates a whole week's labour, just as £100 sets in motion 100 weeks of labour, although it contains only 50. A very essential distinction is thus to be made in regard to variable capital laid out in wages. Its value as the sum of wages, i.e., as a certain amount of materialised labour, is to be distinguished from its value as a mere index of the mass of living labour which it sets in motion. The latter is always greater than the labour which it incorporates and is, therefore, represented by a greater value than that of the variable capital. This greater value is determined, on the one hand, by the number of labourers set in motion by the variable capital and, on the other, by the quantity of surplus-labour performed by them.

It follows from this manner of looking upon variable capital that:

When a capital invested in production sphere A expends only 100 in variable capital for each 700 of total capital, leaving 600 for constant capital, while a capital invested in production sphere B expends 600 for variable and only 100 for constant capital, then capital A of 700 sets in motion only 100 of labour-power, or, in the terms of our previous assumption, 100 weeks of labour, or 6,000 hours of living labour, while the same amount of capital B will set in motion 600 weeks of labour, or 36,000 hours of living labour. The capital in A would then appropriate only 50 weeks of labour, or 3,000 hours of surplus-labour, while the same amount of capital in B would appropriate 300 weeks of labour, or 18,000 hours. Variable capital is not only the index of the labour embodied in it. When the rate of surplus-value is known, it is also an index of the amount of labour set in motion over and above that embodied in itself, i.e., of surplus-labour. Assuming the same intensity of exploitation, the profit in the first case would be 100/700 = 1/7 = $14^2/_7$% and in the second case, 600/700 = 6/7 = $85^5/_7$% or a six-fold rate of profit. In this case, the profit itself would actually be six times as great, 600 in B as against 100 in A, because the same capital set in motion six times as much living labour, which at the same level of exploitation means six times as much surplus value, and thus six times as much profit.

But if the capital invested in A were not 700 but £7,000, while that invested in B were only £700, and the organic composition of both were to remain the same, then the capital in A would employ £1,000 of the £7,000 as variable capital, that is, 1,000 labourers per week = 60,000 hours of living labour, of which 30,000 would be surplus-labour. Yet each £700 of the capital in A would continue to set in motion only 1/6 as much living labour, and hence only 1/6 as much surplus-labour, as the capital in B, and would produce only 1/6 as much profit. If we consider the rate of profit, then in A 1000/7000 = 100/700 = $14^2/_7$%, as compared with 600/700, or $85^5/_7$%, in B. Taking equal amounts of capital, the rates of profit differ because, owing to the different masses of living labour set in motion, the masses of surplus-value, and thus of profit, differ, although the rates of surplus-value are the same.

We get practically the same result if the technical conditions are the same in both spheres of production, but the value of the elements of the employed constant capital is greater or smaller in the one than in the other. Let us assume that both invest £100 as variable capital and therefore employ 100 labourers per week to set in motion the same quantity of machinery and raw materials. But let the latter be more expensive in B than in A. For instance, let the £100 of variable capital set in motion £200 of constant capital in A, and £400 in B. With the same rate of surplus-value, of 100%, the surplus-value produced is in either case equal to £100. Hence, the profit is also equal to £100 in both. But the rate of profit in A is $100/(200_c + 100_v)$ = ⅓ = 33⅓%, while in B it is $100/(400_c + 100_v)$ = 1/5 = 20%. In fact, if we select a certain aliquot part of the total capital in either case, we find that in every £100 of B, only £20, or 1/5, constitute variable capital, while in every £100 of A £33⅓, or ⅓, form variable capital. B produces less profit for each £100, because it sets in motion less living labour than A. The difference in the rates of profit thus resolves itself once more, in this case, into a difference of the masses of profit, because of the masses of surplus-value, produced by each 100 of invested capital.

The difference between this second example and the first is just this: The equalisation between A and B in the second case would require only a change in the value of the constant capital of either A or B, provided the technical basis remained the same. But in the first case, the technical composition itself is different in the two spheres of production and would have to be completely changed to achieve an equalisation.

The different organic composition of various capitals is thus independent of their absolute magnitude. It is always but a question of how much of every 100 is variable and how much constant capital.

Capitals of different magnitude, calculated in percentages, or, what amounts to the same in this case, capitals of the same magnitude operating for the same working-time and with the same degree of exploitation may produce very much different amounts of profit, because of surplus-value, for the reason that a difference in the organic composition of capital in different spheres of production implies a difference in their variable part, thus a difference in the quantities of living labour set in motion by them, and therefore also a difference in the quantities of surplus-labour appropriated by them. And this surplus-labour is the substance of surplus-value, and thus of profit. In different spheres of production, equal portions of the total capital comprise unequal sources of surplus-value, and the sole source of surplus-value is living labour. Assuming the same degree of labour exploitation, the mass of labour set in motion by a capital of 100, and consequently the mass of surplus-labour appropriated by it, depend on the magnitude of its variable component. If a capital, consisting in per cent of $90_c + 10_v$, produced as much surplus-value, or profit, at the same degree of exploitation as a capital consisting of $10_c + 90_v$, it would be as plain as day that the surplus-value, and thus value in general, must have an entirely different source than labour, and that political economy would then be deprived of every rational basis. If we are to assume all the time that £1 stands for the weekly wage of a labourer working 60 hours and that the rate of surplus-value is 100%, then it is evident that the total value product of one labourer in a week is £2. Ten labourers would then produce no more than £20. And since £10 of the £20 replace the wages, the ten labourers cannot produce more surplus-value than £10. On the other hand, 90 labourers, whose total product is £180, and whose wages amount to £90, would produce a surplus-value of £90. The rate of profit in the first case would thus be 10% and in the other 90%. If this were not so, then value and surplus-value would be something else than materialised labour. Since capitals in different spheres of production viewed in percentages—or as capitals of equal magnitude—are divided differently into variable and constant capital, setting in motion unequal quantities of living labour and producing different surplus-values, and therefore profits, it follows that the rate of profit, which consists precisely of the ratio of surplus-value to total capital in per cent, must also differ.

Now, if capitals in different spheres of production, calculated in per cent, i.e., capitals of equal magnitude, produce unequal profits in consequence of their different organic composition, then it follows that the profits of unequal capitals in different spheres of production cannot be proportional to their respective magnitudes, or that profits in different spheres of production are not proportional to the magnitude of the respective capitals invested in them. For if profits were to grow *pro rata* to the magnitude of invested capital, it would mean that in per cent the profits would be the same, so that in different spheres of production capitals of equal magnitude would have equal rates of profit, in spite of their different organic composition. It is only in the same sphere of production, where we have a given organic composition of capital, or in different spheres with the same organic composition of capital that the amounts of profits are directly proportional to the amounts of invested capitals. To say that the profits of unequal capitals are proportional to their magnitudes would only mean that capitals of equal magnitude yield equal profits or that the rate of profit is the same for all capitals, whatever their magnitude and organic composition.

These statements hold good on the assumption that the commodities are sold at their values. The value of a commodity is equal to the value of the constant capital contained in it, plus the value of the variable capital reproduced in it, plus the increment—the surplus-value produced—of this variable capital. At the same rate of surplus-value, its quantity evidently depends on the quantity of the variable capital. The value of the product of an individual capital of 100 is, in one case, $90_c + 10_v + 10_s = 110$; and in the other, $10_c + 90_v + 90_s = 190$. If the commodities go at their values, the first product is sold at 110, of which 10 represent surplus-value, or unpaid labour, and the second at 190, of which 90 represent surplus-value, or unpaid labour.

This is particularly important in comparing rates of profit in different countries. Let us assume that the rate of surplus-value in one European country is 100% so that the labourer works half of the working-day for himself and the other half for his employer. Let us further assume that the rate of profit in an Asian country is 25% so that the labourer works 4/5 of the working-day for himself and 1/5 for his employer. Let $84_c + 16_v$ be the composition of the national capital in the European country, and $16_c + 84_v$ in the Asian country, where little machinery, etc., is used, and where a given quantity of labour-power consumes relatively little raw material productively in a given time. Then we have the following calculation:

In the European country the value of the product $= 84_c + 16_v + 16_s = 116$; rate of profit $= 16/100 = 16\%$.

In the Asian country the value of the product $= 16_c + 84_v + 21_s = 121$; rate of profit $= 21/100 = 21\%$.

The rate of profit in the Asian country is thus more than 25% higher than in the European country, although the rate of surplus-value in the former is one-fourth that of the latter. Men like Carey, Bastiat, and *tutti quanti*, would arrive at the very opposite conclusion.

By the way, different national rates of profit are mostly based on different national rates of surplus-value. But in this chapter we compare unequal rates of profit derived from the same rate of surplus-value.

Aside from differences in the organic composition of capitals, and therefore aside from the different masses of labour—and consequently, other circumstances remaining the same, from different masses of surplus-labour set in motion by capitals of the same magnitude in different spheres of production, there is yet another source of inequality in rates of profit. This is the different period of turnover of capital in different spheres of production. We have seen in Chapter IV that, other conditions being equal, the rates of profit of capitals of the same organic composition are inversely proportional to their periods of turnover. We have also seen that the same variable capital turned over in different periods of time produces different quantities of annual surplus-value. The difference in the periods of turnover is therefore another reason why capitals of equal magnitude in different spheres of production do not produce equal profits in equal periods, and why, consequently, the rates of profit in these different spheres differ.

As far as the ratio of the fixed and circulating capital in the composition of capitals is concerned, however, it does not in itself affect the rate of profit in the least. It can affect the rate of profit only if, in one case, this difference in composition coincides with a different ratio of the variable and constant parts, so that the difference in the rate of profit is due to this latter difference, and not to the different ratio of fixed and circulating capital; and, in the other case, if the difference in the ratio of the fixed and circulating parts of capital is responsible for a difference in the period of turnover in which a certain profit is realised. If capitals are divided into fixed and circulating capital in different proportions, this will naturally always influence the period of turnover and cause differences in it. But this does not imply that the period of turnover, in which the same capitals realise certain profits, is different. For instance, A may continually have to convert the greater part of its product into raw materials, etc., while B may use the same machinery, etc., for a longer time, and may need less raw material, but both A and B, being occupied in production, always have a part of their capital engaged, the one in raw materials, i.e., in circulating capital, and the other in machinery, etc., or in fixed capital. A continually converts a portion of its capital from the form of commodities into that of money, and the latter again into the form of raw material, while B employs a portion of its capital for a longer time as an instrument of labour without any such conversions. If both of them employ the same amount of labour, they will indeed sell quantities of products of unequal value in the course of the year, but both quantities of products will contain equal amounts of surplus-value, and their rates of profit, calculated on the entire capital invested, will be the same, although their composition of fixed and circulating capital, and their periods of turnover, are different. Both capitals realise equal profits in equal periods, although their periods of turnover are different.[1] The difference in the period of turnover is in itself of no importance, except so far as it affects the mass of surplus-labour appropriated and realised by the same capital in a given time. If therefore, a different division into fixed and circulating capital does not necessarily imply a different period of turnover, which would in its turn imply a different rate of profit, it is evident that if there is any such difference in the rates of profit, it is not due to a different ratio of fixed to circulating capital as such, but rather to the fact that this different ratio indicates an inequality in the periods of turnover affecting the rate of profit.

It follows, therefore, that the different composition of constant capital in respect to its fixed and circulating portions in various branches of production has in itself no bearing on the rate of profit, since it is the ratio of variable to constant capital which decides this question, while the value of the constant capital; and therefore also its magnitude in relation to the variable is entirely unrelated to the fixed or circulating nature of its components. Yet it may be found—and this often leads to incorrect conclusions—that wherever fixed capital is considerably advanced, this but expresses the fact that production is on a large scale, so that constant capital greatly outweighs the variable, or that the living labour-power it employs is small compared to the mass of the means of production which it operates.

We have thus demonstrated that different lines of industry have different rates of profit, which correspond to differences in the organic composition of their capitals and, within indicated limits, also to their different periods of turnover; given the same time of turnover, the law (as a general tendency) that profits are related to one another as the magnitudes of the capitals, and that, consequently, capitals of equal magnitude yield equal profits in equal periods, applies only to capitals of the same organic composition, even with the same rate of surplus-value. These statements hold good on the assumption, which has been the basis of all our analyses so far, namely, that the commodities are sold at their values. There is no doubt, on the other hand, that aside from unessential, incidental and mutually compensating distinctions, differences in the average rate of profit in the various branches of industry do not exist in reality and could not exist without abolishing the entire system of capitalist production. It would seem, therefore, that here the theory of value is incompatible with the actual process, incompatible with the real phenomena of production, and that for this reason, any attempt to understand these phenomena should be given up.

It follows from the first part of this volume that the cost-prices of products in different spheres of production are equal if equal portions of capital have been advanced for their production, however different the organic composition of such capitals. The distinction between variable and constant capital escapes the capitalist in the cost-price. A commodity for whose production he must advance £100 costs him just as much, whether he invests $90_c + 10_v$, or $10_c + 90_v$. It costs him £100 in either case—no more and no less. The cost-prices are the same for equal capitals in different spheres, no matter how much the produced values and surplus-values may differ. The equality of cost-prices is the basis for competition among invested capitals, whereby an average profit is brought about.

Note

1. [It follows from Chapter IV that the above statement correctly applies only when capitals A and B are differently composed in respect to their values, but that the percentages of their variable parts are proportionate to their periods of turnover, i.e., inversely proportionate to their number of turnovers. Let capital A have the following percentages of composition: 20_c fixed + 70_c circulating and thus $90_c + 10_v = 100$. At a rate of surplus-value of 100% the 10_v produces 10_s in one turnover, yielding a rate of profit for one turnover = 10%. Let capital B = 60_c fixed + 20_c circulating, and thus $80_c + 20_v = 100$. The 20_v produce 20_s in one turnover at the above rate of surplus-value, yielding a rate of profit for one turnover = 20%, which is double that of A. But if A is turned over twice per year, and B only once, then 2 × 10 also make 20_s per year, and the annual rate of profit is the same for both, namely 20%.—*F.E.*]

9

Formation of a General Rate of Profit (Average Rate of Profit) and Transformation of the Values of Commodities into Prices of Production

The organic composition of capital depends at any given time on two circumstances: first, on the technical relation of labour power employed to the mass of the means of production employed; secondly, on the price of these means of production. This composition, as we have seen, must be examined on the basis of percentage ratios. We express the organic composition of a certain capital consisting 4/5 of constant and 1/5 of variable capital by the formula $80_c + 20_v$. It is furthermore assumed in this comparison that the rate of surplus-value is unchangeable. Let it be any rate picked at random, say, 100%. The capital of 80_c + 20_v then produces a surplus-value of 20_s, and this yields a rate of profit of 20% on the total capital. The magnitude of the actual value of its product depends on the magnitude of the fixed part of the constant capital and on the portion which passes from it through wear and tear into the product. But since this circumstance has absolutely no bearing on the rate of profit, and hence, in the present analysis, we shall assume, for the sake of simplicity, that the constant capital is everywhere uniformly and entirely transferred to the annual product of the capitals. It is further assumed that the capitals in the different spheres of production annually realise the same quantities of surplus-value proportionate to the magnitude of their variable parts. For the present, therefore, we disregard the difference which may be produced in this respect by variations in the duration of turnovers. This point will be discussed later.

Let us take five different spheres of production and let the capital in each have a different organic composition as follows:

Capitals	*Rate of Surplus-Value*	*Surplus-Value*	*Value of Product*	*Rate of Profit*
I. 80c + 20v	100%	20	120	20%
II. 70c + 30v	100%	30	130	30%
III. 60c + 40v	100%	40	140	40%

IV. 85c + 15v	100%	15	115	15%
V. 95c + 5v	100%	5	105	5%

Here, in different spheres of production with the same degree of exploitation, we find considerably different rates of profit corresponding to the different organic composition of these capitals.

The sum total of the capitals invested in these five spheres of production = 500; the sum total of the surplus-value produced by them = 110; the aggregate value of the commodities produced by them = 610. If we consider the 500 as a single capital, and capitals I to V merely as its component parts (as, say, different departments of a cotton mill, which has different ratios of constant to variable capital in its carding, preparatory spinning, spinning, and weaving shops, and in which the average ratio for the factory as a whole has still to be calculated), the mean composition of this capital of 500 would = $390_c + 110_v$, or, in per cent, = $78_c + 22_v$. Should each of the capitals of 100 be regarded as 1/5 of the total capital, its composition would equal this average of $78_c + 22_v$; for every 100, there would be an average surplus-value of 22; thus, the average rate of profit would = 22%, and, finally, the price of every fifth of the total product produced by the 500 would = 122. The product of each fifth of the advanced total capital would then have to be sold at 122.

But to avoid entirely erroneous conclusions, it must not be assumed that all cost-prices = 100.

With $80_c + 20_v$ and a rate of surplus-value = 100%, the total value of commodities produced by capital I = 100 would be $80_c + 20_v + 20_s = 120$, provided the entire constant capital went into the annual product. Now, this may under certain circumstances be the case in some spheres of production. But hardly in cases where the proportion of c : v = 4 : 1. We must, therefore, remember in comparing the values produced by each 100 of the different capitals that they will differ in accordance with the different composition of c as to its fixed and circulating parts, and that, in turn, the fixed portions of each of the different capitals depreciate slowly or rapidly as the case may be, thus transferring unequal quantities of their value to the product in equal periods of time. But this is immaterial to the rate of profit. No matter whether the 80_c give up a value of 80, or 50, or 5, to the annual product, and the annual product consequently = $80_c + 20_v + 20_s = 120$, or $50_c + 20_v + 20_s = 90$, or $5_v + 20_v + 20_s = 45$; in all these cases the redundance of the product's value over its cost-price = 20, and in calculating the rate of profit these 20 are related to the capital of 100 in all of them. The rate of profit of capital I, therefore, is 20% in every case. To make this still plainer, we let different portions of constant capital go into the value of the product of the same five capitals in the following table:

Capitals	*Rate of Surplus-Value*	*Surplus-Value*	*Rate of Profit*	*Used up c*	*Value of commodities*	*Cost-Price*	
I. 80c + 20v	100%	20	20%	50	90	70	
II. 70c + 30v	100%	30	30%	51	111	81	
III. 60c + 40v	100%	40	40%	51	131	91	
IV. 85c + 15v	100%	15	15%	40	70	55	
V. 95c + 5v	100%	5	5%	10	20	15	
390c + 110v	—	110	110%	—	—	—	Total
78c + 22v	—	22	22%	—	—	—	Average

If we now again consider capitals I to V as a single total capital, we shall see that, in this case as well, the composition of the sums of these five capitals = 500 = $390_c + 110_v$, so that we get the same average composition = $78_c + 22_v$, and, similarly, the average surplus-value remains 22. If we divide this surplus-value uniformly among capitals I to V, we get the following commodity-prices:

Capitals	Surplus-Value	Value of Commodities	Cost-Price of Commodities	Price of Commodities	Rate of Profit	Deviation of Price from Value
I. 80c + 20v	20	90	70	92	22%	+2
II. 70c + 30v	30	111	81	103	22%	–8
III. 60c + 40v	40	131	91	113	22%	–18
IV. 85c + 15v	15	70	55	77	22%	+7
V. 95c + 5v	5	20	15	37	22%	+17

Taken together, the commodities are sold at 2 + 7 + 17 = 26 above, and 8 + 18 = 26 below their value so that the deviations of price from value balance out one another through the uniform distribution of surplus-value, or through addition of the average profit of 22 per 100 units of advanced capital to the respective cost-prices of the commodities I to V. One portion of the commodities is sold above its value in the same proportion in which the other is sold below it. And it is only the sale of the commodities at such prices that enables the rate of profit for capitals I to V to be uniformly 22%, regardless of their different organic composition. The prices, which obtain as the average of the various rates of profit in the different spheres of production, added to the cost-prices of the different spheres of production, constitute the prices of production. They have as their prerequisite the existence of a general rate of profit, and this, again, presupposes that the rates of profit in every individual sphere of production taken by itself have previously been reduced to just as many average rates. These particular rates of profit = s/c in every sphere of production and must, as occurs in Part I of this book, be deduced out of the values of the commodities. Without such deduction, the general rate of profit (and consequently the price of production of commodities) remains a vague and senseless conception. Hence, the price of production of a commodity is equal to its cost-price plus the profit allotted to it in percent, in accordance with the general rate of profit, or, in other words, to its cost-price plus the average profit.

Owing to the different organic compositions of capitals invested in different lines of production, and, hence, owing to the circumstance that—depending on the different percentage which the variable part makes up in a total capital of a given magnitude—capitals of equal magnitude put into motion very different quantities of labour, they also appropriate very different quantities of surplus-labour or produce very different quantities of surplus-value. Accordingly, the rates of profit prevailing in the various branches of production are originally very different. These different rates of profit are equalized by competition to a single general rate of profit, which is the average of all these different rates of profit. The profit, accruing in accordance with this general rate of profit to any capital of a given magnitude, whatever its organic composition, is called the average profit. The price of a commodity, which is equal to its cost-price plus the share of the annual average profit on the total capital invested (not merely consumed) in its production that falls to it in accordance with the conditions of turnover, is called its price of production. Take, for example, a capital of 500, of which 100 is fixed capital, and let 10% of this wear out during one turnover of the circulating capital of 400. Let the average profit for the period of turnover be 10%. In that case, the cost-price of the product created during this turnover will be 10_c for wear plus 400 (c + v) circulating capital = 410, and its price of production will be 410 cost-price plus (10% profit on 500) 50 = 460.

Thus, although in selling their commodities the capitalists of the various spheres of production recover the value of the capital consumed in their production, they do not secure the surplus-value, and consequently, the profit, created in their own sphere by the production of these commodities. What they secure is only as much surplus-value, and hence profit, as falls, when uniformly distributed, to the share of every aliquot part of the total social capital from the total social surplus-value, or profit, produced in a given time by the social capital in all spheres of production. Every 100 of an invested capital, whatever its composition, draws as much profit in a year, or any other period of time, as falls to the share of every 100, the Nth part of the total capital, during the same period. So far as profits are concerned, the various capitalists are just so many stockholders in a stock company in which the shares of profit are uniformly divided per 100, so that profits differ in the case of the individual capitalists only in accordance with the amount of capital invested by each in the aggregate enterprise, i.e., according to his investment in social production as a whole, according to the number of his shares. Therefore, the portion of the price of commodities which replaces the elements of capital consumed in the production of these commodities, the portion, therefore, which will have to be used to buy back these consumed capital-values, i.e., their cost-price, depends entirely on the outlay of capital within the respective spheres of production. But the other element of the price of commodities, the profit added to this cost-price, does not depend on the amount of profit produced in a given sphere of production by a given capital in a given period of time. It depends on the mass of profit which falls as an average for any given period to each individual capital as an aliquot part of the total social capital invested in social production.

When a capitalist sells his commodities at their price of production, therefore, he recovers money in proportion to the value of the capital consumed in their production and secures profit in proportion to this advanced capital as the aliquot part in the total social capital. His cost-prices are specific. But the profit added to them is independent of his particular sphere of production, being a simple average per 100 units of invested capital.

Let us assume that the five different investments I to V of the foregoing illustration belong to one man. The quantity of variable and constant capital consumed per 100 of the invested capital in each of the departments I to V in the production of commodities I to V would, needless to say, make up a part of their price since at least this price is required to recover the advanced and consumed portions of the capital. These cost-prices would therefore be different for each class of the commodities I to V, and would as such, be set differently by the owner. But as regards the different quantities of surplus-value, or profit, produced by I to V, they might easily be regarded by the capitalist as profit on his advanced aggregate capital so that every 100 units would get their definite aliquot part. Hence, the cost-prices of the commodities produced in the various departments I to V would be different; but that portion of their selling price derived from the profit added per 100 capital would be the same for all these commodities. The aggregate price of the commodities I to V would therefore equal their aggregate value, i.e., the sum of the cost-prices I to V plus the sum of the surplus-values, or profits, produced in I to V. It would hence actually be the money-expression of the total quantity of past and newly applied labour incorporated in commodities I to V. And in the same way the sum of the prices of production of all commodities produced in society—the totality of all branches of production—is equal to the sum of their values.

This statement seems to conflict with the fact that under capitalist production, the elements of productive capital are, as a rule, bought on the market, and that for this reason, their prices include profit which has already been realised, hence, include the price of production of the respective branch of industry together with the profit contained in it, so that the profit of one branch of industry goes into the cost-price of another. But if we place the sum of the cost-prices of the commodities of an entire country on one side, and the sum of its surplus-values, or profits, on the other, the calculation must evidently be right. For instance, take a certain commodity A. Its cost-price may contain the profits of B, C, D, etc., just as the cost-prices of B, C, D, etc., may contain the profits of A. Now, as we make our calculation the profit of A will not be included in its cost-price, nor will the profits of B, C, D, etc., be included in theirs. Nobody ever includes his own profit in his cost-price. If there are, therefore, n spheres of production, and if each makes a profit amounting to p, then their aggregate cost-price = k - np. Considering the calculation as a whole, we see that since the profits of one sphere of production pass into the cost-price of another, they are therefore included in the calculation as constituents of the total price of the end-product, and so cannot appear a second time on the profit side. If any do appear on this side, however, then only because the commodity in question is itself an ultimate product, whose price of production does not pass into the cost-price of some other commodity.

If the cost-price of a commodity includes a sum = p, which stands for the profits of the producers of the means of production, and if a profit = p_1 is added to this cost-price, the aggregate profit P = p + p_1. The aggregate cost-price of the commodity, considered without the profit portions, is then its own cost-price minus P. Let this cost-price be k. Then, obviously, k + p = k + p + p_1. In dealing with surplus-values, we have seen in Book I that the product of every capital may be so treated, as though a part of it replaces only capital, while the other part represents only surplus-value. In applying this approach to the aggregate product of society, we must make some rectifications. Looking upon society as a whole, the profit contained in, say, the price of flax cannot appear twice—not both as a portion of the linen price and as the profit of the flax.

There is no difference between surplus-value and profit, as long as, e.g., A's surplus-value passes into B's constant capital. It is, after all, quite immaterial to the value of the commodities, whether the labour contained in them is paid or unpaid. This merely shows that B pays for A's surplus-value. A's surplus-value cannot be entered twice in the total calculation.

But the difference is this: Aside from the fact that the price of a particular product, let us say that of capital B, differs from its value because the surplus-value realised in B may be greater or smaller than the profit added to the price of the products of B, the same circumstance applies also to those commodities which form the constant part of capital B, and indirectly also its variable part, as the labourers' necessities of life. So far as the constant portion is concerned, it is itself equal to the cost-price plus the surplus-value, here therefore equal to cost-price plus profit, and this profit may again be greater or smaller than the surplus-value for which it stands. As for the variable capital, the average daily wage is indeed always equal to the value produced in the number of hours the labourer must work to produce the necessities of life. But this number of hours is, in its turn, obscured by the deviation of the prices of production of the necessities of life from their values. However, this always resolves itself to one commodity receiving too little of the surplus-value while another receives too much, so that the deviations from the value which are embodied in the prices of production compensate one another. Under capitalist production, the general law acts as the prevailing tendency only in a very complicated and approximate manner, as a never ascertainable average of ceaseless fluctuations.

Since the general rate of profit is formed by taking the average of the various rates of profit for each 100 of capital invested in a definite period, e.g., a year, it follows that in it the difference brought about by different periods of turnover of different capitals is also effaced. But these differences have a decisive bearing on the different rates of profit in the various spheres of production whose average forms the general rate of profit.

In the preceding illustration concerning the formation of the average rate of profit, we assumed each capital in each sphere of production = 100, and we did so to show the difference in the rates of profit in per cent, and thus also the difference in the values of commodities produced by equal amounts of capital. But it goes without saying that the actual amounts of surplus-value produced in each sphere of production depend on the magnitude of the invested capitals, since the composition of capital is given in each sphere of production. Yet the actual rate of profit in any particular sphere of production is not affected by the fact that the capital invested is 100, or m times 100, or xm times 100. The rate of profit remains 10%, whether the total profit is 10:100, or 1,000:10,000.

However, since the rates of profit differ in the various spheres of production, with very much different quantities of surplus-value, or profit, being produced in them, depending on the proportion of the variable to the total capital, it is evident that the average profit per 100 of the social capital, and hence the average, or general, rate of profit, will differ considerably in accordance with the respective magnitudes of the capitals invested in the various spheres. Let us take four capitals A, B, C, D. Let the rate of surplus-value for all = 100%. Let the variable capital for each 100 of the total be 25 in A, 40 in B, 15 in C, and 10 in D. Then each 100 of the total capital would yield a surplus-value, or profit, of 25 in A, 40 in B, 15 in C, and 10 in D. This would total 90, and if these four capitals are of the same magnitude, the average rate of profit would then be 90/4 or 22½%.

Suppose, however, the total capitals are as follows: A = 200, B = 300, C = 1,000, D = 4,000. The profits produced would then respectively = 50, 120, 150, and 400. This makes a profit of 720 and an average rate of profit of $13^1/_{11}$% for 5,500, the sum of the four capitals.

The masses of the total value produced differ in accordance with the magnitudes of the total capitals invested in A, B, C, D, respectively. The formation of the average rate of profit is, therefore, not merely a matter of obtaining the simple average of the different rates of profit in the various spheres of production, but rather one of the relative weight which these different rates of profit have in forming this average. This, however, depends on the relative magnitude of the capital invested in each particular sphere, or on the aliquot part which the capital invested in each particular sphere forms in the aggregate social capital. There will naturally be a very great difference, depending on whether a greater or smaller part of the total capital produces a higher or lower rate of profit. And this, again, depends on how much capital is invested in spheres, in which the variable capital is relatively small or large compared to the total capital. It is just like the average interest obtained by a usurer who lends various quantities of capital at different interest rates; for instance, at 4, 5, 6, 7%, etc. The average rate will depend entirely on how much of his capital he has loaned out at each of the different rates of interest.

The general rate of profit is, therefore, determined by two factors:

1. The organic composition of the capitals in the different spheres of production, and thus, the different rates of profit in the individual spheres.
2. The distribution of the total social capital in these different spheres, and thus, the relative magnitude of the capital invested in each particular sphere at the specific rate of profit prevailing in it; i.e., the relative share of the total social capital absorbed by each individual sphere of production.

In Books I and II, we dealt only with the *value* of commodities. On the one hand, the *cost-price* has now been singled out as a part of this value, and, on the other, the *price of production* of commodities has been developed as its converted form.

Suppose the composition of the average social capital is $80_c + 20_v$ and the annual rate of surplus-value, s›, is 100%. In that case, the average annual profit for a capital of 100 = 20, and the general annual rate of profit = 20%. Whatever the cost-price, k, of the commodities annually produced by a capital of 100, their price of production would then be k + 20. In those spheres of production in which the composition of capital would = $(80 - x)_c + (20 + x)_v$, the actually produced surplus-value, or the annual profit produced in that particular sphere, would be 20 + x, that is, greater than 20, and the value of the produced commodities = k + 20 + x, that is, greater than k + 20, or greater than their price of production. In those spheres, in which the composition of the capital=$(80 + x)_c + (20 - x)_v$, the annually produced surplus-value, or profit, would = 20 - x, or less than 20, and consequently the value of the commodities k + 20 - x less than the price of production, which = k + 20. Aside from possible differences in the periods of turnover, the price of production of the commodities would then equal their value only in spheres, in which the composition would happen to be $80_c + 20_v$.

The specific development of the social productivity of labour in each particular sphere of production varies in degree, higher or lower, depending on how large a quantity of means of production are set in motion by a definite quantity of labour, hence in a given working-day by a definite number of labourers, and, consequently, on how small a quantity of labour is required for a given quantity of means of production. Such capitals as contain a larger percentage of constant and a smaller percentage of variable capital than the average social capital are, therefore, called capitals of *higher* composition, and, conversely, those capitals in which the constant is relatively smaller, and the variable relatively greater than in the average social capital, are called capitals of *lower* composition. Finally, we call those capitals whose composition coincides with the average, capitals of average composition. Should the average social capital be composed in per cent of $80_c + 20_v$, then a capital of $90_c + 10_v$ is *higher*, and a capital of $70_c + 30_v$ *lower* than the social average. Generally speaking, if the composition of the average social capital=mc + nv, in which m and n are constant magnitudes and m + n = 100, the formula $(m + x)_c + (n - x)_v$ represents the higher composition, and $(m - x)_c + (n + x)_v$ the lower composition of an individual capital or group of capitals. The way in which these capitals perform their functions after establishment of an average rate of profit and assuming one turnover per year, is shown in the following tabulation, in which I represents the average composition with an average rate of profit of 20%.

i. $80_v + 20_v + 20_s$. Rate of profit = 20%.
Price of product = 120. Value = 120.

ii. $90_c + 10_v + 10_s$. Rate of profit = 20%.
Price of product = 120. Value = 110.

iii. $70_c + 30_v + 30_s$. Rate of profit = 20%.
Price of product = 120. Value = 130.

The value of the commodities produced by capital II would, therefore, be smaller than their price of production, the price of production of the commodities of III smaller than their value, and only in the case of capital I in branches of production in which the composition happens to coincide with the social average, would value, and price of production be equal. In applying these terms to any particular cases note must, however, be taken whether a deviation of the ratio between c and v is simply due to a change in the value of the elements of constant capital, rather than to a difference in the technical composition.

The foregoing statements have at any rate modified the original assumption concerning the determination of the cost-price of commodities. We had originally assumed that the cost-price of a commodity equalled the value of the commodities consumed in its production. But for the buyer, the price of production of a specific commodity is its cost-price, and may thus pass as cost-price into the prices of other commodities. Since the price of production may differ from the value of a commodity, it follows that the cost-price of a commodity containing this price of production of another commodity may also stand above or below that portion of its total value derived from the value of the means of production consumed by it. It is necessary to remember this modified significance of the cost-price, and to bear in mind that there is always the possibility of an error if the cost-price of a commodity in any particular sphere is identified with the value of the means of production consumed by it. Our present analysis does not necessitate a closer examination of this point. It remains true, nevertheless, that the cost-price of a commodity is always smaller than its value. For no matter how much the cost-price of a commodity may differ from the value of the means of production consumed by it, this past mistake is immaterial to the capitalist. The cost-price of a particular commodity is a definite condition which is given, and independent of the production of our capitalist, while the result of his production is a commodity containing surplus-value, therefore an excess of value over and above its cost-price. For all other purposes, the statement that the cost-price is smaller than the value of a commodity has now changed practically into the statement that the cost-price is smaller than the price of production. As concerns the total social capital, in which the price of production is equal to the value, this statement is identical with the former, namely that the cost-price is smaller than the value. And while it is modified in the individual spheres of production, the fundamental fact always remains that in the case of the total social capital the cost-price of the commodities produced by it is smaller than their value, or, in the case of the total mass of social commodities, smaller than their price of production, which is identical with their value. The cost-price of a commodity refers only to the quantity of paid labour contained in it, while its value refers to all the paid and unpaid labour contained in it. The price of production refers to the sum of the paid labour plus a certain quantity of unpaid labour determined for any particular sphere of production by conditions over which it has no control.

The formula that the price of production of a commodity = k + p, i.e., equals its cost-price plus profit, is now more precisely defined with p = kp' (p' being the general rate of profit). Hence the price of production = k + kp'. If k = 300 and p' = 15%, then the price of production is k + kp' = 300 + 300 × 15/100, or 345.

The price of production of the commodities in any particular sphere may change in magnitude:

1. If the general rate of profit changes independently of this particular sphere, while the value of the commodities remains the same (the same quantities of congealed and living labour being consumed in their production as before).
2. If there is a change of value, either in this particular sphere in consequence of technical changes, or in consequence of a change in the value of those commodities which form the elements of its constant capital, while the general rate of profit remains unchanged.
3. Finally, if a combination of the two aforementioned circumstances takes place.

In spite of the great changes occurring continually, as we shall see, in the actual rates of profit within the individual spheres of production, any real change in the general rate of profit, unless brought about by way of an exception by extraordinary economic events, is the belated effect of a series of fluctuations extending over very long periods, fluctuations which require much time before consolidating and equalising one another to bring about a change in the general rate of profit. In all shorter periods (quite aside from fluctuations of market-prices), a change in the prices of production is, therefore, always traceable *prima facie* to actual changes in the value of commodities, i.e., to changes in the total amount of labour-time required for their production. Mere changes in the money-expression of the same values are, naturally, not at all considered here.

On the other hand, it is evident that from the point of view of the total social capital the value of the commodities produced by it (or, expressed in money, their price) = value of constant capital + value of variable capital + surplus-value. Assuming the degree of labour exploitation to be constant, the rate of profit cannot change so long as the mass of surplus-value remains the same, unless there is a change in either the value of the constant capital, the value of the variable capital, or the value of both, so that C changes, and thereby s/C, which represents the general rate of profit. In each case, therefore, a change in the general rate of profit implies a change in the value of commodities which form the elements of the constant or variable capital, or of both.

Or, the general rate of profit may change, while the value of the commodities remains the same when the degree of labour exploitation changes.

Or, if the degree of labour exploitation remains the same, the general rate of profit may change through a change in the amount of labour employed relative to the constant capital as a result of technical changes in the labour-process. But such technical changes must always show themselves in, and be attended by, a change in the value of the commodities, whose production would then require more or less labour than before.

We saw in Part I that surplus-value and profit are identical from the standpoint of their mass. But the rate of profit is from the very outset distinct from the rate of surplus-value, which appears at first sight as merely a different form of calculating. But at the same time this serves, also from the outset, to obscure and mystify the actual origin of surplus-value, since the rate of profit can rise or fall while the rate of surplus-value remains the same, and vice versa, and since the capitalist is in practice solely interested in the rate of profit. Yet there was difference of magnitude only between the rate of surplus-value and the rate of profit and not between the surplus-value itself and profit. Since in the rate of profit the surplus-value is calculated in relation to the total capital and the latter is taken as its standard of measurement, the surplus-value itself appears to originate from the total capital, uniformly derived from all its parts, so that the organic difference between constant and variable capital is obliterated in the conception of profit. Disguised as profit, surplus-value actually denies its origin, loses its character, and becomes unrecognisable. However, hitherto the distinction between profit and surplus-value applied solely to a qualitative change, or change of form, while there was no real difference of magnitude in this first stage of the change between surplus-value and profit, but only between the rate of profit and the rate of surplus-value.

But it is different, as soon as a general rate of profit, and thereby an average profit corresponding to the magnitude of invested capital given in the various spheres of production, have been established.

It is then only an accident if the surplus-value, and thus the profit, actually produced in any particular sphere of production, coincides with the profit contained in the selling price of a commodity. As a rule, surplus-value and profit and not their rates alone, are then different magnitudes. At a given degree of exploitation, the mass of surplus-value produced in a particular sphere of production is then more important for the aggregate average profit of social capital, and thus for the capitalist class in general, than for the individual capitalist in any specific branch of production. It is of importance to the latter only in so far as the quantity of surplus-value produced in his branch helps to regulate the average profit. But this is a process which occurs behind his back, one he does not see, nor understand, and which indeed does not interest him. The actual difference of magnitude between profit and surplus-value—not merely between the rate of profit and the rate of surplus-value—in the various spheres of production now completely conceals the true nature and origin of profit not only from the capitalist, who has a special interest in deceiving himself on this score, but also from the labourer. The transformation of values into prices of production serves to obscure the basis for determining value itself. Finally, since the mere transformation of surplus-value into profit distinguishes the portion of the value of a commodity forming the profit from the portion forming its cost-price, it is natural that the conception of value should elude the capitalist at this juncture, for he does not see the total labour put into the commodity, but only that portion of the total labour for which he has paid in the shape of means of production, be they living or not, so that his profit appears to him as something outside the immanent value of the commodity. Now, this idea is fully confirmed, fortified, and ossified in that, from the standpoint of his particular sphere of production, the profit added to the cost-price is not actually determined by the limits of the formation of value within his own sphere, but through completely outside influences.

The fact that this intrinsic connection is here revealed for the first time; that up to the present time, political economy, as we shall see in the following and in Book IV, either forcibly abstracted itself from the distinctions between surplus-value and profit, and their rates, so it could retain value determination as a basis, or else abandoned this value determination and with it all vestiges of a scientific approach, in order to cling to the differences that strike the eye in this phenomenon—this confusion of the theorists best illustrates the utter incapacity of the practical capitalist, blinded by competition as he is, and incapable of penetrating its phenomena, to recognise the inner essence and inner structure of this process behind its outer appearance.

In fact, all the laws evolved in Part I concerning the rise and fall of the rate of profit have the following two-fold meaning:

1. On the one hand, they are the laws of the general rate of profit. In view of the many different causes which make the rate of profit rise or fall, one would think, after everything that has been said and done, that the general rate of profit must change every day. But a trend in one sphere of production compensates for that in another, their effects cross and paralyse one another. We shall later examine to which side these fluctuations ultimately gravitate. But they are slow. The suddenness, multiplicity, and different duration of the fluctuations in the individual spheres of production make them compensate for one another in the order of their succession in time, a fall in prices following a rise, and vice versa, so that they remain limited to local, i.e., individual, spheres. Finally, the various local fluctuations neutralise one another. Within each individual sphere of production, there take place changes, i.e., deviations from the general rate of profit, which counterbalance one another in a definite time on the one hand, and thus have no influence upon the general rate of profit, and which, on the other, do not react upon it, because they are balanced by other simultaneous local fluctuations. Since the general rate of profit is not only determined by the average rate of profit in each sphere, but also by the distribution of the total social capital among the different individual spheres, and since this distribution is continually changing, it becomes another constant cause of change in the general rate of profit. But it is a cause of change which mostly paralyses itself, owing to the uninterrupted and many-sided nature of this movement.
2. Within each sphere, there is some room for play for a longer or shorter space of time, in which the rate of profit of this sphere may fluctuate, before this fluctuation consolidates sufficiently after rising or falling to gain time for influencing the general rate of profit and therefore assuming more than local importance. The laws of the rate of profit, as developed in Part I of this book, likewise remain applicable within these limits of space and time.

The theoretical conception concerning the first transformation of surplus-value into profit, that every part of a capital yields a uniform profit, expresses a practical fact. Whatever the composition of an industrial capital, whether it sets in motion one quarter of congealed labour and three-quarters of living labour, or three-quarters of congealed labour and one-quarter of living labour, whether in one case it absorbs three times as much surplus-labour, or produces three times as much surplus-value than in another—in either case it yields the same profit, given the same degree of labour exploitation and leaving aside individual differences, which, incidentally, disappear because we are dealing in both cases with the average composition of the entire sphere of production. The individual capitalist (or all the capitalists in each individual sphere of production), whose outlook is limited, rightly believes that his profit is not derived solely from the labour employed by him, or in his line of production. This is quite true, as far as his average profit is concerned. To what extent this profit is due to the aggregate exploitation of labour on the part of the total social capital, i.e., by all his capitalist colleagues—this interrelation is a complete mystery to the individual capitalist; all the more so, since no bourgeois theorists, the political economists, have so far revealed it. A saving of labour—not only labour necessary to produce a certain product, but also the number of employed labourers—and the employment of more congealed labour (constant capital), appear to be very sound operations from the economic standpoint and do not seem to exert the least influence on the general rate of profit and the average profit. How could living labour be the sole source of profit, in view of the fact that a reduction in the quantity of labour required for production appears not to exert any influence on profit? Moreover, it even seems in certain circumstances to be the nearest source of an increase of profits, at least for the individual capitalist.

If in any particular sphere of production there is a rise or fall of the portion of the cost-price which represents the value of constant capital, this portion comes from the circulation and, either enlarged or reduced, passes from the very outset into the process of production of the commodity. If, on the other hand, the same number of labourers produces more or less in the same time, so that the quantity of labour required for the production of a definite quantity of commodities varies while the number of labourers remains the same, that portion of the cost-price which represents the value of the variable capital may remain the same, i.e., contribute the same amount to the cost-price of tho total product. But every one of the individual commodities whose sum makes up the total product, shares in more or less labour (paid and therefore also unpaid), and shares consequently in the greater or smaller outlay for this labour, i.e., a larger or smaller portion of the wage. The total wages paid by the capitalist remain the same, but wages differ if calculated per piece of the commodity. Thus, there is a change in this portion of the cost-price of the commodity. But no matter whether the cost-price of the individual commodity (or, perhaps, the cost-price of the sum of commodities produced by a capital of a given magnitude) rises or falls, be it due to such changes in its own value, or in that of its elements, the average profit of, e.g., 10% remains 10%. Still, 10% of an individual commodity may represent very different amounts, depending on the change of magnitude caused in the cost-price of the individual commodity by such changes of value as we have assumed.

So far as the variable capital is concerned—and this is most important, because it is the source of surplus-value, and because anything which conceals its relation to the accumulation of wealth by the capitalist serves to mystify the entire system—matters get cruder or appear to the capitalist in the following light: A variable capital of £100 represents the weekly wage of, say, 100 labourers. If these 100 labourers weekly produce 200 pieces of a commodity = 200C, in a given working-time, then 1C—abstracted from that portion of its cost-price which is added by the constant capital, costs £100/200 = 10 shillings, since £100 = 200C. Now suppose that a change occurs in the productiveness of labour. Suppose it doubles, so that the same number of labourers now produces twice 200C in the time which it previously took to produce 200C. In that case (considering only that part of the cost-price which consists of wages) 1C = £100/400 = 5 shillings, since now £100 = 400C. Should the productiveness decrease one-half, the same labour would produce only 200C/2, and since £100 = 200C/2, 1C = £200/2 = £1. The changes in the labour-time required for the production of the commodities, and hence the changes in their value, thus appear in regard to the cost-price, and hence to the price of production, as a different distribution of the same wage for more or fewer commodities, depending on the greater or smaller quantity of commodities produced in the same working-time for the same wage. What the capitalist, and consequently also the political economist, see is that the part of the paid labour per piece of commodity changes with the productivity of labour, and that the value of each piece also changes accordingly. What they do not see is that the same applies to unpaid labour contained in very piece of the commodity, and this is perceived so much less since the average profit actually is only accidentally determined by the unpaid labour absorbed in the sphere of the individual capitalist. It is only in such crude and meaningless form that we can glimpse that the value of commodities is determined by the labour contained in them.

10

Equalisation of the General Rate of Profit Through Competition Market-Prices and Market-Values. Surplus-Profit

The capital invested in some spheres of production has a mean, or average, composition, that is, it has the same, or almost the same composition as the average social capital.

In these spheres, the price of production is exactly or almost the same as the value of the produced commodity expressed in money. If there were no other way of reaching a mathematical limit, this would be the one. Competition so distributes the social capital among the various spheres of production that the prices of production in each sphere take shape according to the model of the prices of production in these spheres of average composition, i.e., they = k + kp' (cost-price plus the average rate of profit multiplied by the cost price). This average rate of profit, however, is the percentage of profit in that sphere of average composition in which profit, therefore, coincides with surplus-value. Hence, the rate of profit is the same in all spheres of production, for it is equalized on the basis of those average spheres of production which has the average composition of capital. Consequently, the sum of the profits in all spheres of production must equal the sum of the surplus-values, and the sum of the prices of production of the total social product equal the sum of its value. But it is evident that the balance among spheres of production of different composition must tend to equalize them with the spheres of average composition, be it exactly or only approximately the same as the social average. Between the spheres more or less approximating the average, there is again a tendency toward equalization, seeking the ideal average, i.e., an average that does not really exist, i.e., a tendency to take this ideal as a standard. In this way, the tendency necessarily prevails to make the prices of production merely converted forms of value, or to turn profits into mere portions of surplus-value. However, these are not distributed in proportion to the surplus-value produced in each special sphere of production, but rather in proportion to the mass of capital employed in each sphere, so that equal masses of capital, whatever their composition, receive equal aliquot shares of the total surplus-value produced by the total social capital.

In the case of capitals of average, or approximately average, composition, the price of production is thus the same or almost the same as the value, and the profit the same as the surplus-value produced by them. All other capitals, of whatever composition, tend toward this average under pressure of competition. But since the capitals of average composition are of the same, or approximately the same, structure as the average social capital, all capitals have the tendency, regardless of the surplus-value produced by them, to realize the average profit, rather than their own surplus-value in the price of their commodity, i.e., to realize the prices of production.

On the other hand, it may be said that wherever an average profit, and therefore a general rate of profit, is produced—no matter by what means—such an average profit cannot be anything but the profit on the average social capital, whose sum is equal to the sum of surplus-value. Moreover, the prices obtained by adding this average profit to the cost-prices cannot be anything but the values transmuted into prices of production. Nothing would be altered if capitals in certain spheres of production would not, for some reason, be subject to the process of equalization. The average profit would then be computed on that portion of the social capital which enters the equalization process. It is evident that the average profit can be nothing but the total mass of surplus-values allotted to the various quantities of capital proportionally to their magnitudes in their different spheres of production. It is the total realized unpaid labour, and this total mass, like the paid, congealed or living, labour, obtains in the total mass of commodities and money that falls to the capitalists.

The really difficult question is this: how is this equalization of profits into a general rate of profit brought about, since it is obviously a result rather than a point of departure?

To begin with, an estimate of the values of commodities, for instance, in terms of money, can obviously only be the result of their exchange. If therefore, we assume such an estimate, we must regard it as the outcome of an actual exchange of commodity-value for commodity-value. But how does this exchange of commodities at their real value come about?

Let us first assume that all commodities in the different branches of production are sold at their real values. What would then be the outcome? According to the foregoing, very different rates of profit would then reign in the various spheres of production. It is *prima facie* two entirely different matters whether commodities are sold at their values (i.e., exchanged in proportion to the value contained in them at prices corresponding to their value), or whether they are sold at such prices that their sale yields equal profits for equal masses of the capital advanced for their respective production.

The fact that capitals employing unequal amounts of living labour produce unequal amounts of surplus-value, presupposes at least to a certain extent that the degree of exploitation or the rate of surplus-value are the same, or that any existing differences in them are equalized by real or imaginary (conventional) grounds of compensation. This would assume competition among labourers and equalization through their continual migration from one sphere of production to another. Such a general rate of surplus-value—viewed as a tendency, like all other economic laws—has been assumed by us for the sake of theoretical simplification. But in reality, it is an actual premise of the capitalist mode of production, although it is more or less obstructed by practical frictions causing more or less considerable local differences, such as the settlement laws for farm-labourers in Britain. But in theory, it is assumed that the laws of capitalist production operate in their pure form. In reality, there exists only approximation; but, this approximation is the greater, the more developed the capitalist mode of production and the less it is adulterated and amalgamated with survivals of former economic conditions.

The whole difficulty arises from the fact that commodities are not exchanged simply as *commodities*, but as *products of capitals*, which claim participation in the total amount of surplus-value, proportional to their magnitude, or equal if they are of equal magnitude. And this claim is to be satisfied by the total price for commodities produced by a given capital in a certain space of time. This total price is, however, only the sum of the prices of the individual commodities produced by this capital.

The *punctum saliens* will be best brought if we approach the matter as follows: suppose the labourers themselves are in possession of their respective means of production and exchange their commodities with one another. In that case, these commodities would not be products of capital. The value of the various means of labour and raw materials would differ in accordance with the technical nature of the labours performed in the different branches of production. Furthermore, aside from the unequal value of the means of production employed by them, they would require different quantities of means of production for given quantities of labour, depending on whether a certain commodity can be finished in one hour, another in one day, and so forth. Also, suppose the labourers work an equal average length of time, allowing for compensations that arise from the different labour intensities, etc. In such a case, two labourers would, first, both have replaced their outlays, the cost-prices of the consumed means of production, in the commodities which make up the product of their day's work. These outlays would differ, depending on the technical nature of their labour. Secondly, both of them would have created equal amounts of new value, namely the working-day added by them to the means of production. This would comprise their wages plus the surplus-value, the latter representing surplus-labour over and above their necessary wants, the product of which would, however, belong to them. To put it the capitalist way, both of them receive the same wages plus the same profit, or the same value, expressed, say, by the product of a ten-hour working-day. But in the first place, the values of their commodities would have to differ. In commodity I, for instance, the portion of value corresponding to the consumed means of production might be higher than in commodity II. And, to introduce all possible differences, we might assume right now that commodity I absorbs more living labour, and consequently requires more labour-time to be produced, than commodity II. The values of commodities I and II are, therefore, very different. So are the sums of the values of the commodities, which represent the product of the labour performed by labourers I and II in a given time. The rates of profit would also differ considerably for I and II if we take the rate of profit to be the proportion of the surplus-value to the total value of the invested means of production. The means of subsistence daily consumed by I and II during production, which take the place of wages, here form the part of the invested means of production ordinarily called variable capital. But for equal working periods the surplus values would be the same for I and II, or, more precisely, since I and II each receive the value of the product of a day's work, both of them receive equal values after the value of the invested 'constant' elements has been deducted, and one portion of those equal values may be regarded as a substitute for the means of subsistence consumed in production, and the other as surplus-value in excess of it. If labourer I has greater expenses, they are made good by a greater portion of the value of his commodity, which replaces this 'constant ' part, and he, therefore, has to reconvert a larger portion of the total value of his product into the material elements of this constant part, while labourer II, though receiving less for this, has so much less to reconvert. In these circumstances, a difference in the rates of profit would therefore be immaterial, just as it is immaterial to the wage-labourer today what rate of profit may express the amount of surplus-value filched from him, and just as in international commerce, the difference in the various national rates of profit is immaterial to commodity exchange.

The exchange of commodities at their values, or approximately at their values, thus requires a much lower stage than their exchange at their prices of production, which requires a definite level of capitalist development.

Whatever the manner in which the prices of various commodities are first mutually fixed or regulated, their movements are always governed by the law of value. If the labour-time required for their production happens to shrink, prices fall; if it increases, prices rise, provided other conditions remain the same.

Apart from the domination of prices and price movement by the law of value, it is quite appropriate to regard the values of commodities as not only theoretically but also historically *prius* to the prices of production. This applies to conditions in which the labourer owns his means of production, and this is the condition of the land-owning farmer living off his own labour and the craftsman, in the ancient as well as in the modern world. This agrees also with the view we expressed previously that the evolution of products into commodities arises through exchange between different communities, not between the members of the same community. It holds not only for this primitive condition, but also for subsequent conditions, based on slavery and serfdom, and for the guild organisation of handicrafts, so long as the means of production involved in each branch of production can be transferred from one sphere to another only with difficulty and therefore the various spheres of production are related to one another, within certain limits, as foreign countries or communist communities.

For prices at which commodities are exchanged to approximately correspond to their values, nothing more is necessary than 1) for the exchange of the various commodities to cease being purely accidental or only occasional; 2) so far as direct exchange of commodities is concerned, for these commodities to be produced on both sides in approximately sufficient quantities to meet mutual requirements, something learned from mutual experience in trading and therefore a natural outgrowth of continued trading; and 3) so far as selling is concerned, for no natural or artificial monopoly to enable either of the contracting sides to sell commodities above their value or to compel them to undersell. By accidental monopoly we mean a monopoly which a buyer or seller acquires through an accidental state of supply and demand.

The assumption that the commodities of the various spheres of production are sold at their value merely implies, of course, that their value is the centre of gravity around which their prices fluctuate, and their continual rises and drops tend to equalise. There is also the *market-value*—of which later—to be distinguished from the individual value of particular commodities produced by different producers. The individual value of some of these commodities will be below their market-value (that is, less labour time is required for their production than expressed is the market value), while that of others will exceed the market-value. On the one hand, market-value is to be viewed as the average value of commodities produced in a single sphere, and, on the other, as the individual value of the commodities produced under average conditions of their respective sphere and forming the bulk of the products of that sphere. It is only in extraordinary combinations that commodities produced under the worst, or the most favourable, conditions regulate the market-value, which, in turn, forms the centre of fluctuation for market-prices. The latter, however, are the same for commodities of the same kind. If the ordinary demand is satisfied by the supply of commodities of average value, hence of a value midway between the two extremes, then the commodities whose individual value is below the market-value realise an extra surplus-value, or surplus-profit, while those, whose individual value exceeds the market-value, are unable to realise a portion of the surplus-value contained in them.

It does no good to say that the sale of commodities produced under the least favourable conditions proves that they are required to satisfy the demand. If, in the assumed case, the price were higher than the average market-value, the demand would be smaller. At a certain price, a commodity occupies just so much place on the market. This place remains the same in case of a price change only if the higher price is accompanied by a drop in the supply of the commodity, and a lower price by an increase of supply. And if the demand is so great that it does not contract when the price is regulated by the value of commodities produced under the least favourable conditions, then these determine the market-value. This is not possible unless demand is greater than usual, or if supply drops below the usual level. Finally, if the mass of the produced commodities exceeds the quantity disposed of at average market-values, the commodities produced under the most favourable conditions regulate the market-value. They may, for example, be sold exactly or approximately at their individual value, in which case the commodities produced under the least favourable conditions may not even realise their cost-price, while those produced under average conditions realise only a portion of the surplus-value contained in them. What has been said here of market-value applies to the price of production as soon as it takes the place of market-value. The price of production is regulated in each sphere, and likewise regulated by special circumstances. And this price of production is, in its turn, the centre around which the daily market-prices fluctuate and tend to equalise one another within definite periods. (See Ricardo on determining the price of production through those working under the least favourable conditions.)

No matter how the prices are regulated, we arrive at the following:

1. The law of value dominates price movements with reductions or increases in required labour-time making prices of production fall or rise. It is in this sense

that Ricardo (who doubtlessly realised that his prices of production deviated from the value of commodities) says that 'the inquiry to which I wish to draw the reader's attention relates to the effect of the variations in the relative value of commodities, and not in their absolute value'.

2. The average profit determining the prices of production must always be approximately equal to that quantity of surplus-value, which falls to the share of individual capital in its capacity of an aliquot part of the total social capital. Suppose that the general rate of profit, and therefore the average profit, are expressed by money-value greater than the money-value of the actual average surplus-value. So far as the capitalists are concerned, it is then immaterial whether they reciprocally charge 10 or 15% profit. Neither of these percentages covers more actual commodity-value than the other, since the overcharge in money is mutual. As for the labourer (the assumption being that he receives his normal wage and the rise in the average profit does not, therefore, imply an actual deduction from his wage, i.e., it expresses something entirely different from the normal surplus-value of the capitalist), the rise in commodity-prices caused by an increase of the average profit must correspond to the rise of the money-expression of the variable capital. Such a general nominal increase in the rate of profit and the average profit above the limit provided by the ratio of the actual surplus-value to the total invested capital is not, in effect, possible without causing an increase in wages, and also an increase in the prices of commodities forming the constant capital. The reverse is true in case of a reduction. Since the total value of the commodities regulates the total surplus-value, and this in, turn, regulates the level of average profit and thereby the general rate of profit—as a general law or a law governing fluctuations—it follows the law of value regulates the prices of production.

What competition, first in a single sphere, achieves is a single market-value and market-price derived from the various individual values of commodities. And it is competition of capitals in different spheres, which first brings out the price of production, equalizing the rates of profit in the different spheres. The latter process requires a higher development of capitalist production that the previous one.

For commodities of the same sphere of production, the same kind, and approximately the same quality, to be sold at their values, the following two requirements are necessary:

First, the different individual values must be equalized at one social value, the above-named market value, and this implies competition among producers of the same kind of commodities and, likewise, the existence of a common market in which they offer their articles for sale. For the market-price of identical commodities, each, however, produced under different individual circumstances, to correspond to the market-value and not to deviate from it either by rising above or falling below it, it is necessary that the pressure exerted by different sellers upon one another be sufficient to bring enough commodities to market to fill the social requirements, i.e., a quantity for which society is capable of paying the market-value. Should the mass of products exceed this demand, the commodities would have to be sold below their market-value; and conversely, above their market-value if the mass of products were not large enough to meet the demand, or, what amounts to the same, if the pressure of competition among sellers were not strong enough to bring this mass of products to market. Should the market-value change, this would also entail a change in the conditions on which the total mass of commodities could be sold. Should the market-value fall, this would entail a rise in the average social demand (this always taken to mean the effective demand), which could, within certain limits, absorb larger masses of commodities. Should the market-value rise, this would entail a drop in the social demand, and a smaller mass of commodities would be absorbed. Hence, if supply and demand regulate the market-price, or rather the deviations of the market-price from the market-value, then, in turn, the market-value regulates the ratio of supply to demand, or the centre round which fluctuations of supply and demand cause market-prices to oscillate.

Looking closer, we find that the conditions applicable to the value of an individual commodity are here reproduced as conditions governing the value of the aggregate of a certain kind of commodity. Capitalist production is mass production from the very outset. But even in other, less developed, modes of production that which is produced in relatively small quantities as a common product by small-scale, even if numerous, producers, is concentrated in large quantities—at least in the case of the vital commodities—in the hands of relatively few merchants. The latter accumulate them and sell them as the common product of an entire branch of production, or of a more or less considerable contingent of it.

It should be here noted in passing that the 'social demand,' i.e., the factor which regulates the principle of demand, is essentially subject to the mutual relationship of the different classes and their respective economic position, notably therefore to, firstly, the ratio of total surplus-value to wages, and, secondly, to the relation of the various parts into which surplus-value is split up (profit, interest, ground-rent, taxes, etc.). And this, thus again shows how absolutely nothing can be explained by the relation of supply to demand before ascertaining the basis on which this relation rests.

Although both commodity and money represent a unity of exchange-value and use-value, we have already seen that in buying and selling both of these functions are polarised at the two extremes, the commodity (seller) representing the use-value, and the money (buyer) representing the exchange-value. One of the first premises of selling was that a commodity should have use-value and should therefore satisfy a social need. The other premise was that the quantity of labour contained in the commodity should represent socially necessary labour, i.e., its individual value (and, what amounts to the same under the present assumption, its selling price) should coincide with its social value.

Let us apply this to the mass of commodities available in the market, which represents the product of a whole sphere.

The matter will be most readily pictured by regarding this whole mass of commodities, produced by *one* branch of industry, as *one* commodity, and the sum of the prices of the many identical commodities as *one* price. Then, whatever has been said of a single commodity applies literally to the mass of commodities of an entire branch of production available in the market. The requirement that the individual value of a commodity should correspond to its social value is now realised, or further determined, in that the mass contains social labour necessary for its production, and that the value of this mass is equal to its market-value.

Now suppose that the bulk of these commodities is produced under approximately similar normal social conditions, so that this value is at the same time the individual value of the individual commodities which make up this mass. If a relatively small portion of these commodities may now have been produced below, and another above, these conditions, so that the individual value of one portion is greater, and that of the other smaller, than the average value of the bulk of the commodities, but in such proportions that these extremes balance one another, so that the average value of the commodities at these extremes is equal to the value of commodities in the centre, then the market-value is determined by the value of the commodities produced under average conditions. The value of the entire mass of commodities is equal to the actual sum of the values of all individual commodities taken together, whether produced under average conditions, or under conditions above or below the average. In that case, the market-value, or social value, of the mass of commodities—the necessary labour-time contained in them—is determined by the value of the preponderant mean mass.

Suppose, on the contrary, that the total mass of the commodities in question brought to market remains the same, while the value of the commodities produced under less favourable conditions fails to balance out the value of commodities produced under more favourable conditions, so that the part of the mass produced under less favourable conditions forms a relatively weighty quantity as compared with the average mass and with the other extreme. In that case, the mass produced under less favourable conditions regulates the market, or social value.

Suppose, finally, that the mass of commodities produced under better than average conditions considerably exceeds that produced under worse conditions, and is large even compared with that produced under average conditions. In that case, the part produced under the most favourable conditions determines the market-value. We ignore here the overstocked market, in which the part produced under most favourable conditions always regulates the market-price. We are not dealing here with the market-price, in so far as it differs from the market-value, but with the various determinations of the market-value itself.[1]

In fact, strictly speaking (which, of course, occurs in reality only in approximation and with a thousand modifications), the market-value of the entire mass, regulated as it is by the average values, is in case I equal to the sum of their individual values; although, in the case of the commodities produced at the extremes, this value is represented as an average value which is forced upon them. Those who produce at the worst extreme must then sell their commodities below the individual value; those producing at the best extreme sell them above it.

In case II the individual lots of commodity-values produced at the two extremes do not balance one another. Rather, the lot produced under the worse conditions decides the issue. Strictly speaking, the average price, or the market-value, of each individual commodity, or each aliquot part of the total mass, would now be determined by the total value of the mass as obtained by adding up the values of the commodities produced under different conditions, and in accordance with the aliquot part of this total value falling to the share of each individual commodity. The market-value thus obtained would exceed the individual value not only of the commodities belonging to the favourable extreme, but also of those belonging to the average lot. Yet, it would still be below the individual value of those commodities produced at the unfavourable extreme. How close the market-value approaches, or finally coincides with, the latter would depend entirely on the volume occupied by commodities produced at the unfavourable extreme of the commodity sphere in question. If demand is only slightly greater than supply, the individual value of the unfavourably produced commodities regulates the market-price.

Finally, if the lot of commodities produced at the favourable extreme occupies greater place than the other extreme, and also than the average lot, as it does in case III, then the market-value falls below the average value. The average value, computed by adding the sums of values at the two extremes and at the middle, stands here below the value of the middle, which it approaches, or vice versa, depending on the relative place occupied by the favourable extreme. Should demand be weaker than supply, the favourably situated part, whatever its size, makes room for itself forcibly by paring its price down to its individual value? The market-value cannot ever coincide with this individual value of the commodities produced under the most favourable conditions, except when supply far exceeds demand.

This mode of determining market-values, which we have here outlined *abstractly*, is promoted in the real market by competition among the buyers, provided the demand is large enough to absorb the mass of commodities at values so fixed. And this brings us to the other point.

Second, to say that a commodity has a use-value is merely to say that it satisfies some social want. So long as we dealt with individual commodities only, we could assume that there was a need for a particular commodity—its quantity already implied by its price without inquiring further into the quantity required to satisfy this want. This quantity is, however, of essential importance, as soon as the product of an entire branch of production is placed on one side, and the social need for it on the other. It then becomes necessary to consider the extent, i.e., the amount of this social want.

In the foregoing determinations of market-value it was assumed that the mass of the produced commodities is given, i.e., remains the same, and that there is a change only in the proportions of its constituent elements, which are produced under different conditions, and that, hence, the market-value of the same mass of commodities is differently regulated. Suppose, this mass corresponds in size to the usual supply, leaving aside the possibility that a portion of the produced commodities may be temporarily withdrawn from the market. Should demand for this mass now also remain the same, this commodity will be sold at its market-value, no matter which of the three aforementioned cases regulates this market-value. This mass of commodities does not merely satisfy a need, but satisfies it to its full social extent. Should their quantity be smaller or greater, however, than the demand for them, there will be deviations of the market-price from the market-value. And the first deviation is that if the supply is too small, the market-value is always regulated by the commodities produced under the least favourable circumstances and, if the supply is too large, always by the commodities produced under the most favourable conditions; that therefore it is one of the extremes which determines the market-value, in spite of the fact that in accordance with the mere proportion of the commodity masses produced under different conditions, a different result should obtain. If the difference between demand and the available quantity of the product is more considerable, the market-price will likewise be considerably above or below the market-value. Now, the difference between the quantity of the produced commodities and that quantity of them at which they are sold at market-value may be due to two reasons. Either the quantity itself changes, becoming too small or too large, so that reproduction would have taken place on a different scale than that which regulated the given market-value. In that case, the supply changed, although demand remained the same, and there was, therefore, relative over-production or under-production. Or else reproduction, and thus supply, remained the same, while demand shrank or increased, which may be due to several reasons. Although the absolute magnitude of the supply was the same, its relative magnitude, its magnitude relative to, or measured by, the demand, had changed. The effect is the same as in the first case, but in the reverse direction. Finally, if changes take place on both sides, but either in reverse directions, or, if in the same direction, then not to the same extent, if therefore there are changes on both sides, but these alter the former proportion between the two sides, then the final result must always lead to one of the two above-mentioned cases.

The real difficulty in formulating the general definition of supply and demand is that it seems to take on the appearance of a tautology. First, consider the supply—the product available in the market, or that which can be delivered to it. To avoid dwelling upon useless detail, we shall here consider only the mass annually reproduced in every given branch of production and ignore the greater or lesser faculty possessed by the different commodities to be withdrawn from the market and stored away for consumption, say, until next year. This annual reproduction is expressed by a certain quantity—in weight or numbers—depending on whether this mass of commodities is measured in discrete elements or continuously. They are not only use-values satisfying human wants, but these use-values are available in the market in definite quantities. Secondly, however, this quantity of commodities has a specific market-value, which may be expressed by a multiple of the market-value of the commodity, or of its measure, which serves as unit. Thus, there is no necessary connection between the quantitative volume of the commodities in the market and their market-value, since, for instance, many commodities have a specifically high value, and others a specifically low value, so that a given sum of values may be represented by a very large quantity of one commodity, and a very small quantity of another. There is only the following connection between the quantity of the articles available in the market and the market-value of these articles: On a given basis of labour productivity the production of a certain quantity of articles in every particular sphere of production requires a definite quantity of social labour-time; although this proportion varies in different spheres of production and has no inner relation to the usefulness of these articles or the special nature of their use-values. Assuming all other circumstances to be equal, and a certain quantity a of some commodity to cost b labour-time, a quantity na of the same commodity will cost nb labour-time. Further, if society wants to satisfy some want and have an article produced for this purpose, it must pay for it. Indeed, since commodity-production necessitates a division of labour, society pays for this article by devoting a portion of the available labour-time to its production. Therefore, society buys it with a definite quantity of its disposable labour-time. That part of society which through the division of labour happens to employ its labour in producing this particular article, must receive an equivalent in social labour incorporated in articles which satisfy its own wants. However, there exists an accidental rather than a necessary connection between the total amount of social labour applied to a social article, i.e., between the aliquot part of society's total labour-power allocated to producing this article, or between the volume which the production of this article occupies in total production, on the one hand, and the volume whereby society seeks to satisfy the want gratified by the article in question, on the other. Every individual article, or every definite quantity of a commodity may, indeed, contain no more than the social labour required for its production, and from this point of view the market-value of this entire commodity represents only necessary labour, but if this commodity has been produced in excess of the existing social needs, then so much of the social labour-time is squandered and the mass of the commodity comes to represent a much smaller quantity of social labour in the market than is actually incorporated in it. (It is only where production is under the actual, predetermining control of society that the latter establishes a relation between the volume of social labour-time applied in producing definite articles, and the volume of the social want to be satisfied by these articles.) For this reason, these commodities must be sold below their market-value, and a portion of them may even be altogether unsaleable. The reverse applies if the quantity of social labour employed in the production of a certain kind of commodity is too small to meet the social demand for that commodity. But if the quantity of social labour expended in the production of a certain article corresponds to the social demand for that article, so that the produced quantity corresponds to the usual scale of reproduction and the demand remains unchanged, then the article is sold at its market-value. The exchange, or sale, of commodities at their value is the rational state of affairs, i.e., the natural law of their equilibrium. It is this law that explains the deviations, and not vice versa, the deviations that explain the law.

Now let us look at the other side—the demand.

Commodities are bought either as means of production or means of subsistence to enter productive or individual consumption. It does not alter matters that some commodities may serve both purposes. There is, then, a demand for them on the part of producers (here capitalists, since we have assumed that means of production have been transformed into capital) and of consumers. Both appear at first sight to presuppose a given quantity of social want on the side of demand, corresponding on the other side to a definite quantity of social output in the various lines of production. If the cotton industry is to accomplish its annual reproduction on a given scale, it must have the usual supply of cotton, and, other circumstances remaining the same, an additional amount of cotton corresponding to the annual extension of reproduction caused by the accumulation of capital. This is equally true with regard to means of subsistence. The working-class must find at least the same quantity of necessities on hand if it is to continue living in its accustomed average way, although they may be more or less differently distributed among the different kinds of commodities. Moreover, there must be an additional quantity to allow for the annual increase of population. The same, with more or less modification, applies to other classes.

It would seem, then, that there is on the side of demand a certain magnitude of definite social wants which require for their satisfaction a definite quantity of a commodity on the market. But quantitatively, the definite social wants are very elastic and changing. Their fixedness is only apparent. If the means of subsistence were cheaper, or money-wages higher, the labourers would buy more of them, and a greater social need would arise for them, leaving aside the paupers, etc., whose demand is even below the narrowest limits of their physical wants. On the other hand, if cotton were cheaper, for example, the capitalists' demand for it would increase, more additional capital would be thrown into the cotton industry, etc. We must never forget that the demand for productive consumption is, under our assumption, a demand of the capitalist, whose essential purpose is the production of surplus-value, so that he produces a particular commodity to this sole end. Still, this does not hinder the capitalist, so long as he appears in the market as a buyer of, say, cotton, from representing the need for this cotton, just as it is immaterial to the seller of cotton whether the buyer converts it into shirting or gun-cotton, or whether he intends to turn it into wads for his own, and the world's, ears. But this does exert a considerable influence on the kind of buyer the capitalist is. His demand for cotton is substantially modified by the fact that it disguises his real need for making profit. The limits within which the need for commodities in the *market*, the demand, differs quantitatively from the *actual social need*, naturally vary considerably for different commodities; what I mean is the difference between the demanded quantity of commodities and the quantity which would have been in demand at other money-prices or other money or living conditions of the buyers.

Nothing is easier than to realise the inconsistencies of demand and supply, and the resulting deviation of market-prices from market-values. The real difficulty consists in determining what is meant by the equation of supply and demand.

Supply and demand coincide when their mutual proportions are such that the mass of commodities of a definite line of production can be sold at their market-value, neither above nor below it. That is the first thing we hear.

The second is this: If commodities are sold at their market-values, supply and demand coincide.

If supply equals demand, they cease to act, and for this very reason, commodities are sold at their market-values. Whenever two forces operate equally in opposite directions, they balance one another, exert no outside influence, and any phenomena taking place in these circumstances must be explained by causes other than the effect of these two forces. If supply and demand balance one another, they cease to explain anything, do not affect market-values, and therefore leave us so much more in the dark about the reasons why the market-value is expressed in just this sum of money and no other. It is evident that the real inner laws of capitalist production cannot be explained by the interaction of supply and demand (quite aside from a deeper analysis of these two social motive forces, which would be out of place here), because these laws cannot be observed in their pure state, until supply and demand cease to act, i.e., are equated. In reality, supply and demand never coincide, or, if they do, it is by mere accident, hence scientifically = 0, and to be regarded as not having occurred. But political economy assumes that supply and demand coincide with one another. Why? To be able to study phenomena in their fundamental relations, in the form corresponding to their conception, that is, is to study them independent of the appearances caused by the movement of supply and demand. The other reason is to find the actual tendencies of their movements and, to some extent to record them. Since the inconsistencies are of an antagonistic nature, and since they continually succeed one another, they balance out one another through their opposing movements, and their mutual contradiction. Since, therefore, supply and demand never equal one another in any given case, their differences follow one another in such a way—and the result of a deviation in one direction is that it calls forth a deviation in the opposite direction—that supply and demand are always equated when the whole is viewed over a certain period, but only as an average of past movements, and only as the continuous movement of their contradiction. In this way, the market-prices which have deviated from the market-values adjust themselves, as viewed from the standpoint of their average number, to equal the market-values, in that deviations from the latter cancel each other as plus and minus. And this average is not merely of theoretical, but also of practical importance to capital, whose investment is calculated on the fluctuations and compensations of a more or less fixed period.

On the one hand, the relation of demand and supply, therefore, only explains the deviations of market-prices from market-values. On the other, it explains the tendency to eliminate these deviations, i.e., to eliminate the effect of the relation of demand and supply. (Such exceptions as commodities which have a price without having a value are not considered here.) Supply and demand may eliminate the effect caused by their difference in many different ways. For instance, if the demand, and consequently the market-price, fall, capital may be withdrawn, thus causing supply to shrink. It may also be that the market-value itself shrinks and balances with the market-price as a result of inventions which reduce the necessary labour-time. Conversely, if the demand increases, and consequently the market-price rises above the market-value, this may lead to too much capital flowing into this line of production and production may swell to such an extent that the market-price will even fall below the market-value. Or, it may lead to a price increase, which cuts the demand. In some lines of production it may also bring about a rise in the market-value itself for a shorter or longer period, with a portion of the desired products having to be produced under worse conditions during this period.

Supply and demand determine the market-price, and so does the market-price, and the market-value in the further analysis, determine supply and demand. This is obvious in the case of demand, since it moves in a direction opposite to prices, swelling when prices fall, and vice versa. But this is also true of supply. Because the prices of means of production incorporated in the offered commodities determine the demand for these means of production, and thus the supply of commodities whose supply embraces the demand for these means of production. The prices of cotton are determinants in the supply of cotton goods.

To this confusion—determining prices through demand and supply, and, at the same time, determining supply and demand through prices—must be added that demand determines supply, just as supply determines demand, and production determines the market, as well as the market determines production.[2]

Even the ordinary economist (see footnote) agrees that the proportion between supply and demand may vary in consequence of a change in the market-value of commodities, without a change being brought about in demand or supply by extraneous circumstances. Even he must admit that, whatever the market-value, supply and demand must coincide in order for it to be established. In other words, the ratio of supply to demand does not explain the market-value, but conversely, the latter rather explains the fluctuations of supply and demand. The author of the *Observations* continues after the passage quoted in the footnote:

> This proportion [between demand and supply], however, if we still mean by 'demand' and 'natural price', what we meant just now, when referring to Adam Smith, must always be a proportion of equality; for it is only when the supply is equal to the effectual demand, that is, to that demand which will neither more nor less than pay the natural price, that the natural price is in fact paid; consequently, there may be two very different natural prices, at different times, for the same commodity, and yet the

proportion, which the supply bears to the demand, be in both cases the same, namely, the proportion of equality.

It is admitted, then, that with two different natural prices of the same commodity, at different times, demand and supply are always able to, and must, balance one another if the commodity is to be sold at its natural price in both instances. Since there is no difference in the ratio of supply to demand in either case, but a difference in the magnitude of the natural price itself, it follows that this price is obviously determined independently of demand and supply, and thus that it can least of all be determined by them.

For a commodity to be sold at its market-value, i.e., proportionally to the necessary social labour contained in it, the total quantity of social labour used in producing the total mass of this commodity must correspond to the quantity of the social want for it, i.e., the effective social want. Competition, the fluctuations of market-prices which correspond to the fluctuations of demand and supply, tend continually to reduce to this scale the total quantity of labour devoted to each kind of commodity.

The proportion of supply and demand recapitulates, first, the relation of use-value to exchange-value, of commodity to money, and of buyer to seller; and, second, that of producer to consumer, although both of them may be represented by third parties, the merchants. In considering buyer and seller, it suffices to counterpose them individually in order to present their relationship. Three individuals are enough for the complete metamorphosis of a commodity, and therefore for the process of sale and purchase taken as a whole. A converts his commodity into the money of B, to whom he sells his commodity, and reconverts his money again into commodities, when he uses it to make purchases from C; the whole process takes place among these three. Further, in the study of money, it had been assumed that the commodities are sold at their values because there was absolutely no reason to consider prices divergent from values, it being merely a matter of changes of form which commodities undergo in their transformation into money and their reconversion from money into commodities. As soon as a commodity has been sold and a new commodity bought with the receipts, we have before us the entire metamorphosis, and to this process, as such, it is immaterial whether the price of the commodity lies above or below its value. The value of the commodity remains important as a basis, because the concept of money cannot be developed on any other foundation, and price, in its general meaning, is but value in the form of money. At any rate, it is assumed in the study of money as a medium of circulation that there is not just one metamorphosis of a certain commodity. It is rather the social interrelation of these metamorphoses which is studied. Only thus do we arrive at the circulation of money and the development of its function as a medium of circulation. But however important this connection may be for the conversion of money into a circulating medium, and for its resulting change of form, it is of no moment to the transaction between individual buyers and sellers.

In the case of supply and demand, however, the supply is equal to the sum of sellers, or producers, of a certain kind of commodity, and the demand equals the sum of buyers or consumers (both productive and individual) of the same kind of commodity. The sums react on one another as units, as aggregate forces. The individual counts here only as part of a social force, as an atom of the mass, and it is in this form that competition brings out the social character of production and consumption.

The side of competition which happens for the moment to be weaker is also the side in which the individual acts independently of, and often directly against, the mass of his competitors, and precisely in this manner is the dependence of one upon the other impressed upon them, while the stronger side acts always more or less as a united whole against its antagonist. If the demand for this particular kind of commodity is greater than the supply, one buyer outbids another—within certain limits—and so raises the price of the commodity for all of them above the market-value, while on the other hand the sellers unite in trying to sell at a high market-price. If, conversely, the supply exceeds the demand, one begins to dispose of his goods at a cheaper rate and the others must follow, while the buyers unite in their efforts to depress the market-price as much as possible below the market-value. The common interest is appreciated by each only so long as he gains more by it than without it. And unity of action ceases the moment one or the other side becomes the weaker, when each tries to extricate himself on his own as advantageously as he possibly can. Again, if one produces more cheaply and can sell more goods, thus possessing himself of a greater place in the market by selling below the current market-price, or market-value, he will do so, and will thereby begin a movement which gradually compels the others to introduce the cheaper mode of production, and one which reduces the socially necessary labour to a new, and lower, level. If one side has the advantage, all belonging to it gain. It is as though they exerted their common monopoly. If one side is weaker, then one may try on his own hook to become the stronger (for instance, one who works with lower costs of production), or at least to get off as lightly as possible, and in such cases each for himself and the devil take the hindmost, although his actions affect not only himself, but also all his boon companions.[3]

Demand and supply imply the conversion of value into market-value, and so far as they proceed on a capitalist basis, so far as the commodities are products of capital, they are based on capitalist production processes, i.e., on quite different relationships than the mere purchase and sale of goods. Here it is not a question of the formal conversion of the value of commodities into prices, i.e., not of a mere change of form. It is a question of definite deviations in quantity of the market-prices from the market-values, and, further, from the prices of production. In simple purchase and sale it suffices to have the producers of commodities as such counterposed to one another. In further analysis supply and demand presuppose the existence of different classes and sections of classes which divide the total revenue of a society and consume it among themselves as revenue, and, therefore, make up the demand created by revenue. While on the other hand, it requires an insight into the over-all structure of the capitalist production process for an understanding of the supply and demand created among themselves by producers as such.

Under capitalist production, it is not merely a matter of obtaining an equal mass of value in another form—be it that of money or some other commodity—for a mass of values thrown into circulation in the form of a commodity, but it is rather a matter of realising as much surplus-value, or profit, on capital advanced for production, as any other capital of the same magnitude, or *pro rata* to its magnitude in whichever line it is applied. It is, therefore, a matter, at least as a minimum, of selling the commodities at prices which yield the average profit, i.e., at prices of production. In this form, capital becomes conscious of itself as a *social power* in which every capitalist participates proportionally to his share in the total social capital.

First, capitalist production is in itself indifferent to the particular use-value, and distinctive features of any commodity it produces. In every sphere of production it is only concerned with producing surplus-value, and appropriating a certain quantity of unpaid labour incorporated in the product of labour. And it is likewise in the nature of the wage-labour subordinated by capital that it is indifferent to the specific character of its labour and must submit to being transformed in accordance with the requirements of capital and to being transferred from one sphere of production to another.

Second, one sphere of production is, in fact, just as good or just as bad as another. Every one of them yields the same profit, and every one of them would be useless if the commodities it produced did not satisfy some social need.

Now, if the commodities are sold at their values, then, as we have shown, very different rates of profit arise in the various spheres of production, depending on the different organic composition of the masses of capital invested in them. But capital withdraws from a sphere with a low rate of profit and invades others, which yield a higher profit. Through this incessant outflow and influx, or, briefly, through its distribution among the various spheres, which depends on how the rate of profit falls here and rises there, it creates such a ratio of supply to demand that the average profit in the various spheres of production becomes the same, and values are, therefore, converted into prices of production. Capital succeeds in this equalisation, to a greater or lesser degree, depending on the extent of capitalist development in the given nation; i.e., on the extent the conditions in the country in question are adapted for the capitalist mode of production. With the progress of capitalist production, it also develops its own conditions and subordinates to its specific character and its immanent laws all the social prerequisites on which the production process is based.

The incessant equilibration of constant divergences is accomplished so much more quickly, 1) the more mobile the capital, i.e., the more easily it can be shifted from one sphere and from one place to another; 2) the more quickly labour-power can be transferred from one sphere to another and from one production locality to another. The first condition implies complete freedom of trade within the society and the removal of all monopolies with the exception of the natural ones, those, that is, which naturally arise out of the capitalist mode of production. It implies, furthermore, the development of the credit system, which concentrates the inorganic mass of the disposable social capital vis-a-vis the individual capitalist. Finally, it implies the subordination of the various spheres of production to the control of capitalists. This last implication is included in our premises, since we assumed that it was a matter of converting values into prices of production in all capitalistically exploited spheres of production. But this equilibration itself runs into greater obstacles, whenever numerous and large spheres of production not operated on a capitalist basis (such as soil cultivation by small farmers), filter in between the capitalist enterprises and become linked with them. A great density of population is another requirement.— The second condition implies the abolition of all laws preventing the labourers from transferring from one sphere of production to another and from one local centre of production to another; indifference of the labourer to the nature of his labour; the greatest possible reduction of labour in all spheres of production to simple labour; the elimination of all vocational prejudices among labourers; and last but not least, a subjugation of the labourer to the capitalist mode of production. Further reference to this belongs to a special analysis of competition.

It follows from the foregoing that in each particular sphere of production, the individual capitalist, as well as the capitalists as a whole, take direct part in the exploitation of the total working-class by the totality of capital and in the degree of that exploitation, not only out of general class sympathy, but also for direct economic reasons. For, assuming all other conditions—among them the value of the total advanced constant capital—to be given, the average rate of profit depends on the intensity of exploitation of the sum total of labour by the sum total of capital.

The average profit coincides with the average surplus-value produced for each 100 of capital, and so far as the surplus-value is concerned, the foregoing statements apply as a matter of course. In the case of the average profit the value of the advanced capital becomes an additional element determining the rate of profit. In fact, the direct interest taken by the capitalist, or the capital, of any individual sphere of production in the exploitation of the labourers who are directly employed is confined to making an extra gain, a profit exceeding the average, either through exceptional overwork, or reduction of the wage below the average, or through the exceptional productivity of the labour employed. Aside from this, a capitalist who would not in his line of production employ any variable capital, and therefore any labourer (in reality an exaggerated assumption), would nonetheless be as much interested in the exploitation of the working-class by capital, and would derive his profit quite as much from unpaid surplus-labour, as, say, a capitalist who would employ only variable capital (another exaggeration), and who would thus invest his entire capital in wages. But the degree of exploitation of labour depends on the average intensity of labour if the working-day is given, and on the length of the working-day if the intensity of exploitation is given. The degree of exploitation of labour determines the rate of surplus-value, and therefore the mass of surplus-value for a given total mass of variable capital, and consequently the magnitude of the profit. The individual capitalist, as distinct from his sphere as a whole, has the same special interest in exploiting the labourers he personally employs as the capital of a particular sphere, as distinct from the total social capital, has in exploiting the labourers directly employed in that sphere.

On the other hand, every particular sphere of capital, and every individual capitalist, have the same interest in the productivity of the social labour employed by the sum total of capital. For two things depend on this productivity: First, the mass of use-values in which the average profit is expressed; and this is doubly important, since this average profit serves as a fund for the accumulation of new capital and as a fund for revenue to be spent for consumption. Second, the value of the total capital invested (constant and variable), which, the amount of surplus-value, or profit, for the whole capitalist class being given, determines the rate of profit, or the profit on a certain quantity of capital. The special productivity of labour in any particular sphere, or in any individual enterprise of this sphere, is of interest only to those capitalists who are directly engaged in it, since it enables that particular sphere, vis-a-vis the total capital, or that individual capitalist, vis-a-vis his sphere, to make an extra profit.

Here, then, we have a mathematically precise proof why capitalists form a veritable freemason society vis-a-vis the whole working-class, while there is little love lost between them in competition among themselves.

The price of production includes the average profit. We call it price of production. It is really what Adam Smith calls *natural price*, Ricardo calls *price of production*, or *cost of production*, and the physiocrats call *prix nécessaire*, because in the long run it is a prerequisite of supply, of the reproduction of commodities in every individual sphere. But none of them has revealed the difference between price of production and value. We can well understand why the same economists who oppose determining the value of commodities by labour-time, i.e., by the quantity of labour contained in them, why they always speak of prices of production as centres around which market-prices fluctuate. They can afford to do it because the price of production is an utterly external and *prima facie* meaningless form of the value of commodities, a form as it appears in competition, therefore in the mind of the vulgar capitalist, and consequently in that of the vulgar economist.

Our analysis has revealed how the market-value (and everything said concerning it applies with appropriate modifications to the price of production) embraces a surplus-profit for those who produce in any particular sphere of production under the most favourable conditions. With the exception of crises, and of overproduction in general, this applies to all market-prices, no matter how much they may deviate from market-values or market-prices of production. For the market-price signifies that the same price is paid for commodities of the same kind, although they may have been produced under very different individual conditions and hence may have different cost-prices. (We do not speak at this point of any surplus-profits due to monopolies in the usual sense of the term, whether natural or artificial.)

A surplus-profit may also arise if certain spheres of production are in a position to evade the conversion of the values of their commodities into prices of production, and thus the reduction of their profits to the average profit. We shall devote more attention to the further modifications of these two forms of surplus-profit in the part dealing with ground-rent.

Notes

1. The controversy between Storch and Ricardo with regard to ground-rent (a controversy pertaining only to the subject; in fact, the two opponents pay no attention to one another), whether the market-value (or rather what they call market-price and price of production respectively) was regulated by the commodities produced under unfavourable conditions (Ricardo) [*On the Principles of Political Economy, and Taxation, Third edition, London, 1821, pp. 661.—Ed.*], or by those produced under favourable conditions (Storch) [*Cours d'economie politique, ou exposition des principes, qudeterminent la prosperite des nations, tome II, St.-Petersbourg, 1815, pp. 78-79.—Ed.*], resolves itself in the final analysis in that both are right and both wrong, and that both of them have failed to consider the average case. Compare Corbet [*An Inquiry into the Causes and Modes of the Wealth of Individuals, London, 1841, pp. 42-44.—Ed.*] on the cases in which the price is regulated by commodities produced under the most favourable conditions.—'It is not meant to be asserted by him (Ricardo) that two particular lots of two different articles, as a hat and a pair of shoes, exchange with one another when those two particular lots were produced by equal quantities of labour. By "commodity", we must here understand the "description of commodity", not a particular individual hat, pair of shoes etc. The whole labour which produces all the hats in England is to be considered, to this purpose, as divided among all the hats. This seems to me not to have been expressed at first, and in the general statement of this doctrine.' (*Observations on Certain Verbal Disputes in Political Economy, etc., London, 1821, pp. 53-54.*)
2. The following subtility is sheer nonsense: 'Where the quantity of wages, capital, and land, required to produce an article, are become different from what they were, that which Adam Smith calls the natural price of it is also different, and that price, which was previously its natural price becomes, with reference to this alteration, its market-price; because, though neither the supply, nor the quantity wanted, may have been changed'—both of them change here, just because the market-value, or, in the case of Adam Smith, the price of production, changes in consequence of a change of value—'that supply is not now exactly enough for those persons who are able and willing to pay what is now the cost of production, but is either greater or less than that; so that the proportion between the supply and what is with reference to the new cost of production the effectual demand, is different from what it was. An alteration in the rate of supply will then take place if there is no obstacle in the way of it, and at last bring the commodity to its new natural price. It may then seem good to some persons to say that as the commodity gets to its natural price by an alteration in its supply, the natural price is as much owing to one proportion between the demand and supply, as the market-price is to another; and consequently, that the natural price, just as much as the market-price, depends on the proportion that demand and supply bear to each other.' ('The great principle of demand and supply is called into action to determine what A. Smith calls natural prices as well as market-prices.'—Malthus.) [*Principles of Political Economy, London, 1820, p. 75.—Ed.*] (*Observations on Certain Verbal Disputes, etc.*, London, 1821, pp. 60-61.) The good man does not grasp the fact that it is precisely the change in the cost of production, and thus in the value which caused a change in the demand, in the present case, and thus in the proportion between demand and supply, and that this change in the demand may bring about a change in the supply. This would prove just the reverse of what our good thinker wants to prove. It would prove that the change in the cost of production is by no means due to the proportion of demand and supply, but rather regulates this proportion.'
3. 'If each man of a class could never have more than a given share, or aliquot part, of the gains and possessions of the whole, he would readily combine to raise the gain'; (he does it as soon as the proportion of demand to supply permits it) 'this is monopoly. But where each man thinks that he may anyway increase the absolute amount of his own share, though by a process which lessens the whole amount, he will often do it; this is competition.' (*An Inquiry into Those Principles Respecting the Nature of Demand, etc*,, London, 1821, p. 105.)

11

Effects of General Wage Fluctuations on Prices of Production

Let the average composition of social capital be $80_c + 20_v$, and the profit 20%. The rate of surplus-value is then 100%. A general increase of wages, all else remaining the same, is tantamount to a reduction in the rate of surplus-value. In the case of average capital, profit and surplus-value are identical. Let wages rise 25%. Then the same quantity of labour, formerly set in motion with 20, will cost 25. We shall then have a turnover value of $80_c + 25_v + 15_p$, instead of $80_c + 20_v + 20_p$. As before, the labour set in motion by the variable capital produces a value of 40. If v rises from 20 to 25, the surplus s, or p, will amount to only 15. The profit of 15 on a capital of 105 is $14^2/_7$%, and this would be the new average rate of profit. Since the price of production of commodities produced by the average capital coincides with their value, the price of production of these commodities would have remained unchanged. A wage increase would therefore have caused a drop in profit, but no change in the value and price of the commodities. Formerly, as long as the average profit was 20%, the price of production of commodities produced in one period of turnover was equal to their cost-price plus a profit of 20% on this cost-price, therefore = k + kp' = k + 20k/100. In this formula, k is a variable magnitude, changing in accordance with the value of the means of production that go into the commodities, and with the amount of depreciation given up by the fixed capital to the product. The price of production would then amount to k + 14 2/7 k/100. Let us now select a capital, whose composition is lower than the original composition of the average social capital of $80_c + 20_v$ (which has now changed into $76^4/_{21c} + 23^{17}/_{21v}$); say, $50_c + 50_v$. In this case, the price of production of the annual product before the wage increase would have been $50_c + 50_v$ + 20p = 120, assuming for the sake of simplicity that the entire fixed capital passes through depreciation into the product and that the period of turnover is the same as in the first case. For the same quantity of labour set in motion a wage increase of 25% means an increase of the variable capital from 50 to 62½. If the annual product were sold at the former price of production of 120, this would give us $50_c + 62½_v + 7½_p$, or a rate of profit of 6⅔%. But the new average rate of profit is $14^2/_7$%, and since we assume all other circumstances to remain the same, the capital of $50_c + 62½_v$ must also make this profit. Now a capital of 112½ makes a profit of 16 1/14 at a rate of profit of $14^2/_7$%. Therefore, the price of production of the commodities produced by this capital is now $50_c + 62½_v + 16¼_p = 128^8/_{14}$. Owing to a wage rise of 255, the price of production of the same quantity of the same commodities, therefore, has here risen from 120 to $128^8/_{14}$, or more than 7%.

Conversely, suppose we take a sphere of production of a higher composition than the average capital; say, $92_c + 8_v$. The original average profit in this case would still be 20, and if we again assume that the entire fixed capital passes into the annual product and that the period of turnover is the same as in cases I and II, the price of production of the commodity is here also 120.

Owing to the rise in wages of 25% the variable capital for the same quantity of labour rises from 8 to 10, the cost-price of the commodities from 100 to 102, while the average rate of profit falls from 20% to $14^2/_7$%. But 100 : $14^2/_7$ = 102 : $14^4/_7$. The profit now falling to the share of 102 is therefore $14^4/_7$. For this reason, the total product sells at k + kp' = 102 + $14^4/_7$ = $116^4/_7$. The price of production has therefore fallen from 120 to $116^4/_7$, or $3^3/_7$.

Consequently, if wages are raised 25%:

1. the price of production of the commodities of a capital of average social composition does not change;
2. the price of production of the commodities of a capital of lower composition rises, but not in proportion to the fall in profit;
3. the price of production of the commodities of a capital of higher composition falls, but also not in the same proportion as profit.

Since the price of production of the commodities of the average capital remained the same, equal to the value of the product, the sum of the prices of production of the products of all capitals remained the same as well, and equal to the sum total of the values produced by the aggregate capital. The increase on one side and the decrease on the other balance for the aggregate capital on the level of the average social capital.

If the price of production rises in case II and falls in case III, these opposite effects alone, which are brought about by a fall in the rate of surplus-value or by a general wage increase, show that this cannot be a matter of compensation in the price for the rise in wages, since the fall in the price of production in case III cannot compensate the capitalist for the fall in profit, and since the rise of the price in case II does not prevent a fall in profit. Rather, in either case, whether the price rises or falls, the profit remains the same as that of the average capital, in which case the price remains unchanged. It is the same average profit which has fallen by $5^{5}/_{7}$, or somewhat over 25%, in the case of II as well as III. It follows from this that if the price did not rise in II and fall in III, II would have to sell below and III above the new reduced average profit. It is self-evident that, depending on whether 50, 25, or 10 per 100 units of capital are laid out for wages, the effect of a wage increase on a capitalist who has invested 1/10 of his capital in wages must be quite different from that on one who has invested ¼ or ½. An increase in the price of production on the one side, a fall on the other, depending on a capital being below or above the average social composition, occurs solely by virtue of the process of levelling the profit to the new reduced average profit.

How would a general reduction in wages, and a corresponding general rise of the rate of profit, and thus of the average profit, now affect the prices of production of commodities produced by capitals deviating in opposite directions from the average social composition? We have but to reverse the foregoing exposition to obtain the result (which Ricardo fails to analyse).

I. Average capital = $80_c + 20_v$ = 100; rate of surplus-value = 100%; price of production=value of commodities = $80_c + 20_v + 20_p$ = 120; rate of profit = 20%. Suppose wages fall by one-fourth. Then the same constant capital is set in motion by 15_v, instead of 20_v. Then the value of commodities = $80_c + 15_v + 25_p$ = 120. The quantity of labour performed by v remains unchanged, except that the value newly created by it is distributed differently between the capitalist and the labourer. The surplus-value rises from 20 to 25 and the rate of surplus-value from 20/20 to 25/15, or from 100% to 166⅔%. The profit on 95 now = 25, so that the rate of profit per 100 = $26^{6}/_{19}$. The new composition of the capital in per cent is now $84^{4}/_{19c} + 15^{15}/_{19v}$ = 100.

II. Lower composition. Originally $50_c + 50_v$, as above. Due to the fall of wages by one-fourth v is reduced to 37½, and consequently the advanced total capital to 50_c + 37½$_v$ = 87½. If we apply the new rate of profit of 26 6/19% to this, we get 100 : $26^{6}/_{19}$ = 87½: $23^{1}/_{38}$. The same mass of commodities which formerly cost 120, now costs 87½ + $23^{1}/_{38}$ = $110^{10}/_{19}$, this being a price reduction of almost 10%.

III. Higher composition. Originally $92_c + 8_v$ = 100. The reduction of wages by one-fourth reduces 8_v to 6_v, and the total capital to 98. Consequently, 100:26 6/19 = 98 : $25^{16}/_{19}$. The price of production of the commodity, formerly 100 + 20 = 120, is now, after the fall in wages, 98 + $25^{15}/_{19}$ = $123^{15}/_{19}$, this being a rise of almost 4.

It is evident, therefore, that we have but to follow the same development in the opposite direction with the appropriate modifications; that a general reduction of wages is attended by a general rise of surplus-value, of the rate of surplus-value and, other circumstances remaining the same, of the rate of profit, even if expressed in a different proportion; a fall in the prices of production for commodities produced by capitals of lower composition, and a rise in the prices of production for commodities produced by capitals of higher composition. The result is just the reverse of that observed for a general rise of wages.[1] In both cases—rise or fall of wages—it is assumed that the working-day remains the same, and also the prices of the means of subsistence. In these circumstances, a fall in wages is possible only if they stood higher than the normal price of labour, or if they are depressed below this price. The way in which the matter is modified if the rise or fall of wages is due to a change in value, and consequently the price of production of commodities usually consumed by the labourer, will be analysed at some length in the part dealing with ground-rent. At this point, however, the following remarks are to be made once and for all:

Should the rise or fall in wages be due to a change in the value of the necessities of life, a modification of the foregoing findings can take place only to the extent that commodities, whose change of price raises or lowers the variable capital, also go into the constant capital as constituent elements and therefore affect more than just the wages alone. But if they affect only wages, the above analysis contains all that needs to be said.

In this entire chapter, the establishment of the general rate of profit and the average profit, and consequently, the transmutation of values into prices of production, are assumed as given. The question merely was, how a general rise or fall in wages affected the assumed prices of production of commodities. This is but a very secondary question compared with the other important points analysed in this part. But it is the only relevant question treated by Ricardo, and, as we shall see, he treated it one-sidedly and unsatisfactorily.

Note

1. It is very peculiar that Ricardo [On the Principles of Political Economy, and Taxation, Third edition, London, 1821, pp. 36-41.— Ed.] (who naturally proceeds differently from us, since he did not understand the levelling of values to prices of production) did not once consider this eventuality, but only the first case, that of a wage rise and its influence on the prices of production of commodities. And the *servum pecus imitatorum* [Horace, Epistles, Book I, Epistle 19.— Ed.] did not even attempt to make this extremely self-evident, actually tautological, practical application.

12

Supplementary Remarks

Section I. *Causes Implying a Change in the Price of Production*

There are just two causes that can change the price of production of a commodity:

First. A change in the general rate of profit. This can solely be due to a change in the average rate of surplus-value, or, if the average rate of surplus-value remains the same, to a change in the ratio of the sum of the appropriated surplus-values to the sum of the advanced total social capital.

If the change in the rate of surplus-value is not due to a depression of wages below normal, or their rise above normal—and movements of that kind are to be regarded merely as oscillations—it can only occur either through a rise, or fall, in the value of labour-power, the one being just as impossible as the other unless there is a change in the productivity of the labour producing means of subsistence, i.e., in the value of commodities consumed by the labourer.

Or, through a change in the proportion of the sum of appropriated surplus-values to the advanced total capital of society. Since the change, in this case, is not caused by the rate of surplus-value, it must be caused by the total capital, or rather its constant part. The mass of this part, technically considered, increases or decreases in proportion to the quantity of labour-power bought by the variable capital, and the mass of its value thus increases or decreases with the increase or decrease of its own mass. It also increases or decreases, therefore, proportionately to the mass of the value of the variable capital. If the same labour sets more constant capital in motion, it has become more productive. If the reverse, then less productive. Thus, there has been a change in the productivity of labour, and there must have occurred a change in the value of certain commodities.

The following law, then, applies to both cases: If the price of production of a commodity changes in consequence of a change in the general rate of profit, its own value may have remained unchanged. However, a change must have occurred in the value of other commodities.

Second. The general rate of profit remains unchanged. In this case, the price of production of a commodity can change only if its own value has changed. This may be due to more, or less, labour being required to reproduce the commodity in question, either because of a change in the productivity of labour which produces this commodity in its final form, or of the labour which produces those commodities that go into its production. The price of production of cotton yarn may fall, either because raw cotton is produced cheaper than before, or because the labour of spinning has become more productive due to improved machinery.

The price of production, as we have seen, = k + p, equal to cost-price plus profit. This, however, = k + kp', in which k, the cost-price, is a variable magnitude, which changes for different spheres of production and is everywhere equal to the value of the constant and variable capital consumed in the production of the commodity, and p' is the average rate of profit in percentage form. If k = 200, and p' = 20%, the price of production k + kp' = 200 + 200 × 20/100 = 200 + 40 = 240. This price of production may clearly remain the same, in spite of a change in the value of the commodities.

All changes in the price of production of commodities are reduced, in the last analysis, to changes in value. But not all changes in the value of commodities need, express themselves in changes in the price of production. The price of production is not determined by the value of any one commodity alone, but by the aggregate value of all commodities. A change in commodity A may therefore be balanced by an opposite change in commodity B, so that the general relation remains the same.

Section II. *Price of Production of Commodities of Average Composition*

We have seen how a deviation in prices of production from values arises from: 1) adding the average profit instead of the surplus-value contained in a commodity to is cost-price; 2) the price of production, which so deviates from the value of a commodity, entering into the cost-price of other commodities as one of its elements, so that the cost-price of a commodity may already contain a deviation from value in those means of production consumed by it, quite aside from a deviation of its own which may arise through a difference between the average profit and the surplus-value.

It is, therefore, possible that even the cost-price of commodities produced by capitals of average composition may differ from the sum of the values of the elements which make up this component of their price of production. Suppose, the average composition is $80_c + 20_v$. Now, it is possible that in the actual capitals of this composition, 80_c may be greater or smaller than the value of c, i.e., the constant capital, because this c may be made up of commodities whose price of production differs from their value. In the same way, 20_v might diverge from its value if the consumption of the wage includes commodities whose price of production diverges from their value; in which case the labourer would work a longer, or shorter, time to buy them back (to replace them) and would thus perform more, or less, necessary labour than would be required if the price of production of such necessities of life coincided with their value.

However, this possibility does not detract in the least from the correctness of the theorems demonstrated which hold for commodities of average composition. The quantity of profit falling to these commodities is equal to the quantity of surplus-value contained in them. For instance, in a capital of the given composition $80_c + 20_v$, the most important thing in determining surplus-value is not whether these figures are expressions of actual values, but how they are related to one another, i.e., whether v = 1/5 of the total capital, and c = 4/5. Whenever this is the case, the surplus-value produced by v is, as was assumed, equal to the average profit. On the other hand, since it equals the average profit, the price of production = cost-price plus profit = k + p = k + s; i.e., in practice it is equal to the value of the commodity. This implies that a rise or fall in wages would not change the price of production, k + p, any more than it would change the value of the commodities, and would merely effect a corresponding opposite movement, a fall or a rise, in the rate of profit. For if a rise or fall of wages were here to bring about a change in the price of commodities, the rate of profit in these spheres of average composition would rise above, or fall below, the level prevailing in other spheres. The sphere of average composition maintains the same level of profit as the other spheres only so long as the price remains unchanged. The practical result is therefore the same as it would be if its products were sold at their real value. For if commodities are sold at their actual values, it is evident that, other conditions being equal, a rise, or fall, in wages will cause a corresponding fall or rise in profit, but no change in the value of commodities, and that under all circumstances a rise or fall in wages can never affect the value of commodities, but only the magnitude of the surplus-value.

Section III. *The Capitalist's Grounds for Compensating*

It has been said that competition levels the rates of profit of the different spheres of production into an average rate of profit and thereby turns the values of the products of these different spheres into prices of production. This occurs through the continual transfer of capital from one sphere to another, in which, for the moment, the profit happens to lie above average. The fluctuations of profit caused by the cycle of fat and lean years succeeding one another in any given branch of industry within given periods must, however, receive due consideration. This incessant outflow and inflow of capital between the different spheres of production creates trends of rise and fall in the rate of profit, which equalise one another more or less and thus have a tendency to reduce the rate of profit everywhere to the same common and general level.

This movement of capitals is primarily caused by the level of market-prices, which lift profits above the general average in one place and depress them below it in another. Merchant's capital is left out of consideration as it is irrelevant at this point, for we know from the sudden paroxysms of speculation appearing in certain popular articles that it can withdraw masses of capital from one line of business with extraordinary rapidity and throw them with equal rapidity into another. Yet with respect to each sphere of actual production—industry, agriculture, mining, etc.—the transfer of capital from one sphere to another offers considerable difficulties, particularly on account of the existing fixed capital. Experience shows, moreover, that if a branch of industry, such as, say, the cotton industry, yields unusually high profits at one period, it makes very little profit, or even suffers losses, at another, so that in a certain cycle of years the average profit is much the same as in other branches. And capital soon learns to take this experience into account.

What competition does *not* show, however, is the determination of value, which dominates the movement of production; and the values that lie beneath the prices of production and that determine them in the last instance. Competition, on the other hand, shows: 1) the average profits, which are independent of the organic composition of capital in the different spheres of production, and therefore also of the mass of living labour appropriated by any given capital in any given sphere of exploitation; 2) the rise and fall of prices of production caused by changes in the level of wages, a phenomenon which at first glance completely contradicts the value relation of commodities; 3) the fluctuations of market-prices, which reduce the average market-price of commodities in a given period of time, not to the market-*value*, but to a very different market-price of production, which diverges considerably from this market-value. All these phenomena *seem* to contradict the determination of value by labour-time as much as the nature of surplus-value consisting of unpaid surplus-labour. *Thus everything appears reversed in competition.* The final pattern of economic relations as seen on the surface, in their real existence and consequently in the conceptions by which the bearers and agents of these relations seek to understand them, is very much different from, and indeed quite the reverse of, their inner but concealed essential pattern and the conception corresponding to it.

Further, as soon as capitalist production reaches a certain level of development, the equalisation of the different rates of profit in individual spheres to general rate of profit no longer proceeds solely through the play of attraction and repulsion, by which market-prices attract or repel capital. After average prices, and their corresponding market-prices, become stable for a time it reaches the *consciousness* of the individual capitalists that this equalisation balances *definite differences*, so that they include these in their mutual calculations. The differences exist in the mind of the capitalists and are taken into account as grounds for compensating.

Average profit is the basic conception, the conception that capitals of equal magnitude must yield equal profits in equal time spans. This, again, is based on the conception that the capital in each sphere of production must share *pro rata* to its magnitude in the total surplus-value squeezed out of the labourers by the total social capital; or, that every individual capital should be regarded merely as a part of the total social capital, and every capitalist actually as a shareholder in the total social enterprise, each sharing in the total profit *pro rata* to the magnitude of his share of capital.

This conception serves as a basis for the capitalist's calculations, for instance, that a capital whose turnover is slower than another's, because its commodities take longer to be produced, or because they are sold in remoter markets, nevertheless charges the profit it loses in this way, and compensates itself by raising the price. Or else, that investments of capital in lines exposed to greater hazards, for instance, in shipping, are compensated by higher prices. As soon as capitalist production, and with it the insurance business, are developed, the hazards are, in effect, made equal for all spheres of production (cf. Corbet); but the more hazardous lines pay higher insurance rates, and recover them in the prices of their commodities. In practice, all this means that every circumstance, which renders one line of production—and all of them are considered equally necessary within certain limits—less profitable, and another more profitable, is taken into account once and for all as valid ground for compensation, without always requiring the renewed action of competition to justify the motives or factors for calculating this compensation. The capitalist simply forgets—or rather fails to see, because competition does not point it out to him—that all these grounds for compensation mutually advanced by capitalists in calculating the prices of commodities of different lines of production merely come down to the fact that they all have an equal claim, *pro rata* to the magnitude of their respective capitals, to the common loot, the total surplus-value. It rather *seems* to them that since the profit pocketed by them differs from the surplus-value they appropriated, these grounds for compensation do not level out their participation in the total surplus-value, but *create the profit itself*, which seems to be derived from the additions made on one or another ground to the cost-price of their commodities.

In other respects, the statements made in Chapter VII concerning the capitalists' assumptions as to the source of surplus-value, apply also to average profit. The present case appears different only in so far as a saving in cost-price depends on individual business acumen, alertness, etc., assuming the market-price of commodities and the exploitation of labour to be given.

PART III

THE LAW OF THE TENDENCY OF THE RATE OF PROFIT TO FALL

13

The Law As Such

Assuming a given wage and working-day, a variable capital, for instance of 100, represents a certain number of employed labourers. It is the index of this number. Suppose £100 are the wages of 100 labourers for, say, one week. If these labourers perform equal amounts of necessary and surplus-labour, if they work daily as many hours for themselves, *i.e.*, for the reproduction of their wage, as they do for the capitalist, *i.e.*, for the production of surplus-value, then the value of their total product = £200, and the surplus-value they produce would amount to £100. The rate of surplus-value, s/v, would = 100%. But, as we have seen, this rate of surplus-value would nonetheless express itself in very different rates of profit, depending on the different volumes of constant capital c and consequently of the total capital C, because the rate of profit = s/C. The rate of surplus-value is 100%:

If c = 50, and v = 100, then p' = 100/150 = 66⅔%;
c = 100, and v = 100, then p' = 100/200 = 50%;
c = 200, and v = 100, then p' = 100/300 = 33⅓%;
c = 300, and v = 100, then p' = 100/400 = 25%;
c = 400, and v = 100, then p' = 100/500 = 20%.

This is how the same rate of surplus-value would express itself under the same degree of labour exploitation in a falling rate of profit, because the material growth of the constant capital implies also a growth—albeit not in the same proportion—in its value, and consequently in that of the total capital.

If it is further assumed that this gradual change in the composition of capital is not confined only to individual spheres of production, but that it occurs more or less in all, or at least in the key spheres of production, so that it involves changes in the average organic composition of the total capital of a certain society, then the gradual growth of constant capital in relation to variable capital must necessarily lead to *a gradual fall of the general rate of profit*, so long as the rate of surplus-value, or the intensity of exploitation of labour by capital, remain the same. Now we have seen that it is a law of capitalist production that its development is attended by a relative decrease of variable in relation to constant capital, and consequently to the total capital set in motion. This is just another way of saying that owing to the distinctive methods of production developing in the capitalist system, the same number of labourers, *i.e.*, the same quantity of labour-power set in motion by a variable capital of a given value, operate, work up and productively consume in the same time span an ever-increasing quantity of means of labour, machinery and fixed capital of all sorts, raw and auxiliary materials—and consequently a constant capital of an ever-increasing value. This continual relative decrease of the variable capital vis-a-vis the constant, and consequently the total capital, is identical with the progressively higher organic composition of the social capital in its average. It is likewise just another expression for the progressive development of the social productivity of labour, which is demonstrated precisely by the fact that the same number of labourers, in the same time, *i.e.*, with less labour, convert an ever-increasing quantity of raw and auxiliary materials into products, thanks to the growing application of machinery and fixed capital in general. To this growing quantity of value of the constant capital—although indicating the growth of the real mass of use-values of which the constant capital materially consists only approximately—corresponds a progressive cheapening of products. Every individual product, considered by itself, contains a smaller quantity of labour than it did on a lower level of production, where the capital invested in wages occupies a far greater place compared to the capital invested in means of production. The hypothetical series drawn up at the beginning of this chapter expresses, therefore, the actual tendency of capitalist production. This mode of production produces a progressive relative decrease of the variable capital as compared to the constant capital, and consequently a continuously rising organic composition of the total capital. The immediate result of this is that the rate of surplus-value, at the same, or even a rising, degree of labour exploitation, is represented by a continually falling general rate of profit. (We shall see later [Present edition: Ch. XIV.—*Ed.*] why this fall does not manifest itself in an absolute form, but rather as a tendency toward a progressive fall.) The progressive tendency of the general rate of profit to fall is, therefore, just *an expression peculiar to the capitalist mode of production* of the progressive development of the social productivity of labour. This does not mean to say that the rate of profit may not fall temporarily for other reasons. But proceeding from the nature of the capitalist mode of production, it is thereby proved logical necessity that in its development, the general average rate of surplus-value must express itself in a falling general rate of profit. Since the mass of the employed living labour is continually on the decline as compared to the mass of materialised labour set in motion by it, *i.e.*, to the productively consumed means of production, it follows that the portion of living labour, unpaid and congealed in surplus-value, must also be continually on the decrease compared to the amount of value represented by the invested total capital. Since the ratio of the mass of surplus-value to the value of the invested total capital forms the rate of profit, this rate must constantly fall.

Simple as this law appears from the foregoing statements, all of political economy has so far had little success in discovering it, as we shall see in a later part. [K. Marx, *Theorien über den Mehrwert*. K. Marx/F. Engels, *Werke*, Band 26, Teil 2, S. 435-66, 541-43.—*Ed.*] The economists perceived the phenomenon and cudgelled their brains in tortuous attempts to interpret it. Since this law is of great importance to capitalist production, it may be said to be a mystery whose solution has been the goal of all political economy since Adam Smith, the difference between the various schools since Adam Smith having been in the divergent approaches to a solution. When we consider, on the other hand, that up to the present political economy has been running in circles around the distinction between constant and variable capital, but has never known how to define it accurately; that it has never separated surplus-value from profit, and never even considered profit in its pure form as distinct from its different, independent components, such as industrial profit, commercial profit, interest, and ground-rent; that it has never thoroughly analysed the differences in the organic composition of capital, and, for this reason, has never thought of analysing the formation of the general rate of profit—if we consider all this, the failure to solve this riddle is no longer surprising.

We intentionally present this law before going on to the division of profit into different independent categories. The fact that this analysis is made independently of the division of profit into different parts, which fall to the share of different categories of people, shows from the outset that this law is, in its entirety, independent of this division, and just as independent of the mutual relations of the resultant categories of profit. The profit to which we are here referring is but another name for surplus-value itself, which is presented only in its relation to total capital rather than to variable capital, from which it arises. The drop in the rate of profit, therefore, expresses the falling relation of surplus-value to advanced total capital, and is for this reason independent of any division whatsoever of this surplus-value among the various categories.

We have seen that at a certain stage of capitalist development, where the organic composition of capital c : v was 50 : 100, a rate of surplus-value of 100% was expressed in a rate of profit of 66⅔%, and that at a higher stage, where c : v was 400 : 100, the same rate of surplus-value was expressed in a rate of profit of only 20%. What is true of different successive stages of development in one country, is also true of different coexisting stages of development in different countries. In an undeveloped country, in which the former composition of capital is the average, the general rate of profit would = 66⅔%, while in a country with the latter composition and a much higher stage of development, it would = 20%.

The difference between the two national rates of profit might disappear, or even be reversed, if labour were less productive in the less developed country, so that a larger quantity of labour were to be represented in a smaller quantity of the same commodities, and a larger exchange-value were represented in less use-value. The labourer would then spend more of his time in reproducing his own means of subsistence, or their value, and less time in producing surplus-value; consequently, he would perform less surplus-labour, with the result that the rate of surplus-value would be lower. Suppose, the labourer of the less developed country were to work ⅔ of the working-day for himself and ⅓ for the capitalist; in accordance with the above illustration, the same labour-power would then be paid with 133⅓ and would furnish a surplus of only 60⅔. A constant capital of 50 would correspond to a variable capital of 433⅓. The rate of surplus-value would amount to 66⅔ : 133⅓ = 50%, and the rate of profit to 66⅔ : 133⅓, or approximately 36%.

Since we have not so far analysed the different component parts of profit, *i.e.*, they do not for the present exist for us, we make the following remarks beforehand merely to avoid misunderstanding: In comparing countries in different stages of development it would be a big mistake to measure the level of the national rate of profit by, say, the level of the national rate of interest, namely when comparing countries with a developed capitalist production with countries in which labour has not yet been formally subjected to capital, although in reality the labourer is exploited by the capitalist (as, for instance, in India, where the ryot manages his farm as an independent producer whose production as such is not, therefore, as yet subordinated to capital, although the usurer may not only rob him of his entire surplus-labour by means of interest, but may also, to use a capitalist term, hack off a part of his wage). This interest comprises all the profit, and more than the profit, instead of merely expressing an aliquot part of the produced surplus-value, or profit, as it does in countries with a developed capitalist production. On the other hand, the rate of interest is, in this case, mostly determined by relations (loans granted by usurers to owners of larger estates who draw ground-rent) which have nothing to do with profit, and rather indicate to what extent usury appropriates ground-rent.

As regards countries possessing different stages of development of capitalist production, and consequently capitals of different organic composition, a country where the normal working-day is shorter than another's may have a higher rate of surplus-value (one of the factors which determine the rate of profit). *First,* if the English ten-hour working-day is, on account of its higher intensity, equal to an Austrian working-day of 14 hours, then, dividing the working-day equally in both instances, 5 hours of English surplus-labour may represent a greater value on the world-market than 7 hours of Austrian surplus-labour. *Second,* a larger portion of the English working-day than of the Austrian may represent surplus-labour.

The law of the falling rate of profit, which expresses the same, or even a higher, rate of surplus-value, states, in other words, that any quantity of the average social capital, say, a capital of 100, comprises an ever larger portion or means of labour, and an ever smaller portion of living labour. Therefore, since the aggregate mass of living labour operating the means of production decreases in relation to the value of these means of production, it follows that the unpaid labour and the portion of value in which it is expressed must decline as compared to the value of the advanced total capital. Or: An ever smaller aliquot part of invested total capital is converted into living labour, and this total capital, therefore, absorbs in proportion to its magnitude less and less surplus-labour, although the unpaid part of the labour applied may at the same time grow in relation to the paid part. The relative decrease of the variable and increase of the constant capital, however much both parts may grow in absolute magnitude, is, as we have said, but another expression for greater productivity of labour.

Let a capital of 100 consist of $80_c + 20_v$, and the latter = 20 labourers. Let the rate of surplus-value be 100%, *i.e.*, the labourers work half the day for themselves and the other half for the capitalist. Now let the capital of 100 in a less developed country = $20_c + 80_v$, and let the latter = 80 labourers. But these labourers require 2/3 of the day for themselves, and work only 1/3 for the capitalist. Everything else being equal, the labourers in the first case produce a value of 40, and in the second of 120. The first capital produces $80_c + 20_v + 20_s = 120$; rate of profit = 20%. The second capital, $20_c + 80_v + 40_s = 140$; rate of profit 40%. In the second case, the rate of profit is, therefore, double the first, although the rate of surplus-value in the first = 100%, which is double that of the second, where it is only 50%. But then, a capital of the same magnitude appropriates the surplus-labour of only 20 labourers in the first case, and of 80 labourers in the second case.

The law of the progressive falling of the rate of profit, or the relative decline of appropriated surplus-labour compared to the mass of materialised labour set in motion by living labour, does not rule out in any way that the absolute mass of exploited labour set in motion by the social capital, and consequently the absolute mass of the surplus-labour it appropriates, may grow; nor, that the capitals controlled by individual capitalists may dispose of a growing mass of labour and, hence, of surplus-labour, the latter even though the number of labourers they employ does not increase.

Take a certain working population of, say, two million. Assume, furthermore, that the length and intensity of the average working-day, and the level of wages, and thereby the proportion between necessary and surplus-labour, are given. In that case, the aggregate labour of these two million, and their surplus-labour expressed in surplus-value, always produces the same magnitude of value. But with the growth of the mass of the constant (fixed and circulating) capital set in motion by this labour, this produced quantity of value declines in relation to the value of this capital, which value grows with its mass, even if not in quite the same proportion. This ratio, and consequently the rate of profit, shrinks in spite of the fact that the mass of commanded living labour is the same as before, and the same amount of surplus-labour is sucked out of it by the capital. It changes because the mass of materialised labour set in motion by living labour increases, and not because the mass of living labour has shrunk. It is a relative decrease, not an absolute one, and has, in fact, nothing to do with the absolute magnitude of the labour and surplus-labour set in motion. The drop in the rate of profit is not due to an absolute, but only to a relative decrease of the variable part of the total capital, *i.e.*, to its decrease in relation to the constant part.

What applies to any given mass of labour and surplus-labour, also applies to a growing number of labourers, and, thus, under the above assumption, to any growing mass of commanded labour in general, and to its unpaid part, the surplus-labour, in particular. If the working population increases from two million to three, and if the variable capital invested in wages also rises to three million from its former two million, while the constant capital rises from four million to fifteen million, then, under the above assumption of a constant working-day and a constant rate of surplus-value, the mass of surplus-labour, and of surplus-value, rises by one-half, *i.e.*, 50%, from two million to three. Nevertheless, in spite of this growth of the absolute mass of surplus-labour, and hence of surplus-value, by 50%, the ratio of variable to constant capital would fall from 2 : 4 to 3 : 15, and the ratio of surplus-value to total capital would be (in millions)

I. $4_c + 2_v + 2_s$; C = 6, p' = 33⅓%.
II. $15_c + 3_v + 3_s$; C = 18, p' = 16⅔%.

While the mass of surplus-value has increased by one-half, the rate of profit has fallen by one-half. However, the profit is only the surplus-value calculated in relation to the total social capital, and the mass of profit, its absolute magnitude, is socially equal to the absolute magnitude of the surplus-value. The absolute magnitude of the profit, its total amount, would, therefore, have grown by 50%, in spite of its enormous relative decrease compared to the advanced total capital, or in spite of the enormous decrease in the general rate of profit. The number of labourers employed by capital, hence the absolute mass of the labour set in motion by it, and therefore the absolute mass of surplus-labour absorbed by it, the mass of the surplus-value produced by it, and therefore the absolute mass of the profit produced by it, *can*, consequently, increase, and increase progressively, in spite of the progressive drop in the rate of profit. And this not only *can* be so. Aside from temporary fluctuations, it *must* be so, on the basis of capitalist production.

Essentially, the capitalist process of production is simultaneously a process of accumulation. We have shown that with the development of capitalist production, the mass of values to be simply reproduced or maintained increases as the productivity of labour grows, even if the labour-power employed should remain constant. But with the development of social productivity of labour, the mass of produced use-values, of which the means of production form a part, grows still more. And the additional labour, through whose appropriation this additional wealth can be reconverted into capital, does not depend on the value, but on the mass of these means of production (including means of subsistence), because in the production process, the labourers have nothing to do with the value, but with the use-value, of the means of production. Accumulation itself, however, and the concentration of capital that goes with it, is a material means of increasing productiveness. Now, this growth of the means of production includes the growth of the working population, the creation of a working population, which corresponds to the surplus-capital, or even exceeds its general requirements, thus leading to an over-population of workers. A momentary excess of surplus-capital over the working population it has commandeered, would have a two-fold effect. It could, on the one hand, by raising wages, mitigate the adverse conditions which decimate the offspring of the labourers and would make marriages easier among them, so as gradually to increase the population. On the other hand, by applying methods which yield relative surplus-value (introduction and improvement of machinery), it would produce a far more rapid, artificial, relative over-population, which in its turn, would be a breeding ground for a really swift propagation of the population since under capitalist production misery produces population. It, therefore, follows of itself from the nature of the capitalist process of accumulation, which is but one facet of the capitalist production process, that the increased mass of means of production that is to be converted into capital always finds a correspondingly increased, even excessive, exploitable worker population. As the process of production and accumulation advances, therefore, the mass of available and appropriated surplus-labour, and hence the absolute mass of profit appropriated by the social capital, *must* grow. Along with the volume, however, the same laws of production and accumulation increase also the value of the constant capital in a mounting progression more rapidly than that of the variable part of capital, invested as it is in living labour. Hence, the same laws produce for the social capital a growing absolute mass of profit, and a falling rate of profit.

We shall entirely ignore here that with the advance of capitalist production and the attendant development of the productiveness of social labour and multiplication of production branches, hence products, the same amount of value represents a progressively increasing mass of use-values and enjoyments.

The development of capitalist production and accumulation lifts labour-processes to an increasingly enlarged scale and thus imparts to them ever greater dimensions, and involves accordingly larger investments of capital for each individual establishment. A mounting concentration of capitals (accompanied, though on a smaller scale, by an increase in the number of capitalists) is, therefore, one of its material requirements as well as one of its results. Hand in hand with it, mutually interacting, there occurs a progressive expropriation of the more or less direct producers. It is, then, natural for the individual capitalists to command increasingly large armies of labourers (no matter how much the variable capital may decrease in relation to the constant), and natural, too, that the mass of surplus-value, and hence profit, appropriated by them, should grow simultaneously with, and in spite of, the fall in the rate of profit. The causes which concentrate masses of labourers under the command of individual capitalists, are the very same that swell the mass of the invested fixed capital, and auxiliary and raw materials, in mounting proportion as compared to the mass of employed living labour.

It requires no more than a passing remark at this point to indicate that, given a certain labouring population, the mass of surplus-value, hence the absolute mass of profit, must grow if the rate of surplus-value increases, be it through a lengthening or intensification of the working-day, or through a drop in the value of wages due to an increase in the productiveness of labour, and that it must do so in spite of the relative decrease of variable capital in respect to constant.

The same development of the productiveness of social labour, the same laws which express themselves in a relative decrease of variable as compared to total capital, and in the thereby facilitated accumulation, while this accumulation in its turn becomes a starting-point for the further development of the productiveness and for a further relative decrease of variable capital—this same development manifests itself, aside from temporary fluctuations, in a progressive increase of the total employed labour-power and a progressive increase of the absolute mass of surplus-value, and hence of profit.

Now, what must be the form of this double-edged law of a decrease in the *rate* of profit and a simultaneous increase in the absolute *mass* of profit arising from the same causes? As a law based on the fact that under given conditions the appropriated mass of surplus-labour, hence of surplus-value, increases, and that, so far as the total capital is concerned, or the individual capital as an aliquot part of the total capital, profit and surplus-value are identical magnitudes?

Let us take an aliquot part of capital upon which we calculate the rate of profit, *e.g.*, 100. These 100 represent the average composition of the total capital, say, $80_c + 20_v$. We have seen in the second part of this book that the average rate of profit in the various branches of production is determined not by the particular composition of each individual capital, but by the average social composition. As the variable capital decreases relative to the constant, hence the total capital of 100, the rate of profit, or the relative magnitude of surplus-value, *i.e.*, its ratio to the advanced total capital of 100, falls even though the intensity of exploitation were to remain the same, or even to increase. But it is not this relative magnitude alone which falls. The magnitude of the surplus-value or profit absorbed by the total capital of 100 also falls absolutely. At a rate of surplus-value of 100%, a capital of $60_c + 40_v$ produces a mass of surplus-value, and hence of profit, amounting to 40; a capital of $80_c + 20_v$ a mass of profit of 30; and for a capital of $80_c + 20_v$ the profit falls to 20. This falling applies to the mass of surplus-value, and hence of profit, and is due to the fact that the total capital of 100 employs less living labour, and, the intensity of labour exploitation remaining the same, sets in motion less surplus-labour, and therefore produces less surplus-value. Taking any aliquot part of the social capital, *i.e.*, a capital of average composition, as a standard by which to measure surplus-value—and this is done in all profit calculations—a relative fall of surplus-value is generally identical with its absolute fall. In the cases given above, the rate of profit sinks from 40% to 30% and to 20%, because, in fact, the mass of surplus-value, and hence of profit, produced by the same capital falls absolutely from 40 to 30 and to 20. Since the magnitude of the value of the capital, by which the surplus-value is measured, is given as 100, a fall in the proportion of surplus-value to this given magnitude can be only another expression for the decrease of the absolute magnitude of surplus-value and profit. This is, indeed, a tautology. But, as shown, the fact that this decrease occurs at all, arises from the nature of the development of the capitalist process of production.

On the other hand, however, the same causes which bring about an absolute decrease of surplus-value, and hence profit, on a given capital, and consequently of the rate of profit calculated in per cent, produce an increase in the absolute mass of surplus-value, and hence of profit, appropriated by the social capital (*i.e.*, by all capitalists taken as a whole). How does this occur, what is the only way in which this can occur, or what are the conditions obtaining in this seeming contradiction?

If any aliquot part = 100 of the social capital, and hence any 100 of average social composition, is a given magnitude, for which therefore a fall in the rate of profit coincides with a fall in the absolute magnitude of the profit because the capital which here serves as a standard of measurement is a constant magnitude, then the magnitude of the social capital like that of the capital in the hands of individual capitalists, is variable, and in keeping with our assumptions it must vary inversely with the decrease of its variable portion.

In our former illustration, when the percentage of composition was $60_c + 40_v$, the corresponding surplus-value, or profit, was 40, and hence the rate of profit 40%. Suppose, the total capital in this stage of composition was one million. Then the total surplus-value, and hence the total profit, amounted to 400,000. Now, if the composition later = $80_c + 20_v$, while the degree of labour exploitation remained the same, then the surplus-value or profit for each 100 = 20. But since the absolute mass of surplus-value or profit increases, as demonstrated, in spite of the decreasing rate of profit or the decreasing production of surplus-value by every 100 of capital—increases, say, from 400,000 to 440,000, then this occurs solely because the total capital which formed at the time of this new composition has risen to 2,200,000. The mass of the total capital set in motion has risen to 220%, while the rate of profit has fallen by 50%. Had the total capital no more than doubled, it would have to produce as much surplus-value and profit to obtain a rate of profit of 20% as the old capital of 1,000,000 produced at 40%. Had it grown to less than double, it would have produced less surplus-value, or profit, than the old capital of 1,000,000, which, in its former composition, would have had to grow from 1,000,000 to no more than 1,100,000 to raise its surplus-value from 400,000 to 440,000.

We again meet here the previously defined law that the relative decrease of the variable capital, hence the development of the social productiveness of labour, involves an increasingly large mass of total capital to set in motion the same quantity of labour-power and squeeze out the same quantity of surplus-labour. Consequently, the possibility of a relative surplus of labouring people develops proportionately to the advances made by capitalist production, not because the productiveness of social labour *decreases*, but because it *increases*. It does not, therefore, arise out of an absolute disproportion between labour and the means of subsistence, or the means for the production of these means of subsistence, but out of a disproportion occasioned by capitalist exploitation of labour, a disproportion between the progressive growth of capital and its relatively shrinking need for an increasing population.

Should the rate of profit fall by 50%, it would shrink one-half. If the mass of profit is to remain the same, the capital must be doubled. For the mass of profit made at a declining rate of profit to remain the same, the multiplier indicating the growth of the total capital must be equal to the divisor indicating the fall of the rate of profit. If the rate of profit falls from 40 to 20, the total capital must rise inversely at the rate of 20 : 40 to obtain the same result. If the rate of profit falls from 40 to 8, the capital would have to increase at the rate of 8 : 40, or five-fold. A capital of 1,000,000 at 40% produces 400,000, and a capital of 5,000,000 at 8% likewise produces 400,000. This applies if we want the result to remain the same. But if the result is to be higher, then the capital must grow at a greater rate than the rate of profit falls. In other words, for the variable portion of the total capital not to remain the same in absolute terms, but to increase absolutely in spite of its falling in percentage of the total capital, the total capital must grow at a faster rate than the percentage of the variable capital falls. It must grow so considerably that in its new composition it should require more than the old portion of variable capital to purchase labour-power. If the variable portion of a capital = 100 should fall from 40 to 20, the total capital must rise higher than 200 to be able to employ a larger variable capital than 40.

Even if the exploited mass of the working population were to remain constant, and only the length and intensity of the working-day were to increase, the mass of the invested capital would have to increase, since it would have to be greater in order to employ the same mass of labour under the old conditions of exploitation after the composition of capital changes.

Thus, the same development of the social productiveness of labour expresses itself with the progress of capitalist production on the one hand in a tendency of the rate of profit to fall progressively and, on the other, in a progressive growth of the absolute mass of the appropriated surplus-value, or profit; so that on the whole a relative decrease of variable capital and profit is accompanied by an absolute increase of both. This two-fold effect, as we have seen, can express itself only in a growth of the total capital at a pace more rapid than that at which the rate of profit falls. For an absolutely increased variable capital to be employed in a capital of higher composition, or one in which the constant capital has increased relatively more, the total capital must not only grow proportionately to its higher composition, but still more rapidly. It follows, then, that as the capitalist mode of production develops, an ever larger quantity of capital is required to employ the same, let alone an increased, amount of labour-power. Thus, on a capitalist foundation, the increasing productiveness of labour necessarily and permanently creates a seeming over-population of labouring people. If the variable capital forms just 1/6 of the total capital instead of the former ½, the total capital must be trebled to employ the same amount of labour-power. And if twice as much labour-power is to be employed, the total capital must increase six-fold.

Political economy, which has until now been unable to explain the law of the tendency of the rate of profit to fall, pointed self-consolingly to the increasing mass of profit, *i.e.*, to the growth of the absolute magnitude of profit, be it for the individual capitalist or for the social capital, but this was also based on mere platitude and speculation.

To say that the mass of profit is determined by two factors—first, the rate of profit, and, secondly, the mass of capital invested at this rate, is mere tautology. It is, therefore, but a corollary of this tautology to say that there is a possibility for the mass of profit to grow even though the rate of profit may fall at the same time. It does not help us one step farther since it is just as possible for the capital to increase without the mass of profit growing, and for it to increase even while the mass of profit falls. For 100 at 25% yields 25, and 400 at 5% yields only 20.[1] But if the same causes which make the rate of profit fall, entail the accumulation, *i.e.*, the formation of additional capital, and if each additional capital employs additional labour and produces additional surplus-value; if, on the other hand, the mere fall in the rate of profit implies that the constant capital, and with it the total old capital, have increased, then this process ceases to be mysterious. We shall see later [K. Marx, *Theorien über den Mehrwert.* K. Marx/F. Engels, *Werke,* Band 26, Teil 2,. S. 435-66, 541- 43.—*Ed*] to what deliberate falsifications some people resort in their calculations to spirit away the possibility of an increase in the mass of profit simultaneous with a decrease in the rate of profit.

We have shown how the same causes that bring about a tendency for the general rate of profit to fall necessitate an accelerated accumulation of capital and, consequently, an increase in the absolute magnitude, or total mass, of the surplus-labour (surplus-value, profit) appropriated by it. Just as everything appears reversed in competition, and thus in the consciousness of the agents of competition, so also this law, this inner and necessary connection between two seeming contradictions. It is evident that within the proportions indicated above, a capitalist disposing of a large capital will receive a larger mass of profit than a small capitalist making seemingly high profits. Even a cursory examination of competition shows, furthermore, that under certain circumstances, when the greater capitalist wishes to make room for himself on the market, and to crowd out the smaller ones, as happens in times of crises, he makes practical use of this, *i.e.*, he deliberately lowers his rate of profit in order to drive the smaller ones to the wall. Merchants capital, which we shall describe in detail later, also notably exhibits phenomena which appear to attribute a fall in profit to an expansion of business, and thus of capital. The scientific expression for this false conception will be given later. Similar superficial observations result from a comparison of rates of profit in individual lines of business, distinguished either as subject to free competition, or to monopoly. The utterly shallow conception existing in the minds of the agents of competition is found in Roscher, namely, that a reduction in the rate of profit is 'more prudent and humane'. [Roscher, *Die Grundlage der Nationalökonomie*, 3 Auflage, 1858, 108, S. 192.—*Ed.*] The fall in the rate of profit appears in this case as an *effect* of an increase in capital and of the concomitant calculation of the capitalist that the mass of profits pocketed by him will be greater at a smaller rate of profit. This entire conception (with the exception of Adam Smith›s, which we shall mention later) [K. Marx, *Theorien über den Mehrwert.* K. Marx/F. Engels, *Werke,* Band 26, Teil 2, S. 214-28.—*Ed.*] rests on an utter misapprehension of what the general rate of profit is, and on the crude notion that prices are actually determined by adding a more or less arbitrary quota of profit to the true value of commodities. Crude as these ideas are, they arise necessarily out of the inverted aspect which the immanent laws of capitalist production represent in competition.

The law that a fall in the rate of profit due to the development of productiveness is accompanied by an increase in the mass of profit, also expresses itself in the fact that a fall in the price of commodities produced by a capital is accompanied by a relative increase of the masses of profit contained in them and realised by their sale.

Since the development of the productiveness and the correspondingly higher composition of capital sets in motion an ever-increasing quantity of means of production through a constantly decreasing quantity of labour, every aliquot part of the total product, *i.e.*, every single commodity, or each particular lot of commodities in the total mass of products, absorbs less living labour, and also contains less materialised labour, both in the depreciation of the fixed capital applied and in the raw and auxiliary materials consumed. Hence every single commodity contains a smaller sum of labour materialised in means of production and of labour newly added during production. This causes the price of the individual commodity to fall. But the mass of profits contained in the individual commodities may nevertheless increase if the rate of the absolute or relative surplus-value grows. The commodity contains less newly added labour, but its unpaid portion grows in relation to its paid portion. However, this is the case only within certain limits. With the absolute amount of living labour newly incorporated in individual commodities decreasing enormously as production develops, the absolute mass of unpaid labour contained in them will likewise decrease, however much it may have grown as compared to the paid portion. The mass of profit on each individual commodity will shrink considerably with the development of the productiveness of labour, in spite of a growth in the rate of surplus-value. And this reduction, just as the fall in the rate of profit, is only delayed by the cheapening of the elements of constant capital and by the other circumstances set forth in the first part of this book, which increase the rate of profit at a given, or even falling, rate of surplus-value.

That the price of individual commodities whose sum makes up the total product of capital falls, means simply that a certain quantity of labour is realised in a larger quantity of commodities, so that each individual commodity contains less labour than before. This is the case even if the price of one part of constant capital, such as raw material, etc., should rise. Outside of a few cases (for instance, if the productiveness of labour uniformly cheapens all elements of the constant, and the variable, capital), the rate of profit will fall, in spite of the higher rate of surplus-value, 1) because even a larger unpaid portion of the smaller total amount of newly added labour is smaller than a smaller aliquot unpaid portion of the former larger amount and 2) because the higher composition of capital is expressed in the individual commodity by the fact that the portion of its value in which newly added labour is materialised decreases in relation to the portion of its value which represents raw and auxiliary material, and the wear and tear of fixed capital. This change in the proportion of the various component parts in the price of individual commodities, *i.e.*, the decrease of that portion of the price in which newly added living labour is materialised, and the increase of that portion of it in which formerly materialised labour is represented, is the form which expresses the decrease of the variable in relation to the constant capital through the price of the individual commodities. Just as this decrease is absolute for a certain amount of capital, say of 100, it is also absolute for every individual commodity as an aliquot part of the reproduced capital. However, the rate of profit, if calculated merely on the elements of the price of an individual commodity, would be different from what it actually is. And for the following reason:

[The rate of profit is calculated on the total capital invested, but for a definite time, actually a year. The rate of profit is the ratio of the surplus-value, or profit, produced and realised in a year, to the total capital calculated in per cent. It is, therefore, not necessarily equal to a rate of profit calculated for the period of turnover of the invested capital rather than for a year. It is only if the capital is turned over exactly in one year that the two coincide.

On the other hand, the profit made in the course of a year is merely the sum of profits on commodities produced and sold during that same year. Now, if we calculate the profit on the cost-price of commodities, we obtain a rate of profit = p/k in which p stands for the profit realised during one year, and k for the sum of the cost-prices of commodities produced and sold within the same period. It is evident that this rate of profit p/k will not coincide with the actual rate of profit p/C, mass of profit divided by total capital, unless k = C, that is, unless the capital is turned over in exactly one year.

Let us take three different conditions of an industrial capital.

I. A capital of £8,000 produces and sells annually 5,000 pieces of a commodity at 30s. per piece, thus making an annual turnover of £7,500. It makes a profit of 10s. on each piece, or £2,500 per year. Every piece, then, contains 20s. advanced capital and 10s. profit, so that the rate of profit per piece is 10/20 = 50%. The turned-over sum of £7,500 contains £5,000 advanced capital and £2,500 profit. Rate of profit per turnover, p/k, likewise 50%. But calculated on the total capital the rate of profit p/C = 2,500/8,000 = 31¼%

II. The capital rises to £10,000. Owing to increased productivity of labour it is able to produce annually 10,000 pieces of the commodity at a cost-price of 20s. per piece. Suppose the commodity is sold at a profit of 4s., hence at 24s. per piece. In that case the price of the annual product = £12,000, of which £10,000 is advanced capital and £2,000 is profit. The rate of profit p/k = 4/20 per piece, and 2,000/10,000 for the annual turnover, or in both cases = 20%. And since the total capital is equal to the sum of the cost-prices, namely £10,000, it follows that p/C, the actual rate of profit, is in this case also 20%.

III. Let the capital rise to £15,000 owing to a constant growth of the productiveness of labour, and let it annually produce 30,000 pieces of the commodity at a cost-price of 13s. per piece, each piece being sold at a profit of 2s., or at 15s. The annual turnover therefore = 30,000×15s. = £22,500, of which £19,500 is advanced capital and £3,000 profit. The rate of profit p/k then = 2/13 = 3,000/19,500 = 15 5/13%. But p/C = 3,000/15,000 = 20%.

We see, therefore, that only in case II, where the turned-over capital-value is equal to the total capital, the rate of profit per piece, or per total amount of turnover, is the same as the rate of profit calculated on the total capital. In case I, in which the amount of the turnover is smaller than the total capital, the rate of profit calculated on the cost-price of the commodity is higher; and in case III, in which the total capital is smaller than the amount of the turnover, it is lower than the actual rate calculated on the total capital. This is a general rule.

In commercial practice, the turnover is generally calculated inaccurately. It is assumed that the capital has been turned over once as soon as the sum of the realised commodity-prices equals the sum of the invested total capital. But the *capital* can complete one whole turnover only when the sum of the *cost-prices* of the realised commodities equals the sum of the total capital.—*F.E.*]

This again shows how important it is in capitalist production to regard individual commodities, or the commodity-product of a certain period, as products of advanced capital and in relation to the total capital which produces them, rather than in isolation, by themselves, as mere commodities.

The *rate* of profit must be calculated by measuring the mass of produced and realised surplus-value not only in relation to the consumed portion of capital reappearing in the commodities but also to this part plus that portion of unconsumed but applied capital which continues to operate in production. However, the *mass* of profit cannot be equal to anything but the mass of profit or surplus-value contained in the commodities themselves and to be realised by their sale.

If the productivity of industry increases, the price of individual commodities falls. There is less labour in them, less paid and unpaid labour. Suppose, the same labour produces, say, triple its former product. Then ⅔ less labour yields individual product. And since profit can make up but a portion of the amount of labour contained in an individual commodity, the mass of profit in the individual commodity must decrease, and this takes place within certain limits, even if the rate of surplus-value should rise. In any case, the mass of profit on the total product does not fall below the original mass of profit so long as the capital employs the same number of labourers at the same degree of exploitation. (This may also occur if fewer labourers are employed at a higher rate of exploitation.) For the mass of profit on the individual product decreases proportionately to the increase in the number of products. The mass of profit remains the same, but it is distributed differently over the total amount of commodities. Nor does this alter the distribution between the labourers and capitalists of the amount of value created by newly added labour. The mass of profit cannot increase so long as the same amount of labour is employed, unless the unpaid surplus-labour increases, or should intensity of exploitation remain the same unless the number of labourers grows. Or, both these causes may combine to produce this result. In all these cases—which, however, in accordance with our assumption, presuppose an increase of constant capital as compared to variable, and an increase in the magnitude of total capital—the individual commodity contains a smaller mass of profit, and the rate of profit falls even if calculated on the individual commodity. A given quantity of newly added labour materialises in a larger quantity of commodities. The price of the individual commodity falls. Considered abstractly, the rate of profit may remain the same, even though the price of the individual commodity may fall as a result of greater productiveness of labour and a simultaneous increase in the number of this cheaper commodity if, for instance, the increase in productiveness of labour acts uniformly and simultaneously on all the elements of the commodity, so that its total price falls in the same proportion in which the productivity of labour increases, while, on the other hand, the mutual relation of the different elements of the price of the commodity remains the same. The rate of profit could even rise if a rise in the rate of surplus-value were accompanied by a substantial reduction in the value of the elements of constant, and particularly of fixed, capital.

But in reality, as we have seen, the rate of profit will fall in the long run. In no case does a fall in the price of any individual commodity by itself give a clue to the rate of profit. Everything depends on the magnitude of the total capital invested in its production. For instance, if the price of one yard of fabric falls from 3s. to 1⅔s., if we know that before this price reduction it contained 1⅔s. constant capital, yarn, etc., ⅔s. wages, and ⅔s. profit, while after the reduction, it contains 1s. constant capital, $#8531s. wages, and ⅓s. profit, we cannot tell if the rate of profit has remained the same or not. This depends on whether, and by how much, the advanced total capital has increased, and how many yards more it produces in a given time.

The phenomenon, springing from the nature of the capitalist mode of production, that increasing productivity of labour implies a drop in the price of the individual commodity, or of a certain mass of commodities, an increase in the number of commodities, a reduction in the mass of profit on the individual commodity and in the rate of profit on the aggregate of commodities, and an increase in the mass of profit on the total quantity of commodities—this phenomenon appears on the surface only in a reduction of the mass of profit on the individual commodity, a fall in its price, an increase in the mass of profit on the augmented total number of commodities produced by the total social capital or an individual capitalist. It then appears as if the capitalist adds less profit to the price of the individual commodity of his own free will, and makes up for it through the greater number of commodities he produces. This conception rests upon the notion of profit upon alienation, which, in its turn, is deduced from the conception of merchant capital.

We have previously seen in Book I (4 and 7 Abschnitt) [English edition: Parts IV and VII.—*Ed.*] that the mass of commodities growing along with the productivity of labour and the cheapening of the individual commodity as such (as long as these commodities do not enter the price of labour-power as determinants)—that this does not affect the proportion between paid and unpaid labour in the individual commodity, in spite of the falling price.

Since all things appear distorted, namely, reversed in competition, the individual capitalist may imagine: 1) that he is reducing his profit on the individual commodity by cutting its price, but still making a greater profit by selling a larger quantity of commodities; 2) that he fixes the price of the individual commodities and that he determines the price of the total product by multiplication, while the original process is really one of division (see Book I, Kap. X, S. 281 [English edition: Ch. XII.—*Ed*]), and multiplication is only correct secondarily, since it is based on that division. The vulgar economist does practically no more than translate the singular concepts of the capitalists, who are in the thrall of competition, into a seemingly more theoretical and generalised language, and attempt to substantiate the justice of those conceptions.

The fall in commodity-prices and the rise in the mass of profit on the augmented mass of these cheapened commodities is, in fact, but another expression for the law of the falling rate of profit attended by a simultaneously increasing mass of profit.

The analysis of how far a falling rate of profit may coincide with rising prices no more belongs here than that of the point previously discussed in Book I (S. 280-81 [English edition: Ch. XII.—*Ed.*]), concerning relative surplus-value. A capitalist working with improved but not as yet generally adopted methods of production sells below the market-price, but above his individual price of production; his rate of profit rises until competition levels it out. During this equalisation period, the second requisite, expansion of the invested capital, makes its appearance. According to the degree of this expansion, the capitalist will be able to employ a part of his former labourers, actually perhaps all of them, or even more, under the new conditions, and hence to produce the same, or a greater, mass of profit.

Note

1. 'We should also expect that, however the rate of the profits of stock might diminish in consequence of the accumulation of capital on the land and the rise of wages, yet the aggregate amount of profits would increase. Thus, supposing that, with repeated accumulations of £100,000, the rate of profit should fall from 20 to 19, to 48, to 17%, a constantly diminishing rate, we should expect that the whole amount of profits received by those successive owners of capital would be always progressive; that it would be greater when the capital was £200,000, than when £100,000; still greater when £300,000; and so on, increasing, though at a diminishing rate, with every increase of capital. This progression, however, is only true for a certain time; thus 19% on £200,000 is more than 20% on £100,000; again 18% on £300,000 is more than 19% on £200,000; but after capital has accumulated to a large amount, and profits have fallen, the further accumulation diminishes the aggregate of profits. Thus, suppose the accumulation should be £1,000,000, and the profits 7%, the whole amount of profits will be £70,000; now if an addition of £100,000 capital be made to the million, and profits should fall to 6%, £66,000 or a diminution of £4,000 will be received by the owners of the stock, although the whole amount of stock will be increased from £1,000,000 to £1,100,000.'—Ricardo, *Political Economy,* Chap. VI (*Works,* ed. by MacCulloch, 1852, pp. 68-69).—The fact is, that the assumption has here been made that the capital increases from 1,000,000 to 1,100,000, that is, by 10%, while the rate of profit falls from 7 to 6, hence by 14 2/7 %. *Hinc illae lacrimae!* ['Thus these tears'—Publius, Terence, *Andria,* Act I, Scene 1.—*Ed.*]

14

Counteracting Influences

If we consider the enormous development of the productive forces of social labour in the last 30 years alone as compared with all preceding periods; if we consider, in particular, the enormous mass of fixed capital, aside from the actual machinery, which goes into the process of social production as a whole, then the difficulty which has hitherto troubled the economist, namely to explain the falling rate of profit, gives place to its opposite, namely to explain why this fall is not greater and more rapid. There must be some counteracting influences at work, which cross and annul the effect of the general law, and which give it merely the characteristic of a tendency, for which reason we have referred to the fall of the general rate of profit as a tendency to fall.

The following are the most general counterbalancing forces:

Section I. *Increasing Intensity of Exploitation*

The degree of exploitation of labour, the appropriation of surplus-labour and surplus-value, is raised notably by lengthening the working-day and intensifying labour. These two points have been comprehensively treated in Book I as incidental to the production of absolute and relative surplus-value. There are many ways of intensifying labour which imply an increase of constant, as compared to variable, capital, and hence a fall in the rate of profit, such as compelling a labourer to operate a larger number of machines. In such cases—and in most procedures serving the production of relative surplus-values—the same causes which increase the rate of surplus-value, may also, from the standpoint of given quantities of invested total capital, involve a fall in the mass of surplus-value. But there are other aspects of intensification, such as the greater velocities of machinery, which consume more raw material in the same time, but, so far as the fixed capital is concerned, wear out the machinery so much faster, and yet do not in any way affect the relation of its value to the price of the labour which sets it in motion. But notably, it is prolongation of the working-day, this invention of modern industry, which increases the mass of appropriated surplus-labour without essentially altering the proportion of the employed labour-power to the constant capital set in motion by it, and which rather tends to reduce this capital relatively. Moreover, it has already been demonstrated—and this constitutes the real secret of the tendency of the rate of profit to fall—that the manipulations to produce relative surplus-value amount, on the whole, to transforming as much as possible of a certain quantity of labour into surplus-value, on the one hand, and employing as little labour as possible in proportion to the invested capital, on the other, so that the same reasons which permit raising the intensity of exploitation rule out exploiting the same quantity of labour as before by the same capital. These are the counteracting tendencies, which, while effecting a rise in the rate of surplus-value, also tend to decrease the mass of surplus-value, and hence the rate of profit produced by a certain capital. Mention should also be made here of the widespread introduction of female and child labour, in so far as the whole family must now perform more surplus-labour for capital than before, even when the total amount of their wages increases, which is by no means always the case.—Everything that promotes the production of relative surplus-value by mere improvement in methods, as in agriculture, without altering the magnitude of the invested capital, has the same effect. The constant capital, it is true, does not, in such cases, increase in relation to the variable, inasmuch as we regard the variable capital as an index of the amount of labour-power employed, but the mass of the product does increase in proportion to the labour-power employed. The same occurs, if the productiveness of labour (no matter, whether its product goes into the labourer's consumption or into the elements of constant capital) is freed from hindrances in communications, from arbitrary or other restrictions which have become obstacles in the course of time; from fetters of all kinds, without directly affecting the ratio of variable to constant capital.

It might be asked whether the factors that check the fall of the rate of profit, but that always hasten its fall in the last analysis, whether these include the temporary, but always recurring, elevations in surplus-value above the general level, which keep occurring now in this and now in that line of production redounding to the benefit of those individual capitalists, who make use of inventions, etc., before these are introduced elsewhere. This question must be answered in the affirmative.

The mass of surplus-value produced by a capital of a given magnitude is the product of two factors—the rate of surplus-value multiplied by the number of labourers employed at this rate. At a given rate of surplus-value it, therefore, depends on the number of labourers, and it depends on the rate of surplus-value when the number of labourers is given. Generally, therefore, it depends on the composite ratio of the absolute magnitudes of the variable capital and the rate of surplus-value. Now we have seen that, on the average, the same factors which raise the rate of relative surplus-value lower the mass of the employed labour-power. It is evident, however, that this will occur to a greater or lesser extent, depending on the definite proportion in which this conflicting movement obtains, and that the tendency towards a reduction in the rate of profit is notably weakened by a rise in the rate of absolute surplus-value, which originates with the lengthening of the working-day.

We saw in the case of the rate of profit that a drop in the rate was generally accompanied by an increase in the mass of profit, due to the increasing mass of total capital employed. From the standpoint of the total variable capital of society, the surplus-value it has produced is equal to the profit it has produced. Both the absolute mass and the rate of surplus-value have increased; the one because the quantity of labour-power employed by society has grown, and the other, because the intensity of exploitation of this labour-power has increased. But in the case of a capital of a given magnitude, *e.g.*, 100, the rate of surplus-value may increase, while the average mass may decrease; for the rate is determined by the proportion, in which the variable capital produces value, while the mass is determined by the proportion of variable capital to the total capital.

The rise in the rate of surplus-value is a factor which determines the mass of surplus-value, and hence also the rate of profit, for it takes place, especially under conditions, in which, as we have previously seen, the constant capital is either not increased at all, or not proportionately increased, in relation to the variable capital. This factor does not abolish the general law. But it causes that law to act rather as a tendency, *i.e.*, as a law whose absolute action is checked, retarded, and weakened, by counteracting circumstances. But since the same influences which raise the rate of surplus-value (even a lengthening of the working-time is a result of large-scale industry) tend to decrease the labour-power employed by a certain capital, it follows that they also tend to reduce the rate of profit and to retard this reduction. If one labourer is compelled to perform as much labour as would rationally be performed by at least two, and if this is done under circumstances in which this one labourer can replace three, then this one labourer will perform as much surplus-labour as was formerly performed by two, and the rate of surplus-value will have risen accordingly. But he will not perform as much as three had performed, and the mass of surplus-value will have decreased accordingly. But this reduction in mass will be compensated, or limited, by the rise in the rate of surplus-value. If the entire population is employed at a higher rate of surplus-value, the mass of surplus-value will increase, in spite of the population remaining the same. It will increase still more if the population increases. And although this is tied up with a relative reduction of the number of employed labourers in proportion to the magnitude of the total capital, this reduction is moderated, or checked, by the rise in the rate of surplus-value.

Before leaving this point, it is to be emphasised once more that with a capital of a given magnitude the *rate* of surplus-value may rise, while its *mass* is decreasing, and vice versa. The mass of surplus-value is equal to the rate multiplied by the number of labourers; however, the rate is never calculated on the total, but only on the variable capital, actually only for every working-day. On the other hand, with a given magnitude of capital-value, the *rate of profit* can neither rise nor fall without the *mass of surplus-value* also rising or falling.

Section II. *Depression of Wages Below the Value of Labour-Power*

This is mentioned here only empirically, since, like many other things which might be enumerated, it has nothing to do with the general analysis of capital, but belongs in an analysis of competition, which is not presented in this work. However, it is one of the most important factors checking the tendency of the rate of profit to fall.

Section III. *Cheapening of Elements of Constant Capital*

Everything said in Part I of this book about factors which raise the rate of profit while the rate of surplus-value remains the same, or regardless of the rate of surplus-value, belongs here. Hence also, with respect to the total capital, that the value of the constant capital does not increase in the same proportion as its material volume. For instance, the quantity of cotton worked up by a single European spinner in a modern factory has grown tremendously compared to the quantity formerly worked up by a European spinner with a spinning-wheel. Yet, the value of the worked-up cotton has not grown in the same proportion as its mass. The same applies to machinery and other fixed capital. In short, the same development which increases the mass of the constant capital in relation to the variable reduces the value of its elements as a result of the increased productivity of labour, and therefore prevents the value of constant capital, although it continually increases, from increasing at the same rate as its material volume, *i.e.*, the material volume of the means of production set in motion by the same amount of labour-power. In isolated cases, the mass of the elements of constant capital may even increase, while its value remains the same, or falls.

The foregoing is bound up with the depreciation of existing capital (that is, of its material elements), which occurs with the development of industry. This is another continually operating factor which checks the fall of the rate of profit, although it may under certain circumstances encroach on the mass of profit by reducing the mass of the capital yielding a profit. This again shows that the same influences which tend to make the rate of profit fall, also moderate the effects of this tendency.

Section IV. *Relative Over-Population*

Its propagation is inseparable from, and hastened by, the development of the productivity of labour as expressed by a fall in the rate of profit. The relative over-population becomes so much more apparent in a country, the more the capitalist mode of production is developed in it. This, again, is the reason why, on the one hand, the more or less imperfect subordination of labour to capital continues in many branches of production, and continues longer than seems at first glance compatible with the general stage of development. This is due to the cheapness and abundance of disposable or unemployed wage-labourers, and to the greater resistance, which some branches of production, by their very nature, render to the transformation of manual work into machine production. On the other hand, new lines of production are opened up, especially for the production of luxuries, and it is these that take as their basis this relative over-population, often set free in other lines of production through the increase of their constant capital. These new lines start out predominantly with living labour, and by degrees pass through the same evolution as the other lines of production. In either case, the variable capital makes up a considerable portion of the total capital and wages are below the average, so that both the rate and mass of surplus-value in these lines of production are unusually high. Since the general rate of profit is formed by levelling the rates of profit in the individual branches of production, however, the same factor which brings about the tendency in the rate of profit to fall, again produces a counterbalance to this tendency and more or less paralyses its effects.

Section V. *Foreign Trade*

Since foreign trade partly cheapens the elements of constant capital, and partly the necessities of life for which the variable capital is exchanged, it tends to raise the rate of profit by increasing the rate of surplus-value and lowering the value of constant capital. It generally acts in this direction by permitting an expansion of the scale of production. It thereby hastens the process of accumulation, on the one hand, but causes the variable capital to shrink in relation to the constant capital, on the other, and thus hastens a fall in the rate of profit. In the same way, the expansion of foreign trade, although the basis of the capitalist mode of production in its infancy, has become its own product, however, with the further progress of the capitalist mode of production, through the innate necessity of this mode of production, its need for an ever-expanding market. Here we see once more the dual nature of this effect. (Ricardo has entirely overlooked this side of foreign trade. [D. Ricardo, *On the Principles of Political Economy, and Taxation, Third edition, London, 1824, Ch. VII.—Ed.]*)

Another question—really beyond the scope of our analysis because of its special nature—is this: Is the general rate of profit raised by the higher rate of profit produced by capital invested in foreign, and particularly colonial, trade?

Capitals invested in foreign trade can yield a higher rate of profit, because, in the first place, there is competition with commodities produced in other countries with inferior production facilities, so that the more advanced country sells its goods above their value even though cheaper than the competing countries. In so far as the labour of the more advanced country is here realised as labour of a higher specific weight, the rate of profit rises, because labour which has not been paid as being of a higher quality is sold as such. The same may obtain in relation to the country, to which commodities are exported and to that from which commodities are imported; namely, the latter may offer more materialised labour *in kind* than it receives, and yet thereby receive commodities cheaper than it could produce them. Just as a manufacturer who employs a new invention before it becomes generally used, undersells his competitors and yet sells his commodity above its individual value, that is, realises the specifically higher productiveness of the labour he employs as surplus-labour. He thus secures a surplus-profit. As concerns capitals invested in colonies, etc., on the other hand, they may yield higher rates of profit for the simple reason that the rate of profit is higher there due to backward development, and likewise the exploitation of labour, because of the use of slaves, coolies, etc. Why should not these higher rates of profit, realised by capitals invested in certain lines and sent home by them, enter into the equalisation of the general rate of profit and thus tend, *pro tanto*, to raise it, unless it is the monopolies that stand in the way.[1] There is so much less reason for it, since these spheres of investment of capital are subject to the laws of free competition. What Ricardo fancies is mainly this: with the higher prices realised abroad commodities are bought there in return and sent home. These commodities are thus sold on the home market, which fact can at best be but a temporary extra disadvantage of these favoured spheres of production over others. This illusion falls away as soon as it is divested of its money-form. The favoured country recovers more labour in exchange for less labour, although this difference, this excess is pocketed, as in any exchange between labour and capital, by a certain class. Since the rate of profit is higher, therefore, because it is generally higher in a colonial country, it may, provided natural conditions are favourable, go hand in hand with low commodity-prices. A levelling takes place but not a levelling to the old level, as Ricardo feels.

This same foreign trade develops the capitalist mode of production in the home country, which implies the decrease of variable capital in relation to constant, and, on the other hand, causes over-production in respect to foreign markets, so that in the long run it again has an opposite effect.

We have thus seen in a general way that the same influences which produce a tendency in the general rate of profit to fall, also call forth counter-effects, which hamper, retard, and partly paralyse this fall. The latter do not do away with the law, but impair its effect. Otherwise, it would not be the fall of the general rate of profit, but rather its relative slowness, that would be incomprehensible. Thus, the law acts only as a tendency. And it is only under certain circumstances and only after long periods that its effects become strikingly pronounced.

Before we go on, in order to avoid misunderstandings, we should recall two, repeatedly treated, points.

First: The same process which brings about a cheapening of commodities in the course of the development of the capitalist mode of production, causes a change in the organic composition of the social capital invested in the production of commodities, and consequently lowers the rate of profit. We must be careful, therefore, not to identify the reduction in the relative cost of an individual commodity, including that portion of it which represents wear and tear of machinery, with the rise in the value of the constant in relation to variable capital, although, conversely, every reduction in the relative cost of the constant capital assuming the volume of its material elements remains the same, or increases, tends to raise the rate of profit, *i.e.*, to reduce *pro tanto* the value of the constant capital in relation to the shrinking proportions of the employed variable capital.

Second: The fact that the newly added living labour contained in the individual commodities, which taken together make up the product of capital, decreases in relation to the materials they contain and the means of labour consumed by them; the fact, therefore, that an ever-decreasing quantity of additional living labour is materialised in them, because their production requires less labour with the development of the social productiveness—this fact does not affect the ratio, in which the living labour contained in the commodities breaks up into paid and unpaid labour. Quite the contrary. Although the total quantity of additional living labour contained in the commodities decreases, the unpaid portion increases in relation to the paid portion, either by an absolute or a relative shrinking of the paid portion; for the same mode of production which reduces the total quantity of additional living labour in a commodity is accompanied by a rise in the absolute and relative surplus-value. The tendency of the rate of profit to fall is bound up with a tendency of the rate of surplus-value to rise, hence with a tendency for the rate of labour exploitation to rise. Nothing is more absurd, for this reason, than to explain the fall in the rate of profit by a rise in the rate of wages, although this may be the case by way of an exception. Statistics is not able to make actual analyses of the rates of wages in different epochs and countries, until the conditions which shape the rate of profit are thoroughly understood. The rate of profit does not fall because labour becomes less productive, but because it becomes more productive. Both the rise in the rate of surplus-value and the fall in the rate of profit are but specific forms through which growing productivity of labour is expressed under capitalism.

Section VI. *The Increase of Stock Capital*

The foregoing five points may still be supplemented by the following, which, however, cannot be more fully treated for the present. With the progress of capitalist production, which goes hand in hand with accelerated accumulation, a portion of capital is calculated and applied only as interest-bearing capital. Not in the sense in which every capitalist who lends out capital is satisfied with interest, while the industrial capitalist pockets the investor's profit. This has no bearing on the level of the general rate of profit, because for the latter profit = interest + profit of all kinds + ground rent, the division into these particular categories being immaterial to it. But in the sense that these capitals, although invested in large productive enterprises, yield only large or small amounts of interest, so-called dividends, after all costs have been deducted. In railways, for instance. These do not, therefore, go into levelling the general rate of profit, because they yield a lower than average rate of profit. If they did enter into it, the general rate of profit would fall much lower. Theoretically, they may be included in the calculation, and the result would then be a lower rate of profit than the seemingly existing rate, which is decisive for the capitalists; it would be lower, because the constant capital particularly in these enterprises is largest in its relation to the variable capital.

Note

1. Adam Smith was right in this respect, contrary to Ricardo, who said: 'They contend that the equality of profits will be brought about by the general rise of profits; and I am of the opinion that the profits of the favoured trade will speedily submit to the general level.' (*Works*:, ed. by MacCulloch, p. 73.)

15

Exposition of the Internal Contradictions of the Law

Section I. *General*

We have seen in the first part of this book that the rate of profit expresses the rate of surplus-value always lower than it actually is. We have just seen that even a rising rate of surplus-value has a tendency to express itself in a falling rate of profit. The rate of profit would equal the rate of surplus-value only if $c = 0$, *i.e.*, if the total capital were paid out in wages. A falling rate of profit does not express a falling rate of surplus-value, unless the proportion of the value of the constant capital to the quantity of labour-power which sets it in motion remains unchanged or the amount of labour-power increases in relation to the value of the constant capital.

On the plea of analysing the rate of profit, Ricardo actually analyses the rate of surplus-value alone, and this only on the assumption that the working-day is intensively and extensively a constant magnitude.

A fall in the rate of profit and accelerated accumulation are different expressions of the same process only in so far as both reflect the development of productiveness. Accumulation, in turn, hastens the fall of the rate of profit, inasmuch as it implies concentration of labour on a large scale, and thus a higher composition of capital. On the other hand, a fall in the rate of profit again hastens the concentration of capital and its centralisation through expropriation of minor capitalists, the few direct producers who still have anything left to be expropriated. This accelerates accumulation with regard to mass, although the rate of accumulation falls with the rate of profit.

On the other hand, the rate of self-expansion of the total capital, or the rate of profit, being the goad of capitalist production (just as self-expansion of capital is its only purpose), its fall checks the formation of new independent capitals and thus appears as a threat to the development of the capitalist production process. It breeds over-production, speculation, crises, and surplus-capital alongside surplus-population. Those economists, therefore, who, like Ricardo, regard the capitalist mode of production as absolute, feel at this point that it creates a barrier itself, and for this reason attribute the barrier to Nature (in the theory of rent), not to production. But the main thing about their horror of the falling rate of profit is the feeling that capitalist production meets in the development of its productive forces a barrier which has nothing to do with the production of wealth as such; and this peculiar barrier testifies to the limitations and to the merely historical, transitory character of the capitalist mode of production; testifies that for the production of wealth, it is not an absolute mode, moreover, that at a certain stage it rather conflicts with its further development.

True, Ricardo and his school considered only industrial profit, which includes interest. But the rate of ground-rent likewise has a tendency to fall, although its absolute mass increases, and may also increase proportionately more than industrial profit. (E. West, [*Essay on the Application of Capital to Land*, London, 1815.—*Ed*] who developed the law of ground-rent *before* Ricardo.) If we consider the total social capital C, and use p_1 for the industrial profit that remains after deducting interest and ground-rent, i for interest, and r for ground-rent, then $s/C = p/C = p_1 + i + r/C = p_1/C + i/C + r/C$. We have seen that while s, the total amount of surplus-value, is continually increasing in the course of capitalist development, s/C is just as steadily declining, because C grows still more rapidly than s. Therefore it is by no means a contradiction for p_1, i, and r to be steadily increasing, each individually, while $s/C = p/C$, as well as p_1/C, i/C, and r/C, should each by itself be steadily shrinking, or that p_1 should increase in relation to i, or r in relation to p_1 or to p_1 and i. With a rising total surplus-value or profit $s = p$, and a simultaneously falling rate of profit $s/C = p/C$, the proportions of the parts p_1, i, and r, which make up $s = p$, may change at will within the limits set by the total amount of s without thereby affecting the magnitude of s or s/C.

The mutual variation of p_1, i, and r is merely a varying distribution of s among different classes. Consequently, p_1/C, i/C, or r/C, the rate of individual industrial profit, the rate of interest, and the ratio of ground-rent to the total capital, may rise in relation to one another, while s/C, the general rate of profit, falls. The only condition is that the sum of all three = s/C. If the rate of profit falls from 50% to 25%, because the composition of a certain capital with, say, a rate of surplus-value = 100% has changed from $50_c + 50_v$ to $75_c + 25_v$, then a capital of 1,000 will yield a profit of 500 in the first case, and in the second a Capital of 4,000 will yield a profit of 1,000. We see that s or p have doubled, while p' has fallen by one-half. And if that 50% was formerly divided into 20 profit, 10 interest, and 20 rent, then $p_1/C = 20\%$, $i/C = 10\%$, and $r/C = 20\%$. If the proportions had remained the same after the change from 50% to 25%, then $p_1/C = 10\%$, $i/C = 5\%$, and $r/C = 10\%$. If, however, p_1/C should fall to 8% and i/C to 4%, then r/C would rise to 13%. The relative magnitude of r would have risen as against p_1 and i, while p would have remained the same. Under both assumptions, the sum of p_1, i, and r would have increased, because produced by a capital four times as large. Furthermore, Ricardo's assumption that originally industrial profit (plus interest) contains the entire surplus-value is historically and logically false. It is rather the progress of capitalist production which 1) gives the whole profit directly to the industrial and commercial capitalists for further distribution, and 2) reduces rent to the excess over the profit. On this capitalist basis, again, the rent grows, being a portion of profit (*i.e.*, of the surplus-value viewed as the product of the total capital), but not that specific portion of the product, which the capitalist pockets.

Given the necessary means of production, *i.e.*, a sufficient accumulation of capital, the creation of surplus-value is only limited by the labouring population if the rate of surplus-value, *i.e.*, the intensity of exploitation, is given; and no other limit but the intensity of exploitation if the labouring population is given. And the capitalist process of production consists essentially of the production of surplus-value, represented in the surplus-product or that aliquot portion of the produced commodities materialising unpaid labour. It must never be forgotten that the production of this surplus-value—and the reconversion of a portion of it into capital, or the accumulation, forms an integral part of this production of surplus-value—is the immediate purpose and compelling motive of capitalist production. It will never do, therefore, to represent capitalist production as something which it is not, namely as production whose immediate purpose is enjoyment or the manufacture of the means of enjoyment for the capitalist. This would be overlooking its specific character, which is revealed in all its inner essence.

The creation of this surplus-value makes up the direct process of production, which, as we have said, has no other limits but those mentioned above. As soon as all the surplus-labour it was possible to squeeze out has been embodied in commodities, surplus-value has been produced. But this production of surplus-value completes but the first act of the capitalist process of production—the direct production process. Capital has absorbed so and so much unpaid labour. With the development of the process, which expresses itself in a drop in the rate of profit, the mass of surplus-value thus produced swells to immense dimensions. Now comes the second act of the process. The entire mass of commodities, *i.e.*, the total product, including the portion which replaces the constant and variable capital, and that representing surplus-value, must be sold. If this is not done, or done only in part, or only at prices below the prices of production, the labourer has been indeed exploited, but his exploitation is not realised as such for the capitalist, and this can be bound up with a total or partial failure to realise the surplus-value pressed out of him, indeed even with the partial or total loss of the capital. The conditions of direct exploitation, and those of realising it, are not identical. They diverge not only in place and time, but also logically. The first are only limited by the productive power of society, the latter by the proportional relation of the various branches of production and the consumer power of society. But this last-named is not determined either by the absolute productive power, or by the absolute consumer power, but by the consumer power based on antagonistic conditions of distribution, which reduce the consumption of the bulk of society to a minimum varying within more or less narrow limits. It is furthermore restricted by the tendency to accumulate, the drive to expand capital and produce surplus-value on an extended scale. This is law for capitalist production, imposed by incessant revolutions in the methods of production themselves, by the depreciation of existing capital always bound up with them, by the general competitive struggle and the need to improve production and expand its scale merely as a means of self-preservation and under penalty of ruin. The market must, therefore, be continually extended, so that its interrelations and the conditions regulating them assume more and more the form of a natural law working independently of the producer, and become ever more uncontrollable. This internal contradiction seeks to resolve itself through expansion of the outlying field of production. But the more productiveness develops, the more it finds itself at variance with the narrow basis on which the conditions of consumption rest. It is no contradiction at all on this self-contradictory basis that there should be an excess of capital simultaneously with a growing surplus of population. For while a combination of these two would, indeed, increase the mass of produced surplus-value, it would at the same time intensify the contradiction between the conditions under which this surplus-value is produced and those under which it is realised.

If a certain rate of profit is given, the mass of profit will always depend on the magnitude of the advanced capital. The accumulation, however, is then determined by that portion of this mass which is reconverted into capital. As for this portion, being equal to the profit minus the revenue consumed by the capitalists, it will depend not merely on the value of this mass, but also on the cheapness of the commodities which the capitalist can buy with it, commodities which pass partly into his consumption, his revenue, and partly into his constant capital. (Wages are here assumed to be given.)

The mass of capital set in motion by the labourer, whose value he preserves by his labour and reproduces in his product, is quite different from the value which he adds to it. If the mass of the capital = 1,000 and the added labour = 100, the reproduced capital = 1,100. If the mass = 100 and the added labour = 20, the reproduced capital = 120. In the first case, the rate of profit = 10%, in the second = 20%. And yet more can be accumulated out of 100 than out of 20. And thus the river of capital rolls on (aside from its depreciation through increase of the productiveness), or its accumulation does, not in proportion to the rate of profit, but in proportion to the impetus it already possesses. So far as it is based on a high rate of surplus-value, a high rate of profit is possible when the working-day is very long, although labour is not highly productive. It is possible, because the wants of the labourers are very small, hence average wages very low, although the labour itself is unproductive. The low wages will correspond to the labourers' lack of energy. Capital then accumulates slowly, in spite of the high rate of profit. Population is stagnant and the working-time which the product costs, is great, while the wages paid to the labourer etare small.

The rate of profit does not sink because the labourer is exploited any less, but because generally less labour is employed in proportion to the employed capital.

If, as shown, a falling rate of profit is bound up with an increase in the mass of profit, a larger portion of the annual product of labour is appropriated by the capitalist under the category of capital (as a replacement for consumed capital) and a relatively smaller portion under the category of profit. Hence the fantastic idea of priest Chalmers, [Th. Chalmers,

On Political Economy in Connexion with the Moral State and Moral Prospects of Society, Second edition, Glasgow, 1832, p. *88.—Ed*] that the less of the annual product is expended by capitalists as capital, the greater the profits they pocket. In which case, the state church comes to their assistance, to care for the consumption of the greater part of the surplus-product, rather than having it used as capital. The preacher confounds cause with effect. Furthermore, the mass of profit increases in spite of its slower rate with the growth of the invested capital. However, this requires a simultaneous concentration of capital, since the conditions of production then demand employment of capital on a larger scale. It also requires its centralisation, *i.e.*, the swallowing up of the small capitalists by the big and their deprivation of capital. It is again but an instance of separating—raised to the second power—the conditions of production from the producers to whose number these small capitalists still belong, since their own labour continues to play a role in their case. The labour of a capitalist stands altogether in inverse proportion to the size of his capital, *i.e.*, to the degree in which he is a capitalist. It is this same severance of the conditions of production, on the one hand, from the producers, on the other, that forms the conception of capital. It begins with primitive accumulation (Buch I, Kap. XXIV [English edition: Part *VIII.—Ed.*]), appears as a permanent process in the accumulation and concentration of capital, and expresses itself finally as centralisation of existing capitals in a few hands and a deprivation of many of their capital (to which expropriation is now changed). This process would soon bring about the collapse of capitalist production if it were not for counteracting tendencies, which have a continuous decentralising effect alongside the centripetal one.

Section II. *Conflict between Expansion of Production and Production of Surplus-Value*

The development of the social productiveness of labour is manifested in two ways: first, in the magnitude of the already produced productive forces, the value and mass of the conditions of production under which new production is carried on, and in the absolute magnitude of the already accumulated productive capital; secondly, in the relative smallness of the portion of total capital laid out in wages, *i.e.*, in the relatively small quantity of living labour required for the reproduction and self-expansion of a given capital, for mass production. This also implies concentration of capital.

In relation to employed labour-power the development of the productivity again reveals itself in two ways: First, in the increase of surplus-labour, *i.e.*, the reduction of the necessary labour-time required for the reproduction of labour-power. Secondly, in the decrease of the quantity of labour-power (the number of labourers) generally employed to set in motion a given capital.

The two movements not only go hand in hand, but mutually influence one another and are phenomena in which the same law expresses itself. Yet, they affect the rate of profit in opposite ways. The total mass of profit is equal to the total mass of surplus-value, the rate of profit = s/C = surplus-value/advanced total capital. The surplus-value, however, as a total, is determined first by its rate, and second by the mass of labour simultaneously employed at this rate, or, what amounts to the same, by the magnitude of the variable capital. One of these factors, the rate of surplus-value, rises, and the other, the number of labourers, falls (relatively or absolutely). Inasmuch as the development of the productive forces reduces the paid portion of employed labour, it raises the surplus-value, because it raises its rate; but inasmuch as it reduces the total mass of labour employed by a given capital, it reduces the factor of the number by which the rate of surplus-value is multiplied to obtain its mass. Two labourers, each working 12 hours daily, cannot produce the same mass of surplus-value as 24 who work only 2 hours, even if they could live on air and hence did not have to work for themselves at all. In this respect, then, the compensation of the reduced number of labourers by intensifying the degree of exploitation has certain insurmountable limits. It may, for this reason, well check the fall in the rate of profit, but cannot prevent it altogether.

With the development of the capitalist mode of production, therefore, the rate of profit falls, while its mass increases with the growing mass of the capital employed. Given the rate, the absolute increase in the mass of capital depends on its existing magnitude. But, on the other hand, if this magnitude is given, the proportion of its growth, *i.e.*, the rate of its increment, depends on the rate of profit. The increase in the productiveness (which, moreover, we repeat, always goes hand in hand with a depreciation of the available capital) can directly only increase the value of the existing capital if by raising the rate of profit it increases that portion of the value of the annual product which is reconverted into capital. As concerns the productivity of labour, this can only occur (since this productivity has nothing direct to do with the *value* of the existing capital) by raising the relative surplus-value, or reducing the value of the constant capital, so that the commodities which enter either the reproduction of labour-power, or the elements of constant capital, are cheapened. Both imply a depreciation of the existing capital, and both go hand in hand with a reduction of the variable capital in relation to the constant. Both cause a fall in the rate of profit, and both slow it down. Furthermore, inasmuch as an increased rate of profit causes a greater demand for labour, it tends to increase the working population and thus the material, whose exploitation makes real capital out of capital.

Indirectly, however, the development of the productivity of labour contributes to the increase of the value of the existing capital by increasing the mass and variety of use-values in which the same exchange-value is represented and which form the material substance, *i.e.*, the material elements of capital, the material objects making up the constant capital directly, and the variable capital at least indirectly. More products which may be converted into capital, whatever their exchange-value, are created with the same capital and the same labour. These products may serve to absorb additional labour, hence also additional surplus-labour, and therefore create additional capital. The amount of labour which a capital can command does not depend on its value, but on the mass of raw and auxiliary materials, machinery and elements of fixed capital and necessities of life, all of which it comprises, whatever their value may be. As the mass of the labour employed, and thus of surplus-labour increases, there is also a growth in the value of the reproduced capital and in the surplus-value newly added to it.

These two elements embraced by the process of accumulation, however, are not to be regarded merely as existing side by side in repose, as Ricardo does. They contain a contradiction which manifests itself in contradictory tendencies and phenomena. These antagonistic agencies counteract each other simultaneously.

Alongside the stimulants of an actual increase of the labouring population, which spring from the increase of the portion of the total social product serving as capital, there are agencies which create a merely relative over-population.

Alongside the fall in the rate of profit mass of capitals grows, and hand in hand with this, there occurs a depreciation of existing capitals which checks the fall and gives an accelerating motion to the accumulation of capital-values.

Alongside the development of productivity, there develops a higher composition of capital, *i.e.*, the relative decrease of the ratio of variable to constant capital.

These different influences may at one time operate predominantly side by side in space, and at another succeed each other in time. From time to time the conflict of antagonistic agencies finds vent in crises. The crises are always but momentary and forcible solutions of the existing contradictions. They are violent eruptions which for a time, restore the disturbed equilibrium.

The contradiction, to put it in a very general way, consists in that the capitalist mode of production involves a tendency towards absolute development of the productive forces, regardless of the value and surplus-value it contains, and regardless of the social conditions under which capitalist production takes place; while, on the other hand, its aim is to preserve the value of the existing capital and promote its self-expansion to the highest limit (*i.e.*, to promote an ever more rapid growth of this value). The specific feature about it is that it uses the existing value of capital as a means of increasing this value to the utmost. The methods by which it accomplishes this include the fall of the rate of profit, depreciation of existing capital, and development of the productive forces of labour at the expense of already created productive forces.

The periodical depreciation of existing capital—one of the means immanent in capitalist production to check the fall of the rate of profit and hasten accumulation of capital-value through formation of new capital—disturbs the given conditions, within which the process of circulation and reproduction of capital takes place, and is therefore accompanied by sudden stoppages and crises in the production process.

The decrease of variable in relation to constant capital, which goes hand in hand with the development of the productive forces, stimulates the growth of the labouring population, while continually creating an artificial over-population. The accumulation of capital in terms of value is slowed down by the falling rate of profit, to hasten still more the accumulation of use-values, while this, in its turn, adds new momentum to accumulation in terms of value.

Capitalist production seeks continually to overcome these immanent barriers, but overcomes them only by means which again place these barriers in its way and on a more formidable scale.

The *real barrier* of capitalist production is *capital itself.* It is that capital and its self-expansion appear as the starting and the closing point, the motive and the purpose of production; that production is only production for *capital* and not vice versa, the means of production are not mere means for a constant expansion of the living process of the *society* of producers. The limits within which the preservation and self-expansion of the value of capital resting on the expropriation and pauperisation of the great mass of producers can alone move—these limits come continually into conflict with the methods of production employed by capital for its purposes, which drive towards unlimited extension of production, towards production as an end in itself, towards unconditional development of the social productivity of labour. The means—unconditional development of the productive forces of society—comes continually into conflict with the limited purpose, the self-expansion of the existing capital. The capitalist mode of production is, for this reason, a historical means of developing the material forces of production and creating an appropriate world-market and is, at the same time, a continual conflict between this, its historical task and its own corresponding relations of social production.

Section III. *Excess Capital and Excess Population*

A drop in the rate of profit is attended by a rise in the minimum capital required by an individual capitalist for the productive employment of labour; required both for its exploitation generally, and for making the consumed labour-time suffice as the labour-time necessary for the production of the commodities, so that it does not exceed the average social labour-time required for the production of the commodities. Concentration increases simultaneously, because beyond certain limits, a large capital with a small rate of profit accumulates faster than a small capital with a large rate of profit. At a certain high point, this increasing concentration in its turn causes a new fall in the rate of profit. The mass of small dispersed capitals is thereby driven along the adventurous road of speculation, credit frauds, stock swindles, and crises. The so-called plethora of capital always applies essentially to a plethora of the capital for which the fall in the rate of profit is not compensated through the mass of profit—this is always true of newly developing fresh offshoots of capital—or to a plethora which places capitals incapable of action on their own at the disposal of the managers of large enterprises in the form of credit. This plethora of capital arises from the same causes as those which call forth relative over-population, and is, therefore, a phenomenon supplementing the latter, although they stand at opposite poles—unemployed capital at one pole, and unemployed worker population at the other.

Over-production of capital, not of individual commodities—although over-production of capital always includes over-production of commodities—is therefore simply over-accumulation of capital. To appreciate what this over-accumulation is (its closer analysis follows later), one need only assume it to be absolute. When would over-production of capital be absolute? Overproduction which would affect not just one or another, or a few important spheres of production, but would be absolute in its full scope, hence would extend to all fields of production?

There would be absolute over-production of capital as soon as additional capital for purposes of capitalist production = 0. The purpose of capitalist production, however, is self-expansion of capital, *i.e.*, appropriation of surplus-labour, production of surplus-value, of profit. As soon as capital would, therefore, have grown in such a ratio to the labouring population that neither the absolute working-time supplied by this population, nor the relative surplus working-time, could be expanded any further (this last would not be feasible at any rate in the case when the demand for labour were so strong that there were a tendency for wages to rise); at a point, therefore, when the increased capital produced just as much, or even less, surplus-value than it did before its increase, there would be absolute over-production of capital; *i.e.*, the increased capital C + ΔC would produce no more, or even less, profit than capital C before its expansion by ΔC. In both cases there would be a steep and sudden fall in the general rate of profit, but this time due to a change in the composition of capital not caused by the development of the productive forces, but rather by a rise in the money-value of the variable capital (because of increased wages) and the corresponding reduction in the proportion of surplus-labour to necessary labour.

In reality, it would appear that a portion of the capital would lie completely or partially idle (because it would have to crowd out some of the active capital before it could expand its own value), and the other portion would produce values at a lower rate of profit, owing to the pressure of unemployed or but partly employed capital. It would be immaterial in this respect if a part of the additional capital were to take the place of the old capital, and the latter were to take its position in the additional capital. We should still always have the old sum of capital on one side, and the sum of additional capital on the other. The fall in the rate of profit would then be accompanied by an absolute decrease in the mass of profit, since the mass of employed labour-power could not be increased and the rate of surplus-value raised under the conditions we had assumed, so that the mass of surplus-value could not be increased either. And the reduced mass of profit would have to be calculated on an increased total capital. But even if it is assumed that the employed capital continues to self-expand at the old rate of profit, and the mass of profit hence remains the same, this mass would still he calculated on an increased total capital, this likewise implying a fall in the rate of profit. If a total capital of 1,000 yielded a profit of 100, and after being increased to 1,500 still yielded 100, then, in the second case, 1,000 would yield only 66⅔. Self-expansion of the old capital, in the absolute sense, would have been reduced. The capital = 1,000 would yield no more under the new circumstances than formerly a capital = 666⅔.

It is evident, however, that this actual depreciation of the old capital could not occur without a struggle, and that the additional capital ΔC could not assume the functions of capital without a struggle. The rate of profit would not fall under the effect of competition due to over-production of capital. It would rather be the reverse; it would be the competitive struggle which would begin because the fallen rate of profit and over-production of capital originate from the same conditions. The part of ΔC in the hands of old functioning capitalists would be allowed to remain more or less idle to prevent a depreciation of their own original capital and not to narrow its place in the field of production. Or they would employ it, even at a momentary loss, to shift the need of keeping additional capital idle on newcomers and on their competitors in general.

That portion of ΔC which is in new hands would seek to assume a place for itself at the expense of the old capital, and would accomplish this in part by forcing a portion of the old capital to lie idle. It would compel the old capital to give up its old place and withdraw to join completely or partially unemployed additional capital.

A portion of the old capital has to lie unused under all circumstances; it has to give up its characteristic quality as capital, so far as acting as such and producing value is concerned. The competitive struggle would decide what part of it would be particularly affected. So long as things go well, competition effects an operating fraternity of the capitalist class, as we have seen in the case of the equalisation of the general rate of profit, so that each shares in the common loot in proportion to the size of his respective investment. But as soon as it no longer is a question of sharing profits, but of sharing losses, everyone tries to reduce his own share to a minimum and to shove it off upon another. The class, as such, must inevitably lose. How much the individual capitalist must bear of the loss, *i.e.*, to what extent he must share in it at all, is decided by strength and cunning, and competition then becomes a fight among hostile brothers. The antagonism between each individual capitalist's interests and those of the capitalist class as a whole, then comes to the surface, just as previously, the identity of these interests operated in practice through competition.

How is this conflict settled and the conditions restored which correspond to the 'sound' operation of capitalist production? The mode of settlement is already indicated in the very emergence of the conflict whose settlement is under discussion. It implies the withdrawal and even the partial destruction of capital amounting to the full value of additional capital ΔC, or at least a part of it. Although, as the description of this conflict shows, the loss is by no means equally distributed among individual capitals, its distribution being rather decided through a competitive struggle in which the loss is distributed in very different proportions and forms, depending on special advantages or previously captured positions, so that one capital is left unused, another is destroyed, and a third suffers but a relative loss, or is just temporarily depreciated, etc.

But the equilibrium would be restored under all circumstances through the withdrawal or even the destruction of more or less capital. This would extend partly to the material substance of capital, *i.e.*, a part of the means of production, of fixed and circulating capital, would not operate, not act as capital; some of the operating establishments would then be brought to a standstill. Although, in this respect, time attacks and worsens all means of production (except land), the stoppage would, in reality cause far greater damage to the means of production. However, the main effect, in this case, would be that these means of production would cease to function as such, that their function as means of production would be disturbed for a shorter or longer period.

The main damage, and that of the most acute nature, would occur in respect to capital, and in so far as the latter possesses the characteristic of value it would occur in respect to the *values* of capitals. That portion of the value of a capital which exists only in the form of claims on prospective shares of surplus-value, *i.e.*, profit, in fact in the form of promissory notes on production in various forms, is immediately depreciated by the reduction of the receipts on which it is calculated. A part of the gold and silver lies unused, *i.e.*, does not function as capital. Part of the commodities on the market can complete their process of circulation and reproduction only through an immense contraction of their prices, hence through a depreciation of the capital which they represent. The elements of fixed capital are depreciated to a greater or lesser degree in just the same way. It must be added that definite, presupposed, price relations govern the process of reproduction, so that the latter is halted and thrown into confusion by a general drop in prices. This confusion and stagnation paralyses the function of money as a medium of payment, whose development is geared to the development of capital and is based on those presupposed price relations. The chain of payment obligations due at specific dates is broken in a hundred places. The confusion is augmented by the attendant collapse of the credit system, which develops simultaneously with capital, and leads to violent and acute crises, to sudden and forcible depreciations, to the actual stagnation and disruption of the process of reproduction, and thus to a real falling off in reproduction.

But there would have been still other agencies at work at the same time. The stagnation of production would have laid off a part of the working-class and would thereby have placed the employed part in a situation, where it would have to submit to a reduction of wages even below the average. This has the very same effect on capital as an increase of the relative or absolute surplus-value at average wages would have had. Prosperity would have led to more marriages among labourers and reduced the decimation of offspring. While implying a real increase in population, this does not signify an increase in the actual working population. But it affects the relations of the labourer to capital in the same way as an increase of the number of actually working labourers would have affected them. On the other hand, the fall in prices and the competitive struggle would have driven every capitalist to lower the individual value of his total product below its general value by means of new machines, new and improved working methods, new combinations, *i.e.*, to increase the productivity of a given quantity of labour, to lower the proportion of variable to constant capital, and thereby to release some labourers; in short, to create an artificial over-population. Ultimately, the depreciation of the elements of constant capital would itself tend to raise the rate of profit. The mass of employed constant capital would have increased in relation to variable, but its value could have fallen. The ensuing stagnation of production would have prepared—within capitalistic limits—a subsequent expansion of production.

And thus, the cycle would run its course anew. Part of the capital, depreciated by its functional stagnation, would recover its old value. For the rest, the same vicious circle would be described once more under expanded conditions of production, with an expanded market and increased productive forces.

However, even under the extreme conditions assumed by us this absolute over-production of capital is not absolute over-production, not absolute over-production of means of production. It is over-production of means of production only in so far as the latter serve *as capital,* and consequently include a self-expansion of value, must produce an additional value in proportion to the increased mass.

Yet it would still be over-production, because capital would be unable to exploit labour to the degree required by a 'sound', 'normal' development of the process of capitalist production, to a degree which would at least increase the mass of profit along with the growing mass of the employed capital; to a degree which would, therefore, prevent the rate of profit from falling as much as the capital grows, or even more rapidly.

Over-production of capital is never anything more than over-production of means of production—of means of labour and necessities of life—which may serve as capital, *i.e.*, may serve to exploit labour at a given degree of exploitation; a fall in the intensity of exploitation below a certain point, however, calls forth disturbances, and stoppages in the capitalist production process, crises, and destruction of capital. It is no contradiction that this over-production of capital is accompanied by more or less considerable relative over-population. The circumstances which increased the productiveness of labour, augmented the mass of produced commodities, expanded markets, accelerated accumulation of capital both in terms of its mass and its value, and lowered the rate of profit—these same circumstances have also created, and continuously create, a relative overpopulation, an over-population of labourers not employed by the surplus-capital owing to the low degree of exploitation at which alone they could be employed, or at least owing to the low rate of profit which they would yield at the given degree of exploitation.

If capital is sent abroad, this is not done because it absolutely could not be applied at home, but because it can be employed at a higher rate of profit in a foreign country. But such capital is absolute excess capital for the employed labouring population and for the home country in general. It exists as such alongside the relative over-population, and this is an illustration of how both of them exist side by side, and mutually influence one another.

On the other hand, a fall in the rate of profit connected with accumulation necessarily calls forth a competitive struggle. Compensation of a fall in the rate of profit by a rise in the mass of profit applies only to the total social capital and to the big, firmly placed capitalists. The new additional capital operating independently does not enjoy any such compensating conditions. It must still win them, and so it is that a fall in the rate of profit calls forth a competitive struggle among capitalists, not vice versa. To be sure, the competitive struggle is accompanied by a temporary rise in wages and a resultant further temporary fall of the rate of profit. The same occurs when there is an over-production of commodities, when markets are overstocked. Since the aim of capital is not to minister to certain wants, but to produce profit, and since it accomplishes this purpose by methods which adapt the mass of production to the scale of production, not vice versa, a rift must continually ensue between the limited dimensions of consumption under capitalism and a production which forever tends to exceed this immanent barrier. Furthermore, capital consists of commodities, and therefore over-production of capital implies over-production of commodities. Hence the peculiar phenomenon of economists who deny over-production of commodities, admitting over-production of capital. To say that there is no general over-production, but rather a disproportion within the various branches of production, is no more than to say that under capitalist production, the proportionality of the individual branches of production springs as a continual process from disproportionality, because the cohesion of the aggregate production imposes itself as a blind law upon the agents of production, and not as a law which, being understood and hence controlled by their common mind, brings the productive process under their joint control. It amounts furthermore to demanding that countries in which capitalist production is not developed, should consume and produce at a rate which suits the countries with capitalist production. If it is said that over-production is only relative, this is quite correct; but the entire capitalist mode of production is only a relative one, whose barriers are not absolute. They are absolute only for this mode, *i.e.*, on its basis. How could there otherwise be a shortage of demand for the very commodities which the mass of the people lack, and how would it be possible for this demand to be sought abroad, in foreign markets, to pay the labourers at home the average amount of necessities of life? This is possible only because in this specific capitalist interrelation, the surplus-product assumes a form in which its owner cannot offer it for consumption, unless it first reconverts itself into capital for him. If it is finally said that the capitalists have only to exchange and consume their commodities among themselves, then the entire nature of the capitalist mode of production is lost sight of; and also forgotten is the fact that it is a matter of expanding the value of the capital, not consuming it. In short, all these objections to the obvious phenomena of over-production (phenomena which pay no heed to these objections) amount to the contention that the barriers of *capitalist* production are not barriers of *production generally*, and therefore not barriers of this specific, capitalist mode of production. The contradiction of the capitalist mode of production, however, lies precisely in its tendency towards an absolute development of the productive forces, which continually come into conflict with the specific *conditions* of production in which capital moves, and alone can move.

There are not too many necessities of life produced, in proportion to the existing population. Quite the reverse. Too little is produced to decently and humanely satisfy the wants of the great mass.

There are not too many means of production produced to employ the able-bodied portion of the population. Quite the reverse. In the first place, too large a portion of the produced population is not really capable of working, and is through force of circumstances made dependent on exploiting the labour of others, or on labour which can pass under this name only under a miserable mode of production. In the second place, not enough means of production are produced to permit the employment of the entire able-bodied population under the most productive conditions, so that their absolute working period could be shortened by the mass and effectiveness of the constant capital employed during working-hours.

On the other hand, too many means of labour and necessities of life are produced at times to permit of their serving as means for the exploitation of labourers at a certain rate of profit. Too many commodities are produced to permit of a realisation and conversion into new capital of the value and surplus-value contained in them under the conditions of distribution and consumption peculiar to capitalist production, *i.e.*, too many to permit of the consummation of this process without constantly recurring explosions.

Not too much wealth is produced. But at times too much wealth is produced in its capitalistic, self-contradictory forms.

The limitations of the capitalist mode of production come to the surface:

1. In that the development of the productivity of labour creates out of the falling rate of profit a law which at a certain point comes into antagonistic conflict with this development and must be overcome constantly through crises.
2. In that the expansion or contraction of production are determined by the appropriation of unpaid labour and the proportion of this unpaid labour to materialised labour in general, or, to speak the language of the capitalists, by profit and the proportion of this profit to the employed capital, thus by a definite rate of profit, rather than the relation of production to social requirements, *i.e.*, to the requirements of socially developed human beings. It is for this reason that the capitalist mode of production meets with barriers at a certain expanded stage of production which, if viewed from the other premise, would reversely have been altogether inadequate. It comes to a standstill at a point fixed by the production and realisation of profit, and not the satisfaction of requirements.

If the rate of profit falls, there follows, on the one hand, an exertion of capital in order that the individual capitalists, through improved methods, etc., may depress the value of their individual commodity below the social average value and thereby realise an extra profit at the prevailing market-price. On the other hand, there appears swindling and a general promotion of swindling by recourse to frenzied ventures with new methods of production, new investments of capital, new adventures, all for the sake of securing a shred of extra profit which is independent of the general average and rises above it.

The rate of profit, *i.e.*, the relative increment of capital, is above all important to all new offshoots of capital seeking to find an independent place for themselves. And as soon as formation of capital were to fall into the hands of a few established big capitals, for which the mass of profit compensates for the falling rate of profit, the vital flame of production would be altogether extinguished. It would die out. The rate of profit is the motive power of capitalist production. Things are produced only so long as they can be produced with a profit. Hence the concern of the English economists over the decline of the rate of profit. The fact that the bare possibility of this happening should worry Ricardo, shows his profound understanding of the conditions of capitalist production. It is that which is held against him, it is his unconcern about 'human beings,' and his having an eye solely for the development of the productive forces, whatever the cost in human beings and capital-*values*—it is precisely that which is the important thing about him.

Development of the productive forces of social labour is the historical task and justification of capital. This is just the way in which it unconsciously creates the material requirements of a higher mode of production. What worries Ricardo is the fact that the rate of profit, the stimulating principle of capitalist production, the fundamental premise and driving force of accumulation, should be endangered by the development of production itself. And here the quantitative proportion means everything. There is, indeed, something deeper behind it, of which he is only vaguely aware. It comes to the surface here in a purely economic way—*i.e.*, from the bourgeois point of view, within the limitations of capitalist understanding, from the standpoint of capitalist production itself—that it has its barrier, that it is relative, that it is not an absolute, but only a historical mode of production corresponding to a definite limited epoch in the development of the material requirements of production.

Section IV. *Supplementary Remarks*

Since the development of the productivity of labour proceeds very disproportionately in the various lines of industry, and not only disproportionately in degree but frequently also in opposite directions, it follows that the mass of average profit (= surplus-value) must be substantially below the level one would naturally expect after the development of the productiveness in the most advanced branches of industry. The fact that the development of the productivity in different lines of industry proceeds at substantially different rates and frequently even in opposite directions, is not due merely to the anarchy of competition and the peculiarity of the bourgeois mode of production. Productivity of labour is also bound up with natural conditions, which frequently become less productive as productivity grows—inasmuch as the latter depends on social conditions. Hence the opposite movements in these different spheres—progress here, and retrogression there. Consider the mere influence of the seasons, for instance, on which the bulk of raw materials depends for its mass, the exhaustion of forest lands, coal and iron mines, etc.

While the circulating part of constant capital, such as raw materials, etc., continually increases its mass in proportion to the productivity of labour, this is not the case with fixed capital, such as buildings, machinery, and lighting and heating facilities, etc. Although, in absolute terms, a machine becomes dearer with the growth of its bodily mass, it becomes relatively cheaper. If five labourers produce ten times as much of a commodity as before, this does not increase the outlay for fixed capital ten-fold; although the value of this part of constant capital increases with the development of the productiveness, it does not by any means increase in the same proportion. We have frequently pointed out the difference in the ratio of constant to variable capital as expressed in the fall of the rate of profit, and the difference in the same ratio as expressed in relation to the individual commodity and its price with the development of the productivity of labour.

[The value of a commodity is determined by the total labour-time of past and living labour incorporated in it. The increase in labour productivity consists precisely in that the share of living labour is reduced while that of past labour is increased, but in such a way that the total quantity of labour incorporated in that commodity declines; in such a way, therefore, that living labour decreases more than past labour increases. The past labour contained in the value of a commodity—the constant part of capital—consists partly of the wear and tear of fixed, partly of circulating, constant capital entirely consumed by that commodity, such as raw and auxiliary materials. The portion of value deriving from raw and auxiliary materials must decrease with the increased productivity of labour, because with regard to these materials, the productivity expresses itself precisely by reducing their value. On the other hand, it is most characteristic of rising labour productivity that the fixed part of constant capital is strongly augmented, and with it that portion of its value which is transferred by wear and tear to the commodities. For a new method of production to represent a real increase in productivity, it must transfer a smaller additional portion of the value of fixed capital to each unit of the commodity in wear and tear than the portion of value deducted from it through the saving in living labour; in short, it must reduce the value of the commodity. It must obviously do so even if, as it occurs in some cases, an additional value goes into the value of the commodity for more or dearer raw or auxiliary materials over and above the additional portion for wear and tear of the fixed capital. All additions to the value must be more than offset by the reduction in value resulting from the decrease in living labour.

This reduction of the total quantity of labour going into a commodity seems, accordingly, to be the essential criterion of increased productivity of labour, no matter under what social conditions production is carried on. Productivity of labour, indeed, would always be measured by this standard in a society, in which producers regulate their production according to a preconceived plan, or even under simple commodity-production. But how does the matter stand under capitalist production?

Suppose, a certain line of capitalist industry produces a normal unit of its commodity under the following conditions: The wear and tear of fixed capital amounts to ½ shilling per piece; raw and auxiliary materials go into it to the amount of 17½ shillings per piece; wages, 2 shillings; and surplus-value, 2 shillings at a rate of surplus-value of 100%. Total value = 22 shillings. We assume for the sake of simplicity that the capital in this line of production has the average composition of social capital, so that the price of production of the commodity is identical with its value, and the profit of the capitalist with the created surplus-value. Then the cost-price of the commodity = ½ + 17½ + 2 = 20s., the average rate of profit 2/20 = 10%, and the price of production per piece of the commodity, like its value = 22s.

Suppose a machine is invented which reduces by half the living labour required per piece of the commodity, but trebles that portion of its value accounted for by the wear and tear of the fixed capital. In that case, the calculation is: Wear and tear = 1½ s., raw and auxiliary materials, as before, 17½s., wages, 1s., surplus-value 1s., total 21s. The commodity then falls 1s. in value; the new machine has certainly increased the productivity of labour. But the capitalist sees the matter as follows: his cost-price is now 1½s. for wear, 17½s. for raw and auxiliary materials, 1s. for wages, total 20s., as before. Since the rate of profit is not immediately altered by the new machine, he will receive 10% over his cost-price, that is, 2s. The price of production, then, remains unaltered = 22s., but is 1s. above the value. For a society producing under capitalist conditions the commodity has not cheapened. The new machine is *no* improvement for it. The capitalist is, therefore, not interested in introducing it. And since its introduction would make his present, not as yet worn-out, machinery simply worthless, would turn it into scrap-iron, hence would cause a positive loss, he takes good care not to commit this, what is for him a utopian, mistake.

The law of increased productivity of labour is not, therefore, absolutely valid for capital. So far as capital is concerned, productiveness does not increase through a saving in living labour in general, but only through a saving in the *paid* portion of living labour, as compared to labour expended in the past, as we have already indicated in passing in Book I (Kap. XI II, 2, 5. 409/398). [English edition: Ch. XV, 2.—*Ed.*] Here the capitalist mode of production is beset with another contradiction. Its historical mission is unconstrained development in geometrical progression of the productivity of human labour. It goes back on its mission whenever, as here, it checks the development of productivity. It thus demonstrates again that it is becoming senile and that it is more and more outlived.][1]

Under competition, the increasing minimum of capital required with the increase in productivity for the successful operation of an independent industrial establishment, assumes the following aspect: As soon as the new, more expensive equipment has become universally established, smaller capitals are henceforth excluded from this industry. Smaller capitals can carry on independently in the various spheres of industry only in the infancy of mechanical inventions. Very large undertakings, such as railways, on the other hand, which have an unusually high proportion of constant capital, do not yield the average rate of profit, but only a portion of it, only an interest. Otherwise the general rate of profit would have fallen still lower. But this offers direct employment to large concentrations of capital in the form of stocks.

Growth of capital, hence accumulation of capital, does not imply a fall in the rate of profit, unless it is accompanied by the aforementioned changes in the proportion of the organic constituents of capital. Now it so happens that in spite of the constant daily revolutions in the mode of production, now this and now that larger or smaller portion of the total capital continues to accumulate for certain periods on the basis of a given average proportion of those constituents, so that there is no organic change with its growth, and consequently no cause for a fall in the rate of profit. This constant expansion of capital, hence also an expansion of production, on the basis of the old method of production, which goes quietly on while new methods are already being introduced at its side, is another reason, why the rate of profit does not decline as much as the total capital of society grows.

The increase in the absolute number of labourers does not occur in all branches of production, and not uniformly in all, in spite of the relative decrease of variable capital laid out in wages. In agriculture, the decrease of the element of living labour may be absolute.

At any rate, it is but a requirement of the capitalist mode of production that the number of wage-workers should increase absolutely, in spite of its relative decrease. Labour-power becomes redundant for it as soon as it is no longer necessary to employ it for 12 to 15 hours daily. A development of productive forces which would diminish the absolute number of labourers, *i.e.*, enable the entire nation to accomplish its total production in a shorter time span, would cause a revolution, because it would put the bulk of the population out of the running. This is another manifestation of the specific barrier of capitalist production, showing also that capitalist production is by no means an absolute form for the development of the productive forces and for the creation of wealth, but rather that at a certain point, it comes into collision with this development. This collision appears partly in periodical crises, which arise from the circumstance that now this and now that portion of the labouring population becomes redundant under its old mode of employment. The limit of capitalist production is the excess time of the labourers. The absolute spare time gained by society does not concern it. The development of productivity concerns it only in so far as it increases the surplus labour-time of the working-class, not because it decreases the labour-time for material production in general. It moves thus in a contradiction.

We have seen that the growing accumulation of capital implies its growing concentration. Thus grows the power of capital, the alienation of the conditions of social production personified in the capitalist from the real producers. Capital comes more and more to the fore as a social power, whose agent is the capitalist. This social power no longer stands in any possible relation to that which the labour of a single individual can create. It becomes an alienated, independent, social power, which stands opposed to society as an object, and as an object that is the capitalist's source of power. The contradiction between the general social power into which capital develops, on the one hand, and the private power of the individual capitalists over these social conditions of production, on the other, becomes ever more irreconcilable, and yet contains the solution of the problem, because it implies at the same time the transformation of the conditions of production into general, common, social, conditions. This transformation stems from the development of the productive forces under capitalist production, and from the ways and means by which this development takes place.

No capitalist ever voluntarily introduces a new method of production, no matter how much more productive it may be, and how much it may increase the rate of surplus-value, so long as it reduces the rate of profit. Yet every such new method of production cheapens the commodities. Hence, the capitalist sells them originally above their prices of production, or, perhaps, above their value. He pockets the difference between their costs of production and the market-prices of the same commodities produced at higher costs of production. He can do this, because the average labour-time required socially for the production of these latter commodities is higher than the labour-time required for the new methods of production. His method of production stands above the social average. But competition makes it general and subject to the general law. There follows a fall in the rate of profit—perhaps first in this sphere of production, and eventually it achieves a balance with the rest—which is, therefore, wholly independent of the will of the capitalist.

It is still to be added to this point, that this same law also governs those spheres of production, whose product passes neither directly nor indirectly into the consumption of the labourers, or into the conditions under which their necessities are produced; it applies, therefore, also to those spheres of production, in which there is no cheapening of commodities to increase the relative surplus-value or cheapen labour-power. (At any rate, a cheapening of constant capital in all these lines may increase the rate of profit, with the exploitation of labour remaining the same.) As soon as the new production method begins to spread, and thereby to furnish tangible proof that these commodities can actually be produced more cheaply, the capitalists working with the old methods of production must sell their product below its full price of production, because the value of this commodity has fallen, and because the labour-time required by them to produce it is greater than the social average. In one word—and this appears as an effect of competition—these capitalists must also introduce the new method of production, in which the proportion of variable to constant capital has been reduced.

All the circumstances which lead to the use of machinery cheapening the price of a commodity produced by it, come down in the last analysis to a reduction of the quantity of labour absorbed by a single piece of the commodity; and secondly, to a reduction in the wear-and-tear portion of the machinery, whose value goes into a single piece of the commodity. The less rapid the wear of machinery, the more the commodities over which it is distributed, and the more living labour it replaces before its term of reproduction arrives. In both cases, the quantity and value of the fixed constant capital increase in relation to the variable.

> All other things being equal, the power of a nation to save from its profits varies with the rate of profits: is great when they are high, less, when low; but as the rate of profits declines, all other things do not remain equal.... A low rate of profits is ordinarily accompanied by a rapid rate of accumulation, relatively to the numbers of the people, as in England ... a high rate of profit by a slower rate of accumulation, relatively to the numbers of the people. Examples: Poland, Russia, India, etc. (Richard Jones, *An Introductory Lecture on Political Economy*, London, 1833, p. 50 ff.)

Jones emphasises correctly that in spite of the falling rate of profit, the inducements and faculties to accumulate are augmented; first, on account of the growing relative overpopulation; second, because the growing productivity of labour is accompanied by an increase in the mass of use-values represented by the same exchange-value, hence in the material elements of capital; third, because the branches of production become more varied; fourth, due to the development of the credit system, the stock companies, etc., and the resultant case of converting money into capital without becoming an industrial capitalist; fifth, because the wants and the greed for wealth increase; and, sixth, because the mass of investments in fixed capital grows, etc.

Three cardinal facts of capitalist production:

1. Concentration of means of production in few hands, whereby they cease to appear as the property of the immediate labourers and turn into social production

capacities. Even if initially they are the private property of capitalists. These are the trustees of bourgeois society, but they pocket all the proceeds of this trusteeship.

2. Organisation of labour itself into social labour: through co-operation, division of labour, and the uniting of labour with the natural sciences.

   In these two senses, the capitalist mode of production abolishes private property and private labour, even though in contradictory forms.

3. Creation of the world-market.

   The stupendous productivity developing under the capitalist mode of production relative to population, and the increase, if not in the same proportion, of capital-values (not just of their material substance), which grow much more rapidly than the population, contradict the basis, which constantly narrows in relation to the expanding wealth, and for which all this immense productiveness works. They also contradict the conditions under which this swelling capital augments its value. Hence the crises.

Note

1. The foregoing is placed in brackets, because, though a rehash of the notes of the original manuscript, it goes in some points beyond the scope of the material found in the original.—*F.E.*

PART IV

CONVERSION OF COMMODITY-CAPITAL AND MONEY-CAPITAL INTO COMMERCIAL CAPITAL AND MONEY-DEALING CAPITAL (MERCHANT'S CAPITAL)

16

Commercial Capital

Merchant's, or trading, capital breaks up into two forms or sub-divisions, namely, commercial capital and money-dealing capital, which we shall now define more closely, in so far as this is necessary for our analysis of capital in its basic structure. This is all the more necessary, because modern political economy, even in the persons of its best exponents, throws trading capital and industrial capital indiscriminately together and, in effect, wholly overlooks the characteristic peculiarities of the former.

The movements of commodity-capital have been analysed in Book II. To take the total capital of society, one part of it—always made up of different elements and even changing in magnitude—always exists in the form of commodities on the market, to be converted into money. Another part exists on the market in the form of money, to be converted into commodities. It is always in the process of this transition, of this formal metamorphosis. Inasmuch as this function of capital in the process of circulation is at all set apart as a special function of a special capital, as a function established by virtue of the division of labour to a special group of capitalists, commodity-capital becomes commercial capital.

We have explained (Book II, Chapter VI, 'The Costs of Circulation,') to what extent the transport industry, storage and distribution of commodities in a distributable form, may be regarded as production processes continuing within the process of circulation. These episodes incidental to the circulation of commodity-capital are sometimes confused with the distinct functions of merchant's or commercial capital. Sometimes they are, indeed, practically bound up with these distinct, specific functions, although with the development of the social division of labour, the function of merchant's capital evolves in a pure form, *i.e.*, divorced from those real functions, and independent of them. Those functions are therefore irrelevant to our purpose, which is to define the specific difference of this special form of capital. In so far as capital solely employed in the circulation process, special commercial capital, partly combines those functions with its specific ones, it does not appear in its pure form. We obtain its pure form after stripping it of all these incidental functions.

We have seen that the existence of capital as commodity-capital and the metamorphosis it undergoes within the sphere of circulation in the market as commodity-capital—a metamorphosis which resolves itself into buying and selling, converting commodity-capital into money-capital and money-capital into commodity-capital—that this forms a phase in the reproduction process of industrial capital, hence in its process of production as a whole. We have also seen, however, that it is distinguished in its function as a capital of circulation from its function as productive capital. These are two different and separate forms of existence of the same capital. One portion of the total social capital is continually on the market in the form of capital of circulation, passing through this process of transmutation, although for each individual capital its existence as commodity-capital, and its metamorphosis as such, merely represent ever-vanishing and ever renewed nodal points—*i.e.*, stages of transition in the continuity of its production process, and although the elements of commodity-capital in the market vary continuously, for this reason, being constantly withdrawn from the commodity-market and equally periodically returned to it as new products of the process of production.

Commercial capital is nothing but a transmuted form of a part of this capital of circulation constantly to be found in the market, ever in the process of its metamorphosis, and always encompassed by the sphere of circulation. We say a part, because a part of the selling and buying of commodities always takes place directly between industrial capitalists.

We leave this part entirely out of consideration in this analysis, because it contributes nothing to defining the conception, or to understanding the specific nature of merchant's capital, and because it has furthermore been exhaustively treated for our purpose in Book II.

The dealer in commodities, as a capitalist generally, appears on the market primarily as the representative of a certain sum of money, which be advances as a capitalist, *i.e.*, which he wants to turn from x (its original value) into x + Dx (the original sum plus profit). But it is evident to him—not being just a capitalist in general, but rather a special dealer in commodities—that his capital must first enter the market in the form of money-capital, for he does not produce commodities. He merely trades in them, expedites their movement, and to operate with them, he must first buy them, and, therefore, must be in possession of money-capital.

Suppose that a dealer in commodities owns £3,000, which he invests as a trading capital. With these £3,000, he buys, say, 30,000 yards of linen from some linen manufacturer at 2s. per yard. He then sells the 30,000 yards. If the annual average rate of profit = 10% and he makes an annual profit of 10% after deducting all incidental expenses, then by the end of the year he has converted his £3,000 into £3,300. How he makes this profit is a question which we shall discuss later. At present, we intend to consider solely the form of the movements of his capital. With his £3,000 he keeps buying linen and selling it; he constantly repeats this operation of buying in order to sell, M—C—M', the simple form of capital as it obtains entirely in the process of circulation, uninterrupted by the production process, which lies outside its own movement and function.

What is now the relation of this commercial capital to commodity-capital as a mere form of existence of industrial capital? So far as the linen manufacturer is concerned, he has realised the value of his linen with the merchant's money and thereby completed the first phase in the metamorphosis of his commodity-capital—its conversion into money. Other conditions being equal, he can now proceed to reconvert this money into yarn, coal, wages, etc., and into means of existence, etc., for the consumption of his revenue. Hence, leaving aside the revenue expenditure, he can go on with his process of reproduction.

But while the sale of the linen, its metamorphosis into money, has taken place for him, as producer, it has not yet taken place for the linen itself. It is still on the market as commodity-capital awaiting to undergo its first metamorphosis—to be sold. Nothing has happened to this linen besides a change in the person of its owner. As concerns its purpose, as concerns its place in the process, it is still commodity-capital, a saleable commodity, with the only difference that it is now in the merchant's hands instead of the manufacturer's. The function of selling it, of effecting the first phase of its metamorphosis, has passed from the manufacturer to the merchant, has become the special business of the merchant, whereas previously, it was a function which the producer had to perform himself after having completed the function of its production.

Let us assume that the merchant fails to sell the 30,000 yards of linen during the interval required by the linen manufacturer to bring another 30,000 yards to market at a value of £3,000. The merchant cannot buy them again, because he still has in stock the unsold 30,000 yards which have not as yet been reconverted into money-capital. A stoppage ensues, *i.e.*, an interruption of reproduction. The linen producer might, of course, have additional money-capital at his disposal, which he could convert into productive capital, regardless of the sale of the 30,000 yards, in order to continue the production process. But this would not alter the situation. So far as the capital tied up in the 30,000 yards of linen is concerned, its process of reproduction is, and remains, interrupted. It is, indeed, easily seen here that the merchant's operations are really nothing but operations that must be performed at all events to convert the producer's commodity-capital into money. They are operations which effect the functions of commodity-capital in the circulation and reproduction processes. If it devolved upon the producer's clerk to attend exclusively to the sale, and also the purchase, instead of an independent merchant, this connection would not be obscured for a single moment.

Commercial capital is, therefore, nothing but the producer's commodity—capital which has to undergo the process of conversion into money—to perform its function of commodity-capital on the market—the only difference being that instead of representing an incidental function of the producer, it is now the exclusive operation of a special kind of capitalist, the merchant, and is set apart as the business of a special investment of capital.

This becomes evident, furthermore, in the specific form of circulation of commercial capital The merchant buys a commodity and then sells it: M—C—M'. In the simple circulation of commodities, or even in the circulation of commodities as it appears in the circulation process of industrial capital, C'—M—C, circulation is effected by each piece of money changing hands twice. The linen manufacturer sells his commodity-linen, converting it into money; the buyer's money passes into his hands. With this same money he buys yarn, coal, labour, etc.—expends the money for reconverting the value of linen into the commodities which make up its production elements. The commodity he buys is not the same commodity, not the same kind of commodity which he sells. He has sold products and bought means of production. But it is different with respect to the movements of merchant's capital. With his £3,000 the linen merchant buys 30,000 yards of linen; he sells the same 30,000 yards of linen in order to retrieve his money-capital (£3,000 and the profit) from circulation. It is not the same pieces of money, but rather the same commodity which here changes places twice; the commodity passes from the seller into the hands of the buyer, and from the hands of the buyer, who now becomes seller, into those of another buyer. It is sold twice, and may be sold repeatedly through the medium of a series of merchants. And it is precisely through this repeated sale, through this two-fold change of place of the same commodity, that the money advanced for its purchase by the first buyer is retrieved, its reflux to him effected. In one case, C'—M—C effects the two-fold change of place of the same money, the sale of a commodity in one form and the purchase of a commodity in another. In the other case, M—C—M' effects the two-fold change of place of the same commodity, the withdrawal of advanced money from circulation. It is evident that the commodity has not been finally sold when it passes from the producer into the hands of the merchant, in that the latter merely carries on the operation of selling—or effects the function of commodity-capital. But at the same time, it is evident that what is C—M, a mere function of his capital in its transient form of commodity-capital for the productive capitalist, is M—C—M', a specific increase in the value of his advanced money-capital, for the merchant. One phase of the metamorphosis of commodities appears here in respect to the merchant in the form of M—C—M', hence as evolution of a distinct kind of capital.

The merchant finally sells his commodity, that is, the linen, to the consumer, be it a productive consumer (for instance, a bleacher), or an individual who acquires the linen for his private use. The merchant thereby recovers his advanced capital (with a profit), and can repeat his operation anew. Had the money served merely as a means of payment in purchasing the linen, so that the merchant would have had to pay only after six weeks, and had he succeeded in selling before this term was out, he could have paid the linen manufacturer without advancing any money-capital of his own. Had he not sold it, he would have had to advance his £3,000 on the date of expiration, instead of on delivery of the linen. And if a drop in the market-prices had compelled him to sell below the purchase price, he would have had to make good the shortage out of his own capital.

What is it, then, that lends to commercial capital the character of an independently operating capital, whereas in the hands of the producer who does his own selling it is obviously merely a special form of his capital in a specific phase of the reproduction process during its sojourn in the sphere of circulation?

First: The fact that commodity-capital is finally converted into money, that it performs its initial metamorphosis, *i.e.*, its appropriate function on the market qua commodity-capital while in the hands of an agent other than the producer, and that this function of commodity-capital is effected by the merchant in his operations, his buying and selling, so that these operations assume the appearance of a separate undertaking distinct from the other functions of industrial capital—and hence of an independent undertaking. It is a distinct form of the social division of labour, so that part of the function ordinarily performed as a special phase of the reproduction process of capital, in this case—circulation, appears as the exclusive function of specific circulation agent distinct from the producer. But this alone would by no means give this particular business the aspect of a function of a specific capital distinct from, and independent of, industrial capital engaged in the process of reproduction; indeed, it does not so appear in cases where trade is carried on by travelling salesmen or other direct agents of the industrial capitalist. Therefore, there must be a second element involved.

Second: This arises from the fact that in his capacity as an independent circulation agent, the merchant advances money-capital (his own or borrowed). The transaction which for industrial capital in the reproduction process amounts merely to C—M, *i.e.*, converting commodity-capital into money-capital, or mere sale, assumes for the merchant the form of M—C—M', or purchase and sale of the same commodity, and thus of a reflux of money-capital which leaves him in the purchase, and returns to him in the sale.

It is always C—M, the conversion of commodity-capital into money-capital, which for the merchant assumes the form of M—C—M, inasmuch as he advances capital to purchase commodities from their producers; it is always the first metamorphosis of commodity-capital, although for a producer, or for industrial capital in process of reproduction, the same transaction may amount to M—C, to a reconversion of money into commodities (means of production), to the second phase of the metamorphosis. For the linen producer, the first metamorphosis was C—M, the conversion of his commodity-capital into money-capital. For the merchant the same act appears as M—C, as a conversion of his money-capital into commodity-capital. Now, if he sells this linen to a bleacher, it will mean M—C, *i.e.*, the conversion of money capital into productive capital, this being the second metamorphosis of his commodity-capital for the bleacher, while for the merchant it means C—M, the sale of the linen he had bought. But in fact, it is only at this point that the commodity-capital produced by the linen manufacturer has been finally sold. In other words, this M—C—M of the merchant represents no more than a middleman's function for C—M between two manufacturers. Or let us assume that the linen manufacturer buys yarn from a yarn dealer with a portion of the value of the sold linen. This is M—C for him. But for the merchant selling the yarn it is C—M, the resale of the yarn. As concerning the yarn in its capacity of commodity-capital, it is no more than its final sale, whereby it passes from the sphere of circulation into that of consumption; it is C—M, the consummation of its first metamorphosis. Whether the merchant buys, or sells to the industrial capitalist, his M—C—M, the circuit of merchant's capital, always expresses what is just C—M, or simply the completion of its first metamorphosis, with regard to the commodity-capital, a transient form of industrial capital in process of reproduction. The M—C of merchant's capital is C—M only for the industrial capitalist, not for the commodity-capital produced by him. It is but the transfer of commodity-capital from the industrial capitalist to the circulation agent. It is not until the merchant's capital closes C—M that functioning commodity-capital performs its final C—M. M—C—M amounts solely to two C—M's of the same commodity-capital, two successive sales of it, which merely effect its last and final sale.

Thus, commodity-capital assumes in commercial capital the form of an independent type of capital because the merchant advances money-capital, which is realised and functions as capital only by serving exclusively to mediate the metamorphosis of commodity-capital, its function as commodity-capital, *i.e.*, its conversion into money, and it accomplishes this by the continual purchase and sale of commodities. This is its exclusive operation. This activity of effecting the circulation process of industrial capital is the exclusive function of the money-capital with which the merchant operates. By means of this function he converts his money into money-capital, moulds his M into M—C—M, and by the same process converts commodity-capital into commercial capital.

So long and so far as commercial capital exists in the form of commodity-capital, it is obviously nothing else—from the standpoint of the reproduction process of the total social capital—but a portion of industrial capital in the market in process of metamorphosis, which exists and functions as commodity-capital. It is, therefore, only the *money*-capital advanced by the merchant which is exclusively destined for purchase and sale and for this reason never assumes any other form but that of commodity-capital and money-capital, never that of productive capital, and is always confined to the sphere of circulation of capital—it is only this money-capital which is now to be regarded with reference to the entire reproduction process of capital.

As soon as the producer, the linen manufacturer, has sold his 30,000 yards to the merchant for £3,000, he uses the money so obtained to buy the necessary means of production, so that his capital returns to the production process. His process of production continues without interruption. So far as he is concerned, the conversion of his commodity into money is accomplished. But for the linen itself, as we have seen, its metamorphosis has not yet taken place. It has not yet been finally reconverted into money, has not yet passed as a use-value into either productive or individual consumption. It is now the linen merchant who represents on the market the same commodity-capital originally represented by the linen manufacturer. For the latter the process of transformation has been curtailed, only to be continued in the merchant's hands.

Had the linen producer been obliged to wait until his linen had really ceased being a commodity, until it has passed into the hands of its ultimate buyer, its productive or individual consumer, his process of reproduction would have been interrupted. Or, to avoid interrupting it, he would have had to curtail his operations, to convert a smaller portion of his linen into yarn, coal, labour, etc., in short, into the elements of productive capital, and to retain a larger portion of it as a money reserve, so that with one portion of his capital on the market in the shape of commodities, another would continue the process of production; one portion would be on the market in the form of commodities, while the other returned in the form of money. This division of his capital is not abolished by the merchant's intervention. But without it the portion of money reserve in the capital of circulation would always have to be greater in relation to the part employed in the form of productive capital, and the scale of reproduction would have to be restricted accordingly. Instead, however, the manufacturer is enabled to constantly employ a larger portion of his capital in the actual process of production, and a smaller portion as money reserve.

On the other hand, however, another portion of the social capital, in the form of merchant's capital, is kept continually within the sphere of circulation. It is employed all the time for the sole purpose of buying and selling. Hence there seems to have been no more than a replacement of persons holding this capital in their hands.

If, instead of buying £3,000 worth of linen with the purpose of selling it again, the merchant had applied these £3,000 productively, the productive capital of society would have increased. True, the linen manufacturer would then have been obliged to hold back a larger portion of his capital as money reserve, and likewise the merchant, now transformed into an industrial capitalist. On the other hand, if the merchant remains merchant, the manufacturer saves time in selling, which he can devote to supervising the production process, while the merchant must apply all his time to selling.

If merchant's capital does not overstep its necessary proportions, it is to be inferred,

1. that as a result of the division of labour the capital devoted exclusively to buying and selling (and this includes not only the money required to buy commodities, but also the money which must be invested in labour to maintain the merchant's establishment, and in his constant capital-the storehouses, transport, etc.) is smaller than it would be if the industrial capitalist were constrained to carry on the entire commercial part of his business on his own;
2. that because the merchant devotes all his time exclusively to this business, the producer is able to convert his commodities more rapidly into money, and, moreover, the commodity-capital itself passes more rapidly through its metamorphosis than it would in the hands of the producer;
3. that in viewing the aggregate merchant's capital in its relation to industrial capital, one turnover of merchant's capital may represent not only the turnovers of many capitals in one sphere of production, but the turnovers of a number of capitals in different spheres of production. The former is the case when, for instance, the linen merchant, after buying the product of some linen manufacturer with his £3,000, sells it before the same manufacturer brings another lot of the same quantity to market, and buys, and again sells, the product of another, or several other, linen manufacturers, thus effecting the turnovers of different capitals in the same sphere of production. The latter is the case if, for example, the merchant after selling his linen buys silk, thus effecting the turnover of a capital in a different sphere of production.

In general, it may be noted that the turnover of industrial capital is limited not by the time of circulation alone, but also by the time of production. The turnover of merchant's capital dealing in one kind of commodity is not merely limited by the turnover of a single industrial capital, but by that of all industrial capitals in the same branch of production. After the merchant has bought and sold the linen of one producer he can buy and sell that of another, before the first brings another lot to the market. The same merchant's capital may, therefore, successively promote the different turnovers of capitals invested in a certain branch of production, with the effect that its turnover is not identical with the turnovers of a sole industrial capital, and does not, therefore, replace just the single money reserve which that one industrial capitalist would have had to hold *in petto*. The turnover of merchant's capital in one sphere of production is naturally restricted by the total production of that sphere. But it is not restricted by the scale of production, or the period of turnover, of any one capital of the same sphere, so far as its period of turnover is qualified by its time of production. Suppose, A supplies a commodity requiring three months for its production. After the merchant has bought and sold it, say, in one month, he can buy and sell the same product of some other manufacturer. Or after he has sold, say, the corn of one farmer, he can buy and sell that of another with the same money, etc. The turnover of his capital is restricted by the mass of corn he is able to buy and sell successively within a certain period, for instance, in one year, while the turnover of the farmer's capital is, regardless of the time of turnover, restricted by the time of production, which lasts one year.

However, the turnover of the same merchant's capital may equally well effect the turnovers of capitals in different branches of production.

In so far as the same merchant's capital serves in different turnovers to transform different commodity-capitals successively into money, buying and selling them one after another, it performs the same function in its capacity of money-capital with regard to commodity-capital, which money in general performs by means of the number of its turnovers in a given period with regard to commodities.

The turnover of merchant's capital is not identical with the turnover, or a single reproduction, of an industrial capital of equal size; it is rather equal to the sum of the turnovers of a number of such capitals, whether in the same or in different spheres of production. The more quickly merchant's capital is turned over, the smaller the portion of total money capital serving as merchant's capital; and conversely, the more slowly it is turned over, the larger this portion. The less developed production, the larger the sum of merchant's capital in its relation to the sum of the commodities thrown into circulation; but the smaller in absolute terms, or in comparison with more developed conditions, and vice versa. In such undeveloped conditions, therefore, the greater part of the actual money-capital is in the hands of merchants, whose fortune constitutes money wealth vis-à-vis the others.

The velocity of circulation of the money-capital advanced by the merchant depends 1) on the speed with which the process of production is renewed and the different processes of production are linked together; and 2) on the velocity of consumption.

To accomplish the turnover we have examined above, merchant's capital does not first have to buy commodities for its full amount of value, and then to sell them. Instead, the merchant performs both movements simultaneously. His capital then breaks up into two parts. One of them consists of commodity-capital, and the other of money-capital. He buys and converts his money into commodities at one place. Elsewhere, he sells and converts another part of his commodity-capital into money. On one side, his capital returns to him in the form of money-capital, while on the other he gets commodity-capital. The larger the portion in one form, the smaller the portion in the other. This alternates and balances itself. If the use of money as a medium of circulation combines with its use as a means of payment and the attendant development of the credit system, then the money-capital part of merchant's capital is reduced still more in relation to the volume of the transactions this merchant's capital effects. If I buy £3,000 worth of wine on three months' credit and sell all the wine for cash before this term expires, I do not need to advance a single penny for these transactions. In this case it is also quite obvious that the money-capital, which here acts as merchant's capital, is nothing more than industrial capital in its money-capital form, in its process of reflux in the form of money. (The fact that the manufacturer who sold £3,000 worth of wine on three months' credit may discount his promissory note at the banker's does not alter the matter at all and has nothing to do with the merchant's capital.) If market-prices should fall in the meantime by, say, 1/10, the merchant, far from making a profit, would recover only £2,700 instead of £3,000. He would have to put up £300 out of his own pocket. These £300 would serve merely as a reserve to balance the difference in price. But the same applies to the manufacturer. If he himself had sold at falling prices, he would likewise have lost £300, and would not be able to resume production on the same scale without reserve capital.

The linen merchant buys £3,000 worth of linen from the manufacturer. The latter pays, say, £2,000 of the £3,000 for yarn. He buys this yarn from a yarn dealer. The money which the manufacturer pays to the yarn dealer is not the linen dealer's money, for the latter has received commodities to this amount. It is the money-form of the manufacturer's own capital. Now in the hands of the yarn dealer these £2,000 appear as returned money-capital. But to what extent are they that as distinct from the £2,000 representing the discarded money-form of the linen and the assumed money-form of the yarn? If the yarn dealer bought on credit and sold for cash before the expiration of his term of payment, then these £2,000 do not contain one penny of merchant's capital as distinct from the money-form which the industrial capital itself assumes in the course of its circuit. In so far as commercial capital is not, therefore, just a form of industrial capital in the merchant's hands as commodity- or money-capital, it is nothing but that portion of money-capital which belongs directly to the merchant and circulates in the purchase and sale of commodities. On a reduced scale this portion represents that part of capital advanced for production which should always have to be in the hands of the industrialist as money reserve and means of purchase, and which should always have to circulate as his money-capital. This portion, on a reduced scale, is now in the hands of merchant capitalists and performs its functions as such in the process of circulation. It is that portion of the total capital which, aside from what is expended as revenue, must continually circulate on the market as a means of purchase in order to maintain the continuity of the process of reproduction. The more rapid the process of reproduction, and the more developed the function of money as a means of payment, *i.e.*, the more developed the credit system,[1] the smaller that portion is in relation to the total capital.

Merchant's capital is simply capital functioning in the sphere of circulation. The process of circulation is a phase of the total process of reproduction. But no value is produced in the process of circulation, and, therefore, no surplus-value. Only changes of form of the same mass of value take place. In fact, nothing occurs there outside the metamorphosis of commodities, and this has nothing to do as such either with the creation or change of values. If a surplus-value is realised in the sale of produced commodities, then this is only because it already existed in them. In the second act, the re-exchange of money-capital against commodities (elements of production), the buyer, therefore, does not realise any surplus-value either. He merely initiates the production of surplus-value through exchanging his money for means of production and labour-power. But so far as these metamorphoses require circulation time—time during which capital does not produce at all, least of all surplus-value—it restricts the creation of values, and the surplus-value expresses itself through the rate of profit in inverse ratio to the duration of the circulation period. Merchant's capital, therefore, does not create either value or surplus-value, at least not directly. In so far as it contributes to shortening the time of circulation, it may help indirectly to increase the surplus-value produced by the industrial capitalists. In so far as it helps to expand the market and effects the division of labour between capitals, hence enabling capital to operate on a larger scale, its function promotes the productivity of industrial capital, and its accumulation. In so far as it shortens circulation time, it raises the ratio of surplus-value to advanced capital, hence the rate of profit. And to the extent that it confines a smaller portion of capital to the sphere of circulation in the form of money-capital, it increases that portion of capital which is engaged directly in production.

Note

1. To be able to classify merchant's capital as productive capital, Ramsay confounds it with the transportation industry and calls commerce 'the transport of commodities from one place to another.' *(An Essay on the Distribution of Wealth*, p. 19.) The same confusion by Verri (*Meditazioni sulla Economia Politica*, § 4 [In: *Scrittori Classici Italiani di Economia Politica*. Parte Moderna, t. XV, p.32.—*Ed.*]) and by Say (*Traité d'économie politique*, I, 14, 15). In his *Elements of Political Economy* (Andover and New York, 1835) S.P. Newman says: 'In the existing economical arrangements of society, the very act, which is performed by the merchant, of standing between the producer and the consumer, advancing to the former capital and receiving products in return, and then handing over these products to the latter, receiving back capital in return, is a transaction which both facilitates the economical processes of the community, and adds value to the products in relation to which it is performed' (p. 174). Producer and consumer thus save time and money through the intervention of the merchant. This service requires an advance of capital and labour, and must be rewarded, 'since it adds value to products, for the same products in the hands of consumers are worth more than in the hands of producers.' And so commerce appears to him, as it does to M. Say, as 'strictly an act of production' (p. 175). This Newman's view is fundamentally wrong. The *use-value* of a commodity is greater in the hands of the consumer than in those of the producer, because it is first realised by the consumer. For the use-value of a commodity does not serve its end, does not begin to function until the commodity

enters the sphere of consumption. So long as it is in the hands of the producer, it exists only in potential form. But one does not pay twice for a commodity—first for its exchange-value, and then for its use-value. By paying for its exchange-value, I appropriate its use-value. And its exchange-value is not in the least augmented by transferring the commodity from the producer or middleman to the consumer.

17

Commercial Profit

We have seen in Book II that the pure functions of capital in the sphere of circulation—the operations which the industrial capitalist must perform, first, to realise the value of his commodities, and second, to reconvert this value into elements of production, operations effecting the metamorphosis of commodity-capital, C'—M—C, hence the acts of selling and buying-produce neither value nor surplus-value. It was rather seen that the time required for this purpose, objectively in regard to commodities and subjectively in regard to the capitalist, sets the limit to the production of value and surplus-value. What is true of the metamorphosis of commodity-capital in general, is, of course, not in the least altered by the fact that a part of it may assume the shape of commercial capital, or that the operations, effecting the metamorphosis of commodity-capital, appear as the special concern of a special group of capitalists, or as the exclusive function of a portion of the money-capital. If selling and buying commodities—and that is what the metamorphosis of commodity-capital C'—M—C amounts to—by industrial capitalists themselves are not operations which create value or surplus-value, they will certainly not create either of these when carried out by persons other than the industrial capitalists. Furthermore, if that portion of the total social capital, which must continually be on hand as money-capital, in order that the process of reproduction is not interrupted by the process of circulation and proceeds continuously—if this money-capital creates neither value nor surplus-value, it cannot acquire the properties of creating them by being continually thrown into circulation by some section of capitalists other than the industrial capitalists, to perform the same function. We have already indicated to what extent merchant's capital may be indirectly productive, and we shall later discuss this point at greater length.

Commercial capital, therefore—stripped of all heterogeneous functions, such as storing, expressing, transporting, distributing, retailing, which may be connected with it, and confined to its true function of buying in order to sell—creates neither value nor surplus-value, but acts as middleman in their realisation and thereby simultaneously in the actual exchange of commodities, *i.e.*, in their transfer from hand to hand, in the social metabolism. Nevertheless, since the circulation phase of industrial capital is just as much a phase of the reproduction process as production is, the capital operating independently in the process of circulation must yield the average annual profit just as well as capital operating in the various branches of production. Should merchant's capital yield a higher percentage of average profit than industrial capital, then a portion of the latter would transform itself into merchant's capital. Should it yield a lower average profit, then the converse would result. A portion of the merchant's capital would then be transformed into industrial capital. No species of capital changes its purpose, or function, with greater ease than merchant's capital.

Since merchant's capital does not itself produce surplus-value, it is evident that the surplus-value which it pockets in the form of average profit must be a portion of the surplus-value produced by the total productive capital. But now the question arises: How does merchant's capital attract its share of the surplus-value or profit produced by the productive capital?

It is just an illusion that commercial profit is a mere addition to, or a nominal rise of, the prices of commodities in excess of their value.

It is plain that the merchant can draw his profit only out of the price of the commodities he sells, and plainer still that the profit he makes in selling his commodities must be equal to the difference between his purchase price and his selling price, *i.e.*, equal to the excess of the latter over the former.

It is possible that additional costs (costs of circulation) may enter into the commodities after their purchase and before their sale, and it is also possible that this may not happen. If such costs should occur, it is plain that the excess of the selling price over the purchase price would not be all profit. To simplify the analysis, we shall assume at this point that no such costs occur.

For the industrial capitalist, the difference between the selling price and the purchase price of his commodities is equal to the difference between their price of production and their cost-price, or, from the standpoint of the total social capital, equal to the difference between the value of the commodities and their cost-price for the capitalists, which again comes down to the difference between the total quantity of labour and the quantity of paid labour incorporated in them. Before the commodities bought by the industrial capitalist are thrown back on the market as saleable commodities, they pass through the process of production, in which alone the portion of their price to be realised as profit is created. But it is different with the merchant. The commodities are in his hands only so long as they are in the process of circulation. He merely continues their sale, the realisation of their price which was begun by the productive capitalist, and therefore, does not cause them to pass through any intermediate process in which they could again absorb surplus-value. While the industrial capitalist merely realises the previously produced surplus-value, or profit, in the process of circulation, the merchant has not only to realise his profit during and through circulation, but must first make it. There appears to be no other way of doing this outside of selling the commodities bought by him from the industrial capitalist at their prices of production, or, from the standpoint of the total commodity-capital, at their values in excess of their prices of production, making a nominal extra charge to their prices, hence, selling them, from the standpoint of the total commodity-capital, above their value, and pocketing this excess of their nominal value over their real value; in short, selling them for more than they are worth.

This method of adding an extra charge is easy to grasp. For instance, one yard of linen costs 2s. If I want to make a 10% profit in reselling it, I must add 1/10 to the price, hence sell the yard at 2s. 2 2/5 d. The difference between its actual price of production and its selling price is then = 2 2/5d., and this represents a profit of 10% on 2s. This amounts to my selling the yard to the buyer at a price which is in reality the price of 1 1/10 yard. Or, what amounts to the same, it is as though I sold to the buyer only 10/11 of a yard for 2s. and kept 1/11 of a yard for myself. In fact, I can buy back 1/11 of a yard for 2 2/5d. at the price of 2s. 2 2/5d. per yard. This would, therefore, be just a roundabout way of sharing in the surplus-value and surplus-product by a nominal rise in the price of commodities.

This is realisation of commercial profit by raising the price of commodities, as it appears at first glance. And, indeed, this whole notion that profit originates from a nominal rise in the price of commodities, or from their sale above their value, springs from the observations of commercial capital.

But it is quickly apparent on closer inspection that this is mere illusion. Assuming capitalist production to be predominant, commercial profit cannot be realised in this manner. (It is here always a question of averages, not of isolated cases.) Why do we assume that the merchant can realise a profit of no more than, say, 10% on his commodities by selling them 10% above their price of production? Because we assume that the producer of these commodities, the industrial capitalist (who appears as '*the producer*' before the outside world, being the personification of industrial capital), had sold them to the dealer at their prices of production. If the purchase price of commodities paid by the dealer is equal to their price of production, or, in the last instance, equal to their value, so that the price of production or, in the last instance, the value, represent the merchant's cost-price, then, indeed, the excess of his selling price over his purchase price—and this difference alone is the source of his profit—must be an excess of their commercial price over their price of production, so that in the final analysis the merchant sells all commodities above their values. But why was it assumed that the industrial capitalist sells his commodities to the merchant at their prices of production? Or rather, what was taken for granted in that assumption? It was that merchant's capital did not go into forming the general rate of profit (we are dealing with it as yet only in its capacity of commercial capital). We proceeded necessarily from this premise in discussing the general rate of profit, first, because merchant's capital as such did not exist for us at the time, and, second, because average profit, and hence the general rate of profit, had first to be developed as a levelling of profits or surplus-values actually produced by the industrial capitals in the different spheres of production. But in the case of merchant's capital we are dealing with a capital which shares in the profit without participating in its production. Hence, it is now necessary to supplement our earlier exposition.

Suppose, the total industrial capital advanced in the course of the year = $720_c + 180_v$ = 900 (say million £), and that s› = 100%. The product therefore = $720_c + 180_v + 180_s$. Let us call this product or the produced commodity-capital, C, whose value, or price of production (since both are identical for the totality of commodities) = 1,080, and the rate of profit for the total social capital of 900 = 20%. These 20% are, according to our earlier analyses, the average rate of profit, since the surplus-value is not calculated here on this or that capital of any particular composition, but on the total industrial capital of average composition. Thus, C = 1,080, and the rate of profit = 20%. Let us now assume, however, that aside from these £900 of industrial capital, there are still £100 of merchant's capital, which shares in the profit *pro rata* to its magnitude just as the former. According to our assumption, it is 1/10 of the total capital of 1,000. Therefore, it participates to the extent of 1/10 in the total surplus-value of 180, and thus secures a profit of 18%. Actually, then, the profit to be distributed among the other 1/10 of the total capital is only = 162, or on the capital of 900 likewise = 18%. Hence, the price at which C is sold by the owners of the industrial capital of 900 to the merchants = $720_c + 180_v + 162_s$ = 1,062. If the dealer then adds the average profit of 18% to his capital of 100, he sells the commodities at 1,062 + 18 = 1,080, *i.e.*, at their price of production, or, from the standpoint of the total commodity-capital, at their value, although he makes his profit only during and through the circulation process, and only from an excess of his selling price over his purchase price. Yet he does not sell the commodities above their value, or above their price of production, precisely because he has bought them from the industrial capitalist below their value, or below their price of production.

Thus, merchant's capital enters the formation of the general rate of profit as a determinant *pro rata* to its part in the total capital. Hence, if we say in the given case that the average rate of profit = 18%, it would = 20%, if it were not that 1/10 of the total capital was merchant's capital and the general rate of profit thereby lowered by 1/10. This leads to a closer and more comprehensive definition of the price of production. By price of production we mean, just as before, the price of a commodity = its costs (the value of the constant + variable capital contained in it) + the average profit. But this average profit is now determined differently. It is determined by the total profit produced by the total productive capital; but not as calculated on the total productive capital alone, so that if this = 900, as assumed above, and the profit = 180, then the average rate of profit = 180/900 = 20%. But, rather, as calculated on the total productive + merchant's capital, so that with 900 productive and 100 merchant's capital, the average rate of profit = 180/1,000 = 18%. The price of production is, therefore = k (the costs) + 18, instead of k + 20. The share of the total profit falling to merchant's capital is thus included in the average rate of profit. The actual value, or price of production, of the total commodity-capital is, therefore = k + p + m (where m is commercial profit). The price of production, or the price at which the industrial capitalist as such sells his commodities, is thus smaller than the actual price of production of the commodity; or in terms of all commodities taken together, the prices at which the class of industrial capitalists sell their commodities are lower than their value. Hence, in the above case, 900 (costs) + 18% on 900, or 900 + 162= 1,062. It follows, then, that in selling a commodity at 118 for which he paid 100 the merchant does, indeed, add 18% to the price. But since this commodity, for which he paid 100, is really worth 118, he does not sell it above its value. We shall henceforth use the term price of production in this, its more precise, sense. It is evident, therefore, that the profit of the industrial capitalist equals the excess of the price of production of the commodity over its cost-price, and that commercial profit, as distinct from this industrial profit, equals the excess of the selling price over the price of production of the commodity which, for the merchant, is its purchase price; but that the actual price of the commodity = its price of production + the commercial profit. Just as industrial capital realises only such profits as already exist in the value of commodities as surplus-value, so merchant's capital realises profits only because the entire surplus-value, or profit, has not as yet been fully realised in the price charged for the commodities by the industrial capitalist.[1] The merchant's selling price thus exceeds the purchase price not because the former exceeds the total value, but because the latter is below this value.

Merchant's capital, therefore, participates in levelling surplus-value to average profit, although it does not take part in its production. Thus, the general rate of profit contains a deduction from surplus-value due to merchant's capital, hence a deduction from the profit of industrial capital.

It follows from the foregoing:

1. The larger the merchant's capital in proportion to the industrial capital, the smaller the rate of industrial profit, and vice versa.
2. It was demonstrated in the first part that the rate of profit is always lower than the rate of the actual surplus-value, *i.e.*, it always understates the intensity of exploitation, as in the above case, $720_c + 180_v + 180_s$, the rate of surplus-value of 100% and a rate of profit of only 20%. And the difference becomes still greater, inasmuch as the average rate of profit appears smaller again, dropping from 20% to 18%, if the share falling to merchant's capital is also taken into account. The average rate of profit of the direct capitalist exploiter, therefore, expresses a rate of profit smaller than it actually is.

Assuming all other circumstances remaining the same, the relative volume of merchant's capital (with the exception of the small dealer who represents a hybrid form) is in inverse proportion to the velocity of its turnover, hence in inverse proportion to the energy of the process of reproduction in general. In the course of scientific analysis, the formation of a general rate of profit appears to result from industrial capitals and their competition, and is only later corrected, supplemented, and modified by the intervention of merchant's capital. In the course of its historical development, however, the process is really reversed. It is the commercial capital which first determines the prices of commodities more or less in accordance with their values, and it is the sphere of circulation, the sphere that promotes the process of reproduction, in which a general rate of profit initially takes shape. It is originally the commercial profit which determines the industrial profit. Not until the capitalist mode of production has asserted itself and the producer himself has become merchant, is commercial profit reduced to that aliquot part of the total surplus-value falling to the share of merchant's capital as an aliquot part of the total capital engaged in the social process of reproduction.

It was seen in the supplementary equalisation of profit through the intervention of merchant's capital that no additional element entered the value of commodities with the merchant's advanced money-capital, and that the extra charge to the price, whereby the merchant makes his profit, was merely equal to that portion of the value of the commodities, which productive capital had not calculated in the price of production, *i.e.*, had left out. The case of this money-capital is similar to that of the industrial capitalist's fixed capital, since it is not consumed and its value, therefore, does not make up an element of the value of commodity. It is in the purchase price of commodity-capital that the merchant replaces its price of production = M, in money. His own selling price, as previously shown, is = M + ΔM, where ΔM stands for the addition to the price of commodities determined by the general rate of profit. Once he sells the commodities, his original money-capital, which he advanced for their purchase, returns to him together with this ΔM. We see once more that his money-capital is nothing but the industrial capitalist's commodity-capital transformed into money-capital, which affects the magnitude of the value of this commodity-capital no more than would a direct sale of the latter to the ultimate consumer, instead of to the merchant. It, actually, merely anticipates the payment of the consumer. However, this is correct only on the condition hitherto assumed, that the merchant has no overhead expenses, or that aside from the money-capital which he must advance to buy commodities from the producer he need not advance any other capital, circulating or fixed, in the process of commodity metamorphosis., the process of buying and selling. But this is not so in reality, as we have seen in the analysis of the costs of circulation (Book II, Chap. VI). These costs of circulation are partly expenses which the merchant has to reclaim from other agents of circulation, and partly expenses arising directly from his specific business.

No matter what the nature of these costs of circulation—whether they arise from the purely commercial nature of the merchant's establishment as such and hence belong to the merchant's specific costs of circulation, or represent items which are charges for subsequent processes of production added in the process of circulation, such as expressage, transport, storage, etc.—they always require of the merchant, aside from his money-capital, advanced to the purchase of commodities, some additional capital for the purchase and payment of such means of circulation. As much of this element of cost as consists of circulating capital passes wholly as an additional element into the selling price of the commodities; and as much of it as consists of fixed capital only to the extent of its wear and tear. But only as an element which forms a nominal value, even if as the purely commercial costs of circulation, it does not add any real value to the commodities. But whether fixed or circulating, this entire additional capital participates in forming the general rate of profit.

The purely commercial costs of circulation (hence, excluding costs of expressage, shipping, storage, etc.) resolve themselves into costs required to realise the value of commodities, to transform it from commodities into money, or from money into commodities, to effect their exchange. We leave entirely out of consideration all possible processes of production which may continue in the process of circulation, and from which the merchant's business can be altogether separated; as, in fact, the actual transport industry and expressage may be, and are, industrial branches entirely distinct from commercial; and purchaseable and saleable commodities may be stored in docks or in other public premises, with the resultant cost of storage being charged to the merchant by third persons inasmuch as he has to advance it. All this takes place in actual wholesale commerce, where merchant's capital appears in its purest form, unmixed with other functions. The express company owner, the railway director, and the shipowner, are not 'merchants.' The costs which we consider here are those of buying and selling. We have already remarked earlier that these resolve themselves into accounting, book-keeping, marketing, correspondence, etc. The constant capital required for this purpose consists of offices, paper, postage, etc. The other costs break up into variable capital advanced for the employment of mercantile wage-workers. (Expressage, transport costs, advances for customs duties, etc., may partly be considered as being advanced by the merchant in purchasing commodities and thus enter the purchase price as far as he is concerned.)

All these costs are not incurred in producing the use-value of commodities, but in realising their value. They are pure costs of circulation. They do not enter into the immediate process of production, but since they are part of the process of circulation they are also part of the total process of reproduction.

The only portion of these costs of interest to us at this point is that advanced as variable capital. (The following questions should also be analysed: First, how does the law that only necessary labour enters the value of commodities operate in the process of circulation? Second, how does accumulation obtain in merchant's capital? Third, how does merchant's capital function in the actual aggregate reproduction process of society?)

These costs arise due to the product having the economic form of a commodity.

If the labour-time which the industrial capitalists themselves lose while directly selling commodities to one another—hence, speaking objectively, the circulation time of the commodities—does not add value to these commodities, it is evident that this labour-time does not change its nature in the least by falling to the merchant instead of the industrial capitalist. The conversion of commodities (products) into money, and of money into commodities (means of production) is a necessary function of industrial capital and, therefore, a necessary operation of the capitalist—who is actually but personified capital endowed with a consciousness of its own and a will. But these functions neither create value, nor produce surplus-value. By performing these operations and carrying on the functions of capital in the sphere of circulation after the productive capitalist has ceased to be involved the merchant merely takes the place of the industrial capitalist. The labour-time required in these operations is devoted to certain necessary operations of the reproduction process of capital, but yields no additional value. If the merchant did not perform these operations (hence, did not expend the labour-time entailed), he would not be applying his capital as a circulation agent of industrial capital; he would not then be continuing the interrupted function of the industrial capitalist, and consequently could not participate as a capitalist *pro rata* to his advanced capital, in the mass of profit produced by industrial capitalists. In order to share in the mass of surplus-value, to expand the value of his advance as capital, the commercial capitalist need not employ wage-workers. If his business and capital are small, he may be the only worker in it. He is paid with that portion of the profit which falls to him through the difference between the purchase price paid by him for commodities and their actual price of production.

But, on the other hand, the profit realised by the merchant on a small amount of advanced capital may be no larger, or may even be smaller, than the wages of one of the better-paid skilled wage-workers. In fact, he brushes shoulders with many direct commercial agents of the productive capitalist, such as buyers, sellers, travellers, who enjoy the same or a higher income either in the form of wages, or in the form of a share in the profit (percentages, bonuses) made from each sale. In the first case, the merchant pockets the mercantile profit as an independent capitalist; in the other, the salesman, the industrial capitalist's wage-labourer, receives a portion of the profit either in the form of wages, or as a proportional share in the profit of the industrial capitalist, whose direct agent he is, while his employer pockets both the industrial and the commercial profit. But in all these cases, although his income may appear to the circulation agent as an ordinary wage, as payment for work performed, and although, where it does not so appear, the profit may be no larger than the wage of a better-paid labourer, his income is derived solely from the mercantile profit. This follows from his labour not being labour which produces value.

The lengthening of the act of circulation represents for the industrial capitalist 1) a personal loss of time, since it prevents him from performing in person his function as manager of the productive process; 2) a longer stay of his product in money- or commodity-form, in the circulation process, hence in a process where it does not expand value and where the direct production process is interrupted. If this process is not to be interrupted, production must either be curtailed, or more money-capital must be advanced to maintain the process of production on the same scale. This means that each time either a smaller profit is made on the capital hitherto invested, or that additional money-capital must be advanced to make the previous profit. All this remains unchanged when the merchant takes the place of the industrial capitalist. Instead of the industrial capitalist devoting more time to the process of circulation, it is the merchant who is so engaged; instead of the industrial capitalist it is the merchant who advances additional capital for circulation; or, what amounts to the same thing, instead of a large portion of the industrial capital being continually diverted into the process of circulation, it is the merchant's capital which is wholly tied up in it; and instead of making a smaller profit, the industrial capitalist must yield a portion of his profit wholly to the merchant. So long as merchant's capital remains within the bounds in which it is necessary, the only difference is that this division of the functions of capital reduces the time exclusively used up in the process of circulation, that less additional capital is advanced for this purpose, and that the loss in total profit, represented by mercantile profit, is smaller than it would otherwise have been. If in the above example, $720_c + 180_v + 180_s$, assisted by a merchant's capital of 100, produces a profit of 162, or 18%, for the industrial capitalist, hence implying a deduction of 18, then, but for this independent merchant's capital, the additional capital required would probably be 200, and we should have a total advance by the industrial capitalist of 1,100 instead of 900, which, based upon a surplus-value of 180, would yield a rate of profit of only 16 4/11%.

If the industrial capitalist who acts as his own merchant advances not only the additional capital to buy new commodities before his product in the process of circulation has been reconverted into money, but also capital (office expenses and wages for commercial employees) to realise the value of his commodity-capital, or, in other words, for the process of circulation, then these supplements form additional capital, but do not create surplus-value. They must be made good out of the value of the commodities, because a portion of the value of these commodities must be reconverted into these circulation costs. But no additional surplus-value is created thereby. So far as this concerns the total capital of society, it means in fact, that a portion of it must be set aside for secondary operations which are no part of the self-expansion process, and that this portion of the social capital must be continually reproduced for this purpose. This reduces the rate of profit for the individual capitalist and for the entire class of industrial capitalists, an effect arising from every new investment of additional capital whenever such capital is required to set in motion the same mass of variable capital.

In so far as these additional costs connected with the business of circulation are transferred from the industrial to the commercial capitalist, there takes place a similar reduction in the rate of profit, but to a lesser degree and in a different way. It now develops that the merchant advances more capital than would be necessary if these costs did not exist, and that the profit on this additional capital increases the amount of the commercial profit, so that more of the merchant's capital joins industrial capital in levelling the average rate of profit and thereby the average profit falls. If in our above example an additional capital of 50 is advanced besides the merchant's capital of 100 to cover the costs in question, then the total surplus-value of 180 is distributed with respect to a productive capital of 900 plus a merchant's capital of 150, together = 1,050. The average rate of profit, therefore, sinks to $17^{1}/_{7}\%$ The industrial capitalist sells his commodities to the merchant at $900 + 154^{2}/_{7} = 1{,}0542^{1}/_{7}$, and the merchant sells them at 1,130 (1,080 + 50 for costs which he must recover). Moreover, it must be admitted that the division between merchant's and industrial capital is accompanied by a centralisation of the commercial expenses and, consequently, by their reduction.

The question now arises: What about the commercial wage-workers employed by the commercial capitalist, here the merchant?

In one respect, such a commercial employee is a wage-worker like any other. In the first place, his labour-power is bought with the variable capital of the merchant, not with money expended as revenue, and consequently it is not bought for private service, but for the purpose of expanding the value of the capital advanced for it. In the second place, the value of his labour-power, and thus his wages, are determined as those of other wage-workers, *i.e.*, by the cost of production and reproduction of his specific labour-power, not by the product of his labour.

However, we must make the same distinction between him and the wage-workers directly employed by industrial capital which exists between industrial capital and merchant's capital, and thus between the industrial capitalist and the merchant. Since the merchant, as a mere agent of circulation, produces neither value nor surplus-value (for the additional value which he adds to the commodities through his expenses resolves itself into an addition of previously existing values, although the question here poses itself, how he preserves this value of his constant capital?) it follows that the mercantile workers employed by him in these same functions cannot directly create surplus-value for him. Here, as in the case of productive labourers, we assume that wages are determined by the value of the labour-power, and that, hence, the merchant does not enrich himself by depressing wages, so that he does not enter into his cost account an advance for labour which he has paid only in part; in other words, that he does not enrich himself through cheating his clerks, etc.

The difficulty as concerns mercantile wage-workers is by no means to explain how they produce direct profits for their employer without creating any direct surplus-value (of which profit is but a transmuted form). This question has, indeed, already been solved in the general analysis of commercial profits. Just as industrial capital makes profit by selling labour embodied and realised in commodities, for which it has not paid any equivalent, so merchant's capital derives profit from not paying in full to productive capital for all the unpaid labour contained in the commodities (in commodities, in so far as capital invested in their production functions as an aliquot part of the total industrial capital), and by demanding payment for this unpaid portion still contained in the commodities when making a sale. The relation of merchant's capital to surplus-value is different from that of industrial capital. The latter produces surplus-value by directly appropriating the unpaid labour of others. The former appropriates a portion of this surplus-value by having this portion transferred from industrial capital to itself.

It is only through its function of realising values that merchant's capital acts as capital in the process of reproduction, and hence draws on the surplus-value produced by the total capital. The mass of the individual merchant's profits depends on the mass of capital that he can apply in this process, and he can apply so much more of it in buying and selling, the more the unpaid labour of his clerks. The very function, by virtue of which the merchant's money becomes capital, is largely done through his employees. The unpaid labour of these clerks, while it does not create surplus-value, enables him to appropriate surplus-value, which, in effect, amounts to the same thing with respect to his capital. It is, therefore, a source of profit for him. Otherwise commerce could never be conducted on a large scale, capitalistically.

Just as the labourer's unpaid labour directly creates surplus-value for productive capital, so the unpaid labour of the commercial wage-worker secures a share of this surplus-value for merchant's capital.

The difficulty lies here: Since the merchant's labour-time and labour do not create value, although they secure for him a share of already produced surplus-value, how does the matter stand with the variable capital which he lays out in purchasing commercial labour-power? Is this variable capital to be included in the cost outlays of the advanced merchant's capital? If not, this appears to conflict with the law of equalisation of the rate of profit; what capitalist would advance 150 if he could charge only 100 to advanced capital? If so, it seems to conflict with the nature of merchant's capital, since this kind of capital does not act as capital by setting in motion the labour of others, as industrial capital does, but rather by doing its own work, *i.e.*, performing the functions of buying and selling, this being precisely the means and the reason why it receives a portion of the surplus-value produced by the industrial capital.

(We must, therefore, analyse the following points: the merchant's variable capital; the law of necessary labour in the sphere of circulation; how the merchant's labour maintains the value of his constant capital; the part played by merchant's capital in the process of reproduction as a whole; and, finally, the duplication in commodity-capital and money-capital, on the one hand, and in commercial capital and money-dealing capital on the other.)

If every merchant had only as much capital as he himself were able to turn over by his own labour, there would be infinite fragmentation of merchant's capital. This fragmentation would increase in the same proportion as productive capital raised production and operated with greater masses in the forward march of the capitalist mode of production. Hence, an increasing disproportion of the two. Capital in the sphere of circulation would become decentralised in the same proportion as it became centralised in the sphere of production. The purely commercial business of the industrial capitalist, and thus his purely commercial expenses, would expand infinitely thereby, for he would have to deal with, say, 1,000 merchants, instead of 100. Thus, the advantages of independently operating merchant's capital would largely be lost. And not the purely commercial expenses alone, but also the other costs of circulation, such as sorting, expressage, etc., would grow. This, as far as the industrial capital is concerned. Now let us consider merchant's capital. Firstly, the purely commercial operations. It does not take more time to deal with large figures than with small ones. It takes ten times as much time to make 10 purchases at £100 each as it does to make *one* purchase at £1,000. It takes ten times as much correspondence, paper, and postage, to correspond with 10 small merchants as it does with *one* large merchant. The clearly defined division of labour in a commercial office, in which one keeps the books, another looks after money matters, a third has charge of correspondence, one buys, another sells, a third travels, etc., saves immense quantities of labour-time, so that the number of workers employed in wholesale commerce are in no way related to the comparative size of the establishment. This is so, because in commerce much more than in industry the same function requires the same labour-time, whether performed on a large or a small scale. This is the reason why concentration appears earlier historically in the merchant's business than in the industrial workshop. Further, regarding outlays in constant capital. One hundred small offices cost incomparably more than one large office, 100 small warehouses more than a large one, etc. The costs of transport, which enter the accounts of a commercial establishment at least as costs to be advanced, grow with the fragmentation.

The industrial capitalist would have to lay out more in labour and in circulation costs in the commercial part of his business. The same merchant's capital, when divided among many small capitalists, would, owing to this fragmentation, require more labourers to perform its functions, and more merchant's capital would, furthermore, be needed to turn over the same commodity-capital.

Suppose B is the entire merchant's capital directly applied in buying and selling commodities, and b the corresponding variable capital paid out in wages to the commercial employees. Then B + b is smaller than the total merchant's capital, B, would be if every merchant had to get along without assistants, hence would invest nothing in b. However, we have not yet overcome the difficulty.

The selling price of the commodities must suffice 1) to pay the average profit on B + b. This is explained if only by the fact that B + b is generally a reduction of the original B, representing a smaller merchant's capital than would be required without b. But this selling price must suffice 2) to cover not only the additional profit on b, but to replace also the paid wages, the merchant's variable capital = b. This last consideration gives rise to the difficulty. Does b represent a new constituent of the price, or is it merely a part of the profit made by means of B + b, which appears as wages only so far as the mercantile wage-worker is concerned, and as concerns the merchant simply replaces variable capital? In the latter case, the merchant's profit on his advanced capital B + b would just equal the profit due to B by virtue of the general rate, plus b, which he pays out in the form of wages, but which does not itself yield a profit.

The crux of the matter is, indeed, to find the limits (mathematically speaking) of b. Let us first accurately define the problem. Let B stand for capital invested directly in buying and selling commodities, K for the constant capital (actual handling costs) consumed in this function, and b for the variable capital invested by the merchant.

Recovering B offers no difficulties at all. For the merchant it is simply the realised purchase price, and the price of production for the manufacturer. It is the price paid by the merchant, and in reselling he recovers B as part of his selling price; in addition to this B, he makes a profit on B, as previously explained. For example, let the commodity cost £100. Suppose the profit is 10%. In that case, the commodity is sold at 110. The commodity previously cost 100, and the merchant's capital of 100 merely adds 10 to it.

Now if we look at K, it is at most as large as, but in fact smaller than, the portion of constant capital which the producer would use up in buying and selling, but then it would form an addition to the constant capital he requires directly in production. This portion, nonetheless, must be continually recovered in the price of the commodity, or, what amounts to the same, a corresponding portion of the commodity must be continually expended in this form, or, from the standpoint of the total capital of society, must be continually reproduced in this form. This portion of the advanced constant capital would have a limiting effect on the rate of profit, just as the entire mass of it directly invested in production. In so far as the industrial capitalist leaves the commercial part of his business to the merchant, he need not advance this part of the capital. The merchant advances it in his stead. In a way, he does this but nominally, since a merchant neither produces, nor reproduces, the constant capital consumed by him (the actual handling costs). Its production appears a separate business, or at least a part of the business, of some industrial capitalists who thus play a role similar to those who supply constant capital to producers of necessities of life. First, therefore, the merchant has this constant capital recovered for him and, secondly, receives his profit on it. Through both of these, therefore, the industrial capitalist's profit is reduced. But owing to economising and concentration which are bound up with division of labour, it shrinks less than it would if he himself had to advance this capital. The reduction in the rate of profit is less, because the capital thus advanced is less.

So far, then, the selling price is made up of B + K + the profit on B + K. This portion of it offers no further difficulties. But now b, the variable capital advanced by the merchant, enters into it.

The resultant selling price is B + K + b + the profit on B + K + the profit on b.

B merely recovers the purchase price and adds nothing to it but the profit on B. K adds the profit on K, and K itself; but K + the profit on K, the part of the circulation costs advanced in the form of constant capital + the corresponding average profit, would be larger in the hands of the industrial capitalist than in the merchant's. The shrinking of the average profit appears in the form of the full average profit calculated after deducting B + K from the advanced industrial capital, with the deduction from the average profit on B + K paid to the merchant, so that this deduction appears as the profit of a specific capital, merchant's capital.

But the situation is different with respect to b + the profit on b, or, in the present case, where the rate of profit is assumed = 10%, with b + 1/10 b. And the real difficulty lies here.

What the merchant buys with b is, according to our assumption, nothing but commercial labour, hence labour required to perform the functions of circulating capital, C—M and M—C. But commercial labour is the labour generally necessary for a capital to operate as merchant's capital, to help convert commodities into money and money into commodities. It is labour which realises, but does not create, values. And only in so far as a capital performs these functions—hence a capitalist performs these operations, or this work with his capital—does it serve as merchant's capital and participate in regulating the general rate of profit, *i.e.*, draw its dividends out of the total profit. But (b + the profit on b) appears to include, first, payment for labour (for it makes no difference whether the industrial capitalist pays the merchant for his own labour, or the labour of the clerks paid by the merchant), and, secondly, the profit on the payment for this labour, which the merchant would have to perform in person. First, merchant's capital gets its b refunded, and, secondly, he makes the profit on it. This arises from the fact, therefore, that, first, it requires payment for the work whereby it operates as *merchant's* capital, and that, secondly, it demands the profit, because it operates as *capital, i.e.*, because it performs work for which profit is paid to it as functioning capital. This is, therefore, the question to be solved.

Let us assume that B = 100, b = 10, and the rate of profit = 10%. We take it that K = 0, in order to leave out of consideration this element of the purchase price, which does not belong here and has already been accounted for. Hence, the selling price would = B + p + b + p (= B + Bp' + b + bp'; where p stands for the rate of profit) = 100 + 40 + 10 + 1=121.

But if b were not invested by the merchant in wages—since b is paid only for commercial labour, hence labour required, to realise the value of the commodity—capital thrown on the market by industrial capital—the matter would stand as follows: to buy or sell for B = 100, the merchant would devote his time, and we wish to assume that this is the only time at his disposal. The commercial labour represented by b, or 10, if paid for by profit instead of wages, would presuppose another merchant's capital = 100, since at 10% this makes b = 10. This second B = 100 would not additionally go into the price of commodities, but the 10% would. There would, hence, be two operations at 100 = 200, that would buy commodities at 200 + 20 = 220.

Since merchant's capital is absolutely nothing but an individualised form of a portion of industrial capital engaged in the process of circulation, all questions referring to it must be solved by representing the problem primarily in a form; in which the phenomena peculiar to merchant's capital do not yet appear independently, but still in direct connection with industrial capital, as a branch of it. As an office, distinct from a workshop, mercantile capital operates continually in the circulation process. It is here—in the office of the industrial capitalist himself—that we must first analyse the b now under consideration.

The office is from the outset always infinitesimally small compared to the industrial workshop. As for the rest, it is clear that as the scale of production is extended, commercial operations required constantly for the circulation of industrial capital, in order to sell the product existing as commodity-capital, to reconvert the money so received into means of production, and to keep account of the whole process, multiply accordingly. Calculation of prices, book-keeping, managing funds, correspondence—all belong under this head. The more developed the scale of production, the greater, even if not proportionately greater, the commercial operations of the industrial capital, and consequently the labour and other costs of circulation involved in realising value and surplus-value. This necessitates the employment of commercial wage-workers who make up the actual office staff. The outlay for these, although made in the form of wages, differs from the variable capital laid out in purchasing productive labour. It increases the outlay of the industrial capitalist, the mass of the capital to be advanced, without directly increasing surplus-value. Because it is an outlay for labour employed solely in realising value already created. Like every other outlay of this kind, it reduces the rate of profit be-cause the advanced capital increases, but not the surplus-value. If surplus-value s remains constant while advanced capital C increases to C + ΔC, then the rate of profit s/C is replaced by the smaller rate of profit s/C + ΔC. The industrial capitalist endeavours, therefore, to cut these expenses of circulation down to a minimum, just as his expenses for constant capital. Hence, industrial capital does not maintain the same attitude to its commercial wage-labourers as it does to its productive wage-labourers. The more productive wage-labourers it employs under otherwise equal circumstances, the greater the output, and the greater the surplus-value, or profit. Conversely, however, the larger the scale of production, the greater the quantity of value and surplus-value to be realised, the greater the produced commodity-capital, the greater are the absolute, if not relative, office costs, giving rise to a kind of division of labour. To what extent profit is the precondition for these outlays, is seen, among other things, from the fact that with the increase of commercial salaries, a part of them is frequently paid by a share in the profit. It is in the nature of things that labour consisting merely of intermediate operations connected partly with calculating values, partly with realising them, and partly with reconverting the realised money into means of production, is a labour whose magnitude, therefore, depends on the quantity of the produced values that have to he realised, and does not act as the cause, like directly productive labour, but rather as an effect, of the respective magnitudes and masses of these values. The same applies to the other costs of circulation. To do much measuring, weighing, packing, and transporting, much must be on hand. The amount of packing, transporting, etc., depends on the quantity of commodities which are the objects of this activity, not vice versa.

The commercial worker produces no surplus-value directly. But the price of his labour is determined by the value of his labour-power, hence by its costs of production, while the application of this labour-power, its exertion, expenditure of energy, and wear and tear, is as in the ease of every other wage-labourer by no means limited by its value. His wage, therefore, is not necessarily proportionate to the mass of profit which he helps the capitalist to realise. What he costs the capitalist and what he brings in for him, are two different things. He creates no direct surplus-value, but adds to the capitalist's income by helping him to reduce the cost of realising surplus-value, inasmuch as he performs partly unpaid labour. The commercial worker, in the strict sense of the term, belongs to the better-paid class of wage-workers—to those whose labour is classed as skilled and stands above average labour. Yet the wage tends to fall, even in relation to average labour, with the advance of the capitalist mode of production. This is due partly to the division of labour in the office, implying a one-sided development of the labour capacity, the cost of which does not fall entirely on the capitalist, since the labourer's skill develops by itself through the exercise of his function, and all the more rapidly as division of labour makes it more one-sided. Secondly, because the necessary training, knowledge of commercial practices, languages, etc., is more and more rapidly, easily, universally and cheaply reproduced with the progress of science and public education the more the capitalist mode of production directs teaching methods, etc., towards practical purposes. The universality of public education enables capitalists to recruit such labourers from classes that formerly had no access to such trades and were accustomed to a lower standard of living. Moreover, this increases supply, and hence competition. With few exceptions, the labour-power of these people is, therefore, devaluated with the progress of capitalist production. Their wage falls, while their labour capacity increases. The capitalist increases the number of these labourers whenever he has more value and profits to realise. The increase of this labour is always a result, never a cause of more surplus-value.[2]

There is duplication, therefore. On the one hand, the functions as commodity-capital and money-capital (hence further designated as merchant's capital) are general definite forms assumed by industrial capital. On the other hand, specific capitals, and therefore specific groups of capitalists, are exclusively devoted to these functions; and these functions thus develop into specific spheres of self-expansion of capital.

In the case of mercantile capital, the commercial functions and circulation costs are found only in individualised form. That side of industrial capital which is devoted to circulation, continuously exists not only in the shape of commodity-capital and money-capital, but also in the office alongside the workshop. But it becomes independent in the case of mercantile capital. In the latter's case, the office is its only workshop. The portion of capital employed in the form of circulation costs appears much larger in the case of the big merchant than in that of the industrialist, because besides their own offices connected with every industrial workshop, that part of capital which would have to be so applied by the entire class of industrial capitalists is concentrated in the hands of a few merchants, who in carrying out the functions of circulation also provide for the growing expenses incidental to their continuation.

To industrial capital the costs of circulation appear as unproductive expenses, and so they are. To the merchant they appear as a source of his profit, proportional, given the general rate of profit, to their size. The outlay to be made for these circulation costs is, therefore, a productive investment for mercantile capital. And for this reason, the commercial labour which it buys is likewise immediately productive for it.

Notes

1. John Bellers [*Essays about the Poor, Manufactures, Trade, Plantations, and Immorality*, London, 1699, p. 10.—*Ed.*].
2. How well this forecast of the fate of the commercial proletariat, written in 1865, has stood the test of time can be corroborated by hundreds of German clerks, who are trained in all commercial operations and acquainted with three or four languages, and offer their services in vain in London City at 25 shillings per week, which is far below the wages of a good machinist. A blank of two pages in the manuscript indicates that this point was to have been treated at greater length. For the rest, we refer the reader to Book II (Kap. VI.) ('The Costs of Circulation') [English edition: Vol. II, Ch. VI.—*Ed.*], where various matters belonging under this head have already been discussed.—*F.E.*

18

The Turnover of Merchant's Capital Prices

The turnover of industrial capital is a combination of its period of production and time of circulation, and therefore, embraces the entire process of production. The turnover of merchant's capital, on the other hand, being in reality nothing but an alienated movement of commodity-capital, represents only the first phase in the metamorphosis of a commodity, C—M, as the refluent movement of a specific capital; M—C, C—M, is, from the mercantile point of view, the turnover of merchant's capital. The merchant buys, converting his money into commodities, then sells, converting the latter back into money, and so forth in constant repetition. Within circulation, the metamorphosis of industrial capital always presents itself in the form of C_1—M—C_2; the money realised by the sale of the produced commodity C_1 is used to purchase new means of production, C_2. This amounts to a practical exchange of C_1 for C_2, and the same money thus changes hands twice. Its movement mediates the exchange of two different kinds of commodities, C_1 and C_2. But in the case of the merchant, it is, conversely, the same commodity which changes hands twice in M—C—M'. It merely promotes the reflux of his money.

If, for example, a certain merchant's capital is £100, and for these £100 the merchant buys commodities and sells them for £110, then his capital of £100 has completed one turnover, and the number of such turnovers per year depends on the number of times this movement M—C—M' is repeated.

We here leave entirely out of consideration the costs which may be concealed in the difference between the purchase price and the selling price, since these do not alter in any way the form, which we are now analysing.

The number of turnovers of a given merchant's capital, therefore, is analogous in this case to the repeated cycles of money as a mere medium of circulation. Just as the same thaler buys ten times its value in commodities in making ten cycles, so the same money-capital of the merchant, when turned over ten times, buys ten times its value in commodities, or realises a total commodity-capital of ten times its value; a merchant's capital of 100, for instance, a ten-fold value = 1,000. But there is this difference: In the cycle of money as a medium of circulation it is the same piece of money that passes through different hands, thus repeatedly performing the same function and hence making up for the mass of the circulating pieces of money by its velocity. But in the merchant's case, it is the same money capital, the same money-value, regardless of what pieces of money it may be composed, which repeatedly buys and sells commodity-capital to the amount of its value and which therefore, returns to the same hands, the same point of departure as M + ΔM, *i.e.*, value plus surplus-value. This characterises its turnover as a capital turnover. It always withdraws more money from circulation than it throws in. It is self-evident, at any rate, that an accelerated turnover of merchant's capital (given a developed credit system, the function of money as a means of payment predominates) implies a more rapid circulation of the same quantity of money.

A repeated turnover of commercial capital, however, never connotes more than repeated buying and selling; while a repeated turnover of industrial capital connotes the periodicity and renovation of the entire reproduction process (which includes the process of consumption). For merchant's capital this appears merely as an external condition. Industrial capital must continually bring commodities to the market and withdraw them from it, in order that rapid turnover of merchant's capital may remain possible. If the process of reproduction is slow, then so is the turnover of merchant's capital. True, merchant's capital promotes the turnover of productive capital, but only in so far as it shortens its time of circulation. It has no direct influence on the time of production, which is also a barrier to the period of turnover of industrial capital. This is the first barrier for the turnover of merchant's capital. Secondly, aside from the barrier formed by reproductive consumption, the turnover of merchant's capital is ultimately limited by the velocity and volume of the total individual consumption, since all the commodity-capital which is part of the consumption-fund depends on it.

However (aside from the turnovers in the world of commerce, in which one merchant always sells the same commodity to another, and this sort of circulation may appear highly prosperous in times of speculation), the merchant's capital, in the first place, curtails phase C—M for productive capital. Secondly, under the modern credit system it disposes of a large portion of the total social money-capital, so that it can repeat its purchases even before it has definitely sold what has previously been purchased. And it is immaterial in this case, whether our merchant sells directly to the ultimate consumer, or there are a dozen other intermediate merchants between them. Owing to the immense elasticity of the reproduction process, which may always be pushed beyond any given bounds, it does not encounter any obstacle in production itself, or at best a very elastic one. Aside from the separation of C—M and M—C, which follows from the nature of the commodities, a fictitious demand is then created. In spite of its independent status, the movement of merchant's capital is never more than the movement of industrial capital within the sphere of circulation. But by virtue of its independent status it moves, within certain limits, independently of the bounds of the reproduction process and thereby even drives the latter beyond its bounds. This internal dependence and external independence push merchant's capital to a point where the internal connection is violently restored through a crisis.

Hence the phenomenon that crises do not come to the surface, do not break out, in the retail business first, which deals with direct consumption, but in the spheres of wholesale trade, and of banking, which places the money-capital of society at the disposal of the former.

The manufacturer may actually sell to the exporter, and the exporter, in his turn, to his foreign customer; the importer may sell his raw materials to the manufacturer, and the latter may sell his products to the wholesale merchant, etc. But at some particular imperceptible point the goods lie unsold, or else, again, all producers and middlemen may gradually become overstocked. Consumption is then generally at its highest, either because one industrial capitalist sets a succession of others in motion; or because the labourers employed by them are fully employed and have more to spend than usual. The capitalists' expenditures increase together with their growing income. Besides, as we have seen (Book II, Part III), continuous circulation takes place between constant capital and constant capital (even regardless of accelerated accumulation). It is at first independent of individual consumption because it never enters the latter. But this consumption definitely limits it nevertheless, since constant capital is never produced for its own sake but solely because more of it is needed in spheres of production whose products go into individual consumption. However, this may go on undisturbed for some time, stimulated by prospective demand, and in such branches, therefore, the business of merchants and industrialists goes briskly forth. The crisis occurs when the returns of merchants who sell in distant markets (or whose supplies have also accumulated on the home market) become so slow and meagre that the banks press for payment, or promissory notes for purchased commodities become due before the latter have been resold. Then forced sales take place, sales in order to meet payments. Then comes the crash, which brings the illusory prosperity to an abrupt end.

But the superficiality and meaninglessness of the turnover of merchant's capital are still greater, because the turnover of one and the same merchant's capital may simultaneously or successively promote the turnovers of several productive capitals.

The turnover of merchant's capital does not just promote the turnovers of several industrial capitals, it can also expedite the opposite phases of the metamorphosis of commodity-capital. For instance, the merchant buys linen from the manufacturer and sells it to the bleacher. In this case, therefore, the turnover of the same merchant's capital—in fact, the same C—M, a realisation of the linen—represents two opposite phases for two different industrial capitals. Inasmuch as the merchant sells for productive consumption, his C—M is always M—C for one industrial capitalist, and his M—C always C—M for another industrial capitalist.

If we leave out K, the circulation costs, as we do in this chapter, if, in other words, we leave aside that portion of capital which the merchant advances along with the money required to purchase commodities, it follows that we also omit ΔK, the additional profit made on this additional capital. This is thus the strictly logical and mathematically correct mode of analysis if we want to see how profit and turnover of merchant's capital affect prices.

If the price of production of 1 lb. of sugar were £1, the merchant could buy 100 lbs. of sugar with £100. If he buys and sells this quantity in the course of the year, and if the average annual rate of profit is 15%, he would add £15 to the £100, and 3s. to £1, the price of production of 1 lb. of sugar. That is, he would sell 1 lb. of sugar at £1.3s. But if the price of production of 1 lb. of sugar should fall to 1s., the merchant could buy 2,000 lbs. of sugar with £100, and sell the sugar at 1s. 1 4/5d. per lb. The annual profit on capital invested in the sugar business would still be £15 on each £100. But the merchant has to sell 100 lbs. in the first case, and 2,000 lbs. in the second. The high or low level of the price of production has nothing to do with the rate of profit. But it would greatly and decisively affect that aliquot part of the selling price of each lb. of sugar, which resolves itself in mercantile profit, *i.e.*, the addition to the price which the merchant makes on a certain quantity of commodities or products. If the price of production of a commodity is small, so, too, the amount the merchant advances in its purchase price, *i.e.*, for a certain quantity of it. Hence, with a given rate of profit, the amount of profit he makes on this quantity of cheap commodities is small as well. Or, what amounts to the same, he can then buy with a certain amount of capital, say, 100, a larger quantity of these cheap commodities, and the total profit of 15, which he makes per 100, breaks up into small fractions over each individual piece or portion belonging to this mass of commodities. If the opposite takes place, then the reverse is true. This depends entirely on the greater or smaller productivity of the industrial capital in whose products he trades. If we except the cases in which the merchant is a monopolist and simultaneously monopolises production, as did the Dutch East India Company in its day, nothing can be more ridiculous than the current idea that it depends on the merchant whether he sells many commodities at a small profit or few commodities at a large profit on each individual piece of the commodities. The two limits of his selling price are: on the one hand, the price of production of the commodities, over which he has no control; on the other hand, the average rate of profit, over which he has just as little control. The only thing up to him to decide is whether he wants to deal in dear or in cheap commodities, and even here the size of his available capital and other circumstances also have their effect. Therefore, it depends wholly on the degree of development of the capitalist mode of production, not on the merchant's goodwill, what course he shall follow. A purely commercial company like the old Dutch East India Company, which had a monopoly of production, could fancy that it could continue a method adapted at best to the beginnings of capitalist production, under entirely changed conditions.[1]

The following circumstances, among others, help to maintain that popular prejudice, which, like all false conceptions of profit, etc., arises from the observation of pure commerce and merchants' prejudice:

First: phenomena of competition, which, however, apply merely to the distribution of mercantile profit among individual merchants, the shareholders of the total merchant's capital; if one, for example, sells cheaper, in order to drive his competitors off the field.

Secondly: an economist of the calibre of Professor Roscher may still imagine in Leipzig that it was 'common sense and humanitarian' [Roscher, *Die Grundlagen der Nationalökonomie*, 3. Auflage, 1858, S. 192.—*Ed.*] grounds, which produced the change in selling prices, and that it was not a result of a revolutionised mode of production.

Thirdly: if production prices fall due to greater productivity of labour, and selling prices fall for the same reason, the demand, and with it the market-prices, often rise even faster than the supply, so that selling prices yield more than the average profit.

Fourthly: a merchant may reduce his selling price (which is never more than a reduction of the usual profit that he adds to the price) so as to turn over a larger capital more rapidly. All these are matters that only concern competition between the merchants themselves.

We have already shown in Book I [English edition: Vol. 1, pp. 519-20.—*Ed*]. that high or low commodity-prices do not determine either the mass of surplus-value produced by a given capital, or the rate of surplus-value; although the price of a commodity, and with it the share of surplus-value in this price, are greater or smaller, depending on the relative quantity of commodities produced by a given quantity of labour. The prices of every specified quantity of a commodity are, so far as they correspond to the values, determined by the total quantity of labour incorporated in this commodity. If little labour is incorporated in much commodity, the unit price of the commodity is low and the surplus-value in it is small. How this labour incorporated in a commodity breaks up into paid and unpaid labour and what portion of its price, therefore, represents surplus-value, has nothing to do with this total quantity of labour, nor, consequently, with the price of the commodity. But the rate of surplus-value does not depend on the absolute magnitude of the surplus-value contained in the unit price of the commodity. It depends on its relative magnitude, its proportion to the wages contained in the same commodity. The rate of surplus-value may therefore, be large, while the absolute magnitude of surplus-value in each unit of the commodity is small. This absolute magnitude of surplus-value in each piece of the commodity depends primarily on the productivity of labour, and only secondarily on its division into paid and unpaid labour.

Now, in the case of the commercial selling price, the price of production is a given external precondition.

The high commercial commodity-prices in former times were due 1) to the high prices of production, *i.e.*, the unproductiveness of labour; 2) to the absence of a general rate of profit, with merchant's capital absorbing a much larger quota of surplus-value than would have fallen to its share if capitals enjoyed greater general mobility. The ending of this situation, in both its aspects, is therefore, the result of the development of the capitalist mode of production.

The turnovers of merchant's capital vary in duration, their annual number consequently being greater or smaller, in different branches of commerce. Within the same branch the turnover is more or less rapid in the different phases of the economic cycle. Yet there is an average number of turnovers, determined by experience.

We have already seen that the turnover of merchant's capital differs from that of industrial capital. This is in the nature of things. One single phase in the turnover of industrial capital appears as a complete turnover of an independently constituted merchant's capital, or yet of its part. It also stands in a different relation to profit and price determination.

In the case of industrial capital, its turnover expresses, on the one hand, the periodicity of reproduction, and, therefore, the mass of commodities thrown on the market in a certain period depends on it. On the other hand, its time of circulation creates a barrier, an extensible one, and exerts more or less of a restraint on the creation of value and surplus-value, because it affects the volume of the production process. The turnover, therefore, acts as a determining element on the mass of annually produced surplus-value, and hence on the formation of the general rate of profit, but it acts as a limiting, rather than positive, element. For merchant's capital, on the contrary, the average rate of profit is a given magnitude. The merchant's capital does not directly participate in creating profit or surplus-value, and joins in shaping the general rate of profit only in so far as it draws a dividend proportionate to its share in the total capital, out of the mass of profit produced by industrial capital.

The greater the number of turnovers of an industrial capital under conditions described in Book II, Part II, the greater the mass of profit it creates. True, through the formation of a general rate of profit, the total profit is distributed among the different capitals not in proportion to their actual part in its production, but in proportion to the aliquot part they make up of the total capital, *i.e.*, in proportion to their magnitude. But this does not alter the essence of the matter. The greater the number of turnovers of the total industrial capital, the greater the mass of profits, the mass of annually produced surplus-value, and, therefore, other circumstances remaining unchanged, the rate of profit. It is different with merchant's capital. The rate of profit is a given magnitude with respect to it, determined on the one hand by the mass of profit produced by industrial capital, and on the other by the relative magnitude of the total merchant's capital, by its quantitative relation to the sum of capital advanced in the processes of production and circulation. The number of its turnovers does, indeed, decisively affect its relation to the total capital, or the relative magnitude of merchant's capital required for the circulation, for it is evident that the absolute magnitude of the required merchant's capital and the velocity of its turnovers stand in inverse proportion. But, all other conditions remaining equal, the relative magnitude of merchant's capital, or the part it makes up of the total capital, is determined by its absolute magnitude. If the total capital is 10,000, and the merchant's capital 1/10 of that sum, it is = 1,000; if the total capital is 1,000, then 1/10 of it = 100. The absolute magnitude of merchant's capital varies, depending on the magnitude of the total capital, although its relative magnitude remains the same. But here we assume that its relative magnitude, say, 1/10 of the total capital, is given. This relative magnitude, however, is again determined by the turnover. If it is turned over rapidly, its absolute magnitude, for example, will = £1,000 in the first case, = 100 in the second, and hence its relative magnitude = 1/10. With a slower turnover its absolute magnitude is, say, = 2,000 in the first case, and = 200 in the second. Its relative magnitude will then have increased from 1/10 to 1/5 of the total capital. Circumstances which reduce the average turnover of merchant's capital, like the development of means of transportation, for instance, reduce *pro tanto* the absolute magnitude of merchant's capital, and thereby increase the general rate of profit. If the opposite takes place, then the reverse is true. A developed capitalist mode of production, compared with earlier conditions, exerts a two-fold influence on merchant's capital. On the one hand, the same quantity of commodities is turned over with a smaller mass of actually functioning merchant's capital; owing to the more rapid turnover of merchant's capital, and the more rapid reproduction process, on which this depends, the relation of merchant's capital to industrial capital diminishes. On the other hand, with the development of the capitalist mode of production all production becomes the production of commodities, which places all products into the hands of agents of circulation. It is to be added that under the previous mode of production, which produced on a small scale, a very large portion of the producers sold their goods directly to the consumers, or worked on their personal orders, save for the mass of products consumed directly, in kind, by the producer himself, and the mass of services performed in kind. While, therefore, under former modes of production commercial capital was greater in relation to the commodity-capital which it turned over, it was:

1. Absolutely smaller, because a disproportionately smaller part of the total product was produced as commodities, and passed as commodity-capital into circulation, falling into the hands of merchants. It was smaller, because the commodity-capital was smaller. But at the same time it was proportionately larger, not only because its turnover was slower and not only in relation to the mass of commodities turned over by it. It was larger also because the price of this mass of commodities, and hence the merchant's capital to be advanced for it, were greater than under capitalist production on account of a lower productivity of labour, so that the same value was incorporated in a smaller mass of commodities.
2. It is not only that a larger mass of commodities is produced on the basis of capitalist production (taking into account also the reduced value of this mass of commodities), but the same mass of products, for instance, of corn, also forms a greater commodity mass, *i.e.*, more and more of it becomes an object of commerce. As a consequence, there is an increase not only of the mass of

merchant's capital, but of all capital applied in circulation, such as in marine shipping, railways, telegraph, etc.

3. However, and this is an aspect which belongs to the discussion of 'competition among capitals': idle or only half-functioning merchant's capital grows with the progress of the capitalist mode of production, with the ease of entering retail trade, with speculation, and the redundance of released capital.

But, assuming the relative magnitude of merchant's capital to total capital to be given, the difference of turnovers in the various branches of commerce does not affect either the magnitude of the total profit falling to the share of merchant's capital, or the general rate of profit. The merchant's profit is not determined by the mass of commodity-capital turned over by him, but by the dimensions of the money-capital advanced by him to promote this turnover. If the general annual rate of profit is 15%, and the merchant advances £100, which he turns over once a year, he will sell his commodities at 115. If his capital turns over five times a year, he will sell a commodity-capital he bought at 100 at 103 five times a year, hence in a year a commodity-capital of 500 at 515. This gives the same annual profit of 15 on his advanced capital of 100. If this were not so, merchant's capital would yield a much higher profit, proportionate to the number of its turnovers, than industrial capital, which would be in conflict with the law of the general rate of profit.

Hence, the number of turnovers of merchant's capital in the various branches of commerce has a direct influence on the mercantile prices of commodities. The amount added to the mercantile price, the aliquot part of mercantile profit of a given capital, which falls upon the price of production of a commodity, is in inverse proportion to the number of turnovers, or the velocity of turnover, of merchants' capitals in the various lines of commerce. If a certain merchant's capital is turned over five times a year, it will add to a commodity-capital of equal value but 1/5 of what another merchant's capital, which turns over just once a year, adds to a commodity-capital of equal value.

The modification of selling prices by the average period of turnover of capitals in different branches of commerce amounts to this: The same mass of profits, determined for any given magnitude of merchant's capital by the general annual rate of profit, hence determined independently of the specific character of the commercial operations of this capital, is differently distributed—proportionately to the rate of turnover—over masses of commodities of equal value, so that, for instance, if a merchant's capital is turned over five times a year, 15/5 = 3% if once a year, 15%, is added to the price of the commodities.

The same percentage of commercial profit in different branches of commerce, therefore, increases the selling prices of commodities by quite different percentages of their values, all depending on their periods of turnover.

On the other hand, in the case of industrial capital, the period of turnover does not in any way affect the magnitude of the value of individual commodities produced, although it does affect the mass of values and surplus-values produced in a given time by a given capital, because it affects the mass of exploited labour. This is concealed, to be sure, and seems to be otherwise as soon as one turns to prices of production. But this is due solely to the fact that, according to previously analysed laws, the prices of production of various commodities deviate from their values. If we look upon the process of production as a whole, and upon the mass of commodities produced by the total industrial capital, we shall at once find the general law vindicated.

While, therefore, a closer inspection of the influence of the period of turnover on the formation of values by industrial capital leads us back to the general law and to the basis of political economy, that the values of commodities are determined by the labour-time contained in them, the influence of the turnovers of merchant's capital on mercantile prices reveals phenomena which, without benefit of a very far-reaching analysis of the connecting links, seem to point to a purely arbitrary determination of prices; namely, that they are fixed by a capital simply bent upon pocketing a certain quantity of profit in a year. Due particularly to this influence of turnovers, it appears that within certain limits the process of circulation as such determines commodity-prices independently of the process of production. All superficial and false conceptions of the process of reproduction as a whole are derived from examinations of merchant's capital and from the conceptions which its peculiar movements call forth in the minds of circulation agents.

If, as the reader will have realised to his great dismay, the analysis of the actual intrinsic relations of the capitalist process of production is a very complicated matter and very extensive; if it is a work of science to resolve the visible, merely external movement into the true intrinsic movement, it is self-evident that conceptions which arise about the laws of production in the minds of agents of capitalist production and circulation will diverge drastically from these real laws and will merely be the conscious expression of the visible movements. The conceptions of the merchant, stockbroker, and banker, are necessarily quite distorted. Those of the manufacturers are vitiated by the acts of circulation to which their capital is subject, and by the levelling of the general rate of profit.[2] Competition likewise assumes a completely distorted role in their minds. If the limits of value and surplus-value are given, it is easy to grasp how competition of capitals transforms values into prices of production and further into mercantile prices, and surplus-value into average profit. But without these limits, it is absolutely unintelligible why competition should reduce the general rate of profit to one level instead of another, *e.g.*, make it 15% instead of 1,500%. Competition can at best only reduce the general rate of profit to *one* level. But it contains no element by which it could determine this level itself.

From the standpoint of merchant's capital, therefore, it is the turnover which appears to determine prices. On the other hand, while the rate of turnover of industrial capital, in so far as it enables a certain capital to exploit more or less labour, exerts a determining and limiting influence on the mass of profit, and thus on the general rate of profit, this rate of profit obtains for merchant's capital as an external fact, its internal connection with the production of surplus-value being entirely obliterated. If, under otherwise equal circumstances and particularly the same organic composition, the same industrial capital is turned over four times a year instead of twice, it produces twice as much surplus-value and, consequently, profit. And this is apparent as soon, and as long, as this capital has a monopoly on an improved method of production, which makes this accelerated turnover possible. Conversely, differences in the periods of turnover in different branches of commerce manifest themselves in the fact that profit made on the turnover of a given commodity-capital is in inverse proportion to the number of times the money-capital turns over this commodity-capital. Small profits and quick returns appear to the shopkeeper to be the principle which he follows out of sheer principle.

For the rest, it is self-evident that regardless of alternating, mutually compensating, speedier and slower turnovers, this law of turnover of merchant's capital holds good in each branch of commerce only for the average turnovers made by the entire merchant's capital invested in each particular branch. The capital of A, who deals in the same branch as B, may make more or less than the average number of turnovers. In this case, the others make less or more. This does not alter the turnover of the total mass of merchant's capital invested in this line. But it is of decisive moment for the individual merchant or shopkeeper. In this case, he makes an extra profit, just as industrial capitalists make extra profits if they produce under better than average conditions. If competition compels him, he can sell cheaper than his competitors without lowering his profit below the average. If the conditions which would enable him to turn over his capital more rapidly, are themselves for sale, such as a favourable shop location, he can pay extra rent for it, *i.e.*, convert a portion of his surplus-profit into ground-rent.

Notes

1. 'Profit, on the general principle, is always the same, whatever be price; keeping its place like an incumbent body on the swelling or sinking tide. As, therefore, prices rise, a tradesman raises price; as prices fall, a tradesman lowers price.' (Corbet, *An Inquiry into the Causes, etc., of the Wealth of Individuals*, London, 1841, p. 20.) Here, as in the text generally; it is only a matter of ordinary commerce, not of speculation. The analysis of speculation, as well as everything else pertaining to the division of mercantile capital, falls outside the field of our inquiry. 'The profit of trade is a value added to capital which is independent of price, the second' (speculation) 'is founded on the variation in the value of capital or in price itself' (1. c., p. 128).
2. This is a very naive, but also a very correct remark: 'Surely the fact that one and the same commodity may be had from different sellers at considerably different prices is frequently due to mistakes of calculation.' (Feller and Odermann, *Das Ganze der kaufmännischen Arithmetik*, 7th ed., 1859, S.451.) This shows how purely theoretical, that is, abstract, becomes the determination of prices.

19

Money-Dealing Capital

The purely technical movements performed by money in the circulation process of industrial, and, as we may now add, of commercial capital (since it takes over a part of the circulation movement of industrial capital as its own, peculiar movement), if individualised as a function of some particular capital performing just these, and only these, operations as its specific operations, convert this capital into money-dealing capital. A portion of industrial capital, and, more precisely, also of commercial capital, not only obtains all the time in the form of money, as money-capital in general, but as money-capital engaged precisely in these technical functions. A definite part of the total capital dissociates itself from the rest and stands apart in the form of money-capital, whose capitalist function consists exclusively in performing these operations for the entire class of industrial and commercial capitalists. As in the case of commercial capital, a portion of industrial capital engaged in the circulation process in the form of money-capital separates from the rest and performs these operations of the reproduction process for all the other capital. The movements of this money-capital are, therefore, once more merely movements of an individualised part of industrial capital engaged in the reproduction process.

It is only when, and in so far as, capital is newly invested—which also applies to accumulation—that capital in money-form appears as the starting-point and the end result of the movement. But for all capitals already engaged in the process, these first and last points appear merely as points of transit. Since, as already seen in the case of simple commodity-circulation, from the moment of leaving the sphere of production to the moment of its re-entry industrial capital undergoes the metamorphosis C'—M—C, M, in fact, represents the end result of one phase of the metamorphosis, just to become the starting-point of the reverse phase, which supplements it. And although the C—M of industrial capital is always M—C—M for merchant's capital, the actual process for the latter is continually also C—M—C once it has begun to function. But it performs the acts C—M and M—C simultaneously. This is to say that there is not just *one* capital in the stage C—M while another is in the stage M—C, but that the same capital buys continually and sells continually at one and the same time because of the continuity of the production process. It is to be found always in both stages at one and the same time. While one of its parts turns into money, later to be reconverted into commodities, another turns simultaneously into commodities, to be reconverted into money.

It all depends on the form of the commodity exchange whether the money serves here as a means of circulation or of payment. In both cases, the capitalist has to pay out money constantly to many persons, and to receive money continually from many persons. This purely technical operation of disbursing and receiving money is in itself labour which, as long as the money serves as a means of payment, necessitates drawing up payment balances and acts of balancing accounts. This labour is a cost of circulation, *i.e.*, not labour creating value. It is shortened in being carried out by a special section of agents, or capitalists, for the rest of the capitalist class.

A definite portion of the capital must be on hand constantly as a hoard, as potential money-capital—a reserve of means of purchase, a reserve of means of payment, and idle capital in the form of money waiting to be put to work. Another portion streams back continually in this form. Aside from collecting, paying, and book-keeping, this entails safekeeping the hoard, which is an operation all in itself. It is, indeed, a continuous conversion of the hoard into means of circulation and means of payment, and its restoration by means of money secured through sales and from payments due. This constant movement of the part of capital existing as money, dissociated from the function of capital itself, this purely technical function, causes its own labour and expense, classified as costs of circulation.

The division of labour brings it about that these technical operations, dependent upon the functions of capital, should be performed for the entire capitalist class as much as possible by a special section of agents or capitalists as their exclusive function—or that these operations should be concentrated in their hands. We have here, as in merchant's capital, division of labour in a two-fold sense. It becomes a specialised business, and because performed as a specialised business for the money-mechanism of the whole class, it is concentrated and conducted on a large scale. A further division of labour takes place within it, both through division into various independent branches, and through segmentation of work within these branches (large offices, numerous book-keepers and cashiers, and far-reaching division of labour). Paying and receiving money, settling accounts, keeping current accounts, storing money, etc.—all this, dissociated from the acts necessitating these technical operations, makes money-dealing capital of the capital advanced for these functions.

The various operations, whose individualisation into specific businesses gives rise to the money trade, spring from the different purposes of money itself and from its functions, which capital in its money-form must therefore, likewise carry out.

I have pointed out earlier that finance developed originally from the exchange of products between different communities.[1]

Trading in money, commerce in the money-commodity, first developed, therefore, out of international commerce. Ever since different national coins have existed merchants buying in foreign countries have had to exchange their national coins for local coins, and vice versa, or to exchange different coins for uncoined pure silver or gold—the world-money. Hence the exchange business which is to be regarded as one of the natural foundations of modern finance.[2] Out of it developed banks of exchange, in which silver (or gold) serves as world-money—now called bank money or commercial money—as distinct from currency. Exchange transactions, in the sense of mere notes of payment to travellers from a money-changer in one country to a changer in another country, developed back in Rome and Greece out of the actual money-changing.

Trading in gold and silver as commodities (raw materials for the making of luxury articles) is the natural basis of the bullion trade, or the trade which acts as a medium for the functions of money as universal money. These functions, as previously explained (Buch

I, Kap. III, 3, c [English edition: Ch. III, 3, c.—*Ed.*]), are two-fold: currency movement back and forth between the various national spheres of circulation in order to balance international payments and in connection with the migrations of capital in quest of interest; simultaneously, flow of precious metals from their sources of production via the world-market and their distribution among the various national spheres of circulation. Goldsmiths acted as bankers still during the greater part of the 17th century in England. We shall completely disregard the way in which the balancing of international accounts developed further in the bill jobbing, etc., and everything referring to transactions in valuable papers; in short, we shall leave out of consideration all special forms of the credit system, which do not as yet concern us here.

National money discards its local character in the capacity of universal money; one national currency is expressed in another, and thus all of them are finally reduced to their content of gold or silver, while the latter, being the two commodities circulating as world-money, are simultaneously reduced to their reciprocal value-ratio, which changes continually. It is this intermediate operation which the money trader makes his special occupation. Money-changing and the bullion trade are thus the original forms of the money trade, and spring from the two-fold functions of money—as national money and world-money.

The capitalist process of production, just as commerce in general, even under pre-capitalist methods, imply:

First, the accumulation of money as a hoard, *i.e.*, here as that part of capital which must always be on hand in the form of money as a reserve fund of means of payment and purchase. This is the first form of a hoard, as it reappears under the capitalist mode of production, and as it appears generally with the development of merchant's capital, at least for the purposes of this capital. Both remarks apply to national, as well as international, circulation. The hoard is in continuous flux, pours ceaselessly into circulation, and returns ceaselessly from it. The second form of a hoard is that of idle, temporarily unemployed capital in the shape of money, including newly accumulated and not yet invested money-capital. The functions entailed by this formation of a hoard are primarily those of safekeeping, bookkeeping, etc.

Secondly, however, this involves outlays of money for purchases, collecting money from sales, making and receiving payments, balancing payments, etc. The money-dealer performs all these services at first as a simple *cashier* of the merchants and industrial capitalists.[3]

The money trade becomes fully developed, even in its first stages, as soon as its ordinary functions are supplemented by lending and borrowing and by credit. Of this more in the next part, which deals with interest-bearing capital.

The bullion trade itself, the transfer of gold or silver from one country to another, is merely the result of trading in commodities. It is determined by the rate of exchange which expresses the standing of international payments and the interest rates in the different markets. The bullion trader as such acts merely as an intermediary of the results.

In discussing money and the way its movements and forms develop out of simple commodity-circulation, we saw (Book 1 Ch. III) that the movements of the mass of money circulating as means of purchase and payment depend on the metamorphosis of commodities, on the volume and velocity of this metamorphosis, which we now know to be but a phase in the entire process of reproduction. As for securing the money materials—gold and silver—from their sources of production, this resolves itself into a direct exchange of commodities, an exchange of gold and silver as commodities for other commodities. Hence, it is itself as much a phase of the exchange of commodities as the securing of iron or other metals. However, so far as the movement of precious metals on the world-market is concerned (we here leave aside movements expressing the transfer of capital by loans—a type of transfer which also obtains in the shape of commodity-capital), it is quite as much determined by the international exchange of commodities as the movement of money as a national means of purchase and payment is determined by the exchange of commodities in the home market. The inflow and outflow of precious metals from one national sphere of circulation to another, inasmuch as this is caused merely by a depreciation of the national currency, or by a double standard, are alien to money circulation as such and merely represent corrections of deviations brought about arbitrarily by state decrees. Finally, as concerns the formations of hoards which constitute reserve funds for means of purchase and payment, be it for home or foreign trade, and which also merely represent a form of temporarily idle capital, they are in both cases necessary precipitates of the circulation process.

If the entire circulation of money is in volume, form and movement purely a result of commodity-circulation, which, in its turn, from the capitalist point of view, is only the circulation process of capital (also embracing the exchange of capital for revenue, and of revenue for revenue, so far as outlay of revenue is effected through retail trade), it is self-evident that dealing in money does not merely promote the circulation of money, a mere result and phenomenon of commodity-circulation. This circulation of money itself, a phase in commodity-circulation, is taken for granted in money-dealing. What the latter promotes is merely the technical operations of money circulation which it concentrates, shortens, and simplifies. Dealing in money does not form the hoards. It provides the technical means by which the formation of hoards may, so far as it is voluntary (hence, not an expression of unemployed capital or of disturbances in the reproduction process), be reduced to its economic minimum because, if managed for the capitalist class as a whole, the reserve funds of means of purchase and payment need not be as large as they would have to be if each capitalist were to manage his own. The money-dealers do not buy the precious metals. They merely handle their distribution as soon as the commodity trade has bought them. They facilitate the settling of balances, inasmuch as money serves as the means of payment, and reduce through the artificial mechanism of these settlements the amount of money required for this purpose. But they do not determine either the connections, or the volume, of the mutual payments. The bills of exchange and the cheques, for instance, which are exchanged for one another in banks and clearing houses, represent quite independent transactions and are the results of given operations, and it is merely a question of a better technical settlement of these results. So far as money circulates as a means of purchase, the volume and number of purchases and sales have no connection whatever with money-dealing. The latter can do no more than shorten the technical operations that go with buying and selling, and thus reduce the amount of cash money required to turn over the commodities.

Money-dealing in its pure form, which we consider here, *i.e.*, set apart from the credit system, is thus concerned only with the technique of a certain phase of commodity-circulation, namely, that of money circulation and the different functions of money arising in its circulation.

This substantially distinguishes dealing in money from the dealing in commodities, which promotes the metamorphosis of commodities and their exchange, or even gives this process of the commodity-capital the appearance of a process of a capital set apart from industrial capital. While, therefore, commercial capital has its own form of circulation, M—C—M, in which the commodity changes hands twice and thus provides a reflux of money, as distinct from C—M—C, in which money changes hands twice and thus promotes commodity exchange, there is no such special form in the case of money-dealing capital.

In so far as money-capital is advanced by a separate class of capitalists in this technical promotion of money circulation—a capital which on a reduced scale represents the additional capital the merchants and industrial capitalists would otherwise have to advance themselves for these purposes—the general form of capital, M—M', occurs here as well. By advancing M, the advancing capitalist secures M + ΔM. But promotion of M—M' does not here concern the material, but only the technical, processes of the metamorphosis.

It is evident that the mass of money-capital with which the money-dealers operate is the money-capital of merchants and industrial capitalists in the process of circulation, and that the money-dealers' operations are actually operations of merchants and industrial capitalists, in which they act as middlemen.

It is equally evident that the money-dealers' profit is nothing but a deduction from the surplus-value, since they operate with already realised values (even when realised in the form of creditors' claims).

Just as in the commodity trade, there is a duplication of functions, because a part of the technical operations connected with money circulation must be carried out by the dealers and producers of commodities themselves.

Notes

1. *Zur Kritik der politischen Oekonomie*, S. 27.
2. 'The great differences among coins as concerns their grain and coinage by many princes and towns that were privileged to coin money, necessitated the creation of business establishments to enable merchants to use local money wherever compensation for the different coins was required. To be able to make cash payments, merchants who travelled to a foreign market provided themselves with uncoined pure silver, or gold. In the same way they exchanged money received in local markets for uncoined silver or gold when returning home. The business of exchanging money, the exchange of uncoined precious metals for local coins, and vice versa, thus became a widespread and paying business.' (Hüllmann, *Städtewesen des Mittelalters*. Bonn, 1826-29, I, S. 437-38.) 'Banks of exchange do not owe their name to the fact that they issue bills of exchange... but to the fact that they used to exchange coins. Long before the establishment of the Amsterdam Bank of Exchange in 1609, there existed in the Dutch merchant towns money-changers and exchange houses, even exchange banks ... The business of these money-changers consisted in exchanging the numerous varieties of coin brought into the country by foreign traders for the currency of the realm. Gradually their circle of activity extended ... They became the bankers and cashiers of their times. But the government of Amsterdam viewed as dangerous the combination of cashier and exchange businesses, and to meet this danger it was resolved to establish a large chartered institution able to perform both the cashier and exchange operations. This institution was the famous Amsterdam Bank of Exchange of 1609. In like manner, the exchange banks of Venice, Genoa, Stockholm, Hamburg, owe their origin to the continual necessity of changing money. Of all these, the Hamburg Exchange is the only one today still doing business, because the need for such an institution is still felt in that merchants' town, which has no Mint of its own, etc.' (S. Vissering, *Handboek van Praktische Staathuishoudkunde*, Amsterdam, 1860-61, I, 247-48.)
3. 'The institution of cashier has probably nowhere preserved its original independent character so pure as in the Dutch merchant towns' (cf. on the origin of the cashier business in Amsterdam. E. Lusac, *Holland's Rykdom*, Part III). 'Its functions coincide in part with those of the old Amsterdam Bank of Exchange. The cashier receives from the merchants, who employ his services, a certain amount of money, for which he opens a 'credit' for them in his books. Later, they send him their claims, which he collects for them and credits to their account. At the same time, he makes payments on their drafts *(kassiers briefes)* and charges the amounts to their account. He makes a small charge for these receipts and payments, which yields him a remuneration for his labours only corresponding to the size of the turnover accomplished between the two parties. If payments are to be balanced between two merchants, who both deal with the same cashier, such payments are settled very simply by mutual entries in the books, for the cashiers balance their mutual claims from day to day. The cashier's actual business thus consists basically of this mediation in payments. Therefore, it excludes industrial enterprises, speculation, and opening of unlimited credits; for it must be the rule in this business that the cashier makes no payment over and above the credit of any one keeping an account with him.' (Vissering, *loc. cit.*, p. 434.) Re the banking associations of Venice: 'The requirements and locality of Venice, where carrying

bullion was less convenient than in other places, induced the large merchants of that city to found banking associations under due safeguards, supervision and management. Members of such associations deposited certain sums, on which they drew drafts for their creditors, whereupon the paid sum was deducted from the debtor's account on the page of the book reserved for that purpose and added to the sum credited in the same book to the creditor. This is the earliest beginning of the so-called giro banks. These associations are indeed old. But if attributed to the 12th century, they are being confounded with the State Loan Institute established in 1171.' (Hüllmann, *Loc. cit.*, pp. 453-54.)

20

Historical Facts about Merchant's Capital

The particular form in which commercial and money-dealing capitals accumulate money will be discussed in the next part.

It is self-evident from what has gone before that nothing could be more absurd than to regard merchant's capital, whether in the shape of commercial or of money-dealing capital, as a particular variety of industrial capital, such as, say, mining, agriculture, cattle-raising, manufacturing, transport, etc., which are side lines of industrial capital occasioned by the division of social labour, and hence different spheres of investment. The simple observation that in the circulation phase of its reproduction process every industrial capital performs as commodity-capital and as money-capital the very functions which appear as the exclusive functions of the two forms of merchant's capital, should rule out such a crude notion. On the other hand, in commercial and money-dealing capital the differences between industrial capital as productive capital and the same capital in the sphere of circulation are individualised through the fact that the definite forms and functions which capital assumes for the moment appear as independent forms and functions of a separate portion of the capital and are exclusively bound up with it. The transmuted form of industrial capital and the material differences between productive capitals applied in different branches of industry, which arise from the nature of these various branches, are worlds apart.

Aside from the crudity with which the economist generally considers distinctions of form, which really concern him only from their substantive side, this misconception by the vulgar economist is explained on two additional counts. First, his inability to explain the peculiar nature of mercantile profit; and, secondly, his apologetic endeavours to deduce commodity-capital and money-capital, and later commercial capital and money-dealing capital as forms arising necessarily from the process of production as such, whereas they are due to the specific form of the capitalist mode of production, which above all presupposes the circulation of commodities, and hence of money, as its basis.

If commercial capital and money-dealing capital do not differ from grain production any more than this differs from cattle-raising and manufacturing, it is plain as day that production and capitalist production are altogether identical, and that, among other things, the distribution of the social products among the members of a society, be it for productive or individual consumption, must just as consistently be handled by merchants and bankers as the consumption of meat by cattle-raising and that of clothing by their manufacture.[1]

The great economists, such as Smith, Ricardo, etc., are perplexed over mercantile capital being a special variety, since they consider the basic form of capital, capital as industrial capital, and circulation capital (commodity-capital and money-capital) solely because it is a phase in the reproduction process of every capital. The rules concerning the formation of value, profit, etc., immediately deduced by them from their study of industrial capital, do not extend directly to merchant's capital. For this reason, they leave merchant's capital entirely aside and mention it only as a kind of industrial capital. Wherever they make a special analysis of it, as Ricardo does in dealing with foreign trade, they seek to demonstrate that it creates no value (and consequently no surplus-value). But whatever is true of foreign trade, is also true of home trade.

Hitherto we have considered merchant's capital merely from the standpoint, and within the limits, of the capitalist mode of production. However, not commerce alone, but also merchant's capital, is older than the capitalist mode of production, is, in fact, historically the oldest free state of existence of capital.

Since we have already seen that money-dealing and the capital advanced for it require nothing more for their development than the existence of wholesale commerce, and further of commercial capital, it is only the latter which we must occupy ourselves with here.

Since merchant's capital is penned in the sphere of circulation, and since its function consists exclusively of promoting the exchange of commodities, it requires no other conditions for its existence—aside from the undeveloped forms arising from direct barter—outside those necessary for the simple circulation of commodities and money. Or rather, the latter is the condition of *its* existence. No matter what the basis on which products are produced, which are thrown into circulation as commodities—whether the basis of the primitive community, of slave production, of small peasant and petty bourgeois, or the capitalist basis, the character of products as commodities is not altered, and as commodities they must pass through the process of exchange and its attendant changes of form. The extremes between which merchant's capital acts as mediator exist for it as given, just as they are given for money and for its movements. The only necessary thing is that these extremes should be on hand as commodities, regardless of whether production is wholly a production of commodities, or whether only the surplus of the independent producers' immediate needs, satisfied by their own production, is thrown on the market. Merchant's capital promotes only the movements of these extremes, of these commodities, which are preconditions of its own existence.

The extent to which products enter trade and go through the merchants' hands depends on the mode of production, and reaches its maximum in the ultimate development of capitalist production, where the product is produced solely as a commodity, and not as a direct means of subsistence. On the other hand, on the basis of every mode of production, trade facilitates the production of surplus-products destined for exchange, in order to increase the enjoyments, or the wealth, of the producers (here meant are the owners of the products). Hence, commerce imparts to production a character directed more and more towards exchange-value.

The metamorphosis of commodities, their movement, consists 1) materially, of the exchange of different commodities for one another, and 2) formally, of the conversion of commodities into money by sale, and of money into commodities by purchase. And the function of merchant's capital resolves itself into these very acts of buying and selling commodities. It therefore merely promotes the exchange of commodities; yet this exchange is not to be conceived at the outset as a bare exchange of commodities between direct producers. Under slavery, feudalism and vassalage (so far as primitive communities are concerned) it is the slave-owner, the feudal lord, the tribute-collecting state, who are the owners, hence sellers, of the products. The merchant buys and sells for many. Purchases and sales are concentrated in his hands and consequently are no longer bound to the direct requirements of the buyer (as merchant).

But whatever the social organisation of the spheres of production whose commodity exchange the merchant promotes, his wealth exists always in the form of money, and his money always serves as capital. Its form is always M—C—M'. Money, the independent form of exchange-value, is the point of departure, and increasing the exchange-value an end in itself. Commodity exchange as such and the operations effecting it—separated from production and performed by non-producers—are just a means of increasing wealth not as mere wealth, but as wealth in its most universal social form, as exchange-value. The compelling motive and determining purpose are the conversion of M into M + ΔM. The transactions M—C and C—M', which promote M—M', appear merely as stages of transition in this conversion of M into M + ΔM. This M—C—M', the characteristic movement of merchant's capital, distinguishes it from C—M—C, trade in commodities directly between producers, which has for its ultimate end the exchange of use-values.

The less developed the production, the more wealth in money is concentrated in the hands of merchants or appears in the specific form of merchants' wealth.

Within the capitalist mode of production—*i.e.*, as soon as capital has established its sway over production and imparted to it a wholly changed and specific form—merchant's capital appears merely as a capital with a *specific* function. In all previous modes of production, and all the more, wherever production ministers to the immediate wants of the producer, merchant's capital appears to perform the function *par excellence* of capital.

There is, therefore, not the least difficulty in understanding why merchant's capital appears as the historical form of capital long before capital established its own domination over production. Its existence and development to a certain level are in themselves historical premises for the development of capitalist production 1) as premises for the concentration of money wealth, and 2) because the capitalist mode of production presupposes production for trade, selling on a large scale, and not to the individual customer, hence also a merchant who does not buy to satisfy his personal wants but concentrates the purchases of many buyers in his one purchase. On the other hand, all development of merchant's capital tends to give production more and more the character of production for exchange-value and to turn products more and more into commodities. Yet its development, as we shall presently see, is incapable by itself of promoting and explaining the transition from one mode of production to another.

Within capitalist production merchant's capital is reduced from its former independent existence to a special phase in the investment of capital, and the levelling of profits reduces its rate of profit to the general average. It functions only as an agent of productive capital. The special social conditions that take shape with the development of merchant's capital, are here no longer paramount. On the contrary, wherever merchant's capital still predominates we find backward conditions. This is true even within one and the same country, in which, for instance, the specifically merchant towns present far more striking analogies with past conditions than industrial towns.[2]

The independent and predominant development of capital as merchant's capital is tantamount to the non-subjection of production to capital, and hence to capital developing on the basis of an alien social mode of production which is also independent of it. The independent development of merchant's capital, therefore, stands in inverse proportion to the general economic development of society.

Independent mercantile wealth as a predominant form of capital represents the separation of the circulation process from its extremes, and these extremes are the exchanging producers themselves. They remain independent of the circulation process, just as the latter remains independent of them. The product becomes a commodity by way of commerce. It is commerce which here turns products into commodities, not the produced commodity which by its movements gives rise to commerce. Thus, capital appears here first as capital in the process of circulation. It is in the circulation process that money develops into capital. It is in circulation that products first develop as exchange-values, as commodities and as money. Capital can, and must, form in the process of circulation, before it learns to control its extremes—the various spheres of production between which circulation mediates. Money and commodity circulation can mediate between spheres of production of widely different organisation, whose internal structure is still chiefly adjusted to the output of use-values. This individualisation of the circulation process, in which spheres of production are interconnected by means of a third, has a two-fold significance. On the one hand, that circulation has not as yet established a hold on production, but is related to it as to a given premise. On the other hand, that the production process has not as yet absorbed circulation as a mere phase of production. Both, however, are the case in capitalist production. The production process rests wholly upon circulation, and circulation is a mere transitional phase of production, in which the product created as a commodity is realised and its elements of production, likewise created as commodities, are replaced. That form of capital—merchant's capital—which developed directly out of circulation appears here merely as one of the forms of capital occurring in its reproduction process.

The law that the independent development of merchant's capital is inversely proportional to the degree of development of capitalist production is particularly evident in the history of the carrying trade, as among the Venetians, Genoese, Dutch, etc., where the principal gains were not thus made by exporting domestic products, but by promoting the exchange of products of commercially and otherwise economically undeveloped societies, and by exploiting both producing countries.[3] Here, merchant's capital is in its pure form, separated from the extremes—the spheres of production between which it mediates. This is the main source of its development. But this monopoly of the carrying trade disintegrates, and with it this trade itself, proportionately to the economic development of the peoples, whom it exploits at both ends of its course, and whose lack of development was the basis of its existence. In the case of the carrying trade this appears not only as the decline of a special branch of commerce, but also that of the predominance of the purely trading nations, and of their commercial wealth in general, which rested upon the carrying trade. This is but a special form, in which is expressed the subordination of merchants to industrial capital with the advance of capitalist production. The behaviour of merchant's capital wherever it rules over production is strikingly illustrated not only by the colonial economy (the so-called colonial system) in general, but quite specifically by the methods of the old Dutch East India Company.

Since the movement of merchant's capital is M—C—M', the merchant's profit is made, first, in acts which occur only within the circulation process, hence in the two acts of buying and selling; and, secondly, it is realised in the last act, the sale. It is, therefore, profit upon alienation. *Prima facie,* a pure and independent commercial profit seems impossible so long as products are sold at their value. To buy cheap in order to sell dear is the rule of trade. Hence, not the exchange of equivalents. The conception of value is included in it in so far as the various commodities are all values, and therefore, money. In respect to quality they are all expressions of social labour. But they are not values of equal magnitude. The quantitative ratio in which products are exchanged is at first quite arbitrary. They assume the form of commodities inasmuch as they are exchangeables, *i.e.*, expressions of one and the same third. Continued exchange and more regular reproduction for exchange reduces this arbitrariness more and more. But at first not for the producer and consumer, but for their go-between, the merchant, who compares money-prices and pockets the difference. It is through his own movements that he establishes equivalence.

Merchant's capital is originally merely the intervening movement between extremes which it does not control, and between premises which it does not create.

Just as money originates from the bare form of commodity-circulation, C—M—C, not only as a measure of value and a medium of circulation, but also as the absolute form of commodity, and hence of wealth, or hoard, so that its conservation and accumulation as money becomes an end in itself, so, too, does money, the hoard, as something that preserves and increases itself through mere alienation, originate from the bare form of the circulation of merchant's capital, M—C—M'.

The trading nations of ancient times existed like the gods of Epicurus in the intermediate worlds of the universe, or rather like the Jews in the pores of Polish society.

The trade of the first independent flourishing merchant towns and trading nations rested as a pure carrying trade upon the barbarism of the producing nations, between whom they acted the middleman.

In the pre-capitalist stages of society commerce ruled industry. In modern society the reverse is true. Of course, commerce will have more or less of a counter-effect on the communities between which it is carried on. It will subordinate production more and more to exchange-value by making luxuries and subsistence more dependent on sale than on the immediate use of the products. Thereby it dissolves the old relationships. It multiplies money circulation. It encompasses no longer merely the surplus of production, but bites deeper and deeper into the latter, and makes entire branches of production dependent upon it. Nevertheless this disintegrating effect depends very much on the nature of the producing community.

So long as merchant's capital promotes the exchange of products between undeveloped societies, commercial profit not only appears as out-bargaining and cheating, but also largely originates from them. Aside from the fact that it exploits the difference between the prices of production of various countries (and in this respect it tends to level and fix the values of commodities), those modes of production bring it about that merchant's capital appropriates an overwhelming portion of the surplus-product partly as a mediator between communities which still substantially produce for use-value, and for whose economic organisation the sale of the portion of their product entering circulation, or for that matter any sale of products at their value, is of secondary importance; and partly, because under those earlier modes of production the principal owners of the surplus-product with whom the merchant dealt, namely, the slave-owner, the feudal lord, and the state (for instance, the oriental despot) represent the consuming wealth and luxury which the merchant seeks to trap, as Adam Smith correctly scented in the passage on feudal times quoted earlier. Merchant's capital, when it holds a position of dominance, stands everywhere for a system of robbery,[4] so that its development among the trading nations of old and modern times is always directly connected with plundering, piracy, kidnapping slaves, and colonial conquest; as in Carthage, Rome, and later among the Venetians, Portuguese, Dutch, etc.

The development of commerce and merchant's capital gives rise everywhere to the tendency towards production of exchange-values, increases its volume, multiplies it, makes it cosmopolitan, and develops money into world-money. Commerce, therefore, has a more or less dissolving influence everywhere on the producing organisation, which it finds at hand and whose different forms are mainly carried on with a view to use-value. To what extent it brings about a dissolution of the old mode of production depends on its solidity and internal structure. And whither this process of dissolution will lead, in other words, what new mode of production will replace the old, does not depend on commerce, but on the character of the old mode of production itself. In the ancient world the effect of commerce and the development of merchant's capital always resulted in a slave economy; depending on the point of departure, only in the transformation of patriarchal slave system devoted to the production of immediate means of subsistence into one devoted to the production of surplus-value. However, in the modern world, it results in the capitalist mode of production. It follows therefrom that these results spring in themselves from circumstances other than the development of merchant's capital.

It is in the nature of things that as soon as town industry as such separates from agricultural industry, its products are from the outset commodities and thus require the mediation of commerce for their sale. The leaning of commerce towards the development of towns, and, on the other hand, the dependence of towns upon commerce, are so far natural. However, it depends on altogether different circumstances to what measure industrial development will go hand in hand with this development. Ancient Rome, in its later republican days, developed merchant's capital to a higher degree than ever before in the ancient world, without showing any progress in the development of crafts, while in Corinth and other Grecian towns in Europe and Asia Minor the development of commerce was accompanied by highly developed crafts. On the other hand, quite contrary to the growth of towns and attendant conditions, the trading spirit and the development of merchant's capital occur frequently among unsettled nomadic peoples.

There is no doubt—and it is precisely this fact which has led to wholly erroneous conceptions—that in the 16th and 17th centuries the great revolutions, which took place in commerce with the geographical discoveries and speeded the development of merchant's capital, constitute one of the principal elements in furthering the transition from feudal to capitalist mode of production. The sudden expansion of the world-market, the multiplication of circulating commodities, the competitive zeal of the European nations to possess themselves of the products of Asia and the treasures of America, and the colonial system—all contributed materially toward destroying the feudal fetters on production. However, in its first period—the manufacturing period—the modern mode of production developed only where the conditions for it had taken shape within the Middle Ages. Compare, for instance, Holland with Portugal.[5] And when in the 16th, and partially still in the 17th, century the sudden expansion of commerce and emergence of a new world-market overwhelmingly contributed to the fall of the old mode of production and the rise of capitalist production, this was accomplished conversely on the basis of the already existing capitalist mode of production. The world-market itself forms the basis for this mode of production. On the other hand, the immanent necessity of this mode of production to produce on an ever-enlarged scale tends to extend the world-market continually, so that it is not commerce, in this case, which revolutionises industry, but industry which constantly revolutionises commerce. Commercial supremacy itself is now linked with the prevalence to a greater or lesser degree of conditions for a large industry. Compare, for instance, England and Holland. The history of the decline of Holland as the ruling trading nation is the history of the subordination of merchant's capital to industrial capital. The obstacles presented by the internal solidity and organisation of pre-capitalistic, national modes of production to the corrosive influence of commerce are strikingly illustrated in the intercourse of the English with India and China. The broad basis of the mode of production here is formed by the unity of small-scale agriculture and home industry, to which in India we should add the form of village communities built upon the common ownership of land, which, incidentally, was the original form in China as well. In India the English lost no time in exercising their direct political and economic power, as rulers and landlords, to disrupt these small economic communities.[6] English commerce exerted a revolutionary influence on these communities and tore them apart only in so far as the low prices of its goods served to destroy the spinning and weaving industries, which were an ancient integrating element of this unity of industrial and agricultural production. And even so this work of dissolution proceeds very gradually. And still more slowly in China, where it is not reinforced by direct political power. The substantial economy and saving in time afforded by the association of agriculture with manufacture put up a stubborn resistance to the products of the big industries, whose prices include the *faux frais* of the circulation process which pervades them. Unlike the English, Russian commerce, on the other hand, leaves the economic groundwork of Asiatic production untouched.[7]

The transition from the feudal mode of production is two-fold. The producer becomes merchant and capitalist, in contrast to the natural agricultural economy and the guild-bound handicrafts of the medieval urban industries. This is the really revolutionising path. Or else, the merchant establishes direct sway over production. However much this serves historically as a stepping-stone—witness the English 17th-century clothier, who brings the weavers, independent as they are, under his control by selling their wool to them and buying their cloth—it cannot by itself contribute to the overthrow of the old mode of production, but tends rather to preserve and retain it as its precondition. The manufacturer in the French silk industry and in the English hosiery and lace industries, for example, was thus mostly but nominally a manufacturer until the middle of the 19th century. In point of fact, he was merely a merchant, who let the weavers carry on in their old unorganised way and exerted only a merchant's control, for that was for whom they really worked.[8] This system presents everywhere an obstacle to the real capitalist mode of production and goes under with its development. Without revolutionising the mode of production, it only worsens the condition of the direct producers, turns them into mere wage-workers and proletarians under conditions worse than those under the immediate control of capital, and appropriates their surplus-labour on the basis of the old mode of production. The same conditions exist in somewhat modified form in part of the London handicraft furniture industry. It is practised notably in the Tower Hamlets on a very large scale. The whole production is divided into very numerous separate branches of business independent of one another. One establishment makes only chairs, another only tables, a third only bureaus, etc. But these establishments themselves are run more or less like handicrafts by a single minor master and a few journeymen. Nevertheless, production is too large to work directly for private persons. The buyers are the owners of furniture stores. On Saturdays the master visits them and sells his product, the transaction being closed with as much haggling as in a pawnshop over a loan. The masters depend on this weekly sale, if for no other reason than to be able to buy raw materials for the following week and to pay out wages. Under these circumstances, they are really only middlemen between the merchant and their own labourers. The merchant is the actual capitalist who pockets the lion's share of the surplus-value.[9] Almost the same applies in the transition to manufacture of branches formerly carried on as handicrafts or side lines to rural industries. The transition to large-scale industry depends on the technical development of these small owner-operated establishments—wherever they employ machinery that admits of a handicraft-like operation. The machine is driven by steam, instead of by hand. This is of late the case, for instance, in the English hosiery industry.

There is, consequently, a three-fold transition. *First,* the merchant becomes directly an industrial capitalist. This is true in crafts based on trade, especially crafts producing luxuries and imported by merchants together with the raw materials and labourers from foreign lands, as in Italy from Constantinople in the 15th century. *Second,* the merchant turns the small masters into his middlemen, or buys directly from the independent producer, leaving him nominally independent and his mode of production unchanged. *Third,* the industrialist becomes merchant and produces directly for the wholesale market.

In the Middle Ages, the merchant was merely one who, as Poppe rightly says, 'transferred' the goods produced by guilds or peasants [Poppe, *Geschichte der Technologie seit der Wiederherstellung der Wissenschaften bis an das Ende des achtzehnten Jahrhunderts*, Band I, Göttingen. 1807, S. 70.—*Ed.*] The merchant becomes industrialist, or rather, makes craftsmen, particularly the small rural producers, work for him. Conversely, the producer becomes merchant. The master weaver, for instance, buys his wool or yarn himself and sells his cloth to the merchant, instead of receiving his wool from the merchant piecemeal and working for him together with his journeymen. The elements of production pass into the production process as commodities bought by himself. And instead of producing for some individual merchant, or for specified customers, he produces for the world of trade. The producer is himself a merchant. Merchant's capital does no more than carry on the process of circulation. Originally, commerce was the precondition for the transformation of the crafts, the rural domestic industries, and feudal agriculture, into capitalist enterprises. It develops the product into a commodity, partly by creating a market for it, and partly by introducing new commodity equivalents and supplying production with new raw and auxiliary materials, thereby opening new branches of production based from the first upon commerce, both as concerns production for the home and world-market, and as concerns conditions of production originating in the world-market. As soon as manufacture gains sufficient strength, and particularly large-scale industry, it creates in its turn a market for itself, by capturing it through its commodities. At this point commerce becomes the servant of industrial production, for which continued expansion of the market becomes a vital necessity. Ever more extended mass production floods the existing market and thereby works continually for a still greater expansion of this market for breaking out of its limits. What restricts this mass production is not commerce (in so far as it expresses the existing demand), but the magnitude of employed capital and the level of development of the productivity of labour. The industrial capitalist always has the world-market before him, compares, and must constantly compare, his own cost-prices with the market-prices at home, and throughout the world. In the earlier period such comparison fell almost entirely to the merchants, and thus secured the predominance of merchant's capital over industrial capital.

The first theoretical treatment of the modern mode of production—the mercantile system—proceeded necessarily from the superficial phenomena of the circulation process as individualised in the movements of merchant's capital, and therefore, grasped only the appearance of matters. Partly because merchant's capital is the first free state of existence of capital in general. And partly because of the overwhelming influence which it exerted during the first revolutionising period of feudal production—the genesis of modern production. The real science of modern economy only begins when the theoretical analysis passes from the process of circulation to the process of production. Interest-bearing capital is, indeed, likewise a very old form of capital. But we shall see later why mercantilism does not take it as its point of departure, but rather carries on a polemic against it.

Notes

1. The sage Mr Roscher [*Die Grundlagen der Nationalökonomie*, 3. Auflage, 1858, § 60, 5. *103.—Ed.*] has figured out that, since certain people designate trade as *mediation* between producers and consumers, 'one' might just as well designate production itself as *mediation* of consumption (between whom?), and this implies, of course, that merchant's capital is as much a part of productive capital as agricultural and industrial capital. In other words, because I can say, that man can mediate his consumption only by means of production (and he has to do this even without getting his education at Leipzig), or that labour is required for the appropriation of the products of Nature (which might be called *mediation*), it follows, of course, that social *mediation* arising from a specific social form of production—because mediation—has the same absolute character of necessity, and the same rank. The word *mediation* settles everything. By the way, the merchants are not mediators between producers and consumers (consumers as distinct from producers, consumers, that is, who do not produce, are left aside for the moment), but mediators in the exchange of the products of these producers among themselves. They are but middlemen in an exchange, which in thousands of cases proceeds without them.
2. Herr W. Kiesselbach (in his *Der Gang des Welthandels im Mittelalter*, 1860) is indeed still enwrapped in the ideas of a world, in which merchant's capital is the general form of capital. He has not the least idea of the modern meaning of capital, any more than Mommsen when he speaks in his history of Rome of 'capital' and the rule of capital. In modern English history, the commercial estate proper and the merchant towns are also politically reactionary and in league with the landed and moneyed interest against industrial capital. Compare, for instance, the political role of Liverpool with that of Manchester and Birmingham. The complete rule of industrial capital was not acknowledged by English merchant's capital and moneyed interest until after the abolition of the corn tax, etc.
3. 'The inhabitants of trading cities, by importing the improved manufactures and expensive luxuries of richer countries afforded some food to the vanity of the great proprietors, who eagerly purchased them with great quantities of the rude produce of their own lands.

The commerce of a great part of Europe in those times, accordingly consisted chiefly, in the exchange of their own rude produce for the manufactured produce of more civilised nations.... When this taste became so general as to occasion a considerable demand, the merchants, in order to save the expense of carriage, naturally endeavoured to establish some manufactures of the same kind in their own country.' (Adam Smith [*Wealth of Nations*], Book III, Ch. III, London, 1776, pp. 489, 490.)

4. 'Now there is among merchants much complaint about the nobles, or robbers, because they must trade under great danger and run the risk of being kidnapped, beaten, blackmailed, and robbed. If they would suffer these things for the sake of justice, the merchants would be saintly people.... But since such great wrong and unchristian thievery and robbery are committed all over the world by merchants, and even among themselves, is it any wonder that God should procure that such great wealth, gained by wrong, should again be lost or stolen, and they themselves be hit over the head or made prisoner? ... And the princes should punish such unjust bargains with due rigour and take care that their subjects shall not be so outrageously abused by merchants. Because they fail to do so, God employs knights and robbers, and punishes the merchants through them for the wrongs they committed, and uses them as his devils, just as he plagues Egypt and all the world with devils, or destroys through enemies. He thus pits one against the other, without thereby insinuating that knights are any the less robbers than merchants, although the merchants daily rob the whole world, while a knight may rob one or two once or twice a year.' 'Go by the word of Isaiah: Thy princes have become the companions of robbers. For they hang the thieves, who have stolen a gulden or a half gulden, but they associate with those, who rob all the world and steal with greater assurance than all others, so that the proverb remains true: Big thieves hang little thieves; and as the Roman senator Cato said: Mean thieves lie in prisons and stocks, but public thieves are clothed in gold and silks. But what will God say finally? He will do as he said to Ezekiel; he will amalgamate princes and merchants, one thief with another, like lead and iron, as when a city burns down, leaving neither princes nor merchants.' (Martin Luther, *Von Kaufshandlung und Wucher,* 1524, S. 296-97.)
5. How predominant fishery, manufacture and agriculture, aside from other circumstances, were as the basis for Holland's development, has already been explained by 18th-century writers, such as Massie [p. 60]. In contradistinction to the former view, which underrated the volume and importance of commerce in Asia, in Antiquity, and in the Middle Ages, it has now come to be the custom to extremely overrate it. The best antidote against this conception is to study the imports and exports of England in the early 18th century and to compare them with modern imports and exports. And yet they were incomparably greater than those of any former trading nation. (See Anderson, *An Historical and Chronological Deduction of the Origin of Commerce.* [Vol. II, London, 1764, p. 261 et seq.—Ed.])
6. If any nation's history, then the history of the English in India is a string of futile and really absurd (in practice infamous) economic experiments. In Bengal they created a caricature of large-scale English landed estates; in south-eastern India a caricature of small parcelled property; in the north-west they did all they could to transform the Indian economic community with common ownership of the soil into a caricature of itself.
7. Since Russia has been making frantic exertions to develop its own capitalist production, which is exclusively dependent upon its domestic and the neighbouring Asiatic market, this is also beginning to change.—*F.E.*
8. The same is true of the ribbon and basting makers and the silk weavers of the Rhine. Even a railway has been built near Krefeld for the intercourse of these rural hand-weavers with the town 'manufacturer.' But this was later put out of business, together with the hand-weavers, by the mechanical weaving industry.—*F.E.*
9. This system has been developed since 1865 on a still larger scale. For details see the First Report of the Select Committee of the House of Lords on the Sweating System, London, *1888.*—*F.E.*

PART V

DIVISION OF PROFIT INTO INTEREST AND PROFIT OF ENTERPRISE. INTEREST-BEARING CAPITAL

21

Interest-Bearing Capital

In our first discussion of the general, or average, rate of profit (Part II of this book) we did not have this rate before us in its complete form, the equalisation of profit appearing only as equalisation between industrial capitals invested in different spheres. This was supplemented in the preceding part, which dealt with the participation of merchant's capital in this equalisation, and also commercial profit. The general rate of profit and the average profit now appeared in narrower limits than before. It should be remembered in the course of our analysis that in any future reference to the general rate of profit or to average profit we mean this latter connotation, hence only the final form of average rate. And since this rate is the same for mercantile, as well as industrial, capital, it is no longer necessary, so far as this average profit is concerned, to make a distinction between industrial and commercial profit. Whether industrially invested in the sphere of production, or commercially in the sphere of circulation, capital yields the same average annual profit *pro rata* to its magnitude.

Money—here taken as the independent expression of a certain amount of value existing either actually as money or as commodities—may be converted into capital on the basis of capitalist production, and may thereby be transformed from a given value to a self-expanding, or increasing, value. It produces profit, *i.e.*, it enables the capitalist to extract a certain quantity of unpaid labour, surplus-product and surplus-value from the labourers, and to appropriate it. In this way, aside from its use-value as money, it acquires an additional use-value, namely that of serving as capital. Its use-value then consists precisely in the profit it produces when converted into capital. In this capacity of potential capital, as a means of producing profit, it becomes a commodity, but a commodity *sui generis*. Or, what amounts to the same, capital as capital becomes a commodity.[1]

Suppose the annual average rate of profit is 20%. In that case, a machine valued at £100, employed as capital under average conditions and an average amount of intelligence and purposive effort, would yield a profit of £20. A man in possession of £100, therefore, possesses the power to make £120 out of £100, or to produce a profit of £20. He possesses a potential capital of £100. If he gives these £100 to another for one year, so the latter may use them as real capital, he gives him the power to produce a profit of £20—a surplus-value which costs this other nothing, and for which he pays no equivalent. If this other should pay, say, £5 at the close of the year to the owner of the £100 out of the profit produced, he would thereby pay the use-value of the £100—the use-value of its function as capital, the function of producing a profit of £20. The part of the profit paid to the owner is called interest, which is just another name, or special term, for a part of the profit given up by capital in the process of functioning to the owner of the capital, instead of putting it into its own pocket.

It is plain that the possession of £100 gives their owner the power to pocket the interest—that certain portion of profit produced by means of his capital. If he had not given the £100 to the other person, the latter could not have produced any profit, and could not at all have acted as a capitalist with reference to these £100.[2]

To speak here of natural justice, as Gilbart does (see note), is nonsense. The justice of the transactions between agents of production rests on the fact that these arise as natural consequences out of the production relationships. The juristic forms in which these economic transactions appear as wilful acts of the parties concerned, as expressions of their common will and as contracts that may be enforced by law against some individual party, cannot, being mere forms, determine this content. They merely express it. This content is just whenever it corresponds, is appropriate, to the mode of production. It is unjust whenever it contradicts that mode. Slavery on the basis of capitalist production is unjust; likewise fraud in the quality of commodities.

The £100 produce the profit of £20 because they function as capital, be it industrial or mercantile. But the *sine qua non* of this function as capital is that they are expended as capital, *i.e.*, are expended in purchasing means of production (in the case of industrial capital) or commodities (in the case of merchant's capital). But to be expended, they must be available. If A, the owner of the £100, were either to spend them for personal consumption, or to keep them as a hoard, they could not have been invested as capital by B in his capacity of functioning capitalist. B does not expend his own capital, but A's; however, he cannot expend A's capital without A's consent. Therefore, it is really A who originally expends the £100 as capital, albeit his function as capitalist is limited to this outlay of £100 as capital. In respect to these £100, B acts as capitalist only because A lends him the £100, thus expending them as capital.

Let us first consider the singular circulation of interest-bearing capital. We shall then secondly have to analyse the peculiar manner in which it is sold as a commodity, namely loaned instead of relinquished once and for all.

The point of departure is the money which A advances to B. This may be done with or without security. The first-named form, however, is the more ancient, save advances on commodities or paper, such as bills of exchange, shares, etc. These special forms do not concern us at this point. We are dealing here with interest-bearing capital in its usual form.

In B's possession the money is actually converted into capital, passes through M—C—M' and returns to A as M', as M+ΔM, where ΔM represents the interest. For the sake of simplicity we shall not consider here the case, in which capital remains in B's possession for a long term and interest is paid at regular intervals.

The movement, therefore, is

M—M—C—M'—M'.

What appears duplicated here, is 1) the outlay of money as capital, and 2) its reflux as realised capital, as M' or M+ΔM.

In the movement of merchant's capital, M—C—M', the same commodity changes hands twice, or more than twice, if merchant sells to merchant. But every such change of place of the same commodity indicates a metamorphosis, a purchase or sale of the commodity, no matter how often the process may be repeated, until it enters consumption.

On the other hand, the same money changes hands twice in C—M—C, but this indicates the complete metamorphosis of the commodity, which is first converted into money and then from money back into another commodity.

But in interest-bearing capital the first time M changes hands is by no means a phase either of the commodity metamorphosis, or of reproduction of capital. It first becomes one when it is expended a second time, in the hands of the active capitalist who carries on trade with it, or transforms it into productive capital. M's first change of hands does not express anything here, beyond its transfer from A to B—a transfer which usually takes place under certain legal forms and stipulations.

This double outlay of money as capital, of which the first is merely a transfer from A to B, is matched by its double reflux. As M', or M + ΔM, it flows back out of the process to B, the person acting as capitalist. The latter then transfers it back to A, but together with a part of the profit, as realised capital, as M + ΔM, in which ΔM is not the entire profit, but only a portion of the profit—the interest. It flows back to B only as what he had expended, as functioning capital, but as the property of A. To make its reflux complete, B must consequently return it to A. But in addition to the capital, B must also turn over to A a portion of the profit, a part which goes under the name of interest, which he had made with this capital since A had given him the money only as a capital, *i.e.*, as value which is not only preserved in its movement, but also creates surplus-value for its owner. It remains in B's hands only so long as it is functioning capital. And with its reflux—on the stipulated date—it ceases to function as capital. When no longer acting as capital, however, it must again be returned to A, who had never ceased being its legal owner.

The form of lending, which is peculiar to this commodity, to capital as commodity, and which also occurs in other transactions instead of that of sale, follows from the simple definition that capital obtains here as a commodity, or that money as capital becomes a commodity.

A distinction should be made here.

We have seen (Book II, Chap. I), and recall briefly at this point, that in the process of circulation capital serves as commodity-capital and money-capital. But in neither form does capital become a commodity as capital.

As soon as productive capital turns into commodity-capital it must be placed on the market to be sold as a commodity. There it acts simply as a commodity. The capitalist then appears only as the seller of commodities, just as the buyer is only the buyer of commodities. As a commodity the product must realise its value, must assume its transmuted form of money, in the process of circulation by its sale. It is also quite immaterial for this reason, whether this commodity is bought by a consumer as a necessity of life, or by a capitalist as means of production, *i.e.*, as a component part of his capital. In the act of circulation commodity-capital acts only as a commodity, not as a capital. It is commodity-*capital*, as distinct from an ordinary commodity, 1) because it is weighted with surplus-value, the realisation of its value, therefore, being simultaneously the realisation of surplus-value; but this alters nothing about its simple existence as a commodity, as a product with a certain price; 2) because its function as a commodity is a phase in its process of reproduction as capital, and therefore, its movement as a commodity being only a partial movement of its process, is simultaneously its movement as capital. Yet it does not become that through the sale as such, but only through the connection of the sale with the whole movement of this specific quantity of value in the capacity of capital.

In the same way as money-capital it really acts simply as money, *i.e.*, as a means of buying commodities (the elements of production). The fact that this money is simultaneously money-capital, a form of capital, does not emerge from the act of buying, the actual function which it here performs as money, but from the connection of this act with the total movement of capital, since this act, performed by capital as money, initiates the capitalist production process.

But in so far as they actually function, *i.e.*, actually play a role in the process, commodity-capital acts here only as a commodity and money-capital only as money. At no time during the metamorphosis, viewed by itself, does the capitalist sell his commodities as *capital* to the buyer, although to him they represent capital; nor does he give up money as capital to the seller. In both cases, he gives up his commodities simply as commodities, and money simply as money, *i.e.*, as a means of purchasing commodities.

It is only in connection with the entire process, at the moment where the point of departure appears simultaneously as the point of return, in M—M' or C—C', that capital in the process of circulation appears as capital (whereas in the process of production it appears as capital through the subordination of the labourer to the capitalist and the production of surplus value). In this moment of return, however, the connection disappears. What we have then is M', or M + ΔM, a sum of money equal to the sum originally advanced plus an increment—the realised surplus-value (regardless of whether the amount of value increased by ΔM exists in the form of money, or commodities, or elements of production). And it is precisely at this point of return where capital exists as realised capital, as an expanded value, that it never enters the circulation in this form—in so far as this point is fixed as a point of rest, whether real or imaginary—but rather appears to have been withdrawn from circulation as a result of the whole process. Whenever it is again expended, it is never given up to another as *capital*, but is sold to him as an ordinary commodity, or given to him as ordinary money in exchange for commodities. It never appears as capital in its process of circulation, only as commodity or money, and at this point this is the only form of its existence for *others*. Commodities and money are here capital not because commodities change into money, or money into commodities, not in their actual relations to sellers or buyers, but only in their ideal relations to the capitalist himself (subjectively speaking), or as phases in the process of reproduction (objectively speaking). Capital exists as capital in actual movement, not in the process of circulation, but only in the process of production, in the process by which labour-power is exploited.

The matter is different with interest-bearing capital, however, and it is precisely this difference which lends it its specific character. The owner of money who desires to enhance his money as interest-bearing capital, turns it over to a third person, throws it into circulation, turns it into a commodity as *capital*; not just capital for himself, but also for others. It is not capital merely for the man who gives it up, but is from the very first given to the third person as capital, as a value endowed with the use-value of creating surplus-value, of creating profit; a value which preserves itself in its movement and returns to its original owner, in this case, the owner of money, after performing its function. Hence it leaves him only for a specified time, passes but temporarily out of the possession of its owner into the possession of a functioning capitalist, is therefore, neither given up in payment nor sold, but merely loaned, merely relinquished with the understanding that, first, it shall return to its point of departure after a definite time interval, and, second, that it shall return as realised capital—a capital having realised its use-value, its power of creating surplus-value.

Commodities loaned out as capital are loaned either as fixed or as circulating capital, depending on their properties. Money may be loaned out in either form. It may be loaned as fixed capital, for instance, if it is paid back in the form of an annuity, whereby a portion of the capital flows back together with the interest. Certain commodities, such as houses, ships, machines, etc., can be loaned out only as fixed capital by the nature of their use-values. Yet all loaned capital, whatever its form, and no matter how the nature of its use-value may modify its return, is always only a specific form of money-capital. Because what is loaned out is always a definite sum of money, and it is this sum on which interest is calculated. Should whatever is loaned out be neither money nor circulating capital, it is also paid back in the way fixed capital returns. The lender periodically receives interest and a portion of the consumed value of the fixed capital itself, this being an equivalent for the periodic wear and tear. And at the end of the stipulated term the unconsumed portion of the loaned fixed capital is returned in kind. If the loaned capital is circulating capital, it is likewise returned in the manner peculiar to circulating capital.

The *manner* of reflux is, therefore, always determined by the actual circuit described by capital in the act of reproduction and by its specific varieties. But as for loaned capital, its reflux assumes the *form* of return payments, because its advance, by which it is transferred, possesses the form of a loan.

In this chapter we treat only of actual money-capital, from which the other forms of loaned capital are derived.

The loaned capital flows back in two ways. In the process of reproduction it returns to the functioning capitalist, and then its return repeats itself once more as transfer to the lender, the money-capitalist, as return payment to the real owner, its legal point of departure.

In the actual process of circulation, capital appears always as a commodity or as money, and its movement always is broken up into a series of purchases and sales. In short, the process of circulation resolves itself into the metamorphosis of commodities. It is different, when we consider the process of reproduction as a whole. If we start out with money (and the same is true if we start out with commodities, since we begin with their value, hence view them *sub specie* as money), we shall see that a certain sum of money is expended and returns after a certain period with an increment. The advanced sum of money returns together with a surplus-value. It has remained intact and increased in making a certain cycle. But now, being loaned out as capital, money is loaned as just the sum of money which preserves and expands itself, which returns after a certain period with an increment, and is always ready to perform the same process over again. It is expended neither as money nor as a commodity, thus, neither exchanged against a commodity when advanced in the form of money, nor sold in exchange for money when advanced as a commodity; rather, it is expended as capital. This relation to itself, in which capital presents itself when the capitalist production process is viewed as a whole and as a single unity, and in which capital appears as money that begets money, is here imparted to it as its character, its designation, without any intermediary movement. And it is relinquished with this designation when loaned out as money-capital.

A queer conception of the role of money-capital is hold by Proudhon (*Gratuité du Crédit. Discussion entre M. F. Bastiat et M. Proudhon*, Paris, 1850). Loaning seems an evil to Proudhon because it is not selling. Loaning for an interest is

> the faculty of selling the same article over and over again, and of receiving its price again and again, without once relinquishing ownership of the object which is being sold (p. 9). [The cited words belong to Cheve, one of the editors of the newspaper *La Voix du peuple*, and the author of the 'first letter' in the book *Gratuité du Crédit. Discussion entre M. F. Bastiat et M. Proudhon*, Paris, 1850.—*Ed*]

The object—money, a house, etc.—does not change owners as in selling and buying. But Proudhon does not see that no equivalent is received in return for money given away in the form of interest-bearing capital. True, the object is given away in every act of buying and selling, so far as there are processes of exchange at all. Ownership of the sold article is always relinquished. But its value is not given up. In a sale the commodity is given away, but not its value, which is returned in the form of money, or in what is here just another form of it—promissory notes, or titles of payment. When purchasing, the money is given away, but not its value, which is replaced in the form of commodities. The industrial capitalist retains the same value in his hands throughout the process of reproduction (excluding surplus-value), but in different forms.

Inasmuch as there is an exchange, *i.e.*, an exchange of articles, there is no change in the value. The same capitalist always retains the same value. But so long as surplus-value is produced by the capitalist, there is no exchange. As soon as an exchange occurs, the surplus-value is already incorporated in the commodities. If we view the entire circuit made by capital, M—C—M', rather than individual acts of exchange, we shall see that a definite amount of value is continually advanced, and that this same amount plus surplus-value, or profit, is withdrawn from circulation. The actual acts of exchange do not, at any rate, reveal how this process is promoted. And it is precisely this process of M as capital, on which the interest of the money-lending capitalist rests, and from which it is derived.

> 'In fact,' says Proudhon, 'the hat-maker, who sells hats, receives their value, neither more nor less. But the money-lending capitalist ... does not recover just his capital, he recovers more than his capital, more than he throws into the exchange; he receives an interest over and above his capital' (p. 69).

Here the hatter represents the productive capitalist as distinct from the loan capitalist. Proudhon has obviously failed to grasp the secret of how the productive capitalist can sell commodities at their value (equalisation through prices of production is here immaterial to his conception) and receive a profit over and above the capital he flings into exchange. Suppose the price of production of 100 hats = £115, and that this price of production happens to coincide with the value of the hats, which means that the capital producing the hats is of the same composition as the average social capital. Should the profit = 15%, the hatter makes a profit of £15 by selling his commodities at their value of £115. They cost him only £100. If he produced them with his own capital, he pockets the entire surplus of £15 but if with borrowed capital, he may have to give up £5 as interest. This alters nothing in the value of the hats, only in the distribution among different persons of the surplus-value already contained in this value. Since, therefore, the value of the hats is not affected by the payment of interest, it is nonsense on Proudhon's part to say:

> As in commerce the interest on capital is added to the wages of labourers in making up the price of commodities, it is impossible for the labourer to buy back the product of his own labour. *Vivre en travaillant* is a principle which contains a contradiction under the rule of interest. (p. 105)[3]

How little Proudhon understood the nature of capital is shown in the following statement, in which he describes the movement of capital in general as a movement peculiar to interest-bearing capital:

> Since money-capital returns to its source from exchange through the accumulation of interest, it follows that reinvestment always made by the same individual continually brings profit to the same person. (p. 154)

What is it that still puzzles him in the peculiar movement of interest-bearing capital? The categories: buying, price, giving up articles, and the immediate form in which surplus-value appears here; in short, the phenomenon that capital as such has become a commodity, that selling, consequently, has turned into lending and price into a share of the profit.

The return of capital to its point of departure is generally the characteristic movement of capital in its total circuit. This is by no means a feature of interest-bearing capital alone. What singles it out is rather the external form of its return without the intervention of any circuit. The loaning capitalist gives away his capital, transfers it to the industrial capitalist, without receiving any equivalent. His transfer is not an act belonging to the real circulation process of capital at all. It serves merely to introduce this circuit, which is effected by the industrial capitalist. This first change of position of money does not express any act of the metamorphosis—neither buying nor selling. Ownership is not relinquished, because there is no exchange and no equivalent is received. The return of the money from the hands of the industrial capitalist to those of the loaning capitalist merely supplements the first act of giving away the capital. Advanced in the form of money, the capital again returns to the industrial capitalist through the circular process in the form of money. But since it did not belong to him when he invested it, it cannot belong to him on its return. Passing through the process of reproduction cannot by any means turn the capital into his property. He must, therefore, restore it to the lender. The first expenditure, which transfers the capital from the lender to the borrower, is a legal transaction which has nothing to do with the actual process of reproduction. It is merely a prelude to this process. The return payment, which again transfers the capital that has flowed back from the borrower to the lender is another legal transaction, a supplement of the first. One introduces the actual process, the other is an act supplementary to this process. Point of departure and point of return, the giving away and the recovery of the loaned capital, thus appear as arbitrary movements promoted by legal transactions, which take place before and after the actual movement of capital and have nothing to do with it as such. It would have been all the same as concerns this actual movement if the capital had from the first belonged to the industrial capitalist and had returned to him, therefore, as his own.

In the first introductory act the lender gives his capital to the borrower. In the supplemental and closing act the borrower returns the capital to the lender. As concerns the transaction between these two—and aside from the interest for the present—as concerns the movement of the loaned capital between lender and borrower, therefore, the two acts (separated by a longer or shorter time interval, during which the actual reproduction process of the capital takes place) embrace the entire movement. And this movement, disposing on condition of returning, constitutes *per se* the movement of lending and borrowing, that specific form of conditionally alienating money or commodities.

The characteristic movement of capital in general, the return of the money to the capitalist, *i.e.*, the return of capital to its point of departure, assumes in the case of interest-bearing capital a wholly external appearance, separated from the actual movement, of which it is a form. A gives away his money not as money, but as capital. No transformation occurs in the capital. It merely changes hands. Its real transformation into capital does not take place until it is in the hands of B. But for A it becomes capital as soon as he gives it to B. The actual reflux of capital from the processes of production and circulation takes place only for B. But for A the reflux assumes the same form as the alienation. The capital returns from B to A. Giving away, *i.e.*, loaning money for a certain time and receiving it back with interest (surplus-value) is the complete form of the movement peculiar to interest-bearing capital as such. The actual movement of loaned money as capital is an operation lying outside the transactions between lender and borrower. In these the intermediate act is obliterated, invisible, not directly included. A special sort of commodity, capital has its own peculiar mode of alienation. Neither does its return, therefore, express itself as the consequence and result, of some definite series of economic processes, but as the effect of a specific legal agreement between buyer and seller. The time of return depends on the progress of the process of reproduction; in the case of interest-bearing capital, its return as capital *seems* to depend on the mere agreement between lender and borrower. So that in regard to this transaction the return of capital no longer appears as a result arising out of the process of reproduction; it appears as if the loaned capital never lost the form of money. To be sure, these transactions are really determined by the actual reproductive returns. But this is not evident in the transaction itself. Nor is it by any means always the case in practice. If the actual return does not take place in due time, the borrower must look for other resources to meet his obligations vis-à-vis the lender. The bare *form* of capital—money expended as a certain sum, A, which returns as sum A + 1/x A after a given lapse of time without any other intermediate act save this lapse of time—is only a meaningless form of the actual movement of capital.

In the actual movement of capital its return is a phase in the process of circulation. The money is first converted into means of production; production transforms them into commodities; through sale of the commodities they are reconverted into money and return in this form into the hands of the capitalist who had originally advanced the capital in the form of money. But in the case of interest-bearing capital, the return, like alienation, is the result of a legal transaction between the owner of the capital and a second party. We see only the alienation and the return payment. Whatever passes in the interim is obliterated.

But since money advanced as capital has the property of returning to the person who advanced it, to the one who expended it as capital, and since M—C—M' is the immanent form of the movement of capital, the owner of the money can, for this very reason, loan it out as capital, as something that has the property of returning to its point of departure, of preserving, and increasing, its value in the course of its movement. He gives it away as capital, because it returns to its point of departure after having been employed as capital, hence can be restored by the borrower after a certain period precisely because it has come back to him.

Loaning money as capital—its alienation on the condition of it being returned after a certain time-presupposes, therefore, that it will be actually employed as capital, and that it actually flows back to its starting-point. The real cycle made by money as capital is, therefore, the premise for the legal transaction by which the borrower must return the money to the lender. If the borrower does not use the money as capital, that is his own business. The lender loans it as capital, and as such it is supposed to perform the functions of capital, which include the circuit of money-capital until it returns to its starting-point in the form of money.

The acts of circulation, M—C and C—M', in which a certain amount of value functions as money or commodities, are but intermediate processes, mere phases of the total movement. As capital, it performs the entire movement M—M'. It is advanced as money or a sum of values in one form or another, and returns as a sum of values. The lender of money does not expend it in purchasing commodities, or, if this sum of values is in commodity-form, does not sell it for money. He advances it as capital, as M—M', as a value, which returns to its point of departure after a certain term. He lends instead of buying or selling. This lending, therefore, is the appropriate form of alienating value as *capital*, instead of alienating it as money or commodities. It does not follow, however, that lending cannot also take the form of transactions which have nothing to do with the capitalist process of reproduction.

We have so far only considered the movements of loaned *capital* between its owner and the industrial capitalist. Now we must inquire into *interest*.

The lender expends his money as capital; the amount of value, which he relinquishes to another, is capital, and consequently returns to him. But the mere return of it would not be the reflux of the loaned sum of value as *capital*, but merely the return of a loaned sum of value. To return as capital, the advanced sum of value must not only be preserved in the movement but must also expand, must increase in value, *i.e.*, must return with a surplus-value, as M + ΔM, the latter being interest or a portion of the average profit, which does not remain in the hands of the operating capitalist, but falls to the share of the money-capitalist.

The fact that the latter has relinquished it as capital implies that it must be restored to him as M + ΔM. Later, we shall also have to turn our attention to the form in which interest is paid in the meantime at fixed intervals, but without the capital, whose return follows at the end of a lengthy period.

What does the money-capitalist give to the borrower, the industrial capitalist? What does he really turn over to him? It is only this act of handing over money which changes lending money into alienation of money as capital, *i.e.*, alienation of capital as a commodity.

It is only by this act of alienating that capital is loaned by the money-lender as a commodity, or that the commodity at his disposal is given to another as capital.

What is alienated in an ordinary sale? Not the value of the sold commodity, for this merely changes its form. The value exists ideally in a commodity as its price before it actually passes as money into the hands of the seller. The same value and the same amount of value merely change their form. In the one instance they exist in commodity-form, in the other in the form of money. What is really alienated by the seller, and, therefore, passes into the individual or productive consumption of the buyer, is the use-value of the commodity—the commodity as a use-value.

What, now, is the use-value which the money-capitalist gives up for the period of the loan and relinquishes to the productive capitalist—the borrower? It is the use-value which the money acquires by being capable of becoming capital, of performing the functions of capital, and creating a definite surplus-value, the average profit (whatever is above or below it appears here as a mere accident) during its process, besides preserving its original magnitude of value. In the case of the other commodities the use-value is ultimately consumed. Their substance disappears, and with it their value. In contrast, the commodity-capital is peculiar in that its value and use-value not only remain intact but also increase, through consumption of its use-value.

It is this use-value of money as capital—this faculty of producing an average profit—which the money-capitalist relinquishes to the industrial capitalist for the period, during which he places the loaned capital at the latter's disposal.

Money thus loaned has in this respect a certain similarity with labour-power in its relation to the industrial capitalist. With the difference that the latter pays for the value of labour-power, whereas he simply pays back the value of the loaned capital. The use-value of labour-power for the industrial capitalist is that labour-power creates more value (profit) in its consumption than it possesses itself, and than it costs. This additional value is use-value for the industrial capitalist. And in like manner the use-value of loaned capital appears as its faculty of begetting and increasing value.

The money-capitalist, in fact, alienates a use-value, and thus whatever he gives away is given as a commodity. It is to this extent that the analogy with a commodity *per se* is complete. In the first place, it is a value which passes from one hand to another. In the case of an ordinary commodity, a commodity as such, the same value remains in the hands of the buyer and seller, only in different forms; both have the same value which they had before the transaction, and which they had alienated—the one in the form of a commodity, the other in the form of money. The difference is that in a loan the money-capitalist is the only one in the transaction who gives away value; but he preserves it through the prospective return. In the loan transaction just one party receives value, since only one party relinquishes value.—In the second place, a real use-value is relinquished on the one side, and received and consumed on the other. But in contrast to ordinary commodities this use-value is value in itself, namely the excess over the original value realised through the use of money as capital. The profit is this use-value.

The use-value of the loaned money lies in its being able to serve as capital and, as such, to produce the average profit under average conditions.[4]

What, now, does the industrial capitalist pay, and what is, therefore, the price of the loaned capital?

> 'That which men pay as interest for the use of what they borrow' is, according to Massie, 'a part of the profit it is capable of producing.' (1. c., p. 49)[5]

What the buyer of an ordinary commodity buys is its use-value; what he pays for is its value. What the borrower of money buys is likewise its use-value as capital; but what does he pay for? Surely not its price, or value, as in the case of ordinary commodities. No change of form occurs in the value passing between borrower and lender, as occurs between buyer and seller when it exists in one instance in the form of money, and in another in the form of a commodity. The sameness of the alienated and returned value is revealed here in an entirely different way. The sum of value, *i.e.*, the money, is given away without an equivalent, and is returned after a certain period. The lender always remains the owner of the same value, even after it passes from his hands into those of the borrower. In an ordinary exchange of commodities money always comes from the buyer's side; but in a loan it comes from the side of the seller. He is the one who gives away money for a certain period, and the buyer of capital is the one who receives it as a commodity. But this is only possible as long as the money acts as capital and, is therefore, advanced. The borrower borrows money as capital, as a value producing more value. But at the moment when it is advanced it is still only potential capital, like any other capital at its starting-point, the moment it is advanced. It is only through its employment that it expands its value and realises itself as capital. However, it has to be returned by the borrower as *realised* capital, hence as value plus surplus-value (interest). And the latter can only be a portion of the realised profit. Only a portion, not all of it. For the use-value of the loaned capital to the borrower consists in producing profit for him. Otherwise there would not have been any alienation of use-value on the lender's part. On the other hand, not all the profit can fall to the borrower's share. Otherwise he would pay nothing for the alienated use-value, and would return the advanced money to the lender as ordinary money, not as capital, as realised capital, for it is realised capital only as $M + \Delta M$.

Both of them, lender and borrower, expend the same sum of money as capital. But it is only in the hands of the latter that it serves as capital. The profit is not doubled by the double existence of the same sum of money as capital for two persons. It can serve as capital for both of them only by dividing the profit. The portion which falls to the lender is called interest.

The entire transaction, as assumed, takes place between two kinds of capitalists—the money-capitalist and the industrial or merchant capitalist.

It must always be borne in mind that here capital as capital is a commodity, or that the commodity here discussed is capital. All the relations in evidence here would, therefore, be irrational from the standpoint of an ordinary commodity, or from that of capital in so far as it acts as a commodity-capital in the process of reproduction. Lending and borrowing, instead of selling and buying, is a distinction which here springs from the specific nature of the commodity-capital. Similarly, the fact that it is interest, not the price of the commodity, which is paid here. If we want to call interest the price of money-capital, then it is an irrational form of price quite at variance with the conception of the price of commodities.[6] The price is here reduced to its purely abstract and meaningless form, signifying that it is a certain sum of money paid for something serving in one way or another as a use-value; whereas the conception of price really signifies the value of some use-value expressed in money.

Interest, signifying the price of capital, is from the outset quite an irrational expression. The commodity in question has a double value, first a value, and then a price different from this value, while price represents the expression of value in money. Money-capital is nothing but a sum of money, or the value of a certain quantity of commodities fixed in a sum of money. If a commodity is loaned out as capital, it is only a disguised form of a sum of money. Because what is loaned out as capital is not so and so many pounds of cotton, but so much and so much money existing in the form of cotton as its value. The price of capital, therefore, refers to it as to a sum of money, even if not currency, as Mr Torrens thinks (see Footnote 59). How, then, can a sum of value have a price besides its own price, besides the price expressed in its own money-form? Price, after all, is the value of a commodity (this is also true of the market-price, whose difference from value is not one of quality, but only one of quantity, referring only to the magnitude of value) as distinct from its use-value. A price which differs from value in quality is an absurd contradiction.[7]

Capital manifests itself as capital through self-expansion. The degree of its self-expansion expresses the quantitative degree in which it realises itself as capital. The surplus-value or profit produced by it—its rate or magnitude—is measurable only by comparison with the value of the advanced capital. The greater or lesser self-expansion of interest-bearing capital is, therefore, likewise only measurable by comparing the amount of interest, its share in the total profits, with the value of the advanced capital. If, therefore, price expresses the value of the commodity, then interest expresses the self-expansion of money-capital and thus appears as the price paid for it to the lender. This shows how absurd it is from the very first to apply hereto the simple relations of exchange through the medium of money in buying and selling, as Proudhon does. The basic premise is precisely that money functions as capital and may thus be transferred as such, *i.e.*, as potential capital, to a third person.

Capital, however, appears here as a commodity, inasmuch as it is offered on the market, and the use-value of money is actually alienated as capital. Its use-value, however, lies in producing profit. The value of money or of commodities employed as capital does not depend on their value as money or as commodities, but on the quantity of surplus-value they produce for their owner. The product of capital is profit. On the basis of capitalist production it is merely a different use of money—whether it is expended as money; or advanced as capital. Money, or commodities, are in themselves potentially capital, just as labour-power is potential capital. Because, 1) money may be converted into elements of production and is, as is, merely an abstract expression of them—their existence as value; 2) the material elements of wealth have the property of potentially becoming capital, because their supplementary opposite, which makes them into capital, namely wage-labour, is available on the basis of capitalist production.

The contradictory social features of material wealth—its antagonism to labour as wage-labour—are expressed in capitalist property as such independently of the production process. This particular fact, set apart from the process of capitalist production itself, from which it constantly results and as whose constant result it serves as a constant prerequisite, expresses itself in that money and commodities alike are latent, potential, capital, so that they may be sold as capital, and in that they can in this form command the labour of others bestowing a claim to appropriate the labour of others, and therefore, represent self-expanding values. It also becomes clearly apparent that this relationship, and not the labour offered as an equivalent on the part of the capitalist, supplies the title and the means to appropriate the labour of others.

Furthermore, capital appears as a commodity, inasmuch as the division of profit into interest and profit proper is regulated by supply and demand, that is, by competition, just as the market-prices of commodities. But the difference here is just as apparent as the analogy. If supply and demand coincide, the market-price of commodities corresponds to their price of production, *i.e.*, their price then appears to be regulated by the immanent laws of capitalist production, independently of competition, since the fluctuations of supply and demand explain nothing but deviations of market-prices from prices of production. These deviations mutually balance one another, so that in the course of certain longer periods the average market-prices equal the prices of production. As soon as supply and demand coincide, these forces cease to operate, *i.e.*, compensate one another, and the general law determining prices then also comes to apply to individual cases. The market-price then corresponds even in its immediate form, and not only as the average of market-price movements, to the price of production, which is regulated by the immanent laws of the mode of production itself. The same applies to wages. If supply and demand coincide, they neutralise each other's effect, and wages equal the value of labour-power. But it is different with the interest on money-capital. Competition does not, in this case, determine the deviations from the rule. There is rather no law of division except that enforced by competition, because, as we shall later see, no such thing as a 'natural' rate of interest exists. By the natural rate of interest people merely mean the rate fixed by free competition. There are no 'natural' limits for the rate of interest. Whenever competition does not merely determine the deviations and fluctuations, whenever, therefore, the neutralisation of opposing forces puts a stop to any and all determination, the thing to be determined becomes something arbitrary and lawless. More on this in the next chapter.

In the case of interest-bearing capital everything appears superficial: the advance of capital as mere transfer from lender to borrower; the reflux of realised capital as mere transfer back, as a return payment with interest, by borrower to lender. The same is true of the fact, immanent in the capitalist mode of production, that the rate of profit is not only determined by the relation of profit made in one single turnover to advanced capital-value, but also by the length of this period of turnover, hence determined as profit yielded by industrial capital within definite spans of time. In the case of interest-bearing capital this likewise appears on the surface to mean that a definite interest is paid to the lender for a definite time span.

With his usual insight into the internal connection of things, the romantic Adam Müller says (*Elemente der Staatskunst*, Berlin, 1809, Dritter Theil, S. 138);

> In determining the prices of things, time is not considered; while in determining interest, time is the principal factor.

He does not see how the time of production and the time of circulation enter into the determination of commodity-prices, and how this is just what determines the rate of profit for a given period of turnover of capital, whereas interest is determined by precisely this determination of profit for a given period. His sagacity here, as elsewhere, consists in observing the clouds of dust on the surface and presumptuously declaring this dust to be something mysterious and important.

Notes

1. At this point certain passages may be quoted, in which the economists so conceive the matter.—'You (the Bank of England) are very large dealers in the *commodity of capital*?' is the question posed to a director of this bank when he was interrogated for the Report on Bank Acts on the witness stand. (H. of C. 1857, p. 404.)
2. 'That a man who borrows money with a view of making a profit by it, should give some portion of his profit to the lender, is a self-evident principle of natural justice.' (Gilbart, *The History and Principles of Banking*, London, 1834, p.463.)
3. 'A house,' 'money,' etc., are not to be loaned as 'capital' if Proudhon is to have his way, but are to be sold as 'commodities ... cost-price' (p. 44). Luther stood somewhat above Proudhon. He knew that profit-making does not depend on the manner of lending or buying: 'They turn buying also into usury. But this is really too much to bite off at once. We must first confine ourselves to one thing, usury in lending, and after we have stopped that (after judgement-day), we shall not fail to preach against *usury in buying*.' (Martin Luther, *An die Pfarherrn wider den Wucher zu predigen*, Wittenberg, 1540.)
4. 'The equitableness of taking interest depends not upon a man's making or not making profit, but upon its' (the borrowed) 'being capable of producing profit if rightly employed.' (*An Essay on the Governing Causes of the Natural Rate of Interest, wherein the sentiments of Sir W. Petty and Mr Locke, on that head, are considered*, London, 1750, p. 49. The author of this anonymous work is J. Massie.)
5. 'Rich people, instead of employing their money themselves ... let it out to other people for them to make profit of, reserving for the owners a proportion of the profits so made' (l. c., pp. 23-24).
6. 'The term ‹value,› when applied to currency, has three several meanings ... 2) currency, actually in hand... compared with the same amount of currency to be received upon a future day. In this case, the value of currency is measured by the rate of interest, and the rate of interest being determined by the ratio between the amount of liable capital and the demand for it.' (Colonel R. Torrens, *On the Operation of the Bank Charter Act of 1844, etc.*, 2nd ed., 1847, pp. 5, 6.)
7. 'The ambiguity of the term 'value of money' or of the currency, when employed indiscriminately as it is, to signify both value in exchange for commodities and value in use of capital, is a constant source of confusion.' (Tooke, *Inquiry into the Currency Principle*, p. 77.) The main confusion (implied in the matter itself) that value as such (interest) becomes the use-value of capital, has escaped Tooke.

22

Division of Profit Rate of Interest Natural Rate of Interest

The subject of this chapter, like all the other phenomena of credit we shall come across later on, cannot be analysed here in detail. The competition between lenders and borrowers and the resultant minor fluctuations of the money-market fall outside the scope of our inquiry. The circuit described by the rate of interest during the industrial cycle requires for its presentation the analysis of this cycle itself, but this likewise cannot be given here. The same applies to the greater or lesser approximate equalisation of the rate of interest in the world-market. We are here concerned with the independent form of interest-bearing capital and the individualisation of interest, as distinct from profit.

Since interest is merely a part of profit paid, according to our earlier assumption, by the industrial capitalist to the money-capitalist, the maximum limit of interest is the profit itself, in which case the portion pocketed by the productive capitalist would = 0. Aside from exceptional cases, in which interest might actually be larger than profit, but then could not be paid out of the profit, one might consider as the maximum limit of interest the total profit minus the portion (to be subsequently analysed) which resolves itself into wages of superintendence. The minimum limit of interest is altogether indeterminable. It may fall to any low. Yet in that case, there will always be counteracting influences to raise it again above this relative minimum.

> 'The relation between the sum paid for the use of capital and the capital expresses the rate of interest as measured in money.' 'The rate of interest depends 1) on the rate of profit; 2) on the proportion in which the entire profit is divided between the lender and borrower.' (*Economist*, January 22, 1853.) 'If that which men pay as interest for the use of what they borrow, be a part of the profits it is capable of producing, this interest must always be governed by those profits.' (Massie, 1.c., p.49.)

Let us first assume that there is a fixed relation between the total profit and that part of it which has to be paid as interest to the money-capitalist. It is then clear that the interest will rise or fall with the total profit, and the latter is determined by the general rate of profit and its fluctuations. For instance, if the average rate of profit were = 20% and the interest = ¼ of the profit, the rate of interest would = 5%; if the average rate of profit were = 16%, the rate of interest would = 4%. With the rate of profit at 20%, the rate of interest might rise to 8%, and the industrial capitalist would still make the same profit as he would at a rate of profit = 16% and a rate of interest = 4%, namely 12%. Should interest rise only to 6% or 7%, he would still keep a larger share of the profit. If the interest amounted to a constant quota of the average profit, it would follow that the higher the general rate of profit, the greater the absolute difference between the total profit and the interest, and the greater the portion of the total profit pocketed by the productive capitalist, and vice versa. Take it that interest = 1/5 of the average profit. One-fifth of 10 is 2; the difference between total profit and interest = 8. One-fifth of 20 = 4; difference = 20 - 4 = 16; 1/5 of 25 = 5; difference = 25 - 5 = 20; 1/5 of 30 = 6; difference = 30 - 6 = 24; 1/5 of 35 = 7; difference = 35 - 7 = 28. The different rates of interest of 4, 5, 6, 7% would here always represent no more than 1/5, or 20% of the total profit. If the rates of profit are different, therefore, different rates of interest may represent the same aliquot parts of the total profit, or the same percentage of the total profit. With such constant proportions of interest, the industrial profit (the difference between the total profit and the interest) would rise proportionately to the general rate of profit, and conversely.

All other conditions taken as equal, *i.e.*, assuming the proportion between interest and total profit to be more or less constant, the functioning capitalist is able and willing to pay a higher or lower interest directly proportional to the level of the rate of profit.[1]

Since we have seen that the rate of profit is inversely proportional to the development of capitalist production, it follows that the higher or lower rate of interest in a country is in the same inverse proportion to the degree of industrial development, at least in so far as the difference in the rate of interest actually expresses the difference in the rates of profit. It shall later develop that this need not always be the case. In this sense it may be said that interest is regulated through profit, or, more precisely, the general rate of profit. And this mode of regulating interest applies even to its average.

In any event the average rate of profit is to be regarded as the ultimate determinant of the maximum limit of interest.

The fact that interest is to be related to average profit will be considered presently at greater length. Whenever a specified entity, such as profit, is to be divided between two parties, the matter naturally hinges above all on the magnitude of the entity which is to be divided, and this, the magnitude of the profit, is determined by its average rate. Suppose the general rate of profit, hence the magnitude of profit, for a capital of given size, say, = 100, is assumed as given. Then the variations of interest will obviously be inversely proportional to those of the part of profit remaining in the hands of the producing capitalist, working with a borrowed capital. And the circumstances determining the amount of profit to be distributed, of the value produced by unpaid labour, differ widely from those which determine its distribution between these two kinds of capitalists, and frequently produce entirely opposite effects.[2]

If we observe the cycles in which modern industry moves—state of inactivity, mounting revival, prosperity, over-production, crisis, stagnation, state of inactivity, etc., which fall beyond the scope of our analysis—we shall find that a low rate of interest generally corresponds to periods of prosperity or extra profit, a rise in interest separates prosperity and its reverse, and a maximum of interest up to a point of extreme usury corresponds to the period of crisis.[3] The summer of 1843 ushered in a period of remarkable prosperity; the rate of interest, still 4½% in the spring of 1842, fell to 2% in the spring and summer of 1843;[4] in September it fell as low as 1½% (Gilbart, I, p. 166); whereupon it rose to 8% and higher during the crisis of 1847.

It is possible, however, for low interest to go along with stagnation, and for moderately rising interest to go along with revived activity.

The rate of interest reaches its peak during crises, when money is borrowed at any cost to meet payments. Since a rise in interest implies a fall in the price of securities, this simultaneously offers a fine opportunity to people with available money-capital, to acquire at ridiculously low prices such interest-bearing securities as must, in the course of things, at least regain their average price as soon as the rate of interest falls again.[5]

However, the rate of interest also has a tendency to fall quite independently of the fluctuations in the rate of profit. And, indeed, due to two main causes:

> I. 'Were we even to suppose that capital was never borrowed with any view but to productive employment, I think it very possible that interest might vary without any change in the rate of gross profits. For, as a nation advances in the career of wealth, a class of men springs up and increases more and more, who by the labours of their ancestors find themselves in the possession of funds sufficiently ample to afford a handsome maintenance from the interest alone. Very many also who during youth and middle age were actively engaged in business, retire in their latter days' to live quietly on the interest of the sums they have themselves accumulated. This class, as well as the former, has a tendency to increase with the increasing riches of the country, for those who begin with a tolerable stock are likely to make an independence sooner than they who commence with little. Thus it comes to pass, that in old and rich countries, the amount of national capital belonging to those who are unwilling to take the trouble of employing it themselves, bears a larger proportion to the whole productive stock of the society, than in newly settled and poorer districts. How much more numerous in proportion to the population is the class of *rentiers* ... in England! As the class of *rentiers* increases, so also does that of lenders of capital, for they are one and the same.' (Ramsay, *An Essay on the Distribution of Wealth*, pp. 201-02.)

II. The development of the credit system and the attendant ever-growing control of industrialists and merchants over the money savings of all classes of society that is effected through the bankers, and the progressive concentration of these savings in amounts which can serve as money-capital, must also depress the rate of interest. More about this later.

With reference to the determination of the rate of interest, Ramsay says that it

> 'depends partly upon the rate of gross profits, partly on the proportion in which these are separated into profits of capital and those of enterprise. This proportion again depends upon the competition between the lenders of capital and the borrowers; which competition is influenced, though by no means entirely regulated, by the rate of gross profit expected to be realised.[6] And the reason why competition is not exclusively regulated by this cause, is, because on the one hand many borrow without any view to productive employment; and, on the other, because the proportion of the whole capital to be lent, varies with the riches of the country independently of any change in gross profits.' (Ramsay, 1. c., pp. 206-07.)

To determine the average rate of interest we must 1) calculate the average rate of interest during its variations in the major industrial cycles; and 2) find the rate of interest for investments which require long-term loans of capital.

The average rate of interest prevailing in a certain country—as distinct from the continually fluctuating market rates—cannot be determined by any law. In this sphere there is no such thing as a natural rate of interest in the sense in which economists speak of a natural rate of profit and a natural rate of wages. Massie has rightly said in this respect (p.49):

> The only thing which any man can be in doubt about on this occasion, is, what proportion of these profits do of right belong to the borrower, and what to the lender; and this there is no other method of determining than by the opinions of borrowers and lenders in general; for right and wrong, in this respect, are only what common consent makes so.

Equating supply and demand—assuming the average rate of profit as given—means nothing. Wherever else this formula is resorted to (and this is then practically correct), it serves as a formula to find the fundamental rule (the regulating limits or limiting magnitudes) which is independent of, and rather determines, competition; notably as a formula for those who are held captive by the practice of competition, and by its phenomena and the conceptions arising out of them, to arrive at what is again but a superficial idea of the inner connection of economic relations obtaining within competition. It is a method to pass from the variations that go with competition to the limits of these variations. This is not the case with the average rate of interest. There is no good reason why average conditions of competition, the balance between lender and borrower, should give the lender an interest rate of 3, 4, 5%, etc., or else a certain percentage of the gross profits, say 20% or 50%, on his capital. Wherever it is competition as such which determines anything, the determination is accidental, purely empirical, and only pedantry or fantasy would seek to represent this accident as a necessity.[7] Nothing is more amusing in the reports of Parliament for 1857 and 1858 concerning bank legislation and commercial crises than to hear of 'the real rate produced' as the directors of the Bank of England, London bankers, country bankers, and professional theorists chatter back and forth, never getting beyond such commonplaces as that 'the price paid for the use of loanable capital should vary with the supply of such capital,' that 'a high rate and a low profit cannot permanently exist,' and similar specious platitudes.[8] Customs, juristic tradition, etc., have as much to do with determining the average rate of interest as competition itself, in so far as it exists not merely as an average, but rather as actual magnitude. In many law disputes, where interest has to be calculated, an average rate of interest has to be assumed as the legal rate. If we inquire further as to why the limits of a mean rate of interest cannot be deduced from general laws, we find the answer lies simply in the nature of interest. It is merely a part of the average profit. The same capital appears in two roles—as loanable capital in the lender's hands and as industrial, or commercial, capital in the hands of the functioning capitalist. But it functions just once, and produces profit just once. In the production process itself the nature of capital as loanable capital plays no role. How the two parties who have claim to it divide the profit is in itself just as purely empirical a matter belonging to the realm of accident as the distribution of percentage shares of a common profit in a business partnership. Two entirely different elements—labour-power and capital—act as determinants in the division between surplus-value and wages, which division essentially determines the rate of profit; these are functions of two independent variables, which limit one another; and it is their *qualitative difference* that is the source of the *quantitative division* of the produced value. We shall see later that the same occurs in the splitting of surplus-value into rent and profit. Nothing of the kind occurs in the case of interest. Here the *qualitative differentiation* as we shall presently see, proceeds rather from the *purely quantitative division* of the same sum of surplus-value.

It follows from the aforesaid that there is no such thing as a 'natural' rate of interest. But if, unlike the general rate of profit, there is on the one hand no general law to determine the limits of the average interest, or average rate of interest as distinct from the continually fluctuating market rates of interest, because it is merely a question of dividing the gross profit between two owners of capital under different title; on the other hand, the rate of interest—be it the average or the market rate prevalent in each particular case—appears as a uniform, definite and tangible magnitude in a quite different way from the general rate of profit.[9]

The rate of interest is similarly related to the rate of profit as the market-price of a commodity is to its value. In so far as the rate of interest is determined by the rate of profit, this is always the general rate of profit and not any specific rate of profit prevailing in some particular branch of industry, and still less any extra profit which an individual capitalist may make in a particular sphere of business.[10] It is a fact, therefore, that the general rate of profit appears as an empirical, given reality in the average rate of interest, although the latter is not a pure or reliable expression of the former.

It is indeed true that the rate of interest itself varies in accordance with the different classes of securities offered by borrowers, and in accordance with the length of time for which the money is borrowed; but it is uniform in each of these classes at a given moment. This distinction, then, does not militate against a fixed and uniform appearance of the rate of interest.[11]

The average rate of interest appears in every country over fairly long periods as a constant magnitude, because the general rate of profit varies only at longer intervals—in spite of constant variations in specific rates of profit, in which a change in one sphere is offset by an opposite change in another. And its relative constancy is revealed precisely in this more or less constant nature of the average, or common, rate of interest.

As concerns the perpetually fluctuating market rate of interest, however, it exists at any moment as a fixed magnitude, just as the market-price of commodities, because in the money-market all loanable capital continually faces functioning capital as an aggregate mass, so that the relation between the supply of loanable capital on one side, and the demand for it on the other, decides the market level of interest at any given time. This is all the more so, the more the development, and the attendant concentration, of the credit system gives to loanable capital a general social character and throws it all at once on the money-market. On the other hand, the general rate of profit is never anything more than a tendency, a movement to equalise specific rates of profit. The competition between capitalists—which is itself this movement toward equilibrium—consists here of their gradually withdrawing capital from spheres in which profit is for an appreciable length of time below average, and gradually investing capital into spheres in which profit is above average. Or it may also consist in additional capital distributing itself gradually and in varying proportions among these spheres. It is continual variation in supply and withdrawal of capital in regard to these different spheres, and never a simultaneous mass effect, as in the determination of the rate of interest.

We have seen that interest-bearing capital, although a category which differs absolutely from a commodity, becomes a commodity *sui generis*, so that interest becomes its price, fixed at all times by supply and demand like the market-price of an ordinary commodity. The market rate of interest, while fluctuating continually, appears therefore, at any given moment just as constantly fixed and uniform as the market-price of a commodity prevailing in each individual case. Money-capitalists supply this commodity, and functioning capitalists buy it, creating the demand for it. This does not occur when equalisation creates a general rate of profit. If prices of commodities in one sphere are below or above the price of production (wherein we deliberately leave aside the fluctuations attendant upon the various phases of the industrial cycle in each and every enterprise) the balance is effected through the expansion or curtailment of production, *i.e.*, the expansion or curtailment of the masses of commodities thrown on the market by industrial capitals—caused by inflow or outflow of capital to and from individual spheres of production. It is by this equalisation of the average market-prices of commodities to prices of production that deviations of specific rates of profit from the general, or average, rate of profit are corrected. It cannot be that in this process industrial or mercantile capital *as such* should ever assume the appearance of commodities vis-à-vis the buyer, as in the case of interest-bearing capital. If perceptible at all, this process is so only in the fluctuations and equalisations of market-prices of commodities to prices of production, not as a direct fixation of the average profit. The general rate of profit is, indeed, determined 1) by the surplus-value produced by the total capital, 2) by the proportion of this surplus-value to the value of the total capital, and 3) by competition, but only in so far as this is a movement whereby capitals invested in particular production spheres seek to draw equal dividends out of this surplus-value in proportion to their relative magnitudes. The general rate of profit, therefore, derives actually from causes far different and far more complicated than the market rate of interest, which is directly and immediately determined by the proportion between supply and demand, and hence is not as tangible and obvious a fact as the rate of interest. The individual rates of profit in various spheres of production are themselves more or less uncertain; but in so far as they appear, it is not their uniformity but their differences which are perceptible. The general rate of profit, however, appears only as the lowest limit of profit, not as an empirical, directly visible form of the actual rate of profit.

In emphasising this difference between the rate of interest and the rate of profit, we still omit the following two points, which favour consolidation of the rate of interest: 1) the historical pre-existence of interest-bearing capital and the existence of a traditional general rate of interest; 2) the far greater direct influence exerted by the world-market on establishing the rate of interest, irrespective of the economic conditions of a country, as compared with its influence on the rate of profit.

The average profit does not obtain as a directly established fact, but rather is to be determined as an end result of the equalisation of opposite fluctuations. Not so with the rate of interest. It is a thing fixed daily in its general, at least local, validity—a thing which serves industrial and mercantile capitals even as a prerequisite and a factor in the calculation of their operation. It becomes the general endowment of every sum of money of £100 to yield £2, 3, 4, 5. Meteorological reports never denote the readings of the barometer and thermometer with greater accuracy than stock exchange reports denote the rate of interest, not for one or another capital, but for capital in the money-market, *i.e.*, for loanable capital generally.

In the money-market only lenders and borrowers face one another. The commodity has the same form-money. All specific forms of capital in accordance with its investment in particular spheres of production or circulation are here obliterated. It exists in the undifferentiated homogeneous form of independent value-money. The competition of individual spheres does not affect it. They are all thrown together as borrowers of money, and capital confronts them all in a form, in which it is as yet indifferent to the prospective manner of its investment. It obtains most emphatically in the supply and demand of capital as *essentially the common capital of a class*—something industrial capital does only in the movement and competition of capital between the various individual spheres. On the other hand, money-capital in the money-market actually possesses the form, in which, indifferent to its specific employment, it is divided as a common element among the various spheres, among the capitalist class, as the requirements of production in each individual sphere may dictate. Moreover, with the development of large-scale industry money-capital, so far as it appears on the market, is not represented by some individual capitalist, not the owner of one or another fraction of the capital in the market, but assumes the nature of a concentrated, organised mass, which, quite different from actual production, is subject to the control of bankers, *i.e.*, the representatives of social capital. So that, as concerns the form of demand, loanable capital is confronted by the class as a whole, whereas in the province of supply it is loanable capital which obtains *en masse*.

These are some of the reasons why the general rate of profit appears blurred and hazy alongside the definite interest rate, which may fluctuate in magnitude, but always confronts borrowers as given and fixed because it varies uniformly for all of them. Just as variations in the value of money do not prevent it from having the same value vis-à-vis all commodities. Just as the daily fluctuations in market-prices of commodities do not prevent them from being daily reported in the papers. So the rate of interest is regularly reported as 'the price of money.' It is so, because capital itself is being offered here in the form of money as a commodity. The fixation of its price is thus a fixation of its market-price, as with all other commodities. The rate of interest, therefore, always appears as the general rate of interest, as so much money for so much money, as a definite quantity. The rate of profit, on the other hand, may vary even within the same sphere for commodities with the same price, depending on different conditions under which different capitals produce the same commodity, because the rate of profit of an individual capital is not determined by the market-price of a commodity, but rather by the difference between market-price and cost-price. And these different rates of profit can strike a balance—first within the same sphere and then between different spheres—only through continual fluctuation.

(Note for later elaboration.) A specific form of credit: It is known that when money serves as a means of payment instead of a means of purchase, the commodity is alienated, but its value is realised only later. If payment is not made until after the commodity has again been sold, this sale does not appear as the result of the purchase; rather it is through this sale that the purchase is realised. In other words, the sale becomes a means of purchase. Secondly: titles to debts, bills of exchange, etc., become means of payment for the creditor. Thirdly: the compensation of titles to debts replaces money.

Notes

1. 'The natural rate of interest is governed by the profits of trade to particulars.' (Massie, l. c., p. 51.)
2. At this point the manuscript contains the following remark: 'The course of this chapter shows that it is preferable, before analysing the laws of the distribution of profits, to ascertain first the way in which the division of quantity becomes one of quality. To make a transition from the previous chapter, we need but assume that interest is a certain indefinite portion of profit.'
3. 'In the first period, immediately after pressure, money is abundant without speculation;

in the second period, money is abundant and speculations abound; in the third period, speculation begins to decline and money is in demand, in the fourth period, money is scarce and a pressure arrives.' (Gilbart, *A Practical Treatise on Banking*, 5th ed., Vol. I, London, 1849, p. 149.)

4. Tooke explains this 'by the accumulation of surplus-capital necessarily accompanying the scarcity of profitable employment for it in previous years, by the release of hoards, and by the revival of confidence in commercial prospects.' *(History of Prices from 1839 till 1847*, London, 1848, p. 54.

5. 'An old customer of a banker was refused a loan upon a £200,000 bond; when about to leave to make known his suspension of payment, he was told there was no necessity for the step, under the circumstances the banker would buy the bond at £50,000.' ([H. Roy] *The Theory of the Exchanges. The Bank Charter Act of 1844, etc.*, London, 1869, p. 50.)

6. Since the rate of interest is on the whole determined by the average rate of profit, inordinate swindling is often bound up with a low rate of interest. For instance, the railway swindle in the summer of 1844. The rate of interest of the Bank of England was not raised to 3% until 16th October, 1844.

7. J G. Opdyke, for instance, in his *Treatise on Political Economy* (New York, 1851) makes a very unsuccessful attempt to explain the universality of a 5% rate of interest by eternal laws. Mr Karl Arnd is still more naive in *Die naturgemässe Volkswirtschaft gegenüber dem Monopoltengeist und dem Kommunismus, etc.*, Hanau, 1845. It is stated there: 'In the natural course of goods production there is just *one* phenomenon, which, in the fully settled countries, seems in some measure to regulate the rate of interest; this is the proportion, in which the timber in European forests is augmented through their annual growth. This new growth occurs quite independently of their exchange-value, at the rate of 3 or 4 to 100.' (How queer that trees should see to their new growth independently of their exchange-value!) 'According to this a drop in the rate of interest below its present level in the richest countries cannot be expected' (p. 124). (He means, because the new growth of the trees is independent of their exchange-value, however much their exchange-value may depend on their new growth.) This deserves to be called 'the primordial forest rate of interest.' Its discoverer makes a further laudable contribution in this work to 'our science' as the 'philosopher of the dog tax.' [Marx ironically calls K. Arnd the 'philosopher of the dog tax' because in a special paragraph in his book (§ 88, 5.420-24) he advocated that tax.—Ed.]

8. The Bank of England raises and lowers the rate of its discount, always, of course, with due consideration of the rate prevailing in the open market, in accordance with imports and exports of gold. 'By which gambling in discounts, by anticipation of the alterations in the bank-rate, has now become half the trade of the great heads of the money centre'—*i.e.*, of the London money-market. ([H. Roy] *The Theory of the Exchanges, etc.*, p. 113.)

9. 'The price of commodities fluctuates› continually; they are all made for different uses; the money serves for all purposes. The commodities, even those of the same kind, differ according to quality; cash money is always of the same value, or at least is assumed to be so. Thus it is that the price of money, which we designate by the term interest, has a greater stability and uniformity than that of any other thing.' (J. Steuart, *Principles of Political Economy*, French translation, 1789, IV, p. 27.)

10. 'This rule of dividing profits is not, however, to be applied particularly to every lender and borrower, but to lenders and borrowers in general ... remarkably great and small gains are the reward of skill and the want of understanding, which lenders have nothing at all to do with; for as they will not suffer by the one, they ought not to benefit by the other. What has been said of particular men in the same business is applicable to particular sorts of business; if the merchants and tradesmen employed in any one branch of trade get more by what they borrow than the common profits made by other merchants and tradesmen of the same country, the extraordinary gain is theirs, though it required only common skill and understanding to get

it; and not the lenders›, who supplied them with money ... for the lenders would not have lent their money to carry on any branch of trade up on lower terms than would admit of paying so much as the common rate of interest; and therefore, they ought not to receive more than that, whatever advantages may be made by their money.' (Massie, 1. c., pp. 50, 51.)

11. Bank-rate 5%
Market rate of discount, 60 days' drafts 3 5/8%
Ditto, 8 months' 3½%
Ditto, 6 months' 3 5/16%
Loans to bill-brokers, day to day 1 to 2%
Ditto, for one week 3%
Last rate for fortnight, loans to stockbrokers 4¾ to 5%
Deposit allowance (banks) 3½%
Ditto (discount houses) 3 to 3¼ %
How large this difference may be for one and the same day is shown in the preceding figures of the rate of interest of the London money-market on December 9, 1889, taken from the City article of the *Daily News* of December 10.
The minimum is 1%, the maximum 5%. [*F.E.*]

23

Interest and Profit of Enterprise

Interest, as we have seen in the two preceding chapters, appears originally, is originally, and remains, in fact, merely a portion of the profit, *i.e.*, of the surplus-value, which the functioning capitalist, industrialist or merchant has to pay to the owner and lender of money-capital whenever he uses loaned capital instead of his own. If he employs only his own capital, no such division of profit takes place; the latter is then entirely his. Indeed, as long as the owners of the capital employ it on their own in the reproduction process, they do not compete in determining the rate of interest. This alone shows that the category of interest—impossible without determining the rate of interest—is alien to the movements of industrial capital as such.

> 'The rate of interest may be defined to be that proportional sum which the lender is content to receive, and the borrower to pay, annually, or for any longer or shorter period, for the use of a certain amount of moneyed capital.... When the owner of a capital employs it actively in reproduction, he does not come under the head of those capitalists, the proportion of whom, to the number of borrowers, determines the rate of interest.' (Th. Tooke, *History of Prices*, London, 1838, II, pp. 355-56.)

It is indeed only the separation of capitalists into money-capitalists and industrial capitalists that transforms a portion of the profit into interest, that generally creates the category of interest; and it is only the competition between these two kinds of capitalists which creates the rate of interest.

As long as capital functions in the process of reproduction—assuming that it even belongs to the industrial capitalist and he has no need of paying it back to a lender—the capitalist, as a private individual, does not have at his disposal this capital itself, but only the profit, which he may spend as revenue. As long as his capital functions as capital, it belongs to the process of reproduction, is tied up in it. He is, indeed, its owner, but this ownership does not enable him to dispose of it in any other way, so long as he uses it as capital for the exploitation of labour. The same is true of the money-capitalist. So long as his capital is loaned out and thereby serves as money-capital, it brings him interest, a portion of the profit, but he cannot dispose of the principal. This is evident whenever he loans out his capital for, say, a year, or more, and receives interest at certain stipulated times without the return of his principal. But even the return of the principal makes no difference here. If he gets it back, he must always loan it out again, so long as it is to function for him as capital—here as money-capital. As long as he keeps it in his own hands, it does not collect interest and does not act as capital; and as long as it does gather interest and serve as capital, it is out of his hands. Hence the possibility of loaning out capital for all time. The following remarks by Tooke directed against Bosanquet are, therefore, entirely wrong. He quotes Bosanquet (*Metallic, Paper and Credit Currency*, London, 1842, p. 73):

> Were the rate of interest reduced as low as 1%, capital borrowed would be placed nearly on a par with capital possessed.

To this Tooke adds the following marginal note:

> That a capital borrowed at that, or even a lower rate, should be considered nearly on a par with capital possessed, is a proposition so strange as hardly to warrant serious notice were it not advanced by a writer so intelligent, and, on some points of the subject, so well informed. Has he overlooked the circumstance, or does he consider it of little consequence, that there must, by the supposition, be a condition of repayment? (Th. Tooke, *An Inquiry into the Currency Principle*, 2nd ed., London, 1844, p. 80.)

If interest were = 0, the industrial capitalist operating on borrowed capital would stand on a par with a capitalist using his own capital. Both would pocket the same average profit, and capital, whether borrowed or owned, serves as capital only as long as it produces profit. The condition of return payment would alter nothing. The nearer the rate of interest approaches zero, falling, for instance, to 1%, the nearer borrowed capital is to being on a par with owner's capital. So long as money-capital is to exist as money-capital, it must always be loaned out, and indeed at the prevailing rate of interest, say of 1%, and always to the same class of industrial and commercial capitalists. So long as these function as capitalists, the sole difference between the one working with borrowed capital and the other with his own is that the former must pay interest and the latter must not; the one pockets the entire profit p, and the other p - i, the profit minus the interest. The nearer interest approaches zero, the nearer p - i approaches p, and hence the nearer the two capitals are to being on a par. The one must pay back the capital and borrow anew; yet the other must likewise advance it again and again to the production process, so long as his capital is to function, and cannot dispose of it freely, independent of this process. The sole remaining difference between the two is the obvious difference that one is the owner of his capital, and the other is not.

The question which now arises is this. How does this purely quantitative division of profit into net profit and interest turn into a qualitative one? In other words, how is it that a capitalist who employs solely his own, not borrowed capital, classifies a portion of his gross profit under the specific category of interest and as such calculates it separately? And, furthermore, how is it that all capital, whether borrowed or not, is differentiated as interest-bearing capital from itself as capital producing a net profit?

It is understood that not every accidental quantitative division of profit turns in this manner into a qualitative one. For instance, some industrial capitalists join hands to operate a business and then divide the profit among themselves in accordance with some legal agreement. Others do their business, each on his own, without any partners. These last do not calculate their profit under two heads—one part as individual profit, and the other as company profit for their non-existent partners. In this case the quantitative division, therefore, does not become a qualitative one. This occurs whenever ownership happens to be vested in several juridical persons. It does not occur whenever this is not the case.

In order to answer this question, we must dwell somewhat longer on the actual point of departure in the formation of interest; that is, we must proceed from the assumption that the money-capitalist and industrial capitalist really confront one another not just as legally different persons, but as persons playing entirely different roles in the reproduction process, or as persons in whose hands the same capital really performs a two-fold and wholly different movement. The one merely loans it, the other employs it productively.

For the productive capitalist who works on borrowed capital, the gross profit falls into two parts—the interest, which he is to pay the lender, and the surplus over and above the interest, which makes up his own share of the profit. If the general rate of profit is given, this latter portion is determined by the rate of interest; and if the rate of interest is given, then by the general rate of profit. And furthermore: however the gross profit, the actual value of the total profit, may diverge in each individual case, from the average profit, the portion belonging to the functioning capitalist is determined by the interest, since this is fixed by the general rate of interest (leaving aside any special legal stipulations) and assumed to be given beforehand, before the process of production begins, hence before its result, the gross profit, is achieved. We have seen that the actual specific product of capital is surplus-value, or, more precisely, profit. But for the capitalist working on borrowed capital it is not profit, but profit minus interest, that portion of profit which remains to him after paying interest. This portion of the profit, therefore, necessarily appears to him to be the product of a capital as long as it is operative; and this it is, as far as he is concerned, because he represents capital only as functioning capital. He is its personification as long as it functions, and it functions as long as it is profitably invested in industry or commerce and such operations are undertaken with it through its employer as are prescribed by the branch of industry concerned. As distinct from interest, which he has to pay to the lender out of the gross profit, the portion of profit which falls to his share necessarily assumes the form of industrial or commercial profit, or, to use a German term embracing both, the form of *Unternehmergewinn* (profit of enterprise). If the gross profit equals the average profit, the size of the profit of enterprise is determined exclusively by the rate of interest. If the gross profit deviates from the average profit, its difference from the average profit (after interest is deducted from both) is determined by all the circumstances which cause a temporary deviation, be it of the rate of profit in any particular sphere from the general rate of profit, or the profit of some individual capitalist in a certain sphere from the average profit of this sphere. We have seen however that the rate of profit within the production process itself does not depend on surplus-value alone, but also on many other circumstances, such as purchase prices of means of production, methods more productive than the average, on savings of constant capital, etc. And aside from the price of production, it depends on special circumstances, and in every single business transaction on the greater or lesser shrewdness and industry of the capitalist, whether, and to what extent, he buys or sells above or below the price of production and thus appropriates a greater or smaller portion of the total surplus-value in the process of circulation. In any case, the quantitative division of the gross profit turns here into a qualitative one, and all the more so because the quantitative division itself depends on *what* is to be divided, the *manner* in which the active capitalist manages his capital, and what gross profit it yields to him as a functioning capital, *i.e.*, in consequence of his functions as an active capitalist. The functioning capitalist is here assumed as a non-owner of capital. Ownership of the capital is represented in relation to him by the money-capitalist, the lender. The interest he pays to the latter thus appears as that portion of gross profit which is due to the ownership of capital as such. As distinct from this, that portion of profit which falls to the active capitalist appears now as profit of enterprise, deriving solely from the operations, or functions, which he performs with the capital in the process of reproduction, hence particularly those functions which he performs as entrepreneur in industry or commerce. In relation to him interest appears, therefore, as the mere fruit of owning capital, of capital as such abstracted from the reproduction process of capital, inasmuch as it does not 'work,' does not function; while profit of enterprise appears to him as the exclusive fruit of the functions which he performs with the capital, as the fruit of the movement and performance of capital, of a performance which appears to him as his own activity, as opposed to the inactivity, the non-participation of the money-capitalist in the production process. This qualitative distinction between the two portions of gross profit that interest is the fruit of capital as such, of the ownership of capital irrespective of the production process, and that profit of enterprise is the fruit of performing capital, of capital functioning in the production process, and hence of the active role played by the employer of the capital in the reproduction process—this qualitative distinction is by no means merely a subjective notion of the money-capitalist, on the one hand, and the industrial capitalist, on the other. It rests upon an objective fact, for interest flows to the money-capitalist, to the lender, who is the mere owner of capital, hence represents only ownership of capital before the production process and outside of it; while the profit of enterprise flows to the functioning capitalist alone, who is non-owner of the capital.

The merely quantitative division of the gross profit between two different persons who both have different legal claims to the same capital, and hence to the profit produced by it, thus turns into a qualitative division for both the industrial capitalist in so far as he is operating on borrowed capital, and for the money-capitalist, in so far as he does not himself apply his capital. One portion of the profit appears now as fruit due as such to capital in one form, as interest; the other portion appears as a specific fruit of capital in an opposite form, and thus as profit of enterprise. One appears exclusively as the fruit of operating with the capital, the fruit of performing capital, or of the functions performed by the active capitalist. And this ossification and individualisation of the two parts of the gross profit in respect to one another, as though they originated from two essentially different sources, now takes firm shape for the entire capitalist class and the total capital. And, indeed, regardless of whether the capital employed by the active capitalist is borrowed or not, and whether the capital belonging to the money-capitalist is employed by himself or not. The profit of every capital, and consequently also the average profit established by the equalisation of capitals, splits, or is separated, into two qualitatively different, mutually independent and separately individualised parts, to wit—interest and profit of enterprise—both of which are determined by separate laws. The capitalist operating on his own capital, like the one operating on borrowed capital, divides the gross profit into interest due to himself as owner, as his own lender, and into profit of enterprise due to him as to an active capitalist performing his function. As concerns this division, therefore, as a qualitative one, it is immaterial whether the capitalist really has to share with another, or not. The employer of capital, even when working with his own capital, splits into two personalities—the owner of capital and the employer of capital; with reference to the categories of profit which it yields, his capital also splits into capital-*property*, capital *outside* the production process, and yielding interest of itself, and capital *in* the production process which yields a profit of enterprise through its function.

Interest, therefore, becomes firmly established in a way that it no longer appears as a division of gross profit of indifference to production, which occurs occasionally when the industrial capitalist happens to operate with someone else's capital. His profit splits into interest and profit of enterprise even when he operates on his own capital. A merely quantitative division thus turns into a qualitative one. It occurs regardless of the fortuitous circumstance whether the industrial capitalist is, or is not, the owner of his capital. It is not only a matter of different quotas of profit assigned to different persons, but two different categories of profit which are differently related to the capital, hence related to different aspects of the capital.

Now that this division of gross profit into interest and profit of enterprise has become a qualitative one, it is easy to discover the reasons why it acquires this character of a qualitative division for the total capital and the entire class of capitalists.

Firstly, this follows from the simple empirical circumstance that the majority of industrial capitalists, even if in different numerical proportions, work with their own and with borrowed capital, and that at different times the proportion between one's own and borrowed capital changes.

Secondly, the transformation of a portion of the gross profit into the form of interest converts its other portion into profit of enterprise. The latter is, indeed, but the opposite form assumed by the excess of gross profit over interest as soon as this exists as an independent category. The entire analysis of the problem how gross profit is differentiated into interest and profit of enterprise, resolves itself into the inquiry of how a portion of the gross profit becomes universally ossified and individualised as interest. Yet historically interest-bearing capital existed as a completed traditional form, and hence interest as a completed sub-division of surplus-value produced by capital, long before the capitalist mode of production and its attendant conceptions of capital and profit. Thus it is that to the popular mind money-capital, or interest-bearing capital, is still capital as such, as capital *par excellence.* Thus it is, on the other hand, that up to the time of Massie the notion prevailed that it is money as such which is paid in interest. The fact that loaned capital yields interest whether actually employed as capital or not—even when borrowed only for consumption—lends strength to the idea that this form of capital exists independently. The best proof of the independence which interest possessed during the early periods of the capitalist mode of production in reference to profit, and which interest-bearing capital possessed in reference to industrial capital, is that it was discovered (by Massie [[J. Massie] *An Essay on the Governing Causes of the Natural Rate of Interest*, London, 1750.—*Ed.*] and after him by Hume [D. Hume, 'On Interest.' In: 'Essays and Treatises on Several Subjects,' Vol. I, London, 1764.—*Ed.*]) as late as the middle of the 18th century, that interest is but a portion of the gross profit, and that such a discovery was at all necessary.

Thirdly, whether the industrial capitalist operates on his own or on borrowed capital does not alter the fact that the class of money-capitalists confronts him as a special kind of capitalists, money-capital as an independent kind of capital, and interest as an independent form of surplus-value peculiar to this specific capital.

Qualitatively speaking, interest is surplus-value yielded by the mere ownership of capital; it is yielded by capital as such, even though its owner remains outside the reproduction process. Hence it is surplus-value realised by capital outside of its process.

Quantitatively speaking, that portion of profit which forms interest does not seem to be related to industrial or commercial capital as such, but to money-capital, and the rate of this portion of surplus-value, the rate of interest, reinforces this relation. Because, in the first place, the rate of interest is independently determined despite its dependence upon the general rate of profit, and, in the second place, like the market-price of commodities, it appears in contrast to the intangible rate of profit as a fixed, uniform, tangible and always given relation for all its variations. If all capital were in the hands of the industrial capitalists there would be no such thing as interest and rate of interest. The independent form assumed by the quantitative division of gross profit creates the qualitative one. If the industrial capitalist were to compare himself with the money-capitalist, it would be his profit of enterprise alone, the excess of his gross profit over the average interest—the latter appearing to be empirically given by virtue of the rate of interest—that would distinguish him from the other person. If, on the other hand, he compares himself with the industrial capitalist working with his own, instead of borrowed, capital, the latter differs from him only as a money-capitalist in pocketing the interest instead of paying it to someone else. The portion of gross profit distinguished from interest appears to him, in either case, as profit of enterprise, and interest itself as a surplus-value yielded by capital as such, which it would yield even if not applied productively.

This is correct in the practical sense for the individual capitalist. He has the choice of making use of his capital by lending it out as interest-bearing capital, or of expanding its value on his own by using it as productive capital, regardless of whether it exists as money-capital from the very first, or whether it still has to be converted into money-capital. But to apply it to the total capital of society, as some vulgar economists do, and to go so far as to define it as the cause of profit, is, of course, preposterous. The idea of converting all the capital into money-capital, without there being people who buy and put to use means of production, which make up the total capital outside of a relatively small portion of it existing in money, is, of course, sheer nonsense. It would be still more absurd to presume that capital would yield interest on the basis of capitalist production without performing any productive function, *i.e.*, without creating surplus-value, of which interest is just a part; that the capitalist mode of production would run its course without capitalist production. If an untowardly large section of capitalists were to convert their capital into money-capital, the result would be a frightful depreciation of money-capital and a frightful fall in the rate of interest; many would at once face the impossibility of living on their interest, and would hence be compelled to reconvert into industrial capitalists. But we repeat that it is a fact for the individual capitalist. For this reason, even when operating with his own capital, he necessarily considers the part of his average profit which equals the average interest as fruit of his capital as such, set apart from the process of production; and as distinct from this portion singled out as interest, he considers the surplus of the gross profit as mere profit of enterprise.

Fourthly, [A blank in the manuscript].

We have seen, therefore, that the portion of profit which the functioning capitalist has to pay to the owner of borrowed capital is transformed into an independent form for a portion of the profit, which all capital as such, whether borrowed or not, yields under the name of interest. How large this portion is depends on the average rate of interest. Its origin is only still revealed in the fact that the functioning capitalist, when owner of his capital, does not compete—at least not actively—in determining the interest rate. The purely quantitative division of the profit between two persons who have different legal titles to it has turned into a qualitative division, which seems to spring from the very nature of capital and profit. Because, as we have seen, as soon as a portion of profit universally assumes the form of interest, the difference between average profit and interest, or the portion of profit over and above the interest, assumes a form opposite to interest—the form of profit of enterprise. These two forms, interest and profit of enterprise, exist only as opposites. Hence, they are not related to surplus-value, of which they are but parts placed under different categories, heads or names, but rather to one another. It is because one portion of profit turns into interest, that the other appears as profit of enterprise.

By profit we here always mean average profit, since variations do not concern us in this analysis, be they of individual profits or of profits in different spheres—hence variations caused by the competitive struggle and other circumstances affecting the distribution of the average profit, or surplus-value. This applies generally to this entire inquiry.

Interest is then net profit, as Ramsay calls it, which the ownership of capital yields as such, either simply to the lender, who remains outside the reproduction process, or to the owner who employs his capital productively. But in the latter's case, too, capital yields this net profit to him not in his capacity of productive capitalist, but of money-capitalist, of lender of his own capital as interest-bearing capital to himself as to a functioning capitalist. Just as the conversion of money, and of value in general, into capital is the constant result of capitalist production, so is its existence as capital its constant precondition. By its ability to be transformed into means of production it continually commands unpaid labour and thereby transforms the processes of production and circulation of commodities into the production of surplus-value for its owner. Interest is, therefore, the expression of the fact that value in general-materialised labour in its general social form-value which assumes the form of means of production in the actual process of production, confronts living labour-power as an independent power, and is a means of appropriating unpaid labour; and that it is such a power because it confronts the labourer as the property of another. But on the other hand, this antithesis to wage-labour is obliterated in the form of interest, because interest-bearing capital as such has not wage-labour, but productive capital for its opposite. The lending capitalist as such faces the capitalist performing his actual function in the process of reproduction, not the wage-worker, who, precisely under capitalist production, is expropriated of the means of production. Interest-bearing capital is capital as *property* as distinct from capital as a *function*. But so long as capital does not perform its function, it does not exploit labourers and does not come into opposition to labour.

On the other hand, profit of enterprise is not related as an opposite to wage-labour, but only to interest.

Firstly, assuming the average profit to be given, the rate of the profit of enterprise is not determined by wages, but by the rate of interest. It is high or low in inverse proportion to it[1]

Secondly, the functioning capitalist derives his claim to profits of enterprise, hence the profit of enterprise itself, not from his ownership of capital, but from the function of capital, as distinct from the definite form in which it is only inert property. This stands out as an immediately apparent contrast whenever he operates with borrowed capital, and interest and profit of enterprise, therefore, go to different persons. The profit of enterprise springs from the function of capital in the reproduction process, hence as a result of the operations, the acts by which the functioning capitalist promotes this function of industrial and commercial capital. But to represent functioning capital is not a sinecure, like representing interest-bearing capital. On the basis of capitalist production, the capitalist directs the process of production and circulation. Exploiting productive labour entails exertion, whether he exploits it himself or has it exploited by someone else on his behalf. Therefore, his profit of enterprise appears to him as distinct from interest, as independent of the ownership of capital, but rather as the result of his function as a non-proprietor—a *labourer.*

He necessarily conceives the idea for this reason that his profit of enterprise, far from being counterposed to wage-labour and far from being the unpaid labour of others, is itself rather a *wage* or wages of superintendence of labour, higher than a common labourer›s, 1) because the work is far more complicated, and 2) because he pays them to himself. The fact that his function as a capitalist consists in creating surplus-value, *i.e.*, unpaid labour, and creating it under the most economical conditions, is entirely lost sight of in the contrast that interest falls to the share of the capitalist even when he does not perform the function of a capitalist and is merely the owner of capital; and that, on the other hand, profit of enterprise does fall to the share of the functioning capitalist even when he is not the owner of the capital on which he operates. He forgets, due to the antithetical form of the two parts into which profit, hence surplus-value, is divided, that both are merely parts of the surplus-value, and that this division alters nothing in the nature, origin, and way of existence of surplus-value.

In the process of reproduction the functioning capitalist represents capital as the property of another vis-à-vis the wage-labourers, and the money-capitalist, represented by the functioning capitalist, takes a hand in exploiting labour. The fact that the investing capitalist can perform his function of making the labourers work for him, or of employing means of production as capital, only as the personification of the means of production vis-à-vis the labourers, is forgotten in the contradiction between the function of capital in the reproduction process and the mere ownership of capital outside of the reproduction process.

In fact, the form of interest and profit of enterprise assumed by the two parts of profit, *i.e.*, of surplus-value, expresses no relation to labour, because this relation exists only between labour and profit, or rather the surplus-value as a sum, a whole, the unity of these two parts. The proportion in which the profit is divided, and the different legal titles by which this division is sanctioned, are based on the assumption that profit is already in existence. If, therefore, the capitalist is the owner of the capital on which he operates, he pockets the whole profit, or surplus-value. It is absolutely immaterial to the labourer whether the capitalist does this, or whether he has to pay a part of it to a third person as its legal proprietor. The reasons for dividing the profit among two kinds of capitalists thus turn imperceptibly into the reasons for the existence of the profit, the surplus-value, that is to be divided, and which capital as such derives from the reproduction process regardless of any subsequent division. Since interest is opposed to profit of enterprise, and profit of enterprise to interest, and since they are both counterposed to one another, but not to labour, it follows that profit of enterprise plus interest, *i.e.*, profit, and further surplus-value, are derived—from what? From the antithetical form of its two parts! But profit is produced before its division is undertaken, and before there can be any thought of it.

Interest-bearing capital remains as such only so long as the loaned money is actually converted into capital and a surplus is produced with it, of which interest is a part. But this does not rule out that drawing interest, regardless of the process of production, is its organic property. So does labour-power preserve its property of producing value only so long as it is employed and materialised in the labour-process; yet this does not argue against the fact that it is potentially, as a power, an activity which creates value, and that as such it does not spring from the process of production, but rather antecedes it. It is bought as such a capacity for creating value. One might also buy it without setting it to work productively; for purely personal ends, for instance, for personal services, etc. The same applies to capital. It is the borrower's affair whether he employs it as capital, hence actually sets in motion its inherent property of producing surplus-value. What he pays for, is in either case, the potential surplus-value inherently contained in capital as a commodity.

Let us now consider profit of enterprise in greater detail.

Since the specific social attribute of capital under capitalist production—that of being property commanding the labour-power of another—becomes fixed, so that interest appears as a part of surplus-value produced by capital in this interrelation, the other part of surplus-value—profit of enterprise—must necessarily appear as coming not from capital as such, but from the process of production, separated from its specific social attribute, whose distinct mode of existence is already expressed by the term interest on capital. But the process of production, separated from capital, is simply a labour-process. Therefore, the industrial capitalist, as distinct from the owner of capital, does not appear as operating capital, but rather as a functionary irrespective of capital, or, as a simple agent of the labour-process in general, as a labourer, and indeed as a wage-labourer.

Interest as such expresses precisely the existence of the conditions of labour as capital, in their social antithesis to labour, and in their transformation into personal power vis-à-vis and over labour. It represents the ownership of capital as a means of appropriating the products of the labour of others. But it represents this characteristic of capital as something which belongs to it outside the production process and by no means is the result of the specifically capitalist attribute of this production process itself. Interest represents this characteristic not as directly counterposed to labour, but rather as unrelated to labour, and simply as a relationship of one capitalist to another. Hence, as an attribute outside of and irrelevant to the relation of capital to labour. In interest, therefore, in that specific form of profit in which the antithetical character of capital assumes an independent form, this is done in such a way that the antithesis is completely obliterated and abstracted. Interest is a relationship between two capitalists, not between capitalist and labourer.

On the other hand, this form of interest lends the other portion of profit the qualitative form of profit of enterprise, and further of wages of superintendence. The specific functions which the capitalist as such has to perform, and which fall to him as distinct from and opposed to the labourer, are presented as mere functions of labour. He creates surplus-value not because he works as a *capitalist,* but because he *also* works, regardless of his capacity of capitalist. This portion of surplus-value is thus no longer surplus-value, but its opposite, an equivalent for labour performed. Due to the alienated character of capital, its antithesis to labour, being relegated to a place outside the actual process of exploitation, namely to the interest-bearing capital, this process of exploitation itself appears as a simple labour-process in which the functioning capitalist merely performs a different kind of labour than the labourer. So that the labour of exploiting and the exploited labour both appear identical as labour. The labour of exploiting is just as much labour as exploited labour. The social form of capital falls to interest, but expressed in a neutral and indifferent form. The economic function of capital falls to profit of enterprise, but abstracted from the specific capitalist character of this function.

The same thing passes through the mind of the capitalist in this case, as in the case of the reasons indicated in Part II of this book for compensation in the equalisation to average profit. These reasons for compensation which enter the distribution of surplus-value as determinants are distorted in a capitalist's mind to appear as bases of origin and the (subjective) justifications of profit itself.

The conception of profit of enterprise as the wages of supervising labour, arising from the antithesis of profit of enterprise to interest, is further strengthened by the fact that a portion of profit may, indeed, be separated, and is separated in reality, as wages, or rather the reverse, that a portion of wages appears under capitalist production as integral part of profit. This portion, as Adam Smith correctly deduced, presents itself in pure form, independently and wholly separated from profit (as the sum of interest and profit of enterprise), on the one hand, and on the other, from that portion of profit which remains, after interest is deducted, as profit of enterprise in the salary of management of those branches of business whose size, etc., permits of a sufficient division of labour to justify a special salary for a manager.

The labour of supervision and management is naturally required wherever the direct process of production assumes the form of a combined social process, and not of the isolated labour of independent producers.[2] However, it has a double nature.

On the one hand, all labour in which many individuals co-operate necessarily requires a commanding will to co-ordinate and unify the process, and functions which apply not to partial operations but to the total activity of the workshop, much as that of an orchestra conductor. This is a productive job, which must be performed in every combined mode of production.

On the other hand—quite apart from any commercial department—this supervision work necessarily arises in all modes of production based on the antithesis between the labourer, as the direct producer, and the owner of the means of production. The greater this antagonism, the greater the role played by supervision. Hence it reaches its peak in the slave system.[3] But it is indispensable also in the capitalist mode of production, since the production process in it is simultaneously a process by which the capitalist consumes labour-power. Just as in despotic states, supervision and all-round interference by the government involves both the performance of common activities arising from the nature of all communities, and the specific functions arising from the antithesis between the government and the mass of the people.

In the works of ancient writers, who had the slave system before them, both sides of the work of supervision are as inseparably combined in theory as they were in practice. Likewise in the works of modern economists, who regard the capitalist mode of production as absolute. On the other hand, as I shall presently illustrate with an example, the apologists of the modern slave system utilise the work of supervision quite as much as a justification of slavery, as the other economists do to justify the wage system.

The *villicus* in Cato's time:

> 'At the head of the estate with slave economy (*familia rustica*) stands the manager (*villicus*, derived from *villa*), who receives and expends, buys and sells, takes instructions from the master, in whose absence he gives orders and metes out punishment.... The manager naturally had more freedom of action than the other slaves; the Magonian books advise that he be permitted to marry, raise children, and have his own funds, and Cato recommends that he be married to the female manager; he alone probably had the prospect of winning his freedom from the master in the event of good behaviour. As for the rest, all formed a common household.... Every slave, including the manager himself, was supplied his necessities at his master's expense at definite intervals and fixed rates, and had to get along on them... The quantity varied in accordance with labour, which is why the manager, for example, whose work was lighter than the other slaves', received a smaller ration than they.' (Mommsen, *Römische Geschichte*, 2nd ed., 1856, 1, pp. 809-10.)

Aristotle:

> 'Ο γαρ δεσποτηζ ουχ εν κτασθαι τουζ δουλουζ, αλλεν τω χρηθαιυ ουλουζ.' ('For the master'—the capitalist—'proves himself such not by obtaining slaves'—ownership of capital which gives him power to buy labour-power—'but in employing slaves'—using labourers, nowadays wage-labourers, in the production process.) 'Εστι δε αυτη η επιστημη ουδεν μεγα εχουσα ουδε σεμνον.' ('But there is nothing great or sublime about this science.') 'α γαρ τον δουλον επιστασθαι δει ποιειν εχεινον δει ταυτα επιστασθ αι επιταττειν.' 'But whatever the slave must be able to perform, the master must be able to order.') 'Διο οσοιζ εξουσια μη αυτουζ χαχοπαθειν επιστοποζ λαμβανει ταυ– την την τιμην, αυτοι δε πολιτευονται η φιλοσοφοσιν.' ('Whenever the masters are not compelled to plague themselves with supervision, the manager assumes *this honour*, while the masters attend to affairs of state or study philosophy.') (Aristotle, *De republica*, Bekker edition, Book I, 7.)

Aristotle says in just so many words that supremacy in the political and economic fields imposes the functions of government upon the ruling powers, and hence that they must, in the economic field, know the art of consuming labour-power. And he adds that this supervisory work is not a matter of great moment and that for this reason the master leaves the 'honour' of this drudgery to an overseer as soon as he can afford it.

The work of management and supervision—so far as it is not a special function determined by the nature of all combined social labour, but rather by the antithesis between the owner of means of production and the owner of mere labour-power, regardless of whether this labour-power is purchased by buying the labourer himself, as it is under the slave system, or whether the labourer himself sells his labour-power, so that the production process also appears as a process by which capital consumes his labour—this function arising out of the servitude of the direct producers has all too often been quoted to justify this relationship. And exploitation, the appropriation of the unpaid labour of others, has quite as often been represented as the reward justly due to the owner of capital for his work; but never better than by a champion of slavery in the United States, a lawyer named O'Connor, at a meeting held in New York on December 19, 1859, under the slogan of 'Justice for the South.'

> 'Now, gentlemen,' he said amid thunderous applause, 'to that condition of bondage the Negro is assigned by Nature... He has strength, and has the power to labour; but the Nature which created the power denied to him either the intellect to govern, or willingness to work.' (Applause.) 'Both were denied to him. And that Nature which

deprived him of the will to labour, gave him a master to coerce that will, and to make him a useful... servant in the clime in which he was capable of living useful for himself and for the master who governs him... I maintain that it is not injustice to leave the Negro in the condition in which Nature placed him, to give him a master to govern him ... nor is it depriving him of any of his rights to compel him to labour in return, and afford to that master just compensation for the labour and talent employed in governing him and rendering him useful to himself and to the society.' [*New York Daily Tribune*, November 20, 1859, pp. 7-8.—*Ed*]

Now, the wage-labourer, like the slave, must have a master who puts him to work and rules over him. And assuming the existence of this relationship of lordship and servitude, it is quite proper to compel the wage-labourer to produce his own wages and also the wages of supervision, as compensation for the labour of ruling and supervising him, or

> just compensation for the labour and talent employed in governing him and rendering him useful to himself and to the society.

The labour of supervision and management, arising as it does out of an antithesis, out of the supremacy of capital over labour, and being therefore, common to all modes of production based on class contradictions like the capitalist mode, is directly and inseparably connected, also under the capitalist system, with productive functions which all combined social labour assigns to individuals as their special tasks. The wages of an *epitropos,* or *régisseur,* as he was called in feudal France, are entirely divorced from profit and assume the form of wages for skilled labour whenever the business is operated on a sufficiently large scale to warrant paying for such a manager, although, for all that, our industrial capitalists are far from 'attending to affairs of state or studying philosophy.'

It has already been remarked by Mr Ure[4] that it is not the industrial capitalists, but the industrial managers who are 'the soul of our industrial system.' Whatever concerns the commercial part of an establishment we have already said all that is necessary in the preceding part.

The capitalist mode of production has brought matters to a point where the work of supervision, entirely divorced from the ownership of capital, is always readily obtainable. It has, therefore, come to be useless for the capitalist to perform it himself. An orchestra conductor need not own the instruments of his orchestra, nor is it within the scope of his duties as conductor to have anything to do with the 'wages' of the other musicians. Co-operative factories furnish proof that the capitalist has become no less redundant as a functionary in production as he himself, looking down from his high perch, finds the big landowner redundant. Inasmuch as the capitalist's work does not originate in the purely capitalistic process of production, and hence does not cease on its own when capital ceases; inasmuch as it does not confine itself solely to the function of exploiting the labour of others; inasmuch as it, therefore, originates from the social form of the labour-process, from combination and co-operation of many in pursuance of a common result, it is just as independent of capital as that form itself as soon as it has burst its capitalistic shell. To say that this labour is necessary as capitalistic labour, or as a function of the capitalist, only means that the *vulgus* is unable to conceive the forms developed in the lap of capitalist production, separate and free from their antithetical capitalist character. The industrial capitalist is a worker, compared to the money-capitalist, but a worker in the sense of capitalist, *i.e.*, an exploiter of the labour of others. The wage which he claims and pockets for this labour is exactly equal to the appropriated quantity of another's labour and depends directly upon the rate of exploitation of this labour, in so far as he undertakes the effort required for exploitation; it does not, however, depend on the degree of exertion that such exploitation demands, and which he can shift to a manager for moderate pay. After every crisis there are enough ex-manufacturers in the English factory districts who will supervise, for low wages, what were formerly their own factories in the capacity of managers of the new owners, who are frequently their creditors.[5]

The wages of management both for the commercial and industrial manager are completely isolated from the profits of enterprise in the co-operative factories of labourers, as well as in capitalist stock companies. The separation of wages of management from profits of enterprise, purely accidental at other times, is here constant. In a co-operative factory the antagonistic nature of the labour of supervision disappears, because the manager is paid by the labourers instead of representing capital counterposed to them. Stock companies in general—developed with the credit system—have an increasing tendency to separate this work of management as a function from the ownership of capital, be it self-owned or borrowed. Just as the development of bourgeois society witnessed a separation of the functions of judges and administrators from land-ownership, whose attributes they were in feudal times. But since, on the one hand, the mere owner of capital, the money-capitalist, has to face the functioning capitalist, while money-capital itself assumes a social character with the advance of credit, being concentrated in banks and loaned out by them instead of its original owners, and since, on the other hand, the mere manager who has no title whatever to the capital, whether through borrowing it or otherwise, performs all the real functions pertaining to the functioning capitalist as such, only the functionary remains and the capitalist disappears as superfluous from the production process.

It is manifest from the public accounts of the co-operative factories in England[6] that—after deducting the manager's wages, which form a part of the invested variable capital much the same as wages of other labourers—the profit was higher than the average profit, although at times they paid a much higher interest than did private manufacturers. The source of greater profits in all these cases was greater economy in the application of constant capital. What interests us in this, however, is the fact that here the average profit (= interest + profit of enterprise) presents itself actually and palpably as a magnitude wholly independent of the wages of management. Since the profit was higher here than average profit, the profit of enterprise was also higher than usual.

The same situation is observed in relation to some capitalist stock companies, such as joint-stock banks. The London and Westminster Bank paid an annual dividend of 30% in 1863, while the Union Bank of London and others paid 15%. Aside from the directors' salary the interest paid for deposits is here deducted from gross profit. The high profit is to be explained here by the moderate proportion of paid-in capital to deposits. For instance, in the case of the London and Westminster Bank, in 1863: paid-in capital, £1,000,000; deposits, £14,540,275. As for the Union Bank of London, in 1863: paid-in capital, £600,000; deposits, £12,384,173.

Profit of enterprise and wages of supervision, or management, were confused originally due to the antagonistic form assumed in respect to interest by the surplus of profit. This was further promoted by the apologetic aim of representing profit not as a surplus-value derived from unpaid labour, but as the capitalist's wages for work performed by him. This was met on the part of socialists by a demand to reduce profit actually to what it pretended to be theoretically, namely, mere wages of supervision. And this demand was all the more obnoxious to theoretical embellishment, the more these wages of supervision, like any other wage, found their definite level and definite market-price, on the one hand, with the development of a numerous class of industrial and commercial managers,[7] and the more they fell, on the other, like all wages for skilled labour, with the general development which reduces the cost of production of specially trained labour-power.[8] With the development of co-operation on the part of the labourers, and of stock enterprises on the part of the bourgeoisie, even the last pretext for the confusion of profit of enterprise and wages of management was removed, and profit appeared also in practice as it undeniably appeared in theory, as mere surplus-value, a value for which no equivalent was paid, as realised unpaid labour. It was then seen that the functioning capitalist really exploits labour, and that the fruit of his exploitation, when working with borrowed capital, was divided into interest and profit of enterprise, a surplus of profit over interest.

On the basis of capitalist production a new swindle develops in stock enterprises with respect to wages of management, in that boards of numerous managers or directors are placed above the actual director, for whom supervision and management serve only as a pretext to plunder the stockholders and amass wealth. Very curious details concerning this are to be found in *The City or the Physiology of London Business; with Sketches on Change, and the Coffee Houses,* London, 1845.

> 'What bankers and merchants gain by the direction of eight or nine different companies, may be seen from the following illustration: The private balance sheet of Mr Timothy Abraham Curtis, presented to the Court of Bankruptcy when that gentleman failed, exhibited a sample of the income netted from directorship ... between £800 and £900 a year. Mr Curtis having been associated with the Courts of the Bank of England, and the East India House, it was considered quite a plum for a public company to acquire his services in the boardroom' (pp. 81, 82).

The remuneration of the directors of such companies for each weekly meeting is at least one guinea. The proceedings of the Court of Bankruptcy show that these wages of supervision were, as a rule, inversely proportional to the actual supervision performed by these nominal directors.

Notes

1. 'The profits of enterprise depend upon the net profits of capital, not the latter upon the former.' (Ramsay, *Essay on the Distribution of Wealth,* p. 214. For Ramsay net profits always mean interest.)
2. 'Superintendence is here' (in the case of the farm owner) 'completely dispensed with.' (J. E. Cairnes, *The Slave Power,* London, 1862, p. 48.)
3. 'If the nature of the work requires that the workmen' (viz., the slaves) 'should be dispersed over an extended area, the number of overseers, and, therefore, the cost of the labour which requires this supervision, will be proportionately increased.' (Cairnes, 1. c., p. 44.)
4. A. Ure, *Philosophy of Manufactures,* French translation, 1836, I, p. 67, where this Pindar of the manufacturers at the same time testifies that most manufacturers have not the slightest understanding of the mechanism which they set in motion.
5. In a case known to me, following the crisis of 1868, a bankrupt manufacturer became the paid wage-labourer of his own former labourers. The factory was operated after the bankruptcy of its owner by a labourers' co-operative, and its former owner was employed as manager.—*F. E.*
6. The accounts quoted here go no further than 1864, since the above was written in 1865.—*F. E.*
7. 'Masters are labourers as well as their journeymen. In this character their interest is precisely the same as that of their men. But they are also either capitalists, or the agents of the capitalists, and in this respect their interest is decidedly opposed to the interests of the workmen.' (p. 27). 'The wide spread of education among the journeymen mechanics of this country diminishes daily the value of the labour and skill of almost all masters and employers by increasing the number of persons who possess their peculiar knowledge' (p. 30, Hodgskin, *Labour Defended Against the Claims of Capital, etc.,* London, 1825).
8. 'The general relaxation of conventional barriers, the increased facilities of education tend to bring down the wages of skilled labour instead of raising those of the unskilled.' (J. St. Mill, *Principles of Political Economy,* 2nd ed., London, 1849, I, p. 479.)

24

Externalization of the Relations of Capital in the Form of Interest-Bearing Capital

The relations of capital assume their most externalised and most fetish-like form in interest-bearing capital. We have here M—M', money creating more money, self-expanding value, without the process that effectuates these two extremes. In merchant's capital, M—C—M', there is at least the general form of the capitalistic movement, although it confines itself solely to the sphere of circulation, so that profit appears merely as profit derived from alienation; but it is at least seen to be the product of a social *relation*, not the product of a mere *thing*. The form of merchant's capital at least presents a process, a unity of opposing phases, a movement that breaks up into two opposite actions—the purchase and the sale of commodities. This is obliterated in M—M›, the form of interest-bearing capital. For instance, if £1,000 are loaned out by a capitalist at a rate of interest of 5%, the value of £1,000 as a capital for one year = C + Ci›, where C is the capital and i› the rate of interest. Hence, 5% = 5/100 = 1/20, and 1,000 + 1,000 × 1/20 = £1,050. The value of £1,000 as capital = £1,050, *i.e.*, capital is not a simple magnitude. It is a *relationship* of magnitudes, a relationship of the principal sum as a given value to itself as a self-expanding value, as a principal sum which has produced a surplus-value. And capital as such, as we have seen, assumes this form of a directly self-expanding value for all active capitalists, whether they operate on their own or borrowed capital.

M—M'. We have here the original starting-point of capital, money in the formula M—C—M' reduced to its two extremes M—M', in which M' = M + ΔM, money creating more money. It is the primary and general formula of capital reduced to a meaningless condensation. It is ready capital, a unity of the process of production and the process of circulation, and hence capital yielding a definite surplus-value in a particular period of time. In the form of interest-bearing capital this appears directly, unassisted by the processes of production and circulation. Capital appears as a mysterious and self-creating source of interest—the source of its own increase. The *thing* (money, commodity, value) is now capital even as a mere thing, and capital appears as a mere thing. The result of the entire process of reproduction appears as a property inherent in the thing itself. It depends on the owner of the money, *i.e.*, of the commodity in its continually exchangeable form, whether he wants to spend it as money or loan it out as capital. In interest-bearing capital, therefore, this automatic fetish, self-expanding value, money generating money, are brought out in their pure state and in this form it no longer bears the birth-marks of its origin. The social relation is consummated in the relation of a thing, of money, to itself. Instead of the actual transformation of money into capital, we see here only form without content. As in the case of labour-power, the use-value of money here is its capacity of creating value—a value greater than it contains. Money as money is potentially self-expanding value and is loaned out as such—which is the form of sale for this singular commodity. It becomes a property of money to generate value and yield interest, much as it is an attribute of pear-trees to bear pears. And the money-lender sells his money as just such an interest-bearing thing. But that is not all. The actually functioning capital, as we have seen, presents itself in such a light, that it seems to yield interest not as a functioning capital, but as capital in itself, as money-capital.

This, too, becomes distorted. While interest is only a portion of the profit, *i.e.*, of the surplus-value, which the functioning capitalist squeezes out of the labourer, it appears now, on the contrary, as though interest were the typical product of capital, the primary matter, and profit, in the shape of profit of enterprise, were a mere accessory and by-product of the process of reproduction. Thus we get the fetish form of capital and the conception of fetish capital. In M—M' we have the meaningless form of capital, the perversion and objectification of production relations in their highest degree, the interest-bearing form, the simple form of capital, in which it antecedes its own process of reproduction. It is the capacity of money, or of a commodity, to expand its own value independently of reproduction—which is a mystification of capital in its most flagrant form.

For vulgar political economy, which seeks to represent capital as an independent source of value, of value creation, this form is naturally a veritable find, a form in which the source of profit is no longer discernible, and in which the result of the capitalist process of production—divorced from the process—acquires an independent existence.

It is not until capital is money-capital that it becomes a commodity, whose capacity for self-expansion has a definite price quoted every time in every prevailing rate of interest.

As interest-bearing capital, and particularly in its direct form of interest-bearing money-capital (the other forms of interest-bearing capital, which do not concern us here, are derivatives of this form and presuppose its existence), capital assumes its pure fetish form, M—M' being the subject, the saleable thing. *Firstly,* through its continual existence as money, a form, in which all its specific attributes are obliterated and its real elements invisible. For money is precisely that form in which the distinctive features of commodities as use-values are obscured, and hence also the distinctive features of the industrial capitals which consist of these commodities and conditions of their production. It is that form, in which value—in this case, capital—exists as an independent exchange-value. In the reproduction process of capital, the money-form is but transient—a mere point of transit. But in the money-market capital always exists in this form. *Secondly,* the surplus-value produced by it, here again in the form of money, appears as an inherent part of it. As the growing process is to trees, so generating money (τοχοζ) appears innate in capital in its form of money-capital.

In interest-bearing capital the movement of capital is contracted. The intervening process is omitted. In this way, a capital = 1,000 is fixed as a thing, which in itself = 1,400, and which is transformed after a certain period into 1,100 just as wine stored in a cellar improves its use-value after a certain period. Capital is now a thing, but as a thing it is capital. Money is now pregnant. [Goethe, *Faust*, Part I, Scene 5.—*Ed*] As soon as it is loaned out, or invested in the reproduction process (inasmuch as it yields interest to the functioning capitalist as its owner, separate from profit of enterprise), interest on it grows, no matter whether it is awake or asleep, is at home or abroad, by day or by night. Thus interest-bearing money-capital (and all capital is money-capital in terms of its value, or is considered as the expression of money-capital) fulfils the most fervent wish of the hoarder.

It is this ingrown existence of interest in money-capital as in a thing (this is how the production of surplus-value through capital appears here), which occupies Luther's attention so thoroughly in his naive onslaught against usury. After demonstrating that interest may be demanded if the failure to repay a loan on a definite date to a lender who himself required it to make some payment, caused a loss to him, or resulted in his missing an opportunity to make a profit on a bargain, for instance, in buying a garden, Luther continues:

> Now that I have loaned you them (100 gulden), you cause me a double loss due to my not being able to pay on the one hand nor buy on the other, so that I have to lose on both sides, and this is called *duplex interesse, damni emergentis et lucri cessantis....* On hearing that John sustained losses on his loan of 100 gulden and demands just damages, they rush in and charge double on every 100 gulden, such double reimbursement, namely, for the loss due to non-payment and to inability to make a profit on a bargain, just as though these 100 gulden *had the double loss grown*

on to them, so that whenever they have 100 gulden, they loan them out and charge for two losses, which they have not at all sustained... Therefore, you are a usurer, who takes damages out of his neighbour's money for an imaginary loss that you did not sustain at all, and which you can neither prove nor calculate. This sort of loss is called by the jurists *non verum, sed phantasticum interesse*. It is a loss which each conjures up for himself... It will not do to say, therefore, that there could have been losses because I could not have been able to pay or buy. Else it would mean *ex contingente necessarium*, which is making something out of a thing that is not, and a thing that is uncertain into a thing that is absolutely sure. Would not such usury devour the world in a few years? ... If an unhappy accident befalls him against his will, and he must recover from it, he may demand damages for it, but it is different in trade and just the reverse. There they scheme to profit at the expense of their needy neighbours, how to amass wealth and get rich, to be lazy and idle and live in luxury on the labour of others, without any care, danger, and loss. To sit by the stove and let my 100 gulden gather wealth for me in the country and yet keep them in my pocket, because they are only loaned, without any danger or risk; my friend, who would not like that? (Martin Luther, *An die Pfarherrn wider den Wucher zu predigen, etc.*, Wittenberg, 1540.)

The conception of capital as a self-reproducing and self-expanding value, lasting and growing eternally by virtue of its innate properties—hence by virtue of the hidden quality of scholasticists—has led to the fabulous fancies of Dr Price, which outdo by far the fantasies of the alchemists; fancies, in which Pitt believed in all earnest, and which he used as pillars of his financial administration in his laws concerning the sinking fund.

> Money bearing compound interest increases at first slowly. But, the rate of increase being continually accelerated, it becomes in some time so rapid, as to mock all the powers of the imagination. One penny, put out at our Saviour's birth to 5 per cent compound interest, would, before this time, have increased to a greater sum, than would be contained in a hundred and fifty millions of earths, all solid gold. But if put out to simple interest, it would, in the same time, have amounted to no more than seven shillings and four pence half-penny. Our government has hitherto chosen to improve money in the last, rather than the first of these ways.[1]

His fancy flies still higher in his *Observations on Reversionary Payments, etc.*, London, 1772. There we read:

> A shilling put out to 6% compound interest at our Saviour's birth (presumably in the Temple of Jerusalem) 'would ... have increased to a greater sum than the whole solar system could hold, supposing it a sphere equal in diameter to the diameter of Saturn's orbit.' A state need never therefore be under any difficulties; for with the smallest savings it may in as little time as its interest can require pay off the largest debts (pp. XIII, XIV).

What a pretty theoretical introduction to the national debt of England!

Price was simply dazzled by the gargantuan dimensions obtained in a geometrical progression. Since he took no note of the conditions of reproduction and labour, and regarded capital as a self-regulating automaton, as a mere number that increases itself just as Malthus [*An Essay on the Principle of Population*, London, 1798, pp. 25-26.—*Ed*] did with respect to population in his geometrical progression, he was struck by the thought that he had found the law of its growth in the formula $s = c(1 + i)_n$, in which s = the sum of capital + compound interest, c = advanced capital, i = rate of interest (expressed in aliquot parts of 100) and n stands for the number of years in which this process takes place.

Pitt takes Dr Price's mystification quite seriously. In 1786 the House of Commons had resolved to raise £1 million for the public weal. According to Price, in whom Pitt believed, there was, of course, no better way than to tax the people, so as to 'accumulate' this sum after raising it, and thus to spirit away the national debt through the mystery of compound interest. The above resolution of the House of Commons was soon followed up by Pitt with a law which ordered the accumulation of £250,000,

> until, with the expired annuities, the fund should have grown to £4,000,000 annually. (Act 26, George III, Chap. 31.) ['An Act for vesting certain sums in Commissioners, at the End of every Quarter of a Year, to be by them applied to the Reduction of the National Debt' (Anno 26 Georgii III, Regis, cap. 31).—*Ed.*]

In his speech of 1792, in which Pitt proposed that the amount devoted to the sinking fund be increased, he mentioned machines, credit, etc., among the causes of England's commercial supremacy, but as:

> the most wide-spread and enduring cause, that of accumulation. This principle, he said, was completely developed in the work of Smith, that genius ... and this accumulation, he continued, was accomplished by laying aside at least a portion of the annual profit for the purpose of increasing the principal, which was to be employed in the same manner the following year, and which thus yielded a continual profit.

With Dr Price's aid Pitt thus converts Smith's theory of accumulation into enrichment of a nation by means of accumulating debts, and thus arrives at the pleasant progression of an infinity of loans—loans to pay loans.

It had already been noted by Josiah Child, the father of modern banking, that £100 at 10% would produce in 70 years by compound interest £102,400. (*Traité sur le commerce, etc.*, par J. Child, traduit, etc., Amsterdam et Berlin, 1754, p. 115. Written in 1669.)

How thoughtlessly Dr Price's conception is applied by modern economists, is shown in the following passage from the *Economist*:

> Capital, with compound interest on every portion of capital saved, is so all-engrossing that all the wealth in the world from which income is derived, has long ago become the interest of capital... All rent is now the payment of interest on capital previously invested in the land. (*Economist*, July 49, 1851.)

In its capacity of interest-bearing capital, capital claims the ownership of all wealth which can ever be produced, and everything it has received so far is but an instalment for its all-engrossing appetite. By its innate laws, all surplus-labour which the human race can ever perform belongs to it. Moloch.

In conclusion, the following hodge-podge by the romantic Müller:

> Dr Price's immense increase of compound interest, or of the self-accelerating forces of man, presupposes an undivided, or uninterrupted, uniform application for several centuries, if they are to produce such enormous effects. As soon as capital is divided, cut up into several independently growing shoots, the total process of accumulating forces begins anew. Nature has distributed over a span of about 20 to 25 years the progression of energy which falls on an average to the share of every labourer (!). After the lapse of this time the labourer leaves his career and must transfer the capital accumulated by the compound interest of labour to a new labourer, mostly distributing it among several labourers or children. These must first learn to activate and apply their share of capital, before they can draw any actual compound interest on it. Furthermore, an enormous quantity of capital gained by civil society even in the most restless communities, is gradually accumulated over many years and not employed for any immediate expansion of labour. Instead, as soon as an appreciable

sum is gathered together, it is transferred to another individual, a labourer, bank or state, under the head of a loan. And the receiver then sets the capital into actual motion and draws compound interest on it, so that he can easily pledge to pay simple interest to the lender. Finally, the law of consumption, greed, and waste opposes those huge progressions, in which man's powers and their products would multiply if the law of production, or thrift, were alone effective. (A. Müller, *Elemente der Staatskunst*, III, pp. 147-49.)

It is impossible to concoct a more hair-raising absurdity in so few lines. Leaving aside the droll confusion of labourer and capitalist, value of labour-power and interest on capital, etc., the charging of compound interest is supposed to be explained by the fact that capital is loaned out to bring in compound interest. The method employed by our Müller is thoroughly characteristic of the romanticism in all walks of life. It is made up of current prejudices, skimmed from the most superficial semblance of things. This incorrect and trite content should then be 'exalted' and rendered sublime through a mystifying mode of expression.

The process of accumulation of capital may be conceived as an accumulation of compound interest in the sense that the portion of profit (surplus-value) which is reconverted into capital, *i.e.*, serves to absorb more surplus-labour, may be called interest. But:

1. Aside from all incidental interference, a large part of available capital is constantly more or less depreciated in the course of the reproduction process, because the value of commodities is not determined by the labour-time originally expended in their production, but by the labour-time expended in their reproduction, and this decreases continually owing to the development of the social productivity of labour. On a higher level of social productivity, all available capital appears, for this reason, to be the result of a relatively short period of reproduction, instead of a long process of accumulation of capital.[2]
2. As demonstrated in Part III of this book, the rate of profit decreases in proportion to the mounting accumulation of capital and the correspondingly increasing productivity of social labour, which is expressed precisely in the relative and progressive decrease of the variable as compared to the constant portion of capital. To produce the same rate of profit after the constant capital set in motion by one labourer increases ten-fold, the surplus labour-time would have to increase ten-fold, and soon the total labour-time, and finally the entire 24 hours of a day, would not suffice, even if wholly appropriated by capital. The idea that the rate of profit does not shrink is, however, the basis of Price's progression and in general the basis of 'all-engrossing capital with compound interest.'[3]

The identity of surplus-value and surplus-labour imposes a qualitative limit upon the accumulation of capital. This consists of the *total working-day*, and the prevailing development of the productive forces and of the population, which limits the number of simultaneously exploitable working-days. But if one conceives of surplus-value in the meaningless form of interest, the limit is merely quantitative and defies all fantasy.

Now, the concept of capital as a fetish reaches its height in interest-bearing capital, being a conception which attributes to the accumulated product of labour, and at that in the fixed form of money, the inherent secret power, as an automaton, of creating surplus-value in geometrical progression, so that the accumulated product of labour, as the *Economist* thinks, has long discounted all the wealth of the world for all time as belonging to it and rightfully coming to it. The product of past labour, the past labour itself, is here pregnant in itself with a portion of present or future living surplus-labour. We know, however, that in reality the preservation, and to that extent also the reproduction of the value of products of past labour is *only* the result of their contact with living labour; and secondly, that the domination of the products of past labour over living surplus-labour lasts only as long as the relations of capital, which rest on those particular social relations in which past labour independently and overwhelmingly dominates over living labour.

Notes

1. Richard Price, *An Appeal to the Public on the Subject of the National Debt*, 2nd ed., London, 1774, p. 19. He cracks the naive joke: 'It is borrowing money at simple interest, in order to improve it at compound interest.' (R. Hamilton, *An Inquiry into the Rise and Progress of the National Debt of Great Britain*, 2nd ed., Edinburgh, 1814, p. 133.) According to this, borrowing would be the safest means also for private people to gather wealth. But if I borrow £100 at 5% annual interest, I have to pay £5 at the end of the year, and even if the loan lasts for 100 million years, I have meanwhile only £100 to loan every year and £5 to pay every year. I can never manage by this process to loan £105 when borrowing £100. And how am I going to pay 5%? By new loans, or, if it is the state, by new taxes. Now, if the industrial capitalist borrows money, and his profit amounts to, say, 15%, he may pay 5% interest, spend 5% for his private expenses (although his appetite grows with his income), and capitalise 5%. In this case, 15% is the precondition for paying continually 5% interest. If this process continues, the rate of profit, for the reasons indicated in former chapters, will fall from 15% to, say, 10%. But Price entirely forgets that the interest of 5% presupposes a rate of profit of 15%, and assumes it to continue with the accumulation of capital. He has nothing whatsoever to do with the actual process of accumulation, but rather only with lending money and getting it back with compound interest. How that is accomplished is immaterial to him, since it is the innate property of interest-bearing capital.
2. See Mill and Carey, and Roscher's mistaken commentary on this score. [Marx refers to the following works: J. St. Mill, *Principles of Political Economy*, Second edition, Vol. I, London, 1849, pp. 91-92; H. Ch. Carey, *Principles of Social Science*, Vol. III, Philadelphia, 1859, pp. 71.73; W. Roscher, *Die Grundlagen der Nationalökonomie*, 3 Auflage, Stuttgart und Augsburg, 1858, § 45.—*Ed.*]
3. 'It is clear, that no labour, no productive power, no ingenuity, and no art, can answer the overwhelming demand of compound interest. But all saving is made from the revenue of the capitalist, so that actually these demands are constantly made and as constantly the productive power of labour refuses to satisfy them. A sort of balance is, therefore, constantly struck.' *(Labour Defended Against the Claims of Capital*, p. 23. By Hodgskin.)

25

Credit and Fictitious Capital

An exhaustive analysis of the credit system and of the instruments which it creates for its own use (credit-money, etc.) lies beyond our plan. We merely wish to dwell here upon a few particular points, which are required to characterise the capitalist mode of production in general. We shall deal only with commercial and bank credit. The connection between the development of this form of credit and that of public credit will not be considered here.

I have shown earlier (Buch I, Kap. III, 3, b [English edition: Ch. III, 3, b.—*Ed.*]) how the function of money as a means of payment, and therewith a relation of creditor and debtor between the producer and trader of commodities, develop from the simple circulation of commodities. With the development of commerce and of the capitalist mode of production, which produces solely with an eye to circulation, this natural basis of the credit system is extended, generalised, and worked out. Money serves here, by and large, merely as a means of payment, *i.e.*, commodities are not sold for money, but for a written promise to pay for them at a certain date. For brevity's sake, we may put all these promissory notes under the general head of bills of exchange. Such bills of exchange, in their turn, circulate as means of payment until the day on which they fall due; and they form the actual commercial money. Inasmuch as they ultimately neutralise one another through the balancing of claims and debts, they act absolutely as money, although there is no eventual transformation into actual money. Just as these mutual advances of producers and merchants make up the real foundation of credit, so does the instrument of their circulation, the bill of exchange, form the basis of credit-money proper, of banknotes, etc. These do not rest upon the circulation of money, be it metallic or government-issued paper money, but rather upon the circulation of bills of exchange.

W. Leatham (banker of Yorkshire) writes in his *Letters on the Currency*, 2nd ed., London, 1840:

> I find, then, the amount for the whole of the year of 1839 ... to be £528,493,842 (he assumed that the foreign bills of exchange made up about one-fifth of the total) 'and the amount of bills out at one time in the above year, to be £132,123,460' (p. 56). The bills of exchange make up 'one component part greater in amount than all the rest put together' (p. 3). 'This enormous superstructure of bills of exchange rests (!) upon the base formed by the amount of banknotes and gold, and when, by events, this base becomes too much narrowed, its solidity and very existence is endangered' (p. 8). If I estimate the whole currency.

(he means of the banknotes)

> and the amount of the liabilities of the Bank and country bankers, payable on demand, I find a sum of 153 million, which, by law, can be converted into gold ... and the amount of gold to meet this demand' only 14 million (p.11). 'The bills of exchange are not ... placed under any control, except by preventing the abundance of money, excessive and low rates of interest or discount, which create a part of them, and encourage their great and dangerous expansion. It is impossible to decide what part arises out of real *bonâ fide* transactions, such as actual bargain and sale, or what part is fictitious and mere accommodation paper, that is, where one bill of exchange is drawn to take up another running, in order to raise a fictitious capital, by creating so much currency. In times of abundance and cheap money this I know reaches an enormous amount'.

(pp. 43-44). J.W. Bosanquet, *Metallic, Paper and Credit Currency*, London, 1842:

> An average amount of payments to the extent of upwards of £3,000,000 is settled through the Clearing House

(where the London bankers exchange due bills and filed cheques)

> every day of business in the year, and the daily amount of money required for the purpose is little more than £200,000 (p. 86).

(In 1889, the total turnover of the Clearing House amounted to £7,618.75 million, which, in roughly 300 business days, averages £25½ million daily.—*F. E.*]

> Bills of exchange act undoubtedly as currency, independent of money, inasmuch as they transfer property from hand to hand by endorsement (p. 92). It may be assumed that upon an average there are two endorsements upon every bill in circulation, and

> ... each bill performs two payments before it becomes due. Upon this assumption it would appear, that by endorsement alone property changed hands, by means of bills of exchange, to the value of twice five hundred and twenty-eight million, or £1,056,000,000, being at the rate of more than £3,000,000 per day, in the course of the year 1839. We may safely therefore conclude, that deposits and bills of exchange together, perform the functions of money, by transferring property from hand and to hand without the aid of money, to an extent daily of not less than £18,000,000. (p. 93)

Tooke says the following about credit in general:

> Credit, in its most simple expression, is the confidence which, well, or ill-founded, leads a person to entrust another with a certain amount of capital, in money, or in goods computed at a value in money agreed upon, and in each case payable at the expiration of a fixed term. In the case where the capital is lent in money, that is whether in banknotes, or in a cash credit, or in an order upon a correspondent, an addition for the use of the capital of so much upon every £100 is made to the amount to be repaid. In the case of goods the value of which is agreed in terms of money, constituting a sale, the sum stipulated to be repaid includes a consideration for the use of the capital and for the risk, till the expiration of the period fixed for payment. Written obligations of payment at fixed dates mostly accompany these credits, and the obligations or promissory notes after date being transferable, form the means by which the lenders, if they have occasion for the use of their capital, in the shape whether of money or goods, before the expiration of the term of the bills they hold, are mostly enabled to borrow Or to buy on lower terms, by having their own credit strengthened by the names on the bills in addition to their own. *(Inquiry into the Currency Principle,* p. 87.)

Ch. Coquelin, *Du Crédit et des Banques dans L'Industrie, Revue des Deux Mondes,* 1842, Tome 31:

> In every country the majority of credit transactions takes place within the circle of industrial relations... The producer of the raw material advances it to the processing manufacturer, and receives from the latter a promise to pay on a certain day. The manufacturer, having completed his share of the work, in his turn advances his product on similar terms to another manufacturer, who has to process it further, and in this way credit stretches on and on, from one to the other, right up to the consumer. The wholesale dealer gives the retailer commodities on credit, while receiving credit from a manufacturer or commission agent. All borrow with one hand and lend with the other, sometimes money, but more frequently products. In this manner an incessant exchange of advances, which combine and intersect in all directions, takes place in industrial relations. The development of credit consists precisely in this multiplication and growth of mutual advances, and therein is the real seat of its power.

The other side of the credit system is connected with the development of money-dealing, which, of course, keeps step under capitalist production with the development of dealing in commodity. We have seen in the preceding part (Chap. XIX) how the care of the reserve funds of businessmen, the technical operations of receiving and disbursing money, of international payments, and thus of the bullion trade, are concentrated in the hands of the money-dealers. The other side of the credit system—the management of interest-bearing capital, or money-capital, develops alongside this money-dealing as a special function of the money-dealers. Borrowing and lending money becomes their particular business. They act as middlemen between the actual lender and the borrower of money-capital. Generally speaking, this aspect of the banking business consists of concentrating large amounts of the loanable money-capital in the bankers' hands, so that, in place of the individual money-lender, the bankers confront the industrial capitalists and commercial capitalists as representatives of all moneylenders. They become the general managers of money-capital. On the other hand, by borrowing for the entire world of commerce, they concentrate all the borrowers vis-à-vis all the lenders. A bank represents a centralisation of money-capital, of the lenders, on the one hand, and on the other, a centralisation of the borrowers. Its profit is generally made by borrowing at a lower rate of interest than it receives in loaning.

The loanable capital which the banks have at their disposal streams to them in various ways. In the first place, being the cashiers of the industrial capitalists, all the money-capital which every producer and merchant must have as a reserve fund, or receives in payment, is concentrated in their hands. These funds are thus converted into loanable money-capital. In this way, the reserve fund of the commercial world, because it is concentrated in a common treasury, is reduced to its necessary minimum, and a portion of the money-capital which would otherwise have to lie slumbering as a reserve fund, is loaned out and serves as interest-bearing capital. In the second place, the loanable capital of the banks is formed by the deposits of money-capitalists who entrust them with the business of loaning them out. Furthermore, with the development of the banking system, and particularly as soon as banks came to pay interest on deposits, money savings and the temporarily idle money of all classes were deposited with them. Small amounts, each in itself incapable of acting in the capacity of money-capital, merge together into large masses and thus form a money power. This aggregation of small amounts must be distinguished as a specific function of the banking system from its go-between activities between the money-capitalists proper and the borrowers. In the final analysis, the revenues, which are usually but gradually consumed, are also deposited with the banks.

The loan is made (we refer here strictly to commercial credit) by discounting bills of exchange—by converting bills of exchange into money before they come due—and by advances of various kinds: direct advances on personal credit, loans against securities, such as interest-bearing paper, government paper, stocks of all sorts, and, notably, overdrafts against bills of lading, dock warrants, and other certified titles of ownership of commodities and overdrawing deposits, etc.

The credit given by a banker may assume various forms, such as bills of exchange on other banks, cheques on them, credit accounts of the same kind, and finally if the bank is entitled to issue notes—banknotes of the bank itself. A bank-note is nothing but a draft upon a banker, payable at any time to the bearer, and given by the banker in place of private drafts. This last form of credit appears particularly important and striking to the layman, first, because this form of credit-money breaks out of the confines of mere commercial circulation into general circulation, and serves there as money; and because in most countries, the principal banks issuing notes, being a peculiar mixture of national and private banks, actually have the national credit to back them, and their notes are more or less legal tender; because it is apparent here that the banker deals in credit itself, a bank-note being merely a circulating token of credit. But the banker also has to do with credit in all its other forms, even when he advances the cash money deposited with him. In fact, a bank-note simply represents the coin of wholesale trade, and it is always the deposit which carries the most weight with banks. The best proof of this is furnished by the Scottish banks.

Special credit institutions, like special forms of banks, need no further consideration for our purpose.

> The business of bankers ... may be divided into two branches... One branch of the banker's business is to *collect* capital from those who have not immediate employment for it, and to distribute or transfer it to those who have. The other branch is to receive deposits of the *incomes* of their customers, and to pay out the amount, as it is wanted for expenditure by the latter in the objects of their consumption... The former being

a circulation of *capital*, the latter of currency... One relates to the concentration of capital on the one hand and the distribution of it on the other, the other is employed in administering the circulation for local purposes of the district. Tooke, *Inquiry into the Currency Principle*, pp. 36, 37.

We shall revert to this passage later, in Chapter XXVIII.

Reports of Committees, Vol. VIII. Commercial Distress, Vol. 11, Part I, 1847-48, Minutes of Evidence. (Further quoted as Commercial Distress, 1847-48.) In the forties, when discounting bills of exchange in London, 21-day drafts of one bank on another were often accepted in lieu of banknotes. (Testimony of J. Pease, country banker, Nos. 4638 and 4645.) According to the same report, bankers were in the habit of giving such bills of exchange regularly in payment to their customers whenever money was tight. If the receiver wanted banknotes, he had to rediscount this bill. For the banks this amounted to a privilege of coining money. Messrs. Jones, Lloyd and Co. made payments in this way 'from time immemorial,' as soon as money was scarce and the rate of interest rose above 5%. The customer was glad to get such banker's bills because bills from Jones, Loyd and Co. were easier discounted than his own; besides, they often passed through twenty to thirty hands. (*Ibid.*, Nos. 901 to 904, 905, 992.)

All these forms serve to make the payments claim transferable.

> There is scarcely any shape into which credit can be cast, in which it will not at times be called to perform the functions of money; and whether that shape be a bank-note, or a bill of exchange, or a banker's cheque, the process is in every essential particular the same, and the result is the same. Fullarton, *On the Regulation of Currencies*, 2nd ed., London, 1845, p. 38.—'Banknotes are the small change of credit' (p. 51).

The following from J. W. Gilbart's *The History and Principle of Banking*, London, 1834:

> 'The trading capital of a bank may be divided into two parts: the invested capital, and the borrowed banking capital' (p. 117). 'There are three ways of raising a banking or borrowed capital. First, by receiving; secondly, by the issuing of notes; thirdly, by the drawing of bills. If a person will lend me £100 for nothing, and I lend that £100 to another person at four per cent interest, then, in the course of a year, I shall gain £4 by the transaction. Again, if a person will take my "promise to pay" ('I promise to pay' is the usual formula for English banknotes) 'and bring it back to me at the end of the year, and pay me four per cent for it, just the same as though I had lent him 100 sovereigns, then I shall gain £4 by that transaction; and again, if a person in a country town brings me £100 on condition that, twenty-one days afterwards, I shall pay the same amount to a person in London, then whatever interest I can make of the money during the twenty-one days, will be my profit. This is a fair representation of the operations of banking, and of the way in which a banking capital is created by means of deposits, notes, and bills' (p. 117). 'The profits of a banker are generally in proportion to the amount of his banking or borrowed capital... To ascertain the real profit of a bank, the interest upon the invested capital should be deducted from the gross profit, and what remains is the banking profit' (p. 118). '*The advances of bankers to their customers are made with other people's money*' (p. 146). 'Precisely those bankers who do not issue notes, create a banking capital by the discounting of bills. They render their discounts subservient to the increase of their deposits. The London bankers will not discount except for those houses who have deposit accounts with them' (p. 119). 'A party who has had bills discounted, and has paid interest on the whole amount, must leave some portion of that amount in the hands of the banker without interest. By this means the banker obtains more than the current rate of interest on the money actually advanced, and raises a banking capital to the amount of the balance left in his hands' (pp. 119- 20).

Economising on reserve funds, deposits, cheques:

> 'Banks of deposit serve to economise the use of the circulating medium. This is done upon the principle of transfer of titles.... Thus it is that banks of deposit ... are enabled to settle a large amount of transactions with a small amount of money. The money thus liberated, is employed by the banker in making advances, by discount or otherwise, to his customers. Hence the principle of transfer gives additional efficiency to the deposit system...' (p. 123). 'It matters not whether the two parties, who have dealings with each other, keep their accounts with the same banker or with different bankers; for, as the bankers exchange their cheques with each other at the clearing house.... The deposit system might thus, by means of transfers, be carried to such an extent as wholly to supersede the use of a metallic currency. Were every man to keep a deposit account at a bank, and make all his payments by cheques, money might be superseded, and cheques become the sole circulating medium. In this case, however, it must be supposed that the banker has the money in his hands, or the cheques would have no value' (p. 124).

Centralisation of local transactions in the hands of the banks is effected 1) through branch banks. Country banks have branch establishments in the smaller towns of their district, and London banks in different districts of the city. 2) Through agencies.

> 'Each country banker employs a London agent to pay his notes or bills ... and to receive sums that may be lodged by parties residing in London for the use of parties residing in the country' (p.127). 'Each banker accepts the notes of others, but does not reissue them. In all larger cities they come together once or twice a week and exchange their notes. The balance is paid by a draft on London' (p.134). 'It is the object of banking to give facilities to trade, and whatever gives facilities to trade gives facilities to speculation. Trade and speculation are in some cases so nearly allied, that it is impossible to say at what precise point trade ends and speculation begins.... Wherever there are banks, capital is more readily obtained, and at a cheaper rate. The cheapness of capital gives facilities to speculation, just in the same way as the cheapness of beef and of beer gives facilities to gluttony and drunkenness (pp. 137, 438). 'As banks of circulation always issue their own notes, it would seem that their discounting business was carried on exclusively with this last description of capital, but it is not so. It is very possible for a banker to issue his own notes for all the bills he discounts, and yet nine-tenths of the bills in his possession shall represent real capital. For, although in the first instance, the banker's notes are given for the bill, yet these notes may not stay in circulation until the bill becomes due—the bill may have three months to run, the notes may return in three days' (p. 172). 'The overdrawing of a cash credit account is a regular matter of business; it is, in fact, the purpose for which the cash credit has been granted.... Cash credits are granted not only upon personal security, but also upon the security of the Public Funds' (pp. 174, 175). 'Capital advanced, by way of loan, on the securities of merchandise, would produce the same effects as if advanced in the discounting of bills. If a party borrows 1400 on the security of his merchandise, it is the same as though he had sold his merchandise for a 8100 bill, and got it discounted with the banker. By obtaining this advance he is enabled to hold over this merchandise for a better market, and avoids a sacrifice which, otherwise, be might be induced to make, in order to raise the money for urgent purposes' (pp. 180-81).

The Currency Theory Reviewed, etc., pp. 62-63:

> It is unquestionably true that the £1,000 which you deposit at A today may be reissued tomorrow, and form a deposit at B. The day after that, reissued from B, it may form a deposit at C ... and so on to infinitude; and that the same £1,000 in money may thus,

> by a succession of transfers, multiply itself into a sum of deposits absolutely indefinite. It is possible, therefore, that *nine-tenths of all the deposits in the United Kingdom may have no existence beyond their record in the books of the bankers* who are respectively accountable for them ... Thus in Scotland, for instance, currency (mostly paper money at that) has never exceeded £3 million, the deposits in the banks are estimated at £27 million.... Unless a run on the banks be made, the same £1,000 would, if sent back upon its travels, cancel with the same facility a sum equally indefinite. As the same £1,000 with which you cancel your debt to a tradesman today, may cancel his debt to the merchant tomorrow, the merchant's debt to the bank the day following, and so on without end; so the same £1,000 may pass from hand to hand, and bank to bank, and cancel any conceivable sum of deposits.

[We have seen that Gilbart knew even in 1834 that

> Whatever gives facilities to trade gives facilities to speculation. Trade and speculation are in some cases so nearly allied, that it is impossible to say at what precise point trade ends and speculation begins.

The easier it is to obtain advances on unsold commodities, the more such advances are taken, and the greater the temptation to manufacture commodities, or dump already manufactured commodities in distant markets, just to obtain advances of money on them. To what extent the entire business world of a country may be seized by such swindling, and what it finally comes to, is amply illustrated by the history of English business during 1845-47. It shows us what credit can accomplish. Before passing on to the following examples, a few preliminary remarks.

At the close of 1842, the pressure which English industry suffered almost uninterruptedly since 1837, began to lift. During the following two, years foreign demand for English manufactured goods increased still more; 1845 and 1846 marked a period of greatest prosperity. In 1843 the Opium War had opened China to English commerce. The new market gave a new impetus to the further expansion of an expanding industry, particularly the cotton industry. 'How can we ever produce too much? We have to clothe 300 million people,' a Manchester manufacturer said to this writer at the time. But all the newly erected factory buildings, steam-engines, and spinning and weaving machines did not suffice to absorb the surplus-value pouring in from Lancashire. With the same zeal as was shown in expanding production, people engaged in building railways. The thirst for speculation of manufacturers and merchants at first found gratification in this field, and as early as in the summer of 1844. Stock was fully underwritten, *i.e.*, so far as there was money to cover the initial payments. As for the rest, time would show! But when further payments were due—Question 1059, C. D. 1848/57, indicates that the capital invested in railways in 1846-47 amounted to £75 million—recourse had to be taken to credit, and in most cases the basic enterprises of the firm had also to bleed.

And in most cases, these basic enterprises were already over-burdened. The enticingly high profits had led to far more extensive operations than justified by the available liquid resources. Yet there was credit-easy to obtain and cheap. The bank discount rate stood low: 1¾ to 2¾% in 1844, less than 3% until October 1845, rising to 5% for a while (February 1846), then dropping again to 3¼% in December 1846. The Bank of England had an unheard-of supply of gold in its vaults. All inland quotations were higher than ever before. Why then allow this splendid opportunity to escape? Why not go in for all one was worth? Why not send all one could manufacture to foreign markets which pined for English goods? And why should not the manufacturer himself pocket the double gain arising from selling yarn and fabrics in the Far East, and the return cargo in England?

Thus arose the system of mass consignments to India and China against advance payments, and this soon developed into a system of consignments purely for the sake of getting advances, as described in greater detail in the following notes, which led inevitably to over-flooding the markets and a crash.

The crash was precipitated by the crop failure of 1846. England, and particularly Ireland, required enormous imports of foodstuffs, notably corn and potatoes. But the countries which supplied them could be paid with the products of English industry only to a very limited extent. Precious metals had to be given out. Gold worth at least nine million was sent abroad. Of this amount, no less than seven and a half million came from the treasury of the Bank of England, whose freedom of action on the money-market was thereby considerably impaired. Other banks, whose reserves were deposited with the Bank of England and were practically identical with those of that Bank, were thus also compelled to curtail accommodation of money. The rapid and easy flow of payments was obstructed, first here and there, then generally. The banking discount rate, still 3 to 3½% in January 1847, rose to 7% in April, when the first panic broke out. The situation eased somewhat in the summer (6½%, 6%), but when the new crop failed as well, panic broke out afresh and even more violently. The official minimum bank discount rose in October to 7 and in November to 10%; *i.e.*, the overwhelming mass of bills of exchange was discountable only at outrageous rates of interest, or no longer discountable at all. The general cessation of payments caused the failure of several leading and very many medium-sized and small firms. The Bank itself was in danger due to the limitations imposed by the artful Bank Act of 1844. The government yielded to the general clamour and suspended the Bank Act on October 25, thereby eliminating the absurd legal fetters imposed on the Bank. Now it could throw its supply of banknotes into circulation without hindrance. The credit of these banknotes being in practice guaranteed by the credit of the nation, and thus unimpaired, the money stringency was thus instantly and decisively relieved. Naturally, quite a number of hopelessly enmeshed large and small firms failed nevertheless, but the peak of the crisis was overcome, the banking discount dropped to 5% in December, and in the course of 1848, a new wave of business activity began which took the edge off the revolutionary movements on the continent in 1849, and which inaugurated in the fifties an unprecedented industrial prosperity, but then ended again—in the crash of 1857.—*F. E.*]

I. A document issued by the House of Lords in 1848 deals with the colossal depreciation of government paper and bonds during the 1847 crisis. According to it, the depreciation of October 23, 1847, compared with the level in February of the same year, amounted to:

On English government bonds	£93,824,217
On dock and canal stock	£1,358,288
On railway stock	£19,579,820
Total	£114,762,325

II. With reference to the swindle in East Indian trade, in which drafts were no longer drawn because commodities were being bought, but rather commodities were bought to be able to make out discountable drafts convertible into money, the *Manchester Guardian* of November 24, 1847, remarks:

Mr A in London instructs a Mr B to buy from the manufacturer C in Manchester commodities for shipment to a Mr D in East India. B pays C in six months' drafts to be made out by C on B. B secures himself by six months' drafts on A. As soon as the goods are shipped A makes out six months' drafts on D against the mailed bill of lading.

> The shipper and the co-signee were thus both put in possession of funds—months before they actually paid for the goods; and, very commonly, these bills were renewed

at maturity, on pretence of affording time for the returns in a 'long trade'. Unfortunately, losses by such a trade, instead of leading to its contraction, led directly to its increase. The poorer men became, the greater need they had to purchase, in order to make up, by new advances, the capital they had lost on the past adventures. Purchases thus became, not a question of supply and demand, but the most important part of the finance operations of a firm labouring under difficulties. But this is only one side of the picture. What took place in reference to the export of goods at home, was taking place in the purchase and shipment of produce abroad. Houses in India, who had credit to pass their bills, were purchasers of sugar, indigo, silk, or cotton—not because the prices advised from London by the last overland mail promised a profit on the prices current in India, but because former drafts upon the London house would soon fall due, and must be provided for. What was so simple as to purchase a cargo of sugar, pay for it in bills upon the London house at ten months' date, transmit the shipping documents by the overland mail; and, in less than two months, the goods on the high seas, or perhaps not yet passed the mouth of the Hoogly, were pawned in Lombard Street—putting the London house in funds eight months before the drafts against those goods fell due. And all this went on without interruption or difficulty, as long as bill-brokers had abundance of money 'at call,'; to advance on bills of lading and dock warrants, and to discount, without limit, the bills of India houses drawn upon the eminent firms in Mincing Lane.

[This fraudulent procedure remained in vogue so long as goods to and from India had to round the Cape in sailing vessels. But ever since they are being shipped in steamboats via the Suez Canal, this method of fabricating fictitious capital has been deprived of its basis—the long freight voyage. And ever since the telegraph informs the English businessman about the Indian market and the Indian merchant about the English market, on the same day, this method has become totally impracticable.—*F.E.*]

III. The following is taken from the quoted Report on Commercial Distress, 1847-48:

In the last week of April 1847, the Bank of England advised the Royal Bank of Liverpool that it would thereafter reduce its discount business with the latter bank by one-half. The announcement operated with peculiar hardship on this account, that the payments into Liverpool had latterly been much more in bills than in cash; and the merchants who generally brought to the Bank a large proportion of cash with which to pay their acceptances, had latterly been able to bring only bills which they had received for their cotton and other produce, and that Increased very rapidly as the difficulties increased.... The acceptances ... which the Bank had to pay for the merchants, were acceptances drawn chiefly upon them from abroad, and they have been accustomed to meet those acceptances by whatever payment they received for their produce.... The bills that the merchants brought... in lieu of cash, which they usually brought ... were of various dates, and of various descriptions; a considerable number of them were bankers' bills, of three months' date, the large bulk being cotton bills. These bills of exchange, when bankers' bills, were accepted by London bankers, and by merchants in every trade that we could mention—the Brazilian, the American, the Canadian, the West Indian.... The merchants did not draw upon each other; but the parties in the interior, who had purchased produce from the merchants, remitted to the merchants bills on London bankers, or bills on various parties in London, or bills upon anybody. The announcement of the Bank of England caused a reduction of the maturity terms of bills drawn against sales of foreign products, frequently extending to over three months. (pp. 26, 27)

The period of prosperity in England from 1844 to 1847, was, as described above, connected with the first great railway swindle. The above-named report makes the following reference to the effect of this swindle on business in general:

> In April 1847 'almost all mercantile houses had begun to starve their business more or less ... by taking part of their commercial capital for railways' (p.42). 'Loans were made on railway shares at a high rate of interest, say, 8%, by private individuals, by bankers and by fire-offices' (p. 66). 'Loans to so great an extent by commercial houses to railways induced them to lean too much upon banks by the discount of paper, whereby to carry on their commercial operations' (p. 67). (Question:) 'Should you say that the railway calls had had a great effect in producing the pressure which there was' (on the money-market) 'in April and October' (1847)?—(Answer:) 'I should say that they had had hardly any effect at all in producing the pressure in April; I should imagine that up to April, and up, perhaps, to the summer, they had increased the power of bankers in some respects rather than diminished it; for the expenditure had not been nearly so rapid as the calls; the consequence was, that most of the banks had rather a large amount of railway money in their hands in the beginning of the year.'

(This is corroborated in numerous statements made by bankers in C. D. 1848-57.)

> In the summer that melted gradually away, and on the 31st of December it was materially less. One cause ... of the pressure in October was the gradual diminution of the railway money in the bankers' hands; between the 22nd of April and the 31st of December the railway balances in our hands were reduced one-third; and the railway calls have also had this effect throughout the Kingdom; they have been gradually draining the deposits of bankers. (pp. 43, 44)

Samuel Gurney (head of the ill-famed firm of Overend, Gurney and Co.) similarly says:

> During the year 1846 ... there had been a considerable demand for capital, for the establishment of rail-ways ... but it did not increase the value of money.... There was a condensation of small sums into large masses, and those large masses were used in our market; so that, upon the whole, the effect was to throw more money into the money-market of the City than to take it out. (p. 159)

A. Hodgson, Director of the Liverpool Joint-Stock Bank, shows how much bills of exchange may constitute a reserve for bankers:

> It has been our habit to keep at least nine-tenths of all our deposits, and all money we have of other persons, in our bill case, in bills that are falling due from day to day ... so much so, that during the time of the run, the bills falling due were almost equal to the amount of the ran upon us day by day. (p. 53)

Speculative bills.

> '5092. Who were those bills (against sold cotton) generally accepted by?'—(R. Gardner, the cotton manufacturer repeatedly mentioned in this work:) 'Produce brokers: a person buys cotton, and places it in the hands of a broker, and draws upon that broker, and gets the bills discounted.'—'5094. And they are taken to the banks at Liverpool, and discounted?—Yes, and in other parts besides.... I believe if it had not been for the accommodation thus granted, and principally by the Liverpool banks, cotton would never have been so high last year as it was by 1½ d. or 2d. a pound.'—'600. You have stated that a vast amount of bills were put in circulation, drawn by speculators upon cotton brokers in Liverpool; does that system extend to your advance on acceptances upon colonial and foreign produce as well as on cotton?' (A. Hodgson, a Liverpool banker:) 'It refers to all kinds of colonial produce, but to cotton most especially.'—'601. Do you, as a banker, disencourage as far as you can that description of paper?—We do not; we consider it a very legitimate description of paper, when kept in moderation. This description of paper is frequently renewed.'

Swindling in the East Indian and Chinese Market, 1847.—Charles Turner (head of one of the leading East Indian houses in Liverpool):

> 'We are all aware of the events which have taken place as regards the Mauritius trade, and other trades of that kind. The brokers have been in the habit ... not only of advancing upon goods after their arrival to meet the bills drawn against those goods, which is perfectly legitimate, and upon the bills of lading ... but.... they have advanced upon produce before it was shipped, and in some cases before it was manufactured. Now, to speak of my own individual instance: I have bought bills in Calcutta to the extent of six or seven thousand pounds in one particular instance; the proceeds of the bills went down to the Mauritius, to help in the growth of sugar; those bills came to England, and above half of them were protested; for when the shipments of sugar came forward, instead of being held to pay those bills, it had been mortgaged to third parties ... before it was shipped, in fact almost before it was boiled' (p.78). 'Now manufacturers are insisting upon cash but it does not amount to much, because if a buyer has any credit in London, he can draw upon the house, and get the bill discounted; he goes to London, where discounts now are cheap; he gets the bill discounted, and pays cash to the manufacturer.... It takes twelve months, at least, for the shipper of goods to get his return from India ... a man with ten or fifteen thousand pounds would go into the Indian trade; he would open a credit with a house in London, to a considerable extent, giving that house one per cent; he, drawing upon the house in London, on the understanding that the proceeds of the goods that go out are to be returned to the house in London, but it being perfectly understood by both parties that the man in London is to be kept out of a cash advance; that is to say, in other words, the bills are to be renewed till the proceeds come home. The bills were discounted at Liverpool, Manchester ... or in London ... many of them lie in the Scotch banks' (p. 79).—'786. There is one house which failed in London the other day, and in examining their affairs, a transaction of this sort was proved to have taken place; there is a house of business at Manchester, and another at Calcutta; they opened a credit account with a house in London to the extent of £200,000; that is to say, the friends of this house in Manchester, who consigned goods to the East India House from Glasgow and from Manchester, had the power of drawing upon the house in London to the extent of £200,000; at the same time, there was an understanding that the corresponding house in Calcutta were to draw upon the London house to the extent of £200,000; with the proceeds of those bills sold in Calcutta, they were to buy other bills, and remit them to the house in London, to take up the first bills drawn from Glasgow... There would have been £600,000 of bills created upon that transaction.'—'971. At present, if a house in Calcutta purchase a cargo' (for England), 'and give their own bills upon their correspondent in London in payment, and they send the bills of lading home to this country, those bills of lading ... immediately become available to them in Lombard Street for advances, and they have eight months' use of the money before their correspondents are called upon to pay.'

IV. In 1848 a secret committee of the House of Lords investigated the causes of the 1847 crisis. The evidence given to the committee was not published, however, until 1857 (Minutes of Evidence, taken before the Secret Committee of the H. of L. appointed to inquire into the Causes of Distress, etc., 1857; quoted as C.D. 1848/57). Here Mr Lister, Director of the Union Bank of Liverpool, testified, among other things, to the following:

> 2444. In the spring of 1844 there was an undue extension of credit... because a man transferred property from business into railways and was still anxious to carry on the

> same extent of business. He probably first thought that he could sell the railway shares at a profit and replace the money in his business. Perhaps he found that could not be done, and he then got credit in his business where formerly he paid in cash. There was an extension of credit from that circumstance.
>
> 2500. Were those bills ... upon which the banks had sustained a loss by holding them, principally bills upon corn or bills upon cotton?—They were bills upon all kinds of produce, corn and cotton and sugar, all foreign produce of all descriptions. There was scarcely any thing perhaps with the exception of oil, that did not go down.'—2506. A broker who accepts a bill will not accept it without a good margin as to the value.
>
> 2512. There are two kinds of bills drawn against produce; the first is the original bill drawn abroad upon the merchant, who imports it.... The bills which are drawn against produce frequently fall due before the produce arrives. The merchant, therefore, when it arrives, if he has not sufficient capital, has to pledge that produce with the broker till he has time to sell that produce. Then anew species of bill is immediately drawn by the merchant in Liverpool upon the broker, on the security of that produce.... Then it is the business of the banker to ascertain from the broker whether he has the produce, and to what extent he has advanced upon it. It is his business to see that the broker has property to protect himself if he makes a loss.
>
> 2516. We also receive bills from abroad.... A man buys a bill abroad on England, and sends it to a house in England; we cannot tell whether that bill is drawn prudently or imprudently, whether it is drawn for produce or for wind.
>
> 2533. You said that almost every kind of foreign produce was sold at a great loss. Do you think that that was in consequence of undue speculation in that produce?—It arose from a very large import, and there not being an equal consumption to take it off. It appears that consumption fell off a great deal. 2534. In October produce was almost unsaleable.

How a general *sauve qui peut* develops at the height of a crisis is revealed in the same report by a first-rate expert, the esteemed crafty Quaker, Samuel Gurney, of Overend, Gurney and Co.:

> 1262 ... When a panic exists a man does not ask himself what he can get for his banknotes, or whether he shall lose one or two per cent by selling his exchequer bills, or three per cent. If he is under the influence of alarm he does not care for the profit or loss, but makes himself safe and allows the rest of the world to do as they please.

V. Concerning the mutual satiation of the two markets Mr Alexander, a merchant in the East India trade, testifies before the Committee of the, Lower House on the Bank Act of 1857 (quoted as B.C. 1857):

> 4330. At the present moment, if I lay out 6s. in Manchester, I get 5s. back in India; if I lay out 6s. in India, I get 5s. back in London.

So that the Indian market is, therefore, drugged by England, and the English by India. This was, indeed, the case in the summer of 1857, barely ten years after the bitter experience of 1847!

26

Accumulation of Money-Capital Its Influence on the Interest Rate

In England there takes place a steady accumulation of additional wealth, which has a tendency ultimately to assume the form of money. Now next in urgency, perhaps, to the desire to acquire money, is the wish to part with it again for some species of investment that shall yield either interest or profit; for money itself, as money, yields neither. Unless, therefore, concurrently with this ceaseless influx of surplus-capital, there is a gradual and sufficient extension of the field for its employment, we must be subject to periodical accumulations of money seeking investment, of more or less volume, according to the movement of events. For a long series of years, the grand absorbent of the surplus wealth of England was our public debt.... As soon as in 1816 the debt reached its maximum, and operated no longer as an absorbent, a sum of at least seven-and-twenty million per annum was necessarily driven to seek other channels of investment. What was more, various return payments of capital were made.... Enterprises which entail a large capital and create an opening from time to time for the excess of unemployed capital ... are absolutely necessary, at least in our country, so as to take care of the periodical accumulations of the superfluous wealth of society, which is unable to find room in the usual fields of application. (*The Currency Theory Reviewed,* London, 1845, pp. 32-34.)

Of 1845 the same work says:

'Within a very recent period prices have sprung upwards from the lowest point of depression.... Consols touch par.... The bullion in the vaults of the Bank of England has ... exceeded in amount the treasure held by that establishment since its institution. Shares of every description range at prices on the average wholly unprecedented, and interest has declined to rates which are all but nominal. If these be not evidences that another heavy accumulation of unemployed wealth exists at this hour in England, that another period of speculative excitement is at hand.' (*Ibid.*, p. 36.)

'Although ... the import of bullion is no sure sign of gain upon the foreign trade, yet, in the absence of any explanatory cause, it does *prima facie* represent a portion of it.' (J. G. Hubbard, *The Currency and the Country,* London, 1843, pp. 40-411.) 'Suppose ... that at a period of steady trade, fair prices ... and full, but not redundant circulation, a deficient harvest should give occasion for an import of corn, and an export of gold to the value of five million. The circulation'

[meaning, as we shall presently see, idle money-capital rather than means of circulation—*F.E.*]

'would of course be reduced by the same amount. An equal quantity of the circulation might still be held by individuals, but the deposits of merchants at their bankers, the balances of bankers with their money-broker, and the reserve in their till, will all be diminished, and the immediate result of this reduction in the amount of unemployed capital will be a rise in the rate of interest. I will assume from 4 per cent to 6. Trade being in a sound state, confidence will not be shaken, but credit will be more highly valued.' (*Ibid.*, p. 42.) 'But imagine ... that all prices fall.... The superfluous currency returns to the bankers in increased deposits-the abundance of unemployed capital lowers the rate of interest to a minimum, and this state of things lasts until either a

> return of higher prices or a more active trade call the dormant currency into service, or until it is absorbed by investments in foreign stocks or foreign goods' (p. 68).

The following extracts are also taken from the parliamentary Report on Commercial Distress, 1847-48.—Owing to the crop failure and famine of 1846-47 large-scale imports of foodstuffs became necessary.

> These circumstances caused the imports of the country to be very largely in excess over ... exports ... a considerable drain upon the banks, and an increased application to the discount brokers ... for the discount of bills.... They began to scrutinise the bills ... The facilities of houses then began to be very seriously curtailed, and the weak houses began to fail. Those houses which ... relied upon their credit... went down. This increased the alarm that had been previously felt; and the bankers and others finding that they would not rely with the same degree of confidence that they had previously done upon turning their bills and other money securities into banknotes, for the purpose of meeting their engagements, still further curtailed their facilities, and in many cases refused them altogether; they locked up their banknotes, in many instances to meet their own engagements; they were afraid of parting with them.... The alarm and confusion were increased daily; and unless Lord John Russell .... had issued the letter to the Bank ... universal bankruptcy would have been the issue. (pp. 74-75)

Russell's letter suspended the Bank Act.—The previously mentioned Charles Turner testifies:

> Some houses had large means, but not available. The whole of their capital was locked up in estates in the Mauritius, or indigo factories, or sugar factories. Having incurred liabilities to the extent of £500,000 or £600,000 they had no available assets to pay their bills, and eventually it proved that to pay their bills they were entirely dependent upon their credit. (p. 81)

The aforementioned S. Gurney said [1664]:

> At present (1848) there is a limitation of transaction and a great superabundance of money.—'1763. I do not think it was owing to the want of capital; it was owing to the alarm that existed that the rate of interest got so high.'

In 1847 England paid at least £9 million gold to foreign countries for imported foodstuffs. Of this amount £7½ million came from the Bank of England and 1½ million from other sources (p. 245).—Morris, Governor of the Bank of England:

> The public stocks in the country and canal and railway shares had already by the 23rd of October 1847 been depreciated in the aggregate to the amount of £114,752,225. (p. 312)

Again Morris, when questioned by Lord G. Bentinck:

> 'Are you not aware that all property invested in stocks and produce of every description was depreciated in the same way; that raw cotton, raw silk and unmanufactured wool were sent to the continent at the same depreciated price... and that sugar, coffee and tea were sacrificed as at forced sales?—It was ... inevitable that the country should make a considerable sacrifice for the purpose of meeting the efflux of bullion which had taken place in consequence of the large importation of food.'—[3848] 'Do not you think it would have been better to trench upon the £8,000,000 lying in the coffers of the Bank than to have endeavoured to get the gold back again at such a sacrifice?—*No, I do not.*' —

Now to the commentaries on such heroism. Disraeli questions Mr W. Cotton, a Director and former Governor of the Bank of England:

'What was the rate of dividend paid to the Bank proprietors in 1844?—It was 7 per cent for the year.'—'What is the dividend ... for 1847?—Nine per cent.'—'Does the Bank pay the income tax for its proprietors in this year?—It does.'—'Did it do so in 1844?—It did not.'[1]—'Then this Bank Act' (of 1844) 'has worked very well for the proprietors?... The result is, that since the passing of the Act, the dividend to the proprietors has been raised from 7 per cent to 9 per cent, and the income tax, that previously to the Act was paid by the proprietors, is now paid by the Bank?—*It is so.*' (Nos. 4356-61.)

Mr Pease, a country banker, had the following to say concerning hoarding in banks during the crisis of 1847:

> '4605. As the Bank was obliged still to raise its rate of interest, every one seemed apprehensive; country bankers increased the amount of bullion in their hands, and increased their reserve of notes, and many of us who were in the habit of keeping, perhaps, a few hundred pounds of gold and banknotes, immediately laid up thousands in our desks and drawers, as there was an uncertainty about discounts, and about our bills being current in the market, a general hoarding ensued.'

A member of the Committee remarks:

> '4691. Then, whatever may have been the cause during the last 12 years, the result has been rather in favour of the Jew and money-dealer, than the productive classes generally.'

How much a money-dealer takes advantage of times of crisis is revealed by Tooke:

> In the hardware districts of Warwickshire and Staffordshire, a great many orders for goods were declined to be accepted in 1847, because the rate of interest which the manufacturer had to pay for discounting his bills more than absorbed all his profit. (No. 5451)

Let us now take another parliamentary report cited earlier: Report of Select Committee on Bank Acts, communicated from the Commons to the Lords, 1857 (quoted further as B. C. 1857). In it Mr Norman, Director of the Bank of England and a leading figure among the champions of the Currency Principle, is interrogated as follows:

> '3635. You stated, that you consider that the rate of interest depends, not upon the amount of notes, but upon the supply and demand of capital. Will you state what you include in 'capital,' besides notes and coin?—I believe that the ordinary definition of 'capital' is commodities or services used in production.'—'3636. Do you mean to include all commodities in the word 'capital' when you speak of the rate of interest?—All commodities used in production.'—'3637. You include all that in the word 'capital,' when you speak of what regulates the rate of interest?—Yes. Supposing a cotton manufacturer to want cotton for his factory, the way in which he goes to work to obtain it is, probably, by getting an advance from his banker, and with the notes so obtained he goes to Liverpool, and makes a purchase. What he really wants is the cotton; he does not want the notes or the gold, except as a means of getting the cotton. Or he may want the means of paying his workmen; then again, he borrows the notes, and he pays the wages of the workmen with the notes; and the workmen, again, require food and lodging, and the money is the means of paying for those.'—'3638. But interest is paid for the money?—It is, in the first instance; but take another case. Supposing he buys the cotton on credit, without going to the bank for an advance, then the difference between the ready-money price and the credit price at the time at which he is to pay for it is the measure of the interest. Interest would exist if there was no money at all.'

This self-complacent rubbish is quite fitting for this pillar of the Currency Principle. First, the brilliant discovery that banknotes or gold are means of buying something, and that they are not borrowed for their own sake. And this is advanced to explain that the rate of interest is regulated—but by what? By the demand and supply of commodities, which heretofore was known to regulate only the market-prices of commodities. However, very different rates of interest are compatible with the same market-prices of commodities.—But now this cunning. He is confronted with the correct remark: 'But interest is paid for the money,' which, of course, contains the implication: 'What has interest received by the banker, who does not deal in commodities at all, to do with these commodities? And do not manufacturers receive money at the same rate of interest, although they invest it in widely different markets, hence in markets with widely different conditions of demand and supply for the commodities used in production?' All that this celebrated genius has to say in reply to these questions is that if the manufacturer buys cotton on credit 'the difference between the ready-money price and the credit price at the time at which he is to pay for it is the measure of the interest.' Quite the contrary. The prevailing rate of interest whose regulation the great intellect Norman was asked to explain is the measure of the difference between the cash price and the credit price until payment is due. First, the cotton is to be sold at its cash price, and this is determined by the market-price, itself regulated by the state of supply and demand. Say the price £1,000. This concludes the transaction between the manufacturer and the cotton broker so far as buying and selling is concerned. Now comes a second transaction. This is one between lender and borrower. The value of £1,000 is advanced to the manufacturer in cotton, and he has to repay it in money, say, in three months. And three months' interest for £1000, determined by the market rate of interest, makes up the extra charge over and above the cash price. The price of cotton is determined by supply and demand. But the price of the advanced value of cotton, of £1,000 advanced for three months, is determined by the rate of interest. And this fact, that cotton is thus transformed into money-capital, proves to Mr Norman that interest would exist even if there had been no money. If there were no money at all, there would certainly be no general rate of interest.

There is, to begin with, a vulgar conception of capital as 'commodities used in production.' In so far as these commodities serve as capital, their value as *capital*, as distinct from their value as *commodities*, is expressed in the profit which is derived from their productive or mercantile employment. And the rate of profit under all circumstances has something to do with the market-price of the purchased commodities and with their supply and demand, but is determined by entirely different circumstances. And there is no doubt that the interest rate is generally limited by the rate of profit. But Mr Norman should tell us just how this limit is determined. And it is determined by the supply and demand of money-capital *as distinguished* from the other forms of capital. It could be further asked: How are demand and supply of money-capital determined? It is doubtlessly true that a tacit connection exists between the supply of material capital and the supply of money-capital; and, likewise, that the demand of industrial capitalists for money-capital is determined by conditions of actual production. Instead of enlightening us on this point, Norman offers us the sage opinion that the demand for money-capital is not identical with the demand for money as such; and this sagacity alone, because he, Overstone, and the other Currency prophets, constantly have pricks of conscience since they are striving to make capital out of means of circulation as such through the artificial intervention of legislation, and to raise the interest rate.

Now to Lord Overstone, alias Samuel Jones Loyd, as he is asked to explain why he takes 10% for his 'money' because 'capital' is so scarce in his country.

> '3653. The fluctuations in the rate of interest arise from one of two causes: an alteration in the value of capital.'

(excellent! Value of capital, generally speaking, signifies precisely the rate of interest! A change in the rate of interest is thus made to spring from a change in the rate of interest. 'Value of capital,' as we have shown elsewhere, is never conceived otherwise in theory. Or else, if Lord Overstone means the rate of profit by the phrase 'value of capital', then the profound thinker returns to the notion that the interest rate is regulated by the rate of profit!)

> 'or an alteration in the amount of money in the country. All great fluctuations of interest, great either in their duration or in the extent of the fluctuation, may be distinctly traced to alterations in the value of capital. Two more striking practical illustrations of that fact cannot be furnished than the rise in the rate of interest in 1847 and during the last two years (1855-56); the minor fluctuations in the rate of interest, which arise from an alteration in the quantity of money, are small both in extent and in duration. They are frequent, and the more rapid and frequent they are, the more effectual they are for accomplishing their destined purpose',

which is to enrich bankers like Overstone. Friend Samuel Gurney expresses it very naively before the Committee of Lords, C. D. 1848 [1857]:

> '1324. Do you think that the great fluctuations in the rate of interest which have taken place in the last year are advantageous or not to bankers or dealers in money?—I think they are advantageous to dealers in money. All fluctuations in trade are advantageous to the knowing man.'
>
> '1325. May not the banker suffer eventually from the high rates of interest, by impoverishing his best customers?—No; I do not think it has that effect perceptibly.' —

Voilà ce que parler veut dire. [This is what had to be said.—*Ed.*]

We shall eventually return to the influence of the quantity of available money on the rate of interest. But it is to be noted right here that Overstone again makes a *quid pro quo.* The demand for money-capital in 1847 (before October, there was no anxiety over money stringency, or the 'quantity of money,' as he called it) increased for various reasons, such as rising prices for corn and cotton, lack of buyers of sugar due to over-production, railway speculation and the crash, overcrowding of foreign markets with cotton goods, and the forced export to, and import from, India for the purpose of speculation in bills of exchange, which was described above. All these things, over-production in industry and underproduction in agriculture—in other words, greatly differing causes—gave rise to an increased demand for money-capital, *i.e.*, for credit and money. The increased demand for money-capital had its origin in the course of the productive process itself. But whatever may have been the cause, it was the demand for *money*-capital which made the interest rate, the value of money-capital, climb. If Overstone means to say that the value of money-capital rose *because* it rose, then it is tautology. But if, by 'value of capital,' he means a rise in the rate of profit as the cause of the rise in the rate of interest, we shall immediately see that this is wrong. The demand for money-capital, and consequently the 'value of capital,' may rise even though the profit may decrease; as soon as the relative supply of money-capital shrinks, its 'value' increases. What Overstone wished to prove is that the crisis of 1847, and the attendant high interest rate, had nothing to do with the 'quantity of money,' *i.e.*, with the regulations of the Bank Act of 1844 which he had inspired; although it was, indeed, connected with them, inasmuch as the fear of exhausting the bank reserve—a creation of Overstone—contributed a money panic to the crisis of 1847-48. But this is not the issue here. There was a dearth of money-capital, caused by the excessive volume of operations compared to the available means and precipitated by the disturbance in the reproduction process due to a crop failure, over-investment in railways, over-production, particularly of cotton goods, swindling operations in trade with India and China, speculation, superfluous sugar imports, etc. What the people, who had bought corn at 120 shillings per quarter, lacked when it fell to 60 shillings, were the 60 shillings which they had overpaid and the corresponding credit for that amount in Lombard Street advances on the corn. It was by no means a lack of banknotes that prevented them from converting their corn into money at its old price of 120 shillings. The same applied to those who had imported an excess of sugar, which became almost unsaleable. It applied likewise to the gentlemen who had tied up their floating capital in railways and relied on credit to replace it in their 'legitimate' business. To Overstone, all this signifies a 'moral sense of the enhanced value of his money.' But this enhanced value of money-capital corresponded directly, on the other hand, to the depreciated money-value of real capital (commodity-capital and productive capital). The value of capital in the one form rose because the value of capital in the other fell. Overstone, however, seeks to identify these two values of different sorts of capital in a single value of capital in general, and he tries to do so by opposing both of them to a scarcity of the medium of circulation, of available money. But the same amount of money-capital may be loaned with very different quantities of the circulation medium.

Take his example of 1847. The official bank-rate stood at 3 to 3½% in January; 4 to 4½% in February. In March it was generally 4%. April (panic) 4 to 7½%. May 5 to 5½%, June, on the whole, 5%. July 5%. August 5 to 5½%. September 5% with trifling variations of 5¼, 5½, 6%. October 5, 5½, 7%. November 7-10%. December 7 to 5%.—In this case the interest rose because profits decreased and the money-values of commodities fell enormously. If, therefore, Overstone says here that the rate of interest rose in 1847 because the value of capital rose, he cannot mean anything by value of capital but the value of money-capital, and the value of money-capital is the rate of interest, and nothing else. But later he showed the cloven hoof and identified the value of capital with the rate of profit.

As for the high rate of interest paid in 1856, Overstone was indeed ignorant of the fact that this was partially a symptom that the credit jobbers were coming to the fore, who paid interest not from their profit, but with the capital of others; he maintained just a few months before the crisis of 1857 that 'business is quite sound.'

He testified furthermore: [B.C. 1857]

> '3722. That idea of the profits of trade being destroyed by a rise in the rate of interest is most erroneous. In the first place, a rise in the rate of interest is seldom of any long duration; in the second place, if it is of long duration, and of great extent, it is really a rise in the value of capital, and why does value of capital rise? Because the rate of profit is increased.'

Here, then, we learn, at last, what the meaning of 'value of capital' is. Furthermore, the rate of profit may be high for a lengthy period, and yet the profit of enterprise may fall and the rate of interest rise to a point where it swallows the greater portion of the profit.

> '3724. The rise in the rate of interest has been in consequence of the great increase in the trade of the country, and the great rise in the rate of profits; and to complain of the rise in the rate of interest as being destructive of the two things, which have been its own cause, is a sort of logical absurdity, which one does not know how to deal with.'

This is just as logical as if he were to say: The rise in the rate of profit has been in consequence of the rise in commodity-prices by speculation, and to complain that the rise in prices destroys its own cause, namely, speculation, is a logical absurdity, etc. That anything can ultimately destroy its own cause is a logical absurdity only for the usurer enamoured of the high interest rate. The greatness of the Romans was the cause of their conquests, and their conquests destroyed their greatness. Wealth is the cause of luxury and luxury has a destructive effect on wealth. The wiseacre! The idiocy of the present-day bourgeois world cannot be better described than by the respect, which the 'logic' of the millionaire—the dunghill aristocrat—inspired in all England. Furthermore, if a high rate of profit and an expansion of business may be causes of a high interest rate, a high rate of interest is by no means therefore a cause of high profit. The question is precisely whether such a high interest (as was actually discovered during the crisis) continued or, what is more, reached its climax after the high rate of profit had long gone the way of all flesh.

> '3718. With regard to a great rise in the rate of discount, that is a circumstance entirely arising from the increased value of capital, and the cause of that increased value of capital I think any person may discover with perfect clearness. I have already alluded to the fact that during the 13 years this Act has been in operation, the trade of this country has increased from £45,000,000 to £120,000,000. Let any person reflect upon all the events which are involved in that short statement; let him consider the enormous demand upon capital for the purpose of carrying on such a gigantic increase of trade, and let him consider at the same time that the natural source from which that great demand should be supplied, namely, the annual savings of this country, has for the last three or four years been consumed in the unprofitable expenditure of war. I confess that my surprise is, that the rate of interest is not much higher than it is; or, in other words, my surprise is, that the pressure for capital to carry on these gigantic operations, is not far more stringent than you have found it to be.'

What an amazing jumble of words by our logician of usury! Here he comes again with his increased value of capital! He seems to think that this enormous expansion of the reproduction process, hence accumulation of real capital, took place on one side, and that on the other there existed a 'capital', for which there arose an 'enormous demand', in order to accomplish this gigantic increase of commerce! Was not this enormous increase of production an increase of capital itself, and if it created a demand, did it not also create the supply, and, simultaneously, an increased supply of money-capital? If the interest rate rose very high, then merely because the demand for money-capital increased still more rapidly than its supply, which implies, in other words, that with the expansion of industrial production, its operation on a credit basis expanded as well. That is to say, the actual industrial expansion caused an increased demand for 'accommodation,' and the latter demand is evidently what our banker means by the 'enormous demand for capital.' It was surely not the expansion of this *demand* for capital alone, which raised the export business from £45 to £120 million. And furthermore, what does Overstone mean when he says that the country's annual savings swallowed by the Crimean War form the natural source of supply for this big demand? in the first place, how did England achieve accumulation in 1792-1815, which was a far different war from the little Crimean one? In the second place, if the natural source was dry, from what source did capital flow at all? It is well known that England did not request loans from foreign countries. Yet if there is an artificial source besides the natural one, it would have been best for a nation to utilise the natural source in war and the artificial one in business. But if only the old money-capital was available, could it double its effectiveness through a high rate of interest? Mr Overstone evidently thinks that the country's annual savings (which, however, were supposed to have been consumed in this case) are converted only into money-capital. But if no real accumulation, *i.e.*, expansion of production and augmentation of the means of production, had taken place, what good would there be from the accumulation of debtor's money claims on this production?

The increase in the 'value of capital' springing from a high rate of profit is identified by Overstone with an increase caused by a greater demand for money-capital. This demand may climb for reasons quite independent of the rate of profit. He himself cites the example of its rise in 1847 as a result of the depreciation of real capital. Depending on what suits his purpose, he ascribes the value of capital to real capital or money-capital.

The dishonesty of our banking lord, and his narrow-minded banker's point of view with its didactic flavouring are further revealed in the following:

> (3728. Question:) 'You have stated that the rate of discount is of no material moment you think to the merchant; will you be kind enough to state what you consider the ordinary rate of profit?'

Mr Overstone declares that it is 'impossible' to answer this question.

> '3729. Supposing the average rate of profit to be, say, from 7 to 10%, a variation of from 2 to 7 or 8% in the rate of discount must materially affect the rate of profit, must it not?'

(This question itself lumps together the rate of profit of enterprise with the rate of profit, and. passes over the fact that the rate of profit is the common source of interest and profit of enterprise. The interest rate may leave the rate of profit untouched, but not the profit of enterprise. Overstone replied:)

> 'In the first place parties will not pay a rate of discount which seriously interrupts their profits; they will discontinue their business rather than do that.'

(Yes, if they can do so without ruining themselves. So long as their profit is high, they pay the discount because they wish to, and when it is low, because they have to.)

> 'What is the meaning of discount? Why does a person discount a bill? ... Because he wants to obtain the command of a greater quantity of capital.'

(*Halte-là!* because he wants to anticipate the return in money of his tied-up capital and to prevent his business from stopping; because he must meet payments due. He demands more capital only when business is good, or when he speculates on another's capital, though business may be bad. The discount is by no means simply a device to expand business.)

> 'And why does he want to obtain the command of a greater quantity of capital? Because he wants to employ that capital; and why does he want to employ that capital? Because it is profitable to him to do so; it would not be profitable to him to do so if the discount destroyed his profit.'

This smug logician assumes that bills of exchange are discounted only for the purpose of expanding business, and that business is expanded because it is profitable. The first assumption is wrong. The ordinary businessman discounts, in order to anticipate the money-form of his capital and thereby to keep his process of reproduction in flow; not in order to expand his business or secure additional capital, but in order to balance the credit he gives by the credit he receives. And if he wants to expand his business on credit, discounting bills will do him little good because it is merely conversion of the money-capital which he already has in his hands from one form into another; he will rather take a direct loan for a longer period. The credit swindler will get his accommodation bills discounted to expand his business activity, to cover one squalid business deal by another; not to make profits but to obtain possession of another's capital.

After Mr Overstone has thus identified discounting with borrowing additional capital (instead of with converting bills representing capital into hard cash), he beats an instant retreat as soon as the screws are applied to him.

> (3730. Question:) 'Merchants being engaged in business, must they not for a certain period carry on their operations in despite of any temporary increase in the rate of discount?'—(Overstone:) 'There is no doubt that in any particular transaction, if a person can get his command of capital at a low rate of interest rather than at a high rate of interest, taken in that limited view of the matter, that is convenient to him.'

But it is a very unlimited point of view, on the other hand, which enables Mr Overstone quite suddenly to understand only his, banker's capital, as 'capital,' and to assume that the man who discounts a bill of exchange with him is a man without capital, just because his capital exists in the form of commodities, or because the money-form of his capital is a bill of exchange, which Mr Overstone converts into another money-form.

> 3732. 'With reference to the Act of 1844, can you state what has been about the average rate of interest in proportion to the amount of bullion in the Bank; would it be a fact that when the amount of bullion has been about £9,000,000 or £10,000,000 the rate of interest has been 6 or 7 per cent, and that when it has been £16,000,000, the rate of interest has been, say, from 3 to 4 per cent?'

(The examiner wishes to press him to explain the rate of interest, so far as it is influenced by the amount of bullion in the Bank, on the basis of the rate of interest, so far as it is influenced by the value of capital.)

> 'I do not apprehend that that is so... but if it is, then I think we must take still more stringent measures than those adopted by the Act of 1844, because if it be true that the greater the store of bullion, the lower the rate of interest, we ought to set to work, according to that view of the matter, to increase the store of bullion to an indefinite amount, and then we should get the interest down to nothing.'

The examiner, Cayley, unmoved by this poor joke, continues:

> '3733. If that be so, supposing that £5,000,000 of bullion was to be restored to the Bank, in the course of the next six months the bullion then would amount, say, to £16,000,000, and supposing that the rate of interest was thus to fall to 3 or 4 per cent, how could it be stated that that fall in the rate of interest arose from a great decrease of the trade of the country?—I said that the recent rise in the rate of interest, not that the fall in the rate of interest, was closely connected with the great increase in the trade of the country.'

But what Cayley says is this: If a rise of interest rate together with a contraction of the gold reserve, is an indication of an expansion in business, then a fall of the interest rate together with an expansion of the gold reserve, must be an indication of a contraction of business. Overstone has no answer to this.

> (3736. Question:) 'I observed you' (in the text always 'Your Lordship') 'to say that money was the instrument for obtaining capital.'

(Precisely this is the mistake, to conceive money as an instrument; it is a form of capital.)

> 'Under a drain of bullion (of the Bank of England) is not the great strain, on the contrary, for *capitalists* to obtain money?'—(Overstone:) 'No, it is not the capitalists, it is those who are not capitalists, who want to obtain money and why do they want to obtain money? ... Because through the money they obtain the command of the capital of the capitalist to carry on the business of the persons who are not capitalists.'

Here he declares point-blank that manufacturers and merchants are not capitalists, and that the capitalist's capital is only money-capital.

> '3737. Are not the parties who draw bills of exchange capitalists?—The parties who draw bills of exchange may be, and may not be, capitalists.'

Here he is stuck.

He is then asked whether merchants' bills of exchange represent commodities which have been sold or shipped. He denies that these bills represent the value of commodities in the same way that a bank-note represents gold. (3740, 3741.) This is somewhat insolent.

'3742. Is it not the merchant's object to get money?—No; getting money is not the object in drawing the bill; getting money is the object in discounting the bill.'

Drawing bills of exchange is converting commodities into a form of credit-money, just as discounting bills of exchange is converting this credit-money into another, namely banknotes. At any rate, Mr Overstone admits here that the purpose of discounting is to obtain money. A while ago he said that discounting was a way not of converting capital from one form into another, but of obtaining additional capital.

'3743. What is the great desire of the mercantile community under pressure of panic, such as you state to have occurred in 1825, 1837 and 1839; is their object to get possession of capital or the legal tender?—Their object is get the command of capital to support their business.'

Their purpose is to obtain means of payment for due bills of exchange on themselves, on account of the prevailing lack of credit, so that they will not have to let their commodities go below price. If they have no capital at all themselves, they receive it along with the means of payment, because they receive value without an equivalent. The urge to obtain money as such consists always in the wish to convert value from the form of commodities or creditor's claims into the form of money. Hence, even aside from the crises, the great difference between borrowing capital and discount, the latter being a mere conversion of money claims from one form into another, or into real money.

[I take the liberty at this point in my capacity of editor to interpolate a few remarks.

With respect to Norman, as well as Loyd-Overstone, the banker is always the one who 'advances capital' to others, and his customers are those who demand 'capital' from him. Thus, Overstone says that people have bills of exchange discounted through him, 'because they wish to obtain the command of *capital*' (3729), and that it is pleasant for such people if they can 'get *command of capital* at a low rate of interest' (3730). 'Money is the instrument for obtaining *capital*' (3736), and during a panic the great desire of the mercantile community is to 'get the command of *capital*' (3743). For all of Loyd-Overstone's confusion over what capital is, it is at least clear that he designates what the banker gives to his client as capital, as a capital which the client did not formerly possess, but which was advanced to him to supplement what he already possessed.

The banker has become so accustomed to act as distributor (through loans) of the social capital available in money-form that he considers every function whereby he hands out money, as loaning. All the money he pays out appears to him as a loan. If the money is directly loaned, this is literally true. If it is invested in the bill-discounting business, it is, in fact, advanced by himself until the bill becomes due. The notion thus grows on him that all the payments he makes are advances; furthermore, that they are advances not merely in the sense that every investment of money with the object of deriving interest or profit, is economically considered an advance of money which the owner of money concerned, in his capacity of private individual, makes to himself in his capacity as entrepreneur, but advances in the definite sense that the banker lends his client a sum of money which augments the capital already at the latter's disposal.

It is this conception, which, transferred from the banker's office to political economy, has created the confusing controversy, whether that which the banker places at his client's disposal in hard cash is capital or mere money, a medium of circulation, or currency. To decide this—fundamentally simple—controversy, we must put ourselves in the place of a bank client. It all depends on what this customer requests and receives.

If the bank allows its client a loan simply on his personal credit, without any security on his part, then the matter is clear. He then certainly receives an advance of definite value as a supplement to the capital he has already invested. He receives it in the form of money;

hence, not merely money, but also money-*capital.*

If, on the other hand, he receives the advance against securities, etc., then it is an advance in the sense of money paid to him on condition that he pay it back. But it is not an advance of capital. For the securities also represent capital, and a larger amount at that than the advance. The recipient therefore receives less capital-value than he deposits as security; this represents for him no acquisition of additional capital. He does not enter into the transaction because he needs capital—he has that in his securities—but because he needs money. Here we, therefore, have an advance of *money,* not of capital.

If the loan is granted by discounting bills, then even the *form* of an advance disappears. Then it is purely a matter of buying and selling. The bill passes by endorsement into the possession of the bank, while the money passes into the possession of the client. There is no question of any return payment on his part. If the client buys hard cash with a bill of exchange or some similar instrument of credit, it is no more and no less an advance than were he to buy cash money with his other commodities, such as cotton, iron, or corn. Still less can this be called an advance of *capital.* Every purchase and sale between one merchant and another is a transfer of capital. But an advance of capital occurs only when the transfer of capital is not reciprocal, but unilateral and for a period of time. An advance of capital through discount can, therefore, only occur when a bill is a speculative one, which does not represent any sold commodities, and no banker will take such a bill if he is aware of its nature. In the regular discounting business the bank client does not, therefore, receive an advance, either of capital or of money. What he receives is money for sold commodities.

The cases in which the customer demands and receives capital from a bank are thus clearly distinguished from those, in which he merely receives an advance of money, or buys money from the bank. And since least of all Mr Loyd-Overstone ever advanced his funds without collateral except on the rarest occasions (he was the banker of my firm in Manchester), it is likewise evident that his lyric descriptions of the great quantities of capital loaned by generous bankers to manufacturers in need of capital are gross inventions.

By the way, in Chapter XXXII Marx says essentially the same thing: 'The demand for means of payment is a mere demand for *convertibility into money,* so far as merchants and producers have good securities to offer; it is a demand for *money-capital* whenever there is no collateral, so that an advance of means of payment gives them not only the *form of money* but also the *equivalent* they lack, whatever its form, with which to make payment.'—And again in Chapter XXXIII: 'Under a developed system of credit, with the money concentrated in the hands of bankers, it is they, *at least nominally,* who advance it. This advance refers only to money in circulation. It is an advance of *circulation,* not an advance of capitals which it circulates.' Mr Chapman, who should know, likewise corroborates this conception of the discounting business: B. C. 1857:

> 'The banker has the bill, the banker has *bought the bill.*' Evid. Question 5139.

We shall, however, return to this subject in Chapter XXVIII.—*F. E.*]

> '3744. Will you be good enough to describe what you actually mean by the term "capital"?'—(Overstone:) 'Capital consists of various commodities, by means of which trade is carried on; there is fixed capital and there is circulating capital. Your ships, your docks, your wharves ... are fixed capital; your provisions, your clothes, etc., are circulating capital.'
>
> '3745. Is the country oppressed under a drain of bullion?—Not in the rational sense of the word.'

(Then comes the old Ricardian theory of money.)

> 'In the natural state of things the money of the world is distributed amongst the different countries of the world in certain proportions, those proportions being such that under that distribution (of money) the intercourse between any one country and all the other countries of the world jointly will be an intercourse of barter; but disturbing circumstances will arise to affect that distribution, and when those arise, a certain portion of the money of any given country passes to other countries.'—'3746. Your Lordship now uses the term 'money.' I understood you before to say that it was a loss of capital.—That what was a loss of capital?'—'3747. The export of bullion?—No, I did not say so. If you treat bullion as capital, no doubt it is a loss of capital; it is parting with a certain proportion of those precious metals which constitute the money of the world.'—'3748. I understood Your Lordship to say that an alteration in the rate of discount was a mere sign of an alteration in the value of capital?—I did.'—'3749. And that the rate of discount generally alters with the state of the store of bullion in the Bank of England?—Yes, but I have already stated that the fluctuations in the rate of interest, which arise from an alteration in the quantity of money' (what he therefore means here is the quantity of actually existing gold) 'in a country, are very small.'
>
> '3750. Then, does Your Lordship mean that there is a less capital than there was, when there is a more continuous yet temporary increase in the rate of discount than usual?—Less, in one sense of the word. The proportion between capital and the demand for it is altered; it may be by an increased demand, not by a diminution of the quantity of capital.'

(But a moment ago it was capital = money or gold, and a little before that he had explained the rise in interest rate by a high rate of profit, due to an expansion rather than a contraction of business or capital.)

> '3751. What is the capital which you particularly allude to?—That depends entirely upon what the capital is which each person wants. It is the capital which the country has at its command for conducting its business, and when that business is doubled, there must be a great increase in the demand for the capital with which it is to be carried on.'

(This shrewd banker doubles first the business activity and then the demand for capital with which it is to be doubled. All he sees is his client, who asks Mr Loyd for more capital by which to double the volume of his business.)

> 'Capital is like any other commodity' (but according to Mr Loyd capital is nothing but the totality of commodities), 'it will vary in its price' (hence, commodities change their price twice, one time as commodities and the second as capital), 'according to the supply and demand.'
>
> '3752. The changes in the rate of discount are generally connected with the changes in the amount of gold which there is in the coffers of the Bank. Is it that capital to which Your Lordship refers?—No.'—'3753. Can Your Lordship point to any instance in which there has been a large store of capital in the Bank of England connected with a high rate of discount?—The Bank of England is not a place for the deposit of capital, it is a place for the deposit of money.'—'3754. Your Lordship has stated that the rate of interest depends upon the amount of capital; will you be kind enough to state what capital you mean, and whether you can point to any instance in which there has been a large store of bullion in the Bank and at the same time a high rate of interest?—It is very probable (aha!) that the accumulation of bullion in the Bank may be coincident with a low rate of interest, because a period in which there is a diminished demand for capital.'

(namely, money-capital; the period to which reference is made here, 1844 and 1845, was a period of prosperity) 'is a period, during which, of course, the means or instrument through which you command capital may accumulate.'—'3755. Then you think that there is no connection between the rate of discount and the amount of bullion in the coffers of the Bank?—There may be a connection, but it is not a connection of principle' (his Bank Act of 1844, however, made it a principle of the Bank of England to regulate the interest rate by the quantity of bullion in its possession), 'there may be a coincidence of time.'—'3758. Do I rightly understand you to say, that the difficulty of merchants in this country, under a state of pressure, in consequence of a high rate of discount, is in getting capital, and not in getting money?—You are putting two things together which I do not join in that form; their difficulty is in getting capital, and their difficulty also is in getting money.... The difficulty of getting money and the difficulty of getting capital is the same difficulty taken in two successive stages of its progress.'

Here the fish is caught in the net again. The first difficulty is to discount a bill of exchange, or to obtain a loan against the security of commodities. It is the difficulty of converting capital, or a commercial token of capital into money. And this difficulty is manifested, among other things, in a high rate of interest. But as soon as the money is obtained, what is the second difficulty? Does anyone ever find any difficulty in getting rid of his money when it is merely a matter of paying? And if it is a matter of buying, has anyone ever had any difficulty in purchasing during times of crisis? And, for the sake of argument, should this refer to a specific dearth in corn, cotton, etc., this difficulty could only appear in the price of these commodities, not in the value of money-capital, *i.e.*, not in the rate of interest; and this difficulty is overcome, in the final analysis, by the fact that our man now has the money to buy them.

'3760. But a higher rate of discount is an increased difficulty of getting money?—It is an increased difficulty of getting money, but it is not because you want to have the money; it is only the form' (and this form brings profit into the banker's pocket) 'in which the increased difficulty of getting capital presents itself according to the complicated relations of a civilised state.'

'3763. (Overstone's reply:) The banker is the go-between who receives deposits on the one side, and on the other applies those deposits, entrusting them, *in the form of capital,* to the hands of persons, who, etc.'

At last we have what he means by capital. He converts money into capital by 'entrusting' it, less euphemistically, by loaning it at interest.

After Mr Overstone has stated that a change in the rate of discount is not essentially connected with a change in quantity of the gold reserve in a bank, or in the quantity of available money, but that there is at best only a coincidence in time, he repeats:

'3805. When the money in the country is diminished by a drain, its value increases, and the Bank of England must conform to that alteration in the value of money.'

(hence, the value of money *as capital;* in other words, the rate of interest, for the value of money *as money,* compared with commodities, remains the same),

'which is meant by the technical term of raising the rate of interest.'

'3819. I never confound those two.'

Meaning money and capital, and for the simple reason that he never differentiated between them.

'3834. The very large sum, which had to be paid' (for corn in 1847), 'which was *in point of fact capital,* for the supply of the necessary provisions of the country.'

> '3841. The variations in the rate of discount have no doubt a very close relation to the state of the reserve' (of the Bank of England), 'because the state of the reserve is the indicator of the increase or the decrease of the quantity of money in the country; and in proportion as the money in the country increases or decreases, the value of that money will increase or decrease, and the bank-rate of discount will conform to that change.'

Thus, Overstone admits here what he emphatically denied in No. 3755.

> '3842. There is an intimate connection between them.'

Meaning the quantity of bullion in the issue department, on the one hand, and the reserve of notes in the banking department, on the other. Here he explains the change in the rate of interest by the change in the quantity of money. But this statement is wrong. The reserve may shrink because the circulating money in the country increases. This is the case when the public takes more notes and the hoard of metal does not decrease. But in such case the interest rate rises, because then the banking capital of the Bank of England is limited by the Act of 1844. But he dare not mention this, because due to this law the two departments have nothing to do with one another.

> '3859. A high rate of profit will always create a great demand for capital; a great demand for capital will raise the value of it.'

Here, at last, we have the connection between a high rate of profit and a demand for capital as Overstone conceives it. Now, a high rate of profit prevailed in, for example, 1844-45 in the cotton industry, because raw cotton was cheap, and remained so, whereas the demand for cotton goods was strong. The value of capital (and in an earlier statement Overstone calls capital that which everyone needs in his business), in this case therefore the value of raw cotton, was not increased for the manufacturer. The high rate of profit may have induced some cotton manufacturer to obtain money on credit for the purpose of expanding his business. Thereby his demand rose for *money*-capital, but for nothing else.

> '3889. Bullion may or may not be money, just as paper may or may not be a bank-note.'

> '3896. Do I correctly understand Your Lordship that you give up the argument, which you used in 1840, that the fluctuations in the notes out of the Bank of England ought to conform to the fluctuations in the amount of bullion?—I give it up so far as this... that now with the means of information which we possess, the notes out of the Bank of England must have added to them the notes which are in the banking reserve of the Bank of England.'

This is superlative. The arbitrary provision that the Bank may make out as many paper notes as it has gold in the treasury and 14 million more, implies, of course, that its issue of notes fluctuates with the fluctuations of the gold reserve. But since the present 'means of information which we possess' clearly showed that the mass of notes, which the Bank can thus manufacture (and which the issue department transfers to the banking department)—that this circulation between the two departments of the Bank of England, fluctuating with the fluctuations of the gold reserve, does not determine the fluctuations in the circulation of banknotes outside the Bank of England, then the latter—the real circulation—becomes a matter of indifference to the bank administration, and the circulation between the two departments of the Bank, whose difference from the real circulation is mirrored in the reserve, alone becomes decisive. To the outside world this internal circulation is significant only because the reserve indicates how close the Bank is approaching the legal maximum of its note issue, and how much its clients can still receive from the banking department.

The following is a brilliant example of Overstone's *mala fides:*

'4243. Does the quantity of capital, do you think, oscillate from month to month to such a degree as to alter its value in the way exhibited of late years in the oscillations in the rate of discount?—The relation between the demand and the supply of capital may undoubtedly fluctuate even within short periods.... If France tomorrow put out a notice that she wishes to borrow a very large loan, there is no doubt that it would immediately cause a great alteration *in the value of money,* that is to say, *in the value of capital,* in this country.'

'4245. If France announces, that she wants suddenly, for any purpose, 30 million's worth of commodities there will be a great demand for *capital,* to use the more scientific and the simpler term.'

'4246. The *capital,* which France would wish to buy with her loan, is *one* thing, and the *money* with which she buys it is *another,* is it the *money,* which alters in value, or not?—We seem to be reviving the old question, which I think is more fit for the chamber of a student than for this committee room.'

And with this he retires, but not into the chamber of a student.[2]

Notes

1. In other words, formerly they first fixed the dividend, and then deducted the income tax as the dividend was paid to the individual stockholder; after 1844, however, the Bank first paid the income tax on its total profit, and then paid the dividend 'free of income tax.'
   The same nominal percentages are, therefore, higher in the latter case by the amount of the tax.—*F. E.*
2. More on Overstone's confusion of terms in matters concerning capital at the close of Chapter XXXII.—[*F.E.*]

27

The Role of Credit in Capitalist Production

The general remarks, which the credit system so far elicited from us, were the following:

I. Its necessary development to affect the equalisation of the rate of profit, or the movements of this equalisation, upon which the entire capitalist production rests.
II. Reduction of the costs of circulation.

   1. One of the principal costs of circulation is money itself, being value in itself. It is economised through credit in three ways.
      a) By dropping away entirely in a great many transactions.
      b) By the accelerated circulation of the circulating medium.[1] This corresponds in part with what is to be said under 2). On the one hand, the acceleration is technical; *i.e.*, with the same magnitude and number of actual turnovers of commodities for consumption, a smaller quantity of money or money tokens performs the same service. This is bound up with the technique of banking. On the other hand, credit accelerates the velocity of the metamorphoses of commodities and thereby the velocity of money circulation.
      c) Substitution of paper for gold money.

2. Acceleration, by means of credit, of the individual phases of circulation or of the metamorphosis of commodities, later the metamorphosis of capital, and with it an acceleration of the process of reproduction in general. (On the other hand, credit helps to keep the acts of buying and selling longer apart and serves thereby as a basis for speculation.) Contraction of reserve funds, which may be viewed in two ways: as a reduction of the circulating medium, on the one hand, and, on the other, as a reduction of that part of capital which must always exist in the form of money.[2]

III. Formation of stock companies. Thereby:

1. An enormous expansion of the scale of production and of enterprises, that was impossible for individual capitals. At the same time, enterprises that were formerly government enterprises, become public.
2. The capital, which in itself rests on a social mode of production and presupposes a social concentration of means of production and labour-power, is here directly endowed with the form of social capital (capital of directly associated individuals) as distinct from private capital, and its undertakings assume the form of social undertakings as distinct from private undertakings. It is the abolition of capital as private property within the framework of capitalist production itself.
3. Transformation of the actually functioning capitalist into a mere manager, administrator of other people's capital, and of the owner of capital into a mere owner, a mere money-capitalist. Even if the dividends which they receive include the interest and the profit of enterprise, *i.e.*, the total profit (for the salary of the manager is, or should be, simply the wage of a specific type of skilled labour, whose price is regulated in the labour-market like that of any other labour), this total profit is henceforth received only in the form of interest, *i.e.*, as mere compensation for owning capital that now is entirely divorced from the function in the actual process of reproduction, just as this function in the person of the manager is divorced from ownership of capital. Profit thus appears (no longer only that portion of it, the interest, which derives its justification from the profit of the borrower) as a mere appropriation of the surplus-labour of others, arising from the conversion of means of production into capital, *i.e.*, from their alienation vis-à-vis the actual producer, from their antithesis as another's property to every individual actually at work in production, from manager down to the last day-labourer. In stock companies, the function is divorced from capital ownership; hence also labour is entirely divorced from ownership of means of production and surplus-labour. This result of the ultimate development of capitalist production is a necessary transitional phase towards the reconversion of capital into the property of producers, although no longer as the private property of the individual producers, but rather as the property of associated producers, as outright social property. On the other hand, the stock company is a transition toward the conversion of all functions in the reproduction process, which still remain linked with capitalist property, into mere functions of associated producers, into social functions.

   Before we go any further, there is still the following economically important fact to be noted: Since profit here assumes the pure form of interest, undertakings of this sort are still possible if they yield bare interest, and this is one of the causes, stemming the fall of the general rate of profit, since such undertakings, in which the ratio of constant capital to the variable is so enormous, do not necessarily enter into the equalisation of the general rate of profit.

   [Since Marx wrote the above, new forms of industrial enterprises have developed, as we know, representing the second and third degree of stock companies. The daily growing speed with which production may be enlarged in all fields of large-scale industry today, is offset by the ever-greater slowness with which the market for these increased products expands. What the former turns out in months, can scarcely be absorbed by the latter in years. Add to this the protective tariff policy, by which every industrial country shuts itself off from all others, particularly from England, and also artificially increases domestic production capacity. The results are a general chronic over-production, depressed prices, falling and even wholly disappearing profits; in short, the old boasted freedom of competition has reached the end of its tether and must itself announce its obvious, scandalous bankruptcy. And in every country, this is taking place through the big industrialists of a certain branch joining in a cartel for the regulation of production. A committee fixes the quantity to be produced by each establishment and is the final authority for distributing the incoming orders. Occasionally even international cartels were established, as between the English and German iron industries. But even this form of association in production did not suffice. The antagonism of interests between the individual firms broke through it only too often, restoring competition. This led in some branches, where the scale of production permitted, to the concentration of the entire production of that branch of industry in one big joint-stock company under single management. This has been repeatedly effected in America; in Europe, the biggest example so far is the United Alkali Trust, which has brought all British alkali production into the hands of a single business firm. The former owners of the more than thirty individual plants have received shares for the appraised value of their entire establishments, totalling about £5 million, which represent the fixed capital of the trust. The technical management remains in the same hands as before, but business control is concentrated in the hands of the general management. The floating capital, totalling about £1 million, was offered to the public for subscription. The total capital is, therefore, £6 million. Thus, in this branch, which forms the basis of the whole chemical industry, competition has been replaced by monopoly in England, and the road has been paved, most gratifyingly, for future expropriation by the whole of society, the nation.—*F.E.*]

This is the abolition of the capitalist mode of production within the capitalist mode of production itself, and hence a self-dissolving contradiction, which *prima facie* represents a mere phase of transition to a new form of production. It manifests itself as such a contradiction in its effects. It establishes a monopoly in certain spheres and thereby requires state interference. It reproduces a new financial aristocracy, a new variety of parasites in the shape of promoters, speculators and simply nominal directors; a whole system of swindling and cheating by means of corporation promotion, stock issuance, and stock speculation. It is private production without the control of private property.

IV. Aside from the stock-company business, which represents the abolition of capitalist private industry on the basis of the capitalist system itself and destroys private industry as it expands and invades new spheres of production, credit offers to the individual capitalist; or to one who is regarded a capitalist, absolute control within certain limits over the capital and property of others, and thereby over the labour of others.[3] The control over social capital, not the individual capital of his own, gives him control of social labour. The capital itself, which a man really owns or is supposed to own in the opinion of the public, becomes purely a basis for the superstructure of credit. This is particularly true of wholesale commerce, through which the greatest portion of the social product passes. All standards of measurement, all excuses more or less still justified under capitalist production, disappear here. What the speculating wholesale merchant risks is social property, not *his own.* Equally sordid becomes the phrase relating the origin of capital to savings, for what he demands is that *others* should save for him. [Just as all, France recently saved up one and a half billion francs for the Panama Canal swindlers. In fact, a description of the entire Panama swindle is here correctly anticipated, fully twenty years before it occurred.—*F.E.*] The other phrase concerning abstention is squarely refuted by his luxury, which is now itself a means of credit. Conceptions which have some meaning on a less developed stage of capitalist production, become quite meaningless here. Success and failure both lead here to a centralisation of capital, and thus to expropriation on the most enormous scale. Expropriation extends here from the direct producers to the smaller and the medium-sized capitalists themselves. It is the point of departure for the capitalist mode of production; its accomplishment is the goal of this production. In the last instance, it aims at the expropriation of the means of production from all individuals. With the development of social production, the means of production cease to be means of private production and products of private production, and can thereafter be only means of production in the hands of associated producers, *i.e.*, the latter's social property, much as they are their social products. However, this expropriation appears within the capitalist system in a contradictory form, as appropriation of social property by a few; and credit lends the latter more and more the aspect of pure adventurers. Since property here exists in the form of stock, its movement and transfer become purely a result of gambling on the stock exchange, where the little fish are swallowed by the sharks and the lambs by the stock-exchange wolves. There is antagonism against the old form in the stock companies, in which social means of production appear as private property; but the conversion to the form of stock still remains ensnared in the trammels of capitalism; hence, instead of overcoming the antithesis between the character of wealth as social and as private wealth, the stock companies merely develop it in a new form.

The co-operative factories of the labourers themselves represent within the old form the first sprouts of the new, although they naturally reproduce, and must reproduce, everywhere in their actual organisation all the shortcomings of the prevailing system. But the antithesis between capital and labour is overcome within them, if at first only by way of making the associated labourers into their own capitalist, *i.e.*, by enabling them to use the means of production for the employment of their own labour. They show how a new mode of production naturally grows out of an old one, when the development of the material forces of production and of the corresponding forms of social production have reached a particular stage. Without the factory system arising out of the capitalist mode of production, there could have been no co-operative factories. Nor could these have developed without the credit system arising out of the same mode of production. The credit system is not only the principal basis for the gradual transformation of capitalist private enterprises into capitalist stock companies, but equally offers the means for the gradual extension of co-operative enterprises on a more or less national scale. The capitalist stock companies, as much as the co-operative factories, should be considered as transitional forms from the capitalist mode of production to the associated one, with the only distinction that the antagonism is resolved negatively in the one and positively in the other.

So far we have considered the development of the credit system—and the implicit latent abolition of capitalist property—mainly with reference to industrial capital. In the following chapters we shall consider credit with reference to interest-bearing capital as such, and to its effect on this capital, and the form it thereby assumes; and there are generally a few more specifically economic remarks still to be made.

But first this:

The credit system appears as the main lever of over-production and over-speculation

> in commerce solely because the reproduction process, which is elastic by nature, is here forced to its extreme limits, and is so forced because a large part of the social capital is employed by people who do not own it and who consequently tackle things quite differently than the owner, who anxiously weighs the limitations of his private capital in so far as he handles it himself. This simply demonstrates the fact that the self-expansion of capital based on the contradictory nature of capitalist production permits an actual free development only up to a certain point, so that in fact it constitutes an immanent fetter and barrier to production, which are continually broken through by the credit system.[4] Hence, the credit system accelerates the material development of the productive forces and the establishment of the world-market. It is the historical mission of the capitalist system of production to raise these material foundations of the new mode of production to a certain degree of perfection. At the same time credit accelerates the violent eruptions of this contradiction—crises—and thereby the elements of disintegration of the old mode of production.

The two characteristics immanent in the credit system are, on the one hand, to develop the incentive of capitalist production, enrichment through exploitation of the labour of others, to the purest and most colossal form of gambling and swindling, and to reduce more and more the number of the few who exploit the social wealth; on the other hand, to constitute the form of transition to a new mode of production. It is this ambiguous nature, which endows the principal spokesmen of credit from Law to Isaac Péreire with the pleasant character mixture of swindler and prophet.

Notes

1. 'The average of notes in circulation during the year was, in 1812, 106,538,000 francs; in 1818, 101,205,000 francs; whereas the movement of the currency, or the annual aggregate of disbursements and upon all accounts, was, in 1812, 2,837,712,000 francs; in 1818, 9,665,030,000 francs. The activity of the currency in France, therefore, during the year 1818, as compared with its activity in 1812, was in the proportion of three to one. The great regulator of the velocity of circulation is credit.... This explains, why a severe pressure upon the money-market is generally coincident with a full circulation.' (*The Currency Theory Reviewed, etc.*, p. 65)—'Between September 1833 and September 1843 nearly 300 banks were added to the various issuers of notes throughout the United Kingdom; the result was a reduction in the circulation to the extent of two million and a half; it was £36,035,244 at the close of September 1833, and £33,518,554 at the close of September 1843.' (L. c., p. 53)—'The prodigious activity of Scottish circulation enables it, with £100, to effect the same quantity of monetary transactions, which in England it requires £420 to accomplish.' (L. c., p. 55. This last refers only to the technical side of the operation.)
2. Before the establishment of the banks ... the amount of capital withdrawn for the purposes of currency was greater, at all times, than the actual circulation of commodities required.' (*Economist,* 1845, p. 238.)
3. See, for instance, in the *Times* the list of business bankruptcies in a crisis year such as 1857 and compare the private property of those bankrupt with the amount of their debts. 'The truth is that the power of purchase by persons having capital and credit is much beyond anything that those who are unacquainted practically with speculative markets have any idea of.' (Tooke, *Inquiry into the Currency Principle,* p. 79.) 'A person having the reputation of capital enough for his regular business, and enjoying good credit in his trade, if he takes a sanguine view of the prospect of a rise of price of the article in which he deals, and is favoured by circumstances in the outset and progress of his speculation, may effect purchases to an extent perfectly enormous compared with his capital' (*Ibid.*, p. 136). 'Merchants, manufacturers, etc., carry on operations much beyond those which the use of their own

capital alone would enable them to do.... Capital is rather the foundation upon which a good credit is built than the limit of the transactions of any commercial establishment.' (*Economist*, 1847, p. 333.)

4. Th. Chalmers [*On Political Economy, etc.*, Glasgow, 1832.—Ed.].

28

Medium of Circulation and Capital; Views of Tooke and Fullarton

The distinction between currency and capital, as Tooke, Wilson, and others draw it, whereby the differences between medium of circulation as money, as money-capital generally, and as interest-bearing capital (moneyed capital in the English sense) are thrown together pell-mell, comes down to two things.[1]

Currency circulates on the one hand as *coin* (money), so far as it promotes the *expenditure of revenue*, hence the traffic between the individual consumers and the retail merchants, to which category belong all merchants who sell to the consumers—to the individual consumers as distinct from productive consumers or producers. Here money circulates in the function of coin, although it continually *replaces capital.* A certain portion of money in a particular country is continually devoted to this function, although this portion consists of perpetually changing individual coins. In so far as money promotes the *transfer of capital*, however, either as a means of purchase (medium of circulation) or as a means of payment, it is *capital.* It is, therefore, neither its function as a means of purchase, nor that as a means of payment, which distinguishes it from coin, for it may also act as a means of purchase between one dealer and another so far as they buy from one another in hard cash, and also as a means of payment between dealer and consumer so far as credit is given and the revenue consumed before it is paid. The difference is, therefore, that in the second case, this money not only replaces the capital for one side, the seller, but is expended, advanced, by the other side, the buyer, as capital. The difference, then, is, in fact, that between *the money-form of revenue* and *the money-form of capital*, but not that between currency and capital, for a certain quantity of money *circulates* in the transactions between dealers as well as in the transactions between consumers and dealers. It is, therefore, equally *currency* in *both* functions. Tooke's conception introduces confusion into this question in various ways:

1. By confusing the functional distinctions;
2. By introducing the question of the quantity of money circulating together in both functions;
3. By introducing the question of the relative proportions of the quantities of currency circulating in the two functions and thus in the two spheres of the process of reproduction.

Ad 1) Confusing the functional distinctions that money in one form is currency, and capital in the other. In so far as money serves in one or another function, be it to realise revenue or transfer capital, it functions in buying and selling, or in paying, as a means of purchase or a means of payment, and, in the wider sense of the word, as currency. The further purpose which it has in the calculations of its spender or recipient, of being capital or revenue for him, alters absolutely nothing, and this is doubly demonstrated. Although the kinds of money circulating in the two spheres are different, the same piece of money, for instance, a five-pound note, passes from one sphere into the other and alternately performs both functions; which is inevitable, if only because the retail merchant can give his capital the form of money only in the shape of the coin which he receives from his customers. It may be assumed that the actual small change has its circulation centre of gravity in the domain of retail trade; the retail dealer needs it continually to make change and receives it back continually in payment from his customers. But he also receives money, *i.e.*, coin, in that metal which serves as a standard of value, hence in England one-pound coins, or even banknotes, particularly notes of small denominations, such as five- and ten-pound notes. These gold coins and notes, with whatever small change he has to spare, are deposited by the retail dealer every day, or every week, in his bank, and he pays for his purchases by drawing cheques on his bank deposit. But the same gold coins and hank-notes are just as steadily withdrawn from the bank, directly or indirectly (for instance, small change by manufacturers for the payment of wages), as the money-form of its revenue by the entire public in its capacity of consumer, and flow continually back to the retail dealers, for whom they thus again realise a portion of their capital, but at the same time also a portion of their revenue. This last circumstance is important, and is wholly overlooked by Tooke. Only where money is expended as money-capital, early in the reproduction process (Book II, Part 1), does capital-value exist purely as such. For the produced commodities contain not merely capital, but also surplus-value; they are not only capital in themselves, but already capital realised as capital, capital with the source of revenue incorporated in it. What the retail dealer gives away for the money returning to him, his commodities, therefore, is for him capital plus profit, capital plus revenue.

Furthermore, in returning to the retailer, circulating money restores the money-form of his capital.

To reduce the difference between circulation as circulation of revenue and circulation of capital into a difference between currency and capital is, therefore, altogether wrong. This mode of expression is in Tooke's case due to his simply assuming the standpoint of a banker issuing his own banknotes. Those of his notes which are continually in the public's hands (even if consisting of ever different notes) and serving as currency, cost him nothing, save the cost of the paper and the printing. They are circulating certificates of indebtedness (bills of exchange) made out in his own name, but they bring him money and thus serve as a means of expanding his capital. They differ from his capital, however, whether it be his own or borrowed. That is why there is a special distinction for him between currency and capital, which, however, has nothing to do with the definition of these terms as such, least of all with that made by Tooke.

The distinct attribute—whether it serves as the money-form of revenue or of capital—changes nothing in the character of money as a medium of circulation; it retains this character no matter which of the two functions it performs. True, money serves more as an actual medium of circulation (coin, means of purchase) when acting as the money-form of revenue, due to the dispersion of purchases and sales, and because the majority of disbursers of revenue, the labourers, can buy relatively little on credit; whereas in the traffic of the business world, where the medium of circulation is the money-form of capital, money serves mainly as a means of payment, partly on account of the concentration, and partly on account of the prevailing credit system. But the distinction between money as a means of payment and money as a means of purchase (means of circulation) is a distinction that refers to the money itself. It is not a distinction between money and capital. More copper and silver circulate in the retail business, and more gold in the wholesale business. Yet the distinction between silver and copper on the one hand, and gold on the other, is not the distinction between circulation and capital.

Ad 2) Introducing the question of the quantity of money circulating together in both functions: So far as money circulates, be it as a means of purchase or as a means of payment—

no matter in which of the two spheres and independently of its function of realising revenue or capital—the quantity of its circulating mass comes under the laws developed previously in discussing the simple circulation of commodities (Vol. I, Ch. III, 2, b). The velocity of circulation, hence the number of repetitions of the same function as means of purchase and means of payment by the same pieces of money in a given term, the mass of simultaneous purchases and sales, or payments, the sum of the prices of the circulating commodities, and finally the balances of payments to be settled in the same period, determine in either case the mass of circulating money, of currency. Whether money so employed represents capital or revenue for the payer or receiver, is immaterial, and in no way alters the matter. Its mass is simply determined by its function as a medium of purchase and payment.

Ad 3) On the question of the relative proportions of the amounts of currency circulating in both functions and thus in both spheres of the reproduction process. Both spheres of circulation are connected internally, for, on the one hand, the mass of revenues to be spent expresses the volume of consumption, and, on the other, the magnitude of the masses of capital circulating in production and commerce expresses the volume and velocity of the reproduction process. Nevertheless, the same circumstances have a different effect, working even in opposite directions, upon the quantities of money circulating in both functions or spheres, or on the amount of currency, as the English put it in banking parlance. And this gives new cause for Tooke's vulgar distinction between capital and currency. The fact that the gentlemen of the Currency Theory confuse two different things is no reason to present them as two different concepts.

In times of prosperity, intense expansion, acceleration and vigour of the reproduction process, labourers are fully employed. Generally, there is also a rise in wages, which makes up in some measure for their fall below average during other periods of the business cycle. At the same time, the revenues of the capitalists grow considerably. Consumption increases generally. Commodity-prices also rise regularly, at least in the various vital branches of business. Consequently, the quantity of circulating money grows at least within definite limits, since the greater velocity of circulation, in turn, sets up certain barriers to the growth of the amount of currency. Since that portion of the social revenue which consists of wages is originally advanced by the industrial capitalist in the form of variable capital, and always in money-form, it requires more money for its circulation in times of prosperity. But we must not count this twice—first as money required for the circulation of variable capital, and then as money required for the circulation of the labourers' revenue. The money paid to the labourers as wages is spent in retail trade and returns about once a week to the banks as the retailers' deposits, after negotiating miscellaneous intermediary transactions in smaller cycles. In times of prosperity, the reflux of money proceeds smoothly for the industrial capitalists, and thus the need for money accommodation does not increase because more wages have to be paid, and more money is required for the circulation of their variable capital.

The total result is that the mass of circulating media serving the expenditure of revenue grows decidedly in periods of prosperity.

As concerns the circulation required for the transfer of capital, hence required exclusively between capitalists, a period of brisk business is simultaneously a period of the most elastic and easy credit. The velocity of circulation between capitalist and capitalist is regulated directly by credit, and the mass of circulating medium required to settle payments, and even in cash purchases, decreases accordingly. It may increase in absolute terms, but decreases relatively under all circumstances compared to the expansion of the reproduction process. On the one hand, greater mass payments are settled without the mediation of money; on the other, owing to the vigour of the process, there is a quicker movement of the same amounts of money, both as means of purchase and of payment. The same quantity of money promotes the reflux of a greater number of individual capitals.

On the whole, the currency of money in such periods appears full, although its

Department II (transfer of capital) is, at least relatively, contracted, while its Department I (expenditure of revenue) expands in absolute terms.

The refluxes express the reconversion of commodity-capital into money, M—C—M', as we have seen in the discussion of the reproduction process, Book II, Part I. Credit renders the reflux in money-form independent of the time of actual reflux both for the industrial capitalist and the merchant. Both of them sell on credit; their commodities are thus alienated before they are reconverted into money for them, hence before they flow back to them in money-form. On the other hand, they buy on credit, and in this way, the value of their commodities is reconverted, be it into productive capital or commodity-capital, even before this value has really been transformed into money, *i.e.*, before the commodity-price is due and paid for. In such times of prosperity, the reflux passes off smoothly and easily. The retailer securely pays the wholesaler, the wholesaler pays the manufacturer, the manufacturer pays the importer of raw materials, etc. The appearance of rapid and reliable refluxes always keeps up for a longer period after they are over. In reality, by virtue of the credit that is under way, since credit refluxes take the place of the real ones. The banks scent danger as soon as their clients deposit more bills of exchange than money. See the testimony of the Liverpool bank director, p. 398. [Present edition: Ch. XXV.—*Ed.*]

To insert what I have noted earlier: 'In periods of predominant credit, the velocity of the circulation of money increases faster than commodity-prices, whereas in times of declining credit commodity-prices drop slower than the velocity of circulation.' (*Zur Kritik der politischen Oekonomie,* 1859, S. 83, 84.)

The reverse is true in a period of crisis. Circulation No. I contracts, prices fall, similarly wages; the number of employed labourers is reduced, the mass of transactions decreases. On the contrary, the need for money accommodation increases in circulation No. II with the contraction of credit. We shall examine this point in greater detail immediately.

There is no doubt that with the decrease of credit which goes hand in hand with stagnation in the reproduction process, the circulation mass required for No. I, the expenditure of revenue, contracts, while that required for No. II, the transfer of capital, expands. But to what extent this statement coincides with what is maintained by Fullarton and others still remains to he analysed:

> A demand for capital on loan and a demand for additional circulation are quite distinct things, and not often found associated. (Fullarton, 1. c., p. 82, title of Chapter 5.)[2]

In the first place, it is evident that in the first of the two cases mentioned above, during times of prosperity, when the mass of the circulating medium must increase, the demand for it increases. But it is likewise evident that, when a manufacturer draws more or less of his deposit out of a bank in gold or banknotes because he has to expend more capital in the form of money, his demand for capital does not thereby increase. What increases is merely his demand for this particular form in which he expends his capital. The demand refers only to the technical form, in which he throws his capital into circulation. Just as in the case of a different development of the credit system, the same variable capital, for example, or the same quantity of wages, requires a greater mass of means of circulation in one country than in another; in England more than in Scotland, for instance, and in Germany more than in England. Likewise in agriculture, the same capital active in the reproduction process requires different quantities of money in different seasons for the performance of its function.

But the contrast drawn by Fullarton is not correct. It is by no means the strong demand for loans as he says, which distinguishes the period of depression from that of prosperity, but the ease with which this demand is satisfied in periods of prosperity, and the difficulties which it meets in periods of depression. It is precisely the enormous development of the credit system during a prosperity period, hence also the enormous increase in the demand for loan capital and the readiness with which the supply meets it in such periods, which brings about a shortage of credit during a period of depression. It is not, therefore, the difference in volume of demand for loans which characterises both periods.

As we have previously remarked, both periods are primarily distinguished by the fact that the demand for currency between consumers and dealers predominates in periods of prosperity, and the demand for currency between capitalists predominates in periods of depression. During a depression the former decreases, and the latter increases.

What strikes Fullarton and others as decisively important is the phenomenon that in such periods when securities in possession of the Bank of England are on the increase, its circulation of notes decreases, and vice versa. The level of the securities, however, expresses the volume of the pecuniary accommodation, the volume of discounted bills of exchange and of advances made against marketable collateral. Thus Fullarton says in the above passage that the securities in the hands of the Bank of England fluctuate mostly in an opposite direction to its circulation, and this corroborates the view long held by private banks that no bank can increase its issue of banknotes beyond a certain point determined by the needs of its public; but if a bank wants to make advances beyond this limit, it must make them out of its capital; hence it must either realise on securities or utilise deposits which it would otherwise have invested in securities.

This, however, reveals also what Fullarton means by capital. What does capital signify here? That the Bank can no longer make advances with its own banknotes, or promissory notes, which, of course, cost it nothing. But what does it make advances with in that case? With the sums realised from the sale of securities held in reserve, *i.e.*, government bonds, stocks, and other interest-bearing paper. And what does it get in payment for the sale of such paper? Money-gold or banknotes, so far as the latter are legal tender, such as those of the Bank of England. What the bank advances, therefore, is under all circumstances money. This money, however, now constitutes a part of its capital. If it advances gold, this is understandable. If it advances notes, then these notes represent capital, because it has given up some actual value for them, such as interest-bearing paper. In the case of private banks the notes secured by them through the sale of securities cannot be anything else, in the main, but Bank of England notes or their own notes, since others would hardly be taken in payment for securities. If it is the Bank of England itself, then its own notes, which it receives in return, cost it capital, that is, interest-bearing paper. Besides, it thereby withdraws its own notes from circulation. Should it reissue these notes, or issue new notes in their stead to the same amount, they now represent capital. And they do so equally well, when used for advances to capitalists, or when used later, when the demand for such pecuniary accommodation decreases, for reinvestment in securities. In all these cases the term capital is employed only from the banker's point of view, and means that the banker is compelled to loan more than his mere credit.

As is known, the Bank of England makes all its advances in its own notes. Now, if despite this, as a rule, the bank-note circulation of the Bank decreases in proportion as the discounted bills of exchange and collateral in its hands, and thus its advances increase—what becomes of the notes thrown into circulation? How do they return to the Bank?

To begin with, if the demand for money accommodation arises from an unfavourable national balance of payments and thereby implies a drain of gold, the matter is very simple. The bills of exchange are discounted in banknotes. The banknotes are exchanged for gold by the Bank itself, in its issue department, and this gold is exported. It is as though the Bank paid out gold directly, without the mediation of notes, on discounting bills. Such an increased demand, which may in certain cases be £7 to £10 million, naturally does not add a single five-pound note to the country's domestic circulation. If it is now said that the Bank advances capital, and not currency, this means two things. First, that it does not advance credit, but actual values, a part of its own capital or of capital deposited with it. Secondly, that it does not advance money for inland, but for international circulation, that it advances world-money; and for this purpose money must always exist in its form of a hoard, in its metallic state; in the form in which it is not merely a form of value, but value itself, whose money-form it is. Although this gold now represents capital, both for the Bank and the exporting gold-dealer, *i.e.*, banking or commercial capital, the demand for it is not for capital, but for the absolute form of money-capital. This demand arises precisely at the moment when foreign markets are overcrowded with unsaleable English commodity-capital. What is wanted, therefore, is capital, not as *capital,* but capital as *money,* in the form in which money serves as a universal world-market commodity; and this is its original form of precious metal. The drain of gold is not, therefore, as Fullarton, Tooke, etc., claim, 'a mere question of capital.' Rather, it is a 'question of money,' even if in a specific function. The fact that it is not a question of *inland* circulation as the advocates of the Currency Theory maintain, does not prove at all, as Fullarton and others think, that it is merely a question of capital. It is a question of money in the form in which money is an international means of payment.

> Whether that capital (the purchase price for the million of quarters of foreign wheat after a crop failure in the home country) is transmitted in merchandise or in specie, is a point which in no way affects the nature of the transaction. (Fullarton, 1. c., p. 131.)

But it significantly affects the question, whether there is a drain of gold, or not. Capital is transferred in the form of precious metal, because it either cannot be transferred at all, or only at a great loss in the shape of commodities. The fear which the modern banking system has of gold drain exceeds anything ever imagined by the monetary system, which considers precious metals as the only true wealth. Take, for instance, the following evidence of the Governor of the Bank of England, Morris, before the Parliamentary Committee on the crisis of 1847-48:

> (3846. Question:) 'When I spoke of the depreciation of stocks and fixed capital, are you not aware that all property invested in stocks and produce of every description was depreciated in the same way; that raw cotton, raw silk, and unmanufactured wool were sent to the continent at the same depreciated price, and that sugar, coffee and tea were sacrificed as at forced sales?—It was inevitable that the country should make *a considerable sacrifice* for the purpose of meeting the *efflux of bullion* which had taken place in consequence of the large importation of food.'—'3848. Do not you think it would have been better to trench upon the £8 million lying in the coffers of the Bank, than to have endeavoured to get the gold back again at such a sacrifice?—*No, I do not.*' —

It is gold which here stands for the only true wealth.

Fullarton quotes the discovery by Tooke that

> with only one or two exceptions, and those admitting of satisfactory explanation, every remarkable fall of exchange, followed by a drain of gold, that has occurred during the last half-century, has been coincident throughout with a comparatively low state of the circulating medium, and vice versa. (Fullarton, p. 121.)

This discovery proves that such drains of gold occur generally after a period of animation and speculation, as

> the signal of a collapse already commenced an indication of overstocked markets, of a cessation of the foreign demand for our productions, of delayed returns, and, as the necessary sequel of all these, of commercial discredit, manufactories shut up, artisans starving, and a general stagnation of industry and enterprise. (p. 129)

This, naturally, is at once the best refutation of the claim of the advocates of the Currency Theory, that a full circulation drives out bullion and a low circulation attracts it.

On the contrary, while the Bank of England generally carries a strong gold reserve during a period of prosperity, this hoard is generally formed during the slack period, which follows after a storm.

All this sagacity concerning the drain of gold, then, amounts to saying that the demand for *international* media of circulation and payment differs from the demand for *internal* media of circulation and payment (and it goes without saying, therefore, that 'the existence of a drain does not necessarily imply any diminution of the internal demand for circulation,' as Fullarton has it on page 112 of his work) and that the export of precious metal and its being thrown into international circulation is not the same as throwing notes or specie into internal circulation. As for the rest, I have shown on a previous occasion [English edition: Vol. 1.—*Ed.*] that the movements of a hoard concentrated as a reserve fund for international payments have as such nothing to do with the movements of money as a medium of circulation. At any rate, the question is complicated by the fact that the different functions of a hoard, which I have developed from the nature of money—such as its function as a reserve fund of means of payment to cover due bills in domestic business; the function of a reserve fund of currency; and finally, the function of a reserve fund of world-money—are here attributed to one sole reserve fund. It also follows from this that under certain circumstances, a drain of gold from the Bank to the home market may combine with a drain abroad. The question is further complicated, however, by the fact that this hoard is arbitrarily burdened with the additional function of serving as a fund guaranteeing the convertibility of banknotes in countries, in which the credit system and credit-money are developed. And in addition to all this comes 1) the concentration of the national reserve fund in one single central bank, and 2) its reduction to the smallest possible minimum. Hence, also, Fullarton's complaint (p.143):

> One cannot contemplate the perfect silence and facility with which variations of the exchange usually pass off in continental countries, compared with the state of feverish disquiet and alarm always produced in England whenever the treasure at the Bank seems to be at all approaching to exhaustion, without being struck with the great advantage in this respect which a metallic currency possesses.

However, if we now leave aside the drain of gold, how can a bank that issues notes, like the Bank of England, increase the amount of money accommodation granted by it without increasing its issue of banknotes?

So far as the bank itself is concerned, all the notes outside its walls, whether circulating or in private hoards, are in circulation, *i.e.*, are out of its hands. Hence, if the bank extends its discounting and money-lending business, its advances on securities, all the banknotes issued by it for that purpose must return, for otherwise, they would increase the volume of circulation, something which is not supposed to happen. This return may take place in two ways.

First: The bank pays A notes against securities; A uses them to pay for bills of exchange due to B, and B deposits notes once more in the bank. This brings to a close the circulation of these notes, but the loan remains.

> The loan remains, and the currency, if not wanted, finds its way back to the issuer. (Fullarton, p. 97.)

The notes, which the bank advanced to A, have now returned to it; but it is the creditor of A, or whoever may have been the drawer of the bill discounted by A, and the debtor of B for the amount of value expressed in these notes, and B thus disposes of a corresponding portion of the capital of the bank.

Secondly: A pays to B, and B himself, or C, to whom he pays the notes, uses these notes to pay bills due to the bank, directly or indirectly. In that case the bank is paid in its own notes. This concludes the transaction (pending A's return payment to the bank).

To what extent, now, shall the bank's advance to A be regarded as an advance of capital, or as a mere advance of means of payment?[3]

[This depends on the nature of the loan itself. Three cases must be distinguished.

First case.—A receives from the bank amounts loaned on his own personal credit, without giving any security for them. In this case, he does not merely receive means of payment, but also unquestionably a new capital, which he may employ in his business and realise as an additional capital until the maturity date.

Second case.—A has given to the bank securities, national bonds, or stocks as collateral, and received for them, say, up to two-thirds of their momentary value as a cash loan. In this case, he has received the means of payment he needed, but no additional capital, for he entrusted to the bank a larger capital-value than he received from it. But this larger capital-value was, on the one hand, unavailable for his momentary needs (means of payment), because invested in a particular interest-bearing form; on the other hand, A had his own reasons for not wanting to convert this capital-value directly into means of payment by selling it. His securities served, among other things, as a reserve capital, and he set them in motion as such. The transaction between A and the bank, therefore, consists in a temporary mutual transfer of capital, so that A does not receive any additional capital (quite the contrary!) although he receives the desired means of payment. For the bank, on the other hand, this transaction constitutes a temporary lodgement of money-capital in the form of a loan, a conversion of money-capital from one form into another, and this conversion is precisely the essential function of the banking business.

Third case.—A had the bank discount a bill of exchange and received its value in cash after the deduction of discount. In this case, he sold a non-convertible money-capital to the bank for the amount of value in convertible form. He sold his still running bill for cash money. The bill is now the property of the bank. It does not alter the matter that A, as last endorser of the bill, is responsible for it to the bank in default of payment. He shares this responsibility with the other endorsers and with the drawer of the bill, all of whom are duly responsible to him. In this case, therefore, we do not have a loan, but only an ordinary purchase and sale. For this reason, A has nothing to pay back to the bank. It reimburses itself by cashing the bill when it becomes due. Here, too, a transfer of capital has taken place between A and the bank, and in exactly the same manner as in the sale and purchase of any other commodity, and for this very reason, A did not receive any additional capital. What he needed and received were means of payment, and he received them by having the bank convert one form of his money-capital—his bill—into another—money.

It is, therefore, only in the first case that there is any question of a real advance of capital; in the second and third cases, the matter can be so regarded only in the sense that every investment of capital implies an 'advance of capital.' In this sense, the bank advances money-capital to A; but for A it is *money-capital* at best in the sense that it is a portion of his capital in general. And he requires it and uses it not specifically as capital, but rather as specifically a means of payment. Otherwise, every ordinary sale of commodities by which means of payment are secured might be considered as receiving an advance of capital.—*F. E.*]

In the case of private banks which issue their own notes, we have this difference, that if their notes remain neither in local circulation, nor return to them in the form of deposits, or in payment for due bills of exchange, they fall into the hands of persons who compel the private bank to cash these notes in gold or in notes of the Bank of England. In this event, therefore, its loan, in fact, represents an advance of notes of the Bank of England, or, what amounts to the same thing for the private bank, of gold, hence a portion of its bank capital. The same holds good in case the Bank of England itself, or some other bank, which has a fixed legal maximum for its issue of notes, must sell securities to withdraw its own notes from circulation and then issue them once more in the shape of advances; in that case, the bank's own notes represent a portion of its mobilised bank capital.

Even if the circulation were purely metallic, it would be possible 1) for a drain of gold [Marx evidently refers here to a drain of gold that would, at least partially, go abroad—*F. E.*] to empty the treasury, and 2) since gold would be chiefly wanted by the bank to make payments (in settlement of erstwhile transactions), the advance against collateral could grow considerably, but would flow back to it in the form of deposits or in payment of due bills of exchange; so that, on one side, the total treasure of the bank would decrease with an increase of the securities in its hands, while on the other, it would now be holding the same amount, which it possessed formerly as owner, as debtor of its depositors, and finally the total quantity of currency would decrease.

Our assumption so far has been that the loans are made in notes, so that they carry with them at least a fleeting, even if instantly disappearing, increase in the issue of notes. But this is not necessary. Instead of a paper note, the bank may open a credit account for A, in which case this A, the bank's debtor, becomes its imaginary depositor. He pays his creditors with cheques on the bank, and the recipient of these cheques passes them on to his own banker, who exchanges them for the cheques outstanding against him in the clearing house. In this case, no mediation of notes takes place at all, and the entire transaction is confined to the fact that the bank settles its own debt with a cheque drawn on itself, and its actual recompense consists in its claim on A. In this case, the bank has loaned a portion of its own bank capital, because its own debt claims, to A.

In so far as this demand for pecuniary accommodation is a demand for capital, it is so only for money-capital. It is capital only from the standpoint of the banker, namely gold (in the case of gold exports abroad) or notes of the National Bank, which a private bank can obtain only by purchase against an equivalent, and which, therefore, represent capital for it. Or, again, it is a case of interest-bearing papers, government bonds, stocks, etc., which must be sold in order to obtain gold or banknotes. Such papers, however, if in government bonds, are capital only for the buyer, for whom they represent the purchase price, the capital he invested in them. In themselves, they are not capital but merely debt claims. If mortgages, they are mere titles on future ground-rent. And if they are shares of stock, they are mere titles of ownership, which entitle the holder to a share in future surplus-value. All of these are not real capital. They do not form constituent parts of capital, nor are they values in themselves. By way of similar transactions, money belonging to the bank may be transformed into deposits, so that the bank becomes the debtor instead of owner of this money, and holds it under a different title of ownership. However important this may be to the bank, it alters nothing in the mass of reserve capital, or even of money-capital available in a particular country. Capital, therefore, represents here only money-capital, and, if not available in the actual form of money, it represents a mere title on capital. This is very important, since a scarcity of, and pressing demand for, *banking* capital is confounded with a decrease of *actual* capital, which conversely is in such cases rather abundant in the form of means of production and products, and swamps the markets.

It is, therefore, easy to explain how the mass of securities held by a bank as collateral increases, hence how the growing demand for pecuniary accommodation can be satisfied by the bank, while the total mass of currency remains the same or decreases. This total mass is held in check during such periods of money stringency in two ways: 1) by a drain of gold; 2) by a demand for money in its capacity as a mere means of payment, when the issued banknotes return immediately; or when the transactions take place without the mediation of notes by means of book credit; when, therefore, payments are made simply through a credit transaction, the settlement of these payments being the sole purpose of the operation. It is a peculiarity of money, when it serves merely to settle accounts (and in times of crises, loans are taken up to pay, rather than to buy; to wind up previous transactions, not to initiate new ones), that its circulation is no more than fleeting, even where balances are not settled by mere credit operations, without the mediation of money, so that, when there is a strong demand for pecuniary accommodation, an enormous quantity of such transactions can take place without expanding the circulation. But the mere fact that the circulation of the Bank of England remains stable or even decreases simultaneously with an extensive accommodation of money on its part, does not *prima facie* prove, as Fullarton, Tooke and others assume (owing to their erroneous notion that pecuniary accommodation is identical with receiving capital on loan as additional capital), that the circulation of money (of banknotes) in its function as a means of payment is not increased and extended. Since the circulation of notes as means of purchase decreases during a business depression, when such extensive accommodation is necessary, their circulation as means of payment may increase, and the aggregate amount of the circulation, the sum of notes functioning as means of purchase and payment, may remain stable or may even decrease. The circulation as a means of payment of banknotes immediately returning to the bank that issues them is simply not circulation in the eyes of those economists.

Should circulation as a means of payment increase at a higher rate than it decreases as a means of purchase, the aggregate circulation would increase, although the money serving as a means of purchase would decrease considerably in quantity. And this actually occurs in certain periods of crisis, namely, when credit collapses completely and when not only commodities and securities are unsaleable but bills of exchange are undiscountable and nothing counts any more but money payment, or, as the merchant puts it, cash. Since Fullarton *et al.* do not understand that the circulation of notes as means of payment is the characteristic feature of such periods of money shortage, they treat this phenomenon as accidental.

> With respect again to those examples of eager competition for the possession of banknotes, which characterise seasons of panic and which may sometimes, as at the close of 1825, lead to a sudden, though only temporary, enlargement of the issues, even while the efflux of bullion is still going on, these, I apprehend, are not to be regarded as among the natural or necessary concomitants of a low exchange; the demand in such cases is not for circulation (read circulation as a means of purchase), but for hoarding, a demand on the part of alarmed bankers and capitalists which arises generally in the last act of the crisis (hence, for a reserve of means of payment), after a long continuation of the drain, and is the precursor of its termination. (Fullarton, p. 130.)

In the discussion of money as a means of payment (Vol. I, Ch. III, 3, b) we have already explained, in what manner, when the chain of payments is suddenly interrupted, money turns from its ideal form into a material and, at the same time, absolute form of value vis-à-vis the commodities. This was illustrated by some examples (footnotes 100 and 101). This interruption itself is partly an effect, partly a cause of the instability of credit and of the circumstances accompanying it, such as overstocking of markets, depreciation of commodities, interruption of production, etc.

It is evident, however, that Fullarton transforms the distinction between money as a means of purchase and money as a means of payment into a false distinction between currency and capital. This is again due to the narrow-minded banker's conception of circulation.

It might yet be asked: which is it, capital or money in its specific function as a means of payment that is in short supply in such periods of stringency? And this is a well-known controversy.

In the first place, so far as the stringency is marked by a drain of gold, it is evidently international means of payment that are demanded. But money in its specific capacity of international means of payment is gold in its metallic actuality, as a valuable substance in itself, as a quantity of value. It is at the same time capital, not capital as commodity-capital, but as money-capital, capital not in the form of commodities but in the form of money (and, at that, of money in the eminent sense of the word, in which it exists as universal world-market commodity). It is not a contradiction here between a demand for money as a means of payment and a demand for capital. The contradiction is rather between capital in its money-form and capital in its commodity-form; and the form which is here demanded and in which alone it can function, is its money-form.

Aside from this demand for gold (or silver) it cannot be said that there is any dearth whatever of capital in such periods of crisis. Under extraordinary circumstances, such as rise in the price of corn, or a cotton famine, etc., this may be the case; but these phenomena are not necessary or regular accompaniments of such periods; and the existence of such a lack of capital cannot be assumed beforehand without further ado from the mere fact that there is a heavy demand for pecuniary accommodation. On the contrary. The markets are overstocked, swamped with commodity-capital. Hence, it is not, in any case, a lack of *commodity*-capital which causes the stringency. We shall return to this question later.

Notes

1. We here give the related passage from Tooke in the original, which was cited in German on p. 390 [present edition: Ch. XXV:] 'The business of bankers, setting aside the issue of promissory notes payable on demand, may be divided into two branches, corresponding with the distinction pointed out by Dr (Adam) Smith of the transactions between dealers and dealers, and between dealers and consumers. One branch of the bankers' business is to collect *capital* from those who have not immediate employment for it, and to distribute or transfer it to these who have. The other branch is to receive deposits of the *incomes* of their customers, and to pay out the amount, as it is wanted for expenditure by the latter in the objects of their consumption ... the former being a circulation of *capital,* the latter of *currency.* '(Tooke, *Inquiry into the Currency Principle,* London, p. 36.) The first is 'the concentration of capital on the one hand and the distribution of it on the other'; the latter is 'administering the circulation for local purposes of the district.' *(Ibid.,* p. 37.) A far more correct conception is outlined in the following passage by Kinnear: 'Money ... is employed to perform two operations essentially distinct.... As a medium of exchange between dealers and dealers, it is the instrument by which transfers of capital are effected; that is, the exchange of a certain amount of capital in money for an equal amount of capital in commodities. But money employed in the payment of wages and in purchase and sale between dealers and consumers is not capital, but income; that portion of the incomes of the community, which is devoted to daily expenditure. It circulates in constant daily use, and is that alone which can, with strict propriety, be termed currency. Advances of capital depend entirely on the will of the Bank and other possessors of capital, for borrowers are always to be found; but the amount of the currency depends on the wants of the community, among whom the money circulates, for the purposes of daily expenditure.' (J. G. Kinnear, *The Crisis and the Currency,* London, 1847 [pp. 3-4].)
2. 'It is a great error, indeed, to imagine that the demand for pecuniary accommodation' (that is, for the loan of capital) 'is identical with a demand for additional means of circulation, or even that the two are frequently associated. Each demand originates in circumstances peculiarly affecting itself, and very distinct from each other. It is when everything looks prosperous, when wages are high, prices on the rise, and factories busy, that an additional supply of *currency* is usually required to perform the additional functions inseparable

from the necessity of making larger and more numerous payments; whereas it is chiefly in a more advanced stage of the commercial cycle, when difficulties begin to present themselves, when markets are overstocked, and returns delayed, that interest rises, and a pressure comes upon the Bank for advances of *capital.* It is true that there is no medium through which the Bank is accustomed to advance capital except that of its promissory notes; and that to refuse the notes, therefore, is to refuse the accommodation. But the accommodation once granted, everything adjusts itself in conformity with the necessities of the market; the loan remains, and the currency, if not wanted, finds its way hack to the issuer. Accordingly, a very slight examination of the Parliamentary Returns may convince any one, that the securities in the hands of the Bank of England fluctuate more frequently in an opposite direction to its circulation than in concert with it, and that the example, therefore, of that great establishment furnishes no exception to the doctrine so strongly pressed by the country bankers, to the effect that no hank can enlarge its circulation, if that circulation he already adequate to the purposes to which a bank-note currency is commonly applied; but that every addition to its advances, after that limit is passed, must he made from its capital, and supplied by the sale of some of its securities in reserve, or by abstinence from further investment in such securities. The table compiled from the Parliamentary Returns for the interval between 1833 and 1840, to which I have referred in a preceding page, furnishes continued examples of this truth; but two of these are so remarkable that it will be quite unnecessary for me to go beyond them. On the 3rd of January, 1837, when the resources of the Bank were strained to the uttermost to sustain credit and meet the difficulties of the money-market, we find its advances on loan and discount carried to the enormous sum of £17,022,000, an amount scarcely known since the war, and almost equal to the entire aggregate issues which, in the meanwhile, remain unmoved at so low a point as £17,076,000! On the other hand, we have on the 4th of June, 1833, a circulation of £18,892,000, with a return of private securities in hand, nearly, if not the very lowest on record for the last half-century, amounting to no more than £972,000!' (Fullarton, 1. c., pp. 97, 98.) That a demand for pecuniary accommodation need not be identical by any means with a demand for gold (what Wilson, Tooke and others call capital) is seen from the following testimony of Mr Weguelin, Governor of the Bank of England: 'The discounting of bills to that extent' (one million daily for three successive days) 'would not reduce the reserve' (of banknotes), 'unless the public demanded a greater amount of active circulation. The notes issued on the discount of bills would be returned through the medium of the bankers and through deposits. Unless these transactions were for the purpose of exporting bullion, and unless there were an amount of internal panic which induced people to lock up their notes, and not to pay them into the hands of the bankers ... the reserve would not be affected by the magnitude of the transactions.'—'The Bank may discount a million and a half a day, and that is done constantly, without its reserve being in the slightest degree affected, the notes coming back again as deposits, and no other alteration taking place than the mere transfer from one account to another.' (Report on Bank Acts, 1857, Evidence Nos. 241, 500.) The notes therefore serve here merely as means of transferring credits.

3. The passage that follows in the original is unintelligible in this context and has been rewritten by the editor to the end of the brackets. In another context this point has already been touched upon in Chapter XXVI.—*F. E*

29

Component Parts of Bank Capital

It is now necessary to examine the component parts of bank capital in greater detail.

We have just seen that Fullarton and others transform the distinction between money as a medium of circulation and money as a means of payment—also universal money in so far as it concerns a drain of gold—into a distinction between currency and capital.

The peculiar role played by capital in this instance is the reason why bankers' economics teaches that money is indeed capital *par excellence* as insistently as enlightened economics taught that money is not capital.

In subsequent analyses, we shall demonstrate that money-capital is being confused here with moneyed capital in the sense of interest-bearing capital, while in the former sense, money-capital is always merely a transient form of capital—in contradistinction to the other forms of capital, namely, commodity-capital and productive capital.

Bank capital consists of 1) cash money, gold or notes; 2) securities. The latter can be subdivided into two parts: commercial paper or bills of exchange, which run for a period, become due from time to time, and whose discounting constitutes the essential business of the banker; and public securities, such as government bonds, treasury notes, stocks of all kinds, in short, interest-bearing paper which is however significantly different from bills of exchange. Mortgages may also be included here. The capital composed of these tangible component parts can again be divided into the banker's invested capital and into deposits, which constitute his banking capital, or borrowed capital. In the case of banks which issue notes, these must be included. We shall leave the deposits and notes out of consideration for the present. It is evident at any rate that the actual component parts of the banker's capital (money, bills of exchange, deposit currency) remain unaffected whether the various elements represent the banker's own capital or deposits, *i.e.*, the capital of other people. The same division would remain, whether he were to carry on his business with only his own capital or only with deposited capital.

The form of interest-bearing capital is responsible for the fact that every definite and regular money revenue appears as interest on some capital, whether it arises from some capital or not. The money income is first converted into interest, and from the interest, one can determine the capital from which it arises. In like manner, in the case of interest-bearing capital, every sum of value appears as capital as long as it is not expended as revenue; that is, it appears as principal in contrast to possible or actual interest which it may yield.

The matter is simple. Let the average rate of interest be 5% annually. A sum of £500 would then yield £25 annually if converted into interest-bearing capital. Every fixed annual income of £25 may then be considered as interest on a capital of £500. This, however, is and remains a purely illusory conception, except in the case where the source of the £25, whether it be a mere title of ownership or claim, or an actual element of production such as real estate, is directly transferable or assumes a form in which it becomes transferable. Let us take the national debt and wages as illustrations.

The state has to annually pay its creditors a certain amount of interest for the capital borrowed from them. In this case, the creditor cannot recall his investment from his debtor, but can only sell his claim, or his title of ownership. The capital itself has been consumed, *i.e.*, expended by the state. It no longer exists. What the creditor of the state possesses is 1) the state's promissory note, amounting to, say, £100; 2) this promissory note gives the creditor a claim upon the annual revenue of the state, that is, the annual tax proceeds, for a certain amount, *e.g.*, £5 or 5%; 3) the creditor can sell this promissory note of £100 at his discretion to some other person. If the rate of interest is 5%, and the security given by the state is good, the owner A can sell this promissory note, as a rule, to B for £100; for it is the same to B whether he lends £100 at 5% annually, or whether he secures for himself by the payment of £100 an annual tribute from the state amounting to £5. But in all these cases, the capital, as whose offshoot (interest) state payments are considered, is illusory, fictitious capital. Not only that the amount loaned to the state no longer exists, but it was never intended that it be expended as capital, and only by investment as capital could it have been transformed into a self-preserving value. To the original creditor A, the share of annual taxes accruing to him represents interest on his capital, just as the share of the spendthrift's fortune accruing to the usurer appears to the latter, although in both cases, the loaned amount was not invested as capital. The possibility of selling the state's promissory note represents for A the potential means of regaining his principal. As for B, his capital is invested, from his individual point of view, as interest-bearing capital. So far as the transaction is concerned, B has simply taken the place of A by buying the latter's claim on the state's revenue. No matter how often this transaction is repeated, the capital of the state debt remains purely fictitious, and, as soon as the promissory notes become unsaleable, the illusion of this capital disappears. Nevertheless, this fictitious capital has its own laws of motion, as we shall presently see.

We shall now consider labour-power in contrast to the capital of the national debt, where a negative quantity appears as capital—just as interest-bearing capital, in general, is the fountainhead of all manner of insane forms, so that debts, for instance, can appear to the banker as commodities. Wages are conceived here as interest, and therefore labour-power as the capital yielding this interest. For example, if the wage for one year amounts to £50 and the rate of interest is 5%, the annual labour-power is equal to a capital of £1,000. The insanity of the capitalist mode of conception reaches its climax here, for instead of explaining the expansion of capital on the basis of the exploitation of labour-power, the matter is reversed, and the productivity of labour-power is explained by attributing this mystical quality of interest-bearing capital to labour-power itself. In the second half of the 17th century, this used to be a favourite conception (for example, of Petty), but it is used even nowadays in all seriousness by some vulgar economists and more particularly by some German statisticians.[1] Unfortunately, two disagreeably frustrating facts mar this thoughtless conception. In the first place, the labourer must work in order to obtain this interest. In the second place, he cannot transform the capital-value of his labour-power into cash by transferring it. Rather, the annual value of his labour-power is equal to his average annual wage, and what he has to give the buyer in return through his labour is this same value plus a surplus-value, *i.e.*, the increment added by his labour. In a slave society, the labourer has a capital-value, namely, his purchase price. And when he is hired out, the hirer must pay, in the first place, the interest on this purchase price, and, in addition, replace the annual wear and tear on the capital.

The formation of a fictitious capital is called capitalisation. Every periodic income is capitalised by calculating it on the basis of the average rate of interest, as an income which would be realised by a capital loaned at this rate of interest. For example, if the annual income is £100 and the rate of interest 5%, then the £100 would represent the annual interest on £2,000, and the £2,000 is regarded as the capital-value of the legal title of ownership on the £100 annually. For the person who buys this title of ownership, the annual income of £100 represents indeed the interest on his capital invested at 5%. All connection with the actual expansion process of capital is thus completely lost, and the conception of capital as something with automatic self-expansion properties is thereby strengthened.

Even when the promissory note—the security—does not represent a purely fictitious capital, as it does in the case of state debts, the capital-value of such paper is nevertheless wholly illusory. We have previously seen in what manner the credit system creates associated capital. The paper serves as title of ownership which represents this capital. The stocks of railways, mines, navigation companies, and the like, represent actual capital, namely, the capital invested and functioning in such enterprises, or the amount of money advanced by the stockholders for the purpose of being used as capital in such enterprises. This does not preclude the possibility that these may represent pure swindle. But this capital does not exist twice, once as the capital-value of titles of ownership (stocks) on the one hand and on the other hand as the actual capital invested, or to be invested, in those enterprises. It exists only in the latter form, and a share of stock is merely a title of ownership to a corresponding portion of the surplus-value to be realised by it. A may sell this title to B, and B may sell it to C. These transactions do not alter anything in the nature of the problem. A or B then has his title in the form of capital, but C has transformed his capital into a mere title of ownership to the anticipated surplus-value from the stock capital.

The independent movement of the value of these titles of ownership, not only of government bonds but also of stocks, adds weight to the illusion that they constitute real capital alongside of the capital or claim to which they may have title. For they become commodities, whose price has its own characteristic movements and is established in its own way. Their market-value is determined differently from their nominal value, without any change in the value (even though the expansion may change) of the actual capital. On the one hand, their market-value fluctuates with the amount and reliability of the proceeds to which they afford legal title. If the nominal value of a share of stock, that is, the invested sum originally represented by this share, is £100, and the enterprise pays 10% instead of 5%, then its market-value, everything else remaining equal, rises to £200, as long as the rate of interest is 5%, for when capitalised at 5%, it now represents a fictitious capital of £200. Whoever buys it for £200 receives a revenue of 5% on this investment of capital. The converse is true when the proceeds from the enterprise diminish. The market-value of this paper is in part speculative, since it is determined not only by the actual income, but also by the anticipated income, which is calculated in advance. But assuming the expansion of the actual capital as constant, or where no capital exists, as in the case of state debts, the annual income to be fixed by law and otherwise sufficiently secured, the price of these securities rises and falls inversely as the rate of interest. If the rate of interest rises from 5% to 10%, then securities guaranteeing an income of £5 will now represent a capital of only £50. Conversely, if the rate of interest falls to 2½%; the same securities will represent a capital of £200. Their value is always merely capitalised income, that is, the income calculated on the basis of a fictitious capital at the prevailing rate of interest. Therefore, when the money-market is tight, these securities will fall in price for two reasons: first, because the rate of interest rises, and secondly, because they are thrown on the market in large quantities in order to convert them into cash. This drop in price takes place regardless of whether the income that this paper guarantees its owner is constant, as is the case with government bonds, or whether the expansion of the actual capital, which it represents, as in industrial enterprises, is possibly affected by disturbances in the reproduction process. In the latter event, there is only still another depreciation added to that mentioned above. As soon as the storm is over, this paper again rises to its former level, in so far as it does not represent a business failure or swindle. Its depreciation in times of crisis serves as a potent means of centralising fortunes.[2]

To the extent that the depreciation or increase in value of this paper is independent of the movement of value of the actual capital that it represents, the wealth of the nation is just as great before as after its depreciation or increase in value.

> The public stocks and canal and railway shares had already by the 23rd of October, 1847, been depreciated in the aggregate to the amount of £114,752,225. (Morris, Governor of the Bank of England, testimony in the Report on Commercial Distress, 1847-48 [No. 3800].)

Unless this depreciation reflected an actual stoppage of production and of traffic on canals and railways, or a suspension of already initiated enterprises, or squandering capital in positively worthless ventures, the nation did not grow one cent poorer by the bursting of this soap bubble of nominal money-capital.

All this paper actually represents nothing more than accumulated claims, or legal titles, to future production whose money or capital value represents either no capital at all, as in the case of state debts, or is regulated independently of the value of real capital which it represents.

In all countries based on capitalist production, there exists in this form an enormous quantity of so-called interest-bearing capital, or moneyed capital. And by accumulation of money-capital, nothing more, in the main, is connoted than an accumulation of these claims on production, an accumulation of the market-price, the illusory capital-value of these claims.

A part of the banker's capital is now invested in this so-called interest-bearing paper. This is itself a portion of the reserve capital, which does not perform any function in the actual business of banking. The most important portion of this paper consists of bills of exchange, that is, promises to pay made by industrial capitalists or merchants. For the money-lender, these bills of exchange are interest-bearing, in other words, when he buys them, he deducts interest for the time which they still have to run. This is called discounting. It depends on the prevailing rate of interest, how much of a deduction is made from the sum represented by the bill of exchange.

Finally, the last part of the capital of a banker consists of his money reserve in gold and notes. The deposits, unless tied up by agreement for a certain time, are always at the disposal of the depositors. They are in a state of continual fluctuation. But while one depositor draws on his account, another deposits, so that the general average sum total of deposits fluctuates little during periods of normal business.

The reserve funds of the banks, in countries with developed capitalist production, always express on the average the quantity of money existing in the form of a hoard, and a portion of this hoard, in turn, consists of paper, mere drafts upon gold, which have no value in themselves. The greater portion of banker's capital is, therefore, purely fictitious and consists of claims (bills of exchange), government securities (which represent spent capital), and stocks (drafts on future revenue). And it should not be forgotten that the money-value of the capital represented by this paper in the safes of the banker is itself fictitious, in so far as the paper consists of drafts on guaranteed revenue (*e.g.*, government securities), or titles of ownership to real capital (*e.g.*, stocks), and that this value is regulated differently from that of the real capital, which the paper represents at least in part; or, when it represents mere claims on revenue and no capital, the claim on the same revenue is expressed in continually changing fictitious money-capital. In addition to this, it must be noted that this fictitious banker's capital represents largely, not his own capital, but that of the public, which makes deposits with him, either interest-bearing or not.

Deposits are always made in money, in gold or notes, or in drafts upon these. With the exception of the reserve fund, which contracts or expands in accordance with the requirements of actual circulation, these deposits are in fact always in the hands of the industrial capitalists and merchants, on the one hand, whose bills of exchange are thereby discounted and who thus receive advances; on the other hand, they are in the hands of dealers in securities (exchange brokers), or in the hands of private parties who have sold their securities, or in the hands of the government (in the case of treasury notes and new loans). The deposits themselves play a double role. On the one hand, as we have just mentioned, they are loaned out as interest-bearing capital and are, therefore, not in the safes of the banks, but figure merely on their books as credits of the depositors. On the other hand, they function merely as such book entries, in so far as the mutual claims of the depositors are balanced by cheques on their deposits and can be written off against each other. In this connection, it is immaterial whether these deposits are entrusted to the same banker, who can thus balance the various accounts against each other, or whether this is done in different banks, which mutually exchange cheques and pay only the balances to one another.

With the development of interest-bearing capital and the credit system, all capital seems to double itself, and sometimes treble itself, by the various modes in which the same capital, or perhaps even the same claim on a debt, appears in different forms in different hands.[3] The greater portion of this 'money-capital' is purely fictitious. All the deposits, with the exception of the reserve fund, are merely claims on the banker, which, however, never exist as deposits. To the extent that they serve in clearing-house transactions, they perform the function of capital for the bankers—after the latter have loaned them out. They pay one another their mutual drafts upon the non-existing deposits by balancing their mutual accounts.

Adam Smith says with regard to the role played by capital in the loaning of money:

> Even in the moneyed interest, however, the money is, as it were, but the deed of assignment which conveys from one hand to another those capitals which the owners do not care to employ themselves. Those capitals may be greater in almost any proportion than the amount of the money, which serves as the instrument of their conveyance, the same pieces of money successively serving for many different loans, as well as for many different purchases. A, for example, lends to W £1,000, with which W immediately purchases of B £1,000 worth of goods. B, having no occasion for the money himself, lends the identical pieces to X, with which X immediately purchases of C another £1,000 worth of goods. C, in the same manner, and for the same reason, lends them to Y, who again purchases goods with them of D. In this manner the same pieces, either of coin or of paper, may, in the course of a few days, serve as the instrument of three different loans, and of three different purchases, each of which is, in value, equal to the whole amount of those pieces. What the three moneyed men, A, B and C, assign to the three borrowers, W, X and Y, is the power of making those purchases. In this power consist both the value and the use of the loans. The stock lent by the three moneyed men is equal to the value of the goods which can be purchased with it, and is three times greater than that of the money with which the purchases are made. Those loans, however, may be all perfectly well secured, the goods purchased by the different debtors being so employed, as, in due time, to bring back, with a profit, an equal value either of coin or of paper. And as the same pieces of money can thus serve as the instrument of different loans to three, or for the same reason, to thirty times their value, so they may likewise successively serve as the instrument of repayment. ([*An Inquiry into the Nature and Causes o/ the Wealth of Nations,* Aberdeen, London, 1848, p. *236.—Ed.*] Book II, Chap. IV.)

Since the same piece of money can be used for various purchases, corresponding to its velocity of circulation, it can similarly be used for various loans, since the purchases take it from one person to another, and a loan is but a transfer from one person to another without the mediation of a purchase. To every seller, money represents the transformed shape of his commodities. Nowadays, when every value is expressed as capital-value, it represents in the various loans various capitals in succession. This is simply another way of expressing the earlier statement that it can successively realise various commodity-values. At the same time it serves as a medium of circulation, in order to transfer the real capitals from person to person. In the case of loans, it does not pass from person to person as a medium of circulation. As long as it remains in the hands of the lender, it is in his hands not a medium of circulation, but the value existence of his capital. And in this form, he transfers it when lending it to another. If A had lent the money to B, and B to C, without the mediation of purchases, the same money would not represent three capitals, but only one—a *single* capital-value. The number of capitals which it actually represents depends on the number of times that it functions as the value-form of various commodity-capitals.

The same thing that Adam Smith says about loans in general also applies to deposits, which are merely another name for the loans which the public makes to the bankers. The same pieces of money may serve as the instruments for any number of deposits.

> It is unquestionably true that the £1,000 which you deposit at A today may be reissued tomorrow, and form a deposit at B. The day after that, reissued from B, it may form a deposit at C... and so on to infinitude; and that the same £1,000 in money may, thus, by a succession of transfers, multiply itself into a sum of deposits absolutely indefinite. It is possible, therefore, that nine-tenths of all the deposits in the United Kingdom may have no existence beyond their record in the books of the bankers who are respectively accountable for them.... Thus in Scotland, for instance, currency has never exceeded £3 million, the deposits in the banks are estimated at £27 million. Unless a run on the banks be made, the same £1,000 would, if sent back upon its travels, cancel with the same facility a sum equally indefinite. As the same £1,000, with which you cancel your debt to a tradesman today, may cancel his debt to the merchant tomorrow, the merchant's debt to the bank the day following, and so on without end; so the same £1,000 may pass from hand to hand, and bank to bank, and cancel any conceivable sum of deposits. (*The Currency Theory Reviewed*, pp. 62-63.)

Just as everything in this credit system is doubled and trebled and transformed into a mere phantom of the imagination, so it is with the 'reserve fund,' where one would at last hope to grasp on to something solid.

Let us listen once more to Mr Morris, Governor of the Bank of England:

> The reserves of the private bankers are in the hands of the Bank of England in the shape of deposits.... An export of gold acts exclusively, in the first instance, upon the reserve of the Bank of England; but it would also be acting upon the reserves of the bankers, inasmuch as it is a withdrawal of a portion of the reserves which they have in the Bank of England. It would be acting upon the reserves of all the bankers throughout the country. (Commercial Distress, 1847-48, Nos. 3639, 3642.)

Ultimately, then, the reserve funds actually merge with the reserve fund of the Bank of England.[4] However, this reserve fund also has a double existence. The reserve fund of the banking department is equal to the surplus of notes which the Bank is authorised to issue over and above the notes in circulation. The legal maximum of the note issue is £14 million (for which no bullion reserve is required; it is the approximate amount owed by the state to the Bank) plus the amount of the Bank's supply of precious metal. If the supply of precious metal in the Bank amounts to £14 million, the Bank can thus issue £28 million in notes, and if £20 million of these are in circulation, the reserve fund of the banking department is £8 million. These £8 million's worth of notes are then legally the banker's capital at the disposal of the Bank, and at the same time, the reserve fund for its deposits. Now, if a drain of gold takes place, whereby the supply of precious metal in the Bank is reduced by £6 million—requiring the destruction of an equivalent number of notes—the reserve of the banking department would fall from £8 million to £2 million. On the one hand, the Bank would raise its rate of interest considerably; on the other hand, the banks having deposits with it, and the other depositors, would observe a large decrease in the reserve fund covering their own credits in the Bank. In 1857, the four largest stock banks of London threatened to call in their deposits, and thereby bankrupt the banking department, unless the Bank of England would secure a 'government letter' suspending the Bank Act of 1844.[5] In this way, the banking department could fail, as in 1847, while any number of millions (*e.g.*, 8 million in 1847) are held in its issue department to guarantee the convertibility of the circulating notes. But this is again illusory.

That large portion (of deposits) for which the bankers themselves have no immediate demand passes into the hands of the bill-brokers, who give to the banker in return commercial bills already discounted by them for persons in London and in different parts of the country as a security for the sum advanced by the banker. The bill-broker is responsible to the banker for payment of this money at call; and such is the magnitude of these transactions, that Mr Neave, the present Governor of the Bank [of England], stated in evidence, 'We know that one broker had 5 million, and we were led to believe that another had between 8 and 10 million; there was one with 4, another with 3½, and a third with above 8. I speak of deposits with the brokers. (Report of Committee on Bank Acts, 1857-58, p. 5, Section 8.)

The London bill-brokers carried on their enormous transactions without any cash reserve, relying on the run off of their bills falling due, or in extremity, on the power of obtaining advances from the Bank of England on the security of bills under discount.' *Ibid.*, p. VIII, Section 17. 'Two bill-broking houses in London suspended payment in 1847; both afterwards resumed business. In 1857, both suspended again. The liabilities of one house in 1847 were, in round numbers, £2,683,000, with a capital of £180,000; the liabilities of the same house, in 1857, were £5,300,000, the capital probably not more than one-fourth of what it was in 1847. The liabilities of the other firm were between £3,000,000 and £4,000,000 at each period of stoppage, with a capital not exceeding £45,000. *(Ibid.*, p. XXI, Section 52.)

Notes

1. 'The labourer possesses capital-value, which is arrived at by considering the money-value or his annual wage as income from interest.... Capitalising ... the average daily wage at 4%, we obtain the average value of a male agricultural labourer to be: German Austria, 4,500 taler; Prussia, 4,500; England, 3,750; France, 2,000; inner Russia, 750 taler.' (Von Reden, *Vergleichende Kultur-Statistik,* Berlin, 1848, p. 434.)
2. [Immediately after the February Revolution, when commodities and securities were extremely depreciated and utterly unsaleable, a Swiss merchant in Liverpool, Mr B. Zwilchenbart—who told this to my father—cashed all his belongings, travelled with cash in hand to Paris and sought out Rothschild, offering to participate in a joint enterprise with him. Rothschild looked at him fixedly, rushed towards him, grabbed him by his shoulders and asked: *'Avez-vous de l'argent sur vous?'—'Oui, M. le baron.'—'Alors vous êtes mon homme!'* ('Have you money in your possession?'—'Yes, Baron.'—'Then you are my man!')—And they did a thriving business together.—*F.E.*]
3. [This doubling and trebling of capital has developed considerably further in recent years, for instance, through financial trusts, which already occupy a heading of their own in the report of the London Stock Exchange. A company is organised for the purchase of a certain class of interest-bearing of foreign government securities, English municipal or American public bonds, railway stocks, etc. The capital, for example, £2 million, is raised by stock subscriptions. The Board of Directors buys up the values in question or speculates more or less actively therein, and after deducting the expenses distributes among the stockholders the annual interest as dividends. Furthermore, some stock companies have adopted the custom of dividing the common stock into two classes, preferred and deferred. The preferred receive a fixed rate of interest, say, 5%, provided that the total profit permits it; if there is anything left after that, the deferred receive it. In this manner, the 'solid' investment of capital in preferred shares is more or less separated from actual speculation—with deferred shares. Since a few large enterprises have been unwilling to adopt this new custom, the expedient has been resorted to of organising new companies which invest a million or several million pounds sterling in shares of the former companies and then issue new shares amounting to

the nominal value of the purchased shares, but half of them are issued as preferred and the other half as deferred. In such cases the original shares are doubled, since they serve as a basis for a new issue of shares.—*F.E.*]

4. [To what extent this has intensified since then is shown by the following official tabulation of the bank reserves of the fifteen largest London banks in November 1892, taken from the *Daily News* of December 15, 1892:

Name of Bank	*Liabilities*	*Cash Reserves*	*Percentages*
City	£9,317,629	£746,551	8.01
Capital and Counties	11,392,744	1,307,483	11.47
Imperial	3,987,400	447,157	11.22
Lloyds	23,800,937	2,966,806	12.46
Lon. And Westminster	24,671,559	3,818,885	15.50
Lon. And S. Western	5,570,268	812,353	14.58
London Joint Stock	12,127,993	1,288,977	10.62
London and Midland	8,814,499	1,127,280	12.79
London and County	37,111,035	3,600,374	9.70
National	11,163,829	1,426,225	12.77
National Provincial.	41,907,384	4,614,780	41.01
Parrs and the Alliance	12,794,489	1,532,707	11.98
Prescott & Co	4,041,058	538,517	13.07
Union of London.,	15,502,618	2,300,084	14.84
Williams, Deacon & Manchester & Co.	10,452,381	1,317,628	12.60
Total	£232,655,823	£27,845,807	11.97

Of this total reserve of almost 28 million, at least 25 million are deposited in the Bank of England, and at most 3 million are in cash in the safes of the 15 banks themselves. But the cash reserve of the banking department of the Bank of England amounted to less than 16 million during that same month of November 1892!—*F. E.*]

5. The suspension of the Bank Act of 1844 permits the Bank to issue any quantity of banknotes regardless of the gold reserve backing in its possession; thus, to create an arbitrary quantity of fictitious paper money-capital, and to use it for the purpose of making loans to banks, exchange brokers, and through them to commerce.—*F. E.*]

30

Money-Capital and Real Capital I

The only difficult questions, which we are now approaching in connection with the credit system, are the following:

First: The accumulation of the actual money-capital. To what extent is it, and to what extent is it not, an indication of an actual accumulation of capital, *i.e.*, of reproduction on an extended scale? Is the so-called plethora of capital—an expression used only with reference to the interest-bearing capital, *i.e.*, moneyed capital—only a special way of expressing industrial over-production, or does it constitute a separate phenomenon alongside of it?

Does this plethora, or excessive supply of money-capital, coincide with the existence of stagnating masses of money (bullion, gold coin and banknotes), so that this superabundance of actual money is the expression and external form of that plethora of loan capital?

Secondly: To what extent does a scarcity of money, *i.e.*, a shortage of loan capital, express a shortage of real capital (commodity-capital and productive capital)? To what extent does it coincide, on the other hand, with a shortage of money as such, a shortage of the medium of circulation?

In so far as we have hitherto considered the peculiar form of accumulation of money-capital and of money wealth in general, it has resolved itself into an accumulation of claims of ownership upon labour. The accumulation of the capital of the national debt has been revealed to mean merely an increase in a class of state creditors, who have the privilege of a firm claim upon a certain portion of the tax revenue.[1] By means of these facts, whereby even an accumulation of debts may appear as an accumulation of capital, the height of distortion taking place in the credit system becomes apparent. These promissory notes, which are issued for the originally loaned capital long since spent, these paper duplicates of consumed capital, serve for their owners as capital to the extent that they are saleable commodities and may, therefore, be reconverted into capital.

Titles of ownership to public works, railways, mines, etc., are indeed, as we have also seen, titles to real capital. But they do not place this capital at one's disposal. It is not subject to withdrawal. They merely convey legal claims to a portion of the surplus-value to be produced by it. But these titles likewise become paper duplicates of the real capital; it is as though a bill of lading were to acquire a value separate from the cargo, both concomitantly and simultaneously with it. They come to nominally represent non-existent capital. For the real capital exists side by side with them and does not change hands as a result of the transfer of these duplicates from one person to another. They assume the form of interest-bearing capital, not only because they guarantee a certain income, but also because, through their sale, their repayment as capital-values can be obtained. To the extent that the accumulation of this paper expresses the accumulation of railways, mines, steamships, etc., to that extent does it express the extension of the actual reproduction process—just as the extension of, for example, a tax list on movable property indicates the expansion of this property. But as duplicates which are themselves objects of transactions as commodities, and thus able to circulate as capital-values, they are illusory, and their value may fall or rise quite independently of the movement of value of the real capital for which they are titles. Their value, that is, their quotation on the Stock Exchange, necessarily has a tendency to rise with a fall in the rate of interest—in so far as this fall, independent of the characteristic movements of money-capital, is due merely to the tendency for the rate of profit to fall; therefore, this imaginary wealth expands, if for this reason alone, in the course of capitalist production in accordance with the expressed value for each of its aliquot parts of specific original nominal value.[2]

Gain and loss through fluctuations in the price of these titles of ownership, and their centralisation in the hands of railway kings, etc., become, by their very nature, more and more a matter of gamble, which appears to take the place of labour as the original method of acquiring capital wealth and also replaces naked force. This type of imaginary money wealth not only constitutes a very considerable part of the money wealth of private people, but also of banker's capital, as we have already indicated.

In order to quickly settle this question, let us point out that one could also mean by the accumulation of money-capital the accumulation of wealth in the hands of bankers (money-lenders by profession), acting as middlemen between private money-capitalists on the one hand, and the state, communities, and reproducing borrowers on the other. For the entire vast extension of the credit system, and all credit in general, is exploited by them as their private capital. These fellows always possess capital and incomes in money-form or in direct claims on money. The accumulation of the wealth of this class may take place completely differently than actual accumulation, but it proves at any rate that this class pockets a good deal of the real accumulation.

Let us reduce the scope of the problem before us. Government securities, like stocks and other securities of all kinds, are spheres of investment for loanable capital—capital intended for bearing interest. They are forms of loaning such capital. But they themselves are not the loan capital, which is invested in them. On the other hand, in so far as credit plays a direct role in the reproduction process, what the industrialist or merchant needs when he wishes to have a bill discounted or a loan granted is neither stocks nor government securities. What he needs is money. He, therefore, pledges or sells those securities if he cannot secure money in any other way. It is the accumulation of *this* loan capital with which we have to deal here, and more particularly accumulation of loanable money-capital. We are not concerned here with loans of houses, machines, or other fixed capital. Nor are we concerned with the advances industrialists and merchants make to one another in commodities and within the compass of the reproduction process, although we must also investigate this point beforehand in more detail. We are concerned exclusively with money loans, which are made by bankers, as middlemen, to industrialists and merchants.

Let us then, to begin with, analyse commercial credit, that is, the credit which the capitalists engaged in reproduction give to one another. It forms the basis of the credit system. It is represented by the bill of exchange, a promissory note with a definite term of payment, *i.e.*, a document of deferred payment. Everyone gives credit with one hand and receives credit with the other. Let us completely disregard, for the present, banker's credit, which constitutes an entirely different sphere. To the extent that these bills of exchange circulate among the merchants themselves as means of payment again, by endorsement from one to another—without, however, the mediation of discounting—it is merely a transfer of the claim from A to B and does not change the picture in the least. It merely replaces one person by another. And even in this case, the liquidation can take place without the intervention of money. Spinner A, for example, has to pay a bill to cotton broker B, and the latter to importer C. Now, if C also exports yarn, which happens often enough, he may buy yarn from A on a bill of exchange and the spinner A may pay the broker B with the broker's own bill which was received in payment from C. At most, a balance will have to be paid in money. The entire transaction then consists merely in the exchange of cotton and yarn. The exporter represents only the spinner, and the cotton broker, the cotton planter.

Two things are now to be noted in the circuit of this purely commercial credit.

First: The settlement of these mutual claims depends upon the return flow of capital, that is, on C—M, which is merely deferred. If the spinner has received a bill of exchange from a cotton goods manufacturer, then manufacturer can pay if the cotton goods which he has on the market have been sold in the interim. If the corn speculator has a bill of exchange drawn upon his agent, the agent can pay the money if the corn has been sold in the interim at the expected price. These payments, therefore, depend on the fluidity of reproduction, that is, the production and consumption processes. But since the credits are mutual, the solvency of one depends upon the solvency of another; for in drawing his bill of exchange, one may have counted either on the return flow of the capital in his own business or on the return flow of the capital in a third party's business whose bill of exchange is due in the meantime. Aside from the prospect of return flow of capital, payment can only be possible by means of reserve capital at the disposal of the person drawing the bill of exchange, in order to meet his obligations in case the return flow of capital should be delayed.

Secondly: This credit system does not do away with the necessity for cash payments. For one thing, a large portion of expenses must always be paid in cash, *e.g.*, wages, taxes, etc.

Furthermore, capitalist B, who has received from C a bill of exchange in place of cash payment, may have to pay a bill of his own which has fallen due to D before C's bill becomes due, and so he must have ready cash. A complete circuit of reproduction as that assumed above, *i.e.*, from cotton planter to cotton spinner and back again, can only constitute an exception; it will be constantly interrupted at many points. We have seen in the discussion of the reproduction process (Vol II, Part III) that the producers of constant capital exchange, in part, constant capital among themselves. As a result, the bills of exchange can, more or less, balance each other out. Similarly, in the ascending line of production, where the cotton broker draws on the cotton spinner, the spinner on the manufacturer of cotton goods, the manufacturer on the exporter, the exporter on the importer (perhaps of cotton again). But the circuit of transactions, and, therefore, the turn about of the series of claims, does not take place at the same time. For example, the claim of the spinner on the weaver is not settled by the claim of the coal-dealer on the machine-builder. The spinner never has any counter-claims on the machine-builder, in his business, because his product, yarn, never enters as an element in the machine-builder's reproduction process. Such claims must, therefore, be settled by money.

The limits of this commercial credit, considered by themselves, are 1) the wealth of the industrialists and merchants, that is, their command of reserve capital in case of delayed returns; 2) these returns themselves. These returns may be delayed, or the prices of commodities may fall in the meantime, or the commodities may become momentarily unsaleable due to a stagnant market. The longer the bills of exchange run, the larger must be the reserve capital, and the greater the possibility of a diminution or delay of the returns through a fall in prices or a glut on the market. And, furthermore, the returns are so much less secure, the more the original transaction was conditioned upon speculation on the rise or fall of commodity-prices. But it is evident that with the development of the productive power of labour, and thus of production on a large scale: 1) the markets expand and become more distant from the place of production; 2) credits must, therefore, be prolonged; 3) the speculative element must thus more and more dominate the transactions. Production on a large scale and for distant markets throws the total product into the hands of commerce, but it is impossible that the capital of a nation should double itself in such a manner that commerce should itself be able to buy up the entire national product with its own capital and to sell it again. Credit is, therefore, indispensable here; credit, whose volume grows with the growing volume of value of production and whose time duration grows with the increasing distance of the markets. A mutual interaction takes place here. The development of the production process extends the credit, and credit leads to an extension of industrial and commercial operations.

When we examine this credit detached from banker's credit, it is evident that it grows with an increasing volume of industrial capital itself. Loan capital and industrial capital are identical here. The loaned capital is commodity-capital which is intended either for ultimate individual consumption or for the replacement of the constant elements of productive capital. What appears here as loan capital is always capital existing in some definite phase of the reproduction process, but which by means of purchase and sale passes from one person to another, while its equivalent is not paid by the buyer until some later stipulated time. For example, cotton is transferred to the spinner for a bill of exchange, yarn to the manufacturer of cotton goods for a bill of exchange, cotton goods to the merchant for a bill, from whose hands they go to the exporter for a bill, and then, for a bill to some merchant in India, who sells the goods and buys indigo instead, etc. During this transfer from hand to hand, the transformation of cotton into cotton goods is effected, and the cotton goods are finally transported to India and exchanged for indigo, which is shipped to Europe and there enters into the reproduction process again. The various phases of the reproduction process are promoted here by credit, without any payment on the part of the spinner for the cotton, the manufacturer of cotton goods for the yarn, the merchant for the cotton goods, etc. In the first stages of the process, the commodity, cotton, goes through its various production phases, and this transition is promoted by credit. But as soon as the cotton has received in production its ultimate form as a commodity, the same commodity-capital passes only through the hands of various merchants who promote its transportation to distant markets, and the last of whom finally sells these commodities to the consumer and buys other commodities in their stead, which either become consumed or go into the reproduction process. It is necessary, then, to differentiate between two stages here:

In the first stage, credit promotes the actual successive phases in the production of the same article; in the second, credit merely promotes the transfer of the article, including its transportation, from one merchant to another, in other words, the process C—M. But here also the commodity is at least in the process of circulation, that is, in a phase of the reproduction process.

It follows, then, that it is never idle capital which is loaned here, but capital which must change its form in the hands of its owner; it exists in a form that for him is merely commodity-capital, *i.e.*, capital which must be retransformed, and, to begin with, at least converted into money. It is, therefore, the metamorphosis of commodities that is here promoted by credit; not merely C—M, but also M—C and the actual production process. A large quantity of credit within the reproductive circuit (banker's credit excepted) does not signify a large quantity of idle capital, which is being offered for loan and is seeking profitable investment. It means rather a large employment of capital in the reproduction process. Credit, then, promotes here 1) as far as the industrial capitalists are concerned, the transition of industrial capital from one phase into another, the connection of related and dovetailing spheres of production; 2) as far as the merchants are concerned, the transportation and transition of commodities from one person to another until their definite sale for money or their exchange for other commodities.

The maximum of credit is here identical with the fullest employment of industrial capital, that is, the utmost exertion of its reproductive power without regard to the limits of consumption. These limits of consumption are extended by the exertions of the reproduction process itself. On the one hand, this increases the consumption of revenue on the part of labourers and capitalists, on the other hand, it is identical with an exertion of productive consumption.

As long as the reproduction process is continuous and, therefore, the return flow assured, this credit exists and expands, and its expansion is based upon the expansion of the reproduction process itself. As soon as a stoppage takes place, as a result of delayed returns, glutted markets, or fallen prices, a superabundance of industrial capital becomes available, but in a form in which it cannot perform its functions. Huge quantities of commodity-capital but unsaleable. Huge quantities of fixed capital, but largely idle due to stagnant reproduction. Credit is contracted 1) because this capital is idle, *i.e.*, blocked in one of its phases of reproduction because it cannot complete its metamorphosis; 2) because confidence in the continuity of the reproduction process has been shaken; 3) because the demand for this commercial credit diminishes. The spinner, who curtails his production and has a large quantity of unsold yarn in stock, does not need to buy any cotton on credit; the merchant does not need to buy any commodities on credit because he has more than enough of them.

Hence, if there is a disturbance in this expansion or even in the normal flow of the reproduction process, credit also becomes scarce; it is more difficult to obtain commodities on credit. However, the demand for cash payment and the caution observed toward sales on credit are particularly characteristic of the phase of the industrial cycle following a crash. During the crisis itself, since everyone has products to sell, cannot sell them, and yet must sell them in order to meet payments, it is not the mass of idle and investment-seeking capital, but rather the mass of capital impeded in its reproduction process, that is greatest just when the shortage of credit is most acute (and, therefore, the rate of discount highest for banker's credit). The capital already invested is then, indeed, idle in large quantities because the reproduction process is stagnant. Factories are closed, raw materials accumulate, finished products flood the market as commodities. Nothing is more erroneous, therefore, than to blame a scarcity of productive capital for such a condition. It is precisely at such times that there is a superabundance of productive capital, partly in relation to the normal, but temporarily reduced scale of reproduction, and partly in relation to the paralysed consumption.

Let us suppose that the whole of society is composed only of industrial capitalists and wage-workers. Let us furthermore disregard price fluctuations, which prevent large portions of the total capital from replacing themselves in their average proportions and which, owing to the general interrelations of the entire reproduction process as developed in particular by credit, must always call forth general stoppages of a transient nature. Let us also disregard the sham transactions and speculations, which the credit system favours. Then, a crisis could only be explained as the result of a disproportion of production in various branches of the economy, and as a result of a disproportion between the consumption of the capitalists and their accumulation. But as matters stand, the replacement of the capital invested in production depends largely upon the consuming power of the non-producing classes; while the consuming power of the workers is limited partly by the laws of wages, partly by the fact that they are used only as long as they can be profitably employed by the capitalist class. The ultimate reason for all real crises always remains the poverty and restricted consumption of the masses as opposed to the drive of capitalist production to develop the productive forces as though only the absolute consuming power of society constituted their limit.

A real lack of productive capital, at least among capitalistically developed nations, can be said to exist only in times of general crop failures, either in the principal foodstuffs or in the principal industrial raw materials.

However, in addition to this commercial credit we have actual money credit. The advances of the industrialists and merchants among one another are amalgamated with the money advances made to them by the bankers and money-lenders. In discounting bills of exchange the advance is only nominal. A manufacturer sells his product for a bill of exchange and gets this bill discounted by some bill-broker. In reality, the latter advances only the credit of his banker, who in turn advances to the broker the money-capital of his depositors. The depositors consist of the industrial capitalists and merchants themselves and also of workers (through savings-banks)—as well as ground-rent recipients and other unproductive classes. In this way every individual industrial manufacturer and merchant gets around the necessity of keeping a large reserve fund and being dependent upon his actual returns. On the other hand, the whole process becomes so complicated, partly by simply manipulating bills of exchange, partly by commodity transactions for the sole purpose of manufacturing bills of exchange, that the semblance of a very solvent business with a smooth flow of returns can easily persist even long after returns actually come in only at the expense partly of swindled money-lenders and partly of swindled producers. Thus business always appears almost excessively sound right on the eve of a crash. The best proof of this is furnished, for instance, by the Reports on Bank Acts of 1857 and 1858, in which all bank directors, merchants, in short all the invited experts with Lord Overstone at their head, congratulated one another on the prosperity and soundness of business—just one month before the outbreak of the crisis in August 1857. And, strangely enough, Tooke in his *History of Prices* succumbs to this illusion once again as historian for each crisis. Business is always thoroughly sound and the campaign in full swing, until suddenly the debacle takes place.

We revert now to the accumulation of money-capital.

Not every augmentation of loanable money-capital indicates a real accumulation of capital or expansion of the reproduction process. This becomes most evident in the phase of the industrial cycle immediately following a crisis, when loan capital lies around idle in great quantities. At such times, when the production process is curtailed (production in the English industrial districts was reduced by one-third after the crisis of 1847), when the prices of commodities are at their lowest level, when the spirit of enterprise is paralysed, the rate of interest is low, which in this case, indicates nothing more than an increase in loanable capital precisely as a result of contraction and paralysation of industrial capital. It is quite obvious that a smaller quantity of a circulation medium is required when the prices of commodities have fallen, the number of transactions decreased, and the capital laid out for wages reduced; that, on the other hand, no additional money is required to function as world-money after foreign debts have been liquidated either by the export of gold or as a result of bankruptcies; that, finally, the volume of business connected with discounting bills of exchange diminishes in proportion with the reduced number and magnitudes of the bills of exchange them-selves. Hence the demand for loanable money-capital, either to act as a medium of circulation or as a means of payment (the investment of new capital is still out of the question), decreases and this capital, therefore, becomes relatively abundant. Under such circumstances, however, the supply of loanable money-capital also increases, as we shall later see.

Thus, the situation after the crisis of 1847 was characterised by 'a limitation of transaction and a great superabundance of money.' (Commercial Distress, 1847-48, Evidence No. 1664.) The rate of interest was very low because of the 'almost perfect destruction of commerce and the almost total want of means of employing money' (*loc. cit.*, p. 45, testimony of Hodgson, Director of the Royal Bank of Liverpool). What nonsense these gentlemen concocted (and Hodgson is, moreover, one of the best of them) in order to explain these facts, can be seen from the following remark:

> The pressure [1847] arose from the real diminution of the moneyed capital of the country, caused partly by the necessity of paying in gold for imports from all parts of the world, and partly by the absorption of floating into fixed capital. (1. c., p. 39)

How the conversion of floating capital into fixed capital reduces the money-capital of a country is unintelligible. For, in the case of railways, *e.g.*, in which capital was mainly invested at that time, neither gold nor paper is used for viaducts and rails, and the money for the railway stocks, to the extent that it had been deposited solely in payment, performed exactly the same functions as any other money deposited in banks and even increased the loanable money-capital temporarily, as already shown above; but to the extent that it had actually been spent for construction, it circulated in the country as a medium of purchase and of payment. Only in so far as fixed capital cannot be exported, so that with the impossibility of its export the available capital secured from returns for exported articles also drops out of the picture—including the returns in cash or bullion—only to that extent could the money-capital be affected. But at that time English export articles were also piled up in huge quantities on the foreign markets without being able to be sold. It is true, the floating capital of the merchants and manufacturers of Manchester, etc., who had a portion of their normal business capital tied up in railway stocks and were, therefore, dependent upon borrowed capital for running their business, had become fixed, and they, therefore, had to suffer the consequences. But it would have been the same, if the capital belonging to their business, but withdrawn from it, had been invested, say, in mines instead of railways-mining products like iron, coal, copper being themselves in turn floating capital. The actual reduction of available money-capital through crop failures, corn imports, and gold exports constituted, naturally, an event that had nothing to do with the railway swindle.

Almost all mercantile houses had begun to starve their business more or less ... by taking part of their commercial capital for railways.—æLoans to so great an extent by commercial houses to railways [*loc. cit.*, p. 42] induced them to lean too much upon... banks by the discount of paper, whereby to carry on their commercial operations' (the same Hodgson, *loc. cit.*, *p.* 67). 'In Manchester there have been immense losses in consequence of the speculation in railways' (R. Gardner, previously cited in Vol. I, Ch. XIII, 3, c, and in several other places; Evidence No. 4884, *loc. cit.*).

One of the principal causes of the crisis of 1847 was the colossal flooding of the market and the fabulous swindle in the East Indian trade with commodities. But there were also other circumstances which bankrupted very rich firms in this line:

They had large means, but not available. The whole of their capital was locked up in estates in the Mauritius, or indigo factories, or sugar factories. Having incurred liabilities to the extent of £500,000-600,000, they had no available assets to pay their bills, and eventually it proved that to pay their bills they were entirely dependent upon their credit. (Ch. Turner, big East Indian merchant in Liverpool, No. 730, *loc. cit.*)

See also Gardner (No. 4872, *loc. cit.*):

'Immediately after the China treaty, so great a prospect was held out to the country of a great extension of our commerce with China, that there were many large mills built with a view to that trade exclusively, in order to manufacture that class of cloth which is principally taken for the China market, and our previous manufactures had the addition of all those.'—'4874. How has that trade turned out?—Most ruinous, almost beyond description; I do not believe, that of the whole of the shipments that were made in 1844 and 1845 to China, above two-thirds of the amount have ever been returned; in consequence of tea being the principal article of repayment and of the expectation that was held out, we, as manufacturers, fully calculated upon a great reduction in the duty on tea.'

And now, naively expressed, comes the characteristic credo of the English manufacturer:

'Our commerce with no foreign market is limited by their power to purchase the commodity, but it is limited in this country by our capability of consuming that which we receive in return for our manufactures.'

(The relatively poor countries, with whom England trades, are, of course, able to pay for and consume any amount of English products, but unfortunately wealthy England cannot assimilate the products sent in return.)

'4876. I sent out some goods in the first instance, and the goods sold at about 45 per cent loss, from the full conviction that the price, at which my agents could purchase tea, would leave so great a profit in this country as to make up the deficiency... but instead of profit, I lost in some instances 25 and up to 50 per cent.'—'4877. Did the manufacturers generally export on their own account?—Principally; the merchants, I think, very soon saw that the thing would not answer, and they rather encouraged the manufacturers to consign than take a direct interest themselves.'

In 1857, on the other hand, the losses and failures fell mainly upon the merchants, since the manufacturers left them the task of flooding the foreign markets 'on their own account.'

An expansion of money-capital, which arises out of the fact that, in view of the expansion of banking (see, below, the example of Ipswich, where in the course of a few years immediately preceding 1857 the deposits of the capitalist farmers quadrupled), what was formerly a private hoard or coin reserve is always converted into loanable capital for a definite time, does not indicate a growth in productive capital any more than the increasing deposits with the London stock banks when the latter began to pay interest on deposits. As long as the scale of production remains the same, this expansion leads only to an abundance of loanable money-capital as compared with the productive. Hence the low rate of interest.

After the reproduction process has again reached that state of prosperity which precedes that of over-exertion, commercial credit becomes very much extended; this forms, indeed, the 'sound' basis again for a ready flow of returns and extended production. In this state the rate of interest is still low, although it rises above its minimum. This is, in fact, the *only* time that it can be said a low rate of interest, and consequently a relative abundance of loanable capital, coincides with a real expansion of industrial capital. The ready flow and regularity of the returns, linked with extensive commercial credit, ensures the supply of loan capital in spite of the increased demand for it, and prevents the level of the rate of interest from rising. On the other hand, those cavaliers who work without any reserve capital or without any capital at all and who thus operate completely on a money credit basis begin to appear for the first time in considerable numbers. To this is now added the great expansion of fixed capital in all forms, and the opening of new enterprises on a vast and far-reaching scale. The interest now rises to its average level. It reaches its maximum again as soon as the new crisis sets in. Credit suddenly stops then, payments are suspended, the reproduction process is paralysed, and with the previously mentioned exceptions, a superabundance of idle industrial capital appears side by side with an almost absolute absence of loan capital.

On the whole, then, the movement of loan capital, as expressed in the rate of interest, is in the opposite direction to that of industrial capital. The phase wherein a low rate of interest, but above the minimum, coincides with the 'improvement' and growing confidence after a crisis, and particularly the phase wherein the rate of interest reaches its average level, exactly midway between its minimum and maximum, are the only two periods during which an abundance of loan capital is available simultaneously with a great expansion of industrial capital. But at the beginning of the industrial cycle, a low rate of interest coincides with a contraction, and at the end of the industrial cycle, a high rate of interest coincides with a superabundance of industrial capital. The low rate of interest that accompanies the 'improvement' shows that the commercial credit requires bank credit only to a slight extent because it is still self-supporting.

The industrial cycle is of such a nature that the same circuit must periodically reproduce itself, once the first impulse has been given.[8] During a period of slack, production sinks below the level, which it had attained in the preceding cycle and for which the technical basis has now been laid. During prosperity—the middle period—it continues to develop on this basis. In the period of over-production and swindle, it strains the productive forces to the utmost, until it exceeds the capitalistic limits of the production process.

It is clear that there is a shortage of means of payment during a period of crisis. The convertibility of bills of exchange replaces the metamorphosis of commodities themselves, and so much more so exactly at such times the more a portion of the firms operates on pure credit. Ignorant and mistaken bank legislation, such as that of 1844-45, can intensify this money crisis. But no kind of bank legislation can eliminate a crisis.

In a system of production, where the entire continuity of the reproduction process rests upon credit, a crisis must obviously occur—a tremendous rush for means of payment—when credit suddenly ceases and only cash payments have validity. At first glance, therefore, the whole crisis seems to be merely a credit and money crisis. And in fact it is only a question of the convertibility of bills of exchange into money. But the majority of these bills represent actual sales and purchases, whose extension far beyond the needs of society is, after all, the basis of the whole crisis. At the same time, an enormous quantity of these bills of exchange represents plain swindle, which now reaches the light of day and collapses; furthermore, unsuccessful speculation with the capital of other people; finally, commodity-capital which has depreciated or is completely unsaleable, or returns that can never more be realised again. The entire artificial system of forced expansion of the reproduction process cannot, of course, be remedied by having some bank, like the Bank of England, give to all the swindlers the deficient capital by means of its paper and having it buy up all the depreciated commodities at their old nominal values. Incidentally, everything here appears distorted, since in this paper world, the real price and its real basis appear nowhere, but only bullion, metal coin, notes, bills of exchange, securities. Particularly in centres where the entire money business of the country is concentrated, like London, does this distortion become apparent; the entire process becomes incomprehensible; it is less so in centres of production.

Incidentally in connection with the superabundance of industrial capital which appears during crises the following should be noted: commodity-capital is in itself simultaneously money-capital, that is, a definite amount of value expressed in the price of the commodities. As use-value it is a definite quantum of objects of utility, and there is a surplus of these available in times of crises. But as money-capital as such, as potential money-capital, it is subject to continual expansion and contraction. On the eve of a crisis, and during it, commodity-capital in its capacity as potential money-capital is contracted. It represents less money-capital for its owner and his creditors (as well as security for bills of exchange and loans) than it did at the time when it was bought and when the discounts and mortgages based on it were transacted. If this is the meaning of the contention that the money-capital of a country is reduced in times of stringency, this is identical with saying that the prices of commodities have fallen. Such a collapse in prices merely balances out their earlier inflation.

The incomes of the unproductive classes and of those who live on fixed incomes remain in the main stationary during the inflation of prices which goes hand in hand with over-production and over-speculation. Hence their consuming capacity diminishes relatively, and with it their ability to replace that portion of the total reproduction which would normally enter into their consumption. Even when their demand remains nominally the same, it decreases in reality.

It should be noted in regard to imports and exports, that, one after another, all countries become involved in a crisis and that it then becomes evident that all of them, with few exceptions, have exported and imported too much, so that *they all have an unfavourable balance of payments.* The trouble, therefore, does not actually lie with the balance of payments. For example, England suffers from a drain of gold. It has imported too much. But at the same time all other countries are over-supplied with English goods. They have thus also imported too much, or have been made to import too much. (There is, indeed, a difference between a country which exports on credit and those which export little or nothing on credit. But the latter then import on credit; and this is only then not the case when commodities are sent to them on consignment.) The crisis may first break out in England, the country which advances most of the credit and takes the least, because the balance of payments, the balance of payments due, which must be settled immediately, is *unfavourable,* even though the general balance of trade is *favourable.* This is explained partly as a result of the credit which it has granted, and partly as a result of the huge quantity of capital loaned to foreign countries, so that a large quantity of returns flow back to it in commodities, in addition to the actual trade returns. (However, the crisis has at times first broken out in America, which takes most of the commercial and capital credit from England.) The crash in England, initiated and accompanied by a gold drain, settles England's balance of payments, partly by a bankruptcy of its importers (about which more below), partly by disposing of a portion of its commodity-capital at low prices abroad, and partly by the sale of foreign securities, the purchase of English securities, etc. Now comes the turn of some other country. The balance of payments was momentarily in its favour; but now the time lapse normally existing between the balance of payments and balance of trade has been eliminated or at least reduced by the crisis: all payments are now suddenly supposed to be made at once. The same thing is now repeated here. England now has a return flow of gold, the other country a gold drain. What appears in one country as excessive imports, appears in the other as excessive exports, and vice versa. But over-imports and over-exports have taken place in all countries (we are not speaking here about crop failures, etc., but about a general crisis); that is over-production promoted by credit and the general inflation of prices that goes with it.

In 1857, the crisis broke out in the United States. A flow of gold from England to America followed. But as soon as the bubble in America burst, the crisis broke out in England and the gold flowed from America to England. The same took place between England and the continent. The balance of payments is in times of general crisis unfavourable to every nation, at least to every commercially developed nation, but always to each country in succession, as in volley firing, *i.e.*, as soon as each one's turn comes for making payments; and once the crisis has broken out, *e.g.*, in England, it compresses the series of these terms into a very short period. It then becomes evident that all these nations have simultaneously over-exported (thus over-produced) and over-imported (thus over-traded), that prices were inflated in all of them, and credit stretched too far. And the same break-down takes place in all of them. The phenomenon of a gold drain then takes place successively in all of them and proves precisely by its general character 1) that gold drain is just a phenomenon of a crisis, not its cause; 2) that the sequence in which it hits the various countries indicates only when their judgement-day has come, *i.e.*, when the crisis started and its latent elements come to the fore there.

It is characteristic of the English economic writers—and the economic literature worth mentioning since 1830 resolves itself mainly into a literature on currency, credit, and crises—that they look upon the export of precious metals in times of crisis, in spite of the turn in the rates of exchange, only from the standpoint of England, as a purely national phenomenon, and resolutely close their eyes to the fact that all other European banks raise their rate of interest when their bank raises its own in times of crisis, and that, when the cry of distress over the drain of gold is raised in their country today, it is taken up in America tomorrow and in Germany and France the day after.

> In 1847, 'the engagements running upon this country had to be met' [mostly for corn]. 'Unfortunately, they were met to a great extent by failures' [wealthy England secured relief by bankruptcies in its obligations toward the continent and America], 'but to the extent to which they were not met by failures, they were met by the exportation of bullion.' (Report of Committee on Bank Acts, 1857.)

In other words, in so far as a crisis in England is intensified by bank legislation, this legislation is a means of cheating the corn-exporting countries in periods of famine, first on their corn and then on the money for the corn. A prohibition on the export of corn during such periods for countries which are themselves labouring more or less under scarcities, is, therefore, a very rational measure to thwart this plan of the Bank of England to 'meet obligations' for corn imports 'by bankruptcies.' It is after all much better that the corn producers and speculators lose a portion of their profit for the good of their own country than their capital for the good of England.

It follows from the above that commodity-capital, during crises and during periods of business depression in general, loses to a large extent its capacity to represent potential money-capital. The same is true of fictitious capital, interest-bearing paper, in so far as it circulates on the stock exchange as money-capital. Its price falls with rising interest. It falls, furthermore, as a result of the general shortage of credit, which compels its owners to dump it in large quantities on the market in order to secure money. It falls, finally, in the case of stocks, partly as a result of the decrease in revenues for which it constitutes drafts and partly as a result of the spurious character of the enterprises which it often enough represents.

This fictitious money-capital is enormously reduced in times of crisis, and with it the ability of its owners to borrow money on it on the market. However, the reduction of the money equivalents of these securities on the stock exchange list has nothing to do with the actual capital which they represent, but very much indeed with the solvency of their owners.

Notes

1. The public fund is nothing but imaginary capital, which represents that portion of the annual revenue, which is set aside to pay the debt. An equivalent amount of capital has been spent; it is this which serves as a denominator for the loan, but it is not this which is represented by the public fund; for the capital no longer exists. New wealth must be created by the work of industry; a portion of this wealth is annually set aside in advance for those who have loaned that wealth which has been spent; this portion is taken by means of taxes from those who produce it, and is given to the creditors of the state, and, according to the customary proportion between capital and interest in the country, an imaginary capital is assumed equivalent to that which could give rise to the annual income which these creditors are to receive. (Sismondi, *Nouveaux principes* [Seconde édition, Paris, 1827], II, p. 230.)
2. A portion of the accumulated loanable money-capital is indeed merely an expression of industrial capital. For instance, when England, in 1857, had invested 180 million in American railways and other enterprises, this investment was transacted almost completely by the export of English commodities for which the Americans did not have to make payment in return. The English exporter drew bills of exchange for these commodities on America, which the English stock subscribers bought up and which were sent to America for purchasing the stock subscriptions.
3. [As I have already stated elsewhere [English edition: Vol. I.—*Ed.*], a change has taken place here since the last major general crisis. The acute form of the periodic process with its former ten-year cycle, appears to have given way to a more chronic, long drawn out, alternation between a relatively short and slight business improvement and a relatively long, indecisive depression-taking place in the various industrial countries at different times. But perhaps it is only a matter of a prolongation of the duration of the cycle. In the early years of world commerce, 1845-47, it can be shown that these cycles lasted about five years; from 1847 to 1867 the cycle is clearly ten years; is it possible that we are now in the preparatory stage of a new world crash of unparalleled vehemence? Many things seem to point in this direction. Since the last general crisis of 1867 many profound changes have taken place. The colossal expansion of the means of transportation and communication—ocean liners, railways, electrical telegraphy, the Suez Canal—has made a real world-market a fact. The former monopoly of England in industry has been challenged by a number of competing industrial countries; infinitely greater and varied fields have been opened in all parts of the world for the investment of surplus European capital, so that it is far more widely distributed and local over-speculation may be more easily overcome. By means of all this, most of the old breeding-grounds of crises and opportunities for their development have been eliminated or strongly reduced. At the same time, competition in the domestic market recedes before the cartels and trusts, while in the foreign market it is restricted by protective tariffs, with which all major industrial countries, England excepted, surround themselves. But these protective tariffs are nothing but preparations for the ultimate general industrial war, which shall decide who has supremacy on the world-market. Thus every factor, which works against a repetition of the old crises, carries within itself the germ of a far more powerful future crisis.—*F. E.*]

31

Money Capital and Real Capital. II

We are still not finished with this question: to what extent does the accumulation of capital in the form of loanable money-capital coincide with actual accumulation, *i.e.*, the expansion of the reproduction process.

The transformation of money into loanable money-capital is a much simpler matter than the transformation of money into productive capital. But two things should be distinguished here:

1. the mere transformation of money into loan capital;
2. the transformation of capital or revenue into money, which is transformed into loan capital.

It is only the latter point which can involve a positive accumulation of loan capital connected with an actual accumulation of industrial capital.

1. Transformation of Money into Loan Capital

We have already seen that a large build-up or surplus of loan capital can occur, which is connected with productive accumulation only to the extent that it is inversely proportional to it. This is the case in two phases of the industrial cycle, namely, first, when industrial capital in both its forms of productive and commodity-capital is contracted, *i.e.*, at the beginning of the cycle after the crisis; and, secondly, when the improvement begins, but when commercial credit still does not use bank credit to a great extent. In the first case, money-capital, which was formerly employed in production and commerce, appears as idle loan capital; in the second case, it appears used to an increasing extent, but at a very low rate of interest, because the industrial and commercial capitalists now prescribe terms to the money-capitalist. The surplus of loan capital expresses, in the first case, a stagnation of industrial capital, and in the second, a relative independence of commercial credit from banking credit—based on the fluidity of the returns, short-term credit, and a preponderance of operations with one's own capital. The speculators, who count on the credit capital of other people, have not yet appeared on the field; the people who work with their own capital are still far removed from approximately pure credit operations. In the former phase, the surplus of loan capital is directly opposite to expressing actual accumulation. In the second phase, it coincides with a renewed expansion of the reproduction process—it accompanies it, but is not its cause. The surplus of loan capital is already decreasing, *i.e.*, it is still only relative compared to the demand. In both cases, the expansion of the actual process of accumulation is promoted by the fact that the low interest—which coincides in the first case with low prices and in the second, with slowly rising prices—increases that portion of the profit which is transformed into profit of enterprise. This takes place to an even greater extent when interest rises to its average level during the height of the period of prosperity, when it has indeed grown, but not relative to profit.

We have seen, on the other hand, that an accumulation of loan capital can take place without any actual accumulation, *i.e.*, by mere technical means such as an expansion and concentration of the banking system; and a saving in the circulation reserve, or in the reserve fund of private means of payment, which are then always transformed into loan capital for a short time. Although this loan capital, which, for this reason, is also called floating capital, always retains the form of loan capital only for short periods of time (and should indeed also be used for discounting only for short periods of time), there is a continual ebb and flow of it. If one draws some away, another adds to it. The mass of loanable money-capital thus grows quite independently of the actual accumulation (we are not speaking here at all about loans for a number of years but only of short-term ones on bills of exchange and deposits).

> Bank Committee, 1857. Question 501. 'What do you mean by "floating capital"?' [Answer of Mr Weguelin, Governor of the Bank of England:] 'It is capital applicable to loans of money for short periods.... (502) The Bank of England notes ... the country banks circulation, and the amount of coin which is in the country.' [Question:] 'It does not appear from the returns before the Committee, if by floating capital you mean the active circulation' [of the notes of the Bank of England], 'that there is any very great variation in the active circulation?' [But there is a very great difference whether this active circulation is advanced by the money-lender or by the reproductive capitalist himself. Weguelin's answer:] 'I include in floating capital the reserves of the bankers, in which there is a considerable fluctuation.'

That is to say, there is considerable fluctuation in that portion of the deposits which the bankers have not loaned out again, but which figures as their reserve and for the greater part also as the reserve of the Bank of England, where they are deposited. Finally, the same gentleman says: floating capital may be bullion, that is, bar and coin (503). It is truly wonderful how in this credit gibberish of the money-market all categories of political economy receive a different meaning and a different form. Floating capital is the expression there for circulating capital, which is, of course, something quite different, and money is capital, and bullion is capital, and banknotes are circulation, and capital is a commodity, and debts are commodities, and fixed capital is money invested in hard-to-sell paper!

> The joint-stock banks of London ... have increased their deposits from £8,850,774 in *1847* to £43,100,724 in 1857.... The evidence given to your Committee leads to the inference that of this vast amount, a large part has been derived from sources not heretofore made available for this purpose; and that the practice of opening accounts and depositing money with bankers has extended to numerous classes who did not formerly employ their capital (!) in that way. It is stated by Mr Rodwell, the Chairman of the Association of the Private Country Bankers [distinguished from joint-stock banks], and delegated by them to give evidence to your Committee, that in the neighbourhood of Ipswich this practice has lately increased four-fold among the farmers and shopkeepers of that district; that almost every farmer, even those paying only £50 per annum rent, now keeps deposits with bankers. The aggregate of these deposits of course finds its way to the employments of trade, and especially gravitates to London, the centre of commercial activity, where it is employed first in the discount of bills, or in other advances to the customers of the London bankers. That large portion, however, for which the bankers themselves have no immediate demand passes into the hands of the bill-brokers, who give to the banker in return commercial bills already discounted by them for persons in London and in different parts of the country, as a security for the sum advanced by the banker. (Bank Committee, 1858, p. V.)

By making advances to the bill-broker on bills of exchange which this broker has already discounted once, the banker does, in fact, rediscount them; but in reality, very many of these bills have already been rediscounted by the bill-broker, and with the same money that the banker uses to rediscount the bills of the bill-broker, the latter rediscounts new bills. What this leads to is shown by the following:

> Extensive fictitious credits have been created by means of accommodation bills, and open credits, great facilities for which have been afforded by the practice of joint-stock

country banks discounting such bills, and rediscounting them with the bill-brokers in the London market, upon the credit of the bank alone, without reference to the quality of the bills otherwise. (*loc. cit.*, p. XXI)

Concerning this rediscounting and the assistance which this purely technical increase of loanable money-capital gives to credit swindles, the following extract from the *Economist* is of interest:

> For some years past capital [namely, loanable money-capital] has accumulated in some districts of the country more rapidly than it could be used, while, in others, the means of employing capital have increased more rapidly than the capital itself. While the bankers in the purely agricultural districts throughout the kingdom found no sufficient means of profitably and safely employing their deposits in their own districts, those in the large mercantile towns, and in the manufacturing and mining districts, have found a larger demand for capital than their own means could supply. The effect of this relative state of different districts has led, of late years, to the establishment and rapid extension of a new class of houses in the distribution of capital, who, though usually called bill-brokers, are in reality bankers upon an immense scale. The business of these houses has been to receive, for such periods, and at such rates of interest as were agreed upon, the surplus-capital of bankers in those districts where it could not be employed, as well as the temporary unemployed moneys of public companies and extensive mercantile establishments, and advance them at higher rates of interest to banker in those districts where capital was more in demand, generally by rediscounting the bills taken from their customers ... and in this way Lombard Street has become the great centre in which the transfer of spare capital has been made from one part of the country, where it could not be profitably employed, to another, where a demand existed for it, as well as between individuals similarly circumstanced. At first these transactions were confined almost exclusively to borrowing and lending on banking securities. But as the capital of the country rapidly accumulated, and became more economised by the establishment of banks, the funds at the disposal of these 'discount houses' became so large that they were induced to make advances first on dock warrants of merchandise (storage bills on commodities in docks), and next on bills of lading, representing produce not even arrived in this country, though sometimes, if not generally, secured by bills drawn by the merchant upon his broker. This practice rapidly changed the whole character of English commerce. The facilities thus afforded in Lombard Street gave extensive powers to the brokers in Mincing Lane, who on their part ... offered the full advantage of them to the importing merchant; who so far took advantage of them, that, whereas 25 years ago, the fact that a merchant received advances on his bills of lading, or even his dock warrants, would have been fatal to his credit, the practice has become so common of late years that it may be said to be now the general rule, and not the rare exception, as it was 25 years ago. Nay, so much further has this system been carried, that large sums have been raised in Lombard Street on bills drawn against the *forthcoming* crops of distant colonies. The consequence of such facilities being thus granted to the importing merchants led them to extend their transactions abroad, and to invest their floating capital with which their business has hitherto been conducted, in the most objectionable of all fixed securities-foreign plantations—over which they could exercise little or no control. And thus we see the direct change of credit through which the capital of the country, collected in our rural districts, and in small amounts in the shape of deposits in country banks, and centres in Lombard Street for employment, has been, first, made available for the extending operations in our mining and manufacturing districts, by the rediscount of bills to banks in those localities; next, for granting greater facilities for the importation of foreign produce by advances upon

dock warrants and bills of lading, and thus liberating the ‹legitimate› mercantile capital of houses engaged in foreign and colonial trade, and inducing to its most objectionable advances on foreign plantations. (*Economist,*November 20, 1847, p. 1334.)

This is how credits are 'nicely' devoured. The rural depositor fancies that he deposits only with his banker, and fancies furthermore that when his banker lends to others, it is done to private persons whom he knows. He has not the slightest suspicion that this banker places his deposit at the disposal of some London bill-broker, over whose operations neither of them have the slightest control.

We have already seen how large public enterprises, such as railways, may momentarily increase loan capital, owing to the circumstance that the deposited amounts always remain at the disposal of the bankers for a certain length of time until they are really used.

Incidentally, the mass of loan capital is quite different from the quantity of circulation. By the quantity of circulation we mean here the sum of all the banknotes and coin, including bars of precious metals, existing and circulating in a country. A portion of this quantity constitutes the reserve of the banks which continuously vary in magnitude.

> On November 12, 1857' [the date of the suspension of the Bank Act of 1844], 'the entire reserve of the Bank of England was only £580,751 (including London and all its branches); their deposits at the same time amounting to £22,500,000; of which near six and a half million belonged to London bankers. (Bank Acts, 1858, p. LVII.)

The variations in the interest rate (aside from those occurring over longer periods or the variation in the interest rate among various countries; the former are dependent upon variations in the general rate of profit, the latter on differences in the rates of profit and in the development of credit) depend upon the supply of loan capital (all other circumstances, state of confidence, etc. being equal), that is, of capital loaned in the form of money, coin and notes; in contradistinction to industrial capital, which, as such—in commodity-form—is loaned by means of commercial credit among the agents of reproduction themselves.

However, the mass of this loanable money-capital is different from, and independent of, the mass of circulating money.

For example, if £20 were loaned five times per day, a money-capital of £100 would be loaned, and this would imply at the same time that this £20 would have served, moreover, at least four times as a means of purchase or payment; for, if no purchase and payment intervened—so that it would not have represented at least four times the converted form of capital (commodities, including labour-power)—it would not constitute a capital of £100, but only five claims of £20 each.

In countries with a developed credit, we can assume that all money-capital available for lending exists in the form of deposits with banks and money-lenders. This is at least true for business as a whole. Moreover, in times of flourishing business, before the real speculation gets underway—when credit is easy and confidence is growing—most of the functions of circulation are settled by a simple transfer of credit, without the help of coin or paper money.

The mere possibility of large sums of deposits existing when a relatively small quantum of a medium of circulation is available, depends solely on:

1. the number of purchases and payments which the same coin performs;
2 the number of return excursions, whereby it goes back to the banks as deposits, so that its repeated function as a means of purchase and payment is promoted through its renewed transformation into deposits. For example, a small dealer deposits weekly with his banker £100 in money; the banker pays out a portion of the deposit of a manufacturer with this; the latter pays it to his workers; and the workers use it to pay the small dealer, who deposits it in the bank again.

> The £100 deposited by this small dealer have served, therefore, first, to pay the manufacturer a deposit of his; secondly, to pay the workers; thirdly, to pay the dealer himself; fourthly, to deposit another portion of the money-capital of the same small dealer; thus at the end of twenty weeks, if he himself did not have to draw against this money, he would have deposited £2,000 in the bank by means of the same £100.

To what extent this money-capital is idle, is shown only by the ebb and flow in the reserve fund of the banks. Therefore, Mr Weguelin, Governor of the Bank of England in 1857, concludes that the gold of the Bank of England is the 'only' reserve capital:

> '1258. Practically, I think, the rate of discount is governed by the amount of unemployed capital which there is in the country. The amount of unemployed capital is represented by the reserve of the Bank of England, which is practically a reserve of bullion. When, therefore, the bullion is drawn upon, it diminishes the amount of unemployed capital in the country, and consequently raises the value of that which remains.'—[Newmarch]
> '1364. The reserve of bullion in the Bank of England is, in truth, the central reserve, or hoard of treasure, upon which the whole trade of the country is carried on... And it is upon that hoard or reservoir that the action of the foreign exchanges always falls.' (Report on Bank Acts, 1857 [PP. 108, 119].)

The statistics of exports and imports furnish a measure of the accumulation of real, *i.e.*, productive and commodity-capital. These always show that, during the ten-year cyclical periods of development of British industry (1815 to 1870), the maximum of the last prosperity *before* the crisis always reappears as the minimum of the following prosperity, whereupon it rises to a new and far higher peak.

The actual or declared value of the exported products from Great Britain and Ireland in the prosperity year of 1824 was £40,396,300. With the crisis of 1825, the amount of exports then falls below this sum and fluctuates between 35 and 39 million annually. With the return of prosperity in 1834, it rises above the former maximum to *£41,649,191,* and reaches in 1836 the new maximum of £53,368,571. Beginning with 1837, it falls again to 42 million, so that the new minimum is already higher than the old maximum, and then fluctuates between 50 and 53 million. The return of prosperity lifts the amount of exports in 1844 to £58,500,000, whereby the peak of 1836 is again already far exceeded. In 1845, it reaches £60,111,082; it then falls to something over 57 million in 1846, reaches in 1847 almost 59 million, in 1848 almost 53 million, rises in 1849 to 63,500,000, in 1853 to nearly 99 million, in 1854 to 97 million, in 1855 to 94,500,000, in 1856 almost 116 million and reaches a peak of 122 million in 1857. It falls in 1858 to 116 million, rises already in 1859 to 130 million, in 1860 to nearly 136 million, in 1861 only 125 million (the new low is here again higher than the former peak), in 1863 to 146,500,000.

Of course, the same thing could be demonstrated in the case of imports, which shows the expansion of the market; here it is only a matter of the scale of production. [Of course, this holds true of England only for the time of its actual industrial monopoly; but it applies in general to the whole complex of countries with modern large-scale industries, as long as the world-market is still expanding.—*F. E.*]

2. Transformation of Capital or Revenue into Money that is Transformed into Loan Capital

We will consider here the accumulation of money-capital, in so far as it is not an expression either of a stoppage in the flow of commercial credit or of an economy—whether it be an economy in the actual circulating medium or in the reserve capital of the agents engaged in reproduction.

Aside from these two cases, an accumulation of money-capital can arise through an unusual inflow of gold, as in 1852 and 1853 as a result of the new Australian and Californian gold mines. This gold was deposited in the Bank of England. The depositors received notes for it, which they did not directly redeposit with bankers. By this means the Circulating medium was unusually increased. (Testimony of Weguelin, Bank Committee, 1857, No. 1329.) The Bank strove to utilise these deposits by lowering its discount to 2%. The mass of gold accumulated in the Bank rose during six months of 1853 to 22-23 million.

The accumulation of all money-lending capitalists naturally always takes place directly in money-form, whereas we have seen that the actual accumulation of industrial capitalists is accomplished, as a rule, by an increase in the elements of reproductive capital itself. Hence, the development of the credit system and the enormous concentration of the money-lending business in the hands of large banks must, by themselves alone, accelerate the accumulation of loanable capital, as a form distinct from actual accumulation. This rapid development of loan capital is, therefore, a result of actual accumulation, for it is a consequence of the development of the reproduction process, and the profit which forms the source of accumulation for these money-capitalists is only a deduction from the surplus-value which the reproductive ones filch (and it is at the same time the appropriation of a portion of the interest from the savings *of others*). Loan capital accumulates at the expense of both the industrial and commercial capitalists. We have seen that in the unfavourable phases of the industrial cycle the rate of interest may rise so high that it temporarily consumes the whole profit of some lines of business which are particularly handicapped. At the same time, prices of government and other securities fall. It is at such times that the money-capitalists buy this depreciated paper in huge quantities which in the later phases soon regains its former level and rises above it. It is then sold again and a portion of the money-capital of the public is thus appropriated. That portion which is not sold yields a higher interest because it was bought below par. But the money-capitalists convert all profits made, end reconverted by them into capital, first into loanable money-capital. The accumulation of the latter—as distinct from the actual accumulation, although its offshoot—thus takes place, even when we consider only the money-capitalists, bankers, etc., by themselves, as an accumulation of this particular class of capitalists. And it must grow with every expansion of the credit system which accompanies the actual expansion of the reproduction process.

If the interest rate is low, this depreciation of the money-capital falls principally upon the depositors, not upon the banks. Before the development of stock banks, ¾ of all the deposits in England lay in the banks without yielding interest. While interest is now paid on them, it amounts to at least 1% less than the current rate of interest.

As for the money accumulation of the other classes of capitalists, we disregard that portion of it which is invested in interest-bearing paper and accumulates in this form. We consider only that portion which is thrown upon the market as loanable money-capital.

In the first place, we have here that portion of the profit which is not spent as revenue, but is set aside for accumulation—for which, however, the industrial capitalists have no use in their own business at the moment. This profit exists directly in commodity-capital, a part of whose value it constitutes, and along with which it is realised in money. Now, if it is not reconverted into the production elements of commodity-capital (we leave out of consideration for the present the merchant, whom we shall discuss separately), it must remain for a length of time in the form of money. This amount increases with the amount of capital itself, even when the rate of profit declines. That portion which is to be spent as revenue is gradually consumed, but, in the meantime, as deposits, it constitutes loan capital with the banker. Thus, even the growth of that portion of profit which is spent as revenue expresses itself as a gradual and continually repeated accumulation of loan capital. The same is true of the other portion, which is intended for accumulation. Therefore, with the development of the credit system and its organisation, even an increase in revenue, *i.e.*, the consumption of the industrial and commercial capitalists, expresses itself as an accumulation of loan capital. And this holds true for all revenues so far as they are consumed gradually, in other words, for ground-rent, wages in their higher form, incomes of unproductive classes, etc. All of them assume for a certain time the form of money revenue and are, therefore, convertible into deposits and thus into loan capital. All revenue—whether it be intended for consumption or accumulation—as long as it exists in some form of money, is a part of the value of commodity-capital transformed into money, and is, for this reason, an expression and result of actual accumulation, but is not productive capital itself. When a spinner has exchanged his yarn for cotton—that portion which constitutes revenue however for money, the real existence of his industrial capital is the yarn, which has passed into the hands of the weaver or, perhaps, of some private consumer, and the yarn is, in fact, the existence—whether it is for reproduction or consumption—of the capital-value as well as the surplus-value contained in it. The magnitude of the surplus-value transformed into money depends upon the magnitude of the surplus-value contained in the yarn. But as soon as it has been transformed into money, this money is only the value existence of this surplus-value. And as such it becomes a moment of loan capital. For this purpose, nothing more is required than that it be transformed into a deposit, if it has not already been loaned out by its owner. But in order to be retransformed into productive capital, it must, on the other hand, already have reached a certain minimum limit.

32

Money Capital and Real Capital III

The mass of money to be transformed back into capital in this manner is a result of the enormous reproduction process, but considered by itself, as loanable money-capital, it is not itself a mass of reproductive capital.

The most important point of our presentation so far is that the expansion of the part of the revenue intended for consumption (leaving out of consideration the worker, because his revenue is equal to the variable capital) shows itself at first as an accumulation of money-capital. A factor, therefore, enters into the accumulation of money-capital that is essentially different from the actual accumulation of industrial capital; for the portion of the annual product which is intended for consumption does not by any means become capital. A portion of it *replaces* capital, *i.e.*, the constant capital of the producers of means of consumption, but to the extent that it is actually transformed into capital, it exists in the natural form of the revenue of the producers of this constant capital. The same money, which represents the revenue and serves merely for the promotion of consumption, is regularly transformed into loanable money-capital for a period of time. In so far as this money represents wages, it is at the same time the money-form of the variable capital; and in so far as it replaces the constant capital of the producers of means of consumption, it is the money-form temporarily assumed by their constant capital and serves to purchase the components of their constant capital to be replaced in kind. Neither in the one nor in the other form does it express in itself accumulation, although its quantity increases with the growth of the reproduction process. But it performs temporarily the function of loanable money, *i.e.*, of money-capital. In this respect, therefore, the accumulation of money-capital must always reflect a greater accumulation of capital than actually exists, owing to the fact that the extension of individual consumption, because it is promoted by means of money, appears as an accumulation of money-capital, since it furnishes the money-form for actual accumulation, *i.e.*, for money which permits new investments of capital.

Thus, the accumulation of loanable money-capital expresses in part only the fact that all money into which industrial capital is transformed in the course of its circuit assumes the form not of money *advanced* by the reproductive capitalists, but of money *borrowed* by them; so that indeed the advance of money that must take place in the reproduction process appears as an advance of borrowed money. In fact, on the basis of commercial credit, one person lends to another the money required for the reproduction process. But this now assumes the following form: the banker, who receives the money as a loan from one group of the reproductive capitalists, lends it to another group of reproductive capitalists, so that the banker appears in the role of a supreme benefactor; and at the same time, the control over this capital falls completely into the hands of the banker in his capacity as middleman.

A few special forms of accumulation of money-capital still remain to be mentioned. For example, capital is released by a fall in the price of the elements of production, raw materials, etc. If the industrial capitalist cannot expand his reproduction process immediately, a portion of his money-capital is expelled from the circuit as superfluous and is transformed into loanable money-capital. Secondly, however, capital in the form of money is released especially by the merchant, whenever interruptions in his business take place. If the merchant has completed a series of transactions and cannot begin a new series because of such interruptions until later, the money realised represents for him only a hoard, surplus-capital. But at the same time, it represents a direct accumulation of loanable money-capital. In the first case, the accumulation of money-capital expresses a repetition of the reproduction process under more favourable conditions, an actual release of a portion of formerly tied-up capital; in other words, an opportunity for expanding the reproduction process with the same amount of money. But in the other case, it expresses merely an interruption in the flow of transactions. However, in both cases it is converted into loanable money-capital, represents its accumulation, influences equally the money-market and the rate of interest—although it expresses a promotion of the actual accumulation process in one case and its obstruction in the other. Finally, accumulation of money-capital is influenced by the number of people who have feathered their nests and have withdrawn from reproduction. Their number increases as more profits are made in the course of the industrial cycle. In this case, the accumulation of loanable money-capital expresses, on the one hand, an actual accumulation (in accordance with its relative extent), and, on the other hand, only the extent of the transformation of the industrial capitalists into mere money-capitalists.

As for the other portion of profit, which is not intended to be consumed as revenue, it is converted into money-capital only when it is not immediately able to find a place for investment in the expansion of business in the productive sphere in which it has been made. This may be due to two causes. Either because this sphere of production is saturated with capital, or because accumulation must first reach a certain volume before it can serve as capital, depending on the investment magnitudes of new capital required in this particular sphere. Hence it is converted for a while into loanable money-capital and serves in the expansion of production in other spheres. Assuming all other conditions being equal, the quantity of profits intended for transformation back into capital will depend on the quantity of profits made and thus on the extension of the reproduction process itself. But if this new accumulation meets with difficulties in its employment, through a lack of spheres for investment, *i.e.*, due to a surplus in the branches of production and an over-supply of loan capital, this plethora of loanable money-capital merely shows the limitations of *capitalist* production. The subsequent credit swindle proves that no real obstacle stands in the way of the employment of this surplus-capital. However, an obstacle is indeed immanent in its laws of expansion, *i.e.*, in the limits in which capital can realise itself as capital. A plethora of money-capital as such does not necessarily indicate over-production, not even a shortage of spheres of investment for capital.

The accumulation of loan capital consists simply in the fact that money is precipitated as loanable money. This process is very different from an actual transformation into capital; it is merely the accumulation of money in a form in which it can be transformed into capital. But this accumulation can reflect, as we have shown, events which are greatly different from actual accumulation. As long as actual accumulation is continually expanding, this extended accumulation of money-capital may be partly its result, partly the result of circumstances which accompany it but are quite different from it, and, finally, even partly the result of impediments to actual accumulation. If for no other reason than that accumulation of loan capital is inflated by such circumstances, which are independent of actual accumulation but nevertheless accompany it, there must be a continuous plethora of money-capital in definite phases of the cycle and this plethora must develop with the expansion of credit. And simultaneously with it, the necessity of driving the production process beyond its capitalistic limits must also develop: over-trade, over-production, and excessive credit. At the same time, this must always take place in forms that call forth a reaction.

As far as accumulation of money-capital from ground-rent, wages, etc., is concerned, it is not necessary to discuss that matter here. Only one aspect should be emphasised and that is that the business of actual saving and abstinence (by hoarders), to the extent that it furnishes elements of accumulation, is left by the division of labour, which comes with the progress of capitalist production, to those who receive the minimum of such elements, and who frequently enough lose even their savings, as do the labourers when banks fail. On the one hand, the capital of the industrial capitalist is not 'saved' by himself, but he has command of the savings of others in proportion to the magnitude of his capital; on the other hand, the money-capitalist makes of the savings of others his own capital, and of the credit, which the reproductive capitalists give to one another and which the public gives to them, a private source for enriching himself. The last illusion of the capitalist system, that capital is the fruit of one's own labour and savings, is thereby destroyed. Not only does profit consist in the appropriation of other people's labour, but the capital, with which this labour of others is set in motion and exploited, consists of other people's property, which the money-capitalist places at the disposal of the industrial capitalists, and for which he in turn exploits the latter.

A few remarks remain to be made about credit capital.

How often the same piece of money can figure as loan capital, wholly depends, as we have already previously shown, on:

1. how often it realises commodity-values in sale or payment, thus transfers capital, and furthermore how often it realises revenue. How often it gets into other hands as realised value, either of capital or of revenue, obviously depends, therefore, on the extent and magnitude of the actual transactions;
2. this depends on the economy of payments and the development and organisation of the credit system;
3. finally, the concatenation and velocity of action of credits, so that when a deposit is made at one point it immediately starts off as a loan at another.

Even assuming that the form in which loan capital exists is exclusively that of real money, gold or silver—the commodity whose substance serves as a measure of value—a large portion of this money-capital is always necessarily purely fictitious, that is, a title to value—just as paper money. In so far as money functions in the circuit of capital, it constitutes indeed, for a moment, money-capital; but it does not transform itself into loanable money-capital; it is rather exchanged for the elements of productive capital, or paid out as a medium of circulation in the realisation of revenue, and cannot, therefore, transform itself into loan capital for its owner. But in so far as it is transformed into loan capital, and the same money repeatedly represents loan capital, it is evident that it exists only at one point in the form of metallic money; at all other points it exists only in the form of claims to capital. With the assumption made, the accumulation of these claims arises from actual accumulation, that is, from the transformation of the value of commodity-capital, etc., into money; but nevertheless the accumulation of these claims or titles as such differs from the actual accumulation from which it arises, as well as from the future accumulation (the new production process), which is promoted by the lending of this money.

Prima facie loan capital always exists in the form of money,[1] later as a claim to money, since the money in which it originally exists is now in the hands of the borrower in actual money-form. For the lender it has been transformed into a claim to money, into a title of ownership. The same mass of actual money can, therefore, represent very different masses of money-capital. Mere money, whether it represents realised capital or realised revenue, becomes loan capital through the simple act of lending, through its transformation into a deposit, if we consider the general form in a developed credit system. The deposit is money-capital for the depositor. But in the hands of the banker it may be only potential money-capital, which lies idle in his safe instead of in its owner's.[2]

With the growth of material wealth the class of money-capitalists grows; on the one hand, the number and the wealth of retiring capitalists, rentiers, increases; and on the other hand, the development of the credit system is promoted, thereby increasing the number of bankers, money-lenders, financiers, etc. With the development of the available money-capital, the quantity of interest-bearing paper, government securities, stocks, etc., also grows as we have previously shown. However, at the same time the demand for available money-capital also grows, the jobbers, who speculate with this paper, playing a prominent role on the money-market. If all the purchases and sales of this paper were only an expression of actual investments of capital, it would be correct to say that they could have no influence on the demand for loan capital, since when A sells his paper, he draws exactly as much money as B puts into the paper. But even if the paper itself exists though not the capital (at least not as money-capital) originally represented by it, it always creates *pro tanto* a new demand for such money-capital. But at any rate it is then money-capital, which was previously at the disposal of B but is now at the disposal of A.

> B. A. 1857. No. 4886. 'Do you consider that it is a correct description of the causes which determined the rate of discount, to say that it is fixed by the quantity of capital on the market, which is applicable to the discount of mercantile bills, as distinguished from other classes of securities?'—[Chapman:] 'No, I think that the question of interest is affected by all convertible securities of a current character; it would be wrong to limit it simply to the discount of bills, because it would be absurd to say that when there is a great demand for money upon [the deposit of] consols, or even upon Exchequer bills, as has ruled very much of late, at a rate much higher than the commercial rate, our commercial world is not affected by it; it is very materially affected by it.'—'4890. When sound and current securities, such as bankers acknowledge to be so, are on the market, and people want to borrow money upon them, it certainly has its effect upon commercial bills; for instance, I can hardly expect a man to let me have money at 5% upon commercial bills, if he can lend his money at the same moment at 6% upon consols, or whatever it may be; it affects us in the same manner; a man can hardly expect me to discount bills at 5½%, if I can lend my money at 6%.'—'4892. We do not talk of investors who buy their £2,000, or £5,000, or £40,000, as affecting the money-market materially. If you ask me as to the rate of interest upon [a deposit of] consols, I allude to people, who deal in hundreds of thousands of pounds, who are what are called jobbers, who take large portions of loans, or make purchases on the market, and have

to hold that stock till the public take it off their hands at a profit; these men, therefore, want money.'

With the development of the credit system; great concentrated money-markets are created, such as London, which are at the same time the main seats of trade in this paper. The bankers place huge quantities of the public's money-capital at the disposal of this unsavoury crowd of dealers, and thus this brood of gamblers multiplies.

'Money upon the Stock Exchange is, generally speaking, cheaper than it is elsewhere,' says James Morris the incumbent of the Governor's chair of the Bank of England in 1848 before the Secret Committee of Lords (C. D. 1848, printed 1857, No. 219).

In the discussion on interest-bearing capital, we have already shown that the average interest over a long period of years, other conditions remaining equal, is determined by the average rate of profit; not profit of enterprise, which is nothing more than profit minus interest. [Present edition: Ch. XXII.—*Ed.*]

It has also been mentioned, and will be further analysed in another place, that also for the variations in commercial interest, that is, interest calculated by the money-lenders for discounts and loans within the commercial world, a phase is reached, in the course of the industrial cycle, in which the rate of interest exceeds its minimum and reaches its mean level (which it exceeds later) and that this movement is a result of a rise in profits.

In the meantime, two things are to be noted here.

First: When the rate of interest stays up for a long time (we are speaking here of the rate of interest in a given country like England, where the average rate of interest is given over a lengthy period of time, and also shows itself in the interest paid on long-term loans—what could be called private interest), it is *prima facie* proof that the rate of profit is high during this period, but it does not prove necessarily that the rate of profit of enterprise is high. This latter distinction is more or less removed for capitalists, who operate mainly with their own capital; they realise the high rate of profit, since they pay the interest to themselves. The possibility of a high rate of interest of long duration is present when the rate of profit is high; this does not refer, however, to the phase of actual squeeze. But it is possible that this high rate of profit may leave only a low rate of profit of enterprise, after the high rate of interest has been deducted. The rate of profit of enterprise may shrink, while the high rate of profit continues. This is possible because the enterprises must be continued, once they have been started. During this phase, operations are carried on to a large extent with pure credit capital (capital of other people); and the high rate of profit may be partly speculative and prospective. A high rate of interest can be paid with a high rate of profit but decreasing profit of enterprise. It can be paid (and this is done in part during times of speculation), not out of the profit, but out of the borrowed capital itself, and this can continue for a while.

Secondly: The statement that the demand for money-capital, and therefore, the rate of interest, grows, because the rate of profit is high, is not identical with the statement that the demand for industrial capital grows and, therefore, the rate of interest is high.

In times of crisis, the demand for loan capital, and therefore, the rate of interest, reaches its maximum; the rate of profit, and with it the demand for industrial capital, has to all intents and purposes disappeared. During such times, everyone borrows only for the purpose of paying, in order to settle previously contracted obligations. On the other hand, in times of renewed activity after a crisis, loan capital is demanded for the purpose of buying and for the purpose of transforming money-capital into productive or commercial capital. And then it is demanded either by the industrial capitalist or the merchant. The industrial capitalist invests it in means of production and in labour-power.

The rising demand for labour-power can never by itself be a cause for a rising rate of interest, in so far as the latter is determined by the rate of profit. Higher wages are never a cause for higher profits, although they may be one of the consequences of higher profits during some particular phases of the industrial cycle.

The demand for labour-power can increase because the exploitation of labour takes place under especially favourable circumstances, but the rising demand for labour-power, and thus for variable capital, does not in itself increase the profit; it, on the contrary, lowers it *pro tanto.* But the demand for variable capital can nevertheless increase at the same time, thus also the demand for money-capital—which can raise the rate of interest. The market-price of labour-power then rises above its average, more than the average number of labourers are employed, and the rate of interest rises at the same time because under such circumstances the demand for money-capital rises. The rising demand for labour-power raises the price of this commodity, as every other, increases its price; but not the profit, which depends mainly upon the relative cheapness of this commodity in particular. But it raises at the same time—under the assumed conditions—the rate of interest, because it increases the demand for money-capital. If the money-capitalist, instead of lending the money, should transform himself into an industrial capitalist, the fact that he has to pay more for labour-power would not increase his profit but would rather decrease it correspondingly. The state of business may be such that his profit may nevertheless rise, but it would never be so because he pays more for labour. The latter circumstance, in so far as it increases the demand for money-capital, is, however, sufficient to raise the rate of interest. If wages should rise for some reason during an otherwise unfavourable state of business, the rise in wages would lower the rate of profit, but raise the rate of interest to the extent that it increased the demand for money-capital.

Leaving labour aside, the thing called 'demand for capital' by Overstone consists only in a demand for commodities. The demand for commodities raises their price, either because it rises above average, or because the supply of commodities falls below average. If the industrial capitalist or merchant must now pay, *e.g.*, £150 for the same amount of commodities for which he used to pay £100, he would now have to borrow £150 instead of the former £100, and if the rate of interest were 5%, he would now have to pay an interest of £7½ as compared with £5 formerly. The amount of interest to be paid by him would rise because he now has to borrow more capital.

The whole endeavour of Mr Overstone consists in representing the interests of loan capital and industrial capital as being identical, whereas his Bank Act is precisely calculated to exploit this very difference of interests to the advantage of money-capital.

It is possible that the demand for commodities, in case their supply has fallen below average, does not absorb any more money-capital than formerly. The same sum, or perhaps a smaller one, has to be paid for their total value, but a smaller quantity of use-values is received for the same sum. In this case, the demand for loanable capital will be unchanged, and therefore rate of interest will not rise, although the demand for commodities would have risen as compared to their supply, and consequently, the price of commodities would have become higher. The rate of interest cannot be affected, unless the total demand for loan capital increases, and this is not the case under the above assumptions.

The supply of an article can also fall below average, as it does when crop failures in corn, cotton, etc., occur; and the demand for loan capital can increase because speculation in these commodities counts on further rise in prices and the easiest way to make them rise is to temporarily withdraw a portion of the supply from the market. But in order to pay for the purchased commodities without selling them, money is secured by means of the commercial 'bill of exchange operations.' In this case, the demand for loan capital increases, and the rate of interest can rise as a result of this attempt to artificially prevent the supply of this commodity from reaching the market. The higher rate of interest then reflects an artificial reduction in the supply of commodity-capital. On the other hand, the demand for an article can grow because its supply has increased and the article sells below its average price.

In this case, the demand for loan capital can remain the same, or even fall, because more commodities can be had for the same sum of money. Speculative stock-piling could also occur, either for the purpose of taking advantage of the most favourable moment for production purposes, or in expectation of a future rise in prices. In this case, the demand for loan capital could grow, and the rise in the rate of interest would then be a reflection of capital investment in surplus stock-piling of elements of productive capital. We are only considering here the demand for loan capital as it is influenced by the demand for, and supply of, commodity-capital. We have already discussed how the varying state of the reproduction process in the phases of the industrial cycle influences the supply of loan capital. The trivial proposition that the market rate of interest is determined by the supply and demand of (loan) capital is shrewdly jumbled up by Overstone with his own postulate, namely, that loan capital is identical with capital in general; and in this way he tries to transform the usurer into the only capitalist and his capital into the only capital.

In times of stringency, the demand for loan capital is a demand for means of payment and nothing else; it is by no means a demand for money as a means of purchase. At the same time, the rate of interest may rise very high, regardless whether real capital, *i.e.*, productive and commodity capital, exists in abundance or is scarce. The demand for means of payment is a mere demand for convertibility into *money,* so far as merchants and producers have good securities to offer; it is a demand for *money-capital* whenever there is no collateral, so that an advance of means of payment gives them not only the *form of money* but also the *equivalent* they lack, whatever its form, with which to make payment. This is the point where both sides of the controversy on the prevalent theory of crises are at the same time right and wrong. Those who say that there is merely a lack of means of payment, either have only the owners of *bona fide* securities in mind, or they are fools who believe that it is the duty and power of banks to transform all bankrupt swindlers into solvent and respectable capitalists by means of pieces of paper. Those who say that there is merely a lack of capital, are either just quibbling about words, since precisely at such times there is a mass of *inconvertible* capital as a result of over-imports and over-production, or they are referring only to such cavaliers of credit who are now, indeed, placed in the position where they can no longer obtain other people's capital for their operations and now demand that the bank should not only help them to pay for the lost capital, but also enable them to continue with their swindles.

It is a basic principle of capitalist production that money, as an independent form of value, stands in opposition to commodities, or that exchange-value must assume an independent form in money; and this is only possible when a definite commodity becomes the material whose value becomes a measure of all other commodities, so that it thus becomes the general commodity, the commodity *par excellence*—as distinguished from all other commodities. This must manifest itself in two respects, particularly among capitalistically developed nations, which to a large extent replace money, on the one hand, by credit operations, and on the other by credit-money. In times of a squeeze, when credit contracts or ceases entirely, money suddenly stands as the only means of payment and true existence of value in absolute opposition to all other commodities. Hence the universal depreciation of commodities, the difficulty or even impossibility of transforming them into money, *i.e.*, into their own purely fantastic form. Secondly, however, credit-money itself is only money to the extent that it absolutely takes the place of actual money to the amount of its nominal value. With a drain on gold its convertibility, *i.e.*, its identity with actual gold becomes problematic. Hence coercive measures, raising the rate of interest, etc., for the purpose of safeguarding the conditions of this convertibility. This can be carried more or less to extremes by mistaken legislation, based on false theories of money and enforced upon the nation by the interests of the money-dealers, the Overstones and their ilk. The basis, however, is given with the basis of the mode of production itself. A depreciation of credit-money (not to mention, incidentally, a purely imaginary loss of its character as money) would unsettle all existing relations. Therefore, the value of commodities is sacrificed for the purpose of safeguarding the fantastic and independent existence of this value in money. As money-value, it is secure only as long as money is secure. For a few millions in money, many millions in commodities must therefore be sacrificed. This is inevitable under capitalist production and constitutes one of its beauties. In former modes of production, this does not occur because, on the narrow basis upon which they stand, neither credit nor credit-money can develop greatly. As long as the *social* character of labour appears as the *money-existence* of commodities, and thus as a *thing* external to actual production, money crises—independent of or as an intensification of actual crises—are inevitable. On the other hand, it is clear that as long as the credit of a bank is not shaken, it will alleviate the panic in such cases by increasing credit-money and intensify it by contracting the latter. The entire history of modern industry shows that metal would indeed be required only for the balancing of international commerce, whenever its equilibrium is momentarily disturbed, if only domestic production were organised. That the domestic market does not need any metal even now is shown by the suspension of the cash payments of the so-called national banks, which resort to this expedient in all extreme cases as the sole relief.

In the case of two individuals, it would be ridiculous to say that in their transactions with one another both have an unfavourable balance of payments. If they are reciprocally creditor and debtor of one another, it is evident that when their claims do not balance, one must be the creditor and the other the debtor for the balance. With nations this is by no means the case. And that this is not the case is acknowledged by all economists when they admit that the balance of payments can be favourable or unfavourable for a nation, though its trade balance must ultimately be settled. The balance of payments differs from the balance of trade in that it is a balance of trade which must be settled at a definite time. What the crises now accomplish is to narrow the difference between the balance of payments and the balance of trade to a short interval; and the specific conditions which develop in the nation suffering from a crisis and, therefore, having its payments become due—these conditions already lead to such a contraction of the time of settlement. First, shipping away precious metals; then selling consigned commodities at low prices; exporting commodities to dispose of them or to obtain money advances on them at home; increasing the rate of interest, recalling credit, depreciating securities, disposing of foreign securities, attracting foreign capital for investment in these depreciated securities, and finally bankruptcy, which settles a mass of claims. At the same time, metal is still often sent to the country where a crisis has broken out, because the drafts drawn on it are insecure and payment in specie is most trustworthy. Furthermore, in regard to Asia, all capitalist nations are usually simultaneously—directly or indirectly—its debtors. As soon as these various circumstances exert their full effect upon the other involved nation, it likewise begins to export gold and silver, in short, its payments become due and the same phenomena are repeated.

In commercial credit, the interest—as the difference between credit price and cash price—enters into the price of commodities only in so far as the bills of exchange have a longer than ordinary running time. Otherwise it does not. And this is explained by the fact that everyone takes credit with one hand and gives it with the other. [This does not agree with my experience.—*F.E.*] But in so far as discount in this form enters here, it is not regulated by this commercial credit, but by the money-market.

If supply and demand of money-capital, which determine the rate of interest, were identical with supply and demand of actual capital, as Overstone maintains, the interest would be simultaneously low and high, depending on whether various commodities or various phases (raw material, semi-finished product, finished product) of the same commodity were being considered. In 1844, the rate of interest of the Bank of England fluctuated between 4% (from January to September) and 2½ and 3% (from November to the end of the year). In 1845, it was 2½, 2¾, and 3% from January to October, and between 3 and 5% during the remaining months. The average price of fair Orleans cotton was 6¼d. in 1844 and 4 7/8d. in 1845. On March 3, 1844, the cotton supply in Liverpool was 627,042 bales, and on March 3, 1845, it was 773,800 bales. To judge by the low price of cotton, the rate of interest should have been low in 1845, and it was indeed for the greater part of this time. But to judge by the yarn, the rate of interest should have been high, for the prices were relatively high and the profits absolutely high. From cotton at 4d. per pound, yarn could be spun, in 1845 with a spinning cost of 4d. (good secunda mule twist No. 40), or a total cost of 8d. to the spinner, which he could sell in September and October 1845 at 10½ or 11½d. per pound. (See the testimony of Wylie below.)

The entire matter can be resolved as follows:

Supply and demand of loan capital would be identical with supply and demand of capital generally (although this last statement is absurd; for the industrial or commercial capitalist a commodity is a form of his capital, yet he never asks for capital as such, but only for the particular commodity as such, he buys and pays for it as a commodity, *e.g.*, corn or cotton, regardless of the role that it has to play in the circuit of his capital), if there were no money-lenders, and if in their stead the lending capitalists were in possession of machinery, raw materials, etc., which they would lend or hire out, as houses are rented out now, to the industrial capitalists, who are themselves owners of some of these objects. Under such circumstances, the supply of loan capital would be identical with the supply of elements of production for the industrial capitalist and commodities for the merchant. But it is clear that the division of profit between the lender and borrower would then, to begin with, completely depend on the relation of the capital which is lent to that which is the property of the one who employs it.

According to Mr Weguelin (B. A. 1857), the rate of interest is determined by 'the amount of unemployed capital' (252); it is 'but an indication of a large amount of capital seeking employment' (271); later this unemployed capital becomes 'floating capital' (485) and by this he means 'the Bank of England notes and other kinds of circulation in the country, for instance, the country banks circulation and the amount of coin which is in the country. I include in floating capital the reserves of the bankers' (502, 503), and later also gold bullion (503). Thus the same Mr Weguelin says that the Bank of England exerts great influence upon the rate of interest in times, when 'we' [the Bank of England] 'are holders of the greater portion of the unemployed capital' (1198), while, according to the above testimony of Mr Overstone, the Bank of England 'is no place for capital.' Mr Weguelin further says:

> 'I think the rate of discount is governed by the amount of unemployed capital which there is in the country. The amount of unemployed capital is represented by the reserve of the Bank of England, which is practically a reserve of bullion. When, therefore, the bullion is drawn upon, it diminishes the amount of unemployed capital in the country and consequently raises the value of that which remains' (1258).

J. Stuart Mill says (2102):

> 'The Bank is obliged to depend for the solvency of its banking department upon what it can do to replenish the reserve in that department; and therefore as soon as it finds that there is any drain in progress, it is obliged to look to the safety of its reserve, and to commence contracting its discounts or selling securities.'

The reserve, in so far as only the banking department is considered, is a reserve for the deposits only. According to the Overstones, the banking department is supposed to act only as a banker, without regard to the 'automatic' issue of notes. But in times of actual stringency the Bank, independently of the reserve of the banking department which consists only of notes, keeps a sharp eye on the bullion reserve, and must do so if it does not wish to fail. For, to the extent that the bullion reserve dwindles, so the reserve of banknotes also dwindles, and no one should be better informed of this than Mr Overstone, who precisely by his Bank Act of 1844 has so sagaciously arranged this.

Notes

1. B. A. 1857. Testimony of Twells, banker: '4516. As a banker, do you deal in capital or in money?—We deal in money.'—'4517. How are the deposits paid into your bank?—In money.'—'4518. How are they paid out?—In money.'—'4519. Then can they be called anything else but money?—No.'

   Overstone (see Chapter XXVI) confuses continually 'capital' and 'money.' 'Value of money' also means interest to him, but in so far as it is determined by the mass of money, 'value of capital' is supposed to be interest, in so far as it is determined by the demand for productive capital and the profit made by it. He says: '4140. The use of the word 'capital' is very dangerous.'—'4148. The export of bullion from this country is a diminution of the quantity of money in this country, and a diminution of the quantity of money in this country must of course create a pressure upon the money-market generally' [but not in the capital-market, according to this].—'4112. As the money goes out of the country, the quantity in the country is diminished. That diminution of the quantity remaining in the country produces an increased value of that money' [this originally means in his theory an increase in the value of money as such through a contraction of circulation, as compared to the values of commodities; in other words, an increase in the value of money is the same as a fall in the value of commodities. But since in the meantime even he has been convinced beyond peradventure that the mass of circulating money *does not* determine prices, it is now the diminution in money as a medium of circulation which is supposed to raise its value as interest-bearing capital, and thus the rate of interest]. 'And that increased value of what remains stops the exit of money, and is kept up until it has brought back that quantity of money which is necessary to restore the equilibrium.'—More of Overstone's contradictions later on.
2. At this point the confusion starts: both of these things are supposed to be 'money', namely, the deposit as a claim to payment from the banker, and the deposited money in the hands of the banker. Banker Twells, before the Banking Committee of 1857, offers the following example: 'If I begin business with £10,000, I buy with £5,000 commodities and put them into warehouse. I deposit the other £5,000 with a banker, to draw upon it and use it as I require it. I consider it still £10,000 capital to me, though £5,000 is in the shape of deposits or money' (4528).—This now gives rise to the following peculiar debate.—'4531. You have parted with your £5,000 of notes to somebody else?—Yes.'—'4532. Then he has £5,000 of deposits?-Yes.'—'4533. And you have £5,000 of deposits left?—Exactly.'—'4534. He has £5,000 in money, and you have £5,000 in money?—Yes.'—'4535. But it is nothing but money at last?—No.' This confusion is due partly to the circumstance that A, who has deposited £5,000, can draw on it and dispose of it as though he still had it. To that extent it serves him as potential money. However, in all cases in which he draws on it he destroys his deposit *pro tanto*. If he draws out real money, and his own money has already been lent to someone else, he is not paid with his own money, but with that of some other depositor. If he pays a debt to B with a cheque on his banker, and B deposits this cheque with his banker, and the banker of A also has a cheque on the banker of B, so that the two bankers merely exchange cheques, the money deposited by A has performed the function of money twice; first, in the hands of the one who has received the money deposited by A; secondly, in the hands of A himself. In the second function, it is a balancing of claims (the claim of A on his banker, and the claim of the latter on the banker of B) without using money. Here the deposit acts twice as money,

namely, as real money and then as a claim on money. Mere claims to money can take the place of money only by a balancing of claims.

33

The Medium of Circulation in the Credit System

> 'The great regulator of the velocity of the currency is credit. This explains why a severe pressure upon the money-market is generally coincident with a full circulation.' (*The Currency Theory Reviewed*, p. 65.)

This is to be taken in a double sense. On the one hand, all methods which save on medium of circulation are based upon credit. On the other hand, however, take, for example, a 500-pound note. A gives it to B on a certain day in payment for a bill of exchange; B deposits it on the same day with his banker; the latter discounts a bill of exchange with it on the very same day for C; C pays it to his bank, the bank gives it to the bill-broker as an advance, etc. The velocity with which the note circulates here, to serve for purchases and payments, is effected by the velocity with which it repeatedly returns to someone in the form of a deposit and passes over to someone else again in the form of a loan. The pure economy in medium of circulation appears most highly developed in the clearing house—in the simple exchange of bills of exchange that are due—and in the preponderant function of money as a means of payment for merely settling balances. But the very existence of these bills of exchange depends in turn on credit, which the industrialists and merchants mutually give one another. If this credit declines, so does the number of bills, particularly long-term ones, and consequently also the effectiveness of this method of balancing accounts. And this economy, which consists in eliminating money from transactions and rests entirely upon the function of money as a means of payment, which in turn is based upon credit, can only be of two kinds (aside from the more or less developed technique in the concentration of these payments): mutual claims, represented by bills of exchange or cheques, are balanced out either by the same banker, who merely transcribes the claim from the account of one to that of another, or by the various bankers among themselves.[1] The concentration of 8 to 40 million bills of exchange in the hands of one bill-broker, such as the firm of Overend, Gurney & Co., was one of the principal means of expanding the scale of such balancing locally. The effectiveness of the medium of circulation is increased through this economy in so far as a smaller quantity of it is required simply to balance accounts. On the other hand the velocity of the money flowing as medium of circulation (by which it is also economised) depends entirely upon the flow of purchases and sales, and on the chain of payments, in so far as they occur successively in money. But credit effects and thereby increases the velocity of circulation. A single piece of money, for instance, can effect only five moves, and remains longer in the hands of each individual as mere medium of circulation without credit mediating—when A, its original owner, buys from B, B from C, C from D, D from E, and E from F, that is, when its transition from one hand to another is due only to actual purchases and sales. But when B deposits the money received in payment from A with his banker and the latter uses it in discounting bills of exchange for C, C in turn buys from D, D deposits it with his banker and the latter lends it to E, who buys from F, then even its velocity as mere medium of circulation (means of purchase) is effected by several credit operations: B's depositing with his banker and the latter's discounting for C, D's depositing with his banker, and the latter's discounting for E; in other words through four credit operations. Without these credit operations, the same piece of money would not have performed five purchases successively in the given period of time. The fact that it changed bands without mediation of actual sales and purchases, through depositing and discounting, has here accelerated its change of hands in the series of actual transactions.

We have seen previously that one and the same bank-note can constitute deposits in several banks. Similarly, it can also constitute various deposits in the same bank. The banker discounts, with the note which A has deposited, B's bill of exchange, B pays C, and C deposits the same note in the same bank that issued it.

We have already demonstrated in the discussion of simple money circulation (Vol I, Ch. III, 2) that the mass of actual circulating money, assuming the velocity of circulation and economy of payments as given, is determined by the prices of commodities and the quantity of transactions. The same law governs the circulation of notes.

In the following table, the annual average number of notes of the Bank of England, in so far as they were in the hands of the public, are recorded, namely, the 5- and 10-pound notes, the 20- to 100-pound notes, and the larger denominations between 200 and 1,000 pounds sterling; also the percentages of the total circulation that each one of these groupings constitutes. The amounts are in thousands, *i.e.*, the last three figures are omitted.

Year	*£5-10 Notes*	*%*	*£20-100 Notes*	*%*	*£200-1,000 Notes*	*%*	*Total*
1844	9,263	45.7	5,735	28.3	5,253	26.0	20,241
1845	9,698	46.9	6,082	29.3	4,942	23.8	20,722
1846	9,918	48.9	5,778	28.5	4,590	22.6	20,286
1847	9,591	50.1	5,498	28.7	4,066	21.2	19,155
1848	8,732	48.3	5,046	27.9	4,307	23.8	18,085
1849	8,692	47.2	5,234	28.5	4,477	24.3	18,403
1850	9,164	47.2	5,587	28.8	4,646	24.0	19,398
1851	9,362	48.1	5,554	28.5	4,557	23.4	19,473
1852	9,839	45.0	6,161	28.2	5,856	26.8	21,856
1853	10,699	47.3	6,393	28.2	5,541	24.5	22,653
1854	10,565	51.0	5,910	28.5	4,234	20.5	20,709
1855	10,628	53.6	5,706	28.9	3,459	17.5	19,793
1856	10,680	54.4	5,645	28.7	3,323	16.9	19,648
1857	10,659	54.7	5,567	28.6	3,241	16.7	19,467

(B. A. 1858, p. XXVI.) The total sum of circulating banknotes, therefore, positively decreased from 1844 to 1857, although commercial business, as indicated by exports and imports, had more than doubled. The smaller banknotes of £5 and £10 increased, as the table shows, from £9,263,000 in 1844 to £10,659,000 in 1857. And this took place simultaneously with the particularly heavy increase in gold circulation at that time. On the other hand, there was a decrease in the notes of higher denominations (£200 to £1,000) from £5,856,000 in 1852 to £3,241,000 in 1857, *i.e.*, a decrease of more than £2½ million. This is explained as follows:

> 'On the 8th June 1854, the private bankers of London admitted the joint-stock banks to the arrangements of the clearing house, and shortly afterwards the final clearing was adjusted in the Bank of England. The daily clearances are now effected by transfers in the accounts which the several banks keep in that establishment. In consequence of the adoption of this system, the large notes which the bankers formerly employed for the purpose of adjusting their accounts are no longer necessary.' (B. A. 1858, p. V.)

To what small minimum the use of money in wholesale trade has been reduced, can be deduced from the table reprinted in Book I (Ch. III, Footnote), which was presented to the Bank Committee by Morrison, Dillon & Co., one of the largest of those London firms from which a small dealer can buy his entire assortment of commodities.

According to the testimony of W. Newmarch before the Bank Committee 1857, No. 1741, other circumstances also contributed to economy in the circulating medium: penny postage, railways, telegraphy, in short, the improved means of communication; thus England can now carry on five to six times more business with about the same circulation of banknotes. This is also essentially due to the withdrawal from circulation of notes of higher denomination than £10. Here Newmarch sees a natural explanation for the phenomenon that in Scotland and Ireland, where one-pound notes also circulate, note circulation has risen by about 31% (1747). The total circulation of banknotes in the United Kingdom, including one-pound notes, is said to be £39 million (1749). The gold circulation, £70 million (1750). In Scotland, the circulation of notes was £3,120,000 in 1834; £3,020,000 in 1844; and £4,050,000 in 1854 (1752).

From these figures alone, it is evident that banks issuing notes can by no means increase the number of circulating notes at will, as long as these notes are at all times exchangeable for money. [Inconvertible paper money is not considered here at all; inconvertible banknotes can become a universal medium of circulation only where they are actually backed by state credit, as is the case in Russia at present. They then fall under the laws of inconvertible paper money issued by the state, which have already been developed in Book I (Ch. III, 2, c) 'Coin and Symbols of Value.'—*F.E.*]

The quantity of circulating notes is regulated by the turnover requirements, and every superfluous note wends its way back immediately to the issuer. Since in England only the notes of the Bank of England circulate universally as legal means of payment, we can disregard at this point the insignificant, and merely local, note circulation of the country banks.

Before the Bank Committee 1858, Mr Neave, Governor of the Bank of England, testifies:

> 'No. 947. (Question:) Whatever measures you resort to, the amount of notes with the public, you say, remains the same; that is somewhere about £20,000,000?—In ordinary times, the uses of the public seem to want about £20,000,000. There are special periodical moments when, through the year, they rise to another £1,000,000 or £1,500,000. I stated that, if the public wanted more, they could always take it from the Bank of England.'—'948. You stated that during the panic the public would not allow you to diminish the amount of notes; I want you to account for that.—In moments of panic, the public have, as I believe, the full power of helping themselves as to notes; and of course, as long as the Bank has a liability, they may use that liability to take the notes from the Bank.'—'949. Then there seems to be required, at all times, somewhere about £20,000,000 of legal tender?—£20,000,000 of notes with the public; it varies. It is £18,500,000, £19,000,000, £20,000,000, and so on; but taking the average, you may call it from £19,000,000 to £20,000,000.'

Testimony of Thomas Tooke before the Committee of Lords on Commercial Distress (C. D. 1848/57), No. 3094:

> 'The Bank has no power of its own volition to extend the amount of its circulation in the hands of the public; but it has the power of reducing the amount of the notes in the hands of the public, not however without a very violent operation.'

J. C. Wright, a banker for 30 years in Nottingham, having explained at length the impossibility for a country bank to be able to keep more notes in circulation than the public needs and wants, says about notes of the Bank of England (C. D. 1848/57), No. 2844:

> 'I am not aware that there is any check' (for note issue) 'upon the Bank of England, but any excess of circulation will go into the deposits and thus assume a different name.'

The same holds true for Scotland, where almost nothing but paper circulates, because there as well as in Ireland one-pound notes are also in use and 'the Scotch hate gold.' Kennedy, Director of a Scottish bank, declares that banks could not even contract their circulation of notes and

> 'conceives that so long as there are internal transactions requiring notes or gold to perform them, bankers must, either through the demands of their depositors or in one shape or another, furnish as much currency as those transactions require.... The Scottish banks can restrict their transactions, but they cannot control their currency.' (*Ibid.*, Nos. 3446, 3448.)

Similarly, Anderson, Director of the Union Bank of Scotland, states (*ibid.*, No. 3578):

> 'The system of exchanges between yourselves ' [among the Scottish banks] 'prevents any over-issue on the part of any one bank?—Yes; there is a more powerful preventive than the system of exchanges' [which has really nothing to do with this, but does indeed guarantee the ability of the notes of each bank to circulate throughout Scotland], 'the universal practice in Scotland of keeping a bank account; everybody who has any money at all has a bank account and puts in every day the money which he does not immediately want, so that at the close of the business of the day there is no money scarcely out of the banks except what people have in their pockets.'

The same applies to Ireland, as indicated in the testimony of the Governor of the Bank of Ireland, MacDonnell, and the Director of the Provincial Bank of Ireland, Murray, before the same Committee.

Note circulation is just as independent of the state of the gold reserve in the vaults of the bank which guarantees the convertibility of these notes, as it is of the will of the Bank of England.

> 'On September 18, 1846, the circulation of the Bank of England was £20,900,000 and the bullion in the Bank £16,273,000; and on April 5, 1847, the notes in circulation were £20,815,000 and the bullion £10,246,000.... It is evident that six million of gold were exported, without any contraction of the currency of the country.' (J. G. Kinnear, *The Crisis and the Currency*, London, 1847, p. 5.)

Of course, this applies only under present conditions prevailing in England, and even here only in so far as legislation does not decree a different relationship between the note issue and metal reserve.

Hence only the requirements of business itself exert an influence on the quantity of circulating money-notes and gold. To be noted here, in the first instance, are the periodic fluctuations, which repeat themselves annually regardless of the general condition of business, so that for the past 20 years

> 'the circulation is high in one month, and it is low in another month, and in a certain other month occurs a medium point.' (Newmarch, B. A. 1857, No. 1650.)

Thus, in August of every year a few millions, generally in gold, pass from the Bank of England into domestic circulation to pay the harvest expenses; since wages are the principal payments to be made here, banknotes are less serviceable in England for this purpose. By the close of the year this money has streamed back to the Bank. In Scotland, there are almost nothing but one-pound notes instead of sovereigns; here, then, the note circulation is expanded in the corresponding situation, namely, twice a year—in May and November—

from 3 million to 4 million; after a fortnight the return flow begins, and is almost completed in one month. (Anderson, C. D. 1848/57, Nos. 3595-3600.)

The note circulation of the Bank of England also experiences a momentary fluctuation every three months because of the quarter]y payment of 'dividends,' that is, interest on the national debt, whereby banknotes are first withdrawn from circulation and then again released to the public; but they flow back very soon again. Weguelin (B. A. 1857, No. 38) states that this fluctuation in the note circulation amounts to 2½. Mr Chapman of the notorious firm of Overend, Gurney & Co., however, estimates the amount of disturbance thus created in the money-market as being much higher.

> 'When you abstract from the circulation £6,000,000 or £7,000,000 of revenue in anticipation of dividends, somebody must be the medium of supplying that in the intermediate times.' (B. A. 1857, No. 5196.)

Far more significant and enduring are the fluctuations in quantity of circulating medium corresponding to the various phases of the industrial cycle. Let us listen to another *associe* of that firm on this question, the esteemed Quaker Samuel Gurney (C. D. 1848/57, No. 2645):

> 'At the end of October (1847) the amount of banknotes in the hands of the public was £20,800,000. At that period there was great difficulty in getting possession of banknotes in the money-market. This arose from the alarm of not being able to get them in consequence of the restriction of the Act of 1844. At present [March 1848] the amount of banknotes in the hands of the public is ... £17,700,000, but there being now no commercial alarm whatsoever, it is much beyond what is required. There is no banking house or money-dealer in London, but what has a larger amount of banknotes than they can use.'—'2650. The amount of banknotes ... out of the custody of the Bank of England affords a totally insufficient exponent of the active state of the circulation, without taking into consideration likewise ... the state of the commercial world and the state of credit.'—'2651. The feeling of surplus that we have under the present amount of circulation in the hands of the public arises in a large degree from our present state of great stagnation. In a state of high prices and excitement of transaction £17,700,000 would give us a feeling of restriction.'

[As long as the state of business is such that returns of loans made come in regularly and credit thus remains unshaken, the expansion and contraction of circulation depend simply upon the requirements of industrialists and merchants. Since gold, at least in England, does not come into question in the wholesale trade and the circulation of gold, aside from seasonal fluctuations, may be regarded as rather constant over a long period of time, the note circulation of the Bank of England constitutes a sufficiently accurate measure of these changes. In the period of stagnation following a crisis, circulation is smallest; with the renewed demand, a greater need for circulating medium develops, which increases with rising prosperity; the quantity of circulating medium reaches its apex in the period of over-tension and over-speculation—the crisis precipitously breaks out and overnight banknotes which yesterday were still so plentiful disappear from the market and with them the discounters of bills, lenders of money on securities, and buyers of commodities. The Bank of England is called upon for help—but even its powers are soon exhausted, for the Bank Act of 1844 compels it to contract its note circulation at the very moment when the whole world cries out for notes; when owners of commodities cannot sell, yet are called upon to pay and are prepared for any sacrifice, if only they can secure banknotes.

> 'During an alarm,' says the earlier mentioned banker Wright (*loc. cit.*, No. 2930), 'the country requires twice as much circulation as in ordinary times, because the circulation is hoarded by bankers and others.'

Once the crisis has broken out, it becomes from then on only a question of means of payment. But since every one is dependent upon someone else for the receipt of these means of payment, and no one knows whether the next one will be able to meet his payments when due, a regular stampede ensues for those means of payment available on the market, that is, for banknotes. Everyone hoards as many of them as he can lay hand on, and thus the notes disappear from circulation on the very day when they are most needed. Samuel Gurney (C. D. 1848/57, No. 1116) estimates the amount of bank notes brought under lock and key in October 1847, at a time of such alarm, to have reached £4 to £5 million.—*F.E.*)

In this connection, the cross-examination of Chapman, Gurney's associate who has been previously mentioned, before the Bank Committee of 1857 is especially interesting. I present here its principal contents in context, although certain points are touched upon which we shall not examine until later.

Mr Chapman has the following to say:

> '4963. I have also no hesitation in saying that I do not think it is a proper condition of things that the money-market should be under the power of any individual capitalist (such as does exist in London), to create a tremendous scarcity and pressure, when we have a very low state of circulation out. That is possible ... there is more than one capitalist, who can withdraw from the circulating medium £1,000,000 or £2,000,000 of notes, if they have an object to attain by it.'—4965. [In the German 1894 edition this reads: 4995.—*Ed.*] A big speculator can sell £1,000,000 or £2,000,000 of consols and thus take the money out of the market. Something similar to this has happened quite recently, 'it creates a very violent pressure.'

4967. The notes are then indeed unproductive.

> 'But that is nothing, if it effects his great object; his great object is to knock down the funds, to create a scarcity, and he has it perfectly in his power to do so.'

An illustration: One morning there was a great demand for money in the Stock Exchange; nobody knew its cause; somebody asked Chapman to lend him £50,000 at 7%. Chapman was astonished, for his rate of interest was much lower; he accepted. Soon after that the man returned, borrowed another £50,000 at 7½%, then £100,000 at 8%, and wanted still more at 8½%. Then even Chapman became uneasy. Later it turned out that a considerable sum of money had been suddenly withdrawn from the market. But, says Chapman,

> 'I did lend a large sum at 8%; I was afraid to go beyond; I did not know what was coming.'

It must never be forgotten that, although £19 to £20 million in notes are almost constantly supposed to be in the hands of the public, nevertheless, the portion of these notes which actually circulates, and, on the other hand, the portion which is held idle by the banks as a reserve, continually and significantly vary with respect to each other. If this reserve is large, and therefore the actual circulation small, it means, from the point of view of the money-market, that the circulation is full, money is plentiful; if the reserve is small, and therefore the actual circulation full, in the language of the money-market the circulation is low, money is scarce—in other words, the portion representing idle loan capital is small. A real expansion or contraction of the circulation, that is independent of the phases of the industrial cycle—with the amount needed by the public, however, remaining the same—occurs only for technical reasons, for instance, on the dates when taxes or the interest on the national debt are due. When taxes are paid, more notes and gold than usual flow into the Bank of England and, in effect, contract the circulation without regard to its needs. The reverse takes place when the dividends on the national debt are paid out. In the former case, loans are made from the Bank in order to obtain circulating medium. In the latter case, the rate of interest falls in private banks because of the momentary growth of their reserves. This has nothing to do with the absolute quantity of circulating medium; it does, however, concern the banking firm which sets this circulating medium in motion and for which this process consists in the alienation of loan capital and for which it pockets the profits thereby.

In the one case, there is merely a temporary displacement of circulating medium, which the Bank of England balances by short-term loans at low interest shortly before the quarterly taxes and also before the quarterly dividends on the national debt become due; the issue of these supernumerary notes first fills up the gap caused by the payment of taxes, while their return payment to the Bank soon thereafter brings back the excess of notes obtained by the public through the payment of dividends.

In the other case, low or full circulation is always simply a matter of different distribution of the same quantity of circulating medium into active circulation and deposits, *i.e.*, an instrument of loans.

On the other hand, if, for example, the number of notes issued is increased on the basis of a flow of gold into the Bank of England, these notes assist in discounting bills outside of the Bank and return to it through the repayment of loans, so that the absolute quantity of circulating notes is only momentarily increased.

If the circulation is full because of business expansion (which may take place even though prices are relatively low), then the rate of interest can be relatively high because of the demand for loan capital as a result of rising profits and increased new investments. If it is low, because of business contraction, or perhaps because credit is very plentiful, the rate of interest can be low even though prices are high. (See Hubbard. Present edition: Ch. XXXIII.—*Ed*)

The absolute amount of circulation has a determining influence on the rate of interest only in times of stringency. The demand for full circulation can either reflect merely a demand for a hoarding medium (disregarding the reduced velocity of the money circulation and the continuous conversion of the same identical pieces of money into loan capital) owing to lack of credit, as was the case in 1847 when the suspension of the Bank Act did not cause any expansion of the circulation, but sufficed to draw forth the hoarded notes and to channel them into circulation; or it may be that more means of circulation are actually required under the circumstances, as was the case in 1857 when the circulation actually expanded for some time after the suspension of the Bank Act.

Otherwise, the absolute quantity of circulation has no influence whatever upon the rate of interest, since—assuming the economy and velocity of currency to be constant—it is determined in the first place by commodity-prices and the quantity of transactions (whereby one of these generally neutralises the effect of the other), and finally by the state of credit, whereas it by no means exerts the reverse effect upon the latter; and, secondly, since commodity-prices and interest do not necessarily stand in any direct correlation to each other.

During the life of the Bank Restriction Act (1797-1819) a surplus of currency existed and the rate of interest was always much higher than after the resumption of cash payments. Later, it fell rapidly with the restriction of the note issue and rising bill quotations. In 1822, 1823, and 1832, the general circulation was low, and so was the rate of interest. In 1824, 1825, and 1836, the circulation was full and the rate of interest rose. In the summer of 1830 the circulation was full and the rate of interest low. Since the gold discoveries, money circulation throughout Europe has expanded, and the rate of interest risen. Therefore, the rate of interest does not depend upon the quantity of circulating money.

The difference between the issue of circulating medium and the lending of capital is best demonstrated in the actual reproduction process. We have seen (Vol. II, Part III) in what manner the different component parts of production are exchanged for one another. For example, variable capital consists materially of the means of subsistence of the labourers, a portion of their own product. But this is paid out to them piecemeal in money. The capitalist has to advance this, and it is very greatly dependent on the credit system organisation whether he can pay out the new variable capital the following week with the old money which he paid out in the previous week. The same holds for exchange among various component parts of the total social capital, for instance, between means of consumption and means of production of means of consumption. The money for their circulation, as we have seen, must be advanced by one or both of the exchanging parties. It remains thereupon in circulation, but returns after the exchange has been completed to the one who advanced it, since it had been advanced by him over and above his actually employed industrial capital (Vol. II, Ch. XX). Under a developed system of credit, with the money concentrated in the hands of bankers, it is they, at least nominally, who advance it. This advance refers only to money in circulation. It is an advance of circulation, not an advance of capitals which it circulates.

> Chapman: '5062. There may be times, when the notes in the hands of the public, though they may be large, are not to be had. Money also exists during a panic; but everyone takes good care not to convert it into loanable capital, *i.e.*, loanable money; everyone holds on to it for the purpose of meeting real payment needs.'
>
> '5099. The country bankers in rural districts send up their unemployed balances to yourselves and other houses?—Yes.'—'5100. On the other hand, the Lancashire and Yorkshire districts require discounts from you for the use of their trades?—Yes.'—'5101. Then by that means the surplus money of one part of the country is made available for the demands of another part of the country?—Precisely so.'

Chapman states that the custom of banks to invest their surplus money-capital for short periods in consols and treasury notes has decreased considerably of late, ever since it has become customary to lend this money at call, *i.e.*, payable on demand. He personally considers the purchase of such paper for his business very impractical. He, therefore, invests his money in reliable bills of exchange, some of which become due every day, so that he always knows how much ready money he can count on from day to day. [5101 to 5105.]

Even the growth of exports expresses itself more or less for every country, but particularly for the country granting credit, as an increasing demand on the domestic money-market, which is not felt, however, until a period of stringency. When exports increase, British manufacturers usually draw long-term bills of exchange on the export merchants against consignments of British goods (5126).

> '5127. Is it not frequently the case that an understanding exists that those bills are to be redrawn from time to time?—[Chapman:] That is a thing which they keep from us; we should not admit any bill of that sort. ... I dare say it is done, but I cannot speak to a thing of the kind.' [The innocent Chapman.] '5129. If there is a large increase of the exports of the country, as there was last year, of £20 million, will not that naturally lead to a great demand for capital for the discount of bills representing those exports?—No doubt.'—'5130. Inasmuch as this country gives credit, as a general rule, to foreign countries for all exports, it would be an absorption of a corresponding increase of capital for the time being?—This country gives an immense credit; but then it takes credit for its raw material. We are drawn upon from America always at 60 days, and from other parts at 90 days. On the other hand we give credit; if we send goods to Germany, we give two or three months.'

Wilson inquires of Chapman (5131), whether bills of exchange on England are not drawn simultaneously with the loading of these imported raw materials and colonial goods and whether these bills of exchange do not arrive simultaneously with the bills of lading. Chapman believes so, but does not profess to know anything about such 'commercial' transactions and suggests that experts in this field be questioned.—In exporting to America, remarks Chapman, 'the goods are symbolised in transit' 5133; this gibberish is supposed to mean that the English export merchant draws against his commodities bills of exchange with a four-month term on one of the big American banking houses in London and this firm receives collateral from America.

> '5136. As a general rule, are not the more remote transactions conducted by the merchant, who waits for his capital until the goods are sold?—There may be houses of great private wealth, who can afford to lay out their own capital and not take any advance upon the goods; but the most part are converted into advances by the acceptances of some well-known established houses.'—'5137. Those houses are resident in ... London, or Liverpool, or elsewhere.'—'5138. Therefore, it makes no difference, whether the manufacturer lays out his money, or whether he gets a merchant in London or Liverpool to advance it; it is still an advance in this country?—Precisely. The manufacturer in few cases has anything to do with it' [but in 1847 in almost every case]. 'A man dealing in manufactured goods, for instance, at Manchester, will buy his goods and ship them through a house of respectability in London; when the London house is satisfied that they are all packed according to the understanding, he draws upon this London house for six months against these goods to India or China, or wherever they are going; then the banking world comes in and discounts that bill for him; so that, by the time he has to pay for those goods, he has the money all ready by the discount of that bill.'—'5139. Although he has the money, the banker is laying out of his money?—The *banker has the bill; the banker has bought the bill;* he uses his banking capital in that form, namely, in discounting commercial bills.'

[Hence even Chapman does not regard the discounting of bills as an advance of money, but as a purchase of commodities.—*F.E.*]

> '5140. Still that forms part of the demand upon the money-market in London?—No doubt; it is a substantial occupation of the money-market and of the Bank of England. The Bank of England are as glad to get these bills as we are, because they know them to be good property.'—'5141. In that way, as the export trade increases, the demand upon the money-market increases also?—As the prosperity of the country increases, we' [the Chapmans] 'partake of it.'—'5142. Then when these various fields for the employment of capital increase suddenly, of course, the natural consequence is that the rate of interest is higher?—No doubt about it.'
>
> In 5143 Chapman cannot 'quite understand, that under our large exports we have had such occasion for bullion.'

In 5144 the esteemed Wilson asks:

> 'May it not be that we give larger credits upon our exports than we take credits upon our imports?—I rather doubt that point myself. If a man accepts against his Manchester goods sent to India, you cannot accept for less than ten months. We have had to pay America for her cotton (that is perfectly true) some time before India pays us; but still it is rather refined in its operation.'—'5145. If we have had an increase, as we had last year, of £20 million in our exports of manufactures we must have had a very large increase of imports of raw material previously to that' [and in this way over-exports are already identified with over-imports, and over-production with over-trading], 'in order to make up that increased quantity of goods?—No doubt.'—'5146. We should have to pay a very considerable balance, that is to say, the balance, no doubt, would run against us during that time, but in the long run, with America ... the exchanges are in our favour, and we have been receiving for some time past large supplies of bullion from America.'

5148. Wilson asks the arch-usurer Chapman, whether he does not regard his high rate of interest as a sign of great prosperity and a high rate of profit. Chapman, evidently surprised at the naïveté of this sycophant, affirms this, of course, but has enough integrity to add the following:

> 'There are some, who cannot help themselves; they have engagements to meet, and they must fulfil them, whether it is profitable or not; but, for a continuance' [of the high rate of interest], 'it would indicate prosperity.'

Both forget that a high rate of interest can also indicate, as it did in 1857, that the country is undermined by the roving cavaliers of credit who can afford to pay a high interest because they pay it out of other people's pockets (whereby, however, they help to determine the rate of interest for all), and meanwhile they live in grand style on anticipated profits. Simultaneously, precisely this can incidentally provide a very profitable business for manufacturers and others. Returns become wholly deceptive as a result of the loan system. This also explains the following, which should require no explanation so far as the Bank of England is concerned, since it discounts at a lower rate than others when the interest rate is high.

> '5156. I should say,' says Chapman, 'that our discounts, taking the present moment, when we have had for so long a high rate of interest, are at their maximum.'

[Chapman made this statement on July 21, 1857, a couple of months before the crash.]

> '5157. In 1852' [when the interest rate was low] 'they were not nearly so large.'

For business was indeed a great deal sounder then.

> '5159. If there was a great flood of money in the market ... and the bank-rate low, we should get a decrease of bills ... In 1852 there was a totally different phase of things. The exports and imports of the country were as nothing then compared to the present.'—'5161. Under this high rate of discount our discounts are as large as they were in 1854.' [When the rate of interest was between 5 and 5½%.]

A very amusing part of Chapman's testimony reveals how these people really regard public money as their own and assume for themselves the right to constant convertibility of the bills of exchange discounted by them. The questions and replies show great naïveté. It becomes the obligation of legislation to make those bills which are accepted by large firms convertible at all time; to ensure that the Bank of England should under all circumstances continue to rediscount them for bill-brokers. And yet three of such bill-brokers went bankrupt in 1857, owing about 8 million and their own infinitesimally small capital compared with these debts.

> '5177. Do you mean by that that you think that they' [that is bills accepted by Barings or Loyds] 'ought to be discountable on compulsion, in the same way that a Bank of England note is now exchangeable against gold by compulsion?—I think it would be a very lamentable thing, that they should not be discountable; a most extraordinary position, that a man should stop payment, who had the acceptances of Smith, Payne & Co., or Jones, Loyd & Co. in his hands, because he could not get them discounted.'—'5178. Is not the engagement of Messrs. Baring an engagement to pay a certain sum of money when the bill is due?—That is perfectly true; but Messrs. Baring, when they contract that engagement, and every other merchant who contracts an engagement, never dream that they are going to pay it in sovereigns; they expect that they are going to pay it at the Clearing House.'—'5180. Do you think that there should be any machinery contrived by which the public would have a right to claim money before that bill was due by calling upon somebody to discount it?—No, not from the acceptor; but if you mean by that that we are not to have the possibility of getting

> commercial bills discounted, we must alter the whole constitution of things.'—'5182. Then you think that it' [commercial bill] 'ought to be convertible into money, exactly in the same way that a Bank of England note ought to be convertible into gold?—Most decidedly so, under certain circumstances.'—'5184. Then you think that the provisions of the currency should be so shaped that a bill of exchange of undoubted character ought at all times to be as readily exchangeable against money as a bank-note?—I do.'—'5185. You do not mean to say that either the Bank of England or any individual should, by law, be compelled to exchange it?—I mean to say this, that in framing a bill for the currency, we should make provision to prevent the possibility of an inconvertibility of the bills of exchange of the country arising, assuming them to be undoubtedly solid and legitimate.'

This is the convertibility of the commercial bill as compared with the convertibility of banknotes.

> '5190. The money-dealers of the country only, in point of fact, represent the public.'

As did Mr Chapman later before the court of assizes in the Davidson case. See the *Great City Frauds.* [S. Laing, *New Series of the Great City Frauds of Cole, Davison, and Cordon,* London.—*Ed.*]

> '5196. During the quarters' [when the dividends are paid] 'it is ... absolutely necessary that we should go to the Bank of England. When you abstract from the circulation £6,000,000 or £7,000,000 of revenue in anticipation of the dividends, somebody must be the medium of supplying that in the intermediate time.'

[In this case, it is then a question of a supply of money, not of capital or loan capital.]

> '5169. Everybody acquainted with our commercial circle must know that when we are in such a state that we find it impossible to sell Exchequer bills, when India bonds are perfectly useless, when you cannot discount the first commercial bills, there must be great anxiety on the part of those whose business renders them liable to pay the circulating medium of the realm on demand, which is the case with all bankers. Then the effect of that is to make every man double his reserve. Just see what the result of that is throughout the country, that every country banker, of whom there are about 500, has to send up to his London correspondent to remit him £5,000 in banknotes. Taking such a limited sum as that as the average, which is quite absurd, you come to £2,500,000 taken out of the circulation. How is that to be supplied?'

On the other hand, the private capitalists, etc., who have money do not let go of it at any interest, for they say after the manner of Chapman,

> '5195. We would rather have no interest at all, than have a doubt about our getting the money in case we require it.'
>
> '5173. Our system is this: That we have £300,000,000 of liabilities which may be called for at a single moment to be paid in the coin of the realm, and that coin of the realm, if the whole of it is substituted, amounts to £23,000,000, or whatever it may be; is not that a state which may throw us into convulsions at any moment?'

Hence the sudden change of the credit system into a monetary system during crises.

Aside from the domestic panic during crises, one can speak of the quantity of money only in so far as it concerns bullion, universal money. And this is precisely what Chapman excludes; he speaks only of 23 million in *banknotes.*

The same Chapman:

'5218. The primary cause of the derangement of the money-market' [in April and later in October 1847] 'no doubt was in the quantity of money which was required to regulate our exchanges, in consequence of the extraordinary importations of the year.'

In the first place, this reserve of world-market money had then been reduced to its minimum. Secondly, it served at the same time as security for the convertibility of credit-money, banknotes. It combined in this manner two quite different functions, both of which, however, stem from the nature of money, since real money is always world-market money, and credit-money always rests upon world-market money.

In 1847, without the suspension of the Bank Act of 1844,

'the clearing houses could not have been settled.' (5221.)

That Chapman had an inkling of the imminent crisis, after all:

'5236. There are certain conditions of the money-market (and the present is not very far from it), where money is exceedingly difficult, and recourse must he had to the Bank.'

'5239. With reference to the sums which we took from the Bank on the Friday, Saturday and Monday, the 19th, 20th, and 22nd of October, 1847, we should only have been too thankful to have got the bills back on the Wednesday following; the money reflowed to us directly the panic was over.'

On Tuesday, October 23, the Bank Act was suspended and the crisis was thus broken.

Chapman believes (5274) that the bills of exchange running simultaneously on London amount to £100 or £120 million. This does not include local bills made on provincial firms.

'5287. Whereas in October 1856, the amount of the notes in the hands of the public ran up to £21,155,000, there was an extraordinary difficulty in obtaining money; notwithstanding that the public held so much, we could not touch it.'

This was due to the fear caused by the squeeze in which the Eastern Bank found itself for a period of time (March 1856).

5290-92. As soon as the panic is over,

'all bankers deriving their profit from interest begin to employ the money immediately.'

5302. Chapman does not explain the uneasiness that exists when the bank reserve decreases as being due to apprehension concerning deposits, but rather that all those who suddenly may be compelled to pay large sums of money are well aware they may be driven to seek their last refuge in the bank when there is a stringency in the money-market; and

'if the banks have a very small reserve, they are not glad to receive us; but on the contrary.'

It is pretty, incidentally, to observe how the reserve as a real magnitude dwindles away. Bankers hold a minimum for current business needs either in their own hands or the Bank of England. Bill-brokers hold the 'loose bank money of the country' without any reserve. And the Bank of England has nothing to offset its liabilities for deposits but the reserves of bankers and others, together with some public deposits, etc., which it permits to drop to a very low level, for instance, to £2 million. Aside from these £2 million in paper, then, this whole swindle has absolutely no other reserve but the bullion reserve in times of stringency (and this reduces the reserve, because the notes which come in to replace outgoing bullion must be cancelled), and thus every reduction of this reserve by drain on gold increases the crisis.

'5306. If there should not be currency to settle the transactions at the clearing house, the only next alternative which I can see is to meet together, and to make our

> payments in first-class bills, bills upon the Treasury, and Messrs. Smith, Payne, and so forth.'—'5307. Then, if the government failed to supply you with a circulating medium, you would create one for yourselves?—What can we do? The public come in, and take the circulating medium out of our hands; it does not exist.'—'5308. You would only then do in London what they do in Manchester every day of the week?—Yes.'

Particularly clever is Chapman's reply to a question posed by Cayley (a Birmingham man of the Attwood school) regarding Overstone's conception of capital:

> '5315. It has been stated before this Committee, that in a pressure like that of 1847, men are not looking for money, but are looking for capital; what is your opinion in that respect?—I do not understand it; we only deal in money; I do not understand what you mean by it.'—'5316. If you mean thereby' [commercial capital] 'the quantity of money which a man has of his own in his business, if you call that capital, it forms, in most cases, a very small proportion of the money which he wields in his affairs through the credit which is given him by the public'—through the mediation of the Chapmans.

> '5339. Is it the want of property that makes us give up our specie payments?—Not at all.... It is not that we want property, but it is that we are moving under a highly artificial system; and if we have an immense superincumbent demand upon our currency, circumstances may arise to prevent our obtaining that currency. Is the whole commercial industry of the country to be paralysed? Shall we shut up all the avenues of employment?'—'5338. If the question should arise whether we should maintain specie payments, or whether we should maintain the industry of the country, I have no hesitation in saying which I should drop.'

Concerning the hoarding of banknotes 'with a view to aggravate the pressure and to take advantage of the consequences' he says that this can very easily occur. Three large banks would be sufficient.

> '5383. Must it not be within your knowledge, as a man conversant with the great transactions of this metropolis, that capitalists do avail themselves of these crises to make enormous profit out of the ruin of the people who fall victims to them?—There can be no doubt about it.'

And we may well believe Mr Chapman on this score, although he finally broke his own neck, commercially speaking, in an attempt at making 'enormous profit out of the ruin of victims.' For while his associate Gurney says: Every change in business is advantageous for one who is well informed, Chapman says:

> 'The one section of the community knows nothing of the other; one is the manufacturer, for instance; who exports to the continent, or imports his raw commodity; he knows nothing of the man who deals in bullion.' (5046.)

And thus it happened that one fine day Gurney and Chapman themselves 'were not well informed' and went into ill-famed bankruptcy.

We have previously seen that note issue does not in all cases signify an advance of capital. The following testimony by Tooke before the C. D. Committee of Lords, 1848, indicates merely that an advance of capital, even if accomplished by the bank through an issue of new notes, does not unqualifiedly signify an increase in the number of circulating notes:

> '3099. Do you think that the Bank of England for instance might enlarge its advances greatly, and yet lead to no additional issue of notes?—There are facts in abundance to prove it; one of the most striking instances was in 1835, when the Bank made use of the

West India deposits and of the loan from the East India Company in extended advances to the public. At that time the amount of notes in the hands of the public was actually rather diminished. And something like the same discrepancy is observable in 1846 at the time of the payment of the railway deposits into the Bank; the securities [in discount and deposits] were increased to about thirty million, while there was no perceptible effect upon the amount of notes in the hands of the public.'

Aside from banknotes, wholesale trade has another medium of circulation, which is far more important to it, namely, bills of exchange. Mr Chapman showed us how essential it is for the regular flow of business that good hills of exchange be accepted in payment everywhere and under all conditions.

'Gilt nicht mehr der Tausves Jontof, was soll gelten, Zeter, Zeter!' ['If the Tausves-Jontof's nothing, What is left? O vile detractor!'—Heine, *Disputation.*—Ed.]

How are these two media of circulation related to one another?

Gilbart writes on this score:

The reduction of the amount of the note circulation uniformly increases the amount of the bill circulation. These bills are of two classes—commercial bills and bankers' bills ... when money becomes scarce, the money-lenders say, 'draw upon us and we will accept'. And when a country banker discounts a bill for his customer, instead of giving him the cash, he will give him his own draft at twenty-one days upon his London agent. These bills serve the purpose of a currency. (J. W. Gilbart, *An Inquiry into the Causes of the Pressure, etc.*, p. 31.)

This is corroborated in somewhat modified form by Newmarch, B. A. 1857, No. 1426:

There is no connection between the variations in the amount of bill circulation and the variations in the bank-note circulation ... the only pretty uniform result is ...that whenever there is any pressure upon the money-market, as indicated by a rise in the rate of discount, then the volume of the bill circulation is very much increased, and vice versa.

However, the bills of exchange drawn at such times are by no means only the short-term bank-bills mentioned by Gilbart. On the contrary, they are largely bills of accommodation, which represent no real transaction at all, or simply transactions made for the sole purpose of drawing bills of exchange on them; we have presented sufficient illustrations of both. Hence the *Economist* (Wilson) says in comparing the security of such bills with that of banknotes:

'Notes payable on demand can never be kept out in excess, because the excess would always return to the bank for payment, while bills at two months may be issued in great excess, there being no means of checking the issue till they have arrived at maturity, when they may have been replaced by others. For a people to admit the safety of the circulation of bills payable only on a distant day, and to object to the safety of a circulation of paper payable on demand, is, to us, perfectly unaccountable.' *(Economist,* May 22, 1847, p. 575.)

The quantity of circulating bills of exchange, therefore, like that of banknotes, is determined solely by the requirements of commerce; in ordinary times, there circulated in the fifties in the United Kingdom, in addition to 39 million in banknotes, about 300 million in bills of exchange—of which 100-120 million were made out on London alone. The volume of circulating bills of exchange has no influence on note circulation and is influenced by the latter only in times of money tightness, when the quantity of hills increases and their quality deteriorates. Finally, in a period of crisis, the circulation of bills collapses completely; nobody can make use of a promise to pay since everyone will accept only cash payment; only the bank-note retains, at least thus far in England, its ability to circulate, because the nation with its total wealth backs up the Bank of England.

We have seen that even Mr Chapman, who after all was himself a magnate on the money-market in 1857, complains bitterly that there were several large money-capitalists in London strong enough to disrupt the whole money-market at any given moment and thereby bleed white the smaller money-dealers. There were several such money sharks, he said, who could considerably intensify a stringency by selling one or two million's worth of consols and thereby withdrawing an equal amount of banknotes (and simultaneously available loan capital) from the market. The joint action of three large banks would suffice to transform a stringency into a panic by a similar manoeuvre.

The largest capital power in London is, of course, the Bank of England, which, however, is prevented by its status as a semi-government institution from showing its domination in such a brutal manner. Nevertheless, it also knows enough about ways and means of feathering its nest, particularly since the Bank Act of 1844.

The Bank of England has a capital of £14,553,000, and in addition has at its disposal about £3 million 'balance,' that is, undistributed profits, as well as all money collected by the government for taxes, etc., which must be deposited with the Bank until it is needed. If we add to this the sum of other deposits, about £30 million in ordinary times, and the banknotes issued without reserve backing, we shall find that Newmarch made a rather conservative estimate in stating (B. A. 1857, No. 4889):

> 'I satisfied myself that the amount of funds constantly employed in the [London] money-market may be described as something like £420,000,000; and of that £120,000,000 a very considerable proportion, something like 15 or 20 per cent, is wielded by the Bank of England.'

In so far as the Bank issues notes which are not covered by the bullion reserve in its vaults, it creates symbols of value that constitute for it not only circulating medium, but also additional—even if fictitious—capital to the nominal amount of these unbacked notes. And this additional capital yields additional profit.—In B. A. 1857, Wilson questions Newmarch:

> '1563. The circulation of a banker, so far as it is kept out upon the average, is an addition to the effective capital of that banker, is it not?—Certainly.'—'1564. Then whatever profit he derives from that circulation is a profit derived from credit, and not from a capital which he actually possesses?—Certainly.'

The same is true, of course, for private banks issuing notes. In his replies Nos. 1866 to 1868, Newmarch considers two-thirds of all banknotes issued by them (the last third has to be covered by bullion reserve in these banks) as 'the creation of so much capital', because this amount of coin is saved. The profit of the banker as a result of this may not be larger than that of other capitalists. The fact remains that he draws the profit out of this national saving of coin. The fact that a national saving becomes a private profit does not shock the bourgeois economist in the least, since profit is generally the appropriation of national labour. Is there anything more absurd, for instance, than the Bank of England (1797 to 1817)—whose notes have credit only thanks to the state—taking payment from the state, *i.e.*, from the public, in the form of interest on government loans, for the power granted it by the state to transform these same notes from paper into money and then to lend it back to the state?

The banks, incidentally, have still other means of creating capital. Again according to Newmarch, the country banks, as mentioned above, are accustomed to send their superfluous funds (that is, Bank of England notes) to London bill-brokers, in return for discounted bills of exchange. With these bills of exchange, the bank serves its customers, since it follows a rule not to reissue bills of exchange received from its local customers, in order to prevent their business transactions from becoming known in their own neighbourhood. These bills received from London not only serve the purpose of being issued to customers who have to make direct payments in London, in the event they do not prefer to get the bank's own draft on London; they also serve to settle payments locally, since the banker's endorsement secures local credit for them. Thus, in Lancashire, for instance, all the local banks' own notes and a large portion of Bank of England notes have been pushed out of circulation by such bills. (*Ibid.*,1568 to 1574.)

Thus we see here how banks create credit and capital by 1) issuing their own notes, 2) writing out drafts on London running up to 21 days, but paid in cash to them immediately on issue, and 3) paying out discounted bills of exchange, which are endowed with credit primarily and essentially by endorsement through the bank—at least as far as concerns the local district.

The power of the Bank of England is revealed by its regulation of the market rate of interest. In times of normal activity, it may happen that the Bank cannot prevent a moderate drain of gold from its bullion reserve by raising the discount rate[2] because the demand for means of payment is satisfied by private banks, stock banks and bill-brokers, who have gained considerably in capital power during the last thirty years. In such case, the Bank of England must have recourse to other means. But the statement made by banker Glyn (of Glyn, Mills, Currie & Co.) before the C. D. 1848/57 still holds good for critical periods:

> '1709. Under circumstances of great pressure upon the country the Bank of England commands the rate of interest.'—'1740. In times of extraordinary pressure ... whenever the discounts of the private bankers or brokers become comparatively limited, they fall upon the Bank of England, and then it is that the Bank of England has the power of commanding the market rate.'

Nevertheless, the Bank of England, being a public institution under government protection and enjoying corresponding privileges, cannot exploit its power as ruthlessly as does private business. For this reason Hubbard remarks before the Banking Committee (B. A. 1857):

> '2844. [Question:] Is not it the case that when the rate of discount is highest, the Bank is the cheapest place to go, and that when it is the lowest, the bill-brokers are the cheapest parties?—[Hubbard:] That will always be the case, because the Bank of England never goes quite so low as its competitors, and when the rate is highest, it is never quite as high.'

But it is a serious event in business life nevertheless when, in time of stringency, the Bank of England puts on the screw, as the saying goes, that is, when it raises still higher the interest rate which is already above average.

> 'As soon as the Bank puts on the screw, all purchases for foreign exportation immediately cease ... the exporters wait until prices have reached the lowest point of depression; and then, and not till then, they make their purchases. But when this point has arrived, the exchanges have been rectified—gold ceases to be exported before the lowest point of depression has arrived. Purchases of goods for exportation may have the effect of bringing back some of the gold which has been sent abroad, but they come too late to prevent the drain.' (J. W. Gilbart, *An Inquiry into the Causes of the Pressure on the Money-Market*, London, 1840, p. 35.) 'Another effect of regulating the currency by the foreign exchanges is that it leads in seasons of pressure to an enormous rate of interest.' (*Loc. cit.*, p. 40.) 'The cost of rectifying the exchanges falls upon the productive industry of the country, while during the process the profits of the Bank of England are actually augmented in consequence of carrying on her business with a less amount of treasure.' (*Loc. cit.*, p. 52.)

But, says friend Samuel Gurney,

'The great fluctuations in the rate of interest are advantageous to bankers and dealers in money—all fluctuations in trade are advantageous to the knowing man.'

And even though the Gurneys skim off the cream by ruthlessly exploiting the precarious state of business, whereas the Bank of England cannot do so with the same liberty, nevertheless it also makes a very pretty profit—not to mention the personal profits falling into the laps of its directors, as a result of their exceptional opportunity for ascertaining the general state of business. According to data submitted to the Lords' Committee of 1817 when cash payments were resumed, these profits accruing to the Bank of England for the entire period from 1797 to 1817 were as follows:

Bonuses and increased dividends	7,451,136
New stock divided among proprietors	7,276,500
Increased value of capital	14,553,000
Total	29,280,636

This, on a capital of £11,642,400 over a period of 19 years. (D. Hardcastle, *Banks and Bankers,* 2nd ed., London, 1843, p. 120.) If we estimate the total gain of the Bank of Ireland, which also suspended cash payments in 1797, by the same method, we obtain the following result:

Dividends as by returns due 1821	4,736,085
Declared bonus	1,225,000
Increased assets	1,214,800
Increased value of capital	4,185,000
Total	11,360,885

This, on a capital of £3 million. (*Ibid.,* pp. 363-64.)

Talk about centralisation! The credit system, which has its focus in the so-called national banks and the big money-lenders and usurers surrounding them, constitutes enormous centralisation, and gives to this class of parasites the fabulous power, not only to periodically despoil industrial capitalists, but also to interfere in actual production in a most dangerous manner—and this gang knows nothing about production and has nothing to do with it. The Acts of 1844 and 1845 are proof of the growing power of these bandits, who are augmented by financiers and stock-jobbers.

Should anyone still doubt that these esteemed bandits exploit the national and world production solely in the interests of production and the exploited themselves, he will surely learn better from the following homily on the high moral worth of bankers:

> 'Banking establishments are ... moral and religious Institutions.... How often has the fear of being seen by the watchful and reproving eye of his banker deterred the young tradesman from joining the company of riotous and extravagant friends? ... What has been his anxiety to stand well in the estimation of his banker? ... Has not the frown of his banker been of more influence with him than the jeers and discouragements of his friends? Has he not trembled to be supposed guilty of deceit or the slightest misstatement, lest it should give rise to suspicion, and his accommodation be in consequence restricted or discontinued? ... And has not that friendly advice been of more value to him than that of priest?' (G. M. Bell, a Scottish bank director, in *The Philosophy of Joint Stock Banking,* London, 1840, pp. 46, 47.)

Notes

1. Average number of days during which a bank-note remained in circulation:

Year	*£5 Note*	*£10 Note*	*£20-100*	*£200-500*	*£1,000*
1792	?	236	209	31	22
1818	148	137	121	18	13
1846	79	71	34	12	8
1856	70	58	27	9	7

(Compilation by Marshall, Cashier of the Bank of England, in Report on Bank Act, 1857. Appendix II, pp. 300-01.)

2. At the general meeting of stockholders of the Union Bank of London on January 17, 1894, President Ritchie relates that the Bank of England raised the discount in 1893 from 2½% in July to 3 and 4% in August, and since it lost within four weeks fully £4½ million in gold despite this, it raised the bank-rate to 5%, whereupon gold flowed back to it and the bank rate was reduced to 4% in September and then to 3% in October. But this bank-rate was not recognised in the market. 'When the bank-rate was 5%, the discount rate was 3½%, and the rate for money 2½%; when the bank-rate fell to 4%, the discount rate was 2 3/8% and the money rate 1¾%; when the bank-rate was 3%, the discount rate fell to 1½% and the money rate to something below that.' *(Daily News,* January 18, 1894.)—*F.E.*

34

The Currency Principle and the English Bank Legislation of 1844

[In a former work, Ricardo's theory on the value of money as related to commodity-prices has been analysed; we can, therefore, confine ourselves here to the indispensable. According to Ricardo, the value of metallic money is determined by the labour-time incorporated in it, but only as long as the quantity of money stands in correct relationship to the amount and price of commodities to be exchanged. If the quantity of money rises above this ratio, its value falls and commodity-prices rise; if it fails below the correct ratio, its value rises and commodity-prices fall—assuming all other conditions equal. In the first case, the country in which this excess gold exists will export the gold whose value has depreciated and import commodities; in the second case, gold will flow to those countries in which it is assessed above its value, while the under-assessed commodities flow from these countries to other markets, where they command normal prices. Since under these circumstances

> 'gold itself may become, either as coin or bullion, a token of metallic value of greater or smaller magnitude than its own value, it is self-evident that convertible banknotes in circulation must share the same fate. Although banknotes are convertible, and therefore their real value corresponds to their nominal value, the aggregate currency consisting of metal and of convertible notes may appreciate or depreciate in accordance with its aggregate quantity, for reasons already stated, rising above or falling below the level determined by the exchange-value of circulating commodities and the metallic value of gold.... This depreciation, not of paper as compared with gold, but of gold and paper taken

together, or of the aggregate currency of a country, is one of Ricardo's principal discoveries which Lord Overstone and Co. pressed into their service and made a fundamental principle of Sir Robert Peel's bank legislation of 1844 and 1845.' (*Zur Kritik der Politischen Ökonomie*, p.155.)

We need not here repeat a demonstration of the incorrectness of this Ricardian theory which is given in the cited work. We are merely interested in the way Ricardo's theses were elaborated by that school of bank theorists who dictated Peel's above-mentioned Bank Acts.

> The commercial crises of the 19th century, especially the great crises of 1825 and 1836, did not result in any new developments in the Ricardian theory of money, but they did furnish new applications for it. These were no longer isolated economic phenomena, such as the depreciation of precious metals in the 16th and 17th centuries according to Hume, or the depreciation of paper money in the 18th and early 19th centuries according to Ricardo; these were instead the violent storms in the world-market wherein the conflict of all elements of the capitalist production process discharges itself, and whose origin and cure were sought in the most superficial and abstract sphere of this process, the sphere of money circulation. The actual theoretical assumption from which the school of economic weather prophets proceeds, is actually reduced to the dogma that Ricardo discovered the laws governing the purely metallic currency. The only thing remaining for them to do was to subordinate credit and bank-note circulation to these laws.
>
> The most general and palpable phenomenon in commercial crises is the sudden general decline in prices following a prolonged overall rise. The general decline in commodity-prices may be expressed as a rise in the relative value of money with respect to all commodities, and the general price rise as a decline in the relative value of money. In either expression the phenomenon is described but not explained.... The different wording leaves the problem as little changed as would its translation from German into English. Ricardo's theory of money was therefore exceedingly opportune, because it lends to a tautology the semblance of a statement of causal relationship. Whence comes the periodic general fall in commodity-prices? From the periodic rise of the relative value of money. Whence the general periodic rise in prices? From the periodic decline in the relative value of money. It might have been stated with equal truth that the periodic rise and fall of prices is due to their periodic rise and fall. ...Once the tautology is admitted as a causal relationship, the rest follows easily. A rise in commodity-prices is caused by a decline in the value of money and a decline in the value of money is caused, as we know from Ricardo, by an over-supply of currency, *i.e.*, a rise in the volume of currency over the level determined by its own intrinsic value and the intrinsic value of commodities. Similarly, a general decline in commodity-prices is explained by a rise in the value of money above its intrinsic value in consequence of under-supply of currency. Thus, prices rise and fall periodically, because there is periodically too much or too little money in circulation. Should a price rise happen to coincide with contracted money circulation, and a fall in prices with expanded circulation, it may be asserted despite this that the quantity of money in circulation has, though not absolutely, yet relatively increased or declined in consequence of a contraction or expansion of the volume of commodities in the market, even if this cannot be statistically proved. We have seen that according to Ricardo these general price fluctuations must take place even with a purely metallic currency, but that they alternatively balance one another; thus, *e.g.*, an under-supply of currency causes a fall in prices, the export of commodities abroad, but this export causes an import of gold from abroad, which in turn brings about a price rise; the opposite movement taking place in the case of an over-supply of currency, when commodities are imported and gold is exported. But, since despite these general

> price fluctuations which are in perfect accord with Ricardo's metallic currency, their turbulent and violent form, their crisis form, belongs to the period of developed credit system, it is crystal clear that the issue of banknotes is not exactly regulated by the laws of metallic currency. Metallic currency has its remedy in the import and export of precious metal, which immediately enters circulation as coin and thus, by its inflow or outflow, causes commodity-prices to fall or rise. The same effect on prices must now be exerted artificially by banks through imitating the laws of metallic currency. If gold is coming in from abroad it proves that currency is in under-supply, that the value of money is too high and commodity-prices too low, and, consequently, that banknotes must be put into circulation in proportion to the newly imported gold. On the other hand, notes must be withdrawn from circulation in proportion to the gold exported from the country. The issue of banknotes, in other words, must be regulated by the import and export of precious metal or by the rate of exchange. Ricardo's false assumption that gold is only coin, and, therefore, all imported gold swells the currency, causing prices to rise, while all exported gold reduces the currency, leading to a fall in prices—this theoretical assumption is here turned *into the practical experiment of putting an amount of coin in circulation equal in every case to the amount of gold available.* Lord Overstone (banker of Jones Loyd), Colonel Torrens, Norman, Clay, Arbuthnot and a host of other writers, known in England as advocates of the 'Currency Principle', have not only preached this doctrine, but succeeded in 1844 and 1845 with the aid of Sir Robert Peel's Bank Acts in making it the basis of English and Scottish bank legislation. Its ignominious failure, both theoretical as well as practical, following upon experiments on the broadest national scale, can be treated only in connection with the theory of credit. (*Loc. cit.*, pp. 165-68.)

The critique of this school was furnished by Thomas Tooke, James Wilson (in the *Economist* of 1844 to 1847) and John Fullarton. But we have seen on several occasions, particularly in Chapter XXVIII of this book, how incompletely they, too, saw through the nature of gold, and how unclear they were about the relationship of money and capital. We quote here merely a few instances in connection with the transactions of the Committee of the Lower House of 1857 concerning Peel's Bank Acts (B. C. 1857).—*F.E.*]

J. G. Hubbard, former Governor of the Bank of England, testifies:

> '2400. The effect of the export of bullion ... has no reference whatever to the prices of commodities. It has an effect, and a very important one, upon the price of interest-bearing securities, because, as the rate of interest varies, the value of commodities which embodied that interest is necessarily powerfully affected.'

He presents two tables covering the years 1834 to 1843, and 1845 to 1853, which show that the price variations of fifteen major commercial articles were quite independent of the export and import of gold and the interest rate. On the other hand, they show a close connection between the export and import of gold, which is, indeed, the 'representative of our uninvested capital,' and the interest rate.

> '[2402] In 1847, a very large amount of American securities were retransferred to America, and Russian securities to Russia, and other continental securities were transferred to those places from which we drew our supplies of grain.'

The fifteen major articles on which the following tables of Hubbard are based include cotton, cotton yarn, cotton fabrics, wool, woollen cloth, flax, linen, indigo, pig-iron, tin, copper, tallow, sugar, coffee, and silk.

I. 1834-1843

Date	*Bullion Reserve of Bank £*	*Market Rate of Discount**	*Price increase*	*Price Decrease*	*Unchanged*
1834, March 1	9,104,000	2¾%	–	–	–
1835, March 1	6,274,000	3¾%	7	7	1
1836, March 1	7,918,000	3¼%	11	3	1
1837, March 1	4,077,000	5%	5	9	1
1838, March 1	10,471,000	2¾%	4	11	–
1839, Sept. 1	2,684,000	6%	8	5	2
1840, June 1	4,571,000	4¾%	5	9	1
1840, Dec. 1	3,642,000	5¾%	7	6	2
1841, Dec. 1	4,873,000	5%	3	2	–
1842, Dec. 1	10,603,000	2½%	2	13	–
1843, June 1	11,566,000	2¼%	1	14	–

Price changes on 15 major items

II. 1844-1853

Date	*Bullion Reserve of Bank £*	*Market Rate of Discount*	*Price Increase*	*Price Decrease*	*Unchanged*
1844, March 1	16,162,000	2¼%	–	–	–
1845, Dec 1	13,237,000	4½%	11	4	–
1846, Sept. 1	16,366,000	3%	7	8	–
1847, Sept. 1	9,140,000	6%	6	6	3
1850, March 1	17,126,000	2½%	5	9	1
1851, June 1	13,705,000	3%	2	11	2
1852, Sept. 1	21,853,000	1¾%	9	5	1
1853, Dec. 1	15,093,000	5%	14	–	1

Price changes on 15 major items

Hubbard comments in this regard:

> As in the 10 years 1834-43, so in 1844-53, movements in the bullion of the Bank were invariably accompanied by a decrease or increase in the loanable value of money advanced on discount; and the variations in the prices of commodities in this country exhibit an entire independence of the amount of circulation as shown in the fluctuations in bullion at the Bank of England. (Bank Acts Report, 1857, II, pp. 290, 291)

Since the demand and supply of commodities regulate their market-prices, it becomes evident here how wrong Overstone is in identifying the demand for loanable money-capital (or rather the deviations of supply therefrom), as expressed by the discount rate, with the demand for actual 'capital.' The contention that commodity-prices are regulated by fluctuations in the quantity of currency is now concealed by the phrase that discount rate fluctuations express fluctuations in the demand for actual material capital, as distinct from money-capital. We have seen that before the same Committee, both Norman and Overstone actually contended this, and that the latter especially was compelled to resort to very lame subterfuges, until he was finally cornered (Chap. XXVI). It is indeed an old humbug that changes in the existing quantity of gold in a particular country must raise or lower commodity-prices within this country by increasing or decreasing the quantity of the medium of circulation. If gold is exported, then, according to this Currency Theory, commodity-prices must rise in the country importing this gold, and thereby the value of exports from the gold-exporting country on the gold-importing country's market; on the other hand, the value of the gold-importing country's exports would fall on the gold-exporting country's market while it would rise on the domestic market, *i.e.*, the country receiving the gold. But, in fact, a decrease in the quantity of gold raises only the interest rate, whereas an increase in the quantity of gold lowers the interest rate; and if not for the fact that the fluctuations in the interest rate enter into the determination of cost-prices, or in the determination of demand and supply, commodity prices would be wholly unaffected by them.

In the same report, N. Alexander, head of a large firm doing business with India, expresses the following views on the heavy drain of silver to India and China in the mid-fifties. This was partly due to the Chinese Civil War, which checked the sale of English fabrics in China, and partly due to the disease among silkworms in Europe, which sharply reduced silkworm breeding in Italy and France:

> '4337. Is the drain for China or for India?—You send the silver to India, and you buy opium with a great deal of it, all of which goes on to China to lay down funds for the purchase of the silk; and the state of the markets in India' (in spite of the accumulation of silver there) 'makes it a more profitable investment for the merchant to lay down silver than to send piece-goods or English manufactures.'—'4338. In order to obtain the silver, has there not been a great drain from France?—Yes, very large.'—'4344. Instead of bringing in silk from France and Italy, we are sending it there in large quantities, both from Bengal and from China.'

In other words, silver, the money metal of that continent, was sent to Asia instead of commodities, not because commodity-prices had risen in the country which produced them (England), but because prices had fallen, as a result of over-imports in the country which imported them; and this despite the fact that the silver was received by England from France and had to be paid for partly in gold. According to the Currency Theory, prices should have fallen in England and risen in India and China as a result of such imports.

Another illustration. Before the Lords' Committee (C. D. 1848/57), Wylie, one of the first Liverpool merchants, testifies as follows:

> '1994. At the close of 1845 there was no trade that was more remunerating, and in which there were such large profits [than cotton spinning]. The stock of cotton was large and good, useful cotton could be bought at 4d. per pound, and from such cotton good secunda mule twist No. 40 was made at an expense not exceeding a like amount, say at a cost of 8d. per pound in all to the spinner. This yarn was largely sold and contracted for in September and October 1845 at 10½ and 11½d. per pound, and in some instances the spinners realised a profit equal to the first cost of the cotton.'—'1996. The trade continued to be remunerative until the beginning of 1846.'—'2000. On March 3, 1844, the stock of cotton [627,042 bales] was more than double what it is this day [on March 3, 1848, when it was 301,070 bales] and yet the price then was 1¼d. per pound dearer.' [6¼d. as against 5d.]—At the same time yarn, good secunda mule twist No. 40, had fallen from 11½-12d. to 9½d. per lb. in October, and to 7¾d. at the end of December 1847; yarn was sold at the purchase price of the cotton from which it had been spun (*ibid.*, Nos. 2021 and 2022).

This shows the self-interest of Overstone's sagacity according to which money should be 'dear' because capital is 'scarce.' On March 3, 1844, the bank interest rate stood at 3%; in October and November of 1847, it rose to 8 and 9%, and was still 4% on March 3, 1848. The prices of cotton were depressed far below the price, which corresponded to the state of supply by the complete stoppage of sales and the panic with its ensuing high rate of interest. As a result, there was an enormous decrease in imports in 1848, on the one hand, and, on the other, a decrease in production in America; hence a new rise in cotton prices in 1849.

According to Overstone, the commodities were too dear because there was too much money in the country.

> '2002. The late decline in the condition of the cotton manufactories is not to be ascribed to the want of the raw material, as the price seems to have been lower, though the stock of the raw material is very much diminished.'

How nicely Overstone confuses prices, or the value of commodities, with the value of money, that is, the interest rate. In his reply to Question 2026, Wylie sums up his general judgement of the Currency Theory, based on which Cardwell and Sir Charles Wood, in May 1847,

> 'asserted the necessity of carrying out the Bank Act of 1844 in its full and entire integrity.'—'These principles seemed to me to be of a nature that would give an artificial high value to money and an artificial and ruinously low value to all commodities and produce.'

He says, furthermore, concerning the effects of this Bank Act on business in general:

> 'As bills at four months, which is the regular course of drafts, from manufacturing towns on merchants and bankers for the purchase of goods going to the United States, could not be discounted except at great sacrifices, the execution of orders was checked to a great extent, until after the Government Letter of October 25 (suspension of the Bank Act), when those four months' bills became discountable' (2097).

We see, then, that the suspension of this Bank Act was received with relief in the provinces as well.

> '2102. Last October [1847] there was scarcely an American buyer purchasing goods here who did not at once curtail his orders as much as he possibly could; and when our advices of the dearness of money reached America, all fresh orders ceased.'—'2134. Corn and sugar were special. The corn market was affected by the prospects of the harvest, and sugar was affected by the immense stocks and imports.'—'2463. Of our indebtedness to America ... much was liquidated by forced sales of consigned goods, and I fear that much was cancelled by the failures here.'—'2196. If I recollect rightly, *70 per cent was paid on our Stock Exchange in October 1847.*'

[The crisis of 1837, with its protracted aftermath, followed in 1842 by a regular post-crisis, and the self-interested blindness of industrialists and merchants, who absolutely refused to see any over-production—for such a thing was absurd and impossible according to vulgar economy—had ultimately achieved that confusion of thought which enabled the Currency School to put its dogma into practice on a national scale. The bank legislation of 1844 and 1845 was passed.

The Bank Act of 1844 divides the Bank of England into an issue department and a banking department. The former receives securities—principally government obligations—amounting to 14 million, and the entire metal hoard, of which not more than one-quarter is to consist of silver, and issues notes to the full amount of the total. In so far as these notes are not in the hands of the public, they are held in the banking department and, together with the small amount of coin required for daily use (about one million), constitute its ever ready reserve. The issue department gives the public gold for notes and notes for gold; the remaining transactions with the public are carried on by the banking department. Private banks in England and Wales authorised in 1844 to issue their own notes retained this privilege, but their note issue was fixed; if one of these banks ceases to issue its own notes, the Bank of England can increase its unbacked notes by two-thirds of the quota thus made available; in this way, its issue was increased by 1892 from £14 to £16½ million (to be exact, £16,450,000).

Thus, for every five pounds in gold which leave the bank treasury, a five-pound note returns to the issue department and is destroyed; for every five sovereigns going into the treasury, a new five-pound note comes into circulation. In this manner, Overstone's ideal paper circulation, which strictly follows the laws of metallic circulation, is carried out in practice, and by this means, according to the advocates of the Currency Theory, crises are made impossible for all time.

But in reality, the separation of the Bank into two independent departments deprived its management of the possibility of freely utilising its entire available means at critical times, so that situations could arise in which the banking department might be on the verge of bankruptcy while the issue department still had intact several millions in gold and, in addition, its entire 14 million in securities. And this could take place so much more easily since there is a period in almost every crisis when heavy exports of gold take place which must be covered in the main by the metal reserve of the bank. But for every five pounds in gold which then go abroad, the domestic circulation is deprived of a five-pound note, so that the quantity of circulating medium is reduced precisely at a time when the largest quantity is most needed. The Bank Act of 1844 thus directly induces the entire commercial world forthwith to hoard a reserve fund of banknotes at the outbreak of a crisis; in other words, to accelerate and intensify the crisis. By such artificial intensification of demand for money accommodation, that is, for means of payment at the decisive moment, and the simultaneous restriction of the supply, the Bank Act drives the rate of interest to a hitherto unknown height during a crisis. Hence, instead of eliminating crises, the Act, on the contrary, intensifies them to a point where either the entire industrial world must go to pieces, or else the Bank Act. Both on October 25, 1847, and on November 12, 1857, the crisis reached such a point; the government then lifted the restriction for the Bank in issuing notes by suspending the Act of 1844, and this sufficed in both cases to overcome the crisis. In 1847, the assurance that banknotes would again be issued for first-class securities sufficed to bring to light the £4 to £5 million of hoarded notes and put them back into circulation; in 1857, the issue of notes exceeding the legal amount reached almost one million, but this lasted only for a very short time.

It should also be mentioned that the 1844 legislation still shows traces recalling the first twenty years of the 19th century, the period when specie payments were suspended, and notes devaluated. The fear that notes may lose their credit is still plainly in evidence. But this fear is quite groundless, since even in 1825, the issue of a discovered old supply of one-pound notes, which had been taken out of circulation, broke the crisis and proved thereby that the credit of the notes remained unshaken even in times of the most general and deepest mistrust. And this is quite understandable; for, after all, the entire nation backs up these symbols of value with its credit.—*F.E.*]

Let us now turn to a few comments on the effect of the Bank Act. John Stuart Mill believes that the Bank Act of 1844 [In the German 1894 edition this reads: 1847.—*Ed*] kept down over-speculation. Happily, this sage spoke on June 12, 1857. Four months later the crisis broke out. He literally congratulated the 'bank directors and the commercial public generally' on the fact that they

> 'understand much better than they did the nature of a commercial crisis, and the extreme mischief which they do both to themselves and to the public by upholding over-speculation.' (B.C. 1857, No. 2031.)

The sagacious Mr Mill thinks that if one-pound notes are issued

> 'as advances to manufacturers and others, who pay wages ... the notes may get into the hands of others who expend them for consumption, and in that case the notes do constitute in themselves a demand for commodities and may for some time tend to promote a rise of prices' [2066].

Does Mr Mill assume, then, that manufacturers will pay higher wages because they pay them in paper instead of gold? Or does he believe that if a manufacturer receives his loan in £100 notes and exchanges them for gold, these wages would constitute less demand than if paid immediately in one-pound notes? And does he not know that, for instance, in certain mining districts, wages were paid in the notes of local banks, so that several labourers together received one five-pound note? Does this increase their demand? Or will bankers advance money to manufacturers more easily and in larger quantities in small notes than in large ones?

[This singular fear which Mill has for one-pound notes would be inexplicable if his whole work on political economy did not reveal an eclecticism which shows no hesitation in the face of any contradiction. On the one hand, he agrees on many points with Tooke as opposed to Overstone; on the other, he believes that commodity-prices are determined by the quantity of available money. He is thus by no means convinced that, all other conditions being equal, a sovereign will find its way into the coffers of the Bank for every one-pound note issued. He fears that the quantity of circulating medium could be increased and thereby devaluated, that is, commodity-prices might rise. This and nothing more is concealed behind the above-mentioned apprehension.—*F.E.*]

Tooke expresses the following views before the C. D. 1848/57 concerning the division of the Bank into two departments and the excessive precautions taken to safeguard the cashing of notes:

> The greater fluctuations of the interest rate in 1847, as compared with 1837 and 1839, are due solely to the separation of the Bank into two departments (3010).—The safety of banknotes was affected neither in 1825 nor in 1837 and 1839 (3015).—The demand for gold in 1825 was aimed only at filling the vacuum created by the complete discredit of the one-pound notes of country banks; this vacuum could be filled only by gold, until such time as the Bank of England also issued one-pound notes (3022).—In November and December 1825 not the slightest demand existed for gold for export purposes (3023).
>
> 'In point of discredit at home as well as abroad, a failure in paying the dividends and the deposits would be of far greater consequence than the suspending of the payment of the banknotes (3028).'
>
> '3035. Would you not say that any circumstance, which had the effect of ultimately endangering the convertibility of the note, would be one likely to add serious difficulty in a moment of commercial pressure?—Not at all.'
>
> 'In the course of 1847 ... an increased issue from the circulating department might have contributed to replenish the coffers of the Bank, as it did in 1825' (3058).

Before the Committee on B. A. 1857, Newmarch testifies:

> '1357. The first mischievous effect ... of that separation of departments' (of the Bank) ' and ... a necessary consequence from the cutting in two of the reserve of bullion has been that the banking business of the Bank of England, that is to say, the whole of that part of the operation of the Bank of England which brings it more immediately into contact with the commerce of the country, has been carried on upon a moiety only of its former amounts of reserve. Out of that division of the reserve has arisen, therefore, this state of things, that whenever the reserve of the banking department has been diminished, even to a small extent, it has rendered necessary an action by the Bank upon its rate of discount. That diminished reserve, therefore, has produced a frequent succession of changes and jerks in the rate of discount.'—'1358. The alterations since 1844' [until June 1857] 'have been some 60 in number, whereas the alterations prior to 1844 in the same space of time certainly did not amount to a dozen.'

Of special interest is the testimony of Palmer, a Director of the Bank of England since 1811 and for a while its Governor, before the Lords' Committee on C. D. 1848/57:

> '828. In December 1825, there was about £1,100,000 of bullion remaining in the Bank. At that period it must undoubtedly have failed *in toto*, if this Act had been in existence' [meaning the Act of 1844]. 'The issue in December, I think, was 5 or 6 millions of notes in a week, which relieved the panic that existed at that period.'
>
> '825. The first period' [since July 1, 1825] 'when the present Act would have failed, if the Bank had attempted to carry out the transactions then undertaken, was on the 28th of February 1837; at that period there were £3,900,000 to £4,000,000 of bullion in the possession of the Bank, and then the Bank would have been left with £650,000 only in the reserve. Another period is in the year 1839, which continued from the 9th of July to the 5th of December.'—'826. What was the amount of the reserve in that case?—The reserve was minus altogether £200,000 upon the 5th of September. On the 5th of November it rose to about a million or a million and a half.'—'830. The Act of 1844 would have prevented the Bank giving assistance to the American trade in 1837.'—'831. There were three of the principal American houses that failed. ... Almost every house connected with America was in a state of discredit, and unless the Bank had come forward at that period, I do not believe that there would have been more than one or two houses that could have sustained themselves.'—'836. The pressure in 1837 is not to be compared with that of 1847. The pressure in the former year was chiefly confined to the American trade.'—838. (Early in June 1837 the management of the Bank discussed the question of overcoming the pressure.) 'Some gentlemen advocated the opinion ... that the correct principle was to raise the rate of interest, by which the price of commodities would be lowered; in short, to make money dear and commodities cheap, by which the foreign payment would be accomplished.'—'906. The establishment of an artificial limitation of the powers of the Bank under the Act of 1844, instead of the ancient and natural limitation of the Bank's powers, namely, the actual amount of its specie, tends to create artificial difficulty, and therefore an operation upon the prices of merchandise that would have been unnecessary but for the provisions of the Act.'—'968. You cannot, by the working of the Act of 1844, materially reduce the bullion, under ordinary circumstances, below nine million and a half. It would then cause a pressure upon prices and credit which would occasion such an advance in the exchange with foreign countries as 10 increase the import of bullion, and to that extent add to the amount in the issue department.'—'996. Under the limitation that you' [the Bank] 'are now subject to, you have not the command of silver to an extent that you require at a time when silver would be required for an action upon the foreign exchanges.'—'999. What was the object of the regulation restricting the Bank as to the amount of silver to one-fifth?—I cannot answer that question.'

The purpose was to make money dear; aside from the Currency Theory, the separation of the two bank departments and the requirement for Scottish and Irish banks to hold gold in reserve for backing notes issued beyond a certain amount had the same purpose. This brought about a decentralisation of the national metal reserve, which decreased its capability of correcting unfavourable exchange rates. All the following stipulations aim to raise the interest rate: that the Bank of England shall not issue notes exceeding 14 million except against gold reserve; that the banking department shall be administered as an ordinary bank, forcing the interest rate down when money is plentiful and driving it, up when money is scarce; limiting the silver reserve, the principal means of rectifying the rates of exchange with the continent and Asia; the regulations concerning the Scottish and Irish banks, which never require gold for export but must now keep it under the pretence of ensuring an actually illusory convertibility of their notes. The fact is that the Act of 1844 caused a run on the Scottish banks for gold in 1857 for the first time. Nor does the new bank legislation make any distinction between a drain of gold abroad or for domestic purposes, although it goes without saying that their effects are quite different. Hence the continual large fluctuations in the market rate of interest. With reference to silver, Palmer says on two separate occasions, 992 and 994, that the Bank can buy silver for notes only when the rate of exchange is favourable for England, *i.e.*, silver is superfluous; for:

> '1003. The only object in holding a considerable amount of bullion in silver is to facilitate making the foreign payment so long as the exchanges are against the country.'—'1004. Silver is ... a commodity which, being money in every other part of the world, is therefore the most direct commodity for the purpose' [payments abroad]. 'The United States latterly have taken gold alone.'

In his opinion, the Bank did not have to raise the interest rate above its old level of 5% in times of stringency, so long as unfavourable exchange rates do not drain gold to foreign countries. Were it not for the Act of 1844; the Bank would be able to discount all first-class bills presented to it without difficulty. [1018-20] But under the Act of 1844 and in the state in which the Bank found itself in October 1847,

> 'there was no rate of interest which the Bank could have charged to houses of credit, which they would not have been willing to pay to carry on their payments' [1022].

And this high interest rate was precisely the purpose of the Act.

> '1029. ... Great distinction which I wish to draw between the action of the rate of interest upon a foreign demand' [for precious metal] 'and an advance in the rate for the object of checking a demand upon the Bank during a period of internal discredit.'—'4023. Previously to the Act of 1844 ... when the exchanges were in favour of the country, and positive panic and alarm existed through the country, there was no limit put upon the issue, by which alone that state of distress could be relieved.'

So speaks a man who has occupied a post for 39 years in the administration of the Bank of England. Let us now listen to a private banker, Twells, an associate of Spooner, Attwood & Co. since 1801. He is alone among the witnesses before the B. C. 4857 who provides us with an insight into the country's actual state of affairs and who sees the crisis approaching. In other respects, however, he is a sort of little-shilling man from Birmingham, like his associates, the Attwood brothers, who are the founders of this school. (See *Zur Kritik der pol. Oek.*, S. 59.) He testifies:

> '4488. How do you think that the Act of 1844 has operated?—If I were to answer you as a banker, I should say that it has operated exceedingly well, for it has afforded a rich harvest to bankers and [money-]capitalists of all kinds. But it has operated very badly to the honest industrious trades-man who requires steadiness in the rate of discount, that he may be enabled to make his arrangements with confidence.... It has made money-lending a most profitable pursuit.'—'4489. It [the Bank Act,] enables the London joint-stock banks to return from 20 to 22% to their proprietors?—The other day one of them was paying 18% and I think another 20%; they ought to support the Act of 1844 very strongly.'—'4490. The little tradesmen and respectable merchants, who have not a large capital ... it pinches them very much indeed ... The only means that I have of knowing is that I observe such an amazing quantity of their acceptances unpaid. They are always small, perhaps ranging from £20 to £400, a great many of them are unpaid and go back unpaid to all parts of the country, which is always an indication of suffering amongst ... little shopkeepers.'

4494. He declares that business is not profitable now. The following remarks of his are important because they show that he saw the latent existence of the crisis when none of the others had even an inkling of it.

> '4494. Things keep their prices in Mincing Lane, but we sell nothing, we cannot sell upon any terms; we keep the nominal price.'

4495. He relates the following case: A Frenchman sends a broker in Mincing Lane commodities for £3,000 to be sold at a certain price. The broker cannot obtain the requested price, and the Frenchman cannot sell below this price. The commodities remain unsold, but the Frenchman needs money. The broker, therefore, makes him an advance of £1,000 and has the French man draw a bill of exchange of £1,000 for three months on the broker against his commodities as security. At the end of the three months, the bill becomes due, but the commodities still remain unsold. The broker must then pay the bill, and although he possesses security for £3,000, he cannot convert it into cash and, as a result, faces difficulties. In this manner, one person drags another down with him.

> '4496. With regard to the large exports ... where there is a depressed state of trade at home, it necessarily forces large exportation.'—'4497. Do you think that the home consumption has been diminished?—*Very much indeed ... immensely* ... the shopkeepers are the best authorities.'—'4498. Still the importations are very large; does not that indicate a large consumption?—It does, *if you can sell;* but many of the warehouses are full of these things; in this very instance which I have been relating, there is £3,000 worth imported, which cannot be sold.'

> '4514. When money is dear, would you say that capital would be cheap?—Yes.'

This man, then, is by no means of Overstone's opinion that a high rate of interest is the same as dear capital.

The following shows how business is now conducted:

> '4616. Others are going to a very great extent, carrying on a prodigious trade in exports and imports, to an extent far beyond what their capital justifies them in doing; there can be no doubt of all of that. These men may succeed; they may by some lucky venture get large fortunes, and put themselves right. That is very much the system in which a great deal of trade is now carried on. Persons will consent to lose 20, 30, and 40 per cent upon a shipment; the next venture may bring it back to them. If they fail in one after another, then they are broken up; and that is just the case which we have often seen recently; mercantile houses have broken up, without one shilling of property being left.'

> '4791. The low rate of interest' [during the last ten years] 'operates against bankers, it is true, but I should have very great difficulty in explaining to you, unless I could show you the books, how much higher the profits' [his own] ' are now than they used to be formerly. When interest is low, from excessive issues, we have large deposits; when interest is high, we get the advantage in that way.'—'4794. When money is at a moderate rate, we have more demand for it; we lend more; it operates in that way' [for us, the bankers]. 'When it gets higher, we get more than a fair proportion for it; we get more than we ought to do.'

We have seen that the credit of Bank of England notes is considered beyond question by all experts. Nevertheless, the Bank Act completely ties up nine to ten million in gold for the convertibility of these notes. The sacredness and inviolability of this reserve are thereby carried much farther than among hoarders of olden times. Mr Brown (Liverpool) testifies, C. D. 1847/57:

> '2311: This money' [the metal reserve in the issue department] 'might as well have been thrown into the sea from any use that it was of at that time, there being no power to employ any of it without violating the Act of Parliament.'

The building contractor E. Capps, already cited earlier, whose testimony is also used to illustrate the modern building system in London (Vol. II, Ch. XII), sums up his opinion of the Bank Act of 1844 as follows [B. A. 1857]:

> '5508. Then upon the whole ... you think that the present system' [of bank legislation] 'is a somewhat adroit scheme for bringing the profits of industry periodically into the usurer's bag?—I think so. I know that it has operated so in the building trade.'

As mentioned before, the Scottish banks were forced by the Bank Act of 1845 into a system resembling that of the English. They were obliged to hold gold in reserve for their note issue beyond the limit fixed for each bank. The effect of this may be seen from the following testimony before the C. D. 1848/57.

Kennedy, Director of a Scottish bank:

> '3375. Was there anything that you can call a circulation of gold in Scotland previously to the passing of the Act of 1845?—None whatever.'—'3376. Has there been any additional circulation of gold since?—None whatever; the people dislike gold.'—3450.

The sum of about £900,000 in gold, which the Scottish banks are compelled to keep since 1845, can only be injurious in his opinion and

> 'absorbs unprofitably so much of the capital of Scotland.'

Furthermore, Anderson, Director of the Union Bank of Scotland:

> '3588. The only pressure upon the Bank of England by the banks in Scotland for gold was for foreign exchanges?—It was; and that is not to be relieved by holding gold in Edinburgh.'—'3590. Having the same amount of securities in the Bank of England' [or in the private banks of England] 'we have the same power that we had before of making a drain upon the Bank of England.'

Finally, we quote an article from the *Economist* (Wilson):

> The Scotch banks keep unemployed amounts of cash with their London agents; these keep them in the Bank of England. This gives to the Scotch banks, within the limits of these amounts, command over the metal reserve of the Bank, and here it is always in the place where it is needed, when foreign payments are to be made.

This system was disturbed by the Act of 1845:

> In consequence of the Act of 1845 for Scotland of late a large drain of the coin of the Bank has taken place, to supply a mere contingent demand in Scotland, which may never occur... Since that period there has been a large sum uniformly locked up in Scotland, and another considerable sum constantly travelling back and forward between London and Scotland. If a period arrives when a Scotch bank expects an increased demand for its notes, a box of gold is brought down from London; when this period is past, the same box, generally unopened, is sent back to London. (*Economist*, October 23, 1847 [pp. 1214-1215].)

[And what does the father of the Bank Act, banker Samuel Jones Loyd, alias Lord Overstone, say to all this?

Already in 1848 he repeated before the Lords' Committee on Commercial Distress that 'pressure, and a high rate of interest caused by the want of sufficient capital, cannot be relieved by an extra issue of banknotes' (1514),

in spite of the fact that the mere *authority* to increase the note issue, given by the Government's Letter of October 25, 1847, had sufficed to take the edge off the crisis.

He holds to the view that

> 'the high rate of interest and the depression of the manufacturing interests was the necessary result of the diminution of the *material* capital applicable to manufacturing and trading purposes' (1604).

And yet the depressed condition of the manufacturing industry had for months consisted in material commodity-capital filling the warehouses to overflowing and being actually unsaleable; so that for precisely this reason, material productive capital lay wholly or partly idle, in order not to produce still more unsaleable commodity-capital.

And before the Bank Committee of 1857, he says:

> 'By strict and prompt adherence to the principles of the Act of 1844, everything has passed off with regularity and ease, the monetary system is safe and unshaken, the prosperity of the country is undisputed, the public confidence in the wisdom of the Act of 1844 is daily gaining strength, and if the Committee wish for further practical illustration of the soundness of the principles on which it rests, or of the beneficial results which it has ensured, the true and sufficient answer to the Committee is, look around you, look at the present state of the trade of this country, ... look at the contentment of the people, look at the wealth and prosperity which pervades every class of the community, and then having done so, the Committee may be fairly called upon to decide whether they will interfere with the continuance of an Act under which those results have been developed.' (B. C. 1857, No. 4189.)

To this song of praise by Overstone before the Committee on July 14, the antistrophe was given on November 12 of the same year in the shape of a letter to the Bank's management, in which the government suspended the miracle-working law of 1844 to save what could still be saved.—*F. E.*]

35

Precious Metal and Rate of Exchange

Section I. *Movement of the Gold Reserve*

It should be noted in regard to the accumulation of notes in times of stringency, that it is a repetition of the hoarding of precious metal as used to take place in troubled times in the most primitive conditions of society. The Act of 1844 is interesting in its operation because it seeks to transform all precious metal existing in the country into a circulating medium; it seeks to equate a drain of gold with a contraction of the circulating medium and a return flow of gold with an expansion of the circulating medium. As a result, the experiment proved the contrary to be the case. With a single exception, which we shall mention shortly, the quantity of circulating notes of the Bank of England has never, since 1844, reached the maximum which it was authorised to issue. The crisis of 1857 proved, on the other hand, that this maximum does not suffice under certain circumstances. From November 13 to 30, 1857, a daily average of

£488,830 above this maximum was circulating (B. A. 1858, p. XI). The legal maximum was at that time £14,475,000, plus the amount of metal reserve in the vaults of the Bank.

Concerning the outflow and inflow of precious metal, the following is to be noted:

First, a distinction should be made between the back and forth movement of metal within a region which does not produce any gold and silver, on the one hand, and, on the other, the flow of gold and silver from their sources of production to various other countries and the distribution of this additional metal among them.

Before the gold mines of Russia, California and Australia made Their influence felt, the supply since the beginning of the 19th century sufficed only for the replacement of worn-out coins, for general use in articles of luxury, and for the export of silver to Asia.

However, in the first place, silver exports to Asia have since increased extraordinarily, owing to the Asiatic trade of America and Europe. The silver exported from Europe was largely replaced by the additional supply of gold. Secondly, a portion of the newly imported gold was absorbed by internal money circulation. It is estimated that up to 1857, about 30 million in gold were added to England's internal circulation.[1] Furthermore, the average level of metal reserves in all the central banks of Europe and America increased since 1844. The expansion of domestic money circulation resulted at the same time in bank reserves growing more rapidly in the period of stagnation following upon the panic, because of the larger quantity of gold coins thrust out of domestic circulation and immobilised. Finally, the consumption of precious metal for luxury articles increased since the discovery of new gold deposits as a consequence of the increased wealth.

Secondly, precious metal flows back and forth between countries which do not produce any gold or silver, the same country continually importing, and also exporting. It is only the preponderance of this movement in one or another direction which, in the final analysis, determines whether a drain or an augmentation has taken place, since the mere oscillations and frequently parallel movements largely neutralise one another. But for this reason, in so far as the result is concerned, the continuity and, in the main, the parallel course of both movements is overlooked. A greater import or a greater export of precious metal is always interpreted to be solely the effect and expression of the relation between the imports and exports of commodities, whereas it is simultaneously indicative of the relation between exports and imports of precious metal itself, quite independent of commodity trade.

Thirdly, the preponderance of imports over exports, and vice versa, is measured on the whole by the increase or decrease in metal reserves of the central banks. The greater or lesser precision of this criterion naturally depends primarily on the degree of centralization of the banking business in general. For on this depends the extent that precious metal in general accumulated in the so-called national banks represents the national metal reserve. But assuming this to be the case, the criterion is not accurate because an additional import may be absorbed under certain circumstances by domestic circulation and the growing consumption of gold and silver in producing luxury articles; furthermore, because without additional import, a withdrawal of gold coin for domestic circulation could take place, and thus the metal reserve could decrease even without a simultaneous increase in exports.

Fourthly, an export of metal assumes the aspect of a drain when the movement of decrease continues for a long time, so that the decrease represents a tendency of movement and depresses the metal reserve of the bank considerably below its average level, down to approximately its average minimum. This minimum is more or less arbitrarily fixed, in so far as it is differently determined in every individual case by legislation concerning backing for the cashing of notes, etc. Concerning the quantitative limits which such a drain can reach in England, Newmarch testified before the Committee on B. A. 1857, Evidence No. 1494:

> 'Judging from experience, it is very unlikely that the efflux of treasure arising from any oscillation in the foreign trade will proceed beyond £3,000,000 or £4,000,000.'

In 1847, the lowest gold reserve level of the Bank of England, occurring on October 23, showed a decrease of £5,198,156 as compared with that of December 26, 1846, and a decrease of £6,453,748 as compared with the highest level of 1846 (August 29).

Fifthly, the determination of the metal reserve of the so-called national banks, a determination, however, which does not by itself regulate the magnitude of this metal hoard, for it can grow solely by the paralysis of domestic and foreign trade, is threefold: 1) reserve fund for international payments, in other words, reserve fund of world-money; 2) reserve fund for alternately expanding and contracting domestic metal circulation; 3) reserve fund for the payment of deposits and for the convertibility of notes (this is connected with the function of the bank and has nothing to do with the functions of money as such). The reserve fund can, therefore, also be influenced by conditions which affect every one of these three functions. Thus, as an international fund, it can be influenced by the balance of payments, no matter by what factors the latter may be determined and whatever its relation to the balance of trade may be. As a reserve fund for domestic metal circulation, it can be influenced by the latter's expansion or contraction. The third function—that of a security fund—does not, admittedly, determine the independent movement of the metal reserve, but has a two-fold effect. If notes are issued which replace metallic money (also including silver coins in countries where silver is a measure of value) in domestic circulation, the function of the reserve fund under 2) drops away. And a portion of the precious metal, which served to perform this function, will for a long time find its way abroad. In this case, metallic coins are not withdrawn for domestic circulation, and thus the temporary augmentation of the metal reserve by immobilising a part of the circulating coined metal simultaneously falls away. Furthermore, if a minimum metal reserve must be maintained under all circumstances for the payment of deposits and for the convertibility of notes, this affects in its own way the results of a drain or return flow of gold; it affects that part of the reserve which the bank is obliged to maintain under all circumstances, or that part which it seeks to get rid of as useless at certain times. If the circulation were purely metallic and the banking system concentrated, the bank would likewise have to consider its metal reserve as security for the payment of its deposits, and a drain of metal could cause a panic such as was witnessed in Hamburg in 1857.

Sixthly, with the exception of perhaps 1837, the real crisis always broke out only after a change in the rates of exchange, that is, as soon as the import of precious metal had again gained preponderance over its export.

In 1825, the real crash came after the drain on gold had ceased. In 1839, there was a drain on gold, but it did not bring about a crash. In 1847, the drain on gold ceased in April and, the crash came in October. In 1857, the drain on gold to foreign countries had ceased in early November, and the crash did not come until later that same month.

This is particularly evident in the crisis of 1847, when the drain on gold ceased in April after causing a slight preliminary crisis, and the real business crisis did not come until October.

The following testimony was presented at the Secret Committee of the House of Lords on Commercial Distress, 1848. This evidence was not printed until 1857 (also cited as C. D. 1848/57).

Evidence of Tooke:

> In April 1847, a stringency arose, which, strictly speaking, equalled a panic, but was of relatively short duration and not accompanied by any commercial failures of importance. In October the stringency was far more intensive than at any time during April, an almost unheard-of number of commercial failures taking place (2996).—In April the rates of exchange, particularly with America, compelled us to export a considerable amount of gold in payment for unusually large imports; only by an

extreme effort did the Bank stop the drain and drive the rates higher (2997).—In October the rates of exchange favoured England (2998).—The change in the rates of exchange had begun in the third week of April (3000).—They fluctuated in July and August; since the beginning of August they always favoured England (3001).—The drain on gold in August arose from a demand for internal circulation [3003].

J. Morris, Governor of the Bank of England:

> Although the rate of exchange favoured England since August 1847, and an import of gold had taken place in consequence, the bullion reserve of the Bank decreased.
>
> '£2,200,000 went out into the country in consequence of the internal demand' (137).—This is explained on the one hand by an increased employment of labourers in railway construction, and on the other by the 'circumstance of the bankers wishing to provide themselves with gold in times of distress' (147).

Palmer, ex-governor and a Director of the Bank of England since 1811:

> '684. During the whole period from the middle of April 1847 to the day of withdrawing the restrictive clause in the Act of 1844 the foreign exchanges were in favour of this country.'

The drain of bullion, which created an independent money panic in April 1847, was here, therefore, as always, but a precursor of the crisis, and a turn had already taken place before it broke out. In 1839, a heavy drain of bullion took place for grain, etc., while business was strongly depressed, but there was no crisis or money panic.

Seventhly, as soon as general crises have spent themselves, gold and silver—leaving aside the inflow of new precious metal from the producing countries—distribute themselves once more in the proportions in which they existed in a state of equilibrium as individual hoards of the various countries. Other conditions being equal, the relative magnitude of a hoard in each country will be determined by the role of that country in the world-market. They flow from the country which had more than its normal share to those with less than a normal amount. These movements of outgoing and incoming metal merely restore the original distribution among the various national reserves. This redistribution, however, is brought about by the effects of various circumstances, which will be taken up in our treatment of rates of exchange. As soon as the normal distribution is once more restored—beginning with this moment—a stage of growth sets in and then again a drain. [This last statement applies, of course, only to England, as the centre of the world money-market.—*F.E.*]

Eighthly, a drain of metal is generally the symptom of a change in the state of foreign trade, and this change, in turn, is a premonition that conditions are again approaching a crisis.[2]

Ninthly, the balance of payments can favour Asia against Europe and America.[3]

An import of precious metal takes place mainly during two periods. On the one hand, it takes place in the first phase of a low interest rate, which follows upon a crisis and reflects a restriction of production; and then in the second phase, when the interest rate rises, but before it attains its average level. This is the phase during which returns come quickly, commercial credit is abundant, and therefore the demand for loan capital does not grow in proportion to the expansion of production. In both phases, with loan capital relatively abundant, the superfluous addition of capital existing in the form of gold and silver, *i.e.*, a form in which it can primarily serve only as loan capital, must seriously affect the rate of interest and concomitantly the atmosphere of business in general.

On the other hand, a drain, a continued and heavy export of precious metal, takes place as soon as returns no longer flow, markets are overstocked, and an illusory prosperity is maintained only by means of credit; in other words, as soon as a greatly increased demand for loan capital exists and the interest rate, therefore, has reached at least its average level. Under such circumstances, which are reflected precisely in a drain of precious metal, the effect of continued withdrawal of capital, in a form in which it exists directly as loanable money-capital, is considerably intensified. This must have a direct influence on the interest rate. But instead of restricting credit transactions, the rise in interest rate extends them and leads to an over-straining of all their resources. This period, therefore, precedes the crash.

Newmarch is asked, B. A. 1857:

> '1520. But then the volume of bills in circulation increases with the rate of discount?—It seems to do so.'—'1522. In quiet ordinary times the ledger is the real instrument of exchange; but when any difficulty arises; when, for example, under such circumstances as I have suggested, there is a rise in the bank-rate of discount ... then the transactions naturally resolve themselves into drawing bills of exchange, those bills of exchange being not only more convenient as regards legal proof of the transaction which has taken place, but also being more convenient in order to effect purchases elsewhere, and being pre-eminently convenient as a means of credit by which capital can be raised.'

Furthermore, as soon as somewhat threatening conditions induce the bank to raise its discount rate—whereby the probability exists at the same time that the bank will cut down the running time of the bills to be discounted by it—the general apprehension spreads that this will rise in crescendo. Everyone, and above all the credit swindler, will therefore strive to discount the future and have as many means of credit as possible at his command at the given time. These reasons, then, amount to this: it is not that the mere quantity of imported or exported precious metal as such which makes its influence felt, but that it exerts its effect, firstly, by virtue of the specific character of precious metal as capital in money-form, and secondly, by acting like a feather which, when added to the weight on the scales, suffices to tip the oscillating balance definitely to one side; it acts because it arises under conditions when any addition decides in favour of one or the other side. Without these grounds, it would be quite inexplicable why a drain of gold amounting to, say, £5,000,000 to £8,000,000—and this is the limit of experience to date—should have any appreciable effect. This small decrease or increase of capital, which seems insignificant even compared to the £70 million in gold which circulate on an average in England, is really a negligibly small magnitude when compared to production of such volume as that of the English.[5] But it is precisely the development of the credit and banking system, which tends, on the one hand, to press all money-capital into the service of production (or what amounts to the same thing, to transform all money income into capital), and which, on the other hand, reduces the metal reserve to a minimum in a certain phase of the cycle, so that it can no longer perform the functions for which it is intended—it is the developed credit and banking system which creates this over-sensitiveness of the whole organism. At less developed stages of production, the decrease or increase of the hoard below or above its average level is a relatively insignificant matter. Similarly, on the other hand, even a very considerable drain of gold is relatively ineffective if it does not occur in the critical period of the industrial cycle.

In the given explanation we have not considered cases in which a drain of gold takes place as a result of crop failures, etc. In such cases the large and sudden disturbance of the equilibrium of production, which is expressed by this drain, requires no further explanation as to its effect. This effect is that much greater the more such a disturbance occurs in a period when production is in full swing.

We have also omitted from consideration the function of the metal reserve as a security for bank-note convertibility and as the pivot of the entire credit system. The central bank is the pivot of the credit system. And the metal reserve, in turn, is the pivot of the bank.[6] The change-over from the credit system to the monetary system is necessary, as I have already shown in Vol. I (Ch. III) in discussing means of payment. That the greatest sacrifices of real wealth are necessary to maintain the metallic basis in a critical moment has been admitted by both Tooke* and Loyd-Overstone. The controversy revolves merely round a plus or a minus, and round the more or less rational treatment of the inevitable.[7] A certain quantity of metal, insignificant compared with the total production, is admitted to be the pivotal point of the system. Hence the superb theoretical dualism, aside from the appalling manifestation of this characteristic that it possesses as the pivotal point during crises. So long as enlightened economy treats 'of capital' *ex professo,* it looks down upon gold and silver with the greatest disdain, considering them as the most indifferent and useless form of capital. But as soon as it treats of the banking system, everything is reversed, and gold and silver become capital *par excellence,* for whose preservation every other form of capital and labour is to be sacrificed. But how are gold and silver distinguished from other forms of wealth? Not by the magnitude of their value, for this is determined by the quantity of labour incorporated in them; but by the fact that they represent independent incarnations, expressions of the *social* character of wealth. [The wealth of society exists only as the wealth of private individuals, who are its private owners. It preserves its social character only in that these individuals mutually exchange qualitatively different use-values for the satisfaction of their wants. Under capitalist production they can do so only by means of money. Thus the wealth of the individual is realised as social wealth only through the medium of money. It is in money, in this thing, that the social nature of this wealth is incarnated.—*F.E.*] This social existence of wealth, therefore, assumes the aspect of a world beyond, of a thing, matter, commodity, alongside of and external to the real elements of social wealth. So long as production is in a state of flux, this is forgotten. Credit, likewise a social form of wealth, crowds out money and usurps its place. It is faith in the social character of production which allows the money-form of products to assume the aspect of something that is only evanescent and ideal, something merely imaginative. But as soon as credit is shaken—and this phase of necessity always appears in the modern industrial cycle—all the real wealth is to be actually and suddenly transformed into money, into gold and silver—a mad demand, which, however, grows necessarily out of the system itself. And all the gold and silver which is supposed to satisfy these enormous demands amounts to but a few millions in the vaults of the Bank.[8]

Among the effects of the gold drain, then, the fact that production as social production is not really subject to social control, is strikingly emphasised by the existence of the social form of wealth as a thing external to it. The capitalist system of production, in fact, has this feature in common with former systems of production, in so far as they are based on trade in commodities and private exchange. But only in the capitalist system of production does this become apparent in the most striking and grotesque form of absurd contradiction and paradox, because, in the first place, production for direct use-value, for consumption by the producers themselves, is most completely eliminated under the capitalist system, so that wealth exists only as a social process expressed as the intertwining of production and circulation; and secondly, with the development of the credit system, capitalist production continually strives to overcome the metal barrier, which is simultaneously a material and imaginative barrier of wealth and its movement, but again and again it breaks its back on this barrier.

In the crisis, the demand is made that all bills of exchange, securities, and commodities shall be simultaneously convertible into bank money, and all this bank money, in turn, into gold.

Section II. *The Rate of Exchange*

[The rate of exchange is known to be the barometer for the international movement of money metals. If England has more payments to make to Germany than Germany to England, the price of marks, expressed in sterling, rises in London, and the price of sterling, expressed in marks, falls in Hamburg and Berlin. If this preponderance of England's payment obligations towards Germany is not balanced again, for instance, by a preponderance of purchases by Germany in England, the sterling price of bills of exchange in marks on Germany must rise to the point where it will pay to send metal (gold coin or bullion) from England to Germany in payment of obligations, instead of sending bills of exchange. This is the typical course of events.

If this export of precious metal assumes a larger scope and lasts for a longer period, then the English bank reserve is affected, and the English money-market, particularly the Bank of England, must take protective measures. These consist mainly, as we have already seen, in raising the interest rate. When the drain on gold is considerable, the money-market, as a rule, becomes tight, that is, the demand for loan capital in the form of money significantly exceeds the supply, and the higher interest rate follows quite naturally from this; the discount rate fixed by the Bank of England corresponds to this situation and asserts itself on the market. However, there are cases when the drain on bullion is due to other than ordinary combinations of business transactions (for instance, loans to foreign states, investment of capital in foreign countries, etc.), and the London money-market as such does not justify an effective rise in the interest rate; the Bank of England must then first 'make money scarce,' as the phrase goes, through heavy loans in the 'open market' and thus artificially create a situation which justifies, or renders necessary, a rise in the interest rate; such a manoeuvre becomes more difficult from year to year.—*F.E.*]

How this raising of the interest rate affects the rates of exchange is shown by the following testimony before the Committee of the Lower House concerning bank legislation in 1857 (quoted as B. A. or B. C. 1857).

> John Stuart Mill: '2176. When there is a state of commercial difficulty there is always ... a considerable fall in the price of securities ... foreigners send over to buy railway shares in this country, or English holders of foreign railway shares sell their foreign railway shares abroad ... there is so much transfer of bullion prevented.'—'2182. A large and rich class of bankers and dealers in securities, through whom the equalisation of the rate of interest and the equalisation of commercial pressure between different countries usually takes place ... are always on the look out to buy securities which are likely to rise.... The place for them to buy securities will be the country which is sending bullion away.'—'2184. These investments of capital took place to a very considerable extent in 1847, to a sufficient extent to have relieved the drain considerably.'

J. G. Hubbard, ex-Governor, and a Director of the Bank of England since 1838:

> '2545. There are great quantities of European securities ... which have a European currency in all the different money-markets, and those bonds, as soon as their value is reduced by 1 or 2 per cent in one market, are immediately purchased for transmission to those markets where their value is still unimpaired.'—'2565. Are not foreign countries considerably in debt to the merchants of this country?—Very largely.'—'2566. Therefore, the cashment of those debts might be sufficient to account for a very large accumulation of capital in this country?—In 1847, the ultimate restoration of our position was effected by our striking off so many millions previously due by America, and so many millions due by Russia to this country.'

[At the same time, England owed these same countries 'so and so many millions' for grain and also did not fail to 'draw a line' through the greater portion of these millions via the bankruptcy of the English debtors. See the report on Bank Acts, 1857, Chapter XXX above.—*F.E.*]

> '2572. In 1847, the exchange between this country and St. Petersburg was very high. When the Government Letter came out authorising the Bank to issue irrespectively of

the limitation of £14,000,000 [above and beyond the gold reserve—*F.E.*], the stipulation was that the rate of discount should be 8%. At that moment, with the then rate of discount, it was a profitable operation to order gold to be shipped from St. Petersburg to London and on its arrival to lend it at 8% up to the maturity of the three months' bills drawn against the purchase of gold.'—'2573. In all bullion operations there are many points to be taken into consideration; there is the rate of exchange and the rate of interest, which is available for the investment during the period of the maturity of the bill [drawn against it—*F.E.*].'

Rate of Exchange with Asia

The following points are important because, on the one hand, they show how England recoups its losses when its rate of exchange with Asia is unfavourable, at the expense of other countries, whose imports from Asia are paid through English middlemen. On the other hand, they are important because Mr Wilson once again makes the foolish attempt here to identify the effects of the export of precious metal on the rates of exchange with the effect of the export of capital in general upon these rates; the export being in both cases not as a means of paying or buying, but for capital investment. In the first place, it goes without saying that whether so many millions of pounds sterling are sent to India in precious metal or iron rails, to be invested in railways there, these are merely two different forms of transferring the same amount of capital to another country; namely, a transfer which does not enter the calculation of ordinary mercantile business, and for which the exporting country expects no other return than the future annual revenue from the income of these railways. If this export is made in the form of precious metal, it will exert a direct influence upon the money-market and with it upon the interest rate of the country exporting this precious metal; if not necessarily under all circumstances, then under the previously outlined conditions, since it is precious metal and as such is directly loanable money-capital and the basis of the entire money system. Similarly, this export also directly affects the rate of exchange. Precious metal is exported only for the reason, and to the extent, that bills of exchange, say on India, which are offered in the London money-market, do not suffice to make these extra remittances. In other words, there is a demand for Indian bills of exchange which exceeds their supply, and so the rates turn for a time against England, not because it is in debt to India, but because it has to send extraordinary sums to India. In the long run, such a shipment of precious metal to India must have the effect of increasing the Indian demand for English commodities, because it indirectly increases the consuming power of India for European goods. But, if the capital is shipped in the form of rails, etc., it cannot have any influence on the rates of exchange, since India has no return payment to make for it. Precisely for this reason, it need not have any influence on the money-market. Wilson seeks to establish the existence of such an influence by declaring that such an extra expenditure would bring about an additional demand for money accommodation and would thus influence the interest rate. This may be the case; but to maintain that it must take place under all circumstances is totally wrong. No matter where the rails are shipped and whether laid on English or Indian soil, they represent nothing but a definite expansion of English production in a particular sphere. To contend that an expansion of production, even within very broad limits, cannot take place without driving up the interest rate, is absurd. Money accommodation, *i.e.*, the amount of business transacted, which includes credit operations, may grow; but these credit operations can increase while the interest rate remains unchanged. This was actually the case during the railway mania in England in the forties. The interest rate did not rise. And it is evident that, so far as actual capital is concerned, in this case, commodities, the effect on the money-market will he just the same, whether these commodities are destined for foreign countries or for domestic consumption.

It could only make a difference when capital investments by England in foreign countries exerted a restraining influence upon its commercial exports, *i.e.*, exports for which payment must be made, thus giving rise to a return flow, or to the extent that these capital investments are already general symptoms indicating the over-expansion of credit and the initiation of swindling operations.

In the following, Wilson puts the questions and Newmarch replies.

> '1786. On a former day you stated, with reference to the demand for silver for the East, that you believed that the exchanges with India were in favour of this country, notwithstanding the large amount of bullion that is continually transmitted to the East; have you any ground for supposing the exchanges to be in favour of this country?—Yes, I have.... I find that the real value of the exports from the United Kingdom to India in 1851 was £7,420,000; to that is to be added the amount of India House drafts, that is, the funds drawn from India by the East India Company for the purpose of their own expenditure. Those drafts in that year amounted to £3,200,000, making, therefore, the total export from the United Kingdom to India £10,620,000. In 1855... the actual value of the export of goods from the United Kingdom had risen to £10,350,000 and the India House drafts were £3,700,000, making, therefore, the total export from this country £14,050,000. Now as regards 1851, I believe there are no means of stating what was the real value of the import of goods from India to this country, but in 1854 and 1855 we have a statement of the real value; in 1855, the total real value of the imports of goods from India to this country was £12,670,000 and that sum, compared with the £14,050,000 I have mentioned, left a balance in favour of the United Kingdom, as regards the direct trade between the two countries, of £1,380,000' [B. A. 1857].

Thereupon Wilson remarks that the rates of exchange are also affected by indirect commerce. For instance, exports from India to Australia and North America are covered by drafts on London, and therefore, affect the rate of exchange just as though the commodities had gone directly from India to England. Furthermore, when India and China are considered together, the balance is against England, since China has constantly to make heavy payments to India for opium, and England has to make payments to China, so that the sums go by this circuitous route to India (1787, 1788).

1791. Wilson now asks if the effect on the rates of exchange will not be the same whether capital

> 'went in the form of iron rails and locomotives, or whether it went in the form of coin.'

Newmarch correctly answers:

> 'The £12 million which have been sent during the last few years to India for railway construction served to purchase an annuity which India has to pay at regular intervals to England. 'But as far as regards the immediate operation on the bullion market, the investments of the £12 million would only be operative as far as bullion was required to be sent out for actual money disbursements.'

> 1797. (Weguelin asks:) 'If no return is made for this iron (rails), how can it be said to affect the exchanges?—I do not think that that part of the expenditure which is sent out in the form of commodities affects the computation of the exchange.... The computation of the exchange between two countries is affected, one might say, solely by the quantity of obligations or bills offering in one country, as compared with the quantity offering in the other country against it; that is the rationale of the exchange. Now, as regards the transmission of those £12,000,000, the money in the first place is subscribed in this country ... now, if the nature of the transaction was such that the whole of that £12,000,000 was required to be laid down in Calcutta, Bombay, and Madras in treasure

> ... a sudden demand would very violently operate upon the price of silver, and upon the exchange, just the same as if the India Company were to give notice tomorrow that their drafts were to be raised from £3,000,000 to £12,000,000. But half of those £12,000,000 is spent ... in buying commodities in this country ... iron rails and timber, and other materials it is an expenditure in this country of the capital of this country for a particular kind of commodity to be sent out to India, and there is an end of it.'—'1798. [Weguelin:] But the production of those articles of iron and timber necessary for the railways produces a large consumption of foreign articles, which might affect the exchange?—Certainly.'

Wilson now thinks that iron represents labour to a large extent, and that the wage paid for this labour largely represents imported goods (1799), and then questions further:

> '1801. But speaking quite generally, it would have the effect of turning the exchanges against this country if you sent abroad the articles which were produced by the consumption of the imported articles without receiving any remittance for them either in the shape of produce or otherwise?—That principle is exactly what took place in this country during the time of the great railway expenditure [1845]. For three or four or five years, you spent upon railways £30,000,000, nearly the whole of which went in the payment of wages. You sustained in three years a larger population employed in constructing railways, and locomotives, and carriages, and stations than you employed in the whole of the factory districts. The people ... spent those wages in buying tea and sugar and spirits and other foreign commodities; those commodities were imported; but it was a fact, that during the time this great expenditure was going on the foreign exchanges between this country and other countries were not materially deranged. There was no efflux of bullion, on the contrary, there was rather an influx.'

1802. Wilson insists that with an equalised trade balance and par rates between England and India the extra shipment of iron and locomotives 'would affect the exchanges with India.' Newmarch cannot see it that way so long as the rails are sent out as capital investment and India has no payment to make for them in one form or another; he adds:

> 'I agree with the principle that no one country can have permanently against itself an adverse state of exchange with all the other countries, with which it deals; an adverse exchange with one country necessarily produces a favourable exchange with another.'

Wilson retorts with this triviality:

> '1803. But would not a transfer of capital be the same whether it was sent in one form or another?—As regards the obligation it would.'—'1804. The effect therefore of making railways in India, whether you send bullion or whether you send materials, would be the same upon the capital-market here in increasing the value of capital as if the whole was sent out in bullion?'

If iron prices did not rise, it was in any case proof that the 'value' of 'capital' contained in the rails had not been increased. What we are here concerned with is the value of money-capital, *i.e.*, the interest rate. Wilson would like to identify money-capital with capital in general. The simple fact is essentially that 12 million were subscribed in England for Indian railways. This is a matter which has nothing directly to do with the rates of exchange, and the designation of the £12 million is also the same to the money-market. If the money-market is in good shape, it need not produce any effect at all on it, just as the English railway subscriptions in 1844 and 1845 left the money-market unaffected. If the money-market is already in somewhat difficult straits, the interest rate might indeed be affected by it, but certainly only in an upward direction, and this, according to Wilson's theory, would favourably affect the rates of exchange for England, that is, it would work against the tendency to export precious metal; if not to India, then to some other country. Mr Wilson jumps from one thing to another. In Question 1802, it is the rates of exchange that are supposed to be affected, and In Question 1804, the 'value of capital'—which are two very different things. The interest rate may affect the rates of exchange, and the rates of exchange may affect the interest rate, but the latter can be stable while the rates of exchange fluctuate, and the rates of exchange can be stable while the interest rate fluctuates. Wilson cannot get it through his head that the mere form in which capital is shipped abroad makes such a difference in the effect, *i.e.*, that the difference in the form of capital is of such importance, and particularly its money-form, which runs very much counter to enlightened economy. Newmarch replies to Wilson one-sidedly in that he does not indicate that he has jumped so suddenly and without reason from rate of exchange to interest rate. Newmarch answers Question 1804 with uncertainty and equivocation:

> 'No doubt, if there is a demand for £12,000,000 to be raised, it is immaterial, as regards the general rate of interest, whether that £12 million is required to be sent in bullion or in materials. I think, however.'

[a fine transition, this 'however,' when he intends to say the exact opposite]

> 'it is not quite immaterial'

[it is immaterial, but, nevertheless, it is not immaterial]

> 'because in the one case the £6 million would be returned immediately; in the other case it would not be returned so rapidly. Therefore it would make some.'

[what definiteness!]

> 'difference, whether the £6 million was expended in this country or sent wholly out of it.'

What does he mean when he says six million would return immediately? In so far as the £6 million have been expended in England, they exist in rails, locomotives, etc., which are shipped to India, whence they do not return; their value returns very slowly through amortisation, whereas the six million in precious metal may perhaps return very quickly in kind. In so far as the six million have been expended in wages, they have been consumed; but the money used for payment circulates in the country the same as ever, or forms a reserve. The same holds true for the profits of rail producers and that portion of the six million which replaces their constant capital. Thus, this ambiguous statement about returns is used by Newmarch only to avoid saying directly: The money has remained in the country, and in so far as it serves as loanable money-capital the difference for the money-market (aside from the possibility that circulation could have absorbed more coin) is only that it is charged to the account of A instead of B. An investment of this kind, where capital is transferred to other countries in commodities, not in precious metal, can affect the rate of exchange (but not the rate of exchange with the country in which the exported capital is invested) only in so far as the production of these exported commodities requires an additional import of other foreign commodities. This production then cannot balance out the additional import. However, the same thing happens with every export on credit, no matter whether intended for capital investment or ordinary commercial purposes. Moreover, this additional import can also call forth by way of reaction an additional demand for English goods, for instance, on the part of the colonies or the United States.

Previously (1786), Newmarch stated that, owing to drafts of the East India Company, exports from England to India were larger than imports. Sir Charles Wood cross-examines him on this score. This preponderance of English exports to India over imports from

India is actually brought about by imports from India for which England does not pay any equivalent. The drafts of the East India Company (now the East India government) reserve themselves into a tribute levied on India. For instance, in 1855, imports from India to England amounted to £12,670,000; English exports to India amounted to £10,350,000; balance in India's favour £2,250,000. [*i.e*, approximately 2¼ million: more precisely, £2,320,000.—*Ed.*]

> 'If that was the whole state of the case, that £2,250,000 would have to be remitted in some form to India. But then come in the advertisements from the India House. The India House advertise to this effect that they are prepared to grant drafts on the various presidencies in India to the extent of £3,250,000.'

[This amount was levied for the London expenses of the East India Company and for the dividends to be paid to stockholders.]

> 'And that not merely liquidates the £2,250,000 which arose out of the course of trade, but it presents £1,000,000 of surplus' (1917) [B. A. 1857].
>
> '1922. [Wood:] Then the effect of those India House drafts is not to increase the exports to India, but *pro tanto* to diminish them?'

[This should read: to reduce the necessity of covering the imports from India by exports to that country to the same amount.] Mr Newmarch explains this by saying that the British import 'good government' into India for these £3,700,000 (1925). Wood, as a former Minister for India, knows full well the kind of 'good government' which the British import to India, and correctly replies with irony:

> '1926. Then the export, which, you state, is caused by the East India drafts, is an export of good government, and not of produce.'

Since England exports a good deal 'in this way' for 'good government' and as capital investment in foreign countries—thus obtaining imports which are completely independent of the ordinary run of business, tribute partly for exported 'good government' and partly in the form of revenues from capital invested in the colonies or elsewhere, *i.e.*, tribute for which it does not have to pay any equivalent—it is evident that the rates of exchange are not affected when England simply consumes this tribute without exporting anything in return. Hence, it is also evident that the rates of exchange are not affected when it reinvests this tribute, not in England, but productively or unproductively in foreign countries; for instance, when it sends munitions for it to the Crimea. Moreover, to the extent that imports from abroad enter into the revenue of England—of course, they must be paid for in the form of tribute, for which no equivalent return is necessary, or by exchange for this unpaid tribute or in the ordinary course of commerce—England can either consume them or reinvest them as capital. In neither case are the rates of exchange affected, and this is overlooked by the sage Wilson. Whether a domestic or a foreign product constitutes a part of the revenue—whereby the latter case merely requires an exchange of domestic for foreign products—the consumption of this revenue, be it productive or unproductive, alters nothing in the rates of exchange, even though it may alter the scale of production. The following should be read with the foregoing in mind:

1934. Wood asks Newmarch how the shipment of war supplies to the Crimea would affect the rate of exchange with Turkey. Newmarch replies:

> 'I do not see that the mere transmission of warlike stores would necessarily affect the exchange, but certainly the transmission of treasure would affect the exchange.'

In this case he thus distinguishes capital in the form of money from capital in other forms. But now Wilson asks:

> '1935. If you make an export of any article to a great extent, for which there is to be no corresponding import.'

[Mr Wilson forgets that there are very considerable imports into England for which corresponding exports have never taken place, except in the form of 'good government' or of previously exported investment capital; in any case imports which do not enter into normal commercial movement. But these imports are again exchanged, for instance, for American products, and the circumstance that American goods are exported without corresponding imports does not alter the fact that the value of these imports can be consumed without an equivalent flow abroad; they have been received without reciprocal exports and can therefore be consumed without entering into the balance of trade],

> 'you do not discharge the foreign debt you have created by your imports.'

[but, if you have previously paid for these imports, for instance, by credit given abroad, then no debt is contracted thereby, and the question has nothing to do with the international balance; it resolves itself into productive and unproductive expenditures, no matter whether the products so consumed are domestic or foreign],

> 'and therefore you must by that transaction affect the exchanges by not discharging the foreign debt, by reason of your export having no corresponding imports?—That is true as regards countries generally.'

This lecture by Wilson amounts to saying that every export with no corresponding import is simultaneously an import with no corresponding export, because foreign, *i.e.*, imported, commodities enter into the production of the exported article. The assumption is that every export of this kind is based on, or creates, an unpaid import and thus presupposes a debt abroad. This is wrong, even when the following two circumstances are disregarded: 1) England receives certain imports free of charge for which it pays no equivalent, *e.g.*, a portion of its Indian imports. It can exchange these for American imports and export the latter without importing in return; in any case, so far as the value is concerned, it has only exported something that has cost it nothing. 2) England may have paid for imports, for instance, American imports, which constitute additional capital; if it consumes these unproductively, for instance, as war materials, this does not constitute any debt towards America and does not affect the rate of exchange with America. Newmarch contradicts himself in Nos. 1934 and 1935, and Wood calls this to his attention in No. 1938:

> 'If no portion of the goods which are employed in the manufacture of the articles exported without return [war materials], came from the country to which those articles are sent, how is the exchange with that country affected; supposing the trade with Turkey to be in an ordinary state of equilibrium, how is the exchange between this country and Turkey affected by the export of warlike stores to the Crimea?'

Here, Newmarch loses his equanimity; he forgets that he has answered the same simple question correctly in No. 1934, and says:

> 'We seem, I think, to have exhausted the practical question, and to have now attained a very elevated region of metaphysical discussion.'

[Wilson has still another version of his claim that the rate of exchange is affected by every transfer of capital from one country to another, no matter whether in the form of precious metal or commodities. Wilson knows, of course, that the rate of exchange is affected by the interest rate, particularly by the relation of the rates of interest prevailing in the two countries whose mutual rates of exchange are under discussion. If he can now demonstrate that surpluses of capital in general, *i.e.*, in the first place, commodities of all kinds including precious metal, have a hand in influencing the interest rate, then he is a step closer to his goal; a transfer of any considerable portion of this capital to some other country must then change the interest rate in both countries, with the change taking place in opposite directions. Thereby, in a secondary way, the rate of exchange between both countries is also altered.—*F. E.*]

He then says in the *Economist*, May 22, 1847, page 574, which he edited at the time:

> No doubt, however, such abundance of capital as is indicated by large stocks of commodities of all kinds, including bullion, would necessarily lead, not only to low prices of commodities in general, but also to a lower rate of interest for the use of capital. If we have a stock of commodities on hand, which is sufficient to serve the country for two years to come, a command over those commodities would be obtained for a given period, at a much lower rate than if the stocks were barely sufficient to last us two months. All loans of money, in whatever shape they are made, are simply a transfer of a command over commodities from one to another. Whenever, therefore, commodities are abundant, the interest of money must be low, and when they are scarce, the interest of money must be high. As commodities become abundant, the number of sellers, in proportion to the number of buyers, increases, and, in proportion as the quantity is more than is required for immediate consumption, so must a larger portion be kept for future use. Under these circumstances, the terms on which a holder becomes willing to sell for a future payment, or on credit, become lower than if he were certain that his whole stock would be required within a few weeks.

In regard to the statement, it is to be noted that a large *influx* in precious metal can take place simultaneously with a *contraction* in production, as is always the case in the period following a crisis. In the subsequent phase, precious metal may come in from countries which mainly produce precious metal; imports of other commodities are generally balanced by exports during this period. In these two phases, the interest rate is low and rises but slowly; we have already discussed the reason for this. This low interest rate could always be explained without recourse to the influence of any 'large stocks of commodities of all kinds.' And how is this influence to take place? The low price of cotton, for instance, renders possible the high profits of the spinners, etc. Now, why is the interest rate low? Surely not because the profit, which may be made on borrowed capital, is high. But simply and solely because, under existing conditions, the demand for loan capital does not grow in proportion to this profit; in other words, because loan capital has a movement different from industrial capital. What the *Economist* wants to prove is exactly the reverse, namely, that the movements of loan capital are identical with those of industrial capital.

In regard to the statement, if we reduce the absurd assumption of stocks for two years in advance to the point where it begins to take on some meaning, it signifies that the market is overstocked. This would cause a fall in prices. Less would have to be paid for a bale of cotton. This would by no means justify the conclusion that money for the purchase of this cotton is more easily borrowed. This depends on the state of the money-market. If money can be borrowed more easily, it is only because commercial credit is in a state requiring it to make less use than usual of bank credit. The commodities glutting the market are either means of subsistence or means of production. The low price of both increases the industrial capitalist's profit. Why should it depress the interest rate, unless it be through the antithesis, rather than the identity, between the abundance of industrial capital and the demand for money accommodation? Circumstances are such that the merchant and industrial capitalist can more easily advance credit to one another; owing to this facilitation of commercial credit, both industrialist as well as merchant need less bank credit; hence the interest rate can be low. This low interest rate has nothing to do with the influx in precious metal, although both may run parallel to each other, and the same causes bringing about low prices of imported articles may also produce a surplus of imported precious metal. If the import market were really glutted, it would prove that a decrease in the demand for imported articles had taken place, and this would be inexplicable at low prices, unless it were attributed to a contraction of domestic industrial production; but this, again, would be inexplicable, so long as there is excessive importing at low prices. A mass of absurdities—in order to prove that a fall in prices = a fall in the interest rate. Both may simultaneously exist side by side. But if they do, it will be a reflection of the opposition in the directions of the movement of industrial capital and the movement of loanable money-capital. It will not be a reflection of their identity.

In regard to the statement, it is hard to understand even after this exposition why money interest should be low when commodities are available in abundance. If commodities are cheap, then I may need only £1,000 instead of the previous £2,000 to buy a definite quantity. But perhaps I nevertheless invest £2,000, and thus buy twice the quantity which I could have bought formerly. In this way, I expand my business by advancing the same capital, which I may have to borrow. I buy £2,000 worth of commodities, the same as before. My demand on the money-market therefore remains the same, even though my demand on the commodity-market rises with the fall in commodity-prices. But if this demand for commodities should decrease, that is, if production should not expand with the fall in commodity-prices, an event which would contradict all the laws of the *Economist,* then the demand for loanable money-capital would decrease, although the profit would increase. But this increasing profit would create a demand for loan capital. Incidentally, a low level of commodity-prices may be due to three causes. First, to lack of demand. In such a case, the interest rate is low because production is paralysed and not because commodities are cheap, for the low prices are but a rejection of that paralysis. Second, it may be due to supply exceeding demand. This may be the result of a glut on the market, etc., which may lead to a crisis and coincide with a high interest rate during the crisis itself; or, it may be the result of a fall in the value of commodities, so that the same demand can be satisfied at lower prices. Why should the interest rate fall in the last case? Because profits increase? If this were due to less money-capital being required for obtaining the same productive or commodity-capital, it would merely prove that profit and interest are inversely proportional to each other. In any case, the general statement of the *Economist* is false. Low money-prices for commodities and a low interest rate do not necessarily go together. Otherwise, the interest rate would be lowest in the poorest countries, where money-prices for produce are lowest, and highest in the richest countries, where money-prices for agricultural products are highest. In general, the *Economist* admits: If the value of money falls, it exerts no influence on the interest rate. £100 bring £105 the same as ever. If the £100 are worth less, so are the £5 interest. This relation is not affected by the appreciation or depreciation of the original sum. Considered from the point of view of value, a definite quantity of commodities is equal to a definite sum of money. If this value increases, it is equal to a larger sum of money. The opposite is true when it falls. If the value is equal to 2,000, then 5% = 100; if it is equal to 1,000, then 5% = 50. But this does not alter the interest rate in any way. The rational part of this matter is merely that greater money accommodation is required when it takes £2,000 to sell the same quantity of commodities than when only £1,000 are required. But this merely shows that profit and interest are here inversely proportional to each other. For the lower the prices of the components of constant and variable capital, the higher the profit and the lower the interest. But the opposite can also be and is often the case. For instance, cotton may be cheap because no demand exists for yarn and fabrics; and cotton may be relatively expensive because a large profit in the cotton industry creates a great demand for it. On the other hand, the profits of industrialists may be high precisely because the price of cotton is low. Hubbard's table proves that the interest rate and the prices of commodities execute completely independent movements, whereas the movements of the interest rate adhere closely to those of the metal reserve and the rates of exchange.

The *Economist* states:

Whenever, therefore, commodities are abundant, the interest of money must be low.

Precisely the opposite obtains during crises. Commodities are superabundant, inconvertible into money, and therefore the interest rate is high; in another phase of the cycle, the demand for commodities is great, and therefore, quick returns are made, but at the same time, prices are rising, and because of the quick returns the interest rate is low.

When they [the commodities] are scarce, the interest of money must be high.

The opposite is again true in the slack period following a crisis. Commodities are scarce, absolutely speaking, not with reference to demand; and the interest rate is low.

In regard to the statement, it is pretty evident that an owner of commodities, provided he can sell the latter at all, will get rid of them at a lower price when the market is glutted than he would when there is a prospect of the existing supply becoming rapidly exhausted. But why the interest rate should fall because of that is not so clear.

If the market is glutted with imported commodities, the interest rate may rise as a result of an increased demand on the part of the owners for loan capital, in order to avoid dumping their commodities on the market. The interest rate may fall, because the fluidity of commercial credit may keep the demand for bank credit relatively low.

The *Economist* mentions the rapid effect on rates of exchange in 1847 of the raising of the interest rate and other circumstances exerting pressure on the money-market. But it should be borne in mind that the gold drain continued until the end of April in spite of the change in the rates of exchange; a turn did not take place here until early May.

On January 1, 1847, the metal reserve of the Bank was £15,066,691; the interest rate 3½%; three months' rates of exchange on Paris 25.75; on Hamburg 13.10; on Amsterdam 12.3¼. On March 5, the metal reserve had fallen to £11,595,535; the discount had risen to 4%; the rate of exchange fell to 25.67½ on Paris; 13.9¼ on Hamburg; and 12.2½ on Amsterdam. The drain of gold continued. See the following table:

1847	*Bullion Reserve of the Bank of England*	*Money-Market*	*Highest Three-Month Rates*		
			Paris	*Hamburg*	*Amsterdam*
March 20	11,231,630	Bank disc. 4%	25.67½	13.9¾	12.2½
April 3	10,246,410	„ „ 5%	25.80	13.10	12.3½
April 10	9,867,053	Money very scarce	25.90	13.10½	12.4½
April 17	9,329,841	Bank disc. 5.5%	26.02½	13.40¾	12.5½
April 24	9,213,890	Pressure	26.05	13.12	12.6
May 4	9,337,746	Increasing pressure	26.45	13.12¾	12.6½
May 8	9,588,759	Highest pressure	26.27½	13.15½	12.7¾

In 1847, the total export of precious metal from England amounted to £8,602,597.

Of this to the

United States	£3,226,411
France	£2,479,892
Hanse towns	£958,781
Holland	£247,743

In spite of the change in the rates at the end of March, the drain of gold continued for another full month, probably to the United States.

> We thus see [says the *Economist*, August 2, 1847, p. 954] how rapid and striking was the effect of a rise in the rate of interest, and the pressure which ensued in correcting an adverse exchange, and in turning the tide of bullion back to this country. This effect was produced entirely independent of the balance of trade. A higher rate of interest caused a lower price of securities, both foreign and English, and induced large purchases to be made on foreign account, which increased the amount of bills to be drawn from this country, while, on the other hand, the high rate of interest and the difficulty of obtaining money was such that the demand of those bills fell off, while their amount increased.... For the same cause orders for imports were countermanded, and investments of English funds abroad were realised and brought home for employment here. Thus, for example, we read in the *Rio de Janeiro Price Current* of the 10th May, 'Exchange [on England] has experienced a further decline, principally caused by a pressure on the market for remittance of the proceeds of large sales of [Brazilian] government stock, on English account.' Capital belonging to this country, which has been invested in public and other securities abroad, when the interest was very low here, was thus again brought back when the interest became high.

England's Balance of Trade

India alone has to pay 5 million in tribute for 'good government,' interest and dividends on British capital, etc., not counting the sums sent home annually by officials as savings from their salaries, or by English merchants as part of their profit to be invested in England. Every British colony continually has to make large remittances for the same reason. Most of the banks in Australia, the West Indies, and Canada, have been founded with English capital, and the dividends are payable in England. In the same way, England owns many foreign securities—European, North American, and South American—on which it draws interest. In addition to this, it has interests in foreign railways, canals, mines, etc., with corresponding dividends. Remittance on all these items is made almost exclusively in products over and above the amount of English exports. On the other hand, what is sent from England to owners of English securities abroad and for consumption by Englishmen abroad, is insignificant in comparison.

The question, so far as it concerns the balance of trade and the rates of exchange, is 'at any particular moment one of time.'

> Practically speaking ... England gives long credits upon her exports, while the imports are paid for in ready money. At particular moments this difference of practice has a considerable effect upon the exchanges. At a time when our exports are very considerably increasing, *e.g.*, 1850, a continual increase of investment of British capital must be going on ... in this way remittances of 1850 may be made against goods exported in 1849. But if the exports of 1850 exceed those of 1849 by more than 6 million, the practical effect must he that more money is sent abroad, to this amount, than returned in the same year. And in this way an effect is produced on the rates of exchange and the rate of interest. When, on the contrary, our trade is depressed after a commercial crisis, and when our exports are much reduced, the remittances due for the past years of larger exports greatly exceed the value of our imports; the exchanges become correspondingly in our favour, capital rapidly accumulates at home, and the rate of interest becomes less. *(Economist,* January 11, 1851 [p. 30].)

The foreign rates of exchange can change:

1. In consequence of the immediate balance of payments, no matter what the cause—a purely mercantile one, or capital investment abroad, or government expenditures for wars, etc., in so far as cash payments thereby are made to foreign countries.

2. In consequence of money depreciation—whether metal or paper—in a particular country. This is purely nominal. If £1 should represent only half as much money as formerly, it would naturally be counted as 12.5 francs instead of 25 francs.
3. When it is a matter of a rate of exchange between countries, of which one uses silver and the other gold as 'money,' the rate of exchange depends upon the relative fluctuations of the value of these two metals, since these necessarily alter the parity between them. This is illustrated by the rates of exchange in 1850; they were unfavourable to England, although that country's export rose enormously. Yet, no drain of gold took place. This was a result of a momentary rise in the value of silver as against gold. (See *Economist,* November 30, 1850 [pp. 1319-1320].)

Parity for the rate of exchange of £1 is: Paris, 25 francs 20 cent.; Hamburg, 13 marks banko 10.5 shillings; Amsterdam, 11 florins 97 cent. To the extent that the Paris rate of exchange exceeds 25.20 francs, it becomes more favourable to the English debtor of France, or the buyer of French commodities. In both cases, he needs fewer pounds sterling in order to accomplish his purpose.—In remoter countries, where precious metal is not easily obtained when bills of exchange are scarce and insufficient for remittances to be made to England, the natural effect is to drive up the prices of such products as are generally shipped to England since a greater demand arises for them, in order to send them to England in place of bills of exchange; this is often the case in India.

An unfavourable rate of exchange, or even a drain on gold, can take place when there is a great abundance of money in England, the interest rate is low and the price for securities is high.

In the course of 1848, England received large quantities of silver from India, since good bills of exchange were rare and mediocre ones were not readily accepted in consequence of the crisis of 1847 and the general lack of credit in business with India. All this silver had barely arrived before it found its way to the continent, where the revolution led to the formation of many hoards. The bulk of the same silver made the trip back to India in 1850, since the rate of exchange now made this profitable.

The monetary system is essentially a Catholic institution, the credit system essentially Protestant. 'The Scotch hate gold.' In the form of paper the monetary existence of commodities is only a social one. It is *Faith* that brings salvation. Faith in money-value as the immanent spirit of commodities, faith in the mode of production and its predestined order, faith in the individual agents of production as mere personifications of self-expanding capital. But the credit system does not emancipate itself from the basis of the monetary system any more than Protestantism has emancipated itself from the foundations of Catholicism.

Notes

1. The effect this had on the money-market is indicated by the following testimony of Newmarch: '1509. At the close of 1853, there was a considerable apprehension in the public mind, and in September of that year the Bank of England raised its discount on three occasions... In the early part of October there was a considerable degree of apprehension and alarm in the public mind. That apprehension and alarm was relieved to a very great extent before the end of November, and was almost wholly removed, in consequence of the arrival of nearly £5,000,000 of treasure from Australia... The same thing happened in the autumn of 1854, by the arrival in the months of October and November of nearly £6,000,000 of treasure. The same thing happened again in the autumn of 1855, which we know was a period of excitement and alarm, by the arrivals, in the three months of September, October and November, of nearly £8,000,000 of treasure; and then at the close of last year, 1856, we find exactly the same occurrence. In truth, I might appeal to the observation almost of any member of the Committee, whether the natural and complete solvent to which we have got

into the habit of looking for any financial pressure, is not the arrival of a gold ship' [B. A. 1857].

2. According to Newmarch, a drain of gold to foreign countries can arise from three causes: 1) from purely commercial conditions, that is, if imports have exceeded exports, as was the case in 1836 to 1844, and again in 1847—principally a heavy import of grain; 2) in order to secure the means for investing English capital in foreign countries, as in 1857 for railways in India, and 3) for definite expenditures abroad, as in 1853 and 1854 for war purposes in the Orient.

3. 1918. Newmarch. 'When you combine India and China, when you bring into account the transactions between India and Australia, and the still more important transactions between China and the United States, the trade being a triangular one, and the adjustment taking place through us ... then it is true that the balance of trade was not merely against this country, but against France, and against the United States.'—(B. A. 1857.)

4. See, for instance, the ridiculous reply of Weguelin [B.A. 1857] where he states that a drain of five million in gold is so much capital less, and thus attempts to explain certain phenomena which do *not* take place when there is an infinitely greater increase in prices or depreciation, expansion or contraction of real industrial capital. On the other hand, it is just as ridiculous to attempt to explain these phenomena directly as symptoms of an expansion or contraction of the mass of real capital (considered from the viewpoint of its material elements).

5. Newmarch (B. A. 1857): '1364. The reserve of bullion in the Bank of England is, in truth, the central reserve or hoard of treasure upon which the whole trade of the country is made to turn; all the other banks in the country look to the Bank of England as the central hoard or reservoir from which they are to draw their reserve of coin; and it is upon that hoard or reservoir that the action of the foreign exchanges always falls.›

6. 'Practically, then, both Mr Tooke and Mr Loyd would meet an additional demand for gold ... by an early ... contraction of credit by raising the rate of interest, and restricting advances of capital.... But the principles of Mr Loyd lead to certain [legal] restrictions and regulations which produce the most serious inconvenience.' *(Economist* [December 11], 1847, p. 1418.)

7. 'You quite agree that there is no mode by which you can modify the demand for bullion except by raising the rate of interest?›—Chapman [associate member of the great bill-brokers' firm of Overend, Gurney & Co.]: 'I should say so.... When our bullion falls to a certain point, we had better sound the tocsin at once and say we are drooping, and every man sending money abroad must do it at his own peril.' (B. A. 1857, Evidence No. 5057.)

36

Pre-Capitalist Relationships

Interest-bearing capital, or, as we may call it in its antiquated form, usurer's capital, belongs together with its twin brother, merchant's capital, to the antediluvian forms of capital, which long precede the capitalist mode of production and are to be found in the most diverse economic formations of society.

The existence of usurer's capital merely requires that at least a portion of products should be transformed into commodities, and that money should have developed in its various functions along with trade in commodities.

The development of usurer's capital is bound up with the development of merchant's capital and especially that of money-dealing capital. In ancient Rome, beginning with the last years of the Republic, when manufacturing stood far below its average level of development in the ancient world, merchant's capital, money-dealing capital, and usurer's capital developed to their highest point within the ancient form.

We have seen (English edition: Vol. I, pp. 130-34.—*Ed.*) that hoarding necessarily appears along with money. But the professional hoarder does not become important until he is transformed into a usurer.

The merchant borrows money in order to make a profit with it, in order to use it as capital, that is, to expend it. Hence in earlier forms of society the money-lender stands in the same relation to him as to the modern capitalist. This specific relation was also experienced by the Catholic universities.

> The universities of Alcalá, Salamanca, Ingolstadt, Freiburg in Breisgau, Mayence, Cologne, Trèves, one after another recognized the legality of interest for commercial loans. The first five of these approbations were deposited in the archives of the Consulate of the city of Lyons and published in the appendix to the *Traitè de l'usure et des intérêts*, by Bruyset-Ponthus, Lyons. (M. Augier, *Le Crèdit public, etc.*, Paris, 1842, p. 206.)

In all the forms in which slave economy (not the patriarchal kind, but that of later Grecian and Roman times) serves as a means of amassing wealth, where money, therefore, is a means of appropriating the labour of others through the purchase of slaves, land, etc., money can be expanded as capital, i.e., bear interest, for the very reason that it can be so invested.

The characteristic forms, however, in which usurer's capital exists in periods antedating capitalist production are of two kinds. I purposely say characteristic forms. The same forms repeat themselves on the basis of capitalist production, but as mere subordinate forms. They are then no longer the forms which determine the character of interest-bearing capital. These two forms are: first, usury by lending money to extravagant members of the upper classes, particularly landowners; secondly, usury by lending money to small producers who possess their own conditions of labour—this includes the artisan, but mainly the peasant, since particularly under pre-capitalist conditions, in so far as they permit of small independent individual producers, the peasant class necessarily constitutes the overwhelming majority of them.

Both the ruin of rich landowners through usury and the impoverishment of the small producers lead to the formation and concentration of large amounts of money-capital. But to what extent this process does away with the old mode of production, as happened in modern Europe, and whether it puts the capitalist mode of production in its stead, depends entirely upon the stage of historical development and the attendant circumstances.

Usurer's capital as the characteristic form of interest-bearing capital corresponds to the predominance of small-scale production of the self-employed peasant and small master craftsman. When the labourer is confronted by the conditions of labour and by the product of labour in the shape of capital, as under the developed capitalist mode of production, he has no occasion to borrow any money as a producer. When he does any money borrowing, he does so, for instance, at the pawnshop to secure personal necessities. But wherever the labourer is the owner, whether actual or nominal, of his conditions of labour and his product, he stands as a producer in relation to the money-lender's capital, which confronts him as usurer's capital. Newman expresses the matter insipidly when he says the banker is respected, while the usurer is hated and despised, because the banker lends to the rich, whereas the usurer lends to the poor. (F. W. Newman, *Lectures on Political Economy*, London, 1851, p. 44.) He overlooks the fact that a difference between two modes of social production and their corresponding social orders lies at the heart of the matter and that the situation cannot be explained by the distinction between rich and poor. Moreover, the usury which sucks dry the small producer goes hand in hand with the usury which sucks dry the rich owner of a large estate. As soon as the usury of the Roman patricians had completely ruined the Roman plebeians, the small peasants, this form of exploitation came to an end and a pure slave economy replaced the small-peasant economy.

In the form of interest, the entire surplus above the barest means of subsistence (the amount that later becomes wages of the producers) can be consumed by usury (this later assumes the form of profit and ground-rent), and hence it is highly absurd to compare the level of this interest, which assimilates all the surplus-value excepting the share claimed by the state, with the level of the modern interest rate, where interest constitutes at least normally only a part of the surplus-value. Such a comparison overlooks that the wage-worker produces and gives to the capitalist who employs him, profit, interest and ground-rent, i.e., the entire surplus-value. Carey makes this absurd comparison in order to show how advantageous the development of capital, and the fall in the interest rate that accompanies it, are for the labourer. Furthermore, while the usurer, not content with squeezing the surplus-labour out of his victim, gradually acquires possession even of his very conditions of labour, land, house, etc., and is continually engaged in thus expropriating him, it is again forgotten that, on the other hand, this complete expropriation of the labourer from his conditions of labour is not a result which the capitalist mode of production seeks to achieve, but rather the established condition for its point of departure. The wage-slave, just like the real slave, cannot become a creditor's slave due to his position—at least in his capacity as producer; the wage-slave, it is true, can become a creditor's slave in his capacity as consumer. Usurer's capital in the form whereby it indeed appropriates all of the surplus-labour of the direct producers, without altering the mode of production; whereby the ownership or possession by the producers of the conditions of labour and small-scale production corresponding to this—is its essential prerequisite; whereby, in other words, capital does not directly subordinate labour to itself, and does not, therefore, confront it as industrial capital—this usurer's capital impoverishes the mode of production, paralyses the productive forces instead of developing them, and at the same time perpetuates the miserable conditions in which the social productivity of labour is not developed at the expense of labour itself, as in the capitalist mode of production.

Usury thus exerts, on the one hand, an undermining and destructive influence on ancient and feudal wealth and ancient and feudal property. On the other hand, it undermines and ruins small-peasant and small-burgher production, in short, all forms in which the producer still appears as the owner of his means of production. Under the developed capitalist mode of production, the labourer is not the owner of the means of production, i.e., the field which he cultivates, the raw materials which he processes, etc. But under this system separation of the producer from the means of production reflects an actual revolution in the mode of production itself. The isolated labourers are brought together in large workshops for the purpose of carrying out separate but interconnected activities; the tool becomes a machine. The mode of production itself no longer permits the dispersion of the instruments of production associated with small property; nor does it permit the isolation of the labourer himself. Under the capitalist mode of production usury can no longer separate the producer from his means of production, for they have already been separated.

Usury centralizes money wealth where the means of production are dispersed. It does not alter the mode of production, but attaches itself firmly to it like a parasite and makes it wretched. It sucks out its blood, enervates it and compels reproduction to proceed under ever more pitiable conditions. Hence the popular hatred against usurers, which was most pronounced in the ancient world where ownership of means of production by the producer himself was at the same time the basis for political status, the independence of the citizen.

To the extent that slavery prevails, or in so far as the surplus product is consumed by the feudal lord and his retinue, while either the slave-owner or the feudal lord fall into the clutches of the usurer, the mode of production still remains the same; it only becomes harder on the labourer. The indebted slave holder or feudal lord becomes more oppressive because he is himself more oppressed. Or he finally makes way for the usurer, who becomes a landed proprietor or a slave-holder himself, like the knights in ancient Rome. The place of the old exploiter, whose exploitation was more or less patriarchal because it was largely a means of political power, is taken by a hard, money mad parvenu. But the mode of production itself is not altered thereby.

Usury has a revolutionary effect in all pre-capitalist modes of production only in so far as it destroys and dissolves those forms of property on whose solid foundation and continual reproduction in the same form the political organization is based. Under Asian forms, usury can continue a long time, without producing anything more than economic decay and political corruption. Only where and when the other prerequisites of capitalist production are present does usury become one of the means assisting in establishment of the new mode of production by ruining the feudal lord and small-scale producer, on the one hand, and centralizing the conditions of labour into capital, on the other.

> In the Middle Ages no country had a general rate of interest. The Church forbade, from the outset, all lending at interest. Laws and courts offered little protection for loans. Interest was so much the higher in individual cases. The limited circulation of money, the need to make most payments in cash, compelled people to borrow money, and all the more so when the exchange business has still undeveloped. Therefore large divergences both in interest rates and the conceptions of usury. In the time of Charlemagne it was considered usurious to charge 100%. In Lindau on Lake Constance, some local burghers took 216⅔% in 1348. In Zurich, the City Council decreed that 43⅓% should be the legal interest rate. In Italy 40% had to be paid sometimes, although the usual rate from the 12th to the 14th century did not exceed 20%. Verona ordered that 12½% be the legal rate. Emperor Friedrich II fixed the rate at 10%, but only for Jews. He did not deign to speak for Christians. In the German Rhine provinces, 10% was the rule as early as the 13th century. (Hullmann, *Geschichte des Städtewesens*, II, S. 55-57.)

Usurer's capital employs the method of exploitation characteristic of capital yet without the latter's mode of production. This condition also repeats itself within bourgeois economy, in backward branches of industry or in those branches which resist the transition to the modern mode of production. For instance, if we wish to compare the English interest rate with the Indian, we should not take the interest rate of the Bank of England, but rather, e.g., that charged by lenders of small machinery to small producers in domestic industry.

Usury, in contradistinction to consuming wealth, is historically important, inasmuch as it is in itself a process generating capital. Usurer's capital and merchant's wealth promote the formation of moneyed wealth independent of landed property. The less products assume the character of commodities, and the less intensively and extensively exchange-value has taken hold of production, the more does money appear as actual wealth as such, as wealth in general—in contrast to its limited representation in use-values. This is the basis of hoarding. Aside from money as world-money and as hoard, it is, in particular, the form of means of payment whereby it appears as the absolute form of commodities. And it is especially its function as a means of payment which develops interest and thereby money-capital. What squandering and corrupting wealth desires is money as such, money as a means of buying everything (also as a means of paying debts). The small producer needs money above all for making payments. (The transformation of services and taxes in kind to landlords and the state into money-rent and money-taxes plays a great role here.) In either case, money is needed as such. On the other hand, it is in usury that hoarding first becomes reality and that the hoarder fulfills his dream. What is sought from the owner of a hoard is not capital, but money as such; but by means of interest he transforms this hoard of money into capital, that is, into a means of appropriating surplus labour in part or in its entirety, and similarly securing a hold on a part of the means of production themselves, even though they may nominally remain the property of others. Usury lives in the pores of production, as it were, just as the gods of Epicurus lived in the space between worlds. Money is so much harder to obtain, the less the commodity-form constitutes the general form of products. Hence the usurer knows no other barrier but the capacity of those who need money to pay or to resist. In small-peasant and small-burgher production money serves as a means of purchase, mainly, whenever the means of production of the labourer (who is still predominantly their owner under these modes of production) are lost to him either by accident or through extraordinary upheavals, or at least are not replaced in the normal course of reproduction. Means of subsistence and raw materials constitute an essential part of these requirements of production. If these become more expensive, it may make it impossible to replace them out of the returns for the product, just as ordinary crop failures may prevent the peasant from replacing his seed in kind. The same wars through which the Roman patricians ruined the plebe jails by compelling them to serve as soldiers and which prevented them from reproducing their conditions of labour, and therefore, made paupers of them (and pauperization, the crippling or loss of the prerequisites of reproduction is here the predominant form) these same wars filled the store-rooms and coffers of the patricians with looted copper, the money of that time. Instead of directly giving plebeians the necessary commodities, i.e., grain, horses, and cattle, they loaned them this copper for which they had no use themselves, and took advantage of this situation to exact enormous usurious interest, thereby turning the plebeians into their debtor slaves. During the reign of Charlemagne, the Frankish peasants were likewise ruined by wars, so that they faced no choice but to become serfs instead of debtors. In the Roman Empire, as is known, extreme hunger frequently resulted in the sale of children and also in free men selling themselves as slaves to the rich. So much for general turning-points. In individual cases, the maintenance or loss of the means of production on the part of small producers depends on a thousand contingencies, and every one of these contingencies or losses signifies impoverishment and becomes a crevice into which a parasitic usurer may creep. The mere death of his cow may render the small peasant incapable of renewing his reproduction on its former scale. He then falls into the clutches of the usurer, and once in the usurer's power, he can never extricate himself.

The really important and characteristic domain of the usurer, however, is the function of money as a means of payment. Every payment of money, ground-rent, tribute, tax, etc., which becomes due on a certain date, carries with it the need to secure money for such a purpose. Hence from the days of ancient Rome to those of modern times, wholesale usury relies upon tax-collectors, *fermiers gènèraux, receveurs gènèraux*. Then, there develops with commerce and the generalization of commodity- production the separation, in time, of purchase and payment. The money has to be paid on a definite date. How this can lead to circumstances in which the money-capitalist and usurer, even nowadays, merge into one is shown by modern money crises. This same usury, however, becomes one of the principal means of further developing the necessity for money as a means of payment—by driving the producer ever more deeply into debt and destroying his usual means of payment, since the burden of interest alone makes his normal reproduction impossible. At this point, usury sprouts up out of money as a means of payment and extends this function of money as its very own domain.

The credit system develops as a reaction against usury. But this should not be misunderstood, nor by any means interpreted in the manner of the ancient writers, the church fathers, Luther or the early socialists. It signifies no more and no less than the subordination of interest-bearing capital to the conditions and requirements of the capitalist mode of production.

On the whole, interest-bearing capital under the modern credit system is adapted to the conditions of the capitalist mode of production. Usury as such does not only continue to exist, but is even freed, among nations with a developed capitalist production, from the fetters imposed upon it by all previous legislation. Interest-bearing capital retains the form of usurer's capital in relation to persons or classes, or in circumstances where borrowing does not, nor can, take place in the sense corresponding to the capitalist mode of production; where borrowing takes place as a result of individual need, as at the pawnshop; where money is borrowed by wealthy spendthrifts for the purpose of squandering; or where the producer is a non-capitalist producer, such as a small farmer or craftsman, who is thus still, as the immediate producer, the owner of his own means of production; finally where the capitalist producer himself operates on such a small scale that he resembles those self-employed producers.

What distinguishes interest-bearing capital—in so far as it is an essential element of the capitalist mode of production—from usurer's capital is by no means the nature or character of this capital itself. It is merely the altered conditions under which it operates, and consequently also the totally transformed character of the borrower who confronts the money-lender. Even when a man without fortune receives credit in his capacity of industrialist or merchant, it occurs with the expectation that he will function as capitalist and appropriate unpaid labour with the borrowed capital. He receives credit in his capacity of potential capitalist. The circumstance that a man without fortune but possessing energy, solidity, ability and business acumen may become a capitalist in this manner—and the commercial value of each individual is pretty accurately estimated under the capitalist mode of production—is greatly admired by apologists of the capitalist system. Although this circumstance continually brings an unwelcome number of new soldiers of fortune into the field and into competition with the already existing individual capitalists, it also reinforces the supremacy of capital itself, expands its base and enables it to recruit ever new forces for itself out of the substratum of society. In a similar way, the circumstance that the Catholic Church in the Middle Ages formed its hierarchy out of the best brains in the land, regardless of their estate, birth or fortune, was one of the principal means of consolidating ecclesiastical rule and suppressing the laity. The more a ruling class is able to assimilate the foremost minds of a ruled class, the more stable and dangerous becomes its rule.

The initiators of the modern credit system take as their point of departure not an anathema against interest-bearing capital in general, but on the contrary, its explicit recognition.

We are not referring here to such reactions against usury which attempted to protect the poor against it, like the *Monts-de-piètè* (1350 in Sarlins in Franche-Comté, later in Perugia and Savona in Italy, 1400 and 1479). These are noteworthy mainly because they reveal the irony of history, which turns pious wishes into their very opposite during the process of realization. According to a moderate estimate, the English working-class pays 100% to the pawnshops, the modern successors of *Monts-de-piètè*[1] We are also not referring to the credit fantasies of such men as Dr Hugh Chamberleyne or John Briscoe, who attempted during the last decade of the 17th century to emancipate the English aristocracy from usury by means of a farmers' bank using paper money based on real estate.[2]

The credit associations established in the 12th and 14th centuries in Venice and Genoa arose from the need for marine commerce and the wholesale trade associated with it to emancipate themselves from the domination of outmoded usury and the monopolization of the money business. While the actual banks founded in those city-republics assumed simultaneously the shape of public credit institutions from which the state received loans on future tax revenues, it should not be forgotten that the merchants founding those associations were themselves prominent citizens of those states and as much interested in emancipating their government as they were in emancipating themselves from the exactions of usurers,[3] and at the same time in getting tighter and more secure control over the state. Hence, when the Bank of England was to be established, the Tories also protested:

> Banks are republican institutions. Flourishing banks existed in Venice, Genoa, Amsterdam, and Hamburg. But who ever heard of a Bank of France or Spain?

The Bank of Amsterdam, in 1609, was not epoch-making in the development of the modern credit system any more than that of Hamburg in 1619. It was purely a bank for deposits. The checks issued by the bank were indeed merely receipts for the deposited coined and uncoined precious metal, and circulated only with the endorsement of the acceptors. But in Holland commercial credit and dealing in money developed hand in hand with commerce and manufacture, and interest-bearing capital was subordinated to industrial and commercial capital by the course of development itself. This could already be seen in the low interest rate. Holland, however, was considered in the 17th century the model of economic development, as England is now. The monopoly of old-style usury, based on poverty, collapsed in that country of its own weight.

During the entire 18th century there is the cry, with Holland referred to as an example, for a compulsory reduction of the rate of interest (and legislation acts accordingly), in order to subordinate interest-bearing capital to commercial and industrial capital, instead of the reverse. The main spokesman for this movement is Sir Josiah Child, the father of ordinary English private banking. He declaims against the monopoly of usurers in much the same way as the wholesale clothing manufacturers, Moses & Son, do when leading the light against the monopoly of 'private tailors.' This same Josiah Child is simultaneously the father of English stock-jobbing. Thus, this autocrat of the East India Company defends its monopoly in the name of free trade. Versus Thomas Manley *(Interest of Money Mistaken*—Thomas Manley was not the author of this book. It was published anonymously in London in 1668.—*Ed.*) he says:

> 'As the champion of the timid and trembling band of usurers he erects his main batteries at that point which I have declared to be the weakest he denies point-blank that the low rate of interest is the cause of wealth and vows that it is merely its effect.' (*Traitès sur le Commerce, etc.*, 1669, trad. Amsterdam et Berlin, 1754.) 'If it is commerce that enriches a country, and if a lowering of interest increases commerce, then a lowering of interest or a restriction of usury is doubtless a fruitful primary cause of the wealth of a nation. It is not at all absurd to say that the same thing may be simultaneously a cause under certain circumstances, and an effect under others' (l. c., p. 155). 'The egg is the cause of the hen, and the hen is the cause of the egg. The lowering of interest may cause an increase of wealth, and the increase of wealth may cause a still greater reduction of interest' (l. c., p. 156). 'I am the defender of industry and my opponent defends laziness and sloth' (p. 179).

This violent battle against usury, this demand for the subordination of interest-bearing capital to industrial capital, is but the herald of the organic creations that establish these prerequisites of capitalist production in the modern banking system, which on the one hand robs usurer's capital of its monopoly by concentrating all idle money reserves and throwing them on the money market, and on the other hand limits the monopoly of the precious metal itself by creating credit-money.

The same opposition to usury, the demand for the emancipation of commerce, industry and the state from usury, which are observed here in the case of Child, will be found in all writings on banking in England during the last third of the 17th and the early 18th centuries. We also find colossal illusions about the miraculous effects of credit, abolition of the monopoly of precious metal, its displacement by paper, etc. The Scotsman William Paterson, founder of the Bank of England and the Bank of Scotland, is by all odds Law the First.

> Against the Bank of England 'all goldsmiths and pawnbrokers set up a howl of rage.' (Macaulay, *History of England*, IV, p.499.)

'During the first ten years the Bank had to struggle with great difficulties; great foreign feuds; its notes were only accepted far below their nominal value ... the goldsmiths' (in whose hands the trade in precious metals served as a basis of a primitive banking business) 'were jealous of the Bank, because their business was diminished, their discounts were lowered, their transactions with the government had passed to their opponents.' (3. Francis, l. c., p. 73.)

Even before the establishment of the Bank of England a plan was proposed in 1683 for a National Bank of Credit, which had for its purpose, among others,

'that tradesmen, when they have a considerable quantity of goods, may, by the help of this bank, deposit their goods, by raising a credit on their own dead stock, employ their servants, and increase their trade, till they get a good market instead of selling them at a loss' [J. Francis, l. c., pp. 39-40].

After many endeavors this Bank of Credit was established in Devonshire House on Bishopsgate Street. It made loans to industrialists and merchants on the security of deposited goods to the amount of three-quarters of their value, in the form of bills of exchange. In order to make these bills of exchange capable of circulating, a number of people in each branch of business were organized into a society, from which every possessor of such bills would be able to obtain goods with the same facility as if he were to offer them cash payment. This bank's business did not flourish. Its machinery was too complicated, and the risk too great in case of a commodity depreciation.

If we go by the actual content of those records which accompany and theoretically promote the formation of the modern credit system in England, we shall not find anything in them but—as one of its conditions—the demand for a subordination of interest-bearing capital and of loanable means of production in general to the capitalist mode of production. On the other hand, if we simply cling to the phraseology, we shall be frequently surprised by the agreement—including the mode of expression with the illusions of the followers of Saint-Simon about banking and credit.

Just as in the writings of the physiocrats the *cultivateur* does not stand for the actual tiller of the soil, but for the big farmer, so the *travailleur* with Saint-Simon, and continuing on through his disciples, does not stand for the labourer, but for the industrial and commercial capitalist.

'*Un travailleur a besoin d'aides, de seconds, d'ouvriers; il les cherche intelligents, habiles, dèvouès: il les met a l'oeuvre, et leurs travaux sont productifs.*' ([Enfantin] A *travailleur* (worker) needs helpers, supporters, labourers; he looks for such as are intelligent, able, devoted; he puts them to work, and their labour is productive.' (*Religion saint-simonienne, Economie politique et Politique*, Paris, 1831, p. 104.).

In fact, one should bear in mind that only in his last work, *Le Nouveau Christianisme*, Saint-Simon speaks directly for the working-class and declares their emancipation to be the goal of his efforts. All his former writings are, indeed, mere encomiums of modern bourgeois society in contrast to the feudal order, or of industrialists and bankers in contrast to marshals and juristic law-manufacturers of the Napoleonic era. What a difference compared with the contemporaneous writings of Owen![4] For the followers of Saint-Simon, the industrial capitalist likewise remains the *travailleur par excellence*, as the above-quoted passage indicates. After reading their writings critically, one will not be surprised that their credit and bank fantasies materialized in the *credit mobilier*, founded by an ex-follower of Saint-Simon, Emile Péreire. This form, incidentally, could become dominant only in a country like France, where neither the credit system nor large-scale industry had reached the modern level of development. This was not at all possible in England and America. The embryo of

Crédit mobilizer is already contained in the following passages from *Doctrine de Saint-Simon. Exposition. Premiere annèe, 1828-29*, 3me ed., Paris, 1831. It is understandable that bankers can lend money more cheaply than the capitalists and private usurers. These bankers are, therefore,

> able to supply tools to the industrialists far more cheaply, that is, at lower interest, than the real estate owners and capitalists, who may be more easily mistaken in their choice of borrowers (p. 202).

But the authors themselves add in a footnote:

> The advantage that would accrue from the mediation of bankers between the idle rich and the *travailleurs* is often counterbalanced, or even canceled, by the opportunities offered in our disorganized society to egoism, which may manifest itself in various forms of fraud and charlatanism. The bankers often worm their way between the travailleurs and idle rich for the purpose of exploiting both to the detriment of society.

Travailleur here means *capitaliste industriel*. Incidentally, it is wrong to regard the means at the command of the modern banking system merely as the means of idle people. In the first place, it is the portion of capital which industrialists and merchants temporarily hold in the form of idle money, as a money reserve or as capital to be invested. Hence it is idle capital, but not capital of the idle. In the second place, it is the portion of all revenue and savings in general which is to be temporarily or permanently accumulated. Both are essential to the nature of the banking system.

But it should always be borne in mind that, in the first place, money—in the form of precious metal—remains the foundation from which the credit system, by its very nature, can *never* detach itself. Secondly, that the credit system presupposes the monopoly of social means of production by private persons (in the form of capital and landed property), that it is itself, on the one hand, an immanent form of the capitalist mode of production, and on the other, a driving force in its development to its highest and ultimate form.

The banking system, so far as its formal organization and centralization is concerned, is the most artificial and most developed product turned out by the capitalist mode of production, a fact already expressed in 1697 in *Some Thoughts of the Interests of England*. This accounts for the immense power of an institution such as the Bank of England over commerce and industry, although their actual movements remain completely beyond its province and it is passive toward them. The banking system possesses indeed the form of universal book-keeping and distribution of means of production on a social scale, but solely the form. We have seen that the average profit of the individual capitalist, or of every individual capital, is determined not by the surplus-labour appropriated at first hand by each capital, but by the quantity of total surplus-labour appropriated by the total capital, from which each individual capital receives its dividend only proportional to its aliquot part of the total capital. This social character of capital is first promoted and wholly realized through the full development of the credit and banking system. On the other hand this goes farther. It places all the available and even potential capital of society that is not already actively employed at the disposal of the industrial and commercial capitalists so that neither the lenders nor users of this capital are its real owners or producers. It thus does away with the private character of capital and thus contains in itself, but only in itself, the abolition of capital itself. By means of the banking system the distribution of capital as a special business, a social function, is taken out of the hands of the private capitalists and usurers. But at the same time, banking and credit thus become the most potent means of driving capitalist production beyond its own limits, and one of the most effective vehicles of crises and swindle.

The banking system shows, furthermore, by substituting various forms of circulating credit in place of money, that money is in reality nothing but a particular expression of the social character of labour and its products, which, however, as antithetical to the basis of private production, must always appear in the last analysis as a thing, a special commodity, alongside other commodities.

Finally, there is no doubt that the credit system will serve as a powerful lever during the transition from the capitalist mode of production to the mode of production of associated labour; but only as one element in connection with other great organic revolutions of the mode of production itself. On the other hand, the illusions concerning the miraculous power of the credit and banking system, in the socialist sense, arise from a complete lack of familiarity with the capitalist mode of production and the credit system as one of its forms. As soon as the means of production cease being transformed into capital (which also includes the abolition of private property in land), credit as such no longer has any meaning. This, incidentally, was even understood by the followers of Saint-Simon. On the other hand, as long as the capitalist mode of production continues to exist, interest-bearing capital, as one of its forms, also continues to exist and constitutes in fact the basis of its credit system. Only that sensational writer, Proudhon, who wanted to perpetuate commodity-production and abolish money,[5] was capable of dreaming up the monstrous crèdit gratuit, the ostensible realization of the pious wish of the petty-bourgeois estate.

In *Religion saint-simonienne, èconomie politique et Politique*, we read on page 45:

> Credit serves the purpose, in a society in which some own the instruments of industry without the ability or will to employ them, and where other industrious people have no instruments of labour, of transferring these instruments in the easiest manner possible from the hands of the former, their owners, to the hands of the others who know how to use them. Note that this definition regards credit as a result of the way in which *property* is constituted.

Therefore, credit disappears with this constitution of property. We read, furthermore, on page 98, that the present banks

> consider it their business to follow the movement initiated by transactions taking place outside of their domain, but not themselves to provide an impulse to this movement; in other words, the banks perform the role of capitalists in relation to the travailleurs, whom they loan money.

The notion that the banks themselves should take over the management and distinguish themselves

> through the number and usefulness of their managed establishments and of promoted works. (p. 101)

contains the *Crédit mobilier* in embryo. In the same way, Charles Pecqueur demands that the banks (which the followers of Saint-Simon call a *Système general des banques*) 'should rule production.' Pecqueur is essentially a follower of Saint-Simon, but much more radical. He wants

> the credit institution ... to control the entire movement of national production.—'Try to create a national credit institution, which shall advance the wherewithal to needy people of talent and merit, without, however, forcibly tying these borrowers together through close solidarity in production and consumption, but on the contrary enabling them to determine their own exchange and production. In this way, you will only accomplish what the private banks already accomplish now, that is, anarchy, disproportion between production and consumption, the sudden ruin of one person, and the sudden enrichment of another; so that your institution will never get any farther than producing a certain amount of benefits for one person, corresponding

> to an equivalent amount of misfortune to be endured by another ... and you will have only provided the wage-labourers assisted by you with the means to compete with one another just as their capitalist masters now do. (Ch. Pecqueur, *Thèorie Nouvelle èconomie sociale et Politique*, Paris, 1842, p. 434.)

We have seen that merchant's capital and interest-bearing capital are the oldest forms of capital. But it is in the nature of things that interest-bearing capital assumes in popular conception the form of capital *par excellence*. In merchant's capital there takes place the work of the middleman, no matter whether considered as cheating, labour, or anything else. But in the case of interest-bearing capital the self-reproducing character of capital, the self-expanding value, the production of surplus value, appears purely as an occult property. This accounts for the fact that even some political economists, particularly in countries where industrial capital is not yet fully developed, as in France, cling to interest-bearing capital as the fundamental form of capital and regard ground-rent, for example, merely as a modified form of it, since the loan-form also predominates here. In this way, the internal organisation of the capitalist mode of production is completely misunderstood, and the fact is entirely overlooked that land, like capital, is loaned only to capitalists. Of course, means of production in kind, such as machines and business offices, can also be loaned instead of money. But they then represent a definite sum of money, and the fact that in addition to interest a part is paid for wear and tear is due to their use-value, i.e., the specific natural form of these elements of capital. The decisive factor here is again whether they are loaned to direct producers, which would presuppose the non-existence of the capitalist mode of production-at least in the sphere in which this occurs—or whether they are loaned to industrial capitalists, which is precisely the assumption based upon the capitalist mode of production. It is still more irrelevant and meaningless to drag the lending of houses, etc., for individual use into this discussion. That the working-class is also swindled in this form, and to an enormous extent, is self evident; but this is also done by the retail dealer, who sells means of subsistence to the worker. This is secondary exploitation, which runs parallel to the primary exploitation taking place in the production process itself. The distinction between selling and loaning is quite immaterial in this case and merely formal, and, as already indicated, (Present edition: pp. 345-50.—Ed.) cannot appear as essential to anyone, unless he be wholly unfamiliar with the actual nature of the problem.

Usury, like commerce, exploits a given mode of production. It does not create it, but is related to it outwardly. Usury tries to maintain it directly, so as to exploit it ever anew; it is conservative and makes this mode of production only more pitiable. The less elements of production enter into the production process as commodities, and emerge from it as commodities, the more does their origination from money appear as a separate act. The more insignificant the role played by circulation in the social reproduction, the more usury flourishes.

That money wealth develops as a special kind of wealth, means in respect to usurer's capital that it possesses all its claims in the form of money claims. It develops that much more in a given country, the more the main body of production is limited to natural services, etc., that is, to use-values.

Usury is a powerful lever in developing the preconditions for industrial capital in so far as it plays the following double role, first, building up, in general, an independent money wealth alongside that of the merchant, and, secondly, appropriating the conditions of labour, that is, ruining the owners of the old conditions of labour.

Interest in the Middle Ages

> In the Middle Ages the population was purely agricultural. Under such a government as was the feudal system there can be but little traffic, and hence but little profit. Hence the

laws against usury were justified in the Middle Ages. Besides, in an agricultural country a person seldom wants to borrow money except he be reduced to poverty or distress.... In the reign of Henry VIII, interest was limited to 10 per cent. James I reduced it to 8 per cent ... Charles II reduced it to 6 per cent; in the reign of Queen Anne, it was reduced to 5 per cent.... In those times, the lenders ... had, in fact, though not a legal, yet an actual monopoly, and hence it was necessary that they, like other monopolists, should be placed under restraint. In our times, it is the rate of profit which regulates the rate of interest. In those times, it was the rate of interest which regulated the rate of profit. If the money-lender charged a high rate of interest to the merchant, the merchant must have charged a higher rate of profit on his goods. Hence, a large sum of money would be taken from the pockets of the purchasers to be put into the pockets of the money-lenders. (Gilbart, *History and Principles of Banking*, pp. 163, 164, 165.)

I have been told that 10 gulden are now taken annually at every Leipzig Fair, (The author has in mind the loan of 100 gulden with interest payable in three installments at the Leipzig Fair, held three times annually: Easter and St. Michael's Day) that is, 30 on each hundred, some add the Neuenburg Fair, thus making 40 per hundred; whether that is so, I don't know. For shame! What will be the infernal outcome of this? ... Whoever now has 100 florins at Leipzig takes 40 annually, which is the same as devouring one peasant or burgher each year. If one has 1,000 florins, he takes 400 annually which means devouring a knight or a rich nobleman per year. If one has 10,000 florins, he takes 4,000 per year, which means devouring a rich count each year. If one has 100,000 florins, as the big merchants must possess, he takes 40,000 annually, which means devouring one affluent prince each year. If one has 1,000,000 florins, he takes 400,000 annually, which means devouring one mighty king every year. And he does not risk either his person or his wares, does not work, sits near his fire-place and roasts apples; so might a lowly robber sit at home and devour a whole world in ten years. (Quoted from *Bücher vom Kaufhandel und Wucher* vom Jahre 1524, Luther's *Werke*, Wittenberg, 1589, Teil 6, S. 312.)

Fifteen years ago I took pen in hand against usury when it had spread so alarmingly that I could scarcely hope for any improvement. Since then it has become so arrogant that it deigns not to be classed as vice, sin, or shame, but achieves praise as pure virtue and honour, as though it were performing a great favour and Christian service for the people. What will help deliver us now that shame has turned into honour and vice into virtue? (Martin Luther, *An die Pfarherrn wider den Wucher zu predigen*, Wittenberg, 1540.)

Jews, Lombards, usurers and extortioners were our first bankers, our primitive traffickers in money, their character little short of infamous... They were joined by London goldsmiths. As a body ... our primitive bankers ... were a very bad set, they were gripping usurers, iron-hearted extortioners. (D. Hardcastle, *Banks and Bankers*, 2nd ed., London, 1843, pp. 19, 20.)

The example shown by Venice (in establishing a bank) was thus quickly imitated; all sea-coast towns, and in general all towns which had earned fame through their independence and commerce, founded their first banks. The return voyage of their ships, which often was of long duration, inevitably led to the custom of lending on credit. This was further intensified by the discovery of America and the ensuing trade with that continent. (This is the main point.) The chartering of ships made large loans necessary-a procedure already obtaining in ancient Athens and Greece. In 1308, the Hanse town of Bruges possessed an insurance company. (M. Augier, l. c., pp. 202, 203.)

To what extent the granting of loans to landowners, and thus to the pleasure-seeking wealthy in general, still prevailed in the last third of the 17th century, even in England, before the development of modern credit, may be seen, among others, in the works of Sir Dudley North. He was not only one of the first English merchants, but also one of the most prominent theoretical economists of his time:

> The moneys employed at interest in this nation, are not near the tenth part, disposed to trading people, wherewith to manage their trades; but are for the most part lent for the supplying of luxury, and to support the expense of persons, who though great owners of lands, yet spend faster than their lands bring in; and being loath to sell, choose rather to mortgage their estates. (*Discourses upon Trade*, London, 1691, pp. 6-7.)

Poland in the 18th century:

> Warsaw carried on a large bustling business in bills of exchange which, however, had as its principal basis and aim the usury of its bankers. In order to secure money, which they could lend to spendthrift gentry at 8% and more, they sought and obtained abroad open exchange credit, that is, credit that had no commodity trade as its basis, but which the foreign drawee continued to accept as long as the returns from these manipulations did not fail to come in. However, they paid heavily for this through bankruptcies of men like Tapper and other highly respected Warsaw bankers. (J. G. Büsch, *Theoretisch-praktische Darstellung der Handlung, etc.*, 3rd ed., Hamburg, 1808, Vol. II, pp. 232, 233.)

Advantages Derived by the Church from the Prohibition of Interest

> Taking interest had been interdicted by the Church. But selling property for the purpose of finding succour in distress had not been forbidden. It had not even been prohibited to transfer property to the money-lender as security for a certain term, until a debtor repaid his loan, leaving the money-lender free to enjoy the usufruct of the property as a reward for his abstinence from his money.... The Church itself, and its associated communes and *pia corpora*, derived much profit from this practice, particularly during the crusades. This brought a very large portion of national wealth into possession of the so-called 'dead hand,' all the more so because the Jews were barred from engaging in such usury, the possession of such fixed liens not being concealable.... Without the ban on interest churches and cloisters would never have become so affluent. (l. c., p. 55)

Notes

1. 'It is by frequent fluctuations within the month, and by pawning one article to relieve another, where a small sum is obtained, that the premium for money becomes so excessive. There are about 240 licensed pawnbrokers in the metropolis, and nearly 1,450 in the country. The capital employed is supposed somewhat to exceed a million pounds sterling; and this capital is turned round thrice in the course of the year, and yields each time about 33½ per cent on an average; according to which calculation, the inferior orders of society in England pay about one million a year for the use of a temporary loan, exclusive of what they lose by goods being forfeited.' (J. D. Tuckett, *A History of the Past and Present State of the Labouring Population*, London, 1846, 1, p. 114.)
2. Even in the titles of their works they state as their principal purpose 'the general good of the landed men, the great increase of the value of land, the exemption of the nobility, gentry, etc., from taxes, enlarging their yearly estates, etc.' Only the usurers would stand to lose, those worst enemies of the nation who had done more injury to the nobility and yeomanry than an army of invasion from France could have done.
3. 'The rich goldsmith' (the precursor of the banker), 'for example, made Charles II of England pay twenty and thirty per cent for accommodation. A business so profitable, induced the

goldsmith 'more and more to become lender to the King, to anticipate all the revenue, to take every grant of Parliament into pawn as soon as it was given; also to outvie each other in buying and taking to pawn bills, orders, and tallies, so that, in effect, all the revenue passed through their hands.' (John Francis, *History of the Bank of England*, London, 1848, I, p.31.) 'The erection of a bank had been suggested several times before that. It was at last a necessity' (l. c., p. 38). 'The bank was a necessity for the government itself, sucked dry by usurers, in order to obtain money at a reasonable rate, on the security of parliamentary grants' (l. c., pp. 59, 60).

4. Marx would surely have modified this passage considerably, had he reworked his manuscript. It was inspired by the role of the ex-followers of Saint-Simon under France's Second Empire where just at the time that Marx wrote the above, the world redeeming credit fantasies of this school through the irony of history were being realised in the form of a tremendous swindle on a scale never seen before. Later Marx spoke only with admiration of the genius and encyclopaedic mind of Saint Simon. When in his earlier works the latter ignores the antithesis between the bourgeoisie and the proletariat which was just then coming into existence in France when he includes among the *travailleurs* that part of the bourgeoisie which was active in production, this corresponds to Fourier's conception of attempting to reconcile capital and labour and is explained by the economic and political situation of France in those days. The fact that Owen was more far sighted in this respect is due to his different environment, for he lived in a period of industrial revolution and of acutely sharpening class antagonisms.—*F. E.*

5. Karl Marx, *Misère de la Philosophie*, Bruxelles et Paris, 1847.—Karl Marx, *Zur Kritik der politischen Oekonomie*, S. 64.

PART VI

TRANSFORMATION OF SURPLUS-PROFIT INTO GROUND-RENT

37

Introduction

The analysis of landed property in its various historical forms is beyond the scope of this work. We shall be concerned with it only in so far as a portion of the surplus-value produced by capital falls to the share of the landowner. We assume, then, that agriculture is dominated by the capitalist mode of production just as manufacture is; in other words, that agriculture is carried on by capitalists who differ from other capitalists primarily in the manner in which their capital, and the wage-labour set in motion by this capital, are invested. So far as we are concerned, the farmer produces wheat, etc., in much the same way as the manufacturer produces yarn or machines. The assumption that the capitalist mode of production has encompassed agriculture implies that it rules over all spheres of production and bourgeois society, i.e., that its prerequisites, such as free competition among capitals, the possibility of transferring the latter from one production sphere to another, and a uniform level of the average profit, etc., are fully matured. The form of landed property which we shall consider here is a specifically historical one a form *transformed* through the influence of capital and of the capitalist mode of production, either of feudal landownership, or of small-peasant agriculture as a means of livelihood, in which the *possession* of the land and the soil constitutes one of the prerequisites of production for the direct producer, and in which his *ownership* of land appears as the most advantageous condition for the prosperity of *his* mode of production. Just as the capitalist mode of production in general is based on the expropriation of the conditions of labour from the labourers, so does it in agriculture presuppose the expropriation of the rural labourers from the land and their subordination to a capitalist, who carries on agriculture for the sake of profit. Thus, for the purpose of our analysis, the objection that other forms of landed property and of agriculture have existed, or still exist, is quite irrelevant. Such an objection can only apply to those economists who treat the capitalist mode of production in agriculture, and the form of landed property corresponding to it, not as historical but rather as eternal categories.

For our purposes, it is necessary to study the modern form of landed property, because our task is to consider the specific conditions of production and circulation which arise from the investment of capital in agriculture. Without this, our analysis of capital would not be complete. We, therefore, confine ourselves exclusively to the investment of capital in agriculture itself, that is, in producing the principal agricultural crop which feeds a given people. We can use wheat for this purpose, because it is the principal means of subsistence in modern capitalistically developed nations. (Or, instead of agriculture, we can use mining because the laws are the same for both.)

One of the big contributions of Adam Smith was to have shown that ground-rent for capital invested in the production of such agricultural products as flax and dye-stuffs, and in independent cattle-raising, etc., is determined by the ground-rent obtained from capital invested in the production of the principal article of subsistence. [Smith, *An Inquiry into the Nature and Causes of the Wealth of Nations*, Aberdeen, London, 1848, pp. 105-16.—*Ed.*] In fact, no further progress has been made in this regard since then. Any limitations or additions would belong in an independent study of landed property, not here. Hence, we shall not speak of landed property *ex professo*—in so far as it does not refer to land destined for wheat production—but shall merely refer to it on occasion by way of illustration.

It should be noted for the sake of completeness that we also include water, etc., in the term land, in so far as it belongs to someone as an accessory to the land.

Landed property is based on the monopoly by certain persons over definite portions of the globe, as exclusive spheres of their private will to the exclusion of all others.[1] With this in mind, the problem is to ascertain the economic value, that is, the realisation of this monopoly on the basis of capitalist production. With the legal power of these persons to use or misuse certain portions of the globe, nothing is decided. The use of this power depends wholly upon economic conditions, which are independent of their will. The legal view itself only means that the landowner can do with the land what every owner of commodities can do with his commodities. And this view, this legal view of free private ownership of land, arises in the ancient world only with the dissolution of the organic order of society, and in the modern world only with the development of capitalist production. It has been imported by Europeans to Asia only here and there. In the section dealing with primitive accumulation (Buch I, Kap. XXIV [English edition: Part VIII.—*Ed*].), we saw that this mode of production presupposes, on the one hand, the separation of the direct producers from their position as mere accessories to the land (in the form of vassals, serfs, slaves, etc.), and, on the other hand, the expropriation of the mass of the people from the land. To this extent the monopoly of landed property is a historical premise, and continues to remain the basis of the capitalist mode of production, just as in all previous modes of production which are based on the exploitation of the masses in one form or another. But the form of landed property with which the incipient capitalist mode of production is confronted does not suit it. It first creates for itself the form required by subordinating agriculture to capital. It thus transforms feudal landed property, clan property, small peasant property in mark communes—no matter how divergent their juristic forms may be—into the economic form corresponding to the requirements of this mode of production. One of the major results of the capitalist mode of production is that, on the one hand, it transforms agriculture from a mere empirical and mechanical self-perpetuating process employed by the least developed part of society into the conscious scientific application of agronomy, in so far as this is at all feasible under conditions of private property;[2] that it divorces landed property from the relations of dominion and servitude, on the one hand, and, on the other, totally separates land as an instrument of production from landed property and landowner—for whom the land merely represents a certain money assessment which he collects by virtue of his monopoly from the industrial capitalist, the capitalist farmer; it dissolves the connection between landownership and the land so thoroughly that the landowner may spend his whole life in Constantinople, while his estates lie in Scotland. Landed property thus receives its purely economic form by discarding all its former political and social embellishments and associations, in brief all those traditional accessories, which are denounced, as we shall see later, as useless and absurd superfluities by the industrial capitalists themselves, as well as their theoretical spokesmen, in the heat of their struggle with landed property. The rationalising of agriculture, on the one hand, which makes it for the first time capable of operating on a social scale, and the reduction *ad absurdum* of property in land, on the other, are the great achievements of the capitalist mode of production. Like all of its other historical advances, it also attained these by first completely impoverishing the direct producers.

Before we proceed to the problem itself, several more preliminary remarks are necessary to avoid misunderstanding.

The prerequisites for the capitalist mode of production, therefore, are the following: The actual tillers of the soil are wage labourers employed by a capitalist, the capitalist farmer who is engaged in agriculture merely as a particular field of exploitation for capital, as investment for his capital in a particular sphere of production. This capitalist farmer pays the landowner, the owner of the land exploited by him, a sum of money at definite periods fixed by contract, for instance, annually (just as the borrower of money-capital pays a fixed interest), for the right to invest his capital in this specific sphere of production. This sum of money is called ground-rent, no matter whether it is paid for agricultural land, building lots, mines, fishing grounds, or forests, etc. It is paid for the entire time for which the landowner has contracted to rent his land to the capitalist farmer. Ground-rent, therefore, is here that form in which property in land is realised economically, that is, produces value. Here, then, we have all three classes—wage-labourers, industrial capitalists, and landowners constituting together, and in their mutual opposition, the framework of modern society.

Capital may be fixed in the land, incorporated in it either in a transitory manner, as through improvements of a chemical nature, fertilisation, etc., or more permanently, as in drainage canals, irrigation works, leveling, farm buildings, etc. Elsewhere I have called the capital thus applied to land *la terre-capital.*[3] It belongs to the category of fixed capital. The interest on capital incorporated in the land and the improvements thus made in it as an instrument of production can constitute a part of the rent paid by the capitalist farmer to the landowner,[4] but it does not constitute the actual ground-rent, which is paid for the use of the land as such—be it in a natural or cultivated state. In a systematic treatment of landed property, which is not within our scope, this part of the landowner's revenue would have to be discussed at length. But a few words about it will suffice here. The more transitory capital investments, which accompany the ordinary production processes in agriculture, are all made without exception by the capitalist farmer. These investments, like cultivation proper in general, improve the land,[5] increase its output, and transform the land from mere material into land-capital when the cultivation is carried on more or less rationally, i.e., when it is not reduced to a brutal spoliation of the soil, as was in vogue, e.g., among the former slave-holders in the United States; however, the gentlemen landowners secure themselves against such practice by contract. A cultivated field is worth more than an uncultivated one of the same natural quality. The more permanent fixed capital investments, which are incorporated in the soil and used up in a longer period of time, are also in the main, and in some spheres often exclusively, made by the capitalist farmer. But as soon as the time stipulated by contract has expired—and this is one of the reasons why with the development of capitalist production the landowners seek to shorten the contract period as much as possible—the improvements incorporated in the soil become the property of the landowner as an inseparable feature of the substance, the land. In the new contract made by the landowner he adds the interest for capital incorporated in the land to the ground-rent itself. And he does this whether he now leases the land to the capitalist farmer who made these improvements or to some other farmer. His rent is thus inflated; and should he wish to sell his land (we shall see immediately how its price is determined), its value is now higher. He sells not merely the land but the improved land, the capital incorporated in the land for which he paid nothing. Quite aside from the movements of ground-rent itself, here lies one of the secrets of the increasing enrichment of landowners, the continuous inflation of their rents, and the constantly growing money-value of their estates along with progress in economic development. Thus they pocket a product of social development created without their help—*fruges consumere nati.* [Horace, *Epistles*, Book I, *Epistles 2, 27.—Ed*]. But this is at the same time one of the greatest obstacles to a rational development of agriculture, for the tenant farmer avoids all improvements and outlays for which he cannot expect complete returns during the term of his lease. We find this situation denounced as such an obstacle again and again, not only in the 18th century by James Anderson, the actual discoverer of the modern theory of rent [On J. Anderson's theory of rent see K. Marx, *Theorien über den Mehrwert* (K. Marx/F. Engels, *Werke*, Band 26, 2. Teil, S. 103-05, 110-14, 134-39).—*Ed.*]—who was also a practical capitalist farmer and an advanced agronomist for his time—but also in our own day by opponents of the present constitution of landed property in England.

A.A. Walton, in his *History of the Landed Tenures of Great Britain and Ireland*, London, 1865, says on this score (pp.96, 97):

> All the efforts of the numerous agricultural associations throughout the country must fail to produce any very extensive or really appreciable results in the real advancement

of agricultural improvement, so long as such improvements mean in a far higher degree increased value to the estate and rent-roll of the landlord, than bettering the condition of the tenant farmer or the labourer. The farmers, generally, are as well aware as either the landlord or his agent, or even the president of the Agricultural Association, that good drainage, plenty of manure, and good management, combined with the increased employment of labour, to thoroughly cleanse and work the land, will produce wonderful results both in improvement and production. To do all this, however, considerable outlay is required, and the farmers are also aware, that however much they may improve the land or enhance its value, the landlords will, in the long run, reap the principal benefit, in higher rents and the increased value of their estates.... They are shrewd enough to observe what those orators [landowners and their agents speaking at agricultural festivities], by some singular inadvertence, omit to tell them — namely, that the lion's share of any improvements they may make is sure to go into the pockets of the landlords in the long run.... However much the former tenant may have improved the farm, his successor will find that the landlord will always increase the rent in proportion to the increased value of the land from former improvements.

In agriculture proper, this process does not yet appear quite as plainly as when the land is used for building purposes. By far the largest portion of land used in England for building purposes but not sold as a freehold is leased by the landowners for 99 years or, if possible, for a shorter term. After the lapse of this period the buildings fall into the hands of the landowner together with the land itself.

'They' [the tenants] 'are bound to deliver up the house at the expiration of the lease, in good tenantable condition, to the great landlord, after having paid an exorbitant ground-rent up to the expiration of the lease. No sooner is the lease expired, than the agent or surveyor will come and examine your house, and see that you put it into good repair, and then take possession of it, and annex it to his lord's domains.... The fact is, if this system is permitted to be in full operation for any considerable period longer, the whole of the house property in the kingdom will be in the hands of the great landlords, as well as the land. The whole of the West End of London, north and south from Temple Bar, may be said to belong to about half a dozen great landlords, all let at enormous rents, and where the leases have not quite expired they are fast falling due. The same may be said either more or less of every town in the kingdom. Nor does this grasping system of exclusion and monopoly stop even here. Nearly the whole of the dock accommodation in our seaport towns is by the same process of usurpation in the hands of the great leviathans of the land' (1. c., pp.92-93).

It is evident in these circumstances that when the census for England and Wales in 1861 gives the total population as 20,066,224 and the number of landlords as 36,032, the proportion of owners to the number of houses and to population would look completely different if the large landlords were placed on one side and the small ones on the other.

This illustration of ownership in buildings is important. In the first place, it clearly shows the difference between actual ground-rent and interest on fixed capital incorporated in the land, which may constitute an addition to ground-rent. Interest on buildings, like that on capital incorporated in the land by the tenant in agriculture, falls into the hands of the industrial capitalist, the building speculator, or the tenant, so long as the lease lasts, and has in itself nothing to do with ground-rent, which must be paid on stated dates annually for the use of the land. Secondly, it shows that capital incorporated in the land by others ultimately passes into the hands of the landlord together with the land, and that the interest for it inflates his rent.

Some writers, acting either as spokesmen of landlordism and taking up the cudgels against the attacks of bourgeois economists, or in an endeavour to transform the capitalist system of production from a system of contradictions into one of 'harmonies,' like Carey, have tried to represent ground-rent, the specific economic expression of landed property, as identical with interest. This would eliminate the opposition between landlords and capitalists. The opposite method was employed in the early stages of capitalist production. In those days, landed property was still regarded by popular conception as the pristine and respectable form of private property, while interest on capital was decried as usury. Dudley North, Locke and others, therefore, represented interest on capital as a form analogous to ground-rent, just as Turgot deduced the justification for interest from the existence of ground-rent.—Aside from the fact that ground-rent may, and does, exist in its pure form without any addition for interest on capital incorporated in the land, those more recent writers forget that, in this way, the landlord not only receives interest on other persons' capital that costs him nothing, but also pockets this capital of others without recompense. The justification of landed property, like that of all other forms of property corresponding to a certain mode of production, is that the mode of production itself is a transient historical necessity, and this includes the relations of production and exchange which stem from it. It is true, as we shall see later, that landed property differs from other kinds of property in that it appears superfluous and harmful at a certain stage of development, even from the point of view of the capitalist mode of production.

Ground-rent may in another form be confused with interest and thereby its specific character overlooked. Ground-rent assumes the form of a certain sum of money, which the landlord draws annually by leasing a certain plot on our planet. We have seen that every particular sum of money may be capitalised, that is, considered as the interest on an imaginary capital. For instance, if the average rate of interest is 5%, then an annual ground-rent of £200 may be regarded as interest on a capital of £4,000. Ground-rent so capitalised constitutes the purchase price or value of the land, a category which like the price of labour is *prima facie* irrational, since the earth is not the product of labour, and therefore, has no value. But on the other hand, a real relation in production is concealed behind this irrational form. If a capitalist buys land yielding a rent of £200 annually and pays £4,000 for it, then he draws the average annual interest of 5% on his capital of £4,000, just as if he had invested this capital in interest-bearing papers or loaned it directly at 5% interest. It is the expansion of a capital of £4,000 at 5%. On this assumption, he would recover the purchase price of his estate through its revenues in twenty years. In England, therefore, the purchase price of land is calculated in so many years' purchase which is merely another way of expressing the capitalisation of ground-rent. It is in fact the purchase price-not of the land, but of the ground-rent yielded by it—calculated in accordance with the usual interest rate. But this capitalisation of rent assumes the existence of rent, while rent cannot inversely be derived and explained from its own capitalisation. Its existence, independent of its sale, is rather the starting-point for the inquiry.

It follows, then, that the price of land may rise or fall inversely as the interest rate rises or falls if we assume ground-rent to be a constant magnitude. If the ordinary interest rate should fall from 5% to 4%, then the annual ground-rent of £200 would represent the annual realisation from a capital of £5,000 instead of £4,000. The price of the same piece of land would thus have risen from £4,000 to £5,000, or from 20 years' to 25 years' purchase. The converse would take place in the opposite case. This is a movement of the price of land which is independent of the movement of ground-rent itself and regulated only by the interest rate. But as we have seen that the rate of profit has a tendency to fall in the course of social progress, and, therefore, the interest rate has the same tendency, so far as it is regulated by the rate of profit; and that, furthermore, the interest rate shows a tendency to fall in consequence of the growth of loanable capital, apart from the influence of the rate of profit, it follows that the price of land has a tendency to rise, even independently of the movement of ground-rent and the prices of the products of the land, of which rent constitutes a part.

The confusion of ground-rent itself with the interest form which it assumes for the buyer of the land—a confusion resulting from complete lack of familiarity with the nature of ground-rent—must necessarily lead to the most absurd conclusions. Since landed property is considered in all ancient countries as a particularly genteel form of property, and its purchase also as an eminently safe capital investment, the interest rate at which ground-rent is bought is generally lower than that of other long-term investments of capital, so that a buyer of real estate draws, for instance, only 4% on his purchase price, whereas he would draw 5% for the same capital in other investments. In other words, he pays more capital for ground-rent than he would for the same annual amount of income from other investments. This leads Mr Thiers to conclude in his generally very poor work on *La Propriété* (a reprint of his speech in the French National Assembly in 1849 directed against Proudhon) [Proudhon's speech was published in '*Compte rendu des seances de l'Assemblée Nationale*,' Tome II, Paris, 1849, pp. 666-71.—*Ed.*] that ground-rent is low, whereas it merely proves that its purchase price is high.

The fact that capitalised ground-rent appears as the price or value of land, so that land, therefore, is bought and sold like any other commodity, serves some apologists as a justification for landed property since the buyer pays an equivalent for it, the same as for other commodities; and the major portion of landed property has changed hands in this way. The same reason in that case would also serve to justify slavery, since the returns from the labour of the slave, whom the slave-holder has bought, merely represent the interest on the capital invested in this purchase. To derive a justification for the existence of ground-rent from its sale and purchase means in general to justify its existence by its existence.

As important as it may be for a scientific analysis of ground-rent—that is, the independent and specific economic form of landed property on the basis of the capitalist mode of production—study it in its pure form free of all distorting and obfuscating irrelevancies, it is just as important for an understanding of the practical effects of landed property even for a theoretical comprehension of a multitude of facts which contradict the concept and nature of ground-rent and yet appear as modes of existence of ground-rent—to learn the sources which give rise to such muddling in theory.

In practice, naturally, everything appears as ground-rent that is paid as lease money by tenant to landlord for the right to cultivate the soil. No matter what the composition of this tribute and no matter what its sources, it has this in common with the actual ground-rent—that the monopoly of the so-called landed proprietor of a portion of our planet enables him to levy such tribute and impose such an assessment. It has this in common with the actual ground-rent—that it determines the price of land, which, as we have indicated earlier, is nothing but the capitalised income from the lease of the land.

We have already seen that interest for the capital incorporated in the land may constitute such an extraneous component of ground-rent, a component which must become a continually growing extra charge on the total rent of a country as economic development progresses. But aside from this interest, it is possible that the lease money may conceal in part, and in certain cases in its entirety, i.e., in complete absence of the actual ground-rent when the land is, therefore, actually worthless—a deduction from the average profit or from the normal wages, or both. This portion, whether of profit or wages, appears here as ground-rent, because instead of falling to the industrial capitalist or the wage-worker, as would normally be the case, it is paid to the landlord in the form of lease money. Economically speaking, neither the one nor the other of these portions constitutes ground-rent; but, in practice, it constitutes the landlord's revenue, an economic realisation of his monopoly, much as actual ground-rent, and it has just as determining an influence on land prices.

We are not speaking now of conditions in which ground-rent, the manner of expressing landed property in the capitalist mode of production, formally exists without the existence of the capitalist mode of production itself, i.e., without the tenant himself being an industrial capitalist, nor the type of his management being a capitalist one. Such is the case, e.g., in *Ireland*. The tenant there is generally a small farmer. What he pays to the landlord in the form of rent frequently absorbs not merely a part of his profit, that is, his own surplus labour (to which he is entitled as possessor of his own instruments of labour), but also a part of his normal wage, which he would otherwise receive for the same amount of labour. Besides, the landlord, who does nothing at all for the improvement of the land, also expropriates his small capital, which the tenant for the most part incorporates in the land through his own labour. This is precisely what a usurer would do under similar circumstances, with just the difference that the usurer would at least risk his own capital in the operation. This continual plunder is the core of the dispute over the Irish Tenancy Rights Bill. The main purpose of this Bill is to compel the landlord when ordering his tenant off the land to indemnify the latter for his improvements on the land, or for his capital incorporated in the land. Palmerston used to wave this demand aside with the cynical answer;

> 'The House of Commons is a house of landed proprietors.'

Nor are we referring to exceptional circumstances in which the landlord may enforce a high rental—even in countries with capitalist production—that stands in no relation to the yield from the soil. Of such a nature, for example, is the leasing of small patches of land to labourers in English factory districts, either as small gardens or for amateur spare-time farming. (Reports of Inspectors of Factories.)

We are referring to ground-rent in countries with developed capitalist production. Among English tenants, for instance, there are a number of small capitalists who are destined and compelled by education, training, tradition, competition, and other circumstances to invest their capital as tenants in agriculture. They are forced to be satisfied with less than the average profit, and to turn over part of it to the landlords as rent. This is the only condition under which they are permitted to invest their capital in the land, in agriculture. Since landlords everywhere exert considerable, and in England even overwhelming, influence on legislation, they are able to exploit this situation for the purpose of victimising the entire class of tenants. For instance, the Corn Laws of 1815—a bread tax, admittedly imposed upon the country to secure for the idle landlords a continuation of their abnormally increased rentals during the anti-Jacobin war—had indeed the effect, excluding cases of a few extraordinarily rich harvests, of maintaining prices of agricultural products above the level to which they would have fallen had corn imports been unrestricted. But they did not have the effect of maintaining prices at the level decreed by the lawmaking landlords to serve as normal prices in such manner as to constitute the legal limit for imports of foreign corn. But the leaseholds were contracted in an atmosphere created by these normal prices. As soon as the illusion was dispelled, a new law was passed, containing new normal prices, which were as much the impotent expression of a greedy landlord's fantasy as the old ones. In this way, tenants were defrauded from 1815 up to the thirties. Hence the standing problem of agricultural distress during this entire period. Hence the expropriation and the ruin of a whole generation of tenants during this period and their replacement by a new class of capitalists.[6]

A much more general and important fact, however, is the depression of the actual farm-labourer's wage below its normal average, so that part of it is deducted to become part of the lease money and thus, in the guise of ground-rent, it flows into the pocket of the landlord rather than the labourer. This is, for example, quite generally the case in England and Scotland, with the exception of a few favourably situated counties. The inquiries into the level of wages by the parliamentary investigating committees, which were appointed before the passage of the Corn Laws in England—so far the most valuable and almost unexploited contributions to the history of wages in the 19th century, and at the same time a pillory erected for themselves by the English aristocracy and bourgeoisie—proved convincingly and beyond a doubt that the high rates of rent, and the corresponding rise in land prices during the anti-Jacobin war, were due in part to no other cause but deductions from wages and their depression to a level that was even below the physical minimum requirement; in other words, to part of the normal wage being handed over to the landlords. Various circumstances, such as the depreciation of money and the manipulation of the Poor Laws in the agricultural districts, had made this operation possible at a time when the incomes of the tenants were enormously increasing and the landlords were amassing fabulous riches. Indeed, one of the main arguments of both tenants and landlords for the introduction of duties on corn was that it was physically impossible to depress farm labourers' wages any lower. This state of affairs has not significantly changed, and in England, as in all European countries, a portion of the normal wage is absorbed by ground-rent just as ever. When Count Shaftesbury, then Lord Ashley, one of the philanthropic aristocrats, was so extraordinarily moved by the condition of English factory operatives and acted as their spokesman in Parliament during the agitation for a ten-hour day, the spokesmen of the industrialists took their revenge by publishing wage statistics of agricultural labourers in the villages belonging to him (see Buch I, Kap. XXIII, 5, e [English edition: Ch XXV 5 e—Ed]) ('*The British Agricultural Proletariat*'), which clearly showed that a portion of the ground-rent of this philanthropist consisted of loot filched for him by his tenants out of the wages of agricultural labourers. This publication is also interesting for the fact that its revelations may bravely take their place beside the worst exposures made by the committees in 1814 and 1815. As soon as circumstances force a temporary increase in the wage of agricultural labourers a cry goes up from the capitalist tenant farmers that raising wages to the normal level, as done in other branches of industry, would be impossible and would ruin them, unless ground-rent were reduced at the same time. Therein lies the confession that under the head of ground-rent there is a deduction of the labourers' wages which is handed over to the landlords. For instance, from 1849 to 1859 the wages of agricultural labourers rose in England through a combination of momentous events: the exodus from Ireland, which cut off the supply of agricultural labourers coming from there; an extraordinary absorption of the agricultural population by factories; a war-time demand for soldiers; an exceptionally large emigration to Australia and the United States (California), and other circumstances which need not be dwelt upon here. At the same time, average prices of grain fell by more than 16% during this period, with the exception of the poor agricultural years 1854 to 1856. The tenant farmers clamoured for a reduction in rents. They were successful in individual cases, but on the whole failed to achieve this demand. They had recourse to a reduction of production costs, among other things by the mass production of steam-engines and new machinery, which to some extent replaced horses and pushed them out of the economy, but also brought about, in part, an artificial over-population by throwing agricultural day-labourers out of work, and thereby caused a new drop in wages. And this took place in spite of the overall relative decrease in agricultural population during that decade as compared with the growth of total population, and in spite of an absolute decrease in agricultural population in some purely agricultural districts.[7] Thus Fawcett, then professor of political economy at Cambridge [who died in 1884 while Postmaster General], stated at the Social Science Congress on October 12, 1865:

> 'The labourers were beginning to emigrate, and the farmers were already beginning to complain that they would not be able to pay such high rents as they have been accustomed to pay, because labour was becoming dearer in consequence of emigration.'

Here, then, high ground-rent is directly identified with low wages. And in so far as the level of land prices is determined by this circumstance-increasing rent—a rise in the value of land is identical with a depreciation of labour, the high price of land is identical with the low price of labour.

The same is true of France.

> The rental rises because the prices of bread, wine, meat, vegetables and fruit rise, on the one hand, while, on the other hand, the price of labour remains unchanged. If the older people examine the accounts of their fathers, taking us back about 100 years, they will find that the price of a day's labour in rural France was the same as it is now. The price of meat has trebled since then.... Who is the victim of this revolution? Is it the rich man, who is the proprietor of an estate, or the poor man who works it? ... The increase in rental is evidence of a public disaster. (*Du Mécanisime de la Société en France et en Angleterre*, by M. Rubichon, 2nd ed., Paris, 1837, p. 101.)

Illustrations of rent representing deductions, on the one hand, from average profit and, on the other, from average wages:

Morton, [Here Marx quotes John Lockart Morton.—*Ed.*] real estate agent and agricultural mechanic who was previously quoted, states that it has been observed in many localities that rent for large estates is lower than for small ones because

> the competition is usually greater for the latter than for the former, and as few small farmers are able to turn their attention to any other business than that of farming, their anxiety to get a suitable occupation leads them in many instances to give more rent than their judgement can approve of. (John L. Morton, *The Resources of Estates*, London, 1858, p. 116.)

However, this difference is supposed to be gradually disappearing in England; this he attributes largely to the emigration precisely of the class of small tenants. The same Morton illustrates with an example in which clearly the wage of the tenant himself, and even more surely that of his labourers, suffers a deduction for ground-rent. This takes place in the case of leaseholds with less than 70 to 80 acres (30-34 ha.) where a two-horse plough cannot be maintained.

> Unless the tenant works with his own hands as laboriously as any labourer, his farm will not keep him. If he entrusts the performance of his work to workmen while he continues merely to observe them, the chances are, that at no distant period, he will find he is unable to pay his rent (1. c., p. 148).

Morton concludes, therefore, that unless the tenants of a certain locality are very poor, the leaseholds should not be smaller than 70 acres, so that the tenants may keep two or three horses.

Extraordinary sagacity on the part of Monsieur Léonce de Lavergne, *Membre de l'Institut et de la Société Centrale d'Agriculture.* In his Economie Rurale de l'Angleterre (quoted from the English translation, London, 1855), he makes the following comparison of the annual advantage derived from cattle which is employed in France but not in England where it is replaced by horses (p.42):

France	*Milk*	*£4 million*	*England*	*Milk*	*£16 million*
	Meat	£16 million		Meat	£20 million
	Labour	£8 million		Labour	—
	TOTAL:	£28 million		TOTAL:	£36 million

But the greater total for England is obtained here because according to his own testimony milk is twice as expensive in England as in France whereas he assumes the same prices for meat in both countries (p.35); therefore, English milk production shrinks to £8 million and the total to £28 million, which is the same as in France. It is indeed rather too much when Mr Lavergne allows the quantities and price differences to enter simultaneously into his calculations so that when England produces certain articles more dearly than France—this appears to be an advantage of English agriculture, whereas at best it signifies a larger profit for the tenants and landlords.

That Mr Lavergne is not only familiar with the economic achievements of English agriculture, but also subscribes to the prejudices of the English tenants and landlords, is shown on page 48:

> One great drawback attends cereals generally ... they exhaust the soil which bears them.

Not only does Mr Lavergne believe that other plants do not do so, but also believes that fodder crops and root crops enrich the soil:

> Forage plants derive from the atmosphere the principal elements of their growth, while they give to the soil more than they take from it; thus both directly and by their conversion into animal manure contributing in two ways to repair the mischief done by cereals and exhausting crops generally; one principle, therefore, is that they should at least alternate with these crops; in this consists the Norfolk rotation. (pp. 50, 51)

No wonder that Mr Lavergne, who believes these English rustic fairy-tales, also believes that the wages of English farm labourers have lost their former abnormality since the duties on corn have been lifted. (See what has been previously said on this point. Buch I, Kap. XXIII, 5, pp.704 to 729. [English edition: Ch. XXV, 5, pp. 673-96.—*Ed.*] But let us also listen to Mr John Bright's speech in Birmingham, December 14, 1865. After mentioning the 5 million families entirely unrepresented in Parliament, he continues:

> There is among them one million, or rather more than one million, in the United Kingdom who are classed in the unfortunate list of paupers. There is another million just above pauperism, but always in peril lest they should become paupers. Their condition and prospects are not more favourable than that. Now look at the ignorant and lower strata of this portion of the community. Look to their abject condition, to their poverty, to their suffering, to their utter hopelessness of any good. Why, in the United States—even in the Southern States during the reign of slavery every Negro had an idea that there was a day of jubilee for him. But to these people—to this class of the lowest strata in this country—I am here to state that there is neither the belief of anything better nor scarcely an aspiration after it. Have you read a paragraph which lately appeared in the newspapers about John Cross, a Dorsetshire labourer? He worked six days in the week, had an excellent character from his employer for whom he had worked twenty-four years at the rate of eight shillings per week. John Cross had a family of seven children to provide for out of these wages in his hovel—for a feeble wife and an infant child. He took—legally, I believe he stole—a wooden hurdle of the value of sixpence. For this offence he was tried before the magistrates and sentenced to 14 or 20 days' imprisonment.... I can tell you that many thousands of cases like that of John Cross are to be found throughout the country, and especially in the south, and that their condition is such that hitherto the most anxious investigator has been unable to solve the mystery as to how they keep body and soul together. Now cast your eye over the country and look at these five million of families and the desperate condition of this strata of them. Is it not true that the unenfranchised nation may be said to toil and toil and knowing almost no rest? Compare it with the ruling class—but if I do I shall be charged with communism.... But compare this great toiling and unenfranchised nation with the section who may be considered the governing classes. Look at its wealth; look at its ostentation—look at its luxury. Behold its weariness—for there is weariness amongst them, but it is the weariness of satiety—and see how they rush from place to place, as it were, to discover some new pleasure. (*Morning Star*, December 14, 1865.)

It is shown in what follows how surplus-labour, and consequently surplus-product, is generally confused with ground-rent that qualitatively and quantitatively specifically determined, at least on the basis of the capitalist mode of production, part of the surplus-product. The natural basis of surplus-labour in general, that is, a natural prerequisite without which such labour cannot be performed, is that Nature must supply—in the form of animal or vegetable products of the land, in fisheries, etc.—the necessary means of subsistence under conditions of an expenditure of labour which does not consume the entire working day. This natural productivity of agricultural labour (which includes here the labour of simple gathering, hunting, fishing and cattle-raising) is the basis of all surplus-labour, as all labour is primarily and initially directed toward the appropriation and production of food. (Animals also supply at the same time skins for warmth in colder climates; also cave-dwellings, etc.)

The same confusion between surplus-product and ground-rent is found differently expressed by Mr Dove. [P. Dove, *The Elements of Political Science*, Edinburgh, 1854, pp.264, 273.—*Ed.*] Originally agricultural and industrial labour were not separated; the latter was an adjunct of the former. The surplus-labour and the surplus-product of the land-cultivating tribe, house commune, or family included both agricultural and industrial labour. Both went hand in hand. Hunting, fishing and agriculture were impossible without suitable tools. Weaving, spinning, etc., were first carried on as an agrarian side line.

We have previously shown that just as the labour of an individual workman breaks up into necessary and surplus labour, the aggregate labour of the working-class may be so divided that the portion which produces the total means of subsistence for the working-class (including the means of production required for this purpose) performs the necessary labour for the whole of society. The labour performed by the remainder of the working-class may then be regarded as surplus labour. But the necessary labour consists by no means only of agricultural labour, but also of that labour which produces all other products necessarily included in the average consumption of the labourer. Furthermore, from the social standpoint, some perform only necessary labour because others perform only surplus labour, and vice versa. It is but a division of labour between them. The same holds for the division of labour between agricultural and industrial labourers in general. The purely industrial character of labour, on the one hand, corresponds to the purely agricultural character on the other. This purely agricultural labour is by no means natural, but is rather a product—and a very modern one at that, which has not yet been achieved everywhere—of social development and corresponds to a very definite stage of the development of production. Just as a portion of agricultural labour is materialised in products which either minister only to luxury or serve as raw materials in industry, but by no means serve as food, let alone as food for the masses, so on the other hand a portion of industrial labour is materialised in products which serve as necessary means of consumption for both agricultural and nonagricultural labourers. It is a mistake, from a social point of view, to regard this industrial labour as surplus-labour. It is, in part, as much necessary labour as the necessary portion of the agricultural labour. It is also but a form rendered independent of a part of industrial labour which was formerly naturally connected with agricultural labour, a necessary mutual supplement to the specifically agricultural labour now separated from it. (From a purely material point of view, 500 mechanical weavers, e.g., produce surplus-fabrics to a far greater degree, that is, more than is required for their own clothing.)

Finally, it should be borne in mind in considering the various forms of manifestation of ground-rent, that is, the lease money paid under the heading of ground-rent to the landlord for the use of the land for purposes of production or consumption, that the price of things which have in themselves no value, i.e., are not the product of labour, such as land, or which at least cannot be reproduced by labour, such as antiques and works of art by certain masters, etc., may be determined by many fortuitous combinations. In order to sell a thing, nothing more is required than its capacity to be monopolised and alienated.

There are three main errors to be avoided in studying ground-rent, and which obscure its analysis.

1. Confusing the various forms of rent pertaining to different stages of development of the social production process.

   Whatever the specific form of rent may be, all types have this in common: the appropriation of rent is that economic form in which landed property is realised, and ground-rent, in turn, presupposes the existence of landed property, the ownership of certain portions of our planet by certain individuals. The owner may be an individual representing the community, as in Asia, Egypt, etc.; or this landed property may be merely incidental to the ownership of the immediate producers themselves by some individual as under slavery or serfdom; or it may be a purely private ownership of Nature by non-producers, a mere title to land; or, finally, it may be a relationship to the land which, as in the case of colonists and small peasants owning land, seems to be directly included—in the isolated and not socially developed labour—in the appropriation and production of the products of particular plots of land by the direct producers.

   This common element in the various forms of rent, namely that of being the economic realisation of landed property, of legal fiction by grace of which certain individuals have an exclusive right to certain parts of our planet—makes it possible for the differences to escape detection.
2. All ground-rent is surplus-value, the product of surplus-labour. In its undeveloped form as rent in kind it is still directly the surplus-product itself. Hence, the mistaken idea that the rent corresponding to the capitalist mode of production—which is always a surplus over and above profit, i.e., above a value portion of commodities which itself consists of surplus-value (surplus-labour)—that this special and specific component of surplus-value is explained by merely explaining the general conditions for the existence of surplus-value and profit in general. These conditions are: the direct producers must work beyond the time necessary for reproducing their own labour-power, for their own reproduction. They must perform surplus-labour in general. This is the subjective condition. The objective condition is that they must be able to perform surplus-labour. The natural conditions must be such that a part of their available labour-time suffices for their reproduction and self-maintenance as producers, that the production of their necessary means of subsistence shall not consume their whole labour-power. The fertility of Nature establishes a limit here, a starting-point, a basis. On the other hand, the development of the social productive power of their labour forms the other limit. Examined more closely, since the production of means of subsistence is the very first condition of their existence and of all production in general, labour used in this production, that is, agricultural labour in the broadest economic sense, must be fruitful enough so as not to absorb the entire available labour-time in the production of means of subsistence for the direct producers, that is, agricultural surplus-labour, and therefore, agricultural surplus-product must be possible. Developed further, the total agricultural labour, both necessary and surplus labour, of a segment of society must suffice to produce the necessary subsistence for the whole of society, that is, for non-agricultural labourers too. This means therefore, that the major division of labour between agricultural and industrial must be possible; and similarly between tillers of the soil producing means of subsistence and those producing raw materials. Although the labour of the direct producers of means of subsistence breaks up into necessary and surplus labour as far as they themselves are concerned, it represents from the social standpoint only the necessary labour required

to produce the means of subsistence. Incidentally, the same is true for all division of labour within society as a whole, as distinct from the division of labour within individual workshops. It is the labour necessary for the production of particular articles, for the satisfaction of some particular need of society for these particular articles. If this division is proportional, then the products of various groups are sold at their values (at a later stage of development they are sold at their prices of production), or at prices which are certain modifications of these values or prices of production determined by general laws. It is indeed the effect of the law of value, not with reference to individual commodities or articles, but to each total product of the particular social spheres of production made independent by the division of labour; so that not only is no more than the necessary labour-time used up for each specific commodity, but only the necessary proportional quantity of the total social labour-time is used up in the various groups. For the condition remains that the commodity represents use-value. But if the use-value of individual commodities depends on whether they satisfy a particular need then the use-value of the mass of the social product depends on whether it satisfies the quantitatively definite social need for each particular kind of product in an adequate manner, and whether the labour is, therefore, proportionately distributed among the different spheres in keeping with these social needs, which are quantitatively circumscribed. (This point is to be noted in the distribution of capital among the various spheres of production.) The social need, that is, the use-value on a social scale, appears here as a determining factor for the amount of total social labour-time which is expended in various specific spheres of production. But it is merely the same law which is already applied in the case of single commodities, namely, that the use-value of a commodity is the basis of its exchange-value and thus of its value. This point has a bearing upon the relationship between necessary and surplus labour only in so far as a violation of this proportion makes it impossible to realise the value of the commodity and thus the surplus-value contained in it. For instance; let us assume that proportionally too much cotton goods have been produced, although only the labour-time necessary under the prevailing conditions is incorporated in this total cloth production. But in general too much social labour has been expended in this particular line; in other words, a portion of this product is useless. It is, therefore, sold solely as if it had been produced in the necessary proportion. This quantitative limit to the quota of social labour-time available for the various particular spheres of production is but a more developed expression of the law of value in general, although the necessary labour-time assumes a different meaning here. Only just so much of it is required for the satisfaction of social needs. The limitation occurring here is due to the use value. Society can use only so much of its total labour-time for this particular kind of product under prevailing conditions of production. But the subjective and objective conditions of surplus labour and surplus-value in general have nothing to do with the particular form of either the profit or the rent. These conditions apply to surplus-value as such, no matter what special form it may assume. Hence they do not explain ground-rent.

3. It is precisely in the economic realisation of landed property, in the development of ground-rent, that the following characteristic peculiarity comes to the fore, namely that its amount is by no means determined by the actions of its recipient, but is determined rather by the independent development of social labour in which the recipient takes no part. It may easily happen, therefore, that something is regarded as a peculiarity of rent (and of the products of agriculture in general), which is really a common feature of all branches of production and all their products where the basis is commodity-production—and, in particular, capitalist production, which is in its entirety commodity production.

The amount of ground-rent (and with it the value of land) grows with social development as a result of the total social labour. On the one hand, this leads to an expansion of the market and of the demand for products of the soil, and, on the other, it stimulates the demand for land itself, which is a prerequisite of competitive production in all lines of business activity, even those which are not agricultural. More exactly—if one considers only the actual agricultural rent—rent, and thereby the value of the land, develops with the market for the products of the soil, and thus with the increase in the non-agricultural population, with its need and demand for means of subsistence and raw materials. It is in the nature of capitalist production to continually reduce the agricultural population as compared with the non-agricultural, because in industry (in the strict sense) the increase of constant capital in relation to variable capital goes hand in hand with an absolute increase, though relative decrease, in variable capital; on the other hand, in agriculture the variable capital required for the exploitation of a certain plot of land decreases absolutely; it can thus only increase to the extent that new land is taken into cultivation, but this again requires as a prerequisite a still greater growth of the non-agricultural population.

In fact, we are not dealing here with a characteristic peculiarity of agriculture and its products. On the contrary, the same applies to all other branches of production and products where the basis is commodity-production and its absolute form, capitalist production.

These products are commodities, or use-values, which have an exchange-value that is to be realised, to be converted into money, only in so far as other commodities form an equivalent for them, that is, other products confront them as commodities and values; thus, in so far as they are not produced as immediate means of subsistence for the producers themselves, but as commodities, as products which become use-values only by their transformation into exchange-values (money), by their alienation. The market for these commodities develops through the social division of labour; the division of productive labours mutually transforms their respective products into commodities, into equivalents for each other, making them mutually serve as markets. This is in no way peculiar to agricultural products.

Rent can develop as money-rent only on the basis of commodity production, in particular capitalist production, and it develops to the same extent that agricultural production becomes commodity production, that is, to the same extent that non-agricultural production develops independently of agricultural production, for to that degree the agricultural product becomes commodity, exchange-value, and value. In so far as commodity-production and thus the production of value develops with capitalist production so does the production of surplus-value and surplus product. But in the same proportion as the latter develops, landed property acquires the capacity of capturing an ever-increasing portion of this surplus-value by means of its land monopoly and thereby, of raising the value of its rent and the price of the land itself. The capitalist still performs an active function in the development of this surplus-value and surplus-product. But the landowner need only appropriate the growing share in the surplus-product and the surplus-value, without having contributed anything to this growth. This is the characteristic peculiarity of his position, and not the fact that the value of the products of the land, and thus of the land itself, increases to the degree that the market for them expands, the demand grows and with it the world of commodities which confronts the products of the land—in other words, the mass of non-agricultural commodity producers and non-agricultural commodity-production. But since this takes place without any action on his part, it appears to him as something unique that the mass of value, the mass of surplus-value, and the transformation of a portion of surplus value into ground-rent should depend upon the social production process, on the development of commodity-production in general. For this reason,

Dove, for instance, tries to evolve rent from this. He says that rent does not depend upon the mass of the agricultural product, but upon its value, [P. Dove, *The Elements of Political Science*, Edinburgh, 1854, p.279.—*Ed.*] however, this depends upon the mass and productivity of the non-agricultural population. But it is also true of every other product that it can only develop as a commodity partly as the mass and partly as the variety of other commodities which form equivalents for its increase. This has already been demonstrated in connection with the general presentation of value. [English edition: Vol. I, p. 88.—*Ed.*] On the one hand, the exchangeability of a product in general depends on the multiplicity of commodities existing in addition to it. On the other hand, on it depends in particular the quantity in which this product can be produced as a commodity.

No producer, whether industrial or agricultural, when considered by himself alone, produces value or commodities. His product becomes a value and a commodity only in the context of definite social interrelations. In the first place, in so far as it appears as the expression of social labour, hence in so far as the individual producer's labour-time counts as a part of the social labour-time in general; and, secondly, this social character of his labour appears impressed upon his product through its pecuniary character and through its general exchangeability determined by its price.

Therefore, if, on the one hand, surplus-value or, still more narrowly, the surplus-product in general is explained instead of rent, the mistake is made, on the other hand, of ascribing exclusively to agricultural products a characteristic which belongs to all products in their capacity as commodities and values. This is vulgarised still more by those who pass from the general determination of value over to the realisation of the value of a specific commodity. Every commodity can realise its value only in the process of circulation, and whether it realises its value, or to what extent it does so, depends on prevailing market conditions.

It is not a singularity of ground-rent, then, that agricultural products develop into, and as, values, i.e., that they confront other commodities as commodities, and that non-agricultural products confront them as commodities; or that they develop as specific expressions of social labour. The singularity of ground-rent is rather that together with the conditions in which agricultural products develop as values (commodities), and together with the conditions in which their values are realised, there also grows the power of landed property to appropriate an increasing portion of these values, which were created without its assistance; and so an increasing portion of surplus-value is transformed into ground-rent.

Notes

1. Nothing could he more comical than Hegel's development of private landed property. According to this, man as an individual must endow his will with reality as the soul of external nature, and must therefore take possession of this nature and make it his private property. If this were the destiny of the '*individual*', of man as an individual, it would follow that every human being must be a landowner, in order to become a real individual. Free private ownership of land, a very recent product, is according to Hegel, not a definite social relation, but a relation of man as an individual to 'nature,' an absolute right of man to appropriate all things (Hegel *Philosophie des Rechts*, Berlin 1840 p 79) This much at least is evident the individual cannot maintain himself as a landowner by his mere 'will' against the will of another individual, who likewise wants to become a real individual by virtue of the same strip of land. It definitely requires some thing other than goodwill. Furthermore, it is absolutely impossible to determine where the 'individual' draws the line for realising his will —whether this will requires for its realisation a whole country, or whether it requires

a whole group of countries by whose appropriation 'the supremacy of my will over the thing can be manifested.' Here Hegel comes to a complete impasse. 'The appropriation is of a very particular kind; I do not take possession of more than I touch with my body; but it is clear, on the other hand, that external things are more extensive than I can grasp. By thus having possession of such a thing, some other is thereby connected to it. I carry out the act of appropriation by means of my hand, but its scope can be extended' (p.90). But this other thing is again linked with still another and so the boundary within which my will, as the soul, can pour into the soil, disappears. 'When I possess something, my mind at once passes over to the idea that not only this property in my immediate possession, but what is associated with it is also mine. Here positive right must decide, for nothing more can be deduced from the concept' (p. 91). This is an extraordinarily naive admission 'of the concept', and proves that this concept which makes the blunder at the very outset of regarding as absolute a very definite legal view of landed property belonging to bourgeois society—understands 'nothing' of the actual nature of this landed property. This contains at the same time the admission that 'positive right' can, and must, alter its determinations as the requirements of social, i.e., economic, development change.

2. Very conservative agricultural chemists, such as Johnston, admit that a really rational agriculture is confronted everywhere with insurmountable barriers stemming from private property. So do writers who are *ex professo* advocates of the monopoly of private property in the world, for instance, Charles Comte in his two-volume work, which has as its special aim the defence of private property. 'A nation,' he says, 'cannot attain to the degree of prosperity and power compatible with its nature, unless every portion of the soil nourishing it is assigned to that purpose which agrees best with the general interest. In order to give to its wealth a strong development, one sole and above all highly enlightened will should, if possible, take it upon itself to assign each piece of its domain its task and make every piece contribute to the prosperity of all others. But the existence of such a will ... would be incompatible with the division of the land into private plots—and with the authority guaranteed each owner to dispose of his property in an almost absolute manner. [*Traité de la propriété*, Tome I, Paris, 1834, p. 228.—*Ed.*] Johnston, Comte, and others, only have in mind the necessity of tilling the land of a certain country as a whole, when they speak of a contradiction between property and a rational system of agronomy. But the dependence of the cultivation of particular agricultural products upon the fluctuations of market-prices, and the continual changes in this cultivation with these price fluctuations—the whole spirit of capitalist production, which is directed toward the immediate gain of money are in contradiction to agriculture, which has to minister to the entire range of permanent necessities of life required by the chain of successive generations. A striking illustration of this is furnished by the forests, which are only rarely managed in a way more or less corresponding to the interests of society as a whole, *i.e.*, when they are not private property, but subject to the control of the state.

3. *Misère de la Philosophie*, p.165. There I have made a distinction between *terre-matière* and *terre-capital*. 'The mere application of further outlays of capital to land already transformed into means of production increases land as capital without adding anything to land as matter, that is, to the extent of the land.... Land as capital is no more eternal than any other capital... Land as capital is fixed capital; but fixed capital gets used up just as much as circulating capital.'

4. I say 'can' because under certain circumstances this interest is regulated by the law of ground-rent and, therefore, can disappear, as in the case of competition between virgin lands of great natural fertility.

5. See James Anderson [*A Calm Investigation of the Circumstances that have led to the Present Scarcity of Grain in Britain*, London, 1801, pp.35-36, 38.—*Ed.*] and Carey, *The Past, the Present, and the Future*, Philadelphia, 1848, pp. 129-31.—*Ed.*

6. See the *Anti-Corn Law Prize-Essays*. However, the Corn Laws always kept prices at an artificially higher level. For the better placed tenants this was favourable. They profited from the passivity in which the protective duties kept the great mass of tenants who relied, with or without good reason, on the exceptional average price.
7. John C. Morton, *The Forces Used in Agriculture*. Lecture in the London Society of Arts, 1860, based upon authentic documents collected from about 100 tenants in 12 Scottish and 35 English counties.

38

Differential Rent: General Remarks

In the analysis of ground-rent we shall begin with the assumption that products paying such a rent, products in which a portion of the surplus-value, and therefore also a portion of the total price, resolves itself into ground-rent, i.e., that agricultural as well as mining products are sold at their prices of production like all other commodities. (It suffices for our purposes to confine ourselves to agricultural and mining products.) In other words, their selling prices are made up of the elements of their cost (the value of consumed constant and variable capital) plus a profit determined by the general rate of profit and calculated on the total advanced capital, whether consumed or not. We assume, then, that average selling prices of these products are equal to their prices of production. The question now arises how it is possible for ground-rent to develop under these conditions, i.e., how it is possible for a portion of the profit to become transformed into ground-rent, so that a portion of the commodity-price falls to the landlord.

In order to demonstrate the general character of this form of ground-rent, let us assume that most of the factories of a certain country derive their power from steam-engines, while a smaller number derive it from natural waterfalls. Let us further assume that the price of production in the former amounts to 115 for a quantity of commodities which have consumed a capital of 100. The 15% profit is calculated not solely on the consumed capital of 100, but on the total capital employed in the production of this commodity-value. We have previously shown that this price of production is not determined by the individual cost-price of every single industrial producer, but by the average cost-price of the commodity under average conditions of capital in the entire sphere of production. It is, in fact, the market-price of production, the average market-price as distinct from its oscillations. It is in general in the form of the market-price, and, furthermore, in the form of the regulating market-price, or market-price of production, that the nature of the value of commodities asserts itself, its determination not by the labour-time necessary in the case of any individual producer for the production of a certain quantity of commodities, or of some individual commodity, but by the socially necessary labour-time; that is, by the labour-time, required for the production of the socially necessary total quantity of commodity varieties on the market under the existing average conditions of social production

As definite figures are immaterial in this case, we shall assume furthermore that the cost-price in factories run on water-power is only 90 instead of 100. Since the regulating market-price of production of this quantity of commodities = 115, with a profit of 15%, the manufacturers who operate their machines on water power will also sell their commodities at 115, i.e., the average price regulating the market-price. Their profit would then be 25 instead of 15; the regulating price of production would allow them a surplus-profit of 10%

not because they sell their commodities above the price of production, but because they sell them at the price of production, because their commodities are produced, or their capital operates, under exceptionally favourable conditions, i.e., under conditions which are more favourable than the average prevailing in this sphere.

Two things become evident at once:

First, the surplus-profit of the producers who use a natural waterfall as motive power is to begin with in the same class with all surplus-profit (and we have already analysed this category when discussing prices of production) which is not the fortuitous result of transactions in the circulation process, of the fortuitous fluctuations in market-prices. This surplus-profit, then, is likewise equal to the difference between the individual price of production of these favoured producers and the general social price of production regulating the market in this entire production sphere. This difference is equal to the excess of the general price of production of the commodities over their individual price of production. The two regulating limits of this excess are, on the one hand, the individual cost-price, and thus the individual price of production, and, on the other hand, the general price of production. The value of commodities produced with water-power is smaller because a smaller total quantity of labour is required for their production, i.e., less labour—in materialised form—enters into the constant capital as part of the latter.

The labour employed here is more productive, its individual productive power is greater than that employed in the majority of factories of the same kind. Its greater productive power is shown in the fact that in order to produce the same quantity of commodities, it requires a smaller quantity of constant capital, a smaller quantity of materialised labour, than the others. It also requires less living labour, because the water-wheel need not be heated. This greater individual productiveness of employed labour reduces the value, but also the cost-price and thereby the price of production of the commodity. For the individual industrial capitalist this expresses itself in a lower cost-price for his commodities. He has to pay for less materialised labour, and also less wages for less living labour-power employed. Since the cost-price of his commodities is lower, his individual price of production is also lower. His cost-price is 90 instead of 100. His individual price of production would therefore be only 103½ instead of 115 (100:115 = 90:103½) The difference between his individual price of production and the general price of production is limited by the difference between his individual cost- price and the general cost-price. This is one of the magnitudes which form the limits to his surplus-profit. The other is the magnitude of the general price of production into which the general rate of profit enters as one of the regulating factors. Were coal to become cheaper, the difference between his individual cost-price and the general cost-price would decrease, and with it his surplus-profit. Should he be compelled to sell his commodities at their individual value, or at the price of production determined by their individual value, then the difference would disappear. It is, on the one hand, a result of the fact that the commodities are sold at their general market-price, the price brought about by the equalisation of individual prices through competition, and, on the other, a result of the fact that the greater individual productivity of labour set in motion by him does not benefit the labourer, but the employer, as does all productivity of labour, that it appears as the productiveness of capital.

Since the level of the general price of production is one of the limits of this surplus-profit, the level of the general rate of profit being one of its factors, this surplus-profit can only arise from the difference between the general and the individual price of production, and consequently from the difference between the general and the individual rate of profit. An excess above this difference presupposes the sale of products above, not at, the price of production regulated by the market.

Secondly, thus far, the surplus-profit of the manufacturer using natural water-power instead of steam does not differ in any way from any other surplus-profit. All normal surplus-profit, that is, all surplus-profit not due to fortuitous sales or market-price fluctuations is determined by the difference between the individual price of production of the commodities of a particular capital and the general price of production, which regulates the market-prices of the commodities produced by the capital in this sphere of production in general, or, in other words, the market-prices of commodities of the total capital invested in this sphere of production.

But now we come to the difference.

To what circumstance does the industrial capitalist in the present case owe his surplus-profit, the surplus resulting for him personally from the price of production regulated by the general rate of profit?

He owes it in the first instance to a natural force—the motive power of the waterfall—which is found readily available in Nature and is not itself a product of labour like the coal which transforms water into steam. The coal, therefore, has value, must be paid for by an equivalent, and has a cost. The waterfall is a natural production agent in the production of which no labour enters.

But this is not all. The manufacturer who operates with steam also employs natural forces which cost him nothing yet make the labour more productive and increase the surplus-value and thereby the profit, inasmuch as they thus cheapen the manufacture of the means of subsistence required for the labourers. These natural forces are thus quite as much monopolised by capital as the social natural forces of labour arising from co-operation, division of labour, etc. The manufacturer pays for coal, but not for the capacity of water to alter its physical state, to turn into steam, not for the elasticity of the steam, etc. This monopolisation of natural forces, that is, of the increase in labour-power produced by them, is common to all capital operating with steam-engines. It may increase that portion of the product of labour which represents surplus-value in relation to that portion which is transformed into wages. In so far as it does this, it raises the general rate of profit, but it does not create any surplus-profit, for this consists of the excess of individual profit over average profit. The fact that the application of a natural force, a waterfall, creates surplus-profit in this case, cannot therefore, be due solely to the circumstance that the increased productivity of labour here results from the application of a natural force. Other modifying circumstances are necessary.

Conversely, the mere application of natural forces in industry may influence the level of the general rate of profit because it affects the quantity of labour required to produce the necessary means of subsistence. But in itself it does not create any deviation from the general rate of profit, and this is precisely the point in which we are interested here. Furthermore, the surplus-profit which some individual capital otherwise realises in a particular sphere of production—for deviations of the rates of profit in various spheres of production are continually balanced out into an average rate—is due, aside from fortuitous deviations, to a reduction in cost-price, in production costs. This reduction arises either from the fact that capital is used in greater than average quantities, so that *faux frais* of production are reduced, while the general causes increasing the productiveness of labour (cooperation, division of labour, etc.) can become effective to a higher degree, with more intensity, because their field of activity has become larger; or it may arise from the fact that, aside from the amount of functioning capital, better methods of labour, new inventions, improved machinery, chemical manufacturing secrets, etc., in short, new and improved, better than average means of production and methods of production are used. The reduction in cost-price and the surplus-profit arising from it are here the result of the manner in which the functioning capital is invested. They result either from the fact that the capital is concentrated in the hands of one person in extraordinarily large quantities (a condition that is cancelled out as soon as equal magnitudes of capital are used on the average), or from the fact that a certain magnitude of capital functions in a particularly productive manner (a condition that disappears as soon as the exceptional method of production becomes general or is surpassed by a still more developed one).

The cause of the surplus-profit, then, arises here from the capital itself (which includes the labour set in motion by it) whether it be due to the greater magnitude of capital employed or to its more efficient application; and, as a matter of fact, there is no particular reason why all capital in the same production sphere should not be invested in the same manner. On the contrary, the competition between capitals tends to cancel these differences more and more. The determination of value by the socially necessary labour-time asserts itself through the cheapening of commodities and the compulsion to produce commodities under the same favourable conditions. But matters are different with the surplus-profit of an industrial capitalist who makes use of the waterfall. The increased productiveness of the labour used by him comes neither from the capital and labour itself, nor from the mere application of some natural force different from capital and labour but incorporated in the capital. It arises from the greater natural productiveness of labour bound up with the application of a force of Nature, but not a force of Nature that is at the command of all capital in the same sphere of production, as for example the elasticity of steam. In other words, its application is not to be taken for granted whenever capital is generally invested in this sphere of production. On the contrary, it is a monopolisable force of Nature which, like the waterfall, is only at the command of those who have at their disposal particular portions of the earth and its appurtenances. It is by no means within the power of capital to call into existence this natural premise for a greater productivity of labour in the same manner as any capital may transform water into steam. It is found only locally in Nature and, wherever it does not exist, it cannot be established by a definite investment of capital. It is not bound to goods which labour can produce, such as machines and coal, but to specific natural conditions prevailing in certain portions of land. Those manufacturers who own waterfalls exclude those who do not from using this natural force, because land, and particularly land endowed with water-power, is scarce. This does not prevent the amount of water-power available for industrial purposes from being increased, even though the number of natural waterfalls in a given country is limited. The waterfall may be harnessed by man in order to fully exploit its motive force. If such exists, the water-wheel may be improved so as to make use of as much of the water-power as possible; where the ordinary wheel is not suitable for the water-supply, turbines may be used, etc. The possession of this natural force constitutes a monopoly in the hands of its owner; it is a condition for an increase in the productiveness of the invested capital that cannot be established by the production process of the capital itself;[1] this natural force, which can be monopolised in this manner, is always bound to the land. Such a natural force does not belong to the general conditions of the sphere of production in question, nor to those conditions of the latter which may be generally established.

Now let us assume that the waterfalls, along with the land to which they belong, are held by individuals who are regarded as owners of these portions of the earth, i.e., who are landowners. These owners prevent the investment of capital in the waterfalls and their exploitation by capital. They can permit or forbid such utilisation. But a waterfall cannot be created by capital out of itself. Therefore, the surplus-profit which arises from the employment of this waterfall is not due to capital, but to the utilisation of a natural force which can be monopolised, and has been monopolised, by capital. Under these circumstances, the surplus-profit is transformed into ground-rent, that is, it falls into possession of the owner of a waterfall. If the manufacturer pays the owner of a waterfall £10 annually, then his profit is £15, that is, 15% on the £100 which then make up his cost of production; and he is just as well or possibly better off than all other capitalists in his sphere of production who operate with steam. It would not alter matters one bit if the capitalist himself should be the owner of a waterfall. He would, in such a case, pocket as before the surplus-profit of £10 in his capacity as waterfall owner, and not in his capacity as capitalist; and precisely because this surplus does not stem from his capital as such, but rather from the control of a limited natural force distinct from his capital which can be monopolised, is it transformed into ground-rent.

First, it is evident that this rent is always a differential rent, for it does not enter as a determining factor into the general production price of commodities, but rather is based on it. It invariably arises from the difference between the individual production price of a particular capital having command over the monopolised natural force, on the one hand, and the general production price of the total capital invested in the sphere of production concerned, on the other.

Secondly, this ground-rent does not arise from the absolute increase in the productiveness of employed capital, or labour appropriated by it, since this can only reduce the value of commodities; it is due to the greater relative fruitfulness of specific separate capitals invested in a certain production sphere, as compared with investments of capital which are excluded from these exceptional and natural conditions favouring productiveness. For instance, if the use of steam should offer overwhelming advantages not offered by the use of water-power, despite the fact that coal has value and the water-power has not, and if these advantages more than compensated for the expense, then, the water-power would not be used and could not produce any surplus-profit, and therefore could not produce any rent.

Thirdly, the natural force is not the source of surplus-profit, but only its natural basis, because this natural basis permits an exceptional increase in the productiveness of labour. In the same way, use-value is in general the bearer of exchange-value, but not its cause. If the same use-value could be obtained without labour, it would have no exchange-value, yet it would retain, as before, the same natural usefulness as use-value. On the other hand, nothing can have exchange-value unless it has use-value, i.e., unless it is a natural bearer of labour. Were it not for the fact that the various values are averaged out into prices of production, and the various individual prices of production into a general price of production regulating the market, the mere increase in productivity of labour through utilisation of the waterfall would merely lower the price of commodities produced with the aid of this waterfall, without increasing the share of profit contained in these commodities. Similarly, on the other hand, this increased productivity of labour itself would not be converted into surplus-value were it not for the fact that capital appropriates the natural and social productivity of the labour used by it as its own.

Fourthly, the private ownership of the waterfall in itself has nothing to do with the creation of the surplus-value (profit) portion, and therefore, of the price of the commodity in general, which is produced by means of the waterfall. This surplus-profit would also exist if landed property did not exist; for instance, if the land on which the waterfall is situated were used by the manufacturer as unclaimed land. Hence landed property does not create the portion of value which is transformed into surplus-profit, but merely enables the landowner, the owner of the waterfall, to coax this surplus-profit out of the pocket of the manufacturer and into his own. It is not the cause of the creation of such surplus-profit, but is the cause of its transformation into the form of ground-rent, and therefore, of the appropriation of this portion of the profit, or commodity-price, by the owner of the land or waterfall.

Fifthly, it is evident that the price of the waterfall, that is, the price which the landowner would receive were he to sell it to a third party or even to the manufacturer himself, does not immediately enter into the production price of the commodities, although it does enter into the individual cost-price of the manufacturer; because the rent arises here from the price of production of similar commodities produced by steam machinery, and this price is regulated independently of the waterfall. Furthermore, this price of the waterfall on the whole is an irrational expression, but behind it is hidden a real economic relationship. The waterfall, like land in general, and like any natural force, has no value because it does not represent any materialised labour, and therefore, it has no price, which is normally no more than the expression of value in money terms. Where there is no value, there is also *eo ipso* nothing to be expressed in money. This price is nothing more than the capitalised rent. Landownership enables the landowner to appropriate the difference between the individual profit and average profit. The profit thus acquired, which is renewed every year, may be capitalised, and appears then as the price of the natural force itself. If the surplus-profit realised by the manufacturer using the waterfall amounts to £10 per year, and the average interest is 5%, then these £10 represent the annual interest on a capital of £200 and the capitalisation of the annual £10 which the waterfall enables its owner to appropriate from the manufacturer, appears then as the capital-value of the waterfall itself. That it is not the waterfall itself which has value, but that its price is a mere reflection of the appropriated surplus-profit capitalistically calculated, becomes at once evident from the fact that the price of £200 represents merely the product obtained by multiplying a surplus-profit of £10 by 20 years, whereas, other conditions remaining equal, the same waterfall will enable its owner to appropriate these £10 every year for an indefinite number of years—30 years, 100 years, or x years; and, whereas, on the other hand, should some new method of production not applicable with water-power reduce the cost-price of commodities produced by steam machinery from £100 to £90, the surplus-profit, and thereby the rent, and thus the price of the waterfall, would disappear.

Now that we have described the general concept of differential rent, we shall pass on to its consideration in agriculture proper. What applies to agriculture will also apply on the whole to mining.

Note

1. Concerning extra profit, see the Inquiry [into those Principles, Respecting the Nature of Demand and the Necessity of Consumption, lately advocated by Mr Malthus, London, 1821.—*Ed.*] (against Malthus).

39

First Form of Differential Rent (Differential Rent I)

Ricardo is quite right in the following observations:

> Rent is always the difference between the produce obtained by the employment of two equal quantities of capital and labour. (*Principles*, p. 59)

[He means differential rent, for he assumes that no other rent but differential rent exists.] He should have added, 'on equal areas of land' in so far as it is a matter of ground-rent and not surplus-profit in general.

In other words, surplus-profit, if normal and not due to accidental occurrences in the circulation process, is always produced as a difference between the products of two equal quantities of capital and labour, and this surplus-profit is transformed into ground-rent when two equal quantities of capital and labour are employed on equal areas of land with unequal results. Moreover, it is by no means absolutely necessary for this surplus-profit to arise from the unequal results of equal quantities of invested capital. The various investments may also employ unequal quantities of capital. Indeed, this is generally the case. But equal proportions, for instance £100 of each, produce unequal results; that is, their rates of profit are different. This is the general prerequisite for the existence of surplus-profit in any sphere of capital investment. The second prerequisite is the transformation of this surplus-profit into the form of ground-rent (of rent in general as a form distinct from profit); it must be investigated in each case when, how, under what conditions this transformation takes place.

Ricardo is also right in the following observation, provided it is limited to differential rent:

> Whatever diminishes the inequality in the produce obtained on the same or on new land, tends to lower rent, and whatever increases that inequality, necessarily produces an opposite effect and tends to raise it. (p.74)

However, among these causes are not merely the general ones (fertility and location), but also 1) the distribution of taxes, depending on whether it operates uniformly or not; the latter is always the case when, as in England, it is not centralised and when the tax is levied on land, not on rent; 2) the inequalities arising from a difference in agricultural development in different parts of the country, since this line of production, owing to its traditional character, evens out with more difficulty than manufacture; and 3) the inequality in distribution of capital among capitalist tenants. Since the invasion of agriculture by the capitalist mode of production, transformation of independently producing peasants into wage-workers, is in fact the last conquest of this mode of production, these inequalities are greater here than in any other line of production.

Having made these preliminary remarks, I will first present a brief summary of the characteristic features of my analysis in contradistinction to that of Ricardo, etc.

We shall first consider the unequal results of equal quantities of capital applied to different plots of land of equal size; or, in the case of unequal size, results calculated on the basis of equal areas.

The two general causes of these unequal results—quite independent of capital—are: 1) *Fertility*. (With reference to this first point, it will be necessary to discuss what is meant by natural fertility of land and what factors are involved.) 2) The *location* of the land. This is a decisive factor in the case of colonies and in general determines the sequence in which plots of land can be cultivated. Furthermore, it is evident that these two different causes of differential rent—fertility and location—may work in opposite directions. A certain plot of land may be very favourably located and yet be very poor in fertility, and vice versa. This circumstance is important, for it explains how it is possible that bringing into cultivation the land of a certain country may equally well proceed from the better to the worse land as vice versa. Finally, it is clear that the progress of social production in general has, on the one hand, the effect of evening out differences arising from location as a cause of ground-rent, by creating local markets and improving locations by establishing communication and transportation facilities; on the other hand, it increases the differences in individual locations of plots of land by separating agriculture from manufacturing and forming large centres of production, on the one hand, while relatively isolating agricultural districts, on the other.

For the present, however, we shall leave this point concerning location out of consideration and confine ourselves to natural fertility. Aside from climatic factors, etc., the difference in natural fertility depends on the chemical composition of the top soil, that is, on its different plant nutrition content. However, assuming the chemical composition and natural fertility in this respect to be the same for two plots of land, the actual effective fertility differs depending on whether these elements of plant nutrition are in a form which may be more or less easily assimilated and immediately utilised for nourishing the crops. Hence, it will depend partly upon chemical and partly upon mechanical developments in agriculture to what extent the same natural fertility may be made available on plots of land of similar natural fertility. Fertility, although an objective property of the soil, always implies an economic relation, a relation to the existing chemical and mechanical level of development in agriculture, and, therefore, changes with this level of development. Whether by chemical means (such as the use of certain liquid fertilisers on stiff clay soil and calcination of heavy clayey soils), or mechanical means (such as special ploughs for heavy soils), the obstacles which made a soil of equal fertility actually less fertile can be eliminated (drainage also belongs under this head). Or even the sequence in types of soils taken under cultivation may be changed thereby, as was the case, for instance, with light sandy soil and heavy clayey soil at a certain period of development in English agriculture. This shows once again that historically, in the sequence of soils taken under cultivation, one may pass over from more fertile to less fertile soils as well as vice versa. The same results may be obtained by an artificially created improvement in soil composition or by a mere change in agricultural methods. Finally, the same result may be brought about by a change in the hierarchical arrangement of the soil types due to different conditions of the subsoil, as soon as the latter likewise begins to be tilled and turned over into top layers. This is in part dependent on the employment of new agricultural methods (such as the cultivation of fodder-grass) and in part on the employment of mechanical means which either turn the subsoil over into top layers, mix it with top soil, or cultivate the subsoil without turning it up.

All these influences upon the differential fertility of various plots of land are such that from the standpoint of economic fertility, the level of labour productivity, in this case the capacity of agriculture to make the natural soil fertility immediately exploitable—a capacity which differs in various periods of development—is as much a factor in so-called natural soil fertility as its chemical composition and other natural properties.

We assume, then, the existence of a particular stage of development in agriculture. We assume furthermore that the hierarchical arrangement of soil types accords with this stage of development, as is, of course, always the case for simultaneous capital investments on different plots of land. Differential rent may then form either an ascending or a descending sequence, for although the sequence is given for the totality of actually cultivated plots of land, a series of movements leading to its formation has invariably taken place.

Let us assume the existence of four kinds of soil: A, B, C, D. Let us furthermore assume the price of one quarter of wheat = £3, or 60 shillings. Since the rent is solely differential rent, this price of 60 shillings per quarter for the worst soil is equal to the price of production, that is, equal to the capital plus average profit. Let A be this worst soil, which yields 1 quarter = 60 shillings for each 50 shillings spent; hence the profit amounts to 10 shillings, or 20%.

Let B yield 2 quarters = 120 shillings for the same expenditure. This would mean 70 shillings of profit, or a surplus-profit of 60 shillings.

Let C yield 3 quarters = 180 shillings for the same expenditure; total profit = 130 shillings; surplus-profit = 120 shillings.

Let D yield 4 quarters = 240 shillings = 180 shillings of surplus-profit.

We would then have the following sequence:

TABLE I

Type of Soil	*Product*		*Capital Advanced*	*Profit*		*Rent*	
	Quarters	*Shillings*		*Quarters*	*Shillings*	*Quarters*	*Shillings*
A	1	60	50	1/6	10	—	—
B	2	120	50	1 1/6	70	1	60
C	3	180	50	2 1/6	130	2	120
D	4	240	50	3 1/6	190	3	180
Total...	10 qrs	600sh.				6 qrs	360sh.

The respective rents are: D = 190sh.—10sh., or the difference between D and A; C = 130sh.—10sh., or the difference between C and A; B = 70sh.—10sh., or the difference between B and A; and the total rent for B, C, D = 6 quarters = 360 shillings, equal to the sum of the differences between D and A, C and A, B and A.

This sequence, which represents a given product in a given condition may, considered abstractly (we have already offered the reasons why this may be the case in reality), descend from D to A, from fertile to less and less fertile soil, or rise from A to D, from relatively poor to more and more fertile soil, or, finally, may fluctuate, i.e., now rising, now descending—for instance from D to C, from C to A, and from A to B.

The process in the case of a descending sequence was as follows: The price of a quarter of wheat rose gradually from, say, 15 shillings to 60 shillings. As soon as the 4 quarters produced by D (we may consider these 4 quarters as so many million quarters) no longer sufficed, the price of wheat rose to a point where the supply shortage could be produced by C. That is to say, the price of wheat must have risen to 20 shillings per quarter. When it had risen to 30 shillings per quarter, B could be taken under cultivation, and when it reached 60 shillings A could be taken under cultivation; and the capital invested did not have to content itself with a rate of profit lower than 20%. In this manner, a rent was established for D, first of 5 shillings per quarter = 20 shillings for the 4 quarters produced by it; then of 15 shillings per quarter = 60 shillings, then of 45 shillings per quarter = 180 shillings for 4 quarters.

If the rate of profit of D originally was similarly = 20 %, then its total profit on 4 quarters of wheat was also but 10 shillings, but this represented more grain when the price was 15 shillings than it does when the price is 60 shillings. But since the grain enters into the reproduction of labour-power, and part of each quarter has to make good some portion of wages and another constant capital, the surplus-value under these conditions was higher, and thus other things being equal the rate of profit too. (The matter of rate of profit will have to be specially analysed, and in greater detail.)

On the other hand, if the sequence were in the reverse order, that is, if the process initiated from A, then the price of wheat at first would rise above 60 shillings per quarter when new land would have to be taken under cultivation. But since the necessary supply would be produced by B, a supply of 2 quarters, the price would fall to 60 shillings again, for B produced wheat at a cost of 30 shillings per quarter, but sold it at 60 shillings because the supply just sufficed to cover the demand. Thus a rent was formed, first of 60 shillings for B, and in the same way for C and D; it is assumed throughout that the market-price remained at 60 shillings, although C and D produced wheat having an actual value of 20 and 15 shillings per quarter respectively, because the supply of the one quarter produced by A was needed as much as ever to satisfy the total demand. In this case, the increase in demand above supply, which was first satisfied by A, then by A and B, would not have made it possible to cultivate B, C and D successively, but would merely have caused a general extension of the sphere of cultivation, and the more fertile lands might only later come under cultivation.

In the first sequence, an increase in price would raise the rent and decrease the rate of profit. Such a decrease might be entirely or partially checked by counteracting circumstances. This point will have to be treated later in more detail. It should not be forgotten that the general rate of profit is not determined uniformly in all spheres of production by the surplus-value. It is not the agricultural profit which determines industrial profit, but vice versa. But of this more anon.

In the second sequence the rate of profit on invested capital would remain the same. The amount of profit would be represented by less grain; but the relative price of grain, compared with that of other commodities, would have risen. However, the increase in profit wherever such an increase takes place, becomes separated from the profit in the form of rent, instead of flowing into the pockets of the capitalist tenant farmer and appearing as a growing profit. The price of grain, however, could remain unchanged under the conditions assumed here.

The development and growth of differential rent would remain the same for fixed as well as for increasing prices, and for a continuous progression from worse to better soils as well as for a continuous retrogression from better to worse soils.

Thus far we have assumed: 1) that the price rises in one sequence and remains stationary in the other; 2) that there is a continuous progression from better to worse soil, or from worse to better soil.

But now let us assume that the demand for grain rises from its original figure of 10 to 17 quarters; furthermore, that the worst soil A is displaced by another soil A, which produces 1 ⅓ quarters at a price of production of 60 shillings (50sh. cost plus 10sh. for 20% profit), so that its price of production per quarter = 45 shillings; or, perhaps, the old soil A may have improved through continuous rational cultivation, or be cultivated more productively at the same cost, for instance through the introduction of clover, etc., so that its output with the same investment of capital rises to 1⅓ quarters. Let us also assume that soil types B, C and D yield the same output as previously, but that new soil types have been introduced, for instance, A' with a fertility lying between A and B, and also B' and B" with a fertility between B and C. We should then observe the following phenomena:

First: The price of production of a quarter of wheat, or its regulating market-price, falls from 60 shillings to 45 shillings, or by 25%.

Second: The cultivation proceeds simultaneously from more fertile to less fertile soil, and from less fertile to more fertile soil. Soil A' is more fertile than A, but less fertile than the hitherto cultivated soils B, C and D. B' and B" are more fertile than A, A' and B, but less fertile than C and D. The sequence thus proceeds in crisscross fashion. Cultivation does not proceed to soil absolutely less fertile than A, etc., but to relatively less fertile soil with respect to the hitherto most fertile soil types C and on the other hand, cultivation does not proceed to soil absolutely more fertile, but to relatively more fertile soil with respect to the hitherto least fertile soil A, or A and B.

Thirdly: The rent on B falls; likewise the rent on C and D; but the total rental in grain rises from 6 quarters to 7⅔ the amount of cultivated and rent-yielding land increases, and the amount of produce rises from 10 quarters to 17. The profit, although it remains the same for A, rises if expressed in grain, but the rate of profit itself might rise, because the relative surplus-value does. In this case, the wage, i.e., the investment of variable capital and therefore the total outlay, is reduced because of the cheapening of means of subsistence. This total rental expressed in money falls from 360 shillings to 345 shillings.

TABLE II

Type of Soil	*Product*		*Capital Invested*	*Profit*		*Rent*		*Price of Production per Quarter*
	Quarters	*Shillings*		*Quarters*	*Shillings*	*Quarters*	*Shillings*	
A	1⅓	60	50	2/9	10	—	—	45 sh.
A'	1⅔	75	50	5/9	25	⅓	15	36 sh.
B	2	90	50	8/9	40	⅔	30	30 sh.
B'	2⅓	105	50	1 2/9	55	1	45	25 5/7* sh.
B"	2⅔	120	50	1 5/9	70	1⅓	60	22½ sh.
C	3	135	50	1 8/9	85	1⅔	75	20 sh.
D	4	180	50	2 8/9	130	2⅔	120	15 sh.
Total...	17					7⅔	345	

(*In the German 1894 edition this reads: 25 2/7.—Ed.)

Let us draw up the new sequence. [See p. 655—*Ed.*]

Finally, if only soil types A, B, C and D were cultivated as before, but their productiveness rose in such a way that A produced 2 quarters instead of 1 quarter, B—4 quarters instead of 2, C—7 quarters instead of 3, and D—10 quarters instead of 4, so that the same causes affect the various types of soil differently, the total production increases from 10 quarters to 23. Assuming that demand absorbs these 23 quarters through an increase in population and a fall in prices, we should obtain the following result:

TABLE III

Type of Soil	*Product*		*Capital Invested*	*Price of Production per Quarter*	*Profit*		*Rent*	
	Quarters	*Shillings*			*Quarters*	*Shillings*	*Quarters*	*Shillings*
A	2	60	50	30	⅓	10	0	0
B	4	120	50	15	2⅓	70	2	60
C	7	210	50	8 4/7	5⅓	160	5	150
D	10	300	50	6	8⅓	250	8	240
Total	23						15	450

The numerical proportions in this and in other tables are chosen at random but the assumptions are quite rational.

The first and principal assumption is that an improvement in agriculture acts differently upon different soils, and in this case affects the best types of soil, C and D, more than types A and B. Experience has shown that this is generally the case, although the opposite may also take place. If the improvement affected the poorer soils more than the better ones, rent on the latter would have fallen instead of risen. But in our table, we have assumed that the absolute growth in fertility of all soil types is simultaneously accompanied by an increase in greater relative fertility of the better soil types, C and D; this means an increase in the difference between the product at the same capital investment, and thus an increase in differential rent.

The second assumption is that total demand keeps pace with the increase in the total product. *First*, one need not imagine such an increase coming about abruptly, but rather gradually—until sequence III is established. *Secondly*, it is not true that the consumption of necessities of life does not increase as they become cheaper. The abolition of the Corn Laws in England proved the reverse to be the case (F. Newman, *Lectures on Political Economy*, London, 1851, p.158.—*Ed.*); the opposite view stems solely from the fact that large and sudden differences in harvests, which are mere results of weather, bring about at one time an extraordinary fall, at another an extraordinary rise, in grain prices. While in such a case the sudden and short-lived reduction in price does not have time to exert its full effect upon the extension of consumption, the opposite is true when a reduction arises from the lowering of the regulating price of production itself, i.e., is of a long-term nature. *Thirdly*, a part of the grain may be consumed in the form of brandy or beer; and the increasing consumption of both of these items is by no means confined within narrow limits. *Fourthly*, the matter depends in part upon the increase in population and in part on the fact that the country may be grain-exporting, as England still was long after the middle of the 18th century, so that the demand is not solely regulated within the confines of national consumption. *Finally*, the increase and price reduction in wheat production may result in making wheat, instead of rye or oats, the principal article of consumption for the masses, so that the demand for it may grow if only for this reason, just as the opposite may take place when production decreases and prices rise. Thus, under these assumptions, and with the previously selected ratios, sequence III yields the result that the price per quarter falls from 60 to 30 shillings, that is, by 50%; that production, compared to sequence I, increases from 10 to 23 quarters, i.e., by 130%; that the rent remains fixed for soil B, increases by 25% (In the German 1894 edition this reads: doubles.— *Ed.*) for C, and by 33⅓% (*Ibid.*p 22.— *Ed.*) for D; and that the total rental increases from £18 to £22½, (*Ibid.* 22.—*Ed.*), by 25%. (*Ibid.*: 22 1/9%—*Ed.*)

A comparison of these three tables (whereby sequence I is to be taken twice, rising from A to D, and descending from D to A), which may be considered either as given gradations under some stage of society, for instance, as existing side by side in three different countries, or as succeeding one another in different periods of development within the same country, shows:

1. The sequence, when complete, whatever the course of its formative process may have been, invariably appears as being in a descending line; for when analysing rent the point of departure will always be land yielding the maximum rent, and only finally do we come to lànd yielding no rent.
2. The price of production on the worst soil, i.e., which yields no rent, is always the one regulating the market-price, although the latter in Table I, if its sequence were formed in an ascending line, only remained fixed because better and better soil was constantly drawn into cultivation. In such a case, the price of grain produced on the best soil is a regulating one ill so far as it depends upon the quantity produced on such soil to what extent soil type A remains the regulator. If B, C and D should produce more than demand requires, A would cease to be the regulator. Storch has this point hazily in mind when he adopts the best soil type as the regulating one. (H. Storch, *Cours d'économie politique, ou Exposition des principes qui determinent la prospérité des nations*, Tome II, St.-Petersbourg, 1815, pp. 78-79.—Ed.) In this manner, the American price of grain regulates the English price.
3. Differential rent arises from differences in the natural fertility of the soil which is given for every given stage of agricultural development (leaving aside for the present the question of location); in other words, from the limited area of the best land, and from the circumstance that equal amounts of capital must be invested on unequal types of soil, so that an unequal product results from the same amount of capital.
4. The existence of a differential rent and of a graduated differential rent can develop equally well in a descending sequence, which proceeds from better to worse soils, as in an ascending one, which progresses in the opposite direction from worse to better soils; or it may be brought about in checkered fashion by alternating movements. (Sequence I may be formed by proceeding from D to A, or from A to D; sequence II comprises both types of movement.)
5. Depending on its mode of formation, differential rent may develop along with a stationary, rising or falling price of the products of the land. In the case of a falling price, total production and total rental may rise, and rent may develop on hitherto rentless land, even though the worst soil A may have been displaced by a better one or may itself have improved, and even though the rent may decrease on other land which is better, or even the best (Table II); this process may also be connected with a fall in total rent (in money). Finally, at a time when prices fall on account of a general improvement in cultivation, so that the product of the worst soil and its price decrease, the rent on some of the better soils may remain the same, or may fall, while it may rise on the best ones. Nevertheless, the differential rent of every soil, compared with the worst soil, depends, if the difference in quantity of products is given, upon the price, say, of a quarter of wheat. But when the price is given, differential rent depends upon the magnitude of the difference in quantity of products, and if with an increasing absolute fertility of all soils that of the better ones grows relatively more than that of the worse ones, the magnitude of this difference grows proportionately. In this way (see Table I), when the price is 60 shillings, the rent on D is determined by its differential product as compared with

A; in other words, by the surplus of 3 quarters. The rent is therefore = 3 × 60 = 180 shillings. But in Table III, where the price = 30 shillings, the rent is determined by the quantity of surplus-product of D as compared with A = 8 quarters; we therefore obtain 8 × 30 = 240 shillings.

This takes care of the first false assumption regarding differential rent—still found among West, Malthus, and Ricardo—namely, that it necessarily presupposes a movement toward worse and worse soil, or an ever-decreasing fertility of the soil. ([West] *Essay on the Application Of Capital to Land*, London, 1815. Malthus, Principles of Political Economy, London, 1836. Malthus, *An Inquiry into the Nature and Progress of Rent, and the Principles by which it is regulated*, London, 1815. Ricardo, *On the Principles of Political Economy, and Taxation*, Third edition, London, 4824, Chap. 11. —*Ed.*) It can be formed, as we have seen, with a movement toward better and better soil; it can be formed when a better soil takes the lowest position that was formerly occupied by the worst soil; it can be connected with a progressive improvement in agriculture. The precondition is merely the inequality of different kinds of soil. So far as the increase in productivity is concerned, it assumes that the increase in absolute fertility of the total area does not eliminate this inequality, but either increases it, leaves it unchanged, or merely reduces it.

From the beginning to the middle of the 18th century, England's grain prices constantly fell in spite of the falling prices of gold and silver, while at the same time (viewing this entire period as a whole) there was an increase in rent, in the over-all amount of rent, in the area of cultivated land, in agricultural production, and in population. This corresponds to Table I taken in conjunction with Table II in an ascending line, but in such a way that the worst land A is either improved or eliminated from the grain-producing area; however, this does not mean that it was not used for other agricultural or industrial purposes.

From the early 19th century (date to be specified more precisely) until 1815 there is a constant rise in grain prices, accompanied by a steady increase in rent, in the over-all amount of rent, in the area of cultivated land, in agricultural production, and in population. This corresponds to Table I in a descending line. (Cite some sources here on the cultivation of inferior land in that period.)

In Petty's and Davenant's time, farmers and landowners complained about improvements and the bringing into cultivation of new land; the rent on better lands decreased, and the total amount of rent increased through the extension of the area of land yielding rent.

(These three points should be illustrated later by quotations; likewise for the difference in fertility of various cultivated sections of land in a particular country.)

Regarding differential rent in general, it is to be noted that the market-value is always above the total price of production of the total quantity of products. As an example, let us take Table I. Ten quarters of total product are sold for 600 shillings because the market-price is determined by the price of production of A, which amounts to 60 shillings per quarter. But the actual price of production is:

A	1 qr = 60 sh.	1 qr = 60 sh.
B	2 qrs = 60 sh.	1 qr = 30 sh.
C	3 qrs = 60 sh.	1 qr = 20 sh
D	4 qrs = 60 sh.	1 qr = 15 sh.
	10 qrs = 240 sh.	**Average 1 qr = 24 sh.**

The actual price of production of these 10 quarters is 240 shillings; but they are sold for 600 shillings, i.e., at 250% of the price of production. The actual average price for 1 quarter is 24 shillings; the market-price is 60 shillings, i.e., also 250% of the production price.

This is determination by market-value as it asserts itself on the basis of capitalist production through competition; the latter creates a false social value. This arises from the law of market-value, to which the products of the soil are subject. The determination of the market-value of products, including therefore agricultural products, is a social act, albeit a socially unconscious and unintentional one. It is based necessarily upon the exchange-value of the product, not upon the soil and the differences in its fertility. If we suppose the capitalist form of society to be abolished and society organised as a conscious and planned association, then the 10 quarters would represent a quantity of independent labour-time equal to that contained in 240 shillings. Society would not then buy this agricultural product at two and a half times the actual labour-time embodied in it and the basis for a class of landowners would thus be destroyed. This would have the same effect as a reduction in price of the product to the same amount resulting from foreign imports. While it is, therefore, true that, by retaining the present mode of production, but assuming that the differential rent is paid to the state, prices of agricultural products would, everything else being equal, remain the same, it is equally wrong to say that the value of the products would remain the same if capitalist production were superseded by association. The identity of the market-price for commodities of the same kind is the manner whereby the social character of value asserts itself on the basis of capitalist production and, in general, any production based on the exchange of commodities between individuals. What society overpays for agricultural products in its capacity of consumer, what is a minus in the realisation of its labour-time in agricultural production, is now a plus for a portion of society, for the landlords.

A second circumstance, important for the analysis to be given under II of the next chapter, is the following:

It is not merely a matter of rent per acre, or per hectare, nor generally of a difference between the price of production and market-price, nor between the individual and the general price of production per acre, but it is also a question of how many acres of each type of soil are under cultivation. The point of importance here relates directly only to the magnitude of the rental, that is, the total rent of the entire cultivated area; but it serves us at the same time as a stepping-stone to the consideration of a rise in the *rate of rent* although there is no rise in prices, nor increase in the differences in relative fertility of the various types of soil if prices fall.

We had above:

TABLE I

Type of Soil	*Acres*	*Price of Production*	*Product*	*Rent in Grain*	*Rent in Money*
A	1	£3	1 qrs	0	0
B	1	£3	2 qrs	1 qrs	£3
C	1	£3	3 qrs	2 qrs	£6
D	1	£3	4 qrs	3qrs	£9
Total	4 acres		10 qrs	6 qrs	£18

Now let us assume that the number of cultivated acres is doubled in every category. We then have:

TABLE IA

Type of Soil	*Acres*	*Price of Production*	*Product*	*Rent in Grain*	*Rent in Money*
A	2	£6	2 qrs	0	0
B	2	£6	4 qrs	2 qrs	£6
C	2	£6	6 qrs	4 qrs	£12
D	2	£6	8 qrs	6qrs	£18
Total...	8 acres		20 qrs	12 qrs	£ 36

Let us assume two more cases. Suppose in the first case production expands on the two poorest types of soil in the following manner:

TABLE IB

Type of Soil	*Acres*	*Price of Production*		*Product*	*Rent in Grain*	*Rent in Money*
		Per Acre	*Total*			
A	4	£3	£3	4 qr	0	£0
B	4	£3	£6	8 qrs	4 qrs	£12
C	2	£3	£15	6 qrs	4 qrs	£12
D	2	£3	£16	8 qrs	6 qrs	£18
Total...	12 acres		£36	26 qrs	14 qrs	£42

And, finally, let us assume an unequal expansion of production and cultivated area for the four soil categories:

TABLE IC

Type of Soil	*Acres*	*Price of Production*		*Product*	*Rent in Grain*	*Rent in Money*
		Per Acre	*Total*			
A	1	£3	£3	1 qr	0	£0
B	2	£3	£6	4 qrs	2 qrs	£6
C	5	£3	£15	15 qrs	10 qrs	£30
D	4	£3	£12	16 qrs	12 qrs	£18
Total...	12 acres		£ 36	36 qrs	24 qrs	£72

In the first place, the rent per acre remains the same in all these cases—I, Ia, Ib and Ic—for, in fact, the result of the same investment of capital per acre of the same soil type has remained unchanged. We have only assumed what is true of any country at any given moment; namely, that various soil types exist in definite ratios to the total cultivated area. And we also assumed what is always true of any two countries being compared, or of the same country at different periods, namely, that the proportions in which the total cultivated area is distributed among the different soil types vary.

In comparing Ia with I we see that if the cultivation of land in all four categories increases in the same proportion a doubling of the cultivated acreage doubles the total production, and that the same applies to the rent in grain and money.

However, if we compare Ib and then Ic with I, we see that in both cases a tripling of the area under cultivation occurs. It increases in both cases from 4 acres to 12, but in Ib classes A and B contribute most to the increase, with A yielding no rent and B yielding the smallest amount of differential rent. Thus, out of the 8 newly cultivated acres, A and B account for 3 each, i.e., 6 together, whereas C and D account for I each, i.e., 2 together. In other words, three-quarters of the increase is accounted for by A and B, and only one-quarter by C and D. With this premise, in Ib compared with I the trebled area of cultivation does not result in a trebled product, for the product does not increase from 10 to 30, but only to 26. On the other hand, since a considerable part of the increase concerns A, which does not yield any rent, and since the major part of the increase on better soils concerns B, the rent in grain rises only from 6 to 14 quarters, and the rent in money from £18 to £42.

But if we compare Ic with I, where the land yielding no rent does not increase in area and the land yielding a minimum rent increases but slightly, while C and D account for the major part of the increase, we find that when the cultivated area is trebled production increases from 10 to 36 quarters, i.e., to more than three times its original amount. The rent in grain increases from 6 to 24 quarters or to four times its original amount; and similarly money-rent, from £18 to £72.

In all these cases it is in the nature of things that the price of the agricultural product remains unchanged. The total rental increases in all cases with the extension of cultivation, unless it takes place exclusively on the worst soil, which does not yield any rent. But this increase varies. Should this extension involve the better soil types and the total output, consequently, increase not merely in proportion to the expansion of the area, but rather more rapidly, then the rent in grain and money increases to the same extent. Should it be the worst soil, and the types of soil close to it, that are principally involved in the expansion (whereby it is assumed that the worst soil represents a constant type), the total rental does not increase in proportion to the extension of cultivation. Thus, given two countries in which soil A, yielding no rent, is of the same quality, the rental is inversely proportional to the aliquot part represented by the worst soil and the inferior soil types in the total area under cultivation, and therefore inversely proportional to the output, assuming equal capital investments on equal total land areas. A relationship between the quantity of the worst and the quantity of the better cultivated land in the total land area of a given country thus has an opposite influence on the total rental than the relationship between the quality of the worst cultivated land and the quality of the better and best has on the rent per acre and—other circumstances remaining the same—on the total rental. Confusion between these two points has given rise to all kinds of erroneous objections raised against differential rent.

The total rental, then, increases by the mere extension of cultivation, and by the consequent greater investment of capital and labour in the land. But the most important point is this: Although it is our assumption that the ratio of rents per acre for the various kinds of soil remains the same, and therefore, also, the rate of rent considered with reference to capital invested in each acre, yet the following is to be observed: If we compare Ia with I, the case in which the number of cultivated acres and the capital invested in them have been proportionately increased, we find that as the total production has increased proportionately to the expanded cultivated area, i.e., as both have been doubled, so has the rental. It has risen from £18 to £36, just as the number of acres has risen from 4 to 8.

If we take the total area of 4 acres, we find that the total rental amounted to £18 and thus the average rent, including the land which does not yield any rent, is £4½. Such a calculation might be made, say, by a landlord owning all 4 acres; and in this way the average rent is statistically computed for a whole country. The total rental of £18 is obtained by the investment of a capital of £10. We call the ratio of these two figures the rate of rent; in the present case it is therefore, 180%.

The same rate of rent obtains in Ia, where 8 instead of 4 acres are cultivated, but all types of land have contributed to the increase in the same proportion. The total rental of £36 yields for 8 acres and an invested capital of £20 an average rent of £4½ per acre and a rate of rent of 180%.

But if we consider Ib, where the increase has taken place mainly upon two inferior categories of soil, we obtain a rent of £42 for 12 acres, or an average rent of £3½ per acre. The total invested capital is £30, and therefore the rate of rent = 140%. The average rent per acre has thus decreased by £1, and the rate of rent has fallen from 180 to 140%. Here then we have a rise in the total rental from £18 to £42, but a drop in average rent calculated per acre as well as on the basis of capital; the drop takes place parallel to an increase in production, but not proportionately. This occurs even though the rent for all types of soil, calculated per acre as well as on the basis of capital outlay, remains the same. This occurs because three-quarters of the increase is accounted for by soil A, which does not yield any rent, and soil B, which yields only minimum rent.

If the total expansion in Case Ib had taken place solely on soil A, we should have 9 acres on A, I acre on B, I acre on C and I acre on D. The total rental would be £18, the same as before; the average rent for the 12 acres, therefore, would be £1½ per acre; and a rent of £18 on an invested capital of £30 would give a rate of rent of 60%. The average rent, calculated per acre as well as on the basis of invested capital, would have greatly decreased, while the total rental would not have increased.

Finally, let us compare Ic with I and Ib. Compared with I, the area has been trebled, and also the invested capital. The total rental is £72 for 12 acres, or £6 per acre—as against £4½ in Case I. The rate of rent on the invested capital (£72:£30) is 240% instead of 180%. The total output has risen from 10 to 36 quarters.

Compared with Ib, where the total number of cultivated acres, the invested capital, and the differences between the cultivated soil types are the same, but the distribution different, the output is 36 quarters instead of 26 quarters, the average rent per acre is £6 instead of £3½, and the rate of rent with reference to the same invested total capital is 240% instead of 140%.

No matter whether we regard the various conditions in tables Ia, Ib and Ic as existing simultaneously side by side in different countries, or as existing successively in the same country, we come to the following conclusions: So long as the price of grain remains unchanged because the yield on the worst, rentless soil remains the same; so long as the difference in the fertility of the various cultivated types of soil remains the same; so long as the respective outputs remain the same, hence, given equal capital investments on equal aliquot parts (acres) of cultivated area in every type of soil; so long as the ratio, therefore, between the rents per acre on each category of soil is constant, and the rate of rent on the capital invested in each plot of the same kind of soil is constant: *First*, the rental constantly increases with the extension of cultivated area and with the consequent increased capital investment, except for the case where the entire increase is accounted for by rentless land. *Secondly*, the average rent per acre (total rental divided by the total number of cultivated acres) as well as the average rate of rent (total rental divided by the invested total capital) may vary very considerably; and, indeed, both change in the same direction, but in different proportions to each other. If we leave out of consideration the case in which the expansion takes place only on the rentless soil A, we find that the average rent per acre and the average rate of rent on the capital invested in agriculture depend on the proportions which the various classes of soil constitute in the total cultivated area; or, what amounts to the same thing, on the distribution of the total employed capital among the kinds of soil of varying fertility. Whether much or little land is cultivated, and whether the total rental is, therefore, larger or smaller (with the exception of the case in which the expansion is confined to A), the average rent per acre, or the average rate of rent on invested capital, remains the same as long as the proportions of the various categories of soil in the total cultivated area remain unchanged. In spite of an increase, even a very considerable one, in the total rental with the extension of cultivation and expansion of capital investment, the average rent per acre and the average rate of rent on capital decrease when the extension of rentless land, and land yielding only little differential rent, is greater than the extension of the superior one yielding greater rent. Conversely, the average rent per acre and the average rate of rent on capital increase proportionately to the extent that better land constitutes a relatively greater part of the total area, and therefore, employs a relatively greater share of the invested capital.

Hence, if we consider the average rent per acre, or hectare, of the total cultivated land as is generally done in statistical works, in comparing either different countries in the same period, or different periods in the same country, we find that the average level of rent per acre, and consequently total rental, corresponds to a certain extent (although by no means identical, but rather a more rapidly increasing extent) to the absolute, not to the relative, fertility of the soil in a given country; that is, to the average amount of produce which it yields from the same area. For the larger the share of superior soils in the total cultivated area, the greater the output for equal capital investments on equally large areas of land; and the higher the average rent per acre. In the reverse case the opposite takes place. Thus, rent does not appear to be determined by the ratio of differential fertility, but by the absolute fertility, and the law of differential rent appears invalid. For this reason certain phenomena are disputed, or an attempt is made to explain them by non-existing differences in average prices of grain and in the differential fertility of cultivated land, whereas such phenomena are merely due to the fact that the ratio of total rental to total area of cultivated land or to total capital invested in the land—as long as the fertility of the rentless soil remains the same, and therefore, the prices of production, and the differences between the various kinds of soil remain unchanged—is determined not merely by the rent per acre or the rate of rent on capital, but quite as much by the relative number of acres of each type of soil in the total number of cultivated acres; or, what amounts to the same thing, by the distribution of the total invested capital among the various types of soil. Curiously enough, this fact has been completely overlooked thus far. At any rate, we see (and this is important for our further analysis) that the relative level of the average rent per acre, and the average rate of rent (or the ratio of the total rental to the total capital invested in the land), may rise or fall by merely extensively expanding cultivation, as long as prices remain the same, the differential fertilities of the various soils remain unaltered, and the rent per acre, or rate of rent for capital invested per acre in every type of soil actually yielding rent, i.e., for all capital actually yielding rent, remains unchanged.

It is necessary to make the following additional points with reference to the form of differential rent considered under heading I; they also apply in part to differential rent II:

First, it was seen that the average rent per acre, or the average rate of rent on capital, may increase with an extension of cultivation when prices are stationary and the differential fertility of the cultivated plots of land remains unaltered. As soon as all the land in a given country has been appropriated, and investments of capital in land, cultivation, and population have reached a definite level—all given conditions as soon as the capitalist mode of production becomes the prevailing one and also encompasses agriculture—the price of uncultivated land of varying quality (merely assuming differential rent to exist) is determined by the price of the cultivated plots of land of the same quality and equivalent location. The price is the same—after deducting the cost of bringing the new land into cultivation—even though this land does not yield any rent. The price of the land is, indeed, nothing but the capitalised rent. But even in the case of cultivated land, the price pays only for future rents, as, for instance, when the prevalent interest rate is 5% and the rent for twenty years is paid at one time in advance. When land is sold, it is sold as land yielding rent, and the prospective character of the rent (which is here considered as a product of the soil, but it only seems to be that) does not distinguish the uncultivated from the cultivated land. The price of the uncultivated land, like its rent the price of which represents the contracted form of the latter is quite illusory as long as the land is not actually used. But it is thus determined a priori and is realised as soon as a purchaser is found. Hence, while the actual average rent in a given country is determined by its actual average annual rental and the relation of the latter to the total cultivated area, the price of the uncultivated land is determined by the price of the cultivated land, and is therefore but a reflection of the capital invested in the cultivated land and the results obtained therefrom. Since all land with the exception of the worst yields rent (and this rent, as we shall see under the head of differential rent II, increases with the quantity of capital and corresponding intensity of cultivation), the nominal price of uncultivated plots of land is thus formed, and they thus become commodities, a source of wealth for their owners. This explains at the same time, why the price of land increases in a whole region, even in the uncultivated part (Opdyke). Land speculation, for instance, in the United States, is based solely on this reflection thrown by capital and labour on uncultivated land.

Secondly, progress in extending cultivated land generally takes place either toward inferior soil or on the various given types of soil in varying proportions, depending on the manner in which they are met. Extension on inferior soil is naturally never made voluntarily, but can only result from rising prices, assuming a capitalist mode of production, and can only result from necessity under any other mode of production. However, this is not absolutely so. Poor soil may be preferred to a relatively better soil on account of location, which is of decisive importance for every extension of cultivation in young countries; furthermore, even though the soil formation in a certain region may generally be classified as fertile, it may nevertheless consist of a motley confusion of better and worse soils, so that the inferior soil may have to be cultivated if only because it is found in the immediate vicinity of the superior soil. If inferior soil is surrounded by superior soil, then the latter gives it the advantage of location in comparison with more fertile soil which is not yet, or is about to become, part of the cultivated area.

Thus, the State of Michigan was one of the first Western States to become an exporter of grain. Yet its soil on the whole is poor. But its proximity to the State of New York and its water-ways via the Lakes and Erie Canal initially gave it the advantage over the States endowed by Nature with more fertile soil, but situated farther to the West. The example of this State, as compared with the State of New York, also demonstrates the transition from superior to inferior soil. The soil of the State of New York, particularly its western part, is incomparably more fertile, especially for the cultivation of wheat. This fertile soil was transformed into infertile soil by rapacious methods of cultivation, and now the soil of Michigan appeared as the more fertile.

> In 1838, wheaten flour was shipped at Buffalo for the West; and the wheat-region of New York, with that of Upper Canada, were the main sources of its supply. Now, after only twelve years, an enormous supply of wheat and flour is brought from the West, along Lake Erie, and shipped upon the Erie Canal for the East, at Buffalo and the adjoining port of Blackrock... The effect of these large arrivals from the Western States—which were unnaturally stimulated during the years of European famine ... has been to render wheat less valuable in western New York, to make the wheat culture less remunerative, and to turn the attention of the New York farmers more to grazing and dairy husbandry, fruit culture, and other branches of rural economy, in which they think the North-West will be unable so directly to compete with them. (I. W. Johnston, *Notes on North America*, London, 1851, I, pp. 220-23.)

Thirdly, it is a mistaken assumption that the land in colonies and, in general, in young countries which can export grain at cheaper prices, must of necessity be of greater natural fertility. The grain is not only sold below its value in such cases, but below its price of production, i.e., below the price of production determined by the average rate of profit in the older countries.

The fact that we, as Johnston says (p. 223),

> are accustomed to attach the idea of great natural productiveness and of boundless tracts of rich land, to those new States from which come the large supplies of wheat that are annually poured into the port of Buffalo,

is primarily the result of economic conditions. The entire population of such an area as Michigan, for instance, is at first almost exclusively engaged in farming, and particularly in producing agricultural mass products, which alone can be exchanged for industrial products and tropical goods. Its entire surplus production appears, therefore, in the form of grain. This from the outset sets apart the colonial states founded on the basis of the modern world-market from those of earlier, particularly ancient, times. They receive through the world-market finished products, such as clothing and tools which they would have to produce themselves under other circumstances. Only on such a basis were the Southern States of the Union enabled to make cotton their staple crop. The division of labour on the world-market makes this possible. Hence, if they *seem* to have a large surplus production considering their youth and relatively small population, this is not so much due to the fertility of their soil, nor the fruitfulness of their labour, but rather to the one-sided form of their labour, and therefore of the surplus-produce in which such labour is incorporated.

Furthermore, a relatively inferior soil which is newly cultivated and never before touched by civilisation provided the climatic conditions are then not completely unfavourable, has accumulated a great deal of plant food that is easily assimilated—at least in the upper layers of the soil—so that it will yield crops for a long time without the application of fertilisers and even with very superficial cultivation. The western prairies have the additional advantage of hardly requiring any clearing expenses since Nature has made them arable.[1] In less fertile areas of this kind, the surplus is not produced as a result of the high fertility of the soil, i.e., the yield per acre, but as a result of the large acreage which may be superficially cultivated, since such land costs the cultivator nothing, or next to nothing as compared with older countries. This is the case, for instance, where share cropping exists, as in parts of New York, Michigan, Canada, etc. A family superficially cultivates, say, 100 acres, and although the output per acre is not large, the output from 100 acres yields a considerable surplus for sale. In addition to this, cattle may be grazed on natural pastures at almost no cost, without requiring artificial grass meadows. It is the quantity of the land, not its quality, which is decisive here. The possibility of such superficial cultivation is naturally more or less rapidly exhausted, namely, in inverse proportion to the fertility of the new soil and in direct proportion to the export of its products.

> And yet such a country will give excellent first crops, even of wheat, and will supply to those who skim the first cream off the country, a large surplus of this grain to send to market. (1, c., p. 224)

Property relations in countries with maturer civilisations, with their determination of the price of uncultivated soil by that of the cultivated, etc., make such an extensive economy impossible.

That this soil, therefore, need not be exceedingly rich, as Ricardo imagines, nor that soils of equal fertility need be cultivated, may be seen from the following. In the State of Michigan, 465,900 acres were planted in 1848 to wheat which yielded 4,739,300 bushels, or an average of 10 1/5 bushels per acre after deducting seed grain, this leaves less than 9 bushels per acre. Of the 29 counties of this State, 2 produced an average of 7 bushels, 3 an average of 8 bushels, 2—9, 7—10, 6—11, 3—12, 4—13 bushels, and only one county produced an average of 16 bushels, and another 18 bushels per acre (l.c., p. 225).

For practical cultivation higher soil fertility coincides with greater capability of immediate exploitation of such fertility. The latter may be greater in a naturally poor soil than in a naturally rich one; but it is the kind of soil which a colonist will take up first, and must take up when capital is wanting.

Finally, the extension of cultivation to larger areas—aside from the case just mentioned, in which recourse must be had to soil inferior than that cultivated hitherto—to the various kinds of soil from A to D, thus, for instance, the cultivation of larger tracts of B and C does not by any means presuppose a previous rise in grain prices any more than the preceding annual expansion of cotton spinning, for instance, requires a constant rise in yarn prices. Although considerable rise or fall in market-prices affects the volume of production, regardless of it there is in agriculture (just as in all other capitalistically operated lines of production) nevertheless a continuous relative over-production, in itself identical with accumulation, even at those average prices whose level has neither a retarding nor exceptionally stimulating effect on production. Under other modes of production this relative overproduction is effected directly by the population increase, and in colonies by steady immigration. The demand increases constantly, and, in anticipation of this new capital is continually invested in new land, although this varies with the circumstances for different agricultural products. It is the formation of new capitals which in itself brings this about. But so far as the individual capitalist is concerned, he measures the volume of his production by that of his available capital, to the extent that he can still control it himself. His aim is to capture as big a portion as possible of the market. Should there be any over-production, he will not take the blame upon himself, but places it upon his competitors. The individual capitalist may expand his production by appropriating a larger aliquot share of the existing market or by expanding the market itself.

Note

1. [It is precisely the rapidly growing cultivation of such prairie or steppe regions which of late turns the renowned statement of Malthus, that 'the population is a burden upon the means of subsistence,' into ridicule, and produced in its stead the agrarian lament that agriculture, and with it Germany, will be ruined, unless the means of subsistence which are a burden upon the population are forcibly kept away from them. The cultivation of these steppes, prairies, pampas, ilanos, etc., is nevertheless only in its beginning; its revolutionising effect on European agriculture will, therefore, make itself felt in the future even more so than hitherto.—*F. E.]*

40

Second Form of Differential Rent (Differential Rent II)

Thus far we have considered differential rent only as the result of varying productivity of equal amounts of capital invested in equal areas of land of different fertility, so that differential rent was determined by the difference between the yield from the capital invested in the worst, rentless soil and that from the capital invested in superior soil. We had side by side capitals invested in different plots of land, so that every new investment of capital signified a more extensive cultivation of the soil, an expansion of cultivated area. In the last analysis, however, differential rent was by its nature merely the result of the different productivity of equal capitals invested in land. But can it make any difference if capitals of different productivity are invested successively in the same plot of land or side by side in different plots of land, provided the results are the same?

To begin with, there is no denying that, in so far as the formation of surplus-profit is concerned, it is immaterial whether £3 in production price per acre of A yield 1 qr, so that £3 is the price of production and the regulating market-price of 1 qr, while £3 in production price per acre of B yield 2 qrs, and thereby £3 of surplus-profit, similarly, £3 in production price per acre of C yield 3 qrs and £6 of surplus-profit, and, finally, £3 in production price per acre of D yield 4 qrs and £9 of surplus-profit; or whether the same result is achieved by applying these £12 in production price, or £10 of capital, with the same success in the same sequence upon one and the same acre. It is in both cases a capital of £10, whose value portions of £2½ each are successively invested—whether in four acres of varying fertility side by side, or successively in one and the same acre of land—and because of their varying outputs, one portion yields no surplus-profit, whereas the other portions yield surplus-profit proportionate to their difference in yield with respect to rentless investment.

The surplus-profit and the various rates of surplus-profit for the different value portions of capital are formed in the same manner in both cases. And the rent is nothing but a form of this surplus-profit, which constitutes its substance. But at any rate, in the second method, there are some difficulties concerning the transformation of surplus-profit into rent, this change of form, which includes the transfer of surplus-profit from the capitalist tenant to the landowner. This accounts for the obstinate resistance of English tenants to official agricultural statistics. And it accounts for their struggle against the landlords over the determination of actual results derived from their capital investment (Morton). For rent is fixed when land is leased, and after that the surplus-profit arising from successive investments of capital flows into the pockets of the tenant as long as the lease lasts. This is why the tenants have fought for long leases, and, on the other hand, due to the greater power of the landlords, an increase in the number of tenancies at will has taken place, i.e., leases which can be cancelled annually.

It is, therefore, evident from the very outset that, even if immaterial for the law of formation of surplus-profit, it makes a considerable difference for the transformation of surplus-profit into ground-rent whether equal capitals are invested side by side in equal areas of land with unequal results, or whether they are invested successively in the same land. The latter method confines this transformation, on the one hand, within narrower limits, on the other hand, within more variable limits. For this reason, the work of the tax-assessor, as Morton shows in his *Resources of Estates,* becomes a very important, complicated and difficult profession in countries practising intensive cultivation (and, economically speaking, we mean nothing more by intensive cultivation than the concentration of capital upon the same plot rather than its distribution among several adjoining pieces of land). If soil improvements are of a more permanent nature the artificially increased differential fertility of the soil coincides with its natural differential fertility as soon as the lease expires, and therefore the assessment of the rent corresponds to the determination of the rent on plots of different fertilities in general. On the other hand, in so far as the formation of surplus-profit is determined by the magnitude of operating capital, the amount of rent for a certain amount of operating capital is added to the average rent of the country and thus provision is made for the new tenant to command sufficient capital to continue cultivation in the same intensive manner.

In the study of differential rent II, the following points are still to be emphasised.

First, its basis and point of departure, not just historically, but also in so far as concerns its movements at any given period of time, is differential rent I, that is, the simultaneous cultivation side by side of soils of unequal fertility and location; in other words, the simultaneous application, side by side, of unequal portions of the total agricultural capital upon plots of land of unequal quality.

Historically this is self-evident. In the colonies, colonists have but little capital to invest; the principal production agents are labour and land. Every individual head of family seeks for himself and his kin an independent field of employment alongside his fellow-colonists. This must generally be the case in agriculture proper even under pre-capitalist modes of production. In the case of sheep-herding and cattle-raising, in general, as independent lines of production, exploitation of the soil is more or less common and extensive from the very outset. The capitalist mode of production has for its point of departure former modes of production in which the means of production were, in fact or legally, the property of the tiller himself, in a word, from a handicraft-like pursuit of agriculture. It is in the nature of things that the latter gives way but gradually to the concentration of means of production and their transformation into capital, as against direct producers transformed into wage-labourers. In so far as the capitalist mode of production is manifested here typically, it occurs at first particularly in sheep-herding and cattle-raising. But it is thus not manifested in a concentration of capital upon a relatively small area of land, but in production on a larger scale, economising in the expense of keeping horses, and in other production costs; but, in fact, not by investing more capital in the same land. Furthermore, in accordance with the natural laws of field husbandry, capital—used here, at the same time, in the sense of means of production already produced—becomes the decisive element in soil cultivation when cultivation has reached a certain level of development and the soil has been correspondingly exhausted. So long as the tilled area is small in comparison with the untilled, and so long as the soil strength has not been exhausted (and this is the case when cattle-raising and meat consumption prevail in the period before agriculture proper and plant nutrition have become dominant), the new developing mode of production is opposed to peasant production mainly in the extensiveness of the land being tilled for a capitalist, in other words, again in the extensive application of capital to larger areas of land. It should, therefore, be remembered from the outset that differential rent I is the historical basis which serves as a point of departure. On the other hand, the movement of differential rent II at any given moment occurs only within a sphere which is itself but the variegated basis of differential rent I.

Secondly, in the differential rent in form II, the differences in distribution of capital (and ability to obtain credit) among tenants are added to the differences in fertility. In manufacturing proper, each line of business rapidly develops its own minimum volume of business and a corresponding minimum of capital, below which no individual business can be conducted successfully. In the same way, each line of business develops a normal average amount of capital above this minimum, which the bulk of producers should, and do, command. A larger volume of capital can produce extra profit; a smaller volume does not so much as yield the average profit. The capitalist mode of production spreads in agriculture but slowly and unevenly, as may be observed in England, the classic land of the capitalist mode of production in agriculture. In so far as the free importation of grain does not exist, or its effect is but limited because the volume is small, producers working inferior soil, and thus under worse than average conditions of production, determine the market-price. A large portion of the total mass of capital invested in husbandry, and in general available to it, is in their hands.

It is true that the peasant, for example, expends much labour on his small plot of land. But it is labour isolated from objective social and material conditions of productivity, labour robbed and stripped of these conditions.

This circumstance enables the actual capitalist tenants to appropriate a portion of surplus-profit—a fact which would not obtain, at least so far as this point is concerned, if the capitalist mode of production were as evenly developed in agriculture as in manufacture.

Let us first consider just the formation of surplus-profit with differential rent II, without for the present bothering about the conditions under which the transformation of this surplus-profit into ground-rent may take place.

It is then evident that differential rent II is merely differently expressed differential rent I, but identical to it in substance. The variation in fertility of various soil types exerts its influence in the case of differential rent I only in so far as unequal results are attained by capitals invested in the soil, i.e., the amount of products obtained either with respect to equal magnitudes of capital, or proportionate amounts. Whether this inequality takes place for various capitals invested successively in the same land or for capitals invested in several plots of differing soil type—this can change nothing in the difference in fertility nor in its product and can therefore change nothing in the formation of differential rent for the more productively invested portions of capital. It is still the soil which, now as before, shows different fertility with the same investment of capital, save that here the same soil performs for a capital successively invested in different portions what various kinds of soil do in the case of differential rent I for different equal portions of social capital invested in them.

If the same capital of £10, which is shown in Table I to be invested in the form of independent capitals of £2½ each by various tenants in each acre of the four soil types A, B, C and D, were instead successively invested in one and the same acre D, so that the first investment yielded 4 qrs, the second 3, the third 2, and the fourth 1 qr (or in the reverse order), then the price of the quarter furnished by the least productive capital, namely = £3, would not yield any differential rent, but would determine the price of production, so long as the supply of wheat whose price of production is £3 were needed. And since our assumption is that the capitalist mode of production prevails, so that the price of £3 includes the average profit made by a capital of £2½ generally, the other three portions of £2½ each will yield surplus-profit in accordance with the difference in output, since this output is not sold at its own price of production, but at the price of production of the least productive investment of £2½; the latter investment does not yield any rent and the price of its products is determined by the general law of prices of production. The formation of surplus-profit would be the same as in Table I.

Once again it is seen here that differential rent II presupposes differential rent I. The minimum output obtained from a capital of £2½, i.e., from the worst soil, is here assumed to be 4 qr. Assumed, also, is that aside from the £2½ which yield 4 qrs and for which he pays a differential rent of 3 qrs, the tenant operating with soil type D invests in this same soil £2½ which yield only 1 qr, like the same capital upon the worst soil A. This would be an investment of capital which does not yield rent, since it returns to him only average profit. There would be no surplus-profit which could be transformed into rent. On the other hand, this decreasing yield of the second investment of capital in D would have no influence on the rate of profit. It would be the same as though £2½ had been invested anew in an additional acre of soil type A, a circumstance which would in no way affect the surplus-profit and, therefore, the differential rent of soils A, B, C and D. But for the tenant, this additional investment of £2½ in D would have been quite as profitable as, in accordance with our assumption, the investment of the original £2½ per acre of D, although the latter yields 4 qrs. Furthermore, if two other investments of £2½ each should yield an additional output of 3 qrs and 2 qrs respectively, a decrease would have taken place again compared with the output from the first investment of £2½ in D, which yielded 4 qrs, i.e., a surplus-profit of 3 qrs. But it would be merely a decrease in the amount of surplus-profit, and would not affect either the average profit or the regulating price of production. The latter would be the case only if the additional production yielding this decreasing surplus-profit made the production upon A superfluous, and threw acre A out of cultivation. In such case, the decreasing productiveness of the additional investment of capital in acre D would be accompanied by a fall in the price of production, for instance, from £3 to £1½, if acre B would become the rentless soil and regulator of the market-price.

The output from D would now be = 4 + 1 + 3 + 2 = 10 qrs whereas formerly it was = 4 qrs. But the price per quarter as regulated by B would have fallen to £1½. The difference between D and B would be = 10 - 2 = 8 qrs, at £1½ per quarter = £12, whereas the money-rent from D was previously = £9. This should be noted. Calculated per acre, the magnitude of rent would have risen by 33⅓% in spite of the decreasing rate of surplus-profit on the two additional capitals of £2½ each.

We see from this to what highly complicated combinations differential rent in general, and in form II coupled with form I, in particular, may give rise, whereas Ricardo, for instance, treats it very one-sidedly and as though it were a simple matter. As in the above case, a fall in the regulating market-price and at the same time rise in rent from fertile soils may take place so that both the absolute product and the absolute surplus-product increase. (In differential rent I, in descending order, the relative surplus-product and thus the rent per acre may increase, although the absolute surplus-product per acre remains constant or even decreases.) But at the same time, productiveness of the investments of capital made successively in the same soil decreases, although a large portion of them falls to the more fertile soils. From a certain point of view—as concerns both output and prices of production—the productivity of labour has risen. But from another point of view, it has decreased because the rate of surplus-profit and the surplus-product per acre decrease for the various investments of capital in the same land.

Differential rent II, with decreasing productiveness of successive investments of capital, would necessarily be accompanied by a rise in price of production and an absolute decrease in productivity only if investments of capital could be made in none but the worst soil A. If an acre of A, which with an investment of capital of £2½ yielded 1 qr at a price of production of £3, should only yield a total of 1½ qrs with an additional outlay of £2½, i.e., a total investment of £5, then the price of production of this 1½ qrs = £6 or that of 1 qr = £4. Every decrease in productivity with a growing investment of capital would here mean a relative decrease in output per acre, whereas upon superior soils it would only signify a decrease in the superfluous surplus-product.

But by the nature of things, with the development of intensive cultivation, i.e., with successive investments of capital in the same soil, this will take place more advantageously, or to a greater extent on better soils. (We are not referring to permanent improvements by which a hitherto useless soil is converted into useful soil.) The decreasing productiveness of successive investments of capital must, therefore, have principally the effect indicated above. The better soil is selected because it affords the best promise that capital invested in it will be profitable, since it contains the most natural elements of fertility, which need but be utilised.

When, after the abolition of the Corn Laws, cultivation in England became still more intensive, a great deal of former wheat land was devoted to other purposes, particularly cattle pastures, while the fertile land best suited for wheat was drained and otherwise improved. The capital for wheat cultivation was thus concentrated in a more limited area.

In this case—and all possible surplus rates between the greatest surplus-product of the best soil and the output of rentless soil A coincide here with an absolute, rather than a relative, increase in surplus-product per acre—the newly formed surplus-profit (potential rent) does not represent a portion of a former average profit transformed into rent (a portion of the output in which the average profit formerly was expressed) but an additional surplus-profit, which is transformed out of this form into rent.

On the other hand, only in such case where the demand for grain increased to such an extent that the market-price rose above the price of production of A, so that the surplus-product of A, B, or any other kind of soil could be supplied only at a price higher than £3 would the decrease in yield from an additional investment of capital in any of the soil types A, B, C and D be accompanied by a rise in price of production and the regulating market-price. In so far as this lasted for a lengthy period of time without resulting in the cultivation of additional soil A (of at least the quality of A), or without a cheaper supply resulting from other circumstances, wages would rise in consequence of the increase in the price of bread, everything else being equal, and the rate of profit would fall accordingly. In this case, it would be immaterial, whether the increased demand were satisfied by bringing under cultivation soil of inferior quality than A, or by additional investments of capital, in any of the four types of soil. Differential rent would then increase together with a falling rate of profit.

This one case, in which the decreasing productiveness of subsequent additional capitals invested in already cultivated soils may lead to an increase in price of production, a fall in rate of profit, and the formation of higher differential rent—for the latter would increase under the given circumstances upon all kinds of soil just as though soil of inferior quality than A were regulating the market-price—has been labelled by Ricardo as the only case, the normal case—to which he reduces the entire formation of differential rent II.

This would also be the case if only type A soil were cultivated and successive investments of capital in it were not accompanied by a proportional increase in produce.

Here then, in the case of differential rent II, one completely loses sight of differential rent I.

Except for this case, in which the supply from the cultivated soils is either insufficient and the market-price thus continually higher than the price of production until new additional soil of inferior quality is taken under cultivation, or until the total product from the additional capital invested in various kinds of soil can be supplied only at a higher price of production than that hitherto prevailing—save for this case, the proportional drop in productivity of the additional capitals leaves the regulating price of production and the rate of profit unchanged. For the rest, three additional cases are possible:

a) If the additional capital invested in any one of the types of soil A, B, C or D yields only the rate of profit determined by the price of production of A, then no surplus-profit, and therefore no potential rent, is formed, any more than there would be if additional type A soil had been cultivated.

b) If the additional capital yields a larger product, new surplus-profit (potential rent) is, of course, formed provided the regulating price remains the same. This is not necessarily the case; it is not the case, in particular, when this additional production throws soil A out of cultivation and thus out of the sequence of competing soils. In this case, the regulating price of production falls. If this were accompanied by a fall in wages, or if the cheaper product were to enter into the constant capital as one of its elements, the rate of profit would rise. If the increased productivity of the additional capital had taken place upon the best soils C and D, it would depend entirely upon the degree of increased productivity and the amount of additional new capital to what extent the formation of increased surplus-profit (and thus increased rent) would be associated with the fall in prices and the rise in the rate of profit. The latter may also rise without a fall in wages, through a cheapening of the elements of constant capital.

c) If the additional investment of capital takes place with decreasing surplus-profit, but in such manner that the yield from the additional outlay still leaves a surplus above the yield from the same capital invested in A, a new formation of surplus-profit takes place under all circumstances, unless the increased supply excludes soil A from cultivation. This may take place simultaneously upon D, C, B and A. But, on the other hand, if the worst soil A is squeezed out of cultivation, then the regulating price of production falls and it will depend upon the relation between the reduced price of 1 qr and the increased number of quarters forming surplus-profit whether the surplus-profit expressed in money, and consequently the differential rent, rises or falls. But at any rate, it is noteworthy here that with decreasing surplus-profit from successive investments of capital the price of production may fall, instead of rising, which it seemingly should do at first sight.

These additional investments of capital with decreasing surplus yields correspond entirely to the case in which, e.g., four new independent capitals of £2½ each would be invested in soils with fertility between A and B, B and C, C and D, and yielding 1½, 2⅓, 2⅔, and 3 qrs respectively. Surplus-profit (potential rent) would take shape on all these soils for all four additional capitals, although the rate of surplus-profit, compared with that for the same investment of capital on the correspondingly better soil, would have decreased. And it would be immaterial whether these four capitals were invested in D, etc., or distributed between D and A.

We now come to an essential difference between the two forms of differential rent.

Under differential rent I, with constant price of production and constant differences, the average rent per acre, or the average rate of rent on capital, may increase together with the rental. But the average is a mere abstraction. The actual amount of rent, calculated per acre or with respect to capital, remains the same here.

On the other hand, under the same conditions, the amount of rent calculated per acre may increase although the rate of rent, measured relative to invested capital, remains the same.

Let us assume that production is doubled by the investment of £5 instead of £2½ in each of the soils A, B, C and D, i.e., a total of £20 instead of £10, and that the relative fertility remains unchanged. This would be tantamount to cultivating 2 instead of 1 acre of each of these kinds of soil at the same cost. The rate of profit would remain the same; also its relation to surplus-profit or rent. But if A were now to yield 2 qrs, B—4, C—6, and D—8, the price of production would nevertheless remain £3 per quarter because this increase is not due to doubled fertility with the same capital, but to the same proportional fertility with a doubled capital. The two quarters of A would now cost £6 just as 1 qr cost £3 before. The profit would have doubled on all four soils, but only because the invested capital was doubled. In the same proportion, however, the rent would also have been doubled; it would be 2 qrs for B instead of 1, 4 qrs for C instead of 2, and 6 for D instead of 3; and correspondingly, the money-rent for B, C and D would now be £6, £12, and £18 respectively. Like the yield per acre, the rent in money per acre would be doubled, and, consequently, also the price of the land whereby this money-rent is capitalised. Calculated in this manner, the amount of rent in grain and money increases, and thus the price of land, because the standard used in its computation, i.e., the acre, is an area of constant magnitude. On the other hand, calculated as rate of rent on invested capital, there is no change in the proportional amount of rent. The total rental of 36 is to the invested capital of 20 as the rental of 18 is to the invested capital of 10. The same holds true for the ratio of money-rent from each type of soil to the capital invested in it; for instance, in C, £12 rent is to £5 capital as £6 rent was formerly to £2½ capital. No new differences arise here between the invested capitals, but new surplus-profits do, merely because the additional capital is invested in one of the rent-bearing soils, or in all of them, with the same proportional yield as previously. If this double investment took place, for example, only in C, the differential rent between C, B and D, calculated with respect to capital, would remain the same: for when the amount of rent obtained from C is doubled, so is the invested capital.

This shows that the amount of rent in produce and money per acre, and therefore the price of land, may rise, while the price of production, the rate of profit, and the differences remain unchanged (and therefore the rate of surplus-profit or of rent, calculated with respect to capital, remains unchanged).

The same may take place with decreasing rates of surplus-profit, and therefore of rent, that is, with decreasing productivity of the additional outlays of capital that still yield rent. If the second investments of capital of £2½ had not doubled the output, but B had yielded only 3½ qrs, C—5 qrs, and D—7 qrs, [In the German 1894 edition this reads: 6 qrs.—*Ed.*] then the differential rent for the second £2½ of capital in B would be only ½ qr instead of 1, on C—1 qr instead of 2 and on D—2 qrs instead of 3. The proportions between rent and capital for the two successive investments would then be as follows:

	First Investment		*Second Investment*	
B:	Rent £3,	Capital £2½	Rent £1½,	Capital £2½
C:	’ £6,	’ £2½	’ £3,	’ £2½
D:	’ £9,	’ £2½	’ £6,	’ £2½

In spite of this decreased rate of relative productivity of capital, and thus of the surplus-profit calculated on capital, the rent in grain and money would have increased on B from 1 to 1½ qrs (from £3 to £4½), on C—from 2 to 3 qrs (from £6 to £9), and on D—from 3 to 5 qrs (from £9 to £15). In this case, the differences for the additional capitals, compared with the capital invested in A, would have decreased, the price of production would have remained the same, but the rent per acre, and consequently the price of land per acre, would have risen. The combinations of differential rent II, which presupposes differential rent I as its basis, will now be taken up.

41

Differential Rent II First Case: Constant Price of Production

The assumption here implies that the market-price is regulated as before by the capital invested in the worst soil A.

I. If the additional capital invested in any one of the rent-bearing soils—B, C, D—produces only as much as the same capital upon soil A, i.e., if it yields only the average profit at the regulating price of production, but no surplus-profit, then the effect upon the rent is nil. Everything remains as before. It is the same as though an arbitrary number of acres of A quality, i.e., of the worst soil, has been added to the cultivated area.

II. The additional capitals yield additional produce proportional to their magnitude on every one of the various soils; in other words, the volume of production grows according to the specific fertility of each soil type—in proportion to the magnitude of the additional capital. In Chapter XXXIX, we started with the following Table I:

TABLE I

Type of soil	*Acres*	*Capital £*	*Profit £*	*Price of Prod. £*	*Output Qrs*	*Selling price £*	*Proceeds £*	*Rent*		*Rate of Surplus profit*
								Qrs	*£*	
A	1	2½	½	3	1	3	3	0	0	0
B	1	2½	½	3	2	3	6	1	3	120%
C	1	2½	½	3	3	3	9	2	6	240%
D	1	2½	½	3	4	3	12	3	9	360%
Total	4	10		12	10		30	6	18	

This is now transformed into:

TABLE II

Type of soil	*Acres*	*Capital £*	*Profit £*	*Price of Prod.*	*Output Qrs*	*Selling price £*	*Proceeds £*	*Rent*		*Surplus profit*
								Qrs	*£*	
A	1	2½ + 2½=5	1	6	2	3	6	0	0	0
B	1	2½ + 2½=5	1	6	4	3	2	2	6	120%
C	1	2½ + 2½=5	1	6	6	3	18	4	12	240%
D	1	2½ + 2½=5	1	6	8	3	24	6	18	360%
Total	4	20			20		60	12	36	

It is not necessary in this case that the investment of capital be doubled in all soils, as in the table. The law is the same so long as additional capital is invested in one, or several, of the rent-bearing soils, no matter in what proportion. It is only necessary that production should increase upon every soil in the same ratio as the capital. The rent increases here merely in consequence of an increased investment of capital in the soil, and in proportion to this increase. This increase in produce and rent in consequence of, and proportionately to, the increased outlay of capital is just the same as regards the quantity of produce and rent, as when the cultivated area of the rent-bearing plots of land of the same quality had been increased and taken under cultivation with the same outlay of capital as that previously invested in the same types of soils. In the case of Table II, for instance, the result would remain the same, if the additional capital of £2½ per acre were invested in an additional acre of B, C and D.

Furthermore, this assumption does not imply a more productive investment of capital, but only an outlay of more capital upon the same area with the same success as before.

All relative proportions remain the same here. Of course, if we do not consider the proportional differences, but consider the purely arithmetic ones, then the differential rent may change upon the various soils. Let us assume, for instance, that additional capital has been invested only in B and D. The difference between D and A is then = 7 qrs whereas previously it was = 3, the difference between B and A = 3 qrs, whereas previously it was = 1; that between C and B = -1, whereas previously it was = +1, etc. But this arithmetic difference, which is decisive in differential rent I in so far as it expresses the difference in productivity with equal outlays of capital, is here quite immaterial, because it is merely a consequence of different additional investments of capital, or of no additional investment, while the difference for each equal portion of capital upon the various plots of land remains unchanged.

III. The additional capitals yield surplus-produce and thus form surplus-profit, but at a decreasing rate, not in proportion to their increase.

TABLE III

Soil	*Acres*	*Capital £*	*Profit £*	*Price of Prod. £*	*Output Qrs*	*Selling price £*	*Proceeds £*	*Rent*		*Rate of Surplus profit*
								Qrs	*£*	
A	1	2½	½	3	1	3	3	0	0	0
B	1	2½ + 2½ = 5	1	6	2 + 1½ = 3½	3	10½	1½	4½	90%
C	1	2½ + 2½ = 5	1	6	3+2=5	3	15	3	9	180%
D	1	2½ + 2½ = 5	1	6	4 + 3½ = 7½	3	22½	5½	16½	330%
		17½	3½	21	17		51	10	30	

In the case of this third assumption, it is again immaterial whether the additional second investments of capital are uniformly distributed among the various soils or not; whether the decreasing production of surplus-profit takes place proportionately or not; whether the additional investments of capital are all in the same rent-bearing type of soil, or whether they are distributed equally or unequally among rent-bearing plots of land of varying quality. All these circumstances are immaterial for the law that is to be developed. The only assumption is that additional investments of capital yield surplus-profit upon any one of the rent-bearing soils, but in decreasing proportion to the amount of the increase in capital. The limits of this decrease, in the table before us, are between 4 quarters = £12, the output from the first outlay of capital on the best soil D, and 1 quarter = £3, the output from the same outlay of capital in the worst soil A. The output from the best soil in case of the investment of capital I constitutes the top limit, and the output from the same outlay of capital in the worst soil A, which yields neither rent nor surplus-profit, is the bottom limit of output, which successive investments of capital yield upon any of the soil types producing surplus-profit with decreasing productivity of successive investments of capital. Just as assumption II corresponds to the case in which new plots of the same quality are added from the better soils to the cultivated area, in which the quantity of any one of the cultivated soils is increased, so assumption III corresponds to the case in which additional plots are cultivated whose various degrees of fertility are distributed among soils ranging from D to A, i.e., from the best to the worst soils. If the successive outlays of capital are made exclusively in soil D, they may include the existing differences between D and A, then differences between D and C, and likewise between D and B. If they are all made in soil C, then only differences between C and A, and C and B; if exclusively in B, then only differences between B and A.

But this is the law: The rent increases absolutely upon all these soils, even if not in proportion to the additional capital invested.

The rate of surplus-profit, considering both the additional capital and the total capital invested in the soil, decreases; but the absolute magnitude of the surplus-profit increases; just as the decreasing rate of profit on capital in general is, in the main, accompanied by an increase in the absolute amount of profit. Thus the average surplus-profit of a capital invested in B = 90% on the capital, whereas it was = 120% for the first outlay of capital. But the total surplus-profit increases from 1 qr to 1½ qrs, or from £3 to £4½. The total rent—considered by itself rather than in relation to the doubled magnitude of the advanced capital—has risen absolutely. The differences in rents from various soils and their relative proportions may vary here; but this variation in differences is a consequence, not cause, of the increase in rents in relation to one another.

IV. The case in which additional investments of capital in the better soils yield more produce than the original ones requires no further analysis. It goes without saying that under this assumption the rent per acre will increase, and proportionately more than the additional capital, no matter in which kind of soil the outlay has been made. In this case, the additional investment of capital is accompanied by improvements. This includes the cases in which an additional outlay of less capital produces the same or a greater effect than an additional outlay of more capital did formerly. This case is not quite identical with the former one, and the distinction is important in all investments of capital. For instance, if 400 yields a profit of 40, and 200 employed in a certain form yields a profit of 40, then the profit has risen from 10% to 20%, and to that extent it is the same as though 50 employed in a more effective form yields a profit of 10 instead of 5. We assume here that the profit is associated with a proportional increase in output. But the difference is that I must double the capital in the one case, whereas in the other, the effect I produce is doubled with the capital employed hitherto. It is by no means the same whether I produce: 1) the same output as before with half as much living and materialised labour, or 2) twice the output as before with the same labour, or 3) four times the former output with twice the labour. In the first case, labour—in a living or materialised form—is released, and may be employed otherwise; the power to dispose of capital and labour increases. The release of capital (and labour) is in itself an augmentation of wealth; it has exactly the same effect as though this additional capital has been obtained by accumulation, but it saves the labour of accumulation.

Assume that a capital of 100 has produced an output of ten metres. The 100 includes constant capital, living labour and profit. Thus a metre costs 10. Now, if I can produce 20 metres with the same capital of 100, then a metre costs 5. If, on the other hand, I can produce 10 metres with a capital of 50, then a metre likewise costs 5, and should the former supply of commodities suffice a capital of 50 is released. If I have to invest a capital of 200 in order to produce 40 metres, then a metre also costs 5. The determination of value, and also the price, does not permit any difference to be discerned here; no more than the amount of output proportional to the outlay of capital. But in the first case, additional capital is saved [In the German 1894 edition this reads: capital is released.—*Ed.*] to be used perhaps to double production if necessary; in the second case, capital is released, [*Ibid.*: additional capital is saved.—*Ed.*] in the third case, the increased output can only be obtained by augmenting the invested capital, although not in the same proportion as when the increased output was to have been supplied by the old productive power. (This belongs in Part I.)

From the viewpoint of capitalist production, the employment of constant capital is always cheaper than that of variable capital, not as regards increasing the surplus-value, but rather as regards reducing the cost-price—and saving of costs even in the element creating surplus-value, in labour, performs this service for the capitalist and makes profit for him so long as the regulating price of production remains the same. This presupposes, in fact, the development of credit and an abundance of loan capital corresponding to the capitalist mode of production. On the one hand, I employ £100 additional constant capital, if £100 is the output of five labourers during the year; on the other hand, £100 in variable capital. If the rate of surplus-value = 100%, then the value created by the five labourers = £200; on the other hand, the value of £100 constant capital = £100 and as capital it is perhaps = £105, if the interest rate = 5%. The same sums of money express very different values, from the viewpoint of the output they produce, depending on whether they are advanced to production as magnitudes of value of constant or of variable capital. Furthermore, as regards the cost of the commodities from the viewpoint of the capitalist, there is also this difference, that of the £100 constant capital only the wear and tear enters into the value of the commodity in so far as this money is invested in fixed capital, whereas the £100 invested in wages must be completely reproduced in the commodity.

In the case of colonists, and independent small producers in general, who have no access to capital at all or only at high interest rates, that part of the output which represents wages is their revenue, whereas for the capitalist it constitutes an advance of capital. The former, therefore, regards this expenditure of labour as the indispensable prerequisite for the labour-product, which is the thing that interests him above all. But, as regards his surplus-labour, after deducting the necessary labour, it is evidently realised in the surplus-product; and as soon as he can sell the latter, or use it for himself, he looks upon it as something that cost him nothing, because it cost him no materialised labour. It is only the expenditure of the latter which appears to him as alienation of wealth. Of course, he tries to sell as high as possible; but even a sale below value and below the capitalist price of production still appears to him as profit, unless this profit is anticipated by debts, mortgages, etc. For the capitalist, on the other hand, the investment of both variable and constant capital represents an advance of capital. The relatively larger advance of the latter reduces the cost-price, and in fact the value of the commodities, everything else being equal. Hence, although profit arises only from surplus-labour, consequently only from the employment of variable capital, it may still seem to the individual capitalist that living labour is the most expensive element in his price of production which should be reduced to a minimum before all else. This is but a capitalistically distorted form of the fact that the relatively greater use of congealed labour, as compared with living labour, signifies an increase in the productivity of social labour and a greater social wealth. From the viewpoint of competition, everything appears thus distorted and turned topsy-turvy.

Assuming prices of production to remain unchanged, the additional investments of capital in the better soils, that is, in all soils from B upward may be made with unaltered, increasing, or decreasing productivity. For soil A this would only be possible under the conditions assumed by us, if productivity remains the same—whereby the land continues to yield no rent—and also if productivity increases; a portion of the capital invested in A would then yield rent, while the remainder would not. But it would be impossible if productivity on A were to decrease, for then the price of production would not remain unchanged, but would rise. Yet in all these cases, i.e., whether the surplus-product yielded by the additional investments is proportional to the latter or is greater or smaller than this proportion—whether, therefore, the rate of surplus-profit on the capital remains constant, rises or falls, when this capital increases, the surplus-product and the corresponding surplus-profit per acre increases, and hence also the potential rent in grain and money. The growth in the mere quantity of surplus-profit or rent, calculated per acre, that is, an increasing quantity calculated on the basis of some constant unit—in the present case on a definite quantity of land such as an acre or a hectare—expresses itself as an increasing ratio. Hence the magnitude of the rent, calculated per acre, increases under such circumstances simply in consequence of the increase in the capital invested in the land. This takes place, to be sure, assuming the prices of production remain the same, and, on the other hand, regardless of whether the productivity of the additional capital remains unaltered, or whether it decreases or increases. The latter circumstances modify the range in which the magnitude of rent per acre increases but not the existence of this increase itself. This is a phenomenon peculiar to differential rent II, and distinguishing it from differential rent I. If the additional investments of capital were made successively in space, side by side in new additional soil of corresponding quality, rather than successively in time in the same soil, the quantity of the rental would have increased, and, as previously shown, so would the average rent from the total cultivated area, but not the magnitude of the rent per acre. Given the same result so far as quantity and value of total production and surplus-product are concerned, the concentration of capital upon a smaller area of land increases the amount of rent per acre, whereas under the same conditions, its dispersion over a larger area, all other conditions being equal, does not produce this effect. But the more the capitalist mode of production develops, the more does the concentration of capital upon the same area of land develop, and, therefore, the more does the rent, calculated per acre, increase. Consequently, given two countries in which the prices of production are identical, the differences in soil type are identical, and the same amount of capital is invested—but in the one country more in the form of successive outlays upon a limited area of land, whereas in the other more in the form of co-ordinated outlays upon a larger area—then the rent per acre, and thereby the price of land, would be higher in the first country and lower in the second, although the total rent would be the same for both countries. The difference in magnitude of rent could thus not be explained here to be a result of a difference in the natural fertility of the various soils, nor a result of a difference in the quantity of employed labour, but solely a result of different ways in which the capital is invested.

When we refer to surplus-product here, this should always be understood to mean that aliquot part of the output which represents surplus-profit. Ordinarily, we mean by excess product or surplus-product that portion of the output which represents the total surplus-value, or in some cases that portion which represents the average profit. The specific meaning which this term assumes in the case of rent-bearing capital gives rise to misunderstanding, as previously pointed out.

42

Differential Rent II Second Case: Falling Price of Production

The price of production may fall when additional investments of capital take place with an unaltered, falling, or rising rate of productivity.

Section I. *Productivity of the Additional Investment of Capital Remains the Same*

In this case, the assumption, therefore, is that the output increases proportionally to the capital invested in the various soils and in accordance with their respective qualities. This means for constant differences in soils that the surplus-product increases in proportion to the increased investment of capital. This case, then, excludes any additional investment of capital in soil A which might affect the differential rent. For this soil, the rate of surplus-profit = 0; thus, it remains = 0 since we have assumed that the productiveness of the additional capital, and therefore the rate of surplus-profit, remain the same.

But under these conditions the regulating price of production can only fall, because it is the price of production of the next best soil, of B, or any better soil than A, rather than that of A, which becomes the regulator; so that the capital is withdrawn from A, or perhaps from A and B if the price of production of C should become the regulating one, and thus all soils inferior to C would be eliminated from the competition among grain-producing soils. The prerequisite for this is, under the assumed conditions, that the additional yield from the additional investments of capital satisfy the demand, so that the output from the inferior soil A, etc., become superfluous for the re-establishment of a full supply.

Thus, let us take, for instance, Table II, but in such a way that 18 qrs instead of 20 satisfy the demand. Soil A would drop out; B * and its price of production of 30 shillings per quarter would become regulating. The differential rent then assumes the following form:

TABLE IV

Type of soil	*Acres*	*Capital £*	*Profit £*	*Price of Prod.*	*Output Qrs*	*Selling price per qr £*	*Proceeds £*	*Rent*		*Rate of Surplus Profit*
								In Grain Qrs	*In Money £*	
B	1	5	1	6	4	1½	6	0	0	0%
C	1	5	1	6	6	1½	9	2	3	60%
D	1	5	1	6	8	1½	12	4	6	120%
Total	3	15	3	18	18		27	6	9	

[* In the German 1894 edition this reads: D.—Ed.]

Compared with Table II, the ground-rent would hence have fallen from £36 to £9, and in grain from 12 qrs to 6 qrs; total output would have fallen only by 2 qrs, from 20 to 18. The rate of surplus-profit calculated on the capital would have fallen to one-third, i.e., from 180% to 60%. [*Ibid.*: one-half, from 180% to 90%.—*Ed.*] Thus, the fall in the price of production is accompanied here by a decrease of the rent in grain and money.

Compared with Table I, there is merely a decrease in money-rent; the rent in grain is in both cases 6 qrs; but in the one case it = £18, and in the other £9. For soil C, [*Ibid.*: for soil C and D.—*Ed.*] the rent in grain, compared with Table I, has remained the same. In fact, it is owing to the additional production resulting from the uniformly acting additional capital that the yield from A has been excluded from the market, and thereby soil A has been eliminated as a competing producing agent, and it is owing to this fact that a new differential rent I has been formed in which the better soil B plays the same role as did formerly the inferior soil A.

Consequently, on the one hand, the rent from B has disappeared; on the other hand, nothing has been altered in the differences between B, C and D by the investment of additional capital—in accordance with our assumption. For this reason, that part of the output which is transformed into rent is reduced.

If the above result—the satisfaction of the demand with A excluded—had been accomplished, perchance, by the investment of more than double the capital in C or D, or in both, then the matter would assume a different aspect. For example, if the third investment of capital were made in C:

TABLE IVa

Type of soil	*Acres*	*Capital £*	*Profit £*	*Price of Prod. £*	*Output Qrs*	*Selling price £*	*Proceeds £*	*Rent*		*Rate of Surplus Profit*
								In Grain Qrs	*In Money £*	
B	1	5	1	6	4	1½	6	0	0	0%
C	1	7½	1½	9	9	1½	13½	3	4½	60%
D	1	5	1	6	8	1½	12	4	6	120%*
Total	3	17½	3½	21	21		31½	7	10½	

In this case, compared with Table IV, the output from C has risen from 6 to 9 qrs, the surplus-product from 2 to 3 qrs, and the money-rent from £3 to £4½. Compared with Table II, where the latter was £12, and Table I, where it was £6, the money-rent has, on the other hand, decreased. The total rental in grain = 7 qrs and has fallen compared with Table II (12 qrs) and risen compared with Table I (6 qrs); in money (£10½) it has fallen compared with both (£18 and £36).

If the third investment of capital of £2½ had been employed on soil B, it would indeed have altered the quantity of production, but would not have affected the rent, since, according to our assumption, the successive investments do not produce any differences upon the same soil and soil B does not yield any rent.

If we assume, on the other hand, that the third investment of capital takes place upon D instead of C, we have the following, Table IVb

TABLE IVb

Type of soil	*Acres*	*Capital £*	*Profit £*	*Price of Prod. £*	*Output Qrs*	*Selling price £*	*Proceeds £*	*Rent*		*Rate of Surplus Profit*
								In Grain Qr	*In Money £*	
B	1	5	1	6	4	1½	6	0	0	0%
C	1	5	1	6	6	1½	9	2	3	60%
D	1	7½	1½	9	12	1½	18	6	9	120%
Total	3	17½	3½	21	22		33	8	12	

Here the total product is 22 qrs, more than double that of Table I, although the invested capital is only £17½ as against £10, that is, not twice the amount. The total product is also larger by 2 qrs than that of Table II, although the invested capital in the latter is larger—namely, £20.

Compared with Table I, the rent in grain from soil D has increased from 3 [In the German 1894 edition this reads: 2.—*Ed.*] to 6 qrs, whereas the money-rent, £9, has remained the same. Compared with Table II, the grain-rent from D is the same, namely, 6 qrs, but the money-rent has fallen from £18 to £9.

Comparing the total rents, the grain-rent from Table IVb = 8 qrs is larger than that from Table I = 6 qrs and than that from Table IVa = 7 qrs; but it is smaller than that from Table II = 12 qrs. The money-rent from Table IVb = £12 is larger than that from Table IVa = £10½ and smaller than that from Table 1 = £18 and that from Table II = £36.

In order that the total rental may, under the conditions of Table IVb (with the elimination of rent from B), be equal to that of Table I, we need £6 more of surplus-product, that is, 4 qrs at £1½, which is the new price of production. We then have a total rental of £18 again as in Table I. The magnitude of the required additional capital will vary according to whether we invest it in C or D, or divide it between the two.

On C, £5 capital yields 2 qrs of surplus-product; consequently, £10 additional capital yields 4 qrs of additional surplus-product. On D, £5 additional capital would suffice to produce 4 qrs of additional grain-rent under the conditions assumed here, namely that the productivity of the additional investments of capital remains the same. We should then obtain the following results:

TABLE IVc

Type of soil	Acres	Capital £	Profit £	Price of Prod. £	Output Qrs	Selling price £	Proceeds £	Rent		Rate of Surplus Profit
								Qrs	£	
B	1	5	1	6	4	1½	6	0	0	0%
C	1	15	3	18	18	1½	27	6	9	60%
D	1	7½	1½	9	12	1½	18	6	9	120%
Total	3	27½	5½	33	34		51	12	18	

TABLE IVd

Type of soil	Acres	Capital £	Profit £	Price of Prod. £	Output Qrs	Selling price £	Proceeds £	Rent		Rate of Surplus Profit
								Qrs	£	
B	1	5	1	6	4	1½	6	0	0	0%
C	1	5	1	6	6	1½	9	2	3	60%
D	1	12½	2½	15	20	1½	30	10	15	120%
Total	3	22½	4½	27	30		45	12	18	

The total money rental would be exactly one-half of what it was in Table II, where the additional capitals were invested at constant prices of production.

The most important thing is to compare the above tables with Table I.

We find that while the price of production has fallen by one-half, i.e., from 60 shillings to 30 shillings per quarter, the total money rental has remained the same, namely = £18, and the grain-rent has correspondingly doubled from 6 to 12 qrs. Upon B the rent has disappeared; upon C the money-rent has risen by one-half in IVc, but has fallen by one-half in IVd; upon D in IVc, it has remained the same, = £9, and has risen from £9 to £15 in IVd. The production has risen from 10 to 34 qrs in IVc, and to 30 qrs in IVd; the profit from £2 to £5½ in IVc and to £4 in IVd. The total investment of capital has risen in the one case from £10 to £27½, and in the other from £10 to £22½; i.e., in both cases it has more than doubled. The rate of rent, that is, the rent calculated on the invested capital, is in all tables from IV to IVd everywhere the same for each kind of soil—which was already implied in the assumption that the rate of productivity for the two successive investments of capital remains the same for each soil type. But compared with Table I this rate has fallen, both for the average of all kinds of soil and for each one of them individually. In Table I it was = 180% on an average, whereas in IVc it = (18/27½) × 100 = 65 5/11% and in IVd it = (18/22½) × 100 = 80%. The average money-rent per acre has risen. Formerly, in Table I, its average was £4½ per acre from all four acres, whereas in IVc and IVd it is £6 per acre upon the three acres. Its average upon the rent-bearing land was formerly £6, whereas now it is £9 per acre. Hence the money-value of the rent per acre has risen and now represents twice as much grain as it did formerly; but the 12 qrs of grain-rent are now less than one-half of the total output of 34 and 30 [In the German 1894 edition this reads: 33 and 27.—*Ed.*] qrs respectively, whereas in Table I the 6 qrs represent 3/5 of the total output of 10 qrs. Consequently, although the rent as an aliquot part of the total output has fallen, and has also fallen when calculated on the invested capital, its money-value calculated per acre has risen, and still more its value as a product. If we take soil D in Table IVd, we find that the price of production corresponding to the capital outlay here = £15, of which £12½ is invested capital. The money-rent = £15. In Table I, for the same soil D, the price of production was = £3, the invested capital = £2½, and the money-rent = £9; that is, the latter was three times the price of production and almost four times the capital. In Table IVd, the money-rent for D, £15, is exactly equal to the price of production and larger than the capital by only 1/5. Nevertheless, the money-rent per acre is ⅔ larger, namely, £15 instead of £9. In Table I, the grain-rent of 3 qrs = ¾ of the total product of 4 qrs; in Table IVd it is 10 qrs, or one-half the total product (20 qrs) per acre of D. This shows that the money-value and grain value of the rent per acre may rise, although it constitutes a smaller aliquot part of the total yield and has fallen in proportion to the invested capital.

The value of the total product in Table I = £30; the rent = £18, or more than one-half of it. The value of the total product in IVd = £45, of which the rent = £18, or less than one-half.

Now, the reason why in spite of the fall in price by £1½ per quarter, i.e., a fall of 50%, and in spite of the reduction in competing soil from 4 to 3 acres, the total money-rent remains the same and the total grain-rent is doubled, while, calculated per acre, both the grain-rent and money-rent rise, is that more quarters of surplus-product are produced. The price of grain falls by 50%, and the surplus-product increases by 100%. But in order to obtain this result, the total production under the conditions assumed by us must be trebled, and the investment of capital in the superior soils must be more than doubled. At what rate the latter must increase depends in the first place upon the distribution of additional capital investments among the better and best soils, always assuming that the productivity of the capital invested in each soil type increases proportionately to its magnitude.

If the fall in price of production were smaller, less additional capital would be required to produce the same money-rent. If the supply required to throw soil A out of cultivation—and this depends not merely upon the output per acre of A, but also upon the share held by A in the entire cultivated area—thus, if the supply required for this purpose were larger, and thereby also the amount of additional invested capital required in soils better than A, then, other circumstances remaining the same, the money and grain rents would have increased still more, although soil B would have ceased yielding money and grain rents. If the capital eliminated from A had been = £5, the tables to be compared for this case would be tables II and IVd. The total product would have increased from 20 to 30 qrs. The money-rent would be only half as large, or £48 instead of £36; the grain-rent would be the same, namely = 12 qrs.

If a total product of 44 qrs = £66 could be produced upon D with a capital = £27½—corresponding to the old rate for D, 4 qrs per £2½ capital—then the total rental would once more reach the level attained in Table II, and the table would appear as follows:

Type of Soil	*Capital £*	*Output Qrs*	*Grain-Rent Qrs*	*Money-Rent £*
B	5	4	0	0
C	5	6	2	3
D	27½	44	22	33
Total	37½	54	24	36

The total production would be 54 qrs as against 20 qrs in Table II, and the money-rent would be the same, = £36. But the total capital would be £37½, whereas in Table II it was = 20. The total invested capital would be double almost, while production would be nearly treble; the grain-rent would be double and the money-rent would remain the same. Hence, if the price falls—while productivity remains the same—as a result of the investment of additional money-capital in the better soils which yield rent, that is, all soils better than A, then the total capital has a tendency not to increase at the same rate as production and grain-rent; thus the increase in grain-rent may compensate for the loss in money-rent due to the falling price. The same law also manifests itself in that the invested capital must be proportionately larger as more is invested in C than D, i.e., in soils yielding less rent rather than in soils yielding more rent. The point is simply this: in order that the money-rent may remain the same or rise, a definite additional quantity of surplus-product must be produced, and the greater the fertility of the soils yielding surplus-product, the less capital this requires. If the difference between B and C, and C and D, were still greater, still less additional capital would be required. The specific proportion is determined by 1) the ratio of fall in price, in other words, by the difference between soil B, which does not yield rent now, and soil A, which formerly was the soil not yielding rent; 2) the ratio of the differences between the soils better than B upwards; 3) the amount of newly invested additional capital, and 4) its distribution among the soils of varying quality.

In fact, we see that this law merely expresses what was already ascertained in the first case: When the price of production is given, no matter what its magnitude, the rent may increase as a result of additional capital investment. For owing to the elimination of A, we now have a new differential rent I with B as the worst soil and £1½ per quarter as the new price of production. This applies to Table IV as well as to Table II. It is the same law, except that our point of departure is soil B instead of A, and our price of production is taken as £1½ instead of £3.

The important thing here is this: To the extent that so much and so much additional capital was necessary in order to withdraw the capital from soil A and create the supply without it, we find that this may be accompanied by an unaltered, rising, or falling rent per acre, if not from all plots of land then at least from some, and so far as the average of the cultivated plots is concerned. We have seen that grain-rent and money-rent do not maintain a uniform relation to one another. It is merely due to tradition that grain-rent is still of any importance in economics. One might demonstrate equally well that, e.g., a manufacturer can buy much more of his yarn with his profit of £5 than he could formerly with a profit of £10. It shows at any rate, that messieurs landlords, when they are simultaneously owners or shareholders in manufacturing establishments, sugar-refineries, distilleries, etc., may in their capacity as producers of their own raw materials still make a considerable profit when the money-rent is falling.[1]

Section II. *Decreasing Rate of Productivity of the Additional Capital*

This introduces nothing new into the problem, in so far as the price of production may also fall in this case, as in the case just considered, only when additional investments of capital in better soils than A render the output from A superfluous and the capital is, therefore, withdrawn from A, or A is employed for the production of other products. This case has been exhaustively discussed above. It was shown that the rent in grain and money per acre may increase, decrease, or remain unchanged.

For convenience in making comparisons we reproduce the following table:

TABLE IV

Type of Soil	*Acres*	*Capital £*	*Profit £*	*Price of Production. per Qr*	*Output Qrs*	*Grain-Rent Qrs*	*Money-Rent Qrs*	*Rate of Surplus Profit*
A	1	2½	½	3	1	0	0	0
B	1	2½	½	1½	2	1	3	120%
C	1	2½	½	1	3	2	6	240%
D	1	2½	½	¾	4	3	9	360%
Total	4	10			10	6	18	180% average

Now let us assume that a quantity of 16 qrs supplied by B, C, and D at a decreasing rate of productivity suffices to exclude A from cultivation. In such case, Table III is transformed into the following:

TABLE V

Type of Soil	*Acres*	*Investment of Capital £*	*Profit £*	*Output Qrs*	*Selling price £*	*Proceeds £*	*Grain-Rent Qrs*	*Money-Rent £*	*Rate of Surplus Profit*
B	1	2½ + 2½	1	2 + 1½ = 3½	1 5/7	6	0	0	0
C	1	2½ + 2½	1	3+2=5	1 5/7	8 4/7	1½	2 4/7	51 3/7%
D	1	2½ + 2½	1	4 + 3½ = 7½	1 5/7	12 6/7	4	6 6/7	137 1/7%**
Total	3***	15		16		27 3/7	5½	9 3/7	94 2/7% average****

[* In the German 1894 edition this reads 51 2/5.—*Ed.*]
[** *Ibid.* 137 1/5—*Ed.*]
[*** *Ibid.*: 4.—*Ed.*]
[**** Here, as well as in tables VI, VII, VII I, IX and X the land which yields no rent is left out of consideration.—*Ed.*]

Here, at a decreasing rate of productivity of the additional capital, and a varying decrease for the various soil types, the regulating price of production has fallen from £3 to £1 5/7. The investment of capital has risen by one-half-from £10 to £15. The money-rent has fallen by almost one-half-from £18 to £9 3/7, but the grain-rent has fallen by only 1/12—from 6 qrs to 5½ qrs. The total output has risen from 10 to 16, or by 60%. The grain-rent constitutes a little more than one-third of the total product. The advanced capital is to the money-rent as 15:9 3/7, whereas formerly this ratio was 10:18.

Section III. *Rising Rate of Productivity of the Additional Capital*

This differs from Variant I at the beginning of this chapter, where the price of production falls while the rate of productivity remains the same, merely in that when a given amount of additional produce is required to exclude soil A this occurs here more quickly.

The effect may vary in accordance with the distribution of investments among the various soils for a falling, as well as an increasing, productivity of the additional capital investments. In so far as this varying effect balances out the differences, or accentuates them, the differential rent of the better soils, and thereby the total rental too, will fall or rise, as was already the case in differential rent I. In other respects, everything depends upon the magnitude of the land area and capital excluded together with A, and upon the relative magnitude of advanced capital required with a rising productivity in order to produce the additional output to meet the demand.

The only point worthwhile analysing here, and which really takes us back to the investigation of the way in which this differential profit is transformed into differential rent, is the following:

In the first case, where the price of production remains the same the additional capital which may be invested in soil A does not affect the differential rent as such, since soil A, as before, does not yield any rent, the price of its produce remains the same, and it continues to regulate the market.

In the second case, Variant I, where the price of production falls while the rate of productivity remains the same, soil A will necessarily be excluded, and still more so in Variant II (falling price of production with falling rate of productivity), since otherwise the additional capital invested in soil A would have had to raise the price of production. But here, in Variant III of the second case, where the price of production falls because the productivity of the additional capital rises, this additional capital may under certain circumstances be invested in soil A as well as in the better soils.

Let us assume that when invested in soil A an additional capital of £2½ produces 1 1/5 qrs instead of 1 qr.

TABLE VI

Type of Soil	*Acres*	*Capital £*	*Profit £*	*Price of Production £*	*Output Qrs*	*Selling price £*	*Proceeds £*	*Rent*		*Rate of Surplus Profit*
								Qrs	*£*	
A	1	2½ + 2½ = 5	1	6	1 + 1 1/5 =2 1/5	2 8/11	6	0	0	0%
B	1	2½ + 2½ = 5	1	6	2 + 2 2/5 = 4 2/5	2 8/11	12	2 1/5	6	120%
C	1	2½ + 2½ = 5	1	6	3 + 3 3/5 = 6 3/5	2 8/11	18	4 2/5	12	240%
D	1	2½ + 2½ = 5	1	6	4 + 4 4/5 = 8 4/5	2 8/11	24	6 3/5	18	360%
	4	20	4	24	22		60	13 1/5	36	240%

Aside from being compared with the basic Table I, this table should be compared with Table II, where a two-fold investment of capital is associated with a constant productivity, proportional to the investment of capital.

In accordance with our assumption, the regulating price of production falls. If it were to remain constant, = £3, then the worst soil A, which used to yield no rent with an investment of only £2½, would now yield rent without worse soil being brought under cultivation. This would have occurred due to an increase in the productivity of this soil, but only for a part of the capital, not for the original capital invested. The first £3 of production price yield 1 qr; the second yield 1 1/5; qrs; but the entire output of 2 1/5; qrs is now sold at its average price. Since the rate f productivity increases with the additional investment of capital, this presupposes an improvement. The latter may consist of a general increase in capital invested per acre (more fertiliser, more mechanised labour, etc.), or it may be that only through this additional capital it is at all possible to bring about a qualitatively different more productive investment of the capital. In both cases, the investment of £5 of capital per acre yields an output of 2 1/5 qrs, whereas the investment of one-half of this capital, i.e., £2 1/5, yields only 1 qr of produce. The produce from soil A could, regardless of transient market conditions, only continue to be sold at a higher price of production instead of at the new average price, as long as a considerable area of type A soil continued to be cultivated with a capital of only £2½ per acre. But as soon as the new relation of £5 of capital per acre, and thereby the improved management, becomes universal, the regulating price of production would have to fall to £2 8/11. The differencc between the two portions of capital would disappcar, and then, in fact, the cultivation of an acre of soil A with a capital of only £2½ would be abnormal, i.e., would not correspond to the new conditions of production. It would then no longer be a difference between the yields from different portions of capital invested in the same acre, but between a sufficient and an insufficient total investment of capital per acre. This shows, *first of all,* that insufficient capital in the hands of a large number of tenant farmers (it must be a large number, for a small number would simply be compelled to sell below their price of production) produces the same effect as a differentiation of the soils themselves in a descending line. The inferior cultivation of inferior soil increases the rent from superior soils; it may even lead to rent being yielded from better cultivated soil of equally poor quality, which would otherwise not be yielded. It shows, *secondly,* that differential rent, in so far as it arises from successive investments of capital in the same total area, resolves itself in reality into an average, in which the effects of the various investments of capital are no longer recognisable and distinguishable, and therefore do not result in rent being yielded from the worst soil, but rather: 1) make the average price of the total yield for, say, an acre of A, the new regulating price and 2) appear as alteration in the total quantity of capital per acre required under the new conditions for the adequate cultivation of the soil; and in which the individual successive investments of capital, as well as their respective effects, will appear indistinguishably blended together. It is exactly the same with the individual differential rents from the superior soils. In each case, they are determined by the difference between the average output from the soil in question and the output from the worst soil at the increased capital investment—which has now become normal.

No soil yields any produce without an investment of capital. This is the case even for simple differential rent, differential rent I; when it is said that one acre of soil A, which regulates the price of production, yields so much and so much produce at such and such a price, and that superior soils B, C and D yield so much differential produce, and therefore, so much and so much money-rent at the regulating price of production, it is always assumed that a definite amount of capital is invested which, under the prevailing conditions of production, is considered normal. In the same way, a certain minimum capital is required for every individual branch of industry in order that the commodities may be produced at their price of production.

If this minimum is altered as a result of successive investments of capital associated with improvements on the same soil, it occurs gradually. So long as a certain number of acres, say, of A, do not receive this additional working capital, a rent is produced upon the better cultivated acres of A due to the unaltered price of production, and the rent from all superior soils, B, C and D, is increased. But as soon as the new method of cultivation has become general enough to be the normal one, the price of production falls; the rent from the superior plots declines again, and that portion of soil A that does not possess the working capital, which has now become the average, must sell its produce below its individual price of production, i.e., below the average profit.

In the case of a falling price of production, this also occurs even with decreasing productivity of the additional capital—as soon as the required total product is supplied, in consequence of increased investment of capital, by the superior soils, and thus, e.g., the working capital is withdrawn from A, i.e., A no longer competes in the production of this particular product, e.g., wheat. The quantity of capital which is now required, on an average, to be invested in the better soil B, the new regulator, now becomes normal: and when one speaks of the varying fertility of plots of land, it is assumed that this new normal quantity of capital per acre is employed.

On the other hand, it is evident that this average investment of capital, say, in England, of £8 per acre prior to 1848, and £12 subsequent to that year, will constitute the standard in concluding leases. For the farmer expending more than this, the surplus-profit is not transformed into rent for the duration of the contract. Whether this takes place after expiration of the contract or not will depend upon the competition among the farmers who are in a position to make the same extra capital advance. We are not referring here to such permanent soil improvements that continue to provide the increased output with the same or even with a decreasing outlay of capital. Such improvements, although products of capital, have the same effect as natural differences in the quality of the land.

We see, then, that a factor comes into consideration in the case of differential rent II which does not appear in the case of differential rent I as such, since the latter can continue to exist independently of any change in the normal investment of capital per acre. It is, on the one hand, the blurring of results from various investments, of capital in regulating soil A, whose output flow simply appears as a normal average output per acre. It is, on the other hand, the change in the normal minimum, or in the average magnitude of invested capital per acre, so that this change appears as a property of the soil. It is, finally, the difference in the manner of transforming surplus-profit into the form of rent.

Table VI shows, furthermore, compared with tables I and II, that the grain-rent has more than doubled in relation to I, and has increased by 1 1/5 qrs in relation to II; while the money-rent has doubled in relation to I, but has not changed in relation to II. It would have increased considerably if (other conditions remaining the same) more of the additional capital had been allocated to the superior soils, or if on the other hand the effect of the additional capital on A had been less appreciable, and thus the regulating average price per quarter from A had been higher.

If the increase in productiveness by means of additional capital should produce varying results for the various soils, this would produce a change in their differential rents.

In any case, it has been shown that the rent per acre, for instance with a doubled investment of capital, may not only double, but may more than double—while the price of production falls in consequence of an increased rate of productivity of the additional capital invested, i.e., when this productivity grows at a higher rate than the advanced capital. But it may also fall if the price of production should fall much lower as a result of a more rapid increase in productiveness of soil A.

Let us assume that the additional investments of capital, for instance in B and C, do not increase the productivity at the same rate as they do for A, so that the proportional differences decrease for B and C and the increase in output does not make up for the fall in price. Then, compared with Table II, the [money] rent from D would remain unchanged, and that from B and C would fall.

TABLE VIa

Type of Soil	*Acres*	*Capital £*	*Profit £*	*Output Per Acre Qrs*	*Selling price*	*Proceeds £*	*Grain-Rent Qrs*	*Money-Rent £*
A	1	2½+2½	1	1+3=4	1½	6	0	0
B	1	2½ + 2½ = 5	1	2 + 2½ = 4½	1½	6¾	½	¾
C	1	2½ + 2½ = 5	1	3 + 5 = 8	1½	12	4	6
D	1	2½ + 2½ = 5	1	4 + 12 = 16	1½	24	12	18
Total	4	20		32½			16½	24¾

Finally, the money-rent would rise if more additional capital were invested in the superior soils with the same proportional increase in productiveness than in A, or if the additional investments of capital in the superior soils were effective at an increasing rate of productivity. In both cases the differences would increase.

The money-rent falls when the improvement due to additional investment of capital reduces the differences completely, or in part, and affects A more than B and C. The smaller the increase in productivity of the superior soils, the more it falls. It depends upon the extent of inequality produced, whether the grain-rent shall rise, fall or remain stationary.

The money-rent rises, and similarly the grain-rent, either when—the proportional difference in additional fertility of the various soils remaining unaltered—more capital is invested in the rent-bearing soils than in rentless soil A, and more in soils yielding higher rent than in those yielding lower rents; or when the fertility—the additional capital remaining equal—increases more on the better and best soils than on A, i.e., the money and grain rents rise in proportion to this increase in fertility of the better soils above that of the poorer ones.

But under all circumstances, there is a relative rise in rent when increased productive power is the result of an addition of capital, and not merely the result of increased fertility with unaltered investment of capital. This is the absolute point of view, which shows that here, as in all former cases, the rent and increased rent per acre (as in the case of differential rent I on the entire cultivated area—the magnitude of the average rental) are the result of an increased investment of capital in land, no matter whether this capital functions with a constant rate of productivity at constant or decreasing prices or with a decreasing rate of productivity at constant or falling prices, or with an increasing rate of productivity at falling prices. For our assumption: constant prices with a constant, falling, or rising rate of productivity of the additional capital, and falling prices with a constant, falling, or rising rate of productivity, resolves itself into: a constant rate of productivity of the additional capital at constant or falling prices, a falling rate of productivity at constant or falling prices, and a rising rate of productivity at constant and falling prices. Although the rent may remain stationary, or may fall, in all these cases, it would fall more if the additional investment of capital, other circumstances remaining the same, were not a prerequisite for the increased productiveness. The additional capital, then, is always the cause for the relatively high rent, although absolutely it may have decreased.

Note

1. The above tables IVa to IVd had to be recalculated due to an error in computation which ran through all of them. While this did not affect the theoretical conclusions drawn from these tables, it introduced, in part, quite monstrous numerical values for production per acre. Even these are not objectionable in principle. For all relief and topographical maps it is customary to choose a much larger scale for the vertical than for the horizontal. Nevertheless, should anyone feel that his agrarian feelings have been injured thereby, he is at liberty to multiply the number of acres by any numerical value that will satisfy him. One might also choose 10, 12, 14, 16 bushels (8 bushels = 1 quarter) per acre in Table 1 instead of 1, 2, 3, 4 quarters, and the derived numerical values in the other tables would remain within the limits of probability; it will be found that the result, i.e., the ratio of rent increase to capital increase, is exactly the same. This has been done in the tables included by the editor in the next chapter.—*F. E.*

43

Differential Rent II Third Case: Rising Price of Production

[A rising price of production presupposes that the productivity of the poorest quality land yielding no rent decreases. The assumed regulating price of production cannot rise above £3 per quarter unless the £2½ invested in soil A produce less than 1 qr, or the £5—less than 2 qrs, or unless an even poorer soil than A has to be taken under cultivation.

For constant, or even increasing, productivity of the second investment of capital this would only be possible if the productivity of the first investment of capital of ½ had decreased. This case occurs often enough. For instance, when with superficial ploughing the exhausted top soil yields ever smaller crops, under the old method of cultivation, and then the subsoil, turned up through deeper ploughing, produces better crops than before with more rational cultivation. But, strictly speaking, this special case does not apply here. The decrease in productivity of the first £2½ of invested capital signifies for the superior soils, even when the conditions are assumed to be analogous there, a decrease in differential rent I; yet here we are considering only differential rent II. But since this special case cannot occur without presupposing the existence of differential rent II, and represents in fact the reaction of a modification of differential rent I upon II, we shall give an illustration of it [see Table VII—*Ed.*].

The money-rent and proceeds are the same as in Table II. The increased regulating price of production makes good what has been lost in quantity of produce; since this price and the quantity of produce are inversely proportional, it is evident that their mathematical product will remain the same.

TABLE VII

Type of Soil	*Acres*	*Invested Capital £*	*Profit £*	*Price of Prod. £*	*Output Qrs*	*Selling Price £*	*Proceeds £*	*Grain-Rent Qrs*	*Money Rent £*	*Rate of Rent*
A	1	2½ + 2½	1	6	½ + 1¼ = 1¾	3 3/7	6	0	0	0%
B	1	2½ + 2½	1	6	1 + 2½ = 3½	3 3/7	12	1¾	6	120%
C	1	2½ + 2½	1	6	1½ + 3¾ = 5¼	3 3/7	18	3½	12	240%
D	1	2½ + 2½	1	6	2 + 5 = 7	3 3/7	24	5¼	18	360%
		20			17½		60	10½	36	240%

In the above case, it was assumed that the productiveness of the second investment of capital was greater than the original productivity of the first investment. Nothing changes if we assume the second investment to have only the same productivity as the first, as shown in the following table:

TABLE VIII

								Rent		
Type of Soil	*Acres*	*Invested Capital £*	*Profit £*	*Price of Prod. £*	*Output Qrs*	*Selling Price £*	*Proceeds £*	*In Grain Qrs*	*In Money £*	*Rate of Surplus-Profit*
A	1	2½ + 2½ = 5	1	6	½ + 1½ = 2½	4	6	0	0	0%
B	1	2½ + 2½ = 5	1	6	1 + 2 = 3	4	12	1½	6	120%
C	1	2½ + 2½ = 5	1	6	1½ + 3 = 4½	4	18	3	12	240%
D	1	2½ + 2½ = 5	1	6	2 + 4 = 6	4	24	4½	18	360%
		20			15		60	9	36	240%

Here, too, the price of production rising at the same rate compensates in full for the decrease in productivity in the case of yield as well as money-rent.

The third case appears in its pure form only when the productivity of the second investment of capital declines, while that of the first remains constant—which was always assumed in the first and second cases. Here differential rent I is not affected, i.e., the change affects only that part which arises from differential rent II. We shall give two illustrations: in the first we assume that the productivity of the second investment of capital has been reduced to ½, in the second to ¾.

TABLE IX

								Rent		
Type of Soil	*Acres*	*Invested Capital £*	*Profit £*	*Price of Prod.*	*Output Qrs*	*Selling Price £*	*Proceeds £*	*In Grain Qrs*	*In Money £*	*Rate of Rent*
A	1	2½ + 2½ = 5	1	6	1 + ½ = 1½	4	6	0	0	0
B	1	2½ + 2½ = 5	1	6	2 + 1 = 3	4	12	1½	6	120%
C	1	2½ + 2½ = 5	1	6	3 + 1½ = 4½	4	18	3	12	240%
D	1	2½ + 2½ = 5	1	6	4 + 2 = 6	4	24	4½	18	360%
		20			15		60	9	36	240%

Table IX is the same as Table VIII, except for the fact that the decrease in productivity in VIII occurs for the first, and in IX for the second investment of capital.

TABLE X

								Rent		
Type of Soil	*Acres*	*Invested Capital £*	*Profit £*	*Price of Prod.*	*Output Qrs*	*Selling Price £*	*Proceeds £*	*In Grain Qrs*	*In Money £*	*Rate of Rent*
A	1	2½ + 2½ = 5	1	6	1 + ¼ = 1¼	4 4/5	6	0	0	0%
B	1	2½ + 2½ = 5	1	6	2 + ½ = 2½	4 4/5	12	1¼	6	120%
C	1	2½ + 2½ = 5	1	6	3 + ¾ = 3¾	4 4/5	18	2½	12	240%
D	1	2½ + 2½ = 5	1	6	4 + 1 = 5	4 4/5	24	3¾	18	360%
		20		24	12½		60	7½	36	240%

In this table, too, the total proceeds, the money-rent and rate of rent remain the same as in tables II, VII and VIII, because produce and selling price are again inversely proportional, while the invested capital remains the same.

But how do matters stand in the other possible case when the price of production rises, namely, in the case of a poor quality soil not worth cultivating until then that is taken under cultivation?

Let us suppose that a soil of this sort, which we shall designate by a, enters into competition. Then the hitherto rentless soil A would yield rent, and the foregoing tables VII, VIII and X would assume the following forms:

TABLE VIIa

								Rent		
Type of Soil	*Acres*	*Invested Capital £*	*Profit £*	*Price of Prod.*	*Output Qrs*	*Selling Price £*	*Proceeds £*	*In Grain Qrs*	*In Money £*	*Increase*
a	1	5	1	6	1½	4	6	0	0	0
A	1	2½ + 2½	1	6	½ + 1¼ = 1¾	4	7	¼	1	1
B	1	2½ + 2½	1	6	1 + 2½ = 3½	4	14	2	8	1 + 7
C	1	2½ + 2½	1	6	1½ + 3¾ = 5¼	4	21	3¾	15	1 + 2 × 7
D	1	2½ + 2½	1	6	2 + 5 = 7	4	28	5½	22	1 + 3 × 7
				30	19		76	11½	46	

TABLE VIIIa

								Rent		
Type of Soil	*Acres*	*Invested Capital £*	*Profit £*	*Price of Prod.*	*Output Qrs*	*Selling Price £*	*Proceeds £*	*In Grain Qrs*	*In Money £*	*Increase*
a	1	5	1	6	1¼	4 4/5	6	0	0	0
A	1	2½ + 2½	1	6	½ + 1 = 1½	4 4/5	7 1/5	¼	1 1/5	1 1/5
B	1	2½ + 2½	1	6	1 + 2 = 3	4 4/5	14 2/5	1¾	8 2/5	1 1/5 + 7 1/5
C	1	2½ + 2½	1	6	1½ + 3 = 4½	4 4/5	21 3/5	3¼*	15 3/5	1 1/5 + 2 × 7 1/5
D	1	2½ + 2½	1	6	2 + 4 = 6	4 4/5	28 4/5	4¾	22 4/5	1 1/5 + 3 × 7 1/5
	5			30	16¼		78	10**	48	

[* In the German 1894 edition this reads: 2¼.—*Ed.*]
[** *Ibid.*: 9—*Ed.*]

TABLE Xa

								Rent		
Type of Soil	*Acres*	*Invested Capital £*	*Profit £*	*Price of Prod.*	*Output Qrs*	*Selling Price £*	*Proceeds £*	*In Grain Qrs*	*In Money £*	*Increase*
a	1	5	1	6	1 1/8	5⅓	6	0	0	0
A	1	2½ + 2½	1	6	1 + ¼ = 1¼	5⅓	6⅔	⅔	⅔	
B	1	2½ + 2½	1	6	2 + ½ = 2½	5⅓	13⅓	1 3/8	7⅓	⅔ + 6⅔
C	1	2½ + 2½	1	6	3 + ¾ = 3¾	5⅓	20	2 5/8	14	⅔ + 2 × 6⅔
D	1	2½ + 2½	1	6	4 + 1 = 5	5⅓	26⅔	3 7/8	20⅔	⅔ + 3 × 6⅔
				30	13 5/8		72⅔	8	42⅔	

By interpolating soil a there arises a new differential rent I; upon this new basis, differential rent II likewise develops in an altered form. Soil a has different fertility in each of the above three tables; the sequence of proportionally increasing fertilities begins only with soil A. The sequence of rising rents also behaves similarly. The rent of the worst rent-bearing soil, previously rentless, is a constant which is simply added to all higher rents. Only after deducting this constant does the sequence of differences clearly become evident for the higher rents, and similarly its parallel in the fertility sequence of the different soils. In all the tables, the fertilities from A to D are related as 1 : 2 : 3 : 4, and correspondingly the rents:

in VIIa, as 1 : (1 + 7) : (1 + 2 × 7) : (1 + 3 × 7),

in VIIIa, as 1 1/5 : (1 1/5 + 7 1/5) : (1 1/5 + 2 × 7 1/5) : (1 1/5 + 3 × 7 1/5),

and in Xa, as ⅔ : (⅔ + 6⅔) : (⅔ + 2 × 6⅔) : ⅔ + 3 × 6⅔).

In brief, if the rent from A = n, and the rent from the soil of next higher fertility = n + m, then the sequence is as follows: n : (n + m) : (n + 2m) : (n + 3m), etc.—*F. E.*]

[Since the foregoing third case had not been elaborated in the manuscript—only the title is there—it was the task of the editor to fill in the gap, as above, to the best of his ability. However, in addition, it still remains for him to draw the general conclusions from the entire foregoing analysis of differential rent II, consisting of three principal cases and nine subcases. The illustrations presented in the manuscript, however, do not suit this purpose very well. In the first place, they compare plots of land whose yields for equal areas are related as 1 : 2 : 3 : 4; i.e., differences, which exaggerate greatly from the very first, and which lead to utterly monstrous numerical values in the further development of the assumptions and calculations made upon this basis. Secondly, they create a completely erroneous impression. If for degrees of fertility related as 1 : 2 : 3 : 4, etc., rents are obtained in the sequence 0 : 1 : 2 : 3, etc., one feels tempted to derive the second sequence from the first, and to explain the doubling, tripling, etc., of rents by the doubling, tripling, etc., of the total yields. But this would be wholly incorrect. The rents are related as 0 : 1 : 2 : 3 : 4 even when the degrees of fertility are related as n : (n + 1) : (n + 2) : (n + 3) : (n + 4). The rents are not related as the *degrees* of fertility, but as the *differences* of fertility—beginning with the rentless soil as the zero point.

The original tables had to be offered to illustrate the text. But in order to obtain a perceptual basis for the following results of the investigation, I present below a new series of tables in which the yields are indicated in bushels (1/8 quarter, or 36.35 litres) and shillings (= marks).

The first of these, Table XI, corresponds to the former Table I. It shows the yields and rents for soils of five different qualities, A to E, with a first capital investment of 50 shillings, which added to 10 shillings profit = 60 shillings total price of production per acre. The yields in grain are made low: 10, 12, 14, 16, 18 bushels per acre. The resulting regulating price of production is 6 shillings per bushel.

The following 13 tables correspond to the three cases of differential rent II treated in this and the two preceding chapters with an additional invested capital of 50 shillings per acre in the same soil with constant, falling and rising prices of production. Each of these cases, in turn, is presented as it takes shape for:

1) constant, 2) falling, and 3) rising productivity of the second investment of capital in relation to the first. This yields a few other variants, which are especially useful for illustration purposes.

For case I: Constant price of production—we have:

Variant 1:	Productivity of the second investment of capital remains the same (Table XII).
Variant 2:	Productivity declines. This can take place only when no second investment of capital is made in soil A, i.e., in such a way that a) soil B likewise yields no rent (Table XIII) or b) soil B does not become completely rentless (Table XIV).

Variant 3:	Productivity increases (Table XV). This case likewise excludes a second investment of capital in soil A.

For case II: Falling price of production—we have:

Variant 1:	Productivity of the second investment of capital remains the same (Table XVI).
—" —2:	Productivity declines (Table XVII). These two variants require that soil A be eliminated from competition, and that soil B become rentless and regulate the price of production.
—" —3:	Productivity increases (Table XVIII). Here Soil A remains the regulator.

For case III: Rising price of production—two eventualities are possible: soil A may remain rentless and continue to regulate the price, or poorer soil than A enters into competition and regulates the price, in which case A yields rent.
First eventuality: Soil A remains the regulator.

Variant 1:	Productivity of the second investment remains the same (Table XIX). This is admissible under the conditions assumed by us, provided the productivity of the first investment decreases.
—" —2:	Productivity of the second investment decreases (Table XX). This does not exclude the possibility that the first investment may retain the same productivity.
—" —3:	Productivity of the second investment increases (Table XXI [In the German 1894 edition this reads: XIX.—Ed.]). This, again, presupposes falling productivity of the first investment.

Second eventuality: An inferior quality soil (designated as a) enters into competition; soil A yields rent.

Variant 1:	Productivity of the second investment remains the same (Table XXII).
Variant 2:	Productivity declines (Table XXIII).
—’— 3:	Productivity increases (Table XXIV).

These three variants conform to the general conditions of the problem and require no further comment.

The tables now follow:

TABLE XI

Type of Soil	*Price of Production Sh.*	*Output Bushels*	*Selling Price Sh.*	*Proceeds Sh.*	*Rent Sh.*	*Rent Increase*
A	60	10	6	60	0	0
B	60	12	6	72	12	12
C	60	14	6	84	24	2 × 12
D	60	16	6	96	36	3 × 12
E	60	18	6	108	48	4 × 12
					120	10 × 12

For second capital invested in the same soil:
First Case: Price of production remains unaltered.
Variant 1: Productivity of the second investment of capital remains the same.

TABLE XII

Type of Soil	Price of Production Sh.	Output Bushels	Selling Price Sh.	Proceeds Sh.	Rent Sh.	Rent Increase
A	60 + 60 = 120	10 + 10 = 20	6	120	0	0
B	60 + 60 = 120	12 + 12 = 24	6	144	24	24
C	60 + 60 = 120	14 + 14 = 28	6	168	48	2 × 24
D	60 + 60 = 120	16 + 16 = 32	6	192	72	3 × 24
E	60 + 60 = 120	18 + 18 = 36	6	216	96	4 × 24
					240	10 × 24

Variant 2: Productivity of the second investment of capital declines; no second investment in soil A.

1) Soil B ceases to yield rent.

TABLE XIII

Type of Soil	Price of Production Sh.	Output Bushels	Selling Price Sh.	Proceeds Sh.	Rent Sh.	Rent Increase
A	60	10	6	60	0	0
B	60 + 60 = 120	12 + 8 = 20	6	120	0	0
C	60 + 60 = 120	14 + 9⅓ = 23⅓	6	140	20	20
D	60 + 60 = 120	16 + 10⅔ = 26⅔	6	160	40	2 × 20
E	60 + 60 = 120	18 + 12 = 30	6	180	60	3 × 20
					120	6 × 20

[*In the German 1894 edition this reads: 20.—*Ed.*]

2) Soil B does not become completely rentless.

TABLE XIV

Type of Soil	Price of Production Sh.	Output Bushels	Selling Price Sh.	Proceeds Sh.	Rent Sh.	Rent Increase
A	60	10	6	60	0	0
B	60 + 60 = 120	12 + 9 = 21	6	126	6	6
C	60 + 60 = 120	14 + 10½ = 24½	6	147	27	6 + 21
D	60 + 60 = 120	16 + 12 = 28	6	168	48	6 + 2 × 21
E	60 + 60 = 120	18 + 13½ = 31½	6	189	69	6 + 3 × 21
					150	4 × 6 + 6 × 21

Variant 3: Productivity of the second investment of capital increases; here, too, no second investment in Soil A.

TABLE XV

Type of Soil	*Price of Production Sh.*	*Output Bushels*	*Selling Price Sh.*	*Proceeds Sh.*	*Rent Sh.*	*Rent Increase*
A	60	10	6	60	0	0
B	60 + 60 = 120	12 + 15 = 27	6	162	42	42
C	60 + 60 = 120	14 + 17½ = 31½	6	189	69	42 + 27
D	60 + 60 = 120	16 + 20 = 36	6	216	96	42 + 2 × 27
E	60 + 60 = 120	18 + 22½ = 40½	6	243	123	42 + 3 × 27
					330	4 × 42 + 6 × 27

Second Case: Price of production declines.

Variant 1: Productivity of the second investment of capital remains the same. Soil A is excluded from competition and soil B becomes rentless.

TABLE XVI

Type of Soil	*Price of Production Sh.*	*Output Bushels*	*Selling Price Sh.*	*Proceeds Sh.*	*Rent Sh.*	*Rent Increase*
B	60 + 60 = 120	12 + 12 = 24	5	120	0	0
C	60 + 60 = 120	14 + 14 = 28	5	140	20	20
D	60 + 60 = 120	16 + 16 = 32	5	160	40	2 × 20
E	60 + 60 = 120	18 + 18 = 36	5	180	60	3 × 20
					120	6 × 20

Variant 2: Productivity of the second investment of capital declines; soil A is excluded from competition and soil B becomes rentless.

TABLE XVII

Type of Soil	*Price of Production Sh.*	*Output Bushels*	*Selling Price Sh.*	*Proceeds Sh.*	*Rent Sh.*	*Rent Increase*
B	60 + 60 = 120	12 + 9 = 21	5 5/7	120	0	0
C	60 + 60 = 120	14 + 10½ = 24½	5 5/7	140	20	20
D	60 + 60 = 120	16 + 12 = 28	5 5/7	160	40	2 × 20
E	60 + 60 = 120	18 + 13½ = 31½	5 5/7	180	60	3 × 20
					120	6 × 20

Variant 3: Productivity of the second investment of capital increases; soil A remains in competition; soil B yields rent.

TABLE XVIII

Type of Soil	*Price of Production Sh.*	*Output Bushels*	*Selling Price Sh.*	*Proceeds Sh.*	*Rent Sh.*	*Rent Increase*
A	60 + 60 = 120	10 + 15 = 25	4 4/5	120	0	0
B	60 + 60 = 120	12 + 18 = 30	4 4/5	144	24	24
C	60 + 60 = 120	14 + 21 = 35	4 4/5	168	48	2 × 24
D	60 + 60 = 120	16 + 24 = 46	4 4/5	192	72	3 × 24
E	60 + 60 = 120	18 + 27 = 45	4 4/5	216	96	4 × 24
					240	10 × 24

Case: Price of production rises.

A) Soil A remains rentless and continues to regulate the price.

Variant 1: Productivity of the second investment of capital remains the same: this requires decreasing productivity of the first investment of capital.

TABLE XIX

Type of Soil	*Price of Production Sh.*	*Output Bushels*	*Selling Price Sh.*	*Proceeds Sh.*	*Rent Sh.*	*Rent Increase*
A	60 + 60 = 120	7½ + 10 = 17½	6 6/7	120	0	0
B	60 + 60 = 120	9 + 12 = 21	6 6/7	144	24	24
C	60 + 60 = 120	10½ + 14 = 24½	6 6/7	168	48	2 × 24
D	60 + 60 = 120	12 + 16 = 28	6 6/7	192	72	3 × 24
E	60 + 60 = 120	13½ + 18 = 31½	6 6/7	216	96	4 × 24
					240	10 × 24

Variant 2: Productivity of the second investment of capital decreases; which does not exclude constant productivity of the first investment.

TABLE XXI

Type of Soil	*Price of Production Sh.*	*Output Bushels*	*Selling Price Sh.*	*Proceeds Sh.*	*Rent Sh.*	*Rent Increase*
A	60 + 60 = 120	5 + 12½ = 17½	6 6/7	120	0	0
B	60 + 60 = 120	6 + 15 = 21	6 6/7	144	24	24
C	60 + 60 = 120	7 + 17½ = 24½	6 6/7	168	48	2 × 24
D	60 + 60 = 120	8 + 20 = 28	6 6/7	192	72	3 × 24
E	60 + 60 = 120	9 + 22½ = 31½	6 6/7	216	96	4 × 24
					240	10 × 24

B) An inferior soil (designated as a) becomes the price regulator and soil A thus yields rent. This makes admissible for all variants constant productivity of the second investment.

Variant 1: Productivity of the second investment of capital remains the same.

TABLE XXII

Type of Soil	*Price of Production Sh.*	*Output Bushels*	*Selling Price Sh.*	*Proceeds Sh.*	*Rent Sh.*	*Rent Increase*
a	120	16	7½	120	0	0
A	60 + 60 = 120	10 + 10 = 20	7½	150	30	30
B	60 + 60 = 120	12 + 12 = 24	7½	180	60	2 × 30
C	60 + 60 = 120	14 + 14 = 28	7½	210	90	3 × 30
D	60 + 60 = 120	16 + 16 = 32	7½	240	120	4 × 30
E	60 + 60 = 120	18 + 18 = 36	7½	270	150	5 × 30
					450	15 × 30

Variant 2: Productivity of the second investment of capital declines.

TABLE XXIII

Type of Soil	Price of Production Sh.	Output Bushels	Selling Price Sh.	Proceeds Sh.	Rent Sh.	Rent Increase
A	120	15	8	120	0	0
A	60 + 60 = 120	10 + 7½ = 17½	8	140	20	20
B	60 + 60 = 120	12 + 9 = 21	8	168	48	20 + 28
C	60 + 60 = 120	14 + 10½ = 24½	8	196	76	20 + 2 × 28
D	60 + 60 = 120	16 + 12 = 28	8	224	104	20 + 3 × 28
E	60 + 60 = 120	18 + 13½ = 31½	8	252	132	20 + 4 × 28
					380	5 × 20 + 10 × 28

Variant 3: Productivity of the second investment increases.

TABLE XXIV

Type of Soil	Price of Production Sh.	Output Bushels	Selling Price Sh.	Proceeds Sh.	Rent Sh.	Rent Increase
A	120	16	7½	120	0	0
A	60 + 60 = 120	10 + 12½ = 21½	7½	168¾	48¾	15 + 33¾
B	60 + 60 = 120	12 + 15 = 27	7½	202½	82½	15 + 2 × 33¾
C	60 + 60 = 120	14 + 17½ = 31½	7½	236¼	116¼	15 + 3 × 33¾
D	60 + 60 = 120	16 + 20 = 36	7½	270	150	15 + 4 × 33¾
E	60 + 60 = 120	18 + 22½ = 40½	7½	303¾	183¾	15 + 5 × 33¾
					581¼	5 × 15 + 15 × 33¾

These tables lead to the following conclusions:

In the first place, the sequence of rents behaves exactly as the sequence of fertility differences—taking the rentless regulating soil as the zero point. It is not the absolute yield, but only the differences in yield which are the factors determining rent. Whether the various soils yield 1, 2, 3, 4, 5 bushels, or whether they yield 11, 12, 13, 14, 15 bushels per acre, the rents in both cases form the sequence 0, 1, 2, 3, 4 bushels, or their equivalent in money.

But far more important is the result with respect to the total rent yields for repeated investment of capital in the same land.

In five out of the thirteen analysed cases, the total rent doubles when the investment of capital is doubled; instead of l0x12 shillings it becomes 10 × 24 shillings = 240 shillings. These cases are:

Case I, constant price, variant 1: constant production rise (Table XII).

Case II, falling price, variant 3: increasing production rise (Table XVIII).

Case III, increasing price, first eventuality (where soil A remains the regulator), in all three variants (tables XIX, XX and XXI).

In four cases the rent more than doubles, namely:

Case I, variant 3, constant price, but increasing production rise (Table XV) The total rent climbs to 330 shillings.

Case III, second eventuality (where soil A yields rent), in all three variants (Table XXII, rent = 15 × 30 = 450 shillings; Table XXIII, rent = 5 × 20 + 10 × 28 = 380 shillings; Table XXIV, rent = 5 × 15 + 15 × 33¾ = 581¼ shillings).

In one case the rent rises, but not to twice the amount yielded by the first investment of capital:

Case I, constant price, variant 2: falling productivity of the second investment, under conditions whereby B does not become completely rentless (Table XIV, rent = 4 × 6 + 6 × 21 = 150 shillings).

Finally, only in three cases does the total rent remain at the same level with a second investment—for all soils taken together—as with the first investment (Table XI); these are the cases in which soil A is excluded from competition and B becomes the regulator and thereby rentless soil. Thus, the rent for B not only vanishes but is also deducted from every succeeding term of the rent sequence; the result is thus determined. These cases are:

Case I, variant 2, when the conditions are such that soil A is excluded (Table XIII). The total rent is 6 × 20, or 10 × 12 = 120, as in Table XI.

Case II, variants I and 2. Here soil A is necessarily excluded in accordance with the assumptions (tables XVI and XVII) and the total rent is again 6 × 20 = 10 × 12 = 120 shillings.

Thus, this means: In the great majority of all possible cases the rent rises—per acre of rent-bearing land as well as particularly in its total amount—as a result of an increased investment of capital in the land. Only in three out of the thirteen analysed cases does its total remain unaltered. These are the cases in which the lowest quality soil—hitherto the regulator and rentless—is eliminated from competition and the next quality soil takes its place, i.e., becomes rentless. But even in these cases, the rents upon the superior soils rise in comparison with the rents due to the first capital investment; when the rent for C falls from 24 to 20, then those for D and E rise from 36 and 48 to 40 and 60 shillings respectively.

A fall in the total rents below the level for the first investment of capital (Table XI) would be possible only if soil B as well as soil A were to be excluded from competition and soil C were to become regulating and rentless.

Thus, the more capital is invested in the land, and the higher the development of agriculture and civilisation in general in a given country, the more rents rise per acre as well as in total amount, and the more immense becomes the tribute paid by society to the big landowners in the form of surplus-profits—so long as the various soils, once taken under cultivation, are all able to continue competing.

This law accounts for the amazing vitality of the class of big landlords. No social class lives so sumptuously, no other class claims the right it does to traditional luxury in keeping with its 'estate,' regardless of where the money for this purpose may be derived, and no other class piles debt upon debt so lightheartedly. And yet it always lands again on its feet—thanks to the capital invested by other people in the land, which yields it a rent, completely out of proportion to the profits reaped therefrom by the capitalist.

However, the same law also explains why the vitality of the big landlord is gradually being exhausted.

When the English corn duties were abolished in 1846, the English manufacturers believed that they had thereby turned the land-owning aristocracy into paupers. Instead, they became richer than ever. How did this occur? Very simply. In the first place, the farmers were now compelled by contract to invest £12 per acre annually instead of £8. And secondly, the landlords, being strongly represented in the Lower House too, granted themselves a large government subsidy for drainage projects and other permanent improvements on their land. Since no total displacement of the poorest soil took place, but rather, at worst, it became employed for other purposes—and mostly only temporarily—rents rose in proportion to the increased investment of capital, and the landed aristocracy consequently was better off than ever before.

But everything is transitory. Transoceanic steamships and the railways of North and South America and India enabled some very singular tracts of land to compete in European grain markets. These were, on the one hand, the North American prairies and the Argentine pampas—plains cleared for the plough by Nature itself, and virgin soil which offered rich harvests for years to come even with primitive cultivation and without fertilisers. And, on the other hand, there were the land holdings of Russian and Indian communist communities which had to sell a portion of their produce, and a constantly increasing one at that, for the purpose of obtaining money for taxes wrung from them—frequently by means of torture—by a ruthless and despotic state. These products were sold without regard to price of production, they were sold at the price which the dealer offered, because the peasant perforce needed money without fail when taxes became due. And in face of this competition—coming from virgin plains as well as from Russian and Indian peasants ground down by taxation—the European tenant farmer and peasant could not prevail at the old rents. A portion of the land in Europe fell decisively out of competition as regards grain cultivation, and rents fell everywhere; our second case, variant 2—falling prices and falling productivity of the additional investment of capital—became the rule for Europe; and therefore the lament of landlords from Scotland to Italy and from southern France to East Prussia. Fortunately, the plains are far from being entirely brought under cultivation; there are enough left to ruin all the big landlords of Europe and the small ones into the bargain—*F.E.*]

The headings under which rent should be analysed are:

A. Differential rent.

1. Conception of differential rent. Water-power as an illustration. Transition to agricultural rent proper.
2. Differential rent I, arising from the varying fertility of various plots of land.
3. Differential rent II, arising from successive investments of capital in the same land. Differential rent II should be analysed:
   a) with a stationary,
   b) falling,
   c) and rising price of production. And also
   d) transformation of surplus-profit into rent.
4) Influence of this rent upon the rate of profit.

B. Absolute rent.

C. The price of land.

D. Final remarks concerning ground-rent.

Over-all conclusions to be drawn from the consideration of differential rent in general are the following:

First, the formation of surplus-profit may take place in various ways. On the one hand, based on differential rent I, that is, on the investment of the entire agricultural capital in land consisting of soils of varying fertility. Or, in the form of differential rent II, based on the varying differential productivity of successive investments of capital in the same land, i.e., a greater productivity—expressed, e.g., in quarters of wheat—than is secured with the same investment of capital in the worst land—rentless, but which regulates the price of production. But no matter how this surplus-profit may arise, its transformation into rent, i.e., its transfer from farmer to landlord, always presupposes that the various actual individual production prices of the partial outputs of the individual successive investments of capital (i.e., independent of the general price of production by which the market is regulated) have previously been reduced to an individual average price of production. The excess of the general regulating production price of the output per acre over this individual average production price constitutes and is a measure of the rent per acre. In the case of differential rent I, the differential results are in themselves distinguishable because they take place upon different portions of land—distinct from one another and existing side by side—given an investment of capital per acre and a degree of cultivation considered normal. In the case of differential rent II, they must first be made distinguishable; they must in fact be transformed back into differential rent I, and this can only take place in the indicated way. For example, let us take Table III, S. 226.

Soil B yields for the first invested capital of £2½—2 quarters per acre, and for the second investment of equal magnitude—1½ quarters; together—3½ quarters from the same acre. It is not possible to distinguish which part of these 3½ quarters is a product of invested capital I and which part a product of invested capital II, for it is all grown upon the same soil. In fact, the 3½ quarters is the yield from the total capital of £5; and the actual fact of the matter is simply this: a capital of £2½ yielded 2 quarters, and a capital of £5 yielded 3½ quarters rather than 4 quarters. The situation would be just the same if the £5 yielded 4 quarters, i.e., if the yield from both investments of capital were equal; similarly, if the yield were even 5 quarters, i.e., if the second investment of capital were to yield a surplus of 1 quarter. The price of production of the first 2 quarters is £1½ per quarter, and that of the second 1½ quarters is £2 per quarter. Consequently the 3½ quarters together cost £6. This is the individual price of production of the total product, and, on the average, amounts to £1 14 2/7 sh. per quarter, i.e., approximately £1¾. With the general price of production determined by soil A, namely £3, this results in a surplus-profit of £1¼ per quarter, and thus for the 3½ quarters, a total of £4 3/8. At the average price of production of B this corresponds to about 1½ quarters. In other words, the surplus-profit from B is represented by an aliquot portion of the output from B, i.e., by the 1½ quarters, which express the rent in terms of grain, and which sell—in accordance with the general price of production—for £4½. But on the other hand, the excess product from an acre of B over that from an acre of A does not automatically represent surplus-profit, and thereby surplus-product. According to our assumption, an acre of B yields 3½ quarters, whereas an acre of A yields only 1 quarter. Excess product from B is, therefore, 2½ quarters but the surplus-product is only 1½ quarters; for the capital invested in B is twice that invested in A, and thus its price of production is double. If an investment of £5 were also to take place in A, and the rate of productivity were to remain the same, then the output would be 2 quarters instead of 1 quarter, and it would then be seen that the actual surplus-product is determined by comparing 3½ with 2, not 3½ with 1; i.e., it is only 1½ quarters, not 2½ quarters. Furthermore, if a third investment of capital, amounting to £2½, were made in B, and this were to yield only 1 quarter—this quarter would then cost £3 as in A—its selling price of £3 would only cover the price of production, would provide only the average profit, but no surplus-profit, and would thus yield nothing that could be transformed into rent. The comparison of the output per acre from any given soil type with the output per acre from soil A does not show whether it is the output from an equal or from a larger investment of capital, nor whether the additional output only covers the price of production or is due to greater productivity of the additional capital.

Secondly, assuming a decreasing rate of productivity for the additional investments of capital whose limit, so far as the new formation of surplus-profit is concerned, is that investment of capital which just covers the price of production, i.e., which produces a quarter as dearly as the same investment of capital in an acre of soil A, namely, at £3, according to our assumption—it follows from what has just been said: that the limit, where the total investment of capital in an acre of B would no longer yield any rent, is reached when the individual average production price of output per acre of B would rise to the price of production per acre of A.

If only investments of capital are made in B that yield the price of production, i.e., yield no surplus-profit nor new rent, then this indeed raises the individual average price of production per quarter, but does not affect the surplus-profit, and eventually the rent, formed by previous investments of capital. For the average price of production always remains below that of A, and when the price excess per quarter decreases, the number of quarters increases proportionately, so that the total excess in price remains unaltered.

In the case assumed, the first two investments of capital in B amounting to £5 yield 3½ quarters, thus according to our assumption 1½ quarters of rent = £4½. Now, if a third investment of £2½ is made, but one which yields only an additional quarter, then the total price of production (including 20% profit) of the 4½ quarters = £9; thus the average price per quarter = £2. The average price of production per quarter upon B has thus risen from £1 5/7 to £2, and the surplus-profit per quarter, compared with the regulating price of A, has fallen from £1 2/7 to £1. But 1 × 4½ = £4½ just as formerly 1 2/7 × 3½ = £4½.

Let us assume that a fourth and fifth additional investment of capital, amounting to £2½ each, are made in B, which do no more than produce a quarter at its general price of production. The total product per acre would then be 6½ quarters and their price of production £15. The average price of production per quarter for B would have risen again—from £2 [In the German 1894 edition this reads: 1.—*Ed.*] to £2 4/13—and the surplus-profit per quarter, compared with the regulating price of production of A, would have dropped again—from £1 to £ 9/13. But these £9/13 would now have to be calculated upon the basis of 6½ quarters instead of 4½ quarters. And 9/13 × 6½ = 1 × 4½ = 4½.

It follows from this, firstly, that no increase in the regulating price of production is necessary under these circumstances, in order to make possible additional investments of capital in the rent-bearing soil—even to the point where the additional capital completely ceases to produce surplus-profit and continues to yield only the average profit. It follows furthermore that the total surplus-profit per acre remains the same here, no matter how much surplus-profit per quarter may decrease; this decrease is always balanced by a corresponding increase in the number of quarters produced per acre. In order that the average price of production might reach the level of the general price of production (hence £3 for soil B), it is necessary that supplementary investments be made whose output has a higher price of production than the regulating one of £3. But we shall see that this alone does not suffice without further ado to raise the average price of production per quarter of B to the general price of production of £3.

Let us assume that soil B produced:

1. 3½ quarters whose price of production is, as before, £6, i.e., two investments of capital amounting to £2½ each both yielding surplus-profit, but of decreasing amount.
2. 1 quarter at £3, an investment of capital in which the individual price of production is equal to the regulating price of production.
3. 1 quarter at £4, an investment of capital in which the individual price of production is higher by 33% than the regulating price.

We should then have 5½ quarters per acre for £13 with an investment of a capital of £10 7/10; this is four times the original invested capital, but not quite three times the output of the first investment of capital.

5½ quarters at £13 gives an average price of production of £2 4/11 per quarter, i.e., an excess of £7/11 per quarter, assuming the regulating price of production of £3. This excess may be transformed into rent. 5½ quarters sold at the regulating price of production of £3 yield £16½. After deducting the production price of £13, a surplus-profit, or rent, of £3½ remains, which, calculated at the present average price of production per quarter of B, that is, at £24/11 per quarter, represents 1 25/52 quarters. The money-rent would be lower by £1 and the grain-rent by about ½ quarter, but in spite of the fact that the fourth additional investment of capital in B not only fails to yield surplus-profit, but yields less than the average profit, surplus-profit, and rent still continue to exist. Let us assume that, in addition to investment 3), investment 2) also produces at a price exceeding the regulating price of production. Then the total production is: 3½ quarters for £6 + 2 quarters for £8; total 5½ quarters for £14 production price. The average price of production per quarter would be £2 6/11 and would leave an excess of £5/11. The 5½ quarters, sold at £3, give a total of £16½; deducting the £14 production price leaves £2½ for rent. At the present average price of production upon B, this would be equivalent to 55/56 of a quarter. In other words, rent is still yielded although less than before.

This shows, at any rate, that with additional investments of capital in the better soils whose output costs more than the regulating price of production the rent does not disappear—at least not within the bounds of admissible practice—although it must decrease. It will decrease in proportion, on the one hand, to the aliquot part formed by this less productive capital in the total investment of capital, and on the other hand, in proportion to the decrease in its productiveness. The average price of its produce would still lie below the regulating price and would thus still permit surplus-profit to be formed that could be transformed into rent.

Let us now assume that, as a result of four successive investments of capital (£2½, £2½, £5 and £5) with decreasing productivity, the average price per quarter of B coincides with the general price of production.

				Price of Production				*Surplus for Rent*	
Capital £		*Profit £*	*Output Qrs*	*Per Qr £*	*Total £*	*Selling Price £*	*Proceeds £*	*Qrs*	*£*
1)	2½	½	2	1½	3	3	6	1	3
2)	2½	½	1½	2	3	3	4½	½	1½
3)	5	1	1½	4	6	3	4½	-½	-1½
4)	5	1	1	6	6	3	3	-1	-3
	15	3	6		18		18	0	0

The farmer, in this case, sells every quarter at its individual price of production, and consequently the total number of quarters at their average price of production per quarter, which coincides with the regulating price of £3. Hence he still makes a profit of 20% = £3 upon his capital of £15. But the rent is gone. What has become of the excess in this equalisation of the individual prices of production per quarter with the general price of production?

The surplus-profit from the first £2½ was £3, from the second £2½ it was £1½; total surplus-profit from ⅓ of the invested capital, that is, from £5 = £4½ = 90%.

In the case of investment 3), the £5 not only fails to yield surplus-profit, but its output of 1½ quarters, sold at the general price of production, gives a deficit of £1½. Finally, in the case of investment 4), which likewise amounts to £5 its output of I quarter, sold at the general price of production, gives a deficit of £3. Both investments of capital together thus give a deficit of £4½, which is equal to the surplus-profit of £4½, realised from investments 4) and 2).

The surplus-profit and deficit balance out. Therefore the rent disappears. In fact, this is possible only because the elements of surplus-value, which formed surplus-profit or rent, now enter into the formation of the average profit. The farmers makes this average profit of £3 on £15, or 20%, at the expense of the rent.

The equalisation of the individual average price of production of B to the general price of production of A, which regulates the market-price, presupposes that the difference of the individual price of the produce from the first investments of capital below the regulating price is more and more compensated and finally balanced out by the difference of the price of the produce from the subsequent investments of capital above the regulating price. What appears as surplus-profit, so long as the produce from the first investments of capital is sold by itself, thus gradually becomes part of its average price of production, and thereby enters into the formation of the average profit, until it is finally completely absorbed by it.

If only £5 are invested in B instead of £15 and the additional 2½ quarters of the last table are produced by taking 2½ new acres of A under cultivation with an investment of £2½ per acre, then the additional invested capital would amount to only £6¼, i.e., the total investment in A and B for the production of these 6 quarters would be only £11¼, instead of £15, and their total price of production, including profit, £13½. The 6 quarters would still be sold for £18, but the investment of capital would have decreased by £3¾, and the rent from B would be £4½ per acre, as before. It would be different if the production of the additional 2½ quarters required that a soil inferior to A, for instance, A_{-1} and A_{-2}, be taken under cultivation; so that the price of production per quarter would be: for 1½ quarters on soil A_{-1} = £4, and for the last quarter on soil A_{-2} = £6. In this case, £6 would be the regulating price of production per quarter. The 3½ quarters from B would then be sold for £21 instead of £10½, which would mean a rent of £15 instead of £4½, or, a rent in grain of 2½ quarters instead of 1½ quarters. Similarly, a quarter on A would now yield a rent of £3 = ½ quarter.

Before discussing this point further, another observation:

The average price of a quarter from B is equalised, i.e., coincides with the general production price of £3 per quarter, regulated by A, as soon as that portion of the total capital which produces the excess of 1½ quarters is balanced by that portion of the total capital which produces the deficit of 1½ quarters. How soon this equalisation is effected, or how much capital with under-productiveness must be invested in B for this purpose, will depend, assuming the surplus-productivity of the first investments of capital to be given, upon the relative under-productiveness of the later investments compared with an investment of the same amount in the worst, regulating soil A, or upon the individual price of production of their produce, compared with the regulating price.

The following conclusions can now be drawn from the foregoing:

First: So long as the additional capitals are invested in the same land with surplus-productivity, even if the surplus-productivity is decreasing, the absolute rent per acre in grain and money increases, although it decreases relatively, in proportion to the advanced capital (in other words, the rate of surplus-profit or rent). The limit is established here by that additional capital which yields only the average profit, or for whose produce the individual price of production coincides with the general price of production. The price of production remains the same under these circumstances, unless the production from the poorer soils becomes superfluous as a result of increased supply. Even when the price is falling, these additional capitals may within certain limits still produce surplus-profit, though less of it.

Secondly: The investment of additional capital yielding only the average profit, whose surplus-productivity therefore = 0, does not alter in any way the amount of the existing surplus-profit, and consequently of rent. The individual average price per quarter increases thereby upon the superior soils; the excess per quarter decreases, but the number of quarters which contain this decreased excess increases, so that the mathematical product remains the same.

Thirdly: Additional investments of capital, the produce of which has an individual price of production exceeding the regulating price—the surplus-productivity is therefore not merely = 0, but less than zero, or a negative quantity, that is, less than the productivity of an equal investment of capital in the regulating soil A—bring the individual average price of production of the total output from the superior soil closer and closer to the general price of production, i.e., reduce more and more the difference between them which constitutes the surplus-profit, or rent. An increasingly greater part of what constituted surplus-profit or rent enters into the formation of the average profit. But nevertheless, the total capital invested in an acre of B continues to yield surplus-profit, although the latter decreases as the amount of capital with under-productiveness increases and to the extent of this under-productiveness. The rent, with increasing capital and increasing production, in this case decreases absolutely per acre, not merely relatively with reference to the increasing magnitude of the invested capital, as in the second case.

The rent can be eliminated only when the individual average price of production of the total output from the better soil B coincides with the regulating price, so that the entire surplus-profit from the first more productive investments of capital is consumed in the formation of average profit.

The minimum limit of the drop in rent per acre is that point at which it disappears. But this point does not occur as soon as the additional investments of capital are under-productive, but rather as soon as the additional investment of under-productive capital becomes so large in magnitude that its effect is to cancel the over-productiveness of the first investments of capital, so that the productiveness of the total invested capital becomes the same as that of the capital invested in A, and the individual average price per quarter of B becomes, therefore, the same as that per quarter of A.

In this case too, the regulating price of production, £3 per quarter, would remain the same, although the rent had disappeared. Only beyond this point would the price of production have to rise in consequence of an increase either in the extent of under-productiveness of the additional capital or in the magnitude of the additional capital of equal under-productiveness. For instance, if, in the above table 2½ quarters were produced instead of 1½ quarters upon the same soil at £4 per quarter, we would have had a total of 7 quarters for £22 price of production; a quarter would have cost £3 1/7 it would thus be £1/7 above the general price of production, and the latter would therefore, have to rise.

For a long time, then, additional capital with under-productiveness, or even increasing under- productiveness, might be invested until the individual average price per quarter from the best soils became equal to the general price of production, until the excess of the latter over the former—and thereby the surplus-profit and the rent—entirely disappeared.

And even then, the disappearance of rent from the better soils would only signify that the individual average price of their produce coincides with the general price of production, so that an increase in the latter would not yet be required.

In the above illustration, upon better soil B—which is however the lowest in the sequence of better or rent-bearing soils—3½ quarters were produced by a capital of £5 with surplus-productiveness and 2½ quarters by a capital of £10 with under-productiveness, i.e., a total of 6 quarters; 5½ of this total is thus produced by the latter portions of capital with under-productiveness. And it is only at this point that the individual average price of production of the 6 quarters rises to £3 per quarter and thus coincides with the general price of production.

Under the law of landed property, however, the latter 2½ quarters could not have been produced in this way at £3 per quarter, except when they could be produced upon 2½ new acres of soil A. The case in which the additional capital produces only at the general price of production, would have constituted the limit. Beyond this point, the additional investment of capital in the same land would have had to cease.

Indeed, if, the farmer once pays £4½ rent for the first two investments of capital, he must continue to pay it, and every investment of capital which produced a quarter for more than £3 [In the German 1894 edition this reads: for less than £3.—*Ed.*] would result in a deduction from his profit. The equalisation of the individual average price, in the case of under-productiveness, is thereby prevented.

Let us take this case in the previous illustration, where the price of production for soil A, £3 per quarter, regulates the price for B.

					Selling Price			
Capital £	*Profit £*	*Price of Production £*	*Output Qrs*	*Price of Production per Qr £*	*Per Qr £*	*Total £*	*Surplus-Profit £*	*Loss £*
2½	½	3	2	1½	3	6	3	—
2½	½	3	1½	2	3	4½	1½	—
5	1	6	1½	4*	3	4½	—	1½
5	1	6	1	6	3	3	—	3
15	3	18				18	4½	4½

[* In the German 1894 edition this reads: 3.—Ed.]

The price of production for the 3½ quarters in the first two investments of capital is likewise £3 per quarter for the farmer, since he has to pay a rent of £4½; thus the difference between his individual price of production and the general price of production is not pocketed by him. For him, then, the excess in produce price for the first two investments of capital cannot serve to balance out the deficit incurred by the produce in the third and fourth investments of capital.

The 1½ quarters from investment 3 cost the farmer £6, profit included: but at the regulating price of £3 per quarter, he can sell them for only £4½. In other words, he would not only lose his whole profit, but &#163½, or 10% of his invested capital of £5, over and above it. The loss of profit and capital in the case of investment 3 would amount to £4½, and in the case of investment 4 to £3, i.e., a total of £4½, or just as much as the rent from the better investments of capital; the individual price of production for the latter, however, cannot take part in equalising the individual average price of production of the total product from B, because the excess is paid out as rent to a third party.

If it were necessary, to meet the demand, to produce the additional 1½ quarters by the third investment of capital the regulating market-price would have to rise to £4 per quarter. In consequence of this rise in the regulating market-price, the rent from B would rise for the first and second investments, and rent would he formed upon A.

Thus although differential rent is but a formal transformation of surplus-profit into rent, and property in land merely enables the owner in this case to transfer the surplus-profit of the farmer to himself, we find nevertheless that successive investment of capital in the same land, or, what amounts to the same thing, the increase in capital invested in the same land, reaches its limit far more rapidly when the rate of productiveness of the capital decreases and the regulating price remains the same; in fact a more or less artificial barrier is reached as a consequence of the mere formal transformation of surplus-profit into ground-rent, which is the result of landed property. The rise in the general price of production, which becomes necessary here within more narrow limits than otherwise, is in this case not merely the cause of the increase in differential rent, but the existence of differential rent as rent is at the same time the reason for the earlier and more rapid rise in the general price of production—in order to ensure thereby the increased supply of produce that has become necessary.

The following should furthermore be noted:

By an additional investment of capital in soil B, the regulating price could not, as above, rise to £4 if soil A were to supply the additional produce below £4 by a second investment of capital, or if new and worse soil than A, whose price of production were indeed higher than £3 but lower than £4, were to enter into competition. We see, then, that differential rent I and differential rent II, while the first is the basis of the second, serve simultaneously as limits for one another, whereby now a successive investment of capital in the same land, now an investment of capital side by side in new additional land, is made. In like manner they limit each other in other cases; for instance, when better soil is taken up.

44

Differential Rent Also on the Worst Cultivated Soil

Let us assume the demand for grain is rising, and the supply can only result from successive investments of capital under conditions of under-productiveness in the rent-bearing soils, or by additional investment of capital, also with decreasing productivity, in soil A, or by the investment of capital in new lands of inferior quality than A.

Let us take soil B as representative of the rent-bearing soils.

The additional investment of capital demands an increase in the market-price above the hitherto prevailing price of production of £3 per quarter, in order to make possible the increased production upon B of one quarter (which may here stand for one million quarters, just as every acre may stand for one million acres). Increased output may also be yielded by soils C and D, etc., the soils bearing the highest rent, but only with decreasing surplus-productiveness; but it is assumed that the quarter from B is necessary in order to meet the demand. If this quarter is more cheaply produced by investing more capital in B than with the same addition of capital to A, or by descending to soil A - 1, which may, e.g., require £4 to produce a quarter, whereas the addition to capital A might do so for £3¾, then the additional capital on B will regulate the market-price.

A produces a quarter for £3, as heretofore. Similarly B, as before, produces a total of 3½ quarters at an individual price of production of £6 for its total output. Now, if an additional £4 of production price (including profit) becomes necessary on B in order to produce an additional quarter, whereas it could have been produced on A for £3¾, then it would naturally be produced on A, rather than on B. Let us assume, then, that it can be produced on B with the additional price of production of £3½. In this case, £3½ would become the regulating price for the entire output. B would now sell its present output of 4½ quarters for £15¾. Of this £6 is the price of production for the first 3½ quarters and the £3½ for the last quarter, i.e., a total of £9½. This leaves a surplus-profit for rent = £6¼ as against the former £4½. In this case, an acre of A would also yield a rent of £1½; but it would not be the worst soil A, but rather the better soil B that would regulate the price of production of £3½. Of course, we assume here that new soil of quality A and equally favourable location as that hitherto cultivated is not available, but that either a second investment of capital in the already cultivated plot A at a higher price of production, or the cultivation of an even poorer soil A-1, is required. As soon as differential rent II comes into force through successive investments of capital, the limits of the rising price of production may be regulated by better soil; and the worst soil, the basis of differential rent I, may also yield rent. This, even with a single differential rent, all cultivated land would yield rent. We would then have the following two tables, where by price of production we mean the sum of the invested capital plus 20% profit; in other words, on every £2½ of capital £½ of profit or a total of £3.

Type of Soil	*Acres*	*Price of Production £*	*Output Qrs*	*Selling Price £*	*Pro-ceeds £*	*Grain-Rent Qrs*	*Money-Rent £*
A	1	3	1	3	3	0	0
B	1	6	3½	3	10½	1½	4½
C	1	6	5½	3	16½	3½	10½
D	1	6	7½	3	22½	5½	16½
Total	4	21	17½		52½	10½	31½

This is the state of affairs before the new capital of £3½, which yields only one quarter, is invested in B. After this investment, the situation looks as follows:

Type of Soil	*Acres*	*Price of Production £*	*Output Qrs*	*Selling Price £*	*Pro-ceeds £*	*Grain-Rent Qrs*	*Money-Rent £*
A	1	3	1	3½	3½	1/7	½
B	1	9½	4½	3½	15¾	1 11/14	6¼
C	1	6	5½	3½	19¼	3 11/14	13¼
D	1	6	7½	3½	26¼	5 11/14	20¼
Total	4	24½	18½		64¾	11½	40¼

[This, again, is not quite correctly calculated. First of all, the cost of the 4½ qrs for farmer B is, in the first place, £9½: in price of production and, secondly, £4½ in rent, i.e., a total of £14; average per quarter = £3½. This average price of his total production thus becomes the regulating market-price. Thus, the rent on A would amount to £1/9 instead of £½, and that on B would remain £4½ as heretofore; 4½ qrs at £3½ = £14 and, if we deduct £9½ in price of production, £4½ remain for surplus-profit. We see, then, that in spite of the required change in numerical values this illustration shows how, by means of differential rent II, better soil, already yielding rent, may regulate the price and thus transform *all* soil, even hitherto rentless, into rent-bearing soil.—*F. E.*]

The grain-rent must rise as soon as the regulating price of production of the grain rises, i.e., as soon as the price of production of a quarter of grain from the regulating soil, or the regulating invested capital in one of the various soil types, rises. It is the same as though all soils had become less productive and produced, e.g., only 5/7 quarter instead of 1 quarter with every new investment of £2½. Whatever else they produce in grain with the same investment of capital is transformed into surplus-product, which represents the surplus-profit, and therefore, the rent. Assuming the rate of profit remains the same, the farmer can buy less grain with his profit. The rate of profit may remain the same if wages do not rise—either because they are depressed to the physical minimum, i.e., below the normal value of labour-power; or because the other articles of consumption needed by the labourer and supplied by manufacture have become relatively cheaper; or because the working day has become longer or more intensive, so that the rate of profit in non-agricultural lines of production, which, however, regulates the agricultural profit, has remained the same or has risen; or, finally, because more constant and less variable capital is employed in agriculture, even though the amount of capital invested is the same.

We have thus considered the first method by which rent may arise on the hitherto worst soil A without taking still worse soil under cultivation; that is, rent may arise from the difference between its individual, hitherto regulating, price of production and the new, higher price of production, whereby the last additional capital employed under conditions of under-productiveness upon the better soil supplies the necessary additional produce.

If the additional produce had to be supplied by soil A-1, which cannot produce a quarter for less than £4, then the rent per acre of A would have risen to £1. But, in this case, soil A-1 would have taken the place of A as the worst cultivated soil, and the latter would have moved into the lowest position in the sequence of rent-bearing soils. Differential rent I would have changed. This case, then, is not included in the consideration of differential rent II, which arises from the varying productiveness of successive investments of capital in the same piece of land.

But aside from this, differential rent may arise on soil A in two other ways.

With the price unchanged—any given price, even a lower one compared to former ones—when the additional investment of capital results in surplus-productiveness, which *prima facie*, and up to a certain point must always be the case precisely on the worst soil.

Secondly, however, when the productiveness of successive investments of capital in soil A decreases.

It is assumed in both cases that the increased production is required to meet demand.

But from the point of view of differential rent, a peculiar difficulty arises here owing to the previously developed law—according to which it is always the individual average price of production per quarter for the total production (or the total outlay of capital) which acts as the determining factor. In the case of soil A, however, there is not, as in the cases of the better soils, another price of production which limits for new investments of capital the equalisation of the individual with the general price of production. For the individual price of production of A is precisely the general price of production regulating the market-price.

Let us assume:

1. *When the productiveness of successive investments of capital is increasing*, 1 acre of A will produce 3 qrs instead of 2 qrs given an investment of £5—corresponding to a price of production of £6. The first investment of £2½ yielded 1 qr, the second—2 qrs. In this case, a price of production of £6 will yield 3 qrs, so that the average cost of a quarter will be £2; i.e., if the 3 qrs are sold at £2 per quarter, then A, as heretofore, does not yield any rent, but only the basis of differential rent II has been altered; the regulating price of production is now £2 instead of £3; a capital of £2½ now produces an average of 1½ qrs on the worst soil, instead of 1 qr, and now this is the official productivity for all better soils given an investment of £2½. From now on, a portion of their former surplus-product enters into the formation of their necessary output, just as a portion of their surplus-profit enters into forming the average profit.

On the other hand, if the calculation is made upon the basis of better soils, where the average calculation does not alter the absolute surplus at all, because for them the general price of production is the limit for the investment of capital, then a quarter from the first investment of capital costs £3 and the 2 qrs from the second investment cost only £1½ each. This would thereby give rise to a grain-rent of 1 qr and a money-rent of £3 on A, but the 3 qrs would be sold for the old price of £9. If a third investment of £2½ were made under conditions of the same productiveness as the second investment, then the total would be 5 qrs for a price of production of £9. If the individual average price of production of A should remain the regulating price, then a quarter would now be sold at £1 4/5. The average price would have fallen once more—not through a new rise in productiveness of the third investment of capital, but merely through the addition of a new investment of capital having the same additional productiveness as the second. Instead of raising the rent as on the rent-bearing soils, the successive investments of capital in soil A of higher, but constant productiveness would proportionally lower the price of production and thereby, everything else being equal, the differential rent on all other soils. On the other hand, if the first investment of capital which produces 1 qr at a price of production of £3 should in itself remain regulating, then 5 qrs would be sold for £15, and the differential rent of the later investments of capital in soil A would amount to £6. The additional capital per acre of soil A, however it is applied, would be an improvement in this case, and would make the original portion of capital more productive. It would be ridiculous to say that ⅓ of the capital had produced 4 qr and the other ⅔—4 qrs. For £9 per acre would always produce 5 qrs, while £3 would produce only 1 qr. Whether or not a rent would arise here, whether or not a surplus-profit would be derived, would depend wholly upon the circumstances. Normally the regulating price of production would have to fall. This would be the case, if this improved but more expensive cultivation of soil A should occur only because it also takes place on the better soils, in other words, if a general revolution in agriculture should occur; so that when we now refer to the natural fertility of soil A, it is assumed that it is worked with £6 or £9 instead of £3. This would particularly apply if the bulk of cultivated acres of soil A, which furnish the main supply of a given country, should employ this new method. But if the improvement should at first extend only to a small area of A, then this better cultivated portion would yield a surplus-profit, which the landlord would be quick to transform wholly or in part into rent, and to fix in the form of rent. In this way—if the demand kept pace with the increasing supply—as more and more of soil A began to employ the new method of cultivation, rent might be gradually formed on all soil of quality A, and the surplus-productivity might be eliminated wholly or in part, depending on market conditions. The equalisation of the price of production of A to the average price of its produce obtained under conditions of increased outlay of capital might thus be prevented by fixing the surplus-profit of this increased investment of capital in the form of rent. Thus, as was previously seen to be the case for the better soils when the productiveness of the additional capital decreased, it would again be the transformation of surplus-profit into ground-rent, i.e., the intervention of property in land, which would raise the price of production, instead of the differential rent merely being the result of the difference between the individual and the general price of production. It would prevent, in the case of soil A, the coincidence of both prices because it would interfere with the regulation of the price of production by the average price of production on A; it would thus maintain a higher price of production than necessary and thereby create rent. Even if grain were freely imported from abroad, the same result could be brought about or perpetuated by compelling farmers to use soil capable of competing in grain cultivation without yielding rent, at the price of production regulated from abroad, for other purposes, e.g., pasturage, so that only rent-bearing soils would be used for grain cultivation, i.e., only soils whose individual average price of production per quarter were below that determined from abroad. On the whole, it is to be assumed that in the given case, the price of production will fall, but not to the level of its average; it will be higher than the average, but below the price of production of the worst cultivated soil A, so that the competition from new soil A is limited.

2. *When the productiveness of additional capitals is decreasing.* Let us assume that soil A-1 requires £4 to produce the additional quarter, whereas soil A produces it for £3¾, i.e., more cheaply, but still £¾ more dearly than the quarter produced by its first investment of capital. In this case, the total price of the two quarters produced upon A would = £6¾; thus the average price per quarter = £3 3/8. The price of production would rise, but only by £3/8, whereas it would rise by another 3/8 or to £3¾, if the additional capital were invested in new land which produced at £3¾, and it would thus bring about a proportional increase in all other differential rents.

The price of production of £3 3/8 per quarter for A would thus be equalised to its average price of production with an increased investment of capital, and would be the regulating price; thus, it would not yield any rent, since it would not produce any surplus-profit.

However, if this quarter, produced by the second investment of capital, were sold for £3¾, soil A would now yield a rent of £¾, and indeed, on all acres of A in which no additional investment of capital had taken place and which thus would still produce at £3 per quarter. So long as any uncultivated fields of A remain, the price could rise only temporarily to £3¾. Competition from new fields of A would hold the price of production at £3 until all land of type A, whose favourable location enables it to produce a quarter at less than £3¾, would be exhausted. This is then what we would assume, although the landlord, so long as an acre of land yields rent, will not let a tenant farmer have another acre rent-free.

It would again depend to what extent a second investment of capital in the available soil A had become general, whether the price of production is equalised at the average price or whether the individual price of production of the second investment of capital becomes regulating at £3¾. The latter occurs only when the landowner has sufficient time until demand is satisfied to fix as rent the surplus-profit derived at the price of £3¾ per qr.

Concerning decreasing productiveness of the soil with successive investments of capital, see Liebig. [Liebig, *Die Chemie in ihrer Anwendung auf Agricultur und Physiologie*, Braunschweig, 1862.—*Ed.*] We have observed that the successive decrease in surplus-productiveness of invested capital invariably increases the rent per acre, so long as the price of production remains constant, and that this may occur even with a falling price of production.

But, in general, the following is to be noted.

From the standpoint of the capitalist mode of production, a relative increase in the price of products always takes place when these products cannot be secured unless an expenditure or payment not previously made is incurred. For by the replacement of capital consumed in production we mean only the replacement of values represented by certain means of production. Natural elements entering as agents into production, and which cost nothing, no matter what role they play in production, do not enter as components of capital, but as a free gift of Nature to capital, that is, as a free gift of Nature's productive power to labour, which, however, appears as the productiveness of capital, as all other productivity under the capitalist mode of production. Therefore, if such a natural power, which originally costs nothing, takes part in production, it does not enter into the determination of price, so long as the product which it helped to produce suffices to meet the demand. But if in the course of development, a larger output is demanded than that which can be supplied with the help of this natural power, i.e., if this additional output must be created without the help of this natural power, or by assisting it with human labour-power, then a new additional element enters into capital. A relatively larger investment of capital is thus required in order to secure the same output. All other circumstances remaining the same, a rise in the price of production takes place.

(From a note-book 'begun in mid-February 1876.' [*F.E.*])

Differential rent and rent as mere interest on capital incorporated in the soil.

The so-called permanent improvements—which change the physical, and, in part, also the chemical conditions of the soil by means of operations requiring an expenditure of capital, and which may be regarded as an incorporation of capital in the soil—nearly all amount to giving a particular piece of land in a certain limited locality such properties as are naturally possessed by some other piece of land elsewhere, sometimes quite near by. One piece of land is naturally level, another has to be levelled; one possesses natural drainage, another requires artificial drainage; one is endowed by Nature with a deep layer of top soil, another needs artificial deepening; one clay soil is naturally mixed with the proper amount of sand, another has to be treated to obtain this proportion; one meadow is naturally irrigated or covered with layers of silt, another requires labour to obtain this condition, or, in the language of bourgeois economics, it requires capital.

It is indeed a truly amusing theory, whereby here, in the case of one piece of land whose comparative advantages have been acquired, rent is interest, whereas in the case of another piece of land which possesses these advantages naturally, it is not interest. (In fact, this is so distorted in practice that since rent really coincides in the one case with interest, it is falsely also called interest in the other cases, where this is positively not the case.) However, land yields rent after capital is invested not because capital is invested, but because the invested capital makes this land more productive than it formerly was. Assuming that all the land of a given country requires this investment of capital, every piece of land which has not received it must first pass through this stage, and the rent (interest yielded in the given case) borne by land already provided with investment of capital constitutes differential rent just as though it naturally possessed this advantage and the other land had first to acquire it artificially.

This rent too, which may be resolved into interest, becomes pure differential rent as soon as the invested capital is amortised. Otherwise, one and the same capital would have to exist twice as capital.

A most amusing phenomenon is that all opponents of Ricardo who oppose the idea that value determination is based exclusively on labour rather than regarding differential rent as arising from differences in soil, point out that here Nature rather than labour determines value; but at the same time they credit this determination to the location of the land, or—and to an even greater extent—the interest on capital put into the land during its cultivation. The same labour produces the same value in a product created during a given period of time; but the magnitude or quantum of this product, and consequently also the portion of value associated with some aliquot part of this product, depends for a given quantity of labour solely upon the quantum of product, and the latter, in turn, depends upon the productivity of the given quantum of labour rather than the absolute magnitude of this quantum. It is immaterial whether this productivity is due to Nature or to society. Only in the case when the productivity itself costs labour, and consequently capital, does it increase the price of production by a new element—which Nature by itself does not do.

45

Absolute Ground-Rent

In the analysis of differential rent we proceeded from the assumption that the worst soil does not pay any ground-rent; or, to put it more generally, only such land pays ground-rent whose product has an individual price of production below the price of production regulating the market, so that in this manner a surplus-profit arises which is transformed into rent. It is to be noted, to begin with, that the law of differential rent as such is entirely independent of the correctness or incorrectness of this assumption.

Let us call the general price of production, by which the market is regulated, P. Then, P coincides with the individual price of production of the output of the worst soil A; i.e., its price pays for the constant and variable capital consumed in production plus the average profit (= profit of enterprise plus interest).

The rent in this case is equal to zero. The individual price of production of the next better soil B is = P′, and P > P′; that is, P pays for more than the actual price of production of the product of soil B. Let us now assume that P - P′ = d; d, the excess of P over P′, is therefore the surplus-profit which the farmer of soil type B realises. This d is transformed into rent, which must be paid to the landlord. Let P′′ be the actual price of production of the third type of soil C, and $P - P'' = 2d$; then this 2d is converted into rent; similarly, let P''' be the individual price of production of the fourth type of soil D, and $P - P''' = 3d$, which is transformed into ground-rent, etc. Now let us assume the premise for soil A, that rent = 0 and therefore the price of its product = $P + 0$, is erroneous. Assume rather that it, too, yields rent = r. In that case, two different conclusions follow.

First: The price of the product of soil A would not be regulated by the price of production on the latter, but would include an excess above this price, i.e., would be = $P + r$. Because assuming the capitalist mode of production to be functioning normally, that is, assuming that the excess r which the farmer pays to the landlord represents neither a deduction from wages nor from the average profit of capital, the farmer can only pay it by selling the product above its price of production, thus, yielding him surplus-profit if he did not have to turn over this excess to the landlord in the form of rent. The regulating market-price of the total output on the market derived from all soils would then not be the price of production which capital generally yields in all spheres of production, i.e., a price equal to costs plus average profit, but rather the price of production plus the rent, $P + r$, and not P. For the price of the product of soil A represents generally the limit of the regulating general market-price, i.e., the price at which the total product can be supplied, and to that extent it regulates the price of this total product.

But *secondly*: Although the general price of agricultural products would in this case be significantly modified, the law of differential rent would nevertheless in no way lose its force. For if the price of the product of soil A, and thereby the general market-price = $P + r$, the price for soils B, C, D, etc., would likewise = $P + r$. But since $P - P' = d$ for soil B, then $(P + r) - (P' + r)$ would likewise = d, and $P - P'' = (P + r) - (P'' + r) = 2d$ for soil C; and finally $P - P''' = (P + r) - (P''' + r) = 3d$ for soil D, etc. Thus the differential rent would be the same as before and would be regulated by the same law, although the rent would include an element independent of this law and would show a general increase together with the price of the agricultural product. It follows, then, that no matter what the case may be as regards the rent of the least fertile soils, the law of differential rent is not only independent of it, but that the only manner of grasping differential rent in keeping with its character is to let the rent on soil A = 0. Whether this actually = 0 or > 0 is immaterial so far as the differential rent is concerned, and, in fact, does not come into consideration.

The law of differential rent, then, is independent of the results of the following study.

If we were now to inquire more deeply into the basis of the assumption that the product of the worst soil A does not yield any rent, the answer would of necessity be as follows: If the market-price of the agricultural product, say grain, attains that level where an additional investment of capital in soil A results in the usual price of production, i.e., the usual average profit on the capital is yielded, then this condition suffices for investing the additional capital in soil A. In other words, this condition is sufficient for the capitalist to invest new capital yielding the usual profit and to employ it in the normal manner.

It should be noted here that in this case, too, the market-price must be higher than the price of production of A. For as soon as the additional supply is created, it is evident that the relation between supply and demand becomes altered. Formerly the supply was insufficient. Now it is sufficient. Hence the price must fall. In order to fall, it must have been higher than the price of production of A. But due to the fact that soil A newly taken under cultivation is less fertile, the price does not fall again as low as when the price of production of soil B regulated the market. The price of production of A constitutes the limit, not for the temporary but for the relatively permanent rise of the market-price. On the other hand, if the new soil taken under cultivation is more fertile than the hitherto regulating soil A, and yet only suffices to meet the increased demand, then the market-price remains unchanged. The investigation of the question whether the poorest type of soil yields rent, however, coincides in this case too with our present inquiry, for here too the assumption that soil A does not yield any rent would be explained by the fact that the market-price is sufficient for the capitalist farmer to exactly cover, with this price, the invested capital plus the average profit; in brief, it would be explained by the fact that the market-price yields him the price of production of his commodities.

At any rate, the capitalist farmer can cultivate soil A under these conditions, inasmuch as he, as capitalist, has such power of decision. The prerequisite for the normal expansion of capital in soil A is now present. But from the premise that the capitalist farmer can now invest capital in soil A under average conditions for the expansion of capital, even if he did not have to pay any rent, it nowise follows that this land, belonging to category A, is now at the disposal of the farmer without further ado. The fact that the tenant farmer could realise the usual profit on his capital did he not have to pay any rent, is by no means a basis for the landlord to lend his land gratis to the farmer and to become so philanthropic as to grant *crédit gratuit* for the sake of a business friendship. Such an assumption would mean the abstraction of landed property, the elimination of land-ownership, and it is precisely the existence of the latter that constitutes a limitation to the investment of capital and the free expansion of capital in the land. This limitation does not at all disappear before the simple reflection of the farmer that the level of grain prices would enable him to realise the usual profit from the investment of his capital in the exploitation of soil A did he not have to pay any rent; in other words, if he could proceed in effect as though landed property did not exist. But differential rent presupposes the existence of a monopoly in land ownership, landed property as a limitation to capital, for without it surplus-profit would not be transformed into ground-rent nor fall to the share of the landlord instead of the farmer. And landed property as a limitation continues to exist even when rent in the form of differential rent disappears, i.e., on soil A. If we consider the cases in a country with capitalist production, where the investment of capital in the land can take place without payment of rent, we shall find that they are all based on a *de facto* abolition of landed property, if not also the legal abolition; this, however, can only take place under very specific circumstances which are by their very nature accidental.

First: When the landlord is himself a capitalist, or the capitalist is himself a landlord. In this case he may *himself* manage his land as soon as market-price has risen sufficiently to enable him to get, from what is now soil A, the price of production, that is, replacement of capital plus average profit. But why? Because for him landed property does not constitute an obstacle to the investment of capital. He can treat his land simply as an element of Nature, and therefore, be guided solely by considerations of expansion of his capital, by capitalist considerations. Such cases occur in practice, but only as exceptions. Just as capitalist cultivation of the soil presupposes the separation of functioning capital from landed property, so does it as a rule exclude self-management of landed property. It is immediately evident that this case is a purely accidental one. If the increased demand for grain requires the cultivation of a larger area of soil type A than is in the hands of self-managing proprietors, in other words, if a part of it must be rented to be at all cultivated, then this hypothetical lifting of the limitation created by landed property to the investment of capital at once collapses. It is an absurd contradiction to start out with the differentiation under the capitalist mode of production between capital and land, farmers and landlords, and then to turn round and assume that landlords, as a rule, manage their own land wherever and whenever capital would not draw rent from the cultivation of the soil if landed property were not separate and distinct from it. (See the passage by Adam Smith concerning mining rent, quoted below.) This abolition of landed property is fortuitous. It may or may not occur.

Secondly: In the total area of a leasehold there may be certain portions which do not yield any rent at the existing level of market-prices, so that they are in fact loaned gratis; but the landlord does not look upon it in that light, because he sees the total rental of the leased land, not the specific rent of the individual component plots. In this case, as regards the rentless component plots of the leasehold, landed property as a limitation to the investment of capital is eliminated for the capitalist farmer; and this, indeed, by contract with the landlord himself. But he does not pay rent for these plots merely because he pays rent for the land associated with them. A combination is here presupposed whereby poorer soil A does not have to be resorted to as a distinctly new field of production in order to produce the deficit supply, but rather whereby it merely constitutes an inseparable part of the better land. But the case to be investigated is precisely that in which certain pieces of land of soil type A must be independently managed, i.e., for the conditions generally prevailing under the capitalist mode of production, they must be independently leased.

Thirdly: A farmer may invest additional capital in the same leasehold even if the additional product secured in this manner yields him only the price of production at the prevailing market-prices, i.e., provides him with the usual profit but does not enable him to pay any additional rent. He thus pays ground-rent with one portion of the capital invested in the land, but not with the other. How little this assumption helps to solve the problem, however, is seen from the following: If the market-price (and the fertility of the soil) enables him to obtain an additional yield with his additional capital, which, as in the case of the old capital, yields a surplus-profit in addition to the price of production, he is able to pocket this surplus-profit so long as his lease does not expire. But why? Because the limitation placed by landed property on the investment of his capital in land has been eliminated for the duration of the lease. But the simple fact that additional soil of poorer quality must be independently cleared and independently leased in order for him to secure this surplus-profit proves irrefutably that the investment of additional capital in the old soil no longer suffices to produce the required increased supply. One assumption excludes the other. It is true that now one might say: The rent on the worst soil A is itself differential rent—whether the comparison is made with respect to the land cultivated by the owner himself (this occurs, however, as a purely chance exception) or with respect to the additional investment of capital in the old leaseholds which do not yield any rent. However, this would be 1) a differential rent which does not arise from the difference in fertility of the various categories of soil, and which, therefore, would *not* presuppose that soil A does not yield any rent and its produce sells at the price of production; and 2) the circumstance whether additional investments of capital in the same leasehold yield rent or not is just as irrelevant to the question as to whether the new soil of class A to be taken under cultivation pays rent or not, as it is irrelevant to, say, the establishment of a new and independent manufacturing business whether another manufacturer in the same line invests a portion of his capital in interest-bearing paper because he cannot use all of it in his business, or whether he makes certain improvements which do not yield him the full profit, but nevertheless do yield more than interest. This is of secondary importance to him. The additional new establishments, on the other hand, must yield the average profit and are organised in the hope of obtaining this average profit. It is true, to be sure, that the additional investments of capital in the old leaseholds and the additional cultivation of new land of soil type A mutually restrict one another. The limit, up to which additional capital may be invested in the same leasehold under less favourable conditions of production, is determined by the competing new investments in soil A; on the other hand, the rent which this category of soil can yield is limited by the competing additional investments of capital in the old leaseholds.

But all this dubious subterfuge does not solve the problem, which, simply stated, is this: Assume the market-price of grain (which in this inquiry stands for products of the soil in general) to be sufficient to permit taking portions of soil A under cultivation and that the capital invested in these new fields could return the price of production, i.e., replace capital plus average profit. Thus assume that conditions exist for the normal expansion of capital on soil A. Is this sufficient? Can this capital then really be invested? Or must the market-price rise to the point where even the worst soil A yields rent? In other words, does the landowner's monopoly hinder the investment of capital which would not be the case from the purely capitalist standpoint in the absence of this monopoly? It follows from the way in which the question itself is posed that if, e.g., additional capitals are invested in the old leaseholds, yielding the average profit at the given market-price, but no rent, this circumstance in no way answers the question whether capital may now really be invested in soil A, which also yields the average profits but no rent. But this is precisely the question before us. The fact that additional investments of capital not yielding any rent do not satisfy the demand is proved by the necessity of taking new land of soil type A under cultivation. Just two alternatives are possible if the additional cultivation of soil A takes place only in so far as it yields rent, that is, yields more than the price of production. Either the market-price must be such that even the last additional investments of capital in the old leaseholds yield surplus-profit, whether pocketed by the farmer or by the landlord. This rise in price and this surplus-profit from the last additional investments of capital would then result from the fact that soil A cannot be cultivated without yielding rent. For if the price of production were sufficient for cultivation to take place, merely yielding average profit, the price would not have risen so high, and competition from new plots would have been felt as soon as they just yielded this price of production. Competing with the additional investments in old leaseholds not yielding any rent would then be investments in soil A, which likewise do not yield any rent.—Or, the last investments in the old leaseholds do not yield any rent, but nevertheless the market-price has risen sufficiently to make it possible for soil A to be taken under cultivation and to yield rent. In this case, the additional investment of capital not yielding any rent was only possible because soil A cannot be cultivated until the market-price permits it to pay rent. Without this condition, its cultivation would have already begun at a lower price level; and those later investments of capital in the old leaseholds, which require the high market-price in order to yield the usual profit without rent, could not have taken place. At the high market-price, it is true, they yield only the average profit. At a lower market-price, which would have become the regulating price of production from the time soil A came under cultivation, they would thus not have yielded this average profit, i.e., the investments would thus not have taken place at all under such conditions. In this way, the rent from soil A would indeed constitute differential rent compared with the investments in the old leaseholds not yielding any rent. But that such differential rent is formed on the land areas of A is but a consequence of the fact that the latter are not at all available to cultivation, unless they yield rent; i.e., that the necessity for this rent exists, which, in itself, is not determined by any differences in soil types, and which constitutes the barrier to possible investment of additional capitals in the old leaseholds. In either case, the rent from soil A would not be simply a consequence of the rise in grain prices, but, conversely, the fact that the worst soil must yield rent in order to make its cultivation at all possible, would be the cause for the rise in the grain price to the point where this condition may be fulfilled.

Differential rent has the peculiarity that landed property here merely intercepts the surplus-profit which would otherwise flow into the pocket of the farmer, and which the latter may actually pocket under certain circumstances during the period of his lease. Landed property is here merely the cause for transferring a portion of the commodity-price which arises without the property having anything to do with it (indeed, in consequence of the fact that the price of production which regulates the market-price is determined by competition) and which resolves itself into surplus-profit—the cause for transferring this portion of the price from one person to another, from the capitalist to the landlord. But landed property is not the cause which *creates* this portion of the price, or the rise in price upon which this portion of the price is premised. On the other hand, if the worst soil A cannot be cultivated—although its cultivation would yield the price of production—until it produces something in excess of the price of production, rent, then landed property is the creative cause of *this* rise in price. *Landed property itself has created rent.* This fact is not altered, if, as in the second case mentioned, the rent now paid on soil A constitutes differential rent compared with the last additional investment of capital in old leaseholds, which pay only the price of production. For the circumstance that soil A cannot be cultivated until the regulating market-price has risen high enough to permit rent to be yielded from soil A—only this circumstance is the basis here for the fact that the market-price rises to a point which enables the last investments in the old leaseholds to yield, indeed, only their price of production, but a price of production which, at the same time, yields rent on soil A. The fact that the latter has to pay rent at all is, in this case, the cause for the differential rent between soil A and the last investments in the old leaseholds.

When stating, in general, that soil A does not pay any rent—assuming the price of grain is regulated by the price of production—we mean rent in the categorical sense of the word. If the farmer pays 'lease money' which constitutes a deduction from the normal wages of his labourers, or from his own normal average profit, he does not pay rent, i.e., an independent component of the price of his commodities distinct from wages and profit. We have already indicated that this continually takes place in practice. In so far as the wages of the agricultural labourers in a given country are, in general, depressed below the normal average level of wages, so that a deduction from wages, a part of the wages, as a general rule enters into rent, this does not constitute an exceptional case for the farmer cultivating the worst soil. In the same price of production which makes cultivation of the worst soil possible these low wages already form a constituent element, and the sale of the product at the price of production does not, therefore, enable the farmer cultivating this soil to pay any rent. The landlord can also lease his land to some labourer, who may be satisfied to pay to the former in the form of rent, all or the largest part of that which he realises in the selling price over and above the wages. In all these cases, however, no real rent is paid in spite of the fact that lease money is paid. But wherever conditions correspond to those under the capitalist mode of production, rent and lease money must coincide. Yet it is precisely this normal condition which must be analysed here.

Since even the cases considered above—where, under the capitalist mode of production, investments of capital in the land may actually take place without yielding rent—do not contribute to the solution of our problem, so much less does reference to colonial conditions. The criterion establishing a colony as a colony—we are referring here only to true agricultural colonies—is not merely the prevailing vast area of fertile land in a natural state. It is rather the circumstance that this land has not been appropriated, has not been subjected to private ownership. Herein lies the enormous difference, as regards the land, between old countries and colonies: the legal or actual non-existence of landed property, as Wakefield[1] correctly remarks, and as Mirabeau *père*, the physiocrat, and other elder economists, had discovered long before him. It is quite immaterial here whether the colonists simply appropriate the land, or whether they actually pay to the state, in the form of a nominal land price, a fee for a valid legal title to the land. It is also immaterial that the colonists already settled there may be the legal owners of the land. In fact, landed property constitutes no limitation here to the investment of capital—and also of labour without capital; the appropriation of some of the land by the colonists already established there does not prevent the newcomers from employing their capital or their labour upon new land. Therefore, when it is necessary to investigate the influence of landed property upon the prices of products of the land and upon rent—in those cases where landed property restricts land as an investment sphere of capital—it is highly absurd to speak of free bourgeois colonies where, in agriculture, neither the capitalist mode of production exists, nor the form of landed property corresponding to it—which, in fact, does not exist at all. Ricardo, e.g., does so in his chapter on ground-rent.

In the preface he states that he intends to investigate the effect of the appropriation of land upon the value of the products of the soil, and directly thereafter he takes the colonies as an illustration, whereby he assumes that the land exists in a relatively elementary form and that its exploitation is not limited by the monopoly of landed property.

The mere legal ownership of land does not create any ground-rent for the owner. But it does, indeed, give him the power to withdraw his land from exploitation until economic conditions permit him to utilise it in such a manner as to yield him a surplus, be it used for actual agricultural or other production purposes, such as buildings, etc. He cannot increase or decrease the absolute magnitude of this sphere, but he can change the quantity of land placed on the market. Hence, as Fourier already observed, it is a characteristic fact that in all civilised countries a comparatively appreciable portion of land always remains uncultivated.

Thus, assuming the demand requires that new land be taken under cultivation, whose soil, let us say, is less fertile than that hitherto cultivated—will the landlord lease it for nothing, just because the market-price of the product of the land has risen sufficiently to return to the farmer the price of production, and thereby the usual profit, on his investment in this land? By no means. The investment of capital must yield him rent. He does not lease his land until he can be paid lease money for it. Therefore, the market-price must rise to a point above the price of production, i.e., to P + r, so that rent can be paid to the landlord. Since according to our assumption, landed property does not yield anything until it is leased, is economically valueless until then, a small rise in the market-price above the price of production suffices to bring the new land of poorest quality on the market.

The following question now arises: Does it follow from the fact that the worst soil yields ground-rent which cannot be derived from any difference in fertility that the price of the product of the land is necessarily a monopoly price in the usual sense, or a price into which the rent enters like a tax, with the sole distinction that the landlord levies the tax instead of the state? It goes without saying that this tax has its specific economic limits. It is limited by additional investments of capital in the old leaseholds, by competition from products of the land coming from abroad—assuming their import is unrestricted—by competition among the landlords themselves, and finally by the needs of the consumers and their ability to pay. But this is not the question here. The point is whether the rent paid on the worst soil enters into the price of the products of this soil—which price regulates the general market-price according to our assumption—in the same way as a tax placed on a commodity enters into its price, i.e., as an element that is independent of the value of the commodity.

This, by no means, necessarily follows, and the contention that it does has been made only because the distinction between the value of commodities and their price of production has heretofore not been understood. We have seen that the price of production of a commodity is not at all identical with its value, although the prices of production of commodities, considered in their totality, are regulated only by their total value, and although the movement of production prices of various kinds of commodities, all other circumstances being equal, is determined exclusively by the movement of their values. It has been shown that the price of production of a commodity may lie above or below its value, and coincides with its value only by way of exception. Hence, the fact that products of the land are sold above their price of production does not at all prove that they are sold above their value; just as the fact that products of industry, on the average, are sold at their price of production does not prove that they are sold at their value. It is possible for agricultural products to be sold above their price of production and below their value, while, on the other hand, many industrial products yield the price of production only because they are sold above their value.

The relation of the price of production of a commodity to its value is determined solely by the ratio of the variable part of the capital with which the commodity is produced to its constant part, or by the organic composition of the capital producing it. If the composition of the capital in a given sphere of production is lower than that of the average social capital, i.e., if its variable portion, which is used for wages, is larger in its relation to the constant portion, used for the material conditions of labour, than is the case in the average social capital, then the value of its product must lie above the price of production. In other words, because such capital employs more living labour, it produces more surplus-value, and therefore, more profit, assuming equal exploitation of labour, than an equally large aliquot portion of the social average capital. The value of its product, therefore, is above the price of production, since this price of production is equal to capital replacement plus average profit, and the average profit is lower than the profit produced in this commodity. The surplus-value produced by the average social capital is less than the surplus-value produced by a capital of this lower composition. The opposite is the case when the capital invested in a certain sphere of production is of a bigger composition than the social average capital. The value of commodities produced by it lies below their price of production, which is generally the case with products of the most developed industries.

If the capital in a certain sphere of production is of a lower composition than the average social capital, then this is, in the first place, merely another way of saying that the productivity of the social labour in this particular sphere of production is below the average; for the level of productivity attained is manifested in the relative preponderance of constant over variable capital, or in the continual decrease—for the given capital—of the portion used for wages. On the other hand, if the capital in a certain sphere of production is of a higher composition, then this reflects a development of productiveness that is above the average.

Leaving aside actual works of art, whose consideration by their very nature is excluded from our discussion, it is self-evident, moreover, that different spheres of production require different proportions of constant and variable capital in accordance with their specific technical features, and that living labour must play a bigger role in some, and smaller in others. For instance, in the extractive industries, which must be clearly distinguished from agriculture, raw material as an element of constant capital is wholly absent, and even auxiliary material rarely plays an important role. In the mining industry, however, the other part of constant capital, i.e., fixed capital, plays an important role. Nevertheless, here too, progress may be measured by the relative increase of constant capital in relation to variable capital.

If the composition of capital in agriculture proper is lower than that of the average social capital, then, *prima facie*, this expresses the fact that in countries with developed production agriculture has not progressed to the same extent as the processing industries. Such a fact could be explained—aside from all other circumstances, including in part decisive economic ones—by the earlier and more rapid development of the mechanical sciences, and in particular their application compared with the later and in part quite recent development of chemistry, geology and physiology, and again, in particular, their application to agriculture. Incidentally, it is an indubitable and long-known fact[2] that the progress of agriculture itself is constantly expressed by a relative growth of constant capital as compared with variable capital. Whether the composition of agricultural capital is lower than that of the average social capital in a specific country where capitalist production prevails, for instance England, is a question which can only be decided statistically, and for our purposes it is superfluous to go into it in detail. In any case, it is theoretically established that the value of agricultural products can be higher than their price of production only on this assumption. In other words, a capital of a certain size in agriculture produces more surplus-value, or what amounts to the same, sets in motion and commands more surplus-labour (and with it employs more living labour generally) than a capital of the same size of average social composition.

This assumption, then, suffices for that form of rent which we are analysing here, and which can obtain only so long as this assumption holds good. Wherever this assumption no longer holds, the corresponding form of rent likewise no longer holds.

However, the mere existence of an excess in the value of agricultural products over their price of production would not in itself suffice to explain the existence of a ground-rent which is independent of differences in fertility of various soil types and in successive investments of capital on the same land—a rent, in short, which is to be clearly distinguished in concept from differential rent and which we may therefore call *absolute rent.* Quite a number of manufactured products are characterised by the fact that their value is higher than their price of production, without thereby yielding any excess above the average profit, or a surplus-profit, which could be converted into rent. Conversely, the existence and concept of price of production and general rate of profit, which it implies, rest upon the fact that individual commodities are not sold at their value. Prices of production arise from an equalisation of the values of commodities. After replacing the respective capital-values used up in the various spheres of production, this distributes the entire surplus-value, not in proportion to the amount produced in the individual spheres of production and thus incorporated in their commodities, but in proportion to the magnitude of advanced capitals. Only in this manner do average profit and price of production arise, whose characteristic element the former is. It is the perpetual tendency of capitals to bring about through competition this equalisation in the distribution of surplus-value produced by the total capital, and to overcome all obstacles to this equalisation. Hence it is their tendency to tolerate only such surplus-profits as arise, under all circumstances, not from the difference between the values and prices of production of commodities but rather from the difference between the general price of production governing the market and the individual prices of production differing from it; surplus-profits which obtain within a certain sphere of production, therefore, and not between two different spheres, and thus do not affect the general prices of production of the various spheres, i.e., the general rate of profit, but rather presuppose the transformation of values into prices of production and a general rate of profit. This supposition rests, however, as previously discussed, upon the constantly changing proportional distribution of the total social capital among the various spheres of production, upon the perpetual inflow and outflow of capitals, upon their transferability from one sphere to another, in short, upon their free movement between the various spheres of production, which represent so many available fields of investment for the independent components of the total social capital. The premise in this case is that no barrier, or just an accidental and temporary barrier, interferes with the competition of capitals—for instance, in a sphere of production, in which the commodity-values are higher than the prices of production, or where the surplus-value produced exceeds the average profit—to reduce the value to the price of production and thereby proportionally distribute the excess surplus-value of this sphere of production among all spheres exploited by capital. But if the reverse occurs, if capital meets an alien force which it can but partially, or not at all, overcome, and which limits its investment in certain spheres, admitting it only under conditions which wholly or partly exclude that general equalisation of surplus-value to an average profit, then it is evident that the excess of the value of commodities in such spheres of production over their price of production would give rise to a surplus-profit, which could be converted into rent and such made independent with respect to profit. Such an alien force and barrier are presented by landed property, when confronting capital in its endeavour to invest in land; such a force is the landlord vis-à-vis the capitalist.

Landed property is here the barrier which does not permit any new investment of capital in hitherto uncultivated or unrented land without levying a tax, or in other words, without demanding a rent, although the land to be newly brought under cultivation may belong to a category which does not yield any differential rent and which, were it not for landed property, could have been cultivated even at a small increase in market-price, so that the regulating market-price would have netted to the cultivator of this worst soil solely his price of production. But owing to the barrier raised by landed property, the market-price must rise to a level at which the land can yield a surplus over the price of production, i.e., yield a rent. However, since the value of the commodities produced by agricultural capital is higher than their price of production, according to our assumption, this rent (save for one case which we shall discuss forthwith) forms the excess of value over the price of production, or a part of it. Whether the rent equals the entire difference between the value and price of production, or only a greater or lesser part of it, will depend wholly on the relation between supply and demand and on the area of land newly taken under cultivation. So long as the rent does not equal the excess of the value of agricultural products over their price of production, a portion of this excess will always enter into the general equalisation and proportional distribution of all surplus-value among the various individual capitals. As soon as the rent does equal the excess of the value over the price of production, this entire portion of surplus-value over and above the average profit will be withdrawn from this equalisation. But whether this absolute rent equals the whole excess of value over the price of production, or just a part of it, the agricultural products will always be sold at a monopoly price, not because their price exceeds their value, but because it equals their value, or because their price is lower than their value but higher than their price of production. Their monopoly would consist in the fact that, unlike other products of industry whose value is higher than the general price of production, they are not levelled out to the price of production. Since one portion of the value, as well as of price of production, is an actually given constant, namely the cost-price, representing the capital = k used up in production, their difference consists in the other, the variable portion, the surplus-value, which equals p, the profit, in the price of production, i.e., equals the total surplus-value calculated on the social capital and on every individual capital as an aliquot part of the social capital; but which in the value of commodities equals the actual surplus-value created by this particular capital, and forms an integral part of the commodity-values produced by this capital. If the value of commodities is higher than their price of production, then the price of production = k + p, and the value = k + p + d, so that p + d = the surplus-value contained therein. The difference between the value and the price of production, therefore, = d, the excess of surplus-value created by this capital over the surplus-value allocated to it through the general rate of profit. It follows from this that the price of agricultural products may lie higher than their price of production, without reaching their value. It follows, furthermore, that a permanent increase in the price of agricultural products may take place up to a certain point, before their price reaches their value. It follows likewise that the excess in the value of agricultural products over their price of production can become a determining element of their general market-price solely as a consequence of the monopoly in landed property. It follows, finally, that in this case the increase in the price of the product is not the cause of rent, but rather that rent is the cause of the increase in the price of the product. If the price of the product from a unit area of the worst soil = P + r, then all differential rents will rise by corresponding multiples of r, since the assumption is that P + r becomes the regulating market-price.

If the average composition of the non-agricultural social capital were = $85_c + 15_v$, and the rate of surplus-value = 100%, then the price of production would = 115. If the composition of the agricultural capital were = $75_c + 25_v$ and the rate of surplus-value were the same, then the value of the agricultural product and the regulating market-price would = 125. If the agricultural and the non-agricultural product should be equalised to the same average price (we assume for the sake of brevity the total capital in both lines of production to be equal), then the total surplus-value would = 40, or 20%, on the 200 of capital. The product of the one as well as the other would be sold at 120. In an equalisation into prices of production, the average market-prices of the non-agricultural product would thus lie above, and those of the agricultural product below, their value. If the agricultural products were sold at their full value, they would be higher by 5, and the industrial products lower by 5, than they are in the equalisation. If market conditions do not permit the sale of the agricultural products at their full value, to the full surplus above the price of production, then the effect lies between the two extremes; the industrial products are sold somewhat above their value, and the agricultural products somewhat above their price of production.

Although landed property may drive the price of agricultural produce above its price of production, it does not depend on this, but rather on the general state of the market, to what degree market-price exceeds the price of production and approaches the value, and to what extent, therefore, the surplus-value created in agriculture over and above the given average profit shall either be transformed into rent or enter into the general equalisation of the surplus-value to average profit. At any rate, this absolute rent arising out of the excess of value over the price of production is but a portion of the agricultural surplus-value, a conversion of this surplus-value into rent, its being filched by the landlord; just as the differential rent arises out of the conversion of surplus-profit into rent, its being filched by the landlord under a generally regulating price of production. These two forms of rent are the only normal ones. Apart from them the rent can be based only upon an actual monopoly price, which is determined neither by price of production nor by value of commodities, but by the buyers' needs and ability to pay. Its analysis belongs under the theory of competition, where the actual movement of market-prices is considered.

If all the land suitable for agriculture in a certain country were leased—assuming the capitalist mode of production and normal conditions to be general—there would not be any land not paying rent; but there might be some capitals, certain parts of capitals invested in land, that might not yield any rent. For as soon as the land has been rented, landed property ceases to act as an absolute barrier against the investment of necessary capital. Still, it continues to act as a relative barrier even after that, in so far as the reversion to the landlord of the capital incorporated in the land circumscribes the activity of the tenant within very definite limits. Only in this case all rent would be transformed into differential rent, although this would not be a differential rent determined by any difference in soil fertility, but rather by the difference between the surplus-profits arising from the last investments of capital in a particular soil type and the rent paid for the lease of the worst quality land. Landed property acts as an absolute barrier only to the extent that the landlord exacts a tribute for making land at all accessible to the investment of capital. When such access has been gained, he can no longer set any absolute limits to the size of any investment of capital in a given plot of land. In general, housing construction meets a barrier in the ownership by a third party of the land upon which the houses are to be built. But, once this land has been leased for the purpose of housing construction, it depends upon the tenant whether he will build a large or a small house.

If the average composition of agricultural capital were equal to, or higher than, that of the average social capital, then absolute rent—again in the sense just described—would disappear; i.e., rent which differs equally from differential rent as well as that based upon an actual monopoly price. The value of agricultural produce, then, would not lie above its price of production, and the agricultural capital would not set any more labour in motion, and therefore, would also not realise any more surplus-labour than the non-agricultural capital. The same would take place, were the composition of agricultural capital to become equal to that of the average social capital with the progress of civilisation.

It seems to be a contradiction, at first glance, to assume that, on the one hand, the composition of agricultural capital rises, in other words, that its constant component increases with respect to its variable, and, on the other hand, that the price of the agricultural product should rise high enough to permit rent to be yielded by new and worse soil than that previously cultivated, a rent which, in this case, could originate only from an excess of market-price over the value and price of production, in short, a rent derived solely from a monopoly price of the product.

It is necessary to make a distinction here.

In the first place, it was noted in considering the manner in which rate of profit is formed, that capitals, which have the same composition technologically speaking, i.e., which set equivalent amounts of labour in motion relative to machinery and raw materials, may nonetheless have different compositions owing to different values of the constant portions of these capitals. The raw materials or machinery may be dearer in one case than in another. For the same quantity of labour to be set in motion (and this would be required, according to our assumption, to work up the same mass of raw materials), a larger capital would have to be advanced in the one case than in the other, since the same amount of labour cannot be set in motion with, say, a capital of 100 if the cost of raw material, which must be covered out of the 100, is 40 in one case and 20 in another. But it would become immediately evident that these two capitals are of the same technical composition, as soon as the price of the dearer raw material fell to the level of the cheaper one. The value ratio between constant and variable capital would have become the same in that case, although no change had taken place in the technical proportions between the living labour and the mass and nature of the conditions of labour employed by this capital. On the other band, a capital of lower organic composition could assume the appearance of being in the same class with one of a higher organic composition, merely from a rise in the value of its constant portions, solely from the viewpoint of its value-composition. Suppose one capital = $60_c + 40_v$, because it employs much machinery and raw material compared to living labour-power, and another capital = $40_c + 60_v$, because it employs much living labour (60%), little machinery (e.g., 10%) and compared to labour-power less and cheaper raw material (e.g., 30%). Then a simple rise in the value of raw and auxiliary materials from 30 to 80 could equalise the composition, so that now the second capital would consist of 80 raw material and 60 labour-power for 10 in machines, or $90_c + 60_v$, which, in percentages, would also = $60_c + 40_v$, with no change having taken place in the technical composition. In other words, capitals of equal organic composition may be of different value-composition, and capitals with identical percentages of value-composition may show varying degrees of organic composition and thus express different stages in the development of the social productivity of labour. The mere circumstance, then, that agricultural capital might be on the general level of value-composition, would not prove that the social productivity of labour is equally high-developed in it. It would merely show that its own product, which again forms a part of its conditions of production, is dearer, or that auxiliary materials, such as fertiliser, which used to be close by, must now be brought from afar, etc.

But aside from this, the peculiar nature of agriculture must be taken into account.

Suppose labour-saving machinery, chemical aids, etc., are more extensively used in agriculture, and that therefore constant capital increases technically, not merely in value, but also in mass, as compared with the mass of employed labour-power, then in agriculture (as in mining) it is not only a matter of the social, but also of the natural, productivity of labour which depends on the natural conditions of labour. It is possible for the increase of social productivity in agriculture to barely compensate, or not even compensate, for the decrease in natural power—this compensation will nevertheless be effective only for a short time—so that despite technical development there, no cheapening of the product occurs, but only a still greater increase in price is averted. It is also possible that the absolute mass of products decreases with rising grain prices, while the relative surplus-product increases; namely, in the case of a relative increase in constant capital which consists chiefly of machinery or animals requiring only replacement of wear and tear, and with a corresponding decrease in variable capital which is expended in wages requiring constant replacement in full out of the product.

Moreover, it is also possible that with progress in agriculture only a moderate rise in market-price above the average is necessary, in order to cultivate and draw a rent from poorer soil, which would have required a greater rise in market-price if technical aids were less developed.

The fact that in larger-scale cattle-raising, for example, the mass of employed labour-power is very small compared with constant capital as represented in cattle itself, could be taken to refute the assertion that more labour-power, on a percentage basis, is set in motion by agricultural capital than by the average social capital outside of agriculture. But it should be noted here that we have taken as determining for rent analysis that portion of agricultural capital which produces the principal plant foodstuffs providing the chief means of subsistence among civilised nations. Adam Smith—and this is one of his merits—has already demonstrated that a quite different determination of prices is to be observed in cattle-raising, and, for that matter, generally for capitals invested in land which are not engaged in raising the principal means of subsistence, e.g., grain. Namely, in that case, the price is determined in such a way that the price of the product of the land—which is used for cattle-raising, say as an artificial pasture, but which could just as easily have been transformed into cornfields of a certain quality—must rise high enough to produce the same rent as on arable land of the same quality. In other words, the rent of cornfields becomes a determining element in the price of cattle, and for this reason Ramsay has justly remarked that the price of cattle is in this manner artificially raised by the rent, by the economic expression of landed property, in short, through landed property. [G. Ramsay, *An Essay on the Distribution of Wealth*, Edinburgh, 1836, pp. 278-79.—*Ed.*]

> By the extension of cultivation the unimproved wilds become insufficient to supply the demand for butcher's meat. A great part of the cultivated lands must be employed in rearing and fattening cattle, of which the price, therefore, must be sufficient to pay, not only the labour necessary for tending them, but the rent which the landlord and the profit which the farmer could have drawn from such land, employed in tillage. The cattle bred upon the most uncultivated moors, when brought to the same market, are, in proportion to their weight or goodness, sold at the same price as those which are reared upon the most improved land. The proprietors of those moors profit by it, and raise the rent of their land in proportion to the price of their cattle. (Adam Smith, Book I, Ch. XI, Part 1.)

In this case, likewise, as distinct from grain-rent, the differential rent is in favour of the worst soil.

Absolute rent explains some phenomena, which, at first sight, seem to make merely a monopoly price responsible for the rent. To go on with Adam Smith's example, take the owner of some Norwegian forest, for instance, which exists independent of human activity, i.e., it is not a product of silviculture. If the proprietor of this forest receives a rent from a capitalist who has the timber felled, perhaps in consequence of a demand from England, or if this owner has the timber felled himself acting in the capacity of capitalist, then a greater or smaller amount of rent will accrue to him in timber, apart from the profit on invested capital. This appears to be a pure monopoly charge derived from a pure product of Nature. But, as a matter of fact, the capital here consists almost exclusively of a variable component expended in labour, and thus sets more surplus-labour in motion than another capital of the same size. The value of the timber, then, contains a greater surplus of unpaid labour, or of surplus-value, than that of a product of a capital of a higher organic composition. For this reason the average profit can be derived from this timber, and a considerable surplus in the form of rent can fall to the share of the owner of the forest. Conversely, it may be assumed that, owing to the ease with which timber-felling may be extended, in other words, its production rapidly increased, the demand must rise very considerably for the price of timber to equal its value, and thereby for the entire surplus of unpaid labour (over and above that portion which falls to the capitalist as average profit) to accrue to the owner in the form of rent.

We have assumed that the land newly brought under cultivation is of still inferior quality to the worst previously cultivated. If it is better, it yields a differential rent. But here we are analysing precisely the case wherein rent does not appear as a differential rent. There are only two cases possible. The newly cultivated soil is either inferior to, or just as good as the previously cultivated soil. If inferior, then the matter has already been analysed. It remains only to analyse the case in which it is just as good.

As already developed in our analysis of differential rent, the progress of cultivation may just as well bring equally good, or even better soils under the plough as worse soil.

First: Because in differential rent (or any rent in general, since even in the case of non-differential rent the question always arises whether, on the one hand, the soil fertility in general, and, on the other hand, its location, admit of its cultivation at the regulating market-price so as to yield a profit and rent) two conditions work in opposing directions, now cancelling one another, now alternately exerting the determining influence. The rise in market-price—provided the cost-price of cultivation has not fallen, i.e., no technical progress has given a new impetus to further cultivation—may bring under cultivation more fertile soil formerly excluded from competition by virtue of its location. Or it may so enhance the advantage of the location of the inferior soil that its lesser fertility is counterbalanced by it. Or, without any rise in market-price the location may bring better soils into competition through improvement in means of communication, as can be observed on a large scale in the prairie States of North America. In countries of older civilisation the same also takes place constantly if not to the same extent as in the colonies, where, as Wakefield correctly observes, location is decisive. [[E. Wakefield] *England and America. A Comparison of the Social and Political State of both Nations*, Vol. I, London, 1833, pp. 214-15.—*Ed.*] To sum up, then, the contradictory influences of location and fertility, and the variableness of the location factor, which is continually counterbalanced and perpetually passes through progressive changes tending towards equalisation, alternately carry equally good, better or worse land areas into new competition with the older ones under cultivation.

Secondly: With the development of natural science and agronomy the soil fertility is also changed by changing the means through which the soil constituents may be rendered immediately serviceable. In this way, light soil types in France and in the eastern counties of England, which were regarded as inferior at one time, have recently risen to first place. (See Passy. [H. Passy, *Rente du sol.* In: Dictionnaire de l'économie politique, Tome II. Paris. 1854, p. 515.—*Ed.*]) On the other hand, soil considered inferior not for bad chemical composition but for certain mechanical and physical obstacles that hindered its cultivation, is converted into good land as soon as means to overcome these obstacles have been discovered.

Thirdly: In all ancient civilisations, old historical and traditional relations, for instance, in the form of state-owned lands, communal lands, etc., have purely arbitrarily withheld from cultivation large tracts of land, which only return to it little by little. The succession in which they are brought under cultivation depends neither upon their good quality nor siting, but upon wholly external circumstances. In tracing the history of English communal lands turned successively into private property through the Enclosure Bills and brought under the plough, nothing would be more ridiculous than the fantastic idea that a modern agricultural chemist, such as Liebig, had indicated the selection of land in this succession, designating certain fields for cultivation owing to chemical properties and excluding others. What was more decisive, in this case, was the opportunity which makes the thief; the more or less plausible legalistic subterfuges of the big landlords to justify their appropriation.

Fourthly: Apart from the fact that the stage of development reached at any time by the population and capital increase sets certain limits, even though elastic, to the extension of cultivation, and apart from chance effects which temporarily influence the market-price—

such as a series of good or bad seasons—the extension of agriculture over a larger area depends on the overall state of the capital market and business conditions in a country. In periods of stringency it will not suffice for uncultivated soil to yield the tenant an average profit—no matter whether he pays any rent or not—in order that additional capital be invested in agriculture. In other periods when there is a plethora of capital, it will pour into agriculture even without a rise in market-price if only other normal conditions are present. Better soil than hitherto cultivated would in fact be excluded from competition solely on the basis of unfavourable location, or if hitherto insurmountable obstacles to its employment existed, or through chance. For this reason we should only concern ourselves with soils which are just as good as those last cultivated. However, there still exists the difference in cost of clearing for cultivation between the new soil and the one last cultivated. And it depends upon the level of market-prices and credit conditions whether this will be undertaken or not. As soon as this soil then actually enters into competition, the market-price will fall once more to its former level, assuming other conditions to be equal, and the new soil will then yield the same rent as the corresponding old soil. The assumption that it does not yield any rent is proved by its advocates by assuming precisely what they are called upon to prove, namely that the last soil did not yield any rent. One might prove in the same manner that houses which were the last built do not yield any rent for the building outside of house-rent proper, even though they are leased. In fact, however, they do yield rent even before yielding any house-rent, when they frequently remain vacant for a long period. Just as successive investments of capital in a certain piece of land may bring a proportional surplus and thereby the same rent as the first investment, so fields of the same quality as those last cultivated may bring the same proceeds for the same cost. Otherwise it would be altogether inexplicable how fields of the same quality are ever brought successively under cultivation; it seems that either it would be necessary to take all together, or rather not a single one of them, in order not to bring all the remaining ones into competition. The landlord is always ready to draw a rent, i.e., to receive something for nothing. But capital requires certain conditions to fulfil his wish. Competition between pieces of land does not, therefore, depend upon the landlord desiring them to compete, but upon the capital existing which seeks to compete with other capitals in the new fields.

To the extent that the agricultural rent proper is purely a monopoly price, the latter can only be small, just as the absolute rent can only be small here under normal conditions whatever the excess of the product's value over its price of production. The essence of absolute rent, therefore, consists in this: Given the same rate of surplus-value, or degree of labour exploitation, equally large capitals in various spheres of production produce different amounts of surplus-value, in accordance with their varying average composition. In industry these various masses of surplus-value are equalised into an average profit and distributed uniformly among the individual capitals as aliquot parts of the social capital. Landed property hinders such an equalisation among capitals, invested in land, whenever production requires land for either agriculture or extraction of raw materials, and takes hold of a portion of the surplus-value, which would otherwise take part in equalising to the general rate of profit. The rent, then, forms a portion of the value, or, more specifically, surplus-value, of commodities, and instead of falling into the lap of the capitalists, who have extracted it from their labourers, it falls to the share of the landlords, who extract it from the capitalists. It is hereby assumed that the agricultural capital sets more labour in motion than an equally large portion of non-agricultural capital. How far the discrepancy goes, or whether it exists at all, depends upon the relative development of agriculture as compared with industry. It is in the nature of the case that this difference must decrease with the progress of agriculture, unless the proportionate decrease of variable as compared with constant capital is still greater in the case of industrial than in the case of agricultural capital.

This absolute rent plays an even more important role in the extractive industry proper, where one element of constant capital, raw material, is wholly lacking and where, excluding those lines in which capital consisting of machinery and other fixed capital is very considerable, by far the lowest composition of capital prevails. Precisely here, where the rent appears entirely attributable to a monopoly price, unusually favourable market conditions are necessary for commodities to be sold at their value, or for rent to equal the entire excess of a commodity's surplus-value over its price of production. This applies, for instance, to rent from fisheries, stone quarries, natural forests, etc.[3]

Notes

1. Wakefield, *England and America*, London, 1833. Compare also *Das Kapital*, Buch I, Kap. XXV [English edition: Ch. XXXIII.—*Ed.*].
2. See Dombasle [*Annales agricoles de Roville, ou Mélanges d'agriculture, d'économie rurale et de législation agricole*, Paris, 1824-37.—Ed.] and R. Jones [*An Essay on the Distribution of Wealth, and on the Sources of Taxation*, Part I, *Rent*, London, 1831, p. 227.—*Ed.*]. XLV-1018
3. Ricardo deals with this very superficially. See the passage directed against Adam Smith concerning forest rent in Norway, at the very beginning of Chapter 11, in *Principles*.

46

Building Site Rent. Rent in Mining. Price of Land

Wherever rent exists at all, differential rent appears at all times and is governed by the same laws, as agricultural differential rent. Wherever natural forces can be monopolised and guarantee a surplus-profit to the industrial capitalist using them, be it waterfalls, rich mines, waters teeming with fish, or a favourably located building site, there the person who by virtue of title to a portion of the globe has become the proprietor of these natural objects will wrest this surplus-profit from functioning capital in the form of rent. Adam Smith has set forth, as concerns land for building purposes, that the basis of its rent, like that of all non-agricultural land, is regulated by agricultural rent proper (Book I, Ch. XI, 2 and 3). This rent is distinguished, in the first place, by the preponderant influence exerted here by location upon differential rent (very significant, e.g., in vineyards and building sites in large cities); secondly, by the palpable and complete passiveness of the owner, whose sole activity consists (especially in mines) in exploiting the progress of social development, toward which he contributes nothing and for which he risks nothing, unlike the industrial capitalist; and finally by the prevalence of monopoly prices in many cases, particularly through the most shameless exploitation of poverty (for poverty is more lucrative for house-rent than the mines of Potosi ever were for Spain[1]), and the monstrous power wielded by landed property, when united hand in hand with industrial capital, enables it to be used against labourers engaged in their wage struggle as a means of practically expelling them from the earth as a dwelling-place.[2] One part of society thus exacts tribute from another for the permission to inhabit the earth, as landed property in general assigns the landlord the privilege of exploiting the terrestrial body, the bowels of the earth, the air, and thereby the maintenance and development of life. Not only the population increase and with it the growing demand for shelter, but also the development of fixed capital, which is either incorporated in land, or takes root in it and is based upon it, such as all industrial buildings, railways, warehouses, factory buildings, docks, etc., necessarily increase the building rent. A confusion of house-rent, in so far as it constitutes interest and amortisation on capital invested in a house, and rent for the mere land, is not possible in this case, even with all the goodwill of a person like Carey, particularly when landlord and building speculator are different persons, as is true in England. Two elements should be considered here: on the one hand, the exploitation of the earth for the purpose of reproduction or extraction; on the other hand, the space required as an element of all production and all human activity. And property in land demands its tribute in both senses. The demand for building sites raises the value of land as space and foundation, while thereby the demand for elements of the terrestrial body serving as building material grows simultaneously.[3]

That it is the ground-rent, and not the house, which forms the actual object of building speculation in rapidly growing cities, especially where construction is carried on as an industry, e.g., in London, has already been illustrated in Book II, Chapter XII, in the testimony of a big building speculator in London, Edward Capps, given before the Select Committee on Bank Acts of 1857. He stated there, No.5435:

> 'I think a man who wishes to rise in the world can hardly expect to rise by following out a fair trade ...it is necessary for him to add speculative building to it, and that must be done not on a small scale; ...for the builder makes very little profit out of the buildings themselves; he makes the principal part of the profit out of the improved ground-rents. Perhaps he takes a piece of ground, and agrees to give £300 a year for it; by laying it out with care, and putting certain descriptions of buildings upon it, he may succeed in making £400 or £450 a year out of it, and his profit would be the increased ground-rent of £100 or £150 a year, rather than the profit of the buildings at which ...in many instances, he scarcely looks at all.'

And parenthetically it should not be forgotten that after the lapse of the lease, generally at the end of 99 years, the land with all its buildings and its ground-rent—usually increased in the interim twice or three times, reverts from the building speculator or his legal successor to the original last landlord.

Mining rent proper is determined in the same way as agricultural rent.

> There are some mines, of which the produce is barely sufficient to pay the labour and replace, together with its ordinary profits, the stock employed in working them. They afford some profit to the undertaker of the work, but no rent to the landlord. They can be wrought advantageously by nobody but the landlord, who, being himself the undertaker of the work, gets the ordinary profit of the capital which he employs in it. Many coal mines in Scotland are wrought in this manner, and can be wrought in no other. The landlord will allow nobody else to work them without paying some rent, and nobody can afford to pay any. (Adam Smith, Book I, Ch. XI, 2.)

It must be distinguished, whether the rent springs from a monopoly price, because a monopoly price of the product or the land exists independently of it, or whether the products are sold at a monopoly price, because a rent exists. When we refer to a monopoly price, we mean in general a price determined only by the purchasers' eagerness to buy and ability to pay, independent of the price determined by the general price of production, as well as by the value of the products. A vineyard producing wine of very extraordinary quality which can be produced only in relatively small quantities yields a monopoly price. The wine-grower would realise a considerable surplus-profit from this monopoly price, whose excess over the value of the product would be wholly determined by the means and fondness of the discriminating wine-drinker. This surplus-profit, which accrues from a monopoly price, is converted into rent and in this form falls into the lap of the landlord, thanks to his title to this piece of the globe endowed with singular properties. Here, then, the monopoly price creates the rent. On the other hand, the rent would create a monopoly price if grain were sold not merely above its price of production, but also above its value, owing to the limits set by landed property to the investment of capital in uncultivated land without payment of rent. That it is only the title of a number of persons to the possession of the globe enabling them to appropriate to themselves as tribute a portion of the surplus-labour of society and furthermore to a constantly increasing extent with the development of production, is concealed by the fact that the capitalised rent, i.e., precisely this capitalised tribute, appears as the price of land, which may therefore, be sold like any other article of commerce. The buyer, therefore, does not feel that his title to the rent is obtained gratis, and without the labour, risk, and spirit of enterprise of the capitalist, but rather that he has paid for it with an equivalent. To the buyer, as previously indicated, the rent appears merely as interest on the capital with which he has purchased the land and consequently his title to the rent. In the same way, the slave-holder considers a Negro, whom he has purchased, as his property, not because the institution of slavery as such entitles him to that Negro, but because he has acquired him like any other commodity, through sale and purchase. But the title itself is simply transferred, and not created by the sale. The title must exist before it can be sold, and a series of sales can no more create this title through continued repetition than a single sale can. What created it in the first place were the production relations. As soon as these have reached a point where they must shed their skin, the material source of the title, justified economically and historically and arising from the process which creates social life, falls by the wayside, along with all transactions based upon it. From the standpoint of a higher economic form of society, private ownership of the globe by single individuals will appear quite as absurd as private ownership of one man by another. Even a whole society, a nation, or even all simultaneously existing societies taken together, are not the owners of the globe. They are only its possessors, its usufructuaries, and, like *boni patres familias,* they must hand it down to succeeding generations in an improved condition.

In the following analysis of the price of land we leave out of consideration all fluctuations of competition, all land speculation, and also small landed property, in which land forms the principal instrument of producers and must, therefore, be bought by them at any price.

I. The price of land may rise without the rent rising, namely:

   1. by a mere fall in interest rate, which causes the rent to be sold more dearly, and thereby the capitalised rent, or price of land, rises;
   2. because the interest on capital incorporated in the land rises.

II. The price of land may rise, because the rent increases.

The rent may increase, because the price of the product of the land rises, in which case, the rate of differential rent always rises, whether the rent on the worst cultivated soil be large, small or non-existent. By rate we mean the ratio of that portion of surplus-value converted into rent to the invested capital which produces the agricultural product. This differs from the ratio of surplus-product to total product, for the total product does not comprise the entire invested capital, namely, the fixed capital, which continues to exist alongside the product. On the other hand, it covers the fact that on soils yielding differential rent an increasing portion of the product is transformed into an excess of surplus-product. The increase in price of agricultural product of the worst soil first creates rent and thereby the price of land.

The rent, however, may also increase without a rise in price of the agricultural product. This price may remain constant, or even decrease.

If the price remains constant, the rent can grow only (apart from monopoly prices) because, on the one hand, given the same amount of capital invested in the old lands, new lands of better quality are cultivated, which merely suffice, however, to cover the increased demand, so that the regulating market-price remains unchanged. In this case, the price of the old lands does not rise, but the price of the newly cultivated lands rises above that of the old ones.

Or, on the other hand, the rent rises because the mass of capital exploiting the land increases, assuming that the relative productivity and market-price remain the same. Although the rent thus remains the same compared with the invested capital, still its mass, for instance, may be doubled, because the capital itself has doubled. Since no fall in price has occurred, the second investment of capital yields a surplus-profit just as well as the first, and it likewise is transformed into rent after the expiration of the lease. The mass of rent rises here, because the mass of capital producing a rent increases. The contention that various successive investments of capital in the same piece of land can produce rent only in so far as their yield is unequal, so that a differential rent thus arises, is reduced to the contention that when two capitals of £1,000 each are invested in two fields of equal productivity, only one of them can produce a rent, although both fields belong to a better soil type, which produces differential rent. (The mass of rental, the total rent of a country, grows therefore with the mass of capital invested, without the price of the individual pieces of land, or the rate of rent, or even the mass of rent on individual pieces of land, necessarily increasing; the amount of rental grows, in this case, with the extension of cultivation over a wider area. This may even be combined with a decrease in rent on individual holdings.) Otherwise, this contention would lead to the other, namely, that the investment of capital in two different pieces of land existing side by side follows different laws than the successive investment of capital in the same plot, whereas differential rent is derived precisely from the identity of the law in both cases, from the increased productiveness of capital invested either in the same field or in different fields. The only modification which exists here and is overlooked is that successive investments of capital, when applied to different pieces of land, meet the barrier of landed property, which is not the case with successive investments of capital in the same piece of land. This accounts for the opposing tendencies by which these two different forms of investment curb each other in practice. No difference in capital ever appears here. If the composition of the capital remains the same, and similarly the rate of surplus-value, the rate of profit remains unaltered, so that the mass of profit is doubled when the capital is doubled. In like manner the rate of rent remains the same under the assumed conditions. If a capital of £1,000 produces a rent of x, then a capital of £2,000, under the assumed conditions, produces a rent of 2x. But calculated with reference to the area of land, which has remained unaltered, since, according to our assumption, the doubled capital operates in the same field, the level of rent has also risen as a consequence of its increase in mass. The same acre which yielded a rent of £2, now yields £4.[4]

The relation of a portion of the surplus-value, of money-rent—for money is the independent expression of value—to the land is in itself absurd and irrational; for the magnitudes which are here measured by one another are incommensurable—a particular use-value, a piece of land of so many and so many square feet, on the one hand, and value, especially surplus-value, on the other. This expresses in fact nothing more than that, under the given conditions, the ownership of so many square feet of land enables the landowner to wrest a certain quantity of unpaid labour, which the capital wallowing in these square feet like a hog in potatoes has realised. [Written in the manuscript here in brackets, but crossed out, is the name 'Liebig'.] But *prima facie* the expression is the same as if one desired to speak of the relation of a five-pound note to the diameter of the earth. However, the reconciliation of irrational forms in which certain economic relations appear and assert themselves in practice does not concern the active agents of these relations in their everyday life. And since they are accustomed to move about in such relations, they find nothing strange therein. A complete contradiction offers not the least mystery to them.

They feel as much at home as a fish in water among manifestations which are separated from their internal connections and absurd when isolated by themselves. What Hegel says with reference to certain mathematical formulas applies here: that which seems irrational to ordinary common sense is rational, and that which seems rational to it is itself irrational. [Hegel, *Encyclopädie der philosophischen Wissenschaften in Grundrisse,* 1. Teil, *Die Logik.* In: *Werke,* Band 6, Berlin, 1840, S. 404.—*Ed.*] When considered in connection with the land area itself, a rise in the mass of rent is thus expressed in the same way as a rise in the rate of rent, and hence the embarrassment experienced when the conditions which would explain the one case are lacking in the other.

The price of land, however, may also rise even when the price of the agricultural product decreases.

In this case, the differential rent, and with it the price of the better lands, may have risen, owing to further differentiations. Or, if this is not the case, the price of the agricultural product may have fallen by virtue of greater labour productivity but in such a manner that the increased production more than counterbalances this. Let us assume that one quarter cost 60 shillings. Now, if the same acre, with the same capital, should produce two quarters instead of one, and the price of one quarter should fall to 40 shillings, then two quarters would cost 80 shillings, so that the value of the product of the same capital invested in the same acre would have risen by one-third, despite the fall in price per quarter by one-third. How this is possible without selling the product above its price of production or above its value, has been developed in the analysis of differential rent. As a matter of fact it is possible only in two ways. Either bad soil is excluded from competition, but the price of the better soil increases with the increase in differential rent, i.e., the general improvement affects the various soil types differently. Or, the same price of production (and the same value, if absolute rent is paid) expresses itself on the worst soil through a larger mass of products, when labour productivity has become greater. The product represents the same value as before, but the price of its aliquot parts has fallen, while their number has increased. This is impossible when the same capital has been employed; for in this case, the same value always expresses itself through any portion of the product. It is possible, however, when additional capital has been expended for gypsum, guano, etc., in short, for improvements the effects of which extend over several years. The stipulation is that the price of an individual quarter falls, but not to the same extent as the number of quarters increases.

III. These different conditions under which rent may rise, and with it the price of land in general, or of particular kinds of land, may partly compete, or partly exclude one another, and can only act alternately. But it follows from the foregoing that the consequence of a rise in the price of land does not necessarily signify also a rise in rent, or that a rise in rent, which always brings with it a rise in the price of land, is not necessarily contingent upon an increase in the agricultural product.[5]

Rather than tracing to their origin the real natural causes leading to an exhaustion of the soil, which, incidentally, were unknown to all economists writing on differential rent owing to the level of agricultural chemistry in their day, the shallow conception was seized upon that any amount of capital cannot be invested in a limited area of land; as the *Edinburgh Review,* [Tome LIV, August-December 1831, pp. 94-95.—*Ed.*] for instance, argued against Richard Jones that all of England cannot be fed through the cultivation of Soho Square. If this be considered a special disadvantage of agriculture, precisely the opposite is true. It is possible to invest capital here successively with fruitful results, because the soil itself serves as an instrument of production, which is not the case with a factory, or holds only to a limited extent, since it serves only as a foundation, as a place and a space providing a basis of operations. It is true that, compared with scattered handicrafts, large-scale industry may concentrate much production in a small area. Nevertheless a definite amount of space is always required at any given level of productivity, and the construction of tall buildings also has its practical limitations. Beyond this any expansion of production also demands an extension of land area. The fixed capital invested in machinery, etc., does not improve through use, but on the contrary, wears out. New inventions may indeed permit some improvement in this respect, but with any given development in productive power, machines will always deteriorate. If productivity is rapidly developed, all of the old machinery must be replaced by the more advantageous; in other words, it is lost. The soil, however, if properly treated, improves all the time. The advantage of the soil, permitting successive investments of capital to bring gains without loss of previous investments, implies the possibility of differences in yield from these successive investments of capital.

Notes

1. Laing [*National Distress; its Causes and Remedies,* London, 1844.—*Ed.*], Newman [*Lectures on Political Economy,* London, 1857.—*Ed.*].
2. Crowlington Strike. Engels, *Lage der arbeitenden Klasse in England,* S. 307.
3. 'The paving of the streets of London has enabled the owners of some barren rocks on the coast of Scotland to draw a rent from what never afforded any before.' Adam Smith [An *Inquiry into the Nature and Causes of the Wealth of Nations,*] Book 1, Chapter XI, 2.
4. It is one of the merits of Rodbertus whose important work on rent [*Sociale Briefe an von Kirchmann,* Dritter Brief: Widerlegung der Ricardo'schen Lehre von der Grundrente und Begründung einer neuen Rententheorie, Berlin, 1851.—*Ed.*] we shall discuss in Book IV [i.e., *Theorien über den Mehrwert.* K. Marx. Engels, *Werke,* Band 26, 2. Teil, S. 7-102, *139-51.—Ed.*] to have developed this point. He commits the one error, however, of assuming, in the first place, that as regards capital an increase in profit is always expressed by an increase in capital, so that the ratio remains the same when the mass of profit increases. But this is erroneous, since the rate of profit may increase, given a changed composition of capital, even if the exploitation of labour remains the same, precisely because the proportional value of the constant portion of capital compared with its variable portion falls. Secondly, he commits the mistake of dealing with the ratio of money-rent to a quantitatively definite piece of land, e.g., an acre, as though it had been the general premise of classical economics in its analysis of the rise or fall of rent. This, again, is erroneous. Classical economics always treats the rate of rent, in so far as it considers rent in its natural form, with reference to the product, and in so far as it considers rent as money-rent, with reference to the advanced capital, because these are in fact the rational expressions.
5. Concerning the actual fall in the price of land when rent rises, see Passy. [H. Passy, Rente du sol. In: Dictionnaire de l'économie politique, Tome II.]

47

Genesis of Capitalist Ground-Rent

Section I. *Introductory Remarks*

We must clarify in our minds wherein lies the real difficulty in analysing ground-rent from the viewpoint of modern economics, as the theoretical expression of the capitalist mode of production. Even many of the more modern writers have not as yet grasped this, as evidenced by each renewed attempt to 'newly' explain ground-rent. The novelty almost invariably consists in a relapse into long out-of-date views. The difficulty is not to explain the surplus-product produced by agricultural capital and its corresponding surplus-value in general. This question is solved in the analysis of the surplus-value produced by all productive capital, in whatever sphere it may be invested. The difficulty consists rather in showing the source of the excess of surplus-value paid the landlord by capital invested in land in the form of rent, after equalisation of the surplus-value to the average profit among the various capitals, after the various capitals have shared in the total surplus-value produced by the social capital in all spheres of production in proportion to their relative size; in other words, the source subsequent to this equalisation and the apparently already completed distribution of all surplus-value which, in general, is to be distributed. Quite apart from the practical motives, which prodded modern economists as spokesmen of industrial capital against landed property to investigate this question—motives which we shall point out more clearly in the chapter on history of ground-rent—the question was of paramount interest to them as theorists. To admit that the appearance of rent for capital invested in agriculture is due to some particular effect produced by the sphere of investment itself, due to singular qualities of the earth's crust itself, is tantamount to giving up the conception of value as such, thus tantamount to abandoning all attempts at a scientific understanding of this field. Even the simple observation that rent is paid out of the price of agricultural produce—which takes place even where rent is paid in kind if the farmer is to recover his price of production—showed the absurdity of attempting to explain the excess of this price over the ordinary price of production; in other words, to explain the relative dearness of agricultural products on the basis of the excess of natural productivity of agricultural production over the productivity of other lines of production. For the reverse is true: the more productive labour is, the cheaper is every aliquot part of its product, because so much greater is the mass of use-values incorporating the same quantity of labour, i.e., the same value.

The whole difficulty in analysing rent, therefore, consists in explaining the excess of agricultural profit over the average profit, not the surplus-value, but the excess of surplus-value characteristic of this sphere of production; in other words, not the 'net product', but the excess of this net product over the net product of other branches of industry. The average profit itself is a product formed under very definite historical production relations by the movement of social processes, a product which, as we have seen, requires very complex adjustment. To be able to speak at all of a surplus over the average profit, this average profit itself must already be established as a standard and as a regulator of production in general as is the case under capitalist production. For this reason there can be no talk of rent in the modern sense, a rent consisting of a surplus over the average profit, i.e., over and above the proportional share of each individual capital in the surplus-value produced by the total social capital, in social formations where it is not capital which performs the function of enforcing all surplus-labour and appropriating directly all surplus-value. And where, therefore, capital has not yet completely, or only sporadically, brought social labour under its control. It reflects naïveté, e.g., of a person like Passy (see below), when he speaks of rent in primitive society as a surplus over profit [Passy, *Rente du sol.* In: Dictionnaire de l'économie politique, Tome II. Paris, 1854, p. 511.—*Ed.*]—a historically defined social form of surplus-value, but which, according to Passy, might almost as well exist without any society.

For the older economists, who in general merely begin analysing the capitalist mode of production, still undeveloped in their day, the analysis of rent offers either no difficulty at all, or only a difficulty of a completely different kind. Petty, Cantillon, and in general those writers who are closer to feudal times, assume ground-rent to be the normal form of surplus-value in general, [[Petty] *A Treatise on Taxes and Contributions,* London, 1667, pp. 23-24; [Richard Cantillon] *Essai sur la nature du commerce en géneral,* Amsterdam, 1756.—*Ed.*] whereas profit to them is still amorphously combined with wages, or at best appears to be a portion of surplus-value extorted by the capitalist from the landlord. These writers thus take as their point of departure a situation where, in the first place, the agricultural population still constitutes the overwhelming majority of the nation, and, secondly, the landlord still appears as the person appropriating at first hand the surplus-labour of the direct producers by virtue of his monopoly of landed property, where landed property, therefore, still appears as the main condition of production. For these writers the question could not yet be posed, which, inversely, seeks to investigate from the viewpoint of capitalist production how landed property manages to wrest back again from capital a portion of the surplus-value produced by it (that is, filched by it from the direct producers) and already appropriated directly.

The *physiocrats* are troubled by difficulties of another nature. As the actually first systematic spokesmen of capital, they attempt to analyse the nature of surplus-value in general. For them, this analysis coincides with the analysis of rent, the only form of surplus-value which they recognise. Therefore, they consider rent-yielding, or agricultural, capital to be the only capital producing surplus-value, and the agricultural labour set in motion by it, the only labour producing surplus-value, which from a capitalist viewpoint is quite properly considered the only productive labour. They are quite right in considering the creation of surplus-value as decisive. Apart from other merits to be set forth in Book IV, they deserve credit primarily for going back from merchant's capital, which functions solely in the sphere of circulation, to productive capital, in opposition to the mercantile system, which, with its crude realism, constitutes the actual vulgar economy of that period, pushing into the background in favour of its own practical interests the beginnings of scientific analysis made by Petty and his successors. In this critique of the mercantile system, incidentally, only its conceptions of capital and surplus-value are dealt with. It has already been indicated previously that the monetary system correctly proclaims production for the world-market and the transformation of the output into commodities, and thus into money, as the prerequisite and condition of capitalist production. In this system's further development into the mercantile system, it is no longer the transformation of commodity-value into money, but the creation of surplus-value which is decisive—but from the meaningless viewpoint of the circulation sphere and, at the same time, in such manner that this surplus value is represented as surplus money, as the balance of trade surplus. At the same time, however, the characteristic feature of the interested merchants and manufacturers of that period, which is in keeping with the stage of capitalist development represented by them, is that the transformation of feudal agricultural societies into industrial ones and the corresponding industrial struggle of nations on the world-market depends on an accelerated development of capital, which is not to be arrived at along the so-called natural path, but rather by means of coercive measures. It makes a tremendous difference whether national capital is gradually and slowly transformed into industrial capital, or whether this development is accelerated by means of a tax which they impose through protective duties mainly upon landowners, middle and small peasants, and handicraftsmen, by way of accelerated expropriation of the independent direct producers, and through the violently accelerated accumulation and concentration of capital, in short by means of the accelerated establishment of conditions of capitalist production. It simultaneously makes an enormous difference in the capitalist and industrial exploitation of the natural national productive power. Hence the national character of the mercantile system is not merely a phrase on the lips of its spokesmen. Under the pretext of concern solely for the wealth of the nation and the resources of the state, they, in fact, pronounce the interests of the capitalist class and the amassing of riches in general to be the ultimate aim of the state, and thus proclaim bourgeois society in place of the old divine state. But at the same time they are consciously aware that the development of the interests of capital and of the capitalist class, of capitalist production, forms the foundation of national power and national ascendancy in modern society.

The physiocrats, furthermore, are correct in stating that in fact all production of surplus-value, and thus all development of capital, has for its natural basis the productiveness of agricultural labour. If man were not capable of producing in one working-day more means of subsistence, which signifies in the strictest sense more agricultural products than every labourer needs for his own reproduction, if the daily expenditure of his entire labour power sufficed merely to produce the means of subsistence indispensable for his own individual requirements, then one could not speak at all either of surplus-product or surplus-value. An agricultural labour productivity exceeding the individual requirements of the labourer is the basis of all societies, and is above all the basis of capitalist production, which disengages a constantly increasing portion of society from the production of basic foodstuffs and transforms them into 'free heads,' as Steuart [Steuart, *An Inquiry Into the Principles of Political Economy*, Vol. I, Dublin, 1770, p. 396.—*Ed.*] has it, making them available for exploitation in other spheres.

But what can be said of more recent writers on economics, such as Daire, Passy, etc., who parrot the most primitive conceptions concerning the natural conditions of surplus-labour and thereby surplus-value in general, in the twilight of classical economy, indeed on its very death-bed, and who imagine that they are thus propounding something new and striking on ground-rent [Daire, *Introduction. In: Physiocrats, 1.* Teil, Paris, 1846; Passy, *Rente du sol.* In: Dictionnaire de l'économie politique, Tome II, Paris, 1854, p. 511.—*Ed.*] long after this ground-rent has been investigated as a special form and become a specific portion of surplus-value? It is particularly characteristic of vulgar economy that it echoes what was new, original, profound and justified during a specific outgrown stage of development, in a period when it has turned platitudinous, stale, and false. It thus confesses its complete ignorance of the problems which concerned classical economy. It confounds them with questions that could only have been posed on a lower level of development of bourgeois society. The same holds true of its incessant and self-complacent rumination of the physiocratic phrases concerning free trade. These phrases have long since lost all theoretical interest, no matter how much they may engage the practical attention of this or that state.

In natural economy proper, when no part of the agricultural product, or but a very insignificant portion, enters into the process of circulation, and then only a relatively small portion of that part of the product which represents the landlord's revenue, as, e.g., in many Roman latifundia, or upon the villas of Charlemagne, or more or less during the entire Middle Ages (see Vinçard, *Histoire du travail*), the product and surplus-product of the large estates consists by no means purely of products of agricultural labour. It encompasses equally well the products of industrial labour. Domestic handicrafts and manufacturing labour as secondary occupations of agriculture, which forms the basis, are the prerequisite of that mode of production upon which natural economy rests—in European antiquity and the Middle Ages as well as in the present-day Indian community, in which the traditional organisation has not yet been destroyed. The capitalist mode of production completely abolishes this relationship; a process which may be studied on a large scale particularly in England during the last third of the 18th century. Thinkers like Herrenschwand, who had grown up in more or less semi-feudal societies, still consider, e.g., as late as the close of the 18th century, this separation of manufacture from agriculture as a foolhardy social adventure, as an unthinkably risky mode of existence. And even in the agricultural economies of antiquity showing the greatest analogy to capitalist agriculture, namely Carthage and Rome, the similarity to a plantation economy is greater than to a form corresponding to the really capitalist mode of exploitation.[1] A formal analogy, which, simultaneously, however, turns out to be completely illusory in all essential points to a person familiar with the capitalist mode of production, who does not, like Herr Mommsen,[2] discover a capitalist mode of production in every monetary economy, is not to be found at all in continental Italy during antiquity, but at best only in Sicily, since this island served Rome as an agricultural tributary so that its agriculture was aimed chiefly at export. Farmers in the modern sense existed there.

An erroneous conception of the nature of rent is based upon the fact that rent in kind, partly as tithes to the church and partly as a curiosity perpetuated by long-established contracts, has been dragged over into modern times from the natural economy of the Middle Ages, completely in contradiction to the conditions of the capitalist mode of production. It thereby creates the impression that rent does not arise from the price of the agricultural product, but from its mass, thus not from social conditions, but from the earth. We have previously shown that although surplus-value is manifested in a surplus-product the converse does not hold that a surplus-product, representing a mere increase in the mass of product, constitutes surplus-value. It may represent a minus quantity in value. Otherwise the cotton industry of 1860, compared with that of 1840, would show an enormous surplus-value, whereas on the contrary the price of the yarn has fallen. Rent may increase enormously as a result of a succession of crop failures, because the price of grain rises, although this surplus-value appears as an absolutely decreasing mass of dearer wheat. Conversely, the rent may fall in consequence of a succession of bountiful years, because the price falls, although the reduced rent appears as a greater mass of cheaper wheat. As regards rent in kind, it should be noted now that, in the first place, it is a mere tradition carried over from an obsolete mode of production and managing to prolong its existence as a survival. Its contradiction to the capitalist mode of production is shown by its disappearance of itself from private contracts, and its being forcibly shaken off as an anachronism, wherever legislation was able to intervene as in the case of church tithes in England. Secondly, however, where rent in kind persisted on the basis of capitalist production, it was no more, and could be no more, than an expression of money-rent in medieval garb. Wheat, for instance, is quoted at 40 shillings per quarter. One portion of this wheat must replace the wages contained therein, and must be sold to become available for renewed expenditure. Another portion must be sold to pay its proportionate share of taxes. Seed and even a portion of fertiliser enter as commodities into the process of reproduction, wherever the capitalist mode of production and with it division of social labour are developed, i.e., they must be purchased for replacement purposes; and therefore another portion of this quarter must be sold to obtain money for this. In so far as they need not be bought as actual commodities, but are taken out of the product itself in kind, in order to enter into its reproduction anew as conditions of production—as occurs not only in agriculture, but in many other lines of production producing constant capital—they figure in the books as money of account and are deducted as elements of the cost-price. The wear and tear of machinery, and of fixed capital in general, must be made good in money. And finally comes profit, which is calculated on this sum, expressed as costs either in actual money or in money of account. This profit is represented by a definite portion of the gross product, which is determined by its price. And the excess portion which then remains forms rent. If the rent in kind stipulated by contract is greater than this remainder determined by the price, then it does not constitute rent, but a deduction from profit. Owing to this possibility alone, rent in kind is an obsolete form, in so far as it does not reflect the price of the product, but may be greater or smaller than the real rent, and thus may comprise not only a deduction from profit, but also from those elements required for capital replacement. In fact, this rent in kind, so far as it is rent not merely in name but also in essence, is exclusively determined by the excess of the price of the product over its price of production. Only it presupposes that this variable is a constant magnitude. But it is such a comforting reflection that the product in kind should suffice, first, to maintain the labourer, secondly, to leave the capitalist tenant farmer more food than he needs, and finally, that the remainder should constitute the natural rent. Quite like a manufacturer producing 200,000 yards of cotton goods. These yards of goods not only suffice to clothe his labourers; to clothe his wife, all his offspring and himself abundantly; but also leave over enough cotton for sale, in addition to paying an enormous rent in terms of cotton goods. It is all so simple! Deduct the price of production from 200,000 yards of cotton goods, and a surplus of cotton goods must remain for rent. But it is indeed a naive conception to deduct the price of production of, say, £10,000 from 200,000 yards of cotton goods, without knowing the selling price, to deduct money from cotton goods, to deduct an exchange-value from a use-value as such, and thus to determine the surplus of yards of cotton goods over pounds sterling. It is worse than squaring the circle, which is at least based upon the conception that there is a limit at which straight lines and curves imperceptibly flow together. But such is the prescription of M. Passy. Deduct money from cotton goods, before the cotton goods have been converted into money, either in one's mind or in reality! What remains is the rent, which, however, is to be grasped *naturaliter* (see, for instance, Karl Arnd [K. Arnd, *Die naturgemässe Volkswirtschaft, gegenüber dem Monopoliengeiste und dem Communismus*, Hanau, 1845, S. 461-62.—*Ed.*]) and not by deviltries of sophistry. The entire restoration of rent in kind is finally reduced to this foolishness, the deduction of the price of production from so many and so many bushels of wheat, and the subtraction of a sum of money from a cubic measure.

Section II. *Labour Rent*

If we consider ground-rent in its simplest form, that of *labour rent*, where the direct producer, using instruments of labour (plough, cattle, etc.) which actually or legally belong to him, cultivates soil actually owned by him during part of the week, and works during the remaining days upon the estate of the feudal lord without any compensation from the feudal lord, the situation here is still quite clear, for in this case, rent and surplus-value are identical. Rent, not profit, is the form here through which unpaid surplus-labour expresses itself. To what extent the labourer (a self-sustaining serf) can secure, in this case, a surplus above his indispensable necessities of life, i.e., a surplus above that which we would call wages under the capitalist mode of production, depends, other circumstances remaining unchanged, upon the proportion in which his labour-time is divided into labour-time for himself and enforced labour-time for his feudal lord. This surplus above the indispensable requirements of life, the germ of what appears as profit under the capitalist mode of production, is therefore, wholly determined by the amount of ground-rent, which, in this case, is not only directly unpaid surplus-labour, but also appears as such. It is unpaid surplus-labour for the 'owner' of the means of production, which here coincide with the land, and so far as they differ from it, are mere accessories to it. That the product of the serf must here suffice to reproduce his conditions of labour, in addition to his subsistence, is a circumstance which remains the same under all modes of production. For it is not the result of their specific form, but a natural requisite of all continuous and reproductive labour in general, of any continuing production, which is always simultaneously reproduction, i.e., including reproduction of its own operating conditions. It is furthermore evident that in all forms in which the direct labourer remains the 'possessor' of the means of production and labour conditions necessary for the production of his own means of subsistence, the property relationship must simultaneously appear as a direct relation of lordship and servitude, so that the direct producer is not free; a lack of freedom which may be reduced from serfdom with enforced labour to a mere tributary relationship. The direct producer, according to our assumption, is to be found here in possession of his own means of production, the necessary material labour conditions required for the realisation of his labour and the production of his means of subsistence. He conducts his agricultural activity and the rural home industries connected with it independently. This independence is not undermined by the circumstance that the small peasants may form among themselves a more or less natural production community, as they do in India, since it is here merely a question of independence from the nominal lord of the manor. Under such conditions the surplus-labour for the nominal owner of the land can only be extorted from them by other than economic pressure, whatever the form assumed may be.[3] This differs from slave or plantation economy in that the slave works under alien conditions of production and not independently. Thus, conditions of personal dependence are requisite, a lack of personal freedom, no matter to what extent, and being tied to the soil as its accessory, bondage in the true sense of the word. Should the direct producers not be confronted by a private landowner, but rather, as in Asia, under direct subordination to a state which stands over them as their landlord and simultaneously as sovereign, then rent and taxes coincide, or rather, there exists no tax which differs from this form of ground-rent. Under such circumstances, there need exist no stronger political or economic pressure than that common to all subjection to that state. The state is then the supreme lord. Sovereignty here consists in the ownership of land concentrated on a national scale. But, on the other hand, no private ownership of land exists, although there is both private and common possession and use of land.

The specific economic form, in which unpaid surplus-labour is pumped out of direct producers, determines the relationship of rulers and ruled, as it grows directly out of production itself and, in turn, reacts upon it as a determining element. Upon this, however, is founded the entire formation of the economic community which grows up out of the production relations themselves, thereby simultaneously its specific political form. It is always the direct relationship of the owners of the conditions of production to the direct producers—a relation always naturally corresponding to a definite stage in the development of the methods of labour and thereby its social productivity—which reveals the innermost secret, the hidden basis of the entire social structure and with it the political form of the relation of sovereignty and dependence, in short, the corresponding specific form of the state. This does not prevent the same economic basis—the same from the standpoint of its main conditions—due to innumerable different empirical circumstances, natural environment, racial relations, external historical influences, etc. from showing infinite variations and gradations in appearance, which can be ascertained only by analysis of the empirically given circumstances.

So much is evident with respect to labour rent, the simplest and most primitive form of rent: Rent is here the primeval form of surplus-labour and coincides with it. But this identity of surplus-value with unpaid labour of others need not be analysed here because it still exists in its visible, palpable form, since the labour of the direct producer for himself is still separated in space and time from his labour for the landlord and the latter appears directly in the brutal form of enforced labour for a third person. In the same way the 'attribute' possessed by the soil to produce rent is here reduced to a tangibly open secret, for the disposition to furnish rent here also includes human labour-power bound to the soil, and the property relation which compels the owner of labour-power to drive it on and activate it beyond such measure as is required to satisfy his own indispensable needs. Rent consists directly in the appropriation of this surplus expenditure of labour-power by the landlord; for the direct producer pays him no additional rent. Here, where surplus-value and rent are not only identical but where surplus-value has the tangible form of surplus-labour, the natural conditions or limits of rent, being those of surplus-value in general, are plainly clear. The direct producer must 1) possess enough labour-power, and 2) the natural conditions of his labour, above all the soil cultivated by him, must be productive enough, in a word, the natural productivity of his labour must be big enough to give him the possibility of retaining some surplus-labour over and above that required for the satisfaction of his own indispensable needs. It is not this possibility which creates the rent, but rather compulsion which turns this possibility into reality. But the possibility itself is conditioned by subjective and objective natural circumstances. And here too lies nothing at all mysterious. Should labour-power be minute, and the natural conditions of labour scanty, then the surplus-labour is small, but in such a case so are the wants of the producers on the one hand and the relative number of exploiters of surplus-labour on the other, and finally so is the surplus-product, whereby this barely productive surplus-labour is realised for those few exploiting landowners.

Finally, labour rent in itself implies that, all other circumstances remaining equal, it will depend wholly upon the relative amount of surplus-labour, or enforced labour, to what extent the direct producer shall be enabled to improve his own condition, to acquire wealth, to produce an excess over and above his indispensable means of subsistence, or, if we wish to anticipate the capitalist mode of expression, whether he shall be able to produce a profit for himself, and how much of a profit, i.e., an excess over his wages which have been produced by himself. Rent here is the normal, all-absorbing, so to say legitimate form of surplus-labour, and far from being excess over profit, which means, in this case, being above any other excess over wages, it is rather that the amount of such profit, and even its very existence, depends, other circumstances being equal, upon the amount of rent, i.e., the enforced surplus-labour to be surrendered to the landowners.

Since the direct producer is not the owner, but only a possessor, and since all his surplus-labour *de jure* actually belongs to the landlord, some historians have expressed astonishment that it should be at all possible for those subject to enforced labour, or serfs, to acquire any independent property, or relatively speaking, wealth, under such circumstances. However, it is evident that tradition must play a dominant role in the primitive and undeveloped circumstances on which these social production relations and the corresponding mode of production are based. It is furthermore clear that here as always it is in the interest of the ruling section of society to sanction the existing order as law and to legally establish its limits given through usage and tradition. Apart from all else, this, by the way, comes about of itself as soon as the constant reproduction of the basis of the existing order and its fundamental relations assumes a regulated and orderly form in the course of time. And such regulation and order are themselves indispensable elements of any mode of production, if it is to assume social stability and independence from mere chance and arbitrariness. These are precisely the form of its social stability, and therefore, its relative freedom from mere arbitrariness and mere chance. Under backward conditions of the production process as well as the corresponding social relations, it achieves this form by mere repetition of their very reproduction. If this has continued on for some time, it entrenches itself as custom and tradition and is finally sanctioned as an explicit law. However, since the form of this surplus-labour, enforced labour, is based upon the imperfect development of all social productive powers and the crudeness of the methods of labour itself, it will naturally absorb a relatively much smaller portion of the direct producer's total labour than under developed modes of production, particularly the capitalist mode of production. Take it, for instance, that the enforced labour for the landlord originally amounted to two days per week. These two days of enforced labour per week are thereby fixed, are a constant magnitude, legally regulated by prescriptive or written law. But the productivity of the remaining days of the week, which are at the disposal of the direct producer himself, is a variable magnitude, which must develop in the course of his experience, just as the new wants he acquires, and just as the expansion of the market for his product and the increasing assurance with which he disposes of this portion of his labour-power will spur him on to a greater exertion of his labour-power, whereby it should not be forgotten that the employment of his labour-power is by no means confined to agriculture, but includes rural home industry. The possibility is here presented for definite economic development taking place, depending, of course, upon favourable circumstances, inborn racial characteristics, etc.

Section III. *Rent In Kind*

The transformation of labour rent into rent in kind changes nothing from the economic standpoint in the nature of ground-rent. The latter consists, in the forms considered here, in that rent is the sole prevailing and normal form of surplus-value, or surplus-labour. This is further expressed in the fact that it is the only surplus-labour, or the only surplus-product, which the direct producer, who is in *possession* of the labour conditions needed for his own reproduction, must give up to the *owner* of the land, which in this situation is the all-embracing condition of labour. And, furthermore, that land is the only condition of labour which confronts the direct producer as alien property, independent of him, and personified by the landlord. To whatever extent rent in kind is the prevailing and dominant form of ground-rent, it is further-more always more or less accompanied by survivals of the earlier form, i.e., of rent paid directly in labour, corvée-labour, no matter whether the landlord be a private person or the state. Rent in kind presupposes a higher stage of civilisation for the direct producer, i.e., a higher level of development of his labour and of society in general. And it is distinct from the preceding form in that surplus-labour needs no longer be performed in its natural form, thus no longer under the direct supervision and compulsion of the landlord or his representatives: the direct producer is driven rather by force of circumstances than by direct coercion, through legal enactment rather than the whip, to perform it on his own responsibility. Surplus-production, in the sense of production beyond the indispensable needs of the direct producer, and within the field of production actually belonging to him, upon the land exploited by himself instead of, as earlier, upon the nearby lord's estate beyond his own land, has already become a self-understood rule here. In this relation the direct producer more or less disposes of his entire labour-time, although, as previously, a part of this labour-time, at first practically the entire surplus portion of it, belongs to the landlord without compensation; except that the landlord no longer directly receives this surplus-labour in its natural form, but rather in the products' natural form in which it is realised. The burdensome, and according to the way in which enforced labour is regulated, more or less disturbing interruption by work for the landlord (see Buch I, Kap. VIII, 2) [English edition Ch X, 2—*Ed*] ('Manufacturer and Boyard') stops wherever rent in kind appears in pure form, or at least it is reduced to a few short intervals during the year, when a continuation of some corvée-labour side by side with rent in kind takes place. The labour of the producer for himself and his labour for the landlord are no longer palpably separated by time and space. This rent in kind, in its pure form, while it may drag fragments along into more highly developed modes of production and production relations, still presupposes for its existence a natural economy, i.e., that the conditions of the economy are either wholly or for the overwhelming part produced by the economy itself, directly replaced and reproduced out of its gross product. It furthermore presupposes the combination of rural home industry with agriculture. The surplus-product, which forms the rent, is the product of this combined agricultural and industrial family labour, no matter whether rent in kind contains more or less of the industrial product, as is often the case in the Middle Ages, or whether it is paid only in the form of actual products of the land. In this form of rent it is by no means necessary for rent in kind, which represents the surplus-labour, to fully exhaust the entire surplus-labour of the rural family. Compared with labour rent, the producer rather has more room for action to gain time for surplus-labour whose product shall belong to himself, as well as the product of his labour which satisfies his indispensable needs. Similarly, this form will give rise to greater differences in the economic position of the individual direct producers. At least the possibility for such a differentiation exists, and the possibility for the direct producer to have in turn acquired the means to exploit other labourers directly. This, however, does not concern us here, since we are dealing with rent in kind in its pure form; just as in general we cannot enter into the endless variety of combinations wherein the various forms of rent may be united, adulterated and amalgamated. The form of rent in kind, by being bound to a definite type of product and production itself and through its indispensable combination of agriculture and domestic industry, through its almost complete self-sufficiency whereby the peasant family supports itself through its independence from the market and the movement of production and history of that section of society lying outside of its sphere, in short owing to the character of natural economy in general, this form is quite adapted to furnishing the basis for stationary social conditions as we see, e.g., in Asia. Here, as in the earlier form of labour rent, ground-rent is the normal form of surplus-value, and thus of surplus-labour, i.e., of the entire excess labour which the direct producer must perform gratis, hence actually under compulsion although this compulsion no longer confronts him in the old brutal form—for the benefit of the owner of his essential condition of labour, the land. The profit, if by erroneously anticipating we may thus call that portion of the direct producer's labour excess over his necessary labour, which he retains for himself, has so little to do with determining rent in kind, that this profit, on the contrary, grows up behind the back of rent and finds its natural limit in the size of rent in kind. The latter may assume dimensions which seriously imperil reproduction of the conditions of labour, the means of production themselves, rendering the expansion of production more or less impossible and reducing the direct producers to the physical minimum of means of subsistence. This is particularly the case, when this form is met with and exploited by a conquering commercial nation, e.g., the English in India.

Section IV. *Money-Rent*

By money-rent—as distinct from industrial and commercial ground-rent based upon the capitalist mode of production, which is but an excess over average profit—we here mean the ground-rent which arises from a mere change in form of rent in kind, just as the latter in turn is but a modification of labour rent. The direct producer here turns over instead of the product, its price to the landlord (who may be either the state or a private individual). An excess of products in their natural form no longer suffices; it must be converted from its natural form into money-form. Although the direct producer still continues to produce at least the greater part of his means of subsistence himself, a certain portion of this product must now be converted into commodities, must be produced as commodities. The character of the entire mode of production is thus more or less changed. It loses its independence, its detachment from social connection. The ratio of cost of production, which now comprises greater or lesser expenditures of money, becomes decisive; at any rate, the excess of that portion of gross product to be converted into money over that portion which must serve, on the one hand, as means of reproduction again, and, on the other, as means of direct subsistence, assumes a determining role. However, the basis of this type of rent, although approaching its dissolution, remains the same as that of rent in kind, which constitutes its point of departure. The direct producer as before is still possessor of the land either through inheritance or some other traditional right, and must perform for his lord, as owner of his most essential condition of production, excess corvée-labour, that is, unpaid labour for which no equivalent is returned, in the form of a surplus-product transformed into money. Ownership of the conditions of labour as distinct from land, such as agricultural implements and other goods and chattels, is transformed into the property of the direct producer even under the earlier forms of rent, first in fact, and then also legally, and even more so is this the precondition for the form of money-rent. The transformation of rent in kind into money-rent, taking place first sporadically and then on a more or less national scale, presupposes a considerable development of commerce, of urban industry, of commodity-production in general, and thereby of money circulation. It furthermore assumes a market-price for products, and that they be sold at prices roughly approximating their values, which need not at all be the case under earlier forms. In Eastern Europe we may still partly observe this transformation taking place under our very eyes. How unfeasible it can be without a certain development of social labour productivity is proved by various unsuccessful attempts to carry it through under the Roman Empire, and by relapses into rent in kind after seeking to convert at least the state tax portion of this rent into money-rent. The same transitional difficulties are evidenced, e.g., in pre-revolutionary France, when money-rent was combined with and adulterated by, survivals of its earlier forms.

Money-rent, as a transmuted form of rent in kind, and in antithesis to it, is, nevertheless, the final form, and simultaneously the form of dissolution of the type of ground-rent which we have heretofore considered, namely ground-rent as the normal form of surplus-value and of the unpaid surplus-labour to be performed for the owner of the conditions of production. In its pure form, this rent, like labour rent and rent in kind, represents no excess over profit. It absorbs the profit, as it is understood. In so far as profit arises beside it practically as a separate portion of excess labour, money-rent like rent in its earlier forms still constitutes the normal limit of such embryonic profit, which can only develop in relation to the possibilities of exploitation, be it of one's own excess labour or that of another, which remains after the performance of the surplus-labour represented by money-rent. Should any profit actually arise along with this rent, then this profit does not constitute the limit of rent, but rather conversely, the rent is the limit of the profit. However, as already indicated, money-rent is simultaneously the form of dissolution of the ground-rent considered thus far, coinciding *prima facie* with surplus-value and surplus-labour, i.e., ground-rent as the normal and dominant form of surplus-value.

In its further development money-rent must lead—aside from all intermediate forms, e.g., the small peasant tenant farmer—either to the transformation of land into peasants' freehold, or to the form corresponding to the capitalist mode of production, that is, to rent paid by the capitalist tenant farmer.

With money-rent prevailing, the traditional and customary legal relationship between landlord and subjects who possess and cultivate a part of the land, is necessarily turned into a pure money relationship fixed contractually in accordance with the rules of positive law. The possessor engaged in cultivation thus becomes virtually a mere tenant. This transformation serves on the one hand, provided other general production relations permit, to expropriate more and more the old peasant possessors and to substitute capitalist tenants in their stead. On the other hand, it leads to the former possessor buying himself free from his rent obligation and to his transformation into an independent peasant with complete ownership of the land he tills. The transformation of rent in kind into money-rent is furthermore not only inevitably accompanied, but even anticipated, by the formation of a class of propertyless day-labourers, who hire themselves out for money. During their genesis, when this new class appears but sporadically, the custom necessarily develops among the more prosperous peasants subject to rent payments of exploiting agricultural wage-labourers for their own account, much as in feudal times, when the more well-to-do peasant serfs themselves also held serfs. In this way, they gradually acquire the possibility of accumulating a certain amount of wealth and themselves becoming transformed into future capitalists. The old self-employed possessors of land themselves thus give rise to a nursery school for capitalist tenants, whose development is conditioned by the general development of capitalist production beyond the bounds of the country-side. This class shoots up very rapidly when particularly favourable circumstances come to its aid, as in England in the 16th century, where the then progressive depreciation of money enriched them under the customary long leases at the expense of the landlords.

Furthermore: as soon as rent assumes the form of money-rent, and thereby the relationship between rent-paying peasant and landlord becomes a relationship fixed by contract—a development which is only possible generally when the world-market, commerce and manufacture have reached a certain relatively high level—the leasing of land to capitalists inevitably also makes its appearance. The latter hitherto stood beyond the rural limits and now carry over to the countryside and agriculture the capital acquired in the cities and with it the capitalist mode of operation developed—i.e., creating a product as a mere commodity and solely as a means of appropriating surplus-value. This form can become the general rule only in those countries which dominate the world-market in the period of transition from the feudal to the capitalist mode of production. When the capitalist tenant farmer steps in between landlord and actual tiller of the soil, all relations which arose out of the old rural mode of production are torn asunder. The farmer becomes the actual commander of these agricultural labourers and the actual exploiter of their surplus-labour, whereas the landlord maintains a direct relationship, and indeed simply a money and contractual relationship, solely with this capitalist tenant. Thus, the nature of rent is also transformed, not merely in fact and by chance, as occurred in part even under earlier forms, but normally, in its recognised and prevailing form. From the normal form of surplus-value and surplus-labour, it descends to a mere excess of this surplus-labour over that portion of it appropriated by the exploiting capitalist in the form of profit; just as the total surplus-labour, profit and excess over profit, is extracted directly by him, collected in the form of the total surplus-product, and turned into cash. It is only the excess portion of this surplus-value which is extracted by him from the agricultural labourer by direct exploitation, by means of his capital, which he turns over to the landlord as rent. How much or how little he turns over to the latter depends, on the average, upon the limits set by the average profit which is realised by capital in the non-agricultural spheres of production, and by the prices of non-agricultural production regulated by this average profit. From a normal form of surplus-value and surplus-labour, rent has now become transformed into an excess over that portion of the surplus-labour claimed in advance by capital as its legitimate and normal share, and characteristic of this particular sphere of production, the agricultural sphere of production. Profit, instead of rent, has now become the normal form of surplus-value and rent still exists solely as a form, not of surplus-value in general, but of one of its offshoots, surplus-profit, which assumes an independent form under particular circumstances. It is not necessary to elaborate the manner in which a gradual transformation in the mode of production itself corresponds to this transformation. This already follows from the fact that it is normal for the capitalist tenant farmer to produce agricultural products as commodities, and that, while formerly only the excess over his means of subsistence was converted into commodities, now but a relatively insignificant part of these commodities is directly used by him as means of subsistence. It is no longer the land, but rather capital, which has now brought even agricultural labour under its direct sway and productiveness.

The average profit and the price of production regulated thereby are formed outside of relations in the country-side and within the sphere of urban trade and manufacture. The profit of the rent-paying peasant does not enter into it as an equalising factor, for his relation to the landlord is not a capitalist one. In so far as he makes profit, i.e., realises an excess above his necessary means of subsistence, either by his own labour or through exploiting other people's labour, it is done behind the back of the normal relationship, and other circumstances being equal, the size of this profit does not determine rent, but on the contrary, it is determined by the rent as its limit. The high rate of profit in the Middle Ages is not entirely due to the low composition of capital, in which the variable component invested in wages predominates. It is due to swindling on the land, the appropriation of a portion of the landlord's rent and of the income of his vassals. If the country-side exploits the town politically in the Middle Ages, wherever feudalism has not been broken down by exceptional urban development—as in Italy, the town, on the other hand, exploits the land economically everywhere and without exception, through its monopoly prices, its system of taxation, its guild organisation, its direct commercial fraudulence and its usury.

One might imagine that the mere appearance of the capitalist farmer in agricultural production would prove that the price of agricultural products, which from time immemorial have paid rent in one form or another, must be higher, at least at the time of this appearance, than the prices of production of manufacture whether it be because the price of such agricultural products has reached a monopoly price level, or has risen as high as the value of the agricultural products, and their value actually is above the price of production regulated by the average profit. For were this not so, the capitalist farmer could not at all realise, at the existing prices of agricultural produce, first the average profit out of the price of these products, and then pay out of the same price an excess above this profit in the form of rent. One might conclude from this that the general rate of profit, which guides the capitalist farmer in his contract with the landlord, has been formed without including rent, and, therefore, as soon as it assumes a regulating role in agricultural production, it finds this excess at hand and pays it to the landlord. It is in this traditional manner that, for instance, Herr Rodbertus explains the matter. [J. Rodbertus, *Sociale Briefe an von Kirchmann, Dritter Brief: Widerlegung der Ricardo'schen Lehre von der Grundrente und Begründung einer neuen Rententheorie.* See also K. Marx, *Theorien über den Mehrwert.* 2. Teil, *1957, pp.* 3-106, 142-54.—*Ed.*] But:

First: This appearance of capital as an independent and leading force in agriculture does not take place all at once and generally, but gradually and in particular lines of production. It encompasses at first, not agriculture proper, but such branches of production as cattle-breeding, especially sheep-raising, whose principal product, wool, offers at the early stages a constant excess of market-price over price of production during the rise of industry, and this does not level out until later. Thus in England during the 16th century.

Secondly: Since this capitalist production appears at first but sporadically, the assumption cannot be disputed that it first extends only to such land categories as are able, through their particular fertility, or their exceptionally favourable location, to generally pay a differential rent.

Thirdly: Let us even assume that at the time this mode of production appeared—and this indeed presupposes an increasing preponderance of urban demand—the prices of agricultural products were higher than the price of production, as was doubtless the case in England during the last third of the 17th century. Nevertheless, as soon as this mode of production has somewhat extricated itself from the mere subordination of agriculture to capital, and as soon as agricultural improvement and the reduction of production costs, which necessarily accompany its development, have taken place, the balance will be restored by a reaction, a fall in the price of agricultural produce, as happened in England in the first half of the 18th century.

Rent, thus, as an excess over the average profit cannot be explained in this traditional way. Whatever may be the existing historical circumstances at the time rent first appears, once it has struck root it cannot exist except under the modern conditions earlier described.

Finally, it should be noted in the transformation of rent in kind into money-rent that along with it capitalised rent, or the price of land, and thus its alienability and alienation become essential factors, and that thereby not only can the former peasant subject to payment of rent be transformed into an independent peasant proprietor, but also urban and other moneyed people can buy real estate in order to lease it either to peasants or capitalists and thus enjoy rent as a form of interest on their capital so invested; that, therefore, this circumstance likewise facilitates the transformation of the former mode of exploitation, the relation between owner and actual cultivator of the land, and of rent itself.

Section V. *Métayage and Peasant Proprietorship of Land Parcels*

We have now arrived at the end of our elaboration of ground-rent.

In all these forms of ground-rent, whether labour rent, rent in kind, or money-rent (as merely a changed form of rent in kind), the one paying rent is always supposed to be the actual cultivator and possessor of the land, whose unpaid surplus-labour passes directly into the hands of the landlord. Even in the last form, money-rent in so far as it is 'pure,' i.e., merely a changed form of rent in kind—this is not only possible, but actually takes place.

As a transitory form from the original form of rent to capitalist rent, we may consider the metayer system, or share-cropping, under which the manager (farmer) furnishes labour (his own or another's), and also a portion of working capital, and the landlord furnishes, aside from land, another portion of working capital (e.g., cattle), and the product is divided between tenant and landlord in definite proportions which vary from country to country. On the one hand, the farmer here lacks sufficient capital required for complete capitalist management. On the other hand, the share here appropriated by the landlord does not bear the pure form of rent. It may actually include interest on the capital advanced by him and an excess rent. It may also absorb practically the entire surplus-labour of the farmer, or leave him a greater or smaller portion of this surplus-labour. But, essentially, rent no longer appears here as the normal form of surplus-value in general. On the one hand, the sharecropper, whether he employs his own or another's labour, is to lay claim to a portion of the product not in his capacity as labourer, but as possessor of part of the instruments of labour, as his own capitalist. On the other hand, the landlord claims his share not exclusively on the basis of his land-ownership, but also as lender of capital.[4]

A survival of the old communal ownership of land, which had endured after the transition to independent peasant farming, e.g., in Poland and Rumania, served there as a subterfuge for effecting a transition to the lower forms of ground-rent. A portion of the land belongs to the individual peasant and is tilled independently by him. Another portion is tilled in common and creates a surplus-product, which serves partly to cover community expenses, partly as a reserve in cases of crop failure, etc. These last two parts of the surplus-product, and ultimately the entire surplus-product including the land upon which it has been grown, are more and more usurped by state officials and private individuals, and thus the originally free peasant proprietors, whose obligation to till this land in common is maintained, are transformed into vassals subject either to corvée-labour or rent in kind; while the usurpers of common land are transformed into owners, not only of the usurped common lands, but even the very lands of the peasants themselves.

We need not further investigate slave economy proper (which likewise passes through a metamorphosis from the patriarchal system mainly for home use to the plantation system for the world-market) nor the management of estates under which the landlords themselves are independent cultivators, possessing all instruments of production, and exploiting the labour of free or unfree bondsmen, who are paid either in kind or money. Landlord and owner of the instruments of production, and thus the direct exploiter of labourers included among these elements of production, are in this case one and the same person. Rent and profit likewise coincide then, there occurring no separation of the different forms of surplus-value. The entire surplus-labour of the labourers, which is manifested here in the surplus-product, is extracted from them directly by the owner of all instruments of production, to which belong the land and, under the original form of slavery, the immediate producers themselves. Where the capitalist outlook prevails, as on American plantations, this entire surplus-value is regarded as profit; where neither the capitalist mode of production itself exists, nor the corresponding outlook has been transferred from capitalist countries, it appears as rent. At any rate, this form presents no difficulties. The income of the landlord, whatever it may be called, the available surplus-product appropriated by him, is here the normal and prevailing form, whereby the entire unpaid surplus-labour is directly appropriated, and landed property forms the basis of such appropriation.

Further, *proprietorship of land parcels*. The peasant here is simultaneously the free owner of his land, which appears as his principal instrument of production, the indispensable field of employment for his labour and his capital. No lease money is paid under this form. Rent, therefore, does not appear as a separate form of surplus-value, although in countries in which otherwise the capitalist mode of production is developed, it appears as a surplus-profit compared with other lines of production; but as surplus-profit which, like all proceeds of his labour in general, accrues to the peasant.

This form of landed property presupposes, as in the earlier older forms, that the rural population greatly predominates numerically over the town population, so that, even if the capitalist mode of production otherwise prevails, it is but relatively little developed, and thus also in the other lines of production the concentration of capital is restricted to narrow limits and a fragmentation of capital predominates. In the nature of things, the greater portion of agricultural produce must be consumed as direct means of subsistence by the producers themselves, the peasants, and only the excess above that will find its way as commodities into urban commerce. No matter how the average market-price of agricultural products may here be regulated, differential rent, an excess portion of commodity-prices from superior or more favourably located land, must evidently exist here much as under the capitalist mode of production. This differential rent exists, even where this form appears under social conditions, under which no general market-price has as yet been developed; it appears then in the excess surplus-product. Only then it flows into the pockets of the peasant whose labour is realised under more favourable natural conditions. The assumption here is generally to be made that no absolute rent exists, i.e., that the worst soil does not pay any rent—precisely under this form where the price of land enters as a factor in the peasant's actual cost of production whether because in the course of this form's further development either the price of land has been computed at a certain money-value, in dividing up an inheritance, or, during the constant change in ownership of an entire estate, or of its component parts, the land has been bought by the cultivator himself, largely by raising money on mortgage; and, therefore, where the price of land, representing nothing more than capitalised rent, is a factor assumed in advance, and where rent thus seems to exist independently of any differentiation in fertility and location of the land. For, absolute rent presupposes either realised excess in product value above its price of production, or a monopoly price exceeding the value of the product. But since agriculture here is carried on largely as cultivation for direct subsistence, and the land exists as an indispensable field of employment for the labour and capital of the majority of the population, the regulating market-price of the product will reach its value only under extraordinary circumstances. But this value will, generally, be higher than its price of production owing to the preponderant element of living labour, although this excess of value over price of production will in turn be limited by the low composition even of non-agricultural capital in countries with an economy composed predominantly of land parcels. For the peasant owning a parcel, the limit of exploitation is not set by the average profit of capital, in so far as he is a small capitalist; nor, on the other hand, by the necessity of rent, in so far as he is a landowner. The absolute limit for him as a small capitalist is no more than the wages he pays to himself, after deducting his actual costs. So long as the price of the product covers these wages, he will cultivate his land, and often at wages down to a physical minimum. As for his capacity as land proprietor, the barrier of ownership is eliminated for him, since it can make itself felt only *vis-à-vis* a capital (including labour) separated from land-ownership, by erecting an obstacle to the investment of capital. It is true, to be sure, that interest on the price of land—which generally has to be paid to still another individual, the mortgage creditor—is a barrier. But this interest can be paid precisely out of that portion of surplus-labour which would constitute profit under capitalist conditions. The rent anticipated in the price of land and in the interest paid for it can, therefore be nothing but a portion of the peasant's capitalised surplus-labour over and above the labour indispensable for his subsistence, without this surplus-labour being realised in a part of the commodity-value equal to the entire average profit, and still less in an excess above the surplus-labour realised in the average profit, i.e., in a surplus-profit. The rent may be a deduction from the average profit, or even the only portion of it which is realised. For the peasant parcel holder to cultivate his land, or to buy land for cultivation, it is, therefore, not necessary, as under the normal capitalist mode of production, that the market-price of the agricultural products rise high enough to afford him the average profit, and still less a fixed excess above this average profit in the form of rent. It is not necessary, therefore, that the market-price rise, either up to the value or the price of production of his product. This is one of the reasons why grain prices are lower in countries with predominant small peasant land proprietorship than in countries with a capitalist mode of production. One portion of the surplus-labour of the peasants, who work under the least favourable conditions, is bestowed gratis upon society and does not at all enter into the regulation of price of production or into the creation of value in general. This lower price is consequently a result of the producers' poverty and by no means of their labour productivity.

This form of free self-managing peasant proprietorship of land parcels as the prevailing, normal form constitutes, on the one hand, the economic foundation of society during the best periods of classical antiquity, and on the other hand, it is found among modern nations as one of the forms arising from the dissolution of feudal land ownership. Thus, the yeomanry in England, the peasantry in Sweden, the French and West German peasants. We do not include colonies here, since the independent peasant there develops under different conditions.

The free ownership of the self-managing peasant is evidently the most normal form of landed property for small-scale operation, i.e., for a mode of production, in which possession of the land is a prerequisite for the labourer's ownership of the product of his own labour, and in which the cultivator, be he free owner or vassal, always must produce his own means of subsistence independently, as an isolated labourer with his family. Ownership of the land is as necessary for full development of this mode of production as ownership of tools is for free development of handicraft production. Here is the basis for the development of personal independence. It is a necessary transitional stage for the development of agriculture itself. The causes which bring about its downfall show its limitations. These are: Destruction of rural domestic industry, which forms its normal supplement as a result of the development of large-scale industry; a gradual impoverishment and exhaustion of the soil subjected to this cultivation; usurpation by big landowners of the common lands, which constitute the second supplement of the management of land parcels everywhere and which alone enable it to raise cattle; competition, either of the plantation system or large-scale capitalist agriculture. Improvements in agriculture, which on the one hand cause a fall in agricultural prices and, on the other, require greater outlays and more extensive material conditions of production, also contribute towards this, as in England during the first half of the 18th century.

Proprietorship of land parcels by its very nature excludes the development of social productive forces of labour, social forms of labour, social concentration of capital, large-scale cattle-raising, and the progressive application of science.

Usury and a taxation system must impoverish it everywhere. The expenditure of capital in the price of the land withdraws this capital from cultivation. An infinite fragmentation of means of production, and isolation of the producers themselves. Monstrous waste of human energy. Progressive deterioration of conditions of production and increased prices of means of production—an inevitable law of proprietorship of parcels. Calamity of seasonal abundance for this mode of production.[5]

One of the specific evils of small-scale agriculture where it is combined with free land-ownership arises from the cultivator's investing capital in the purchase of land. (The same applies also to the transitory form, in which the big landowner invests capital, first, to buy land, and second, to manage it as his own tenant farmer.) Owing to the changeable nature which the land here assumes as a mere commodity, the changes of ownership increase,[6] so that the land, from the peasant's viewpoint, enters anew as an investment of capital with each successive generation and division of estates, i.e., it becomes land purchased by him. The price of land here forms a weighty element of the individual unproductive costs of production or cost-price of the product for the individual producer.

The price of land is nothing but capitalised and therefore anticipated rent. If capitalist methods are employed by agriculture, so that the landlord receives only rent, and the farmer pays nothing for land except this annual rent, then it is evident that the capital invested by the landowner himself in purchasing the land constitutes indeed an interest-bearing investment of capital for him, but has absolutely nothing to do with capital invested in agriculture itself. It forms neither a part of the fixed, nor of the circulating, capital employed here;[7] it merely secures for the buyer a claim to receive annual rent, but has absolutely nothing to do with the production of the rent itself. The buyer of land just pays his capital out to the one who sells the land, and the seller in return relinquishes his ownership of the land. Thus this capital no longer exists as the capital of the purchaser; he no longer has it; therefore it does not belong to the capital which he can invest in any way in the land itself. Whether he bought the land dear or cheap, or whether he received it for nothing, alters nothing in the capital invested by the farmer in his establishment, and changes nothing in the rent, but merely alters the question whether it appears to him as interest or not, or as higher or lower interest respectively.

Take, for instance, the slave economy. The price paid for a slave is nothing but the anticipated and capitalised surplus-value or profit to be wrung out of the slave. But the capital paid for the purchase of a slave does not belong to the capital by means of which profit, surplus-labour, is extracted from him. On the contrary. It is capital which the slave-holder has parted with, it is a deduction from the capital which be has available for actual production. It has ceased to exist for him, just as capital invested in purchasing land has ceased to exist for agriculture. The best proof of this is that it does not reappear for the slave-holder or the landowner except when he, in turn, sells his slaves or land. But then the same situation prevails for the buyer. The fact that he has bought the slave does not enable him to exploit the slave without further ado. He is only able to do so when he invests some additional capital in the slave economy itself.

The same capital does not exist twice, once in the hands of the seller, and a second time in the hands of the buyer of the land. It passes from the hands of the buyer to those of the seller, and there the matter ends. The buyer now no longer has capital, but in its stead a piece of land. The circumstance that the rent produced by a real investment of capital in this land is calculated by the new landowner as interest on capital which he has not invested in the land, but given away to acquire the land, does not in the least alter the economic nature of the land factor, any more than the circumstance that someone has paid £1,000 for 3% consols has anything to do with the capital out of whose revenue the interest on the national debt is paid.

In fact, the money expended in purchasing land, like that in purchasing government bonds, is merely capital *in itself*, just as any value sum is capital in itself, potential capital, on the basis of the capitalist mode of production. What is paid for land, like that for government bonds or any other purchased commodity, is a sum of money. This is capital in itself, because it can be converted into capital. It depends upon the use put to it by the seller whether the money obtained by him is really transformed into capital or not. For the buyer, it can never again function as such, no more than any other money which he has definitely paid out. It figures in his accounts as interest-bearing capital, because he considers the income, received as rent from the land or as interest on state indebtedness, as interest on the money which the purchase of the claim to this revenue has cost him. He can only realise it as capital through resale. But then another, the new buyer, enters the same relationship maintained by the former, and the money thus expended cannot be transformed into actual capital for the expender through any change of hands.

In the case of small landed property the illusion is fostered still more that land itself possesses value and thus enters as capital into the price of production of the product, much as machines or raw materials. But we have seen that rent, and therefore, capitalised rent, the price of land, can enter as a determining factor into the price of agricultural products in only two cases. First, when as a consequence of the composition of agricultural capital—a capital which has nothing to do with the capital invested in purchasing land—the value of the products of the soil is higher than their price of production, and market conditions enable the landlord to realise this difference. Second, when there is a monopoly price. And both are least of all the case under the management of land parcels and small land-ownership because precisely here production to a large extent satisfies the producers' own wants and is carried on independently of regulation by the average rate of profit. Even where cultivation of land parcels is conducted upon leased land, the lease money comprises, far more so than under any other conditions, a portion of the profit and even a deduction from wages; this money is then only a nominal rent, not rent as an independent category as opposed to wages and profit.

The expenditure of money-capital for the purchase of land, then, is not an investment of agricultural capital. It is a decrease *pro tanto* in the capital which small peasants can employ in their own sphere of production. It reduces *pro tanto* the size of their means of production and thereby narrows the economic basis of reproduction. It subjects the small peasant to the money-lender, since credit proper occurs but rarely in this sphere in general. It is a hindrance to agriculture, even where such purchase takes place in the case of large estates. It contradicts in fact the capitalist mode of production, which is on the whole indifferent to whether the landowner is in debt, no matter whether he has inherited or purchased his estate. The nature of management of the leased estate itself is not altered whether the landowner pockets the rent himself or whether he must pay it out to the holder of his mortgage.

We have seen that, in the case of a given ground-rent, the price of land is regulated by the interest rate. If the rate is low, then the price of land is high, and vice versa. Normally, then, a high price of land and a low interest rate should go hand in hand, so that if the peasant paid a high price for the land in consequence of a low interest rate, the same low rate of interest should also secure his working capital for him on easy credit terms. But in reality, things turn out differently when peasant proprietorship of land parcels is the prevailing form. In the first place, the general laws of credit are not adapted to the farmer, since these laws presuppose a capitalist as the producer. Secondly, where proprietorship of land parcels predominates—we are not referring to colonies here—and the small peasant constitutes the backbone of the nation, the formation of capital, i.e., social reproduction, is relatively weak, and still weaker is the formation of loanable money-capital, in the sense previously elaborated. This presupposes the concentration and existence of a class of idle rich capitalists (Massie). [[Massie] *An Essay on the Governing Causes of the Natural Rate of Interest,* London, 1750, pp 23-24.—*Ed*] Thirdly, here where the ownership of the land is a necessary condition for the existence of most producers, and an indispensable field of investment for their capital, the price of land is raised independently of the interest rate, and often in inverse ratio to it, through the preponderance of the demand for landed property over its supply. Land sold in parcels brings a far higher price in such a case than when sold in large tracts, because here the number of small buyers is large and that of large buyers is small (Bandes Noires, [Associations of profiteers.—*Ed.*] Rubichon; Newman [Newman, *Lectures on Political Economy,* London, 1851, pp. 180-81.—*Ed.*]). For all these reasons, the price of land rises here with a relatively high rate of interest. The relatively low interest, which the peasant derives here from the outlay of capital for the purchase of land (Mounier), corresponds here, on the other side, to the high usurious interest rate which he himself has to pay to his mortgage creditors. The Irish system bears out the same thing, only in another form.

The price of land, this element foreign to production in itself, may therefore, rise here to such a point that it makes production impossible (Dombasle).

The fact that the price of land plays such a role, that purchase and sale, the circulation of land as a commodity, develops to this degree, is practically a result of the development of the capitalist mode of production in so far as a commodity is here the general form of all products and all instruments of production. On the other hand, this development takes place only where the capitalist mode of production has a limited development and does not unfold all of its peculiarities, because this rests precisely upon the fact that agriculture is no longer, or not yet, subject to the capitalist mode of production, but rather to one handed down from extinct forms of society. The disadvantages of the capitalist mode of production, with its dependence of the producer upon the money-price of his product, coincide here, therefore, with the disadvantages occasioned by the imperfect development of the capitalist mode of production. The peasant turns merchant and industrialist without the conditions enabling him to produce his products as commodities.

The conflict between the price of land as an element in the producers' cost-price and no element in the price of production (even though the rent enters as a determining factor into the price of the agricultural product, the capitalised rent, which is advanced for 20 years or more, by no means enters as a determinant) is but one of the forms manifesting the general contradiction between private land-ownership and a rational agriculture, the normal social utilisation of the soil. But on the other hand, private land ownership, and thereby expropriation of the direct producers from the land—private land-ownership by the one, which implies lack of ownership by others—is the basis of the capitalist mode of production.

Here, in small-scale agriculture, the price of land, a form and result of private land-ownership, appears as a barrier to production itself. In large-scale agriculture, and large estates operating on a capitalist basis, ownership likewise acts as a barrier, because it limits the tenant farmer in his productive investment of capital, which in the final analysis benefits not him, but the landlord. In both forms, exploitation and squandering of the vitality of the soil (apart from making exploitation dependent upon the accidental and unequal circumstances of individual producers rather than the attained level of social development) takes the place of conscious rational cultivation of the soil as eternal communal property, an inalienable condition for the existence and reproduction of a chain of successive generations of the human race. In the case of small property, this results from the lack of means and knowledge of applying the social labour productivity. In the case of large property, it results from the exploitation of such means for the most rapid enrichment of farmer and proprietor. In the case of both through dependence on the market-price.

All critique of small landed property resolves itself in the final analysis into a criticism of private ownership as a barrier and hindrance to agriculture. And similarly all counter-criticism of large landed property. In either case, of course, we leave aside all secondary political considerations. This barrier and hindrance, which are erected by all private landed property vis-à-vis agricultural production and the rational cultivation, maintenance and improvement of the soil itself, develop on both sides merely in different forms, and in wrangling over the specific forms of this evil its ultimate cause is forgotten.

Small landed property presupposes that the overwhelming majority of the population is rural, and that not social, but isolated labour predominates; and that, therefore, under such conditions wealth and development of reproduction, both of its material and spiritual prerequisites, are out of the question, and thereby also the prerequisites for rational cultivation. On the other hand, large landed property reduces the agricultural population to a constantly falling minimum, and confronts it with a constantly growing industrial population crowded together in large cities. It thereby creates conditions which cause an irreparable break in the coherence of social interchange prescribed by the natural laws of life. As a result, the vitality of the soil is squandered, and this prodigality is carried by commerce far beyond the borders of a particular state (Liebig). [Liebig, *Die Chemie in ihrer Anwendung auf Agricultur und Physiologie*, Braunschweig, 1862.—*Ed.*]

While small landed property creates a class of barbarians standing halfway outside of society, a class combining all the crudeness of primitive forms of society with the anguish and misery of civilised countries, large landed property undermines labour-power in the last region, where its prime energy seeks refuge and stores up its strength as a reserve fund for the regeneration of the vital force of nations—on the land itself. Large-scale industry and large-scale mechanised agriculture work together. If originally distinguished by the fact that the former lays waste and destroys principally labour-power, hence the natural force of human beings, whereas the latter more directly exhausts the natural vitality of the soil, they join hands in the further course of development in that the industrial system in the countryside also enervates the labourers, and industry and commerce on their part supply agriculture with the means for exhausting the soil.

Notes

1. Adam Smith emphasises how, in his time (and this applies also to the plantations in tropical and subtropical countries in our own day), rent and profit were not yet divorced from one another [Smith, *An Inquiry into the Nature and Causes of the Wealth of Nations*, Aberdeen, London, 1848, p. 44.—*Ed.*], for the landlord was simultaneously a capitalist, just as Cato, for instance, was on his estates. But this separation is precisely the prerequisite for the capitalist mode of production, to whose conception the basis of slavery moreover stands in direct contradiction.
2. Herr Mommsen, in his 'Roman History,' by no means uses the term capitalist in the sense employed by modern economics and modern society, but rather in the manner of popular conception, such as still continues to thrive, though not in England or America, but nevertheless on the European continent, as an ancient tradition reflecting bygone conditions.
3. Following the conquest of a country, the immediate aim of a conqueror was also to convert its people to his own use. Cf. Linguet [*Théorie des loi civiles, ou Principes fondamentaux de la société*, Tomes I-II, Londres, 1767.—*Ed.*]. See also Möser [*Osnabrükische Geschichte*, 1. Theil, Berlin und Stettin, S. 178.—*Ed.*].
4. Cf Buvet [*Cours d'économie politique*, Bruxelles, 1842.—*Ed.*] Tocqueville [*L'ancien régime et la révolution*, Paris, 1856.—*Ed.*], Sismondi [*Nouveaux principes d'économie politique.—Seconde édition*, Tome I, Paris, 1827.—*Ed.*]
5. See the speech from the throne of the King of France in Tooke. [New-march, *A History of Prices, and of the State of the Circulation, during the nine years 1848-56*, Vol. VI, London. 1857, pp. 29-30.—*Ed.*]
6. See Mounier [*De l'agriculture en France*, Paris, 1846.—*Ed.*] and Rubichon [*Du méchanisme de la société en France et en Angleterre*, Paris. 1837.—*Ed.*].
7. Dr H. Maron *(Extensiv oder Intensiv?)* [no further information given about this pamphlet] starts from the false assumption of the adversaries he opposes. He assumes that capital invested in the purchase of land is 'investment capital,' and then engages in a controversy about the respective definitions of investment capital and working capital, that is, fixed and circulating capital. His wholly amateurish conceptions of capital in general, which may be excused incidentally in one who is not an economist in view of the state of German political economy, conceal from him that this capital is neither investment nor working capital, any more than the capital which someone invests at the Stock Exchange in purchasing stocks or government securities, and which, for him, represents a personal investment of capital, is 'invested' in any branch of production.

PART VII

REVENUES AND THEIR SOURCES

48

The Trinity Formula

I[1]

Capital—profit (profit of enterprise plus interest), land—ground-rent, labour—wages, this is the trinity formula which comprises all the secrets of the social production process.

Furthermore, since as previously [Present edition: Ch. XXIII.—*Ed.*] demonstrated interest appears as the specific characteristic product of capital and profit of enterprise on the contrary appears as wages independent of capital, the above trinity formula reduces itself more specifically to the following:

Capital—interest, land—ground-rent, labour—wages, where profit, the specific characteristic form of surplus-value belonging to the capitalist mode of production, is fortunately eliminated.

On closer examination of this economic trinity, we find the following:

First, the alleged sources of the annually available wealth belong to widely dissimilar spheres and are not at all analogous with one another. They have about the same relation to each other as lawyer's fees, red beets and music.

Capital, land, labour! However, capital is not a thing, but rather a definite social production relation, belonging to a definite historical formation of society, which is manifested in a thing and lends this thing a specific social character. Capital is not the sum of the material and produced means of production. Capital is rather the means of production transformed into capital, which in themselves are no more capital than gold or silver in itself is money. It is the means of production monopolised by a certain section of society, confronting living labour-power as products and working conditions rendered independent of this very labour-power, which are personified through this antithesis in capital. It is not merely the products of labourers turned into independent powers, products as rulers and buyers of their producers, but rather also the social forces and the future [? illegible] [A later collation with the manuscript showed that the text reads as follows: 'die Gesellschaftlichen Kräfte und Zusammenhängende Form dieser Arbeit' (the social forces of their labour and socialised form of this labour).—*Ed.*] form of this labour, which confront the labourers as properties of their products. Here, then, we have a definite and, at first glance, very mystical, social form, of one of the factors in a historically produced social production process.

And now alongside of this we have the land, inorganic nature as such, *rudis indigestaque moles,* ['A rude and undigested mass', Ovid, *Metamorphoses,* Book I, 7.—*Ed*] in all its primeval wildness. Value is labour. Therefore surplus-value cannot be earth. Absolute fertility of the soil effects nothing more than the following: a certain quantity of labour produces a certain product—in accordance with the natural fertility of the soil. The difference in soil fertility causes the same quantities of labour and capital, hence the same value, to be manifested in different quantities of agricultural products; that is, causes these products to have different individual values. The equalisation of these individual values into market-values is responsible for the fact that the 'advantages of fertile over inferior soil ... are transferred from the cultivator or consumer to the landlord'. (Ricardo, *Principles,* London, 1821, p.62.)

And finally, as third party in this union, a mere ghost—Labour, which is no more than an abstraction and taken by itself does not exist at all, or, if we take... [illegible] [As has been established by later reading of the manuscript, it reads here: 'wenn wir das Gemeinte nehmen' (if we take that which is behind it).—*Ed.*], the productive activity of human beings in general, by which they promote the interchange with Nature, divested not only of every social form and well-defined character, but even in its bare natural existence, independent of society, removed from all societies, and as an expression and confirmation of life which the still non-social man in general has in common with the one who is in any way social.

II

Capital—interest; landed property, private ownership of the Earth, and, to be sure, modern and corresponding to the capitalist mode of production—rent; wage-labour—wages. The connection between the sources of revenue is supposed to be represented in this form. Wage-labour and landed property, like capital, are historically determined social forms; one of labour, the other of monopolised terrestrial globe, and indeed both forms corresponding to capital and belonging to the same economic formation of society.

The first striking thing about this formula is that side by side with capital, with this form of an element of production belonging to a definite mode of production, to a definite historical form of social process of production, side by side with an element of production amalgamated with and represented by a definite social form are indiscriminately placed: the land on the one hand and labour on the other, two elements of the real labour process, which in this material form are common to all modes of production, which are the material elements of every process of production and have nothing to do with its social form.

Secondly. In the formula: capital—interest, land—ground-rent, labour—wages, capital, land and labour appear respectively as sources of interest (instead of profit), ground-rent and wages, as their products, or fruits; the former are the basis, the latter the consequence, the former are the cause, the latter the effect; and indeed, in such a manner that each individual source is related to its product as to that which is ejected and produced by it. All the proceeds, interest (instead of profit), rent, and wages, are three components of the value of the products, i.e., generally speaking, components of value or expressed in money, certain money components, price components. The formula: capital—interest is now indeed the most meaningless formula of capital, but still one of its formulas. But how should land create value, i.e., a socially defined quantity of labour, and moreover that particular portion of the value of its own products which forms the rent? Land, e.g., takes part as an agent of production in creating a use-value, a material product, wheat. But it has nothing to do with the production of the *value of wheat.* In so far as value is represented by wheat, the latter is merely considered as a definite quantity of materialised social labour, regardless of the particular substance in which this labour is manifested or of the particular use-value of this substance. This nowise contradicts that 1) other circumstances being equal, the cheapness or dearness of wheat depends upon the productivity of the soil. The productivity of agricultural labour is dependent on natural conditions, and the same quantity of labour is represented by more or fewer products, use-values, in accordance with such productivity. How large the quantity of labour represented in one bushel of wheat depends upon the number of bushels yielded by the same quantity of labour. It depends, in this case, upon the soil productivity in what quantities of product the value shall be manifested. But this value is given, independent of this distribution. Value is represented in use-value; and use-value is a prerequisite for the creation of value; but it is folly to create an antithesis by placing a use-value, like land, on one side and on the other side value, and a particular portion of value at that. 2)... [here the manuscript breaks off].

III

Vulgar economy actually does no more than interpret, systematise and defend in doctrinaire fashion the conceptions of the agents of bourgeois production who are entrapped in bourgeois production relations. It should not astonish us, then, that vulgar economy feels particularly at home in the estranged outward appearances of economic relations in which these *prima facie* absurd and perfect contradictions appear and that these relations seem the more self-evident the more their internal relationships are concealed from it, although they are understandable to the popular mind. But all science would be superfluous if the outward appearance and the essence of things directly coincided. Thus, vulgar economy has not the slightest suspicion that the trinity which it takes as its point of departure, namely, land—rent, capital—interest, labour—wages or the price of labour, are *prima facie* three impossible combinations. First we have the use-value *land,* which has no value, and the exchange-value *rent:* so that a social relation conceived as a thing is made proportional to Nature, i.e., two incommensurable magnitudes are supposed to stand in a given ratio to one another. Then *capital—interest.* If capital is conceived as a certain sum of values represented independently by money, then it is *prima facie* nonsense to say that a certain value should be worth more than it is worth. It is precisely in the form: capital—interest that all intermediate links are eliminated, and capital is reduced to its most general formula, which therefore, in itself is also inexplicable and absurd. The vulgar economist prefers the formula capital—interest, with its occult quality of making a value unequal to itself, to the formula capital—profit, precisely for the reason that this already more nearly approaches actual capitalist relations. Then again, driven by the disturbing thought that 4 is not 5 and that 100 taler cannot possibly be 110 taler, he flees from capital as value to the material substance of capital; to its use-value as a condition of production of labour, to machinery, raw materials, etc. Thus, he is able once more to substitute in place of the first incomprehensible relation, whereby 4 = 5, a wholly incommensurable one between a use-value, a thing on one side, and a definite social production relation, surplus-value, on the other, as in the case of landed property. As soon as the vulgar economist arrives at this incommensurable relation, everything becomes clear to him, and he no longer feels the need for further thought. For he has arrived precisely at the 'rational' in bourgeois conception. Finally, *labour—wages,* or price of labour, is an expression, as shown in Book I, which *prima facie* contradicts the conception of value as well as of price—the latter generally being but a definite expression of value. And 'price of labour' is just as irrational as a yellow logarithm. But here the vulgar economist is all the more satisfied, because he has gained the profound insight of the bourgeois, namely, that he pays money for labour, and since precisely the contradiction between the formula and the conception of value relieves him from all obligation to understand the latter.

We[2] have seen that the capitalist process of production is a historically determined form of the social process of production in general. The latter is as much a production process of material conditions of human life as a process taking place under specific historical and economic production relations, producing and reproducing these production relations themselves, and thereby also the bearers of this process, their material conditions of existence and their mutual relations, i.e., their particular socio-economic form. For the aggregate of these relations, in which the agents of this production stand with respect to Nature and to one another, and in which they produce, is precisely society, considered from the standpoint of its economic structure. Like all its predecessors, the capitalist process of production proceeds under definite material conditions, which are, however, simultaneously the bearers of definite social relations entered into by individuals in the process of reproducing their life. Those conditions, like these relations, are on the one hand prerequisites, on the other hand results and creations of the capitalist process of production; they are produced and reproduced by it. We saw also that capital—and the capitalist is merely capital personified and functions in the process of production solely as the agent of capital—in its corresponding social process of production, pumps a definite quantity of surplus-labour out of the direct producers, or labourers; capital obtains this surplus-labour without an equivalent, and in essence it always remains forced labour—no matter how much it may seem to result from free contractual agreement. This surplus-labour appears as surplus-value, and this surplus-value exists as a surplus-product. Surplus-labour in general, as labour performed over and above the given requirements, must always remain. In the capitalist as well as in the slave system, etc., it merely assumes an antagonistic form and is supplemented by complete idleness of a stratum of society. A definite quantity of surplus-labour is required as insurance against accidents, and by the necessary and progressive expansion of the process of reproduction in keeping with the development of the needs and the growth of population, which is called accumulation from the viewpoint of the capitalist. It is one of the civilising aspects of capital that it enforces this surplus-labour in a manner and under conditions which are more advantageous to the development of the productive forces, social relations, and the creation of the elements for a new and higher form than under the preceding forms of slavery, serfdom, etc. Thus it gives rise to a stage, on the one hand, in which coercion and monopolisation of social development (including its material and intellectual advantages) by one portion of society at the expense of the other are eliminated; on the other hand, it creates the material means and embryonic conditions, making it possible in a higher form of society to combine this surplus-labour with a greater reduction of time devoted to material labour in general. For, depending on the development of labour productivity, surplus-labour may be large in a small total working-day, and relatively small in a large total working-day. If the necessary labour-time = 3 and the surplus-labour = 3, then the total working-day = 6 and the rate of surplus-labour = 100%. If the necessary labour = 9 and the surplus-labour = 3, then the total working-day = 12 and the rate of surplus-labour only = 33⅓%. In that case, it depends upon the labour productivity how much use-value shall be produced in a definite time, hence also in a definite surplus labour-time. The actual wealth of society, and the possibility of constantly expanding its reproduction process, therefore, do not depend upon the duration of surplus-labour, but upon its productivity and the more or less copious conditions of production under which it is performed. In fact, the realm of freedom actually begins only where labour which is determined by necessity and mundane considerations ceases; thus in the very nature of things it lies beyond the sphere of actual material production. Just as the savage must wrestle with Nature to satisfy his wants, to maintain and reproduce life, so must civilised man, and he must do so in all social formations and under all possible modes of production. With his development this realm of physical necessity expands as a result of his wants; but, at the same time, the forces of production which satisfy these wants also increase. Freedom in this field can only consist in socialised man, the associated producers, rationally regulating their interchange with Nature, bringing it under their common control, instead of being ruled by it as by the blind forces of Nature; and achieving this with the least expenditure of energy and under conditions most favourable to, and worthy of, their human nature. But it nonetheless still remains a realm of necessity. Beyond it begins that development of human energy which is an end in itself, the true realm of freedom, which, however, can blossom forth only with this realm of necessity as its basis. The shortening of the working-day is its basic prerequisite.

In a capitalist society, this surplus-value, or this surplus-product (leaving aside chance fluctuations in its distribution and considering only its regulating law, its standardising limits), is divided among capitalists as dividends proportionate to the share of the social capital each holds. In this form surplus-value appears as average profit which falls to the share of capital, an average profit which in turn divides into profit of enterprise and interest, and which under these two categories may fall into the laps of different kinds of capitalists. This appropriation and distribution of surplus-value, or surplus-product, on the part of capital, however, has its barrier in landed property. Just as the operating capitalist pumps surplus-labour, and thereby surplus value and surplus-product in the form of profit, out of the labourer, so the landlord in turn pumps a portion of this surplus-value, or surplus-product, out of the capitalist in the form of rent in accordance with the laws already elaborated.

Hence, when speaking here of profit as that portion of surplus-value falling to the share of capital, we mean average profit (equal to profit of enterprise plus interest) which is already limited by the deduction of rent from the aggregate profit (identical in mass with aggregate surplus-value); the deduction of rent is assumed. Profit of capital (profit of enterprise plus interest) and ground-rent are thus no more than particular components of surplus-value, categories by which surplus-value is differentiated depending on whether it falls to the share of capital or landed property, headings which in no whit however alter its nature. Added together, these form the sum of social surplus-value. Capital pumps the surplus-labour, which is represented by surplus-value and surplus-product, directly out of the labourers. Thus, in this sense, it may be regarded as the producer of surplus-value. Landed property has nothing to do with the actual process of production. Its role is confined to transferring a portion of the produced surplus-value from the pockets of capital to its own. However, the landlord plays a role in the capitalist process of production not merely through the pressure he exerts upon capital, nor merely because large landed property is a prerequisite and condition of capitalist production since it is a prerequisite and condition of the expropriation of the labourer from the means of production, but particularly because he appears as the personification of one of the most essential conditions of production.

Finally, the labourer in the capacity of owner and seller of his individual labour-power receives a portion of the product under the label of wages, in which that portion of his labour appears which we call necessary labour, i.e., that required for the maintenance and reproduction of this labour-power, be the conditions of this maintenance and reproduction scanty or bountiful, favourable or unfavourable.

Whatever may be the disparity of these relations in other respects, they all have this in common: Capital yields a profit year after year to the capitalist, land a ground-rent to the landlord, and labour-power, under normal conditions and so long as it remains useful labour-power, a wage to the labourer. These three portions of total value annually produced, and the corresponding portions of the annually created total product (leaving aside for the present any consideration of accumulation), may be annually consumed by their respective owners, without exhausting the source of their reproduction. They are like the annually consumable fruits of a perennial tree, or rather three trees; they form the annual incomes of three classes, capitalist, landowner and labourer, revenues distributed by the functioning capitalist in his capacity as direct extorter of surplus-labour and employer of labour in general. Thus, capital appears to the capitalist, land to the landlord, and labour-power, or rather labour itself, to the labourer (since he actually sells labour-power only as it is manifested, and since the price of labour-power, as previously shown, inevitably appears as the price of labour under the capitalist mode of production), as three different sources of their specific revenues, namely, profit, ground-rent and wages. They are really so in the sense that capital is a perennial pumping-machine of surplus-labour for the capitalist, land a perennial magnet for the landlord, attracting a portion of the surplus-value pumped out by capital, and finally, labour the constantly self-renewing condition and ever self-renewing means of acquiring under the title of wages a portion of the value created by the labourer and thus a part of the social product measured by this portion of value, i.e., the necessities of life. They are so, furthermore, in the sense that capital fixes a portion of the value and thereby of the product of the annual labour in the form of profit; landed property fixes another portion in the form of rent; and wage-labour fixes a third portion in the form of wages, and precisely by this transformation converts them into revenues of the capitalist, landowner, and labourer, without, however, creating the substance itself which is transformed into these various categories. The distribution rather presupposes the existence of this substance, namely, the total value of the annual product, which is nothing but materialised social labour. Nevertheless, it is not in this form that the matter appears to the agents of production, the bearers of the various functions in the production process, but rather in a distorted form. Why this takes place will be developed in the further course of our analysis. Capital landed property and labour appear to those agents of production as three different, independent sources, from which as such there arise three different components of the annually produced value—and thereby the product in which it exists; thus, from which there arise not merely the different forms of this value as revenues falling to the share of particular factors in the social process of production, but from which this value itself arises, and thereby the substance of these forms of revenue.

[Here one folio sheet of the manuscript is missing.]

... Differential rent is bound up with the relative soil fertility, in other words, with properties arising from the soil as such. But, in the first place, in so far as it is based upon the different individual values of the products of different soil types, it is but the determination just mentioned; secondly, in so far as it is based upon the regulating general market-value, which differs from these individual values, it is a social law carried through by means of competition, which has to do neither with the soil nor the different degrees of its fertility.

It might seem as if a rational relation were expressed at least in 'labour—wages.' But this is no more the case than with 'land—ground-rent.' In so far as labour is value-creating, and is manifested in the value of commodities, it has nothing to do with the distribution of this value among various categories. In so far as it has the specifically social character of wage-labour, it is not value-creating. It has already been shown in general that wages of labour, or price of labour, is but an irrational expression for the value, or price of labour-power; and the specific social conditions, under which this labour-power is sold, have nothing to do with labour as a general agent in production. Labour is also materialised in that value component of a commodity which as wages forms the price of labour-power; it creates this portion just as much as the other portions of the product; but it is materialised in this portion no more and no differently than in the portions forming rent or profit. And, in general, when we establish labour as value-creating, we do not consider it in its concrete form as a condition of production, but in its social delimitation which differs from that of wage-labour.

Even the expression 'capital—profit' is incorrect here. If capital is viewed in the only relation in which it produces surplus-value, namely, its relation to the labourer whereby it extorts surplus-labour by compulsion exerted upon labour-power, i.e., the wage-labourer, then this surplus-value comprises, outside of profit (profit of enterprise plus interest), also rent, in short the entire undivided surplus-value. Here, on the other hand, as a source of revenue, it is placed only in relation to that portion falling to the share of the capitalist. This is not the surplus-value which it extracts generally but only that portion which it extracts for the capitalist. Still more does all connection vanish no sooner the formula is transformed into 'capital—interest.'

If we at first considered the disparity of the above three sources, we now note that their products, their offshoots, or revenues, on the other band, all belong to the same sphere, that of value. However, this is compensated for (this relation not only between incommensurable magnitudes, but also between wholly unlike, mutually unrelated, and non-comparable things) in that capital, like land and labour, is simply considered as a material substance, that is, simply as a produced means of production, and thus is abstracted both as a relation to the labourer and as value.

Thirdly, if understood in this way, the formula, capital—interest (profit), land—rent, labour—wages, presents a uniform and symmetrical incongruity. In fact, since wage-labour does not appear as a socially determined form of labour, but rather all labour appears by its nature as wage-labour (thus appearing to those in the grip of capitalist production relations), the definite specific social forms assumed by the material conditions of labour—the produced means of production and the land—with respect to wage-labour (just as they, in turn, conversely presuppose wage-labour), directly coincide with the material existence of these conditions of labour or with the form possessed by them generally in the actual labour-process, independent of its concrete historically determined social form, or indeed independent of *any* social form. The changed form of the conditions of labour, i.e., alienated from labour and confronting it independently, whereby the produced means of production are thus transformed into capital, and the land into monopolised land, or landed property—this form belonging to a definite historical period thereby coincides with the existence and function of the produced means of production and of the land in the process of production in general. These means of production are in themselves capital by nature; capital is merely an 'economic appellation' for these means of production; and so, in itself land is by nature the earth monopolised by a certain number of landowners. Just as products confront the producer as an independent force in capital and capitalists—who actually are but the personification of capital—so land becomes personified in the landlord and likewise gets on its hind legs to demand, as an independent force, its share of the product created with its help. Thus, not the land receives its due portion of the product for the restoration and improvement of its productivity, but instead the landlord takes a share of this product to chaffer away or squander. It is clear that capital presupposes labour as wage-labour. But it is just as clear that if labour as wage-labour is taken as the point of departure, so that the identity of labour in general with wage-labour appears to be self-evident, then capital and monopolised land must also appear as the natural form of the conditions of labour in relation to labour in general. To be capital, then, appears as the natural form of the means of labour and thereby as the purely real character arising from their function in the labour-process in general. Capital and produced means of production thus become identical terms. Similarly, land and land monopolised through private ownership become identical. The means of labour as such, which are by nature capital, thus become the source of profit, much as the land as such becomes the source of rent.

Labour as such, in its simple capacity as purposive productive activity, relates to the means of production, not in their social determinate form, but rather in their concrete substance, as material and means of labour; the latter likewise are distinguished from one another merely materially, as use-values, i.e., the land as unproduced, the others as produced, means of labour. If, then, labour coincides with wage-labour, so does the particular social form in which the conditions of labour confront labour coincide with their material existence. The means of labour as such are then capital, and the land as such is landed property. The formal independence of these conditions of labour in relation to labour, the unique form of this independence with respect to wage-labour, is then a property inseparable from them as things, as material conditions of production, an inherent, immanent, intrinsic character of them as elements of production. Their definite social character in the process of capitalist production bearing the stamp of a definite historical epoch is a natural, and intrinsic substantive character belonging to them, as it were, from time immemorial, as elements of the production process. Therefore, the respective part played by the earth as the original field of activity of labour, as the realm of forces of Nature, as the pre-existing arsenal of all objects of labour, and the other respective part played by the produced means of production (instruments, raw materials, etc.) in the general process of production, must seem to be expressed in the respective shares claimed by them as capital and landed property, i.e., which fall to the share of their social representatives in the form of profit (interest) and rent, like to the labourer—the part his labour plays in the process of production is expressed in wages. Rent, profit and wages thus seem to grow out of the role played by the land, produced means of production, and labour in the simple labour-process, even when we consider this labour-process as one carried on merely between man and Nature, leaving aside any historical determination. It is merely the same thing again, in another form, when it is argued: the product in which a wage-labourer's labour for himself is manifested, his proceeds or revenue, is simply wages, the portion of value (and thereby the social product measured by this value) which his wages represent. Thus, if wage-labour coincides with labour generally, then so do wages with the produce of labour, and the value portion representing wages with the value created by labour generally. But in this way the other portions of value, profit and rent also appear independent with respect to wages, and must arise from sources of their own, which are specifically different and independent of labour; they must arise from the participating elements of production, to the share of whose owners they fall; i.e., profit arises from the means of production, the material elements of capital, and rent arises from the land, or Nature, as represented by the landlord (Roscher). [Roscher, *System der Volkswirtschaft,* Band I, *Die Grundlagen der Nationalökonomie,* Stuttgart und Augsburg, 1858.—*Ed.*]

Landed property, capital and wage-labour are thus transformed from sources of revenue—in the sense that capital attracts to the capitalist, in the form of profit, a portion of the surplus-value extracted by him from labour, that monopoly in land attracts for the landlord another portion in the form of rent; and that labour grants the labourer the remaining portion of value in the form of wages—from sources by means of which one portion of value is transformed into the form of profit, another into the form of rent, and a third into the form of wages—into actual sources from which these value portions and respective portions of the product in which they exist, or for which they are exchangeable, arise themselves, and from which, therefore, in the final analysis, the value of the product itself arises.[3]

In the case of the simplest categories of the capitalist mode of production, and even of commodity-production, in the case of commodities and money, we have already pointed out the mystifying character that transforms the social relations, for which the material elements of wealth serve as bearers in production, into properties of these things themselves (commodities) and still more pronouncedly transforms the production relation itself into a thing (money). All forms of society, in so far as they reach the stage of commodity-production and money circulation, take part in this perversion. But under the capitalist mode of production and in the case of capital, which forms its dominant category, its determining production relation, this enchanted and perverted world develops still more. If one considers capital, to begin with, in the actual process of production as a means of extracting surplus-labour, then this relationship is still very simple, and the actual connection impresses itself upon the bearers of this process, the capitalists themselves, and remains in their consciousness. The violent struggle over the limits of the working-day demonstrates this strikingly. But even within this non-mediated sphere, the sphere of direct action between labour and capital, matters do not rest in this simplicity. With the development of relative surplus-value in the actual specifically capitalist mode of production, whereby the productive powers of social labour are developed, these productive powers and the social interrelations of labour in the direct labour-process seem transferred from labour to capital. Capital thus becomes a very mystic being since all of labour's social productive forces appear to be due to capital, rather than labour as such, and seem to issue from the womb of capital itself. Then the process of circulation intervenes, with its changes of substance and form, on which all parts of capital, even agricultural capital, devolve to the same degree that the specifically capitalist mode of production develops. This is a sphere where the relations under which value is originally produced are pushed completely into the background. In the direct process of production the capitalist already acts simultaneously as producer of commodities and manager of commodity-production. Hence this process of production appears to him by no means simply as a process of producing surplus-value. But whatever may be the surplus-value extorted by capital in the actual production process and appearing in commodities, the value and surplus-value contained in the commodities must first be realised in the circulation process. And both the restitution of the values advanced in production and, particularly, the surplus-value contained in the commodities seem not merely to be realised in the circulation, but actually to arise from it; an appearance which is especially reinforced by two circumstances: first, the profit made in selling depends on cheating, deceit, inside knowledge, skill and a thousand favourable market opportunities; and then by the circumstance that added here to labour-time is a second determining element—time of circulation. This acts, in fact, only as a negative barrier against the formation of value and surplus-value, but it has the appearance of being as definite a basis as labour itself and of introducing a determining element that is independent of labour and resulting from the nature of capital. In Book II we naturally had to present this sphere of circulation merely with reference to the form determinations which it created and to demonstrate the further development of the structure of capital taking place in this sphere. But in reality this sphere is the sphere of competition, which, considered in each individual case, is dominated by chance; where, then, the inner law, which prevails in these accidents and regulates them, is only visible when these accidents are grouped together in large numbers, where it remains, therefore, invisible and unintelligible to the individual agents in production. But furthermore: the actual process of production, as a unity of the direct production process and the circulation process, gives rise to new formations, in which the vein of internal connections is increasingly lost, the production relations are rendered independent of one another, and the component values become ossified into forms independent of one another.

The conversion of surplus-value into profit, as we have seen, is determined as much by the process of circulation as by the process of production. Surplus-value, in the form of profit, is no longer related back to that portion of capital invested in labour from which it arises, but to the total capital. The rate of profit is regulated by laws of its own, which permit, or even require, it to change while the rate of surplus-value remains unaltered. All this obscures more and more the true nature of surplus-value and thus the actual mechanism of capital. Still more is this achieved through the transformation of profit into average profit and of values into prices of production, into the regulating averages of market-prices. A complicated social process intervenes here, the equalisation process of capitals, which divorces the relative average prices of the commodities from their values, as well as the average profits in the various spheres of production (quite aside from the individual investments of capital in each particular sphere of production) from the actual exploitation of labour by the particular capitals. Not only does it appear so, but it is true in fact that the average price of commodities differs from their value, thus from the labour realised in them, and the average profit of a particular capital differs from the surplus-value which this capital has extracted from the labourers employed by it. The value of commodities appears, directly, solely in the influence of fluctuating productivity of labour upon the rise and fall of the prices of production, upon their movement and not upon their ultimate limits. Profit seems to be determined only secondarily by direct exploitation of labour, in so far as the latter permits the capitalist to realise a profit deviating from the average profit at the regulating market-prices, which apparently prevail independent of such exploitation. Normal average profits themselves seem immanent in capital and independent of exploitation; abnormal exploitation, or even average exploitation under favourable, exceptional conditions, seems to determine only the deviations from average profit, not this profit itself. The division of profit into profit of enterprise and interest (not to mention the intervention of commercial profit and profit from money-dealing, which are founded upon circulation and appear to arise completely from it, and not from the process of production itself) consummates the individualisation of the form of surplus-value, the ossification of its form as opposed to its substance, its essence. One portion of profit, as opposed to the other, separates itself entirely from the relationship of capital as such and appears as arising not out of the function of exploiting wage-labour, but out of the wage-labour of the capitalist himself. In contrast thereto, interest then seems to be independent both of the labourer's wage-labour and the capitalist's own labour, and to arise from capital as its own independent source. If capital originally appeared on the surface of circulation as a fetishism of capital, as a value-creating value, so it now appears again in the form of interest-bearing capital, as in its most estranged and characteristic form. Wherefore also the formula capital—interest, as the third to land—rent and labour—wages, is much more consistent than capital—profit, since in profit there still remains a recollection of its origin, which is not only extinguished in interest, but is also placed in a form thoroughly antithetical to this origin.

Finally, capital as an independent source of surplus-value is joined by landed property, which acts as a barrier to average profit and transfers a portion of surplus-value to a class that neither works itself, nor directly exploits labour, nor can find morally edifying rationalisations, as in the case of interest-bearing capital, e.g., risk and sacrifice of lending capital to others. Since here a part of the surplus-value seems to be bound up directly with a natural element, the land, rather than with social relations, the form of mutual estrangement and ossification of the various parts of surplus-value is completed, the inner connection completely disrupted, and its source entirely buried, precisely because the relations of production, which are bound to the various material elements of the production process, have been rendered mutually independent.

In capital—profit, or still better capital—interest, land—rent, labour—wages, in this economic trinity represented as the connection between the component parts of value and wealth in general and its sources, we have the complete mystification of the capitalist mode of production, the conversion of social relations into things, the direct coalescence of the material production relations with their historical and social determination. It is an enchanted, perverted, topsy-turvy world, in which Monsieur le Capital and Madame la Terre do their ghost-walking as social characters and at the same time directly as mere things. It is the great merit of classical economy to have destroyed this false appearance and illusion, this mutual independence and ossification of the various social elements of wealth, this personification of things and conversion of production relations into entities, this religion of everyday life. It did so by reducing interest to a portion of profit, and rent to the surplus above average profit, so that both of them converge in surplus-value; and by representing the process of circulation as a mere metamorphosis of forms, and finally reducing value and surplus-value of commodities to labour in the direct production process. Nevertheless even the best spokesmen of classical economy remain more or less in the grip of the world of illusion which their criticism had dissolved, as cannot be otherwise from a bourgeois standpoint, and thus they all fall more or less into inconsistencies, half-truths and unsolved contradictions. On the other hand, it is just as natural for the actual agents of production to feel completely at home in these estranged and irrational forms of capital—interest, land—rent, labour—wages, since these are precisely the forms of illusion in which they move about and find their daily occupation. It is, therefore, just as natural that vulgar economy, which is no more than a didactic, more or less dogmatic, translation of everyday conceptions of the actual agents of production, and which arranges them in a certain rational order, should see precisely in this trinity, which is devoid of all inner connection, the natural and indubitable lofty basis for its shallow pompousness. This formula simultaneously corresponds to the interests of the ruling classes by proclaiming the physical necessity and eternal justification of their sources of revenue and elevating them to a dogma.

In our description of how production relations are converted into entities and rendered independent in relation to the agents of production, we leave aside the manner in which the interrelations, due to the world-market, its conjunctures, movements of market-prices, periods of credit, industrial and commercial cycles, alternations of prosperity and crisis, appear to them as overwhelming natural laws that irresistibly enforce their will over them, and confront them as blind necessity. We leave this aside because the actual movement of competition belongs beyond our scope, and we need present only the inner organisation of the capitalist mode of production, in its ideal average, as it were.

In preceding forms of society this economic mystification arose principally with respect to money and interest-bearing capital. In the nature of things it is excluded, in the first place, where production for the use-value, for immediate personal requirements, predominates; and, secondly, where slavery or serfdom form the broad foundation of social production, as in antiquity and during the Middle Ages. Here, the domination of the producers by the conditions of production is concealed by the relations of dominion and servitude, which appear and are evident as the direct motive power of the process of production. In early communal societies in which primitive communism prevailed, and even in the ancient communal towns, it was this communal society itself with its conditions which appeared as the basis of production, and its reproduction appeared as its ultimate purpose. Even in the medieval guild system neither capital nor labour appear untrammelled, but their relations are rather defined by the corporate rules, and by the same associated relations, and corresponding conceptions of professional duty, craftsmanship, etc. Only when the capitalist mode of production—[The manuscript breaks off here—*Ed.*]

Notes

1. The following three fragments were found in different parts of the manuscript for Part VI.—*F. E.*
2. Beginning of Chapter XLVIII according to the manuscript.—*F. E.*
3. Wages, profit, and rent are the three original sources of all revenue, as well as of all exchangeable value (A. Smith) [*An Inquiry into the Nature and Causes of the Wealth of Nations,* Aberdeen, London, 1848, S. 43.—*Ed.*]—It is thus that the causes of material production are at the same time the sources of the original revenues which exist. (Storch [*Cours d'économie politique,* St.-Pétersbourg, 1815.—*Ed.*], I, p. 259.—*Ed.*)

49

Concerning the Analysis of the Process of Production

For the purposes of the following analysis we may leave out of consideration the distinction between price of production and value, since this distinction disappears altogether when, as here, the value of the total annual product of labour is considered, i.e., the product of the total social capital.

Profit (profit of enterprise plus interest) and rent are nothing but peculiar forms assumed by particular parts of the surplus-value of commodities. The magnitude of surplus-value is the limit of the total size of the parts into which it may be divided. Average profit plus rent are, therefore, equal to the surplus-value. It is possible for part of the surplus-labour, and thus surplus-value, contained in the commodities, not to take part directly in the equalisation of an average profit, so that part of the commodity-value is not expressed at all in its price. But first, this is balanced either by the fact that the rate of profit increases, when the commodities sold below their value form an element of the constant capital, or by profit and rent being represented by a larger product, when commodities sold below their value enter into the portion of value consumed as revenue in the form of articles for individual consumption. Secondly, this is eliminated in the average movement. At any rate, even if a portion of surplus-value not expressed in the price of the commodity is lost for the price formation, the sum of average profit plus rent in its normal form can never be larger than the total surplus-value, although it may be smaller. Its normal form presupposes wages corresponding to the value of labour-power. Even monopoly rent, in so far as it is not a deduction from wages, i.e., does not constitute a special category, must always indirectly be a part of the surplus-value. If it is not part of the price excess above the price of production of the commodity itself, of which it is a constituent part (as in differential rent), or an excess portion of the surplus-value of the commodity itself, of which it is a constituent part, above that portion of its own surplus-value measured by the average profit (as in absolute rent), it is at least part of the surplus-value of other commodities, i.e., of commodities which are exchanged for this commodity having a monopoly price. The sum of average profit plus ground-rent can never be greater than the magnitude of which they are components and which exists before this division. It is, therefore, immaterial for our discussion whether the entire surplus-value of the commodities, i.e., all the surplus-labour contained in the commodities, is realised in their price or not. The surplus-labour is not entirely realised if only for the reason that due to a continual change in the amount of labour socially necessary to produce a certain commodity, resulting from the constant change in the productiveness of labour, some commodities are always produced under abnormal conditions and must, therefore, be sold below their individual value. At any rate, profit plus rent equal the total realised surplus-value (surplus-labour), and for purposes of this discussion the realised surplus-value may be equated to all surplus-value; for profit and rent are realised surplus-value, or, generally speaking, the surplus-value which passes into the prices of commodities, thus in practice all the surplus-value forming a constituent part of this price.

On the other hand, wages, which form the third specific form of revenue, are always equal to the variable component part of capital, i.e., the component part which is laid out in purchasing living labour-power, paying labourers rather than in means of labour. (The labour which is paid in the expenditure of revenue is itself paid in wages, profit, or rent, and therefore does not form any value portion of commodities by which it is paid. Hence it is not considered in the analysis of commodity-value and of the component parts into which it is divided.) It is the materialisation of that portion of the total working-day of the labourer in which the value of variable capital and thus the price of labour is reproduced; that portion of commodity-value in which the labourer reproduces the value of his own labour-power, or the price of his labour. The total working-day of the labourer is divided into two parts. One portion in which he performs the amount of labour necessary to reproduce the value of his own means of subsistence; the paid portion of his total labour, the portion necessary for his own maintenance and reproduction. The entire remaining portion of the working-day, the entire excess quantity of labour performed above the value of the labour realised in his wages, is surplus-labour, unpaid labour, represented in the surplus-value of his total commodity-production (and thus in an excess quantity of commodities), surplus-value which in turn is divided into differently named parts, into profit (profit of enterprise plus interest) and rent.

The entire value portion of commodities, then, in which the total labour of the labourers added during one day, or one year, is realised, the total value of the annual product, created by this labour, is divided into the value of wages, into profit and into rent. For this total labour is divided into necessary labour, by which the labourer creates that value portion of the product with which he is himself paid, that is, his wages, and into unpaid surplus-labour, by which he creates that value portion of the product which represents surplus-value and which is later divided into profit and rent. Aside from this labour, the labourer performs no labour, and aside from the total value of the product, which assumes the forms of wages, profit and rent, he creates no value. The value of the annual product, in which the new labour added by the labourer during the year is incorporated, is equal to the wage, or the value of the variable capital plus the surplus-value, which in turn is divided into profit and rent.

The entire value portion of the annual product, then, which the labourer creates in the course of the year, is expressed in the annual value sum of the three revenues, the value of wages, profit, and rent. Evidently, therefore, the value of the constant portion of capital is not reproduced in the annually created value of product, for the wages are only equal to the value of the variable portion of capital advanced in production, and rent and profit are only equal to the surplus-value, the excess of value produced above the total value of advanced capital, which equals the value of the constant capital plus the value of the variable capital.

It is completely irrelevant to the problem to be solved here that a portion of the surplus-value converted into the form of profit and rent is not consumed as revenue, but is accumulated. That portion which is saved up as an accumulation fund serves to create new, additional capital, but not to replace the old capital, be it the component part of old capital laid out for labour-power or for means of labour. We may, therefore, assume here, for the sake of simplicity, that the revenue passes wholly into individual consumption. The difficulty is two-fold. On the one hand the value of the annual product, in which the revenues, wages, profit and rent, are consumed, contains a portion of value equal to the portion of value of constant capital used up in it. It contains this portion of value in addition to that portion which resolves itself into wages and that which resolves itself into profit and rent. Its value is therefore = wages + profit + rent + C (its constant portion of value). How can an annually produced value, which only = wages + profit + rent, buy a product the value of which = (wages + profit + rent) + C? How can the annually produced value buy a product which has a higher value than its own?

On the other hand, if we leave aside that portion of constant capital which did not pass over into the product, and which therefore continues to exist, although with reduced value, as before the annual production of commodities; in other words, temporarily leaving out of consideration the employed, but not consumed, fixed capital, then the constant portion of advanced capital is seen to have been wholly transferred to the new product in the form of raw and auxiliary materials, whereas a part of the means of labour has been wholly consumed and another part only partially, and thus only a part of its value has been consumed in production. This entire portion of constant capital consumed in production must be replaced in kind. Assuming all other circumstances, particularly the productive power of labour, to remain unchanged, this portion requires the same amount of labour for its replacement as before, i.e., it must be replaced by an equivalent value. If not, then reproduction itself cannot take place on the former scale. But who is obliged to perform this labour, and who does perform it?

As to the first difficulty: Who is obliged to pay for the constant portion of value contained in the product, and with what?—It is assumed that the value of constant capital consumed in production reappears as a part of the value of the product. This does not contradict the assumptions of the second difficulty. For it has already been demonstrated in Book I (Kap. V) [English edition: Ch. VII.—*Ed.*] ('The Labour Process and the Process of Producing Surplus-Value') how the old value remains simultaneously preserved in the product through the mere addition of new labour, although this does not reproduce the old value and does no more than add to it, creates merely additional value; but that this results from labour, not in so far as it is value-creating, i.e., labour in general, but in its function as definite productive labour. Therefore, no additional labour was necessary to preserve the value of the constant portion in the product in which the revenue, i.e., the entire value created during the year, is expended. But to be sure, new additional labour is required to replace the value and use-value of constant capital consumed during the preceding year, without the replacement of which no reproduction at all is possible.

All newly added labour is represented in the value newly created during the year, and this in turn is divided into the three revenues: wages, profit and rent.—Thus, on the one hand, no excess social labour remains for the replacement of the consumed constant capital, which must be replaced partially in kind and according to its value, and partially merely according to its value (for pure wear and tear on fixed capital). On the other hand, the value annually created by labour, divided into wages, profit and rent, and to be expended in this form, appears not to suffice to pay for, or buy, the constant portion of capital, which must be contained, outside their own value, in the annual product.

It is seen that the problem presented here has already been solved in the consideration of reproduction of the total social capital—Book II, Part III. We return to it here, in the first place, because surplus-value had not been developed there in its revenue forms: profit (profit of enterprise plus interest) and rent, and could not, therefore, be treated in these forms; and then, also because precisely in the form of wages, profit and rent there is contained an incredible blunder in analysis, which pervades all political economy since Adam Smith.

We divided all capital there into two big classes: Class I, producing means of production, and Class II, producing articles of individual consumption. The fact that certain products may serve equally well both for personal consumption and as means of production (a horse, grain, etc.) does not invalidate the absolute correctness of this division in any way. It is actually no hypothesis, but merely an expression of fact. Take the annual product of a country. One portion of the product, whatever its ability to serve as means of production, passes over into individual consumption. It is the product for which wages, profit and rent are expended. This product is the product of a definite department of the social capital. It is possible that this same capital may also produce products belonging to Class I. In so far as it does so, it is not the portion of this capital consumed in the products of Class II, products belonging actually to individual consumption, which supplies the productively consumed products belonging to Class I. This entire product II, which passes into individual consumption, and for which, therefore, the revenue is spent, is the existent form of the capital consumed in it plus the produced surplus. It is thus the product of a capital invested solely in the production of articles of consumption. And in the same way Department I of the annual product, which serves as means of reproduction—raw materials and instruments of labour—whatever capacity this product may otherwise possess *naturaliter* to serve as means of consumption, is the product of a capital invested solely in the production of means of production. By far the greater part of products forming constant capital exists also materially in a form in which it cannot pass into individual consumption. In so far as this could be done, e.g., in so far as a farmer could eat his seed-corn, butcher his draught animals, etc., the economic barrier works the same for him as if this portion did not exist in consumable form.

As already indicated, we leave out of consideration in both classes the fixed portion of constant capital, which continues to exist in kind and, so far as its value is concerned, independently of the annual product of both classes.

In Class II, for the products of which wages, profit and rent are expended, in short, the revenues consumed, the product itself consists of three components so far as its value is concerned. One component is equal to the value of the constant portion of capital consumed in production; a second component is equal to the value of the variable advanced capital laid out in wages; finally, a third component is equal to the produced surplus-value, thus = profit + rent. The first component of the product of Class II, the value of the constant portion of capital, can be consumed neither by the capitalists of Class II, nor by the labourers of this class, nor by the landowners. It forms no part of their revenues, but must be replaced in kind and must be sold for this to occur. On the other hand, the other two components of this product are equal to the value of the revenues created in this class, = wages + profit + rent. In Class I the product consists of the same constituents, as regards form. But that part which here forms revenue, wages + profit + rent, in short, the variable portion of capital + surplus-value, is not consumed here in the natural form of products of this Class I, but in products of Class II. The value of the revenues of Class I must, therefore, be consumed in that portion of products of Class II which forms the constant capital of II to be replaced. The portion of the product of Class II which must replace its constant capital is consumed in its natural form by the labourers, capitalists and landlords of Class I. They spend their revenue for this product of II. On the other hand, the product of I, to the extent that it represents a revenue of Class I, is productively consumed in its natural form by Class II, whose constant capital it replaces in kind. Finally, the used-up constant portion of capital of Class I is replaced out of the very products of this class, which consist precisely of means of labour, raw and auxiliary materials, etc., partly through exchange by capitalists of I among themselves, partly so that some of these capitalists can directly use their own product once more as means of production.

Let us take the previous scheme (Book II, Chapter XX, II) for simple reproduction:

$$\left.\begin{array}{l} \text{I. } 4{,}000c + 1{,}000v + 1{,}000s = 6{,}000 \\ \text{II. } 2{,}000c + 500v + 500s = 3{,}000 \end{array}\right\} = 9{,}000$$

According to this, the producers and landlords of II consume $500_v + 500_s = 1{,}000$ as revenue; $2{,}000_c$ remains to be replaced. This is consumed by the labourers, capitalists and those who draw rent from I, whose income $= 1{,}000_v + 1{,}000_s = 2{,}000$. The consumed product of II is consumed as revenue by I, and the portion of the revenue of I representing an unconsumable product is consumed as constant capital by II. It remains then to account for the $4{,}000_c$ of I. This is replaced out of the product of I itself, which = 6,000, or rather = 6,000 - 2,000; for these 2,000 have already been converted into constant capital for II. It should be noted, of course, that these numbers have been chosen arbitrarily, and so the relation between the value of the revenues of I and the value of the constant capital of II appears arbitrary. It is evident, however, that so far as the process of reproduction is normal and takes place under otherwise equal circumstances, i.e., leaving aside the accumulation, the sum of the values of wages, profit and rent in Class I must equal the value of the constant portion of capital of Class II. Otherwise either Class II will not be able to replace its constant capital, or Class I will not be able to convert its revenue from unconsumable into consumable form.

Thus, the value of the annual commodity-product, just like the value of the commodity-product produced by some particular investment of capital, and like the value of any individual commodity, resolves itself into two component parts: A, which replaces the value of the advanced constant capital, and B, which is represented in the form of revenue—wages, profit and rent. The latter component part of value, B, is counterposed to the former A, in so far as A, under otherwise equal circumstances: 1) never assumes the form of revenue and 2) always flows back in the form of capital, and indeed constant capital. The other component, B, however, carries within itself, in turn, an antithesis. Profit and rent have this in common with wages: all three are forms of revenue. Nevertheless they differ essentially in that profit and rent represent surplus-value, i.e., unpaid labour, whereas wages represent paid labour. The portion of the value of the product which represents wages expended thus replaces wages, and, under the conditions assumed by us, where reproduction takes place on the same scale and under the same conditions, is again reconverted into wages, flows back first as variable capital, as a component of the capital that must be advanced anew for reproduction. This portion has a two-fold function. It exists first in the form of capital and is exchanged as such for labour-power. In the hands of the labourer, it is transformed into revenue which he draws out of the sale of his labour-power, is converted as revenue into means of subsistence and consumed. This double process is revealed through the mediation of money circulation. The variable capital is advanced in money, paid out as wages. This is its first function as capital. It is exchanged for labour-power and transformed into the manifestation of this labour-power, into labour. This is the process as regards the capitalist. Secondly, however: with this money the labourers buy a part of the commodities produced by them, which is measured by this money, and is consumed by them as revenue. If we imagine the circulation of money to be eliminated, then a part of the labourer's product is in the hands of the capitalist in the form of available capital. He advances this part as capital, gives it to the labourer for new labour-power, while the labourer consumes it as revenue directly or indirectly through exchange for other commodities. That portion of the value of the product, then, which is destined in the course of reproduction to be converted into wages, into revenue for the labourers, first flows back into the hands of the capitalist in the form of capital, or more accurately variable capital. It is an essential requirement that it should flow back in this form in order for labour as wage-labour, the means of production as capital, and the process of production itself as a capitalist process, to be continually reproduced anew.

In order to avoid unnecessary difficulty, one should distinguish gross output and net output from gross income and net income.

The gross output, or gross product, is the total reproduced product. With the exception of the employed but not consumed portion of fixed capital, the value of the gross output, or gross product, equals the value of capital advanced and consumed in production, that is, constant and variable capital plus surplus-value, which resolves itself into profit and rent. Or, if we consider the product of the total social capital instead of that of an individual capital, the gross output equals the material elements forming the constant and variable capital, plus the material elements of the surplus-product in which profit and rent are represented.

The gross income is that portion of value and that portion of the gross product measured by it which remains after deducting that portion of value and that portion of the product of total production measured by it which replaces the constant capital advanced and consumed in production. The gross income, then, is equal to wages (or the portion of the product destined to again become the income of the labourer) + profit + rent. The net income, on the other hand, is the surplus-value, and thus the surplus-product, which remains after deducting wages, and which, in fact, thus represents the surplus-value realised by capital and to be divided with the landlord, and the surplus-product measured by it.

Thus, we saw that the value of each individual commodity and the value of the total commodity-product of each individual capital is divided into two parts: one replaces only constant capital, and the other, although a fraction of it flows back as variable capital—thus also flows back in the *form* of capital—nevertheless is destined to be wholly transformed into gross income, and to assume the form of wages, profit and rent, the sum of which makes up the gross income. Furthermore, we saw that the same is true of the value of the annual total product of a society. A difference between the product of the individual capitalist and that of society exists only in so far as: from the standpoint of the individual capitalist the net income differs from the gross income, for the latter includes the wages, whereas the former excludes them. Viewing the income of the whole society, national income consists of wages plus profit plus rent, thus, of the gross income. But even this is an abstraction to the extent that the entire society, on the basis of capitalist production, bases itself on the capitalist standpoint and thereby considers only the income resolved into profit and rent as net income.

On the other hand, the fantasy of men like Say, to the effect that the entire yield, the entire gross output, resolves itself into the net income of the nation or cannot be distinguished from it, that this distinction therefore disappears from the national viewpoint, is but the inevitable and ultimate expression of the absurd dogma pervading political economy since Adam Smith, that in the final analysis the value of commodities resolves itself completely into income, into wages, profit and rent.[1]

To comprehend, in the case of each individual capitalist, that a portion of his product must be transformed again into capital (even aside from the expansion of reproduction, or accumulation), indeed not only into variable capital, which is destined to again become in its turn income for the labourers, thus a form of revenue, but also into constant capital, which can never be transformed into revenue—such discernment is naturally extraordinarily easy. The simplest observation of the process of production shows this clearly. The difficulty first begins as soon as the process of production is viewed as a whole. The value of the entire portion of the product which is consumed as revenue in the form of wages, profit and rent (it is entirely immaterial whether the consumption is individual or productive), indeed, completely resolves itself under analysis into the sum of values consisting of wages plus profit plus rent, that is, into the total value of the three revenues, although the value of this portion of the product, just like that which does not enter into revenue, contains a value portion = C, equal to the value of the constant capital contained in these portions, and thus *prima facie* cannot be limited by the value of the revenue. This circumstance which, on the one hand, is a practically irrefutable fact, on the other hand, an equally undeniable theoretical contradiction presents a difficulty which is most easily circumvented by the assertion that commodity-value contains another portion of value, merely appearing to differ, from the standpoint of the individual capitalist, from the portion existing in the form of revenue. The phrase: that which appears as revenue for one constitutes capital for another, relieves one of the necessity for any further reflection. But how, then, the old capital can be replaced when the value of the entire product is consumable in the form of revenue; and how the value of the product of each individual capital can be equal to the value sum of the three revenues plus C, constant capital, whereas the sum of the values of the products of all capitals is equal to the value sum of the three revenues plus 0—this appears, of course, as an insoluble riddle and must be solved by declaring that the analysis is completely incapable of unravelling the simple elements of price, and must be content to go around in a vicious circle making a spurious advance *ad infinitum*. Thus, that which appears as constant capital may be resolved into wages, profit and rent, but the commodity-values in which wages, profit and rent appear, are determined in their turn by wages, profit and rent, and so forth *ad infinitum*.[2]

The fundamentally erroneous dogma to the effect that the value of commodities in the last analysis may be resolved into wages + profit + rent also expresses itself in the proposition that the consumer must ultimately pay for the total value of the total product; or also that the money circulation between producers and consumers must ultimately be equal to the money circulation between the producers themselves (Tooke); all these propositions are as false as the axiom upon which they are based.

The difficulties, which lead to this erroneous and *prima facie* absurd analysis, are briefly these:

1. The fundamental relationship of constant and variable capital, hence also the nature of surplus-value, and thereby the entire basis of the capitalist mode of production, are not understood. The value of each partial product of capital, each individual commodity, contains a portion of value = constant capital, a portion of value = variable capital (transformed into wages for labourers), and a portion of value = surplus-value (later split into profit and rent). Thus, how is it possible for the labourer with his wages, the capitalist with his profit, the landlord with his rent, to be able to buy commodities, each of which contains not only one of these constituent elements, but all three of them; and how is it possible for the sum of the values of wages, profit and rent, that is, the three sources of revenue together, to be able to buy

the commodities which go to make up the total consumption of the recipients of these incomes—commodities containing an additional component of value, namely constant capital, outside these three components of value? How should they buy a value of four with a value of three?[3]

We presented our analysis in Book II, Part III.

2. The method is not grasped whereby labour, in adding a new value, preserves the old value in a new form without producing this old value anew.

3 The pattern of the process of reproduction is not understood—how it appears not from the standpoint of individual capital, but rather from that of the total capital; the difficulty is not understood how it is that the product in which wages and surplus-value, in short, the entire value produced by all the labour newly added during the year, is realised, replaces the constant part of its value and yet at the same time resolves itself into value limited solely by the revenues; and furthermore how it is that the constant capital consumed in production can be replaced in substance and value by new capital, although the total sum of newly added labour is realised only in wages and surplus-value, and is fully represented in the sum of the values of both. It is precisely here that the main difficulty lies, in the analysis of reproduction and the relations of its various component parts, both as concerns their material character and their value relationships.

4. To these difficulties is added still another, which increases even more as soon as the various component parts of surplus-value appear in the form of mutually independent revenues. This difficulty consists in the definite designations of revenue and capital interchanging, and altering their position, so that they seem to be merely relative determinations from the point of view of the individual capitalist and to disappear when the total process of production is viewed as a whole. For instance, the revenue of the labourers and capitalists of Class I, which produces constant capital, replaces in value and substance the constant capital of the capitalists of Class II, which produces articles of consumption. One may, therefore, squeeze out of the dilemma by remonstrating that what is revenue for one is capital for another and that these designations thus have nothing to do with the actual peculiarities of the value components of commodities. Furthermore: commodities which are ultimately destined to form the substantive elements of revenue expenditure, that is, articles of consumption, pass through various stages during the year, e.g., woollen yarn, cloth. In one stage they form a portion of constant capital, in the other they are consumed individually, and thus pass wholly into the revenue. One may therefore imagine along with Adam Smith that constant capital is but an apparent element of commodity-value, which disappears in the total pattern. Thus, a further exchange takes place of variable capital for revenue. The labourer buys with his wages that portion of commodities which form his revenue. In this way he simultaneously replaces for the capitalist the money-form of variable capital. Finally: one portion of products which form constant capital is replaced in kind or through exchange by the producers of constant capital themselves; a process with which the consumers have nothing to do. When this is overlooked the impression is created that the revenue of consumers replaces the entire product, i.e., including the constant portion of value.

5. Aside from the confusion which the transformation of values into prices of production brings about, another arises due to the transformation of surplus-value into different, special, mutually independent forms of revenue applying to the various elements of production, i.e., into profit and rent. It is forgotten that the fact that the values of commodities are the basis, and that the division of these

commodity-values into distinct constituent parts, and the further development of these constituents of value into forms of revenue, their transmutation into relations of various owners of different factors of production to these individual components of value, their distribution among these owners according to definite categories and titles, itself alters nothing in value determination and its law. Just as little is the law of value changed by the circumstance that the equalisation of profit, i.e., the distribution of the total surplus-value among the various capitals, and the obstacles which landed property partially (in absolute rent) puts in the way of this equalisation, bring about a divergence between the regulating average prices and the individual values of commodities. This again affects merely the addition of surplus-value to the various commodity-prices, but does not abolish surplus-value itself, nor the total value of commodities as the source of these various component parts of price.

This is the *quid pro quo* which we shall consider in the next chapter, and which is inevitably linked with the illusion that value arises out of its own component parts. And namely, the various component values of the commodity acquire independent forms as revenues, and as such revenues they are related back to the particular material elements of production as their sources of origin instead of to the value of the commodity as their source. They are actually related back to those sources—however, not as components of value, but rather as revenues, as components of value falling to the share of these particular categories of agents in production: the labourer, the capitalist and the landlord. But then one might fancy that these constituents of value, rather than arising out of the division of commodity-value, conversely form it instead only through their combination, which leads to the pretty and vicious circle, whereby the value of commodities arises out of the sum of the values of wages, profit and rent, and the value of wages, profit and rent, in its turn, is determined by the value of commodities, etc.[4]

Considering reproduction in its normal state, only a part of newly added labour is employed for production, and thus for replacement of constant capital; precisely that part which replaces the constant capital used up in the production of articles of consumption, of material elements of revenue. This is balanced by the fact that this constant portion of Class II costs no additional labour. But, now, this constant capital (looking upon the total process of reproduction, in which then the above-mentioned equalisation of Classes I and II is included), not representing a product of newly added labour, although this product could not be created without it—this constant capital, in the process of reproduction, considered from the standpoint of substance, is exposed to certain accidents and dangers which could decimate it. (Furthermore, however, considered from the point of view of value as well, it may be depreciated through a change in the productiveness of labour; but this refers only to the individual capitalist.) Accordingly, a portion of the profit, therefore of surplus-value and thereby also surplus-product, in which (as concerns value) only newly added labour is represented, serves as an insurance fund. And it matters not whether this insurance fund is managed by insurance companies as a separate business or not. This is the sole portion of revenue which is neither consumed as such nor serves necessarily as a fund for accumulation. Whether it actually serves as such, or covers merely a loss in reproduction, depends upon chance. This is also the only portion of surplus-value and surplus-product, and thus of surplus-labour, which would continue to exist, outside of that portion serving for accumulation, and hence expansion of the process of reproduction, even after the abolition of the capitalist mode of production. This, of course, presupposes that the portion regularly consumed by direct producers does not remain limited to its present minimum. Apart from surplus-labour for those who on account of age are not yet, or no longer, able to take part in production, all labour to support those who do not work would cease. If we think back to the beginnings of society, we find no produced means of production, hence no constant capital, the value of which could pass into the product, and which, in reproduction on the same scale, would have to be replaced in kind out of the product and to a degree measured by its value. But Nature there directly provides the means of subsistence, which need not first be produced. Nature thereby also gives to the savage who has but few wants to satisfy the time, not to use the as yet non-existent means of production in new production, but to transform, alongside the labour required to appropriate naturally existing means of production, other products of Nature into means of production: bows, stone knives, boats, etc. This process among savages, considered merely from the substantive side, corresponds to the reconversion of surplus-labour into new capital. In the process of accumulation, the conversion of such products of excess labour into capital obtains continually; and the circumstance that all new capital arises out of profit, rent, or other forms of revenue, i.e., out of surplus-labour, leads to the mistaken idea that all value of commodities arises from some revenue. This reconversion of profit into capital shows rather upon closer analysis that, conversely, the additional labour—which is always represented in the form of revenue—does not serve for the maintenance, or reproduction respectively, of the old capital value, but for the creation of new excess capital so far as it is not consumed as revenue.

The whole difficulty arises from the fact that all newly added labour, in so far as the value created by it is not resolved into wages, appears as profit—interpreted here as a form of surplus-value in general—i.e., as a value which costs the capitalist nothing and which, of course, therefore does not have to replace for him anything advanced, any capital whatever. This value thus exists in the form of available additional wealth, in short, from the viewpoint of the individual capitalist, in the form of his revenue. But this newly created value can just as well be consumed productively as individually, equally well as capital or revenue. As a consequence of its natural form, some of it must be productively consumed. It is, therefore, evident that the annually added labour creates capital as well as revenue; as becomes evident in the process of accumulation. However, the portion of labour-power employed in the creation of new capital (thus analogous to that portion of the working-day employed by a savage, not for acquiring subsistence, but to fashion tools with which to acquire his subsistence) becomes invisible in that the entire product of surplus-labour first appears in the form of profit; a designation which indeed has nothing to do with this surplus-product itself, but refers merely to the individual relation of the capitalist to the surplus-value pocketed by him. In fact, the surplus-value created by the labourer is divided into revenue and capital; i.e., into articles of consumption and additional means of production. But former constant capital taken over from the previous year (leaving aside the portion impaired and thus *pro tanto* destroyed, thus so far as it does not have to be reproduced—and such disturbances in the process of reproduction fall under insurance) is not reproduced as concerns value by the newly added labour.

We see, furthermore, that a portion of the newly added labour is continually absorbed in the reproduction and replacement of consumed constant capital, although this newly added labour resolves itself solely into revenue, into wages, profit and rent. But it is thereby overlooked 1) that one value portion of the product of this labour *is no* product of this new additional labour, but rather pre-existing and consumed constant capital; that the portion of the product in which this part of value appears is thus also not transformed into revenue, but replaces the means of production of this constant capital in kind; 2) that the portion of value in which this newly added labour actually appears is not consumed as revenue in kind, but replaces the constant capital in another sphere, where it is transformed into a natural form, in which it may be consumed as revenue, but which in its turn is again not entirely a product of newly added labour.

In so far as reproduction obtains on the same scale, every consumed element of constant capital must be replaced in kind by a new specimen of the same kind, if not in quantity and form, then at least in effectiveness. If the productiveness of labour remains the same, then this replacement in kind implies replacing the same value which the constant capital had in its old form. But should the productiveness of labour increase, so that the same material elements may be reproduced with less labour, then a smaller portion of the value of the product can completely replace the constant part in kind. The excess may then be employed to form new additional capital or a larger portion of the product may be given the form of articles of consumption, or the surplus-labour may be reduced. On the other hand, should the productiveness of labour decrease, then a larger portion of the product must be used for the replacement of the former capital, and the surplus-product decreases.

The reconversion of profit, or generally of any form of surplus-value, into capital shows—leaving aside the historically defined economic form and considering it merely as the simple formation of new means of production—that the situation still prevails whereby the labourer performs labour to produce means of production beyond the labour for acquiring his immediate means of subsistence. Transformation of profit into capital is no more than employing a portion of excess labour to form new, additional means of production. That this takes place in the shape of a transformation of profit into capital signifies merely that it is the capitalist rather than the labourer who disposes of excess labour. That this excess labour must first pass through a stage in which it appears as revenue (whereas, e.g., in the case of a savage it appears as excess labour directly destined for the production of means of production) means simply that this labour, or its product, is appropriated by the non-worker. However, what is actually transformed into capital is not profit as such. Transformation of surplus-value into capital signifies merely that the surplus-value and surplus-product are not consumed individually as revenue by the capitalist. But, what is actually so transformed is value, materialised labour, or the product in which this value is directly manifested, or for which it is exchanged after having been previously transformed into money. And when the profit is transformed back into capital, this definite form of surplus-value, or profit, does not form the source of the new capital. The surplus-value is thereby merely changed from one form into another. But it is not this change of form which turns it into capital. It is the commodity and its value which now function as capital. However, that the value of the commodity is not paid for—and only by this means does it become surplus-value—is quite irrelevant for the materialisation of labour, the value itself.

The misunderstanding is expressed in various forms. For instance, that the commodities which compose the constant capital also contain elements of wages, profit and rent. Or, on the other hand, that what is revenue for the one is capital for another, and that therefore these are but subjective relations. Thus the yarn of the spinner contains a portion of value representing profit for him, Should the weaver buy the yarn, he realises the profit of the spinner, but for himself this yarn is merely a part of his constant capital.

Aside from the previous remarks made concerning the relations between revenue and capital, the following is to be noted: That which, as regards value, passes along with the yarn as a constituent element into the capital of the weaver, is the value of the yarn. In what manner the parts of this value have been resolved for the spinner himself into capital and revenue, or, in other words, into paid and unpaid labour, is completely irrelevant for the value determination of the commodity itself (aside from modifications through the average profit). Back of this still lurks the idea that the profit, or surplus-value in general, is an excess above the value of the commodity, which can only be made by an extra charge, mutual cheating, or gain through selling. When the price of production is paid, or even the value of the commodity, the component values of the commodity which appear to the seller in the form of revenue are naturally also paid. Monopoly prices, of course, are not referred to here.

Secondly, it is quite correct to say that the component parts of commodities which make up the constant capital, like any other commodity-value, may be reduced to portions of value which resolve themselves for the producers and the owners of the means of production into wages, profit and rent. This is merely a capitalist form of expression for the fact that all commodity-value is but the measure of the socially necessary labour contained in a commodity. But it has already been shown in Book I that this nowise prevents the commodity-product of any capital from being split into separate parts, of which one represents exclusively the constant portion of capital, another the variable portion of capital, and a third solely surplus-value.

Storch expresses the opinion of many others when he says:

> The saleable products which make up the national revenue must be considered in political economy in two different ways: relative to individuals as values, and relative to the nation as goods; for the revenue of a nation is not appraised, like that of an individual, by its value, but by its utility or by the wants which it can satisfy. (*Considérations sur le revenu national,* p. 19.)

In the first place, it is a false abstraction to regard a nation whose mode of production is based upon value, and furthermore is capitalistically organised, as an aggregate body working merely for the satisfaction of the national wants.

Secondly, after the abolition of the capitalist mode of production, but still retaining social production, the determination of value continues to prevail in the sense that the regulation of labour-time and the distribution of social labour among the various production groups, ultimately the book-keeping encompassing all this, become more essential than ever.

Notes

1. Ricardo makes the following very apt comment on thoughtless Say: 'Of net produce and gross produce, M. Say speaks as follows: 'The whole value produced is the gross produce; this value, after deducting from it the cost of production, is the net produce.' (Vol. II, p. 491.) There can, then, be no net produce, because the cost of production, according to M. Say, consists of rent, wages and profits. On page 508 he says: 'The value of a product, the value of a productive service, the value of the cost of production, are all, then, similar values, whenever things are left to their natural course.' Take a whole from a whole, and nothing remains.' (Ricardo, *Principles,* Chapter XXII, p.512, Note.)—By the way we shall see later that Ricardo now refuted Smith's false analysis of commodity-price, its reduction to the sum of the values of the revenues. He does not bother with it, and accepts its correctness so far in his analysis that he 'abstracts' from the constant portion of the value of commodities. He also falls back into the same way of looking at things from time to time.
2. 'In every society the price of every commodity finally resolves itself into some one or other, or all of those three parts [viz., wages, profits, rent] ... A fourth part, it may perhaps be thought, is necessary for replacing the stock of the farmer or for compensating the wear and tear of his labouring cattle, and other instruments of husbandry. But it must be considered that the price of any instrument of husbandry, such as a labouring horse, is itself made up of the same three parts: the rent of the land upon which he is reared, the labour of tending and rearing him, and the profits of the farmer, who advances both the rent of his land and the wages of his labour. Though the price of the corn, therefore, may pay the price as well as the maintenance of the horse, the whole price still resolves itself either immediately or ultimately into the same three parts of rent, labour [meaning wages] and profit.' (Adam Smith.)—We shall show later on how Adam Smith himself feels the inconsistency and insufficiency of this subterfuge, for it is nothing but a subterfuge on his part to send us from Pontius to Pilate while nowhere does he indicate the real investment of capital, in which case the price of the product resolves itself ultimately into these three parts, without any further *progressus.*
3. Proudhon exposes his inability to grasp this in the ignorant formulation: *L'ouvrier ne peut pas racheter son propre produit* (the labourer cannot buy back his own product), because

the interest which is added to the *prix-de-revient* (cost-price) is contained in the product. But how does M. Eugène Forcade teach him to know better? 'If Proudhon's objection were correct, it would strike not only the profits of capital, but would eliminate the possibility even of industry. If the labourer is compelled to pay 100 for each article for which he has received only 80, if his wages can buy back only the value which he has put into a product, it could be said that the labourer cannot buy back anything, that wages cannot pay for anything. In fact, there is always something more than the wages of the labourer contained in the cost-price, and always more than the profits of enterprise in the selling price, for instance, the price of raw materials, often paid to foreign countries. ... Proudhon has forgotten about the continual growth of national capital; he has forgotten that this growth refers to all labourers, whether in an enterprise or in handicrafts.' *(Revue des deux Mondes,* 1848, Tome 24, p. 998.) Here we have the optimism of bourgeois thoughtlessness in the form of sagacity that most corresponds to it. M. Forcade first believes that the labourer could not live did he not receive a higher value than that which he produces, whereas conversely the capitalist mode of production could not exist were he really to receive all the value which he produces. Secondly, he correctly generalises the difficulty, which Proudhon expressed only from a narrow viewpoint. The price of commodities contains not only an excess over wages, but also over profit, namely, the constant portion of value. According to Proudhon's reasoning, then, the capitalist too could not buy back the commodities with his profit. And how does Forcade solve this riddle? By means of a meaningless phrase: the growth of capital. Thus the continual growth of capital is also supposed to be substantiated, among other things, in that the analysis of commodity-prices, which is impossible for the political economist as regards a capital of 100, becomes superfluous in the case of a capital of 10,000. What would be said of a chemist, who, on being asked, How is it that the product of the soil contains more carbon than the soil? would answer: It comes from the continual increase in agricultural production. The well-meaning desire to discover in the bourgeois world the best of all possible worlds replaces in vulgar economy all need for love of truth and inclination for scientific investigation.

4. 'The circulating capital invested in materials, raw materials and finished goods is itself composed of goods, the necessary price of which is formed of the same elements; so that, viewing the total goods in one country, it would mean duplication to count this portion of circulating capital among the elements of the necessary price.' (Storch, *Cours d'économie politique,* II, p. 140.)—By these elements of circulating capital Storch means the value of constant capital (fixed capital is merely circulating in a different form. 'It is true that the wages of the labourer, like that portion of profit of enterprise which consists of wages, if we consider them as a part of the means of subsistence, also consist of goods bought at current prices and which likewise comprise wages, interest on capital, ground-rent and profit of enterprise.... This observation merely serves to prove that it is impossible to resolve the necessary price into its simplest elements.', (*ibid,* Note.)—In his *Considérations sur la nature du revenu national* (Paris, 1824), Storch indeed realises in his controversy with Say to what absurdity the erroneous analysis of commodity-value leads—when it resolves value into mere revenues. He correctly points out the folly of such results—not from the viewpoint of the individual capitalist, but from that of a nation—but himself goes no step further in his analysis of the *prix nécessaire* from that presented in his *Cours,* that it is impossible to resolve it into its actual elements, without resolving it into a spurious advance *ad infinitum.* 'It is evident that the value of' the annual product is divided partly into capitals and partly into profits, and that each one of these portions of value of the annual product regularly goes to buy the products needed by the nation, as much to preserve its capital as to renew its consumption fund (pp. 134, 135).... Can it' (a self-employed peasant family) 'live in its barns or stables, eat its seed and forage, clothe itself with its draught cattle, dispense with its agricultural implements? According to the thesis of M. Say one must answer all these

questions in the affirmative (pp. 135, 136) .... If it is admitted that the revenue of a nation is equal to its gross product, i.e., if no capital has to be deducted from it, then it must also be admitted that a nation can spend the entire value of its annual product unproductively without impairing its future income in the least (147). The products which constitute the capital of a nation are not consumable' (p.150).

50

Illusions Created by Competition

It has been shown that the value of commodities, or the price of production regulated by their total value, resolves itself into:

1) A portion of value replacing constant capital, or representing past labour, which was used up in the form of means of production in making the commodity; in a word, the value, or price, which these means of production carried into the production process of the commodities. We are not referring at all here to individual commodities, but to commodity-capital, that is, the form in which the product of the capital during a definite period of time, say a year, manifests itself; the individual commodity forms one element of commodity-capital, which, moreover, so far as its value is concerned, resolves itself into the same analogous constituents.

2) The portion of value representing variable capital, which measures the income of the labourer and is transformed into wages for him; i.e., the labourer has reproduced these wages in this variable portion of value; in short, the portion of value which represents the paid portion of new labour added to the above constant portion in the production of the commodities.

3) Surplus-value, i.e., the portion of value of the produced commodities in which the unpaid labour, or surplus-labour, is incorporated. This last portion of value, in its turn, assumes the independent forms which are at the same time forms of revenue: the forms of profit on capital (interest on capital as such and profit of enterprise on capital as functioning capital) and ground-rent, which is claimed by the owner of the land participating in the production process. The components 2) and 3), that is, the portion of value which always assumes the revenue forms of wages (of course only after the latter have first gone through the form of variable capital), profit and rent, is distinguished from the constant component 1) by the fact that in it is embodied that entire value in which the new additional labour added to the constant part, to the means of production of the commodities, is materialised. Now, apart from the constant portion, it is correct to say that the value of a commodity, i.e., to the extent that it represents newly added labour, continually resolves itself into three parts, which constitute three forms of revenue, namely, wages, profit and rent,[1] the respective magnitudes of whose value, that is, the aliquot portions which they constitute in the total value, are determined by various specific laws developed above. But, it would be a mistake to state the converse, namely, that the value of wages, rate of profit and rate of rent form independent constituent elements of value, whose synthesis gives rise to the value of commodities, apart from the constant component; in other words, it would be a mistake to say that they are constituent elements of the value of commodities, or of the price of production.[2]

The difference is easily seen.

Let us assume that the value of the product of a capital of 500 is equal to 400_c +

$100_v + 150_s = 650$; let the 150_s in turn, be divided into 75 profit + 75 rent. We will also assume, in order to forestall useless difficulties, that this is a capital of average composition, so that its price of production and its value coincide; this coincidence always takes place whenever the product of such an individual capital may be considered as the product of some portion—corresponding to its magnitude—of the total capital.

Here wages, measured by variable capital, form 20% of the advanced capital; surplus-value, calculated on the total capital, forms 30%, namely 15% profit and 15% rent. The entire value component of the commodity representing the newly added labour is equal to $100_v + 150_s = 250$. Its magnitude does not depend upon its division into wages, profit and rent. We see from the relation of these parts to each other that labour-power, which is paid with 100 in money, say £100, has supplied a quantity of labour represented by money to the amount of £250. We see from this that the labourer performed 1½ times as much surplus-labour as he did labour for himself. If the working-day = 10 hours, then he worked 4 hours for himself and 6 hours for the capitalist. Therefore, the labour of the labourers paid with £100 is expressed in a money-value of £250. Apart from this value of £250, there is nothing to divide between labourer and capitalist, between capitalist and landlord. It is the total value newly added to the value of the means of production, i.e., 400. The specific commodity-value of 250 thus produced and determined by the quantity of labour materialised in it constitutes the limit, therefore, for the dividends which the labourer, capitalist and landlord will be able to draw from this value in the form of revenue—wages, profit and rent.

Let us assume that a capital of the same organic composition, that is, the same proportion between employed living labour-power and constant capital set in motion, is compelled to pay £150 instead of £100 for the same labour-power which sets in motion the constant capital of 400. And let us further assume that profit and rent share in the surplus-value in different proportions. Since we have assumed that the variable capital of £150 sets the same quantity of labour in motion as did the variable capital of £100, the newly produced value would = 250, as before, and the value of the total product would be 650, also as before, but we would then have $400_c + 150_v + 100_s$ and these 100_s would divide, say, into 45 profit and 55 rent. The proportion in which the newly produced total value would be distributed as wages, profit and rent would now be very different; similarly, the magnitude of the advanced total capital would be different, although it only sets the same total quantity of labour in motion. Wages would amount to 27 3/11%, profit—8 2/11%, and rent—10% of the advanced capital; thus, the total surplus-value would be somewhat over 18%.

As a result of the increase in wages, the unpaid portion of total labour would be different and thereby the surplus-value too. If the working-day contained 10 hours, the labourer would have worked 6 hours for himself and only 4 hours for the capitalist. The proportions of profit and rent would also be different; the reduced surplus-value would be divided in a different proportion between the capitalist and the landlord. Finally, since the value of the constant capital would have remained the same and the value of the advanced variable capital would have risen, the reduced surplus-value would express itself in a still more reduced rate of gross profit, by which we mean in this case the ratio of the total surplus-value to the total advanced capital.

The change in the value of wages, in the rate of profit, and in the rate of rent, whatever the effect of the laws regulating the proportions of these parts to each other, could only move within the limits set by the newly produced commodity-value of 250. An exception could only take place if rent should be based on a monopoly price. This would nowise alter the law, but merely complicate the analysis. For if we consider only the product itself in this case, then only the division of surplus-value would be different. But if we consider its relative value as compared with other commodities, then we should find solely this difference—that a portion of the surplus-value had been transferred from them to this particular commodity.

To recapitulate:

Value of the Product		New Value	Rate of Surplus Value	Rate of Gross Profit
First Case:	$400_c + 100_v + 1505 = 650$	250	150%	30%
Second Case:	$400_c + 150_v + 100_s = 650$	250	66⅔%	18 2/11%

In the first place, the surplus-value falls one-third of what it was, i.e., from 150 to 100. The rate of profit falls by a little more than one-third, i.e., from 30% to 18%, because the reduced surplus-value must be calculated on an increased total advanced capital. But it by no means falls in the same proportion as the rate of surplus-value. The latter falls from 150/100 to 100/150, that is, from 150% to 66⅔%, whereas the rate of profit only falls from 150/500 to 100/550, or from 30% to 18 2/11%. The rate of profit, then, falls proportionately more than the mass of surplus-value, but less than the rate of surplus-value. We find, furthermore, that value, as well as mass of products, remains the same, so long as the same quantity of labour is employed, although the advanced capital has increased due to the augmentation of its variable component. This increase in advanced capital would indeed be very much felt by a capitalist undertaking a new enterprise. But considering reproduction as a whole, augmentation of the variable capital merely means that a larger portion of the value newly created by newly added labour is converted into wages, and thus, in the first place, into variable capital instead of into surplus-value and surplus-product. The value of the product thus remains the same, because it is limited on the one hand by the value of the constant capital = 400, and on the other by the number 250, in which the newly added labour is represented. Both, however, remain unaltered. This product would, as before, represent the same amount of use-value in the same magnitude of value, to the extent that it would itself again enter into the constant capital; thus, the same mass of elements of constant capital would retain the same value. The matter would be different if wages were to rise not because the labourer received a larger share of his own labour, but if he received a larger portion of his own labour because the labour productivity had decreased. In this case, the total value in which the same labour, paid and unpaid, would be incorporated, would remain the same. But the mass of products in which this quantity of labour would be incorporated would have decreased so that the price of each aliquot portion of this product would rise, because each portion would contain more labour. The increased wages of 150 would not represent any more product than the wages of 100 did before; the reduced surplus-value of 100 would represent merely ⅔ the former product, i.e., 66⅔% of the mass of use-values formerly represented by 100. In this case, the constant capital would also become dearer to the extent that this product would enter into it. However, this would not be the result of the increase in wages, but rather the increase in wages would be a result of the increase in the price of commodities and a result of the diminished productivity of the same quantity of labour. It appears here as though the increase in wages had made the product dearer; however, this increase is not the cause, but rather the result, of a change in the value of the commodities, due to the decreased productivity of labour.

On the other hand, all other circumstances remaining the same, i.e., if the same quantity of employed labour is still represented by 250, then, if the value of the means of production employed should rise or fall, the value of the same quantity of products would rise or fall by the same magnitude. $450_c + 100_v + 150_s$ gives a product-value = 700; but $350_c + 100_v + 150_s$ gives a value for the same quantity of products of only 600, as against a former 650. Hence, if the advanced capital, set in motion by the same quantity of labour, increases or decreases, then the value of the product rises or falls, other circumstances remaining the same, if the increase or decrease in advanced capital is due to a change in the magnitude of the value of the constant portion of capital. On the other hand, the value of the product remains unchanged if the increase or decrease in advanced capital is caused by a change in the magnitude of the value of the variable portion of capital, assuming the labour productivity remains the same. In the case of the constant capital, the increase or decrease in its value is not compensated for by any opposite movement. But in the case of the variable capital, assuming the labour productivity remains the same, an increase or decrease in its value is compensated for by the opposite movement on the part of the surplus-value, so that the value of the variable capital plus the surplus-value, i.e., the value newly added by labour to the means of production and newly incorporated in the product, remains the same.

But if the increase or decrease in the value of the variable capital or wages is due to a rise or fall in the price of commodities, i.e., a decrease or increase in the productiveness of the labour employed by this investment of capital then the value of the product is affected. But the rise or fall in wages, in this case, is not a cause, but merely an effect.

On the other hand, assuming the constant capital in the above illustration to remain = 400_c, if the change from $100_v + 150_s$ to $150_v + 100_s$, i.e., the increase in variable capital, should be due to a decrease in the productiveness of labour, not in this particular branch of industry, say, cotton spinning, but perhaps in agriculture which provides the labourer's foodstuffs, i.e., due to a rise in the price of these foodstuffs, then the value of the product would remain unchanged. The value of 650 would still be represented by the same quantity of cotton yarn.

It follows, furthermore, from the above: If the decrease in the expenditure of constant capital is due to economies, etc., in lines of production whose products enter into the labourer's consumption, then this, just like the direct increase in the productivity of the employed labour itself, may lead to a decrease in wages due to a cheapening of the means of subsistence of the labourer, and may lead, therefore, to an increase in the surplus-value; so that the rate of profit, in this case, would grow for two reasons, namely, on the one hand, because the value of the constant capital decreases, and on the other hand, because the surplus-value increases. In our consideration of the transformation of surplus-value into profit, we assumed that wages do not fall, but remain constant, because there we had to investigate the fluctuations in the rate of profit, independent of the changes in the rate of surplus-value. Moreover, the laws developed there are general ones, and also apply to investments of capital whose products do not enter into the labourer's consumption, whereby changes in the value of the product, therefore, are without influence upon the wages.

Thus, the separation and resolution of new value annually added by new labour to the means of production, or to the constant part of capital, into the various forms of revenue, viz., wages, profit and rent, do not at all alter the limits of the value itself, the total value to be distributed among these various categories; any more than a change in the mutual relations of these individual parts can change their total, this given magnitude of value. The given number 100 always remains the same, whether it is divided into 50 + 50, or into 20 + 70 + 10, or into 40 + 30 + 30. The portion of the value of the product which is resolved into these revenues is determined, just like the constant portion of the value of capital, by the value of the commodities, i.e., by the quantity of labour incorporated in them in each case. Given first, then, is the quantity of value of commodities to be divided among wages, profit and rent; in other words, the absolute limit of the sum of the portions of value of these commodities. Secondly, as concerns the individual categories themselves, their average and regulating limits are likewise given. Wages form the basis in this limitation. They are regulated on the one hand by a natural law; their lower limit is determined by the physical minimum of means of subsistence required by the labourer for the conservation of his labour-power and for its reproduction; i.e., by a definite quantity of commodities. The value of these commodities is determined by the labour-time required for their reproduction; and thus by the portion of new labour added to the means of production, or by the portion of each working-day required by the labourer for the production and reproduction of an equivalent for the value of these necessary means of subsistence. For instance, if his average daily means of subsistence have a value = 6 hours of average labour, then he must work on an average six hours per day for himself. The actual value of his labour-power deviates from this physical minimum; it differs according to climate and level of social development; it depends not merely upon the physical, but also upon the historically developed social needs, which become second nature. But in every country, at a given time, this regulating average wage is a given magnitude. The value of all other revenue thus has its limit. It is always equal to the value in which the total working-day (which coincides in the present case with the average working-day, since it comprises the total quantity of labour set in motion by the total social capital) is incorporated minus the portion of the working-day incorporated in wages. Its limit is therefore determined by the limit of the value in which the unpaid labour is expressed, that is, by the quantity of this unpaid labour. While the portion of the working-day which is required by the labourer for the reproduction of the value of his wages finds its ultimate limit in the physical minimum of wages, the other portion of the working-day, in which surplus-labour is incorporated, and thus the portion of value representing surplus-value, finds its limit in the physical maximum of the working-day, i.e., in the total quantity of daily labour-time during which the labourer can, in general, be active and still preserve and reproduce his labour-power. Since we are here concerned with the distribution of the value which represents the total labour newly added per year, the working-day may be regarded here as a constant magnitude, and is assumed as such, no matter how much or how little it may deviate from its physical maximum. The absolute limit of the portion of value which forms surplus-value, and which resolves itself into profit and ground-rent, is thus given. It is determined by the excess of the unpaid portion of the working-day over its paid portion, i.e., by the portion of the value of the total product in which this surplus-labour exists. If we call the surplus-value thus limited and calculated on the advanced total capital—the profit, as I have done, then this profit, so far as its absolute magnitude is concerned, is equal to the surplus-value and, therefore, its limits are just as much determined by law as the latter. On the other hand, the level of the rate of profit is likewise a magnitude held within certain specific limits determined by the value of commodities. It is the ratio of the total surplus-value to the total social capital advanced in production. If this capital = 500 (say millions) and the surplus-value = 100, then 20% constitutes the absolute limit of the rate of profit. The distribution of the social profit according to this rate among the capitals invested in the various spheres of production creates prices of production which deviate from the values of commodities and which are the real regulating average market-prices. But this deviation abolishes neither the determination of prices by values nor the regular limits of profit. Instead of the value of a commodity being equal to the capital consumed in its production plus the surplus-value contained in it, its price of production is now equal to the capital, c, consumed in its production plus the surplus-value falling to its share as a result of the general rate of profit, for instance, 20% on the capital advanced in its production, counting both the consumed and the merely employed capital. But this additional amount of 20% is itself determined by the surplus-value created by the total social capital and its relation to the value of this capital; and for this reason it is 20% and not 10 or 100. The transformation of values into prices of production, then, does not remove the limits on profit, but merely alters its distribution among the various particular capitals which make up the social capital, i.e., it distributes it uniformly among them in the proportion in which they form parts of the value of this total capital. The market-prices rise above and fall below these regulating prices of production, but these fluctuations mutually balance each other. If one examines price lists over a more or less long period of time, and if one disregards those cases in which the actual value of commodities is altered by a change in the productivity of labour, and likewise those cases in which the process of production has been disturbed by natural or social accidents, one will be surprised, in the first place, by the relatively narrow limits of the deviations, and, secondly, by the regularity of their mutual compensation. The same domination of the regulating averages will be found here that Quetelet pointed out in the case of social phenomena. If the equalisation of the values of commodities into prices of production does not meet any obstacles, then the rent resolves itself into differential rent, i.e., it is limited to the equalisation of the surplus-profits which would he given to some capitalists by the regulating prices of production and which are now appropriated by the landlord. Here, then, rent has its definite limit of value in the deviations of the individual rates of profit, which are caused by the regulation of prices of production by the general rate of profit. If landed property obstructs equalisation of the values of commodities into prices of production, and appropriates absolute rent, then the latter is limited by the excess of the value of the agricultural products over their price of production, i.e., by the excess of the surplus-value contained in them over the rate of profit assigned to the capitals by the general rate of profit. This difference, then, forms the limit of the rent, which, as before, is but a definite portion of the given surplus-value contained in the commodities.

Finally, if equalisation of surplus-value into average profit meets with obstacles in the various spheres of production in the form of artificial or natural monopolies, and particularly monopoly in landed property, so that a monopoly price becomes possible, which rises above the price of production and above the value of the commodities affected by such a monopoly, then the limits imposed by the value of the commodities would not thereby be removed. The monopoly price of certain commodities would merely transfer a portion of the profit of the other commodity-producers to the commodities having the monopoly price. A local disturbance in the distribution of the surplus-value among the various spheres of production would indirectly take place, but it would leave the limit of this surplus-value itself unaltered. Should the commodity having the monopoly price enter into the necessary consumption of the labourer, it would increase the wage and thereby reduce the surplus-value, assuming the labourer receives the value of his labour-power as before. It could depress wages below the value of labour-power, but only to the extent that the former exceed the limit of their physical minimum. In this case the monopoly price would be paid by a deduction from real wages (i.e.. the quantity of use-values received by the labourer for the same quantity of labour) and from the profit of the other capitalists. The limits within which the monopoly price would affect the normal regulation of the prices of commodities would be firmly fixed and accurately calculable.

Thus just as the division of the newly added value of commodities, and, in general, value resolvable into revenue, finds its given and regulating limits in the relation between necessary and surplus labour, wages and surplus-value, so does the division of surplus-value itself into profit and ground-rent find its limits in the laws regulating the equalisation of the rate of profit. As regards the division into interest and profit of enterprise, the average profit itself forms the limit for both taken together. It furnishes the given magnitude of value which they may split among themselves and which alone can be so divided. The specific ratio of this division is here fortuitous, i.e., it is determined exclusively by conditions of competition. Whereas, in other cases, the balancing of supply and demand is equivalent to elimination of the deviations in market-prices from their regulating average prices, i.e., elimination of the influence of competition, it is here the only determinant. But why? Because the same production factor, capital, has to divide its share of the surplus-value between two owners of the same production factor. But the fact that there is no definite, regular limit here for the division of the average profit does not remove its limit as part of the commodity-value; just as the fact that two partners in a certain business divide their profit unequally due to different external circumstances does not affect the limits of this profit in any way.

Hence, although the portion of the commodity-value in which the new labour added to the value of the means of production is incorporated is divided into various parts, which in the form of revenue assume mutually independent forms, this is no reason for now considering wages, profit and ground-rent as the constituent elements which, in combination or taken all together, are the source of the regulating price (natural price, *prix necessaire*) of the commodities themselves; so that it is not the commodity-value, after deducting the constant portion of value, which would be the original unit that divides into these three parts, but rather, conversely, the price of each of these three parts would be independently determined, and the price of the commodities would then be formed by adding these three independent magnitudes together. In reality, the commodity-value is the magnitude which precedes the sum of the total values of wages, profit and rent, regardless of the relative magnitudes of the latter. In the above erroneous conception, wages, profit and rent are three independent magnitudes of value, whose total magnitude produces, limits and determines the magnitude of the commodity-value.

In the first place it is evident that if wages, profit and rent were to form the price of commodities, this would apply as much to the constant portion of the commodity-value as to the other portion, in which variable capital and surplus-value are incorporated. Thus, this constant portion may here be left entirely out of consideration, since the value of the commodities of which it is composed would likewise resolve itself into the sum of the values of wages, profit and rent. As already noted, this conception, then, denies the very existence of such a constant portion of value.

It is furthermore evident that value loses all meaning here. Only the conception of price still remains, in the sense that a certain amount of money is paid to the owner of labour-power, capital and land. But what is money? Money is not a thing, but a definite form of value, hence, value is again presupposed. Let us say, then, that a definite amount of gold or silver is paid for these elements of production, or that it is mentally equated to them. But gold and silver (and the enlightened economist is proud of this discovery) are themselves commodities like all other commodities. The price of gold and silver is therefore likewise determined by wages, profit and rent. Hence we cannot determine wages, profit and rent by equating them to a certain amount of gold and silver, for the value of this gold and silver, by means of which they should be evaluated as in their equivalent, should be first determined precisely by them, independently of gold and silver, i.e., independently of the value of any commodity, which value is precisely the product of the above three factors. Thus, to say that the value of wages, profit and rent consists in their being equivalent to a certain quantity of gold and silver, would merely be saying that they are equal to a certain quantity of wages, profit and rent.

Take wages first. For it is necessary to make labour the point of departure, even in this view of the matter. How, then, is the regulating price of wages determined, the price about which its market-prices oscillate?

Let us say that it is determined by the supply and demand of labour-power. But what sort of labour-power demand is this? It is a demand made by capital. The demand for labour is therefore tantamount to the supply of capital. In order to speak of a supply of capital, we should know above all what capital is. Of what does capital consist? If we take its simplest aspect, it consists of money and commodities. But money is merely a commodity-form. Capital, then, consists of commodities. But the value of commodities, according to our assumption, is determined, in the first instance, by the price of the labour producing the commodities, by wages. Wages are here presupposed and are treated as a constituent element of the price of commodities. This price then should be determined by the ratio of available labour to capital. The price of the capital itself is equal to the price of the commodities of which it is composed. The demand by capital for labour is equal to the supply of capital. And the supply of capital is equal to the supply of a quantity of commodities of given price, and this price is regulated in the first place by the price of labour, and the price of labour in turn is equal to that portion of the commodity-price constituting the variable capital, which is granted to the labourer in exchange for his labour; and the price of the commodities constituting this variable capital is again determined, in turn, primarily by the price of labour; for it is determined by the prices of wages, profit and rent. In order to determine wages, we cannot, therefore, presuppose capital, for the value of the capital is itself determined in part by wages.

Moreover, dragging competition into this problem does not help at all. Competition makes the market-prices of labour rise or fall. But suppose supply and demand of labour are balanced. How are wages then determined? By competition. But we have just assumed that competition ceases to act as a determinant, that its influence is cancelled due to equilibrium between its two mutually opposing forces. Indeed, it is precisely the natural price of wages that we wish to find, i.e., the price of labour that is not regulated by competition, but which, on the contrary, regulates the latter.

Nothing remains but to determine the necessary price of labour by the necessary means of subsistence of the labourer. But these means of subsistence are commodities, which have a price. The price of labour is therefore determined by the price of the necessary means of subsistence and the price of the means of subsistence, like that of all other commodities, is determined primarily by the price of labour. Therefore, the price of labour determined by the price of the means of subsistence is determined by the price of labour. The price of labour is determined by itself. In other words, we do not know how the price of labour is determined. Labour, in this case, has a price in general, because it is considered as a commodity. In order, therefore, to speak of the price of labour, we must know what price in general is. But we do not learn at all in this way what price in general is.

Nevertheless, let us assume that the necessary price of labour is determined in this agreeable manner. Then how is the average profit determined, the profit of every capital under normal conditions, which constitutes the second element in the price of commodities? The average profit must be determined by an average rate of profit; how is this rate determined? By competition among the capitalists? But the competition already presupposes the existence of profit. It presupposes various rates of profit, and thus various profits—either in the same or in different spheres of production. Competition can influence the rate of profit only to the extent that it affects the prices of commodities. Competition can only make the producers within the same sphere of production sell their commodities at the same prices, and make them sell their commodities in different spheres of production at prices which will give them the same profit, the same proportional addition to the price of commodities which has already been partially determined by wages. Hence competition can only equalise inequalities in the rate of profit. In order to equalise unequal rates of profit, profit must exist as an element in the price of commodities. Competition does not create it. It lowers or raises its level, but does not create the level which is established when equalisation has been achieved. And when we speak of a necessary rate of profit, what we wish to know is precisely the rate of profit independent of the movements of competition, which in turn regulates competition itself. The average rate of profit sets in when there is an equilibrium of forces among the competing capitalists. Competition may establish this equilibrium but not the rate of profit which makes its appearance with this equilibrium. When this equilibrium is established, why is the general rate of profit now 10, or 20, or 100%? Because of competition? No, on the contrary, competition has eliminated the causes producing deviations from 10, 20, or 100%. It has brought about a commodity-price whereby every capital yields the same profit in proportion to its magnitude. The magnitude of this profit itself, however, is independent of competition. The latter merely reduces, again and again, all deviations to this magnitude. One person competes with another, and competition compels him to sell his commodities at the same price as the other. But why is this price 10 or 20 or 100?

Thus, nothing remains but to declare rate of profit, and therefore profit, to be in some unaccountable manner a definite extra charge added to the price of commodities, which up to this point was determined by wages. The only thing that competition tells us is that this rate of profit must be a given magnitude. But we knew this before—when we dealt with general rate of profit and 'necessary price' of profit.

It is quite unnecessary to wade through this absurd process anew in the case of ground-rent. One can see without doing this that, when carried out more or less consistently, it makes profit and rent merely appear as definite extra charges added by unaccountable laws to the price of commodities, a price primarily determined by wages. In short, competition has to shoulder the responsibility of explaining all the meaningless ideas of the economists, whereas it should rather be the economists who explain competition.

Now, disregarding here the illusion of a profit and rent being created by circulation, i.e., price components arising through sale—and circulation can never give what it did not first receive—the matter simply amounts to this:

Let the price of a commodity determined by wages = 100; let the rate of profit be 10% of wages, and the rent 15% of wages. Then the price of the commodity determined by the sum of wages, profit and rent = 125. This additional 25 cannot arise from the sale of the commodity. For all who sell one another commodities sell at 125 that which costs 100 in wages; which is the same as if they had all sold at 100. Thus, the operation must be considered independently of the circulation process.

If the three share the commodity itself, which now costs 125—and it does not alter matters any if the capitalist first sells at 125, and then pays 100 to the labourer, 10 to himself, and 15 to the landlord—the labourer receives 4/5 = 100 of the value and of the product. The capitalist receives 2/25 of the value and of the product, and the landlord 3/25. Since the capitalist sells at 125 instead of 100, he gives the labourer only 4/5 of the product incorporating the latter's labour. Thus, it would be just the same as if he had given 80 to the labourer and retained 20—of which 8 would fall to his share and 12 to the landlord. In this case, he would have sold the commodity at its value, since in fact the additions to the price represent increases that are independent of the value of the commodity, which under the assumption made above is determined by the value of wages. This, in a roundabout way, amounts to saying that according to this conception the term 'wages,' here 100, means the value of the product, i.e., the sum of money in which this definite quantity of labour is represented; but that this value in turn differs from the real wage and therefore leaves a surplus. But, here the surplus is realised by a nominal addition to the price. Hence, if wages were equal to 110 instead of 100, the profit would have to be = 11 and the ground-rent = 16½, so that the price of the commodity would = 137½. This would leave the proportions unaltered. But since the division would always be obtained by way of a nominal addition of definite percentages to wages, the price would rise and fall with the wages. Wages are here first set equal to the value of the commodity, and then divorced from it again. In fact, however, this amounts to saying in a roundabout and meaningless way that the value of the commodity is determined by the quantity of labour contained in it, whereas the value of wages is determined by the price of the necessary means of subsistence, and the excess of value above the wage forms profit and rent.

The splitting of the value of commodities after subtracting the value of the means of production consumed in their creation; the splitting of this given quantity of value, determined by the quantity of labour incorporated in the produced commodities, into three component parts, which assume, as wages, profit and rent, independent and mutually unrelated forms of revenue—this splitting appears in a perverted form on the surface of capitalist production, and consequently in the minds of those captivated by the latter.

Let the total value of a certain commodity = 300, of which 200 is the value of the means of production, or elements of constant capital, consumed in its production. This leaves 100 as the amount of new value added to the commodity during its process of production. This new value of 100 is all that is available for division among the three forms of revenue. If we let wages = x, profit = y and ground-rent = z, then the sum of x + y +

z will always = 100 in our case. But to the industrialists, merchants and bankers, and to the vulgar economists, this appears quite different. For them, the value of the commodity, after subtracting the value of the means of production consumed by it, is not given = 100, this 100 then being divided into x, y and z. But rather, the price of the commodity simply consists of the value of wages, the value of profit and the value of rent, which magnitudes are determined independently of the value of the commodity and of each other, so that x, y and z are each given and determined independently, and only from the sum of these magnitudes, which the may be smaller or larger than 100, is the magnitude of value of the commodity itself obtained by adding these component values together. This *quid pro quo* is inevitable because:

First: The component parts of the value of a commodity, appear as independent revenues in relation to one another, and as such are related to three very dissimilar production factors, namely labour, capital and land, and therefore they seem to arise from the latter. Ownership of labour-power, capital and land is the cause for these various component values of commodities falling to the share of the respective owners, and thus transforming themselves into revenue for them. But the value does not arise from a transformation into revenue; it must rather exist before it can be converted into revenue, before it can assume this form. The illusion that the opposite is true is strengthened all the more as the determination of the relative magnitudes of these three components in relation to one another follows different laws, whose connection with, and limitation by, the value of the commodities themselves nowise appear on the surface.

Secondly: We have seen that a general rise or fall in wages, by causing a movement of the general rate of profit in the opposite direction—other circumstances remaining the same—changes the prices of production of the various commodities, i.e., raises some and lowers others, depending on the average composition of capital in the respective spheres of production. Thus, experience shows here that in some spheres of production, at any rate, the average price of a commodity rises because wages have risen, and falls because wages have fallen. But 'experience' does not show that the value of commodities, which is independent of wages, secretly regulates these changes. However, if the rise in wages is local, if it only takes place in particular spheres of production as a result of special circumstances, then a corresponding nominal rise in the prices of these commodities may occur. This rise in the relative value of one kind of commodity in relation to the others, for which wages have remained unchanged, is then merely a reaction against the local disturbance in the uniform distribution of surplus-value among the various spheres of production, a means of equalising the particular rates of profit into the general rate. 'Experience' shows in this case, that wages again determine the price. Thus, in both of these cases experience shows that wages determine the prices of commodities. But 'experience' does not show the hidden cause of this interrelation. Furthermore: The average price of labour, i.e., the value of labour-power, is determined by the production price of the necessary means of subsistence. If the latter rises or falls, the former rises or falls accordingly. Thus, experience again shows the existence of a connection between wages and the price of commodities. But the cause may appear as an effect, and the effect as a cause, which is also the case in the movements of market-prices, where a rise of wages above their average corresponds to the rise of market-prices above the prices of production during periods of prosperity, and the subsequent fall of wages below their average corresponds to a fall of market-prices below the prices of production. To the dependence of prices of production upon the values of commodities *prima facie* there would always have to correspond, apart from the oscillatory movements of market-prices, the experience that whenever wages rise the rate of profit falls, and vice versa. But we have seen that the rate of profit may be determined by movements in the value of constant capital, independently of the movements of wages; so that wages and rate of profit, instead of moving in opposite directions, may move in the same direction, may rise or fall together. If the rate of surplus-value were to directly coincide with the rate of profit, this would not be possible. Similarly if wages should rise as a result of a rise in the prices of the means of subsistence, the rate of profit may remain the same, or even rise, due to greater intensity of labour or prolongation of the working-day. All these experiences bear out the illusion created by the independent and distorted form of the component values, namely, that either wages alone, or wages and profit together, determine the value of commodities. Once such an illusion appears with respect to wages, once the price of labour and the value created by labour seem to coincide, the same automatically applies to profit and rent. Their prices, i.e., their money-expression, must then be regulated independently of labour and of the value created by the latter.

Thirdly: Let us assume that according to direct experience the values of a commodity, or the prices of production—which merely appear to be independent of the values—always coincide with the market-prices of the commodity rather than merely prevailing as the regulating average prices by constant compensation of the continual fluctuations in market-price. Let us assume, furthermore, that reproduction always takes place under the same unaltered conditions, i.e., labour productivity remains constant in all elements of capital. Finally, let us assume that the component value of the commodity-product, which is formed in every sphere of production by the addition of a new quantity of labour—i.e., a newly produced value—to the value of the means of production, always split into constant proportions of wages, profit and rent, so that the wage actually paid always directly coincides with the value of labour-power, the profit actually realised—with the portion of the total surplus-value which falls to the share of every independently functioning part of the total capital by virtue of the average rate of profit, and the actual rent is always limited by the bounds within which ground-rent on this basis is normally confined. In a word, let us assume that the division of the socially produced values and the regulation of the prices of production takes place on a capitalist basis, but that competition is eliminated.

Thus, under these assumptions, namely, if the value of commodities were constant and appeared so, if the component value of the commodity-product which resolves itself into revenues were to remain a constant magnitude and always appeared as such, and finally, if this given and constant component value always split into constant proportions of wages, profit and rent—even under these assumptions, the real movement would necessarily appear in distorted form; not as the splitting of a previously given magnitude of value into three parts which assume mutually independent forms of revenue, but, on the contrary, as the formation of this magnitude of value from the sum of the independent and separately determined, each by itself, constituent elements—wages, profit and ground-rent. This illusion would necessarily arise, because in the actual movement of individual capitals, and the commodities produced by them, not the value of commodities would appear to be a precondition of its splitting but, conversely, the components into which it is split function as a precondition of the value of the commodities. In the first place, we have seen that to every capitalist the cost-price of his commodities appears as a given magnitude and continually appears as such in the actual price of production. The cost-price, however, is equal to the value of the constant capital, the advanced means of production, plus the value of labour-power, which, however, appears to the agent of production in the irrational form of the price of labour, so that wages simultaneously appear as revenue of the labourer. The average price of labour is a given magnitude, because the value of labour-power, like that of any other commodity, is determined by the necessary labour-time required for its reproduction. But as concerns that portion of the value of commodities which is embodied in wages, it does not arise from the fact that it assumes this form of wages, that the capitalist advances to the labourer his share of his own product in the form of wages, but from the fact that the labourer produces an equivalent for his wages, i.e., that a portion of his daily or annual labour produces the value contained in the price of his labour-power. But wages are stipulated by contract, before their corresponding value equivalent has been produced. As an element of price, whose magnitude is given before the commodity and its value have been produced, as a constituent part of the cost-price, wages thereby do not appear as a portion which detaches itself in independent form from the total value of the commodity, but rather, conversely, as a given magnitude, which predetermines this value, i.e., as a creator of price and value. A role similar to that of wages in the cost-price of commodities is played by the average profit in their price of production, for the price of production is equal to cost-price plus average profit on the advanced capital. This average profit figures practically, in the mind and calculation of the capitalist himself, as a regulating element, not merely in so far as it determines the transfer of capitals from one sphere of investment into another, but also in all sales and contracts which embrace a process of reproduction extending over long periods. But so far as it figures in this manner, it is a pre-existent magnitude, which is in fact independent of the value and surplus-value produced in any particular sphere of production, and thus even more so in the case of any individual investment of capital in any sphere of production. Rather than appearing as a result of a splitting of value, it manifests itself much more as a magnitude independent of the value of the produced commodities, as pre-existing in the process of production of commodities and itself determining the average price of the commodities, i.e., as a creator of value. Indeed, the surplus-value, owing to the separation of its various portions into mutually, completely unrelated forms, appears in still more concrete form as a prerequisite for creating commodity-value. A part of the average profit in the form of interest confronts the functioning capitalist independently as an assumed element in the production of commodities and of their value. No matter how much the magnitude of the interest fluctuates, at each moment and for every capitalist it is a given magnitude entering into the cost-price of the commodities produced by him as individual capitalist. The same role is played by ground-rent in the form of lease money fixed by contract for the agricultural capitalist, and in the form of rent for business premises in the case of other entrepreneurs. These portions into which surplus-value is split, being given as elements of cost-price for the individual capitalist, appear conversely therefore as creators of surplus-value; creators of a portion of the price of commodities, just as wages create the other. The secret wherefore these products of the splitting of commodity-value constantly appear as prerequisites for the formation of value itself is simply this, that the capitalist mode of production, like any other, does not merely constantly reproduce the material product, but also the social and economic relations, the characteristic economic forms of its creation. Its result, therefore, appears just as constantly presupposed by it, as its presuppositions appear as its results. And it is this continual reproduction of the same relations which the individual capitalist anticipates as self-evident, as an indubitable fact. So long as the capitalist mode of production persists as such, a portion of the newly added labour continually resolves itself into wages, another into profit (interest and profit of enterprise), and a third into rent. In contracts between the owners of various agencies of production this is always assumed, and this assumption is correct, however much the relative proportions may fluctuate in individual cases. The definite form in which the parts of value confront each other is presupposed because it is continually reproduced, and it is continually reproduced because it is continually presupposed.

To be sure, experience and appearance now also demonstrate that market-prices, in whose influence the capitalist actually sees the only determination of value, are by no means dependent upon such anticipation, so far as their magnitude is concerned; that they do not correspond to whether the interest or rent were set high or low. But the market-prices are constant only in their variation, and their average over longer periods results precisely in the respective averages of wages, profit and rent as the constant magnitudes, and therefore, in the last analysis, those dominating the market-prices.

On the other hand, it seems plain on reflection that if wages, profit and rent are creators of value since they seem to be presupposed in the production of value, and are assumed by the individual capitalist in his cost-price and price of production, then the constant portion, whose value enters as given into the production of every commodity, is also a creator of value. But the constant portion of capital is no more than a sum of commodities and, therefore, of commodity-values. Thus we should arrive at the absurd tautology that commodity-value is the creator and cause of commodity-value.

However, if the capitalist were at all interested in reflecting about this—and his reflections as capitalist are dictated exclusively by his interests and self-interested motives—experience would show him that the product which he himself produces enters into other spheres of production as a constant portion of capital, and that products of these other production spheres enter into his own product as constant portions of capital. Since the additional value, so far as his new production is concerned, seems to be formed, from his point of view, by the magnitudes of wages, profit and rent, then this also holds good for the constant portion consisting of the products of other capitalists. And thus, the price of the constant portion of capital, and thereby the total value of the commodities, reduces itself in the final analysis, although in a manner which is somewhat unaccountable, to a sum of values resulting from the addition of independent creators of value—wages, profit and rent—which are regulated according to different laws and arise from different sources.

Fourthly: Whether the commodities are sold at their values or not, and hence the determination of value itself, is quite immaterial for the individual capitalist. It is, from the very outset, a process that takes place behind his back and is controlled by the force of circumstances independent of himself, because it is not the values, but the divergent prices of production, which form the regulating average prices in every sphere of production. The determination of value as such interests and has a determining effect on the individual capitalist and the capital in each particular sphere of production only in so far as the reduced or increased quantity of labour required to produce commodities, as a consequence of a rise or fall in productiveness of labour, enables him in one instance to make an extra profit, at the prevailing market-prices, and compels him in another to raise the price of his commodities, because more wages, more constant capital, and thus more interest, fall upon each portion of the product, or individual commodity. It interests him only in so far as it raises or lowers the cost of production of commodities for himself, thus only in so far as it makes his position exceptional.

On the other hand, wages, interest and rent appear to him as regulating limits not only of the price at which he can realise the profit of enterprise, the portion of profit falling to his share as functioning capitalist, but also at which he must generally be able to sell his commodities, if continued reproduction is to take place. It is quite immaterial to him whether or not he realises, through sale, the value and surplus-value incorporated in his commodities, provided only that he makes the customary, or larger, profit of enterprise at given prices, over and above his individual cost-price determined by wages, interest and rent. Apart from the constant portion of capital-wages, interest and rent appear to him, therefore, as the limiting and thereby productive determining elements of the commodity-price. Should he succeed, e.g., in depressing wages below the value of labour-power, i.e., below its normal level, in obtaining capital at a lower interest rate, and in paying less lease money than the normal amount for rent, then it is completely irrelevant to him whether he sells his product below its value, or even below the general price of production, thereby giving away gratis a portion of the surplus-labour contained in the commodities. This also applies to the constant portion of capital. If an industrialist, e.g., can buy his raw material below its price of production, then this buffers him against loss, even should he sell it in the finished product under its price of production. His profit of enterprise may remain the same, or even increase, if only the excess of the commodity-price over its elements, which must he paid, replaced by an equivalent, remains the same or increases. But aside from the value of the means of production which enter into the production of his commodities as a given price magnitude, it is precisely wages, interest and rent which enter into this production as limiting and regulating price magnitudes. Consequently they appear to him as the elements determining the price of the commodities. Profit of enterprise, from this standpoint, seems to be either determined by the excess of market-prices, dependent upon accidental conditions of competition, over the immanent value of commodities determined by the above-mentioned elements of price; or, to the extent that this profit itself exerts a determining influence upon market-prices, it seems itself, in turn, dependent upon the competition between buyers and sellers.

In the competition of individual capitalists among themselves as well as in the competition on the world-market, it is the given and assumed magnitudes of wages, interest and rent which enter into the calculation as constant and regulating magnitudes; constant not in the sense of being unalterable magnitudes, but in the sense that they are given in each individual case and constitute the constant limit for the continually fluctuating market-prices. For instance, in competition on the world-market it is solely a question of whether commodities can be sold advantageously with existing wages, interest and rent at, or below, existing general market-prices, i.e., realising a corresponding profit of enterprise. If wages and the price of land are low in one country, while interest on capital is high, because the capitalist mode of production has not been developed generally, whereas in another country, wages and the price of land are nominally high, while interest on capital is low, then the capitalist employs more labour and land in the one country, and in the other relatively more capital. These factors enter into calculation as determining elements in so far as competition between these two capitalists is possible. Here, then, experience shows theoretically, and the self-interested calculation of the capitalist shows practically, that the prices of commodities are determined by wages, interest and rent, by the price of labour, capital and land, and that these elements of price are indeed the regulating constituent factors of price.

Of course, there always remains an element here which is not assumed, but which results from the market-price of commodities, namely, the excess above the cost-price formed by the addition of the aforementioned elements: wages, interest and rent. This fourth element seems to be determined by competition in each individual case, and in the average case by the average profit, which in its turn is regulated by this same competition, only over longer periods.

Fifthly: On the basis of the capitalist mode of production, it becomes so much a matter of course to split up the value, in which newly added labour is represented, into the forms of revenue, of wages, profit and ground-rent, that this method is applied (leaving aside earlier stages of history, from which we gave illustrations in our study of ground-rent) even where the preconditions for these forms of revenue are missing. That is, all is subsumed by analogy under these forms of revenue.

When an independent labourer—let us take a small farmer, since all three forms of revenue may here be applied—works for himself and sells his own product, he is first considered as his own employer (capitalist), who makes use of himself as a labourer, and second as his own landlord, who makes use of himself as his own tenant. To himself as wage-worker he pays wages, to himself as capitalist he gives the profit, and to himself as landlord he pays rent. Assuming the capitalist mode of production and the relations corresponding to it to be the general basis of society, this subsumption is correct, in so far as it is not thanks to his labour, but to his ownership of means of production—which have assumed here the general form of capital—that he is in a position to appropriate his own surplus-labour. And furthermore, to the extent that he produces his product as commodities, and thus depends upon its price (and even if not, this price is calculable), the quantity of surplus-labour which he can realise depends not on its own magnitude, but on the general rate of profit; and likewise any eventual excess above the amount of surplus-value determined by the general rate of profit is, in turn, not determined by the quantity of labour performed by him, but can be appropriated by him only because he is owner of the land. Since such a form of production not corresponding to the capitalist mode of production may thus be subsumed under its forms of revenue—and to a certain extent not incorrectly—the illusion is all the more strengthened that capitalist relations are the natural relations of every mode of production.

Of course, if wages are reduced to their general basis, namely, to that portion of the product of the producer's own labour which passes over into the individual consumption of the labourer; if we relieve this portion of its capitalist limitations and extend it to that volume of consumption which is permitted, on the one hand, by the existing productivity of society (that is, the social productivity of his own individual labour as actually social), and which, on the other hand, the full development of the individuality requires; if, furthermore, we reduce the surplus-labour and surplus-product to that measure which is required under prevailing conditions of production of society, on the one side to create an insurance and reserve fund, and on the other to constantly expand reproduction to the extent dictated by social needs; finally, if we include in No. 1 the necessary labour, and in No. 2 the surplus-labour, the quantity of labour which must always be performed by the able-bodied in behalf of the immature or incapacitated members of society, i.e., if we strip both wages and surplus-value, both necessary and surplus labour, of their specifically capitalist character, then certainly there remain not these forms, but merely their rudiments, which are common to all social modes of production.

Moreover, this method of subsumption was also characteristic of previous dominant modes of production, e.g., feudalism. Production relations which nowise corresponded to it, standing entirely beyond it, were subsumed under feudal relations, e.g., in England, the tenures in common socage (as distinct from tenures on knight's service), which comprised merely monetary obligations and were feudal in name only.

Notes

1. In breaking down the value added to the constant portion of capital into wages, profit and ground-rent, it goes without saying that these are portions of value. One may, indeed, conceive of them as existing in the direct product in which this value appears, i.e., in the direct product produced by labourers and capitalists in some particular sphere of production—for instance, yarn produced in the spinning industry. But in fact they do not materialise in this product any more or any less than in any other commodity, in any other component of the material wealth having the same value. And in practice wages are indeed paid in money, that is, in the pure expression of value, likewise interest and rent. For the capitalist, the transformation of his product into the pure expression of value is indeed very important; in the distribution itself this transformation is already assumed. Whether these values are reconverted into the same product, the same commodity, out of whose production they arose, whether the labourer buys back a part of the product directly produced by himself or buys the product of some other labour of a different kind, has nothing to do with the matter itself. Herr Rodbertus quite unnecessarily flies into a passion about this.
2. 'It will be sufficient to remark that the same general rule which regulates the value of raw produce and manufactured commodities is applicable also to the metals; their value depending not on the rate of profits, nor on the rate of wages, nor on the rent paid for mines, but on the total quantity of labour necessary to obtain the metal and to bring it to market.' (Ricardo, *Principles,* Ch. III, p. 77.)

51

Distribution Relations and Production Relations

The new value added by the annual newly added labour—and thus also that portion of the annual product in which this value is represented and which may be drawn out of the total output and separated from it—is thus split into three parts, which assume three different forms of revenue, into forms which express one portion of this value as belonging or falling to the share of the owner of labour-power, another portion to the owner of capital, and a third portion to the owner of landed property. These, then, are relations, or forms of distribution, for they express the relations under which the newly produced total value is distributed among the owners of the various production factors.

From the common viewpoint these distribution relations appear as natural relations, as relations arising directly from the nature of all social production, from the laws of human production in general. It cannot, indeed, be denied that pre-capitalist societies disclose other modes of distribution, but the latter are interpreted as undeveloped, unperfected and disguised, not reduced to their purest expression and their highest form and differently shaded modes of the natural distribution relations.

The only correct aspect of this conception is: Assuming some form of social production to exist (e.g., primitive Indian communities, or the more ingeniously developed communism of the Peruvians), a distinction can always be made between that portion of labour whose product is directly consumed individually by the producers and their families and—aside from the part which is productively consumed—that portion of labour which is invariably surplus-labour, whose product serves constantly to satisfy the general social needs no matter how this surplus-product may be divided, and no matter who may function as representative of these social needs. Thus, the identity of the various modes of distribution amounts merely to this: they are identical if we abstract from their differences and specific forms and keep in mind only their unity as distinct from their dissimilarity.

A more advanced, more critical mind, however, admits the historically developed character of distribution relations,[1] but nevertheless clings all the more tenaciously to the unchanging character of production relations themselves, arising from human nature and thus independent of all historical development.

On the other hand, scientific analysis of the capitalist mode of production demonstrates the contrary, that it is a mode of production of a special kind, with specific historical features; that, like any other specific mode of production, it presupposes a given level of the social productive forces and their forms of development as its historical precondition: a precondition which is itself the historical result and product of a preceding process, and from which the new mode of production proceeds as its given basis; that the production relations corresponding to this specific, historically determined mode of production—relations which human beings enter into during the process of social life, in the creation of their social life—possess a specific, historical and transitory character; and, finally, that the distribution relations essentially coincident with these production relations are their opposite side, so that both share the same historically transitory character.

In the study of distribution relations, the initial point of departure is the alleged fact that the annual product is apportioned among wages, profit and rent. But if so expressed, it is a misstatement. The product is apportioned on one side to capital, on the other to revenue. One of these revenues, wages, never itself assumes the form of revenue, revenue of the labourer, until after it has first confronted this labourer in the *form of capital*. The confrontation of produced conditions of labour and of the products of labour generally, as capital, with the direct producers implies from the outset a definite social character of the material conditions of labour in relation to the labourers, and thereby a definite relationship into which they enter with the owners of the means of production and among themselves during production itself. The transformation of these conditions of labour into capital implies in turn the expropriation of the direct producers from the land, and thus a definite form of landed property.

If one portion of the product were not transformed into capital, the other would not assume the forms of wages, profit and rent.

On the other hand, if the capitalist mode of production presupposes this definite social form of the conditions of production, so does it reproduce it continually. It produces not merely the material products, but reproduces continually the production relations in which the former are produced, and thereby also the corresponding distribution relations.

It may be said, of course, that capital itself (and landed property which it includes as its antithesis) already presupposes a distribution: the expropriation of the labourer from the conditions of labour, the concentration of these conditions in the hands of a minority of individuals, the exclusive ownership of land by other individuals, in short, all the relations which have been described in the part dealing with primitive accumulation (Buch I, Kap. XXIV) [English edition: Part VIII—*Ed*]. But this distribution differs altogether from what is understood by distribution relations when the latter are endowed with a historical character in contradistinction to production relations. What is meant thereby are the various titles to that portion of the product which goes into individual consumption. The aforementioned distribution relations, on the contrary, are the basis of special social functions performed within the production relations by certain of their agents, as opposed to the direct producers. They imbue the conditions of production themselves and their representatives with a specific social quality. They determine the entire character and the entire movement of production.

Capitalist production is distinguished from the outset by two characteristic features.

First. It produces its products as commodities. The fact that it produces commodities does not differentiate it from other modes of production; but rather the fact that being a commodity is the dominant and determining characteristic of its products. This implies, first and foremost, that the labourer himself comes forward merely as a seller of commodities, and thus as a free wage-labourer, so that labour appears in general as wage-labour. In view of what has already been said, it is superfluous to demonstrate anew that the relation between capital and wage-labour determines the entire character of the mode of production. The principal agents of this mode of production itself, the capitalist and the wage-labourer, are as such merely embodiments, personifications of capital and wage-labour; definite social characteristics stamped upon individuals by the process of social production; the products of these definite social production relations.

The characteristic 1) of the product as a commodity, and 2) of the commodity as a product of capital, already implies all circulation relations, i.e., a definite social process through which the products must pass and in which they assume definite social characteristics; it likewise implies definite relations of the production agents, by which the value-expansion of their product and its reconversion, either into means of subsistence or into means of production, are determined. But even apart from this, the entire determination of value and the regulation of the total production by value results from the above two characteristics of the product as a commodity, or of the commodity as a capitalistically produced commodity. In this entirely specific form of value, labour prevails on the one hand solely as social labour; on the other hand, the distribution of this social labour and the mutual supplementing and interchanging of its products, the subordination under, and introduction into, the social mechanism, are left to the accidental and mutually nullifying motives of individual capitalists. Since these latter confront one another only as commodity-owners, and everyone seeks to sell his commodity as dearly as possible (apparently even guided in the regulation of production itself solely by his own free will), the inner law enforces itself only through their competition, their mutual pressure upon each other, whereby the deviations are mutually cancelled. Only as an inner law, vis-à-vis the individual agents, as a blind law of Nature, does the law of value exert its influence here and maintain the social equilibrium of production amidst its accidental fluctuations.

Furthermore, already implicit in the commodity, and even more so in the commodity as a product of capital, is the materialisation of the social features of production and the personification of the material foundations of production, which characterise the entire capitalist mode of production.

The *second* distinctive feature of the capitalist mode of production is the production of surplus-value as the direct aim and determining motive of production. Capital produces essentially capital, and does so only to the extent that it produces surplus-value. We have seen in our discussion of relative surplus-value, and further in considering the transformation of surplus-value into profit, how a mode of production peculiar to the capitalist period is founded hereon—a special form of development of the social productive powers of labour, but confronting the labourer as powers of capital rendered independent, and standing in direct opposition therefore to the labourer's own development. Production for value and surplus-value implies, as has been shown in the course of our analysis, the constantly operating tendency to reduce the labour-time necessary for the production of a commodity, i.e., its value, below the actually prevailing social average. The pressure to reduce cost-price to its minimum becomes the strongest lever for raising the social productiveness of labour, which, however, appears here only as a continual increase in the productiveness of capital.

The authority assumed by the capitalist as the personification of capital in the direct process of production, the social function performed by him in his capacity as manager and ruler of production, is essentially different from the authority exercised on the basis of production by means of slaves, serfs, etc.

Whereas, on the basis of capitalist production, the mass of direct producers is confronted by the social character of their production in the form of strictly regulating authority and a social mechanism of the labour-process organised as a complete hierarchy—this authority reaching its bearers, however, only as the personification of the conditions of labour in contrast to labour, and not as political or theocratic rulers as under earlier modes of production—among the bearers of this authority, the capitalists themselves, who confront one another only as commodity-owners, there reigns complete anarchy within which the social interrelations of production assert themselves only as an overwhelming natural law in relation to individual free will.

Only because labour pre-exists in the form of wage-labour, and the means of production in the form of capital—i.e., solely because of this specific social form of these essential production factors—does a part of the value (product) appear as surplus-value and this surplus-value as profit (rent), as the gain of the capitalist, as additional available wealth belonging to him. But only because this surplus-value thus appears as *his profit* do the additional means of production, which are intended for the expansion of reproduction, and which constitute a part of this profit, present themselves as new additional capital, and the expansion of the process of reproduction in general as a process of capitalist accumulation.

Although the form of labour as wage-labour is decisive for the form of the entire process and the specific mode of production itself, it is not wage-labour which determines value. In the determination of value, it is a question of social labour-time in general, the quantity of labour which society generally has at its disposal, and whose relative absorption by the various products determines, as it were, their respective social importance. The definite form in which the social labour-time prevails as decisive in the determination of the value of commodities is of course connected with the form of labour as wage-labour and with the corresponding form of the means of production as capital, in so far as solely on this basis does commodity-production become the general form of production.

Let us moreover consider the so-called distribution relations themselves. The wage presupposes wage-labour, and profit—capital. These definite forms of distribution thus presuppose definite social characteristics of production conditions, and definite social relations of production agents. The specific distribution relations are thus merely the expression of the specific historical production relations.

And now let us consider profit. This specific form of surplus-value is the precondition for the fact that the new creation of means of production takes place in the form of capitalist production; thus, a relation dominating reproduction, although it seems to the individual capitalist as if he could in reality consume his entire profit as revenue. However, he thereby meets barriers even in the form of insurance and reserve funds laws of competition, etc., which hamper him and prove to him in practice that profit is not a mere distribution category of the individually consumable product. The entire process of capitalist production is furthermore regulated by the prices of the products. But the regulating prices of production are themselves in turn regulated by the equalisation of the rate of profit and its corresponding distribution of capital among the various social spheres of production. Profit, then, appears here as the main factor, not of the distribution of products, but of their production itself, as a factor in the distribution of capitals and labour itself among the various spheres of production. The division of profit into profit of enterprise and interest appears as the distribution of the same revenue. But it arises, to begin with, from the development of capital as a self-expanding value, a creator of surplus-value, i.e., from this specific social form of the prevailing process of production. It evolves credit and credit institutions out of itself, and thereby the form of production. As interest, etc., the ostensible distribution forms enter into the price as determining production factors.

Ground-rent might seem to be a mere form of distribution, because landed property as such does not perform any, or at least any normal, function in the process of production itself. But the circumstance that 1) rent is limited to the excess above the average profit, and that 2) the landlord is reduced from the manager and master of the process of production and of the entire process of social life to the position of mere lessor of land, usurer in land and mere collector of rent, is a specific historical result of the capitalist mode of production. The fact that the earth received the form of landed property is a historical precondition for this. The fact that landed property assumes forms which permit the capitalist mode of operation in agriculture is a product of the specific character of this mode of production. The income of the landlord may be called rent, even under other forms of society. But it differs essentially from rent as it appears in this mode of production.

The so-called distribution relations, then, correspond to and arise from historically determined specific social forms of the process of production and mutual relations entered into by men in the reproduction process of human life. The historical character of these distribution relations is the historical character of production relations, of which they express merely one aspect. Capitalist distribution differs from those forms of distribution which arise from other modes of production, and every form of distribution disappears with the specific form of production from which it is descended and to which it corresponds.

The view which regards only distribution relations as historical, but not production relations, is, on the one hand, solely the view of the initial, but still handicapped, criticism of bourgeois economy. On the other hand, it rests on the confusion and identification of the process of social production with the simple labour-process, such as might even be performed by an abnormally isolated human being without any social assistance. To the extent that the labour-process is solely a process between man and Nature, its simple elements remain common to all social forms of development. But each specific historical form of this process further develops its material foundations and social forms. Whenever a certain stage of maturity has been reached, the specific historical form is discarded and makes way for a higher one. The moment of arrival of such a crisis is disclosed by the depth and breadth attained by the contradictions and antagonisms between the distribution relations, and thus the specific historical form of their corresponding production relations, on the one hand, and the productive forces, the production powers and the development of their agencies, on the other hand. A conflict then ensues between the material development of production and its social form.[2]

Notes

1. J. Stuart Mill, *Some Unsettled Questions in Political Economy*, London, 1844.
2. See the work on *Competition and Co-operation* (1832?).

52

Classes

The owners merely of labour-power, owners of capital, and land-owners, whose respective sources of income are wages, profit and ground-rent, in other words, wage-labourers, capitalists and land-owners, constitute then three big classes of modern society based upon the capitalist mode of production.

In England, modern society is indisputably most highly and classically developed in economic structure. Nevertheless, even here the stratification of classes does not appear in its pure form. Middle and intermediate strata even here obliterate lines of demarcation everywhere (although incomparably less in rural districts than in the cities). However, this is immaterial for our analysis. We have seen that the continual tendency and law of development of the capitalist mode of production is more and more to divorce the means of production from labour, and more and more to concentrate the scattered means of production into large groups, thereby transforming labour into wage-labour and the means of production into capital. And to this tendency, on the other hand, corresponds the independent separation of landed property from capital and labour,[1] or the transformation of all landed property into the form of landed property corresponding to the capitalist mode of production.

The first question to he answered is this: What constitutes a class?—and the reply to this follows naturally from the reply to another question, namely: What makes wage-labourers, capitalists and landlords constitute the three great social classes?

At first glance—the identity of revenues and sources of revenue. There are three great social groups whose members, the individuals forming them, live on wages, profit and ground-rent respectively, on the realisation of their labour-power, their capital, and their landed property.

However, from this standpoint, physicians and officials, e.g., would also constitute two classes, for they belong to two distinct social groups, the members of each of these groups receiving their revenue from one and the same source. The same would also be true of the infinite fragmentation of interest and rank into which the division of social labour splits labourers as well as capitalists and landlords-the latter, e.g., into owners of vineyards, farm owners, owners of forests, mine owners and owners of fisheries.

[Here the manuscript breaks off.]

Notes

1. F. List remarks correctly: 'The prevalence of a self-sufficient economy on large estates demonstrates solely the lack of civilisation, means of communication, domestic trades and wealthy cities. It is to be encountered, therefore, throughout Russia, Poland, Hungary and Mecklenburg. Formerly, it was also prevalent in England; with the advance of trades and commerce, however, this was replaced by the breaking up into middle estates and the leasing of land.' (*Die Ackerverfassung, die Zwergwirtschaft und die Auswanderung,* 1842, p.10.)

Supplement by Frederick Engels

Introduction

The third book of *Capital* is receiving many and various interpretations ever since it has been subject to public judgement. It was not to be otherwise expected. In publishing it, what I was chiefly concerned with was to produce as authentic a text as possible, to demonstrate the new results obtained by Marx in Marx's own words as far as possible, to intervene myself only where absolutely unavoidable, and even then to leave the reader in no doubt as to who was talking to him. This has been deprecated. It has been said that I should have converted the material available to me into a systematically written book, *en faire un livre,* as the French say; in other words, sacrifice the authenticity of the text to the reader's convenience. But this was not how I conceived my task. I lacked all justification for such a revision, a man like Marx has the right to be heard himself, to pass on his scientific discoveries to posterity in the full genuineness of his own presentation. Moreover, I had no desire thus to infringe—as it must seem to me—upon the legacy of so pre-eminent a man; it would have meant to me a breach of faith. And third, it would have been quite useless. For the people who cannot or do not want to read, who, even in Volume I, took more trouble to understand it wrongly than was necessary to understand it correctly—for such people it is altogether useless to put oneself out in any way. But for those who are interested in a real understanding, the original text itself was precisely the most important thing; for them my recasting would have had at most the value of a commentary, and, what is more, a commentary on something unpublished and inaccessible. The original text would have had to be referred to at the first controversy, and at the second and third its publication *in extenso* would have become quite unavoidable.

Such controversies are a matter of course in a work that contains so much that is new, and in a hastily sketched and partly incomplete first draft to boot. And here my intervention, of course, can be of use: to eliminate difficulties in understanding, to bring more to the fore important aspects whose significance is not strikingly enough evident in the text, and to make some important additions to the text written in 1865 to fit the state of affairs in 1895. Indeed, there are already two points which seem to me to require a brief discussion.

Section I. *Law of Value and Rate of Profit*

It was to be expected that the solution of the apparent contradiction between these two factors would lead to debates just as much after, as before, the publication of Marx's text. Some were prepared for a complete miracle, and find themselves disappointed because they see a simple, rational, prosaically-sober solution of the contradiction, instead of the hocus-pocus they had expected. Most joyfully disappointed, of course, is the well-known, illustrious Loria. He has at last found the Archimedian fulcrum from which even a gnome of his calibre can lift the solidly built, gigantic Marxian structure into the air and explode it. What! he declaims indignantly. Is that supposed to be a solution? That is pure mystification! When economists speak of value, they mean value that is actually established in exchange.

> No economist with any trace of sense has ever concerned himself or will ever want to concern himself with a value which commodities do not sell for and never can sell for *(ne possono vendersi mai)*.... In asserting that the value for which commodities *never* sell is proportional to the labour they contain, what does Marx do except repeat in an inverted form the thesis of the orthodox economists, that the value for which

commodities sell is *not* proportional to the labour expended on them? ... Matters are not helped by Marx's saying that despite the divergency of individual prices from individual values, the total price of all commodities always coincides with their total value, or the amount of labour contained in the totality of the commodities. For inasmuch as value is nothing more than the exchange ratio between one commodity and another, the very concept of a total value is an absurdity, nonsense ... a contradiction *in abjecto*....

At the very beginning of the book, he argues, Marx says that exchange can equate two commodities only by virtue of a similar and equally large element contained in them—namely, the equal amount of labour. And now he most solemnly repudiates himself by asserting that commodities exchange with one another in a totally different ratio than that of the amount of labour contained in them.

Was there ever such an utter *reductio ad absurdum*, such complete theoretical bankruptcy? Was ever scientific suicide committed with greater pomp and more solemnity! (*Nouva Antologia*, Feb. 1, 1895, pp. 478-79.)

We see: our Loria is more than happy. Wasn't he right in treating Marx as one of his own, as an ordinary charlatan? There you see it—Marx sneers at his public just like Loria; he lives on mystification just like the most insignificant Italian professor of economics. But, whereas Dulcamara can afford that because he knows his trade, the clumsy Northerner, Marx, commits nothing but ineptitudes, writes nonsense and absurdities, so that there is nothing left finally for him but solemn suicide.

Let us save for later the statement that commodities have never been sold, nor can ever be sold, at the values determined by labour. Let us deal here merely with Mr Loria's assurance that:

'value is nothing more than the exchange ratio between one commodity and another,' and that therefore 'the very concept of a total value is an absurdity, nonsense...'

The ratio in which two commodities are exchanged for each other, their value, is therefore something purely accidental, stuck on to the commodities from the outside, which can be one thing today and something else tomorrow. Whether a metric hundredweight of wheat is exchanged for a gramme or a kilogramme of gold does not in the least depend upon conditions inherent in that wheat or gold. For otherwise these conditions would also have to assert themselves in the exchange, dominate the latter on the whole, and also have an independent existence apart from exchange, so that one could speak of a total value of commodities. That is nonsense, says the illustrious Loria. No matter in what ratio two commodities may be exchanged for each other, that is their value—and that's all there is to it. Hence, value is identical with price, and every commodity has as many values as the prices it can get. And price is determined by supply and demand; and any one asking any more questions is a fool to expect an answer.

But there is a little hitch to the matter. In the normal state, supply and demand balance. Therefore, let us divide all the commodities in the world into two halves, the supply group and the equally large demand group. Let us assume that each represents a price of 1,000 billion marks, francs, pounds, or what you will. According to elementary arithmetic, that makes a price of 2,000 billions. Nonsense, absurd, says Mr Loria. The two groups together may represent a price of 2,000 billions. But it is otherwise with value. If we say price: 1,000 + 1,000 = 2,000. But if we say value: 1,000 + 1,000 = 0. At least in this case, where the totality of commodities is involved. For here the commodities of each of the two groups are worth 1,000 billion only because each of the two can and will give this sum for the commodities of the other. But if we unite the totality of the commodities of the two in the hands of a third person, the first has no value in his hand any longer, nor the second, and the third certainly not—in the end, no one has anything. And again we marvel at the superiority with which our southern Cagliostro has manhandled the concept of value in such a fashion that not the slightest trace of it has been left. This is the acme of vulgar economics![1]

In Braun's *Archiv für soziale Gesetzgebung*, Vol. VII, No.4, Werner Sombart gives an outline of the Marxian system which, taken all in all, is excellent. It is the first time that a German university professor succeeds on the whole in seeing in Marx's writings what Marx really says, stating that the criticism of the Marxian system cannot consist of a refutation—

let the political careerist deal with that

—but merely in a further development. Sombart, too, deals with our subject, as is to be expected. He investigates the importance of value in the Marxian system, and arrives at the following results. Value is not manifest in the exchange relation of capitalistically produced commodities; it does not live in the consciousness of the agents of capitalist production; it is not an empirical, but a mental, a logical fact; the concept of value in its material definiteness in Marx is nothing but the economic expression for the fact of the social productive power of labour as the basis of economic existence; in the final analysis, the law of value dominates economic processes in a capitalist economic system, and for this economic system quite generally has the following content: the value of commodities is the specific and historical form in which the productive power of labour, in the last analysis dominating all economic processes, asserts itself as a determining factor. So, says Sombart, it cannot be said that this conception of the significance of the law of value for the capitalist form of production is wrong. But it does seem to me to be too broad, and susceptible of a narrower, more precise formulation: in my opinion it by no means exhausts the entire significance of the law of value for the economic stages of society's development dominated by this law.

There is a likewise excellent article by Conrad Schmidt on the third volume of *Capital* in Braun's *Sozialpolitisches Zentralblatt*, February 25, 1895, No.22. Especially to be emphasized here is the proof of how the Marxian derivation of average profit from surplus-value for the first time gives an answer to the question not even posed by economics up to now: how the magnitude of this average rate of profit is determined, and how it comes about that it is, say, 10 or 15 per cent and not 50 or 100 per cent. Since we know that the surplus-value first appropriated by the industrial capitalist is the sole and exclusive source from which profit and rent flow, this question solves itself. This passage of Schmidt's article might be directly written for economists a la Loria, if it were not labour in vain to open the eyes of those who do not want to see.

Schmidt, too, has his formal misgivings regarding the law of value. He calls it a scientific *hypothesis*, set up to explain the actual exchange process, which proves to be the necessary theoretical starting point, illuminating and indispensable, even in respect of the phenomena of competitive prices which seem in absolute contradiction to it. According to him, without the law of value all theoretical insight into the economic machinery of capitalist reality ceases. And in a private letter that he permits me to quote, Schmidt declares the law of value within the capitalist form of production to be a pure, although theoretically necessary, fiction. This view, however, is quite incorrect in my opinion. The law of value has a far greater and more definite significance for capitalist production than that of a mere hypothesis, not to mention a fiction, even though a necessary one.

Sombart, as well as Schmidt,—I mention the illustrious Loria merely as an amusing vulgar-economist foil—does not make sufficient allowance for the fact that we are dealing here not only with a purely logical process, but with a historical process, and its explanatory reflection in thought, the logical pursuance of its inner connections.

The decisive passage is to be found in Marx, Vol. III,:

> The whole difficulty arises from the fact that commodities are not exchanged simply as *commodities*, but as *products of capitals*, which claim participation in the total amount of surplus-value, proportional to their magnitude, or equal if they are of equal magnitude.

To illustrate this difference, it is supposed that the workers are in possession of their means of production, that they work on the average for equally long periods of time and with equal intensity, and exchange their commodities with one another directly. Then, in one day, two workers would have added by their labour an equal amount of new value to their products, but the product of each would have different value, depending on the labour already embodied in the means of production. This latter part of the value would represent the constant capital of capitalist economy, while that part of the newly-added value employed for the worker's means of subsistence would represent the variable capital, and the portion of the new value still remaining would represent the surplus-value, which in this case would belong to the worker. Thus, after deducting the amount to replace the 'constant' part of value only advanced by them, both workers would get equal values; but the ratio of the part representing surplus-value to the value of the means of production—which correspond to the capitalist rate of profit—would be different in each case. But since each of them gets the value of the means of production replaced through the exchange, this would be a wholly immaterial circumstance.

> The exchange of commodities at their values, or approximately at their values, thus requires a *much lower stage* than their exchange at their prices of production, which requires a definite level of capitalist development.... Apart from the domination of prices and price movement by the law of value, it is quite appropriate to regard the values of commodities as not only *theoretically* but also *historically* antecedent (prius) to the prices of production. This applies to conditions *in which the labourer owns his own means of production*, and this is the condition of the land-owning working farmer and the craftsman, in the ancient as well as in the modern world. This agrees also with the view we expressed previously, that the evolution of products into commodities arises through exchange between different communities, not between the members of the same community. It holds not only for this primitive condition, but also for subsequent conditions, based on slavery and serfdom, and for the guild organization of handicrafts, so long as the means of production involved in each branch of production can be transferred from one sphere to another only with difficulty and therefore the various spheres of production are related to one another, within certain limits, as foreign countries or communist communities.

Had Marx an opportunity to go over the third volume once more, he would doubtless have extended this passage considerably. As it stands, it gives only a sketchy outline of what is to be said on the point in question. Let us, therefore, examine it somewhat closer.

We all know that at the beginning of society, products are consumed by the producers themselves, and that these producers are spontaneously organized in more or less communistic communities; that the exchange of the surplus of these products with strangers, which ushers in the conversion of products into commodities, is of a later date; that it takes places at first only between individual communities of different tribes, but later also prevails within the community, and contributes considerably to the latter's dissolution into bigger or smaller family groups. But even after this dissolution, the exchanging family heads remain working peasants, who produce almost all they require with the aid of their families on their own farmsteads, and get only a slight portion of the required necessities from the outside in exchange for surplus products of their own. The family is engaged not only in agriculture and livestock-raising; it also works their products up into finished articles of consumption; now and then it even does its own milling with the hand-mill; it bakes bread, spins, dyes, weaves flax and wool, tans leather, builds and repairs wooden buildings, makes tools and utensils, and not infrequently does joinery and blacksmithing; so that the family, or family group, is in the main self-sufficient.

The little that such a family had to obtain by barter or buy from outside, even up to the beginning of the 19th century in Germany, consisted principally of the objects of handicraft production—that is, such things the nature of whose manufacture was by no means unknown to the peasant, and which he did not produce himself only because he lacked the raw material or because the purchased article was much better or very much cheaper. Hence, the peasant of the Middle Ages knew fairly accurately the labour-time required for the manufacture of the articles obtained by him in barter. The smith and the cartwright of the village worked under his eyes; likewise, the tailor and shoemaker—who in my youth still paid their visits to our Rhine peasants, one after another, turning home-made materials into shoes and clothing. The peasants, as well as the people from whom they bought, were themselves workers; the exchanged articles were each one's own products. What had they expended in making these products? Labour and labour alone: to replace tools, to produce raw material, and to process it, they spent nothing but their own labour-power; how then could they exchange these products of theirs for those of other labouring producers otherwise than in the ratio of labour expended on them? Not only was the labour-time spent on these products the only suitable measure for the quantitative determination of the values to be exchanged: no other way was at all possible. Or is it believed that the peasant and the artisan were so stupid as to give up the product of 10 hours' labour of one person for that of a single hours' labour of another? No other exchange is possible in the whole period of peasant natural economy than that in which the exchanged quantities of commodities tend to be measured more and more according to the amounts of labour embodied in them. From the moment money penetrates into this mode of economy, the tendency towards adaptation to the law of value (in the Marxian formulation, *nota bene*!) grows more pronounced on the one hand, while on the other it is already interrupted by the interference of usurers' capital and fleecing by taxation; the periods for which prices, on average, approach to within a negligible margin of values, begin to grow longer.

The same holds good for exchange between peasant products and those of the urban artisans. At the beginning, this barter takes places directly, without the medium of the merchant, on the cities' market days, when the peasant sells and makes his purchases. Here, too, not only does the peasant know the artisan's working conditions, but the latter knows those of the peasant as well. For the artisan is himself still a bit of a peasant—he not only has a vegetable and fruit garden, but very often also has a small piece of land, one or two cows, pigs, poultry, etc. People in the Middle Ages were thus able to check up with considerable accuracy on each other's production costs for raw material, auxiliary material, and labour-time—at least in respect of articles of daily general use.

But how, in this barter on the basis of the quantity of labour, was the latter to be calculated, even if only indirectly and relatively, for products requiring a longer labour, interrupted at regular intervals, and uncertain in yield—grain or cattle, for example? And among people, to boot, who could not calculate? Obviously, only by means of a lengthy process of zigzag approximation, often feeling the way here and there in the dark, and, as is usual, learning only through mistakes. But each one's necessity for covering his own outlay on the whole always helped to return to the right direction; and the small number of kinds of articles in circulation, as well as the often century-long stable nature of their production, facilitated the attaining of this goal. And that it by no means took so long for the relative amount of value of these products to be fixed fairly closely is already proved by the fact that cattle, the commodity for which this appears to be most difficult because of the long time of production of the individual head, became the first rather generally accepted money commodity. To accomplish this, the value of cattle, its exchange ratio to a large number of other commodities, must already have attained a relatively unusual stabilization, acknowledged without contradiction in the territories of many tribes. And the people of that time were certainly clever enough—both the cattlebreeders and their customers—not to give away the labour-time expended by them without an equivalent in barter. On the contrary, the closer people are to the primitive state of commodity production—the Russians and Orientals, for example—the more time do they still waste today, in order to squeeze out, through long tenacious bargaining, the full compensation for their labour-time expended on a product.

Starting with this determination of value by labour-time, the whole of commodity production developed, and with it, the multifarious relations in which the various aspects of the law of value assert themselves, as described in the first part of Vol. I of *Capital*; that is, in particular, the conditions under which labour alone is value-creating. These are conditions which assert themselves without entering the consciousness of the participants and can themselves be abstracted from daily practice only through laborious, theoretical investigation; which act, therefore, like natural laws, as Marx proved to follow necessarily from the nature of commodity production. The most important and most incisive advance was the transition to metallic money, the consequence of which, however, was that the determination of value by labour-time was no longer visible upon the surface of commodity exchange. From the practical point of view, money became the decisive measure of value, all the more as the commodities entering trade became more varied, the more they came from distant countries, and the less, therefore, the labour-time necessary for their production could be checked. Money itself usually came first from foreign parts; even when precious metals were obtained within the country, the peasant and artisan were partly unable to estimate approximately the labour employed therein, and partly their own consciousness of the value-measuring property of labour had been fairly well dimmed by the habit of reckoning with money; in the popular mind, money began to represent absolute value.

In a word: the Marxian law of value holds generally, as far as economic laws are valid at all, for the whole period of simple commodity production—that is, up to the time when the latter suffers a modification through the appearance of the capitalist form of production. Up to that time, prices gravitate towards the values fixed according to the Marxian law and oscillate around those values, so that the more fully simple commodity production develops, the more the average prices over long periods uninterrupted by external violent disturbances coincide with values within a negligible margin. Thus, the Marxian law of value has general economic validity for a period lasting from the beginning of exchange, which transforms products into commodities, down to the 15th century of the present era. But the exchange of commodities dates from a time before all written history—which in Egypt goes back to at least 2500 B.C., and perhaps 5000 B.C., and in Babylon to 4000 B.C., perhaps to 6000 B.C.; thus, the law of value has prevailed during a period of from five to seven thousand years. And now, let us admire the thoroughness of Mr Loria, who calls the value generally and directly valid during this period a value at which commodities are never sold nor can ever be sold, and with which no economist having a spark of common sense would ever occupy himself!

We have not spoken of the merchant up to now. We could save the consideration of this intervention for now, when we pass to the transformation of simple into capitalist commodity production. The merchant was the revolutionary element in this society where everything else was stable—stable, as it were, through inheritance; where the peasant obtained not only his hide of land, but his status as a freehold proprietor, as a free or enthralled quit-rent peasant or serf, and the urban artisan his trade and guild privileges by inheritance and almost inalienably, and each of them, in addition, his customer, his market, as well as his skill, trained from childhood for the inherited craft. Into this world then entered the merchant, with whom its revolution was to start. But not as a conscious revolutionary; on the contrary, as flesh of its flesh, bone of its bone. The merchant of the Middle Ages was by no means an individualist; he was essentially an associate like all his contemporaries. The mark association, grown out of primitive communism, prevailed in the countryside. Each peasant originally had an equal hide, with equal pieces of land of each quality, and a corresponding, equal share in the rights of the mark. After the mark had become a closed association, and no new hides were allocated any longer, subdivision of the hides occurred through inheritance, etc., with corresponding subdivisions of the common rights in the mark; but the full hide remained the unit, so that there were half, quarter and eighth-hides with half, quarter and eighth-rights in the mark. All later productive associations, particularly the guilds in the cities, whose statutes were nothing but the application of the mark constitution to a craft privilege instead of to a restricted area of land, followed the pattern of the mark association. The central point of the whole organization was the equal participation of every member in the privileges and produce assured to the guild, as is strikingly expressed in the 1527 licence of the Elberfeld and Barmen yarn trade. (Thun: *Industrie am Niederrhein*, Vol. II, 164 ff.) The same holds true of the mine guilds, where each share participated equally and was also divisible, together with its rights and obligations, like the hide of the mark member. And the same holds good in no less degree of the merchant companies, which initiated overseas trade. The Venetians and the Genoese in the harbor of Alexandria or Constantinople, each 'nation' in its own *fondaco*—dwelling, inn, warehouse, exhibition and salesrooms, together with central offices—formed complete trade associations; they were closed to competitors and customers; they sold at prices fixed among themselves; their commodities had a definite quality guaranteed by public inspection and often by stamp; they deliberated in common on the prices to be paid by the natives for their products, etc. Nor did Hanseatic merchants act otherwise on the German Bridge (Tydske Bryggen) in Bergen, Norway; the same holds true of their Dutch and English competitors. Woe to the man who sold under the price or bought above the price! The boycott that struck him meant at that time inevitable ruin, not counting the direct penalties imposed by the association upon the guilty. And even close associations were founded for definite purposes, such as the Maona of Genoa in the 14th and 15th centuries, for years the ruler of the alum mines in Phocaea in Asia Minor, as well as of the Island of Chios; furthermore, the great Ravensberg Trading Company, which dealt with Italy and Spain since the end of the 14th century, founding branches in those countries; the German company of the Augsburgers: Fugger, Welser, Vöhlin, Höchstetter, etc; that of the Nürnbergers: Hirschvogel and others, which participated with a capital of 66,000 ducats and three ships in the 1505-06 Portuguese expedition to India, making a net profit of 150 per cent, according to others 175 per cent (Heyd; *Levantehandel*, Vol. II, p.524); and a large number of other companies, 'Monopolia,' over which Luther waxes so indignant.

Here, for the first time, we meet with a profit and a rate of profit. The merchant's efforts are deliberately and consciously aimed at making this rate of profit equal for all participants. The Venetians in the Levant, and the Hanseatics in the North, each paid the same prices for his commodities as his neighbor; his transport charges were the same, he got the same prices as every other merchant of his 'nation'. Thus, the rate of profit was equal for all. In the big trading companies, the allocation of profit *pro rata* of the paid-in capital share is as much a matter of course as the participation in mark rights *pro rata* of the entitled hide share, or as the mining profit *pro rata* of the mining share. The equal rate of profit, which in its fully developed form is one of the final results of capitalist production, thus manifests itself here in its simplest form as one of the points from which capital started historically, as a direct offshoot in fact of the mark association, which in turn is a direct offshoot of primitive communism.

This original rate of profit was necessarily very high. The business was very risky, not only because of wide-spread piracy; the competing nations also permitted themselves all sorts of acts of violence when the opportunity arose; finally, sales and marketing conditions were based upon licences granted by foreign prices, which were broken or revoked often enough. Hence, the profit had to include a high insurance premium. The turnover was slow, the handling of transactions protracted, and in the best periods—which, admittedly, were seldom of long duration—the business was a monopoly trade with monopoly profit. The very high interest rates prevailing at the time, which always had to be lower on the whole than the percentage of usual commercial profit, also prove that the rate of profit was on the average very high.

But this high rate of profit, equal for all participants and obtained through joint labour of the community, held only locally within the associations—that is, in this case, the 'nation,' Venetians, Genoese, Hanseatics, and Dutchmen each had a special rate of profit, and at the beginning more or less each individual market areas, as well. Equalization of these different company profit rates took place in the opposite way, through competition. First, the profit rates of the different markets for one and the same nation. If Alexandria offered more profit for Venetian goods than Cyprus, Constantinople, or Trebizond, the Venetians would start more capital moving towards Alexandria, withdrawing it from trade with other markets. Then, the gradual equalization of profit rates among the different nations, exporting the same or similar goods to the same markets, had to follow, and some of these nations were very often squeezed to the wall and disappeared from the scene. But this process was being continually interrupted by political events, just as all Levantine trade collapsed owing to the Mongolian and Turkish invasions; the great geographic-commercial discoveries after 1492 only accelerated this decline and then made it final.

The sudden expansion of the market area that followed the revolution in communications connected with it, introduced no essential change at first in the nature of trade operations. At the beginning, co-operative companies also dominated trade with India and America. But in the first place, bigger nations stood behind these companies. In trade with America, the whole of great united Spain took the place of the Catalonians trading with the Levant; alongside it, two countries like England and France; and even Holland and Portugal, the smallest, were still at least as large and strong as Venice, the greatest and strongest trading nation of the preceding period. This gave the traveling merchant, the merchant adventurer of the 16th and 17th centuries, a backing that made the company, which protected its companions with arms, also, more and more superfluous, and its expenses an outright burden. Moreover, the wealth in a single hand grew considerably faster, so that single merchants soon could invest as large sums in an enterprise as formerly an entire company. The trading companies, wherever still existent, were usually converted into armed corporations, which conquered and monopolistically exploited whole newly discovered countries under the protection and the sovereignty of the mother country. But the more colonies were founded in the new areas, largely by the state, the more did company trade recede before that of the individual merchant, and the equalization of the profit rate became therewith more and more a matter of competition exclusively.

Up to now, wc have become acquainted with a rate of profit only for merchant capital. For only merchant and usurers' capital had existed up to that time; industrial capital was yet to be developed. Production was still predominantly in the hands of workers owning their own means of production, whose work therefore yielded no surplus-value to any capital. If they had to surrender a part of the product to third parties without compensation, it was in the form of tribute to feudal lords. Merchant capital, therefore, could only make its profit, at least at the beginning, out of the foreign buyers of domestic products, or the domestic buyers of foreign products; only toward the end of this period—for Italy, that is, with the decline of Levantine trade—were foreign competition and the difficulty of marketing able to compel the handicraft producers of export commodities to sell the commodity under its value to the exporting merchant. And thus we find here that commodities are sold at their value, on the average, in the domestic retail trade of individual producers with one another, but, for the reasons given, not in international trade as a rule. Quite the opposite of the present-day world, where the production prices hold good in international and wholesale trade, while the formations of prices in urban retail trade is governed by quite other rates of profit. So that the meat of an ox, for example, experiences today a greater rise in price on its way from the London wholesaler to the individual London consumer than from the wholesaler in Chicago, including transport, to the London wholesaler.

The instrument that gradually brought about this revolution in price formation was industrial capital. Rudiments of the latter had been formed as early as the Middle Ages, in three fields—shipping, mining, and textiles. Shipping on the scale practiced by the Italian and Hanseatic maritime republics was impossible without sailors, i.e., wage-labourers (whose wage relationship may have been concealed under association forms with profit-sharing), or without oarsmen—wage-labourers or slaves—for the galleys of that day. The guilds in the ore mines, originally associated workers, had already been converted, in almost every case, into stock companies for exploiting the deposits by means of wage-labourers. And in the textile industry, the merchant had begun to place the little master-weaver directly in his service, by supplying him with yarn and having it made into cloth for his account in return for a fixed wage—in short, by himself changing from a mere buyer into a so-called *contractor*.

Here, we have the first beginnings of the formation of capitalist surplus-value. We can ignore the mining guilds as closed monopoly corporations. With regard to the ship-owners, it is obvious that their profit had to be at least as high as the customary one in the country, plus an extra increment for insurance, depreciation of ships, etc. But how were matters with the textile contractors, who first brought commodities, directly manufactured for capitalist account, into competition with the commodities of the same sort made for handicraft account?

Merchant capital's rate of profit was at hand to start with. Likewise, it had already been equalized to an approximate average rate, at least for the locality in question. Now, what could induce the merchant to take on the extra business of a contractor? Only one thing: the prospect of greater profit at the same selling price as the others. And he had this prospect. By taking the little master into his service, he broke through the traditional bonds of production within which the producer sold his finished product and nothing else. The merchant capitalist bought the labour-power, which still owned its production instruments but no longer the raw material. By thus guaranteeing the weaver regular employment, he could depress the weaver's wage to such a degree that a part of the labour-time furnished remained unpaid for. The contractor thus became an appropriator of surplus-value over and above his commercial profit. Admittedly, he had to employ additional capital to buy yarn, etc., and leave it in the weaver's hands until the article for which he formerly had to pay full price only upon purchasing it, was finished. But, in the first place, he had already used extra capital in most cases for advances to the weaver, who as a rule submitted to the new production conditions only under the pressure of debt. And, secondly, apart from that, the calculation took the following form:

Assume that our merchant operates his export business with capital of 30,000 ducats, sequins, pounds sterling or whatever is the case. Of that, say 10,000 are engaged in the purchase of domestic goods, whereas 20,000 are used in the overseas market. Say the capital is turned over once in two years. Annual turnover = 15,000. Now, our merchant wants to become a contractor, to have cloth woven for his own account. How much additional capital must he invest? Let us assume that the production time of the piece of cloth, such as he sells, averages two months—which is certainly very high. Let us further assume that he has to pay for everything in cash. Hence, he must advance enough capital to supply his weavers with yarn for two months. Since his turnover is 15,000 a year, he buys cloth for

2,500 in two months. Let us say that 2,000 of that represents the value of yarn, and 500 weavers' wages; then our merchant requires an additional capital of 2,000. We assume that the surplus-value he appropriates from the weaver by the new method totals only 5 per cent of the value of the cloth, which constitutes the certainly very modest surplus-value rate of 25 per cent. (2,000c + 500v + 125s; s' = 125/500 = 25%, p' = 125/2,500 = 5%). Our man then makes an extra profit of 750 on his annual turnover of 15,000, and has thus got his additional capital back in 2⅔ years.

But in order to accelerate his sales and hence his turnover, thus making the same profit with the same capital in a shorter period of time, and hence a greater profit in the same time, he will donate a small portion of his surplus-value to the buyer—he will sell cheaper than his competitors. These will also gradually be converted into contractors, and then the extra profit for all of them will be reduced to the ordinary profit, or even to a lower profit on the capital that has been increased for all of them. The equality of the profit rate is re-established, although possibly on another level, by a part of the surplus-value made at home being turned over to the foreign buyers.

The next step in the subjugation of industry by capital takes place through the introduction of manufacture. This, too, enable the manufacturer, who is most often his own export trader in the 17th and 18th centuries—generally in Germany down to 1850, and still today here and there—to produce cheaper than his old-fashioned competitor, the handicraftsman. The same process is repeated; the surplus-value appropriated by the manufacturing capitalist enables him (or the export merchant who shares with him) to sell cheaper than his competitors, until the general introduction of the new mode of production, when equalization against takes place. The already existing mercantile rate of profit, even if it is levelled out only locally, remains the Procrustean bed in which the excessive industrial surplus-value is lopped off without mercy.

If manufacturing sprung ahead by cheapening its products, this is even more true of modern industry, which forces the production costs of commodities lower and lower through its repeated revolutions in production, relentlessly eliminating all former modes of production. It is large-scale industry, too, that thus finally conquers the domestic market for capital, puts an end to the small-scale production and natural economy of the self-sufficient peasant family, and places the entire nation in service of capital. Likewise, it equalizes the profit rate of the different commercial and industrial branches of business into *one* general rate of profit, and finally ensures industry the position of power due to it in this equalization by eliminating most of the obstacles formerly hindering the transfer of capital from one branch to another. Thereby the conversion of values into production prices is accomplished for all exchange as a whole. This conversion therefore proceeds according to objective laws, without the consciousness or the intent of the participants. Theoretically, there is no difficulty at all in the fact that competition reduces to the general level profits which exceed the general rate, thus again depriving the first industrial appropriator of the surplus-value exceeding the average. All the more so in practice, however, for the spheres of production with excessive surplus-value, with high variable and low constant capital—i.e., with low capital composition—are by their very nature the ones that are last and least completely subjected to capitalist production, especially agriculture. On the other hand, the rise of production prices above commodity values, which is required to raise the below-average surplus-value, contained in the products of the spheres of high capital composition, to the level of the average rate of profit, appears to be extremely difficult theoretically, but is soonest and most easily effected in practice, as we have seen. For when commodities of this class are first produced capitalistically and enter capitalist commerce, they compete with commodities of the same nature produced by per-capitalist methods and hence dearer. Thus, even if the capitalist producer renounces a part of the surplus-value, he can still obtain the rate of profit prevailing in his locality, which originally had no direct connection with surplus-value because it had arisen from merchant capital long before there was any capitalist production at all, and therefore before an industrial rate of profit was possible.

Section II. *The Stock Exchange*

1. The position of the stock exchange in capitalist production in general is clear from Vol. III, Part 5, especially Chapter [27]. But since 1865, when the book was written, a change has taken place which today assigns a considerably increased and constantly growing role to the stock exchange, and which, as it develops, tends to concentrate all production, industrial as well as agricultural, and all commerce, the means of communication as well as the functions of exchange, in the hands of stock exchange operators, so that the stock exchange becomes the most prominent representative of capitalist production itself.
2. In 1865 the stock exchange was still a *secondary* element in the capitalist system. Government bonds represented the bulk of exchange securities, and even their sum-total was still relatively small. Besides, there were joint-stock banks, predominant on the continent and in America, and just beginning to absorb the aristocratic private banks in England, but still relatively insignificant *en masse*. Railway shares were still comparatively weak compared to the present time. There were still only few directly productive establishments in stock company form—and, like the banks, most of all in the *poorer* countries: Germany, Austria, America, etc. The 'minister's eye' was still an unconquered superstition.

   At that time, the stock exchange was still a place where the capitalists took away each other's accumulated capital, and which directly concerned the workers only as new proof of the demoralising general effect of capitalist economy and as confirmation of the Calvinist doctrine that predestination (alias chance) decides, even in this life, blessedness and damnation, wealth, i.e., enjoyment and power, and poverty, i.e., privation and servitude.
3. Now it is otherwise. Since the crisis of 1866 accumulation has proceeded with ever-increasing rapidity, so that in no industrial country, least of all in England, could the expansion of production keep up with that of accumulation, or the accumulation of the individual capitalist be completely utilised in the enlargement of his own business; English cotton industry as early as 1845; the railway swindles. But with this accumulation the number of *rentiers*, people who were fed up with the regular tension in business and therefore wanted merely to amuse themselves or to follow a mild pursuit as directors or governors of companies, also rose. And third, in order to facilitate the investment of this mass floating around as money-capital, new legal forms of limited liability companies were established wherever that had not yet been done, and the liability of the shareholder, formerly unlimited, was also reduced ± [more or less] (joint-stock companies in Germany, 1890. Subscription 40 per cent!).
4. Thereafter, gradual conversion of industry into stock companies. One branch after another suffers this fate. First iron, where giant plants are now necessary (before that, mines, where not already organised on shares). Then the chemical industry, likewise machinery plants. On the continent, the textile industry; in England, only in a few areas in Lancashire (Oldham Spinning Mill, Burnley Weaving Mill, etc., tailor co-operatives, but this is only a preliminary stage which will again fall into the masters' hands at the next crisis), breweries (the American ones sold a few years ago to English capital, then Guinness, Bass, Allsopp). Then the trusts, which create gigantic enterprises under common management (such as United Alkali). The ordinary individual firm is more and more only a preliminary stage to bring the business to the point where it is big enough to be 'founded.'

Likewise in trade: Leafs, Parsons, Morleys, Morrison, Dillon—all founded. The same in retail stores by now, and not merely under the cloak of co-operation *à la* 'stores.'

Likewise banks and other credit establishments even in England. A tremendous number of new banks, all shares delimited. Even old banks etc., are converted, with seven private shareholders, into limited companies.

5. The same in the field of agriculture. The enormously expanded banks, especially in Germany under all sorts of bureaucratic names, more and more the holders of mortgages; with their shares the actual higher ownership of landed property is transferred to the stock exchange, and this is even more true when the farms fall into the creditors' hands. Here the agricultural revolution of prairie cultivation is very impressive; if it continues, the time can be foreseen when England's and France's land will also be in the hands of the stock exchange.
6. Now all foreign investments in the form of shares. To mention England alone: American railways, North and South (consult the stock exchange list), Goldberger, etc.
7. Then colonisation. Today this is purely a subsidiary of the stock exchange, in whose interests the European powers divided Africa a few years ago, and the French conquered Tunis and Tonkin. Africa leased directly to companies (Niger, South Africa, German South-West and German East Africa), and Mashonaland and Natal seized by Rhodes for the stock exchange.